Official

BASEBALL REGISTER

1987 EDITION

Editor/Baseball Register
BARRY SIEGEL

Contributing Editors/Baseball Register
CRAIG CARTER
JOHN DUXBURY
BILL RABINOWITZ

President-Chief Executive Officer
RICHARD WATERS

Editor
TOM BARNIDGE

Director of Books and Periodicals
RON SMITH

Published by

The Sporting News

1212 North Lindbergh Boulevard
P.O. Box 56 — St. Louis, MO 63166

Copyright © 1987
The Sporting News Publishing Company

A Times Mirror
Company

ISBN 0-89204-238-9   ISSN 0067-4281

Table
of
CONTENTS

⚔☻⚔

Players included are those who played in at least one game in the major leagues in 1986, those who were part of a team's 40-man roster and selected invitees to spring training.

◆

ON THE COVER: Philadelphia Phillies third baseman Mike Schmidt captured his third National League Most Valuable Player award, hitting .290 with 37 home runs and 119 RBIs.

—Photo by Photo Editor Rich Pilling

◆

EXPLANATION OF ABBREVIATIONS

G—Games played. Pos.—Position. AB—At Bats. R—Runs. H—Hits. 2B—Two-Base Hits. 3B—Three-Base Hits. HR—Home Runs. RBI—Runs Batted In. B.A.—Batting Average. PO—Putouts. A—Assists. E—Errors. F.A.—Fielding Average. IP—Innings Pitched. W—Won. L—Lost. Pct.—Percentage. R—Runs. ER—Earned Runs. SO—Strikeouts. BB—Bases on Balls. ERA—Earned-Run Average.

Players

*Denotes led league. ●Tied for lead. Mark before position (where more than one position is given) denotes where played as leader in department shown.

DONALD WILLIAM AASE

Name pronounced AH-see.

(Don)

Born September 8, 1954, at Orange, Calif.
Height, 6.03. Weight, 210.
Throws and bats righthanded.
Attended California State University, Fullerton, Calif.

Major League saves: 1979 (2), 1980 (2), 1981 (11), 1982 (4), 1984 (8), 1985 (14), 1986 (34). Total—75.
Led International League pitchers in games started with 29 in 1975.
Led Carolina League pitchers in games started with 30, complete games with 18 and tied for lead in shutouts with 4 in 1974.
Named Carolina League Pitcher of the Year, 1974.

Year Club	League	G.	IP.	W.	L.	Pct.	H.	R.	ER.	SO.	BB.	ERA.
1972—Williamsport	NYP	12	62	0	*10	.000	60	48	40	40	34	5.81
1973—Winter Haven	Florida St.	29	170	12	●15	.444	153	82	68	127	73	3.60
1974—Winston-Salem	Carolina	32	*230	*17	8	.680	185	72	62	*176	84	*2.43
1975—Pawtucket	Int'national	29	186	8	13	.381	173	85	75	125	88	3.63
1976—Rhode Island†	Int'national	10	54	5	2	.714	42	23	20	40	34	3.33
1977—Pawtucket	Int'national	18	109	6	6	.500	118	67	61	64	60	5.04
1977—Boston‡	American	13	92	6	2	.750	85	36	32	49	19	3.13
1978—California	American	29	179	11	8	.579	185	88	80	93	80	4.02
1979—California	American	37	185	9	10	.474	200	104	99	96	77	4.82
1980—California	American	40	175	8	13	.381	193	83	79	74	66	4.06
1981—California	American	39	65	4	4	.500	56	17	17	38	24	2.35
1982—California§	American	24	52	3	3	.500	45	20	20	40	23	3.46
1983—California x	American					(Did not play)						
1984—Redwood y	California	4	12⅓	0	1	.000	9	9	7	10	7	5.11
1984—California z	American	23	39	4	1	.800	30	7	7	28	19	1.62
1985—Baltimore	American	54	88	10	6	.625	83	44	37	67	35	3.78
1986—Baltimore	American	66	81⅔	6	7	.462	71	29	27	67	28	2.98
Major League Totals—9 Years		325	956⅔	61	54	.530	948	428	398	552	371	3.74

Selected by Boston Red Sox' organization in 6th round of free-agent draft, June 6, 1972.
†On disabled list, June 23, 1976 through remainder of season.
‡Traded with cash to California Angels for Second Baseman Jerry Remy, December 8, 1977.
§On disabled list, June 3 to June 27 and July 20 to September 7, 1982.
xOn disabled list, March 30, 1983 through remainder of season.
yOn California disabled list, March 27 to June 13, 1984; included rehabilitation disability assignment to Redwood, May 10 to May 30, 1984.
zGranted free agency, November 8, 1984; signed by Baltimore Orioles, December 13, 1984.

CHAMPIONSHIP SERIES RECORD

Year Club	League	G.	IP.	W.	L.	Pct.	H.	R.	ER.	SO.	BB.	ERA.
1979—California	American	2	5	1	0	1.000	4	1	1	6	2	1.80

ALL-STAR GAME RECORD

Year League	IP.	W.	L.	Pct.	H.	R.	ER.	SO.	BB.	ERA.
1986—American	⅔	0	0	.000	0	0	0	0	0	0.00

SHAWN WESLEY ABNER

Born June 17, 1966, at Hamilton, O.
Height, 6.01. Weight, 190.
Throws and bats righthanded.
Brother of Ben Abner, outfielder in Pittsburgh Pirates' organization.

Tied for Texas League lead in being hit by pitch with 7 in 1986.
Led Texas League outfielders in total chances with 352 in 1986.
Led Carolina League outfielders in total chances with 352 in 1985.
Named Carolina League Player of the Year, 1985.

Year Club	League	Pos.	G.	AB.	R.	H.	2B.	3B.	HR.	RBI.	B.A.	PO.	A.	E.	F.A.
1984—Kingsport	Appal.	OF	46	183	32	50	8	0	10	35	.273	87	1	1	.989
1984—Little Falls	NYP	OF	18	68	7	18	2	0	1	5	.265	40	2	1	.977
1985—Lynchburg	Carol.	OF	139	*542	71	*163	*30	*11	16	*89	.301	*332	8	12	.966
1986—Jackson†	Texas	OF	*134	511	80	136	29	●8	14	76	.266	*338	10	4	.989

Selected by New York Mets' organization in 1st round (first player selected) of free-agent draft, June 4, 1984.
†Traded with Outfielders Stanley Jefferson and Kevin Mitchell and Pitchers Kevin Armstrong and Kevin Brown to San Diego Padres for Outfielder Kevin McReynolds, Pitcher Gene Walter and Infielder Adam Ging, December 11, 1986.

—DID YOU KNOW—

That the only players to play complete All-Star Games for both the American and National leagues were Johnny Temple and Dave Winfield?

JOHNNY RAY ABREGO

Name pronounced Uh-BRAY-goh.
Born July 4, 1962, at Corpus Christi, Tex.
Height, 6.00. Weight, 185.
Throws and bats righthanded.

Pitched 1-0 no-hit victory against Nashua, August 1, 1985.
Led Northwest League in hit batsmen with 14 and tied for lead in games started by pitchers with 14 in 1983.
Tied for Eastern League lead in hit batsmen with 12 in 1985.

Year Club	League	G.	IP.	W.	L.	Pct.	H.	R.	ER.	SO.	BB.	ERA.
1981—Helena	Pioneer	12	67	3	4	.429	60	40	35	52	52	4.70
1982—Helena†	Pioneer					(Did not play)						
1983—Bend†	Northwest	14	88⅓	7	5	.583	81	58	39	59	40	3.97
1984—Lodi	California	23	150⅓	9	9	.500	111	57	35	139	66	2.10
1984—Iowa	Am. Assoc.	5	26⅔	1	1	.500	28	16	15	17	9	5.06
1985—Iowa	Am. Assoc.	5	25	0	5	.000	29	24	22	12	15	7.92
1985—Pittsfield	Eastern	22	156⅓	6	6	.500	119	60	48	92	72	2.76
1985—Chicago	National	6	24	1	1	.500	32	18	17	13	12	6.38
1986—Iowa	Am. Assoc.	6	29	3	2	.600	32	19	19	13	18	5.90
Major League Totals—1 Year		6	24	1	1	.500	32	18	17	13	12	6.38

Selected by Philadelphia Phillies' organization in 1st round (20th player selected) of free-agent draft, June 11, 1981.
†Drafted by Chicago Cubs, December 5, 1983.

JAMES JUSTIN ACKER
(Jim)

Born September 24, 1958, at Freer, Tex.
Height, 6.02. Weight, 212.
Throws and bats righthanded.
Attended University of Texas, Austin, Tex.
Brother of Bill Acker, nose tackle with St. Louis Cardinals, Kansas City Chiefs, Cincinnati Bengals and
Buffalo Bills, 1980 through 1984.

Major League saves: 1983 (1), 1984 (1), 1985 (10). Total—12.

Year Club	League	G.	IP.	W.	L.	Pct.	H.	R.	ER.	SO.	BB.	ERA.
1980—Bradenton Braves	Gulf Coast	1	5	1	0	1.000	1	0	0	5	0	0.00
1980—Savannah	Southern	13	95	5	5	.500	84	33	28	47	29	2.65
1981—Savannah	Southern	10	77	5	5	.500	57	34	23	37	34	2.69
1981—Richmond	Int'national	21	118	8	7	.533	112	63	55	72	74	4.19
1982—Savannah†‡	Southern	26	142	9	14	.391	120	96	70	96	86	4.44
1983—Toronto	American	38	97⅔	5	1	.833	103	52	47	44	38	4.33
1984—Toronto§	American	32	72	3	5	.375	79	39	35	33	25	4.38
1985—Toronto	American	61	86⅓	7	2	.778	86	35	31	42	43	3.23
1986—Toronto x	American	23	60	2	4	.333	63	34	29	32	22	4.35
1986—Atlanta	National	21	95	3	8	.273	100	47	40	37	26	3.79
American League Totals—4 Years		154	316	17	12	.586	331	160	142	151	128	4.04
National League Totals—1 Year		21	95	3	8	.273	100	47	40	37	26	3.79
Major League Totals—4 Years		175	411	20	20	.500	431	207	182	188	154	3.99

Selected by Atlanta Braves' organization in 1st round (21st player selected) of free-agent draft, June 3, 1980.
†On disabled list, April 9 to April 20, 1982.
‡Drafted by Toronto Blue Jays, December 6, 1982.
§On disabled list, August 16 to September 1, 1984.
xTraded to Atlanta Braves for Pitcher Joe Johnson, July 6, 1986.

CHAMPIONSHIP SERIES RECORD

Year Club	League	G.	IP.	W.	L.	Pct.	H.	R.	ER.	SO.	BB.	ERA.
1985—Toronto	American	2	6	0	0	.000	2	0	0	5	0	0.00

JAMES DAVID ADDUCI

Name pronounced Uh-DOO-see.

(Jim)

Born August 9, 1959, at Chicago, Ill.
Height, 6.04. Weight, 200.
Throws and bats lefthanded.
Attended Southern Illinois University, Carbondale, Ill.

Led American Association batters in game-winning RBIs with 14 and tied for lead in strikeouts with 103 in 1983.
Led Texas League in game-winning RBIs with 14 in 1982.
Tied for Pacific Coast League lead in errors by first basemen with 15 in 1985.

Year Club	League	Pos.	G.	AB.	R.	H.	2B.	3B.	HR.	RBI.	B.A.	PO.	A.	E.	F.A.
1980—Johnson City	Appal.	OF	17	63	15	21	4	0	5	16	.333	27	2	1	.967
1980—St. Petersburg	Fla. St.	OF	37	118	29	32	4	0	2	13	.271	62	3	2	.970
1981—St. Petersburg	Fla. St.	OF	92	321	44	87	12	7	7	45	.271	185	4	7	.964
1981—Arkansas	Texas	OF	40	131	16	36	8	3	5	14	.275	55	3	1	.983
1982—Arkansas	Texas	OF	121	392	64	117	28	5	22	92	.298	178	6	3	.984
1983—Louisville	A. A.	OF-1B	129	467	81	131	29	7	25	★101	.281	327	17	14	.961
1983—St. Louis	Nat.	1B-OF	10	20	0	1	0	0	0	0	.050	47	4	0	1.000
1984—Louisville†‡	A. A.	OF-1B	113	412	62	119	25	6	12	58	.289	252	13	5	.981
1985—Vancouver	P. C.	1B-OF	112	393	63	109	28	2	20	77	.277	788	65	16	.982

Year	Club	League	Pos.	G.	AB.	R.	H.	2B.	3B.	HR.	RBI.	B.A.	PO.	A.	E.	F.A.
1986—Vancouver	P. C.	OF-1B	113	425	71	144	26	5	4	53	.339	418	31	7	.985
1986—Milwaukee	Amer.	1B	3	11	2	1	1	0	0	0	.091	25	3	0	1.000
American League Totals—1 Year			3	11	2	1	1	0	0	0	.091	25	3	0	1.000
National League Totals—1 Year			10	20	0	1	0	0	0	0	.050	47	4	0	1.000
Major League Totals—2 Years			13	31	2	2	1	0	0	0	.065	72	7	0	1.000

Selected by Philadelphia Phillies' organization in 28th round of free-agent draft, June 7, 1977.

Selected by St. Louis Cardinals' organization in 7th round of free-agent draft, June 3, 1980.

†On disabled list, April 25 to May 22, 1984.

‡Traded with Outfielder Paul Householder to Milwaukee Brewers for Pitchers Rich Buonantony and Jim Koontz and Infielder Ron Koenigsfeld, October 3, 1984.

MICHAEL TROY AFENIR
(Known by middle name.)

Name pronounced AFF-nur.

Born September 21, 1963, at Escondido, Calif.

Height, 6.04. Weight, 185.

Throws and bats righthanded.

Attended Palomar College, San Marcos, Calif.

Led South Atlantic League in passed balls with 32 in 1984.

Year	Club	League	Pos.	G.	AB.	R.	H.	2B.	3B.	HR.	RBI.	B.A.	PO.	A.	E.	F.A.
1983—Sarasota Astros	Gulf C.	C	27	89	16	26	5	1	5	24	.292	101	19	3	.976
1983—Auburn	NYP	C	7	26	2	3	0	0	0	0	.115	48	2	0	1.000
1984—Asheville	S. Atl.	C-1B	115	358	44	69	16	0	16	69	.193	656	61	12	.984
1985—Osceola	Fla. St.	*C-SS	99	323	38	80	19	1	6	41	.248	557	72	*16	.975
1986—Columbus	South.	C-1B	91	313	50	68	15	3	14	45	.217	492	38	14	.974

Selected by Chicago Cubs' organization in 1st round (second player selected) of free-agent draft, January 12, 1982.

Selected by Baltimore Orioles' organization in secondary phase of free-agent draft, June 7, 1982.

Selected by Houston Astros' organization in secondary phase of free-agent draft, January 11, 1983.

JUAN ROBERTO AGOSTO

Born February 23, 1958, at Rio Piedras, P.R.

Height, 6.02. Weight, 187.

Throws and bats lefthanded.

Major League saves: 1983 (7), 1984 (7), 1985 (1), 1986 (1). Total—16.

Led Carolina League in balks with 4 in 1977 and 5 in 1978.

Year	Club	League	G.	IP.	W.	L.	Pct.	H.	R.	ER.	SO.	BB.	ERA.
1975—Winter Haven	Florida St.	6	28	0	4	.000	35	23	18	19	24	5.79
1975—Elmira	NYP	9	23	1	4	.200	27	37	22	22	34	8.61
1976—Winter Haven	Florida St.	28	107	5	11	.313	97	70	55	80	69	4.63
1977—Winston-Salem	Carolina	30	119	4	9	.308	128	106	79	98	*111	5.97
1978—Winter Haven	Florida St.	1	1	0	0	.000	5	2	2	0	0	27.00
1978—Winston-Salem†	Carolina	23	120	5	11	.313	114	76	51	74	89	3.83
1979—Puerto Rico‡	Int.-Amer.	10	31	3	2	.600	31	13	9	9	17	2.61
1980—Glens Falls	Eastern	8	22	1	0	1.000	26	18	17	8	18	6.95
1980—Appleton	Midwest	23	144	11	6	.647	118	60	43	93	52	2.69
1981—Edmonton	P. Coast	48	120	7	10	.412	128	61	52	57	49	3.90
1981—Chicago	American	2	6	0	0	.000	5	3	3	3	0	4.50
1982—Edmonton	P. Coast	50	95⅓	3	4	.429	101	63	53	39	49	5.00
1982—Chicago	American	1	2	0	0	.000	7	4	4	1	0	18.00
1983—Denver	Am. Assoc.	19	26	4	1	.800	19	8	6	19	10	2.08
1983—Chicago	American	39	41⅔	2	2	.500	41	20	19	29	11	4.10
1984—Chicago	American	49	55⅓	2	1	.667	54	20	19	26	34	3.09
1985—Chicago	American	54	60⅓	4	3	.571	45	27	24	39	23	3.58
1985—Buffalo	Am. Assoc.	6	12⅔	0	0	.000	13	3	3	11	2	2.13
1986—Chicago§-Minnesota	American	26	25	1	4	.200	49	30	24	12	18	8.64
1986—Toledo x	Int'national	21	35	4	3	.571	33	11	9	29	14	2.31
Major League Totals—6 Years		171	190⅓	9	10	.474	201	104	93	110	86	4.40

Signed as free agent by Boston Red Sox' organization, August 29, 1974.

†Released, September 21, 1978; signed by Puerto Rico of Inter-American League, March 10, 1979.

‡Declared free agent when Inter-American League folded, June 15, 1979; signed by Chicago White Sox' organization, January 18, 1980.

§Sold to Minnesota Twins in exchange for loaning Pitcher Pete Filson to Buffalo (Chicago White Sox' organization), April 30, 1986; Filson was returned to Minnesota and traded to Chicago White Sox for Pitcher Kurt Walker, September 3, 1986.

xReleased, December 19, 1986.

CHAMPIONSHIP SERIES RECORD

Year	Club	League	G.	IP.	W.	L.	Pct.	H.	R.	ER.	SO.	BB.	ERA.
1983—Chicago	American	1	⅓	0	0	.000	0	0	0	0	0	0.00

—DID YOU KNOW—

That Boston's Dwight Evans hit a home run on the first pitch of the 1986 season off Detroit's Jack Morris?

LUIS AGUAYO (MURIEL)

Name pronounced Uh-GWY-oh.

Born March 13, 1959, at Vega Baja, P.R.
Height, 5.09. Weight, 190.
Throws and bats righthanded

Major League stolen bases: 1980 (1), 1981 (1), 1982 (1), 1985 (1), 1986 (1). Total—5.
Led Carolina League second basemen in assists with 365, errors with 30 and fielding percentage with .953 in 1977.

Year Club	League	Pos.	G.	AB.	R.	H.	2B.	3B.	HR.	RBI.	B.A.	PO.	A.	E.	F.A.
1976—Spartanburg	W. Car.	2B	3	11	0	1	0	0	0	0	.091	5	2	1	.875
1976—Auburn	NYP	2B-3B-SS	51	197	27	49	9	2	0	23	.249	79	99	10	.947
1977—Peninsula	Carol.	2B-SS	130	497	73	127	28	2	9	41	.256	271	409	34	.952
1978—Reading	East.	SS-2B	115	378	49	74	19	5	4	33	.196	198	341	25	.956
1979—Oklahoma City	A. A.	SS-2B	113	370	54	101	21	1	8	46	.273	191	320	27	.950
1980—Philadelphia†	Nat.	2B-SS	20	47	7	13	1	2	1	8	.277	44	44	3	.967
1980—Oklahoma City‡	A. A.	SS	84	291	37	71	19	2	9	40	.244	154	268	★28	.938
1981—Philadelphia	Nat.	2B-SS-3B	45	84	11	18	4	0	1	7	.214	39	63	5	.953
1982—Philadelphia	Nat.	2B-SS-3B	50	56	11	15	1	2	3	7	.268	27	49	4	.950
1983—Philadelphia§	Nat.	SS	2	4	1	1	0	0	0	0	.250	3	0	0	1.000
1983—Portland	P. C.	SS-2B	71	229	38	65	14	3	5	33	.284	121	216	10	.971
1984—Philadelphia	Nat.	3B-2B-SS	58	72	15	20	4	0	3	11	.278	18	55	3	.161
1984—Portland	P. C.	SS	3	13	3	7	1	0	1	2	.538	6	7	1	.929
1985—Philadelphia	Nat.	SS-2B-3B	91	165	27	46	7	3	6	21	.279	92	158	9	.965
1986—Philadelphia	Nat.	2B-SS-3B	62	133	17	28	6	1	4	13	.211	57	90	5	.967
Major League Totals—7 Years			328	561	89	141	23	8	18	67	.251	280	459	29	.962

Signed as free agent by Philadelphia Phillies' organization, December 27, 1975.
†On disabled list, May 7 to May 22, 1980.
‡On disabled list, May 22 to August 30, 1980.
§On disabled list, March 23 to June 13, 1983.

DIVISION SERIES RECORD

Year Club	League	Pos.	G.	AB.	R.	H.	2B.	3B.	HR.	RBI.	B.A.	PO.	A.	E.	F.A.
1981—Philadelphia	Nat.	PR	2	0	1	0	0	0	0	0	.000	0	0	0	.000

RICHARD WARREN AGUILERA

Name pronounced Ag-ah-lair-uh.

(Rick)

Born December 31, 1961, at San Gabriel, Calif.
Height, 6.05. Weight, 195.
Throws and bats righthanded.
Attended Brigham Young University, Provo, Utah.

Tied for Carolina League lead in shutouts with 3 in 1984.
Tied for New York-Pennsylvania League lead in shutouts with 2 in 1983.

Year Club	League	G.	IP.	W.	L.	Pct.	H.	R.	ER.	SO.	BB.	ERA.
1983—Little Falls	NYP	16	104	5	6	.455	★109	55	43	84	26	3.72
1984—Lynchburg	Carolina	13	88⅓	8	3	.727	72	29	23	101	28	2.34
1984—Jackson†	Texas	11	67	4	4	.500	68	37	34	71	19	4.57
1985—Tidewater	Int'national	11	79	6	4	.600	64	24	22	55	17	2.51
1985—New York	National	21	122⅓	10	7	.588	118	49	44	74	37	3.24
1986—New York	National	28	141⅔	10	7	.588	145	70	61	104	36	3.88
Major League Totals—2 Years		49	264	20	14	.588	263	119	105	178	73	3.58

Selected by St. Louis Cardinals' organization in 37th round of free-agent draft, June 3, 1980.
Selected by New York Mets' organization in 3rd round of free-agent draft, June 6, 1983.
†On disabled list, September 3 to September 15, 1985.

CHAMPIONSHIP SERIES RECORD

Year Club	League	G.	IP.	W.	L.	Pct.	H.	R.	ER.	SO.	BB.	ERA.
1986—New York	National	2	5	0	0	.000	2	1	0	2	2	0.00

WORLD SERIES RECORD

Year Club	League	G.	IP.	W.	L.	Pct.	H.	R.	ER.	SO.	BB.	ERA.
1986—New York	National	2	3	1	0	1.000	8	4	4	4	1	12.00

DARREL WAYNE AKERFELDS

Born June 12, 1962, at Denver, Colo.
Height, 6.02. Weight, 210.
Throws and bats righthanded.
Attended Mesa College, Grand Junction, Colo., and
University of Arkansas, Fayetteville, Ark.

Tied for Midwest League lead in wild pitches with 19 in 1984.

Year Club	League	G.	IP.	W.	L.	Pct.	H.	R.	ER.	SO.	BB.	ERA.
1983—Bellingham†	Northwest	12	68⅓	5	3	.625	62	36	34	85	36	4.48
1984—Madison	Midwest	24	151	11	6	.647	156	86	74	137	74	4.41
1985—Huntsville‡	Southern	17	96⅓	9	6	.600	75	42	37	56	64	3.46
1986—Tacoma	P. Coast	25	150	8	12	.400	158	91	79	91	62	4.74
1986—Oakland	American	2	5⅓	0	0	.000	7	5	4	5	3	6.75
Major League Totals—1 Year		2	5⅓	0	0	.000	7	5	4	5	3	6.75

Selected by Atlanta Braves' organization in 9th round of free-agent draft, June 3, 1980.
Selected by Seattle Mariners' organization in 1st round (seventh player selected) of free-agent draft, June 6, 1983.
†Traded to Oakland A's, December 7, 1983, completing deal in which Seattle Mariners traded Pitcher Bill Caudill and a player to be named later to Oakland for Pitcher Dave Beard and Catcher Bob Kearney, November 21, 1983.
‡On disabled list, May 22 to June 13 and July 5 to August 20, 1985.

MICHAEL PETER ALDRETE

(Mike)

Born January 29, 1961, at Carmel, Calif.
Height, 5.11. Weight, 180.
Throws and bats lefthanded.
Received bachelor of arts degree in communication from
Stanford University, Stanford, Calif.

Major League stolen bases: 1986 (1).
Led California League in total bases with 225 in 1984.

Year	Club	League	Pos.	G.	AB.	R.	H.	2B.	3B.	HR.	RBI.	B.A.	PO.	A.	E.	F.A.
1983—Great Falls	Pion.	1B-OF	38	132	30	55	11	2	4	31	.417	257	17	4	.986
1983—Fresno	Calif.	1B	20	68	5	14	4	0	1	12	.206	189	9	2	.990
1984—Fresno	Calif.	1B	136	457	89	155	28	3	12	72	.339	1180	74	8	★.994
1985—Shreveport	Texas	1B-OF	127	441	80	147	32	1	15	77	.333	854	41	9	.990
1985—Phoenix	P. C.	OF	3	8	0	1	1	0	0	1	.125	3	0	0	1.000
1986—Phoenix	P. C.	OF-1B	47	159	36	59	14	0	6	35	.371	131	8	1	.993
1986—San Francisco	Nat.	1B-OF	84	216	27	54	18	3	2	25	.250	317	36	1	.997
Major League Totals—1 Year			84	216	27	54	18	3	2	25	.250	317	36	1	.997

Selected by San Francisco Giants' organization in 7th round of free-agent draft, June 6, 1983.

JAY ROBERT ALDRICH

Born April 14, 1961, at Alexandria, La.
Height, 6.03. Wight, 205.
Throws and bats righthanded.
Attended Monclair State College, Upper Montclair, N.J.

Tied for California League lead in intentional bases on balls issued with 10 in 1984.

Year	Club	League	G.	IP.	W.	L.	Pct.	H.	R.	ER.	SO.	BB.	ERA.
1982—Pikeville	Ap'lachian	11	53⅔	1	2	.333	44	33	25	37	28	4.19
1983—Beloit	Midwest	28	103⅔	7	4	.636	114	59	48	96	35	4.17
1984—Stockton	California	54	105⅔	11	●14	.440	107	46	34	78	44	2.90
1985—El Paso	Texas	42	63⅓	4	1	.800	61	28	25	35	13	3.55
1986—El Paso	Texas	40	54⅓	3	3	.500	60	24	21	34	18	3.48

Selected by Milwaukee Brewers' organization in 10th round of free-agent draft, June 7, 1982.

DOYLE LAFAYETTE ALEXANDER

Born September 4, 1950, at Cordova, Ala.
Height, 6.03. Weight, 200.
Throws and bats righthanded.
Attended Jefferson State Junior College, Birmingham, Ala.

Major League saves: 1972 (2), 1975 (1). Total—3.

Year	Club	League	G.	IP.	W.	L.	Pct.	H.	R.	ER.	SO.	BB.	ERA.
1968—Tri-City	Northwest	13	70	3	★9	.250	66	47	32	58	47	4.11
1969—Daytona Beach	Florida St.	30	185	13	9	.591	154	75	56	140	100	2.72
1969—Albuquerque	Texas	3	15	0	3	.000	19	10	10	3	12	6.00
1970—Albuquerque	Texas	10	80	4	3	.571	72	29	28	60	20	3.15
1970—Spokane	P. Coast	19	137	9	7	.563	137	66	55	78	26	3.61
1971—Spokane	P. Coast	15	110	6	3	.667	114	49	42	65	31	3.44
1971—Los Angeles†	National	17	92	6	6	.500	105	45	39	30	18	3.82
1972—Baltimore	American	35	106	6	8	.429	78	36	29	49	30	2.46
1973—Baltimore‡	American	29	175	12	8	.600	169	85	75	63	52	3.86
1974—Baltimore	American	30	114	6	9	.400	127	65	51	40	43	4.03
1975—Baltimore	American	32	133	8	8	.500	127	47	45	46	47	3.05
1976—Baltimore§-New York x	American	30	201	13	9	.591	172	81	75	58	63	3.36
1977—Texas	American	34	237	17	11	.607	221	103	96	82	82	3.65
1978—Texas	American	31	191	9	10	.474	198	84	82	81	71	3.86
1979—Texas y	American	23	113	5	7	.417	114	65	56	50	69	4.46
1980—Atlanta z	National	35	232	14	11	.560	227	120	108	114	74	4.19
1981—San Francisco a	National	24	152	11	7	.611	156	51	49	77	44	2.90
1982—Fort Lauderdale	Florida St.	2	11	0	1	.000	12	5	5	4	2	4.09
1982—New York bc	American	16	66⅔	1	7	.125	81	52	45	26	14	6.08
1982—Columbus	Int'national	1	3⅔	0	0	.000	5	4	4	1	2	9.82
1983—New York d-Toronto	American	25	145	7	8	.467	157	76	71	63	33	4.41
1983—Kinston	Carolina	1	6	0	0	.000	3	0	0	4	0	0.00
1984—Toronto	American	36	261⅔	17	6	★.739	238	99	91	139	59	3.13
1985—Toronto	American	36	260⅔	17	10	.630	268	105	100	142	67	3.45
1986—Toronto e	American	17	111	5	4	.556	120	56	55	65	20	4.46
1986—Atlanta f	National	17	117⅓	6	6	.500	135	58	50	74	17	3.84
National League Totals—4 Years		93	593⅓	37	30	.552	623	274	246	295	153	3.73
American League Totals—13 Years		374	2115	123	105	.539	2070	954	871	904	650	3.71
Major League Totals—16 Years		467	2708⅓	160	135	.542	2693	1228	1117	1199	803	3.71

Selected by Los Angeles Dodgers' organization in 44th round of free-agent draft, June 7, 1968.

†Traded with Pitcher Bob O'Brien, Catcher Sergio Robles and First Baseman-Outfielder Royle Stillman to Baltimore Orioles for Pitcher Pete Richert and Outfielder Frank Robinson, December 2, 1971.

‡On disabled list, July 10 to August 6, 1973.

§Traded with Pitchers Ken Holtzman and Grant Jackson, Catcher Elrod Hendricks and Pitcher Jimmy Freeman to New York Yankees for Pitchers Rudy May, Tippy Martinez, Dave Pagan, Scott McGregor and Catcher Rick Dempsey, June 15, 1976.

xPlayed out option year and granted free agency, November 1, 1976; signed as free agent by Texas Rangers, November 23, 1976.

yTraded with Shortstop Larvell Blanks to Atlanta Braves for Pitcher Adrian Devine, Shortstop Pepe Frias and a player to be named later, December 7, 1979; Atlanta received $50,000 to complete deal when Outfielder Jeff Burroughs exercised no-trade clause.

zTraded to San Francisco Giants for Pitcher John Montefusco and Outfielder Craig Landis, December 12, 1980.

aTraded to New York Yankees for Pitcher Andy McGaffigan and Outfielder Ted Wilborn, March 30, 1982.

bOn disabled list, May 10 to July 8, 1982; included rehabilitation disability assignment to Columbus, June 22 to July 8, 1982.

cOn disabled list, August 11 to September 10, 1982.

dReleased, May 31, 1983; signed by Toronto Blue Jays' organization, June 21, 1983.

eTraded to Atlanta Braves for Pitcher Duane Ward, July 6, 1986.

fGranted free agency, November 12, 1986.

CHAMPIONSHIP SERIES RECORD

Established American League Championship Series record for most runs and most earned runs allowed, seven-game Series (10), 1985.

Year Club	League	G.	IP.	W.	L.	Pct.	H.	R.	ER.	SO.	BB.	ERA.
1973—Baltimore	American	1	3⅔	0	1	.000	5	3	2	1	0	4.91
1985—Toronto	American	2	10⅓	0	1	.000	14	10	10	9	3	8.71
Championship Series Total—2 Years		3	14	0	2	.000	19	13	12	10	3	7.71

WORLD SERIES RECORD

Year Club	League	G.	IP.	W.	L.	Pct.	H.	R.	ER.	SO.	BB.	ERA.
1976—New York	American	1	6	0	1	.000	9	5	5	1	2	7.50

ANDREW NEAL ALLANSON
(Andy)

Born December 22, 1961, at Richmond, Va.
Height, 6.05. Weight, 220.
Throws and bats righthanded.
Attended University of Richmond, Richmond, Va.

Major League stolen bases: 1986 (10).

Year Club	League	Pos.	G.	AB.	R.	H.	2B.	3B.	HR.	RBI.	B.A.	PO.	A.	E.	F.A.
1983—Waterloo	Midw.	C	17	50	4	10	0	0	0	0	.200	99	8	3	.973
1983—Batavia	NYP	C	51	145	27	38	3	0	0	6	.262	372	27	5	.988
1984—Buffalo†	East.	C	39	111	12	28	4	0	0	11	.252	154	15	3	.983
1984—Waterloo	Midw.	C	46	144	14	39	5	0	0	10	.271	68	9	1	.987
1985—Waterbury	East.	C	120	420	69	131	17	1	0	47	★.312	578	64	10	.985
1986—Cleveland	Amer.	C	101	293	30	66	7	3	1	29	.225	446	33	★20	.960
Major League Totals—1 Year			101	293	30	66	7	3	1	29	.225	446	33	20	.960

Selected by Cleveland Indians' organization in 2nd round of free-agent draft, June 6, 1983.

†On disabled list, June 19 to June 29, 1984.

NEIL PATRICK ALLEN

Born January 24, 1958, at Kansas City, Kan.
Height, 6.02. Weight, 190.
Throws and bats righthanded.

Major League saves: 1979 (8), 1980 (22), 1981 (18), 1982 (19), 1983 (2), 1984 (3), 1985 (3). Total—75.
Tied for Carolina League lead in complete games with 11 in 1977.

Year Club	League	G.	IP.	W.	L.	Pct.	H.	R.	ER.	SO.	BB.	ERA.
1976—Marion	Ap'lachian	6	33	2	0	1.000	23	8	7	29	6	1.91
1976—Wausau	Midwest	6	48	4	2	.667	51	27	20	34	20	3.75
1977—Lynchburg†	Carolina	20	142	10	2	.833	136	55	44	★126	43	2.79
1978—Jackson	Texas	16	120	5	9	.357	88	38	28	111	38	★2.10
1978—Tidewater	Int'national	10	57	2	7	.222	65	35	28	30	12	4.42
1979—New York‡	National	50	99	6	10	.375	100	46	39	65	47	3.55
1980—New York	National	59	97	7	10	.412	87	43	40	79	40	3.71
1981—New York	National	43	67	7	6	.538	64	26	22	50	26	2.96
1982—New York	National	50	64⅔	3	7	.300	65	22	22	59	30	3.06
1983—New York§-St. Louis	National	46	175⅔	12	13	.480	179	84	77	106	84	3.94
1984—St. Louis x	National	57	119	9	6	.600	105	54	47	66	49	3.55
1985—St. Louis x	National	23	29	1	4	.200	32	22	18	10	17	5.59
1985—New York y	American	17	29⅓	1	0	1.000	26	9	9	16	13	2.76
1986—Chicago z	American	22	113	7	2	.778	101	50	48	57	38	3.82
National League Totals—7 Years		328	651⅓	45	56	.446	632	297	265	435	293	3.66
American League Totals—2 Years		39	142⅓	8	2	.800	127	59	57	73	51	3.60
Major League Totals—8 Years		367	793⅔	53	58	.477	759	356	322	508	344	3.65

Selected by New York Mets' organization in 11th round of free-agent draft, June 8, 1976.

†On disabled list, July 26 to September 1, 1977.

‡On disabled list, June 1 to June 25, 1979.
§Traded with Pitcher Rick Ownbey to St. Louis Cardinals for First Baseman Keith Hernandez, June 15, 1983.
xTraded to New York Yankees for a player to be named later, July 17, 1985; deal settled with cash.
yTraded with Catcher Scott Bradley, Outfielder Glen Braxton and cash to Chicago White Sox for Catchers Ron Hassey and Chris Alvarez, Pitcher Eric Schmidt and Outfielder Matt Winters, February 13, 1986.
zOn disabled list, August 6 to September 10, 1986.

WILLIAM FRANCIS ALMON
(Bill)

Born November 21, 1952, at Providence, R. I.
Height, 6.03. Weight, 170.
Throws and bats righthanded.
Received bachelor of arts degree from Brown University, Providence, R. I., in 1979.
Brother of John Almon, outfielder in San Diego Padres' organization, 1977 through 1979.
Major League stolen bases: 1974 (1), 1976 (3), 1977 (20), 1978 (17), 1979 (6), 1980 (2), 1981 (16), 1982 (10), 1983 (26), 1984 (5), 1985 (10), 1986 (11). Total—127.
Led National League in sacrifice hits with 20 in 1977.
Led National League shortstops in total chances with 882 in 1977.
Led Pacific Coast League shortstops in total chances with 792 in 1975.
Tied for Pacific Coast League lead in stolen bases with 33 in 1975.
Named College Player of the Year by THE SPORTING NEWS, 1974.
Received reported $100,000 bonus to sign with San Diego Padres, 1974.
Named shortstop on THE SPORTING NEWS College Baseball All-America Team, 1974.

Year Club	League	Pos.	G.	AB.	R.	H.	2B.	3B.	HR.	RBI.	B.A.	PO.	A.	E.	F.A.
1974—Hawaii	P. C.	SS	14	36	6	8	0	0	0	3	.222	16	33	7	.875
1974—Alexandria	Texas	SS	25	97	9	18	2	2	0	5	.186	48	70	8	.937
1974—San Diego	Nat.	SS	16	38	4	12	1	0	0	3	.316	13	30	4	.915
1975—Hawaii	P. C.	SS	●144	496	76	113	22	0	1	47	.228	★288	456	★48	.939
1975—San Diego	Nat.	SS	6	10	0	4	0	0	0	0	.400	6	5	0	1.000
1976—Hawaii	P. C.	SS	129	454	67	132	16	2	3	44	.291	★248	395	★36	.947
1976—San Diego	Nat.	SS	14	57	6	14	3	0	1	6	.246	23	52	3	.962
1977—San Diego	Nat.	SS	155	613	75	160	18	11	2	43	.261	★303	538	★41	.954
1978—San Diego	Nat.	3B-SS-2B	138	405	39	102	19	2	0	21	.252	102	255	23	.939
1979—San Diego†	Nat.	2B-SS-OF	100	198	20	45	3	0	1	8	.227	142	193	7	.980
1980—Mtl.‡-N.Y.§	Nat.	SS-2B-3B	66	150	15	29	4	3	0	7	.193	79	134	12	.947
1981—Chicago	Amer.	SS	103	349	46	105	10	2	4	41	.301	190	340	17	.969
1982—Chicago x	Amer.	SS	111	308	40	79	10	4	4	26	.256	164	317	●26	.949
1983—Oakland	Amer.	S-3-1-O-2	143	451	45	120	29	1	4	63	.266	327	176	20	.962
1984—Oakland y	Amer.	O-1-3-S-C	106	211	24	47	11	0	7	16	.223	255	15	2	.993
1985—Pittsburgh	Nat.	S-O-1-3	88	244	33	66	17	0	6	29	.270	104	108	5	.977
1986—Pittsburgh	Nat.	O-3-S-1	102	196	29	43	7	2	7	27	.219	80	45	8	.940
National League Totals—9 Years			685	1911	221	475	72	18	17	144	.249	852	1360	103	.956
American League Totals—4 Years			463	1319	155	351	60	7	19	146	.266	936	848	65	.965
Major League Totals—13 Years			1148	3230	376	826	132	25	36	290	.256	1788	2208	168	.960

Selected by San Diego Padres' organization in 10th round of free-agent draft, June 8, 1971.
Selected by San Diego Padres' organization in 1st round (first player selected) of free-agent draft, June 5, 1974.
†Traded with First Baseman-Outfielder Dan Briggs to Montreal Expos for Second Baseman Dave Cash, November 27, 1979.
‡Became free agent after refusing option to Denver, July 7, 1980; signed by New York Mets, July 11, 1980.
§Released, December 19, 1980; signed by Chicago White Sox' organization, February 4, 1981.
xGranted free agency, November 10, 1982; signed by Oakland A's, January 18, 1983.
yGranted free agency, November 8, 1984; signed by Pittsburgh Pirates, April 8, 1985.

ROBERTO ALOMAR

Born February 5, 1968, at Salinas, Puerto Rico.
Height, 6.00. Weight, 155.
Throws right and bats left and righthanded.
Son of Sandy Alomar, Sr., infielder with Milwaukee-Atlanta Braves, New York Mets, Chicago White Sox, California Angels, New York Yankees and Texas Rangers, 1964 through 1978; and minor league instructor, San Diego Padres' organization, 1985; and brother of Sandy Alomar, Jr., catcher in San Diego Padres' organization.
Led South Atlantic League second basemen in errors with 35 in 1985.

Year Club	League	Pos.	G.	AB.	R.	H.	2B.	3B.	HR.	RBI.	B.A.	PO.	A.	E.	F.A.
1985—Charleston	S. Atl.	2B-SS	★137	★546	89	160	14	3	0	54	.293	298	339	36	.947
1986—Reno	Calif.	2B	90	356	53	123	16	4	4	49	★.346	198	265	18	.963

Signed as free agent by San Diego Padres' organization, February 16, 1985.

SANTOS ALOMAR JR. (VELAZQUEZ)
(Sandy)

Born June 30, 1967, at Salinas, Puerto Rico.
Height, 6.05. Weight, 200.
Throws right and bats left and righthanded.
Son of Sandy Alomar, Sr., infielder with Milwaukee-Atlanta Braves, New York Mets, Chicago White Sox, California Angels, New York Yankees and Texas Rangers, 1964 through 1978; and minor league instructor, San Diego Padres' organization, 1985; and brother of Roberto Alomar, infielder in San Diego Padres' organization.

Led Northwest League catchers in putouts with 421 in 1984.

Year—Club	League	Pos.	G.	AB.	R.	H.	2B.	3B.	HR.	RBI.	B.A.	PO.	A.	E.	F.A.
1984—Spokane	N'west	*C-1B	59	219	13	47	5	0	0	21	.215	465	51	8	*.985
1985—Charleston	S. Atl.	C-OF	100	352	38	73	7	0	3	43	.207	779	75	18	.979
1986—Beaumont	Texas	C	100	346	36	83	15	1	4	27	.240	505	60	*18	.969

Signed as free agent by San Diego Padres' organization, October 21, 1983.

EDWARD ALLEN AMELUNG
(Ed)

Born April 13, 1959, at Fullerton, Calif.
Height, 6.00. Weight, 185.
Throws and bats lefthanded.
Attended Santa Ana College, Santa Ana, Calif., and San Diego State University, San Diego, Calif.

Major League stolen bases: 1984 (3).
Led Florida State League in total bases with 224 in 1981.

Year—Club	League	Pos.	G.	AB.	R.	H.	2B.	3B.	HR.	RBI.	B.A.	PO.	A.	E.	F.A.
1981—Vero Beach	Fla. St.	OF	*136	*522	84	*155	17	*14	8	75	.297	237	*22	*13	.952
1981—San Antonio	Texas	OF	4	15	1	2	0	0	0	1	.133	9	0	0	1.000
1982—San Antonio	Texas	OF	135	529	96	160	27	4	24	91	.302	301	17	7	.978
1982—Albuquerque	P. C.	OF	2	9	1	2	0	0	0	2	.222	5	0	0	1.000
1983—Albuquerque	P. C.	OF	135	534	90	157	37	8	10	85	.294	256	15	7	.975
1984—Albuquerque	P. C.	OF	107	433	89	152	35	4	15	63	.351	216	8	3	.987
1984—Los Angeles	Nat.	OF	34	46	7	10	0	0	0	4	.217	31	0	0	1.000
1985—Albuquerque	P. C.	OF	137	561	70	163	29	3	8	61	.291	288	*17	5	.984
1986—Albuquerque†	P. C.	OF-1B	82	291	48	82	12	2	6	45	.282	178	4	4	.978
1986—Los Angeles	Nat.	OF	8	11	0	1	0	0	0	0	.091	5	0	0	1.000
Major League Totals—2 Years			42	57	7	11	0	0	0	4	.193	36	0	0	1.000

Signed as free agent by Los Angeles Dodgers' organization, August 20, 1980.
†On disabled list, April 15 to May 28, 1986.

LARRY EUGENE ANDERSEN

Born May 6, 1953, at Portland, Ore.
Height, 6.03. Weight, 205.
Throws and bats righthanded.
Attended Bellevue Community College, Bellevue, Wash.

Pitched 6-0 no-hit victory against Victoria, June 1, 1974.
Major League saves: 1981 (5), 1982 (1), 1984 (4), 1985 (3), 1986 (1). Total—14.
Led Pacific Coast League in saves with 25 in 1978 and 22 in 1983.
Led American Association in balks with 4 in 1975.

Year—Club	League	G.	IP.	W.	L.	Pct.	H.	R.	ER.	SO.	BB.	ERA.
1971—Reno	California	7	24	1	0	1.000	37	20	18	10	9	6.75
1971—Sarasota Indians	Gulf Coast	4	15	0	3	.000	15	7	5	10	7	3.00
1972—Reno	California	27	124	4	14	.222	166	102	90	79	57	6.53
1973—Reno	California	29	164	10	8	.556	173	91	72	115	67	3.95
1974—San Antonio	Texas	25	169	10	6	.625	176	84	72	64	51	3.83
1975—Oklahoma City	Am. Assoc.	25	156	10	11	.476	179	87	73	64	52	4.21
1975—Cleveland	American	3	6	0	0	.000	4	3	3	4	2	4.50
1976—Toledo	Int'national	6	23	0	2	.000	47	33	33	8	6	12.91
1976—Williamsport	Eastern	21	133	9	6	.600	117	47	40	74	34	2.71
1977—Toledo†	Int'national	45	65	5	6	.455	52	20	14	40	37	1.94
1977—Cleveland	American	11	14	0	1	.000	10	7	5	8	9	3.21
1978—Portland	P. Coast	57	99	10	7	.588	92	42	38	65	45	3.45
1979—Tacoma	P. Coast	27	112	10	6	.625	124	59	50	52	32	4.02
1979—Cleveland‡	American	8	17	0	0	.000	25	14	14	7	4	7.41
1980—Portland§	P. Coast	52	93	5	7	.417	78	24	18	65	16	1.74
1981—Seattle	American	41	68	3	3	.500	57	27	20	40	18	2.65
1982—Seattle x	American	40	79⅔	0	0	.000	100	56	53	32	23	5.99
1982—Salt Lake City y	P. Coast	5	6⅔	1	0	1.000	2	0	0	8	3	0.00
1983—Portland	P. Coast	52	70⅓	7	8	.467	63	35	16	64	30	2.05
1983—Philadelphia	National	17	26⅓	1	0	1.000	19	7	7	14	9	2.39
1984—Philadelphia	National	64	90⅔	3	7	.300	85	32	24	54	25	2.38
1985—Philadelphia	National	57	73	3	3	.500	78	41	35	50	26	4.32
1986—Philadelphia z-Houston a	National	48	77⅓	2	1	.667	83	30	26	42	26	3.03
American League Totals—5 Years		103	184⅔	3	4	.429	196	107	95	91	56	4.63
National League Totals—4 Years		186	267⅓	9	11	.450	265	110	92	160	86	3.10
Major League Totals—9 Years		289	452	12	15	.444	461	217	187	251	142	3.72

Selected by Cleveland Indians' organization in 7th round of free-agent draft, June 8, 1971.
†Appeared as first baseman with no chances.
‡Traded to Pittsburgh Pirates for Outfielder Larry Littleton and Pitcher John Burden, December 21, 1979.
§Traded to Seattle Mariners, October 29, 1980, completing deal in which Seattle traded Pitcher Odell Jones to Pittsburgh Pirates for a player to be named later, April 1, 1980.
xOn disabled list, August 11 to September 1, 1982; included rehabilitation disability assignment to Salt Lake City, August 11 to August 31, 1982.
yLoaned to Portland (Philadelphia Phillies' organization), April 1, 1983; sold to Philadelphia Phillies, July 29, 1983.
zReleased, May 13, 1986; signed by Houston Astros, May 16, 1986.
aGranted free agency, November 12, 1986; re-signed by Astros, December 19, 1986.

Year	Club	League	G.	IP.	W.	L.	Pct.	H.	R.	ER.	SO.	BB.	ERA.
1986—Houston	National	2	5	0	0	.000	1	0	0	3	2	0.00

WORLD SERIES RECORD

Year	Club	League	G.	IP.	W.	L.	Pct.	H.	R.	ER.	SO.	BB.	ERA.
1983—Philadelphia	National	2	4	0	0	.000	4	1	1	1	0	2.25

ALLAN LEE ANDERSON

Born January 7, 1964, at Lancaster, Ohio.
Height, 5.11. Weight, 169.
Throws and bats lefthanded.

Led California League in shutouts with 5 in 1984.

Year	Club	League	G.	IP.	W.	L.	Pct.	H.	R.	ER.	SO.	BB.	ERA.
1983—Wisconsin Rapids	Midwest	7	30⅓	0	4	.000	36	28	23	46	17	6.82
1983—Elizabethton	Ap'lachian	6	12⅔	1	3	.250	17	12	12	12	7	8.53
1984—Visalia	California	26	188⅔	12	7	.632	152	80	60	151	105	2.86
1985—Toledo	Int'national	27	176	7	11	.389	176	81	67	94	79	3.43
1986—Toledo	Int'national	11	67	2	5	.286	78	39	34	37	31	4.57
1986—Minnesota†	American	21	84⅓	3	6	.333	106	54	52	51	30	5.55
Major League Totals—1 Year		21	84⅓	3	6	.333	106	54	52	51	30	5.55

Selected by Minnesota Twins' organization in 2nd round of free-agent draft, June 7, 1982.
†Appeared in one game as a pinch-runner.

DAVID CARTER ANDERSON
(Dave)

Born August 1, 1960, at Louisville, Ky.
Height, 6.02. Weight, 185.
Throws and bats righthanded.
Attended Memphis State University, Memphis, Tenn.

Major League stolen bases: 1983 (6), 1984 (15), 1985 (5), 1986 (5). Total—31.
Led Pacific Coast League shortstops in double plays with 81 in 1982.

Year	Club	League	Pos.	G.	AB.	R.	H.	2B.	3B.	HR.	RBI.	B.A.	PO.	A.	E.	F.A.
1981—Vero Beach	Fla. St.	SS	65	200	44	54	8	1	0	18	.270	109	218	23	.934
1982—Albuquerque	P. C.	SS	132	507	100	174	19	7	5	76	.343	223	397	*34	.948
1983—Albuquerque	P. C.	SS	9	27	10	11	1	1	0	3	.407	17	26	1	.977
1983—Los Angeles	Nat.	SS-3B	61	115	12	19	4	2	1	2	.165	56	100	5	.969
1984—Los Angeles	Nat.	SS-3B	121	374	51	94	16	2	3	34	.251	176	359	19	.966
1985—Los Angeles†	Nat.	3B-SS-2B	77	221	24	44	6	0	4	18	.199	61	187	9	.965
1985—Albuquerque	P. C.	SS-3B-2B	28	97	23	28	7	0	3	16	.289	29	62	11	.892
1986—Los Angeles‡	Nat.	3B-SS-2B	92	216	31	53	9	0	1	15	.245	77	159	11	.955
Major League Totals—4 Years			351	926	118	210	35	4	9	69	.227	370	805	44	.964

Selected by Los Angeles Dodgers' organization in 1st round (22nd player selected) of free-agent draft, June 8, 1981.
†On disabled list, April 29 to June 2 and July 31 to September 1, 1985; included rehabilitation disability assignment to Albuquerque, May 17 to June 1 and August 17 to August 31, 1985.
‡On disabled list, June 22 to August 19, 1986.

CHAMPIONSHIP SERIES RECORD

Year	Club	League	Pos.	G.	AB.	R.	H.	2B.	3B.	HR.	RBI.	B.A.	PO.	A.	E.	F.A.
1985—Los Angeles	Nat.	PR-SS-3B	4	5	1	0	0	0	0	0	.000	3	4	0	1.000

RICHARD ARLEN ANDERSON
(Rich)

Born November 29, 1956, at Everett, Wash.
Height, 6.00. Weight, 175.
Throws and bats righthanded.
Attended Everett Community College, Everett, Wash., and University of Washington, Seattle, Wash.

Pitched 8-0 no-hit victory against Shreveport, May 12, 1979.
Major League saves: 1986 (1).

Year	Club	League	G.	IP.	W.	L.	Pct.	H.	R.	ER.	SO.	BB.	ERA.
1978—Little Falls	NYP	14	40	2	3	.400	48	25	10	40	20	2.25
1979—Jackson	Texas	25	131	8	11	.421	124	72	56	71	43	3.85
1980—Jackson	Texas	25	64	3	2	.600	57	24	23	48	17	3.23
1980—Tidewater	Int'national	14	40	1	3	.250	36	18	17	25	15	3.83
1981—Tidewater	Int'national	37	89	3	5	.375	68	34	33	41	45	3.34
1982—Tidewater	Int'national	31	80	4	2	.667	84	35	29	49	23	3.26
1983—Jackson	Texas	13	77⅔	5	1	.833	77	40	31	48	29	3.59
1983—Tidewater	Int'national	15	40	2	1	.667	37	19	18	23	22	4.05
1984—Tidewater†	Int'national	26	130⅓	6	9	.400	118	59	49	93	48	3.38
1985—Tidewater	Int'national	48	95⅓	6	3	.667	79	28	21	54	33	1.98
1986—Tidewater	Int'national	22	84	7	2	.778	76	26	25	56	16	2.68
1986—New York	National	15	49⅔	2	1	.667	45	17	15	21	11	2.72
Major League Totals—1 Year		15	49⅔	2	1	.667	45	17	15	21	11	2.72

Selected by New York Mets' organization in 24th round of free-agent draft, June 6, 1978.
†Granted free agency, October 15, 1984; re-signed by Mets' organization, February 2, 1985.

SCOTT RICHARD ANDERSON

Born August 1, 1962, at Corvallis, Ore.
Height, 6.06. Weight, 190.
Throws and bats righthanded.
Attended Oregon State University, Corvallis, Ore.
Tied for Texas League lead in games started by pitchers with 27 in 1985.

Year Club	League	G.	IP.	W.	L.	Pct.	H.	R.	ER.	SO.	BB.	ERA.
1984—Burlington	Midwest	14	86⅓	3	6	.333	79	33	24	81	28	2.50
1985—Tulsa	Texas	28	174⅓	9	6	.600	177	87	71	123	51	3.67
1986—Tulsa	Texas	10	18⅔	0	0	.000	11	4	3	13	8	1.45
1986—Oklahoma City	Am. Assoc.	48	82	5	7	.417	82	36	27	51	28	2.96

Selected by Texas Rangers' organization in 7th round of free-agent draft, June 4, 1984.

JOAQUIN ANDUJAR

Name pronounced Wah-KEEN AHN-doo-hahr.

Born December 21, 1952, at San Pedro de Macoris, Dominican Republic.
Height, 6.00. Weight, 180.
Throws right and bats left and righthanded.
Major League saves: 1978 (1), 1979 (4), 1980 (2), 1983 (1), 1986 (1). Total—9.
Led National League in hit batsmen with 11 in 1985 and tied for lead with 7 in 1984.
Tied for National League lead in shutouts with 4 in 1984.
Tied for National League lead in balks with 5 in 1976.
Named National League Comeback Player of the Year by THE SPORTING NEWS, 1984.
Named pitcher on THE SPORTING NEWS National League All-Star fielding team, 1984.

Year Club	League	G.	IP.	W.	L.	Pct.	H.	R.	ER.	SO.	BB.	ERA.
1970—Bradenton Reds	Gulf Coast	12	82	3	5	.375	*86	*58	*38	88	56	4.17
1971—Sioux Falls	Northern	19	75	4	7	.364	61	67	53	82	63	6.36
1972—Three Rivers	Eastern	22	112	7	6	.538	87	59	44	101	73	3.54
1973—Indianapolis	Am. Assoc.	11	40	2	5	.286	42	45	40	23	45	9.00
1973—Three Rivers†	Eastern	10	59	5	2	.714	38	29	13	39	38	1.98
1974—Indianapolis	Am. Assoc.	33	111	8	8	.500	85	62	44	92	93	3.57
1975—Three Rivers‡§	Eastern	18	62	4	8	.333	57	36	28	44	40	4.06
1976—Houston	National	28	172	9	10	.474	163	74	69	59	75	3.61
1977—Houston	National	26	159	11	8	.579	149	80	65	69	64	3.68
1978—Houston x	National	35	111	5	7	.417	88	45	42	55	58	3.41
1979—Houston	National	46	194	12	12	.500	168	86	74	77	88	3.43
1980—Houston	National	35	122	3	8	.273	132	59	53	75	43	3.91
1981—Houston y-St. Louis z	National	20	79	8	4	.667	85	41	36	37	23	4.10
1982—St. Louis	National	38	265⅔	15	10	.600	237	85	73	137	50	2.47
1983—St. Louis	National	39	225	6	16	.273	215	112	104	125	75	4.16
1984—St. Louis	National	36	*261⅓	*20	14	.588	218	104	97	147	70	3.34
1985—St. Louis a	National	38	269⅔	21	12	.636	265	113	102	112	82	3.40
1986—Oakland bc	American	28	155⅓	12	7	.632	139	70	66	72	56	3.82
National League Totals—10 Years		341	1858⅔	110	101	.521	1720	799	715	893	628	3.46
American League Totals—1 Year		28	155⅓	12	7	.632	139	70	66	72	56	3.82
Major League Totals—11 Years		369	2014	122	108	.530	1859	869	781	965	684	3.49

Signed as free agent by Cincinnati Reds' organization, November 14, 1969.
†On disabled list, August 5 to August 15, 1973.
‡On disabled list, May 11 to July 4, 1975.
§Traded to Houston Astros for two minor league players to be named later, October 24, 1975; Cincinnati Reds' organization acquired Pitchers Carlos Alfonso and Luis Sanchez to complete deal, December 12, 1975.
xOn disabled list, July 8 to July 30, 1978.
yTraded to St. Louis Cardinals for Outfielder Tony Scott, June 7, 1981.
zGranted free agency, November 13, 1981; re-signed by Cardinals, December 29, 1981.
aTraded to Oakland A's for Catcher Mike Heath and Pitcher Tim Conroy, December 10, 1985.
bOn suspended list, April 7 to April 12, 1986.
cOn disabled list, June 7 to July 18, 1986.

CHAMPIONSHIP SERIES RECORD

Established National League Championship Series record for most runs allowed (10) and most earned runs allowed (8), six-game Series, 1985.

Year Club	League	G.	IP.	W.	L.	Pct.	H.	R.	ER.	SO.	BB.	ERA.
1980—Houston	National	1	1	0	0	.000	0	0	0	0	1	0.00
1982—St. Louis	National	1	6⅔	1	0	1.000	6	2	2	4	2	2.70
1985—St. Louis	National	2	10⅓	0	1	.000	14	10	8	9	4	6.97
Championship Series Totals—3 Years		4	18	1	1	.500	20	12	10	13	7	5.00

WORLD SERIES RECORD

Year Club	League	G.	IP.	W.	L.	Pct.	H.	R.	ER.	SO.	BB.	ERA.
1982—St. Louis	National	2	13⅓	2	0	1.000	10	3	2	4	1	1.35
1985—St. Louis	National	2	4	0	1	.000	10	4	4	3	4	9.00
World Series Totals—2 Years		4	17⅓	2	1	.667	20	7	6	7	5	3.12

ALL-STAR GAME RECORD

Year League		IP.	W.	L.	Pct.	H.	R.	ER.	SO.	BB.	ERA.
1979—National		2	0	0	.000	2	2	1	0	1	4.50

Named to National League All-Star Team for 1985 game; declined and replaced by Ron Darling.
Named to National League All-Star Team for 1984 game; replaced due to injury by Fernando Valenzuela.
Member of National League All-Star Team in 1977; did not play.

LUIS ANTONIO AQUINO (COLON)

Name pronounced A-Keno.

Born May 19, 1965, at Rio Piedras, Puerto Rico.
Height, 6.00. Weight, 155.
Throws and bats righthanded.

Led Southern League in saves with 20 and tied for lead in games finished in relief with 42 in 1985.
Led Carolina League in games finished in relief with 42 in 1984.

Year	Club	League	G.	IP.	W.	L.	Pct.	H.	R.	ER.	SO.	BB.	ERA.
1982—Bradenton Blue Jays		Gulf Coast	13	73⅓	4	7	.364	60	33	27	52	17	3.31
1983—Florence		S. Atlantic	29	133⅔	7	9	.438	128	91	78	104	61	5.25
1984—Kinston		Carolina	★53	70	5	6	.455	50	21	21	78	37	2.70
1984—Knoxville		Southern	3	4	0	0	.000	3	4	4	7	3	9.00
1985—Knoxville		Southern	50	83	5	7	.417	58	29	24	82	32	2.60
1986—Syracuse		Int'national	43	84⅓	3	7	.300	70	30	27	60	34	2.88
1986—Toronto		American	7	11⅓	1	1	.500	14	8	8	5	3	6.35
Major League Totals—1 Year			7	11⅓	1	1	.500	14	8	8	5	3	6.35

Signed as free agent by Toronto Blue Jays' organization, June 15, 1981.

ANTONIO RAFAEL ARMAS (MACHADO)

(Tony)

Born July 2, 1953, at Anzoategui, Venezuela.
Height, 6.01. Weight, 200.
Throws and bats righthanded.

Established major league records for most putouts (11) and chances accepted by right fielder, game (12), June 12, 1982.
Tied major league record for fewest double plays by outfielder, season, for leader in most double plays (4), 1977.
Major League stolen bases: 1977 (1), 1978 (1), 1979 (1), 1980 (5), 1981 (5), 1982 (2), 1984 (1). Total—16.
Led American League in total bases with 339 in 1984.
Led American League batters in strikeouts with 115 in 1981 and 156 in 1984.
Tied for American League lead in grounding into double plays with 31 in 1983.
Tied for American League lead in double plays by outfielders with 4 in 1977.
Named American League Player of the Year by THE SPORTING NEWS, 1981.
Named outfielder on THE SPORTING NEWS American League All-Star Team, 1981 and 1984.
Named outfielder on THE SPORTING NEWS American League Silver Slugger team, 1984.

Year	Club	League	Pos.	G.	AB.	R.	H.	2B.	3B.	HR.	RBI.	B.A.	PO.	A.	E.	F.A.
1971—Monroe		W. Car.	OF	31	88	7	20	3	0	1	10	.227	37	3	6	.870
1971—Bradenton Pir.		Gulf C.	OF	43	169	12	39	3	3	0	17	.231	★98	5	3	.972
1972—Gastonia		W. Car.	OF	117	399	50	106	18	4	9	51	.266	165	7	8	.956
1973—Sherbrooke†		East.	OF	84	302	46	91	15	5	11	45	.301	150	6	8	.951
1974—Thetford Mines		East.	OF	★137	476	64	132	26	3	15	81	.277	★329	18	10	.972
1975—Charleston		Int.	OF	128	450	65	135	28	4	12	72	.300	220	4	3	.987
1976—Charleston		Int.	OF-1B	114	409	62	96	24	1	21	67	.235	210	8	7	.969
1976—Pittsburgh‡		Nat.	OF	4	6	0	2	0	0	0	1	.333	3	0	0	1.000
1977—Oakland§		Amer.	OF-SS	118	363	26	87	8	2	13	53	.240	294	9	6	.981
1978—Oakland x		Amer.	OF	91	239	17	51	6	1	2	13	.213	214	3	2	.991
1979—Oakland y		Amer.	OF	80	278	29	69	9	3	11	34	.248	194	7	5	.976
1980—Oakland		Amer.	OF	158	628	87	175	18	8	35	109	.279	374	17	10	.975
1981—Oakland		Amer.	OF	●109	440	51	115	24	3	●22	76	.261	259	8	2	.993
1982—Oakland za		Amer.	OF	138	536	58	125	19	2	28	89	.233	333	9	6	.983
1983—Boston		Amer.	OF	145	574	77	125	23	2	36	107	.218	326	5	5	.985
1984—Boston		Amer.	OF	157	639	107	171	29	5	★43	★123	.268	329	4	9	.974
1985—Boston b		Amer.	OF	103	385	50	102	17	5	23	64	.265	173	3	3	.983
1986—Boston cd		Amer.	OF	121	425	40	112	21	4	11	58	.264	247	4	8	.969
National League Totals—1 Year				4	6	0	2	0	0	0	1	.333	3	0	0	1.000
American League Totals—10 Years				1220	4507	542	1132	174	35	224	726	.251	2743	69	56	.980
Major League Totals—11 Years				1224	4513	542	1134	174	35	224	727	.251	2746	69	56	.980

Signed as free agent by Pittsburgh Pirates' organization, January 18, 1971.
†On disabled list, May 27 to July 12, 1973.
‡Traded with Pitchers Dave Giusti, Doc Medich, Doug Bair and Rick Langford and Outfielder Mitchell Page to Oakland A's for Infielders Tommy Helms and Phil Garner and Pitcher Chris Batton, March 15, 1977.
§On disabled list, August 5 to September 1, 1977.
xOn disabled list, April 28 to June 2, 1978.
yOn disabled list, April 15 to June 5, 1979.
zOn disabled list, May 13 to May 28, 1982.
aTraded with Catcher Jeff Newman to Boston Red Sox for Third Baseman Carney Lansford, Outfielder Garry Hancock and a player to be named later, December 6, 1982; Oakland A's acquired Pitcher Jerry King to complete deal, December 20, 1982.
bOn disabled list, June 17 to July 26, 1985.
cOn disabled list, July 12 to July 27, 1986.
dGranted free agency, November 12, 1986.

DIVISION SERIES RECORD

Year Club League	Pos.	G.	AB.	R.	H.	2B.	3B.	HR.	RBI.	B.A.	PO.	A.	E.	F.A.
1981—Oakland.................. Amer.	OF	3	11	1	6	2	0	0	3	.545	6	0	1	.857

CHAMPIONSHIP SERIES RECORD

Year Club League	Pos.	G.	AB.	R.	H.	2B.	3B.	HR.	RBI.	B.A.	PO.	A.	E.	F.A.
1981—Oakland.................. Amer.	OF	3	12	0	2	0	0	0	0	.167	5	2	0	1.000
1986—Boston.................... Amer.	OF	5	16	1	2	1	0	0	0	.125	12	0	0	1.000
Championship Series Totals—2 Years.....		8	28	1	4	1	0	0	0	.143	17	2	0	1.000

WORLD SERIES RECORD

Year Club League	Pos.	G.	AB.	R.	H.	2B.	3B.	HR.	RBI.	B.A.	PO.	A.	E.	F.A.
1986—Boston.................... Amer.	PH	1	1	0	0	0	0	0	0	.000	0	0	0	.000

ALL-STAR GAME RECORD

Year League	Pos.	AB.	R.	H.	2B.	3B.	HR.	RBI.	B.A.	PO.	A.	E.	F.A.
1981—American	OF	1	0	0	0	0	0	0	.000	0	0	0	.000

Member of American League All-Star Team in 1984; did not play.

MICHAEL DENNIS ARMSTRONG
(Mike)

Born March 7, 1954, at Glen Cove, N.Y.
Height, 6.03. Weight, 206.
Throws and bats righthanded.
Attended University of Miami, Coral Gables, Fla.

Major League saves: 1982 (6), 1983 (3), 1984 (1). Total—10.
Led Eastern League pitchers in games started with 29 in 1977.

Year Club	League	G.	IP.	W.	L.	Pct.	H.	R.	ER.	SO.	BB.	ERA.
1974—Tampa...............................	Florida St.	6	16	0	2	.000	26	17	17	14	18	9.56
1974—Seattle...............................	Northwest	15	102	6	7	.462	85	45	30	86	47	2.65
1975—Three Rivers	Eastern	25	150	5	10	.333	116	55	45	86	44	2.70
1976—Three Rivers	Eastern	24	146	10	10	.500	143	77	57	91	52	3.51
1977—Three Rivers	Eastern	30	184	*16	10	.615	185	91	77	107	83	3.77
1978—Chattanooga	Southern	31	74	9	6	.600	61	34	25	54	37	3.04
1978—Indianapolis	Am. Assoc.	16	23	1	2	.333	26	18	17	17	17	6.65
1979—Nashville†	Southern	32	64	5	1	.833	58	30	24	53	29	3.38
1979—Amarillo............................	Texas	7	31	2	3	.400	32	15	12	34	14	3.48
1979—Hawaii...............................	P. Coast	3	7	0	0	.000	6	2	2	4	5	2.57
1980—Hawaii...............................	P. Coast	42	74	4	4	.500	48	18	16	67	26	1.95
1980—San Diego	National	11	14	0	0	.000	16	10	9	14	13	5.79
1981—Hawaii...............................	P. Coast	22	36	5	2	.714	21	7	6	39	12	1.50
1981—San Diego‡	National	10	12	0	2	.000	14	9	8	9	11	6.00
1982—Omaha...............................	Am. Assoc.	15	28	4	2	.667	19	12	10	27	20	3.21
1982—Kansas City.......................	American	52	112⅔	5	5	.500	88	45	40	75	43	3.20
1983—Kansas City§	American	58	102⅔	10	7	.588	86	53	44	52	45	3.86
1984—Fort Lauderdale x	Florida St.	8	11⅔	1	0	1.000	9	2	1	15	5	0.77
1984—New York	American	36	54⅓	3	2	.600	47	21	21	43	26	3.48
1985—Columbus...........................	Int'national	21	40⅔	2	2	.500	49	31	30	40	26	6.64
1985—New York	American	9	14⅔	0	0	.000	9	5	5	11	2	3.07
1986—Columbus...........................	Int'national	31	106	6	9	.400	103	54	48	103	53	4.08
1986—New York y	American	7	8⅔	0	1	.000	13	9	9	8	5	9.35
National League Totals—2 Years		21	26	0	2	.000	30	19	17	23	24	5.88
American League Totals—5 Years ...		162	293	18	15	.545	243	133	119	189	121	3.66
Major League Totals—7 Years		183	319	18	17	.514	273	152	136	212	145	3.84

Selected by Cleveland Indians' organization in 9th round of free-agent draft, June 6, 1972.
Selected by Cincinnati Reds' organization in 1st round (24th player selected) of free-agent draft, January 9, 1974.
†Traded to San Diego Padres' organization for Third Baseman Paul O'Neill, July 25, 1979.
‡Traded to Kansas City Royals' organization for a player to be named later, April 4, 1982; San Diego Padres' organization acquired Pitcher Walt Vanderbush to complete deal, December 8, 1982.
§Traded with Catcher Duane Dewey to New York Yankees for First Baseman Steve Balboni and Pitcher Roger Erickson, December 8, 1983.
xOn New York Yankees disabled list, March 27 to June 16, 1984; included rehabilitation disability assignment to Fort Lauderdale, May 31 to June 16, 1984.
yReleased, December 22, 1986.

SCOTT GENTRY ARNOLD

Born August 18, 1962, at Lexington, Ky.
Height, 6.02. Weight, 210.
Throws and bats righthanded.
Attended Miami University, Oxford, O.

Tied for Appalachian League lead in games started by pitchers with 13 in 1984.

Year Club	League	G.	IP.	W.	L.	Pct.	H.	R.	ER.	SO.	BB.	ERA.
1984—Johnson City	Ap'lachian	14	91⅓	4	5	.444	80	38	31	90	38	3.05
1984—Springfield	Midwest	1	6	0	1	.000	6	6	6	9	0	9.00
1985—Savannah...........................	S. Atlantic	24	169	8	9	.471	131	76	62	169	70	3.30
1986—St. Petersburg...................	Florida St.	22	136⅓	10	5	.667	121	57	41	85	39	2.71
1986—Arkansas...........................	Texas	5	28⅓	4	1	.800	24	15	12	23	14	3.81

Selected by New York Yankees' organization in 40th round of free-agent draft, June 6, 1983.
Selected by St. Louis Cardinals' organization in 5th round of free-agent draft, June 4, 1984.

TONY DALE ARNOLD

Born May 3, 1959, at El Paso, Tex.
Height, 6.00. Weight, 185.
Throws and bats righthanded.
Attended University of Texas, Austin, Tex.

Year Club	League	G.	IP.	W.	L.	Pct.	H.	R.	ER.	SO.	BB.	ERA.
1981—Bluefield	Ap'lachian	5	23	2	1	.667	32	22	21	15	11	8.22
1981—Miami	Florida St.	6	22	2	1	.667	21	4	3	8	3	1.23
1982—Hagerstown	Carolina	12	80⅓	8	2	.800	78	38	34	48	16	3.81
1982—Charlotte	Southern	15	88	5	6	.455	103	55	51	49	29	5.22
1983—Charlotte	Southern	44	106⅔	7	5	.583	122	47	39	48	36	3.29
1983—Rochester	Int'national	3	7⅔	0	1	.000	10	5	3	5	5	3.52
1984—Charlotte	Southern	16	83	7	5	.583	93	35	29	25	25	3.14
1984—Rochester	Int'national	14	91⅓	5	6	.455	92	50	46	55	24	4.53
1985—Charlotte	Southern	31	160⅔	11	7	.611	163	74	69	85	21	3.87
1986—Rochester†	Int'national	38	87⅔	4	3	.571	92	25	19	49	14	1.95
1986—Baltimore	American	11	25⅓	0	2	.000	25	15	10	7	11	3.55
Major League Totals—1 Year		11	25⅓	0	2	.000	25	15	10	7	11	3.55

Selected by Baltimore Orioles' organization in 10th round of free-agent draft, June 8, 1981.
†On disabled list, April 17 to April 30, 1986.

BRADLEY JAMES ARNSBERG
(Brad)

Born August 20, 1963, at Seattle, Wash.
Height, 6.04. Weight, 205.
Throws and bats righthanded.
Attended Merced College, Merced, Calif.
Brother of Tim Arnsberg, pitcher in Houston Astros' organization.

Pitched 5-0 no-hit victory against Savannah, May 24, 1984.
Led International League pitchers in games started with 28 and balks with 5 in 1986.
Tied for South Atlantic League lead in complete games with 10 and shutouts with 4 in 1984.
Named Eastern League Pitcher of the Year, 1985.

Year Club	League	G.	IP.	W.	L.	Pct.	H.	R.	ER.	SO.	BB.	ERA.
1984—Greensboro	S. Atlantic	23	158⅔	12	5	.706	121	61	52	112	59	2.95
1985—Albany†	Eastern	20	141⅓	●14	2	★.875	105	34	25	82	35	★1.59
1986—Columbus	Int'national	28	★177⅓	8	●12	.400	168	●106	●83	96	53	4.21
1986—New York	American	2	8	0	0	.000	13	3	3	3	1	3.38
Major League Totals—1 Year		2	8	0	0	.000	13	3	3	3	1	3.38

Selected by Cleveland Indians' organization in 19th round of free-agent draft, June 8, 1981.
Selected by St. Louis Cardinals' organization in secondary phase of free-agent draft, January 12, 1982.
Selected by Baltimore Orioles' organization in secondary phase of free-agent draft, June 7, 1982.
Selected by California Angels' organization in secondary phase of free-agent draft, January 11, 1983.
Selected by New York Yankees' organization in secondary phase of free-agent draft, June 6, 1983.
†On disabled list, May 12 to May 24 and June 23 to July 22, 1985.

FERNANDO ARROYO

Born March 21, 1952, at Sacramento, Calif.
Height, 6.02. Weight, 190.
Throws and bats righthanded.

Pitched seven-inning 5-0 perfect game against West Palm Beach, July 8, 1971.

Year Club	League	G.	IP.	W.	L.	Pct.	H.	R.	ER.	SO.	BB.	ERA.
1970—Bristol	Appalachian	9	61	4	1	.800	45	28	14	53	21	2.07
1971—Lakeland	Fla. State	25	193	11	11	.500	153	71	54	117	53	2.52
1972—Montgomery	Southern	28	157	8	9	.471	142	81	67	82	55	3.84
1973—Montgomery	Southern	23	159	9	8	.529	153	71	54	74	50	3.06
1974—Evansville	Am. Assoc.	35	87	6	4	.600	93	50	41	45	45	4.24
1975—Evansville	Am. Assoc.	11	86	5	4	.556	82	37	25	44	18	2.62
1975—Detroit	American	14	53	2	1	.667	56	28	27	25	22	4.58
1976—Evansville	Am. Assoc.	44	102	5	8	.385	120	74	54	56	41	4.76
1977—Detroit	American	38	209	8	18	.308	227	102	97	60	52	4.18
1978—Evansville	Am. Assoc.	20	105	4	10	.286	124	56	48	45	30	4.11
1978—Detroit†	American	2	4	0	0	.000	8	4	4	1	0	9.00
1979—Evansville	Am. Assoc.	19	114	7	4	.636	113	50	38	39	34	3.00
1979—Detroit‡	American	6	12	1	1	.500	17	11	11	7	4	8.25
1980—Toledo	Int'national	9	72	6	1	.857	56	22	13	36	14	1.63
1980—Minnesota	American	21	92	6	6	.500	97	55	48	27	32	4.70
1981—Minnesota	American	23	128	7	10	.412	144	66	56	39	34	3.94
1982—Minnesota§-Oakland	American	16	36	0	1	.000	40	22	21	13	13	5.25
1982—Tacoma x-Edmonton	P. Coast	18	48	2	3	.400	57	31	21	22	17	3.94
1983—Denver y	Am. Assoc.	23	162⅔	★14	4	★.778	188	80	75	43	30	4.15
1984—Denver z	Am. Assoc.	5	30⅔	4	1	.800	30	16	15	11	8	4.40
1984—Yucatan a	Mexican	11	87⅓	8	3	.727	64	20	15	29	7	1.55
1985—Yucatan b	Mexican	7	38	2	3	.400	42	18	18	10	8	4.26
1986—San Jose c-Modesto	California	6	33⅔	2	4	.333	33	17	15	17	4	4.01
1986—Tacoma	P. Coast	15	101⅔	7	4	.636	112	56	49	24	22	4.34
1986—Oakland d	American	1	0	0	0	.000	0	0	0	0	3	.....
Major League Totals—8 Years		121	534	24	37	.393	589	288	264	172	160	4.45

Selected by Detroit Tigers' organization in 9th round of free-agent draft, June 4, 1970.
†On disabled list, March 27 to May 3, 1978.
‡Traded to Minnesota Twins' organization for Pitcher Jeff Holly, December 5, 1979.
§Released, May 18, 1982; signed by Oakland A's organization, May 25, 1982.
xReleased, July 27, 1982; signed by Edmonton (Chicago White Sox' organization), July 29, 1982.
yReleased, February 7, 1984; re-signed by Denver (Chicago White Sox' organization), February 29, 1984.
zLoaned to Yucatan of Mexican League, May 11, 1984; returned, August 20, 1984.
aSold to Yucatan of Mexican League, December 5, 1984.
bGranted free agency, October 15, 1985; signed by San Jose (Independent), April 11, 1986.
cReleased, May 5, 1986; signed by Modesto (Oakland A's organization), May 29, 1986.
dGranted free agency, October 15, 1986.

RANDALL CARL ASADOOR
(Randy)

Born October 20, 1962, at Fresno, Calif.
Height, 6.01. Weight, 185.
Throws and bats righthanded.
Received degree from Fresno State University, Fresno, Calif.

Major League stolen bases: 1986 (1).
Led Pacific Coast League third basemen in putouts with 90, assists with 195 and total chances with 308 in 1985.

Year	Club	League	Pos.	G.	AB.	R.	H.	2B.	3B.	HR.	RBI.	B.A.	PO.	A.	E.	F.A.
1983—Tulsa	Texas		3B-SS	46	157	15	43	12	0	8	28	.274	26	65	12	.883
1984—Tulsa†	Texas		3B-SS	124	425	65	106	22	3	16	53	.249	70	208	28	.908
1985—Las Vegas	P. C.		3B-1B	126	413	57	105	27	0	17	58	.254	107	199	23	.930
1986—Las Vegas	P. C.		3B-OF	125	396	69	111	16	10	13	52	.280	93	214	24	.927
1986—San Diego	Nat.		3B-2B	15	55	9	20	5	0	0	7	.364	12	31	5	.896
Major League Totals—1 Year				15	55	9	20	5	0	0	7	.364	12	31	5	.896

Selected by Baltimore Orioles' organization in 11th round of free-agent draft, June 3, 1980.
Selected by Texas Rangers' organization in 3rd round of free-agent draft, June 6, 1983.
†Traded to San Diego Padres for Pitcher Mitch Williams, April 6, 1985.

ALAN DEAN ASHBY

Born July 8, 1951, at Long Beach, Calif.
Height, 6.02. Weight, 195.
Throws right and bats left and righthanded.
Attended Los Angeles Harbor Junior College, Wilmington, Calif.

Tied National League record for most games, switch-hit home runs, season (1), September 27, 1982.
Major League stolen bases: 1975 (3), 1978 (1), 1982 (2), 1986 (1). Total—7.
Led National League in passed balls with 14 in 1980.
Led California League catchers in double plays with 12 in 1971.

Year	Club	League	Pos.	G.	AB.	R.	H.	2B.	3B.	HR.	RBI.	B.A.	PO.	A.	E.	F.A.
1969—Sarasota Indians	Gulf C.		C	48	117	10	28	3	1	0	14	.239	219	20	2	*.992
1970—Reno†	Calif.		C	40	121	15	23	5	1	3	18	.190	321	27	7	.980
1971—Jacksonville	South.		C	13	35	4	7	2	0	0	8	.200	76	6	1	.988
1971—Reno‡	Calif.		C-3B	77	239	52	70	14	1	18	60	.293	492	59	10	.982
1972—Portland	P. C.		C	95	291	33	65	9	2	9	28	.223	601	50	8	.988
1973—Ok.C.§-Evan.	A. A.		C-OF	41	124	20	28	8	0	3	16	.226	253	26	2	.993
1973—Cleveland	Amer.		C	11	29	4	5	1	0	1	3	.172	45	0	1	.978
1974—Oklahoma City	A. A		C	66	211	26	60	19	1	2	24	.284	405	33	8	.982
1974—Cleveland	Amer.		C	10	7	1	1	0	0	0	0	.143	12	0	0	1.000
1975—Cleveland	Amer.		C-1B-3B	90	254	32	57	10	1	5	32	.224	450	43	6	.988
1976—Cleveland xy	Amer.		C-1B-3B	89	247	26	59	5	1	4	32	.239	476	52	7	.987
1977—Toronto	Amer.		C	124	396	25	83	16	3	2	29	.210	619	71	11	.984
1978—Toronto z	Amer.		C	81	264	27	69	15	0	9	29	.261	399	38	6	.986
1979—Houston a	Nat.		C	108	336	25	68	15	2	2	35	.202	548	57	8	.988
1980—Houston	Nat.		C	116	352	30	90	19	2	3	48	.256	608	60	6	.991
1981—Houston	Nat.		C	83	255	20	69	13	0	4	33	.271	434	58	9	.982
1982—Houston b	Nat.		C	100	339	40	87	14	2	12	49	.257	530	55	14	.977
1983—Houston c	Nat.		C	87	275	31	63	18	1	8	34	.229	435	56	13	.974
1984—Houston d	Nat.		C	66	191	16	50	7	0	4	27	.262	303	42	5	.986
1985—Houston e	Nat.		C	65	189	20	53	8	0	8	25	.280	312	37	8	.978
1986—Houston f	Nat.		C	120	315	24	81	15	0	7	38	.257	632	43	10	.985
American League Totals—6 Years				405	1197	115	274	47	5	21	125	.229	2001	204	31	.986
National League Totals—8 Years				745	2252	206	561	109	7	48	289	.249	3802	408	73	.983
Major League Totals—14 Years				1150	3449	321	835	156	12	69	414	.242	5803	612	104	.984

Selected by Cleveland Indians' organization in 3rd round of free-agent draft, June 5, 1969.
†On military list, January 1 to May 23, 1970.
‡On temporary inactive list, August 27 to September 13, 1971.
§Loaned to Evansville (Milwaukee Brewers' organization), May 22, 1973; returned, July 2, 1973.
xOn disabled list, August 9, 1976 through remainder of season.
yTraded with Outfielder-First Baseman Doug Howard to Toronto Blue Jays for Pitcher Al Fitzmorris, November 5, 1976.
zTraded to Houston Astros for Pitcher Mark Lemongello, Outfielder Joe Cannon and Shortstop Pedro Hernandez, November 27, 1978.
aOn disabled list, August 30 to September 17, 1979.
bGranted free agency, November 10, 1982; re-signed by Astros, December 21, 1982.
cOn disabled list, June 27 to July 24, 1983.
dOn disabled list, April 25 to May 31, 1984.

eOn disabled list, July 29 to September 7, 1985.
fGranted free agency, November 12, 1986; re-signed by Astros, December 19, 1986.

DIVISION SERIES RECORD

Year	Club	League	Pos.	G.	AB.	R.	H.	2B.	3B.	HR.	RBI.	B.A.	PO.	A.	E.	F.A.
1981—Houston		Nat.	C	3	9	1	1	0	0	1	2	.111	24	2	0	1.000

CHAMPIONSHIP SERIES RECORD

Year	Club	League	Pos.	G.	AB.	R.	H.	2B.	3B.	HR.	RBI.	B.A.	PO.	A.	E.	F.A.
1980—Houston		Nat.	C-PH	2	8	0	1	0	0	0	1	.125	11	2	0	1.000
1986—Houston		Nat.	C	6	23	2	3	1	0	1	2	.130	59	1	0	1.000
Championship Series Totals—2 Years				8	31	2	4	1	0	1	3	.129	70	3	0	1.000

PAUL ANDRE ASSENMACHER

Born December 10, 1960, at Detroit, Mich.
Height, 6.03. Weight, 195.
Throws and bats lefthanded.
Attended Aquinas College, Grand Rapids, Mich.

Major League saves: 1986 (7).

Year	Club	League	G.	IP.	W.	L.	Pct.	H.	R.	ER.	SO.	BB.	ERA.
1983—Bradenton Braves		Gulf Coast	10	36⅔	1	0	1.000	35	14	9	44	4	2.21
1984—Durham		Carolina	26	147⅓	6	11	.353	153	78	70	147	52	4.28
1985—Durham		Carolina	14	38⅓	3	2	.600	38	16	14	36	13	3.29
1985—Greenville		Southern	29	52⅔	6	0	1.000	47	16	15	59	11	2.56
1986—Atlanta		National	61	68⅓	7	3	.700	61	23	19	56	26	2.50
Major League Totals—1 Year			61	68⅓	7	3	.700	61	23	19	56	26	2.50

Signed as free agent by Atlanta Braves' organization, July 10, 1983.

KEITH ROWE ATHERTON

Born February 19, 1959, at Mathews, Va.
Height, 6.04. Weight, 200.
Throws and bats righthanded.

Major League saves: 1983 (4), 1984 (2), 1985 (3), 1986 (10). Total—19.
Led Eastern League in complete games with 13 in 1980.
Tied for Northwest League lead in shutouts with 2 in 1978.

Year	Club	League	G.	IP.	W.	L.	Pct.	H.	R.	ER.	SO.	BB.	ERA.
1978—Bend		Northwest	12	92	7	3	.700	86	44	35	81	40	3.42
1979—Waterbury		Eastern	4	21	0	3	.000	28	23	13	7	13	5.57
1979—Modesto		California	21	146	9	8	.529	190	107	97	103	51	5.98
1980—West Haven		Eastern	27	190	11	12	.478	185	101	87	117	58	4.12
1981—West Haven		Eastern	27	175	11	13	.458	174	83	70	116	64	3.60
1982—Tacoma		P. Coast	28	★200	12	9	.571	214	108	97	128	54	4.37
1983—Tacoma		P. Coast	26	120⅓	3	8	.273	117	60	53	93	44	3.96
1983—Oakland†		American	29	68⅓	2	5	.286	53	22	21	40	23	2.77
1984—Oakland		American	57	104	7	6	.538	110	51	50	58	39	4.33
1985—Oakland‡		American	56	104⅔	4	7	.364	89	51	50	77	42	4.30
1986—Oakland§-Minnesota		American	60	97	6	10	.375	100	47	44	67	46	4.08
Major League Totals—4 Years			202	374	19	28	.404	352	171	165	242	150	3.97

Selected by Oakland A's organization in 2nd round of free-agent draft, June 6, 1978.
†Struck out in only at bat during season when designated hitter took the field.
‡On disabled list, July 24 to August 13, 1985.
§Traded to Minnesota Twins for a player to be named later and cash, May 20, 1986; Oakland A's organization acquired Pitcher Eric Broersma to complete deal, May 23, 1986.

DONALD GLENN AUGUST
(Don)

Born July 3, 1963, at Inglewood, Calif.
Height, 6.03. Weight, 190.
Throws and bats righthanded.
Attended Chapman College, Orange, Calif.

Tied for Pacific Coast League lead in games started by pitchers with 27 in 1986.
Member of 1984 U.S. Olympic baseball team.

Year	Club	League	G.	IP.	W.	L.	Pct.	H.	R.	ER.	SO.	BB.	ERA.
1985—Columbus		Southern	27	176⅓	14	8	.636	183	77	58	78	49	2.96
1986—Tucson†-Vancouver		P. Coast	27	179	10	10	.500	192	88	67	70	51	3.37

Selected by Houston Astros' organization in 1st round (17th player selected) of free-agent draft, June 4, 1984.
†Traded with a player to be named later to Milwaukee Brewers for Pitcher Danny Darwin, August 15, 1986; Milwaukee organization acquired Pitcher Mark Knudson to complete deal, August 21, 1986.

WALTER WAYNE BACKMAN
(Wally)

Born September 22, 1959, at Hillsboro, Ore.
Height, 5.09. Weight, 160.
Throws right and bats right and lefthanded.

Major League stolen bases: 1980 (2), 1981 (1), 1982 (8), 1984 (32), 1985 (30), 1986 (13). Total—86.
Tied for National League lead in sacrifice hits with 14 in 1985.
Led International League in bases on balls received with 87 in 1980.
Led Carolina League in caught stealing with 17 in 1978.

Year Club	League	Pos.	G.	AB.	R.	H.	2B.	3B.	HR.	RBI.	B.A.	PO.	A.	E.	F.A.
1977—Little Falls	NYP	SS-3B	69	255	44	83	10	2	6	30	.325	96	185	19	.937
1978—Lynchburg	Carol.	SS	132	494	86	149	19	●9	3	38	.302	★202	★329	30	★.947
1979—Jackson	Texas	SS-2B	110	404	63	114	11	5	2	19	.282	184	259	31	.935
1980—Tidewater	Int.	2B-SS	125	400	53	117	15	5	1	51	.293	237	320	22	.962
1980—New York	Nat.	2B-SS	27	93	12	30	1	1	0	9	.323	62	55	1	.992
1981—New York	Nat.	2B-3B	26	36	5	10	2	0	0	0	.278	14	21	2	.946
1981—Tidewater†‡	Int.	SS-3B-2B	21	59	6	9	3	1	0	6	.153	12	38	1	.980
1982—New York§	Nat.	2B-3B-SS	96	261	37	71	13	2	3	22	.272	173	209	16	.960
1983—New York	Nat.	2B-3B	26	42	6	7	0	1	0	3	.167	16	15	2	.939
1983—Tidewater	Int.	2B-SS-3B	101	361	69	114	11	3	1	28	.316	175	278	13	.972
1984—New York	Nat.	2B-SS	128	436	68	122	19	2	1	26	.280	223	306	10	.981
1985—New York	Nat.	★2B-SS	145	520	77	142	24	5	1	38	.275	273	370	7	★.989
1986—New York	Nat.	2B	124	387	67	124	18	2	1	27	.320	186	290	17	.966
Major League Totals—7 Years			572	1775	272	506	77	13	6	125	.285	947	1266	55	.976

Selected by New York Mets' organization in 1st round (16th player selected) of free-agent draft, June 7, 1977.
†On suspended list, June 18 to June 20, 1981.
‡On disabled list, July 9 to September 1, 1981.
§On disabled list, August 15 to September 8, 1982.

CHAMPIONSHIP SERIES RECORD

Year Club	League	Pos.	G.	AB.	R.	H.	2B.	3B.	HR.	RBI.	B.A.	PO.	A.	E.	F.A.
1986—New York	Nat.	2B-PH	6	21	5	5	0	0	0	2	.238	9	17	0	1.000

WORLD SERIES RECORD

Year Club	League	Pos.	G.	AB.	R.	H.	2B.	3B.	HR.	RBI.	B.A.	PO.	A.	E.	F.A.
1986—New York	Nat.	PR-2B	6	18	4	6	0	0	0	1	.333	9	13	0	1.000

SCOTT BAILES

Born December 18, 1961, at Chillicothe, O.
Height, 6.02. Weight, 170.
Throws and bats lefthanded.
Attended St. Louis Community College at Meramec, St. Louis, Mo.

Major League saves: 1986 (7).

Year Club	League	G.	IP.	W.	L.	Pct.	H.	R.	ER.	SO.	BB.	ERA.
1982—Greenwood†	S. Atlantic	3	13⅔	0	1	.000	17	12	11	8	6	7.24
1983—Alexandria	Carolina	52	75	5	2	.714	67	38	28	101	45	3.36
1984—Nashua	Eastern	54	87	6	8	.429	80	43	33	61	46	3.41
1985—Nashua‡-Waterbury	Eastern	42	126⅓	9	6	.600	123	58	38	93	43	2.71
1986—Cleveland	American	62	112⅔	10	10	.500	123	70	62	60	43	4.95
Major League Totals—1 Year		62	112⅔	10	10	.500	123	70	62	60	43	4.95

Selected by Texas Rangers' organization in 7th round of free-agent draft, January 12, 1982.
Selected by Pittsburgh Pirates' organization in secondary phase of free-agent draft, June 7, 1982.
†On disabled list, August 12, 1982 through remainder of season.
‡Traded to Cleveland Indians' organization, July 3, 1985, completing deal in which Cleveland traded Shortstop Johnnie LeMaster to Pittsburgh Pirates for a player to be named later, May 30, 1985.

JOHN MARK BAILEY

(Known by middle name.)

Born November 4, 1961, at Springfield, Mo.
Height, 6.05. Weight, 195.
Throws right and bats right and lefthanded.
Attended Southwest Missouri State University, Springfield, Mo.

Major League stolen bases: 1986 (1).
Switch-hit home runs in one game, September 16, 1984.
Led National League in passed balls with 17 in 1984 and 19 in 1985.
Led South Atlantic League catchers in fielding percentage with .989 in 1983.

Year Club	League	Pos.	G.	AB.	R.	H.	2B.	3B.	HR.	RBI.	B.A.	PO.	A.	E.	F.A.
1982—Auburn	NYP	1B-3B-OF	65	230	46	69	10	1	11	40	.300	195	29	5	.978
1983—Asheville	S. Atl.	C-1B	122	410	68	108	23	1	19	62	.263	767	77	7	.992
1984—Columbus	South.	C-1B-OF	17	53	5	15	3	2	0	9	.283	83	11	0	1.000
1984—Houston	Nat.	C	108	344	38	73	16	1	9	34	.212	629	56	12	.983
1985—Houston	Nat.	●C-1B	114	332	47	88	14	0	10	45	.265	566	52	●13	.979
1986—Houston	Nat.	C-1B	57	153	9	27	5	0	4	15	.176	322	33	4	.989
1986—Tucson	P. C.	C-1B	35	123	22	42	8	1	1	19	.341	120	10	3	.977
Major League Totals—3 Years			279	829	94	188	35	1	23	94	.227	1517	141	29	.983

Selected by Houston Astros' organization in 6th round of free-agent draft, June 7, 1982.

HAROLD DOUGLAS BAINES

Born March 15, 1959, at St. Michaels, Md.
Height, 6.02. Weight, 195.
Throws and bats lefthanded.

Tied major league record for most plate appearances, game (12), May 8, finished May 9, 1984 (25 innings).
Established American League record for most game-winning runs batted in, season (22), 1985.
Tied American League records for longest errorless game and most innings by outfielder, game (25), May 8, finished May 9, 1984.
Major League stolen bases: 1980 (2), 1981 (6), 1982 (10), 1983 (7), 1984 (1), 1985 (1), 1986 (2). Total—29.
Hit three home runs in a game, July 7, 1982 and September 17, 1984.
Led American League in slugging percentage with .541 in 1984.
Led American League in game-winning RBIs with 22 in 1983.
Tied for American Association lead in double plays by outfielders with 4 in 1979.
Named outfielder on THE SPORTING NEWS American League All-Star Team, 1985.

Year Club	League	Pos.	G.	AB.	R.	H.	2B.	3B.	HR.	RBI.	B.A.	PO.	A.	E.	F.A.
1977—Appleton	Midw.	OF	69	222	37	58	11	2	5	29	.261	94	10	7	.937
1978—Knoxville	South.	OF-1B	137	502	70	138	16	6	13	72	.275	291	22	13	.960
1979—Iowa	A. A.	OF	125	466	87	139	25	8	22	87	.298	222	•16	11	.956
1980—Chicago	Amer.	OF	141	491	55	125	23	6	13	49	.255	229	6	9	.963
1981—Chicago	Amer.	OF	82	280	42	80	11	7	10	41	.286	120	10	2	.985
1982—Chicago	Amer.	OF	161	608	89	165	29	8	25	105	.271	326	10	7	.980
1983—Chicago	Amer.	OF	156	596	76	167	33	2	20	99	.280	312	10	9	.973
1984—Chicago	Amer.	OF	147	569	72	173	28	10	29	94	.304	307	8	6	.981
1985—Chicago	Amer.	OF	160	640	86	198	29	3	22	113	.309	318	8	2	.994
1986—Chicago	Amer.	OF	145	570	72	169	29	2	21	88	.296	295	15	5	.984
Major League Totals—7 Years			992	3754	492	1077	182	38	140	589	.287	1907	67	40	.980

Selected by Chicago White Sox' organization in 1st round (first player selected) of free-agent draft, June 7, 1977.

CHAMPIONSHIP SERIES RECORD

Year Club	League	Pos.	G.	AB.	R.	H.	2B.	3B.	HR.	RBI.	B.A.	PO.	A.	E.	F.A.
1983—Chicago	Amer.	OF	4	16	0	2	0	0	0	0	.125	5	1	0	1.000

ALL-STAR GAME RECORD

Year League	Pos.	AB.	R.	H.	2B.	3B.	HR.	RBI.	B.A.	PO.	A.	E.	F.A.
1985—American	PH	1	0	1	0	0	0	0	1.000	0	0	0	.000
1986—American	PH	1	0	0	0	0	0	0	.000	0	0	0	.000
All-Star Game Totals—2 Years		2	0	1	0	0	0	0	.500	0	0	0	.000

CHARLES DOUGLAS BAIR
(Doug)

Born August 22, 1949, at Defiance, O.
Height, 6.00. Weight, 180.
Throws and bats righthanded.
Received bachelor of science degree in industrial education from
Bowling Green State University, Bowling Green, O.

Major League saves: 1977 (8), 1978 (28), 1979 (16), 1980 (6), 1981 (1), 1982 (8), 1983 (5), 1984 (4), 1986 (4). Total—80.
Led Carolina League in complete games with 15 in 1972.
Named Carolina League Pitcher of the Year, 1972.

Year Club	League	G.	IP.	W.	L.	Pct.	H.	R.	ER.	SO.	BB.	ERA.
1971—Salem†	Carolina	6	29	2	3	.400	35	22	19	18	26	5.90
1971—Waterbury	Eastern	1	7	1	0	1.000	5	0	0	2	0	0.00
1972—Salem	Carolina	24	180	15	7	.682	170	•86	57	186	★95	2.85
1972—Charleston	Int'national	1	4	0	1	.000	5	3	3	5	0	6.75
1973—Charleston	Int'national	26	158	7	11	.389	173	103	77	94	87	4.39
1974—Charleston‡	Int'national	26	170	7	★16	.304	166	87	77	117	91	4.08
1975—Charleston	Int'national	26	167	9	12	.429	157	72	56	113	58	3.02
1976—Charleston	Int'national	45	122	7	10	.412	102	48	43	108	57	3.17
1976—Pittsburgh§	National	4	6	0	0	.000	4	4	4	4	5	6.00
1977—San Jose	P. Coast	20	33	5	2	.714	24	8	8	49	17	2.18
1977—Oakland x	American	45	83	4	6	.400	78	39	32	68	57	3.47
1978—Cincinnati	National	70	100	7	6	.538	87	23	22	91	38	1.98
1979—Cincinnati	National	65	94	11	7	.611	93	47	45	86	51	4.31
1980—Cincinnati	National	61	85	3	6	.333	91	42	40	62	39	4.24
1981—Cincinnati y-St. Louis	National	35	55	4	2	.667	55	34	31	30	19	5.07
1982—St. Louis	National	63	91⅔	5	3	.625	69	27	26	68	36	2.55
1983—St. Louis z	National	26	29⅔	1	1	.500	24	11	10	21	13	3.03
1983—Detroit a	American	27	55⅔	7	3	.700	51	27	24	39	19	3.88
1984—Detroit	American	47	93⅔	5	3	.625	82	42	39	57	36	3.75
1985—Detroit b	American	21	49	2	0	1.000	54	38	34	30	25	6.24
1985—St. Louis c	National	2	2	0	0	.000	1	0	0	0	2	0.00
1986—Tacoma	P. Coast	8	12	3	1	.750	8	3	0	13	6	0.00
1986—Oakland d	American	31	45	2	3	.400	37	15	15	40	18	3.00
National League Totals—8 Years		326	463¼	31	25	.554	424	188	178	362	203	3.46
American League Totals—5 Years		171	326⅓	20	15	.571	302	161	144	234	155	3.97
Major League Totals—11 Years		497	789⅔	51	40	.560	726	349	322	596	358	3.67

Selected by Pittsburgh Pirates' organization in 2nd round of free-agent draft, June 8, 1971.
†On temporary inactive list, June 23 to July 22, 1971.
‡Conditionally released to Detroit Tigers' organization, December 17, 1974; returned, March 28, 1975.
§Traded with Pitchers Doc Medich, Dave Giusti and Rick Langford, Outfielders Mitchell Page and Tony Armas to Oakland A's for Infielders Phil Garner and Tommy Helms, and Pitcher Chris Batton, March 15, 1977.
xTraded to Cincinnati Reds for First Baseman Dave Revering and cash, February 25, 1978.
yTraded to St. Louis Cardinals for Pitcher Joe Edelen and Second Baseman Neil Fiala, September 10, 1981.

zTraded to Detroit Tigers for a player to be named later, June 21, 1983; St. Louis Cardinals acquired Pitcher Dave Rucker to complete deal, July 5, 1983.
aGranted free agency, November 7, 1983; re-signed by Tigers, December 23, 1983.
bReleased, August 22, 1985; signed by St. Louis Cardinals, September 2, 1985.
cGranted free agency, November 12, 1985; signed by Oakland A's organization, May 19, 1986.
dGranted free agency, November 10, 1986.

CHAMPIONSHIP SERIES RECORD

Year Club	League	G.	IP.	W.	L.	Pct.	H.	R.	ER.	SO.	BB.	ERA.
1979—Cincinnati	National	1	1	0	1	.000	2	1	1	0	1	9.00
1982—St. Louis	National	1	1	0	0	.000	2	0	0	0	3	0.00
Championship Series Totals—2 Years		2	2	0	1	.000	4	1	1	0	4	4.50

WORLD SERIES RECORD

Year Club	League	G.	IP.	W.	L.	Pct.	H.	R.	ER.	SO.	BB.	ERA.
1982—St. Louis	National	3	2	0	1	.000	2	2	2	3	2	9.00
1984—Detroit	American	1	⅔	0	0	.000	0	0	0	1	0	0.00
World Series Totals—2 Years		4	2⅔	0	1	.000	2	2	2	4	2	6.75

DOUGLAS LEE BAKER
(Doug)

Born April 3, 1961, at Fullerton, Calif.
Height, 5.09. Weight, 165.
Throws right and bats left and righthanded.
Attended Arizona State University, Tempe, Ariz.
Brother of Dave Baker, third baseman with Toronto Blue Jays, 1982.

Major League stolen bases: 1984 (3).
Led Southern League in sacrifice hits with 18 and being hit by pitch with 13 in 1983.
Led Southern League shortstops in total chances with 747 in 1983.

Year Club	League	Pos.	G.	AB.	R.	H.	2B.	3B.	HR.	RBI.	B.A.	PO.	A.	E.	F.A.
1982—Birmingham	South.	SS	70	213	28	48	3	4	1	21	.225	115	190	14	.956
1983—Birmingham	South.	SS	*146	452	72	109	18	3	5	51	.241	238	*482	27	.964
1984—Evansville†	A. A.	SS	77	243	34	63	21	1	8	30	.259	152	270	16	.963
1984—Detroit	Amer.	SS-2B	43	108	15	20	4	1	0	12	.185	56	86	5	.966
1985—Detroit	Amer.	SS-2B	15	27	4	5	1	0	0	1	.185	12	12	1	.960
1985—Nashville	A. A.	SS	107	325	42	71	9	4	2	30	.218	179	318	22	.958
1986—Detroit	Amer.	SS-2B	13	24	1	3	1	0	0	0	.125	17	21	1	.974
1986—Nashville	A. A.	SS	112	369	46	101	14	6	2	40	.274	*208	291	15	*.971
Major League Totals—3 Years			71	159	20	28	6	1	0	13	.176	85	119	7	.967

Selected by Oakland A's organization in 9th round of free-agent draft, January 13, 1981.
Selected by Detroit Tigers' organization in 9th round of free-agent draft, June 7, 1982.
†On disabled list, June 10 to June 21, 1984.

CHAMPIONSHIP SERIES RECORD

Year Club	League	Pos.	G.	AB.	R.	H.	2B.	3B.	HR.	RBI.	B.A.	PO.	A.	E.	F.A.
1984—Detroit	Amer.	SS	1	0	0	0	0	0	0	0	.000	0	0	0	.000

JOHNNIE B. BAKER JR.
(Dusty)

Born June 15, 1949, at Riverside, Calif.
Height, 6.02. Weight, 200.
Throws and bats righthanded.
Attended American River Junior College, Sacramento, Calif.

Tied major league records for most plate appearances, most at bats and most times faced pitcher as batsman, inning (3), September 20, second game, 1972; most stolen bases, inning (3), June 27, 1984, third inning.
Established National League record for fewest chances accepted by outfielder, season, 150 or more games (235), 1977.
Major League stolen bases: 1972 (4), 1973 (24), 1974 (18), 1975 (12), 1976 (2), 1977 (2), 1978 (12), 1979 (11), 1980 (12), 1981 (10), 1982 (17), 1983 (7), 1984 (4), 1985 (2). Total—137.
Led National League outfielders in total chances with 407 in 1973.
Named outfielder on THE SPORTING NEWS National League All-Star Team, 1980.
Named outfielder on THE SPORTING NEWS National League All-Star fielding team, 1981.
Named outfielder on THE SPORTING NEWS National League Silver Slugger team, 1980 and 1981.

Year Club	League	Pos.	G.	AB.	R.	H.	2B.	3B.	HR.	RBI.	B.A.	PO.	A.	E.	F.A.
1967—Austin	Texas	OF	9	39	6	9	1	0	0	1	.231	17	0	1	.944
1968—W. Palm B'ch†	Fla. St.	OF	6	21	2	4	0	0	0	2	.190	6	2	0	1.000
1968—Greenwood	W. Car.	OF	52	199	45	68	11	3	6	39	.342	82	1	3	.965
1968—Atlanta	Nat.	OF	6	5	0	2	0	0	0	0	.400	0	0	0	.000
1969—Shreveport	Texas	OF	73	265	40	68	5	1	9	31	.257	135	10	3	.980
1969—Richmond	Int.	OF-3B	25	89	7	22	4	0	0	8	.247	40	9	4	.925
1969—Atlanta	Nat.	OF	3	7	0	0	0	0	0	0	.000	2	0	0	1.000
1970—Richmond	Int.	OF	118	461	97	150	29	3	11	51	.325	236	10	7	.972
1970—Atlanta	Nat.	OF	13	24	3	7	0	0	0	4	.292	11	1	3	.800
1971—Richmond	Int.	OF-3B	80	341	62	106	23	2	11	41	.311	136	13	4	.974
1971—Atlanta	Nat.	OF	29	62	2	14	2	0	0	4	.226	29	1	0	1.000
1972—Atlanta‡	Nat.	OF	127	446	62	143	27	2	17	76	.321	344	8	4	.989
1973—Atlanta	Nat.	OF	159	604	101	174	29	4	21	99	.288	*390	10	7	.983

Year	Club	League	Pos.	G.	AB.	R.	H.	2B.	3B.	HR.	RBI.	B.A.	PO.	A.	E.	F.A.
1974—Atlanta	Nat.		OF	149	574	80	147	35	0	20	69	.256	359	10	7	.981
1975—Atlanta§	Nat.		OF	142	494	63	129	18	2	19	72	.261	287	10	3	.990
1976—Los Angeles	Nat.		OF	112	384	36	93	13	0	4	39	.242	254	3	1	.996
1977—Los Angeles	Nat.		OF	153	533	86	155	26	1	30	86	.291	227	8	3	.987
1978—Los Angeles	Nat.		OF	149	522	62	137	24	1	11	66	.262	250	13	4	.985
1979—Los Angeles	Nat.		OF	151	554	86	152	29	1	23	88	.274	289	14	3	.990
1980—Los Angeles	Nat.		OF	153	579	80	170	26	4	29	97	.294	308	5	3	.991
1981—Los Angeles	Nat.		OF	103	400	48	128	17	3	9	49	.320	181	8	2	.990
1982—Los Angeles	Nat.		OF	147	570	80	171	19	1	23	88	.300	226	7	6	.975
1983—Los Angeles xy.....	Nat.		OF	149	531	71	138	25	1	15	73	.260	249	4	5	.981
1984—San Francisco za.	Nat.		OF	100	243	31	71	7	2	3	32	.292	112	1	3	.974
1985—Oakland..............	Amer.		1B-OF	111	343	48	92	15	1	14	52	.268	465	29	5	.990
1986—Oakland b	Amer.		OF-1B	83	242	25	58	8	0	4	19	.240	90	4	0	1.000
National League Totals—17 Years.........				1845	6532	891	1831	297	22	224	942	.280	3518	103	54	.985
American League Totals—2 Years.........				194	585	73	150	23	1	18	71	.256	555	33	5	.992
Major League Totals—19 Years...............				2039	7117	964	1981	320	23	242	1013	.278	4073	136	59	.986

Selected by Atlanta Braves' organization in 26th round of free-agent draft, June 6, 1967.

†On restricted list, April 5 to June 13, 1968.

‡On military list, June 17 to July 3, 1972.

§Traded with First Baseman-Third Baseman Ed Goodson to Los Angeles Dodgers for Outfielder Jimmy Wynn, Second Baseman Lee Lacy, First Baseman-Outfielder Tom Paciorek and Infielder Jerry Royster, November 17, 1975.

xReleased on waivers, February 10, 1984; San Francisco Giants claim rejected, February 16, 1984.

yGranted free agency, February 21, 1984; signed by San Francisco Giants, April 1, 1984.

zOn restricted list, April 2 to April 11, 1984.

aTraded to Oakland A's for Pitcher Ed Puikunas and Catcher Dan Winters, March 24, 1985.

bGranted free agency, November 10, 1986.

DIVISION SERIES RECORD

Year	Club	League	Pos.	G.	AB.	R.	H.	2B.	3B.	HR.	RBI.	B.A.	PO.	A.	E.	F.A.
1981—Los Angeles	Nat.		OF	5	18	2	3	1	0	0	1	.167	12	0	0	1.000

CHAMPIONSHIP SERIES RECORD

Tied Championship Series records for highest batting average, four-game Series (.467), 1978; most home runs with bases filled, game (1), October 5, 1977; most runs batted in, four-game Series (8), 1977; most runs batted in, inning (4), October 5, 1977 (fourth inning).

Tied National League Championship Series record for most hits, game (4), October 7, 1978.

Year	Club	League	Pos.	G.	AB.	R.	H.	2B.	3B.	HR.	RBI.	B.A.	PO.	A.	E.	F.A.
1977—Los Angeles	Nat.		OF	4	14	4	5	1	0	2	8	.357	3	0	0	1.000
1978—Los Angeles	Nat.		OF	4	15	1	7	2	0	0	1	.467	5	0	0	1.000
1981—Los Angeles	Nat.		OF	5	19	3	6	1	0	0	3	.316	10	0	1	.909
1983—Los Angeles	Nat.		OF	4	14	4	5	1	0	1	1	.357	9	0	0	1.000
Championship Series Totals—4 Years.....				17	62	12	23	5	0	3	13	.371	27	0	1	.964

WORLD SERIES RECORD

Year	Club	League	Pos.	G.	AB.	R.	H.	2B.	3B.	HR.	RBI.	B.A.	PO.	A.	E.	F.A.
1977—Los Angeles	Nat.		OF	6	24	4	7	0	0	1	5	.292	11	0	1	.917
1978—Los Angeles	Nat.		OF	6	21	2	5	0	0	1	1	.238	12	0	0	1.000
1981—Los Angeles	Nat.		OF	6	24	3	4	0	0	0	1	.167	13	0	0	1.000
World Series Totals—3 Years				18	69	9	16	0	0	2	7	.232	36	0	1	.973

ALL-STAR GAME RECORD

Year	League	Pos.	AB.	R.	H.	2B.	3B.	HR.	RBI.	B.A.	PO.	A.	E.	F.A.
1981—National		OF	2	0	1	0	0	0	0	.500	2	0	0	1.000
1982—National		OF	2	0	0	0	0	0	0	.000	0	0	0	.000
All-Star Game Totals—2 Years....................			4	0	1	0	0	0	0	.250	2	0	0	1.000

STEPHEN CHARLES BALBONI
(Steve)

Born January 16, 1957, at Brockton, Mass.
Height, 6.03. Weight, 225.
Throws and bats righthanded.
Attended Eckerd College, St. Petersburg, Fla.

Major League stolen bases: 1985 (1).

Led American League batters in strikeouts with 166 in 1985.

Led American League first basemen in total chances with 1,686 in 1985.

Led International League batters in strikeouts with 146 in 1981.

Led Southern League in total bases with 288 and intentional bases on balls received with 17 in 1980.

Led Florida State League batters in strikeouts with 154 in 1979.

Led Florida State League first basemen in double plays with 106 in 1979 and Southern League first basemen with 125 in 1980.

Named Southern League Most Valuable Player, 1980.

Named Florida State League Most Valuable Player, 1979.

Named designated hitter on THE SPORTING NEWS College Baseball All-America Team, 1978.

Year	Club	League	Pos.	G.	AB.	R.	H.	2B.	3B.	HR.	RBI.	B.A.	PO.	A.	E.	F.A.
1978—West Haven	East.		DH	2	2	0	0	0	0	0	0	.000	0	0	0	.000
1978—Fort Lauderdale ..	Fla. St.		1B	60	176	19	36	5	0	1	19	.205	475	19	4	.992

Year Club League	Pos.	G.	AB.	R.	H.	2B.	3B.	HR.	RBI.	B.A.	PO.	A.	E.	F.A.
1979—Fort Lauderdale .. Fla. St.	1B	*140	*504	69	127	19	2	*26	*91	.252	*1297	*97	11	*.992
1980—Nashville............... South.	1B	141	521	*101	157	25	2	*34	*122	.301	*1218	76	13	*.990
1981—Columbus......... Int.	1B	125	434	68	107	21	2	*33	*98	.247	631	55	*14	.980
1981—New York........... Amer.	1B	4	7	2	2	1	1	0	2	.286	14	1	0	1.000
1982—Columbus......... Int.	1B	83	313	57	89	17	1	*32	86	.284	426	38	8	.983
1982—New York........... Amer.	1B	33	107	8	20	2	1	2	4	.187	194	13	2	.990
1983—Columbus......... Int.	1B	84	317	72	87	14	0	27	81	.274	479	47	11	.980
1983—New York†.......... Amer.	1B	32	86	8	20	2	0	5	17	.233	178	9	3	.984
1984—Kansas City......... Amer.	1B	126	438	58	107	23	2	28	77	.244	1102	79	●15	.987
1985—Kansas City......... Amer.	1B	160	600	74	146	28	2	36	88	.243	*1573	101	12	.993
1986—Kansas City......... Amer.	1B	138	512	54	117	25	1	29	88	.229	1236	98	*18	.987
Major League Totals—6 Years...............		493	1750	204	412	81	7	100	276	.235	4297	301	50	.989

Selected by New York Yankees' organization in 4th round of free-agent draft, June 6, 1978.

†Traded with Pitcher Roger Erickson to Kansas City Royals for Pitcher Mike Armstrong and Catcher Duane Dewey, December 8, 1983.

CHAMPIONSHIP SERIES RECORD

Tied American League Championship Series record for most strikeouts, seven-game Series (8), 1985.

Year Club League	Pos.	G.	AB.	R.	H.	2B.	3B.	HR.	RBI.	B.A.	PO.	A.	E.	F.A.
1984—Kansas City.......... Amer.	1B	3	11	0	1	0	0	0	0	.091	20	3	1	.958
1985—Kansas City.......... Amer.	1B	7	25	1	3	0	0	0	1	.120	72	7	2	.975
Championship Series Totals—2 Years.....		10	36	1	4	0	0	0	1	.111	92	10	3	.971

WORLD SERIES RECORD

Tied World Series record for most at-bats, inning (2), October 27, 1985 (fifth inning).

Year Club League	Pos.	G.	AB.	R.	H.	2B.	3B.	HR.	RBI.	B.A.	PO.	A.	E.	F.A.
1985—Kansas City.......... Amer.	1B	7	25	2	8	0	0	0	3	.320	70	3	0	1.000

JEFFREY SCOTT BALLARD
(Jeff)

Born August 13, 1963, at Billings, Mont.
Height, 6.03. Weight, 195.
Throws and bats lefthanded.
Attended Stanford University, Stanford, Calif.

Tied for New York-Pennsylvania League lead in shutouts with 3 in 1985.

Year Club	League	G.	IP.	W.	L.	Pct.	H.	R.	ER.	SO.	BB.	ERA.
1985—Newark	NYP	13	96	●10	2	.833	78	20	15	91	20	1.41
1986—Hagerstown	Carolina	17	112	9	5	.643	106	39	23	115	32	*1.85
1986—Charlotte.....................	Southern	10	59⅔	5	2	.714	70	29	22	35	20	3.32
1986—Rochester.....................	Int'national	2	6⅓	0	2	.000	11	6	5	7	3	7.11

Selected by Milwaukee Brewers' organization in 16th round of free-agent draft, June 8, 1981.

Selected by Baltimore Orioles' organization in 27th round of free-agent draft, June 4, 1984.

Selected by Baltimore Orioles' organizaton in 7th round of free-agent draft, June 3, 1985.

JAY SCOT BALLER

Born October 6, 1960, at Stayton, Ore.
Height, 6.06. Weight, 215.
Throws and bats righthanded.

Major League saves: 1985 (1), 1986 (5). Total—6.
Led International League in hit batsmen with 12 in 1983.
Led Eastern League in hit batsmen with 12 in 1982.
Led South Atlantic League in hit batsmen with 10 in 1980.
Led Pioneer League in home runs allowed with 9 in 1979.

Year Club	League	G.	IP.	W.	L.	Pct.	H.	R.	ER.	SO.	BB.	ERA.
1979—Helena	Pioneer	13	67	5	6	.455	89	59	43	68	34	5.78
1980—Spartanburg..................	S. Atlantic	26	139	10	5	.667	132	69	55	95	72	3.56
1981—Peninsula.....................	Carolina	27	147	9	14	.391	119	85	64	166	78	3.92
1982—Reading	Eastern	50	151⅓	9	8	.529	110	64	45	155	85	*2.68
1982—Philadelphia†	National	4	8	0	0	.000	7	4	3	7	2	3.38
1983—Charleston...................	Int'national	20	78⅔	4	12	.250	91	79	77	62	66	8.81
1983—Buffalo........................	Eastern	16	34⅔	1	2	.333	32	34	29	35	35	7.53
1984—Buffalo........................	Eastern	14	79⅓	4	5	.444	73	50	40	74	48	4.54
1984—Maine‡........................	Int'national	15	83⅔	9	4	.692	82	57	50	52	48	5.38
1985—Iowa	Am. Assoc.	24	149	8	9	.471	140	77	70	119	63	4.23
1985—Chicago.......................	National	20	52	2	3	.400	52	21	20	31	17	3.46
1986—Chicago.......................	National	36	53⅔	2	4	.333	58	37	32	42	28	5.37
1986—Iowa	Am. Assoc.	27	59⅓	3	7	.300	63	32	29	51	32	4.40
Major League Totals—3 Years............................		60	113⅔	4	7	.364	117	62	55	80	47	4.35

Selected by Philadelphia Phillies' organization in 3rd round of free-agent draft, June 5, 1979.

†Traded with Second Baseman Manny Trillo, Outfielder George Vukovich, Infielder Julio Franco and Catcher Jerry Willard to Cleveland Indians for Outfielder Von Hayes, December 9, 1982.

‡Traded to Chicago Cubs' organization for Infielder Dan Rohn, April 1, 1985.

CHRISTOPHER MICHAEL BANDO
(Chris)

Born February 4, 1956, at Cleveland, O.
Height, 6.00. Weight, 195.
Throws right and bats left and righthanded
Attended Arizona State University, Tempe, Ariz.
Brother of Sal Bando, infielder with Kansas City Athletics, Oakland A's and
Milwaukee Brewers, 1966 through 1981; Milwaukee Brewers' Special Assistant
to the General Manager since 1982; and coach with Milwaukee Brewers, 1983.

Major League stolen bases: 1984 (1).
Received reported $25,000 bonus to sign with Cleveland Indians, 1978.

Year	Club	League	Pos.	G.	AB.	R.	H.	2B.	3B.	HR.	RBI.	B.A.	PO.	A.	E.	F.A.
1978—Chattanooga	South.		C	76	241	30	55	12	0	4	21	.228	285	51	10	.971
1979—Chattanooga†	South.		C-3B	21	62	5	15	4	1	0	7	.242	61	13	0	1.000
1980—Chattanooga‡	South.		C-3B	121	404	78	141	31	3	12	73	★.349	480	97	12	.980
1981—Charleston	Int.		C-3B	96	320	47	98	16	2	11	45	.306	414	51	10	.979
1981—Cleveland	Amer.		C	21	47	3	10	3	0	0	6	.213	53	5	2	.967
1982—Cleveland§	Amer.		C-3B	66	184	13	39	6	1	3	16	.212	268	23	3	.990
1983—Cleveland	Amer.		C	48	121	15	31	3	0	4	15	.256	170	19	1	.995
1984—Maine x	Int.		C-1B	29	92	18	24	2	0	3	13	.261	138	12	5	.968
1984—Cleveland	Amer.		C-1B-3B	75	220	38	64	11	0	12	41	.291	307	30	6	.983
1985—Cleveland	Amer.		C	73	173	11	24	4	1	0	13	.139	251	28	4	.986
1986—Cleveland	Amer.		C	92	254	28	68	9	0	2	26	.268	359	30	4	.990
Major League Totals—6 Years				375	999	108	236	36	2	21	117	.236	1408	135	20	.987

Selected by Milwaukee Brewers' organization in 22nd round of free-agent draft, June 7, 1977.
Selected by Cleveland Indians' organization in 2nd round of free-agent draft, June 6, 1978.
†On disabled list, April 16 to August 9, 1979.
‡On disabled list, April 24 to May 6, 1980.
§On disabled list, May 2 to June 17, 1982.
xOn Cleveland disabled list, March 28 to April 20, 1984.

MICHAEL SCOTT BANKHEAD
(Known by middle name.)

Born July 31, 1963, at Raleigh, N.C.
Height, 5.10. Weight, 175.
Throws and bats righthanded.
Attended University of North Carolina, Chapel Hill, N.C.

Member of 1984 U.S. Olympic baseball team.

Year	Club	League	G.	IP.	W.	L.	Pct.	H.	R.	ER.	SO.	BB.	ERA.
1985—Memphis	Southern	24	140⅓	8	6	.571	117	63	56	●128	56	3.59
1986—Omaha	Am. Assoc.	7	48⅓	2	2	.500	31	11	8	34	14	1.49
1986—Kansas City†	American	24	121	8	9	.471	121	66	62	94	37	4.61
Major League Totals—1 Year		24	121	8	9	.471	121	66	62	94	37	4.61

Selected by Pittsburgh Pirates' organization in 17th round of free-agent draft, June 8, 1981.
Selected by Kansas City Royals' organization in 1st round (16th player selected) of free-agent draft, June 4, 1984.
†Traded with Pitcher Steve Shields and Outfielder Mike Kingery to Seattle Mariners for Outfielder Danny Tartabull and Pitcher Rick Luecken, December 10, 1986.

FLOYD FRANKLIN BANNISTER

Born June 10, 1955, at Pierre, S. Dakota.
Height, 6.01. Weight, 203.
Throws and bats lefthanded.
Attended Arizona State University, Tempe, Ariz.
Brother-in-law of Greg Cochran, pitcher in Oakland A's and New York Yankees'
organizations, 1975 through 1982.

Named College Player of the Year by THE SPORTING NEWS, 1976.
Named lefthanded pitcher on THE SPORTING NEWS College Baseball All-America Team, 1975 and 1976.

Year	Club	League	G.	IP.	W.	L.	Pct.	H.	R.	ER.	SO.	BB.	ERA.
1976—Covington	Ap'lachian	3	13	0	0	.000	3	0	0	27	2	0.00
1976—Columbus	Southern	3	24	1	0	1.000	16	4	4	20	14	1.50
1976—Memphis	Int'national	1	6	1	0	1.000	7	1	1	6	3	1.50
1977—Houston†	National	24	143	8	9	.471	138	70	64	112	68	4.03
1978—Houston‡	National	28	110	3	9	.250	120	59	59	94	63	4.83
1979—Seattle	American	30	182	10	15	.400	185	92	82	115	68	4.05
1980—Seattle	American	32	218	9	13	.409	200	96	84	155	66	3.47
1981—Seattle§	American	21	121	9	9	.500	128	62	60	85	39	4.46
1982—Seattle x	American	35	247	12	13	.480	225	112	94	★209	77	3.43
1983—Chicago	American	34	217⅓	16	10	.615	191	88	81	193	71	3.35
1984—Chicago y	American	34	218	14	11	.560	211	127	117	152	80	4.83
1985—Chicago	American	34	210⅔	10	14	.417	211	121	114	198	100	4.87
1986—Chicago z	American	28	165⅓	10	14	.417	162	81	65	92	48	3.54
National League Totals—2 Years		52	253	11	18	.379	258	129	123	206	131	4.38
American League Totals—8 Years		248	1579⅓	90	99	.476	1513	779	697	1199	549	3.97
Major League Totals—10 Years		300	1832⅓	101	117	.463	1771	908	820	1405	680	4.03

Selected by Oakland A's organization in 3rd round of free-agent draft, June 5, 1973.
Selected by Houston Astros' organization in 1st round (first player selected) of free-agent draft, June 8, 1976.

†On disabled list, July 26 to August 22, 1977.
‡Traded to Seattle Mariners for Shortstop Craig Reynolds, December 8, 1978.
§On disabled list, August 8 to August 29, 1981.
xGranted free agency, November 10, 1982; signed by Chicago White Sox, December 13, 1982.
yHad one at-bat with no hits.
zOn disabled list, May 19 to June 17, 1986.

CHAMPIONSHIP SERIES RECORD

Year Club	League	G.	IP.	W.	L.	Pct.	H.	R.	ER.	SO.	BB.	ERA.
1983—Chicago	American	1	6	0	1	.000	5	4	3	5	1	4.50

ALL-STAR GAME RECORD

Year League	IP.	W.	L.	Pct.	H.	R.	ER.	SO.	BB.	ERA.
1982—American	1	0	0	.000	1	0	0	0	0	0.00

JESSE LEE BARFIELD

Born October 29, 1959, at Joliet, Ill.
Height, 6.01. Weight, 200.
Throws and bats righthanded.

Major League stolen bases: 1981 (4), 1982 (1), 1983 (2), 1984 (8), 1985 (22), 1986 (8). Total—45.
Led American League outfielders in double plays with 8 in 1985 and 1986.
Led Florida State League batters in strikeouts with 125 in 1978.
Named outfielder on THE SPORTING NEWS American League All-Star fielding team, 1986.
Named outfielder on THE SPORTING NEWS American League Silver Slugger team, 1986.

Year Club	League	Pos.	G.	AB.	R.	H.	2B.	3B.	HR.	RBI.	B.A.	PO.	A.	E.	F.A.
1977—Utica	NYP	OF	70	234	37	53	9	3	5	35	.226	122	6	●13	.908
1978—Dunedin	Fla. St.	OF	133	441	40	91	12	3	2	34	.206	229	★22	★15	.944
1979—Kinston	Carol.	OF	136	477	66	126	24	5	8	71	.264	284	19	17	.947
1980—Knoxville†	South.	OF	124	433	63	104	12	8	14	65	.240	309	14	12	.964
1981—Knoxville	South.	OF	141	524	83	137	24	13	16	70	.261	270	★23	6	.980
1981—Toronto	Amer.	OF	25	95	7	22	3	2	2	9	.232	71	2	0	1.000
1982—Toronto	Amer.	OF	139	394	54	97	13	2	18	58	.246	217	15	9	.963
1983—Toronto	Amer.	OF	128	388	58	98	13	3	27	68	.253	213	16	8	.966
1984—Toronto	Amer.	OF	110	320	51	91	14	1	14	49	.284	190	9	10	.952
1985—Toronto	Amer.	OF	155	539	94	156	34	9	27	84	.289	349	★22	4	.989
1986—Toronto	Amer.	OF	158	589	107	170	35	2	★40	108	.289	368	★20	3	.992
Major League Totals—6 Years			715	2325	371	634	112	19	128	376	.273	1408	84	34	.978

Selected by Toronto Blue Jays' organization in 9th round of free-agent draft, June 7, 1977.
†On disabled list, August 15 to August 29, 1980.

CHAMPIONSHIP SERIES RECORD

Year Club	League	Pos.	G.	AB.	R.	H.	2B.	3B.	HR.	RBI.	B.A.	PO.	A.	E.	F.A.
1985—Toronto	Amer.	OF	7	25	3	7	1	0	1	4	.280	21	0	1	.955

ALL-STAR GAME RECORD

Year League	Pos.	AB.	R.	H.	2B.	3B.	HR.	RBI.	B.A.	PO.	A.	E.	F.A.
1986—American	PH-OF	3	0	0	0	0	0	0	.000	2	0	0	1.000

GREGORY ROBERT BARGAR
(Greg)

Born January 27, 1959, at Inglewood, Calif.
Height, 6.02. Weight, 185.
Throws and bats righthanded.
Attended El Camino College, Torrance, Calif., and University of Arizona, Tucson, Ariz.

Tied for American Association lead in home runs allowed with 17 in 1985.
Tied for American Association lead in games started by pitchers with 29 in 1984.

Year Club	League	G.	IP.	W.	L.	Pct.	H.	R.	ER.	SO.	BB.	ERA.
1980—Memphis	Southern	14	86	5	5	.500	95	52	48	54	48	5.02
1981—Memphis	Southern	9	65	5	2	.714	58	29	26	52	27	3.60
1981—Denver	Am. Assoc.	23	91	5	6	.455	108	63	61	58	58	6.03
1982—Wichita	Am. Assoc.	9	31⅓	0	4	.000	53	45	39	18	22	11.20
1982—Memphis	Southern	16	118⅔	5	6	.455	100	61	54	124	63	4.10
1983—Memphis	Southern	8	59	4	4	.500	51	25	20	50	28	3.05
1983—Wichita	Am. Assoc.	12	73⅓	6	2	.750	78	41	38	53	32	4.66
1983—Montreal	National	8	20	2	0	1.000	23	15	15	9	8	6.75
1984—Indianapolis	Am. Assoc.	31	180⅓	9	8	.529	156	101	93	121	83	4.64
1984—Montreal	National	3	8	0	1	.000	8	7	7	2	7	7.88
1985—Indianapolis†	Am. Assoc.	38	162⅔	5	★17	.227	150	97	84	119	85	4.65
1986—Louisville	Am. Assoc.	25	68⅓	3	4	.429	56	31	27	65	35	3.56
1986—St. Louis	National	22	27⅓	0	2	.000	36	19	17	12	10	5.60
Major League Totals—3 Years		33	55⅓	2	3	.400	67	41	39	23	25	6.34

Selected by St. Louis Cardinals' organization in 10th round of free-agent draft, January 9, 1979.
Selected by Montreal Expos' organization in 3rd round of free-agent draft, June 3, 1980.
†Sold to St. Louis Cardinals' organization, February 10, 1986.

RICKY VERNARD BARLOW

Born March 21, 1963, at Woodville, Tex.
Height, 6.02. Weight, 170.
Throws and bats righthanded.

Year Club	League	G.	IP.	W.	L.	Pct.	H.	R.	ER.	SO.	BB.	ERA.
1981—Bristol	Ap'lachian	11	58	6	3	.667	63	38	28	24	36	4.34
1982—Macon	S. Atlantic	13	64⅓	2	4	.333	64	41	39	36	49	5.46
1982—Bristol	Ap'lachian	10	57⅔	4	4	.500	46	31	24	56	37	3.75
1983—Lakeland†	Florida St.	2	3⅓	0	1	.000	9	9	9	2	6	24.30
1984—Lakeland	Florida St.	25	122	1	*17	.056	134	*116	*92	65	101	6.79
1985—Lakeland	Florida St.	9	50⅓	1	7	.125	51	34	31	35	27	5.54
1985—Birmingham	Southern	18	63⅓	1	5	.167	88	74	59	39	55	8.38
1986—Glens Falls	Eastern	28	89	5	8	.385	82	37	26	73	47	2.63

Selected by Detroit Tigers' organization in 1st round (17th player selected) of free-agent draft, June 8, 1981.
†On disabled list, April 8 to August 15, 1983.

MARTIN GLENN BARRETT
(Marty)

Born June 23, 1958, at Arcadia, Calif.
Height, 5.10. Weight, 175.
Throws and bats righthanded.
Attended Mesa Community College, Mesa, Ariz. and Arizona State University, Tempe, Ariz.
Brother of Charlie Barrett, pitcher in Los Angeles Dodgers' organization, 1973 through 1978;
and Tom Barrett, infielder in Philadelphia Phillies' organization.

Major League stolen bases: 1984 (5), 1985 (7), 1986 (15). Total—27.
Led American League in sacrifice hits with 18 in 1986.
Led American League second basemen in double plays with 110 in 1985.
Led Eastern League in sacrifice hits with 15 in 1980.
Led Florida State League in sacrifice flies with 9 in 1979.
Led International League second basemen in double plays with 99 in 1982.

Year Club	League	Pos.	G.	AB.	R.	H.	2B.	3B.	HR.	RBI.	B.A.	PO.	A.	E.	F.A.
1979—Winter Haven	Fla. St.	2B	57	178	25	53	7	0	1	28	.298	124	144	6	.978
1980—Bristol	East.	*2B-SS	128	475	72	130	17	2	1	41	.274	279	372	10	*.985
1981—Pawtucket†	Int.	2B	88	343	36	91	12	2	1	28	.265	186	254	10	.978
1982—Pawtucket	Int.	2B	131	477	72	143	27	1	5	57	.300	303	*415	11	*.985
1982—Boston	Amer.	2B	8	18	0	1	0	0	0	0	.056	11	21	0	1.000
1983—Boston	Amer.	2B	33	44	7	10	1	1	0	2	.227	32	28	1	.984
1983—Pawtucket	Int.	2B	36	119	24	41	4	2	1	18	.345	70	115	1	.995
1984—Boston	Amer.	2B	139	475	56	144	23	3	3	45	.303	245	417	9	*.987
1985—Boston	Amer.	2B	156	534	59	142	26	0	5	56	.266	*355	479	11	.987
1986—Boston	Amer.	2B	158	625	94	179	39	4	4	60	.286	303	*450	14	.982
Major League Totals—5 Years			494	1696	216	476	89	8	12	163	.281	946	1395	35	.985

Selected by California Angels' organization in 11th round of free-agent draft, January 11, 1977.
Selected by New York Mets' organization in 3rd round of free-agent draft, January 10, 1978.
Selected by Boston Red Sox' organization in secondary phase of free-agent draft, June 5, 1979.
†On disabled list, June 25 to July 15 and July 17 to August 4, 1981.

CHAMPIONSHIP SERIES RECORD

Established American League Championship Series record for most hits, seven-game Series (11), 1986.
Tied American League Championship Series record for most singles, seven-game Series (9), 1986.

Year Club	League	Pos.	G.	AB.	R.	H.	2B.	3B.	HR.	RBI.	B.A.	PO.	A.	E.	F.A.
1986—Boston	Amer.	2B	7	30	4	11	2	0	0	5	.367	19	21	0	1.000

WORLD SERIES RECORD

Tied World Series record for most assists by second baseman, inning (3), October 23, 1986 (first inning).

Year Club	League	Pos.	G.	AB.	R.	H.	2B.	3B.	HR.	RBI.	B.A.	PO.	A.	E.	F.A.
1986—Boston	Amer.	2B	7	30	1	13	2	0	0	4	.433	13	25	0	1.000

KEVIN CHARLES BASS

Born May 12, 1959, at Menlo Park, Calif.
Height, 6.00. Weight, 180.
Throws right and bats right and lefthanded.
Brother of Richard Bass, minor league outfielder, 1976 and 1977;
cousin of James Lofton, wide receiver with Green Bay Packers.

Major League stolen bases: 1983 (2), 1984 (5), 1985 (19), 1986 (22). Total—48.
Led Midwest League in being hit by pitch with 10 in 1978.
Led Eastern League outfielders in double plays with 7 in 1980.

Year Club	League	Pos.	G.	AB.	R.	H.	2B.	3B.	HR.	RBI.	B.A.	PO.	A.	E.	F.A.
1977—Newark	NYP	OF	48	189	30	56	11	●7	1	33	.296	56	2	3	.951
1978—Burlington	Midw.	OF	129	499	81	132	27	5	18	69	.265	*281	14	11	.964
1979—Holyoke	East.	OF	135	490	69	129	15	4	8	54	.263	280	●16	*17	.946
1980—Holyoke	East.	OF	136	490	79	147	*31	7	4	51	.300	305	14	*18	.947
1981—Vancouver†	P. C.	OF	97	339	40	87	10	5	2	30	.257	175	14	7	.964
1982—Milwaukee	Amer.	OF	18	9	4	0	0	0	0	0	.000	7	0	0	1.000
1982—Vancouver‡	P. C.	OF	102	413	70	130	23	7	17	65	.315	199	15	10	.955
1982—Houston	Nat.	OF	12	24	2	1	0	0	0	1	.042	11	0	1	.917

Year Club	League	Pos.	G.	AB.	R.	H.	2B.	3B.	HR.	RBI.	B.A.	PO.	A.	E.	F.A.
1983—Houston	Nat.	OF	88	195	25	46	7	3	2	18	.236	68	1	4	.945
1984—Houston§	Nat.	OF	121	331	33	86	17	5	2	29	.260	149	4	4	.975
1985—Houston	Nat.	OF	150	539	72	145	27	5	16	68	.269	328	10	1	*.997
1986—Houston	Nat.	OF	157	591	83	184	33	5	20	79	.311	303	12	5	.984
American League Totals—1 Year			18	9	4	0	0	0	0	0	.000	7	0	0	1.000
National League Totals—5 Years			528	1680	215	462	84	18	40	195	.275	859	27	15	.983
Major League Totals—5 Years			546	1689	219	462	84	18	40	195	.274	866	27	15	.983

Selected by Milwaukee Brewers' organization in 2nd round of free-agent draft, June 7, 1977.
†On disabled list, July 29 to September 1, 1981.
‡Traded with Pitchers Mike Madden and Frank DiPino to Houston Astros, September 3, 1982, completing deal in which Houston traded Pitcher Don Sutton to Milwaukee Brewers for three players to be named later, August 30, 1982.
§On disabled list, March 29 to April 13, 1984.

CHAMPIONSHIP SERIES RECORD

Year Club	League	Pos.	G.	AB.	R.	H.	2B.	3B.	HR.	RBI.	B.A.	PO.	A.	E.	F.A.
1986—Houston	Nat.	OF	6	24	0	7	2	0	0	0	.292	16	0	1	.941

ALL-STAR GAME RECORD

Year League	Pos.	AB.	R.	H.	2B.	3B.	HR.	RBI.	B.A.	PO.	A.	E.	F.A.
1986—National	PH	1	0	0	0	0	0	0	.000	0	0	0	.000

WILLIAM DAVID BATHE
(Bill)

Born October 14, 1960, at Downey, Calif.
Height, 6.02. Weight, 200.
Throws and bats righthanded.
Attended Rio Hondo College, Whittier, Calif.; California State University
Fullerton, Calif.; and Pepperdine University, Malibu, Calif.
Twin brother of Bob Bathe, third baseman in Chicago Cubs' organization.

Led Pacific Coast League catchers in total chances with 702 in 1983 and 684 in 1985.
Led Pacific Coast League catchers in putouts with 632 and tied for lead in double plays with 9 in 1983.

Year Club	League	Pos.	G.	AB.	R.	H.	2B.	3B.	HR.	RBI.	B.A.	PO.	A.	E.	F.A.
1981—San José†	Calif.	C-OF	51	177	20	45	9	1	4	22	.254	234	42	8	.972
1982—West Haven	East.	C	128	370	57	104	22	0	17	57	.281	*763	55	9	*.989
1983—Tacoma	P. C.	C-1B	116	399	56	101	18	1	16	62	.253	633	55	15	.979
1984—Tacoma	P. C.	C-3B-1B	84	245	27	63	12	1	3	42	.257	381	29	7	.983
1985—Tacoma	P. C.	C	108	359	43	100	26	0	6	45	.279	*613	64	7	.990
1986—Oakland	Amer.	C	39	103	9	19	3	0	5	11	.184	211	11	2	991
1986—Tacoma	P. C.	C	40	135	13	26	7	1	1	13	.193	120	21	2	.986
Major League Totals—1 Year			39	103	9	19	3	0	5	11	.184	211	11	2	.991

Selected by Pittsburgh Pirates' organization in 10th round of free-agent draft, January 8, 1980.
Selected by Oakland A's organization in 8th round of free-agent draft, June 8, 1981.
†Loaned to San Jose (Co-op), June 23, 1981; returned, October 22, 1981.

JOSE JOAQUIN BAUTISTA

Name pronounced Bough-TEES-tuh.
Born July 25, 1964, at Bani, Dominican Republic.
Height, 6.01. Weight, 177.
Throws and bats righthanded.

Pitched 6-0 no-hit victory against Prince William, May 26, 1985 (first game).

Year Club	League	G.	IP.	W.	L.	Pct.	H.	R.	ER.	SO.	BB.	ERA.
1981—Kingsport	Ap'lachian	13	66	3	6	.333	84	54	34	34	17	4.64
1982—Kingsport	Ap'lachian	14	38⅓	0	4	.000	61	44	38	13	19	8.92
1983—Sarasota Mets	Gulf Coast	13	81⅔	4	3	.571	66	31	21	44	32	2.31
1984—Columbia	S. Atlantic	19	135	13	4	.765	121	52	47	96	35	3.13
1985—Lynchburg	Carolina	27	169	15	8	.652	145	49	44	109	33	2.34
1986—Jackson	Texas	7	21⅔	0	1	.000	36	22	20	13	8	8.31
1986—Lynchburg	Carolina	18	118⅔	8	8	.500	120	58	52	62	24	3.94

Signed as free agent by New York Mets' organization, April 25, 1981.

CHRISTOPHER R. BAYER
(Chris)

Born April 9, 1964, at Bay Shore, N. Y.
Height, 6.02. Weight, 195.
Throws right and bats left and righthanded.
Attended Pace University, Pace Plaza, N.Y.

Year Club	League	G.	IP.	W.	L.	Pct.	H.	R.	ER.	SO.	BB.	ERA.
1985—Elmira†	NYP	14	53⅔	1	5	.167	44	30	20	48	26	3.35
1986—Columbia	S. Atlantic	20	78⅔	9	1	*.900	59	27	22	80	32	2.52
1986—Jackson	Texas	2	4⅓	0	0	.000	9	7	5	2	2	10.38

Selected by Boston Red Sox' organization in 11th round of free-agent draft, June 3, 1985.
†Traded with Pitchers Bob Ojeda, Tom McCarthy and John Mitchell to New York Mets for Pitchers Calvin Schiraldi and Wes Gardner and Outfielders John Christensen and LaSchell Tarver, November 13, 1985.

DONALD EDWARD BAYLOR
(Don)

Born June 28, 1949, at Austin, Tex.
Height, 6.01. Weight, 210.
Throws and bats righthanded.
Attended Miami-Dade Junior College, Miami, Fla., and
Blinn Junior College, Brenham, Tex.

Established major league record for most times caught stealing, inning, (2), June 15, 1974 (9th inning).

Tied major league records for most long hits, opening game of season (4), April 6, 1973 (2 doubles, 1 triple, 1 home run); most consecutive home runs, two consecutive games (4), July 1 and 2, 1975 (bases on balls included).

Tied modern major league record for most at bats, game (7), August 25, 1979.

Established American League records for most times hit by pitch, lifetime (227); most times hit by pitch, season (35), 1986.

Tied American League records for most hits, two consecutive games (9), August 13 and 14, 1973; most times hit by pitch, season (24), 1985.

Major League stolen bases: 1970 (1), 1972 (24), 1973 (32), 1974 (29), 1975 (32), 1976 (52), 1977 (26), 1978 (22), 1979 (22), 1980 (6), 1981 (3), 1982 (10), 1983 (17), 1984 (1), 1986 (3). Total—280.

Hit three home runs in a game, July 2, 1975.

Led American League in game-winning RBIs with 21 in 1982.

Led American League in sacrifice flies with 12 in 1978.

Led American League in being hit by pitch with 13 in 1973, 20 in 1976, 18 in 1978, 23 in 1984, 24 in 1985, 35 in 1986 and tied for lead with 13 in 1975.

Led International League in being hit by pitch with 19 in 1970 and 16 in 1971.

Led International League in total bases with 296 in 1970.

Led Texas League in being hit by pitch with 13 in 1969.

Led Appalachian League in stolen bases with 26, total bases with 135 and tied for lead in caught stealing with 6 in 1967.

Named American League Most Valuable Player by Baseball Writers' Association of America, 1979.

Named American League Player of the Year by THE SPORTING NEWS, 1979.

Named designated hitter on THE SPORTING NEWS American League All-Star Team, 1979, 1985 and 1986.

Named designated hitter on THE SPORTING NEWS American League Silver Slugger team, 1983, 1985 and 1986.

Named Appalachian League Player of the Year, 1967.

Named Minor League Player of the Year by THE SPORTING NEWS, 1970.

Year	Club	League	Pos.	G.	AB.	R.	H.	2B.	3B.	HR.	RBI.	B.A.	PO.	A.	E.	F.A.
1967—Bluefield	Appal.	OF	●67	246	50	★85	10	★8	8	47	★.346	106	5	5	.957
1968—Stockton	Calif.	OF	68	244	52	90	6	3	7	40	.369	135	3	7	.952
1968—Elmira	East.	OF	6	24	4	8	1	1	1	3	.333	10	1	0	1.000
1968—Rochester	Int.	OF	15	46	4	10	2	0	0	4	.217	29	1	4	.882
1969—Miami	Fla. St.	OF	17	56	13	21	5	4	3	24	.375	30	2	3	.914
1969—Dal.-Ft. Worth	Texas	OF	109	406	71	122	17	●10	11	57	.300	241	7	★13	.950
1970—Rochester	Int.	OF	●140	508	★127	166	★34	★15	22	107	.327	286	5	7	.977
1970—Baltimore	Amer.	OF	8	17	4	4	0	0	0	4	.235	15	0	0	1.000
1971—Rochester	Int.	OF	136	492	104	154	●31	10	20	95	.313	210	4	9	.960
1971—Baltimore	Amer.	OF	1	2	0	0	0	0	0	1	.000	4	0	0	1.000
1972—Baltimore	Amer.	OF-1B	102	320	33	81	13	3	11	38	.253	206	4	5	.977
1973—Baltimore	Amer.	OF-1B	118	405	64	116	20	4	11	51	.286	228	10	6	.975
1974—Baltimore	Amer.	OF-1B	137	489	66	133	22	1	10	59	.272	260	2	5	.981
1975—Baltimore†	Amer.	OF-1B	145	524	79	148	21	6	25	76	.282	286	8	5	.983
1976—Oakland‡	Amer.	OF-1B	157	595	85	147	25	1	15	68	.247	781	45	12	.986
1977—California	Amer.	OF-1B	154	561	87	141	27	0	25	75	.251	280	16	7	.977
1978—California	Amer.	OF-1B	158	591	103	151	26	0	34	99	.255	194	9	6	.971
1979—California	Amer.	OF-1B	●162	628	★120	186	33	3	36	★139	.296	203	3	5	.976
1980—California§	Amer.	OF	90	340	39	85	12	2	5	51	.250	119	4	4	.969
1981—California	Amer.	1B-OF	103	377	52	90	18	1	17	66	.239	38	3	0	1.000
1982—California x	Amer.	DH	157	608	80	160	24	1	24	93	.263	0	0	0	.000
1983—New York	Amer.	OF-1B	144	534	82	162	33	3	21	85	.303	23	2	1	.962
1984—New York	Amer.	OF	134	493	84	129	29	1	27	89	.262	8	0	1	.889
1985—New York y	Amer.	DH	142	477	70	110	24	1	23	91	.231	0	0	0	.000
1986—Boston	Amer.	1B-OF	160	585	93	139	23	1	31	94	.238	71	4	1	.987
Major League Totals—17 Years				2072	7546	1141	1982	350	26	315	1179	.263	2716	110	58	.980

Selected by Baltimore Orioles' organization in 2nd round of free-agent draft, June 6, 1967.

†Traded with Pitchers Mike Torrez and Paul Mitchell to Oakland Athletics for Outfielder Reggie Jackson and Pitchers Ken Holtzman and Bill Van Bommel, April 2, 1976.

‡Played out option year and granted free agency, November 1, 1976; signed as free agent by California Angels, November 16, 1976.

§On disabled list, May 11 to June 26, 1980.

xGranted free agency, November 10, 1982; signed by New York Yankees, December 1, 1982.

yTraded to Boston Red Sox for Designated Hitter Mike Easler, March 28, 1986.

CHAMPIONSHIP SERIES RECORD

Established Championship Series record for most runs batted in, five-game Series (10), 1982.

Tied Championship Series records for most clubs, total Series (3); most times reached first base safely, game (5), October 8, 1986; most home runs with bases filled, game (1), October 9, 1982; most runs batted in, game (5), October 5, 1982; most runs batted in, inning (4), October 9, 1982 (eighth inning).

Established American League Championship Series record for most consecutive games, one or more hits (10).

Year	Club	League	Pos.	G.	AB.	R.	H.	2B.	3B.	HR.	RBI.	B.A.	PO.	A.	E.	F.A.
1973—Baltimore	Amer.	OF-PH	4	11	3	3	0	0	0	1	.273	7	0	0	1.000
1974—Baltimore	Amer.	OF	4	15	0	4	0	0	0	0	.267	9	0	0	1.000
1979—California	Amer.	DH-OF	4	16	2	3	0	0	1	2	.188	4	0	0	1.000

Year Club	League	Pos.	G.	AB.	R.	H.	2B.	3B.	HR.	RBI.	B.A.	PO.	A.	E.	F.A.
1982—California	Amer.	DH	5	17	2	5	1	1	1	10	.294	0	0	0	.000
1986—Boston	Amer.	DH	7	26	6	9	3	0	1	2	.346	0	0	0	.000
Championship Series Totals—5 Years			24	85	13	24	4	1	3	15	.282	20	0	0	1.000

WORLD SERIES RECORD

Year Club	League	Pos.	G.	AB.	R.	H.	2B.	3B.	HR.	RBI.	B.A.	PO.	A.	E.	F.A.
1986—Boston	Amer.	DH-PH	4	11	1	2	1	0	0	1	.182	0	0	0	.000

ALL-STAR GAME RECORD

Year League	Pos.	AB.	R.	H.	2B.	3B.	HR.	RBI.	B.A.	PO.	A.	E.	F.A.
1979—American	OF	4	2	2	1	0	0	1	.500	1	0	0	1.000

WILLIAM LAMAR BEANE
Name pronounced Been.
(Billy)

Born March 29, 1962, at Orlando, Fla.
Height, 6.04. Weight, 195.
Throws and bats righthanded.
Attended University of California at San Diego, La Jolla, Calif.

Major League stolen bases: 1986 (2).
Led International League batters in strikeouts with 130 in 1985.
Tied for Carolina League lead in sacrifice flies with 8 in 1981.
Led Texas League outfielders in fielding percentage with .994 in 1983.

Year Club	League	Pos.	G.	AB.	R.	H.	2B.	3B.	HR.	RBI.	B.A.	PO.	A.	E.	F.A.
1980—Little Falls	NYP	OF	43	138	10	29	3	2	1	14	.210	93	5	3	.970
1981—Lynchburg	Carol.	OF	114	403	47	108	13	●9	9	59	.268	233	8	11	.956
1982—Jackson	Texas	OF	126	418	39	88	13	4	5	36	.211	200	6	10	.954
1983—Jackson	Texas	OF-1B	121	423	53	104	14	1	11	75	.246	382	24	8	.981
1984—Jackson	Texas	OF	123	455	78	128	29	3	20	72	.281	180	5	7	.964
1984—New York	Nat.	OF	5	10	0	1	0	0	0	0	.100	2	0	0	1.000
1985—Tidewater	Int.	OF	135	504	63	143	★34	4	19	77	.284	255	10	6	.978
1985—New York†	Nat.	OF	8	8	0	2	1	0	0	1	.250	1	0	0	1.000
1986—Minnesota‡	Amer.	OF	80	183	20	39	6	0	3	15	.213	118	0	0	1.000
1986—Toledo	Int.	OF	32	126	17	37	5	0	5	17	.294	68	0	4	.944
National League Totals—2 Years			13	18	0	3	1	0	0	1	.167	3	0	0	1.000
American League Totals—1 Year			80	183	20	39	6	0	3	15	.213	118	0	0	1.000
Major League Totals—3 Years			93	201	20	42	7	0	3	16	.209	121	0	0	1.000

Selected by New York Mets' organization in 1st round (23rd player selected) of free-agent draft, June 3, 1980.
†Traded with Pitchers Bill Latham and Joe Klink to Minnesota Twins for Second Baseman Tim Teufel and Outfielder Pat Crosby, January 16, 1986.
‡On disabled list, April 1 to April 21, 1986.

JAMES LOUIS BEATTIE
Name pronounced BEE-tee.
(Jim)

Born July 4, 1954, at Langeley AFB, Hampton, Va.
Height, 6.06. Weight, 225.
Throws and bats righthanded.
Received bachelor of arts degree in art from Dartmouth College, Hanover, N. H., in 1976.

Tied major league records for most putouts by pitcher, inning (3), September 13, 1978 (second inning); most putouts by pitcher, nine-inning game (5), September 13, 1978.
Pitched seven-inning, 2-0 no-hit victory against Spokane, July 9, 1978.
Major League saves: 1981 (1).

Year Club	League	G.	IP.	W.	L.	Pct.	H.	R.	ER.	SO.	BB.	ERA.
1975—Oneonta†	NYP	5	24	2	0	1.000	15	11	5	22	7	1.88
1975—Syracuse	Int'national	5	33	2	2	.500	25	14	12	30	21	3.27
1976—Syracuse	Int'national	17	100	5	5	.500	106	76	67	74	80	6.03
1976—West Haven	Eastern	8	60	5	2	.714	47	19	15	48	33	2.25
1977—West Haven‡	Eastern	3	27	2	0	1.000	14	5	1	22	8	0.33
1977—Fort Lauderdale	Florida St.	9	38	1	3	.250	52	27	25	28	17	5.92
1977—Syracuse	Int'national	12	80	6	5	.545	70	41	37	53	43	4.16
1978—Tacoma	P. Coast	4	23	3	0	1.000	17	5	4	15	12	1.57
1978—New York	American	25	128	6	9	.400	123	60	53	65	51	3.73
1979—Columbus	Int'national	8	53	5	1	.833	31	9	8	47	25	1.36
1979—New York§x	American	15	76	3	6	.333	85	45	44	32	41	5.21
1980—Seattle	American	33	187	5	15	.250	205	115	101	67	98	4.86
1981—Seattle	American	13	67	3	2	.600	59	24	22	36	18	2.96
1981—Spokane	P. Coast	18	120	6	9	.400	115	60	42	70	48	3.15
1982—Seattle	American	28	172⅓	8	12	.400	149	73	64	140	65	3.34
1983—Salt Lake City y	P. Coast	3	16⅔	2	1	.667	19	12	11	13	8	5.94
1983—Seattle	American	30	196⅔	10	15	.400	197	89	84	132	66	3.84
1984—Seattle	American	32	211	12	16	.429	206	86	80	119	75	3.41
1985—Seattle z	American	18	70⅓	6	5	.455	93	61	57	45	33	7.29
1986—Calgary a	P. Coast	3	13⅔	1	1	.500	17	8	8	14	6	5.27
1986—Seattle b	American	9	40⅓	0	6	.000	57	28	27	24	14	6.02
Major League Totals—9 Years		203	1148⅔	52	87	.374	1174	581	532	660	461	4.17

Selected by New York Yankees' organization in 4th round of free-agent draft, June 4, 1975.
†On disabled list, July 13 to July 29, 1975.
‡On disabled list, April 15 to May 2, 1977.
§On disabled list, June 25 to July 22, 1979.
xTraded with Outfielder Juan Beniquez, Catcher Jerry Narron and Pitcher Rick Anderson to Seattle Mariners for Outfielder Ruppert Jones and Pitcher Jim Lewis, November 1, 1979.
yOn Seattle disabled list, March 24 to April 27, 1983; included rehabilitation disability assignment to Salt Lake City, April 12 to April 27, 1983.
zOn disabled list, June 12 to July 26 and August 28, 1985 through remainder of season.
aOn Seattle disabled list, April 3 to June 12 and August 8, 1986 through remainder of season; included rehabilitation disability assignment to Calgary, May 23 to June 11, 1986.
bGranted free agency, November 12, 1986.

CHAMPIONSHIP SERIES RECORD

Year Club	League	G.	IP.	W.	L.	Pct.	H.	R.	ER.	SO.	BB.	ERA.
1978—New York	American	1	5⅓	1	0	1.000	2	1	1	3	5	1.69

WORLD SERIES RECORD

Year Club	League	G.	IP.	W.	L.	Pct.	H.	R.	ER.	SO.	BB.	ERA.
1978—New York	American	1	9	1	0	1.000	9	2	2	8	4	2.00

THOMAS JOSEPH BECKWITH
(Joe)

Born January 28, 1955, at Auburn, Ala.
Height, 6.02. Weight, 200.
Throws right and bats lefthanded.
Attended Auburn University, Auburn, Ala.

Major League saves: 1979 (2), 1982 (1), 1983 (1), 1984 (2), 1985 (1). Total—7.

Year Club	League	G.	IP.	W.	L.	Pct.	H.	R.	ER.	SO.	BB.	ERA.
1977—San Antonio	Texas	12	78	5	5	.500	88	40	29	31	20	3.35
1978—Albuquerque	P. Coast	28	150	8	9	.471	186	118	97	59	80	5.82
1979—Albuquerque	P. Coast	27	113	8	8	.500	119	74	58	64	46	4.62
1979—Los Angeles	National	17	37	1	2	.333	42	18	18	28	15	4.38
1980—Albuquerque	P. Coast	7	14	2	1	.667	15	8	4	12	5	2.57
1980—Los Angeles	National	38	60	3	3	.500	60	17	13	40	23	1.95
1981—Los Angeles†	National					(Did not play)						
1982—Albuquerque	P. Coast	26	101⅓	5	6	.455	138	90	76	80	55	6.68
1982—Los Angeles	National	19	40	2	1	.667	38	14	12	33	14	2.70
1983—Los Angeles‡	National	42	71	3	4	.429	73	40	28	50	35	3.55
1984—Kansas City	American	49	100⅔	8	4	.667	92	39	38	75	25	3.40
1985—Kansas City§	American	49	95	1	5	.167	99	45	43	80	32	4.07
1986—Syracuse x	Int'national	23	125⅓	9	6	.600	123	59	54	97	46	3.88
1986—Los Angeles y	National	15	18⅓	0	0	.000	28	16	14	13	6	6.87
National League Totals—6 Years		131	226⅓	9	10	.474	241	105	85	164	93	3.38
American League Totals—2 Years		98	195⅔	9	9	.500	191	84	81	155	57	3.73
Major League Totals—8 Years		229	422	18	19	.486	432	189	166	319	150	3.54

Selected by Cleveland Indians' organization in 12th round of free-agent draft, June 8, 1976.
Selected by Los Angeles Dodgers' organization in 2nd round of free-agent draft, June 7, 1977.
†On disabled list, April 8, 1981 through remainder of season.
‡Traded to Kansas City Royals for Catcher Joe Szekely and Pitchers Jose Torres and John Serritella, December 8, 1983.
§Released, March 28, 1986; signed by Syracuse (Toronto Blue Jays' organization), April 8, 1986.
xSold to Los Angeles Dodgers, July 31, 1986.
yReleased, November 1, 1986.

CHAMPIONSHIP SERIES RECORD

Year Club	League	G.	IP.	W.	L.	Pct.	H.	R.	ER.	SO.	BB.	ERA.
1983—Los Angeles	National	2	2⅓	0	0	.000	1	0	0	3	2	0.00

WORLD SERIES RECORD

Year Club	League	G.	IP.	W.	L.	Pct.	H.	R.	ER.	SO.	BB.	ERA.
1985—Kansas City	American	1	2	0	0	.000	1	0	0	3	0	0.00

STEPHEN WAYNE BEDROSIAN

Name pronounced Bed-ROHZ-ee-un.

(Steve)

Born December 6, 1957, at Methuen, Mass.
Height, 6.03. Weight, 195.
Throws and bats righthanded.
Attended North Essex Community College, Haverhill, Mass., and
University of New Haven, New Haven, Conn.

Established major league record for most games taken out as starting pitcher, season (37), 1985.
Major League saves: 1982 (11), 1983 (19), 1984 (11), 1986 (29). Total—70.
Tied for Southern League lead in games started by pitchers with 29 in 1980.
Named National League Rookie Pitcher of the Year by THE SPORTING NEWS, 1982.

Year	Club	League	G.	IP.	W.	L.	Pct.	H.	R.	ER.	SO.	BB.	ERA.
1978—Kingsport	Ap'lachian	6	38	2	2	.500	38	18	13	29	25	3.08
1978—Greenwood	W. Carol.	8	55	5	1	.833	45	17	13	58	34	2.13
1979—Savannah†	Southern	13	89	5	5	.500	71	36	30	73	58	3.03
1980—Savannah	Southern	29	★203	14	10	.583	167	91	72	★161	96	3.19
1981—Richmond	Int'national	26	184	10	10	.500	143	76	55	144	99	2.69
1981—Atlanta	National	15	24	1	2	.333	15	14	12	9	15	4.50
1982—Atlanta	National	64	137⅔	8	6	.571	102	39	37	123	57	2.42
1983—Atlanta	National	70	120	9	10	.474	100	50	48	114	51	3.60
1984—Atlanta‡	National	40	83⅔	9	6	.600	65	23	22	81	33	2.37
1985—Atlanta§	National	37	206⅔	7	15	.318	198	101	88	134	111	3.83
1986—Philadelphia	National	68	90⅓	8	6	.571	79	39	34	82	34	3.39
Major League Totals—6 Years		294	662⅓	42	45	.483	559	266	241	543	301	3.27

Selected by Atlanta Braves' organization in 3rd round of free-agent draft, June 6, 1978.
†On disabled list, June 24 to September 18, 1979.
‡On disabled list, August 20 to September 4, 1984.
§Traded with Outfielder Milt Thompson to Philadelphia Phillies for Catcher Ozzie Virgil and Pitcher Pete Smith, December 10, 1985.

CHAMPIONSHIP SERIES RECORD

Year	Club	League	G.	IP.	W.	L.	Pct.	H.	R.	ER.	SO.	BB.	ERA.
1982—Atlanta	National	2	1	0	0	.000	3	2	2	2	1	18.00

TIMOTHY WAYNE BELCHER
(Tim)

Born October 19, 1961, at Mount Gilead, O.
Height, 6.03. Weight, 210.
Throws and bats righthanded.
Attended Mt. Vernon Nazarene College, Mt. Vernon, O.
Named righthanded pitcher on THE SPORTING NEWS College Baseball All-America Team, 1983.

Year	Club	League	G.	IP.	W.	L.	Pct.	H.	R.	ER.	SO.	BB.	ERA.
1984—Madison	Midwest	16	98⅓	9	4	.692	80	45	39	111	48	3.57
1984—Albany	Eastern	10	54	3	4	.429	37	30	20	40	41	3.33
1985—Huntsville	Southern	29	149⅔	11	10	.524	145	99	78	90	99	4.69
1986—Huntsville†	Southern	9	37	2	5	.286	50	28	27	25	22	6.57

Selected by Minnesota Twins' organization in 1st round (first player selected) of free-agent draft, June 6, 1983.
Selected by New York Yankees' organization in secondary phase of free-agent draft, January 17, 1984.
Selected by Oakland A's organization in player compensation pool draft, February 8, 1984. (Oakland received compensation for Baltimore Orioles' signing of free-agent Pitcher Tom Underwood, a Type A player, February 7, 1984.)
†On disabled list, April 10 to May 4 and May 5 to July 23, 1986.

DAVID GUS BELL
(Buddy)

Born August 27, 1951, at Pittsburgh, Pa.
Height, 6.02. Weight, 185.
Throws and bats righthanded.
Attended Xavier University, Cincinnati, O., and Miami University, Oxford, O.
Son of Gus Bell, outfielder with Pittsburgh Pirates, Cincinnati Reds, New York Mets and Milwaukee Braves, 1950 through 1964; scout, Cleveland Indians, 1966, 1968 and 1969; and scout, Texas Rangers, 1985.

Tied major league record for most home runs, opening day of season (2), April 8, 1982.
Major League stolen bases: 1972 (5), 1973 (7), 1974 (1), 1975 (6), 1976 (3), 1977 (1), 1978 (1), 1979 (5), 1980 (3), 1981 (3), 1982 (5), 1983 (3), 1984 (2), 1985 (3), 1986 (2). Total—50.
Led American League in sacrifice flies with 10 in 1981.
Led American League third basemen in total chances with 495 in 1978, 361 in 1981, 540 in 1982 and 523 in 1983.
Led American League third basemen in assists with 364 in 1979 and 281 in 1981.
Led American League third basemen in putouts with 144 and double plays with 44 in 1973.
Tied for American League lead in game-winning RBIs with 16 in 1979.
Tied for American League lead in double plays by third basemen with 30 in 1978.
Led Gulf Coast League second basemen in double plays with 26 in 1969.
Named third baseman on THE SPORTING NEWS American League All-Star Team, 1981 and 1984.
Named third baseman on THE SPORTING NEWS American League All-Star fielding team, 1979 through 1984.
Named third baseman on THE SPORTING NEWS American League Silver Slugger team, 1984.

Year	Club	League	Pos.	G.	AB.	R.	H.	2B.	3B.	HR.	RBI.	B.A.	PO.	A.	E.	F.A.
1969—Sarasota Ind	Gulf C.	2B	51	170	18	39	4	●3	3	24	.229	119	108	7	★.970
1970—Sumter	W. Car.	3B-2B-SS	121	442	81	117	19	3	12	75	.265	116	189	27	.919
1971—Wichita	A. A.	★3-2-S-O	129	470	65	136	23	1	11	59	.289	★139	203	16	.955
1972—Cleveland	Amer.	OF-3B	132	466	49	119	21	1	9	36	.255	284	23	3	.990
1973—Cleveland	Amer.	3B-OF	156	631	86	169	23	7	14	59	.268	146	363	22	.959
1974—Cleveland†	Amer.	3B	116	423	51	111	15	1	7	46	.262	112	274	15	.963
1975—Cleveland	Amer.	3B	153	553	66	150	20	4	10	59	.271	★146	330	25	.950
1976—Cleveland	Amer.	3B-1B	159	604	75	170	26	2	7	60	.281	109	331	20	.957
1977—Cleveland	Amer.	3B-OF	129	479	64	140	23	4	11	64	.292	134	253	16	.960
1978—Cleveland‡	Amer.	3B	142	556	71	157	27	8	6	62	.282	125	★355	15	.970
1979—Texas	Amer.	3B-SS	●162	★670	89	200	42	3	18	101	.299	147	429	17	.971
1980—Texas§	Amer.	★3B-SS	129	490	76	161	24	4	17	83	.329	125	282	8	★.981
1981—Texas	Amer.	3B-SS	97	360	44	106	16	1	10	64	.294	67	284	14	.962

Year Club	League	Pos.	G.	AB.	R.	H.	2B.	3B.	HR.	RBI.	B.A.	PO.	A.	E.	F.A.
1982—Texas	Amer.	★3B-SS	148	537	62	159	27	2	13	67	.296	★131	397	13	★.976
1983—Texas	Amer.	3B	156	618	75	171	35	3	14	66	.277	123	★383	17	.967
1984—Texas	Amer.	3B	148	553	88	174	36	5	11	83	.315	129	323	●20	.958
1985—Texas x	Amer.	3B	84	313	33	74	13	3	4	32	.236	70	192	16	.942
1985—Cincinnati	Nat.	3B	67	247	28	54	15	2	6	36	.219	54	105	9	.946
1986—Cincinnati	Nat.	3B-2B	155	568	89	158	29	3	20	75	.278	105	291	10	.975
American League Totals—14 Years			1911	7253	929	2061	348	48	151	882	.284	1843	4218	221	.965
National League Totals—2 Years			222	815	117	212	44	5	26	111	.260	159	396	19	.967
Major League Totals—15 Years			2133	8068	1046	2273	392	53	177	993	.282	2002	4614	240	.965

Selected by Cleveland Indians' organization in 16th round of free-agent draft, June 5, 1969.
†On disabled list, May 27 to June 17 and August 8 to September 1, 1974.
‡Traded to Texas Rangers for Third Baseman Toby Harrah, December 8, 1978.
§On disabled list, June 9 to June 24, 1980.
xTraded to Cincinnati Reds for Outfielder Duane Walker and a player to be named later, July 19, 1985; Texas Rangers' organization acquired Pitcher Jeff Russell to complete deal, July 23, 1985.

ALL-STAR GAME RECORD

Year League	Pos.	AB.	R.	H.	2B.	3B.	HR.	RBI.	B.A.	PO.	A.	E.	F.A.
1973—American	PH	1	0	1	0	1	0	0	1.000	0	0	0	.000
1980—American	3B	2	0	0	0	0	0	0	.000	0	2	0	1.000
1981—American	3B	1	0	0	0	0	0	1	.000	1	2	0	1.000
1982—American	PH-3B	3	0	0	0	0	0	0	.000	0	1	1	.500
1984—American	3B	1	0	0	0	0	0	0	.000	0	1	0	1.000
All-Star Game Totals—5 Years		8	0	1	0	1	0	1	.125	1	6	1	.875

ERIC ALVIN BELL

Born October 27, 1963, at Modesto, Calif.
Height, 6.00. Weight, 165.
Throws and bats lefthanded.
Tied for Carolina League lead in games started by pitchers with 26 in 1985.

Year Club	League	G.	IP.	W.	L.	Pct.	H.	R.	ER.	SO.	BB.	ERA.
1982—Bluefield	Ap'lachian	11	51⅓	4	1	.800	42	19	12	30	36	2.10
1983—Newark	NYP	18	60	3	2	.600	71	44	33	56	30	4.95
1984—Hagerstown†	Carolina	3	3⅔	0	0	.000	6	4	4	6	5	9.82
1984—Newark	NYP	15	102⅓	8	3	.727	82	40	28	114	26	2.46
1985—Hagerstown	Carolina	26	158⅓	11	6	.647	141	73	55	★162	63	3.13
1985—Baltimore	American	4	5⅔	0	0	.000	4	3	3	4	4	4.76
1986—Charlotte	Southern	18	129⅔	9	6	.600	109	49	44	104	66	★3.05
1986—Rochester	Int'national	11	76⅔	7	3	★.700	68	26	26	59	35	3.05
1986—Baltimore	American	4	23⅓	1	2	.333	23	14	13	18	14	5.01
Major League Totals—2 Years		8	29	1	2	.333	27	17	16	22	18	4.97

Selected by Baltimore Orioles' organization in 9th round of free-agent draft, June 7, 1982.
†On disabled list, May 3 to June 18, 1984.

GEORGE ANTONIO BELL (MATHY)

Born October 21, 1959, at San Pedro de Macoris, Dominican Republic.
Height, 6.01. Weight, 190.
Throws and bats righthanded.
Brother of Rolando and Juan Bell, both shortstops in Los Angeles Dodgers' organization.
Major League stolen bases: 1981 (3), 1983 (1), 1984 (11), 1985 (21), 1986 (7). Total—43.
Tied for American League lead in game-winning RBIs with 15 in 1986.
Tied for International League lead in double plays by outfielders with 4 in 1983.
Led Western Carolinas League in total bases with 270 in 1979.
Named outfielder on THE SPORTING NEWS American League All-Star Team, 1986.
Named outfielder on THE SPORTING NEWS American League Silver Slugger team, 1985 and 1986.

Year Club	League	Pos.	G.	AB.	R.	H.	2B.	3B.	HR.	RBI.	B.A.	PO.	A.	E.	F.A.
1978—Helena	Pion.	OF	33	106	20	33	6	1	0	14	.311	39	4	4	.915
1979—Spartanburg	W. Car.	OF	130	491	78	150	24	★15	22	★102	.305	206	14	8	.965
1980—Reading†‡	East.	OF	22	55	11	17	5	2	0	11	.309	24	0	1	.960
1981—Toronto	Amer.	OF	60	163	19	38	2	1	5	12	.233	92	3	3	.969
1982—Syracuse§	Int.	OF	37	125	11	25	5	4	3	19	.200	72	3	1	.987
1983—Syracuse	Int.	OF	85	317	37	86	11	4	15	59	.271	135	12	6	.961
1983—Toronto	Amer.	OF	39	112	5	30	5	4	2	17	.268	61	1	3	.954
1984—Toronto	Amer.	OF-3B	159	606	85	177	39	4	26	87	.292	289	13	9	.971
1985—Toronto	Amer.	●OF-1B	157	607	87	167	28	6	28	95	.275	320	14	●11	.968
1986—Toronto	Amer.	OF-3B	159	641	101	198	38	6	31	108	.309	270	17	10	.966
Major League Totals—5 Years			574	2129	297	610	112	21	92	319	.287	1032	48	36	.968

Signed as free agent by Philadelphia Phillies' organization, June 23, 1978.
†On disabled list, June 22, 1980 through remainder of season.
‡Drafted by Toronto Blue Jays, December 8, 1980.
§On disabled list, April 20 to May 1, June 14 to June 30 and July 8, 1982 through remainder of season.

CHAMPIONSHIP SERIES RECORD

Year Club	League	Pos.	G.	AB.	R.	H.	2B.	3B.	HR.	RBI.	B.A.	PO.	A.	E.	F.A.
1985—Toronto	Amer.	OF	7	28	4	9	3	0	0	1	.321	13	0	0	1.000

JAY STUART BELL

Born December 11, 1965, at Pensacola, Fla.
Height, 6.01. Weight, 180.
Throws and bats righthanded.

Tied major league record by hitting home run in first major league at-bat, September 29, 1986.
Led Eastern League shortstops in total chances with 613 in 1986.
Led California League shortstops in double plays with 84 in 1985.
Led Appalachian League shortstops in double plays with 43 and total chances with 352 in 1984.

Year Club	League	Pos.	G.	AB.	R.	H.	2B.	3B.	HR.	RBI.	B.A.	PO.	A.	E.	F.A.
1984—Elizabethton	Appal.	SS	66	245	43	54	12	1	6	30	.220	★109	★218	25	.929
1985—Visalia†	Calif.	SS	106	376	56	106	16	6	9	59	.282	176	330	53	.905
1985—Waterbury	East.	SS	29	114	13	34	11	2	1	14	.298	41	79	6	.952
1986—Waterbury	East.	SS	138	494	86	137	28	4	7	74	.277	197	★371	★45	.927
1986—Cleveland	Amer.	2B	5	14	3	5	2	0	1	4	.357	1	6	2	.778
Major League Totals—1 Year			5	14	3	5	2	0	1	4	.357	1	6	2	.778

Selected by Minnesota Twins' organization in 1st round (eighth player selected) of free-agent draft, June 4, 1984.
†Traded with Pitcher Curt Wardle, Outfielder Jim Weaver and a player to be named later to Cleveland Indians for Pitcher Bert Blyleven, August 1, 1985; Cleveland organization acquired Pitcher Rich Yett to complete deal, September 17, 1985.

TERENCE WILLIAM BELL
(Terry)

Born October 27, 1962, at Dayton, O.
Height. 6.00. Weight, 195.
Throws and bats righthanded.
Attended Old Dominion University, Norfolk, Va.

Year Club	League	Pos.	G.	AB.	R.	H.	2B.	3B.	HR.	RBI.	B.A.	PO.	A.	E.	F.A.
1983—Wausau	Midw.	C	17	51	4	9	0	0	0	1	.176	93	12	1	.991
1984—Wausau	Midw.	C	83	253	30	62	10	1	1	23	.245	496	53	4	★.993
1984—Chattanooga	South.	C	2	7	1	1	0	0	0	0	.143	12	1	1	.929
1985—Salinas	Calif.	C	92	263	40	62	15	1	1	40	.236	495	67	16	.972
1986—Chatt.††-Memp.	South.	C-1B	52	136	21	32	9	0	0	15	.235	277	26	9	.971
1986—Kansas City	Amer.	C	8	3	0	0	0	0	0	0	.000	7	0	0	1.000
Major League Totals—1 Year			8	3	0	0	0	0	0	0	.000	7	0	0	1.000

Selected by Oakland A's organization in 6th round of free-agent draft, June 3, 1980.
Selected by Seattle Mariners' organization in 1st round (17th player selected) of free-agent draft, June 6, 1983.
†On disabled list, April 16 to May 21, 1986.
‡Traded to Kansas City Royals' organization for Pitcher Mark Huismann, May 21, 1986.

RAFAEL LEONIDAS BELLIARD (MATIAS)

Name pronounced BELL-ee-ard.

Born October 24, 1961, at Pueblo Nuevo, Mao, D.R.
Height, 5.06. Weight, 150.
Throws and bats righthanded.

Major League stolen bases: 1982 (1), 1984 (4), 1986 (12). Total—17.
Led Carolina League in sacrifice hits with 12 and tied for lead in caught stealing with 15 in 1981.
Tied for Eastern League lead in double plays by shortstops with 69 in 1983.

Year Club	League	Pos.	G.	AB.	R.	H.	2B.	3B.	HR.	RBI.	B.A.	PO.	A.	E.	F.A.
1980—Bradenton Pir.	Gulf C.	SS-2B-3B	12	42	6	9	1	0	0	2	.214	24	39	1	.984
1980—Shelby	S. Atl.	SS	8	24	1	3	0	0	0	2	.125	10	27	5	.881
1981—Alexandria	Carol.	SS	127	472	58	102	6	5	0	33	.216	●205	330	29	.949
1982—Buffalo†	East.	SS	40	124	14	34	1	1	0	19	.274	56	87	5	.966
1982—Pittsburgh	Nat.	SS	9	2	3	1	0	0	0	0	.500	2	2	0	1.000
1983—Lynn	East.	SS-2B	127	431	63	113	13	2	2	37	.262	203	307	26	.951
1983—Pittsburgh	Nat.	SS	4	1	1	0	0	0	0	0	.000	1	3	0	1.000
1984—Pittsburgh‡	Nat.	SS-2B	20	22	3	5	0	0	0	0	.227	12	13	3	.893
1985—Pittsburgh	Nat.	SS	17	20	1	4	0	0	0	1	.200	13	23	2	.947
1985—Hawaii	P. C.	SS-2B	100	341	35	84	12	4	1	18	.246	172	289	5	.989
1986—Pittsburgh§	Nat.	SS-2B	117	309	33	72	5	2	0	31	.233	147	317	12	.975
Major League Totals—5 Years			167	354	41	82	5	2	0	32	.232	175	358	17	.969

Signed as free agent by Pittsburgh Pirates' organization, July 10, 1980.
†On disabled list, April 19 to July 24, 1982.
‡On disabled list, June 28 to August 28, 1984.
§On disabled list, July 28 to August 12, 1986.

ESTEBAN VALERA BELTRE

Born December 26, 1967, at Ingenio Quisfuella, D. R.
Height, 5.10. Weight, 155.
Throws and bats righthanded.

Year Club	League	Pos.	G.	AB.	R.	H.	2B.	3B.	HR.	RBI.	B.A.	PO.	A.	E.	F.A.
1984—Calgary	Pion.	SS	18	20	1	4	0	0	0	2	.200	13	13	10	.722
1985—Utica	NYP	SS	72	241	19	48	6	2	0	22	.199	106	206	26	.923
1986—W. Palm Beach	Fla. St.	SS	97	285	24	69	11	1	1	20	.242	116	273	23	.944

Signed as free agent by Montreal Expos' organization, May 9, 1984.

BRUCE EDWIN BENEDICT

Born August 18, 1955, at Birmingham, Ala.
Height, 6.01. Weight, 185.
Throws and bats righthanded.
Attended University of Nebraska, Omaha, Neb.
Son of David Benedict, pitcher in New York Yankees', Washington Senators'
and St. Louis Cardinals' organizations, 1950 through 1958.
Major League stolen bases: 1979 (1), 1980 (3), 1981 (1), 1982 (4), 1983 (1), 1984 (1), 1986 (1). Total—12.

Year Club	League	Pos.	G.	AB.	R.	H.	2B.	3B.	HR.	RBI.	B.A.	PO.	A.	E.	F.A.
1976—Kingsport	Appal.	C	17	63	10	18	1	0	0	4	.286	98	25	3	.976
1976—Greenwood	W. Car.	C	21	54	7	13	1	0	1	10	.241	93	12	5	.955
1976—Savannah	South.	C	24	73	10	21	1	0	0	7	.288	107	12	2	.983
1977—Savannah	South.	C	124	395	55	104	15	0	7	40	.263	★770	★112	13	.985
1978—Richmond	Int.	C	111	348	41	97	13	0	2	34	.279	592	56	4	★.994
1978—Atlanta	Nat.	C	22	52	3	13	2	0	0	1	.250	81	14	1	.990
1979—Atlanta	Nat.	C	76	204	14	46	11	0	0	15	.225	344	35	6	.984
1980—Richmond	Int.	C	3	10	0	3	0	0	0	0	.300	10	5	0	1.000
1980—Atlanta	Nat.	C	120	359	18	91	14	1	2	34	.253	502	76	7	.988
1981—Atlanta	Nat.	C	90	295	26	78	12	1	5	35	.264	404	★73	7	.986
1982—Atlanta	Nat.	C	118	386	34	95	11	1	3	44	.246	602	73	5	★.993
1983—Atlanta	Nat.	C	134	423	43	126	13	1	2	43	.298	738	91	7	.992
1984—Atlanta	Nat.	C	95	300	26	67	8	1	4	25	.223	504	37	5	.991
1985—Atlanta	Nat.	C	70	208	12	42	6	0	0	20	.202	314	35	4	.989
1986—Atlanta	Nat.	C	64	160	11	36	10	1	0	13	.225	252	28	2	.993
Major League Totals—9 Years			789	2387	187	594	87	6	16	230	.249	3741	462	44	.990

Selected by Atlanta Braves' organization in 5th round of free-agent draft, June 8, 1976.

CHAMPIONSHIP SERIES RECORD

Year Club	League	Pos.	G.	AB.	R.	H.	2B.	3B.	HR.	RBI.	B.A.	PO.	A.	E.	F.A.
1982—Atlanta	Nat.	C	3	8	1	2	1	0	0	0	.250	16	2	0	1.000

ALL-STAR GAME RECORD

Year League	Pos.	AB.	R.	H.	2B.	3B.	HR.	RBI.	B.A.	PO.	A.	E.	F.A.
1981—National	C	1	0	0	0	0	0	0	.000	3	0	0	1.000
1983—National	C	1	0	1	0	0	0	0	1.000	5	0	0	1.000
All-Star Game Totals—2 Years		2	0	1	0	0	0	0	.500	8	0	0	1.000

JUAN JOSE BENIQUEZ (TORRES)

Name pronounced Be-NEE-kez.

Born May 13, 1950, at San Sebastian, Puerto Rico.
Height, 5.11. Weight, 175.
Throws and bats righthanded.

Established modern major league record for most errors, shortstop, two consecutive games (6), July 13 and 14, 1972.
Major League stolen bases: 1971 (3), 1972 (2), 1974 (19), 1975 (7), 1976 (17), 1977 (26), 1978 (10), 1979 (3), 1980 (2), 1981 (2), 1982 (3), 1983 (4), 1985 (4), 1986 (2). Total—104.
Hit three home runs in a game, June 12, 1986.
Led American League outfielders in putouts with 410 and total chances with 434 in 1976.
Led International League in sacrifice hits with 11 in 1971.
Led Florida State League shortstops in assists with 372 and double plays with 51 in 1969.
Named outfielder on The Sporting News American League All-Star fielding team, 1977.

Year Club	League	Pos.	G.	AB.	R.	H.	2B.	3B.	HR.	RBI.	B.A.	PO.	A.	E.	F.A.
1969—Winter Haven	Fla. St.	★SS-2B	120	426	59	111	15	★14	2	59	.261	175	373	★49	.918
1969—Winston-Salem	Carol.	SS	2	10	0	2	0	0	0	0	.200	2	6	0	1.000
1970—Winston-Salem	Carol.	SS	92	335	53	91	12	2	9	37	.272	144	275	35	.923
1970—Pawtucket	East.	SS	56	233	29	58	5	3	4	25	.249	105	167	29	.904
1971—Louisville	Int.	SS	132	534	82	149	12	★16	4	51	.279	205	364	★55	.912
1971—Boston	Amer.	SS	16	57	8	17	2	0	0	4	.298	24	27	6	.895
1972—Louisville	Int.	SS	66	277	40	82	14	7	5	32	.296	114	172	21	.932
1972—Boston	Amer.	SS	33	99	10	24	4	1	1	8	.242	38	88	14	.900
1973—Pawtucket	Int.	O-S-2-3	131	440	80	131	24	4	13	52	★.298	196	176	26	.934
1974—Boston†	Amer.	OF	106	389	60	104	14	3	5	33	.267	264	4	6	.978
1975—Boston‡§	Amer.	OF-3B	78	254	43	74	14	4	2	17	.291	110	17	1	.992
1976—Texas	Amer.	★OF-2B	145	478	49	122	14	4	0	33	.255	411	★18	7	.984
1977—Texas x	Amer.	OF	123	424	56	114	19	6	10	50	.269	311	10	4	.988
1978—Texas yz	Amer.	OF	127	473	61	123	17	3	11	50	.260	309	8	9	.972
1979—New York ab	Amer.	OF-3B	62	142	19	36	6	1	4	17	.254	100	15	2	.983
1980—Seattle cde	Amer.	OF	70	237	26	54	10	0	6	21	.228	176	3	8	.957
1981—California	Amer.	OF	58	166	18	30	5	0	3	13	.181	117	0	5	.959
1982—California	Amer.	OF	112	196	25	52	11	2	3	24	.265	113	4	2	.983
1983—California f	Amer.	OF	92	315	44	96	11	0	3	34	.305	174	8	6	.968
1984—California	Amer.	OF	110	354	60	119	17	0	8	39	.336	197	5	6	.971
1985—California g	Amer.	O-1-3-S	132	411	54	125	13	5	8	42	.304	439	26	4	.991
1986—Baltimore h	Amer.	OF-3B-1B	113	343	48	103	15	0	6	36	.300	211	56	13	.954
Major League Totals—15 Years			1377	4338	581	1193	176	29	70	421	.275	2994	289	94	.972

Signed as free agent by Boston Red Sox' organization, October 1, 1968.
†On disabled list, July 3 to July 28, 1974.
‡On disabled list, July 2 to July 18, 1975.
§Traded with Pitcher Steve Barr, a minor league player to be named later and an estimated $200,000 to Texas

Rangers for Pitcher Ferguson Jenkins, November 17, 1975; Texas acquired Pitcher Craig Skok to complete deal, December 12, 1975.

xOn disabled list, July 31 to August 15, 1977.

yOn disabled list, June 13 to July 13, 1978.

zTraded with Pitchers Paul Mirabella, Mike Griffin and Dave Righetti and Outfielder Greg Jemison to New York Yankees for Pitchers Sparky Lyle, Larry McCall and Dave Rajsich, Catcher Mike Heath, Shortstop Domingo Ramos and cash, November 10, 1978.

aOn disabled list, July 9 to September 1, 1979.

bTraded with Catcher Jerry Narron and Pitchers Jim Beattie and Rick Anderson to Seattle Mariners for Outfielder Ruppert Jones and Pitcher Jim Lewis, November 1, 1979.

cOn disabled list, April 9 to June 2 and July 19 to August 8, 1980.

dOn suspended list, September 2 to September 7, 1980.

eGranted free agency, October 24, 1980; signed by California Angels, December 29, 1980.

fOn disabled list, June 20 to August 9, 1983.

gGranted free agency, November 12, 1985; signed by Baltimore Orioles, January 28, 1986.

hTraded to Kansas City Royals for Shortstop Joe Jarrell and Pitcher Jimmy Daniels, December 17, 1986.

CHAMPIONSHIP SERIES RECORD

Tied American League Championship Series record for most stolen bases, three-game Series (2), 1975.

Year Club	League	Pos.	G.	AB.	R.	H.	2B.	3B.	HR.	RBI.	B.A.	PO.	A.	E.	F.A.
1975—Boston	Amer.	DH	3	12	2	3	0	0	0	1	.250	0	0	0	.000
1982—California	Amer.	OF	2	0	0	0	0	0	0	0	.000	1	0	0	1.000
Championship Series Totals—2 Years			5	12	2	3	0	0	0	1	.250	1	0	0	1.000

WORLD SERIES RECORD

Year Club	League	Pos.	G.	AB.	R.	H.	2B.	3B.	HR.	RBI.	B.A.	PO.	A.	E.	F.A.
1975—Boston	Amer.	OF-PH	3	8	0	1	0	0	0	1	.125	6	1	0	1.000

TODD ERIC BENZINGER

Born February 11, 1963, at Dayton, Ky.

Height, 6.01. Weight, 180.

Throws right and bats left and righthanded.

Year Club	League	Pos.	G.	AB.	R.	H.	2B.	3B.	HR.	RBI.	B.A.	PO.	A.	E.	F.A.
1981—Elmira	NYP	OF-1B	41	141	21	34	10	1	2	8	.241	131	9	2	.986
1982—Winston-Salem	Carol.	OF-1B	121	443	54	97	19	1	5	46	.219	438	28	8	.983
1983—Winter Haven	Fla. St.	OF-1B-3B	125	480	56	134	34	5	7	68	.279	206	10	8	.964
1984—New Britain†	East.	OF-1B	110	391	49	101	25	5	10	60	.258	465	29	14	.972
1985—Pawtucket‡	Int.	OF	70	256	31	64	13	1	11	47	.250	106	3	3	.973
1986—Pawtucket§	Int.	OF-1B	90	314	41	79	13	2	11	32	.252	156	4	2	.988

Selected by Boston Red Sox' organization in 4th round of free-agent draft, June 8, 1981.

†On disabled list, August 10, 1984 through remainder of season.

‡On disabled list, April 10 to June 11, 1985.

§On disabled list, April 11 to April 21, 1986.

JUAN BAUTISTA BERENGUER

Name pronounced Bare-en-GARE.

Born November 30, 1954, at Aguadulce, Panama.

Height, 5.11. Weight, 215.

Throws and bats righthanded.

Major League saves: 1983 (1), 1986 (4). Total—5.

Led Carolina League pitchers in games started with 28 and hit batsmen with 13 in 1976.

Tied for American Association lead in complete games with 9 in 1982.

Tied for Texas League pitchers lead in games started with 26 in 1977.

Tied for Midwest League lead in hit batsmen with 8 in 1975.

Named International League Pitcher of the Year, 1978.

Year Club	League	G.	IP.	W.	L.	Pct.	H.	R.	ER.	SO.	BB.	ERA.
1975—Wausau	Midwest	18	95	5	4	.556	83	41	31	58	50	2.94
1976—Lynchburg	Carolina	28	187	10	13	.435	★175	89	★75	114	★118	3.61
1977—Jackson	Texas	26	181	9	8	.529	143	89	69	★160	★126	3.43
1978—Tidewater	Int'national	24	147	10	7	.588	117	60	60	130	91	3.67
1978—New York†	National	5	13	0	2	.000	17	12	12	8	11	8.31
1979—Tacoma	P. Coast	26	166	8	8	.500	128	101	90	★220	129	4.88
1979—New York	National	5	31	1	1	.500	28	13	10	25	12	2.90
1980—Tidewater	Int'national	27	157	9	●15	.375	122	78	67	★178	76	3.84
1980—New York‡	National	6	9	0	1	1.000	9	9	6	7	10	6.00
1981—Kansas City§-Toronto x	American	20	91	2	★13	.133	84	62	53	49	51	5.24
1982—Evansville	Am. Assoc.	25	156⅓	11	10	.524	152	85	80	127	80	4.61
1982—Detroit	American	2	6⅔	0	0	.000	5	5	5	8	9	6.75
1983—Detroit	American	37	157⅔	9	5	.643	110	58	55	129	71	3.14
1984—Detroit	American	31	168⅓	11	10	.524	146	75	65	118	79	3.48
1985—Detroit y	American	31	95	5	6	.455	96	67	59	82	48	5.59
1986—San Francisco za	National	46	73⅓	2	3	.400	64	23	22	72	44	2.70
National League Totals—4 Years		62	126⅓	3	7	.300	118	57	50	112	77	3.56
American League Totals—5 Years		121	518⅔	27	34	.443	441	267	237	386	258	4.11
Major League Totals—9 Years		183	645	30	41	.423	559	324	287	498	335	4.00

Signed as free agent by New York Mets' organization, February 22, 1975.

†Loaned to Tacoma (Cleveland Indians' organization), March 24, 1979; returned August 29, 1979.

‡Traded to Kansas City for Outfielder Marvell Wynne and Pitcher John Skinner, March 31, 1981.
§Sold on waivers to Toronto Blue Jays, August 8, 1981.
xReleased, March 28, 1982; signed by Evansville (Detroit Tigers' organization), April 4, 1982.
yTraded with Catcher Bob Melvin and a player to be named later to San Francisco Giants for Pitchers Dave LaPoint and Eric King and Catcher Matt Nokes, October 7, 1985; San Francisco acquired Pitcher Scott Medvin to complete deal, December 11, 1985.
zOn disabled list, April 7 to April 28, 1986.
aReleased, December 19, 1986.

BRUCE MICHAEL BERENYI

Name pronounced Buh-RENN-ee.

Born August 21, 1954, at Bryan, O.
Height, 6.03. Weight, 215.
Throws and bats righthanded.
Attended Glen Oaks Community College, Centerville, Mich. and
Northeast Missouri State University, Kirksville, Mo.
Nephew of Ned Garver, pitcher with St. Louis Browns, Detroit Tigers,
Kansas City A's and Los Angeles Angels, 1948 through 1961.

Led American Association in shutouts with 3 and wild pitches with 13 in 1979.
Named Southern League Pitcher of the Year, 1978.

Year Club	League	G.	IP.	W.	L.	Pct.	H.	R.	ER.	SO.	BB.	ERA.
1976—Eugene	Northwest	12	49	3	1	.750	50	37	26	39	55	4.78
1977—Shelby	W. Carol.	25	145	10	8	.556	102	55	37	120	75	★2.30
1978—Nashville†	Southern	23	135	10	5	.667	107	44	37	103	63	2.47
1979—Indianapolis	Am. Assoc.	25	166	9	9	.500	134	64	52	★136	98	★2.82
1980—Indianapolis	Am. Assoc.	20	123	5	8	.385	111	66	59	★121	●100	4.32
1980—Cincinnati	National	6	28	2	2	.500	34	26	24	19	23	7.71
1981—Cincinnati	National	21	126	9	6	.600	97	55	49	106	★77	3.50
1982—Cincinnati	National	34	221⅓	9	★18	.333	208	90	83	157	96	3.36
1983—Cincinnati	National	32	186⅓	9	14	.391	173	92	80	151	102	3.86
1984—Cincinnati‡-New York	National	32	166	12	13	.480	163	93	82	134	95	4.45
1985—New York§	National	3	13⅔	1	0	1.000	8	6	4	10	10	2.63
1985—Tidewater	Int'national	1	1	0	0	.000	3	1	1	1	0	9.00
1986—New York	National	14	39⅔	2	2	.500	47	30	28	30	22	6.35
1986—Tidewater	Int'national	10	49	2	6	.250	55	46	36	48	27	6.61
Major League Totals—7 Years		142	782	44	55	.444	730	392	350	607	425	4.03

Selected by Detroit Tigers' organization in 19th round of free-agent draft, June 4, 1975.
Selected by Cincinnati Reds' organization in secondary phase of free-agent draft, June 8, 1976.
†On disabled list, June 30 to July 27, 1978.
‡Traded to New York Mets for Third Baseman Eddie Williams and Pitchers Jay Tibbs and Matt Bullinger, June 15, 1984.
§On disabled list, April 24 to September 1, 1985; included rehabilitation disability assignment to Tidewater, May 18 to May 21, 1985.

DAVID BRUCE BERGMAN
(Dave)

Born June 6, 1953, at Evanston, Ill.
Height, 6.02. Weight, 180.
Throws and bats lefthanded.
Received bachelor of arts degree in business administration
from Illinois State University, Normal, Ill., in 1974.

Major League stolen bases: 1978 (2), 1980 (1), 1981 (2), 1982 (3), 1983 (2), 1984 (3). Total—13.
Led International League in bases on balls received with 95 in 1979.
Led International League first basemen in putouts with 1,199 in 1976.
Led Eastern League first basemen in assists with 58 in 1975.
Named Eastern League Most Valuable Player, 1975.
Named outfielder on THE SPORTING NEWS College Baseball All-America Team, 1974.

Year Club	League	Pos.	G.	AB.	R.	H.	2B.	3B.	HR.	RBI.	B.A.	PO.	A.	E.	F.A.
1974—Oneonta	NYP	1B	56	201	60	70	6	●7	10	48	★.348	494	★29	8	★.985
1975—West Haven	East.	1B-OF	124	399	76	124	15	6	11	60	★.311	610	61	5	.993
1975—New York	Amer.	OF	7	17	0	0	0	0	0	0	.000	10	1	1	.917
1976—Syracuse	Int.	★1B-OF	134	455	68	134	23	2	7	65	.295	1201	82	10	★.992
1977—Syracuse	Int.	OF-1B	132	468	88	146	29	4	16	59	.312	534	39	8	.986
1977—New York†	Amer.	OF-1B	5	4	1	1	0	0	0	1	.250	8	0	0	1.000
1978—Houston	Nat.	1B-OF	104	186	15	43	5	1	0	12	.231	328	16	4	.989
1979—Charleston	Int.	1B-OF	138	461	78	129	23	3	6	58	.280	910	61	11	.989
1979—Houston	Nat.	1B	13	15	4	6	0	0	1	2	.400	8	0	0	1.000
1980—Houston	Nat.	1B-OF	90	78	12	20	6	1	0	3	.256	187	16	1	.995
1981—Hou.‡-S.F.	Nat.	1B-OF	69	151	17	38	9	0	4	14	.252	255	25	3	.989
1982—San Francisco	Nat.	1B-OF	100	121	22	33	3	1	4	14	.273	321	20	4	.988
1983—San Francisco§	Nat.	1B-OF	90	140	16	40	4	1	6	24	.286	299	27	2	.994
1984—Detroit	Amer.	1B-OF	120	271	42	74	8	5	7	44	.273	658	75	8	.989
1985—Detroit x	Amer.	1B-OF	69	140	8	25	2	0	3	7	.179	306	25	3	.991
1985—Nashville	A. A.	1B	11	39	6	9	1	0	1	6	.231	87	8	1	.990
1986—Detroit	Amer.	1B-OF	65	130	14	30	6	1	1	9	.231	255	29	4	.986
National League Totals—6 Years			466	691	86	180	27	4	15	69	.260	1398	104	14	.991
American League Totals—5 Years			266	562	65	130	16	6	11	61	.231	1237	130	16	.988
Major League Totals—11 Years			732	1253	151	310	43	10	26	130	.247	2635	234	30	.990

Selected by Chicago Cubs' organization in 12th round of free-agent draft, June 8, 1971.
Selected by New York Yankees' organization in 2nd round of free-agent draft, June 5, 1974.
†Traded to Houston Astros, November 23, 1977, completing deal in which Houston traded First Baseman-Catcher Cliff Johnson to New York Yankees for Infielder Mike Fischlin, Pitcher Randy Niemann and a player to be named later, June 15, 1977.
‡Traded with Outfielder Jeff Leonard to San Francisco Giants for First Baseman Mike Ivie, April 20, 1981.
§Traded to Philadelphia Phillies for Outfielder Alejandro Sanchez, March 24, 1984; Traded by Philadelphia with Pitcher Willie Hernandez to Detroit Tigers for Outfielder Glenn Wilson and Catcher-First Baseman John Wockenfuss, March 24, 1984.
xOn disabled list, April 22 to May 29, 1985; included rehabilitation disability assignment to Nashville, May 15 to May 29, 1985.

CHAMPIONSHIP SERIES RECORD

Year—Club	League	Pos.	G.	AB.	R.	H.	2B.	3B.	HR.	RBI.	B.A.	PO.	A.	E.	F.A.
1980—Houston	Nat.	PR-1B	4	3	0	1	0	1	0	2	.333	8	2	1	.909
1984—Detroit	Amer.	PR-1B	2	1	1	1	0	0	0	0	1.000	5	0	0	1.000
Championship Series Totals—2 Years			6	4	1	2	0	1	0	2	.500	13	2	1	.938

WORLD SERIES RECORD

Year—Club	League	Pos.	G.	AB.	R.	H.	2B.	3B.	HR.	RBI.	B.A.	PO.	A.	E.	F.A.
1984—Detroit	Amer.	PR-1B	5	5	0	0	0	0	0	0	.000	22	4	0	1.000

ANTONIO BERNAZARD (GARCIA)
(Tony)

Born August 24, 1956, at Caguas, P.R.
Height, 5.09. Weight, 160.
Throws right and bats right and lefthanded.
Attended University of Florida, Gainesville, Fla., and Humacao College, Humacao, P.R.
Brother of Oscar Bernazard, outfielder in Pittsburgh Pirates'
and Montreal Expos' organizations, 1975 through 1978.

Major League stolen bases: 1979 (1), 1980 (9), 1981 (4), 1982 (11), 1983 (23), 1984 (20), 1985 (17), 1986 (17). Total—102.
Switch-hit home runs in one game, July 1, 1986.
Led American League second basemen in total chances with 810 in 1986.
Led Eastern League in caught stealing with 20 in 1977.
Led American Association second basemen in putouts with 297, assists with 386 and double plays with 101 in 1978.
Led Eastern League second basemen in double plays with 70 in 1976.
Led Florida State League second basemen in assists with 386 in 1975.
Named second baseman on THE SPORTING NEWS American League All-Star Team, 1986.

Year—Club	League	Pos.	G.	AB.	R.	H.	2B.	3B.	HR.	RBI.	B.A.	PO.	A.	E.	F.A.
1974—Kinston†	Carol.	2B	56	225	22	45	3	1	0	16	.200	129	142	19	.934
1974—Sarasota Expos‡	Gulf C.	2B	34	109	11	18	2	1	1	6	.165	95	71	7	.960
1975—W. Palm Beach	Fla. St.	2B-SS	★134	★509	65	121	16	2	6	50	.238	282	389	28	.960
1976—Quebec City	East.	2B	106	334	35	72	8	3	1	26	.216	227	257	18	.964
1977—Quebec City	East.	2B	125	425	68	119	11	6	1	34	.280	273	379	25	.963
1978—Denver	A. A.	★2-3-O	128	479	★107	137	30	9	9	65	.286	302	390	★32	.956
1979—Denver	A. A.	2B	82	273	58	82	15	2	3	29	.300	178	275	●19	.960
1979—Montreal	Nat.	2B	22	40	11	12	2	0	1	8	.300	22	34	1	.982
1980—Montreal§	Nat.	2B-SS	82	183	26	41	7	1	5	18	.224	82	151	9	.963
1981—Chicago	Amer.	2B-SS	106	384	53	106	14	4	6	34	.276	228	320	7	.987
1982—Chicago x	Amer.	2B	137	540	90	138	25	9	11	56	.256	353	443	12	.985
1983—Chi. y-Sea. z	Amer.	2B	139	533	65	141	34	3	8	56	.265	262	422	19	.973
1984—Cleveland	Amer.	2B	140	439	44	97	15	4	2	38	.221	264	397	★20	.971
1985—Cleveland a	Amer.	2B-SS	153	500	73	137	26	3	11	59	.274	313	399	16	.978
1986—Cleveland	Amer.	2B	146	562	88	169	28	4	17	73	.301	★351	442	17	.979
National League Totals—2 Years			104	223	37	53	9	1	6	26	.238	104	185	10	.967
American League Totals—6 Years			821	2958	413	788	142	27	55	316	.266	1771	2423	91	.979
Major League Totals—8 Years			925	3181	450	841	151	28	61	342	.264	1875	2608	101	.978

Signed as free agent by Montreal Expos' organization, November 13, 1973.
†On disabled list, June 10 to June 17, 1974.
‡On temporary inactive list, August 15 to September 25, 1974.
§Traded to Chicago White Sox for Pitcher Richard Wortham, December 12, 1980.
xOn disabled list, September 13, 1982 through remainder of season.
yTraded to Seattle Mariners for Second Baseman Julio Cruz, June 15, 1983.
zTraded to Cleveland Indians for Outfielder Gorman Thomas and Second Baseman Jack Perconte, December 7, 1983.
aGranted free agency, November 12, 1985; re-signed by Indians, January 8, 1986.

NEHAMES BERNSTINE JR.
(Pookie)

Born November 20, 1960, at Bryan, Tex.
Height, 5.10. Weight, 175.
Throws right and bats right and lefthanded.
Attended Lewis-Clark State College, Lewiston, Ida.

Year—Club	League	Pos.	G.	AB.	R.	H.	2B.	3B.	HR.	RBI.	B.A.	PO.	A.	E.	F.A.
1982—Batavia†	NYP	OF-2B	71	263	48	82	13	2	2	18	.312	74	26	2	.980
1983—Waterloo	Midw.	OF-2B	130	455	83	106	14	8	6	29	.233	60	7	5	.931
1984—Buffalo‡	East.	OF	126	479	88	137	16	9	8	52	.286	219	7	4	.983

Year	Club	League	Pos.	G.	AB.	R.	H.	2B.	3B.	HR.	RBI.	B.A.	PO.	A.	E.	F.A.
1985—Pittsfield	East.	OF	50	202	33	63	6	5	1	17	.312	120	5	6	.954
1985—Iowa	A. A.	OF	83	302	52	96	11	4	2	18	.318	168	6	1	.994
1986—Iowa§	A. A.	OF	85	255	34	61	1	3	2	20	.239	130	2	3	.978
1986—Pittsfield	East.	OF	21	69	12	23	7	1	3	4	.333	43	0	0	1.000

Selected by Cleveland Indians' organization in 5th round of free-agent draft, June 7, 1982.

†Batted righthanded.

‡Sold to Chicago Cubs' organization, April 14, 1985, after replacing Infielder-Outfielder Glenn Edwards, who was sold to Chicago organization on April 1, 1985 but was returned due to injury.

§On disabled list, April 11 to April 22, 1986.

DALE ANTHONY BERRA

Born December 13, 1956, at Ridgewood, N. J.
Height, 6.00. Weight, 190.
Throws and bats righthanded.
Son of Yogi Berra, Hall of Fame catcher with New York Yankees and New York
Mets, 1946 through 1963 and 1965; manager, New York Yankees, 1964, 1984 and 1985; manager,
New York Mets, 1972 through 1975; coach, New York Yankees, 1976 through 1983;
and currently coach with Houston Astros; Brother of Larry Berra Jr., catcher in New York Mets'
organization, 1971 and 1972; and Tim Berra, wide receiver with Baltimore Colts, 1974.

Established major league record for most times awarded first base on catcher's interference, season (7), 1983.
Major League stolen bases: 1978 (3), 1980 (2), 1981 (11), 1982 (6), 1983 (8), 1984 (1), 1985 (1). Total—32.
Led National League in intentional bases on balls received with 19 in 1983.
Led New York-Pennsylvania League in sacrifice flies with 8 in 1975.
Led Western Carolinas League third basemen in double plays with 27 in 1976.
Tied for New York-Pennsylvania League lead in double plays by third basemen with 13 in 1975.

Year	Club	League	Pos.	G.	AB.	R.	H.	2B.	3B.	HR.	RBI.	B.A.	PO.	A.	E.	F.A.
1975—Niagara Falls	NYP	3B	36	*269	36	69	6	4	3	*49	.257	67	*137	*24	.895
1976—Charleston	W. Car.	3B	*139	527	78	157	28	5	16	89	.298	129	*269	*41	.907
1977—Columbus	Int.	*3B-SS	125	438	68	127	18	7	18	54	.290	97	252	*29	.923
1977—Pittsburgh	Nat.	3B	17	40	0	7	1	0	0	3	.175	14	22	1	.973
1978—Columbus	Int.	SS-3B	99	361	58	101	18	5	18	63	.280	142	280	22	.950
1978—Pittsburgh	Nat.	3B-SS	56	135	16	28	2	0	6	14	.207	31	84	11	.913
1979—Portland	P. C.	SS-3B	56	210	37	68	13	2	6	32	.324	68	158	8	.966
1979—Pittsburgh	Nat.	SS-3B	44	123	11	26	5	0	3	15	.211	43	86	12	.915
1980—Pittsburgh	Nat.	3B-SS-2B	93	245	21	54	8	2	6	31	.220	88	171	11	.959
1981—Pittsburgh	Nat.	3B-SS-2B	81	232	21	56	12	0	2	27	.241	89	167	8	.970
1982—Pittsburgh	Nat.	SS-3B	156	529	64	139	25	5	10	61	.263	241	505	30	.961
1983—Pittsburgh	Nat.	SS	161	537	51	135	25	1	10	52	.251	286	505	30	.963
1984—Pittsburgh†‡	Nat.	●SS-3B	136	450	31	100	16	0	9	52	.222	186	449	●30	.955
1985—New York	Amer.	3B-SS	48	109	8	25	5	1	1	8	.229	22	74	9	.914
1986—New York§	Amer.	SS-3B	42	108	10	25	7	0	2	13	.231	40	67	4	.964
1986—Tucson	P. C.	3-2-0-S	22	82	8	20	3	0	1	9	.244	25	45	4	.946
National League Totals—8 Years			744	2291	215	545	94	8	46	255	.238	978	1989	133	.957
American League Totals—2 Years			90	217	18	50	12	1	3	21	.230	62	141	13	.940
Major League Totals—10 Years			834	2508	233	595	106	9	49	276	.237	1040	2130	146	.956

Selected by Pittsburgh Pirates' organization in 1st round (20th player selected) of free-agent draft, June 4, 1975.

†On disabled list, August 30 to September 14, 1984.

‡Traded with Pitcher Alfonso Pulido and Outfielder Jay Buhner to New York Yankees for Outfielder Steve Kemp, Infielder Tim Foli and $800,000, December 20, 1984.

§Released, July 27, 1986; signed by Houston Astros' organization, August 4, 1986.

MARK WILLIAM BERRY

Born September 22, 1962, at Lynnwood, Calif.
Height, 6.00. Weight, 180.
Throws and bats righthanded.
Attended Oxnard College, Oxnard, Calif., and University of Arkansas, Fayetteville, Ark.

Tied for Florida State League lead in sacrifice flies with 10 in 1986.
Tied for Pioneer League lead in errors by catchers with 12 and double plays with 4 in 1984.

Year	Club	League	Pos.	G.	AB.	R.	H.	2B.	3B.	HR.	RBI.	B.A.	PO.	A.	E.	F.A.
1984—Billings	Pion.	C-3B	52	191	53	63	15	3	7	43	.330	325	35	13	.965
1985—Cedar Rapids†	Midw.	C	93	319	35	85	16	2	7	38	.266	475	35	5	*.990
1986—Tampa	Fla. St.	C-3B-SS	132	444	76	140	20	4	4	73	.315	476	146	25	.961

Selected by Kansas City Royals' organization in 11th round of free-agent draft, January 12, 1982.
Selected by Kansas City Royals' organization in secondary phase of free-agent draft, June 7, 1982.
Selected by Cincinnati Reds' organization in 6th round of free-agent draft, June 4, 1984.

†On disabled list, June 4 to June 14, 1985.

DAMON SCOTT BERRYHILL

Born December 3, 1963, at South Laguna, Calif.
Height, 6.00. Weight, 210.
Throws right and bats right and lefthanded.
Attended Orange Coast College, Costa Mesa, Calif.

Led Carolina League in passed balls with 18 in 1985.

Year	Club	League	Pos.	G.	AB.	R.	H.	2B.	3B.	HR.	RBI.	B.A.	PO.	A.	E.	F.A.
1984—Quad Cities†	Midw.	C-1B	62	217	30	60	14	0	0	31	.276	314	31	8	.977

Year Club	League	Pos.	G.	AB.	R.	H.	2B.	3B.	HR.	RBI.	B.A.	PO.	A.	E.	F.A.
1985—Winston-Salem ..... Carol.		C-1B	117	386	31	90	25	1	9	50	.233	625	71	11	.984
1986—Pittsfield .... East.		C-OF	112	345	33	71	13	1	6	35	.206	449	61	12	.977

Selected by Chicago White Sox' organization in 13th round of free-agent draft, January 11, 1983.
Selected by Chicago Cubs' organization in 1st round (fourth player selected) of free-agent draft, January 17, 1984.
†Batted righthanded.

KARL JON BEST

Born March 6, 1959, at Aberdeen, Wash.
Height, 6.04. Weight, 210.
Throws and bats righthanded.

Major League saves: 1985 (4), 1986 (1). Total—5.

Year Club	League	G.	IP.	W.	L.	Pct.	H.	R.	ER.	SO.	BB.	ERA.
1978—Stockton	California	12	40	1	5	.167	42	37	21	32	33	4.73
1978—Bellingham	Northwest	10	54	3	3	.500	58	32	30	47	32	5.00
1979—Alexandria	Carolina	24	167	8	11	.421	150	74	60	108	85	3.23
1980—Lynn..................................	Eastern	26	154	9	14	.391	144	116	95	92	*106	5.55
1981—Lynn†.................................	Eastern	13	71	4	4	.500	73	37	30	50	31	3.80
1982—Lynn..................................	Eastern	21	138⅓	9	4	.692	104	63	53	125	90	3.45
1983—Salt Lake City.................	P. Coast	51	84	7	4	.636	86	51	45	108	64	4.82
1983—Seattle..............................	American	4	5⅓	0	1	.000	14	9	8	3	5	13.50
1984—Salt Lake City.................	P. Coast	46	76	6	5	.545	69	52	44	77	55	5.21
1984—Seattle..............................	American	5	6	1	1	.500	7	2	2	6	0	3.00
1985—Calgary............................	P. Coast	4	5⅓	0	0	.000	2	1	0	8	4	0.00
1985—Seattle‡............................	American	15	32⅓	2	1	.667	25	9	7	32	6	1.95
1986—Seattle§............................	American	26	35⅔	2	3	.400	35	19	16	23	21	4.04
1986—Calgary............................	P. Coast	16	17	0	1	.000	16	6	3	20	12	1.59
Major League Totals—4 Years		50	79⅓	5	6	.455	81	39	33	64	32	3.74

Selected by Seattle Mariners' organization in 12th round of free-agent draft, June 7, 1977.
†On disabled list, May 9 to July 25, 1981.
‡On disabled list, June 24, 1985 through remainder of season.
§On disabled list, March 30 to April 18, 1986.

ROLAND AMERICO BIANCALANA JR.

Name pronounced Bee-AHN-ka-la-na.

(Buddy)

Born February 2, 1960, at Larkspur, Calif.
Height, 5.11. Weight, 160.
Throws right and bats right and lefthanded.
Attended College of Marin, Kentfield, Calif., and University of San Francisco, San Francisco, Calif.

Major League stolen bases: 1983 (1), 1984 (1), 1985 (1), 1986 (5). Total—8.
Led American Association shortstops in double plays with 79 in 1982.

Year Club	League	Pos.	G.	AB.	R.	H.	2B.	3B.	HR.	RBI.	B.A.	PO.	A.	E.	F.A.
1978—Sarasota Royals... Gulf C.		SS	32	76	12	13	1	1	0	2	.171	36	81	6	.951
1979—Fort Myers........... Fla. St.		SS	125	357	44	71	7	4	2	32	.199	*236	342	36	.941
1980—Fort Myers........... Fla. St.		SS	92	258	30	44	5	2	0	28	.171	189	232	23	.948
1981—Jacksonville......... South.		SS	132	385	47	81	7	2	2	27	.210	208	374	48	.924
1982—Omaha................... A. A.		SS	130	415	56	104	16	9	2	36	.251	204	●357	18	*.969
1982—Kansas City.......... Amer.		SS	3	2	0	1	0	1	0	0	.500	2	8	0	1.000
1983—Omaha................... A. A.		SS	113	367	41	82	13	3	5	39	.223	184	341	23	.958
1983—Kansas City.......... Amer.		SS	6	15	2	3	0	0	0	0	.200	11	21	3	.914
1984—Kansas City.......... Amer.		SS-2B	66	134	18	26	6	1	2	9	.194	62	144	8	.963
1984—Omaha................... A. A.		2B-SS-3B	58	204	33	53	11	9	7	25	.260	78	128	2	.990
1985—Kansas City†........ Amer.		SS-2B	81	138	21	26	5	1	1	6	.188	83	169	10	.962
1986—Kansas City.......... Amer.		SS-2B	100	190	24	46	4	4	2	8	.242	108	190	16	.949
Major League Totals—5 Years			256	479	65	102	15	7	5	23	.213	266	532	37	.956

Selected by Kansas City Royals' organization in 1st round (25th player selected) or free-agent draft, June 6, 1978.
†On disabled list, July 25 to August 12, 1985.

CHAMPIONSHIP SERIES RECORD

Year Club	League	Pos.	G.	AB.	R.	H.	2B.	3B.	HR.	RBI.	B.A.	PO.	A.	E.	F.A.
1984—Kansas City.......... Amer.		PR-SS	2	1	0	0	0	0	0	0	.000	1	2	0	1.000
1985—Kansas City.......... Amer.		SS	7	18	2	4	1	0	0	1	.222	9	20	0	1.000
Championship Series Total—2 Years			9	19	2	4	1	0	0	1	.211	10	22	0	1.000

WORLD SERIES RECORD

Year Club	League	Pos.	G.	AB.	R.	H.	2B.	3B.	HR.	RBI.	B.A.	PO.	A.	E.	F.A.
1985—Kansas City.......... Amer.		SS	7	18	2	5	0	0	0	2	.278	6	20	0	1.000

BEN AMON BIANCHI

Born August 15, 1961, at Ely, Nev.
Height, 6.04. Weight, 200.
Throws and bats righthanded.
Attended Treasure Valley Community College, Ontario, Ore.,
and Portland State University, Portland, Ore.

Year	Club	League	G.	IP.	W.	L.	Pct.	H.	R.	ER.	SO.	BB.	ERA.
1983—Newark		NYP	19	43	3	2	.600	59	32	24	35	20	5.02
1984—Hagerstown†		Carolina	19	76	2	8	.200	78	44	33	40	57	3.91
1985—Hagerstown‡		Carolina	17	63⅓	2	7	.222	58	24	19	53	35	2.70
1985—Daytona Beach§		Florida St.	7	38⅓	0	4	.000	30	30	29	32	31	6.81
1986—Visalia		California	14	66	7	2	.778	46	26	21	68	38	2.86
1986—Orlando		Southern	16	101⅓	5	4	.556	97	68	55	58	65	4.88

Selected by Baltimore Orioles' organization in 17th round of free-agent draft, June 6, 1983.

†On disabled list, July 2 to August 15, 1984.

‡On disabled list, April 16 to April 28, 1985.

§Traded with Catcher Steve Padia and a player to be named later to Minnesota Twins for Outfielder Mike Hart, March 31, 1986; Minnesota organization acquired Infielder Jeff Hubbard to complete deal, April 23, 1986.

ALPHONSE DANTE BICHETTE

(Known by middle name.)

Born November 18, 1963, at West Palm Beach, Fla.

Height, 6.03. Weight, 210.

Throws and bats righthanded.

Attended Palm Beach Junior College, Lake Worth, Fla.

Led Midwest League in game-winning RBIs with 13 in 1985.

Year	Club	League	Pos.	G.	AB.	R.	H.	2B.	3B.	HR.	RBI.	B.A.	PO.	A.	E.	F.A.
1984—Salem		N'west	OF-1B-3B	64	250	27	58	9	2	4	30	.232	224	24	11	.958
1985—Quad Cities		Midw.	1B-OF-C	137	547	58	145	28	4	11	78	.265	300	21	15	.955
1986—Midland		Texas	OF-3B	62	243	43	69	16	2	12	36	.284	131	30	11	.936

Selected by California Angels' organization in 16th round of free-agent draft, June 4, 1984.

MICHAEL JOSEPH BIELECKI

Name pronounced Bill-LECK-ee.

(Mike)

Born July 31, 1959, at Baltimore, Md.

Height, 6.03. Weight, 200.

Throws and bats righthanded.

Attended Loyola College, Baltimore, Md. and Valencia Community College, Orlando, Fla.

Tied for Eastern League lead in home runs allowed with 24 in 1982.

Tied for South Atlantic League lead in games started with 28 in 1981.

Year	Club	League	G.	IP.	W.	L.	Pct.	H.	R.	ER.	SO.	BB.	ERA.
1979—Bradenton Pirates		Gulf Coast	9	51	1	4	.200	48	21	13	35	21	2.29
1980—Shelby		S. Atlantic	29	99	3	5	.375	106	60	50	78	58	4.55
1981—Greenwood		S. Atlantic	28	192	12	11	.522	172	95	73	163	82	3.42
1982—Buffalo		Eastern	25	157⅓	7	12	.368	165	96	●85	135	75	4.86
1983—Lynn		Eastern	25	163⅔	●15	7	.682	126	73	58	★143	69	3.19
1984—Hawaii		P. Coast	28	187⅔	★19	3	★.864	162	70	62	★162	88	2.97
1984—Pittsburgh		National	4	4⅓	0	0	.000	4	0	0	1	0	0.00
1985—Pittsburgh		National	12	45⅔	2	3	.400	45	26	23	22	31	4.53
1985—Hawaii		P. Coast	20	129⅓	8	6	.571	117	58	55	111	56	3.83
1986—Pittsburgh		National	31	148⅔	6	11	.353	149	87	77	83	83	4.66
Major League Totals—3 Years			47	198⅔	8	14	.364	198	113	100	106	114	4.53

Selected by Kansas City Royals' organization in 6th round of free-agent draft, January 9, 1979.

Selected by Pittsburgh Pirates' organization in secondary phase of free-agent draft, June 5, 1979.

DANN JAMES BILARDELLO

Name pronounced Bill-ar-DELL-oh.

Born May 26, 1959, at Santa Cruz, Calif.

Height, 6.00. Weight, 190.

Throws and bats righthanded.

Attended Cabrillo College, Aptos, Calif.

Major League stolen bases: 1983 (2), 1986 (1). Total—3.

Led Texas League catchers in double plays with 15 in 1982.

Led Pioneer League catchers in double plays with 5 in 1978.

Year	Club	League	Pos.	G.	AB.	R.	H.	2B.	3B.	HR.	RBI.	B.A.	PO.	A.	E.	F.A.
1978—Lethbridge		Pion.	C	42	133	21	33	8	1	2	20	.248	210	36	7	.972
1979—Clinton†		Midw.	C	52	142	18	34	4	0	2	15	.239	283	31	3	.991
1980—Lodi‡		Calif.	C	41	117	22	36	4	0	6	15	.308	169	30	8	.961
1981—Lodi		Calif.	C	105	352	72	108	19	2	21	80	.307	203	39	9	.964
1981—San Antonio		Texas	C	6	19	0	1	0	0	0	1	.053	34	2	1	.973
1982—San Antonio§		Texas	C	103	347	49	99	14	2	17	48	.285	546	★80	15	.977
1983—Cincinnati		Nat.	C	109	298	27	71	18	0	9	38	.238	494	72	5	.991
1984—Cincinnati		Nat.	C	68	182	16	38	7	0	2	10	.209	323	34	3	.992
1984—Wichita		A. A.	C	49	167	21	40	9	0	5	17	.240	290	31	3	.991
1985—Cincinnati		Nat.	C	42	102	6	17	0	0	1	9	.167	198	20	3	.986
1985—Denver x		A. A.	C-1B-3B	67	236	41	57	5	3	10	37	.242	365	50	6	.986
1986—Montreal		Nat.	C	79	191	12	37	5	0	4	11	.194	391	38	8	.982
1986—Indianapolis y		A. A.	C	2	5	1	3	0	1	0	0	.600	6	0	0	1.000
Major League Totals—4 Years				298	773	61	163	30	0	16	74	.211	1406	164	19	.988

Selected by Seattle Mariners' organization in 3rd round of free-agent draft, January 10, 1978.

Selected by Los Angeles Dodgers' organization in secondary phase of free-agent draft, June 6, 1978.

†On disabled list, May 9 to June 14, 1979.
‡On disabled list, June 12 to August 13, 1980.
§Drafted by Cincinnati Reds, December 6, 1982.
xTraded with Pitchers Jay Tibbs, Andy McGaffigan and John Stuper to Montreal Expos for Pitcher Bill Gullickson and Catcher Sal Butera, December 19, 1985.
yReleased, December 19, 1986.

MICHAEL LAWRENCE BIRKBECK
(Mike)

Born March 10, 1961, at Orrville, O.
Height, 6.01. Weight, 190.
Throws and bats righthanded.
Attended University of Akron, Akron, O.

Year Club	League	G.	IP.	W.	L.	Pct.	H.	R.	ER.	SO.	BB.	ERA.
1983—Paintsville	Ap'lachian	7	28⅔	3	1	.750	17	12	6	38	17	1.88
1983—Beloit	Midwest	7	42	2	4	.333	35	22	16	38	17	3.43
1984—Beloit	Midwest	26	177⅔	14	3	.824	134	57	43	164	64	2.18
1985—El Paso	Texas	24	155	9	9	.500	154	67	59	103	64	3.43
1986—Vancouver	P. Coast	23	134⅓	12	6	.667	160	82	69	81	39	4.62
1986—Milwaukee	American	7	22	1	1	.500	24	12	11	13	12	4.50
Major League Totals—1 Year		7	22	1	1	.500	24	12	11	13	12	4.50

Selected by Chicago Cubs' organization in 11th round of free-agent draft, June 7, 1982.
Selected by Milwaukee Brewers' organization in 4th round of free-agent draft, June 8, 1983.

TIMOTHY DEAN BIRTSAS
(Tim)

Born September 5, 1960, at Clarkston, Mich.
Height, 6.07. Weight, 225.
Throws and bats lefthanded.
Received bachelor of science degree in recreation from Michigan State University, East Lansing, Mich.

Year Club	League	G.	IP.	W.	L.	Pct.	H.	R.	ER.	SO.	BB.	ERA.
1982—Oneonta	NYP	6	16⅓	1	1	.500	19	13	7	24	17	3.86
1983—Fort Lauderdale	Florida St.	23	167⅔	12	8	.600	120	57	44	★160	88	2.36
1984—Fort Lauderdale†	Florida St.	11	57⅔	5	1	.833	51	23	23	62	37	3.59
1985—Tacoma	P. Coast	4	26⅔	2	2	.500	21	10	9	25	14	3.04
1985—Oakland	American	29	141⅓	10	6	.625	124	72	63	94	91	4.01
1986—Oakland	American	2	2	0	0	.000	2	5	5	1	4	22.50
1986—Tacoma	P. Coast	19	92⅓	3	7	.300	94	59	52	75	71	5.07
Major League Totals—2 Years		31	143⅓	10	6	.625	126	77	68	95	95	4.27

Selected by New York Yankees' organization in 2nd round of free-agent draft, June 7, 1982.
†Traded with Outfielder Stan Javier and Pitchers Jay Howell, Eric Plunk and Jose Rijo to Oakland A's for Outfielder Rickey Henderson, Pitcher Bert Bradley and cash, December 5, 1984.

JOSEPH ANTHONY BITKER

Born February 12, 1964, at Glendale, Calif.
Height, 6.01. Weight, 175.
Throws and bats righthanded.
Attended Sacramento City College, Sacramento, Calif.
Tied for South Atlantic League lead in shutouts with 4 in 1985.

Year Club	League	G.	IP.	W.	L.	Pct.	H.	R.	ER.	SO.	BB.	ERA.
1984—Spokane	Northwest	14	87	4	4	.500	85	48	33	60	33	3.41
1985—Charleston	S. Atlantic	13	90⅓	9	3	.750	74	35	26	85	31	2.59
1985—Beaumont	Texas	15	98	8	1	.889	91	43	34	64	41	3.12
1986—Beaumont	Texas	18	114⅔	7	7	.500	114	55	45	91	52	3.53
1986—Las Vegas	P. Coast	5	27⅓	2	0	1.000	24	10	10	19	9	3.29

Selected by Detroit Tigers' organization in 3rd round of free-agent draft, January 11, 1983.
Selected by Minnesota Twins' organization in 6th round of free-agent draft, January 17, 1984.
Selected by San Diego Padres' organization in secondary phase of free-agent draft, June 4, 1984.

JEFFREY SCOTT BITTIGER
(Jeff)

Born April 13, 1962, at Jersey City, N.J.
Height, 5.10. Weight, 175.
Throws and bats righthanded.
Attended Montclair State College, Upper Montclair, N.J., and
Jersey City State College, Jersey City, N.J.
Tied for International League lead in games started by pitchers with 28 in 1983.
Named Texas League Pitcher of the Year, 1982.

Year Club	League	G.	IP.	W.	L.	Pct.	H.	R.	ER.	SO.	BB.	ERA.
1980—Little Falls	NYP	7	26	0	1	.000	10	6	3	33	20	1.04
1981—Lynchburg	Carolina	24	137	11	7	.611	121	72	60	★168	79	3.94
1981—Jackson	Texas	4	33	2	1	.667	24	4	4	27	8	1.09
1982—Jackson	Texas	25	164	12	5	.706	106	59	54	★190	94	2.96
1983—Tidewater	Int'national	28	163	12	10	.545	175	90	79	110	★111	4.36
1984—Tidewater†	Int'national	24	134⅔	8	8	.500	124	72	58	70	53	3.88

Year Club	League	G.	IP.	W.	L.	Pct.	H.	R.	ER.	SO.	BB.	ERA.
1985—Tidewater‡	Int'national	24	131⅔	11	7	.611	131	62	54	66	52	3.69
1986—Portland	P. Coast	27	171⅓	13	8	.619	181	83	79	101	58	4.15
1986—Philadelphia	National	3	14⅔	1	1	.500	16	10	9	8	7	5.52
Major League Totals—1 Year		3	14⅔	1	1	.500	16	10	9	8	7	5.52

Selected by New York Mets' organization in 7th round of free-agent draft, June 3, 1980.

†On disabled list, June 13 to June 24, 1984.

‡Traded with Catcher Ronn Reynolds to Philadelphia Phillies for Pitcher Rodger Cole and First Baseman Ronnie Gideon, January 16, 1986.

RECORD AS THIRD BASEMAN

Year Club	League	Pos.	G.	AB.	R.	H.	2B.	3B.	HR.	RBI.	B.A.	PO.	A.	E.	F.A.
1980—Little Falls	NYP	3B-P	22	37	4	7	0	1	0	3	.189	11	24	8	.814

HARRY RALSTON BLACK
(Bud)

Born June 30, 1957, at San Mateo, Calif.
Height, 6.01. Weight, 180.
Throws and bats lefthanded.
Attended Lower Columbia College, Longview, Wash. and received bachelor of arts degree
in finance from San Diego State University, San Diego, Calif. in 1979.
Son of Harry Black, Sr., former minor league hockey player.

Major League saves: 1986 (9).
Led American League in balks with 7 in 1982.

Year Club	League	G.	IP.	W.	L.	Pct.	H.	R.	ER.	SO.	BB.	ERA.
1979—Bellingham	Northwest	2	5	0	0	.000	3	0	0	8	5	0.00
1979—San Jose	California	17	27	0	1	.000	17	11	9	24	16	3.00
1980—San Jose	California	32	86	5	3	.625	67	34	33	73	49	3.45
1981—Lynn	Eastern	22	87	2	6	.250	78	38	29	86	23	3.00
1981—Spokane	P. Coast	4	8	1	0	1.000	12	4	4	4	2	4.50
1981—Seattle†	American	2	1	0	0	.000	2	0	0	0	3	0.00
1982—Kansas City	American	22	88⅓	4	6	.400	92	48	45	40	34	4.58
1982—Omaha	Am. Assoc.	4	29	3	1	.750	23	9	8	20	10	2.48
1983—Omaha	Am. Assoc.	5	35	3	1	.750	31	13	13	32	13	3.34
1983—Kansas City	American	24	161⅓	10	7	.588	159	75	68	58	43	3.79
1984—Kansas City	American	35	257	17	12	.586	226	99	89	140	64	3.12
1985—Kansas City	American	33	205⅔	10	15	.400	216	111	99	122	59	4.33
1986—Kansas City	American	56	121	5	10	.333	100	49	43	68	43	3.20
Major League Totals—6 Years		172	834⅓	46	50	.479	795	382	344	428	246	3.71

Selected by San Francisco Giants' organization in 3rd round of free-agent draft, January 11, 1977.
Selected by New York Mets' organization in secondary phase of free-agent draft, June 7, 1977.
Selected by Seattle Mariners' organization in 17th round of free-agent draft, June 5, 1979.

†Traded to Kansas City Royals, March 2, 1982, completing deal in which Kansas City traded Infielder Manny Castillo to Seattle Mariners for a player to be named later, October 23, 1981.

CHAMPIONSHIP SERIES RECORD

Year Club	League	G.	IP.	W.	L.	Pct.	H.	R.	ER.	SO.	BB.	ERA.
1984—Kansas City	American	1	5	0	1	.000	7	4	4	3	1	7.20
1985—Kansas City	American	3	10⅔	0	0	.000	11	3	2	8	4	1.69
Championship Series Totals—2 Years		4	15⅔	0	1	.000	18	7	6	11	5	3.45

WORLD SERIES RECORD

Year Club	League	G.	IP.	W.	L.	Pct.	H.	R.	ER.	SO.	BB.	ERA.
1985—Kansas City	American	2	5⅓	0	1	.000	4	3	3	4	5	5.06

LARRY MORGAN BLACKWELL

Born October 7, 1964, at Petersburg, Va.
Height, 5.10. Weight, 165.
Throws and bats righthanded.

Tied for Appalachian League lead in bases on balls received with 47 in 1985.

Year Club	League	Pos.	G.	AB.	R.	H.	2B.	3B.	HR.	RBI.	B.A.	PO.	A.	E.	F.A.
1984—Elizabethton	Appal.	OF	63	227	44	53	7	2	0	14	.233	120	7	4	.969
1985—Elizabethton	Appal.	SS	63	221	55	52	7	3	5	24	.246	73	133	*34	.858
1986—Kenosha†	Midw.	OF	75	265	40	64	8	1	5	35	.242	157	8	9	.948

Selected by Minnesota Twins' organization in 4th round of free-agent draft, June 4, 1984.

†On disabled list, May 15 to July 6, 1986.

JEFFREY MICHAEL BLAUSER
(Jeff)

Born November 8, 1965, at Los Gatos, Calif.
Height, 6.00. Weight, 170.
Throws and bats righthanded.
Attended Sacramento City College, Sacramento, Calif.

Led Carolina League shortstops in total chances with 506 in 1986.

Year Club	League	Pos.	G.	AB.	R.	H.	2B.	3B.	HR.	RBI.	B.A.	PO.	A.	E.	F.A.
1984—Pulaski	Appal.	SS	62	217	41	54	6	1	3	24	.249	61	162	24	.903
1985—Sumter	S. Atl.	SS	125	422	74	99	19	0	5	49	.235	150	306	35	.929
1986—Durham	Carol.	SS	123	447	94	128	27	3	13	52	.286	167	★314	25	★.951

Selected by St. Louis Cardinals' organization in 1st round (eighth player selected) of free-agent draft, January 17, 1984.

Selected by Atlanta Braves' organization in secondary phase of free-agent draft, June 4, 1984.

TERRY FENNELL BLOCKER

Born August 18, 1959, at Columbia, S.C.
Height, 6.02. Weight, 195.
Throws and bats lefthanded.
Received degree in health and recreation from Tennessee State University, Nashville, Tenn. in 1981.

Year Club	League	Pos.	G.	AB.	R.	H.	2B.	3B.	HR.	RBI.	B.A.	PO.	A.	E.	F.A.
1981—Little Falls	NYP	OF	36	135	28	46	8	1	7	16	.341	72	6	7	.918
1982—Jackson	Texas	OF	118	438	69	114	20	2	5	38	.260	248	7	3	★.988
1983—Jackson	Texas	OF	66	263	38	81	16	7	3	54	.308	92	5	5	.951
1983—Tidewater	Int.	OF	72	239	26	73	7	2	2	32	.305	133	4	6	.958
1984—Tidewater	Int.	OF	115	386	45	85	10	1	3	31	.220	215	2	6	.973
1985—New York†	Nat.	OF	18	15	1	1	0	0	0	0	.067	4	0	0	1.000
1985—Tidewater	Int.	OF	75	267	40	82	8	4	5	38	.307	183	5	5	.974
1986—Tidewater	Int.	OF	117	434	53	125	13	5	9	47	.288	249	11	7	.974
Major League Totals—1 Year			18	15	1	1	0	0	0	0	.067	4	0	0	1.000

Selected by New York Mets' organization in 1st round (fourth player selected) of free-agent draft, June 8, 1981.
†On disabled list, June 10 to June 25, 1985.

VIDA ROCHELLE BLUE JR.

Born July 28, 1949, at Mansfield, La.
Height, 6.00. Weight, 200.
Throws left and bats left and righthanded.
Attended Southern University, Baton Rouge, La.

Tied American League record for most strikeouts by lefthanded pitcher, extra-inning game (17), July 9, 1971 (pitched 11 of 20 innings).
Pitched 6-0 no-hit victory against Minnesota Twins, September 21, 1970.
Pitched seven-inning, 4-0 no-hit victory against Appleton, June 19, 1968.
Major League saves: 1969 (1), 1975 (1). Total—2.
Led American League in shutouts with 8 in 1971.
Named National League Pitcher of the Year by THE SPORTING NEWS, 1978.
Named American League Pitcher of the Year by THE SPORTING NEWS, 1971.
Named American League Most Valuable Player by Baseball Writers' Association of America, 1971.
Won American League Cy Young Memorial Award, 1971.
Named lefthanded pitcher on THE SPORTING NEWS National League All-Star Team, 1978.
Named lefthanded pitcher on THE SPORTING NEWS American League All-Star Team, 1971.

Year Club	League	G.	IP.	W.	L.	Pct.	H.	R.	ER.	SO.	BB.	ERA.
1968—Burlington	Midwest	24	152	8	●11	.421	102	67	42	★231	80	2.49
1969—Birmingham	Southern	15	104	10	3	.769	80	40	37	112	52	3.20
1969—Oakland	American	12	42	1	1	.500	49	34	31	24	18	6.64
1970—Iowa	Am. Assoc.	17	133	12	3	★.800	88	40	32	★165	55	2.17
1970—Oakland	American	6	39	2	0	1.000	20	12	9	35	12	2.08
1971—Oakland	American	39	312	24	8	.750	209	73	63	301	88	★1.82
1972—Oakland†	American	25	151	6	10	.375	117	55	47	111	48	2.80
1973—Oakland	American	37	264	20	9	.690	214	108	96	158	105	3.27
1974—Oakland	American	40	282	17	15	.531	246	118	102	174	98	3.26
1975—Oakland	American	39	278	22	11	.667	243	103	93	189	99	3.01
1976—Oakland	American	37	298	18	13	.581	268	90	78	166	63	2.36
1977—Oakland‡§	American	38	280	14	●19	.424	●284	138	●119	157	86	3.83
1978—San Francisco	National	35	258	18	10	.643	233	87	80	171	70	2.79
1979—San Francisco	National	34	237	14	14	.500	246	143	★132	138	111	5.01
1980—San Francisco x	National	31	224	14	10	.583	202	79	74	129	61	2.97
1981—San Francisco y	National	18	125	8	6	.571	97	40	34	63	54	2.45
1982—Kansas City	American	31	181	13	12	.520	163	80	76	103	80	3.78
1983—Kansas City z	American	19	85⅓	0	5	.000	96	62	57	53	35	6.01
1984—						(Out of Organized Baseball)						
1985—San Francisco a	National	33	131	8	8	.500	115	70	65	103	80	4.47
1986—San Francisco bc	National	28	156⅔	10	10	.500	137	65	57	100	77	3.27
National League Totals—6 Years		179	1131⅔	72	58	.554	1030	484	442	704	453	3.52
American League Totals—11 Years		323	2212⅓	137	103	.571	1909	873	771	1471	732	3.14
Major League Totals—17 Years		502	3344	209	161	.565	2939	1357	1213	2175	1185	3.26

Selected by Kansas City A's organization in 2nd round of free-agent draft, June 6, 1967.
†On restricted list, March 30 to April 27, 1972.
‡On disqualified list, April 5 to April 16, 1977.
§Traded to San Francisco Giants for Outfielder Gary Thomasson, Catcher Gary Alexander, Pitchers Dave Heaverlo, Alan Wirth, John Johnson and Phillip Huffman, a player to be named later and cash estimated at $390,000, March 15, 1978; Oakland acquired Shortstop Mario Guerrero to to complete deal, April 7, 1978.
xOn disabled list, June 28 to August 2, 1980.
yTraded with Pitcher Bob Tufts to Kansas City Royals for Pitchers Atlee Hammaker, Craig Chamberlain and Renie Martin and a player to be named later, March 30, 1982; San Francisco Giants' organization acquired Second Baseman Brad Wellman to complete deal, April 19, 1982.

zReleased, August 5, 1983; signed by San Francisco Giants, April 6, 1985.
aGranted free agency, November 12, 1985; re-signed by Giants, December 17, 1985.
bOn disabled list, April 28 to May 24, 1986.
cGranted free agency, November 12, 1986.

CHAMPIONSHIP SERIES RECORD

Tied Championship Series records for fewest hits allowed, game (2), October 8, 1974; most earned runs allowed, five-game Series (8), 1973.
Established American League Championship Series record for most games pitched, five game Series (4), 1972.

Year	Club	League	G.	IP.	W.	L.	Pct.	H.	R.	ER.	SO.	BB.	ERA.
1971—Oakland	American	1	7	0	1	.000	7	5	5	8	2	6.43
1972—Oakland	American	4	5⅓	0	0	.000	4	0	0	5	1	0.00
1973—Oakland	American	2	7	0	1	.000	8	8	8	3	5	10.29
1974—Oakland	American	1	9	1	0	1.000	2	0	0	7	0	0.00
1975—Oakland	American	1	3	0	0	.000	6	3	3	2	0	9.00
Championship Series Totals—5 Years		9	31⅓	1	2	.333	27	16	16	25	8	4.60

WORLD SERIES RECORD

Year	Club	League	G.	IP.	W.	L.	Pct.	H.	R.	ER.	SO.	BB.	ERA.
1972—Oakland	American	4	8⅔	0	1	.000	8	4	4	5	5	4.15
1973—Oakland	American	2	11	0	1	.000	10	6	6	8	3	4.91
1974—Oakland	American	2	13⅔	0	1	.000	10	5	5	9	7	3.29
World Series Totals—3 Years		8	33⅓	0	3	.000	28	15	15	22	15	4.05

ALL-STAR GAME RECORD

Only pitcher in All-Star Game history to start in each league: American League, 1971; National League, 1978.
Tied All-Star Game records for most home runs allowed, total games (4); most home runs allowed, inning (2), July 15, 1975 (second inning).

Year	League	IP.	W.	L.	Pct.	H.	R.	ER.	SO.	BB.	ERA.
1971—American		3	1	0	1.000	2	3	3	3	0	9.00
1975—American		2	0	0	.000	5	2	2	1	0	9.00
1978—National		3	0	0	.000	5	3	3	2	1	9.00
1981—National		1	1	0	1.000	0	0	0	1	0	0.00
All-Star Game Totals—4 Years		9	2	0	1.000	12	8	8	7	1	8.00

Named to American League All-Star Team in 1977; replaced due to injury.
Named to National League All-Star Team in 1980; replaced due to injury by Ed Whitson.

RIK AALBERT BLYLEVEN
(Bert)

Born April 6, 1951, at Zeist, The Netherlands.
Height, 6.03. Weight, 205.
Throws and bats righthanded.

Established major league record for most home runs allowed, season (50), 1986.
Tied major league record for most putouts by pitcher, nine-inning game (6), June 24, 1984.
Established American League record for most years, 200 or more strikeouts (8).
Tied American League records for longest one-hit complete game (10 innings), June 21, 1976; most seasons, 200 or more strikeouts (7).
Pitched 6-0 no-hit victory against California Angels, September 22, 1977.
Led American League in home runs allowed with 50 in 1986.
Led American League pitchers in complete games with 24 and tied for lead in games started with 37 in 1985.
Led American League in hit batsmen with 12 in 1976.
Led American League in shutouts with 9 in 1973 and 5 in 1985.
Tied for American League lead in balks with 3 in 1970.
Named American League Rookie Pitcher of the Year by THE SPORTING NEWS, 1970.

Year	Club	League	G.	IP.	W.	L.	Pct.	H.	R.	ER.	SO.	BB.	ERA.
1969—Sarasota Twins	Gulf Coast	7	32	2	2	.500	31	13	10	39	11	2.81
1969—Orlando	Florida St.	6	37	5	0	1.000	36	6	6	41	14	1.46
1970—Evansville	Am. Assoc.	8	54	4	2	.667	48	18	15	63	12	2.50
1970—Minnesota	American	27	164	10	9	.526	143	66	58	135	47	3.18
1971—Minnesota	American	38	278	16	15	.516	267	95	87	224	59	2.82
1972—Minnesota	American	39	287	17	17	.500	247	93	87	228	69	2.73
1973—Minnesota	American	40	325	20	17	.541	296	109	91	258	67	2.52
1974—Minnesota	American	37	281	17	17	.500	244	99	83	249	77	2.66
1975—Minnesota	American	35	276	15	10	.600	219	104	92	233	84	3.00
1976—Minnesota†-Texas	American	36	298	13	16	.448	283	106	95	219	81	2.87
1977—Texas‡	American	30	235	14	12	.538	181	81	71	182	69	2.72
1978—Pittsburgh	National	34	244	14	10	.583	217	94	82	182	66	3.02
1979—Pittsburgh	National	37	237	12	5	.706	238	102	95	172	92	3.61
1980—Pittsburgh§	National	34	217	8	13	.381	219	102	92	168	59	3.82
1981—Cleveland	American	20	159	11	7	.611	145	52	51	107	40	2.89
1982—Cleveland x	American	4	20⅓	2	2	.500	16	14	11	19	11	4.87
1983—Cleveland	American	24	156⅓	7	10	.412	160	74	68	123	44	3.91
1984—Cleveland y	American	33	245	19	7	.731	204	86	78	170	74	2.87
1985—Cleveland z-Minnesota	American	37	★293⅔	17	16	.515	264	121	103	★206	75	3.16
1986—Minnesota	American	36	★271⅔	17	14	.548	262	134	121	215	58	4.01
National League Totals—3 Years		105	698	34	28	.548	674	298	269	522	217	3.47
American League Totals—14 Years		436	3290	195	169	.536	2931	1234	1096	2568	855	3.00
Major League Totals—17 Years		541	3988	229	197	.538	3605	1532	1365	3090	1072	3.08

Selected by Minnesota Twins' organization in 3rd round of free-agent draft, June 5, 1969.
†Traded with Shortstop Danny Thompson to Texas Rangers for Pitcher Bill Singer, Infielders Roy Smalley and Mike Cubbage, Pitcher Jim Gideon and a reported $250,000 cash, June 1, 1976.
‡Traded with First Baseman-Outfielder John Milner to Pittsburgh Pirates for Outfielder-First Baseman Al Oliver and Infielder Nelson Norman, December 8, 1977.
§Traded with Catcher Manny Sanguillen to Cleveland Indians for Pitchers Bob Owchinko, Rafael Vasquez and Victor Cruz and Catcher Gary Alexander, December 9, 1980.
xOn disabled list, May 2, 1982 through remainder of season.
yOn disabled list, May 23 to June 10, 1984.
zTraded to Minnesota Twins for Pitcher Curt Wardle, Outfielder Jim Weaver, Infielder Jay Bell and a player to be named later, August 1, 1986; Cleveland Indians' organization acquired Pitcher Rich Yett to complete deal, September 17, 1985.

CHAMPIONSHIP SERIES RECORD

Year Club	League	G.	IP.	W.	L.	Pct.	H.	R.	ER.	SO.	BB.	ERA.
1970—Minnesota	American	1	2	0	0	.000	2	1	0	2	0	0.00
1979—Pittsburgh	National	1	9	1	0	1.000	8	1	1	9	0	1.00
Championship Series Totals—2 Years		2	11	1	0	1.000	10	2	1	11	0	0.82

WORLD SERIES RECORD

Year Club	League	G.	IP.	W.	L.	Pct.	H.	R.	ER.	SO.	BB.	ERA.
1979—Pittsburgh	National	2	10	1	0	1.000	8	2	2	4	3	1.80

ALL-STAR GAME RECORD

Year League	IP.	W.	L.	Pct.	H.	R.	ER.	SO.	BB.	ERA.
1973—American	1	0	1	.000	2	2	2	0	2	18.00
1985—American	2	0	0	.000	3	2	2	1	1	9.00
All-Star Game Totals—2 Years	3	0	1	.000	5	4	4	1	3	12.00

BRUCE ANTON BOCHTE
Name pronounced BOCK-tee.

Born November 12, 1950, at Pasadena, Calif.
Height, 6.03. Weight, 205.
Throws and bats lefthanded.
Received bachelor of science degree in commerce from
University of Santa Clara, Santa Clara, Calif.

Major League stolen bases: 1974 (6), 1975 (3), 1976 (4), 1977 (6), 1978 (3), 1979 (2), 1980 (2), 1981 (1), 1982 (8), 1984 (2), 1985 (3), 1986 (3). Total—43.
Led American League in grounding into double plays with 27 in 1979.

Year Club	League	Pos.	G.	AB.	R.	H.	2B.	3B.	HR.	RBI.	B.A.	PO.	A.	E.	F.A.
1972—Stockton	Calif.	1B-OF	72	266	36	87	14	2	11	42	.327	470	27	9	.982
1973—El Paso	Texas	1B-OF	122	417	57	133	32	4	10	79	.319	775	41	11	.987
1974—Salt Lake City	P. C.	OF-1B	92	332	55	118	15	2	9	56	.355	218	12	6	.975
1974—California	Amer.	OF-1B	57	196	24	53	4	1	5	26	.270	248	9	5	.981
1975—California†	Amer.	1B	107	375	41	107	19	3	3	48	.285	850	51	12	.987
1976—California	Amer.	OF-1B	146	466	53	120	17	1	2	49	.258	651	42	7	.990
1977—Calif.‡-Cleve.§	Amer.	OF-1B	137	492	64	148	23	1	7	51	.301	486	33	9	.983
1978—Seattle	Amer.	OF-1B	140	486	58	128	25	3	11	51	.263	180	7	3	.984
1979—Seattle	Amer.	1B	150	554	81	175	38	6	16	100	.316	1361	114	*14	.991
1980—Seattle	Amer.	1B	148	520	62	156	34	4	13	78	.300	1273	98	6	.996
1981—Seattle	Amer.	1B-OF	99	335	39	87	16	0	6	30	.260	766	49	4	.995
1982—Seattle x	Amer.	OF-1B	144	509	58	151	21	0	12	70	.297	428	26	3	.993
1983—					(Out of Organized Baseball)										
1984—Oakland y	Amer.	1B	148	469	58	124	23	0	5	52	.264	1048	66	8	.993
1985—Oakland z	Amer.	1B	137	424	48	125	17	1	14	60	.295	942	60	10	.990
1986—Oakland a	Amer.	1B	125	407	57	104	13	1	6	43	.256	912	88	9	.991
Major League Totals—12 Years			1538	5233	643	1478	250	21	100	658	.282	9145	643	90	.991

Selected by California Angels' organization in 2nd round of free-agent draft, June 6, 1972.
†On disabled list, June 24 to August 13, 1975.
‡Traded with Pitcher Sid Monge and cash estimated at $250,000 to Cleveland Indians for Pitchers Dave Schuler and Dave LaRoche, May 11, 1977.
§Granted free agency, November 2, 1977; signed by Seattle Mariners, December 20, 1977.
xGranted free agency, November 10, 1982; signed by Oakland A's, November 14, 1983.
yGranted free agency after not being tendered a contract, December 20, 1984; re-signed by A's, December 24, 1984.
zGranted free agency, November 12, 1985; re-signed by A's, December 4, 1985.
aGranted free agency, November 10, 1986.

ALL-STAR GAME RECORD

Year League	Pos.	AB.	R.	H.	2B.	3B.	HR.	RBI.	B.A.	PO.	A.	E.	F.A.
1979—American	PH-1B	1	0	1	0	0	0	1	1.000	2	0	0	1.000

—DID YOU KNOW—

That Dwight Gooden's 3-2 loss to the Reds on May 11 was the first loss suffered by a Mets starting pitcher in 1986? The starting four of Gooden, Bob Ojeda, Sid Fernandez and Ron Darling were a combined 17-0 to that point.

BRUCE DOUGLAS BOCHY

Name pronounced BOW-chee.

Born April 16, 1955, At Landes de Bussac, France.
Height, 6.04. Weight, 229.
Throws and bats righthanded.
Attended Brevard Community College, Cocoa, Fla., and
Florida State University, Tallahassee, Fla.
Brother of Joe Bochy, catcher in Minnesota Twins' organization, 1969 through 1972.

Major League stolen bases: 1986 (1).
Tied for Florida State League lead in passed balls with 12 in 1977.

Year Club League	Pos.	G.	AB.	R.	H.	2B.	3B.	HR.	RBI.	B.A.	PO.	A.	E.	F.A.
1975—Covington .... Appal.	C	37	145	31	49	9	0	4	34	.338	231	36	4	.985
1976—Columbus .... South.	C	69	230	9	53	6	0	0	16	.230	266	45	6	.981
1976—Dubuque................. Midw.	C-1B	30	103	9	25	4	0	1	8	.243	165	25	5	.974
1977—Cocoa .... Fla. St.	C	128	430	40	109	18	2	3	35	.253	★492	67	12	.979
1978—Columbus .... South.	C	79	261	25	70	10	2	7	34	.268	419	49	7	.985
1978—Houston .... Nat.	C	54	154	8	41	8	0	3	15	.266	268	35	8	.974
1979—Houston .... Nat.	C	56	129	11	28	4	0	1	6	.217	198	29	7	.970
1980—Houston† .... Nat.	C-1B	22	22	0	4	1	0	0	0	.182	19	1	0	1.000
1981—Tidewater............. Int.	C	85	269	23	61	11	2	8	38	.227	253	35	3	.990
1982—Tidewater............. Int.	C	81	251	32	57	11	0	15	52	.227	427	57	5	★.990
1982—New York‡............ Nat.	C-1B	17	49	4	15	4	0	2	8	.306	92	8	4	.962
1983—Las Vegas............. P. C.	C	42	145	28	44	8	1	11	33	.303	157	21	3	.983
1983—San Diego .... Nat.	C	23	42	2	9	1	1	0	3	.214	51	5	0	1.000
1984—Las Vegas............. P. C.	C	34	121	18	32	7	0	7	22	.264	189	17	2	.990
1984—San Diego .... Nat.	C	37	92	10	21	5	1	4	15	.228	147	12	2	.988
1985—San Diego .... Nat.	C	48	112	16	30	2	0	6	13	.268	148	11	2	.988
1986—San Diego .... Nat.	C	63	127	16	32	9	0	8	22	.252	202	22	2	.991
Major League Totals—8 Years.................		320	727	67	180	34	2	24	82	.248	1125	123	25	.980

Selected by Chicago White Sox' organization in 8th round of free-agent draft, January 9, 1975.
Selected by Houston Astros' organization in secondary phase of free-agent draft, June 4, 1975.
†Traded to New York Mets' organization for two players to be named later, February 11, 1981; Houston Astros acquired Infielder Randy Rogers and Catcher Stan Hough to complete deal, April 3, 1981.
‡Released, January 21, 1983; signed by Las Vegas (San Diego Padres' organization), February 23, 1983.

CHAMPIONSHIP SERIES RECORD

Year Club League	Pos.	G.	AB.	R.	H.	2B.	3B.	HR.	RBI.	B.A.	PO.	A.	E.	F.A.
1980—Houston .... Nat.	C	1	1	0	0	0	0	0	0	.000	5	1	0	1.000

WORLD SERIES RECORD

Year Club League	Pos.	G.	AB.	R.	H.	2B.	3B.	HR.	RBI.	B.A.	PO.	A.	E.	F.A.
1984—San Diego .... Nat.	PH	1	1	0	1	0	0	0	0	1.000	0	0	0	.000

RANDY WALTER BOCKUS

Born October 5, 1960, at Canton, O.
Height, 6.02. Weight, 190.
Throws right and bats lefthanded.
Attended Kent State University, Kent, O.

Led Texas League pitchers in complete games with 15 and tied for lead in games started with 27 in 1985.
Led California League pitchers in games started with 30 in 1983.
Tied for Texas League in shutouts with 3 in 1984.

Year Club	League	G.	IP.	W.	L.	Pct.	H.	R.	ER.	SO.	BB.	ERA.
1982—Great Falls.....................	Pioneer	18	53	2	0	1.000	60	38	27	42	22	4.58
1983—Fresno............................	California	30	196	14	6	.700	185	89	78	★144	78	3.58
1984—Shreveport	Texas	18	128⅓	8	5	.615	106	44	40	93	54	2.81
1985—Shreveport	Texas	28	★201	★14	11	.560	196	85	61	126	44	★2.73
1986—Phoenix..........................	P. Coast	42	122⅔	11	6	.647	139	69	58	55	54	4.26
1986—San Francisco†	National	5	7	0	0	.000	7	5	2	4	6	2.57
Major League Totals—1 Year.................................		5	7	0	0	.000	7	5	2	4	6	2.57

Selected by San Francisco Giants' organization in 34th round of free-agent draft, June 7, 1982.
†Appeared in one game as an outfielder with no chances.

MICHAEL JAMES BODDICKER

Name pronounced BOD-dick-er

(Mike)

Born August 23, 1957, at Cedar Rapids, Iowa.
Height, 5.11. Weight, 172.
Throws and bats righthanded.
Attended University of Iowa, Iowa City, Iowa.

Tied modern major league record for most putouts by pitcher, season (49), 1984.
Led American League in shutouts with 5 in 1983.
Named American League Rookie Pitcher of the Year by THE SPORTING NEWS, 1983.
Named righthanded pitcher on THE SPORTING NEWS American League All-Star Team, 1984.

Year Club	League	G.	IP.	W.	L.	Pct.	H.	R.	ER.	SO.	BB.	ERA.
1978—Bluefield	Ap'lachian	8	19	2	1	.667	9	2	1	28	10	0.47
1978—Charlotte	Southern	10	65	4	3	.571	42	15	14	48	17	1.94
1978—Rochester	Int'national	1	5	1	0	1.000	4	1	1	3	2	1.80
1979—Charlotte	Southern	14	102	9	3	.750	82	40	34	89	36	3.00
1979—Rochester	Int'national	15	72	4	6	.400	88	48	48	48	27	6.00
1980—Rochester	Int'national	25	190	12	9	.571	149	57	46	109	35	2.18
1980—Baltimore	American	1	7	0	1	.000	6	6	5	4	5	6.43
1981—Rochester	Int'national	30	182	10	10	.500	182	91	85	109	66	4.20
1981—Baltimore	American	2	6	0	0	.000	6	4	3	2	2	4.50
1982—Rochester	Int'national	20	133⅓	10	5	.667	121	59	53	82	36	3.58
1982—Baltimore	American	7	25⅔	1	0	1.000	25	10	10	20	12	3.51
1983—Rochester	Int'national	4	23⅔	3	1	.750	17	6	5	18	13	1.90
1983—Baltimore	American	27	179	16	8	.667	141	65	55	120	52	2.77
1984—Baltimore†	American	34	261⅓	*20	11	.645	218	95	81	128	81	*2.79
1985—Baltimore‡	American	32	203⅓	12	17	.414	227	104	92	135	89	4.07
1986—Baltimore§	American	33	218⅓	14	12	.538	214	125	114	175	74	4.70
Major League Totals—7 Years		136	900⅔	63	49	.563	837	409	360	584	315	3.60

Selected by Montreal Expos' organization in 8th round of free-agent draft, June 4, 1975.
Selected by Baltimore Orioles' organization in 6th round of free-agent draft, June 6, 1978.
†Appeared in one game as a pinch-runner.
‡Appeared in two games as a pinch-runner.
§On disabled list, April 20 to May 10, 1986.

CHAMPIONSHIP SERIES RECORD

Established Championship Series record for most strikeouts, four-game Series (14), 1983.
Tied Championship Series record for most strikeouts, game (14), October 6, 1983.

Year Club	League	G.	IP.	W.	L.	Pct.	H.	R.	ER.	SO.	BB.	ERA.
1983—Baltimore	American	1	9	1	0	1.000	5	0	0	14	3	0.00

WORLD SERIES RECORD

Year Club	League	G.	IP.	W.	L.	Pct.	H.	R.	ER.	SO.	BB.	ERA.
1983—Baltimore	American	1	9	1	0	1.000	3	1	0	6	0	0.00

ALL-STAR GAME RECORD

Member of American League All-Star Team in 1984; did not play.

DANIEL RAYMOND BOEVER

(Name pronounced Beaver.)

(Dan)

Born May 8, 1961, at Vermillion, S.D.
Height, 6.02. Weight, 190.
Throws and bats righthanded.
Attended Westark Community College, Fort Smith, Ark., and
University of Nebraska, Lincoln, Neb.

Year Club	League	Pos.	G.	AB.	R.	H.	2B.	3B.	HR.	RBI.	B.A.	PO.	A.	E.	F.A.
1983—Billings	Pion.	OF	22	85	24	25	8	1	3	20	.294	34	1	5	.875
1984—Tampa	Fla. St.	OF	10	23	3	5	0	0	0	0	.217	3	1	0	1.000
1984—Cedar Rapids	Midw.	OF	66	208	20	54	10	0	6	34	.260	95	9	5	.954
1985—Cedar Rapids	Midw.	OF-1B	134	481	61	136	30	5	11	70	.283	198	16	6	.973
1986—Denver	A. A.	OF	11	26	2	5	1	0	0	2	.192	15	0	1	.938
1986—Vermont	East.	OF	124	437	66	131	26	2	13	80	.300	248	12	9	.967

Selected by Cincinnati Reds' organization in 5th round of free-agent draft, January 8, 1980.
Selected by Atlanta Braves' organization in 5th round of free-agent draft, January 13, 1981.
Selected by Toronto Blue Jays' organization in 23rd round of free-agent draft, June 7, 1982.
Selected by Cincinnati Reds' organization in 8th round of free-agent draft, June 6, 1983.

JOSEPH MARTIN BOEVER

Name pronounced BAY-vur.

(Joe)

Born October 4, 1960, at St. Louis, Mo.
Height, 6.01. Weight, 200.
Throws and bats righthanded.
Attended Crowder College, Neosho, Mo., St. Louis Community College at
Meramec, St. Louis, Mo., and University of Nevada, Las Vegas, Nev.

Led Florida State League in games finished in relief with 38 and tied for lead in saves with 14 in 1984.
Led Florida State League in games finished in relief with 46, saves with 26 and intentional bases on balls issued with 12 in 1983.
Tied for New York-Pennsylvania League lead in intentional bases on balls issued with 5 in 1982.

Year Club	League	G.	IP.	W.	L.	Pct.	H.	R.	ER.	SO.	BB.	ERA.
1982—Erie	NYP	19	32⅔	2	3	.400	20	8	7	63	12	1.93
1982—Springfield	Midwest	3	4	0	0	.000	3	1	1	7	2	2.25
1983—St. Petersburg	Florida St.	53	80⅓	5	6	.455	61	29	27	57	37	3.02
1984—Arkansas	Texas	8	11	0	1	.000	10	11	10	12	12	8.18
1984—St. Petersburg	Florida St.	48	77⅔	6	4	.600	52	31	26	81	45	3.01

Year Club	League	G.	IP.	W.	L.	Pct.	H.	R.	ER.	SO.	BB.	ERA.
1985—Arkansas	Texas	27	37⅔	3	1	.750	21	5	5	45	23	1.19
1985—Louisville	Am. Assoc.	21	35⅓	3	2	.600	28	11	8	37	22	2.04
1985—St. Louis	National	13	16⅓	0	0	.000	17	8	8	20	4	4.41
1986—St. Louis	National	11	21⅔	0	1	.000	19	5	4	8	11	1.66
1986—Louisville	Am. Assoc.	51	88	4	5	.444	71	25	22	75	48	2.25
Major League Totals—2 Years		24	38	0	1	.000	36	13	12	28	15	2.84

Signed as free agent by St. Louis Cardinals' organization, June 25, 1982.

WADE ANTHONY BOGGS

Born June 15, 1958, at Omaha, Neb.
Height, 6.02. Weight, 190.
Throws right and bats lefthanded.
Attended Hillsborough Community College, Tampa, Fla.

Tied major league record for most games, one or more hits, season (135), 1985.
Established American League records for highest batting average, rookie season, 100 or more games (.349), 1982; most singles, season (187), 1985.
Major League stolen bases: 1982 (1), 1983 (3), 1984 (3), 1985 (2). Total—9.
Led American League in bases on balls received with 105 in 1986.
Led American league third basemen in total chances with 486 in 1985.
Led American League third basemen in double plays with 30 in 1984.
Named third baseman on THE SPORTING NEWS American League All-Star Team, 1983, 1985 and 1986.
Named third baseman on THE SPORTING NEWS American League Silver Slugger team, 1983 and 1986.

Year—Club	League	Pos.	G.	AB.	R.	H.	2B.	3B.	HR.	RBI.	B.A.	PO.	A.	E.	F.A.
1976—Elmira	NYP	3B	57	179	29	47	6	0	0	15	.263	36	75	16	.874
1977—Winston-Salem	Carol.	3B-2B-SS	117	422	67	140	13	1	2	55	.332	145	223	27	.932
1978—Bristol	East.	3-S-2-O	109	354	63	110	14	2	1	32	.311	62	107	7	.960
1979—Bristol†	East.	★3-S-2	113	406	56	132	17	2	0	41	.325	94	213	15	★.953
1980—Pawtucket	Int.	3B-1B	129	418	51	128	21	0	1	45	.306	108	156	12	.957
1981—Pawtucket	Int.	3B-1B	137	498	67	★167	★41	3	5	60	★.335	359	238	26	.958
1982—Boston	Amer.	1B-3B-OF	104	338	51	118	14	1	5	44	.349	489	168	8	.988
1983—Boston	Amer.	3B	153	582	100	210	44	7	5	74	★.361	118	368	★27	.947
1984—Boston	Amer.	3B	158	625	109	203	31	4	6	55	.325	141	330	●20	.959
1985—Boston	Amer.	3B	161	653	107	★240	42	3	8	78	★.368	134	335	17	.965
1986—Boston	Amer.	3B	149	580	107	207	47	2	8	71	★.357	★121	267	19	.953
Major League Totals—5 Years			725	2778	474	978	178	17	32	322	.352	1003	1468	91	.964

Selected by Boston Red Sox' organization in 7th round of free-agent draft, June 8, 1976.
†On disabled list, April 20 to May 2, 1979.

CHAMPIONSHIP SERIES RECORD

Year Club	League	Pos.	G.	AB.	R.	H.	2B.	3B.	HR.	RBI.	B.A.	PO.	A.	E.	F.A.
1986—Boston	Amer.	3B	7	30	3	7	1	1	0	2	.233	7	13	2	.909

WORLD SERIES RECORD

Tied World Series record for most assists by third baseman, inning (3), October 19, 1986 (third inning).

Year Club	League	Pos.	G.	AB.	R.	H.	2B.	3B.	HR.	RBI.	B.A.	PO.	A.	E.	F.A.
1986—Boston	Amer.	3B	7	31	3	9	3	0	0	3	.290	4	15	0	1.000

ALL-STAR GAME RECORD

Year League	Pos.	AB.	R.	H.	2B.	3B.	HR.	RBI.	B.A.	PO.	A.	E.	F.A.
1985—American	3B	0	0	0	0	0	0	0	.000	0	0	0	.000
1986—American	3B	3	0	1	0	0	0	0	.333	0	1	0	1.000
All-Star Game Totals—2 Years		3	0	1	0	0	0	0	.333	0	1	0	1.000

BARRY LAMAR BONDS

Born July 24, 1964, at Riverside, Calif.
Height, 6.01. Weight, 185.
Throws and bats lefthanded.
Attended Arizona State University, Tempe, Ariz.
Son of Bobby Bonds, outfielder with San Francisco, New York Yankees, California,
Chicago White Sox, Texas, Cleveland, St. Louis and Chicago Cubs,
1968 through 1981; and coach with Cleveland Indians since 1984.

Major League stolen bases: 1986 (36).
Named outfielder on THE SPORTING NEWS College Baseball All-America Team, 1985.

Year Club	League	Pos.	G.	AB.	R.	H.	2B.	3B.	HR.	RBI.	B.A.	PO.	A.	E.	F.A.
1985—Prince William	Carol.	OF	71	254	49	76	16	4	13	37	.299	202	4	5	.976
1986—Hawaii	P. C.	OF	44	148	30	46	7	2	7	37	.311	109	4	2	.983
1986—Pittsburgh	Nat.	OF	113	413	72	92	26	3	16	48	.223	280	9	5	.983
Major League Totals—1 Year		113	413	72	92	26	3	16	48	.223	280	9	5	.983

Selected by San Francisco Giants' organization in 2nd round of free-agent draft, June 7, 1982.
Selected by Pittsburgh Pirates' organization in 1st round (sixth player selected) of free-agent draft, June 3, 1985.

JUAN GUILLERMO BONILLA

Name pronounced Boh-NEE-yah.

Born February 12, 1956, at Santurce, Puerto Rico.
Height, 5.09. Weight, 170.
Throws and bats righthanded.
Attended Florida State University, Tallahassee, Fla.

Major League stolen bases: 1981 (4), 1983 (3). Total—7.
Led Midwest League in sacrifice flies with 13 in 1978.
Led Midwest League second basemen in double plays with 84 in 1978, Southern League second basemen with 104 in 1979 and Pacific Coast League second basemen with 110 in 1980.

Year Club	League	Pos.	G.	AB.	R.	H.	2B.	3B.	HR.	RBI.	B.A.	PO.	A.	E.	F.A.
1978—Waterloo	Midw.	2B	130	470	81	137	32	1	13	78	.291	*285	*381	21	*.969
1979—Chattanooga	South.	2B	138	550	80	150	26	0	5	59	.273	332	360	18	.975
1980—Tacoma†	P. C.	2B	139	502	66	152	27	2	4	55	.303	*366	*422	15	.981
1981—San Diego	Nat.	2B	99	369	30	107	13	2	1	25	.290	229	290	*13	.976
1982—San Diego‡	Nat.	2B	45	182	21	51	6	2	0	8	.280	99	134	6	.975
1983—San Diego§	Nat.	2B	152	556	55	132	17	4	4	45	.237	335	414	11	.986
1984—..................................					(Out of Organized Baseball)										
1985—New York	Amer.	2B	8	16	0	2	1	0	0	2	.125	7	14	1	.955
1985—Columbus x	Int.	2B-SS-3B	102	388	60	128	22	0	1	52	*.330	155	215	15	.961
1986—Baltimore y	Amer.	2B-3B	102	284	33	69	10	1	1	18	.243	143	175	10	.970
National League Totals—3 Years			296	1107	106	290	36	8	5	78	.262	663	838	30	.980
American League Totals—2 Years			110	300	33	71	11	1	1	20	.237	150	189	11	.969
Major League Totals—5 Years			406	1407	139	361	47	9	6	98	.257	813	1027	41	.978

Selected by New York Yankees' organization in 24th round of free-agent draft, June 7, 1977.
Signed as free agent by Cleveland Indians' organization, January 6, 1978.
†Traded to San Diego Padres for Pitcher Bob Lacey, April 1, 1981.
‡On disabled list, May 20 to September 21, 1982.
§Released, March 26, 1984; signed by Columbus (New York Yankees' organization), February 26, 1985.
xReleased, December 11, 1985; signed by Baltimore Orioles, January 15, 1986.
yReleased, November 12, 1986.

ROBERTO MARTIN ANTONIO BONILLA

Name pronounced Boh-NEE-yah.

(Bobby)

Born February 23, 1963, at New York, N.Y.
Height, 6.03. Weight, 210.
Throw right and bats left and righthanded.
Attended New York Technical College, Westbury, N.Y.

Major League stolen bases: 1986 (8).

Year Club	League	Pos.	G.	AB.	R.	H.	2B.	3B.	HR.	RBI.	B.A.	PO.	A.	E.	F.A.
1981—Bradenton Pir.	Gulf C.	1B-C-3B	22	69	6	15	5	0	0	7	.217	124	23	5	.967
1982—Bradenton Pir.	Gulf C.	1B	47	167	20	38	3	0	5	26	.228	318	36	*14	.962
1983—Alexandria	Carol.	OF-1B	●136	504	88	129	19	7	11	59	.256	259	12	15	.948
1984—Nashua	East.	*OF-1B	136	484	74	128	19	5	11	71	.264	312	8	*15	.955
1985—Prince William†‡	Carol.	1B-3B	39	130	15	34	4	1	3	11	.262	180	9	2	.990
1986—Chicago§	Amer.	OF-1B	75	234	27	63	10	2	2	26	.269	361	22	2	.995
1986—Pittsburgh	Nat.	OF-1B-3B	63	192	28	46	6	2	1	17	.240	90	16	3	.972
American League Totals—1 Year			75	234	27	63	10	2	2	26	.269	361	22	2	.995
National League Totals—1 Year			63	192	28	46	6	2	1	17	.240	90	16	3	.972
Major League Totals—1 Year			138	426	55	109	16	4	3	43	.256	451	38	5	.990

Signed as free agent by Pittsburgh Pirates' organization, July 11, 1981.
†On Pittsburgh disabled list, March 25 to July 19, 1985.
‡Drafted by Chicago White Sox, December 10, 1985.
§Traded to Pittsburgh Pirates for Pitcher Jose DeLeon, July 23, 1986.

ROBERT BARRY BONNELL

Name pronounced Buh-NELL.

(Known by middle name.)

Born October 27, 1953, at Cincinnati, O.
Height, 6.03. Weight, 205.
Throws and bats righthanded.
Attended Ohio State University, Columbus, O.
Brother of Glenn Bonnell, infielder in Cincinnati Reds' organization, 1976.

Major League stolen bases: 1977 (7), 1978 (12), 1979 (8), 1980 (3), 1981 (4), 1982 (14), 1983 (10), 1984 (5), 1985 (1). Total—64.

Year Club	League	Pos.	G.	AB.	R.	H.	2B.	3B.	HR.	RBI.	B.A.	PO.	A.	E.	F.A.
1975—Spart.†-Green.	W. Car.	OF	124	457	86	148	20	●6	12	80	*.324	276	19	12	.961
1976—Savannah	South.	OF	51	188	31	42	6	2	6	23	.223	117	6	5	.961
1976—Richmond	Int.	OF	66	227	36	64	13	2	5	31	.282	134	4	3	.979
1977—Richmond	Int.	OF	14	50	8	19	3	0	0	10	.380	42	2	1	.978
1977—Atlanta‡	Nat.	OF-3B	100	360	41	108	11	0	1	45	.300	203	65	8	.971
1978—Atlanta	Nat.	OF-3B	117	304	36	73	11	3	1	16	.240	187	35	6	.974
1979—Atlanta§	Nat.	OF-3B	127	375	47	97	20	3	12	45	.259	221	8	4	.983

Year Club League	Pos.	G.	AB.	R.	H.	2B.	3B.	HR.	RBI.	B.A.	PO.	A.	E.	F.A.
1980—Toronto x............ Amer.	OF	130	463	55	124	22	4	13	56	.268	271	15	8	.973
1981—Toronto .... Amer.	OF	66	227	21	50	7	4	4	28	.220	148	5	4	.975
1982—Toronto .... Amer.	OF-3B	140	437	59	128	26	3	6	49	.293	234	7	5	.980
1983—Toronto y............. Amer.	OF-3B	121	377	49	120	21	3	10	54	.318	213	13	3	.987
1984—Seattle.................. Amer.	OF-3B-1B	110	363	42	96	15	4	8	48	.264	171	23	6	.970
1985—Seattle z .... Amer.	OF-1B	48	111	9	27	8	0	1	10	.243	61	2	1	.984
1986—Seattle a .... Amer.	OF-1B	17	51	4	10	2	0	0	4	.196	46	6	2	.963
National League Totals—3 Years		344	1039	124	278	42	6	14	106	.268	611	108	18	.976
American League Totals—7 Years		632	2029	239	555	101	18	42	249	.274	1144	71	29	.977
Major League Totals—10 Years		976	3068	363	833	143	24	56	355	.272	1755	179	47	.976

Selected by Chicago White Sox' organization in 8th round of free-agent draft, June 8, 1971.
Selected by Philadelphia Phillies' organization in secondary phase of free-agent draft, January 9, 1975.
†Traded with Catcher Jim Essian and cash to Atlanta Braves for First Baseman Dick Allen and Catcher Johnny Oates, May 7, 1975.
‡On disabled list, June 29 to July 21, 1977.
§Traded with Pitcher Joey McLaughlin and Shortstop Pat Rockett to Toronto Blue Jays for First Baseman Chris Chambliss and Shortstop Luis Gomez, December 5, 1979.
xOn disabled list, August 13 to September 2, 1980.
yTraded to Seattle Mariners for Pitcher Bryan Clark, December 9, 1983.
zOn disabled list, August 15 to September 14, 1985.
aReleased, July 21, 1986.

GREGORY SCOTT BOOKER
(Greg)

Born June 22, 1960, at Lynchburg, Va.
Height, 6.06. Weight, 233.
Throws and bats righthanded.
Attended Elon College, Elon College, N.C.
Son-in-law of Jack McKeon, minor league catcher, 1949 through 1959;
minor league manager, 1955 through 1964, 1968 through 1972 and 1976;
manager, Kansas City Royals, 1973 through 1975; manager,
Oakland A's, 1977 and 1978; and Vice-President/Baseball Operations with
San Diego Padres since 1980; related to Richard 'Buddy' Booker,
catcher with Cleveland Indians and Chicago White Sox, 1966 and 1968.

Led California League in wild pitches with 20 in 1982.

Year Club	League	G.	IP.	W.	L.	Pct.	H.	R.	ER.	SO.	BB.	ERA.
1981—Walla Walla	Northwest	11	53	2	3	.400	55	41	31	25	35	5.26
1982—Reno	California	27	161⅔	8	*13	.381	160	*133	*114	81	*157	6.35
1983—Las Vegas....................	P. Coast	46	102⅓	5	6	.455	120	77	63	58	68	5.54
1983—San Diego	National	6	11⅔	0	1	.000	18	10	10	5	9	7.71
1984—Las Vegas....................	P. Coast	9	55⅔	4	3	.571	66	39	34	23	24	5.50
1984—San Diego	National	32	57⅓	1	1	.500	67	27	21	28	27	3.30
1985—San Diego	National	17	22⅓	0	1	.000	20	17	17	7	17	6.85
1985—Las Vegas†	P. Coast	10	45	1	1	.500	46	34	27	16	34	5.40
1986—Las Vegas....................	P. Coast	36	128⅔	8	9	.471	148	89	75	71	65	5.25
1986—San Diego	National	9	11	1	0	1.000	10	5	2	7	4	1.64
Major League Totals—4 Years		64	102⅓	2	3	.400	115	59	50	47	57	4.40

Selected by Oakland A's organization in 32nd round of free-agent draft, June 6, 1978.
Selected by San Diego Padres' organization in 10th round of free-agent draft, June 8, 1981.
†On disabled list, July 18 to August 21, 1985.

CHAMPIONSHIP SERIES RECORD

Year Club	League	G.	IP.	W.	L.	Pct.	H.	R.	ER.	SO.	BB.	ERA.
1984—San Diego	National	1	2	0	0	.000	2	0	0	2	1	0.00

WORLD SERIES RECORD

Year Club	League	G.	IP.	W.	L.	Pct.	H.	R.	ER.	SO.	BB.	ERA.
1984—San Diego	National	1	1	0	0	.000	0	1	1	0	4	9.00

RECORD AS INFIELDER

Year Club	League	Pos.	G.	AB.	R.	H.	2B.	3B.	HR.	RBI.	B.A.	PO.	A.	E.	F.A.
1981—Walla Walla .... N'west		*P-1B	31	64	8	12	0	0	4	15	.188	26	14	0	*1.000

RODERICK STEWART BOOKER
(Rod)

Born September 4, 1958, at Los Angeles, Calif.
Height, 6.00. Weight, 175.
Throws right and bats lefthanded.
Attended Pasadena City College, Pasadena, Calif., and
University of California, Berkeley, Calif.

Year Club	League	Pos.	G.	AB.	R.	H.	2B.	3B.	HR.	RBI.	B.A.	PO.	A.	E.	F.A.
1980—Visalia .... Calif.		SS	69	242	45	68	5	4	0	26	.281	91	198	18	.941
1981—Orlando .... South.		SS-3B	111	331	56	85	8	3	0	33	.257	145	304	30	.937
1982—Toledo† .... Int.		SS-2B-3B	104	292	38	73	8	1	0	19	.250	177	272	36	.926
1983—Arkansas .... Texas		SS-3B-2B	127	469	75	128	15	3	3	60	.273	153	343	19	.963
1984—Louisville .... A. A.		2B-SS-3B	63	185	19	47	3	1	0	14	.254	100	167	8	.971

Year	Club	League	Pos.	G.	AB.	R.	H.	2B.	3B.	HR.	RBI.	B.A.	PO.	A.	E.	F.A.
1984—Arkansas...............	Texas	SS	52	209	10	43	4	3	0	22	.206	87	160	15	.943
1985—Arkansas...............	Texas	SS	129	466	59	123	18	3	1	47	.264	198	362	26	*.956
1986—Arkansas...............	Texas	SS	36	151	20	48	7	2	0	20	.318	66	121	10	.949
1986—Louisville	A. A.	2B-SS-3B	78	289	51	81	11	5	1	30	.280	151	205	10	.973

Selected by Detroit Tigers' organization in 14th round of free-agent draft, June 8, 1976.
Selected by Baltimore Orioles' organization in 10th round of free-agent draft, June 5, 1979.
Selected by Minnesota Twins' organization in 4th round of free-agent draft, June 3, 1980.
†Sold to St. Louis Cardinals' organization, April 5, 1983.

ROBERT RAYMOND BOONE
(Bob)

Born November 19, 1947, at San Diego, Calif.
Height, 6.02. Weight, 202.
Throws and bats righthanded.
Received bachelor of arts degree in psychology from Stanford University, Palo Alto, Calif. in 1969.
Son of Ray Boone, infielder with Cleveland, Detroit, Chicago A.L., Kansas City,
Milwaukee and Boston, 1948 through 1960; and scout with Boston Red Sox since 1961;
brother of Rodney Alan Boone, catcher-outfielder in Kansas City Royals' and
Houston Astros' organization, 1972 through 1975.

Major League stolen bases: 1972 (1), 1973 (3), 1974 (3), 1975 (1), 1976 (2), 1977 (5), 1978 (2), 1979 (1), 1980 (3), 1981 (2), 1983 (4), 1984 (3), 1985 (1), 1986 (1). Total—32.
Led American League catchers in double plays with 12 in 1983, 15 in 1985 and 16 in 1986.
Led American League catchers in total chances with 745 in 1982.
Led National League catchers in fielding percentage with .991 in 1978.
Led National League catchers in total chances with 924 in 1974.
Led Pacific Coast League catchers in passed balls with 18 and double plays with 13 in 1972.
Tied for Carolina League lead in double plays by third basemen with 18 in 1969.
Named catcher on The Sporting News National League All-Star Team, 1976.
Named catcher on The Sporting News American League All-Star fielding team, 1982 and 1986.
Named catcher on The Sporting News National League All-Star fielding team, 1978 and 1979.

Year	Club	League	Pos.	G.	AB.	R.	H.	2B.	3B.	HR.	RBI.	B.A.	PO.	A.	E.	F.A.
1969—Raleigh-Dur.	Carol.	3B	80	300	45	90	13	1	5	46	.300	71	160	20	.920
1970—Reading†	East.	3B	20	80	12	23	2	0	2	10	.288	28	38	7	.904
1971—Reading‡	East.	3B-C-SS	92	328	41	87	14	3	4	37	.265	206	138	17	.953
1972—Eugene	P. C.	C	138	513	77	158	32	4	17	67	.308	*699	*77	*24	.970
1972—Philadelphia ...	Nat.	C	16	51	4	14	1	0	1	4	.275	66	7	5	.936
1973—Philadelphia ...	Nat.	C	145	521	42	136	20	2	10	61	.261	868	*89	10	.990
1974—Philadelphia ...	Nat.	C	146	488	41	118	24	3	3	52	.242	*825	77	*22	.976
1975—Philadelphia ...	Nat.	C-3B	97	289	28	71	14	2	2	20	.246	459	48	5	.990
1976—Philadelphia ...	Nat.	C-1B	121	361	40	98	18	2	4	54	.271	587	39	6	.990
1977—Philadelphia ...	Nat.	C-3B	132	440	55	125	26	4	11	66	.284	654	83	8	.989
1978—Philadelphia ...	Nat.	C-1B-OF	132	435	48	123	18	4	12	62	.283	650	55	8	.989
1979—Philadelphia ...	Nat.	C-3B	119	398	38	114	21	3	9	58	.286	527	66	8	.987
1980—Philadelphia ...	Nat.	C	141	480	34	110	23	1	9	55	.229	741	88	*18	.979
1981—Philadelphia§	Nat.	C	76	227	19	48	7	0	4	24	.211	365	32	6	.985
1982—California..............	Amer.	C	143	472	42	121	17	0	7	58	.256	*650	*87	8	.989
1983—California..............	Amer.	C	142	468	46	120	18	0	9	52	.256	606	*83	*14	.980
1984—California..............	Amer.	C	139	450	33	91	16	1	3	32	.202	660	*71	12	.984
1985—California..............	Amer.	C	150	460	37	114	17	0	5	55	.248	670	71	10	.987
1986—California x	Amer.	C	144	442	48	98	12	2	7	49	.222	812	*84	11	.988
National League Totals—10 Years.........			1125	3690	349	957	172	21	65	456	.259	5742	584	96	.958
American League Totals—5 Years			718	2292	206	544	80	3	31	246	.237	3398	396	55	.986
Major League Totals—15 Years			1843	5982	555	1501	252	24	96	702	.251	9140	980	151	.985

Selected by Philadelphia Phillies' organization in 20th round of free-agent draft, June 5, 1969.
†On military list, May 26, 1970 through remainder of season.
‡On disabled list, April 10 to June 4, 1971.
§Sold to California Angels, December 6, 1981.
xGranted free agency, November 12, 1986.

DIVISION SERIES RECORD

Year	Club	League	Pos.	G.	AB.	R.	H.	2B.	3B.	HR.	RBI.	B.A.	PO.	A.	E.	F.A.
1981—Philadelphia	Nat.	C	3	5	0	0	0	0	0	0	.000	10	2	0	1.000

CHAMPIONSHIP SERIES RECORD

Tied Championship Series record for most consecutive hits, one Series (5), 1986.
Established American League Championship Series record for highest batting average, seven-game Series (.455), 1986.
Tied American League Championship Series records for most consecutive hits, total Series (5); most singles, seven-game Series (9), 1986.

Year	Club	League	Pos.	G.	AB.	R.	H.	2B.	3B.	HR.	RBI.	B.A.	PO.	A.	E.	F.A.
1976—Philadelphia	Nat.	C	3	7	0	2	0	0	0	1	.286	8	2	0	1.000
1977—Philadelphia	Nat.	C	4	10	1	4	0	0	0	0	.400	18	2	0	1.000
1978—Philadelphia	Nat.	C	3	11	0	2	0	0	0	0	.182	16	2	1	.947
1980—Philadelphia	Nat.	C	5	18	1	4	0	0	0	2	.222	22	3	0	1.000
1982—California..............	Amer.	C	5	16	3	4	0	0	1	4	.250	30	3	0	1.000
1986—California..............	Amer.	C	7	22	4	10	0	0	1	2	.455	33	3	0	1.000
Championship Series Totals—6 Years.....			27	84	9	26	0	0	2	9	.310	127	15	1	.993

Year	Club	League	Pos.	G.	AB.	R.	H.	2B.	3B.	HR.	RBI.	B.A.	PO.	A.	E.	F.A.
1980—Philadelphia		Nat.	C	6	17	3	7	2	0	0	4	.412	49	3	0	1.000

ALL-STAR GAME RECORD

Year	League	Pos.	AB.	R.	H.	2B.	3B.	HR.	RBI.	B.A.	PO.	A.	E.	F.A.
1976—National		C	2	0	0	0	0	0	0	.000	5	0	0	1.000
1978—National		C	1	1	1	0	0	0	2	1.000	3	1	0	1.000
1979—National		C	2	1	1	0	0	0	0	.500	0	0	0	.000
1983—American		C	0	0	0	0	0	0	0	.000	1	0	0	1.000
All-Star Game Totals—4 Years			5	2	2	0	0	0	2	.400	9	1	0	1.000

RICHARD ALBERT BORDI

Name pronounced BORD-ee.

(Rich)

Born April 18, 1959, at South San Francisco, Calif.
Height, 6.07. Weight, 220.
Throws and bats righthanded.
Attended Fresno State University, Fresno, Calif.

Major League saves: 1983 (1), 1984 (4), 1985 (2), 1986 (3). Total—10.
Tied for Pacific Coast League lead in complete games with 15 in 1981.

Year	Club	League	G.	IP.	W.	L.	Pct.	H.	R.	ER.	SO.	BB.	ERA.
1980—West Haven		Eastern	11	76	4	6	.400	75	42	35	49	30	4.14
1980—Oakland		American	1	2	0	0	.000	4	1	1	0	0	4.50
1981—Tacoma		P. Coast	27	191	9	11	.450	197	98	78	101	66	3.68
1981—Oakland†		American	2	2	0	0	.000	1	0	0	0	1	0.00
1982—Salt Lake City		P. Coast	25	168⅓	12	9	.571	212	105	84	118	31	4.49
1982—Seattle‡		American	7	13	0	2	.000	18	12	12	10	1	8.31
1983—Iowa§		Am. Assoc.	18	111⅓	7	2	.778	134	62	57	80	21	4.61
1983—Chicago		National	11	25⅓	0	2	.000	34	15	14	20	12	4.97
1984—Chicago xy		National	31	83⅓	5	2	.714	78	37	32	41	20	3.46
1985—New York za		American	51	98	6	8	.429	95	41	35	64	29	3.21
1986—Baltimore		American	52	107	6	4	.600	105	56	53	83	41	4.46
American League Totals—5 Years			113	222	12	14	.462	223	110	101	157	72	4.09
National League Totals—2 Years			42	108⅔	5	4	.556	112	52	46	61	32	3.81
Major League Totals—7 Years			155	330⅔	17	18	.486	335	162	147	218	104	4.00

Selected by Minnesota Twins' organization in 5th round of free-agent draft, June 7, 1977.
Selected by Oakland A's organization in 3rd round of free-agent draft, June 3, 1980.
†Traded to Seattle Mariners for Third Baseman-Outfielder Dan Meyer, December 9, 1981.
‡Traded to Chicago Cubs for Outfielder Steve Henderson, December 9, 1982.
§On disabled list, April 25 to May 10, 1983.
xOn disabled list, August 8 to August 23, 1984.
yTraded with Catcher Ron Hassey, Outfielder Henry Cotto and Pitcher Porfi Altamirano to New York Yankees for Pitcher Ray Fontenot and Outfielder Brian Dayett, December 4, 1984.
zOn disabled list, April 30 to May 15, 1985.
aTraded with Infielder Rex Hudler to Baltimore Orioles for Outfielder Gary Roenicke and a player to be named later, December 12, 1985; New York Yankees acquired Outfielder Leo Hernandez to complete deal, December 16, 1985.

CHRISTOPHER LOUIS BOSIO

Name pronounced Boz-e-o.

(Chris)

Born April 3, 1963, at Rancho Cordova, Calif.
Height, 6.03. Weight, 220.
Throws and bats righthanded.
Attended Sacramento City College, Sacramento, Calif.

Tied for Pacific Coast League lead in saves with 16 in 1986.

Year	Club	League	G.	IP.	W.	L.	Pct.	H.	R.	ER.	SO.	BB.	ERA.
1982—Pikeville		Ap'lachian	13	51⅓	3	2	.600	60	31	28	53	17	4.91
1983—Beloit		Midwest	17	107⅔	3	10	.231	125	82	67	71	41	5.60
1983—Paintsville		Ap'lachian	7	44⅓	2	2	.500	30	18	14	43	18	2.84
1984—Beloit		Midwest	26	181	∗17	6	.739	159	83	55	156	56	2.73
1985—El Paso		Texas	28	181⅓	11	6	.647	186	108	77	∗155	49	3.82
1986—Vancouver		P. Coast	44	67	7	3	.700	47	18	17	60	13	2.28
1986—Milwaukee		American	10	34⅔	0	4	.000	41	27	27	29	13	7.01
Major League Totals—1 Year			10	34⅔	0	4	.000	41	27	27	29	13	7.01

Selected by Pittsburgh Pirates' organization in 29th round of free-agent draft, June 8, 1981.
Selected by Milwaukee Brewers' organization in secondary phase of free-agent draft, January 12, 1982.

THADDIS BOSLEY JR.

Name pronounced BAHZ-lee.

(Thad)

Born September 17, 1956, at Oceanside, Calif.
Height, 6.03. Weight, 175.
Throws and bats lefthanded.
Attended Mira Costa Community College, Oceanside, Calif.

Major League stolen bases: 1977 (5), 1978 (12), 1979 (4), 1980 (3), 1981 (2), 1982 (3), 1983 (1), 1984 (5), 1985 (5), 1986 (3). Total—43.
Led California League in stolen bases with 90 and caught stealing with 17 in 1976.
Led Pioneer League in bases on balls received with 71 in 1974.
Named California League Most Valuable Player, 1976.

Year Club	League	Pos.	G.	AB.	R.	H.	2B.	3B.	HR.	RBI.	B.A.	PO.	A.	E.	F.A.
1974—Idaho Falls	Pion.	OF	68	223	55	54	3	4	0	14	.242	101	4	*11	.905
1975—Quad Cities†	Midw.	OF	108	379	67	113	12	3	1	50	.298	206	2	4	*.981
1976—Salinas	Calif.	OF	134	527	105	171	26	4	2	72	*.324	285	13	7	*.977
1977—Salt Lake City	P. C.	OF	69	298	55	97	22	2	2	38	.326	169	6	5	.972
1977—California‡§	Amer.	OF	58	212	19	63	10	2	0	19	.297	130	1	5	.963
1978—Iowa	A. A.	OF	47	179	27	52	3	0	3	15	.291	77	5	2	.976
1978—Chicago x	Amer.	OF	66	219	25	59	5	1	2	13	.269	155	3	4	.975
1979—Iowa y	A. A.	OF	95	382	62	101	14	5	1	24	.264	140	6	5	.967
1979—Chicago	Amer.	OF	36	77	13	24	1	1	1	8	.312	57	2	2	.967
1980—Chicago za	Amer.	OF	70	147	12	33	2	0	2	14	.224	91	1	4	.958
1981—Vancouver	P. C.	OF	34	122	15	39	5	2	0	14	.320	75	0	5	.938
1981—Milwaukee b	Amer.	OF	42	105	11	24	2	0	0	3	.229	55	1	2	.966
1982—Seattle	Amer.	OF	22	46	3	8	1	0	0	2	.174	12	1	0	1.000
1982—Salt Lake C. cdef	P. C.	OF	22	84	15	25	2	2	3	9	.298	24	2	0	1.000
1983—Mexico City	Mex.	OF	31	107	24	35	7	3	4	18	.327	24	1	0	1.000
1983—Iowa	A. A.	OF	39	124	22	36	11	0	7	24	.290	3	0	1	.750
1983—Chicago	Nat.	OF	43	72	12	21	4	1	2	12	.292	27	1	0	1.000
1984—Iowa	A. A.	OF	51	162	23	58	16	1	6	43	.358	31	4	2	.946
1984—Chicago	Nat.	OF	55	98	17	29	2	2	2	14	.296	39	2	1	.976
1985—Chicago	Nat.	OF	108	180	25	59	6	3	7	27	.328	84	0	1	.988
1986—Chicago	Nat.	OF	87	120	15	33	4	1	1	9	.275	31	0	1	.969
American League Totals—6 Years			294	806	83	211	21	4	5	59	.262	500	9	17	.968
National League Totals—4 Years			293	470	69	142	16	7	12	62	.302	181	3	3	.984
Major League Totals—10 Years			587	1276	152	353	37	11	17	121	.277	681	12	20	.972

Selected by California Angels' organization in 4th round of free-agent draft, June 5, 1974.
†On disabled list, April 19 to May 6, 1975.
‡On disabled list, June 29 to July 10, 1977.
§Traded with Outfielder Bobby Bonds and Pitcher Dick Dotson to Chicago White Sox for Pitchers Chris Knapp and Dave Frost and Catcher Brian Downing, December 5, 1977.
xOn disabled list, June 29 to July 17, 1978.
yOn disabled list, July 15 to July 25, 1979.
zOn disabled list, August 12, 1980 through remainder of season.
aTraded to Milwaukee Brewers' organization for First Baseman-Outfielder John Poff, April 1, 1981.
bTraded to Seattle Mariners for Pitcher Mike Parrott, March 5, 1982.
cOn disabled list, June 6 to July 1 and August 3 to September 2, 1982.
dGranted free agency, September 5, 1982; signed by Tacoma (Oakland A's organization), February 14, 1983.
eSold to Iowa (Chicago Cubs' organization), March 30, 1983.
fLoaned to Mexico City Tigers, April 3, 1983; returned, May 28, 1983.

DIVISION SERIES RECORD

Year Club	League	Pos.	G.	AB.	R.	H.	2B.	3B.	HR.	RBI.	B.A.	PO.	A.	E.	F.A.
1981—Milwaukee	Amer.	PR-DH	1	0	0	0	0	0	0	0	.000	0	0	0	.000

CHAMPIONSHIP SERIES RECORD

Year Club	League	Pos.	G.	AB.	R.	H.	2B.	3B.	HR.	RBI.	B.A.	PO.	A.	E.	F.A.
1984—Chicago	Nat.	PH	2	2	0	0	0	0	0	0	.000	0	0	0	.000

DARYL LAMONT BOSTON

Born January 4, 1963, at Cincinnati, O.
Height, 6.03. Weight, 193.
Throws and bats lefthanded.

Major League stolen bases: 1984 (6), 1985 (8), 1986 (9). Total—23.
Led Eastern League batters in strikeouts with 133 in 1983.
Led Midwest League outfielders in total chances with 312 in 1982.
Tied for American Association lead in sacrifice flies with 11 in 1984.
Tied for American Association lead in double plays by outfielders with 4 in 1984.

Year Club	League	Pos.	G.	AB.	R.	H.	2B.	3B.	HR.	RBI.	B.A.	PO.	A.	E.	F.A.
1981—Sarasota W. S.	Gulf C.	OF	56	189	30	55	6	3	1	30	.291	84	9	3	.969
1982—Appleton	Midw.	OF	*139	512	86	143	19	9	15	77	.279	*293	9	10	.968
1983—Glens Falls	East.	OF	113	435	65	104	15	1	18	50	.239	271	8	13	.955
1983—Denver	A. A.	OF	14	51	11	13	4	1	2	7	.255	26	1	5	.844
1984—Denver	A. A.	OF	127	471	94	147	21	*19	15	82	.312	311	11	●10	.970
1984—Chicago	Amer.	OF	35	83	8	14	3	1	0	3	.169	59	2	6	.910
1985—Chicago	Amer.	OF	95	232	20	53	13	1	3	15	.228	179	7	2	.989
1985—Buffalo	A. A.	OF	63	241	45	66	12	1	10	36	.274	151	3	3	.981
1986—Buffalo	A. A.	OF	96	360	57	109	16	3	5	41	.303	210	1	5	.977
1986—Chicago	Amer.	OF	56	199	29	53	11	3	5	22	.266	152	3	5	.969
Major League Totals—3 Years			186	514	57	120	27	5	8	40	.233	390	12	13	.969

Selected by Chicago White Sox' organization in 1st round (seventh player selected) of free-agent draft, June 8, 1981.

DEREK WAYNE BOTELHO

Name pronounced Boh-TELL-oh.

Born August 2, 1956, at Long Beach, Calif.
Height, 6.02. Weight, 165.
Throws and bats righthanded.
Attended Miami Dade Community College (South), Miami, Fla.

Pitched seven-inning, 8-0 no-hit victory against Miami, June 17, 1981 (first game).
Tied for Eastern League lead in shutouts with 4 in 1978.

Year	Club	League	G.	IP.	W.	L.	Pct.	H.	R.	ER.	SO.	BB.	ERA.
1976—Spartanburg	W. Carol	20	134	9	9	.500	120	69	54	90	49	3.63
1977—Peninsula	Carolina	26	173	13	5	*.722	167	86	72	107	67	3.75
1978—Reading†	Eastern	27	178	15	7	.682	175	77	70	130	65	3.54
1979—Wichita‡§x	Am. Assoc.	4	19	1	2	.333	30	20	18	18	8	8.53
1980—						(Out of Organized Baseball)						
1981—Fort Myers	Florida St.	8	39	2	3	.400	25	10	7	32	9	1.62
1981—Jacksonville y	Southern	7	37	2	2	.500	27	9	8	15	4	1.95
1982—Jacksonville	Southern	9	65	3	4	.429	54	35	33	35	25	4.57
1982—Omaha	Am. Assoc.	15	105⅓	7	5	.583	86	51	49	74	37	4.19
1982—Kansas City	American	8	24	2	1	.667	25	11	11	12	8	4.13
1983—Omaha z	Am. Assoc.	25	152⅔	10	*14	.417	155	105	92	101	73	5.42
1984—Iowa	Am. Assoc.	28	171½	10	11	.476	179	89	75	136	65	3.81
1985—Iowa	Am. Assoc.	20	125⅔	11	7	.611	117	64	60	94	53	4.30
1985—Chicago a	National	11	44	1	3	.250	52	27	26	23	23	5.32
1986—Denver	Am. Assoc.	23	147	11	7	.611	131	70	60	91	59	3.67
American League Totals—1 Year		8	24	2	1	.667	25	11	11	12	8	4.13
National League Totals—1 Year		11	44	1	3	.250	52	27	26	23	23	5.32
Major League Totals—2 Years		19	68	3	4	.429	77	38	37	35	31	4.90

Selected by Philadelphia Phillies' organization in 26th round of free-agent draft, June 5, 1974.
Selected by California Angels' organization in secondary phase of free-agent draft, June 9, 1975.
Selected by Philadelphia Phillies' organization in 2nd round of free-agent draft, January 7, 1976.
†Traded with Outfielder Jerry Martin, Catcher Barry Foote, Second Baseman Ted Sizemore and Pitcher Henry Mack to Chicago Cubs for Second Baseman Manny Trillo, Outfielder Greg Gross and Catcher Dave Rader, February 23, 1979.
‡On temporary inactive list, April 11 to April 26, 1979.
§On disabled list, June 4 to August 31, 1979.
xReleased February 5, 1980; signed by Jacksonville (Kansas City Royals' organization), January 6, 1981.
yOn disabled list, April 9 to May 17, 1981.
zTraded to Chicago Cubs for Pitcher Alan Hargesheimer, March 30, 1984.
aReleased, December 20, 1985; signed by Cincinnati Reds' organization, January 16, 1986.

DENNIS RAY BOYD
(Oil Can)

(Given nickname from beer drinking friends in Meridian, Miss.
where beer is referred to as oil.)

Born October 6, 1959, at Meridian, Miss.
Height, 6.01. Weight, 155.
Throws and bats righthanded.
Attended Jackson State University, Jackson, Miss.
Brother of Don Boyd, outfielder in St. Louis Cardinals' organization, 1973.

Led Florida State League pitchers in games started with 28 and home runs allowed with 11 in 1981.
Tied for Eastern League lead in games started by pitchers with 27 and complete games with 13 in 1982.

Year	Club	League	G.	IP.	W.	L.	Pct.	H.	R.	ER.	SO.	BB.	ERA.
1980—Elmira	NYP	12	69	7	1	.875	54	20	19	79	30	2.48
1981—Winter Haven	Florida St.	28	186	14	8	.636	*195	90	75	154	54	3.63
1982—Bristol	Eastern	27	*205	14	8	.636	190	71	64	*191	49	2.81
1982—Boston	American	3	8⅓	0	1	.000	11	5	5	2	2	5.40
1983—Pawtucket	Int'national	20	122⅔	5	8	.385	119	69	55	129	41	4.04
1983—Boston	American	15	98⅔	4	8	.333	103	46	36	43	23	3.28
1984—Boston	American	29	197⅔	12	12	.500	207	109	96	134	53	4.37
1984—Pawtucket	Int'national	5	37⅓	3	1	.750	30	12	12	45	12	2.89
1985—Boston	American	35	272⅓	15	13	.536	*273	117	112	154	67	3.70
1986—Boston	American	30	214⅓	16	10	.615	222	99	90	129	45	3.78
Major League Totals—5 Years		112	791⅓	47	44	.516	816	376	339	462	190	3.86

Selected by Boston Red Sox' organization in 16th round of free-agent draft, June 3, 1980.

CHAMPIONSHIP SERIES RECORD

Year	Club	League	G.	IP.	W.	L.	Pct.	H.	R.	ER.	SO.	BB.	ERA.
1986—Boston	American	2	13⅔	1	1	.500	17	7	7	8	3	4.61

WORLD SERIES RECORD

Year	Club	League	G.	IP.	W.	L.	Pct.	H.	R.	ER.	SO.	BB.	ERA.
1986—Boston	American	1	7	0	1	.000	9	6	6	3	1	7.71

PHILIP POOLE BRADLEY
(Phil)

Born March 11, 1959, at Bloomington, Ind.
Height, 6.00. Weight, 175.
Throws and bats righthanded.
Received bachelor of science degree in personnel management from
University of Missouri, Columbia, Mo., in 1982.

Major League stolen bases: 1983 (3), 1984 (21), 1985 (22), 1986 (21). Total—67.
Named outfielder on THE SPORTING NEWS American League All-Star Team, 1985.

Year Club	League	Pos.	G.	AB.	R.	H.	2B.	3B.	HR.	RBI.	B.A.	PO.	A.	E.	F.A.
1981—Bellingham	N'west	OF	53	193	38	58	12	5	1	20	.301	94	3	1	★.990
1982—Bakersfield............	Calif.	OF	109	405	98	134	17	10	0	37	.331	226	13	6	.976
1983—Salt Lake City.......	P. Coast	OF	130	458	100	148	14	4	2	41	.323	284	13	1	★.997
1983—Seattle...................	Amer.	OF	23	67	8	18	2	0	0	5	.269	36	1	1	.974
1984—Seattle...................	Amer.	OF	124	322	49	97	12	4	0	24	.301	235	3	2	.992
1985—Seattle...................	Amer.	OF	159	641	100	192	33	8	26	88	.300	336	10	5	.986
1986—Seattle†	Amer.	OF	143	526	88	163	27	4	12	50	.310	250	11	1	.996
Major League Totals—4 Years................			449	1556	245	470	74	16	38	167	.302	857	25	9	.990

Selected by Seattle Mariners' organization in 3rd round of free-agent draft, June 8, 1981.
†On disabled list, May 26 to June 12, 1986.

ALL-STAR GAME RECORD

Year League	Pos.	AB.	R.	H.	2B.	3B.	HR.	RBI.	B.A.	PO.	A.	E.	F.A.
1985—American	OF	1	0	0	0	0	0	0	.000	1	0	0	1.000

SCOTT WILLIAM BRADLEY

Born March 22, 1960, at Essex Fells, N.J.
Height, 5.11. Weight, 185.
Throws right and bats lefthanded.
Received bachelor of science degree in business administration
from University of North Carolina, Chapel Hill, N.C.

Major League stolen bases: 1986 (1).
Tied for International League lead in game-winning RBIs with 14 in 1984.
Tied for Florida State League lead in game-winning RBIs with 13 in 1982.
Named International League Player of the Year, 1984.

Year Club	League	Pos.	G.	AB.	R.	H.	2B.	3B.	HR.	RBI.	B.A.	PO.	A.	E.	F.A.
1981—Oneonta.................	NYP	C-OF	71	276	48	85	17	4	4	54	.308	323	40	9	.976
1982—Nashville...............	South.	C	5	19	2	2	1	0	0	0	.105	44	2	2	.958
1982—Fort Lauderdale ..	Fla. St.	C-1B-3B	121	439	52	130	28	4	3	66	.296	407	57	10	.979
1983—Nashville...............	South.	C-3B	137	525	83	142	33	4	8	76	.270	475	88	13	.977
1984—Columbus..............	Int.	C-OF-3B	★138	★538	84	★180	31	2	6	●84	★.335	432	50	9	.982
1984—New York	Amer.	OF-C	9	21	3	6	1	0	0	2	.286	10	0	0	1.000
1985—New York†	Amer.	C	19	49	4	8	2	1	0	1	.163	12	0	1	.923
1985—Albany	East.	3B	6	24	2	3	1	0	0	2	.125	8	14	4	.846
1985—Columbus‡	Int.	C-3B	43	163	17	49	10	0	4	27	.301	118	53	4	.977
1986—Buffalo..................	A. A.	C-OF	33	126	14	42	3	3	5	20	.333	165	9	0	1.000
1986—Chi.§-Sea...............	Amer.	C-OF	77	220	20	66	8	3	5	28	.300	281	21	3	.990
Major League Totals—3 Years................			105	290	27	80	11	4	5	31	.276	303	21	4	.988

Selected by Minnesota Twins' organization in 12th round of free-agent draft, June 6, 1978.
Selected by New York Yankees' organization in 3rd round of free-agent draft, June 8, 1981.
†On disabled list, April 24 to June 17, 1985; included rehabilitation disability assignment to Sarasota, June 5 and June 6, 1985, and Albany, June 7 to June 17, 1985.
‡Traded with Pitcher Neil Allen, Outfielder Glen Braxton and cash to Chicago White Sox for Catchers Ron Hassey and Chris Alvarez, Pitcher Eric Schmidt and Outfielder Matt Winters, February 13, 1986.
§Traded to Seattle Mariners for a player to be named later, June 26, 1986; Chicago White Sox' organization acquired Outfielder Ivan Calderon to complete deal, July 1, 1986.

GLENN ERICK BRAGGS

Born October 17, 1962, at San Bernardino, Calif.
Height, 6.03. Weight, 210.
Throws and bats righthanded.
Attended University of Hawaii, Honolulu, Hawaii.

Major League stolen bases: 1986 (1).
Led Texas League in being hit by pitch with 10 in 1985.
Led Appalachian League in total bases with 164, bases on balls received with 54 and intentional bases on balls received with 6 in 1983.
Named California League Most Valuable Player, 1984.
Named Appalachian League Player of the Year, 1983.
Received reported $50,000 bonus to sign with Milwaukee Brewers, 1983.

Year Club	League	Pos.	G.	AB.	R.	H.	2B.	3B.	HR.	RBI.	B.A.	PO.	A.	E.	F.A.
1983—Paintsville	Appal.	OF	●73	241	★65	★94	★20	1	●16	★74	★.390	115	8	6	.953
1984—Stockton	Calif.	OF	108	399	76	118	29	2	15	86	.296	158	4	6	.964
1985—El Paso..................	Texas	OF	117	448	105	139	26	4	20	103	.310	239	10	11	.958
1986—Vancouver.............	P. C.	OF	90	325	80	117	26	6	15	75	.360	218	8	2	.991
1986—Milwaukee.............	Amer.	OF	58	215	19	51	8	2	4	18	.237	116	5	12	.910
Major League Totals—1 Year................			58	215	19	51	8	2	4	18	.237	116	5	12	.910

Selected by New York Yankees' organization in 6th round of free-agent draft, June 3, 1980.
Selected by Milwaukee Brewers' organization in 2nd round of free-agent draft, June 6, 1983.

MICHAEL CHARLES BRANTLEY
(Mickey)

Born June 17, 1961, at Catskill, N.Y.
Height, 5.10. Weight, 180.
Throws and bats righthanded.
Attended Columbia-Greene Community College, Hudson, N.Y., and
Coastal Carolina Community College, Jacksonville, N.C.

Major League stolen bases: 1986 (1).
Tied for Southern League lead in sacrifice flies with 10 in 1984.

Year	Club	League	Pos.	G.	AB.	R.	H.	2B.	3B.	HR.	RBI.	B.A.	PO.	A.	E.	F.A.
1983—Bakersfield	Calif.		OF	53	185	33	55	9	3	6	29	.297	59	3	1	.984
1984—Chattanooga	South.		OF-3B	131	472	73	149	21	9	11	76	.316	211	14	8	.966
1984—Salt Lake City	P. C.		OF	4	17	2	4	0	0	0	1	.235	8	0	0	1.000
1985—Calgary†	P. C.		OF	74	279	52	68	13	6	11	45	.244	165	1	3	.982
1986—Calgary	P. C.		OF	106	396	*104	126	18	4	30	92	.318	201	9	4	.981
1986—Seattle	Amer.		OF	27	102	12	20	3	2	3	7	.196	54	3	1	.983
Major League Totals—1 Year				27	102	12	20	3	2	3	7	.196	54	3	1	.983

Selected by Cincinnati Reds' organization in 8th round of free-agent draft, June 7, 1982.
Selected by Seattle Mariners' organization in 2nd round of free-agent draft, June 6, 1983.
†On disabled list, August 20 to September 9, 1985.

SIDNEY EUGENE BREAM
(Sid)

Born August 3, 1960, at Carlisle, Pa.
Height, 6.04. Weight, 215.
Throws and bats lefthanded.
Attended Liberty Baptist College, Lynchburg, Va.

Established National League record for most assists by first baseman, season (166), 1986.
Major League stolen bases: 1984 (1), 1986 (13). Total—14.
Led National League first basemen in total chances with 1,503 in 1986.
Led Pacific Coast League first basemen in total chances with 1,411 in 1983 and 1,200 in 1984.
Led Pacific Coast League first basemen in double plays with 106 in 1984.

Year	Club	League	Pos.	G.	AB.	R.	H.	2B.	3B.	HR.	RBI.	B.A.	PO.	A.	E.	F.A.
1981—Vero Beach	Fla. St.		1B	70	260	35	85	12	5	1	47	.327	613	45	10	.985
1982—Vero Beach	Fla. St.		1B	63	226	41	70	13	5	4	43	.310	523	40	5	.991
1982—San Antonio	Texas		1B	70	259	43	83	18	0	8	50	.320	621	40	12	.982
1982—Albuquerque	P. C.		1B	3	8	3	3	1	0	1	2	.375	11	0	0	1.000
1983—Albuquerque	P. C.		1B	138	485	115	149	23	4	●32	*118	.307	1264	*123	24	.983
1983—Los Angeles	Nat.		1B	15	11	0	2	0	0	0	2	.182	8	0	0	1.000
1984—Albuquerque	P. C.		1B	114	429	82	147	25	4	20	90	.343	1071	*112	17	.986
1984—Los Angeles	Nat.		1B	27	49	2	9	3	0	0	6	.184	95	11	0	1.000
1985—L.A.†-Pitt.	Nat.		1B	50	148	18	34	7	0	6	21	.230	367	35	3	.993
1985—Albuquerque	P. C.		1B-OF	85	297	51	110	25	3	17	57	.370	381	51	2	.995
1986—Pittsburgh	Nat.		*1B-OF	154	522	73	140	37	5	16	77	.268	1320	*166	*17	.989
Major League Totals—4 Years				246	730	93	185	47	5	22	106	.253	1790	212	20	.990

Selected by Los Angeles Dodgers' organization in 2nd round of free-agent draft, June 8, 1981.
†Traded with Outfielder Cecil Espy, September 9, 1985, completing deal in which Los Angeles Dodgers acquired Third Baseman Bill Madlock for three players to be named later, August 31, 1985. Pittsburgh Pirates acquired Outfielder R. J. Reynolds as partial completion of deal, September 3, 1985.

ROBERT EARL BRENLY
(Bob)

Born February 25, 1954, at Coshocton, Ohio.
Height, 6.02. Weight, 210.
Throws and bats righthanded.
Received bachelor of science degree in health education from
Ohio University, Athens, Ohio in 1976.

Tied major league record for most errors by third baseman, inning (4), September 14, 1986 (fourth inning).
Major League stolen bases: 1982 (6), 1983 (10), 1984 (6), 1986 (10). Total—33.
Led National League catchers in fielding percentage with .995 in 1986.
Led California League third basemen in double plays with 30 in 1978.
Led Midwest League third basemen in double plays with 21 in 1977.

Year	Club	League	Pos.	G.	AB.	R.	H.	2B.	3B.	HR.	RBI.	B.A.	PO.	A.	E.	F.A.
1976—Great Falls	Pion.		3B	25	86	16	27	5	1	1	17	.314	10	16	2	.929
1976—Fresno	Calif.		3B	17	60	16	22	3	1	1	9	.367	2	6	1	.889
1977—Cedar Rapids	Midw.		*●3B-OF	136	499	85	135	16	1	22	73	.271	90	*263	●31	.919
1978—Fresno	Calif.		3B	135	489	102	139	34	5	17	89	.284	*118	247	27	.931
1979—Fresno	Calif.		3B	56	212	49	65	11	2	9	37	.307	39	133	17	.910
1979—Shreveport	Texas		C-3-0-1	64	193	33	57	8	1	9	30	.295	199	55	7	.973
1980—Shreveport	Texas		3B	2	10	2	3	0	0	1	3	.300	1	2	0	1.000
1980—Phoenix	P. C.		3-C-S-O	84	287	34	74	9	6	7	45	.258	183	110	20	.936
1981—Phoenix	P. C.		C-OF-3B	76	257	42	75	11	3	7	41	.292	177	41	9	.960

Year	Club	League	Pos.	G.	AB.	R.	H.	2B.	3B.	HR.	RBI.	B.A.	PO.	A.	E.	F.A.
1981—San Francisco	Nat.	C-3B-OF	19	45	5	15	2	1	1	4	.333	52	6	4	.935
1982—San Francisco† ...	Nat.	C-3B	65	180	26	51	4	1	4	15	.283	265	32	12	.961
1983—San Francisco	Nat.	C-1B-OF	104	281	36	63	12	2	7	34	.224	465	73	9	.984
1984—San Francisco	Nat.	C-1B-OF	145	506	74	147	28	0	20	80	.291	807	76	13	.985
1985—San Francisco	Nat.	C-3B-1B	133	440	41	97	16	1	19	56	.220	719	85	17	.979
1986—San Francisco	Nat.	C-3B-1B	149	472	60	116	26	0	16	62	.246	688	118	16	.981
Major League Totals—6 Years			615	1924	242	489	88	5	67	251	.254	2996	390	71	.979

Signed as free agent by San Francisco Giants' organization, June 21, 1976.
†On disabled list, March 25 to May 13, 1982.

ALL-STAR GAME RECORD

Year	League	Pos.	AB.	R.	H.	2B.	3B.	HR.	RBI.	B.A.	PO.	A.	E.	F.A.
1984—National		PH	1	0	0	0	0	0	0	.000	0	0	0	.000

GEORGE HOWARD BRETT

Born May 15, 1953, at Glen Dale, W. Va.
Height, 6.00.   Weight, 195.
Throws right and bats lefthanded.
Attended Longview Community College, Lee's Summit, Mo. and
El Camino College, Torrance, Calif.
Brother of Ken Brett, pitcher with Boston, Milwaukee, Philadelphia, Pittsburgh, New York AL,
Chicago AL, California, Minnesota, Los Angeles and Kansas City, 1967 and 1969 through 1981;
and manager of Utica (Co-op) in New York-Pennsylvania League, 1985;
John Brett, third baseman in Boston Red Sox' organization, 1968;
and Bob Brett, outfielder in Kansas City Royals' organization, 1972.

Established major league record for most consecutive games, three or more hits, season (6), May 8 through 13, 1976.
Tied major league records for most consecutive seasons leading major league in triples (2), 1975 and 1976; most home runs, month of October (4), 1985.
Established American League record for fewest putouts by third baseman for leader in most putouts, season (140), 1976.
Became sixth major-league player to collect 20 or more doubles, triples and home runs in one season, 1979.
Hit three home runs in a game, July 22, 1979 and April 20, 1983.
Hit for the cycle, May 28, 1979.
Major League stolen bases: 1974 (8), 1975 (13), 1976 (21), 1977 (14), 1978 (23), 1979 (17), 1980 (15), 1981 (14), 1982 (6), 1985 (9), 1986 (1). Total—141.
Led American League in intentional bases on balls received with 31 in 1985 and 18 in 1986.
Led American League in slugging percentage with .664 in 1980, .563 in 1983 and .585 in 1985.
Led American League in total bases with 298 in 1976.
Led American League third basemen in double plays with 33 in 1985.
Led American League third basemen in assists with 373, errors with 30 and total chances with 532 in 1979.
Led American League third baseman in putouts with 140 in 1976.
Led California League in sacrifice hits with 8 in 1972.
Led California League third basemen in assists with 172 in 1972.
Named Man of the Year by THE SPORTING NEWS, 1980.
Named Major League Player of the Year by THE SPORTING NEWS, 1980.
Named American League Player of the Year by THE SPORTING NEWS, 1980.
Named American League Most Valuable Player by Baseball Writers' Association of America, 1980.
Named third baseman on THE SPORTING NEWS American League All-Star Team, 1976, 1979 and 1980.
Named third baseman on THE SPORTING NEWS American League All-Star fielding team, 1985.
Named third baseman on THE SPORTING NEWS Silver Slugger team, 1980 and 1985.

Year	Club	League	Pos.	G.	AB.	R.	H.	2B.	3B.	HR.	RBI.	B.A.	PO.	A.	E.	F.A.
1971—Billings	Pion.	SS-3B	68	258	44	75	8	5	5	44	.291	87	140	28	.890
1972—San José†	Calif.	*3-S-2	117	431	66	118	13	5	10	68	.274	101	213	*30	.913
1973—Omaha	A. A.	3B-OF	117	405	66	115	16	4	8	64	.284	92	219	26	.923
1973—Kansas City	Amer.	3B	13	40	2	5	2	0	0	0	.125	9	28	1	.974
1974—Omaha	A. A.	3B	16	64	9	17	2	0	2	14	.266	8	31	4	.907
1974—Kansas City	Amer.	3B-SS	133	457	49	129	21	5	2	47	.282	102	279	21	.948
1975—Kansas City	Amer.	3B-SS	159	*634	84	*195	35	●13	11	89	.308	132	356	●26	.949
1976—Kansas City	Amer.	3B-SS	159	*645	94	*215	34	*14	7	67	*.333	146	350	26	.950
1977—Kansas City	Amer.	3B-SS	139	564	105	176	32	13	22	88	.312	115	325	21	.954
1978—Kansas City‡	Amer.	3B-SS	128	510	79	150	*45	8	9	62	.294	104	289	16	.961
1979—Kansas City§	Amer.	3B-1B	154	645	119	*212	42	*20	23	107	.329	176	378	31	.947
1980—Kansas City§	Amer.	3B-1B	117	449	87	175	33	9	24	118	*.390	107	256	17	.955
1981—Kansas City	Amer.	3B	89	347	42	109	27	7	6	43	.314	74	170	14	.946
1982—Kansas City	Amer.	3B-OF	144	552	101	166	32	9	21	82	.301	130	295	17	.962
1983—Kansas City x	Amer.	3B-1B-OF	123	464	90	144	38	2	25	93	.310	210	192	25	.941
1984—Kansas City y	Amer.	3B	104	377	42	107	21	3	13	69	.284	59	201	14	.949
1985—Kansas City	Amer.	3B	155	550	108	184	38	5	30	112	.335	107	*339	15	.967
1986—Kansas City	Amer.	3B-SS	124	441	70	128	28	4	16	73	.290	97	218	16	.952
Major League Totals—14 Years			1741	6675	1072	2095	428	112	209	1050	.314	1568	3676	260	.953

Selected by Kansas City Royals' organization in 2nd round of free-agent draft, June 8, 1971.
†On disabled list, April 29 to May 11, 1972.
‡On disabled list, May 4 to May 19 and July 27 to August 14, 1978.
§On disabled list, June 11 to July 10, 1980.
xOn disabled list, June 8 to June 29, 1983.
yOn disabled list, April 1 to May 18, 1984.

DIVISION SERIES RECORD

Year	Club	League	Pos.	G.	AB.	R.	H.	2B.	3B.	HR.	RBI.	B.A.	PO.	A.	E.	F.A.
1981—Kansas City		Amer.	3B	3	12	0	2	0	0	0	0	.167	1	6	1	.876

CHAMPIONSHIP SERIES RECORD

Established Championship Series records for most games with one club (27); highest slugging average, total Series, 10 or more games and 30 or more at-bats (.728); most runs, total Series (22); most three-base hits, total Series (4); most runs, four-game Series (7), 1978; most home runs, total Series (9); most Series, two or more home runs (3); most total bases, total Series (75); most long hits, total Series (18).

Tied Championship Series records for most runs, game (4), October 11, 1985; most three-base hits, Series (2), 1977; most home runs, game (3), October 6, 1978; most times hitting home run as leadoff batter, start of game (1), October 6, 1978.

Established American League Championship Series records for highest slugging average, seven-game Series (.826), 1985; most runs, total Series (16); most home runs, four-game Series (3), 1978; highest slugging average, four-game Series (1.056), 1978; most hits, four-game Series (7), 1978; most home runs, seven-game Series (3), 1985; most total bases, four-game Series (19), 1978; most long hits, four-game Series (5), 1978 and seven-game Series (5), 1985; most long hits, two consecutive games, one series (4), October 6 and 7, 1978; most total bases (19) and most bases on balls (7), seven-game Series, 1985; most total bases, game (12), October 6, 1978.

Tied American League Championship Series records for most at-bats, four-game Series (18), 1978; most Series, one or more home runs (4); most long hits, game (3), October 6, 1978 and October 11, 1985; most consecutive games, one or more hits (9); most home runs, three-game Series (2), 1980.

Year	Club	League	Pos.	G.	AB.	R.	H.	2B.	3B.	HR.	RBI.	B.A.	PO.	A.	E.	F.A.
1976—Kansas City		Amer.	3B	5	18	4	8	1	1	1	5	.444	3	7	3	.769
1977—Kansas City		Amer.	3B	5	20	2	6	0	2	0	2	.300	5	12	2	.895
1978—Kansas City		Amer.	3B	4	18	7	7	1	1	3	3	.389	3	8	1	.917
1980—Kansas City		Amer.	3B	3	11	3	3	1	0	2	4	.273	2	7	0	1.000
1984—Kansas City		Amer.	3B	3	13	0	3	0	0	0	0	.231	2	7	0	1.000
1985—Kansas City		Amer.	3B	7	23	6	8	2	0	3	5	.348	7	8	2	.882
Championship Series Totals—6 Years				27	103	22	35	5	4	9	19	.340	22	49	8	.899

WORLD SERIES RECORD

Tied World Series record for most times reached first base safely, game (batting 1.000) (5), October 22, 1985.

Year	Club	League	Pos.	G.	AB.	R.	H.	2B.	3B.	HR.	RBI.	B.A.	PO.	A.	E.	F.A.
1980—Kansas City		Amer.	3B	6	24	3	9	2	1	1	3	.375	4	17	1	.955
1985—Kansas City		Amer.	3B	7	27	5	10	1	0	0	1	.370	10	19	1	.967
World Series Totals—2 Years				13	51	8	19	3	1	1	4	.373	14	36	2	.962

ALL-STAR GAME RECORD

Year	League	Pos.	AB.	R.	H.	2B.	3B.	HR.	RBI.	B.A.	PO.	A.	E.	F.A.
1976—American		3B	2	0	0	0	0	0	0	.000	0	1	0	1.000
1977—American		3B	2	0	0	0	0	0	0	.000	2	1	0	1.000
1978—American		3B	3	1	2	1	0	0	2	.667	0	2	0	1.000
1979—American		3B	3	1	0	0	0	0	0	.000	1	2	0	1.000
1981—American		3B	3	0	0	0	0	0	0	.000	0	1	0	1.000
1982—American		3B	2	0	2	0	0	0	0	1.000	0	0	0	.000
1983—American		3B	4	2	2	1	1	0	1	.500	1	5	0	1.000
1984—American		3B	3	1	1	0	0	0	1	.333	3	0	0	1.000
1985—American		3B	1	0	0	0	0	0	1	.000	2	1	0	1.000
All-Star Game Totals—9 Years			23	5	7	2	1	1	5	.304	9	13	0	1.000

Named to American League All-Star Team in 1980; replaced due to injury.
Named to American League All-Star Team for 1986 game; replaced due to injury by Brook Jacoby.

MICHAEL QUINN BREWER
(Mike)

Born October 24, 1959, at Shreveport, La.
Height, 6.05. Weight, 190.
Throws and bats righthanded.
Attended Foothill College, Los Altos Hills, Calif.
Brother of Tony Brewer, outfielder in Los Angeles Dodgers' organization, 1980 through 1985.

Led Gulf Coast League in total bases with 105 and tied for lead in caught stealing with 7 in 1979.
Named Gulf Coast League Most Valuable Player, 1979.

Year	Club	League	Pos.	G.	AB.	R.	H.	2B.	3B.	HR.	RBI.	B.A.	PO.	A.	E.	F.A.
1979—Sarasota Gold		Gulf C.	OF	51	★205	38	★76	7	5	4	★47	★.371	72	5	●5	.939
1980—Fort Myers		Fla. St.	OF	123	426	54	102	13	4	6	63	.239	199	8	★11	.950
1981—Fort Myers		Fla. St.	OF	128	459	69	132	16	9	16	84	.288	209	12	9	.961
1982—Jacksonville		South.	OF	121	438	74	109	15	4	20	68	.249	269	13	11	.962
1982—Omaha		A. A.	OF	18	56	10	16	5	0	1	7	.286	37	3	1	.976
1983—Omaha		A. A.	OF	120	412	63	104	23	3	9	42	.252	233	10	11	.957
1984—Omaha		A. A.	OF	104	330	46	67	10	4	11	41	.203	181	6	●10	.949
1984—Memphis†		South.	OF	35	129	17	29	4	0	2	23	.225	73	3	4	.950
1985—Maine		Int.	OF	119	413	58	97	17	2	17	53	.235	264	11	7	.975
1986—Omaha		A. A.	OF	108	389	47	99	20	4	12	57	.254	240	6	5	.980
1986—Kansas City		Amer.	OF	12	18	0	3	1	0	0	0	.167	9	0	0	1.000
Major League Totals—1 Year				12	18	0	3	1	0	0	0	.167	9	0	0	1.000

Selected by Kansas City Royals' organization in 1st round (22nd player selected) of free-agent draft, January 9, 1979.

†Traded to Cleveland Indians' organization for a player to be named later or cash, April 5, 1985; returned, September 17, 1985.

BERNARDO BRITO

Born December 4, 1963, at Sabana Pelenque, Dominican Republic.
Height, 6.01. Weight, 190.
Throws and bats righthanded.

Led Eastern League batters in strikeouts with 127 in 1986.
Led Midwest League in total bases with 244 in 1985.
Led New York-Pennsylvania League in total bases with 171 in 1984.

Year Club	League	Pos.	G.	AB.	R.	H.	2B.	3B.	HR.	RBI.	B.A.	PO.	A.	E.	F.A.
1981—Batavia	NYP	OF	12	29	1	6	0	0	0	2	.207	2	0	0	1.000
1982—Batavia	NYP	OF	41	123	10	29	2	0	4	15	.236	40	0	6	.870
1983—Waterloo	Midw.	OF	35	119	13	24	4	0	4	17	.202	41	2	3	.935
1983—Batavia	NYP	OF	60	206	18	50	10	3	7	34	.243	54	7	8	.884
1984—Batavia	NYP	OF	●76	★297	41	89	●19	3	★19	57	.300	100	8	8	.931
1985—Waterloo	Midw.	OF	135	498	66	128	27	1	★29	78	.257	160	15	9	.951
1986—Waterbury	East.	OF-SS	129	479	61	118	17	1	★18	75	.246	67	1	1	.986

Signed as free agent by Cleveland Indians' organization, October 8, 1980.

GREGORY ALLEN BROCK

(Greg)

Born June 14, 1957, at McMinnville, Ore.
Height, 6.03. Weight, 205.
Throws right and bats lefthanded.
Attended University of Wyoming, Laramie, Wyo.
Brother of Eric Brock, shortstop in Los Angeles Dodgers' organization, 1983 and 1984.

Major League stolen bases: 1983 (5), 1984 (8), 1985 (4), 1986 (2). Total—19.
Led Pacific Coast League in bases on balls received with 105 and intentional bases on balls received with 15 in 1982.
Led Pioneer League in bases on balls received with 54 in 1979.
Led Pacific Coast League first basemen in double plays with 106 in 1982.

Year Club	League	Pos.	G.	AB.	R.	H.	2B.	3B.	HR.	RBI.	B.A.	PO.	A.	E.	F.A.
1979—Lethbridge	Pion.	1B	66	247	61	88	18	2	16	77	.356	543	★36	8	★.986
1980—Lodi	Calif.	1B	121	418	72	125	19	3	★29	95	.299	906	★79	5	★.995
1981—San Antonio	Texas	1B	128	499	86	147	25	3	★32	106	.295	1071	★90	9	.992
1982—Albuquerque	P. C.	1B	135	480	118	149	21	8	44	138	.310	★1076	★106	★20	.983
1982—Los Angeles	Nat.	1B	18	17	1	2	1	0	0	1	.118	9	0	0	1.000
1983—Los Angeles	Nat.	1B	146	455	64	102	14	2	20	66	.224	1162	106	12	.991
1984—Los Angeles†	Nat.	1B	88	271	33	61	6	0	14	34	.225	703	65	4	.995
1984—Albuquerque	P. C.	1B-3B	24	93	19	29	7	0	6	15	.312	134	38	11	.940
1985—Los Angeles	Nat.	1B	129	438	64	110	19	0	21	66	.251	1113	84	7	.994
1986—Los Angeles‡§	Nat.	1B	115	325	33	76	13	0	16	52	.234	726	87	3	.996
Major League Totals—5 Years			496	1506	195	351	53	2	71	219	.233	3713	342	26	.994

Selected by Los Angeles Dodgers' organization in 13th round of free-agent draft, June 5, 1979.
†On disabled list, May 12 to June 7, 1984.
‡On disabled list, June 19 to July 10, 1986.
§Traded to Milwaukee Brewers for Pitchers Tim Leary and Tim Crews, December 10, 1986.

CHAMPIONSHIP SERIES RECORD

Year Club	League	Pos.	G.	AB.	R.	H.	2B.	3B.	HR.	RBI.	B.A.	PO.	A.	E.	F.A.
1983—Los Angeles	Nat.	1B	3	9	1	0	0	0	0	0	.000	13	0	0	1.000
1985—Los Angeles	Nat.	1B-PH	5	12	2	1	0	0	1	2	.083	35	4	0	1.000
Championship Series Totals—2 Years			8	21	3	1	0	0	1	2	.048	48	4	0	1.000

THOMAS DALE BROOKENS

(Tom)

Born August 10, 1953, at Chambersburg, Pa.
Height, 5.10. Weight, 170.
Throws and bats righthanded.
Attended Mansfield State College, Mansfield, Pa.

Twin brother of Tim Brookens, infielder-outfielder in Detroit Tigers' organization, 1975 through 1978; cousin of Ike Brookens, pitcher with Detroit Tigers, 1975.

Tied American League record for most errors by third baseman, game (4), September 6, 1980.
Major League stolen bases: 1979 (10), 1980 (13), 1981 (5), 1982 (5), 1983 (10), 1984 (6), 1985 (14), 1986 (11). Total—74.
Tied for American League lead in errors by third basemen with 23 in 1985.

Year Club	League	Pos.	G.	AB.	R.	H.	2B.	3B.	HR.	RBI.	B.A.	PO.	A.	E.	F.A.
1975—Montgomery	South.	SS	100	329	37	73	11	2	7	36	.222	139	298	31	.934
1976—Montgomery	South.	2B	137	492	76	127	22	5	11	56	.258	310	★389	★25	.965
1977—Evansville	A. A.	3B-2B	118	440	70	127	22	5	8	52	.289	132	250	25	.939
1978—Evansville†	A. A.	3B-2B-1B	65	206	27	58	11	1	6	25	.282	76	100	20	.898
1979—Evansville	A. A.	3B-2B	77	265	51	81	23	2	14	46	.306	71	166	16	.937
1979—Detroit	Amer.	3B-2B	60	190	23	50	5	2	4	21	.263	76	141	11	.952
1980—Detroit	Amer.	★3-2-S	151	509	64	140	25	9	10	66	.275	127	307	★29	.937
1981—Detroit‡	Amer.	3B	71	239	19	58	10	1	4	25	.243	58	139	10	.952
1982—Detroit	Amer.	3-2-S-O	140	398	40	92	15	3	9	58	.231	119	276	20	.952
1983—Detroit	Amer.	3B-SS-2B	138	332	50	71	13	3	6	32	.214	97	254	22	.941
1984—Detroit§	Amer.	3B-SS-2B	113	224	32	55	11	4	5	26	.246	98	187	12	.960

Year Club	League	Pos.	G.	AB.	R.	H.	2B.	3B.	HR.	RBI.	B.A.	PO.	A.	E.	F.A.
1985—Detroit x................	Amer.	3-S-2-C	156	485	54	115	34	6	7	47	.237	135	277	24	.944
1986—Detroit..................	Amer.	3-2-S-O	98	281	42	76	11	2	3	25	.270	106	144	7	.973
Major League Totals—8 Years.................			927	2658	324	657	124	30	48	300	.247	816	1725	135	.950

Selected by Detroit Tigers' organization in 1st round (fourth player selected) of free-agent draft, January 9, 1975.
†On disabled list, April 14 to May 9 and June 4 to June 21, 1978.
‡On disabled list, March 30 to May 4, 1981.
§On disabled list, August 19 to September 4, 1984.
xGranted free agency, November 12, 1985; re-signed by Tigers, January 8, 1986.

CHAMPIONSHIP SERIES RECORD

Year Club	League	Pos.	G.	AB.	R.	H.	2B.	3B.	HR.	RBI.	B.A.	PO.	A.	E.	F.A.
1984—Detroit...................	Amer.	2B-3B	2	2	0	0	0	0	0	0	.000	0	2	1	.667

WORLD SERIES RECORD

Year Club	League	Pos.	G.	AB.	R.	H.	2B.	3B.	HR.	RBI.	B.A.	PO.	A.	E.	F.A.
1984—Detroit...................	Amer.	PH-3B	3	3	0	0	0	0	0	0	.000	0	3	0	1.000

HUBERT BROOKS JR.
(Hubie)

Born September 24, 1956, at Los Angeles, Calif.
Height, 6.00. Weight, 188.
Throws and bats righthanded.
Attended Mesa Community College, Mesa, Ariz., and received bachelor of science
degree in health science from Arizona State University, Tempe, Ariz.
Grandson of Leandrus Brooks, player with Philadelphia of Negro National League;
cousin of Donnie Moore, pitcher with California Angels.

Tied modern National League record for most errors in inning by third baseman (3), May 10, 1981 (fourth inning).
Major League stolen bases: 1980 (1), 1981 (9), 1982 (6), 1983 (6), 1984 (6), 1985 (6), 1986 (4). Total—38.
Led International League in game-winning RBIs with 12 in 1980.
Named shortstop on THE SPORTING NEWS National League Silver Slugger team, 1985 and 1986.
Named shortstop on THE SPORTING NEWS College Baseball All-America Team, 1978.
Named outfielder on THE SPORTING NEWS College Baseball All-America Team, 1977.

Year Club	League	Pos.	G.	AB.	R.	H.	2B.	3B.	HR.	RBI.	B.A.	PO.	A.	E.	F.A.
1978—Jackson	Texas	SS-OF-3B	45	153	19	33	8	1	3	16	.216	49	84	14	.905
1979—Jackson	Texas	3B-SS	112	406	68	124	21	2	3	28	.305	92	218	29	.942
1979—Tidewater.............	Int.	SS-3B-OF	5	15	1	6	1	0	1	3	.400	4	8	1	.923
1980—Tidewater.............	Int.	OF-3B-SS	113	417	50	124	18	5	3	50	.297	152	90	18	.931
1980—New York.............	Nat.	3B	24	81	8	25	2	1	1	10	.309	16	40	2	.966
1981—New York.............	Nat.	★3-O-S	98	358	34	110	21	2	4	38	.307	67	193	★21	.925
1982—New York†...........	Nat.	3B	126	457	40	114	21	2	2	40	.249	89	237	24	.931
1983—New York.............	Nat.	3B-2B	150	586	53	147	18	4	5	58	.251	116	303	21	.952
1984—New York‡...........	Nat.	3B-SS	153	561	61	159	23	2	16	73	.283	112	284	29	.932
1985—Montreal	Nat.	SS	156	605	67	163	34	7	13	100	.269	203	441	28	.958
1986—Montreal §	Nat.	SS	80	306	50	104	18	5	14	58	.340	116	222	15	.958
Major League Totals—7 Years.................			787	2954	313	822	137	23	55	377	.278	719	1720	140	.946

Selected by Montreal Expos' organization in 19th round of free-agent draft, June 5, 1974.
Selected by Kansas City Royals' organization in secondary phase of free-agent draft, January 7, 1976.
Selected by Chicago White Sox' organization in secondary phase of free-agent draft, June 8, 1976.
Selected by Oakland A's organization in secondary phase of free-agent draft, January 11, 1977.
Selected by Chicago White Sox' organization in secondary phase of free-agent draft, June 7, 1977.
Selected by New York Mets' organization in 1st round (third player selected) of free-agent draft, June 6, 1978.
†On disabled list, June 28 to July 22, 1982.
‡Traded with Catcher Mike Fitzgerald, Outfielder Herm Winningham and Pitcher Floyd Youmans to Montreal Expos for Catcher Gary Carter, December 10, 1984.
§On disabled list, August 2, 1986 through remainder of season.

ALL-STAR GAME RECORD

Year League	Pos.	AB.	R.	H.	2B.	3B.	HR.	RBI.	B.A.	PO.	A.	E.	F.A.
1986—National.............................	PH-SS	2	1	0	0	0	0	0	.000	1	0	0	1.000

ROBERT RICHARD BROWER
(Bob)

Born January 10, 1960, at Queens, N.Y.
Height, 5.11. Weight, 185.
Throws and bats righthanded.
Attended Duke University, Durham, N.C.

Major League stolen bases: 1986 (1).
Led American Association in bases on balls received with 94 in 1986.
Led American Association outfielders in total chances with 382 in 1986.

Year Club	League	Pos.	G.	AB.	R.	H.	2B.	3B.	HR.	RBI.	B.A.	PO.	A.	E.	F.A.
1982—Sarasota Rangers	Gulf C.	OF	36	122	25	35	7	2	0	7	.287	53	3	0	1.000
1983—Burlington	Midw.	OF	43	138	35	43	4	6	5	28	.312	60	4	4	.941
1983—Tulsa	Texas	OF	69	252	41	59	4	1	3	17	.234	138	4	4	.973
1984—Tulsa	Texas	OF	96	344	69	98	14	9	7	30	.285	209	10	3	.986
1984—Oklahoma City	A. A.	OF	35	107	18	24	2	2	1	8	.224	69	7	2	.974
1985—Oklahoma City	A. A.	OF	133	445	56	111	13	★18	5	50	.249	282	8	3	.990

Year Club League	Pos.	G.	AB.	R.	H.	2B.	3B.	HR.	RBI.	B.A.	PO.	A.	E.	F.A.
1986—Oklahoma City ..... A. A.	OF	●140	*550	*130	●158	25	7	13	72	.287	*366	8	8	.979
1986—Texas .... Amer.	OF	21	9	3	1	1	0	0	0	.111	9	0	0	1.000
Major League Totals—1 Year		21	9	3	1	1	0	0	0	.111	9	0	0	1.000

Signed as free agent by Texas Rangers' organization, July 1, 1982.

CURTIS STEVEN BROWN
(Curt)

Born January 15, 1960, at Ft. Lauderdale, Fla.
Height, 6.03. Weight, 165.
Throws and bats righthanded.
Attended Broward Community College Central, Ft. Lauderdale, Fla.

Led Pacific Coast League in saves with 15 in 1982.

Year Club	League	G.	IP.	W.	L.	Pct.	H.	R.	ER.	SO.	BB.	ERA.
1979—Idaho Falls	Pioneer	12	72	2	6	.250	86	49	37	47	13	4.63
1980—Salinas†	California	20	73	7	3	.700	80	32	24	28	19	2.96
1981—Redwood	California	5	9	1	0	1.000	10	6	6	2	2	6.00
1981—Holyoke	Eastern	32	67	5	3	.625	55	15	11	32	19	1.48
1982—Spokane	P. Coast	50	72⅔	3	4	.429	85	40	36	36	23	4.46
1983—Edmonton	P. Coast	40	57⅓	3	4	.429	66	37	26	32	16	4.08
1983—California‡	American	10	16	1	1	.500	25	13	13	7	4	7.31
1984—Columbus	Int'national	32	72⅓	4	4	.500	58	28	19	26	18	2.36
1984—New York	American	13	16⅔	1	1	.500	18	5	5	10	4	2.70
1985—Columbus §	Int'national	47	86⅔	8	3	.727	110	57	47	40	28	4.88
1986—Indianapolis	Am. Assoc.	48	95⅓	11	3	.786	101	37	34	51	22	3.21
1986—Montreal	National	6	12	0	1	.000	15	6	4	4	2	3.00
American League Totals—2 Years		23	32⅔	2	2	.500	43	18	18	17	8	4.96
National League Totals—1 Year		6	12	0	1	.000	15	6	4	4	2	3.00
Major League Totals—3 Years		29	44⅔	2	3	.400	58	24	22	21	10	4.43

Signed as free agent by California Angels' organization, April 19, 1979.
†On disabled list, July 25 to August 4 and August 13 to August 23, 1980.
‡Traded to New York Yankees for Pitcher Mike Browning, December 16, 1983.
§Granted free agency, October 15, 1985; signed by Indianapolis (Montreal Expos' organization), December 27, 1985.

JAMES KEVIN BROWN

(Known by middle name.)
Born March 14, 1965, at McIntyre, Ga.
Height, 6.04. Weight, 195.
Throws and bats righthanded.
Attended Georgia Tech, Atlanta, Ga.

Named as righthanded pitcher on THE SPORTING NEWS College Baseball All-America Team, 1986.

Year Club	League	G.	IP.	W.	L.	Pct.	H.	R.	ER.	SO.	BB.	ERA.
1986—Tulsa	Texas	3	10	0	0	.000	9	7	5	10	5	4.50
1986—Texas	American	1	5	1	0	1.000	6	2	2	4	0	3.60
Major League Totals—1 Year		1	5	1	0	1.000	6	2	2	4	0	3.60

Selected by Texas Rangers' organization in 1st round (fourth player selected) of free-agent draft, June 2, 1986.

JOHN CHRISTOPHER BROWN
(Chris)

Born August 15, 1961, at Jackson, Miss.
Height, 6.00. Weight, 185.
Throws and bats righthanded.

Major League stolen bases: 1984 (2), 1985 (2), 1986 (13). Total—17.
Led National League in being hit by pitch with 11 in 1985.

Year Club	League	Pos.	G.	AB.	R.	H.	2B.	3B.	HR.	RBI.	B.A.	PO.	A.	E.	F.A.
1979—Great Falls	Pion.	3B	47	171	24	46	5	3	5	30	.269	31	77	11	.908
1980—Clinton	Midw.	3B-1B	103	337	38	80	5	3	7	35	.237	352	132	19	.962
1981—Fresno	Calif.	3B-OF-1B	85	291	37	84	11	2	8	44	.289	89	156	23	.914
1982—Shreveport	Texas	3B-2B	58	185	26	49	14	0	1	21	.265	51	82	9	.937
1982—Fresno	Calif.	3B-1B-SS	41	133	22	39	9	1	4	31	.293	41	71	6	.949
1983—Shreveport	Texas	3B	102	322	44	88	21	0	10	58	.273	63	182	17	.935
1984—Phoenix†	P. C.	3B	84	283	41	80	13	5	9	64	.283	43	119	17	.905
1984—San Francisco	Nat.	3B	23	84	6	24	7	0	1	11	.286	23	40	7	.900
1985—San Francisco	Nat.	3B	131	432	50	117	20	3	16	61	.271	94	243	10	*.971
1986—San Francisco	Nat.	3B-SS	116	416	57	132	16	3	7	49	.317	73	181	18	.934
Major League Totals—3 Years			270	932	107	273	43	6	24	121	.293	190	464	35	.949

Selected by San Francisco Giants' organization in 2nd round of free-agent draft, June 5, 1979.
†On disabled list, April 11 to April 21 and July 30 to August 11, 1984.

ALL-STAR GAME RECORD

Year League	Pos.	AB.	R.	H.	2B.	3B.	HR.	RBI.	B.A.	PO.	A.	E.	F.A.
1986—National	3B	2	1	1	1	0	0	0	.500	1	0	0	1.000

MICHAEL CHARLES BROWN
(Mike)

Born December 29, 1959, at San Francisco, Calif.
Height, 6.02. Weight, 195.
Throws and bats righthanded.
Attended San Jose State University, San Jose, Calif.

Major League stolen bases: 1983 (1), 1985 (2), 1986 (2). Total—5.

Year Club	League	Pos.	G.	AB.	R.	H.	2B.	3B.	HR.	RBI.	B.A.	PO.	A.	E.	F.A.
1980—Salinas	Calif.	OF-C	47	152	24	40	7	0	5	35	.263	72	4	5	.938
1981—Holyoke	East.	OF	135	499	64	160	25	8	6	83	.321	182	9	9	.955
1982—Spokane	P. C.	OF	134	476	74	135	30	7	11	73	.284	261	20	14	.957
1983—Edmonton	P. C.	OF	115	442	91	157	39	6	22	106	.355	190	11	2	.990
1983—California	Amer.	OF	31	104	12	24	5	1	3	9	.231	52	4	3	.949
1984—Edmonton	P. C.	OF	26	102	22	35	9	4	4	24	.343	50	5	0	1.000
1984—California	Amer.	OF	62	148	19	42	8	3	7	22	.284	57	4	2	.968
1985—California†	Amer.	OF	60	153	23	41	9	1	4	20	.268	78	3	0	1.000
1985—Pittsburgh	Nat.	OF	57	205	29	68	18	2	5	33	.332	87	3	6	.938
1986—Pittsburgh	Nat.	OF	87	243	18	53	7	0	4	26	.218	107	3	3	.973
1986—Hawaii	P. C.	OF	24	87	14	33	8	0	1	12	.379	38	2	1	.976
American League Totals—3 Years			153	405	54	107	22	5	14	51	.264	187	11	5	.975
National League Totals—2 Years			144	448	47	121	25	2	9	59	.270	194	6	9	.957
Major League Totals—4 Years			297	853	101	228	47	7	23	110	.267	381	17	14	.966

Selected by California Angels' organization in 7th round of free-agent draft, June 3, 1980.

†Traded with Pitcher Pat Clements and a player to be named later to Pittsburgh Pirates for Pitchers John Candelaria and Al Holland and Outfielder George Hendrick, August 2, 1985; Pittsburgh organization acquired Pitcher Bob Kipper to complete deal, August 16, 1985.

MICHAEL GARY BROWN
(Mike)

Born March 4, 1959, at Haddon Township, N.J.
Height, 6.02. Weight, 195.
Throws and bats righthanded.
Attended Clemson University, Clemson, S.C.

Led Carolina League in complete games with 12 and shutouts with 6 in 1981.
Tied for International League lead in hit basemen with 8 in 1985.
Named Carolina League Pitcher of the Year, 1981.

Year Club	League	G.	IP.	W.	L.	Pct.	H.	R.	ER.	SO.	BB.	ERA.
1980—Winter Haven	Florida St.	17	71	3	4	.429	79	37	34	50	32	4.31
1981—Winston-Salem	Carolina	21	145	★14	4	.778	94	32	24	144	39	★1.49
1982—Bristol†	Eastern	16	110	9	6	.600	92	39	30	113	35	2.45
1982—Boston	American	3	6	1	0	1.000	7	0	0	4	1	0.00
1983—Boston‡	American	19	104	6	6	.500	110	62	54	35	43	4.67
1984—Boston	American	15	67	1	8	.111	104	63	51	32	19	6.85
1984—Pawtucket	Int'national	12	87⅓	6	3	.667	90	44	33	54	27	3.40
1985—Pawtucket§	Int'national	20	70⅔	2	5	.286	78	52	44	51	25	5.60
1985—Boston	American	2	3⅓	0	0	.000	9	8	8	3	3	21.60
1986—Pawtucket	Int'national	7	42⅓	1	4	.200	51	27	22	27	16	4.68
1986—Boston x -Seattle	American	21	73	4	6	.400	91	49	47	41	36	5.79
Major League Totals—5 Years		60	253⅓	12	20	.375	321	182	160	115	102	5.68

Selected by Atlanta Braves' organization in 20th round of free-agent draft, June 7, 1977.
Selected by Boston Red Sox' organization in 2nd round of free-agent draft, June 3, 1980.

†On disabled list, April 27 to June 16, 1982.
‡On disabled list, July 28 to August 19, 1983.
§On suspended list, July 9 to July 26, 1985.

xClaimed with Pitcher Mike Trujillo on waivers by Seattle Mariners from Boston Red Sox, August 22, 1986, as part of deal in which Seattle traded Infielder Spike Owen and Outfielder Dave Henderson to Boston for Infielder Rey Quinones, a player to be named later and cash, August 19, 1986. Seattle acquired Outfielder John Christensen to complete deal, September 25, 1986.

JEROME A. BROWNE
(Jerry)

Born February 13, 1966, at St. Croix, Virgin Islands.
Height, 5.10. Weight, 140.
Throws right and bats left and righthanded.

Led Texas League second basemen in fielding percentage with .984 in 1986.
Led Carolina League second basemen in total chances with 675 in 1985.

Year Club	League	Pos.	G.	AB.	R.	H.	2B.	3B.	HR.	RBI.	B.A.	PO.	A.	E.	F.A.
1983—Sarasota Rangers	Gulf C.	2B	48	181	34	51	2	2	0	20	.282	92	123	14	.939
1984—Burlington	Midw.	SS-2B	127	420	70	99	10	1	0	18	.236	231	311	43	.926
1985—Salem	Carol.	2B	122	460	69	123	18	4	3	58	.267	★265	★390	20	.970
1986—Tulsa	Texas	2B-SS	128	491	82	149	15	7	2	57	.303	282	307	19	.969
1986—Texas	Amer.	2B	12	24	6	10	2	0	0	3	.417	9	15	2	.923
Major League Totals—1 Year			12	24	6	10	2	0	0	3	.417	9	15	2	.923

Signed as free agent by Texas Rangers' organization, March 3, 1983.

THOMAS LEO BROWNING
(Tom)

Born April 28, 1960, at Casper, Wyo.
Height, 6.01. Weight, 190.
Throws and bats lefthanded.
Attended Tennessee Wesleyan College, Athens, Tenn., and
Le Moyne College, Syracuse, N.Y.

Pitched seven-inning, 2-0 no-hit victory against Iowa, July 31, 1984.
Tied for National League lead in games started by pitchers with 39 in 1986.
Tied for American Association lead in home runs allowed with 24 in 1984.
Named National League Rookie Pitcher of the Year by THE SPORTING NEWS, 1985.

Year Club	League	G.	IP.	W.	L.	Pct.	H.	R.	ER.	SO.	BB.	ERA.
1982—Billings	Pioneer	14	88	4	●8	.333	96	53	38	*87	41	3.89
1983—Tampa	Florida St.	11	78⅔	8	1	.889	53	19	13	101	36	1.49
1983—Waterbury	Eastern	18	117⅓	4	10	.286	100	62	46	101	63	3.53
1984—Wichita	Am. Assoc.	30	189⅓	12	10	.545	169	88	83	*160	73	3.95
1984—Cincinnati	National	3	23⅓	1	0	1.000	27	4	4	14	5	1.54
1985—Cincinnati	National	38	261⅓	20	9	.690	242	111	103	155	73	3.55
1986—Cincinnati	National	39	243⅓	14	13	.519	225	123	103	147	70	3.81
Major League Totals—3 Years		80	528	35	22	.614	494	238	210	316	148	3.58

Selected by Cincinnati Reds' organization in 9th round of free-agent draft, June 7, 1982.

ANTHONY MICHAEL BRUMLEY
(Mike)

Born April 9, 1963, at Oklahoma City, Okla.
Height, 5.10. Weight, 165.
Throws right and bats left and righthanded.
Attended University of Texas, Austin, Tex.
Son of Mike Brumley, catcher with Washington Senators, 1964 through 1966.

Led American Association shortstops in total chances with 597 in 1986.

Year Club	League	Pos.	G.	AB.	R.	H.	2B.	3B.	HR.	RBI.	B.A.	PO.	A.	E.	F.A.
1983—Winter Haven	Fla. St.	SS-OF	44	153	25	48	6	4	1	18	.314	51	92	20	.877
1984—New Britain†	East.	OF-SS	34	121	14	28	6	2	0	9	.231	71	6	6	.928
1984—Midland	Texas	OF	73	255	37	55	11	3	6	21	.216	128	4	5	.964
1985—Pittsfield	East.	SS-OF	131	460	66	127	23	*14	3	58	.276	182	333	33	.940
1986—Iowa	A. A.	SS	139	458	74	103	21	5	10	44	.225	177	*400	20	.966

Selected by Philadelphia Phillies' organization in 16th round of free-agent draft, June 3, 1980.
Selected by Boston Red Sox' organization in 2nd round of free-agent draft, June 6, 1983.
†Traded with Pitcher Dennis Eckersley to Chicago Cubs for First Baseman-Outfielder Bill Buckner, May 25, 1984.

THOMAS ANDREW BRUNANSKY
(Tom)

Born August 20, 1960, at West Covina, Calif.
Height, 6.04. Weight, 210.
Throws and bats righthanded.

Major League stolen bases: 1981 (1), 1982 (1), 1983 (2), 1984 (4), 1985 (5), 1986 (12). Total—25.
Led American League outfielders in double plays with 8 in 1983 and 6 in 1984.
Tied for Texas League lead in double plays by outfielders with 4 in 1980.
Received reported $100,000 bonus to sign with California Angels, 1978.

Year Club	League	Pos.	G.	AB.	R.	H.	2B.	3B.	HR.	RBI.	B.A.	PO.	A.	E.	F.A.
1978—Idaho Falls	Pioneer	OF	48	190	55	63	14	4	6	45	.332	85	1	8	.915
1979—Salinas	Calif.	OF	*140	485	85	131	23	1	23	76	.270	279	11	6	.980
1980—El Paso	Texas	OF	128	495	103	160	24	8	24	97	.323	306	17	*14	.958
1980—Salt Lake City	P. C.	OF	9	32	7	11	2	2	1	8	.344	28	1	0	1.000
1981—Salt Lake City†	P. C.	OF	96	343	61	114	17	10	22	81	.332	250	14	5	.981
1981—California	Amer.	OF	11	33	7	5	0	0	3	6	.152	27	3	2	.938
1982—Spokane‡	P. C.	OF	25	88	12	18	6	1	1	6	.205	44	7	1	.981
1982—Minnesota	Amer.	OF	127	463	77	126	30	1	20	46	.272	343	8	5	.986
1983—Minnesota	Amer.	OF	151	542	70	123	24	5	28	82	.227	375	16	6	.985
1984—Minnesota	Amer.	OF	155	567	75	144	21	0	32	85	.254	304	13	5	.984
1985—Minnesota	Amer.	OF	157	567	71	137	28	4	27	90	.242	300	14	5	.984
1986—Minnesota	Amer.	OF	157	593	69	152	28	1	23	75	.256	315	10	6	.982
Major League Totals—6 Years			758	2765	369	687	131	11	133	384	.248	1664	64	29	.983

Selected by California Angels' organization in 1st round (14th player selected) of free-agent draft, June 6, 1978.
†On disabled list, August 8 to August 31, 1981.
‡Traded with Pitcher Mike Walters and cash to Minnesota Twins for Pitcher Doug Corbett and Second Baseman Rob Wilfong, May 12, 1982.

ALL-STAR GAME RECORD

Year League	Pos.	AB.	R.	H.	2B.	3B.	HR.	RBI.	B.A.	PO.	A.	E.	F.A.
1985—American	OF	1	0	0	0	0	0	0	.000	0	0	0	.000

RALPH WENDALL BRYANT

Born May 20, 1961, at Fort Gaines, Ga.
Height, 6.02. Weight, 200.
Throws right and bats lefthanded.
Attended Abraham Baldwin Agriculture College, Tifton, Ga.

Led Texas League in slugging percentage with .581 in 1984.
Led Florida State League batters in strikeouts with 104 in 1982.

Year Club	League	Pos.	G.	AB.	R.	H.	2B.	3B.	HR.	RBI.	B.A.	PO.	A.	E.	F.A.
1981—Lethbridge	Pion.	OF	50	181	31	48	12	4	5	29	.265	34	4	3	.927
1982—Vero Beach	Fla. St.	OF	122	409	71	125	22	7	9	71	.306	91	6	5	.951
1983—Vero Beach	Fla. St.	OF	130	489	74	129	27	11	10	65	.264	231	12	10	.960
1984—San Antonio	Texas	OF	115	434	71	130	21	4	*31	86	.300	191	11	*12	.944
1985—Albuquerque	P. C.	OF	120	400	62	107	27	3	15	64	.268	171	11	*13	.933
1985—Los Angeles	Nat.	OF	6	6	0	2	0	0	0	1	.333	0	0	0	.000
1986—Albuquerque	P. C.	OF	107	338	56	80	17	2	19	55	.237	158	10	*13	.928
1986—Los Angeles	Nat.	OF	27	75	15	19	4	2	6	13	.253	39	2	2	.953
Major League Totals—2 Years			33	81	15	21	4	2	6	14	.259	39	2	2	.953

Selected by Los Angeles Dodgers' organization in 6th round of free-agent draft, January 8, 1980.
Selected by Minnesota Twins' organization in 13th round of free-agent draft, January 13, 1981.
Selected by Los Angeles Dodgers' organization in secondary phase of free-agent draft, June 8, 1981.

THOMAS RAY BRYDEN
(T. R.)

Born January 17, 1959, at Moses Lake, Wash.
Height, 6.04. Weight, 190.
Throws and bats righthanded.
Attended Centralia Junior College, Spokane, Wash.;
and Gonzaga University, Spokane, Wash.

Led California League in hit batsmen with 13 in 1983.
Led Midwest League in hit batsmen with 15 in 1982.

Year Club	League	G.	IP.	W.	L.	Pct.	H.	R.	ER.	SO.	BB.	ERA.
1981—Idaho Falls	Pioneer	14	66	2	5	.286	62	42	36	51	47	4.91
1982—Danville	Midwest	22	135⅔	10	9	.526	125	87	66	101	79	4.38
1983—Redwood	California	44	69⅔	6	5	.545	53	34	26	42	55	3.36
1984—Redwood	California	20	30⅓	1	3	.250	26	12	10	34	10	2.97
1984—Waterbury	Eastern	25	43	2	3	.400	35	22	14	38	25	2.93
1985—Midland	Texas	7	10⅓	1	2	.333	13	11	8	4	4	6.97
1985—Edmonton	P. Coast	36	73⅔	5	6	.455	73	45	39	52	36	4.76
1986—California	American	16	34⅓	2	1	.667	38	25	25	25	21	6.55
1986—Edmonton	P. Coast	22	38⅔	1	0	1.000	42	16	15	34	22	3.49
Major League Totals—1 Year		16	34⅓	2	1	.667	38	25	25	25	21	6.55

Signed as free agent by California Angels' organization, June 18, 1981.

WILLIAM JOSEPH BUCKNER
(Bill)

Born December 14, 1949, at Vallejo, Calif.
Height, 6.01. Weight, 185.
Throws and bats lefthanded.
Attended University of Southern California, Los Angeles, Calif., and
Arizona State University, Tempe, Ariz.
Brother of Jim Buckner, minor league outfielder, 1972 through 1981;
and Bob Buckner, minor league infielder, 1966 through 1970;
and part-time scout with Chicago Cubs, 1977 through 1979.

Established major league record for most assists, first baseman, season (184), 1985.
Tied major league record for most games, first baseman, season (162), 1985.
Established National League record for fewest double plays, first baseman, season, 150 or more games (89), 1982.
Tied National League record for fewest errors by first baseman for leader in errors, season (13), 1983.
Major League stolen bases: 1971 (4), 1972 (10), 1973 (12), 1974 (31), 1975 (8), 1976 (28), 1977 (7), 1978 (7), 1979 (9), 1980 (1), 1981 (5), 1982 (15), 1983 (12), 1984 (2), 1985 (18), 1986 (6). Total—175.
Led Pioneer League first basemen in double plays with 37 in 1968.

Year Club	League	Pos.	G.	AB.	R.	H.	2B.	3B.	HR.	RBI.	B.A.	PO.	A.	E.	F.A.
1968—Ogden	Pion.	1B	*64	*256	54	*88	10	*8	4	41	*.344	468	28	4	*.992
1969—Albuquerque	Texas	OF-1B	70	257	44	79	7	3	7	50	.307	220	15	3	.987
1969—Spokane	P. C.	OF-1B	36	143	21	45	1	1	2	27	.315	128	12	5	.966
1969—Los Angeles	Nat.	PH	1	1	0	0	0	0	0	0	.000	0	0	0	.000
1970—Spokane	P. C.	1B-OF	111	465	78	156	33	2	3	74	.335	582	22	7	.989
1970—Los Angeles	Nat.	OF-1B	28	68	6	13	3	1	0	4	.191	37	1	0	1.000
1971—Los Angeles	Nat.	OF-1B	108	358	37	99	15	1	5	41	.277	235	11	1	.996
1972—Los Angeles	Nat.	OF-1B	105	383	47	122	14	3	5	37	.319	434	22	4	.991
1973—Los Angeles	Nat.	1B-OF	140	575	68	158	20	0	8	46	.275	981	50	3	.997
1974—Los Angeles	Nat.	OF-1B	145	580	83	182	30	3	7	58	.314	284	5	7	.976
1975—Los Angeles†	Nat.	OF	92	288	30	70	11	2	6	31	.243	138	4	2	.986
1976—Los Angeles‡	Nat.	OF-1B	154	642	76	193	28	4	7	60	.301	315	7	5	.985
1977—Chicago§	Nat.	1B	122	426	40	121	27	0	11	60	.284	966	58	10	.990
1978—Chicago x	Nat.	1B	117	446	47	144	26	1	5	74	.323	1075	83	6	.995
1979—Chicago	Nat.	1B	149	591	72	168	34	7	14	66	.284	1258	124	7	.995

Year Club League	Pos.	G.	AB.	R.	H.	2B.	3B.	HR.	RBI.	B.A.	PO.	A.	E.	F.A.
1980—Chicago .... Nat.	1B-OF	145	578	69	187	41	3	10	68	*.324	916	78	8	.992
1981—Chicago .... Nat.	1B	106	421	45	131	*35	3	10	75	.311	996	81	*17	.984
1982—Chicago .... Nat.	1B	161	*657	93	201	34	5	15	105	.306	1547	*159	12	.993
1983—Chicago .... Nat.	*●1B-OF	153	626	79	175	●38	6	16	66	.280	1391	*161	●13	.992
1984—Chicago y .... Nat.	1B-OF	21	43	3	9	0	0	0	2	.209	71	6	0	1.000
1984—Boston .... Amer.	1B	114	439	51	122	21	2	11	67	.278	974	96	●15	.986
1985—Boston .... Amer.	1B	162	673	89	201	46	3	16	110	.299	1384	*184	12	.992
1986—Boston .... Amer.	1B	153	629	73	168	39	2	18	102	.267	1067	*157	14	.989
National League Totals—16 Years		1747	6683	795	1973	356	39	119	793	.295	10644	850	95	.992
American League Totals—3 Years		429	1741	213	491	106	7	45	279	.282	3425	437	41	.989
Major League Totals—18 Years		2176	8424	1008	2464	462	46	164	1072	.292	14069	1287	136	.991

Selected by Los Angeles Dodgers' organization in 2nd round of free-agent draft, June 7, 1968.

†On disabled list, April 21 to May 12, 1975.

‡Traded with Infielder Ivan DeJesus and Pitcher Jeff Albert to Chicago Cubs for Outfielder Rick Monday and Pitcher Mike Garman, January 11, 1977.

§On disabled list, March 28 to April 19, 1977.

xOn disabled list, June 22 to July 7, 1978.

yTraded to Boston Red Sox for Pitcher Dennis Eckersley and Outfielder Mike Brumley, May 25, 1984.

CHAMPIONSHIP SERIES RECORD

Year Club League	Pos.	G.	AB.	R.	H.	2B.	3B.	HR.	RBI.	B.A.	PO.	A.	E.	F.A.
1974—Los Angeles .... Nat.	OF	4	18	0	3	1	0	0	0	.167	6	0	0	1.000
1986—Boston .... Amer.	1B	7	28	3	6	1	0	0	3	.214	49	5	0	1.000
Championship Series Totals—2 Years		11	46	3	9	2	0	0	3	.196	55	5	0	1.000

WORLD SERIES RECORD

Year Club League	Pos.	G.	AB.	R.	H.	2B.	3B.	HR.	RBI.	B.A.	PO.	A.	E.	F.A.
1974—Los Angeles .... Nat.	OF	5	20	1	5	1	0	1	1	.250	11	0	0	1.000
1986—Boston .... Amer.	1B	7	32	2	6	0	0	0	1	.188	53	7	1	.984
World Series Totals—2 Years		12	52	3	11	1	0	1	2	.212	64	7	1	.986

ALL-STAR GAME RECORD

Year League	Pos.	AB.	R.	H.	2B.	3B.	HR.	RBI.	B.A.	PO.	A.	E.	F.A.
1981—National	PH	1	0	0	0	0	0	0	.000	0	0	0	.000

STEVEN BERNARD BUECHELE

Name pronounced BOO-shell.

(Steve)

Born September 26, 1961, at Lancaster, Calif.
Height, 6.02. Weight, 190.
Throws and bats righthanded.
Attended Stanford University, Stanford, Calif.

Major League stolen bases: 1985 (3), 1986 (5). Total—8.

Named American Association Most Valuable Player, 1985.

Year Club League	Pos.	G.	AB.	R.	H.	2B.	3B.	HR.	RBI.	B.A.	PO.	A.	E.	F.A.
1982—Tulsa .... Texas	2B-3B	62	213	21	63	12	2	5	33	.296	111	174	8	.973
1983—Tulsa .... Texas	2B-3B	117	437	62	121	12	4	14	62	.277	182	259	18	.961
1983—Oklahoma City ..... A. A.	2B-3B	9	34	6	9	5	0	1	4	.265	17	22	1	.975
1984—Oklahoma City ..... A. A.	2B-3B	131	447	48	118	25	3	7	59	.264	236	329	17	.971
1985—Oklahoma City ..... A. A.	3B-2B	89	350	56	104	20	7	9	64	.297	84	170	7	.973
1985—Texas .... Amer.	3B-2B	69	219	22	48	6	3	6	21	.219	52	138	6	.969
1986—Texas .... Amer.	3B-2B-OF	153	461	54	112	19	2	18	54	.243	174	292	12	.975
Major League Totals—2 Years		222	680	76	160	25	5	24	75	.235	226	430	18	.973

Selected by Chicago White Sox' organization in 1st round (ninth player selected) of free-agent draft, June 5, 1979.

Selected by Texas Rangers' organization in 5th round of free-agent draft, June 7, 1982.

JAY CAMPBELL BUHNER

Born August 13, 1964, at Louisville, Ky.
Height, 6.03. Weight, 205.
Throws and bats righthanded.
Attended McLennan Community College, Waco, Tex.

Led Florida State League in game-winning RBIs with 15 in 1985.

Year Club League	Pos.	G.	AB.	R.	H.	2B.	3B.	HR.	RBI.	B.A.	PO.	A.	E.	F.A.
1984—Watertown† .... NYP	OF	65	229	43	74	16	3	9	●58	.323	106	8	1	.991
1985—Fort Lauderdale .. Fla. St.	OF	117	409	65	121	18	10	11	76	.296	235	12	7	.972
1986—Fort Lauderdale‡ Fla. St.	OF	36	139	24	42	9	1	7	31	.302	84	7	3	.968

Selected by Atlanta Braves' organization in 9th round of free-agent draft, June 6, 1983.

Selected by Pittsburgh Pirates' organization in secondary phase of free-agent draft, January 17, 1984.

†Traded with Infielder Dale Berra and Pitcher Alfonso Pulido to New York Yankees for Outfielder Steve Kemp, Infielder Tim Foli and $800,000, December 20, 1984.

‡On disabled list, April 11 to July 28, 1986.

DeWAYNE ALLISON BUICE

Born August 20, 1957, at Lynwood, Calif.
Height, 6.00. Weight, 170.
Throws and bats righthanded.
Attended California State University at Dominguez Hills, Carson, Calif.;
Los Angeles Harbor Junior College, Wilmington, Calif.,
and Cypress College, Cypress, Calif.

Year Club	League	G.	IP.	W.	L.	Pct.	H.	R.	ER.	SO.	BB.	ERA.
1977—Great Falls	Pioneer	15	37	1	4	.200	48	34	15	30	24	3.65
1978—Cedar Rapids	Midwest	36	74	3	5	.375	58	30	14	68	41	1.70
1979—Fresno	California	46	97	7	5	.583	83	51	40	86	44	3.71
1980—Fresno†	California	36	100	7	4	.636	101	42	37	88	38	3.33
1981—West Haven	Eastern	*58	82	8	3	.727	75	24	19	88	41	2.09
1981—Tacoma	P. Coast	2	3	1	0	1.000	0	0	0	2	3	0.00
1982—Tacoma‡	P. Coast	19	41	4	2	.667	51	22	19	36	19	4.17
1982—West Haven	Eastern	8	23⅔	1	1	.500	18	11	9	40	8	3.42
1983—Tacoma § x y	P. Coast	32	52⅓	5	3	.625	44	27	20	41	22	3.44
1984—						(Out of Organized Baseball)						
1985—						(Out of Organized Baseball)						
1986—Midland	Texas	45	78⅓	8	6	.571	70	34	30	73	22	3.45
1986—Edmonton	P. Coast	8	12⅓	2	1	.667	6	2	1	11	3	0.73

Signed as free agent by San Francisco Giants' organization, May 19, 1977.
†Drafted by West Haven (Oakland A's organization), December 9, 1980.
‡On disabled list, July 3 to July 13 and August 12, 1982 through remainder of season.
§On disabled list, June 8 to June 28 and July 13, 1983 through remainder of season.
x Granted free agency, October 15, 1983; signed by Maine (Cleveland Indians' organization), January 14, 1984.
y Released, April 7, 1984; signed by Edmonton (California Angels' organization), November 19, 1985.

ERIC GERALD BULLOCK

Born February 16, 1960, at Los Angeles, Calif.
Height, 5.11. Weight, 185.
Throws and bats lefthanded.
Attended Los Angeles Harbor Junior College, Woodland Hills, Calif. and
California State University, Fullerton, Calif.
Son of Eddie Bullock, minor league outfielder, 1955.

Major League stolen bases: 1986 (2).
Tied for Pacific Coast League lead in being hit by pitch with 7 in 1985.

Year Club	League	Pos.	G.	AB.	R.	H.	2B.	3B.	HR.	RBI.	B.A.	PO.	A.	E.	F.A.
1981—Sarasota Orange	Gulf C.	OF	56	184	38	54	8	3	1	15	.293	67	6	3	.961
1981—Daytona Beach	Fla. St.	DH	1	2	1	1	0	0	0	1	.500	0	0	0	.000
1982—Daytona Beach	Fla. St.	OF	117	442	90	150	24	11	5	●85	.339	180	11	5	.974
1982—Columbus	South.	OF	18	66	6	20	1	0	2	13	.303	21	1	0	1.000
1983—Columbus	South.	OF	130	475	65	131	15	6	9	59	.276	196	9	3	.986
1984—Columbus	South.	OF	71	265	47	77	15	2	3	41	.291	133	3	4	.971
1984—Tucson	P. C.	OF	60	185	22	51	6	2	1	16	.276	96	2	5	.951
1985—Tucson	P. C.	OF	124	467	81	149	26	8	4	57	.319	199	5	7	.967
1985—Houston	Nat.	OF	18	25	3	7	2	0	0	2	.280	4	0	2	.750
1986—Houston	Nat.	OF	6	21	0	1	0	0	0	1	.048	7	0	1	.875
1986—Tucson†	P. C.	OF	42	151	28	58	8	2	3	21	.384	73	2	1	.987
Major League Totals—2 Years			24	46	3	8	2	0	0	3	.174	11	0	3	.813

Selected by Los Angeles Dodgers' organization in 18th round of free-agent draft, June 6, 1978.
Selected by San Diego Padres' organization in 1st round (fifth player selected) of free-agent draft, January 13, 1981.
Selected by Houston Astros' organization in secondary phase of free-agent draft, June 8, 1981.
†On disabled list, May 6 to July 7, 1986.

RICHARD SCOTT BUONANTONY

Name pronounced Bohn-ANN-tohn-ee.

(Rich)

Born November 28, 1962, at Hoboken, N.J.
Height, 6.04. Weight, 205.
Throws and bats righthanded.
Attended University of Nevada, Las Vegas, Nev.

Tied for Texas League lead in hit batsmen with 8 in 1985.

Year Club	League	G.	IP.	W.	L.	Pct.	H.	R.	ER.	SO.	BB.	ERA.
1980—Sarasota Cubs	Gulf Coast	12	63	3	*8	.273	66	40	28	37	26	4.00
1981—Sarasota Cubs	Gulf Coast	13	64	2	6	.250	70	50	36	50	38	5.06
1982—Quad Cities	Midwest	26	161	12	4	.750	151	79	70	103	79	3.91
1983—Salinas	California	22	138	6	7	.462	136	73	53	97	62	3.46
1983—Midland†	Texas	4	24⅔	1	1	.500	24	15	15	13	20	5.47
1984—El Paso	Texas	8	34⅓	2	2	.500	46	39	36	17	31	9.44
1984—Stockton‡	California	20	129⅔	6	7	.462	127	61	55	121	72	3.82
1985—Arkansas	Texas	27	147⅓	10	11	.476	141	90	76	121	92	4.64
1986—Louisville	Am. Assoc.	23	108	7	6	.538	106	74	67	81	53	5.58

Selected by Chicago Cubs' organization in 14th round of free-agent draft, June 3, 1980.
†Traded to Milwaukee Brewers, October 24, 1983, completing deal in which Milwaukee traded Catcher Steve Lake to Chicago Cubs for player to be named later, April 1, 1983.

‡Traded with Pitcher Jim Koontz and Infielder Ron Koenigsfield to St. Louis Cardinals for Outfielders Paul Householder and Jim Adduci, October 2, 1984.

TIMOTHY PHILIP BURKE
(Tim)

Born February 19, 1959, at Omaha, Neb.
Height, 6.03. Weight, 190.
Throws and bats righthanded.
Attended University of Nebraska, Lincoln, Neb.

Established National League record for most games pitched by rookie, season (78), 1985.
Major League saves: 1985 (8), 1986 (4). Total—12.

Year Club	League	G.	IP.	W.	L.	Pct.	H.	R.	ER.	SO.	BB.	ERA.
1980—Salem†	Carolina					(Did not play)						
1981—Alexandria	Carolina	23	149	8	10	.444	139	67	57	111	48	3.44
1982—Buffalo‡	Eastern	25	144	7	10	.412	162	93	83	93	57	5.19
1983—Columbus	Eastern	4	12	1	0	1.000	15	9	9	6	8	6.75
1983—Nashville§x	Southern	20	129	12	4	.750	124	63	46	64	37	3.21
1984—Indianapolis	Am. Assoc.	35	180⅔	11	8	.579	192	81	70	108	61	3.49
1985—Montreal	National	★78	120⅓	9	4	.692	86	32	32	87	44	2.39
1986—Montreal	National	68	101⅓	9	7	.563	103	37	33	82	46	2.93
Major League Totals—2 Years		146	221⅔	18	11	.621	189	69	65	169	90	2.64

Selected by Pittsburgh Pirates' organization in 2nd round of free-agent draft, June 3, 1980.
†On disabled list, July 12, 1980 through remainder of season.
‡Traded with Catcher John Holland, Infielder Jose Rivera and Outfielder Don Aubin to New York Yankees' organization for Outfielder Lee Mazzilli, December 22, 1982.
§On disabled list, May 4 to May 23, 1983.
xTraded to Montreal Expos' organization for Outfielder Pat Rooney, December 19, 1983.

JOHN DAVID BURKETT

Born November 28, 1964, at New Brighton, Pa.
Height, 6.02. Weight, 172.
Throws and bats righthanded.

Year Club	League	G.	IP.	W.	L.	Pct.	H.	R.	ER.	SO.	BB.	ERA.
1983—Great Falls	Pioneer	13	50⅓	2	6	.250	73	44	35	38	30	6.26
1984—Clinton	Midwest	20	126⅔	7	6	.538	128	81	61	83	38	4.33
1985—Fresno	California	20	109⅔	7	4	.636	98	43	35	72	46	2.87
1986—Fresno	California	4	24⅔	0	3	.000	34	19	15	14	8	5.47
1986—Shreveport	Texas	22	128⅔	10	6	.625	99	46	38	73	42	2.66

Selected by San Francisco Giants' organization in 6th round of free-agent draft, June 6, 1983.

ELLIS RENA BURKS

Born September 11, 1964, at Vicksburg, Miss.
Height, 6.02. Weight, 175.
Throws and bats righthanded.
Attended Ranger Junior College, Ranger, Tex.

Tied for Florida State League lead in double plays by outfielders with 6 in 1984.

Year Club	League	Pos.	G.	AB.	R.	H.	2B.	3B.	HR.	RBI.	B.A.	PO.	A.	E.	F.A.
1983—Elmira	NYP	OF	53	174	30	42	9	0	2	23	.241	89	5	2	.979
1984—Winter Haven	Fla. St.	OF	112	375	52	96	15	4	6	43	.256	196	12	5	.977
1985—New Britain	East.	OF	133	476	66	121	25	7	10	61	.254	306	9	8	.975
1986—New Britain	East.	OF	124	462	70	126	20	3	14	55	.273	318	5	5	.985

Selected by Boston Red Sox' organization in 1st round (20th player selected) of free agent draft, January 11, 1983.

RICHARD PAUL BURLESON
(Rick)

Born April 29, 1951, at Lynwood, Calif.
Height, 5.10. Weight, 160.
Throws and bats righthanded.
Attended Cerritos Junior College, Norwalk, Calif.

Established major league records for most double plays by shortstop, season (147), 1980; most assists by shortstop, game (15), April 13, 1982 (20 innings).
Major League stolen bases: 1974 (3), 1975 (8), 1976 (14), 1977 (13), 1978 (8), 1979 (9), 1980 (12), 1981 (4), 1986 (1). Total—72.
Led American League shortstops in total chances with 851 in 1980 and 615 in 1981.
Led American League shortstops in double plays with 147 in 1980 and 88 in 1981.
Led International League shortstops in fielding percentage with .961 in 1973.
Led Eastern League shortstops in double plays with 80 in 1972.
Named shortstop on THE SPORTING NEWS American League All-Star Team, 1977 and 1981.
Named shortstop on THE SPORTING NEWS American League All-Star fielding team, 1979.
Named shortstop on THE SPORTING NEWS American League Silver Slugger team, 1981.

Year Club	League	Pos.	G.	AB.	R.	H.	2B.	3B.	HR.	RBI.	B.A.	PO.	A.	E.	F.A.
1970—Winter Haven	Fla. St.	SS	118	419	42	92	13	4	1	29	.220	188	★400	38	.939
1971—Greenville	W. Car.	SS	29	118	24	31	4	2	2	12	.263	32	68	11	.901
1971—Winston-Salem†	Carol.	SS	77	299	35	82	14	2	4	30	.274	118	262	23	.943
1972—Pawtucket	East.	SS	136	488	59	115	26	0	9	51	.236	★191	380	23	★.961

Year	Club	League	Pos.	G.	AB.	R.	H.	2B.	3B.	HR.	RBI.	B.A.	PO.	A.	E.	F.A.
1973—Pawtucket	Int.		SS-2B	★146	477	58	120	20	1	6	45	.252	241	431	25	.964
1974—Pawtucket	Int.		SS	10	41	7	14	4	0	1	4	.341	10	36	3	.939
1974—Boston	Amer.		SS-2B-3B	114	384	36	109	22	0	4	44	.284	209	329	21	.962
1975—Boston	Amer.		SS	158	580	66	146	25	1	6	62	.252	267	498	29	.963
1976—Boston	Amer.		SS	152	540	75	157	27	1	7	42	.291	274	478	34	.957
1977—Boston	Amer.		SS	154	★663	80	194	36	7	3	52	.293	★285	482	24	.970
1978—Boston‡	Amer.		SS	145	626	75	155	32	5	5	49	.248	285	482	15	.981
1979—Boston	Amer.		SS	153	627	93	174	32	5	5	60	.278	272	523	16	★.980
1980—Boston§	Amer.		SS	155	644	89	179	29	2	8	51	.278	★301	★528	22	.974
1981—California	Amer.		SS	●109	430	53	126	17	1	5	33	.293	★208	★394	13	.979
1982—California x	Amer.		SS	11	45	4	7	1	0	0	2	.156	19	51	1	.986
1983—California yz	Amer.		SS	33	119	22	34	7	0	0	11	.286	54	102	5	.969
1983—Edmonton	P. C.		SS	14	51	3	10	3	0	0	4	.196	17	16	3	.917
1984—California a	Amer.		PH-PR	7	4	2	0	0	0	0	0	.000	0	0	0	.000
1985—California b	Amer.										(Did not play)					
1986—California c	Amer.		SS-2B-3B	93	271	35	77	14	0	5	29	.284	62	90	3	.981
Major League Totals—12 Years				1284	4933	630	1358	242	22	48	435	.275	2236	3957	183	.971

Selected by Minnesota Twins' organization in 8th round of free-agent draft, June 5, 1969.
Selected by Boston Red Sox' organization in secondary phase of free-agent draft, January 17, 1970.
†On disabled list, June 1 to June 19, 1971.
‡On disabled list, July 14 to July 28, 1978.
§Traded with Third Baseman Butch Hobson to California Angels for Third Baseman Carney Lansford, Pitcher Mark Clear and Outfielder Rick Miller, December 10, 1980.
xOn disabled list, April 18, 1982 through remainder of season.
yOn disabled list, March 30 to June 30, 1983; included rehabilitation disability assignment to Edmonton, June 10 to June 27, 1983.
zOn disabled list, August 19 to September 3, 1983.
aOn disabled list, March 29 to September 1, 1984.
bOn disabled list, April 8, 1985 through remainder of season.
cGranted free agency, November 12, 1986.

CHAMPIONSHIP SERIES RECORD

Year	Club	League	Pos.	G.	AB.	R.	H.	2B.	3B.	HR.	RBI.	B.A.	PO.	A.	E.	F.A.
1975—Boston	Amer.		SS	3	9	2	4	2	0	0	1	.444	4	12	1	.941
1986—California	Amer.		PH-DH-2B	4	11	0	3	0	0	0	0	.273	3	5	0	1.000
Championship Series Totals—2 Years				7	20	2	7	2	0	0	1	.350	7	17	1	.960

WORLD SERIES RECORD

Year	Club	League	Pos.	G.	AB.	R.	H.	2B.	3B.	HR.	RBI.	B.A.	PO.	A.	E.	F.A.
1975—Boston	Amer.		SS	7	24	1	7	1	0	0	2	.292	9	19	1	.966

ALL-STAR GAME RECORD

Year	League	Pos.	AB.	R.	H.	2B.	3B.	HR.	RBI.	B.A.	PO.	A.	E.	F.A.
1977—American		SS	2	0	0	0	0	0	0	.000	0	0	0	.000
1979—American		PR-SS	2	1	0	0	0	0	0	.000	0	1	0	1.000
1981—American		SS	1	0	0	0	0	0	0	.000	1	3	0	1.000
All-Star Game Totals—3 Years			5	1	0	0	0	0	0	.000	1	4	0	1.000

Named to American League All-Star Team for 1978 game; replaced due to injury by Jerry Remy.

ROBERT BRITT BURNS

(Known by middle name.)
Born June 8, 1959, at Houston, Tex.
Height, 6.05. Weight, 218.
Throws left and bats righthanded.

Major League saves: 1984 (3).
Tied for American League lead in balks with 4 in 1980.
Named American League Rookie Pitcher of the Year by THE SPORTING NEWS, 1980.

Year	Club	League	G.	IP.	W.	L.	Pct.	H.	R.	ER.	SO.	BB.	ERA.
1978—Appleton	Midwest		6	30	3	2	.600	25	8	8	28	2	2.40
1978—Chicago	American		2	8	0	2	.000	14	12	11	3	3	12.38
1978—Knoxville	Southern		4	21	1	1	.500	24	16	10	17	4	4.29
1979—Knoxville	Southern		20	110	6	10	.375	126	68	59	92	37	4.83
1979—Iowa	Am. Assoc.		7	41	2	3	.400	41	17	15	34	15	3.29
1979—Chicago	American		6	5	0	0	.000	10	5	3	2	1	5.40
1980—Chicago	American		34	238	15	13	.536	213	83	75	133	63	2.84
1981—Chicago	American		24	157	10	6	.625	139	52	46	108	49	2.64
1982—Chicago	American		28	169⅓	13	5	.722	168	89	76	116	67	4.04
1983—Chicago†	American		29	173⅔	10	11	.476	165	79	69	115	55	3.58
1984—Chicago‡	American		34	117	4	12	.250	130	74	65	85	45	5.00
1984—Appleton	Midwest		1	5	1	0	1.000	4	1	1	5	1	1.80
1984—Denver	Am. Assoc.		1	6	1	0	1.000	6	3	3	5	3	4.50
1985—Chicago§	American		36	227	18	11	.621	206	105	100	172	79	3.96
1986—New York x y	American							(Did not play)					
Major League Totals—8 Years			193	1095	70	60	.538	1045	499	445	734	362	3.66

Selected by Chicago White Sox' organization in 3rd round of free-agent draft, June 6, 1978.
†On disabled list, March 29 to May 9, 1983.
‡On disabled list, July 19 to August 20, 1984; included rehabilitation disability assignment to Appleton, August 10 to August 15, 1984, and Denver, August 16 to August 20, 1984.

xOn disabled list, March 31, 1986 through entire 1986 season.
yGranted free agency, November 12, 1986.

CHAMPIONSHIP SERIES RECORD

Year Club	League	G.	IP.	W.	L.	Pct.	H.	R.	ER.	SO.	BB.	ERA.
1983—Chicago	American	1	9⅓	0	1	.000	6	1	1	8	5	0.96

ALL-STAR GAME RECORD

Member of American League All-Star Team in 1981; did not play.

TODD EDWARD BURNS

Born July 6, 1963, at Maywood, Calif.
Height, 6.02. Weight, 186.
Throws and bats righthanded.
Attended Oral Roberts University, Tulsa, Okla.

Tied for Southern League lead in shutouts with 3 in 1986.

Year Club	League	G.	IP.	W.	L.	Pct.	H.	R.	ER.	SO.	BB.	ERA.
1984—Medford	Northwest	22	36⅓	3	0	1.000	21	4	2	63	12	0.50
1984—Madison	Midwest	10	14	3	2	.600	11	4	4	20	3	2.57
1985—Madison	Midwest	20	123	8	8	.500	109	55	50	94	40	3.66
1985—Huntsville	Southern	4	22⅔	3	1	.750	16	6	3	8	13	1.19
1986—Huntsville	Southern	20	124⅔	7	7	.500	122	59	52	77	39	3.75
1986—Tacoma	P. Coast	11	16⅔	0	1	.000	11	4	4	14	12	2.16

Selected by Oakland A's organization in 7th round of free-agent draft, June 4, 1984.

BERTRAM RAY BURRIS

(Known by middle name.)

Born August 22, 1950, at Idabel, Okla.
Height, 6.05. Weight, 210.
Throws and bats righthanded.
Received bachelor of arts degree in recreational leadership from Southwestern State, Weatherford, Okla.

Major League saves: 1974 (1), 1978 (1), 1982 (2). Total—4.
Tied for National League lead in home runs allowed with 29 in 1977.

Year Club	League	G.	IP.	W.	L.	Pct.	H.	R.	ER.	SO.	BB.	ERA.
1972—Midland	Texas	14	95	7	5	.583	98	43	37	91	20	3.51
1973—Wichita	Am. Assoc.	8	59	4	3	.571	72	45	37	34	19	5.64
1973—Chicago	National	31	65	1	1	.500	65	22	21	57	27	2.91
1974—Wichita	Am. Assoc.	7	46	2	3	.400	52	33	26	34	23	5.09
1974—Chicago	National	40	75	3	5	.375	91	61	55	40	26	6.60
1975—Chicago	National	36	238	15	10	.600	259	121	109	108	73	4.12
1976—Chicago	National	37	249	15	13	.536	251	102	86	112	70	3.11
1977—Chicago	National	39	221	14	16	.467	270	132	116	105	67	4.72
1978—Chicago	National	40	199	7	13	.350	210	112	105	94	79	4.75
1979—Chicago†-New York§	National	18	43	0	2	.000	44	27	23	24	21	4.81
1979—New York‡	American	15	28	1	3	.250	40	22	19	19	10	6.11
1980—New York xy	National	29	170	7	13	.350	181	86	76	83	54	4.02
1981—Montreal	National	22	136	9	7	.563	117	56	46	52	41	3.04
1982—Montreal	National	37	123⅔	4	14	.222	143	77	65	55	53	4.73
1983—Montreal z	National	40	154	4	7	.364	139	68	63	100	56	3.68
1984—Oakland ab	American	34	211⅔	13	10	.565	193	84	74	93	90	3.15
1985—Milwaukee c	American	29	170⅓	9	13	.409	182	95	91	81	53	4.81
1986—Louisville	Am. Assoc.	4	18⅔	1	1	.500	18	5	5	9	2	2.41
1986—St. Louis d	National	23	82	4	5	.444	92	52	51	34	32	5.60
American League Totals—3 Years		78	410	23	26	.469	415	201	184	193	153	4.04
National League Totals—12 Years		392	1755⅔	83	106	.439	1862	916	816	864	599	4.18
Major League Totals—14 Years		470	2165⅔	106	132	.445	2277	1117	1000	1057	752	4.16

Selected by Chicago Cubs' organization in 17th round of free-agent draft, June 6, 1972.
†Traded to New York Yankees for Pitcher Dick Tidrow, May 23, 1979.
‡Sold on waivers to New York Mets, August 20, 1979.
§On disabled list, September 15 to October 3, 1979.
xOn disabled list, July 3 to August 4, 1980.
yGranted free agency, October 27, 1980; signed by Montreal Expos, February 18, 1981.
zTraded to Oakland A's for Outfielder Rusty McNealy and cash, December 8, 1983.
aAppeared in three games as a pinch-runner.
bTraded with Pitcher Eric Barry and a player to be named later to Milwaukee Brewers for Pitcher Don Sutton December 7, 1984; Milwaukee organization acquired Pitcher Ed Myers to complete deal, March 25, 1985.
cReleased, April 1, 1986; signed by Louisville (St. Louis Cardinals' organization), April 11, 1986.
dReleased, August 27, 1986.

DIVISION SERIES RECORD

Year Club	League	G.	IP.	W.	L.	Pct.	H.	R.	ER.	SO.	BB.	ERA.
1981—Montreal	National	1	5⅓	0	1	.000	7	4	3	4	4	5.06

CHAMPIONSHIP SERIES RECORD

Established National League Championship Series record for most innings pitched, five-game Series (17), 1981.

Year	Club	League	G.	IP.	W.	L.	Pct.	H.	R.	ER.	SO.	BB.	ERA.
1981—Montreal	National	2	17	1	0	1.000	10	1	1	4	3	0.53

DENNIS ALLEN BURTT

Born November 29, 1957, at San Diego, Calif.
Height, 6.00. Weight, 187.
Throws right and bats left and righthanded.
Attended Santa Ana Junior College, Santa Ana, Calif.

Tied for International League lead in intentional bases on balls issued with 9 in 1982 and shutouts with 3 in 1985.

Year	Club	League	G.	IP.	W.	L.	Pct.	H.	R.	ER.	SO.	BB.	ERA.
1976—Elmira	NYP	8	44	5	0	1.000	22	7	6	34	20	1.23
1977—Winter Haven†	Florida St.	7	32	2	1	.667	20	13	3	12	18	0.84
1978—Winter Haven	Florida St.	29	100	8	4	.667	76	35	29	76	39	2.61
1979—Winter Haven	Florida St.	35	152	11	10	.524	113	53	40	109	74	2.37
1980—Bristol	Eastern	31	165	11	8	.579	141	74	65	102	93	3.55
1981—Bristol	Eastern	27	170	10	8	.556	134	77	53	108	80	2.81
1982—Pawtucket	Int'national	25	150⅓	13	7	.650	163	96	80	79	98	4.79
1983—Pawtucket‡	Int'national	23	110½	4	5	.444	109	72	65	66	75	5.30
1984—Pawtucket§	Int'national	26	131⅓	6	8	.429	151	89	72	70	67	4.93
1985—Toledo	Int'national	27	172⅓	●14	8	.636	182	96	79	95	67	4.13
1985—Minnesota	American	5	28⅓	2	2	.500	20	13	12	9	7	3.81
1986—Minnesota	American	3	2	0	0	.000	7	7	7	1	3	31.50
1986—Toledo	Int'national	24	134⅓	9	10	.474	151	78	69	46	52	4.62
Major League Totals—2 Years		8	30⅓	2	2	.500	27	20	19	10	10	5.64

Selected by Boston Red Sox' organization in 2nd round of free-agent draft, January 7, 1976.
†On disabled list, June 13 to August 8, 1977.
‡On disabled list, May 1 to May 31 and July 26 to August 5, 1983.
§Granted free agency, October 15, 1984; signed by Minnesota Twins' organization, December 31, 1984.

ROBERT RANDALL BUSH
(Randy)

Born October 5, 1958, at Dover, Del.
Height, 6.01. Weight, 184.
Throws and bats lefthanded.
Attended Miami-Dade North Community College, Miami, Fla.,
and University of New Orleans, New Orleans, La.

Tied American League record for most home runs by pinch-hitter, consecutive at-bats (2), June 20 and 23, 1986.
Major League stolen bases: 1984 (1), 1985 (3), 1986 (5). Total—9.
Led Southern League in being hit by pitch with 8 in 1979 and 12 in 1981.

Year	Club	League	Pos.	G.	AB.	R.	H.	2B.	3B.	HR.	RBI.	B.A.	PO.	A.	E.	F.A.
1979—Orlando	South.	1B	76	243	33	62	12	2	6	34	.255	653	38	13	.982
1980—Toledo†	Int.	OF-1B	40	108	11	21	1	0	1	7	.194	112	6	1	.992
1980—Orlando	South.	1B	51	175	32	41	2	1	7	26	.234	458	28	4	.992
1981—Orlando	South.	OF-1B	136	482	98	140	26	3	22	94	.290	174	7	5	.973
1982—Toledo	Int.	OF	49	160	21	52	14	0	8	27	.325	68	0	1	.986
1982—Minnesota	Amer.	OF	55	119	13	29	6	1	4	13	.244	7	0	0	1.000
1983—Minnesota	Amer.	1B	124	373	43	93	24	3	11	56	.249	21	3	0	1.000
1984—Minnesota	Amer.	1B	113	311	46	69	17	1	11	43	.222	5	0	0	1.000
1985—Minnesota	Amer.	OF-1B	97	234	26	56	13	3	10	35	.239	79	0	2	.975
1986—Minnesota	Amer.	OF-1B	130	357	50	96	19	7	7	45	.269	182	2	4	.979
Major League Totals—5 Years			519	1394	178	343	79	15	43	192	.246	294	5	6	.980

Selected by Minnesota Twins' organization in 2nd round of free-agent draft, June 5, 1979.
†On disabled list, May 25 to June 27, 1980.

JOHN DANIEL BUTCHER

Born March 8, 1957, at Glendale, Calif.
Height, 6.04. Weight, 190.
Throws and bats righthanded.
Attended Yavapai College, Prescott, Ariz.

Major League saves: 1982 (1), 1983 (5). Total—6.
Led International League in complete games with 14 in 1980.

Year	Club	League	G.	IP.	W.	L.	Pct.	H.	R.	ER.	SO.	BB.	ERA.
1977—Sarasota Rangers	Gulf Coast	6	42	3	2	.600	28	10	6	23	11	1.29
1977—Asheville	W. Carol.	2	16	1	0	1.000	13	4	2	13	6	1.13
1978—Asheville	W. Carol.	24	154	10	9	.526	150	81	57	103	77	3.33
1979—Tulsa†	Texas	26	155	9	12	.429	197	106	88	82	53	5.11
1980—Charleston	Int'national	22	152	10	7	.588	141	57	56	71	50	3.32
1980—Texas	American	6	35	3	3	.500	34	19	16	27	13	4.11
1981—Wichita	Am. Assoc.	24	136	8	10	.444	171	100	85	87	60	5.63
1981—Texas	American	5	28	1	2	.333	18	6	5	19	8	1.61
1982—Denver	Am. Assoc.	8	59	5	1	.833	54	20	18	31	14	2.75
1982—Texas	American	18	94⅓	5	1	.167	102	53	51	39	34	4.87
1983—Texas‡	American	38	123	6	6	.500	128	50	48	58	41	3.51
1984—Minnesota	American	34	225	13	11	.542	242	98	86	83	53	3.44
1985—Minnesota	American	34	207⅔	11	14	.440	239	125	115	92	43	4.98
1986—Minnesota§-Cleveland xy	American	29	120⅔	1	8	.111	168	93	88	45	37	6.56
Major League Totals—7 Years		164	833⅔	36	49	.424	931	444	409	363	229	4.42

Selected by St. Louis Cardinals' organization in 2nd round of free-agent draft, January 7, 1976.
Selected by Atlanta Braves' organization in secondary phase of free-agent draft, June 8, 1976.
Selected by Houston Astros' organization in secondary phase of free-agent draft, January 11, 1977.
Selected by Texas Rangers' organization in secondary phase of free-agent draft, June 7, 1977.
†On disabled list, July 30 to August 10, 1979.
‡Traded with Pitcher Mike Smithson and Catcher Sam Sorce to Minnesota Twins for Outfielder Gary Ward, December 7, 1983.
§Traded to Cleveland Indians for Pitcher Neal Heaton, June 20, 1986.
xOn disabled list, August 21 to September 5, 1986.
yReleased, December 23, 1986.

SALVATORE PHILIP BUTERA
(Sal)

Born September 25, 1952, at Richmond Hill, N.Y.
Height, 6.00. Weight, 189.
Throws and bats righthanded.
Attended Suffolk Community College, Selden, N.Y.

Led Carolina League in passed balls with 20 in 1974.
Tied for Carolina League lead in double plays by catchers with 9 in 1974.

Year	Club	League	Pos.	G.	AB.	R.	H.	2B.	3B.	HR.	RBI.	B.A.	PO.	A.	E.	F.A.
1972—Sarasota W. Sox†	Gulf C.	C	36	114	18	28	7	0	0	16	.246	253	20	10	.965
1973—Fort Lauderdale	Fla. St.	C	99	319	21	76	12	1	1	32	.238	503	★86	10	.983
1974—Lynchburg	Carol.	C	124	417	35	90	16	2	3	55	.216	589	★102	7	★.990
1975—Orlando	South.	C	20	51	8	9	2	0	0	4	.176	61	14	0	1.000
1975—Tacoma	P. C.	C	73	215	21	52	9	0	2	26	.242	376	36	6	.986
1976—Orlando	South.	C	90	267	45	73	8	0	3	28	.273	326	41	6	.984
1977—Tacoma	P. C.	C	87	252	27	70	13	0	4	45	.278	257	49	9	.971
1978—Toledo	Int.	C	74	206	20	52	7	0	4	28	.252	334	32	5	.987
1979—Toledo	Int.	C	78	236	20	70	13	0	2	29	.297	392	33	11	.975
1980—Minnesota	Amer.	C	34	85	4	23	1	0	0	2	.271	106	9	6	.950
1981—Minnesota	Amer.	C-1B	62	167	13	40	7	1	0	18	.240	256	41	9	.971
1982—Minnesota‡	Amer.	C	54	126	9	32	2	0	0	8	.254	230	26	3	.988
1983—Detroit	Amer.	C	4	5	1	1	0	0	0	0	.200	12	1	1	.929
1983—Evansville§	A. A.	C	67	219	23	65	11	0	2	21	.297	300	26	11	.967
1984—Indianapolis	A. A.	C	111	283	36	76	11	0	7	41	.269	588	54	6	★.991
1984—Montreal	Nat.	C	3	3	0	0	0	0	0	0	.000	9	0	0	1.000
1985—Indianapolis	A. A.	C	5	18	2	4	0	0	1	4	.222	27	4	0	1.000
1985—Montreal x	Nat.	C-P	67	120	11	24	1	0	3	12	.200	227	20	4	.984
1986—Cincinnati	Nat.	C-P	56	113	14	27	6	1	2	16	.239	215	17	5	.979
American League Totals—4 Years			154	383	27	96	10	1	0	28	.251	604	77	19	.973
National League Totals—3 Years			126	236	25	51	7	1	5	28	.216	451	37	9	.982
Major League Totals—7 Years			280	619	52	147	17	2	5	56	.237	1055	114	28	.977

Signed as free agent by Minnesota Twins' organization, May 15, 1972.
†Loaned to Sarasota White Sox (Chicago White Sox' organization), June 26, 1972; returned, September 14, 1972.
‡Traded to Detroit Tigers for Catcher Stine Poole, March 25, 1983.
§Released, October 21, 1983; signed by Indianapolis (Montreal Expos' organization), December 23, 1983.
xTraded with Pitcher Bill Gullickson to Cincinnati Reds for Pitchers Jay Tibbs, Andy McGaffigan and John Stuper and Catcher Dann Bilardello, December 19, 1985.

PITCHING RECORD

Year	Club	League	G.	IP.	W.	L.	Pct.	H.	R.	ER.	SO.	BB.	ERA.
1985—Montreal	National	1	1	0	0	.000	0	0	0	0	0	0.00
1986—Cincinnati	National	1	1	0	0	.000	0	0	0	1	1	0.00
Major League Totals—2 Years		2	2	0	0	.000	0	0	0	1	1	0.00

BRETT MORGAN BUTLER

Born June 15, 1957, at Los Angeles, Calif.
Height, 5.10. Weight, 160.
Throws and bats lefthanded.
Attended Arizona State University, Tempe, Ariz., and received bachelor of science degree in education from Southeastern Oklahoma State University, Durant, Okla., in 1979.

Tied major league record for fewest double plays by outfielder, season, for leader in most double plays (4), 1983.
Major League stolen bases: 1981 (9), 1982 (21), 1983 (39), 1984 (52), 1985 (47), 1986 (32). Total—200.
Led American League in caught stealing with 22 in 1984 and 20 in 1985.
Tied for National League lead in double plays by outfielders with 4 in 1983.
Led International League in bases on balls received with 103 in 1981.
Named International League Most Valuable Player, 1981.

Year	Club	League	Pos.	G.	AB.	R.	H.	2B.	3B.	HR.	RBI.	B.A.	PO.	A.	E.	F.A.
1979—Greenwood	W. Car.	OF	35	117	26	37	2	4	1	11	.316	45	2	0	1.000
1979—Bradenton	Gulf C.	OF	30	111	36	41	7	5	3	20	.369	66	5	0	1.000
1980—Anderson	S. Atl.	OF	70	255	73	76	12	6	1	26	.298	190	5	1	.995
1980—Durham	Carol.	OF	66	224	47	82	15	6	2	39	.366	156	4	3	.982
1981—Richmond	Int.	OF	125	466	★93	156	19	4	3	36	.335	286	15	3	.990
1981—Atlanta	Nat.	OF	40	126	17	32	2	3	0	4	.254	76	2	1	.987
1982—Atlanta	Nat.	OF	89	240	35	52	2	0	0	7	.217	129	2	0	1.000
1982—Richmond	Int.	OF	41	157	22	57	8	3	1	22	.363	101	2	1	.990
1983—Atlanta†	Nat.	OF	151	549	84	154	21	★13	5	37	.281	284	13	4	.987
1984—Cleveland	Amer.	OF	159	602	108	162	25	9	3	49	.269	448	13	4	.991

Year	Club	League	Pos.	G.	AB.	R.	H.	2B.	3B.	HR.	RBI.	B.A.	PO.	A.	E.	F.A.
1985—Cleveland	Amer.	OF	152	591	106	184	28	14	5	50	.311	437	19	1	*.998
1986—Cleveland	Amer.	OF	161	587	92	163	17	*14	4	51	.278	434	9	3	.993
National League Totals—3 Years			280	915	136	238	25	16	5	48	.260	489	17	5	.990
American League Totals—3 Years			472	1780	306	509	70	37	12	150	.286	1319	41	8	.994
Major League Totals—6 Years			752	2695	442	747	95	53	17	198	.277	1808	58	13	.993

Selected by Atlanta Braves' organization in 23rd round of free-agent draft, June 5, 1979.

†Traded with Infielder Brook Jacoby to Cleveland Indians, October 21, 1983, completing deal in which Atlanta Braves acquired Pitcher Len Barker for three players to be named later, August 28, 1983. Cleveland acquired Pitcher Rick Behenna as partial completion of deal, September 2, 1983.

CHAMPIONSHIP SERIES RECORD

Year	Club	League	Pos.	G.	AB.	R.	H.	2B.	3B.	HR.	RBI.	B.A.	PO.	A.	E.	F.A.
1982—Atlanta	Nat.	OF-PH	2	1	0	0	0	0	0	0	.000	0	0	0	.000

RANDALL PARKER BYERS

Born October 2, 1964, at Bridgeton, N.J.
Height, 6.02. Weight, 180.
Throws right and bats lefthanded.
Attended Community College of Baltimore, Baltimore, Md.

Led South Atlantic League in game-winning RBIs with 22 in 1985.

Year	Club	League	Pos.	G.	AB.	R.	H.	2B.	3B.	HR.	RBI.	B.A.	PO.	A.	E.	F.A.
1984—Spokane	N'west	OF	67	273	34	63	9	●4	4	43	.231	146	6	9	.944
1985—Charleston	S. Atl.	*3B-OF	133	501	79	160	32	●9	7	94	.319	72	181	*44	.852
1986—Beaumont	Texas	OF	121	463	60	123	23	4	11	50	.266	204	●14	10	.956

Selected by Toronto Blue Jays' organization in 22nd round of free-agent draft, June 7, 1982.
Selected by Detroit Tigers' organization in secondary phase of free-agent draft, January 11, 1983.
Selected by Boston Red Sox' organization in secondary phase of free-agent draft, June 6, 1983.
Selected by San Diego Padres' organization in secondary phase of free-agent draft, January 17, 1984.

ENOS MILTON CABELL JR.

Name pronounced Kuh-BELL.

Born October 8, 1949, at Fort Riley, Kan.
Height, 6.05. Weight, 185.
Throws and bats righthanded.
Attended Los Angeles Harbor Junior College, Wilmington, Calif.
Cousin of Dick Davis, outfielder with Milwaukee Brewers, Philadelphia Phillies, Pittsburgh Pirates and Toronto Blue Jays, 1977 through 1982, and currently with Kintetsu Buffaloes of Japanese Baseball; and Ken Landreaux, outfielder with Los Angeles Dodgers.

Major League stolen bases: 1973 (1), 1974 (5), 1975 (12), 1976 (35), 1977 (42), 1978 (33), 1979 (37), 1980 (21), 1981 (6), 1982 (15), 1983 (3), 1984 (8), 1985 (9), 1986 (10). Total—237.
Led National League third basemen in putouts with 140 and errors with 23 in 1977.
Led Appalachian League in total bases with 149 in 1969.
Led International League first basemen in assists with 90 and fielding percentage with .990 in 1972.
Led Texas League first basemen in assists with 121 in 1971.
Led California League first basemen in assists with 80 and errors with 26 in 1970.
Named Texas League Player of the Year, 1971.
Named Appalachian League Player of the Year, 1969.

Year	Club	League	Pos.	G.	AB.	R.	H.	2B.	3B.	HR.	RBI.	B.A.	PO.	A.	E.	F.A.
1969—Bluefield	Appal.	1B	●69	*270	*62	*101	14	2	10	43	.374	*471	30	9	.982
1970—Stockton	Calif.	1B-OF	138	517	78	147	25	6	10	67	.284	844	81	33	.966
1971—Dall-Ft. Worth	Texas	●1-3-O	140	521	65	*162	24	6	6	79	*.311	1135	122	●20	.984
1972—Rochester	Int.	1-O-3-S	141	*540	82	145	26	9	8	66	.269	893	110	11	.989
1972—Baltimore	Amer.	1B	3	5	0	0	0	0	0	1	.000	7	0	0	1.000
1973—Rochester	Int.	1B-3B-2B	60	229	43	81	9	1	2	24	.354	510	47	10	.982
1973—Baltimore	Amer.	1B-3B	32	47	12	10	2	0	1	3	.213	111	4	1	.991
1974—Baltimore†	Amer.	1-O-3-2	80	174	24	42	4	2	3	17	.241	223	45	4	.985
1975—Houston	Nat.	OF-1B-3B	117	348	43	92	17	6	2	43	.264	197	58	6	.977
1976—Houston	Nat.	3B-1B	144	586	85	160	13	7	2	43	.273	131	263	17	.959
1977—Houston	Nat.	3B-1B-SS	150	625	101	176	36	7	16	68	.282	176	288	24	.951
1978—Houston	Nat.	3B-1B-SS	●162	*660	92	195	31	8	7	71	.295	211	277	18	.964
1979—Houston	Nat.	3B-1B	155	603	60	164	30	5	6	67	.272	396	199	14	.977
1980—Houston‡	Nat.	*3B-1B	152	604	69	167	23	8	2	55	.276	118	250	*29	.927
1981—San Francisco§	Nat.	1B-3B	96	396	41	101	20	1	2	36	.255	634	90	16	.978
1982—Detroit	Amer.	1B-3B-OF	125	464	45	121	17	3	2	37	.261	592	143	16	.979
1983—Detroit x	Amer.	1B-3B-SS	121	392	62	122	23	5	5	46	.311	830	79	3	.997
1984—Houston	Nat.	1B	127	436	52	135	17	3	8	44	.310	971	66	7	.993
1985—Hous.y-L.A.	Nat.	1B-3B-OF	117	335	40	91	19	1	2	36	.272	456	97	11	.980
1986—Los Angeles z	Nat.	1B-OF-3B	107	277	27	71	11	0	2	29	.256	389	49	9	.980
American League Totals—5 Years			361	1082	143	295	46	10	11	104	.273	1763	271	24	.988
National League Totals—10 Years			1327	4870	610	1352	217	46	49	492	.278	3679	1637	151	.972
Major League Totals—15 Years			1688	5952	753	1647	263	56	60	596	.277	5442	1908	175	.977

Signed as free agent by Baltimore Orioles' organization, September 22, 1968.

†Traded with Second Baseman Rob Andrews to Houston Astros for First Baseman Lee May and Outfielder Jay Schlueter, December 3, 1974.

‡Traded to San Francisco Giants for Outfielder Chris Bourjos and Pitcher Bob Knepper, December 8, 1980.

§Traded with cash to Detroit Tigers for Outfielder Champ Summers, March 4, 1982.

xGranted free agency, November 7, 1983; signed by Houston Astros, February 14, 1984.
yTraded to Los Angeles Dodgers for Pitcher Rafael Montalvo and a player to be named later, July 10, 1985; Houston Astros' organization acquired Third Baseman German Rivera to complete deal, July 15, 1985.
zGranted free agency, November 12, 1986.

CHAMPIONSHIP SERIES RECORD

Tied Championship Series record for most clubs, total Series (3).

Year	Club	League	Pos.	G.	AB.	R.	H.	2B.	3B.	HR.	RBI.	B.A.	PO.	A.	E.	F.A.
1974—Baltimore	Amer.		O-PH-PR	3	4	0	1	0	0	0	0	.250	2	0	0	1.000
1980—Houston	Nat.		3B	5	21	1	5	1	0	0	0	.238	1	9	0	1.000
1985—Los Angeles	Nat.		1B-PH	5	13	1	1	0	0	0	0	.077	20	3	0	1.000
Championship Series Totals—3 Years				13	38	2	7	1	0	0	0	.184	23	12	0	1.000

IVAN CALDERON (PEREZ)

Name pronounced Call-durh-OWN.

Born March 19, 1962, at Fajardo, Puerto Rico.
Height, 5.11. Weight, 160.
Throws and bats righthanded.

Major League stolen bases: 1984 (1), 1985 (4), 1986 (3). Total—8.
Tied for Southern League lead in total bases with 267 in 1983.

Year	Club	League	Pos.	G.	AB.	R.	H.	2B.	3B.	HR.	RBI.	B.A.	PO.	A.	E.	F.A.
1980—Bellingham	N'west		OF	57	195	44	62	7	★9	4	32	.318	56	4	7	.896
1981—Wausau	Midw.		OF-SS	117	402	79	123	19	1	20	62	.306	130	17	6	.961
1982—Wausau	Midw.		S-O-3-1	126	461	91	132	22	5	24	89	.286	215	202	45	.903
1983—Chattanooga	South.		OF	139	546	92	●170	34	★15	11	80	★.311	251	10	13	.953
1984—Salt Lake City†	P. C.		OF	66	255	61	93	7	9	4	45	.365	132	9	8	.946
1984—Seattle‡	Amer.		OF	11	24	2	5	1	0	1	1	.208	22	0	0	1.000
1985—Seattle	Amer.		OF-1B	67	210	37	60	16	4	8	28	.286	108	5	2	.983
1986—Sea.§-Chi.	Amer.		OF	50	164	16	41	7	1	2	15	.250	64	4	5	.932
1986—Calgary	P. C.		OF	24	81	17	27	3	0	3	18	.333	34	2	1	.973
1986—Buffalo	A. A.		OF	27	105	11	23	9	0	5	22	.219	30	1	5	.861
Major League Totals—3 Years				128	398	55	106	24	5	11	44	.266	194	9	7	.967

Signed as free agent by Seattle Mariners' organization, July 30, 1979.
†On disabled list, May 25 to July 2, 1984.
‡On disabled list, August 26 to September 12, 1984.
§Traded to Chicago White Sox' organization, July 1, 1986, completing deal in which Chicago traded Catcher Scott Bradley to Seattle Mariners for a player to be named later, June 26, 1986.

JEFFREY WILTON CALHOUN
(Jeff)

Born April 11, 1958, at LaGrange, Ga.
Height, 6.02. Weight, 190.
Throws and bats lefthanded.
Received degree from University of Mississippi, University, Miss. in 1980.

Major League saves: 1985 (4).
Led Florida State League in wild pitches with 17 in 1982.

Year	Club	League	G.	IP.	W.	L.	Pct.	H.	R.	ER.	SO.	BB.	ERA.
1980—Sarasota Astros	Gulf Coast		8	50	2	2	.500	38	18	10	41	21	1.80
1981—Daytona Beach†	Florida St.		21	111	6	6	.500	106	55	46	94	71	3.73
1982—Columbus	Southern		7	34⅔	1	3	.250	44	35	22	32	28	5.71
1982—Daytona Beach	Florida St.		21	116⅓	9	6	.600	126	71	60	62	55	4.64
1983—Columbus	Southern		27	151⅓	6	11	.353	157	103	78	93	83	4.64
1984—Columbus	Southern		37	63⅔	4	2	.667	52	21	20	51	26	2.83
1984—Tucson	P. Coast		14	21⅔	1	1	.500	16	4	4	20	12	1.66
1984—Houston	National		9	15⅓	0	1	.000	5	3	2	11	2	1.17
1985—Houston‡	National		44	63⅔	2	5	.286	56	21	18	47	24	2.54
1986—Houston	National		20	26⅔	1	0	1.000	28	16	11	14	12	3.71
1986—Tucson	P. Coast		22	39	1	3	.250	29	20	19	28	19	4.38
Major League Totals—3 Years			73	105⅔	3	6	.333	89	40	31	72	38	2.64

Selected by California Angels' organization in 28th round of free-agent draft, June 8, 1976.
Selected by Houston Astros' organization in 3rd round of free-agent draft, June 3, 1980.
†On disabled list, May 4 to May 16, 1981.
‡On disabled list, June 7 to June 22, 1985.

CHAMPIONSHIP SERIES RECORD

Year	Club	League	G.	IP.	W.	L.	Pct.	H.	R.	ER.	SO.	BB.	ERA.
1986—Houston	National		1	1	0	0	.000	1	1	1	0	1	9.00

ERNIE CARLOS CAMACHO

Born February 1, 1956, at Salinas, Calif.
Height, 6.01. Weight, 180.
Throws and bats righthanded.
Attended Hartnell Junior College, Salinas, Calif.

Major League saves: 1984 (23), 1986 (20). Total—43.

Year Club	League	G.	IP.	W.	L.	Pct.	H.	R.	ER.	SO.	BB.	ERA.
1976—Modesto	California	10	56	3	4	.429	69	47	35	29	39	5.63
1977—Modesto†	California	5	32	2	1	.667	30	19	14	21	23	3.94
1977—Chattanooga	Southern	11	60	3	8	.273	74	50	43	20	28	6.45
1978—Modesto‡	California	1	2	0	0	.000	0	0	0	2	2	0.00
1979—Ogden	P. Coast	21	97	7	9	.438	102	86	71	60	70	6.59
1980—Ogden	P. Coast	33	64	5	3	.625	60	29	28	58	26	3.94
1980—Oakland§	American	5	12	0	0	.000	20	9	9	9	5	6.75
1981—Portland x	P. Coast	18	38	2	3	.400	45	24	20	31	22	4.74
1981—Pittsburgh y	National	7	22	0	1	.000	23	13	12	11	15	4.91
1982—Edmonton zab	P. Coast	7	19⅔	0	0	.000	10	8	7	18	16	3.20
1982—Mexico City Reds	Mexican	15	20⅓	3	1	.750	21	12	12	15	6	5.31
1982—Rochester c	Int'national	8	17⅔	0	1	.000	16	7	4	11	10	2.04
1983—Vancouver d	P. Coast	11	23⅔	0	2	.000	31	21	18	16	12	6.85
1983—Charleston	Int'national	24	33⅓	4	0	1.000	19	5	5	27	17	1.35
1983—Cleveland	American	4	5⅓	0	1	.000	5	3	3	2	2	5.06
1984—Cleveland	American	69	100	5	9	.357	83	31	27	48	37	2.43
1985—Cleveland e	American	2	3⅓	0	1	.000	4	3	3	2	1	8.10
1986—Cleveland f	American	51	57⅓	2	4	.333	60	26	26	36	31	4.08
American League Totals—5 Years		131	178	7	15	.318	172	72	68	97	76	3.44
National League Totals—1 Year		7	22	0	1	.000	23	13	12	11	15	4.91
Major League Totals—6 Years		138	200	7	16	.304	195	85	80	108	91	3.60

Selected by Pittsburgh Pirates' organization in 12th round of free-agent draft, June 4, 1975.
Selected by California Angels' organization in secondary phase of free-agent draft, January 7, 1976.
Selected by Oakland A's organization in secondary phase of free-agent draft, June 8, 1976.
†On disabled list, April 23 to June 14, 1977.
‡On Jersey City temporary inactive list, April 14 to July 18, 1978; on Modesto temporary inactive list, July 18 to August 30, 1978.
§Traded to Pittsburgh Pirates, April 10, 1981, completing deal in which Pittsburgh traded Pitcher Bob Owchinko to Oakland A's for cash and player to be named later, April 6, 1981.
xOn disabled list, June 23 to July 15, 1981.
yTraded with Infielder Vance Law to Chicago White Sox for Pitchers Ross Baumgarten and Butch Edge, March 21, 1982.
zOn suspended list, April 5 to April 25, 1982.
aLoaned to Mexico City Reds, May 16, 1982; returned, August 2, 1982.
bLoaned to Rochester (Baltimore Orioles' organization), August 5, 1982; returned, September 17, 1982.
cGranted free agency, October 22, 1982; signed by Vancouver (Milwaukee Brewers' organization), December 19, 1982.
dTraded with Outfielder Gorman Thomas and Pitcher Jamie Easterly to Cleveland Indians for Outfielder Rick Manning and Pitcher Rick Waits, June 6, 1983.
eOn disabled list, April 13, 1985 through remainder of season.
fOn disabled list, May 14 to May 29, 1986.

MICHAEL THOMAS CAMPBELL
(Mike)

Born February 17, 1964, at Seattle, Wash.
Height, 6.03. Weight, 210.
Throws and bats righthanded.
Attended University of Hawaii, Honolulu, Haw.

Year Club	League	G.	IP.	W.	L.	Pct.	H.	R.	ER.	SO.	BB.	ERA.
1985—Salinas	California	10	50	4	4	.500	41	22	18	50	22	3.24
1986—Chattanooga	Southern	12	75	9	1	*.900	69	32	29	80	22	3.48
1986—Calgary	P. Coast	1	3	0	1	.000	1	3	3	3	2	9.00

Selected by Atlanta Braves' organization in 5th round of free-agent draft, June 7, 1982.
Selected by Seattle Mariners' organization in 1st round (seventh player selected) of free-agent draft, June 3, 1985.

WILLIAM RICHARD CAMPBELL
(Bill)

Born August 9, 1948, at Highland Park, Mich.
Height, 6.04. Weight, 200.
Throws and bats righthanded.
Attended Mount San Antonio Junior College, Walnut, Calif.

Tied American League record for most games won, season, all as relief pitcher (17), 1976.
Major League saves: 1973 (7), 1974 (19), 1975 (5), 1976 (20), 1977 (31), 1978 (4), 1979 (9), 1981 (7), 1982 (8), 1983 (8), 1984 (1), 1985 (4), 1986 (3). Total—126.
Led National League in intentional bases on balls issued with 18 in 1983.
Led American League in saves with 31 in 1977.
Led American League in games finished in relief with 68 in 1976 and tied for lead with 60 in 1977.
Led Southern League in complete games with 14 and tied for lead in games started by pitchers with 29 in 1972.
Named American League Fireman of the Year by THE SPORTING NEWS, 1976 and 1977.
Named Southern League Pitcher of the Year, 1972.

Year Club	League	G.	IP.	W.	L.	Pct.	H.	R.	ER.	SO.	BB.	ERA.
1971—Wisconsin Rapids†	Midwest	9	63	5	3	.625	42	43	8	91	19	1.14
1972—Charlotte	Southern	29	219	13	10	.565	181	74	59	*204	69	2.42
1973—Tacoma	P. Coast	18	133	10	5	.667	123	63	54	110	46	3.65
1973—Minnesota	American	28	52	3	3	.500	44	20	18	42	20	3.12
1974—Minnesota	American	63	120	8	7	.533	109	37	35	89	55	2.63

Year Club	League	G.	IP.	W.	L.	Pct.	H.	R.	ER.	SO.	BB.	ERA.
1975—Minnesota	American	47	121	4	6	.400	119	58	51	76	46	3.79
1976—Minnesota‡	American	★78	168	17	5	★.773	145	63	56	115	62	3.00
1977—Boston	American	69	140	13	9	.591	112	48	46	114	60	2.96
1978—Boston	American	29	51	7	5	.583	62	25	22	47	17	3.88
1979—Boston	American	41	55	3	4	.429	55	28	26	25	23	4.25
1980—Boston§	American	23	41	4	0	1.000	44	26	22	17	22	4.83
1981—Boston x	American	30	48	1	1	.500	45	23	17	37	20	3.19
1982—Chicago	National	62	100	3	6	.333	89	44	41	71	40	3.69
1983—Chicago y	National	★82	121⅓	6	8	.429	128	65	61	97	49	4.49
1984—Philadelphia z	National	57	81⅓	6	5	.545	68	43	31	52	35	3.43
1985—St. Louis a	National	50	64⅓	5	3	.625	55	32	25	41	21	3.50
1986—Detroit bc	American	34	55⅔	3	6	.333	46	26	24	37	21	3.88
American League Totals—10 Years		442	851⅔	63	46	.578	781	354	317	599	346	3.35
National League Totals—4 Years		251	368	20	22	.476	340	184	158	261	145	3.86
Major League Totals—14 Years		693	1219⅔	83	68	.550	1121	538	475	860	491	3.51

Signed as free agent by Minnesota Twins' organization, September 25, 1970.
†On disabled list, June 14, 1971 through remainder of season.
‡Granted free agency, November 1, 1976; signed by Boston Red Sox, November 6, 1976.
§On disabled list, March 25 to June 20, 1980.
xGranted free agency, November 13, 1981; signed by Chicago Cubs, December 8, 1981.
yTraded with Catcher Mike Diaz to Philadelphia Phillies for Outfielders Bob Dernier and Gary Matthews and Pitcher Porfi Altamirano, March 27, 1984.
zTraded with Shortstop Ivan DeJesus to St. Louis Cardinals for Pitcher Dave Rucker, April 6, 1985.
aReleased, November 14, 1985; signed by Detroit Tigers, January 31, 1986.
bOn disabled list, May 17 to June 18, 1986.
cReleased, October 15, 1986.

CHAMPIONSHIP SERIES RECORD

Year Club	League	G.	IP.	W.	L.	Pct.	H.	R.	ER.	SO.	BB.	ERA.
1985—St. Louis	National	3	2⅓	0	0	.000	3	0	0	2	0	0.00

WORLD SERIES RECORD

Year Club	League	G.	IP.	W.	L.	Pct.	H.	R.	ER.	SO.	BB.	ERA.
1985—St. Louis	National	3	4	0	0	.000	4	1	1	5	2	2.25

ALL-STAR GAME RECORD

Year League	IP.	W.	L.	Pct.	H.	R.	ER.	SO.	BB.	ERA.
1977—American	1	0	0	.000	0	0	0	0	2	1	0.00

SILVESTRE CAMPUSANO
(Sil)

Born December 31, 1966, at Mano Guayabo, D.R.
Height, 6.00. Weight, 160.
Throws and bats righthanded.

Tied for Gulf Coast League lead in stolen bases with 21 in 1984.
Led Southern League outfielders in total chances with 437 and tied for lead in double plays with 6 in 1986.
Led South Atlantic League outfielders in double plays with 5 in 1985.
Named South Atlantic League Most Valuable Player, 1985.

Year Club	League	Pos.	G.	AB.	R.	H.	2B.	3B.	HR.	RBI.	B.A.	PO.	A.	E.	F.A.
1984—Bradenton Jays	Appal.	OF	●63	236	42	63	17	2	0	22	.267	128	7	★8	.944
1985—Florence	S. Atl.	OF	88	348	80	109	31	1	15	56	.313	188	12	4	.980
1985—Knoxville	South.	OF	45	178	30	54	9	0	6	29	.303	135	3	4	.972
1986—Knoxville	South.	OF	132	493	89	126	32	6	14	59	.256	★401	21	15	.966

Signed as free agent by Toronto Blue Jays' organization, November 14, 1983.

CASEY TODD CANDAELE

Born January 12, 1961, at Lompoc, Calif.
Height, 5.09. Weight, 165.
Throws right and bats right and lefthanded.
Attended University of Arizona, Tucson, Ariz.

Major League stolen bases: 1986 (3).
Led American Association in sacrifice hits with 11 in 1986.
Led Florida State League second basemen in assists with 391, double plays with 87 and errors with 30 in 1983.
Tied for American Association lead in double plays by second basemen with 68 in 1986.

Year Club	League	Pos.	G.	AB.	R.	H.	2B.	3B.	HR.	RBI.	B.A.	PO.	A.	E.	F.A.
1983—W. Palm Beach	Fla. St.	2-O-3-S	127	★511	77	156	26	9	0	45	.305	271	403	32	.955
1983—Memphis	South.	3B	5	19	4	4	1	0	0	1	.211	2	11	0	1.000
1984—Jacksonville	South.	S-O-2-3	132	532	68	145	23	2	2	53	.273	224	352	18	.970
1985—Indianapolis	A. A.	O-2-S-3	127	390	55	101	13	5	0	35	.259	266	160	6	.986
1986—Indianapolis	A. A.	2B-OF	119	480	77	145	32	6	2	42	.302	240	319	13	.977
1986—Montreal	Nat.	2B-3B	30	104	9	24	4	1	0	6	.231	45	74	2	.983
Major League Totals—1 Year			30	104	9	24	4	1	0	6	.231	45	74	2	.983

Signed as free agent by Montreal Expos' organization, August 15, 1982.

JOHN ROBERT CANDELARIA

Born November 6, 1953, at Brooklyn, N.Y.
Height, 6.07. Weight, 250.
Throws left and bats right and lefthanded.

Pitched 2-0 no-hit victory against Los Angeles Dodgers, August 9, 1976.
Major League saves: 1976 (1), 1978 (1), 1980 (1), 1982 (1), 1984 (2), 1985 (9). Total—15.
Tied for National League lead in home runs allowed with 29 in 1977.
Led Carolina League in home runs allowed with 17 in 1974.
Named American League Comeback Player of the Year by THE SPORTING NEWS, 1986.
Received reported $40,000 bonus to sign with Pittsburgh Pirates, 1973.

Year Club	League	G.	IP.	W.	L.	Pct.	H.	R.	ER.	SO.	BB.	ERA.
1973—Charleston	W. Carol.	18	95	10	2	*.833	84	45	40	60	38	3.79
1974—Salem	Carolina	25	154	11	8	.579	146	80	63	147	63	3.68
1974—Charleston	Int'national	1	11	0	0	.000	7	2	2	10	1	1.64
1975—Charleston	Int'national	10	61	7	1	.875	53	15	12	48	17	1.77
1975—Pittsburgh	National	18	121	8	6	.571	95	47	37	95	36	2.75
1976—Pittsburgh	National	32	220	16	7	.696	173	87	77	138	60	3.15
1977—Pittsburgh	National	33	231	20	5	*.800	197	64	60	133	52	*2.34
1978—Pittsburgh	National	30	189	12	11	.522	191	73	68	94	49	3.24
1979—Pittsburgh	National	33	207	14	9	.609	201	83	74	101	41	3.22
1980—Pittsburgh	National	35	233	11	14	.440	246	114	104	97	50	4.02
1981—Pittsburgh†	National	6	41	2	2	.500	42	17	16	14	11	3.51
1982—Pittsburgh	National	31	174⅔	12	7	.632	166	62	57	133	37	2.94
1983—Pittsburgh	National	33	197⅔	15	8	.652	191	73	71	157	45	3.23
1984—Pittsburgh	National	33	185⅓	12	11	.522	179	69	56	133	34	2.72
1985—Pittsburgh‡	National	37	54⅓	2	4	.333	57	23	22	47	14	3.64
1985—California	American	13	71	7	3	.700	70	33	30	53	24	3.80
1986—California§	American	16	91⅔	10	2	.833	68	30	26	81	26	2.55
1986—Palm Springs	California	2	7	0	0	.000	4	2	2	8	2	2.57
National League Totals—11 Years		321	1854	124	84	.596	1738	712	642	1142	427	3.12
American League Totals—2 Years		29	162⅔	17	5	.773	138	63	56	134	50	3.10
Major League Totals—12 Years		350	2016⅔	141	89	.613	1876	775	698	1276	477	3.12

Selected by Pittsburgh Pirates' organization in 2nd round of free-agent draft, June 6, 1972.
†On disabled list, May 11, 1981 through remainder of season.
‡Traded with Pitcher Al Holland and Outfielder George Hendrick to California Angels for Pitcher Pat Clements, Outfielder Mike Brown and a player to be named later, August 2, 1985; Pittsburgh Pirates' organization acquired Pitcher Bob Kipper to complete deal, August 16, 1985.
§On disabled list, April 15 to July 8, 1986; included rehabilitation disability assignment to Palm Springs, June 26 to July 2, 1986.

CHAMPIONSHIP SERIES RECORD

Established Championship Series record for most strikeouts, three-game Series (14), 1975.
Tied Championship Series records for most strikeouts, game (14), October 7, 1975; most consecutive strikeouts, start of game (4), October 7, 1975.

Year Club	League	G.	IP.	W.	L.	Pct.	H.	R.	ER.	SO.	BB.	ERA.
1975—Pittsburgh	National	1	7⅔	0	0	.000	3	3	3	14	2	3.52
1979—Pittsburgh	National	1	7	0	0	.000	5	2	2	4	1	2.57
1986—California	American	2	10⅔	1	1	.500	11	8	1	7	6	0.84
Championship Series Totals—3 Years		4	25⅓	1	1	.500	19	13	6	25	9	2.13

WORLD SERIES RECORD

Year Club	League	G.	IP.	W.	L.	Pct.	H.	R.	ER.	SO.	BB.	ERA.
1979—Pittsburgh	National	2	9	1	1	.500	14	6	5	4	2	5.00

ALL-STAR GAME RECORD

Member of National League All-Star Team in 1977; did not play.

THOMAS CAESAR CANDIOTTI
(Tom)

Born August 31, 1957, at Walnut Creek, Calif.
Height, 6.03. Weight, 205.
Throws and bats righthanded.
Received bachelor of science degree in business administration
from St. Mary's College, Moraga, Calif., in 1979.

Led American League in complete games with 17 in 1986.

Year Club	League	G.	IP.	W.	L.	Pct.	H.	R.	ER.	SO.	BB.	ERA.
1979—Victoria†	Northwest	12	70	5	1	.833	63	23	19	66	16	2.44
1980—Fort Myers	Florida St.	7	44	3	2	.600	32	16	11	31	9	2.25
1980—Jacksonville‡§	Southern	17	117	7	8	.467	98	45	36	93	40	2.77
1981—El Paso x	Texas	21	119	7	6	.538	137	51	37	68	27	2.80
1982—Vancouver y	P. Coast					(Did not play)						
1983—El Paso	Texas	7	24⅔	1	0	1.000	23	10	8	18	7	2.92
1983—Vancouver	P. Coast	15	99⅓	6	4	.600	87	35	31	61	16	2.81
1983—Milwaukee	American	10	55⅔	4	4	.500	62	21	20	21	16	3.23
1984—Vancouver z	P. Coast	15	96⅔	8	4	.667	96	36	31	53	22	2.89
1984—Milwaukee a	American	8	32⅓	2	2	.500	38	21	19	23	10	5.29
1984—Beloit	Midwest	2	10	0	1	.000	12	5	3	12	5	2.70

Year Club	League	G.	IP.	W.	L.	Pct.	H.	R.	ER.	SO.	BB.	ERA.
1985—El Paso	Texas	4	29½	1	0	1.000	29	11	9	16	7	2.76
1985—Vancouver b	P. Coast	24	150⅔	9	13	.409	178	83	66	97	36	3.94
1986—Cleveland	American	36	252⅓	16	12	.571	234	112	100	167	106	3.57
Major League Totals—3 Years		54	340⅓	22	18	.550	334	154	139	211	132	3.68

Signed as free-agent by Victoria (Independent), July 17, 1979.

†Released, January 4, 1980; signed by Ft. Myers (Kansas City Royals' organization), January 5, 1980.

‡On disabled list, June 7 to June 26, 1980.

§Drafted by Vancouver (Milwaukee Brewers' organization), December 9, 1980.

xOn disabled list, April 10 to May 12, 1981.

yOn disabled list, April 13, 1982 through remainder of season.

zOn disabled list, May 30 to June 15, 1984.

aOn disabled list, August 2 to September 1, 1984; included rehabilitation disability assignment to Beloit, August 24 to August 31, 1984.

bGranted free agency, October 15, 1985; signed by Cleveland Indians, December 12, 1985.

JOHN ANTHONY CANGELOSI

Born March 10, 1963, at Brooklyn, N.Y.
Height, 5.08. Weight, 150.
Throws left and bats right and lefthanded.
Attended Miami-Dade Community College (North), Miami, Fla.

Established American League record for most stolen bases by rookie (50), 1986.
Major League stolen bases: 1986 (50).
Led Eastern League in bases on balls received with 101 in 1984.
Led Midwest League in stolen bases with 87 and caught stealing with 35 in 1983.
Tied for New York-Pennsylvania League lead in bases on balls received with 56 in 1982.

Year Club	League	Pos.	G.	AB.	R.	H.	2B.	3B.	HR.	RBI.	B.A.	PO.	A.	E.	F.A.
1982—Niagara Falls	NYP	OF	●76	277	60	80	15	4	5	38	.289	118	5	4	.969
1983—Appleton	Midw.	OF	128	439	87	124	12	4	1	48	.282	262	10	6	.978
1984—Glens Falls†	East.	OF	138	464	91	133	17	1	1	38	.287	310	11	11	.967
1985—Mex. City Reds	Mex.	OF	61	201	46	71	9	4	1	30	.353	127	7	6	.957
1985—Chicago	Amer.	OF	5	2	2	0	0	0	0	0	.000	1	0	0	1.000
1985—Buffalo	A. A.	OF	78	244	34	58	8	5	1	21	.238	148	9	2	.987
1986—Chicago	Amer.	OF	137	438	65	103	16	3	2	32	.235	276	7	9	.969
Major League Totals—2 Years			142	440	67	103	16	3	2	32	.234	277	7	9	.969

Selected by Chicago White Sox' organization in 4th round of free-agent draft, January 12, 1982.

†Loaned with Infielder Manny Salinas to Mexico City Reds, March 4, 1985, as part of deal in which Infielder Nelson Barrera was purchased by Chicago White Sox; returned, June 1, 1985.

JOSE CANSECO

Name pronounced CON-seko.

Born July 2, 1964, at Havana, Cuba.
Height, 6.03. Weight, 215.
Throws and bats righthanded.
Identical twin brother of Ozzie Canseco, outfielder in Oakland A's organization.

Major League stolen bases: 1985 (1), 1986 (15). Total—16.
Led Northwest League batters in strikeouts with 78 in 1983.
Led California League outfielders in double plays with 8 in 1984.
Named American League Rookie Player of the Year by THE SPORTING NEWS, 1986.
Named American League Rookie of the Year by Baseball Writers' Association of America, 1986.
Named Minor League Player of the Year by THE SPORTING NEWS, 1985.
Named Southern League Most Valuable Player, 1985.

Year Club	League	Pos.	G.	AB.	R.	H.	2B.	3B.	HR.	RBI.	B.A.	PO.	A.	E.	F.A.
1982—Miami	Fla. St.	3B	6	9	0	1	0	0	0	0	.111	3	1	1	.800
1982—Idaho Falls	Pion.	3B-OF	28	57	13	15	3	0	2	7	.263	6	17	3	.885
1983—Madison	Midw.	OF	34	88	8	14	4	0	3	10	.159	23	2	1	.962
1983—Medford	N'west	OF	59	197	34	53	15	2	11	40	.269	46	5	5	.911
1984—Modesto	Calif.	OF	116	410	61	113	21	2	15	73	.276	216	17	9	.963
1985—Huntsville†	South.	OF	58	211	47	67	10	2	25	80	.318	117	9	7	.947
1985—Tacoma	P.C.	OF	60	233	41	81	16	1	11	47	.348	81	7	2	.978
1985—Oakland	Amer.	OF	29	96	16	29	3	0	5	13	.302	56	2	3	.951
1986—Oakland	Amer.	OF	157	600	85	144	29	1	33	117	.240	319	4	●14	.958
Major League Total—2 Years			186	696	101	173	32	1	38	130	.249	375	6	17	.957

Selected by Oakland A's organization in 15th round of free-agent draft, June 7, 1982.

†On disabled list, May 14 to June 3, 1985.

ALL-STAR GAME RECORD

Member of American League All-Star Team in 1986; did not play.

STEVEN NORMAN CARLTON
(Steve)

Born December 22, 1944, at Miami, Fla.
Height, 6.05. Weight, 210.
Throws and bats lefthanded.
Attended Miami-Dade Community College, Miami, Fla.

Established major league records for most consecutive starting assignments, lifetime (544); most strikeouts, game by lefthanded pitcher and losing pitcher (19), September 15, 1969; most balks, season (11), 1979.

Established National League records for most years and most consecutive years pitched (22); most games started, lifetime (677); most consecutive starting assignments, lifetime (534); most years, 100 or more strikeouts (18); most consecutive years, 100 or more strikeouts (18); most strikeouts, lifetime (4,000); most bases on balls issued, lifetime (1,717).

Tied National League record for most strikeouts, game (19), September 15, 1969.

Tied modern National League record for most games won, season, by lefthander (27), 1972.

Led National League pitchers in games started with 41 in 1972, 38 in 1982 and tied for lead with 40 in 1973 and 38 in 1980.

Led National League in shutouts with 6 in 1982.

Led National League in complete games with 30 in 1972, 19 in 1982 and tied for lead with 18 in 1973.

Led National League in balks with 7 in 1977, 11 in 1979, 7 in 1980 and 9 in 1982 and 1983 and tied for lead with 7 in 1975, 1978 and 1984.

Led National League in wild pitches with 17 in 1980.

Led National League in home runs allowed with 30 in 1978.

Won National League Cy Young Memorial Award, 1972, 1977, 1980 and 1982.

Named National League Pitcher of the Year by THE SPORTING NEWS, 1972, 1977, 1980 and 1982.

Named lefthanded pitcher on THE SPORTING NEWS National League All-Star Team, 1969, 1971, 1972, 1977, 1979, 1980 and 1982.

Named pitcher on THE SPORTING NEWS National League All-Star fielding team, 1981.

Year—Club	League	G.	IP.	W.	L.	Pct.	H.	R.	ER.	SO.	BB.	ERA.
1964—Rock Hill	W. Carol.	11	79	10	1	.909	39	17	9	91	36	1.03
1964—Winnipeg	Northern	12	75	4	4	.500	63	40	28	79	48	3.36
1964—Tulsa	Texas	4	24	1	1	.500	16	13	7	21	18	2.63
1965—St. Louis	National	15	25	0	0	.000	27	7	7	21	8	2.52
1966—Tulsa	P. Coast	19	128	9	5	.643	110	65	51	108	54	3.59
1966—St. Louis	National	9	52	3	3	.500	56	22	18	25	18	3.12
1967—St. Louis	National	30	193	14	9	.609	173	71	64	168	62	2.98
1968—St. Louis	National	34	232	13	11	.542	214	87	77	162	61	2.99
1969—St. Louis	National	31	236	17	11	.607	185	66	57	210	93	2.17
1970—St. Louis	National	34	254	10	★19	.345	239	123	105	193	109	3.72
1971—St. Louis†	National	37	273	20	9	.690	275	120	108	172	98	3.56
1972—Philadelphia	National	41	★346	★27	10	.730	★257	84	76	★310	87	★1.98
1973—Philadelphia	National	40	●293	13	★20	.394	★293	★146	★127	223	113	3.90
1974—Philadelphia	National	39	291	16	13	.552	249	118	104	★240	★136	3.22
1975—Philadelphia	National	37	255	15	14	.517	217	116	101	192	104	3.56
1976—Philadelphia	National	35	253	20	7	★.741	224	94	88	195	72	3.13
1977—Philadelphia	National	36	283	★23	10	.697	229	99	83	198	89	2.64
1978—Philadelphia	National	34	247	16	13	.552	228	91	78	161	63	2.84
1979—Philadelphia	National	35	251	18	11	.621	202	112	101	213	89	3.62
1980—Philadelphia	National	38	★304	★24	9	.727	243	87	79	★286	90	2.34
1981—Philadelphia	National	24	190	13	4	.765	152	59	51	179	62	2.42
1982—Philadelphia	National	38	★295⅔	★23	11	.676	253	114	102	★286	86	3.10
1983—Philadelphia	National	37	★283⅔	15	16	.484	★277	117	98	★275	84	3.11
1984—Philadelphia	National	33	229	13	7	.650	214	104	91	163	79	3.58
1985—Philadelphia‡	National	16	92	1	8	.111	84	43	34	48	53	3.33
1986—Philadelphia§-San Francisco x	National	22	113	5	11	.313	138	90	74	80	61	5.89
1986—Chicago y	American	10	63⅓	4	3	.571	58	30	26	40	25	3.69
National League Totals—22 Years		695	4991⅓	319	226	.585	4429	1970	1723	4000	1717	3.11
American League Totals—1 Year		10	63⅓	4	3	.571	58	30	26	40	25	3.69
Major League Totals—22 Years		705	5054⅔	323	229	.585	4487	2000	1749	4040	1742	3.11

Signed as free agent by St. Louis Cardinals' organization, October 8, 1963.

†Traded to Philadelphia Phillies for Pitcher Rick Wise, February 25, 1972.

‡On disabled list, June 21 to September 2, 1985.

§Released, June 24, 1986; signed by San Francisco Giants, July 4, 1986.

xReleased, August 7, 1986; signed by Chicago White Sox, August 12, 1986.

yGranted free agency, November 12, 1986.

DIVISION SERIES RECORD

Year—Club	League	G.	IP.	W.	L.	Pct.	H.	R.	ER.	SO.	BB.	ERA.
1981—Philadelphia	National	2	14	0	2	.000	14	6	6	13	8	3.86

CHAMPIONSHIP SERIES RECORD

Established Championship Series record for most bases on balls, total Series (28).

Tied Championship Series records for most games won, total Series (4); most games won, Series (2); most home runs hit by pitcher, total Series (1); most bases on balls, four-game Series (8), 1977; most bases on balls, five-game series (8), 1980.

Established National League Championship Series records for most strikeouts, total Series (39); most games started, total Series (8); most innings pitched, total Series (53⅔); most hits allowed, total Series (53); most earned runs allowed, total Series (21).

Tied National League Championship Series records for most strikeouts, four-game Series (13), 1983; most bases on balls, three-game Series (5), 1976.

Year—Club	League	G.	IP.	W.	L.	Pct.	H.	R.	ER.	SO.	BB.	ERA.
1976—Philadelphia	National	1	7	0	1	.000	8	5	4	6	5	5.14
1977—Philadelphia	National	2	11⅔	0	1	.000	13	9	9	6	8	6.94
1978—Philadelphia	National	1	9	1	0	1.000	8	4	4	8	2	4.00
1980—Philadelphia	National	2	12⅓	1	0	1.000	11	3	3	6	8	2.19
1983—Philadelphia	National	2	13⅔	2	0	1.000	13	1	1	13	5	0.66
Championship Series Totals—5 Years		8	53⅔	4	2	.667	53	22	21	39	28	3.52

WORLD SERIES RECORD

Tied World Series record for most games won, losing none, six-game Series (2), 1980.

Year Club	League	G.	IP.	W.	L.	Pct.	H.	R.	ER.	SO.	BB.	ERA.
1967—St. Louis	National	1	6	0	1	.000	3	1	0	5	2	0.00
1968—St. Louis	National	2	4	0	0	.000	7	3	3	3	1	6.75
1980—Philadelphia	National	2	15	2	0	1.000	14	5	4	17	9	2.40
1983—Philadelphia	National	1	6⅔	0	1	.000	5	3	2	7	3	2.70
World Series Total—4 Years		6	31⅓	2	2	.500	29	12	9	32	15	2.56

ALL-STAR GAME RECORD

Year League	IP.	W.	L.	Pct.	H.	R.	ER.	SO.	BB.	ERA.
1968—National	1	0	0	.000	0	0	0	1	0	0.00
1969—National	3	1	0	1.000	2	2	2	2	1	6.00
1972—National	1	0	0	.000	0	0	0	0	1	0.00
1979—National	1	0	0	.000	2	3	3	0	1	27.00
1982—National	2	0	0	.000	1	0	0	4	2	0.00
All-Star Game Totals—5 Years	8	1	0	1.000	5	5	5	7	5	5.63

Member of National League All-Star Team in 1971, 1974, 1977, 1980 and 1981; did not play.

DONALD WAYNE CARMAN

(Don)

Born August 14, 1959, at Oklahoma City, Okla.
Height, 6.03. Weight, 190.
Throws and bats lefthanded.
Attended Seminole Junior College, Seminole, Okla.,
and University of Oklahoma, Norman, Okla.

Major League saves: 1983 (1), 1985 (7), 1986 (1). Total—9.

Year Club	League	G.	IP.	W.	L.	Pct.	H.	R.	ER.	SO.	BB.	ERA.
1979—Spartanburg	W. Carol.	37	78	6	3	.667	72	36	34	70	28	3.92
1980—Peninsula	Carolina	27	150	14	5	.737	149	73	57	★141	53	3.42
1981—Reading	Eastern	28	176	12	13	.480	167	93	79	105	75	4.04
1982—Oklahoma City	Am. Assoc.	10	33	0	1	.000	37	29	25	29	23	6.82
1982—Reading	Eastern	20	97⅓	6	7	.462	99	58	45	81	62	4.16
1983—Reading	Eastern	★56	124⅓	8	5	.615	85	51	41	93	71	2.97
1983—Philadelphia	National	1	1	0	0	.000	0	0	0	0	0	0.00
1984—Portland	P. Coast	39	55⅔	3	3	.500	66	36	33	53	22	5.34
1984—Philadelphia	National	11	13⅓	0	1	.000	14	9	8	16	6	5.40
1985—Philadelphia	National	71	86⅓	9	4	.692	52	25	20	87	38	2.08
1986—Philadelphia	National	50	134⅓	10	5	.667	113	50	48	98	52	3.22
Major League Totals—4 Years		133	235	19	10	.655	179	84	76	201	96	2.91

Signed as free agent by Philadelphia Phillies' organization, August 25, 1978.

NORMAN RAFAEL CARRASCO

(Norm)

Born August 6, 1962, at Caracas, Venezuela.
Height, 5.09. Weight, 170.
Throws and bats righthanded.

Led Eastern League in grounding into double plays with 19 in 1984.
Led Eastern League second basemen in total chances with 648 and tied for lead in double plays with 79 in 1984.
Led Midwest League second basemen in total chances with 720 and double plays with 85 in 1982.
Led Pioneer League second basemen in double plays with 52 in 1981.

Year Club	League	Pos.	G.	AB.	R.	H.	2B.	3B.	HR.	RBI.	B.A.	PO.	A.	E.	F.A.
1981—Idaho Falls	Pion.	2B	68	262	44	98	22	4	3	57	.374	★145	197	16	★.955
1982—Danville	Midw.	2B	136	★553	★115	154	★34	2	10	51	.278	★313	★379	28	.961
1983—Redwood	Calif.	2B	132	473	56	112	29	4	6	59	.237	★287	●363	28	.959
1984—Waterbury	East.	2B	134	516	78	147	23	3	9	64	.285	★286	346	16	.975
1985—Edmonton	P. C.	2B	114	402	41	95	13	3	3	47	.236	245	326	13	.978
1986—Edmonton	P. C.	2B-3B-C	86	302	38	91	14	1	3	34	.301	118	159	10	.965

Signed as free agent by California Angels' organization, March 18, 1981.

MARK STEVEN CARREON

Born July 19, 1963, at Chicago, Ill.
Height, 6.00. Weight, 170.
Throws left and bats righthanded.

Led Carolina League in sacrifice flies with 11 in 1983.
Tied for South Atlantic League lead in game-winning RBIs with 12 in 1982.

Year Club	League	Pos.	G.	AB.	R.	H.	2B.	3B.	HR.	RBI.	B.A.	PO.	A.	E.	F.A.
1981—Kingsport	Appal.	OF-C	64	232	30	67	8	0	1	36	.289	101	7	4	.964
1982—Shelby	S. Atl.	OF	133	486	★120	160	29	6	2	79	.329	183	8	5	.974
1983—Lynchburg	Carol.	OF	128	491	94	164	13	8	1	67	.334	173	8	14	.928
1984—Jackson	Texas	OF	119	435	64	122	14	3	1	43	.280	146	1	4	.974
1985—Tidewater	Int.	OF	7	15	1	2	1	0	1	2	.133	2	0	0	1.000
1985—Jackson	Texas	OF	123	447	96	140	23	5	6	51	.313	201	8	1	.995
1986—Tidewater	Int.	OF	115	426	62	123	23	2	10	64	.289	192	6	6	.971

Selected by New York Mets' organization in 8th round of free-agent draft, June 8, 1981.

DENNIS MAURICE CARTER

Born November 20, 1964, in Hinds County, Miss.
Height, 6.04. Weight, 200.
Throws and bats righthanded.
Attended Middle Georgia College, Cochran, Ga., and Chipola Junior College, Marianna, Fla.

Led New York-Pennsylvania League batters in total bases with 152, game-winning RBIs with 10, sacrifice flies with 8 and strikeouts with 93 in 1985.

Year Club	League	Pos.	G.	AB.	R.	H.	2B.	3B.	HR.	RBI.	B.A.	PO.	A.	E.	F.A.
1984—Johnson City	Appal.	OF	38	135	33	40	7	1	6	34	.296	60	2	0	1.000
1985—Savannah	S. Atl.	OF	15	39	2	5	1	0	0	2	.128	27	2	1	.967
1985—Erie	NYP	OF	●77	282	45	80	●20	2	●16	★77	.284	119	10	2	.985
1986—Springfield	Midw.	OF	138	518	82	140	27	6	13	82	.270	237	●17	7	.973

Selected by San Diego Padres' organization in 7th round of free-agent draft, January 11, 1983.
Selected by Seattle Mariners' organization in secondary phase of free-agent draft, June 6, 1983.
Selected by St. Louis Cardinals' organization in secondary phase of free-agent draft, January 17, 1984.

GARY EDMUND CARTER

Born April 8, 1954, at Culver City, Calif.
Height, 6.02. Weight, 210.
Throws and bats righthanded.
Brother of Gordon Carter, outfielder in San Francisco Giants'
organization, 1972 and 1973.

Established major league record for fewest passed balls, season, 150 or more games (1), 1978.
Tied major league record for most home runs, two consecutive games (5), September 3 and 4, 1985.
Established National League records for most seasons leading league in games by catcher (6); most years leading league in putouts by catcher (7); most years leading league in chances accepted by catcher (7).
Major League stolen bases: 1974 (2), 1975 (5), 1977 (5), 1978 (10), 1979 (3), 1980 (3), 1981 (1), 1982 (2), 1983 (1), 1984 (2), 1985 (1), 1986 (1). Total—36.
Hit three home runs in a game, April 20, 1977 and September 3, 1985.
Led National League in sacrifice flies with 15 and tied for lead in game-winning RBIs with 16 and grounding into double plays with 21 in 1986.
Led National League catchers in assists with 107 in 1983.
Led National League catchers in total chances with 921 in 1977, 874 in 1978, 848 in 1979, 937 in 1980, 571 in 1981 and 1,068 in 1982.
Led National League in passed balls with 12 in 1979.
Led National League catchers in putouts with 811 in 1977, 781 in 1978, 509 in 1981, and 956 in 1985.
Led National League catchers in double plays with 14 in 1977, 9 in 1978, 12 in 1979 and 14 in 1983.
Led International League catchers in putouts with 794, assists with 65, double plays with 15 and fielding percentage with .990 in 1974.
Named National League Rookie Player of the Year by THE SPORTING NEWS, 1975.
Named catcher on THE SPORTING NEWS National League All-Star Team, 1980 through 1982 and 1984 through 1986.
Named catcher on THE SPORTING NEWS National League All-Star fielding team, 1980 through 1982.
Named catcher on THE SPORTING NEWS National League Silver Slugger team, 1981, 1982 and 1984 through 1986.

Year Club	League	Pos.	G.	AB.	R.	H.	2B.	3B.	HR.	RBI.	B.A.	PO.	A.	E.	F.A.
1972—Cocoa Expos	Fla.E.C.	C-1B-3B	18	71	6	17	3	0	2	9	.239	111	12	10	.925
1972—W. Palm Beach	Fla. St.	C	20	50	9	16	2	2	0	5	.320	84	12	2	.980
1973—Quebec City	East.	C-1B-OF	130	439	65	111	16	1	15	68	.253	823	75	20	.978
1973—Peninsula	Int.	C	8	25	2	7	2	0	0	1	.280	5	1	0	1.000
1974—Memphis	Int.	C-1B-3B	135	441	62	118	14	7	23	83	.268	908	76	12	.988
1974—Montreal	Nat.	C-OF	9	27	5	11	0	1	1	6	.407	28	4	0	1.000
1975—Montreal	Nat.	OF-C-3B	144	503	58	136	20	1	17	68	.270	430	38	9	.981
1976—Montreal†	Nat.	C-OF	91	311	31	68	8	1	6	38	.219	364	42	2	.995
1977—Montreal	Nat.	★C-OF	154	522	86	148	29	2	31	84	.284	813	★101	9	.990
1978—Montreal	Nat.	C-1B	157	533	76	136	27	1	20	72	.255	787	83	10	.989
1979—Montreal	Nat.	C	141	505	74	143	26	5	22	75	.283	★751	★88	9	.989
1980—Montreal	Nat.	C	154	549	76	145	25	5	29	101	.264	★822	★108	7	★.993
1981—Montreal	Nat.	C-1B	100	374	48	94	20	2	16	68	.251	515	58	4	.993
1982—Montreal	Nat.	C	154	557	91	163	32	1	29	97	.293	★954	★104	10	.991
1983—Montreal	Nat.	★C-1B	145	541	63	146	37	3	17	79	.270	855	108	5	★.995
1984—Montreal‡	Nat.	C-1B	159	596	75	175	32	1	27	●106	.294	990	78	7	.993
1985—New York	Nat.	C-1B-OF	149	555	83	156	17	1	32	100	.281	987	70	8	.992
1986—New York§	Nat.	C-1-O-3	132	490	81	125	14	2	24	105	.255	943	70	9	.991
Major League Totals—13 Years			1689	6063	847	1646	287	26	271	999	.271	9239	952	89	.991

Selected by Montreal Expos' organization in 3rd round of free-agent draft, June 6, 1972.
†On disabled list, June 6 to July 22, 1976.
‡Traded to New York Mets for Infielder Hubie Brooks, Catcher Mike Fitzgerald, Outfielder Herm Winningham and Pitcher Floyd Youmans, December 10, 1984.
§On disabled list, August 17 to September 1, 1986.

DIVISION SERIES RECORD

Year Club	League	Pos.	G.	AB.	R.	H.	2B.	3B.	HR.	RBI.	B.A.	PO.	A.	E.	F.A.
1981—Montreal	Nat.	C	5	19	3	8	3	0	2	6	.421	21	5	0	1.000

CHAMPIONSHIP SERIES RECORD

Tied National League Championship Series record for most at-bats, six-game Series (27), 1986.

Year Club	League	Pos.	G.	AB.	R.	H.	2B.	3B.	HR.	RBI.	B.A.	PO.	A.	E.	F.A.
1981—Montreal	Nat.	C	5	16	3	7	1	0	0	0	.438	27	3	0	1.000
1986—New York	Nat.	C	6	27	1	4	1	0	0	2	.148	42	5	0	1.000
Championship Series Totals—2 Years			11	43	4	11	2	0	0	2	.256	69	8	0	1.000

Year	Club	League	Pos.	G.	AB.	R.	H.	2B.	3B.	HR.	RBI.	B.A.	PO.	A.	E.	F.A.
1986—New York		Nat.	C	7	29	4	8	2	0	2	9	.276	57	1	0	1.000

ALL-STAR GAME RECORD

Tied All-Star Game record for most home runs, game (2), August 9, 1981.

Year	League	Pos.	AB.	R.	H.	2B.	3B.	HR.	RBI.	B.A.	PO.	A.	E.	F.A.
1975—National		OF	0	0	0	0	0	0	0	.000	1	0	0	1.000
1979—National		C	2	0	1	0	0	0	1	.500	6	1	0	1.000
1980—National		C	1	0	0	0	0	0	0	.000	1	0	0	1.000
1981—National		C	3	2	2	0	0	2	2	.667	5	1	0	1.000
1982—National		C	3	0	1	0	0	0	1	.333	7	0	0	1.000
1983—National		C	2	0	0	0	0	0	0	.000	3	0	0	1.000
1984—National		C	2	1	1	0	0	1	1	.500	9	0	0	1.000
1986—National		C	3	0	0	0	0	0	0	.000	9	0	0	1.000
All-Star Game Totals—8 Years			16	3	5	0	0	3	5	.313	41	2	0	1.000

Named to National League All-Star Team for 1985 game; replaced due to injury by Terry Kennedy.

JOSEPH CHRIS CARTER
(Joe)

Born March 7, 1960, at Oklahoma City, Okla.
Height, 6.03. Weight, 215.
Throws and bats righthanded.
Attended Wichita State University, Wichita, Kan.
Brother of Fred Carter, outfielder in New York Yankees' organization.

Major League stolen bases: 1983 (1), 1984 (2), 1985 (24), 1986 (29). Total—56.
Hit three home runs in a game, August 29, 1986.
Led American Association in total bases with 265 and tied for lead in strikeouts by batters with 103 in 1983.
Named College Player of the Year by THE SPORTING NEWS, 1981.
Named outfielder on THE SPORTING NEWS College Baseball All-America Team, 1980 and 1981.
Received reported $150,000 bonus to sign with Chicago Cubs, 1981.

Year	Club	League	Pos.	G.	AB.	R.	H.	2B.	3B.	HR.	RBI.	B.A.	PO.	A.	E.	F.A.
1981—Midland		Texas	OF	67	249	42	67	15	3	5	35	.269	100	10	4	.965
1982—Midland†		Texas	OF	110	427	84	136	22	8	25	98	.319	182	6	5	.974
1983—Iowa		A. A.	OF	124	*522	82	160	27	6	22	83	.307	204	9	12	.947
1983—Chicago		Nat.	OF	23	51	6	9	1	1	0	1	.176	26	0	0	1.000
1984—Iowa‡		A. A.	OF	61	248	45	77	12	7	14	67	.310	142	6	2	.987
1984—Cleveland§		Amer.	OF-1B	66	244	32	67	6	1	13	41	.275	169	11	6	.968
1985—Cleveland		Amer.	O-1-2-3	143	489	64	128	27	0	15	59	.262	311	17	6	.982
1986—Cleveland		Amer.	OF-1B	162	663	108	200	36	9	29	*121	.302	800	55	10	.988
National League Totals—1 Year				23	51	6	9	1	1	0	1	.176	26	0	0	1.000
American League Totals—3 Years				371	1396	204	395	69	10	57	221	.283	1280	83	22	.984
Major League Totals—4 Years				394	1447	210	404	70	11	57	222	.279	1306	83	22	.984

Selected by Chicago Cubs' organization in 1st round (second player selected) of free-agent draft, June 8, 1981.
†On disabled list, April 9 to April 19, 1984.
‡Traded with Outfielder Mel Hall and Pitchers Don Schulze and Darryl Banks to Cleveland Indians for Catcher Ron Hassey and Pitchers Rick Sutcliffe and George Frazier, June 13, 1984.
§On disabled list, July 2 to July 17, 1984.

CHARLES DOUGLAS CARY
(Chuck)

Born March 3, 1960, at Whittier, Calif.
Height, 6.04. Weight, 210.
Bats and throws lefthanded.
Attended University of California, Berkeley, Calif.

Major League saves: 1985 (2).
Tied for Southern League lead in balks with 3 in 1982.

Year	Club	League	G.	IP.	W.	L.	Pct.	H.	R.	ER.	SO.	BB.	ERA.
1981—Macon		S. Atlantic	13	87	5	5	.500	77	32	25	55	19	2.59
1982—Birmingham		Southern	28	166	8	14	.364	162	93	77	125	64	4.17
1983—Birmingham†		Southern	17	104⅔	6	8	.429	103	50	42	69	42	3.61
1983—Evansville		Am. Assoc.	15	16⅓	1	1	.500	21	10	8	8	8	4.41
1984—Birmingham‡		Southern	22	108⅓	6	4	.600	118	61	58	62	46	4.82
1985—Nashville		Am. Assoc.	48	66	2	1	.667	55	27	22	54	27	3.00
1985—Detroit		American	16	23⅔	0	1	.000	16	9	9	22	8	3.42
1986—Detroit		American	22	31⅔	1	2	.333	33	18	12	21	15	3.41
1986—Nashville		Am. Assoc.	22	26⅓	1	4	.200	29	21	16	19	15	5.47
Major League Totals—2 Years			38	55⅓	1	3	.250	49	27	21	43	23	3.42

Selected by Detroit Tigers' organization in 7th round of free-agent draft, June 8, 1981.
†On disabled list, April 18 to May 12, 1983.
‡On disabled list, June 24 to July 11 and August 4 to August 17, 1984.

JUAN CASTILLO

Name pronounced Cas-TEE-yo.
Born January 25, 1962, at San Pedro de Macoris, Dominican Republic.
Height, 5.11. Weight, 162.
Throws right and bats left and righthanded.

Major league stolen bases: 1986 (1).
Led Texas League in caught stealing with 17 in 1983.
Led Texas League second basemen in assists with 359 in 1984.
Led Texas League second basemen in putouts with 247, assists with 360, errors with 27, double plays with 79 and total chances with 634 in 1983.
Led California League second basemen in double plays with 88 in 1982.

Year	Club	League	Pos.	G.	AB.	R.	H.	2B.	3B.	HR.	RBI.	B.A.	PO.	A.	E.	F.A.
1980—Burlington	Midw.	2B	30	103	12	22	0	0	0	6	.214	60	72	3	.978
1980—Butte	Pion.	2B	59	183	28	53	9	3	0	20	.290	87	99	18	.912
1981—Burlington	Midw.	2B	110	365	36	90	8	4	4	34	.247	244	284	18	*.967
1982—Stockton	Calif.	2B	134	483	60	130	9	8	0	42	.269	273	*428	23	.968
1983—El Paso	Texas	2B-SS-OF	123	461	79	125	24	2	8	62	.271	250	363	28	.956
1984—El Paso	Texas	2B-OF-SS	119	448	78	129	21	7	4	59	.288	273	360	17	.974
1984—Vancouver	P. C.	2B	8	30	6	10	0	0	0	2	.333	16	18	1	.971
1985—Vancouver	P. C.	SS-2B	118	440	71	119	17	3	1	32	.270	222	367	26	.958
1986—Milwaukee	Amer.	2-S-3-O	26	54	6	9	0	1	0	5	.167	41	46	4	.956
1986—Vancouver	P. C.	2B	26	73	10	14	3	0	0	4	.192	34	95	5	.963
Major League Totals—1 Year				26	54	6	9	0	1	0	5	.167	41	46	4	.956

Signed as free agent by Milwaukee Brewers' organization, October 11, 1979.

MONTE CARMELO CASTILLO

Name pronounced Cas-TEE-yo.

(Carmen)

Born June 8, 1958, at San Francisco de Macoris, Dominican Republic.
Height, 6.01. Weight, 185.
Throws and bats righthanded.

Major League stolen bases: 1983 (1), 1984 (1), 1985 (3), 1986 (2). Total—7.

Year	Club	League	Pos.	G.	AB.	R.	H.	2B.	3B.	HR.	RBI.	B.A.	PO.	A.	E.	F.A.
1978—Auburn†	NYP	OF	53	174	37	41	10	2	4	21	.236	109	6	11	.913
1978—Helena	Pion.	OF	5	15	1	6	2	0	0	2	.400	2	0	1	.667
1979—Waterloo	Midw.	OF	49	138	25	28	5	1	3	12	.203	54	1	7	.887
1979—Batavia	NYP	OF	36	128	29	43	8	1	8	28	.336	56	4	5	.923
1980—Waterloo	Midw.	OF	117	390	69	103	14	1	11	64	.264	173	10	14	.929
1981—Chattanooga	South.	OF	119	441	63	124	17	6	11	58	.281	236	13	15	.943
1982—Charleston	Int.	OF	71	281	46	78	12	1	9	39	.278	159	10	11	.939
1982—Cleveland	Amer.	OF	47	120	11	25	4	0	2	11	.208	91	0	2	.978
1983—Charleston‡	Int.	OF	36	148	29	40	5	2	4	22	.270	85	6	6	.938
1983—Cleveland	Amer.	OF	23	36	9	10	2	1	1	3	.278	23	3	2	.929
1984—Cleveland	Amer.	OF	87	211	36	55	9	2	10	36	.261	123	2	9	.933
1985—Cleveland	Amer.	OF	67	184	27	45	5	1	11	25	.245	101	0	5	.953
1985—Maine	Int.	OF	26	96	12	23	2	2	2	18	.240	9	0	0	1.000
1986—Cleveland	Amer.	OF	85	205	34	57	9	0	8	32	.278	58	4	4	.939
Major League Totals—5 Years				309	756	117	192	29	4	32	107	.254	396	9	22	.948

Signed as free agent by Philadelphia Phillies' organization, June 30, 1978.
†Drafted by Chattanooga (Cleveland Indians' organization), December 5, 1978.
‡On disabled list, May 5 to July 4, 1983.

WILLIAM HOLLAND CAUDILL

Name pronounced KAH-dull.

(Bill)

Born July 13, 1956, at Santa Monica, Calif.
Height, 6.01. Weight, 210.
Throws and bats righthanded.

Pitched six-inning, 4-0 no-hit victory against Winter Haven, May 14, 1975.
Major League saves: 1980 (1), 1982 (26), 1984 (36), 1985 (14), 1986 (2). Total—105.
Led Florida State League in complete games with 12 in 1975.

Year	Club	League	G.	IP.	W.	L.	Pct.	H.	R.	ER.	SO.	BB.	ERA.
1974—Sarasota Cardinals	Gulf Coast	8	30	1	0	1.000	18	9	6	35	13	1.80
1975—St. Petersburg	Florida St.	25	163	●14	8	.636	123	63	57	*153	87	3.15
1976—Arkansas†	Texas	27	140	6	15	.286	128	79	69	*140	84	4.44
1977—Three Rivers‡	Eastern	19	114	13	4	*.765	97	56	53	93	72	4.18
1977—Indianapolis	Am. Assoc.	8	44	2	2	.500	31	20	18	25	31	3.68
1978—Wichita	Am. Assoc.	29	158	8	9	.471	151	103	97	124	105	5.53
1979—Wichita	Am. Assoc.	6	36	3	1	.750	27	11	11	36	17	2.75
1979—Chicago	National	29	90	1	7	.125	89	57	48	104	41	4.80
1980—Chicago	National	72	128	4	6	.400	100	37	31	112	59	2.18
1981—Chicago§x	National	30	71	1	5	.167	87	50	46	45	31	5.83
1982—Seattle	American	70	95⅔	12	9	.571	65	25	25	111	35	2.35
1983—Seattle yz	American	63	72⅔	2	8	.200	70	39	38	73	38	4.71
1984—Oakland ab	American	68	96⅓	9	7	.563	77	30	29	89	31	2.71

Year Club	League	G.	IP.	W.	L.	Pct.	H.	R.	ER.	SO.	BB.	ERA.
1985—Toronto	American	67	69⅓	4	6	.400	53	26	23	46	35	2.99
1986—Toronto c	American	40	36⅓	2	4	.333	36	25	25	32	17	6.19
National League Totals—3 Years		131	289	6	18	.250	276	144	125	261	131	3.89
American League Totals—5 Years		308	370⅓	29	34	.460	301	145	140	351	156	3.40
Major League Totals—8 Years		439	659⅓	35	52	.402	577	289	265	612	287	3.62

Selected by St. Louis Cardinals' organization in 8th round of free-agent draft, June 5, 1974.
†Traded to Cincinnati Reds' organization for Infielder-Outfielder Joel Youngblood, March 28, 1977.
‡Traded with Pitcher Woodie Fryman to Chicago Cubs for Pitcher Bill Bonham, October 31, 1977.
§Traded to New York Yankees, April 1, 1982, as partial completion of deal in which Chicago Cubs acquired Second Baseman Pat Tabler from New York on waivers for two players to be named later, August 19, 1981; New York organization acquired Pitcher Jay Howell to complete deal, August 2, 1982.
xTraded with Pitcher Gene Nelson, a player to be named later and cash by New York Yankees to Seattle Mariners for Pitcher Shane Rawley, April 1, 1982; Seattle organization acquired Outfielder Bobby Brown to complete deal, April 6, 1982.
yOn disabled list, August 17 to September 4, 1983.
zTraded with a player to be named later to Oakland A's for Pitcher Dave Beard and Catcher Bob Kearney, November 21, 1983; Oakland acquired Pitcher Darrel Akerfelds to complete deal, December 7, 1983.
aHad one at-bat with a strikeout.
bTraded to Toronto Blue Jays for Outfielder Dave Collins, Shortstop Alfredo Griffin and cash, December 8, 1984.
cOn disabled list, April 8 to April 23, 1986.

ALL-STAR GAME RECORD

Year League	IP.	W.	L.	Pct.	H.	R.	ER.	SO.	BB.	ERA.
1984—American	1	0	0	.000	0	0	0	3	0	0.00

CESAR CEDENO

Name pronounced Suh-DAYN-yoh.

Born February 25, 1951, at Santo Domingo, Dominican Republic.
Height, 6.02. Weight, 200.
Throw and bats righthanded.

Tied major league record for most doubles, inning (2), April 9, 1973 (1st game, 6th inning).
Hit for the cycle, August 2, 1972 and August 9, 1976.
Major League stolen bases: 1970 (17), 1971 (20), 1972 (55), 1973 (56), 1974 (57), 1975 (50), 1976 (58), 1977 (61), 1978 (23), 1979 (30), 1980 (48), 1981 (12), 1982 (16), 1983 (13), 1984 (19), 1985 (14), 1986 (1). Total—550.
Led National League in caught stealing with 21 in 1972 and 17 in 1975.
Led National League outfielders in double plays with 5 in 1976.
Led National League outfielders in total chances with 460 in 1974.
Tied for National League lead in sacrifice flies with 9 in 1979.
Tied for Carolina League lead in being hit by pitch with 14 in 1969.
Named outfielder on THE SPORTING NEWS National League All-Star Team, 1972, 1973, 1976 and 1980.
Named outfielder on THE SPORTING NEWS National League All-Star fielding team, 1972 through 1976.

Year Club	League	Pos.	G.	AB.	R.	H.	2B.	3B.	HR.	RBI.	B.A.	PO.	A.	E.	F.A.
1968—Covington	Appal.	OF	36	131	23	49	5	6	0	21	.374	49	●8	7	.891
1968—Cocoa	Fla. St.	OF	69	180	19	46	8	2	0	16	.256	70	4	7	.914
1969—Peninsula	Carol.	1B-OF	142	497	62	136	★32	3	5	39	.274	761	52	17	.980
1970—Okla. City	A. A.	OF	54	233	47	87	14	9	14	61	.373	113	6	4	.967
1970—Houston	Nat.	OF	90	355	46	110	21	4	7	42	.310	211	1	7	.968
1971—Houston	Nat.	OF-1B	161	611	85	161	★40	6	10	81	.264	348	6	4	.989
1972—Houston	Nat.	OF	139	559	103	179	●39	8	22	82	.320	345	9	7	.981
1973—Houston	Nat.	OF	139	525	86	168	35	2	25	70	.320	357	10	7	.981
1974—Houston†	Nat.	OF	160	610	95	164	29	5	26	102	.269	★446	11	3	.993
1975—Houston	Nat.	OF	131	500	93	144	31	3	13	63	.288	322	8	6	.982
1976—Houston	Nat.	OF	150	575	89	171	26	5	18	83	.297	377	11	8	.980
1977—Houston‡	Nat.	OF	141	530	92	148	36	8	14	71	.279	335	14	1	★.997
1978—Houston§	Nat.	OF	50	192	31	54	8	2	7	23	.281	149	2	2	.987
1979—Houston	Nat.	★1B-OF	132	470	57	123	27	4	6	54	.262	948	35	★17	.983
1980—Houston	Nat.	OF	137	499	71	154	32	8	10	73	.309	338	9	8	.977
1981—Houston x	Nat.	1B-OF	82	306	42	83	19	0	5	34	.271	510	28	5	.991
1982—Cincinnati	Nat.	OF-1B	138	492	52	142	35	1	8	57	.289	301	5	3	.990
1983—Cincinnati	Nat.	OF-1B	98	332	40	77	16	0	9	39	.232	258	10	1	.996
1984—Cincinnati y	Nat.	OF-1B	110	380	59	105	24	2	10	47	.276	355	21	7	.982
1985—Cinc.z-St.L.ab	Nat.	1B-OF	111	296	38	86	16	1	9	49	.291	351	14	3	.992
1986—Los Angeles c	Nat.	OF	37	78	5	18	2	1	0	6	.231	33	1	2	.944
1986—Louisville	A. A.	OF	20	65	5	11	3	0	1	4	.169	10	0	0	1.000
Major League Totals—17 Years			2006	7310	1084	2087	436	60	199	976	.285	5984	195	91	.985

Signed as free agent by Houston Astros' organization, October 25, 1967.
†On disabled list, July 20 to August 8, 1975.
‡On disabled list, March 23 to April 13, 1977.
§On disabled list, June 17 to September 29, 1978.
xTraded to Cincinnati Reds for Third Baseman Ray Knight, December 18, 1981.
yOn disabled list, May 29 to June 13, 1984.
zTraded to St. Louis Cardinals for Outfielder Mark Jackson, August 29, 1985.
aGranted free agency, November 12, 1985; signed by Syracuse (Toronto Blue Jays' organization), March 14, 1986.
bReleased, April 3, 1986; signed by Los Angeles Dodgers, April 10, 1986.
cReleased, June 5, 1986; signed by Louisville (St. Louis Cardinals' organization), July 19, 1986.

DIVISION SERIES RECORD

Year Club	League	Pos.	G.	AB.	R.	H.	2B.	3B.	HR.	RBI.	B.A.	PO.	A.	E.	F.A.
1981—Houston	Nat.	1B	4	13	0	3	1	0	0	0	.231	36	2	1	.974

CHAMPIONSHIP SERIES RECORD

Year Club	League	Pos.	G.	AB.	R.	H.	2B.	3B.	HR.	RBI.	B.A.	PO.	A.	E.	F.A.
1980—Houston	Nat.	OF	3	11	1	2	0	0	0	1	.182	5	0	0	1.000
1985—St. Louis	Nat.	OF-PH	5	12	2	2	1	0	0	0	.167	5	0	0	1.000
Championship Series Totals—2 Years			8	23	3	4	1	0	0	1	.174	10	0	0	1.000

WORLD SERIES RECORD

Year Club	League	Pos.	G.	AB.	R.	H.	2B.	3B.	HR.	RBI.	B.A.	PO.	A.	E.	F.A.
1985—St. Louis	Nat.	OF	5	15	1	2	1	0	0	1	.133	9	0	0	1.000

ALL-STAR GAME RECORD

Year League	Pos.	AB.	R.	H.	2B.	3B.	HR.	RBI.	B.A.	PO.	A.	E.	F.A.
1972—National	OF	2	1	1	0	0	0	0	.500	0	0	0	.000
1973—National	OF	3	0	1	0	0	0	1	.333	3	0	0	1.000
1974—National	OF	2	0	0	0	0	0	0	.000	2	0	0	1.000
1976—National	OF	2	1	1	0	0	1	2	.500	1	0	0	1.000
All-Star Game Totals—4 Years		9	2	3	0	0	1	3	.333	6	0	0	1.000

RICHARD ALDO CERONE
Name pronounced Ce-RONE.

(Rick)

Born May 19, 1954, at Newark, N. J.
Height, 5.11. Weight, 185.
Throws and bats righthanded.
Received bachelor of science degree in physical education from
Seton Hall University, South Orange, N. J. in 1975.

Major League stolen bases: 1979 (1), 1980 (1), 1984 (1), 1985 (1). Total—4.
Named catcher on THE SPORTING NEWS American League All-Star Team, 1980.
Received reported $60,000 bonus to sign with Cleveland Indians, 1975.

Year Club	League	Pos.	G.	AB.	R.	H.	2B.	3B.	HR.	RBI.	B.A.	PO.	A.	E.	F.A.
1975—Okla. City	A. A.	C-OF	46	140	22	35	6	1	2	13	.250	178	30	3	.986
1975—Cleveland	Amer.	C	7	12	1	3	1	0	0	0	.250	18	1	0	1.000
1976—Toledo†	Int.	C	96	339	38	86	19	0	11	49	.254	351	50	*18	.957
1976—Cleveland‡	Amer.	C	7	16	1	2	0	0	0	1	.125	25	1	1	.963
1977—Charleston	Int.	C-OF	70	231	30	54	10	1	6	40	.234	254	32	5	.983
1977—Toronto	Amer.	C	31	100	7	20	4	0	1	10	.200	146	15	1	.944
1978—Toronto	Amer.	C	88	282	25	63	8	2	3	20	.223	426	44	4	.992
1979—Toronto§	Amer.	C	136	469	47	112	27	4	7	61	.239	560	68	13	.980
1980—New York	Amer.	C	147	519	70	144	30	4	14	85	.277	800	73	9	.990
1981—New York x	Amer.	C	71	234	23	57	13	2	2	21	.244	353	26	3	.992
1982—New York y	Amer.	C	89	300	29	68	10	0	5	28	.227	509	25	6	.989
1983—New York	Amer.	C-3B	80	246	18	54	7	0	2	22	.220	412	18	4	.991
1984—New York z	Amer.	C	38	120	8	25	3	0	2	13	.208	230	9	1	.996
1984—Columbus a	Int.	C	8	25	2	5	2	0	0	1	.200	42	5	1	.979
1985—Atlanta bc	Nat.	C	96	282	15	61	9	0	3	25	.216	384	48	6	.986
1986—Milwaukee d	Amer.	C	68	216	22	56	14	0	4	18	.259	391	44	4	.991
American League Totals—11 Years			762	2514	251	604	117	12	40	279	.240	3870	324	46	.989
National League Total—1 Year			96	282	15	61	9	0	3	25	.216	384	48	6	.986
Major League Totals—12 Years			858	2796	266	665	126	12	43	304	.238	4254	372	52	.989

Selected by Cleveland Indians' organization in 1st round (seventh player selected) of free-agent draft, June 4, 1975.
†On disabled list, May 13 to May 24, 1976.
‡Traded with Infielder-Outfielder John Lowenstein to Toronto Blue Jays for Outfielder Rico Carty, December 6, 1976.
§Traded with Pitcher Tom Underwood and Outfielder Ted Wilborn to New York Yankees for First Baseman Chris Chambliss, Infielder Damaso Garcia and Pitcher Paul Mirabella, November 1, 1979.
xOn disabled list, April 19 to May 24, 1981.
yOn disabled list, May 12 to July 15, 1982.
zOn disabled list, May 7 to July 5, 1984; included rehabilitation disability assignment to Columbus, June 25 to July 5, 1984.
aTraded to Atlanta Braves for Pitcher Brian Fisher, December 5, 1984.
bOn disabled list, June 17 to July 2, 1985.
cTraded with Pitcher David Clay and Shortstop Flavio Alfaro to Milwaukee Brewers for Catcher Ted Simmons, March 5, 1986.
dGranted free agency, November 12, 1986.

DIVISION SERIES RECORD

Year Club	League	Pos.	G.	AB.	R.	H.	2B.	3B.	HR.	RBI.	B.A.	PO.	A.	E.	F.A.
1981—New York	Amer.	C	5	18	1	6	2	0	1	5	.333	42	1	1	.977

CHAMPIONSHIP SERIES RECORD

Tied Championsip Series record for hitting home run in first Series at-bat, October 8, 1980.

Year Club	League	Pos.	G.	AB.	R.	H.	2B.	3B.	HR.	RBI.	B.A.	PO.	A.	E.	F.A.
1980—New York	Amer.	C	3	12	1	4	0	0	1	2	.333	14	4	0	1.000
1981—New York	Amer.	C	3	10	1	1	0	0	0	0	.100	23	2	0	1.000
Championship Series Totals—2 Years			6	22	2	5	0	0	1	2	.227	37	6	0	1.000

Year	Club	League	Pos.	G.	AB.	R.	H.	2B.	3B.	HR.	RBI.	B.A.	PO.	A.	E.	F.A.
1981—New York		Amer.	C	6	21	2	4	1	0	1	3	.190	42	4	0	1.000

JOHN JOSEPH CERUTTI

Born April 28, 1960, at Albany, N. Y.
Height, 6.02. Weight, 195.
Throws and bats lefthanded.
Received bachelor of arts degree in economics from Amherst College, Amherst, Mass.

Major League saves: 1986 (1).
Tied for Southern League lead in shutouts with 3 in 1983.
Tied for Pioneer League lead in home runs allowed with 8 and games started by pitchers with 14 in 1981.

Year	Club	League	G.	IP.	W.	L.	Pct.	H.	R.	ER.	SO.	BB.	ERA.
1981—Medicine Hat		Pioneer	14	*107	8	4	.667	87	45	36	120	43	3.03
1982—Kinston		Carolina	16	113	10	5	.667	88	47	40	136	49	3.19
1982—Knoxville		Southern	4	32⅓	4	0	1.000	18	4	4	17	10	1.11
1982—Syracuse		Int'national	6	30	0	3	.000	42	25	22	20	16	6.60
1983—Knoxville		Southern	29	188⅔	9	13	.409	182	89	72	131	65	3.43
1984—Syracuse		Int'national	29	148	7	●13	.350	152	89	73	114	52	4.44
1985—Syracuse		Int'national	28	182	11	9	.550	165	84	60	110	60	2.97
1985—Toronto		American	4	6⅔	0	2	.000	10	7	4	5	4	5.40
1986—Syracuse		Int'national	7	43⅔	1	3	.250	44	27	20	22	16	4.12
1986—Toronto		American	34	145⅓	9	4	.692	150	73	67	89	47	4.15
Major League Totals—2 Years			38	152	9	6	.600	160	80	71	94	51	4.20

Selected by Toronto Blue Jays' organization in 1st round (21st player selected) of free-agent draft, June 8, 1981.

RONALD CHARLES CEY

Name pronounced Say.

(Ron)

Born February 15, 1948, at Tacoma, Wash.
Height, 5.09. Weight, 185.
Throws and bats righthanded.
Attended Washington State University, Pullman, Wash., and Western
Washington State College, Bellingham, Wash.

Major League stolen bases: 1973 (1), 1974 (1), 1975 (5), 1977 (3), 1978 (2), 1979 (3), 1980 (2), 1982 (3), 1984 (3), 1985 (1). Total—24.
Led National League third basemen in double plays with 39 in 1973.
Led Pacific Coast League in bases on balls received with 117 in 1972.
Led Northwest League in sacrifice flies with 7 in 1968.
Led Pacific Coast League third baseman in putouts with 106, assists with 274 and tied for lead in double plays with 24 in 1972.
Led California League third basemen in double plays with 22 in 1969.
Tied for Pacific Coast League lead in being hit by pitch with 9 in 1971.

Year	Club	League	Pos.	G.	AB.	R.	H.	2B.	3B.	HR.	RBI.	B.A.	PO.	A.	E.	F.A.
1968—Tri-City		N'west	3B	74	254	50	76	11	4	9	*62	.299	46	*175	10	*.957
1969—Albuquerque		Texas	3B	13	32	8	5	1	0	0	2	.156	13	19	1	.970
1969—Bakersfield		Calif.	3B	98	353	68	117	16	1	22	56	.331	82	197	22	.927
1970—Albuquerque		Texas	3B	71	239	31	79	22	1	4	56	.331	44	132	10	.946
1971—Spokane		P. C.	3B	137	500	85	164	26	4	32	*123	.328	95	283	24	*.940
1971—Los Angeles		Nat.	PH	2	2	0	0	0	0	0	0	.000	0	0	0	.000
1972—Albuquerque		P. C.	3B-2B	142	496	99	163	25	7	23	103	.329	108	279	21	.949
1972—Los Angeles		Nat.	3B	11	37	3	10	1	0	1	3	.270	7	20	3	.900
1973—Los Angeles		Nat.	3B	152	507	60	124	18	4	15	80	.245	111	*328	18	.961
1974—Los Angeles		Nat.	3B	159	577	88	151	20	2	18	97	.262	155	365	22	.959
1975—Los Angeles		Nat.	3B	158	566	72	160	29	2	25	101	.283	144	309	19	.960
1976—Los Angeles		Nat.	3B	145	502	69	139	18	3	23	80	.277	111	334	16	.965
1977—Los Angeles		Nat.	3B	153	564	77	136	22	3	30	110	.241	138	346	18	.964
1978—Los Angeles		Nat.	3B	159	555	84	150	32	0	23	84	.270	116	336	16	.966
1979—Los Angeles		Nat.	3B	150	487	77	137	20	1	28	81	.281	123	265	9	*.977
1980—Los Angeles		Nat.	3B	157	551	81	140	25	0	28	77	.254	*127	317	13	.972
1981—Los Angeles		Nat.	3B	85	312	42	90	15	2	13	50	.288	71	184	16	.941
1982—Los Angeles†		Nat.	3B	150	556	62	141	23	1	24	79	.254	93	320	16	.963
1983—Chicago		Nat.	3B	159	581	73	160	33	1	24	90	.275	90	270	17	.955
1984—Chicago		Nat.	3B	146	505	71	121	27	0	25	97	.240	97	230	11	*.967
1985—Chicago		Nat.	3B	145	500	64	116	18	2	22	63	.232	75	273	*21	.943
1986—Chicago		Nat.	3B	97	256	42	70	21	0	13	36	.273	41	118	8	.952
Major League Totals—16 Years				2028	7058	965	1845	322	21	312	1128	.261	1499	4015	223	.961

Selected by New York Mets' organization in 24th round of free-agent draft, June 6, 1966.
Selected by Los Angeles Dodgers' organization in 3rd round of free-agent draft, June 7, 1968.
†Traded to Chicago Cubs for Outfielder Dan Cataline and Pitcher Vance Lovelace, January 19, 1983.

CHAMPIONSHIP SERIES RECORD

Tied Championship Series records for most two-base hits, total Series (7); most home runs with bases filled, game (1), October 4, 1977; most runs batted in, inning (4), October 4, 1977 (seventh inning); most two-base hits, four-game Series (3), 1974.
Tied National League Championship record for most hits, game (4), October 6, 1974.

Year Club League	Pos.	G.	AB.	R.	H.	2B.	3B.	HR.	RBI.	B.A.	PO.	A.	E.	F.A.
1974—Los Angeles .... Nat.	3B	4	16	2	5	3	0	1	1	.313	2	4	2	.750
1977—Los Angeles .... Nat.	3B	4	13	4	4	1	0	1	4	.308	7	14	1	.955
1978—Los Angeles .... Nat.	3B	4	16	4	5	1	0	1	3	.313	2	13	0	1.000
1981—Los Angeles .... Nat.	3B	5	18	1	5	1	0	0	3	.278	5	16	1	.955
1984—Chicago .... Nat.	3B	5	19	3	3	1	0	1	3	.158	1	6	0	1.000
Championship Series Totals—5 Years....		22	82	14	22	7	0	4	14	.268	17	53	4	.946

WORLD SERIES RECORD

Tied World Series record for batting in all club's runs, game, most (4), October 11, 1978.

Year Club League	Pos.	G.	AB.	R.	H.	2B.	3B.	HR.	RBI.	B.A.	PO.	A.	E.	F.A.
1974—Los Angeles .... Nat.	3B	5	17	1	3	0	0	0	0	.176	5	9	1	.933
1977—Los Angeles .... Nat.	3B	6	21	2	4	1	0	1	3	.190	5	7	0	1.000
1978—Los Angeles .... Nat.	3B	6	21	2	6	0	0	1	4	.286	2	12	0	1.000
1981—Los Angeles .... Nat.	3B	6	20	3	7	0	0	1	6	.350	4	11	0	1.000
World Series Totals—4 Years		23	79	8	20	1	0	3	13	.253	16	39	1	.982

ALL-STAR GAME RECORD

Year League	Pos.	AB.	R.	H.	2B.	3B.	HR.	RBI.	B.A.	PO.	A.	E.	F.A.
1974—National	3B	2	0	1	1	0	0	2	.500	0	0	0	.000
1975—National	3B	3	0	1	0	0	0	0	.333	0	1	0	1.000
1976—National	3B	0	0	0	0	0	0	0	.000	0	0	0	.000
1977—National	3B	2	0	0	0	0	0	0	.000	0	0	0	.000
1978—National	3B	1	0	0	0	0	0	0	.000	1	0	0	1.000
1979—National	3B	1	0	0	0	0	0	0	.000	2	1	0	1.000
All-Star Game Totals—6 Years..................		9	0	2	1	0	0	2	.222	3	2	0	1.000

RAY CHARLES CHADWICK

Born November 17, 1962, at Durham, N.C.
Height, 6.02. Weight, 180.
Throws right and bats left and righthanded.
Attended Winston-Salem State University, Winston-Salem, N.C.

Led Midwest League in balks with 5 in 1984.
Tied for Pacific Coast League lead in shutouts with 3 in 1986.

Year Club	League	G.	IP.	W.	L.	Pct.	H.	R.	ER.	SO.	BB.	ERA.
1983—Salem................................	Northwest	16	83⅓	3	5	.375	72	*63	●46	82	51	4.97
1984—Peoria†..............................	Midwest	26	153⅓	11	9	.550	138	87	68	133	85	3.99
1985—Redwood‡..........................	California	4	14	0	1	.000	13	14	10	10	11	6.43
1985—Midland.............................	Texas	10	60	5	2	.714	53	36	35	44	47	5.25
1985—Edmonton..........................	P. Coast	2	11⅔	1	1	.500	9	7	4	9	6	3.09
1986—Edmonton..........................	P. Coast	20	124	9	9	.500	116	66	65	89	66	4.72
1986—California...........................	American	7	27⅓	0	5	.000	39	26	22	9	15	7.24
Major League Totals—1 Year........		7	27⅓	0	5	.000	39	26	22	9	15	7.24

Selected by California Angels' organization in 16th round of free-agent draft, June 6, 1983.
†On disabled list, May 17 to June 2, 1984.
‡On disabled list, April 9 to June 6, 1985.

CARROLL CHRISTOPHER CHAMBLISS
(Chris)

Born December 26, 1948, at Dayton, O.
Height, 6.01. Weight, 220.
Throws right and bats lefthanded.
Attended Mira Costa Junior College, Oceanside, Calif., and University of California,
Los Angeles, Calif.; and received degree in physical education and recreation from
Montclair State College, Upper Montclair, N.J.
Cousin of Jo Jo White, guard with Boston Celtics, Golden State Warriors
and Kansas City Kings, 1969-70 through 1980-81.

Tied major league record for fewest caught stealing, season, 150 or more games (0), 1976 and 1977.
Major League stolen bases: 1971 (2), 1972 (3), 1973 (4), 1976 (1), 1977 (4), 1978 (2), 1979 (3), 1980 (7), 1981 (4), 1982 (7), 1983 (2), 1984 (1). Total—40.
Led National League first basemen in double plays with 144 in 1982.
Led National League first basemen in total chances with 1,739 in 1980 and 1,144 in 1981.
Led American League first basemen in total chances with 1,565 in 1973.
Named American League Rookie Player of the Year by THE SPORTING NEWS, 1971.
Named American League Rookie of the Year by Baseball Writers' Association of America, 1971.
Named first baseman on THE SPORTING NEWS American League All-Star Team, 1976.
Named first baseman on THE SPORTING NEWS American League All-Star fielding team, 1978.

Year Club League	Pos.	G.	AB.	R.	H.	2B.	3B.	HR.	RBI.	B.A.	PO.	A.	E.	F.A.
1970—Wichita†................ A. A.	OF-1B	105	383	60	131	17	8	7	52	*.342	413	21	13	.971
1971—Wichita.................. A. A.	OF-1B	13	42	8	12	3	0	2	6	.286	42	3	0	1.000
1971—Cleveland.............. Amer.	1B	111	415	49	114	20	4	9	48	.275	943	55	8	.992
1972—Cleveland‡............. Amer.	1B	121	466	51	136	27	2	6	44	.292	1109	56	8	.993
1973—Cleveland.............. Amer.	1B	155	572	70	156	30	2	11	53	.273	1437	114	14	.991
1974—Cleve.§-N.Y. .... Amer.	1B	127	467	46	119	20	3	6	50	.255	1035	84	11	.990
1975—New York.............. Amer.	1B	150	562	66	171	38	4	9	72	.304	1222	106	12	.991
1976—New York.............. Amer.	1B	156	641	79	188	32	6	17	96	.293	1440	109	9	.994
1977—New York.............. Amer.	1B	157	600	90	172	32	6	17	90	.287	1368	98	16	.989

Year	Club	League	Pos.	G	AB	R	H	2B	3B	HR	RBI	B.A.	PO	A	E	F.A.
1978—New York	Amer.		1B	162	625	81	171	26	3	12	90	.274	1366	111	4	*.997
1979—New York xy	Amer.		1B	149	554	61	155	27	3	18	63	.280	1299	95	7	.995
1980—Atlanta	Nat.		1B	158	602	83	170	37	2	18	72	.282	*1626	101	12	.993
1981—Atlanta	Nat.		1B	107	404	44	110	25	2	8	51	.272	1046	*94	4	.997
1982—Atlanta	Nat.		1B	157	534	57	144	25	2	20	86	.270	1352	138	10	.993
1983—Atlanta z	Nat.		1B	131	447	59	125	24	3	20	78	.280	1092	89	5	.996
1984—Atlanta	Nat.		1B	135	389	47	100	14	0	9	44	.257	996	70	8	.993
1985—Atlanta	Nat.		1B	101	170	16	40	7	0	3	21	.235	299	25	1	.997
1986—Atlanta a	Nat.		1B	97	122	13	38	8	0	2	14	.311	141	6	1	.993
American League Totals—9 Years				1288	4902	593	1382	252	33	105	606	.282	11219	828	89	.993
National League Totals—7 Years				886	2668	319	727	140	9	80	366	.272	6552	523	41	.994
Major League Totals—16 Years				2174	7570	912	2109	392	42	185	972	.279	17771	1351	130	.993

Selected by Cincinnati Reds' organization in 31st round of free-agent draft, June 6, 1967.

Selected by Cincinnati Reds' organization in secondary phase of free-agent draft, January 27, 1968.

Selected by Cleveland Indians' organization in 1st round (first player selected) of free-agent draft, January 17, 1970.

†On disabled list, May 25 to June 16, 1970.

‡On military list, June 23 to June 30, 1972.

§Traded with Pitchers Dick Tidrow and Cecil Upshaw to New York Yankees for Fritz Peterson, Steve Kline, Fred Beene and Tom Buskey, April 26, 1974.

xTraded with Infielder Damaso Garcia and Pitcher Paul Mirabella to Toronto Blue Jays for Catcher Rick Cerone, Pitcher Tom Underwood and Outfielder Ted Wilborn, November 1, 1979.

yTraded with Shortstop Luis Gomez to Atlanta Braves for Outfielder Barry Bonnell and Pitcher Joey McLaughlin, December 5, 1979.

zOn disabled list, August 8 to August 23, 1983.

aGranted free agency, November 12, 1986.

CHAMPIONSHIP SERIES RECORD

Established Championship Series records for highest slugging average, five-game Series (.952), 1976; most total bases, five-game Series (20), 1976.

Tied Championship Series records for most hits, five-game Series (11), 1976; most hits, two consecutive games, one Series (6), October 3 and 4, 1978; most consecutive hits, one Series (5), 1978.

Tied American League Championship Series records for most consecutive hits, total Series (5); most one-base hits, four-game Series (6), 1978; most home runs, five-game Series (2), 1976.

Year	Club	League	Pos.	G	AB	R	H	2B	3B	HR	RBI	B.A.	PO	A	E	F.A.
1976—New York	Amer.		1B	5	21	5	11	1	1	2	8	.524	50	3	1	.981
1977—New York	Amer.		1B	5	17	0	1	0	0	0	0	.059	35	7	0	1.000
1978—New York	Amer.		1B	4	15	1	6	0	0	0	2	.400	28	1	0	1.000
1982—Atlanta	Nat.		1B	3	10	0	0	0	0	0	0	.000	30	5	0	1.000
Championship Series Totals—4 Years				17	63	6	18	1	1	2	10	.286	143	16	1	.994

WORLD SERIES RECORD

Tied World Series records for most errors by first baseman, four-game Series (1), 1976; one or more hits, each game, four-game Series, 1976.

Year	Club	League	Pos.	G	AB	R	H	2B	3B	HR	RBI	B.A.	PO	A	E	F.A.
1976—New York	Amer.		1B	4	16	1	5	1	0	0	1	.313	26	3	1	.967
1977—New York	Amer.		1B	6	24	4	7	2	0	0	4	.292	55	5	0	1.000
1978—New York	Amer.		1B	3	11	1	2	0	0	0	0	.182	17	1	0	1.000
World Series Totals—3 Years				13	51	6	14	3	0	1	5	.275	98	9	1	.991

ALL-STAR GAME RECORD

Year	League	Pos.	AB	R	H	2B	3B	HR	RBI	B.A.	PO	A	E	F.A.
1976—American		PH	1	0	0	0	0	0	0	.000	0	0	0	.000

NORMAN WOOD CHARLTON
(Norm)

Born January 6, 1963, at Fort Polk, La.
Height, 6.02. Weight, 175.
Throws left and bats left and righthanded.
Attended Rice University, Houston, Tex.

Year	Club	League	G	IP	W	L	Pct.	H	R	ER	SO	BB	ERA
1984—West Palm Beach	Florida St.		8	39⅓	1	4	.200	51	27	20	27	22	4.58
1985—West Palm Beach†	Florida St.		24	128	7	10	.412	135	79	65	71	79	4.57
1986—Vermont	Eastern		22	136⅔	10	6	.625	109	55	43	96	74	2.83

Selected by Montreal Expos' organization in 1st round (27th player selected) of free-agent draft, June 4, 1984.

†Traded with a player to be named later to Cincinnati Reds for Infielder Wayne Krenchicki, March 31, 1986; Cincinnati acquired Second Baseman Tim Barker to complete deal, April 2, 1986.

PEDRO JOSE CHAVEZ

Born February 23, 1962, at Los Teques, Venezuela.
Height 5.11. Weight, 162.
Throws and bats righthanded.

Year	Club	League	Pos.	G	AB	R	H	2B	3B	HR	RBI	B.A.	PO	A	E	F.A.
1981—Macon	S. Atl.		SS	99	324	42	80	10	2	2	24	.247	147	303	36	.926
1982—Lakeland†	Fla. St.		SS-3B	83	254	27	68	11	1	2	29	.268	71	174	22	.918

Year Club	League	Pos.	G.	AB.	R.	H.	2B.	3B.	HR.	RBI.	B.A.	PO.	A.	E.	F.A.
1983—Birmingham‡ .... South.	3-2-S-1	20	49	7	11	1	0	0	3	.224	23	37	7	.896
1983—San Jose .... Calif.	SS	107	401	56	111	12	3	6	42	.277	159	303	41	.918
1984—Birmingham .... South.	SS	60	228	26	54	8	0	1	25	.237	128	167	13	.958
1984—Evansville .... A. A.	SS-3B-2B	88	334	47	90	18	4	1	27	.269	135	254	16	.960
1985—Nashville................ A. A.	SS-2B-3B	51	154	14	35	3	1	2	14	.227	74	118	10	.950
1985—Birmingham .... South.	SS-2B-3B	55	189	20	42	2	1	0	18	.222	89	131	11	.952
1986—Nashville................ A. A.	2B-SS-3B	122	414	55	107	20	3	2	43	.258	176	277	21	.956

Signed as free agent by Detroit Tigers' organization, August 20, 1980.

†On disabled list, April 9 to May 7, 1982.

‡Loaned to San Jose (Co-op), May 9, 1983; returned, September 8, 1983.

RODNEY OSBORNE CHILDRESS
(Rocky)

Born February 18, 1962, at Santa Rosa, Calif.
Height, 6.02. Weight, 195.
Throws and bats righthanded.
Attended Santa Rosa Junior College, Santa Rosa, Calif.

Led Eastern League in intentional bases on balls issued with 13 in 1984.
Led Carolina League in saves with 16 and tied for lead in games finished in relief with 50 in 1983.

Year Club	League	G.	IP.	W.	L.	Pct.	H.	R.	ER.	SO.	BB.	ERA.
1980—Helena..............................	Pioneer	15	68	3	4	.429	79	32	19	43	20	2.51
1981—Bend.................................	Northwest	25	46	4	5	.444	56	36	23	38	21	4.50
1982—Spartanburg....................	S. Atlantic	46	92	4	4	.500	101	53	41	54	44	4.01
1983—Peninsula........................	Carolina	★58	74⅓	4	7	.364	87	47	36	43	31	4.36
1984—Reading...........................	Eastern	●62	103⅓	7	6	.538	107	38	34	50	40	2.96
1985—Portland..........................	P. Coast	34	56⅔	5	2	.714	48	12	8	30	23	1.27
1985—Philadelphia	National	16	33⅓	0	1	.000	45	23	23	14	9	6.21
1986—Portland†-Tucson	P. Coast	61	83⅓	5	10	.333	99	69	63	40	46	6.80
1986—Philadelphia‡	National	2	2⅔	0	0	.000	4	3	2	1	1	6.75
Major League Totals—2 Years..............................		18	36	0	1	.000	49	26	25	15	10	6.25

Selected by Philadelphia Phillies' organization in 21st round of free-agent draft, June 3, 1980.

†Traded to Houston Astros' organization for Pitcher Mike Madden, June 20, 1986; deal voided, June 27, 1986.

‡Traded to Houston Astros for a player to be named later, November 16, 1986.

JOHN LAWRENCE CHRISTENSEN

Born September 5, 1960, at Downey, Calif.
Height, 6.00. Weight, 180.
Throws and bats righthanded.
Attended California State University, Fullerton, Calif.
Brother of Jim Christensen, second baseman with Minnesota Twins' and
Oakland A's organizations, 1977 through 1983.

Major League stolen bases: 1985 (1).
Led International League outfielders in fielding percentage with .994 in 1984.

Year Club	League	Pos.	G.	AB.	R.	H.	2B.	3B.	HR.	RBI.	B.A.	PO.	A.	E.	F.A.
1982—Shelby.................... S. Atl.	OF	125	440	100	147	24	2	22	★97	.334	156	9	2	.988
1982—Lynchburg............ Carol.	OF	8	31	7	10	1	1	0	4	.323	11	1	1	.923
1983—Jackson .... Texas	OF-1B-3B	109	405	76	135	26	2	12	72	.333	417	49	11	.977
1983—Tidewater............. Int.	OF	20	80	12	21	0	0	2	15	.263	28	1	2	.935
1984—Tidewater............. Int.	OF-1B	129	421	57	133	12	0	15	71	.316	177	7	1	.995
1984—New York............. Nat.	OF	5	11	2	3	2	0	0	3	.273	1	0	1	.500
1985—New York............. Nat.	OF	51	113	10	21	4	1	3	13	.186	41	2	2	.956
1985—Tidewater†........... Int.	OF	43	156	14	33	4	1	1	13	.212	65	7	4	.947
1986—Pawtucket‡ .... Int.	OF	62	175	27	41	0	0	5	22	.234	83	2	0	1.000
Major League Totals—2 Years.................		56	124	12	24	6	1	3	16	.194	42	2	3	.936

Selected by California Angels' organization in 16th round of free-agent draft, June 6, 1978.

Selected by New York Mets' organization in 2nd round of free-agent draft, June 8, 1981.

†Traded with Pitchers Calvin Schiraldi and Wes Gardner and Outfielder LaSchelle Tarver to Boston Red Sox for Pitchers Bob Ojeda, Tom McCarthy, John Mitchell and Chris Bayer, November 13, 1985.

‡Traded to Seattle Mariners, September 25, 1986, completing deal in which Seattle traded Shortstop Spike Owen and Outfielder Dave Henderson to Boston Red Sox for Infielder Rey Quinones, a player to be named later and cash, August 19, 1986. As part of deal, Seattle claimed Pitchers Mike Brown and Mike Trujillo on waivers from Boston, August 22, 1986.

STEPHEN RANDALL CHRISTMAS
(Steve)

Born December 9, 1957, at Orlando, Fla.
Height, 6.00. Weight, 190.
Throws right and bats lefthanded.
Attended Oklahoma City Southwestern Junior College, Oklahoma City, Okla.

Tied for American Association lead in sacrifice flies with 7 and grounded into double plays with 16 in 1985.
Led Eastern League catchers in total chances with 702 in 1981.
Led Eastern League catchers in fielding percentage with .984 in 1980.
Led Florida State League catchers in putouts with 646 and assists with 113 in 1979.
Led Western Carolinas League catchers in total chances with 627 in 1978.
Tied for Eastern League lead in passed balls with 15 in 1981.

Tied for Florida State League lead in passed balls with 17 in 1979.

Year Club	League	Pos.	G.	AB.	R.	H.	2B.	3B.	HR.	RBI.	B.A.	PO.	A.	E.	F.A.
1977—Eugene	N'west	C-3B-1B	46	173	30	53	13	1	6	30	.306	214	24	7	.971
1978—Shelby	W. Car.	C	106	352	53	88	10	0	9	40	.250	*532	*77	18	.971
1979—Tampa	Fla. St.	●C-1B	122	377	50	99	18	2	6	39	.263	684	119	●17	.979
1980—Waterbury	East.	C-1B	115	347	44	84	15	2	7	44	.242	621	81	11	.985
1981—Waterbury	East.	C	126	395	40	104	21	0	7	63	.263	594	*95	13	.982
1982—Indianapolis†	A. A.	C-1B	85	252	31	77	14	1	7	37	.306	409	39	12	.974
1983—Tucson	P. C.	C-1B	48	164	18	47	6	0	2	18	.287	159	21	6	.968
1983—Indianapolis‡	A. A.	C-1B	31	98	14	24	6	1	4	20	.245	187	16	3	.985
1983—Cincinnati§	Nat.	C	9	17	0	1	0	0	0	1	.059	28	3	0	1.000
1984—Denver	A. A.	C-1B-OF	74	198	24	55	9	3	4	29	.278	248	22	3	.989
1984—Chicago x	Amer.	C	12	11	1	4	1	0	1	4	.364	2	0	0	1.000
1985—Buffalo y	A. A.	3B-1B-C	127	409	50	122	12	0	16	56	.298	360	119	11	.978
1986—Iowa	A. A.	1B-C-3B	62	180	22	54	11	0	4	25	.300	233	20	3	.988
1986—Chicago z	Nat.	C-1B	3	9	0	1	1	0	0	2	.111	11	2	0	1.000
National League Totals—2 Years			12	26	0	2	1	0	0	3	.077	39	5	0	1.000
American League Totals—1 Year			12	11	1	4	1	0	1	4	.364	2	0	0	1.000
Major League Totals—3 Years			24	37	1	6	2	0	1	7	.162	41	5	0	1.000

Selected by Minnesota Twins' organization in 33rd round of free-agent draft, June 4, 1975.
Signed as free agent by Cincinnati Reds' organization, February 13, 1977.
†Loaned to Tucson (Houston Astros' organization), April 2, 1983; returned, June 27, 1983.
‡On disabled list, June 26 to July 22, 1983.
§Traded to Chicago White Sox for Infielder Fran Mullins, November 21, 1983.
xReleased, December 10, 1984; re-signed by Chicago White Sox' organization, January 14, 1985.
yGranted free agency, October 15, 1985; signed by Chicago Cubs, January 15, 1986.
zOn disabled list, May 2 to July 10, 1986; included rehabilitation disability assignment to Iowa, June 30 to July 10, 1986.

MARK THOMAS CIARDI

Name pronounced See-r-dee.

Born August 19, 1961, at New Brunswick, N.J.
Height, 6.00. Weight, 180.
Throws and bats righthanded.
Attended University of Maryland, College Park, Md.

Year Club	League	G.	IP.	W.	L.	Pct.	H.	R.	ER.	SO.	BB.	ERA.
1983—Paintsville	Ap'lachian	13	69⅔	7	2	.778	62	33	25	80	17	3.23
1984—Beloit	Midwest	25	176	10	7	.588	160	76	59	*166	41	3.02
1985—Stockton	California	18	129⅓	10	6	.625	116	59	53	119	39	3.69
1985—El Paso	Texas	10	67⅔	8	1	.889	55	27	20	50	13	2.66
1986—Vancouver	P. Coast	26	168⅓	9	8	.529	194	80	76	106	35	4.06

Selected by Milwaukee Brewers' organization in 27th round of free-agent draft, June 7, 1982.
Selected by Milwaukee Brewers' organization in 15th round of free-agent draft, June 6, 1983.

JOSEPH JOHN CIPOLLONI

Name pronounced Sip-uh-LOHN-ee.

(Joe)

Born August 12, 1960, at Philadelphia, Pa.
Height, 5.08. Weight, 180.
Throws and bats righthanded.
Attended Phoenix College, Phoenix, Ariz., and University of Arizona, Tucson, Ariz.

Led Carolina League catchers in double plays with 10 in 1983.

Year Club	League	Pos.	G.	AB.	R.	H.	2B.	3B.	HR.	RBI.	B.A.	PO.	A.	E.	F.A.
1981—Helena	Pion.	C	15	46	5	10	2	0	1	4	.217	85	14	2	.980
1982—Spartanburg	S. Atl.	C-3B	73	230	33	59	16	0	2	29	.257	422	64	12	.976
1983—Peninsula	Carol.	C	98	347	41	80	14	1	5	39	.231	625	76	14	.980
1984—Reading	East.	C	95	283	30	57	10	0	5	31	.201	440	61	10	.980
1985—Reading	East.	C	87	287	21	70	11	1	4	34	.244	437	67	7	.986
1986—Portland†	P. C.	C	10	31	4	6	0	0	1	2	.194	42	1	1	.977

Selected by Pittsburgh Pirates' organization in 25th round of free-agent draft, June 3, 1980.
Signed as free agent by Philadelphia Phillies' oganization, August 8, 1981.
†On disabled list, May 1, 1986 through remainder of season.

JAMES CLANCY

(Jim)

Born December 18, 1955, at Chicago, Ill.
Height, 6.04. Weight, 220.
Throws and bats righthanded.
Led American League pitchers in games started with 40 in 1982 and tied for lead with 36 in 1984.
Tied for Gulf Coast League lead in shutouts with 2 in 1974.

Year Club	League	G.	IP.	W.	L.	Pct.	H.	R.	ER.	SO.	BB.	ERA.
1974—Sarasota Rangers	Gulf Coast	9	53	3	3	.500	40	21	16	58	28	2.72
1975—Anderson	W. Carol.	23	148	6	13	.316	139	85	63	109	91	3.83
1976—San Antonio†‡	Texas	23	125	6	8	.429	133	94	*89	77	98	6.41

Year Club	League	G.	IP.	W.	L.	Pct.	H.	R.	ER.	SO.	BB.	ERA.
1977—Jersey City	Eastern	20	118	5	13	.278	116	87	64	99	75	4.88
1977—Toronto	American	13	77	4	9	.308	80	47	43	44	47	5.03
1978—Toronto	American	31	194	10	12	.455	199	96	88	106	91	4.08
1979—Toronto§	American	12	64	2	7	.222	65	44	39	33	31	5.48
1980—Toronto	American	34	251	13	16	.448	217	108	92	152	★128	3.30
1981—Toronto	American	22	125	6	12	.333	126	77	68	56	64	4.90
1982—Toronto	American	40	266⅔	16	14	.533	251	122	110	139	77	3.71
1983—Toronto	American	34	223	15	11	.577	238	115	97	99	61	3.91
1984—Toronto	American	36	219⅔	13	15	.464	249	★132	★125	118	88	5.12
1985—Toronto x	American	23	128⅔	9	6	.600	117	54	54	66	37	3.78
1985—Knoxville	Southern	2	8	1	0	1.000	7	3	3	2	2	3.38
1986—Toronto y	American	34	219⅓	14	14	.500	202	100	96	126	63	3.94
Major League Totals—10 Years		279	1768⅓	102	116	.468	1744	895	812	939	687	4.13

Selected by Texas Rangers' organization in 4th round of free-agent draft, June 5, 1974.

†On disabled list, June 15 to June 26, 1976.

‡Selected by Toronto Blue Jays from Texas Rangers in American League expansion draft, November 5, 1976.

§On disabled list, May 12 to July 4 and August 5, 1979 through remainder of season.

xOn disabled list, March 25 to April 30 and July 27 to September 2, 1985; included rehabilitation disability assignment to Knoxville, April 21 to April 30, 1985.

yGranted free agency, November 12, 1986.

CHAMPIONSHIP SERIES RECORD

Year Club	League	G.	IP.	W.	L.	Pct.	H.	R.	ER.	SO.	BB.	ERA.
1985—Toronto	American	1	1	0	1	.000	2	1	1	0	1	9.00

ALL-STAR GAME RECORD

Year League	IP.	W.	L.	Pct.	H.	R.	ER.	SO.	BB.	ERA.
1982—American	1	0	0	.000	0	0	0	0	0	0.00

BRYAN DONALD CLARK

Born July 12, 1956, at Madera, Calif.
Height, 6.02. Weight, 200.
Throws and bats lefthanded.
Attended Fresno City College, Fresno, Calif.

Major League saves: 1981 (2), 1985 (2). Total—4.
Led Carolina League in wild pitches with 24 in 1977 and 27 in 1979.
Led Western Carolinas League in wild pitches with 31 in 1976.
Led New York-Pennsylvania League in wild pitches with 24 in 1975.
Tied for American Association lead in shutouts with 2 in 1986.
Tied for Carolina League lead in shutouts with 3 in 1979.
Tied for Gulf Coast League lead in shutouts with 2 in 1974.

Year Club	League	G.	IP.	W.	L.	Pct.	H.	R.	ER.	SO.	BB.	ERA.
1974—Bradenton Pirates	Gulf Coast	11	62	4	6	.400	49	35	23	47	★40	3.34
1975—Charleston	W. Carol.	12	57	4	7	.364	56	48	34	38	67	5.37
1975—Niagara Falls	NYP	13	74	3	★10	.231	47	49	37	59	★71	4.50
1976—Charleston	W. Carol.	22	103	1	13	.071	97	87	70	79	104	6.12
1977—Salem	Carolina	26	125	5	★13	.278	135	105	66	108	105	4.75
1978—Charleston†	W. Carol.	12	56	1	6	.143	55	53	38	44	55	6.11
1978—Bellingham	Northwest	2	4	0	0	.000	4	1	1	6	3	2.25
1978—Stockton	California	11	27	0	4	.000	30	32	22	18	39	7.33
1979—Alexandria	Carolina	23	167	●14	5	.737	124	57	49	116	★112	2.64
1980—Spokane	P. Coast	8	41	2	5	.286	43	35	24	19	37	5.27
1980—Lynn	Eastern	16	116	9	5	.643	102	49	40	93	50	3.10
1981—Seattle	American	29	93	2	5	.286	92	54	45	52	55	4.35
1982—Salt Lake City	P. Coast	4	5⅓	1	1	.500	5	6	6	2	5	10.13
1982—Seattle	American	37	114⅔	5	2	.714	104	44	35	70	58	2.75
1983—Seattle‡	American	41	162⅓	7	10	.412	160	82	71	76	72	3.94
1984—Syracuse	Int'national	6	34	3	1	.750	32	16	13	26	26	3.44
1984—Toronto§	American	20	45⅔	1	2	.333	66	33	30	21	22	5.91
1985—Maine	Int'national	4	18⅔	1	0	1.000	15	2	2	9	8	0.96
1985—Cleveland x	American	31	62⅔	3	4	.429	78	47	44	24	34	6.32
1986—Buffalo	Am. Assoc.	34	122	7	6	.538	124	54	44	85	54	3.25
1986—Chicago	American	5	8	0	0	.000	8	4	4	5	2	4.50
Major League Totals—6 Years		163	486⅓	18	23	.439	508	264	229	248	243	4.24

Selected by Pittsburgh Pirates' organization in 10th round of free-agent draft, June 5, 1974.

†Sold to Seattle Mariners' organization, June 12, 1978.

‡Traded to Toronto Blue Jays for Outfielder Barry Bonnell, December 9, 1983.

§Released, April 1, 1985; signed by Cleveland Indians' organization, April 15, 1985.

xReleased, November 12, 1985; signed by Buffalo (Chicago White Sox' organization), February 25, 1986.

DAVID EARL CLARK
(Dave)

Born September 3, 1962, at Tupelo, Miss.
Height, 6.02. Weight, 200.
Throws right and bats lefthanded.
Attended Jackson State University, Jackson, Miss.

Major League stolen bases: 1986 (1).

Named outfielder on THE SPORTING NEWS College Baseball All-America Team, 1983.

Year	Club	League	Pos.	G.	AB.	R.	H.	2B.	3B.	HR.	RBI.	B.A.	PO.	A.	E.	F.A.
1983—Waterloo		Midw.	OF	58	159	20	44	8	1	4	20	.277	37	4	1	.976
1984—Waterloo		Midw.	OF	110	363	74	112	16	3	15	63	.309	128	10	4	.972
1984—Buffalo		East.	OF	17	56	12	10	1	0	3	10	.179	23	2	1	.962
1985—Waterbury		East.	OF	132	463	75	140	24	7	12	64	.302	204	11	11	.951
1986—Maine		Int.	OF	106	355	56	99	17	2	19	58	.279	150	4	6	.963
1986—Cleveland		Amer.	OF	18	58	10	16	1	0	3	9	.276	26	0	0	1.000
Major League Totals—1 Year				18	58	10	16	1	0	3	9	.276	26	0	0	1.000

Selected by Cleveland Indians' organization in 1st round (11th player selected) of free-agent draft, June 6, 1983.

JACK ANTHONY CLARK

Born November 10, 1955, at New Brighton, Pa.
Height, 6.03.   Weight, 205.
Throws and bats righthanded.

Major League stolen bases: 1975 (1), 1976 (6), 1977 (12), 1978 (15), 1979 (11), 1980 (2), 1981 (1), 1982 (6), 1983 (5), 1984 (1), 1985 (1), 1986 (1). Total—62.
Led National League in game-winning RBIs with 18 in 1980 and tied for lead with 21 in 1982.
Tied for National League lead in double plays by outfielders with 5 in 1978, 7 in 1979 and 4 in 1981.
Led California League in total bases with 254 in 1974 and Texas League with 239 in 1975.
Led Texas League third basemen in putouts with 102, assists with 278, double plays with 29 and fielding percentage with .872 in 1975.
Named outfielder on THE SPORTING NEWS National League All-Star Team, 1978.
Named first baseman on THE SPORTING NEWS National League Silver Slugger team, 1985.

Year	Club	League	Pos.	G.	AB.	R.	H.	2B.	3B.	HR.	RBI.	B.A.	PO.	A.	E.	F.A.
1973—Great Falls		Pion.	OF-P-3B	65	234	46	75	20	1	9	54	.321	73	9	1	.988
1974—Fresno		Calif.	3B	131	495	88	156	23	9	19	★117	.315	100	204	★53	.852
1975—Lafayette		Texas	★3B-OF	126	466	94	141	25	2	●23	77	.303	107	279	★56	.873
1975—San Francisco		Nat.	OF-3B	8	17	3	4	0	0	0	2	.235	8	1	0	1.000
1976—Phoenix		P. C.	OF-3B	131	470	111	152	29	★16	17	86	.323	188	23	9	.959
1976—San Francisco		Nat.	OF	26	102	14	23	6	2	2	10	.225	71	3	1	.987
1977—San Francisco		Nat.	OF	136	413	64	104	17	4	13	51	.252	226	11	6	.975
1978—San Francisco		Nat.	OF	156	592	90	181	46	8	25	98	.306	320	16	6	.982
1979—San Francisco		Nat.	OF-3B	143	527	84	144	25	2	26	86	.273	262	13	5	.971
1980—San Francisco†		Nat.	OF	127	437	77	124	20	8	22	82	.284	229	7	8	.967
1981—San Francisco		Nat.	OF	99	385	60	103	19	2	17	53	.268	193	●14	4	.981
1982—San Francisco		Nat.	OF	157	563	90	154	30	3	27	103	.274	281	10	6	.980
1983—San Francisco		Nat.	OF-1B	135	492	82	132	25	0	20	66	.268	262	20	9	.969
1984—San Francisco‡§		Nat.	OF-1B	57	203	33	65	9	1	11	44	.320	120	9	2	.985
1985—St. Louis x		Nat.	★1B-OF	126	442	71	124	26	3	22	87	.281	1128	66	★14	.988
1986—St. Louis y		Nat.	1B	65	232	34	55	12	2	9	23	.237	623	35	3	.995
Major League Totals—12 Years				1235	4405	702	1213	235	35	194	705	.275	3723	205	64	.984

Selected by San Francisco Giants' organization in 13th round of free-agent draft, June 5, 1973.
†On disabled list, August 23 to September 8, 1980.
‡On disabled list, June 25 to September 5, 1984.
§Traded to St. Louis Cardinals for First Basemen David Green and Gary Rajsich, Pitcher Dave LaPoint and Shortstop Jose Gonzalez (Jose Uribe), February 1, 1985.
xOn disabled list, August 24 to September 8, 1985.
yOn disabled list, June 25, 1986 through remainder of season.

CHAMPIONSHIP SERIES RECORD

Tied Championship Series record for most hits, inning (2), October 13, 1985 (second inning).
Tied National League Championship Series records for most singles (7) and most bases on balls (5), six-game Series, 1985.

Year	Club	League	Pos.	G.	AB.	R.	H.	2B.	3B.	HR.	RBI.	B.A.	PO.	A.	E.	F.A.
1985—St. Louis		Nat.	1B	6	21	4	8	0	0	1	4	.381	55	0	0	1.000

WORLD SERIES RECORD

Year	Club	League	Pos.	G.	AB.	R.	H.	2B.	3B.	HR.	RBI.	B.A.	PO.	A.	E.	F.A.
1985—St. Louis		Nat.	1B	7	25	1	6	2	0	0	4	.240	49	4	0	1.000

ALL-STAR GAME RECORD

Year	League	Pos.	AB.	R.	H.	2B.	3B.	HR.	RBI.	B.A.	PO.	A.	E.	F.A.
1978—National		OF	1	0	0	0	0	0	0	.000	0	0	0	.000
1979—National		PH	1	0	0	0	0	0	0	.000	0	0	0	.000
1985—National		1B	1	0	0	0	0	0	0	.000	4	0	0	1.000
All-Star Game Totals—3 Years			3	0	0	0	0	0	0	.000	4	0	0	1.000

PITCHING RECORD

Year	Club	League	G.	IP.	W.	L.	Pct.	H.	R.	ER.	SO.	BB.	ERA.
1973—Great Falls		Pioneer	5	15	0	2	.000	24	24	10	17	19	6.00

WILLIAM NUSCHLER CLARK JR.

(Will)

Born March 17, 1964, at New Orleans, La.
Height, 6.02. Weight, 190.
Throws and bats lefthanded.
Received degree in petroleum engineering from Mississippi State University, Mississippi State, Miss.

Tied major league record by hitting home run in first major league at-bat, April 8, 1986.
Major League stolen bases: 1986 (4).
Named first baseman on THE SPORTING NEWS College Baseball All-America Team, 1985.
Member of 1984 U.S. Olympic baseball team.
Named designated hitter on THE SPORTING NEWS College Baseball All-America Team, 1984.

Year	Club	League	Pos.	G.	AB.	R.	H.	2B.	3B.	HR.	RBI.	B.A.	PO.	A.	E.	F.A.
1985—Fresno	Calif.	1B-OF	65	217	41	67	14	0	10	48	.309	523	51	6	.990
1986—San Francisco†	Nat.	1B	111	408	66	117	27	2	11	41	.287	942	72	11	.989
1986—Phoenix	P. C.	DH	6	20	3	5	0	0	0	1	.250	0	0	0	.000
Major League Totals—1 Year			111	408	66	117	27	2	11	41	.287	942	72	11	.989

Selected by Kansas City Royals' organization in 4th round of free-agent draft, June 7, 1982.
Selected by San Francisco Giants' organization in 1st round (second player selected) of free-agent draft, June 3, 1985.
†On disabled list, June 4 to July 24, 1986; included rehabilitation disability assignment to Phoenix, July 7 to July 24, 1986.

STANLEY MARTEN CLARKE
(Stan)

Born August 9, 1960, at Toledo, O.
Height, 6.01. Weight, 180.
Throws and bats lefthanded.
Attended University of Toledo, Toledo, O.

Led Pioneer League in balks with 6 and tied for lead in complete games with 6 in 1981.

Year	Club	League	G.	IP.	W.	L.	Pct.	H.	R.	ER.	SO.	BB.	ERA.
1981—Medicine Hat	Pioneer	17	94	8	4	.667	96	54	42	112	35	4.02
1982—Florence	S. Atlantic	50	95	6	4	.600	60	26	20	136	52	1.89
1982—Knoxville	Southern	11	16	0	1	.000	11	3	3	12	3	1.69
1983—Knoxville	Southern	26	43⅓	2	4	.333	30	18	12	51	20	2.49
1983—Toronto	American	10	11	1	1	.500	10	4	4	7	5	3.27
1983—Syracuse	Int'national	33	53	0	3	.000	39	26	17	58	34	2.89
1984—Syracuse†	Int'national	29	56⅔	2	3	.400	40	32	26	55	46	4.13
1985—Syracuse	Int'national	43	117⅔	●14	4	★.778	106	52	44	98	66	3.37
1985—Toronto	American	4	4	0	0	.000	3	2	2	2	2	4.50
1986—Syracuse	Int'national	31	138⅔	8	9	.471	138	68	60	64	57	3.89
1986—Toronto‡	American	10	12⅔	0	1	.000	18	13	13	9	10	9.24
Major League Totals—3 Years		24	27⅔	1	2	.333	31	19	19	18	17	6.18

Selected by Toronto Blue Jays' organization in 6th round of free-agent draft, June 8, 1981.
†On disabled list, June 6 to July 3 and August 23, 1984 through remainder of season.
‡Drafted by Seattle Mariners, December 9, 1986.

DANNY BRUCE CLAY

Born October 24, 1961, at Sun Valley, Ida.
Height, 6.01. Weight, 190.
Throws and bats righthanded.
Attended Los Angeles Pierce Junior College, Woodland Hills, Calif.,
and Loyola Marymount University, Los Angeles, Calif.

Tied for Appalachian League lead in shutouts with 2 in 1983.

Year	Club	League	G.	IP.	W.	L.	Pct.	H.	R.	ER.	SO.	BB.	ERA.
1983—Wisconsin Rapids	Midwest	4	21	0	4	.000	18	17	14	15	12	6.00
1983—Elizabethton	Ap'lachian	15	★97⅔	6	7	.462	82	47	34	80	42	3.13
1984—Kenosha	Midwest	26	171⅔	9	8	.529	146	73	52	96	64	2.73
1985—Orlando	Southern	31	190⅔	13	9	.591	★195	112	95	79	89	4.48
1986—Toledo	Int'national	29	151⅔	8	11	.421	147	92	●83	105	★93	4.93

Selected by San Francisco Giants' organization in 30th round of free-agent draft, June 3, 1980.
Signed as free agent by Minnesota Twins' organization, November 27, 1982.

MARK ALAN CLEAR

Born May 27, 1956, at Los Angeles, Calif.
Height, 6.04. Weight, 215.
Throws and bats righthanded.
Attended Mount San Antonio College, Walnut, Calif.
Nephew of Bob Clear, minor league pitcher, 1945 through 1955; minor league player-manager, 1956 through 1961; minor league manager, 1962 through 1973; scout with California Angels, 1974 and 1975; and coach with California Angels since 1976.

Major League saves: 1979 (14), 1980 (9), 1981 (9), 1982 (14), 1983 (4), 1984 (8), 1985 (3), 1986 (16). Total—77.
Led Appalachian League in hit batsmen with 11 in 1974.
Named American League Rookie Pitcher of the Year by THE SPORTING NEWS, 1979.

Year	Club	League	G.	IP.	W.	L.	Pct.	H.	R.	ER.	SO.	BB.	ERA.
1974—Pulaski†	Ap'lachian	14	51	0	7	.000	73	★69	49	38	43	8.65
1975—Idaho Falls	Pioneer	13	28	1	2	.333	24	14	6	29	30	1.93
1976—Quad Cities	Midwest	30	144	8	10	.444	135	84	63	109	111	3.94
1977—Quad Cities	Midwest	13	74	6	3	.667	64	47	40	48	50	4.86
1977—Salinas	California	13	44	1	4	.200	49	36	32	26	45	6.55
1978—Salinas	California	10	53	3	5	.375	51	38	32	55	40	5.43
1978—El Paso	Texas	31	52	4	2	.667	28	14	14	80	32	2.42
1979—California	American	52	109	11	5	.688	87	48	44	98	68	3.63

Year Club	League	G.	IP.	W.	L.	Pct.	H.	R.	ER.	SO.	BB.	ERA.
1980—California‡	American	58	106	11	11	.500	82	51	39	105	65	3.31
1981—Boston	American	34	77	8	3	.727	69	36	35	82	51	4.09
1982—Boston	American	55	105	14	9	.609	92	39	35	109	61	3.00
1983—Boston	American	48	96	4	5	.444	101	71	67	81	68	6.28
1984—Boston	American	47	67	8	3	.727	47	38	30	76	70	4.03
1985—Boston§	American	41	55⅔	1	3	.250	45	26	23	55	50	3.72
1986—Milwaukee	American	59	73⅔	5	5	.500	53	23	18	85	36	2.20
Major League Totals—8 Years		394	689⅓	62	44	.585	576	332	291	691	469	3.80

Selected by Philadelphia Phillies' organization in 8th round of free-agent draft, June 5, 1974.
†Released, April 2, 1975; signed by California Angels' organization, June 16, 1975.
‡Traded with Third Baseman Carney Lansford and Outfielder Rick Miller to Boston Red Sox for Shortstop Rick Burleson and Third Baseman Butch Hobson, December 10, 1980.
§Traded to Milwaukee Brewers for Infielder Ed Romero, December 11, 1985.

CHAMPIONSHIP SERIES RECORD

Year Club	League	G.	IP.	W.	L.	Pct.	H.	R.	ER.	SO.	BB.	ERA.
1979—California	American	1	5⅔	0	0	.000	4	3	3	3	2	4.76

ALL-STAR GAME RECORD

Year League	IP.	W.	L.	Pct.	H.	R.	ER.	SO.	BB.	ERA.
1979—American	2	0	0	.000	2	1	1	0	1	4.50

Member of American League All-Star Team in 1982; did not play.

WILLIAM ROGER CLEMENS

(Known by middle name.)
Born August 4, 1962, at Dayton, O.
Height, 6.04. Weight, 205.
Throws and bats righthanded.
Attended San Jacinto College (North), Houston, Tex.,
and University of Texas, Austin, Tex.

Established major league record for most strikeouts, nine-inning game (20), April 29, 1986.
Tied American League record for most consecutive strikeouts, game (8), April 29, 1986.
Named Major League Player of the Year by THE SPORTING NEWS, 1986.
Named American League Pitcher of the Year by THE SPORTING NEWS, 1986.
Won American League Cy Young Memorial Award, 1986.
Named American League Most Valuable Player by Baseball Writers' Association of America, 1986.
Named righthanded pitcher on THE SPORTING NEWS American League All-Star Team, 1986.

Year Club	League	G.	IP.	W.	L.	Pct.	H.	R.	ER.	SO.	BB.	ERA.
1983—Winter Haven	Florida St.	4	29	3	1	.750	22	4	4	36	0	1.24
1983—New Britain	Eastern	7	52	4	1	.800	31	8	8	59	12	1.38
1984—Pawtucket	Int'national	7	46⅔	2	3	.400	39	12	10	50	14	1.93
1984—Boston	American	21	133⅓	9	4	.692	146	67	64	126	29	4.32
1985—Boston†	American	15	98⅓	7	5	.583	83	38	36	74	37	3.29
1986—Boston	American	33	254	★24	4	★.857	179	77	70	238	67	★2.48
Major League Totals—3 Years		69	485⅔	40	13	.755	408	182	170	438	133	3.15

Selected by New York Mets' organization in 12th round of free-agent draft, June 8, 1981.
Selected by Boston Red Sox' organization in 1st round (19th player selected) of free-agent draft, June 6, 1983.
†On disabled list, July 8 to August 3 and August 21, 1985 through remainder of season.

CHAMPIONSHIP SERIES RECORD

Tied Championship Series record for most games started, Series (3), 1986.
Established American League Championship Series records for most innings pitched, seven-game Series (22⅔), 1986; most hits allowed, Series (22), 1986.
Tied American League Championship Series records for most runs (8) and earned runs (7) allowed, game, October 7, 1986.

Year Club	League	G.	IP.	W.	L.	Pct.	H.	R.	ER.	SO.	BB.	ERA.
1986—Boston	American	3	22⅔	1	1	.500	22	12	11	17	7	4.37

WORLD SERIES RECORD

Year Club	League	G.	IP.	W.	L.	Pct.	H.	R.	ER.	SO.	BB.	ERA.
1986—Boston	American	2	11⅓	0	0	.000	9	5	4	11	6	3.18

ALL-STAR GAME RECORD

Year League	IP.	W.	L.	Pct.	H.	R.	ER.	SO.	BB.	ERA.
1986—American	3	1	0	1.000	0	0	0	2	0	0.00

PATRICK BRIAN CLEMENTS

(Pat)

Born February 2, 1962, at McCloud, Calif.
Height, 6.00. Weight, 175.
Throws left and bats righthanded.
Attended University of California, Los Angeles, Calif.

Major League saves: 1985 (3), 1986 (2). Total—5.

Year Club	League	G.	IP.	W.	L.	Pct.	H.	R.	ER.	SO.	BB.	ERA.
1983—Peoria	Midwest	15	92⅓	4	7	.364	113	56	46	67	24	4.48
1984—Waterbury	Eastern	43	67	4	2	.667	59	28	20	44	29	2.69
1985—California†	American	41	62	5	0	1.000	47	23	23	19	25	3.34
1985—Pittsburgh	National	27	34⅓	0	2	.000	39	14	14	17	15	3.67
1986—Pittsburgh‡	National	65	61	0	4	.000	53	20	19	31	32	2.80
American League Totals—1 Year		41	62	5	0	1.000	47	23	23	19	25	3.34
National League Totals—2 Years		92	95⅓	0	6	.000	92	34	33	48	47	3.12
Major League Totals—2 Years		133	157⅓	5	6	.455	139	57	56	67	72	3.20

Selected by New York Yankees' organization in 32nd round of free-agent draft, June 3, 1980.
Selected by California Angels' organization in 4th round of free-agent draft, June 6, 1983.
†Traded with Outfielder Mike Brown and a player to be named later to Pittsburgh Pirates for Pitchers John Candelaria and Al Holland and Outfielder George Hendrick, August 2, 1985; Pittsburgh organization acquired Pitcher Bob Kipper to complete deal, August 16, 1985.
‡Traded with Pitchers Rick Rhoden and Cecilio Guante to New York Yankees for Pitchers Doug Drabek, Brian Fisher and Logan Easley, November 26, 1986.

STEWART WALKER CLIBURN
(Stu)

Born December 19, 1956, at Jackson, Miss.
Height, 6.00. Weight, 187.
Throws and bats righthanded.
Attended Delta State University, Cleveland, Miss.
Identical twin of Stan Cliburn, catcher in California Angels' organization.

Major League saves: 1985 (6).

Year Club	League	G.	IP.	W.	L.	Pct.	H.	R.	ER.	SO.	BB.	ERA.
1977—Salem	Carolina	15	97	8	5	.615	108	50	35	48	33	3.25
1978—Shreveport†	Texas	9	42	1	0	1.000	37	13	9	30	17	1.93
1979—Buffalo	Eastern	15	103	6	6	.500	110	50	37	62	43	3.23
1979—Portland‡	P. Coast	7	33	3	2	.600	43	19	18	17	17	4.91
1980—Buffalo§	Eastern	1	6	1	0	1.000	5	0	0	2	3	0.00
1980—Portland	P. Coast	17	82	2	9	.182	97	56	50	44	39	5.49
1981—Buffalo x	Eastern	28	85	5	8	.385	77	45	41	53	35	4.34
1981—Portland y	P. Coast	6	17	0	1	.000	32	18	18	7	6	9.53
1982—Holyoke	Eastern	22	103⅔	5	3	.625	91	48	41	78	42	3.56
1982—Spokane	P. Coast	8	38⅔	1	6	.143	51	37	33	28	17	7.68
1983—Nashua	Eastern	39	98⅔	6	7	.462	94	45	41	40	31	3.74
1984—Edmonton	P. Coast	45	75	7	7	.500	71	30	24	48	28	2.88
1984—California	American	1	2	0	0	.000	3	3	3	1	1	13.50
1985—Edmonton	P. Coast	2	3⅔	0	0	.000	3	0	0	2	0	0.00
1985—California	American	44	99	9	3	.750	87	25	23	48	26	2.09
1986—Edmonton z	P. Coast	20	23⅓	1	2	.333	36	18	18	17	7	6.94
Major League Totals—2 Years		45	101	9	3	.750	90	28	26	49	27	2.32

Selected by San Francisco Giants' organization in 16th round of free-agent draft, June 5, 1974.
Selected by Pittsburgh Pirates' organization in 4th round of free-agent draft, June 7, 1977.
†On disabled list, May 9 to May 24, May 26 to June 15 and July 2 to August 22, 1978.
‡On disabled list, July 22 to August 8, 1979.
§On disabled list, April 14 to April 26, 1980.
xOn disabled list, May 11 to May 27, 1981.
yReleased, April 8, 1982; signed by Holyoke (California Angels' organization), April 29, 1982.
zOn disabled list, April 22 to July 16, 1986.

BRYAN RICHARD CLUTTERBUCK

Born December 17, 1959, at Detroit, Mich.
Height, 6.04. Weight, 223.
Throws and bats righthanded.
Attended Eastern Michigan University, Ypsilanti, Mich.

Tied for Texas League lead in games started by pitchers with 27 in 1983 and 1984.
Tied for Midwest League lead in shutouts with 4 in 1982.

Year Club	League	G.	IP.	W.	L.	Pct.	H.	R.	ER.	SO.	BB.	ERA.
1981—Butte	Pioneer	6	16	1	1	.500	22	13	13	4	7	7.31
1982—Beloit	Midwest	26	173⅔	13	6	.684	165	84	70	138	56	3.63
1983—El Paso	Texas	27	166⅓	11	7	.611	204	118	96	86	78	5.19
1984—El Paso	Texas	27	179	10	9	.526	⋆198	⋆103	⋆79	112	52	3.97
1985—Vancouver	P. Coast	29	147⅔	11	7	.611	156	68	58	101	41	3.53
1986—Vancouver	P. Coast	17	115⅓	8	5	.615	121	60	59	63	30	4.60
1986—Milwaukee	American	20	56⅔	0	1	.000	68	32	27	38	16	4.29
Major League Totals—1 Year		20	56⅔	0	1	.000	68	32	27	38	16	4.29

Selected by Milwaukee Brewers' organization in 7th round of free-agent draft, June 8, 1981.

—DID YOU KNOW—

That Tony Perez collected 32 doubles, six triples, 19 home runs and 91 RBIs for the Cincinnati Reds in 1976 and then proceeded to match those numbers in 1977 for the Montreal Expos?

JAMES STANLEY COCANOWER
(Jaime)
Nickname pronounced HI-me.

Born February 14, 1957, at Balboa Heights, Canal Zone
Height, 6.04. Weight, 200.
Throws and bats righthanded.
Received bachelor of business administration degree in accounting
from Baylor University, Waco, Tex., in 1980.

Led California League in balks with 6 in 1980.
Named California League co-Most Valuable Player, 1980.

Year Club	League	G.	IP.	W.	L.	Pct.	H.	R.	ER.	SO.	BB.	ERA.
1978—Burlington†	Midwest						(Did not play)					
1979—Stockton‡	California	20	78	2	4	.333	73	42	36	36	45	4.15
1980—Stockton	California	27	●198	17	5	.773	143	74	48	132	105	2.18
1981—Vancouver	P. Coast	26	137	6	12	.333	144	95	86	78	102	5.65
1982—Vancouver	P. Coast	14	74	4	3	.571	81	49	40	32	59	4.86
1982—El Paso§	Texas	9	61⅓	3	1	.750	73	36	23	29	30	3.32
1983—Vancouver x	P. Coast	23	153⅓	10	10	.500	177	100	82	79	59	4.81
1983—Milwaukee	American	5	30	2	0	1.000	21	8	6	8	12	1.80
1984—Milwaukee	American	33	174⅔	8	16	.333	188	99	78	65	78	4.02
1985—Vancouver	P. Coast	9	62⅔	5	2	.714	59	27	22	19	23	3.16
1985—Milwaukee	American	24	116⅓	6	8	.429	122	72	56	44	73	4.33
1986—Milwaukee y	American	17	44⅔	0	1	.000	40	29	22	22	38	4.43
Major League Totals—4 Years		79	365⅔	16	25	.390	371	208	162	139	201	3.99

Signed as free agent by Milwaukee Brewers' organization, June 7, 1978.
†On disabled list, June 17 to September 27, 1978.
‡On temporary inactive list, August 16 to September 8, 1979.
§On temporary inactive list, June 30 to July 15, 1982.
xOn disabled list, July 15 to July 24, 1983.
yReleased, December 23, 1986.

DAVID CARTER COCHRANE
(Dave)

Born January 31, 1963, at Riverside, Calif.
Height, 6.02. Weight, 180.
Throws right and bats left and righthanded.
Attended California State University, Fullerton, Calif.

Led Texas League batters in strikeouts with 133 in 1984.
Led Carolina League in game-winning RBIs with 18 in 1983.
Led New York-Pennsylvania League batters in strikeouts with 117 and intentional bases on balls received with 7 in 1982.

Year Club	League	Pos.	G.	AB.	R.	H.	2B.	3B.	HR.	RBI.	B.A.	PO.	A.	E.	F.A.
1982—Little Falls	NYP	3B	70	269	51	81	16	2	22	62	.301	49	110	★29	.846
1983—Lynchburg	Carol.	3B	120	445	73	117	16	1	25	★102	.263	66	167	26	.900
1984—Jackson	Texas	3B-SS	129	454	66	121	29	3	22	77	.267	79	167	32	.885
1985—Jackson†‡§	Texas	SS	33	103	14	23	1	0	4	20	.223	39	87	14	.900
1986—Birmingham	South.	3B-SS	93	349	66	95	23	5	17	74	.272	82	201	36	.887
1986—Buffalo	A. A.	3B-SS-OF	38	124	15	28	7	0	6	16	.226	25	58	4	.954
1986—Chicago	Amer.	3B-SS	19	62	4	12	2	0	1	2	.194	10	31	6	.872
Major League Totals—1 Year			19	62	4	12	2	0	1	2	.194	10	31	6	.872

Selected by New York Mets' organization in 4th round of free-agent draft, June 8, 1981.
†On disabled list, May 25 to July 16, 1985.
‡Traded to Chicago White Sox' organization for Outfielder Tom Paciorek, July 16, 1985.
§On Glens Falls disabled list, July 16, 1985 through remainder of season.

ATLEE ALAN COCKRELL
(Known by middle name.)

Born December 5, 1962, at Joplin, Mo.
Height, 6.02. Weight, 210.
Throws and bats righthanded.
Attended University of Tennessee, Knoxville, Tenn.

Led Texas League batters in strikeouts with 137 in 1985 and 126 in 1986.
Received reported $100,000 bonus to sign with San Francisco Giants, 1984.
Named outfielder on THE SPORTING NEWS College Baseball All-America Team, 1984.

Year Club	League	Pos.	G.	AB.	R.	H.	2B.	3B.	HR.	RBI.	B.A.	PO.	A.	E.	F.A.
1984—Everett	N'west	OF	2	8	1	3	0	0	0	3	.375	6	0	0	1.000
1984—Fresno	Calif.	OF	61	214	20	46	6	0	1	32	.215	96	9	5	.955
1985—Shreveport	Texas	OF	126	455	53	115	25	3	11	68	.253	177	10	10	.949
1986—Shreveport	Texas	OF-1B	124	438	66	113	31	3	14	78	.258	203	5	7	.967

Selected by Toronto Blue Jays' organization in 8th round of free-agent draft, June 8, 1981.
Selected by San Francisco Giants' organization in 1st round (ninth player selected) of free-agent draft, June 4, 1984.

CHRISTOPHER ALLEN CODIROLI

Name pronounced Coda-RO-lee.

(Chris)

Born March 26, 1958, at Oxnard, Calif.
Height, 6.01. Weight, 160.
Throws and bats righthanded.
Attended San Jose City College, San Jose, Calif., and San Jose State University, San Jose, Calif.

Major League saves: 1983 (1), 1984 (1). Total—2.
Tied for American League lead in games started by pitchers with 37 in 1985.

Year Club	League	G.	IP.	W.	L.	Pct.	H.	R.	ER.	SO.	BB.	ERA.
1978—Lakeland	Florida St.	16	102	4	6	.400	93	44	37	72	40	3.26
1978—Montgomery	Southern	10	78	5	2	.714	60	20	17	57	24	1.96
1979—Montgomery†	Southern	8	49	2	3	.400	41	24	18	34	27	3.31
1980—Lakeland‡	Florida St.	9	50	1	1	.500	33	13	10	26	19	1.80
1980—Montgomery§	Southern	2	4	0	1	.000	6	7	6	1	4	13.50
1981—San Jose	California	14	35	3	2	.600	23	8	6	26	24	1.54
1981—West Haven	Eastern	21	50	3	2	.600	35	25	15	47	25	2.70
1982—West Haven x	Eastern	12	45	6	1	.857	37	14	12	45	19	2.40
1982—Tacoma	P. Coast	16	123⅓	10	3	*.769	100	36	26	85	21	*1.90
1982—Oakland	American	3	16⅔	1	2	.333	16	8	8	5	4	4.32
1983—Oakland	American	37	205⅔	12	12	.500	208	115	102	85	72	4.46
1984—Oakland	American	28	89⅓	6	4	.600	111	67	58	44	34	5.84
1984—Tacoma	P. Coast	9	57	2	1	.667	49	35	24	52	30	3.79
1985—Oakland	American	37	226	14	14	.500	228	125	112	111	78	4.46
1986—Oakland y	American	16	91⅔	5	8	.385	91	54	41	43	38	4.03
Major League Totals—5 Years		121	629⅓	38	40	.487	654	369	321	288	226	4.59

Selected by Detroit Tigers' organization in 1st round (11th player selected) of free-agent draft, January 10, 1978.
†On disabled list, May 25, 1979 through remainder of season.
‡On disabled list, April 11 to June 10, 1980.
§Released, April 3, 1981; signed by Oakland A's organization, April 14, 1981.
xOn disabled list, April 19 to April 29, 1982.
yOn disabled list, June 28, 1986 through remainder of season.

KEVIN REESE COFFMAN

Born January 19, 1965, at Austin, Tex.
Height, 6.02. Weight, 175.
Throws and bats righthanded.

Year Club	League	G.	IP.	W.	L.	Pct.	H.	R.	ER.	SO.	BB.	ERA.
1983—Bradenton Braves	Gulf Coast	6	28⅔	2	4	.333	27	29	21	25	39	6.59
1984—Anderson	S. Atlantic	7	32⅔	1	4	.200	37	23	17	23	26	4.68
1984—Pulaski	Ap'lachian	11	48	1	4	.200	41	26	22	41	33	4.13
1985—Durham†	Carolina	3	4⅓	0	1	.000	4	5	5	1	11	10.38
1985—Sumter‡	S. Atlantic	24	62⅔	1	3	.250	42	25	22	43	26	3.16
1986—Durham	Carolina	3	13⅓	1	2	.333	11	12	11	7	17	7.43
1986—Sumter	S. Atlantic	18	114⅓	10	3	.769	99	56	39	120	64	3.07
1986—Greenville	Southern	8	48⅔	3	4	.429	43	24	24	43	30	4.44

Selected by Atlanta Braves' organization in 11th round of free-agent draft, June 6, 1983.
†On disabled list, April 24 to May 4, 1985.
‡On disabled list, May 4 to May 28, 1985.

ALEXANDER COLE JR.

(Alex)

Born August 17, 1965, at Fayetteville, N.C.
Height, 6.02. Weight, 170.
Throws and bats lefthanded.
Attended Manatee Junior College, Bradenton, Fla.

Led Florida State League in caught stealing with 22 in 1986.
Led Appalachian League in stolen bases with 46 and caught stealing with 8 in 1985.
Led Appalachian League outfielders in total chances with 142 in 1985.

Year Club	League	Pos.	G.	AB.	R.	H.	2B.	3B.	HR.	RBI.	B.A.	PO.	A.	E.	F.A.
1985—Johnson City	Appal.	OF	66	232	*60	61	5	1	1	13	.263	*127	*12	3	.979
1986—St. Petersburg	Fla. St.	OF	74	286	76	98	9	1	0	26	.343	201	4	8	.962
1986—Louisville	A. A.	OF	63	200	25	50	2	4	1	16	.250	135	6	9	.940

Selected by Pittsburgh Pirates' organization in 11th round of free-agent draft, January 17, 1984.
Selected by St. Louis Cardinals' organization in 2nd round of free-agent draft, January 9, 1985.

WILLIAM RODGERS COLE

(Rodger)

Born March 21, 1961, at Ann Arbor, Mich.
Height, 5.07. Weight, 160.
Throws and bats righthanded.
Attended Cochise County Community College, Douglas, Ariz.,
and Wiley College, Marshall, Tex.

Year Club	League	G.	IP.	W.	L.	Pct.	H.	R.	ER.	SO.	BB.	ERA.
1982—Helena	Pioneer	13	86⅔	7	3	.700	76	43	31	69	27	3.22

Year Club	League	G.	IP.	W.	L.	Pct.	H.	R.	ER.	SO.	BB.	ERA.
1983—Peninsula	Carolina	25	167⅓	9	13	.409	173	91	72	105	73	3.87
1983—Reading	Eastern	1	7	1	0	1.000	4	0	0	3	0	0.00
1984—Reading	Eastern	10	63⅔	3	4	.429	64	26	14	38	21	1.98
1984—Portland	P. Coast	17	96⅓	3	5	.375	110	66	57	46	41	5.33
1985—Portland†‡§	P. Coast	40	86⅓	3	6	.333	101	57	45	47	50	4.69
1986—Indianapolis	Am. Assoc.	25	158⅔	12	4	.750	145	74	58	75	64	3.29

Selected by Philadelphia Phillies' organization in 27th round of free-agent draft, June 7, 1982.

†On disabled list, May 7 to June 1, 1985.

‡Traded with First Baseman Ronnie Gideon to New York Mets for Catcher Ronn Reynolds and Pitcher Jeff Bittiger, January 16, 1986.

§Traded to Montreal Expos for Outfielder Doug Frobel, April 5, 1986.

VINCENT MAURICE COLEMAN
(Vince)

Born September 22, 1961, at Jacksonville, Fla.
Height, 6.00. Weight, 170.
Throws right and bats left and righthanded.
Received degree in physical education from Florida A&M University, Tallahassee, Fla.
Cousin of Greg Coleman, punter with Minnesota Vikings.

Established major league records for most stolen bases (110) and most caught stealing (25), rookie season, 1985.
Tied major league records for most sacrifice flies, game (3), May 1, 1986; fewest errors by outfielder, season, for leader in errors (9), 1986.
Established National League record for most strikeouts by switch-hitter, season (115), 1985.
Major League stolen bases: 1985 (110), 1986 (107). Total—217.
Led National League in stolen bases with 107 in 1986.
Led National League in stolen bases with 110 and caught stealing with 25 in 1985.
Led American Association in stolen bases with 101 and caught stealing with 36 in 1984.
Led South Atlantic League in stolen bases with 145 and caught stealing with 31 in 1983.
Tied for Appalachian League lead in stolen bases with 43 in 1982.
Led American Association outfielders in total chances with 381 in 1984.
Named National League Rookie Player of the Year by THE SPORTING NEWS, 1985.
Named National League Rookie of the Year by Baseball Writers' Association of America, 1985.
Named South Atlantic League Most Valuable Player, 1983.

Year Club	League	Pos.	G.	AB.	R.	H.	2B.	3B.	HR.	RBI.	B.A.	PO.	A.	E.	F.A.
1982—Johnson City	Appal.	OF	58	212	40	53	2	1	0	16	.250	123	7	8	.942
1983—Macon	S. Atl.	OF	113	446	99	156	8	7	0	53	★.350	225	18	8	.968
1984—Louisville	A. A.	OF	152	★608	★97	156	21	7	4	48	.257	357	14	●10	.974
1985—Louisville	A. A.	OF	5	21	1	3	0	0	0	0	.143	8	0	0	1.000
1985—St. Louis	Nat.	OF	151	636	107	170	20	10	1	40	.267	305	16	7	.979
1986—St. Louis	Nat.	OF	154	600	94	139	13	8	0	29	.232	300	12	●9	.972
Major League Totals—2 Years			305	1236	201	309	33	18	1	69	.250	605	28	16	.975

Selected by Philadelphia Phillies' organization in 20th round of free-agent draft, June 8, 1981.
Selected by St. Louis Cardinals' organization in 10th round of free-agent draft, June 7, 1982.

CHAMPIONSHIP SERIES RECORD

Year Club	League	Pos.	G.	AB.	R.	H.	2B.	3B.	HR.	RBI.	B.A.	PO.	A.	E.	F.A.
1985—St. Louis	Nat.	OF	3	14	2	4	0	0	0	1	.286	8	0	0	1.000

DARNELL COLES

First name pronounced Darr-NELL.

Born June 2, 1962, at San Bernardino, Calif.
Height, 6.01. Weight, 185.
Throws and bats righthanded.
Attended Orange Coast College, Costa Mesa, Calif.

Major League stolen bases: 1984 (2), 1986 (6). Total—8.
Led Midwest League shortstops in double plays with 66 in 1981.

Year Club	League	Pos.	G.	AB.	R.	H.	2B.	3B.	HR.	RBI.	B.A.	PO.	A.	E.	F.A.
1980—Bellingham	N'west	SS	35	117	23	25	3	1	2	12	.214	37	80	★28	.807
1981—Wausau	Midw.	SS	111	354	53	97	20	3	9	48	.274	154	335	52	.904
1982—Bakersfield	Calif.	SS	136	482	91	146	24	4	11	55	.303	200	419	★73	.895
1983—Chattanooga	South.	SS	72	261	49	75	10	4	5	24	.287	131	232	30	.924
1983—Salt Lake City	P. C.	SS	61	234	43	74	12	5	10	41	.316	100	178	25	.917
1983—Seattle	Amer.	3B	27	92	9	26	7	0	1	6	.283	17	47	4	.941
1984—Salt Lake City†	P. C.	3B	69	242	57	77	22	3	14	68	.318	45	164	16	.929
1984—Seattle	Amer.	3B-OF	48	143	15	23	3	1	0	6	.161	31	63	8	.922
1985—Calgary‡	P. C.	3B-SS-OF	31	97	16	31	8	0	4	24	.320	16	49	5	.929
1985—Seattle§	Amer.	SS-3B-OF	27	59	8	14	4	0	1	5	.237	25	44	6	.920
1986—Detroit x	Amer.	3B-OF-SS	142	521	67	142	30	2	20	86	.273	111	242	23	.939
Major League Totals—4 Years			244	815	99	205	44	3	22	103	.252	184	396	41	.934

Selected by Seattle Mariners' organization in 1st round (sixth player selected) of free-agent draft, June 3, 1980.

†On Seattle disabled list, March 29 to April 24, 1984; included rehabilitation disability assignment to Salt Lake City, April 12 to April 24, 1984.

‡On disabled list, August 8 to September 9, 1985.

§Traded to Detroit Tigers for Pitcher Rich Monteleone, December 12, 1985.

xOn disabled list, June 16 to July 1, 1986.

DAVID S. COLLINS
(Dave)

Born October 20, 1952, at Rapid City, S. D.
Height, 5.10. Weight, 175.
Throws left and bats left and righthanded.
Attended Mesa Community College, Mesa, Ariz.

Major League stolen bases: 1975 (24), 1976 (32), 1977 (25), 1978 (7), 1979 (16), 1980 (79), 1981 (26), 1982 (13), 1983 (31), 1984 (60), 1985 (29), 1986 (27). Total—369.
Led Pioneer League outfielders in double plays with 3 in 1972.
Named Pioneer League Most Valuable Player, 1972.

Year Club	League	Pos.	G.	AB.	R.	H.	2B.	3B.	HR.	RBI.	B.A.	PO.	A.	E.	F.A.
1972—Idaho Falls	Pion.	★OF-1B	68	252	40	69	8	★8	1	27	.274	101	★11	3	.974
1973—Quad Cities†	Midw.	OF	110	387	61	100	15	7	4	49	.258	229	10	11	.956
1974—Salinas	Calif.	OF-1B	39	143	30	49	3	5	1	21	.343	109	0	5	.956
1974—El Paso	Texas	1B-OF	82	324	64	114	15	4	4	49	★.352	381	14	12	.971
1975—Salt Lake City	P. C.	OF	51	193	41	60	7	6	0	24	.311	58	2	1	.984
1975—California	Amer.	OF	93	319	41	85	13	4	3	29	.266	159	3	2	.988
1976—Salt Lake City	P. C.	OF	35	136	28	49	13	4	0	12	.360	50	3	2	.964
1976—California‡	Amer.	OF	99	365	45	96	12	1	4	28	.263	160	3	1	.994
1977—Seattle§	Amer.	OF	120	402	46	96	9	3	5	28	.239	124	6	2	.985
1978—Cincinnati	Nat.	OF	102	102	13	22	1	0	0	7	.216	30	1	1	.969
1979—Cincinnati	Nat.	OF-1B	122	396	59	126	16	4	3	35	.318	223	3	4	.983
1980—Cincinnati	Nat.	OF	144	551	94	167	20	4	3	35	.303	337	5	5	.986
1981—Cincinnati x	Nat.	OF	95	360	63	98	18	6	3	23	.272	167	4	4	.977
1982—New York y	Amer.	OF-1B	111	348	41	88	12	3	3	25	.253	498	28	7	.987
1983—Toronto z	Amer.	OF-1B	118	402	55	109	12	4	1	34	.271	270	9	3	.989
1984—Toronto a	Amer.	OF-1B	128	441	59	136	24	●15	2	44	.308	237	11	2	.992
1985—Oakland b	Amer.	OF	112	379	52	95	16	4	4	29	.251	221	1	5	.978
1986—Detroit c	Amer.	OF	124	419	44	113	18	2	1	27	.270	211	2	1	.995
National League Totals—4 Years			463	1409	229	413	55	14	9	100	.293	757	13	14	.982
American League Totals—8 Years			905	3075	383	818	116	36	23	244	.266	1880	63	23	.988
Major League Totals—12 Years			1368	4484	612	1231	171	50	32	344	.275	2637	76	37	.987

Selected by Cincinnati Reds' organization in 23rd round of free-agent draft, June 8, 1971.
Selected by Kansas City Royals' organization in secondary phase of free-agent draft, January 12, 1972.
Selected by California Angels' organization in secondary phase of free-agent draft, June 6, 1972.
†On disabled list, May 21 to May 31, 1973.
‡Selected by Seattle Mariners in special American League expansion draft, November 5, 1976.
§Traded to Cincinnati Reds for Pitcher Shane Rawley, December 9, 1977.
xGranted free agency, November 13, 1981; signed by New York Yankees, December 23, 1981.
yTraded with Pitcher Mike Morgan, First Baseman Fred McGriff and a reported $400,000 to Toronto Blue Jays for Pitcher Dale Murray and Outfielder-Catcher Tom Dodd, December 9, 1982.
zOn disabled list, June 4 to June 22, 1983.
aTraded with Shortstop Alfredo Griffin and cash to Oakland A's for Pitcher Bill Caudill, December 8, 1984.
bTraded to Detroit Tigers for Infielder Barbaro Garbey, November 13, 1985.
cReleased, October 16, 1986; signed by Montreal Expos, November 13, 1986.

CHAMPIONSHIP SERIES RECORD

Year Club	League	Pos.	G.	AB.	R.	H.	2B.	3B.	HR.	RBI.	B.A.	PO.	A.	E.	F.A.
1979—Cincinnati	Nat.	OF	3	14	0	5	1	0	0	1	.357	5	0	0	1.000

DAVID ISMAEL CONCEPCION (BONITEZ)

Name pronounced Con-sep-see-OHN.

(Dave)

Born June 17, 1948, at Ocumare de la Costa, Aragua, Venezuela.
Height, 6.01. Weight, 190.
Throws and bats righthanded.
Attended College Augustin Codazzi, Aragua, Venezuela.

Tied major league records for most stolen bases by pinch-runner, inning, (2), July 7, 1974 (1st game, 7th inning); most double plays by shortstop, game, (5), June 25, 1975.
Established National League record for fewest chances accepted by shortstop, season, 150 or more games (616), 1985.
Tied National League record for fewest double plays by shortstop, season, 150 or more games (64), 1985.
Major League stolen bases: 1970 (10), 1971 (9), 1972 (13), 1973 (22), 1974 (41), 1975 (33), 1976 (21), 1977 (29), 1978 (23), 1979 (19), 1980 (12), 1981 (4), 1982 (13), 1983 (14), 1984 (22), 1985 (16), 1986 (9). Total—314.
Led National League in game-winning RBIs with 14 in 1981.
Tied for National League lead in grounding into double plays with 21 in 1983.
Led National League shortstops in total chances with 805 in 1974 and 837 in 1976.
Tied for National League lead in double plays by shortstops with 102 in 1979.
Led Southern League in double plays with 64 in 1969.
Led Florida State League shortstops in fielding percentage with .953 in 1968.
Named shortstop on THE SPORTING NEWS National League All-Star Team, 1974, 1976, 1977 and 1981.
Named shortstop on THE SPORTING NEWS National League All-Star fielding team, 1977 through 1979.
Named shortstop on THE SPORTING NEWS National League Silver Slugger team, 1981 and 1982.

Year Club	League	Pos.	G.	AB.	R.	H.	2B.	3B.	HR.	RBI.	B.A.	PO.	A.	E.	F.A.
1968—Tampa	Fla. St.	SS-2B	120	329	47	77	11	1	0	22	.234	151	239	20	.951
1969—Asheville	South.	SS	96	340	47	100	11	5	1	37	.294	★157	★292	★29	★.939
1969—Indianapolis	A. A.	S-2-3-O	42	167	29	57	7	1	0	17	.341	76	128	9	.958

Year	Club	League	Pos.	G.	AB.	R.	H.	2B.	3B.	HR.	RBI.	B.A.	PO.	A.	E.	F.A.
1970—Cincinnati	Nat.		SS-2B	101	265	38	69	6	3	1	19	.260	144	247	22	.947
1971—Cincinnati†	Nat.		S-2-3-O	130	327	24	67	4	4	1	20	.205	182	310	13	.974
1972—Cincinnati	Nat.		SS-3B-2B	119	378	40	79	13	2	2	29	.209	197	372	19	.968
1973—Cincinnati‡	Nat.		SS-OF	89	328	39	94	18	3	8	46	.287	167	292	12	.975
1974—Cincinnati	Nat.		*SS-OF	160	594	70	167	25	1	14	82	.281	239	*536	30	.963
1975—Cincinnati	Nat.		SS-3B	140	507	62	139	23	1	5	49	.274	241	446	16	.977
1976—Cincinnati	Nat.		SS	152	576	74	162	28	7	9	69	.281	*304	*506	27	.968
1977—Cincinnati	Nat.		SS	156	572	59	155	26	3	8	64	.271	280	490	11	*.986
1978—Cincinnati	Nat.		SS	153	565	75	170	33	4	6	67	.301	255	459	23	.969
1979—Cincinnati	Nat.		SS	149	590	91	166	25	3	16	84	.281	284	495	27	.967
1980—Cincinnati	Nat.		SS-2B	156	622	72	162	31	8	5	77	.260	265	451	16	.978
1981—Cincinnati	Nat.		SS	106	421	57	129	28	0	5	67	.306	208	322	22	.960
1982—Cincinnati	Nat.		SS-1B-3B	147	572	48	164	25	4	5	53	.287	271	459	17	.977
1983—Cincinnati	Nat.		SS-3B-1B	143	528	54	123	22	0	1	47	.233	227	387	13	.979
1984—Cincinnati	Nat.		SS-3B-1B	154	531	46	130	26	1	4	58	.245	213	324	17	.969
1985—Cincinnati	Nat.		SS-3B	155	560	59	141	19	2	7	48	.252	214	405	24	.963
1986—Cincinnati§ x	Nat.		S-1-2-3	90	311	42	81	13	2	3	30	.260	153	223	10	.974
Major League Totals—17 Years				2300	8247	950	2198	365	48	100	909	.267	3844	6724	319	.971

Signed as free agent by Cincinnati Reds' organization, September 12, 1967.
†On disabled list March 21 to April 20, 1971.
‡On disabled list July 22, 1973 through remainder of season.
§On disabled list, July 11 to September 1, 1986.
xGranted free agency, November 12, 1986; re-signed by Reds, December 5, 1986.

CHAMPIONSHIP SERIES RECORD

Year	Club	League	Pos.	G.	AB.	R.	H.	2B.	3B.	HR.	RBI.	B.A.	PO.	A.	E.	F.A.
1970—Cincinnati	Nat.		PR-SS	3	0	0	0	0	0	0	0	.000	1	1	0	1.000
1972—Cincinnati	Nat.		PH-S-PR	3	2	0	0	0	0	0	0	.000	0	0	0	.000
1975—Cincinnati	Nat.		SS	3	11	2	5	0	0	1	1	.455	6	8	1	.933
1976—Cincinnati	Nat.		SS	3	10	4	2	1	0	0	0	.200	2	12	0	1.000
1979—Cincinnati	Nat.		SS	3	14	1	6	1	0	0	0	.429	3	14	0	1.000
Championship Series Totals—5 Years				15	37	7	13	2	0	1	1	.351	12	35	1	.979

WORLD SERIES RECORD

Tied World Series records for most sacrifice flies, total Series (3); fewest chances accepted by shortstop, game (0), October 16, 1975; one or more hits, each game, four-game Series, 1976.

Year	Club	League	Pos.	G.	AB.	R.	H.	2B.	3B.	HR.	RBI.	B.A.	PO.	A.	E.	F.A.
1970—Cincinnati	Nat.		SS	3	9	0	3	0	1	0	3	.333	2	2	0	1.000
1972—Cincinnati	Nat.		S-PR-PH	6	13	2	4	0	1	0	2	.308	4	11	1	.938
1975—Cincinnati	Nat.		SS	7	28	3	5	1	0	1	4	.179	12	22	1	.971
1976—Cincinnati	Nat.		SS	4	14	1	5	1	1	0	3	.357	6	11	1	.944
World Series Totals—4 Years				20	64	6	17	2	3	1	12	.266	24	46	3	.959

ALL STAR GAME RECORD

Year	League	Pos.	AB.	R.	H.	2B.	3B.	HR.	RBI.	B.A.	PO.	A.	E.	F.A.
1975—National		SS	2	0	1	0	0	0	0	.500	1	1	1	.667
1976—National		SS	2	0	1	0	0	0	0	.500	2	3	0	1.000
1977—National		SS	1	0	0	0	0	0	0	.000	1	1	0	1.000
1978—National		SS	0	1	0	0	0	0	0	.000	2	0	0	1.000
1980—National		SS	1	1	0	0	0	0	0	.000	2	0	0	1.000
1981—National		SS	3	0	0	0	0	0	0	.000	0	0	0	.000
1982—National		SS	3	1	1	0	0	1	2	.333	1	1	0	1.000
All-Star Game Totals—7 Years			12	3	3	0	0	1	2	.250	7	8	1	.938

Named to National League All-Star Team for 1973 game; replaced due to injury.
Named to National League All-Star Team for 1979 game; replaced due to injury by Larry Parrish.

ONIX CARDONA CONCEPCION (CARDONA)

Name pronounced Con-CEP-see-own.
Born October 5, 1958, at Dorado, Puerto Rico.
Height, 5.06. Weight, 180.
Throws and bats righthanded.

Major League stolen bases: 1982 (2), 1983 (10), 1984 (9), 1985 (4). Total—25.
Led California League shortstops in double plays with 85 in 1979.

Year	Club	League	Pos.	G.	AB.	R.	H.	2B.	3B.	HR.	RBI.	B.A.	PO.	A.	E.	F.A.
1976—Jacksonville	South.		2B-SS	5	13	1	4	0	0	0	4	.308	10	18	2	.933
1976—Sarasota Royals	Gulf C.		SS	18	47	13	11	3	0	0	4	.234	16	40	8	.875
1977—Sarasota Royals	Gulf C.		2B-SS-1B	28	59	7	11	1	0	0	0	.186	45	37	5	.943
1978—Fort Myers	Fla. St.		SS-2B	79	213	29	50	7	0	0	13	.235	120	223	24	.935
1979—Bakersfield	Calif.		SS	127	504	88	151	25	3	14	75	.300	*227	*454	*55	.925
1980—Jacksonville	South.		SS	74	273	48	88	13	3	12	44	.322	117	249	16	.958
1980—Omaha	A. A.		SS	58	210	22	59	9	3	4	34	.281	74	135	11	.950
1980—Kansas City	Amer.		SS	12	15	1	2	0	0	0	2	.133	5	10	3	.833
1981—Omaha	A. A.		SS	118	438	62	112	15	2	6	57	.256	126	211	23	.936
1981—Kansas City	Amer.		SS	2	0	0	0	0	0	0	0	.000	0	0	0	.000
1982—Kansas City†	Amer.		SS-2B	74	205	17	48	9	1	0	15	.234	92	168	11	.959
1983—Kansas City	Amer.		3B-2B-SS	80	219	22	53	11	3	0	20	.242	92	175	15	.947
1984—Kansas City‡	Amer.		SS-2B-3B	90	287	36	81	9	2	1	23	.282	116	295	11	.974

Year	Club	League	Pos.	G.	AB.	R.	H.	2B.	3B.	HR.	RBI.	B.A.	PO.	A.	E.	F.A.
1985—Kansas City§		Amer.	SS-2B	131	314	32	64	5	1	2	20	.204	127	370	21	.959
1986—Omaha xy		A. A.	SS-2B	57	183	14	52	6	2	0	20	.284	54	98	7	.956
Major League Totals—6 Years				389	1040	108	248	34	7	3	80	.238	432	1018	61	.960

Signed as free agent by Kansas City Royals' organization, March 10, 1976.
†On disabled list, April 2 to April 23, 1982.
‡On disabled list, June 21 to July 8 and August 11 to September 4, 1984.
§Released, April 1, 1986; re-signed by Royals' organization, May 15, 1986.
xOn Kansas City disabled list, May 15 to June 29, 1986; included rehabilitation disability assignment to Omaha, June 9 to June 29, 1986.
yReleased, October 28, 1986.

CHAMPIONSHIP SERIES RECORD

Year	Club	League	Pos.	G.	AB.	R.	H.	2B.	3B.	HR.	RBI.	B.A.	PO.	A.	E.	F.A.
1984—Kansas City		Amer.	SS	3	7	0	0	0	0	0	0	.000	0	6	1	.857
1985—Kansas City		Amer.	SS-PR	4	1	0	0	0	0	0	0	.000	2	4	0	1.000
Championship Series Totals—2 Years				7	8	0	0	0	0	0	0	.000	2	10	1	.923

WORLD SERIES RECORD

Year	Club	League	Pos.	G.	AB.	R.	H.	2B.	3B.	HR.	RBI.	B.A.	PO.	A.	E.	F.A.
1980—Kansas City		Amer.	PR	3	0	0	0	0	0	0	0	.000	0	0	0	.000
1985—Kansas City		Amer.	PR-SS	3	0	1	0	0	0	0	0	.000	0	2	0	1.000
World Series Totals—2 Years				6	0	1	0	0	0	0	0	.000	0	2	0	1.000

DAVID BRIAN CONE

Born January 2, 1963, at Kansas City, Mo.
Height, 6.01. Weight, 180.
Throws right and bats lefthanded.

Led Southern League in wild pitches with 27 in 1984.

Year	Club	League	G.	IP.	W.	L.	Pct.	H.	R.	ER.	SO.	BB.	ERA.
1981—Sarasota Royals-Blue		Gulf Coast	14	67	6	4	.600	52	24	19	45	33	2.55
1982—Charleston		S. Atlantic	16	104⅔	9	2	.818	84	38	24	87	47	2.06
1982—Fort Myers		Florida St.	10	72⅓	7	1	.875	56	21	17	57	25	2.12
1983—Jacksonville†		Southern					(Did not play)						
1984—Memphis		Southern	29	178⅔	8	12	.400	162	103	85	110	114	4.28
1985—Omaha		Am. Assoc.	28	158⅔	9	15	.375	157	90	82	115	★93	4.65
1986—Omaha		Am. Assoc.	39	71	8	4	.667	60	23	22	63	25	2.79
1986—Kansas City		American	11	22⅔	0	0	.000	29	14	14	21	13	5.56
Major League Totals—1 Year			11	22⅔	0	0	.000	29	14	14	21	13	5.56

Selected by Kansas City Royals' organization in 3rd round of free-agent draft, June 8, 1981.
†On disabled list, April 8, 1983 through entire season.

TIMOTHY JAMES CONROY
(Tim)

Born April 3, 1960, at Monroeville, Pa.
Height, 5.11. Weight, 185.
Throws and bats lefthanded.

Pitched seven-inning, 1-0 no-hit victory against Tucson, May 14, 1985 (first game).
Led Eastern League in wild pitches with 22 in 1979 and tied for lead with 16 in 1980.

Year	Club	League	G.	IP.	W.	L.	Pct.	H.	R.	ER.	SO.	BB.	ERA.
1978—Oakland		American	2	5	0	0	.000	3	6	4	0	9	7.20
1978—Vancouver†		P. Coast	3	9	0	1	.000	13	16	16	3	10	16.00
1979—Waterbury		Eastern	25	138	7	●14	.333	115	95	80	106	★119	5.22
1980—West Haven		Eastern	25	147	8	14	.364	160	119	101	72	93	6.18
1981—West Haven		Eastern	14	57	2	6	.250	59	50	38	51	43	6.00
1981—Modesto		California	8	39	1	3	.250	50	37	34	46	23	7.85
1982—Modesto		California	27	171⅔	15	4	.789	139	59	43	★184	62	2.25
1982—Oakland		American	5	25⅓	2	2	.500	20	13	10	17	18	3.55
1983—Oakland		American	39	162⅓	7	10	.412	141	89	71	112	98	3.94
1984—Oakland		American	38	93	1	6	.143	82	58	54	69	63	5.23
1985—Oakland		American	16	25⅓	0	1	.000	22	15	12	8	15	4.26
1985—Tacoma‡		P. Coast	22	129⅓	11	3	.786	106	52	47	166	71	3.27
1986—St. Louis§		National	25	115⅓	5	11	.313	122	72	67	79	56	5.23
1986—Louisville		Am. Assoc.	2	8	1	0	1.000	6	2	2	6	6	2.25
National League Totals—1 Year			25	115⅓	5	11	.313	122	72	67	79	56	5.23
American League Totals—5 Years			100	311	10	19	.345	268	181	151	206	203	4.37
Major League Totals—6 Years			125	426⅓	15	30	.333	390	253	218	285	259	4.60

Selected by Oakland A's organization in 1st round (20th player selected) of free-agent draft, June 6, 1978.
†On disabled list, July 16 to September 1, 1978.
‡Traded with Catcher Mike Heath to St. Louis Cardinals for Pitcher Joaquin Andujar, December 10, 1985.
§On disabled list, March 24 to April 17 and May 26 to July 8, 1986; included rehabilitation disability assignment to Louisville, June 27 to July 8, 1986.

MICHAEL HORACE COOK
(Mike)

Born August 14, 1963, at Charleston, S. C.
Height, 6.03. Weight, 200.
Throws and bats righthanded.
Attended University of South Carolina, Columbia, S. C.

Year	Club	League	G.	IP.	W.	L.	Pct.	H.	R.	ER.	SO.	BB.	ERA.
1985—Quad Cities†	Midwest		2	10	0	0	.000	6	3	2	10	7	1.80
1986—Midland	Texas		15	105⅓	4	6	.400	101	54	41	82	52	3.50
1986—California	American		5	9	0	2	.000	13	12	9	6	7	9.00
1986—Edmonton	P. Coast		9	55⅓	4	1	.800	49	42	33	35	24	5.37
Major League Totals—1 Year			5	9	0	2	.000	13	12	9	6	7	9.00

Selected by Philadelphia Phillies' organization in 6th round of free-agent draft, June 7, 1982.
Selected by California Angels' organization in 1st round (19th player selected) of free-agent draft, June 3, 1985.
†On temporary inactive list, July 9, 1985 through remainder of season.

CECIL CELESTER COOPER

Born December 20, 1949, at Brenham, Tex.
Height, 6.02. Weight, 190.
Throws and bats lefthanded.
Attended Blinn College, Brenham, Tex., and Prairie View A&M College, Prairie View, Tex.

Tied major league records for most strikeouts, extra-inning game (6), June 14, 1974 (15 innings); most at-bats, game (11), May 8, finished May 9, 1984 (25 innings).
Major League stolen bases: 1971 (1), 1973 (1), 1974 (2), 1975 (1), 1976 (7), 1977 (13), 1978 (3), 1979 (15), 1980 (17), 1981 (5), 1982 (2), 1983 (2), 1984 (8), 1985 (10), 1986 (1). Total—88.
Hit three home runs in a game, July 27, 1979.
Led American League in total bases with 335 in 1980.
Led American League first basemen in total chances with 1,068 in 1981 and 1,550 in 1983.
Led American League first basemen in double plays with 160 in 1980, 111 in 1981, 156 in 1982 and 144 in 1983.
Tied for American League lead in game-winning RBIs with 16 in 1979.
Named first baseman on THE SPORTING NEWS American League All-Star Team, 1979 through 1982.
Named first baseman on THE SPORTING NEWS American League All-Star fielding team, 1979 and 1980.
Named first baseman on THE SPORTING NEWS American League Silver Slugger team, 1980 through 1982.
Named Midwest League Player of the Year, 1970.

Year	Club	League	Pos.	G.	AB.	R.	H.	2B.	3B.	HR.	RBI.	B.A.	PO.	A.	E.	F.A.
1968—Jamestown	NYP	1B	26	84	16	38	6	0	0	6	.452	130	0	1	.992
1969—Greenville†	W. Car.	1B-OF	62	212	27	63	12	2	1	18	.297	434	32	8	.983
1970—Danville‡	Midw.	1B-OF	114	420	86	141	16	8	3	39	★.336	535	33	12	.979
1971—Winston-Salem	Carol.	1B	42	153	31	58	6	3	6	26	.379	359	21	5	.987
1971—Pawtucket	East.	1B-OF	98	367	55	126	21	2	10	60	.343	740	35	12	.985
1971—Boston	Amer.	1B	14	42	9	13	4	1	0	3	.310	82	3	1	.988
1972—Louisville	Int.	1B	134	515	86	★162	★31	9	10	78	.315	1102	78	★17	.986
1972—Boston	Amer.	1B	12	17	0	4	1	0	0	2	.235	19	0	0	1.000
1973—Pawtucket	Int.	1B	128	450	68	132	27	1	15	77	.293	1082	84	12	.990
1973—Boston	Amer.	1B	30	101	12	24	2	0	3	11	.238	227	17	4	.984
1974—Boston	Amer.	1B	121	414	55	114	24	1	8	43	.275	637	40	12	.983
1975—Boston	Amer.	1B	106	305	49	95	17	6	14	44	.311	197	20	1	.995
1976—Boston§	Amer.	1B	123	451	66	127	22	6	15	78	.282	600	42	4	.994
1977—Milwaukee	Amer.	1B	160	643	86	193	31	7	20	78	.300	1386	118	12	.992
1978—Milwaukee x	Amer.	1B	107	407	60	127	23	2	13	54	.312	842	66	11	.988
1979—Milwaukee	Amer.	1B	150	590	83	182	●44	1	24	106	.308	1323	78	10	.993
1980—Milwaukee	Amer.	1B	153	622	96	219	33	4	25	★122	.352	1336	★106	5	★.997
1981—Milwaukee	Amer.	1B	106	416	70	133	★35	1	12	60	.320	★987	72	●9	.992
1982—Milwaukee	Amer.	1B	155	654	104	205	38	3	32	121	.313	1428	98	5	.997
1983—Milwaukee	Amer.	1B	160	661	106	203	37	3	30	●126	.307	★1452	87	11	.993
1984—Milwaukee	Amer.	1B	148	603	63	166	28	3	11	67	.275	1061	98	10	.991
1985—Milwaukee	Amer.	1B	154	631	82	185	39	4	16	99	.293	1087	94	17	.986
1986—Milwaukee y	Amer.	1B	134	542	46	140	24	1	12	75	.258	697	61	9	.988
Major League Totals—16 Years			1833	7099	987	2130	402	47	235	1089	.300	13361	1000	121	.992

Selected by Boston Red Sox' organization in 27th round of free-agent draft, June 7, 1968.
†On temporary inactive list, April 13 to June 4, 1969.
‡Drafted by St. Louis Cardinals, November 30, 1970; returned, April 5, 1971.
§Traded to Milwaukee Brewers for First Baseman George Scott and Outfielder Bernie Carbo, December 6, 1976.
xOn disabled list, June 9 to July 21, 1978.
yOn disabled list, April 3 to April 18, 1986.

DIVISION SERIES RECORD

Year	Club	League	Pos.	G.	AB.	R.	H.	2B.	3B.	HR.	RBI.	B.A.	PO.	A.	E.	F.A.
1981—Milwaukee	Amer.	1B	5	18	1	4	0	0	0	3	.222	47	4	1	.981

CHAMPIONSHIP SERIES RECORD

Year	Club	League	Pos.	G.	AB.	R.	H.	2B.	3B.	HR.	RBI.	B.A.	PO.	A.	E.	F.A.
1975—Boston	Amer.	1B	3	10	0	4	2	0	0	1	.400	24	1	1	.962
1982—Milwaukee	Amer.	1B	5	20	1	3	2	0	0	4	.150	37	3	2	.952
Championship Series Totals—2 Years			8	30	1	7	4	0	0	5	.233	61	4	3	.956

Established World Series records for most assists by first baseman, seven-game Series (10), 1982; most chances accepted by first baseman, seven-game Series (81), 1982.

Year	Club	League	Pos.	G.	AB.	R.	H.	2B.	3B.	HR.	RBI.	B.A.	PO.	A.	E.	F.A.
1975—Boston		Amer.	1B-PH	5	19	0	1	1	0	0	1	.053	40	1	0	1.000
1982—Milwaukee		Amer.	1B	7	28	3	8	1	0	1	6	.286	71	10	1	.988
World Series Totals—2 Years				12	47	3	9	2	0	1	7	.191	111	11	1	.992

ALL-STAR GAME RECORD

Year	League	Pos.	AB.	R.	H.	2B.	3B.	HR.	RBI.	B.A.	PO.	A.	E.	F.A.
1979—American		PH	0	0	0	0	0	0	0	.000	0	0	0	.000
1980—American		1B	1	0	0	0	0	0	0	.000	6	0	0	1.000
1982—American		1B	2	0	1	0	0	0	0	.500	5	0	0	1.000
1983—American		PH	1	1	1	0	0	0	0	1.000	0	0	0	.000
1985—American		PH	0	0	0	0	0	0	0	.000	0	0	0	.000
All-Star Game Totals—5 Years			4	1	2	0	0	0	0	.500	11	0	0	1.000

JOSE MANUEL CORA
(Joey)

Born May 14, 1965, at Cuguas, Puerto Rico.
Height, 5.08. Weight, 150.
Throws right and bats left and righthanded.
Attended Vanderbilt University, Nashville, Tenn.

Year	Club	League	Pos.	G.	AB.	R.	H.	2B.	3B.	HR.	RBI.	B.A.	PO.	A.	E.	F.A.
1985—Spokane		N'west	2B	43	170	48	55	11	2	3	26	.324	92	123	9	.960
1986—Beaumont		Texas	2B-SS	81	315	54	96	5	5	3	41	.305	217	267	19	.962

Selected by San Diego Padres' organization in 1st round (23rd player selected) of free-agent draft, June 3, 1985.

CHARLES DEAN CORBELL JR.
(Charlie)

Born November 30, 1960, at Baytown, Tex.
Height, 6.01. Weight, 180.
Throws and bats righthanded.
Attended Blinn College, Brenham, Tex., and University of Arkansas, Fayetteville, Ark.

Led Texas League in shutouts with 5 and tied for lead in complete games with 8 in 1986.
Tied for California League lead in shutouts with 3 in 1985.

Year	Club	League	G.	IP.	W.	L.	Pct.	H.	R.	ER.	SO.	BB.	ERA.
1983—Great Falls		Pioneer	8	54⅓	3	3	.500	47	23	18	43	14	2.98
1983—Clinton		Midwest	6	31⅓	0	2	.000	38	22	17	23	11	4.88
1984—Clinton		Midwest	25	177	9	11	.450	148	71	52	101	52	2.64
1985—Fresno		California	26	181⅓	*17	4	*.810	174	77	65	89	61	3.23
1986—Shreveport†		Texas	26	*176⅔	11	6	.647	163	67	58	69	36	2.95

Selected by Chicago White Sox' organization in 8th round of free-agent draft, January 13, 1981.
Selected by San Francisco Giants' organization in 21st round of free-agent draft, June 6, 1983.
†Drafted by New York Mets, December 9, 1986.

DOUGLAS MITCHELL CORBETT
(Doug)

Born November 4, 1952, at Sarasota, Fla.
Height, 6.01. Weight, 185.
Throws and bats righthanded.
Received bachelor of science degree in physical education from University of Florida, Gainesville, Fla.

Established American League record for most saves by rookie (23), 1980.
Major League saves: 1980 (23), 1981 (17), 1982 (11), 1984 (4), 1986 (10). Total—65.
Led American League in games finished in relief with 45 and intentional bases on balls issued with 13 in 1981.
Led American Association in saves with 12 in 1978.
Led Gulf Coast League in intentional bases on balls issued with 3 in 1974.

Year	Club	League	G.	IP.	W.	L.	Pct.	H.	R.	ER.	SO.	BB.	ERA.
1974—Sarasota Royals†		Gulf Coast	11	42	4	2	.667	36	22	14	32	18	3.00
1975—Tampa		Florida St.	27	61	2	3	.400	42	11	10	48	21	1.48
1976—Tampa		Florida St.	45	85	10	5	.667	86	25	21	37	22	2.22
1977—Three Rivers		Eastern	39	88	4	5	.444	72	35	27	65	40	2.76
1978—Nashville		Southern	15	25	2	1	.667	18	11	7	33	7	2.52
1978—Indianapolis		Am. Assoc.	38	68	4	4	.500	54	22	15	46	17	1.99
1979—Indianapolis‡		Am. Assoc.	*69	110	3	6	.333	94	38	36	77	39	2.95
1980—Minnesota		American	73	136	8	6	.571	102	31	30	89	42	1.99
1981—Minnesota		American	*54	88	2	6	.250	80	29	25	60	34	2.56
1982—Minnesota§-California		American	43	79	1	9	.100	73	45	45	52	35	5.13
1982—Spokane		P. Coast	8	19	1	0	1.000	16	11	8	19	4	3.79
1983—California		American	11	17⅓	1	1	.500	26	10	7	18	4	3.63
1983—Edmonton		P. Coast	32	83	6	6	.500	95	55	43	61	29	4.66
1984—Edmonton		P. Coast	2	4⅔	1	0	1.000	2	0	0	5	0	0.00
1984—California		American	45	85	5	1	.833	76	22	20	48	30	2.12
1985—California x		American	30	46	3	3	.500	49	33	25	24	20	4.89

Year Club	League	G.	IP.	W.	L.	Pct.	H.	R.	ER.	SO.	BB.	ERA.
1985—Edmonton	P. Coast	1	3	0	1	.000	3	1	1	1	0	3.00
1986—California y	American	46	78⅔	4	2	.667	66	36	32	36	22	3.66
Major League Totals—7 Years		302	530	24	28	.462	472	206	184	327	187	3.12

Signed as free agent by Kansas City Royals' organization, June 11, 1974.
†Released, April 10, 1975; signed by Cincinnati Reds' organization, May 6, 1975.
‡Drafted by Minnesota Twins, December 3, 1979.
§Traded with Second Baseman Rob Wilfong to California Angels for Outfielder Tom Brunansky, Pitcher Mike Walters and cash, May 12, 1982.
xOn disabled list, July 25 to August 29, 1985; included rehabilitation disability assignment to Edmonton, August 27 to August 29, 1985.
yGranted free agency, November 12, 1986.

CHAMPIONSHIP SERIES RECORD

Year Club	League	G.	IP.	W.	L.	Pct.	H.	R.	ER.	SO.	BB.	ERA.
1986—California	American	3	6⅔	1	0	1.000	9	4	4	2	2	5.40

ALL-STAR GAME RECORD

Member of American League All-Star team in 1981; did not play.

TIMOTHY MICHAEL CORCORAN
(Tim)

Born March 19, 1953, at Glendale, Calif.
Height, 5.11. Weight, 180.
Throws and bats lefthanded.
Attended Mount San Antonio Junior College, Walnut, Calif. and California
State University, Los Angeles, Calif.
Brother of Pat Corcoran, infielder in Oakland A's organization, 1976 through 1978.

Major League stolen bases: 1978 (3), 1979 (1). Total—4.

Year Club	League	Pos.	G.	AB.	R.	H.	2B.	3B.	HR.	RBI.	B.A.	PO.	A.	E.	F.A.
1974—Bristol	Appal.	OF	27	92	20	34	6	0	3	25	.370	32	0	0	1.000
1974—Lakeland	Fla. St.	OF	36	126	15	34	1	3	1	16	.270	71	3	1	.987
1975—Montgomery	South.	OF-1B	122	388	42	95	20	3	3	.245	60	.245	283	21	4	.987
1976—Montgomery	South.	OF-1B	129	437	66	135	25	5	5	60	.309	607	49	5	.992
1977—Evansville	A. A.	1B-OF-P	39	136	27	47	11	3	7	33	.346	303	21	8	.976
1977—Detroit	Amer.	OF	55	103	13	29	3	0	3	15	.282	38	0	0	1.000
1978—Detroit	Amer.	OF	116	324	37	86	13	1	1	27	.265	186	6	3	.985
1979—Evansville	A. A.	OF-1B	87	287	40	97	15	0	4	50	.338	292	23	2	.994
1979—Detroit	Amer.	OF-1B	18	22	4	5	1	0	0	6	.227	45	2	0	1.000
1980—Detroit	Amer.	1B-OF	84	153	20	44	7	1	3	18	.288	274	19	5	.983
1981—Evansville†‡	A. A.	1B-OF	106	336	48	100	17	1	8	63	.298	644	41	12	.983
1981—Minnesota§	Amer.	1B	22	51	4	9	3	0	0	4	.176	108	9	0	1.000
1982—Oklahoma City	A. A.	OF-1B	120	433	60	125	28	5	7	69	.289	330	11	9	.974
1983—Portland	P. C.	OF-1B	128	454	75	141	30	7	9	93	.311	437	32	6	.987
1983—Philadelphia	Nat.	1B	3	0	0	0	0	0	0	0	.000	4	0	0	1.000
1984—Philadelphia x	Nat.	1B-OF	102	208	30	71	13	1	5	36	.341	338	21	1	.997
1985—Philadelphia y	Nat.	1B-OF	103	182	11	39	6	1	0	22	.214	389	25	3	.993
1986—New York	Nat.	1B	6	7	1	0	0	0	0	0	.000	8	1	0	1.000
1986—Tidewater z	Int.	1B-OF	86	273	21	71	10	2	1	24	.260	515	34	1	.998
American League Totals—5 Years			295	653	78	173	27	2	7	70	.265	651	36	8	.988
National League Totals—4 Years			214	397	42	110	19	2	5	58	.277	739	47	4	.995
Major League Totals—9 Years			509	1050	120	283	46	4	12	128	.270	1390	83	12	.992

Signed as free agent by Detroit Tigers' organization, June 10, 1974.
†On disabled list, July 14 to July 24 and July 27 to August 10, 1981.
‡Traded to Minnesota Twins, September 4, 1981, completing deal in which Minnesota traded First Baseman-Outfielder Ron Jackson to Detroit Tigers for a player to be named later, August 23, 1981.
§Released, March 26, 1982; signed by Oklahoma City (Philadelphia Phillies' organization), April 13, 1982.
xOn disabled list, August 19 to September 3, 1984.
yReleased, December 22, 1985; signed by New York Mets' organization, March 4, 1986.
zReleased, June 9, 1986.

PITCHING RECORD

Year Club	League	G.	IP.	W.	L.	Pct.	H.	R.	ER.	SO.	BB.	ERA.
1977—Evansville	Am. Assoc.	1	3	0	0	.000	2	2	2	2	1	6.00
1983—Portland	P. Coast	1	1	0	0	.000	3	2	2	0	0	18.00

EDWIN JOSUE CORREA
(Ed)

Born April 29, 1966, at Hato Rey, Puerto Rico.
Height, 6.02. Weight, 190.
Throws and bats righthanded.

Year Club	League	G.	IP.	W.	L.	Pct.	H.	R.	ER.	SO.	BB.	ERA.
1982—Sarasota White Sox	Gulf Coast	10	59	5	2	.714	40	23	18	53	27	2.75
1983—Appleton†	Midwest	19	95	3	9	.250	81	59	47	87	61	4.45
1984—Appleton	Midwest	26	149⅓	10	6	.625	127	71	57	135	87	3.44
1985—Glens Falls	Eastern	8	40	1	5	.167	37	41	30	34	35	6.75

Year Club	League	G.	IP.	W.	L.	Pct.	H.	R.	ER.	SO.	BB.	ERA.
1985—Appleton	Midwest	18	139	13	3	●.813	93	45	39	128	56	2.53
1985—Chicago‡	American	5	10⅓	1	0	1.000	11	9	8	10	11	6.97
1986—Texas	American	32	202⅓	12	14	.462	167	102	95	189	126	4.23
Major League Totals—2 Years		37	212⅔	13	14	.481	178	111	103	199	137	4.36

Signed as free agent by Chicago White Sox' organization, July 11, 1982.

†On disabled list, May 22 to June 12, 1983.

‡Traded with Infielder Scott Fletcher and a player to be named later to Texas Rangers for Infielder Wayne Tolleson and Pitcher Dave Schmidt, November 25, 1985; Texas acquired Infielder Jose Mota to complete deal, December 12, 1985.

HENRY COTTO (SUAREZ)

Name pronounced KOTT-oh.

Born January 5, 1961, at New York, N. Y.
Height, 6.02. Weight, 180.
Throws and bats righthanded.

Major League stolen bases: 1984 (9), 1985 (1), 1986 (3). Total—13.
Led Texas League in stolen bases with 52 in 1982.
Tied for American Association lead in caught stealing with 17 in 1983.
Led Texas League outfielders in total chances with 333 in 1982.
Tied for International League lead in double plays by outfielders with 3 in 1986.

Year Club	League	Pos.	G.	AB.	R.	H.	2B.	3B.	HR.	RBI.	B.A.	PO.	A.	E.	F.A.
1980—Sarasota Cubs	Gulf C.	OF	43	166	24	47	7	5	0	30	.283	93	6	3	.971
1980—Quad Cities	Midw.	OF	19	78	9	22	1	1	0	5	.282	27	2	4	.879
1981—Quad Cities	Midw.	OF	128	493	80	144	15	6	1	46	.292	249	★23	13	.954
1982—Midland	Texas	OF	130	524	103	161	12	5	1	36	.307	★310	16	7	.979
1983—Iowa†	A. A.	OF	104	426	52	111	7	10	0	35	.261	253	8	7	.974
1984—Chicago	Nat.	OF	105	146	24	40	5	0	0	8	.274	117	3	2	.984
1984—Iowa‡	A. A.	OF	8	30	3	6	2	0	0	1	.200	12	3	0	1.000
1985—New York§	Amer.	OF	34	56	4	17	1	0	1	6	.304	41	2	1	.977
1985—Columbus	Int.	OF	75	272	38	70	16	2	7	36	.257	158	5	2	.988
1986—New York	Amer.	OF	35	80	11	17	3	0	1	6	.213	59	1	0	1.000
1986—Columbus	Int.	OF	97	359	45	89	17	6	7	48	.248	215	5	8	.965
National League Totals—1 Year			105	146	24	40	5	0	0	8	.274	117	3	2	.984
American League Totals—2 Years			69	136	15	34	4	0	2	12	.250	100	3	1	.990
Major League Totals—3 Years			174	282	39	74	9	0	2	20	.262	217	6	3	.987

Signed as free agent by Chicago Cubs' organization, June 7, 1980.

†On disabled list, May 10 to May 30, 1983.

‡Traded with Catcher Ron Hassey and Pitchers Rich Bordi and Porfi Altamirano to New York Yankees for Pitcher Ray Fontenot and Outfielder Brian Dayett, December 4, 1984.

§On disabled list, May 25 to July 5, 1985; included rehabilitation disability assignment to Columbus, June 19 to July 5, 1985.

CHAMPIONSHIP SERIES RECORD

Year Club	League	Pos.	G.	AB.	R.	H.	2B.	3B.	HR.	RBI.	B.A.	PO.	A.	E.	F.A.
1984—Chicago	Nat.	OF-PR	3	1	1	1	0	0	0	0	1.000	2	0	0	1.000

ALFRED EDWARD COWENS JR.

(Al)

Born October 25, 1951, at Los Angeles, Calif.
Height, 6.02. Weight, 205.
Throws and bats righthanded.

Major League stolen bases: 1974 (5), 1975 (12), 1976 (23), 1977 (16), 1978 (14), 1979 (10), 1980 (6), 1981 (3), 1982 (11), 1983 (10), 1984 (9), 1986 (1). Total—120.
Named outfielder on THE SPORTING NEWS American League All-Star fielding team, 1977.
Named Southern League Player of the Year, 1973.

Year Club	League	Pos.	G.	AB.	R.	H.	2B.	3B.	HR.	RBI.	B.A.	PO.	A.	E.	F.A.
1969—Kingsport	Appal.	3B-SS-OF	51	180	30	53	6	1	2	30	.294	48	85	16	.893
1970—Billings	Pion.	OF-SS	62	237	45	67	9	5	7	47	.283	82	20	5	.953
1971—Waterloo	Midw.	3B-1B-OF	16	48	5	14	5	0	0	5	.292	37	12	3	.942
1971—San Jose	Calif.	OF	99	380	60	108	14	5	8	66	.284	138	14	3	★.981
1972—Waterloo	Midw.	3B	8	31	5	7	1	0	0	3	.226	5	17	2	.917
1972—San Jose	Calif.	OF-3B-1B	83	307	36	86	17	2	5	53	.280	134	53	10	.949
1972—Jacksonville	South.	OF	35	120	17	24	2	1	4	9	.200	48	5	2	.964
1973—Jacksonville	South.	OF-1B-3B	135	491	91	142	25	7	16	81	.289	444	52	18	.965
1974—Kansas City	Amer.	OF-3B	110	269	28	65	7	1	1	25	.242	151	14	3	.982
1975—Kansas City	Amer.	OF	120	328	44	91	13	8	4	42	.277	214	4	5	.978
1976—Kansas City	Amer.	OF	152	581	71	154	23	6	3	59	.265	329	13	5	.986
1977—Kansas City	Amer.	OF	●162	606	98	189	32	14	23	112	.312	307	14	6	.982
1978—Kansas City†	Amer.	OF-3B	132	485	63	133	24	8	5	63	.274	280	20	4	.987
1979—Kansas City‡§	Amer.	OF	136	516	69	152	18	7	9	73	.295	288	3	4	.986
1980—Calif.x-Det.	Amer.	OF	142	522	69	140	20	3	6	59	.268	263	11	3	.989
1981—Detroit y	Amer.	OF	85	253	27	66	11	4	1	18	.261	166	3	1	.994
1982—Seattle z	Amer.	OF	146	560	72	151	39	8	20	78	.270	280	14	4	.987
1983—Seattle a	Amer.	OF	110	356	39	73	19	2	7	35	.205	124	7	2	.985
1984—Seattle	Amer.	OF	139	524	60	145	34	2	15	78	.277	228	8	3	.987

Year Club	League	Pos.	G.	AB.	R.	H.	2B.	3B.	HR.	RBI.	B.A.	PO.	A.	E.	F.A.
1985—Seattle b	Amer.	OF	122	452	59	120	32	5	14	69	.265	198	10	7	.967
1986—Seattle c	Amer.	OF	28	82	5	15	4	0	0	6	.183	31	2	1	.971
Major League Totals—13 Years			1584	5534	704	1494	276	68	108	717	.270	2859	123	48	.984

Selected by Kansas City Royals' organization in 84th round of free agent draft, June 5, 1969.
†On disabled list, June 29 to July 24, 1978.
‡On disabled list, May 9 to May 30, 1979.
§Traded with Shortstop Todd Cruz and a player to be named later to California Angels for First Baseman Willie Aikens and Shortstop Rance Mulliniks, December 6, 1979; California organization acquired Pitcher Craig Eaton to complete deal, April 1, 1980.
xTraded to Detroit Tigers for First Baseman Jason Thompson, May 27, 1980.
ySold to Seattle Mariners, March 28, 1982.
zGranted free agency, November 10, 1982; re-signed by Mariners, January 14, 1983.
aOn disabled list, July 23 to August 21, 1983.
bReleased, December 20, 1985; re-signed by Mariners, February 7, 1986.
cReleased, June 12, 1986.

CHAMPIONSHIP SERIES RECORD

Year Club	League	Pos.	G.	AB.	R.	H.	2B.	3B.	HR.	RBI.	B.A.	PO.	A.	E.	F.A.
1976—Kansas City	Amer.	OF	5	21	3	4	0	1	0	0	.190	15	0	0	1.000
1977—Kansas City	Amer.	OF	5	19	2	5	0	0	1	5	.263	14	0	0	1.000
1978—Kansas City	Amer.	OF	4	15	2	2	0	0	0	1	.133	5	0	0	1.000
Championship Series Totals—3 Years			14	55	7	11	0	1	1	6	.200	34	0	0	1.000

JOSEPH ALAN COWLEY

(Joe)

Born August 15, 1958, at Lexington, Ky.
Height, 6.05. Weight, 210.
Throws and bats righthanded.

Established American League record for most consecutive strikeouts at start of game (7), May 28, 1986.
Pitched 7-1 no-hit victory against California Angels, September 19, 1986.
Led International League in shutouts with 4 in 1983.
Led Western Carolinas League in hit batsmen with 19 and tied for lead in balks with 3 in 1978.
Tied for Southern League lead in hit batsmen with 13 in 1979.

Year Club	League	G.	IP.	W.	L.	Pct.	H.	R.	ER.	SO.	BB.	ERA.
1976—Bradenton Braves	Gulf Coast	5	13	0	4	.000	17	16	13	12	19	9.00
1977—Greenwood	W. Carol.	10	32	1	0	1.000	31	29	29	25	43	8.16
1977—Kingsport	Ap'lachian	14	70	6	5	.545	72	59	48	59	50	6.17
1978—Greenwood	W. Carol.	25	161	11	7	.611	133	85	*71	141	*113	3.97
1979—Savannah	Southern	25	144	7	9	.438	115	74	60	103	81	3.75
1980—Savannah†	Southern	4	12	1	3	.250	24	18	17	13	9	12.75
1980—Durham	Carolina	10	64	6	0	1.000	57	26	20	44	25	2.81
1981—Savannah	Southern	11	69	6	0	1.000	47	22	21	56	16	2.74
1981—Richmond	Int'national	18	45	3	2	.600	33	15	14	39	16	2.80
1982—Atlanta‡	National	17	52⅓	1	2	.333	53	27	26	27	16	4.47
1982—Richmond	Int'national	9	51⅓	4	2	.667	46	24	23	33	30	4.03
1983—Richmond§	Int'national	28	124⅔	9	7	.563	106	69	61	108	72	4.40
1984—Columbus	Int'national	17	113	10	3	.769	100	59	46	96	50	3.66
1984—New York	American	16	83⅓	9	2	.818	75	34	33	71	31	3.56
1985—New York x	American	30	159⅔	12	6	.667	132	75	70	97	85	3.95
1986—Chicago y	American	27	162⅓	11	11	.500	133	81	70	132	83	3.88
1986—Buffalo	Am. Assoc.	6	36⅓	1	3	.250	34	18	16	30	26	3.96
National League Totals—1 Year		17	52⅓	1	2	.333	53	27	26	27	16	4.47
American League Totals—3 Years		73	405⅓	32	19	.627	340	190	173	300	199	3.84
Major League Totals—4 Years		90	457⅔	33	21	.611	393	217	199	327	215	3.91

Signed as free agent by Atlanta Braves' organization, July 22, 1976.
†On disabled list, April 26 to July 3, 1980.
‡On disabled list, May 10 to June 12, 1982.
§Granted free agency, October 20, 1983; signed by New York Yankees, November 22, 1983.
xTraded with Catcher Ron Hassey to Chicago White Sox for Pitcher Britt Burns, Shortstop Mike Soper and Outfielder Glen Braxton, December 12, 1985.
yAppeared in one game as a pinch-runner.

DANNY BRADFORD COX

Born September 21, 1959, at Northhampton, England.
Height, 6.04. Weight, 230.
Throws and bats righthanded.
Attended Chattahoochee Valley Community College, Phenix City, Ala.,
and Troy State University, Troy, Ala.

Pitched 11-0 no-hit victory against Bristol, August 9, 1981.
Tied for National League lead in hit batsmen with 7 in 1984.
Led Appalachian League in complete games with 10 and shutouts with 4 in 1981.
Named Appalachian League Player of the Year, 1981.

Year Club	League	G.	IP.	W.	L.	Pct.	H.	R.	ER.	SO.	BB.	ERA.
1981—Johnson City	Ap'lachian	13	*109	9	4	.692	80	27	25	*87	36	*2.06
1982—Springfield	Midwest	15	84⅓	5	3	.625	82	46	24	68	29	2.56
1983—St. Petersburg†	Florida St.	5	32	2	2	.500	26	10	9	22	14	2.53

Year Club	League	G.	IP.	W.	L.	Pct.	H.	R.	ER.	SO.	BB.	ERA.
1983—Arkansas	Texas	11	86⅓	8	3	.727	60	31	22	73	24	2.29
1983—Louisville	Am. Assoc.	2	11	0	0	.000	10	3	3	8	0	2.45
1983—St. Louis	National	12	83	3	6	.333	92	38	30	36	23	3.25
1984—St. Louis	National	29	156⅓	9	11	.450	171	81	70	70	54	4.03
1984—Louisville	Am. Assoc.	6	42⅓	4	1	.800	34	16	10	34	7	2.13
1985—St. Louis	National	35	241	18	9	.667	226	91	77	131	64	2.88
1986—St. Louis‡	National	32	220	12	13	.480	189	85	71	108	60	2.90
Major League Totals—4 Years		108	700⅓	42	39	.519	678	295	248	345	201	3.19

Selected by St. Louis Cardinals' organization in 13th round of free-agent draft, June 8, 1981.

†On Arkansas disabled list, April 8 to April 21, 1983.

‡On disabled list, March 30 to April 24, 1986; included rehabilitation disability assignment to Louisville, April 17 to April 24, 1986.

CHAMPIONSHIP SERIES RECORD

Year Club	League	G.	IP.	W.	L.	Pct.	H.	R.	ER.	SO.	BB.	ERA.
1985—St. Louis	National	1	6	1	0	1.000	4	1	1	4	5	1.50

WORLD SERIES RECORD

Year Club	League	G.	IP.	W.	L.	Pct.	H.	R.	ER.	SO.	BB.	ERA.
1985—St. Louis	National	2	14	0	0	.000	14	2	2	13	4	1.29

RODNEY PAUL CRAIG

Born January 12, 1958, at Los Angeles, Calif.
Height, 6.01. Weight, 195.
Throws right and bats right and lefthanded.
Attended Jan Jacinto College, Pasadena, Tex.

Major League stolen bases: 1979 (1), 1980 (3), 1982 (3). Total—7.

Year Club	League	Pos.	G.	AB.	R.	H.	2B.	3B.	HR.	RBI.	B.A.	PO.	A.	E.	F.A.
1977—Bellingham	N'west	OF-3B	54	208	29	59	11	2	4	22	.284	63	6	5	.932
1978—Stockton	Calif.	OF	90	342	58	93	12	0	1	21	.272	121	10	7	.949
1979—Spokane	P. C.	OF	46	181	36	57	8	2	2	13	.315	113	2	1	.991
1979—San Jose	Calif.	OF	64	238	51	75	7	5	3	27	.315	54	1	2	.965
1979—Seattle	Amer.	OF	16	52	9	20	8	1	0	6	.385	24	0	2	.923
1980—Seattle†	Amer.	OF	70	240	30	57	15	1	3	20	.238	155	2	2	.987
1980—Spokane‡§	P. C.	OF	36	131	19	39	5	5	1	15	.298	58	1	1	.983
1981—Charleston x	Int.	OF	23	78	14	20	3	1	2	5	.256	38	0	1	.974
1982—Cleveland	Amer.	OF	49	65	7	15	2	0	0	1	.231	28	0	1	.966
1983—Charleston	Int.	OF	121	413	86	110	20	0	11	56	.266	270	4	8	.972
1984—Maine y	Int.	OF	122	416	71	111	16	0	14	63	.267	251	14	3	.989
1985—Tidewater z	Int.	OF	9	23	1	6	1	0	0	2	.261	16	0	0	1.000
1986—Buffalo	A. A.	OF	112	402	79	109	28	8	11	60	.271	208	6	6	.973
1986—Chicago a	Amer.	OF	10	10	3	2	0	0	0	0	.200	0	0	0	.000
Major League Totals—4 Years			145	367	49	94	25	2	3	27	.256	207	2	5	.977

Signed as free agent by Seattle Mariners' organization, May 20, 1977.

†On disabled list, June 12 to June 27, 1980.

‡On disabled list, July 10 to August 3, 1980.

§Traded to Cleveland Indians' organization for First Baseman Wayne Cage, March 26, 1981.

xOn disabled list, May 13 to September 4, 1981.

yReleased, January 9, 1985; signed by Tidewater (New York Mets' organization), August 25, 1985.

zGranted free agency, October 15, 1985; signed by Buffalo (Chicago White Sox' organization), January 16, 1986.

aGranted free agency, October 15, 1986.

STEVEN RAY CRAWFORD
(Steve)

Born April 29, 1958, at Pryor, Okla.
Height, 6.05. Weight, 225.
Throws and bats righthanded.
Attended Claremore Junior College, Claremore, Okla. and
Northeastern Oklahoma State University, Tahlequah, Okla.

Major League saves: 1984 (1), 1985 (12), 1986 (4). Total—17.
Led Carolina League pitchers in games started with 28 and complete games with 15 in 1979.
Tied for Carolina League lead in shutouts with 3 in 1979.

Year Club	League	G.	IP.	W.	L.	Pct.	H.	R.	ER.	SO.	BB.	ERA.
1978—Winston-Salem	Carolina	19	110	9	5	.643	109	53	42	60	48	3.44
1979—Winston-Salem	Carolina	29	★211	11	11	.500	★208	88	●69	127	67	2.94
1980—Bristol†	Eastern	24	177	9	7	.563	170	68	52	97	64	2.64
1980—Boston	American	6	32	2	0	1.000	41	14	13	10	8	3.66
1981—Boston	American	14	58	0	5	.000	69	38	32	29	18	4.97
1982—Boston‡	American	5	9	1	0	1.000	14	3	2	2	0	2.00
1982—Pawtucket	Int'national	10	46	1	4	.200	55	25	21	20	15	4.11
1983—Pawtucket§	Int'national	27	154⅔	8	11	.421	181	98	89	104	80	5.18
1984—Pawtucket	Int'national	7	18⅓	2	1	.667	11	10	4	8	9	1.96
1984—Boston	American	35	62	5	0	1.000	69	31	23	21	21	3.34
1985—Boston x	American	44	91	6	5	.545	103	47	38	58	28	3.76
1986—Boston y	American	40	57⅓	0	2	.000	69	29	25	32	19	3.92
1986—Pawtucket	Int'national	5	6	1	1	.500	10	4	4	2	1	6.00
Major League Totals—6 Years		144	309⅓	14	12	.538	365	162	133	152	94	3.87

Signed as free agent by Boston Red Sox' organization, May 6, 1978.

†On disabled list, April 14 to May 2, 1980.

‡On disabled list, April 1 to August 12, 1982; included rehabilitation disability assignment to Pawtucket, July 21 to August 9, 1982.

§On disabled list, July 26 to August 5, 1983.

xOn disabled list, May 7 to May 22 and June 23 to July 8, 1985.

yOn disabled list, July 18 to September 1, 1986; included rehabilitation disability assignment to Pawtucket, August 15 to September 1, 1986.

CHAMPIONSHIP SERIES RECORD

Year Club	League	G.	IP.	W.	L.	Pct.	H.	R.	ER.	SO.	BB.	ERA.
1986—Boston	American	1	1⅔	1	0	1.000	1	0	0	1	2	0.00

WORLD SERIES RECORD

Year Club	League	G.	IP.	W.	L.	Pct.	H.	R.	ER.	SO.	BB.	ERA.
1986—Boston	American	3	4⅓	1	0	1.000	5	3	3	4	0	6.23

JOSE CRUZ (DILAN)

Born August 8, 1947, at Arroyo, Puerto Rico.

Height, 6.00. Weight, 185.

Throws and bats lefthanded.

Brother of Hector Cruz, third baseman-outfielder with St. Louis, Chicago N.L., San Francisco and Cincinnati, 1973 and 1975 through 1982, and Yomiuri Giants of Japanese baseball, 1983; and Cirilo (Tommy) Cruz, outfielder with St. Louis Cardinals and Chicago White Sox, 1973 and 1977, and currently with Nippon Ham Fighters in Japanese baseball.

Tied major league record for fewest double plays by outfielder, season, 150 or more games (0), 1978.

Major League stolen bases: 1971 (6), 1972 (9), 1973 (10), 1974 (4), 1975 (6), 1976 (28), 1977 (44), 1978 (37), 1979 (36), 1980 (36), 1981 (5), 1982 (21), 1983 (30), 1984 (22), 1985 (16), 1986 (3). Total—313.

Led National League outfielders in double plays with 5 in 1972.

Tied for National League lead in sacrifice flies with 10 in 1977 and 1984.

Named outfielder on THE SPORTING NEWS National League All-Star Team, 1984.

Named outfielder on THE SPORTING NEWS National League Silver Slugger team, 1983 and 1984.

Led Texas League in total bases with 254 in 1970.

Year Club	League	Pos.	G.	AB.	R.	H.	2B.	3B.	HR.	RBI.	B.A.	PO.	A.	E.	F.A.
1967—St. Petersburg	Fla. St.	OF-1B	78	205	33	57	8	9	1	20	.278	113	5	7	.944
1968—Modesto	Calif.	OF-SS	133	504	101	144	24	10	13	53	.286	219	10	11	.954
1969—Arkansas†	Texas	OF	102	400	56	109	18	9	6	49	.273	235	16	9	.965
1970—Arkansas	Texas	OF	133	493	89	148	★29	7	21	90	.300	★276	10	12	.960
1970—St. Louis	Nat.	OF	6	17	2	6	1	0	0	1	.353	16	0	0	1.000
1971—Tulsa	A. A.	OF	67	254	56	83	15	7	15	49	.327	146	1	7	.955
1971—St. Louis	Nat.	OF	83	292	46	80	13	2	9	27	.274	197	2	5	.975
1972—St. Louis	Nat.	OF	117	332	33	78	14	4	2	23	.235	220	9	5	.979
1973—St. Louis	Nat.	OF	132	406	51	92	22	5	10	57	.227	276	2	6	.979
1974—St. Louis‡	Nat.	OF-1B	107	161	24	42	4	3	5	20	.261	81	2	2	.976
1975—Houston	Nat.	OF	120	315	44	81	15	2	9	49	.257	187	6	4	.980
1976—Houston	Nat.	OF	133	439	49	133	21	5	4	61	.303	265	10	8	.972
1977—Houston	Nat.	OF	157	579	87	173	31	10	17	87	.299	311	11	9	.973
1978—Houston	Nat.	OF-1B	153	565	79	178	34	9	10	83	.315	328	5	8	.977
1979—Houston	Nat.	OF	157	558	73	161	33	7	9	72	.289	320	7	14	.959
1980—Houston	Nat.	OF	160	612	79	185	29	7	11	91	.302	323	16	●11	.969
1981—Houston	Nat.	OF	107	409	53	109	16	5	13	55	.267	237	5	4	.984
1982—Houston	Nat.	OF	155	570	62	157	27	2	9	68	.275	340	9	★13	.964
1983—Houston	Nat.	OF	160	594	85	●189	28	8	14	92	.318	322	9	7	.979
1984—Houston	Nat.	OF	160	600	96	187	28	13	12	95	.312	310	11	8	.976
1985—Houston	Nat.	OF	141	544	69	163	34	4	9	79	.300	257	12	8	.971
1986—Houston§	Nat.	OF	141	479	48	133	22	4	10	72	.278	237	5	4	.984
Major League Totals—17 Years			2189	7472	980	2147	372	90	153	1032	.287	4227	121	116	.974

Signed as free agent by St. Louis Cardinals' organization, October 27, 1966.

†On disabled list, April 8 to May 12, 1969.

‡Sold to Houston Astros, October 24, 1974.

§On disabled list, March 30 to April 19, 1986.

DIVISION SERIES RECORD

Year Club	League	Pos.	G.	AB.	R.	H.	2B.	3B.	HR.	RBI.	B.A.	PO.	A.	E.	F.A.
1981—Houston	Nat.	OF	5	20	0	6	1	0	0	0	.300	15	0	1	.938

CHAMPIONSHIP SERIES RECORD

Established Championship Series record for most walks, five-game series (8), 1980.

Year Club	League	Pos.	G.	AB.	R.	H.	2B.	3B.	HR.	RBI.	B.A.	PO.	A.	E.	F.A.
1980—Houston	Nat.	OF	5	15	3	6	1	1	0	4	.400	19	0	0	1.000
1986—Houston	Nat.	OF	6	26	0	5	0	0	0	2	.192	11	0	0	1.000
Championship Series Totals—2 Years			11	41	3	11	1	1	0	6	.268	30	0	0	1.000

ALL-STAR GAME RECORD

Year League		Pos.	AB.	R.	H.	2B.	3B.	HR.	RBI.	B.A.	PO.	A.	E.	F.A.
1985—National		OF	1	0	0	0	0	0	0	.000	2	0	0	1.000

Member of National League All-Star Team in 1980; did not play.

JULIO LUIS CRUZ

Born December 2, 1954, at Brooklyn, N. Y.
Height, 5.09. Weight, 167.
Throws right and bats right and lefthanded.
Attended San Bernardino Valley College, San Bernardino, Calif.

Tied major league records for most chances accepted by second baseman, nine-inning game (18), June 7, 1981; most at-bats, game (11), May 8, finished May 9, 1984 (25 innings); longest errorless game by second baseman (25 innings), May 8, finished May 9, 1984.

Established American League record for most games played with two clubs, season (160), Seattle (61), Chicago (99), 1983.

Tied American League records for most consecutive stolen bases without caught stealing (32); most innings played by second baseman, game (25), May 8, finished May 9, 1984.

Major league stolen bases: 1977 (15), 1978 (59), 1979 (49), 1980 (45), 1981 (43), 1982 (46), 1983 (57), 1984 (14), 1985 (8), 1986 (7). Total—343.

Led American League second basemen in fielding percentage with .987 in 1978.

Led Pioneer League in stolen bases with 34, in being hit by pitch with 7 and tied for lead in caught stealing with 11 in 1974.

Tied for Pacific Coast League lead in sacrifice hits with 9 in 1977.

Tied for Midwest League lead in sacrifice hits with 11 in 1975.

Year	Club	League	Pos.	G.	AB.	R.	H.	2B.	3B.	HR.	RBI.	B.A.	PO.	A.	E.	F.A.
1974—Idaho Falls	Pioneer	2B-SS-3B	72	237	44	57	4	1	0	27	.241	137	185	22	.936
1975—Quad Cities	Midw.	2B	108	368	79	96	6	6	0	35	.261	228	259	14	.972
1976—Salinas	Calif.	2B	96	348	92	107	12	3	1	45	.307	234	314	10	*.982
1976—El Paso	Texas	2B	13	49	9	16	4	1	0	9	.327	23	21	0	1.000
1976—Salt Lake City†	P. C.	2B-3B-OF	20	69	11	17	2	2	0	6	.246	30	47	1	.987
1977—Hawaii	P. C.	2B	75	303	71	111	9	9	0	33	.366	189	237	7	.984
1977—Seattle	Amer.	2B	60	199	25	51	3	1	1	7	.256	114	171	5	.983
1978—Seattle	Amer.	2B-SS	147	550	77	129	14	1	1	25	.235	295	482	11	.986
1979—Seattle‡	Amer.	2B	107	414	70	112	16	2	1	29	.271	258	361	13	.979
1980—Seattle§	Amer.	2B	119	422	66	88	9	3	2	16	.209	269	355	11	.983
1981—Seattle	Amer.	2B-SS	94	352	57	90	12	3	2	24	.256	240	297	11	.980
1982—Seattle	Amer.	2B-SS-3B	154	549	83	133	22	5	8	49	.242	322	438	10	.987
1983—Sea. x-Chi. y	Amer.	2B	160	515	71	130	19	5	3	52	.252	344	471	14	.983
1984—Chicago	Amer.	2B	143	415	42	92	14	4	5	43	.222	273	452	18	.976
1985—Chicago z	Amer.	2B	91	234	28	46	2	3	0	15	.197	158	220	7	.982
1986—Chicago a	Amer.	2B	81	209	38	45	2	0	0	19	.215	132	205	5	.985
Major League Totals—10 Years			1156	3859	557	916	113	27	23	279	.237	2405	3452	105	.982

Signed as free agent by California Angels' organization, May 7, 1974.
†Selected by Seattle Mariners from California Angels in American League expansion draft, November 5, 1976.
‡On disabled list, June 5 to August 3, 1979.
§On disabled list, April 24 to May 9, 1980.
xTraded to Chicago White Sox for Second Baseman Tony Bernazard, June 15, 1983.
yGranted free agency, November 7, 1983; re-signed by White Sox, January 8, 1984.
zOn disabled list, May 17 to June 3, 1985.
aOn disabled list, April 8 to April 25 and September 8, 1986 through remainder of season.

CHAMPIONSHIP SERIES RECORD

Year	Club	League	Pos.	G.	AB.	R.	H.	2B.	3B.	HR.	RBI.	B.A.	PO.	A.	E.	F.A.
1983—Chicago	Amer.	2B	4	12	0	4	0	0	0	0	.333	10	14	0	1.000

STEPHEN T. CURRY

Born September 13, 1965, at Winter Park, Fla.
Height, 6.06. Weight, 195.
Throws and bats righthanded.
Attended Manatee Junior College, Bradenton, Fla.

Led Eastern League in complete games with 12 and tied for lead in balks with 5 in 1986.
Led Florida State League in balks with 11 in 1985.

Year	Club	League	G.	IP.	W.	L.	Pct.	H.	R.	ER.	SO.	BB.	ERA.
1984—Elmira	NYP	14	83⅓	6	4	.600	83	51	37	82	35	4.00
1985—Winter Haven	Florida St.	27	161	9	10	.474	157	75	66	81	63	3.69
1986—New Britain	Eastern	24	*177⅓	11	9	.550	163	66	55	94	76	2.79

Selected by Boston Red Sox' organization in 7th round of free-agent draft, June 4, 1984.

TY COWAN DABNEY

Born August 23, 1962, at San Diego, Calif.
Height, 6.00. Weight, 170.
Throws right and bats lefthanded.
Attended University of California, Riverside, Calif.

Named California League Most Valuable Player, 1986.

Year	Club	League	Pos.	G.	AB.	R.	H.	2B.	3B.	HR.	RBI.	B.A.	PO.	A.	E.	F.A.
1985—Everett	N'west	2B-3B	57	210	36	69	13	5	6	31	.329	61	114	9	.951
1986—Fresno	Calif.	3B-1B	121	446	75	153	*36	2	15	107	.343	135	110	24	.911
1986—Phoenix	P. C.	3B	11	36	5	12	3	1	1	4	.333	2	12	2	.875

Selected by California Angels' organization in 10th round of free-agent draft, January 12, 1982.
Selected by New York Yankees' organization in 50th round of free-agent draft, June 4, 1984.
Selected by San Francisco Giants' organization in 13th round of free-agent draft, June 3, 1985.

KALVOSKI DANIELS
(Kal)

Born August 20, 1963, at Vienna, Ga.
Height, 5.11. Weight, 185.
Throws right and bats lefthanded.
Attended Middle Georgia College, Cochran, Ga.

Major League stolen bases: 1986 (15).
Led Eastern League in slugging percentage with .525 in 1984.
Tied for Pioneer League lead in game-winning RBIs with 9 and stolen bases with 27 in 1982.

Year Club	League	Pos.	G.	AB.	R.	H.	2B.	3B.	HR.	RBI.	B.A.	PO.	A.	E.	F.A.
1982—Billings	Pion.	OF	67	240	43	88	19	4	3	38	.367	104	4	5	.956
1983—Cedar Rapids	Midw.	OF	101	342	51	86	14	5	5	28	.251	130	5	2	.985
1984—Vermont	East.	OF	122	415	81	130	29	4	17	62	.313	143	2	5	.967
1985—Denver†	A. A.	OF	76	285	59	86	12	9	15	43	.302	83	5	4	.957
1986—Cincinnati	Nat.	OF	74	181	34	58	10	4	6	23	.320	88	0	3	.967
1986—Denver†	A. A.	OF	42	132	33	49	12	2	8	32	.371	78	4	3	.965
Major League Totals—1 Year			74	181	34	58	10	4	6	23	.320	88	0	3	.967

Selected by New York Mets' organization in 3rd round of free-agent draft, January 12, 1982.
Selected by Cincinnati Reds' organization in secondary phase of free-agent draft, June 7, 1982.
†On disabled list, July 7, 1985 through remainder of season.

RONALD MAURICE DARLING JR.
(Ron)

Born August 19, 1960, at Honolulu, Hawaii.
Height, 6.03. Weight, 195.
Throws and bats righthanded.
Attended Yale University, New Haven, Conn.
Brother of Eddie Darling, first baseman in New York Yankees' organization, 1981 and 1982.
Tied National League record for fewest assists by pitcher, season, for leader in assists (47), 1985 and 1986.

Year Club	League	G.	IP.	W.	L.	Pct.	H.	R.	ER.	SO.	BB.	ERA.
1981—Tulsa†	Texas	13	71	4	2	.667	72	43	35	53	33	4.44
1982—Tidewater	Int'national	26	152	7	9	.438	143	76	63	114	95	3.73
1983—Tidewater	Int'national	27	159	10	9	.526	137	83	71	107	102	4.02
1983—New York	National	5	35⅓	1	3	.250	31	11	11	23	17	2.80
1984—New York	National	33	205⅔	12	9	.571	179	97	87	136	104	3.81
1985—New York	National	36	248	16	6	.727	214	93	80	167	*114	2.90
1986—New York	National	34	237	15	6	.714	203	84	74	184	81	2.81
Major League Totals—4 Years		108	726	44	24	.647	627	285	252	510	316	3.12

Selected by Texas Rangers' organization in 1st round (ninth player selected) of free-agent draft, June 8, 1981.
†Traded with Pitcher Walt Terrell to New York Mets' organization for Outfielder Lee Mazzilli, April 1, 1982.

CHAMPIONSHIP SERIES RECORD

Year Club	League	G.	IP.	W.	L.	Pct.	H.	R.	ER.	SO.	BB.	ERA.
1986—New York	National	1	5	0	0	.000	6	4	4	5	2	7.20

WORLD SERIES RECORD

Tied World Series records for most consecutive home runs allowed, inning (2), October 27, 1986 (second inning);
most wild pitches, game (2), October 18, 1986.

Year Club	League	G.	IP.	W.	L.	Pct.	H.	R.	ER.	SO.	BB.	ERA.
1986—New York	National	3	17⅔	1	1	.500	13	4	3	12	10	1.53

ALL-STAR GAME RECORD

Member of National League All-Star Team in 1985; did not play.

DANNY WAYNE DARWIN

Born October 25, 1955, at Bonham, Tex.
Height, 6.03. Weight, 190.
Throws and bats righthanded.
Attended Grayson County College, Denison, Tex.

Major League saves: 1980 (8), 1982 (7), 1985 (2). Total—17.
Tied for American League lead in home runs allowed with 34 in 1985.
Tied for Texas League lead in shutouts with 4 and hit batsmen with 8 in 1977.
Tied for Western Carolinas League lead in balks with 5 in 1976.

Year Club	League	G.	IP.	W.	L.	Pct.	H.	R.	ER.	SO.	BB.	ERA.
1976—Asheville	W. Carol.	16	102	6	3	.667	96	54	41	76	48	3.62
1977—Tulsa†	Texas	23	154	13	4	.765	130	53	43	129	72	2.51
1978—Tucson	P. Coast	23	125	8	9	.471	147	100	87	126	83	6.26
1978—Texas	American	3	9	1	0	1.000	11	4	4	8	1	4.00
1979—Tucson	P. Coast	13	95	6	6	.500	89	43	38	65	42	3.60
1979—Texas	American	20	78	4	4	.500	50	36	35	58	30	4.04
1980—Texas‡	American	53	110	13	4	.765	98	37	32	104	50	2.62
1981—Texas	American	22	146	9	9	.500	115	67	59	98	57	3.64
1982—Texas§	American	56	89	10	8	.556	95	38	34	61	37	3.44
1983—Texas§	American	28	183	8	13	.381	175	86	71	92	62	3.49
1984—Texas x	American x	35	223⅔	8	12	.400	249	110	98	123	54	3.94

Year	Club	League	G.	IP.	W.	L.	Pct.	H.	R.	ER.	SO.	BB.	ERA.
1985—Milwaukee y		American	39	217⅔	8	18	.308	212	112	92	125	65	3.80
1986—Milwaukee z		American	27	130⅓	6	8	.429	120	62	51	80	35	3.52
1986—Houston		National	12	54⅓	5	2	.714	50	19	14	40	9	2.32
American League Totals—9 Years			283	1186⅔	67	76	.469	1125	552	476	749	391	3.61
National League Totals—1 Year			12	54⅓	5	2	.714	50	19	14	40	9	2.32
Major League Totals—9 Years			295	1241	72	78	.480	1175	571	490	789	400	3.55

Signed as free agent by Texas Rangers' organization, May 10, 1976.
†On disabled list, April 25 to May 4 and May 22 to June 11, 1977.
‡On disabled list, June 5 to June 26, 1980.
§On disabled list, March 25 to April 10 and August 9 to September 1, 1983.
xTraded with a player to be named later to Milwaukee Brewers as part of a six-player, four-team deal in which Kansas City Royals acquired Catcher Jim Sundberg from Milwaukee, Texas Rangers acquired Catcher Don Slaught from Kansas City, New York Mets' organization acquired Pitcher Frank Wills from Kansas City and Milwaukee organization acquired Pitcher Tim Leary from New York, January 18, 1985; Milwaukee organization acquired Catcher Bill Hance from Texas to complete deal, January 30, 1985.
yGranted free agency, November 12, 1985; re-signed by Brewers, December 22, 1985.
zTraded to Houston Astros for Pitcher Don August and a player to be named later, August 15, 1986; Milwaukee Brewers' organization acquired Pitcher Mark Knudson to complete deal, August 21, 1986.

DARREN ARTHUR DAULTON

Born January 3, 1962, at Arkansas City, Kan.
Height, 6.02. Weight, 190.
Throws right and bats lefthanded.
Attended Cowley County Community College, Arkansas City, Kan.

Major League stolen bases: 1985 (3), 1986 (2). Total—5.
Tied for Eastern League lead in sacrifice flies with 10 in 1983.

Year	Club	League	Pos.	G.	AB.	R.	H.	2B.	3B.	HR.	RBI.	B.A.	PO.	A.	E.	F.A.
1980—Helena		Pion.	C	37	100	13	20	2	1	1	10	.200	224	17	4	.984
1981—Spartanburg		S. Atl.	C-OF-3B	98	270	44	62	11	1	3	29	.230	378	34	4	.990
1982—Peninsula		Carol.	C-1B	110	324	65	78	21	2	11	44	.241	654	63	9	.990
1983—Reading		East.	C-1B-OF	113	362	77	95	16	4	19	83	.262	557	57	14	.978
1983—Philadelphia		Nat.	C	2	3	1	1	0	0	0	0	.333	8	0	0	1.000
1984—Portland†		P. C.	C	80	252	45	75	19	4	7	38	.298	322	26	6	.983
1985—Portland		P. C.	C	23	64	13	19	5	3	2	10	.297	110	9	0	1.000
1985—Philadelphia‡		Nat.	C	36	103	14	21	3	1	4	11	.204	160	15	1	.994
1986—Philadelphia§		Nat.	C	49	138	18	31	4	0	8	21	.225	244	21	4	.985
Major League Totals—3 Years				87	244	33	53	7	1	12	32	.217	412	36	5	.989

Selected by Philadelphia Phillies' organization in 25th round of free-agent draft, June 3, 1980.
†On disabled list, July 20 to August 28, 1984.
‡On disabled list, May 17 to August 9, 1985; included rehabilitation disability assignment to Portland, July 20 to August 7, 1985.
§On disabled list, June 22, 1986 through remainder of season.

ANDRE ANTER DAVID

Born May 18, 1958, at Hollywood, Calif.
Height, 6.00. Weight, 170.
Throws and bats lefthanded.
Attended Los Angeles Valley College, Van Nuys, Calif. and California State University, Fullerton, Calif.

Tied major league record by hitting home run in first major league at-bat, June 29, 1984, first game.
Tied for International League lead in intentional bases on balls received with 8 in 1986.

Year	Club	League	Pos.	G.	AB.	R.	H.	2B.	3B.	HR.	RBI.	B.A.	PO.	A.	E.	F.A.
1980—Visalia		Calif.	OF	63	210	33	68	9	2	0	32	.324	99	10	3	.973
1981—Orlando		South.	OF	133	475	57	111	13	5	10	54	.234	253	17	9	.968
1982—Toledo		Int.	OF	15	43	4	6	1	1	0	0	.140	26	1	2	.931
1982—Orlando		South.	OF-1B-3B	107	366	61	102	17	7	5	49	.279	195	9	7	.967
1983—Toledo		Int.	OF-1B	116	403	59	117	15	1	6	54	.290	107	7	4	.966
1984—Toledo		Int.	OF-1B	61	194	30	57	14	1	7	24	.294	87	4	3	.968
1984—Minnesota		Amer.	OF	33	48	5	12	2	0	1	5	.250	14	0	0	1.000
1985—Toledo†		Int.	1B-OF	102	331	40	88	15	1	8	48	.266	332	17	5	.986
1986—Toledo		Int.	OF-1B	111	348	55	114	18	1	10	44	★.328	152	9	3	.982
1986—Minnesota‡		Amer.	PH	5	5	0	1	0	0	0	0	.200	0	0	0	.000
Major League Totals—2 Years				38	53	5	13	2	0	1	5	.245	14	0	0	1.000

Selected by Minnesota Twins' organization in 14th round of free-agent draft, June 5, 1979.
Selected by Minnesota Twins' organization in 8th round of free-agent draft, June 3, 1980.
†On disabled list, July 31 to August 9, 1985.
‡Granted free agency, October 15, 1986.

JACKIE GLENN DAVIDSON JR.

Born September 20, 1964, at Fort Worth, Tex.
Height, 6.00. Weight, 175.
Throws right and bats left and righthanded.

Tied for Midwest League lead in games started by pitchers with 27 and home runs allowed with 16 in 1985.

Year	Club	League	G.	IP.	W.	L.	Pct.	H.	R.	ER.	SO.	BB.	ERA.
1983—Pikeville		Ap'lachian	2	6⅔	0	1	.000	10	14	11	5	7	14.85

Year Club	League	G.	IP.	W.	L.	Pct.	H.	R.	ER.	SO.	BB.	ERA.
1984—Quad Cities	Midwest	27	149⅔	7	13	.350	145	102	●95	109	103	5.71
1985—Peoria	Midwest	25	166⅓	10	6	.625	153	88	62	152	76	3.35
1986—Pittsfield	Eastern	12	77⅔	8	3	.727	67	35	28	47	27	3.24
1986—Iowa	Am. Assoc.	15	92⅓	4	5	.444	117	58	50	48	32	4.87

Selected by Chicago Cubs' organization in 1st round (sixth player selected) of free-agent draft, June 6, 1983.

JOHN MARK DAVIDSON

(Known by middle name.)

Born February 15, 1961, at Knoxville, Tenn.
Height, 6.02. Weight, 180.
Throws and bats righthanded.
Attended University of North Carolina, Charlotte, N.C.,
and Clemson University, Clemson, S.C.
Son of Max Davidson, minor league outfielder, 1947 through 1954.

Major League stolen bases: 1986 (2).
Led Southern League in game-winning RBIs with 16 in 1985.

Year Club	League	Pos.	G.	AB.	R.	H.	2B.	3B.	HR.	RBI.	B.A.	PO.	A.	E.	F.A.
1982—Wis. Rapids	Midw.	OF	79	247	54	74	11	0	10	41	.300	166	13	5	.973
1983—Wis. Rapids†	Midw.	OF	111	363	63	80	15	1	13	48	.220	181	6	6	.969
1984—Orlando‡	South.	OF-1B-3B	114	348	55	99	11	6	4	37	.284	243	13	3	.988
1985—Orlando	South.	OF-3B	134	453	93	137	17	2	25	106	.302	305	14	6	.982
1986—Toledo	Int.	OF	108	383	55	95	16	1	10	38	.248	290	8	8	.974
1986—Minnesota	Amer.	OF	36	68	5	8	3	0	0	2	.118	48	0	1	.980
Major League Totals—1 Year			36	68	5	8	3	0	0	2	.118	48	0	1	.980

Selected by Minnesota Twins' organization in 11th round of free-agent draft, June 7, 1982.
†On disabled list, April 15 to May 4, 1983.
‡On disabled list, July 16 to July 26, 1984.

ALVIN GLENN DAVIS

(Al)

Born September 9, 1960, at Riverside, Calif.
Height, 6.01. Weight, 190.
Throws right and bats lefthanded.
Received bachelor of science degree in finance from Arizona State University, Tempe, Ariz.

Major League stolen bases: 1984 (5), 1985 (1). Total—6.
Led Southern League in bases on balls received with 120 and sacrifice flies with 12 in 1983.
Led Southern League first basemen in total chances with 1,348 and double plays with 118 in 1983.
Named American League Rookie Player of the Year by THE SPORTING NEWS, 1984.
Named American League Rookie of the Year by Baseball Writers' Association of America, 1984.

Year Club	League	Pos.	G.	AB.	R.	H.	2B.	3B.	HR.	RBI.	B.A.	PO.	A.	E.	F.A.
1982—Lynn	East	1B	74	225	37	64	10	1	12	56	.284	579	51	6	.991
1983—Chattanooga†	South.	★●1B-OF	131	422	87	125	24	3	18	83	.296	★1233	★99	●16	.988
1984—Salt Lake City	P. C.	1B	1	3	2	2	0	0	0	1	.667	2	0	0	1.000
1984—Seattle	Amer.	1B	152	567	80	161	34	3	27	116	.284	1271	94	11	.992
1985—Seattle	Amer.	1B	155	578	78	166	33	1	18	78	.287	1438	103	13	.992
1986—Seattle‡	Amer.	1B	135	479	66	130	18	1	18	72	.271	880	82	14	.986
Major League Totals—3 Years			442	1624	224	457	85	5	63	266	.281	3589	279	38	.990

Selected by San Francisco Giants' organization in 8th round of free-agent draft, June 6, 1978.
Selected by Oakland A's organization in 6th round of free-agent draft, June 8, 1981.
Selected by Seattle Mariners' organization in 6th round of free-agent draft, June 7, 1982.
†On disabled list, July 21 to July 31, 1983.
‡On disabled list, June 25 to July 17, 1986.

ALL-STAR GAME RECORD

Year League	Pos.	AB.	R.	H.	2B.	3B.	HR.	RBI.	B.A.	PO.	A.	E.	F.A.
1984—American	PH	1	0	0	0	0	0	0	.000	0	0	0	.000

CHARLES THEODORE DAVIS

(Chili)

(Original nickname was Chili Bowl, which was prompted by a friend who saw Davis
after he received a haircut back in the sixth grade. The nickname was later shortened to Chili.)

Born January 17, 1960, at Kingston, Jamaica.
Height, 6.03. Weight, 195.
Throws right and bats left and righthanded.

Tied major league record for fewest errors by outfielder, season, for leader in errors (9), 1986.
Tied National League record for most games, switch-hit home runs, season (1), June 5, 1983.
Major League stolen bases: 1981 (2), 1982 (24), 1983 (10), 1984 (12), 1985 (15), 1986 (16). Total—79.

Year Club	League	Pos.	G.	AB.	R.	H.	2B.	3B.	HR.	RBI.	B.A.	PO.	A.	E.	F.A.
1978—Cedar Rapids	Midw.	C-OF	124	424	63	119	18	5	16	73	.281	365	45	25	.943
1979—Fresno	Calif.	OF-C	134	490	91	132	24	5	21	95	.269	339	43	20	.950
1980—Shreveport	Texas	OF-C	129	442	50	130	30	4	12	67	.294	184	20	12	.944
1981—San Francisco	Nat.	OF	8	15	1	2	0	0	0	0	.133	7	0	0	1.000
1981—Phoenix†	P. C.	OF	88	334	76	117	16	6	19	75	.350	175	7	6	.968
1982—San Francisco	Nat.	OF	154	641	86	167	27	6	19	76	.261	404	●16	12	.972

Year Club League	Pos.	G.	AB.	R.	H.	2B.	3B.	HR.	RBI.	B.A.	PO.	A.	E.	F.A.
1983—San Francisco ...... Nat.	OF	137	486	54	113	21	2	11	59	.233	357	7	9	.976
1983—Phoenix................. P. C.	OF	10	44	12	13	2	0	2	9	.295	15	0	2	.882
1984—San Francisco ...... Nat.	OF	137	499	87	157	21	6	21	81	.315	292	9	9	.971
1985—San Francisco ...... Nat.	OF	136	481	53	130	25	2	13	56	.270	279	10	6	.980
1986—San Francisco ...... Nat.	OF	153	526	71	146	28	3	13	70	.278	303	9	●9	.972
Major League Totals—6 Years.................		725	2648	352	715	122	19	77	342	.270	1642	51	45	.974

Selected by San Francisco Giants' organization in 11th round of free-agent draft, June 7, 1977.

†On disabled list, August 19 to August 28, 1982.

ALL-STAR GAME RECORD

Year League	Pos.	AB.	R.	H.	2B.	3B.	HR.	RBI.	B.A.	PO.	A.	E.	F.A.
1984—National	PH	1	0	0	0	0	0	0	.000	0	0	0	.000
1986—National	OF	1	0	0	0	0	0	0	.000	0	0	0	.000
All-Star Game Totals—2 Years....................		2	0	0	0	0	0	0	.000	0	0	0	.000

ERIC KEITH DAVIS

Born May 29, 1962, at Los Angeles, Calif.
Height, 6.02. Weight, 170.
Throws and bats righthanded.

Major League stolen bases: 1984 (10), 1985 (16), 1986 (80). Total—106.
Hit three home runs in a game, September 10, 1986.
Led Northwest League in stolen bases with 40 in 1981.

Year Club League	Pos.	G.	AB.	R.	H.	2B.	3B.	HR.	RBI.	B.A.	PO.	A.	E.	F.A.
1980—Eugene .... N'west	SS-2B	33	73	12	16	1	0	1	11	.219	24	35	11	.843
1981—Eugene .... N'west	OF	62	214	*67	69	10	4	11	39	.322	94	11	4	.963
1982—Cedar Rapids........ Midw.	OF	111	434	80	120	20	5	15	56	.276	239	9	9	.965
1983—Waterbury........... East.	OF	89	293	56	85	13	1	15	43	.290	214	8	2	.991
1983—Indianapolis......... A. A.	OF	19	77	18	23	4	0	7	19	.299	61	1	1	.984
1984—Wichita................ A. A.	OF	52	194	42	61	9	5	14	34	.314	110	5	5	.958
1984—Cincinnati†........... Nat.	OF	57	174	33	39	10	1	10	30	.224	125	4	1	.992
1985—Cincinnati............. Nat.	OF	56	122	26	30	3	3	8	18	.246	75	3	1	.987
1985—Denver .... A. A.	OF	64	206	48	57	10	2	15	38	.277	94	5	3	.971
1986—Cincinnati............. Nat.	OF	132	415	97	115	15	3	27	71	.277	274	2	7	.975
Major League Totals—3 Years.................		245	711	156	184	28	7	45	119	.259	474	9	9	.982

Selected by Cincinnati Reds' organization in 8th round of free-agent draft, June 3, 1980.

†On disabled list, August 16 to September 1, 1984.

GEORGE EARL DAVIS JR.
(Storm)

(Nicknamed by mother after character in book she was reading while pregnant with Storm.)
Born December 26, 1961, at Dallas, Tex.
Height, 6.04. Weight, 210.
Throws and bats righthanded.

Major League saves: 1984 (1).

Year Club League	G.	IP.	W.	L.	Pct.	H.	R.	ER.	SO.	BB.	ERA.
1979—Bluefield................ Ap'lachian.	10	58	4	4	.500	44	34	25	54	30	3.88
1980—Miami.................... Florida St.	25	151	9	12	.429	157	85	59	90	55	3.52
1981—Charlotte............... Southern	28	187	14	10	.583	*215	86	72	119	65	3.47
1982—Rochester.............. Int'national	4	26⅔	2	1	.667	25	13	11	27	7	3.71
1982—Baltimore .... American	29	100⅔	8	4	.667	96	40	39	67	28	3.49
1983—Baltimore .... American	34	200⅓	13	7	.650	180	90	80	125	64	3.59
1984—Baltimore .... American	35	225	14	9	.609	205	86	78	105	71	3.12
1985—Baltimore .... American	31	175	10	8	.556	172	92	88	93	70	4.53
1986—Baltimore†............. American	25	154	9	12	.429	166	70	62	96	49	3.62
1986—Hagerstown‡........... Carolina	1	4	0	0	.000	3	0	0	6	3	0.00
Major League Totals—5 Years......................	154	855	54	40	.574	819	378	347	486	282	3.65

Selected by Baltimore Orioles' organization in 7th round of free-agent draft, June 5, 1979.

†On disabled list, July 4 to July 22, 1986; included rehabilitation disability assignment to Hagerstown, July 18 to July 22, 1986.

‡Traded to San Diego Padres for Catcher Terry Kennedy and Pitcher Mark Williamson, October 30, 1986.

CHAMPIONSHIP SERIES RECORD

Year Club League	G.	IP.	W.	L.	Pct.	H.	R.	ER.	SO.	BB.	ERA.
1983—Baltimore .... American	1	6	0	0	.000	5	0	0	2	2	0.00

WORLD SERIES RECORD

Year Club League	G.	IP.	W.	L.	Pct.	H.	R.	ER.	SO.	BB.	ERA.
1983—Baltimore .... American	1	5	1	0	1.000	6	3	3	3	1	5.40

GLENN EARL DAVIS

Born March 28, 1961, at Jacksonville, Fla.
Height, 6.03. Weight, 210.
Throws and bats righthanded.
Attended Manatee Junior College, Bradenton, Fla.,
and University of Georgia, Athens, Ga.

Major League stolen bases: 1986 (3).
Tied for National League lead in game-winning RBIs with 16 in 1986.
Led Gulf Coast League first basemen in total chances with 520 and tied for lead in double plays with 35 in 1981.
Named first baseman on THE SPORTING NEWS National League Silver Slugger team, 1986.

Year Club League	Pos.	G.	AB.	R.	H.	2B.	3B.	HR.	RBI.	B.A.	PO.	A.	E.	F.A.
1981—Sara. Astros-Or..... Gulf C.	★1B-OF	54	188	27	49	7	1	6	35	.261	★469	★37	★14	.973
1982—Daytona Beach .... Fla. St.	1B-3B	103	378	70	119	28	3	●19	79	.315	759	70	16	.981
1982—Columbus.............. South.	1B	26	97	14	24	6	1	4	8	.247	257	11	2	.993
1983—Columbus.............. South.	OF	118	445	68	133	19	3	●25	85	.299	186	17	9	.958
1983—Tucson................... P. C.	OF-1B-3B	15	57	5	12	3	0	1	8	.211	52	4	2	.966
1984—Tucson................... P. C.	1B-OF	131	471	66	140	28	7	16	94	.297	922	94	22	.979
1984—Houston................. Nat.	1B	18	61	6	13	5	0	2	8	.213	151	15	2	.988
1985—Tucson................... P. C.	1B-OF	60	220	22	67	24	2	5	35	.305	420	29	5	.989
1985—Houston................. Nat.	1B-OF	100	350	51	95	11	0	20	64	.271	766	57	12	.986
1986—Houston................. Nat.	1B	158	574	91	152	32	3	31	101	.265	1253	111	11	.992
Major League Totals—3 Years.................		276	985	148	260	48	3	53	173	.264	2170	183	25	.989

Selected by Baltimore Orioles' organization in 32nd round of free-agent draft, June 5, 1979.
Selected by Houston Astros' organization in secondary phase of free-agent draft, January 13, 1981.

CHAMPIONSHIP SERIES RECORD

Tied Championship Series records for most at-bats, game (7), October 15, 1986 (16 innings); hitting home run in first Series at-bat, October 8, 1986.

Year Club League	Pos.	G.	AB.	R.	H.	2B.	3B.	HR.	RBI.	B.A.	PO.	A.	E.	F.A.
1986—Houston................. Nat.	1B	6	26	3	7	1	0	1	3	.269	62	3	1	.985

ALL-STAR GAME RECORD

Year League	Pos.	AB.	R.	H.	2B.	3B.	HR.	RBI.	B.A.	PO.	A.	E.	F.A.
1986—National..............................	PH	1	0	0	0	0	0	0	.000	0	0	0	.000

JODY RICHARD DAVIS

Born November 12, 1956, at Gainesville, Ga.
Height, 6.03. Weight, 210.
Throws and bats righthanded.
Attended Middle Georgia College, Cochran, Ga.

Major League stolen bases: 1984 (5), 1985 (1). Total—6.
Led National League catchers in total chances with 998 and double plays with 14 in 1986.
Led National League in passed balls with 21 in 1983.
Tied for National League lead in double plays by catchers with 11 in 1982.
Led Carolina League in sacrifice flies with 13 in 1978.
Led Carolina League catchers in double plays with 8 in 1978.
Named catcher on THE SPORTING NEWS National League All-Star fielding team, 1986.

Year Club League	Pos.	G.	AB.	R.	H.	2B.	3B.	HR.	RBI.	B.A.	PO.	A.	E.	F.A.
1976—Marion................... Appal.	C	50	164	20	38	5	1	5	19	.232	290	30	★13	.961
1977—Little Falls............ NYP	C-1B	64	214	37	62	11	2	11	46	.290	369	50	12	.972
1978—Lynchburg............ Carol.	C-1B-3B	120	408	57	107	24	2	16	94	.262	595	79	15	.978
1979—Jackson†.............. Texas	C-1B	132	433	57	128	23	4	21	91	.296	661	81	15	.980
1980—St. Petersburg...... Fla. St.	C-1B	45	155	27	43	4	0	6	27	.277	171	20	5	.974
1980—Springfield‡§......... A. A.	C-1B	13	36	3	6	1	0	0	2	.167	59	7	1	.985
1981—Chicago .... Nat.	C	56	180	14	46	5	1	4	21	.256	274	44	9	.972
1982—Chicago .... Nat.	C	130	418	41	109	20	2	12	52	.261	598	89	11	.984
1983—Chicago .... Nat.	C	151	510	56	138	31	2	24	84	.271	730	75	13	.984
1984—Chicago .... Nat.	C	150	523	55	134	25	2	19	94	.256	811	89	★15	.984
1985—Chicago .... Nat.	C	142	482	47	112	30	0	17	58	.232	694	84	8	.990
1986—Chicago .... Nat.	★C-1B	148	528	61	132	27	2	21	74	.250	★885	★105	8	.992
Major League Totals—6 Years.................		777	2641	274	671	138	9	97	383	.254	3992	486	64	.986

Selected by New York Mets' organization in 3rd round of free-agent draft, January 7, 1976.
†Traded to St. Louis Cardinals' organization for Pitcher Ray Searage, December 10, 1979.
‡On disabled list, April 14 to June 20, 1980.
§Drafted by Chicago Cubs, December 8, 1980.

CHAMPIONSHIP SERIES RECORD

Established National League Championship Series record for highest slugging average, five-game Series (.833), 1984.
Tied National League Championship Series record for most total bases, five-game Series (15), 1984.

Year Club League	Pos.	G.	AB.	R.	H.	2B.	3B.	HR.	RBI.	B.A.	PO.	A.	E.	F.A.
1984—Chicago .... Nat.	C	5	18	3	7	2	0	2	6	.389	23	2	0	1.000

ALL-STAR GAME RECORD

Year League	Pos.	AB.	R.	H.	2B.	3B.	HR.	RBI.	B.A.	PO.	A.	E.	F.A.
1984—National..............................	C	1	0	0	0	0	0	0	.000	1	0	0	1.000
1986—National..............................	C	1	0	1	0	0	0	0	1.000	3	0	0	1.000
All-Star Game Totals—2 Years....................		2	0	1	0	0	0	0	.500	4	0	0	1.000

—DID YOU KNOW—

That all seven American League East Division teams were playing at least .500 baseball on July 1, 1986?

JOEL CLARK DAVIS

Born January 30, 1965, at Jacksonville, Fla.
Height, 6.05. Weight, 205.
Throws right and bats lefthanded.

Year Club	League	G.	IP.	W.	L.	Pct.	H.	R.	ER.	SO.	BB.	ERA.
1983—Sarasota White Sox	Gulf Coast	12	75⅓	6	2	.750	51	23	16	95	26	1.91
1984—Appleton	Midwest	11	40⅓	1	2	.333	40	27	27	38	38	6.02
1984—Niagara Falls	NYP	11	69	3	4	.429	57	35	18	72	37	2.35
1984—Glens Falls	Eastern	4	11⅔	1	2	.333	12	13	10	9	14	7.71
1985—Glens Falls†	Eastern	4	25⅓	1	1	.500	21	8	8	20	16	2.84
1985—Buffalo	Am. Assoc.	10	56⅓	2	5	.286	61	39	29	31	35	4.63
1985—Chicago	American	12	71⅓	3	3	.500	71	34	33	37	26	4.16
1986—Chicago	American	19	105⅓	4	5	.444	115	64	55	54	51	4.70
1986—Buffalo	Am. Assoc.	6	39⅓	1	4	.200	41	24	20	30	11	4.58
Major League Totals—2 Years		31	176⅔	7	8	.467	186	98	88	91	77	4.48

Selected by Chicago White Sox' organization in 1st round (13th player selected) of free-agent draft, June 6, 1983.
†On disabled list, April 12 to May 28, 1985.

JOHN KIRK DAVIS

Born January 5, 1963, at Chicago, Ill.
Height, 6.07. Weight 215.
Throws and bats righthanded.

Led Pioneer League in wild pitches with 12 in 1982.

Year Club	League	G.	IP.	W.	L.	Pct.	H.	R.	ER.	SO.	BB.	ERA.
1981—Sarasota Royals Blue	Gulf Coast	10	30	2	2	.500	28	21	17	13	23	5.10
1982—Butte	Pioneer	14	80⅔	7	1	.875	100	62	★55	38	37	6.14
1983—Charleston	S. Atlantic	20	78	5	6	.455	104	64	57	48	40	6.58
1984—Fort Myers	Florida St.	25	153	7	11	.389	170	91	77	84	70	4.53
1985—Memphis	Southern	27	160⅓	6	15	.286	186	113	96	103	75	5.39
1986—Memphis	Southern	41	111⅓	6	6	.500	99	63	58	70	69	4.69
1986—Omaha	Am. Assoc.	2	2	0	0	.000	2	1	1	1	1	4.50

Selected by Kansas City Royals' organization in 7th round of free-agent draft, June 8, 1981.

MARK WILLIAM DAVIS

Born October 19, 1960, at Livermore, Calif.
Height, 6.04. Weight, 195.
Throws and bats lefthanded.
Attended Chabot College, Hayward, Calif.

Major League saves: 1985 (7), 1986 (4). Total—11.
Led Western Carolinas League in shutouts with 5, home runs allowed with 18 and tied for lead in balks with 5 in 1979.
Tied for Eastern League lead in shutouts with 4 and in games started by pitchers with 28 in 1980.
Named Eastern League Most Valuable Player, 1980.

Year Club	League	G.	IP.	W.	L.	Pct.	H.	R.	ER.	SO.	BB.	ERA.
1979—Spartanburg	W. Carol.	26	166	11	9	.550	147	76	59	135	49	3.20
1980—Reading	Eastern	28	★193	★19	6	★.760	140	63	53	★185	75	★2.47
1980—Philadelphia	National	2	7	0	0	.000	4	2	2	5	5	2.57
1981—Oklahoma City†	Am. Assoc.	13	65	5	2	.714	66	34	28	56	47	3.88
1981—Philadelphia	National	9	43	1	4	.200	49	37	37	29	24	7.74
1982—Oklahoma City†§	Am. Assoc.	21	96⅔	5	12	.294	111	75	67	95	50	6.24
1983—Phoenix	P. Coast	13	72⅔	6	3	.667	89	57	51	64	33	6.32
1983—San Francisco	National	20	111	6	4	.600	93	51	43	83	50	3.49
1984—San Francisco	National	46	174⅔	5	17	.227	201	113	★104	124	54	5.36
1985—San Francisco	National	77	114⅓	5	12	.294	89	49	45	131	41	3.54
1986—San Francisco	National	67	84⅓	5	7	.417	63	33	28	90	34	2.99
Major League Totals—6 Years		221	534⅓	22	44	.333	499	285	259	462	208	4.36

Selected by New York Mets' organization in 21st round of free-agent draft, June 6, 1978.
Selected by Philadelphia Phillies' organization in secondary phase of free-agent draft, January 9, 1979.
†On disabled list, April 14 to June 11, 1981.
‡On disabled list, August 3 to August 30, 1982.
§Traded with Pitcher Mike Krukow and Outfielder Charles Penigar to San Francisco Giants for Second Baseman Joe Morgan and Pitcher Al Holland, December 14, 1982.

MICHAEL DWAYNE DAVIS
(Mike)

Born June 11, 1959, at San Diego, Calif.
Height, 6.03. Weight, 185.
Throws and bats lefthanded.
Attended San Diego Mesa College, San Diego, Calif.
Brother of Mark A. Davis, outfielder in Chicago White Sox' organization; and cousin of Dave Grayson, defensive back with Dallas Texans, Kansas City Chiefs and Oakland Raiders, 1961 through 1970.

Major League stolen bases: 1980 (2), 1982 (3), 1983 (32), 1984 (14), 1985 (24), 1986 (27). Total—102.

Year Club	League	Pos.	G.	AB.	R.	H.	2B.	3B.	HR.	RBI.	B.A.	PO.	A.	E.	F.A.
1977—Medicine Hat	Pion.	★OF-1-2	59	213	53	67	5	3	2	18	.315	82	6	★15	.854

Year Club	League	Pos.	G.	AB.	R.	H.	2B.	3B.	HR.	RBI.	B.A.	PO.	A.	E.	F.A.
1978—Modesto	Calif.	OF-1B	106	406	74	136	12	4	2	35	.335	201	10	13	.942
1979—Modesto	Calif.	OF	41	161	48	63	10	4	0	19	.391	76	3	7	.919
1979—Waterbury	East.	OF	97	351	51	77	9	5	6	39	.219	208	7	15	.935
1980—Ogden	P. C.	OF	19	69	14	21	7	2	1	14	.304	34	2	1	.973
1980—Oakland	Amer.	OF-1B	51	95	11	20	2	1	1	8	.211	76	7	1	.988
1981—Tacoma	P. C.	OF-1B	133	515	84	148	28	6	6	71	.287	286	7	7	.977
1981—Oakland	Amer.	OF-1B	17	20	0	1	1	0	0	0	.050	3	0	0	1.000
1982—Tacoma†	P. C.	OF-1B	100	374	71	118	23	3	12	68	.316	197	13	9	.959
1982—Oakland	Amer.	OF-1B	23	75	12	30	4	0	1	10	.400	65	4	5	.932
1983—Oakland‡	Amer.	OF	128	443	61	122	24	4	8	62	.275	278	16	8	.974
1984—Oakland	Amer.	OF	134	382	47	88	18	3	9	46	.230	287	6	●12	.961
1985—Oakland	Amer.	OF	154	547	92	157	34	1	24	82	.287	370	6	8	.979
1986—Oakland	Amer.	OF	142	489	77	131	28	3	19	55	.268	310	9	9	.973
Major League Totals—7 Years			649	2051	300	549	111	12	62	263	.268	1389	48	43	.971

Selected by Minnesota Twins' organization in 31st round of free agent draft, June 8, 1976.
Selected by Oakland A's organization in 3rd round of free agent draft, June 7, 1977.
†On disabled list, April 13 to May 24, 1982.
‡On disabled list, July 13 to July 31, 1983.

CHAMPIONSHIP SERIES RECORD

Year Club	League	Pos.	G.	AB.	R.	H.	2B.	3B.	HR.	RBI.	B.A.	PO.	A.	E.	F.A.
1981—Oakland	Amer.	PH	1	1	0	1	0	0	0	0	1.000	0	0	0	.000

RONALD GENE DAVIS
(Ron)

Born August 6, 1955, at Houston Tex.
Height, 6.04. Weight, 198.
Throws and bats righthanded.
Attended Blinn Junior College, Brenham, Tex.

Established major league record for most consecutive strikeouts by relief pitcher, game (8), May 4, 1981.
Established American League record for most wins by rookie relief pitcher, season (14), 1979.
Tied American League record for most consecutive strikeouts, game (8), May 4, 1981.
Major League saves: 1979 (9), 1980 (7), 1981 (6), 1982 (22), 1983 (30), 1984 (29), 1985 (25), 1986 (2). Total—130.
Led American League in intentional bases on balls issued with 12 in 1982.

Year Club	League	G.	IP.	W.	L.	Pct.	H.	R.	ER.	SO.	BB.	ERA.
1976—Pompano Beach	Florida St.	18	115	8	8	.500	110	62	48	78	51	3.76
1977—Midland†	Texas					(Did not play)						
1977—Pompano Beach	Florida St.	21	111	8	7	.533	119	63	51	58	59	4.14
1978—Midland‡	Texas	12	68	3	3	.500	80	51	48	45	33	6.35
1978—West Haven	Eastern	21	60	9	2	.818	41	14	10	39	27	1.50
1978—New York	American	4	2	0	0	.000	3	4	3	0	3	13.50
1979—Columbus	Int'national	11	19	0	1	.000	13	9	9	10	15	4.26
1979—New York	American	44	85	14	2	*.875	84	29	27	43	28	2.86
1980—New York	American	53	131	9	3	.750	121	50	43	65	32	2.95
1981—New York§	American	43	73	4	5	.444	47	22	22	83	25	2.71
1982—Minnesota	American	63	106	3	9	.250	106	53	52	89	47	4.42
1983—Minnesota	American	66	89	5	8	.385	89	34	33	84	33	3.34
1984—Minnesota	American	64	83	7	11	.389	79	44	42	74	41	4.55
1985—Minnesota	American	57	64⅔	2	6	.250	55	28	25	72	35	3.48
1986—Minnesota x	American	36	38⅔	2	6	.250	55	42	39	30	29	9.08
1986—Chicago	National	17	20	0	2	.000	31	18	17	10	3	7.65
American League Totals—9 Years		430	672⅓	46	50	.479	639	306	286	540	273	3.83
National League Totals—1 Year		17	20	0	2	.000	31	18	17	10	3	7.65
Major League Totals—9 Years		447	692⅓	46	52	.469	670	324	303	550	276	3.94

Selected by Chicago Cubs' organization in 3rd round of free-agent draft, January 7, 1976.
†On disabled list, April 9 to May 6, 1977.
‡Traded to New York Yankees' organization, June 12, 1978; completing deal in which New York traded Pitcher Ken Holtzman to Chicago Cubs for a player to be named later, June 10, 1978.
§Traded with Pitcher Paul Boris and Shortstop Greg Gagne and a reported $400,000 to Minnesota Twins for Shortstop Roy Smalley, April 10, 1982.
xTraded with Pitcher Dewayne Coleman to Chicago Cubs for Pitchers George Frazier and Ray Fontenot and Shortstop Julius McDougal, August 13, 1986.

DIVISION SERIES RECORD

Year Club	League	G.	IP.	W.	L.	Pct.	H.	R.	ER.	SO.	BB.	ERA.
1981—New York	American	3	6	1	0	1.000	1	0	0	6	2	0.00

CHAMPIONSHIP SERIES RECORD

Year Club	League	G.	IP.	W.	L.	Pct.	H.	R.	ER.	SO.	BB.	ERA.
1980—New York	American	1	4	0	0	.000	3	1	1	3	1	2.25
1981—New York	American	2	3⅓	0	0	.000	0	0	0	4	2	0.00
Championship Series Totals—2 Years		3	7⅓	0	0	.000	3	1	1	7	3	1.23

WORLD SERIES RECORD

Year Club	League	G.	IP.	W.	L.	Pct.	H.	R.	ER.	SO.	BB.	ERA.
1981—New York	American	4	2⅓	0	0	.000	4	8	6	4	5	23.14

Year League	IP.	W.	L.	Pct.	H.	R.	ER.	SO.	BB.	ERA.
1981—American	1	0	0	.000	1	1	1	1	0	9.00

STEVEN KENNON DAVIS
(Steve)

Born August 4, 1960, at San Antonio, Tex.
Height, 6.01. Weight, 170.
Throws and bats lefthanded.
Attended Texas A&M University, College Station, Tex.

Tied for Southern League lead in shutouts with 3 in 1985.
Named Southern League Pitcher of the Year, 1985.

Year—Club	League	G.	IP.	W.	L.	Pct.	H.	R.	ER.	SO.	BB.	ERA.
1982—Medicine Hat..................	Pioneer	13	36⅔	5	1	.833	38	15	14	46	17	3.44
1983—Florence	S. Atlantic	23	153⅔	10	7	.588	129	66	55	167	52	3.22
1983—Knoxville	Southern	4	22	1	3	.250	26	17	17	18	14	6.95
1984—Knoxville	Southern	27	154⅔	9	6	.600	123	71	60	77	96	3.49
1985—Knoxville	Southern	27	154	★17	6	.739	114	49	42	107	72	★2.45
1985—Syracuse	Int'national	6	36	3	2	.600	19	11	10	34	17	2.50
1985—Toronto	American	10	28	2	1	.667	23	14	11	22	13	3.54
1986—Toronto	American	3	3⅔	0	0	.000	8	7	7	5	5	17.18
1986—Syracuse	Int'national	23	104⅔	5	7	.417	104	67	65	80	57	5.59
Major League Totals—2 Years		13	31⅔	2	1	.667	31	21	18	27	18	5.12

Selected by Toronto Blue Jays' organization in 21st round of free-agent draft, June 7, 1982.

TRENCH NEAL DAVIS

Born September 12, 1960, at Baltimore, Md.
Height, 6.03. Weight, 171.
Throws and bats lefthanded.

Major League stolen bases: 1985 (1).
Led Pacific Coast League in stolen bases with 53 in 1984.
Led Pacific Coast League in caught stealing with 22 in 1982.

Year—Club	League	Pos.	G.	AB.	R.	H.	2B.	3B.	HR.	RBI.	B.A.	PO.	A.	E.	F.A.
1980—Bradenton Pir.	Gulf C.	1B	43	142	16	39	3	3	1	12	.275	184	15	10	.952
1981—Greenwood............	S. Atl.	1B-OF	●141	●530	70	★158	24	9	4	73	.298	917	31	31	.968
1982—Portland.................	P. C.	OF	141	★571	80	153	16	5	2	46	.268	333	16	★14	.961
1983—Hawaii...................	P. C.	OF-1B	79	277	41	71	6	9	0	23	.256	147	9	3	.981
1983—Lynn...................	East.	OF-1B	59	219	37	61	7	4	2	16	.279	110	7	5	.959
1984—Hawaii...................	P. C.	OF	141	553	79	143	23	8	1	39	.259	311	18	★13	.962
1985—Hawaii...................	P. C.	OF	132	534	59	144	16	★12	2	56	.270	293	10	8	.974
1985—Pittsburgh............	Nat.	OF	2	7	1	1	0	0	0	0	.143	2	0	1	.667
1986—Hawaii...................	P. C.	OF	104	411	41	128	8	7	0	30	.311	216	9	9	.962
1986—Pittsburgh†...........	Nat.	OF	15	23	2	3	0	0	0	1	.130	10	1	1	.917
Major League Totals—2 Years...............			17	30	3	4	0	0	0	1	.133	12	1	2	.867

Signed as free agent by Pittsburgh Pirates' organization, June 23, 1980.
†Granted free agency, October 15, 1986; signed by Atlanta Braves' organization, November 17, 1986.

WILLIAM CHESTER DAWLEY
(Bill)

Born February 6, 1958, at Norwich, Conn.
Height, 6.04. Weight, 240.
Throws and bats righthanded.

Major League saves: 1983 (14), 1984 (5), 1985 (2), 1986 (2). Total—23.
Led American Association pitchers in games started with 28 in 1982.

Year—Club	League	G.	IP.	W.	L.	Pct.	H.	R.	ER.	SO.	BB.	ERA.
1976—Billings	Pioneer	13	78	6	4	.600	62	42	24	80	37	2.77
1977—Tampa..............................	Florida St.	24	181	10	8	.556	151	69	57	110	69	2.83
1978—Nashville..........................	Southern	27	141	7	13	.350	135	78	63	86	55	4.02
1979—Nashville†........................	Southern	25	140	9	9	.500	144	72	62	84	41	3.99
1980—Indianapolis.....................	Am. Assoc.	25	77	4	6	.400	90	46	39	28	31	4.56
1980—Waterbury........................	Eastern	7	49	2	2	.500	43	18	16	33	25	2.94
1981—Indianapolis.....................	Am. Assoc.	26	133	6	8	.429	141	77	73	109	69	4.94
1982—Indianapolis‡§.................	Am. Assoc.	29	★179	11	7	.611	196	86	76	106	48	3.82
1983—Houston	National	48	79⅔	5	6	.500	51	26	25	60	22	2.82
1984—Houston	National	60	98	11	4	.733	82	24	21	47	35	1.93
1985—Houston xy.......................	National	49	81	5	3	.625	76	35	32	48	37	3.56
1986—Chicago z.........................	American	46	97⅔	0	7	.000	91	38	36	66	28	3.32
National League Totals—3 Years.......................		157	258⅔	22	13	.629	209	85	78	155	94	2.71
American League Totals—1 Year		46	97⅔	0	7	.000	91	38	36	66	28	3.32
Major League Totals—4 Years............................		203	356⅓	22	20	.524	300	123	114	221	122	2.88

Selected by Cincinnati Reds' organization in 7th round of free-agent draft, June 8, 1976.
†On temporary inactive list, May 21 to May 31, 1979.
‡Appeared in one game as an outfielder with no chances.
§Traded with Outfielder Anthony Walker to Houston Astros' organization for Catcher Alan Knicely, March 31, 1983.

xOn disabled list, July 6 to July 24, 1985.
yReleased, April 1, 1986; signed by Chicago White Sox, April 15, 1986.
zTraded to St. Louis Cardinals for Infielder Fred Manrique, December 22, 1986.

ALL-STAR GAME RECORD

Year League	IP.	W.	L.	Pct.	H.	R.	ER.	SO.	BB.	ERA.
1983—National	1⅓	0	0	.000	1	0	0	1	0	0.00

ANDRE FERNANDO DAWSON

Born July 10, 1954, at Miami, Fla.
Height, 6.03. Weight, 195.
Throws and bats righthanded.
Attended Florida A&M University, Tallahassee, Fla.
Nephew of Theodore Taylor, third baseman-outfielder in Pittsburgh Pirates' organization, 1967 through 1969.

Tied major league records for most total bases, inning (8) and most home runs, inning (2), July 30, 1978 (third inning) and September 24, 1985 (fifth inning); most runs batted in, inning (6), September 24, 1985 (fifth inning).

Major League stolen bases: 1976 (1), 1977 (21), 1978 (28), 1979 (35), 1980 (34), 1981 (26), 1982 (39), 1983 (25), 1984 (13), 1985 (13), 1986 (18). Total—253.

Hit three home runs in a game, September 24, 1985.
Led National League in being hit by pitch with 12 in 1978 and 7 in 1981.
Led National League in total bases with 341 and sacrifice flies with 18 in 1983.
Led National League outfielders in total chances with 344 in 1981, 435 in 1982 and 450 in 1983.
Tied for National League lead in being hit by pitch with 6 in 1980 and 9 in 1983.
Led Pioneer League in total bases with 166, in being hit by pitch with 6 and tied for lead in sacrifice flies with 5 in 1975.

Named National League Player of the Year by THE SPORTING NEWS, 1981.
Named National League Rookie Player of the Year by THE SPORTING NEWS, 1977.
Named National League Rookie of the Year by Baseball Writers' Association of America, 1977.
Named outfielder on THE SPORTING NEWS National League All-Star Team, 1981 and 1983.
Named outfielder on THE SPORTING NEWS National League All-Star fielding team, 1980 through 1985.
Named outfielder on THE SPORTING NEWS National League Silver Slugger team, 1980, 1981 and 1983.

Year Club	League	Pos.	G.	AB.	R.	H.	2B.	3B.	HR.	RBI.	B.A.	PO.	A.	E.	F.A.
1975—Lethbridge	Pion.	OF	●72	★300	52	★99	14	7	★13	50	.330	★142	7	★10	.937
1976—Quebec City	East.	OF	40	143	27	51	6	0	8	27	.357	89	3	6	.939
1976—Denver	A. A.	OF	74	240	51	84	19	4	20	46	.350	97	2	2	.980
1976—Montreal	Nat.	OF	24	85	9	20	4	1	0	7	.235	61	1	2	.969
1977—Montreal	Nat.	OF	139	525	64	148	26	9	19	65	.282	352	9	4	.989
1978—Montreal	Nat.	OF	157	609	84	154	24	8	25	72	.253	411	17	5	.988
1979—Montreal	Nat.	OF	155	639	90	176	24	12	25	92	.275	394	7	5	.988
1980—Montreal	Nat.	OF	151	577	96	178	41	7	17	87	.308	410	14	6	.986
1981—Montreal	Nat.	OF	103	394	71	119	21	3	24	64	.302	★327	10	7	.980
1982—Montreal	Nat.	OF	148	608	107	183	37	7	23	83	.301	★419	8	8	.982
1983—Montreal	Nat.	OF	159	633	104	●189	36	10	32	113	.299	★435	6	9	.980
1984—Montreal	Nat.	OF	138	533	73	132	23	6	17	86	.248	297	11	8	.975
1985—Montreal	Nat.	OF	139	529	65	135	27	2	23	91	.255	248	9	7	.973
1986—Montreal†‡	Nat.	OF	130	496	65	141	32	2	20	78	.284	200	11	3	.986
Major League Totals—11 Years			1443	5628	828	1575	295	67	225	838	.280	3554	103	64	.983

Selected by Montreal Expos' organization in 11th round of free-agent draft, June 4, 1975.
†On disabled list, June 5 to June 30, 1986.
‡Granted free agency, November 12, 1986.

DIVISION SERIES RECORD

Year Club	League	Pos.	G.	AB.	R.	H.	2B.	3B.	HR.	RBI.	B.A.	PO.	A.	E.	F.A.
1981—Montreal	Nat.	OF	5	20	1	6	0	1	0	0	.300	12	1	1	.929

CHAMPIONSHIP SERIES RECORD

Year Club	League	Pos.	G.	AB.	R.	H.	2B.	3B.	HR.	RBI.	B.A.	PO.	A.	E.	F.A.
1981—Montreal	Nat.	OF	5	20	2	3	0	0	0	0	.150	12	0	0	1.000

ALL-STAR GAME RECORD

Year League	Pos.	AB.	R.	H.	2B.	3B.	HR.	RBI.	B.A.	PO.	A.	E.	F.A.
1981—National	OF	4	0	1	0	0	0	0	.250	4	0	0	1.000
1982—National	OF	4	0	1	0	0	0	0	.250	4	0	0	1.000
1983—National	OF	3	0	0	0	0	0	0	.000	3	0	0	1.000
All-Star Game Totals—3 Years		11	0	2	0	0	0	0	.182	11	0	0	1.000

BRIAN KELLY DAYETT

Born January 22, 1957, at New London, Conn.
Height, 5.10. Weight, 180.
Throws and bats righthanded.
Attended St. Leo College, St. Leo, Fla.

Led American Association in sacrifice flies with 11 and tied for lead in game-winning RBIs with 11 in 1986.
Led International League in total bases with 281 in 1983.
Led Southern League in total bases with 285 and game-winning RBIs with 15 in 1982.
Tied for New York-Pennsylvania League lead in double plays by third basemen with 20 in 1978.
Named Southern League Most Valuable Player, 1982.

Year Club League	Pos.	G.	AB.	R.	H.	2B.	3B.	HR.	RBI.	B.A.	PO.	A.	E.	F.A.
1978—Oneonta................NYP	3B-C-1B	68	256	53	79	●20	4	11	63	.309	207	106	14	.957
1979—West Haven .... East.	3B	135	465	58	119	21	4	11	74	.256	86	226	24	.929
1980—Nashville............... South.	3B	35	100	15	21	8	0	0	9	.210	16	60	6	.927
1980—Alexandria .... Carol.	3B-2B	13	48	12	21	5	1	3	17	.438	7	17	3	.889
1980—Fort Lauderdale .. Fla. St.	3B	52	174	31	43	8	2	4	21	.247	51	103	11	.933
1981—Nashville............... South.	3B-OF	112	338	53	91	15	3	18	62	.269	55	125	15	.923
1982—Nashville............... South.	OF-3B	●144	536	89	150	29	2	34	96	.280	201	9	12	.946
1983—Columbus............... Int.	OF-1B-3B	128	479	105	138	28	5	★35	★108	.288	224	10	6	.975
1983—New York............. Amer.	OF	11	29	3	6	0	1	0	5	.207	22	1	0	1.000
1984—Columbus............... Int.	OF	45	166	26	50	8	2	5	24	.301	91	1	2	.979
1984—New York†............ Amer.	OF	64	127	14	31	8	0	4	23	.244	80	3	1	.988
1985—Chicago‡ .... Nat.	OF	22	26	1	6	0	0	1	4	.231	8	0	0	1.000
1985—Iowa .... A. A.	OF-3B	14	37	5	14	4	0	1	11	.378	21	2	2	.920
1986—Chicago .... Nat.	OF	24	67	7	18	4	0	4	11	.269	31	1	0	1.000
1986—Iowa .... A. A.	OF	121	409	69	115	29	6	19	87	.281	193	10	4	.981
American League Totals—2 Years		75	156	17	37	8	1	4	28	.237	102	4	1	.991
National League Totals—2 Years		46	93	8	24	4	0	5	15	.258	39	1	0	1.000
Major League Totals—4 Years		121	249	25	61	12	1	9	43	.245	141	5	1	.993

Selected by New York Yankees' organization in 16th round of free-agent draft, June 6, 1978.

†Traded with Pitcher Ray Fontenot to Chicago Cubs for Catcher Ron Hassey, Outfielder Henry Cotto and Pitcher Rich Bordi and Porfi Altamirano, December 4, 1984.

‡On disabled list, June 20, 1985 through remainder of season.

KENNETH GRANT DAYLEY II
(Ken)

Born February 25, 1959, at Jerome, Ida.
Height, 6.00. Weight, 171.
Throws and bats lefthanded.
Attended University of Portland, Portland, Ore.

Major League saves: 1985 (11), 1986 (5). Total—16.
Led International League pitchers in games started with 31 in 1981.
Received reported $100,000 bonus to sign with Atlanta Braves, 1980.
Named lefthanded pitcher on THE SPORTING NEWS College Baseball All-America Team, 1980.

Year Club League	G.	IP.	W.	L.	Pct.	H.	R.	ER.	SO.	BB.	ERA.
1980—Savannah...................... Southern	16	105	8	3	.727	86	38	30	104	54	2.57
1981—Richmond...................... Int'national	31	★200	●13	8	.619	180	82	74	★162	★117	3.33
1982—Richmond...................... Int'national	13	98⅓	8	3	.727	89	43	34	79	47	3.11
1982—Atlanta........................... National	20	71⅓	5	6	.455	79	39	36	34	25	4.54
1983—Richmond...................... Int'national	14	90⅔	9	3	.750	79	39	33	74	49	3.28
1983—Atlanta........................... National	24	104⅔	5	8	.385	100	59	50	70	39	4.30
1984—Atlanta†-St. Louis........ National	7	23⅔	0	5	.000	44	28	21	10	11	7.99
1984—Richmond...................... Int'national	9	62⅓	5	1	.833	66	31	28	45	24	4.04
1984—Louisville..................... Am. Assoc.	13	96⅓	4	6	.400	86	42	35	79	22	3.27
1985—St. Louis........................ National	57	65⅓	4	4	.500	65	24	20	62	18	2.76
1986—St. Louis‡§................... National	31	38⅔	0	3	.000	42	19	14	33	11	3.26
Major League Totals—5 Years	139	303⅔	14	26	.350	330	169	141	209	104	4.18

Selected by Atlanta Braves' organization in 1st round (third player selected) of free-agent draft, June 3, 1980.

†Traded with First Baseman Mike Jorgensen to St. Louis Cardinals for Third Baseman Ken Oberkfell, June 15, 1984.

‡On disabled list, July 13, 1986 through remainder of season.

§Released, December 17, 1986.

CHAMPIONSHIP SERIES RECORD

Established National League Championship Series records for most games pitched (5) and most saves (2), six-game Series, 1985.

Year Club League	G.	IP.	W.	L.	Pct.	H.	R.	ER.	SO.	BB.	ERA.
1985—St. Louis............................. National	5	6	0	0	.000	2	0	0	3	1	0.00

WORLD SERIES RECORD

Year Club League	G.	IP.	W.	L.	Pct.	H.	R.	ER.	SO.	BB.	ERA.
1985—St. Louis............................. National	4	6	1	0	1.000	1	0	0	5	3	0.00

JON ERIC DEBUS

Born August 31, 1958, at Chicago Heights, Ill.
Height, 6.03. Weight, 215.
Throws and bats righthanded.
Received bachelor of arts degree in American history
from College of St. Francis, Joliet, Ill.

Tied for California League lead in total bases with 245 in 1982.
Led California League in passed balls with 42 in 1983.

Year Club League	Pos.	G.	AB.	R.	H.	2B.	3B.	HR.	RBI.	B.A.	PO.	A.	E.	F.A.
1980—Lethbridge .... Pion.	OF	62	246	49	82	16	3	8	58	.333	77	5	9	.901
1981—Vero Beach........... Fla. St.	3B-OF	121	425	50	103	19	5	3	54	.242	92	154	24	.911
1982—Lodi........................ Calif.	3B	138	498	73	162	23	6	16	94	.325	★101	219	★48	.870
1983—Lodi........................ Calif.	C	104	354	64	97	22	2	7	56	.274	322	45	12	.968
1983—San Antonio........... Texas	C	7	26	2	7	1	0	0	4	.269	29	5	1	.971

Year—Club	League	Pos.	G.	AB.	R.	H.	2B.	3B.	HR.	RBI.	B.A.	PO.	A.	E.	F.A.
1983—Albuquerque	P. C.	C	14	47	10	14	3	1	1	6	.298	45	1	0	1.000
1984—Albuquerque	P. C.	C-3-O-2	77	165	21	44	3	0	3	26	.267	125	30	14	.917
1985—San Antonio	Texas	C-1-O-3	110	390	49	112	23	2	7	64	.287	482	59	18	.968
1986—Albuquerque	P. C.	C-1-O-3-P	93	233	34	61	9	1	14	50	.262	239	25	3	.989

Selected by Los Angeles Dodgers' organization in 21st round of free-agent draft, June 3, 1980.

PITCHING RECORD

Year—Club	League	G.	IP.	W.	L.	Pct.	H.	R.	ER.	SO.	BB.	ERA.
1986—Albuquerque	P. Coast	2	3	0	0	.000	4	3	3	0	2	9.00

DOUGLAS VERNON DeCINCES
Name pronounced Duh-SIN-say.
(Doug)

Born August 29, 1950, at Burbank, Calif.
Height, 6.02. Weight, 195.
Throws and bats righthanded.
Attended Pierce Junior College, Woodland Hills, Calif., and University of
California, Los Angeles, Calif.

Tied major league record for most times, three or more home runs, game, season (2), August 3 and August 8, 1982.
Tied American League record for most assists, third baseman, game (11), May 7, 1983, 12 innings.
Major League stolen bases: 1976 (8), 1977 (8), 1978 (7), 1979 (5), 1980 (11), 1982 (7), 1983 (2), 1984 (4), 1985 (1), 1986 (2). Total—55.
Hit three home runs in a game, August 3 and August 8, 1982.
Led American League third basemen in assists with 330 in 1977 and 399 in 1982.
Led American League third basemen in total chances with 474 in 1977 and 479 in 1980.
Led American League third basemen in double plays with 34 in 1977, 41 in 1980 and 31 in 1981.
Tied for American League lead in putouts by third basemen with 86 in 1981.
Led Southern League second basemen in errors with 26 in 1972.
Named third baseman on THE SPORTING NEWS American League All-Star Team, 1982.
Named third baseman on THE SPORTING NEWS American League Silver Slugger team, 1982.

Year—Club	League	Pos.	G.	AB.	R.	H.	2B.	3B.	HR.	RBI.	B.A.	PO.	A.	E.	F.A.
1970—Bluefield	Appal.	S-1-2-3-P	54	164	28	48	10	0	4	27	.293	105	98	18	.919
1970—Dallas-Ft. W.	Texas	SS	11	35	3	6	1	0	0	2	.171	25	19	3	.936
1971—Dallas-Ft. W.†	Texas	2B-SS	78	235	29	61	10	1	5	29	.260	154	164	12	.964
1972—Asheville	South.	2B-SS	123	396	71	104	23	7	10	60	.263	254	314	28	.953
1973—Rochester	Int.	★3B-S-2	131	438	79	117	25	3	19	79	.267	150	264	17	★.961
1973—Baltimore	Amer.	3B-2B-SS	10	18	2	2	0	0	0	3	.111	4	19	2	.920
1974—Rochester	Int.	3B	132	444	70	125	17	4	11	66	.282	98	255	★32	.917
1974—Baltimore	Amer.	3B	1	1	0	0	0	0	0	0	.000	0	2	0	1.000
1975—Baltimore	Amer.	3-S-2-1	61	167	20	42	6	3	4	23	.251	92	115	7	.967
1976—Baltimore	Amer.	3-2-1-S	129	440	36	103	17	2	11	42	.234	191	257	20	.957
1977—Baltimore	Amer.	3B-1B-2B	150	522	63	135	28	3	19	69	.259	125	331	20	.958
1978—Baltimore	Amer.	3B-2B	142	511	72	146	37	1	28	80	.286	138	308	14	.970
1979—Baltimore‡	Amer.	3B	120	422	67	97	27	1	16	61	.230	99	247	13	.964
1980—Baltimore	Amer.	●3B-1B	145	489	64	122	23	2	16	64	.249	122	●340	19	.960
1981—Baltimore§	Amer.	●3-1-O	100	346	49	91	23	2	13	55	.263	91	191	●17	.943
1982—California	Amer.	3B-SS	153	575	94	173	42	5	30	97	.301	113	400	22	.959
1983—California x	Amer.	3B	95	370	49	104	19	3	18	65	.281	79	216	14	.955
1984—California	Amer.	3B	146	547	77	147	23	3	20	82	.269	107	266	14	.964
1985—California y	Amer.	3B	120	427	50	104	22	1	20	78	.244	95	202	13	.958
1986—California z	Amer.	3B-SS	140	512	69	131	20	3	26	96	.256	119	216	12	.965
Major League Totals—14 Years			1512	5347	712	1397	287	29	221	815	.261	1375	3110	187	.960

Selected by San Diego Padres' organization in 3rd round of free-agent draft, June 5, 1969.
Selected by Baltimore Orioles' organization in secondary phase of free-agent draft, January 17, 1970.
†On disabled list, June 25 to July 27, 1971.
‡On disabled list, April 27 to June 5, 1979.
§Traded with Pitcher Jeff Schneider to California Angels for Outfielder Dan Ford, January 28, 1982.
xOn disabled list, July 14 to August 19, 1983.
yOn disabled list, May 15 to June 3, 1985.
zGranted free agency, November 12, 1986.

CHAMPIONSHIP SERIES RECORD

Established American League Championship Series record for most at-bats, seven-game Series (32), 1986.
Tied American League record for hits, two consecutive Series (15), 1982 and 1986.

Year—Club	League	Pos.	G.	AB.	R.	H.	2B.	3B.	HR.	RBI.	B.A.	PO.	A.	E.	F.A.
1979—Baltimore	Amer.	3B	4	13	4	4	1	0	0	3	.308	5	8	0	1.000
1982—California	Amer.	3B	5	19	5	6	2	0	0	0	.316	9	12	3	.875
1986—California	Amer.	3B	7	32	2	9	3	0	1	3	.281	6	18	2	.923
Championship Series Totals—3 Years			16	64	11	19	6	0	1	6	.297	20	38	5	.921

WORLD SERIES RECORD

Tied World Series records for hitting home run in first series at bat, October 10, 1979; most errors by third baseman, inning (2), October 10, 1979 (sixth inning); most bases on balls, game (4), October 13, 1979.

Year—Club	League	Pos.	G.	AB.	R.	H.	2B.	3B.	HR.	RBI.	B.A.	PO.	A.	E.	F.A.
1979—Baltimore	Amer.	3B	7	25	2	5	0	0	1	3	.200	7	21	3	.903

ALL-STAR GAME RECORD

Year League	Pos.	AB.	R.	H.	2B.	3B.	HR.	RBI.	B.A.	PO.	A.	E.	F.A.
1983—American	PH	1	0	0	0	0	0	0	.000	0	0	0	.000

PITCHING RECORD

Year Club	League	G.	IP.	W.	L.	Pct.	H.	R.	ER.	SO.	BB.	ERA.
1970—Bluefield	Ap'lachian	1	2	0	1	.000	3	2	1	1	1	4.50

JEFFREY LINDEN DEDMON
(Jeff)

Born March 4, 1960, at Torrance, Calif.
Height, 6.02. Weight, 200.
Throws right and bats lefthanded.
Attended West Los Angeles College, Culver City, Calif.

Major League saves: 1984 (4), 1986 (3). Total—7.

Year Club	League	G.	IP.	W.	L.	Pct.	H.	R.	ER.	SO.	BB.	ERA.
1980—Bradenton Braves	Gulf Coast	10	64	3	4	.429	55	26	21	28	11	2.95
1980—Anderson	S. Atlantic	2	11	1	0	1.000	10	3	1	8	3	0.82
1981—Durham	Carolina	28	165	7	8	.467	178	97	79	115	50	4.31
1982—Durham	Carolina	31	121⅓	5	6	.455	113	57	37	102	54	2.74
1983—Savannah	Southern	21	50	4	1	.800	46	18	16	26	16	2.88
1983—Richmond	Int'national	21	36	2	2	.500	28	9	7	33	14	1.75
1983—Atlanta	National	5	4	0	0	.000	10	6	6	3	0	13.50
1984—Atlanta	National	54	81	4	3	.571	86	39	34	51	35	3.78
1984—Richmond	Int'national	6	10	1	2	.333	11	10	9	10	13	8.10
1985—Richmond	Int'national	10	12	1	1	.500	12	2	2	7	3	1.50
1985—Atlanta	National	60	86	6	3	.667	84	52	39	41	49	4.08
1986—Atlanta†	National	57	99⅔	6	6	.500	90	43	33	58	39	2.98
Major League Totals—4 Years		176	270⅔	16	12	.571	270	140	112	153	123	3.72

Selected by Houston Astros' organization in 1st round (seventh player selected), of free-agent draft, January 9, 1979.
Selected by Oakland A's organization in secondary phase of free-agent draft, June 5, 1979.
Selected by San Francisco Giants' organization in secondary phase of free-agent draft, January 8, 1980.
Selected by Atlanta Braves' organization in secondary phase of free-agent draft, June 3, 1980.
†Appeared in one game as an outfielder with no chances.

ROBERT GEORGE DEER
(Rob)

Born September 29, 1960, at Orange, Calif.
Height, 6.03. Weight, 210.
Throws and bats righthanded.
Attended Fresno City College, Fresno, Calif.

Major League stolen bases: 1984 (1), 1986 (5). Total—6.
Led Pacific Coast League batters in strikeouts with 175 in 1984.
Led Texas League batters in strikeouts with 177 in 1982 and 185 in 1983.
Tied for Texas League lead in game-winning RBIs with 13 in 1983.
Led California League batters in strikeouts with 146 in 1981.

Year Club	League	Pos.	G.	AB.	R.	H.	2B.	3B.	HR.	RBI.	B.A.	PO.	A.	E.	F.A.
1978—Great Falls	Pion.	OF	48	137	20	34	6	5	0	18	.248	83	3	4	.956
1979—Cedar Rapids	Midw.	OF	29	86	7	18	0	1	1	16	.209	35	1	4	.900
1979—Great Falls	Pion.	OF	63	218	49	69	18	7	7	44	.317	95	10	5	.955
1980—Clinton	Midw.	OF	127	434	60	114	31	5	13	58	.263	184	●17	11	.948
1981—Fresno	Calif.	OF	135	479	86	137	24	4	★33	107	.286	211	14	6	.974
1982—Shreveport	Texas	OF-1B	128	410	58	85	26	0	27	73	.207	184	10	11	.946
1983—Shreveport	Texas	OF	132	448	89	97	15	1	★35	99	.217	252	13	7	.974
1984—Phoenix	P. C.	OF	133	449	88	102	21	1	★31	69	.227	251	★19	9	.968
1984—San Francisco	Nat.	OF	13	24	5	4	0	0	3	3	.167	19	0	2	.905
1985—San Francisco†	Nat.	OF-1B	78	162	22	30	5	1	8	20	.185	127	2	2	.985
1986—Milwaukee	Amer.	OF-1B	134	466	75	108	17	3	33	86	.232	312	8	8	.976
National League Totals—2 Years			91	186	27	34	5	1	11	23	.183	146	2	4	.974
American League Totals—1 Year			134	466	75	108	17	3	33	86	.232	312	8	8	.976
Major League Totals—3 Years			225	652	102	142	22	4	44	109	.218	458	10	12	.975

Selected by San Francisco Giants' organization in 4th round of free-agent draft, June 6, 1978.
†Traded to Milwaukee Brewers for Pitchers Dean Freeland and Eric Pilkington, December 18, 1985.

IVAN DeJESUS (ALVAREZ)

Name pronounced Day-HAY-soos.

Born January 9, 1953, at Santurce, Puerto Rico.
Height, 5.11. Weight, 185.
Throws and bats righthanded.
Attended University of Puerto Rico, Rio Piedras, Puerto Rico.

Tied Major League record for fewest double plays by shortstop, season, 150 or more games (64), 1983.
Major League stolen bases: 1975 (1), 1977 (24), 1978 (41), 1979 (24), 1980 (44), 1981 (21), 1982 (14), 1983 (11), 1984 (12), 1985 (2). Total—194.
Hit for the cycle, April 22, 1980.

Led National League shortstops in double plays with 81 in 1981.
Led Pacific Coast League shortstops in double plays with 114 in 1974.
Led California League shortstops in double plays with 87 in 1973.
Led California League shortstops in assists with 311, errors with 48 and double plays with 53 in 1971.
Led Florida State League shortstops in double plays with 56 in 1970.

Year	Club	League	Pos.	G.	AB.	R.	H.	2B.	3B.	HR.	RBI.	B.A.	PO.	A.	E.	F.A.
1970—Daytona Beach	Fla. St.		SS	123	396	51	92	12	7	2	38	.232	164	361	38	.933
1971—Bakersfield	Calif.		SS-2B	126	462	77	108	16	2	6	30	.234	159	323	49	.908
1972—Daytona Beach	Fla. St.		SS	131	442	56	108	15	4	7	39	.244	187	*452	37	.945
1973—Bakersfield	Calif.		SS	132	519	77	125	17	1	7	57	.241	221	*403	*47	.930
1974—Albuquerque	P. C.		SS	140	510	81	152	17	5	7	55	.298	*268	*479	38	.952
1974—Los Angeles	Nat.		SS	3	3	1	1	0	0	0	0	.333	1	0	0	1.000
1975—Albuquerque	P. C.		SS	62	221	24	60	10	2	1	21	.271	97	265	24	.938
1975—Los Angeles	Nat.		SS	63	87	10	16	2	1	0	2	.184	45	107	4	.974
1976—Albuquerque	P. C.		SS-3B	108	405	69	123	27	7	7	64	.304	161	341	35	.935
1976—Los Angeles†	Nat.		SS-3B	22	41	4	7	2	1	0	2	.171	20	47	3	.957
1977—Chicago	Nat.		SS	155	624	91	166	31	7	3	40	.266	234	*595	33	.962
1978—Chicago	Nat.		SS	160	619	*104	172	24	7	3	35	.278	232	*558	27	.967
1979—Chicago	Nat.		SS	160	636	92	180	26	10	5	52	.283	235	507	32	.959
1980—Chicago	Nat.		SS	157	618	78	160	26	3	3	33	.259	229	529	24	.969
1981—Chicago‡	Nat.		SS	106	403	49	78	8	4	0	13	.194	*221	343	24	.959
1982—Philadelphia	Nat.		SS-3B	161	536	53	128	21	5	3	59	.239	222	488	21	.971
1983—Philadelphia	Nat.		SS	158	497	60	126	15	7	4	45	.254	214	438	23	.966
1984—Philadelphia§	Nat.		SS	144	435	40	112	15	3	0	35	.257	166	400	29	.951
1985—St. Louis x	Nat.		3B-SS	59	72	11	16	5	0	0	7	.222	15	40	2	.965
1986—Columbus	Int.		SS-2B	25	84	10	22	3	1	0	15	.262	36	72	6	.947
1986—New York y	Amer.		SS	7	4	1	0	0	0	0	0	.000	5	4	1	.900
1986—Vermont z	East.		SS-3B	10	36	4	10	1	0	1	5	.278	9	23	0	1.000
National League Totals—12 Years				1348	4571	593	1162	175	48	21	323	.254	1834	4052	222	.964
American League Totals—1 Year				7	4	1	0	0	0	0	0	.000	5	4	1	.900
Major League Totals—13 Years				1355	4575	594	1162	175	48	21	323	.254	1839	4056	223	.964

Signed as free agent by Los Angeles Dodgers' organization, May 23, 1969.

†Traded with First Baseman Bill Buckner and Pitcher Jeff Albert to Chicago Cubs for Outfielder Rick Monday and Pitcher Mike Garman, January 11, 1977.

‡Traded to Philadelphia Phillies for Shortstop Larry Bowa and Infielder Ryne Sandberg, January 27, 1982.

§Traded with Pitcher Bill Campbell to St. Louis Cardinals for Pitcher Dave Rucker, April 6, 1985.

xGranted free agency, November 12, 1985; signed by Columbus (New York Yankees' organization), May 1, 1986.

yReleased, June 24, 1986; signed by Vermont (Cincinnati Reds' organization), July 16, 1986.

zReleased, July 28, 1986.

CHAMPIONSHIP SERIES RECORD

Year	Club	League	Pos.	G.	AB.	R.	H.	2B.	3B.	HR.	RBI.	B.A.	PO.	A.	E.	F.A.
1983—Philadelphia	Nat.		SS	4	12	0	3	0	0	0	1	.250	4	11	2	.882

WORLD SERIES RECORD

Year	Club	League	Pos.	G.	AB.	R.	H.	2B.	3B.	HR.	RBI.	B.A.	PO.	A.	E.	F.A.
1983—Philadelphia	Nat.		SS	5	16	0	2	0	0	0	0	.125	5	14	1	.950
1985—St. Louis	Nat.		PH	1	1	0	0	0	0	0	0	.000	0	0	0	.000
World Series Totals—2 Years				6	17	0	2	0	0	0	0	.118	5	14	1	.950

JOSE DeLEON (CHESTARO)

Born December 20, 1960, at LaVega, D.R.
Height, 6.03. Weight, 219.
Throws and bats righthanded.

Major League saves: 1985 (3), 1986 (1). Total—4.
Led Gulf Coast League in home runs allowed with 7 in 1979.
Tied for South Atlantic League lead in home runs allowed with 19 in 1980.
Tied for Gulf Coast League lead in wild pitches with 9 in 1979.

Year	Club	League	G.	IP.	W.	L.	Pct.	H.	R.	ER.	SO.	BB.	ERA.
1979—Bradenton Pirates	Gulf Coast		11	59	2	4	.333	76	47	42	33	38	6.41
1980—Shelby	S. Atlantic		26	168	10	15	.400	160	108	*90	118	69	4.82
1981—Buffalo	Eastern		25	159	12	6	.667	136	72	55	158	94	3.11
1982—Portland†	P. Coast		24	119	10	7	.588	138	81	79	94	65	5.97
1983—Hawaii	P. Coast		20	127⅓	11	6	.647	90	50	43	128	68	*3.04
1983—Pittsburgh	National		15	108	7	3	.700	75	34	34	118	47	2.83
1984—Pittsburgh	National		30	192⅓	7	13	.350	147	86	80	153	92	3.74
1985—Pittsburgh	National		31	162⅔	2	*19	.095	138	93	85	149	89	4.70
1985—Hawaii	P. Coast		5	41	4	0	1.000	15	4	4	45	10	0.88
1986—Hawaii	P. Coast		15	106	5	8	.385	87	32	29	83	44	2.46
1986—Pittsburgh‡	National		9	16⅓	1	3	.250	17	16	15	11	17	8.27
1986—Chicago	American		13	79	4	5	.444	49	30	26	68	42	2.96
National League Totals—4 Years			85	479⅓	17	38	.309	377	231	214	431	245	4.02
American League Totals—1 Year			13	79	4	5	.444	49	30	26	68	42	2.96
Major League Totals—4 Years			98	558⅓	21	43	.328	426	245	225	499	287	3.63

Selected by Pittsburgh Pirates' organization in 3rd round of free-agent draft June 5, 1979.

†On disabled list, July 5 to July 29, 1982.

‡Traded to Chicago White Sox for Outfielder Bobby Bonilla, July 23, 1986.

LUIS M. DE LOS SANTOS

Born December 29, 1966, at San Cristobal, D.R.
Height, 6.05. Weight, 190.
Throws and bats righthanded.

Year Club	League	Pos.	G.	AB.	R.	H.	2B.	3B.	HR.	RBI.	B.A.	PO.	A.	E.	F.A.
1984—Eugene	N'west	3B	67	257	27	69	10	2	2	30	.268	67	93	22	.879
1985—Fort Myers	Fla. St.	3B	123	454	44	120	18	2	0	48	.264	87	141	32	.877
1986—Memphis	South.	3B	135	525	72	159	21	5	3	84	.303	★136	244	★50	.884

Selected by Kansas City Royals' organization in 2nd round of free-agent draft, June 4, 1984.

JOHN RIKARD DEMPSEY
(Rick)

Born September 13, 1949, at Fayetteville, Tenn.
Height, 6.00. Weight, 184.
Throws and bats righthanded.
Attended Pierce Junior College, Woodland Hills, Calif.
Brother of Pat Dempsey, catcher in Minnesota Twins' organization.
Tied major league record for most double plays by catcher, game (3), June 1, 1977.
Major league stolen bases: 1974 (1), 1976 (1), 1977 (2), 1978 (7), 1980 (3), 1983 (1), 1984 (1), 1986 (1). Total—17.
Tied for American League lead in double plays by catchers with 14 in 1978.
Led International League in passed balls with 14 in 1973.
Led New York-Pennsylvania League catchers in putouts with 468, assists with 35, fielding percentage with .990 and tied for lead in double plays with 4 in 1968.

Year Club	League	Pos.	G.	AB.	R.	H.	2B.	3B.	HR.	RBI.	B.A.	PO.	A.	E.	F.A.
1967—Sarasota Twins	Gulf C.	C-OF-1B	40	102	9	21	4	3	0	9	.206	133	16	2	.987
1968—Wis. Rapids	Midw.	C	11	35	12	8	2	0	1	6	.229	68	2	1	.986
1968—Auburn	NYP	C-1B-OF	73	270	48	79	10	7	7	61	.293	505	38	7	.987
1969—Wis. Rapids	Midw.	C	50	151	35	55	11	2	6	31	.364	341	30	●13	.966
1969—Minnesota	Amer.	C	5	6	1	3	1	0	0	0	.500	5	0	1	.833
1970—Charlotte	South	C-OF-2B	105	351	28	86	20	6	4	42	.245	506	76	18	.970
1970—Minnesota	Amer.	C	5	7	1	0	0	0	0	0	.000	12	0	1	.923
1971—Charlotte	South	C-OF	105	338	39	82	16	2	8	47	.243	599	65	8	.988
1971—Minnesota	Amer.	C	6	13	2	4	1	0	0	0	.308	30	4	2	.944
1972—Minnesota†	Amer.	C	25	40	0	8	1	0	0	0	.200	67	5	1	.986
1972—Tacoma	P. C.	C-OF	48	161	13	38	6	2	3	18	.236	284	33	5	.984
1973—Syracuse	Int.	C-OF-3B	122	387	53	96	14	4	6	47	.248	585	69	9	.986
1973—New York	Amer.	C	6	11	0	2	0	0	0	0	.182	9	0	2	.818
1974—New York	Amer.	C-OF	43	109	12	26	3	0	2	12	.239	152	22	4	.978
1975—New York	Amer.	C-OF-3B	71	145	18	38	8	0	1	11	.262	92	9	3	.971
1976—N.Y.‡-Balt.	Amer.	C-OF	80	216	12	42	2	0	0	12	.194	302	39	4	.988
1977—Baltimore§	Amer.	C	91	270	27	61	7	4	3	34	.226	416	52	11	.977
1978—Baltimore	Amer.	C	136	441	41	114	25	0	6	32	.259	636	79	11	.985
1979—Baltimore	Amer.	C	124	368	48	88	23	0	6	41	.239	615	★81	7	.990
1980—Baltimore	Amer.	C-OF-1B	119	362	51	95	26	3	9	40	.262	544	55	8	.987
1981—Baltimore	Amer.	C	92	251	24	54	10	1	6	15	.215	384	35	1	★.998
1982—Baltimore	Amer.	C	125	344	35	88	15	1	5	36	.256	491	46	5	.991
1983—Baltimore	Amer.	C	128	347	33	80	16	2	4	32	.231	591	65	2	★.997
1984—Baltimore	Amer.	C	109	330	37	76	11	0	11	34	.230	453	43	4	.992
1985—Baltimore	Amer.	C	132	362	54	92	19	0	12	52	.254	575	49	8	.987
1986—Baltimore x	Amer.	C	122	327	42	68	15	1	13	29	.208	659	53	7	.990
Major League Totals—18 Years			1419	3949	438	939	183	12	78	380	.238	6033	637	82	.988

Selected by Minnesota Twins' organization in 12th round of free-agent draft, June 6, 1967.
†Traded to New York Yankees' organization for Outfielder Danny Walton, October 27, 1972.
‡Traded with Pitchers Rudy May, Tippy Martinez, Dave Pagan and Scott McGregor to Baltimore Orioles for Pitchers Ken Holtzman, Doyle Alexander and Grant Jackson, Catcher Ellie Hendricks and Pitcher Jimmy Freeman, June 15, 1976.
§On disabled list, July 9 to August 21, 1977.
xGranted free agency, November 12, 1986.

CHAMPIONSHIP SERIES RECORD

Year Club	League	Pos.	G.	AB.	R.	H.	2B.	3B.	HR.	RBI.	B.A.	PO.	A.	E.	F.A.
1979—Baltimore	Amer.	C	3	10	3	4	2	0	0	2	.400	10	1	0	1.000
1983—Baltimore	Amer.	C	4	12	1	2	0	0	0	0	.167	29	5	1	.971
Championship Series Totals—2 Years			7	22	4	6	2	0	0	2	.273	39	6	1	.978

WORLD SERIES RECORD

Established World Series record for most long hits, five-game Series (5), 1983.
Tied World Series record for most two-base hits, five-game Series (4), 1983.

Year Club	League	Pos.	G.	AB.	R.	H.	2B.	3B.	HR.	RBI.	B.A.	PO.	A.	E.	F.A.
1979—Baltimore	Amer.	C-PR	7	21	3	6	2	0	0	0	.286	38	2	0	1.000
1983—Baltimore	Amer.	C	5	13	3	5	4	0	1	2	.385	27	4	0	1.000
World Series Totals—2 Years			12	34	6	11	6	0	1	2	.324	65	6	0	1.000

—DID YOU KNOW—

That the Cincinnati Reds opening-day crowd of 54,960 was the largest regular-season turnout in Riverfront Stadium history?

JOHN ALLEN DENNY

Born November 8, 1952, at Prescott, Ariz.
Height, 6.03. Weight, 190.
Throws and bats righthanded.
Attended Yavapai College, Prescott, Ariz., and Southern Illinois University, Edwardsville, Ill.

Tied National League record for fewest games won, season, for leader in games won (19), 1983.
Pitched 8-1 no-hit victory against Midland, May 17, 1973.
Named National League Pitcher of the Year by THE SPORTING NEWS, 1983.
Won National League Cy Young Memorial Award, 1983.
Named National League Comeback Player of the Year by THE SPORTING NEWS, 1983.
Named righthanded pitcher on THE SPORTING NEWS National League All-Star Team, 1983.

Year Club	League	G.	IP.	W.	L.	Pct.	H.	R.	ER.	SO.	BB.	ERA.
1970—Sarasota Cardinals	Gulf Coast	11	42	2	2	.500	32	14	6	43	9	1.29
1971—St. Petersburg	Florida St.	26	139	8	13	.381	123	58	47	77	62	3.04
1972—Modesto†	California	14	92	7	5	.583	95	54	45	65	39	4.40
1973—Arkansas‡	Texas	20	147	10	6	.625	128	57	51	81	52	3.12
1974—Tulsa	Am. Assoc.	21	132	9	8	.529	127	66	55	79	57	3.75
1974—St. Louis	National	2	2	0	0	.000	3	2	0	1	0	0.00
1975—Tulsa	Am. Assoc.	7	60	3	1	.750	47	12	12	44	32	1.80
1975—St. Louis	National	25	136	10	7	.588	149	73	60	72	51	3.97
1976—St. Louis	National	30	207	11	9	.550	189	71	58	74	74	★2.52
1977—St. Louis§	National	26	150	8	8	.500	165	85	75	60	62	4.50
1978—St. Louis	National	33	234	14	11	.560	200	81	77	103	74	2.96
1979—St. Louis x	National	31	206	8	11	.421	206	116	111	99	100	4.85
1980—Cleveland y	American	16	109	8	6	.571	116	54	53	59	47	4.38
1981—Cleveland z	American	19	146	10	6	.625	139	62	51	94	66	3.14
1982—Cleveland a	American	21	138⅓	6	11	.353	126	80	77	94	73	5.01
1982—Philadelphia	National	4	22⅓	0	2	.000	18	12	10	19	10	4.03
1983—Philadelphia	National	36	242⅔	★19	6	★.760	229	77	64	139	53	2.37
1984—Philadelphia b	National	22	154⅓	7	7	.500	122	53	42	94	29	2.45
1985—Philadelphia c	National	33	230⅔	11	14	.440	252	112	98	123	83	3.82
1986—Cincinnati d	National	27	171⅓	11	10	.524	179	89	80	115	56	4.20
National League Totals—11 Years		269	1756⅓	99	85	.538	1712	771	675	899	592	3.46
American League Totals—3 Years		56	393⅓	24	23	.511	381	196	181	247	186	4.14
Major League Totals—13 Years		325	2149⅔	123	108	.532	2093	967	856	1146	778	3.58

Selected by St. Louis Cardinals' organization in 29th round of free-agent draft, June 4, 1970.
†On disabled list, July 17, 1972 through remainder of season.
‡On disabled list, August 11, 1973 through remainder of season.
§On disabled list, June 22 to July 29, 1977.
xTraded with Outfielder Jerry Mumphrey to Cleveland Indians for Outfielder Bobby Bonds, December 7, 1979.
yOn disabled list, July 15 to September 8, 1980.
zGranted free agency, November 13, 1981; re-signed by Indians, February 13, 1982.
aTraded to Philadelphia Phillies for Pitchers Jerry Reed and Roy Smith and Outfielder Wil Culmer, September 11, 1982.
bOn disabled list, May 31 to July 30, 1984.
cTraded with Pitcher Jeff Gray to Cincinnati Reds for Outfielder Gary Redus and Pitcher Tom Hume, December 11, 1985.
dGranted free agency, November 12, 1986.

CHAMPIONSHIP SERIES RECORD

Year Club	League	G.	IP.	W.	L.	Pct.	H.	R.	ER.	SO.	BB.	ERA.
1983—Philadelphia	National	1	6	0	1	.000	5	3	0	3	3	0.00

WORLD SERIES RECORD

Tied World Series record for most putouts, pitcher, inning (2), October 15, 1983 (fifth inning).

Year Club	League	G.	IP.	W.	L.	Pct.	H.	R.	ER.	SO.	BB.	ERA.
1983—Philadelphia	National	2	13	1	1	.500	12	5	5	9	3	3.46

ANDREW DENSON JR.

(Drew)

Born November 16, 1965, at Cincinnati, O.
Height, 6.05. Weight, 210.
Throws and bats righthanded.

Led Gulf Coast League in total bases with 133 and slugging percentage with .556 in 1984.

Year Club	League	Pos.	G.	AB.	R.	H.	2B.	3B.	HR.	RBI.	B.A.	PO.	A.	E.	F.A.
1984—Bradenton Brav	Gulf C.	OF	62	239	43	★77	★20	3	●10	★45	★.322	65	6	2	.973
1985—Sumter†	S. Atl.	OF	111	383	59	115	18	4	14	74	.300	119	5	3	.976
1986—Durham	Carol.	OF	72	231	31	54	6	3	4	23	.234	86	3	11	.890

Selected by Atlanta Braves' organization in 1st round (19th player selected) of free-agent draft, June 4, 1984.
†On disabled list, April 24 to May 4, 1985.

—DID YOU KNOW—

That when Detroit's Eric King tied a major league record by making six putouts July 8 in a nine-inning game against Minnesota, the opposing starting pitcher—Bert Blyleven—held the record he tied?

ROBERT EUGENE DERNIER

Name pronounced Dur-NEER.

(Bob)

Born January 5, 1957, at Kansas City, Mo.
Height, 6.00. Weight, 165.
Throws and bats righthanded.
Attended Longview Community College, Lee's Summit, Mo.

Major League stolen bases: 1980 (3), 1981 (2), 1982 (42), 1983 (35), 1984 (45), 1985 (31), 1986 (27). Total—185.
Led Carolina League in stolen bases with 77 in 1979, Eastern League with 71 in 1980 and American Association with 72 in 1981.
Led Carolina League outfielders in putouts with 315 in 1979.
Tied for Carolina League lead in sacrifice hits with 12 in 1979.
Tied for Pioneer League lead in double plays by third basemen with 9 in 1978.
Named outfielder on THE SPORTING NEWS National League All-Star fielding team, 1984.
Named Carolina League Most Valuable Player, 1979.

Year—Club	League	Pos.	G.	AB.	R.	H.	2B.	3B.	HR.	RBI.	B.A.	PO.	A.	E.	F.A.
1978—Spartanburg	W. Car.	SS	22	57	9	8	1	0	0	5	.140	23	61	16	.840
1978—Helena	Pion.	3B	53	186	49	56	6	2	4	27	.301	38	104	22	.866
1979—Peninsula	Carol.	OF-3B	135	491	102	143	19	2	4	42	.291	331	23	10	.973
1980—Reading	East.	OF	136	*536	*111	160	29	4	10	57	.299	*325	9	9	.974
1980—Philadelphia	Nat.	OF	10	7	5	4	0	0	0	1	.571	9	0	0	1.000
1981—Oklahoma City	A. A.	OF	127	497	*105	150	26	7	5	35	.302	*317	7	5	.985
1981—Philadelphia	Nat.	OF	10	4	0	3	0	0	0	0	.750	2	0	0	1.000
1982—Philadelphia	Nat.	OF	122	370	56	92	10	2	4	21	.249	255	5	5	.981
1983—Philadelphia	Nat.	OF	122	221	41	51	10	0	1	15	.231	164	3	2	.988
1983—Reading†	East.	OF	14	56	8	13	1	1	1	4	.232	36	0	0	1.000
1984—Chicago	Nat.	OF	143	536	94	149	26	5	3	32	.278	355	5	5	.986
1985—Chicago‡	Nat.	OF	121	469	63	119	20	3	1	21	.254	310	4	9	.972
1986—Chicago§	Nat.	OF	108	324	32	73	14	1	4	18	.225	222	3	3	.987
Major League Totals—7 Years			636	1931	291	491	80	11	13	108	.254	1317	20	24	.982

Selected by Cincinnati Reds' organization in 12th round of free-agent draft, January 11, 1977.
Signed as free agent by Philadelphia Phillies' organization, August 5, 1977.
†Traded with Outfielder Gary Matthews and Pitcher Porfi Altamirano to Chicago Cubs for Pitcher Bill Campbell and Catcher Mike Diaz, March 27, 1984.
‡On disabled list, June 15 to July 7, 1985.
§On disabled list, June 15 to July 23, 1986.

CHAMPIONSHIP SERIES RECORD

Tied Championship Series record for most times hitting home run as leadoff batter, start of game (1), October 2, 1984.

Year—Club	League	Pos.	G.	AB.	R.	H.	2B.	3B.	HR.	RBI.	B.A.	PO.	A.	E.	F.A.
1983—Philadelphia	Nat.	OF	1	0	0	0	0	0	0	0	.000	0	0	0	.000
1984—Chicago	Nat.	OF	5	17	5	4	2	0	1	1	.235	12	1	0	1.000
Championship Series Totals—2 Years			6	17	5	4	2	0	1	1	.235	12	1	0	1.000

WORLD SERIES RECORD

Year—Club	League	Pos.	G.	AB.	R.	H.	2B.	3B.	HR.	RBI.	B.A.	PO.	A.	E.	F.A.
1983—Philadelphia	Nat.	PR	1	0	1	0	0	0	0	0	.000	0	0	0	.000

JAMES JOSEPH DESHAIES

Name pronounced De-SHAYS.

(Jim)

Born June 23, 1960, at Massena, N.Y.
Height, 6.04. Weight, 222.
Throws and bats lefthanded.
Received bachelor of arts degree from Le Moyne College, Syracuse, N.Y., in 1982.

Established modern major league record for most consecutive strikeouts at start of game (8), September 23, 1986.
Pitched seven-inning, 5-1 no-hit victory against Columbus, May 4, 1984.
Led National League in balks with 7 in 1986.
Led International League in balks with 4 in 1985.
Tied for International League lead in shutouts with 4 in 1984.

Year—Club	League	G.	IP.	W.	L.	Pct.	H.	R.	ER.	SO.	BB.	ERA.
1982—Oneonta	NYP	15	108⅓	6	5	.545	93	50	40	*137	40	3.32
1983—Fort Lauderdale	Florida St.	20	117⅔	11	3	.786	105	44	33	128	58	2.52
1984—Nashville	Southern	7	45	3	2	.600	33	20	14	42	29	2.80
1984—Columbus	Int'national	18	135⅔	10	5	.667	99	45	36	117	62	*2.39
1984—New York	American	2	7	0	1	.000	14	9	9	5	7	11.57
1985—Columbus†‡	Int'national	21	131⅔	8	6	.571	124	67	63	106	59	4.31
1985—Houston	National	2	3	0	0	.000	1	0	0	2	0	0.00
1986—Houston§	National	26	144	12	5	.706	124	58	52	128	59	3.25
American League Totals—1 Year		2	7	0	1	.000	14	9	9	5	7	11.57
National League Totals—2 Years		28	147	12	5	.706	125	58	52	130	59	3.18
Major League Totals—3 Years		30	154	12	6	.667	139	67	61	135	66	3.56

Selected by Montreal Expos' organization in 13th round of free-agent draft, June 6, 1978.
Selected by New York Yankees' organization in 21st round of free-agent draft, June 7, 1982.

†On disabled list, April 10 to April 26 and August 4 to August 14, 1985.
‡Traded with a player to be named later to Houston Astros for Pitcher Joe Niekro, September 15, 1985; Houston organization acquired Infielder Neder Horta, September 24, 1985, and Pitcher Dody Rather, January 11, 1986, to complete deal.
§On disabled list, April 21 to May 7, 1986.

ORESTES DESTRADE

Name pronounced Des-TRAD-a.
Born May 8, 1962, at Santiago, Cuba.
Height, 6.04. Weight, 210.
Throws right and bats right and lefthanded.
Attended Florida College, Temple Terrace, Fla.
Led Eastern League batters in strikeouts with 129 in 1985.
Tied for Florida State League lead in bases on balls received with 82 and game-winning RBIs with 15 in 1983.
Led Eastern League first basemen in total chances with 1,194 and double plays with 99 in 1985.
Tied for Appalachian League lead in double plays by first basemen with 42 in 1981.

Year Club League	Pos.	G.	AB.	R.	H.	2B.	3B.	HR.	RBI.	B.A.	PO.	A.	E.	F.A.
1981—Paintsville .... Appal.	1B	63	208	51	57	12	1	★14	46	.274	461	22	11	.978
1982—Greensboro .... S. Atl.	1B	43	122	9	22	4	1	1	14	.180	359	15	4	.989
1982—Oneonta................. NYP	1B	64	194	44	45	12	1	4	30	.232	298	33	10	.971
1983—Fort Lauderdale .. Fla. St.	OF-1B	127	425	61	124	24	5	18	74	.292	425	24	9	.980
1984—Nashville................ South.	OF-1B	35	121	15	29	6	0	6	12	.240	56	2	3	.951
1984—Fort Lauderdale .. Fla. St.	1B	95	308	40	68	14	2	12	57	.221	764	41	●16	.981
1985—Albany .... East.	1B	136	471	82	119	24	5	23	72	.253	★1103	73	18	.985
1986—Columbus.............. Int.	1B	98	359	59	99	21	4	19	56	.276	697	63	11	.986

Selected by California Angels' organization in 23rd round of free-agent draft, June 3, 1980.
Signed as free agent by New York Yankees' organization, May 17, 1981.

MICHAEL DEVEREAUX

(Mike)

Born April 10, 1963, at Casper, Wyo.
Height, 6.00. Weight, 195.
Throws and bats righthanded.
Attended Mesa Community College, Mesa, Ariz., and received bachelor of arts degree in finance from Arizona State University, Tempe, Ariz.
Led Pioneer League in total bases with 152 and stolen bases with 40 in 1985.

Year Club League	Pos.	G.	AB.	R.	H.	2B.	3B.	HR.	RBI.	B.A.	PO.	A.	E.	F.A.
1985—Great Falls............ Pion.	OF	●70	★289	★73	★103	17	10	4	★67	.356	100	4	5	.954
1986—San Antonio.......... Texas	OF	115	431	69	130	22	2	10	53	.302	292	13	4	.987

Selected by Cleveland Indians' organization in 26th round of free-agent draft, June 4, 1984.
Selected by Los Angeles Dodgers' organization in 5th round of free-agent draft, June 3, 1985.

JEFFREY ALLEN DeWILLIS

(Jeff)

Born April 13, 1965, at Houston, Tex.
Height, 6.02. Weight, 170.
Throws and bats righthanded.
Led Carolina League catchers in total chances with 932 and double plays with 8 in 1984.

Year Club League	Pos.	G.	AB.	R.	H.	2B.	3B.	HR.	RBI.	B.A.	PO.	A.	E.	F.A.
1983—Medicine Hat........ Pion.	C-OF-1B	56	190	34	46	8	0	5	21	.242	317	26	8	.977
1984—Kinston................... Carol.	C	122	356	47	84	11	1	1	31	.236	★848	69	15	.984
1984—Knoxville .... South.	C	1	2	1	0	0	0	0	0	.000	2	2	0	1.000
1985—Kinston................... Carol.	C	27	87	12	16	3	1	1	8	.184	206	26	3	.987
1985—Knoxville .... South.	C	68	196	22	43	7	1	2	22	.219	377	45	3	.993
1985—Syracuse† .... Int.	C	19	48	3	11	1	0	1	3	.229	106	9	3	.975
1986—Memp.-Knox........ South.	C-1B-SS	75	160	26	32	5	0	1	14	.200	367	43	7	.983

Selected by Toronto Blue Jays' organization in 3rd round of free-agent draft, June 6, 1983.
†Loaned to Memphis (Kansas City Royals' organization), April 1, 1986; returned, June 22, 1986.

BAUDILIO JOSE DIAZ (SEIJAS)

Name pronounced DEE-az.

(Bo)

Born March 23, 1953, at Cua, Miranda, Venezuela.
Height, 5.11. Weight, 200.
Throws and bats righthanded.
Major League stolen bases: 1980 (1), 1981 (2), 1982 (3), 1983 (1), 1986 (1). Total—8.
Tied for International League lead in double plays by catchers with 7 in 1977.

Year Club League	Pos.	G.	AB.	R.	H.	2B.	3B.	HR.	RBI.	B.A.	PO.	A.	E.	F.A.
1971—Winter Haven....... Fla. St.	C	4	10	1	0	0	0	0	0	.000	25	1	0	1.000
1971—Williamsport .... NYP	PH	1	1	0	0	0	0	0	0	.000	0	0	0	.000
1971—Pawtucket............. East.	C	1	2	0	0	0	0	0	0	.000	4	0	0	1.000
1971—Greenville............. W. Car.	C	10	25	2	5	1	0	0	0	.200	35	2	2	.949
1972—Winter Haven....... Fla. St.	C	14	44	3	7	1	0	0	0	.159	72	7	0	1.000
1973—Elmira.................... NYP	C	25	69	3	17	3	0	0	9	.246	107	16	1	.992

Year Club League	Pos.	G.	AB.	R.	H.	2B.	3B.	HR.	RBI.	B.A.	PO.	A.	E.	F.A.
1974—Winter Haven....... Fla. St.	C-3B	97	327	31	79	20	1	1	38	.242	476	75	14	.975
1975—Winston-Salem ..... Carol.	C	59	179	22	47	8	1	6	29	.263	271	45	9	.972
1976—Rhode Island .... Int.	C-OF	62	117	10	29	1	0	4	18	.248	222	28	3	.988
1977—Pawtucket............. Int.	★C-3B	105	308	37	81	14	1	7	54	.263	459	67	6	★.989
1977—Boston†.............. Amer.	C	2	1	0	0	0	0	0	0	.000	5	0	0	1.000
1978—Cleveland‡............. Amer.	C	44	127	12	30	4	0	2	11	.236	183	18	6	.971
1979—Tacoma .... P. C.	C	34	115	5	28	7	0	2	11	.243	223	24	5	.980
1979—Cleveland§............. Amer.	C	15	32	0	5	2	0	0	1	.156	63	6	3	.958
1980—Cleveland............. Amer.	C	76	207	15	47	11	2	3	32	.227	317	35	4	.989
1981—Cleveland x .... Amer.	C	63	182	25	57	19	0	7	38	.313	247	27	7	.975
1982—Philadelphia .... Nat.	C	144	525	69	151	29	1	18	85	.288	850	80	10	.989
1983—Philadelphia .... Nat.	C	136	471	49	111	17	0	15	64	.236	903	97	★14	.986
1984—Philadelphia y...... Nat.	C	27	75	5	16	4	0	1	9	.213	114	9	1	.992
1984—Reading............... East.	C	3	7	2	3	0	0	1	3	.429	11	4	1	.938
1985—Phil. za-Cinc......... Nat.	C	77	237	21	58	13	1	5	31	.245	428	42	8	.983
1986—Cincinnati............. Nat.	C	134	474	50	129	21	0	10	56	.272	732	83	13	.984
American League Totals—5 Years		200	549	52	139	36	2	12	82	.253	815	86	20	.978
National League Totals—5 Years........		518	1782	194	465	84	2	49	245	.261	3027	311	46	.986
Major League Totals—10 Years...............		718	2331	246	604	120	4	61	327	.259	3842	397	66	.985

Signed as free agent by Boston Red Sox' organization, November 25, 1970.

†Traded with Pitchers Rick Wise and Mike Paxton and Third Baseman Ted Cox to Cleveland Indians for Pitcher Dennis Eckersley and Catcher Fred Kendall, March 30, 1978.

‡On disabled list, April 16 to June 16, 1978.

§On disabled list, March 31 to April 17 and June 8 to July 20, 1979.

xTraded to Philadelphia Phillies for Outfielder Lonnie Smith and a player to be named later, November 20, 1981; Cleveland organization acquired Pitcher Scott Munninghoff to complete deal, December 9, 1981.

yOn disabled list, May 1 to May 31, June 21 to July 16 and August 20, 1984 through remainder of season; included rehabilitation disability assignment to Reading, July 11 to July 16, 1984.

zOn disabled list, April 19 to June 1, 1985.

aTraded with Pitcher Greg Simpson to Cincinnati Reds for Shortstop Tom Foley, Catcher Alan Knicely, a player to be named later and cash, August 8, 1985; Philadelphia Phillies acquired Pitcher Freddie Toliver to complete deal, August 27, 1985.

CHAMPIONSHIP SERIES RECORD

Year Club League	Pos.	G.	AB.	R.	H.	2B.	3B.	HR.	RBI.	B.A.	PO.	A.	E.	F.A.
1983—Philadelphia .... Nat.	C	4	13	0	2	1	0	0	0	.154	32	2	0	1.000

WORLD SERIES RECORD

Year Club League	Pos.	G.	AB.	R.	H.	2B.	3B.	HR.	RBI.	B.A.	PO.	A.	E.	F.A.
1983—Philadelphia .... Nat.	C	5	15	1	5	1	0	0	0	.333	37	1	1	.974

ALL-STAR GAME RECORD

Year League	Pos.	AB.	R.	H.	2B.	3B.	HR.	RBI.	B.A.	PO.	A.	E.	F.A.
1981—American	C	1	0	0	0	0	0	0	.000	2	0	0	1.000

CARLOS ANTONIO DIAZ JR.

Name pronounced DEE-az.

Born January 7, 1958, at Kaneohe, Haw.
Height, 6.00. Weight, 170.
Throws left and bats righthanded.
Attended Allan Hancock Junior College, Santa Maria, Calif.

Major League saves: 1982 (1), 1983 (2), 1984 (1). Total—4.

Year Club League	G.	IP.	W.	L.	Pct.	H.	R.	ER.	SO.	BB.	ERA.
1979—Bellingham .... Northwest	2	8	0	0	.000	5	0	0	8	2	0.00
1979—San Jose .... California	26	24	4	1	.800	26	18	17	36	13	6.38
1980—Spokane† .... P. Coast	★58	64	3	5	.375	72	31	28	51	27	3.94
1981—Richmond........................ Int'national	35	49	3	3	.500	32	17	15	29	20	2.81
1982—Richmond........................ Int'national	31	53⅓	3	4	.429	52	21	16	52	17	2.70
1982—Atlanta‡-New York............National	23	29	3	2	.600	37	17	13	16	13	4.03
1983—New York§...................... National	54	83⅓	3	1	.750	62	22	19	64	35	2.05
1984—Los Angeles .... National	37	41	1	0	1.000	47	26	25	36	24	5.49
1984—Albuquerque .... P. Coast	20	46⅓	1	2	.333	48	30	23	35	20	4.47
1985—Los Angeles .... National	46	79⅓	6	3	.667	70	28	23	73	18	2.61
1986—Los Angeles x .... National	19	25⅓	0	0	.000	33	14	12	18	7	4.26
1986—Albuquerque y.................. P. Coast	14	22⅓	1	4	.200	26	17	14	10	9	5.64
Major League Totals—5 Years.............................	179	258	13	6	.684	249	107	92	207	97	3.21

Selected by Seattle Mariners' organization in 3rd round of free-agent draft, January 9, 1979.

Selected by Seattle Mariners' organization in secondary phase of free-agent draft, June 5, 1979.

†Traded to Atlanta Braves' organization for Outfielder Jeff Burroughs, March 6, 1981.

‡Traded to New York Mets for Pitcher Tom Hausman, September 10, 1982.

§Traded with a player to be named later to Los Angeles Dodgers for Pitcher Sid Fernandez and Infielder Ross Jones, December 8, 1983; Los Angeles acquired Infielder Bob Bailor to complete deal, December 12, 1983.

xOn disabled list, May 10 to May 26, 1986.

yReleased, October 20, 1986; signed by Oakland A's, December 22, 1986.

CHAMPIONSHIP SERIES RECORD

Year Club League	G.	IP.	W.	L.	Pct.	H.	R.	ER.	SO.	BB.	ERA.
1985—Los Angeles .... National	2	3	0	0	.000	5	1	1	2	1	3.00

EDGAR SERRANO DIAZ

Born February 8, 1964, at Santurce, Puerto Rico.
Height, 6.00. Weight, 165.
Throws and bats righthanded.

Led Texas League shortstops in total chances with 743 and double plays with 101 in 1985.

Year Club	League	Pos.	G.	AB.	R.	H.	2B.	3B.	HR.	RBI.	B.A.	PO.	A.	E.	F.A.
1982—Pikeville	Appal.	SS	15	24	4	2	0	0	0	0	.083	12	30	3	.933
1983—Beloit	Midw.	SS	107	307	29	64	2	0	0	15	.208	173	258	42	.911
1984—Stockton	Calif.	SS	123	419	58	108	1	7	0	35	.258	189	381	40	.934
1985—El Paso	Texas	SS	132	501	90	134	14	4	0	55	.267	★217	★489	37	.950
1986—Vancouver	P. C.	★SS-2B	108	346	44	109	2	4	0	43	.315	173	311	★31	.940
1986—Milwaukee	Amer.	SS	5	13	0	3	0	0	0	0	.231	6	8	2	.875
Major League Totals—1 Year			5	13	0	3	0	0	0	0	.231	6	8	2	.875

Signed as free agent by Milwaukee Brewers' organization, March 3, 1982.

MICHAEL ANTHONY DIAZ

Name pronounced DEE-az.

(Mike)

Born April 15, 1960, at San Francisco, Calif.
Height, 6.02. Weight, 195.
Throws and bats righthanded.

Tied for Pacific Coast League lead in being hit by pitch with 7 in 1985.
Led Texas League catchers in total chances with 684 in 1981.

Year Club	League	Pos.	G.	AB.	R.	H.	2B.	3B.	HR.	RBI.	B.A.	PO.	A.	E.	F.A.
1978—Bradenton Cubs	Gulf C.	C-OF	26	68	10	19	3	0	1	7	.279	54	8	3	.954
1979—Geneva	NYP	C	63	237	45	74	★19	1	7	36	.312	★423	35	7	.985
1980—Davenport	Midw.	C	105	386	51	113	17	1	8	47	.293	★627	63	★16	.977
1981—Midland	Texas	C	110	390	56	103	19	2	10	60	.264	★593	★75	16	.977
1982—Midland	Texas	C	121	443	54	128	23	4	22	75	.289	417	42	15	.968
1983—Iowa	A. A.	C-1B-OF	74	238	43	77	13	3	15	47	.324	223	14	12	.952
1983—Chicago†	Nat.	C	6	7	2	2	1	0	0	1	.286	5	0	0	1.000
1984—Portland	P. C.	C-OF-1B	105	341	52	92	15	1	14	46	.270	373	16	14	.965
1985—Port.‡-Haw.	P. C.	C-O-1-3	128	445	65	139	29	4	22	85	.312	698	37	7	.991
1986—Pittsburgh	Nat.	OF-1B-3B	97	209	22	56	9	0	12	36	.268	202	8	3	.986
Major League Totals—2 Years			103	216	24	58	10	0	12	37	.269	207	8	3	.986

Selected by Chicago Cubs' organization in 30th round of free-agent draft, June 6, 1978.

†Traded with Pitcher Bill Campbell to Philadelphia Phillies for Outfielders Bob Dernier and Gary Matthews and Pitcher Porfi Altamirano, March 27, 1984.

‡Traded to Pittsburgh Pirates' organization for Catcher Steve Herz, April 27, 1985.

ROBERT KEITH DIBBLE

(Rob)

Born January 24, 1964, at Bridgeport, Conn.
Height, 6.04. Weight, 220.
Throws right and bats lefthanded.
Attended Florida Southern College, Lakeland, Fla.

Year Club	League	G.	IP.	W.	L.	Pct.	H.	R.	ER.	SO.	BB.	ERA.
1983—Billings	Pioneer	5	12⅔	1	1	.000	18	13	11	7	11	7.82
1983—Eugene	Northwest	7	37⅔	3	2	.600	38	28	24	17	18	5.73
1984—Tampa	Florida St.	15	64⅔	5	2	.714	59	31	21	39	29	2.92
1985—Cedar Rapids	Midwest	45	65⅓	5	5	.500	67	37	28	73	28	3.84
1986—Vermont	Eastern	31	55⅓	3	2	.600	53	29	19	37	28	3.09
1986—Denver	Am. Assoc.	5	6⅔	1	0	1.000	9	4	4	3	2	5.40

Selected by St. Louis Cardinals' organization in 11th round of free-agent draft, June 7, 1982.
Selected by Cincinnati Reds' organization in secondary phase of free-agent draft, June 6, 1983.

FRANK MICHAEL DiPINO

Born October 22, 1956, at Syracuse, N.Y.
Height, 6.00. Weight, 180.
Throws and bats lefthanded.
Attended St. Leo College, St. Leo, Fla.

Pitched seven-inning, 6-0 no-hit victory against Reading, June 8, 1980 (second game).
Major League saves: 1983 (20), 1984 (14), 1985 (6), 1986 (3). Total—43.

Year Club	League	G.	IP.	W.	L.	Pct.	H.	R.	ER.	SO.	BB.	ERA.
1977—Newark	NYP	14	29	1	3	.250	14	12	8	41	22	2.48
1978—Burlington	Midwest	15	88	5	4	.556	98	58	46	68	36	4.70
1979—Stockton†	California	16	99	5	3	.625	92	45	38	67	46	3.45
1980—Holyoke	Eastern	16	76	7	0	1.000	46	13	11	58	27	1.30
1980—Vancouver	P. Coast	24	28	3	1	.750	24	10	7	32	14	2.25
1981—Vancouver‡	P. Coast	27	81	3	5	.375	83	45	39	81	39	4.33
1981—Milwaukee	American	2	2	0	0	.000	0	0	0	3	3	0.00
1982—Vancouver§	P. Coast	26	189⅔	13	9	.591	187	102	85	115	86	4.03
1982—Houston	National	6	28⅓	2	2	.500	32	20	19	25	11	6.04

Year Club	League	G.	IP.	W.	L.	Pct.	H.	R.	ER.	SO.	BB.	ERA.
1983—Houston	National	53	71⅓	3	4	.429	52	21	21	67	20	2.65
1984—Houston	National	57	75⅓	4	9	.308	74	32	28	65	36	3.35
1985—Houston	National	54	76	3	7	.300	69	44	34	49	43	4.03
1986—Houston x-Chicago	National	61	80⅓	3	7	.300	74	45	39	70	30	4.37
American League Totals—1 Year		2	2	0	0	.000	0	0	0	3	3	0.00
National League Totals—5 Years		231	331⅓	15	29	.341	301	162	141	276	140	3.83
Major League Totals—6 Years		233	333⅓	15	29	.341	301	162	141	279	143	3.81

Signed as free agent by Milwaukee Brewers' organization, July 11, 1977.
†On disabled list, May 19 to June 11, 1979.
‡On disabled list, May 9 to June 10, 1981.
§Traded with Outfielder Kevin Bass and Pitcher Mike Madden to Houston Astros, September 3, 1982, completing deal in which Houston traded Pitcher Don Sutton to Milwaukee Brewers for three players to be named later, August 30, 1982.
xTraded to Chicago Cubs for Outfielder Davey Lopes, July 21, 1986.

BENITO JAMES DISTEFANO JR.

Name pronounced Dis-tuh-FAHN-oh.

(Benny)

Born January 23, 1962, at Brooklyn, N.Y.
Height, 6.01. Weight, 205.
Throws and bats lefthanded.
Attended Alvin Community College, Alvin, Tex.

Year Club	League	Pos.	G.	AB.	R.	H.	2B.	3B.	HR.	RBI.	B.A.	PO.	A.	E.	F.A.
1982—Greenwood	S. Atl.	1B	136	477	74	138	23	●8	15	89	.289	★1184	★104	19	.985
1983—Lynn	East.	OF-1B	★137	480	71	130	19	7	25	92	.271	271	13	13	.956
1984—Hawaii	P. C.	1B-OF	66	240	40	73	13	8	6	33	.304	334	30	0	1.000
1984—Pittsburgh	Nat.	OF-1B	45	78	10	13	1	2	3	9	.167	88	9	3	.970
1985—Hawaii	P. C.	OF-1B	136	480	74	114	27	8	14	67	.238	375	18	8	.980
1986—Hawaii	P. C.	OF-1B	111	402	58	104	25	9	13	57	.259	564	37	9	.985
1986—Pittsburgh	Nat.	OF-1B	31	39	3	7	1	0	1	5	.179	13	0	0	1.000
Major League Totals—2 Years			76	117	13	20	2	2	4	14	.171	101	9	3	.973

Selected by Los Angeles Dodgers' organization in 16th round of free-agent draft, January 13, 1981.
Selected by Toronto Blue Jays' organization in secondary phase of free-agent draft, June 8, 1981.
Selected by Pittsburgh Pirates' organization in secondary phase of free-agent draft, January 12, 1982.

KENNETH JOHN DIXON

(Ken)

Born October 17, 1960, at Monroe, Va.
Height, 5.11. Weight, 166.
Throws right and bats left and righthanded.

Major League saves: 1985 (1).
Led Southern League in complete games with 20 and tied for lead in home runs allowed with 20 in 1984.
Tied for Appalachian League lead in hit batsmen with 5 in 1980.
Named Southern League Pitcher of the Year, 1984.

Year Club	League	G.	IP.	W.	L.	Pct.	H.	R.	ER.	SO.	BB.	ERA.
1980—Bluefield	Ap'lachian	13	78	4	5	.444	69	46	40	62	★48	4.62
1981—Miami	Florida St.	11	60	1	8	.111	57	41	29	40	42	4.35
1981—Bluefield	Ap'lachian	3	18	2	1	.667	23	12	12	22	11	6.00
1981—Hagerstown	Carolina	9	65	3	5	.375	44	25	21	73	30	2.91
1982—Hagerstown	Carolina	15	97⅔	7	8	.467	97	59	50	71	50	4.61
1982—Charlotte	Southern	13	76⅔	3	8	.273	72	44	39	61	42	4.58
1983—Charlotte	Southern	20	130	8	7	.533	123	64	57	73	70	3.95
1983—Rochester	Int'national	11	64⅓	3	6	.333	65	41	32	34	26	4.48
1984—Charlotte	Southern	31	★240	●16	8	.667	198	92	76	★211	78	2.85
1984—Baltimore	American	2	13	0	1	.000	14	6	6	8	4	4.15
1985—Baltimore†	American	34	162	8	4	.667	144	68	66	108	64	3.67
1986—Baltimore	American	35	202⅓	11	13	.458	194	111	103	170	83	4.58
Major League Totals—3 Years		71	377⅓	19	18	.514	352	185	175	286	151	4.17

Selected by Baltimore Orioles' organization in 3rd round of free-agent draft, June 3, 1980.
†Appeared in three games as pinch-runner.

REGINALD TERRENCE DOBIE

(Reggie)

Born August 17, 1964, at Rosedale, Miss.
Height, 6.01. Weight, 175.
Throws and bats righthanded.
Attended Triton College, River Grove, Ill., and
Chicago State University, Chicago, Ill.

Tied for Texas League lead in games started by pitchers with 27 and wild pitches with 15 in 1986.
Tied for Carolina League lead in games started by pitchers with 26 in 1985.
Tied for Gulf Coast League lead in balks with 3 in 1983.

Year — Club	League	G.	IP.	W.	L.	Pct.	H.	R.	ER.	SO.	BB.	ERA.
1983—Sarasota Mets	Gulf Coast	12	44	0	4	.000	47	21	16	44	31	3.27
1984—Columbia	S. Atlantic	25	171⅓	10	9	.526	123	75	58	*128	*119	3.03
1985—Lynchburg	Carolina	26	167⅔	12	5	.706	118	61	49	144	77	2.63
1986—Jackson	Texas	28	155	13	7	.650	113	70	63	123	94	3.66

Selected by New York Mets' organization in 8th round of free-agent draft, January 11, 1983.

THOMAS MARION DODD
(Tom)

Born August 15, 1958, at Portland, Ore.
Height, 6.00. Weight, 190.
Throws and bats righthanded.
Attended University of Oregon, Eugene, Ore.

Led Southern League in slugging percentage with .596 in 1986.
Tied for Southern League lead in double plays by outfielders with 5 in 1982.

Year — Club	League	Pos.	G.	AB.	R.	H.	2B.	3B.	HR.	RBI.	B.A.	PO.	A.	E.	F.A.
1980—Fort Lauderdale	Fla. St.	OF-3B	103	269	45	68	10	3	7	29	.253	117	3	4	.968
1981—Greensboro	S. Atl.	OF	103	351	77	96	15	5	*29	95	.274	105	3	4	.964
1981—Fort Lauderdale	Fla. St.	OF	12	25	5	6	0	0	1	1	.240	10	0	1	.909
1982—Nash.†-Knox.‡	South.	OF-C	123	387	49	91	20	7	14	51	.235	186	14	7	.966
1983—Nashville§	South.	OF-C	22	71	10	16	2	0	3	11	.225	41	2	0	1.000
1983—Glens Falls	East.	OF-C-P	94	314	38	76	15	2	13	56	.242	255	28	6	.979
1984—Glens Falls xy	East.	OF-C-1B	135	448	72	116	19	4	17	75	.259	343	41	11	.972
1985—Hagerstown	Carol.	OF	10	30	3	8	2	1	1	3	.267	12	1	0	1.000
1985—Charlotte	South.	3-O-2-C	85	287	51	88	18	2	17	52	.307	79	90	23	.880
1986—Charlotte	South.	3B-OF-1B	105	399	75	129	19	3	28	100	.323	49	90	14	.908
1986—Baltimore	Amer.	3B	8	13	1	3	0	0	1	2	.231	0	0	0	.000
1986—Rochester	Int.	OF	17	49	7	8	1	1	2	6	.163	8	0	0	1.000
Major League Totals—1 Year			8	13	1	3	0	0	1	2	.231	0	0	0	.000

Selected by Oakland A's organization in 2nd round of free-agent draft, June 7, 1979.
Selected by New York Yankees' organization in secondary phase of free-agent draft, January 8, 1980.
†Traded with First Baseman Dave Revering and Third Baseman Jeff Reynolds to Toronto Blue Jays for First Baseman John Mayberry, May 5, 1982.
‡Traded with Pitcher Dale Murray to New York Yankees for Outfielder Dave Collins, Pitcher Mike Morgan, First Basemen Fred McGriff and $400,000, December 9, 1982.
§Released, May 9, 1983; signed by Chicago White Sox' organization, May 12, 1983.
xOn voluntarily retired list, January 13 to May 7, 1985.
yReleased, May 8, 1985; signed by Baltimore Orioles' organization, May 26, 1985.

PITCHING RECORD

Year — Club	League	G.	IP.	W.	L.	Pct.	H.	R.	ER.	SO.	BB.	ERA.
1983—Glens Falls	Eastern	2	3⅓	0	0	.000	1	0	0	1	0	0.00

PATRICK NEAL DODSON
(Pat)

Born October 11, 1959, at Santa Monica, Calif.
Height, 6.04. Weight, 210.
Throws and bats lefthanded.
Attended University of California, Los Angeles, Calif.

Led International League in slugging percentage with .524 in 1986.
Led Florida State League in bases on balls received with 95 in 1981.
Led Florida State League first basemen in double plays with 100 and total chances with 1,223 in 1981.
Named International League Player of the Year, 1986.

Year — Club	League	Pos.	G.	AB.	R.	H.	2B.	3B.	HR.	RBI.	B.A.	PO.	A.	E.	F.A.
1980—Winter Haven	Fla. St.	1B-OF	61	190	26	52	18	0	1	36	.274	437	28	3	.994
1981—Winter Haven	Fla. St.	1B	127	413	54	104	17	3	4	42	.252	*1134	76	13	*.989
1982—Winter Haven†	Fla. St.	1B-OF	104	345	50	87	16	0	15	69	.252	786	54	6	.993
1983—New Britain	East.	1B-OF	118	383	55	100	25	1	12	70	.261	815	54	11	.988
1984—Pawtucket	Int.	1B-OF	114	292	51	75	17	0	16	51	.257	681	48	9	.988
1985—Pawtucket	Int.	*1B-OF-P	123	400	51	89	14	0	18	47	.223	942	83	8	*.992
1986—Pawtucket	Int.	1B	120	416	60	112	23	1	27	*102	.269	983	77	*14	.987
1986—Boston	Amer.	1B	9	12	3	5	2	0	1	3	.417	25	1	0	1.000
Major League Totals—1 Year			9	12	3	5	2	0	1	3	.417	25	1	0	1.000

Selected by Boston Red Sox' organization in 6th round of free-agent draft, June 3, 1980.
†On disabled list, August 17, 1982 through remainder of season.

PITCHNG RECORD

Year — Club	League	G.	IP.	W.	L.	Pct.	H.	R.	ER.	SO.	BB.	ERA.
1985—Pawtucket	Int'national	3	3⅔	0	0	.000	2	0	0	1	4	0.00

—DID YOU KNOW—

That outfielder Vince Coleman hit three sacrifice flies and shortstop Ozzie Smith scored all three runs in the St. Louis Cardinals' 4-3 loss to San Diego on May 1, 1986?

WILLIAM DONALD DORAN

Name pronounced DOOR-un.

(Bill)

Born May 28, 1958, at Cincinnati, Ohio.
Height, 6.00. Weight, 175.
Throws right and bats right and lefthanded.
Attended Miami University, Oxford, Ohio.

Major League stolen bases: 1982 (5), 1983 (12), 1984 (21), 1985 (23), 1986 (42). Total—103.
Led National League in caught stealing with 19 in 1986.
Led Pacific Coast League second basemen in double plays with 123 in 1982.
Led Gulf Coast League second basemen in double plays with 33 in 1979.

Year	Club	League	Pos.	G.	AB.	R.	H.	2B.	3B.	HR.	RBI.	B.A.	PO.	A.	E.	F.A.
1979—Sarasota Astros	Gulf C.	2B	44	164	21	42	6	0	1	16	.256	107	*144	11	.958
1980—Daytona Beach	Fla. St.	2B-SS	102	369	62	90	11	3	2	45	.244	232	259	21	.959
1981—Columbus	South.	2B-SS	124	427	83	120	17	7	5	56	.281	263	355	17	.973
1982—Tucson	P. C.	2B	*142	559	100	169	32	7	1	65	.302	*361	*424	*23	.972
1982—Houston	Nat.	2B	26	97	11	27	3	0	0	6	.278	41	78	3	.975
1983—Houston	Nat.	2B	154	535	70	145	12	7	8	39	.271	*347	461	17	.979
1984—Houston	Nat.	2B-SS	147	548	92	143	18	11	4	41	.261	274	440	12	.983
1985—Houston	Nat.	2B	148	578	84	166	31	6	14	59	.287	345	440	16	.980
1986—Houston	Nat.	2B	145	550	92	152	29	3	6	37	.276	262	329	16	.974
Major League Totals—5 Years				620	2308	349	633	93	27	32	182	.274	1269	1748	64	.979

Selected by Houston Astros' organization in 6th round of free-agent draft, June 5, 1979.

CHAMPIONSHIP SERIES RECORD

Tied Championship Series record for most at-bats, game (7), October 15, 1986 (16 innings).
Tied National League Championship Series record for most at-bats, six-game Series (27), 1986.

Year	Club	League	Pos.	G.	AB.	R.	H.	2B.	3B.	HR.	RBI.	B.A.	PO.	A.	E.	F.A.
1986—Houston	Nat.	2B	6	27	3	6	0	0	1	3	.222	9	17	0	1.000

BRIAN RICHARD DORSETT

Born April 9, 1961, at Terre Haute, Ind.
Height, 6.03. Weight, 215.
Throws and bats righthanded.
Attended Indiana State University, Terre Haute, Ind.

Year	Club	League	Pos.	G.	AB.	R.	H.	2B.	3B.	HR.	RBI.	B.A.	PO.	A.	E.	F.A.
1983—Medford	N'west	C	14	48	11	13	2	1	1	10	.271	85	8	2	.979
1983—Madison	Midw.	C	58	204	16	52	7	0	3	27	.255	337	51	6	.985
1984—Modesto†	Calif.	C-1B	99	375	39	99	19	0	8	52	.264	511	76	13	.978
1985—Madison	Midw.	C	40	161	15	43	11	0	2	30	.267	194	40	5	.979
1985—Huntsville	South.	C	88	313	38	84	18	3	11	43	.268	437	51	10	.980
1986—Tacoma	P. C.	C	117	426	49	111	33	1	10	51	.261	420	54	18	.963

Selected by Oakland A's organization in 10th round of free-agent draft, June 6, 1983.
†On disabled list, June 18 to July 24, 1984.

RICHARD ELLIOTT DOTSON

Born January 10, 1959, at Cincinnati, O.
Height, 6.00. Weight, 203.
Throws and bats righthanded.

Tied for American League lead in shutouts with 4 in 1981.

Year	Club	League	G.	IP.	W.	L.	Pct.	H.	R.	ER.	SO.	BB.	ERA.
1977—Idaho Falls†	Pioneer	13	66	4	5	.444	65	61	42	83	63	5.73
1978—Knoxville	Southern	26	145	11	10	.524	128	85	69	152	*105	4.28
1979—Knoxville	Southern	25	163	9	9	.500	133	81	67	133	88	3.70
1979—Chicago	American	5	24	2	0	1.000	28	13	10	13	6	3.75
1980—Chicago	American	33	198	12	10	.545	185	105	94	109	87	4.27
1981—Chicago	American	24	141	9	8	.529	145	67	59	73	49	3.77
1982—Chicago	American	34	196⅔	11	15	.423	219	97	84	109	73	3.84
1983—Chicago	American	35	240	22	7	*.759	209	92	86	137	*106	3.23
1984—Chicago‡	American	32	245⅔	14	15	.483	216	110	98	120	103	3.59
1985—Chicago§	American	9	52⅓	3	4	.429	53	30	26	33	17	4.47
1986—Chicago	American	34	197	10	●17	.370	226	125	120	110	69	5.48
Major League Totals—8 Years		206	1294⅔	83	76	.522	1281	639	577	704	510	4.01

Selected by California Angels' organization in 1st round (seventh player selected) of free-agent draft, June 7, 1977.
†Traded with Outfielders Bobby Bonds and Thad Bosley to Chicago White Sox for Catcher Brian Downing and Pitchers Chris Knapp and Dave Frost, December 5, 1977.
‡Appeared in one game as a pinch-runner.
§On disabled list, April 7 to April 22 and June 11, 1985 through remainder of season.

CHAMPIONSHIP SERIES RECORD

Year	Club	League	G.	IP.	W.	L.	Pct.	H.	R.	ER.	SO.	BB.	ERA.
1983—Chicago	American	1	5	0	1	.000	6	6	6	3	3	10.80

ALL-STAR GAME RECORD

Year	League		IP.	W.	L.	Pct.	H.	R.	ER.	SO.	BB.	ERA.
1984—American			2	0	0	.000	2	0	0	2	1	0.00

KENNETH ALLEN DOWELL
(Ken)

Born January 19, 1961, at Sacramento, Calif.
Height, 5.09. Weight, 160.
Throws and bats righthanded.
Attended Sacramento City College, Sacramento, Calif.

Led South Atlantic League in bases on balls received with 114 in 1981.
Tied for Carolina League lead in sacrifice flies with 9 in 1982.
Led Pacific Coast League shortstops in assists with 450, total chances with 675 and tied for lead in putouts with 206 and double plays with 92 in 1986.
Led Eastern League shortstops in fielding percentage with .957 in 1983.
Tied for Pioneer League lead in double plays by shortstops with 32 in 1980.

Year	Club	League	Pos.	G.	AB.	R.	H.	2B.	3B.	HR.	RBI.	B.A.	PO.	A.	E.	F.A.
1980—Helena		Pion.	SS	47	154	17	35	1	0	1	24	.227	74	163	17	.933
1981—Spartanburg		S. Atl.	3-S-2-O	137	451	70	102	19	5	2	51	.226	136	357	36	.932
1982—Peninsula		Carol.	SS-3B-2B	114	381	55	84	14	2	0	35	.220	126	305	32	.931
1983—Reading		East.	SS-2B-3B	126	367	64	108	13	1	2	42	.294	199	377	24	.960
1984—Portland†		P. C.	SS	50	145	15	30	3	1	0	8	.207	72	146	13	.944
1985—Portland		P. C.	SS-2B-3B	114	303	32	64	6	3	1	23	.211	183	351	14	.974
1986—Portland		P. C.	SS-2B	141	439	66	132	11	5	1	44	.301	219	469	19	.973

Selected by San Diego Padres' organization in 1st round (sixth player selected) of free-agent draft, January 8, 1980.
Selected by Philadelphia Phillies' organization in secondary phase of free-agent draft, June 3, 1980.
†On disabled list, June 24 to August 15, 1984.

BRIAN JAY DOWNING

Born October 9, 1950, at Los Angeles, Calif.
Height, 5.10. Weight, 200.
Throws and bats righthanded.
Attended Cypress Junior College, Cypress, Calif.

Tied major league records for highest fielding percentage by outfielder, season, 150 or more games (1.000), 1982; fewest errors by outfielder, season, 150 or more games (0), 1982; fewest double plays by outfielder, season, 150 or more games (0), 1982.
Established American League record for most consecutive errorless games by an outfielder (244), May 25, 1981 through July 21, second game, 1983.
Major League stolen bases: 1975 (13), 1976 (7), 1977 (1), 1978 (3), 1979 (3), 1981 (1), 1982 (2), 1983 (1), 1985 (5), 1986 (4). Total—40.

Year	Club	League	Pos.	G.	AB.	R.	H.	2B.	3B.	HR.	RBI.	B.A.	PO.	A.	E.	F.A.
1970—Sarasota W. S.		Gulf C.	C-OF	34	96	16	21	1	1	0	14	.219	167	11	1	.994
1971—Appleton		Midw.	3B-C-OF	99	333	51	82	6	3	3	22	.246	353	98	13	.972
1972—Knoxville		South.	OF-3B-C	135	442	75	123	24	7	15	67	.278	250	123	21	.947
1973—Iowa		A. A.	3B-OF-C	68	228	34	56	6	1	7	27	.246	84	90	8	.956
1973—Chicago†		Amer.	OF-C-3B	34	73	5	13	1	0	2	4	.178	72	17	5	.947
1974—Chicago		Amer.	C-OF	108	293	41	66	12	1	10	39	.225	337	30	2	.995
1975—Chicago		Amer.	C	138	420	58	101	12	1	7	41	.240	730	84	8	.990
1976—Chicago‡		Amer.	C	104	317	38	81	14	0	3	30	.256	450	38	6	.988
1977—Chicago§		Amer.	C-OF	69	169	28	48	4	2	4	25	.284	325	28	6	.983
1978—California		Amer.	C	133	412	42	105	15	0	7	46	.255	681	82	5	.993
1979—California		Amer.	C	148	509	87	166	27	3	12	75	.326	669	35	11	.985
1980—California x		Amer.	C	30	93	5	27	6	0	2	25	.290	69	6	0	1.000
1981—California		Amer.	OF-C	93	317	47	79	14	0	9	41	.249	237	18	2	.992
1982—California		Amer.	OF	158	623	109	175	37	2	28	84	.281	321	9	0	●1.000
1983—California y		Amer.	OF	113	403	68	99	15	1	19	53	.246	160	9	1	.994
1984—California		Amer.	OF	156	539	65	148	28	2	23	91	.275	272	5	0	★1.000
1985—California		Amer.	OF	150	520	80	137	23	1	20	85	.263	244	5	2	.992
1986—California z		Amer.	OF	152	513	90	137	27	4	20	95	.267	267	5	3	.989
Major League Totals—14 Years				1586	5201	763	1382	235	17	166	734	.266	4834	389	51	.990

Signed as free-agent by Chicago White Sox' organization, August 19, 1969.
†On disabled list, June 1 to July 9, 1973.
‡On disabled list, July 30 to August 15, 1976.
§Traded with Pitchers Chris Knapp and Dave Frost to California Angels for Outfielders Bobby Bonds and Thad Bosley and Pitcher Dick Dotson, December 5, 1977.
xOn disabled list, April 20 to September 1, 1980.
yOn disabled list, May 10 to June 20, 1983.
zGranted free agency, November 12, 1986.

CHAMPIONSHIP SERIES RECORD

Established American League Championship Series record for most runs batted in, seven-game Series (7), 1986.

Year	Club	League	Pos.	G.	AB.	R.	H.	2B.	3B.	HR.	RBI.	B.A.	PO.	A.	E.	F.A.
1979—California		Amer.	C	4	15	1	3	0	0	0	1	.200	27	0	0	1.000
1982—California		Amer.	C	5	19	3	3	1	0	0	0	.158	5	0	0	1.000
1986—California		Amer.	OF	7	27	2	6	0	0	1	7	.222	18	0	0	1.000
Championship Series Totals—3 Years				16	61	6	12	1	0	1	8	.197	50	0	0	1.000

ALL-STAR GAME RECORD

Year	League	Pos.	AB.	R.	H.	2B.	3B.	HR.	RBI.	B.A.	PO.	A.	E.	F.A.
1979—American		C	1	0	1	0	0	0	0	1.000	3	0	0	1.000

KELLY ROBERT DOWNS

Born October 25, 1960, at Ogden, Utah.
Height, 6.04. Weight, 195.
Throws and bats righthanded.
Brother of Dave Downs, pitcher with Philadelphia Phillies, 1972.
Tied for Pacific Coast League lead in games started by pitchers with 29 in 1983.

Year	Club	League	G.	IP.	W.	L.	Pct.	H.	R.	ER.	SO.	BB.	ERA.
1980—Spartanburg	W. Carol.	14	90	5	7	.417	85	41	26	40	17	2.60
1981—Peninsula	Carolina	25	175	13	7	.650	176	79	58	124	35	2.98
1982—Oklahoma City	Am. Assoc.	32	156⅔	2	★15	.118	182	★116	93	70	72	5.34
1983—Portland	P. Coast	29	159⅓	9	●13	.409	186	98	79	71	61	4.46
1984—Portland†	P. Coast	30	163	7	12	.368	166	106	96	104	65	5.30
1985—Phoenix	P. Coast	37	137	9	10	.474	138	69	61	109	56	4.01
1986—Phoenix	P. Coast	18	108	8	5	.615	116	54	41	68	28	3.42
1986—San Francisco	National	14	88⅓	4	4	.500	78	29	27	64	30	2.75
Major League Totals—1 Year		14	88⅓	4	4	.500	78	29	27	64	30	2.75

Selected by Philadelphia Phillies' organization in 26th round of free-agent draft, June 5, 1979.
†Traded with Pitcher George Riley to San Francisco Giants for First Baseman Al Oliver and a player to be named later, August 20, 1984; Philadelphia Phillies acquired Pitcher Renie Martin to complete deal, August 30, 1984.

THOMAS DEAN DOZIER
(Tom)

Born September 5, 1961, at Richmond, Calif.
Height, 6.02. Weight, 190.
Throws and bats righthanded.

Year	Club	League	G.	IP.	W.	L.	Pct.	H.	R.	ER.	SO.	BB.	ERA.
1979—Johnson City	Ap'lachian	11	35	1	3	.250	48	28	20	12	15	5.14
1980—Johnson City	Ap'lachian	11	40	3	2	.600	38	25	22	19	14	4.95
1981—St. Petersburg	Florida St.	15	37	2	2	.500	38	23	23	13	21	5.59
1981—Gastonia	S. Atlantic	11	43	1	0	1.000	26	8	7	26	10	1.47
1982—Springfield	Midwest	26	133	11	6	.647	131	74	62	87	52	4.20
1983—St. Petersburg	Florida St.	26	153	11	7	.611	133	63	50	109	60	2.94
1983—Springfield†	Midwest	1	6⅔	0	0	.000	3	2	1	9	5	1.35
1984—Albany	Eastern	44	89⅓	6	5	.545	74	37	29	57	34	2.92
1985—Tacoma‡	P. Coast	6	34	0	0	.000	27	18	16	22	14	4.24
1985—Huntsville	Southern	12	59⅔	5	2	.714	42	28	21	54	26	3.17
1986—Tacoma	P. Coast	19	74⅓	5	3	.625	65	31	28	49	38	3.39
1986—Oakland	American	4	6⅓	0	0	.000	6	6	4	4	5	5.68
Major League Totals—1 Year		4	6⅓	0	0	.000	6	6	4	4	5	5.68

Selected by St. Louis Cardinals' organization in 11th round of free-agent draft, June 5, 1979.
†Traded with pitcher Jim Strichek to Oakland A's organization, September 14, 1983, completing deal in which Oakland traded Pitcher Steve Baker to St. Louis Cardinals for two players to be named later, September 2, 1983.
‡On disabled list, April 22 to June 18, 1985.

DOUGLAS DEAN DRABEK
(Doug)

Born July 25, 1962, at Victoria, Tex.
Height, 6.01. Weight, 185.
Throws and bats righthanded.
Attended University of Houston, Houston, Tex.

Year	Club	League	G.	IP.	W.	L.	Pct.	H.	R.	ER.	SO.	BB.	ERA.
1983—Niagara Falls	NYP	16	103⅔	6	7	.462	99	52	42	103	48	3.65
1984—Appleton	Midwest	1	5	1	0	1.000	3	1	1	6	3	1.80
1984—Glens Falls†	Eastern	19	124⅔	12	5	.706	90	34	31	75	44	2.24
1984—Nashville	Southern	4	31	1	2	.333	30	11	8	22	10	2.32
1985—Albany	Eastern	26	★192⅔	13	7	.650	153	71	64	★153	55	2.99
1986—Columbus	Int'national	8	42	1	4	.200	50	36	34	23	25	7.29
1986—New York‡	American	27	131⅔	7	8	.467	126	64	60	76	50	4.10
Major League Totals—1 Year		27	131⅔	7	8	.467	126	64	60	76	50	4.10

Selected by Cleveland Indians' organization in 4th round of free-agent draft, June 3, 1980.
Selected by Chicago White Sox' organization in 11th round of free-agent draft, June 6, 1983.
†Traded with Pitcher Kevin Hickey to New York Yankees' organization, August 13, 1984, completing deal in which New York traded Infielder Roy Smalley to Chicago White Sox for two players to be named later, July 18, 1984.
‡Traded with Pitchers Brian Fisher and Logan Easley to Pittsburgh Pirates for Pitchers Rick Rhoden, Cecilio Guante and Pat Clements, November 26, 1986.

DAVID FRANCIS DRAVECKY
(Dave)

Born February 14, 1956, at Youngstown, O.
Height, 6.01. Weight, 193.
Throws left and bats righthanded.
Attended Youngstown State University, Youngstown, Ohio.
Major League saves: 1982 (2), 1983 (8). Total—10.
Led Texas League in shutouts with 4 in 1981.

Year Club	League	G.	IP.	W.	L.	Pct.	H.	R.	ER.	SO.	BB.	ERA.
1978—Charleston	W. Carol.	20	52	4	2	.667	54	30	24	31	32	4.15
1979—Buffalo	Eastern	35	114	6	7	.462	125	71	54	81	59	4.26
1980—Buffalo†	Eastern	27	161	13	7	.650	165	76	60	64	60	3.35
1981—Amarillo	Texas	30	172	●15	5	.750	157	69	51	141	45	2.67
1982—Hawaii	P. Coast	16	36⅓	4	1	.800	28	15	10	26	14	2.48
1982—San Diego	National	31	105	5	3	.625	86	37	30	59	33	2.57
1983—San Diego	National	28	183⅓	14	10	.583	181	78	73	74	44	3.58
1984—San Diego	National	50	156⅔	9	8	.529	125	53	51	71	51	2.93
1985—San Diego	National	34	214⅔	13	11	.542	200	79	70	105	57	2.93
1986—San Diego	National	26	161⅓	9	11	.450	149	68	55	87	54	3.07
Major League Totals—5 Years		169	821⅓	50	43	.538	741	315	279	396	239	3.06

Selected by Pittsburgh Pirates' organization in 21st round of free-agent draft, June 6, 1978.
†Traded to San Diego Padres' organization for Outfielder Robert D. (Bobby) Mitchell, April 5, 1981.

CHAMPIONSHIP SERIES RECORD

Year Club	League	G.	IP.	W.	L.	Pct.	H.	R.	ER.	SO.	BB.	ERA.
1984—San Diego	National	3	6	0	0	.000	2	0	0	5	0	0.00

WORLD SERIES RECORD

Year Club	League	G.	IP.	W.	L.	Pct.	H.	R.	ER.	SO.	BB.	ERA.
1984—San Diego	National	2	4⅔	0	0	.000	3	0	0	5	1	0.00

ALL-STAR GAME RECORD

Year League	IP.	W.	L.	Pct.	H.	R.	ER.	SO.	BB.	ERA.
1983—National	2	0	0	.000	1	0	0	2	0	0.00

DANIEL DRIESSEN
(Dan)

Born July 29, 1951, at Hilton Head, S. C.
Height, 5.11. Weight, 200.
Throws right and bats lefthanded.
Uncle of Gerald Perry, first baseman-outfielder with Atlanta Braves; cousin of Reggie Kinlaw, nose guard with Seattle Seahawks; and Marcus Kinlaw, offensive lineman at University of Miami (Fla.).

Major League stolen bases: 1973 (8), 1974 (10), 1975 (10), 1976 (14), 1977 (31), 1978 (28), 1979 (11), 1980 (19), 1981 (2), 1982 (11), 1983 (6), 1984 (2), 1985 (2). Total—154.
Tied for National League lead in bases on balls received with 93 and in being hit by pitch with 6 in 1980.
Led Eastern League first basemen in fielding percentage with .994 in 1972.

Year Club	League	Pos.	G.	AB.	R.	H.	2B.	3B.	HR.	RBI.	B.A.	PO.	A.	E.	F.A.
1970—Tampa	Fla. St.	1B	93	242	28	54	2	1	0	20	.223	473	37	5	.990
1971—Tampa	Fla. St.	1B	136	468	72	153	27	9	4	62	.327	1064	86	15	.987
1972—Three Rivers	East.	1B-3B	136	481	62	155	37	4	4	65	.322	805	138	9	.991
1973—Indianapolis	A. A.	3B-1B	47	181	42	74	14	4	6	46	.409	50	97	6	.961
1973—Cincinnati	Nat.	3B-1B-OF	102	366	49	110	15	2	4	47	.301	160	157	12	.964
1974—Cincinnati	Nat.	3B-1B-OF	150	470	63	132	23	6	7	56	.281	186	206	26	.938
1975—Cincinnati†	Nat.	1B-OF	88	210	38	59	8	1	7	38	.281	309	20	5	.985
1976—Cincinnati	Nat.	1B-OF	98	219	32	54	11	1	7	44	.247	314	23	2	.994
1977—Cincinnati	Nat.	1B	151	536	75	161	31	4	17	91	.300	1182	75	7	.994
1978—Cincinnati	Nat.	1B	153	524	68	131	23	3	16	70	.250	1264	93	6	★.996
1979—Cincinnati	Nat.	1B	150	515	72	129	24	3	18	75	.250	1289	79	9	.993
1980—Cincinnati	Nat.	1B	154	524	81	139	36	1	14	74	.265	1349	85	7	.995
1981—Cincinnati	Nat.	1B	82	233	35	55	14	0	7	33	.236	558	30	3	.995
1982—Cincinnati	Nat.	1B	149	516	64	139	25	1	17	57	.269	1239	78	3	★.998
1983—Cincinnati‡	Nat.	1B	122	386	57	107	17	1	12	57	.277	917	71	4	★.996
1984—Cinc.§-Mont.	Nat.	1B	132	387	47	104	24	0	16	60	.269	870	52	7	.992
1985—Mont.x-S.F.	Nat.	1B	145	493	53	120	26	0	9	44	.243	1203	91	4	.997
1986—S.F.y-Hou.z	Nat.	1B	32	40	7	10	3	0	1	3	.250	77	6	0	1.000
1986—Tucson	P. C.	1B	70	237	35	70	21	0	5	35	.295	495	30	8	.985
Major League Totals—14 Years			1708	5419	741	1450	280	23	152	752	.268	10920	1066	95	.992

Signed as free agent by Cincinnati Reds' organization, August 28, 1969.
†On disabled list, March 23 to April 15, 1975.
‡On disabled list, June 11 to July 1, 1983.
§Traded to Montreal Expos for Pitchers Andy McGaffigan and Jim Jefferson, July 26, 1984.
xTraded to San Francisco Giants for Pitcher Bill Laskey, First Baseman Scot Thompson and a player to be named later, August 1, 1985; deal settled when Laskey was traded back to San Francisco for Pitcher George Riley and Outfielder Alonzo Powell, October 24, 1985.
yReleased, May 1, 1986; signed by Houston Astros' organization, June 2, 1986.
zReleased, October 24, 1986.

CHAMPIONSHIP SERIES RECORD

Year Club	League	Pos.	G.	AB.	R.	H.	2B.	3B.	HR.	RBI.	B.A.	PO.	A.	E.	F.A.
1973—Cincinnati	Nat.	3B-PR	4	12	0	2	1	0	0	1	.167	3	2	1	.833
1976—Cincinnati	Nat.	PH	1	1	0	0	0	0	0	0	.000	0	0	0	.000
1979—Cincinnati	Nat.	1B	3	12	1	1	0	0	0	0	.083	32	0	0	1.000
Championship Series Totals—3 Years			8	25	1	3	1	0	0	1	.120	35	2	1	.974

Year	Club	League	Pos.	G.	AB.	R.	H.	2B.	3B.	HR.	RBI.	B.A.	PO.	A.	E.	F.A.
1975—Cincinnati	Nat.		PH	2	2	0	0	0	0	0	0	.000	0	0	0	.000
1976—Cincinnati	Nat.		DH	4	14	4	5	2	0	1	1	.357	0	0	0	.000
World Series Totals—2 Years				6	16	4	5	2	0	1	1	.313	0	0	0	.000

TIMOTHY DARNELL DRUMMOND
(Tim)

Born December 24, 1964, at La Plata, Md.
Height, 6.03. Weight, 170.
Throws and bats righthanded.
Attended Charles County Community College, La Plata, Md.

Year	Club	League	G.	IP.	W.	L.	Pct.	H.	R.	ER.	SO.	BB.	ERA.
1983—Bradenton Pirates		Gulf Coast	14	88	7	2	.778	73	20	14	40	21	1.43
1984—Macon		S. Atlantic	27	154⅔	7	★15	.318	139	93	67	76	81	3.90
1985—Macon		S. Atlantic	27	168⅓	8	11	.421	171	100	77	91	73	4.12
1986—Prince William		Carolina	47	73⅔	6	4	.600	71	39	31	55	34	3.79

Selected by Pittsburgh Pirates' organization in 12th round of free-agent draft, January 11, 1983.

ROBERT THOMAS DUCEY
(Rob)

Born May 24, 1965, at Toronto, Canada.
Height, 6.02. Weight, 175.
Throws right and bats lefthanded.
Attended Seminole Community College, Sanford, Fla.

Tied for Southern League lead in double plays by outfielders with 6 in 1986.

Year	Club	League	Pos.	G.	AB.	R.	H.	2B.	3B.	HR.	RBI.	B.A.	PO.	A.	E.	F.A.
1984—Medicine Hat		Pion.	OF-1B	63	235	49	71	10	3	12	49	.302	185	11	6	.970
1985—Florence		S. Atl.	OF-1B	134	529	78	133	22	2	13	86	.251	228	8	9	.963
1986—Ventura		Calif.	OF-1B	47	178	36	60	11	3	12	38	.337	97	3	2	.980
1986—Knoxville		South.	OF	88	344	49	106	22	3	11	58	.308	186	10	6	.970

Signed as free agent by Toronto Blue Jays' organization, May 16, 1984.

MARIANO DUNCAN

Born March 13, 1963, at San Pedro de Macoris, Dominican Republic.
Height, 6.00. Weight, 160.
Throws right and bats left and righthanded.

Major League stolen bases: 1985 (38), 1986 (48). Total—86.
Led Florida State League in stolen bases with 56 in 1983.
Led Texas League second basemen in double plays with 84 in 1984.

Year	Club	League	Pos.	G.	AB.	R.	H.	2B.	3B.	HR.	RBI.	B.A.	PO.	A.	E.	F.A.
1982—Lethbridge		Pion.	SS-2B	30	55	9	13	3	1	1	8	.236	23	35	15	.795
1983—Vero Beach		Fla. St.	OF-SS-2B	109	384	73	102	10	★15	0	42	.266	169	157	37	.898
1984—San Antonio		Texas	2B-OF-SS	125	502	80	127	14	●11	2	44	.253	283	335	22	.966
1985—Los Angeles		Nat.	SS-2B	142	562	74	137	24	6	6	39	.244	224	430	30	.956
1986—Los Angeles†		Nat.	SS	109	407	47	93	7	0	8	30	.229	172	317	25	.951
Major League Totals—2 Years				251	969	121	230	31	6	14	69	.237	396	747	55	.954

Signed as free agent by Los Angeles Dodgers' organization, January 17, 1982.
†On disabled list, August 19 to September 17, 1986.

Year	Club	League	Pos.	G.	AB.	R.	H.	2B.	3B.	HR.	RBI.	B.A.	PO.	A.	E.	F.A.
1985—Los Angeles		Nat.	SS	5	18	2	4	2	1	0	1	.222	7	16	1	.958

GREGORY JON DUNN
(Greg)

Born January 7, 1962, at Atwater, Calif.
Height, 6.00. Weight, 180.
Throws and bats righthanded.

Pitched 11-1 no-hit victory against Batavia, August 3, 1981.

Year	Club	League	G.	IP.	W.	L.	Pct.	H.	R.	ER.	SO.	BB.	ERA.
1981—Erie		NYP	13	75	7	1	●.875	50	42	34	84	54	4.08
1982—Springfield		Midwest	27	162⅔	12	7	.632	149	92	78	116	90	4.32
1983—Springfield†		Midwest	27	95	2	7	.222	86	66	47	84	52	4.45
1984—St. Petersburg		Florida St.	30	126⅔	5	12	.294	120	75	60	99	90	4.26
1985—Springfield		Midwest	55	80	4	9	.308	56	29	22	115	62	2.48
1986—Louisville‡		Am. Assoc.	10	11	0	0	.000	8	4	4	12	15	3.27

Selected by St. Louis Cardinals' organization in 21st round of free-agent draft, June 3, 1980.
†On disabled list, September 1 to September 12, 1983.
‡On disabled list, May 19 to September 2, 1986.

MICHAEL DENNIS DUNNE
(Mike)

Born October 27, 1962, at Peoria, Ill.
Height, 6.04. Weight, 190.
Throws and bats righthanded.
Attended Bradley University, Peoria, Ill.

Led American Association pitchers in balks with 9 and tied for lead in games started with 28 in 1986.
Member of 1984 U.S. Olympic baseball team.
Named righthanded pitcher on THE SPORTING NEWS College Baseball All-America Team, 1984.

Year Club	League	G.	IP.	W.	L.	Pct.	H.	R.	ER.	SO.	BB.	ERA.
1985—Arkansas†	Texas	23	146	4	9	.308	133	72	50	91	57	3.08
1986—Louisville	Am. Assoc.	28	*185⅔	9	●12	.429	182	102	*94	94	82	4.56

Selected by St. Louis Cardinals' organization in 1st round (seventh player selected) of free-agent draft, June 4, 1984.
†On disabled list, May 31 to June 10, 1985.

SHAWON DONNELL DUNSTON

Born March 21, 1963, at Brooklyn, N.Y.
Height, 6.01. Weight, 175.
Throws and bats righthanded.

Major League stolen bases: 1985 (11), 1986 (13). Total—24.
Led National League shortstops in total chances with 817 and tied for lead in double plays with 96 in 1986.
Received reported $150,000 bonus to sign with Chicago Cubs, 1982.

Year Club	League	Pos.	G.	AB.	R.	H.	2B.	3B.	HR.	RBI.	B.A.	PO.	A.	E.	F.A.
1982—Sarasota Cubs	Gulf C.	SS-3B	53	190	27	61	11	0	2	28	.321	61	129	24	.888
1983—Quad Cities†	Midw.	SS	117	455	65	141	17	8	4	62	.310	172	326	47	.914
1984—Midland	Texas	SS	73	298	44	98	13	3	3	34	.329	164	203	32	.920
1984—Iowa	A. A.	SS	61	210	25	49	11	1	7	27	.233	90	165	26	.907
1985—Chicago	Nat.	SS	74	250	40	65	12	4	4	18	.260	144	248	17	.958
1985—Iowa	A. A.	SS	73	272	24	73	9	6	2	28	.268	138	176	12	.963
1986—Chicago	Nat.	SS	150	581	66	145	36	3	17	68	.250	*320	*465	*32	.961
Major League Totals—2 Years			224	831	106	210	48	7	21	86	.253	464	713	49	.960

Selected by Chicago Cubs' organization in 1st round (first player selected) of free-agent draft, June 7, 1982.
†On disabled list, May 31 to June 10, 1983.

LEON DURHAM

Born July 31, 1957, at Cincinnati, O.
Height, 6.02. Weight, 210.
Throws and bats lefthanded.

Major League stolen bases: 1980 (8), 1981 (25), 1982 (28), 1983 (12), 1984 (16), 1985 (7), 1986 (8). Total—104.
Tied for National League lead in intentional bases on balls received with 24 in 1985.
Led Texas League first basemen in double plays with 96 in 1978.
Led Gulf Coast League first basemen in errors with 10 in 1976.
Named outfielder on THE SPORTING NEWS National League Silver Slugger team, 1982.

Year Club	League	Pos.	G.	AB.	R.	H.	2B.	3B.	HR.	RBI.	B.A.	PO.	A.	E.	F.A.
1976—Sarasota Cards	Gulf C.	1B-OF	44	156	25	35	3	5	2	18	.224	296	5	12	.962
1977—Gastonia	W. Car.	1B	63	239	45	88	18	3	4	44	.368	492	28	8	.985
1977—St. Petersburg	Fla. St.	1B	63	209	26	60	3	6	0	25	.287	533	27	9	.984
1978—Arkansas†	Texas	1B	102	367	72	116	21	5	12	70	.316	931	42	8	*.992
1979—Springfield	A. A.	OF-1B	127	449	84	139	33	4	23	88	.310	304	19	6	.982
1980—Springfield	A. A.	OF-1B	32	128	20	33	5	5	5	23	.258	96	8	4	.963
1980—St. Louis‡	Nat.	OF-1B	96	303	42	82	15	4	8	42	.271	180	22	3	.985
1981—Chicago§	Nat.	OF-1B	87	328	42	95	14	6	10	35	.290	175	4	5	.973
1982—Chicago	Nat.	OF-1B	148	539	84	168	33	7	22	90	.312	311	12	12	.964
1983—Chicago x	Nat.	OF-1B	100	337	58	87	18	8	12	55	.258	203	4	6	.972
1984—Chicago y	Nat.	1B	137	473	86	132	30	4	23	96	.279	1162	96	7	.994
1985—Chicago	Nat.	1B	153	542	58	153	32	2	21	75	.282	1421	107	7	.995
1986—Chicago	Nat.	1B	141	484	66	127	18	7	20	65	.262	1231	80	7	.995
Major League Totals—7 Years			862	3006	436	844	160	38	116	458	.281	4683	325	47	.991

Selected by St. Louis Cardinals' organization in 1st round (15th player selected) of free-agent draft, June 8, 1976.
†On disabled list, April 23 to May 25, 1978.
‡Traded with Third Baseman Ken Reitz and a player to be named later to Chicago Cubs for Pitcher Bruce Sutter, December 9, 1980; Chicago acquired Third Baseman Tye Waller to complete deal, December 22, 1980.
§On disabled list, June 2 to August 9, 1981.
xOn disabled list, June 9 to June 24, 1983.
yOn disabled list, June 24 to July 12, 1984.

CHAMPIONSHIP SERIES RECORD

Year Club	League	Pos.	G.	AB.	R.	H.	2B.	3B.	HR.	RBI.	B.A.	PO.	A.	E.	F.A.
1984—Chicago	Nat.	1B	5	20	2	3	0	0	2	4	.150	47	3	1	.980

ALL-STAR GAME RECORD

Year League	Pos.	AB.	R.	H.	2B.	3B.	HR.	RBI.	B.A.	PO.	A.	E.	F.A.
1983—National	OF	2	0	0	0	0	0	0	.000	0	0	0	.000

Member of National League All-Star Team in 1982; did not play.

JAMES EDWARD DWYER
(Jimmy)

Born January 3, 1950, at Evergreen Park, Ill.
Height, 5.10. Weight, 175.
Throws and bats lefthanded.
Received bachelor of arts degree in accounting from Southern Illinois University, Carbondale, Ill., in 1973.
Nephew of Don Dwyer, second baseman in New York Giants' organization, 1947.

Major League stolen bases: 1975 (4), 1978 (7), 1979 (3), 1980 (3), 1982 (2), 1983 (1). Total—20.
Tied for American Association lead in caught stealing with 13 in 1977.

Year	Club	League	Pos.	G.	AB.	R.	H.	2B.	3B.	HR.	RBI.	B.A.	PO.	A.	E.	F.A.
1971—Cedar Rapids	Midw.	OF	58	201	30	63	6	6	2	15	.313	73	3	3	.962
1972—Modesto	Calif.	OF	92	354	87	115	15	★13	9	45	.325	149	8	4	.975
1972—Arkansas	Texas	OF	44	162	16	41	1	0	2	14	.253	101	6	2	.982
1973—Tulsa	A. A.	OF	87	349	63	135	22	8	1	40	★.387	127	8	5	.964
1973—St. Louis	Nat.	OF	28	57	7	11	1	1	0	0	.193	32	0	0	1.000
1974—Tulsa	A. A.	OF-1B	36	119	20	40	7	2	1	15	.336	120	13	3	.978
1974—St. Louis	Nat.	OF-1B	74	86	13	24	1	0	2	11	.279	31	3	0	1.000
1975—Tulsa	A. A.	OF	33	109	17	44	8	2	1	17	.404	49	2	2	.962
1975—St.L.†-Mont.	Nat.	OF	81	206	26	56	8	1	3	21	.272	104	8	4	.966
1976—Mont.‡-N.Y.§	Nat.	OF-PH	61	105	9	19	3	1	0	5	.181	35	0	1	.972
1976—Tidewater	Int.	OF	8	26	0	5	1	0	0	1	.192	14	0	1	.933
1977—Wichita x	A. A.	OF	130	464	★113	★154	★38	12	18	70	★.332	245	6	8	.969
1977—St. Louis	Nat.	OF	13	31	3	7	1	0	0	2	.226	16	0	0	1.000
1978—St.L. y-S.F. z	Nat.	OF-1B	107	238	30	53	12	2	6	26	.223	216	15	3	.987
1979—Boston	Amer.	1B-OF	76	113	19	30	7	0	2	14	.265	167	16	4	.979
1980—Boston a	Amer.	OF-1B	93	260	41	74	11	1	9	38	.285	143	15	4	.975
1981—Baltimore	Amer.	OF-1B	68	134	16	30	0	1	3	10	.224	97	2	2	.980
1982—Baltimore	Amer.	OF-1B	71	148	28	45	4	3	6	15	.304	87	0	2	.978
1983—Baltimore	Amer.	OF-1B	100	196	37	56	17	1	8	38	.286	123	2	4	.969
1984—Baltimore b	Amer.	OF	76	161	22	41	9	1	2	21	.255	83	3	3	.966
1985—Baltimore c	Amer.	OF	101	233	35	58	8	3	7	36	.249	131	4	1	.993
1986—Baltimore d	Amer.	OF-1B	94	160	18	39	13	1	8	31	.244	33	4	0	1.000
National League Totals—6 Years			364	723	88	170	26	5	11	65	.235	434	26	8	.983
American League Totals—8 Years			679	1405	216	373	69	11	45	203	.265	864	46	20	.978
Major League Totals—14 Years			1043	2128	304	543	95	16	56	268	.255	1298	72	28	.980

Selected by St. Louis Cardinals' organization in 11th round of free-agent draft, June 8, 1971.
†Traded to Montreal Expos for Infielder Larry Lintz, July 25, 1975.
‡Traded with Outfielder Jose (Pepe) Mangual to New York Mets for Outfielder Del Unser and Infielder Wayne Garrett, July 21, 1976.
§In three-club deal, Chicago Cubs traded Outfielder-First Baseman Pete LaCock to Kansas City Royals, the New York Mets traded Outfielder Jim Dwyer to Chicago Cubs' organization, and New York received a player to be named later, December 8, 1976; New York acquired Outfielder Sheldon Mallory from Kansas City to complete deal, December 13, 1976.
xReleased, September 7, 1977, signed by St. Louis Cardinals, September 13, 1977.
yTraded to San Francisco Giants, June 15, 1978, completing deal in which San Francisco traded Pitcher Frank Riccelli to St. Louis Cardinals for a player to be named later, October 25, 1977.
zSold to Boston Red Sox, March 15, 1979.
aGranted free agency, October 22, 1980; signed by Baltimore Orioles, December 23, 1980.
bOn disabled list, July 19 to August 29, 1984.
cGranted free agency, November 12, 1985; re-signed by Orioles, February 5, 1986.
dGranted free agency, November 12, 1986; re-signed by Orioles, November 20, 1986.

CHAMPIONSHIP SERIES RECORD

Year	Club	League	Pos.	G.	AB.	R.	H.	2B.	3B.	HR.	RBI.	B.A.	PO.	A.	E.	F.A.
1983—Baltimore	Amer.	PH-OF	2	4	1	1	1	0	0	0	.250	4	0	0	1.000

WORLD SERIES RECORD

Tied World Series record for hitting home run in first Series at-bat, October 11, 1983 (first inning).

Year	Club	League	Pos.	G.	AB.	R.	H.	2B.	3B.	HR.	RBI.	B.A.	PO.	A.	E.	F.A.
1983—Baltimore	Amer.	OF	2	8	3	3	1	0	1	1	.375	2	0	0	1.000

LEONARD KYLE DYKSTRA

Name pronounced DYK-struh.

(Lenny)

Born February 10, 1963, at Santa Ana, Calif.
Height, 5.10. Weight, 160.
Throws and bats lefthanded.
Grandson of Pete Leswick, forward with New York Americans and Boston Bruins
of NHL, 1936-37 and 1944-45; nephew of Tony Leswick, forward with
New York Rangers, Detroit Red Wings and Chicago Black
Hawks of NHL, 1945-46 through 1955-56 and 1957-58.

Major League stolen bases: 1985 (15), 1986 (31). Total—46.
Led Carolina League in bases on balls received with 107, stolen bases with 105 and caught stealing with 23 in 1983.
Named Carolina League Player of the Year, 1983.

Year	Club	League	Pos.	G.	AB.	R.	H.	2B.	3B.	HR.	RBI.	B.A.	PO.	A.	E.	F.A.
1981—Shelby	S. Atl.	OF-SS	48	157	34	41	7	2	0	18	.261	86	3	4	.957
1982—Shelby	S. Atl.	OF	120	413	95	120	13	7	3	38	.291	239	11	14	.947

Year Club League	Pos.	G.	AB.	R.	H.	2B.	3B.	HR.	RBI.	B.A.	PO.	A.	E.	F.A.
1983—Lynchburg............ Carol.	OF	●136	*525	*132	*188	24	*14	8	81	*.358	268	9	7	.975
1984—Jackson................. Texas	OF	131	501	*100	138	25	7	6	52	.275	256	5	2	*.992
1985—Tidewater............. Int.	OF	58	229	44	71	8	6	1	25	.310	184	4	5	.974
1985—New York............. Nat.	OF	83	236	40	60	9	3	1	19	.254	165	6	1	.994
1986—New York............. Nat.	OF	147	431	77	127	27	7	8	45	.295	283	8	3	.990
Major League Totals—2 Years.................		230	667	117	187	36	10	9	64	.280	448	14	4	.991

Selected by New York Mets' organization in 12th round of free-agent draft, June 8, 1981.

CHAMPIONSHIP SERIES RECORD

Year Club League	Pos.	G.	AB.	R.	H.	2B.	3B.	HR.	RBI.	B.A.	PO.	A.	E.	F.A.
1986—New York............. Nat.	OF-PH	6	23	3	7	1	1	1	3	.304	10	0	0	1.000

WORLD SERIES RECORD

Tied World Series record for most times home run as leadoff batter, start of game (1), October 21, 1986.

Year Club League	Pos.	G.	AB.	R.	H.	2B.	3B.	HR.	RBI.	B.A.	PO.	A.	E.	F.A.
1986—New York............. Nat.	OF-PH	7	27	4	8	0	0	2	3	.296	14	0	0	1.000

WILLIAM ALBERT EARLEY
(Bill)

Born January 30, 1956, at Cincinnati, O.
Height, 6.04. Weight, 200.
Throws left and bats righthanded.
Attendedn Miami University, Oxford, O.

Led American Association in games finished in relief with 42 in 1986.
Tied for American Association lead in games started by pitchers with 26 in 1981.

Year Club	League	G.	IP.	W.	L.	Pct.	H.	R.	ER.	SO.	BB.	ERA.
1978—Geneva..............................	NYP	13	95	10	3	.769	88	36	23	94	35	2.18
1979—Midland...........................	Texas	30	164	13	6	.684	180	87	74	94	62	4.06
1980—Midland...........................	Texas	8	21	0	2	.000	27	18	11	20	10	4.71
1980—Wichita............................	Am. Assoc.	21	98	7	4	.636	103	44	42	51	37	3.86
1981—Iowa†..............................	Am. Assoc.	29	154	4	*16	.200	164	94	83	75	*90	4.85
1982—Tabasco...........................	Mexican	14	77⅔	4	4	.500	63	22	18	43	26	2.09
1982—Iowa..............................	Am. Assoc.	28	66	4	2	.667	61	28	25	33	27	3.41
1983—Iowa..............................	Am. Assoc.	46	80	5	6	.455	87	39	35	56	34	3.94
1984—Iowa‡.............................	Am. Assoc.	54	86	6	6	.500	93	44	36	61	34	3.77
1985—Oklahoma City§	Am. Assoc.	41	77	7	5	.583	68	29	28	43	18	3.27
1986—Louisville	Am. Assoc.	52	70⅓	4	6	.400	60	29	25	43	32	3.20
1986—St. Louis.........................	National	3	3	0	0	.000	0	0	0	2	2	0.00
Major League Totals—1 Year.....................		3	3	0	0	.000	0	0	0	2	2	0.00

Selected by Kansas City Royals' organization in 11th round of free-agent draft, June 7, 1977.
Signed as free agent by Chicago Cubs' organization, June 19, 1978.
†Loaned to Tabasco of Mexican League, April 7, 1982; returned, June 26, 1982.
‡Granted free agency, October 15, 1984; signed by Oklahoma City (Texas Rangers' organization), February 11, 1985.
§Granted free agency, October 15, 1985; signed by Louisville (St. Louis Cardinals' organization), January 18, 1986.

MICHAEL ANTHONY EASLER
(Mike)

Born November 29, 1950, at Cleveland, O.
Height, 6.01. Weight, 196.
Throws right and bats lefthanded.
Attended Cleveland State University, Cleveland, O.

Brother-in-law of Cliff Johnson, first baseman-designated hitter with Houston Astros, New York Yankees, Cleveland Indians, Chicago Cubs, Oakland A's, Toronto Blue Jays and Texas Rangers, 1972 through 1986.
Major League stolen bases: 1976 (1), 1980 (5), 1981 (4), 1982 (1), 1983 (4), 1984 (1), 1986 (3). Total—19.
Hit for the cycle, June 12, 1980.
Tied for Southern League lead in being hit by pitch with 8 in 1972.
Tied for American Association lead in double plays by outfielders with 4 in 1976.

Year Club	League	Pos.	G.	AB.	R.	H.	2B.	3B.	HR.	RBI.	B.A.	PO.	A.	E.	F.A.
1969—Covington	Appal.	OF-3B	33	113	21	36	7	2	0	11	.319	25	10	4	.897
1970—Cocoa†...................	Fla. St.	OF	96	314	30	79	11	4	1	24	.252	142	5	7	.955
1971—Cocoa‡...................	Fla. St.	OF	109	392	61	115	15	5	11	68	.293	153	14	8	.954
1972—Columbus..............	South.	OF	106	372	52	100	11	4	13	46	.269	149	7	8	.951
1973—Columbus..............	South.	OF	48	168	27	52	11	1	6	32	.310	81	2	1	.988
1973—Denver	A. A.	OF	48	176	24	50	11	2	7	26	.284	74	2	6	.927
1973—Houston	Nat.	OF	6	7	1	0	0	0	0	0	.000	1	0	1	.500
1974—Denver	A. A.	OF	100	367	75	104	18	8	19	63	.283	172	7	5	.973
1974—Houston	Nat.	PH	15	15	0	1	0	0	0	0	.067	0	0	0	.000
1975—Iowa§-Tulsa...........	A. A.	OF	113	415	69	130	31	6	15	69	.313	161	6	8	.954
1975—Houston x	Nat.	PH	5	5	0	0	0	0	0	0	.000	0	0	0	.000
1976—Tulsa y	A. A.	OF	118	378	75	133	31	2	26	77	*.352	172	*16	8	.959
1976—California z............	Amer.	DH	21	54	6	13	1	1	0	4	.241	0	0	0	.000
1977—Columbus..............	Int.	OF	127	451	83	136	29	5	18	75	.302	171	7	3	.983
1977—Pittsburgh	Nat.	OF	10	18	3	8	2	0	1	5	.444	7	0	0	1.000
1978—Columbus ab.........	Int.	OF-1B	126	448	84	148	26	3	18	84	*.330	378	31	5	.988

Year Club League	Pos.	G.	AB.	R.	H.	2B.	3B.	HR.	RBI.	B.A.	PO.	A.	E.	F.A.
1979—Pittsburgh............. Nat.	OF	55	54	8	15	1	1	2	11	.278	0	0	0	.000
1980—Pittsburgh............. Nat.	OF	132	393	66	133	27	3	21	74	.338	201	6	3	.986
1981—Pittsburgh............. Nat.	OF	95	339	43	97	18	5	7	42	.286	188	13	4	.980
1982—Pittsburgh............. Nat.	OF	142	475	52	131	27	2	15	58	.276	243	8	7	.973
1983—Pittsburgh cd....... Nat.	OF	115	381	44	117	17	2	10	54	.307	158	6	6	.965
1984—Boston............... Amer.	1B	156	601	87	188	31	5	27	91	.313	256	29	7	.976
1985—Boston e .... Amer.	OF	155	568	71	149	29	4	16	74	.262	32	0	3	.914
1986—New York f .... Amer.	OF	146	490	64	148	26	2	14	78	.302	23	0	1	.958
National League Totals—9 Years...........		575	1687	217	502	92	13	56	244	.298	798	33	21	.975
American League Totals—4 Years		478	1713	228	498	87	12	57	247	.291	311	29	11	.969
Major League Totals—13 Years		1053	3400	445	1000	179	25	113	491	.294	1109	62	32	.973

Selected by Houston Astros' organization in 6th round of free-agent draft, June 5, 1969.

†On temporary inactive list, May 13 to May 25, 1970.

‡On temporary inactive list, May 25 to June 14, 1971.

§Loaned to St. Louis Cardinals' organization, June 25, 1975.

xTraded to St. Louis Cardinals for Pitcher Mike Barlow, September 30, 1975.

yTraded to California Angels for a player to be named later, September 3, 1976; St. Louis Cardinals acquired Infielder Ron Farkas to complete deal, September 7, 1976.

zTraded to Pittsburgh Pirates for Pitcher Randy Sealy, April 4, 1977.

aSold to Boston Red Sox, October 27, 1978.

bTraded to Pittsburgh Pirates for Outfielder George Hill and Pitcher Martin Rivas, March 15, 1979.

cOn disabled list, August 11 to September 2, 1983.

dTraded to Boston Red Sox for Pitcher John Tudor, December 6, 1983.

eTraded to New York Yankees for Designated Hitter Don Baylor, March 28, 1986.

fTraded with Infielder Tom Barrett to Philadelphia Phillies for Pitchers Charles Hudson and Jeff Knox, December 11, 1986.

CHAMPIONSHIP SERIES RECORD

Year Club League	Pos.	G.	AB.	R.	H.	2B.	3B.	HR.	RBI.	B.A.	PO.	A.	E.	F.A.
1979—Pittsburgh............. Nat.	PH	1	1	0	0	0	0	0	0	.000	0	0	0	.000

WORLD SERIES RECORD

Year Club League	Pos.	G.	AB.	R.	H.	2B.	3B.	HR.	RBI.	B.A.	PO.	A.	E.	F.A.
1979—Pittsburgh............. Nat.	PH	2	1	0	0	0	0	0	0	.000	0	0	0	.000

ALL-STAR GAME RECORD

Year League	Pos.	AB.	R.	H.	2B.	3B.	HR.	RBI.	B.A.	PO.	A.	E.	F.A.
1981—National..............................	OF	1	1	0	0	0	0	0	.000	0	0	0	.000

KENNETH LOGAN EASLEY

(Known by middle name.)

Born November 4, 1961, at Salt Lake City, Utah.

Height, 6.01. Weight, 185.

Throws and bats righthanded.

Attended College of Southern Idaho, Twins Falls, Ida.

Led Eastern League in games finished in relief with 45 and tied for lead in saves with 18 in 1986.

Led South Atlantic League in shutouts with 4 in 1983.

Year Club League		G.	IP.	W.	L.	Pct.	H.	R.	ER.	SO.	BB.	ERA.
1981—Paintsville	Ap'lachian	22	53	2	2	.500	60	36	23	26	24	3.91
1982—Paintsville	Ap'lachian	13	84⅓	7	4	.636	77	31	24	59	28	2.56
1983—Greensboro	S. Atlantic	29	158⅓	14	8	.636	157	82	71	116	62	4.04
1984—Fort Lauderdale	Florida St.	32	131	5	7	.417	150	76	56	57	44	3.85
1985—Fort Lauderdale	Florida St.	17	19	1	1	.500	19	6	2	16	6	0.95
1985—Albany	Eastern	29	85	5	3	.625	85	40	30	58	38	3.18
1986—Albany†	Eastern	49	77⅔	8	7	.533	70	25	13	73	20	1.51

Selected by New York Yankees' organization in 20th round of free-agent draft, June 8, 1981.

†Traded with Pitchers Doug Drabek and Brian Fisher to Pittsburgh Pirates for Pitchers Rick Rhoden, Cecilio Guante and Pat Clements, November 26, 1986.

JAMES MORRIS EASTERLY

(Jamie)

Born February 17, 1953, at Houston, Tex.

Height, 5.10. Weight, 180.

Throws and bats lefthanded.

Attended Sam Houston State University, Huntsville, Tex.

Pitched seven-inning, 10-0 perfect game against Iowa, July 14, 1979.

Major League saves: 1977 (1), 1978 (1), 1981 (4), 1982 (2), 1983 (4), 1984 (2). Total—14.

Year Club League		G.	IP.	W.	L.	Pct.	H.	R.	ER.	SO.	BB.	ERA.
1971—Greenwood................................	W. Carol.	8	29	3	0	1.000	14	3	2	33	9	0.62
1972—Greenwood................................	W. Carol.	7	24	1	0	1.000	11	0	0	29	13	0.00
1972—Savannah†	Southern	2	4	0	1	.000	7	2	2	4	4	4.50
1973—Savannah‡	Southern	15	67	5	3	.625	62	40	28	53	41	3.76
1974—Richmond..................................	Int'national	26	138	9	6	.600	115	48	39	84	75	2.54
1974—Atlanta......................................	National	3	3	0	0	.000	6	7	5	0	4	15.00
1975—Richmond..................................	Int'national	2	10	1	1	.500	11	3	2	4	6	1.80
1975—Atlanta......................................	National	21	69	2	9	.182	73	47	38	34	42	4.96

Year Club	League	G.	IP.	W.	L.	Pct.	H.	R.	ER.	SO.	BB.	ERA.
1976—Richmond	Int'national	33	137	7	6	.583	133	56	45	91	88	2.96
1976—Atlanta	National	4	22	1	1	.500	23	12	12	11	13	4.91
1977—Atlanta§	National	22	59	2	4	.333	72	46	40	37	30	6.10
1978—Atlanta	National	37	78	3	6	.333	91	52	49	42	45	5.65
1979—Richmond	Int'national	10	13	0	0	.000	5	0	0	12	7	0.00
1979—Atlanta xy	National	4	3	0	0	.000	7	6	4	3	3	12.00
1979—Denver	Am. Assoc.	20	88	5	6	.455	100	40	32	55	39	3.27
1980—Denver z	Am. Assoc.	56	134	9	8	.529	118	64	54	105	56	3.63
1981—Milwaukee	American	44	62	3	3	.500	46	23	22	31	34	3.19
1982—Milwaukee a	American	28	30⅔	0	2	.000	39	19	16	16	15	4.70
1983—Milwaukee bc-Cleveland d	American	53	68⅔	4	3	.571	83	32	28	45	32	3.67
1984—Cleveland e	American	26	69⅓	3	1	.750	74	31	26	42	23	3.38
1985—Cleveland f	American	50	98⅔	4	1	.800	96	52	43	58	53	3.92
1986—Cleveland g	American	13	17⅔	0	2	.000	27	16	15	9	12	7.64
National League Totals—6 Years		91	234	8	20	.286	272	170	148	127	137	5.69
American League Totals—6 Years		214	347	14	12	.538	365	173	150	201	169	3.89
Major League Totals—12 Years		305	581	22	32	.407	637	343	298	328	306	4.62

Selected by Atlanta Braves' organization in 2nd round of free-agent draft, June 8, 1971.

†On disabled list, April 11 to April 27, July 7 to July 28 and August 5, 1972 through remainder of season.

‡On disabled list, April 24 to May 12 and May 24 to July 9, 1973.

§On disabled list, June 6 to July 4 and July 21 to September 19, 1977.

xLoaned to Denver (Montreal Expos' organization), June 6, 1979; returned, August 31, 1979.

ySold to Montreal Expos, October 17, 1979.

zSold to Milwaukee Brewers, September 22, 1980.

aOn disabled list, July 12 to September 1, 1982.

bHad a sacrifice bunt and a ground out in only plate appearances during season when designated hitter took the field.

cTraded with Outfielder Gorman Thomas and Pitcher Ernie Camacho to Cleveland Indians for Outfielder Rick Manning and Pitcher Rick Waits, June 6, 1983.

dGranted free agency, November 7, 1983; re-signed by Indians, January 17, 1984.

eOn disabled list, March 25 to June 15, 1984.

fGranted free agency, November 12, 1985; re-signed by Indians, January 8, 1986.

gOn disabled list, June 1, 1986 through remainder of season.

DIVISION SERIES RECORD

Year Club	League	G.	IP.	W.	L.	Pct.	H.	R.	ER.	SO.	BB.	ERA.
1981—Milwaukee	American	2	1⅓	0	0	.000	2	1	1	1	0	6.75

DENNIS LEE ECKERSLEY

Born October 3, 1954, at Oakland, Calif.
Height, 6.02. Weight, 195.
Throws and bats righthanded.
Son-in-law of Al Jacinto, second baseman in Chicago White Sox' organization, 1947 through 1954.

Tied American League record for most low-hit (no-hit and one-hit) games, season (3), 1977.
Pitched 1-0 no-hit victory against California Angels, May 30, 1977.
Major League saves: 1975 (2), 1976 (1). Total—3.
Led American League in home runs allowed with 30 in 1978.
Tied for American League lead in intentional bases on balls issued with 11 in 1977.
Led Texas League in hit batsmen with 10 in 1974.
Led California League pitchers in games started with 31 and tied for lead in shutouts with 5 in 1973.
Named American League Rookie Pitcher of the Year by THE SPORTING NEWS, 1975.
Received reported $32,000 bonus to sign with Cleveland Indians, 1972.

Year Club	League	G.	IP.	W.	L.	Pct.	H.	R.	ER.	SO.	BB.	ERA.
1972—Reno	California	12	75	5	5	.500	87	46	40	56	33	4.80
1973—Reno	California	31	202	12	8	.600	182	97	82	218	91	3.65
1974—San Antonio	Texas	23	167	●14	3	*.824	141	66	63	*163	60	3.40
1975—Cleveland	American	34	187	13	7	.650	147	61	54	152	90	2.60
1976—Cleveland	American	36	199	13	12	.520	155	82	76	200	78	3.44
1977—Cleveland†	American	33	247	14	13	.519	214	100	97	191	54	3.53
1978—Boston	American	35	268	20	8	.714	258	99	89	162	71	2.99
1979—Boston	American	33	247	17	10	.630	234	89	82	150	59	2.99
1980—Boston	American	30	198	12	14	.462	188	101	94	121	44	4.27
1981—Boston	American	23	154	9	8	.529	160	82	73	79	35	4.27
1982—Boston	American	33	224⅓	13	13	.500	228	101	93	127	43	3.73
1983—Boston	American	28	176⅓	9	13	.409	223	119	110	77	39	5.61
1984—Boston‡	American	9	64⅔	4	4	.500	71	38	36	33	13	5.01
1984—Chicago§	National	24	160⅓	10	8	.556	152	59	54	81	36	3.03
1985—Chicago x	National	25	169⅓	11	7	.611	145	61	58	117	19	3.08
1986—Chicago	National	33	201	6	11	.353	226	109	102	137	43	4.57
American League Totals—10 Years		294	1965⅓	124	102	.549	1878	872	804	1292	526	3.68
National League Totals—3 Years		82	530⅔	27	26	.509	523	229	214	335	98	3.63
Major League Totals—12 Years		376	2496	151	128	.541	2401	1101	1018	1627	624	3.67

Selected by Cleveland Indians' organization in 3rd round of free-agent draft, June 6, 1972.

†Traded with Catcher Fred Kendall to Boston Red Sox for Pitchers Rick Wise and Mike Paxton, Third Baseman Ted Cox and Catcher Bo Diaz, March 30, 1978.

‡Traded with Outfielder Mike Brumley to Chicago Cubs for First Baseman-Outfielder Bill Buckner, May 25, 1984.

§Granted free agency, November 8, 1984; re-signed by Cubs, November 28, 1984.

xOn disabled list, August 11 to September 7, 1985.

CHAMPIONSHIP SERIES RECORD

Year Club	League	G.	IP.	W.	L.	Pct.	H.	R.	ER.	SO.	BB.	ERA.
1984—Chicago	National	1	5⅓	0	1	.000	9	5	5	0	0	8.44

ALL-STAR GAME RECORD

Year League	IP.	W.	L.	Pct.	H.	R.	ER.	SO.	BB.	ERA.
1977—American	2	0	0	.000	0	0	0	1	0	0.00
1982—American	3	0	1	.000	2	3	3	1	2	9.00
All-Star Game Totals—2 Years	5	0	1	.000	2	3	3	2	2	5.40

JEFFREY ALLEN EDWARDS
(Jeff)

Born June 27, 1963, at Nashville, Tenn.
Height, 6.02. Weight, 190.
Throws and bats lefthanded.
Attended Vanderbilt University, Nashville, Tenn.

Tied for Pioneer League lead in shutouts with 2 in 1984.

Year Club	League	G.	IP.	W.	L.	Pct.	H.	R.	ER.	SO.	BB.	ERA.
1984—Great Falls	Pioneer	13	66	4	5	.444	83	42	26	75	26	3.55
1985—Bakersfield†	California	16	88⅓	3	3	.500	80	44	38	73	49	3.87
1986—San Antonio‡	Texas	33	140⅔	9	10	.474	128	63	59	123	55	3.77

Selected by St. Louis Cardinals' organization in 21st round of free-agent draft, June 8, 1981.
Selected by Los Angeles Dodgers' organization in 7th round of free-agent draft, June 7, 1984.
†On disabled list, June 29 to August 12, 1985.
‡Drafted by Houston Astros, December 9, 1986.

MARK ANTHONY EICHHORN

Name pronounced IKE-horn

Born November 21, 1960, at San Jose, Calif.
Height, 6.03. Weight, 200.
Throws and bats righthanded.
Attended Cabrillo Junior College, Aptos, Calif.

Major League saves: 1986 (10).
Led American League in intentional bases on balls issued with 14 in 1986.
Tied for Southern League lead in games started by pitchers with 29 in 1981.
Named American League Rookie Pitcher of the Year by THE SPORTING NEWS, 1986.

Year Club	League	G.	IP.	W.	L.	Pct.	H.	R.	ER.	SO.	BB.	ERA.
1979—Medicine Hat	Pioneer	16	93	7	6	.538	101	62	35	66	26	3.39
1980—Kinston	Carolina	26	183	14	10	.583	158	72	59	119	56	2.90
1981—Knoxville	Southern	30	192	10	14	.417	202	112	85	99	57	3.98
1982—Syracuse	Int'national	27	156⅔	10	11	.476	158	92	79	71	83	4.54
1982—Toronto	American	7	38	0	3	.000	40	28	23	16	14	5.45
1983—Syracuse	Int'national	7	30⅔	0	5	.000	36	32	27	12	21	7.92
1983—Knoxville	Southern	21	120⅔	6	12	.333	124	65	58	54	47	4.33
1984—Syracuse	Int'national	36	117⅔	5	9	.357	147	92	78	54	51	5.97
1985—Knoxville	Southern	26	116⅓	5	1	.833	101	49	39	76	34	3.02
1985—Int'national	Int'national	8	37⅓	2	5	.286	38	24	20	27	7	4.82
1986—Toronto†	American	69	157	14	6	.700	105	32	30	166	45	1.72
Major League Totals—2 Years		76	195	14	9	.609	145	60	53	182	59	2.45

Selected by Toronto Blue Jays' organization in 2nd round of free-agent draft, January 9, 1979.
†On disabled list, June 16 to July 1, 1986.

JAMES MICHAEL EISENREICH

Name pronounced EYES-en-rike.

(Jim)

Born April 18, 1959, at St. Cloud, Minn.
Height, 5.11. Weight, 180.
Throws and bats lefthanded.
Attended St. Cloud State University, St. Cloud, Minn.

Major League stolen bases: 1984 (2).
Named Appalachian League Co-Player of the Year, 1980.

Year Club	League	Pos.	G.	AB.	R.	H.	2B.	3B.	HR.	RBI.	B.A.	PO.	A.	E.	F.A.
1980—Elizabethton	Appal.	OF	67	258	47	77	12	●4	3	41	.298	151	7	3	.981
1980—Wis. Rapids	Midw.	DH	5	16	4	7	0	0	0	5	.438	0	0	0	.000
1981—Wis. Rapids	Midw.	OF	★134	489	101	●152	★27	0	23	99	.311	★295	17	9	.972
1982—Minnesota†	Amer.	OF	34	99	10	30	6	0	2	9	.303	72	0	2	.973
1983—Minnesota‡	Amer.	OF	2	7	1	2	1	0	0	0	.286	6	1	0	1.000
1984—Minnesota§x	Amer.	OF	12	32	1	7	1	0	0	3	.219	5	0	0	1.000
1985—								(Out of Organized Baseball)							
1986—y								(Out of Organized Baseball)							
Major League Totals—3 Years			48	138	12	39	8	0	2	12	.283	83	1	2	.977

Selected by Minnesota Twins' organization in 16th round of free-agent draft, June 3, 1980.
†On disabled list, May 6 to May 28 and June 18 to September 1, 1982.

‡On disabled list, April 7, 1983; then transferred to voluntarily retired list, May 27, 1983 through remainder of season.
§On disabled list, April 26 to May 18, 1984.
xOn voluntarily retired list, June 4, 1984 through September 29, 1986.
yClaimed on waivers by Kansas City Royals, October 2, 1986.

KEVIN DANIEL ELSTER

Born August 3, 1964, at San Pedro, Calif.
Height, 6.02. Weight, 180.
Throws and bats righthanded.
Attended Golden West College, Huntington Beach, Calif.

Led Texas League shortstops in total chances with 589 and double plays with 83 in 1986.
Led New York-Pennsylvania League shortstops in double plays with 45 and total chances with 358 in 1984.

Year	Club	League	Pos.	G.	AB.	R.	H.	2B.	3B.	HR.	RBI.	B.A.	PO.	A.	E.	F.A.
1984—Little Falls	NYP	SS	71	257	35	66	7	3	3	35	.257	★128	214	16	★.955
1985—Lynchburg	Carol.	SS	59	224	41	66	9	0	7	26	.295	82	195	16	.945
1985—Jackson†	Texas	SS	59	214	30	55	13	0	2	22	.257	107	220	10	.970
1986—Jackson	Texas	SS	127	435	69	117	19	3	2	52	.269	★196	★365	28	★.952
1986—New York	Nat.	SS	19	30	3	5	1	0	0	0	.167	16	35	2	.962
Major League Totals—1 Year			19	30	3	5	1	0	0	0	.167	16	35	2	.962

Selected by New York Mets' organization in 2nd round of free-agent draft, January 17, 1984.
†On disabled list, August 11, 1985 through remainder of season.

CHAMPIONSHIP SERIES RECORD

Year	Club	League	Pos.	G.	AB.	R.	H.	2B.	3B.	HR.	RBI.	B.A.	PO.	A.	E.	F.A.
1986—New York	Nat.	PR-SS	4	3	0	0	0	0	0	0	.000	2	3	0	1.000

WORLD SERIES RECORD

Year	Club	League	Pos.	G.	AB.	R.	H.	2B.	3B.	HR.	RBI.	B.A.	PO.	A.	E.	F.A.
1986—New York	Nat.	SS	1	1	0	0	0	0	0	0	.000	3	3	1	.857

RALPH DAVID ENGLE
(Dave)

Born November 30, 1956, at San Diego, Calif.
Height, 6.03. Weight, 216.
Throws and bats righthanded.
Attended University of Southern California, Los Angeles, Calif.

Major League stolen bases: 1983 (2), 1985 (2). Total—4.

Year	Club	League	Pos.	G.	AB.	R.	H.	2B.	3B.	HR.	RBI.	B.A.	PO.	A.	E.	F.A.
1978—Salinas†	Calif.	3B	53	203	34	62	11	0	6	40	.305	20	65	10	.895
1979—Toledo	Int.	3B	106	363	46	104	17	1	7	51	.287	72	197	23	.921
1980—Toledo	Int.	OF	133	489	74	150	27	3	7	73	★.307	225	16	5	.980
1981—Minnesota	Amer.	OF-3B	82	248	29	64	14	4	5	32	.258	144	4	3	.980
1982—Minnesota	Amer.	OF	58	186	20	42	7	2	4	16	.226	63	3	1	.985
1982—Toledo	Int.	OF	9	34	14	15	1	1	5	12	.441	15	4	0	1.000
1983—Minnesota	Amer.	C-OF	120	374	46	114	22	4	8	43	.305	306	26	9	.974
1984—Minnesota	Amer.	C	109	391	56	104	20	1	4	38	.266	376	34	8	.981
1985—Minnesota‡	Amer.	C-OF	70	172	28	44	8	2	7	25	.256	66	4	1	.986
1986—Detroit§	Amer.	1B-OF-C	35	86	6	22	7	0	0	4	.256	185	14	0	1.000
1986—Nashville x	A. A.	OF-C	8	24	5	4	0	0	2	7	.167	17	2	0	1.000
Major League Totals—6 Years			474	1457	185	390	78	13	28	158	.268	1140	85	22	.982

Selected by California Angels' organization in 2nd round of free-agent draft, June 6, 1978.
†Traded with Outfielder Ken Landreaux and Pitchers Paul Hartzell and Brad Havens to Minnesota Twins for First Baseman Rod Carew, February 3, 1979.
‡Traded to Detroit Tigers for Infielder Chris Pittaro and Outfielder Alex Sanchez, January 16, 1986.
§On disabled list, April 29 to August 10, 1986; included rehabilitation disability assignment to Nashville, May 28 to June 6, 1986.
xReleased, August 10, 1986.

ALL-STAR GAME RECORD
Member of American League All-Star Team in 1984; did not play.

NICHOLAS ANDREW ESASKY

Name pronounced Ee-SASS-kee.
(Nick)

Born February 24, 1960, at Hialeah, Fla.
Height, 6.03. Weight, 200.
Throws and bats righthanded.

Major League stolen bases: 1983 (6), 1984 (1), 1985 (3). Total—10.
Led Eastern League batters in strikeouts with 131 and game-winning RBIs with 14 in 1980.

Year	Club	League	Pos.	G.	AB.	R.	H.	2B.	3B.	HR.	RBI.	B.A.	PO.	A.	E.	F.A.
1978—Billings	Pion.	3B	64	213	38	65	10	5	4	48	.305	★62	88	22	.872
1979—Tampa	Fla. St.	3B	124	439	52	118	16	3	10	66	.269	91	234	27	.923
1980—Waterbury	East.	3B	135	425	79	115	18	4	★30	79	.271	98	241	23	.936
1981—Indianapolis	A. A.	3B	121	423	55	112	22	4	17	62	.265	99	220	★37	.896

Year	Club	League	Pos.	G.	AB.	R.	H.	2B.	3B.	HR.	RBI.	B.A.	PO.	A.	E.	F.A.
1982—Indianapolis	A. A.		3B	105	341	59	90	15	3	27	62	.264	77	150	21	★.915
1983—Indianapolis	A. A.		3B	49	158	33	44	5	0	14	37	.278	27	71	14	.875
1983—Cincinnati	Nat.		3B	85	302	41	80	10	5	12	46	.265	53	133	13	.935
1984—Cincinnati	Nat.		3B-1B	113	322	30	62	10	5	10	45	.193	220	137	18	.952
1985—Cincinnati	Nat.		3B-OF-1B	125	413	61	108	21	0	21	66	.262	169	106	8	.972
1986—Cincinnati†	Nat.		1B-OF-3B	102	330	35	76	17	2	12	41	.230	585	33	5	.992
Major League Totals—4 Years				425	1367	167	326	58	12	55	198	.238	1027	409	44	.970

Selected by Cincinnati Reds' organization in 1st round (17th player selected) of free-agent draft, June 6, 1978.
†On disabled list, June 15 to July 17, 1986.

ANGEL RUBEN ESCOBAR (RIVAS)

Born May 12, 1965, at La Sabana, Venezuela.
Height, 6.01. Weight, 160.
Throws right and bats left and righthanded.

Led Texas League in sacrifice hits with 11 in 1986.
Led Midwest League shortstops in double plays with 71 in 1984.

Year	Club	League	Pos.	G.	AB.	R.	H.	2B.	3B.	HR.	RBI.	B.A.	PO.	A.	E.	F.A.
1983—Great Falls	Pion.		SS-2B	44	109	15	23	3	1	0	6	.211	50	64	17	.870
1984—Clinton	Midw.		SS	99	311	47	70	16	2	2	25	.225	175	295	★48	.907
1985—Fresno	Calif.		SS-2B	109	386	62	97	13	2	1	34	.251	174	290	36	.928
1986—Shreveport	Texas		★SS-2B	131	439	58	121	14	4	2	46	.276	185	349	★33	.942

Signed as free agent by San Francisco Giants' organization, June 10, 1982.

JUAN ESPINO (REYES)

Born March 16, 1956, at Bonao, Dominican Republic.
Height, 6.00. Weight, 185.
Throws and bats righthanded.

Led New York-Pennsylvania League batters in strikeouts with 61 in 1975.
Led International League in passed balls with 13 in 1985 and tied for lead with 10 in 1983.

Year	Club	League	Pos.	G.	AB.	R.	H.	2B.	3B.	HR.	RBI.	B.A.	PO.	A.	E.	F.A.
1975—Oneonta	NYP		C-OF	48	157	24	36	5	5	2	23	.229	26	3	2	.935
1976—Fort Lauderdale†	Fla. St.		C	39	118	18	30	5	3	4	20	.254	170	20	3	.984
1977—Fort Lauderdale	Fla. St.		C	52	141	8	28	8	0	0	16	.199	266	40	9	.971
1978—West Haven	East.		C	82	261	32	73	14	0	6	37	.280	426	44	6	★.987
1979—West Haven	East.		C	95	296	40	70	11	1	8	44	.236	509	57	13	.978
1980—Nashville	South.		C	17	56	3	9	1	0	0	9	.161	115	6	2	.984
1980—Columbus	Int.		C	48	129	11	27	7	1	1	16	.209	238	29	5	.982
1981—Columbus	Int.		C	80	253	22	59	8	2	7	32	.233	434	53	8	.984
1982—Columbus‡	Int.		C	54	163	30	46	10	1	3	27	.282	264	34	5	.983
1982—New York	Amer.		C	3	2	0	0	0	0	0	0	.000	4	0	0	1.000
1983—Columbus	Int.		C	77	211	35	59	10	1	10	42	.280	326	42	7	.981
1983—New York§	Amer.		C	10	23	1	6	0	0	1	3	.261	38	1	0	1.000
1984—Maine x	Int.		C	97	327	38	82	6	1	7	41	.251	432	47	11	.978
1985—Columbus	Int.		C	74	224	30	56	11	0	3	20	.250	349	46	7	.983
1985—New York	Amer.		C	9	11	0	4	0	0	0	0	.364	16	4	0	1.000
1986—Columbus y	Int.		C	53	179	21	54	5	1	5	21	.302	227	16	5	.980
1986—New York	Amer.		C	27	37	1	6	2	0	0	5	.162	72	6	1	.987
Major League Totals—4 Years				49	73	2	16	2	0	1	8	.219	130	11	1	.993

Signed as free agent by New York Yankees' organization, December 26, 1974.
†On disabled list, May 26 to June 9, 1976.
‡On disabled list, August 3 to August 23, 1982.
§Sold to Cleveland Indians' organization, March 31, 1984.
xSold to Columbus (New York Yankees' organization), January 8, 1985.
yOn disabled list, April 12 to April 26, 1986.

ALVARO ALBERTO ESPINOZA (RAMIREZ)

Name pronounced Ess-pin-OH-zuh.

Born February 19, 1962, at Valencia, Carabobo, Venezuela.
Height, 6.00. Weight, 170.
Throws and bats righthanded.

Tied for International League lead in sacrifice hits with 16 in 1984.
Led International League shortstops in putouts with 159 in 1986.
Led California League shortstops in total chances with 660 in 1983.
Led Gulf Coast League shortstops in assists with 217, double plays with 33 and total chances with 356 in 1980.

Year	Club	League	Pos.	G.	AB.	R.	H.	2B.	3B.	HR.	RBI.	B.A.	PO.	A.	E.	F.A.
1979—Sarasota Astros	Gulf C.		SS-2B-3B	11	32	3	7	0	0	0	5	.219	18	27	1	.978
1980—Sara. Astros-O.†	Gulf C.		★SS-3B	59	200	24	43	5	0	0	14	.215	★114	219	★25	.930
1981—			(Out of Organized Baseball)													
1982—Wis. Rapids	Midw.		SS-3B-1B	112	379	41	101	9	0	5	29	.266	237	241	33	.935
1983—Visalia	Calif.		SS	130	486	57	155	20	1	4	57	.319	★256	364	40	.939
1984—Toledo‡	Int.		SS	104	344	22	80	12	5	0	30	.233	157	293	19	.959
1985—Toledo§	Int.		SS	82	266	24	61	11	0	1	33	.229	132	245	16	.959
1985—Minnesota	Amer.		SS	32	57	5	15	2	0	0	9	.263	25	69	5	.949
1986—Toledo	Int.		SS-2B	73	253	18	71	8	1	2	27	.281	170	205	12	.969
1986—Minnesota	Amer.		2B-SS	37	42	4	9	1	0	0	1	.214	23	52	4	.949
Major League Totals—2 Years				69	99	9	24	3	0	0	10	.242	48	121	9	.949

Signed as free agent by Houston Astros' organization, October 30, 1978.
†Released, September 30, 1980; signed by Wisconsin Rapids (Minnesota Twins' organization), March 18, 1982.
‡On disabled list, June 7 to June 25, 1984.
§On disabled list, June 6 to July 2, 1985.

CECIL EDWARD ESPY

Born January 20, 1963, at San Diego, Calif.
Height, 6.03. Weight, 190.
Throws right and bats left and righthanded.
Son of Cecil Espy, scout with St. Louis Cardinals since 1979.

Led Florida State League in stolen bases with 74 in 1982.
Tied for Texas League lead in caught stealing with 17 in 1985.
Led Texas League shortstops in errors with 50 in 1985.
Led Texas League outfielders in total chances with 365 in 1984.

Year Club	League	Pos.	G.	AB.	R.	H.	2B.	3B.	HR.	RBI.	B.A.	PO.	A.	E.	F.A.
1980—Sarasota W. Sox ...	Gulf C.	OF	58	212	33	58	7	3	0	26	.274	138	4	7	.953
1981—Appleton ...	Midw.	OF	72	273	37	55	2	2	1	19	.201	143	5	5	.967
1981—Sarasota W. Sox† .	Gulf C.	OF	43	142	24	40	3	1	0	16	.282	54	1	4	.932
1982—Vero Beach ...	Fla. St.	OF	131	*523	*100	*166	14	7	1	34	.317	275	9	10	.966
1983—San Antonio ...	Texas	OF	133	*564	88	151	16	11	4	38	.268	258	12	10	.964
1983—Los Angeles ...	Nat.	OF	20	11	4	3	1	0	0	1	.273	11	0	0	1.000
1984—San Antonio ...	Texas	*O-2-S	*133	*535	99	146	19	8	8	60	.273	*348	16	5	.986
1985—San Antonio‡ ...	Texas	SS-OF	124	461	64	129	24	3	5	49	.280	183	346	51	.912
1986—Hawaii§ ...	P. C.	OF-2B-SS	106	384	49	101	19	3	4	38	.263	172	8	5	.973
Major League Totals—1 Year			20	11	4	3	1	0	0	1	.273	11	0	0	1.000

Selected by Chicago White Sox' organization in 1st round (eighth player selected) of free-agent draft, June 3, 1980.
†Traded with Pitcher Burt Geiger to Los Angeles Dodgers' organization for Outfielder Rudy Law, March 30, 1982.
‡Traded with First Baseman Sid Bream to Pittsburgh Pirates, September 9, 1985, completing deal in which Los Angeles Dodgers acquired Third Baseman Bill Madlock for three players to be named later, R. J. Reynolds as partial completion of deal, September 3, 1985.
§Drafted by Texas Rangers, December 9, 1986.

DARRELL WAYNE EVANS

Born May 26, 1947, at Pasadena, Calif.
Height, 6.02. Weight, 205.
Throws right and bats lefthanded.
Attended Pasadena City College, Pasadena, Calif. and
California State University, Los Angeles, Calif.
Grandson of David Salazar, former minor league player.

Established National League records for most double plays, third baseman, (45), 1974; most games, consecutive, one or more bases on balls (15), April 9 through 27, 1976.
Tied modern National League record for most errors in inning by third baseman (3), April 11, 1980 (7th inning).
Major League stolen bases: 1971 (2), 1972 (4), 1973 (6), 1974 (4), 1975 (12), 1976 (9), 1977 (9), 1978 (4), 1979 (6), 1980 (17), 1981 (2), 1982 (5), 1983 (6), 1984 (2), 1986 (3). Total—91.
Hit three home runs in a game, June 15, 1983.
Led National League in bases on balls received with 124 in 1973 and 126 in 1974.
Led National League third basemen in putouts with 161 and assists with 381 in 1975.
Led National League third basemen in double plays with 45 in 1974 and 41 in 1975.
Led National League third basemen in total chances with 471 in 1973, 578 in 1974, 578 in 1975, 520 in 1978 and 528 in 1979.
Led International League third basemen in fielding percentage with .951 in 1970.
Named third baseman on THE SPORTING NEWS National League All-Star Team, 1973.
Named Player of the Year in Gulf Coast League, 1967.

Year Club	League	Pos.	G.	AB.	R.	H.	2B.	3B.	HR.	RBI.	B.A.	PO.	A.	E.	F.A.
1967—Peninsula ...	Carol.	3B	8	28	4	11	1	1	0	6	.393	6	13	2	.905
1967—Bradenton A's ...	Gulf C.	3B-SS	14	45	13	22	3	3	2	11	.489	25	30	2	.965
1967—Leesburg ...	Fla. St.	3B-SS	39	142	18	37	4	2	0	12	.261	49	81	11	.922
1968—Birmingham† ...	South.	3B-1B-2B	56	187	18	45	6	3	3	25	.241	103	101	10	.953
1969—Richmond ...	Int.	3B	59	211	43	76	12	4	7	45	.360	51	103	19	.890
1969—Shreveport ...	Texas	3B-SS-OF	24	79	14	22	5	4	2	14	.278	25	40	3	.956
1969—Atlanta ...	Nat.	3B	12	26	3	6	0	0	0	1	.231	4	7	1	.917
1970—Richmond ...	Int.	3B-1B-OF	120	447	92	134	20	7	20	83	.300	99	220	16	.952
1970—Atlanta ...	Nat.	3B	12	44	4	14	1	1	0	9	.318	6	26	2	.941
1971—Richmond ...	Int.	OF-3B	31	101	20	31	2	2	6	30	.307	59	11	1	.986
1971—Atlanta ...	Nat.	3B-OF	89	260	42	63	11	1	12	38	.242	77	138	14	.939
1972—Atlanta‡ ...	Nat.	3B	125	418	67	106	12	0	19	71	.254	126	273	25	.941
1973—Atlanta ...	Nat.	3B-1B	161	595	114	167	25	8	41	104	.281	266	335	24	.962
1974—Atlanta ...	Nat.	3B	160	571	99	137	21	3	25	79	.240	*185	367	26	.955
1975—Atlanta ...	Nat.	*3B-1B	156	567	82	138	22	2	22	73	.243	164	382	*36	.938
1976—Atl.§-S.F. ...	Nat.	1B-3B	136	396	53	81	9	1	11	46	.205	978	110	10	.991
1977—San Francisco ...	Nat.	OF-1B-3B	144	461	64	117	18	3	17	72	.254	324	83	13	.969
1978—San Francisco x..	Nat.	3B	159	547	82	133	24	2	20	78	.243	*147	*348	*25	.952
1979—San Francisco ...	Nat.	3B	160	562	68	142	23	2	17	70	.253	*129	*369	*30	.943
1980—San Francisco ...	Nat.	3B-1B	154	556	69	147	23	0	20	78	.264	232	340	27	.955
1981—San Francisco ...	Nat.	3B-1B	102	357	51	92	13	4	12	48	.258	188	202	14	.965
1982—San Francisco ...	Nat.	3B-1B-SS	141	465	64	119	20	4	16	61	.256	471	233	21	.971
1983—San Francisco y..	Nat.	1B-3B-SS	142	523	94	145	29	3	30	82	.277	1001	164	19	.984
1984—Detroit ...	Amer.	1B-3B	131	401	60	93	11	1	16	63	.232	331	62	2	.995

Year Club	League	Pos.	G.	AB.	R.	H.	2B.	3B.	HR.	RBI.	B.A.	PO.	A.	E.	F.A.
1985—Detroit	Amer.	1B-3B	151	505	81	125	17	0	*40	94	.248	831	125	20	.980
1986—Detroit	Amer.	1B-3B	151	507	78	122	15	0	29	85	.241	809	109	2	.998
National League Totals—15 Years			1853	6348	956	1607	251	34	262	910	.253	4298	3377	287	.964
American League Totals—3 Years			433	1413	219	340	43	1	85	242	.241	1971	296	24	.990
Major League Totals—18 Years			2286	7761	1175	1947	294	35	347	1152	.251	6269	3673	311	.970

Selected by Chicago Cubs' organization in 8th round of free-agent draft, June 22, 1965.
Selected by New York Yankees' organization in secondary phase of free-agent draft, January 29, 1966.
Selected by Detroit Tigers' organization in 5th round of free-agent draft, June 6, 1966.
Selected by Philadelphia Phillies' organization in 3rd round of free-agent draft, January 28, 1967.
Selected by Kansas City A's organization in secondary phase of free-agent draft, June 7, 1967.
†Drafted by Atlanta Braves, December 2, 1968.
‡On military list, June 17 to July 3, 1972.
§Traded with Shortstop Marty Perez to San Francisco Giants for First Baseman-Outfielder Willie Montanez, Shortstop Craig Robinson, Infielder Mike Eden and Outfielder Jake Brown, June 13, 1976.
xGranted free agency, November 2, 1978; re-signed by Giants, December 5, 1978.
yGranted free agency, November 7, 1983; signed by Detroit Tigers, December 17, 1983.

CHAMPIONSHIP SERIES RECORD

Year Club	League	Pos.	G.	AB.	R.	H.	2B.	3B.	HR.	RBI.	B.A.	PO.	A.	E.	F.A.
1984—Detroit	Amer.	1B-3B	3	10	1	3	1	0	0	1	.300	22	4	0	1.000

WORLD SERIES RECORD

Year Club	League	Pos.	G.	AB.	R.	H.	2B.	3B.	HR.	RBI.	B.A.	PO.	A.	E.	F.A.
1984—Detroit	Amer.	1B-3B	5	15	1	1	0	0	0	1	.067	18	5	0	1.000

ALL-STAR GAME RECORD

Year League	Pos.	AB.	R.	H.	2B.	3B.	HR.	RBI.	B.A.	PO.	A.	E.	F.A.
1973—National	PH	0	0	0	0	0	0	0	.000	0	0	0	.000
1983—National	1B	1	0	0	0	0	0	0	.000	2	1	0	1.000
All-Star Game Totals—2 Years		1	0	0	0	0	0	0	.000	2	1	0	1.000

DWIGHT MICHAEL EVANS

Born November 3, 1951, at Santa Monica, Calif.
Height, 6.03. Weight, 205.
Throws and bats righthanded.

Major League stolen bases: 1973 (5), 1974 (4), 1975 (3), 1976 (6), 1977 (4), 1978 (8), 1979 (6), 1980 (3), 1981 (3), 1982 (3), 1983 (3), 1984 (3), 1985 (7), 1986 (3). Total—61.
Hit for the cycle, June 28, 1984.
Led American League in bases on balls received with 85 in 1981 and 114 in 1985.
Led American League in total bases with 215 in 1981.
Led American League outfielders in double plays with 8 in 1975 and 7 in 1980.
Led Western Carolinas League in sacrifice flies with 8 in 1970.
Tied for Carolina League lead in double plays by outfielders with 3 in 1971.
Named outfielder on THE SPORTING NEWS American League All-Star Team, 1982 and 1984.
Named outfielder on THE SPORTING NEWS American League All-Star fielding team, 1976, 1978, 1979 and 1981 through 1985.
Named outfielder on THE SPORTING NEWS American League Silver Slugger team, 1981.
Named International League Most Valuable Player, 1972.

Year Club	League	Pos.	G.	AB.	R.	H.	2B.	3B.	HR.	RBI.	B.A.	PO.	A.	E.	F.A.
1969—Jamestown	NYP	OF-3B	34	100	13	28	3	2	1	12	.280	44	10	3	.947
1970—Greenville	W. Car.	OF-3B	108	355	69	98	14	*11	7	68	.276	130	11	7	.953
1971—Winston-Salem	Carol.	OF-1B	118	402	63	115	20	4	12	63	.286	219	17	10	.959
1972—Louisville	Int.	OF	●144	496	90	149	23	8	17	*95	.300	270	12	6	.979
1972—Boston	Amer.	OF	18	57	2	15	3	1	1	6	.263	25	3	0	1.000
1973—Boston	Amer.	OF	119	282	46	63	13	1	10	32	.223	178	4	1	.995
1974—Boston	Amer.	OF	133	463	60	130	19	8	10	70	.281	294	8	3	.990
1975—Boston	Amer.	OF	128	412	61	113	24	6	13	56	.274	281	15	4	.987
1976—Boston	Amer.	OF	146	501	61	121	34	5	17	62	.242	324	15	2	*.994
1977—Boston†	Amer.	OF	73	230	39	66	9	2	14	36	.287	126	2	1	.992
1978—Boston	Amer.	OF	147	497	75	123	24	2	24	63	.247	305	14	6	.982
1979—Boston	Amer.	OF	152	489	69	134	24	1	21	58	.274	307	15	4	.988
1980—Boston	Amer.	OF	148	463	72	123	37	5	18	60	.266	268	11	5	.982
1981—Boston	Amer.	OF	108	412	84	122	19	4	●22	71	.296	259	9	2	.993
1982—Boston	Amer.	OF	●162	609	122	178	37	7	32	98	.292	346	9	10	.973
1983—Boston‡	Amer.	OF	126	470	74	112	19	4	22	58	.238	222	6	3	.987
1984—Boston	Amer.	OF	●162	630	*121	186	37	8	32	104	.295	311	7	2	.994
1985—Boston	Amer.	OF	159	617	110	162	29	1	29	78	.263	291	9	3	.990
1986—Boston	Amer.	OF	152	529	86	137	33	2	26	97	.259	280	10	5	.983
Major League Totals—15 Years			1933	6661	1082	1785	361	57	291	949	.268	3817	137	51	.987

Selected by Boston Red Sox' organization in 5th round of free-agent draft, June 5, 1969.
†On disabled list, June 21 to July 8 and August 25 to September 21, 1977.
‡On disabled list, August 13 to September 1, 1983.

CHAMPIONSHIP SERIES RECORD

Year Club	League	Pos.	G.	AB.	R.	H.	2B.	3B.	HR.	RBI.	B.A.	PO.	A.	E.	F.A.
1975—Boston	Amer.	OF	3	10	1	1	1	0	0	0	.100	7	0	0	1.000
1986—Boston	Amer.	OF	7	28	2	6	1	0	1	4	.214	11	0	0	1.000
Championship Series Totals—2 Years			10	38	3	7	2	0	1	4	.184	18	0	0	1.000

Tied World Series record for highest fielding average by outfielder, seven-game Series (1.000 with 24 chances), 1975.

Year Club	League	Pos.	G.	AB.	R.	H.	2B.	3B.	HR.	RBI.	B.A.	PO.	A.	E.	F.A.
1975—Boston	Amer.	OF	7	24	3	7	1	1	1	5	.292	23	1	0	1.000
1986—Boston	Amer.	OF	7	26	4	8	2	0	2	9	.308	16	1	1	.944
World Series Totals—2 Years			14	50	7	15	3	1	3	14	.300	39	2	1	.976

ALL-STAR GAME RECORD

Year League	Pos.	AB.	R.	H.	2B.	3B.	HR.	RBI.	B.A.	PO.	A.	E.	F.A.
1978—American	OF	1	0	0	0	0	0	0	.000	3	0	0	1.000
1981—American	PH-OF	2	1	1	0	0	0	0	.500	2	0	0	1.000
All-Star Game Totals—2 Years		3	1	1	0	0	0	0	.333	5	0	0	1.000

STANLEY ROBERT FANSLER
(Stan)

Born February 12, 1965, at Elkins, W. Va.
Height, 5.11. Weight, 180.
Throws and bats righthanded.

Year Club	League	G.	IP.	W.	L.	Pct.	H.	R.	ER.	SO.	BB.	ERA.
1983—Watertown	NYP	14	57	0	*10	.000	79	●69	51	49	28	8.05
1984—Watertown	NYP	14	98⅔	5	1	.833	68	32	22	78	38	2.01
1985—Nashua	Eastern	24	158⅔	9	7	.563	137	67	53	74	75	3.01
1986—Hawaii	P. Coast	29	156	8	9	.471	139	83	63	77	65	3.63
1986—Pittsburgh	National	5	24	0	3	.000	20	12	10	13	15	3.75
Major League Totals—1 Year		5	24	0	3	.000	20	12	10	13	15	3.75

Selected by Pittsburgh Pirates' organization in 2nd round of free-agent draft, June 6, 1983.

EDWARD JOSEPH FARMER
(Ed)

Born October 18, 1949, at Evergreen Park, Ill.
Height, 6.05. Weight, 212.
Throws and bats righthanded.
Attended Chicago State College, Chicago, Ill.

Major League saves: 1971 (4), 1972 (7), 1973 (3), 1978 (1), 1979 (14), 1980 (30), 1981 (10), 1982 (6). Total—75.
Led International League in wild pitches with 13 in 1977.

Year Club	League	G.	IP.	W.	L.	Pct.	H.	R.	ER.	SO.	BB.	ERA.
1967—Sarasota Indians	Gulf Coast	7	32	3	0	1.000	12	13	7	29	30	1.97
1968—Waterbury	Eastern	4	14	0	3	.000	12	15	11	9	13	7.07
1968—Reno	California	23	125	8	5	.615	132	74	65	122	69	4.68
1969—Waterbury	Eastern	7	26	0	4	.000	36	26	20	12	19	6.92
1969—Monroe	W. Carol.	10	46	3	5	.375	44	39	30	30	43	5.87
1970—Wichita†	Am. Assoc.	23	121	5	7	.417	114	64	54	69	70	4.02
1971—Wichita	Am. Assoc.	7	40	2	2	.500	35	22	20	19	15	4.50
1971—Cleveland	American	43	79	5	4	.556	77	42	38	48	41	4.33
1972—Cleveland	American	46	61	2	5	.286	51	32	30	33	27	4.43
1973—Cleveland‡-Detroit§x	American	40	62	3	2	.600	77	38	34	38	32	4.94
1974—Toledo	Int'national	7	47	2	3	.400	33	18	14	34	23	2.68
1974—Philadelphia y	National	14	31	2	1	.667	41	32	29	20	27	8.42
1975—Sacramento	P. Coast	14	61	2	8	.200	69	59	53	53	67	7.82
1975—Union Laguna	Mexican	2	1	0	1	.000	1	4	3	0	4	27.00
1976—Salt Lake City z	P. Coast					(Did not play)						
1977—Rochester	Int'national	24	131	11	5	.688	127	72	65	96	★89	4.47
1977—Baltimore a	American	1	0	0	0	.000	1	1	1	0	1	.....
1978—Spokane	P.Coast	55	90	9	7	.563	103	73	60	50	53	6.00
1978—Milwaukee b	American	3	11	1	0	1.000	7	1	1	6	4	0.82
1979—Texas c-Chicago	American	53	114	5	7	.417	96	57	38	73	53	3.00
1980—Chicago	American	64	100	7	9	.438	92	37	37	54	56	3.33
1981—Chicago d	American	42	53	3	3	.500	53	33	27	42	34	4.58
1982—Philadelphia	National	47	76	2	6	.250	66	44	41	58	50	4.86
1983—Philadelphia e	National	12	26⅔	0	6	.000	35	22	18	16	20	6.08
1983—Portland f-Tacoma	P. Coast	15	23⅔	1	1	.500	29	18	13	16	8	4.94
1983—Oakland g	American	5	10⅓	0	0	.000	15	4	4	7	0	3.48
1984—Tacoma h	P. Coast	21	28⅓	3	4	.429	27	28	19	29	22	6.04
1985—Miami ijk	Florida St.	48	66	7	5	.583	73	30	20	54	35	2.73
1986—Hawaii	P. Coast	40	80⅔	4	7	.364	63	35	23	61	33	2.57
American League Totals—9 Years		297	490⅓	26	30	.464	469	245	210	301	248	3.85
National League Totals—3 Years		73	133⅔	4	13	.235	142	98	88	94	97	5.93
Major League Totals—11 Years		370	624	30	43	.411	611	343	298	395	345	4.30

Selected by Cleveland Indians' organization in 5th round of free-agent draft, June 6, 1967.
†On disabled list, July 23 to August 21, 1970.
‡Traded to Detroit Tigers for Pitcher Tom Timmerman and Infielder Kevin Collins, June 15, 1973.
§Traded to New York Yankees for Catcher Jerry Moses in three-team deal in which Cleveland Indians acquired Pitcher Jim Perry from Detroit Tigers and Cleveland sent Outfielder Walt Williams and Pitcher Rick Sawyer to New York, March 19, 1974.
xSold to Philadelphia Phillies, March 21, 1974.

yTraded to Milwaukee Brewers for Infielder-Outfielder Steve McCartney, December 3, 1974.
zReleased, April 4, 1976; signed by Baltimore Orioles' organization, March 2, 1977.
aReleased, March 28, 1978; signed by Milwaukee Brewers' organization, April 1, 1978.
bTraded with First Baseman Gary Holle and cash to Texas Rangers for Pitcher Reggie Cleveland, December 15, 1978.
cTraded with First Baseman Gary Holle to Chicago White Sox for Third Baseman Eric Soderholm, June 15, 1979.
dGranted free agency, November 13, 1981; signed by Philadelphia Phillies as Type A player, January 28, 1982. (Catcher Joel Skinner selected from player compensation pool by Chicago White Sox, February 2, 1982.)
eOn disabled list, July 3 to August 13, 1983; included rehabilitation disability assignment to Portland, July 27 to August 13, 1983.
fReleased, August 13, 1983; signed by Tacoma (Oakland A's organization), August 23, 1983.
gReleased, March 26, 1984; signed by Tacoma (Oakland A's organization), April 1, 1984.
hReleased, May 31, 1984; signed by Miami (Independent), April 12, 1985.
iOn disabled list, May 3 to May 15, 1985.
jOn temporary inactive list, August 8, 1985 through remainder of season.
kReleased, December 19, 1985; signed by Hawaii (Pittsburgh Pirates' organization), February 13, 1986.

ALL-STAR GAME RECORD

Year	League	IP.	W.	L.	Pct.	H.	R.	ER.	SO.	BB.	ERA.
1980—American		⅔	0	0	.000	1	0	0	0	0	0.00

STEVEN MICHAEL FARR
(Steve)

Born December 12, 1956, at Cheverly, Md.
Height, 5.11. Weight, 190.
Throws and bats righthanded.
Attended American University, Washington, D.C.

Major League saves: 1984 (1), 1985 (1), 1986 (8). Total—10.

Year	Club	League	G.	IP.	W.	L.	Pct.	H.	R.	ER.	SO.	BB.	ERA.
1977—Niagara Falls		NYP	10	52	1	5	.167	53	30	23	43	30	3.98
1978—Charleston		W. Carol.	21	77	5	3	.625	72	45	36	54	63	4.21
1978—Salem		Ap'lacian	2	16	2	0	1.000	13	2	1	12	1	0.56
1979—Salem†		Carolina	26	119	3	10	.231	138	81	66	105	47	4.99
1980—Buffalo		Eastern	23	161	11	6	.647	158	84	71	71	64	3.97
1980—Portland		P. Coast	2	7	0	1	.000	11	9	8	0	2	10.29
1981—Buffalo		Eastern	29	106	8	3	.727	102	50	44	82	48	3.74
1981—Portland		P. Coast	4	23	0	3	.000	39	28	20	19	12	7.83
1982—Buffalo‡§		Eastern	25	76⅓	5	8	.385	72	40	34	84	38	4.01
1983—Buffalo		Eastern	18	112	13	1	*.929	88	28	20	108	50	*1.61
1984—Maine		Int'national	6	45	4	0	1.000	37	14	13	40	8	2.60
1984—Cleveland xy		American	31	116	3	11	.214	106	61	59	83	46	4.58
1985—Omaha		Am. Assoc.	17	133⅔	10	4	.714	105	36	30	98	41	*2.02
1985—Kansas City		American	16	37⅔	2	1	.667	34	15	13	36	20	3.11
1986—Kansas City		American	56	109⅓	8	4	.667	90	39	38	83	39	3.13
Major League Totals—3 Years			103	263	13	16	.448	230	115	110	202	105	3.76

Signed as a free agent by Pittsburgh Pirates' organization, December 13, 1976.
†On disabled list, June 6 to June 22, 1979.
‡On Lynn suspended list, April 16, 1982; then transferred to restricted list, April 27 to June 8, 1983.
§Traded to Buffalo (Cleveland Indians' organization) for Catcher John Malkin, June 8, 1983.
xOn disabled list, June 20 to July 5, 1984.
yReleased, March 31, 1985; signed by Kansas City Royals' organization, May 9, 1985.

CHAMPIONSHIP SERIES RECORD

Year	Club	League	G.	IP.	W.	L.	Pct.	H.	R.	ER.	SO.	BB.	ERA.
1985—Kansas City		American	2	6⅓	1	0	1.000	4	1	1	3	1	1.42

JOHN EDWARD FARRELL

Born August 4, 1962, at Neptune, N.J.
Height, 6.04. Weight, 210.
Throws and bats righthanded.
Attended Oklahoma State University, Stillwater, Okla.

Tied for Eastern League lead in shutouts with 3 and hit batsmen with 10 in 1986.

Year	Club	League	G.	IP.	W.	L.	Pct.	H.	R.	ER.	SO.	BB.	ERA.
1984—Waterloo		Midwest	9	43⅓	0	5	.000	59	34	31	29	33	6.44
1984—Maine		Int'national	5	26⅓	2	1	.667	20	11	11	12	20	3.76
1985—Waterbury		Eastern	25	149	7	13	.350	161	*106	86	75	76	5.19
1986—Waterbury		Eastern	26	173⅓	9	10	.474	158	82	59	104	54	3.06

Selected by Oakland A's organization in 9th round of free-agent draft, June 3, 1980.
Selected by Cleveland Indians' organization in 16th round of free-agent draft, June 6, 1983.
Selected by Cleveland Indians' organization in 2nd round of free-agent draft, June 4, 1984.

—DID YOU KNOW—

That the 1986 Orioles and Yankees played the longest nine-inning game in baseball history, a four-hour, 16-minute June 8 marathon that Baltimore won, 18-9?

JEFFREY JOSEPH FASSERO
(Jeff)

Born January 5, 1963, at Springfield, Ill.
Height, 6.01. Weight, 180.
Throws and bats lefthanded.
Attended Lincoln Land Community College, Springfield, Ill.,
and University of Mississippi, University, Miss.

Tied for Florida State League lead in games started by pitchers with 26 in 1986.

Year Club	League	G.	IP.	W.	L.	Pct.	H.	R.	ER.	SO.	BB.	ERA.
1984—Johnson City	Ap'lachian	13	66⅔	4	7	.364	65	42	34	59	39	4.59
1985—Springfield	Midwest	29	119	4	8	.333	125	78	53	65	45	4.01
1986—St. Petersburg	Florida St.	26	*176	13	7	.650	156	63	48	112	56	2.45

Selected by St. Louis Cardinals' organization in 22nd round of free-agent draft, June 4, 1984.

MICHAEL OTIS FELDER
(Mike)

Born November 18, 1962, at Vallejo, Calif.
Height, 5.08. Weight, 160.
Throws right and bats left and righthanded.
Attended Contra Costa College, San Pablo, Calif.

Major League stolen bases: 1985 (4), 1986 (16). Total—20.
Led Pacific Coast League in stolen bases with 61 in 1985.
Led Texas League in sacrifice flies with 9 in 1984.
Led Texas League in stolen bases with 71 in 1983 and 58 in 1984.
Led California League in stolen bases with 92 in 1982.
Led Texas League outfielders in putouts with 332, total chances with 363 and tied for lead in assists with 18 in 1983.

Year Club	League	Pos.	G.	AB.	R.	H.	2B.	3B.	HR.	RBI.	B.A.	PO.	A.	E.	F.A.
1981—Stockton	Calif.	2B-OF	91	338	66	91	8	1	3	30	.269	172	162	13	.963
1982—Stockton	Calif.	OF	137	524	102	138	18	11	7	47	.263	314	9	10	.970
1983—El Paso	Texas	●OF-2B	133	554	108	156	23	10	9	78	.282	334	24	●13	.965
1984—El Paso†	Texas	OF	122	496	98	144	19	2	9	72	.290	321	13	6	.982
1985—Vancouver	P. C.	OF-2B	137	563	91	177	16	11	2	43	.314	294	15	4	.987
1985—Milwaukee	Amer.	OF	15	56	8	11	1	0	0	0	.196	32	1	0	1.000
1986—Milwaukee‡	Amer.	OF	44	155	24	37	2	4	1	13	.239	98	0	0	1.000
1986—El Paso	Texas	OF	8	31	10	14	3	0	0	2	.452	14	0	0	1.000
1986—Vancouver	P. C.	OF	39	153	21	40	3	4	1	15	.261	83	4	4	.956
Major League Totals—2 Years			59	211	32	48	3	4	1	13	.227	130	1	0	1.000

Selected by Milwaukee Brewers' organization in 3rd round of free-agent draft, January 13, 1981.
†On disabled list, April 15 to April 26, 1984.
‡On disabled list, May 3 to June 5, 1986; included rehabilitation disability assignment to El Paso, May 23 to June 5, 1986.

CHARLES SIDNEY FERNANDEZ
(Sid)

Born October 12, 1962, at Honolulu, Haw.
Height, 6.01. Weight, 220.
Throws and bats lefthanded.

Pitched 1-0 no-hit victory against Fort Lauderdale, June 8, 1982.
Pitched 5-0 no-hit victory against Winter Haven, April 24, 1982.
Major League saves: 1986 (1).
Named Texas League Pitcher of the Year, 1983.

Year Club	League	G.	IP.	W.	L.	Pct.	H.	R.	ER.	SO.	BB.	ERA.
1981—Lethbridge	Pioneer	11	76	5	1	.833	43	21	13	*128	31	*1.54
1982—Vero Beach	Florida St.	12	84⅔	8	1	.889	38	19	18	*137	38	1.91
1982—Albuquerque	P. Coast	13	88	6	5	.545	76	54	53	86	52	5.42
1983—San Antonio	Texas	24	153	●13	4	.765	111	61	48	*209	96	*2.82
1983—Los Angeles†	National	2	6	0	1	.000	7	4	4	9	7	6.00
1984—Tidewater	Int'national	17	105⅔	6	5	.545	69	39	30	123	63	2.56
1984—New York	National	15	90	6	6	.500	74	40	35	62	34	3.50
1985—Tidewater	Int'national	5	35⅓	4	1	.800	17	8	8	42	21	2.04
1985—New York	National	26	170⅓	9	9	.500	108	56	53	180	80	2.80
1986—New York	National	32	204⅓	16	6	.727	161	82	80	200	91	3.52
Major League Totals—4 Years		75	470⅔	31	22	.585	350	182	172	451	212	3.29

Selected by Los Angeles Dodgers' organization in 3rd round of free-agent draft, June 8, 1981.
†Traded with Infielder Ross Jones to New York Mets for Pitcher Carlos Diaz and a player to be named later, December 8, 1983; Los Angeles Dodgers acquired Infielder Bob Bailor to complete deal, December 12, 1983.

CHAMPIONSHIP SERIES RECORD

Year Club	League	G.	IP.	W.	L.	Pct.	H.	R.	ER.	SO.	BB.	ERA.
1986—New York	National	1	6	0	1	.000	3	3	3	5	1	4.50

WORLD SERIES RECORD

Year Club	League	G.	IP.	W.	L.	Pct.	H.	R.	ER.	SO.	BB.	ERA.
1986—New York	National	3	6⅔	0	0	.000	6	1	1	10	1	1.35

Year	League	IP	W.	L.	Pct.	H.	R.	ER.	SO.	BB.	ERA.
1986—National		1	0	0	.000	0	0	0	3	2	0.00

OCTAVIO ANTONIO FERNANDEZ (CASTRO)
(Tony)

Born August 6, 1962, at San Pedro de Macoris, D. R.
Height, 6.02. Weight, 165.
Throws right and bats right and lefthanded.

Established American League record for most games by shortstop, season (163), 1986.
Tied American League record for most games by switch-hitter, season (163), 1986.
Major League stolen bases: 1984 (5), 1985 (13), 1986 (25). Total—43.
Led American League shortstops in total chances with 791 in 1985.
Led International League shortstops in double plays with 87 in 1983.
Named shortstop on THE SPORTING NEWS American League All-Star Team, 1986.
Named shortstop on THE SPORTING NEWS American League All-Star fielding team, 1986.

Year	Club	League	Pos.	G.	AB.	R.	H.	2B.	3B.	HR.	RBI.	B.A.	PO.	A.	E.	F.A.
1980—Kinston	Carol.		SS	62	187	28	52	6	2	0	12	.278	93	205	28	.914
1981—Kinston	Carol.		SS	75	280	57	89	10	6	1	13	.318	121	227	19	.948
1981—Syracuse†	Int.		SS	31	115	13	32	6	2	1	9	.278	69	80	3	.980
1982—Syracuse	Int.		SS	134	523	78	158	21	6	4	56	.302	★246	364	23	★.964
1983—Syracuse	Int.		SS	117	437	65	131	18	6	5	38	.300	★211	361	26	.957
1983—Toronto	Amer.		SS	15	34	5	9	1	1	0	2	.265	16	17	0	1.000
1984—Syracuse	Int.		SS	26	94	12	24	1	0	0	6	.255	46	72	5	.959
1984—Toronto	Amer.		SS-3B	88	233	29	63	5	3	3	19	.269	119	195	9	.972
1985—Toronto	Amer.		SS	161	564	71	163	31	10	2	51	.289	283	★478	30	.962
1986—Toronto	Amer.		SS	★163	★687	91	213	33	9	10	65	.310	★294	445	13	★.983
Major League Totals—4 Years				427	1518	196	448	70	23	15	137	.295	712	1135	52	.973

Signed as free agent by Toronto Blue Jays' organization, April 24, 1979.
†On disabled list, August 10 to August 27, 1981.

CHAMPIONSHIP SERIES RECORD

Year	Club	League	Pos.	G.	AB.	R.	H.	2B.	3B.	HR.	RBI.	B.A.	PO.	A.	E.	F.A.
1985—Toronto	Amer.		SS	7	24	2	8	2	0	0	2	.333	11	15	2	.929

ALL-STAR GAME RECORD

Year	League	Pos.	AB.	R.	H.	2B.	3B.	HR.	RBI.	B.A.	PO.	A.	E.	F.A.
1986—American		SS	0	0	0	0	0	0	0	.000	0	0	0	.000

GEORGE PAUL FERRAN

Born August 27, 1964, at Boston, Mass.
Height, 6.01. Weight, 165.
Throws and bats righthanded.
Attended Los Angeles Mission College, San Fernando, Calif.

Year	Club	League	G.	IP.	W.	L.	Pct.	H.	R.	ER.	SO.	BB.	ERA.
1983—Great Falls†	Pioneer	7	16⅔	0	1	.000	19	11	8	10	10	4.32
1984—Clinton	Midwest	41	90⅔	5	10	.333	73	32	26	87	42	2.58
1985—San Jose	California	23	126	8	9	.471	112	57	48	74	74	3.43
1985—Shreveport	Texas	6	42	4	1	.800	38	18	15	44	14	3.21
1986—Shreveport	Texas	46	153⅓	★16	1	★.941	114	45	39	★147	64	★2.29

Selected by San Francisco Giants' organization in 23rd round of free-agent draft, June 6, 1983.
†On suspended list, August 3, 1983 through remainder of season.

ANTHONY ROSS FERREIRA

Name pronounced Fer-AIR-a.

(Tony)

Born October 4, 1962, at Riverside, Calif.
Height, 6.02. Weight, 160.
Throws and bats lefthanded.
Cousin of Derek Diaz, pitcher in Milwaukee Brewers' organization.

Pitched 6-0 no-hit victory against Knoxville, July 9, 1983.

Year	Club	League	G.	IP.	W.	L.	Pct.	H.	R.	ER.	SO.	BB.	ERA.
1981—Sarasota Royals-Gold	Gulf Coast	12	48	4	0	1.000	40	19	12	45	22	2.25
1982—Fort Myers	Florida St.	22	150⅓	12	7	.632	144	64	48	120	66	2.87
1982—Jacksonville	Southern	6	37⅓	2	4	.333	38	20	17	30	14	4.10
1983—Jacksonville	Southern	35	136⅓	7	11	.389	122	77	64	85	68	4.22
1984—Omaha	Am. Assoc.	40	114⅓	7	10	.412	128	65	58	69	52	4.57
1985—Omaha	Am. Assoc.	27	173⅔	11	10	.524	142	73	62	105	89	3.21
1985—Kansas City†	American	2	5⅔	0	0	.000	6	5	5	5	2	7.94
1986—Tidewater‡	Int'national	24	112⅓	7	5	.583	123	59	46	65	40	3.69
Major League Totals—1 Year		2	5⅔	0	0	.000	6	5	5	5	2	7.94

Selected by Kansas City Royals' organization in 2nd round of free-agent draft, June 8, 1981.
†Traded to New York Mets' organization for Shortstop Argenis Salazar, April 1, 1986.
‡Drafted by Seattle Mariners, December 9, 1986.

CECIL GRANT FIELDER

Born September 21, 1963, at Los Angeles, Calif.
Height, 6.03. Weight, 230.
Throws and bats righthanded.
Attended University of Nevada, Las Vegas, Nev.

Led Pioneer League in total bases with 176 and being hit by pitch with 8 in 1982.

Year—Club	League	Pos.	G.	AB.	R.	H.	2B.	3B.	HR.	RBI.	B.A.	PO.	A.	E.	F.A.
1982—Butte†	Pion.	1B	69	273	73	88	★28	0	★20	68	.322	247	18	4	.985
1983—Florence	S. Atl.	1B	140	500	81	156	28	2	16	94	.312	957	64	16	.985
1984—Kinston	Carol.	1B	61	222	42	63	12	1	19	49	.284	533	24	9	.984
1984—Knoxville	South.	1B	64	236	33	60	12	2	9	44	.254	173	10	4	.979
1985—Knoxville	South.	1B	96	361	52	106	26	2	18	81	.294	444	26	6	.987
1985—Toronto	Amer.	1B	30	74	6	23	4	0	4	16	.311	171	17	4	.979
1986—Toronto	Amer.	1B-3B-OF	34	83	7	13	2	0	4	13	.157	37	4	1	.976
1986—Syracuse	Int.	OF-1B	88	325	47	91	13	3	18	68	.280	117	5	1	.992
Major League Totals—2 Years			64	157	13	36	6	0	8	29	.229	208	21	5	.979

Selected by Baltimore Orioles' organization in 31st round of free-agent draft, June 8, 1981.
Selected by Kansas City Royals' organization in secondary phase of free-agent draft, June 7, 1982.
†Traded to Toronto Blue Jays' organization for Outfielder Leon Roberts, February 4, 1983.

BRUCE ALAN FIELDS

Born October 6, 1960, at Cleveland, O.
Height, 6.00. Weight, 185.
Throws right and bats lefthanded.
Attended Lansing Community College, Lansing, Mich.

Major League stolen bases: 1986 (1).

Year—Club	League	Pos.	G.	AB.	R.	H.	2B.	3B.	HR.	RBI.	B.A.	PO.	A.	E.	F.A.
1978—Bristol	Appal.	OF-3B	46	159	15	32	6	2	0	11	.201	77	4	3	.964
1979—Lakeland	Fla. St.	OF	70	220	30	52	4	2	0	17	.236	120	2	3	.976
1979—Bristol	Appal.	OF-2B	41	138	23	32	4	1	1	7	.232	81	5	2	.977
1980—Lakeland	Fla. St.	OF	53	162	22	37	5	2	1	15	.228	113	1	4	.966
1980—Macon	S. Atl.	OF	67	240	40	71	7	1	2	27	.296	118	2	2	.984
1981—Lakeland	Fla. St.	OF	103	377	54	112	14	3	1	37	.297	225	11	4	★.983
1982—Birmingham	South.	OF	43	162	26	37	3	2	0	14	.228	102	0	6	.944
1982—Macon†	S. Atl.	OF	80	312	61	105	13	3	6	38	.337	162	4	3	.982
1983—San Jose	Calif.	OF	123	450	80	123	21	6	2	45	.273	234	6	7	.972
1984—Birmingham	South.	OF	93	307	49	92	11	3	4	38	.300	169	8	4	.978
1985—Birmingham‡	South.	OF	114	421	59	136	24	4	2	41	★.323	228	10	5	.979
1986—Nashville	A. A.	OF	116	383	57	141	31	5	1	53	★.368	177	10	4	.979
1986—Detroit	Amer.	OF	16	43	4	12	1	1	0	6	.279	25	0	1	.962
Major League Totals—1 Year			16	43	4	12	1	1	0	6	.279	25	0	1	.962

Selected by Detroit Tigers' organization in 7th round of free-agent draft, June 6, 1978.
†Loaned to San Jose (Baltimore Orioles' organization), April 7, 1983; returned, September 8, 1983.
‡On disabled list, April 12 to April 22, 1985.

CHAMPIONSHIP SERIES RECORD

Year—Club	League	Pos.	G.	AB.	R.	H.	2B.	3B.	HR.	RBI.	B.A.	PO.	A.	E.	F.A.
1985—Toronto	Amer.	PH	3	3	0	1	1	0	0	0	.333	0	0	0	.000

THOMAS CARSON FILER
(Tom)

Born December 1, 1956, at Philadelphia, Pa.
Height, 6.01. Weight, 198.
Throws and bats righthanded.
Received bachelor of science degree in marketing from
La Salle College, Philadelphia, Pa., in 1978.

Tied for American Association lead in wild pitches with 11 in 1981.

Year—Club	League	G.	IP.	W.	L.	Pct.	H.	R.	ER.	SO.	BB.	ERA.
1978—Oneonta	NYP	9	43	2	3	.400	30	14	8	34	14	1.67
1979—West Haven	Eastern	24	154	12	8	.600	132	73	62	80	53	3.62
1980—Nashville†	Southern	27	187	13	9	.591	168	94	61	112	86	2.94
1981—Columbus‡	Int'national	1	3	0	1	.000	6	5	5	3	4	15.00
1981—Iowa	Am. Assoc.	21	109	4	9	.308	123	64	58	61	57	4.79
1982—Iowa	Am. Assoc.	17	92⅓	6	7	.462	109	74	69	51	31	6.73
1982—Chicago	National	8	40⅔	1	2	.333	50	25	25	15	18	5.53
1983—Iowa	Am. Assoc.	27	108	5	6	.455	128	56	50	56	44	4.17
1984—Iowa §x	Am. Assoc.	26	123⅓	9	7	.563	149	86	67	80	48	4.89
1985—Syracuse y	Int'national	12	78⅓	7	2	.778	67	24	22	31	22	2.53
1985—Toronto z	American	11	48⅔	7	0	1.000	38	21	21	24	18	3.88
1986—Toronto a	American						(Did not play)					
National League Totals—1 Year		8	40⅔	1	2	.333	50	25	25	15	18	5.53
American League Totals—1 Year		11	48⅔	7	0	1.000	38	21	21	24	18	3.88
Major League Totals—2 Years		19	89⅓	8	2	.800	88	46	46	39	36	4.63

Signed as free agent by New York Yankees' organization, June 28, 1978.
†Drafted by Oakland A's, December 8, 1980; returned, April 9, 1981.
‡Traded with cash to Chicago Cubs' organization for Catcher Barry Foote, April 27, 1981.

§On disabled list, April 20 to May 12 and August 11 to August 22, 1984.
xGranted free agency, October 15, 1984; signed by Syracuse (Toronto Blue Jays' organization), November 21, 1984.
yOn disabled list, April 24 to May 4 and May 16 to May 26, 1985.
zOn disabled list, August 28 to September 12, 1985.
aOn disabled list, March 27, 1986 through entire season.

WILLIAM PETER FILSON
(Pete)

Born September 28, 1958, at Darby, Pa.
Height, 6.02. Weight, 195.
Throws left and bats left and righthanded.
Attended Temple University, Philadelphia, Pa.

Pitched seven-inning, 4-0 no-hit victory against Gastonia, April 25, 1980 (first game).
Pitched seven-inning, 10-0 no-hit victory against Kingsport, August 7, 1979 (second game).
Major League saves: 1983 (1), 1984 (1), 1985 (2). Total—4.
Led International League in complete games with 11 and balks with 8 in 1982.
Led Appalachian League in complete games with 9, shutouts with 3 and balks with 4 in 1979.
Named American Association Pitcher of the Year, 1986.

Year Club	League	G.	IP.	W.	L.	Pct.	H.	R.	ER.	SO.	BB.	ERA.
1979—Paintsville	Ap'lachian	13	★91	★9	0	★1.000	51	19	17	★118	39	★1.68
1979—Oneonta	NYP	1	1	0	0	.000	0	0	0	1	0	0.00
1980—Greensboro	S. Atlantic	4	27	3	0	1.000	13	5	5	34	14	1.67
1980—Fort Lauderdale	Florida St.	23	144	10	9	.526	105	56	48	86	69	3.00
1981—Fort Lauderdale	Florida St.	11	68	7	1	.875	56	20	15	68	20	1.99
1981—Nashville	Southern	14	99	10	2	●.833	73	30	20	77	28	1.82
1982—Columbus†-Toledo	Int'national	23	150⅔	8	10	.444	168	87	77	84	53	4.60
1982—Minnesota	American	5	12⅓	0	2	.000	17	12	12	10	8	8.76
1983—Minnesota‡	American	26	90	4	1	.800	87	34	34	49	29	3.40
1983—Toledo	Int'national	2	7	0	1	.000	8	6	6	6	3	7.71
1984—Minnesota	American	55	118⅔	6	5	.545	106	56	54	59	54	4.10
1985—Minnesota	American	40	95⅔	4	5	.444	93	42	39	42	30	3.67
1986—Minnesota§-Chicago	American	7	18	0	1	.000	27	13	12	8	7	6.00
1986—Buffalo	Am. Assoc.	36	139	★14	3	.824	116	46	35	81	32	★2.27
Major League Totals—5 Years		133	334⅔	14	14	.500	330	157	151	168	128	4.06

Selected by New York Yankees' organization in 8th round of free-agent draft, June 5, 1979.
†Traded with Infielder Larry Milbourne and Pitcher John Pacella to Minnesota Twins for Catcher Butch Wynegar and Pitcher Roger Erickson, May 12, 1982.
‡On disabled list, July 13 to August 3, 1983.
§Loaned to Buffalo (Chicago White Sox' organization) in exchange for sale of Pitcher Juan Agosto to Minnesota Twins and traded to Chicago White Sox for Pitcher Kurt Walker, September 3, 1986.

JOHN JOSEPH FIMPLE
(Jack)

Born February 10, 1959, at Darby, Pa.
Height, 6.02. Weight, 185.
Throws and bats righthanded.
Attended Humboldt State University, Arcata, Calif.

Major League stolen bases: 1983 (1).
Led Midwest League in sacrifice flies with 8 in 1981.
Led Pacific Coast League in passed balls with 16 in 1984.
Led Florida State League catchers in putouts with 542 and assists with 54 in 1982.
Led Midwest League in passed balls with 36 in 1981.

Year Club	League	Pos.	G.	AB.	R.	H.	2B.	3B.	HR.	RBI.	B.A.	PO.	A.	E.	F.A.
1980—Bat.†-Auburn	NYP	2B-3B	61	215	27	52	7	0	5	24	.242	113	121	14	.944
1981—Waterloo‡	Midw.	C-1B	108	371	53	107	21	2	10	76	.288	676	92	10	.987
1982—Vero Beach	Fla. St.	C-1B	111	359	53	101	14	5	9	54	.281	610	58	11	.984
1983—Albuquerque	P. C.	C	80	235	44	58	12	3	10	51	.247	397	★73	14	.971
1983—Los Angeles	Nat.	C	54	148	16	37	8	1	2	22	.250	336	32	4	.989
1984—Albuquerque	P. C.	C	107	334	39	83	15	3	11	60	.249	481	45	8	.985
1984—Los Angeles	Nat.	C	12	26	2	5	1	0	0	3	.192	54	4	1	.983
1985—Albuquerque	P. C.	C-3B	95	231	25	53	11	0	5	29	.229	304	63	4	.989
1986—Albuquerque	P. C.	C-3-1-O	92	297	39	85	17	3	2	35	.286	310	78	5	.987
1986—Los Angeles§	Nat.	C-1B-2B	13	13	2	1	0	0	0	2	.077	30	4	0	1.000
Major League Totals—3 Years			79	187	20	43	9	1	2	27	.230	420	40	5	.989

Selected by Cleveland Indians' organization in 29th round of free-agent draft, June 3, 1980.
†Loaned to Auburn (Co-op), July 27, 1980; returned, September 5, 1980.
‡Traded with Pitcher Larry White and Outfielder Jorge Orta to Los Angeles Dodgers for Pitcher Rick Sutcliffe and Second Baseman Jack Perconte, December 9, 1981.
§Released, December 17, 1986.

CHAMPIONSHIP SERIES RECORD

Year Club	League	Pos.	G.	AB.	R.	H.	2B.	3B.	HR.	RBI.	B.A.	PO.	A.	E.	F.A.
1983—Los Angeles	Nat.	C	3	7	0	1	0	0	0	1	.143	14	2	0	1.000

CHARLES EDWARD FINLEY
(Chuck)

Born November 26, 1962 at Monroe, La.
Height, 6.06. Weight, 220.
Throws and bats lefthanded.
Attended Northeast Louisiana State University, Monroe, La.

Year Club	League	G.	IP.	W.	L.	Pct.	H.	R.	ER.	SO.	BB.	ERA.
1985—Salem	Northwest	18	29	3	1	.750	34	21	15	32	10	4.66
1986—Quad Cities	Midwest	10	12	1	0	1.000	4	0	0	16	3	0.00
1986—California	American	25	46⅓	3	1	.750	40	17	17	37	23	3.30
Major League Totals—1 Year		25	46⅓	3	1	.750	40	17	17	37	23	3.30

Selected by California Angels' organization in 15th round of free-agent draft, June 4, 1984.
Selected by California Angels' organization in secondary phase of free-agent draft, January 9, 1985.

CHAMPIONSHIP SERIES RECORD

Year Club	League	G.	IP.	W.	L.	Pct.	H.	R.	ER.	SO.	BB.	ERA.
1986—California	American	3	2	0	0	.000	1	0	0	1	0	0.00

STEPHEN JOHN FIREOVID

Name pronounced FYR-oh-vid.

(Steve)

Born June 6, 1957, at Bryan, O.
Height, 6.02. Weight, 195.
Throws right and bats left and righthanded.
Attended Miami University, Oxford, O.

Year Club	League	G.	IP.	W.	L.	Pct.	H.	R.	ER.	SO.	BB.	ERA.
1978—Walla Walla	Northwest	14	106	9	2	.818	82	45	29	99	52	2.46
1979—Reno	California	26	168	13	9	.591	182	92	76	135	65	4.07
1980—Amarillo	Texas	27	164	12	6	.667	196	100	86	106	52	4.72
1981—Hawaii	P. Coast	25	162	11	7	.611	173	77	57	57	55	3.17
1981—San Diego	National	5	26	0	1	.000	30	8	8	11	7	2.77
1982—Hawaii	P. Coast	25	135⅔	10	8	.556	171	87	81	56	39	5.37
1983—Las Vegas	P. Coast	28	184⅔	14	10	.583	*212	124	98	80	63	4.78
1983—San Diego†	National	3	5	0	0	.000	4	2	1	1	2	1.80
1984—Portland	P. Coast	46	111⅔	5	9	.357	133	71	54	45	44	4.35
1984—Philadelphia‡	National	6	5⅔	0	0	.000	4	1	1	3	0	1.59
1985—Buffalo	Am. Assoc.	24	137⅓	8	7	.533	154	50	46	57	34	3.01
1985—Chicago§	American	4	7	0	0	.000	17	4	4	2	2	5.14
1986—Seattle	American	10	21	2	0	1.000	28	11	10	10	4	4.29
1986—Calgary	P. Coast	14	82⅓	6	3	.667	93	49	43	29	29	4.70
National League Totals—3 Years		14	36⅔	0	1	.000	38	11	10	15	9	2.45
American League Totals—2 Years		14	28	2	0	1.000	45	15	14	12	6	4.50
Major League Totals—5 Years		28	64⅔	2	1	.667	83	26	24	27	15	3.34

Selected by San Diego Padres' organization in 7th round of free-agent draft, June 6, 1978.
†Traded to Philadelphia Phillies' organization, October 11, 1983, completing deal in which San Diego Padres traded Outfielder Sixto Lezcano and a player to be named later to Philadelphia for four players to be named later, August 31, 1983; San Diego acquired Pitchers Marty Decker, Ed Wojna, Darren Burroughs and Lance McCullers as partial completion of deal, September 20, 1983.
‡Released, November 9, 1984; signed by Buffalo (Chicago White Sox' organization), January 12, 1985.
§Granted free agency, October 15, 1985; signed by Seattle Mariners' organization, January 18, 1986.

TODD RICHARD FISCHER

Born September 15, 1960, at Columbus, O.
Height, 5.10. Weight, 160.
Throws and bats righthanded.
Attended Edison Community College, Fort Myers, Fla.

Led Texas League in saves with 15 in 1985.
Led Pioneer League in games finished in relief with 34 in 1982.

Year Club	League	G.	IP.	W.	L.	Pct.	H.	R.	ER.	SO.	BB.	ERA.
1982—Idaho Falls	Pioneer	*36	56⅓	8	2	.800	39	11	7	63	23	*1.12
1983—Madison	Midwest	49	114⅓	13	9	.591	100	35	29	110	35	2.28
1984—Albany	Eastern	30	85⅔	2	9	.182	105	56	45	56	45	4.73
1985—Mexico City Tigers†‡	Mexican	8	10⅔	0	2	.000	15	6	6	4	4	5.06
1985—Midland	Texas	43	76	6	3	.667	69	32	29	43	29	3.43
1986—California	American	9	17	0	0	.000	18	8	8	7	8	4.24
1986—Edmonton	P. Coast	34	47	4	0	1.000	36	23	20	31	29	3.83
Major League Totals—1 Year		9	17	0	0	.000	18	8	8	7	8	4.24

Signed as free agent by Oakland A's organization, June 3, 1982.
†Loaned to Mexico City Tigers, April 12, 1985; returned to Oakland A's organization, May 14, 1985.
‡Sold to California Angels' organization, May 14, 1985.

MICHAEL THOMAS FISCHLIN

(Mike)

Born September 13, 1955, at Sacramento, Calif.
Height, 6.01. Weight, 165.
Throws and bats righthanded.
Attended Cosumnes River Junior College, Sacramento, Calif.,
and Sacramento State University, Sacramento, Calif.

Major League stolen bases: 1978 (1), 1981 (3), 1982 (9), 1983 (9), 1984 (2). Total—24.
Tied National League record for fewest chances offered by shortstop, two consecutive games (1), June 18 and 20, 1978.
Led International League in sacrifice hits with 15 in 1981.
Led Pacific Coast League shortstops in putouts with 200 and double plays with 88 in 1980.

Year Club	League	Pos.	G.	AB.	R.	H.	2B.	3B.	HR.	RBI.	B.A.	PO.	A.	E.	F.A.
1975—Oneonta	NYP	SS	35	135	22	31	4	3	0	6	.230	34	128	15	.915
1975—Fort Lauderdale	Fla. St.	SS	29	104	7	19	4	0	0	7	.183	54	90	10	.935
1976—West Haven	East.	SS-3B-2B	91	248	16	38	7	1	2	20	.153	149	243	27	.936
1976—Oneonta	NYP	SS	14	55	13	14	3	0	0	5	.255	36	48	7	.923
1977—Fort Lauderdale†	Fla. St.	SS-2B	53	201	28	59	6	4	0	20	.294	84	188	16	.944
1977—Columbus	South.	SS	66	223	23	54	5	0	1	16	.242	104	204	16	.951
1977—Houston	Nat.	SS	13	15	0	3	0	0	0	0	.200	3	17	0	1.000
1978—Charleston	Int.	SS	82	280	38	59	10	2	0	19	.211	141	279	13	.970
1978—Houston	Nat.	SS	44	86	3	10	1	0	0	0	.116	49	67	9	.928
1979—Charleston‡	Int.	SS	44	138	13	31	4	1	0	8	.225	73	134	8	.963
1980—Tucson	P. C.	★SS-OF	131	417	65	117	24	7	3	49	.281	201	★437	★40	★.941
1980—Houston§	Nat.	SS	1	1	0	0	0	0	0	0	.000	0	0	0	.000
1981—Charleston	Int.	SS-2B	136	463	83	110	14	7	5	43	.238	224	433	31	.955
1981—Cleveland	Amer.	SS-2B	22	43	3	10	1	0	0	5	.233	33	39	4	.947
1982—Cleveland	Amer.	S-3-2-C	112	276	34	74	12	1	0	21	.268	142	257	13	.968
1983—Cleveland	Amer.	2B-SS-3B	95	225	31	47	5	2	2	23	.209	169	226	14	.966
1984—Cleveland	Amer.	2B-3B-SS	85	133	17	30	4	2	1	14	.226	104	146	8	.969
1985—Cleveland x	Amer.	2-S-1-3	73	60	12	12	4	1	0	2	.200	73	89	4	.976
1986—New York y	Amer.	SS-2B	71	102	9	21	2	0	0	3	.206	63	107	7	.960
National League Totals—3 Years			58	102	3	13	1	0	0	0	.127	52	84	9	.938
American League Totals—6 Years			458	839	106	194	28	6	3	68	.231	584	864	50	.967
Major League Totals—9 Years			516	941	109	207	29	6	3	68	.222	636	948	59	.964

Selected by New York Yankees' organization in 7th round of free-agent draft, June 4, 1975.
†Traded with Pitcher Randy Niemann and a player to be named later to Houston Astros' organization for Catcher-First Baseman Cliff Johnson, June 15, 1977; Houston acquired First Baseman-Outfielder Dave Bergman to complete deal, November 23, 1977.
‡On disabled list, June 18 to August 28, 1979.
§Traded to Cleveland Indians' organization for cash and a player to be named later, April 3, 1981; Houston Astros' organization acquired Outfielder Jim Lentine to complete deal, September 28, 1981.
xTraded to New York Yankees for a player to be named later, December 11, 1985; Cleveland Indians' organization acquired Pitcher Kevin Trudeau to complete deal, April 11, 1986.
yGranted free agency, November 12, 1986.

BRIAN KEVIN FISHER

Born March 18, 1962, at Honolulu, Hawaii.
Height, 6.04. Weight, 210.
Throws and bats righthanded.
Attended Columbia College, Aurora, Col.

Major League saves: 1985 (14), 1986 (6). Total—20.
Led International League pitchers in games started with 29 in 1984.
Tied for South Atlantic League lead in balks with 4 in 1981.

Year Club	League	G.	IP.	W.	L.	Pct.	H.	R.	ER.	SO.	BB.	ERA.
1980—Bradenton Braves	Gulf Coast	12	61	5	3	.625	55	34	26	48	★53	3.84
1981—Anderson	S. Atlantic	25	152	6	8	.429	139	96	72	152	94	4.26
1982—Durham†	Carolina	18	104	6	6	.500	72	43	32	129	43	2.77
1983—Savannah	Southern	27	150	8	11	.421	172	101	87	103	56	5.22
1984—Richmond‡	Int'national	29	183	9	11	.450	188	●101	★87	122	●100	4.28
1985—Columbus	Int'national	7	11⅓	0	0	.000	8	4	3	12	7	2.38
1985—New York	American	55	98⅓	4	4	.500	77	32	26	85	29	2.38
1986—New York	American	62	96⅔	9	5	.643	105	61	53	67	37	4.93
1986—Columbus§	Int'national	6	8⅔	0	0	.000	8	4	4	4	3	4.15
Major League Totals—2 Years		117	195	13	9	.591	182	93	79	152	66	3.65

Selected by Atlanta Braves' organization in 2nd round of free-agent draft, June 3, 1980.
†On disabled list, May 18 to July 1, 1982.
‡Traded to New York Yankees for Catcher Rick Cerone, December 5, 1984.
§Traded with Pitchers Doug Drabek and Logan Easley to Pittsburgh Pirates for Pitchers Rick Rhoden, Cecilio Guante and Pat Clements, November 26, 1986.

—DID YOU KNOW—

That Minnesota's Kirby Puckett set a personal one-season major league home run high in 1986 when he hit No. 5 on April 23?

CARLTON ERNEST FISK

Born December 26, 1947, at Bellows Falls, Vt.
Height, 6.02. Weight, 217.
Throws and bats righthanded.
Attended University of New Hampshire, Durham, N. H.
Brother of Calvin Fisk, former catcher in Baltimore Orioles' organization;
brother-in-law of Rick Miller, outfielder with Boston Red Sox and California Angels, 1971 through 1985;
cousin of Dave Jennings, punter with New York Jets.

Established major league records for longest game with no passed balls (25 innings), and most innings played by catcher, game (25), May 8, finished May 9, 1984.

Tied major league records for most at-bats (11) and plate appearances (12), game, May 8, finished May 9, 1984 (25 innings); most home runs, opening game of season (2), April 6, 1973.

Tied modern major league record for most long hits, inning (2), May 15, 1975 (eighth inning) and June 30, 1977 (eighth inning).

Established American League record for most home runs by catcher, season (33), 1985.

Tied American League record for fewest passed balls, season, 150 or more games (4), 1977.

Major League stolen bases: 1972 (5), 1973 (7), 1974 (5), 1975 (4), 1976 (12), 1977 (7), 1978 (7), 1979 (3), 1980 (11), 1981 (3), 1982 (17), 1983 (9), 1984 (6), 1985 (17), 1986 (2). Total—115.

Hit for the cycle, May 16, 1984.

Led American League in being hit by pitch with 13 in 1980.

Led American League catchers in passed balls with 11 in 1983.

Led American League catches in putouts with 470 and double plays with 10 in 1981.

Led American League catchers in errors with 10 in 1980.

Led American League catchers in total chances with 933 in 1972, 803 in 1973, 519 in 1981 and 871 in 1985.

Led International League catchers in double plays with 12 in 1971.

Named THE SPORTING NEWS American League Rookie Player of the Year, 1972.

Named American League Rookie of the Year by Baseball Writers' Association of America, 1972.

Named catcher on THE SPORTING NEWS American League All-Star Team, 1972, 1977, 1983 and 1985.

Named catcher on THE SPORTING NEWS American League All-Star fielding team, 1972.

Named catcher on THE SPORTING NEWS American League Silver Slugger team, 1981 and 1985.

Year	Club	League	Pos.	G.	AB.	R.	H.	2B.	3B.	HR.	RBI.	B.A.	PO.	A.	E.	F.A.
1967—Greenville†		W. Car.					(In Military Service)									
1968—Waterloo‡		Midw.	C	62	195	31	66	11	2	12	34	.338	385	42	8	.982
1969—Pittsfield		East.	C	97	309	38	75	18	3	10	41	.243	551	65	★22	.966
1969—Boston		Amer.	C	2	5	0	0	0	0	0	0	.000	2	0	0	1.000
1970—Pawtucket		East.	C-OF-1B	93	284	43	65	18	1	12	44	.229	482	50	7	.987
1971—Louisville		Int.	C-OF-3B	94	308	45	81	10	4	10	43	.263	588	51	13	.980
1971—Boston		Amer.	C	14	48	7	15	2	1	2	6	.313	72	6	2	.975
1972—Boston		Amer.	C	131	457	74	134	28	●9	22	61	.293	★846	★72	●15	.984
1973—Boston		Amer.	C	135	508	65	125	21	0	26	71	.246	★739	50	★14	.983
1974—Boston§		Amer.	C	52	187	36	56	12	1	11	26	.299	267	26	6	.980
1975—Boston x		Amer.	C	79	263	47	87	14	4	10	52	.331	347	30	8	.979
1976—Boston		Amer.	C	134	487	76	124	17	5	17	58	.255	649	73	12	.984
1977—Boston		Amer.	C	152	536	106	169	26	3	26	102	.315	779	69	11	.987
1978—Boston		Amer.	★C-OF	157	571	94	162	39	5	20	88	.284	734	90	★17	.980
1979—Boston y		Amer.	C-OF	91	320	49	87	23	2	10	42	.272	155	8	3	.982
1980—Boston z		Amer.	C-1-O-3	131	478	73	138	25	3	18	62	.289	543	56	11	.982
1981—Chicago		Amer.	C-1-3-O	96	338	44	89	12	0	7	45	.263	479	46	6	.989
1982—Chicago		Amer.	C-1B	135	476	66	127	17	3	14	65	.267	648	63	5	.993
1983—Chicago		Amer.	C	138	488	85	141	26	4	26	86	.289	★709	46	7	.991
1984—Chicago a		Amer.	C	102	359	54	83	20	1	21	43	.231	421	38	6	.987
1985—Chicago b		Amer.	C	153	543	85	129	23	1	37	107	.238	★801	60	10	.989
1986—Chicago		Amer.	C-OF	125	457	42	101	11	0	14	63	.221	455	44	8	.984
Major League Totals—17 Years				1827	6521	1003	1767	316	42	281	977	.271	8646	777	141	.985

Selected by Baltimore Orioles' organization in 36th round of free-agent draft, June, 1965.
Selected by Boston Red Sox' organization in 1st round (fourth player selected) of free-agent draft, January, 1967.
†On temporary inactive list, April 17, 1967; transferred to military list, May 18, 1967 through April 9, 1968.
‡On temporary inactive list, August 5 to August 20, 1968.
§On disabled list, March 21 to April 26 and June 28, 1974 through remainder of season.
xOn disabled list, March 24 to June 23, 1975.
yOn disabled list, April 14 to May 21, 1979.
zGranted free agency by arbitrator's ruling, February 12, 1981; signed by Chicago White Sox, March 18, 1981.
aOn disabled list, June 13 to July 5, 1984.
bGranted free agency, November 12, 1985; re-signed by White Sox, January 8, 1986.

CHAMPIONSHIP SERIES RECORD

Year	Club	League	Pos.	G.	AB.	R.	H.	2B.	3B.	HR.	RBI.	B.A.	PO.	A.	E.	F.A.
1975—Boston		Amer.	C	3	12	4	5	1	0	0	2	.417	15	0	0	1.000
1983—Chicago		Amer.	C	4	17	0	3	1	0	0	0	.176	27	3	0	1.000
Championship Series Totals—2 Years				7	29	4	8	2	0	0	2	.276	42	3	0	1.000

WORLD SERIES RECORD

Tied World Series records for most at bats inning and most times faced pitcher inning (2), October 15, 1975 (fourth inning); most errors by catcher, game (2), October 14, 1975.

Year	Club	League	Pos.	G.	AB.	R.	H.	2B.	3B.	HR.	RBI.	B.A.	PO.	A.	E.	F.A.
1975—Boston		Amer.	C	7	25	5	6	0	0	2	4	.240	37	3	2	.952

ALL-STAR GAME RECORD

Year	League	Pos.	AB.	R.	H.	2B.	3B.	HR.	RBI.	B.A.	PO.	A.	E.	F.A.
1972—American		C	2	1	1	0	0	0	0	.500	2	0	0	1.000

Year	League	Pos.	AB.	R.	H.	2B.	3B.	HR.	RBI.	B.A.	PO.	A.	E.	F.A.
1973—American		C	2	0	0	0	0	0	0	.000	3	0	0	1.000
1976—American		C	1	0	0	0	0	0	0	.000	1	0	0	1.000
1977—American		C	2	0	0	0	0	0	0	.000	6	1	0	1.000
1978—American		C	2	0	0	0	0	0	1	.000	4	0	0	1.000
1980—American		C	2	0	0	0	0	0	0	.000	5	0	0	1.000
1981—American		C	3	1	1	0	0	0	0	.333	4	0	0	1.000
1982—American		C	2	0	0	0	0	0	0	.000	2	0	0	1.000
1985—American		C	2	0	0	0	0	0	0	.000	2	0	0	1.000
All-Star Game Totals—9 Years			18	2	2	0	0	0	1	.111	29	1	0	1.000

Named to American League All-Star Team for 1974 game; replaced due to injury.

MICHAEL PATRICK FITZGERALD
(Mike)

Born March 28, 1964, at Savannah, Ga.
Height, 6.01. Weight, 200.
Throws and bats righthanded.
Attended Middle Georgia College, Cochran, Ga.

Led Midwest League in game-winning RBIs with 17 and sacrifice flies with 10 in 1986.
Led Midwest League in passed balls with 23 in 1985.
Led Appalachian League catchers in double plays with 4 and tied for lead in errors with 11 in 1984.

Year	Club	League	Pos.	G.	AB.	R.	H.	2B.	3B.	HR.	RBI.	B.A.	PO.	A.	E.	F.A.
1984—Johnson City	Appal.	C-OF	51	171	31	59	11	0	7	31	★.345	245	35	13	.956
1985—Springfield	Midw.	C	113	413	58	105	21	0	16	62	.254	673	56	17	.977
1986—Springfield	Midw.	1B-C	126	498	74	148	30	4	19	93	.297	819	63	22	.976

Selected by San Francisco Giants' organization in 1st round (15th player selected) of free-agent draft, January 11, 1983.
Selected by Cleveland Indians' organization in 10th round of free-agent draft, January 17, 1984.
Selected by St. Louis Cardinals' organization in secondary phase of free-agent draft, June 4, 1984.

MICHAEL ROY FITZGERALD
(Mike)

Born July 13, 1960, at Long Beach, Calif.
Height, 6.00. Weight, 185.
Throws and bats righthanded.
Nephew of Dan Gausepohl, outfielder in San Diego
Padres' organization, 1979 through 1982.

Tied major league record by hitting home run in first major league at-bat, September 13, 1983.
Major League stolen bases: 1984 (1), 1985 (5), 1986 (3). Total—9.
Led Carolina League in sacrifice flies with 11 in 1979.

Year	Club	League	Pos.	G.	AB.	R.	H.	2B.	3B.	HR.	RBI.	B.A.	PO.	A.	E.	F.A.
1978—Little Falls	NYP	C	48	140	25	36	10	0	5	21	.257	230	37	1	.996
1979—Lynchburg	Carol.	C	117	368	55	93	16	4	13	★75	.253	424	60	10	.980
1980—Alex.†-Lynch.	Carol.	C-1B-OF	105	338	36	71	10	2	10	44	.210	438	45	7	.986
1981—Jackson	Texas	C-1-O-3	66	218	28	68	14	2	4	29	.312	344	52	3	.992
1981—Tidewater	Int.	C-OF	24	58	9	9	2	0	1	3	.155	124	9	2	.985
1982—Tidewater	Int.	C-1-O-3	94	302	33	74	9	2	4	36	.245	451	34	7	.986
1983—Tidewater	Int.	C-1-3-O	111	370	64	105	17	1	14	65	.284	588	62	8	.988
1983—New York	Nat.	C	8	20	1	2	0	0	1	2	.100	37	8	2	.957
1984—New York‡	Nat.	C	112	360	20	87	15	1	2	33	.242	715	47	4	★.995
1985—Montreal	Nat.	C	108	295	25	61	7	1	5	34	.207	542	46	8	.987
1986—Indianapolis	A. A.	C	10	32	4	11	3	0	0	4	.344	58	5	1	.984
1986—Montreal§	Nat.	C	73	209	20	59	13	1	6	37	.282	415	35	3	.993
Major League Totals—4 Years			301	884	66	209	35	3	14	106	.236	1709	136	17	.991

Selected by New York Mets' organization in 6th round of free-agent draft, June 6, 1978.
†Loaned to Alexandria (Co-op), April 8, 1980; returned, May 31, 1980.
‡Traded with Infielder Hubie Brooks, Outfielder Herm Winningham and Pitcher Floyd Youmans to Montreal Expos for Catcher Gary Carter, December 10, 1984.
§On disabled list, August 2, 1986 through remainder of season.

MICHAEL KENDALL FLANAGAN
(Mike)

Born December 16, 1951, at Manchester, N. H.
Height, 6.00. Weight, 195.
Throws and bats lefthanded.
Attended University of Massachusetts, Amherst, Mass.
Son of Ed Flanagan, Jr., minor league pitcher, 1947 through 1952.

Major League saves: 1977 (1).
Tied for American League lead in shutouts with 5 in 1979.
Tied for American League lead in games started by pitchers with 40 in 1978.
Tied for International League lead in shutouts with 4 in 1975.
Tied for Southern League lead in shutouts with 3 in 1974.
Named American League Pitcher of the Year by THE SPORTING NEWS, 1979.
Won American League Cy Young Memorial Award, 1979.
Named lefthanded pitcher on THE SPORTING NEWS American League All-Star Team, 1979.

Year Club	League	G	IP	W	L	Pct.	H	R	ER	SO	BB	ERA.
1973—Miami	Florida St.	11	61	4	1	.800	39	21	15	61	25	2.21
1974—Miami	Florida St.	14	103	6	6	.500	67	32	24	119	48	2.10
1974—Asheville	Southern	11	84	6	4	.600	61	19	17	62	18	1.82
1975—Rochester	Int'national	27	173	13	4	*.765	155	58	48	135	56	2.50
1975—Baltimore	American	2	10	0	1	.000	9	4	3	7	6	2.70
1976—Baltimore	American	20	85	3	5	.375	83	41	39	56	33	4.13
1976—Rochester	Int'national	7	51	6	1	.857	40	16	12	24	14	2.12
1977—Baltimore	American	36	235	15	10	.600	235	100	95	149	70	3.64
1978—Baltimore	American	40	281	19	15	.559	271	128	*126	167	87	4.04
1979—Baltimore	American	39	266	*23	9	.719	245	107	91	190	70	3.08
1980—Baltimore	American	37	251	16	13	.552	*278	121	115	128	71	4.12
1981—Baltimore	American	20	116	9	6	.600	108	55	54	72	37	4.19
1982—Baltimore	American	36	236	15	11	.577	233	110	104	103	76	3.97
1983—Baltimore†	American	20	125⅓	12	4	.750	135	53	46	50	31	3.30
1984—Baltimore	American	34	226⅔	13	13	.500	213	103	89	115	81	3.53
1985—Hagerstown‡	Carolina	1	6	0	0	.000	1	0	0	5	4	0.00
1985—Baltimore	American	15	86	4	5	.444	101	49	49	42	28	5.13
1986—Baltimore§	American	29	172	7	11	.389	179	95	81	96	66	4.24
Major League Totals—12 Years		328	2090	136	103	.569	2090	966	892	1175	656	3.84

Selected by Houston Astros' organization in 15th round of free-agent draft, June 8, 1971.
Selected by Baltimore Orioles' organization in 7th round of free-agent draft, June 5, 1973.
†On disabled list, May 18 to August 7, 1983.
‡On Baltimore disabled list, March 26 to July 20, 1985; included rehabilitation disability assignment to Hagerstown, July 10 to July 20, 1985.
§On disabled list, May 31 to June 19, 1986.

CHAMPIONSHIP SERIES RECORD

Year Club	League	G	IP	W	L	Pct.	H	R	ER	SO	BB	ERA.
1979—Baltimore	American	1	7	1	0	1.000	6	6	4	2	1	5.14
1983—Baltimore	American	1	5	1	0	1.000	5	1	1	1	0	1.80
Championship Series Total—2 Years		2	12	2	0	1.000	11	7	5	3	1	3.75

WORLD SERIES RECORD

Year Club	League	G	IP	W	L	Pct.	H	R	ER	SO	BB	ERA.
1979—Baltimore	American	3	15	1	1	.500	18	7	5	13	2	3.00
1983—Baltimore	American	1	4	0	0	.000	6	2	2	1	1	4.50
World Series Totals—2 Years		4	19	1	1	.500	24	9	7	14	3	3.32

ALL-STAR GAME RECORD

Named to American League All-Star Team for 1978 game; did not play.

TIMOTHY EARL FLANNERY
(Tim)

Born September 29, 1957, at Tulsa, Okla.
Height, 5.11. Weight, 176.
Throws right and bats lefthanded.
Attended Chapman College, Orange, Calif.
Nephew of Hal Smith, catcher with St. Louis Cardinals and Pittsburgh Pirates, 1956 through 1961 and 1965;
minor league manager, 1966; coach, Pittsburgh Pirates, 1967; coach, Cincinnati Reds, 1968 and 1969;
and scout with St. Louis Cardinals, 1970 through 1975 and since 1978.
Major League stolen bases: 1980 (2), 1981 (1), 1982 (1), 1983 (2), 1984 (4), 1985 (2), 1986 (3). Total—15.

Year Club	League	Pos.	G	AB	R	H	2B	3B	HR	RBI.	B.A.	PO.	A.	E.	F.A.
1978—Reno	Calif.	2B-P	84	340	65	119	11	5	2	49	.350	213	269	19	.962
1979—Amarillo	Texas	2B-SS	125	524	88	●181	23	6	6	71	.345	287	374	28	.959
1979—San Diego	Nat.	2B	22	65	2	10	0	1	0	4	.154	45	60	1	.991
1980—Hawaii	P. C.	2B	47	182	27	63	10	3	1	16	.346	102	146	5	.980
1980—San Diego	Nat.	2B-3B	95	292	15	70	12	0	0	25	.240	140	204	8	.977
1981—Hawaii	P. C.	2B	21	78	16	22	3	1	0	10	.282	47	62	2	.982
1981—San Diego	Nat.	3B-2B	37	67	4	17	4	1	0	6	.254	16	32	2	.960
1982—San Diego	Nat.	2B-3B-SS	122	379	40	100	11	7	0	30	.264	226	278	14	.973
1983—San Diego	Nat.	3B-2B-SS	92	214	24	50	7	3	3	19	.234	63	156	4	.982
1984—San Diego	Nat.	2B-SS-3B	86	128	24	35	3	3	2	10	.273	36	69	5	.955
1985—San Diego	Nat.	2B-3B	126	384	50	108	14	3	1	40	.281	261	287	13	.977
1986—San Diego	Nat.	2B-3B-SS	134	368	48	103	11	2	3	28	.280	226	275	5	.990
Major League Totals—8 Years			714	1897	207	493	62	20	9	162	.260	1013	1361	52	.979

Selected by San Diego Padres' organization in 6th round of free-agent draft, June 6, 1978.

CHAMPIONSHIP SERIES RECORD

Year Club	League	Pos.	G	AB	R	H	2B	3B	HR	RBI.	B.A.	PO.	A.	E.	F.A.
1984—San Diego	Nat.	PH	3	2	2	1	0	0	0	0	.500	0	0	0	.000

WORLD SERIES RECORD

Year Club	League	Pos.	G	AB	R	H	2B	3B	HR	RBI.	B.A.	PO.	A.	E.	F.A.
1984—San Diego	Nat.	PH-2B	1	1	0	1	0	0	0	0	1.000	1	0	0	1.000

PITCHING RECORD

Year—Club	League	G.	IP.	W.	L.	Pct.	H.	R.	ER.	SO.	BB.	ERA.
1978—Reno	California	1	⅓	0	1	.000	3	6	5	0	1	135.00

SCOTT BRIAN FLETCHER

Born July 30, 1958, at Fort Walton Beach, Fla.
Height, 5.11. Weight, 173.
Throws and bats righthanded.
Attended University of Toledo, Toledo, Ohio; Valencia Community College,
Orlando, Fla., and Georgia Southern College, Statesboro, Ga.
Son of Richard W. Fletcher, minor league pitcher, 1952 through 1959.

Major League stolen bases: 1982 (1), 1983 (5), 1984 (10), 1985 (5), 1986 (12). Total—33.
Led American Association in being hit by pitch with 9 and grounding into double plays with 20 in 1981.
Led American Association shortstops in total chances with 607 in 1982.
Led Texas League second basemen in double plays with 112 in 1980.

Year—Club	League	Pos.	G.	AB.	R.	H.	2B.	3B.	HR.	RBI.	B.A.	PO.	A.	E.	F.A.
1979—Geneva	NYP	SS	67	261	59	81	12	3	4	43	.310	99	195	18	*.942
1980—Midland	Texas	*2B-SS	130	501	*111	164	16	*11	6	65	.327	*354	*390	*29	.962
1981—Iowa	A. A.	SS	119	458	66	117	26	4	4	33	.255	*222	337	28	.952
1981—Chicago	Nat.	2B-SS-3B	19	46	6	10	4	0	0	1	.217	34	44	3	.963
1982—Iowa	A. A.	SS	129	502	90	157	26	3	4	60	.313	224	●357	26	.957
1982—Chicago†	Nat.	SS	11	24	4	4	0	0	0	1	.167	11	23	0	1.000
1983—Chicago	Amer.	SS-2B-3B	114	262	42	62	16	5	3	31	.237	126	308	16	.964
1984—Chicago	Amer.	SS-2B-3B	149	456	46	114	13	3	3	35	.250	234	439	19	.973
1985—Chicago‡	Amer.	3B-SS-2B	119	301	38	77	8	1	2	31	.256	123	208	8	.976
1986—Texas	Amer.	SS-3B-2B	147	530	82	159	34	5	3	50	.300	216	388	16	.974
National League Totals—2 Years			30	70	10	14	4	0	0	2	.200	45	67	3	.974
American League Totals—4 Years			529	1549	208	412	71	14	11	147	.266	699	1343	59	.972
Major League Totals—6 Years			559	1619	218	426	75	14	11	149	.263	744	1410	62	.972

Selected by Los Angeles Dodgers' organization in 33rd round of free-agent draft, June 8, 1976.
Selected by Oakland A's organization in secondary phase of free-agent draft, January 10, 1978.
Selected by Houston Astros' organization in secondary phase of free-agent draft, June 6, 1978.
Selected by Chicago Cubs' organization in secondary phase of free-agent draft, June 5, 1979.
†Traded with Pitchers Dick Tidrow and Randy Martz and Infielder Pat Tabler to Chicago White Sox for Pitchers Steve Trout and Warren Brusstar, January 25, 1983.
‡Traded with Pitcher Ed Correa and a player to be named later to Texas Rangers for Infielder Wayne Tolleson and Pitcher Dave Schmidt, November 25, 1985; Texas acquired Infielder Jose Mota to complete deal, December 12, 1985.

CHAMPIONSHIP SERIES RECORD

Year—Club	League	Pos.	G.	AB.	R.	H.	2B.	3B.	HR.	RBI.	B.A.	PO.	A.	E.	F.A.
1983—Chicago	Amer.	SS	3	7	0	0	0	0	0	0	.000	3	8	0	1.000

THOMAS MICHAEL FOLEY
(Tom)

Born September 9, 1959, at Columbus, Ga.
Height, 6.01. Weight, 171.
Throws right and bats lefthanded.
Attended Miami-Dade Community College South, Miami, Fla.

Major League stolen bases: 1983 (1), 1984 (3), 1985 (2), 1986 (10). Total—16.
Led Pioneer League in caught stealing with 10 in 1977.
Led Florida State League shortstops in double plays with 71 in 1979.
Led Western Carolinas League shortstops in double plays with 98 in 1978.

Year—Club	League	Pos.	G.	AB.	R.	H.	2B.	3B.	HR.	RBI.	B.A.	PO.	A.	E.	F.A.
1977—Billings	Pion.	3B-SS	59	209	37	53	7	1	2	21	.254	53	109	24	.871
1978—Shelby	W. Car.	SS	124	424	55	98	19	1	2	41	.231	*217	●352	30	*.950
1979—Tampa	Fla. St.	SS	125	414	38	95	12	6	0	37	.229	223	*394	35	.946
1980—Waterbury	East.	2B	131	477	49	119	16	4	4	41	.249	*222	329	31	.947
1981—Indianapolis	A. A.	SS	103	347	47	81	12	2	6	27	.233	175	267	27	.942
1982—Indianapolis	A. A.	SS	129	427	65	115	20	9	8	63	.269	*227	343	27	.955
1983—Cincinnati	Nat.	SS-2B	68	98	7	20	4	1	0	9	.204	54	76	2	.985
1984—Cincinnati	Nat.	SS-2B-3B	106	277	26	70	8	3	5	27	.253	119	228	11	.969
1985—Cinc.† - Phil.	Nat.	SS-2B-3B	89	250	24	60	13	1	3	23	.240	127	202	7	.979
1986—Reading‡	East.	SS-2B	3	11	2	2	2	0	0	0	.182	2	11	0	1.000
1986—Phil.§ - Montreal	Nat.	SS-2B-3B	103	263	26	70	15	3	1	23	.266	117	190	6	.981
Major League Totals—4 Years			366	888	83	220	40	8	9	82	.248	417	696	26	.977

Selected by Cincinnati Reds' organization in 7th round of free-agent draft, June 7, 1977.
†Traded with Catcher Alan Knicely, a player to be named later and cash to Philadelphia Phillies for Catcher Bo Diaz and Pitcher Greg Simpson, August 8, 1985; Philadelphia acquired Pitcher Freddie Toliver to complete deal, August 27, 1985.
‡On Philadelphia disabled list, March 23 to April 29, 1986; included rehabilitation disability assignment to Reading, April 25 to April 29, 1986.
§Traded with Pitcher Lary Sorensen to Montreal Expos for Pitcher Dan Schatzeder and Infielder Skeeter Barnes, July 24, 1986.

SILTON RAY FONTENOT

Name pronounced FON-ten-oh.
(Known by middle name.)
Born August 8, 1957, at Lake Charles, La.
Height, 6.00. Weight, 175.
Throws and bats lefthanded.
Attended McNeese State University, Lake Charles, La.

Major League saves: 1986 (2).

Year Club	League	G.	IP.	W.	L.	Pct.	H.	R.	ER.	SO.	BB.	ERA.
1979—Sarasota Rangers†	Gulf Coast	8	31	3	1	.750	28	20	14	42	12	4.06
1980—Greensboro‡	S. Atlantic	11	49	2	2	.500	41	27	20	50	19	3.67
1981—Greensboro§	S. Atlantic	9	59	4	2	.667	53	22	18	62	23	2.75
1981—Fort Lauderdale x	Florida St.	8	45	1	4	.200	50	34	28	37	31	5.60
1982—Fort Lauderdale	Florida St.	12	74	6	5	.545	57	29	24	72	31	2.92
1982—Nashville	Southern	14	91⅓	5	6	.455	85	34	22	69	17	2.17
1983—Columbus	Int'national	26	35	3	2	.600	25	16	11	36	17	2.83
1983—New York §	American	15	97⅓	8	2	.800	101	41	36	27	25	3.33
1984—New York y	American	35	169⅓	8	9	.471	189	77	68	85	58	3.61
1985—Chicago	National	38	154⅔	6	10	.375	177	86	75	70	45	4.36
1986—Iowa	Am. Assoc.	2	15	1	0	1.000	10	3	3	9	8	1.80
1986—Chicago z	National	42	56	3	5	.375	57	30	24	24	21	3.86
1986—Minnesota a	American	15	16⅓	0	0	.000	27	19	18	10	4	9.92
American League Totals—3 Years		65	283	16	11	.593	317	137	122	122	87	3.88
National League Totals—2 Years		80	210⅔	9	15	.375	234	116	99	94	66	4.23
Major League Totals—4 Years		145	493⅔	25	26	.490	551	253	221	216	153	4.03

Selected by Texas Rangers' organization in 34th round of free-agent draft, June 5, 1979.

†Traded with Pitcher Gene Nelson to New York Yankees' organization for Pitchers Bob Polinsky, Neal Mersch and Mark Softy, October 8, 1979; completing deal in which New York traded Outfielder Mickey Rivers and three players to be named later to Texas Rangers for Third Baseman Amos Lewis and two players to be named later, August 1, 1979.

‡On disabled list, April 22 to May 12 and July 14, 1980 through remainder of season.

§On disabled list, April 9 to May 5, 1981.

xOn disabled list, August 27, 1981 through remainder of season.

yTraded with Outfielder Brian Dayett to Chicago Cubs for Catcher Ron Hassey, Outfielder Henry Cotto and Pitchers Rich Bordi and Porfi Altamirano, December 4, 1984.

zTraded with Pitcher George Frazier and Shortstop Julius McDougal to Minnesota Twins for Pitchers Ron Davis and Dewayne Coleman, August 13, 1986.

aReleased, December 19, 1986.

CURTIS GLENN FORD

(Curt)

Born October 11, 1960, at Jackson, Miss.
Height, 5.10. Weight, 150.
Throws right and bats lefthanded.
Attended Jackson State University, Jackson, Miss.

Major League stolen bases: 1985 (1), 1986 (13). Total—14.
Led American Association in stolen bases with 45 and tied for lead in caught stealing with 17 in 1985.
Led Midwest League in total bases with 236 in 1983.
Named Midwest League Most Valuable Player, 1983.

Year Club	League	Pos.	G.	AB.	R.	H.	2B.	3B.	HR.	RBI.	B.A.	PO.	A.	E.	F.A.
1981—Johnson City	Appal.	★2B-1B	63	218	36	65	11	2	5	38	.298	115	149	★18	.936
1982—St. Petersburg	Fla. St.	2B-OF	133	447	59	123	18	8	1	49	.275	292	294	22	.964
1983—Springfield	Midw.	OF-2B	126	465	80	135	27	7	20	★91	.290	181	7	8	.960
1984—Arkansas	Texas	OF-2B-3B	118	442	62	143	23	1	10	78	.324	224	102	8	.976
1984—Louisville	A. A.	OF-2B	13	38	5	10	2	0	0	1	.263	13	2	0	1.000
1985—Louisville	A. A.	OF-3B	127	475	73	121	20	6	7	45	.255	243	25	8	.971
1985—St. Louis	Nat.	OF	11	12	2	6	2	0	0	3	.500	3	0	1	.750
1986—Louisville	A. A.	OF	53	200	47	59	9	2	4	31	.295	120	2	1	.992
1986—St. Louis	Nat.	OF	85	214	30	53	15	2	2	29	.248	109	7	3	.975
Major League Totals—2 Years			96	226	32	59	17	2	2	32	.261	112	7	4	.967

Selected by St. Louis Cardinals' organization in 4th round of free-agent draft, June 8, 1981.

WILLIAM RUSSELL FORD JR.

(Rusty)

Born February 20, 1961, at Lufkin, Tex.
Height, 6.04. Weight, 200.
Throws and bats righthanded.
Attended Wesleyan College, Fort Worth, Tex.

Led Texas League in games finished in relief with 54 in 1986.
Led South Atlantic League in saves with 24 and games finished in relief with 60 in 1985.
Led Northwest League in intentional bases on balls issued with 6 in 1984.

Year Club	League	G.	IP.	W.	L.	Pct.	H.	R.	ER.	SO.	BB.	ERA.
1984—Spokane	Northwest	25	40⅓	2	3	.400	28	19	16	48	28	3.57
1985—Charleston	S. Atlantic	★66	91	7	6	.538	77	33	27	93	40	2.67
1986—Beaumont	Texas	★67	82⅓	2	9	.182	83	45	34	64	56	3.72

Selected by San Diego Padres' organization in 17th round of free-agent draft, June 4, 1984.

KENNETH ROTH FORSCH
(Ken)

Born September 8, 1946, at Sacramento, Calif.
Height, 6.04. Weight, 215.
Throws and bats righthanded.
Attended Sacramento City College, Sacramento, Calif., and Oregon
State University, Corvallis, Ore.
Brother of Bob Forsch, pitcher with St. Louis Cardinals.

Pitched 6-0 no-hit victory against Atlanta Braves, April 7, 1979.
Major League saves: 1973 (4), 1974 (10), 1975 (2), 1976 (19), 1977 (8), 1978 (7), 1986 (1). Total—51.
Led American League in hit batsmen with 11 in 1982.
Tied for American League lead in shutouts with 4 in 1981.
Led Southern League in shutouts with 5 in 1970.

Year Club	League	G.	IP.	W.	L.	Pct.	H.	R.	ER.	SO.	BB.	ERA.
1968—Greensboro	Carolina	3	6	0	0	.000	6	2	2	6	3	3.00
1968—Williamsport	NYP	4	26	1	2	.333	14	6	4	40	9	1.38
1969—Peninsula†	Carolina	17	94	6	5	.545	67	40	33	100	53	3.16
1970—Columbus	Southern	22	167	●13	8	.619	135	48	38	152	39	2.05
1970—Oklahoma City	Am. Assoc.	5	40	4	0	1.000	25	7	7	37	10	1.58
1970—Houston	National	4	24	1	2	.333	28	15	15	13	5	5.63
1971—Houston	National	33	188	8	8	.500	162	60	53	131	53	2.54
1972—Houston	National	30	156	6	8	.429	163	75	68	113	62	3.92
1973—Houston	National	46	201	9	12	.429	197	101	94	149	74	4.21
1974—Houston	National	70	103	8	7	.533	98	38	32	48	37	2.80
1975—Houston‡	National	34	109	4	8	.333	114	42	39	54	30	3.22
1976—Houston	National	52	92	4	3	.571	76	23	22	49	26	2.15
1977—Houston	National	42	86	5	8	.385	80	32	26	45	28	2.72
1978—Houston	National	52	133	10	6	.625	136	44	40	71	37	2.71
1979—Houston§	National	26	178	11	6	.647	155	67	60	58	35	3.03
1980—Houston x	National	32	222	12	13	.480	230	90	79	84	41	3.20
1981—California	American	20	153	11	7	.611	143	54	49	55	27	2.88
1982—California	American	37	228	13	11	.542	225	108	98	73	57	3.87
1983—California	American	31	219⅓	11	12	.478	226	107	99	81	61	4.06
1984—California y	American	2	16⅓	1	1	.500	14	4	4	10	3	2.20
1985—California za	American					(Did not play)						
1986—California b	American	10	17	0	1	.000	24	21	18	13	10	9.53
1986—Calgary	P. Coast	13	55	4	3	.571	67	31	30	23	23	4.91
American League Totals—5 Years		100	633⅔	36	32	.529	632	294	268	232	158	3.81
National League Totals—11 Years		421	1492	78	81	.491	1439	587	528	815	428	3.18
Major League Totals—16 Years		521	2125⅔	114	113	.502	2071	881	796	1047	586	3.37

Selected by California Angels' organization in 13th round of free-agent draft, June, 1966.
Selected by Chicago Cubs' organization in secondary phase of free-agent draft, June 7, 1967.
Selected by Houston Astros' organization in 18th round of free-agent draft, June, 1968.
†On disabled list, June 11 to July 11, 1969.
‡On disabled list, July 31 to September 22, 1975.
§On disabled list, May 23 to June 26, 1979.
xTraded to California Angels for Second Baseman Dickie Thon, April 1, 1981.
yOn disabled list, April 11, 1984 through remainder of season.
zOn disabled list, April 1, 1985 through entire season.
aReleased, December 20, 1985; re-signed by Angels, March 18, 1986.
bReleased, May 25, 1986; signed by Calgary (Seattle Mariners' organization), July 12, 1986.

CHAMPIONSHIP SERIES RECORD

Year Club	League	G.	IP.	W.	L.	Pct.	H.	R.	ER.	SO.	BB.	ERA.
1980—Houston	National	2	8⅔	0	1	.000	10	4	4	6	1	4.15

ALL-STAR GAME RECORD

Year League	IP.	W.	L.	Pct.	H.	R.	ER.	SO.	BB.	ERA.
1976—National	1	0	0	.000	0	0	0	1	0	0.00
1981—American	1	0	0	.000	1	1	1	0	0	9.00
All-Star Game Totals—2 Years	2	0	0	.000	1	1	1	1	0	4.50

ROBERT HERBERT FORSCH
(Bob)

Born January 13, 1950, at Sacramento, Calif.
Height, 6.03. Weight, 215.
Throws and bats righthanded.
Attended Sacramento City College, Sacramento, Calif.
Brother of Ken Forsch, pitcher in Seattle Mariners' organization.

Pitched 3-0 no-hit victory against Montreal Expos, September 26, 1983.
Pitched 5-0 no-hit victory against Philadelphia Phillies, April 16, 1978.
Pitched 5-0 no-hit victory against Denver, May 25, 1973.
Pitched seven-inning, 4-0 no-hit victory against Memphis, May 13, 1972.
Major League saves: 1982 (1), 1985 (2). Total—3.
Led Midwest League in hit batsmen with 11 in 1971.
Tied for Texas League lead in hit batsmen with 10 in 1972.
Named pitcher on THE SPORTING NEWS National League Silver Slugger team, 1980.
Received reported $25,000 bonus to sign with St. Louis Cardinals, 1968.

Year Club	League	G.	IP.	W.	L.	Pct.	H.	R.	ER.	SO.	BB.	ERA.
1970—Cedar Rapids	Midwest	1	3	0	0	.000	6	4	4	1	2	12.00
1970—Lewiston	Northwest	7	28	2	3	.400	32	22	13	15	17	4.18
1971—Cedar Rapids	Midwest	23	158	11	7	.611	140	74	55	134	41	3.13
1972—Arkansas	Texas	24	153	8	10	.444	158	85	*74	109	47	4.35
1973—Tulsa	Am. Assoc.	27	166	12	12	.500	169	91	81	124	66	4.36
1974—Tulsa	Am. Assoc.	15	103	8	5	.615	95	49	42	71	33	3.67
1974—St. Louis	National	19	100	7	4	.636	84	38	33	39	34	2.97
1975—St. Louis	National	34	230	15	10	.600	213	89	73	108	70	2.86
1976—St. Louis	National	33	194	8	10	.444	209	112	85	76	71	3.94
1977—St. Louis	National	35	217	20	7	.741	210	97	84	95	69	3.48
1978—St. Louis	National	34	234	11	17	.393	205	110	96	114	97	3.69
1979—St. Louis	National	33	219	11	11	.500	215	102	93	92	52	3.82
1980—St. Louis	National	31	215	11	10	.524	225	102	90	87	33	3.77
1981—St. Louis	National	20	124	10	5	.667	106	47	44	41	29	3.19
1982—St. Louis	National	36	233	15	9	.625	238	95	90	69	54	3.48
1983—St. Louis	National	34	187	10	12	.455	190	104	89	56	54	4.28
1984—St. Louis†	National	16	52⅓	2	5	.286	64	38	35	21	19	6.02
1985—St. Louis	National	34	136	9	6	.600	132	63	59	48	47	3.90
1986—St. Louis‡	National	33	230	14	10	.583	221	91	83	104	68	3.25
Major League Totals—13 Years		392	2371⅓	143	116	.552	2302	1088	954	950	697	3.62

Selected by St. Louis Cardinals' organization in 38th round of free-agent draft, June 7, 1968.
†On disabled list, June 1 to September 3, 1984.
‡Granted free agency, November 12, 1986; re-signed by Cardinals, December 19, 1986.

CHAMPIONSHIP SERIES RECORD

Year Club	League	G.	IP.	W.	L.	Pct.	H.	R.	ER.	SO.	BB.	ERA.
1982—St. Louis	National	1	9	1	0	1.000	3	0	0	6	0	0.00
1985—St. Louis	National	1	3⅓	0	0	.000	3	2	2	0	2	5.40
Championship Series Totals—2 Years		2	12⅓	1	0	1.000	6	2	2	6	2	1.46

WORLD SERIES RECORD

Tied World Series record for most games lost, seven-game Series (2), 1982.

Year Club	League	G.	IP.	W.	L.	Pct.	H.	R.	ER.	SO.	BB.	ERA.
1982—St. Louis	National	2	12⅔	0	2	.000	18	10	7	4	3	4.97
1985—St. Louis	National	2	3	0	1	.000	6	4	4	3	1	12.00
World Series Totals—2 Years		4	15⅔	0	3	.000	24	14	11	7	4	6.32

RECORD AS INFIELDER

Year Club	League	Pos.	G.	AB.	R.	H.	2B.	3B.	HR.	RBI.	B.A.	PO.	A.	E.	F.A.
1968—Sarasota Cards	Gulf C.	3B	44	143	17	32	5	0	0	16	.224	29	80	12	*.901
1969—Lewiston	N'west	3B-OF-2B	26	74	11	15	3	0	3	10	.203	12	45	13	.814
1969—Modesto	Calif.	3B-OF	33	119	8	28	2	0	1	7	.235	33	58	6	.938
1970—Modesto	Calif.	3B-OF	20	47	4	7	3	0	1	1	.149	19	20	3	.929
1970—Cedar Rapids	Midw.	3B-1B-P	19	34	2	3	2	0	0	1	.088	9	19	3	.903
1970—Lewiston	N'west	P-S-2-3	18	30	5	4	0	1	0	3	.133	9	13	6	.786

TERRY JAY FORSTER

Born January 14, 1952, at Sioux Falls, S. D.
Height, 6.04. Weight, 220.
Throws and bats lefthanded.
Attended Grossmont College, El Cajon, Calif.; and San Diego State University, San Diego, Calif.

Major League saves: 1971 (1), 1972 (29), 1973 (16), 1974 (24), 1975 (4), 1976 (1), 1977 (1), 1978 (22), 1979 (2), 1982 (3), 1983 (13), 1984 (5), 1985 (1), 1986 (5). Total—127.
Led American League in saves with 24 in 1974.
Named American League Fireman of the Year by THE SPORTING NEWS, 1974.

Year Club	League	G.	IP.	W.	L.	Pct.	H.	R.	ER.	SO.	BB.	ERA.
1970—Appleton	Midwest	10	54	6	1	.857	30	11	8	42	29	1.33
1971—Chicago	American	45	50	2	3	.400	46	23	22	48	23	3.96
1972—Chicago	American	62	100	6	5	.545	75	31	25	104	44	2.25
1973—Chicago	American	51	173	6	11	.353	174	69	62	120	78	3.23
1974—Chicago	American	59	134	7	8	.467	120	57	54	105	48	3.63
1975—Chicago†	American	17	37	3	3	.500	30	12	9	32	24	2.19
1976—Chicago‡	American	29	111	2	12	.143	126	61	54	70	41	4.38
1977—Pittsburgh§	National	33	87	6	4	.600	90	47	43	58	32	4.45
1978—Los Angeles x	National	47	65	5	4	.556	56	19	14	46	23	1.94
1979—Los Angeles x	National	17	16	1	2	.333	18	11	10	8	11	5.63
1980—Los Angeles y	National	9	12	0	0	.000	10	4	4	2	4	3.00
1981—Los Angeles	National	21	31	0	1	.000	37	14	14	17	15	4.06
1982—Los Angeles z	National	56	83	5	6	.455	66	38	28	52	31	3.04
1983—Atlanta	National	56	79⅓	3	2	.600	60	19	19	54	31	2.16
1984—Atlanta a	National	25	26⅔	2	0	1.000	30	9	8	10	7	2.70
1985—Atlanta b	National	46	59⅓	2	3	.400	49	22	15	37	28	2.28
1986—California c	American	41	41	4	1	.800	47	18	16	28	17	3.51
1986—Edmonton d	P. Coast	4	3	0	1	.000	9	7	7	4	3	21.00
American League Totals—7 Years		304	646	30	43	.411	618	271	242	507	275	3.37
National League Totals—9 Years		310	459⅓	24	22	.522	416	183	155	284	182	3.04
Major League Totals—16 Years		614	1105⅓	54	65	.454	1034	454	397	791	457	3.23

Selected by Chicago White Sox' organization in 2nd round of free-agent draft, June 4, 1970.
†On disabled list, May 25 to July 1, July 26 to August 17 and August 18 to September 29, 1975.
‡Traded with Pitcher Rich Gossage to Pittsburgh Pirates for Outfielder Richie Zisk and Pitcher Silvio Martinez, December 10, 1976.
§Granted free agency, October 20, 1977; signed by Los Angeles Dodgers, November 22, 1977.
xOn disabled list, March 21 to May 25 and August 13, 1979 through remainder of season.
yOn disabled list, April 2 to July 14 and August 5 to September 15, 1980.
zGranted free agency, November 10, 1982; signed by Atlanta Braves, December 1, 1982.
aOn disabled list, March 28 to April 19, June 24 to August 4 and August 11 to September 1, 1984.
bReleased, April 1, 1986; signed by California Angels, April 16, 1986.
cOn disabled list, July 8 to September 1, 1986; included rehabilitation disability assignment to Edmonton, August 17 to August 29, 1986.
dGranted free agency, November 12, 1986.

DIVISION SERIES RECORD

Year Club	League	G.	IP.	W.	L.	Pct.	H.	R.	ER.	SO.	BB.	ERA.
1981—Los Angeles	National	1	⅓	0	0	.000	0	0	0	0	0	0.00

CHAMPIONSHIP SERIES RECORD

Year Club	League	G.	IP.	W.	L.	Pct.	H.	R.	ER.	SO.	BB.	ERA.
1978—Los Angeles	National	1	1	1	0	1.000	1	0	0	2	0	0.00
1981—Los Angeles	National	1	⅓	0	0	.000	0	0	0	1	0	0.00
Championship Series Totals—2 Years................		2	1⅓	1	0	1.000	1	0	0	3	0	0.00

WORLD SERIES RECORD

Year Club	League	G.	IP.	W.	L.	Pct.	H.	R.	ER.	SO.	BB.	ERA.
1978—Los Angeles	National	3	4	0	0	.000	5	0	0	6	1	0.00
1981—Los Angeles	National	2	2	0	0	.000	1	0	0	0	3	0.00
World Series Totals—2 Years		5	6	0	0	.000	6	0	0	6	4	0.00

GEORGE ARTHUR FOSTER

Born December 1, 1948, at Tuscaloosa, Ala.
Height, 6.01. Weight, 198.
Throws and bats righthanded.
Attended El Camino College, Torrance, Calif.

Established major league record for most home runs, righthanded batter on road (31), 1977.
Tied major league record for most consecutive seasons leading league in runs batted in (3), 1976, 1977 and 1978.
Tied National League record for most home runs, bases filled, month (2), August, 1983.
Major League stolen bases: 1971 (7), 1972 (2), 1974 (3), 1975 (2), 1976 (17), 1977 (6), 1978 (4), 1980 (1), 1981 (4), 1982 (1), 1983 (1), 1984 (2), 1986 (1). Total—51.
Hit three home runs in a game, July 14, 1977.
Led National League in total bases with 388 and slugging percentage with .631 in 1977.
Led California League outfielders in total chances with 285 in 1969.
Led Northwest League outfielders in double plays with 4 in 1968.
Named National League Player of the Year by The Sporting News, 1976 and 1977.
Named National League Most Valuable Player by Baseball Writers' Association of America, 1977.
Named outfielder on The Sporting News National League All-Star Team, 1976 through 1978 and 1981.
Named outfielder on The Sporting News National League Silver Slugger team, 1981.

Year Club	League	Pos.	G.	AB.	R.	H.	2B.	3B.	HR.	RBI.	B.A.	PO.	A.	E.	F.A.
1968—Medford	N'west	OF	72	253	47	70	9	5	3	30	.277	*142	6	5	.967
1969—Fresno	Calif.	OF	121	449	68	144	5	8	14	85	.321	*267	14	4	*.986
1969—San Francisco	Nat.	OF	9	5	1	2	0	0	0	1	.400	3	0	0	1.000
1970—Phoenix†	P. C.	OF	114	403	54	124	18	6	8	66	.308	202	5	9	.958
1970—San Francisco	Nat.	OF	9	19	2	6	1	1	1	4	.316	10	0	0	1.000
1971—S.F.‡-Cin.	Nat.	OF	140	473	50	114	23	4	13	58	.241	315	9	5	.985
1972—Cincinnati	Nat.	OF	59	145	15	29	4	1	2	12	.200	71	1	2	.973
1973—Indianapolis	A. A.	OF	134	496	77	130	26	1	15	60	.262	*332	7	10	.971
1973—Cincinnati	Nat.	OF	17	39	6	11	3	0	4	9	.282	19	1	0	1.000
1974—Cincinnati	Nat.	OF	106	276	31	73	18	0	7	41	.264	172	2	2	.989
1975—Cincinnati	Nat.	OF-1B	134	463	71	139	24	4	23	78	.300	299	11	3	.990
1976—Cincinnati	Nat.	*OF-1B	144	562	86	172	21	9	29	*121	.306	322	9	2	*.994
1977—Cincinnati	Nat.	OF	158	615	*124	197	31	2	*52	*149	.320	352	12	3	.992
1978—Cincinnati	Nat.	OF	158	604	97	170	26	7	*40	*120	.281	319	10	10	.971
1979—Cincinnati§	Nat.	OF	121	440	68	133	18	3	30	98	.302	214	7	4	.982
1980—Cincinnati	Nat.	OF	144	528	79	144	21	5	25	93	.273	295	6	1	.997
1981—Cincinnati x	Nat.	OF	108	414	64	122	23	2	22	90	.295	224	8	2	.991
1982—New York	Nat.	OF	151	550	64	136	23	2	13	70	.247	289	12	8	.974
1983—New York	Nat.	OF	157	601	74	145	19	2	28	90	.241	314	12	4	.988
1984—New York	Nat.	OF	146	553	67	149	22	1	24	86	.269	278	6	7	.976
1985—New York	Nat.	OF	129	452	57	119	24	1	21	77	.263	198	7	5	.976
1986—New York z	Nat.	OF	72	233	28	53	6	1	13	38	.227	96	4	4	.962
1986—Chicago z	Amer.	OF	15	51	2	11	0	2	1	4	.216	19	2	0	1.000
National League Totals—18 Years			1962	6972	984	1914	307	45	347	1235	.275	3790	117	62	.984
American League Totals—1 Year			15	51	2	11	0	2	1	4	.216	19	2	0	1.000
Major League Totals—18 Years			1977	7023	986	1925	307	47	348	1239	.274	3809	119	62	.984

Selected by San Francisco Giants' organization in 3rd round of free-agent draft, January 27, 1968.
†On disabled list, June 10 to June 30, 1970.
‡Traded to Cincinnati Reds for Shortstop Frank Duffy and Pitcher Vern Geishert, May 29, 1971.
§On disabled list, July 22 to August 12, 1979.

xTraded to New York Mets for Catcher Alex Trevino and Pitchers Jim Kern and Greg Harris, February 10, 1982.
yReleased, August 7, 1986; signed by Chicago White Sox, August 15, 1986.
zReleased, September 7, 1986.

CHAMPIONSHIP SERIES RECORD

Tied Championship Series record for most consecutive games, one or more runs batted in (4).

Year	Club	League	Pos.	G.	AB.	R.	H.	2B.	3B.	HR.	RBI.	B.A.	PO.	A.	E.	F.A.
1972—Cincinnati	Nat.	PR	1	0	1	0	0	0	0	0	.000	0	0	0	.000
1975—Cincinnati	Nat.	OF	3	11	3	4	0	0	0	0	.364	7	0	0	1.000
1976—Cincinnati	Nat.	OF	3	12	2	2	0	0	2	4	.167	7	0	0	1.000
1979—Cincinnati	Nat.	OF	3	10	1	2	0	0	1	2	.200	6	2	0	1.000
Championships Series Totals—4 Years			10	33	7	8	0	0	3	6	.242	20	2	0	1.000

WORLD SERIES RECORD

Established World Series records for most putouts by left fielder, game (8), October 21, 1976; most chances accepted by left fielder, game (8), October 21, 1976.

Tied World Series record for most times caught stealing, four-game Series (2), 1976; one or more hits, each game, four-game Series, 1976; most putouts by outfielder, game (8), October 21, 1976.

Year	Club	League	Pos.	G.	AB.	R.	H.	2B.	3B.	HR.	RBI.	B.A.	PO.	A.	E.	F.A.
1972—Cincinnati	Nat.	PR-OF	2	0	0	0	0	0	0	0	.000	0	0	0	.000
1975—Cincinnati	Nat.	OF	7	29	1	8	1	0	0	2	.276	13	1	0	1.000
1976—Cincinnati	Nat.	OF	4	14	3	6	1	0	0	4	.429	14	0	0	1.000
World Series Totals—3 Years			13	43	4	14	2	0	0	6	.326	27	1	0	1.000

ALL-STAR GAME RECORD

Year	League	Pos.	AB.	R.	H.	2B.	3B.	HR.	RBI.	B.A.	PO.	A.	E.	F.A.
1976—National		OF	3	1	1	0	0	1	3	.333	0	0	0	.000
1977—National		OF	3	1	1	1	0	0	1	.333	2	0	0	1.000
1978—National		OF	2	1	0	0	0	0	0	.000	2	0	0	1.000
1979—National		OF	1	0	1	1	0	0	1	1.000	0	0	0	.000
1981—National		OF	2	0	0	0	0	0	0	.000	0	0	0	.000
All-Star Game Totals—5 Years			11	3	3	2	0	1	5	.273	4	0	0	1.000

JOHN ANTHONY FRANCO

Born September 17, 1960, at Brooklyn, N.Y.
Height, 5.10. Weight, 175.
Throws and bats lefthanded.
Attended St. John's University, Jamaica, N.Y.

Major League saves: 1984 (4), 1985 (12), 1986 (29). Total—45.

Year	Club	League	G.	IP.	W.	L.	Pct.	H.	R.	ER.	SO.	BB.	ERA.
1981—Vero Beach	Florida St.	13	79	7	4	.636	78	41	31	60	41	3.53
1982—Albuquerque	P. Coast	5	27⅓	1	2	.333	41	22	22	24	15	7.24
1982—San Antonio	Texas	17	105⅓	10	5	.667	137	70	58	76	46	4.96
1983—Albuquerque†	P. Coast	11	15	0	0	.000	10	11	9	8	11	5.40
1983—Indianapolis	Am. Assoc.	23	115	6	10	.375	148	69	62	54	42	4.85
1984—Wichita	Am. Assoc.	6	9⅓	1	0	1.000	8	6	6	11	4	5.79
1984—Cincinnati	National	54	79⅓	6	2	.750	74	28	23	55	36	2.61
1985—Cincinnati	National	67	99	12	3	.800	83	27	24	61	40	2.18
1986—Cincinnati	National	74	101	6	6	.500	90	40	33	84	44	2.94
Major League Totals—3 Years		195	279⅓	24	11	.686	247	95	80	200	120	2.58

Selected by Los Angeles Dodgers' organization in 5th round of free-agent draft, June 8, 1981.
†Traded with Pitcher Brett Wise to Cincinnati Reds' organization for Infielder Rafael Landestoy, May 9, 1983.

ALL-STAR GAME RECORD

Member of National League All-Star Team in 1986; did not play.

JULIO CESAR FRANCO

Name pronounced FRANHK-oh.
Born August 23, 1961, at San Pedro de Macoris, D.R.
Height, 6.00. Weight, 160.
Throws and bats righthanded.

Major League stolen bases: 1983 (32), 1984 (19), 1985 (13), 1986 (10). Total—74.
Led American League in grounding into double plays with 28 in 1986.
Led American League shortstops in errors with 35 in 1985.
Led Northwest League in total bases with 153 in 1979.
Led Carolina League shortstops in double plays with 73 in 1980.
Led Northwest League shortstops in double plays with 45 in 1979.
Named Carolina League Most Valuable Player, 1980.

Year	Club	League	Pos.	G.	AB.	R.	H.	2B.	3B.	HR.	RBI.	B.A.	PO.	A.	E.	F.A.
1978—Butte	Pion.	SS	47	141	34	43	5	2	3	28	.305	37	52	25	.781
1979—Central Ore.	N'west	SS	●71	299	57	★98	15	5	●10	45	.328	103	★256	31	.921
1980—Peninsula	Carol.	SS	●140	★555	105	178	25	6	11	★99	.321	179	★412	42	.934
1981—Reading	East.	SS	★139	★532	70	160	17	3	8	74	.301	246	437	30	.958
1982—Oklahoma City	A. A.	★SS-3B	120	463	80	139	19	5	21	66	.300	211	350	★42	.930
1982—Philadelphia†	Nat.	SS-3B	16	29	3	8	1	0	0	3	.276	8	25	0	1.000
1983—Cleveland	Amer.	SS	149	560	68	153	24	8	8	80	.273	247	438	28	.961

Year	Club	League	Pos.	G.	AB.	R.	H.	2B.	3B.	HR.	RBI.	B.A.	PO.	A.	E.	F.A.
1984—Cleveland	Amer.		SS	160	*658	82	188	22	5	3	79	.286	280	481	*36	.955
1985—Cleveland	Amer.		SS-2B	160	636	97	183	33	4	6	90	.288	252	437	36	.950
1986—Cleveland	Amer		SS-2B	149	599	80	183	30	5	10	74	.306	248	413	19	.972
National League Totals—1 Year				16	29	3	8	1	0	0	3	.276	8	25	0	1.000
American League Totals—4 Years				618	2453	327	707	109	22	27	323	.288	1027	1769	119	.959
Major League Totals—5 Years				634	2482	330	715	110	22	27	326	.288	1035	1794	119	.960

Signed as free agent by Philadelphia Phillies' organization, June 23, 1978.

†Traded with Second Baseman Manny Trillo, Outfielder George Vukovich, Pitcher Jay Baller and Catcher Jerry Willard to Cleveland Indians for Outfielder Von Hayes, December 9, 1982.

MANUEL ANTONIO FRANCOIS (MOIS)
(Manny)

Born May 28, 1966, at San Pedro de Macoris, D. R.
Height, 5.11. Weight, 165.
Throws right and bats left and righthanded.

Led Florida State League in being hit by pitch with 17 in 1985.

Year	Club	League	Pos.	G.	AB.	R.	H.	2B.	3B.	HR.	RBI.	B.A.	PO.	A.	E.	F.A.
1984—Great Falls†	Pion.		SS	51	174	37	52	7	3	1	22	.299	70	114	*37	.833
1985—Vero Beach†	Fla. St.		SS	115	390	70	108	13	9	1	38	.277	151	283	*54	.889
1986—San Antonio‡	Texas		SS	9	19	3	5	0	0	0	1	.263	8	13	4	.840

Signed as free agent by Los Angeles Dodgers' organization, July 30, 1983.

†Batted righthanded.

‡On disabled list, April 22 to July 22, 1986.

TERRY JON FRANCONA

Born April 22, 1959, at New Brighton, Pa.
Height, 6.01. Weight, 175.
Throws and bats lefthanded.
Attended University of Arizona, Tucson, Ariz.
Son of John (Tito) Francona, outfielder-first baseman with Baltimore, Chicago A.L., Detroit, Cleveland, St. Louis, Philadelphia, Atlanta, Oakland and Milwaukee, 1956 through 1970.

Major League stolen bases: 1981 (1), 1982 (2), 1985 (5). Total—8.

Named College Player of the Year by THE SPORTING NEWS, 1980.

Named outfielder on THE SPORTING NEWS College Baseball All-America Team, 1980.

Year	Club	League	Pos.	G.	AB.	R.	H.	2B.	3B.	HR.	RBI.	B.A.	PO.	A.	E.	F.A.
1980—Memphis	South.		OF	60	210	20	63	13	2	1	23	.300	59	4	4	.940
1981—Memphis	South.		OF-1B	41	161	20	56	8	1	0	18	.348	102	7	5	.956
1981—Denver	A. A.		OF	93	355	53	125	17	*9	1	58	.352	158	7	3	.982
1981—Montreal	Nat.		OF-1B	34	95	11	26	0	1	1	8	.274	41	5	0	1.000
1982—Montreal†	Nat.		OF-1B	46	131	14	42	3	0	0	9	.321	65	0	3	.956
1983—Montreal	Nat.		OF-1B	120	230	21	59	11	1	3	22	.257	172	10	3	.984
1984—Montreal‡	Nat.		1B-OF	58	214	18	74	19	2	1	18	.346	431	50	3	.994
1985—Montreal§	Nat.		1B-OF-3B	107	281	19	75	15	1	2	31	.267	431	40	6	.987
1986—Chicago	Nat.		OF-1B	86	124	13	31	3	0	2	8	.250	123	7	0	1.000
1986—Iowa	A. A.		1B-OF	17	60	7	15	3	2	0	8	.250	82	3	1	.988
Major League Totals—6 Years				451	1075	96	307	51	5	9	96	.286	1263	112	15	.989

Selected by Chicago Cubs' organization in 2nd round of free-agent draft, June 7, 1977.

Selected by Montreal Expos' organization in 1st round (22nd player selected) of free-agent draft, June 3, 1980.

†On disabled list, June 17 to September 27, 1982.

‡On disabled list, June 15 to September 5, 1984.

§Released, April 1, 1986; signed by Chicago Cubs' organization, May 2, 1986.

DIVISION SERIES RECORD

Year	Club	League	Pos.	G.	AB.	R.	H.	2B.	3B.	HR.	RBI.	B.A.	PO.	A.	E.	F.A.
1981—Montreal	Nat.		OF	5	12	0	4	0	0	0	0	.333	8	0	0	1.000

CHAMPIONSHIP SERIES RECORD

Year	Club	League	Pos.	G.	AB.	R.	H.	2B.	3B.	HR.	RBI.	B.A.	PO.	A.	E.	F.A.
1981—Montreal	Nat.		PH-OF	2	1	0	0	0	0	0	0	.000	0	0	0	.000

WILLIAM PATRICK FRASER
(Willie)

Born May 26, 1964, at New York, N.Y.
Height, 6.03. Weight, 200.
Throws and bats righthanded.
Attended Concordia College, Bronxville, N.Y.

Year	Club	League	G.	IP.	W.	L.	Pct.	H.	R.	ER.	SO.	BB.	ERA.
1985—Quad Cities	Midwest	13	81⅔	2	6	.250	95	53	49	72	32	5.40
1986—Palm Springs	California	19	124⅓	9	2	.818	115	60	49	99	29	3.55
1986—Edmonton	P. Coast	6	40	4	1	.800	25	15	14	24	8	3.15
1986—California	American	1	4⅓	0	0	.000	6	4	4	2	1	8.31
Major League Totals—1 Year		1	4⅓	0	0	.000	6	4	4	2	1	8.31

Selected by California Angels' organization in 1st round (15th player selected) of free-agent draft, June 3, 1985.

GEORGE ALLEN FRAZIER

Born October 13, 1954, at Oklahoma City, Okla.
Height, 6.05. Weight, 200.
Throws and bats righthanded.
Attended University of Oklahoma, Norman, Okla.

Major League saves: 1980 (3), 1981 (3), 1982 (1), 1983 (8), 1984 (4), 1985 (2), 1986 (6). Total—27.

Year Club	League	G.	IP.	W.	L.	Pct.	H.	R.	ER.	SO.	BB.	ERA.
1976—Newark	NYP	6	15	2	1	.667	11	3	3	17	4	1.80
1976—Burlington	Midwest	20	36	7	2	.778	30	9	7	28	14	1.75
1977—Spokane	P. Coast	7	11	2	2	.500	9	5	5	9	5	4.09
1977—Holyoke†	Eastern	45	98	12	7	.632	94	44	36	71	29	3.31
1978—Springfield	Am. Assoc.	32	69	6	5	.545	59	33	26	52	25	3.39
1978—St. Louis	National	14	22	0	3	.000	22	14	10	8	6	4.09
1979—Springfield	Am. Assoc.	24	56	1	2	.333	40	17	15	56	23	2.41
1979—St. Louis	National	25	32	2	4	.333	35	19	16	14	12	4.50
1980—Springfield	Am. Assoc.	35	60	1	3	.250	44	22	20	55	23	3.00
1980—St. Louis	National	22	23	1	4	.200	24	10	7	11	7	2.74
1981—Springfield‡	Am. Assoc.	21	31	1	2	.333	35	14	11	28	11	3.19
1981—Columbus	Int'national	27	59	4	1	.800	58	23	21	50	12	3.20
1981—New York	American	16	28	0	1	.000	26	7	5	17	11	1.61
1982—New York	American	63	111⅔	4	4	.500	103	51	43	69	39	3.47
1983—New York§	American	61	115⅓	4	4	.500	94	44	44	78	45	3.43
1984—Cleveland x	American	22	44⅓	4	5	.600	45	19	18	24	14	3.65
1984—Chicago	National	37	63⅔	6	3	.667	53	30	29	58	26	4.10
1985—Chicago	National	51	76	7	8	.467	88	57	54	46	52	6.39
1986—Chicago y	National	35	51⅔	2	4	.333	63	36	31	41	34	5.40
1986—Minnesota	American	15	26⅔	1	1	.500	23	13	13	25	16	4.39
National League Totals—6 Years		184	268⅓	18	26	.409	285	166	147	178	137	4.93
American League Totals—5 Years		177	326	12	12	.500	291	134	123	213	125	3.40
Major League Totals—9 Years		361	594⅓	30	38	.441	576	300	270	391	262	4.09

Selected by Texas Rangers' organization in 13th round of free-agent draft, June 6, 1976.
Selected by Milwaukee Brewers' organization in 9th round of free-agent draft, June 8, 1976.
†Traded to St. Louis Cardinals' organization for Catcher Buck Martinez, December 9, 1977.
‡Traded to New York Yankees' organization, June 7, 1981, completing deal in which New York organization traded Shortstop Rafael Santana to St. Louis Cardinals for a player to be named later, February 16, 1981.
§Traded with Outfielder Otis Nixon and a player to be named later to Cleveland Indians for Third Baseman Toby Harrah and a player to be named later, February 5, 1984; New York organization acquired Pitcher Rick Browne and Cleveland organization acquired Pitcher Guy Elston to complete deal, February 8, 1984.
xTraded with Catcher Ron Hassey and Pitcher Rick Sutcliffe to Chicago Cubs for Outfielders Mel Hall and Joe Carter and Pitchers Don Schulze and Darryl Banks, June 13, 1984.
yTraded with Pitcher Ray Fontenot and Shortstop Julius McDougal to Minnesota Twins for Pitchers Ron Davis and Dewayne Coleman, August 13, 1986.

CHAMPIONSHIP SERIES RECORD

Tied American League Championship Series record for most strikeouts by a relief pitcher, game (5), October 14, 1981.

Year Club	League	G.	IP.	W.	L.	Pct.	H.	R.	ER.	SO.	BB.	ERA.
1981—New York	American	1	5⅔	1	0	1.000	5	0	0	5	1	0.00
1984—Chicago	National	1	1⅔	0	0	.000	2	2	2	1	0	10.80
Championship Series Totals—2 Years		2	7⅓	1	0	1.000	7	2	2	6	1	2.45

WORLD SERIES RECORD

Established World Series record for most games lost, six-game Series (3), 1981.

Year Club	League	G.	IP.	W.	L.	Pct.	H.	R.	ER.	SO.	BB.	ERA.
1981—New York	American	3	3⅔	0	3	.000	9	7	7	2	3	17.18

DEAN EMMONS FREELAND

Born February 25, 1965, at Milwaukee, Wis.
Height, 6.00. Weight, 185.
Throws and bats righthanded.

Year Club	League	G.	IP.	W.	L.	Pct.	H.	R.	ER.	SO.	BB.	ERA.
1984—Paintsville	Ap'lachian	10	61⅔	5	2	.714	50	24	14	51	27	2.04
1985—Beloit	Midwest	12	64	1	6	.143	78	53	46	37	33	6.47
1985—Helena†	Pioneer	13	84⅓	4	6	.400	93	54	36	60	36	3.84
1986—Clinton	Midwest	20	142	7	7	.500	101	53	45	129	76	2.85
1986—Shreveport	Texas	7	33⅓	1	2	.333	31	21	14	21	13	3.78

Signed as free agent by Milwaukee Brewers' organization, August 12, 1983.
†Traded with Pitcher Eric Pilkington to San Francisco Giants for Outfielder Rob Deer, December 18, 1985.

MARVIN FREEMAN

Born April 10, 1963, at Chicago, Ill.
Height, 6.06. Weight, 182.
Throws and bats righthanded.
Attended Jackson State University, Jackson, Miss.

Tied for Eastern League lead in games started by pitchers with 27 in 1986.
Tied for Northwest League lead in games started by pitchers with 15 in 1984.

Year	Club	League	G.	IP.	W.	L.	Pct.	H.	R.	ER.	SO.	BB.	ERA.
1984—Bend	Northwest	15	89⅔	8	5	.615	64	41	26	79	52	2.61
1985—Clearwater	Florida St.	14	88⅓	6	5	.545	72	32	30	55	36	3.06
1985—Reading	Eastern	11	65⅓	1	7	.125	51	41	39	35	52	5.37
1986—Reading	Eastern	27	163	13	6	.684	130	89	73	113	⋆111	4.03
1986—Philadelphia	National	3	16	2	0	1.000	6	4	4	8	10	2.25
Major League Totals—1 Year		3	16	2	0	1.000	6	4	4	8	10	2.25

Selected by Montreal Expos' organization in 9th round of free-agent draft, June 8, 1981.
Selected by Philadelphia Phillies' organization in 2nd round of free-agent draft, June 4, 1984.

MICHAEL EUGENE FRIEDERICH

Name pronounced FREED-uh-rick.

(Mike)

Born February 26, 1965, in Winfield, Ill.
Height, 6.05. Weight, 225.
Throws right and bats left and righthanded.

Pitched 2-0 no-hit victory against Lakeland, August 4, 1985 (first game).

Year	Club	League	G.	IP.	W.	L.	Pct.	H.	R.	ER.	SO.	BB.	ERA.
1983—Sarasota Astros	Gulf Coast	3	21	3	0	1.000	11	4	4	20	3	1.71
1983—Auburn	NYP	9	70⅓	6	2	.750	58	20	14	75	12	⋆1.79
1984—Daytona Beach	Florida St.	25	147⅓	12	9	.571	121	69	57	80	94	3.48
1985—Osceola	Florida St.	24	142⅓	8	9	.471	130	74	52	125	62	3.29
1986—Columbus	Southern	29	165⅓	8	9	.471	161	98	80	108	80	4.35

Selected by Houston Astros' organization in 3rd round of free-agent draft, June 6, 1983.

TODD GERALD FROHWIRTH

Born September 28, 1962, at Milwaukee, Wis.
Height, 6.04. Weight, 190.
Throws and bats righthanded.
Attended Northwest Missouri State University, Maryville, Mo.

Led Carolina League in games finished in relief with 48 and saves with 18 in 1985.
Led Northwest League in games finished in relief with 25 and tied for lead in saves with 11 in 1984.

Year	Club	League	G.	IP.	W.	L.	Pct.	H.	R.	ER.	SO.	BB.	ERA.
1984—Bend	Northwest	29	49⅔	4	4	.500	26	17	9	60	31	1.63
1985—Peninsula	Carolina	⋆54	82	7	5	.583	70	33	20	74	48	2.20
1986—Clearwater	Florida St.	32	52	3	3	.500	54	29	23	39	18	3.98

Selected by Philadelphia Phillies' organization in 13th round of free-agent draft, June 4, 1984.

WILLIAM DAVID FULTON

(Bill)

Born October 22, 1963, at Pittsburgh, Pa.
Height, 6.03. Weight, 195.
Throws and bats righthanded.
Attended Pensacola Junior College, Pensacola, Fla.

Pitched 5-0 no-hit victory against Lakeland, July 2, 1985 (first game).
Pitched 1-0 no-hit victory against Geneva, July 25, 1983.

Year	Club	League	G.	IP.	W.	L.	Pct.	H.	R.	ER.	SO.	BB.	ERA.
1983—Oneonta	NYP	14	84⅓	4	7	.364	73	49	35	77	35	3.74
1984—Greensboro†	S. Atlantic	10	52	2	3	.400	45	26	24	29	26	4.15
1985—Fort Lauderdale	Florida St.	15	112	11	2	.846	91	31	20	71	30	1.61
1986—Albany	Eastern	14	80	6	6	.500	90	46	42	46	24	4.73
1986—Columbus	Int'national	12	75	4	6	.400	89	42	32	36	25	3.84

Selected by Baltimore Orioles' organization in 1st round (25th player selected) of free-agent draft, January 11, 1983.
Selected by New York Yankees' organization in secondary phase of free-agent draft, June 6, 1983.
†On disabled list, June 12 to July 13, 1984.

THOMAS JAMES FUNK

(Tom)

Born March 13, 1962, at Gladstone, Mo.
Height, 6.02. Weight, 203.
Throws and bats lefthanded.
Attended Northwest Missouri State University, Maryville, Mo.

Year	Club	League	G.	IP.	W.	L.	Pct.	H.	R.	ER.	SO.	BB.	ERA.
1983—Auburn	NYP	25	53⅓	5	4	.556	42	20	12	46	18	2.03
1984—Asheville	S. Atlantic	⋆54	74⅔	6	2	.750	54	26	23	80	33	2.77
1985—Asheville	S. Atlantic	40	72⅓	9	2	●.818	51	17	14	69	28	1.74
1986—Columbus	Southern	44	64⅓	6	2	.750	50	23	19	58	30	2.66
1986—Houston	National	8	8⅓	0	0	.000	10	6	6	2	6	6.48
Major League Totals—1 Year		8	8⅓	0	0	.000	10	6	6	2	6	6.48

Selected by Baltimore Orioles' organization in 23rd round of free-agent draft, June 3, 1980.
Selected by Houston Astros' organization in 28th round of free-agent draft, June 6, 1983.

GARY JOSEPH GAETTI

Name pronounced Guy-ETT-ee.

Born August 19, 1958, at Centralia, Ill.
Height, 6.00. Weight, 192.
Throws and bats righthanded.
Attended Lake Land College, Mattoon, Ill., and Northwest
Missouri State University, Maryville, Mo.

Tied major league records by hitting home run in first major league at-bat, September 20, 1981; most home runs, opening day of season (2), April 6, 1982; most sacrifice flies, rookie season (13), 1982.
Major League stolen bases: 1983 (7), 1984 (11), 1985 (13), 1986 (14). Total—45.
Led American League in sacrifice flies with 13 in 1982.
Led American League third basemen in putouts with 142 in 1984 and 146 in 1985.
Led American League third basemen in total chances with 496 in 1984 and 473 in 1986.
Led American League third basemen in assists with 334 in 1984 and 1986.
Led American League third basemen in double plays with 46 in 1983 and 36 in 1986.
Tied for American League lead in errors by third basemen with 20 in 1984.
Led Southern League third basemen in putouts with 122 and assists with 281 in 1981.
Led Midwest League third basemen in double plays with 35 in 1980.
Tied for Appalachian League lead in errors by third basemen with 18 in 1979.
Named third baseman on THE SPORTING NEWS American League All-Star fielding team, 1986.

Year	Club	League	Pos.	G.	AB.	R.	H.	2B.	3B.	HR.	RBI.	B.A.	PO.	A.	E.	F.A.
1979—Elizabethton	Appal.	3B-SS	66	230	50	59	15	2	14	42	.257	70	134	21	.907
1980—Wis. Rapids	Midw.	3B	138	503	77	134	27	3	★22	82	.266	★94	★363	●35	.929
1981—Orlando	South.	★3B-1B	137	561	92	137	19	2	30	93	.277	143	283	★32	.930
1981—Minnesota	Amer.	3B	9	26	4	5	0	0	2	3	.192	5	17	0	1.000
1982—Minnesota	Amer.	3B-SS	145	508	59	117	25	4	25	84	.230	106	291	17	.959
1983—Minnesota	Amer.	3B-SS	157	584	81	143	30	3	21	78	.245	★131	361	17	.967
1984—Minnesota	Amer.	3B-OF-SS	●162	588	55	154	29	4	5	65	.262	163	335	21	.960
1985—Minnesota	Amer.	3B-OF-1B	160	560	71	138	31	0	20	63	.246	162	316	18	.964
1986—Minnesota	Amer.	3-S-O-2	157	596	91	171	34	1	34	108	.287	120	335	21	.956
Major League Totals—6 Years			790	2862	361	728	149	12	107	401	.254	687	1655	94	.961

Selected by St. Louis Cardinals' organization in 4th round of free-agent draft, January 10, 1978.
Selected by Chicago White Sox' organization in secondary phase of free-agent draft, June 6, 1978.
Selected by Minnesota Twins' organization in secondary phase of free-agent draft, June 5, 1979.

GREGORY CARPENTER GAGNE

Name pronounced GAG-nee.

(Greg)

Born November 12, 1961, at Fall River, Mass.
Height, 5.11. Weight, 185.
Throws and bats righthanded.

Tied Major League record for most inside-the-park home runs, game (2), October 4, 1986.
Major League stolen bases: 1985 (10), 1986 (12). Total—22.
Led International League shortstops in total chances with 599 in 1983.

Year	Club	League	Pos.	G.	AB.	R.	H.	2B.	3B.	HR.	RBI.	B.A.	PO.	A.	E.	F.A.
1979—Paintsville	Appal.	SS	41	106	10	19	2	3	0	7	.179	28	62	14	.865
1980—Greensboro†	S. Atl.	SS-3B-2B	98	337	39	91	20	5	3	32	.270	133	233	35	.913
1981—Greensboro	S. Atl.	2B-SS-3B	104	364	71	108	21	3	9	48	.297	172	280	25	.948
1982—Fort Lauderdale‡	Fla. St.	SS	1	3	0	1	0	0	0	0	.333	3	5	0	1.000
1982—Orlando	South.	SS-2B	136	504	73	117	23	5	11	57	.232	185	403	39	.938
1983—Toledo	Int.	SS	119	392	61	100	22	4	17	66	.255	201	★364	★34	.943
1983—Minnesota	Amer.	SS	10	27	2	3	1	0	0	3	.111	10	14	2	.923
1984—Toledo§	Int.	3B-SS-2B	70	236	31	66	7	2	9	27	.280	58	168	20	.926
1984—Minnesota	Amer.	PR-PH	2	1	0	0	0	0	0	0	.000	0	0	0	.000
1985—Minnesota x	Amer.	SS	114	293	37	66	15	3	2	23	.225	149	269	14	.968
1986—Minnesota	Amer.	★SS-2B	156	472	63	118	22	6	12	54	.250	228	381	★26	.959
Major League Totals—4 Years			282	793	102	187	38	9	14	80	.236	387	664	42	.962

Selected by New York Yankees' organization in 5th round of free-agent draft, June 5, 1979.

†On disabled list, September 4 to September 22, 1980.

‡Traded with Pitchers Ron Davis and Paul Boris and a reported $400,000 to Minnesota Twins for Shortstop Roy Smalley, April 10, 1982.

§On disabled list, June 13 to July 18, 1984.

xOn disabled list, August 10 to September 1, 1985.

TELMANCH GAINEY

(Ty)

Born December 25, 1960, at Cheraw, S. C.
Height, 6.01. Weight, 190.
Throws and bats lefthanded.

Major League stolen bases: 1986 (3).
Led Pacific Coast League in slugging percentage with .616 in 1986.

Year	Club	League	Pos.	G.	AB.	R.	H.	2B.	3B.	HR.	RBI.	B.A.	PO.	A.	E.	F.A.
1979—Sarasota Astros	Gulf C.	OF	21	61	5	14	1	1	0	7	.230	13	1	1	.933
1980—Sarasota Astros	Gulf C.	OF	47	167	41	47	4	2	2	26	.281	48	2	3	.943
1980—Daytona Beach	Fla. St.	OF	5	12	3	1	0	0	0	0	.083	4	0	0	1.000
1981—Daytona Beach	Fla. St.	OF	114	347	40	86	11	8	6	38	.248	127	7	3	.978

Year Club League	Pos.	G.	AB.	R.	H.	2B.	3B.	HR.	RBI.	B.A.	PO.	A.	E.	F.A.
1982—Daytona Beach .... Fla. St.	OF	106	425	92	145	20	11	10	58	⋆.341	161	6	9	.949
1982—Columbus .... South.	OF	16	58	9	17	5	0	1	5	.293	19	1	0	1.000
1983—Columbus .... South.	OF	110	397	65	107	15	1	9	43	.270	56	1	0	1.000
1984—Columbus .... South.	OF	133	467	85	129	28	2	13	78	.276	240	8	4	.984
1985—Tucson† .... P. C.	OF	68	232	42	78	14	2	5	46	.336	119	4	4	.969
1985—Houston .... Nat.	OF	13	37	5	6	0	0	0	0	.162	21	0	2	.913
1986—Tucson .... P. C.	OF	104	359	72	126	22	⋆11	17	63	⋆.351	163	4	9	.949
1986—Houston .... Nat.	OF	26	50	6	15	3	1	1	6	.300	30	0	0	1.000
Major League Totals—2 Years		39	87	11	21	3	1	1	6	.241	51	0	2	.962

Selected by Houston Astros' organization in 2nd round of free-agent draft, June 5, 1979.
†On disabled list, May 24 to June 14, 1985.

ANDRES JOSE GALARRAGA

Name pronounced Gahl-ah-RAH-guh.

Born June 18, 1961, at Caracas, Venezuela.
Height, 6.03. Weight, 209.
Throws and bats righthanded.

Major League stolen bases: 1985 (1), 1986 (6). Total—7.
Led Southern League in total bases with 271, slugging percentage with .508, intentional bases on balls received with 10 and tied for lead in being hit by pitch with 9 in 1984.
Tied for American Association lead in game-winning RBIs with 13 in 1985.
Led Southern League first basemen in total chances with 1,428 and double plays with 130 in 1984.
Named Southern League Most Valuable Player, 1984.

Year Club League	Pos.	G.	AB.	R.	H.	2B.	3B.	HR.	RBI.	B.A.	PO.	A.	E.	F.A.
1979—W. Palm Beach .... Fla. St.	1B	7	23	3	3	0	0	0	1	.130	2	1	0	1.000
1979—Calgary .... Pion.	1B-3B-C	42	112	14	24	3	1	4	16	.214	187	21	5	.976
1980—Calgary .... Pion.	1-3-C-O	59	190	27	50	11	4	4	22	.263	287	52	21	.942
1981—Jamestown .... NYP	C-1-O-3	47	154	24	40	5	4	6	26	.260	154	15	0	1.000
1982—W. Palm Beach .... Fla. St.	1B-OF	105	338	39	95	20	2	14	51	.281	462	36	9	.982
1983—W. Palm Beach .... Fla. St.	1B-OF-3B	104	401	55	116	18	3	10	66	.289	861	77	13	.986
1984—Jacksonville .... South.	1B	143	533	81	154	28	4	27	87	.289	⋆1302	⋆110	16	.989
1985—Indianapolis .... A. A.	1B-OF	121	439	⋆75	118	15	8	25	87	.269	930	63	14	.986
1985—Montreal .... Nat.	1B	24	75	9	14	1	0	2	4	.187	173	22	1	.995
1986—Montreal† .... Nat.	1B	105	321	39	87	13	0	10	42	.271	805	40	4	.995
Major League Totals—2 Years		129	396	48	101	14	0	12	46	.255	978	62	5	.995

Signed as free agent by Montreal Expos' organization, January 19, 1979.
†On disabled list, July 10 to August 19 and August 20 to September 4, 1986.

DAVID THOMAS GALLAGHER
(Dave)

Born September 20, 1960, at Trenton, N.J.
Height, 6.00. Weight, 180.
Throws and bats righthanded.
Attended Mercer County Community College, Trenton, N.J.

Led International League in sacrifice hits with 12 in 1986.
Led Midwest League in sacrifice hits with 21 in 1982.
Led International League outfielders in total chances with 369 in 1985.
Tied for Eastern League lead in double plays by outfielders with 4 in 1983.

Year Club League	Pos.	G.	AB.	R.	H.	2B.	3B.	HR.	RBI.	B.A.	PO.	A.	E.	F.A.
1980—Batavia .... NYP	OF	69	241	33	66	6	3	5	36	.274	114	4	2	.983
1981—Waterloo .... Midw.	OF-3B	127	435	55	102	22	1	3	34	.234	224	22	7	.972
1982—Chattanooga .... South.	OF	15	54	10	12	2	1	0	4	.222	32	1	0	1.000
1982—Waterloo .... Midw.	OF	110	409	61	118	25	7	6	47	.289	232	15	4	⋆.984
1983—Buffalo† .... East.	OF-3B	107	376	64	127	21	3	2	47	⋆.338	223	13	5	.979
1984—Maine .... Int.	OF	116	380	49	94	19	5	6	49	.247	208	7	3	.986
1985—Maine .... Int.	OF	132	488	71	118	22	3	9	55	.242	⋆357	9	3	⋆.992
1986—Maine .... Int.	OF	132	497	59	145	23	5	8	44	.292	341	⋆14	1	⋆.997

Selected by Oakland A's organization in 1st round (third player selected) of free-agent draft, January 8, 1980.
Selected by Cleveland Indians' organization in secondary phase of free-agent draft, June 3, 1980.
†On disabled list, May 2 to June 6, 1983.

MICHAEL ANTHONY GALLEGO
(Mike)

Born October 31, 1960, at Whittier, Calif.
Height, 5.08. Weight, 160.
Throws and bats righthanded.
Attended University of California, Los Angeles, Calif.

Major League stolen bases: 1985 (1).
Led Pacific Coast League in being hit by pitch with 8 in 1986.

Year Club League	Pos.	G.	AB.	R.	H.	2B.	3B.	HR.	RBI.	B.A.	PO.	A.	E.	F.A.
1981—Modesto .... Calif.	2B	60	202	38	55	9	3	0	23	.272	127	161	13	.957
1982—West Haven .... East.	2B-SS	54	139	17	25	1	0	0	5	.180	85	111	4	.980
1982—Tacoma .... P. C.	2B-3B-SS	44	136	12	30	3	1	0	11	.221	73	111	8	.958
1983—Tacoma† .... P. C.	2B	2	2	0	0	0	0	0	0	.000	0	1	0	1.000

Year	Club	League	Pos.	G.	AB.	R.	H.	2B.	3B.	HR.	RBI.	B.A.	PO.	A.	E.	F.A.
1983—Albany	East.	2B-SS-3B	90	274	31	61	6	0	0	18	.223	184	260	4	.991
1984—Tacoma	P. C.	2B-SS-3B	101	288	29	70	8	1	0	18	.243	167	231	13	.968
1985—Oakland	Amer.	2B-SS-3B	76	77	13	16	5	1	1	9	.208	57	94	1	.993
1985—Modesto	Calif.	2B-SS-3B	6	25	1	5	1	0	0	2	.200	12	11	1	.958
1986—Tacoma	P. C.	SS-3B-2B	132	443	58	122	16	5	4	46	.275	197	417	23	.964
1986—Oakland	Amer.	2B-3B-SS	20	37	2	10	2	0	0	4	.270	24	51	1	.987
Major League Totals—2 Years				96	114	15	26	7	1	1	13	.228	81	145	2	.991

Selected by Oakland A's organization in 2nd round of free-agent draft., June 8, 1981.
†On temporary inactive list, April 10 to May 20, 1983.

BALVINO GALVEZ

Name pronounced Gal-VEZ.
Born March 31, 1964, at San Pedro de Macoris, D. R.
Height, 6.00. Weight, 170.
Throws and bats righthanded.

Year	Club	League	G.	IP.	W.	L.	Pct.	H.	R.	ER.	SO.	BB.	ERA.
1982—Lethbridge	Pioneer	10	20⅓	0	0	.000	33	21	13	11	17	5.75
1983—Bradenton Dodgers	Gulf Coast	13	66⅓	4	3	.571	62	33	22	51	19	2.98
1984—Vero Beach	Florida St.	26	156⅔	12	11	.522	152	68	63	76	62	3.62
1985—San Antonio	Texas	26	170⅔	10	9	.526	181	99	86	111	79	4.54
1986—Albuquerque	P. Coast	18	81	3	6	.333	82	50	44	32	43	4.89
1986—Los Angeles	National	10	20⅔	0	1	.000	19	10	9	11	12	3.92
Major League Totals—1 Year		10	20⅔	0	1	.000	19	10	9	11	12	3.92

Signed as free agent by Los Angeles Dodgers' organization, September 10, 1981.

RONALD EDWIN GANT

(Ronnie)

Born March 2, 1965, at Victoria, Tex.
Height, 6.00. Weight, 172.
Throws and bats righthanded.

Led Carolina League in total bases with 271 in 1986.
Led South Atlantic League second basemen in double plays with 75 in 1984.

Year	Club	League	Pos.	G.	AB.	R.	H.	2B.	3B.	HR.	RBI.	B.A.	PO.	A.	E.	F.A.
1983—Bradenton Brav.	Gulf C.	SS	56	193	32	45	2	2	1	14	.233	68	134	22	.902
1984—Anderson	S. Atl.	2B	105	359	44	85	14	6	3	38	.237	248	263	31	.943
1985—Sumter	S. Atl.	2B-SS	102	305	46	78	14	4	7	37	.256	160	200	10	.973
1986—Durham	Carol.	2B	137	512	108	142	31	10	★26	102	.277	240	384	26	.960

Selected by Atlanta Braves' organization in 4th round of free-agent draft, June 6, 1983.

JAMES ELMER GANTNER

(Jim)

Born January 5, 1954, at Fond du Lac, Wis.
Height, 5.11. Weight, 175.
Throws right and bats lefthanded.
Attended University of Wisconsin, Oshkosh, Wis.

Tied major league record for longest errorless game by second baseman (25 innings), May 8, finished May 9, 1984; fielded 24⅓ innings.
Tied American League record for most innings played by second baseman, game (25), May 8, finished May 9, 1984; fielded 24⅓ innings.
Major League stolen bases: 1976 (1), 1977 (2), 1978 (2), 1979 (3), 1980 (11), 1981 (3), 1982 (6), 1983 (5), 1984 (6), 1985 (11), 1986 (13). Total—63.
Led American League second basemen in total chances with 613 in 1981, 900 in 1983 and 844 in 1984.
Led American League second basemen in double plays with 95 in 1981 and 128 in 1983.
Led Pacific Coast League third basemen in putouts with 136 and in fielding percentage with .936 in 1977.
Led Eastern League third basemen in fielding percentage with .953 in 1976.
Led Eastern League third basemen in putouts with 118 and assists with 310 in 1975.

Year	Club	League	Pos.	G.	AB.	R.	H.	2B.	3B.	HR.	RBI.	B.A.	PO.	A.	E.	F.A.
1974—Newark	NYP	SS-3B	62	177	35	54	6	2	5	21	.305	64	134	14	.934
1975—Thetford Mines	East.	3B-SS	●138	456	61	117	17	0	12	48	.257	129	317	33	.931
1976—Berkshire	East.	3B-SS	126	403	56	118	21	1	6	53	.293	120	294	20	.954
1976—Milwaukee	Amer.	3B	26	69	6	17	1	0	0	7	.246	17	37	1	.982
1977—Spokane	P. C.	★3B-OF	●143	541	98	152	35	5	15	80	.281	137	★321	31	.937
1977—Milwaukee	Amer.	3B	14	47	4	14	1	0	1	2	.298	8	29	4	.902
1978—Milwaukee	Amer.	2-3-S-1	43	97	14	21	1	0	1	8	.216	46	82	5	.962
1979—Milwaukee	Amer.	3-2-S-P	70	208	29	59	10	3	2	22	.284	80	161	7	.972
1980—Milwaukee	Amer.	3B-2B-SS	132	415	47	117	21	3	4	40	.282	159	335	15	.971
1981—Milwaukee	Amer.	2B	107	352	35	94	14	1	2	33	.267	251	352	10	.984
1982—Milwaukee	Amer.	2B	132	447	48	132	17	2	4	43	.295	307	398	13	.982
1983—Milwaukee	Amer.	2B	161	603	85	170	23	8	11	74	.282	374	★512	14	.984
1984—Milwaukee	Amer.	2B	153	613	61	173	27	1	3	56	.282	★362	469	13	.985
1985—Milwaukee	Amer.	2B-3B-SS	143	523	63	133	15	4	5	44	.254	278	436	11	.985
1986—Milwaukee	Amer.	2B-3B-SS	139	497	58	136	25	1	7	38	.274	309	353	10	.985
Major League Totals—11 Years			1120	3871	450	1066	155	23	40	367	.275	2191	3164	103	.981

Selected by Milwaukee Brewers' organization in 12th round of free-agent draft, June 5, 1974.

Year	Club	League	Pos.	G.	AB.	R.	H.	2B.	3B.	HR.	RBI.	B.A.	PO.	A.	E.	F.A.
1981—Milwaukee		Amer.	2B	4	14	1	2	1	0	0	0	.143	3	15	2	.900

CHAMPIONSHIP SERIES RECORD

Year	Club	League	Pos.	G.	AB.	R.	H.	2B.	3B.	HR.	RBI.	B.A.	PO.	A.	E.	F.A.
1982—Milwaukee		Amer.	2B	5	16	1	3	0	0	0	2	.188	12	8	0	1.000

WORLD SERIES RECORD

Established World Series records for most assists by second baseman, seven-game Series (33), 1982; most errors by second baseman, seven-game Series (5), 1982.

Year	Club	League	Pos.	G.	AB.	R.	H.	2B.	3B.	HR.	RBI.	B.A.	PO.	A.	E.	F.A.
1982—Milwaukee		Amer.	2B	7	24	5	8	4	1	0	4	.333	9	33	5	.894

PITCHING RECORD

Year	Club	League	G.	IP.	W.	L.	Pct.	H.	R.	ER.	SO.	BB.	ERA.
1979—Milwaukee		American	1	1	0	0	.000	2	0	0	0	0	0.00

HENRY EUGENE GARBER
(Gene)

Born November 13, 1947, at Lancaster, Pa.
Height, 5.10. Weight, 172.
Throws and bats righthanded.
Received bachelor of arts degree in history and political science from
Elizabethtown College, Elizabethtown, Pa. in 1969.

Established major league record for most games lost by relief pitcher, season (16), 1979.
Tied major league record for most consecutive games won by relief pitcher, three consecutive games (3), May 15 through 17, 1975.
Major League saves: 1973 (11), 1974 (5), 1975 (14), 1976 (11), 1977 (19), 1978 (25), 1979 (25), 1980 (7), 1981 (2), 1982 (30), 1983 (9), 1984 (11), 1985 (1), 1986 (24). Total—194.
Led National League in games finished in relief with 47 in 1975.
Tied for International League lead in complete games with 13 in 1972.
Named International League Pitcher of the Year, 1972.

Year	Club	League	G.	IP.	W.	L.	Pct.	H.	R.	ER.	SO.	BB.	ERA.
1965—Salem		Ap'lachian	1	⅔	0	0	.000	0	0	0	2	2	0.00
1965—Batavia		NYP	11	72	4	3	.571	71	42	28	40	31	3.50
1966—Raleigh		Carolina	16	94	4	4	.500	106	53	48	76	28	4.60
1967—Raleigh		Carolina	18	138	8	6	.571	103	41	29	68	47	1.89
1968—York		Eastern	16	118	7	2	.778	79	33	21	86	30	1.60
1968—Columbus		Int'national	23	59	5	1	.833	62	21	16	32	17	2.44
1969—York		Eastern	11	73	5	3	.625	61	40	25	57	40	3.08
1969—Pittsburgh		National	2	5	0	0	.000	6	3	3	3	1	5.40
1969—Columbus†		Int'national	17	123	7	6	.538	116	51	42	74	37	3.07
1970—Columbus		Int'national	30	95	5	2	.714	96	57	50	75	38	4.74
1970—Pittsburgh		National	14	22	0	3	.000	22	13	13	7	10	5.32
1971—Charleston‡		Int'national	24	170	14	6	.700	★184	85	79	105	54	4.18
1972—Charleston		Int'national	20	163	14	3	★.824	131	49	41	103	45	★2.26
1972—Pittsburgh§		National	4	6	0	0	.000	7	5	5	3	3	7.50
1973—Kansas City		American	48	153	9	9	.500	164	78	72	60	49	4.24
1974—Kansas City x		American	17	28	1	2	.333	35	21	15	14	13	4.82
1974—Toledo		Int'national	3	22	2	1	.667	19	7	1	17	3	0.41
1974—Philadelphia		National	34	48	4	0	1.000	39	15	11	27	31	2.06
1975—Philadelphia		National	★71	110	10	12	.455	104	48	44	69	27	3.60
1976—Philadelphia		National	59	93	9	3	.750	78	33	29	92	30	2.81
1977—Philadelphia		National	64	103	8	6	.571	82	30	27	78	23	2.36
1978—Philadelphia y-Atlanta		National	65	117	6	5	.545	84	32	28	85	24	2.15
1979—Atlanta		National	68	106	6	16	.273	121	66	51	56	24	4.33
1980—Atlanta		National	68	82	5	5	.500	95	42	35	51	24	3.84
1981—Atlanta z		National	35	59	4	6	.400	49	23	17	34	20	2.59
1982—Atlanta		National	69	119⅓	8	10	.444	100	40	31	68	32	2.34
1983—Atlanta a		National	43	60⅔	4	5	.444	72	37	31	45	23	4.60
1984—Atlanta		National	62	106	3	6	.333	103	45	36	55	24	3.06
1985—Atlanta		National	59	97⅓	6	6	.500	98	41	39	66	25	3.61
1986—Atlanta		National	61	78	5	5	.500	76	23	22	56	20	2.54
American League Totals—2 Years			65	181	10	11	.476	199	99	87	74	62	4.33
National League Totals—16 Years			778	1212⅓	78	88	.470	1136	496	422	795	341	3.13
Major League Totals—17 Years			843	1393⅓	88	99	.471	1335	595	509	869	403	3.29

Selected by Pittsburgh Pirates' organization in 13th round of free-agent draft, June 14, 1965.
†On military list, September 2, 1969, through February 18, 1970.
‡On temporary inactive list, June 24 to July 12, 1971.
§Traded to Kansas City Royals for Pitcher Jim Rooker, October 25, 1972.
xSold to Philadelphia Phillies, July 12, 1974.
yTraded to Atlanta Braves for Pitcher Dick Ruthven, June 15, 1978.
zOn disabled list, May 4 to August 9, 1981.
aOn disabled list, June 25 to July 27, 1983.

CHAMPIONSHIP SERIES RECORD

Year	Club	League	G.	IP.	W.	L.	Pct.	H.	R.	ER.	SO.	BB.	ERA.
1976—Philadelphia		National	2	⅔	0	1	.000	2	2	1	0	1	13.50

Year Club	League	G.	IP.	W.	L.	Pct.	H.	R.	ER.	SO.	BB.	ERA.
1977—Philadelphia	National	3	5⅓	1	1	.500	4	3	2	3	0	3.38
1982—Atlanta	National	2	3⅓	0	1	.000	4	3	3	3	1	8.10
Championship Series Totals—3 Years		7	9⅓	1	3	.250	10	8	6	6	2	5.79

DAMASO DOMINGO GARCIA

First name pronounced Da-MAH-so.

Born February 7, 1957, at Moca, Dominican Republic.
Height, 6.00. Weight, 175.
Throws and bats righthanded.
Attended Madre y Maestra University, Santiago, Dominican Republic.

Major League stolen bases: 1978 (1), 1979 (2), 1980 (13), 1981 (13), 1982 (54), 1983 (31), 1984 (46), 1985 (28), 1986 (9). Total—197.

Tied major league record for most doubles, game (4), June 27, 1986.
Led Florida State League second baseman in double plays with 83 in 1976.
Tied for New York-Pennsylvania League lead in double plays by second basemen with 33 in 1975.
Named second baseman on THE SPORTING NEWS American League All-Star Team, 1982 and 1985.
Named second baseman on THE SPORTING NEWS American League Silver Slugger team, 1982.

Year Club	League	Pos.	G.	AB.	R.	H.	2B.	3B.	HR.	RBI.	B.A.	PO.	A.	E.	F.A.
1975—Oneonta	NYP	2B	50	157	28	42	4	2	0	17	.268	103	118	★17	.929
1976—Fort Lauderdale†	Fla.St.	2B	124	412	55	109	●22	4	1	41	.265	★273	353	21	★.968
1977—West Haven	East.	2B	129	445	62	118	13	9	0	53	.265	263	382	19	.971
1978—Tacoma	P. C.	2B-SS	102	385	51	103	18	6	1	53	.268	217	345	25	.957
1978—New York	Amer.	2B-SS	18	41	5	8	0	0	0	1	.195	36	35	4	.947
1979—Columbus ‡	Int.	SS-1B	39	118	18	32	1	0	1	3	.271	53	85	6	.958
1979—New York §	Amer.	SS-3B	11	38	3	10	1	0	0	4	.263	9	28	4	.902
1980—Toronto	Amer.	2B	140	543	50	151	30	7	4	46	.278	316	471	16	.980
1981—Toronto x	Amer.	2B	64	250	24	63	8	1	1	13	.252	132	181	9	.972
1982—Toronto	Amer.	2B	147	597	89	185	32	3	5	42	.310	273	461	15	.980
1983—Toronto	Amer.	2B	131	525	84	161	23	6	3	38	.307	266	360	12	.981
1984—Toronto	Amer.	2B	152	633	79	180	32	5	5	46	.284	267	427	14	.980
1985—Toronto	Amer.	2B	146	600	70	169	25	4	8	65	.282	302	371	13	.981
1986—Toronto	Amer.	2B-1B	122	424	57	119	22	0	6	46	.281	225	286	8	.985
Major League Totals—9 Years			931	3651	461	1046	173	26	32	301	.286	1826	2620	95	.979

Signed as free agent by New York Yankees' organization, March 10, 1975.
†On suspended list, June 4 to June 7, 1976.
‡On disabled list, May 14 to July 24 and July 31 to August 13, 1979.
§Traded with First Baseman Chris Chambliss and Pitcher Paul Mirabella to Toronto Blue Jays for Catcher Rick Cerone, Pitcher Tom Underwood and Outfielder Ted Wilborn, November 1, 1979.
xOn disabled list, August 22, 1981 through remainder of season.

CHAMPIONSHIP SERIES RECORD

Established American League Championship Series record for most doubles, seven-game Series (4), 1985.

Year Club	League	Pos.	G.	AB.	R.	H.	2B.	3B.	HR.	RBI.	B.A.	PO.	A.	E.	F.A.
1985—Toronto	Amer.	2B	7	30	4	7	4	0	0	1	.233	10	12	0	1.000

ALL-STAR GAME RECORD

Year League	Pos.	AB.	R.	H.	2B.	3B.	HR.	RBI.	B.A.	PO.	A.	E.	F.A.
1984—American	2B	1	0	0	0	0	0	0	.000	1	0	0	1.000
1985—American	2B	2	0	1	0	0	0	0	.500	0	3	0	1.000
All-Star Game Totals—2 Years		3	0	1	0	0	0	0	.333	1	3	0	1.000

LEONARDO ANTONIO GARCIA
(Leo)

Born November 6, 1962, at Santiago, D. R.
Height, 5.08. Weight, 160.
Throws and bats lefthanded.

Year Club	League	Pos.	G.	AB.	R.	H.	2B.	3B.	HR.	RBI.	B.A.	PO.	A.	E.	F.A.
1980—Sarasota W.S.	Gulf C.	OF	32	108	8	26	0	0	0	7	.241	60	3	2	.969
1981—Appleton†	Midw.	OF	107	395	55	103	14	6	1	38	.261	192	13	11	.949
1982—Appleton‡	Midw.	OF	117	435	56	115	17	6	2	37	.264	207	15	10	.957
1983—Waterbury	East.	OF	131	498	65	128	25	★11	5	47	.257	233	13	5	.980
1984—Wichita	A. A.	OF	117	336	47	95	12	6	3	39	.283	147	13	3	.982
1985—Denver	A. A.	OF	118	385	53	112	19	3	4	25	.291	198	14	★11	.951
1986—Denver	A. A.	OF	139	528	81	147	32	6	4	57	.278	317	10	6	.982

Signed as free agent by Chicago White Sox' organization after Inter-American League folded, January 26, 1980.
†On disabled list, July 6 to July 21, 1981.
‡Traded with Third Baseman Wade Rowdon to Cincinnati Reds' organization, September 7, 1982, completing deal in which Cincinnati traded Pitcher Jim Kern to Chicago White Sox for two players to be named later, August 23, 1982.

SANTIAGO GARCIA

Born December 8, 1965, at Barrio Filipina, D. R.
Height, 6.00. Weight, 165.
Throws and bats righthanded.

Led Gulf Coast League shortstops in putouts with 85, assists with 205, double plays with 30 and total chances with 323 in 1984.

Year—Club	League	Pos.	G.	AB.	R.	H.	2B.	3B.	HR.	RBI.	B.A.	PO.	A.	E.	F.A.
1984—Bradenton Jays....	Gulf C.	SS-2B-3B	58	210	31	58	12	0	0	25	.276	104	237	41	.893
1985—Florence	S. Atl.	SS	128	514	86	153	*35	2	8	79	.298	165	390	*59	.904
1986—Ventura†	Calif.	2B	105	405	78	124	25	3	9	61	.306	205	277	24	.953

Signed as free agent by Toronto Blue Jays' organization, September 5, 1983.

†On disabled list, April 11 to May 6, 1986.

RONALD CLYDE GARDENHIRE
(Ron)

Born October 24, 1957, at Butzbach, Germany.
Height, 6.00. Weight, 174.
Throws and bats righthanded.
Attended Paris Junior College, Paris, Tex., and University of Texas, Austin, Tex.

Major League stolen bases: 1981 (2), 1982 (5), 1984 (6). Total—13.

Led Texas League shortstops in assists with 406 and errors with 40 in 1980.

Year—Club	League	Pos.	G.	AB.	R.	H.	2B.	3B.	HR.	RBI.	B.A.	PO.	A.	E.	F.A.
1979—Lynchburg	Carol.	SS	70	277	36	82	13	3	4	27	.296	120	252	21	.947
1980—Jackson	Texas	SS-2B	127	458	58	118	16	6	6	64	.258	168	411	41	.934
1981—Tidewater	Int.	SS-2B-3B	125	414	52	105	17	8	2	40	.254	206	373	33	.946
1981—New York	Nat.	SS-2B-3B	27	48	2	13	1	0	0	3	.271	28	50	2	.975
1982—New York	Nat.	SS-2B-3B	141	384	29	92	17	1	3	33	.240	235	399	29	.956
1983—New York	Nat.	SS	17	32	1	2	0	0	0	1	.063	13	30	0	1.000
1983—Tidewater†	Int.	SS	102	387	63	111	20	6	4	39	.287	202	321	27	.951
1984—New York‡	Nat.	SS-2B-3B	74	207	20	51	7	1	1	10	.246	98	154	12	.955
1985—New York§	Nat.	SS-2B-3B	26	39	5	7	2	1	0	2	.179	21	32	4	.930
1985—Tidewater	Int.	3B-SS-2B	22	71	3	15	2	0	1	10	.211	20	36	5	.918
1986—Tidewater x	Int.	2B-SS	96	323	41	89	10	4	4	33	.276	161	288	19	.959
Major League Totals—5 Years			285	710	57	165	27	3	4	49	.232	395	665	47	.958

Selected by New York Mets' organization in 6th round of free-agent draft, June 5, 1979.

†On disabled list, July 21 to July 31, 1983.

‡On disabled list, July 20 to August 9 and August 20 to September 10, 1984.

§On disabled list, May 2 to May 17, May 25 to July 19 and August 16 to September 1, 1985; included rehabilitation disability assignment to Tidewater, June 25 to July 13, 1985.

xTraded to Minnesota Twins for a player to be named later, November 12, 1986.

WESLEY BRIAN GARDNER
(Wes)

Born April 29, 1961, at Benton, Ark.
Height, 6.04. Weight, 197.
Throws and bats righthanded.
Attended University of Central Arkansas, Conway, Ark.

Major League saves: 1984 (1).

Led International League in saves with 20 in 1984 and tied for lead with 18 in 1985.

Led International League in games finished in relief with 37 in 1984.

Year—Club	League	G.	IP.	W.	L.	Pct.	H.	R.	ER.	SO.	BB.	ERA.
1982—Little Falls	NYP	23	77⅔	3	6	.333	73	48	32	77	29	3.71
1983—Lynchburg	Carolina	49	62⅔	6	3	.667	55	16	13	67	32	1.87
1984—Tidewater	Int'national	40	56	1	2	.333	40	11	10	36	19	1.61
1984—New York	National	21	25⅓	1	1	.500	34	19	18	19	8	6.39
1985—Tidewater	Int'national	53	76⅔	7	6	.538	57	31	24	75	34	2.82
1985—New York†	National	9	12	0	2	.000	18	14	7	11	8	5.25
1986—Boston‡	American	1	1	0	0	.000	1	1	1	1	0	9.00
National League Totals—2 Years		30	37⅓	1	3	.250	52	33	25	30	16	6.03
American League Totals—1 Year		1	1	0	0	.000	1	1	1	1	0	9.00
Major League Totals—3 Years		31	38⅓	1	3	.250	53	34	26	31	16	6.10

Selected by New York Mets' organization in 22nd round of free-agent draft, June 7, 1982.

†Traded with Pitcher Calvin Schiraldi and Outfielders John Christensen and LaSchelle Tarver to Boston Red Sox for Pitchers Bob Ojeda, Tom McCarthy, John Mitchell and Chris Bayer, November 13, 1985.

‡On disabled list, April 14, 1986 through remainder of season; included rehabilitation disability assignment to Pawtucket, June 24 to July 1, 1986.

PHILIP MASON GARNER
(Phil)

Born April 30, 1949, at Jefferson City, Tenn.
Height, 5.10. Weight, 177.
Throws and bats righthanded.
Received bachelor of science degree in general business from
University of Tennessee, Knoxville, Tenn., in 1973.

Tied major league record for most home runs, bases filled, two consecutive games (2), September 14 and 15, 1978.

Tied National League record for most home runs, bases filled, month (2), September, 1978.

Major League stolen bases: 1974 (1), 1975 (4), 1976 (35), 1977 (32), 1978 (27), 1979 (17), 1980 (32), 1981 (10), 1982 (24), 1983 (18), 1984 (3), 1985 (4), 1986 (12). Total—219.

Led American League second basemen in total chances with 865 in 1976.

Led National League second basemen in assists with 499, total chances with 869 and double plays with 116 in 1980.

Led Pacific Coast League third basemen in putouts with 104, assists with 261 and double plays with 23 in 1973.

Year Club	League	Pos.	G.	AB.	R.	H.	2B.	3B.	HR.	RBI.	B.A.	PO.	A.	E.	F.A.
1971—Burlington	Midw.	3B	116	439	73	122	22	4	11	70	.278	*122	203	29	.918
1972—Birmingham	South.	3B	71	264	45	74	10	6	12	40	.280	74	116	13	.936
1972—Iowa	A. A.	3B	70	247	33	60	18	4	9	22	.243	50	140	10	.950
1973—Tucson	P. C.	*3B-2B	138	516	87	149	23	12	14	73	.289	107	270	*35	.915
1973—Oakland	Amer.	3B	9	5	0	0	0	0	0	0	.000	2	3	0	1.000
1974—Tucson	P. C.	3B-SS	96	388	78	128	29	10	11	51	.330	92	182	15	.948
1974—Oakland	Amer.	3B-SS-2B	30	28	4	5	1	0	0	1	.179	11	24	1	.972
1975—Oakland	Amer.	*2B-SS	•160	488	46	120	21	5	6	54	.246	355	427	*26	.968
1976—Oakland†	Amer.	2B	159	555	54	145	29	12	8	74	.261	378	*465	22	.975
1977—Pittsburgh	Nat.	3B-2B-SS	153	585	99	152	35	10	17	77	.260	223	351	17	.971
1978—Pittsburgh	Nat.	3B-2B-SS	154	528	66	138	25	9	10	66	.261	258	389	28	.959
1979—Pittsburgh	Nat.	3B-2B-SS	150	549	76	161	32	8	11	59	.293	234	396	22	.966
1980—Pittsburgh	Nat.	*2B-SS	151	548	62	142	27	6	5	58	.259	349	500	*21	.976
1981—Pitt‡§-Hou.	Nat.	2B	87	294	35	73	9	3	1	26	.248	183	250	12	.973
1982—Houston	Nat.	2B-3B	155	588	65	161	33	8	13	83	.274	285	464	17	.978
1983—Houston	Nat.	2B	154	567	76	135	24	2	14	79	.238	100	311	24	.945
1984—Houston	Nat.	3B-2B	128	374	60	104	17	6	4	45	.278	136	251	12	.970
1985—Houston	Nat.	3B-2B	135	463	65	124	23	10	6	51	.268	101	229	21	.940
1986—Houston x	Nat.	3B-2B	107	313	43	83	14	3	9	41	.265	66	152	23	.905
American League Totals—4 Years			358	1076	104	270	51	17	14	129	.251	746	919	49	.971
National League Totals—10 Years			1374	4809	647	1273	239	65	90	585	.265	1935	3293	197	.964
Major League Totals—14 Years			1732	5885	751	1543	290	82	104	714	.262	2681	4212	246	.966

Selected by Montreal Expos' organization in 8th round of free-agent draft, June 4, 1970.
Selected by Oakland A's organization in secondary phase of free-agent draft, January 13, 1971.
†Traded with Infielder Tommy Helms and Pitcher Chris Batton to Pittsburgh Pirates for Pitchers Doc Medich, Dave Giusti, Rick Langford and Doug Bair and Outfielders Mitchell Page and Tony Armas, March 15, 1977.
‡On disabled list, April 2 to April 23, 1981.
§Traded to Houston Astros for Second Baseman Johnny Ray and two players to be named later, August 31, 1981; Pittsburgh Pirates' organization acquired Outfielder Kevin Houston and Pitcher Randy Niemann to complete deal, September 9, 1981.
xGranted free agency, November 12, 1986.

DIVISION SERIES RECORD

Year Club	League	Pos.	G.	AB.	R.	H.	2B.	3B.	HR.	RBI.	B.A.	PO.	A.	E.	F.A.
1981—Houston	Nat.	2B	5	18	1	2	0	0	0	0	.111	6	8	1	.933

CHAMPIONSHIP SERIES RECORD

Tied Championship Series record for most clubs, total Series (3).

Year Club	League	Pos.	G.	AB.	R.	H.	2B.	3B.	HR.	RBI.	B.A.	PO.	A.	E.	F.A.
1975—Oakland	Amer.	2B	3	5	0	0	0	0	0	0	.000	7	4	1	.917
1979—Pittsburgh	Nat.	2B-SS	3	12	4	5	0	1	1	1	.417	8	9	0	1.000
1986—Houston	Nat.	3B	3	9	1	2	1	0	0	2	.222	1	9	0	1.000
Championship Series Totals—3 Years			9	26	5	7	1	1	1	3	.269	16	22	1	.974

WORLD SERIES RECORD

Established World Series record for most double plays by second baseman, seven-game Series (9), 1979.
Tied World Series records for highest batting average, seven-game Series (.500), 1979; one or more hits, each game, seven-game Series, 1979; most assists by second baseman, inning (3), October 13, 1979 (ninth inning).

Year Club	League	Pos.	G.	AB.	R.	H.	2B.	3B.	HR.	RBI.	B.A.	PO.	A.	E.	F.A.
1979—Pittsburgh	Nat.	2B	7	24	4	12	4	0	0	5	.500	21	23	2	.957

ALL-STAR GAME RECORD

Year League	Pos.	AB.	R.	H.	2B.	3B.	HR.	RBI.	B.A.	PO.	A.	E.	F.A.
1976—American	2B	1	0	0	0	0	0	0	.000	1	1	0	1.000
1980—National	2B	2	1	1	0	0	0	0	.500	1	3	0	1.000
1981—National	2B	0	0	0	0	0	0	0	.000	0	0	0	.000
All-Star Game Totals—3 Years		3	1	1	0	0	0	0	.333	2	4	0	1.000

SCOTT WILLIAM GARRELTS
Name pronounced Guh-RELTZ.

Born October 30, 1961, at Urbana, Ill.
Height, 6.04. Weight, 195.
Throws and bats righthanded.

Pitched seven-inning, 1-0 no-hit victory against Tacoma, August 20, 1983.
Major League saves: 1985 (13), 1986 (10). Total—23.
Tied for Midwest League lead in games started by pitchers with 27 in 1980.

Year Club	League	G.	IP.	W.	L.	Pct.	H.	R.	ER.	SO.	BB.	ERA.
1979—Great Falls	Pioneer	8	43	1	4	.200	45	37	28	26	40	5.86
1980—Clinton	Midwest	27	176	11	11	.500	155	98	76	*159	*149	3.89
1981—Shreveport†	Texas	14	71	3	8	.273	56	43	35	73	43	4.44
1982—Shreveport	Texas	27	151⅓	9	10	.474	131	76	64	159	90	3.81
1982—San Francisco	National	1	2	0	0	.000	3	3	3	4	2	13.50
1983—Phoenix‡	P. Coast	21	97⅔	5	5	.500	86	64	50	89	81	4.61
1983—San Francisco	National	5	35⅔	2	2	.500	33	11	10	16	19	2.52
1984—Phoenix	P. Coast	21	97⅔	5	7	.417	97	75	64	69	82	5.90
1984—San Francisco	National	21	43	2	3	.400	45	33	27	32	34	5.65

Year	Club	League	G.	IP.	W.	L.	Pct.	H.	R.	ER.	SO.	BB.	ERA.
1985—San Francisco	National		74	105⅔	9	6	.600	76	37	27	106	58	2.30
1986—San Francisco	National		53	173⅔	13	9	.591	144	65	60	125	74	3.11
Major League Totals—5 Years			154	360	26	20	.565	301	149	127	283	187	3.18

Selected by San Francisco Giants' organization in 1st round (15th player selected) of free-agent draft, June 5, 1979.

†On disabled list, July 15 to August 16, 1981.

‡On disabled list, May 12 to June 6 and July 8 to July 24, 1983.

ALL-STAR GAME RECORD

Member of National League All-Star Team in 1985; did not play.

STEVEN PATRICK GARVEY
(Steve)

Born December 22, 1948, at Tampa, Fla.
Height, 5.10. Weight, 190.
Throws and bats righthanded.
Received bachelor of science degree in education from
Michigan State University, East Lansing, Mich. in 1971.

Established major league records for most seasons leading league in games by first baseman (9); highest fielding percentage by first baseman, season, 100 and 150 or more games (1.000), 1984; fewest errors by first baseman, season, 150 or more games (0), 1984; highest lifetime fielding percentage by first baseman (.996); most consecutive errorless games by first baseman, season (159), April 3 through September 29, 1984; most consecutive errorless games by first baseman, lifetime (193), June 26, second game, 1983 through April 14, 1985; most consecutive chances accepted, season, no errors, by first baseman (1,319), April 3 through September 29, 1984.

Tied major league records for most games, first baseman, season (162), 1976, 1979, 1980 and 1985; most unassisted double plays, first baseman, game (2), August 31, 1976; most long hits, consecutive, game (5), August 28, 1977; most long hits, game (5), August 28, 1977.

Established National League records for most consecutive years playing in all clubs' games (7); most consecutive games played (1,207); most consecutive chances accepted, lifetime, no errors, by first baseman (1,633), June 26, first game, 1983, through April 15, 1985.

Tied National League records for most long hits, consecutive, season (5), August 28, 1977; most years leading league in games played (6).

Major league stolen bases: 1970 (1), 1971 (1), 1972 (4), 1974 (5), 1975 (11), 1976 (19), 1977 (9), 1978 (10), 1979 (3), 1980 (6), 1981 (3), 1982 (5), 1983 (4), 1984 (1), 1986 (1). Total—83.

Led National League in grounding into double plays with 25 in 1979 and 1984.

Tied for National League lead in sacrifice flies with 10 in 1984.

Led National League first basemen in double plays with 138 in 1985.

Led National League first basemen in total chances with 1,606 in 1974, 1,585 in 1975, 1,669 in 1977, 1,629 in 1978 and 1,539 in 1985.

Led Pacific Coast League third basemen in errors with 24 in 1970.

Led Pioneer League in total bases with 151 and tied for league lead in sacrifice flies with 4 in 1968.

Led Pioneer League third basemen in double plays with 10 in 1968.

Named National League Most Valuable Player by Baseball Writers' Association of America, 1974.

Named first baseman on THE SPORTING NEWS National League All-Star Team, 1974, 1975, 1977 and 1978.

Named first baseman on THE SPORTING NEWS National League All-Star fielding team, 1974 through 1977.

Named third baseman on THE SPORTING NEWS College Baseball All-America Team, 1968.

Year	Club	League	Pos.	G.	AB.	R.	H.	2B.	3B.	HR.	RBI.	B.A.	PO.	A.	E.	F.A.
1968—Ogden	Pion.		3B	62	216	49	73	12	3	★20	★59	.338	★51	★109	★23	.874
1969—Albuquerque	Texas		3B-1B	83	316	51	118	18	2	14	85	.373	348	86	20	.956
1969—Los Angeles	Nat.		PH	3	3	0	1	0	0	0	0	.333	0	0	0	.000
1970—Spokane	P. C.		3B-2B-OF	95	376	71	120	26	5	15	87	.319	103	178	26	.915
1970—Los Angeles	Nat.		3B-2B	34	93	8	25	5	0	1	6	.269	23	59	5	.943
1971—Los Angeles†	Nat.		3B	81	225	27	51	12	1	7	26	.227	53	161	14	.939
1972—Los Angeles	Nat.		★3B-1B	96	294	36	79	14	2	9	30	.269	104	189	★28	.913
1973—Los Angeles	Nat.		1B-OF	114	349	37	106	17	3	8	50	.304	731	27	7	.991
1974—Los Angeles	Nat.		1B	156	642	95	200	32	3	21	111	.312	★1536	62	8	.995
1975—Los Angeles	Nat.		1B	160	659	85	210	38	6	18	95	.319	★1500	77	8	★.995
1976—Los Angeles	Nat.		1B	162	631	85	200	37	4	13	80	.317	★1583	67	3	★.998
1977—Los Angeles	Nat.		1B	●162	646	91	192	25	3	33	115	.297	★1606	55	8	★.995
1978—Los Angeles	Nat.		1B	●162	639	89	★202	36	9	21	113	.316	★1546	74	9	.994
1979—Los Angeles	Nat.		1B	162	648	92	204	32	1	28	110	.315	1402	93	7	.995
1980—Los Angeles	Nat.		1B	★163	658	78	★200	27	1	26	106	.304	1502	112	6	.996
1981—Los Angeles	Nat.		1B	●110	431	63	122	23	1	10	64	.283	1019	55	1	★.999
1982—Los Angeles‡	Nat.		1B	●162	625	66	176	35	1	16	86	.282	1539	111	8	.995
1983—San Diego§	Nat.		1B	100	388	76	114	22	0	14	59	.294	888	49	6	.994
1984—San Diego	Nat.		1B	161	617	72	175	27	2	8	86	.284	1232	87	0	★1.000
1985—San Diego	Nat.		1B	●162	654	80	184	34	6	17	81	.281	★1442	92	5	.997
1986—San Diego	Nat.		1B	155	557	58	142	22	0	21	81	.255	1160	53	7	.994
Major League Totals—18 Years				2305	8759	1138	2583	438	43	271	1299	.295	18866	1423	130	.994

Selected by Minnesota Twins' organization in 3rd round of free-agent draft, June, 1966.

Selected by Los Angeles Dodgers' organization in secondary phase of free-agent draft, June 7, 1968.

†On disabled list, June 23 to July 26, 1971.

‡Granted free agency, November 10, 1982; signed by San Diego Padres, December 21, 1982.

§On disabled list, July 30, 1983 through remainder of season.

DIVISION SERIES RECORD

Year	Club	League	Pos.	G.	AB.	R.	H.	2B.	3B.	HR.	RBI.	B.A.	PO.	A.	E.	F.A.
1981—Los Angeles	Nat.		1B	5	19	4	7	0	1	2	4	.368	49	5	0	1.000

CHAMPIONSHIP SERIES RECORD

Established Championship Series records for most consecutive hits, total Series (6); most long hits, Series (6), 1978; most total bases, four-game Series (22), 1978; most runs batted in, total Series (21).

Tied Championship Series records for most home runs, four-game Series (4), 1978; most runs, game (4), October 9, 1974; most Series, two or more home runs (2); most runs batted in, game (5), October 6, 1984.

Established National League Championship Series records for most runs, four-game Series (6), 1978; highest slugging average, total Series, 10 or more games and 30 or more at bats (.678); most home runs, total Series (8); most runs batted in, five-game Series (7), 1984; most long hits, total Series (12).

Tied National League Championship Series record for most hits, game (4), October 9, 1974 and October 6, 1984.

Year Club League	Pos.	G.	AB.	R.	H.	2B.	3B.	HR.	RBI.	B.A.	PO.	A.	E.	F.A.
1974—Los Angeles .... Nat.	1B	4	18	4	7	1	0	2	5	.389	40	2	1	.977
1977—Los Angeles .... Nat.	1B	4	13	2	4	0	0	0	0	.308	40	1	0	1.000
1978—Los Angeles .... Nat.	1B	4	18	6	7	1	1	4	7	.389	44	5	0	1.000
1981—Los Angeles .... Nat.	1B	5	21	2	6	0	0	1	2	.286	49	2	0	1.000
1984—San Diego .... Nat.	1B	5	20	1	8	1	0	1	7	.400	35	3	0	1.000
Championship Series Totals—5 Years....		22	90	15	32	3	1	8	21	.356	208	13	1	.995

WORLD SERIES RECORD

Tied World Series record for most unassisted double plays by first baseman, game (1), October 9, 1984.

Tied World Series record for most singles, five-game Series, (8), 1974; one or more hits, each game, five-game Series, 1974.

Year Club League	Pos.	G.	AB.	R.	H.	2B.	3B.	HR.	RBI.	B.A.	PO.	A.	E.	F.A.
1974—Los Angeles .... Nat.	1B	5	21	2	8	0	0	0	1	.381	34	3	0	1.000
1977—Los Angeles .... Nat.	1B	6	24	5	9	1	1	1	3	.375	59	6	0	1.000
1978—Los Angeles .... Nat.	1B	6	24	1	5	1	0	0	0	.208	58	3	1	.984
1981—Los Angeles .... Nat.	1B	6	24	3	10	1	0	0	0	.417	44	3	0	1.000
1984—San Diego .... Nat.	1B	5	20	2	4	2	0	0	2	.200	34	3	0	1.000
World Series Totals—5 Years		28	113	13	36	5	1	1	6	.319	229	18	1	.996

ALL-STAR GAME RECORD

Tied All-Star game record for most games played at first base (8).

Year League	Pos.	AB.	R.	H.	2B.	3B.	HR.	RBI.	B.A.	PO.	A.	E.	F.A.
1974—National	1B	4	1	2	1	0	0	1	.500	6	2	0	1.000
1975—National	1B	3	1	2	0	0	1	1	.667	4	1	0	1.000
1976—National	1B	3	1	1	0	1	0	1	.333	6	0	0	1.000
1977—National	1B	3	1	1	0	0	1	1	.333	1	0	0	1.000
1978—National	1B	3	1	2	0	1	0	2	.667	7	1	0	1.000
1979—National	1B	2	1	0	0	0	0	0	.000	5	0	0	1.000
1980—National	1B	2	0	0	0	0	0	0	.000	7	0	0	1.000
1981—National	1B	2	0	1	1	0	0	0	.500	3	1	0	1.000
1984—National	1B	3	1	1	0	0	0	0	.333	5	1	0	1.000
1985—National	1B	3	0	1	0	0	0	1	.333	5	0	0	1.000
All-Star Game Totals—10 Years		28	7	11	2	2	2	7	.393	49	6	0	1.000

RICHARD LEO GEDMAN JR.
(Rich)

Born September 26, 1959, at Worcester, Mass.
Height, 6.00. Weight, 215.
Throws right and bats lefthanded.

Established major league records for most putouts (36) and chances accepted (37) by catcher, two consecutive nine-inning games, April 29, 30, 1986.

Tied major league record for most putouts by catcher, nine-inning game (20), April 29, 1986.

Tied American League record for most chances accepted by catcher, nine-inning game (20), April 29, 1986.

Major League stolen bases: 1985 (2), 1986 (1). Total—3.

Hit for the cycle, September 18, 1985.

Led American League catchers in total chances with 937 and passed balls with 14 in 1986.

Led International League catchers in double plays with 13 in 1980.

Named catcher on The Sporting News American League All-Star Team, 1986.

Named American League Rookie Player of the Year by The Sporting News, 1981.

Year Club League	Pos.	G.	AB.	R.	H.	2B.	3B.	HR.	RBI.	B.A.	PO.	A.	E.	F.A.
1978—Winter Haven....... Fla. St.	C	98	297	35	89	17	3	3	32	.300	377	39	2	∗.995
1979—Bristol .... East.	C	130	470	48	129	25	1	12	63	.274	497	58	11	∗.981
1980—Pawtucket .... Int.	C	111	347	43	82	18	2	11	29	.236	367	∗65	7	.984
1980—Boston..................... Amer.	C	9	24	2	5	0	0	0	1	.208	13	0	2	.867
1981—Pawtucket .... Int.	C	25	81	8	24	3	0	2	11	.296	176	20	6	.969
1981—Boston..................... Amer.	C	62	205	22	59	15	0	5	26	.288	275	30	3	.990
1982—Boston..................... Amer.	C	92	289	30	72	17	2	4	26	.249	397	29	10	.977
1983—Boston..................... Amer.	C	81	204	21	60	16	1	2	18	.294	274	26	6	.980
1984—Boston..................... Amer.	C	133	449	54	121	26	4	24	72	.269	693	58	∗18	.977
1985—Boston..................... Amer.	C	144	498	66	147	30	5	18	80	.295	768	∗78	∗15	.983
1986—Boston†.................. Amer.	C	135	462	49	119	29	0	16	65	.258	∗866	65	6	.994
Major League Totals—7 Years		656	2131	244	583	133	12	69	288	.274	3286	286	60	.983

Signed as free agent by Boston Red Sox' organization, August 5, 1977.

†Granted free agency, November 12, 1986.

CHAMPIONSHIP SERIES RECORD

Tied Championship Series records for most hits, two consecutive games, one Series (6), October 12 (11 innings) and 14, 1986; most times reached first base safely, game (5), October 12, 1986 (11 innings).

Year	Club	League	Pos.	G.	AB.	R.	H.	2B.	3B.	HR.	RBI.	B.A.	PO.	A.	E.	F.A.
1986—Boston		Amer.	C	7	28	4	10	1	0	1	6	.357	45	4	0	1.000

WORLD SERIES RECORD

Tied World Series record for most double plays by catcher, game (2), October 22, 1986.

Year	Club	League	Pos.	G.	AB.	R.	H.	2B.	3B.	HR.	RBI.	B.A.	PO.	A.	E.	F.A.
1986—Boston		Amer.	C	7	30	1	6	1	0	1	1	.200	46	3	2	.961

ALL-STAR GAME RECORD

Year	League	Pos.	AB.	R.	H.	2B.	3B.	HR.	RBI.	B.A.	PO.	A.	E.	F.A.
1985—American		C	1	0	0	0	0	0	0	.000	4	0	0	1.000
1986—American		C	0	0	0	0	0	0	0	.000	1	1	0	1.000
All-Star Game Totals—2 Years			1	0	0	0	0	0	0	.000	5	1	0	1.000

STEPHEN EDWARD GEORGE
(Steve)

Born October 18, 1961, at St. Louis, Mo.
Height, 6.00. Weight, 160.
Throws left and bats left and righthanded.
Attended Broward Community College, Fort Lauderdale,
Fla., and Florida Southern College, Lakeland, Fla.

Pitched five-inning, 6-0 no-hit victory against Miami, August 14, 1985.
Led Florida State League in shutouts with 5 and complete games with 12 in 1985.

Year	Club	League	G.	IP.	W.	L.	Pct.	H.	R.	ER.	SO.	BB.	ERA.
1982—Paintsville		Ap'lachian	13	63⅓	3	4	.429	62	45	35	64	38	4.97
1983—Greensboro		S. Atlantic	35	84	5	4	.556	93	65	47	78	64	5.04
1984—Greensboro†		S. Atlantic	24	48⅔	2	4	.333	30	31	28	46	55	5.18
1985—Fort Lauderdale		Florida St.	24	164⅔	13	7	.650	120	48	32	141	76	1.75
1986—Albany		Eastern	10	57	1	6	.143	62	49	36	34	37	5.68
1986—Fort Lauderdale		Florida St.	15	89⅓	6	6	.500	83	40	32	48	47	3.22

Selected by New York Yankees' organization in 15th round of free-agent draft, June 7, 1982.
†On temporarily inactive list, April 9 to April 19, 1984.

CRAIG STUART GERBER

Born January 8, 1959, at Chicago, Ill.
Height, 6.00. Weight, 175.
Throws right and bats lefthanded.
Attended California State Poly University, San Luis Obispo, Calif.

Tied for California League lead in caught stealing with 20 in 1982.
Tied for Pioneer League lead in caught stealing with 9 in 1981.
Led Pacific Coast League shortstops in fielding percentage with .976 in 1984.
Led Eastern League second basemen in putouts with 311, assists with 441, double plays with 107 and total chances with 762 in 1983.
Led Pioneer League third basemen in putouts with 61 and double plays with 23 in 1981.

Year	Club	League	Pos.	G.	AB.	R.	H.	2B.	3B.	HR.	RBI.	B.A.	PO.	A.	E.	F.A.
1981—Idaho Falls		Pion.	3B-2B-SS	•70	★288	52	77	13	1	0	15	.267	73	145	11	.952
1982—Redwood		Calif.	S-2-3-O	131	493	71	145	21	6	0	39	.294	178	385	23	.961
1982—Spokane		P. C.	2B-3B	2	8	2	5	2	0	0	0	.625	4	6	0	1.000
1983—Nashua		East.	★2B-C-SS	132	502	65	119	18	9	1	40	.237	316	442	10	★.987
1983—Edmonton		P. C.	3B	2	6	2	1	0	0	0	0	.167	1	6	0	1.000
1984—Edmonton		P. C.	SS-2B-OF	114	365	55	84	18	7	1	40	.230	186	339	14	.974
1985—California		Amer.	SS-3B-2B	65	91	8	24	1	2	0	6	.264	56	112	5	.971
1986—Edmonton		P. C.	S-2-3-1	74	243	32	58	5	1	0	15	.239	99	143	14	.945
Major League Totals—1 Year				65	91	8	24	1	2	0	6	.264	56	112	5	.971

Selected by California Angels' organization in 20th round of free-agent draft, June 8, 1981.

HAROLD KENNETH GERHART
(Ken)

Born May 19, 1961, at Charleston, S.C.
Height, 6.00. Weight, 190.
Throws and bats righthanded.
Attended Middle Tennessee State University, Murfreesboro, Tenn.

Led International League in total bases with 232 in 1986.
Led Carolina League in total bases with 275 in 1983.
Led Appalachian League in sacrifice flies with 8 in 1982.

Year	Club	League	Pos.	G.	AB.	R.	H.	2B.	3B.	HR.	RBI.	B.A.	PO.	A.	E.	F.A.
1982—Bluefield		Appal.	OF	66	228	57	59	13	0	12	43	.259	105	3	2	.982
1983—Hagerstown		Carol.	OF	130	501	131	137	29	8	★31	86	.273	274	11	13	.956
1984—Charlotte		South.	OF	85	264	40	53	8	3	13	40	.201	183	5	4	.979
1984—Hagerstown		Carol.	OF	47	168	39	54	18	3	6	21	.321	108	1	5	.956
1985—Charlotte†		South.	OF	68	222	55	61	16	1	17	52	.275	177	4	1	.995
1986—Rochester		Int.	OF	124	453	73	124	18	3	★28	72	.274	216	11	7	.970
1986—Baltimore		Amer.	OF	20	69	4	16	2	0	1	7	.232	34	0	1	.971
Major League Totals—1 Year				20	69	4	16	2	0	1	7	.232	34	0	1	.971

Selected by Baltimore Orioles' organization in 5th round of free-agent draft, June 7, 1982.
†On disabled list, July 8 to September 3, 1985.

JOHN MICHAEL GIBBONS

Born June 8, 1962, at Great Falls, Mont.
Height, 5.11. Weight, 185.
Throws and bats righthanded.

Tied for Appalachian League lead in being hit by pitch with 7 in 1980.
Led South Atlantic League catchers in double plays with 8 in 1982.
Tied for Appalachian League lead in passed balls with 11 in 1980.

Year	Club	League	Pos.	G.	AB.	R.	H.	2B.	3B.	HR.	RBI.	B.A.	PO.	A.	E.	F.A.
1980—Kingsport	Appal.	C	53	181	28	50	7	1	7	34	.276	177	11	7	.964
1981—Shelby	S. Atl.	C	109	360	33	68	11	4	8	57	.189	629	65	18	.975
1982—Shelby	S. Atl.	C-1B	99	321	60	85	13	2	12	67	.265	559	72	17	.974
1982—Jackson	Texas	C	6	18	1	5	0	1	0	3	.278	21	1	0	1.000
1983—Jackson	Texas	C	110	373	63	111	25	1	18	67	.298	575	62	12	.982
1984—New York†	Nat.	C	10	31	1	2	0	0	0	1	.065	54	5	1	.983
1984—Tidewater	Int.	C	65	211	31	54	9	1	6	27	.256	199	20	4	.982
1985—Tidewater	Int.	C	108	370	35	96	10	2	9	30	.259	531	36	6	★.990
1986—Tidewater	Int.	C	96	317	42	78	16	0	3	27	.246	483	51	4	★.993
1986—New York	Nat.	C	8	19	4	9	4	0	1	1	.474	33	5	0	1.000
Major League Totals—2 Years				18	50	5	11	4	0	1	2	.220	87	10	1	.990

Selected by New York Mets' organization in 1st round (24th player selected) of free-agent draft, June 3, 1980.
†On disabled list, March 26 to April 10 and May 2 to June 4, 1984.

KIRK HAROLD GIBSON

Born May 28, 1957, at Pontiac, Mich.
Height, 6.03. Weight, 215.
Throws and bats lefthanded.
Attended Michigan State University, East Lansing, Mich.

Tied major league record for most home runs, opening day of season (2), April 7, 1986.
Major League stolen bases: 1979 (3), 1980 (4), 1981 (17), 1982 (9), 1983 (14), 1984 (29), 1985 (30), 1986 (34). Total—140.
Named as wide receiver on THE SPORTING NEWS College Football All-America Team, 1978.
Selected by St. Louis Cardinals in 7th round (173rd player selected) of 1979 NFL draft.
Received reported $200,000 bonus to sign with Detroit Tigers, 1978.
Named outfielder on THE SPORTING NEWS College Baseball All-America Team, 1978.

Year	Club	League	Pos.	G.	AB.	R.	H.	2B.	3B.	HR.	RBI.	B.A.	PO.	A.	E.	F.A.
1978—Lakeland†	Fla. St.	OF	54	175	27	42	5	4	8	40	.240	115	2	6	.951
1979—Evansville‡	A. A.	OF	89	327	50	80	13	5	9	42	.245	100	5	9	.921
1979—Detroit	Amer.	OF	12	38	3	9	3	0	1	4	.237	15	0	0	1.000
1980—Detroit§	Amer.	OF	51	175	23	46	2	1	9	16	.263	122	1	1	.992
1981—Detroit	Amer.	OF	83	290	41	95	11	3	9	40	.328	142	1	4	.973
1982—Detroit x	Amer.	OF	69	266	34	74	16	2	8	35	.278	167	4	1	.994
1983—Detroit	Amer.	OF	128	401	60	91	12	9	15	51	.227	116	2	3	.975
1984—Detroit	Amer.	OF	149	531	92	150	23	10	27	91	.282	245	4	●12	.954
1985—Detroit y	Amer.	OF	154	581	96	167	37	5	29	97	.287	286	1	●11	.963
1986—Detroit z	Amer.	OF	119	441	84	118	11	2	28	86	.268	190	2	2	.990
Major League Totals—8 Years				765	2723	433	750	115	32	126	420	.275	1283	15	34	.974

Selected by Detroit Tigers' organization in 1st round (12th player selected) of free-agent draft, June 6, 1978.
†On restricted list, August 15, 1978, to March 1, 1979.
‡On disabled list, April 13 to May 21, 1979.
§On disabled list, June 18 to October 6, 1980.
xOn disabled list, July 11, 1982 through remainder of season.
yGranted free agency, November 12, 1985; re-signed by Tigers, January 8, 1986.
zOn disabled list, April 23 to June 2, 1986.

CHAMPIONSHIP SERIES RECORD

Year	Club	League	Pos.	G.	AB.	R.	H.	2B.	3B.	HR.	RBI.	B.A.	PO.	A.	E.	F.A.
1984—Detroit	Amer.	OF	3	12	2	5	1	0	1	2	.417	7	0	0	1.000

WORLD SERIES RECORD

Year	Club	League	Pos.	G.	AB.	R.	H.	2B.	3B.	HR.	RBI.	B.A.	PO.	A.	E.	F.A.
1984—Detroit	Amer.	OF	5	18	4	6	0	0	2	7	.333	5	1	2	.750

PAUL MARSHALL GIBSON

Born January 4, 1960, at Southampton, N.Y.
Height, 6.00. Weight, 165.
Throws left and bats righthanded.
Attended Suffolk County Community College, Selden, N.Y.

Year	Club	League	G.	IP.	W.	L.	Pct.	H.	R.	ER.	SO.	BB.	ERA.
1978—Shelby	W. Carol.	24	140	9	6	.600	106	57	47	71	71	3.02
1979—Tampa	Florida St.	24	129	3	8	.273	121	56	44	58	46	3.07
1980—Cedar Rapids†	Midwest	28	146	6	●15	.286	171	97	80	74	53	4.93
1981—Lakeland	Florida St.	20	64	4	3	.571	64	25	21	38	21	2.95
1982—Birmingham‡	Southern	44	77⅓	3	3	.500	60	25	23	71	39	2.68
1983—Orlando§	Southern	40	76⅔	1	7	.125	91	59	52	45	56	6.10
1984—Orlando x	Southern	27	121	7	7	.500	125	71	52	64	54	3.87

Year Club	League	G.	IP.	W.	L.	Pct.	H.	R.	ER.	SO.	BB.	ERA.
1985—Birmingham	Southern	36	144⅓	8	8	.500	135	73	66	79	63	4.12
1986—Nashville	Am. Assoc.	30	113⅓	5	6	.455	121	58	50	91	40	3.97
1986—Glens Falls	Eastern	9	19⅔	3	1	.750	16	3	3	21	7	1.37

Selected by Cincinnati Reds' organization in 3rd round of free-agent draft, January 10, 1978.
†Released, April 8, 1981; signed by Lakeland (Detroit Tigers' organization), May 23, 1981.
‡Drafted by Minnesota Twins, December 6, 1982.
§On disabled list, August 4 to August 14, 1983.
xGranted free agency, October 15, 1984; signed by Birmingham (Detroit Tigers' organization), November 9, 1984.

ROBERT LOUIS GIBSON JR.
(Bob)

Born June 19, 1957, at Philadelphia, Pa.
Height, 6.00. Weight, 195.
Throws and bats righthanded.
Attended Bloomsburg University, Bloomsburg, Pa.

Major League saves: 1983 (2), 1985 (11). Total—13.

Year Club	League	G.	IP.	W.	L.	Pct.	H.	R.	ER.	SO.	BB.	ERA.
1979—Burlington	Midwest	25	137	5	12	.294	152	99	84	111	81	5.52
1980—Stockton	California	33	67	6	3	.667	45	32	29	59	58	3.90
1981—Stockton	California	49	66	6	8	.429	61	31	22	67	38	3.00
1982—El Paso	Texas	47	66⅓	6	2	.750	55	23	16	66	39	2.17
1982—Vancouver	P. Coast	6	8	1	1	.500	3	2	1	6	10	1.13
1983—Milwaukee	American	27	80⅔	3	4	.429	71	40	35	46	46	3.90
1984—Vancouver†	P. Coast	14	73⅓	3	4	.429	50	40	37	75	39	4.54
1984—Milwaukee	American	18	69	2	5	.286	61	43	38	54	47	4.96
1985—Milwaukee	American	41	92⅓	6	7	.462	86	44	40	53	49	3.90
1986—Vancouver	P. Coast	16	90⅔	10	4	.714	81	30	28	59	37	2.78
1986—Milwaukee‡	American	11	26⅔	1	2	.333	23	18	14	11	23	4.72
Major League Totals—4 Years		97	268⅔	12	18	.400	241	145	127	164	165	4.25

Signed as free agent by Milwaukee Brewers' organization, March 7, 1979.
†On temporary inactive list, July 17 to August 10, 1984.
‡Drafted by Chicago White Sox, December 9, 1986.

BRIAN JEFFREY GILES

Born April 27, 1960, at Manhattan, Kan.
Height, 6.01. Weight, 162.
Throws and bats righthanded.
Grandson of George F. Giles, first baseman in Negro National and American Leagues,
1927 through 1938; son of George F. Giles, Jr., minor league infielder, 1953 through 1955.

Major League stolen bases: 1982 (6), 1983 (17), 1985 (2). Total—25.

Year Club	League	Pos.	G.	AB.	R.	H.	2B.	3B.	HR.	RBI.	B.A.	PO.	A.	E.	F.A.
1978—Little Falls	NYP	2B	61	195	36	44	5	5	4	21	.226	★135	144	16	.946
1979—Lynchburg†	Carol.	2B	86	278	40	83	16	2	2	33	.299	180	271	13	.972
1980—Jackson	Texas	2B	132	448	76	128	30	8	10	57	.286	291	325	26	.960
1981—Tidewater	Int.	2B-SS	121	400	60	107	17	3	7	40	.268	267	384	24	.964
1981—New York	Nat.	SS-2B	9	7	0	0	0	0	0	0	.000	5	8	0	1.000
1982—Tidewater	Int.	2B-SS	108	352	48	98	32	4	11	54	.278	240	354	17	.972
1982—New York	Nat.	2B-SS	45	138	14	29	5	0	3	10	.210	122	133	2	.992
1983—New York	Nat.	2B-SS	145	400	39	98	15	0	2	27	.245	309	390	14	.980
1984—Tidewater†	Int.	2B-SS-3B	118	384	59	93	24	1	6	37	.242	248	344	16	.974
1985—Milwaukee	Amer.	SS-2B	34	58	6	10	1	0	1	1	.172	48	58	2	.981
1985—Vancouver§	P. C.	SS	40	128	21	30	7	1	2	15	.234	47	125	9	.950
1986—Buffalo x	A. A.	SS	30	98	10	28	5	1	3	9	.286	44	82	7	.947
1986—Chicago y	Amer.	2B-SS	9	11	0	3	0	0	0	1	.273	15	11	0	1.000
National League Totals—3 Years			199	545	53	127	20	0	5	37	.233	436	531	16	.984
American League Totals—2 Years			43	69	6	13	1	0	1	2	.188	63	69	2	.985
Major League Totals—5 Years			242	614	59	140	21	0	6	39	.228	499	600	18	.984

Selected by New York Mets' organization in 2nd round of free-agent draft, June 6, 1978.
†On disabled list, July 10 to August 11, 1979.
‡Drafted by Milwaukee Brewers, December 3, 1984.
§Granted free agency, October 15, 1985; signed by Buffalo (Chicago White Sox' organization), December 12, 1985.
xOn disabled list, May 6 to July 17, 1986.
yOn disabled list, August 25, 1986 through remainder of season.

BRIAN ALLEN GIVENS

Born November 6, 1965, at Lompoc, Calif.
Height, 6.05. Weight, 195.
Throws left and bats righthanded.
Attended Trinidad State Junior College, Trinidad, Colo.

Led Appalachian League in wild pitches with 20 in 1984.

Year Club	League	G.	IP.	W.	L.	Pct.	H.	R.	ER.	SO.	BB.	ERA.
1984—Kingsport	Ap'lachian	14	44⅓	4	1	.800	41	36	32	52	52	6.50
1985—Little Falls	NYP	11	73⅔	3	4	.429	54	28	24	81	43	2.93
1985—Columbia	S. Atlantic	3	21⅓	1	2	.333	15	7	7	25	13	2.95
1986—Columbia	S. Atlantic	27	172	8	7	.533	147	89	72	★189	100	3.77

Selected by New York Mets' organization in 10th round of free-agent draft, January 17, 1984.

CLINTON DANIEL GLADDEN III
(Dan)

Born July 7, 1957, at San Jose, Calif.
Height, 5.11. Weight, 180.
Throws and bats righthanded.
Attended DeAnza College, Cupertino, Calif., and
Fresno State University, Fresno, Calif.
Brother of Jeff Gladden, pitcher in Kansas City Royals'
and San Francisco Giants' organization, 1980 through 1984.

Major League stolen bases: 1983 (4), 1984 (31), 1985 (32), 1986 (27). Total—94.
Led Texas League in stolen bases with 52 and caught stealing with 26 in 1981.

Year Club	League	Pos.	G.	AB.	R.	H.	2B.	3B.	HR.	RBI.	B.A.	PO.	A.	E.	F.A.
1979—Fresno	Calif.	OF-2B-SS	60	228	41	70	9	1	3	31	.307	56	16	3	.960
1980—Fresno	Calif.	OF	62	237	46	72	10	2	9	41	.304	68	3	1	.986
1980—Shreveport	Texas	OF-SS	74	292	51	86	11	2	9	35	.295	169	14	5	.973
1981—Shreveport	Texas	OF-SS-2B	124	472	81	148	23	9	8	44	.314	211	12	3	.987
1982—Phoenix	P. C.	OF	130	503	93	155	40	5	10	74	.308	264	16	7	.976
1983—Phoenix	P. C.	OF	127	505	113	153	30	9	12	80	.303	319	6	7	.979
1983—San Francisco	Nat.	OF	18	63	6	14	2	0	1	9	.222	53	0	0	1.000
1984—Phoenix†	P. C.	OF	59	234	70	93	11	7	3	27	.397	130	4	2	.985
1984—San Francisco	Nat.	OF	86	342	71	120	17	2	4	31	.351	232	8	3	.988
1985—San Francisco	Nat.	OF	142	502	64	122	15	8	7	41	.243	273	3	7	.975
1986—San Francisco‡	Nat.	OF	102	351	55	97	16	1	4	29	.276	226	7	3	.987
1986—Phoenix§	P. C.	OF	7	27	5	9	4	0	0	0	.333	11	0	0	1.000
Major League Totals—4 Years			348	1258	196	353	50	11	16	110	.281	784	18	13	.984

Signed as free agent by San Francisco Giants' organization, June 17, 1979.
†On disabled list, April 19 to May 1, 1984.
‡On disabled list, June 4 to July 23, 1986; included rehabilitation disability assignment to Phoenix, July 14 to July 23, 1986.
§Switch-hitter.

THOMAS MICHAEL GLAVINE
(Tom)

Born March 25, 1966, at Concord, Mass.
Height, 6.00. Weight, 175.
Throws and bats lefthanded.

Led Gulf Coast League in wild pitches with 12 in 1984.
Drafted by Los Angeles Kings in 1984 NHL entry draft. Fourth Kings pick, 69th player overall, fourth round.

Year Club	League	G.	IP.	W.	L.	Pct.	H.	R.	ER.	SO.	BB.	ERA.
1984—Bradenton Braves	Gulf Coast	8	32⅓	2	3	.400	29	17	12	34	13	3.34
1985—Sumter	S. Atlantic	26	168⅔	9	6	.600	114	58	44	174	73	*2.35
1986—Greenville	Southern	22	145⅓	11	6	.647	129	62	55	114	70	3.41
1986—Richmond	Int'national	7	40	1	5	.167	40	29	25	12	27	5.63

Selected by Atlanta Braves' organization in 2nd round of free-agent draft, June 4, 1984.

JERRY DON GLEATON
(Jerry Don)

Born September 14, 1957, at Brownwood, Tex.
Height, 6.03. Weight, 210.
Throws and bats lefthanded.
Attended University of Texas, Austin, Tex.

Major League saves: 1984 (2), 1985 (1). Total—3.
Tied for Eastern League lead in complete games with 13 in 1982.
Tied for Texas League lead in home runs allowed with 17 in 1980.

Year Club	League	G.	IP.	W.	L.	Pct.	H.	R.	ER.	SO.	BB.	ERA.
1979—Tulsa	Texas	5	35	3	2	.600	37	19	19	21	15	4.89
1979—Texas	American	5	10	0	1	.000	15	7	7	2	2	6.30
1980—Tulsa	Texas	25	178	13	7	.650	179	83	72	138	68	3.64
1980—Texas†	American	5	7	0	0	.000	5	2	2	2	4	2.57
1981—Seattle	American	20	85	4	7	.364	88	50	45	31	38	4.76
1981—Spokane	P. Coast	13	91	5	7	.417	104	53	42	57	39	4.15
1982—Lynn	Eastern	24	182	15	7	.682	175	71	55	132	54	2.72
1982—Seattle	American	3	4⅔	0	0	.000	7	7	7	1	2	13.50
1983—Salt Lake City	P. Coast	24	137⅓	9	9	.500	189	112	102	73	81	6.68
1984—Salt Lake City‡	P. Coast	29	49⅔	4	1	.800	62	39	32	39	17	5.80
1984—Denver	Am. Assoc.	12	20	1	1	.500	20	5	4	10	4	1.80
1984—Chicago	American	11	18⅓	1	2	.333	20	12	7	4	6	3.44
1985—Buffalo	Am. Assoc.	38	55⅓	8	2	*.800	62	17	15	37	21	2.44
1985—Chicago	American	31	29⅔	1	0	1.000	37	19	19	22	13	5.76
1986—Buffalo§	Am. Assoc.	46	78⅓	4	3	.571	79	34	28	77	35	3.22
Major League Totals—6 Years		75	154⅔	6	10	.375	172	97	87	62	65	5.06

Selected by Baltimore Orioles' organization in 2nd round of free-agent draft, June 8, 1976.
Selected by Texas Rangers' organization in 1st round (17th player selected) of free-agent draft, June 5, 1979.
†Traded with Pitchers Brian Allard, Ken Clay and Steve Finch, Shortstop Rick Auerbach and Outfielder Richie Zisk to Seattle Mariners for Catcher Larry Cox, Pitcher Rick Honeycutt, Outfielders Willie Horton and Leon Roberts and Shortstop Mario Mendoza, December 12, 1980.

RENE ADRIAN GONZALES

Born September 3, 1961, at Austin, Tex.
Height, 6.03. Weight, 180.
Throws and bats righthanded.
Attended Glendale College, Glendale, Calif.; and California State University, Los Angeles, Calif.

Led American Association shortstops in double plays with 79 in 1985.
Led Southern League shortstops in double plays with 102 in 1983.

Year Club	League	Pos.	G.	AB.	R.	H.	2B.	3B.	HR.	RBI.	B.A.	PO.	A.	E.	F.A.
1982—Memphis	South.	SS	56	183	10	39	3	1	1	11	.213	77	183	14	.949
1983—Memphis	South.	SS	144	476	67	128	12	2	2	44	.269	★258	449	20	★.972
1984—Indianapolis	A. A.	SS-3B-2B	114	359	41	84	12	2	2	32	.234	161	349	13	.975
1984—Montreal	Nat.	SS	29	30	5	7	1	0	0	2	.233	17	28	2	.957
1985—Indianapolis	A. A.	SS	130	340	21	77	11	1	0	25	.226	203	★345	23	.960
1986—Indianapolis	A. A.	3B-SS-2B	116	395	57	108	14	2	3	43	.273	208	297	23	.956
1986—Montreal†	Nat.	SS-3B	11	26	1	3	0	0	0	0	.115	7	19	0	1.000
Major League Totals—2 Years			40	56	6	10	1	0	0	2	.179	24	47	2	.973

Selected by Montreal Expos' organization in 5th round of free-agent draft, June 7, 1982.
†Traded to Baltimore Orioles, December 16, 1986, completing deals in which Baltimore traded Pitcher Dennis Martinez to Montreal Expos on June 16, 1986 and Catcher John Stefero to Montreal on December 8, 1986, both for a player to be named later.

DENIO MARIANO GONZALEZ (MANZUETA)
(Denny)

Born July 22, 1963, at Sabana Grande Boya, D.R.
Height 5.11. Weight, 165.
Throws and bats righthanded.

Major League stolen bases: 1984 (1), 1985 (2). Total—3.

Year Club	League	Pos.	G.	AB.	R.	H.	2B.	3B.	HR.	RBI.	B.A.	PO.	A.	E.	F.A.
1981—Bradenton Pir.	Gulf C.	2B-3B	50	179	32	62	5	3	2	24	.346	102	113	14	.939
1982—Portland	P. C.	2B-3B	51	164	23	37	4	6	0	9	.226	106	133	20	.923
1982—Buffalo	East.	2B	68	252	28	70	5	4	3	21	.278	137	176	11	.966
1983—Hawaii	P. C.	SS-2B	125	449	76	121	18	8	9	48	.269	193	319	34	.938
1984—Hawaii	P. C.	OF-3B-2B	113	380	61	114	22	7	15	67	.300	121	84	5	.976
1984—Pittsburgh	Nat.	3B-SS-OF	26	82	9	15	3	1	0	4	.183	26	53	3	.963
1985—Hawaii	P. C.	3-O-2-S	106	365	68	105	21	6	12	57	.288	97	183	15	.949
1985—Pittsburgh	Nat.	3B-OF-2B	35	124	11	28	4	0	4	12	.226	44	42	8	.915
1986—Hawaii	P. C.	3B-SS	109	379	48	84	10	2	10	45	.222	64	157	18	.925
Major League Totals—2 Years			61	206	20	43	7	1	4	16	.209	70	95	11	.938

Signed as free agent by Pittsburgh Pirates' organization, June 25, 1981.

JOSE RAFAEL GONZALEZ

Born November 23, 1964, at Puerto Plata, Dominican Republic.
Height, 6.03. Weight, 190.
Throws and bats righthanded.

Major League stolen bases: 1985 (1), 1986 (4). Total—5.
Tied for Texas League lead in caught stealing with 17 in 1985.
Led Texas League outfielders in total chances with 320 in 1985.

Year Club	League	Pos.	G.	AB.	R.	H.	2B.	3B.	HR.	RBI.	B.A.	PO.	A.	E.	F.A.
1981—Lethbridge	Pion.	OF	34	103	11	14	1	1	0	7	.136	65	6	5	.934
1982—Lethbridge	Pion.	OF	55	209	35	63	14	1	4	47	.301	112	7	1	.992
1983—Lodi†	Calif.	OF	76	310	48	91	17	4	6	36	.294	182	7	4	.979
1984—Bakersfield	Calif.	OF	129	484	86	107	26	1	11	59	.221	264	13	9	.969
1985—San Antonio	Texas	OF	128	448	82	137	22	6	13	62	.306	★294	15	11	.966
1985—Los Angeles	Nat.	OF	23	11	6	3	2	0	0	0	.273	10	0	0	1.000
1986—Albuquerque	P. C.	OF	89	303	39	84	20	3	6	37	.277	171	10	6	.968
1986—Los Angeles	Nat.	OF	57	93	15	20	5	1	2	6	.215	73	0	6	.924
Major League Totals—2 Years			80	104	21	23	7	1	2	6	.221	83	0	6	.933

Signed as free agent by Los Angeles Dodgers' organization, August 12, 1980.
†On disabled list, July 7, 1983 through remainder of season.

DWIGHT EUGENE GOODEN

Born November 16, 1964, at Tampa, Fla.
Height, 6.03. Weight, 198.
Throws and bats righthanded
Uncle of Gary Sheffield, shortstop in Milwaukee Brewers' organization.

Established major league record for most strikeouts by rookie, season (276), 1984.
Tied modern major league record for most strikeouts, two consecutive games (32), September 12, 17, 1984.
Established National League record for most strikeouts, three consecutive games (43), September 7, 12, 17, 1984.
Led National League in complete games with 16 in 1985.
Tied for National League lead in balks with 7 in 1984.
Led Carolina League in shutouts with 6 in 1983.

Named National League Pitcher of the Year by THE SPORTING NEWS, 1985.
Won National League Cy Young Memorial Award, 1985.
Named righthanded pitcher on THE SPORTING NEWS National League All-Star Team, 1985.
Named National League Rookie Pitcher of the Year by THE SPORTING NEWS, 1984.
Named National League Rookie of the Year by Baseball Writers' Association of America, 1984.
Named Carolina League Pitcher of the Year, 1983.
Received reported $125,000 bonus to sign with New York Mets, 1982.

Year	Club	League	G.	IP.	W.	L.	Pct.	H.	R.	ER.	SO.	BB.	ERA.
1982—Kingsport	Ap'lachian	9	65⅔	5	4	.556	53	34	18	66	25	2.47
1982—Little Falls	NYP	2	13	0	1	.000	11	6	6	18	3	4.15
1983—Lynchburg	Carolina	27	191	*19	4	.826	121	58	53	*300	*112	*2.50
1984—New York	National	31	218	17	9	.654	161	72	63	*276	73	2.60
1985—New York	National	35	*276⅔	*24	4	.857	198	51	47	*268	69	*1.53
1986—New York	National	33	250	17	6	.739	197	92	79	200	80	2.84
Major League Totals—3 Years		99	744⅔	58	19	.753	556	215	189	744	222	2.28

Selected by New York Mets' organization in 1st round (fifth player selected) of free-agent draft, June 7, 1982.

CHAMPIONSHIP SERIES RECORD

Tied National League Championship Series record for most innings pitched, game (10), October 14, 1986.

Year	Club	League	G.	IP.	W.	L.	Pct.	H.	R.	ER.	SO.	BB.	ERA.
1986—New York	National	2	17	0	1	.000	16	2	2	9	5	1.06

WORLD SERIES RECORD

Tied World Series record for most games lost, seven-game Series (2), 1986.

Year	Club	League	G.	IP.	W.	L.	Pct.	H.	R.	ER.	SO.	BB.	ERA.
1986—New York	National	2	9	0	2	.000	17	10	8	9	4	8.00

ALL-STAR GAME RECORD

Year	League	IP.	W.	L.	Pct.	H.	R.	ER.	SO.	BB.	ERA.
1984—National		2	0	0	.000	1	0	0	3	0	0.00
1986—National		3	0	1	.000	3	2	2	2	0	6.00
All-Star Game Totals—2 Years		5	0	1	.000	4	2	2	5	0	3.60

Member of National League All-Star Team in 1985; did not play.

DONALD THOMAS GORDON
(Don)

Born October 10, 1959, at New York, N.Y.
Height, 6.01. Weight, 175.
Throws and bats righthanded.
Attended The Citadel, Charleston, S.C., and University
of South Carolina, Columbia, S.C.

Major League saves: 1986 (1).

Year	Club	League	G.	IP.	W.	L.	Pct.	H.	R.	ER.	SO.	BB.	ERA.
1982—Bristol	Ap'lachian	22	65⅔	4	4	.500	48	17	16	42	14	2.19
1983—Birmingham	Southern	43	102⅔	9	5	.643	104	50	39	50	23	3.42
1984—Birmingham†-Knoxville	Southern	54	109⅔	6	4	.600	103	47	41	51	21	3.36
1985—Syracuse	Int'national	51	113	8	5	.615	93	39	26	43	21	*2.07
1986—Toronto	American	14	21⅔	0	1	.000	28	20	17	13	8	7.06
1986—Syracuse	Int'national	25	109	8	5	.615	105	42	35	62	21	2.89
Major League Totals—1 Year		14	21⅔	0	1	.000	28	20	17	13	8	7.06

Selected by Detroit Tigers' organization in 31st round of free-agent draft, June 7, 1982.
†Released, June 23, 1984; signed by Knoxville (Toronto Blue Jays' organization), June 25, 1984.

THOMAS PATRICK GORMAN
(Tom)

Born December 16, 1957, at Woodburn, Ore.
Height, 6.04. Weight, 200.
Throws and bats lefthanded.
Received degree from Gonzaga University, Spokane, Wash.

Tied for Southern League lead in saves with 22 in 1981.

Year	Club	League	G.	IP.	W.	L.	Pct.	H.	R.	ER.	SO.	BB.	ERA.
1980—Memphis	Southern	25	69	6	4	.600	64	34	21	45	22	2.74
1981—Memphis	Southern	52	91	12	9	.571	82	39	31	91	30	3.07
1981—Montreal	National	9	15	0	0	.000	12	7	7	13	6	4.20
1982—Wichita	Am. Assoc.	23	119⅓	8	7	.533	131	77	69	69	35	5.20
1982—Montreal†-New York	National	8	16⅓	1	1	.500	16	5	5	13	4	2.76
1982—Tidewater	Int'national	4	11⅓	1	1	.500	12	8	8	6	4	6.35
1983—Tidewater	Int'national	10	61⅔	6	1	.857	54	25	20	58	18	2.92
1983—New York	National	25	49⅓	1	4	.200	45	29	27	30	15	4.93
1984—Tidewater	Int'national	3	18	1	2	.333	17	8	6	13	4	3.00
1984—New York	National	36	57⅔	6	0	1.000	51	20	19	40	13	2.97
1985—New York‡	National	34	52⅔	4	4	.500	56	32	30	32	18	5.13
1986—Portland	P. Coast	43	54	4	2	.667	44	14	13	44	27	2.17
1986—Philadelphia	National	8	11⅔	0	1	.000	21	10	10	8	5	7.71
Major League Totals—6 Years		120	202⅔	12	10	.545	201	103	98	136	61	4.35

Selected by Montreal Expos' organization in 4th round of free-agent draft, June 3, 1980.
†Traded to New York Mets' organization, August 14, 1982, completing deal in which New York traded Outfielder Joel Youngblood to Montreal Expos for a player to be named later, August 4, 1982.
‡Released, April 1, 1986; signed by Philadelphia Phillies' organization, April 19, 1986.

RICHARD MICHAEL GOSSAGE
(Rich or Goose)

Born July 5, 1951, at Colorado Springs, Colo.
Height, 6.03. Weight, 220.
Throws and bats righthanded.
Attended Southern Colorado State College, Pueblo, Colo.

Established National League record for most strikeouts by relief pitcher, season (151), 1977.
Major League saves: 1972 (2), 1974 (1), 1975 (26), 1976 (1), 1977 (26), 1978 (27), 1979 (18), 1980 (33), 1981 (20), 1982 (30), 1983 (22), 1984 (25), 1985 (26), 1986 (21). Total—278.
Led American League in saves with 26 in 1975 and 27 in 1978.
Led American League in games finished in relief with 55 in 1978.
Tied for American League lead in saves with 33 in 1980.
Tied for American League lead in intentional bases on balls issued with 15 in 1975.
Led Midwest League in complete games with 15 and shutouts with 7 in 1971.
Named American League Fireman of the Year by THE SPORTING NEWS, 1975 and 1978.
Named Midwest League Player of the Year, 1971.

Year	Club	League	G.	IP.	W.	L.	Pct.	H.	R.	ER.	SO.	BB.	ERA.
1970—Sarasota White Sox	Gulf Coast	3	16	0	0	.000	11	6	5	21	4	2.81
1970—Appleton	Midwest	10	35	0	3	.000	41	27	23	21	19	5.91
1971—Appleton	Midwest	25	187	*18	2	*.900	141	48	38	149	50	*1.83
1972—Chicago	American	36	80	7	1	.875	72	44	38	57	44	4.28
1973—Iowa	Am. Assoc.	12	71	5	4	.556	59	32	29	66	28	3.68
1973—Chicago	American	20	50	0	4	.000	57	44	41	33	37	7.38
1974—Appleton	Midwest	2	8	0	2	.000	8	6	3	5	4	3.38
1974—Chicago	American	39	89	4	6	.400	92	45	41	64	47	4.15
1975—Chicago	American	61	142	9	8	.529	99	32	29	130	70	1.84
1976—Chicago†	American	31	224	9	17	.346	214	104	98	135	90	3.94
1977—Pittsburgh‡	National	72	133	11	9	.550	78	27	24	151	49	1.62
1978—New York	American	63	134	10	11	.476	87	41	30	122	59	2.01
1979—New York§	American	36	58	5	3	.625	48	18	17	41	19	2.64
1980—New York	American	64	99	6	2	.750	74	29	25	103	37	2.27
1981—New York	American	32	47	3	2	.600	22	6	4	48	14	0.77
1982—New York	American	56	93	4	5	.444	63	23	23	102	28	2.23
1983—New York x	American	57	87⅓	13	5	.722	82	27	22	90	25	2.27
1984—San Diego	National	62	102⅓	10	6	.625	75	34	33	84	36	2.90
1985—San Diego y	National	50	79	5	3	.625	64	21	16	52	17	1.82
1986—San Diego z	National	45	64⅔	5	7	.417	69	36	32	63	20	4.45
National League Totals—4 Years		229	379	31	25	.554	286	118	105	350	122	2.49
American League Totals—11 Years		496	1103⅓	70	64	.522	910	413	368	925	470	3.00
Major League Totals—15 Years		725	1482⅓	101	89	.532	1196	531	473	1275	592	2.87

Selected by Chicago White Sox' organization in 9th round of free-agent draft, June 4, 1970.
†Traded with Pitcher Terry Forster to Pittsburgh Pirates for Outfielder Richie Zisk and Pitcher Silvio Martinez, December 10, 1976.
‡Granted free agency, October 28, 1977; signed by New York Yankees, November 23, 1977.
§On disabled list, April 21 to July 9, 1979.
xGranted free agency, November 7, 1983; signed by San Diego Padres, January 6, 1984.
yOn disabled list, August 8 to September 1, 1985.
zOn suspended list, August 29 to September 18, 1986.

DIVISION SERIES RECORD

Year	Club	League	G.	IP.	W.	L.	Pct.	H.	R.	ER.	SO.	BB.	ERA.
1981—New York	American	3	6⅔	0	0	.000	3	0	0	8	2	0.00

CHAMPIONSHIP SERIES RECORD

Tied American League Championship Series record for most saves, total Series (2).

Year	Club	League	G.	IP.	W.	L.	Pct.	H.	R.	ER.	SO.	BB.	ERA.
1978—New York	American	2	4	1	0	1.000	3	2	2	3	0	4.50
1980—New York	American	1	⅓	0	1	.000	3	2	2	0	0	54.00
1981—New York	American	2	2⅔	0	0	.000	1	0	0	2	0	0.00
1984—San Diego	National	3	4	0	0	.000	5	2	2	5	1	4.50
Championship Series Totals—4 Years		8	11	1	1	.500	12	6	6	10	1	4.91

WORLD SERIES RECORD

Tied World Series record for most saves, six-game Series (2), 1981.

Year	Club	League	G.	IP.	W.	L.	Pct.	H.	R.	ER.	SO.	BB.	ERA.
1978—New York	American	3	6	1	0	1.000	1	0	0	4	1	0.00
1981—New York	American	3	5	0	0	.000	2	0	0	5	2	0.00
1984—San Diego	National	2	2⅔	0	0	.000	3	4	4	2	1	13.50
World Series Totals—3 Years		8	13⅔	1	0	1.000	6	4	4	11	4	2.63

ALL-STAR GAME RECORD

Established All-Star game record for most games finished (5).

Year League	IP.	W.	L.	Pct.	H.	R.	ER.	SO.	BB.	ERA.
1975—American	1	0	0	.000	1	1	1	0	0	9.00
1977—National	1	0	0	.000	1	2	2	2	1	18.00
1978—American	1	0	0	.000	1	2	2	2	1	18.00
1980—American	1	0	1	.000	4	4	4	1	1	36.00
1984—National	1	0	0	.000	1	0	0	0	0	0.00
1985—National	1	0	0	.000	1	0	0	2	0	0.00
All-Star Game Totals—6 Years	6	0	1	.000	8	7	7	7	3	10.50

Named to American League All-Star Team for 1981 game; replaced due to injury.
Member of American League All-Star Team in 1976 and 1982; did not play.

JAMES WILLIAM GOTT
(Jim)

Born August 3, 1959, at Hollywood, Calif.
Height, 6.04. Weight, 210.
Throws and bats righthanded.

Major League saves: 1984 (2), 1986 (1). Total—3.
Led Western Carolinas League in wild pitches with 21 in 1979.
Tied for Pioneer League lead in games started by pitchers with 14 in 1978.

Year Club	League	G.	IP.	W.	L.	Pct.	H.	R.	ER.	SO.	BB.	ERA.
1977—Calgary	Pioneer	14	65	3	4	.429	71	*82	*69	60	*83	9.55
1978—Gastonia	W. Carol.	22	145	9	6	.600	100	67	64	130	●113	3.97
1978—St. Petersburg	Floria St.	5	28	1	3	.250	23	9	4	15	12	1.29
1979—St. Petersburg	Florida St.	4	18	0	3	.000	18	13	13	9	13	6.50
1979—Gastonia	W. Carol.	19	77	5	5	.500	63	57	48	102	88	5.61
1979—Arkansas†	Texas	2	5	0	1	.000	3	6	3	7	13	5.40
1980—St. Petersburg	Florida St.	25	137	5	11	.313	138	96	70	103	113	4.60
1981—Arkansas‡	Texas	28	131	5	9	.357	68	50	93	65	3.44
1982—Toronto	American	30	136	5	10	.333	134	76	67	82	66	4.43
1983—Toronto	American	34	176⅔	9	14	.391	195	103	93	121	68	4.74
1984—Toronto§	American	35	109⅔	7	6	.538	94	54	49	73	49	4.02
1985—San Francisco x	National	26	148⅓	7	10	.412	144	73	64	78	51	3.88
1986—San Francisco x	National	9	13	0	0	.000	16	12	11	9	13	7.62
1986—Phoenix	P. Coast	2	2⅔	0	0	.000	2	2	2	2	3	6.75
American League Totals—3 Years		99	422⅓	21	30	.412	422	233	209	276	183	4.45
National League Totals—2 Years		35	161⅓	7	10	.412	160	85	75	87	64	4.18
Major League Totals—5 Years		134	583⅔	28	40	.412	582	318	284	363	247	4.38

Selected by St. Louis Cardinals' organization in 4th round of free-agent draft, June 7, 1977.
†On disabled list, August 16 to September 1, 1979.
‡Drafted by Toronto Blue Jays, December 7, 1981.
§Traded with Pitcher Jack McKnight and Infielder Augie Schmidt to San Francisco Giants for Pitcher Gary Lavelle, January 26, 1985.
xOn disabled list, May 9, 1986 through remainder of season; included rehabilitation disability assignment to Phoenix, June 9 to June 24, 1986.

MARK ANDREW GRANT

Born October 24, 1963, at Aurora, Ill.
Height, 6.02. Weight, 195.
Throws and bats righthanded.
Cousin of Rick Ramos, pitcher in Montreal Expos' organization, 1978 through 1983; and nephew of Richard Ramos, pitcher in Chicago White Sox' organization, 1953 through 1958.

Pitched 9-0 no-hit victory against Danville, August 12, 1982.
Major League saves: 1984 (1).
Led Pacific Coast League pitchers in complete games with 10 and tied for lead in games started with 27 in 1986.
Led Pacific Coast League pitchers in wild pitches with 18 and tied for league lead in games started with 29 in 1985.
Tied for Pacific Coast League lead in shutouts with 3 in 1985 and 1986.
Tied for Midwest League lead in shutouts with 4 in 1982.

Year Club	League	G.	IP.	W.	L.	Pct.	H.	R.	ER.	SO.	BB.	ERA.
1981—Great Falls	Pioneer	10	64	2	6	.250	63	36	31	50	35	4.36
1982—Clinton	Midwest	27	*198⅔	*16	5	*.762	139	63	52	*243	60	2.36
1983—Shreveport	Texas	26	*186⅔	10	8	.556	182	83	76	159	71	3.66
1984—Phoenix	P. Coast	17	111⅓	5	7	.417	102	64	49	78	61	3.96
1984—San Francisco†	National	11	53⅔	1	4	.200	56	40	38	32	19	6.37
1985—Phoenix	P. Coast	29	183	8	●15	.348	182	101	92	133	90	4.52
1986—Phoenix	P. Coast	28	181⅓	*14	7	.667	204	105	99	93	46	4.90
1986—San Francisco	National	4	10	0	1	.000	6	4	4	5	5	3.60
Major League Totals—2 Years		15	63⅓	1	5	.167	62	44	42	37	24	5.97

Selected by San Francisco Giants' organization in 1st round (10th player selected) of free-agent draft, June 8, 1981.
†On disabled list, May 4 to May 23, 1984.

JEFFREY EDWARD GRAY
(Jeff)

Born April 10, 1963, at Richmond, Va.
Height, 6.01. Weight, 175.
Throws and bats righthanded.
Attended Florida State University, Tallahassee, Fla.

Led Florida State League in games finished in relief with 47 in 1985.
Tied for Gulf Coast League lead in intentional bases on balls issued with 5 in 1984.

Year Club	League	G.	IP.	W.	L.	Pct.	H.	R.	ER.	SO.	BB.	ERA.
1984—Sarasota Phillies	Gulf Coast	26	41⅓	6	4	.600	35	9	6	26	10	1.31
1985—Clearwater†	Florida St.	55	87⅔	5	9	.357	80	38	31	80	33	3.18
1986—Vermont	Eastern	*55	84⅓	*14	2	*.875	71	24	22	65	26	2.35

Signed as free agent by Philadelphia Phillies' organization, June 14, 1984.
†Traded with Pitcher John Denny to Cincinnati Reds for Outfielder Gary Redus and Pitcher Tom Hume, December 11, 1985.

CHRISTOPHER DeWAYNE GREEN
(Chris)
Born September 5, 1960, at Los Angeles, Calif.
Height, 6.04. Weight, 207.
Throws and bats lefthanded.

Led Pacific Coast League in games finished in relief with 38 in 1986.
Led Carolina League in balks with 4 in 1982.

Year Club	League	G.	IP.	W.	L.	Pct.	H.	R.	ER.	SO.	BB.	ERA.
1979—Bradenton Pirates	Gulf Coast	9	32	1	2	.333	28	28	22	31	40	6.19
1980—Shelby†‡	W. Carol.	19	95	6	7	.462	103	57	45	57	28	4.26
1981—Greenwood	S. Atlantic	27	184	15	7	.682	148	87	63	128	86	3.08
1982—Alexandria	Carolina	14	86⅓	9	1	*.900	76	29	24	84	33	2.50
1982—Buffalo	Eastern	13	99⅓	7	5	.583	71	41	36	82	52	3.26
1983—Hawaii	P. Coast	13	77⅓	0	9	.000	94	53	45	49	36	5.24
1983—Lynn	Eastern	23	74⅔	5	6	.455	76	38	33	73	31	3.98
1984—Pittsburgh	National	4	3	0	0	.000	5	2	2	3	1	6.00
1984—Hawaii§	P. Coast	13	16⅔	2	2	.500	15	15	11	18	8	5.94
1985—Hawaii xy	P. Coast	35	97⅔	3	6	.333	108	50	46	91	28	4.24
1986—Edmonton	P. Coast	46	63⅔	4	5	.444	74	37	31	44	22	4.38
Major League Totals—1 Year		4	3	0	0	.000	5	2	2	3	1	6.00

Selected by Pittsburgh Pirates' organization in 4th round of free-agent draft, June 5, 1979.
†On disabled list, April 21 to May 9, 1980.
‡On suspended list, May 9 to May 13, 1980.
§On temporary inactive list, June 12 to July 26, 1984.
xOn disabled list, April 11 to April 23, 1985.
yTraded to California Angels' organization for Infielder Kevin Davis, April 4, 1986.

GARY ALLAN GREEN
Born January 14, 1962, at Pittsburgh, Pa.
Height, 6.03. Weight, 175.
Throws and bats righthanded.
Attended Oklahoma State University, Stillwater, Okla.
Son of Freddie Green, pitcher with Pittsburgh Pirates and
Washington Senators, 1959 through 1962 and 1964.

Led Texas League in sacrifice hits with 15 in 1985.
Member of 1984 U.S. Olympic baseball team.

Year Club	League	Pos.	G.	AB.	R.	H.	2B.	3B.	HR.	RBI.	B.A.	PO.	A.	E.	F.A.
1985—Beaumont†	Texas	SS	119	409	44	105	17	1	1	51	.257	157	405	30	.949
1986—Las Vegas	P. C.	SS	129	416	42	104	11	3	0	41	.250	158	390	24	.958
1986—San Diego	Nat.	SS	13	33	2	7	1	0	0	2	.212	16	35	0	1.000
Major League Totals—1 Year			13	33	2	7	1	0	0	2	.212	16	35	0	1.000

Selected by San Francisco Giants' organization in 29th round of free-agent draft, June 3, 1980.
Selected by St. Louis Cardinals' organization in 2nd round of free-agent draft, June 6, 1983.
Selected by San Diego Padres' organization in 1st round (26th player selected) of free-agent draft, June 4, 1984.
†On disabled list, July 19 to July 28, 1985.

OTIS ANDRE GREEN
Born March 11, 1964, at Miami, Fla.
Height, 6.02. Weight, 180.
Throws and bats lefthanded.
Attended Miami-Dade Community College (North), Miami, Fla.

Tied for International League lead in double plays by outfielders with 3 in 1986.

Year Club	League	Pos.	G.	AB.	R.	H.	2B.	3B.	HR.	RBI.	B.A.	PO.	A.	E.	F.A.
1983—Medicine Hat	Pion.	OF	59	241	44	76	8	2	10	37	.315	102	1	7	.936
1984—Florence	S. Atl.	OF	43	158	31	42	6	4	5	26	.266	70	4	2	.974
1984—Kinston	Carol.	OF	84	305	40	79	18	3	6	34	.259	120	7	5	.962
1985—Knoxville†	South.	OF	115	442	68	128	19	5	11	68	.290	221	4	3	.987
1986—Syracuse	Int.	OF	122	480	66	135	24	8	5	53	.281	226	13	8	.968

Selected by Chicago White Sox' organization in 5th round of free-agent draft, June 7, 1982.
Selected by Chicago White Sox' organization in secondary phase of free-agent draft, January 11, 1983.
Selected by Toronto Blue Jays' organization in secondary phase of free-agent draft, June 6, 1983.
†On disabled list, July 18 to August 14, 1985.

MICHAEL LEWIS GREENWELL
(Mike)

Born July 18, 1963, at Louisville, Ky.
Height, 6.00. Weight, 170.
Throws right and bats lefthanded.

Major League stolen bases: 1985 (1).
Led Carolina League in being hit by pitch with 15 in 1984.

Year Club	League	Pos.	G.	AB.	R.	H.	2B.	3B.	HR.	RBI.	B.A.	PO.	A.	E.	F.A.
1982—Elmira	NYP	3B-2B	72	268	57	72	10	1	6	36	.269	96	151	31	.888
1983—Winston-Salem†	Carol.	OF	48	158	23	44	8	0	3	21	.278	28	1	1	.967
1984—Winston-Salem	Carol.	3B-OF	130	454	70	139	23	6	16	84	.306	126	132	30	.896
1985—Pawtucket	Int.	OF	117	418	47	107	21	1	13	52	.256	178	8	7	.964
1985—Boston	Amer.	OF	17	31	7	10	1	0	4	8	.323	14	0	0	1.000
1986—Pawtucket	Int.	OF-3B	89	320	62	96	21	1	18	59	.300	130	20	8	.949
1986—Boston	Amer.	OF	31	35	4	11	2	0	0	4	.314	18	1	0	1.000
Major League Totals—2 Years			48	66	11	21	3	0	4	12	.318	32	1	0	1.000

Selected by Boston Red Sox' organization in 3rd round of free-agent draft, June 7, 1982.
†On disabled list, April 21 to May 2 and May 13 to July 25, 1983.

CHAMPIONSHIP SERIES RECORD

Year Club	League	Pos.	G.	AB.	R.	H.	2B.	3B.	HR.	RBI.	B.A.	PO.	A.	E.	F.A.
1986—Boston	Amer.	PH	2	2	0	1	0	0	0	0	.500	0	0	0	.000

WORLD SERIES RECORD

Year Club	League	Pos.	G.	AB.	R.	H.	2B.	3B.	HR.	RBI.	B.A.	PO.	A.	E.	F.A.
1986—Boston	Amer.	PH	4	3	0	0	0	0	0	0	.000	0	0	0	.000

ROBERT ANTHONY GRICH
(Bobby)

Born January 15, 1949, at Muskegon, Mich.
Height, 6.02. Weight, 190.
Throws and bats righthanded.
Attended University of California, Los Angeles, Calif., and
Fresno State University, Fresno, Calif.

Established major league records for highest fielding average by second baseman, season, 100 or more games (.9967), 1985; most putouts, second baseman, season (484), 1974.
Tied major league records for fewest errors by second baseman, 150 or more games, season (5), 1973; highest fielding average, second baseman, lifetime (.984).
Tied American League record for most games, second baseman, season (162), 1973.
Major League stolen bases: 1970 (1), 1971 (1), 1972 (13), 1973 (17), 1974 (17), 1975 (14), 1976 (14), 1977 (6), 1978 (4), 1979 (1), 1980 (3), 1981 (2), 1982 (3), 1983 (2), 1984 (2), 1985 (3), 1986 (1). Total—104.
Hit three home runs in a game, June 18, 1974.
Led American League in slugging percentage with .543 in 1981.
Led American League in being hit by pitch with 20 in 1974.
Led American League second basemen in fielding percentage with .997 in 1985.
Led American League second basemen in double plays with 130 in 1973, 132 in 1974 and 122 in 1975.
Led American League second basemen in total chances with 945 in 1973, 957 in 1974 and 928 in 1975.
Led International League in total bases with 299 in 1971.
Led International League shortstops in double plays with 81 in 1971.
Named Minor League Player of the Year by THE SPORTING NEWS, 1971.
Named International League Most Valuable Player, 1971.
Named Texas League co-Most Valuable Player, 1969.
Named second baseman on THE SPORTING NEWS American League All-Star Team, 1976, 1979 and 1981.
Named second baseman on THE SPORTING NEWS American League All-Star fielding team, 1973 through 1976.
Named second baseman on THE SPORTING NEWS American League Silver Slugger team, 1981.
Received reported $40,000 bonus to sign with Baltimore Orioles, 1967.

Year Club	League	Pos.	G.	AB.	R.	H.	2B.	3B.	HR.	RBI.	B.A.	PO.	A.	E.	F.A.
1967—Bluefield	Appal.	SS	58	213	43	54	10	4	3	26	.254	74	126	24	.893
1968—Stockton	Calif.	SS	113	426	63	97	18	2	8	44	.228	205	★379	35	.943
1969—Dal.-Ft. Worth†	Texas	SS	121	413	60	128	16	8	2	50	.310	★199	368	29	.951
1970—Rochester	Int.	2B-SS	63	235	67	90	11	3	9	42	.383	144	199	9	.974
1970—Baltimore	Amer.	SS-2-3	30	95	11	20	1	3	0	8	.211	56	79	7	.951
1971—Rochester	Int.	SS	130	473	★124	159	26	9	★32	83	★.336	★238	★394	17	★.974
1971—Baltimore	Amer.	SS-2	7	30	7	9	0	0	1	6	.300	11	31	0	1.000
1972—Baltimore	Amer.	S-2-1-3	133	460	66	128	21	3	12	50	.278	299	338	20	.970
1973—Baltimore	Amer.	2B	●162	581	82	146	29	7	12	50	.251	★431	★509	5	★.995
1974—Baltimore	Amer.	2B	160	582	92	153	29	6	19	82	.263	★484	★453	20	.979
1975—Baltimore	Amer.	2B	150	524	81	136	26	4	13	57	.260	★423	★484	21	.977
1976—Baltimore‡	Amer.	★2B-3B	144	518	93	138	31	4	13	54	.266	★389	400	12	.985
1977—California§	Amer.	SS	52	181	24	44	6	0	7	23	.243	88	141	4	.983
1978—California	Amer.	2B	144	487	68	122	16	2	6	42	.251	325	419	13	.983
1979—California	Amer.	2B	153	534	78	157	30	5	30	101	.294	340	438	13	.984
1980—California	Amer.	2B-1B	150	498	60	135	22	2	14	62	.271	353	464	9	.989
1981—California x	Amer.	2B	100	352	56	107	14	2	●22	61	.304	230	349	10	.983
1982—California y	Amer.	2B	145	506	74	132	28	5	19	65	.261	338	450	11	.986
1983—California	Amer.	★2B-SS	120	387	65	113	17	0	16	62	.292	271	415	★22	.969
1984—California	Amer.	2B-1B-3B	116	363	60	93	15	1	18	58	.256	311	282	12	.980

Year	Club	League	Pos.	G.	AB.	R.	H.	2B.	3B.	HR.	RBI.	B.A.	PO.	A.	E.	F.A.
1985—California z		Amer.	2B-1B-3B	144	479	74	116	17	3	13	53	.242	331	408	3	.996
1986—California a		Amer.	2B-1B-3B	98	313	42	84	18	0	9	30	.268	202	231	7	.984
Major League Totals—17 Years				2008	6890	1039	1833	320	47	224	864	.266	4882	5891	189	.983

Selected by Baltimore Orioles' organization in 1st round (18th player selected) of free-agent draft, June 6, 1967.

†On military list, September 2, 1969 through April 1, 1970.

‡Granted free agency, November 1, 1976; signed by California Angels, November 24, 1976.

§On disabled list, June 9, 1977 through remainder of season.

xOn disabled list, June 10 to August 8, 1981.

yOn disabled list, August 30, 1983 through remainder of season.

zGranted free agency, November 12, 1985; re-signed by Angels, November 26, 1985.

aReleased, December 19, 1986.

CHAMPIONSHIP SERIES RECORD

Tied American League Championship Series records for most times on losing club (5); most at-bats, game (6), October 11, 1986 (11 innings); most strikeouts, five-game Series (7), 1982; most strikeouts, seven-game Series (8), 1986; most consecutive strikeouts, one Series, consecutive at-bats and plate appearances (4), 1982.

Year	Club	League	Pos.	G.	AB.	R.	H.	2B.	3B.	HR.	RBI.	B.A.	PO.	A.	E.	F.A.
1973—Baltimore		Amer.	2B	5	20	1	2	0	0	1	1	.100	16	9	0	1.000
1974—Baltimore		Amer.	2B	4	16	2	4	1	0	1	2	.250	13	12	1	.962
1979—California		Amer.	2B	4	13	0	2	1	0	0	2	.154	4	12	1	.941
1982—California		Amer.	2B	5	15	1	3	1	0	0	1	.200	10	17	0	1.000
1986—California		Amer.	2B-1B	6	24	1	5	0	0	1	3	.208	29	9	3	.927
Championship Series Totals—5 Years				24	88	5	16	3	0	3	9	.182	72	59	5	.963

ALL-STAR GAME RECORD

Year	League	Pos.	AB.	R.	H.	2B.	3B.	HR.	RBI.	B.A.	PO.	A.	E.	F.A.
1972—American		SS	4	0	0	0	0	0	0	.000	0	3	0	1.000
1974—American		2B	3	0	1	0	0	0	0	.333	0	2	0	1.000
1976—American		2B	2	0	0	0	0	0	0	.000	1	1	0	1.000
1979—American		2B	1	0	0	0	0	0	0	.000	2	0	0	1.000
1980—American		2B	0	0	0	0	0	0	0	.000	0	1	0	1.000
1982—American		2B	1	0	0	0	0	0	0	.000	2	2	0	1.000
All-Star Game Totals—6 Years			11	0	1	0	0	0	0	.091	5	9	0	1.000

GEORGE KENNETH GRIFFEY
(Ken)

Born April 10, 1950, at Donora, Pa.

Height, 6.00. Weight, 200.

Throws and bats lefthanded.

Tied major league record for most at bats, game, since 1900 (7), June 13, 1975.

Major League stolen bases: 1973 (4), 1974 (9), 1975 (16), 1976 (34), 1977 (17), 1978 (23), 1979 (12), 1980 (23), 1981 (12), 1982 (10), 1983 (5), 1984 (2), 1985 (7), 1986 (14). Total—188.

Hit three home runs in a game, July 22, 1986.

Led American Association in stolen bases with 43 in 1973.

Tied for Eastern League lead in double plays by outfielders with 6 in 1972.

Named as outfielder on THE SPORTING NEWS National League All-Star Team, 1976.

Year	Club	League	Pos.	G.	AB.	R.	H.	2B.	3B.	HR.	RBI.	B.A.	PO.	A.	E.	F.A.
1969—Bradenton Reds	Gulf C.	*OF-1B	49	153	22	43	*11	1	1	12	.281	57	4	*10	.859
1970—Sioux Falls	North.	OF	51	164	20	40	2	1	2	24	.244	76	2	7	.918
1971—Tampa	Fla. St.	OF	88	281	60	96	7	11	3	33	.342	137	13	8	.949
1971—Three Rivers	East.	OF	9	32	1	13	1	2	0	4	.406	17	0	1	.944
1972—Three Rivers	East.	●OF-SS	128	472	*96	150	21	3	14	52	.318	212	10	●15	.937
1973—Indianapolis	A. A.	OF	107	397	88	130	18	5	10	58	.327	171	11	6	.968
1973—Cincinnati	Nat.	OF	25	86	19	33	5	1	3	14	.384	25	1	0	1.000
1974—Indianapolis	A. A.	OF	43	162	34	54	6	4	5	18	.333	70	4	1	.987
1974—Cincinnati	Nat.	OF	88	227	24	57	9	5	2	19	.251	115	5	0	1.000
1975—Cincinnati	Nat.	OF	132	463	95	141	15	9	4	46	.305	202	6	7	.967
1976—Cincinnati	Nat.	OF	148	562	111	189	28	9	6	74	.336	270	10	6	.976
1977—Cincinnati	Nat.	OF	154	585	117	186	35	8	12	57	.318	298	10	3	.990
1978—Cincinnati	Nat.	OF	158	614	90	177	33	8	10	63	.288	296	13	10	.969
1979—Cincinnati†	Nat.	OF	95	380	62	120	27	4	8	32	.316	175	8	3	.984
1980—Cincinnati	Nat.	OF	146	544	89	160	28	10	13	85	.294	266	5	6	.978
1981—Cincinnati‡	Nat.	OF	101	396	65	123	21	6	2	34	.311	268	8	3	.989
1982—New York	Amer.	OF	127	484	70	134	23	2	12	54	.277	282	8	5	.983
1983—New York§	Amer.	1B-OF	118	458	60	140	21	3	11	46	.306	870	57	8	.991
1984—New York	Amer.	OF-1B	120	399	44	109	20	1	7	56	.273	422	22	16	.965
1985—New York x	Amer.	OF-1B	127	438	68	120	28	4	10	69	.274	227	8	7	.971
1986—New York y	Amer.	OF	59	198	33	60	7	0	9	26	.303	96	5	3	.971
1986—Atlanta	Nat.	OF-1B	80	292	36	90	15	3	12	32	.308	136	2	2	.986
National League Totals—10 Years			1127	4149	708	1276	216	63	72	456	.308	2051	68	40	.981
American League Totals—5 Years			551	1977	275	563	99	10	49	251	.285	1897	100	39	.981
Major League Totals—14 Years			1678	6126	983	1839	315	73	121	707	.300	3948	168	79	.981

Selected by Cincinnati Reds' organization in 29th round of free-agent draft, June 5, 1969.

†On disabled list, August 14 to September 7, 1979.

‡Traded to New York Yankees for Pitcher Brian Ryder and a player to be named later, November 4, 1981; Cincinnati Reds' organization acquired Pitcher Freddie Toliver to complete deal, December 10, 1981.

§On disabled list, July 2 to August 2, 1983.
xOn disabled list, May 28 to June 12, 1985.
yTraded to Atlanta Braves for Outfielder Claudell Washington and Shortstop Paul Zuvella, June 30, 1986.

CHAMPIONSHIP SERIES RECORD

Tied Championship Series record for most stolen bases, game (3), October 5, 1975.

Year Club	League	Pos.	G.	AB.	R.	H.	2B.	3B.	HR.	RBI.	B.A.	PO.	A.	E.	F.A.
1973—Cincinnati	Nat.	OF-PH	3	7	0	1	1	0	0	0	.143	2	0	0	1.000
1975—Cincinnati	Nat.	OF	3	12	3	4	1	0	0	4	.333	4	1	0	1.000
1976—Cincinnati	Nat.	OF	3	13	2	5	0	1	0	2	.385	11	0	0	1.000
Championship Series Totals—3 Years....			9	32	5	10	2	1	0	6	.313	17	1	0	1.000

WORLD SERIES RECORD

Tied World Series record for fewest chances accepted by outfielder, extra-inning game (0), October 21, 1975 (12 innings); most at-bats, game, no hits (5), October 21, 1976.

Year Club	League	Pos.	G.	AB.	R.	H.	2B.	3B.	HR.	RBI.	B.A.	PO.	A.	E.	F.A.
1975—Cincinnati	Nat.	OF	7	26	4	7	3	1	0	4	.269	10	1	0	1.000
1976—Cincinnati	Nat.	OF	4	17	2	1	0	0	0	1	.059	5	0	0	1.000
World Series Totals—2 Years			11	43	6	8	3	1	0	5	.186	15	1	0	1.000

ALL-STAR GAME RECORD

Year League	Pos.	AB.	R.	H.	2B.	3B.	HR.	RBI.	B.A.	PO.	A.	E.	F.A.
1976—National	OF	1	1	1	0	0	0	1	1.000	1	0	0	1.000
1980—National	OF	3	1	2	0	0	1	1	.667	0	0	0	.000
All-Star Game Totals—2 Years		4	2	3	0	0	1	2	.750	1	0	0	1.000

Member of National League All-Star Team in 1977; did not play.

ALFREDO CLAUDINO GRIFFIN

Born March 6, 1957, at Dominican Republic City, Dominican Republic.
Height, 5.11. Weight, 165.
Throws right and bats left and righthanded.

Major League stolen bases: 1977 (2), 1979 (21), 1980 (18), 1981 (8), 1982 (10), 1983 (8), 1984 (11), 1985 (24), 1986 (33). Total—135.

Led American League shortstops in putouts with 280 in 1983.
Led American League shortstops in total chances with 824 in 1982.
Named shortstop on THE SPORTING NEWS American League All-Star fielding team, 1985.
Named American League Co-Rookie of the Year by the Baseball Writers' Association of America, 1979.

Year Club	League	Pos.	G.	AB.	R.	H.	2B.	3B.	HR.	RBI.	B.A.	PO.	A.	E.	F.A.
1974—Reno	Calif.	SS	11	35	4	9	0	0	0	1	.257	10	22	9	.780
1974—Sarasota Ind.	Gulf C.	SS	49	158	17	41	1	0	0	11	.259	67	133	★25	.889
1975—San Jose	Calif.	SS	124	358	42	82	4	3	0	25	.229	189	281	47	.909
1976—San Jose	Calif.	SS	64	224	40	58	3	1	0	17	.259	91	145	24	.908
1976—Williamsport	East.	SS	58	200	22	55	3	0	0	17	.275	86	172	17	.938
1976—Toledo	Int.	SS	22	88	5	19	7	1	0	6	.216	44	71	7	.943
1976—Cleveland	Amer.	SS	12	4	0	1	0	0	0	0	.250	1	2	1	.750
1977—Toledo	Int.	SS	125	457	60	114	14	5	1	32	.249	★223	398	★49	.927
1977—Cleveland	Amer.	SS	14	41	5	6	1	0	0	3	.146	17	30	3	.940
1978—Portland	P. C.	★SS-OF	133	474	82	138	22	10	5	48	.291	201	395	★40	.937
1978—Cleveland†	Amer.	SS	5	4	1	2	1	0	0	0	.500	4	7	1	.917
1979—Toronto	Amer.	SS	153	624	81	179	22	10	2	31	.287	272	501	★36	.956
1980—Toronto	Amer.	SS	155	653	63	166	26	●15	2	41	.254	295	489	★37	.955
1981—Toronto	Amer.	★SS-3B-2B	101	388	30	81	19	6	0	21	.209	191	279	★31	.938
1982—Toronto	Amer.	SS	●162	539	57	130	20	8	1	48	.241	★319	479	●26	.968
1983—Toronto	Amer.	SS-2B	●162	528	62	132	22	9	4	47	.250	287	422	25	.966
1984—Toronto‡	Amer.	SS-2B	140	419	53	101	8	2	4	30	.241	230	320	21	.963
1985—Oakland	Amer.	SS	162	614	75	166	18	7	2	64	.270	278	440	30	.960
1986—Oakland	Amer.	SS	162	594	74	169	23	6	4	51	.285	282	421	25	.966
Major League Totals—11 Years			1228	4408	501	1133	160	63	19	336	.257	2176	3390	236	.959

Signed as free agent by Cleveland Indians' organization, August 22, 1973.
†Traded with Third Baseman Phil Lansford to Toronto Blue Jays for Pitcher Victor Cruz, December 6, 1978.
‡Traded with Outfielder Dave Collins and cash to Oakland A's for Pitcher Bill Caudill, December 8, 1984.

ALL-STAR GAME RECORD

Year League	Pos.	AB.	R.	H.	2B.	3B.	HR.	RBI.	B.A.	PO.	A.	E.	F.A.
1984—American	SS	0	0	0	0	0	0	0	.000	0	1	0	1.000

GREGORY EUGENE GROSS
(Greg)

Born August 1, 1952, at York, Pa.
Height, 5.11. Weight, 175.
Throws and bats lefthanded.

Major League stolen bases: 1973 (2), 1974 (12), 1975 (2), 1976 (2), 1978 (3), 1979 (5), 1980 (1), 1981 (2), 1982 (4), 1983 (3), 1984 (1), 1985 (1), 1986 (1). Total—39.
Tied for Appalachian League lead in double plays by outfielders with 3 in 1970.
Named National League Rookie Player of the Year by THE SPORTING NEWS, 1974.
Named Appalachian League Player of the Year, 1970.

Year Club League	Pos.	G.	AB.	R.	H.	2B.	3B.	HR.	RBI.	B.A.	PO.	A.	E.	F.A.
1970—Covington .... Appal.	OF	54	211	40	★74	8	3	2	27	.351	93	★10	3	.972
1971—Columbus............... South.	OF-1B	132	494	57	144	14	4	2	33	.291	244	13	9	.966
1972—Columbus............... South.	OF	101	367	55	111	14	2	0	25	.302	172	9	3	.984
1972—Okla. City.............. A. A.	OF	28	109	15	27	4	0	0	8	.248	64	4	1	.986
1973—Denver .... A. A.	OF	131	528	98	★174	25	6	0	55	.330	226	11	10	.960
1973—Houston .... Nat.	OF	14	39	5	9	2	1	0	1	.231	13	2	0	1.000
1974—Houston .... Nat.	OF	156	589	78	185	21	8	0	36	.314	296	15	2	.994
1975—Houston† .... Nat.	OF	132	483	67	142	14	10	0	41	.294	216	14	10	.958
1976—Houston‡ .... Nat.	OF	128	426	52	122	12	3	0	27	.286	208	13	5	.978
1977—Chicago .... Nat.	OF	115	239	43	77	10	4	5	32	.322	109	3	1	.991
1978—Chicago§ .... Nat.	OF	124	347	34	92	12	7	1	39	.265	182	6	4	.979
1979—Philadelphia x ...... Nat.	OF	111	174	21	58	6	3	0	15	.333	82	5	2	.978
1980—Philadelphia .... Nat.	OF-1B	127	154	19	37	7	2	0	12	.240	69	5	2	.974
1981—Philadelphia .... Nat.	OF	83	102	14	23	6	1	0	7	.225	48	7	1	.982
1982—Philadelphia .... Nat.	OF	119	134	14	40	4	0	0	10	.299	55	3	1	.983
1983—Philadelphia .... Nat.	OF-1B	136	245	25	74	12	3	0	29	.302	105	1	1	.991
1984—Philadelphia .... Nat.	OF-1B	112	202	19	65	9	1	0	16	.322	195	13	2	.990
1985—Philadelphia y ..... Nat.	OF-1B	93	169	21	44	5	2	0	14	.260	66	8	0	1.000
1986—Philadelphia .... Nat.	OF-1B-P	87	101	11	25	5	0	0	8	.248	40	3	0	1.000
Major League Totals—14 Years...............		1537	3404	423	993	125	45	6	287	.292	1684	98	31	.983

Selected by Houston Astros' organization in 4th round of free-agent draft, June 4, 1970.

†On disabled list, April 2 to April 24, 1975.

‡Traded to Chicago Cubs for Infielder Julio Gonzalez, December 8, 1976.

§Traded with Second Baseman Manny Trillo and Catcher Dave Rader to Philadelphia Phillies for Outfielder Jerry Martin, Catcher Barry Foote, Second Baseman Ted Sizemore and Pitchers Derek Botelho and Henry Mack, February 23, 1979.

xGranted free agency, November 1, 1979; re-signed by Phillies, December 13, 1979.

yOn disabled list, September 6, 1985 through remainder of season.

DIVISION SERIES RECORD

Year Club League	Pos.	G.	AB.	R.	H.	2B.	3B.	HR.	RBI.	B.A.	PO.	A.	E.	F.A.
1981—Philadelphia .... Nat.	PH-OF	4	4	0	0	0	0	0	0	.000	0	0	0	.000

CHAMPIONSHIP SERIES RECORD

Year Club League	Pos.	G.	AB.	R.	H.	2B.	3B.	HR.	RBI.	B.A.	PO.	A.	E.	F.A.
1980—Philadelphia .... Nat.	PH-OF	4	4	2	3	0	0	0	1	.750	1	0	0	1.000
1983—Philadelphia .... Nat.	OF-PH	4	5	1	0	0	0	0	0	.000	4	0	0	1.000
Championship Series Totals—2 Years.....		8	9	3	3	0	0	0	1	.333	5	0	0	1.000

WORLD SERIES RECORD

Year Club League	Pos.	G.	AB.	R.	H.	2B.	3B.	HR.	RBI.	B.A.	PO.	A.	E.	F.A.
1980—Philadelphia .... Nat.	PH-OF	4	2	0	0	0	0	0	0	.000	1	0	0	1.000
1983—Philadelphia .... Nat.	OF	2	6	0	0	0	0	0	0	.000	8	0	0	1.000
World Series Totals—2 Years		6	8	0	0	0	0	0	0	.000	9	0	0	1.000

PITCHING RECORD

Year Club	League	G.	IP.	W.	L.	Pct.	H.	R.	ER.	SO.	BB.	ERA.
1986—Philadelphia	National	1	⅔	0	0	.000	1	0	0	2	1	0.00

KEVIN FRANK GROSS

Born June 8, 1961, at Downey, Calif.
Height, 6.05. Weight, 203.
Throws and bats righthanded.
Attended Oxnard College, Oxnard, Calif.,
and California Lutheran College, Thousand Oaks, Calif.

Major League saves: 1984 (1).

Led National League in home runs allowed with 28 and tied for lead in hit batsmen with 8 in 1986.

Tied for South Atlantic League lead in games started by pitchers with 28 in 1981.

Year Club	League	G.	IP.	W.	L.	Pct.	H.	R.	ER.	SO.	BB.	ERA.
1981—Spartanburg..................... S. Atlantic	28	192	13	12	.520	173	94	76	123	62	3.56
1982—Reading............................. Eastern	26	151	10	15	.400	138	81	71	136	89	4.23
1983—Portland............................. P. Coast	15	80	3	5	.375	82	60	60	61	45	6.75
1983—Philadelphia .... National	17	96	4	6	.400	100	46	38	66	35	3.56
1984—Philadelphia .... National	44	129	8	5	.615	140	66	59	84	44	4.12
1985—Philadelphia .... National	38	205⅔	15	13	.536	194	86	78	151	81	3.41
1986—Philadelphia .... National	37	241⅔	12	12	.500	240	115	108	154	94	4.02
Major League Totals—4 Years.............................		136	672⅓	39	36	.520	674	313	283	455	254	3.79

Selected by Baltimore Orioles' organization in 32nd round of free-agent draft, June 5, 1979.

Selected by Philadelphia Phillies' organization in secondary phase of free-agent draft, January 13, 1981.

WAYNE DALE GROSS

Born January 14, 1952, at Riverside, Calif.
Height, 6.02. Weight, 205.
Throws right and bats lefthanded.
Attended California Poly State University, Pomona, Calif.

Major League stolen bases: 1977 (5), 1979 (4), 1980 (5), 1981 (2), 1982 (3), 1983 (3), 1984 (1), 1985 (1). Total—24.

Year Club	League	Pos.	G.	AB.	R.	H.	2B.	3B.	HR.	RBI.	B.A.	PO.	A.	E.	F.A.
1973—Lewiston	N'west.	1B	8	29	4	7	2	0	1	1	.241	58	4	0	1.000
1973—Burlington	Midw.	1B-OF	56	187	27	44	8	3	4	36	.235	426	19	4	.991
1974—Birmingham	South.	1B-OF-3B	105	316	36	77	12	2	14	54	.244	503	42	15	.973
1975—Birmingham	South.	OF-1B	130	435	69	121	23	2	19	71	.278	193	16	13	.941
1976—Tucson	P. C.	3B-1B-OF	115	395	77	128	30	7	19	75	.324	273	164	16	.965
1976—Oakland	Amer.	1B-OF	10	18	0	4	0	0	0	1	.222	30	1	1	.969
1977—Oakland	Amer.	*3B-1B	146	485	66	113	21	1	22	63	.233	127	242	*27	.932
1978—Vancouver	P. C.	3B-1B-OF	17	56	20	23	5	0	3	10	.411	32	33	5	.929
1978—Oakland	Amer.	3B-1B	118	285	18	57	10	2	7	23	.200	120	150	22	.925
1979—Oakland	Amer.	3B-1B-OF	138	442	54	99	19	1	14	50	.224	252	225	21	.958
1980—Oakland	Amer.	3B-1B	113	366	45	103	20	3	14	61	.281	125	136	11	.960
1981—Oakland	Amer.	3B-1B	82	243	29	50	7	1	10	31	.206	68	127	12	.942
1982—Oakland	Amer.	3B-1B	129	386	43	97	14	0	9	41	.251	203	189	11	.973
1983—Oakland†	Amer.	1B-3B-P	137	339	34	79	18	0	12	44	.233	473	113	9	.985
1984—Baltimore	Amer.	3B-1B	127	342	53	74	9	1	22	64	.216	69	205	18	.938
1985—Baltimore‡	Amer.	3B-1B	103	217	31	51	8	0	11	18	.235	81	102	10	.948
1986—Tacoma	P. C.	3B-1B	62	185	30	47	9	0	9	35	.254	16	21	4	.902
1986—Oakland§	Amer.	3B	3	2	0	0	0	0	0	0	.000	0	0	1	.000
Major League Totals—11 Years			1106	3125	373	727	126	9	121	396	.233	1548	1490	143	.955

Selected by Oakland A's organization in 9th round of free-agent draft, June 5, 1973.
†Traded to Baltimore Orioles for Pitcher Tim Stoddard, December 9, 1983.
‡Released, April 3, 1986; signed by Tacoma (Oakland A's organization), May 12, 1986.
§Released, December 8, 1986.

DIVISION SERIES RECORD

Year Club	League	Pos.	G.	AB.	R.	H.	2B.	3B.	HR.	RBI.	B.A.	PO.	A.	E.	F.A.
1981—Oakland	Amer.	3B-PH	2	5	1	2	0	0	1	3	.400	1	4	0	1.000

CHAMPIONSHIP SERIES RECORD

Year Club	League	Pos.	G.	AB.	R.	H.	2B.	3B.	HR.	RBI.	B.A.	PO.	A.	E.	F.A.
1981—Oakland	Amer.	PH-3B	3	5	0	0	0	0	0	0	.000	2	0	0	1.000

ALL-STAR GAME RECORD

Member of American League All-Star Team in 1977; did not play.

PITCHING RECORD

Year Club	League	G.	IP.	W.	L.	Pct.	H.	R.	ER.	SO.	BB.	ERA.
1983—Oakland	American	1	2⅓	0	0	.000	2	0	0	0	1	0.00

JOHN MAYWOOD GRUBB JR.

Born August 4, 1948, at Richmond, Va.
Height, 6.03. Weight, 180.
Throws right and bats lefthanded.
Attended Manatee Junior College, West Bradenton, Fla., and received degree from
Florida State University, Tallahassee, Fla.

Major League stolen bases: 1973 (9), 1974 (4), 1975 (2), 1976 (1), 1978 (6), 1979 (2), 1980 (2), 1984 (1). Total—27.
Tied for Texas League lead in double plays by outfielders with 4 in 1972.

Year Club	League	Pos.	G.	AB.	R.	H.	2B.	3B.	HR.	RBI.	B.A.	PO.	A.	E.	F.A.
1971—Lodi	Calif.	OF-3B-2B	116	409	69	126	23	5	12	56	.308	158	84	14	.945
1972—Alexandria	Texas	*OF-1B	126	446	66	132	25	2	10	61	.296	205	12	2	*.991
1972—San Diego	Nat.	OF	7	21	4	7	1	1	0	1	.333	16	0	0	1.000
1973—San Diego	Nat.	OF-3B	113	389	52	121	22	3	8	37	.311	229	11	3	.988
1974—San Diego	Nat.	OF-3B	140	444	53	127	20	4	8	42	.286	321	8	8	.976
1975—San Diego	Nat.	OF	144	553	72	149	36	2	4	38	.269	334	3	3	.991
1976—San Diego†‡	Nat.	OF-1B-2B	109	384	54	109	22	1	5	27	.284	248	7	6	.977
1977—Cleveland§	Amer.	OF	34	93	8	28	3	3	2	14	.301	47	2	0	1.000
1978—Cleve. x-Tex.	Amer.	OF	134	411	62	113	19	6	15	67	.275	213	16	6	.974
1979—Texas y	Amer.	OF	102	289	42	79	14	0	10	37	.273	135	8	2	.986
1980—Texas	Amer.	OF	110	274	40	76	12	1	9	32	.277	112	6	6	.952
1981—Texas	Amer.	OF	67	199	26	46	9	1	3	26	.231	95	2	1	.990
1982—Texas za	Amer.	OF	103	308	35	86	13	3	3	26	.279	135	4	5	.965
1983—Detroit b	Amer.	OF	57	134	20	34	5	2	4	22	.254	34	1	0	1.000
1984—Detroit c	Amer.	OF	86	176	25	47	5	0	8	17	.267	47	0	0	1.000
1985—Detroit d	Amer.	OF	78	155	19	38	7	1	5	25	.245	23	0	0	1.000
1986—Nashville e	A. A.	OF	8	28	4	5	1	0	1	3	.179	7	2	1	.900
1986—Detroit	Amer.	OF	81	210	32	70	13	1	13	51	.333	26	1	0	1.000
National League Totals—5 Years			513	1791	235	513	101	11	25	145	.286	1148	29	20	.983
American League Totals—10 Years			852	2249	309	617	100	18	72	317	.274	867	40	20	.978
Major League Totals—15 Years			1365	4040	544	1130	201	29	97	462	.280	2015	69	40	.981

Selected by Boston Red Sox' organization in 3rd round of free-agent draft, February 1, 1969.
Selected by Cincinnati Reds' organization in secondary phase of free-agent draft, June 5, 1969.
Selected by Atlanta Braves' organization in secondary phase of free-agent draft, June 4, 1970.
Selected by San Diego Padres' organization in secondary phase of free-agent draft, January 13, 1971.
†On disabled list, April 26 to May 28, 1976.
‡Traded with Catcher Fred Kendall and Shortstop Hector Torres to Cleveland Indians for Outfielder George Hendrick, December 8, 1976.
§On disabled list, April 1 to April 23 and July 8, 1977 through remainder of season.

xTraded to Texas Rangers for a player to be named later, August 31, 1978; Cleveland Indians acquired Pitcher Bobby Cuellar and Outfielder David Rivera to complete deal, October 3, 1978.

yOn disabled list, August 6 to September 1, 1979.

zOn disabled list, March 27 to April 26, 1982.

aTraded to Detroit Tigers for Pitcher Dave Tobik, March 24, 1983.

bOn disabled list, July 27 to September 13, 1983.

cGranted free agency, November 8, 1984; re-signed by Tigers, December 23, 1984.

dOn disabled list, July 5 to July 20, 1985.

eOn Detroit disabled list, April 6 to May 15, 1986; included rehabilitation disability assignment to Nashville, May 5 to May 15, 1986.

CHAMPIONSHIP SERIES RECORD

Year Club	League	Pos.	G.	AB.	R.	H.	2B.	3B.	HR.	RBI.	B.A.	PO.	A.	E.	F.A.
1984—Detroit	Amer.	DH	1	4	0	1	1	0	0	2	.250	0	0	0	.000

WORLD SERIES RECORD

Year Club	League	Pos.	G.	AB.	R.	H.	2B.	3B.	HR.	RBI.	B.A.	PO.	A.	E.	F.A.
1984—Detroit	Amer.	PH-DH	4	3	0	1	0	0	0	0	.333	0	0	0	.000

ALL-STAR GAME RECORD

Year League	Pos.	AB.	R.	H.	2B.	3B.	HR.	RBI.	B.A.	PO.	A.	E.	F.A.
1974—National	OF	1	0	0	0	0	0	0	.000	0	20	0	.000

KELLY WAYNE GRUBER

Born February 26, 1962, at Bellaire, Tex.
Height, 6.00. Weight, 180.
Throws and bats righthanded.
Attended University of Texas, Austin, Tex.

Major League stolen bases: 1986 (2).
Led International League in slugging percentage with .500 in 1984.
Led International League third basemen in total chances with 309 in 1985.
Led Southern League shortstops in errors with 43 in 1982.

Year Club	League	Pos.	G.	AB.	R.	H.	2B.	3B.	HR.	RBI.	B.A.	PO.	A.	E.	F.A.
1980—Batavia	NYP	SS	61	212	27	46	3	2	2	19	.217	87	155	21	.920
1981—Waterloo	Midw.	SS	127	458	64	133	25	4	14	59	.290	*180	*389	*56	.910
1982—Chattanooga	South.	SS-3B	128	441	53	107	18	4	13	54	.243	161	333	44	.918
1983—Buffalo†	East.	3B-SS-OF	111	403	60	106	20	4	15	54	.263	98	170	27	.908
1984—Toronto	Amer.	3B-OF-SS	15	16	1	1	0	0	1	2	.063	6	12	2	.900
1984—Syracuse	Int.	3B-OF	97	342	53	92	12	2	21	55	.269	76	156	18	.928
1985—Syracuse	Int.	3B	121	473	71	118	16	5	21	69	.249	78	*217	14	.955
1985—Toronto	Amer.	3B-2B	5	13	0	3	0	0	0	1	.231	2	6	0	1.000
1986—Toronto	Amer.	3-2-O-S	87	143	20	28	4	1	5	15	.196	43	77	7	.945
Major League Totals—3 Years			107	172	21	32	4	1	6	18	.186	51	95	9	.942

Selected by Cleveland Indians' organization in 1st round (10th player selected) of free-agent draft, June 3, 1980.

†Drafted by Toronto Blue Jays, December 5, 1983.

CECILIO GUANTE (MAGALLANES)

Name pronounced Goo-AHN-tay.

Born February 2, 1960, at Villa Mella, D.R.
Height, 6.03. Weight, 200.
Throws and bats righthanded.

Major League saves: 1983 (9), 1984 (2), 1985 (5), 1986 (4). Total—20.
Led South Atlantic League in saves with 19 in 1980.

Year Club	League	G.	IP.	W.	L.	Pct.	H.	R.	ER.	SO.	BB.	ERA.
1980—Shelby	S. Atlantic	39	90	6	6	.500	58	32	29	114	25	2.90
1980—Salem	Carolina	6	14	0	0	.000	7	2	2	18	8	1.29
1981—Buffalo	Eastern	10	14	1	1	.500	8	3	1	17	9	0.64
1981—Portland†	P. Coast	19	104	6	6	.500	110	64	62	70	58	5.37
1982—Portland	P. Coast	21	35	3	2	.600	34	17	15	29	26	3.86
1982—Pittsburgh	National	10	27	0	0	.000	28	16	10	26	5	3.33
1983—Hawaii	P. Coast	15	25⅔	2	1	.667	22	12	10	24	12	3.51
1983—Pittsburgh	National	49	100⅓	2	6	.250	90	45	37	82	46	3.32
1984—Pittsburgh‡	National	27	41⅓	2	3	.400	32	12	12	30	16	2.61
1984—Nashua	Eastern	1	3	0	0	.000	5	1	1	2	0	3.00
1985—Pittsburgh	National	63	109	4	6	.400	84	34	33	92	40	2.72
1986—Pittsburgh§x	National	52	78	5	2	.714	65	32	29	63	29	3.35
Major League Totals—5 Years		201	355⅔	13	17	.433	299	139	121	293	136	3.06

Signed as free agent by Pittsburgh Pirates' organization, November 24, 1979.

†On disabled list, July 25 to August 5, 1981.

‡On disabled list, July 13 to July 30, 1984.

§On disabled list, August 25 to September 23, 1986.

xTraded with Pitchers Rick Rhoden and Pat Clements to New York Yankees for Pitchers Doug Drabek, Brian Fisher and Logan Easley, November 26, 1986.

MARK STEVEN GUBICZA

Name pronounced GOO-ba-zah.

Born August 14, 1962, at Philadelphia, Pa.
Height, 6.05. Weight, 210.
Throws and bats righthanded.
Son of Anthony F. Gubicza, minor league pitcher, 1950 and 1951.

Year Club	League	G.	IP.	W.	L.	Pct.	H.	R.	ER.	SO.	BB.	ERA.
1981—Sarasota Royals-Gold	Gulf Coast	11	56	●8	1	*.889	39	18	14	40	23	2.25
1982—Fort Myers†	Florida St.	11	48	2	5	.286	49	33	22	36	25	4.13
1983—Jacksonville	Southern	28	196	14	12	.538	146	81	67	*146	93	3.08
1984—Kansas City	American	29	189	10	14	.417	172	90	85	111	75	4.05
1985—Kansas City	American	29	177⅓	14	10	.583	160	88	80	99	77	4.06
1986—Kansas City‡	American	35	180⅔	12	6	.667	155	77	73	118	84	3.64
Major League Totals—3 Years		93	547	36	30	.545	487	255	238	328	236	3.92

Selected by Kansas City Royals' organization in 2nd round of free-agent draft, June 8, 1981.
†On disabled list, June 29, 1982 through remainder of season.
‡On disabled list, June 6 to June 21, 1986.

CHAMPIONSHIP SERIES RECORD

Year Club	League	G.	IP.	W.	L.	Pct.	H.	R.	ER.	SO.	BB.	ERA.
1985—Kansas City	American	2	8⅓	1	0	1.000	4	3	3	4	4	3.24

PEDRO GUERRERO

Name pronounced Guh-RAIR-oh.

Born June 29, 1956, at San Pedro de Macoris, Dominican Republic.
Height, 6.00. Weight, 195.
Throws and bats righthanded.
Cousin of Domingo Michel, second baseman in Los Angeles Dodgers' organization.

Established National League record for most home runs, month of June (15), 1985.
Major League stolen bases: 1979 (2), 1980 (2), 1981 (5), 1982 (22), 1983 (23), 1984 (9), 1985 (12). Total—75.
Led National League in slugging percentage with .577 in 1985.
Led National League third basemen in errors with 30 and tied for lead in total chances with 458 in 1983.
Led Pacific Coast League in sacrifice flies with 15 in 1978.
Tied for Northwest League lead in double plays by third basemen with 13 in 1974.
Named outfielder on THE SPORTING NEWS National League All-Star Team, 1981 and 1982.
Named outfielder on THE SPORTING NEWS National League Silver Slugger team, 1982.

Year Club	League	Pos.	G.	AB.	R.	H.	2B.	3B.	HR.	RBI.	B.A.	PO.	A.	E.	F.A.
1973—Sarasota Ind.†	Gulf C.	3B-SS	44	153	13	39	2	3	2	22	.255	32	82	11	.912
1974—Orangeburg	W. Car.	3B	19	55	3	8	1	0	0	1	.145	11	22	5	.868
1974—Bellingham	N'west	3B	82	297	49	94	●23	2	3	55	.316	*69	124	23	.894
1975—Danville	Midw.	3B-OF	104	351	81	121	25	5	10	76	*.345	111	168	31	.900
1976—Waterbury	East.	1B	132	495	73	151	*30	10	5	66	.305	1129	*96	*19	.985
1977—Albuquerque‡	P. C.	1B	32	129	30	52	11	4	4	39	.403	329	17	10	.972
1978—Albuquerque	P. C.	1B-3B	134	492	92	166	28	4	14	*116	.337	982	80	10	.991
1978—Los Angeles	Nat.	1B	5	8	3	5	0	1	0	1	.625	25	1	0	1.000
1979—Albuquerque	P. C.	OF-3B-1B	113	453	94	151	33	9	22	*103	.333	188	9	5	.975
1979—Los Angeles	Nat.	OF-3B-3B	25	62	7	15	2	0	2	9	.242	53	4	1	.983
1980—Los Angeles§	Nat.	O-2-3-1	75	183	27	59	9	1	7	31	.322	103	110	3	.986
1981—Los Angeles	Nat.	OF-3B-1B	98	347	46	104	17	2	12	48	.300	165	55	11	.952
1982—Los Angeles	Nat.	OF-3B	150	575	87	175	27	5	32	100	.304	282	53	12	.965
1983—Los Angeles	Nat.	3B-1B	160	584	87	174	28	6	32	103	.298	130	308	31	.934
1984—Los Angeles x	Nat.	3B-OF-1B	144	535	85	162	29	4	16	72	.303	271	151	22	.950
1985—Los Angeles	Nat.	OF-3B-1B	137	487	99	156	22	2	33	87	.320	251	123	13	.966
1986—Los Angeles y	Nat.	OF-1B	31	61	7	15	3	0	5	10	.246	39	1	0	1.000
Major League Totals—9 Years			825	2842	448	865	137	21	139	461	.304	1319	806	93	.958

Signed as free agent by Cleveland Indians' organization, January 15, 1973.
†Traded to Los Angeles Dodgers for Pitcher Bruce Ellingsen, April 4, 1974.
‡On disabled list, May 19 to August 30, 1977.
§On disabled list, August 23 to September 15, 1980.
xOn disabled list, July 22 to August 6, 1984.
yOn disabled list, April 4 to July 30 and August 11 to September 3, 1986.

DIVISION SERIES RECORD

Year Club	League	Pos.	G.	AB.	R.	H.	2B.	3B.	HR.	RBI.	B.A.	PO.	A.	E.	F.A.
1981—Los Angeles	Nat.	3B	5	17	1	3	1	0	1	1	.176	3	15	0	1.000

CHAMPIONSHIP SERIES RECORD

Tied National League Championship Series record for most bases on balls, six-game Series (5), 1985.

Year Club	League	Pos.	G.	AB.	R.	H.	2B.	3B.	HR.	RBI.	B.A.	PO.	A.	E.	F.A.
1981—Los Angeles	Nat.	OF	5	19	1	2	0	0	1	2	.105	9	2	0	1.000
1983—Los Angeles	Nat.	3B	4	12	1	3	1	1	0	2	.250	0	9	0	1.000
1985—Los Angeles	Nat.	OF	6	20	2	5	1	0	0	4	.250	11	0	0	1.000
Championship Series Totals—3 Years			15	51	4	10	2	1	1	8	.196	20	11	0	1.000

WORLD SERIES RECORD

Year Club	League	Pos.	G.	AB.	R.	H.	2B.	3B.	HR.	RBI.	B.A.	PO.	A.	E.	F.A.
1981—Los Angeles	Nat.	OF	6	21	2	7	1	1	2	7	.333	17	1	0	1.000

Year League	Pos.	AB.	R.	H.	2B.	3B.	HR.	RBI.	B.A.	PO.	A.	E.	F.A.
1981—National.............................	PH	1	0	0	0	0	0	0	.000	0	0	0	.000
1983—National.............................	3B-OF	1	0	0	0	0	0	0	.000	0	0	1	.000
All-Star Game Totals—2 Years....................		2	0	0	0	0	0	0	.000	0	0	1	.000

Named to National League All-Star Team for 1985 game; replaced due to injury by Glenn Wilson.

ARTHUR LEE GUETTERMAN
(Known by middle name.)

Born November 22, 1958, at Chattanooga, Tenn.
Height, 6.08. Weight, 225.
Throws and bats lefthanded.
Received bachelor of science degree in physical education from
Liberty Baptist College, Lynchburg, Va. in 1981.

Year Club	League	G.	IP.	W.	L.	Pct.	H.	R.	ER.	SO.	BB.	ERA.
1981—Bellingham	Northwest	13	84	6	4	.600	85	36	25	55	42	2.68
1982—Bakersfield.................................	California	26	154	7	11	.389	172	100	76	82	69	4.44
1983—Bakersfield.................................	California	25	156⅓	12	6	.667	164	72	56	93	45	3.22
1984—Chattanooga†	Southern	24	157	11	7	.611	174	68	59	47	38	3.38
1984—Seattle..	American	3	4⅓	0	0	.000	9	2	2	2	2	4.15
1985—Calgary‡	P. Coast	20	110⅓	5	8	.385	138	86	71	48	44	5.79
1986—Seattle..	American	41	76	0	4	.000	108	67	62	38	30	7.34
1986—Calgary	P. Coast	4	19⅓	1	0	1.000	24	12	12	8	7	5.59
Major League Totals—2 Years............................		44	80⅓	0	4	.000	117	69	64	40	32	7.17

Selected by Seattle Mariners' organization in 4th round of free-agent draft, June 8, 1981.
†On disabled list, August 1 to August 15, 1984.
‡On disabled list, April 11 to May 31, 1985.

RONALD AMES GUIDRY
Name pronounced GID-ree.
(Ron)

Born August 28, 1950, at Lafayette, La.
Height, 5.11. Weight, 160.
Throws and bats lefthanded.
Attended University of Southwestern Louisiana, Lafayette, La.

Established major league record for highest winning percentage, season, 20 or more wins (.893), 1978.
Tied major league record for striking out side on nine pitches, August 7, 1984, second game (ninth inning).
Established American League record for most strikeouts by lefthanded pitcher, game (18), June 17, 1978.
Tied American League record for most shutouts by lefthanded pitcher, season (9), 1978.
Major League saves: 1977 (1), 1979 (2), 1980 (1). Total—4.
Led American League in complete games with 21 in 1983.
Led American League in shutouts with 9 in 1978.
Named Man of the Year by THE SPORTING NEWS, 1978.
Named Major League Player of the Year by THE SPORTING NEWS, 1978.
Named American League Pitcher of the Year by THE SPORTING NEWS, 1978.
Won American League Cy Young Memorial Award, 1978.
Named lefthanded pitcher on THE SPORTING NEWS American League All-Star Team, 1978, 1981, 1983 and 1985.
Named pitcher on THE SPORTING NEWS American League All-Star fielding team, 1982 through 1986.

Year Club	League	G.	IP.	W.	L.	Pct.	H.	R.	ER.	SO.	BB.	ERA.
1971—Johnson City	Ap'lachian	7	47	2	2	.500	34	13	11	61	27	2.11
1972—Fort Lauderdale†	Florida St.	15	66	2	4	.333	53	35	28	61	50	3.82
1973—Kinston‡....................................	Carolina	20	101	7	6	.538	85	53	36	97	70	3.21
1974—West Haven§.............................	Eastern	37	77	2	4	.333	80	48	45	79	53	5.26
1975—Syracuse.....................................	Int'national	42	62	6	5	.545	46	24	20	76	37	2.90
1975—New York..................................	American	10	16	0	1	.000	15	6	6	15	9	3.38
1976—New York..................................	American	7	16	0	0	.000	20	12	10	12	4	5.63
1976—Syracuse.....................................	Int'national	22	40	5	1	.833	16	5	3	50	13	0.68
1977—New York..................................	American	31	211	16	7	.696	174	72	66	176	65	2.82
1978—New York..................................	American	35	274	★25	3	★.893	187	61	53	248	72	★1.74
1979—New York x	American	33	236	18	8	.692	203	83	73	201	71	★2.78
1980—New York..................................	American	37	220	17	10	.630	215	97	87	166	80	3.56
1981—New York y	American	23	127	11	5	.688	100	41	39	104	26	2.76
1982—New York..................................	American	34	222	14	8	.636	216	104	94	162	69	3.81
1983—New York x	American	31	250⅓	21	9	.700	232	99	95	156	60	3.42
1984—New York za..............................	American	29	195⅔	10	11	.476	223	102	98	127	44	4.51
1985—New York..................................	American	34	259	★22	6	★.786	243	104	94	143	42	3.27
1986—New York b	American	30	192⅓	9	12	.429	202	94	85	140	38	3.98
1986—Albany c.....................................	Eastern	1	3	0	0	.000	1	1	1	3	2	3.00
Major League Totals—12 Years............................		334	2219⅓	163	80	.671	2030	875	800	1650	580	3.24

Selected by New York Yankees' organization in 3rd round of free-agent draft, June 8, 1971.
†Appeared as outfielder in one game with one putout.
‡On temporary inactive list, July 13 to August 3, 1973.
§Appeared as outfielder with no chances.
xAppeared as outfielder in one game with no chances.
yGranted free agency, November 10, 1981; re-signed by Yankees, December 15, 1981.
zOn disabled list, August 16 to September 3, 1984.
aAppeared in one game as a pinch-runner.

bOn disabled list, July 3 to July 27, 1986; included rehabilitation disability assignment to Albany, July 23 to July 27, 1986.

cGranted free agency, November 12, 1986.

DIVISION SERIES RECORD

Year Club	League	G.	IP.	W.	L.	Pct.	H.	R.	ER.	SO.	BB.	ERA.
1981—New York	American	2	8⅓	0	0	.000	11	5	5	8	3	5.40

CHAMPIONSHIP SERIES RECORD

Year Club	League	G.	IP.	W.	L.	Pct.	H.	R.	ER.	SO.	BB.	ERA.
1977—New York	American	2	11⅓	1	0	1.000	9	5	5	8	3	3.97
1978—New York	American	1	8	1	0	1.000	7	1	1	7	1	1.13
1980—New York	American	1	3	0	1	.000	5	4	4	2	4	12.00
Championship Series Totals—3 Years		4	22⅓	2	1	.667	21	10	10	17	8	4.03

Appeared as pinch-runner for New York Yankees in one game of 1976 Championship Series.

WORLD SERIES RECORD

Tied World Series record for most consecutive home runs allowed, inning (2), October 25, 1981 (seventh inning).

Year Club	League	G.	IP.	W.	L.	Pct.	H.	R.	ER.	SO.	BB.	ERA.
1977—New York	American	1	9	1	0	1.000	4	2	2	7	3	2.00
1978—New York	American	1	9	1	0	1.000	8	1	1	4	7	1.00
1981—New York	American	2	14	1	1	.500	8	3	3	15	4	1.93
World Series Totals—3 Years		4	32	3	1	.750	20	6	6	26	14	1.69

ALL-STAR GAME RECORD

Year League	IP.	W.	L.	Pct.	H.	R.	ER.	SO.	BB.	ERA.
1978—American	⅓	0	0	.000	0	0	0	0	0	0.00
1979—American	⅓	0	0	.000	0	0	0	0	1	0.00
All-Star Game Totals—2 Years	⅔	0	0	.000	0	0	0	0	1	0.00

Member of American League All-Star Team in 1982; did not play.
Named to American League All-Star Team for 1983 game; replaced due to injury by Tippy Martinez.

OSWALDO JOSE GUILLEN (BARRIOS)
Name pronounced GEY-un.
(Ozzie)

Born January 20, 1964, at Ocumare del Tuy, Miranda, Venezuela.
Height, 5.10. Weight, 160.
Throws right and bats lefthanded.

Tied major league record for fewest bases on balls received, 150 or more games, season (12), 1985, 1986.
Established American League record for fewest putouts, shortstop, season, 150 or more games (220), 1985.
Major League stolen bases: 1985 (7), 1986 (8). Total—15.
Led Pacific Coast League shortstops in assists with 362 and total chances with 549 in 1984.
Tied for California League lead in sacrifice hits with 14 in 1982.
Named American League Rookie Player of the Year by The Sporting News, 1985.
Named American League Rookie of the Year by Baseball Writers' Association of America, 1985.

Year Club	League	Pos.	G.	AB.	R.	H.	2B.	3B.	HR.	RBI.	B.A.	PO.	A.	E.	F.A.
1981—Bradenton Padr.†	Gulf C.	SS-2B	55	189	26	49	4	1	0	16	.259	105	135	15	.941
1982—Reno†	Calif.	SS	130	528	*103	*183	33	1	2	54	.347	*240	399	41	.940
1983—Beaumont†‡	Texas	SS	114	427	62	126	20	4	2	48	.295	185	327	*38	.931
1984—Las Vegas†‡	P. C.	SS-2B	122	463	81	137	26	6	5	53	.296	172	364	17	.969
1985—Chicago	Amer.	SS	150	491	71	134	21	9	1	33	.273	220	382	12	*.980
1986—Chicago	Amer.	SS	159	547	58	137	19	4	2	47	.250	261	459	22	.970
Major League Totals—2 Years			309	1038	129	271	40	13	3	80	.261	481	841	34	.975

Signed as free agent by San Diego Padres' organization, December 17, 1980.
†Switch-hitter.
‡Traded with Pitchers Tim Lollar and Bill Long and Third Baseman Luis Salazar to Chicago White Sox for Pitchers LaMarr Hoyt, Kevin Kristan and Todd Simmons, December 6, 1984.

BRADLEY LEE GULDEN
(Brad)

Born June 10, 1956, at New Ulm, Minn.
Height, 5.11. Weight, 182.
Throws right and bats lefthanded.

Major League stolen bases: 1984 (2).
Led Pacific Coast League in passed balls with 22 and tied for lead in double plays by catchers with 11 in 1978.
Led California League in passed balls with 18 in 1977.
Led Northwest League catchers in double plays with 9 and passed balls with 23 in 1975.

Year Club	League	Pos.	G.	AB.	R.	H.	2B.	3B.	HR.	RBI.	B.A.	PO.	A.	E.	F.A.
1975—Bellingham	N'west	C	66	203	25	33	4	0	2	15	.163	*319	*70	*33	.922
1976—Danville	Midw.	*C-OF	103	334	42	95	20	2	3	51	.284	521	90	*39	.939
1977—Lodi	Calif.	C	118	423	76	127	23	2	15	86	.300	*704	*66	*24	.970
1978—Albuquerque	P. C.	C	125	436	69	128	21	4	8	72	.294	*610	*88	*23	.968
1978—Los Angeles†	Nat.	C	3	4	0	0	0	0	0	0	.000	8	1	0	1.000
1979—Columbus	Int.	C	80	230	28	57	10	0	6	34	.248	326	22	3	.991
1979—New York	Amer.	C	40	92	10	15	4	0	0	6	.163	178	24	1	.995

Year Club	League	Pos.	G.	AB.	R.	H.	2B.	3B.	HR.	RBI.	B.A.	PO.	A.	E.	F.A.
1980—Columbus	Int.	C	14	51	6	8	2	0	2	10	.157	54	13	4	.944
1980—Nashville‡	South.	C-OF	85	295	34	70	13	6	6	46	.237	543	80	12	.981
1980—New York§	Amer.	C	2	3	1	1	0	0	1	2	.333	3	0	0	1.000
1981—Seattle	Amer.	C	8	16	0	3	2	0	0	1	.188	24	3	0	1.000
1981—Spokane	P. C	C	15	51	9	14	5	0	2	9	.275	37	3	5	.889
1981—Columbus x	Int.	C-OF	73	237	37	70	13	4	17	42	.295	362	39	7	.983
1982—Wichita	A. A.	C-OF	64	212	37	61	16	2	7	35	.288	219	20	6	.976
1982—Montreal y	Nat.	C	5	6	1	0	0	0	0	0	.000	6	2	0	1.000
1983—Columbus z	Int.	C	94	275	45	87	16	1	9	47	.316	512	45	●13	.977
1984—Cincinnati	Nat.	C	107	292	31	66	8	2	4	33	.226	485	53	14	.975
1985—Denver a	A. A.	C-1B	45	143	20	35	7	0	4	16	.245	263	24	5	.983
1985—Tucson bc	P. C.	C-1B	47	153	20	41	10	2	3	21	.268	203	25	5	.979
1986—Phoenix	P. C.	C	20	46	3	12	3	0	0	9	.261	56	4	1	.984
1986—San Francisco d	Nat.	C	17	22	2	2	0	0	0	1	.091	26	1	0	1.000
National League Totals—4 Years			132	324	34	68	8	2	4	34	.210	525	57	14	.977
American League Totals—3 Years			50	111	11	19	6	0	1	9	.171	205	27	1	.996
Major League Totals—7 Years			182	435	45	87	14	2	5	43	.200	730	84	15	.982

Selected by Los Angeles Dodgers' organization in 17th round of free-agent draft, June 4, 1975.

†Traded to New York Yankees for Outfielder Gary Thomasson, February 15, 1979.

‡On disabled list, August 7 to August 17, 1980.

§Traded with cash to Seattle Mariners for Infielder Larry Milbourne and a player to be named later, November 18, 1980; Seattle traded Gulden back to New York Yankees to complete deal, May 18, 1981.

xTraded to Montreal Expos' organization for Catcher Bobby Ramos, April 5, 1982.

ySold to New York Yankees, October 26, 1982.

zGranted free agency, October 20, 1983; signed by Cincinnati Reds, November 4, 1983.

aSold to Tucson (Houston Astros' organization), June 12, 1985.

bOn disabled list, August 16 to August 27, 1985.

cGranted free agency, October 15, 1985; signed by San Francisco Giants, December 12, 1985.

dReleased, October 16, 1986.

WILLIAM LEE GULLICKSON
(Bill)

Born February 20, 1959, at Marshall, Minn.
Height, 6.03. Weight, 220.
Throws and bats righthanded.

Tied modern major league record for most wild pitches, game (6), April 10, 1982.
Led National League in home runs allowed with 27 in 1984.
Named National League Rookie Pitcher of the Year by THE SPORTING NEWS, 1980.

Year Club	League	G.	IP.	W.	L.	Pct.	H.	R.	ER.	SO.	BB.	ERA.
1977—West Palm Beach	Florida St.	10	56	3	3	.500	67	30	25	35	17	4.02
1978—West Palm Beach	Florida St.	20	148	9	9	.500	121	45	30	127	52	1.82
1978—Memphis	Southern	8	50	1	4	.200	44	19	17	43	19	3.06
1979—Denver	Am. Assoc.	11	54	3	3	.500	65	44	40	31	26	6.67
1979—Memphis	Southern	16	116	10	3	.769	110	52	47	115	42	3.65
1979—Montreal	National	1	1	0	0	.000	2	0	0	0	0	0.00
1980—Denver	Am. Assoc.	9	66	6	2	.750	47	14	14	64	29	1.91
1980—Montreal	National	24	141	10	5	.667	127	53	47	120	50	3.00
1981—Montreal	National	22	157	7	9	.438	142	54	49	115	34	2.81
1982—Montreal	National	34	236⅔	12	14	.462	231	101	94	155	61	3.57
1983—Montreal	National	34	242⅓	17	12	.586	230	108	101	120	59	3.75
1984—Montreal†	National	32	226⅔	12	9	.571	230	100	91	100	37	3.61
1985—Montreal‡§	National	29	181½	14	12	.538	187	78	71	68	47	3.52
1986—Cincinnati	National	37	244⅔	15	12	.556	245	103	92	121	60	3.38
Major League Totals—8 Years		213	1430⅔	87	73	.544	1394	597	545	799	348	3.43

Selected by Montreal Expos' organization in 1st round (second player selected) of free-agent draft, June 7, 1977.

†On disabled list, April 20 to May 8, 1984.

‡On disabled list, June 17 to July 8, 1985.

§Traded with Catcher Sal Butera to Cincinnati Reds for Pitchers Jay Tibbs, Andy McGaffigan and John Stuper and Catcher Dann Bilardello, December 19, 1985.

DIVISION SERIES RECORD

Year Club	League	G.	IP.	W.	L.	Pct.	H.	R.	ER.	SO.	BB.	ERA.
1981—Montreal	National	1	7⅔	1	0	1.000	6	1	1	3	1	1.17

CHAMPIONSHIP SERIES RECORD

Tied Championship Series record for most games lost, Series (2), 1981.

Year Club	League	G.	IP.	W.	L.	Pct.	H.	R.	ER.	SO.	BB.	ERA.
1981—Montreal	National	2	14⅓	0	2	.000	12	5	4	12	6	2.51

DAVID LAWRENCE GUMPERT
(Dave)

Born May 5, 1958, at South Haven, Mich.
Height, 6.03. Weight, 190.
Throws and bats righthanded.
Received degree from Aquinas College, Grand Rapids, Mich.

Major League saves: 1982 (1), 1983 (2), 1986 (2). Total—5.

Tied for American Association lead in intentional bases on balls issued with 7 in 1985.

Year Club	League	G.	IP.	W.	L.	Pct.	H.	R.	ER.	SO.	BB.	ERA.
1981—Lakeland	Florida St.	14	108	8	5	.615	97	33	30	75	26	2.50
1981—Birmingham	Southern	11	74	6	3	.667	78	39	34	25	16	4.14
1981—Evansville	Am. Assoc.	1	4	0	0	.000	5	2	2	3	2	4.50
1982—Birmingham	Southern	42	70⅔	9	6	.600	56	20	17	52	23	2.17
1982—Evansville	Am. Assoc.	2	5⅔	1	0	1.000	0	0	0	2	3	0.00
1982—Detroit	American	5	2	0	0	.000	7	6	6	0	2	27.00
1983—Evansville	Am. Assoc.	14	27⅓	5	1	.833	23	8	7	17	9	2.28
1983—Detroit	American	26	44⅓	0	2	.000	43	16	13	14	7	2.64
1984—Evansville†	Am. Assoc.	56	87⅓	7	4	.636	105	51	48	48	40	4.95
1985—Iowa	Am. Assoc.	42	66⅔	3	4	.429	74	36	31	33	23	4.19
1985—Chicago‡	National	9	10⅓	1	0	1.000	12	7	4	4	7	3.48
1986—Iowa	Am. Assoc.	28	44⅓	2	1	.667	36	13	11	33	7	2.23
1986—Chicago	National	38	59⅔	2	0	1.000	60	32	29	45	28	4.37
American League Totals—2 Years		31	46⅓	0	2	.000	50	22	19	14	9	3.69
National League Totals—2 Years		47	70	3	0	1.000	72	39	33	49	35	4.24
Major League Totals—4 Years		78	116⅓	3	2	.600	122	61	52	63	44	4.02

Signed as free agent by Detroit Tigers' organization, November 4, 1980.
†Released, March 30, 1985; signed by Iowa (Chicago Cubs' organization), April 7, 1985.
‡On disabled list, August 23 to September 18, 1985.

JOAQUIN FERNANDO GUTIERREZ

Name pronounced Wah-KEEN Goo-TEE-erz.

(Jackie)

Born June 27, 1960, at Cartagena, Colombia.
Height, 6.01. Weight, 175.
Throws and bats righthanded.
Brother-in-law of Orlando Ramirez, shortstop with California Angels, 1974 through 1977 and 1979;
son of Campo Gutierrez, who competed in javelin event for Columbia in 1936 Olympics;
and brother of Freddie Gutierrez, who competed in 100 meter race in 1964 Olympics.

Established major league records for fewest assists (347), and chances accepted (575) by shortstop, season, 150 or more games, 1984.
Major League stolen bases: 1984 (12), 1985 (10), 1986 (3). Total—25.
Led Carolina League shortstops in assists with 423 and tied for lead in putouts with 205 and errors with 53 in 1981.

Year Club	League	Pos.	G.	AB.	R.	H.	2B.	3B.	HR.	RBI.	B.A.	PO.	A.	E.	F.A.
1978—Elmira	NYP	SS	63	216	23	42	8	0	0	18	*.194	*131	197	20	*.943
1979—Elmira	NYP	SS-2B	63	183	29	46	4	2	0	14	.251	97	157	12	.955
1980—Winter Haven	Fla. St.	3B-SS-2B	111	368	46	94	4	1	1	40	.255	103	179	19	.937
1981—Winston-Salem	Carol.	SS-3B	137	507	56	126	14	5	1	45	.249	207	428	55	.920
1982—Bristol	East.	SS	138	468	64	130	20	2	1	44	.278	*199	368	37	*.939
1983—New Britain	East.	SS	67	248	36	69	7	2	4	25	.278	116	194	13	.960
1983—Pawtucket	Int.	SS	66	233	30	62	11	1	1	17	.266	109	211	20	.941
1983—Boston	Amer.	SS	5	10	2	3	0	0	0	0	.300	9	6	1	.938
1984—Boston	Amer.	SS	151	449	55	118	12	3	2	29	.263	228	347	31	.949
1985—Boston†	Amer.	SS	103	275	33	60	5	2	2	21	.218	143	238	23	.943
1986—Baltimore‡	Amer.	2B-3B	61	145	8	27	3	0	0	4	.186	96	108	4	.981
1986—Rochester	Int.	SS	54	198	29	60	7	2	1	22	.303	93	146	13	.948
Major League Totals—4 Years			320	879	98	208	20	5	4	54	.237	476	699	59	.952

Signed as free agent by Boston Red Sox' organization, January 14, 1978.
†Traded to Baltimore Orioles for Pitcher Sammy Stewart, December 17, 1985.
‡On disabled list, May 12 to June 20, 1986; included rehabilitation disability assignment to Rochester, June 1 to June 20, 1986.

JOSE ALBERTO GUZMAN (MIRABEL)

Born April 9, 1963, at Santa Isabel, Puerto Rico.
Height, 6.03. Weight, 185.
Throws and bats righthanded.

Year Club	League	G.	IP.	W.	L.	Pct.	H.	R.	ER.	SO.	BB.	ERA.
1981—Sarasota Rangers	Gulf Coast	14	39	3	3	.500	44	30	23	13	14	5.31
1982—Sarasota Rangers	Gulf Coast	12	66	5	4	.556	51	21	16	42	13	2.18
1983—Burlington	Midwest	25	154⅔	12	8	.600	135	68	51	146	52	2.97
1984—Tulsa	Texas	25	140⅓	7	9	.438	137	75	65	82	55	4.17
1985—Oklahoma City	Am. Assoc.	25	149⅔	10	5	.667	131	60	52	76	40	3.13
1985—Texas	American	5	32⅔	2	2	.600	27	13	10	24	14	2.76
1986—Texas	American	29	172⅓	9	15	.375	199	101	87	87	60	4.54
Major League Totals—2 Years		34	205	12	17	.414	226	114	97	111	74	4.26

Signed as free agent by Texas Rangers' organization, February 10, 1981.

ANTHONY KEITH GWYNN

(Tony)

Born May 9, 1960, at Los Angeles, Calif.
Height, 5.11. Weight, 206.
Throws and bats lefthanded.
Attended San Diego State University, San Diego, Calif.
Brother of Chris Gwynn, outfielder in Los Angeles Dodgers' organization.

Tied modern National League record for most stolen bases, game (5), September 20, 1986.
Major League stolen bases: 1982 (8), 1983 (7), 1984 (33), 1985 (14), 1986 (37). Total—99.
Led National League outfielders in total chances with 360 in 1986.
Named outfielder on THE SPORTING NEWS National League All-Star Team, 1984 and 1986.
Named outfielder on THE SPORTING NEWS National League All-Star fielding team, 1986.
Named outfielder on THE SPORTING NEWS National League Silver Slugger team, 1984 and 1986.
Named Northwest League Most Valuable Player, 1981.
Drafted by San Diego Clippers in 10th round (210th player selected) of NBA draft, June 9, 1981.

Year	Club	League	Pos.	G.	AB.	R.	H.	2B.	3B.	HR.	RBI.	B.A.	PO.	A.	E.	F.A.
1981—Walla Walla	N'west	OF	42	178	46	59	12	1	12	37	★.331	76	2	3	.963
1981—Amarillo	Texas	OF	23	91	22	42	8	2	4	19	.462	41	1	0	1.000
1982—Hawaii	P. C.	OF	93	366	65	120	23	2	5	46	.328	208	11	4	.982
1982—San Diego†	Nat.	OF	54	190	33	55	12	2	1	17	.289	110	1	1	.991
1983—Las Vegas‡	P. C.	OF	17	73	15	25	6	0	0	7	.342	23	2	3	.893
1983—San Diego	Nat.	OF	86	304	34	94	12	2	1	37	.309	163	9	1	.994
1984—San Diego	Nat.	OF	158	606	88	★213	21	10	5	71	★.351	345	11	4	.989
1985—San Diego	Nat.	OF	154	622	90	197	29	5	6	46	.317	337	14	4	.989
1986—San Diego	Nat.	OF	160	★642	●107	★211	33	7	14	59	.329	★337	19	4	.989
Major League Totals—5 Years			612	2364	352	770	107	26	27	230	.326	1292	54	14	.990

Selected by San Diego Padres' organization in 3rd round of free-agent draft, June 8, 1981.
†On disabled list, August 26 to September 10, 1982.
‡On San Diego disabled list, March 26 to June 21, 1983; included rehabilitation assignment to Las Vegas, May 31 to June 20, 1983.

CHAMPIONSHIP SERIES RECORD

Tied Championship Series record for most runs, five-game Series (6), 1984.

Year	Club	League	Pos.	G.	AB.	R.	H.	2B.	3B.	HR.	RBI.	B.A.	PO.	A.	E.	F.A.
1984—San Diego	Nat.	OF	5	19	6	7	3	0	0	3	.368	9	0	0	1.000

WORLD SERIES RECORD

Year	Club	League	Pos.	G.	AB.	R.	H.	2B.	3B.	HR.	RBI.	B.A.	PO.	A.	E.	F.A.
1984—San Diego	Nat.	OF	5	19	1	5	0	0	0	0	.263	12	1	1	.929

ALL-STAR GAME RECORD

Year	League	Pos.	AB.	R.	H.	2B.	3B.	HR.	RBI.	B.A.	PO.	A.	E.	F.A.
1984—National		OF	3	0	1	0	0	0	0	.333	0	0	0	.000
1985—National		OF	1	0	0	0	0	0	0	.000	1	0	0	1.000
1986—National		OF	3	0	0	0	0	0	0	.000	1	0	0	1.000
All-Star Game Totals—3 Years			7	0	1	0	0	0	0	.143	2	0	0	1.000

CHRISTOPHER KARLTON GWYNN

(Chris)

Born October 13, 1964, at Long Beach, Calif.
Height, 6.00. Weight, 201.
Throws and bats lefthanded.
Attended San Diego State University, San Diego, Calif.
Brother of Tony Gwynn, outfielder with San Diego Padres.

Named outfielder on THE SPORTING NEWS College Baseball All-America Team, 1985.
Member of 1984 U.S. Olympic baseball team.

Year	Club	League	Pos.	G.	AB.	R.	H.	2B.	3B.	HR.	RBI.	B.A.	PO.	A.	E.	F.A.
1985—Vero Beach	Fla. St.	OF	52	179	19	46	8	6	0	17	.257	43	2	0	1.000
1986—San Antonio	Texas	OF	111	401	46	115	22	1	6	67	.287	186	11	2	.990

Selected by California Angels' organization in 5th round of free-agent draft, June 7, 1982.
Selected by Los Angeles Dodgers' organization in 1st round (10th player selected) of free-agent draft, June 3, 1985.

BRYAN EDMUND HAAS

(Moose)

Born April 22, 1956, at Baltimore, Md.
Height, 6.00. Weight, 170.
Throws and bats righthanded.
Attended Catonsville Junior College, Catonsville, Md.

Major League saves: 1978 (1), 1982 (1). Total—2.

Year	Club	League	G.	IP.	W.	L.	Pct.	H.	R.	ER.	SO.	BB.	ERA.
1974—Newark	NYP	13	96	5	5	.500	91	43	34	89	41	3.19
1975—Burlington	Midwest	25	171	11	8	.579	149	66	39	146	49	2.05
1976—Spokane	P. Coast	30	172	13	9	.591	208	116	★106	130	86	5.55
1976—Milwaukee	American	5	16	0	1	.000	12	8	7	9	12	3.94
1977—Milwaukee	American	32	198	10	12	.455	195	104	95	113	84	4.32
1978—Milwaukee†	American	7	31	2	3	.400	33	22	21	32	8	6.10
1979—Milwaukee	American	29	185	11	11	.500	198	112	98	95	59	4.77
1980—Milwaukee	American	33	252	16	15	.516	246	96	87	146	56	3.11
1981—Milwaukee	American	24	137	11	7	.611	146	69	68	64	40	4.47
1982—Milwaukee	American	32	193⅓	11	8	.517	232	101	96	104	39	4.47
1983—Milwaukee‡	American	25	179	13	3	.813	170	66	65	75	42	3.27
1984—Milwaukee	American	31	189⅓	9	11	.450	205	91	84	84	43	3.99

Year Club	League	G.	IP.	W.	L.	Pct.	H.	R.	ER.	SO.	BB.	ERA.
1985—Milwaukee§	American	27	161⅔	8	8	.500	165	85	69	78	25	3.84
1986—Oakland x	American	12	72⅓	7	2	.778	58	23	22	40	19	2.74
Major League Totals—11 Years		257	1614⅔	98	81	.547	1660	777	712	840	427	3.97

Selected by Milwaukee Brewers' organization in 2nd round of free-agent draft, June 5, 1974.
†On disabled list, April 20 to June 21 and June 27 to September 15, 1978.
‡Appeared in one game as a pinch-runner.
§Traded to Oakland A's for Infielder Steve Kiefer, Pitchers Mike Fulmer and Pete Kendrick and Catcher Charlie O'Brien, March 30, 1986.
xOn disabled list, July 20 to September 23, 1986.

DIVISION SERIES RECORD

Year Club	League	G.	IP.	W.	L.	Pct.	H.	R.	ER.	SO.	BB.	ERA.
1981—Milwaukee	American	2	6⅔	0	2	.000	13	7	7	1	1	9.45

CHAMPIONSHIP SERIES RECORD

Year Club	League	G.	IP.	W.	L.	Pct.	H.	R.	ER.	SO.	BB.	ERA.
1982—Milwaukee	American	1	7⅓	1	0	1.000	5	5	4	7	5	4.91

WORLD SERIES RECORD

Year Club	League	G.	IP.	W.	L.	Pct.	H.	R.	ER.	SO.	BB.	ERA.
1982—Milwaukee	American	2	7⅓	0	0	.000	8	7	6	4	3	7.36

JOHN GABRIEL HABYAN

Name pronounced HAY-bee-un.
Born January 29, 1964, at Bayshore, N.Y.
Height, 6.01. Weight, 195.
Throws and bats righthanded.

Pitched 6-0 no-hit victory against Columbus, May 13, 1985.

Year Club	League	G.	IP.	W.	L.	Pct.	H.	R.	ER.	SO.	BB.	ERA.
1982—Bluefield	Ap'lachian	12	81⅓	●9	2	.818	68	35	32	55	24	3.54
1982—Hagerstown	Carolina	1	⅔	0	0	.000	5	5	5	1	2	67.50
1983—Hagerstown	Carolina	11	48	2	3	.400	54	41	31	42	29	5.81
1983—Newark	NYP	11	71⅔	5	3	.625	68	34	27	64	29	3.39
1984—Hagerstown	Carolina	13	81⅓	9	4	.692	64	41	32	81	33	3.54
1984—Charlotte	Southern	13	77	4	7	.364	84	46	38	55	34	4.44
1985—Charlotte	Southern	28	189⅔	13	5	.722	157	73	69	123	90	3.27
1985—Baltimore	American	2	2⅓	1	0	1.000	3	1	0	2	0	0.00
1986—Rochester	Int'national	26	157⅓	12	7	.632	168	82	75	93	69	4.29
1986—Baltimore	American	6	26⅓	1	3	.250	24	17	13	14	18	4.44
Major League Totals—2 Years		8	29	2	3	.400	27	18	13	16	18	4.03

Selected by Baltimore Orioles' organization in 3rd round of free-agent draft, June 7, 1982.

JERRY WAYNE HAIRSTON

Born February 16, 1952, at Birmingham, Ala.
Height, 5.10. Weight, 190.
Throws right and bats left and righthanded.
Attended Lawson State Junior College, Birmingham, Ala.
Son of Sam Hairston, Sr., catcher with Chicago White Sox, 1951; and scout and minor league instructor with Chicago White Sox, 1961 through 1982 and 1985; brother of John Hairston, catcher-outfielder with Chicago Cubs, 1969; and Sam Hairston, Jr., second baseman in Chicago White Sox' organization, 1966.

Major League stolen bases: 1975 (1), 1976 (1), 1984 (2). Total—4.
Led Mexican League in bases on balls received with 122 in 1978, 77 in 1980 and 122 in 1981.
Led Midwest League second baseman in double plays with 77 in 1971.
Tied for Mexican League lead in double plays by outfielders with 4 in 1981.

Year Club	League	Pos.	G.	AB.	R.	H.	2B.	3B.	HR.	RBI.	B.A.	PO.	A.	E.	F.A.
1970—Sarasota W. Sox	Gulf C.	2B	56	183	37	61	8	2	1	36	.333	129	130	★19	.932
1971—Appleton	Midw.	2B	121	448	86	120	15	4	0	39	.268	★260	★333	★31	.950
1972—Knoxville	South.	2-1-O-3	132	459	82	134	19	●9	10	64	.292	591	225	27	.968
1973—Iowa	A. A.	O-2-3-1	84	274	51	95	18	6	9	65	.347	70	36	7	.938
1973—Chicago	Amer.	OF-1B	60	210	25	57	11	1	0	23	.271	194	13	5	.976
1974—Iowa	A. A.	OF	42	140	31	53	10	2	5	42	.379	48	1	2	.961
1974—Chicago†	Amer.	OF	45	109	8	25	7	0	0	8	.229	24	1	2	.926
1975—Denver	A. A.	DH	40	139	28	51	9	0	3	31	.367	0	0	0	.000
1975—Chicago	Amer.	OF	69	219	26	62	8	0	0	23	.283	111	6	6	.951
1976—Iowa	A. A.	OF-INF	94	325	53	94	24	3	5	64	.289	199	13	5	.977
1976—Chicago	Amer.	OF	44	119	20	27	2	2	0	10	.227	71	1	2	.973
1977—Knoxville‡	Amer.	OF	13	26	3	8	2	0	0	4	.308	15	1	0	1.000
1977—Pittsburgh§	Nat.	OF-2B	51	52	5	10	2	0	2	6	.192	13	0	1	.929
1978—Durango	Mex.	OF	144	488	97	177	21	7	9	77	.363	297	19	11	.966
1979—Durango	Mex.	OF	128	427	87	151	22	5	12	56	.354	295	8	6	.981
1980—Campeche	Mex.	OF-1B	77	235	50	74	15	2	7	28	.315	189	11	3	.985
1981—Mex. C. Reds x	Mex.	OF	123	536	74	118	14	8	7	73	.296	★334	11	6	.983
1981—Chicago	Amer.	OF	9	25	5	7	1	0	1	6	.280	14	0	1	.933
1982—Chicago	Amer.	OF	85	90	11	21	5	0	5	18	.233	34	2	0	1.000

Year	Club	League	Pos.	G.	AB.	R.	H.	2B.	3B.	HR.	RBI.	B.A.	PO.	A.	E.	F.A.
1983—Chicago	Amer.	OF	101	126	17	37	9	1	5	22	.294	29	1	1	.968
1984—Chicago	Amer.	OF	115	227	41	59	13	2	5	19	.260	57	2	2	.967
1985—Chicago	Amer.	OF	95	140	9	34	8	0	2	20	.243	5	0	0	1.000
1986—Chicago	Amer.	1B-OF	101	225	32	61	15	0	5	26	.271	132	9	0	1.000
American League Totals—11 Years			737	1516	197	398	81	6	23	179	.263	686	36	19	.974
National League Totals—1 Year			51	52	5	10	2	0	2	6	.192	13	0	1	.929
Major League Totals—11 Years			788	1568	202	408	83	6	25	185	.260	699	36	20	.974

Selected by Chicago White Sox' organization in 3rd round of free-agent draft, June 4, 1970.
†On disabled list, June 27 to July 12, 1974.
‡Sold to Pittsburgh Pirates, June 13, 1977.
§Sold to Durango of Mexican League, March 2, 1978.
xSold to Chicago White Sox, September 10, 1981.

CHAMPIONSHIP SERIES RECORD

Year	Club	League	Pos.	G.	AB.	R.	H.	2B.	3B.	HR.	RBI.	B.A.	PO.	A.	E.	F.A.
1983—Chicago	Amer.	PH-OF	2	3	0	0	0	0	0	0	.000	0	0	1	.000

ALBERT HALL

Born March 7, 1959, at Birmingham, Ala.
Height, 5.11. Weight, 155.
Throws right and bats left and righthanded.
Major League stolen bases: 1983 (1), 1984 (6), 1985 (1), 1986 (8). Total—16.
Led International League in stolen bases with 62 in 1982 and 72 in 1986.
Led International League in caught stealing with 16 in 1986.
Led Carolina League in being hit by pitch with 9, stolen bases with 100 and caught stealing with 27 in 1980.
Led Western Carolinas League in stolen bases with 66 in 1979.
Led Gulf Coast League shortstops in double plays with 23 in 1978.
Tied for Southern League lead in caught stealing with 17 in 1981.

Year	Club	League	Pos.	G.	AB.	R.	H.	2B.	3B.	HR.	RBI.	B.A.	PO.	A.	E.	F.A.
1977—Kingsport	Appal.	SS	35	68	11	11	0	0	0	3	.162	10	28	10	.792
1978—Bradenton Brav...	Gulf C.	SS	34	123	15	36	4	2	0	14	.293	55	100	●15	.912
1979—Greenwood	W. Car.	SS	105	368	84	106	10	3	0	38	.288	120	288	★72	.850
1980—Durham	Carol.	OF-SS	125	491	95	139	16	7	4	41	.283	166	32	16	.925
1981—Savannah	South.	OF	133	487	83	150	28	10	5	27	.308	263	16	10	.965
1981—Atlanta	Nat.	OF	6	2	1	0	0	0	0	0	.000	0	0	0	.000
1982—Richmond	Int.	OF	129	528	97	139	18	★15	3	42	.263	297	6	7	.977
1982—Atlanta	Nat.	PR	5	0	1	0	0	0	0	0	.000	0	0	0	.000
1983—Richmond	Int.	★OF-SS	130	521	120	153	28	★11	1	42	.294	280	10	★12	.960
1983—Atlanta	Nat.	OF	10	8	2	0	0	0	0	0	.000	3	0	1	.750
1984—Atlanta	Nat.	OF	87	142	25	37	6	1	1	9	.261	64	4	5	.932
1985—Atlanta	Nat.	OF	54	47	5	7	0	1	0	3	.149	7	2	1	.900
1985—Richmond†	Int.	OF	38	98	12	22	0	3	0	5	.224	77	2	3	.963
1986—Richmond	Int.	OF	125	441	73	119	18	3	3	41	.270	264	8	7	.975
1986—Atlanta	Nat.	OF	16	50	6	12	2	0	0	1	.240	26	1	3	.900
Major League Totals—6 Years			178	249	40	56	8	2	1	13	.225	100	7	10	.915

Selected by Atlanta Braves' organization in 6th round of free-agent draft, June 7, 1977.
†On disabled list, July 12 to July 26, 1985.

ANDREW CLARK HALL
(Drew)

Born March 27, 1963, at Louisville, Ky.
Height, 6.04. Weight, 205.
Throws and bats lefthanded.
Attended Morehead State University, Morehead, Ky.

Major League saves: 1986 (1).
Tied for Eastern League lead in shutouts with 3 in 1986.
Named lefthanded pitcher on THE SPORTING NEWS College Baseball All-America Team, 1984.

Year	Club	League	G.	IP.	W.	L.	Pct.	H.	R.	ER.	SO.	BB.	ERA.
1984—Lodi	California	8	48	3	3	.500	43	31	26	43	44	4.88
1985—Winston-Salem	Carolina	24	140⅔	10	7	.588	131	92	73	135	83	4.67
1986—Pittsfield	Eastern	24	158⅓	8	11	.421	130	77	63	115	84	3.58
1986—Chicago	National	5	23⅔	1	2	.333	24	12	12	21	10	4.56
Major League Totals—1 Year			5	23⅔	1	2	.333	24	12	12	21	10	4.56

Selected by Chicago Cubs' organization in 1st round (third player selected) of free-agent draft, June 4, 1984.

MELVIN HALL JR.
(Mel)

Born September 16, 1960, at Lyons, N.Y.
Height, 6.01. Weight, 185.
Throws and bats lefthanded.
Son of Melvin Hall Sr., minor league player in Cincinnati Reds' organization, 1949.
Major League stolen bases: 1983 (6), 1984 (3), 1986 (6). Total—15.
Led American Association in game-winning RBIs with 17 in 1982.
Led Texas League in total bases with 286 in 1981.

Led American Association outfielders in total chances with 339 in 1982.
Led Texas League outfielders in total chances with 324 and double plays with 5 in 1981.

Year	Club	League	Pos.	G.	AB.	R.	H.	2B.	3B.	HR.	RBI.	B.A.	PO.	A.	E.	F.A.
1978—Bradenton Cubs	Gulf C.	OF	43	145	30	42	7	3	2	17	.290	*97	5	4	.962
1979—Geneva	NYP	OF	66	251	49	79	18	5	3	53	.315	113	5	7	.944
1980—Midland	Texas	OF	37	128	17	34	7	3	1	14	.266	58	3	3	.953
1980—Quad Cities	Midw.	OF	97	347	54	102	14	4	6	42	.294	171	9	5	.973
1981—Midland	Texas	OF	131	533	●98	*170	34	5	24	95	.319	*302	14	8	.975
1981—Chicago	Nat.	OF	10	11	1	1	0	0	1	2	.091	0	0	0	.000
1982—Iowa	A. A.	OF	133	502	*116	165	*34	6	32	125	.329	*317	13	●9	.973
1982—Chicago	Nat.	OF	24	80	6	21	3	2	0	4	.263	42	4	3	.939
1983—Chicago†	Nat.	OF	112	410	60	116	23	5	17	56	.283	239	8	3	.988
1983—Midland	Texas	OF	6	19	9	9	2	1	3	7	.474	8	0	0	1.000
1984—Chicago‡	Nat.	OF	48	150	25	42	11	3	4	22	.280	69	5	3	.961
1984—Cleveland	Amer.	OF	83	257	43	66	13	1	7	30	.257	143	3	1	.993
1985—Cleveland§	Amer.	OF	23	66	7	21	6	0	0	12	.318	18	0	0	1.000
1986—Cleveland	Amer.	OF	140	442	68	131	29	2	18	77	.296	233	7	7	.972
National League Totals—4 Years			194	651	92	180	37	10	22	84	.276	350	17	9	.976
American League Totals—3 Years			246	765	118	218	48	3	25	119	.285	394	10	8	.981
Major League Totals—6 Years			440	1416	210	398	85	13	47	203	.281	744	27	17	.978

Selected by Chicago Cubs' organization in 2nd round of free-agent draft, June 6, 1978.

†On disabled list, April 15 to May 31, 1983; included rehabilitation disability assignment to Midland, May 25 to May 31, 1983.

‡Traded with Outfielder Joe Carter and Pitchers Don Schulze and Darryl Banks to Cleveland Indians for Catcher Ron Hassey and Pitchers Rick Sutcliffe and George Frazier, June 13, 1984.

§On disabled list, May 10, 1985 through remainder of season.

CARLTON BYRON HAMILTON
(Carl)

Born November 4, 1964, at Gary, Ind.
Height, 6.02. Weight, 175.
Throws and bats lefthanded.
Attended Triton College, River Grove, Ill.

Led Carolina League in complete games with 11 in 1985.
Tied for Eastern League lead in hit batsmen with 10 in 1986.

Year	Club	League	G.	IP.	W.	L.	Pct.	H.	R.	ER.	SO.	BB.	ERA.
1983—Pikesville	Ap'lachian	5	13	0	2	.000	12	11	9	16	18	6.23
1984—Quad Cities	Midwest	18	109	5	7	.417	69	48	34	104	76	2.81
1985—Winston-Salem	Carolina	25	155⅔	11	10	.524	110	61	47	152	108	2.72
1986—Pittsfield	Eastern	27	155⅓	10	10	.500	132	*92	72	92	110	4.17

Selected by Chicago Cubs' organization in 8th round of free-agent draft, January 11, 1983.
Selected by Chicago Cubs' organization in secondary phase of free-agent draft, June 6, 1983.

JEFFREY ROBERT HAMILTON
(Jeff)

Born March 19, 1964, at Flint, Mich.
Height, 6.03. Weight, 190.
Throws and bats righthanded.

Led Florida State League third basemen in total chances with 395 and double plays with 25 in 1984.
Led Pioneer League third basemen in double plays with 16 in 1983.

Year	Club	League	Pos.	G.	AB.	R.	H.	2B.	3B.	HR.	RBI.	B.A.	PO.	A.	E.	F.A.
1983—Lodi	Calif.	3B-OF	44	141	15	28	4	0	0	10	.199	26	62	17	.838
1983—Lethbridge	Pion.	3B	68	*281	48	●94	*23	2	3	61	.335	38	118	17	.902
1984—Vero Beach	Fla. St.	3B	127	466	51	121	31	4	4	59	.260	*109	*259	*27	*.932
1985—San Antonio	Texas	3B-OF	101	377	48	125	14	3	13	59	.332	69	186	16	.941
1986—Albuquerque	P. C.	3B	71	288	40	90	21	3	10	42	.313	39	151	19	.909
1986—Los Angeles	Nat.	3B-SS	71	147	22	33	5	0	5	19	.224	40	87	4	.969
Major League Totals—1 Year			71	147	22	33	5	0	5	19	.224	40	87	4	.969

Selected by Los Angeles Dodgers' organization in 29th round of free-agent draft, June 7, 1982.

CHARLTON ATLEE HAMMAKER
(Known by middle name.)

Born January 24, 1958, at Carmel, Calif.
Height, 6.02. Weight, 195.
Throws and bats lefthanded.
Attended East Tennessee State University, Johnson City, Tenn.

Year	Club	League	G.	IP.	W.	L.	Pct.	H.	R.	ER.	SO.	BB.	ERA.
1979—Sarasota Royals-Gold	Gulf Coast	1	5	1	0	1.000	3	1	1	6	1	1.80
1979—Fort Myers†	Florida St.	1	5	0	1	.000	9	5	1	5	0	1.80
1980—Jacksonville‡	Southern	20	137	8	9	.471	131	64	51	88	37	3.35
1981—Omaha	Am. Assoc.	21	146	11	5	.688	147	70	59	63	40	3.64
1981—Kansas City§	American	10	39	1	3	.250	44	24	24	11	12	5.54
1982—Phoenix	P. Coast	1	5⅔	0	1	.000	13	5	4	6	2	6.35
1982—San Francisco	National	29	175	12	8	.600	189	86	80	102	28	4.11
1983—San Francisco x	National	23	172⅓	10	9	.526	147	57	43	127	32	*2.25

Year Club	League	G.	IP.	W.	L.	Pct.	H.	R.	ER.	SO.	BB.	ERA.
1984—Phoenix y	P. Coast	2	8	0	1	.000	14	7	4	5	2	4.50
1984—San Francisco	National	6	33	2	0	1.000	32	10	8	24	9	2.18
1985—San Francisco	National	29	170⅔	5	12	.294	161	81	71	100	47	3.74
1986—San Francisco za	National					(Did not play)						
American League Totals—1 Year		10	39	1	3	.250	44	24	24	11	12	5.54
National League Totals—4 Years		87	551	29	29	.500	529	234	202	353	116	3.30
Major League Totals—5 Years		97	590	30	32	.484	573	258	226	364	128	3.45

Selected by Kansas City Royals' organization in 1st round (21st player selected) of free-agent draft, June 5, 1979.

†On disabled list, July 6 to October 26, 1979.

‡On disabled list, August 3 to August 22, 1980.

§Traded with Pitchers Craig Chamberlain and Renie Martin and a player to be named later to San Francisco Giants for Pitchers Vida Blue and Bob Tufts, March 30, 1982; San Francisco organization acquired Second Baseman Brad Wellman to complete deal, April 19, 1982.

xOn disabled list, July 26 to August 21, 1983.

yOn San Francisco disabled list, April 2 to June 26 and August 4 to September 1, 1984; included rehabilitation disability assignment to Phoenix, June 16 to June 25, 1984.

zOn disabled list, April 7, 1986 through entire season.

aReleased, December 19, 1986.

ALL-STAR GAME RECORD

Established All-Star Game and inning records for most runs and earned runs allowed (7), July 6, 1983 (third inning).

Tied All-Star Game record for most home runs allowed, inning (2), July 6, 1983 (third inning).

Year League	IP.	W.	L.	Pct.	H.	R.	ER.	SO.	BB.	ERA.
1983—National	⅔	0	0	.000	6	7	7	0	1	94.50

ALAN ROBERT HARGESHEIMER

Name pronounced HAHR-guh-shy-mer.

(Al)

Born November 21, 1956, at Chicago, Ill.
Height, 6.03. Weight, 200.
Throws and bats righthanded.
Attended Mayfair Junior College, Chicago, Ill. and received bachelor of arts degree
in physical education from Northeastern Illinois University, Chicago, Ill.

Tied for American Association lead in complete games with 8 in 1986.
Tied for California League lead in games started by pitchers with 28 in 1978.

Year Club	League	G.	IP.	W.	L.	Pct.	H.	R.	ER.	SO.	BB.	ERA.
1978—Fresno	California	29	176	7	11	.389	★216	117	96	109	82	4.91
1979—Shreveport	Texas	24	141	6	10	.375	165	96	71	80	60	4.53
1980—Shreveport	Texas	12	81	2	6	.250	67	28	16	40	30	1.78
1980—Phoenix	P. Coast	2	17	1	1	.500	18	8	8	13	13	4.24
1980—San Francisco	National	15	75	4	6	.400	82	38	36	40	32	4.32
1981—Phoenix†	P. Coast	20	118	6	8	.429	127	58	48	64	41	3.66
1981—San Francisco	National	6	19	1	2	.333	20	9	9	8	9	4.26
1982—Phoenix‡	P. Coast	29	152⅔	6	12	.333	214	★136	111	89	95	6.54
1983—Iowa	Am. Assoc.	49	78⅓	7	4	.636	78	35	30	50	48	3.45
1983—Chicago§	National	5	4	0	0	.000	6	4	4	5	2	9.00
1984—Omaha x	Am. Assoc.	11	14⅔	1	2	.333	13	7	5	9	10	3.07
1985—Omaha	Am. Assoc.	32	151⅔	11	10	.524	136	60	49	91	72	2.91
1986—Kansas City y	American	5	13	0	1	.000	18	9	9	4	7	6.23
1986—Omaha	Am. Assoc.	23	150⅓	13	6	.684	131	63	55	71	59	3.29
Major League Totals—4 Years		31	111	5	9	.357	126	60	58	55	50	4.70

Signed as free agent by San Francisco Giants' organization, March 21, 1978.

†On disabled list, June 13 to July 12, 1981.

‡Traded to Chicago Cubs' organization for Pitcher Herman Segelke, October 15, 1982.

§Traded to Kansas City Royals for Pitcher Derek Botelho, March 30, 1984.

xOn disabled list, May 16, 1984 through remainder of season.

yOn disabled list, August 25 to September 8, 1986.

BRIAN DAVID HARPER

Born October 16, 1959, at Los Angeles, Calif.
Height, 6.02. Weight, 195.
Throws and bats righthanded.

Major League stolen bases: 1981 (1).
Led Pacific Coast League in total bases with 339 in 1981.
Led American Association catchers in errors with 13 in 1986.
Led Pacific Coast League catchers in errors with 19 in 1981.
Led Texas League in passed balls with 19 in 1979.

Year Club	League	Pos.	G.	AB.	R.	H.	2B.	3B.	HR.	RBI.	B.A.	PO.	A.	E.	F.A.
1977—Idaho Falls	Pion.	C	52	186	28	60	9	3	1	33	.323	352	36	13	.968
1978—Quad Cities	Midw.	C	129	508	80	149	31	2	24	★101	.293	430	46	16	.967
1979—El Paso	Texas	C	132	531	85	167	★37	3	14	90	.315	443	66	★29	.946
1979—California	Amer.	DH	1	2	0	0	0	0	0	0	.000	0	0	0	.000
1980—El Paso†	Texas	C	105	400	61	114	23	3	12	66	.285	214	30	7	.972
1981—Salt Lake City	P. C.	C-OF-1B	134	549	99	★192	45	9	28	122	.350	421	30	24	.949
1981—California‡	Amer.	OF	4	11	1	3	0	0	0	1	.273	5	0	1	.833

Year Club League	Pos.	G.	AB.	R.	H.	2B.	3B.	HR.	RBI.	B.A.	PO.	A.	E.	F.A.
1982—Pittsburgh............ Nat.	OF	20	29	4	8	1	0	2	4	.276	10	0	0	1.000
1982—Portland................ P. C.	OF-3B-C	101	395	71	112	29	8	17	73	.284	164	36	8	.962
1983—Pittsburgh............ Nat.	OF-1B	61	131	16	29	4	1	7	20	.221	40	0	0	1.000
1984—Pittsburgh§ x ... Nat.	OF-C	46	112	4	29	4	0	2	11	.259	57	3	1	.984
1985—St. Louis y .... Nat.	O-3-C-1	43	52	5	13	4	0	0	8	.250	15	5	0	1.000
1986—Nashville .... A. A.	C-OF-1B	95	317	41	83	11	1	11	45	.262	377	55	15	.966
1986—Detroit................... Amer.	OF-1B-C	19	36	2	5	1	0	0	3	.139	25	2	1	.964
American League Totals—3 Years		24	49	3	8	1	0	0	4	.163	30	2	2	.941
National League Totals—4 Years		170	324	29	79	13	1	11	43	.244	122	8	1	.992
Major League Totals—7 Years		194	373	32	87	14	1	11	47	.233	152	10	3	.982

Selected by California Angels' organization in 4th round of free-agent draft, June 7, 1977.
†On disabled list, July 1 to July 17, 1980.
‡Traded to Pittsburgh Pirates for Shortstop Tim Foli, December 11, 1981.
§On disabled list, April 12 to May 10 and May 16 to June 4, 1984.
xTraded with Pitcher John Tudor to St. Louis Cardinals for Outfielder-First Baseman George Hendrick and Catcher Steve Barnard, December 12, 1984.
yReleased, April 1, 1986; signed by Detroit Tigers, April 25, 1986.

CHAMPIONSHIP SERIES RECORD

Year Club League	Pos.	G.	AB.	R.	H.	2B.	3B.	HR.	RBI.	B.A.	PO.	A.	E.	F.A.
1985—St. Louis................. Nat.	PH	1	1	0	0	0	0	0	0	.000	0	0	0	.000

WORLD SERIES RECORD

Year Club League	Pos.	G.	AB.	R.	H.	2B.	3B.	HR.	RBI.	B.A.	PO.	A.	E.	F.A.
1985—St. Louis................. Nat.	PH	4	4	0	1	0	0	0	1	.250	0	0	0	.000

TERRY JOE HARPER

Born August 19, 1955, at Douglasville, Ga.
Height, 6.01. Weight, 202.
Throws and bats righthanded.

Major League stolen bases: 1980 (2), 1981 (5), 1982 (7), 1983 (6), 1984 (4), 1985 (9), 1986 (3). Total—36.
Led International League in caught stealing with 18 in 1980.
Led International League outfielders in double plays with 5 in 1980.

Year Club League	Pos.	G.	AB.	R.	H.	2B.	3B.	HR.	RBI.	B.A.	PO.	A.	E.	F.A.
1973—Wytheville............ Appal.	P	13	17	3	4	0	0	0	2	.235	3	7	4	.714
1974—Greenwood†........ W. Car.	P	15	15	0	4	0	1	0	1	.267	1	11	2	.857
1975—Greenwood‡......... W. Car.	P	14	0	0	0	0	0	0	0	.000	6	17	0	1.000
1976—Greenwood§......... W. Car.	P	2	0	0	0	0	0	0	0	.000	1	0	0	1.000
1976—Brad. Braves........ Gulf C.	OF-3B-1B	51	185	21	48	6	6	1	37	.259	87	8	6	.941
1977—Greenwood........... W. Car.	OF-3B-1B	70	251	45	74	12	3	4	43	.295	200	10	4	.981
1977—Savannah.............. South.	OF	54	149	14	36	3	5	1	18	.242	94	8	2	.981
1978—Savannah.............. South.	OF	47	174	17	46	9	1	4	21	.264	85	10	2	.979
1978—Richmond.............. Int.	OF	73	205	21	52	5	3	0	24	.254	137	5	2	.896
1979—Richmond x .... Int.	OF	108	327	49	99	18	3	10	58	.303	164	9	9	.951
1980—Richmond.............. Int.	OF	★140	512	66	143	19	8	13	72	.279	315	19	6	.982
1980—Atlanta .... Nat.	OF	21	54	3	10	2	1	0	3	.185	30	0	1	.968
1981—Atlanta .... Nat.	OF	40	73	9	19	1	0	2	8	.260	38	2	1	.976
1981—Richmond.............. Int.	OF	10	44	3	10	3	0	2	4	.227	22	0	0	1.000
1982—Richmond.............. Int.	OF	37	146	25	56	12	2	9	42	.384	77	8	1	.988
1982—Atlanta yz .... Nat.	OF	48	150	16	43	3	0	2	16	.287	74	4	1	.987
1983—Atlanta .... Nat.	OF	80	201	19	53	13	1	3	26	.264	95	5	5	.952
1984—Atlanta a............... Nat.	OF	40	102	4	16	3	1	0	8	.157	60	3	0	1.000
1984—Richmond.............. Int.	OF	59	216	41	70	3	3	10	38	.324	118	7	4	.969
1985—Atlanta .... Nat.	OF	138	492	58	130	15	2	17	72	.264	215	10	5	.978
1986—Atlanta .... Nat.	OF	106	265	26	68	12	0	8	30	.257	92	5	3	.970
Major League Totals—7 Years		473	1337	135	339	49	5	32	163	.254	604	29	16	.975

Selected by Atlanta Braves' organization in 16th round of free-agent draft, June 5, 1973.
†On disabled list, May 5 to May 31 and June 24 to July 9, 1974.
‡On disabled list, June 18 to July 7 and August 2 to August 16, 1975.
§On disabled list, April 27 to June 25, 1976.
xOn disabled list, August 20 to September 26, 1979.
yOn disabled list, June 1 to July 1 and July 23 to July 31, 1982.
zOn disabled list, July 8 to July 23, 1982.
aOn disabled list, March 25 to April 24, 1984.

CHAMPIONSHIP SERIES RECORD

Year Club League	Pos.	G.	AB.	R.	H.	2B.	3B.	HR.	RBI.	B.A.	PO.	A.	E.	F.A.
1982—Atlanta .... Nat.	PR-OF	1	1	1	0	0	0	0	0	.000	0	0	0	.000

PITCHING RECORD

Year Club	League	G.	IP.	W.	L.	Pct.	H.	R.	ER.	SO.	BB.	ERA.
1973—Wytheville...............	Ap'lachian	12	58	3	3	.500	60	36	25	42	36	3.88
1974—Greenwood................	W. Carol.	15	43	4	2	.667	44	23	19	37	25	3.98
1975—Greenwood................	W. Carol.	14	69	1	5	.167	95	48	40	27	39	5.22
1976—Greenwood................	W. Carol.	2	8	1	1	.500	9	10	10	4	7	11.25

COLBERT DALE HARRAH
Name pronounced HAIR-uh.
(Toby)

Born October 26, 1948, at Sissonville, W. Va.
Height, 6.00. Weight, 180.
Throws and bats righthanded.
Attended Ohio Northern University, Ada, O.

Established major league records for most innings by third baseman, no assists, game (17), September 17, 1977; fewest chances offered by shortstop, doubleheader (0), June 25, 1976.

Tied major league record for fewest chances offered by shortstop, two consecutive games (0), June 25, 1976 (doubleheader).

Major League stolen bases: 1971 (10), 1972 (16), 1973 (10), 1974 (15), 1975 (23), 1976 (8), 1977 (27), 1978 (31), 1979 (20), 1980 (17), 1981 (12), 1982 (17), 1983 (16), 1984 (3), 1985 (11), 1986 (2). Total—238.

Led American League in bases on balls received with 109 in 1977.

Led American League shortstops in putouts with 281 in 1974 and tied for lead with 290 in 1976.

Led American League shortstops in errors with 36 in 1976.

Named shortstop on THE SPORTING NEWS American League All-Star Team, 1975.

Year Club	League	Pos.	G.	AB.	R.	H.	2B.	3B.	HR.	RBI.	B.A.	PO.	A.	E.	F.A.
1967—Huron†	North.	2B-SS	63	207	34	53	6	0	3	22	.256	136	163	23	.929
1968—Burlington	Carol.	SS	135	468	73	112	16	3	6	39	.239	217	356	★50	.920
1969—Burlington‡	Carol.	SS-2B	46	147	27	45	4	2	4	12	.306	76	152	10	.958
1969—Savannah	South.	SS	28	80	8	19	2	0	2	7	.238	36	78	11	.912
1969—Washington	Amer.	SS	8	1	4	0	0	0	0	0	.000	0	0	0	.000
1970—Pittsfield§	East.	SS-3B	95	359	57	99	18	1	3	37	.276	159	293	27	.944
1971—Washington	Amer.	SS-3B	127	383	45	88	11	3	2	22	.230	187	321	24	.955
1972—Texas x	Amer.	SS	116	374	47	97	14	3	1	31	.259	166	308	20	.960
1973—Texas y	Amer.	SS-3B	118	461	64	120	16	1	10	50	.260	155	332	27	.947
1974—Texas	Amer.	●SS-3B	161	573	79	149	23	2	21	74	.260	283	474	●29	.963
1975—Texas	Amer.	SS-3B-2B	151	522	81	153	24	1	20	93	.293	253	481	29	.962
1976—Texas	Amer.	SS-3B	155	584	64	152	21	1	15	67	.260	294	481	37	.954
1977—Texas	Amer.	3B-SS	159	539	90	142	25	5	27	87	.263	108	278	15	.963
1978—Texas z	Amer.	3B-SS	139	450	56	103	17	3	12	59	.229	129	330	11	.977
1979—Cleveland	Amer.	3B-SS	149	527	99	147	25	1	20	77	.279	113	215	19	.947
1980—Cleveland	Amer.	3B-SS	160	561	100	150	22	4	11	72	.267	121	319	13	.971
1981—Cleveland	Amer.	3B-SS	103	361	64	105	12	4	5	44	.291	64	180	13	.949
1982—Cleveland	Amer.	3B-2B-SS	●162	602	100	183	29	4	25	78	.304	126	279	12	.971
1983—Cleveland ab	Amer.	★3B-2B	138	526	81	140	23	1	9	53	.266	101	273	11	★.971
1984—New York cd	Amer.	3B-2B-OF	88	253	40	55	9	4	1	26	.217	52	132	6	.968
1985—Texas	Amer.	2B-SS	126	396	65	107	18	1	9	44	.270	212	351	6	.989
1986—Texas ef	Amer.	2B	95	289	36	63	18	2	7	41	.218	166	211	7	.982
Major League Totals—17 Years			2155	7402	1115	1954	307	40	195	918	.264	2530	4965	279	.964

Signed as free agent by Philadelphia Phillies' organization, December 27, 1966.

†Drafted by Washington Senators' organization, November 28, 1967.

‡On military list, January 28 to June 2, 1969.

§On temporary inactive list, July 24 to August 11, 1970.

xOn disabled list, August 14 to September 6, 1972.

yOn disabled list, July 2 to August 7, 1973.

zTraded to Cleveland Indians for Third Baseman Buddy Bell, December 8, 1978.

aOn disabled list, April 17 to May 14, 1983.

bTraded with a player to be named later to New York Yankees for Pitcher George Frazier, Outfielder Otis Nixon and a player to be named later, February 5, 1984; New York organization acquired Pitcher Rick Browne and Cleveland organization acquired Pitcher Guy Elston to complete deal, February 8, 1984.

cOn disabled list, July 3 to July 20, 1984.

dTraded to Texas Rangers for Outfielder Billy Sample and a player to be named later, February 27, 1985; New York Yankees' organization acquired Pitcher Eric Dersin to complete deal, July 14, 1985.

eOn disabled list, June 24 to July 9, 1986.

fGranted free agency, November 12, 1986.

ALL-STAR GAME RECORD

Year League	Pos.	AB.	R.	H.	2B.	3B.	HR.	RBI.	B.A.	PO.	A.	E.	F.A.
1976—American	SS	2	0	0	0	0	0	0	.000	0	0	0	.000

Named to American League All-Star Team for the 1972 game; replaced due to an injury.

Member of American League All-Star Team in 1975 and 1982; did not play.

GREG ALLEN HARRIS

Born November 2, 1955, at Lynwood, Calif.
Height, 6.00. Weight, 165.
Throws right and bats left and righthanded.
Attended Long Beach City College, Long Beach, Calif.

Major League saves: 1981 (1), 1982 (1), 1984 (3), 1985 (11), 1986 (20). Total—36.

Year Club	League	G.	IP.	W.	L.	Pct.	H.	R.	ER.	SO.	BB.	ERA.
1977—Jackson	Texas	30	83	3	6	.333	96	63	50	56	36	5.42
1978—Lynchburg	Carolina	21	154	8	9	.471	114	52	37	102	74	2.16
1978—Jackson	Texas	6	33	2	3	.400	24	13	11	18	10	3.00
1979—Jackson	Texas	25	163	9	11	.450	125	58	41	89	81	★2.26
1980—Tidewater	Int'national	39	110	2	9	.182	99	45	33	92	40	2.70
1981—Tidewater	Int'national	7	48	4	0	1.000	37	14	11	26	16	2.06

Year Club	League	G.	IP.	W.	L.	Pct.	H.	R.	ER.	SO.	BB.	ERA.
1981—New York†	National	16	69	3	5	.375	65	36	34	54	28	4.43
1982—Indianapolis	Am. Assoc.	8	48	4	1	.800	27	18	16	44	24	3.00
1982—Cincinnati	National	34	91⅓	2	6	.250	96	56	49	67	37	4.83
1983—Indianapolis	Am. Assoc.	28	152⅓	9	12	.429	155	83	70	*146	66	4.14
1983—Cincinnati‡	National	1	1	0	0	.000	2	3	3	1	3	27.00
1984—Montreal§-San Diego	National	34	54⅓	2	2	.500	38	18	15	45	25	2.48
1984—Indianapolis x	Am. Assoc.	14	44⅔	4	4	.500	44	27	22	45	29	4.43
1985—Texas	American	58	113	5	4	.556	74	35	31	111	43	2.47
1986—Texas	American	73	111⅓	10	8	.556	103	40	35	95	42	2.83
National League Totals—4 Years		85	215⅔	7	13	.350	201	113	101	167	93	4.21
American League Totals—2 Years		131	224⅓	15	12	.556	177	75	66	206	85	2.65
Major League Totals—6 Years		216	440	22	25	.468	378	188	167	373	178	3.42

Selected by California Angels' organization in 10th round of free-agent draft, June 5, 1974.
Selected by New York Mets' organization in secondary phase of free-agent draft, January 9, 1975.
Selected by New York Mets' organization in 7th round of free-agent draft, January 7, 1976.
Signed as free agent by New York Mets' organization, September 17, 1976.
†Traded with Catcher Alex Trevino and Pitcher Jim Kern to Cincinnati Reds for Outfielder George Foster, February 10, 1982.
‡Claimed on waivers by Montreal Expos, September 27, 1983.
§Traded to San Diego Padres for Infielder Al Newman, July 20, 1984.
xSold to Texas Rangers, February 13, 1985.

CHAMPIONSHIP SERIES RECORD

Tied Championship Series records for most runs, most earned runs and most hits allowed, inning (6), October 2, 1984 (fifth inning); most earned runs allowed, game (7), October 2, 1984.
Tied National League Championship Series record for most runs allowed, five-game Series (8), 1984.

Year Club	League	G.	IP.	W.	L.	Pct.	H.	R.	ER.	SO.	BB.	ERA.
1984—San Diego	National	1	2	0	0	.000	9	8	7	2	3	31.50

WORLD SERIES RECORD

Year Club	League	G.	IP.	W.	L.	Pct.	H.	R.	ER.	SO.	BB.	ERA.
1984—San Diego	National	1	5⅓	0	0	.000	3	0	0	5	3	0.00

LEONARD ANTHONY HARRIS
(Lenny)

Born October 28, 1964, at Miami, Fla.
Height, 5.11. Weight, 180.
Throws right and bats lefthanded.
Attended Miami-Dade Community College (North), Miami, Fla.

Led Eastern League in game-winning RBIs with 13 in 1986.
Led Eastern League third basemen in putouts with 116 and total chances with 360 in 1986.
Led Florida State League third basemen in double plays with 34 in 1985.

Year Club	League	Pos.	G.	AB.	R.	H.	2B.	3B.	HR.	RBI.	B.A.	PO.	A.	E.	F.A.
1983—Billings	Pion.	3B	56	224	37	63	8	1	1	26	.281	34	95	22	.854
1984—Cedar Rapids	Midw.	3B	132	468	52	115	15	3	6	53	.246	111	204	*34	.903
1985—Tampa	Fla. St.	3B	132	499	66	129	11	8	3	51	.259	89	*277	*35	.913
1986—Vermont	East.	*3B-SS	119	450	68	114	17	2	10	52	.253	119	220	*28	.924

Selected by Cincinnati Reds' organization in 5th round of free-agent draft, June 6, 1983.

RONALD KYLE HARTSHORN
(Known by middle name.)

Born October 3, 1964, at Trenton, N.J.
Height, 6.02. Weight, 185.
Throws right and bats lefthanded.
Attended Mercer County Community College, Trenton, N.J.

Tied for Carolina League lead in hit batsmen with 9 in 1985.
Tied for South Atlantic League lead in complete games with 10 and shutouts with 4 in 1984.
Named Carolina League Pitcher of the Year, 1985.

Year Club	League	G.	IP.	W.	L.	Pct.	H.	R.	ER.	SO.	BB.	ERA.
1982—Little Falls	NYP	13	54	5	2	.714	65	53	41	52	30	6.83
1983—Columbia	S. Atlantic	9	32⅔	1	3	.250	46	32	25	20	22	6.89
1983—Little Falls	NYP	15	80⅓	4	7	.364	83	53	40	63	36	4.48
1984—Columbia	S. Atlantic	24	160	14	4	*.778	126	64	44	100	83	*2.48
1985—Lynchburg	Carolina	25	170⅔	*17	4	*.810	125	45	32	98	53	*1.69
1985—Jackson	Texas	3	15⅔	0	2	.000	22	12	12	6	5	6.89
1986—Jackson	Texas	27	153⅓	11	4	.733	169	82	64	86	58	3.76

Selected by New York Mets' organization in 6th round of free-agent draft, June 7, 1982.

—DID YOU KNOW—

That Willie Mays holds the record for the most complete All-Star Games played with 11? Stan Musial is second with 10.

RONALD WILLIAM HASSEY
(Ron)

Born February 27, 1953, at Tucson, Ariz.
Height, 6.02. Weight, 195.
Throws right and bats lefthanded.
Received degree in public administration from University of Arizona, Tucson, Ariz.
Son of Bill Hassey, minor league outfielder, 1949 through 1952.

Major League stolen bases: 1978 (2), 1979 (1), 1982 (3), 1983 (2), 1984 (1), 1986 (1). Total—10.
Led American League in passed balls with 15 in 1985.

Year Club	League	Pos.	G.	AB.	R.	H.	2B.	3B.	HR.	RBI.	B.A.	PO.	A.	E.	F.A.
1976—San Jose	Calif.	C-3B	22	62	7	19	4	0	1	7	.306	55	2	2	.966
1976—Williamsport	East.	C	21	68	6	19	3	0	0	8	.279	63	10	4	.948
1977—Toledo	Int.	C-3-1-O	129	446	50	132	21	1	10	57	.296	484	82	21	.964
1978—Portland	P. C.	C-3B	72	235	42	76	12	1	12	52	.323	312	32	7	.980
1978—Cleveland	Amer.	C	25	74	5	15	0	0	2	9	.203	130	15	1	.993
1979—Tacoma	P. C.	C-3B	44	157	25	53	10	0	3	27	.338	282	44	2	.994
1979—Cleveland	Amer.	C-1B	75	223	20	64	14	0	4	32	.287	368	29	3	.993
1980—Cleveland	Amer.	C-1B	130	390	43	124	18	4	8	65	.318	564	52	4	.994
1981—Cleveland	Amer.	C-1B	61	190	8	44	4	0	1	25	.232	327	44	3	.992
1982—Cleveland	Amer.	C-1B	113	323	33	81	18	0	5	34	.251	566	38	4	.993
1983—Cleveland	Amer.	C	117	341	48	92	21	0	6	42	.270	514	43	3	.995
1984—Cleveland†	Amer.	C-1B	48	149	11	38	5	1	0	19	.255	210	16	1	.996
1984—Chicago‡§	Nat.	C-1B	19	33	5	11	0	0	2	5	.333	53	2	1	.982
1985—New York xy	Amer.	C-1B	92	267	31	79	16	1	13	42	.296	420	20	7	.984
1986—N.Y.z-Chi.	Amer.	C	113	341	45	110	25	1	9	49	.323	318	14	4	.988
American League Totals—9 Years			774	2298	244	647	121	7	48	317	.282	3417	271	30	.992
National League Totals—1 Year			19	33	5	11	0	0	2	5	.333	53	2	1	.982
Major League Totals—10 Years			793	2331	249	658	121	7	50	322	.282	3470	273	31	.992

Selected by Cincinnati Reds' organization in 23rd round of free-agent draft, June 6, 1972.
Selected by Kansas City Royals' organization in 22nd round of free-agent draft, June 4, 1975.
Selected by Cleveland Indians' organization in 18th round of free-agent draft, June 8, 1976.
†Traded with Pitchers Rick Sutcliffe and George Frazier to Chicago Cubs for Outfielders Mel Hall and Joe Carter and Pitchers Don Schulze and Darryl Banks, June 13, 1984.
‡On disabled list, July 5 to September 1, 1984.
§Traded with Outfielder Henry Cotto and Pitchers Rich Bordi and Porfi Altamirano to New York Yankees for Pitcher Ray Fontenot and Outfielder Brian Dayett, December 4, 1984.
xTraded with Pitcher Joe Cowley to Chicago White Sox for Pitcher Britt Burns, Shortstop Mike Soper and Outfielder Glen Braxton, December 12, 1985.
yTraded with Catcher Chris Alvarez, Pitcher Eric Schmidt and Outfielder Matt Winters to New York Yankees for Pitcher Neil Allen, Catcher Scott Bradley, Outfielder Glen Braxton and cash, February 13, 1986.
zTraded with Shortstop Carlos Martinez and a player to be named later to Chicago White Sox for Outfielder Ron Kittle, Infielder Wayne Tolleson and Catcher Joel Skinner, July 30, 1986; New York Yankees traded Catcher Bill Lindsey to Chicago organization to complete deal, December 24, 1986.

MICHAEL VAUGHN HATCHER JR.
(Mickey)

Born March 15, 1955, at Cleveland, O.
Height, 6.02. Weight, 199.
Throws and bats righthanded.
Attended Mesa Community College, Mesa, Ariz., and
University of Oklahoma, Norman, Okla.
Brother of Hal Hatcher, catcher in Kansas City Royals' organization, 1980 through 1985.

Tied American League record for most hits, two consecutive games (9), April 27 and 28, 1985.
Major League stolen bases: 1979 (1), 1981 (3), 1983 (2), 1986 (2). Total—8.

Year Club	League	Pos.	G.	AB.	R.	H.	2B.	3B.	HR.	RBI.	B.A.	PO.	A.	E.	F.A.
1977—Clinton	Midw.	OF	78	288	47	89	12	4	11	53	.309	126	9	4	.971
1978—San Antonio†	Texas	3B	83	334	60	111	12	6	8	62	.332	55	124	22	.891
1978—Albuquerque	P. C.	3B-OF	41	155	25	51	11	5	7	39	.329	24	63	8	.916
1979—Albuquerque	P. C.	3B-OF	103	420	88	156	29	12	10	93	*.371	127	156	12	.959
1979—Los Angeles	Nat.	OF-3B	33	93	9	25	4	1	1	5	.269	47	24	5	.934
1980—Albuquerque	P. C.	OF-3B	43	181	28	65	7	2	7	40	.359	52	32	9	.903
1980—Los Angeles‡	Nat.	3B-OF	57	84	4	19	2	0	1	5	.226	31	23	3	.947
1981—Minnesota	Amer.	OF-1B-3B	99	377	36	96	23	2	3	37	.255	296	11	3	.990
1982—Minnesota	Amer.	OF-3B	84	277	23	69	13	2	3	26	.249	81	17	1	.990
1983—Minnesota§	Amer.	OF-1B-3B	106	375	50	119	15	3	9	47	.317	199	11	3	.986
1984—Minnesota	Amer.	OF-1B-3B	152	576	61	174	35	5	5	69	.302	364	20	9	.977
1985—Minnesota x	Amer.	OF-1B	116	444	46	125	28	0	3	49	.282	246	7	3	.988
1986—Minnesota	Amer.	OF-1B-3B	115	317	40	88	13	3	3	32	.278	220	16	4	.983
National League Totals—2 Years			90	177	13	44	6	1	2	10	.249	78	47	8	.940
American League Totals—6 Years			672	2366	256	671	127	15	26	260	.284	1406	82	23	.985
Major League Totals—8 Years			762	2543	269	715	133	16	28	270	.281	1484	129	31	.981

Selected by Houston Astros' organization in 14th round of free-agent draft, June 5, 1974.
Selected by New York Mets' organization in 2nd round of free-agent draft, January 7, 1976.
Selected by Los Angeles Dodgers' organization in 5th round of free-agent draft, June 7, 1977.
†On disabled list, July 13 to July 23, 1978.
‡Traded with First Baseman Kelly Snider and Pitcher Matt Reeves to Minnesota Twins for Outfielder Ken Landreaux, March 30, 1981.
§On disabled list, June 21 to July 8 and August 1 to August 23, 1983.
xOn disabled list, July 10 to July 25, 1985.

WILLIAM AUGUSTUS HATCHER
(Billy)

Born October 4, 1960, at Williams, Ariz.
Height, 5.09. Weight, 175.
Throws and bats righthanded.
Attended Yavapai Community College, Prescott, Ariz.

Major League stolen bases: 1984 (2), 1985 (2), 1986 (38). Total—42.
Led American Association in being hit by pitch with 9 in 1984.
Led New York-Pennsylvania League in being hit by pitch with 8 in 1981.

Year Club	League	Pos.	G.	AB.	R.	H.	2B.	3B.	HR.	RBI.	B.A.	PO.	A.	E.	F.A.
1981—Geneva	NYP	OF	•75	289	57	81	15	3	4	40	.280	138	7	11	.930
1982—Salinas	Calif.	OF	138	549	92	171	18	8	8	59	.311	235	10	12	.953
1983—Midland	Texas	OF	135	545	★132	163	33	11	10	80	.299	286	17	•13	.959
1984—Iowa	A. A.	OF	150	595	96	164	27	18	9	59	.276	303	15	7	.978
1984—Chicago	Nat.	OF	8	9	1	1	0	0	0	0	.111	2	1	0	1.000
1985—Iowa	A. A.	OF	67	279	39	78	14	5	5	19	.280	157	4	4	.976
1985—Chicago†‡	Nat.	OF	53	163	24	40	12	1	2	10	.245	77	2	1	.988
1986—Houston§	Nat.	OF	127	419	55	108	15	4	6	36	.258	226	7	4	.983
Major League Totals—3 Years			188	591	80	149	27	5	8	46	.252	305	10	5	.984

Selected by Chicago Cubs' organization in 6th round of free-agent draft, January 13, 1981.
†On disabled list, August 19 to September 3, 1985.
‡Traded with a player to be named later to Houston Astros for Outfielder Jerry Mumphrey, December 16, 1985; Houston organization acquired Pitcher Steve Engel to complete deal, July 24, 1986.
§On disabled list, June 28 to July 13, 1986.

CHAMPIONSHIP SERIES RECORD

Tied Championship Series record for most at-bats, game (7), October 15, 1986 (16 innings).
Established National League Championship Series record for most stolen bases, six-game Series (3), 1986.

Year Club	League	Pos.	G.	AB.	R.	H.	2B.	3B.	HR.	RBI.	B.A.	PO.	A.	E.	F.A.
1986—Houston	Nat.	OF	6	25	4	7	0	0	1	2	.280	11	0	1	.917

BRADLEY DAVID HAVENS
(Brad)

Born November 17, 1959, at Highland Park, Mich.
Height, 6.01. Weight, 190.
Throws and bats lefthanded.

Major League saves: 1986 (1).
Led International League in complete games with 12 in 1984.
Led California League in complete games with 12 in 1980.
Led Midwest League in complete games with 17 in 1978.
Tied for California League lead in games started by pitchers with 28 in 1980.
Named International League Pitcher of the Year, 1984.

Year Club	League	G.	IP.	W.	L.	Pct.	H.	R.	ER.	SO.	BB.	ERA.
1978—Quad Cities†	Midwest	26	★200	13	10	.565	171	80	59	★197	74	2.66
1979—Orlando	Southern	19	94	4	10	.286	128	85	76	63	50	7.28
1979—Wisconsin Rapids	Midwest	10	73	6	1	.857	62	35	34	80	18	4.19
1980—Visalia	California	28	195	14	9	.609	186	90	72	★179	82	3.32
1981—Orlando	Southern	11	74	6	2	.750	81	38	29	58	20	3.53
1981—Minnesota	American	14	78	3	6	.333	76	33	31	43	24	3.58
1982—Minnesota	American	33	208⅔	10	14	.417	201	112	100	129	80	4.31
1983—Minnesota	American	16	80⅓	5	8	.385	110	75	73	40	38	8.18
1983—Toledo	Int'national	11	69⅔	6	3	.667	60	34	30	64	37	3.88
1984—Toledo‡	Int'national	25	169	11	10	.524	142	56	49	★169	70	2.61
1985—Rochester	Int'national	34	133⅔	8	10	.444	135	79	72	★129	52	4.85
1985—Baltimore	American	8	14⅓	0	1	.000	20	14	14	19	10	8.79
1986—Baltimore	American	46	71	3	3	.500	64	37	36	57	29	4.56
Major League Totals—5 Years		117	452⅓	21	32	.396	471	271	254	288	181	5.05

Selected by California Angels' organization in 8th round of free-agent draft, June 7, 1977.
†Traded with Outfielder Ken Landreaux, Pitcher Paul Hartzell and Third Baseman Dave Engle to Minnesota Twins for First Baseman Rod Carew, February 3, 1979.
‡Traded to Baltimore Orioles' organization for Pitcher Mark Brown, March 27, 1985.

MELTON ANDREW HAWKINS
(Andy)

Born January 21, 1960, at Waco, Tex.
Height, 6.03. Weight, 205.
Throws and bats righthanded.

Led Pacific Coast League in shutouts with 6 in 1982.
Led Texas League in complete games with 14 and tied for lead in games started by pitchers with 27 in 1981.
Led Northwest League in balks with 4 in 1978.

Year Club	League	G.	IP.	W.	L.	Pct.	H.	R.	ER.	SO.	BB.	ERA.
1978—Walla Walla	Northwest	14	102	8	3	.727	95	52	24	73	45	2.12
1979—Reno	California	27	188	8	13	.381	★232	143	★117	130	97	5.60
1980—Reno	California	26	171	13	10	.565	183	108	81	124	79	4.26
1981—Amarillo	Texas	27	200	11	10	.524	★209	100	★93	144	48	4.19

Year Club	League	G.	IP.	W.	L.	Pct.	H.	R.	ER.	SO.	BB.	ERA.
1982—Hawaii	P. Coast	18	132⅔	9	7	.563	108	49	32	91	47	2.17
1982—San Diego	National	15	63⅓	2	5	.286	66	33	29	25	27	4.10
1983—Las Vegas	P. Coast	14	85⅓	6	4	.600	110	67	61	50	27	6.43
1983—San Diego	National	21	119⅔	5	7	.417	106	50	39	59	48	2.93
1984—San Diego	National	36	146	8	9	.471	143	90	76	77	72	4.68
1985—San Diego	National	33	228⅔	18	8	.692	229	88	80	69	65	3.15
1986—San Diego	National	37	209⅓	10	8	.556	218	111	100	117	75	4.30
Major League Totals—5 Years		142	767⅓	43	37	.538	762	372	324	347	287	3.80

Selected by San Diego Padres' organization in 1st round (fifth player selected) of free-agent draft, June 6, 1978.

CHAMPIONSHIP SERIES RECORD

Year Club	League	G.	IP.	W.	L.	Pct.	H.	R.	ER.	SO.	BB.	ERA.
1984—San Diego	National	3	3⅔	0	0	.000	0	0	0	1	2	0.00

WORLD SERIES RECORD

Year Club	League	G.	IP.	W.	L.	Pct.	H.	R.	ER.	SO.	BB.	ERA.
1984—San Diego	National	3	12	1	1	.500	4	1	1	4	6	0.75

VON FRANCIS HAYES

Born August 31, 1958, at Stockton, Calif.
Height, 6.05. Weight, 180.
Throws right and bats lefthanded.
Attended St. Mary's College, Moraga, Calif.

Tied major league record for most home runs (2) and most total bases (8), inning, June 11, 1985 (first inning).
Major League stolen bases: 1981 (8), 1982 (32), 1983 (20), 1984 (48), 1985 (21), 1986 (24). Total—153.
Led Midwest League third basemen in fielding percentage with .930 in 1980.
Named Midwest League Most Valuable Player, 1980.

Year Club	League	Pos.	G.	AB.	R.	H.	2B.	3B.	HR.	RBI.	B.A.	PO.	A.	E.	F.A.
1980—Waterloo	Midw.	3B-SS	134	492	105	★162	★33	3	15	90	★.329	94	291	30	.928
1981—Cleveland	Amer.	OF-3B	43	109	21	28	8	2	1	17	.257	30	4	3	.919
1981—Charleston	Int.	3B-1B	105	382	58	120	19	6	10	73	.314	96	222	19	.944
1982—Cleveland†	Amer.	OF-3B-1B	150	527	65	132	25	3	14	82	.250	323	17	6	.983
1983—Philadelphia‡	Nat.	OF	124	351	45	93	9	5	6	32	.265	165	7	5	.972
1984—Philadelphia	Nat.	OF	152	561	85	164	27	6	16	67	.292	341	2	4	.988
1985—Philadelphia	Nat.	OF	152	570	76	150	30	4	13	70	.263	368	9	6	.984
1986—Philadelphia	Nat.	1B-OF	158	610	●107	186	★46	2	19	98	.305	1247	100	13	.990
American League Totals—2 Years			193	636	86	160	33	5	15	99	.252	353	21	9	.977
National League Totals—4 Years			586	2092	313	593	112	17	54	267	.283	2121	118	28	.988
Major League Totals—6 Years			779	2728	399	753	145	22	69	366	.276	2474	139	37	.986

Selected by Cleveland Indians' organization in 7th round of free-agent draft, June 5, 1979.
†Traded to Philadelphia Phillies for Second Baseman Manny Trillo, Outfielder George Vukovich, Infielder Julio Franco, Pitcher Jay Baller and Catcher Jerry Willard, December 9, 1982.
‡On disabled list, March 27 to April 12, 1983.

CHAMPIONSHIP SERIES RECORD

Year Club	League	Pos.	G.	AB.	R.	H.	2B.	3B.	HR.	RBI.	B.A.	PO.	A.	E.	F.A.
1983—Philadelphia	Nat.	PH-OF	2	2	0	0	0	0	0	0	.000	0	0	0	.000

WORLD SERIES RECORD

Year Club	League	Pos.	G.	AB.	R.	H.	2B.	3B.	HR.	RBI.	B.A.	PO.	A.	E.	F.A.
1983—Philadelphia	Nat.	PH-OF	4	3	0	0	0	0	0	0	.000	1	0	0	1.000

RAYMOND ALTON HAYWARD JR.
(Ray)

Born April 27, 1961, at Enid, Okla.
Height, 6.01. Weight, 190.
Throws and bats lefthanded.
Received degree in finance from University of Oklahoma, Norman, Okla., in 1983.

Tied for Pacific Coast League lead in hit batsmen with 6 in 1985.
Tied for Pacific Coast League lead in wild pitches with 16 in 1984.
Named lefthanded pitcher on THE SPORTING NEWS College Baseball All-America Team, 1983.

Year Club	League	G.	IP.	W.	L.	Pct.	H.	R.	ER.	SO.	BB.	ERA.
1983—Beaumont	Texas	10	66⅓	5	1	.833	45	16	13	71	30	1.76
1984—Las Vegas	P. Coast	26	129⅓	9	6	.600	129	78	70	91	79	4.87
1985—Las Vegas	P. Coast	28	★191⅓	11	10	.524	198	104	85	150	79	4.00
1986—Las Vegas	P. Coast	26	136	9	11	.450	156	87	70	100	65	4.63
1986—San Diego	National	3	10	0	2	.000	16	12	10	6	4	9.00
Major League Totals—1 Year		3	10	0	2	.000	16	12	10	6	4	9.00

Selected by Pittsburgh Pirates' organization in 12th round of free-agent draft, June 7, 1982.
Selected by San Diego Padres' organization in 1st round (10th player selected) of free-agent draft, June 6, 1983.

EDWARD JOHN HEARN
(Ed)

Born August 23, 1960, at Stuart, Fla.
Height, 6.03. Weight, 215.
Throws and bats righthanded.

Year Club	League	Pos.	G.	AB.	R.	H.	2B.	3B.	HR.	RBI.	B.A.	PO.	A.	E.	F.A.
1978—Helena	Pion.	C	47	173	34	49	3	1	13	45	.283	274	35	9	.972
1979—Helena†	Pion.					(Did not play)									
1980—Spartanburg	S. Atl.	1B	66	217	25	65	12	2	3	32	.300	68	7	1	.987
1981—Peninsula	Carol.	1B	101	317	61	96	29	2	10	44	.303	538	25	12	.979
1982—Peninsula	Carol.	C-1B	21	76	15	25	2	0	6	14	.329	69	2	2	.973
1982—Reading‡§	East.	1B-C	43	135	16	37	6	2	3	27	.274	204	16	7	.969
1983—Jackson	Texas	1B-C	5	20	4	6	1	0	0	2	.300	40	1	1	.976
1983—Lynchburg	Carol.	C-1-3-O	91	290	37	79	16	1	5	47	.272	333	37	9	.976
1984—Jackson x	Texas	C-1B	86	311	46	97	19	2	11	51	.312	613	54	6	.991
1985—Tidewater	Int.	C-1B	112	418	35	110	29	1	5	57	.263	543	45	5	.992
1986—Tidewater	Int.	1B-C	22	83	7	22	4	0	1	12	.265	170	15	1	.995
1986—New York	Nat.	C	49	136	16	36	5	0	4	10	.265	223	11	3	.987
Major League Totals—1 Year			49	136	16	36	5	0	4	10	.265	223	11	3	.987

Selected by Philadelphia Phillies' organization in 4th round of free-agent draft, June 6, 1978.
†On temporary inactive list, June 22, 1979 through remainder of season.
‡On disabled list, June 15 to July 6, 1982.
§Released, January 7, 1983; signed by Lynchburg (New York Mets' organization), February 3, 1983.
xGranted free agency, October 15, 1984; re-signed by Mets' organization, December 13, 1984.

JEFFREY VERNON HEARRON
(Jeff)

Born November 19, 1961, at Long Beach, Calif.
Height, 6.02. Weight, 190.
Throws and bats righthanded.
Attended University of Texas, Austin, Tex.

Year Club	League	Pos.	G.	AB.	R.	H.	2B.	3B.	HR.	RBI.	B.A.	PO.	A.	E.	F.A.
1983—Florence	S. Atl.	C	47	144	19	41	11	0	5	20	.285	235	40	7	.975
1984—Knoxville†	South.	C	81	240	30	60	9	0	7	28	.250	387	45	14	.969
1985—Knoxville‡	South	C	45	130	17	29	6	1	5	15	.223	190	20	3	.986
1985—Toronto	Amer.	C	4	7	0	1	0	0	0	0	.143	16	1	0	1.000
1986—Syracuse	Int.	C	92	320	31	79	19	1	7	36	.247	502	53	9	.984
1986—Toronto	Amer.	C	12	23	2	5	1	0	0	4	.217	47	3	1	.980
Major League Totals—2 Years			16	30	2	6	1	0	0	4	.200	63	4	1	.985

Selected by Toronto Blue Jays' organization in 4th round of free-agent draft, June 6, 1983.
†On disabled list, May 2 to May 12, July 2 to July 17 and September 2 to September 14, 1984.
‡On disabled list, April 11 to April 28, 1985.

CHAMPIONSHIP SERIES RECORD

Year Club	League	Pos.	G.	AB.	R.	H.	2B.	3B.	HR.	RBI.	B.A.	PO.	A.	E.	F.A.
1985—Toronto	Amer.	C	2	0	0	0	0	0	0	0	.000	2	0	0	1.000

MICHAEL THOMAS HEATH
(Mike)

Born February 5, 1955, at Tampa, Fla.
Height, 5.11. Weight, 190.
Throws and bats righthanded.

Major League stolen bases: 1979 (1), 1980 (3), 1981 (3), 1982 (8), 1983 (3), 1984 (7), 1985 (7), 1986 (6). Total—38.
Led New York-Pennsylvania League shortstops in double plays with 42 in 1974.
Tied for Appalachian League lead in sacrifice hits with 7 in 1973.

Year Club	League	Pos.	G.	AB.	R.	H.	2B.	3B.	HR.	RBI.	B.A.	PO.	A.	E.	F.A.
1973—Johnson City	Appal.	SS-2B-3B	48	166	17	29	5	2	0	10	.175	83	137	24	.902
1974—Oneonta	NYP	SS	65	234	51	66	6	3	3	34	.282	114	170	★27	.913
1975—Fort Lauderdale†	Fla. St.	SS	98	376	43	87	7	3	1	23	.231	184	256	31	.934
1976—Fort Lauderdale‡	Fla. St.	SS-3B-C-P	80	267	28	71	16	3	2	30	.266	143	121	16	.943
1977—West Haven	East.	C-3B	98	352	58	94	13	5	8	42	.267	492	72	16	.972
1978—West Haven	East.	C-SS	66	217	43	64	16	1	8	27	.295	335	53	10	.975
1978—New York§	Amer.	C	33	92	6	21	3	1	0	8	.228	151	11	5	.970
1979—Tucson x	P. C.	C	54	196	21	53	8	2	1	28	.270	183	24	7	.967
1979—Oakland	Amer.	OF-C-3B	74	258	19	66	8	0	3	27	.256	167	32	5	.975
1980—Oakland	Amer.	C-OF	92	305	27	74	10	2	1	33	.243	292	20	4	.987
1981—Oakland	Amer.	★C-OF	84	301	26	71	7	1	8	30	.236	399	45	★10	.978
1982—Oakland y	Amer.	C-OF-3B	101	318	43	77	18	4	3	39	.242	368	54	12	.972
1983—Oakland z	Amer.	C-OF-3B	96	345	45	97	17	0	6	33	.281	362	47	11	.974
1984—Oakland	Amer.	C-O-3-S	140	475	49	118	21	5	13	64	.248	495	56	8	.986
1985—Oakland a	Amer.	C-OF-3B	138	436	71	109	18	6	13	55	.250	539	67	12	.981
1986—St. Louis b	Nat.	C-OF	65	190	19	39	8	1	4	25	.205	260	30	10	.967
1986—Detroit	Amer.	C-3B	30	98	11	26	3	0	4	11	.265	145	9	3	.981
American League Totals—9 Years			788	2628	297	659	105	19	51	300	.251	2918	341	70	.979
National League Totals—1 Year			65	190	19	39	8	1	4	25	.205	260	30	10	.967
Major League Totals—9 Years			853	2818	316	698	113	20	55	325	.248	3178	371	80	.978

Selected by New York Yankees' organization in 2nd round of free-agent draft, June 5, 1973.
†On Syracuse disabled list, August 2 to September 16, 1975.
‡On disabled list, June 29 to July 13, 1976.
§Traded with Pitchers Sparky Lyle, Larry McCall and Dave Rajsich, Shortstop Domingo Ramos and cash to Texas Rangers for Outfielders Juan Beniquez and Greg Jemison and Pitchers Mike Griffin, Paul Mirabella and Dave Righetti, November 10, 1978.
xTraded with Third Baseman Dave Chalk and cash to Oakland A's for Pitcher John Henry Johnson, June 15, 1979.
yOn disabled list, March 28 to April 20, 1982.
zOn disabled list, April 25 to May 25, 1983.
aTraded with Pitcher Tim Conroy to St. Louis Cardinals for Pitcher Joaquin Andujar, December 10, 1985.
bTraded to Detroit Tigers for Pitcher Ken Hill and a player to be named later, August 10, 1986; St. Louis Cardinals acquired First Baseman Mike Laga to complete deal, September 2, 1986.

DIVISION SERIES RECORD

Year Club	League	Pos.	G.	AB.	R.	H.	2B.	3B.	HR.	RBI.	B.A.	PO.	A.	E.	F.A.
1981—Oakland	Amer.	C	2	8	0	0	0	0	0	0	.000	9	1	0	1.000

CHAMPIONSHIP SERIES RECORD

Year Club	League	Pos.	G.	AB.	R.	H.	2B.	3B.	HR.	RBI.	B.A.	PO.	A.	E.	F.A.
1981—Oakland	Amer.	C-OF	3	6	1	2	0	0	0	0	.333	3	1	0	1.000

WORLD SERIES RECORD

Year Club	League	Pos.	G.	AB.	R.	H.	2B.	3B.	HR.	RBI.	B.A.	PO.	A.	E.	F.A.
1978—New York	Amer.	C	1	0	0	0	0	0	0	0	.000	0	0	0	.000

PITCHING RECORD

Year Club	League	G.	IP.	W.	L.	Pct.	H.	R.	ER.	SO.	BB.	ERA.
1976—Fort Lauderdale	Florida St.	1	1	0	0	.000	1	0	0	1	0	0.00

NEAL HEATON

Born March 3, 1960, at Jamaica, N.Y.
Height, 6.01. Weight, 205.
Throws and bats lefthanded.
Attended University of Miami, Coral Gables, Fla.

Major League saves: 1983 (7), 1986 (1). Total—8.
Named lefthanded pitcher on THE SPORTING NEWS College Baseball All-America Team, 1981.

Year Club	League	G.	IP.	W.	L.	Pct.	H.	R.	ER.	SO.	BB.	ERA.
1981—Chattanooga	Southern	11	77	4	4	.500	61	42	34	50	27	3.97
1982—Charleston	Int'national	29	172⅔	10	5	.667	194	97	77	105	66	4.01
1982—Cleveland	American	8	31	0	2	.000	32	21	18	14	16	5.23
1983—Cleveland	American	39	149⅓	11	7	.611	157	79	69	75	44	4.16
1984—Cleveland	American	38	198⅔	12	15	.444	231	128	115	75	75	5.21
1985—Cleveland	American	36	207½	9	17	.346	244	119	113	82	80	4.90
1986—Cleveland†-Minnesota	American	33	198⅔	7	15	.318	201	102	90	90	81	4.08
Major League Totals—5 Years		154	785⅓	39	56	.411	865	449	405	336	296	4.64

Selected by New York Mets' organization in 1st round (first player selected) of free-agent draft, January 9, 1979.
Selected by Cleveland Indians' organization in 2nd round of free-agent draft, June 8, 1981.
†Traded to Minnesota Twins for Pitcher John Butcher, June 20, 1986.

DANIEL WILLIAM HEEP
(Danny)

Born July 3, 1957, at San Antonio, Tex.
Height, 5.11. Weight, 185.
Throws and bats lefthanded.
Received degree in teaching and political science from St. Mary's University, San Antonio, Tex.

Major League stolen bases: 1983 (3), 1984 (3), 1985 (2), 1986 (1). Total—9.
Led Southern League in total bases with 274 in 1979.
Named Southern League co-Most Valuable Player, 1979.

Year Club	League	Pos.	G.	AB.	R.	H.	2B.	3B.	HR.	RBI.	B.A.	PO.	A.	E.	F.A.
1978—Daytona Beach	Fla. St.	OF	66	212	29	72	18	2	2	24	.340	89	9	2	.980
1979—Columbus	South.	OF	138	523	103	*171	30	5	21	84	.327	211	12	6	.974
1979—Houston	Nat.	OF	14	14	0	2	0	0	0	2	.143	7	0	0	1.000
1980—Tucson	P. C.	1B-OF	96	376	63	129	28	5	17	69	*.343	810	53	8	.991
1980—Houston	Nat.	1B	33	87	6	24	8	0	0	6	.276	188	8	2	.990
1981—Houston†	Nat.	1B-OF	33	96	6	24	3	0	0	11	.250	198	9	2	.990
1981—Tuscon	P. C.	1B-OF	78	285	55	96	23	5	11	60	.337	635	44	12	.983
1982—Houston‡	Nat.	OF-1B	85	198	16	47	14	1	4	22	.237	192	6	1	.995
1983—New York	Nat.	OF-1B	115	253	30	64	12	0	8	21	.253	159	11	0	1.000
1984—New York	Nat.	OF-1B	99	199	36	46	9	2	1	12	.231	137	7	4	.973
1985—New York	Nat.	OF-1B	95	271	26	76	17	0	7	42	.280	154	5	4	.975
1986—New York§	Nat.	OF	86	195	24	55	8	2	5	33	.282	83	2	1	.988
Major League Totals—8 Years		560	1313	144	338	71	5	25	149	.257	1118	48	14	.988

Selected by Houston Astros' organization in 2nd round of free-agent draft, June 6, 1978.
†On disabled list, April 19 to May 4, 1981.
‡Traded to New York Mets for Pitcher Mike Scott, December 10, 1982.
§Granted free agency, November 12, 1986.

CHAMPIONSHIP SERIES RECORD

Year Club	League	Pos.	G.	AB.	R.	H.	2B.	3B.	HR.	RBI.	B.A.	PO.	A.	E.	F.A.
1980—Houston	Nat.	PH	1	1	0	0	0	0	0	0	.000	0	0	0	.000
1986—New York	Nat.	PH-OF	5	4	0	1	0	0	0	1	.250	0	0	0	.000
Championship Series Totals—2 Years			6	5	0	1	0	0	0	1	.200	0	0	0	.000

WORLD SERIES TOTALS

Year Club	League	Pos.	G.	AB.	R.	H.	2B.	3B.	HR.	RBI.	B.A.	PO.	A.	E.	F.A.
1986—New York	Nat.	PH-O-DH	5	11	0	1	0	0	0	2	.091	1	0	0	1.000

DAVID LEE HENDERSON
(Dave)

Born July 21, 1958, at Dos Palos, Calif.
Height, 6.02. Weight, 210.
Throws and bats righthanded.
Nephew of Joe Henderson, pitcher with Chicago
White Sox and Cincinnati Reds, 1974, 1976 and 1977.

Major League stolen bases: 1981 (2), 1982 (2), 1983 (9), 1984 (5), 1985 (6), 1986 (2). Total—26.

Year Club	League	Pos.	G.	AB.	R.	H.	2B.	3B.	HR.	RBI.	B.A.	PO.	A.	E.	F.A.
1977—Bellingham	N'west	OF	65	251	47	79	14	2	●16	63	.315	136	5	★11	.928
1978—Stockton	Calif.	OF	117	409	48	95	16	4	7	63	.232	204	12	14	.939
1979—San Jose	Calif.	OF	136	507	103	152	23	3	27	99	.300	264	18	4	.986
1980—Spokane†	P. C.	OF	109	341	48	95	26	1	7	50	.279	258	9	7	.974
1981—Seattle	Amer.	OF	59	126	17	21	3	0	6	13	.167	105	4	0	1.000
1981—Spokane	P. C.	OF	80	272	47	76	23	1	12	50	.279	146	7	3	.981
1982—Seattle‡	Amer.	OF	104	324	47	82	17	1	14	48	.253	249	11	4	.985
1983—Seattle	Amer.	OF	137	484	50	130	24	5	17	55	.269	304	17	6	.982
1984—Seattle§	Amer.	OF	112	350	42	98	23	0	14	43	.280	242	11	3	.988
1985—Seattle	Amer.	OF	139	502	70	121	28	2	14	68	.241	335	8	5	.986
1986—Sea. x-Bos.	Amer.	OF	139	388	59	103	22	4	15	47	.265	231	11	5	.980
Major League Totals—6 Years			690	2174	285	555	117	12	80	274	.255	1466	62	23	.985

Selected by Seattle Mariners' organization in 1st round (26th player selected) of free-agent draft, June 7, 1977.
†On disabled list, June 26 to July 22, 1980.
‡On disabled list, May 3 to May 18, 1982.
§On disabled list, August 10 to August 29, 1984.
xTraded with Infielder Spike Owen to Boston Red Sox for Infielder Rey Quinones, a player to be named later and cash, August 19, 1986; as part of deal, Seattle Mariners claimed Pitchers Mike Brown and Mike Trujillo on waivers from Boston, August 22, 1986. Seattle acquired Outfielder John Christensen to complete deal, September 25, 1986.

CHAMPIONSHIP SERIES RECORD

Year Club	League	Pos.	G.	AB.	R.	H.	2B.	3B.	HR.	RBI.	B.A.	PO.	A.	E.	F.A.
1986—Boston	Amer.	OF	5	9	3	1	0	0	1	4	.111	11	0	0	1.000

WORLD SERIES RECORD

Year Club	League	Pos.	G.	AB.	R.	H.	2B.	3B.	HR.	RBI.	B.A.	PO.	A.	E.	F.A.
1986—Boston	Amer.	OF	7	25	6	10	1	1	2	5	.400	22	0	0	1.000

RICKEY HENLEY HENDERSON

Born December 25, 1958, at Chicago, Ill.
Height, 5.10. Weight, 195.
Throws left and bats righthanded.

Established modern major league record for most stolen bases, season (130), 1982.
Established major league record for most times caught stealing, season (42), 1982.
Established American League records for most home runs as leadoff batter, season (9), 1986; most consecutive years, 50 or more stolen bases (7).
Tied American League record for most stolen bases, two consecutive games (7), July 3, 4, 1983.
Major League stolen bases: 1979 (33), 1980 (100), 1981 (56), 1982 (130), 1983 (108), 1984 (66), 1985 (80), 1986 (87). Total—660.
Led American League in bases on balls received with 116 in 1982 and 103 in 1983.
Led American League in stolen bases with 100 in 1980, 56 in 1981, 130 in 1982, 108 in 1983, 66 in 1984, 80 in 1985 and 87 in 1986.
Led American League in caught stealing with 26 in 1980, 22 in 1981, 42 in 1982, 19 in 1983 and tied for lead with 18 in 1986.
Led American League outfielders in total chances with 341 in 1981.
Led Eastern League in stolen bases with 81 and caught stealing with 28 in 1978.
Led California League in stolen bases with 95 and caught stealing with 22 in 1977.
Led Eastern League outfielders in double plays with 4 in 1978.
Won THE SPORTING NEWS Golden Shoe Award, 1983.
Won THE SPORTING NEWS Silver Shoe Award, 1982.
Named outfielder on THE SPORTING NEWS American League All-Star Team, 1981 and 1985.
Named outfielder on THE SPORTING NEWS American League fielding team, 1981.
Named outfielder on THE SPORTING NEWS American League Silver Slugger team, 1981 and 1985.

Year Club	League	Pos.	G.	AB.	R.	H.	2B.	3B.	HR.	RBI.	B.A.	PO.	A.	E.	F.A.
1976—Boise	N'west.	OF	46	140	34	47	13	2	3	23	.336	99	3	★12	.895
1977—Modesto	Calif.	OF	134	481	120	166	18	4	11	69	.345	278	15	★20	.936
1978—Jersey City	East.	OF	133	455	81	141	14	4	0	34	.310	305	●15	7	.979
1979—Ogden	P. C.	OF	71	259	66	80	11	8	3	26	.309	149	6	6	.963

Year	Club	League	Pos.	G.	AB.	R.	H.	2B.	3B.	HR.	RBI.	B.A.	PO.	A.	E.	F.A.
1979—Oakland	Amer.	OF	89	351	49	96	13	3	1	26	.274	215	5	6	.973
1980—Oakland	Amer.	OF	158	591	111	179	22	4	9	53	.303	407	15	7	.984
1981—Oakland	Amer.	OF	108	423	★89	★135	18	7	6	35	.319	★327	7	7	.979
1982—Oakland	Amer.	OF	149	536	119	143	24	4	10	51	.267	379	2	9	.977
1983—Oakland	Amer.	OF	145	513	105	150	25	7	9	48	.292	349	9	3	.992
1984—Oakland†	Amer.	OF	142	502	113	147	27	4	16	58	.293	341	7	11	.969
1985—Fort Lauderdale‡	Fla. St.	OF	3	6	5	1	0	1	0	3	.167	6	0	0	1.000
1985—New York	Amer.	OF	143	547	★146	172	28	5	24	72	.314	439	7	9	.980
1986—New York	Amer.	OF	153	608	★130	160	31	5	28	74	.263	426	4	6	.986
Major League Totals—8 Years			1087	4071	862	1182	188	39	103	417	.290	2883	56	58	.981

Selected by Oakland A's organization in 4th round of free-agent draft, June 8, 1976.

†Traded with Pitcher Bert Bradley and cash to New York Yankees for Outfielder Stan Javier and Pitchers Jay Howell, Jose Rijo, Eric Plunk and Tim Birtsas, December 5, 1984.

‡On New York disabled list, March 30 to April 22, 1985; included rehabilitation disability assignment to Fort Lauderdale, April 19 to April 22, 1985.

DIVISION SERIES RECORD

Year	Club	League	Pos.	G.	AB.	R.	H.	2B.	3B.	HR.	RBI.	B.A.	PO.	A.	E.	F.A.
1981—Oakland	Amer.	OF	3	11	3	2	0	0	0	0	.182	8	0	0	1.000

CHAMPIONSHIP SERIES RECORD

Tied American League Championship Series record for most stolen bases, three-game Series (2), 1981.

Year	Club	League	Pos.	G.	AB.	R.	H.	2B.	3B.	HR.	RBI.	B.A.	PO.	A.	E.	F.A.
1981—Oakland	Amer.	OF	3	11	0	4	2	1	0	1	.364	6	0	1	.857

ALL-STAR GAME RECORD

Tied All-Star Game record for most one-base hits, game (3), July 13, 1982.

Year	League	Pos.	AB.	R.	H.	2B.	3B.	HR.	RBI.	B.A.	PO.	A.	E.	F.A.
1980—American	OF	1	0	0	0	0	0	0	.000	0	0	0	.000
1982—American	OF	4	1	3	0	0	0	0	.750	3	0	1	.750
1983—American	OF	1	0	0	0	0	0	1	.000	0	0	0	.000
1984—American	OF	2	0	0	0	0	0	0	.000	0	0	0	.000
1985—American	OF	3	1	1	0	0	0	0	.333	1	0	0	1.000
1986—American	OF	3	0	0	0	0	0	0	.000	2	0	0	1.000
All-Star Game Totals—6 Years		14	2	4	0	0	0	1	.286	6	0	1	.857

STEPHEN CURTIS HENDERSON

(Steve)

Born November 18, 1952, at Houston, Tex.
Height, 6.01. Weight, 185.
Throws and bats righthanded.
Attended Prairie View A & M University, Prairie View, Tex.

Major League stolen bases: 1977 (6), 1978 (13), 1979 (13), 1980 (23), 1981 (5), 1982 (6), 1983 (10), 1984 (2). Total—78.
Led National League in grounding into double plays with 24 in 1978.
Led Eastern League in total bases with 255 and caught stealing with 17 in 1976.

Year	Club	League	Pos.	G.	AB.	R.	H.	2B.	3B.	HR.	RBI.	B.A.	PO.	A.	E.	F.A.
1974—Billings	Pion.	OF	72	249	★60	72	19	5	●8	●44	.289	114	6	6	★.952
1975—Tampa	Fla. St.	OF-SS	123	413	59	115	9	★16	0	54	.278	263	7	8	.971
1976—Three Rivers	East.	OF	134	506	90	●158	24	★11	17	61	.312	260	12	8	.971
1977—Indianapolis†	A. A.	OF	60	233	35	76	12	6	7	25	.326	107	3	3	.973
1977—New York	Nat.	OF	99	350	67	104	16	6	12	65	.297	189	4	4	.980
1978—New York	Nat.	OF	157	587	83	156	30	9	10	65	.266	315	18	11	.968
1979—New York‡	Nat.	OF	98	350	42	107	16	8	5	39	.306	201	6	2	.990
1980—New York§	Nat.	OF	143	513	75	149	17	8	8	58	.290	299	7	6	.981
1981—Chicago x	Nat.	OF	82	287	32	84	9	5	5	35	.293	152	4	★8	.951
1982—Chicago y	Nat.	OF	92	257	23	60	12	4	2	29	.233	126	5	6	.956
1983—Seattle z	Amer.	OF	121	436	50	128	32	3	10	54	.294	182	15	6	.970
1984—Seattle ab	Amer.	OF	109	325	42	85	12	3	10	35	.262	84	4	6	.936
1985—Oakland	Amer.	OF	85	193	25	58	8	3	3	31	.301	79	3	4	.953
1986—Oakland c	Amer.	OF	11	26	2	2	1	0	0	3	.077	8	0	2	.800
1986—Buffalo	A. A.	OF	72	240	37	69	8	1	5	39	.288	60	1	2	.968
National League Totals—6 Years			671	2344	322	660	100	40	42	291	.282	1282	44	37	.973
American League Totals—4 Years			326	980	119	273	53	9	23	123	.279	353	22	18	.954
Major League Totals—10 Years			997	3324	441	933	153	49	65	414	.281	1635	66	55	.969

Selected by Cincinnati Reds' organization in 5th round of free-agent draft, June 5, 1974.

†Traded with Infielder Doug Flynn, Outfielder Dan Norman and Pitcher Pat Zachry to New York Mets for Pitcher Tom Seaver, June 15, 1977.

‡On disabled list, July 31 to September 17, 1979.

§Traded with cash to Chicago Cubs for Outfielder Dave Kingman, February 28, 1981.

xOn disabled list, May 29 to August 11, 1981.

yTraded to Seattle Mariners for Pitcher Rich Bordi, December 9, 1982.

zGranted free agency, November 7, 1983; re-signed by Mariners, January 26, 1984.

aOn disabled list, June 10 to June 25, 1984.

bGranted free agency, November 8, 1984; signed by Oakland A's, March 31, 1985.

cReleased, May 29, 1986; signed by Buffalo (Chicago White Sox' organization), June 20, 1986.

GEORGE ANDREW HENDRICK JR.

Born October 18, 1949, at Los Angeles, Calif.
Height, 6.03. Weight, 195.
Throws and bats righthanded.
Attended East Los Angeles Junior College, Los Angeles, Calif.

Major League stolen bases: 1972 (3), 1973 (7), 1974 (6), 1975 (6), 1976 (4), 1977 (11), 1978 (2), 1979 (2), 1980 (6), 1981 (4), 1982 (3), 1983 (3), 1985 (1), 1986 (1). Total—59.
Hit three home runs in a game, June 19, 1973.
Led National League in sacrifice flies with 14 in 1982.
Led American League outfielders in double plays with 6 in 1976.
Tied for National League lead in double plays by outfielders with 7 in 1979.
Named first baseman on THE SPORTING NEWS National League All-Star Team, 1983.
Named outfielder on THE SPORTING NEWS National League All-Star Team, 1980.
Named first baseman on THE SPORTING NEWS National League Silver Slugger team, 1983.
Named outfielder on THE SPORTING NEWS National League Silver Slugger team, 1980.

Year Club	League	Pos.	G.	AB.	R.	H.	2B.	3B.	HR.	RBI.	B.A.	PO.	A.	E.	F.A.
1968—Burlington	Midw.	OF	103	364	58	119	●25	4	5	60	★.327	134	8	8	.947
1969—Lodi	Calif.	OF	86	316	47	97	13	2	4	28	.307	121	5	4	.969
1970—Burlington	Midw.	OF	54	198	37	61	9	3	12	43	.308	80	1	5	.942
1970—Birmingham	South.	OF	54	199	30	57	12	0	6	20	.286	115	4	5	.960
1971—Iowa	A. A.	OF	63	249	57	83	9	2	21	63	.333	113	5	3	.975
1971—Oakland	Amer.	OF	42	114	8	27	4	1	0	8	.237	52	1	1	.981
1972—Iowa	A. A.	OF	8	33	0	9	0	0	0	4	.273	14	2	0	1.000
1972—Oakland†	Amer.	OF	58	121	10	22	1	1	4	15	.182	68	0	0	1.000
1973—Cleveland‡	Amer.	OF	113	440	64	118	18	0	21	61	.268	242	7	3	.988
1974—Cleveland	Amer.	OF	139	495	65	138	23	1	19	67	.279	355	9	4	.989
1975—Cleveland	Amer.	OF	145	561	82	145	21	2	24	86	.258	338	4	6	.983
1976—Cleveland§	Amer.	OF	149	551	72	146	20	3	25	81	.265	288	13	4	.987
1977—San Diego	Nat.	OF	152	541	75	168	25	2	23	81	.311	386	11	7	.983
1978—S.D. x-St.L.	Nat.	OF	138	493	64	137	31	1	20	75	.278	313	6	2	.994
1979—St. Louis	Nat.	OF	140	493	67	148	27	1	16	75	.300	254	★20	2	.993
1980—St. Louis	Nat.	OF	150	572	73	173	33	2	25	109	.302	322	10	2	.994
1981—St. Louis	Nat.	OF	101	394	67	112	19	3	18	61	.284	227	6	4	.983
1982—St. Louis	Nat.	OF	136	515	65	145	20	5	19	104	.282	238	6	5	.980
1983—St. Louis	Nat.	1B-OF	144	529	73	168	33	3	18	97	.318	904	79	8	.992
1984—St. Louis y	Nat.	OF-1B	120	441	57	122	28	1	9	69	.277	189	9	2	.990
1985—Pittsburgh z	Nat.	OF	69	256	23	59	15	0	2	25	.230	133	2	4	.971
1985—California	Amer.	OF	16	41	5	5	1	0	2	6	.122	18	1	0	1.000
1986—California	Amer.	OF-1B	102	283	45	77	13	1	14	47	.272	188	9	5	.975
American League Totals—8 Years			764	2606	351	678	101	9	109	371	.260	1549	44	23	.986
National League Totals—9 Years			1150	4234	564	1232	231	18	150	696	.291	2966	149	36	.989
Major League Totals—16 Years			1914	6840	915	1910	332	27	259	1067	.279	4515	193	59	.988

Selected by Oakland A's organization in 1st round (first player selected) of free-agent draft, January 27, 1968.
†Traded with Catcher Dave Duncan to Cleveland Indians for Catcher Ray Fosse and Infielder Jack Heidemann, March 24, 1973.
‡On disabled list, August 14 to September 29, 1973.
§Traded to San Diego Padres for Outfielder John Grubb, Catcher Fred Kendall and Shortstop Hector Torres, December 8, 1976.
xTraded to St. Louis Cardinals for Pitcher Eric Rasmussen, May 26, 1978.
yTraded with Catcher Steve Barnard to Pittsburgh Pirates for Pitcher John Tudor and Outfielder Brian Harper, December 12, 1984.
zTraded with Pitchers John Candelaria and Al Holland to California Angels for Pitcher Pat Clements, Outfielder Mike Brown and a player to be named later, August 2, 1985; Pittsburgh Pirates' organization acquired Pitcher Bob Kipper to complete deal, August 16, 1985.

CHAMPIONSHIP SERIES RECORD

Tied Championship Series record for most clubs, total Series (3).
Tied American League Championship Series record for most positions played, total Series (3).

Year Club	League	Pos.	G.	AB.	R.	H.	2B.	3B.	HR.	RBI.	B.A.	PO.	A.	E.	F.A.
1972—Oakland	Amer.	PH-OF	5	7	2	1	0	0	0	0	.143	1	0	0	1.000
1982—St. Louis	Nat.	OF	3	13	2	4	0	0	0	2	.308	5	0	0	1.000
1986—California	Amer.	OF-1B	3	12	0	1	0	0	0	0	.083	16	2	0	1.000
Championship Series Totals—3 Years			11	32	4	6	0	0	0	2	.188	22	2	0	1.000

WORLD SERIES RECORD

Tied World Series record for most times awarded first base on catcher's interference, game (1), October 15, 1982.

Year Club	League	Pos.	G.	AB.	R.	H.	2B.	3B.	HR.	RBI.	B.A.	PO.	A.	E.	F.A.
1972—Oakland	Amer.	OF	5	15	3	2	0	0	0	0	.133	12	0	0	1.000
1982—St. Louis	Nat.	OF	7	28	5	9	0	0	0	5	.321	10	1	0	1.000
World Series Totals—2 Years			12	43	8	11	0	0	0	5	.256	22	1	0	1.000

ALL-STAR GAME RECORD

Year League	Pos.	AB.	R.	H.	2B.	3B.	HR.	RBI.	B.A.	PO.	A.	E.	F.A.
1974—American	OF	2	0	1	0	0	0	0	.500	3	0	0	1.000
1975—American	PR-OF	1	1	1	0	0	0	0	1.000	0	0	0	.000
1980—National	OF	2	0	1	0	0	0	1	.500	0	0	0	.000
All-Star Game Totals—3 Years		5	1	3	0	0	0	1	.600	3	0	0	1.000

Member of National League All-Star Team in 1983; did not play.

DAVID LEE HENGEL
(Dave)

Born December 18, 1961, at Oakland, Calif.
Height, 6.00. Weight, 185.
Throws and bats righthanded.
Attended University of California, Berkeley, Calif.

Led Midwest League in slugging percentage with .565 in 1984.
Led Pacific Coast League outfielders in double plays with 5 in 1986.

Year	Club	League	Pos.	G.	AB.	R.	H.	2B.	3B.	HR.	RBI.	B.A.	PO.	A.	E.	F.A.
1983—Bellingham	N'west	OF	9	27	4	9	4	0	0	6	.333	10	0	0	1.000
1984—Wausau	Midw.	OF	120	441	68	136	31	2	26	98	.308	109	9	9	.929
1985—Chattanooga	South.	OF	122	460	71	132	30	5	17	89	.287	277	14	6	.980
1985—Calgary	P. C.	OF	6	23	1	2	1	0	0	3	.087	13	0	0	1.000
1986—Calgary	P. C.	OF	113	407	73	116	22	1	27	94	.285	217	●16	8	.967
1986—Seattle	Amer.	OF	21	63	3	12	1	0	1	6	.190	9	1	0	1.000
Major League Totals—1 Year			21	63	3	12	1	0	1	6	.190	9	1	0	1.000

Selected by San Francisco Giants' organization in 6th round of free-agent draft, June 3, 1980.
Selected by Seattle Mariners' organization in 3rd round of free-agent draft, June 6, 1983.

THOMAS ANTHONY HENKE
Name pronounced HEN-key.
(Tom)

Born December 21, 1957, at Kansas City, Mo.
Height, 6.05. Weight, 215.
Throws and bats righthanded.
Attended East Central College, Union, Mo.

Major League saves: 1983 (1), 1984 (2), 1985 (13), 1986 (27). Total—43.
Tied for International League lead in saves with 18 in 1985.
Named International League Pitcher of the Year, 1985.

Year	Club	League	G.	IP.	W.	L.	Pct.	H.	R.	ER.	SO.	BB.	ERA.
1980—Sarasota Rangers	Gulf Coast	8	38	3	3	.500	33	11	4	34	12	0.95
1980—Asheville	S. Atlantic	5	23	0	2	.000	25	21	20	19	20	7.83
1981—Asheville	S. Atlantic	28	92	8	6	.571	77	36	30	67	35	2.93
1981—Tulsa	Texas	15	32	4	3	.571	31	16	14	37	14	3.94
1982—Tulsa	Texas	★52	87⅔	3	6	.333	69	35	26	100	40	2.67
1982—Texas	American	8	15⅔	1	0	1.000	14	2	2	9	8	1.15
1983—Oklahoma City	Am. Assoc.	47	77⅔	9	6	.600	71	33	26	90	33	3.01
1983—Texas	American	8	16	1	0	1.000	16	6	6	17	4	3.38
1984—Texas	American	25	28⅓	1	1	.500	36	21	20	25	20	6.35
1984—Oklahoma City†	Am. Assoc.	39	64⅔	6	2	.750	59	21	19	65	25	2.64
1985—Syracuse	Int'national	39	51⅓	2	1	.667	13	5	5	60	18	0.88
1985—Toronto	American	28	40	3	3	.500	29	12	9	42	8	2.03
1986—Toronto	American	63	91⅓	9	5	.643	63	39	34	118	32	3.35
Major League Totals—5 Years		132	191⅓	15	9	.625	158	80	71	211	72	3.34

Selected by Seattle Mariners' organization in 20th round of free-agent draft, June 5, 1979.
Selected by Chicago Cubs' organization in secondary phase of free-agent draft, January 8, 1980.
Selected by Texas Rangers' organization in secondary phase of free-agent draft, June 3, 1980.
†Selected by Toronto Blue Jays' organization in player compensation pool draft, January 24, 1985. (Toronto received compensation for Texas Rangers' signing of free agent Designated Hitter Cliff Johnson, a Type A player, December 5, 1984.

CHAMPIONSHIP SERIES RECORD

Tied Championship Series record for most games won, seven-game Series (2), 1985.

Year	Club	League	G.	IP.	W.	L.	Pct.	H.	R.	ER.	SO.	BB.	ERA.
1985—Toronto	American	3	6⅓	2	0	1.000	5	3	3	4	4	4.26

MICHAEL ALAN HENNEMAN
(Mike)

Born December 11, 1961, at St. Charles, Mo.
Height, 6.04. Weight, 195.
Throws and bats righthanded.
Attended Oklahoma State University, Stillwater, Okla.

Year	Club	League	G.	IP.	W.	L.	Pct.	H.	R.	ER.	SO.	BB.	ERA.
1984—Birmingham	Southern	29	59⅓	4	2	.667	48	22	16	39	33	2.43
1985—Birmingham	Southern	46	70⅓	3	5	.375	88	50	45	40	28	5.76
1986—Nashville	Am. Assoc.	31	58	2	5	.286	57	27	19	39	23	2.95

Selected by Toronto Blue Jays' organization in 27th round of free-agent draft, June 7, 1982.
Selected by Philadelphia Phillies' organization in secondary phase of free-agent draft, June 6, 1983.
Selected by Detroit Tigers' organization in 4th round of free-agent draft, June 4, 1984.

DWAYNE ALLEN HENRY

Born February 16, 1962, at Elkton, Md.
Height, 6.03. Weight, 205.
Throws and bats righthanded.

Major League saves: 1985 (3).

Year—Club	League	G.	IP.	W.	L.	Pct.	H.	R.	ER.	SO.	BB.	ERA.
1980—Sarasota Rangers	Gulf Coast	11	54	5	1	.833	36	23	16	47	28	2.67
1981—Asheville	S. Atlantic	25	134	8	7	.533	120	81	66	86	58	4.43
1982—Burlington†	Midwest	4	18⅔	2	0	1.000	6	0	0	25	6	0.00
1983—Tulsa‡	Texas	9	14	0	0	.000	16	14	9	14	19	5.79
1983—Sarasota Rangers	Gulf Coast	3	9	0	0	.000	10	6	4	11	1	4.00
1984—Tulsa	Texas	33	85	5	8	.385	65	42	32	79	60	3.39
1984—Texas	American	3	4⅓	0	1	.000	5	4	4	2	7	8.31
1985—Tulsa	Texas	34	81⅓	7	6	.538	51	32	24	97	44	2.66
1985—Texas	American	16	21	2	2	.500	16	7	6	20	7	2.57
1986—Texas§	American	19	19⅓	1	0	1.000	14	11	10	17	22	4.66
1986—Oklahoma City	Am. Assoc.	28	44⅓	2	1	.667	51	30	29	41	27	5.89
Major League Totals—3 Years		38	44⅔	3	3	.500	35	22	20	39	36	4.03

Selected by Texas Rangers' organization in 2nd round of free-agent draft, June 3, 1980.
†On disabled list, May 4, 1982 through remainder of season.
‡On disabled list, April 8 to July 9, 1983.
§On disabled list, May 31 to July 8, 1986; included rehabilitation disability assignment to Oklahoma City, June 18 to July 8, 1986.

CHARLES FLOYD HENSLEY JR.
(Chuck)

Born March 11, 1959, at Tulare, Calif.
Height, 6.03. Weight, 190.
Throws and bats lefthanded.
Attended University of California, Berkeley, Calif.

Major League saves: 1986 (1).

Year—Club	League	G.	IP.	W.	L.	Pct.	H.	R.	ER.	SO.	BB.	ERA.
1980—Lakeland†	Florida St.	28	59	3	2	.600	67	27	22	42	27	3.36
1981—Modesto	California	19	136	8	8	.500	153	75	56	83	57	3.71
1981—West Haven	Eastern	5	26	1	2	.333	32	15	14	13	8	4.85
1982—West Haven	Eastern	37	145	10	4	.714	149	82	63	108	49	3.91
1983—Tacoma‡	P. Coast	59	76⅔	4	8	.333	88	58	47	40	29	5.52
1984—Tacoma§-Vancouver x	P. Coast	14	38	0	4	.000	58	36	28	24	16	6.63
1985—Phoenix	P. Coast	35	74⅓	3	1	.750	75	30	26	52	27	3.15
1985—Shreveport	Texas	13	25⅔	4	3	.571	20	9	8	20	5	2.81
1986—Phoenix	P. Coast	44	51	0	3	.000	42	16	14	50	27	2.47
1986—San Francisco y	National	11	7⅓	0	0	.000	5	2	2	6	2	2.45
Major League Totals—1 Year		11	7⅓	0	0	.000	5	2	2	6	2	2.45

Selected by New York Yankees' organization in 10th round of free-agent draft, June 7, 1977.
Selected by Detroit Tigers' organization in 10th round of free-agent draft, June 3, 1980.
†Released, April 3, 1981; signed by Modesto (Oakland A's organization), April 22, 1981.
‡On disabled list, July 3 to July 13, 1983.
§Sold to Vancouver (Milwaukee Brewers' organization), June 9, 1984.
xReleased, July 2, 1984; signed by Phoenix (San Francisco Giants' organization), April 15, 1985.
yReleased, October 16, 1986; signed by Atlanta Braves' organization, November 17, 1986.

JEFFREY JOHN HERMANN
(Jeff)

Born October 8, 1963, at Joliet, Ill.
Height, 6.05. Weight, 220.
Throws right and bats lefthanded.
Attended College of St. Francis, Joliet, Ill.

Year—Club	League	Pos.	G.	AB.	R.	H.	2B.	3B.	HR.	RBI.	B.A.	PO.	A.	E.	F.A.
1984—Bristol	Appal.	1-C-O-2	62	183	37	48	8	*6	3	37	.262	418	36	6	.987
1985—Lakeland	Fla. St.	1B-OF	101	340	37	88	20	2	5	49	.259	697	51	13	.983
1986—Glens Falls	East.	1B	76	247	28	58	12	4	2	31	.235	570	54	8	.987

Selected by Detroit Tigers' organization in 9th round of free-agent draft, June 4, 1984.

GUILLERMO HERNANDEZ (VILLANUEVA)
(Willie)

Born November 14, 1955, at Aguada, Puerto Rico.
Height, 6.02. Weight, 185.
Throws and bats lefthanded.

Tied National League record for most consecutive strikeouts by relief pitcher, game (6), July 3, 1983.
Major League saves: 1977 (4), 1978 (3), 1981 (2), 1982 (10), 1983 (8), 1984 (32), 1985 (31), 1986 (24). Total—114.
Led American League in games finished in relief with 68 in 1984.
Led Western Carolinas League pitchers in games started with 26 and complete games with 13 in 1977.
Named American League Most Valuable Player by Baseball Writers' Association of America, 1984.
Named American League Pitcher of the Year by THE SPORTING NEWS, 1984.
Won American League Cy Young Memorial Award, 1984.
Named lefthanded pitcher on THE SPORTING NEWS American League All-Star Team, 1984.
Received reported $25,000 bonus to sign with Philadelphia Phillies, 1974.

Year—Club	League	G.	IP.	W.	L.	Pct.	H.	R.	ER.	SO.	BB.	ERA.
1974—Spartanburg	W. Carol.	26	*190	11	11	.500	169	82	58	*179	49	2.75
1975—Reading	Eastern	13	91	8	2	.800	79	32	30	46	25	2.97

Year Club	League	G.	IP.	W.	L.	Pct.	H.	R.	ER.	SO.	BB.	ERA.
1975—Toledo	Int'national	13	80	6	4	.600	86	43	29	46	26	3.26
1976—Oklahoma City†	Am. Assoc.	25	135	8	9	.471	154	82	68	88	30	4.53
1977—Chicago	National	67	110	8	7	.533	94	42	37	78	28	3.03
1978—Chicago	National	54	60	8	2	.800	57	26	25	38	35	3.75
1979—Chicago	National	51	79	4	4	.500	85	50	44	53	39	5.01
1980—Chicago	National	53	108	1	9	.100	115	58	53	75	45	4.42
1981—Iowa	Am. Assoc.	18	74	4	5	.444	84	39	32	41	27	3.89
1981—Chicago	National	12	14	0	0	.000	14	7	6	13	8	3.86
1982—Chicago	National	75	75	4	6	.400	74	26	25	54	24	3.00
1983—Chicago‡-Philadelphia§	National	74	115⅓	9	4	.692	109	47	42	93	32	3.28
1984—Detroit	American	*80	140⅓	9	3	.750	96	30	30	112	36	1.92
1985—Detroit x	American	74	106⅔	8	10	.444	82	38	32	76	14	2.70
1986—Detroit	American	64	88⅔	8	7	.533	87	35	35	77	21	3.55
National League Totals—7 Years		386	561⅓	34	32	.515	548	256	232	404	211	3.72
American League Totals—3 Years		218	335⅔	25	20	.556	265	103	97	265	71	2.60
Major League Totals—10 Years		604	897	59	52	.532	813	359	329	669	282	3.30

Signed as free agent by Philadelphia Phillies' organization, September 11, 1973.
†Drafted by Chicago Cubs, December 6, 1976.
‡Traded to Philadelphia Phillies for Pitchers Dick Ruthven and Bill Johnson, May 22, 1983.
§Traded with First Baseman Dave Bergman to Detroit Tigers for Outfielder Glenn Wilson and Catcher-First Baseman John Wockenfuss, March 24, 1984.
xGrounded out on only at-bat.

CHAMPIONSHIP SERIES RECORD

Tied Championship Series record for most games pitched, three-game Series (3), 1984.

Year Club	League	G.	IP.	W.	L.	Pct.	H.	R.	ER.	SO.	BB.	ERA.
1984—Detroit	American	3	4	0	0	.000	3	1	1	3	1	2.25

WORLD SERIES RECORD

Tied World Series record for most saves, five-game Series (2), 1984.

Year Club	League	G.	IP.	W.	L.	Pct.	H.	R.	ER.	SO.	BB.	ERA.
1983—Philadelphia	National	3	4	0	0	.000	0	0	0	4	1	0.00
1984—Detroit	American	3	5⅓	0	0	.000	4	1	1	0	0	1.69
World Series Totals—2 Years		6	9⅓	0	0	.000	4	1	1	4	1	0.96

ALL-STAR GAME RECORD

Year League	IP.	W.	L.	Pct.	H.	R.	ER.	SO.	BB.	ERA.
1984—American	1	0	0	.000	1	1	1	1	0	9.00
1985—American	⅔	0	0	.000	1	0	0	2	1	0.00
All-Star Game Totals—2 Years	1⅔	0	0	.000	2	1	1	3	1	5.40

Member of American League All-Star Team in 1986; did not play.

KEITH HERNANDEZ

Born October 20, 1953, at San Francisco, Calif.
Height, 6.00. Weight, 195.
Throws and bats lefthanded.
Attended College of San Mateo, San Mateo, Calif.
Son of John Hernandez, minor league infielder, 1941 through 1950; and brother of Gary Hernandez,
first baseman-outfielder in St. Louis Cardinals' organization, 1972 through 1975.

Established major league records for most game-winning RBIs, season (24), 1985; most game-winning RBIs, lifetime (107); most years leading league in double plays by first baseman (6).
Tied National League records for most home runs with bases filled, month (2), September, 1977; fewest errors by first baseman for leader in errors, season (13), 1983.
Major League stolen bases: 1976 (4), 1977 (7), 1978 (13), 1979 (11), 1980 (14), 1981 (12), 1982 (19), 1983 (9), 1984 (2), 1985 (3), 1986 (2). Total—96.
Hit for the cycle, July 4, 1985.
Led National League in bases on balls received with 94 in 1986.
Led National League in intentional bases on balls received with 19 in 1982.
Led National League first basemen in putouts with 1,054 in 1981 and 1,586 in 1982.
Led National League first basemen in double plays with 146 in 1977, 145 in 1979, 146 in 1980, 99 in 1981, 147 in 1983 and 127 in 1984.
Led National League first basemen in total chances with 1,643 in 1979, 1,732 in 1982 and 1,578 in 1983.
Led National League in game-winning RBIs with 24 in 1985 and tied for lead with 21 in 1982.
Led Texas League first basemen in double plays with 101 in 1973.
Named National League Player of the Year by THE SPORTING NEWS, 1979.
Named National League co-Most Valuable Player by Baseball Writers' Association of America, 1979.
Named first baseman on THE SPORTING NEWS National League All-Star Team, 1979, 1980 and 1984 through 1986.
Named first baseman on THE SPORTING NEWS National League All-Star fielding team, 1978 through 1986.
Named first baseman on THE SPORTING NEWS National League Silver Slugger team, 1980 and 1984.

Year Club	League	Pos.	G.	AB.	R.	H.	2B.	3B.	HR.	RBI.	B.A.	PO.	A.	E.	F.A.
1972—St. Petersburg†	Fla. St.	1B	84	309	38	79	16	5	5	41	.256	682	52	7	.991
1972—Tulsa	A. A.	1B	11	29	5	7	1	0	0	1	.241	54	2	0	1.000
1973—Arkansas	Texas	1B	105	388	62	101	20	2	3	52	.260	960	61	9	*.991
1973—Tulsa	A. A.	1B	31	120	20	40	6	1	5	25	.333	289	15	1	.997
1974—Tulsa‡	A. A.	1B-OF	102	353	67	124	18	6	14	63	*.351	690	50	12	.984
1974—St. Louis	Nat.	1B	14	34	3	10	1	2	0	2	.294	70	1	2	.973
1975—Tulsa	A. A.	●1B-OF	85	324	70	107	29	3	10	48	.330	597	53	●13	.980

Year Club League	Pos.	G.	AB.	R.	H.	2B.	3B.	HR.	RBI.	B.A.	PO.	A.	E.	F.A.
1975—St. Louis.............. Nat.	1B	64	188	20	47	8	2	3	20	.250	469	36	2	.996
1976—St. Louis.............. Nat.	1B	129	374	54	108	21	5	7	46	.289	862	●107	10	.990
1977—St. Louis.............. Nat.	1B	161	560	90	163	41	4	15	91	.291	1453	106	12	.992
1978—St. Louis.............. Nat.	1B	159	542	90	138	32	4	11	64	.255	1436	96	10	.994
1979—St. Louis.............. Nat.	1B	161	610	*116	210	*48	11	11	105	*.344	*1489	*146	8	.995
1980—St. Louis.............. Nat.	1B	159	595	*111	191	39	8	16	99	.321	1572	115	9	.995
1981—St. Louis.............. Nat.	1B-OF	103	376	65	115	27	4	8	48	.306	1056	86	3	.997
1982—St. Louis.............. Nat.	1B-OF	160	579	79	173	33	6	7	94	.299	1591	135	11	.994
1983—St.L.§-N.Y............ Nat.	1B	150	538	77	160	23	7	12	63	.297	*1418	147	●13	.992
1984—New York............. Nat.	1B	154	550	83	171	31	0	15	94	.311	1214	*142	8	.994
1985—New York............. Nat.	1B	158	593	87	183	34	4	10	91	.309	1310	*139	4	*.997
1986—New York............. Nat.	1B	149	551	94	171	34	1	13	83	.310	1199	149	5	*.996
Major League Totals—13 Years..............		1721	6090	969	1840	372	58	128	900	.302	15139	1405	97	.994

Selected by St. Louis Cardinals' organization in 42nd round of free-agent draft, June 8, 1971.
†On disabled list, April 10 to May 30, 1972.
‡On disabled list, April 16 to May 20, 1974.
§Traded to New York Mets for Pitchers Neil Allen and Rick Ownbey, June 15, 1983.

CHAMPIONSHIP SERIES RECORD

Tied Championship Series record for most at-bats, game (7), October 15, 1986 (16 innings).

Year Club League	Pos.	G.	AB.	R.	H.	2B.	3B.	HR.	RBI.	B.A.	PO.	A.	E.	F.A.
1982—St. Louis.............. Nat.	1B	3	12	3	4	0	0	0	1	.333	35	1	0	1.000
1986—New York............. Nat.	1B	6	26	3	7	1	1	0	3	.269	67	12	0	1.000
Championship Series Totals—2 Years.....		9	38	6	11	1	1	0	4	.289	102	13	0	1.000

WORLD SERIES RECORD

Year Club League	Pos.	G.	AB.	R.	H.	2B.	3B.	HR.	RBI.	B.A.	PO.	A.	E.	F.A.
1982—St. Louis.............. Nat.	1B	7	27	4	7	2	0	1	8	.259	62	7	2	.972
1986—New York............. Nat.	1B	7	26	1	6	0	0	0	4	.231	48	4	1	.981
World Series Totals—2 Years...................		14	53	5	13	2	0	1	12	.245	110	11	3	.976

ALL-STAR GAME RECORD

Year League	Pos.	AB.	R.	H.	2B.	3B.	HR.	RBI.	B.A.	PO.	A.	E.	F.A.
1979—National..	PH	1	0	0	0	0	0	0	.000	0	0	0	.000
1980—National..	PH-1B	2	0	2	0	0	0	0	1.000	5	0	0	1.000
1984—National..	1B	1	0	0	0	0	0	0	.000	1	0	0	1.000
1986—National..	1B	4	0	0	0	0	0	0	.000	5	0	0	1.000
All-Star Game Totals—4 Years....................		8	0	2	0	0	0	0	.250	11	0	0	1.000

LEONARDO JESUS HERNANDEZ
(Leo)

Born November 6, 1959, at Santa Lucia, Estado Miranda, Venezuela.
Height, 5.11. Weight, 170.
Throws and bats righthanded.

Major League stolen bases: 1983 (1).
Led International League in total bases with 237 in 1984.
Tied for Texas League lead in game-winning RBIs with 12 in 1981.
Led International League third basemen in total chances with 394 in 1986.
Led International League outfielders in errors with 12 in 1984.

Year Club League	Pos.	G.	AB.	R.	H.	2B.	3B.	HR.	RBI.	B.A.	PO.	A.	E.	F.A.
1978—Clinton................... Midw.	3B	112	444	65	123	21	4	17	73	.277	86	222	20	*.939
1979—Clinton................... Midw.	3B	29	113	24	38	8	1	2	23	.336	22	66	6	.936
1979—Lodi........................ Calif.	3B	61	257	48	82	12	2	8	52	.319	52	143	29	.871
1979—San Antonio.......... Texas	3B	36	128	19	32	7	0	2	11	.250	19	51	8	.897
1980—San Antonio.......... Texas	3B	41	136	27	33	9	2	2	26	.243	23	77	14	.877
1980—Vero Beach.......... Fla. St.	3B-OF-1B	82	307	53	95	13	3	10	46	.309	99	102	9	.957
1981—San Antonio.......... Texas	3B	131	497	90	148	34	3	25	91	.298	*107	271	*25	.938
1982—San Antonio†........ Texas	3B-1B	19	75	8	24	4	1	3	14	.320	39	35	6	.925
1982—Charlotte.............. South.	3-1-O-2	68	270	46	78	18	2	20	62	.289	159	104	11	.960
1982—Rochester............. Int.	3B-OF-2B	53	202	29	64	10	3	11	43	.317	41	98	6	.959
1982—Baltimore .... Amer.	PH	2	2	0	0	0	0	0	0	.000	0	0	0	.000
1983—Baltimore .... Amer.	3B	64	203	21	50	6	1	6	26	.246	44	109	13	.922
1983—Rochester............. Int.	3B-OF-2B	57	201	24	69	13	2	8	25	.343	57	66	10	.925
1984—Rochester............. Int.	OF-3B-1B	136	512	66	141	25	4	21	83	.275	248	42	15	.951
1985—Rochester............. Int.	OF-3B-1B	124	475	59	128	31	2	17	69	.269	182	75	10	.963
1985—Baltimore‡........... Amer.	1B-OF	12	21	0	1	0	0	0	0	.048	2	0	0	1.000
1986—Columbus............. Int.	3B	136	*522	62	142	*35	1	11	64	.272	*102	265	27	.931
1986—New York§............ Amer.	3B-2B	7	22	2	5	2	0	1	4	.227	4	10	0	1.000
Major League Totals—4 Years................		85	248	23	56	8	1	7	30	.226	50	119	13	.929

Signed as free agent by Los Angeles Dodgers' organization, January 18, 1978.
†Traded to Baltimore Orioles' organization for Catcher-First Baseman Jose Morales, April 28, 1982.
‡Traded to New York Yankees, December 16, 1985, completing deal in which New York traded Pitcher Rich Bordi and Infielder Rex Hudler to Baltimore Orioles for Outfielder Gary Roenicke and a player to be named later, December 12, 1985.
§Released, October 15, 1986.

MANUEL ANTONIO HERNANDEZ
(Manny)

Born May 7, 1961, at La Romana, Dominican Republic.
Height, 6.00. Weight, 150.
Throws and bats righthanded.

Tied for Pacific Coast League lead in balks with 5 in 1984.

Year	Club	League	G.	IP.	W.	L.	Pct.	H.	R.	ER.	SO.	BB.	ERA.
1979—Sarasota Astros	Gulf Coast	9	14	2	0	1.000	17	6	4	10	10	2.57
1980—Sarasota Astros Blue	Gulf Coast	11	62	5	2	.714	65	26	21	37	15	3.05
1981—Daytona Beach	Florida St.	13	79	6	5	.545	67	36	30	61	24	3.42
1982—Daytona Beach	Florida St.	21	99⅓	6	6	.500	114	70	55	50	52	4.98
1983—Daytona Beach	Florida St.	18	102⅓	10	3	.769	86	46	34	73	27	2.99
1984—Tucson	P. Coast	28	146⅔	6	9	.400	153	96	80	107	65	4.91
1985—Tucson†	P. Coast	11	37⅔	1	1	.500	35	19	15	25	10	3.58
1986—Tucson	P. Coast	22	128	8	7	.533	139	79	67	84	27	4.71
1986—Houston	National	9	27⅔	2	3	.400	33	15	12	9	12	3.90
Major League Totals—1 Year		9	27⅔	2	3	.400	33	15	12	9	12	3.90

Signed as free agent by Houston Astros' organization, November 23, 1978.
†On disabled list, May 9 to July 18, 1985.

MARTIN HERNANDEZ (MORENO)

Born January 30, 1965, at La Tuna Sinaloa, Mexico.
Height, 6.02. Weight, 175.
Throws and bats righthanded.

Tied for Carolina League lead in balks with 7 in 1986.

Year	Club	League	G.	IP.	W.	L.	Pct.	H.	R.	ER.	SO.	BB.	ERA.
1983—Mexico City Reds	Mexican	1	1⅓	0	0	.000	2	3	3	0	2	20.25
1984—Mexico City Reds†	Mexican					(Did Not Play)						
1985—Mexico City Reds†	Mexican	28	108	6	7	.462	94	67	49	38	68	4.08
1986—Nashua	Eastern	3	7⅓	1	1	.500	7	7	4	8	10	4.91
1986—Prince William	Carolina	22	111⅔	6	11	.353	118	63	56	65	42	4.51

Signed as free agent by Mexico City Reds (Mexican League), April 6, 1983.
†Sold to Pittsburgh Pirates' organization, December 12, 1985.

LARRY LEE HERNDON

Born November 3, 1953, at Sunflower, Miss.
Height, 6.03. Weight, 200.
Throws and bats righthanded.
Attended Tennessee State University, Nashville, Tenn. and Skyline College, San Bruno, Calif.

Tied major league record for most consecutive home runs, two consecutive games (4), May 16 and 18, 1982.
Major League stolen bases: 1976 (12), 1977 (4), 1978 (13), 1979 (8), 1980 (8), 1981 (15), 1982 (12), 1983 (9), 1984 (6), 1985 (2), 1986 (2). Total—91.
Hit three home runs in a game, May 18, 1982.
Led Texas League in stolen bases with 50 and caught stealing with 16 in 1974.
Tied for Texas League lead in double plays by outfielders with 4 in 1974.
Named National League Rookie Player of the Year by THE SPORTING NEWS, 1976.

Year	Club	League	Pos.	G.	AB.	R.	H.	2B.	3B.	HR.	RBI.	B.A.	PO.	A.	E.	F.A.
1971—Sarasota Cards	Gulf C.	OF	40	138	13	33	2	0	0	8	.239	68	4	3	.960
1972—St. Petersburg	Fla. St.	OF	7	28	2	4	0	0	0	0	.143	12	1	2	.867
1972—Sarasota R. B.	Gulf C.	OF	31	113	16	29	5	3	0	9	.257	50	5	3	.948
1972—Cedar Rapids†	Midw.	OF	7	21	1	6	0	0	0	1	.286	10	0	0	1.000
1973—St. Petersburg	Fla. St.	OF	141	485	83	139	9	5	3	41	.287	233	10	8	.968
1974—Arkansas	Texas	OF	132	498	74	142	16	●10	2	41	.285	325	*24	16	.956
1974—St. Louis	Nat.	OF	12	1	3	1	0	0	0	0	1.000	1	0	0	1.000
1975—Tulsa‡	A. A.	OF	22	96	13	23	5	0	1	5	.240	35	2	3	.925
1975—Phoenix	P. C.	OF	115	427	49	115	6	4	2	44	.269	287	10	10	.967
1976—Phoenix	P. C.	OF	14	57	8	14	2	1	1	5	.246	38	3	0	1.000
1976—San Francisco	Nat.	OF	115	337	42	97	11	3	2	23	.288	226	8	8	.967
1977—San Francisco§x	Nat.	OF	49	109	13	26	4	3	1	5	.239	87	2	4	.957
1978—San Francisco	Nat.	OF	151	471	52	122	15	9	1	32	.259	369	3	10	.974
1979—San Francisco	Nat.	OF	132	354	35	91	14	5	7	36	.257	196	10	8	.963
1980—San Francisco	Nat.	OF	139	493	54	127	17	11	8	49	.258	247	8	●11	.959
1981—San Francisco y	Nat.	OF	96	364	48	105	15	8	5	41	.288	207	8	5	.977
1982—Detroit	Amer.	OF	157	614	92	179	21	13	23	88	.292	328	11	6	.983
1983—Detroit	Amer.	OF	153	603	88	182	28	9	20	92	.302	283	6	*15	.951
1984—Detroit	Amer.	OF	125	407	52	114	18	5	7	43	.280	199	7	3	.986
1985—Detroit	Amer.	OF	137	442	45	108	12	7	12	37	.244	273	7	7	.976
1986—Detroit z	Amer.	OF	106	283	33	70	13	1	8	37	.247	156	2	2	.988
National League Totals—7 Years			694	2129	247	569	76	39	24	186	.267	1333	39	46	.968
American League Totals—5 Years			678	2349	310	653	92	35	70	297	.278	1239	33	33	.975
Major League Totals—12 Years			1372	4478	557	1222	168	74	94	483	.273	2572	72	79	.971

Selected by St. Louis Cardinals' organization in 3rd round of free-agent draft, June 8, 1971.
†On disabled list, August 11, 1972 through remainder of season.
‡Traded with Pitcher Tony Gonzalez to San Francisco Giants for Pitcher Ron Bryant, May 9, 1975.
§On disabled list, June 19 to August 26, 1977.
xOn disqualified list, August 26, 1977 through remainder of season.

yTraded to Detroit Tigers for Pitchers Dan Schatzeder and Mike Chris, December 9, 1981.
zGranted free agency, November 12, 1986; re-signed by Tigers, December 8, 1986.

CHAMPIONSHIP SERIES RECORD

Year Club League	Pos.	G.	AB.	R.	H.	2B.	3B.	HR.	RBI.	B.A.	PO.	A.	E.	F.A.
1984—Detroit.............. Amer.	OF	2	5	1	1	0	0	1	1	.200	6	0	0	1.000

WORLD SERIES RECORD

Year Club League	Pos.	G.	AB.	R.	H.	2B.	3B.	HR.	RBI.	B.A.	PO.	A.	E.	F.A.
1984—Detroit.............. Amer.	OF-PH	5	15	1	5	0	0	1	3	.333	6	0	0	1.000

THOMAS MITCHELL HERR
(Tom)

Born April 4, 1956, at Lancaster, Pa.
Height, 6.00. Weight, 185.
Throws right and bats left and righthanded.
Attended University of Delaware, Newark, Del.

Tied National League record for most sacrifice flies by switch-hitter, season (13), 1985.
Major League stolen bases: 1979 (1), 1980 (9), 1981 (23), 1982 (25), 1983 (6), 1984 (13), 1985 (31), 1986 (22). Total—130.
Led National League in sacrifice flies with 13 in 1985.
Led National League second basemen in double plays with 74 in 1985, 106 in 1984 and 121 in 1986.
Led National League second basemen in total chances with 590 in 1981.
Led Florida State League in stolen bases with 50 in 1977.
Led Florida State League second basemen in double plays with 91 in 1977.
Named second baseman on THE SPORTING NEWS National League All-Star Team, 1985.

Year Club League	Pos.	G.	AB.	R.	H.	2B.	3B.	HR.	RBI.	B.A.	PO.	A.	E.	F.A.
1975—Johnson City........ Appal.	2B-SS	42	133	29	41	8	1	0	15	.308	74	125	5	.975
1976—St. Petersburg...... Fla. St.	SS-2B	82	275	47	74	6	1	0	21	.269	133	211	18	.950
1977—St. Petersburg...... Fla. St.	2B	136	*515	*80	*156	13	7	1	53	.303	*348	*430	21	*.974
1978—Arkansas.............. Texas	2B	89	335	70	98	23	4	3	45	.293	207	280	13	.974
1978—Springfield............ A. A.	2B	33	86	16	24	6	1	0	8	.279	45	63	7	.939
1979—Springfield............ A. A.	2B	109	423	74	124	20	6	6	48	.293	225	324	10	*.982
1979—St. Louis................ Nat.	2B	14	10	4	2	0	0	0	1	.200	12	11	0	1.000
1980—Springfield............ A. A.	2B-3B	37	141	29	44	6	2	1	16	.312	29	52	1	.988
1980—St. Louis................ Nat.	2B-SS	76	222	29	55	12	5	0	15	.248	124	184	7	.978
1981—St. Louis................ Nat.	2B	103	411	50	110	14	9	0	46	.268	211	*374	5	*.992
1982—St. Louis................ Nat.	2B	135	493	83	131	19	4	0	36	.266	263	427	9	.987
1983—St. Louis†.............. Nat.	2B	89	313	43	101	14	4	2	31	.323	178	245	6	.986
1983—Arkansas.............. Texas	2B	3	9	0	4	3	0	0	1	.444	4	9	0	1.000
1984—St. Louis................ Nat.	2B	145	558	67	154	23	2	4	49	.276	328	452	6	.992
1985—St. Louis................ Nat.	2B	159	596	97	180	38	3	8	110	.302	337	448	12	.985
1986—St. Louis................ Nat.	2B	152	559	48	141	30	4	2	61	.252	352	414	9	.988
Major League Totals—8 Years................		873	3162	421	874	150	31	16	349	.276	1805	2555	54	.988

Signed as free agent by St. Louis Cardinals' organization, August 22, 1974.

†On disabled list, March 25 to April 29 and August 9, 1983 through remainder of season; included rehabilitation disability assignment to Arkansas, April 18 to April 29, 1983.

CHAMPIONSHIP SERIES RECORD

Tied Championship Series record for most consecutive games, one or more runs batted in (4), 1985.
Established National League Championship Series records for most doubles (4) and most long hits (5), six-game Series, 1985.
Tied National League Championship Series record for most bases on balls, six-game Series (5), 1985.

Year Club League	Pos.	G.	AB.	R.	H.	2B.	3B.	HR.	RBI.	B.A.	PO.	A.	E.	F.A.
1982—St. Louis................ Nat.	2B	3	13	1	3	1	0	0	0	.231	6	10	0	1.000
1985—St. Louis................ Nat.	2B	6	21	2	7	4	0	1	6	.333	13	12	0	1.000
Championship Series Totals—2 Years.....		9	34	3	10	5	0	1	6	.294	19	22	0	1.000

WORLD SERIES RECORD

Established World Series record for most double plays started, second baseman, seven-game Series (5), 1985.
Established World Series record for most runs batted in on sacrifice fly (2), October 16, 1982 (second inning).

Year Club League	Pos.	G.	AB.	R.	H.	2B.	3B.	HR.	RBI.	B.A.	PO.	A.	E.	F.A.
1982—St. Louis................ Nat.	2B	7	25	2	4	2	0	0	5	.160	11	19	1	.968
1985—St. Louis................ Nat.	2B	7	26	2	4	2	0	0	0	.154	11	13	0	1.000
World Series Totals—2 Years................		14	51	4	8	4	0	0	5	.157	22	32	1	.982

ALL-STAR GAME RECORD

Year League	Pos.	AB.	R.	H.	2B.	3B.	HR.	RBI.	B.A.	PO.	A.	E.	F.A.
1985—National...	2B	3	1	1	1	0	0	0	.333	0	1	0	1.000

OREL LEONARD HERSHISER IV

Name pronounced Hersh-HYZ-ur.
Born September 16, 1958, at Buffalo, N.Y.
Height, 6.03. Weight, 190.
Throws and bats righthanded.
Attended Bowling Green State University, Bowling Green, O.

Major League saves: 1983 (1), 1984 (2). Total—3.
Tied for National League lead in shutouts with 4 in 1984.
Led Pacific Coast League in intentional bases on balls issued with 8 in 1983.

Year Club	League	G.	IP.	W.	L.	Pct.	H.	R.	ER.	SO.	BB.	ERA.
1979—Clinton	Midwest	15	43	4	0	1.000	33	15	10	33	17	2.09
1980—San Antonio	Texas	49	109	5	9	.357	120	59	43	75	59	3.55
1981—San Antonio	Texas	42	102	7	6	.538	94	54	53	95	50	4.68
1982—Albuquerque	P. Coast	47	123⅔	9	6	.600	121	73	51	93	63	3.71
1983—Albuquerque	P. Coast	49	134⅓	10	8	.556	132	73	61	95	57	4.09
1983—Los Angeles	National	8	8	0	0	.000	7	6	3	5	6	3.38
1984—Los Angeles	National	45	189⅔	11	8	.579	160	65	56	150	50	2.66
1985—Los Angeles	National	36	239⅔	19	3	★.864	179	72	54	157	68	2.03
1986—Los Angeles	National	35	231⅓	14	14	.500	213	112	99	153	86	3.85
Major League Totals—4 Years		124	668⅔	44	25	.638	559	255	212	465	210	2.85

Selected by Los Angeles Dodgers' organization in 17th round of free-agent draft, June 5, 1979.

CHAMPIONSHIP SERIES RECORD

Established National League Championship Series record for most hits allowed (17), six-game Series, 1985.

Year Club	League	G.	IP.	W.	L.	Pct.	H.	R.	ER.	SO.	BB.	ERA.
1985—Los Angeles	National	2	15⅓	1	0	1.000	17	6	6	5	6	3.52

JOSEPH THOMAS HESKETH
(Joe)

Born February 15, 1959, at Lackawanna, N.Y.
Height, 6.02. Weight, 170.
Throws and bats lefthanded.
Attended State University of New York, Buffalo, N.Y.

Major League saves: 1984 (1).
Tied for American Association lead in shutouts with 2 in 1983.
Named American Association Pitcher of the Year, 1984.

Year Club	League	G.	IP.	W.	L.	Pct.	H.	R.	ER.	SO.	BB.	ERA.
1980—West Palm Beach	Florida St.	11	75	8	2	.800	71	30	16	43	32	1.92
1980—Memphis	Southern	3	20	1	0	1.000	20	13	9	20	7	4.05
1981—Memphis†	Southern					(Did Not Play)						
1982—Memphis‡	Southern					(Did Not Play)						
1982—West Palm Beach	Florida St.	8	45⅔	3	2	.600	41	16	14	24	16	2.76
1983—Memphis	Southern	11	74	6	4	.600	82	38	25	22	25	3.04
1983—Wichita	Am. Assoc.	15	88⅓	5	5	.500	98	53	50	41	46	5.09
1984—Indianapolis	Am. Assoc.	22	147⅔	12	3	.800	120	60	50	135	54	3.05
1984—Montreal	National	11	45	2	2	.500	38	12	9	32	15	1.80
1985—Montreal§	National	25	155⅓	10	5	.667	125	52	43	113	45	2.49
1986—Montreal x	National	15	82⅔	6	5	.545	92	46	46	67	31	5.01
Major League Totals—3 Years		51	283	18	12	.600	255	110	98	212	91	3.12

Selected by Montreal Expos' organization in 2nd round of free-agent draft, June 3, 1980.
†On disabled list, April 9, 1981, through remainder of season.
‡On disabled list, April 8 to July 8, 1982.
§On disabled list, August 24, 1985 through remainder of season.
xOn disabled list, July 4, 1986 through remainder of season.

TEODORO HIGUERA (VALENZUELA)
Name pronounced Tea-O-door-RO Hugh-gare-a Val-en-ZWAY-luh.
(Ted)

Born November 9, 1958, at Las Mochis, Mexico.
Height, 5.10. Weight, 180.
Throws left and bats left and righthanded.

Tied for Mexican League lead in games started by pitchers with 27 and complete games with 18 in 1983.
Named lefthanded pitcher on THE SPORTING NEWS American League All-Star Team, 1986.
Named American League Rookie Pitcher of the Year by THE SPORTING NEWS, 1985.

Year Club	League	G.	IP.	W.	L.	Pct.	H.	R.	ER.	SO.	BB.	ERA.
1979—Ciudad Juarez	Mexican	2	1	0	1	.000	4	5	5	1	4	45.00
1980—Ciudad Juarez†	Mexican	19	117	8	3	.727	111	30	24	76	59	1.85
1980—Ciudad Juarez‡	Mexican	8	49	2	5	.286	44	22	20	29	17	3.67
1981—Ciudad Juarez	Mexican	28	203	16	9	.640	207	81	70	157	69	3.10
1982—Ciudad Juarez	Mexican	24	142⅓	9	12	.429	163	77	64	74	53	4.05
1983—Ciudad Juarez§	Mexican	27	★222	●17	8	.680	177	61	50	★165	68	2.03
1984—El Paso	Texas	19	121	8	7	.533	116	57	35	99	43	★2.60
1984—Vancouver	P. Coast	8	40	1	4	.200	49	26	21	29	14	4.73
1985—Milwaukee	American	32	212⅓	15	8	.652	186	105	92	127	63	3.90
1986—Milwaukee	American	34	248⅓	20	11	.645	226	84	77	207	74	2.79
Major League Totals—2 Years		66	460⅔	35	19	.648	412	189	169	334	137	3.30

†20-team season.
‡6-team season.
§Sold to Vancouver (Milwaukee Brewers' organization), September 13, 1983.

Year League	IP.	W.	L.	Pct.	H.	R.	ER.	SO.	BB.	ERA.
1986—American	3	0	0	.000	1	0	0	2	1	0.00

DONALD EARL HILL
(Donnie)

Born November 20, 1960, at Pomona, Calif.
Height, 5.10. Weight, 160.
Throws right and bats left and righthanded.
Attended Orange Coast College, Costa Mesa, Calif.; and Arizona State University, Tempe, Ariz.
Major League stolen bases: 1983 (1), 1984 (1), 1985 (9), 1986 (5). Total—16.
Tied for Eastern League lead in sacrifice flies with 8 in 1982.

Year Club	League	Pos.	G.	AB.	R.	H.	2B.	3B.	HR.	RBI.	B.A.	PO.	A.	E.	F.A.
1981—Modesto	Calif.	SS-2B	46	149	21	29	3	0	6	22	.195	44	84	22	.853
1982—West Haven†	East.	SS-3B	132	405	66	103	21	3	10	59	.254	141	301	29	.938
1983—Tacoma‡	P. C.	SS	93	322	45	101	19	2	14	63	.314	148	256	18	.957
1983—Oakland	Amer.	SS	53	158	20	42	7	0	2	15	.266	87	136	9	.961
1984—Oakland§	Amer.	SS-2B-3B	73	174	21	40	6	0	2	16	.230	102	128	12	.950
1984—Tacoma	P. C.	SS-2B	42	141	28	46	12	3	2	24	.326	71	92	4	.976
1985—Oakland	Amer.	2B	123	393	45	112	13	2	3	48	.285	228	320	15	.973
1986—Oakland x	Amer.	2B-3B-SS	108	339	37	96	16	2	4	29	.283	104	213	9	.972
Major League Totals—4 Years			357	1064	123	290	42	4	11	108	.273	521	797	45	.967

Selected by Houston Astros' organization in 5th round of free-agent draft, January 8, 1980.
Selected by San Francisco Giants' organization in secondary phase of free-agent draft, June 3, 1980.
Selected by Oakland A's organization in secondary phase of free-agent draft, June 8, 1981.
†On temporary inactive list, April 13 to April 23, 1982.
‡On disabled list, April 30 to May 10, 1983.
§On disabled list, May 3 to May 18, 1984.
xTraded to Chicago White Sox for Pitcher Gene Nelson and a player to be named later, December 11, 1986; Oakland A's acquired Pitcher Bruce Tanner to complete deal, December 18, 1986.

GLENALLEN HILL
(Glen)

Born March 22, 1965, at Santa Cruz, Calif.
Height, 6.02. Weight, 190.
Throws and bats righthanded.
Led Southern League in total bases with 287, strikeouts with 153 and tied for lead in sacrifice flies with 13 in 1986.
Led Carolina League batters in strikeouts with 211 in 1985.
Led South Atlantic League batters in strikeouts with 150 in 1984.

Year Club	League	Pos.	G.	AB.	R.	H.	2B.	3B.	HR.	RBI.	B.A.	PO.	A.	E.	F.A.
1983—Medicine Hat	Pion.	OF	46	133	34	63	3	4	6	27	.256	63	3	6	.917
1984—Florence	S. Atl.	OF	129	440	75	105	19	5	16	64	.239	281	9	16	.948
1985—Kinston	Carol.	OF	131	466	57	98	13	0	20	56	.210	234	12	13	.950
1986—Knoxville	South.	OF	141	★570	87	159	23	6	★31	96	.279	230	9	★21	.919

Selected by Toronto Blue Jays' organization in 9th round of free-agent draft, June 6, 1983.

MARC KEVIN HILL

Born February 18, 1952, at Louisiana, Mo.
Height, 6.03. Weight, 240.
Throws and bats righthanded.
Major League stolen bases: 1978 (1).
Led American Association catchers in double plays with 18 in 1974.
Led Florida State League catchers in total chances with 983 and double plays with 14 in 1972.
Led Gulf Coast League catchers in double plays with 5 in 1970.

Year Club	League	Pos.	G.	AB.	R.	H.	2B.	3B.	HR.	RBI.	B.A.	PO.	A.	E.	F.A.
1970—Sarasota Cards	Gulf C.	C	28	78	6	15	3	0	0	6	.192	176	24	2	.990
1971—Cedar Rapids	Midw.	C	87	272	21	63	9	1	1	27	.232	572	57	8	.987
1972—St. Petersburg	Fla. St.	C	124	421	34	104	12	1	8	65	.247	★876	★92	15	.985
1972—Modesto	Calif.	C-1B	7	24	2	8	2	0	0	4	.333	39	3	0	1.000
1973—Arkansas	Texas	C	122	403	41	97	19	2	9	49	.241	★670	64	8	.989
1973—Tulsa	A. A.	C	9	29	4	12	1	0	3	8	.414	61	5	0	1.000
1973—St. Louis	Nat.	C	1	3	0	0	0	0	0	0	.000	5	0	0	1.000
1974—Tulsa	A. A.	C-1B	96	327	46	91	16	1	14	58	.278	553	61	9	.986
1974—St. Louis†	Nat.	C	10	21	2	5	1	0	0	2	.238	41	5	0	1.000
1975—San Francisco	Nat.	C-3B	72	182	14	39	4	0	5	23	.214	282	27	2	.994
1976—San Francisco‡	Nat.	C-1B	54	131	11	24	5	0	3	15	.183	186	24	1	.995
1977—San Francisco	Nat.	C	108	320	28	80	10	0	9	50	.250	505	57	6	.989
1978—San Francisco	Nat.	C-1B	117	358	20	87	15	1	3	36	.243	592	56	9	.986
1979—San Francisco§	Nat.	C-1B	63	169	20	35	3	0	3	15	.207	285	31	3	.991
1980—San Francisco x	Nat.	C	17	41	1	7	2	0	0	0	.171	61	8	2	.972
1980—Seattle y	Amer.	C	29	70	8	16	2	1	2	9	.229	101	10	1	.991
1981—Chicago	Amer.	C-1B-3B	16	6	0	0	0	0	0	0	.000	11	1	0	1.000
1981—Glens Falls	East.	C	2	7	1	3	0	0	0	3	.429	6	1	0	1.000
1982—Chicago	Amer.	C-1B-3B	53	88	9	23	2	0	3	13	.261	136	16	1	.993
1983—Chicago	Amer.	C-1B	58	133	11	30	6	0	1	11	.226	215	12	2	.991
1984—Chicago	Amer.	C-1B	77	193	15	45	10	1	5	20	.233	315	17	3	.991

Year Club	League	Pos.	G.	AB.	R.	H.	2B.	3B.	HR.	RBI.	B.A.	PO.	A.	E.	F.A.
1985—Chicago	Amer.	C-3B	40	75	5	10	2	0	0	4	.133	185	13	3	.985
1986—Chicago za	Amer.	C	22	19	2	3	0	0	0	0	.158	59	7	0	1.000
National League Totals—8 Years			442	1225	96	277	40	1	23	141	.226	1957	208	23	.989
American League Totals—7 Years			295	584	50	127	22	2	11	57	.217	1022	76	10	.991
Major League Totals—14 Years			737	1809	146	404	62	3	34	198	.223	2979	284	33	.990

Selected by St. Louis Cardinals' organization in 10th round of free-agent draft, June 4, 1970.
†Traded to San Francisco Giants for Pitcher Elias Sosa and Catcher Ken Rudolph, October 14, 1974.
‡On disabled list, August 4, 1976 through remainder of season.
§On disabled list, July 25, 1979 through remainder of season.
xSold on waivers to Seattle Mariners, June 20, 1980.
yGranted free agency, October 28, 1980; signed by Chicago White Sox, February 12, 1981.
zReleased, May 27, 1986; re-signed by White Sox, October 2, 1986.
aReleased, October 8, 1986.

SHAWN PATRICK HILLEGAS

Born August 21, 1964, at Dos Palos, Calif.
Height, 6.03. Weight, 190.
Throws and bats righthanded.

Year Club	League	G.	IP.	W.	L.	Pct.	H.	R.	ER.	SO.	BB.	ERA.
1984—Vero Beach	Florida St.	13	93⅓	5	3	.625	71	25	19	64	33	1.83
1985—San Antonio	Texas	23	139⅓	4	10	.286	134	72	49	56	67	3.17
1986—San Antonio	Texas	17	132⅓	9	5	.643	107	60	45	97	58	3.06
1986—Albuquerque	P. Coast	9	46⅔	1	5	.167	48	35	32	43	31	6.17

Selected by California Angels' organization in 26th round of free-agent draft, June 6, 1983.
Selected by Los Angeles Dodgers' organization in secondary phase of free-agent draft, January 17, 1984.

GLENN EDWARD HOFFMAN

Born July 7, 1958, at Orange, Calif.
Height, 6.02. Weight, 190.
Throws and bats righthanded.

Major League stolen bases: 1980 (2), 1983 (1), 1985 (2). Total—5.
Led International League shortstops in double plays with 87 in 1978.
Tied for Florida State League lead in putouts by shortstops with 220 in 1977.

Year Club	League	Pos.	G.	AB.	R.	H.	2B.	3B.	HR.	RBI.	B.A.	PO.	A.	E.	F.A.
1976—Elmira	NYP	SS	60	191	29	52	7	2	3	34	.272	★83	139	17	.925
1977—Winter Haven	Fla. St.	SS-3B-1B	126	425	51	123	17	2	3	61	.289	225	377	36	.944
1977—Pawtucket	Int.	SS	4	9	2	4	1	0	0	2	.444	4	10	1	.933
1978—Pawtucket	Int.	★SS-P	131	411	27	116	17	1	2	48	.282	★211	★391	45	.930
1979—Pawtucket	Int.	3B-SS-P	139	520	70	148	13	3	11	54	.285	172	286	19	.960
1980—Boston	Amer.	3B-SS-2B	114	312	37	89	15	4	4	42	.285	78	202	17	.943
1981—Boston	Amer.	SS-3B	78	242	28	56	10	0	1	20	.231	132	234	15	.961
1982—Boston	Amer.	SS	150	469	53	98	23	2	7	49	.209	246	439	20	.972
1983—Boston	Amer.	SS	143	473	56	123	24	1	4	41	.260	240	417	26	.962
1984—Boston	Amer.	SS-3B-2B	64	74	8	14	4	0	0	4	.189	43	74	5	.959
1985—Boston†	Amer.	SS-3B-2B	96	279	40	77	17	2	6	34	.276	157	232	11	.973
1986—Boston‡§	Amer.	SS-3B	12	23	1	5	2	0	0	1	.217	15	11	2	.929
Major League Totals—7 Years			657	1872	223	462	95	9	22	191	.247	911	1609	96	.963

Selected by Boston Red Sox' organization in 2nd round of free-agent draft, June 8, 1976.
†On disabled list, July 25 to August 21, 1985.
‡On disabled list, May 17 to September 5, 1986; included rehabilitation disability assignment to New Britain, July 13 to August 1, 1986.
§Granted free agency, November 12, 1986.

PITCHING RECORD

Year Club	League	G.	IP.	W.	L.	Pct.	H.	R.	ER.	SO.	BB.	ERA.
1978—Pawtucket	Int'national	1	⅓	0	0	.000	0	0	0	0	0	0.00
1979—Pawtucket	Int'national	1	1	0	0	.000	1	1	1	0	1	9.00

GUY ALAN HOFFMAN

Born July 9, 1956, at Ottawa, Ill.
Height, 5.09. Weight, 175.
Throws and bats lefthanded.
Attended Bradley University, Peoria, Ill.

Major League saves: 1979 (2), 1980 (1). Total—3.

Year Club	League	G.	IP.	W.	L.	Pct.	H.	R.	ER.	SO.	BB.	ERA.
1978—Appleton	Midwest	7	34	2	0	1.000	22	10	9	31	15	2.38
1979—Appleton	Midwest	2	5	0	0	.000	2	0	0	4	1	0.00
1979—Iowa	Am. Assoc.	13	70	6	0	1.000	62	30	26	34	40	3.34
1979—Chicago	American	24	30	0	5	.000	30	18	18	18	23	5.40
1980—Iowa	Am. Assoc.	15	75	6	3	.667	59	31	30	56	34	3.60
1980—Chicago	American	23	38	1	0	1.000	38	12	11	24	17	2.61
1981—Edmonton	P. Coast	20	111	4	6	.400	117	70	53	71	60	4.30
1982—Edmonton	P. Coast	28	138⅓	8	●14	.364	186	129	106	72	67	6.90
1983—Denver	Am. Assoc.	32	52⅔	5	3	.625	49	23	22	50	23	3.76
1983—Chicago	American	11	6	1	0	1.000	14	5	5	2	2	7.50

Year Club	League	G.	IP.	W.	L.	Pct.	H.	R.	ER.	SO.	BB.	ERA.
1984—Denver†	Am. Assoc.	35	112	4	8	.333	124	71	59	76	40	4.74
1985—Iowa‡	Am. Assoc.	9	36	4	0	1.000	23	9	6	37	17	1.50
1986—Iowa‡	Am. Assoc.	9	59⅓	4	0	1.000	50	14	14	48	20	2.12
1986—Chicago	National	32	84	6	2	.750	92	37	36	47	29	3.86
American League Totals—3 Years		58	74	2	5	.286	82	35	34	44	42	4.14
National League Totals—1 Year		32	84	6	2	.750	92	37	36	47	29	3.86
Major League Totals—4 Years		90	158	8	7	.533	174	72	70	91	71	3.99

Signed as free agent by Chicago White Sox' organization, July 17, 1978.
†Released, October 19, 1984; signed by Chicago Cubs' organization, January 3, 1985.
‡On disabled list, April 12 to May 31 and June 1 to July 12, 1985.

ALFRED WILLIS HOLLAND
(Al)

Born August 16, 1952, at Roanoke, Va.
Height, 5.11. Weight, 210.
Throws left and bats righthanded.
Received bachelor of science degree in recreation from
North Carolina A&T University, Greensboro, N. C. in 1975.

Major League saves: 1980 (7), 1981 (7), 1982 (5), 1983 (25), 1984 (29), 1985 (5). Total—78.
Led New York-Pennsylvania League in balks with 5 and tied for lead in shutouts with 2 in 1975.
Named National League co-Fireman of the Year by THE SPORTING NEWS, 1983.

Year Club	League	G.	IP.	W.	L.	Pct.	H.	R.	ER.	SO.	BB.	ERA.
1975—Bradenton Pirates	Gulf Coast	5	40	2	2	.500	24	6	5	39	20	1.13
1975—Niagara Falls	NYP	6	49	4	2	.667	44	20	14	50	14	2.57
1976—Salem	Carolina	39	76	4	2	.667	59	32	25	72	45	2.96
1977—Shreveport	Texas	21	36	4	1	.800	23	7	5	25	17	1.25
1977—Columbus	Int'national	27	86	6	4	.600	83	44	34	73	36	3.56
1977—Pittsburgh	National	2	2	0	0	.000	4	2	2	1	0	9.00
1978—Columbus†	Int'national	20	91	8	5	.615	102	59	54	65	34	5.34
1979—Portland‡-Phoenix	P. Coast	29	174	10	10	.500	173	99	87	140	87	4.50
1979—San Francisco	National	3	7	0	0	.000	3	0	0	7	5	0.00
1980—San Francisco	National	54	82	5	3	.625	71	21	16	65	34	1.76
1981—San Francisco	National	47	101	7	5	.583	87	31	27	78	44	2.41
1982—San Francisco§x	National	58	129⅔	7	3	.700	115	56	48	97	40	3.33
1983—Philadelphia y	National	68	91⅔	4	4	.667	63	26	23	100	30	2.26
1984—Philadelphia	National	68	98⅓	5	10	.333	82	38	37	61	30	3.39
1985—Philadelphia z-Pittsburgh a	National	41	62⅔	1	4	.200	53	24	24	48	21	3.45
1985—California bc	American	15	24⅓	0	1	.000	17	4	4	14	10	1.48
1986—Columbus	Int'national	11	18⅔	1	1	.500	15	5	3	13	7	1.45
1986—New York de	American	25	40⅔	1	0	1.000	44	29	23	37	9	5.09
National League Totals—8 Years		341	574⅓	33	29	.532	478	198	177	457	204	2.77
American League Totals—2 Years		40	65	1	1	.500	61	33	27	51	19	3.74
Major League Totals—9 Years		381	639⅓	34	30	.531	539	231	204	508	223	2.87

Selected by Texas Rangers' organization in 30th round of free-agent draft, June 5, 1974.
Selected by San Diego Padres' organization in secondary phase of free-agent draft, January 9, 1975.
Signed as free agent by Pittsburgh Pirates' organization, June 28, 1975.
†On disabled list, April 14 to May 28 and July 20 to July 31, 1978.
‡Traded with Pitchers Ed Whitson and Fred Breining to San Francisco Giants for Third Basemen Bill Madlock and Lenny Randle and Pitcher Dave Roberts, June 28, 1979.
§On disabled list, May 11 to June 4, 1982.
xTraded with Second Baseman Joe Morgan to Philadelphia Phillies for Pitchers Mike Krukow and Mark Davis and Outfielder Charles Penigar, December 14, 1982.
yOn disabled list, March 31 to April 29, 1983.
zTraded with Pitcher Frankie Griffin to Pittsburgh Pirates for Pitcher Kent Tekulve, April 20, 1985.
aTraded with Pitcher John Candelaria and Outfielder George Hendrick to California Angels for Pitcher Pat Clements, Outfielder Mike Brown and a player to be named later, August 2, 1985; Pittsburgh Pirates' organization acquired Pitcher Bob Kipper to complete deal, August 16, 1985.
bGranted free agency, November 12, 1985; signed by New York Yankees' organization February 6, 1986.
cReleased, April 4, 1986; re-signed by Yankees' organization, April 10, 1986.
dOn disabled list, June 9 to June 24, 1986.
eReleased, August 8, 1986.

CHAMPIONSHIP SERIES RECORD

Year Club	League	G.	IP.	W.	L.	Pct.	H.	R.	ER.	SO.	BB.	ERA.
1983—Philadelphia	National	2	3	0	0	.000	1	0	0	3	0	0.00

WORLD SERIES RECORD

Year Club	League	G.	IP.	W.	L.	Pct.	H.	R.	ER.	SO.	BB.	ERA.
1983—Philadelphia	National	2	3⅔	0	0	.000	1	0	0	5	0	0.00

ALL-STAR GAME RECORD

Member of National League All-Star Team in 1984; did not play.

BRIAN SCOTT HOLMAN

Born January 25, 1965, at Denver, Colo.
Height, 6.04. Weight, 185.
Throws and bats righthanded.

Year	Club	League	G.	IP.	W.	L.	Pct.	H.	R.	ER.	SO.	BB.	ERA.
1983—Jamestown†	NYP	2	5⅓	0	0	.000	7	7	7	5	4	11.81
1984—West Palm Beach	Florida St.	4	8	0	3	.000	14	19	16	14	21	18.00
1984—Gastonia	S. Atlantic	20	90⅔	5	8	.385	76	58	48	94	98	4.76
1985—West Palm Beach	Florida St.	25	143⅓	9	9	.500	124	79	63	103	90	3.96
1986—Jacksonville	Southern	27	157⅔	11	9	.550	146	111	90	118	★122	5.14

Selected by Montreal Expos' organization in 1st round (16th player selected) of free-agent draft, June 6, 1983.

†On disabled list, August 3, 1983 through remainder of season.

BRIAN JOHN HOLTON

Born November 29, 1959, at McKeesport, Pa.
Height, 6.02. Weight, 190.
Throws and bats righthanded.
Attended Louisburg College, Louisburg, N.C.

Tied for Pacific Coast League lead in games started by pitchers with 27 in 1986.
Tied for Texas League lead in complete games with 16 in 1980.
Tied for California League lead in shutouts with 3 in 1979.

Year	Club	League	G.	IP.	W.	L.	Pct.	H.	R.	ER.	SO.	BB.	ERA.
1978—Clinton†	Midwest	14	79	6	4	.600	94	51	38	54	23	4.33
1979—Lodi	California	10	72	7	0	1.000	47	26	21	72	32	2.63
1979—San Antonio	Texas	13	51	3	5	.375	50	24	21	40	25	3.71
1980—San Antonio	Texas	27	207	●15	10	.600	204	93	79	139	65	3.43
1981—Albuquerque	P. Coast	26	191	16	6	.727	215	94	73	73	51	3.44
1982—Albuquerque	P. Coast	32	161⅓	12	8	.600	191	102	92	76	60	5.13
1983—Albuquerque‡	P. Coast	20	97⅔	7	5	.583	113	76	69	70	50	6.36
1984—Albuquerque §x	P. Coast	12	32	0	0	.000	39	23	20	15	9	5.63
1985—Albuquerque	P. Coast	27	179⅔	9	10	.474	183	83	72	86	40	3.61
1985—Los Angeles	National	3	4	1	1	.500	9	7	4	1	1	9.00
1986—Albuquerque	P. Coast	27	★182⅔	10	10	.500	200	90	74	105	20	3.78
1986—Los Angeles	National	12	24⅓	2	3	.400	28	13	12	24	6	4.44
Major League Totals—2 Years		15	28⅓	3	4	.429	37	20	16	25	7	5.08

Selected by Los Angeles Dodgers' organization in 1st round (22nd player selected) of free-agent draft, January 10, 1978.

†On temporary inactive list, June 12 to July 7, 1978.
‡On disabled list, June 28 to July 15, 1983.
§On disabled list, April 7 to July 11, 1984.
xGranted free agency, October 15, 1984; re-signed by Dodgers' organization, October 22, 1984.

FREDERICK WAYNE HONEYCUTT
(Rick)

Born June 29, 1954, at Chattanooga, Tenn.
Height, 5.11. Weight, 190.
Throws and bats lefthanded.
Received bachelor of science degree in health education from
University of Tennessee, Knoxville, Tenn.

Major League saves: 1985 (1).
Tied for New York-Pennsylvania League lead in complete games with 7 in 1976.

Year	Club	League	G.	IP.	W.	L.	Pct.	H.	R.	ER.	SO.	BB.	ERA.
1976—Niagara Falls†	NYP	13	★97	5	3	.625	91	36	28	★98	20	2.60
1977—Shreveport‡§	Texas	21	135	10	6	.625	144	53	37	82	42	★2.47
1977—Seattle	American	10	29	0	1	.000	26	16	14	17	11	4.34
1978—Seattle x	American	26	134	5	11	.313	150	81	73	50	49	4.90
1979—Seattle	American	33	194	11	12	.478	201	103	87	83	67	4.04
1980—Seattle y	American	30	203	10	17	.370	221	99	89	79	60	3.95
1981—Texas	American	20	128	11	6	.647	120	49	47	40	17	3.30
1982—Texas	American	30	164	5	17	.227	201	103	96	64	54	5.27
1983—Texas z	American	25	174⅔	14	8	.636	168	59	47	56	37	★2.42
1983—Los Angeles	National	9	39	2	3	.400	46	26	25	18	13	5.77
1984—Los Angeles	National	29	183⅔	10	9	.526	180	72	58	75	51	2.84
1985—Los Angeles	National	31	142	8	12	.400	141	71	54	67	49	3.42
1986—Los Angeles	National	32	171	11	9	.550	164	71	63	100	45	3.32
American League Totals—7 Years		174	1026⅔	56	72	.438	1087	510	453	389	295	3.97
National League Totals—4 Years		101	535⅔	31	33	.484	531	240	200	260	158	3.36
Major League Totals—10 Years		275	1562⅓	87	105	.453	1618	750	653	649	453	3.76

Selected by Baltimore Orioles' organization in 14th round of free-agent draft, June 6, 1972.
Selected by Pittsburgh Pirates' organization in 17th round of free-agent draft, June 8, 1976.
†Played two games as first baseman and one game as shortstop.
‡Traded to Seattle Mariners, August 22, 1977, completing deal in which Seattle traded Pitcher Dave Pagan to Pittsburgh Pirates for a player to be named later, July 27, 1977.
§Appeared as shortstop with no chances.
xOn disabled list, May 20 to June 26, 1978.
yTraded with Catcher Larry Cox, Outfielders Willie Horton and Leon Roberts and Shortstop Mario Mendoza to Texas Rangers for Pitchers Brian Allard, Ken Clay, Steve Finch and Jerry Don Gleaton, Shortstop Rick Auerbach and Outfielder Richie Zisk, December 12, 1980.
zTraded to Los Angeles Dodgers for Pitcher Dave Stewart and a player to be named later, August 19, 1983; Texas Rangers acquired Pitcher Ricky Wright to complete deal, September 16, 1983.

Year	Club	League	G.	IP.	W.	L.	Pct.	H.	R.	ER.	SO.	BB.	ERA.
1983—Los Angeles		National	2	1⅔	0	0	.000	4	4	4	2	0	21.60
1985—Los Angeles		National	2	1⅓	0	0	.000	4	2	2	1	2	13.50
Championship Series Totals—2 Years			4	3	0	0	.000	8	6	6	3	2	18.00

ALL-STAR GAME RECORD

Year	League		IP.	W.	L.	Pct.	H.	R.	ER.	SO.	BB.	ERA.
1983—American			2	0	0	.000	5	2	2	0	0	9.00

Member of American League All-Star Team in 1980; did not play.

DENNIS RAY HOOD

Born July 3, 1966, at Glendale, Calif.
Height, 6.02. Weight, 165.
Throws and bats righthanded.
Led South Atlantic League outfielders in total chances with 328 in 1986.

Year	Club	League	Pos.	G.	AB.	R.	H.	2B.	3B.	HR.	RBI.	B.A.	PO.	A.	E.	F.A.
1984—Bradenton Brav...		Gulf C.	OF	49	155	16	31	7	0	1	18	.200	96	3	3	.971
1985—Bradenton Brav...		Gulf C.	OF	59	204	19	49	14	0	1	17	.240	103	8	●6	.949
1986—Sumter		S. Atl.	OF	★135	★562	104	142	25	3	7	42	.253	★305	11	12	.963

Selected by Atlanta Braves' organization in 12th round of free-agent draft, June 4, 1984.

SAMUEL LEE HORN

(Sam)

Born November 2, 1963, at Fort Thomas, Ky.
Height, 6.05. Weight, 215.
Throws and bats lefthanded.
Led Carolina League in slugging percentage with .538 in 1984.

Year	Club	League	Pos.	G.	AB.	R.	H.	2B.	3B.	HR.	RBI.	B.A.	PO.	A.	E.	F.A.
1982—Elmira		NYP	1B	61	213	47	64	13	1	11	48	.300	368	29	11	.973
1983—Winston-Salem† ...		Carol.	1B	68	217	33	52	9	0	9	29	.240	363	24	10	.975
1984—Winston-Salem		Carol.	1B	127	403	67	126	22	3	21	89	.313	978	★70	★29	.973
1985—New Britain		East.	1B	134	457	64	129	★32	0	11	82	.282	751	63	★23	.973
1986—New Britain		East.	1B	100	345	41	85	13	0	8	46	.246	356	28	9	.977
1986—Pawtucket		Int.	1B	20	77	8	15	2	0	3	14	.195	61	4	0	1.000

Selected by Boston Red Sox' organization in 1st round (16th player selected) of free-agent draft, June 7, 1982.
†On disabled list, April 28 to June 23, 1983.

JAMES ROBERT HORNER

(Bob)

Born August 6, 1957, at Junction City, Kan.
Height, 6.01. Weight, 215.
Throws and bats righthanded.
Attended Arizona State University, Tempe, Ariz.
Tied major league record for most home runs, game (4), July 6, 1986.
Major League stolen bases: 1980 (3), 1981 (2), 1982 (3), 1983 (4), 1985 (1), 1986 (1). Total—14.
Hit four home runs in a game, July 6, 1986.
Led National League first basemen in double plays with 138 in 1986.
Named National League Rookie Player of the Year by THE SPORTING NEWS, 1978.
Named National League Rookie of the Year by Baseball Writers' Association of America, 1978.
Named College Player of the Year by THE SPORTING NEWS, 1978.
Received reported $175,000 bonus to sign with Atlanta Braves, 1978.
Named second baseman on THE SPORTING NEWS College Baseball All-America Team, 1977 and 1978.

Year	Club	League	Pos.	G.	AB.	R.	H.	2B.	3B.	HR.	RBI.	B.A.	PO.	A.	E.	F.A.
1978—Atlanta		Nat.	3B	89	323	50	86	17	1	23	63	.266	81	199	13	.956
1979—Atlanta†		Nat.	3B-1B	121	487	66	153	15	1	33	98	.314	470	167	22	.967
1980—Atlanta‡		Nat.	3B-1B	124	463	81	124	14	1	35	89	.268	80	253	23	.935
1981—Atlanta		Nat.	3B	79	300	42	83	10	0	15	42	.277	51	129	12	.938
1982—Atlanta		Nat.	3B	140	499	85	130	24	0	32	97	.261	102	217	10	.970
1983—Atlanta§		Nat.	3B-1B	104	386	75	117	21	1	20	68	.303	78	153	10	.959
1984—Atlanta x		Nat.	3B	32	113	15	31	8	0	3	19	.274	21	61	3	.965
1985—Atlanta		Nat.	1B-3B	130	483	61	129	25	3	27	89	.267	917	119	11	.989
1986—Atlanta y		Nat.	1B	141	517	70	141	22	0	27	87	.273	★1378	102	8	.995
Major League Totals—9 Years				960	3571	545	994	160	7	215	652	.278	3178	1400	112	.976

Selected by Oakland A's organization in 15th round of free-agent draft, June 4, 1975.
Selected by Atlanta Braves' organization in 1st round (first player selected) of free-agent draft, June 6, 1978.
†On disabled list, April 11 to April 26, 1979.
‡On disqualified list when refused option to Richmond (International), April 28, 1980; reinstated May 10, 1980.
§On disabled list, August 16, 1983 through remainder of season.
xOn disabled list, April 28 to May 17 and June 4, 1984 through remainder of season.
yGranted free agency, November 12, 1986

CHAMPIONSHIP SERIES RECORD

Year	Club	League	Pos.	G.	AB.	R.	H.	2B.	3B.	HR.	RBI.	B.A.	PO.	A.	E.	F.A.
1982—Atlanta		Nat.	3B	3	11	0	1	0	0	0	0	.091	2	5	0	1.000

Year League	Pos.	AB.	R.	H.	2B.	3B.	HR.	RBI.	B.A.	PO.	A.	E.	F.A.
1982—National	PH	1	0	0	0	0	0	0	.000	0	0	0	.000

RICKY NEAL HORTON
(Rick)

Born July 30, 1959, at Poughkeepsie, N.Y.
Height, 6.02. Weight, 197.
Throws and bats lefthanded.
Received bachelor of science degree in engineering from
University of Virginia, Charlottesville, Va. in 1982.

Major League saves: 1984 (1), 1985 (1), 1986 (3). Total—5.
Led American Association in balks with 7 in 1983.

Year Club	League	G.	IP.	W.	L.	Pct.	H.	R.	ER.	SO.	BB.	ERA.
1980—St. Petersburg	Florida St.	6	25	0	2	.000	29	18	17	13	17	6.12
1980—Gastonia	S. Atlantic	14	42	2	4	.333	30	21	17	30	25	3.64
1981—St. Petersburg	Florida St.	28	100	7	3	.700	101	52	49	66	49	4.41
1982—Arkansas	Texas	16	108⅔	9	6	.600	83	45	38	90	52	3.15
1982—Louisville	Am. Assoc.	8	36⅓	2	3	.400	47	31	27	37	11	6.69
1983—Louisville	Am. Assoc.	30	157	10	6	.625	177	99	84	92	58	4.82
1984—St. Louis	National	37	125⅔	9	4	.692	140	53	48	76	39	3.44
1985—St. Louis	National	49	89⅔	3	2	.600	84	30	29	59	34	2.91
1986—St. Louis†	National	42	100⅓	4	3	.571	77	25	25	49	26	2.24
1986—Springfield	Midwest	1	2	0	0	.000	2	0	0	2	0	0.00
Major League Totals—3 Years		128	315⅔	16	9	.640	301	108	102	184	99	2.91

Selected by San Francisco Giants' organization in 20th round of free-agent draft, June 7, 1977.
Selected by St. Louis Cardinals' organization in 4th round of free-agent draft, June 3, 1980.
†On disabled list, May 25 to June 24, 1986; included rehabilitation disability assignment to Springfield, June 20 to June 24, 1986.

CHAMPIONSHIP SERIES RECORD

Year Club	League	G.	IP.	W.	L.	Pct.	H.	R.	ER.	SO.	BB.	ERA.
1985—St. Louis	National	3	3	0	0	.000	4	4	4	1	2	12.00

WORLD SERIES RECORD

Year Club	League	G.	IP.	W.	L.	Pct.	H.	R.	ER.	SO.	BB.	ERA.
1985—St. Louis	National	3	4	0	0	.000	4	3	3	5	5	6.75

CHARLES OLIVER HOUGH

Name pronounced Huff.

(Charlie)

Born January 5, 1948, at Honolulu, Hawaii.
Height, 6.02. Weight, 190.
Throws and bats righthanded.

Major League saves: 1970 (2), 1973 (5), 1974 (1), 1975 (4), 1976 (18), 1977 (22), 1978 (7), 1980 (1), 1981 (1). Total—61.
Led American League pitchers in complete games with 17 and tied for lead in games started with 36 in 1984.
Led Pacific Coast League in intentional bases on balls issued with 13 in 1972.
Led Pacific Coast League in saves with 18 in 1970.
Led Texas League in home runs allowed with 17 in 1969.
Named Pacific Coast League Pitcher of the Year, 1972.

Year Club	League	G.	IP.	W.	L.	Pct.	H.	R.	ER.	SO.	BB.	ERA.
1966—Ogden	Pioneer	21	68	5	●7	.417	82	56	36	68	29	4.76
1967—Santa Barbara	California	20	165	14	4	★.778	129	50	41	138	43	2.24
1967—Albuquerque	Texas	7	36	2	1	.667	57	31	28	25	10	7.00
1968—Albuquerque†	Texas	27	121	6	10	.375	145	72	53	74	26	3.94
1969—Albuquerque	Texas	27	163	10	9	.526	190	87	74	113	42	4.09
1970—Spokane	P. Coast	49	134	12	8	.600	98	43	29	90	44	1.95
1970—Los Angeles	National	8	17	0	0	.000	18	11	10	8	11	5.29
1971—Spokane‡	P. Coast	47	117	10	8	.556	95	56	51	104	52	3.92
1971—Los Angeles	National	4	4	0	0	.000	3	3	2	4	3	4.50
1972—Albuquerque§	P. Coast	58	125	14	5	.737	109	47	33	95	60	2.38
1972—Los Angeles	National	2	3	0	0	.000	2	1	1	4	2	3.00
1973—Los Angeles	National	37	72	4	2	.667	52	24	22	70	45	2.75
1974—Los Angeles	National	49	96	9	4	.692	65	45	40	63	40	3.75
1975—Los Angeles	National	38	61	3	7	.300	43	25	20	34	34	2.95
1976—Los Angeles	National	77	143	12	8	.600	102	53	47	81	77	3.33
1977—Los Angeles	National	70	127	6	12	.333	98	53	47	105	70	3.33
1978—Los Angeles	National	55	93	5	5	.500	69	38	34	66	48	3.29
1979—Los Angeles	National	42	151	7	5	.583	152	88	80	76	66	4.77
1980—Los Angeles x	National	19	32	1	3	.250	37	21	20	25	21	5.63
1980—Texas	American	16	61	2	2	.500	54	30	27	47	37	3.98
1981—Texas	American	21	82	4	1	.800	61	30	27	69	31	2.96
1982—Texas	American	34	228	16	13	.552	217	111	100	128	72	3.95
1983—Texas	American	34	252	15	13	.536	219	96	89	152	95	3.18
1984—Texas	American	36	266	16	14	.533	★260	127	111	164	94	3.76
1985—Texas	American	34	250⅓	14	16	.467	198	102	92	141	83	3.31

Year Club	League	G.	IP.	W.	L.	Pct.	H.	R.	ER.	SO.	BB.	ERA.
1986—Oklahoma City y	Am. Assoc.	1	5	0	1	.000	7	5	5	3	1	9.00
1986—Texas	American	33	230⅓	17	10	.630	188	115	97	146	89	3.79
National League Totals—11 Years		401	799	47	46	.505	641	352	311	536	417	3.50
American League Totals—7 Years		208	1369⅔	84	69	.549	1197	611	543	847	501	3.57
Major League Totals—17 Years		609	2168⅔	131	115	.533	1838	963	854	1383	918	3.54

Selected by Los Angeles Dodgers' organization in 8th round of free-agent draft, June 9, 1966.
†On temporary inactive list, June 19 to July 1, 1968.
‡On temporary inactive list, July 10 to July 24, 1971.
§On temporary inactive list June 12 to June 15, July 22 to July 24 and August 7 to August 12, 1972.
xSold to Texas Rangers, July 11, 1980.
yOn Texas disabled list, March 25 to May 6, 1986; included rehabilitation disability assignment to Oklahoma City, May 2 to May 6, 1986.

CHAMPIONSHIP SERIES RECORD

Year Club	League	G.	IP.	W.	L.	Pct.	H.	R.	ER.	SO.	BB.	ERA.
1974—Los Angeles	National	1	2⅓	0	0	.000	4	2	2	2	0	7.71
1977—Los Angeles	National	1	2	0	0	.000	2	1	1	3	0	4.50
1978—Los Angeles	National	1	2	0	0	.000	1	1	1	1	0	4.50
Championship Series Totals—3 Years		3	6⅓	0	0	.000	7	4	4	6	0	5.68

WORLD SERIES RECORD

Tied World Series record for most wild pitches, inning and game (2), October 15, 1978 (seventh inning).

Year Club	League	G.	IP.	W.	L.	Pct.	H.	R.	ER.	SO.	BB.	ERA.
1974—Los Angeles	National	1	2	0	0	.000	0	0	0	4	1	0.00
1977—Los Angeles	National	2	5	0	0	.000	3	1	1	5	0	1.80
1978—Los Angeles	National	2	5⅓	0	0	.000	10	5	5	5	2	8.44
World Series Totals—3 Years		5	12⅓	0	0	.000	13	6	6	14	3	4.38

ALL-STAR GAME RECORD

Year League	IP.	W.	L.	Pct.	H.	R.	ER.	SO.	BB.	ERA.
1986—American	1⅔	0	0	.000	2	2	1	3	1	5.40

BATTING RECORD

Year Club	League	Pos.	G.	AB.	R.	H.	2B.	3B.	HR.	RBI.	B.A.	PO.	A.	E.	F.A.
1967—Santa Barbara	Calif.	P-1B	28	72	8	14	2	0	0	4	.194	15	25	2	.953
1968—Albuquerque	Texas	P-1B-3B	56	83	10	21	4	0	0	6	.253	43	25	4	.944
1969—Albuquerque	Texas	P-3B	31	57	10	12	0	0	1	9	.211	10	19	2	.935
1970—Spokane	P. C.	P-OF-1B	49	33	1	6	0	0	1	3	.182	7	28	3	.921
1971—Spokane	P. C.	P-OF	48	36	2	10	0	0	0	3	.278	6	20	1	.963
1972—Albuquerque	P. C.	P-OF	58	34	4	9	1	0	0	3	.265	3	27	0	1.000

PAUL WESLEY HOUSEHOLDER

Born September 4, 1958, at Columbus, O.
Height, 6.00. Weight, 185.
Throws right and bats right and lefthanded.

Major League stolen bases: 1980 (1), 1981 (3), 1982 (17), 1983 (12), 1984 (1), 1985 (1), 1986 (1). Total—36.
Led Western Carolinas League batters in strikeouts with 130 in 1977.
Led American Association outfielders in total chances with 332 in 1981.
Led Southern League outfielders in fielding percentage with .989 and double plays with 5 in 1979.
Tied for American Association lead in game-winning RBIs with 11 in 1981.

Year Club	League	Pos.	G.	AB.	R.	H.	2B.	3B.	HR.	RBI.	B.A.	PO.	A.	E.	F.A.
1976—Billings	Pion.	OF-3B	50	149	23	38	3	2	2	19	.255	74	8	6	.932
1977—Shelby	W. Car.	OF	137	500	72	116	15	●9	10	63	.232	278	10	8	.973
1978—Tampa	Fla. St.	OF	123	415	59	103	8	10	10	42	.248	213	8	11	.953
1979—Nashville	South.	OF-3B	142	488	93	138	24	7	20	95	.283	247	18	4	.985
1980—Indianapolis	A. A.	OF-3B	125	464	74	137	26	5	9	50	.295	249	10	8	.970
1980—Cincinnati	Nat.	OF	20	45	3	11	1	0	1	7	.244	16	2	0	1.000
1981—Indianapolis	A. A.	OF	124	453	72	136	19	6	19	77	.300	315	10	7	.979
1981—Cincinnati	Nat.	OF	23	69	12	19	4	0	2	9	.275	32	1	0	1.000
1982—Cincinnati	Nat.	OF	138	417	40	88	11	5	9	34	.211	220	14	2	.992
1983—Cincinnati†	Nat.	OF	123	380	40	97	24	4	6	43	.255	221	5	2	★.991
1984—Cinc.‡-St.L.	Nat.	OF	27	26	4	3	1	0	0	0	.115	9	1	0	1.000
1984—Wichita§	A. A.	OF	118	408	64	101	14	7	18	64	.248	209	9	4	.982
1985—Milwaukee	Amer.	OF	95	299	41	77	15	0	11	34	.258	202	5	3	.986
1986—Milwaukee	Amer.	OF	26	78	4	17	3	1	1	16	.218	35	1	0	1.000
1986—Vancouver x	P. C.	OF	60	212	25	44	7	0	4	31	.208	96	4	4	.962
National League Totals—5 Years			331	937	99	218	41	10	17	93	.233	498	23	4	.992
American League Totals—2 Years			121	377	45	94	18	1	12	50	.249	237	6	3	.988
Major League Totals—7 Years			452	1314	144	312	59	11	29	143	.237	735	29	7	.991

Selected by Cincinnati Reds' organization in 2nd round of free-agent draft, June 8, 1976.
†On disabled list, March 23 to April 26, 1983.
‡Traded to St. Louis Cardinals for a player to be named later, September 9, 1984; Cincinnati Reds acquired Pitcher John Stuper to complete deal, September 10, 1984.
§Traded with Outfielder Jim Adduci to Milwaukee Brewers for Pitchers Rich Buonantony and Jim Koontz and Infielder Ron Koenigsfeld, October 3, 1984.
xGranted free agency, October 15, 1986.

JACK ROBERT HOWELL

Born August 18, 1961, at Tucson, Ariz.
Height, 6.00. Weight, 185.
Throws right and bats lefthanded.

Major League stolen bases: 1985 (1), 1986 (2). Total—3.
Led California League third basemen in fielding percentage with .943, assists with 259, double plays with 23 and total chances with 368 in 1984.

Year Club	League	Pos.	G.	AB.	R.	H.	2B.	3B.	HR.	RBI.	B.A.	PO.	A.	E.	F.A.
1983—Salem	N'west	3B-2B	21	76	23	30	2	5	3	12	.395	19	32	11	.823
1984—Redwood	Calif.	3B-1B	135	451	62	111	21	5	5	64	.246	96	260	21	.944
1985—Edmonton†	P. C.	3B-SS	79	284	55	106	22	3	13	48	.373	67	130	12	.943
1985—California	Amer.	3B	43	137	19	27	4	0	5	18	.197	33	75	8	.931
1986—Edmonton	P. C.	3B	44	156	39	56	17	3	3	28	.359	28	84	8	.933
1986—California	Amer.	3B-OF	63	151	26	41	14	2	4	21	.272	38	57	2	.979
Major League Totals—2 Years			106	288	45	68	18	2	9	39	.236	71	132	10	.953

Signed as free agent by California Angels' organization, August 6, 1983.
†On disabled list, June 21 to July 7, 1985.

CHAMPIONSHIP SERIES RECORD

Year Club	League	Pos.	G.	AB.	R.	H.	2B.	3B.	HR.	RBI.	B.A.	PO.	A.	E.	F.A.
1986—California	Amer.	PH	2	1	0	0	0	0	0	0	.000	0	0	0	.000

JAY CANFIELD HOWELL

Born November 26, 1955, at Miami, Fla.
Height, 6.03. Weight, 205.
Throws and bats righthanded.
Attended University of Colorado, Boulder, Colo.

Major League saves: 1984 (7), 1985 (29), 1986 (16). Total—52.
Tied for American Association lead in shutouts with 2 in 1982.
Tied for American Association lead in balks with 6 in 1981.
Named American Association Pitcher of the Year, 1982.

Year Club	League	G.	IP.	W.	L.	Pct.	H.	R.	ER.	SO.	BB.	ERA.
1976—Eugene	Northwest	13	73	5	4	.556	65	30	24	79	34	2.96
1977—Tampa	Florida St.	23	158	7	13	.350	141	60	52	99	52	2.96
1978—Nashville	Southern	28	166	9	14	.391	134	70	57	*173	55	3.09
1979—Indianapolis	Am. Assoc.	24	128	10	10	.500	121	82	73	79	84	5.13
1980—Indianapolis	Am. Assoc.	25	98	5	11	.313	95	70	55	73	73	5.05
1980—Cincinnati†	National	5	3	0	0	.000	8	5	5	1	0	15.00
1981—Iowa	Am. Assoc.	23	144	5	10	.333	141	74	60	90	62	3.75
1981—Chicago	National	10	22	2	0	1.000	23	13	12	10	10	4.91
1982—Iowa‡	Am. Assoc.	20	141⅓	13	4	*.765	102	45	37	139	48	*2.36
1982—Columbus	Int'national	5	37⅓	2	1	.667	18	13	10	33	19	2.41
1982—New York	American	6	28	2	3	.400	42	25	24	21	13	7.71
1983—New York§	American	19	82	1	5	.167	89	53	49	61	35	5.38
1984—New York x	American	61	103⅔	9	4	.692	86	33	31	109	34	2.69
1985—Oakland	American	63	98	9	8	.529	98	32	31	68	31	2.85
1986—Oakland y	American	38	53⅓	3	6	.333	53	23	20	42	23	3.38
1986—Modesto	California	2	2	0	0	.000	5	3	3	1	1	13.50
National League Totals—2 Years		15	25	2	0	1.000	31	18	17	11	10	6.12
American League Totals—5 Years		187	365	24	26	.480	368	166	155	301	136	3.82
Major League Totals—7 Years		202	390	26	26	.500	399	184	172	312	146	3.97

Selected by Cincinnati Reds' organization in 12th round of free-agent draft, June 5, 1973.
Selected by Cincinnati Reds' organization in 31st round of free-agent draft, June 8, 1976.
†Traded to Chicago Cubs for Catcher Mike O'Berry, October 17, 1980.
‡Traded to New York Yankees' organization, August 2, 1982, completing deal in which Chicago Cubs acquired Second Baseman Pat Tabler from New York on waivers for two players to be named later, August 19, 1981; New York acquired Pitcher Bill Caudill as partial completion of deal, April 1, 1982.
§On disabled list, August 3, 1983 through remainder of season.
xTraded with Outfielder Stan Javier and Pitchers Jose Rijo, Eric Plunk and Tim Birtsas to Oakland A's for Outfielder Rickey Henderson, Pitcher Bert Bradley and cash, December 5, 1984.
yOn disabled list, April 30 to May 18 and May 27 to July 20, 1986; included rehabilitation disability assignment to Modesto, July 11 to July 16, 1986.

ALL-STAR GAME RECORD

Member of American League All-Star Team in 1985; did not play.

KENNETH HOWELL JR.
(Ken)

Born November 28, 1960, at Detroit, Mich.
Height, 6.03. Weight, 200.
Throws and bats righthanded.
Attended Tuskegee Institute, Tuskegee Institute, Ala.

Major League saves: 1984 (6), 1985 (12), 1986 (12). Total—30.
Tied for Texas League lead in games started by pitchers with 27 in 1983.

Year Club	League	G.	IP.	W.	L.	Pct.	H.	R.	ER.	SO.	BB.	ERA.
1982—Vero Beach	Florida St.	11	59⅔	5	4	.556	58	40	28	37	36	4.22

Year Club	League	G.	IP.	W.	L.	Pct.	H.	R.	ER.	SO.	BB.	ERA.
1983—San Antonio	Texas	27	169⅓	8	11	.421	171	98	83	116	101	4.41
1983—Albuquerque	P. Coast	1	3	0	0	.000	4	3	3	1	1	9.00
1984—Albuquerque†	P. Coast	18	72⅓	8	2	.800	79	48	37	58	37	4.60
1984—Los Angeles	National	32	51⅓	5	5	.500	51	21	19	54	9	3.33
1985—Los Angeles	National	56	86	4	7	.364	66	41	36	85	35	3.77
1986—Los Angeles	National	62	97⅔	6	12	.333	86	48	42	104	63	3.87
Major League Totals—3 Years		150	235	15	24	.385	203	110	97	243	107	3.71

Selected by Los Angeles Dodgers' organization in 3rd round of free-agent draft, June 7, 1982.
†On disabled list, April 7 to April 17, 1984.

CHAMPIONSHIP SERIES RECORD

Year Club	League	G.	IP.	W.	L.	Pct.	H.	R.	ER.	SO.	BB.	ERA.
1985—Los Angeles	National	1	2	0	0	.000	0	0	0	2	0	0.00

MARK WILLIAM HOWIE

Born December 27, 1962, at Baton Rouge, La.
Height, 6.00. Weight, 170.
Throws and bats righthanded.
Attended Louisiana State University, Baton Rouge, La.

Year Club	League	Pos.	G.	AB.	R.	H.	2B.	3B.	HR.	RBI.	B.A.	PO.	A.	E.	F.A.
1984—Medford	N'west	SS	71	256	39	68	12	0	0	25	.266	*107	187	22	*.930
1985—Madison	Midw.	SS-OF-3B	130	486	72	129	13	5	2	46	.265	185	298	29	.943
1986—Madison	Midw.	2B-OF	130	466	92	144	24	4	4	54	.309	241	240	18	.964

Selected by Oakland A's organization in 3rd round of free-agent draft, June 4, 1984.

DEWEY LaMARR HOYT

(Known by middle name.)

Born January 1, 1955, at Columbia, S. C.
Height, 6.02. Weight, 244.
Throws and bats righthanded.
Son of Dewey Hoyt, minor league pitcher, 1947 and 1948.

Major League saves: 1981 (10).
Led Midwest League pitchers in games started with 27 and tied for lead in shutouts with 3 in 1978.
Tied for Florida State League lead in balks with 3 in 1974.
Named American League Pitcher of the Year by THE SPORTING NEWS, 1983.
Won American League Cy Young Memorial Award, 1983.
Named righthanded pitcher on THE SPORTING NEWS American League All-Star Team, 1983.

Year Club	League	G.	IP.	W.	L.	Pct.	H.	R.	ER.	SO.	BB.	ERA.
1973—Johnson City	Ap'lachian	12	76	6	6	.500	73	44	33	58	40	3.91
1974—Fort Lauderdale	Florida St.	23	161	13	4	.765	143	66	43	77	60	2.40
1975—Fort Lauderdale†	Florida St.	7	26	2	1	.667	24	14	13	12	8	4.50
1975—West Haven	Eastern	8	44	2	4	.333	45	25	15	22	13	3.07
1976—West Haven‡	Eastern	25	180	15	8	.652	169	66	50	103	46	2.50
1977—Knoxville	Southern	25	132	4	●13	.235	160	70	62	67	35	4.23
1977—Iowa	Am. Assoc.	6	25	1	2	.333	30	20	20	14	9	7.20
1978—Appleton	Midwest	28	189	*18	4	*.818	*187	74	61	115	60	2.90
1979—Iowa	Am. Assoc.	9	43	1	4	.200	50	29	22	27	24	4.60
1979—Knoxville	Southern	37	82	9	5	.643	80	29	27	60	35	2.96
1979—Chicago	American	2	3	0	0	.000	2	0	0	0	0	0.00
1980—Iowa	Am. Assoc.	18	62	5	2	.714	61	22	20	36	22	2.90
1980—Chicago	American	24	112	9	3	.750	123	66	57	55	41	4.58
1981—Chicago	American	43	91	9	3	.750	80	40	36	60	28	3.56
1982—Chicago	American	39	239⅔	*19	15	.559	248	104	94	124	48	3.53
1983—Chicago	American	36	260⅔	*24	10	.706	236	115	106	148	31	3.66
1984—Chicago§x	American	34	235⅔	13	*18	.419	244	127	117	126	43	4.47
1985—San Diego	National	31	210½	16	8	.667	210	85	81	83	20	3.47
1986—San Diego	National	35	159	8	11	.421	170	100	91	85	68	5.15
American League Totals—6 Years		178	942	74	49	.602	933	452	410	513	191	3.92
National League Totals—2 Years		66	369⅓	24	19	.558	380	185	172	168	88	4.19
Major League Totals—8 Years		244	1311⅓	98	68	.590	1313	637	582	681	279	3.99

Selected by New York Yankees' organization in 5th round of free-agent draft, June 5, 1973.
†On disabled list, April 16 to June 6, 1975.
‡Traded with Outfielder Oscar Gamble, Pitcher Bob Polinsky and cash estimated at $250,000 to Chicago White Sox for Shortstop Bucky Dent, April 5, 1977.
§Appeared in one game as an outfielder with no chances.
xTraded with Pitchers Kevin Kristan and Todd Simmons to San Diego Padres for Pitchers Tim Lollar and Bill Long, Third Baseman Luis Salazar and Shortstop Ozzie Guillen, December 6, 1984.

CHAMPIONSHIP SERIES RECORD

Year Club	League	G.	IP.	W.	L.	Pct.	H.	R.	ER.	SO.	BB.	ERA.
1983—Chicago	American	1	9	1	0	1.000	5	1	1	4	0	1.00

ALL-STAR GAME RECORD

Year League			IP.	W.	L.	Pct.	H.	R.	ER.	SO.	BB.	ERA.
1985—National			3	1	0	1.000	2	1	0	0	0	0.00

KENT ALAN HRBEK

Name pronounced HER-beck.

Born May 21, 1960, at Bloomington, Minn.
Height, 6.04. Weight, 229.
Throws right and bats lefthanded.

Major League stolen bases: 1982 (3), 1983 (4), 1984 (1), 1985 (1), 1986 (2). Total—11.
Led California League in slugging percentage with .630 and tied for lead in sacrifice flies with 9 in 1981.
Named California League Most Valuable Player, 1981.

Year	Club	League	Pos.	G.	AB.	R.	H.	2B.	3B.	HR.	RBI.	B.A.	PO.	A.	E.	F.A.
1979—Elizabethton†‡		Appal.	1B	17	59	5	12	2	0	1	11	.203	126	11	2	.986
1980—Wisc. Rapids§		Midw.	1B	115	419	74	112	16	0	19	76	.267	1005	81	★20	.982
1981—Visalia		Calif.	1B	121	462	119	175	25	5	27	111	★.379	1034	53	11	★.989
1981—Minnesota		Amer.	1B	24	67	5	16	5	0	1	7	.239	124	4	0	1.000
1982—Minnesota		Amer.	1B	140	532	82	160	21	4	23	92	.301	1174	88	9	.993
1983—Minnesota		Amer.	1B	141	515	75	153	41	5	16	84	.297	1151	89	13	.990
1984—Minnesota		Amer.	1B	149	559	80	174	31	3	27	107	.311	1320	99	14	.990
1985—Minnesota		Amer.	1B	158	593	78	165	31	2	21	93	.278	1339	114	8	.995
1986—Minnesota		Amer.	1B	149	550	85	147	27	1	29	91	.267	1218	104	10	.992
Major League Totals—6 Years				761	2816	405	815	156	15	117	474	.289	6326	498	54	.992

Selected by Minnesota Twins' organization in 17th round of free-agent draft, June 6, 1978.
†On Wisconsin Rapids disabled list, April 13 to June 21, 1979.
‡On Elizabethton disabled list, July 22 to September 6, 1979.
§On disabled list, May 27 to June 6, 1980.

ALL-STAR GAME RECORD

Year	League	Pos.	AB.	R.	H.	2B.	3B.	HR.	RBI.	B.A.	PO.	A.	E.	F.A.
1982—American		PH	1	0	0	0	0	0	0	.000	0	0	0	.000

GLENN DEE HUBBARD

Born September 25, 1957, at Hann Air Force Base, Germany.
Height, 5.08, Weight, 169.
Throws and bats righthanded.

Tied major league record for most assists by second baseman, nine-inning game (12), April 14, 1985.
Major League stolen bases: 1978 (2), 1980 (7), 1981 (4), 1982 (4), 1983 (3), 1984 (4), 1985 (4), 1986 (3). Total—31.
Led National League in sacrifice hits with 20 in 1982.
Led National League second basemen in total chances with 888 in 1985.
Led National League second basemen in double plays with 111 in 1982 and 127 in 1985.
Led Appalachian League third basemen in fielding percentage with .932 in 1975.
Named second baseman on THE SPORTING NEWS National League All-Star Team, 1983.

Year	Club	League	Pos.	G.	AB.	R.	H.	2B.	3B.	HR.	RBI.	B.A.	PO.	A.	E.	F.A.
1975—Kingsport		Appal.	3B-SS-2B	53	136	31	39	6	4	2	21	.287	44	88	9	.936
1976—Kingsport		Appal.	2B	37	136	29	40	8	0	2	15	.294	96	122	1	.995
1976—Greenwood†		W. Car.	2B	33	126	26	40	8	1	4	21	.317	62	83	6	.960
1977—Greenwood		W. Car.	2B	45	182	39	70	10	1	5	44	.385	114	133	4	.984
1977—Savannah		South.	2B	87	298	49	67	15	2	6	32	.225	209	239	10	.978
1978—Richmond		Int.	2B	80	301	58	101	12	3	14	36	.336	208	243	11	.976
1978—Atlanta‡		Nat.	2B	44	163	15	42	4	0	2	13	.258	102	130	5	.979
1979—Richmond		Int.	3B-2B	34	125	21	42	5	1	2	17	.336	83	109	7	.965
1979—Atlanta		Nat.	2B	97	325	34	75	12	0	3	29	.231	193	268	●15	.968
1980—Richmond		Int.	2B	38	143	23	45	11	2	2	25	.315	89	127	4	.982
1980—Atlanta		Nat.	2B	117	431	55	107	21	3	9	43	.248	268	405	15	.978
1981—Atlanta		Nat.	2B	99	361	39	85	13	5	6	33	.235	188	344	5	.991
1982—Atlanta		Nat.	2B	145	532	75	132	25	1	9	59	.248	312	505	14	.983
1983—Atlanta		Nat.	2B	148	517	65	136	24	6	12	70	.263	313	484	12	.985
1984—Atlanta		Nat.	2B	120	397	53	93	27	2	9	43	.234	237	405	8	.988
1985—Atlanta		Nat.	2B	142	439	51	102	21	0	5	39	.232	339	★539	10	.989
1986—Atlanta		Nat.	2B	143	408	42	94	16	1	4	36	.230	282	487	19	.976
Major League Totals—9 Years				1055	3573	429	866	163	18	59	365	.242	2234	3567	103	.983

Selected by Atlanta Braves' organization in 20th round of free-agent draft, June 4, 1975.
†On temporary inactive list, May 17 to June 22, 1976.
‡On disabled list, July 22 to August 23, 1978.

CHAMPIONSHIP SERIES RECORD

Year	Club	League	Pos.	G.	AB.	R.	H.	2B.	3B.	HR.	RBI.	B.A.	PO.	A.	E.	F.A.
1982—Atlanta		Nat.	2B	3	9	1	2	0	0	0	1	.222	4	11	0	1.000

ALL-STAR GAME RECORD

Year	League	Pos.	AB.	R.	H.	2B.	3B.	HR.	RBI.	B.A.	PO.	A.	E.	F.A.
1983—National		2B	1	0	1	0	0	0	0	1.000	0	0	0	.000

REX ALLEN HUDLER

Born September 2, 1960, at Tempe, Ariz.
Height, 6.02. Weight, 180.
Throws and bats righthanded.

Major League stolen bases: 1986 (1).
Led International League second basemen in double plays with 95 in 1984.

Year Club	League	Pos.	G.	AB.	R.	H.	2B.	3B.	HR.	RBI.	B.A.	PO.	A.	E.	F.A.
1978—Oneonta	NYP	SS	58	221	33	62	5	5	0	24	.281	123	21	22	.906
1979—Fort Lauderdale†	Fla. St.	S-3-2-O	116	414	37	104	14	1	1	25	.251	164	314	45	.914
1980—Fort Lauderdale‡	Fla. St.	3-2-O-1	37	125	14	26	4	0	0	6	.208	55	71	5	.962
1980—Greensboro	S. Atl.	2B	20	75	7	17	3	1	2	9	.227	51	52	5	.954
1981—Fort Lauderdale§	Fla. St.	2-S-3-O	79	259	35	77	11	1	2	26	.297	104	238	19	.947
1982—Nashville	South.	2B-SS-OF	89	299	27	71	14	1	0	24	.237	136	219	20	.947
1982—Fort Lauderdale	Fla. St.	2B	9	32	2	8	1	0	1	6	.250	23	25	2	.960
1983—Fort Lauderdale	Fla. St.	2B-SS	91	345	55	93	15	2	2	50	.270	195	245	15	.967
1983—Columbus	Int.	2B-3B-SS	40	118	17	36	5	0	1	11	.305	55	95	4	.974
1984—Columbus	Int.	2B	114	394	49	115	26	1	1	35	.292	266	348	16	.975
1984—New York	Amer.	2B	9	7	2	1	1	0	0	0	.143	4	7	0	1.000
1985—Columbus	Int.	2-S-O-3-1	106	380	62	95	13	4	3	18	.250	192	234	17	.962
1985—New York x	Amer.	2B-1B-SS	20	51	4	8	0	1	0	1	.157	42	51	2	.979
1986—Rochester	Int.	2-3-O-S	77	219	29	57	12	3	2	13	.260	135	191	15	.956
1986—Baltimore	Amer.	2B-3B	14	1	1	0	0	0	0	0	.000	2	3	1	.833
Major League Totals—3 Years			43	59	7	9	1	1	0	1	.153	48	61	3	.973

Selected by New York Yankees' organization in 1st round (18th player selected) of free-agent draft, June 6, 1978.
†On disabled list, May 18 to May 31, 1979.
‡On disabled list, May 10 to June 15, 1980.
§On disabled list, May 11 to June 11, 1981.
xTraded with Pitcher Rich Bordi to Baltimore Orioles for Outfielder Gary Roenicke and a player to be named later, December 12, 1985; New York Yankees acquired Outfielder Leo Hernandez to complete deal, December 16, 1985.

CHARLES LYNN HUDSON

Born March 16, 1959, at Ennis, Tex.
Height, 6.03. Weight, 185.
Throws right and bats left and righthanded.
Received bachelor of business administration degree in management from
Prairie View A&M University, Prairie View, Tex., in 1981.
Tied for Carolina League lead in shutouts with 3 in 1982.
Tied for Carolina League lead in games started by pitchers with 14 in 1981.
Named Carolina League Pitcher of the Year, 1982.

Year Club	League	G.	IP.	W.	L.	Pct.	H.	R.	ER.	SO.	BB.	ERA.
1981—Helena	Pioneer	14	87	5	5	.500	92	53	37	67	27	3.83
1982—Peninsula	Carolina	27	185	●15	5	.750	143	56	38	147	64	*1.85
1983—Portland	P. Coast	10	64	6	3	.667	48	19	19	51	16	2.67
1983—Philadelphia	National	26	169⅓	8	8	.500	158	73	63	101	53	3.35
1984—Philadelphia†	National	30	173⅔	9	11	.450	181	101	78	94	52	4.04
1985—Philadelphia	National	38	193	8	13	.381	188	92	81	122	74	3.78
1986—Philadelphia‡	National	33	144	7	10	.412	165	87	79	82	58	4.94
Major League Totals—4 Years		127	680	32	42	.432	692	353	301	399	237	3.98

Selected by Philadelphia Phillies' organization in 12th round of free-agent draft, June 8, 1981.
†On disabled list, August 10 to September 1, 1984.
‡Traded with Pitcher Jeff Knox to New York Yankees for Outfielder Mike Easler and Infielder Tom Barrett, December 11, 1986.

CHAMPIONSHIP SERIES RECORD

Year Club	League	G.	IP.	W.	L.	Pct.	H.	R.	ER.	SO.	BB.	ERA.
1983—Philadelphia	National	1	9	1	0	1.000	4	2	2	9	2	2.00

WORLD SERIES RECORD

Tied World Series records for most games lost, five-game Series (2), 1983; most home runs allowed, five-game Series (4), 1983.

Year Club	League	G.	IP.	W.	L.	Pct.	H.	R.	ER.	SO.	BB.	ERA.
1983—Philadelphia	National	2	8⅓	0	2	.000	9	8	8	6	1	8.64

KEITH WILLS HUGHES

Born September 12, 1963, at Bryn Mawr, Pa.
Height, 6.03. Weight, 210.
Throws and bats lefthanded.
Tied for South Atlantic League lead in intentional bases on balls received with 5 in 1983.

Year Club	League	Pos.	G.	AB.	R.	H.	2B.	3B.	HR.	RBI.	B.A.	PO.	A.	E.	F.A.
1982—Bend	N'west	OF	55	179	29	46	10	2	3	26	.257	90	6	5	.950
1983—Spartanburg	S. Atl.	OF-1B	131	484	80	159	31	4	15	90	.329	171	5	7	.962
1984—Reading†	East.	OF-1B	70	230	35	60	7	5	2	20	.261	117	7	9	.932
1984—Nashville	South.	OF	21	50	6	9	0	0	0	5	.180	19	0	0	1.000
1985—Albany	East.	OF-2B	104	361	53	97	22	5	10	54	.269	218	18	3	.988
1985—Columbus	Int.	OF	18	54	7	16	4	0	3	8	.296	25	0	2	.926
1986—Albany	East.	OF-1B	94	323	44	99	21	3	7	37	.307	247	17	7	.974
1986—Columbus	Int.	OF	2	8	0	1	0	0	0	0	.125	6	0	1	.857

Signed as free agent by Philadelphia Phillies' organization, August 24, 1981.
†Traded with Pitcher Marty Bystrom to New York Yankees for Pitcher Shane Rawley, June 30, 1984.

MARK LAWRENCE HUISMANN

Born May 11, 1958, at Lincoln, Neb.
Height, 6.03. Weight, 195.
Throws and bats righthanded.
Received bachelor of science degree in business and finance from
Colorado State University, Fort Collins, Colo., in 1980.

Major League saves: 1984 (3), 1986 (5). Total—8.
Led American Association in saves with 33 and games finished in relief with 56 in 1985.
Named American Association Pitcher of the Year, 1985.

Year Club	League	G.	IP.	W.	L.	Pct.	H.	R.	ER.	SO.	BB.	ERA.
1980—Sarasota Royals Blue	Gulf Coast	28	59	1	2	.333	50	20	16	46	14	2.44
1981—Charleston	S. Atlantic	28	44	3	2	.600	36	16	8	42	17	1.64
1981—Fort Myers	Florida St.	14	21	3	1	.750	15	9	8	19	16	3.43
1982—Fort Myers	Florida St.	14	23	3	1	.750	16	1	1	21	4	0.39
1982—Jacksonville	Southern	36	54⅔	4	4	.500	52	18	13	60	15	2.14
1983—Jacksonville	Southern	37	61⅓	6	3	.667	60	25	22	46	25	3.23
1983—Omaha	Am. Assoc.	17	24⅓	0	2	.000	16	7	5	25	9	1.85
1983—Kansas City	American	13	30⅔	2	1	.667	29	20	19	20	17	5.58
1984—Kansas City	American	38	75	3	3	.500	84	38	35	54	21	4.20
1984—Omaha	Am. Assoc.	15	19	2	0	1.000	11	0	0	18	5	0.00
1985—Omaha	Am. Assoc.	★59	89½	5	5	.500	70	20	20	70	14	2.01
1985—Kansas City	American	9	18⅔	1	0	1.000	14	4	4	9	3	1.93
1986—Kansas City†-Seattle	American	46	97⅓	3	4	.429	98	47	41	72	25	3.79
Major League Totals—4 Years		106	221⅔	9	8	.529	225	109	99	155	66	4.02

Selected by Chicago Cubs' organization in 23rd round of free-agent draft, June 5, 1979.
Signed as free agent by Kansas City Royals' organization, June 16, 1980.
†Traded to Seattle Mariners for Catcher Terry Bell, May 21, 1986.

CHAMPIONSHIP SERIES RECORD

Year Club	League	G.	IP.	W.	L.	Pct.	H.	R.	ER.	SO.	BB.	ERA.
1984—Kansas City	American	1	2⅔	0	0	.000	6	3	2	2	1	6.75

TIMOTHY CRAIG HULETT

Name pronounced HUGH-lit.

(Tim)

Born January 12, 1960, at Springfield, Ill.
Height, 6.00. Weight, 185.
Throws and bats righthanded.
Attended Miami-Dade Community College (North), Miami, Fla.,
and University of South Florida, Tampa, Fla.

Major League stolen bases: 1983 (1), 1984 (1), 1985 (6), 1986 (4). Total—12.
Tied for American League lead in errors by third basemen with 23 in 1985.
Led American Association in sacrifice flies with 9 in 1983.
Led American Association second basemen in total chances with 730 in 1983.
Led Eastern League second basemen in putouts with 343, assists with 386, double plays with 95, fielding percentage with .975 and total chances with 748 in 1982.
Led Eastern League second basemen in putouts with 332, assists with 415, double plays with 112 and total chances with 763 in 1981.

Year Club	League	Pos.	G.	AB.	R.	H.	2B.	3B.	HR.	RBI.	B.A.	PO.	A.	E.	F.A.
1980—Glens Falls	East.	SS	6	23	2	4	0	0	0	0	.174	14	13	2	.931
1980—Iowa	A. A.	3B	3	8	1	2	0	0	0	0	.250	0	6	3	.667
1980—Appleton	Midw.	2B-3B-SS	79	278	49	72	11	1	13	47	.259	162	258	17	.961
1981—Glens Falls	East.	2B-3B	134	437	59	99	27	1	10	55	.227	333	422	16	.979
1982—Glens Falls	East.	2B-SS	●140	★536	★113	145	28	5	22	87	.271	352	398	21	.973
1983—Denver	A. A.	2B	133	477	77	130	19	4	21	88	.273	★286	★424	★20	.973
1983—Chicago	Amer.	2B	6	5	0	1	0	0	0	0	.200	8	6	2	.875
1984—Chicago	Amer.	3B-2B	8	7	1	0	0	0	0	0	.000	4	15	0	1.000
1984—Denver	A. A.	2B-3B-SS	139	475	72	125	32	6	16	80	.263	269	371	28	.958
1985—Chicago	Amer.	3B-2B-OF	141	395	52	106	19	4	5	37	.268	117	256	24	.940
1986—Chicago	Amer.	3B-2B	150	520	53	120	16	5	17	44	.231	179	331	15	.971
Major League Totals—4 Years			305	927	106	227	35	9	22	81	.245	308	608	41	.957

Selected by Texas Rangers' organization in 39th round of free-agent draft, June 6, 1978.
Selected by Chicago White Sox' organization in secondary phase of free-agent draft, January 8, 1980.

THOMAS HUBERT HUME JR.

Name pronounced Hyoom.

(Tom)

Born March 29, 1953, at Cincinnati, O.
Height, 6.01. Weight, 185.
Throws and bats righthanded.
Attended Manatee Junior College, West Bradenton, Fla.

Major League saves: 1978 (1), 1979 (17), 1980 (25), 1981 (13), 1982 (17), 1983 (9), 1984 (3), 1985 (3), 1986 (4). Total—92.
Led National League in games finished in relief with 62 in 1980.
Tied for Eastern League lead in games started by pitchers with 27 in 1973.
Named National League co-Fireman of the Year by THE SPORTING NEWS, 1980.

Year Club	League	G.	IP.	W.	L.	Pct.	H.	R.	ER.	SO.	BB.	ERA.
1972—Tampa†	Florida St.	23	141	7	11	.389	135	69	54	112	68	3.45
1973—Three Rivers	Eastern	27	170	7	8	.467	186	97	81	103	99	4.29
1974—Three Rivers	Eastern	26	157	7	12	.368	⋆167	91	77	109	90	4.41
1975—Three Rivers	Eastern	7	45	3	2	.600	43	20	15	19	15	3.00
1975—Indianapolis	Am. Assoc.	17	100	6	6	.500	106	49	45	56	36	4.05
1976—Indianapolis	Am. Assoc.	27	182	9	12	.429	178	91	83	111	62	4.10
1977—Indianapolis	Am. Assoc.	28	106	5	6	.455	99	40	30	76	37	2.55
1977—Cincinnati	National	14	43	3	3	.500	54	36	34	22	17	7.12
1978—Cincinnati	National	42	174	8	11	.421	198	89	80	90	50	4.41
1979—Cincinnati	National	57	163	10	9	.526	162	54	50	80	33	2.76
1980—Cincinnati	National	78	137	9	10	.474	121	44	39	68	38	2.56
1981—Cincinnati	National	51	68	9	4	.692	63	27	26	27	31	3.44
1982—Cincinnati‡	National	46	63⅔	2	6	.250	57	24	22	22	21	3.11
1983—Cincinnati§	National	48	66	3	5	.375	66	40	35	34	41	4.77
1984—Cincinnati	National	54	113⅓	4	13	.235	142	83	71	59	41	5.64
1985—Cincinnati x	National	56	80	3	5	.375	65	33	29	50	35	3.26
1986—Clearwater y	Florida St.	9	24	0	1	.000	20	13	8	15	8	3.00
1986—Philadelphia z	National	48	94⅓	4	1	.800	89	37	29	51	34	2.77
Major League Totals—10 Years		494	1002⅓	55	67	.451	1017	467	415	503	341	3.73

Selected by Los Angeles Dodgers' organization in 35th round of free-agent draft, June 8, 1971.

Selected by Cincinnati Reds' organization in secondary phase of free-agent draft, January 12, 1972.

†Appeared in one game as a second basemen with three putouts and two assists and in one game as a third basemen with one assist.

‡On disabled list, July 27, 1982 through remainder of season.

§On disabled list, May 25 to June 19, 1983.

xTraded with Outfielder Gary Redus to Philadelphia Phillies for Pitchers John Denny and Jeff Gray, December 11, 1985.

yOn Philadelphia disabled list, April 3 to May 7, 1986; included rehabilitation disability assignment to Clearwater, April 11 to May 1, 1986.

zGranted free agency, November 12, 1986; re-signed by Phillies, December 26, 1986.

CHAMPIONSHIP SERIES RECORD

Year Club	League	G.	IP.	W.	L.	Pct.	H.	R.	ER.	SO.	BB.	ERA.
1979—Cincinnati	National	3	4	0	1	.000	6	3	3	2	0	6.75

ALL-STAR GAME RECORD

Year League	IP.	W.	L.	Pct.	H.	R.	ER.	SO.	BB.	ERA.
1982—National	⅓	0	0	.000	0	0	0	0	0	0.00

JAMES RANDALL HUNT
(Randy)

Born January 3, 1960, at Montgomery, Ala.
Height, 6.00. Weight, 185.
Throws and bats righthanded.
Attended Chattahoochee Valley Community College, Phenix City,
Ala., and University of Alabama, University, Ala.

Led Florida State League in sacrifice flies with 10 in 1984.

Tied for Midwest League lead in game-winning RBIs with 14 in 1982.

Led New York-Pennsylvania League catchers in double plays with 6 and tied for lead in passed balls with 13 in 1981.

Tied for Midwest League lead in passed balls with 23 in 1982.

Year Club	League	Pos.	G.	AB.	R.	H.	2B.	3B.	HR.	RBI.	B.A.	PO.	A.	E.	F.A.
1981—Erie	NYP	C	60	195	43	58	6	2	8	27	.297	345	●46	9	.978
1982—Springfield	Midw.	C-OF	134	494	72	143	17	3	15	79	.289	557	90	18	.973
1983—Arkansas	Texas	⋆C-OF	105	338	36	76	21	2	4	51	.225	543	67	⋆20	.968
1984—St. Petersburg	Fla. St.	C-OF-1B	100	336	43	92	15	3	5	59	.274	577	78	17	.975
1984—Arkansas	Texas	C	27	90	7	20	6	0	0	4	.222	143	8	4	.974
1985—Louis.†-Okla. C.	A. A.	C	63	182	18	49	14	2	1	23	.269	333	38	5	.987
1985—St. Louis‡	Nat.	C	14	19	1	3	0	0	0	1	.158	33	1	0	1.000
1986—Indianapolis	A. A.	C-OF	68	206	34	51	9	2	4	30	.248	375	42	9	.979
1986—Montreal	Nat.	C	21	48	4	10	0	0	2	5	.208	135	8	6	.960
Major League Totals—2 Years			35	67	5	13	0	0	2	6	.194	168	9	6	.967

Selected by Detroit Tigers' organization in 5th round of free-agent draft, January 8, 1980.

Selected by New York Yankees' organization in secondary phase of free-agent draft, June 3, 1980.

Selected by St. Louis Cardinals' organization in secondary phase of free-agent draft, June 8, 1981.

†Loaned to Oklahoma City (Texas Rangers' organization), July 28, 1985; returned, September 2, 1985.

‡Sold to Montreal Expos, February 27, 1986.

CLINTON MERRICK HURDLE
(Clint)

Born July 30, 1957, at Big Rapids, Mich.
Height, 6.03. Weight, 195.
Throws right and bats lefthanded.

Major League stolen bases: 1978 (1).

Led International League in intentional bases on balls received with 12 and tied for lead in game-winning hits with 14 in 1983.

Led American Association outfielders in double plays with 4 in 1977.
Tied for Gulf Coast League lead in being hit by pitch with 6 in 1975.
Tied for American Association lead in double plays by outfielders with 4 in 1979.
Received reported $50,000 bonus to sign with Kansas City Royals, 1975.

Year	Club	League	Pos.	G.	AB.	R.	H.	2B.	3B.	HR.	RBI.	B.A.	PO.	A.	E.	F.A.
1975—Sarasota Royals	Gulf C.		OF	49	175	34	48	4	4	1	*31	.274	94	5	2	.980
1976—Waterloo	Midw.		OF	127	429	89	101	22	5	19	89	.235	179	12	7	.965
1977—Omaha	A. A.		OF	129	442	85	145	35	3	16	66	.328	198	*17	6	.973
1977—Kansas City	Amer.		OF	9	26	5	8	0	0	2	7	.308	17	0	0	1.000
1978—Kansas City	Amer.		OF-1B-3B	133	417	48	110	25	5	7	56	.264	544	30	12	.980
1979—Omaha	A. A.		OF	68	220	30	52	13	0	6	29	.236	124	14	4	.972
1979—Kansas City	Amer.		OF-3B	59	171	16	41	10	3	3	30	.240	89	2	3	.968
1980—Kansas City	Amer.		OF	130	395	50	116	31	2	10	60	.294	233	8	10	.960
1981—Kansas City†‡	Amer.		OF	28	76	12	25	3	1	4	15	.329	59	1	0	1.000
1982—Cincinnati	Nat.		OF	19	34	2	7	1	0	0	1	.206	17	2	1	.950
1982—Indianapolis§x	A. A.		OF-1B	88	261	38	64	18	0	12	58	.245	113	7	4	.968
1983—Tidewater	Int.		3B-1B-OF	139	477	82	136	*33	4	22	105	.285	130	149	22	.927
1983—New York	Nat.		3B-OF	13	33	3	6	2	0	0	2	.182	1	15	4	.800
1984—Tidewater	Int.		1-C-3-O	128	412	60	100	15	1	21	64	.243	1036	60	9	.992
1985—New York y	Nat.		C-OF	43	82	7	16	4	0	3	7	.195	89	7	1	.990
1986—St. Louis z	Nat.		1-O-C-3	78	154	18	30	5	1	3	15	.195	334	31	3	.992
American League Totals—5 Years				359	1085	131	300	69	11	26	168	.276	942	41	25	.975
National League Totals—4 Years				153	303	30	59	12	1	6	25	.195	441	55	9	.982
Major League Totals—9 Years				512	1388	161	359	81	12	32	193	.259	1383	96	34	.978

Selected by Kansas City Royals' organization in 1st round (ninth player selected) of free-agent draft, June 4, 1975.
†On disabled list, April 20 to May 30 and August 9 to September 13, 1981.
‡Traded to Cincinnati Reds for Pitcher Scott Brown, December 11, 1981.
§Released, November 15, 1982; invited to Seattle Mariners' spring training, February, 1983.
xReleased, April 4, 1983; signed by New York Mets' organization, April 7, 1983.
yDrafted by St. Louis Cardinals, December 10, 1985.
zGranted free agency, November 12, 1986.

DIVISION SERIES RECORD

Year	Club	League	Pos.	G.	AB.	R.	H.	2B.	3B.	HR.	RBI.	B.A.	PO.	A.	E.	F.A.
1981—Kansas City	Amer.		OF	3	11	0	3	0	0	0	0	.273	6	0	0	1.000

CHAMPIONSHIP SERIES RECORD

Year	Club	League	Pos.	G.	AB.	R.	H.	2B.	3B.	HR.	RBI.	B.A.	PO.	A.	E.	F.A.
1978—Kansas City	Amer.		PH-OF	4	8	1	3	0	1	0	1	.375	6	1	0	1.000
1980—Kansas City	Amer.		OF	3	2	0	0	0	0	0	0	.000	1	0	0	1.000
Championship Series Totals—2 Years				7	10	1	3	0	1	0	1	.300	7	1	0	1.000

WORLD SERIES RECORD

Year	Club	League	Pos.	G.	AB.	R.	H.	2B.	3B.	HR.	RBI.	B.A.	PO.	A.	E.	F.A.
1980—Kansas City	Amer.		OF	4	12	1	5	1	0	0	0	.417	8	0	0	1.000

BRUCE VEE HURST

Born March 24, 1958, at St. George, Utah.
Height, 6.03. Weight, 215.
Throws and bats lefthanded.
Attended Dixie College, St. George, Utah.

Led American League in balks with 4 in 1985.

Year	Club	League	G.	IP.	W.	L.	Pct.	H.	R.	ER.	SO.	BB.	ERA.
1976—Elmira	NYP	9	42	3	2	.600	25	18	14	40	38	3.00
1977—Winter Haven†	Florida St.	13	91	5	4	.556	77	28	21	69	25	2.08
1978—Bristol‡	Eastern	6	33	1	3	.250	32	15	10	35	17	2.73
1979—Winter Haven	Florida St.	12	84	8	2	.800	57	22	18	64	20	1.93
1979—Bristol	Eastern	16	113	9	4	.692	108	56	45	91	49	3.58
1980—Pawtucket	Int'national	17	105	8	6	.571	101	52	46	54	50	3.94
1980—Boston	American	12	31	2	2	.500	39	33	31	16	16	9.00
1981—Pawtucket	Int'national	32	157	12	7	.632	143	68	50	99	71	2.87
1981—Boston	American	5	23	2	0	1.000	23	11	11	11	12	4.30
1982—Boston	American	28	117	3	7	.300	161	87	75	53	40	5.77
1983—Boston	American	33	211⅓	12	12	.500	241	102	96	115	62	4.09
1984—Boston	American	33	218	12	12	.500	232	106	95	136	88	3.92
1985—Boston	American	35	229⅓	11	13	.458	243	123	115	189	70	4.51
1986—Boston§	American	25	174⅓	13	8	.619	169	63	58	167	50	2.99
Major League Totals—7 Years		171	1004	55	54	.505	1108	525	481	687	338	4.31

Selected by Boston Red Sox' organization in 1st round (22nd player selected) of free-agent draft, June 8, 1976.
†On disabled list, August 8 to September 14, 1977.
‡On disabled list, May 23 to September 21, 1978.
§On disabled list, June 3 to July 18, 1986.

CHAMPIONSHIP SERIES RECORD

Year	Club	League	G.	IP.	W.	L.	Pct.	H.	R.	ER.	SO.	BB.	ERA.
1986—Boston	American	2	15	1	0	1.000	18	5	4	8	1	2.40

Year Club	League	G.	IP.	W.	L.	Pct.	H.	R.	ER.	SO.	BB.	ERA.
1986—Boston	American	3	23	2	0	1.000	18	5	5	17	6	1.96

PETER JOSEPH INCAVIGLIA
(Pete)

Born April 2, 1964, at Pebble Beach, Calif.
Height, 6.01. Weight, 225.
Throws and bats righthanded.
Attended Oklahoma State University, Stillwater, Okla.
Son of Tom Incaviglia, minor league infielder, 1948 through 1950 and 1955; and
brother of Tony Incaviglia, minor league third baseman, 1979 through 1983.

Tied major league record for most doubles, inning (2), May 11, 1986, second game (fourth inning).
Established American League record for most strikeouts, season (185), 1986.
Major League stolen bases: 1986 (3).
Led American League batters in strikeouts with 185 in 1986.
Received reported $175,000 bonus to sign with Texas Rangers, 1985.
Named designated hitter on THE SPORTING NEWS College Baseball All-America Team, 1985.

Year Club	League	Pos.	G.	AB.	R.	H.	2B.	3B.	HR.	RBI.	B.A.	PO.	A.	E.	F.A.
1986—Texas	Amer.	OF	153	540	82	135	21	2	30	88	.250	157	6	●14	.921
Major League Totals—1 Year			153	540	82	135	21	2	30	88	.250	157	6	14	.921

Selected by San Francisco Giants' organization in 10th round of free-agent draft, June 7, 1982.
Selected by Montreal Expos' organization in 1st round (eighth player selected) of free-agent draft, June 3, 1985.
Traded to Texas Rangers' organization for Pitcher Bob Sebra and Infielder Jim Anderson, November 2, 1985.

FERMIN ALEXIS INFANTE

Name pronounced En-fawn-tay.
(Known by middle name.)
Born December 4, 1962, at Lara, Venezuela.
Height, 5.10. Weight, 175.
Throws and bats righthanded.

Led International League shortstops in total chances with 699 and double plays with 84 in 1985.
Led South Atlantic League shortstops in total chances with 646 in 1983.

Year Club	League	Pos.	G.	AB.	R.	H.	2B.	3B.	HR.	RBI.	B.A.	PO.	A.	E.	F.A.
1982—Bradenton Jays	Gulf C.	SS	37	137	17	40	7	2	0	15	.292	47	117	5	.970
1983—Florence	S. Atl.	SS	128	480	88	134	25	3	4	56	.279	★197	393	★56	.913
1984—Knoxville	South.	SS	67	253	28	67	13	1	2	29	.265	92	204	18	.943
1984—Syracuse	Int.	SS	72	225	27	50	6	1	0	7	.222	88	229	21	.938
1985—Syracuse	Int.	SS	136	453	63	109	10	5	2	39	.241	★225	★432	★42	.940
1986—Syracuse	Int.	SS	57	193	27	53	6	2	0	15	.275	73	172	14	.946

Signed as free agent by Toronto Blue Jays' organization, December 8, 1981.

DANE CHARLES IORG

Name pronounced Orj.
Born May 11, 1950, at Eureka, Calif.
Height, 6.00. Weight, 180.
Throws right and bats lefthanded.
Attended Brigham Young University, Provo, Utah.
Brother of Garth Iorg, third baseman with Toronto Blue Jays; and
Lee Iorg, outfielder in New York Mets' organization, 1974 through 1977.

Major League stolen bases: 1979 (1), 1980 (1), 1981 (2), 1983 (1). Total—5.
Tied for Northwest League lead in sacrifice flies with 6 in 1971.
Led Eastern League first basemen in double plays with 78 in 1975.
Tied for Northwest League lead in double plays by outfielders with 2 in 1971.
Named Northwest League Most Valuable Player, 1971.
Named outfielder on THE SPORTING NEWS College Baseball All-America Team, 1971.

Year Club	League	Pos.	G.	AB.	R.	H.	2B.	3B.	HR.	RBI.	B.A.	PO.	A.	E.	F.A.
1971—Walla Walla	N'west	OF	77	275	64	101	●15	6	7	65	★.367	135	10	6	.960
1972—Reading	East.	OF	15	43	2	6	2	0	0	1	.140	18	0	1	.947
1972—Burlington	Carol.	OF-P	92	324	61	104	20	3	8	37	.321	119	5	5	.961
1973—Reading	East.	OF	116	386	64	119	21	6	7	49	.308	149	8	5	.969
1974—Toledo	Int.	★1B-OF	133	444	53	110	19	3	10	59	.248	947	★91	9	.991
1975—Toledo	Int.	1B-3B	13	36	7	7	2	0	0	2	.194	76	2	0	1.000
1975—Reading	East.	1B	97	319	47	88	19	5	6	59	.276	★827	44	9	★.990
1976—Oklahoma City	A. A.	1B-OF-C	120	396	65	129	25	11	11	68	.326	741	68	11	.987
1977—Okla. City-N.O.	A. A.	OF-1B-3B	75	273	47	90	14	4	9	48	.330	246	20	6	.978
1977—Phil.†-St.L.	Nat.	1B-OF	42	62	5	15	2	0	0	6	.242	71	4	2	.974
1978—Springfield	A. A.	1B-OF-3B	89	345	73	128	20	0	24	87	★.371	643	64	12	.983
1978—St. Louis	Nat.	OF	35	85	6	23	4	1	0	4	.271	33	5	0	1.000
1979—St. Louis	Nat.	OF-1B	79	179	12	52	11	1	1	21	.291	121	7	2	.985
1980—St. Louis	Nat.	OF-1B	105	251	33	76	23	1	3	36	.303	133	2	1	.993
1981—St. Louis	Nat.	OF-1B-3B	75	217	23	71	11	2	2	39	.327	125	7	3	.978
1982—St. Louis	Nat.	OF-1B-3B	102	238	17	70	14	1	0	34	.294	177	10	3	.984
1983—St. Louis‡	Nat.	OF-1B	58	116	6	31	9	1	0	11	.267	127	5	3	.978
1983—Louisville	A. A.	1B	3	10	2	2	0	0	0	0	.200	21	0	0	1.000

Year—Club	League	Pos.	G.	AB.	R.	H.	2B.	3B.	HR.	RBI.	B.A.	PO.	A.	E.	F.A.
1984—St. Louis§	Nat.	1B-OF	15	28	3	4	2	0	0	3	.143	35	2	0	1.000
1984—Kansas City	Amer.	1B-OF-3B	78	235	27	60	16	2	5	30	.255	399	22	3	.993
1985—Kansas City xy	Amer.	OF-1B-3B	64	130	7	29	9	1	1	21	.223	55	4	0	1.000
1986—San Diego z	Nat.	1-3-O-P	90	106	10	24	2	1	2	11	.226	43	2	0	1.000
National League Totals—9 Years			601	1282	115	366	78	8	8	165	.285	865	44	14	.985
American League Totals—2 Years			142	365	34	89	25	3	6	51	.244	454	26	3	.994
Major League Totals—10 Years			743	1647	149	455	103	11	14	216	.276	1319	70	17	.988

Selected by Kansas City Royals' organization in 13th round of free-agent draft, June 7, 1968.
Selected by Philadelphia Phillies' organization in secondary phase of free-agent draft, June 8, 1971.
†Traded with Outfielder Rick Bosetti and Pitcher Tom Underwood to St. Louis Cardinals for Outfielder Bake McBride and Pitcher Steve Waterbury, June 15, 1977.
‡On disabled list, July 17 to August 15, 1983; included rehabilitation disability assignment to Louisville, August 11 to August 15, 1983.
§Sold to Kansas City Royals, May 9, 1984.
xOn disabled list, August 25 to September 9, 1985.
yGranted free agency, November 12, 1985; signed by San Diego Padres, January 28, 1986.
zReleased, October 9, 1986.

CHAMPIONSHIP SERIES RECORD

Year—Club	League	Pos.	G.	AB.	R.	H.	2B.	3B.	HR.	RBI.	B.A.	PO.	A.	E.	F.A.
1984—Kansas City	Amer.	PH	2	2	0	1	0	0	0	1	.500	0	0	0	.000
1985—Kansas City	Amer.	PH	4	2	0	1	1	0	0	0	.500	0	0	0	.000
Championship Series Totals—2 Years			6	4	0	2	1	0	0	1	.500	0	0	0	.000

WORLD SERIES RECORD

Tied World Series record for most at-bats, inning (2), October 19, 1982 (sixth inning).

Year—Club	League	Pos.	G.	AB.	R.	H.	2B.	3B.	HR.	RBI.	B.A.	PO.	A.	E.	F.A.
1982—St. Louis	Nat.	DH	5	17	4	9	4	1	0	1	.529	0	0	0	.000
1985—Kansas City	Amer.	PH	2	2	0	1	0	0	0	2	.500	0	0	0	.000
World Series Totals—2 Years			7	19	4	10	4	1	0	3	.526	0	0	0	.000

PITCHING RECORD

Year—Club	League	G.	IP.	W.	L.	Pct.	H.	R.	ER.	SO.	BB.	ERA.
1972—Burlington	Carolina	1	1	0	0	.000	3	3	3	0	1	27.00
1986—San Diego	National	2	3	0	0	.000	5	4	4	2	1	12.00
Major League Totals—1 Year		2	3	0	0	.000	5	4	4	2	1	12.00

GARTH RAY IORG

Name pronounced Orj.

Born October 12, 1954, at Arcata, Calif.
Height, 5.11. Weight, 175.
Throws and bats righthanded.
Attended College of the Redwoods, Eureka, Calif.
Brother of Dane Iorg, first baseman-outfielder with Philadelphia Phillies, St. Louis Cardinals, Kansas City Royals and San Diego Padres, 1977 through 1986; and Lee Iorg, outfielder in New York Mets' organization, 1974 through 1977.

Major League stolen bases: 1980 (2), 1981 (2), 1982 (3), 1983 (7), 1984 (1), 1985 (3), 1986 (3). Total—21.
Led Florida State League in sacrifice hits with 20 in 1974.

Year—Club	League	Pos.	G.	AB.	R.	H.	2B.	3B.	HR.	RBI.	B.A.	PO.	A.	E.	F.A.
1973—Johnson City	Appal.	SS-2B	51	169	20	40	3	0	3	13	.237	88	120	20	.912
1974—Fort Lauderdale	Fla. St.	SS-2B-3B	102	325	30	70	11	4	0	38	.215	134	245	28	.931
1975—Fort Lauderdale	Fla. St.	3-2-O-S	50	186	10	47	4	2	0	16	.253	67	78	11	.929
1975—West Haven	East.	3B-SS-2B	76	236	19	59	6	2	0	21	.250	79	202	26	.915
1976—West Haven†	East.	2B	78	273	31	75	17	1	1	24	.275	172	236	18	.958
1977—Charleston‡	Int.	2B-SS	70	262	35	77	8	3	1	34	.294	158	234	18	.956
1978—Syracuse§	Int.	3B-2B-SS	89	324	29	70	16	2	6	25	.216	141	204	11	.969
1978—Toronto	Amer.	2B	19	49	3	8	0	0	0	3	.163	34	51	3	.966
1979—Syracuse	Int.	2-3-S-O	121	430	65	121	23	4	5	39	.281	150	250	20	.952
1980—Syracuse	Int.	2B-3B	32	134	17	40	6	3	1	14	.299	60	99	4	.975
1980—Toronto	Amer.	2-3-O-1-S	80	222	24	55	10	1	2	14	.248	122	155	3	.989
1981—Toronto	Amer.	2-3-S-1	70	215	17	52	11	0	0	10	.242	99	182	12	.959
1982—Toronto	Amer.	3B-2B	129	417	45	119	20	5	1	36	.285	114	236	14	.962
1983—Toronto	Amer.	3B-2B-SS	122	375	40	103	22	5	2	39	.275	106	223	9	.973
1984—Toronto	Amer.	3B-2B-SS	121	247	24	56	10	3	1	25	.227	66	117	10	.948
1985—Toronto	Amer.	3B-2B	131	288	33	90	22	1	7	37	.313	71	192	9	.967
1986—Toronto	Amer.	3B-2B-SS	137	327	30	85	19	1	3	44	.260	92	185	12	.958
Major League Totals—8 Years			809	2140	216	568	114	16	16	208	.265	704	1341	72	.966

Selected by New York Yankees' organization in 8th round of free-agent draft, June 5, 1973.
†Selected by Toronto Blue Jays in American League expansion draft, November 5, 1976.
‡On disabled list, June 29 to September 1, 1977.
§On disabled list, June 18 to June 28, 1978.

CHAMPIONSHIP SERIES RECORD

Year—Club	League	Pos.	G.	AB.	R.	H.	2B.	3B.	HR.	RBI.	B.A.	PO.	A.	E.	F.A.
1985—Toronto	Amer.	3B-PH	6	15	1	2	0	0	0	0	.133	5	10	0	1.000

CHARLES LEO JACKSON
(Chuck)

Born March 19, 1963, at Seattle, Wash.
Height, 6.00. Weight, 185.
Throws and bats righthanded.
Attended University of Hawaii, Honolulu, Haw.

Led Southern League third basemen in errors with 30 in 1985.

Year	Club	League	Pos.	G.	AB.	R.	H.	2B.	3B.	HR.	RBI.	B.A.	PO.	A.	E.	F.A.
1984—Auburn	NYP	OF	10	38	4	14	0	2	1	4	.368	9	3	0	1.000
1984—Asheville	S. Atl.	OF	59	199	42	52	12	0	5	32	.261	98	6	4	.963
1985—Tucson	P. C.	OF	19	61	7	11	2	1	1	4	.180	43	3	1	.979
1985—Columbus	South.	3B-OF	108	361	62	112	10	8	8	46	.310	98	232	32	.912
1986—Tucson	P. C.	*3B-OF	127	448	83	137	27	5	11	62	.306	91	202	*29	.910

Selected by Cleveland Indians' organization in 21st round of free-agent draft, June 8, 1981.
Selected by Houston Astros' organization in 7th round of free-agent draft, June 4, 1984.

DANNY LYNN JACKSON

Born January 5, 1962, at San Antonio, Tex.
Height, 6.00. Weight, 190.
Throws left and bats righthanded.
Attended University of Oklahoma, Norman, Okla., and
Trinidad State Junior College, Trinidad, Colo.
Brother of Mike Jackson, fourth-round selection of Kansas City Kings in 1983 NBA draft.

Major League saves: 1986 (1).
Tied for American Association lead in complete games with 10 in 1984.
Tied for American Association lead in shutouts with 2 in 1983 and 3 in 1984.

Year	Club	League	G.	IP.	W.	L.	Pct.	H.	R.	ER.	SO.	BB.	ERA.
1982—Charleston	S. Atlantic	13	96⅓	10	1	.909	80	37	28	62	39	2.62
1982—Jacksonville†	Southern	14	98	7	2	.778	78	30	26	74	42	2.39
1983—Omaha	Am. Assoc.	23	136	7	8	.467	126	74	60	93	73	3.97
1983—Kansas City	American	4	19	1	1	.500	26	12	11	9	6	5.21
1984—Kansas City	American	15	76	2	6	.250	84	41	36	40	35	4.26
1984—Omaha	Am. Assoc.	16	110⅓	5	8	.385	91	50	45	82	45	3.67
1985—Kansas City	American	32	208	14	12	.538	209	94	79	114	76	3.42
1986—Kansas City ‡	American	32	185⅔	11	12	.478	177	83	66	115	79	3.20
Major League Totals—4 Years		83	488⅔	28	31	.475	496	230	192	278	196	3.54

Selected by Oakland A's organization in 24th round of free-agent draft, June 3, 1980.
Selected by Kansas City Royals' organization in secondary phase of free-agent draft, January 17, 1982.
†On disabled list, September 8, 1982 through remainder of season.
‡On disabled list, April 4 to April 21, 1986.

CHAMPIONSHIP SERIES RECORD

Year	Club	League	G.	IP.	W.	L.	Pct.	H.	R.	ER.	SO.	BB.	ERA.
1985—Kansas City	American	2	10	1	0	1.000	10	0	0	7	1	0.00

WORLD SERIES RECORD

Tied World Series record for most consecutive times striking out, Series (5), 1985.

Year	Club	League	G.	IP.	W.	L.	Pct.	H.	R.	ER.	SO.	BB.	ERA.
1985—Kansas City	American	2	16	1	1	.500	9	3	3	12	5	1.69

DARRIN JAY JACKSON

Born August 22, 1962, at Los Angeles, Calif.
Height, 6.00. Weight, 175.
Throws and bats righthanded.

Led Gulf Coast League outfielders in total chances with 127 in 1981.
Tied for Texas League lead in double plays with 6 in 1984.

Year	Club	League	Pos.	G.	AB.	R.	H.	2B.	3B.	HR.	RBI.	B.A.	PO.	A.	E.	F.A.
1981—Sarasota Cubs	Gulf C.	OF	62	210	29	39	5	0	1	15	.186	*121	5	1	.992
1982—Quad Cities	Midw.	OF	132	529	86	146	23	5	5	48	.276	266	9	8	.972
1983—Salinas	Calif.	OF	129	509	70	126	18	5	6	54	.248	237	15	13	.951
1984—Midland	Texas	OF	132	496	63	134	18	2	15	54	.270	286	*19	8	.974
1985—Iowa	A. A.	OF	10	40	0	7	2	1	0	1	.175	19	0	0	1.000
1985—Pittsfield	East.	OF	91	325	38	82	10	1	3	30	.252	221	5	0	1.000
1985—Chicago	Nat.	OF	5	11	0	1	0	0	0	0	.091	7	0	0	1.000
1986—Pittsfield	East.	OF	137	•520	82	139	28	2	15	64	.267	320	*16	7	.980
Major League Totals—1 Year		5	11	0	1	0	0	0	0	.091	7	0	0	1.000

Selected by Chicago Cubs' organization in 2nd round of free-agent draft, June 8, 1981.

KENNETH BERNARD JACKSON
(Ken)

Born August 21, 1963, at Shreveport, La.
Height, 6.01. Weight, 190.
Throws and bats righthanded.
Attended Angelina College, Lufkin, Tex.

Led South Atlantic League in bases on balls received with 114 in 1983.
Led Eastern League shortstops in fielding percentage with .949 and double plays with 68 in 1986.

Year Club	League	Pos.	G.	AB.	R.	H.	2B.	3B.	HR.	RBI.	B.A.	PO.	A.	E.	F.A.
1982—Helena	Pion.	SS	62	218	38	55	11	0	5	28	.252	95	191	*43	.869
1983—Spartanburg	S. Atl.	SS	131	449	95	106	21	3	5	49	.236	167	*430	44	.931
1984—Peninsula	Carol.	SS-2B	71	222	37	50	10	1	3	22	.225	108	179	21	.932
1984—Reading	East.	2B-SS	72	225	31	54	9	2	1	19	.240	146	203	14	.961
1985—Reading	East.	SS	121	423	66	99	15	2	3	34	.234	169	305	33	.935
1986—Reading	East.	SS-2B-3B	134	407	76	93	16	8	4	33	.229	189	360	30	.948

Selected by Toronto Blue Jays' organization in 3rd round of free-agent draft, January 12, 1982.
Selected by Philadelphia Phillies' organization in secondary phase of free-agent draft, June 7, 1982.

MICHAEL RAY JACKSON
(Mike)

Born December 22, 1964, at Houston, Tex.
Height, 6.00. Weight, 185.
Throws and bats righthanded.
Attended Hill Junior College, Hillsboro, Tex.

Led Carolina League in balks with 7 in 1985.

Year Club	League	G.	IP.	W.	L.	Pct.	H.	R.	ER.	SO.	BB.	ERA.
1984—Spartanburg	S. Atlantic	14	80⅔	7	2	.778	53	35	24	77	50	2.68
1985—Peninsula	Carolina	31	125⅓	7	9	.438	127	71	64	96	53	4.60
1986—Reading	Eastern	30	43½	2	3	.400	25	9	8	42	22	1.66
1986—Portland	P. Coast	17	22⅔	3	1	.750	18	8	8	23	13	3.18
1986—Philadelphia	National	9	13⅓	0	0	.000	12	5	5	3	4	3.38
Major League Totals—1 Year		9	13⅓	0	0	.000	12	5	5	3	4	3.38

Selected by Philadelphia Phillies' organization in 29th round of free-agent draft, June 6, 1983.
Selected by Philadelphia Phillies' organization in secondary phase of free-agent draft, January 17, 1984.

REGINALD MARTINEZ JACKSON
(Reggie)

Born May 18, 1946, at Wyncote, Pa.
Height, 6.00. Weight, 206.
Throws and bats lefthanded.
Attended Arizona State University, Tempe, Ariz.

Established major league records for most strikeouts, lifetime (2,500); most strikeouts by lefthanded batter, season (171), 1968; most years, 100 or more strikeouts (18); most consecutive years, 100 or more strikeouts (13).
Tied major league records for most consecutive years leading league in strikeouts (4), 1968 through 1971; most strikeouts, nine-inning game (5), September 27, 1968.
Tied American League records for most years, 20 or more home runs (16); most times, four or more strikeouts, game, season (5), April 7 (second game)—April 21—May 18—June 4—September 21 (first game), 1971; most consecutive games, one or more home runs (6), July 18 through 23, 1976; most seasons leading league, errors, outfielder (5), 1968, 1970, 1972, 1975 and 1976; fewest errors by outfielder, season, for leader in most errors (9), 1972.
Hit three home runs in a game, July 2, 1969 and September 18, 1986.
Hit home runs in all 12 parks, 1975.
Major League stolen bases: 1967 (1), 1968 (14), 1969 (13), 1970 (26), 1971 (16), 1972 (9), 1973 (22), 1974 (25), 1975 (17), 1976 (28), 1977 (17), 1978 (14), 1979 (9), 1980 (1), 1982 (4), 1984 (8), 1985 (1), 1986 (1). Total—226.
Led American League batters in strikeouts with 171 in 1968, 142 in 1969, 135 in 1970, 161 in 1971 and 156 in 1982.
Led American League in slugging percentage with .608 in 1969, .531 in 1973 and .502 in 1976.
Led American League in intentional bases on balls received with 20 in 1974 and tied for lead with 20 in 1969.
Led American League in caught stealing with 17 in 1970.
Tied for American League lead in double plays by outfielders with 5 in 1972.
Led Southern League in total bases with 232 in 1967.
Named Major League Player of the Year by THE SPORTING NEWS, 1973.
Named American League Player of the Year by THE SPORTING NEWS, 1973.
Named American League Most Valuable Player by Baseball Writers' Association of America, 1973.
Named outfielder on THE SPORTING NEWS American League All-Star Team, 1969, 1973, 1975, 1976 and 1980.
Named outfielder on THE SPORTING NEWS American League Silver Slugger Team, 1982.
Named designated hitter on THE SPORTING NEWS American League Silver Slugger team, 1980.
Named Southern League Player of the Year, 1967.
Named College Player of the Year by THE SPORTING NEWS, 1966.
Received reported $85,000 bonus to sign with Kansas City Athletics, 1966.
Named outfielder on THE SPORTING NEWS College Baseball All-America Team, 1966.

Year Club	League	Pos.	G.	AB.	R.	H.	2B.	3B.	HR.	RBI.	B.A.	PO.	A.	E.	F.A.
1966—Lewiston	N'west	OF	12	48	14	14	3	2	2	11	.292	23	0	1	.958
1966—Modesto	Calif.	OF	56	221	50	66	6	0	21	60	.299	108	3	9	.925
1967—Birmingham	South.	OF	114	413	*84	121	26	*17	17	58	.293	228	3	*18	.928
1967—Kansas City	Amer.	OF	35	118	13	21	4	4	1	6	.178	55	1	4	.933
1968—Oakland	Amer.	OF	154	553	82	138	13	6	29	74	.250	269	14	*12	.959
1969—Oakland	Amer.	OF	152	549	*123	151	36	3	47	118	.275	278	14	11	.964
1970—Oakland	Amer.	OF	149	426	57	101	21	2	23	66	.237	251	8	●12	.956
1971—Oakland	Amer.	OF	150	567	87	157	29	3	32	80	.277	285	15	7	.977
1972—Oakland†	Amer.	OF	135	499	72	132	25	2	25	75	.265	301	5	*9	.971
1973—Oakland	Amer.	OF	151	539	*99	158	28	2	*32	*117	.293	302	4	9	.971
1974—Oakland	Amer.	OF	148	506	90	146	25	1	29	93	.289	296	8	10	.968
1975—Oakland‡	Amer.	OF	157	593	91	150	39	3	●36	104	.253	315	13	*12	.965
1976—Baltimore§x	Amer.	OF	134	498	84	138	27	2	27	91	.277	284	8	*11	.964

Year Club League	Pos.	G.	AB.	R.	H.	2B.	3B.	HR.	RBI.	B.A.	PO.	A.	E.	F.A.
1977—New York............... Amer.	OF	146	525	93	150	39	2	32	110	.286	236	7	13	.949
1978—New York............... Amer.	OF	139	511	82	140	13	5	27	97	.274	212	6	3	.986
1979—New York y .... Amer.	OF	131	465	78	138	24	2	29	89	.297	274	7	4	.986
1980—New York............... Amer.	OF ·	143	514	94	154	22	4	●41	111	.300	174	3	7	.962
1981—New York za........ Amer.	OF	94	334	33	79	17	1	15	54	.237	111	3	3	.974
1982—California............... Amer.	OF	153	530	92	146	17	1	●39	101	.275	200	6	6	.972
1983—California............... Amer.	OF	116	397	43	77	14	1	14	49	.194	66	4	1	.986
1984—California............... Amer.	OF	143	525	67	117	17	2	25	81	.223	7	0	0	1.000
1985—California............... Amer.	OF	143	460	64	116	27	0	27	85	.252	112	6	7	.944
1986—California b.......... Amer.	OF	132	419	65	101	12	2	18	58	.241	4	1	1	.833
Major League Totals—20 Years..............		2705	9528	1509	2510	449	48	548	1659	.263	4032	133	142	.967

Selected by Kansas City A's organization in 1st round (second player selected) of free-agent draft, June 13, 1966.
†On disabled list, August 10 to August 25, 1972.
‡Traded with Pitchers Ken Holtzman and Bill Van Bommel to Baltimore Orioles for Outfielder Don Baylor and Pitchers Mike Torrez and Paul Mitchell, April 2, 1976.
§On disqualified list, April 9 to May 2, 1976.
xPlayed out option year and granted free agency, November 1, 1976; signed as free agent with New York Yankees, November 29, 1976.
yOn disabled list, June 3 to June 27, 1979.
zOn disabled list, April 2 to April 17, 1981.
aGranted free agency, November 13, 1981; signed by California Angels, January 22, 1982.
bGranted free agency, November 12, 1986; signed by Oakland A's, December 24, 1986.

DIVISION SERIES RECORD

Year Club League	Pos.	G.	AB.	R.	H.	2B.	3B.	HR.	RBI.	B.A.	PO.	A.	E.	F.A.
1981—New York............... Amer.	OF	5	20	4	6	0	0	2	4	.300	7	0	0	1.000

CHAMPIONSHIP SERIES RECORD

Established Championship Series records for most Series played (11); most Series, one or more hits (10); most Series played all games (9); most games, total Series (45); most at-bats, total Series (163); most times stealing home, game (1), October 12, 1972; most strikeouts, total Series (41).

Tied Championship Series records for most clubs, total Series (3); most times on winning club (6); most times reached first base safely, game (5), October 3, 1978; most doubles, total Series (7).

Established American League Championship Series records for most hits, total Series (37); most singles, total Series (24); highest batting average, four-game Series (.462), 1978; most runs batted in, total Series (20); most runs batted in, four-game Series (6), 1978; most bases on balls, total Series (17).

Tied American League Championship Series records for most times on losing club (5); most home runs, three-game Series (2), 1971; most Series, one or more home runs (4); most total bases, three-game Series (11), 1971; highest slugging average, three-game Series (.917), 1971; most strikeouts, five-game Series (7), 1982; most bases on balls, four-game Series (5), 1974.

Year Club League	Pos.	G.	AB.	R.	H.	2B.	3B.	HR.	RBI.	B.A.	PO.	A.	E.	F.A.
1971—Oakland................. Amer.	OF	3	12	2	4	1	0	2	2	.333	9	1	0	1.000
1972—Oakland................. Amer.	OF	5	18	1	5	1	0	0	2	.278	14	0	1	.933
1973—Oakland................. Amer.	OF	5	21	0	3	0	0	0	0	.143	19	0	0	1.000
1974—Oakland................. Amer.	DH-OF	4	12	0	2	1	0	0	1	.167	0	0	0	.000
1975—Oakland................. Amer.	OF	3	12	1	5	0	0	1	3	.417	5	1	0	1.000
1977—New York............... Amer.	O-D-PH	5	16	1	2	0	0	0	1	.125	10	1	0	1.000
1978—New York............... Amer.	DH-OF	4	13	5	6	1	0	2	6	.462	4	0	0	1.000
1980—New York............... Amer.	OF	3	11	1	3	1	0	0	0	.273	5	0	0	1.000
1981—New York............... Amer.	OF	2	4	1	0	0	0	0	1	.000	1	0	0	1.000
1982—California............... Amer.	OF	5	18	2	2	0	0	1	2	.111	2	0	0	1.000
1986—California............... Amer.	DH	6	26	2	5	2	0	2	2	.192	0	0	0	.000
Championship Series Totals—11 Years...		45	163	16	37	7	0	6	20	.227	69	3	1	.986

WORLD SERIES RECORD

Established World Series records for most home runs, two consecutive Series, two consecutive years (7), 1977 and 1978; highest slugging percentage, six-game Series (1.250), 1977; most home runs, Series (5), 1977; most total bases, Series (25), 1977; most runs, Series (10), 1977; most long hits, six-game Series (6), 1977 (tied record for any length Series); most extra bases on long hits, Series (16), 1977; most home runs, three consecutive games, one Series (5), 1977; most home runs, two consecutive games, Series (4), October 16 and 18, 1977; most consecutive home runs, two consecutive games (4), October 16 and 18, 1977; most home runs, four consecutive games, one in each game (6); highest slugging average, total Series, 20 or more games (.755).

Tied World Series records for most times reached first base safely, game (batting 1.000) (5), October 24, 1981; most home runs, game (3), October 18, 1977 (consecutive, each on first pitch); most home runs, two consecutive innings (2), October 18, 1977 (fourth and fifth inning); most total bases, game (12), October 18, 1977; most runs, game (4), October 18, 1977; most consecutive games, one or more runs batted in (6); one or more hits, each game, six-game Series, 1978; most times hit by pitch, total Series (3).

Year Club League	Pos.	G.	AB.	R.	H.	2B.	3B.	HR.	RBI.	B.A.	PO.	A.	E.	F.A.
1973—Oakland................. Amer.	OF	7	29	3	9	3	1	1	6	.310	17	0	0	1.000
1974—Oakland................. Amer.	OF	5	14	3	4	1	0	1	1	.286	6	1	1	.875
1977—New York............... Amer.	OF	6	20	10	9	1	0	5	8	.450	9	0	0	1.000
1978—New York............... Amer.	DH	6	23	2	9	1	0	2	8	.391	0	0	0	.000
1981—New York............... Amer.	OF	3	12	3	4	1	0	1	1	.333	5	0	1	.832
World Series Totals—5 Years		27	98	21	35	7	1	10	24	.357	37	1	2	.950

ALL-STAR GAME RECORD

Tied All-Star Game record for most home runs by pinch-hitter, game (1), July 13, 1971.

Year	League	Pos.	AB.	R.	H.	2B.	3B.	HR.	RBI.	B.A.	PO.	A.	E.	F.A.
1969—American		OF	2	0	0	0	0	0	0	.000	2	0	0	1.000
1971—American		PH	1	1	1	0	0	1	2	1.000	0	0	0	.000
1972—American		OF	4	0	2	1	0	0	0	.500	5	0	0	1.000
1973—American		OF	4	1	1	1	0	0	0	.250	0	0	0	.000
1974—American		OF	3	0	0	0	0	0	0	.000	3	0	0	1.000
1975—American		OF	3	0	1	0	0	0	0	.333	2	0	0	1.000
1977—American		OF	2	0	1	0	0	0	0	.500	0	0	0	.000
1979—American		PH-OF	1	0	0	0	0	0	0	.000	0	0	0	.000
1980—American		OF	2	0	1	0	0	0	0	.500	0	0	0	.000
1981—American		OF	1	0	0	0	0	0	0	.000	0	0	0	.000
1982—American		OF	1	0	0	0	0	0	1	.000	3	0	0	1.000
1984—American		OF	2	0	0	0	0	0	0	.000	0	0	1	.000
All-Star Game Totals—12 Years			26	2	7	2	0	1	3	.269	15	0	1	.938

Named to American League All-Star Team for 1978 game; replaced due to injury by Graig Nettles.
Named to American League All-Star Team for 1983 game; replaced due to injury by Ben Oglivie.

ROY LEE JACKSON

Born May 1, 1954, at Opelika, Ala.
Height, 6.02. Weight, 205.
Throws and bats righthanded.
Attended Tuskegee Institute, Tuskegee, Ala.

Major league saves: 1980 (1), 1981 (7), 1982 (6), 1983 (7), 1984 (10), 1985 (2), 1986 (1). Total—34.

Year	Club	League	G.	IP.	W.	L.	Pct.	H.	R.	ER.	SO.	BB.	ERA.
1975—Marion		Ap'lachian	8	50	4	2	.667	35	10	8	35	14	1.44
1975—Wausau		Midwest	5	38	1	3	.250	29	12	10	35	7	2.37
1976—Lynchburg		Carolina	7	55	2	3	.400	51	26	21	19	15	3.44
1976—Jackson		Texas	20	132	8	6	.571	136	51	44	82	39	3.00
1977—Tidewater		Int'national	28	168	13	7	.650	174	78	69	110	73	3.70
1977—New York		National	4	24	0	2	.000	25	16	16	13	15	6.00
1978—Tidewater		Int'national	27	176	11	10	.524	176	91	73	132	51	3.73
1978—New York		National	4	13	0	0	.000	21	13	13	6	6	9.00
1979—Tidewater		Int'national	33	137	12	7	.632	143	63	57	89	33	3.74
1979—New York		National	8	16	1	0	1.000	11	4	4	10	5	2.25
1980—Tidewater		Int'national	22	78	3	5	.375	63	33	20	56	51	2.31
1980—New York†		National	24	71	1	7	.125	78	37	33	58	20	4.18
1981—Toronto		American	39	62	1	2	.333	65	23	18	27	25	2.61
1982—Toronto		American	48	97	8	8	.500	77	37	33	71	31	3.06
1983—Toronto		American	49	92	8	3	.727	92	48	46	48	41	4.50
1984—Toronto‡		American	54	86	7	8	.467	73	40	34	58	31	3.56
1985—Rochester§		Int'national	15	27	1	1	.500	26	12	9	25	8	3.00
1985—Las Vegas		P. Coast	3	5⅔	1	0	1.000	3	1	1	3	0	1.59
1985—San Diego x		National	22	40	2	3	.400	32	13	12	28	13	2.70
1986—Minnesota y		American	28	58⅓	0	1	.000	57	29	25	32	16	3.86
National League Totals—5 Years			62	164	4	12	.250	167	83	78	115	59	4.28
American League Totals—5 Years			218	395⅓	24	22	.522	364	177	156	236	144	3.55
Major League Totals—10 Years			280	559⅓	28	34	.452	531	260	234	351	203	3.77

Selected by Houston Astros' organization in 12th round of free-agent draft, June 6, 1972.
Signed as free agent by New York Mets' organization, June 27, 1975.
†Traded to Toronto Blue Jays for Outfielder Bob Bailor, December 12, 1980.
‡Released, April 1, 1985; signed by Rochester (Baltimore Orioles' organization), May 1, 1985.
§Traded with a player to be named later to San Diego Padres' organization for Second Baseman Alan Wiggins, June 27, 1985; San Diego acquired Pitcher Rich Caldwell to complete deal, September 16, 1985.
xReleased, March 23, 1986; signed by Minnesota Twins' organization, March 23, 1986.
yGranted free agency, November 12, 1986.

VINCENT EDWARD JACKSON

(Bo)

Born November 30, 1962, at Bessemer, Ala.
Height, 6.01. Weight, 222.
Throws and bats righthanded.
Attended Auburn University.

Major League stolen bases: 1986 (3).
Heisman Trophy winner, 1985.
Named college football Player of the Year by THE SPORTING NEWS, 1985.
Named as running back on THE SPORTING NEWS College All-America Team, 1985.
Selected by Tampa Bay in 1st round (1st player selected) of 1986 NFL draft.
Selected by Birmingham in 1986 USFL territorial draft.

Year	Club	League	Pos.	G.	AB.	R.	H.	2B.	3B.	HR.	RBI.	B.A.	PO.	A.	E.	F.A.
1986—Memphis		South.	OF	53	184	30	51	9	3	7	25	.277	116	8	7	.947
1986—Kansas City		Amer.	OF	25	82	9	17	2	1	2	9	.207	29	2	4	.886
Major League Totals—1 Year				25	82	9	17	2	1	2	9	.207	29	2	4	.886

Selected by New York Yankees' organization in 2nd round of free-agent draft, June 7, 1982.
Selected by California Angels' organization in 20th round of free-agent draft, June 3, 1985.
Selected by Kansas City Royals' organization in 4th round of free-agent draft, June 2, 1986.

BROOK WALLACE JACOBY JR.

Born November 23, 1959, at Philadelphia, Pa.
Height, 5.11. Weight, 175.
Throws and bats righthanded.
Attended Ventura College, Ventura, Calif.
Son of Brook Jacoby Sr., minor league pitcher, 1956 through 1958.

Major League stolen bases—1984 (3), 1985 (2), 1986 (2). Total—7.
Led International League third basemen in total chances with 331 and double plays with 22 in 1982.

Year Club	League	Pos.	G.	AB.	R.	H.	2B.	3B.	HR.	RBI.	B.A.	PO.	A.	E.	F.A.
1979—Kingsport	Appal.	OF	8	28	3	7	2	0	0	1	.250	9	0	0	1.000
1979—Bradenton	Gulf C.	OF	42	160	24	43	11	1	3	35	.269	65	7	4	.947
1980—Anderson	S. Atl.	OF-3B	132	496	82	147	*40	4	19	*108	.296	219	30	10	.961
1980—Savannah	South.	3B	3	8	0	1	0	0	0	0	.125	0	2	0	1.000
1981—Savannah	South.	3B-OF	140	507	59	148	28	3	24	82	.292	103	232	31	.915
1981—Atlanta	Nat.	3B	11	10	0	2	0	0	0	1	.200	3	4	0	1.000
1982—Richmond	Int.	3B	134	501	74	150	21	3	18	58	.299	83	*229	*19	*.943
1983—Richmond	Int.	3B	133	489	88	154	32	2	25	100	.315	62	247	18	.945
1983—Atlanta†	Nat.	3B	4	8	0	0	0	0	0	0	.000	0	2	0	1.000
1984—Cleveland‡	Amer.	3B-SS	126	439	64	116	19	3	7	40	.264	86	188	14	.951
1985—Cleveland	Amer.	3B-2B	161	606	72	166	26	3	20	87	.274	114	319	19	.958
1986—Cleveland	Amer.	3B	158	583	83	168	30	4	17	80	.288	109	292	25	.941
National League Totals—2 Years			15	18	0	2	0	0	0	1	.111	3	6	0	1.000
American League Totals—3 Years			445	1628	219	450	75	10	44	207	.276	309	799	58	.950
Major League Totals—5 Years			460	1646	219	452	75	10	44	208	.275	312	805	58	.951

Selected by Atlanta Braves' organization in 7th round of free-agent draft, January 9, 1979.
†Traded with Outfielder Brett Butler to Cleveland Indians, October 21, 1983, completing deal in which Atlanta Braves acquired Pitcher Len Barker for three players to be named later, August 28, 1983. Cleveland acquired Pitcher Rick Behenna as partial completion of deal, September 2, 1983.
‡On disabled list, August 20, 1984 through remainder of season.

ALL-STAR GAME RECORD

Year League	Pos.	AB.	R.	H.	2B.	3B.	HR.	RBI.	B.A.	PO.	A.	E.	F.A.
1986—American	PH-3B	1	0	0	0	0	0	0	.000	1	1	0	1.000

DION JAMES

Born November 9, 1962, at Philadelphia, Pa.
Height, 6.01. Weight, 170.
Throws and bats lefthanded.

Major League stolen bases: 1983 (1), 1984 (10). Total—11.
Led California League outfielders in fielding percentage with .988 in 1981.

Year Club	League	Pos.	G.	AB.	R.	H.	2B.	3B.	HR.	RBI.	B.A.	PO.	A.	E.	F.A.
1980—Butte	Pion.	OF-1B	59	224	57	71	14	1	0	27	.317	80	4	7	.923
1980—Burlington	Midw.	OF	3	10	0	1	0	0	0	1	.100	8	1	0	1.000
1981—Stockton	Calif.	OF-1B	124	451	70	137	17	3	2	49	.304	250	10	3	.989
1982—El Paso†	Texas	OF	106	422	103	136	25	3	9	72	.322	237	9	7	.972
1983—Vancouver	P. C.	OF	129	467	84	157	29	5	8	68	.336	289	6	2	.993
1983—Milwaukee	Amer.	OF	11	20	1	2	0	0	0	1	.100	12	1	0	1.000
1984—Milwaukee	Amer.	OF	128	387	52	114	19	5	1	30	.295	252	7	3	.989
1985—Vancouver‡	P. C.	OF	10	37	2	4	2	0	0	5	.108	17	0	0	1.000
1985—Milwaukee	Amer.	OF	18	49	5	11	1	0	0	3	.224	20	0	0	1.000
1986—Vancouver	P. C.	OF-1B	130	485	85	157	25	6	6	55	.282	348	7	5	.986
Major League Totals—3 Years			157	456	58	127	20	5	1	34	.279	284	8	3	.990

Selected by Milwaukee Brewers' organization in 1st round (25th player selected) of free-agent draft, June 3, 1980.
†On disabled list, July 1 to August 1, 1982.
‡On Milwaukee disabled list, March 31 to April 28 and May 20 to September 1, 1985; included rehabilitation disability assignment to Vancouver, April 12 to April 28, 1985.

DONALD CHRISTOPHER JAMES

(Chris)

Born October 4, 1962, at Rusk, Tex.
Height, 6.01. Weight, 190.
Throws and bats righthanded.
Attended Blinn College, Brenham, Tex.
Brother of Craig James, running back with New England Patriots.

Tied for Pacific Coast League lead in being hit by pitch with 7 in 1985.
Led South Atlantic League in total bases with 257 and tied for lead in being hit by pitch with 12 in 1983.
Led Pacific Coast League outfielders in total chances with 351 in 1985.

Year Club	League	Pos.	G.	AB.	R.	H.	2B.	3B.	HR.	RBI.	B.A.	PO.	A.	E.	F.A.
1982—Bend	N'west	3B-OF	63	227	47	72	*19	3	12	50	.317	93	54	10	.936
1983—Spartanburg	S. Atl.	OF-3B	129	499	94	148	23	4	26	*121	.297	150	88	16	.937
1984—Reading	East.	*3B-OF	128	457	66	117	19	*12	8	57	.256	104	209	*39	.889
1985—Portland	P. C.	OF	135	507	78	160	35	8	11	73	.316	*328	16	7	.980
1986—Portland	P. C.	OF-3B	69	266	30	64	6	2	12	41	.241	83	44	8	.941
1986—Philadelphia†	Nat.	OF	16	46	5	13	3	0	1	5	.283	19	0	0	1.000
Major League Totals—1 Year			16	46	5	13	3	0	1	5	.283	19	0	0	1.000

Signed as free agent by Philadelphia Phillies' organization, October 30, 1981.

†On disabled list, May 6 to July 21, 1986; included rehabilitation disability assignment to Portland, July 3 to July 21, 1986.

ROBERT HARVEY JAMES
(Bob)

Born August 15, 1958, at Glendale, Calif.
Height, 6.04. Weight, 230.
Throws and bats righthanded.

Major League saves: 1983 (7), 1984 (10), 1985 (32), 1986 (14). Total—63.
Led American Association in balks with 7 in 1980.
Led Florida State League in wild pitches with 19 in 1978.
Tied for American Association lead in games started by pitchers with 26 in 1979.

Year	Club	League	G.	IP.	W.	L.	Pct.	H.	R.	ER.	SO.	BB.	ERA.
1976—Lethbridge	Pioneer	3	8	0	1	.000	7	8	4	11	9	4.50
1977—West Palm Beach†	Florida St.	21	100	5	5	.500	99	51	37	83	76	3.33
1978—West Palm Beach‡	Florida St.	21	127	10	7	.588	99	53	44	139	86	3.11
1978—Memphis	Southern	3	20	2	1	.667	14	5	1	25	11	0.45
1978—Montreal	National	4	4	0	1	.000	4	4	4	3	4	9.00
1979—Denver	Am. Assoc.	26	132	8	13	.381	139	★112	★98	122	★123	6.68
1979—Montreal	National	2	2	0	0	.000	2	3	3	1	3	13.50
1980—Denver§	Am. Assoc.	17	87	9	2	.818	66	42	37	79	74	3.83
1981—Denver	Am. Assoc.	20	57	1	2	.333	43	43	36	46	69	5.68
1982—Montreal x	National	7	9	0	0	.000	10	6	6	11	8	6.00
1982—Evansville	Am. Assoc.	9	21⅔	1	1	.500	9	6	5	30	14	2.08
1982—Detroit	American	12	19⅔	0	2	.000	22	13	11	20	8	5.03
1983—Detroit y	American	4	4	0	0	.000	5	5	5	4	3	11.25
1983—Wichita	Am. Assoc.	22	31	4	2	.667	27	17	16	40	25	4.65
1983—Montreal	National	27	50	1	0	1.000	37	17	16	56	23	2.88
1984—Montreal z	National	62	96	6	6	.500	92	47	39	91	45	3.66
1985—Chicago	American	69	110	8	7	.533	90	31	26	88	23	2.13
1986—Chicago a	American	49	58⅓	5	4	.556	61	36	34	32	23	5.25
National League Totals—5 Years		102	161	7	7	.500	145	77	68	162	83	3.80
American League Totals—4 Years		134	192	13	13	.500	178	85	76	144	57	3.56
Major League Totals—7 Years		236	353	20	20	.500	323	162	144	306	140	3.67

Selected by Montreal Expos' organization in 1st round (ninth player selected) of free-agent draft, June 8, 1976.

†On temporary inactive list, April 13 to May 6, 1977.
‡On disabled list, April 10 to April 21, 1978.
§On disabled list, July 13 to September 1, 1980.
xSold to Evansville (Detroit Tigers' organization), June 10, 1982.
ySold to Wichita (Montreal Expos' organization), May 3, 1983.
zTraded to Chicago White Sox for Infielder Vance Law, December 7, 1984.
aOn disabled list, August 5 to September 23, 1986.

STANLEY JULIAN JAVIER

Name pronounced HAAV-e-AIR.

(Stan)

Born January 9, 1965, at San Francisco Macoris, Dominican Republic.
Height, 6.00. Weight, 180.
Throws right and bats left and righthanded.
Son of Julian Javier, infielder with St. Louis Cardinals and Cincinnati Reds, 1960 through 1972.

Major League stolen bases: 1986 (8).
Led Southern League in bases on balls received with 112 in 1985.

Year	Club	League	Pos.	G.	AB.	R.	H.	2B.	3B.	HR.	RBI.	B.A.	PO.	A.	E.	F.A.
1981—Johnson City	Appal.	OF	53	144	30	36	5	4	3	19	.250	53	2	3	.948
1982—Johnson City†	Appal.	OF	57	185	45	51	3	●4	8	36	.276	94	8	4	.962
1983—Greensboro	S. Atl.	OF	129	489	109	152	★34	6	12	77	.311	250	10	15	.945
1984—New York	Amer.	OF	7	7	1	1	0	0	0	0	.143	3	0	0	1.000
1984—Nashville‡	South.	OF	76	262	40	76	17	4	7	38	.290	202	4	7	.967
1984—Columbus	Int.	OF	32	99	12	22	3	1	0	7	.222	77	4	2	.976
1985—Huntsville	South.	OF	140	486	105	138	22	8	9	64	.284	363	8	7	.981
1986—Tacoma	P. C.	OF-1B	69	248	50	81	16	2	4	51	.327	172	9	6	.968
1986—Oakland	Amer.	OF	59	114	13	23	8	0	0	8	.202	118	1	0	1.000
Major League Totals—2 Years			66	121	14	24	8	0	0	8	.198	121	1	0	1.000

Signed as free agent by St. Louis Cardinals' organization, March 26, 1981.

†Traded with shortstop Bob Meacham to New York Yankees' organization for Outfielder Bob Helsom and Pitchers Marty Mason and Steve Fincher, December 14, 1982.

‡Traded with Pitchers Jay Howell, Jose Rijo, Eric Plunk and Tim Birtsas to Oakland A's for Outfielder Rickey Henderson, Pitcher Bert Bradley and cash, December 5, 1984.

GREGORY SCOTT JEFFERIES
(Gregg)

Born August 1, 1967, at Burlingame, Calif.
Height, 5.11. Weight, 175.
Throws right and bats left and righthanded.

Led Carolina League in slugging percentage with .549 in 1986.
Named Carolina League Most Valuable Player, 1986.
Named Appalachian League Player of the Year, 1985.

Year Club	League	Pos.	G.	AB.	R.	H.	2B.	3B.	HR.	RBI.	B.A.	PO.	A.	E.	F.A.
1985—Kingsport..............	Appal.	SS-2B	47	166	27	57	18	2	3	29	.343	78	130	21	.908
1985—Columbia	S. Atl.	2B-SS	20	64	7	18	2	2	1	12	.281	28	26	2	.964
1986—Columbia	S. Atl.	SS	25	112	29	38	6	1	5	24	.339	36	83	7	.944
1986—Lynchburg............	Carol.	SS	95	390	66	138	25	9	11	80	★.354	138	273	20	.954
1986—Jackson	Texas	SS-3B	5	19	1	8	1	1	0	7	.421	7	9	1	.941

Selected by New York Mets' organization in 1st round (20th player selected) of free-agent draft, June 3, 1985.

STANLEY JEFFERSON
(Stan)

Born December 4, 1962, at New York, N.Y.
Height, 5.11. Weight, 175.
Throws right and bats left and righthanded.
Attended Bethune-Cookman College, Daytona Beach, Fla.

Led Texas League in stolen bases with 39 in 1985.
Led New York-Pennsylvania League in stolen bases with 35 in 1983.
Named outfielder on THE SPORTING NEWS College Baseball All-America Team, 1983.

Year Club	League	Pos.	G.	AB.	R.	H.	2B.	3B.	HR.	RBI.	B.A.	PO.	A.	E.	F.A.
1983—Little Falls †	NYP	OF	71	281	57	90	5	1	9	36	.320	★153	7	4	.976
1984—Lynchburg †.........	Carol.	OF	128	493	★113	142	20	●9	5	47	.288	265	11	8	.972
1985—Jackson	Texas	OF	133	524	97	145	21	6	8	30	.277	276	9	7	.976
1986—Tidewater.............	Int.	OF	95	369	60	107	19	4	2	37	.290	219	5	2	.991
1986—New York‡...........	Nat.	OF	14	24	6	5	1	0	1	3	.208	13	0	0	1.000
Major League Totals—1 Year.................			14	24	6	5	1	0	1	3	.208	13	0	0	1.000

Selected by New York Mets' organization in 1st round (20th player selected) of free-agent draft, June 6, 1983.
†Batted righthanded.
‡Traded with Outfielders Shawn Abner and Kevin Mitchell and Pitchers Kevin Armstrong and Kevin Brown to San Diego Padres for Outfielder Kevin McReynolds, Pitcher Gene Walter and Infielder Adam Ging, December 11, 1986.

GREGORY DION JELKS
(Greg)

Born August 16, 1961, at Cherokee, Ala.
Height, 6.02. Weight, 190.
Throws and bats righthanded.
Attended Gadsden State Junior College, Gadsden, Ala.

Led South Atlantic League first basemen in double plays with 100 in 1983.
Led Eastern League third basemen in errors with 38 in 1985.

Year Club	League	Pos.	G.	AB.	R.	H.	2B.	3B.	HR.	RBI.	B.A.	PO.	A.	E.	F.A.
1982—Bend......................	N'west	1B	42	140	18	25	3	1	7	30	.179	341	13	9	.975
1983—Spartanburg.........	S. Atl.	1B	123	418	81	109	24	2	24	75	.261	1078	59	●21	.982
1984—Reading.................	East.	1B-OF	92	329	35	74	13	1	6	42	.225	438	32	7	.985
1985—Reading.................	East.	3B-1B	127	447	63	119	15	2	8	55	.266	321	188	43	.905
1986—Portland................	P. C.	OF-3B-1B	63	206	37	54	10	2	8	28	.262	93	39	6	.957

Signed as free agent by Philadelphia Phillies' organization, August 11, 1981.

LARRY STEVEN JELTZ
(Steve)

Born May 28, 1959, at Paris, France.
Height, 5.11. Weight, 170.
Throws right and bats left and righthanded.
Attended University of Kansas, Lawrence, Kan.

Major League stolen bases: 1984 (2), 1985 (1), 1986 (6). Total—9.
Led Carolina League second basemen in double plays with 84 in 1981.
Tied for Carolina League lead in caught stealing with 15 in 1981.

Year Club	League	Pos.	G.	AB.	R.	H.	2B.	3B.	HR.	RBI.	B.A.	PO.	A.	E.	F.A.
1980—Spartanburg†........	S. Atl.	2B	31	107	19	31	2	1	0	8	.290	51	61	4	.966
1981—Peninsula..............	Carol.	2B	133	482	81	112	18	0	2	32	.232	★293	★369	25	.964
1982—Reading.................	East.	2B-SS-3B	126	380	61	92	10	3	7	28	.242	251	297	22	.961
1983—Portland................	P. C.	3-2-S-O	71	181	34	48	6	1	0	16	.265	106	113	11	.952
1983—Philadelphia	Nat.	2B-SS-3B	13	8	0	1	0	1	0	1	.125	4	5	0	1.000
1984—Portland................	P. C.	S-2-O-3	134	436	68	96	10	9	2	46	.220	270	349	28	.957
1984—Philadelphia	Nat.	SS-3B	28	68	7	14	0	1	1	7	.206	37	93	1	.992
1985—Philadelphia	Nat.	SS	89	196	17	37	4	1	0	12	.189	106	215	14	.958
1985—Portland................	P. C.	SS	21	71	6	21	4	1	1	9	.296	28	66	4	.959
1986—Philadelphia	Nat.	SS	145	439	44	96	11	4	0	36	.219	229	406	22	.967
Major League Totals—4 Years.................			275	711	68	148	15	7	1	56	.208	376	719	37	.967

Selected by Philadelphia Phillies' organization in 9th round of free-agent draft, June 3, 1980.
†On disabled list, July 27, 1980 through remainder of season.

THOMAS EDWARD JOHN
(Tommy)

Born May 22, 1943, at Terre Haute, Ind.
Height, 6.03. Weight, 203.
Throws left and bats righthanded.
Attended Indiana State College, Terre Haute, Ind.

Tied American League record for most hit batsmen, game, nine-innings (4), June 15, 1968.
Major League saves: 1978 (1).
Led American League in shutouts with 6 in 1980.
Tied for American League lead in shutouts with 5 in 1966 and 6 in 1967.
Tied for American League lead in wild pitches with 17 and in intentional bases on balls issued with 16 in 1970.
Named National League Comeback Player of the Year by THE SPORTING NEWS, 1976.
Named lefthanded pitcher on THE SPORTING NEWS American League All-Star Team, 1980.
Received reported $40,000 bonus to sign with Cleveland Indians, 1961.

Year—Club	League	G.	IP.	W.	L.	Pct.	H.	R.	ER.	SO.	BB.	ERA.
1961—Dubuque	Midwest	14	88	10	4	.714	74	47	31	99	59	3.17
1962—Charleston	Eastern	21	128	6	8	.429	129	67	55	114	71	3.87
1962—Jacksonville	Int'national	8	34	2	2	.500	29	20	18	27	16	4.76
1963—Charleston	Eastern	12	95	9	2	.818	85	25	17	45	12	1.61
1963—Jacksonville	Int'national	18	102	6	8	.429	115	53	40	63	39	3.53
1963—Cleveland	American	6	20	0	2	.000	23	10	5	9	6	2.25
1964—Cleveland	American	25	94	2	9	.182	97	53	41	65	35	3.93
1964—Portland†	P. Coast	13	74	6	6	.500	75	38	35	72	24	4.26
1965—Chicago	American	39	184	14	7	.667	162	67	63	126	58	3.08
1966—Chicago	American	34	223	14	11	.560	195	76	65	138	57	2.62
1967—Chicago	American	31	178	10	13	.435	143	62	49	110	47	2.48
1968—Chicago‡	American	25	177	10	5	.667	135	45	39	117	49	1.98
1969—Chicago	American	33	232	9	11	.450	230	91	84	128	90	3.26
1970—Chicago	American	37	269	12	17	.414	253	117	98	138	101	3.28
1971—Chicago§	American	38	229	13	16	.448	244	115	92	131	58	3.62
1972—Los Angeles	National	29	187	11	5	.688	172	68	60	117	40	2.89
1973—Los Angeles	National	36	218	16	7	★.696	202	88	75	116	50	3.10
1974—Los Angeles x	National	22	153	13	3	.813	133	51	44	78	42	2.59
1975—Los Angeles y	National					(Did not play)						
1976—Los Angeles	National	31	207	10	10	.500	207	76	71	91	61	3.09
1977—Los Angeles	National	31	220	20	7	.741	225	82	68	123	50	2.78
1978—Los Angeles z	National	33	213	17	10	.630	230	95	78	124	53	3.30
1979—New York	American	37	276	21	9	.700	268	109	91	111	65	2.97
1980—New York	American	36	265	22	9	.710	270	115	101	78	56	3.43
1981—New York a	American	20	140	9	8	.529	135	50	41	50	39	2.64
1982—New York b-California	American	37	221⅔	14	12	.538	239	102	91	68	39	3.69
1983—California	American	34	234⅔	11	13	.458	★287	126	113	65	49	4.33
1984—California	American	32	181⅓	7	13	.350	223	97	91	47	56	4.52
1985—California c-Oakland	American	23	86⅓	4	10	.286	117	59	53	25	28	5.53
1985—Modesto	California	2	4	0	0	.000	12	8	7	11	6	5.73
1985—Madison d	Midwest	1	6	0	0	.000	4	2	2	3	4	3.00
1986—New York e	American	13	70⅔	5	3	.625	73	27	23	28	15	2.93
1986—Fort Lauderdale f	Florida St.	3	13⅔	2	0	1.000	7	2	0	7	1	0.00
American League Totals—17 Years		500	308⅔	177	168	.513	3094	1321	1140	1434	848	3.33
National League Totals—6 Years		182	1198	87	42	.674	1169	460	396	649	296	2.97
Major League Totals—23 Years		682	4279⅔	264	210	.557	4263	1781	1536	2083	1144	3.23

Signed as free agent by Cleveland Indians' organization, June 12, 1961.

†Traded to Chicago White Sox with Catcher John Romano and Outfielder Tommie Agee for Catcher Camilo Carreon and Outfielder Rocky Colavito, January 20, 1965, as part of three-way deal which saw Chicago obtain Colavito from Kansas City Athletics earlier same day for Outfielders Jim Landis and Mike Hershberger and a pitcher to be named later; Kansas City acquired Pitcher Fred Talbot to complete deal, February 10, 1965.

‡On disabled list, August 22, 1968 through remainder of season.

§Traded with Infielder Steve Huntz to Los Angeles Dodgers for Infielder-Outfielder Richie Allen, December 2, 1971.

xOn disabled list, July 17, 1974 through remainder of season.

yOn disabled list, April 6, 1975 through remainder of season.

zGranted free agency, November 17, 1978; signed by New York Yankees, November 21, 1978.

aOn disabled list, June 1 to August 5, 1981.

bTraded to California Angels for a player to be named later, August 31, 1982; New York Yankees acquired Pitcher Dennis Rasmussen to complete deal, November 24 1982.

cReleased, June 19, 1985; signed by Modesto (Oakland A's organization), July 12, 1985.

dGranted free agency, November 12, 1985; signed by New York Yankees, May 2, 1986.

eOn disabled list, June 9 to August 8, 1986; included rehabilitation disability assignment to Fort Lauderdale, July 27 to August 8, 1986.

fGranted free agency, November 12, 1986.

DIVISION SERIES RECORD

Year—Club	League	G.	IP.	W.	L.	Pct.	H.	R.	ER.	SO.	BB.	ERA.
1981—New York	American	1	7	0	1	.000	8	5	5	0	2	6.43

CHAMPIONSHIP SERIES RECORD

Established Championship Series record for most runs allowed, five-game Series (9), 1982.
Tied Championship Series record for most games won, total Series (4).
Tied National League Championship Series record for most complete games, total Series (2).

Year—Club	League	G.	IP.	W.	L.	Pct.	H.	R.	ER.	SO.	BB.	ERA.
1977—Los Angeles	National	2	13⅔	1	0	1.000	11	5	1	11	5	0.66

Year Club	League	G.	IP.	W.	L.	Pct.	H.	R.	ER.	SO.	BB.	ERA.
1978—Los Angeles	National	1	9	1	0	1.000	4	0	0	4	2	0.00
1980—New York	American	1	6⅔	0	0	.000	8	2	2	3	1	2.70
1981—New York	American	1	6	1	0	1.000	6	1	1	3	1	1.50
1982—California	American	2	12⅓	1	1	.500	11	9	7	6	6	5.11
Championship Series Totals—5 Years		7	47⅔	4	1	.800	40	17	11	27	15	2.08

WORLD SERIES RECORD

Year Club	League	G.	IP.	W.	L.	Pct.	H.	R.	ER.	SO.	BB.	ERA.
1977—Los Angeles	National	1	6	0	1	.000	9	5	4	7	3	6.00
1978—Los Angeles	National	2	14⅔	1	0	1.000	14	8	5	6	4	3.07
1981—New York	American	3	13	1	0	1.000	11	1	1	8	0	0.69
World Series Totals—3 Years		6	33⅔	2	1	.667	34	14	10	21	7	2.67

ALL-STAR GAME RECORD

Year League	IP.	W.	L.	Pct.	H.	R.	ER.	SO.	BB.	ERA.
1968—American	⅔	0	0	.000	1	0	0	0	0	0.00
1980—American	2⅓	0	1	.000	4	3	3	1	0	11.57
All-Star Game Totals—2 Years	3	0	1	.000	5	3	3	1	0	9.00

Member of National League All-Star Team for 1978 game; did not play.
Member of American League All-Star Team for 1979 game; did not play.

CLIFFORD JOHNSON JR.
(Cliff)

Born July 22, 1947, at San Antonio, Tex.
Height, 6.04. Weight, 225.
Throws and bats righthanded.
Brother-in-law of Mike Easler, outfielder with Philadelphia Phillies;
Cousin of Elijah Johnson, infielder-outfielder in Houston Astros' and Baltimore Orioles'
organizations, 1961 through 1970 and 1972.

Established major league record for most home runs by pinch-hitter, lifetime (20).
Tied major league records for most home runs, inning (2) and most total bases, inning (8), June 30, 1977 (eighth inning).
Tied modern major league record for most long hits, inning (2), May 31, 1975 (eighth inning) and June 30, 1977 (eighth inning).
Major League stolen bases: 1975 (1), 1979 (2), 1981 (5), 1982 (1). Total—9.
Hit three home runs in a game, June 30, 1977.
Led National League in passed balls with 12 in 1976.
Led American Association in total bases with 285 and being hit by pitch with 16 in 1973.
Led American Association in passed balls with 17 and tied for lead in errors with 13 in 1972.
Tied for Southern League lead in being hit by pitch with 8 in 1972.
Tied for Southern League lead in passed balls with 15 in 1972.
Tied for Appalachian League lead in double plays by catchers with 3 in 1967.
Named American Association Most Valuable Player, 1973.
Named Carolina League Most Valuable Player, 1970.

Year Club	League	Pos.	G.	AB.	R.	H.	2B.	3B.	HR.	RBI.	B.A.	PO.	A.	E.	F.A.
1967—Cocoa	Fla. St.	C-OF	53	156	13	41	5	1	4	20	.263	168	13	10	.948
1967—Covington	Appal.	OF-C-1B	36	110	21	34	7	2	5	24	.309	103	10	6	.950
1968—Cocoa	Fla. St.	★C-OF-1B	117	353	60	102	17	3	10	61	.289	641	55	★26	.964
1969—Peninsula	Carol.	C	103	327	37	75	16	1	11	54	.229	615	68	21	.970
1970—Raleigh-Durham	Carol.	C-OF	102	343	74	114	24	0	★27	★91	.332	474	40	9	.983
1970—Oklahoma City	A. A.	C-OF-1B	22	55	12	21	4	1	1	5	.382	63	9	2	.973
1971—Oklahoma City	A. A.	C-1B	31	105	16	26	5	2	5	15	.248	219	20	2	.992
1971—Columbus	South.	C-1B	58	164	16	30	10	0	4	21	.183	350	35	5	.987
1972—Columbus	South.	C-3B-1B	42	160	28	46	11	2	10	38	.288	235	36	8	.971
1972—Oklahoma City	A. A.	C-1B	89	313	55	88	12	5	17	59	.281	600	59	15	.978
1972—Houston	Nat.	C	5	4	0	1	0	0	0	0	.250	6	0	0	1.000
1973—Denver	A. A.	1B	133	490	★105	148	30	4	★33	★117	.302	132	15	4	.974
1973—Houston	Nat.	1B	7	20	6	6	2	0	2	6	.300	47	2	0	1.000
1974—Houston	Nat.	1B	83	171	26	39	4	1	10	29	.228	270	18	4	.986
1975—Houston	Nat.	1B-C-OF	122	340	52	94	16	1	20	65	.276	604	38	12	.982
1976—Houston	Nat.	C-OF-1B	108	318	36	72	21	2	10	49	.226	468	35	9	.982
1977—Houston†	Nat.	OF-1B	51	144	22	43	8	0	10	23	.299	113	11	3	.976
1977—New York	Amer.	C-1B	56	142	24	42	8	0	12	31	.296	145	14	1	¢994
1978—New York	Amer.	C-1B	76	174	20	32	9	1	6	19	.184	71	10	2	.976
1979—N.Y.‡-Cleve.	Amer.	C	100	304	48	82	16	0	20	67	.270	10	1	0	1.000
1980—Cleveland§	Amer.	DH	54	174	25	40	3	1	6	28	.230	0	0	0	.000
1980—Chicago x	Nat.	1B-C	68	196	28	46	8	0	10	34	.235	469	16	4	.992
1981—Oakland	Amer.	1B	84	273	40	71	8	0	17	59	.260	42	1	0	1.000
1982—Oakland yz	Amer.	1B	73	214	19	51	10	0	7	31	.238	66	8	1	.987
1983—Toronto	Amer.	1B	142	407	59	108	23	1	22	76	.265	47	4	0	1.000
1984—Toronto a	Amer.	1B	127	359	51	109	23	1	16	61	.304	26	0	0	1.000
1985—Tex.bc-Tor.	Amer.	1B	106	369	35	96	11	1	13	66	.260	17	1	1	.947
1986—Toronto de	Amer.	1B	107	336	48	84	12	1	15	55	.250	8	1	0	1.000
National League Totals—7 Years			444	1193	170	301	59	4	62	206	.252	1977	120	32	.985
American League Totals—10 Years			925	2752	369	715	129	6	134	493	.260	432	40	5	.990
Major League Totals—15 Years			1369	3945	539	1016	188	10	196	699	.258	2409	160	37	.986

Selected by Houston Astros' organization in 5th round of free-agent draft, June 7, 1966.

†Traded to New York Yankees for Infielder Mike Fischlin, Pitcher Randy Niemann and a player to be named later, June 15, 1977; Houston Astros acquired First Baseman-Outfielder Dave Bergman to complete deal, November 23, 1977.

‡Traded to Cleveland Indians for Pitcher Don Hood, June 15, 1979.

§Traded to Chicago Cubs for two players to be named later, June 23, 1980; Cleveland Indians acquired Outfielder-First Baseman Karl Pagel and cash to complete deal, June 30, 1980.

xTraded with Infielder Keith Drumright to Oakland A's for Pitcher Mike King, December 11, 1980.

yOn disabled list, August 5 to September 1, 1982.

zTraded to Toronto Blue Jays for Outfielder Al Woods, November 5, 1982.

aGranted free agency, November 8, 1984; signed by Texas Rangers, December 20, 1984 (Pitcher Tom Henke selected from player compensation pool by Texas Rangers' organization, January 24, 1985.)

bOn disabled list, June 15 to July 22, 1985.

cTraded to Toronto Blue Jays for three players to be named later, August 28, 1985; Texas Rangers acquired Pitchers Matt Williams and Jeff Mays, August 29, 1985, and Pitcher Greg Ferlenda, November 14, 1985, to complete deal.

dOn disabled list, July 23 to August 7, 1986.

eGranted free agency, November 12, 1986.

DIVISION SERIES RECORD

Year Club	League	Pos.	G.	AB.	R.	H.	2B.	3B.	HR.	RBI.	B.A.	PO.	A.	E.	F.A.
1981—Oakland	Amer.	DH	2	7	0	2	1	0	0	0	.286	0	0	0	.000

CHAMPIONSHIP SERIES RECORD

Tied Championship Series record for most clubs, total Series (3).

Year Club	League	Pos.	G.	AB.	R.	H.	2B.	3B.	HR.	RBI.	B.A.	PO.	A.	E.	F.A.
1977—New York	Amer.	DH-PH	5	15	2	6	2	0	1	2	.400	0	0	0	.000
1978—New York	Amer.	PH	1	1	0	0	0	0	0	0	.000	0	0	0	.000
1981—Oakland	Amer.	DH	2	6	0	0	0	0	0	0	.000	0	0	0	.000
1985—Toronto	Amer.	DH-PH	7	19	1	7	2	0	0	2	.368	0	0	0	.000
Championship Series Totals—4 Years			15	41	3	13	4	0	1	4	.317	0	0	0	.000

WORLD SERIES RECORD

Year Club	League	Pos.	G.	AB.	R.	H.	2B.	3B.	HR.	RBI.	B.A.	PO.	A.	E.	F.A.
1977—New York	Amer.	PH-C	2	1	0	0	0	0	0	0	.000	0	0	0	.000
1978—New York	Amer.	PH	2	2	0	0	0	0	0	0	.000	0	0	0	.000
World Series Totals—2 Years			4	3	0	0	0	0	0	0	.000	0	0	0	.000

DAVID WAYNE JOHNSON
(Dave)

Born October 24, 1959, at Baltimore, Md.
Height, 5.10. Weight, 179.
Throws and bats righthanded.
Attended Community College of Baltimore, Baltimore, Md.

Year Club	League	G.	IP.	W.	L.	Pct.	H.	R.	ER.	SO.	BB.	ERA.
1982—Greenwood	S. Atlantic	16	58⅓	4	4	.500	50	32	25	41	41	3.86
1983—Alexandria	Carolina	46	113⅔	7	5	.583	100	52	38	95	42	3.01
1984—Prince William	Carolina	13	88⅓	7	5	.583	60	22	13	48	35	1.32
1984—Nashua	Eastern	12	83⅔	1	8	.111	95	52	45	47	31	4.84
1985—Nashua	Eastern	34	153	6	9	.400	129	66	53	84	45	3.12
1986—Hawaii	P. Coast	22	150⅓	8	7	.533	150	68	53	71	35	*3.17

Selected by Kansas City Royals' organization in 5th round of free-agent draft, January 13, 1981.
Signed as free agent by Pittsburgh Pirates' organization, June 10, 1982.

HOWARD MICHAEL JOHNSON

Born November 29, 1960, at Clearwater, Fla.
Height, 5.10. Weight, 175.
Throws right and bats right and lefthanded.
Attended St. Petersburg Junior College, St. Petersburg, Fla.

Major League stolen bases: 1982 (7), 1984 (10), 1985 (6), 1986 (8). Total—31.
Led Florida State League in sacrifice hits with 16 in 1980.
Led American Association third basemen in double plays with 19 in 1982.
Led Florida State League third basemen in double plays with 21 in 1980.

Year Club	League	Pos.	G.	AB.	R.	H.	2B.	3B.	HR.	RBI.	B.A.	PO.	A.	E.	F.A.
1979—Lakeland	Fla. St.	3B-SS-OF	132	456	49	107	9	6	3	49	.235	130	240	36	.911
1980—Lakeland	Fla. St.	3B	130	474	83	135	*28	1	10	69	.285	*110	*264	13	*.966
1981—Birmingham	South.	3B	138	488	84	130	28	7	22	83	.266	103	218	26	.925
1982—Evansville	A. A.	3B-OF	98	366	70	116	16	4	23	67	.317	69	139	23	.900
1982—Detroit	Amer.	3B-OF	54	155	23	49	5	0	4	14	.316	36	40	7	.916
1983—Detroit	Amer.	3B	27	66	11	14	0	0	3	5	.212	10	30	7	.851
1983—Evansville†	A. A.	3B	3	9	1	2	1	0	0	0	.222	1	11	2	.857
1984—Detroit‡	Amer.	3-S-1-O	116	355	43	88	14	1	12	50	.248	63	150	14	.938
1985—New York	Nat.	3B-SS-OF	126	389	38	94	18	4	11	46	.242	78	190	18	.937
1986—New York§	Nat.	3B-SS-OF	88	220	30	54	14	0	10	39	.245	52	136	20	.904
American League Totals—3 Years			197	576	77	151	19	1	19	69	.262	109	220	28	.922
National League Totals—2 Years			214	609	68	148	32	4	21	85	.243	130	326	38	.923
Major League Totals—5 Years			411	1185	145	299	51	5	40	154	.252	239	546	66	.922

Selected by New York Yankees' organization in 23rd round of free-agent draft, June 6, 1978.
Selected by Detroit Tigers' organization in secondary phase of free-agent draft, January 9, 1979.
†On disabled list, June 2 to August 8, 1983.
‡Traded to New York Mets for Pitcher Walt Terrell, December 7, 1984.
§On disabled list, June 2 to June 23, 1986.

CHAMPIONSHIP SERIES RECORD

Year Club	League	Pos.	G.	AB.	R.	H.	2B.	3B.	HR.	RBI.	B.A.	PO.	A.	E.	F.A.
1986—New York	Nat.	PH	2	2	0	0	0	0	0	0	.000	0	0	0	.000

WORLD SERIES RECORD

Year Club	League	Pos.	G.	AB.	R.	H.	2B.	3B.	HR.	RBI.	B.A.	PO.	A.	E.	F.A.
1984—Detroit	Amer.	PH	1	1	0	0	0	0	0	0	.000	0	0	0	.000
1986—New York	Nat.	3B-PH-SS	2	5	0	0	0	0	0	0	.000	1	0	0	1.000
World Series Totals—2 Years			3	6	0	0	0	0	0	0	.000	1	0	0	1.000

JOHN HENRY JOHNSON

Born August 21, 1956, at Houston, Tex.
Height, 6.02. Weight, 210.
Throws and bats lefthanded.

Pitched 5-0 no-hit victory against Calgary, May 2, 1985.
Major League saves: 1980 (4), 1981 (2), 1983 (1), 1984 (1), 1986 (1). Total—9.

Year Club	League	G.	IP.	W.	L.	Pct.	H.	R.	ER.	SO.	BB.	ERA.
1974—Great Falls	Pioneer	14	33	2	1	.667	25	12	10	33	25	2.73
1975—Cedar Rapids	Midwest	22	127	4	12	.250	127	72	53	89	49	3.76
1976—Cedar Rapids	Midwest	20	131	13	2	.867	93	42	28	94	50	1.92
1977—Fresno†	California	23	149	14	2	*.875	142	79	56	155	64	*3.38
1978—Oakland	American	33	186	11	10	.524	164	81	70	91	82	3.39
1979—Oakland‡-Texas	American	31	167	4	14	.222	168	95	86	96	72	4.63
1980—Charleston	Int'national	16	77	3	9	.250	84	49	33	55	35	3.86
1980—Texas	American	33	39	2	2	.500	27	12	10	44	15	2.31
1981—Texas	American	24	24	3	1	.750	19	7	7	8	6	2.63
1982—Pawtucket§ x	Int'national	29	41⅓	3	1	.750	37	21	19	45	23	4.04
1983—Boston	American	34	53⅓	3	2	.600	58	28	22	51	20	3.71
1984—Boston yz	American	30	63⅔	1	2	.333	64	26	25	57	27	3.53
1985—Hawaii a—Vancouver	P. Coast	23	109	4	7	.364	116	64	60	70	44	4.95
1986—Vancouver b	P. Coast	22	32⅓	2	0	1.000	13	1	1	35	16	0.28
1986—Milwaukee	American	19	44	2	1	.667	43	15	13	42	10	2.66
Major League Totals—7 Years		204	577	26	32	.448	543	264	233	389	232	3.63

Selected by San Francisco Giants' organization in 15th round of free-agent draft, June 5, 1974.
†Traded with Outfielder Gary Thomasson, Catcher Gary Alexander, Pitchers Dave Heaverlo, Alan Wirth and Phillip Huffman, a player to be named later and cash estimated at $390,000 to Oakland A's for Pitcher Vida Blue, March 15, 1978; Oakland acquired Shortstop Mario Guerrero to complete deal, April 7, 1978.
‡Traded to Texas Rangers for Third Baseman Dave Chalk and Catcher Mike Heath, June 15, 1979.
§Traded to Pawtucket (Boston Red Sox' organization) for Pitcher Mike Smithson, April 9, 1982.
xOn disabled list, May 30 to June 28 and August 11 to August 21, 1982.
yOn disabled list, June 18 to July 3, 1984.
zReleased, April 1, 1985; signed by Hawaii (Pittsburgh Pirates' organization), April 11, 1985.
aReleased, July 26, 1985; signed by Vancouver (Milwaukee Brewers' organization), August 26, 1985.
bOn disabled list, April 11 to April 30, 1986.

JOSEPH RICHARD JOHNSON
(Joe)

Born October 30, 1961, at Brookline, Mass.
Height, 6.02. Weight, 195.
Throws and bats righthanded.
Attended University of Maine, Orono, Me.

Year Club	League	G.	IP.	W.	L.	Pct.	H.	R.	ER.	SO.	BB.	ERA.
1982—Savannah	Southern	6	28⅔	2	1	.667	32	14	12	15	10	3.77
1983—Savannah	Southern	26	157⅓	10	9	.526	162	82	66	94	59	3.78
1983—Richmond	Int'national	1	5	0	0	.000	7	4	4	2	3	7.20
1984—Richmond	Int'national	4	20⅓	0	2	.000	27	18	13	11	4	5.75
1984—Greenville	Southern	24	151	8	10	.444	155	70	63	72	41	3.75
1985—Greenville	Southern	12	59⅔	6	3	.667	78	30	27	29	12	4.07
1985—Richmond	Int'national	9	72	7	1	.875	60	22	17	50	10	2.13
1985—Atlanta	National	15	85⅔	4	4	.500	95	44	39	34	24	4.10
1986—Atlanta†	National	17	87	6	7	.462	101	58	48	49	35	4.97
1986—Toronto	American	16	88	7	2	.778	94	39	38	39	22	3.89
National League Totals—2 Years		32	172⅔	10	11	.476	196	102	87	83	59	4.53
American League Totals—1 Year		16	88	7	2	.778	94	39	38	39	22	3.89
Major League Totals—2 Years		48	260⅔	17	13	.567	290	141	125	122	81	4.32

Selected by Atlanta Braves' organization in 2nd round of free-agent draft, June 7, 1982.
†Traded to Toronto Blue Jays for Pitcher Jim Acker, July 6, 1986.

MITCHELL DREW JOHNSON
(Mitch)

Born August 2, 1962, at Columbia, Pa.
Height, 6.05. Weight, 218.
Throws and bats righthanded.
Attending Penn State University, York, Pa.

Led Carolina League in complete games with 14 in 1983.
Tied for Florida State League lead in wild pitches with 18 in 1981.
Tied for New York-Pennsylvania League lead in games started by pitchers with 14 in 1980.

Year	Club	League	G.	IP.	W.	L.	Pct.	H.	R.	ER.	SO.	BB.	ERA.
1980—Elmira		NYP	15	69	5	3	.625	69	32	20	28	35	2.61
1981—Winter Haven		Florida St.	32	118	4	8	.333	130	73	52	79	58	3.97
1982—Winter Haven		Florida St.	34	118⅓	6	9	.400	122	70	62	65	65	4.72
1983—Winston-Salem		Carolina	31	★214	15	8	.652	197	97	74	146	59	3.11
1984—New Britain		Eastern	26	174⅓	11	10	.524	160	60	56	94	30	2.89
1985—Pawtucket		Int'national	30	156⅔	5	●13	.278	174	93	78	63	37	4.48
1986—Pawtucket		Int'national	18	84⅔	4	5	.444	101	53	49	36	28	5.21

Selected by Boston Red Sox' organization in 3rd round of free-agent draft, June 3, 1980.

RONDIN ALLEN JOHNSON

Born December 16, 1958, at Bremerton, Wash.
Height, 5.10, Weight, 160.
Throws right and bats left and righthanded.
Attended University of Washington, Seattle, Wash.

Tied for Gulf Coast League lead in caught stealing with 10 in 1980.
Led American Association second basemen in total chances with 581 in 1986.
Led Florida State League second basemen in fielding percentage with .979 in 1981.
Led Southern League second basemen in double plays with 89 in 1983.

Year	Club	League	Pos.	G.	AB.	R.	H.	2B.	3B.	HR.	RBI.	B.A.	PO.	A.	E.	F.A.
1980—Sarasota Royals	Gulf C.		2B	★63	★266	43	70	5	2	0	21	.263	154	★183	12	★.966
1981—Fort Myers†	Fla. St.		2B-SS	107	424	49	92	16	3	0	29	.217	183	339	14	.974
1982—Jacksonville	South.		2B	128	494	59	109	8	3	1	28	.221	268	315	9	★.985
1983—Jacksonville	South.		2B	140	555	74	147	12	5	0	30	.265	274	●416	18	★.975
1984—Omaha	A. A.		2B	131	488	60	123	18	4	1	49	.252	219	342	17	.971
1985—Omaha‡	A. A.		2B	99	366	44	86	8	1	0	22	.235	181	257	10	.978
1986—Omaha§	A. A.		2B	127	484	57	140	15	★14	1	60	.289	★239	★333	9	★.985
1986—Kansas City	Amer.		2B	11	31	1	8	0	1	0	2	.258	14	32	0	1.000
Major League Total—1 Year				11	31	1	8	0	1	0	2	.258	14	32	0	1.000

Selected by Kansas City Royals' organization in 6th round of free-agent draft, June 3, 1980.
†Batted righthanded.
‡On disabled list, April 29 to May 10 and July 9 to July 26, 1985.
§On disabled list, April 11 to April 21, 1986.

ROY EDWARD JOHNSON

Born June 27, 1959, at Parkin, Ark.
Height, 6.04. Weight, 220.
Throws and bats lefthanded.
Attended Tennessee State University, Nashville, Tenn.

Major League stolen bases: 1984 (1).
Tied for New York-Pennsylvania League lead in caught stealing with 6 in 1980.

Year	Club	League	Pos.	G.	AB.	R.	H.	2B.	3B.	HR.	RBI.	B.A.	PO.	A.	E.	F.A.
1980—Jamestown	NYP		OF	36	126	29	41	6	3	6	19	.325	63	1	3	.955
1980—W. Palm Beach	Fla. St.		OF	24	85	11	19	4	1	1	12	.224	44	1	1	.978
1981—Memphis	South.		OF	130	477	83	126	19	10	18	90	.264	★340	8	11	.969
1982—Wichita	A. A.		OF	102	376	73	138	19	6	14	76	★.367	238	4	8	.968
1982—Montreal	Nat.		OF	17	32	2	7	2	0	0	2	.219	18	0	0	1.000
1983—Wichita†	A. A.		OF	79	248	39	72	13	1	5	43	.290	89	1	3	.968
1984—Indianapolis‡	A. A.		OF	107	356	48	96	17	4	9	49	.270	160	3	4	.976
1984—Montreal	Nat.		OF	16	33	2	5	2	0	1	2	.152	15	0	1	.938
1985—Montreal	Nat.		OF	3	5	0	0	0	0	0	0	.000	0	0	0	.000
1985—Indianapolis§x	A. A.		OF	26	90	15	25	6	0	3	12	.278	51	3	4	.931
1985—Jacksonville yz	South.		OF	78	274	39	69	13	1	11	37	.252	144	3	2	.987
1986—Huntsville	South.		OF	52	183	33	63	12	1	5	27	.344	91	3	4	.959
1986—Tacoma	P. C.		OF	68	248	47	85	16	6	9	44	.343	95	1	5	.950
Major League Totals—3 Years				36	70	4	12	4	0	1	4	.171	33	0	1	.971

Selected by Montreal Expos' organization in 5th round of free-agent draft, June 3, 1980.
†On temporary inactive list, April 19 to May 21, 1983.
‡On disabled list, May 24 to June 15, 1984.
§On suspended list, May 16 to May 23, 1985.
xOn disabled list, May 25 to June 5, 1985.
yDrafted by Buffalo (Chicago White Sox' organization), December 11, 1985.
zReleased, April 5, 1986; signed by Huntsville (Oakland A's organization), April 23, 1986.

WALLACE DARNELL JOHNSON
(Wally)

Born December 25, 1956, at Gary, Ind.
Height, 5.11. Weight, 173.
Throws right and bats righthanded.
Attended Indiana State University, Terre Haute, Ind.

Major League stolen bases: 1981 (1), 1982 (4), 1983 (1), 1986 (6). Total—12.
Led Florida State League in stolen bases with 58 and caught stealing with 22 in 1980.
Named Florida State League Southern Division Most Valuable Player, 1980.

Year Club	League	Pos.	G.	AB.	R.	H.	2B.	3B.	HR.	RBI.	B.A.	PO.	A.	E.	F.A.
1979—Jamestown	NYP	2B	70	*284	60	96	11	6	6	42	.338	157	155	17	.948
1980—W. Palm Beach	Fla. St.	2B-OF	126	488	86	*163	17	5	3	49	*.334	294	350	31	.954
1980—Memphis	South.	2B	4	13	1	1	1	0	0	0	.077	5	12	0	1.000
1981—Memphis†	South.	2B-OF	28	102	15	37	9	0	1	18	.363	44	52	10	.906
1981—Denver	A. A.	2B-OF	59	215	39	64	13	4	0	16	.298	72	116	7	.964
1981—Montreal	Nat.	PH	11	9	1	2	0	1	0	3	.222	1	2	0	1.000
1982—Montreal	Nat.	2B	36	57	5	11	0	2	0	2	.193	22	18	2	.952
1982—Wichita	A. A.	2B-OF	76	298	62	105	12	4	6	36	.352	128	79	12	.945
1983—Wichita	A. A.	OF	16	53	7	14	3	1	0	6	.264	26	0	2	.929
1983—Mont.‡-S. F.	Nat.	2B	10	10	1	2	0	0	0	1	.200	3	2	0	1.000
1983—Phoenix§	P. C.	2B	63	229	42	66	8	2	2	26	.288	105	150	15	.944
1984—Jacksonville	South.	DH	31	117	18	35	5	0	1	12	.299	0	0	0	.000
1984—Indianapolis	A. A.	OF-1B-2B	97	357	50	101	12	2	3	38	.283	350	39	5	.987
1984—Montreal	Nat.	1B	17	24	3	5	0	0	0	4	.208	27	3	1	.968
1985—Indianapolis x	A. A.	OF-1B-2B	127	431	68	133	13	3	3	36	.309	240	14	5	.981
1986—Indianapolis	A. A.	1B-OF	61	225	27	58	15	4	0	26	.258	188	14	3	.985
1986—Montreal	Nat.	1B	61	127	13	36	3	1	1	10	.283	204	17	2	.991
Major League Totals—5 Years			135	227	23	56	3	4	1	20	.247	257	42	5	.984

Selected by Montreal Expos' organization in 6th round of free-agent draft, June 5, 1979.
†On disabled list, April 29 to May 15, 1981.
‡Traded to San Francisco Giants for Outfielder Mike Vail, May 25, 1983.
§Released, March 27, 1984; signed by Jacksonville (Montreal Expos' organization), April 1, 1984.
xGranted free agency, October 15, 1985; re-signed by Expos, January 22, 1986.

DIVISION SERIES RECORD

Year Club	League	Pos.	G.	AB.	R.	H.	2B.	3B.	HR.	RBI.	B.A.	PO.	A.	E.	F.A.
1981—Montreal	Nat.	PH	2	2	0	1	0	0	0	1	.500	0	0	0	.000

ALFORNIA JONES
(Al)

Born February 10, 1959, at Charleston, Miss.
Height, 5.11. Weight, 178.
Throws and bats righthanded.
Attended Alcorn State University, Lorman, Miss.

Major League saves: 1984 (5).
Led Midwest League in games finished in relief with 50 in 1983.

Year Club	League	G.	IP.	W.	L.	Pct.	H.	R.	ER.	SO.	BB.	ERA.
1981—Sarasota White Sox	Gulf Coast	11	58	3	5	.375	50	19	9	41	20	1.40
1982—Appleton	Midwest	26	57	2	4	.333	53	27	21	64	34	3.32
1983—Appleton	Midwest	*55	102	11	1	*.917	54	13	11	124	39	0.97
1983—Chicago	American	2	2⅓	0	0	.000	3	1	1	2	2	3.86
1984—Denver	Am. Assoc.	24	28⅔	2	3	.400	26	16	15	20	20	4.71
1984—Chicago	American	20	20⅓	1	1	.500	23	10	10	15	11	4.43
1985—Chicago†	American	5	6	1	0	1.000	3	2	1	2	3	1.50
1985—Buffalo	Am. Assoc.	4	2⅔	0	1	.000	3	3	3	1	3	10.13
1986—Buffalo‡§	Am. Assoc.	27	47⅓	2	4	.333	52	27	24	31	25	4.56
1986—Vancouver	P. Coast	17	24	2	0	1.000	20	6	4	21	11	1.50
Major League Totals—3 Years		27	28⅔	2	1	.667	29	13	12	19	16	3.77

Selected by Chicago White Sox' organization in 13th round of free-agent draft, June 8, 1981.
†On disabled list, April 22 to September 3, 1985; included rehabilitation disability assignment to Buffalo, August 19 to September 3, 1985.
‡Loaned to Vancouver (Milwaukee Brewers' organization), July 17, 1986; returned, July 23, 1986.
§Traded with Outfielder Tom Hartley to Milwaukee Brewers for Pitcher Ray Searage, July 23, 1986.

BARRY LOUIS JONES

Born February 15, 1963, at Centerville, Ind.
Height, 6.02. Weight, 215.
Throws and bats righthanded.
Attended Indiana University, Bloomington, Ind.

Major League saves: 1986 (3).

Year Club	League	G.	IP.	W.	L.	Pct.	H.	R.	ER.	SO.	BB.	ERA.
1984—Watertown	NYP	14	86⅔	6	3	.667	75	41	33	61	49	3.43
1985—Prince William	Carolina	28	37⅓	3	2	.600	26	7	5	42	19	1.21
1985—Nashua	Eastern	23	29	3	2	.600	19	6	5	24	10	1.55
1985—Hawaii	P. Coast	1	3	0	0	.000	5	5	3	2	1	9.00

Year Club	League	G.	IP.	W.	L.	Pct.	H.	R.	ER.	SO.	BB.	ERA.
1986—Hawaii	P. Coast	35	48	3	6	.333	41	20	19	28	20	3.56
1986—Pittsburgh	National	26	37⅓	3	4	.429	29	16	12	29	21	2.89
Major League Totals—1 Year		26	37⅓	3	4	.429	29	16	12	29	21	2.89

Selected by Texas Rangers' organization in 6th round of free-agent draft, June 8, 1981.
Selected by Pittsburgh Pirates' organization in 3rd round of free-agent draft, June 4, 1984.

CHRISTOPHER CARLOS JONES
(Chris)

Born December 16, 1965, at Utica, N. Y.
Height, 6.02. Weight, 190.
Throws and bats righthanded.

Year Club	League	Pos.	G.	AB.	R.	H.	2B.	3B.	HR.	RBI.	B.A.	PO.	A.	E.	F.A.
1984—Billings	Pion.	3B	21	73	8	11	2	0	2	13	.151	6	27	5	.868
1985—Billings	Pion.	OF	63	240	43	62	12	5	4	33	.258	112	4	★13	.899
1986—Cedar Rapids	Midw.	OF	128	473	65	117	13	9	20	78	.247	218	15	11	.955

Selected by Cincinnati Reds' organization in 3rd round of free-agent draft, June 4, 1984.

CHRISTOPHER DALE JONES
(Chris)

Born July 13, 1957, at Los Angeles, Calif.
Height, 6.00. Weight, 183.
Throws and bats lefthanded.
Attended San Diego State University, San Diego, Calif.

Major League stolen bases: 1986 (1).

Year Club	League	Pos.	G.	AB.	R.	H.	2B.	3B.	HR.	RBI.	B.A.	PO.	A.	E.	F.A.
1979—Sarasota Astros	Gulf C.	OF-1B	31	93	15	24	3	1	0	6	.258	76	3	4	.952
1980—Daytona Beach	Fla. St.	OF-1B	124	413	77	103	9	9	5	54	.249	133	6	4	.972
1981—Columbus	South.	OF	●143	535	102	171	25	9	7	65	.320	178	9	2	★.989
1982—Tucson†	P. C.	OF	36	115	17	26	6	2	0	9	.226	58	1	2	.967
1983—Tucson	P. C.	OF	86	234	41	66	8	5	3	21	.282	119	2	0	1.000
1984—Tucson	P. C.	OF	120	452	78	138	29	10	6	49	.305	262	6	2	.993
1985—Tucson	P. C.	OF	76	281	44	95	21	8	2	33	.338	142	7	1	.993
1985—Houston‡	Nat.	OF	31	25	0	5	0	0	0	1	.200	15	0	0	1.000
1986—Phoenix	P. C.	OF	112	364	76	106	24	7	8	55	.291	177	1	3	.983
1986—San Francisco	Nat.	PR-PH	3	1	0	0	0	0	0	0	.000	0	0	0	.000
Major League Totals—2 Years			34	26	0	5	0	0	0	1	.192	15	0	0	1.000

Selected by Baltimore Orioles' organization in 23rd round of free-agent draft, June 7, 1977.
Selected by Houston Astros' organization in 25th round of free-agent draft, June 5, 1979.
†On disabled list, May 5 to August 4, 1982.
‡Released, November 13, 1985; signed by San Francisco Giants' organization, February 3, 1986.

DOUGLAS REID JONES
(Doug)

Born June 24, 1957, at Lebanon, Ind.
Height, 6.02. Weight, 190.
Throws and bats righthanded.
Attended Central Arizona College, Coolidge, Ariz.

Major League saves: 1986 (1).
Led Midwest League in complete games with 16 and tied for lead in shutouts with 3 in 1979.
Tied for Eastern League lead in intentional bases on balls issued with 8 in 1985.

Year Club	League	G.	IP.	W.	L.	Pct.	H.	R.	ER.	SO.	BB.	ERA.
1978—Newark†	NYP	15	38	2	4	.333	49	30	22	27	15	5.21
1979—Burlington	Midwest	28	★190	10	10	.500	144	63	37	115	73	★1.75
1980—Stockton	California	11	76	6	2	.750	63	32	24	54	31	2.84
1980—Vancouver	P. Coast	8	53	3	2	.600	52	19	19	28	15	3.23
1980—Holyoke	Eastern	8	62	5	3	.625	57	23	20	39	26	2.90
1981—El Paso	Texas	15	90	5	7	.417	121	67	58	62	28	5.80
1981—Vancouver	P. Coast	11	80	5	3	.625	79	29	27	38	22	3.04
1982—Milwaukee	American	4	2⅔	0	0	.000	5	3	3	1	1	10.13
1982—Vancouver	P. Coast	23	106	5	8	.385	109	48	35	60	31	2.97
1983—Vancouver‡	P. Coast	3	7	0	1	.000	10	8	8	4	5	10.29
1984—Vancouver§	P. Coast	3	8	1	0	1.000	9	9	9	2	3	10.13
1984—El Paso x	Texas	16	109⅓	6	8	.429	120	61	52	62	35	4.28
1985—Waterbury	Eastern	39	116	9	4	.692	123	59	47	113	36	3.65
1986—Maine	Int'national	43	116⅓	5	6	.455	105	35	27	98	27	★2.09
1986—Cleveland	American	11	18	1	0	1.000	18	5	5	12	6	2.50
Major League Totals—2 Years		15	20⅔	1	0	1.000	23	8	8	13	7	3.48

Selected by Milwaukee Brewers' organization in 3rd round of free-agent draft, January 10, 1978.
†On disabled list, June 20 to July 12, 1978.
‡On disabled list, April 11 to September 1, 1983.
§On disabled list, April 25 to May 30, 1984.
xGranted free agency, October 15, 1984; signed by Waterbury (Cleveland Indians' organization), April 3, 1985.

JAMES CONDIA JONES
(Jimmy)

Born April 20, 1964, at Dallas, Tex.
Height, 6.02. Weight, 175.
Throws and bats righthanded.

Tied modern major league record for fewest hits allowed, first major league game, nine innings (1), September 21, 1986.

Tied for Pacific Coast League lead in games started by pitchers with 27 in 1986.

Year Club	League	G.	IP.	W.	L.	Pct.	H.	R.	ER.	SO.	BB.	ERA.
1982—Walla Walla	Northwest	14	78⅓	4	6	.400	64	49	28	78	71	3.22
1983—Reno	California	17	116⅔	7	5	.583	96	50	35	79	49	2.70
1984—Beaumont†	Texas	13	85⅔	7	2	.778	63	28	20	49	39	2.10
1985—Beaumont‡	Texas	16	85	7	5	.583	84	51	44	57	66	4.66
1986—Las Vegas	P. Coast	28	157⅔	9	10	.474	168	84	77	114	72	4.40
1986—San Diego	National	3	18	2	0	1.000	10	6	5	15	3	2.50
Major League Totals—1 Year		3	18	2	0	1.000	10	6	5	15	3	2.50

Selected by San Diego Padres' organization in 1st round (third player selected) of free-agent draft, June 7, 1982.

†On disabled list, July 13, 1984 through remainder of season.

‡On disabled list, June 29 to July 11 and July 28, 1985 through remainder of season.

LYNN MORRIS JONES

Born January 1, 1953, at Meadville, Pa.
Height, 5.09. Weight, 170.
Throws and bats righthanded.
Received bachelor of arts degree in sociology from Thiel College, Greenville, Pa.
Brother of Darryl Jones, outfielder with New York Yankees, 1979.

Major League stolen bases: 1979 (9), 1980 (1), 1981 (1), 1983 (1), 1984 (1). Total—13.

Tied for Eastern League lead in sacrifice flies with 8 in 1976.

Year Club	League	Pos.	G.	AB.	R.	H.	2B.	3B.	HR.	RBI.	B.A.	PO.	A.	E.	F.A.
1974—Seattle	N'west.	OF	76	282	53	74	15	2	2	37	.262	166	*13	4	.978
1975—Three Rivers	East.	OF-SS	53	141	12	29	3	1	1	14	.206	89	25	6	.950
1975—Eugene	N'west.	OF-3B	62	211	53	71	13	3	13	63	.336	90	9	6	.943
1976—Three Rivers	East.	OF	131	418	41	105	17	0	2	36	.251	196	5	8	.962
1977—Three Rivers†	East.	OF	94	324	49	87	14	2	5	32	.269	229	14	1	*.996
1978—Indianapolis‡	A. A.	OF-2B	126	482	81	158	28	4	9	62	.328	246	14	3	.989
1979—Detroit	Amer.	OF	95	213	33	63	8	0	4	26	.296	142	3	3	.980
1980—Evansville	A. A.	OF	34	121	10	33	4	0	0	11	.273	29	1	1	.968
1980—Detroit§	Amer.	OF	30	55	9	14	2	2	0	6	.255	31	0	0	1.000
1981—Detroit	Amer.	OF	71	174	19	45	5	0	2	19	.259	85	5	1	.989
1982—Detroit	Amer.	OF	58	139	15	31	3	1	0	14	.223	86	3	0	1.000
1983—Detroit x	Amer.	OF	49	64	9	17	1	2	0	6	.266	28	2	1	.968
1984—Kansas City y	Amer.	OF	47	103	11	31	6	0	1	10	.301	51	0	2	.962
1984—Omaha	A. A.	OF	17	63	8	16	6	0	1	3	.254	38	0	0	1.000
1985—Kansas City z	Amer.	OF	110	152	12	32	7	0	0	9	.211	115	2	2	.983
1986—Kansas City a	Amer.	OF-2B	67	47	1	6	2	0	0	1	.128	34	0	1	.971
Major League Totals—8 Years			527	947	109	239	34	5	7	91	.252	572	15	10	.983

Selected by Cincinnati Reds' organization in 10th round of free-agent draft, June 5, 1974.

†On disabled list, July 8 to August 8, 1977.

‡Drafted by Detroit Tigers, December 4, 1978.

§On disabled list, April 30 to July 25, 1980.

xGranted free agency when he refused option to minors, December 1, 1983; signed by Kansas City Royals, December 6, 1983.

yOn disabled list, March 28 to May 2 and June 6 to August 1, 1984; included rehabilitation disability assignment to Omaha, July 12 to August 1, 1984.

zGranted free agency, November 12, 1985; re-signed by Royals, December 2, 1985.

aGranted free agency, November 12, 1986.

CHAMPIONSHIP SERIES RECORD

Year Club	League	Pos.	G.	AB.	R.	H.	2B.	3B.	HR.	RBI.	B.A.	PO.	A.	E.	F.A.
1984—Kansas City	Amer.	PH-OF	3	5	1	1	0	0	0	0	.200	2	0	0	1.000
1985—Kansas City	Amer.	OF	5	0	0	0	0	0	0	0	.000	2	0	0	1.000
Championship Series Totals—2 Years			8	5	1	1	0	0	0	0	.200	4	0	0	1.000

WORLD SERIES RECORD

Year Club	League	Pos.	G.	AB.	R.	H.	2B.	3B.	HR.	RBI.	B.A.	PO.	A.	E.	F.A.
1985—Kansas City	Amer.	PH-OF	6	3	0	2	1	1	0	0	.667	4	0	0	1.000

ODELL JONES JR.

Born January 13, 1953, at Tulare, Calif.
Height, 6.03. Weight, 175.
Throws and bats righthanded.
Attended Compton College, Compton, Calif.
Cousin of Charles Jackson, linebacker with New York Jets.

Pitched 7-0 no-hit victory against Pittsfield, April 29, 1974.

Major League saves: 1983 (10), 1984 (2). Total—12.

Led Eastern League in balks with 3 in 1974.

Year Club	League	G.	IP.	W.	L.	Pct.	H.	R.	ER.	SO.	BB.	ERA.
1972—Niagara Falls	NYP	11	79	7	3	.700	78	34	27	53	20	3.08
1973—Charleston	W. Carol.	10	62	2	3	.400	42	22	10	62	29	1.45
1973—Salem	Carolina	11	67	5	4	.556	64	40	36	55	38	4.84
1974—Thetford Mines	Eastern	24	161	11	8	.579	103	63	58	153	★120	3.24
1975—Charleston	Int'national	26	★188	●14	9	.609	133	67	56	★157	88	2.68
1975—Pittsburgh	National	2	3	0	0	.000	1	0	0	2	0	0.00
1976—Charleston†	Int'national	16	84	2	7	.222	81	49	46	47	43	4.93
1977—Pittsburgh	National	34	108	3	7	.300	118	63	61	66	31	5.08
1978—Columbus	Int'national	28	181	12	9	.571	174	100	★92	★169	69	4.57
1978—Pittsburgh‡	National	3	9	2	0	1.000	7	3	2	10	4	2.00
1979—Seattle§	American	25	119	3	11	.214	151	90	80	72	58	6.05
1980—Portland x	P. Coast	19	98	6	7	.462	96	49	45	89	46	4.13
1981—Portland	P. Coast	23	153	12	6	.667	138	73	60	★135	68	3.53
1981—Pittsburgh	National	13	54	4	5	.444	51	23	20	30	23	3.33
1982—Portland y	P. Coast	28	190⅓	★16	9	.640	162	103	90	★172	94	4.26
1983—Texas z	American	42	67	3	6	.333	56	28	23	50	22	3.09
1984—Texas a	American	33	59⅓	2	4	.333	62	28	24	28	23	3.64
1985—Rochester	Int'national	41	105	4	6	.400	97	52	49	104	45	4.20
1986—Rochester	Int'national	17	83⅔	7	3	★.700	73	38	34	69	42	3.66
1986—Baltimore	American	21	49⅓	2	2	.500	58	22	21	32	23	3.83
National League Totals—4 Years		52	174	9	12	.429	177	89	83	108	58	4.29
American League Totals—4 Years		121	294⅔	10	23	.303	327	168	148	182	126	4.52
Major League Totals—8 Years		173	468⅔	19	35	.352	504	257	231	290	184	4.44

Signed as free agent by Pittsburgh Pirates' organization, November 25, 1971.

†On disabled list, July 13 to August 24, 1976.

‡Traded with Shortstop Mario Mendoza and Pitcher Rafael Vasquez to Seattle Mariners for Pitchers Enrique Romo and Rick Jones and Shortstop Tom McMillan, December 5, 1978.

§Traded to Pittsburgh Pirates' organization for a player to be named later, April 1, 1980; Seattle Mariners acquired Pitcher Larry Andersen to complete deal, October 29, 1980.

xOn disabled list, June 16 to July 6 and July 13 to August 3, 1980.

yDrafted by Texas Rangers, December 6, 1982.

zOn disabled list, August 19 to September 9, 1983.

aGranted free agency, December 20, 1984; signed by Baltimore Orioles, February 1, 1985.

RICHARD MIRON JONES
(Ricky)

Born June 4, 1959, at Tupelo, Miss.
Height, 6.03. Weight, 186.
Throws and bats righthanded.
Attended Chipola Junior College, Marianna, Fla., and West
Georgia College, Carrollton, Ga.

Led International League shortstops in double plays with 101 and total chances with 689 in 1982.
Led Southern League shortstops in double plays with 75 in 1981.

Year Club	League	Pos.	G.	AB.	R.	H.	2B.	3B.	HR.	RBI.	B.A.	PO.	A.	E.	F.A.
1980—Bluefield	Appal.	OF-SS	59	199	27	55	9	3	6	33	.276	78	68	12	.924
1981—Charlotte	South.	SS	134	479	66	125	17	2	11	56	.261	175	402	38	.938
1982—Rochester	Int.	SS	★139	457	66	105	15	2	13	51	.230	221	★440	28	.959
1983—Rochester†	Int.	SS	95	339	28	78	16	1	7	38	.230	151	265	22	.950
1984—Hagerstown	Carol.	SS	5	10	0	1	0	0	0	0	.100	1	4	1	.833
1984—Rochester‡	Int.	SS-3B	38	107	13	24	4	0	6	16	.224	28	63	6	.938
1985—Rochester	Int.	SS	14	52	3	9	1	0	0	4	.173	24	37	3	.953
1985—Charlotte	South.	SS	108	386	64	108	20	1	22	64	.280	161	316	17	★.966
1986—Rochester	Int.	2B-SS-1B	123	443	49	111	25	3	9	56	.251	225	364	24	.961
1986—Baltimore	Amer.	2B-3B	16	33	2	6	2	0	0	4	.182	19	38	0	1.000
Major League Totals—1 Year			16	33	2	6	2	0	0	4	.182	19	38	0	1.000

Selected by Atlanta Braves' organization in 18th round of free-agent draft, June 8, 1976.

Selected by Baltimore Orioles' organization in 15th round of free-agent draft, June 3, 1980.

†On disabled list, May 18 to June 5, July 17 to July 27 and August 3 to August 13, 1983.

‡On disabled list, April 10 to May 3, June 21 to July 2 and August 3, 1984 through remainder of season.

ROBERT OLIVER JONES JR.
(Bobby)

Born October 11, 1949, at Elkton, Md.
Height, 6.03. Weight, 215.
Throws and bats lefthanded.

Tied major league record for most doubles, inning (2), July 3, 1983 (fifteenth inning).
Major League stolen bases: 1976 (3), 1984 (1), 1985 (1). Total—5.
Tied for American Association lead in game-winning RBIs with 11 in 1981.

Year Club	League	Pos.	G.	AB.	R.	H.	2B.	3B.	HR.	RBI.	B.A.	PO.	A.	E.	F.A.
1967—Geneva	NYP	1B	19	60	5	13	2	1	0	2	.217	115	5	0	1.000
1968—Salisbury	W. Car.	OF-1B	102	354	33	87	11	5	5	39	.246	327	24	17	.954
1969—Burlington	Carol.	OF-1B	39	111	7	22	1	0	1	6	.198	73	3	3	.962
1969—Shelby†	W. Car.	OF-1B	20	74	9	20	3	0	1	7	.270	50	2	1	.981
1970—						(In Military Service)									
1971—Anderson	W. Car.	1B-OF	116	424	82	136	19	5	23	77	.321	721	27	10	.987
1972—Denver	A. A.	OF	118	345	46	99	15	6	5	46	.287	159	6	4	.976

Year Club	League	Pos.	G.	AB.	R.	H.	2B.	3B.	HR.	RBI.	B.A.	PO.	A.	E.	F.A.
1973—Spokane	P. C.	OF	121	437	57	121	25	7	9	71	.277	186	6	1	*.995
1974—Spokane	P. C.	OF	131	466	87	140	18	5	16	91	.300	221	9	5	.979
1974—Texas	Amer.	OF	2	5	0	0	0	0	0	0	.000	5	0	0	1.000
1975—Spokane	P. C.	OF-1B	109	404	69	112	12	6	17	67	.277	210	4	3	.986
1975—Texas	Amer.	OF	9	11	2	1	0	0	0	0	.091	6	0	0	1.000
1976—Sacramento‡	P. C.	OF	26	93	16	33	5	2	10	29	.355	51	4	1	.982
1976—California	Amer.	OF-DH	78	166	22	35	6	0	6	17	.211	98	6	1	.990
1977—California	Amer.	DH	14	17	3	3	0	0	1	3	.176	0	0	0	.000
1977—Salt Lake City	P. C.	OF-1B	94	353	71	120	28	10	18	85	.340	224	4	5	.979
1978—Salt Lake City§x	P. C.	OF-1B	122	460	79	141	31	6	14	102	.307	344	13	5	.986
1979—Chunichi	Cent.		110	367	48	105	...	...	16	56	.286	Figures unavailable			
1980—Chunichi	Cent.		64	178	....	50	...	...	4	19	.281	Figures unavailable			
1981—Wichita	A. A.	OF-1B	117	352	53	111	15	3	20	72	.315	332	19	2	.994
1981—Texas	Amer.	OF	10	34	4	9	1	0	3	7	.265	20	4	0	1.000
1982—Denver	A. A.	OF	82	261	44	83	19	5	12	51	.318	120	5	2	.984
1983—Oklahoma City	A. A.	1B	46	171	25	61	14	3	4	29	.357	268	22	2	.993
1983—Texas	Amer.	OF-1B	41	72	5	16	4	0	1	11	.222	24	0	0	1.000
1984—Texas y	Amer.	OF-1B	64	143	14	37	4	0	4	22	.259	139	7	1	.993
1985—Texas	Amer.	OF-1B	83	134	14	30	2	0	5	23	.224	44	0	0	1.000
1986—Oklahoma City	A. A.	1B-OF	90	318	31	80	16	1	6	50	.252	222	16	2	.992
1986—Texas	Amer.	OF-1B	13	21	1	2	0	0	0	3	.095	29	1	1	.968
Major League Totals—9 Years			314	603	65	133	17	0	20	86	.221	365	18	3	.992

Selected by Washington Senators' organization in 36th round of free-agent draft, June 6, 1967.
†On military list, August 18, 1969 through February 15, 1971.
‡Sold on waivers to California Angels, May 17, 1976.
§On disabled list, July 11 to July 21, 1978.
xReleased, January 29, 1979; signed by Wichita (Texas Rangers' organization), December 18, 1980.
yOn disabled list, July 23 to August 10, 1984.

RONALD GLEN JONES

(Ron)

Born June 11, 1964, at Seguin, Tex.
Height, 5.10. Weight, 200.
Throws right and bats lefthanded.
Attended Wharton County Junior College, Wharton, Tex.
Nephew of Alvin Jones, outfielder in Atlanta Braves'
organization, 1973 through 1976.

Led Florida State League in total bases with 216 and slugging percentage with .524 in 1986.
Led Northwest League in game-winning RBIs with 10 in 1985.
Named Florida State League Most Valuable Player, 1986.

Year Club	League	Pos.	G.	AB.	R.	H.	2B.	3B.	HR.	RBI.	B.A.	PO.	A.	E.	F.A.
1985—Bend	N'west	OF	73	286	54	90	13	1	10	60	.315	88	4	*11	.893
1986—Clearwater	Fla. St.	OF	108	412	76	●153	18	*12	7	73	*.371	196	9	2	.990
1986—Portland	P. C.	OF	11	34	4	4	1	0	0	2	.118	11	2	0	1.000

Selected by Toronto Blue Jays' organization in 14th round of free-agent draft, June 7, 1982.
Selected by Montreal Expos' organization in secondary phase of free-agent draft, January 11, 1983.
Signed as free agent by Philadelphia Phillies' organization, October 20, 1984.

ROSS A. JONES

Born January 14, 1960, at Miami, Fla.
Height, 6.02. Weight, 180.
Throws and bats righthanded.
Attended Miami-Dade Community College-New World Center, Miami, Fla.,
and University of Miami, Coral Gables, Fla.

Named shortstop on THE SPORTING NEWS College Baseball All-America Team, 1980.

Year Club	League	Pos.	G.	AB.	R.	H.	2B.	3B.	HR.	RBI.	B.A.	PO.	A.	E.	F.A.
1980—Vero Beach	Fla. St.	SS	70	223	35	59	14	3	4	37	.253	122	215	16	.955
1981—San Antonio	Texas	SS	129	444	75	118	17	2	5	43	.266	185	328	39	.929
1982—Albuquerque	P. C.	2B-SS	128	459	84	132	19	3	9	74	.288	273	350	24	.963
1983—Albuquerque†	P. C.	SS-2B	131	469	67	128	18	8	3	56	.273	217	434	36	.948
1984—New York	Nat.	SS-2B-3B	17	10	2	1	1	0	0	1	.100	0	7	1	.875
1984—Tidewater	Int.	S-3-2-O-1	95	290	35	64	14	0	5	40	.221	177	211	9	.977
1985—Tidewater‡	Int.	O-I-P	50	82	14	19	2	0	1	3	.232	57	24	5	.942
1985—Jackson§	Texas	SS-3B-OF	19	63	4	9	1	0	0	6	.143	26	44	4	.946
1986—Chattanooga	South.	SS-2B-OF	70	230	41	72	9	2	5	42	.313	93	162	9	.966
1986—Calgary	P. C.	2-S-3-O	53	187	23	49	12	1	4	24	.262	83	157	7	.972
1986—Seattle	Amer.	SS-2B-3B	11	21	0	2	0	0	0	0	.095	9	11	0	1.000
American League Totals—1 Year			11	21	0	2	0	0	0	0	.095	9	11	0	1.000
National League Totals—1 Year			17	10	2	1	1	0	0	1	.100	0	7	1	.875
Major League Totals—2 Years			28	31	2	3	1	0	0	1	.097	9	18	1	.964

Selected by Los Angeles Dodgers' organization in 1st round (ninth player selected) of free-agent draft, June 3, 1980.
†Traded with Pitcher Sid Fernandez to New York Mets for Pitcher Carlos Diaz and a player to be named later, December 8, 1983; Los Angeles Dodgers acquired Infielder Bob Bailor to complete deal, December 12, 1983.

PITCHING RECORD

Year Club	League	G.	IP.	W.	L.	Pct.	H.	R.	ER.	SO.	BB.	ERA.
1985—Tidewater	Int'national	1	1	0	0	.000	4	2	2	0	0	18.00

RUPPERT SANDERSON JONES

Born March 12, 1955, at Dallas, Tex.
Height, 5.10. Weight, 171.
Throws and bats lefthanded.

Tied major league records for most strikeouts, two consecutive games (8), July 16 and 17, 1982; most putouts by outfielder, game (12), May 16, 1978, 16 innings.

Tied American League record for most chances accepted by outfielder, game (12), May 16, 1978, 16 innings.

Major League stolen bases: 1977 (13), 1978 (22), 1979 (33), 1980 (18), 1981 (7), 1982 (18), 1983 (11), 1984 (2), 1985 (7), 1986 (10). Total—141.

Tied for Pioneer League lead in double plays by outfielders with 1 in 1973.

Year Club	League	Pos.	G.	AB.	R.	H.	2B.	3B.	HR.	RBI.	B.A.	PO.	A.	E.	F.A.
1973—Billings	Pion.	OF	61	193	45	58	10	4	4	31	.301	55	5	5	.923
1974—Waterloo	Midw.	OF	68	249	44	88	15	0	13	43	.353	94	7	3	.971
1974—San Jose	Calif.	OF	53	191	29	53	7	3	8	45	.277	101	2	4	.963
1975—Omaha	A. A.	OF	119	403	62	98	25	5	13	54	.243	171	15	★13	.935
1976—Omaha	A. A.	OF	102	359	65	94	15	9	19	73	.262	243	2	8	.968
1976—Kansas City†	Amer.	OF	28	51	9	11	1	1	1	7	.216	21	0	0	1.000
1977—Seattle	Amer.	OF	160	597	85	157	26	8	24	76	.263	465	11	9	.981
1978—Seattle‡	Amer.	OF	129	472	48	111	24	3	6	46	.235	393	10	6	.985
1979—Seattle§	Amer.	OF	●162	622	109	166	29	9	21	78	.267	453	13	5	.989
1980—New York xy	Amer.	OF	83	328	38	73	11	3	9	42	.223	246	4	3	.988
1981—San Diego	Nat.	OF	105	397	53	99	34	1	4	39	.249	295	9	2	.993
1982—San Diego z	Nat.	OF	116	424	69	120	20	2	12	61	.283	314	3	5	.984
1983—San Diego a	Nat.	OF-1B	133	335	42	78	12	3	12	49	.233	268	6	6	.979
1984—Evansville	A. A.	OF	48	160	30	50	9	3	9	45	.313	97	1	4	.961
1984—Detroit b	Amer.	OF	79	215	26	61	12	1	12	37	.284	150	4	0	1.000
1985—California	Amer.	OF	125	389	66	90	17	2	21	67	.231	179	12	1	.995
1986—California	Amer.	OF	126	393	73	90	21	3	17	49	.229	205	5	4	.981
American League Totals—8 Years			892	3067	454	759	141	30	111	402	.247	2112	59	28	.987
National League Totals—3 Years			354	1156	164	297	66	6	28	149	.257	877	18	13	.986
Major League Totals—11 Years			1246	4223	618	1056	207	36	139	551	.250	2989	77	41	.987

Selected by Kansas City Royals' organization in 3rd round of free-agent draft, June 5, 1973.

†Selected by Seattle Mariners in American League expansion draft, November 5, 1976.

‡On disabled list, June 16 to July 20, 1978.

§Traded with Pitcher Jim Lewis to New York Yankees for Outfielder Juan Beniquez, Pitchers Jim Beattie and Rick Anderson and Catcher Jerry Narron, November 1, 1979.

xOn disabled list, May 27 to July 10 and August 26, 1980 through remainder of season.

yTraded with Outfielder Joe Lefebvre and Pitchers Tim Lollar and Chris Welsh to San Diego Padres for Outfielder Jerry Mumphrey and Pitcher John Pacella, April 1, 1981.

zOn disabled list, August 6 to August 21, 1982.

aGranted free agency, November 7, 1983; signed by Detroit Tigers, April 10, 1984.

bGranted free agency, November 8, 1984; signed by California Angels, January 30, 1985.

CHAMPIONSHIP SERIES RECORD

Established Championship Series record for most bases on balls, game (4), October 11, 1986 (11 innings).

Year Club	League	Pos.	G.	AB.	R.	H.	2B.	3B.	HR.	RBI.	B.A.	PO.	A.	E.	F.A.
1984—Detroit	Amer.	PH-OF	2	5	1	0	0	0	0	0	.000	5	0	0	1.000
1986—California	Amer.	OF-PR	6	17	4	3	1	0	0	2	.176	6	0	0	1.000
Major League Totals—2 Years			8	22	5	3	1	0	0	2	.136	11	0	0	1.000

WORLD SERIES RECORD

Year Club	League	Pos.	G.	AB.	R.	H.	2B.	3B.	HR.	RBI.	B.A.	PO.	A.	E.	F.A.
1984—Detroit	Amer.	OF	2	3	0	0	0	0	0	0	.000	3	0	0	1.000

ALL-STAR GAME RECORD

Year League		Pos.	AB.	R.	H.	2B.	3B.	HR.	RBI.	B.A.	PO.	A.	E.	F.A.
1977—American		PH	1	0	0	0	0	0	0	.000	0	0	0	.000
1982—National		PH	1	1	1	0	1	0	0	1.000	0	0	0	.000
All-Star Game Totals—2 Years			2	1	1	0	1	0	0	.500	0	0	0	.000

TRACY DONALD JONES

Born March 31, 1961, at Inglewood, Calif.
Height, 6.03. Weight, 180.
Throws and bats righthanded.
Attended Loyola Marymount University, Los Angeles, Calif.

Major League stolen bases: 1986 (7).

Year Club	League	Pos.	G.	AB.	R.	H.	2B.	3B.	HR.	RBI.	B.A.	PO.	A.	E.	F.A.
1983—Tampa	Fla. St.	O-3-1-S	53	118	27	32	5	3	1	15	.271	54	12	11	.857
1983—Eugene	N'west	2B-3B-OF	55	203	42	54	12	0	1	26	.266	81	68	12	.925
1984—Tampa†	Fla. St.	OF	86	307	50	95	14	3	4	41	.309	150	6	0	1.000

Year	Club	League	Pos.	G.	AB.	R.	H.	2B.	3B.	HR.	RBI.	B.A.	PO.	A.	E.	F.A.
1985—Vermont	East.		OF	75	284	40	90	12	3	4	31	.317	117	4	1	.992
1985—Denver	A. A.		OF	51	205	43	69	12	0	10	31	.337	93	2	0	1.000
1986—Cincinnati‡	Nat.		OF-1B	46	86	16	30	3	0	2	10	.349	46	1	0	1.000
Major League Totals—1 Year				46	86	16	30	3	0	2	10	.349	46	1	0	1.000

Selected by New York Mets' organization in 4th round of free-agent draft, June 7, 1982.
Selected by Cincinnati Reds' organization in secondary phase of free-agent draft, January 11, 1983.
†On disabled list, July 18 to September 18, 1984.
‡On disabled list, May 23 to June 15 and July 10 to September 1, 1986.

PAUL SCOTT JORDAN
(Ricky)

Born May 26, 1965, at Richmond, Calif.
Height, 6.03. Weight, 185.
Throws and bats righthanded.

Year	Club	League	Pos.	G.	AB.	R.	H.	2B.	3B.	HR.	RBI.	B.A.	PO.	A.	E.	F.A.
1983—Helena	Pion.		1B	60	247	32	73	7	1	5	33	.296	486	35	7	.986
1984—Spartanburg	S. Atl.		1B	128	490	72	143	23	4	10	76	.292	1129	69	14	.988
1985—Clearwater	Fla. St.		1B	★139	528	60	146	22	8	7	62	.277	1252	86	★20	.985
1986—Reading	East.		★1B-OF	133	478	44	131	19	3	2	60	.274	1052	87	★17	.985

Selected by Philadelphia Phillies' organization in 1st round (22nd player selected) of free-agent draft, June 6, 1983.

DOMINGO FELIX JOSE

(Known by middle name.)

Born May 8, 1965, at Santo Domingo, D. R.
Height, 6.01. Weight, 184.
Throws right and bats left and righthanded.

Year	Club	League	Pos.	G.	AB.	R.	H.	2B.	3B.	HR.	RBI.	B.A.	PO.	A.	E.	F.A.
1984—Idaho Falls	Pion.		OF	45	152	16	33	6	0	1	18	.217	48	6	1	.982
1985—Madison	Midw.		OF	117	409	46	89	13	3	3	33	.218	187	9	12	.942
1986—Modesto	Calif.		OF	127	516	77	147	22	8	14	77	.285	215	12	14	.942

Signed as free agent by Oakland A's organization, January 3, 1984.

WALLACE KEITH JOYNER
(Wally)

Born June 16, 1962, at Atlanta, Ga.
Height, 6.02. Weight, 185.
Throws and bats lefthanded.
Attended Brigham Young University, Provo, Utah.

Major League stolen bases: 1986 (5).
Led American League in sacrifice flies with 12 in 1986.
Tied for Eastern League lead in intentional bases on balls received with 8 in 1984.
Led Pacific Coast League first basemen in total chances with 1,229 and double plays with 121 in 1985.

Year	Club	League	Pos.	G.	AB.	R.	H.	2B.	3B.	HR.	RBI.	B.A.	PO.	A.	E.	F.A.
1983—Peoria	Midw.		1B	54	192	25	63	16	2	3	33	.328	480	45	6	.989
1984—Waterbury	East.		1B-OF	134	467	81	148	24	7	12	72	.317	906	86	9	.991
1985—Edmonton	P. C.		1B	126	477	68	135	29	5	12	73	.283	★1107	★107	●15	.988
1986—California	Amer.		1B	154	593	82	172	27	3	22	100	.290	1222	139	15	.989
Major League Totals—1 Year				154	593	82	172	27	3	22	100	.290	1222	139	15	.989

CHAMPIONSHIP SERIES RECORD

Year	Club	League	Pos.	G.	AB.	R.	H.	2B.	3B.	HR.	RBI.	B.A.	PO.	A.	E.	F.A.
1986—California	Amer.		1B	3	11	3	5	2	0	1	2	.455	24	1	0	1.000

ALL-STAR GAME RECORD

Year	League		Pos.	AB.	R.	H.	2B.	3B.	HR.	RBI.	B.A.	PO.	A.	E.	F.A.
1986—American			1B	1	0	0	0	0	0	0	.000	3	1	0	1.000

Selected by California Angels' organization in 3rd round of free-agent draft, June 6, 1983.

RONALD JOSEPH KARKOVICE

Name pronounced CAR-koh-vice.

(Ron)

Born August 8, 1963, at Union, N.J.
Height, 6.01. Weight, 215.
Throws and bats righthanded.

Major League stolen bases: 1986 (1).
Led Gulf Coast League batters in strikeouts with 73 in 1982.
Led Eastern League catchers in double plays with 13 in 1985.
Led Midwest League catchers in fielding percentage with .996 in 1983.
Led Gulf Coast League catchers in total chances with 394 and tied for lead in double plays with 5 in 1982.

Year Club	League	Pos.	G.	AB.	R.	H.	2B.	3B.	HR.	RBI.	B.A.	PO.	A.	E.	F.A.
1982—Sarasota W.S.	Gulf C.	C	60	214	34	56	6	0	7	32	.262	★331	★51	12	.970
1983—Appleton	Midw.	C-OF	97	326	54	78	17	3	13	48	.239	682	91	4	.995
1984—Glens Falls	East.	C	88	260	37	56	9	1	13	39	.215	442	★68	11	.979
1984—Denver	A. A.	C	31	86	7	19	1	0	2	10	.221	149	28	3	.983
1985—Glens Falls	East.	C	99	324	37	70	9	3	11	37	.216	573	★103	★14	.980
1986—Birmingham	South.	C	97	319	63	90	13	1	20	53	.282	463	72	10	.982
1986—Chicago	Amer.	C	37	97	13	24	7	0	4	13	.247	227	19	1	.996
Major League Totals—1 Year			37	97	13	24	7	0	4	13	.247	227	19	1	.996

Selected by Chicago White Sox' organization in 1st round (14th player selected) of free-agent draft, June 7, 1982.

ROBERT HENRY KEARNEY

Name pronounced KERN-ee.

(Bob)

Born October 3, 1956, at San Antonio, Tex.
Height, 6.00. Weight, 185.
Throws and bats righthanded.
Attended University of Texas, Austin, Tex.

Major League stolen bases: 1983 (1), 1984 (7), 1985 (1). Total—9.
Led American League catchers in total chances with 897 in 1984.
Tied for Pioneer League lead in double plays by catchers with 4 in 1977.

Year Club	League	Pos.	G.	AB.	R.	H.	2B.	3B.	HR.	RBI.	B.A.	PO.	A.	E.	F.A.
1977—Great Falls	Pion.	C	58	211	49	50	7	0	7	34	.237	★417	★56	10	.979
1978—Cedar Rapids	Midw.	C	28	89	8	24	3	0	1	15	.270	182	23	2	.990
1978—Waterbury	East.	C	38	125	10	21	3	0	1	8	.168	195	33	9	.962
1979—Shreveport	Texas	C	63	224	27	60	9	1	4	24	.268	312	49	7	.981
1979—Phoenix	P. C.	C	38	124	11	17	2	1	2	10	.137	183	27	7	.968
1979—San Francisco	Nat.	C	2	0	0	0	0	0	0	0	.000	0	0	0	.000
1980—Phoenix†	P. C.	C	92	298	42	68	8	3	2	24	.228	358	68	11	.975
1981—Tacoma	P. C.	C	86	278	38	70	13	2	3	29	.252	487	73	9	.984
1981—Oakland	Amer.	C	1	0	0	0	0	0	0	0	.000	0	0	0	.000
1982—Oakland	Amer.	C	22	71	7	12	3	0	0	5	.169	114	14	4	.970
1982—Tacoma	P. C.	C	115	388	41	98	13	3	7	55	.253	589	93	9	.987
1983—Oakland‡	Amer.	C	108	298	33	76	11	0	8	32	.255	437	41	9	.982
1984—Seattle	Amer.	C	133	431	39	97	24	1	7	43	.225	★823	63	11	.988
1985—Seattle	Amer.	C	108	305	24	74	14	1	6	27	.243	529	50	3	★.995
1986—Seattle	Amer.	C	81	204	23	49	10	0	6	25	.240	419	46	5	.989
National League Totals—1 Year			2	0	0	0	0	0	0	0	.000	0	0	0	.000
American League Totals—6 Years			453	1309	126	308	62	2	27	132	.235	2322	214	32	.988
Major League Totals—7 Years			455	1309	126	308	62	2	27	132	.235	2322	214	32	.988

Selected by San Francisco Giants' organization in 14th round of free-agent draft, June 7, 1977.
†Drafted by Tacoma (Oakland A's organization), December 9, 1980.
‡Traded with Pitcher Dave Beard to Seattle Mariners for Pitcher Bill Caudill and a player to be named later, November 21, 1983; Oakland A's acquired Pitcher Darrel Akerfelds to complete deal, December 7, 1983.

ANTHONY KELLEY

Born March 4, 1962, at Chicago, Ill.
Height, 6.02. Weight, 205.
Throws and bats righthanded.
Attended University of Nebraska, Lincoln, Neb.

Led Southern League in complete games with 8 and tied for lead in shutouts with 3 in 1986.
Tied for South Atlantic League Lead in shutouts with 4 in 1984.
Named Southern League Pitcher of the Year, 1986.

Year Club	League	G.	IP.	W.	L.	Pct.	H.	R.	ER.	SO.	BB.	ERA.
1983—Auburn	NYP	14	82⅓	5	2	.714	88	40	35	49	17	3.83
1984—Asheville	S. Atlantic	26	★174⅔	14	9	.609	160	68	50	121	56	2.58
1985—Osceola	Florida St.	6	51	5	1	.833	45	11	6	29	6	1.06
1985—Columbus	Southern	22	133	10	8	.556	119	75	57	60	39	3.86
1986—Columbus	Southern	29	193⅓	★14	4	.778	196	92	78	126	35	3.63

Selected by New York Mets' organization in 9th round of free-agent draft, June 3, 1980.
Selected by Houston Astros' organization in 18th round of free-agent draft, June 6, 1983.

BRYAN KEITH KELLY

Born February 24, 1959, at Silver Springs, Md.
Height, 6.02. Weight, 195.
Throws and bats righthanded.
Attended Valencia Community College, Orlando, Fla., and
University of Alabama, Tuscaloosa, Ala.

Pitched 6-0 no-hit victory against Oklahoma City, July 17, 1985.
Led Southern League in hit batsmen with 12 in 1984.
Tied for American Association lead in hit batsmen with 10 and wild pitches with 14 in 1985.

Year Club	League	G.	IP.	W.	L.	Pct.	H.	R.	ER.	SO.	BB.	ERA.
1981—Macon	S. Atlantic	11	53	4	3	.571	50	30	27	46	45	4.58
1981—Lakeland	Florida St.	2	11	1	1	.500	10	3	3	8	7	2.45
1982—Lakeland	Florida St.	11	64	5	6	.455	55	36	30	39	51	4.22
1982—Birmingham	Southern	16	95⅓	8	3	.727	78	44	38	91	74	3.59

Year Club	League	G.	IP.	W.	L.	Pct.	H.	R.	ER.	SO.	BB.	ERA.
1983—Evansville†	Am. Assoc.	14	57	2	4	.333	64	50	39	41	60	6.16
1983—Birmingham	Southern	4	25	1	2	.333	23	17	13	20	22	4.68
1984—Birmingham‡	Southern	28	172	7	10	.412	149	103	82	119	*145	4.29
1985—Nashville	Am. Assoc.	27	112⅔	8	8	.500	86	51	47	93	89	3.75
1986—Nashville	Am. Assoc.	21	101⅓	5	5	.500	106	72	52	74	77	4.62
1986—Detroit	American	6	20	1	2	.333	21	11	10	18	10	4.50
Major League Totals—1 Year		6	20	1	2	.333	21	11	10	18	10	4.50

Selected by Montreal Expos' organization in 8th round of free-agent draft, January 8, 1980.
Selected by Detroit Tigers' organization in 6th round of free-agent draft, June 8, 1981.
†On disabled list, April 15 to May 31, 1983.
‡On Evansville disabled list, April 6 to April 16, 1984.

ROBERTO CONRADO KELLY

Born October 1, 1964, at Panama.
Height, 6.02. Weight, 180.
Throws and bats righthanded.

Year Club	League	Pos.	G.	AB.	R.	H.	2B.	3B.	HR.	RBI.	B.A.	PO.	A.	E.	F.A.
1982—Bradenton Yanks	Gulf C.	SS-OF	31	86	13	17	1	1	1	18	.198	47	79	19	.869
1983—Oneonta	NYP	OF-3B	48	167	17	36	1	2	2	17	.216	70	3	5	.936
1983—Greensboro	S. Atl.	OF	20	49	6	13	0	0	0	3	.265	30	2	0	1.000
1984—Greensboro	S. Atl.	Of-1B	111	361	68	86	13	2	1	26	.238	228	5	4	.983
1985—Fort Lauderdale†	Fla. St.	OF	114	417	86	103	4	*13	3	38	.247	187	1	1	.995
1986—Albany	East.	OF	86	299	42	87	11	4	2	43	.291	206	8	7	.968

Signed as free agent by New York Yankees' organization, February 21, 1982.
†Batted left and righthanded.

GERALD HUBERT KEMP
(Hugh)

Born December 13, 1960, at Nashville, Tenn.
Height, 6.03. Weight, 180.
Throws right and bats lefthanded.
Attended DeKalb Community College Central, Clarkston, Ga.,
and University of Georgia, Athens, Ga.

Tied for American Association lead in games started with 28 in 1986.
Led Pioneer League pitchers in shutouts with 3 and in complete games with 8 and tied for lead in games started with 14 in 1983.

Year Club	League	G.	IP.	W.	L.	Pct.	H.	R.	ER.	SO.	BB.	ERA.
1983—Billings	Pioneer	14	*110	●9	3	.750	82	39	27	*138	46	*2.21
1984—Cedar Rapids	Midwest	27	164⅓	11	9	.550	139	65	51	143	69	2.79
1985—Tampa	Florida St.	9	69⅓	5	1	.833	47	14	12	54	22	1.56
1985—Vermont	Eastern	12	78½	5	3	.625	63	33	29	67	28	3.33
1985—Denver	Am. Assoc.	7	40⅓	2	3	.400	41	20	14	33	20	3.12
1986—Denver	Am. Assoc.	29	171	10	7	.588	180	89	78	106	80	4.11

Selected by Cincinnati Reds' organization in 13th round of free-agent draft, June 6, 1983.

STEVEN F. KEMP
(Steve)

Born August 7, 1954, at San Angelo, Tex.
Height, 6.00. Weight, 190.
Throws and bats lefthanded.
Attended University of Southern California, Los Angeles, Calif.

Major League stolen bases: 1977 (3), 1978 (2), 1979 (5), 1980 (5), 1981 (9), 1982 (7), 1983 (1), 1984 (4), 1985 (1), 1986 (1). Total—38.
Received reported $50,000 bonus to sign with Detroit Tigers, 1976.
Named outfielder on THE SPORTING NEWS College Baseball All-America Team, 1975.

Year Club	League	Pos.	G.	AB.	R.	H.	2B.	3B.	HR.	RBI.	B.A.	PO.	A.	E.	F.A.
1976—Montgomery	South.	OF-1B	73	256	41	74	17	2	8	43	.289	91	4	2	.979
1976—Evansville	A. A.	OF	52	171	37	66	14	3	11	38	.386	91	2	5	.945
1977—Detroit	Amer.	OF	151	552	75	142	29	4	18	88	.257	252	10	5	.981
1978—Detroit	Amer.	OF	159	582	75	161	18	4	15	79	.277	325	11	8	.977
1979—Detroit	Amer.	OF	134	490	88	156	26	3	26	105	.318	229	12	6	.976
1980—Detroit	Amer.	OF	135	508	88	149	23	3	21	101	.293	197	4	1	.995
1981—Detroit†	Amer.	OF	105	372	52	103	18	4	9	49	.277	207	4	3	.986
1982—Chicago‡	Amer.	OF	160	580	91	166	23	1	19	98	.286	280	6	7	.976
1983—New York§	Amer.	OF	109	373	53	90	17	3	12	49	.241	215	5	3	.987
1984—New York xy	Amer.	OF	94	313	37	91	12	1	7	41	.291	138	2	4	.972
1985—Pittsburgh z	Nat.	OF	92	236	19	59	13	2	2	21	.250	105	1	0	1.000
1986—Pittsburgh a	Nat.	OF	13	16	1	3	0	0	1	1	.188	9	0	0	1.000
1986—Las Vegas	P. C.	OF	48	160	27	43	10	2	5	27	.269	32	0	0	1.000
American League Totals—8 Years		1047	3770	559	1058	166	23	127	610	.281	1843	54	37	.981
National League Totals—2 Years		105	252	20	62	13	2	3	22	.246	114	1	0	1.000
Major League Totals—10 Years		1152	4022	579	1120	179	25	130	632	.278	1957	55	37	.982

Selected by Detroit Tigers' organization in 1st round (first player selected) of free-agent draft, January 7, 1976.
†Traded to Chicago White Sox for Outfielder Chet Lemon, November 27, 1981.

‡Granted free agency, November 10, 1982; signed by New York Yankees as Type A player, December 8, 1982. (Pitcher Steve Mura was selected from player compensation pool by Chicago White Sox, January 26, 1983.)
§On disabled list, September 15, 1983 through remainder of season.
xOn disabled list, April 4 to April 20, 1984.
yTraded with Infielder Tim Foli and $800,000 to Pittsburgh Pirates for Infielder Dale Berra, Pitcher Alfonso Pulido and Outfielder Jay Buhner, December 20, 1984.
zOn disabled list, April 6 to April 21, 1985.
aReleased, May 8, 1986; signed by Las Vegas (San Diego Padres' organization), June 23, 1986.

ALL-STAR GAME RECORD

Year League	Pos.	AB.	R.	H.	2B.	3B.	HR.	RBI.	B.A.	PO.	A.	E.	F.A.
1979—American	PH	1	0	0	0	0	0	0	.000	0	0	0	.000

TERRENCE EDWARD KENNEDY
(Terry)

Born June 4, 1956, at Euclid, O.
Height, 6.04. Weight, 224.
Throws right and bats lefthanded.
Attended Florida State University, Tallahassee, Fla.
Son of Bob Kennedy, third baseman-outfielder with Chicago AL, Cleveland, Baltimore, Detroit and Brooklyn, 1939 through 1957; scout, Cleveland, 1958 through 1961; minor league manager, Chicago Cubs' organization, 1962; coach, Chicago Cubs, 1963 and 1964; Chicago Cubs executive, 1965; minor league manager, Los Angeles Dodgers' organization, 1966; coach, Atlanta Braves, 1967; manager, Oakland A's, 1968; Director of Player Development, St. Louis Cardinals, 1969 through 1976; Executive Vice President, Chicago Cubs, 1977 through 1981; Houston Astros Vice-President-Baseball Operations 1982 through 1985; and San Francisco Giants Vice-President-Baseball Operations since 1986; brother of Bob Kennedy Jr., pitcher in St. Louis Cardinals' organization, 1971 through 1975; scout, Seattle Mariners, 1976; scout, Chicago Cubs, 1977 through 1981, and scout with Houston Astros, 1982 through 1985.
Tied National League record for most two-base hits by catcher, season (40), 1982.
Major League stolen bases: 1982 (1), 1983 (1), 1984 (1). Total—3.
Led National League catchers in double plays with 12 in 1981 and tied for lead with 11 in 1982 and 12 in 1985.
Named catcher on THE SPORTING NEWS National League Silver Slugger team, 1983.
Named College Player of the Year by THE SPORTING NEWS, 1977.
Received reported $100,000 bonus to sign with St. Louis Cardinals, 1977.
Named catcher on THE SPORTING NEWS College Baseball All-America Team, 1976 and 1977.

Year Club	League	Pos.	G.	AB.	R.	H.	2B.	3B.	HR.	RBI.	B.A.	PO.	A.	E.	F.A.
1977—Johnson City	Appal.	C-1B	12	39	14	23	7	2	3	15	.590	66	3	1	.986
1977—St. Petersburg	Fla. St.	C	45	166	22	41	8	0	4	22	.247	168	22	6	.969
1978—Arkansas	Texas	C-OF	69	239	55	69	14	0	10	54	.289	365	30	7	.983
1978—Springfield	A. A.	C-1B	64	230	35	76	13	0	10	46	.330	331	26	7	.981
1978—St. Louis	Nat.	C	10	29	0	5	0	0	0	2	.172	46	4	1	.980
1979—Springfield	A. A.	C	84	294	35	86	18	1	13	64	.293	434	38	13	.973
1979—St. Louis	Nat.	C	33	109	11	31	7	0	2	17	.284	135	7	1	.993
1980—St. Louis†	Nat.	C-OF	84	248	28	63	12	3	4	34	.254	231	22	7	.973
1981—San Diego	Nat.	C	101	382	32	115	24	1	2	41	.301	465	63	*20	.964
1982—San Diego	Nat.	C-1B	153	562	75	166	42	1	21	97	.295	777	66	9	.989
1983—San Diego	Nat.	C-1B	149	549	47	156	27	2	17	98	.284	807	82	12	.987
1984—San Diego	Nat.	C	148	530	54	127	16	1	14	57	.240	708	54	14	.982
1985—San Diego	Nat.	C-1B	143	532	54	139	27	1	10	74	.261	662	68	10	.986
1986—San Diego‡	Nat.	C	141	432	46	114	22	1	12	57	.264	692	70	8	.990
Major League Totals—9 Years			962	3373	347	916	177	10	82	477	.272	4523	436	82	.984

Selected by St. Louis Cardinals' organization in 1st round (sixth player selected) of free-agent draft, June 7, 1977.
†Traded with Catcher Steve Swisher, Pitchers John Littlefield, Al Olmsted, Kim Seaman and John Urrea and Infielder Mike Phillips to San Diego Padres for Pitchers Rollie Fingers and Bob Shirley, Catcher-First Baseman Gene Tenace and a player to be named later, December 8, 1980; St. Louis Cardinals' organization acquired catcher Bob Geren to complete deal, December 10, 1980.
‡Traded with Pitcher Mark Williamson to Baltimore Orioles for Pitcher Storm Davis, October 30, 1986.

CHAMPIONSHIP SERIES RECORD

Year Club	League	Pos.	G.	AB.	R.	H.	2B.	3B.	HR.	RBI.	B.A.	PO.	A.	E.	F.A.
1984—San Diego	Nat.	C	5	18	2	4	0	0	0	1	.222	28	4	0	1.000

WORLD SERIES RECORD

Year Club	League	Pos.	G.	AB.	R.	H.	2B.	3B.	HR.	RBI.	B.A.	PO.	A.	E.	F.A.
1984—San Diego	Nat.	C	5	19	2	4	1	0	1	3	.211	30	2	0	1.000

ALL-STAR GAME RECORD

Year League	Pos.	AB.	R.	H.	2B.	3B.	HR.	RBI.	B.A.	PO.	A.	E.	F.A.
1981—National	PH	1	0	0	0	0	0	0	.000	0	0	0	.000
1985—National	C	2	0	1	0	0	0	1	.500	0	0	1	.000
All-Star Game Totals—2 Years		3	0	1	0	0	0	1	.333	0	0	1	.000

Member of National League All-Star Team in 1983; did not play.

MATTHEW LON KEOUGH
Name pronounced KEE-oh.
(Matt)

Born July 3, 1955, at Pomona, Calif.
Height, 6.02. Weight, 175.
Throws and bats righthanded.
Attended University of California, Los Angeles, Calif.
Son of Marty Keough, outfielder-first baseman with Boston, Cleveland, Washington, Cincinnati, Atlanta and Chicago N.L., 1956 through 1966; minor league manager, San Diego Padres' organization, 1970; scout, San Diego Padres, 1969 through 1976; scout, Los Angeles Dodgers, 1977 through 1979; and scout with St. Louis Cardinals since 1980; nephew of Joe Keough, outfielder with Oakland A's, Kansas City Royals and Chicago White Sox, 1968 through 1973.

Tied major league record for most consecutive games lost, start of season (14), 1979.
Led American League in home runs allowed with 38 in 1982.
Tied for California League lead in sacrifice flies with 9 in 1975.
Named American League Comeback Player of the Year by THE SPORTING NEWS, 1980.

Year Club	League	G.	IP.	W.	L.	Pct.	H.	R.	ER.	SO.	BB.	ERA.
1976—Chattanooga	Southern	2	2	0	0	.000	1	0	0	2	0	0.00
1977—Chattanooga	Southern	26	175	9	12	.429	162	87	74	★153	67	3.81
1977—Oakland	American	7	43	1	3	.250	39	25	23	23	22	4.81
1978—Oakland	American	32	197	8	15	.348	178	90	71	108	85	3.24
1979—Oakland	American	30	177	2	17	.105	220	115	99	95	78	5.03
1980—Oakland	American	34	250	16	13	.552	218	94	81	121	94	2.92
1981—Oakland	American	19	140	10	6	.625	125	56	53	60	45	3.41
1982—Oakland	American	34	209⅓	11	●18	.379	233	★144	★133	75	101	5.72
1983—Oakland†-New York	American	26	99⅔	5	7	.417	109	71	59	54	51	5.33
1984—Nashville‡§	Southern	7	40	2	4	.333	41	32	30	32	32	6.75
1985—Louisville xy	Am. Assoc.	19	110	3	7	.300	88	44	41	92	42	3.35
1985—St. Louis z	National	4	10	0	1	.000	10	5	5	10	4	4.50
1986—Chicago a-Houston	National	29	64	5	4	.556	58	31	28	44	30	3.94
1986—Tucson b	P. Coast	8	50⅔	3	3	.500	56	31	22	42	21	3.91
American League Totals—7 Years		182	1116	53	79	.402	1122	595	519	536	476	4.19
National League Totals—2 Years		33	74	5	5	.500	68	36	33	54	34	4.01
Major League Totals—9 Years		215	1190	58	84	.408	1190	631	552	590	510	4.17

Selected by Oakland A's organization in 7th round of free-agent draft, June 5, 1973.
†Traded to New York Yankees for First Baseman Marshall Brant and Pitcher Ben Callahan, June 15, 1983.
‡On disabled list, May 22 to September 10, 1984.
§Released, November 5, 1984; signed by St. Louis Cardinals' organization, April 21, 1985.
xOn temporary inactive list, April 21 to May 7, 1985.
yOn disabled list, June 3 to June 21, 1985.
zGranted free agency, November 12, 1985; signed by Chicago Cubs, February 1, 1986.
aReleased, June 14, 1986; signed by Tucson (Houston Astros' organization), June 30, 1986.
bReleased, October 24, 1986.

CHAMPIONSHIP SERIES RECORD

Year Club	League	G.	IP.	W.	L.	Pct.	H.	R.	ER.	SO.	BB.	ERA.
1981—Oakland	American	1	8⅓	0	1	.000	7	2	1	4	6	1.08

ALL-STAR GAME RECORD

Year League	IP.	W.	L.	Pct.	H.	R.	ER.	SO.	BB.	ERA.
1978—American	⅓	0	0	.000	1	0	0	0	0	0.00

RECORD AS INFIELDER

Led Southern League third basemen in putouts with 110 and assists with 252 in 1976.
Led California League shortstops in errors with 56 in 1975.

Year Club	League	Pos.	G.	AB.	R.	H.	2B.	3B.	HR.	RBI.	B.A.	PO.	A.	E.	F.A.
1974—Burlington	Midw.	SS-1B	98	323	31	64	14	2	4	24	.198	143	207	34	.911
1975—Modesto	Calif.	SS-3B	123	445	73	135	★34	2	13	81	.303	191	312	57	.898
1976—Chattanooga	South.	3-S-O-1-P	124	420	43	88	13	3	6	52	.210	125	274	25	.941

KURT DAVID KEPSHIRE

Born July 3, 1959, at Bridgeport, Conn.
Height, 6.01. Weight, 180.
Throws right and bats lefthanded.
Attended University of New Haven, New Haven, Conn.

Tied for Pioneer League lead in intentional bases on balls issued with 4 in 1979.

Year Club	League	G.	IP.	W.	L.	Pct.	H.	R.	ER.	SO.	BB.	ERA.
1979—Billings	Pioneer	24	50	4	0	1.000	30	16	14	57	27	2.52
1980—Tampa	Florida St.	29	54	5	4	.556	48	20	12	26	19	2.00
1980—Eugene	Northwest	8	42	3	3	.500	54	36	29	18	15	6.21
1981—Cedar Rapids	Midwest	39	98	7	5	.583	98	63	47	94	32	4.32
1982—Cedar Rapids	Midwest	21	33	3	1	.750	23	11	8	29	10	2.18
1982—Waterbury	Eastern	30	46⅓	1	4	.200	35	22	21	31	22	4.08
1982—Indianapolis†	Am. Assoc.	5	9	0	0	.000	7	5	5	5	2	5.00
1983—Arkansas	Texas	19	35⅔	3	2	.600	35	17	14	23	5	3.53

Year Club	League	G.	IP.	W.	L.	Pct.	H.	R.	ER.	SO.	BB.	ERA.
1983—Louisville	Am. Assoc.	21	83⅓	6	2	.750	88	44	34	52	24	3.67
1984—Louisville	Am. Assoc.	16	107⅔	7	5	.583	87	56	55	85	63	4.60
1984—St. Louis	National	17	109	6	5	.545	100	47	40	71	44	3.30
1985—St. Louis	National	32	153⅓	10	9	.526	155	89	81	67	71	4.75
1986—St. Louis	National	2	8	0	1	.000	8	4	4	6	4	4.50
1986—Louisville	Am. Assoc.	13	66⅔	1	9	.100	82	57	48	46	35	6.48
1986—Arkansas‡	Texas	9	51⅔	2	4	.333	58	34	25	28	14	4.35
Major League Totals—3 Years		51	270⅓	16	15	.516	263	140	125	144	119	4.16

Selected by Cincinnati Reds' organization in 24th round of free-agent draft, June 5, 1979.
†Drafted by St. Louis Cardinals, December 6, 1982.
‡Granted free agency, October 15, 1986.

CHARLES PATRICK KERFELD
(Charlie)

Born September 28, 1963, at Knob Noster, Mo.
Height, 6.06. Weight, 225.
Throws and bats righthanded.
Attended Yavapai College, Prescott, Ariz.

Major League saves: 1986 (7)
Led South Atlantic League pitchers in complete games with 12 and tied for lead in games started with 28 in 1983.
Named South Atlantic League Pitcher of the Year, 1983.

Year Club	League	G.	IP.	W.	L.	Pct.	H.	R.	ER.	SO.	BB.	ERA.
1983—Asheville	S. Atlantic	28	★192	★16	10	.615	171	84	62	189	85	2.91
1984—Columbus†	Southern	24	162⅔	14	9	.609	140	80	54	118	79	2.99
1984—Tucson	P. Coast	1	3⅔	0	1	.000	6	4	4	3	1	9.82
1985—Tucson	P. Coast	26	163⅓	10	11	.476	176	95	80	123	74	4.41
1985—Houston	National	11	44⅓	4	2	.667	44	22	20	30	25	4.06
1986—Houston‡	National	61	93⅔	11	2	.846	71	32	27	77	42	2.59
Major League Totals—2 Years		72	138	15	4	.789	115	54	47	107	67	3.07

Selected by Philadelphia Phillies' organization in 24th round of free-agent draft, June 8, 1981.
Selected by Seattle Mariners' organization in secondary phase of free-agent draft, January 12, 1982.
Selected by Houston Astros' organization in secondary phase of free-agent draft, June 7, 1982.
†On disabled list, June 4 to June 28, 1984.
‡On disabled list, June 14 to July 2, 1986.

CHAMPIONSHIP SERIES RECORD

Year Club	League	G.	IP.	W.	L.	Pct.	H.	R.	ER.	SO.	BB.	ERA.
1986—Houston	National	3	4	0	1	.000	2	1	1	4	1	2.25

JAMES LESTER KERN
(Jim)

Born March 15, 1949, at Gladwin, Mich.
Height, 6.05. Weight, 195.
Throws and bats righthanded.
Attended Delta Junior College, University Center, Mich., and
Michigan State University, East Lansing, Mich.

Pitched seven-inning, 2-0 no-hit victory against San Jose, May 29, 1971.
Major League saves: 1976 (15), 1977 (18), 1978 (13), 1979 (29), 1980 (2), 1981 (6), 1982 (5). Total—88.
Led Western Carolinas League in wild pitches with 25 in 1970.
Tied for American Association lead in wild pitches with 17 and balks with 2 in 1974.
Tied for California League lead in balks with 2 in 1971.
Named American League co-Fireman of the Year by THE SPORTING NEWS, 1979.
Named righthanded pitcher on THE SPORTING NEWS American League All-Star Team, 1979.
Named American Association Pitcher of the Year, 1974.

Year Club	League	G.	IP.	W.	L.	Pct.	H.	R.	ER.	SO.	BB.	ERA.
1968—Rock Hill	W. Carol.	12	28	0	3	.000	29	30	21	25	26	6.75
1968—Sarasota Indians	Gulf Coast	12	45	4	4	.500	44	32	19	48	32	3.80
1969—†						(In Military Service)						
1970—Reno	California	4	15	0	0	.000	9	12	10	20	20	6.00
1970—Sumter	W. Carol.	14	72	5	6	.455	57	47	39	71	70	4.88
1971—Reno	California	24	100	7	9	.438	99	91	73	109	100	6.57
1972—Elmira	Eastern	22	104	3	11	.214	87	55	50	90	73	4.33
1973—San Antonio	Texas	25	166	11	7	.611	130	76	55	182	★129	2.98
1974—Oklahoma City	Am. Assoc.	25	189	★17	7	.708	139	63	53	★220	104	2.52
1974—Cleveland	American	4	15	0	1	.000	16	9	8	11	14	4.80
1975—Oklahoma City	Am. Assoc.	3	14	1	1	.500	12	10	10	11	11	6.43
1975—Cleveland	American	13	72	1	2	.333	60	31	30	55	45	3.75
1976—Cleveland	American	50	118	10	7	.588	91	38	31	111	50	2.36
1977—Cleveland	American	60	92	8	10	.444	85	39	35	91	47	3.42
1978—Cleveland‡	American	58	99	10	10	.500	77	36	34	95	58	3.09
1979—Texas	American	71	143	13	5	.722	99	35	25	136	62	1.57
1980—Texas§	American	38	63	3	11	.214	65	38	34	40	45	4.86
1981—Texas xyz	American	23	30	1	2	.333	21	10	9	20	22	2.70
1981—Wichita	Am. Assoc.	2	6	0	0	.000	2	0	0	6	5	0.00
1982—Cincinnati a	National	50	76	3	5	.375	61	27	24	43	48	2.84
1982—Chicago	American	13	28	2	1	.667	20	16	16	23	12	5.14

Year Club	League	G.	IP.	W.	L.	Pct.	H.	R.	ER.	SO.	BB.	ERA.
1983—Chicago bc	American	1	⅔	0	0	.000	1	1	0	0	0	0.00
1984—Philadelphia d	National	8	13⅓	0	1	.000	20	16	15	8	10	10.13
1984—El Paso	Texas	8	15	2	0	1.000	19	10	10	13	8	6.00
1984—Milwaukee e	American	6	4⅔	1	0	1.000	6	0	0	4	3	0.00
1985—Vancouver	P. Coast	5	9⅓	0	0	.000	3	3	3	4	8	2.89
1985—Milwaukee f	American	5	11	0	1	.000	14	8	8	3	5	6.55
1986—Cleveland g	American	16	27⅓	1	1	.500	34	28	24	11	23	7.90
American League Totals—13 Years		358	703⅔	50	51	.495	589	289	254	600	386	3.25
National League Totals—2 Years		58	89⅓	3	6	.333	81	43	39	51	58	3.93
Major League Totals—13 Years		416	793	53	57	.482	670	332	293	651	444	3.33

Signed as free agent by Cleveland Indians' organization, September 4, 1967.
†On military list, May 11, 1969 through January 7, 1970.
‡Traded with Infielder Larvell Blanks to Texas Rangers for Outfielder Bobby Bonds and Pitcher Len Barker, October 3, 1978.
§On disabled list, August 19 to September 15, 1980.
xOn disabled list, April 30 to June 2, 1981; included rehabilitation disability assignment to Wichita, May 26 to June 2, 1981.
yTraded to New York Mets for Second Baseman Doug Flynn and Pitcher Dan Boitano, December 11, 1981.
zTraded with Catcher Alex Trevino and Pitcher Greg Harris by New York Mets to Cincinnati Reds for Outfielder George Foster, February 10, 1982.
aTraded to Chicago White Sox for two players to be named later, August 23, 1982; Cincinnati Reds' organization acquired Third Baseman Wade Rowdon and Outfielder Leo Garcia to complete deal, September 7, 1982.
bOn disabled list, April 6, 1983 through remainder of season.
cReleased, March 1, 1984; signed by Philadelphia Phillies, June 3, 1984.
dReleased, July 27, 1984; signed by El Paso (Milwaukee Brewers' organization), August 8, 1984.
eGranted free agency, November 8, 1984; re-signed by Brewers' organization, January 8, 1985.
fReleased, June 17, 1985; signed by Maine (Cleveland Indians' organization), February 25, 1986.
gReleased, June 17, 1986.

ALL-STAR GAME RECORD

Year League	IP.	W.	L.	Pct.	H.	R.	ER.	SO.	BB.	ERA.
1977—American	1	0	0	.000	0	0	0	2	0	0.00
1978—American	⅔	0	0	.000	1	0	0	1	1	0.00
1979—American	2⅔	0	1	.000	2	2	2	3	3	6.75
All-Star Game Totals—3 Years	4⅓	0	1	.000	3	2	2	6	4	4.15

JAMES EDWARD KEY
(Jimmy)

Born April 22, 1961, at Huntsville, Ala.
Height, 6.01. Weight, 185.
Throws left and bats righthanded.
Attended Clemson University, Clemson, S.C.

Major League saves: 1984 (10).

Year Club	League	G.	IP.	W.	L.	Pct.	H.	R.	ER.	SO.	BB.	ERA.
1982—Medicine Hat	Pioneer	5	31⅓	2	1	.667	27	12	8	25	10	2.30
1982—Florence	S. Atlantic	9	58	5	2	.714	59	33	24	49	18	3.72
1983—Knoxville	Southern	14	101	6	5	.545	86	35	32	57	40	2.85
1983—Syracuse	Int'national	16	89⅓	4	8	.333	87	58	41	71	33	4.13
1984—Toronto	American	63	62	4	5	.444	70	37	32	44	32	4.65
1985—Toronto†	American	35	212⅔	14	6	.700	188	77	71	85	50	3.00
1986—Toronto	American	36	232	14	11	.560	222	98	92	141	74	3.57
Major League Totals—3 Years		134	506⅔	32	22	.593	480	212	195	270	156	3.46

Selected by Chicago White Sox' organization in 10th round of free-agent draft, June 5, 1979.
Selected by Toronto Blue Jays' organization in 3rd round of free-agent draft, June 7, 1982.
†Appeared in one game as a pinch-runner.

CHAMPIONSHIP SERIES RECORD

Year Club	League	G.	IP.	W.	L.	Pct.	H.	R.	ER.	SO.	BB.	ERA.
1985—Toronto	American	2	8⅔	0	1	.000	15	5	5	5	2	5.19

ALL-STAR GAME RECORD

Year League	IP.	W.	L.	Pct.	H.	R.	ER.	SO.	BB.	ERA.
1985—American	⅓	0	0	.000	0	0	0	0	0	0.00

SAM KHALIFA
Name pronounced Kuh-LEE-fuh.

(Sammy)

Born December 5, 1963, at Fontana, Calif.
Height, 5.11. Weight, 170.
Throws and bats righthanded.

Major League stolen bases: 1985 (5).

Year Club	League	Pos.	G.	AB.	R.	H.	2B.	3B.	HR.	RBI.	B.A.	PO.	A.	E.	F.A.
1982—Bradenton Pir.	Gulf. C.	SS	6	25	1	2	0	0	0	0	.080	12	26	4	.905
1982—Greenwood	S. Atl.	SS	48	177	29	54	6	1	0	19	.305	69	136	19	.915

Year	Club	League	Pos.	G.	AB.	R.	H.	2B.	3B.	HR.	RBI.	B.A.	PO.	A.	E.	F.A.
1983—Alexandria†	Carol.	★SS-2B	103	356	42	96	19	6	1	49	.270	156	279	★33	.929
1983—Lynn	East.	SS	5	15	1	3	0	0	0	1	.200	8	9	0	1.000
1984—Nashua‡	East.	SS	91	344	39	82	12	4	1	36	.238	151	266	24	.946
1985—Hawaii	P. C.	SS-2B	67	217	36	61	14	5	1	22	.281	89	193	11	.962
1985—Pittsburgh	Nat.	SS	95	320	30	76	14	3	2	31	.238	156	316	16	.967
1986—Pittsburgh	Nat.	SS-2B	64	151	8	28	6	0	0	4	.185	94	168	10	.963
1986—Hawaii	P. C.	SS-2B	50	200	30	63	9	4	1	26	.315	82	165	7	.972
Major League Totals—2 Years			159	471	38	104	20	3	2	35	.221	250	484	26	.966

Selected by Pittsburgh Pirates' organization in 1st round (seventh player selected) of free-agent draft, June 7, 1982.
†On disabled list, May 6 to May 21, 1983.
‡On disabled list, April 13 to May 9 and August 11, 1984 through remainder of season.

STEVEN GEORGE KIEFER
(Steve)

Born October 18, 1960, at Chicago, Ill.
Height, 6.01. Weight, 180.
Throws and bats righthanded.
Attended Cerritos College, Norwalk, Calif. and Fullerton College, Fullerton, Calif.

Led Pacific Coast League shortstops in errors with 35 in 1984.
Tied for Eastern League lead in sacrifice hits with 12 in 1983.

Year	Club	League	Pos.	G.	AB.	R.	H.	2B.	3B.	HR.	RBI.	B.A.	PO.	A.	E.	F.A.
1981—Medford	N'west	SS-3B	55	192	38	47	7	5	4	22	.245	68	175	17	.935
1982—Madison	Midw.	SS	124	415	72	97	24	1	15	58	.234	173	395	44	.928
1983—Albany	East.	SS-3B-OF	123	415	68	102	18	1	19	81	.246	186	306	38	.928
1984—Tacoma	P. C.	SS-3B	125	455	63	122	18	3	16	54	.268	189	328	38	.932
1984—Oakland	Amer.	SS-3B	23	40	7	7	1	2	0	2	.175	15	35	5	.909
1985—Tacoma†	P. C.	3B-SS	85	331	41	87	25	2	12	53	.263	80	171	13	.951
1985—Oakland‡	Amer.	3B	40	66	8	13	1	1	1	10	.197	15	37	7	.881
1986—Vancouver	P. C.	3B-2B-SS	126	426	67	114	22	6	15	69	.268	123	266	24	.942
1986—Milwaukee	Amer.	SS	2	6	0	0	0	0	0	0	.000	7	8	0	1.000
Major League Totals—3 Years			65	112	15	20	2	3	1	12	.179	37	80	12	.907

Selected by Oakland A's organization in 1st round (16th player selected) of free-agent draft, January 13, 1981.
†On disabled list, May 6 to May 20, 1985.
‡Traded with Pitchers Mike Fulmer and Pete Kendrick and Catcher Charlie O'Brien to Milwaukee Brewers for Pitcher Moose Haas, March 30, 1986.

PAUL NELSON KILGUS

Born February 2, 1962, at Bowling Green, Ky.
Height, 6.01. Weight, 175.
Throws and bats lefthanded.
Attended University of Kentucky, Lexington, Ky.

Year	Club	League	G.	IP.	W.	L.	Pct.	H.	R.	ER.	SO.	BB.	ERA.
1984—Tri-Cities	Northwest	14	78⅓	7	5	.583	87	38	25	60	31	2.87
1985—Salem	Carolina	38	84⅓	3	1	.750	69	28	19	67	26	2.03
1986—Tulsa	Texas	41	103⅔	3	7	.300	102	56	43	59	36	3.73

Selected by Texas Rangers' organization in 43rd round of free-agent draft, June 4, 1984.

JOHN STEVEN KILNER

Born June 20, 1965, at Cleveland, O.
Height, 6.00. Weight, 175.
Throws and bats lefthanded.

Led Appalachian League pitchers in balks with 4 and tied for lead in games started with 13 in 1984.

Year	Club	League	G.	IP.	W.	L.	Pct.	H.	R.	ER.	SO.	BB.	ERA.
1984—Pulaski	Ap'lachian	14	72	4	3	.571	66	35	27	72	40	3.38
1985—Sumter	S. Atlantic	23	130⅓	8	5	.615	111	67	55	163	60	3.80
1986—Durham	Carolina	23	141	6	8	.429	133	79	71	89	63	4.53

Signed as free agent by Atlanta Braves' organization, September 16, 1983.

ERIC STEVEN KING

Born April 10, 1964, at Oxnard, Calif.
Height, 6.02. Weight, 180.
Throws and bats righthanded.

Tied major league record for most putouts by pitcher, nine-inning game (6), July 8, 1986.
Major League saves: 1986 (3).

Year	Club	League	G.	IP.	W.	L.	Pct.	H.	R.	ER.	SO.	BB.	ERA.
1983—Great Falls	Pioneer	20	56⅓	3	4	.429	58	31	27	61	14	4.31
1984—Clinton	Midwest	35	147⅓	5	10	.333	142	74	55	124	76	3.36
1985—Shreveport†‡	Texas	15	104⅔	5	3	.625	74	34	27	80	30	2.32
1986—Nashville	Am. Assoc.	6	38⅓	3	2	.600	29	16	15	38	16	3.52
1986—Detroit	American	33	138⅓	11	4	.733	108	54	54	79	63	3.51
Major League Totals—1 Year		33	138⅓	11	4	.733	108	54	54	79	63	3.51

Signed as free agent by San Francisco Giants' organization, June 11, 1983.
†On suspended list, July 3 to July 13, 1985, then transferred to disabled list, July 13 to July 27, 1985.

‡Traded with Pitcher Dave LaPoint and Catcher Matt Nokes to Detroit Tigers for Pitcher Juan Berenguer, Catcher Bob Melvin and a player to be named later, October 7, 1985; San Francisco Giants acquired Pitcher Scott Medvin to complete deal, December 11, 1985.

JEFFREY WAYNE KING
(Jeff)

Born December 26, 1964, at Marion, Ind.
Height, 6.01. Weight, 175.
Throws and bats righthanded.
Attended University of Arkansas, Fayetteville, Ark.
Son of Jack King, minor league catcher, 1954 and 1955; and brother of James King, shortstop drafted
by Philadelphia Phillies' organization in 1982 and Seattle Mariners' organization in 1984.

Received reported $180,000 bonus to sign with Pittsburgh Pirates, 1986.
Named College Player of the Year by THE SPORTING NEWS, 1986.
Named third baseman on THE SPORTING NEWS College Baseball All-America Team, 1986.

Year	Club	League	Pos.	G.	AB.	R.	H.	2B.	3B.	HR.	RBI.	B.A.	PO.	A.	E.	F.A.
1986—Prince William	Carol.		3B	37	132	18	31	4	1	6	20	.235	25	50	8	.904

Selected by Chicago Cubs' organization in 23rd round of free-agent draft, June 6, 1983.
Selected by Pittsburgh Pirates' organization in 1st round (first player selected) of free-agent draft, June 2, 1986.

MICHAEL SCOTT KINGERY
(Mike)

Born March 29, 1961, at St. James, Minn.
Height, 6.00. Weight, 180.
Throws and bats lefthanded.
Attended Willmar Community College, Willmar, Minn.;
and St. Cloud State University, St. Cloud, Minn.

Major League stolen bases: 1986 (7).
Led Florida State League in intentional bases on balls received with 11 in 1983.
Tied for South Atlantic League lead in double plays by outfielders with 5 in 1982.

Year	Club	League	Pos.	G.	AB.	R.	H.	2B.	3B.	HR.	RBI.	B.A.	PO.	A.	E.	F.A.
1980—Royals—Gold	Gulf C.		OF	44	143	12	32	3	3	0	13	.224	78	5	2	.976
1981—Charleston†	S. Atl.		OF	69	213	33	57	3	4	3	25	.268	80	7	4	.956
1982—Charleston	S. Atl.		OF	140	513	65	163	19	4	8	75	.318	250	21	7	.975
1983—Fort Myers	Fla. St.		OF	123	436	68	116	9	7	2	51	.266	200	16	5	.977
1984—Memphis	South.		OF	139	455	65	135	19	3	4	58	.297	291	18	6	.981
1985—Omaha	A. A.		OF	132	444	51	113	25	6	2	49	.255	247	17	5	.981
1986—Omaha	A. A.		OF	79	298	47	99	14	8	3	47	.332	171	10	1	.995
1986—Kansas City‡	Amer.		OF	62	209	25	54	8	5	3	14	.258	102	6	3	.973
Major League Totals—1 Year				62	209	25	54	8	5	3	14	.258	102	6	3	.973

Signed as free agent by Kansas City Royals' organization, August 27, 1979.
†On disabled list, July 29 to August 15, 1981.
‡Traded with Pitchers Scott Bankhead and Steve Shields to Seattle Mariners for Outfielder Danny Tartabull and Pitcher Rick Luecken, December 10, 1986.

DAVID ARTHUR KINGMAN
(Dave)

Born December 21, 1948, at Pendleton, Ore.
Height, 6.06. Weight, 215.
Throws and bats righthanded.
Attended Harper College, Palatine, Ill., and University of Southern
California, Los Angeles, Calif.

Tied major league records for most home runs, two consecutive games (5), July 27 and 28, 1979; most times, three or more home runs, game, season (2), May 17 and July 28, 1979; most strikeouts, nine-inning game (5), May 28, 1982; most unassisted double plays by first baseman, game (2), July 25, 1982.
Tied modern major league record for most clubs played on, season, major leagues (4), 1977.
Tied National League record for fewest errors by first baseman for leader in errors, season (13), 1974.
Major League stolen bases: 1971 (5), 1972 (16), 1973 (8), 1974 (8), 1975 (7), 1976 (7), 1977 (5), 1978 (3), 1979 (4), 1980 (2), 1981 (6), 1982 (4), 1983 (2), 1984 (2), 1985 (3), 1986 (3). Total—85.
Hit three home runs in a game June 4, 1976, May 14, 1978 and May 17, July 28, 1979 and April 16, 1984.
Hit for the cycle, April 16, 1972.
Led American League in sacrifice flies with 14 in 1984.
Led National League batters in strikeouts with 131 in 1979, 105 in 1981 and 156 in 1982.
Led National League in slugging percentage with .613 in 1979.
Led National League first basemen in errors with 13 in 1974.
Named American League Comeback Player of the Year by THE SPORTING NEWS, 1984.
Named designated hitter on THE SPORTING NEWS American League All-Star Team, 1984.
Named outfielder on THE SPORTING NEWS National League All-Star Team, 1979.
Named outfielder on THE SPORTING NEWS College Baseball All-America Team, 1970.

Year	Club	League	Pos.	G.	AB.	R.	H.	2B.	3B.	HR.	RBI.	B.A.	PO.	A.	E.	F.A.
1970—Amarillo	Texas		1B-OF	60	210	41	62	9	1	15	41	.295	226	9	9	.963
1971—Phoenix	P. C.		OF-1B	105	392	89	109	29	5	26	99	.278	785	40	8	.990
1971—San Francisco	Nat.		1B	41	115	17	32	10	2	6	24	.278	168	9	4	.978
1972—San Francisco	Nat.		3B-1B-OF	135	472	65	106	17	4	29	83	.225	496	159	22	.968
1973—San Francisco	Nat.		3B-1B-P	112	305	54	62	10	1	24	55	.203	313	146	22	.954
1974—San Francisco†	Nat.		1B-3B-OF	121	350	41	78	18	2	18	55	.223	696	98	25	.969

Year	Club	League	Pos.	G.	AB.	R.	H.	2B.	3B.	HR.	RBI.	B.A.	PO.	A.	E.	F.A.
1975—New York	Nat.	OF-1B-3B	134	502	65	116	22	1	36	88	.231	526	69	14	.977
1976—New York‡	Nat.	OF-1B	123	474	70	113	14	1	37	86	.238	293	18	9	.972
1977—N.Y.§-S.D. x	Nat.	OF-1B-3B	114	379	38	84	16	0	20	67	.222	333	24	7	.981
1977—Cal. y-N.Y. z	Amer.	1B-OF	18	60	9	13	4	0	6	11	.217	73	5	2	.975
1978—Chicago a	Nat.	OF-1B	119	395	65	105	17	4	28	79	.266	226	10	6	.975
1979—Chicago	Nat.	OF	145	532	97	153	19	5	★48	115	.288	240	11	12	.954
1980—Chicago bcd	Nat.	OF-1B	81	255	31	71	8	0	18	57	.278	119	10	8	.942
1981—New York	Nat.	1B-OF	100	353	40	78	11	3	22	59	.221	548	34	20	.967
1982—New York	Nat.	1B	149	535	80	109	9	1	★37	99	.204	1232	69	18	.986
1983—New York e	Nat.	1B-OF	100	248	25	49	7	0	13	29	.198	450	28	3	.994
1984—Oakland f	Amer.	1B	147	549	68	147	23	1	35	118	.268	55	2	0	1.000
1985—Oakland g	Amer.	1B	158	592	66	141	16	0	30	91	.238	50	1	0	1.000
1986—Oakland h	Amer.	1B	144	561	70	118	19	0	35	94	.210	17	0	2	.895
National League Totals—13 Years			1474	4915	688	1156	178	24	336	896	.235	5640	685	170	.974
American League Totals—4 Years			467	1762	213	419	62	1	106	314	.238	195	8	4	.981
Major League Totals—16 Years			1941	6677	901	1575	240	25	442	1210	.236	5835	693	174	.974

Selected by California Angels' organization in 2nd round of free-agent draft, June 6, 1967.
Selected by Baltimore Orioles' organization in secondary phase of free-agent draft, January 27, 1968.
Selected by San Francisco Giants' organization in secondary phase of free-agent draft, June 4, 1970.
†Sold to New York Mets for an estimated $125,000, February 28, 1975.
‡On disabled list, July 20 to August 27, 1976.
§Traded to San Diego Padres for Third Baseman-Outfielder Bobby Valentine and Pitcher Paul Siebert, June 15, 1977.
xSold on waivers to California Angels, September 6, 1977.
ySold to New York Yankees, September 15, 1977.
zGranted free agency, November 2, 1977; signed by Chicago Cubs, November 30, 1977.
aOn disabled list, July 1 to July 26, 1978.
bOn supplemental disabled list, June 13 to June 28 and July 10 to August 6, 1980.
cOn disabled list, August 6 to August 12, 1980.
dTraded to New York Mets for Outfielder Steve Henderson and cash, February 28, 1981.
eReleased, January 30, 1984; signed by Oakland A's, March 29, 1984.
fGranted free agency, November 8, 1984; re-signed by A's, December 19, 1984.
gReleased, December 20, 1985; re-signed by A's, January 20, 1986.
hGranted free agency, November 12, 1986.

CHAMPIONSHIP SERIES RECORD

Year	Club	League	Pos.	G.	AB.	R.	H.	2B.	3B.	HR.	RBI.	B.A.	PO.	A.	E.	F.A.
1971—San Francisco	Nat.	PH-OF	4	9	0	1	0	0	0	0	.111	5	0	0	1.000

ALL-STAR GAME RECORD

Year	League	Pos.	AB.	R.	H.	2B.	3B.	HR.	RBI.	B.A.	PO.	A.	E.	F.A.
1976—National		OF	2	0	0	0	0	0	0	.000	1	0	0	1.000
1980—National		OF	1	0	0	0	0	0	0	.000	0	0	0	.000
All-Star Game Totals—2 Years			3	0	0	0	0	0	0	.000	1	0	0	1.000

Named to National League All-Star Team for 1979 game; replaced due to injury by Keith Hernandez.

PITCHING RECORD

Year	Club	League	G.	IP.	W.	L.	Pct.	H.	R.	ER.	SO.	BB.	ERA.
1973—San Francisco	National	2	4	0	0	.000	3	4	4	4	6	9.00

MICHAEL JOHN KINNUNEN

Name pronounced KIN-nu-nen.

(Mike)

Born April 1, 1958, at Seattle, Wash.
Height, 6.01. Weight, 205.
Throws and bats lefthanded.
Attended Washington State University, Pullman, Wash.

Year	Club	League	G.	IP.	W.	L.	Pct.	H.	R.	ER.	SO.	BB.	ERA.
1979—Orlando	Southern	17	118	6	6	.500	129	63	54	55	45	4.12
1980—Toledo	Int'national	15	14	2	2	.500	13	5	4	9	5	2.57
1980—Minnesota	American	21	25	0	0	.000	29	18	14	8	9	5.04
1981—Toledo†	Int'national	50	72	4	4	.500	94	53	44	36	35	5.50
1982—Louisville‡	Am. Assoc.	16	47⅔	2	3	.400	50	29	25	21	21	4.72
1982—Arkansas§	Texas	18	30⅔	4	2	.667	28	6	6	18	17	1.76
1983—Memphis	Southern	38	63	6	4	.600	52	29	18	46	27	2.57
1983—Wichita	Am. Assoc.	13	20⅓	0	1	.000	24	20	18	9	13	7.97
1984—Jacksonville	Southern	38	75	6	2	.750	61	33	31	42	56	3.72
1984—Indianapolis x	Am. Assoc.	16	37	3	1	.750	35	20	19	32	19	4.62
1985—Omaha y	Am. Assoc.	53	52	2	0	1.000	41	24	20	30	41	3.46
1986—Rochester	Int'national	47	53⅔	1	3	.250	41	18	14	43	29	2.35
1986—Baltimore	American	9	7	0	0	.000	8	6	5	1	5	6.43
Major League Totals—2 Years		30	32	0	0	.000	37	24	19	9	14	5.34

Selected by Minnesota Twins' organization in 10th round of free-agent draft, June 5, 1979.
†Traded to St. Louis Cardinals' organization for Pitcher Jeff Little, October 21, 1981.
‡On disabled list, April 13 to April 23, 1982.
§Released, April 4, 1983; signed by Memphis (Montreal Expos' organization), April 27, 1983.

ROBERT WAYNE KIPPER
(Bob)

Born July 8, 1964, at Aurora, Ill.
Height, 6.02. Weight, 200.
Throws left and bats righthanded.

Pitched seven-inning, 9-0 no-hit victory against San Jose, June 10, 1984 (second game).
Named California League Pitcher of the Year, 1984.

Year Club	League	G.	IP.	W.	L.	Pct.	H.	R.	ER.	SO.	BB.	ERA.
1982—Salem	Northwest	13	76⅔	6	5	.545	62	46	38	65	52	4.46
1983—Peoria†	Midwest	22	127⅔	5	8	.385	112	77	66	105	52	4.65
1984—Redwood	California	26	185	*18	8	.692	147	61	42	98	65	*2.04
1985—California	American	2	3⅓	0	1	.000	7	8	8	0	3	21.60
1985—Midland‡	Texas	9	49⅔	3	3	.500	52	22	17	31	10	3.08
1985—Edmonton§x-Hawaii	P. Coast	7	49⅔	3	0	1.000	36	15	11	42	12	1.99
1985—Pittsburgh	National	5	24⅔	1	2	.333	21	16	14	13	7	5.11
1986—Pittsburgh y	National	20	114	6	8	.429	123	60	51	81	34	4.03
1986—Nashua	Eastern	4	18⅓	0	1	.000	14	7	7	19	3	3.44
American League Totals—1 Year		2	3⅓	0	1	.000	7	8	8	0	3	21.60
National League Totals—2 Years		25	138⅔	7	10	.412	144	76	65	94	41	4.22
Major League Totals—2 Years		27	142	7	11	.389	151	84	73	94	44	4.63

Selected by California Angels' organization in 1st round (eighth player selected) of free-agent draft, June 7, 1982.
†On disabled list, July 20 to August 8, 1983.
‡On disabled list, May 31 to June 10, 1985.
§Loaned to Hawaii (Pittsburgh Pirates' organization), August 2, 1985; returned, August 16, 1985.
xTraded to Pittsburgh Pirates' organization, August 16, 1985, completing deal in which Pittsburgh traded Pitchers John Candelaria and Al Holland and Outfielder George Hendrick to California Angels for Pitcher Pat Clements, Outfielder Mike Brown and a player to be named later, August 2, 1985.
yOn disabled list, June 29 to September 1, 1986; included rehabilitation disability assignment to Nashua, August 14 to September 1, 1986.

RONALD DALE KITTLE
(Ron)

Born January 5, 1958, at Gary, Indiana.
Height, 6.04. Weight, 220.
Throws and bats righthanded.

Tied major league record for most home runs, month of October (4), 1985.
Major League stolen bases: 1983 (8), 1984 (3), 1985 (1), 1986 (4). Total—16.
Led American League batters in strikeouts with 150 in 1983.
Led Pacific Coast League in total bases with 355, slugging percentage with .752 and tied for lead in being hit by pitch with 10 in 1982.
Led Eastern League in total bases with 270 and slugging percentage with .694 in 1981.
Named American League Rookie Player of the Year by THE SPORTING NEWS, 1983.
Named American League Rookie of the Year by Baseball Writers' Association of America, 1983.
Named Minor League Player of the Year by THE SPORTING NEWS, 1982.
Named Pacific Coast League Most Valuable Player, 1982.
Named Eastern League Most Valuable Player, 1981.

Year Club	League	Pos.	G.	AB.	R.	H.	2B.	3B.	HR.	RBI.	B.A.	PO.	A.	E.	F.A.
1977—Clinton†	Midw.	OF	22	53	9	10	4	0	0	3	.189	16	0	0	1.000
1977—Lethbridge	Pion.	OF	34	100	22	25	3	0	7	21	.250	29	2	6	.838
1978—Clinton‡	Midw.	OF	13	35	2	5	2	1	0	4	.143	4	1	1	.833
1979—Knoxville	South.	OF-C	53	157	28	43	9	1	6	26	.274	44	1	6	.980
1979—Appleton	Midw.	OF-C	35	120	18	31	3	1	2	12	.258	33	1	2	.972
1980—Appleton	Midw.	C-OF	61	209	31	66	15	3	12	56	.316	56	9	1	.985
1980—Glens Falls§	East.	OF	17	65	11	20	3	1	4	9	.308	24	4	3	.903
1981—Glens Falls x	East.	OF	109	389	97	127	17	3	*40	*103	.326	28	0	3	.903
1982—Edmonton	P. C.	OF-C	127	472	*121	163	22	10	*50	*144	.345	149	15	8	.953
1982—Chicago	Amer.	OF	20	29	3	7	2	0	1	7	.241	3	0	0	1.000
1983—Chicago	Amer.	OF	145	520	75	132	19	3	35	100	.254	234	7	9	.964
1984—Chicago	Amer.	OF	139	466	67	100	15	0	32	74	.215	226	14	7	.972
1985—Chicago y	Amer.	OF	116	379	51	87	12	0	26	58	.230	88	2	1	.989
1985—Buffalo	A. A.	OF	6	21	3	7	2	0	2	5	.333	2	0	0	1.000
1986—Chi. z-N.Y.	Amer.	OF	116	376	42	82	13	0	21	60	.218	39	3	0	1.000
Major League Totals—5 Years			536	1770	238	408	61	3	115	299	.231	590	26	17	.973

Signed as free agent by Los Angeles Dodgers' organization, July 5, 1977.
†On disabled list, April 30 to May 14, 1977.
‡Released, July 7, 1978; signed by Knoxville (Chicago White Sox' organization), September 4, 1978.
§On disabled list, July 27 to August 31, 1980.
xOn disabled list, April 21 to May 10, 1981.
yOn disabled list, July 4 to July 25, 1985; included rehabilitation disability assignment to Buffalo, July 19 to July 25, 1985.
zTraded with Infielder Wayne Tolleson and Catcher Joel Skinner to New York Yankees for Catcher Ron Hassey, Shortstop Carlos Martinez and a player to be named later, July 30, 1986; New York traded Catcher Bill Lindsey to Chicago White Sox' organization to complete deal, December 24, 1986.

CHAMPIONSHIP SERIES RECORD

Year	Club	League	Pos.	G.	AB.	R.	H.	2B.	3B.	HR.	RBI.	B.A.	PO.	A.	E.	F.A.
1983—Chicago		Amer.	OF	3	7	1	2	1	0	0	0	.286	3	0	0	1.000

ALL-STAR GAME RECORD

Year	League	Pos.	AB.	R.	H.	2B.	3B.	HR.	RBI.	B.A.	PO.	A.	E.	F.A.
1983—American		OF	2	1	1	0	0	0	0	.500	1	0	0	1.000

JOSEPH CHARLES KLINK
(Joe)

Born February 3, 1962, at Johnstown, Pa.
Height, 5.11. Weight, 170.
Throws and bats lefthanded.
Attended Biscayne College, Miami, Fla.

Year	Club	League	G.	IP.	W.	L.	Pct.	H.	R.	ER.	SO.	BB.	ERA.
1983—Columbia		S. Atlantic	12	25⅓	2	2	.500	24	16	13	14	14	4.62
1984—Columbia		S. Atlantic	31	38⅔	5	4	.556	30	19	15	49	28	3.49
1985—Lynchburg†		Carolina	44	51⅔	3	3	.500	41	16	13	59	26	2.26
1986—Orlando		Southern	45	68	4	5	.444	59	24	19	63	37	2.51

Selected by New York Mets' organization in 36th round of free-agent draft, June 6, 1983.

†Traded with Pitcher Bill Latham and Outfielder Billy Beane to Minnesota Twins for Second Baseman Tim Teufel and Outfielder Pat Crosby, January 16, 1986.

ROBERT WESLEY KNEPPER
Name pronounced NEPP-ur.
(Bob)

Born May 25, 1954, at Akron, O.
Height, 6.02. Weight, 210.
Throws and bats lefthanded.

Tied National League record for fewest assists by pitcher, season, for leader in assists (47), 1986.
Major League saves: 1982 (1).
Led National League in shutouts with 6 in 1978 and tied for lead with 5 in 1986.
Tied for National League lead in hit batsmen with 8 in 1980.
Led California League pitchers in games started with 30 and tied for lead in complete games with 16 in 1974.
Tied for Pacific Coast League lead in shutouts with 3 in 1976.
Named National League Comeback Player of the Year by THE SPORTING NEWS, 1981.

Year	Club	League	G.	IP.	W.	L.	Pct.	H.	R.	ER.	SO.	BB.	ERA.
1972—Great Falls		Pioneer	12	68	7	1	.875	53	20	11	75	19	1.46
1973—Decatur		Midwest	11	79	7	2	.778	65	28	17	68	23	1.94
1973—Fresno		California	13	71	2	8	.200	78	54	32	66	35	4.06
1974—Fresno		California	30	*238	*20	5	●.800	*239	103	84	*247	80	3.18
1975—Phoenix		P. Coast	26	155	11	11	.500	169	101	79	94	78	4.59
1976—Phoenix		P. Coast	29	205	14	10	.583	209	105	98	130	64	4.30
1976—San Francisco		National	4	25	1	2	.333	26	9	9	11	7	3.24
1977—Phoenix		P. Coast	10	51	3	6	.333	58	51	42	24	25	7.41
1977—San Francisco		National	27	166	11	9	.550	151	73	62	100	72	3.36
1978—San Francisco		National	36	260	17	11	.607	218	85	76	147	85	2.63
1979—San Francisco		National	34	207	9	12	.429	241	117	107	123	77	4.65
1980—San Francisco†		National	35	215	9	16	.360	242	114	98	103	61	4.10
1981—Houston		National	22	157	9	5	.643	128	41	38	75	38	2.18
1982—Houston		National	33	180	5	15	.250	193	100	89	108	60	4.45
1983—Houston		National	35	203	6	13	.316	202	93	72	125	71	3.19
1984—Houston		National	35	233⅔	15	10	.600	223	93	83	140	55	3.20
1985—Houston		National	37	241	15	13	.536	253	●119	95	131	54	3.55
1986—Houston		National	40	258	17	12	.586	232	100	90	143	62	3.14
Major League Totals—11 Years			338	2145⅔	114	118	.491	2109	944	819	1206	642	3.44

Selected by San Francisco Giants' organization in 2nd round of free-agent draft, June 6, 1972.

†Traded with Outfielder Chris Bourjos to Houston Astros for Third Baseman Enos Cabell, December 8, 1980.

DIVISION SERIES RECORD

Year	Club	League	G.	IP.	W.	L.	Pct.	H.	R.	ER.	SO.	BB.	ERA.
1981—Houston		National	1	5	0	1	.000	6	3	3	4	2	5.40

CHAMPIONSHIP SERIES RECORD

Year	Club	League	G.	IP.	W.	L.	Pct.	H.	R.	ER.	SO.	BB.	ERA.
1986—Houston		National	2	15⅓	0	0	.000	13	7	6	9	1	3.52

ALL-STAR GAME RECORD

Year	League	IP.	W.	L.	Pct.	H.	R.	ER.	SO.	BB.	ERA.
1981—National		2	0	0	.000	1	0	0	3	2	0.00

—DID YOU KNOW—

That Philadelphia's Don Carman and Detroit's Walt Terrell both lost no-hit bids in the ninth inning on August 20, 1986?

ALAN LEE KNICELY
Name pronounced NYSS-lee.

Born May 19, 1955, at Harrisonburg, Va.
Height, 6.00. Weight, 194.
Throws and bats righthanded.
Brother of Harold Knicely, catcher in Houston Astros' organization, 1974.

Major League stolen bases: 1986 (1).
Led American Association in total bases with 326 and tied for lead in sacrifice flies with 11 in 1984.
Led Pacific Coast League in passed balls with 16 in 1980.
Tied for Southern League lead in strikeouts by batters with 112 in 1978.
Tied for Pacific Coast League lead in double plays by catchers with 8 in 1980.
Named Minor League Player of the Year by THE SPORTING NEWS, 1984.
Named American Association Most Valuable Player, 1984.
Named Southern League co-Most Valuable Player, 1979.

Year	Club	League	Pos.	G.	AB.	R.	H.	2B.	3B.	HR.	RBI.	B.A.	PO.	A.	E.	F.A.
1974—Covington	Appal.	P	15	41	5	9	2	1	0	6	.220	3	*19	3	.880
1975—Dubuque	Midw.	P	27	35	5	11	1	0	1	9	.314	11	15	1	.963
1976—Dubuque	Midw.	P-1B	77	156	23	45	9	1	4	20	.288	84	23	3	.973
1977—Columbus	South.	3B-P	99	277	28	73	10	3	6	35	.264	84	140	24	.903
1978—Columbus	South.	OF	140	427	51	97	13	2	15	50	.227	262	22	10	.966
1979—Columbus	South.	C	120	422	77	122	12	3	*33	76	.289	446	51	15	.971
1979—Houston	Nat.	C-3B	7	6	0	0	0	0	0	0	.000	2	0	0	1.000
1980—Tucson	P. C.	C	133	468	69	149	18	4	22	*105	.318	511	*93	●23	.963
1980—Houston	Nat.	PH	1	1	0	0	0	0	0	0	.000	0	0	0	.000
1981—Tucson	P. C.	C-OF	138	490	81	150	32	5	18	96	.306	549	81	15	.977
1981—Houston	Nat.	C-OF	3	7	2	4	0	0	2	2	.571	11	2	0	1.000
1982—Houston†	Nat.	C-OF-3B	59	133	10	25	2	0	2	12	.188	128	15	4	.973
1983—Cincinnati	Nat.	C-OF-1B	59	98	11	22	3	0	2	10	.224	124	13	0	1.000
1984—Wichita	A. A.	*1-C-3	152	570	94	*190	29	4	33	*126	.333	967	92	*18	.983
1984—Cincinnati	Nat.	1B-C	10	29	0	4	0	0	0	5	.138	60	5	1	.985
1985—Denver	A. A.	C-1B	29	109	20	45	10	0	7	29	.413	106	15	4	.968
1985—Cinc.‡-Phil.	Nat.	C-1B	55	165	17	40	9	0	5	26	.242	235	13	8	.969
1985—Portland§	P. C.	C-1B	21	77	11	22	2	0	3	11	.286	127	8	4	.971
1986—Louisville	A. A.	1B	67	233	36	66	8	0	9	52	.283	539	64	9	.985
1986—St. Louis x	Nat.	1B-C	34	82	8	16	3	0	1	6	.195	187	16	1	.995
Major League Totals—8 Years			228	521	48	111	17	0	12	61	.213	747	64	14	.983

Selected by Houston Astros' organization in 3rd round of free-agent draft, June 5, 1974.
†Traded to Cincinnati Reds for Pitcher Bill Dawley and Outfielder Anthony Walker, March 31, 1983.
‡Traded with Shortstop Tom Foley, a player to be named later and cash to Philadelphia Phillies for Catcher Bo Diaz and Pitcher Greg Simpson, August 8, 1985; Philadelphia acquired Pitcher Freddie Toliver to complete deal, August 27, 1985.
§Released, March 17, 1986; signed by Louisville (St. Louis Cardinals' organization), March 21, 1986.
xReleased, October 31, 1986; signed by Texas Rangers' organization, December 3, 1986.

PITCHING RECORD

Year	Club	League	G.	IP.	W.	L.	Pct.	H.	R.	ER.	SO.	BB.	ERA.
1974—Covington	Ap'lachian	12	81	7	3	.700	78	35	31	53	42	3.44
1975—Dubuque	Midwest	26	122	4	10	.286	113	59	49	87	62	3.61
1976—Dubuque	Midwest	24	107	7	3	.700	100	58	47	87	62	3.95
1977—Columbus	Southern	14	42	1	5	.167	40	32	24	25	25	5.14

CHARLES RAY KNIGHT
(Known by middle name.)

Born December 28, 1952, at Albany, Ga.
Height, 6.02. Weight, 190.
Throws and bats righthanded.
Attended Albany Junior College, Albany, Ga.
Husband of Nancy Lopez Knight, professional golfer.

Tied major league records for most home runs, inning (2) and most total bases, inning (8), May 13, 1980 (fifth inning).
Major League stolen bases: 1977 (1), 1979 (4), 1980 (1), 1981 (2), 1982 (2), 1985 (1), 1986 (2). Total—13.
Led National League in grounding into double plays with 18 in 1981 and tied for lead with 24 in 1980.
Led American Association third basemen in putouts with 102 in 1976.
Tied for American Association lead in double plays by third basemen with 24 in 1974.
Named National League Comeback Player of the Year by THE SPORTING NEWS, 1986.

Year	Club	League	Pos.	G.	AB.	R.	H.	2B.	3B.	HR.	RBI.	B.A.	PO.	A.	E.	F.A.
1971—Sioux Falls	North.	O-INF-P	64	239	34	68	5	2	6	31	.285	69	79	17	.897
1972—Three Rivers	East.	O-INF-P	97	302	25	64	8	1	2	35	.212	102	142	20	.924
1973—Three Rivers	East.	O-3-1-2	57	193	41	54	14	2	2	22	.280	76	57	7	.950
1973—Indianapolis	A. A.	3-O-1-P	78	253	20	55	10	4	1	16	.217	72	126	11	.947
1974—Indianapolis	A. A.	*3B-OF	107	352	36	80	13	4	5	37	.227	94	177	11	*.961
1974—Cincinnati	Nat.	3B	14	11	1	2	1	0	0	2	.182	2	8	0	1.000
1975—Indianapolis	A. A.	*3B-1B	123	434	58	118	16	5	4	48	.272	*116	227	17	.953
1976—Indianapolis†	A. A.	3B-1B	110	396	47	106	24	3	10	41	.268	136	181	13	.961
1977—Cincinnati	Nat.	3-2-O-S	80	92	8	24	5	1	1	13	.261	45	45	4	.957
1978—Cincinnati‡	Nat.	3-2-O-S-1	83	65	7	13	3	0	1	4	.200	13	41	7	.885
1979—Cincinnati	Nat.	3B	150	551	64	175	37	4	10	79	.318	120	262	15	.962
1980—Cincinnati	Nat.	3B	162	618	71	163	39	7	14	78	.264	120	291	13	.969

Year	Club	League	Pos.	G.	AB.	R.	H.	2B.	3B.	HR.	RBI.	B.A.	PO.	A.	E.	F.A.
1981—Cincinnati§	Nat.	3B	106	386	43	100	23	1	6	34	.259	69	176	11	.957
1982—Houston	Nat.	1B-3B	158	609	72	179	36	6	6	70	.294	1002	186	17	.986
1983—Houston	Nat.	1B	145	507	43	154	36	4	9	70	.304	1285	73	9	.993
1984—Hou. x-N.Y.	Nat.	3B-1B	115	371	28	88	14	0	3	35	.237	256	132	9	.977
1985—New York y	Nat.	3B-2B-1B	90	271	22	59	12	0	6	36	.218	56	113	7	.960
1986—New York z	Nat.	3B-1B	137	486	51	145	24	2	11	76	.298	94	204	16	.949
Major League Totals—11 Years			1240	3967	410	1102	230	25	67	497	.278	3062	1531	108	.977

Selected by Cincinnati Reds' organization in 10th round of free-agent draft, June 4, 1970.

†On disabled list, June 21 to July 2, 1976.

‡On disabled list, April 17 to May 8, 1978.

§Traded to Houston Astros for First Baseman-Outfielder Cesar Cedeno, December 18, 1981.

xTraded to New York Mets for three players to be named later, August 28, 1984; Houston Astros acquired Outfielder Gerald Young and Infielder Manny Lee, August 31, 1984, and Pitcher Mitch Cook, September 10, 1984, to complete deal.

yOn disabled list, March 30 to April 20, 1985.

zGranted free agency, November 12, 1986.

CHAMPIONSHIP SERIES RECORD

Year	Club	League	Pos.	G.	AB.	R.	H.	2B.	3B.	HR.	RBI.	B.A.	PO.	A.	E.	F.A.
1979—Cincinnati	Nat.	3B	3	14	0	4	1	0	0	0	.286	0	5	0	1.000
1986—New York	Nat.	3B	6	24	1	4	0	0	0	2	.167	5	19	1	.960
Championship Series Totals—2 Years			9	38	1	8	1	0	0	2	.211	5	24	1	.967

WORLD SERIES RECORD

Year	Club	League	Pos.	G.	AB.	R.	H.	2B.	3B.	HR.	RBI.	B.A.	PO.	A.	E.	F.A.
1986—New York	Nat.	3B	6	23	4	9	1	0	1	5	.391	5	6	1	.917

ALL-STAR GAME RECORD

Year	League	Pos.	AB.	R.	H.	2B.	3B.	HR.	RBI.	B.A.	PO.	A.	E.	F.A.
1980—National		3B	1	1	1	0	0	0	0	1.000	0	1	0	1.000
1982—National		3B	3	0	0	0	0	0	0	.000	1	4	0	1.000
All-Star Game Totals—2 Years			4	1	1	0	0	0	0	.250	1	5	0	1.000

PITCHING RECORD

Year	Club	League	G.	IP.	W.	L.	Pct.	H.	R.	ER.	SO.	BB.	ERA.
1971—Sioux Falls	Northern	3	4	1	1	.500	5	6	5	4	5	11.25
1972—Three Rivers	Eastern	2	4	0	0	.000	3	1	1	2	4	2.25
1973—Indianapolis	Am. Assoc.	1	2	0	0	.000	2	1	1	0	4	4.50

MARK RICHARD KNUDSON

Name pronounced NOOD-sun.

Born October 28, 1960, at Denver, Colo.
Height, 6.05. Weight, 215.
Throws and bats righthanded.
Attended Colorado State University, Fort Collins, Colo.

Year	Club	League	G.	IP.	W.	L.	Pct.	H.	R.	ER.	SO.	BB.	ERA.
1982—Daytona Beach	Florida St.	12	60⅓	2	6	.250	75	35	32	15	23	4.77
1983—Daytona Beach	Florida St.	12	78⅔	5	3	.625	80	29	21	47	22	2.40
1983—Columbus	Southern	13	69⅔	4	5	.444	82	40	33	28	21	4.26
1984—Columbus	Southern	14	101	4	5	.444	100	32	25	54	27	2.23
1984—Tucson	P. Coast	13	84	4	6	.400	93	41	34	42	20	3.64
1985—Tucson	P. Coast	24	146	8	5	.615	171	69	65	68	37	4.01
1985—Houston†	National	2	11	0	2	.000	21	11	11	4	3	9.00
1986—Tucson‡-Vancouver	P. Coast	17	106⅔	6	6	.500	124	54	49	63	26	4.13
1986—Houston	National	9	42⅔	1	5	.167	48	23	20	20	15	4.22
1986—Milwaukee	American	4	17⅔	0	1	.000	22	15	15	9	5	7.64
National League Totals—2 Years		11	53⅔	1	7	.167	69	34	31	24	18	5.20
American League Totals—1 Year		4	17⅔	0	1	.000	22	15	15	9	5	7.64
Major League Totals—2 Years		15	71⅓	1	8	.111	91	49	46	33	23	5.80

Selected by Houston Astros' organization in 3rd round of free-agent draft, June 7, 1982.

†On disabled list, July 15 to August 5, 1985.

‡Traded to Milwaukee Brewers' organization, August 21, 1986, completing deal in which Milwaukee traded Pitcher Danny Darwin to Houston Astros for Pitcher Don August and a player to be named later, August 15, 1986.

BRAD LYNN KOMMINSK

Name pronounced KOMM-insk.

Born April 4, 1961, at Lima, Ohio.
Height, 6.02. Weight, 205.
Throws and bats righthanded.

Major League stolen bases: 1984 (18), 1985 (10). Total—28.
Led International League batters in strikeouts with 124 in 1986.
Led International League in slugging percentage with .596 and tied for lead in game-winning RBIs with 14 in 1983.
Led Carolina League in total bases with 278 and grounding into double plays with 24 in 1981.
Led Appalachian League batters in strikeouts with 74 and stolen bases with 20 in 1979.
Led International League third basemen in errors with 28 in 1986.

Named Carolina League Most Valuable Player, 1981.
Received reported $72,000 bonus to sign with Atlanta Braves, 1979.

Year Club	League	Pos.	G.	AB.	R.	H.	2B.	3B.	HR.	RBI.	B.A.	PO.	A.	E.	F.A.
1979—Kingsport	Appal.	OF	59	185	37	41	9	1	7	34	.222	112	1	2	.983
1980—Anderson	S. Atl.	OF	121	425	86	111	17	5	20	67	.261	217	5	12	.949
1981—Durham	Carol.	OF	132	459	108	●148	27	2	33	★104	.322	154	7	10	.942
1982—Savannah	South.	OF	133	454	88	124	18	7	26	78	.273	158	6	10	.943
1982—Richmond	Int.	OF	5	17	4	6	1	0	2	5	.353	10	0	0	1.000
1983—Richmond	Int.	OF	117	413	94	138	24	6	24	103	.334	179	4	3	.984
1983—Atlanta	Nat.	OF	19	36	2	8	2	0	0	4	.222	16	1	1	.944
1984—Richmond	Int.	OF	42	144	23	37	11	3	5	28	.257	66	4	3	.959
1984—Atlanta	Nat.	OF	90	301	37	61	10	0	8	36	.203	135	2	1	.993
1985—Atlanta	Nat.	OF	106	300	52	68	12	3	4	21	.227	161	2	7	.959
1986—Richmond	Int.	3B-OF-1B	133	465	67	109	22	4	13	65	.234	127	200	30	.916
1986—Atlanta	Nat.	3B-OF	5	5	1	2	0	0	0	1	.400	1	2	0	1.000
Major League Totals—4 Years			220	642	92	139	24	3	12	62	.217	313	7	9	.973

Selected by Atlanta Braves' organization in 1st round (fourth player selected) of free-agent draft, June 5, 1979.

RAYMOND ALLEN KRAWCZYK

Name pronounced KRAH-sick.

(Ray)

Born October 9, 1959, at Pittsburgh, Pa.
Height, 6.01. Weight, 184.
Throws and bats righthanded.
Attended Golden West College, Huntington Beach, Calif.,
and Oral Roberts University, Tulsa, Okla.

Led Pacific Coast League in saves with 20 in 1985.

Year Club	League	G.	IP.	W.	L.	Pct.	H.	R.	ER.	SO.	BB.	ERA.
1981—Bradenton Pirates	Gulf Coast	4	18	0	1	.000	11	5	3	14	7	1.50
1981—Alexandria	Carolina	8	46	2	4	.333	48	32	25	41	14	4.89
1982—Alexandria	Carolina	6	18⅔	1	0	1.000	10	1	1	25	13	0.48
1982—Buffalo	Eastern	38	101⅓	3	5	.375	93	59	53	102	59	4.71
1983—Hawaii	P. Coast	41	88⅔	5	7	.417	80	46	37	88	33	3.76
1984—Hawaii	P. Coast	43	72	4	5	.444	57	21	17	77	36	2.13
1984—Pittsburgh	National	4	5⅓	0	0	.000	7	2	2	3	4	3.38
1985—Hawaii†‡	P. Coast	38	55⅔	5	3	.625	35	15	14	54	22	2.26
1985—Pittsburgh	National	8	8⅓	0	2	.000	20	13	13	9	6	14.04
1986—Hawaii	P. Coast	32	47⅓	3	6	.333	51	29	26	40	21	4.94
1986—Pittsburgh §x	National	12	12⅓	0	1	.000	17	13	10	7	10	7.30
Major League Totals—3 Years		24	26	0	3	.000	44	28	25	19	20	8.65

Selected by Boston Red Sox' organization in 1st round (23rd player selected) of free-agent draft, January 8, 1980.
Selected by St. Louis Cardinals' organization in secondary phase of free-agent draft, June 3, 1980.
Selected by Pittsburgh Pirates' organization in secondary phase of free-agent draft, June 8, 1981.
†Appeared in one game as a first baseman with no chances.
‡On disabled list, June 10 to June 20, 1985.
§On disabled list, April 23 to June 18, 1986; included rehabilitation disability assignment to Prince William, June 1 to June 18, 1986.
xReleased, November 12, 1986.

WAYNE RICHARD KRENCHICKI

Name pronounced Kren-CHIK-ee.

Born September 17, 1954, at Trenton, N.J.
Height, 6.01. Weight, 180.
Throws right and bats lefthanded
Attended University of Miami, Miami, Fla.
Brother of Tom Krenchicki, shortstop in Los Angeles Dodgers' organization, 1968.

Major League stolen bases: 1982 (5), 1986 (2). Total—7.
Led Southern League second basemen in double plays with 114 in 1977.
Led Florida State League shortstops in assists with 378, double plays with 60 and fielding percentage with .968 in 1976.

Year Club	League	Pos.	G.	AB.	R.	H.	2B.	3B.	HR.	RBI.	B.A.	PO.	A.	E.	F.A.
1976—Miami	Fla. St.	SS-3B	133	459	38	109	14	1	0	35	.237	190	439	19	.971
1977—Charlotte	South.	2B	131	510	69	140	17	9	3	42	.275	★325	★455	25	.969
1978—Rochester	Int.	3B-2B-SS	★140	520	*93	154	26	1	12	71	.296	204	389	32	.949
1979—Rochester†	Int.	2B-SS-3B	66	249	21	65	7	2	0	22	.261	129	173	9	.971
1979—Baltimore	Amer.	3B-2B	16	21	1	4	1	0	0	0	.190	12	12	2	.923
1980—Rochester‡	Int.	2B-3B-SS	87	311	42	82	13	3	2	39	.264	137	230	10	.973
1980—Baltimore	Amer.	SS-2B	9	14	1	2	0	0	0	0	.143	9	9	0	1.000
1981—Baltimore	Amer.	2B-3B-SS	33	56	7	12	4	0	0	6	.214	23	56	3	.963
1981—Rochester§	Int.	2B-3B-SS	16	56	5	10	0	0	0	4	.179	28	58	1	.988
1982—Cincinnati	Nat.	3B-2B	94	187	19	53	6	1	2	21	.283	40	103	6	.960
1983—Cincinnati x	Nat.	3B-2B	51	77	6	21	2	0	0	11	.273	7	41	1	.980
1983—Detroit y	Amer.	3-2-S-1	59	133	18	37	7	0	1	16	.278	43	75	8	.937
1984—Wichita	A. A.	2B-3B	18	64	14	18	7	0	2	5	.281	38	44	3	.965
1984—Cincinnati	Nat.	3B-1B-2B	97	181	18	54	9	2	6	22	.298	35	92	5	.962

Year Club	League	Pos.	G.	AB.	R.	H.	2B.	3B.	HR.	RBI.	B.A.	PO.	A.	E.	F.A.
1985—Cincinnati z	Nat.	3B-2B	90	173	16	47	9	0	4	25	.272	35	87	4	.968
1986—Montreal a	Nat.	1-3-2-O	101	221	21	53	6	2	2	23	.240	325	59	6	.985
American League Totals—4 Years			117	224	27	55	12	0	1	22	.246	87	152	13	.948
National League Totals—5 Years			433	839	80	228	32	5	14	102	.272	442	382	22	.974
Major League Totals—8 Years			550	1063	107	283	44	5	15	124	.266	529	534	35	.968

Selected by Philadelphia Phillies' organization in 8th round of free-agent draft, June 6, 1972.
Selected by Baltimore Orioles' organization in secondary phase of free-agent draft, January 7, 1976.
†On disabled list, May 10 to June 1 and August 5 to August 15, 1979.
‡On disabled list, July 12 to August 1, 1980.
§Traded to Cincinnati Reds, February 16, 1982, completing deal in which Cincinnati traded Pitcher Paul Moskau to Baltimore Orioles for a player to be named later, February 9, 1982.
xTraded to Detroit Tigers for Pitcher Pat Underwood, June 30, 1983.
ySold to Cincinnati Reds, November 18, 1983.
zTraded to Montreal Expos for Pitcher Norm Charlton and a player to be named later, March 31, 1986; Cincinnati Reds acquired Second Baseman Tim Barker to complete deal, April 2, 1986.
aGranted free agency, November 12, 1986.

WILLIAM CULP KRUEGER

Name pronounced KREW-ger.

(Bill)

Born April 24, 1958, at Waukegan, Ill.
Height, 6.05. Weight, 210.
Throws and bats lefthanded.
Received bachelor of arts degree in business administration from
University of Portland, Portland, Ore. in 1979.

Major League saves: 1986 (1).
Tied for Eastern League lead in games started by pitchers with 27 and shutouts with 3 in 1982.

Year Club	League	G.	IP.	W.	L.	Pct.	H.	R.	ER.	SO.	BB.	ERA.
1980—Medford	Northwest	9	44	0	4	.000	54	38	25	48	29	5.11
1981—Modesto	California	16	98	3	5	.375	87	49	40	76	52	3.67
1981—West Haven	Eastern	11	68	3	6	.333	74	36	27	36	31	3.57
1982—West Haven	Eastern	28	181	15	9	.625	160	69	57	163	81	2.83
1983—Oakland	American	17	109⅔	7	6	.538	104	54	44	58	53	3.61
1984—Tacoma†	P. Coast	5	31⅔	2	2	.500	29	17	13	20	21	3.69
1984—Oakland	American	26	142	10	10	.500	156	95	75	61	85	4.75
1985—Oakland	American	32	151⅓	9	10	.474	165	95	76	56	69	4.52
1985—Tacoma	P. Coast	2	9⅔	0	1	.000	12	10	10	10	6	9.31
1986—Oakland‡	American	11	34⅓	1	2	.333	40	25	23	10	13	6.03
1986—Madison	Midwest	1	2	0	0	.000	1	0	0	1	1	0.00
1986—Tacoma	P. Coast	8	52⅓	3	3	.500	53	32	27	41	27	4.64
Major League Totals—4 Years		86	437⅓	27	28	.491	465	269	218	185	220	4.49

Signed as free agent by Oakland A's organization, July 12, 1980.
†On disabled list, August 5, 1983 through remainder of season.
‡On disabled list, May 6 to August 8, 1986; included rehabilitation disability assignment to Madison, July 4 to July 8, and to Tacoma, July 10 to July 18 and July 21 to July 27, 1986.

JOHN MARTIN KRUK

Born February 9, 1961, at Charleston, W. Va.
Height, 5.10. Weight, 170.
Throws and bats lefthanded.
Attended Allegany Community College, Cumberland, Md.

Major League stolen bases: 1986 (2).
Led Texas League in sacrifice flies with 13 in 1983.
Led Pacific Coast League outfielders in double plays with 4 in 1984.

Year Club	League	Pos.	G.	AB.	R.	H.	2B.	3B.	HR.	RBI.	B.A.	PO.	A.	E.	F.A.
1981—Walla Walla	N'west	OF-1B	63	157	31	38	10	0	1	13	.242	108	5	2	.983
1982—Reno	Calif.	OF-1B	125	441	82	137	30	8	11	92	.311	253	11	7	.974
1983—Beaumont	Texas	OF-1B-P	133	498	94	170	41	9	10	88	.341	304	22	8	.976
1984—Las Vegas	P. C.	OF	115	340	56	111	25	6	11	57	.326	183	7	2	.990
1985—Las Vegas	P. C.	OF-1B	123	422	61	148	29	4	7	59	★.351	356	18	7	.982
1986—San Diego	Nat.	OF-1B	122	278	33	86	16	2	4	38	.309	139	6	3	.980
1986—Las Vegas	P. C.	OF-1B	6	28	6	13	3	1	0	9	.464	22	1	0	1.000
Major League Totals—1 Year			122	278	33	86	16	2	4	38	.309	139	6	3	.980

Selected by Pittsburgh Pirates' organization in 3rd round of free-agent draft, January 13, 1981.
Selected by San Diego Padres' organization in secondary phase of free-agent draft, June 8, 1981.

PITCHING RECORD

Year Club	League	G.	IP.	W.	L.	Pct.	H.	R.	ER.	SO.	BB.	ERA.
1983—Beaumont	Texas	3	5	0	0	.000	5	0	0	3	2	0.00

—DID YOU KNOW—

That New York Mets lefthander Sid Fernandez recorded nine strikeouts in the first three innings of a July 30 game against Chicago, but trailed the Cubs, 4-1?

MICHAEL EDWARD KRUKOW

Name pronounced KROO-koh.

(Mike)

Born January 21, 1952, at Long Beach, Calif.
Height, 6.04. Weight, 205.
Throws and bats righthanded.
Attended California Poly State University, San Luis Obispo, Calif.

Major League saves: 1984 (1).
Tied for National League lead in games started by pitchers with 25 in 1981.
Tied for National League lead in hit batsmen with 8 in 1980.
Led Gulf Coast League in intentional bases on balls issued with 4 and tied for lead in complete games with 4 in 1973.

Year Club	League	G.	IP.	W.	L.	Pct.	H.	R.	ER.	SO.	BB.	ERA.
1973—Bradenton Cubs	Gulf Coast	13	77	4	3	.571	76	32	27	*80	28	3.16
1974—Midland	Texas	6	30	1	1	.500	42	24	17	21	19	5.10
1974—Key West	Florida St.	20	130	5	10	.333	121	66	46	94	47	3.18
1975—Midland†	Texas	24	153	13	6	.684	143	65	58	100	66	3.41
1976—Wichita	Am. Assoc.	26	144	7	9	.438	142	61	53	108	47	3.31
1976—Chicago	National	2	4	0	0	.000	6	4	4	1	2	9.00
1977—Chicago	National	34	172	8	14	.364	195	96	84	106	61	4.40
1978—Wichita	Am. Assoc.	7	53	2	3	.400	51	27	23	29	21	3.91
1978—Chicago	National	27	138	9	3	.750	125	62	60	81	53	3.91
1979—Chicago	National	28	165	9	9	.500	172	84	77	119	81	4.20
1980—Chicago	National	34	205	10	15	.400	200	117	100	130	80	4.39
1981—Chicago‡	National	25	144	9	9	.500	146	68	59	101	55	3.69
1982—Philadelphia§	National	33	208	13	11	.542	211	87	72	138	82	3.12
1983—San Francisco x	National	31	184⅓	11	11	.500	189	95	81	136	76	3.95
1984—San Francisco	National	35	199⅓	11	12	.478	*234	*117	101	141	78	4.56
1985—San Francisco	National	28	194⅔	8	11	.421	176	80	73	150	49	3.38
1986—San Francisco y	National	34	245	20	9	.690	204	90	83	178	55	3.05
Major League Totals—11 Years		311	1859⅓	108	104	.509	1858	900	794	1281	672	3.84

Selected by California Angels' organization in 32nd round of free-agent draft, June 4, 1970.
Selected by Chicago Cubs' organization in 8th round of free-agent draft, June 5, 1973.
†On disabled list, May 19 to June 7, 1975.
‡Traded with cash to Philadelphia Phillies for Catcher Keith Moreland and Pitchers Dan Larson and Dickie Noles, December 8, 1981.
§Traded with Pitcher Mark Davis and Outfielder Charles Penigar to San Francisco Giants for Second Baseman Joe Morgan and Pitcher Al Holland, December 14, 1982.
xOn disabled list, April 11 to May 8, 1983.
yOn disabled list, July 23 to August 7, 1986.

ALL—STAR GAME RECORD

Year League	IP.	W.	L.	Pct.	H.	R.	ER.	SO.	BB.	ERA.
1986—National	1	0	0	.000	0	0	0	0	0	0.00

JEFFREY WILLIAM KUNKEL

(Jeff)

Born March 25, 1962, at West Palm Beach, Fla.
Height, 6.02. Weight, 180.
Throws and bats righthanded.
Attended Rider College, Lawrenceville, N.J.
Son of Bill Kunkel, pitcher with Kansas City A's and New York Yankees, 1961 through 1963; umpire, Florida State League, 1966; Southern League, 1967 and 1968; and American League umpire, 1968 through 1984.

Major League stolen bases: 1984 (4).
Named shortstop on THE SPORTING NEWS College Baseball All-America Team, 1983.

Year Club	League	Pos.	G.	AB.	R.	H.	2B.	3B.	HR.	RBI.	B.A.	PO.	A.	E.	F.A.
1983—Burlington	Midw.	SS	31	122	22	35	7	1	6	18	.287	38	88	13	.906
1983—Tulsa	Texas	SS-2B	37	130	21	37	14	0	5	25	.285	68	106	9	.951
1984—Tulsa†	Texas	SS	47	177	30	56	16	1	4	22	.316	64	103	16	.913
1984—Texas	Amer.	SS	50	142	13	29	2	3	3	7	.204	81	120	17	.922
1985—Oklahoma City	A. A.	SS-OF	99	370	40	72	8	6	5	43	.195	152	308	26	.947
1985—Texas	Amer.	SS	2	4	1	1	0	0	0	0	.250	2	5	0	1.000
1986—Oklahoma City	A. A.	SS	55	111	409	50	100	16	4	11	51	.244	135	272	19	.955
1986—Texas	Amer.	SS	8	13	3	3	0	0	1	2	.231	4	6	3	.769
Major League Totals—3 Years			60	159	17	33	2	3	4	9	.208	87	131	20	.916

Selected by Texas Rangers' organization in 1st round (third player selected) of free-agent draft, June 6, 1983.
†On disabled list, April 10 to May 12 and May 17 to June 4, 1984.

RANDY SCOTT KUTCHER

Born April 20, 1960, at Anchorage, Alaska.
Height, 5.11. Weight, 170.
Throws and bats righthanded.

Major League stolen bases: 1986 (6).

Year Club	League	Pos.	G.	AB.	R.	H.	2B.	3B.	HR.	RBI.	B.A.	PO.	A.	E.	F.A.
1979—Great Falls	Pion.	SS	65	245	55	62	8	2	2	25	.253	79	109	29	.866

Year Club	League	Pos.	G.	AB.	R.	H.	2B.	3B.	HR.	RBI.	B.A.	PO.	A.	E.	F.A.
1980—Clinton	Midw.	SS-3B	138	525	72	133	17	●8	3	46	.253	204	365	39	.936
1981—Fresno	Calif.	S-O-2-3	41	161	28	44	10	2	3	26	.273	66	80	18	.890
1981—Shreveport	Texas	SS	77	249	36	71	13	4	4	20	.285	112	212	18	.947
1982—Shreveport	Texas	SS-OF	116	397	56	98	18	2	3	31	.247	183	142	18	.948
1983—Phoenix	P. C.	S-O-2-3-C	104	275	45	75	11	4	3	45	.273	152	138	15	.951
1984—Phoenix	P. C.	O-S-3-2-C	103	336	37	93	17	3	2	31	.277	177	80	11	.959
1985—Phoenix†	P. C.	OF-2B	97	228	36	54	15	2	1	20	.237	143	9	4	.974
1986—Phoenix	P. C.	S-O-2-3-C	55	208	47	72	14	4	11	39	.346	93	89	16	.919
1986—San Francisco	Nat.	O-S-3-2	71	186	28	44	9	1	7	16	.237	111	11	1	.992
Major League Totals—1 Year			71	186	28	44	9	1	7	16	.237	111	11	1	.992

Selected by San Francisco Giants' organization in 4th round of free-agent draft, June 5, 1979.

†Granted free agency, October 15, 1985; re-signed by Giants, February 3, 1986.

STANLEY KYLES
(Stan)

Born February 26, 1961, at Chicago, Ill.
Height, 6.01. Weight, 165.
Throws and bats righthanded.
Brother of Mack Payne, pitcher in Kansas City Royals' organization, 1970 through 1972.

Year Club	League	G.	IP.	W.	L.	Pct.	H.	R.	ER.	SO.	BB.	ERA.
1979—Sarasota Cubs	Gulf Coast	7	16	1	4	.200	23	18	15	10	21	8.44
1980—Geneva	NYP	9	47	2	5	.286	46	34	28	29	40	5.36
1981—Quad Cities	Midwest	8	18	0	2	.000	29	29	24	12	16	12.00
1981—Geneva	NYP	12	61	1	8	.111	66	46	31	24	38	4.57
1982—Salinas	California	26	172	11	5	.688	160	71	48	118	66	2.51
1983—Midland	Texas	23	155⅓	7	11	.389	164	79	66	74	67	3.82
1983—Iowa†	Am. Assoc.	4	25	2	1	.667	16	9	9	9	10	3.24
1984—Albany‡	Eastern	25	64⅓	4	4	.500	58	28	25	29	30	3.50
1985—Tacoma§	P. Coast	43	72	1	7	.125	92	47	41	31	39	5.13
1986—Tacoma	P. Coast	13	52⅓	5	2	.714	53	22	19	30	29	3.27

Selected by Chicago Cubs' organization in 4th round of free-agent draft, June 5, 1979.

†Traded with a player to be named later to Oakland A's for Pitcher Tim Stoddard, March 26, 1984; Oakland acquired Outfielder Stan Boderick to complete deal, March 31, 1984.

‡On disabled list, July 6, 1984 through remainder of season.

§On disabled list, August 12 to August 29, 1985.

MICHAEL JAMES LaCOSS
(Mike)

Born May 30, 1956, at Glendale, Calif.
Height, 6.04. Weight, 190.
Throws and bats righthanded.
Major League saves: 1981 (1), 1983 (1), 1984 (3), 1985 (1). Total—6.
Tied for American Association lead in shutouts with 3 in 1978.

Year Club	League	G.	IP.	W.	L.	Pct.	H.	R.	ER.	SO.	BB.	ERA.
1974—Billings	Pioneer	13	87	6	5	.545	81	40	27	58	38	2.79
1975—Tampa	Florida St.	23	151	4	7	.412	131	61	48	72	41	2.86
1976—Three Rivers	Eastern	25	162	12	10	.545	148	66	53	80	53	2.94
1977—Indianapolis	Am. Assoc.	27	186	11	*13	.458	181	93	80	104	65	3.87
1978—Indianapolis	Am. Assoc.	19	130	11	5	.688	129	62	50	67	49	3.46
1978—Cincinnati	National	16	96	4	8	.333	104	56	48	31	46	4.50
1979—Cincinnati	National	35	206	14	8	.636	202	92	80	73	79	3.50
1980—Cincinnati	National	34	169	10	12	.455	207	101	87	59	68	4.63
1981—Cincinnati†	National	20	78	4	7	.364	102	55	53	22	30	6.12
1982—Houston	National	41	115	6	6	.500	107	41	37	51	54	2.90
1983—Houston‡	National	38	138	5	7	.417	142	81	68	53	56	4.43
1984—Houston§	National	39	132	7	5	.583	132	64	59	86	55	4.02
1985—Kansas City	American	21	40⅔	1	1	.500	49	25	23	26	29	5.09
1985—Omaha x	Am. Assoc.	4	22⅓	2	2	.333	23	12	8	11	15	3.22
1986—San Francisco y	National	37	204⅓	10	13	.435	179	99	81	86	70	3.57
National League Totals—8 Years		260	1138⅓	60	66	.476	1175	589	513	461	458	4.06
American League Totals—1 Year		21	40⅔	1	1	.500	49	25	23	26	29	5.09
Major League Totals—9 Years		281	1179	61	67	.477	1224	614	536	487	487	4.09

Selected by Cincinnati Reds' organization in 3rd round of free-agent draft, June 5, 1974.

†Sold on waivers to Houston Astros, April 4, 1982.

‡On disabled list, June 17 to July 8, 1983.

§Granted free agency, November 8, 1984; signed by Kansas City Royals' organization, February 19, 1985.

xReleased, November 6, 1985; signed by San Francisco Giants' organization, February 3, 1986.

yGranted free agency, November 12, 1986; re-signed by Giants, December 9, 1986.

CHAMPIONSHIP SERIES RECORD

Year Club	League	G.	IP.	W.	L.	Pct.	H.	R.	ER.	SO.	BB.	ERA.
1979—Cincinnati	National	1	1⅔	0	1	.000	1	2	2	0	4	10.80

ALL-STAR GAME RECORD

Year League		IP.	W.	L.	Pct.	H.	R.	ER.	SO.	BB.	ERA.
1979—National		1⅓	0	0	.000	1	0	0	0	0	0.00

LEONDAUS LACY
(Lee)

Born April 10, 1949, at Longview, Tex.
Height, 6.01. Weight, 185.
Throws and bats righthanded.
Attended Laney Junior College, Oakland, Calif.

Tied major league record for most home runs by pinch-hitter, consecutive at-bats (3), May 2, 6 and 17, 1978 (includes one base on balls during streak).

Hit three home runs in a game, June 8, 1986.

Major League stolen bases: 1972 (5), 1973 (2), 1974 (2), 1975 (5), 1976 (3), 1977 (4), 1978 (7), 1979 (6), 1980 (18), 1981 (24), 1982 (40), 1983 (31), 1984 (21), 1985 (10), 1986 (4). Total—182.

Led National League outfielders in fielding percentage with .996 in 1984.

Led California League shortstops in errors with 63 in 1970.

Led Pioneer League third basemen in putouts with 50, assists with 116, errors with 26 and double plays with 9 in 1969.

Year Club	League	Pos.	G.	AB.	R.	H.	2B.	3B.	HR.	RBI.	B.A.	PO.	A.	E.	F.A.
1969—Ogden	Pion	3B-SS-2B	71	239	43	70	6	7	1	38	.293	54	121	27	.866
1970—Bakersfield	Calif.	SS-3B	124	502	96	151	19	5	4	49	.301	189	291	66	.879
1971—Albuquerque	Texas	2-3-S-O	132	488	54	150	17	7	0	57	.307	263	358	31	.952
1972—El Paso	Texas	2B-SS	68	258	39	96	22	4	1	35	.372	123	191	7	.978
1972—Los Angeles	Nat.	2B	60	243	34	63	7	3	0	12	.259	125	161	8	.973
1973—Los Angeles	Nat.	2B	57	135	14	28	2	0	0	8	.207	80	85	6	.965
1974—Los Angeles	Nat.	2B-3B	48	78	13	22	6	0	0	8	.282	38	53	3	.968
1975—Los Angeles†	Nat.	2B-OF-SS	101	306	44	96	11	5	7	40	.314	152	75	13	.946
1976—Atl.‡-L.A.	Nat.	2B-OF-3B	103	338	42	91	11	3	3	34	.269	193	111	9	.971
1977—Los Angeles§	Nat.	OF-2B-3B	75	169	28	45	7	0	6	21	.266	56	69	4	.969
1978—Los Angeles x	Nat.	O-2-3-S	103	245	29	64	16	4	13	40	.261	114	64	9	.952
1979—Pittsburgh	Nat.	OF-2B	84	182	17	45	9	3	5	15	.247	77	8	3	.966
1980—Pittsburgh	Nat.	OF-3B	109	278	45	93	20	4	7	33	.335	175	11	3	.984
1981—Pittsburgh	Nat.	OF-3B	78	213	31	57	11	4	2	10	.268	121	8	3	.977
1982—Pittsburgh	Nat.	OF-3B	121	359	66	112	16	3	5	31	.312	186	9	7	.965
1983—Pittsburgh	Nat.	OF	108	288	40	87	12	3	4	13	.302	167	2	0	1.000
1984—Pittsburgh y	Nat.	OF-2B	138	474	66	152	26	3	12	70	.321	272	18	2	.993
1985—Baltimore z	Amer.	OF	121	492	69	144	22	4	9	48	.293	231	9	4	.984
1986—Baltimore	Amer.	OF	130	491	77	141	18	0	11	47	.287	239	8	2	.992
National League Totals—13 Years			1185	3308	469	955	154	35	64	335	.289	1756	674	70	.972
American League Totals—2 Years			251	983	146	285	40	4	20	95	.290	470	17	6	.988
Major League Totals—15 Years			1436	4291	615	1240	194	39	84	430	.289	2226	691	76	.975

Selected by Los Angeles Dodgers' organization in 2nd round of free-agent draft, February 1, 1969.

†Traded with Outfielder Jimmy Wynn, First Baseman-Outfielder Tom Paciorek and Infielder Jerry Royster to Atlanta Braves for Outfielder Dusty Baker and First Baseman-Third Baseman Ed Goodson, November 17, 1975.

‡Traded with Pitcher Elias Sosa to Los Angeles Dodgers for Pitcher Mike Marshall, June 23, 1976.

§On disabled list, June 20 to July 15, 1977.

xGranted free agency, November 2, 1978; signed by Pittsburgh Pirates, January 19, 1979.

yGranted free agency, November 8, 1984; signed by Baltimore Orioles, December 7, 1984.

zOn disabled list, March 28 to May 13, 1985.

CHAMPIONSHIP SERIES RECORD

Year Club	League	Pos.	G.	AB.	R.	H.	2B.	3B.	HR.	RBI.	B.A.	PO.	A.	E.	F.A.
1974—Los Angeles	Nat.	PR	1	0	0	0	0	0	0	0	.000	0	0	0	.000
1977—Los Angeles	Nat.	PH	1	1	1	1	0	0	0	0	1.000	0	0	0	.000
1978—Los Angeles	Nat.	PH	2	2	0	0	0	0	0	0	.000	0	0	0	.000
Championship Series Totals—3 Years			4	3	1	1	0	0	0	0	.333	0	0	0	.000

WORLD SERIES RECORD

Year Club	League	Pos.	G.	AB.	R.	H.	2B.	3B.	HR.	RBI.	B.A.	PO.	A.	E.	F.A.
1974—Los Angeles	Nat.	PH	1	1	0	0	0	0	0	0	.000	0	0	0	.000
1977—Los Angeles	Nat.	PH-OF	4	7	1	3	0	0	0	2	.429	2	0	0	1.000
1978—Los Angeles	Nat.	DH	4	14	0	2	0	0	0	1	.143	0	0	0	.000
1979—Pittsburgh	Nat.	PH	4	4	0	1	0	0	0	0	.250	0	0	0	.000
World Series Totals—4 Years			13	26	1	6	0	0	0	3	.231	2	0	0	1.000

PETER LINWOOD LADD
(Pete)

Born July 17, 1956, at Portland, Me.
Height, 6.03. Weight, 235.
Throws and bats righthanded.
Attended University of Mississippi, University, Miss.

Major League saves: 1982 (3), 1983 (25), 1984 (3), 1985 (2), 1986 (6). Total—39.

Led Florida State League in saves with 18 in 1978.

Year Club	League	G.	IP.	W.	L.	Pct.	H.	R.	ER.	SO.	BB.	ERA.
1977—Winter Haven	Florida St.	19	27	4	1	.800	19	8	5	27	7	1.67
1978—Winter Haven	Florida St.	44	85	8	2	.800	69	36	30	66	30	3.18
1979—Bristol†	Eastern	18	29	3	1	.750	11	2	2	26	8	0.62
1979—Columbus‡	Southern	13	41	6	1	.857	24	13	12	31	23	2.63
1979—Houston	National	10	12	1	1	.500	8	5	4	6	8	3.00
1980—Columbus	Southern	33	55	6	5	.545	47	27	21	38	29	3.44

Year	Club	League	G.	IP.	W.	L.	Pct.	H.	R.	ER.	SO.	BB.	ERA.
1980—Tucson	P. Coast	18	21	1	2	.333	18	7	6	24	4	2.57
1981—Tucson§	P. Coast	47	96	5	4	.556	90	43	36	68	44	3.38
1982—Vancouver	P. Coast	34	55⅔	10	2	.833	42	19	18	63	18	2.91
1982—Milwaukee	American	16	18	1	3	.250	16	8	8	12	6	4.00
1983—Milwaukee	American	44	49⅓	3	4	.429	30	17	14	41	16	2.55
1983—Vancouver	P. Coast	12	13⅓	0	0	.000	10	2	2	16	4	1.35
1984—Milwaukee	American	54	91	4	9	.308	94	58	53	75	38	5.24
1985—Milwaukee	American	29	45⅔	0	0	.000	58	26	23	22	10	4.53
1985—Vancouver x	P. Coast	5	9	0	0	.000	6	2	2	5	1	2.00
1986—Seattle	American	52	70⅔	8	6	.571	69	33	30	30	18	3.82
National League Totals—1 Year		10	12	1	1	.500	8	5	4	6	8	3.00
American League Totals—5 Years		195	274⅔	16	22	.421	267	142	128	203	88	4.19
Major League Totals—6 Years		205	286⅔	17	23	.425	275	147	132	209	96	4.14

Selected by Boston Red Sox' organization in 25th round of free-agent draft, June 7, 1977.

†Traded with cash and a player to be named later to Houston Astros' organization for First Baseman Bob Watson, June 13, 1979; Houston acquired Pitcher Bob Sprowl to complete deal, June 19, 1979.

‡On disabled list, July 4 to July 18, 1979.

§Traded to Milwaukee Brewers' organization for Pitcher Rickey (Buster) Keeton, October 23, 1981.

xReleased, November 25, 1985; signed by Seattle Mariners' organization, January 18, 1986.

CHAMPIONSHIP SERIES RECORD

Tied Championship Series record for most saves, five-game Series (2), 1982.
Tied American League Championship Series record for most saves, total Series (2), 1982.

Year	Club	League	G.	IP.	W.	L.	Pct.	H.	R.	ER.	SO.	BB.	ERA.
1982—Milwaukee	American	3	3⅓	0	0	.000	0	0	0	5	0	0.00

WORLD SERIES RECORD

Year	Club	League	G.	IP.	W.	L.	Pct.	H.	R.	ER.	SO.	BB.	ERA.
1982—Milwaukee	American	1	⅔	0	0	.000	1	0	0	0	2	0.00

MICHAEL RUSSELL LAGA
(Mike)

Born June 14, 1960, at Ridgewood, N. J.
Height, 6.02. Weight, 210.
Throws and bats lefthanded.
Attended Bergen Community College, Paramus, N. J.,
and Fairleigh Dickinson University, Teaneck, N. J.

Major League stolen bases: 1982 (1).
Led American Association in sacrifice flies with 7 in 1985.
Led American Association first basemen in total chances with 1,146 and double plays with 101 in 1985.
Led American Association in being hit by pitch with 13 in 1982.
Led American Association first basemen in total chances with 1,221 in 1982.

Year	Club	League	Pos.	G.	AB.	R.	H.	2B.	3B.	HR.	RBI.	B.A.	PO.	A.	E.	F.A.
1980—Lakeland	Fla. St.	1B	122	407	60	111	14	6	12	74	.273	1025	84	★18	.984
1981—Birmingham	South.	1B	142	547	89	158	28	7	31	86	.289	1193	★105	★23	.983
1982—Evansville	A. A.	1B	126	444	77	111	15	3	34	90	.250	★1135	68	18	.985
1982—Detroit	Amer.	1B	27	88	6	23	9	0	3	11	.261	163	4	1	.994
1983—Evansville	A. A.	1B	105	355	46	82	24	1	16	58	.231	835	62	★11	.988
1983—Detroit	Amer.	1B	12	21	2	4	0	0	0	2	.190	9	1	0	1.000
1984—Evansville	A. A.	1B	●153	569	86	151	30	9	30	94	.265	1008	92	14	.987
1984—Detroit	Amer.	1B	9	11	1	6	0	0	1	1	.545	12	1	0	1.000
1985—Nashville	A. A.	1B	117	430	58	113	30	2	20	79	.263	★1024	★111	11	.990
1985—Detroit	Amer.	1B	9	36	3	6	1	0	2	6	.167	33	5	1	.974
1986—Detroit †	Amer.	1B	15	45	6	9	1	0	3	8	.200	98	7	0	1.000
1986—Nashville	A. A.	1B	12	41	4	9	3	0	2	7	.220	109	16	2	.984
1986—St. Louis ‡	Nat.	1B	18	46	7	10	4	0	3	8	.217	109	14	0	1.000
American League Totals—5 Years			72	201	18	48	11	0	8	28	.239	315	18	2	.994
National League Totals—1 Year			18	46	7	10	4	0	3	8	.217	109	14	0	1.000
Major League Totals—5 Years			90	247	25	58	15	0	11	36	.235	424	32	2	.996

Selected by Detroit Tigers' organization in 1st round (17th player selected) of free-agent draft, January 8, 1980.

†On disabled list, May 15 to September 1, 1986; included rehabilitation disability assignment to Nashville, August 8 to August 27, 1986.

‡Traded to St. Louis Cardinals, September 2, 1986, completing deal in which St. Louis traded Catcher Mike Heath to Detroit Tigers for Pitcher Ken Hill and a player to be named later, August 10, 1986.

JEFFREY ALLEN LAHTI
Name pronounced LOT-ee.
(Jeff)

Born October 8, 1956, at Oregon City, Ore.
Height, 6.00. Weight, 180.
Throws and bats righthanded.
Attended Treasure Valley Community College, Ontario, Ore. and
Portland State University, Portland, Ore.

Major League saves: 1984 (1), 1985 (19). Total—20.
Tied for Western Carolinas League lead in saves with 13 in 1979.

Year Club	League	G.	IP.	W.	L.	Pct.	H.	R.	ER.	SO.	BB.	ERA.
1978—Eugene	Northwest	16	53	1	5	.167	58	34	26	32	21	4.42
1979—Greensboro	W. Carol.	53	92	7	2	.778	83	43	29	89	33	2.84
1979—Nashville	Southern	6	16	2	0	1.000	10	4	3	12	5	1.69
1980—Waterbury	Eastern	55	91	7	8	.467	75	34	28	78	40	2.77
1981—Indianapolis†	Am. Assoc.	50	100	6	6	.500	78	38	33	70	31	2.97
1982—Louisville	Am. Assoc.	21	30⅓	3	2	.600	27	15	15	17	7	4.45
1982—St. Louis	National	33	56⅔	5	4	.556	53	27	24	22	21	3.81
1983—St. Louis‡	National	53	74	3	3	.500	64	31	26	26	29	3.16
1983—Louisville	Am. Assoc.	1	2	0	0	.000	2	1	1	0	0	4.50
1984—St. Louis	National	63	84⅓	4	2	.667	69	36	35	45	34	3.72
1985—St. Louis§	National	52	68⅓	5	2	.714	63	15	14	41	26	1.84
1986—St. Louis x	National	4	2⅓	0	0	.000	3	0	0	3	1	0.00
Major League Totals—5 Years		205	286	17	11	.607	252	109	99	137	111	3.12

Selected by Philadelphia Phillies' organization in 12th round of free-agent draft, January 7, 1976.
Selected by San Francisco Giants' organization in 7th round of free-agent draft, January 11, 1977.
Selected by Cincinnati Reds' organization in 5th round of free-agent draft, June 6, 1978.
†Traded with Pitcher Jose Brito to St. Louis Cardinals' organization for Pitcher Bob Shirley, April 1, 1982.
‡On disabled list, June 1 to June 22, 1983; included rehabilitation disability assignment to Louisville, June 19 to June 22, 1983.
§On disabled list, April 3 to April 21, 1985.
xOn disabled list, April 27, 1986 through remainder of season.

CHAMPIONSHIP SERIES RECORD

Year Club	League	G.	IP.	W.	L.	Pct.	H.	R.	ER.	SO.	BB.	ERA.
1985—St. Louis	National	2	2	1	0	1.000	2	0	0	1	0	0.00

WORLD SERIES RECORD

Year Club	League	G.	IP.	W.	L.	Pct.	H.	R.	ER.	SO.	BB.	ERA.
1982—St. Louis	National	2	1⅔	0	0	.000	4	2	2	1	1	10.80
1985—St. Louis	National	3	3⅔	0	0	.000	10	6	5	2	0	12.27
World Series Totals—2 Years		5	5⅓	0	0	.000	14	8	7	3	1	11.81

STEVEN MICHAEL LAKE
(Steve)

Born March 14, 1957, at Inglewood, Calif.
Height, 6.01. Weight, 190.
Throws and bats righthanded.
Cousin of Mike Lake, minor league pitcher, 1941 through 1946.

Major League stolen bases: 1985 (1).
Led Appalachian League in passed balls with 15 in 1975.

Year Club	League	Pos.	G.	AB.	R.	H.	2B.	3B.	HR.	RBI.	B.A.	PO.	A.	E.	F.A.
1975—Bluefield	Appal.	C	49	162	17	45	12	0	3	24	.278	254	★39	9	.970
1976—Miami	Fla. St.	PH	1	1	0	1	0	0	0	1	1.000	0	0	0	.000
1977—Miami	Fla. St.	C	79	232	25	55	10	1	2	24	.237	357	47	6	.985
1978—Miami†‡	Fla. St.	C	69	223	19	57	10	0	2	26	.256	300	49	6	.983
1979—Stockton§	Calif.	C	94	329	36	93	12	3	6	40	.283	504	73	8	.986
1980—Holyoke	East.	C-OF	102	325	26	84	9	2	2	44	.258	445	107	10	.982
1981—Vancouver x	P. C.	C	109	348	27	80	14	1	2	38	.230	502	102	7	.989
1982—Tucson y	P. C.	C	112	378	42	100	15	4	3	45	.265	504	91	12	.980
1983—Chicago	Nat.	C	38	85	9	22	4	1	1	7	.259	115	22	0	1.000
1984—Chicago z	Nat.	C	25	54	4	12	4	0	2	7	.222	72	13	4	.955
1984—Midland	Texas	C	9	25	2	4	0	0	1	1	.160	46	7	0	1.000
1985—Chicago	Nat.	C	58	119	5	18	2	0	1	11	.151	182	25	1	.995
1986—Chi. a-St.L.	Nat.	C	36	68	8	20	2	0	2	14	.294	105	9	2	.983
1986—Iowa-Louisville	A. A.	C	33	98	5	24	6	0	0	13	.245	140	21	2	.988
Major League Totals—4 Years			157	326	26	72	12	1	6	39	.221	474	69	7	.987

Selected by Baltimore Orioles' organization in 3rd round of free-agent draft, June 4, 1975.
†On disabled list, April 17 to May 16, 1978.
‡Sold to Milwaukee Brewers' organization, December 21, 1978.
§On disabled list, June 20 to July 6, 1979.
xLoaned to Tucson (Houston Astros' organization), April 5, 1982; returned, September 7, 1982.
yTraded to Chicago Cubs for a player to be named later, April 1, 1983; Milwaukee Brewers' organization acquired Pitcher Rich Buonantony to complete deal, October 24, 1983.
zOn disabled list, May 14 to August 3, 1984; included rehabilitation disability assignment to Midland, July 23 to August 3, 1984.
aReleased, July 15, 1986; signed by Louisville (St. Louis Cardinals' organization), July 24, 1986.

CHAMPIONSHIP SERIES RECORD

Year Club	League	Pos.	G.	AB.	R.	H.	2B.	3B.	HR.	RBI.	B.A.	PO.	A.	E.	F.A.
1984—Chicago	Nat.	C	1	1	0	1	1	0	0	0	1.000	0	0	0	.000

DENNIS PATRICK LAMP

Born September 23, 1952, at Los Angeles, Calif.
Height, 6.03. Weight, 215.
Throws and bats righthanded.
Established National League record for most games taken out as starting pitcher, season (35), 1980.

Major League saves: 1982 (5), 1983 (15), 1984 (9), 1985 (2), 1986 (2). Total—33.

Year Club	League	G.	IP.	W.	L.	Pct.	H.	R.	ER.	SO.	BB.	ERA.
1971—Caldwell	Pioneer	14	46	1	2	.333	51	39	33	43	32	6.46
1972—Bradenton Cubs	Gulf Coast	14	70	7	2	.778	56	20	15	56	21	1.93
1973—Quincy	Midwest	13	89	6	4	.600	67	32	26	71	29	2.63
1973—Midland	Texas	9	48	2	4	.333	54	29	25	23	11	4.69
1974—Key West	Florida St.	8	49	1	5	.167	39	15	8	20	14	1.47
1974—Midland	Texas	24	60	1	1	.500	70	38	31	42	22	4.65
1975—Midland	Texas	37	127	7	5	.583	112	52	47	71	54	3.33
1976—Wichita	Am. Assoc.	30	153	8	*14	.364	182	94	69	98	52	4.06
1977—Wichita	Am. Assoc.	20	129	11	4	*.733	116	54	42	52	23	2.93
1977—Chicago	National	11	30	0	2	.000	43	21	21	12	8	6.30
1978—Chicago	National	37	224	7	15	.318	221	96	82	73	56	3.29
1979—Chicago	National	38	200	11	10	.524	223	96	78	86	46	3.51
1980—Chicago†	National	41	203	10	14	.417	259	*123	*117	83	82	5.19
1981—Chicago	American	27	127	7	6	.538	103	41	34	71	43	2.41
1982—Chicago	American	44	189⅔	11	8	.579	206	96	84	78	59	3.99
1983—Chicago‡	American	49	116⅓	7	7	.500	123	52	48	44	29	3.71
1984—Toronto	American	56	85	8	8	.500	97	53	43	45	38	4.55
1985—Toronto	American	53	105⅔	11	0	1.000	96	42	39	68	27	3.32
1986—Toronto§	American	40	73	2	6	.250	93	50	41	30	23	5.05
National League Totals—4 Years		127	657	28	41	.406	746	336	298	254	192	4.08
American League Totals—6 Years		269	696⅔	46	35	.568	718	334	289	336	219	3.73
Major League Totals—10 Years		396	1353⅔	74	76	.493	1464	670	587	590	411	3.90

Selected by Chicago Cubs' organization in 3rd round of free-agent draft, June 8, 1971.

†Traded to Chicago White Sox for Pitcher Ken Kravec, March 28, 1981.

‡Granted free agency, November 7, 1983; signed by Toronto Blue Jays as Type A player, January 10, 1984. (Pitcher Tom Seaver selected from player compensation pool by Chicago White Sox, January 20, 1984.)

§Released, October 20, 1986.

CHAMPIONSHIP SERIES RECORD

Tied American League Championship Series records for most games pitched, four-game Series (3), 1983; most strikeouts by a relief pitcher, game (5), October 15, 1985.

Year Club	League	G.	IP.	W.	L.	Pct.	H.	R.	ER.	SO.	BB.	ERA.
1983—Chicago	American	3	2	0	0	.000	0	1	0	1	2	0.00
1985—Toronto	American	3	9⅓	0	0	.000	2	0	0	10	1	0.00
Championship Series Totals—2 Years		6	11⅓	0	0	.000	2	1	0	11	3	0.00

RICHARD ANTHONY LANCELLOTTI
(Rick)

Born July 5, 1957, at Providence, R.I.
Height, 6.02. Weight, 200.
Throws and bats lefthanded.
Attended Glassboro State College, Glassboro, N. J.

Led Pacific Coast League in game-winning RBIs with 19 and being hit by pitch with 11 in 1984.
Led Eastern League in total bases with 296 in 1979.
Named Eastern League Most Valuable Player, 1979.

Year Club	League	Pos.	G.	AB.	R.	H.	2B.	3B.	HR.	RBI.	B.A.	PO.	A.	E.	F.A.
1977—Charleston	W. Car.	OF	73	239	37	63	14	4	9	31	.264	103	5	7	.939
1978—Salem	Carol.	OF	133	439	67	106	15	3	15	60	.241	198	15	*13	.942
1979—Buffalo	East.	OF	138	506	95	145	14	7	*41	●107	.287	190	13	16	.927
1980—Portland	P. C.	OF	61	199	25	44	8	0	7	29	.221	62	3	1	.985
1980—Buffalo†	East.	OF	30	107	19	28	1	0	10	21	.262	61	3	3	.955
1980—Amarillo	Texas	OF	22	79	15	30	8	1	4	15	.380	24	0	0	1.000
1981—Hawaii	P. C.	OF-1B	132	482	67	122	23	5	19	84	.253	404	17	5	.988
1982—Hawaii	P. C.	1B-OF	136	500	76	136	31	4	20	95	.272	304	16	4	.988
1982—San Diego‡	Nat.	1B-OF	17	39	2	7	2	0	0	4	.179	63	2	1	.985
1983—Wich.§-Ok. C.x	A. A.	1B-OF	64	218	27	45	11	0	8	35	.206	334	25	5	.986
1983—Las Vegas	P. C.	1B-OF	30	116	21	35	8	0	9	32	.302	47	3	2	.962
1984—Las Vegas y	P. C.	OF-1B	133	522	88	150	29	6	29	*131	.287	340	23	12	.968
1985—Tidewater z	Int.	1B	91	316	32	57	9	0	10	28	.180	701	38	10	.987
1985—Phoenix a	P. C.	OF-1B	33	119	17	25	4	2	6	29	.210	136	3	1	.993
1986—Phoenix	P. C.	OF-1B	122	440	81	121	20	3	*31	106	.275	501	33	12	.978
1986—San Francisco b	Nat.	OF-1B	15	18	2	4	0	0	2	6	.222	7	0	0	1.000
Major League Totals—2 Years			32	57	4	11	2	0	2	10	.193	70	2	1	.986

Selected by Pittsburgh Pirates' organization in 11th round of free-agent draft, June 7, 1977.

†Traded with Outfielder Luis Salazar to San Diego Padres' organization for Infielder Kurt Bevacqua and a player to be named later, August 5, 1980; Pittsburgh Pirates' organization acquired Pitcher Mark Lee to complete deal, August 12, 1980.

‡Sold to Wichita (Montreal Expos' organization), October 7, 1982.

§Released, May 30, 1983; signed by Oklahoma City (Texas Rangers' organization), June 10, 1983.

xReleased, July 26, 1983; signed by Las Vegas (San Diego Padres' organization), August 2, 1983.

yGranted free agency, October 15, 1984; signed by Tidewater (New York Mets' organization), March 31, 1985.

zSold to Phoenix (San Francisco Giants' organization), July 31, 1985.

aGranted free agency, October 15, 1985; re-signed by Giants' organization, February 7, 1986.

bReleased, November 10, 1986.

KENNETH FRANCIS LANDREAUX

Name pronounced LAN-droh.

(Ken)

Born December 22, 1954, at Los Angeles, Calif.
Height, 5.11. Weight, 190.
Throws right and bats lefthanded.
Attended Arizona State University, Tempe, Ariz.
Cousin of Enos Cabell, infielder with Baltimore Orioles, Houston Astros, San Francisco Giants,
Detroit Tigers and Los Angeles Dodgers, 1972 through 1986.

Tied major league record for most two-base hits, inning (2), July 3, 1979 (seventh inning).
Tied modern major league record for most three-base hits, game (3), July 3, 1980.
Major League stolen bases: 1977 (1), 1978 (7), 1979 (10), 1980 (8), 1981 (18), 1982 (31), 1983 (30), 1984 (10), 1985 (15), 1986 (10). Total—140.
Named Minor League Player of the Year by THE SPORTING NEWS, 1977.
Named outfielder on THE SPORTING NEWS College Baseball All-America Team, 1976.

Year Club	League	Pos.	G.	AB.	R.	H.	2B.	3B.	HR.	RBI.	B.A.	PO.	A.	E.	F.A.
1976—El Paso†	Texas	OF	21	59	15	13	3	1	2	11	.220	32	4	0	1.000
1977—El Paso	Texas	OF	57	209	57	74	17	4	16	59	.354	117	6	6	.953
1977—Salt Lake City	P. C.	OF	62	256	67	92	16	4	11	57	.359	164	3	4	.977
1977—California	Amer.	OF	23	76	6	19	5	1	0	5	.250	59	5	2	.970
1978—California‡	Amer.	OF	93	260	37	58	7	5	5	23	.223	138	6	2	.986
1979—Minnesota	Amer.	OF	151	564	81	172	27	5	15	83	.305	292	10	6	.981
1980—Minnesota§	Amer.	OF	129	484	56	136	23	11	7	62	.281	231	8	6	.976
1981—Los Angeles	Nat.	OF	99	390	48	98	16	4	7	41	.251	210	4	0	●1.000
1982—Los Angeles	Nat.	OF	129	461	71	131	23	7	7	50	.284	281	3	4	.986
1983—Los Angeles	Nat.	OF	141	481	63	135	25	3	17	66	.281	299	4	3	.990
1984—Los Angeles x	Nat.	OF	134	438	39	110	11	5	11	47	.251	212	3	3	.986
1985—Los Angeles	Nat.	OF	147	482	70	129	26	2	12	50	.268	267	4	7	.975
1986—Los Angeles y	Nat.	OF	103	283	34	74	13	2	4	29	.261	145	5	7	.955
American League Totals—4 Years			396	1384	180	385	62	22	27	173	.278	720	29	16	.979
National League Totals—6 Years			753	2535	325	677	114	23	58	283	.267	1414	23	24	.984
Major League Totals—10 Years			1149	3919	505	1062	176	45	85	456	.271	2134	52	40	.982

Selected by Houston Astros' organization in 8th round of free-agent draft, June 5, 1973.
Selected by California Angels' organization in 1st round (sixth player selected) of free-agent draft, June 8, 1976.
†On disabled list, July 17 to August 4, 1976.
‡Traded with Pitchers Paul Hartzell and Brad Havens and Third Baseman Dave Engle to Minnesota Twins for First Baseman Rod Carew, February 3, 1979.
§Traded to Los Angeles Dodgers for Third Baseman-Outfielder Mickey Hatcher, First Baseman Kelly Snider and Pitcher Matt Reeves, March 30, 1981.
xOn disabled list, April 27 to May 12, 1984.
yOn disabled list, July 28 to September 3, 1986.

DIVISION SERIES RECORD

Year Club	League	Pos.	G.	AB.	R.	H.	2B.	3B.	HR.	RBI.	B.A.	PO.	A.	E.	F.A.
1981—Los Angeles	Nat.	OF	5	20	1	4	1	0	0	1	.200	16	0	0	1.000

CHAMPIONSHIP SERIES RECORD

Year Club	League	Pos.	G.	AB.	R.	H.	2B.	3B.	HR.	RBI.	B.A.	PO.	A.	E.	F.A.
1981—Los Angeles	Nat.	OF	5	10	0	1	1	0	0	0	.100	4	0	0	1.000
1983—Los Angeles	Nat.	OF	4	14	0	2	0	0	0	1	.143	12	0	0	1.000
1985—Los Angeles	Nat.	PH-OF	5	18	4	7	3	0	0	2	.389	7	0	0	1.000
Championship Series Totals—3 Years			14	42	4	10	4	0	0	3	.238	23	0	0	1.000

WORLD SERIES RECORD

Year Club	League	Pos.	G.	AB.	R.	H.	2B.	3B.	HR.	RBI.	B.A.	PO.	A.	E.	F.A.
1981—Los Angeles	Nat.	PH-O-PR	5	6	1	1	1	0	0	0	.167	6	0	0	1.000

ALL-STAR GAME RECORD

Year League	Pos.	AB.	R.	H.	2B.	3B.	HR.	RBI.	B.A.	PO.	A.	E.	F.A.
1980—American	PH-OF	1	0	0	0	0	0	0	.000	1	0	0	1.000

TERRY LEE LANDRUM

(Tito)

Born October 25, 1954, at Joplin, Mo.
Height, 5.11. Weight, 175.
Throws and bats righthanded.
Attended Eastern Oklahoma State, Wilburton, Okla.

Major League stolen bases: 1980 (3), 1981 (4), 1983 (1), 1984 (3), 1985 (1), 1986 (3). Total—15.
Led Florida State League in stolen bases with 68 in 1978.

Year Club	League	Pos.	G.	AB.	R.	H.	2B.	3B.	HR.	RBI.	B.A.	PO.	A.	E.	F.A.
1973—Orangeburg	W. Car.	OF	70	262	30	73	7	3	1	27	.279	168	7	1	.994
1974—St. Petersburg†	Fla. St.	OF	87	309	38	73	5	9	3	39	.236	214	7	8	.965
1975—St. Petersburg	Fla. St.	OF	132	435	76	96	21	4	11	45	.221	★313	5	7	.978
1976—Arkansas‡	Texas	OF	99	359	49	99	13	3	7	45	.276	201	12	7	.968
1976—Tulsa	A. A.	OF	9	24	1	6	1	0	0	1	.250	17	0	0	1.000
1977—Arkansas	Texas	OF	26	84	11	18	3	1	2	13	.214	50	5	1	.982

Year Club	League	Pos.	G.	AB.	R.	H.	2B.	3B.	HR.	RBI.	B.A.	PO.	A.	E.	F.A.
1977—St. Petersburg.......	Fla. St.	OF	67	249	40	61	15	3	4	40	.245	157	7	1	.994
1978—St. Petersburg.......	Fla. St.	OF	117	434	66	129	*25	1	4	45	.297	*305	8	3	.991
1979—Arkansas................	Texas	OF	71	265	44	71	20	5	3	33	.268	134	7	4	.972
1979—Springfield.............	A. A.	OF	61	193	28	50	8	2	6	34	.259	126	5	2	.985
1980—Springfield.............	A. A.	OF	93	350	55	106	23	6	12	46	.303	193	6	4	.980
1980—St. Louis.................	Nat.	OF	35	77	6	19	2	2	0	7	.247	40	1	1	.976
1981—St. Louis.................	Nat.	OF	81	119	13	31	5	4	0	10	.261	72	6	0	1.000
1982—St. Louis.................	Nat.	OF	79	72	12	20	3	0	2	14	.278	50	2	0	1.000
1982—Louisville	A. A.	OF	25	94	10	19	2	1	0	6	.202	46	0	2	.958
1983—St. Louis.................	Nat.	OF	6	5	0	1	0	1	0	0	.200	1	0	0	1.000
1983—Louisville§.............	A. A.	OF	111	431	79	126	23	*12	18	77	.292	286	8	8	.974
1983—Baltimore x...........	Amer.	OF	26	42	8	13	2	0	1	4	.310	39	0	0	1.000
1984—St. Louis.................	Nat.	OF	105	173	21	47	9	1	3	26	.272	93	1	2	.979
1985—St. Louis y	Nat.	OF	85	161	21	45	8	2	4	21	.280	91	2	0	1.000
1986—St. Louis.................	Nat.	OF	96	205	24	43	7	1	2	17	.210	131	6	1	.993
National League Totals—7 Years...........			487	812	97	206	34	11	11	95	.254	478	18	4	.992
American League Totals—1 Year			26	42	8	13	2	0	1	4	.310	39	0	0	1.000
Major League Totals—8 Years.................			513	854	105	219	36	11	12	99	.256	517	18	4	.993

Signed as free agent by St. Louis Cardinals' organization, October 10, 1972.

†On disabled list, July 19 to September 20, 1974.

‡On disabled list, April 24 to May 10, 1976.

§Sold to Baltimore Orioles, August 31, 1983, completing deal in which Baltimore traded Infielder-Catcher Floyd Rayford to St. Louis Cardinals for a player to be named later, June 13, 1983.

xTraded to St. Louis Cardinals for Pitcher Jose Brito and cash, March 25, 1984.

yOn disabled list, April 17 to May 8, 1985.

CHAMPIONSHIP SERIES RECORD

Tied Championship Series record for most hits, inning (2), October 13, 1985 (second inning).
Tied National League Championship Series record for most hits, game (4), October 13, 1985.

Year Club	League	Pos.	G.	AB.	R.	H.	2B.	3B.	HR.	RBI.	B.A.	PO.	A.	E.	F.A.
1983—Baltimore	Amer.	PR-O-PH	4	10	2	2	0	0	1	1	.200	5	0	0	1.000
1985—St. Louis.................	Nat.	PH-OF	5	14	2	6	0	0	0	4	.429	6	0	0	1.000
Championship Series Totals—2 Years.....			9	24	4	8	0	0	1	5	.333	11	0	0	1.000

WORLD SERIES RECORD

Year Club	League	Pos.	G.	AB.	R.	H.	2B.	3B.	HR.	RBI.	B.A.	PO.	A.	E.	F.A.
1983—Baltimore	Amer.	PR-OF	3	0	0	0	0	0	0	0	.000	1	0	0	1.000
1985—St. Louis.................	Nat.	OF	7	25	3	9	2	0	1	1	.360	12	1	0	1.000
World Series Totals—2 Years			10	25	3	9	2	0	1	1	.360	13	1	0	1.000

THOMAS WILLIAM LANDRUM
(Bill)

Born August 17, 1957, at Columbia, S.C.
Height, 6.02. Weight, 185.
Throws and bats righthanded.
Attended Spartanburg Methodist College, Spartanburg, S.C., and received bachelor of science
degree from University of South Carolina, Columbia, S.C. in 1980.
Son of Joe Landrum, pitcher with Brooklyn Dodgers, 1950 and 1952.

Year Club	League	G.	IP.	W.	L.	Pct.	H.	R.	ER.	SO.	BB.	ERA.
1980—Sarasota Cubs†	Gulf Coast	11	37	2	0	1.000	37	21	17	27	11	4.14
1981—Tampa	Florida St.	17	83	6	8	.42	87	44	35	52	22	3.80
1982—Waterbury....................................	Eastern	*58	112⅓	10	6	.625	109	63	51	104	65	4.09
1983—Waterbury....................................	Eastern	17	29⅔	1	1	.500	17	5	5	33	14	1.52
1983—Indianapolis‡	Am. Assoc.	15	17⅔	1	3	.250	20	6	6	21	6	3.06
1984—Wichita§	Am. Assoc.	47	130⅓	7	4	.636	12	58	50	120	52	3.45
1985—Denver	Am. Assoc.	29	138	6	6	.500	148	72	61	88	49	3.98
1986—Denver x	Am. Assoc.	24	36⅓	1	3	.250	36	20	14	36	25	3.47
1986—Cincinnati	National	10	13⅓	0	0	.000	23	11	10	14	4	6.75
Major League Totals—1 Year..................		10	13⅓	0	0	.000	23	11	10	14	4	6.75

Signed as free agent by Chicago Cubs' organization, June 22, 1980.

†Released, October 20, 1980; signed by Billings (Cincinnati Reds' organization), February 7, 1981.

‡On disabled list, July 19 to August 4, 1983.

§Drafted by Chicago White Sox, December 3, 1984; returned, March 30, 1985.

xOn disabled list, April 29 to June 21, 1986.

JAMES RICK LANGFORD
(Known by middle name.)

Born March 20, 1952, at Farmville, Va.
Height, 6.00. Weight, 185.
Throws and bats righthanded.
Attended Manatee Junior College, Bradenton, Fla., and
Florida State University, Tallahassee, Fla.

Pitched 11-0 no-hit victory against Memphis, May 30, 1976.
Led American League in wild pitches with 16 in 1979.
Led American League in complete games with 28 in 1980 and 18 in 1981.

Year Club	League	G	IP	W	L	Pct.	H	R	ER	SO	BB	ERA
1973—Bradenton Pirates†	Gulf Coast	3	10	1	0	1.000	5	3	0	10	7	0.00
1974—Salem	Carolina	26	174	11	7	.611	143	63	52	125	74	2.69
1975—Shreveport	Texas	16	42	5	2	.714	40	25	17	39	22	3.64
1975—Charleston	Int'national	13	65	7	2	.778	55	26	24	41	20	3.32
1976—Charleston	Int'national	16	121	9	5	.643	106	51	43	95	48	3.20
1976—Pittsburgh‡	National	12	23	0	1	.000	27	17	16	17	14	6.26
1977—Oakland	American	37	208	8	●19	.296	223	107	93	141	73	4.02
1978—Oakland	American	37	176	7	13	.350	169	77	67	92	56	3.43
1979—Oakland	American	34	219	12	16	.429	233	114	104	101	57	4.27
1980—Oakland	American	35	★290	19	12	.613	276	119	105	102	64	3.26
1981—Oakland	American	24	195	12	10	.545	190	81	65	84	58	3.00
1982—Oakland§	American	32	237⅓	11	16	.407	265	121	111	79	49	4.21
1983—Oakland x	American	7	20	0	4	.000	43	28	27	2	10	12.15
1983—Modesto	California	1	6	0	0	.000	4	2	2	2	2	3.00
1984—Tacoma y	P. Coast	3	15	0	2	.000	22	11	10	3	2	6.00
1984—Oakland	American	3	8⅔	0	0	.000	15	8	8	2	2	8.31
1985—Modesto z	California	1	6	0	0	.000	10	5	4	3	2	6.00
1985—Oakland	American	23	59	3	5	.375	60	24	23	21	15	3.51
1986—Oakland abc	American	16	55	1	10	.091	69	49	45	30	18	7.36
National League Totals—1 Year		12	23	0	1	.000	27	17	16	17	14	6.26
American League Totals—10 Years		248	1468	73	105	.410	1543	728	648	654	402	3.97
Major League Totals—11 Years		260	1491	73	106	.408	1570	745	664	671	416	4.01

Selected by St. Louis Cardinals' organization in 11th round of free-agent draft, January 13, 1971.
Selected by Cleveland Indians' organization in 36th round of free-agent draft, June 6, 1972.
Signed as free agent by Pittsburgh Pirates' organization, June 17, 1973.
†On suspended list, July 17, 1973 through remainder of season.
‡Traded with Pitchers Doc Medich, Dave Giusti and Doug Bair, and Outfielders Mitchell Page and Tony Armas to Oakland A's for Infielders Phil Garner and Tommy Helms, and Pitcher Chris Batton, March 15, 1977.
§Appeared in one game as outfielder with one putout and had one at-bat with no hits.
xOn disabled list, April 5 to May 2, May 20 to July 17 and July 31, 1983 through remainder of season.
yOn Oakland disabled list, March 31 to September 1, 1984; included rehabilitation disability assignment to Tacoma, June 5 to June 18, 1984.
zOn Oakland disabled list, April 9 to June 13, 1985; included rehabilitation disability assignment to Modesto, June 9 to June 13, 1985.
aAppeared in one game as a pinch-runner.
bOn disabled list, May 18 to June 2, 1986.
cReleased, July 18, 1986.

DIVISION SERIES RECORD

Year Club	League	G	IP	W	L	Pct.	H	R	ER	SO	BB	ERA
1981—Oakland	American	1	7⅓	1	0	1.000	10	1	1	3	0	1.23

MARK EDWARD LANGSTON

Born August 20, 1960, at San Diego, Calif.
Height, 6.02. Weight, 183.
Throws left and bats righthanded.
Attended San Jose State University, San Jose, Calif.
Named American League Rookie Pitcher of the Year by THE SPORTING NEWS, 1984.

Year Club	League	G	IP	W	L	Pct.	H	R	ER	SO	BB	ERA
1981—Bellingham	Northwest	13	85	7	3	.700	81	37	32	97	46	3.39
1982—Bakersfield	California	26	177⅓	12	7	.632	143	71	50	161	102	2.54
1983—Chattanooga	Southern	28	198	14	9	.609	187	104	79	142	102	3.59
1984—Seattle	American	35	225	17	10	.630	188	99	85	★204	★118	3.40
1985—Seattle†	American	24	126⅔	7	14	.333	122	85	77	72	91	5.47
1986—Seattle	American	37	239⅓	12	14	.462	234	★142	★129	★245	123	4.85
Major League Totals—3 Years		96	591	36	38	.486	544	326	291	521	332	4.43

Selected by Chicago Cubs' organization in 15th round of free-agent draft, June 6, 1978.
Selected by Seattle Mariners' organization in 3rd round of free-agent draft, June 8, 1981.
†On disabled list, June 7 to July 22, 1985.

CARNEY RAY LANSFORD

Born February 7, 1957, at San Jose, Calif.
Height, 6.02. Weight, 195.
Throws and bats righthanded.
Brother of Phil Lansford, infielder in Cleveland Indians' and Toronto Blue Jays' organizations, 1978 through 1981; and Joe Lansford, first baseman with San Diego Padres, 1982 and 1983.
Major League stolen bases: 1978 (20), 1979 (20), 1980 (14), 1981 (15), 1982 (9), 1983 (3), 1984 (9), 1985 (2), 1986 (16). Total—108.
Hit three home runs in a game, September 1, 1979.
Led American League in sacrifice flies with 11 in 1980.
Led Texas League third basemen in double plays with 16 in 1977.
Named third baseman on THE SPORTING NEWS American League Silver Slugger team, 1981.

Year Club	League	Pos.	G.	AB.	R.	H.	2B.	3B.	HR.	RBI.	B.A.	PO.	A.	E.	F.A.
1975—Idaho Falls†	Pion.	3B-SS	8	27	5	6	2	0	1	1	.222	8	14	9	.710
1976—Quad Cities	Midw.	3B-OF-SS	121	418	87	120	19	5	14	86	.287	130	215	36	.906
1977—El Paso	Texas	3B	120	443	98	147	17	3	18	94	.332	★110	★210	15	★.955

Year	Club	League	Pos.	G.	AB.	R.	H.	2B.	3B.	HR.	RBI.	B.A.	PO.	A.	E.	F.A.
1978—California‡	Amer.		3B-SS	121	453	63	133	23	2	8	52	.294	94	186	18	.940
1979—California	Amer.		3B	157	654	114	188	30	5	19	79	.287	★135	263	7	★.983
1980—California§	Amer.		3B	151	602	87	157	27	3	15	80	.261	★151	250	19	.955
1981—Boston	Amer.		3B	102	399	61	134	23	3	4	52	★.336	70	180	13	.951
1982—Boston xy	Amer.		3B	128	482	65	145	28	4	11	63	.301	83	216	10	.968
1983—Oakland z	Amer.		3B-SS	80	299	43	92	16	2	10	45	.308	60	163	10	.957
1984—Oakland	Amer.		3B	151	597	70	179	31	5	14	74	.300	137	268	18	.957
1985—Oakland a	Amer.		3B	98	401	51	111	18	2	13	46	.277	85	119	5	.976
1986—Oakland	Amer.		3B-1B-2B	151	591	80	168	16	4	19	72	.284	480	170	6	.991
Major League Totals—9 Years				1139	4478	634	1307	212	30	113	563	.292	1295	1815	106	.967

Selected by California Angels' organization in 3rd round of free-agent draft, June 4, 1975.

†On disabled list, July 21 to September 30, 1975.

‡On disabled list, June 11 to July 7, 1978.

§Traded with Pitcher Mark Clear and Outfielder Rick Miller to Boston Red Sox for Shortstop Rick Burleson and Third Baseman Butch Hobson, December 10, 1980.

xOn disabled list, June 24 to July 21, 1982.

yTraded with Outfielder Garry Hancock and a player to be named later to Oakland A's for Outfielder Tony Armas and Catcher Jeff Newman, December 6, 1982; Oakland acquired Pitcher Jerry King to complete deal, December 20, 1982.

zOn disabled list, May 19 to June 7, 1983.

aOn disabled list, July 26 to August 28, 1985.

CHAMPIONSHIP SERIES RECORD

Year	Club	League	Pos.	G.	AB.	R.	H.	2B.	3B.	HR.	RBI.	B.A.	PO.	A.	E.	F.A.
1979—California	Amer.		3B	4	17	2	5	0	0	0	3	.294	4	8	0	1.000

DAVID JEFFREY LaPOINT
(Dave)

Born July 29, 1959, at Glens Falls, N. Y.
Height, 6.03. Weight, 215.
Throws and bats lefthanded.

Pitched 4-0 no-hit victory against Reno, July 25, 1979.
Major League saves: 1980 (1).
Led National League in wild pitches with 15 in 1984.
Tied for American Association lead in complete games with 9 in 1981.
Tied for California League lead in shutouts with 3 and complete games with 11 in 1979.
Tied for Midwest League lead in home runs allowed with 20 in 1978.

Year	Club	League	G.	IP.	W.	L.	Pct.	H.	R.	ER.	SO.	BB.	ERA.
1977—Newark	NYP	13	69	5	2	.714	73	40	36	60	22	4.70
1978—Burlington	Midwest	25	161	12	12	.500	177	98	72	134	41	4.02
1979—Stockton	California	27	180	12	10	.545	144	74	63	★208	85	3.15
1980—Vancouver†	P. Coast	17	93	7	4	.636	71	48	29	64	45	2.81
1980—Milwaukee‡	American	5	15	1	0	1.000	17	14	10	5	13	6.00
1981—Springfield	Am. Assoc.	25	172	13	9	.591	160	83	61	★129	66	3.19
1981—St. Louis	National	3	11	1	0	1.000	12	5	5	4	2	4.09
1982—St. Louis	National	42	152⅔	9	3	.750	170	63	58	81	52	3.42
1983—St. Louis	National	37	191⅓	12	9	.571	191	92	84	84	84	3.95
1984—St. Louis§x	National	33	193	12	10	.545	205	94	85	130	77	3.96
1985—San Francisco y	National	31	206⅔	7	17	.292	215	99	82	122	74	3.57
1986—Detroit z	American	16	67⅔	3	6	.333	85	49	43	36	32	5.72
1986—San Diego a	National	24	61⅓	1	4	.200	67	37	29	41	24	4.26
American League Totals—2 Years		21	82⅔	4	6	.400	102	63	53	41	45	5.77
National League Totals—6 Years		170	816	42	43	.494	860	390	343	491	313	3.78
Major League Totals—7 Years		191	898⅔	46	49	.484	962	453	396	532	358	3.97

Selected by Milwaukee Brewers' organization in 10th round of free-agent draft, June 7, 1977.

†On disabled list, May 6 to May 17 and June 6 to July 15, 1980.

‡Traded with Pitcher Lary Sorensen and Outfielders Sixto Lezcano and David Green to St. Louis Cardinals for Pitchers Pete Vuckovich and Rollie Fingers and Catcher Ted Simmons, December 12, 1980.

§On disabled list, June 15 to June 30, 1984.

xTraded with First Basemen David Green and Gary Rajsich and Shortstop Jose Gonzalez (Jose Uribe) to San Francisco Giants for Outfielder-First Baseman Jack Clark, February 1, 1985.

yTraded with Catcher Matt Nokes and Pitcher Eric King to Detroit Tigers for Pitcher Juan Berenguer, Catcher Bob Melvin and a player to be named later, October 7, 1985; San Francisco Giants acquired Pitcher Scott Medvin to complete deal, December 11, 1985.

zTraded to San Diego Padres for Pitcher Mark Thurmond, July 9, 1986.

aReleased, December 18, 1986.

WORLD SERIES RECORD

Year	Club	League	G.	IP.	W.	L.	Pct.	H.	R.	ER.	SO.	BB.	ERA.
1982—St. Louis	National	2	8⅓	0	0	.000	10	6	3	3	2	3.24

—DID YOU KNOW—

That Texas rookie Pete Incaviglia drove in two runs with an October 1 sacrifice fly against Oakland?

BARRY LOUIS LARKIN

Born April 28, 1964, at Cincinnati, O.
Height, 6.00. Weight, 180.
Throws and bats righthanded.
Attended University of Michigan, Ann Arbor, Mich.
Brother of Byron Larkin, guard at Xavier University.

Named American Association Most Valuable Player, 1986.
Major League stolen bases: 1986 (8).
Led American Association in slugging percentage with .525 in 1986.
Named shortstop on THE SPORTING NEWS College Baseball All-America Team, 1985.
Member of 1984 U.S. Olympic baseball team.

Year	Club	League	Pos.	G.	AB.	R.	H.	2B.	3B.	HR.	RBI.	B.A.	PO.	A.	E.	F.A.
1985—Vermont		East.	SS	72	255	42	68	13	2	1	31	.267	110	166	17	.942
1986—Denver		A. A.	SS-2B	103	413	67	136	31	10	10	51	.329	172	287	18	.962
1986—Cincinnati		Nat.	SS-2B	41	159	27	45	4	3	3	19	.283	51	125	4	.978
Major League Totals—1 Year				41	159	27	45	4	3	3	19	.283	51	125	4	.978

Selected by Cincinnati Reds' organization in 2nd round of free-agent draft, June 7, 1982.
Selected by Cincinnati Reds' organization in 1st round (fourth player selected) of free-agent draft, June 3, 1985.

EUGENE THOMAS LARKIN
(Gene)

Born October 24, 1962, at Flushing, N. Y.
Height, 6.03. Weight, 195.
Throws right and bats left and righthanded.
Attended Columbia University, New York, N. Y.

Led California League in sacrifice flies with 14 in 1985.
Tied for Southern League lead in sacrifice flies with 13 in 1986.
Led California League first basemen in double plays with 140 in 1985.
Led Appalachian League first basemen in double plays with 54 in 1984.

Year	Club	League	Pos.	G.	AB.	R.	H.	2B.	3B.	HR.	RBI.	B.A.	PO.	A.	E.	F.A.
1984—Elizabethton		Appal.	1B	57	193	29	63	13	1	6	37	.326	478	19	6	★.988
1985—Visalia		Calif.	1B	●142	528	90	161	25	3	13	●106	.305	★1227	62	12	.991
1986—Orlando		South.	1B-3B	142	529	85	●170	29	6	15	104	.321	923	53	13	.987

Selected by Minnesota Twins' organization in 20th round of free-agent draft, June 4, 1984.

WILLIAM ALAN LASKEY
(Bill)

Born December 20, 1957, at Toledo, O.
Height, 6.05. Weight, 190.
Throws and bats righthanded.
Attended Monroe County Community College, Monroe, Mich., and
Kent State University, Kent, O.

Major League saves: 1986 (1).

Year	Club	League	G.	IP.	W.	L.	Pct.	H.	R.	ER.	SO.	BB.	ERA.
1978—Sarasota Royals		Gulf Coast	4	23	1	2	.333	13	7	5	9	11	1.96
1978—Jacksonville		Southern	7	27	3	2	.600	23	14	13	13	15	4.33
1979—Fort Myers		Florida St.	13	93	7	4	.636	71	24	23	72	35	2.23
1979—Jacksonville		Southern	15	97	4	3	.571	78	44	38	53	46	3.53
1980—Omaha		Am. Assoc.	27	145	5	8	.385	155	81	67	77	72	4.16
1981—Omaha†		Am. Assoc.	23	138	10	8	.556	136	67	60	87	52	3.91
1982—Phoenix		P. Coast	2	14	1	0	1.000	12	5	2	10	2	1.29
1982—San Francisco		National	32	189⅓	13	12	.520	186	74	66	88	43	3.14
1983—San Francisco		National	25	148⅓	13	10	.565	151	75	69	81	45	4.19
1984—San Francisco		National	35	207⅔	9	14	.391	222	112	100	71	50	4.33
1985—San Francisco‡-Montreal§		National	30	148⅓	5	16	.238	165	91	81	60	53	4.91
1986—San Francisco		National	20	27⅓	1	1	.500	28	14	13	8	13	4.28
1986—Phoenix x		P. Coast	14	86⅔	5	5	.500	101	40	33	47	22	3.43
Major League Totals—5 Years			142	721	41	53	.436	752	366	329	308	204	4.11

Selected by Detroit Tigers' organization in 8th round of free-agent draft, January 11, 1977.
Selected by Detroit Tigers' organization in secondary phase of free-agent draft, June 7, 1977.
Selected by Kansas City Royals' organization in secondary phase of free-agent draft, June 6, 1978.
†Traded with Pitcher Rich Gale to San Francisco Giants for Outfielder Jerry Martin, December 10, 1981.
‡Traded with First Baseman Scot Thompson and a player to be named later to Montreal Expos for First Baseman Dan Driessen, August 1, 1985.
§Traded to San Francisco Giants for Pitcher George Riley and Outfielder Alonzo Powell, October 24, 1985 (this deal settled earlier deal of Laskey going from San Francisco to Montreal on August 1, 1985).
xReleased, November 10, 1986.

WILLIAM CAROL LATHAM JR.
(Bill)

Born August 29, 1960, at Birmingham, Ala.
Height, 6.02. Weight, 190.
Throws and bats lefthanded.
Received bachelor of science degree in transportation
from Auburn University, Auburn, Ala. in 1981.

Year Club	League	G.	IP.	W.	L.	Pct.	H.	R.	ER.	SO.	BB.	ERA.
1981—Little Falls	NYP	13	88	5	5	.500	91	52	38	70	38	3.89
1982—Shelby	S. Atlantic	24	143⅓	9	7	.563	145	81	70	114	53	4.40
1983—Lynchburg	Carolina	13	84⅓	8	4	.667	81	34	20	54	22	2.13
1983—Jackson	Texas	12	72⅔	4	4	.500	72	38	35	37	35	4.33
1984—Jackson	Texas	7	44⅔	2	2	.500	38	15	11	27	9	2.22
1984—Tidewater	Int'national	21	132⅓	11	3	.786	119	49	45	57	42	3.06
1985—New York	National	7	22⅔	1	3	.250	21	10	10	10	7	3.97
1985—Tidewater†	Int'national	24	157⅔	13	8	.619	144	61	47	66	57	2.68
1986—Minnesota	American	7	16	0	1	.000	24	14	13	8	6	7.31
1986—Toledo	Int'national	21	133⅔	6	5	.545	155	64	53	48	43	3.57
National League Totals—1 Year		7	22⅔	1	3	.250	21	10	10	10	7	3.97
American League Totals—1 Year		7	16	0	1	.000	24	14	13	8	6	7.31
Major League Totals—2 Years		14	38⅔	1	4	.200	45	24	23	18	13	5.35

Selected by Seattle Mariners' organization in 11th round of free-agent draft, June 7, 1977.
Signed as free agent by New York Mets' organization, June 15, 1981.
†Traded with Outfielder Billy Beane and Pitcher Joe Klink to Minnesota Twins for Second Baseman Tim Teufel and Outfielder Pat Crosby, January 16, 1986.

TIMOTHY JON LAUDNER

Name pronounced LAWD-ner.

(Tim)

Born June 7, 1958, at Mason City, Ia.
Height, 6.03. Weight, 208.
Throws and bats righthanded.
Attended University of Missouri, Columbia, Mo.

Tied American League record for most home runs, first two major league games (2), August 28 and 29, 1981.
Major League stolen bases: 1986 (1).
Led Southern League in slugging percentage with .628 and game-winning RBIs with 14 in 1981.
Named Southern League Most Valuable Player, 1981.

Year Club	League	Pos.	G.	AB.	R.	H.	2B.	3B.	HR.	RBI.	B.A.	PO.	A.	E.	F.A.
1979—Orlando	South.	C	45	141	17	34	7	0	3	20	.241	224	29	6	.977
1980—Orlando†	South.	C	17	61	7	14	5	0	2	5	.230	81	10	1	.989
1980—Visalia	Calif.	C	56	186	23	42	13	0	10	29	.226	251	36	5	.983
1981—Orlando	South.	C-1B	130	433	87	123	21	1	*42	104	.284	631	66	15	.979
1981—Minnesota	Amer.	C	14	43	4	7	2	0	2	5	.163	49	5	0	1.000
1982—Toledo	Int.	C	20	71	4	12	2	0	2	12	.169	121	9	0	1.000
1982—Minnesota	Amer.	C	93	306	37	78	19	1	7	33	.255	454	41	*12	.976
1983—Minnesota	Amer.	C	62	168	20	31	9	0	6	18	.185	259	22	4	.986
1984—Minnesota	Amer.	C	87	262	31	54	16	1	10	35	.206	362	38	9	.978
1985—Minnesota	Amer.	C-1B	72	164	16	39	5	0	7	19	.238	236	19	8	.970
1986—Minnesota	Amer.	C	76	193	21	47	10	0	10	29	.244	299	13	5	.984
Major League Totals—6 Years			404	1136	129	256	61	2	42	139	.225	1659	138	38	.979

Selected by Cincinnati Reds' organization in 33rd round of free-agent draft, June 8, 1976.
Selected by Minnesota Twins' organization in 3rd round of free-agent draft, June 5, 1979.
†On disabled list, April 11 to April 21, 1980.

MICHAEL EUGENE LaVALLIERE

Name pronounced Luh-VAHL-yur.

(Mike)

Born August 18, 1960, at Charlotte, N.C.
Height, 5.10. Weight, 200.
Throws right and bats lefthanded.
Attended University of Lowell, Lowell, Mass.
Son of Guy Lavalliere, minor league catcher, 1952 and 1955 through 1961.

Year Club	League	Pos.	G.	AB.	R.	H.	2B.	3B.	HR.	RBI.	B.A.	PO.	A.	E.	F.A.
1981—Spartanburg	S. Atl.	3B-OF	39	123	15	33	9	0	2	23	.268	16	32	5	.906
1982—Peninsula	Carol.	C-3B	66	178	20	49	4	2	2	23	.275	306	35	6	.983
1983—Reading	East.	C-3B-P	81	218	24	64	16	2	4	43	.294	243	59	4	.987
1984—Reading	East.	C-3-2-P	55	147	19	37	6	0	6	22	.252	113	45	2	.988
1984—Portland	P. C.	C	37	122	20	38	6	3	5	21	.311	186	16	1	.995
1984—Philadelphia†‡	Nat.	C	6	7	0	0	0	0	0	0	.000	20	2	0	1.000
1985—St. Louis	Nat.	C	12	34	2	5	1	0	0	6	.147	48	5	0	1.000
1985—Louisville§	A. A.	C	83	231	19	47	12	1	4	26	.203	420	53	5	.990
1986—St. Louis	Nat.	C	110	303	18	71	10	2	3	30	.234	468	47	6	.988
Major League Totals—3 Years			128	344	20	76	11	2	3	36	.221	536	54	6	.990

Signed as free agent by Philadelphia Phillies' organization, July 12, 1981.
†Traded to St. Louis Cardinals for a player to be named later, December 3, 1984; returned due to injured status, December 13, 1984.
‡Granted free agency, December 23, 1984; signed by Louisville (St. Louis Cardinals' organization), January 23, 1985.
§On disabled list, July 18 to July 29, 1985.

PITCHING RECORD

Year Club	League	G.	IP.	W.	L.	Pct.	H.	R.	ER.	SO.	BB.	ERA.
1983—Reading	Eastern	4	3⅓	0	0	.000	3	3	2	2	2	5.40
1984—Reading	Eastern	1	1	0	0	.000	3	2	2	1	1	18.00

GARY ROBERT LAVELLE

Born January 3, 1949, at Scranton, Pa.
Height, 6.01. Weight, 200.
Throws left and bats righthanded.

Pitched seven-inning, 4-0 no-hit game against Clinton, August 15, 1969.
Major League saves: 1975 (8), 1976 (12), 1977 (20), 1978 (14), 1979 (20), 1980 (9), 1981 (4), 1982 (8), 1983 (20), 1984 (12), 1985 (8). Total—135.
Led National League in intentional bases on balls issued with 18 in 1977.
Tied for Pacific Coast League lead in shutouts with 3 in 1974.

Year Club	League	G.	IP.	W.	L.	Pct.	H.	R.	ER.	SO.	BB.	ERA.
1967—Salt Lake City	Pioneer	17	37	3	2	.600	37	18	12	32	23	2.92
1968—Medford	Northwest	13	60	3	3	.500	53	33	23	67	42	3.45
1969—Decatur†	Midwest	7	48	4	2	.667	41	17	9	30	24	1.69
1970—Amarillo	Texas	21	100	6	12	.333	99	75	60	64	72	5.40
1971—Amarillo	Texas	23	136	11	8	.579	132	65	53	77	56	3.50
1972—Phoenix	P. Coast	37	147	11	14	.440	161	91	69	107	55	4.22
1973—Phoenix‡	P. Coast	36	101	5	7	.417	112	56	51	61	43	4.54
1974—Phoenix	P. Coast	35	182	8	●16	.333	228	119	106	105	76	5.24
1974—San Francisco	National	10	17	0	3	.000	14	7	4	12	10	2.12
1975—San Francisco	National	65	82	6	3	.667	80	30	27	51	48	2.96
1976—San Francisco	National	65	110	10	6	.625	102	37	33	71	52	2.70
1977—San Francisco	National	73	118	7	7	.500	106	35	27	93	37	2.06
1978—San Francisco	National	67	98	13	10	.565	96	41	36	63	44	3.31
1979—San Francisco	National	70	97	7	9	.438	86	31	27	80	42	2.51
1980—San Francisco	National	62	100	6	8	.429	106	43	38	66	36	3.42
1981—San Francisco	National	34	66	2	6	.250	58	33	28	45	23	3.82
1982—San Francisco	National	68	104⅔	10	7	.588	97	35	31	76	29	2.67
1983—San Francisco§	National	56	87	7	4	.636	73	33	25	68	19	2.59
1984—San Francisco x	National	77	101	5	4	.556	92	34	31	71	42	2.76
1985—Toronto	American	69	72⅔	5	7	.417	54	30	25	50	36	3.10
1986—Toronto y	American					(Did not play)						
National League Totals—11 Years		647	980⅔	73	67	.521	910	359	307	696	382	2.82
American League Totals—1 Year		69	72⅔	5	7	.417	54	30	25	50	36	3.10
Major League Totals—12 Years		716	1053⅓	78	74	.513	964	389	332	746	418	2.84

Selected by San Francisco Giants' organization in 34th round of free-agent draft, June 6, 1967.
†On suspended list, April 11, 1969; transferred to military list through July 5, 1969.
‡On temporary inactive list, June 2 to June 20, 1973.
§On disabled list, July 15 to August 5, 1983.
xTraded to Toronto Blue Jays for Pitchers Jim Gott and Jack McKnight and Infielder Augie Schmidt, January 26, 1985.
yOn disabled list, March 24, 1986 through entire season.

CHAMPIONSHIP SERIES RECORD

Year Club	League	G.	IP.	W.	L.	Pct.	H.	R.	ER.	SO.	BB.	ERA.
1985—Toronto	American	1	0	0	0	.000	0	0	0	0	1	0.00

ALL-STAR GAME RECORD

Year League	IP.	W.	L.	Pct.	H.	R.	ER.	SO.	BB.	ERA.
1977—National	2	0	0	.000	1	0	0	2	0	0.00

Member of National League All-Star Team in 1983; did not play.

RUDY KARL LAW

Born October 7, 1956, at Waco, Tex.
Height, 6.02. Weight, 180.
Throws and bats lefthanded.

Tied major league records for most at-bats (11) and plate appearances (12), game, May 8, finished May 9, 1984 (25 innings).
Tied American League records for longest errorless game and most innings by outfielder, game (25), May 8, finished May 9, 1984.
Major League stolen bases: 1978 (3), 1980 (40), 1982 (36), 1983 (77), 1984 (29), 1985 (29), 1986 (14). Total—228.
Led Pacific Coast League in stolen bases with 79 and caught stealing with 20 in 1978.

Year Club	League	Pos.	G.	AB.	R.	H.	2B.	3B.	HR.	RBI.	B.A.	PO.	A.	E.	F.A.
1976—Bellingham	N'west.	OF-1B	54	161	40	54	7	1	1	16	.335	58	2	4	.938
1977—Lodi	Calif.	OF	122	451	124	174	22	5	9	88	★.386	107	2	6	.948
1978—Albuquerque	P. C.	OF	138	★573	118	179	21	9	4	72	.312	236	10	10	.961
1978—Los Angeles	Nat.	OF	11	12	2	3	0	0	0	1	.250	3	0	0	1.000
1979—Albuquerque†	P. C.	OF	72	270	46	80	4	2	0	28	.296	142	2	3	.980
1980—Los Angeles	Nat.	OF	128	388	55	101	5	4	1	23	.260	233	6	3	.988
1981—Albuquerque‡	P. C.	OF	107	397	75	133	16	9	0	39	.335	158	5	5	.970
1982—Chicago	Amer.	OF	121	336	55	107	15	8	3	32	.318	215	2	6	.973
1983—Chicago	Amer.	OF	141	501	95	142	20	7	3	34	.283	302	5	2	★.994
1984—Chicago§	Amer.	OF	136	487	68	122	14	7	6	37	.251	322	5	5	.985
1985—Chicago§x	Amer.	OF	125	390	62	101	21	6	4	36	.259	226	7	3	.987
1986—Kansas City yz	Amer.	OF	87	307	42	80	26	5	1	36	.261	145	2	2	.987
National League Totals—2 Years			139	400	57	104	5	4	1	24	.260	236	6	3	.988
American League Totals—5 Years			610	2021	322	552	96	33	17	175	.273	1210	21	18	.986
Major League Totals—7 Years			749	2421	379	656	101	37	18	199	.271	1446	27	21	.986

Signed as free agent by Los Angeles Dodgers' organization, September 1, 1975.
†On disabled list, June 22 to August 31, 1979.
‡Traded to Chicago White Sox for Outfielder Cecil Espy and Pitcher Bert Geiger, March 30, 1982.
§On disabled list, July 20 to August 4, 1985.
xReleased, April 1, 1986; signed by Kansas City Royals, April 4, 1986.
yOn disabled list, July 7 to September 1, 1986.
zGranted free agency, November 12, 1986; re-signed by Royals, December 8, 1986.

CHAMPIONSHIP SERIES RECORD

Tied American League Championship Series records for most at-bats, four-game Series (18), 1983; most hits, four-game Series (7), 1983; most one-base hits, four-game Series (6), 1983.

Year Club	League	Pos.	G.	AB.	R.	H.	2B.	3B.	HR.	RBI.	B.A.	PO.	A.	E.	F.A.
1983—Chicago	Amer.	OF	4	18	1	7	1	0	0	0	.389	10	0	0	1.000

VANCE AARON LAW

Born October 1, 1956, at Boise, Ida.
Height, 6.02. Weight, 190.
Throws and bats righthanded.
Attended Brigham Young University, Provo, Utah.
Son of Vern Law, pitcher with Pittsburgh Pirates, 1950, 1951 and 1954 through 1967.

Established American League record for longest errorless game by third baseman (25 innings), May 8, finished May 9, 1984.
Tied American League record for most innings played by third baseman, game (25), May 8, finished May 9, 1984.
Major League stolen bases: 1980 (2), 1981 (1), 1982 (4), 1983 (3), 1984 (4), 1985 (6), 1986 (3). Total—23.
Led Pacific Coast League in sacrifice hits with 14 in 1979.

Year Club	League	Pos.	G.	AB.	R.	H.	2B.	3B.	HR.	RBI.	B.A.	PO.	A.	E.	F.A.
1978—Bradenton Pir.	Gulf C.	SS	1	3	0	1	0	0	0	0	.333	2	5	0	1.000
1978—Salem	Carol.	SS	60	213	48	68	13	7	2	30	.319	96	180	22	.926
1979—Portland	P. C.	SS-3B-2B	131	448	62	139	16	8	2	52	.310	201	308	22	.959
1980—Portland	P. C.	SS	96	339	59	100	23	5	5	54	.295	169	295	14	.971
1980—Pittsburgh	Nat.	2B-SS-3B	25	74	11	17	2	2	0	3	.230	31	54	3	.966
1981—Pittsburgh	Nat.	2B-SS-3B	30	67	1	9	0	1	0	3	.134	50	58	0	1.000
1981—Portland†‡	P. C.	2B-SS-3B	88	310	55	86	14	9	5	43	.277	168	218	9	.977
1982—Chicago	Amer.	S-3-2-O	114	359	40	101	20	1	5	54	.281	156	313	26	.947
1983—Chicago	Amer.	3-2-S-O	145	408	55	99	21	5	4	42	.243	94	311	14	.967
1984—Chicago§	Amer.	3-2-O-S	151	481	60	121	18	2	17	59	.252	119	246	16	.958
1985—Montreal	Nat.	2-1-3-O	147	519	75	138	30	6	10	52	.266	420	402	12	.986
1986—Montreal	Nat.	2-1-3-P-O	112	360	37	81	17	2	5	44	.225	273	299	4	.993
National League Totals—4 Years			314	1020	124	245	49	11	15	102	.240	774	813	19	.988
American League Totals—3 Years			410	1248	155	321	59	8	26	155	.257	369	870	56	.957
Major League Totals—7 Years			724	2268	279	566	108	19	41	257	.250	1143	1683	75	.974

Selected by Pittsburgh Pirates' organization in 38th round of free-agent draft, June 6, 1978.
†On disabled list, July 5 to July 15, 1981.
‡Traded with Pitcher Ernie Camacho to Chicago White Sox for Pitchers Ross Baumgarten and Butch Edge, March 21, 1982.
§Traded to Montreal Expos for Pitcher Bob James, December 7, 1984.

CHAMPIONSHIP SERIES RECORD

Year Club	League	Pos.	G.	AB.	R.	H.	2B.	3B.	HR.	RBI.	B.A.	PO.	A.	E.	F.A.
1983—Chicago	Amer.	3B	4	11	0	2	0	0	0	1	.182	1	9	1	.909

PITCHING RECORD

Year Club	League	G.	IP.	W.	L.	Pct.	H.	R.	ER.	SO.	BB.	ERA.
1986—Montreal	National	3	4	0	0	.000	3	2	1	0	2	2.25

THOMAS JAMES LAWLESS
(Tom)

Born December 19, 1956, at Erie, Pa.
Height, 5.11. Weight, 170.
Throws and bats righthanded.
Received bachelor of arts degree in political science from
Pennsylvania State University-Behrend, Erie, Pa.

Major League stolen bases: 1982 (16), 1984 (7), 1985 (2), 1986 (8). Total—33.
Led American Association in stolen bases with 46 in 1983.
Led Florida State League in sacrifice hits with 13 and stolen bases with 60 in 1979.
Led Pioneer League shortstops in putouts with 116 in 1978.

Year Club	League	Pos.	G.	AB.	R.	H.	2B.	3B.	HR.	RBI.	B.A.	PO.	A.	E.	F.A.
1978—Billings	Pioneer	SS-2B	63	254	64	70	5	●7	5	35	.276	117	186	24	.927
1979—Tampa	Fla. St.	2B	131	469	66	126	9	5	1	39	.269	★296	376	17	★.975
1980—Waterbury	East.	2B	130	498	83	137	20	7	2	29	.275	★316	333	14	.979
1981—Waterbury	East.	2B	136	522	77	152	20	10	8	50	.291	323	379	15	.979
1982—Indianapolis	A. A.	2B-SS	86	351	76	108	18	6	2	28	.308	185	251	13	.971
1982—Cincinnati	Nat.	2B	49	165	19	35	6	0	0	4	.212	87	136	5	.978
1983—Indianapolis	A. A.	2B	115	423	93	118	23	3	13	35	.279	255	303	17	.970
1984—Cinc.†-Mont.	Nat.	2B-3B	54	97	11	23	3	0	1	2	.237	50	52	1	.990
1984—Wich.-Ind.‡	A. A.	3B-2B-SS	50	173	36	47	5	5	4	23	.272	53	103	4	.975
1985—Louisville	A. A.	3B-OF	31	124	16	36	9	1	1	12	.290	20	58	3	.963

Year	Club	League	Pos.	G.	AB.	R.	H.	2B.	3B.	HR.	RBI.	B.A.	PO.	A.	E.	F.A.
1985—St. Louis................	Nat.		3B-2B	47	58	8	12	3	1	0	8	.207	19	44	1	.984
1986—St. Louis................	Nat.		3B-2B-OF	46	39	5	11	1	0	0	3	.282	11	15	2	.929
Major League Totals—4 Years................				196	359	43	81	13	1	1	17	.226	167	247	9	.979

Selected by Cincinnati Reds' organization in 17th round of free-agent draft, June 6, 1978.
†Traded to Montreal Expos' organization for First Baseman-Outfielder Pete Rose, August 16, 1984.
‡Sold to Louisville (St. Louis Cardinals' organization), March 25, 1985, completing deal in which St. Louis traded Pitcher Mickey Mahler to Montreal Expos for a player to be named later, February 6, 1985.

WORLD SERIES RECORD

Year	Club	League	Pos.	G.	AB.	R.	H.	2B.	3B.	HR.	RBI.	B.A.	PO.	A.	E.	F.A.
1985—St. Louis................	Nat.		PR	1	0	0	0	0	0	0	0	.000	0	0	0	.000

MARCUS DWAYNE LAWTON

Born August 18, 1965, at Gulfport, Miss.
Height, 6.01. Weight, 160.
Throws right and bats left and righthanded.
Led Carolina League in bases on balls received with 102 in 1986.
Led South Atlantic League in stolen bases with 111 in 1985.
Led Carolina League outfielders in total chances with 359 in 1986.

Year	Club	League	Pos.	G.	AB.	R.	H.	2B.	3B.	HR.	RBI.	B.A.	PO.	A.	E.	F.A.
1983—Sarasota Mets†.....	Gulf C.		SS-3B	51	187	25	48	3	1	0	16	.257	75	128	24	.894
1984—Kingsport†............	Appal.		SS	54	191	43	57	10	1	1	15	.298	86	126	20	.914
1984—Lynchburg†..........	Carol.		2B	3	9	3	2	0	0	0	1	.222	3	8	1	.917
1985—Columbia	S. Atl.		OF-SS-2B	128	470	113	126	11	5	1	53	.268	223	129	39	.900
1986—Lynchburg............	Carol.		OF	*141	*567	*118	158	22	*16	4	66	.279	*336	17	6	*.983

Selected by New York Mets' organization in 6th round of free-agent draft, June 6, 1983.
†Batted righthanded.

JACK THOMAS LAZORKO

Name pronounced La-ZOR-ko.

Born March 30, 1956, at Hoboken, N.J.
Height, 5.11. Weight, 200.
Throws and bats righthanded.
Attended Miami-Dade Community College (South), Miami, Fla.; and received bachelor
of science degree in business administration and management
from Mississippi State University, Mississippi State, Miss. in 1978.
Major League saves: 1984 (1), 1985 (1). Total—2.
Led Texas League in intentional bases on balls issued with 12 in 1980.
Led Texas League in games finished in relief with 37 in 1981.
Tied for American Association lead in shutouts with 2 in 1986.
Tied for Pacific Coast League lead in hit batsmen with 6 in 1985.

Year	Club	League	G.	IP.	W.	L.	Pct.	H.	R.	ER.	SO.	BB.	ERA.
1978—Sarasota Astros............................	Gulf Coast	3	4	0	1	.000	7	2	1	5	2	2.25
1978—Daytona Beach...........................	Florida St.	13	27	3	0	1.000	21	8	8	8	10	2.67
1979—Daytona Beach†.........................	Florida St.	17	29	2	1	.667	38	15	15	17	12	4.66
1979—Asheville................................	W. Carolinas	23	37	4	3	.571	33	19	13	22	12	3.16
1980—Tulsa....................................	Texas	55	82	6	5	.545	78	50	34	47	53	3.73
1981—Tulsa....................................	Texas	47	67	4	8	.333	54	31	25	36	23	3.36
1981—Wichita..................................	Am. Assoc.	8	13	1	0	1.000	14	4	4	9	8	2.77
1982—Denver..................................	Am. Assoc.	23	43⅓	1	2	.333	63	38	33	32	23	6.85
1982—Tulsa‡..................................	Texas	15	39⅔	2	2	.500	27	9	9	40	7	2.04
1983—El Paso§...............................	Texas	46	80⅓	7	1	.875	102	62	53	55	34	5.94
1984—Vancouver..............................	P. Coast	28	52⅔	2	3	.400	43	24	22	35	15	3.76
1984—Milwaukee x	American	15	39⅔	0	1	.000	37	19	19	24	22	4.31
1985—Phoenix y-Calgary z..................	P. Coast	44	74⅓	5	5	.500	56	20	17	52	21	2.06
1985—Seattle a...............................	American	15	20⅓	0	0	.000	23	10	8	7	8	3.54
1986—Nashville...............................	Am. Assoc.	29	154⅔	8	6	.571	146	63	55	*119	72	3.20
1986—Detroit b...............................	American	3	6⅔	0	0	.000	8	3	3	3	4	4.05
Major League Totals—3 Years.............		33	66⅔	0	1	.000	68	32	30	34	34	4.05

Selected by Philadelphia Phillies' organization in 8th round of free-agnt draft, January 9, 1975.
Selected by Philadelphia Phillies' organization in 1st round (18th player selected) of free-agent draft, January 7, 1976.
Selected by Philadelphia Phillies' organization in secondary phase of free-agent draft, June 8, 1976.
Selected by New York Yankees' organization in secondary phase of free-agent draft, June 7, 1977.
Selected by Houston Astros' organization in 11th round of free-agent draft, June 6, 1978.
†Sold to Texas Rangers' organization, June 27, 1979.
‡Released, April 5, 1983; signed by El Paso (Milwaukee Brewers' organization), April 10, 1984.
§On disabled list, April 27 to May 5, 1984.
xGranted free agency, October 15, 1984; signed by Phoenix (San Francisco Giants' organization), April 10, 1985.
ySold to Calgary (Seattle Mariners' organization), June 13, 1985.
zAppeared in one game as a third baseman and outfielder with no chances.
aReleased, November 1, 1985; signed by Nashville (Detroit Tigers' organization), February 7, 1986.
bGranted free agency, October 15, 1986.

CHARLES WILLIAM LEA

Name pronounced Lee.

(Charlie)

Born December 25, 1956, at Orleans, France.
Height, 6.04. Weight, 200.
Throws and bats righthanded.
Attended University of Mississippi, University, Miss., Shelby State Community College,
Memphis, Tenn., and Memphis State University, Memphis, Tenn.

Pitched 4-0 no-hit victory against San Francisco Giants, May 10, 1981 (second game).

Year	Club	League	G.	IP.	W.	L.	Pct.	H.	R.	ER.	SO.	BB.	ERA.
1978—Memphis		Southern	12	68	3	3	.500	57	34	27	37	32	3.57
1979—Memphis		Southern	24	162	8	8	.500	161	88	79	81	71	4.39
1980—Memphis		Southern	9	75	9	0	1.000	34	10	7	54	21	0.84
1980—Denver		Am. Assoc.	2	12	0	0	.000	8	2	2	9	5	1.50
1980—Montreal		National	21	104	7	5	.583	103	51	43	56	55	3.72
1981—Montreal		National	16	64	5	4	.556	63	34	33	31	26	4.64
1982—Montreal‡		National	27	177⅔	12	10	.545	145	70	64	115	56	3.24
1983—Montreal		National	33	222	16	11	.593	195	87	77	137	84	3.12
1984—Montreal		National	30	224⅓	15	10	.600	198	82	72	123	68	2.89
1985—Montreal†		National					(Did not play)						
1986—Montreal‡§		National					(Did not play)						
Major League Totals—5 Years			127	792	55	40	.579	704	324	289	462	289	3.28

Selected by New York Mets' organization in 15th round of free-agent draft, June 4, 1975.
Selected by St. Louis Cardinals' organization in secondary phase of free-agent draft, June 8, 1976.
Selected by Chicago White Sox' organization in secondary phase of free-agent draft, January 11, 1977.
Selected by Montreal Expos' organization in 9th round of free-agent draft, June 6, 1978.
†On disabled list, March 24, 1985 through entire season.
‡On disabled list, March 24, 1986 through entire season.
§Granted free agency, November 12, 1986.

ALL-STAR GAME RECORD

Year	League	IP.	W.	L.	Pct.	H.	R.	ER.	SO.	BB.	ERA.
1984—National		2	1	0	1.000	3	1	1	2	0	4.50

RICHARD MAX LEACH JR.

(Rick)

Born May 4, 1957, at Ann Arbor, Mich.
Height, 6.00. Weight, 195.
Throws and bats lefthanded.
Attended University of Michigan, Ann Arbor, Mich.

Major League stolen bases: 1982 (4), 1983 (2). Total—6.
Led International League in sacrifice flies with 12 in 1985.
Tied for International League lead in assists by outfielders with 13 in 1985.
Selected by Denver Broncos in 5th round of 1979 NFL draft.
Received reported $200,000 bonus to sign with Detroit Tigers, 1979.
Named outfielder on THE SPORTING NEWS College Baseball All-America Team, 1979.

Year	Club	League	Pos.	G.	AB.	R.	H.	2B.	3B.	HR.	RBI.	B.A.	PO.	A.	E.	F.A.
1979—Lakeland†	Fla. St.	OF	48	168	21	51	10	1	2	23	.304	104	8	3	.974
1980—Evansville	A. A.	1B-OF	126	430	69	117	14	1	5	58	.272	767	62	9	.989
1981—Evansville	A. A.	1B	13	44	8	18	5	0	2	16	.409	129	16	2	.986
1981—Detroit	Amer.	1B-OF	54	83	9	16	3	1	1	11	.193	149	14	0	1.000
1982—Detroit‡	Amer.	1B-OF	82	218	23	52	7	2	3	12	.239	430	29	2	.996
1982—Evansville	A. A.	DH	11	38	6	11	2	0	0	2	.289	0	0	0	.000
1983—Detroit§	Amer.	1B-OF	99	242	22	60	17	0	3	26	.248	465	45	4	.992
1984—Syracuse	Int.	OF-1B	23	79	16	24	6	2	3	8	.304	70	4	2	.974
1984—Toronto	Amer.	OF-1B-P	65	88	11	23	6	2	0	7	.261	92	14	0	1.000
1985—Syracuse	Int.	OF-1B	136	533	77	151	24	2	15	79	.283	675	66	10	.987
1985—Toronto	Amer.	1B-OF	16	35	2	7	0	1	0	1	.200	78	6	1	.988
1986—Toronto	Amer.	OF-1B	110	246	35	76	14	1	5	39	.309	107	5	3	.974
Major League Totals—6 Years			426	912	102	234	47	7	12	96	.257	1321	113	10	.993

Selected by Philadelphia Phillies' organization in 11th round of free-agent draft, June 4, 1975.
Selected by Philadelphia Phillies' organization in 24th round of free-agent draft, June 6, 1978.
Selected by Detroit Tigers' organization in 1st round (13th player selected) of free-agent draft, June 5, 1979.
†On disabled list, June 18 to June 29, 1979.
‡On disabled list, April 12 to May 17, 1982; included rehabilitation disability assignment to Evansville, May 6 to May 17, 1982.
§Released, March 24, 1984; signed by Toronto Blue Jays' organization, April 3, 1984.

PITCHING RECORD

Year	Club	League	G.	IP.	W.	L.	Pct.	H.	R.	ER.	SO.	BB.	ERA.
1984—Toronto		American	1	1	0	0	.000	2	3	3	0	2	27.00

—DID YOU KNOW—

That Wally Berger, center fielder on the 1934 National League All-Star team, was the only starter for either squad that did not win election into baseball's Hall of Fame?

TERRY HESTER LEACH

Born March 13, 1954, at Selma, Ala.
Height, 6.00. Weight, 205.
Throws and bats righthanded.
Received business administration degree in personnel management-industrial relations
from Auburn University, Auburn University, Ala.

Major League saves: 1982 (3), 1985 (1). Total—4.
Led Gulf States League in home runs allowed with 12 in 1976.

Year Club	League	G.	IP.	W.	L.	Pct.	H.	R.	ER.	SO.	BB.	ERA.
1976—Baton Rouge†‡	Gulf States	5	19	2	0	1.000	43	21	13	15	14	6.16
1977—Greenwood	W. Carol.	20	67	3	2	.600	47	25	19	67	24	2.55
1978—Savannah§	Southern	9	25	1	0	1.000	24	17	14	21	13	5.04
1978—Kinston	Carolina	34	66	5	4	.556	57	29	24	46	25	3.27
1979—Savannah	Southern	40	92	2	9	.182	77	33	20	68	26	1.96
1979—Richmond	Int'national	7	14	3	1	.750	14	3	3	12	4	1.93
1980—Savannah xy	Southern	22	87	5	1	.833	83	36	31	58	17	3.21
1980—Jackson	Texas	8	54	5	1	.833	50	16	9	30	15	1.50
1981—Tidewater	Int'national	15	76	5	2	.714	63	27	23	42	19	2.72
1981—Jackson	Texas	8	58	5	1	.833	47	14	11	43	12	1.71
1981—New York	National	21	35	1	1	.500	26	11	10	16	12	2.57
1982—Tidewater	Int'national	30	48⅔	4	1	.800	48	20	16	34	19	2.96
1982—New York	National	21	45⅓	2	1	.667	46	22	21	30	18	4.17
1983—Tidewater za	Int'national	37	113	5	7	.417	120	66	56	66	42	4.46
1984—Richmond b-Tidewater	Int'national	43	95	11	4	.733	98	42	32	59	30	3.03
1985—Tidewater	Int'national	24	45⅓	1	0	1.000	33	12	8	25	8	1.59
1985—New York	National	22	55⅔	3	4	.429	48	19	18	30	14	2.91
1986—Tidewater	Int'national	34	79⅔	4	4	.500	69	30	22	55	21	2.49
1986—New York	National	6	6⅔	0	0	.000	6	3	2	4	3	2.70
Major League Totals—4 Years		70	142⅔	6	6	.500	126	55	51	80	47	3.22

Selected by Boston Red Sox' organization in 7th round of free-agent draft, January 7, 1976.
†Signed as free agent by Baton Rouge (Independent), June 29, 1976; released when Baton Rouge withdrew from league, August 13, 1976.
‡Signed by Greenwood (Atlanta Braves' organization) as free agent, May 28, 1977.
§Loaned to Kinston (Independent), June 3, 1978; returned, October 25, 1978.
xOn disabled list, June 12 to July 23, 1980.
yReleased, July 23, 1980; signed by Jackson (New York Mets' organization), July 27, 1980.
zTraded to Chicago Cubs' organization for Pitchers Jim Adamczak and Mitch Cook, September 26, 1983.
aTraded by Chicago Cubs' organization to Atlanta Braves' organization for Pitcher Ron Meridith, April 4, 1984.
bReleased, May 25, 1984; signed by New York Mets' organization, May 26, 1984.

TIMOTHY JAMES LEARY
(Tim)

Born December 23, 1958, at Santa Monica, Calif.
Height, 6.03. Weight, 190.
Throws and bats righthanded.
Attended University of California, Los Angeles, Calif.

Led Texas League in shutouts with 6 in 1980.
Named Texas League Most Valuable Player, 1980.
Named righthanded pitcher on THE SPORTING NEWS College Baseball All-America Team, 1979.

Year Club	League	G.	IP.	W.	L.	Pct.	H.	R.	ER.	SO.	BB.	ERA.
1979—Jackson†	Texas					(Did not play)						
1980—Jackson	Texas	26	173	●15	8	.652	150	67	53	138	62	2.76
1981—New York‡	National	1	2	0	0	.000	0	0	0	3	1	0.00
1981—Tidewater	Int'national	6	34	1	3	.250	27	16	14	15	27	3.71
1982—Tidewater§	Int'national					(Did not play)						
1983—Tidewater	Int'national	27	160⅓	8	★16	.333	170	100	78	106	73	4.38
1983—New York	National	2	10⅔	1	1	.500	15	10	4	9	4	3.38
1984—New York	National	20	53⅔	3	3	.500	61	28	24	29	18	4.02
1984—Tidewater x	Int'national	10	53⅓	4	4	.500	47	26	24	27	42	4.05
1985—Vancouver	P. Coast	27	177⅔	10	7	.588	174	85	79	136	57	4.00
1985—Milwaukee	American	5	33⅓	1	4	.200	40	18	15	29	8	4.05
1986—Milwaukee y	American	33	188⅓	12	12	.500	216	97	88	110	53	4.21
National League Totals—3 Years		23	66⅓	4	4	.500	76	38	28	41	23	3.80
American League Totals—2 Years		38	221⅔	13	16	.448	256	115	103	139	61	4.18
Major League Totals—5 Years		61	288	17	20	.459	332	153	131	180	84	4.09

Selected by New York Mets' organization in 1st round (second player selected) of free-agent draft, June 5, 1979.
†On disabled list, July 19 to October 1, 1979.
‡On disabled list, April 16 to August 1, 1981.
§On disabled list, April 13, 1982 through remainder of season.
xTraded to Milwaukee Brewers' organization as part of a six-player, four-team deal in which Kansas City Royals acquired Catcher Jim Sundberg from Milwaukee, Texas Rangers acquired Catcher Don Slaught from Kansas City, New York Mets' organization acquired Pitcher Frank Wills from Kansas City and Milwaukee acquired Pitcher Danny Darwin and a player to be named later from Texas, January 18, 1985; Milwaukee organization acquired Catcher Bill Hance from Texas to complete deal, January 30, 1985.
yTraded with Pitcher Tim Crews to Los Angeles Dodgers for First Baseman Greg Brock, December 10, 1986.

MANUEL LORA LEE
(Manny)

Born June 17, 1965, at San Pedro de Macoris, D. R.
Height, 5.09. Weight, 150.
Throws right and bats left and righthanded.

Major League stolen bases: 1985 (1).

Year Club	League	Pos.	G.	AB.	R.	H.	2B.	3B.	HR.	RBI.	B.A.	PO.	A.	E.	F.A.
1982—Kingsport..............	Appal.	2B-SS	16	54	2	12	1	0	0	3	.222	34	34	6	.919
1983—Sarasota Mets.......	Gulf C.	2B-SS	32	97	8	24	2	1	0	12	.247	44	79	8	.939
1983—Little Falls............	NYP	2B	17	45	10	13	0	0	0	5	.289	34	40	3	.961
1984—Columbia†‡§	S. Atl.	SS-2B	102	346	84	114	12	5	2	33	★.329	126	277	34	.922
1985—Toronto	Amer.	2B-SS-3B	64	40	9	8	0	0	0	0	.200	34	56	3	.968
1986—Syracuse	Int.	SS-2B	76	236	34	58	6	1	1	19	.246	132	237	18	.953
1986—Knoxville	South.	SS-2B	41	158	21	43	1	2	0	11	.272	70	117	8	.959
1986—Toronto	Amer.	2B-SS-3B	35	78	8	16	0	1	1	7	.205	36	76	2	.982
Major League Totals—2 Years................			99	118	17	24	0	1	1	7	.203	70	132	5	.976

Signed as free agent by New York Mets' organization, May 10, 1982.
†On disabled list, April 9 to April 22, 1984.
‡Traded with Outfielder Gerald Young to Houston Astros, August 31, 1984, as partial completion of deal in which New York Mets acquired Infielder Ray Knight for three players to be named later, August 28, 1984; Houston acquired Pitcher Mitch Cook to complete deal, September 10, 1984.
§Drafted by Toronto Blue Jays, December 3, 1984.

CHAMPIONSHIP SERIES RECORD

Year Club	League	Pos.	G.	AB.	R.	H.	2B.	3B.	HR.	RBI.	B.A.	PO.	A.	E.	F.A.
1985—Toronto	Amer.	PR-2B	1	0	0	0	0	0	0	0	.000	0	0	0	.000

JOSEPH HENRY LEFEBVRE
Name pronounced Luh-FAY.
(Joe)

Born Feburary 22, 1956, at Penacook, N.H.
Height, 5.10. Weight, 180.
Throws right and bats lefthanded.
Attended Eckerd College, St. Petersburg, Fla.

Tied American League record for most home runs, first two major league games (2), May 22 and 23, 1980.
Major League stolen bases: 1981 (6), 1983 (5). Total—11.
Collected six hits in one game, September 13, 1982 (16 innings).
Tied for Eastern League lead in assists by outfielders with 16 in 1979.

Year Club	League	Pos.	G.	AB.	R.	H.	2B.	3B.	HR.	RBI.	B.A.	PO.	A.	E.	F.A.
1977—Fort Lauderdale ..	Fla. St.	OF-P	48	172	20	53	6	9	2	29	.308	76	4	2	.976
1977—West Haven	East.	OF	6	22	8	8	2	0	0	3	.364	7	2	0	1.000
1978—West Haven	East.	OF-3B-C	134	459	★102	122	21	●11	19	70	.266	240	48	14	.954
1979—West Haven	East.	O-I-P-C	138	487	85	142	28	10	21	●107	.292	248	31	10	.965
1980—Columbus..............	Int.	OF-3B	56	198	37	55	11	3	10	26	.278	89	3	5	.948
1980—New York†...........	Amer.	OF	74	150	26	34	1	1	8	21	.227	75	3	2	.975
1981—San Diego	Nat.	OF	86	246	31	63	13	4	8	31	.256	167	6	1	.994
1982—San Diego	Nat.	3B-OF-C	102	239	25	57	9	0	4	21	.238	72	74	3	.980
1982—Hawaii	P. C.	OF-3B	8	32	7	11	3	1	0	5	.344	14	6	1	.952
1983—S. D.‡-Phila..........	Nat.	OF-3B-C	119	278	35	85	20	8	8	39	.306	105	22	5	.962
1984—Philadelphia§	Nat.	OF-3B	52	160	22	40	9	0	3	18	.250	83	4	3	.967
1984—Reading.................	East.	OF	6	12	5	4	1	0	0	0	.333	11	1	0	1.000
1985—Philadelphia x......	Nat.					(Did not play)									
1986—Philadelphia	Nat.	OF	14	18	0	2	0	0	0	0	.111	4	0	0	1.000
1986—Portland y............	P. C.	OF	2	5	1	1	0	0	0	1	.200	2	0	0	1.000
American League Totals—1 Year...........			74	150	26	34	1	1	8	21	.227	75	3	2	.975
National League Totals—5 Years.............			373	941	113	247	51	12	23	109	.262	431	106	12	.978
Major League Totals—6 Years.................			447	1091	139	281	52	13	31	130	.258	506	109	14	.978

Selected by New York Yankees' organization in 3rd round of free-agent draft, June 7, 1977.
†Traded with Outfielder Ruppert Jones and Pitchers Tim Lollar and Chris Welsh to San Diego Padres for Outfielder Jerry Mumphrey and Pitcher John Pacella, April 1, 1981.
‡Traded to Philadelphia Phillies for Pitcher Sid Monge, May 22, 1983.
§On disabled list, June 18, 1984 through remainder of season; included rehabilitation disability assignment to Reading, July 31 to August 10, 1984.
xOn disabled list, March 26, 1985 through entire season.
yOn voluntarily retired list, May 27, 1986.

CHAMPIONSHIP SERIES RECORD

Year Club	League	Pos.	G.	AB.	R.	H.	2B.	3B.	HR.	RBI.	B.A.	PO.	A.	E.	F.A.
1980—New York..............	Amer.	OF	1	0	0	0	0	0	0	0	.000	0	0	0	.000
1983—Philadelphia	Nat.	PH-OF	2	2	0	0	0	0	0	1	.000	2	0	0	1.000
Championship Series Totals—2 Years.....			3	2	0	0	0	0	0	1	.000	2	0	0	1.000

WORLD SERIES RECORD

Year Club	League	Pos.	G.	AB.	R.	H.	2B.	3B.	HR.	RBI.	B.A.	PO.	A.	E.	F.A.
1983—Philadelphia	Nat.	PH-OF	3	5	0	1	1	0	0	2	.200	3	0	0	1.000

PITCHING RECORD

Year Club	League	G.	IP.	W.	L.	Pct.	H.	R.	ER.	SO.	BB.	ERA.
1977—Fort Lauderdale	Florida St.	1	1	0	0	.000	1	1	1	1	2	9.00
1979—West Haven	Eastern	2	5	0	0	.000	5	2	2	4	1	3.60

CRAIG LINDSAY LEFFERTS

Born September 29, 1957, in Munich, West Germany.
Height, 6.01. Weight, 196.
Throws and bats lefthanded.
Attended University of Arizona, Tucson, Ariz.

Major League saves: 1983 (1), 1984 (10), 1985 (2), 1986 (4). Total—17.

Year Club	League	G.	IP.	W.	L.	Pct.	H.	R.	ER.	SO.	BB.	ERA.
1980—Geneva	NYP	12	94	9	1	★.900	74	35	29	★99	24	2.78
1981—Midland	Texas	26	185	12	●12	.500	203	95	85	135	36	4.14
1982—Iowa†	Am. Assoc.	18	97⅓	8	5	.615	97	50	33	71	25	3.05
1983—Chicago‡	National	56	89	3	4	.429	80	35	31	60	29	3.13
1984—San Diego	National	62	105⅔	3	4	.429	88	29	25	56	24	2.13
1985—San Diego	National	60	83⅓	7	6	.538	75	34	31	48	30	3.35
1986—San Diego	National	★83	107⅔	9	8	.529	98	41	37	72	44	3.09
Major League Totals—4 Years		261	385⅔	22	22	.500	341	139	124	236	127	2.89

Selected by Kansas City Royals' organization in 6th round of free-agent draft, June 5, 1979.
Selected by Chicago Cubs' organization in 9th round of free-agent draft, June 3, 1980.
†On disabled list, April 24 to June 4, 1982.
‡Traded with First Baseman Carmelo Martinez and Third Baseman Fritz Connally to San Diego Padres for Pitcher Scott Sanderson, December 7, 1983.

CHAMPIONSHIP SERIES RECORD

Tied Championship Series record for most games won, Series (2), 1984.

Year Club	League	G.	IP.	W.	L.	Pct.	H.	R.	ER.	SO.	BB.	ERA.
1984—San Diego	National	3	4	2	0	1.000	1	0	0	1	1	0.00

WORLD SERIES RECORD

Year Club	League	G.	IP.	W.	L.	Pct.	H.	R.	ER.	SO.	BB.	ERA.
1984—San Diego	National	3	6	0	0	.000	2	0	0	7	1	0.00

GREGORY LYNN LEGG
(Greg)

Born April 21, 1960, at San Jose, Calif.
Height, 6.01. Weight, 185.
Throws and bats righthanded.
Attended Southeastern Oklahoma University, Durant, Okla.

Year Club	League	Pos.	G.	AB.	R.	H.	2B.	3B.	HR.	RBI.	B.A.	PO.	A.	E.	F.A.
1982—Peninsula	Carol.	SS	44	134	20	46	9	0	0	20	.343	56	130	15	.925
1983—Reading	East.	S-3-2-1	90	284	44	87	14	1	4	49	.306	75	163	13	.948
1984—Reading	East.	2B-SS-3B	64	224	16	54	11	1	2	27	.241	111	167	14	.952
1984—Portland	P. C.	2B-SS	50	141	17	34	8	0	1	15	.241	61	95	3	.981
1985—Portland	P. C.	2B	115	420	48	119	11	7	7	50	.283	203	339	13	.977
1986—Portland	P. C.	2B	120	461	72	149	27	5	6	66	.323	265	356	4	★.994
1986—Philadelphia	Nat.	2B-SS	11	20	2	9	1	0	0	1	.450	4	16	1	.952
Major League Totals—1 Year			11	20	2	9	1	0	0	1	.450	4	16	1	.952

Selected by Philadelphia Phillies' organization in 22nd round of free-agent draft, June 7, 1982.

CHARLES LOUIS LEIBRANDT JR.
(Charlie)

Born October 4, 1956, at Chicago, Ill.
Height, 6.03. Weight, 200.
Throws left and bats righthanded.
Received bachelor of science degree in management from
Miami University, Oxford, O.

Established major league record for fewest assists by pitcher, for leader in assists (43), 1986.
Major League saves: 1982 (2).
Tied for American Association lead in shutouts with 3 in 1984.
Tied for American Association lead in games started by pitchers with 26 in 1979.

Year Club	League	G.	IP.	W.	L.	Pct.	H.	R.	ER.	SO.	BB.	ERA.
1978—Eugene	Northwest	3	20	2	0	1.000	24	13	9	18	5	4.05
1978—Tampa	Florida St.	6	47	4	1	.800	26	4	4	40	17	0.77
1978—Indianapolis	Am. Assoc	4	29	2	1	.667	20	9	9	12	12	2.79
1979—Indianapolis	Am. Assoc.	27	162	8	★14	.364	146	67	53	100	65	2.94
1979—Cincinnati	National	3	4	0	0	.000	2	2	0	1	2	0.00
1980—Cincinnati	National	36	174	10	9	.526	200	84	82	62	54	4.24
1981—Indianapolis	Am. Assoc.	25	169	9	7	.563	149	76	55	101	75	2.93
1981—Cincinnati	National	7	30	1	1	.500	28	12	12	9	15	3.60
1982—Cincinnati	National	36	107⅔	5	7	.417	130	68	61	34	48	5.10
1983—Indianapolis†-Omaha	Am. Assoc.	27	185⅓	9	10	.474	181	113	88	128	77	4.27

Year Club	League	G.	IP.	W.	L.	Pct.	H.	R.	ER.	SO.	BB.	ERA.
1984—Omaha	Am. Assoc.	9	72⅔	7	1	.875	51	14	10	38	16	1.24
1984—Kansas City	American	23	143⅔	11	7	.611	158	65	58	53	38	3.63
1985—Kansas City	American	33	237⅔	17	9	.654	223	86	71	108	68	2.69
1986—Kansas City	American	35	231⅓	14	11	.560	238	112	105	108	63	4.09
National League Totals—4 Years		82	315⅔	16	17	.485	360	166	155	106	119	4.42
American League Totals—3 Years		91	612⅔	42	27	.609	619	263	234	269	169	3.44
Major League Totals—7 Years		173	928⅓	58	44	.569	979	429	389	375	288	3.77

Selected by Cincinnati Reds' organization in 9th round of free-agent draft, June 6, 1978.
†Traded to Kansas City Royals for Pitcher Bob Tufts, June 7, 1983.

CHAMPIONSHIP SERIES RECORD

Established American League Championship Series record for most hits allowed, seven-game Series (17), 1985.
Tied Championship Series record for most games lost, Series (2), 1985.
Tied American League Championship Series records for most games lost, total Series (3); most strikeouts by a relief pitcher, game (5), October 16, 1985.

Year Club	League	G.	IP.	W.	L.	Pct.	H.	R.	ER.	SO.	BB.	ERA.
1979—Cincinnati	National	1	⅓	0	0	.000	0	0	0	0	0	0.00
1984—Kansas City	American	1	8	0	1	.000	3	1	1	6	4	1.13
1985—Kansas City	American	3	15⅓	1	2	.333	17	9	9	6	4	5.28
Championship Series Totals—3 Years		5	23⅔	1	3	.250	20	10	10	12	8	3.80

WORLD SERIES RECORD

Year Club	League	G.	IP.	W.	L.	Pct.	H.	R.	ER.	SO.	BB.	ERA.
1985—Kansas City	American	2	16⅓	0	1	.000	10	5	5	10	4	2.76

DAVID PAUL LEIPER
(Dave)

Born June 18, 1962, at Whittier, Calif.
Height, 6.01. Weight, 160.
Throws and bats lefthanded.
Attended Fullerton College, Fullerton, Calif.

Major League saves: 1986 (1).

Year Club	League	G.	IP.	W.	L.	Pct.	H.	R.	ER.	SO.	BB.	ERA.
1982—Idaho Falls	Pioneer	14	85⅓	9	3	.750	94	49	39	77	27	4.11
1983—Madison	Midwest	16	79⅓	5	4	.556	89	43	33	60	37	3.74
1984—Modesto	California	19	35⅓	5	0	1.000	12	2	1	30	14	0.25
1984—Tacoma	P. Coast	28	32⅔	2	3	.400	33	11	11	13	14	3.03
1984—Oakland	American	8	7	1	0	1.000	12	7	7	3	5	9.00
1985—Tacoma†	P. Coast	15	23⅓	0	1	.000	29	16	14	7	12	5.40
1985—Modesto	California	21	30	1	0	1.000	53	31	26	24	19	7.80
1986—Tacoma	P. Coast	20	26	2	1	.667	30	17	14	13	9	4.85
1986—Oakland	American	33	31⅔	2	2	.500	28	17	17	15	18	4.83
Major League Totals—2 Years		41	38⅔	3	2	.600	40	24	24	18	23	5.59

Selected by Texas Rangers' organization in 2nd round of free-agent draft, January 13, 1981.
Selected by San Francisco Giants' organization in secondary phase of free-agent draft, June 8, 1981.
Selected by Oakland A's organization in secondary phase of free-agent draft, January 12, 1982.
†On disabled list, April 11 to May 13, 1985.

JOHN WILLIAM LEISTER

Born January 3, 1961, at San Antonio, Tex.
Height, 6.02. Weight, 200.
Throws and bats righthanded.
Attended Michigan State University, East Lansing, Mich.

Year Club	League	G.	IP.	W.	L.	Pct.	H.	R.	ER.	SO.	BB.	ERA.
1984—Winter Haven	Florida St.	31	175⅓	12	12	.500	173	90	66	103	93	3.39
1985—New Britain	Eastern	27	105	8	6	.571	91	48	37	68	49	3.17
1986—Pawtucket	Int'national	23	134⅔	8	7	.533	125	68	61	78	81	4.08

Selected by New York Mets' organization in 20th round of free-agent draft, June 5, 1979.
Selected by Oakland A's organization in 6th round of free-agent draft, June 6, 1983.
Selected by Boston Red Sox' organization in secondary phase of free-agent draft, January 17, 1984.

ALOIS TERRY LEITER
(Al)

Born October 23, 1965, at Toms River, N. J.
Height, 6.02. Weight, 200.
Throws and bats lefthanded.

Year Club	League	G.	IP.	W.	L.	Pct.	H.	R.	ER.	SO.	BB.	ERA.
1984—Oneonta	NYP	10	57	3	2	.600	52	32	23	48	26	3.63
1985—Oneonta	NYP	6	38	3	2	.600	27	14	10	34	25	2.37
1985—Fort Lauderdale	Florida St.	17	82	1	6	.143	87	70	59	44	57	6.48
1986—Fort Lauderdale	Florida St.	22	117⅔	4	8	.333	96	64	53	101	90	4.05

Selected by New York Yankees' organization in 2nd round of free-agent draft, June 4, 1984.

CHESTER EARL LEMON
(Chet)

Born February 12, 1955, at Jackson, Miss.
Height, 6.00. Weight, 190.
Throws and bats righthanded.
Attended Pepperdine University, Malibu, Calif., and Cerritos College, Norwalk, Calif.

Established American League records for most chances accepted by outfielder, season (524), 1977; most putouts by outfielder, season (512), 1977; most years by outfielder, 400 or more putouts (5).

Tied American League record for most years by outfielder, 500 or more putouts (1), 1977.

Major League stolen bases: 1975 (1), 1976 (13), 1977 (8), 1978 (5), 1979 (7), 1980 (6), 1981 (5), 1982 (1), 1984 (5), 1986 (2). Total—53.

Led American League in being hit by pitch with 13 in 1979, 13 in 1981, 15 in 1982 and 20 in 1983.

Led American League outfielders in total chances with 536 in 1977.

Year Club	League	Pos.	G.	AB.	R.	H.	2B.	3B.	HR.	RBI.	B.A.	PO.	A.	E.	F.A.
1972—Coos Bay-N. B.	N'west	SS-3B	38	140	33	40	8	1	2	16	.286	56	94	16	.904
1972—Burlington	Midw.	3B-SS	33	129	18	33	5	0	1	8	.256	24	62	13	.869
1973—Burlington	Midw.	3B-SS	113	392	73	121	21	1	19	★88	.309	102	215	36	.898
1974—Birmingham†	South.	3B-SS	79	272	52	79	22	2	10	61	.290	84	135	23	.905
1975—Tucson‡...............	P. C.	3B-OF	65	243	43	68	7	2	5	33	.280	60	70	19	.872
1975—Denver	A. A.	3B-OF	70	254	40	78	15	6	8	49	.307	39	76	19	.858
1975—Chicago	Amer.	3B-OF	9	35	2	9	2	0	0	1	.257	5	7	1	.923
1976—Chicago	Amer.	OF	132	451	46	111	15	5	4	38	.246	353	12	3	.992
1977—Chicago	Amer.	OF	150	553	99	151	38	4	19	67	.273	★512	12	12	.978
1978—Chicago§	Amer.	OF	105	357	51	107	24	6	13	55	.300	284	8	5	.983
1979—Chicago	Amer.	OF	148	556	79	177	●44	2	17	86	.318	411	10	10	.977
1980—Chicago	Amer.	OF-2B	147	514	76	150	32	6	11	51	.292	347	11	7	.981
1981—Chicago x.............	Amer.	OF	94	328	50	99	23	6	9	50	.302	240	2	4	.984
1982—Detroit	Amer.	OF	125	436	75	116	20	1	19	52	.266	242	11	4	.984
1983—Detroit	Amer.	OF	145	491	78	125	21	5	24	69	.255	406	6	5	.988
1984—Detroit	Amer.	OF	141	509	77	146	34	6	20	76	.287	427	6	2	.995
1985—Detroit	Amer.	OF	145	517	69	137	28	4	18	68	.265	411	6	4	.990
1986—Detroit	Amer.	OF	126	403	45	101	21	3	12	53	.251	316	6	5	.985
Major League Totals—12 Years...............			1467	5150	747	1429	302	48	166	666	.277	3954	97	62	.985

Selected by Oakland A's organization in 1st round (20th player selected) of free-agent draft, June 6, 1972.

†On disabled list, July 16 to September 16, 1974.

‡Traded with Pitcher Dave Hamilton to Chicago White Sox for Pitchers Stan Bahnsen and Lee (Skip) Pitlock, June 15, 1975.

§On disabled list, August 12 to August 27, 1978.

xTraded to Detroit Tigers for Outfielder Steve Kemp, November 27, 1981.

CHAMPIONSHIP SERIES RECORD

Year Club	League	Pos.	G.	AB.	R.	H.	2B.	3B.	HR.	RBI.	B.A.	PO.	A.	E.	F.A.
1984—Detroit...................	Amer.	OF	3	13	1	0	0	0	0	0	.000	9	0	0	1.000

WORLD SERIES RECORD

Year Club	League	Pos.	G.	AB.	R.	H.	2B.	3B.	HR.	RBI.	B.A.	PO.	A.	E.	F.A.
1984—Detroit................	Amer.	OF	5	17	1	5	0	0	0	1	.294	15	0	0	1.000

ALL-STAR GAME RECORD

Year League	Pos.	AB.	R.	H.	2B.	3B.	HR.	RBI.	B.A.	PO.	A.	E.	F.A.
1978—American	OF	0	0	0	0	0	0	0	.000	0	0	1	.000
1979—American	OF	2	1	0	0	0	0	0	.000	2	0	0	1.000
1984—American	OF	2	0	1	0	0	0	0	.500	0	0	0	.000
All-Star Game Totals—3 Years...................		4	1	1	0	0	0	0	.250	2	0	1	.667

DENNIS PATRICK LEONARD

Born May 8, 1951, at Brooklyn, N. Y.
Height, 6.01. Weight, 195.
Throws and bats righthanded.
Attended Iona College, New Rochelle, N. Y.

Pitched 2-0 no-hit victory against Visalia, April 26, 1973.

Pitched seven-inning, 3-0 no-hit victory against Quincy, July 15, 1972.

Major League saves: 1977 (1).

Led American League in home runs allowed with 30 in 1980.

Led American League pitchers in games started with 38 in 1980, 26 in 1981 and tied for lead with 40 in 1978.

Tied for American League lead in shutouts with 5 in 1979.

Led American Association in complete games with 18, shutouts with 4 and tied for lead in games started by pitchers with 29 in 1974.

Tied for California League lead in complete games with 16 and shutouts with 5 in 1973.

Year Club	League	G.	IP.	W.	L.	Pct.	H.	R.	ER.	SO.	BB.	ERA.
1972—Kingsport.........................	Ap'lachian	4	22	2	1	.667	19	9	8	31	6	3.27
1972—Waterloo	Midwest	10	67	4	3	.571	58	28	23	63	26	3.09
1973—San Jose	California	29	206	★15	9	.625	152	70	59	212	81	2.58
1974—Omaha	Am. Assoc.	29	★223	12	13	.480	178	96	86	193	91	3.47
1974—Kansas City	American	5	22	0	4	.000	28	15	13	8	12	5.32
1975—Omaha	Am. Assoc.	3	19	0	2	.000	19	11	9	14	10	4.26
1975—Kansas City	American	32	212	15	7	.682	212	98	89	146	90	3.78

Year Club	League	G	IP	W	L	Pct.	H	R	ER	SO	BB	ERA.
1976—Kansas City	American	35	259	17	10	.630	247	113	101	150	70	3.51
1977—Kansas City	American	38	293	•20	12	.625	246	117	99	244	79	3.04
1978—Kansas City	American	40	295	21	17	.553	★283	125	109	183	78	3.33
1979—Kansas City	American	32	236	14	12	.538	226	117	107	126	56	4.08
1980—Kansas City	American	38	280	20	11	.645	271	127	★118	155	80	3.79
1981—Kansas City	American	26	★202	13	11	.542	★202	79	67	107	41	2.99
1982—Kansas City†	American	21	130⅔	10	6	.625	145	82	74	58	46	5.10
1982—Fort Myers	Florida St.	1	5	0	0	.000	4	0	0	3	2	0.00
1982—Sarasota Royals	Gulf Coast	1	5	0	1	.000	5	3	3	2	1	5.40
1982—Omaha	Am. Assoc.	3	20⅔	1	2	.333	19	17	17	13	9	7.40
1983—Kansas City‡	American	10	63	6	3	.667	69	29	26	31	19	3.71
1984—Kansas City§	American					(Did not play)						
1985—Fort Myers x	Florida St.	3	16⅓	2	0	1.000	5	3	2	10	2	1.10
1985—Memphis	Southern	1	5	0	0	.000	9	4	4	1	1	7.20
1985—Kansas City	American	2	2	0	0	.000	1	0	0	1	0	0.00
1986—Kansas City	American	33	192⅔	8	13	.381	207	106	95	114	51	4.44
Major League Totals—12 Years		312	2187⅓	144	106	.576	2137	1008	898	1323	622	3.69

Selected by Kansas City Royals' organization in 2nd round of free-agent draft, June 6, 1972.

†On disabled list, May 22 to August 8, 1982; included rehabilitation disability assignment to Ft. Myers, July 8 to July 12, 1982; Sarasota, July 13 to July 14, 1982, and Omaha, July 23 to August 4, 1982.

‡On disabled list, May 29, 1983 through remainder of season.

§On disabled list, March 29, 1984 through entire season.

xOn Kansas City disabled list, April 8 to September 3, 1985; included rehabilitation disability assignment to Fort Myers, August 12 to August 28, and Memphis, August 29, 1985.

DIVISION SERIES RECORD

Year Club	League	G	IP	W	L	Pct.	H	R	ER	SO	BB	ERA.
1981—Kansas City	American	1	8	0	1	.000	7	4	1	3	1	1.13

CHAMPIONSHIP SERIES RECORD

Tied Championship Series record for most games lost, Series (2), 1978.
Established American League Championship Series record for most hits allowed, four-game Series (13), 1978.
Tied American League Championship Series record for most games lost, total Series (3).

Year Club	League	G	IP	W	L	Pct.	H	R	ER	SO	BB	ERA.
1976—Kansas City	American	2	2⅓	0	0	.000	9	5	5	0	2	19.29
1977—Kansas City	American	2	9	1	1	.500	5	4	3	4	2	3.00
1978—Kansas City	American	2	12	0	2	.000	13	5	5	11	2	3.75
1980—Kansas City	American	1	8	1	0	1.000	7	2	2	8	1	2.25
Championship Series Totals—4 Years		7	31⅓	2	3	.400	34	16	15	23	7	4.31

WORLD SERIES RECORD

Year Club	League	G	IP	W	L	Pct.	H	R	ER	SO	BB	ERA.
1980—Kansas City	American	2	10⅔	1	1	.500	15	9	8	5	2	6.75

JEFFREY N. LEONARD

Born September 22, 1955, at Philadelphia, Pa.
Height, 6.04. Weight, 200.
Throws and bats righthanded.

Major League stolen bases: 1979 (23), 1980 (4), 1981 (5), 1982 (18), 1983 (26), 1984 (17), 1985 (11), 1986 (16). Total—120.

Hit for the cycle, June 27, 1985.

Named National League Rookie Player of the Year by THE SPORTING NEWS, 1979.

Year Club	League	Pos.	G	AB	R	H	2B	3B	HR	RBI	B.A.	PO	A	E	F.A.
1973—Bellingham	N'west	OF	55	187	30	52	4	3	2	20	.278	46	2	5	.906
1974—Orangeburg	W. Car.	OF	8	15	0	1	0	0	0	1	.067	5	1	1	.857
1974—Bellingham	N'west	OF	78	278	47	90	12	4	3	43	.324	115	7	6	.953
1975—Bakersfield	Calif.	OF	106	320	44	89	11	3	4	37	.278	137	5	7	.953
1976—Lodi	Calif.	OF	133	509	93	168	29	9	8	85	.330	214	13	★15	.938
1976—Albuquerque	P. C.	OF	7	27	2	8	2	1	1	6	.296	14	0	0	1.000
1977—San Antonio	Texas	OF	122	468	75	147	17	10	12	70	.314	241	12	8	.969
1977—Los Angeles	Nat.	OF	11	10	1	3	0	1	0	2	.300	7	0	0	1.000
1978—Albuquerque†	P. C.	OF	133	502	111	★183	23	14	11	93	★.365	216	8	6	.974
1978—Houston	Nat.	OF	8	26	2	10	2	0	0	4	.385	16	1	0	1.000
1979—Houston	Nat.	OF	134	411	47	119	15	5	0	47	.290	227	6	10	.959
1980—Houston	Nat.	OF	88	216	29	46	7	5	3	20	.213	161	9	3	.983
1981—Hou.†-S.F.	Nat.	OF-1B	44	145	21	42	12	4	4	29	.290	152	5	1	.994
1981—Phoenix	P. C.	OF	47	187	38	75	17	3	7	45	.401	90	2	2	.979
1982—San Francisco§	Nat.	OF-1B	80	278	32	72	16	1	9	49	.259	137	2	9	.939
1982—Phoenix	P. C.	OF	17	59	14	21	5	0	4	12	.356	5	0	0	1.000
1983—San Francisco	Nat.	OF	139	516	74	144	17	7	21	87	.279	253	17	7	.975
1984—San Francisco	Nat.	OF	136	514	76	155	27	2	21	86	.302	247	14	8	.970
1985—San Francisco	Nat.	OF	133	507	49	122	20	3	17	62	.241	203	10	5	.977
1986—San Francisco x	Nat.	OF	89	341	48	95	11	3	6	42	.279	158	4	5	.970
Major League Totals—10 Years			862	2964	379	808	127	31	81	428	.273	1561	68	48	.971

Signed as free agent by Los Angeles Dodgers' organization, June 7, 1973.

†Traded to Houston Astros, September 11, 1978, completing deal in which Los Angeles Dodgers acquired Catcher Joe Ferguson for two players to be named later, July 1, 1978; Houston acquired Shortstop Rafael Landestoy as partial completion of deal, July 7, 1978.

‡Traded with First Baseman-Outfielder Dave Bergman to San Francisco Giants for First Baseman Mike Ivie, April 20, 1981.

§On disabled list, May 23 to July 19, 1982; included rehabilitation disability assignment to Phoenix, July 1 to July 19, 1982.

xOn disabled list, July 31, 1986 through remainder of season.

CHAMPIONSHIP SERIES RECORD

Year Club	League	Pos.	G.	AB.	R.	H.	2B.	3B.	HR.	RBI.	B.A.	PO.	A.	E.	F.A.
1980—Houston	Nat.	PH-OF	3	3	0	0	0	0	0	0	.000	2	1	0	1.000

RANDY LOUIS LERCH

Born October 9, 1954, at Sacramento, Calif.
Height, 6.03. Weight, 195.
Throws and bats lefthanded.

Tied major league record for most sacrifice flies allowed, season (15), 1979.
Major League saves: 1976 (1), 1984 (2). Total—3.
Led American Association pitchers in games started with 29 and tied for lead in complete games with 11 in 1976.

Year Club	League	G.	IP.	W.	L.	Pct.	H.	R.	ER.	SO.	BB.	ERA.
1973—Auburn	NYP	16	96	9	2	.818	88	41	31	75	29	2.91
1974—Rocky Mount	Carolina	22	143	7	7	.500	150	73	58	114	54	3.65
1975—Reading	Eastern	25	177	★16	6	★.727	173	66	53	108	45	2.69
1975—Philadelphia	National	3	7	0	0	.000	6	5	5	8	1	6.43
1976—Oklahoma City	Am. Assoc.	29	★207	13	11	.542	★203	91	77	★152	47	3.35
1976—Philadelphia	National	1	3	0	0	.000	3	1	1	0	0	3.00
1977—Philadelphia	National	32	169	10	6	.625	207	102	95	81	75	5.06
1978—Philadelphia	National	33	184	11	8	.579	183	89	81	96	70	3.96
1979—Philadelphia	National	37	214	10	13	.435	228	98	89	92	60	3.74
1980—Philadelphia†	National	30	150	4	14	.222	178	98	86	57	55	5.16
1981—Milwaukee	American	23	111	7	9	.438	134	63	53	53	43	4.30
1982—Milwaukee‡	American	21	108⅔	8	7	.533	123	68	60	33	51	4.97
1982—Montreal	National	6	23⅔	2	0	1.000	26	11	9	4	8	3.42
1983—Montreal§-San Francisco	National	26	49⅓	2	3	.400	54	33	33	30	26	6.02
1983—Phoenix	P. Coast	5	8⅓	0	0	.000	8	5	3	7	3	3.24
1984—San Francisco xy	National	37	72⅓	5	3	.625	80	36	34	48	36	4.23
1985—Portland	P. Coast	20	108	6	6	.500	84	44	33	68	56	2.75
1986—Portland	P. Coast	12	74⅔	6	5	.545	67	35	25	39	27	3.01
1986—Philadelphia z	National	4	8	1	1	.500	10	8	7	5	7	7.88
National League Totals—10 Years		209	880⅓	45	48	.484	975	481	440	421	338	4.50
American League Totals—2 Years		44	219⅔	15	16	.484	257	131	113	86	94	4.63
Major League Totals—11 Years		253	1100	60	64	.484	1232	612	553	507	432	4.52

Selected by Philadelphia Phillies' organization in 8th round of free-agent draft, June 5, 1973.
†Traded to Milwaukee Brewers for Outfielder Dick Davis, March 1, 1981.
‡Sold to Montreal Expos, August 14, 1982.
§Released, July 28, 1983; signed by Phoenix (San Francisco Giants' organization), August 9, 1983.
xOn disabled list, May 23 to June 7 and July 7 to August 17, 1984.
yGranted free agency, November 8, 1984; signed by Portland (Philadelphia Phillies' organization), May 21, 1985.
zReleased, June 26, 1986.

DIVISION SERIES RECORD

Year Club	League	G.	IP.	W.	L.	Pct.	H.	R.	ER.	SO.	BB.	ERA.
1981—Milwaukee	American	1	6	0	0	.000	3	1	1	3	4	1.50

CHAMPIONSHIP SERIES RECORD

Year Club	League	G.	IP.	W.	L.	Pct.	H.	R.	ER.	SO.	BB.	ERA.
1978—Philadelphia	National	1	5⅓	0	0	.000	7	3	3	0	0	5.06

RUFINO AUGUSTO LINARES

Name pronounced Luh-NAHR-ess.

Born February 28, 1951, at San Pedro de Macoris, D. R.
Height 6.01. Weight, 190.
Throws and bats righthanded.

Brother of Felix Linares, first baseman-pitcher in Atlanta Braves' organization, 1977, 1978 and 1982.

Major League stolen bases: 1981 (8), 1982 (5), 1985 (2). Total—15.

Year Club	League	Pos.	G.	AB.	R.	H.	2B.	3B.	HR.	RBI.	B.A.	PO.	A.	E.	F.A.
1974—Kingsport	Appal.	OF	56	220	32	64	7	1	6	41	.291	106	5	6	.949
1975—Greenwood	W. Car.	OF	106	302	36	77	12	2	2	35	.255	178	6	10	.948
1976—Greenwood	W. Car.	OF-1B	109	389	57	127	20	4	3	54	.326	52	4	1	.982
1977—Savannah	South.	OF	85	262	32	76	12	5	2	29	.290	93	9	5	.953
1978—Savannah	South.	OF	116	400	49	121	15	5	8	51	.303	158	12	3	.983
1978—Richmond	Int.	DH	4	9	1	1	0	1	0	3	.111	0	0	0	.000
1979—Savannah	South.	OF	53	198	35	65	11	1	8	37	.328	40	1	2	.953
1979—Richmond†	Int.	OF	36	104	9	31	4	1	1	13	.298	22	1	5	.821
1980—Richmond	Int.	OF	63	234	31	77	12	4	3	41	.329	56	5	0	1.000
1980—Savannah	South.	OF	51	200	37	85	18	6	2	38	.425	100	4	5	.954
1981—Atlanta	Nat.	OF	78	253	27	67	9	2	5	25	.265	124	6	5	.963
1982—Atlanta	Nat.	OF	77	191	28	57	7	1	2	17	.298	92	4	0	1.000
1983—Richmond‡	Int.	OF	29	107	10	24	6	2	1	24	.224	20	1	1	.955

Year	Club	League	Pos.	G.	AB.	R.	H.	2B.	3B.	HR.	RBI.	B.A.	PO.	A.	E.	F.A.
1984—Richmond.............	Int.		OF	57	216	26	64	13	5	3	39	.296	24	0	1	.960
1984—Atlanta§ x............	Nat.		OF	34	58	4	12	3	0	1	10	.207	21	2	1	.958
1985—Edmonton...........	P. C.		OF	98	383	64	119	13	8	16	65	.311	52	1	2	.964
1985—California.............	Amer.		OF	18	43	7	11	2	0	3	11	.256	1	0	0	1.000
1986—Edmonton y	P. C.		OF	85	316	52	88	15	7	7	54	.278	4	1	1	.833
National League Totals—3 Years..........				189	502	59	136	19	3	8	52	.271	237	12	6	.976
American League Totals—1 Year				18	43	7	11	2	0	3	11	.256	1	0	0	1.000
Major League Totals—4 Years................				207	545	66	147	21	3	11	63	.270	238	12	6	.977

Signed as free agent by Atlanta Braves' organization, December 30, 1973.

†On disabled list, August 3 to August 13, 1979.

‡On Atlanta disabled list, March 24 to August 15, 1983; included rehabilitation disability assignment to Richmond, July 26 to August 15, 1983.

§Released, November 13, 1984; signed by Edmonton (California Angels' organization) as a non-player coach, April 12, 1985.

xReleased, May 4, 1985; re-signed by Edmonton as a player, May 20, 1985.

yReleased, December 19, 1986.

JOSE LIND (SALGADO)

Name pronounced Leend.
Born May 1, 1964, at Toabaja, P. R.
Height, 5.11. Weight, 155.
Throws and bats righthanded.
Brother of Orlando Lind, pitcher in Pittsburgh Pirates' organization.

Led Eastern League second basemen in total chances with 705 and double plays with 84 in 1986.

Year	Club	League	Pos.	G.	AB.	R.	H.	2B.	3B.	HR.	RBI.	B.A.	PO.	A.	E.	F.A.
1983—Bradenton Pir.	Gulf C.		2B-SS	45	163	26	49	3	4	0	18	.301	102	125	9	.962
1984—Macon..................	S. Atl.		2B-SS	121	396	39	82	5	2	0	30	.207	271	306	32	.947
1985—Prince William	Carol.		2-S-3-O	105	377	42	104	9	4	0	28	.276	164	221	14	.965
1986—Nashua	East.		2B	134	•520	58	137	18	5	1	33	.263	★314	★378	13	★.982

Signed as free agent by Pittsburgh Pirates' organization, December 3, 1982.

ORLANDO LIND (SALGADO)

Name pronounced Leend.
Born January 30, 1965, at Dorado, P. R.
Height, 6.01. Weight, 200.
Throws and bats righthanded.
Brother of Jose Lind, infielder in Pittsburgh Pirates' organization.

Year	Club	League	G.	IP.	W.	L.	Pct.	H.	R.	ER.	SO.	BB.	ERA.
1983—Watertown	NYP		10	33⅔	1	4	.200	40	33	29	24	22	7.75
1984—Watertown	NYP		13	33	1	1	.500	34	11	8	29	11	2.18
1985—Prince William	Carolina		36	148	11	7	.611	93	38	30	149	64	1.82
1986—Nashua†	Eastern		15	52⅔	4	3	.571	56	22	21	35	27	3.59

Signed as free agent by Pittsburgh Pirates' organization, July 7, 1982.

†On disabled list, May 13, 1986 through remainder of season.

JAMES WILLIAM LINDEMAN
(Jim)

Born January 10, 1962, at Evanston, Ill.
Height, 6.01. Weight, 200.
Throws and bats righthanded.
Attended Bradley University, Peoria, Ill.

Major League stolen bases: 1986 (1).

Year	Club	League	Pos.	G.	AB.	R.	H.	2B.	3B.	HR.	RBI.	B.A.	PO.	A.	E.	F.A.
1983—St. Petersburg.......	Fla. St.		3B	70	232	45	64	13	1	8	37	.276	36	98	26	.838
1984—Springfield............	Midw.		3B-SS	94	354	69	169	15	2	18	66	.271	78	175	30	.894
1984—Arkansas...............	Texas		3B	40	137	14	26	4	3	0	13	.190	26	67	6	.939
1985—Arkansas...............	Texas		3B	128	450	54	127	30	6	10	63	.282	74	238	24	.929
1986—Louisville	A. A.		1B-3B-OF	139	509	82	128	38	5	20	★96	.251	718	110	19	.978
1986—St. Louis................	Nat.		1B-3B-OF	19	55	7	14	1	0	1	6	.255	118	10	1	.992
Major League Totals—1 Year................				19	55	7	14	1	0	1	6	.255	118	10	1	.992

Selected by St. Louis Cardinals' organization in 1st round (24th player selected) of free-agent draft, June 6, 1983.

NELSON ARTURO LIRIANO

Born June 3, 1964, at Puerto Plata, D. R.
Height, 5.10. Weight, 165.
Throws right and bats left and righthanded.

Led Carolina League second basemen in double plays with 79 in 1985.

Year	Club	League	Pos.	G.	AB.	R.	H.	2B.	3B.	HR.	RBI.	B.A.	PO.	A.	E.	F.A.
1983—Florence	S. Atl.		2B	129	478	87	124	24	5	6	57	.259	214	323	34	.940
1984—Kinston.................	Carol.		2B	132	★512	68	126	22	4	5	50	.246	260	★357	★21	.967
1985—Kinston.................	Carol.		2B	134	451	68	130	23	1	6	36	.288	★261	328	•25	.959
1986—Knoxville	South.		2B-3B-SS	135	557	88	159	25	★15	7	59	.285	239	324	22	.962

Signed as free agent by Toronto Blue Jays' organization, November 1, 1982.

RICHARD BRYAN LITTLE

(Known by middle name.)
Born October 8, 1959, at Houston, Tex.
Height, 5.10. Weight, 160.
Throws right and bats right and lefthanded.
Attended Louisburg College, Louisburg, N.C., and
Texas A & M University, College Station, Tex.
Brother of Grady Little, catcher in Atlanta Braves' and Los Angeles Dodgers' organizations, 1968 through 1973;
minor league manager, Baltimore Orioles' organization, 1980 through 1984; Toronto Blue Jays' organization,
1985; and manager in Atlanta Braves' organization since 1986;
brother of Tom Little, pitcher in Oakland A's organization, 1976.
Major League stolen bases: 1982 (2), 1983 (4), 1984 (2). Total—8.

Year Club	League	Pos.	G.	AB.	R.	H.	2B.	3B.	HR.	RBI.	B.A.	PO.	A.	E.	F.A.
1980—Jamestown	NYP	2B-SS	7	27	6	8	0	0	0	3	.296	11	21	2	.941
1980—W. Palm Beach	Fla. St.	SS	64	195	23	43	2	0	0	11	.221	95	212	12	.962
1981—Memphis	South.	SS •143		553	98	162	15	3	1	46	.293	*237	399	24	*.964
1982—Wichita	A. A.	SS-2B	99	388	67	111	13	3	1	35	.286	165	305	17	.965
1982—Montreal	Nat.	2B-3B	29	42	6	9	0	0	0	3	.214	21	32	1	.981
1983—Montreal	Nat.	SS-2B	106	350	48	91	15	3	1	36	.260	181	248	9	.979
1984—Montreal	Nat.	2B-SS	85	266	31	65	11	1	0	9	.244	137	199	6	.982
1984—Indianapolis†	A. A.	2B-SS-SS	35	106	15	31	2	1	0	5	.292	57	84	3	.979
1985—Buffalo	A. A.	2B	49	183	30	56	13	2	1	20	.306	98	145	3	.988
1985—Chicago	Amer.	2B-3B-SS	73	188	35	47	9	1	2	27	.250	101	165	5	.982
1986—Chi.‡-N.Y	Amer.	2B-SS-3B	34	76	6	14	2	0	0	2	.184	59	69	2	.985
1986—Buffalo	A. A.	SS-2B-3B	30	109	20	31	3	0	3	17	.284	47	76	4	.969
1986—Columbus§	Int.	2B-SS	50	176	16	47	8	0	1	17	.267	90	127	4	.982
National League Totals—3 Years			220	658	85	165	26	4	1	48	.251	339	479	16	.981
American League Totals—2 Years			107	264	41	61	11	1	2	29	.231	160	234	7	.983
Major League Totals—5 Years			327	922	126	226	37	5	3	77	.245	499	713	23	.981

Selected by Los Angeles Dodgers' organization in 5th round of free-agent draft, January 10, 1978.
Selected by Montreal Expos' organization in 9th round of free-agent draft, June 3, 1980.
†Traded to Chicago White Sox for Pitcher Bert Roberge, December 7, 1984.
‡Sold to New York Yankees' organization, July 2, 1986.
§Released, October 15, 1986.

DENNIS WILLIAM LIVINGSTON JR.

Born December 23, 1962, at Somerville, Mass.
Height, 6.00. Weight, 185.
Throws left and bats righthanded.
Attended Oklahoma State University, Stillwater, Okla.

Year Club	League	G.	IP.	W.	L.	Pct.	H.	R.	ER.	SO.	BB.	ERA.
1984—Vero Beach	Florida St.	13	68⅔	5	3	.625	67	42	37	61	39	4.85
1985—Bakersfield	California	27	168⅔	10	11	.476	173	111	*98	*166	117	5.23
1986—Albuquerque	P. Coast	11	49⅓	3	5	.375	39	34	27	40	57	4.93

Selected by San Francisco Giants' organization in 5th round of free-agent draft, June 8, 1981.
Selected by Los Angeles Dodgers' organization in 1st round (23rd player selected) of free-agent draft, June 4, 1984.

WILLIAM TIMOTHY LOLLAR

(Tim)

Born March 17, 1956, at Poplar Bluff, Mo.
Height, 6.03. Weight, 195.
Throws and bats lefthanded.
Attended Mineral Area Community College, Flat River, Mo.,
and University of Arkansas, Fayetteville, Ark.
Major League saves: 1980 (2), 1981 (1), 1985 (1). Total—4.

Year Club	League	G.	IP.	W.	L.	Pct.	H.	R.	ER.	SO.	BB.	ERA.
1978—West Haven†	Eastern	8	31	1	1	.500	40	24	20	20	14	5.81
1979—West Haven	Eastern	22	119	8	5	.615	122	55	42	60	36	3.18
1980—Columbus	Int'national	21	49	2	1	.667	29	15	14	50	27	2.57
1980—New York‡	American	14	32	1	0	1.000	33	14	12	13	20	3.38
1981—San Diego	National	24	77	2	8	.200	87	56	52	38	51	6.08
1982—San Diego	National	34	232⅔	16	9	.640	192	82	81	150	87	3.13
1983—San Diego	National	30	175⅔	7	12	.368	170	98	90	135	85	4.61
1984—San Diego§	National	31	195⅔	11	13	.458	168	89	85	131	105	3.91
1985—Chicago x-Boston y	American	34	150	8	10	.444	140	85	77	105	98	4.62
1986—Boston z	American	32	43	2	0	1.000	51	35	33	28	34	6.91
American League Totals—3 Years		80	225	11	10	.524	224	134	122	146	152	4.88
National League Totals—4 Years		119	681	36	42	.462	617	325	308	454	328	4.07
Major League Totals—7 Years		199	906	47	52	.475	841	459	430	600	480	4.27

Selected by Cleveland Indians' organization in 5th round of free-agent draft, June 6, 1977.
Selected by New York Yankees' organization in 4th round of free-agent draft, June 6, 1978.
†On disabled list, August 2 to August 14, 1978.
‡Traded with Outfielder Ruppert Jones and Joe Lefebvre and Pitcher Chris Welsh to San Diego Padres for
Outfielder Jerry Mumphrey and Pitcher John Pacella, April 1, 1981.
§Traded with Pitcher Bill Long, Third Baseman Luis Salazar and Shortstop Ozzie Guillen to Chicago White Sox for

Pitchers LaMarr Hoyt, Kevin Kristan and Todd Simmons, December 6, 1984.
xTraded to Boston Red Sox for Outfielder Reid Nichols and a player to be named later, July 11, 1985.
yHad one at-bat with no hits.
zAppeared in one game as a pinch-hitter with one hit.

CHAMPIONSHIP SERIES RECORD

Year Club	League	G.	IP.	W.	L.	Pct.	H.	R.	ER.	SO.	BB.	ERA.
1984—San Diego	National	1	4⅓	0	0	.000	3	3	3	3	4	6.23

WORLD SERIES RECORD

Year Club	League	G.	IP.	W.	L.	Pct.	H.	R.	ER.	SO.	BB.	ERA.
1984—San Diego	National	1	1⅔	0	1	.000	4	4	4	0	4	21.60

RECORD AS INFIELDER

Year Club	League	Pos.	G.	AB.	R.	H.	2B.	3B.	HR.	RBI.	B.A.	PO.	A.	E.	F.A.
1978—West Haven	East.	P-1B	28	55	11	14	2	1	2	7	.255	16	3	0	1.000
1979—West Haven	East.	P-1B	65	122	16	28	3	0	5	15	.230	137	9	1	.993

PHILLIP ARDEN LOMBARDI
(Phil)

Born February 20, 1963, at Granada Hills, Calif.
Height, 6.02. Weight, 200.
Throws and bats righthanded.

Led Florida State League catchers in fielding percentage with .985 in 1984.

Year Club	League	Pos.	G.	AB.	R.	H.	2B.	3B.	HR.	RBI.	B.A.	PO.	A.	E.	F.A.
1981—Bradenton Yanks	Gulf C.	C	20	53	9	13	3	0	0	6	.245	94	17	4	.965
1982—Paintsville	Appal.	C	50	180	26	45	8	0	0	14	.250	323	★50	8	.979
1983—Greensboro	S. Atl.	C-OF	94	330	63	99	15	0	7	43	.300	564	52	14	.978
1983—Fort Lauderdale	Fla. St.	C	17	49	1	11	2	0	0	3	.224	77	6	5	.943
1984—Fort Lauderdale	Fla. St.	C-O-1-3	127	393	58	115	20	2	8	70	.293	669	61	14	.990
1985—Albany†	East.	C-O-3-S	76	250	44	64	13	2	5	32	.256	390	48	11	.976
1986—Columbus	Int.	C-OF	75	277	43	81	12	4	8	28	.292	222	16	7	.971
1986—New York	Amer.	OF-C	20	36	6	10	3	0	2	6	.278	22	3	3	.893
Major League Totals—1 Year			20	36	6	10	3	0	2	6	.278	22	3	3	.893

Selected by New York Yankees' organization in 3rd round of free-agent draft, June 8, 1981.
†On disabled list, July 20 to September 16, 1985.

STEPHEN PAUL LOMBARDOZZI
(Steve)

Born April 26, 1960, at Malden, Mass.
Height, 6.00. Weight, 175.
Throws and bats righthanded.
Attended Gulf Coast Community College, Panama City, Fla.,
and University of Florida, Gainesville, Fla.
Brother of Chris Lombardozzi, shortstop in New York Yankees' organization.

Major League stolen bases: 1985 (3), 1986 (3). Total—6.
Led California League shortstops in fielding percentage with .947 in 1982.

Year Club	League	Pos.	G.	AB.	R.	H.	2B.	3B.	HR.	RBI.	B.A.	PO.	A.	E.	F.A.
1981—Elizabethton	Appal.	SS	65	246	48	79	13	2	6	38	.321	89	192	14	★.953
1982—Visalia	Calif.	SS-OF-P	122	441	81	131	24	1	6	67	.297	185	393	33	.946
1983—Orlando	South.	SS-2B	137	492	76	143	23	6	3	52	.291	203	364	33	.945
1984—Toledo	Int.	2B-SS	119	385	57	96	15	1	9	31	.249	237	310	14	.975
1985—Toledo	Int.	2B-3B-SS	118	451	55	119	21	3	14	48	.264	272	324	17	.972
1985—Minnesota	Amer.	2B	28	54	10	20	4	1	0	6	.370	31	80	2	.982
1986—Minnesota	Amer.	2B	156	453	53	103	20	5	8	33	.227	289	407	6	★.991
Major League Totals—2 Years			184	507	63	123	24	6	8	39	.243	320	487	8	.990

Selected by Minnesota Twins' organization in 9th round of free-agent draft, June 8, 1981.

PITCHING RECORD

Year Club	League	G.	IP.	W.	L.	Pct.	H.	R.	ER.	SO.	BB.	ERA.
1982—Visalia	California	1	1	0	1	.000	5	4	4	2	0	36.00

DAVID EARL LOPES
Name rhymes with Ropes.
(Davey)

Born May 3, 1946, at East Providence, R. I.
Height, 5.09. Weight, 170.
Throws and bats righthanded.
Attended Iowa Wesleyan College, Mt. Pleasant, Iowa, and received bachelor of science degree
in education from Washburn University, Topeka, Kan. in 1969.

Established major league record for most consecutive stolen bases, season (38), June 10 through August 24, 1975.
Tied major league record for most errors, inning, second baseman, (3), June 2, 1973 (1st inning).
Tied National League records for most stolen bases, game, since 1900 (5), August 24, 1974; most double plays, second baseman, game (5), May 18, 1975.

Hit three home runs in a game, August 20, 1974.
Major League stolen bases: 1972 (4), 1973 (36), 1974 (59), 1975 (77), 1976 (63), 1977 (47), 1978 (45), 1979 (44), 1980 (23), 1981 (20), 1982 (28), 1983 (22), 1984 (15), 1985 (47), 1986 (25). Total—555.
Led National League in stolen bases with 77 in 1975 and 63 in 1976.
Led Pacific Coast League in stolen bases with 48 in 1972.
Led Pacific Coast League second basemen in errors with 18 in 1972.
Tied for Pacific Coast League lead in errors by outfielders with 10 in 1970.
Named second baseman on THE SPORTING NEWS National League All-Star Team, 1978 and 1979.
Named second baseman on THE SPORTING NEWS National League All-Star fielding team, 1978.

Year	Club	League	Pos.	G.	AB.	R.	H.	2B.	3B.	HR.	RBI.	B.A.	PO.	A.	E.	F.A.
1968—Daytona Beach†...	Fla. St.	OF	82	271	39	67	6	6	5	33	.247	109	7	4	.967
1969—Daytona Bea.‡§....	Fla. St.	OF	72	264	53	74	7	4	9	33	.280	138	16	7	.957
1970—Spokane x......	P. C.	OF-2B	100	343	48	90	15	4	6	35	.262	202	19	12	.948
1971—Spokane y......	P. C.	OF-2B	94	353	78	108	9	9	6	36	.306	157	103	11	.959
1972—Albuquerque z......	P. C.	2B-OF-SS	104	397	94	126	18	6	11	53	.317	213	270	21	.958
1972—Los Angeles	Nat.	2B	11	42	6	9	4	0	0	1	.214	27	27	2	.964
1973—Los Angeles	Nat.	2-O-S-3	142	535	77	147	13	5	6	37	.275	323	380	11	.985
1974—Los Angeles	Nat.	2B	145	530	95	141	26	3	10	35	.266	309	360	*24	.965
1975—Los Angeles	Nat.	2B-OF-SS	155	618	108	162	24	6	8	41	.262	360	386	16	.979
1976—Los Angeles a......	Nat.	2B-OF	117	427	72	103	17	7	4	20	.241	254	268	19	.965
1977—Los Angeles	Nat.	2B	134	502	85	142	19	5	11	53	.283	287	380	14	.979
1978—Los Angeles	Nat.	*2B-OF	151	587	93	163	25	4	17	58	.278	340	424	*20	.974
1979—Los Angeles	Nat.	2B	153	582	109	154	20	6	28	73	.265	341	*384	14	.981
1980—Los Angeles	Nat.	2B	141	553	79	139	15	3	10	49	.251	304	416	15	.980
1981—Los Angeles bc.....	Nat.	2B	58	214	35	44	2	0	5	17	.206	129	161	2	.993
1982—Oakland.................	Amer.	2B-OF	128	450	58	109	19	3	11	42	.242	295	338	15	.977
1983—Oakland.................	Amer.	2B-OF-3B	147	494	64	137	13	4	17	67	.277	267	287	9	.984
1984—Oakland de...........	Amer.	OF-2B-3B	72	230	32	59	11	1	9	36	.257	99	47	6	.961
1984—Chicago	Nat.	OF-2B	16	17	5	4	1	0	0	0	.235	6	2	0	1.000
1985—Chicago	Nat.	OF-3B-2B	99	275	52	78	11	0	11	44	.284	115	6	1	.992
1986—Chi. f-Hou. g	Nat.	OF-3B	96	255	49	70	10	3	7	35	.275	96	65	8	.953
National League Totals—13 Years.........				1418	5137	865	1356	187	42	117	463	.264	2891	3259	146	.977
American League Totals—3 Years				347	1174	154	305	43	8	37	145	.260	661	672	30	.978
Major League Totals—15 Years				1765	6311	1019	1661	230	50	154	608	.263	3552	3931	176	.977

Selected by San Francisco Giants' organization in 28th round of free-agent draft, June 6, 1967.
Selected by Los Angeles Dodgers' organization in secondary phase of free-agent draft, January 27, 1968.
†On restricted list, April 11 to June 13, 1968.
‡On temporary inactive list, April 11 to April 27, 1969.
§On military list, July 22, 1969 to April 8, 1970.
xOn temporary inactive list, June 9 to June 30, 1970.
yOn temporary inactive list, April 26 to April 29 and June 8 to July 2, 1971.
zOn temporary inactive list, June 16 to June 30 and August 28 to September 1, 1972.
aOn disabled list, March 31 to May 3, 1976.
bOn disabled list, August 18 to September 2, 1981.
cTraded to Oakland A's for Second Baseman Lance Hudson, February 8, 1982.
dOn disabled list, July 7 to August 8, 1984.
eTraded to Chicago Cubs, August 31, 1984, as partial completion of deal in which Chicago traded Pitcher Chuck Rainey and a player to be named later to Oakland A's for a player to be named later, July 15, 1984; Oakland organization acquired Outfielder Damon Farmar to complete deal, March 18, 1985.
fTraded to Houston Astros for Pitcher Frank DiPino, July 21, 1986.
gGranted free agency, November 12, 1986; re-signed by Astros, December 15, 1986.

DIVISION SERIES RECORD

Year	Club	League	Pos.	G.	AB.	R.	H.	2B.	3B.	HR.	RBI.	B.A.	PO.	A.	E.	F.A.
1981—Los Angeles	Nat.	2B	5	20	1	4	1	0	0	0	.200	7	12	0	1.000

CHAMPIONSHIP SERIES RECORD

Established Championship Series records for most stolen bases, total Series (9); most stolen bases, four-game Series (3), 1974 and five-game Series (5), 1981.
Tied Championship Series records for most clubs, total Series (3); most consecutive games, one or more runs batted in, total Series (4); most hits, two consecutive games, one Series (6), October 4 and 5, 1978.
Tied National League Championship Series record for most three-base hits, total Series (2).

Year	Club	League	Pos.	G.	AB.	R.	H.	2B.	3B.	HR.	RBI.	B.A.	PO.	A.	E.	F.A.
1974—Los Angeles	Nat.	2B	4	15	4	4	0	1	0	3	.267	9	18	1	.964
1977—Los Angeles	Nat.	2B	4	17	2	4	0	0	0	3	.235	9	10	1	.950
1978—Los Angeles	Nat.	2B	4	18	3	7	1	1	2	5	.389	10	10	2	.909
1981—Los Angeles	Nat.	2B	5	18	0	5	0	0	0	0	.278	13	13	0	1.000
1984—Chicago	Nat.	OF-PH	2	1	0	0	0	0	0	0	.000	0	0	0	.000
1986—Houston	Nat.	PH	3	2	1	0	0	0	0	0	.000	0	0	0	.000
Championship Series Totals—6 Years....			22	71	10	20	1	2	2	11	.282	41	51	4	.958

WORLD SERIES RECORD

Established World Series records for most stolen bases, six-game Series (4), 1981; most putouts by second baseman, six-game Series (26), 1981; most chances accepted by second baseman, six-game Series (40), 1981; most errors by second baseman, six-game Series (6), 1981.
Tied World Series records for most stolen bases, inning (2), October 15, 1974 (first inning); most putouts by second baseman, game (8), October 16, 1974; most chances accepted by second baseman, game (13), October 16, 1974; most putouts by second baseman, inning (3), October 16, 1974 (sixth inning) and October 21 1981 (fourth inning); most times home run as leadoff batter, start of game (1), October 17, 1978; most errors by second baseman, game (3), October 25, 1981; most errors by second baseman, inning (2), October 25, 1981 (fourth inning).

Year Club League	Pos.	G.	AB.	R.	H.	2B.	3B.	HR.	RBI.	B.A.	PO.	A.	E.	F.A.
1974—Los Angeles .... Nat.	2B	5	18	2	2	0	0	0	0	.111	19	9	0	1.000
1977—Los Angeles .... Nat.	2B	6	24	3	4	0	1	1	2	.167	12	22	0	1.000
1978—Los Angeles .... Nat.	2B	6	26	7	8	0	0	3	7	.308	10	19	1	.967
1981—Los Angeles .... Nat.	2B	6	22	6	5	1	0	0	2	.227	26	14	6	.870
World Series Totals—4 Years		23	90	18	19	1	1	4	11	.211	67	64	7	.949

ALL-STAR GAME RECORD

Year League	Pos.	AB.	R.	H.	2B.	3B.	HR.	RBI.	B.A.	PO.	A.	E.	F.A.
1978—National	PH-2B	1	0	1	0	0	0	1	1.000	0	1	0	1.000
1979—National	2B	3	0	1	0	0	0	0	.333	4	1	0	1.000
1980—National	2B	1	0	0	0	0	0	0	.000	0	2	0	1.000
1981—National	2B	0	0	0	0	0	0	0	.000	1	0	0	.000
All-Star Game Totals—4 Years		5	0	2	0	0	0	1	.400	5	4	0	1.000

AURELIO ALEJANDRO LOPEZ (RIOS)

Born October 5, 1948, at Tecamachalco, Puebla, Mexico.
Height, 6.00. Weight, 225.
Throws and bats righthanded.

Pitched 1-0 no-hit victory against Carmen, May 24, 1969.
Major League saves: 1979 (21), 1980 (21), 1981 (3), 1982 (3), 1983 (18), 1984 (14), 1985 (5), 1986 (7). Total—92.
Led Mexican League in wild pitches with 18 in 1975.
Led Mexican League in saves with 20 in 1974, 23 in 1975 and 16 in 1976.
Named Mexican League Most Valuable Player, 1977.

Year Club League	G.	IP.	W.	L.	Pct.	H.	R.	ER.	SO.	BB.	ERA.
1967—Las Choapas .... Mex. SE.	27	96	5	3	.625	93	62	46	80	66	4.31
1968—Mexico City Reds .... Mexican	31	162	10	10	.500	154	73	47	99	64	2.61
1969—Minatitlan .... Mex. SE.	16	83	7	4	.636	56	29	18	64	40	1.95
1969—Mexico City Reds .... Mexican	21	105	10	4	.714	131	53	45	76	49	3.86
1970—Mexico City Reds .... Mexican	37	172	16	11	.593	153	64	57	127	100	2.98
1971—Mexico City Reds† .... Mexican	21	83	4	7	.364	86	49	45	36	59	4.88
1972—Mexico City Reds .... Mexican	46	121	5	7	.417	109	57	49	89	58	3.64
1973—Mexico City Reds‡ .... Mexican	53	127	12	10	.545	115	58	47	117	82	3.33
1974—Mexico City Reds§ .... Mexican	★60	113	7	7	.500	94	50	32	134	70	2.55
1974—Kansas City .... American	8	16	0	0	.000	21	12	10	5	10	5.63
1975—Mexico City Reds .... Mexican	★71	114	10	8	.556	97	46	36	114	68	2.84
1976—Mexico City Reds .... Mexican	★59	98	4	11	.267	111	61	49	65	49	4.50
1977—Mexico City Reds x .... Mexican	★73	157	19	8	.704	132	39	35	165	49	2.01
1978—Springfield .... Am. Assoc.	34	76	6	6	.500	72	37	30	81	39	3.55
1978—St. Louis y .... National	25	65	4	2	.667	52	35	31	46	32	4.29
1979—Detroit .... American	61	127	10	5	.667	95	37	34	106	51	2.41
1980—Detroit .... American	67	124	13	6	.684	125	56	52	97	45	3.77
1981—Detroit .... American	29	82	5	2	.714	70	34	33	53	31	3.62
1982—Detroit z .... American	19	41	3	1	.750	41	27	24	26	19	5.27
1982—Evansville .... Am. Assoc.	12	30⅔	4	0	1.000	23	6	6	30	10	1.76
1983—Detroit .... American	57	115⅓	9	8	.529	87	36	36	90	49	2.81
1984—Detroit .... American	71	137⅔	10	1	.909	109	51	45	94	52	2.94
1985—Detroit a .... American	51	86⅓	3	7	.300	82	50	46	53	41	4.80
1986—Houston .... National	45	78	3	3	.500	64	32	30	44	25	3.46
American League Totals—8 Years	363	729⅓	53	30	.639	630	303	280	524	298	3.46
National League Totals—2 Years	70	143	7	5	.583	116	67	61	90	57	3.84
Major League Totals—10 Years	433	872⅓	60	35	.632	746	370	341	614	355	3.52

Signed as free agent by Las Choapas, March 28, 1967.
†On disabled list, April 30 to May 27 and June 28 to July 12, 1971.
‡Sold to Kansas City Royals, August 29, 1974.
§Sold to Mexico City Reds, March 27, 1975.
xSold to St. Louis Cardinals, October 26, 1977.
yTraded with Outfielder Jerry Morales to Detroit Tigers for Pitchers Bob Sykes and Jack Murphy, December 4, 1978.
zOn disabled list, March 23 to May 13, 1982; included rehabilitation disability assignment to Evansville, April 19 to May 11, 1982.
aGranted free agency, November 12, 1985; signed by Houston Astros, June 3, 1986.

CHAMPIONSHIP SERIES RECORD

Year Club League	G.	IP.	W.	L.	Pct.	H.	R.	ER.	SO.	BB.	ERA.
1984—Detroit .... American	1	3	1	0	1.000	4	0	0	2	1	0.00
1986—Houston .... National	2	3⅓	0	1	.000	7	3	3	3	4	8.10
Championship Series Totals—2 Years	3	6⅓	1	1	.500	11	3	3	5	5	4.26

WORLD SERIES RECORD

Year Club League	G.	IP.	W.	L.	Pct.	H.	R.	ER.	SO.	BB.	ERA.
1984—Detroit .... American	2	3	1	0	1.000	1	0	0	4	1	0.00

ALL-STAR GAME RECORD

Member of American League All-Star Team in 1983; did not play.

DWIGHT LOWRY

Born October 23, 1957, in Robeson County, N. C.
Height, 6.03. Weight, 210.
Throws right and bats lefthanded.
Received degree in industrial relations from University of North Carolina, Chapel Hill, N. C.
Led Florida State League catchers in double plays with 8 in 1982.

Year Club	League	Pos.	G.	AB.	R.	H.	2B.	3B.	HR.	RBI.	B.A.	PO.	A.	E.	F.A.
1980—Lakeland	Fla. St.	C	45	142	18	28	5	0	0	16	.197	171	25	4	.980
1981—Birmingham	South.	C	19	52	3	8	2	0	0	4	.154	108	11	3	.975
1981—Macon	S. Atl.	C	67	231	30	58	6	0	2	32	.251	225	22	5	.980
1982—Lakeland	Fla. St.	C	93	278	33	77	11	2	7	28	.277	350	53	3	*.993
1983—Birmingham	South.	C-OF	90	288	42	77	9	2	9	44	.267	424	51	6	.988
1984—Detroit	Amer.	C	32	45	8	11	2	0	2	7	.244	87	8	0	1.000
1984—Evansville	A. A.	C	61	177	23	39	5	1	5	28	.220	240	45	6	.979
1985—Nashville	A. A.	C	74	203	20	37	7	1	2	13	.182	318	45	12	.968
1986—Nashville	A. A.	C-1B	18	57	5	14	1	0	1	6	.246	91	6	1	.990
1986—Detroit	Amer.	C-1B-OF	56	150	21	46	4	0	3	18	.307	250	17	2	.993
Major League Totals—2 Years			88	195	29	57	6	0	5	25	.292	337	25	2	.995

Selected by Detroit Tigers' organization in 11th round of free-agent draft, June 3, 1980.

MICHAEL W. LOYND
(Mike)

Born March 26, 1964, at St. Louis, Mo.
Height, 6.05. Weight, 215.
Throws and bats righthanded.
Attended Florida State University.

Major League saves: 1986 (1).

Year Club	League	G.	IP.	W.	L.	Pct.	H.	R.	ER.	SO.	BB.	ERA.
1986—Tulsa	Texas	5	29⅓	2	1	.667	32	12	12	31	3	3.68
1986—Texas	American	9	42	2	2	.500	49	30	25	33	19	5.36
Major League Totals—1 Year		9	42	2	2	.500	49	30	25	33	19	5.36

Selected by Baltimore Orioles' organization in 11th round of free-agent draft, June 3, 1985.
Selected by Texas Rangers' organization in 7th round of free-agent draft, June 2, 1986.

GARY PAUL LUCAS

Born November 8, 1954, at Riverside, Calif.
Height, 6.05. Weight, 200.
Throws and bats lefthanded.
Attended Chapman College, Orange, Calif.

Major League saves: 1980 (3), 1981 (13), 1982 (16), 1983 (17), 1984 (8), 1985 (1), 1986 (2). Total—60.
Tied for National League lead in intentional bases on balls issued with 15 in 1981.

Year Club	League	G.	IP.	W.	L.	Pct.	H.	R.	ER.	SO.	BB.	ERA.
1976—Walla Walla	Northwest	14	93	7	3	.700	91	40	32	49	30	3.10
1977—Reno	California	28	176	13	7	.650	205	114	90	98	48	4.60
1978—Amarillo	Texas	25	159	8	17	.320	182	104	86	115	26	4.87
1979—Hawaii†	P. Coast	24	178	10	7	.588	151	64	55	98	58	2.78
1980—San Diego	National	46	150	5	8	.385	138	59	54	85	43	3.24
1981—San Diego	National	*57	90	7	7	.500	78	26	20	53	36	2.00
1982—San Diego	National	65	97⅓	1	10	.091	89	42	35	64	29	3.24
1983—San Diego‡	National	62	91	5	8	.385	85	38	29	60	34	2.87
1984—Montreal	National	55	53	0	3	.000	54	20	16	42	20	2.72
1985—West Palm Beach§	Florida St.	3	5	0	0	.000	4	5	4	3	1	7.20
1985—Indianapolis	Am. Assoc.	1	2	0	0	.000	1	0	0	2	2	0.00
1985—Montreal x	National	49	67⅔	6	2	.750	63	29	24	31	24	3.19
1986—Palm Springs y	California	7	12⅓	2	0	.000	15	8	7	9	1	5.11
1986—California	American	27	45⅔	4	1	.800	45	19	16	31	6	3.15
National League Totals—6 Years		334	549	24	38	.387	507	214	178	335	186	2.92
American League Totals—1 Year		27	45⅔	4	1	.800	45	19	16	31	6	3.15
Major League Totals—7 Years		361	594⅔	28	39	.418	552	233	194	366	192	2.94

Selected by Cincinnati Reds' organization in 1st round (21st player selected) of free-agent draft, January 10, 1973.
Selected by Cincinnati Reds' organization in secondary phase of free-agent draft, June 5, 1973.
Selected by San Diego Padres' organization in 19th round of free-agent draft, June 8, 1976.
†On disabled list, August 5 to August 30, 1979.
‡Traded to Montreal Expos for Pitcher Scott Sanderson and Infielder Al Newman, December 7, 1983.
§On Montreal disabled list, March 27 to May 19, 1985; included rehabilitation disability assignment to West Palm Beach, May 1 to May 14, and Indianapolis, May 15 to May 19, 1985.
xTraded to California Angels for Pitcher Luis Sanchez and Catcher Tim Arnold, December 27, 1985.
yOn California disabled list, March 31 to July 17, 1986; included rehabilitation disability assignment to Palm Springs, June 26 to July 17, 1986.

CHAMPIONSHIP SERIES RECORD

Tied American League Championship Series record for most games pitched, seven-game Series (4), 1986.

Year Club	League	G.	IP.	W.	L.	Pct.	H.	R.	ER.	SO.	BB.	ERA.
1986—California	American	4	2⅓	0	0	.000	3	3	3	2	1	11.57

URBANO RAFAEL LUGO

Born August 12, 1962, at Caracas, Venezuela.
Height, 6.00. Weight, 185.
Throws and bats righthanded.
Son of Urbano Lugo, pitcher in Mexican League, 1967 through 1970 and 1973.

Year Club	League	G.	IP.	W.	L.	Pct.	H.	R.	ER.	SO.	BB.	ERA.
1982—Danville	Midwest	10	24	0	2	.000	35	30	27	13	16	10.13
1982—Salem	Northwest	14	90⅔	7	3	.700	74	45	29	62	61	2.88
1983—Peoria	Midwest	15	107	8	5	.615	82	39	30	96	28	2.52
1983—Redwood	California	11	64⅔	5	5	.500	59	36	28	58	31	3.90
1984—Waterbury	Eastern	24	164⅓	13	8	.619	135	63	51	117	68	2.79
1985—Edmonton	P. Coast	4	25⅔	2	0	1.000	20	14	13	19	14	4.56
1985—California†	American	20	83	3	4	.429	86	36	34	42	29	3.69
1986—Midland‡	Texas	2	11	1	1	.500	9	2	2	4	4	1.64
1986—Edmonton	P. Coast	16	100⅓	8	6	.571	110	58	52	53	41	4.66
1986—California	American	6	21⅓	1	1	.500	21	9	9	9	6	3.80
Major League Totals—2 Years		26	104⅓	4	5	.444	107	45	43	51	35	3.71

Signed as free agent by California Angels' organization, January 31, 1982.
†On disabled list, August 22 to September 6, 1985.
‡On California disabled list, March 31 to June 5, 1986; included rehabilitation disability assignment to Midland, May 15 to June 4, 1986.

MITCHELL SCOTT LYDEN
(Mitch)

Born December 14, 1964, at Portland, Ore.
Height, 6.03. Weight, 200.
Throws and bats righthanded.
Led Florida State League catchers in total chances with 678 in 1985.

Year Club	League	Pos.	G.	AB.	R.	H.	2B.	3B.	HR.	RBI.	B.A.	PO.	A.	E.	F.A.
1983—Oneonta	NYP	C	47	128	14	19	1	0	0	7	.148	310	28	3	★.991
1984—Greensboro	S. Atl.	C	14	32	3	7	1	0	1	2	.219	28	5	1	.971
1984—Sarasota Yankees	Gulf C.	C	54	200	21	47	4	0	1	21	.235	254	49	7	.977
1985—Fort Lauderdale	Fla. St.	C	116	400	43	102	21	1	10	58	.255	★607	63	8	★.988
1986—Albany†	East.	C	46	159	19	48	14	1	8	29	.302	131	25	3	.981
1986—Columbus	Int.	C	2	7	0	0	0	0	0	0	.000	1	0	0	1.000

Selected by New York Yankees' organization in 4th round of free-agent draft, June 6, 1983.
†On disabled list, April 11 to July 13, 1986.

EDWARD FRANCIS LYNCH
(Ed)

Born February 25, 1956, at Brooklyn, N.Y.
Height, 6.05. Weight, 210.
Throws and bats righthanded.
Received bachelor of science degree in finance from University of South Carolina, Columbia, S.C.,
and master's degree in business administration from University of Miami, Coral Gables, Fla.
Major League saves: 1982 (2), 1984 (2). Total—4.

Year Club	League	G.	IP.	W.	L.	Pct.	H.	R.	ER.	SO.	BB.	ERA.
1977—Sarasota Rangers	Gulf Coast	13	56	1	4	.200	61	31	23	36	15	3.70
1978—Asheville	W. Carol.	18	123	7	9	.438	122	55	45	79	33	3.29
1978—Tulsa	Texas	7	54	4	3	.571	61	25	16	44	14	2.67
1979—Tucson†	P. Coast	27	156	10	11	.476	184	96	84	65	37	4.85
1980—Tidewater	Int'national	24	163	13	6	.684	151	69	57	91	42	3.15
1980—New York	National	5	19	1	1	.500	24	12	11	9	5	5.21
1981—Tidewater	Int'national	15	99	7	6	.538	93	46	43	54	29	3.91
1981—New York	National	17	80	4	5	.444	79	32	26	27	21	2.93
1982—New York	National	43	139½	4	8	.333	145	57	55	51	40	3.55
1983—New York	National	30	174⅔	10	10	.500	208	94	83	44	41	4.28
1984—New York	National	40	124	9	8	.529	169	77	62	62	24	4.50
1985—New York	National	31	191	10	8	.556	188	76	73	65	27	3.44
1986—New York‡§-Chicago	National	24	101⅓	7	5	.583	107	48	42	53	23	3.73
1986—Tidewater	Int'national	4	18	1	0	1.000	22	10	10	7	5	5.00
Major League Totals—7 Years		190	829⅓	45	45	.500	920	396	352	311	181	3.82

Selected by Texas Rangers' organization in 22nd round of free-agent draft, June 7, 1977.
†Traded to New York Mets' organization, September 18, 1979, as partial completion of deal in which Texas Rangers acquired First Baseman Willie Montanez for two players to be named later, August 12, 1979; New York acquired First Baseman Mike Jorgensen to complete deal, October 23, 1979.
‡On disabled list, April 13 to June 30, 1986; included rehabilitation disability assignment to Tidewater, June 11 to June 30, 1986.
§Traded to Chicago Cubs for Pitcher Dave Lenderman and Catcher David Liddell, June 30, 1986.

FREDRIC MICHAEL LYNN
(Fred)

Born February 3, 1952, at Chicago, Ill.
Height, 6.01. Weight, 190.
Throws and bats lefthanded.
Attended University of Southern California, Los Angeles, Calif.

Established American League record for most doubles, rookie season (47), 1975.
Tied American League record for most total bases, game (16), June 18, 1975.
Major League stolen bases: 1975 (10), 1976 (14), 1977 (2), 1978 (3), 1979 (2), 1980 (12), 1981 (1), 1982 (7), 1983 (2), 1984 (2), 1985 (7), 1986 (2). Total—64.
Hit three home runs in a game, June 18, 1975.
Hit for the cycle, May 13, 1980.
Led American League in slugging percentage with .566 in 1975 and .637 in 1979.
Named American League Player of the Year by THE SPORTING NEWS, 1975.
Named American League Most Valuable Player by Baseball Writers' Association of America, 1975.
Named American League Rookie of the Year by Baseball Writers' Association of America, 1975.
Named American League Rookie Player of the Year by THE SPORTING NEWS, 1975.
Named outfielder on THE SPORTING NEWS American League All-Star Team, 1975, 1978 and 1979.
Named outfielder on THE SPORTING NEWS American League All-Star fielding team, 1975 and 1978 through 1980.
Received reported $40,000 bonus to sign with Boston Red Sox, 1973.
Named outfielder on THE SPORTING NEWS College Baseball All-America Team, 1972 and 1973.

Year	Club	League	Pos.	G.	AB.	R.	H.	2B.	3B.	HR.	RBI.	B.A.	PO.	A.	E.	F.A.
1973—Bristol	East.	OF	53	162	26	42	9	4	6	36	.259	79	3	5	.943
1974—Pawtucket	Int.	OF	124	415	65	117	19	2	21	68	.282	247	12	7	.974
1974—Boston	Amer.	OF	15	43	5	18	2	2	2	10	.419	18	2	0	1.000
1975—Boston	Amer.	OF	145	528	*103	175	*47	7	21	105	.331	404	11	7	.983
1976—Boston	Amer.	OF	132	507	76	159	32	8	10	65	.314	367	13	6	.984
1977—Boston†	Amer.	OF	129	497	81	129	29	5	18	76	.260	333	7	2	.994
1978—Boston	Amer.	OF	150	541	75	161	33	3	22	82	.298	408	11	7	.984
1979—Boston	Amer.	OF	147	531	116	177	42	1	39	122	*.333	381	10	5	.987
1980—Boston‡	Amer.	OF	110	415	67	125	32	3	12	61	.301	302	11	2	.994
1981—California	Amer.	OF	76	256	28	56	8	1	5	31	.219	176	4	4	.978
1982—California	Amer.	OF	138	472	89	141	38	1	21	86	.299	317	6	3	.991
1983—California	Amer.	OF	117	437	56	119	20	3	22	74	.272	274	8	2	.993
1984—California§	Amer.	OF	142	517	84	140	28	4	23	79	.271	321	12	6	.982
1985—Baltimore	Amer.	OF	124	448	59	118	12	1	23	68	.263	314	6	2	.994
1986—Baltimore x	Amer.	OF	112	397	67	114	13	1	23	67	.287	244	2	4	.984
Major League Totals—13 Years			1537	5589	906	1632	336	40	241	926	.292	3859	103	50	.988

Selected by New York Yankees' organization in 3rd round of free-agent draft, June 4, 1970.
Selected by Boston Red Sox' organization in 2nd round of free-agent draft, June 5, 1973.
†On disabled list, March 24 to May 6, 1977.
‡Traded with Pitcher Steve Renko to California Angels for Pitchers Frank Tanana and Jim Dorsey and Outfielder Joe Rudi, January 23, 1981.
§Granted free agency, November 8, 1984; signed by Baltimore Orioles, December 11, 1984. (Pitcher Donnie Moore selected from player compensation pool by California Angels, January 24, 1985.)
xOn disabled list, June 11 to June 27, 1986.

CHAMPIONSHIP SERIES RECORD

Established Championship Series record for highest batting average, five-game Series (.611), 1982.
Tied Championship Series records for most hits, five-game Series (11), 1982; most one-base hits, five-game Series (8), 1982.
Tied American League Championship Series record for most hits, two consecutive Series (15), 1975 and 1982.

Year	Club	League	Pos.	G.	AB.	R.	H.	2B.	3B.	HR.	RBI.	B.A.	PO.	A.	E.	F.A.
1975—Boston	Amer.	OF	3	11	1	4	1	0	0	3	.364	12	1	1	.929
1982—California	Amer.	OF	5	18	5	11	2	0	1	5	.611	16	0	1	.941
Championship Series Totals—2 Years			8	29	6	15	3	0	1	8	.517	28	1	2	.935

WORLD SERIES RECORD

Tied World Series record for highest fielding average by outfielder, seven-game Series (1.000 with 24 chances), 1975.

Year	Club	League	Pos.	G.	AB.	R.	H.	2B.	3B.	HR.	RBI.	B.A.	PO.	A.	E.	F.A.
1975—Boston	Amer.	OF	7	25	3	7	1	0	1	5	.280	23	1	0	1.000

ALL-STAR GAME RECORD

Hit only All-Star Game home run with bases loaded, July 6, 1983.
Established All-Star Game record for most runs batted in, inning (4), July 6, 1983.

Year	League	Pos.	AB.	R.	H.	2B.	3B.	HR.	RBI.	B.A.	PO.	A.	E.	F.A.
1975—American		PH-OF	2	0	0	0	0	0	0	.000	1	0	0	1.000
1976—American		OF	3	1	1	0	0	1	1	.333	0	0	0	1.000
1977—American		OF	1	1	0	0	0	0	0	.000	2	0	0	1.000
1978—American		OF	4	0	1	0	0	0	0	.250	3	0	0	1.000
1979—American		OF	1	1	1	0	0	1	2	1.000	0	0	0	.000
1980—American		OF	3	1	1	0	0	1	2	.333	2	0	0	1.000
1981—American		PH	1	0	1	0	0	0	1	1.000	0	0	0	.000
1982—American		OF	2	0	0	0	0	0	0	.000	0	0	0	.000
1983—American		OF	3	1	1	0	0	1	4	.333	1	0	0	1.000
All-Star Game Totals—9 Years			20	5	6	0	0	4	10	.300	9	0	0	1.000

BARRY STEPHEN LYONS

Born June 3, 1960, at Biloxi, Miss.
Height, 6.01. Weight, 205.
Throws and bats righthanded.
Attended Delta State University, Cleveland, Miss.

Led Texas League in grounding into double plays with 19 and tied for lead in game-winning RBIs with 16 in 1985.

Led Texas League catchers in errors with 19 in 1985.
Led Carolina League catchers in assists with 72 and fielding percentage with .989 in 1984.
Named Carolina League Player of the Year, 1984.

Year	Club	League	Pos.	G.	AB.	R.	H.	2B.	3B.	HR.	RBI.	B.A.	PO.	A.	E.	F.A.
1982—Shelby	S. Atl.	C-1B	45	164	23	46	12	0	4	46	.280	226	21	8	.969
1983—Lynchburg	Carol.	C	2	7	0	1	0	0	0	2	.143	21	4	0	1.000
1983—Columbia	S. Atl.	C-1B-OF	92	316	55	94	9	2	5	45	.297	387	33	17	.961
1984—Lynchburg	Carol.	C-1B-OF	115	412	59	130	17	3	12	87	.316	894	86	13	.987
1985—Jackson	Texas	C-1B	126	486	69	149	34	6	11	108	.307	834	65	23	.975
1986—New York	Nat.	C	6	9	1	0	0	0	0	2	.000	16	0	1	.941
1986—Tidewater	Int.	1B-C	61	234	28	69	16	0	4	46	.295	423	25	6	.987
Major League Totals—1 Year				6	9	1	0	0	0	0	2	.000	16	0	1	.941

Selected by Detroit Tigers' organization in 25th round of free-agent draft, June 8, 1981.
Selected by New York Mets' organization in 15th round of free-agent draft, June 7, 1982.

STEPHEN JOHN LYONS
(Steve)

Born June 3, 1960, at Tacoma, Wash.
Height, 6.03. Weight, 190.
Throws right and bats lefthanded.
Attended Oregon State University, Corvallis, Ore.

Major League stolen bases: 1985 (12), 1986 (4). Total—16.
Led International League third basemen in putouts with 98, errors with 25 and total chances with 332 in 1984.

Year	Club	League	Pos.	G.	AB.	R.	H.	2B.	3B.	HR.	RBI.	B.A.	PO.	A.	E.	F.A.
1981—Winston-Salem	Carol.	OF-SS	64	252	43	61	9	3	6	40	.242	137	23	8	.952
1982—Bristol	East.	OF-SS	135	460	86	112	23	3	13	58	.243	275	11	9	.969
1983—New Britain	East.	3-O-S-P	132	456	83	112	24	7	7	62	.246	145	207	17	.954
1984—Pawtucket	Int.	3B-OF-SS	131	444	80	119	21	2	17	62	.268	141	211	26	.931
1985—Boston	Amer.	OF-3B-SS	133	371	52	98	14	3	5	30	.264	253	6	7	.974
1986—Bos.†-Chi.	Amer.	OF-3B-1B	101	247	30	56	9	3	1	20	.227	175	11	4	.979
1986—Buffalo	A. A.	3-S-O-1	20	74	18	22	5	1	3	8	.297	36	41	4	.951
Major League Totals—2 Years				234	618	82	154	23	6	6	50	.249	428	17	11	.976

Selected by Boston Red Sox' organization in 1st round (19th player selected) of free-agent draft, June 8, 1981.
†Traded to Chicago White Sox for Pitcher Tom Seaver, June 29, 1986.

PITCHING RECORD

Year	Club	League	G.	IP.	W.	L.	Pct.	H.	R.	ER.	SO.	BB.	ERA.
1983—New Britain	Eastern	3	3⅔	1	0	1.000	3	1	1	2	1	2.45

SHANE LEE MACK

Born December 7, 1963, at Los Angeles, Calif.
Height, 6.00. Weight, 185.
Throws and bats righthanded.
Attended University of California, Los Angeles, Calif.

Tied for Texas League lead in being hit by pitch with 7 in 1986.
Led Texas League outfielders in double plays with 4 in 1986.
Member of 1984 U.S. Olympic baseball team.
Named outfielder on THE SPORTING NEWS College Baseball All-America Team, 1984.

Year	Club	League	Pos.	G.	AB.	R.	H.	2B.	3B.	HR.	RBI.	B.A.	PO.	A.	E.	F.A.
1985—Beaumont	Texas	OF-3B	125	430	59	112	23	3	6	55	.260	252	12	7	.974
1986—Beaumont	Texas	OF	115	452	61	127	26	3	15	68	.281	255	•14	8	.971
1986—Las Vegas	P. C.	OF	19	69	13	25	1	6	0	6	.362	43	0	2	.956

Selected by Kansas City Royals' organization in 4th round of free-agent draft, June 8, 1981.
Selected by San Diego Padres' organization in 1st round (11th player selected) of free-agent draft, June 4, 1984.

MICHAEL ANTHONY MADDEN
(Mike)

Born January 13, 1958, at Denver, Colo.
Height, 6.01. Weight, 190.
Throws and bats lefthanded.
Attended University of Northern Colorado, Greeley, Colo.

Year	Club	League	G.	IP.	W.	L.	Pct.	H.	R.	ER.	SO.	BB.	ERA.
1979—Burlington	Midwest	5	32	2	1	.667	21	11	7	23	15	1.97
1980—Stockton	California	29	134	12	4	.750	88	46	29	92	63	•1.95
1981—El Paso†	Texas	22	125	6	8	.429	154	94	79	140	40	5.69
1982—Vancouver‡	P. Coast	18	80⅔	3	8	.273	92	69	63	41	60	7.03
1983—Houston§	National	28	94⅔	9	5	.643	76	37	33	44	45	3.14
1983—Tucson	P. Coast	4	22	1	1	.500	25	9	9	15	8	3.68
1984—Houston	National	17	40⅔	2	3	.400	46	27	25	29	35	5.53
1984—Tucson	P. Coast	11	60⅔	4	3	.571	60	29	29	38	30	4.30
1985—Tucson x	P. Coast	6	23	2	0	1.000	24	11	9	14	11	3.52
1985—Houston	National	13	19	0	0	.000	29	15	9	16	11	4.26
1986—Houston yz	National	13	39⅔	1	2	.333	47	20	18	30	22	4.08
Major League Totals—4 Years			71	194	12	10	.545	198	99	85	119	113	3.94

Selected by Pittsburgh Pirates' organization in 3rd round of free-agent draft, June 8, 1976.

Signed as free agent by Milwaukee Brewers' organization, July 18, 1979.
†On disabled list, July 9 to August 5, 1981.
‡Traded with Outfielder Kevin Bass and Pitcher Frank DiPino to Houston Astros, September 3, 1982, completing deal in which Houston traded Pitcher Don Sutton to Milwaukee Brewers for three players to be named later, August 30, 1982.
§On disabled list, June 1 to June 22, 1983.
xOn Houston disabled list, April 4 to June 28, 1985; included rehabilitation disability assignment to Tucson, June 9 to June 28, 1985.
yTraded to Philadelphia Phillies' organization for Pitcher Rocky Childress, June 20, 1986; deal voided, June 27, 1986.
zGranted free agency, October 15, 1986; signed by Montreal Expos' organization, December 9, 1986.

MORRIS DeWAYNE MADDEN

Born August 31, 1960, at Laurens, S. C.
Height, 6.00. Weight, 155.
Throws and bats lefthanded.
Attended Spartanburg Methodist College, Spartanburg, S. C.

Year Club	League	G.	IP.	W.	L.	Pct.	H.	R.	ER.	SO.	BB.	ERA.
1979—Lethbridge	Pioneer	13	83	6	1	.857	62	44	27	106	45	2.93
1980—Vero Beach	Florida St.	27	171	11	9	.550	129	79	64	141	*127	3.37
1981—San Antonio	Texas	4	11	0	3	.000	22	17	17	6	14	13.91
1981—Vero Beach	Florida St.	21	146	6	12	.333	148	76	60	108	79	3.70
1982—San Antonio	Texas	4	19	1	1	.500	26	19	18	18	15	8.53
1982—Lodi†	California	12	72⅔	3	7	.300	67	32	21	47	36	2.60
1983—Vero Beach	Florida St.	16	46	2	4	.333	50	33	22	44	25	4.30
1983—San Antonio‡	Texas	27	72⅓	6	5	.545	77	49	44	60	59	5.47
1984—Tampa	Florida St.	29	132	6	9	.400	123	71	64	103	98	4.36
1985—Tampa	Florida St.	23	82½	6	8	.429	76	48	31	78	64	3.39
1985—Vermont§	Eastern	6	32⅓	1	3	.250	25	11	11	31	19	3.06
1986—Glens Falls	Eastern	35	91⅓	7	5	.583	87	52	41	64	55	4.04

Selected by Los Angeles Dodgers' organization in 24th round of free-agent draft, June 5, 1979.
†On disabled list, May 22 to July 4, 1982.
‡Drafted by Indianapolis (Cincinnati Reds' organization), December 6, 1983.
§Granted free agency, October 15, 1985; signed by Nashville (Detroit Tigers' organization), November 23, 1985.

GARRY LEE MADDOX

Born September 1, 1949, at Cincinnati, O.
Height, 6.03. Weight, 190.
Throws and bats righthanded.
Attended Harbor College, Wilmington, Calif.

Tied major league record for most putouts by outfielder, game (12), (12 innings), June 10, 1984.
Major League stolen bases: 1972 (13), 1973 (24), 1974 (21), 1975 (25), 1976 (29), 1977 (22), 1978 (33), 1979 (26), 1980 (25), 1981 (9), 1982 (7), 1983 (7), 1984 (3), 1985 (4). Total—248.
Led National League in sacrifice flies with 8 in 1981.
Led National League outfielders in total chances with 456 in 1976 and 459 in 1978.
Tied for National League lead in double plays by outfielders with 4 in 1981.
Led Pioneer League batters in strikeouts with 68 in 1968.
Led Pioneer League outfielders in double plays with 2 in 1968.
Named outfielder on THE SPORTING NEWS National League All-Star fielding team, 1975 through 1982.

Year Club	League	Pos.	G.	AB.	R.	H.	2B.	3B.	HR.	RBI.	B.A.	PO.	A.	E.	F.A.
1968—Salt Lake City	Pion.	OF	58	206	34	52	11	2	5	29	.252	98	6	*10	.912
1968—Fresno†	Calif.	OF	5	19	2	6	0	0	0	5	.316	7	0	0	1.000
1969-70—						(In Military Service)									
1971—Fresno	Calif.	OF	120	475	105	142	25	5	30	106	.299	215	13	0	.962
1972—Phoenix	P. C.	OF	11	48	16	21	3	2	9	22	.438	22	1	2	.920
1972—San Francisco	Nat.	OF	125	458	62	122	26	7	12	58	.266	279	7	6	.979
1973—San Francisco	Nat.	OF	144	587	81	187	30	10	11	76	.319	370	4	●12	.969
1974—San Francisco	Nat.	OF	135	538	74	153	31	3	8	50	.284	345	3	5	.986
1975—S.F.‡-Phil.§	Nat.	OF	116	426	54	116	26	8	5	50	.272	325	13	5	.985
1976—Philadelphia	Nat.	OF	146	531	75	175	37	6	6	68	.330	*441	10	5	.989
1977—Philadelphia x	Nat.	OF	139	571	85	167	27	10	14	74	.292	383	7	9	.977
1978—Philadelphia	Nat.	OF	155	598	62	172	34	3	11	68	.288	*444	7	8	.983
1979—Philadelphia	Nat.	OF	148	548	70	154	28	6	13	61	.281	433	13	2	.996
1980—Philadelphia	Nat.	OF	143	549	59	142	31	3	11	73	.259	405	7	10	.976
1981—Philadelphia	Nat.	OF	94	323	37	85	7	1	5	40	.263	249	8	6	.977
1982—Philadelphia y	Nat.	OF	119	412	39	117	27	2	8	61	.284	253	8	2	*.992
1983—Philadelphia z	Nat.	OF	97	324	27	89	14	2	4	32	.275	216	1	5	.977
1984—Philadelphia a	Nat.	OF	77	241	29	68	11	0	5	19	.282	160	3	0	1.000
1985—Philadelphia b	Nat.	OF	105	218	22	52	8	1	4	23	.239	143	3	3	.980
1986—Philadelphia cd	Nat.	OF	6	7	1	3	0	0	0	1	.429	1	0	0	1.000
Major League Totals—15 Years			1749	6331	777	1802	337	62	117	754	.285	4447	94	78	.983

Selected by San Francisco Giants' organization in 2nd round of free-agent draft, January 27, 1968.
†On military list, October 31, 1968 through February 21, 1971.
‡Traded to Philadelphia Phillies for First Baseman Willie Montanez, May 4, 1975.
§On disabled list, May 25 to June 30, 1975.
xOn disabled list, August 13 to August 28, 1977.
yOn disabled list, June 20 to July 5 and July 18 to August 5, 1982.
zOn disabled list, June 23 to July 8, 1983.
aOn disabled list, August 3 to August 18 and August 20, 1984 through remainder of season.

bGranted free agency, November 12, 1985; re-signed by Phillies, December 6, 1985.
cOn disabled list, April 23 to May 7, 1986.
dOn voluntarily retired list, May 7, 1986.

DIVISION SERIES RECORD

Year	Club	League	Pos.	G.	AB.	R.	H.	2B.	3B.	HR.	RBI.	B.A.	PO.	A.	E.	F.A.
1981—Philadelphia	....	Nat.	OF	2	3	0	1	1	0	0	0	.333	3	0	0	1.000

CHAMPIONSHIP SERIES RECORD

Tied Championship Series records for most consecutive games, one or more runs batted in, total Series (4); most at bats, four-game Series (19), 1978.

Year	Club	League	Pos.	G.	AB.	R.	H.	2B.	3B.	HR.	RBI.	B.A.	PO.	A.	E.	F.A.
1976—Philadelphia	....	Nat.	OF	3	13	2	3	1	0	0	1	.231	9	0	0	1.000
1977—Philadelphia	....	Nat.	OF	2	7	1	3	0	0	0	2	.429	6	0	0	1.000
1978—Philadelphia	....	Nat.	OF	4	19	1	5	0	0	0	2	.263	16	0	1	.941
1980—Philadelphia	....	Nat.	OF	5	20	2	6	2	0	0	3	.300	23	0	0	1.000
1983—Philadelphia	....	Nat.	OF	3	11	0	3	1	0	0	1	.273	8	0	1	.889
Championship Series Totals—5 Years....				17	70	6	20	4	0	0	9	.286	62	0	2	.969

WORLD SERIES RECORD

Year	Club	League	Pos.	G.	AB.	R.	H.	2B.	3B.	HR.	RBI.	B.A.	PO.	A.	E.	F.A.
1980—Philadelphia	....	Nat.	OF	6	22	1	5	2	0	0	1	.227	11	1	0	1.000
1983—Philadelphia	....	Nat.	PH-OF	4	12	1	3	1	0	1	1	.250	7	0	0	1.000
World Series Totals—2 Years				10	34	2	8	3	0	1	2	.235	18	1	0	1.000

GREGORY ALAN MADDUX
(Greg)

Born April 14, 1966, at San Angelo, Tex.
Height, 6.00. Weight, 150.
Throws and bats righthanded.
Brother of Mike Maddux, pitcher with Philadelphia Phillies.

Led American Association in hit batsmen with 12 and tied for lead in shutouts with 2 in 1986.
Led Appalachian League in hit batsmen with 8 and tied for lead in shutouts with 2 in 1984.

Year	Club	League	G.	IP.	W.	L.	Pct.	H.	R.	ER.	SO.	BB.	ERA.
1984—Pikeville.................................	Ap'lachian	14	85⅔	6	2	.750	63	35	25	62	41	2.63
1985—Peoria.................................	Midland	27	186	13	9	.591	176	86	66	125	52	3.19
1986—Pittsfield.................................	Eastern	8	62⅔	4	3	.571	49	22	19	35	15	2.69
1986—Iowa.................................	Am. Assoc.	18	128⅓	10	1	*.909	127	49	43	65	30	3.02
1986—Chicago.................................	National	6	31	2	4	.333	44	20	19	20	11	5.52
Major League Totals—1 Year..............................		6	31	2	4	.333	44	20	19	20	11	5.52

Selected by Chicago Cubs' organization in 2nd round of free-agent draft, June 4, 1984.

MICHAEL AUSLEY MADDUX
(Mike)

Born August 27, 1961, at Dayton, O.
Height, 6.02. Weight, 180.
Throws and bats righthanded.
Brother of Greg Maddux, pitcher with Chicago Cubs.

Year	Club	League	G.	IP.	W.	L.	Pct.	H.	R.	ER.	SO.	BB.	ERA.
1982—Bend..................................	Northwest	11	65⅓	3	6	.333	68	35	29	59	26	3.99
1983—Spartanburg..................................	S. Atlantic	13	84⅓	4	6	.400	98	62	51	85	47	5.44
1983—Peninsula..................................	Carolina	14	99⅓	8	4	.667	92	46	40	78	35	3.62
1983—Reading..................................	Eastern	1	3	0	0	.000	4	2	2	2	1	6.00
1984—Reading..................................	Eastern	20	116	3	●12	.200	143	82	65	77	49	5.04
1984—Portland..................................	P. Coast	8	44⅔	2	4	.333	58	32	29	22	17	5.84
1985—Portland..................................	P. Coast	27	166	9	12	.429	195	106	98	96	51	5.31
1986—Portland..................................	P. Coast	12	84	5	2	.714	70	26	22	65	22	2.36
1986—Philadelphia	National	16	78	3	7	.300	88	56	47	44	34	5.42
Major League Totals—1 Year..............................		16	78	3	7	.300	88	56	47	44	34	5.42

Selected by Cincinnati Reds' organization in 36th round of free-agent draft, June 5, 1979.
Selected by Philadelphia Phillies' organization in 5th round of free-agent draft, June 7, 1982.

CHARLES SCOTT MADISON
(Scotti)

Born September 12, 1958, at Pensacola, Fla.
Height, 5.11. Weight, 185.
Throws right and bats left and righthanded.
Attended Vanderbilt University, Nashville, Tenn.

Led American Association in slugging percentage with .590 in 1985.
Named catcher on THE SPORTING NEWS College Baseball All-America Team, 1980.

Year	Club	League	Pos.	G.	AB.	R.	H.	2B.	3B.	HR.	RBI.	B.A.	PO.	A.	E.	F.A.
1980—Orlando	South.	C-1B-OF	81	282	31	65	9	4	6	32	.230	185	24	4	.981
1981—Visalia†	Calif.	*C-1B	133	459	109	157	*32	3	26	110	.342	542	66	11	*.982

Year Club	League	Pos.	G.	AB.	R.	H.	2B.	3B.	HR.	RBI.	B.A.	PO.	A.	E.	F.A.
1982—San Antonio‡	Texas	3-C-2-O	88	294	39	69	11	2	7	35	.235	167	75	16	.938
1982—Albuquerque	P. C.	C	11	36	5	8	1	0	0	2	.222	6	0	0	1.000
1983—San Antonio	Texas	C-3B	80	259	54	79	11	4	11	57	.305	423	55	11	.978
1983—Albuquerque§	P. C.	C-3B	23	65	10	19	2	0	2	12	.292	103	18	7	.945
1984—Birmingham	South.	C-1-3-2	133	473	82	129	23	4	15	83	.273	773	109	18	.980
1985—Birmingham	South	C-1B-3B	37	121	28	39	8	1	5	25	.322	205	27	2	.991
1985—Nashville	A. A.	C-3-1-O	86	317	59	108	23	4	16	54	*.341	352	74	11	.975
1985—Detroit	Amer.	C	6	11	0	0	0	0	0	1	.000	1	0	0	1.000
1986—Detroit x	Amer.	3B	2	7	0	0	0	0	0	1	.000	1	1	1	.667
1986—Nashville yz	A. A.	1-3-C-O	106	354	52	91	15	4	10	41	.257	425	95	10	.981
Major League Totals—2 Years			8	18	0	0	0	0	0	2	.000	2	1	1	.750

Selected by Cincinnati Reds' organization in 35th round of free-agent draft, June 8, 1976.
Selected by San Francisco Giants' organization in 10th round of free-agent draft, June 5, 1979.
Selected by Minnesota Twins' organization in 3rd round of free-agent draft, June 3, 1980.
†Traded with Pitcher Paul Voigt to Los Angeles Dodgers' organization for Pitcher Bobby Castillo and Outfielder Bobby Mitchell, January 7, 1982.
‡On disabled list, June 25 to July 16, 1982.
§Sold to Birmingham (Detroit Tigers' organization), March 19, 1984.
xOn disabled list, March 26 to April 29, 1986.
yOn suspended list, May 15 to May 17, 1986.
zGranted free agency, October 15, 1986.

BILL MADLOCK JR.

Born January 12, 1951, at Memphis, Tenn.
Height, 5.11. Weight, 206.
Throws and bats righthanded.
Attended Southeastern Community College, Keokuk, Ia.

Collected six hits in one game, July 26, 1975 (10 innings).
Major League stolen bases: 1973 (3), 1974 (11), 1975 (9), 1976 (15), 1977 (13), 1978 (16), 1979 (32), 1980 (16), 1981 (18), 1982 (18), 1983 (3), 1984 (3), 1985 (10), 1986 (3). Total—170.
Tied for National League lead in grounding into double plays with 25 in 1977.
Tied for National League lead in being hit by pitch with 11 in 1976.
Led National League third basemen in errors with 24 in 1986.
Led Pacific Coast League in total bases with 268 in 1973.
Led Eastern League third basemen in errors with 33 in 1971.
Led New York-Pennsylvania League shortstops in putouts with 107 in 1970.
Named third baseman on THE SPORTING NEWS National League All-Star Team, 1975.

Year Club	League	Pos.	G.	AB.	R.	H.	2B.	3B.	HR.	RBI.	B.A.	PO.	A.	E.	F.A.
1970—Geneva	NYP	SS-3B	66	234	44	63	5	1	6	29	.269	123	132	25	.911
1971—Pittsfield	East.	3-2-S-O	112	376	62	88	14	2	10	37	.234	100	214	34	.902
1972—Pittsfield	East.	2B-3B	42	131	29	43	13	3	4	26	.328	81	88	7	.960
1972—Denver	A. A.	3B-2B	26	61	7	13	3	0	1	9	.213	10	30	2	.952
1973—Spokane	P. C.	2-3-O	123	491	*119	166	22	7	22	90	.338	172	245	25	.943
1973—Texas†	Amer.	3B	21	77	16	27	5	3	1	5	.351	13	32	4	.918
1974—Chicago‡	Nat.	3B	128	453	65	142	21	5	9	54	.313	84	229	18	.946
1975—Chicago	Nat.	3B	130	514	77	182	29	7	7	64	*.354	79	250	20	.943
1976—Chicago§	Nat.	3B	142	514	68	174	36	1	15	84	*.339	107	234	14	.961
1977—San Francisco	Nat.	3B-2B	140	533	70	161	28	1	12	46	.302	101	234	18	.949
1978—San Francisco	Nat.	2B-1B	122	447	76	138	26	3	15	44	.309	234	300	14	.974
1979—S. F.x-Pitts.	Nat.	3B-2B-1B	154	560	85	167	26	5	14	85	.298	209	297	14	.973
1980—Pittsburgh y	Nat.	3B-1B	137	494	62	137	22	4	10	53	.277	159	217	7	.982
1981—Pittsburgh	Nat.	3B	82	279	35	95	23	1	6	45	*.341	50	147	9	.956
1982—Pittsburgh	Nat.	3B-1B	154	568	92	181	33	3	19	95	.319	114	267	18	.955
1983—Pittsburgh	Nat.	3B	130	473	68	153	21	0	12	68	*.323	59	193	11	.958
1984—Pittsburgh z	Nat.	3B-1B	103	403	38	102	16	0	4	44	.253	76	176	15	.944
1985—Pitts. a-L.A.	Nat.	3B-1B	144	513	69	141	27	1	12	56	.275	155	243	19	.954
1986—Los Angeles d	Nat.	3B-1B	111	379	38	106	17	0	10	60	.280	79	171	26	.906
American League Totals—1 Year			21	77	16	27	5	3	1	5	.351	13	32	4	.918
National League Totals—13 Years			1677	6130	843	1879	325	31	145	798	.307	1506	2958	203	.957
Major League Totals—14 Years			1698	6207	859	1906	330	34	146	803	.307	1519	2990	207	.956

Selected by St. Louis Cardinals' organization in 14th round of free-agent draft, June 5, 1969.
Selected by Washington Senators' organization in secondary phase of free-agent draft, January 17, 1970.
†Traded with Infielder-Outfielder Vic Harris to Chicago Cubs for Pitcher Ferguson Jenkins, October 25, 1973.
‡On disabled list, May 4 to June 4, 1974.
§Traded with Infielder Rob Sperring to San Francisco Giants for Outfielder Bobby Murcer, Infielder Steve Ontiveros and Pitcher Andrew Muhlstock, February 11, 1977.
xTraded with Third Baseman Lenny Randle and Pitcher Dave Roberts to Pittsburgh Pirates for Pitchers Ed Whitson, Fred Breining and Al Holland, June 28, 1979.
yOn suspended list, June 5 to June 20, 1980.
zOn disabled list, August 13, 1984 through remainder of season.
aTraded to Los Angeles Dodgers for three players to be named later, August 31, 1985; Pittsburgh Pirates acquired Outfielder R. J. Reynolds, September 3, 1985, and Outfielder Cecil Espy and First Baseman Sid Bream, September 9, 1985, to complete deal.
bOn disabled list, April 25 to May 10 and June 25 to July 15, 1986.

CHAMPIONSHIP SERIES RECORD

Established National League Championship Series records for highest slugging average (.750), most home runs (3), most total bases (18) and most runs batted in (7), six-game Series, 1985.

Year Club	League	Pos.	G.	AB.	R.	H.	2B.	3B.	HR.	RBI.	B.A.	PO.	A.	E.	F.A.
1979—Pittsburgh...............	Nat.	3B	3	12	1	3	0	0	1	2	.250	1	7	0	1.000
1985—Los Angeles	Nat.	3B	6	24	5	8	1	0	3	7	.333	6	9	0	1.000
Championship Series Totals—2 Years.....			9	36	6	11	1	0	4	9	.306	7	16	0	1.000

WORLD SERIES RECORD

Tied World Series records for most double plays by third baseman, seven-game Series (4), 1979; fewest chances offered by third baseman, game (0), October 12, 1979.

Year Club	League	Pos.	G.	AB.	R.	H.	2B.	3B.	HR.	RBI.	B.A.	PO.	A.	E.	F.A.
1979—Pittsburgh...............	Nat.	3B	7	24	2	9	1	0	0	3	.375	3	10	1	.929

ALL-STAR GAME RECORD

Year League	Pos.	AB.	R.	H.	2B.	3B.	HR.	RBI.	B.A.	PO.	A.	E.	F.A.
1975—National..	3B	2	0	1	0	0	0	2	.500	0	0	0	.000
1981—National..	3B	1	0	0	0	0	0	0	.000	0	1	0	.000
1983—National..	PH-3B	1	0	0	0	0	0	0	.000	0	0	0	.000
All-Star Game Totals—3 Years..................		4	0	1	0	0	0	2	.250	0	1	0	1.000

ALEXANDER MADRID JR.
(Alex)

Born April 18, 1963, at Springerville, Ariz.
Height, 6.03. Weight, 200.
Throws and bats righthanded.
Attended Yavapai College, Prescott, Ariz.

Tied for Texas League lead in games started by pitchers with 27 in 1986.

Year Club	League	G.	IP.	W.	L.	Pct.	H.	R.	ER.	SO.	BB.	ERA.
1984—Beloit†..	Midwest	22	118	6	7	.462	113	59	55	92	49	4.19
1985—Beloit...	Midwest	19	135⅔	8	5	.615	144	55	43	99	26	2.85
1985—Stockton...	California	8	59⅓	7	0	1.000	53	16	13	52	15	1.97
1986—El Paso..	Texas	27	158⅓	12	9	.571	★213	★119	★106	99	51	6.03

Selected by Chicago Cubs' organization in 2nd round of free-agent draft, January 12, 1982.
Selected by Cincinnati Reds' organization in secondary phase of free-agent draft, June 7, 1982.
Selected by Texas Rangers' organization in secondary phase of free-agent draft, January 11, 1983.
Selected by Milwaukee Brewers' organization in secondary phase of free-agent draft, June 6, 1983.
†On disabled list, June 15 to June 29, 1984.

DAVID JOSEPH MAGADAN
(Dave)

Born September 30, 1962, at Tampa, Fla.
Height, 6.03. Weight, 190.
Throws right and bats lefthanded.
Attended University of Alabama, University, Ala.
Cousin of Lou Piniella, manager of New York Yankees.

Led Texas League in bases on balls received with 106 in 1985.
Led Carolina League in intentional bases on balls received with 10 in 1984.
Led International League third basemen in fielding percentage with .934 and double plays with 31 in 1986.
Led Texas League third basemen in putouts with 87, assists with 275 and total chances with 393 in 1985.
Named designated hitter on THE SPORTING NEWS College Baseball All-America Team, 1983.

Year Club	League	Pos.	G.	AB.	R.	H.	2B.	3B.	HR.	RBI.	B.A.	PO.	A.	E.	F.A.
1983—Columbia	S. Atl.	1B	64	220	41	74	13	1	3	32	.336	520	37	7	.988
1984—Lynchburg†..........	Carol.	1B	112	371	78	130	22	4	0	62	★.350	896	64	16	.984
1985—Jackson	Texas	★3B-1B	134	466	84	144	22	0	0	76	.309	106	276	★31	.925
1986—Tidewater..............	Int.	3B-1B	133	473	68	147	33	6	1	64	.311	78	284	25	.935
1986—New York..............	Nat.	1B	10	18	3	8	0	0	0	3	.444	48	5	0	1.000
Major League Totals—1 Year..................			10	18	3	8	0	0	0	3	.444	48	5	0	1.000

Selected by Boston Red Sox' organization in 12th round of free-agent draft, June 3, 1980.
Selected by New York Mets' organization in 2nd round of free-agent draft, June 6, 1983.
†On disabled list, August 7 to September 10, 1984.

JOSEPH DAVID MAGRANE
(Joe)

Born July 2, 1964, at Des Moines, Ia.
Height, 6.06. Weight, 225.
Throws left and bats righthanded.
Attended University of Arizona, Tucson, Ariz.

Tied for American Association lead in shutouts with 2 and complete games with 8 in 1986.

Year Club	League	G.	IP.	W.	L.	Pct.	H.	R.	ER.	SO.	BB.	ERA.
1985—Johnson City...................	Ap'lachian	6	30	2	1	.667	15	4	2	31	11	0.60
1985—St. Petersburg................	Florida St.	5	34⅔	3	1	.750	21	8	4	17	14	1.04
1986—Arkansas............................	Texas	13	89⅓	8	4	.667	66	29	24	66	31	2.42
1986—Louisville	Am. Assoc.	15	113⅓	9	6	.600	93	34	26	72	33	2.06

Selected by Pittsburgh Pirates' organization in 3rd round of free-agent draft, June 7, 1982.
Selected by St. Louis Cardinals' organization in 1st round (18th player selected) of free-agent draft, June 3, 1985.

MICHAEL JAMES MAHLER

Name pronounced MAY-ler.

(Mickey)

Born July 30, 1952, at Montgomery, Ala.
Height, 6.03. Weight, 190.
Throws left and bats right and lefthanded.
Attended Trinity University, San Antonio, Tex.
Brother of Rick Mahler, pitcher with Atlanta Braves.

Pitched seven-inning, 6-0 no-hit victory against Birmingham, July 25, 1974.
Pitched 7-0 no-hit victory against Toledo, June 1, 1977.
Major League saves: 1985 (1), 1986 (3). Total—4.
Led Pacific Coast League in complete games with 14 in 1980.
Led International League pitchers in games started with 31 in 1977.
Tied for American Association lead in wild pitches with 15 in 1984.
Tied for International League lead in home runs allowed with 15 in 1975.

Year Club	League	G.	IP.	W.	L.	Pct.	H.	R.	ER.	SO.	BB.	ERA.
1974—Savannah	Southern	14	77	8	1	.889	38	13	11	62	35	1.29
1975—Richmond	Int'national	27	166	6	14	.300	167	82	71	129	70	3.85
1976—Richmond	Int'national	17	84	5	9	.357	95	63	54	52	40	5.79
1976—Savannah	Southern	8	53	3	5	.375	44	21	19	38	20	3.23
1977—Richmond	Int'national	31	⋆217	13	10	.565	202	101	85	145	80	3.53
1977—Atlanta	National	5	23	1	2	.333	31	19	16	14	9	6.26
1978—Atlanta	National	34	135	4	11	.267	130	82	70	92	66	4.67
1979—Atlanta†	National	26	100	5	11	.313	123	72	65	71	47	5.85
1980—Portland	P. Coast	25	173	14	8	.636	143	67	51	⋆140	85	2.65
1980—Pittsburgh‡	National	2	1	0	0	.000	4	7	7	1	3	63.00
1981—Salt Lake City§	P. Coast	23	127	10	4	.714	164	75	70	63	47	4.96
1981—California	American	6	6	0	0	.000	1	0	0	5	2	0.00
1982—Spokane x	P. Coast	20	134⅔	9	7	.563	156	90	85	116	75	5.68
1982—California	American	6	8	2	0	1.000	9	1	1	5	6	1.13
1983—Edmonton yza	P. Coast	1	5	1	0	1.000	3	2	2	3	2	3.60
1984—Louisville b	Am. Assoc.	26	153⅓	8	12	.400	149	83	73	142	88	4.28
1985—Indianapolis-Nashville	Am. Assoc.	14	98	7	2	.778	93	38	35	92	39	3.21
1985—Montreal c	National	9	48⅓	1	4	.200	40	22	19	32	24	3.54
1985—Detroit d	American	3	20⅔	1	2	.333	19	8	4	14	4	1.74
1986—Texas e-Toronto	American	31	64	0	2	.000	72	31	29	28	29	4.08
1986—Oklahoma City f	Am. Assoc.	6	35⅔	1	4	.200	38	20	19	20	17	4.79
National League Totals—5 Years		76	307⅓	11	28	.282	328	202	177	210	149	5.18
American League Totals—4 Years		46	98⅔	3	4	.429	101	40	34	52	41	3.10
Major League Totals—8 Years		122	406	14	32	.304	429	242	211	262	190	4.68

Selected by Atlanta Braves' organization in 10th round of free-agent draft, June 5, 1974.
†Released, March 29, 1980; signed by Pittsburgh Pirates' organization, April 10, 1980.
‡Traded with Catcher Ed Ott to California Angels for First Baseman Jason Thompson, April 1, 1981.
§On suspended list, April 14, 1981.
xOn suspended list, August 5 and August 6, 1982.
yOn California disabled list, April 6, 1983 through remainder of season; included rehabilitation disability assignment to Edmonton, April 9 to April 28, 1983.
zReleased, November 8, 1983; signed by Tidewater (New York Mets' organization), January 25, 1984.
aReleased, March 16, 1984; signed by Louisville (St. Louis Cardinals' organization), March 17, 1984.
bTraded to Montreal Expos for a player to be named later, February 6, 1985; Louisville (St. Louis Cardinals' organization) purchased Infielder Tom Lawless to complete deal, March 25, 1985.
cReleased, July 23, 1985; signed by Nashville (Detroit Tigers' organization), August 3, 1985.
dReleased, October 9, 1985; signed by Texas Rangers, January 16, 1986.
eSold to Toronto Blue Jays, September 1, 1986.
fReleased, October 8, 1986.

RICHARD KEITH MAHLER

Name pronounced MAY-ler.

(Rick)

Born August 5, 1953, at Austin, Tex.
Height, 6.01. Weight, 202.
Throws and bats righthanded.
Attended Trinity University, San Antonio, Tex.
Brother of Mickey Mahler, pitcher with Atlanta Braves,
Pittsburgh Pirates, California Angels, Montreal Expos, Detroit Tigers,
Texas Rangers and Toronto Blue Jays, 1977 through 1982, 1985 and 1986.

Established major league record for most game-winning runs batted in by pitcher, season (3), 1985.
Major League saves: 1981 (2).
Led National League pitchers in games started with 39 in 1985 and tied for lead with 39 in 1986.

Year Club	League	G.	IP.	W.	L.	Pct.	H.	R.	ER.	SO.	BB.	ERA.
1975—Kingsport	Ap'lachian	26	64	2	2	.500	52	23	21	58	26	2.95
1976—Greenwood	W. Carol.	31	105	6	6	.500	96	49	34	68	49	2.91
1977—Savannah	Southern	17	86	6	2	.750	71	31	22	53	38	2.30
1977—Richmond	Int'national	14	40	0	2	.000	45	29	27	25	23	6.08
1978—Richmond	Int'national	32	126	9	5	.643	130	65	55	66	53	3.93
1979—Richmond	Int'national	24	54	4	6	.400	46	26	20	40	18	3.33

Year—Club	League	G.	IP.	W.	L.	Pct.	H.	R.	ER.	SO.	BB.	ERA.
1979—Atlanta	National	15	22	0	0	.000	28	16	15	12	11	6.14
1980—Richmond	Int'national	29	188	12	6	.667	172	68	54	101	80	2.59
1980—Atlanta	National	2	4	0	0	.000	2	1	1	1	0	2.25
1981—Atlanta	National	34	112	8	6	.571	109	41	35	54	43	2.81
1982—Atlanta	National	39	205⅓	9	10	.474	213	105	96	105	62	4.21
1983—Atlanta	National	10	14⅓	0	0	.000	16	8	8	7	9	5.02
1983—Richmond	In'national	24	162⅔	12	7	.632	165	102	89	103	85	4.92
1984—Atlanta	National	38	222	13	10	.565	209	86	77	106	62	3.12
1985—Atlanta	National	39	266⅔	17	15	.531	*272	116	103	107	79	3.48
1986—Atlanta	National	39	237⅔	14	*18	.438	*283	*139	*129	137	95	4.88
Major League Totals—8 Years		216	1084	61	59	.508	1132	512	464	529	361	3.85

Signed as free agent by Atlanta Braves' organization, June 16, 1975.

CHAMPIONSHIP SERIES RECORD

Year—Club	League	G.	IP.	W.	L.	Pct.	H.	R.	ER.	SO.	BB.	ERA.
1982—Atlanta	National	1	1⅔	0	0	.000	3	0	0	0	2	0.00

CANDIDO MALDONADO (GUADARRAMA)
(Candy)

Born September 5, 1960, at Humacao, Puerto Rico.
Height, 5.11. Weight, 195.
Throws and bats righthanded.

Major League stolen bases: 1985 (1), 1986 (4). Total—5.
Led California League in total bases with 247 in 1980.
Tied for Pioneer League lead in sacrifice flies with 6 in 1978.
Named California League co-Most Valuable Player, 1980.

Year—Club	League	Pos.	G.	AB.	R.	H.	2B.	3B.	HR.	RBI.	B.A.	PO.	A.	E.	F.A.
1978—Lethbridge	Pion.	OF	57	210	45	61	15	5	12	48	.290	112	6	8	.937
1979—Clinton	Midw.	OF	50	158	25	37	13	1	2	26	.234	81	5	2	.977
1979—Lethbridge	Pion.	OF	59	234	42	70	*20	3	5	33	.299	81	5	4	.956
1980—Lodi†	Calif.	OF	121	456	75	139	27	3	25	*102	.305	211	13	11	.953
1981—Albuquerque	P. C.	OF	126	460	96	154	40	9	21	104	.335	221	21	8	.968
1981—Los Angeles	Nat.	OF	11	12	0	1	0	0	0	0	.083	8	0	0	1.000
1982—Albuquerque	P. C.	OF	138	541	91	163	28	6	24	96	.301	303	15	10	.970
1982—Los Angeles	Nat.	OF	6	4	0	0	0	0	0	0	.000	5	0	0	1.000
1983—Los Angeles	Nat.	OF	42	62	5	12	1	1	1	6	.194	26	0	0	1.000
1983—Albuquerque	P. C.	OF-3B	38	144	23	46	6	1	4	20	.319	66	11	4	.951
1984—Los Angeles	Nat.	OF-3B	116	254	25	68	14	0	5	28	.268	124	5	8	.942
1985—Los Angeles‡	Nat.	OF	121	213	20	48	7	1	5	19	.225	121	6	2	.984
1986—San Francisco	Nat.	OF-1B	133	405	49	102	31	3	18	85	.252	161	11	3	.983
Major League Totals—6 Years			429	950	99	231	53	5	29	138	.243	445	22	13	.973

Signed as free agent by Los Angeles Dodgers' organization, June 6, 1978.
†On disabled list, August 16 to September 16, 1980.
‡Traded to San Francisco Giants for Catcher Alex Trevino, December 11, 1985.

CHAMPIONSHIP SERIES RECORD

Year—Club	League	Pos.	G.	AB.	R.	H.	2B.	3B.	HR.	RBI.	B.A.	PO.	A.	E.	F.A.
1983—Los Angeles	Nat.	PH	2	2	0	0	0	0	0	0	.000	0	0	0	.000
1985—Los Angeles	Nat.	OF-PH	4	7	0	1	0	0	0	1	.143	4	0	1	.800
Championship Series Totals—2 Years			6	9	0	1	0	0	0	1	.111	4	0	1	.800

ROBIN DALE MALLICOAT
(Rob)

Born November 16, 1964, at St. Helens, Ore.
Height, 6.03. Weight, 178.
Throws and bats lefthanded.
Attended Taft College, Taft, Calif.

Year—Club	League	G.	IP.	W.	L.	Pct.	H.	R.	ER.	SO.	BB.	ERA.
1984—Auburn	NYP	1	5	0	0	.000	8	3	3	6	3	5.40
1984—Asheville	S. Atlantic	11	64⅓	3	4	.429	49	30	28	57	36	3.92
1985—Osceola	Florida St.	26	178⅔	*16	6	.727	119	41	27	*158	74	1.36
1986—Tucson	P. Coast	3	14	0	2	.000	18	14	10	9	8	6.43
1986—Columbus	Southern	10	58	6	6	.000	61	38	31	52	45	4.81

Selected by Detroit Tigers' organization in 8th round of free-agent draft, June 6, 1983.
Selected by Houston Astros' organization in secondary phase of free-agent draft, January 17, 1984.

RICHARD EUGENE MANNING
(Rick)

Born September 2, 1954, at Niagara Falls, N. Y.
Height, 6.01. Weight, 180.
Throws right and bats lefthanded.

Tied major league records for most strikeouts, nine-inning game (5), May 15, 1977; most putouts by outfielder, game (12), July 11, 1983, 15 innings; fewest double plays by outfielder, season, 150 or more games (0), 1983.

Tied American League record for most chances accepted by outfielder, game (12), July 11, 1983, 15 innings.
Major League stolen bases: 1975 (19), 1976 (16), 1977 (9), 1978 (12), 1979 (30), 1980 (12), 1981 (25), 1982 (12), 1983 (18), 1984 (5), 1985 (1), 1986 (5). Total—164.
Led American League outfielders in total chances with 478 in 1983.
Named outfielder on THE SPORTING NEWS American League All-Star fielding team, 1976.
Received reported $65,000 bonus to sign with Cleveland Indians, 1972.

Year Club	League	Pos.	G.	AB.	R.	H.	2B.	3B.	HR.	RBI.	B.A.	PO.	A.	E.	F.A.
1972—Reno	Calif.	OF-SS	57	216	45	52	4	4	3	23	.241	71	45	19	.859
1973—Reno	Calif.	OF-SS	137	486	*101	136	40	*14	6	67	.280	184	8	7	.965
1974—Oklahoma City.....	A. A.	OF	122	402	58	108	16	5	5	39	.269	207	12	8	.965
1975—Oklahoma City.....	A. A.	OF	30	117	18	37	5	2	0	15	.316	62	4	0	1.000
1975—Cleveland..............	Amer.	OF	120	480	69	137	16	5	3	35	.285	331	12	9	.974
1976—Cleveland..............	Amer.	OF	138	552	73	161	24	7	6	43	.292	359	8	5	.987
1977—Cleveland†............	Amer.	OF	68	252	33	57	7	3	5	18	.226	191	2	2	.990
1978—Cleveland..............	Amer.	OF	148	566	65	149	27	3	3	50	.263	377	7	2	.995
1979—Cleveland..............	Amer.	OF	144	560	67	145	12	2	3	51	.259	417	9	6	.986
1980—Cleveland..............	Amer.	OF	140	471	55	110	17	4	3	52	.234	379	7	4	.990
1981—Cleveland..............	Amer.	OF	103	360	47	88	15	3	4	33	.244	305	6	4	.987
1982—Cleveland‡............	Amer.	OF	152	562	71	152	18	2	8	44	.270	387	10	9	.978
1983—Clev.§-Milw........	Amer.	OF	158	569	60	140	20	4	4	43	.246	*471	2	5	.990
1984—Milwaukee............	Amer.	OF	119	341	53	85	10	5	7	31	.249	231	2	3	.987
1985—Milwaukee x.........	Amer.	OF	79	216	19	47	9	1	2	18	.218	160	2	4	.976
1986—Milwaukee............	Amer.	OF	89	205	31	52	7	3	8	27	.254	155	3	2	.988
Major League Totals—12 Years			1458	5134	643	1323	182	42	56	445	.258	3763	70	55	.986

Selected by Cleveland Indians' organization in 1st round (second player selected) of free-agent draft, June 6, 1972.
†On disabled list, June 21 to September 1, 1977.
‡Granted free agency, November 10, 1982; re-signed with Indians, December 15, 1982.
§Traded with Pitcher Rick Waits to Milwaukee Brewers for Outfielder Gorman Thomas and Pitchers Jamie Easterly and Ernie Camacho, June 6, 1983.
xOn disabled list, April 28 to May 17, 1985.

REYES FRED ELOY MANRIQUE
(Fred)

Name pronounced Man-ree-KEE.
Born November 5, 1961, at Bolivar, Venezuela.
Height, 6.01. Weight, 175.
Throws and bats righthanded.

Major League stolen bases: 1986 (1).
Led American Association in grounding into double plays with 19 in 1986.
Led American Association shortstops in errors with 25 and double plays with 86 in 1986.
Led International League second basemen in errors with 22 in 1983 and 24 in 1984.

Year Club	League	Pos.	G.	AB.	R.	H.	2B.	3B.	HR.	RBI.	B.A.	PO.	A.	E.	F.A.
1979—Dunedin	Fla. St.	SS	5	15	0	2	0	0	0	0	.133	4	7	3	.786
1979—Medicine Hat.......	Pion.	SS	66	270	47	81	8	●10	2	30	.300	103	208	*37	.894
1980—Kinston	Carol.	SS-OF	111	390	49	108	9	5	7	50	.277	120	192	37	.894
1981—Knoxville†	South.	SS	115	469	62	131	15	6	5	42	.279	161	330	45	.916
1981—Toronto	Amer.	SS-3B	14	28	1	4	0	0	0	1	.143	10	27	3	.925
1982—Syracuse‡	Int.	2B-3B-SS	103	362	41	91	9	2	4	37	.251	186	255	24	.948
1983—Syracuse	Int.	2-S-3-O	128	485	55	130	22	8	10	50	.268	211	351	36	.940
1984—Syracuse	Int.	2B-SS-3B	129	517	63	146	15	5	6	45	.282	233	389	28	.957
1984—Toronto§	Amer.	2B	10	9	0	3	0	0	0	1	.333	5	10	1	.938
1985—Indianapolis.........	A. A.	3B-SS-2B	123	409	46	98	21	5	8	37	.240	126	249	19	.952
1985—Montreal x	Nat.	2B3-SS-2B	9	13	5	4	1	1	1	1	.308	5	10	0	1.000
1986—Louisville.............	A. A.	SS-2B	133	520	79	148	19	6	9	51	.285	208	421	26	.960
1986—St. Louis y............	Nat.	3B-2B	13	17	2	3	0	0	1	1	.176	1	3	0	1.000
American League Totals—2 Years			24	37	1	7	0	0	0	2	.189	15	37	4	.929
National League Totals—2 Years............			22	30	7	7	1	1	2	2	.233	6	13	0	1.000
Major League Totals—4 Years.................			46	67	8	14	1	1	2	4	.209	21	50	4	.947

Signed as free agent by Toronto Blue Jays' organization, November 24, 1978.
†On disabled list, April 9 to April 19, 1981.
‡On disabled list, June 27 to July 12, 1982.
§Sold to Montreal Expos, April 7, 1985.
xTraded to St. Louis Cardinals for Catcher Tom Nieto, March 31, 1986.
yTraded to Chicago White Sox for Pitcher Bill Dawley, December 22, 1986.

JOSIA MANZANILLO

Born October 16, 1967, at San Pedro de Macoris, D. R.
Height, 5.11. Weight, 150.
Throws and bats righthanded.

Year Club	League	G.	IP.	W.	L.	Pct.	H.	R.	ER.	SO.	BB.	ERA.
1983—Elmira...............	NYP	12	38⅓	1	5	.667	52	44	34	19	20	7.98
1984—Elmira...............	NYP	14	25⅔	2	3	.400	27	24	15	26	26	5.26
1985—Greensboro.......	S. Atlantic	7	12	1	1	.500	12	13	13	10	18	9.75
1985—Elmira...............	NYP	19	39⅔	2	4	.333	36	19	17	43	36	3.86
1986—Winter Haven....	Florida St.	23	142⅔	13	5	.722	110	51	36	102	81	2.27

Signed as free agent by Boston Red Sox' organization, January 10, 1983.

MICHAEL ALLEN MARSHALL
(Mike)

Born January 12, 1960, at Libertyville, Ill.
Height, 6.05. Weight, 220.
Throws and bats righthanded.

Major League stolen bases: 1982 (2), 1983 (7), 1984 (4), 1985 (3), 1986 (4). Total—20.
Led California League in total bases with 301 in 1979.
Led Pacific Coast League first basemen in double plays with 136 in 1981.
Led Texas League first basemen in double plays with 120 in 1980.
Named Minor League Player of the Year by THE SPORTING NEWS, 1981.
Named Pacific Coast League Most Valuable Player, 1981.
Named California League co-Most Valuable Player, 1979.

Year Club	League	Pos.	G.	AB.	R.	H.	2B.	3B.	HR.	RBI.	B.A.	PO.	A.	E.	F.A.
1978—Lethbridge	Pion.	1B-OF	65	256	48	83	15	2	12	70	.324	308	16	7	.979
1979—Lodi	Calif.	1B	137	525	101	*186	*37	3	24	116	*.354	1173	71	20	.984
1980—San Antonio..........	Texas	1B	134	470	95	151	21	6	16	82	.321	*1157	64	●16	.987
1981—Albuquerque	P. C.	1B	128	467	*114	174	25	7	*34	*137	*.373	1127	54	9	.992
1981—Los Angeles	Nat.	1B-3B-OF	14	25	2	5	3	0	0	1	.200	14	2	0	1.000
1982—Albuquerque	P. C.	OF-1B-3B	66	255	74	99	20	1	14	58	.388	113	3	4	.966
1982—Los Angeles	Nat.	OF-1B	49	95	10	23	3	0	5	9	.242	122	5	2	.984
1983—Los Angeles	Nat.	OF-1B	140	465	47	132	17	1	17	65	.284	395	21	6	.986
1984—Los Angeles†	Nat.	OF-1B	134	495	68	127	27	0	21	65	.257	331	17	5	.986
1985—Los Angeles‡	Nat.	OF-1B	135	518	72	152	27	2	28	95	.293	265	12	4	.986
1986—Los Angeles§........	Nat.	OF	103	330	47	77	11	0	19	53	.233	149	8	6	.963
Major League Totals—6 Years................			575	1928	246	516	88	3	90	288	.268	1276	65	23	.983

Selected by Los Angeles Dodgers' organization in 6th round of free-agent draft, June 6, 1978.
†On disabled list, May 13 to June 3, 1984.
‡On disabled list, June 20 to July 18, 1985.
§On disabled list, July 20 to August 4, 1986.

DIVISION SERIES RECORD

Year Club	League	Pos.	G.	AB.	R.	H.	2B.	3B.	HR.	RBI.	B.A.	PO.	A.	E.	F.A.
1981—Los Angeles	Nat.	PH	1	1	0	0	0	0	0	0	.000	0	0	0	.000

CHAMPIONSHIP SERIES RECORD

Year Club	League	Pos.	G.	AB.	R.	H.	2B.	3B.	HR.	RBI.	B.A.	PO.	A.	E.	F.A.
1983—Los Angeles	Nat.	1B-OF	4	15	1	2	1	0	1	2	.133	22	2	0	1.000
1985—Los Angeles	Nat.	OF	6	23	1	5	2	0	1	3	.217	8	0	0	1.000
Championship Series Totals—2 Years.....			10	38	2	7	3	0	2	5	.184	30	2	0	1.000

ALL-STAR GAME RECORD

Member of National League All-Star Team in 1984; did not play.

ALEXIS DeJESUS MARTE (PEGUERO)
(Alex)

Born December 12, 1962, at Santo Domingo, D.R.
Height, 6.00. Weight, 160.
Throws and bats lefthanded.

Led Southern League in stolen bases with 64 and caught stealing with 21 in 1985.
Led Gulf Coast League in stolen bases with 50 in 1981.

Year Club	League	Pos.	G.	AB.	R.	H.	2B.	3B.	HR.	RBI.	B.A.	PO.	A.	E.	F.A.
1981—Bradenton Jays....	Gulf C.	OF	49	157	35	46	4	2	0	15	.293	92	5	4	.960
1981—Florence	S. Atl.	OF	14	51	9	16	0	0	0	0	.314	18	0	2	.900
1982—Florence†	S. Atl.	OF-1B	83	264	47	67	8	3	1	22	.254	102	4	4	.964
1983—Kinston‡...............	Carol.	OF	116	409	53	105	7	3	2	36	.257	180	13	8	.960
1984—Visalia	Calif.	OF	127	510	80	140	11	5	0	30	.275	286	7	6	.980
1985—Orlando	South.	OF	141	534	*117	*171	15	9	0	33	.320	320	*18	12	.966
1986—Toledo	Int.	OF	36	94	13	19	0	0	1	3	.202	55	1	2	.966
1986—Orlando	South.	OF	70	284	55	91	7	2	1	28	.320	142	11	3	.981

Signed as free agent by Toronto Blue Jays' organization, May 13, 1980.
†On disabled list, April 20 to May 10 and May 18 to June 2, 1982.
‡Drafted by Orlando (Minnesota Twins' organization), December 6, 1983.

JOSEPH MICHAEL MARTIN
(Mike)

Born December 3, 1958, at Portland, Ore.
Height, 6.02. Weight, 193.
Throws right and bats lefthanded.
Attended Linn-Benton Community College, Albany, Ore.;
and Mt. Hood Community College, Gresham, Ore.

Led California League catchers in putouts with 582 and total chances with 699 in 1981.

Year Club	League	Pos.	G.	AB.	R.	H.	2B.	3B.	HR.	RBI.	B.A.	PO.	A.	E.	F.A.
1978—Walla Walla	N'west	C-1B	52	167	19	37	11	0	2	26	.222	127	12	4	.972
1979—Reno†‡	Calif.	C	83	255	38	62	7	0	7	30	.243	439	36	13	.973
1980—Red.-Reno..............	Calif.	C	114	363	48	97	13	1	7	47	.267	430	75	*21	.960

Year Club	League	Pos.	G.	AB.	R.	H.	2B.	3B.	HR.	RBI.	B.A.	PO.	A.	E.	F.A.
1981—Reno	Calif.	*C-1B	112	384	83	119	14	2	28	93	.310	587	91	*26	.963
1982—Amarillo.................	Texas	C	110	373	67	101	14	2	11	63	.271	505	53	10	.982
1983—Beaumont.............	Texas	C-1B	57	220	41	70	21	1	5	32	.318	294	23	11	.966
1983—Las Vegas.............	P. C.	C	36	120	14	31	5	0	3	19	.258	175	17	2	.990
1984—Las Vegas§..........	P. C.	C-1B	71	209	28	54	10	0	6	35	.258	335	15	12	.967
1985—Vancouver xy.......	P. C.	C	77	248	24	57	9	3	1	25	.230	400	40	3	*.993
1986—Pittsfield	East.	C-3B	56	144	10	28	6	0	1	13	.194	219	32	4	.984
1986—Chicago	Nat.	C	8	13	1	1	1	0	0	0	.077	18	5	0	1.000
Major League Totals—1 Year..................			8	13	1	1	1	0	0	0	.077	18	5	0	1.000

Selected by Baltimore Orioles' organization in 15th round of free-agent draft, June 7, 1977.
Selected by San Diego Padres' organization in secondary phase of free-agent draft, January 10, 1978.
†On disabled list, May 15 to May 25, 1979.
‡Loaned to Redwood (Co-op), April 8, 1980; returned, July 17, 1980.
§Granted free agency, October 15, 1984; signed by Vancouver (Milwaukee Brewers' organization), November 13, 1984.
xOn disabled list, August 29 to September 11, 1985.
yTraded to Chicago Cubs for Shortstop Rich Rembielak and Pitcher Larry Whitford, January 13, 1986.

CARLOS ALBERTO MARTINEZ

Born August 11, 1965, at La Guaira, Venezuela.
Height, 6.05. Weight, 175.
Throws and bats righthanded.

Year Club	League	Pos.	G.	AB.	R.	H.	2B.	3B.	HR.	RBI.	B.A.	PO.	A.	E.	F.A.
1984—Sara. Yankees......	Gulf C.	SS	31	91	9	14	1	1	0	4	.154	53	103	14	.918
1985—Fort Lauderdale ..	Fla. St.	SS	93	311	39	77	15	7	6	44	.248	123	254	25	.938
1986—Fort Lauderdale†	Fla. St.	SS	5	16	1	1	0	0	0	0	.063	7	18	0	1.000
1986—Albany‡	East.	SS-3B	69	253	34	70	18	2	8	39	.277	120	161	32	.898
1986—Buffalo...................	A. A.	SS-3B	17	54	6	16	1	0	2	6	.296	24	20	5	.898

Signed as free agent by New York Yankees' organization, November 17, 1983.
†On disabled list, April 11 to May 1, 1986.
‡Traded with Catcher Ron Hassey and a player to be named later to Chicago White Sox for Catcher Joel Skinner, Infielder Wayne Tolleson and Outfielder-Designated Hitter Ron Kittle, July 30, 1986; New York Yankees traded Catcher Bill Lindsey to Chicago organization to complete deal, December 24, 1986.

CARMELO MARTINEZ (SALGADO)

Born July 28, 1960, at Dorado, Puerto Rico.
Height, 6.02. Weight, 210.
Throws and bats righthanded.
Attended Central College of Bayamon, Bayamon, Puerto Rico.
Cousin of Edgar Martinez, third baseman in Seattle Mariners' organization.
Tied major league record by hitting home run in first major league at-bat, August 22, 1983.
Major League stolen bases: 1984 (1), 1986 (1). Total—2.
Tied for National League lead in sacrifice flies with 10 in 1984.
Led American Association first basemen in total chances with 1,283 and tied for lead in double plays with 99 in 1983.
Led Texas League first basemen in putouts with 1,087, total chances with 1,180 and double plays with 102 in 1982.

Year Club	League	Pos.	G.	AB.	R.	H.	2B.	3B.	HR.	RBI.	B.A.	PO.	A.	E.	F.A.
1979—Sarasota Cubs.......	Gulf C.	OF-1B	40	143	18	29	4	0	1	23	.203	139	9	6	.961
1980—Quad Cities...........	Midw.	O-1-3-2-S	128	460	65	118	23	0	12	64	.257	433	99	13	.976
1981—Midland.................	Texas	3-O-2-1	116	392	65	116	22	1	21	84	.296	61	80	24	.855
1982—Midland.................	Texas	1B-OF	131	467	100	156	35	4	27	93	.334	1098	78	17	.986
1983—Iowa	A. A.	*1B-2B	123	458	76	115	25	1	*31	94	.251	*1191	*83	9	.993
1983—Chicago†	Nat.	1B-3B-OF	29	89	8	23	3	0	6	16	.258	233	17	2	.992
1984—San Diego	Nat.	OF-1B	149	488	64	122	28	2	13	66	.250	317	15	8	.976
1985—San Diego‡	Nat.	OF-1B	150	514	64	130	28	1	21	72	.253	302	14	7	.978
1986—San Diego	Nat.	OF-1B-3B	113	244	28	58	10	0	9	25	.238	142	14	2	.987
Major League Totals—4 Years..................			441	1335	164	333	69	3	49	179	.249	994	60	19	.982

Signed as free agent by Chicago Cubs' organization, December 9, 1978.
†Traded with Pitcher Craig Lefferts and Third Baseman Fritz Connally to San Diego Padres for Pitcher Scott Sanderson, December 7, 1983.
‡On disabled list, March 31 to April 15, 1985.

CHAMPIONSHIP SERIES RECORD

Year Club	League	Pos.	G.	AB.	R.	H.	2B.	3B.	HR.	RBI.	B.A.	PO.	A.	E.	F.A.
1984—San Diego	Nat.	OF	5	17	1	3	0	0	0	0	.176	6	0	0	1.000

WORLD SERIES RECORD

Established World Series record for most strikeouts, five-game Series (9), 1984.

Year Club	League	Pos.	G.	AB.	R.	H.	2B.	3B.	HR.	RBI.	B.A.	PO.	A.	E.	F.A.
1984—San Diego	Nat.	OF	5	17	0	3	0	0	0	0	.176	7	0	1	.875

—DID YOU KNOW—

That Milwaukee's Ben Oglivie hit five 1986 home runs and three of those came off Minnesota righthander Bert Blyleven?

DAVID MARTINEZ
(Dave)

Born September 26, 1964, at New York, N.Y.
Height, 5.10, Weight, 160.
Throws and bats lefthanded.
Attended Valencia Community College, Orlando, Fla.

Major League stolen bases: 1986 (4).

Year Club	League	Pos.	G.	AB.	R.	H.	2B.	3B.	HR.	RBI.	B.A.	PO.	A.	E.	F.A.
1983—Quad Cities	Midw.	OF	44	119	17	29	6	2	0	10	.244	47	8	1	.982
1983—Geneva	NYP	OF	64	241	35	63	15	2	5	33	.261	132	6	8	.945
1984—Quad Cities†	Midw.	OF	12	41	6	9	2	2	0	5	.220	13	2	1	.938
1985—Winston-Salem	Carol.	OF	115	386	52	132	14	4	5	54	★.342	206	11	7	.969
1986—Iowa	A. A.	OF	83	318	52	92	11	5	5	32	.289	214	7	2	.991
1986—Chicago	Nat.	OF	53	108	13	15	1	1	1	7	.139	77	2	1	.988
Major League Totals—1 Year			53	108	13	15	1	1	1	7	.139	77	2	1	.988

Selected by Texas Rangers' organization in 40th round of free-agent draft, June 7, 1982.
Selected by Chicago Cubs' organization in secondary phase of free-agent draft, January 11, 1983.
†On disabled list, April 27, 1984 through remainder of season.

DAVID De LEON MARTINEZ

Born September 18, 1963, at Austin, Tex.
Height, 6.02, Weight, 195.
Throws and bats righthanded.
Attended Blinn College, Brenham, Tex.

Tied for Northwest League lead in games started by pitchers with 15 in 1984.

Year Club	League	G.	IP.	W.	L.	Pct.	H.	R.	ER.	SO.	BB.	ERA.
1984—Salem	Northwest	15	90	3	8	.273	88	53	43	62	43	4.30
1985—Quad Cities†	Midwest	18	100⅓	5	7	.417	101	67	56	75	61	5.02
1986—Palm Springs	California	18	94⅓	6	4	.600	106	63	55	41	58	5.25

Selected by California Angels' organization in 1st round (fifth player selected) of free-agent draft, January 17, 1984.
†On disabled list, May 13 to June 14, 1985.

FELIX ANTHONY MARTINEZ
(Tippy)

Born May 31, 1950, at La Junta, Colo.
Height, 5.10, Weight, 175.
Throws and bats lefthanded.
Attended Colorado State University, Fort Collins, Colo.

Major League saves: 1975 (8), 1976 (10), 1977 (9), 1978 (5), 1979 (3), 1980 (10), 1981 (11), 1982 (16), 1983 (21), 1984 (17), 1985 (4), 1986 (1). Total—115.
Led American League in intentional bases on balls issued with 13 in 1984.
Tied for Carolina League lead in saves with 15 and wild pitches with 17 in 1973.

Year Club	League	G.	IP.	W.	L.	Pct.	H.	R.	ER.	SO.	BB.	ERA.
1972—Oneonta	NYP	2	9	1	0	1.000	3	2	2	9	10	2.00
1972—Kinston	Carolina	5	20	0	0	.000	22	10	10	18	13	4.50
1973—Kinston	Carolina	54	105	13	8	.619	74	38	31	160	61	2.66
1974—Syracuse	Int'national	36	64	7	5	.583	49	29	27	70	32	3.80
1974—New York	American	10	13	0	0	.000	14	7	6	10	9	4.15
1975—Syracuse	Int'national	14	110	8	2	.800	91	39	25	105	35	2.05
1975—New York	American	23	37	1	2	.333	27	15	11	20	32	2.68
1976—New York†-Baltimore	American	39	70	5	1	.833	50	19	18	45	42	2.31
1977—Baltimore	American	41	50	5	1	.833	47	17	15	29	27	2.70
1978—Baltimore	American	42	69	3	3	.500	77	41	37	57	40	4.83
1979—Baltimore	American	39	78	10	3	.769	59	29	25	61	31	2.88
1980—Baltimore	American	53	81	4	4	.500	69	30	27	68	34	3.00
1981—Baltimore	American	37	59	3	3	.500	48	21	19	50	32	2.90
1982—Baltimore	American	76	95	8	8	.500	81	39	36	78	37	3.41
1983—Baltimore‡	American	65	103⅓	9	3	.750	76	30	27	81	37	2.35
1984—Baltimore	American	55	89⅔	4	9	.308	88	42	39	72	51	3.91
1985—Baltimore	American	49	70	3	3	.500	70	48	42	47	37	5.40
1986—Baltimore§	American	14	16	0	2	.000	18	10	10	11	12	5.63
1986—Rochester	Int'national	3	6	0	1	.000	7	4	4	4	3	6.00
Major League Totals—13 Years		543	831	55	42	.567	724	348	312	629	421	3.38

Selected by Washington Senators' organization in 35th round of free-agent draft, June 5, 1969.
Signed as free agent by New York Yankees' organization, July 22, 1972.
†Traded with Pitchers Rudy May, Dave Pagan and Scott McGregor and Catcher Rick Dempsey to Baltimore Orioles for Pitchers Ken Holtzman, Doyle Alexander and Grant Jackson, Catcher Ellie Hendricks and Pitcher Jimmy Freeman, June 15, 1976.
‡On disabled list, July 9 to July 31, 1983.
§On disabled list, April 20 to May 29, June 19 to July 4 and July 14, 1986 through remainder of season; included rehabilitation disability assignment to Rochester, May 19 to May 29, 1986.

CHAMPIONSHIP SERIES RECORD

Year Club	League	G.	IP.	W.	L.	Pct.	H.	R.	ER.	SO.	BB.	ERA.
1983—Baltimore	American	2	6	1	0	1.000	5	0	0	5	3	0.00

Tied World Series record for most saves, five-game Series (2), 1983.

Year Club	League	G.	IP.	W.	L.	Pct.	H.	R.	ER.	SO.	BB.	ERA.
1979—Baltimore	American	3	1⅓	0	0	.000	3	1	1	1	0	6.75
1983—Baltimore	American	3	3	0	0	.000	3	1	1	0	0	3.00
World Series Totals—2 Years		6	4⅓	0	0	.000	6	2	2	1	0	4.15

ALL-STAR GAME RECORD
Member of American League All-Star Team in 1983; did not play.

JOHN ALBERT MARTINEZ
(Buck)

Born November 7, 1948, at Redding, Calif.
Height, 5.11. Weight, 200.
Throws and bats righthanded.
Attended Sacramento City College, Sacramento, Calif., and
Sacramento State College, Sacramento, Calif.

Major League stolen bases: 1975 (1), 1978 (1), 1980 (1), 1981 (1), 1982 (1). Total—5.
Led American Association catchers in fielding percentage with .994 in 1973.

Year Club	League	Pos.	G.	AB.	R.	H.	2B.	3B.	HR.	RBI.	B.A.	PO.	A.	E.	F.A.
1967—Eugene	N'west	●C-OF-3B	77	269	53	96	16	4	2	46	.357	294	●48	8	.977
1968—Spartanburg	W. Car.	C	8	28	6	11	4	0	0	11	.393	51	2	0	1.000
1968—Tidewater†‡	Carol.	C	36	110	10	31	12	1	1	14	.282	272	16	1	.997
1969—Kansas City§	Amer.	C-OF	72	205	14	47	6	1	4	23	.229	292	26	9	.972
1970—Kansas City x	Amer.	C	6	9	1	1	0	0	0	0	.111	20	3	1	.958
1971—Omaha	A. A.	C	75	269	34	77	23	1	5	39	.286	502	37	8	.985
1971—Kansas City	Amer.	C	22	46	3	7	2	0	0	1	.152	84	6	3	.968
1972—Omaha y	A. A.	C	67	195	23	34	9	0	4	12	.174	493	47	6	.989
1973—Omaha	A. A.	C-1B	82	254	24	69	13	0	5	38	.272	522	47	3	.995
1973—Kansas City	Amer.	C	14	32	2	8	1	0	1	6	.250	52	4	2	.966
1974—Kansas City	Amer.	C	43	107	10	23	3	1	1	8	.215	151	16	4	.977
1975—Kansas City	Amer.	C	80	226	15	51	9	2	3	23	.226	361	39	8	.980
1976—Kansas City z	Amer.	C	95	267	24	61	13	3	5	34	.228	420	40	4	.991
1977—Kansas City a	Amer.	C	29	80	3	18	4	0	1	9	.225	133	8	1	.993
1978—Milwaukee	Amer.	C	89	256	26	56	10	1	1	20	.219	327	32	8	.978
1979—Milwaukee	Amer.	C-P	69	196	17	53	8	0	4	26	.270	198	39	8	.967
1980—Milwaukee b	Amer.	C	76	219	16	49	9	0	3	17	.224	293	33	5	.985
1981—Toronto c	Amer.	C	45	128	13	29	8	1	4	21	.227	192	22	2	.991
1982—Toronto	Amer.	C	96	260	26	63	17	0	10	37	.242	382	35	5	.988
1983—Toronto	Amer.	C	88	221	27	56	14	0	10	33	.253	331	25	4	.989
1984—Toronto	Amer.	C	102	232	24	51	13	1	5	37	.220	360	34	2	.995
1985—Toronto d	Amer.	C	42	99	11	16	3	0	4	14	.162	155	16	2	.988
1986—Toronto e	Amer.	C	81	160	13	29	8	0	2	12	.181	289	19	2	.994
Major League Totals—17 Years			1049	2743	245	618	128	10	58	321	.225	4040	397	70	.984

Selected by Philadelphia Phillies' organization in 7th round of free-agent draft, January 28, 1967.
†Drafted by Houston Astros, December 2, 1968.
‡Traded with Infielder Mickey Sinnerud and Catcher Tommie Smith by Houston Astros to Kansas City Royals for Catcher John Jones, December 16, 1968.
§On restricted list, April 7 to June 17, 1969.
xOn military list, April 2 to August 10, 1970.
yOn disabled list, July 9 to August 25, 1972.
zOn disabled list, May 20 to June 5, 1976.
aTraded with Pitcher Mark Littell to St. Louis Cardinals for Pitcher Al Hrabosky, December 8, 1977; traded by St. Louis to Milwaukee Brewers for Pitcher George Frazier, December 8, 1977.
bTraded to Toronto Blue Jays for Outfielder Gil Kubski, May 10, 1981 (appeared in no games with Milwaukee).
cGranted free agency, November 13, 1981; re-signed by Blue Jays, December 6, 1981.
dOn disabled list, July 10, 1985 through remainder of season.
eGranted free agency, November 12, 1986.

CHAMPIONSHIP SERIES RECORD

Year Club	League	Pos.	G.	AB.	R.	H.	2B.	3B.	HR.	RBI.	B.A.	PO.	A.	E.	F.A.
1976—Kansas City	Amer.	C	5	15	0	5	0	0	0	4	.333	15	4	0	1.000

PITCHING RECORD

Year Club	League	G.	IP.	W.	L.	Pct.	H.	R.	ER.	SO.	BB.	ERA.
1979—Milwaukee	American	1	1	0	0	.000	1	1	1	0	1	9.00

JOSE DENNIS MARTINEZ
(Known by middle name.)

Born May 14, 1955, at Granada, Nicaragua.
Height, 6.01. Weight, 183.
Throws and bats righthanded.

Major League saves: 1977 (4), 1980 (1). Total—5.
Led American League pitchers in games started with 39 and complete games with 18 in 1979.
Led International League in complete games with 16 in 1976.

Named International League Pitcher of the Year, 1976.

Year—Club	League	G.	IP.	W.	L.	Pct.	H.	R.	ER.	SO.	BB.	ERA.
1974—Miami	Florida St.	25	179	15	6	.714	124	48	41	162	53	2.06
1975—Miami	Florida St.	20	145	12	4	.750	125	54	42	114	35	2.61
1975—Asheville	Southern	6	45	4	1	.800	45	16	13	18	12	2.60
1975—Rochester	Int'national	2	5	0	0	.000	7	4	3	4	2	5.40
1976—Rochester	Int'national	25	180	*14	8	.636	148	64	50	*140	50	*2.50
1976—Baltimore	American	4	28	1	2	.333	23	8	8	18	8	2.57
1977—Baltimore	American	42	167	14	7	.667	157	86	76	107	64	4.10
1978—Baltimore	American	40	276	16	11	.593	257	121	108	142	93	3.25
1979—Baltimore	American	40	*292	15	16	.484	279	129	119	132	78	3.67
1980—Baltimore†	American	25	100	6	4	.600	103	44	44	42	44	3.96
1980—Miami	Florida St.	2	12	0	0	.000	3	1	0	7	5	0.00
1981—Baltimore	American	25	179	●14	5	.737	173	84	66	88	62	3.32
1982—Baltimore	American	40	252	16	12	.571	262	123	118	111	87	4.21
1983—Baltimore	American	32	153	7	16	.304	209	108	94	71	45	5.53
1984—Baltimore	American	34	141⅔	6	9	.400	145	81	79	77	37	5.02
1985—Baltimore	American	33	180	13	11	.542	203	110	103	68	63	5.15
1986—Baltimore‡	American	4	6⅔	0	0	.000	11	5	5	2	2	6.75
1986—Rochester§	Int'national	4	19⅓	2	1	.667	18	14	13	14	9	6.05
1986—Montreal x	National	19	98	3	6	.333	103	52	50	63	28	4.59
American League Totals—11 Years		319	1775⅓	108	93	.537	1822	899	820	858	583	4.16
National League Totals—1 Year		19	98	3	6	.333	103	52	50	63	28	4.59
Major League Totals—11 Years		338	1873⅓	111	99	.529	1925	951	870	921	611	4.18

Signed as free agent by Baltimore Orioles' organization, December 10, 1973.

†On disabled list, March 28 to April 20 and June 3 to July 10, 1980; included rehabilitation disability assignment to Miami, July 1 to July 10, 1980.

‡On disabled list, April 28 to June 16, 1986; included rehabilitation disability assignment to Rochester, May 21 to June 10, 1986.

§Traded to Montreal Expos for a player to be named later, June 16, 1986; Baltimore Orioles acquired Infielder Rene Gonzales to complete deal, December 16, 1986.

xGranted free agency, November 12, 1986.

CHAMPIONSHIP SERIES RECORD

Year—Club	League	G.	IP.	W.	L.	Pct.	H.	R.	ER.	SO.	BB.	ERA.
1979—Baltimore	American	1	8⅓	0	0	.000	8	3	3	4	0	3.24

WORLD SERIES RECORD

Year—Club	League	G.	IP.	W.	L.	Pct.	H.	R.	ER.	SO.	BB.	ERA.
1979—Baltimore	American	2	2	0	0	.000	6	4	4	0	0	18.00

REYNALDO IGNACIO MARTINEZ
(Chito)

Born December 19, 1965, in Belize, Central America.
Height, 5.11. Weight, 169.
Throws and bats lefthanded.

Year—Club	League	Pos.	G.	AB.	R.	H.	2B.	3B.	HR.	RBI.	B.A.	PO.	A.	E.	F.A.
1984—Eugene	N'west	OF	59	176	18	53	12	3	0	26	.301	78	2	8	.909
1985—Fort Myers	Fla. St.	OF	76	248	35	65	9	5	0	29	.262	71	161	7	.977
1986—Memphis	South.	OF	93	283	48	86	16	5	11	44	.304	115	6	8	.938

Selected by Kansas City Royals' organization in 6th round of free-agent draft, June 4, 1984.

JOHN ROBERT MARZANO

Born February 14, 1963, at Philadelphia, Pa.
Height, 5.11. Weight, 185.
Throws and bats righthanded.
Attended Temple University, Philadelphia, Pa.

Led Eastern League in being hit by pitch with 12 in 1986.
Member of 1984 U.S. Olympic baseball team.
Named catcher on THE SPORTING NEWS College Baseball All-America Team, 1984.

Year—Club	League	Pos.	G.	AB.	R.	H.	2B.	3B.	HR.	RBI.	B.A.	PO.	A.	E.	F.A.
1985—New Britain	East.	C	103	350	36	86	14	6	4	51	.246	530	70	12	.980
1986—New Britain	East.	C-3B	118	445	55	126	28	2	10	62	.283	509	76	14	.977

Selected by Minnesota Twins' organization in 3rd round of free-agent draft, June 8, 1981.
Selected by Boston Red Sox' organization in 1st round (14th player selected) of free-agent draft, June 4, 1984.

MICHAEL PAUL MASON
(Mike)

Born November 21, 1958, at Fairbault, Minn.
Height, 6.02. Weight, 205.
Throws and bats lefthanded.
Attended Normandale Community College, Bloomington, Minn., and
Oral Roberts University, Tulsa, Okla.

Tied for Texas League lead in balks with 4 in 1982.

Year Club	League	G	IP	W	L	Pct.	H	R	ER	SO	BB	ERA.
1980—Sarasota Rangers	Gulf Coast	12	61	6	1	.857	40	17	14	*55	46	2.07
1981—Asheville†	S. Atlantic	12	85	8	3	.727	58	28	20	39	35	2.12
1982—Tulsa	Texas	26	155	10	9	.526	153	84	67	111	46	3.89
1982—Texas	American	4	23	1	2	.333	21	13	13	8	9	5.09
1983—Texas	American	5	10⅔	0	2	.000	10	7	7	9	6	5.91
1983—Oklahoma City‡	Am. Assoc.	16	88⅔	5	5	.500	100	50	41	50	26	4.16
1984—Texas	American	36	184⅓	9	13	.409	159	78	74	113	51	3.61
1985—Texas	American	38	179	8	15	.348	212	113	96	92	73	4.83
1986—Texas§	American	27	135	7	3	.700	135	71	65	85	56	4.33
1986—Oklahoma City	Am. Assoc.	1	3	0	1	.000	2	5	1	1	3	3.00
Major League Totals—5 Years		110	532	25	35	.417	537	282	255	307	195	4.31

Selected by Detroit Tigers' organization in 14th round of free-agent draft, June 6, 1978.
Selected by Minnesota Twins' organization in secondary phase of free-agent draft, January 9, 1979.
Selected by St. Louis Cardinals' organization in secondary phase of free-agent draft, June 5, 1979.
Selected by Texas Rangers' organization in secondary phase of free-agent draft, June 3, 1980.
†On disabled list, July 26, 1981 through remainder of season.
‡On disabled list, June 17 to July 15, 1983.
§On disabled list, June 7 to June 26 and July 21 to August 6, 1986; included rehabilitation disability assignment to Oklahoma City, June 24 to June 26, 1986.

ROGER LeROY MASON

Born September 18, 1958, at Bellaire, Mich.
Height, 6.06. Weight, 215.
Throws and bats righthanded.
Attended Saginaw Valley State College, University Center, Mich.

Major League saves: 1984 (1).

Year Club	League	G	IP	W	L	Pct.	H	R	ER	SO	BB	ERA.
1981—Macon	S. Atlantic	26	148	10	10	.500	153	77	64	105	50	3.89
1982—Lakeland	Florida St.	22	132⅔	7	7	.500	124	60	51	72	52	3.46
1983—Birmingham	Southern	17	126⅔	7	4	.636	116	45	29	83	43	*2.06
1983—Evansville	Am. Assoc.	11	78⅔	5	5	.500	84	39	37	43	21	4.23
1984—Evansville†	Am. Assoc.	25	151⅔	9	7	.563	175	78	64	88	64	3.80
1984—Detroit‡	American	5	22	1	1	.500	23	11	11	15	10	4.50
1985—Phoenix§	P. Coast	24	167⅓	12	1	*.923	145	67	62	120	72	3.33
1985—San Francisco	National	5	29⅔	1	3	.250	28	13	7	26	11	2.12
1986—San Francisco x	National	11	60	3	4	.429	56	35	32	43	30	4.80
1986—Phoenix	P. Coast	1	6	1	0	1.000	2	0	0	2	1	0.00
American League Totals—1 Year		5	22	1	1	.500	23	11	11	15	10	4.50
National League Totals—2 Years		16	89⅔	4	7	.364	84	48	39	69	41	3.91
Major League Totals—3 Years		21	111⅔	5	8	.385	107	59	50	84	51	4.03

Signed as free agent by Detroit Tigers' organization, September 21, 1980.
†On disabled list, May 3 to May 19, 1984.
‡Traded to San Francisco Giants' organization for Outfielder Alejandro Sanchez, April 5, 1985.
§On disabled list, May 2 to May 23, 1985.
xOn disabled list, May 30 to July 20 and July 26, 1986 through remainder of season; included rehabilitation disability assignment to Phoenix, July 9 to July 17, 1986.

GREGORY INMAN MATHEWS
(Greg)

Born May 17, 1963, at Harbor City, Calif.
Height, 6.02. Weight, 180.
Throws left and bats left and righthanded.
Attended Santa Ana College, Santa Ana, Calif.; and
California State University, Fullerton, Calif.

Tied for American Association lead in shutouts with 2 in 1986.

Year Club	League	G	IP	W	L	Pct.	H	R	ER	SO	BB	ERA.
1984—Erie	NYP	3	15	0	1	.000	16	15	15	9	8	9.00
1984—Johnson City	Ap'lachian	5	31⅓	2	3	.400	27	12	9	21	13	2.59
1984—Savannah	S. Atlantic	6	27⅓	1	0	1.000	24	10	9	21	15	2.96
1985—St. Petersburg	Florida St.	16	122	13	1	*.929	76	17	15	96	47	*1.11
1985—Louisville	Am. Assoc.	12	74	6	4	.600	61	33	24	47	26	2.92
1986—Louisville†	Am. Assoc.	7	45⅓	3	3	.500	44	19	13	20	14	2.58
1986—St. Louis	National	23	145⅓	11	8	.579	139	61	59	67	44	3.65
Major League Totals—1 Year		23	145⅓	11	8	.579	139	61	59	67	44	3.65

Selected by Minnesota Twins' organization in 9th round of free-agent draft, January 12, 1982.
Selected by St. Louis Cardinals' organization in 10th round of free-agent draft, June 4, 1984.
†On disabled list, April 25 to May 12, 1986.

GARY NATHANIEL MATTHEWS

Born July 5, 1950, at San Fernando, Calif.
Height, 6.03. Weight, 205.
Throws and bats righthanded.

Tied major league record for fewest errors by outfielder, season, for leader in errors (9), 1986.
Hit three home runs in a game, September 25, 1976.

Major League stolen bases: 1973 (17), 1974 (11), 1975 (13), 1976 (12), 1977 (22), 1978 (8), 1979 (18), 1980 (11), 1981 (15), 1982 (21), 1983 (13), 1984 (17), 1985 (2), 1986 (3). Total—183.

Led National League in grounding into double plays with 23 in 1982.

Led National League in bases on balls received with 103, game-winning RBIs with 19 and tied for lead in sacrifice flies with 10 in 1984.

Led Texas League in total bases with 232 and tied for lead in sacrifice flies with 10 in 1971.

Tied for California League lead in double plays by outfielders with 3 in 1970.

Named National League Rookie Player of the Year by THE SPORTING NEWS, 1973.

Named National League Rookie of the Year by Baseball Writers' Association of America, 1973.

Year	Club	League	Pos.	G.	AB.	R.	H.	2B.	3B.	HR.	RBI.	B.A.	PO.	A.	E.	F.A.
1969—Decatur	Midw.		OF	53	174	31	56	11	2	8	30	.322	63	7	8	.897
1970—Fresno	Calif.		OF	117	380	77	106	11	5	23	74	.279	133	15	*15	.908
1971—Amarillo	Texas		OF	●142	493	82	138	*37	6	15	*86	.280	290	10	5	*.984
1972—Phoenix	P. C.		OF	136	480	101	150	27	8	21	108	.313	218	●16	*13	.947
1972—San Francisco	Nat.		OF	20	62	11	18	1	1	4	14	.290	34	0	1	.971
1973—San Francisco	Nat.		OF	148	540	74	162	22	10	12	58	.300	277	11	5	.983
1974—San Francisco	Nat.		OF	154	561	87	161	27	6	16	82	.287	281	9	9	.970
1975—San Francisco†	Nat.		OF	116	425	67	119	23	3	12	58	.280	225	11	8	.967
1976—San Francisco‡	Nat.		OF	156	587	79	164	28	4	20	84	.279	265	8	7	.975
1977—Atlanta	Nat.		OF	148	555	89	157	25	5	17	64	.283	262	11	10	.965
1978—Atlanta§	Nat.		OF	129	474	75	135	20	5	18	62	.285	238	10	8	.969
1979—Atlanta	Nat.		OF	156	631	97	192	34	5	27	90	.304	292	12	8	.974
1980—Atlanta x	Nat.		OF	155	571	79	159	17	3	19	75	.278	258	8	●11	.960
1981—Philadelphia	Nat.		OF	101	359	62	108	21	3	9	67	.301	170	11	7	.963
1982—Philadelphia	Nat.		OF	●162	616	89	173	31	1	19	83	.281	268	14	10	.966
1983—Philadelphia y	Nat.		OF	132	446	66	115	18	2	10	50	.258	174	11	5	.974
1984—Chicago	Nat.		OF	147	491	101	143	21	2	14	82	.291	224	7	●11	.955
1985—Chicago z	Nat.		OF	97	298	45	70	12	0	13	40	.235	119	7	3	.977
1986—Chicago	Nat.		OF	123	370	49	96	16	1	21	46	.259	137	5	●9	.940
Major League Totals—15 Years				1944	6986	1070	1972	315	51	231	955	.282	3224	135	112	.968

Selected by San Francisco Giants' organization in 1st round (17th player selected) of free-agent draft, June 7, 1968.

†On disabled list, June 5 to July 18, 1975.

‡Granted free agency, November 1, 1976; signed by Atlanta Braves, November 17, 1976.

§On disabled list, April 15 to May 2, 1978.

xTraded to Philadelphia Phillies for Pitcher Bob Walk, March 25, 1981.

yTraded with Outfielder Bob Dernier and Pitcher Porfi Altamirano to Chicago Cubs for Pitcher Bill Campbell and Catcher Mike Diaz, March 27, 1984.

zOn disabled list, May 27 to June 20 and July 8 to July 23, 1985.

DIVISION SERIES RECORD

Year	Club	League	Pos.	G.	AB.	R.	H.	2B.	3B.	HR.	RBI.	B.A.	PO.	A.	E.	F.A.
1981—Philadelphia	Nat.		OF	5	20	3	8	0	1	1	1	.400	6	0	0	1.000

CHAMPIONSHIP SERIES RECORD

Tied Championship Series records for most runs batted in, four-game Series (8), 1983; most Series, two or more home runs (2); most consecutive hits, one Series (5), 1983.

Year	Club	League	Pos.	G.	AB.	R.	H.	2B.	3B.	HR.	RBI.	B.A.	PO.	A.	E.	F.A.
1983—Philadelphia	Nat.		OF	4	14	4	6	0	0	3	8	.429	6	0	0	1.000
1984—Chicago	Nat.		OF	5	15	4	3	0	0	2	5	.200	10	0	0	1.000
Championship Series Totals—2 Years				9	29	8	9	0	0	5	13	.310	16	0	0	1.000

WORLD SERIES RECORD

Year	Club	League	Pos.	G.	AB.	R.	H.	2B.	3B.	HR.	RBI.	B.A.	PO.	A.	E.	F.A.
1983—Philadelphia	Nat.		OF	5	16	1	4	0	0	1	1	.250	15	0	0	1.000

ALL-STAR GAME RECORD

Year	League	Pos.	AB.	R.	H.	2B.	3B.	HR.	RBI.	B.A.	PO.	A.	E.	F.A.
1979—National		OF	2	0	0	0	0	0	0	.000	2	0	0	1.000

DONALD ARTHUR MATTINGLY

(Don)

Born April 20, 1962, at Evansville, Ind.
Height, 5.11. Weight, 185.
Throws and bats lefthanded.

Tied major league record for most sacrifice flies, game (3), May 3, 1986.

Established American League record for most at-bats by lefthander, season (677), 1986.

Major League stolen bases: 1984 (1), 1985 (2). Total—3.

Led American League in total bases with 370 in 1985 and 388 in 1986.

Led American League in slugging percentage with .573 in 1986.

Led American League in game-winning RBIs with 21 in 1985 and tied for lead with 15 in 1986.

Led American League in sacrifice flies with 15 in 1985.

Led American League first basemen in fielding percentage with .996 in 1984 and 1986.

Led American League first basemen in putouts with 1,377 and total chances with 1,483 in 1986.

Tied for American League lead in double plays by first basemen with 154 in 1985.

Led South Atlantic League in sacrifice flies with 12 in 1980.

Named Major League Player of the Year by THE SPORTING NEWS, 1985.

Named American League Player of the Year by THE SPORTING NEWS, 1984 through 1986.

Named American League Most Valuable Player by Baseball Writers' Association of America, 1985.

Named first baseman on The Sporting News American League All-Star Team, 1984 through 1986.
Named first baseman on The Sporting News American League All-Star fielding team, 1985 and 1986.
Named first baseman on The Sporting News American League Silver Slugger team, 1985 and 1986.
Named South Atlantic League Most Valuable Player, 1980.
Received reported $22,000 bonus to sign with New York Yankees, 1979.

Year Club	League	Pos.	G.	AB.	R.	H.	2B.	3B.	HR.	RBI.	B.A.	PO.	A.	E.	F.A.
1979—Oneonta	NYP	OF-1B	53	166	20	58	10	2	3	31	.349	29	2	2	.939
1980—Greensboro	S. Atl.	OF-1B	133	494	92	*177	32	5	9	105	*.358	205	16	8	.976
1981—Nashville	South.	OF-1B	141	547	74	173	*35	4	7	98	.316	846	69	12	.987
1982—Columbus	Int.	OF-1B	130	476	67	150	24	2	10	75	.315	271	17	5	.983
1982—New York	Amer.	OF-1B	7	12	0	2	0	0	0	1	.167	15	1	0	1.000
1983—New York	Amer.	OF-1B-2B	91	279	34	79	15	4	4	32	.283	350	15	3	.992
1983—Columbus	Int.	1B-OF	43	159	35	54	11	3	8	37	.340	325	29	1	.997
1984—New York	Amer.	1B-OF	153	603	91	*207	*44	2	23	110	*.343	1143	126	6	.995
1985—New York	Amer.	1B	159	652	107	211	*48	3	35	*145	.324	1318	87	7	*.995
1986—New York	Amer.	1B-3B	162	677	117	*238	*53	2	31	113	.352	1378	111	7	.995
Major League Totals—5 Years			572	2223	349	737	160	11	93	401	.332	4204	340	23	.995

Selected by New York Yankees' organization in 19th round of free-agent draft, June 5, 1979.

ALL-STAR GAME RECORD

Year League	Pos.	AB.	R.	H.	2B.	3B.	HR.	RBI.	B.A.	PO.	A.	E.	F.A.
1984—American	PH	1	0	0	0	0	0	0	.000	0	0	0	.000
1985—American	1B	1	0	0	0	0	0	0	.000	4	0	0	1.000
1986—American	PH-1B	3	0	0	0	0	0	0	.000	7	0	0	1.000
All-Star Game Totals—3 Years		5	0	0	0	0	0	0	.000	11	0	0	1.000

LEONARD JAMES MATUSZEK

Named pronounced Mu-TU-zek.

(Len)

Born September 27, 1954, at Toledo, O.
Height, 6.02. Weight, 195.
Throws right and bats lefthanded.
Attended University of Toledo, Toledo, O.

Tied major league record for fewest putouts by first baseman, game (0), June 1, 1984.
Major League stolen bases: 1984 (4), 1985 (2), 1986 (2). Total—8.
Led American Association in intentional bases on balls received with 22 in 1981.

Year Club	League	Pos.	G.	AB.	R.	H.	2B.	3B.	HR.	RBI.	B.A.	PO.	A.	E.	F.A.
1976—Peninsula	Carol.	1B	47	166	23	46	9	1	3	21	.277	426	34	1	.998
1977—Peninsula	Carol.	1B	122	410	56	94	18	4	10	56	.229	1051	74	12	*.989
1978—Reading†	East.	1B-3B	92	294	41	80	16	4	5	36	.272	556	85	13	.980
1979—Reading	East.	1B-3B	32	108	19	31	9	4	3	16	.287	145	42	5	.974
1979—Oklahoma City	A. A.	1B-3B	72	228	31	60	9	3	4	31	.263	421	55	10	.979
1980—Oklahoma City‡	A. A.	1B-3B	67	256	38	78	16	5	7	35	.305	580	55	6	.991
1981—Oklahoma City	A. A.	*1B-3B	129	463	87	146	27	2	21	91	.315	1146	101	6	*.995
1981—Philadelphia	Nat.	1B-3B	13	11	1	3	1	0	0	1	.273	5	4	0	1.000
1982—Philadelphia§	Nat.	3B-1B	25	39	1	3	1	0	0	3	.077	12	8	3	.870
1982—Oklahoma City	A. A.	1B	67	231	41	67	16	4	7	46	.290	560	59	8	.987
1983—Philadelphia	Nat.	1B	28	80	12	22	6	1	4	16	.275	144	9	0	1.000
1983—Portland	P. C.	1B-OF	113	412	82	136	28	6	24	92	.330	811	67	10	.989
1984—Philadelphia xy	Nat.	1B-OF	101	262	40	65	17	1	12	43	.248	644	55	8	.989
1985—Toronto z	Amer.	1B	62	151	23	32	6	2	2	15	.212	19	2	0	1.000
1985—Los Angeles	Nat.	OF-1B-3B	43	63	10	14	2	1	3	13	.222	47	2	0	1.000
1986—Los Angeles a	Nat.	OF-1B	91	199	26	52	7	0	9	28	.261	235	22	5	.981
National League Totals—6 Years			301	654	90	159	34	3	28	104	.243	1087	100	16	.987
American League Totals—1 Year			62	151	23	32	6	2	2	15	.212	19	2	0	1.000
Major League Totals—6 Years			363	805	113	191	40	5	30	119	.237	1106	102	16	.987

Selected by Philadelphia Phillies' organization in 5th round of free-agent draft, June 8, 1976.
†On disabled list, June 23 to July 26, 1978.
‡On disabled list, April 14 to May 16 and May 17 to June 21, 1980.
§On disabled list, April 29 to May 15, 1982.
xOn disabled list, June 9 to July 22, 1984.
yTraded to Toronto Blue Jays for Infielder Jose Escobar, Outfielder Ken Kinnard and Pitcher Dave Shipanoff, April 1, 1985.
zTraded to Los Angeles Dodgers for First Baseman-Outfielder Al Oliver, July 9, 1985.
aOn disabled list, April 2 to May 24, 1986.

CHAMPIONSHIP SERIES RECORD

Year Club	League	Pos.	G.	AB.	R.	H.	2B.	3B.	HR.	RBI.	B.A.	PO.	A.	E.	F.A.
1985—Los Angeles	Nat.	PH-OF-1B	3	1	1	1	0	0	0	0	1.000	0	0	0	.000

GREGORY SCOTT MAYBERRY

(Greg)

Born September 11, 1965, at Lynchburg, Va.
Height, 6.02. Weight, 210.
Throws right and bats lefthanded.
Attended Ferrum College, Ferrum, Va.

Year	Club	League	G.	IP.	W.	L.	Pct.	H.	R.	ER.	SO.	BB.	ERA.
1984—Great Falls	Pioneer	13	89⅓	7	4	.636	75	47	32	★89	39	3.22
1984—Bakersfield	California	1	7	0	1	.000	5	2	2	7	2	2.57
1985—Vero Beach	Florida St.	17	118⅔	11	4	.733	101	40	31	97	37	2.35
1985—San Antonio	Texas	8	41	2	4	.333	35	28	20	31	18	4.39
1986—San Antonio†	Texas	3	17⅔	1	2	.333	12	9	9	10	13	4.58

Selected by Boston Red Sox' organization in 1st round (13th player selected) of free-agent draft, January 17, 1984.
Selected by Los Angeles Dodgers' organization in secondary phase of free-agent draft, June 4, 1984.
†On disabled list, April 24, 1986 through remainder of season.

LEE LOUIS MAZZILLI

Born March 25, 1955, at Brooklyn, N.Y.
Height, 6.01. Weight, 190.
Throws right and bats left and righthanded.
Son of Libero Mazzilli, former professional welterweight boxer.

Major League stolen bases: 1976 (5), 1977 (22), 1978 (20), 1979 (34), 1980 (41), 1981 (17), 1982 (13), 1983 (15), 1984 (8), 1985 (4), 1986 (4). Total—183.
Led Texas League in bases on balls received with 111, caught stealing with 15 and tied for lead in being hit by pitch with 7 in 1976.
Led California League in caught stealing with 16 in 1975.
Received reported $50,000 bonus to sign with New York Mets, 1973.

Year	Club	League	Pos.	G.	AB.	R.	H.	2B.	3B.	HR.	RBI.	B.A.	PO.	A.	E.	F.A.
1974—Anderson	W. Car.	OF	132	472	82	127	24	3	11	48	.269	227	9	9	.963
1975—Visalia	Calif.	OF-1B	125	430	103	121	10	4	13	52	.281	185	9	9	.956
1976—Jackson	Texas	OF	131	439	91	128	21	6	13	43	.292	262	8	8	.971
1976—New York	Nat.	OF	24	77	9	15	2	0	2	7	.195	55	2	1	.983
1977—New York	Nat.	OF	159	537	66	134	24	3	6	46	.250	386	9	3	.992
1978—New York	Nat.	OF	148	542	78	148	28	5	16	61	.273	386	8	5	.987
1979—New York	Nat.	OF-1B	158	597	78	181	34	4	15	79	.303	480	24	5	.990
1980—New York†	Nat.	1B-OF	152	578	82	162	31	4	16	76	.280	874	53	14	.985
1981—New York†	Nat.	OF	95	324	36	74	14	5	6	34	.228	192	5	6	.970
1982—Tex.‡§-N.Y. x	Amer.	OF-1B	95	323	43	81	10	0	10	34	.251	234	8	4	.984
1983—Pittsburgh	Nat.	OF-1B	109	246	37	59	9	0	5	24	.240	173	3	4	.978
1984—Pittsburgh y	Nat.	OF-1B	111	266	37	63	11	1	4	21	.237	103	2	1	.991
1985—Pittsburgh	Nat.	1B-OF	92	117	20	33	8	0	1	9	.282	152	6	3	.981
1986—Pit. z-N.Y.	Nat.	OF-1B	100	151	28	37	5	1	3	15	.245	128	2	0	1.000
1986—Tidewater	Int.	1B-OF	6	20	3	6	1	0	1	1	.300	28	1	0	1.000
National League Totals—10 Years			1148	3435	471	906	166	23	74	372	.264	2929	114	42	.986
American League Totals—1 Year			95	323	43	81	10	0	10	34	.251	234	8	4	.984
Major League Totals—11 Years			1243	3758	514	987	176	23	84	406	.263	3163	122	46	.986

Selected by New York Mets' organization in 1st round (14th player selected) of free-agent draft, June 5, 1973.
†Traded to Texas Rangers for Pitchers Ron Darling and Walt Terrell, April 1, 1982.
‡On disabled list, May 20 to June 29, 1982.
§Traded to New York Yankees for Shortstop Bucky Dent, August 8, 1982.
xTraded to Pittsburgh Pirates for Outfielder Don Aubin, Pitcher Tim Burke, Catcher John Holland and Infielder Jose Rivera, December 22, 1982.
yOn disabled list, August 28 to September 11, 1984.
zReleased, July 23, 1986; signed by New York Mets' organization, August 3, 1986.

CHAMPIONSHIP SERIES RECORD

Year	Club	League	Pos.	G.	AB.	R.	H.	2B.	3B.	HR.	RBI.	B.A.	PO.	A.	E.	F.A.
1986—New York	Nat.	PH	5	5	0	1	0	0	0	0	.200	0	0	0	.000

WORLD SERIES RECORD

Year	Club	League	Pos.	G.	AB.	R.	H.	2B.	3B.	HR.	RBI.	B.A.	PO.	A.	E.	F.A.
1986—New York	Nat.	PH-OF	4	5	2	2	0	0	0	0	.400	1	0	0	1.000

ALL-STAR GAME RECORD

Tied All-Star Game record for most home runs by pinch-hitter, game (1), July 17, 1979.

Year	League	Pos.	AB.	R.	H.	2B.	3B.	HR.	RBI.	B.A.	PO.	A.	E.	F.A.
1979—National		PH-OF	1	1	1	0	0	1	2	1.000	0	0	0	.000

THOMAS MICHAEL McCARTHY
(Tom)

Born June 18, 1961, at Lundstahl, W. Germany.
Height, 6.00. Weight, 180.
Throws and bats righthanded.

Year	Club	League	G.	IP.	W.	L.	Pct.	H.	R.	ER.	SO.	BB.	ERA.
1979—Elmira	NYP	18	46	2	6	.250	67	50	36	26	37	7.04
1980—Elmira	NYP	3	20	2	1	.667	10	7	7	14	13	3.15
1980—Winston-Salem	Carolina	11	61	4	4	.500	55	32	27	28	46	3.98
1981—Winston-Salem	Carolina	28	105	3	7	.300	123	99	85	75	99	7.29
1982—Winston-Salem	Carolina	30	103⅓	3	11	.214	128	95	75	75	65	6.53
1983—Winston-Salem	Carolina	35	98	8	6	.571	91	56	45	100	54	4.13
1984—New Britain	Eastern	38	79⅓	8	5	.615	71	35	27	65	56	3.06
1985—Pawtucket	Int'national	26	85⅓	5	6	.455	72	48	34	65	62	3.59

Year Club	League	G.	IP.	W.	L.	Pct.	H.	R.	ER.	SO.	BB.	ERA.
1985—Boston†	American	3	5	0	0	.000	7	6	6	2	4	10.80
1986—Tidewater	Int'national	22	84⅔	3	2	.600	89	43	38	30	37	4.04
Major League Totals—1 Year		3	5	0	0	.000	7	6	6	2	4	10.80

Selected by Boston Red Sox' organization in 7th round of free-agent draft, June 5, 1979.

†Traded with Pitchers Bob Ojeda, John Mitchell and Chris Bayer to New York Mets for Pitchers Calvin Schiraldi and Wes Gardner and Outfielders John Christensen and LaSchelle Tarver, November 13, 1985.

KIRK EDWARD McCASKILL

Born April 9, 1961, at Kapuskasing, Ontario, Canada.
Height, 6.01. Weight, 195.
Throws and bats righthanded.
Attended University of Vermont, Burlington, Vt.
Son of Ted McCaskill, center with Minnesota North Stars (NHL)
and Los Angeles Sharks (WHA), 1967-68, 1972-73 and 1973-74.

Year Club	League	G.	IP.	W.	L.	Pct.	H.	R.	ER.	SO.	BB.	ERA.
1982—Salem	Northwest	11	71⅓	5	5	.500	63	43	34	87	51	4.29
1983—Redwood	California	16	108⅓	6	5	.545	78	39	28	100	60	2.33
1983—Nashua†	Eastern	13	87	4	8	.333	90	47	43	63	43	4.45
1984—Edmonton	P. Coast	24	143	7	11	.389	162	104	91	75	74	5.73
1985—Edmonton	P. Coast	3	17⅔	1	1	.500	17	7	4	18	6	2.04
1985—California	American	30	189⅔	12	12	.500	189	105	99	102	64	4.70
1986—California	American	34	246⅓	17	10	.630	207	98	92	202	92	3.36
Major League Totals—2 Years		64	436	29	22	.569	396	203	191	304	156	3.94

Selected by California Angels' organization in 4th round of free-agent draft, June 7, 1982.

†On suspended list, August 30, 1983; then transferred to disqualified list, September 26, 1983 through April 25, 1984.

CHAMPIONSHIP SERIES RECORD

Tied Championship Series records for most games lost, Series (2), 1986; most hits allowed, inning (6), October 14, 1986 (third inning).

Established American League Championship Series record for most runs (13) and earned runs (11) allowed, seven-game Series, 1986.

Year Club	League	G.	IP.	W.	L.	Pct.	H.	R.	ER.	SO.	BB.	ERA.
1986—California	American	2	9⅓	0	2	.000	16	13	8	7	5	7.71

RECORD AS HOCKEY PLAYER

Year Team	League	Games	G.	A.	Pts.	Pen.
1983-84—Sherbrooke Jets (a)	AHL	78	10	12	22	21

(a)—June, 1981—Drafted by Winnipeg Jets in 1981 NHL entry draft. Fourth Jets pick, 64th overall, fourth round.

LLOYD GLENN McCLENDON

Born January 11, 1959, at Gary, Ind.
Height, 5.10. Weight, 195.
Throws and bats righthanded.
Attended Valparaiso University, Valparaiso, Ind.

Year Club	League	Pos.	G.	AB.	R.	H.	2B.	3B.	HR.	RBI.	B.A.	PO.	A.	E.	F.A.
1980—Kingsport	Appal.	C	14	46	7	15	2	0	1	9	.326	19	5	3	.889
1980—Little Falls	NYP	C	40	117	25	32	9	1	3	20	.274	203	20	7	.970
1981—Lynchburg	Carol.	C-3B	103	363	55	91	12	6	7	57	.251	437	74	17	.968
1982—Lynchburg†‡	Carol.	C-3B	108	384	61	105	25	1	18	78	.273	492	87	15	.975
1983—Waterbury	East.	C-3B-1B	123	434	58	114	19	2	15	57	.263	466	99	8	.986
1984—Vermont	East.	C-1-3-O	60	202	36	56	16	0	7	27	.277	174	24	3	.985
1984—Wichita	A.A.	3B-1B-C	48	152	28	45	13	1	6	28	.296	143	45	4	.979
1985—Denver	A.A.	1-3-C-O	114	379	57	105	18	5	16	79	.277	470	104	17	.971
1986—Denver	A.A.	1-O-C-3	132	433	75	112	30	1	∗24	88	.259	656	45	11	.985

Selected by New York Mets' organization in 8th round of free-agent draft, June 3, 1980.

†On disabled list, April 4 to April 27, 1982.

‡Traded with Pitcher Charlie Puleo and Outfielder Jason Felice to Cincinnati Reds for Pitcher Tom Seaver, December 16, 1982.

ROBERT CRAIG McCLURE
(Bob)

Born April 29, 1952, at Oakland, Calif.
Height, 5.11. Weight, 170.
Throws left and bats left and righthanded.
Attended College of San Mateo, San Mateo, Calif.

Major League saves: 1975 (1), 1977 (6), 1978 (9), 1979 (5), 1980 (10), 1984 (1), 1985 (3), 1986 (6). Total—41.
Led American League in balks with 6 in 1983.
Tied for Pioneer League lead in shutouts with 3 in 1973.

Year Club	League	G.	IP.	W.	L.	Pct.	H.	R.	ER.	SO.	BB.	ERA.
1973—Billings	Pioneer	14	94	∗10	2	.833	64	41	22	110	67	2.11
1974—Omaha	Am. Assoc.	21	136	5	8	.385	140	71	58	88	65	3.84
1975—Jacksonville†	Southern	9	42	3	2	.600	31	18	11	39	23	2.36
1975—Kansas City	American	12	15	1	0	1.000	4	0	0	15	14	0.00

Year Club	League	G.	IP.	W.	L.	Pct.	H.	R.	ER.	SO.	BB.	ERA.
1976—Omaha	Am. Assoc.	21	133	9	8	.529	133	61	44	91	41	2.98
1976—Kansas City‡	American	8	4	0	0	.000	3	4	4	3	8	9.00
1977—Milwaukee	American	68	71	2	1	.667	64	25	20	57	34	2.54
1978—Milwaukee	American	44	65	2	6	.250	53	30	27	47	30	3.74
1979—Milwaukee	American	36	51	5	2	.714	53	29	22	37	24	3.88
1980—Milwaukee	American	52	91	5	8	.385	83	34	31	47	37	3.07
1981—Burlington	Midwest	4	14	0	2	.000	19	15	15	11	11	9.64
1981—Milwaukee§	American	4	8	0	0	.000	7	3	3	6	4	3.38
1982—Milwaukee x	American	34	172⅔	12	7	.632	160	90	81	99	74	4.22
1983—Milwaukee y	American	24	142	9	9	.500	152	75	71	68	68	4.50
1984—Milwaukee	American	39	139⅔	4	8	.333	154	76	68	68	52	4.38
1985—Milwaukee z	American	38	85⅔	4	1	.800	91	43	41	57	30	4.31
1986—Milwaukee z	American	13	16⅓	2	1	.667	18	7	7	11	10	3.86
1986—Montreal	National	52	62⅔	2	5	.286	53	22	21	42	23	3.02
American League Totals—12 Years		372	861⅓	46	43	.517	842	416	375	515	385	3.92
National League Totals—1 Year		52	62⅔	2	5	.286	53	22	21	42	23	3.02
Major League Totals—12 Years		424	924	48	48	.500	895	438	396	557	408	3.86

Selected by Los Angeles Dodgers' organization in 3rd round of free-agent draft, January 10, 1973.
Selected by Kansas City Royals' organization in secondary phase of free-agent draft, June 5, 1973.
†On disabled list, April 15 to May 13 and June 5 to July 25, 1975.
‡Traded to Milwaukee Brewers, March 15, 1977; completing deal in which Kansas City Royals traded Infielder Jamie Quirk, Outfielder Jim Wohlford and a player to be named later to Milwaukee for Pitcher Jim Colborn and Catcher Darrell Porter, December 6, 1976.
§On disabled list, March 28 to September 1, 1981; included rehabilitation disability assignment to Burlington, August 7 to August 24, 1981.
xGranted free agency, November 10, 1982; re-signed by Brewers, December 6, 1982.
yOn disabled list, August 22 to September 12, 1983.
zSold to Montreal Expos, June 8, 1986.

DIVISION SERIES RECORD

Year Club	League	G.	IP.	W.	L.	Pct.	H.	R.	ER.	SO.	BB.	ERA.
1981—Milwaukee	American	3	3⅓	0	0	.000	4	0	0	2	0	0.00

CHAMPIONSHIP SERIES RECORD

Year Club	League	G.	IP.	W.	L.	Pct.	H.	R.	ER.	SO.	BB.	ERA.
1982—Milwaukee	American	1	1⅔	1	0	1.000	2	0	0	0	0	0.00

WORLD SERIES RECORD

Tied World Series record for most games lost, seven-game Series (2), 1982.

Year Club	League	G.	IP.	W.	L.	Pct.	H.	R.	ER.	SO.	BB.	ERA.
1982—Milwaukee	American	5	4⅓	0	2	.000	5	2	2	5	3	4.15

LANCE GRAYE McCULLERS

Born March 8, 1964, at Tampa, Fla.
Height, 6.01. Weight, 185.
Throws right and bats right and lefthanded.

Major League saves: 1985 (5), 1986 (5). Total—10.
Tied for Pacific Coast League lead in hit batsmen with 6 in 1985.

Year Club	League	G.	IP.	W.	L.	Pct.	H.	R.	ER.	SO.	BB.	ERA.
1982—Helena	Pioneer	13	87	6	4	.600	89	44	36	62	33	3.72
1983—Spartanburg†	S. Atlantic	22	136⅓	9	6	.600	139	79	61	87	57	4.03
1984—Miami	Florida St.	22	106⅓	6	4	.600	92	37	30	94	45	2.54
1984—Beaumont‡	Texas	8	55⅓	4	1	.800	38	13	13	48	35	2.11
1985—Las Vegas	P. Coast	24	149⅓	11	8	.579	135	75	66	148	83	3.98
1985—San Diego	National	21	35	0	2	.000	23	15	9	27	16	2.31
1986—San Diego	National	70	136	10	10	.500	103	46	42	92	58	2.78
Major League Totals—2 Years		91	171	10	12	.455	126	61	51	119	74	2.68

Selected by Philadelphia Phillies' organization in 2nd round of free-agent draft, June 7, 1982.
†Traded with Pitchers Marty Decker, Darren Burroughs and Ed Wojna to San Diego Padres, September 20, 1983, as partial completion of deal in which San Diego traded Outfielder Sixto Lezcano and a player to be named later to Philadelphia Phillies for four players to be named later, August 31, 1983; Philadelphia organization acquired Pitcher Steve Fireovid to complete deal, October 11, 1983.
‡On disabled list, September 7, 1984 through remainder of season.

JULIUS McDOUGAL

Born May 3, 1963, at Jackson, Miss.
Height, 6.02. Weight, 185.
Throws right and bats left and righthanded.
Attended Jackson State University, Jackson, Miss.

Year Club	League	Pos.	G.	AB.	R.	H.	2B.	3B.	HR.	RBI.	B.A.	PO.	A.	E.	F.A.
1984—Lodi	Calif.	SS	62	220	15	41	5	0	0	11	.186	92	189	31	.901
1985—Peoria	Midw.	SS	125	441	66	107	17	2	5	38	.243	196	★356	36	.939
1986—Winston-Salem†	Carol.	SS	103	346	51	100	21	4	1	43	.289	★171	282	★43	.913
1986—Orlando	South.	SS	17	61	9	23	2	0	1	7	.377	31	45	11	.874

Selected by Atlanta Braves' organization in 15th round of free-agent draft, June 8, 1981.
Selected by Chicago Cubs' organization in 3rd round of free-agent draft, June 4, 1984.
†Traded with Pitchers Ray Fontenot and George Frazier to Minnesota Twins for Pitchers Ron Davis and DeWayne Coleman, August 13, 1986.

ODDIBE McDOWELL JR.

First name pronounced OH-da-bee.

Born August 25, 1962, at Hollywood, Fla.
Height, 5.09. Weight, 160.
Throws and bats lefthanded.
Attended Miami-Dade Community College (North), Miami, Fla., and
Arizona State University, Tempe, Ariz.

Tied major league record for most putouts by outfielder, game (12), July 20, 1985, 15 innings.
Tied American League record for most chances accepted by outfielder, game (12), July 20, 1985, 15 innings.
Major League stolen bases: 1985 (25), 1986 (33). Total—58.
Hit for the cycle, July 23, 1985.
Member of 1984 U.S. Olympic baseball team.
Named outfielder on THE SPORTING NEWS College Baseball All-America Team, 1983 and 1984.

Year Club	League	Pos.	G.	AB.	R.	H.	2B.	3B.	HR.	RBI.	B.A.	PO.	A.	E.	F.A.
1985—Oklahoma City	A. A.	OF	31	.125	32	50	7	8	2	18	.400	72	4	1	.987
1985—Texas	Amer.	OF	111	406	63	97	14	5	18	42	.239	282	9	2	.993
1986—Texas	Amer.	OF	154	572	105	152	24	7	18	49	.266	325	13	3	.991
Major League Totals—2 Years			265	978	168	249	38	12	36	91	.255	607	22	5	.992

Selected by St. Louis Cardinals' organization in 4th round of free-agent draft, January 13, 1981.
Selected by Texas Rangers' organization in secondary phase of free-agent draft, June 8, 1981.
Selected by New York Yankees' organization in secondary phase of free-agent draft, January 12, 1982.
Selected by Toronto Blue Jays' organization in secondary phase of free-agent draft, June 7, 1982.
Selected by Minnesota Twins' organization in secondary phase of free-agent draft, June 6, 1983.
Selected by Texas Rangers' organization in 1st round (12th player selected) of free-agent draft, June 4, 1984.

ROGER ALAN McDOWELL

Born December 21, 1960, at Cincinnati, O.
Height, 6.01. Weight, 175.
Throws and bats righthanded.
Attended Bowling Green State University, Bowling Green, O.

Major League saves: 1985 (17), 1986 (22). Total—39.

Year Club	League	G.	IP.	W.	L.	Pct.	H.	R.	ER.	SO.	BB.	ERA.
1982—Shelby	S. Atlantic	12	71⅓	6	4	.600	61	34	26	40	30	3.28
1982—Lynchburg	Carolina	4	29⅓	2	0	1.000	26	12	7	23	11	2.15
1983—Jackson	Texas	27	172⅔	11	12	.478	203	111	93	115	71	4.86
1984—Jackson†	Texas	3	7⅓	0	0	.000	9	3	3	8	1	3.68
1985—New York	National	62	127⅓	6	5	.545	108	43	40	70	37	2.83
1986—New York‡	National	75	128	14	9	.609	107	48	43	65	42	3.02
Major League Totals—2 Years		137	255⅓	20	14	.588	215	91	83	135	79	2.93

Selected by New York Mets' organization in 3rd round of free-agent draft, June 7, 1982.
†On disabled list, April 10 to August 14, 1984.
‡Appeared in one game as an outfielder with no chances.

CHAMPIONSHIP SERIES RECORD

Year Club	League	G.	IP.	W.	L.	Pct.	H.	R.	ER.	SO.	BB.	ERA.
1986—New York	National	2	7	0	0	.000	1	0	0	3	0	0.00

WORLD SERIES RECORD

Year Club	League	G.	IP.	W.	L.	Pct.	H.	R.	ER.	SO.	BB.	ERA.
1986—New York	National	5	7⅓	1	0	1.000	10	5	4	2	6	4.91

ANDREW JOSEPH McGAFFIGAN
(Andy)

Born October 25, 1956, at West Palm Beach, Fla.
Height, 6.03. Weight, 195.
Throws and bats righthanded.
Attended Palm Beach Junior College, Lake Worth, Fla., and
received degree from Florida Southern College, Lakeland, Fla., in 1978.

Major League saves: 1983 (2), 1984 (1), 1986 (2). Total—5.
Named Southern League Pitcher of the Year, 1980.

Year Club	League	G.	IP.	W.	L.	Pct.	H.	R.	ER.	SO.	BB.	ERA.
1978—Oneonta	NYP	2	12	0	1	.000	14	8	6	13	9	4.50
1978—Fort Lauderdale	Florida St.	11	66	4	5	.444	45	28	21	36	20	2.86
1979—West Haven	Eastern	23	144	10	6	.625	136	75	61	113	54	3.81
1980—Nashville†	Southern	31	170	15	5	.750	139	62	45	125	62	*2.38
1981—Columbus‡	Int'national	17	103	8	6	.571	85	45	37	57	37	3.23
1981—New York§	American	2	7	0	0	.000	5	3	2	2	3	2.57
1982—Phoenix x	P. Coast	18	96	1	6	.143	115	72	64	64	51	6.00
1982—San Francisco	National	4	8	1	0	1.000	5	1	0	4	1	0.00
1983—San Francisco y	National	43	134⅓	3	9	.250	131	67	64	93	39	4.29
1984—Montreal z-Cincinnati	National	30	69	3	6	.333	60	28	27	57	23	3.52
1985—Denver	Am. Assoc.	26	106⅔	11	5	.688	105	43	35	91	37	2.95
1985—Cincinnati a	National	15	94⅓	3	3	.500	84	40	39	83	30	3.72
1986—Montreal	National	48	142⅔	10	5	.667	114	49	42	104	55	2.65
American League Totals—1 Year		2	7	0	0	.000	5	3	2	2	3	2.57
National League Totals—5 Years		140	448⅓	20	23	.465	398	185	172	341	148	3.45
Major League Totals—6 Years		142	455⅓	20	23	.465	403	188	174	343	151	3.44

Selected by Cincinnati Reds' organization in 36th round of free-agent draft, June 5, 1974.
Selected by Chicago White Sox' organization in 5th round of free-agent draft, January 7, 1976.
Selected by New York Yankees' organization in 6th round of free-agent draft, June 6, 1978.
†On disabled list, September 1 to September 22, 1980.
‡On disabled list, April 10 to June 14, 1981.
§Traded with Outfielder Ted Wilborn to San Francisco Giants' organization for Pitcher Doyle Alexander, March 30, 1982.
xOn disabled list, June 20 to August 13, 1982.
yTraded to Montreal Expos, March 31, 1984, as compensation for the injury that Pitcher Fred Breining arrived with in trade of February 27, 1984, which sent Breining and Outfielder Max Venable to Montreal for First Baseman Al Oliver. (Breining remained with Montreal.)
zTraded with Pitcher Jim Jefferson to Cincinnati Reds for First Baseman Dan Driessen, July 26, 1984.
aTraded with Pitchers Jay Tibbs and John Stuper and Catcher Dann Bilardello to Montreal Expos for Pitcher Bill Gullickson and Catcher Sal Butera, December 19, 1985.

WILLIE DEAN McGEE

Born November 2, 1958, at San Francisco, Calif.
Height, 6.01. Weight, 176.
Throws right and bats right and lefthanded.
Attended Diablo Valley College, Pleasant Hill, Calif.

Established modern National League record for highest batting average, switch-hitter, season, 100 or more games (.353), 1985.
Major League stolen bases: 1982 (24), 1983 (39), 1984 (43), 1985 (56), 1986 (19). Total—181.
Hit for the cycle, June 23, 1984.
Named National League Player of the Year by THE SPORTING NEWS, 1985.
Named National League Most Valuable Player by Baseball Writers' Association of America, 1985.
Named outfielder on THE SPORTING NEWS National League All-Star Team, 1985.
Named outfielder on THE SPORTING NEWS National League All-Star fielding team, 1983, 1985 and 1986.
Named outfielder on THE SPORTING NEWS National League Silver Slugger team, 1985.

Year	Club	League	Pos.	G.	AB.	R.	H.	2B.	3B.	HR.	RBI.	B.A.	PO.	A.	E.	F.A.
1977—Oneonta		NYP	OF	65	225	31	53	4	3	2	22	.236	103	5	10	.915
1978—Fort Lauderdale	Fla. St.		OF	124	423	62	106	6	6	0	37	.251	243	12	9	.966
1979—West Haven	East.		OF	49	115	21	28	3	1	1	8	.243	88	3	3	.968
1979—Fort Lauderdale	Fla. St.		OF	46	176	25	56	8	3	1	18	.318	103	3	2	.981
1980—Nashville†	South.		OF	78	223	35	63	4	5	1	22	.283	127	6	6	.957
1981—Nashville‡§	South.		OF	100	388	77	125	20	5	7	63	.322	203	10	6	.973
1982—Louisville x	A. A.		OF	13	55	11	16	2	2	1	3	.291	40	0	1	.976
1982—St. Louis	Nat.		OF	123	422	43	125	12	8	4	56	.296	245	3	11	.958
1983—St. Louis y	Nat.		OF	147	601	75	172	22	8	5	75	.286	385	7	5	.987
1983—Arkansas	Texas		OF	7	29	5	8	1	1	0	2	.276	7	0	0	1.000
1984—St. Louis z	Nat.		OF	145	571	82	166	19	11	6	50	.291	374	10	6	.985
1985—St. Louis	Nat.		OF	152	612	114	★216	26	★18	10	82	★.353	382	11	9	.978
1986—St. Louis a	Nat.		OF	124	497	65	127	22	7	7	48	.256	325	9	3	★.991
Major League Totals—5 Years				691	2703	379	806	101	52	32	311	.298	1711	40	34	.981

Selected by Chicago White Sox' organization in 7th round of free-agent draft, June 8, 1976.
Selected by New York Yankees' organization in secondary phase of free-agent draft, January 11, 1977.
†On disabled list, May 22 to June 7 and July 14 to August 7, 1980.
‡On disabled list, April 24 to June 4, 1981.
§Traded to St. Louis Cardinals' organization for Pitcher Bob Sykes, October 21, 1981.
xOn disabled list, April 13 to April 23, 1982.
yOn disabled list, March 30 to April 29, 1983; included rehabilitation disability assignment to Arkansas, April 18 to April 29, 1983.
zOn disabled list, July 12 to July 27, 1984.
aOn disabled list, August 3 to August 27, 1986.

CHAMPIONSHIP SERIES RECORD

Tied Championship Series record for most three-base hits, Series (2), 1982.
Established National League Championship Series record for most runs, six-game Series (6), 1985.
Tied National League Championship Series record for most three-base hits, total Series (2).

Year	Club	League	Pos.	G.	AB.	R.	H.	2B.	3B.	HR.	RBI.	B.A.	PO.	A.	E.	F.A.
1982—St. Louis	Nat.		OF	3	13	4	4	0	2	1	5	.308	12	0	1	.923
1985—St. Louis	Nat.		OF	6	26	6	7	1	0	0	3	.269	18	0	0	1.000
Championship Series Totals—2 Years				9	39	10	11	1	2	1	8	.282	30	0	1	.968

WORLD SERIES RECORD

Tied World Series records for most home runs, game, by rookie (2), October 15, 1982; highest fielding average by outfielder, seven-game Series (1.000 with 24 chances), 1982; most putouts by outfielder, seven-game Series (24), 1982.

Year	Club	League	Pos.	G.	AB.	R.	H.	2B.	3B.	HR.	RBI.	B.A.	PO.	A.	E.	F.A.
1982—St. Louis	Nat.		OF	6	25	6	6	0	0	2	5	.240	24	0	0	1.000
1985—St. Louis	Nat.		OF	7	27	2	7	2	0	1	2	.259	15	0	0	1.000
World Series Totals—2 Years				13	52	8	13	2	0	3	7	.250	39	0	0	1.000

ALL-STAR GAME RECORD

Year	League	Pos.	AB.	R.	H.	2B.	3B.	HR.	RBI.	B.A.	PO.	A.	E.	F.A.
1983—National		OF	2	0	1	0	0	0	0	.500	2	0	0	1.000
1985—National		OF	2	0	1	1	0	0	2	.500	1	0	0	1.000
All-Star Game Totals—2 Years			4	0	2	1	0	0	2	.500	3	0	0	1.000

SCOTT HOUSTON McGREGOR

Born January 18, 1954, at Inglewood, Calif.
Height, 6.01. Weight, 190.
Throws left and bats right and lefthanded.
Attended El Camino Junior College, Torrance, Calif. and Loyola Marymount University, Los Angeles, Calif.

Major League saves: 1977 (4), 1978 (1). Total—5.
Tied for American League lead in home runs allowed with 34 in 1985.
Led International League in complete games with 12 and tied for lead in balks with 3 in 1974.
Led Eastern League pitchers in complete games with 14 and tied for lead in games started with 27 in 1973.
Led International League in shutouts with 6 in 1976.
Named International League Pitcher of the Year, 1974.
Received reported $80,000 bonus to sign with New York Yankees, 1972.

Year Club	League	G.	IP.	W.	L.	Pct.	H.	R.	ER.	SO.	BB.	ERA.
1972—Fort Lauderdale	Florida St.	11	79	7	3	.700	66	30	24	54	25	2.73
1973—West Haven	Eastern	27	★197	●12	●13	.480	★197	95	72	126	63	3.29
1974—Syracuse	Int'national	27	★199	13	10	.565	204	88	76	124	75	3.44
1975—Syracuse†	Int'national	21	124	6	9	.400	134	73	55	72	60	3.99
1976—Syracuse‡-Rochester	Int'national	24	162	12	6	.667	159	59	55	83	40	3.06
1976—Baltimore	American	3	15	0	1	.000	17	7	6	6	5	3.60
1977—Baltimore	American	29	114	3	5	.375	119	57	56	55	30	4.42
1978—Baltimore	American	35	233	15	13	.536	217	98	86	94	47	3.32
1979—Baltimore	American	27	175	13	6	.684	165	70	65	81	23	3.34
1980—Baltimore	American	36	252	20	8	.714	254	101	93	119	58	3.32
1981—Baltimore	American	24	160	13	5	.722	167	63	58	82	40	3.26
1982—Baltimore	American	37	226⅓	14	12	.538	238	126	116	84	52	4.61
1983—Baltimore	American	36	260	18	7	.720	271	101	92	86	45	3.18
1984—Baltimore§	American	30	196⅓	15	12	.556	216	93	86	67	54	3.94
1985—Baltimore	American	35	204	14	14	.500	226	118	109	86	65	4.81
1986—Baltimore	American	34	203	11	15	.423	216	110	102	95	57	4.52
Major League Totals—11 Years		326	2038⅔	136	98	.581	2106	944	869	855	476	3.84

Selected by New York Yankees' organization in 1st round (14th player selected) of free-agent draft, June 6, 1972.
†On disabled list, August 1 to August 29, 1975.
‡Traded with Pitchers Rudy May, Tippy Martinez and Dave Pagan, and Catcher Rick Dempsey to Baltimore Orioles for Pitchers Ken Holtzman, Doyle Alexander and Grant Jackson, Catcher Ellie Hendricks and Pitcher Jimmy Freeman, June 15, 1976.
§On disabled list, August 29, 1984 through remainder of season.

CHAMPIONSHIP SERIES RECORD

Year Club	League	G.	IP.	W.	L.	Pct.	H.	R.	ER.	SO.	BB.	ERA.
1979—Baltimore	American	1	9	1	0	1.000	6	0	0	4	1	0.00
1983—Baltimore	American	1	6⅔	0	1	.000	6	2	1	2	3	1.35
Championship Series Totals—2 Years		2	15⅔	1	1	.500	12	2	1	6	4	0.57

WORLD SERIES RECORD

Year Club	League	G.	IP.	W.	L.	Pct.	H.	R.	ER.	SO.	BB.	ERA.
1979—Baltimore	American	2	17	1	1	.500	16	6	6	8	2	3.18
1983—Baltimore	American	2	17	1	1	.500	9	2	2	12	2	1.06
World Series Totals—2 Years		4	34	2	2	.500	25	8	8	20	4	2.12

ALL-STAR GAME RECORD

Member of American League All-Star Team in 1981; did not play.

FREDERICK STANLEY McGRIFF
(Fred)

Born October 31, 1963, at Tampa, Fla.
Height, 6.03. Weight, 200.
Throws and bats lefthanded.

Tied for International League lead in intentional bases on balls received with 8 and grounding into double plays with 16 in 1986.
Led Gulf Coast League in bases on balls received with 48 and tied for lead in game-winning RBIs with 6 in 1982.
Led International League first basemen in total chances with 1,314 and double plays with 108 in 1986.

Year Club	League	Pos.	G.	AB.	R.	H.	2B.	3B.	HR.	RBI.	B.A.	PO.	A.	E.	F.A.
1981—Bradenton Yanks	Gulf C.	1B	29	81	6	12	2	0	0	9	.148	176	8	7	.963
1982—Braden. Yanks†	Gulf C.	1B	62	217	38	59	11	1	★9	●41	.272	514	★56	8	.986
1983—Florence	S. Atl.	1B	33	119	26	37	3	1	7	26	.311	250	14	6	.978
1983—Kinston	Carol.	1B	94	350	53	85	14	1	21	57	.243	784	57	10	.988
1984—Knoxville	South.	1B	56	189	29	47	13	2	9	25	.249	481	45	10	.981
1984—Syracuse	Int.	1B	70	238	28	56	10	1	13	28	.235	644	45	3	.996
1985—Syracuse‡	Int.	1B	51	176	19	40	8	2	5	20	.227	433	37	5	.989
1986—Syracuse	Int.	★1B-OF	133	468	69	121	23	4	19	74	.259	★1219	★85	10	★.992
1986—Toronto	Amer.	1B	3	5	1	1	0	0	0	0	.200	3	0	0	1.000
Major League Totals—1 Year			3	5	1	1	0	0	0	0	.200	3	0	0	1.000

Selected by New York Yankees' organization in 9th round of free-agent draft, June 8, 1981.
†Traded with Outfielder Dave Collins, Pitcher Mike Morgan and a reported $400,000 to Toronto Blue Jays for Outfielder-Catcher Tom Dodd and Pitcher Dale Murray, December 9, 1982.
‡On disabled list, June 5 to August 14, 1985.

TERENCE ROY McGRIFF
(Terry)

Born September 23, 1963, at Fort Pierce, Fla.
Height, 6.02. Weight, 180.
Throws and bats righthanded.

Led American Association catchers in total chances with 481, double plays with 8 and passed balls with 10 in 1986.
Led Eastern League catchers in total chances with 731 in 1985.

Year	Club	League	Pos.	G.	AB.	R.	H.	2B.	3B.	HR.	RBI.	B.A.	PO.	A.	E.	F.A.
1981—Billings		Pion.	C-1B	42	96	15	26	3	0	1	15	.271	166	14	7	.963
1982—Eugene		N'west	C	53	190	23	46	10	2	4	31	.242	320	★43	8	.978
1983—Tampa		Fla. St.	C	87	260	21	66	11	3	5	45	.254	403	67	7	.985
1984—Tampa		Fla. St.	C	110	345	48	96	19	0	7	41	.278	576	88	16	.976
1985—Vermont		East.	C	110	363	52	92	10	4	13	60	.253	★636	89	6	★.992
1986—Denver		A. A.	C	108	340	54	99	22	1	9	54	.291	411	★59	11	.977

Selected by Cincinnati Reds' organization in 8th round of free-agent draft, June 8, 1981.

MARK DAVID McGWIRE

Born October 1, 1963, at Claremont, Calif.
Height, 6.05. Weight, 215.
Throws and bats righthanded.
Attended University of Southern California, Los Angeles, Calif.

Led California League third basemen in assists with 239 and total chances with 354 in 1985.
Member of 1984 U.S. Olympic baseball team.
Named College Player of the Year by THE SPORTING NEWS, 1984.
Named first baseman on THE SPORTING NEWS College Baseball All-America Team, 1984.

Year	Club	League	Pos.	G.	AB.	R.	H.	2B.	3B.	HR.	RBI.	B.A.	PO.	A.	E.	F.A.
1984—Modesto		Calif.	1B	16	55	7	11	3	0	1	1	.200	107	6	1	.991
1985—Modesto		Calif.	3B-1B	138	489	95	134	23	3	●24	●106	.274	105	240	33	.913
1986—Huntsville		South	3B	55	195	40	59	15	0	10	53	.303	34	124	16	.908
1986—Tacoma		P. C.	3B	78	280	42	89	21	5	13	59	.318	53	126	25	.877
1986—Oakland		Amer.	3B	18	53	10	10	1	0	3	9	.189	10	20	6	.833
Major League Totals—1 Year				18	53	10	10	1	0	3	9	.189	10	20	6	.833

Selected by Montreal Expos' organization in 8th round of free-agent draft, June 8, 1981.
Selected by Oakland A's organization in 1st round (10th player selected) of free-agent draft, June 4, 1984.

JOEL JACOB McKEON

Born February 25, 1963, at Covington, Ky.
Height, 6.00. Weight, 185.
Throws and bats lefthanded.
Attended Miami-Dade Community College (North), Miami, Fla.

Major League saves: 1986 (1).

Year	Club	League	G.	IP.	W.	L.	Pct.	H.	R.	ER.	SO.	BB.	ERA.
1982—Sarasota White Sox		Gulf Coast	4	29	3	1	.750	22	7	6	43	2	1.86
1982—Glens Falls		Eastern	7	45	5	2	.714	44	19	15	23	15	3.00
1983—Appleton		Midwest	19	99⅔	5	5	.500	74	34	29	110	58	2.62
1984—Glens Falls		Eastern	45	66⅔	2	3	.400	53	33	27	56	46	3.65
1985—Buffalo		Am. Assoc.	49	82⅓	6	4	.600	85	40	34	62	36	3.72
1986—Buffalo		Am. Assoc.	5	8⅓	1	0	1.000	1	4	0	8	6	0.00
1986—Chicago†		American	30	33	3	1	.750	18	10	9	18	17	2.45
Major League Totals—1 Year			30	33	3	1	.750	18	10	9	18	17	2.45

Selected by San Francisco Giants' organization in 4th round of free-agent draft, January 12, 1982.
Selected by Chicago White Sox' organization in secondary phase of free-agent draft, June 7, 1982.
†On disabled list, July 23, 1986 through remainder of season.

MARK TREMELL McLEMORE

Born October 4, 1964, at San Diego, Calif.
Height, 5.11. Weight, 175.
Throws right and bats left and righthanded.

Led California League second basemen in assists with 400 and double plays with 84 in 1984.

Year	Club	League	Pos.	G.	AB.	R.	H.	2B.	3B.	HR.	RBI.	B.A.	PO.	A.	E.	F.A.
1982—Salem		N'west	2B-SS	55	165	42	49	6	2	0	25	.297	81	125	11	.947
1983—Peoria		Midw.	2B-SS	95	329	42	79	7	3	0	18	.240	170	250	24	.946
1984—Redwood		Calif.	2B-SS	134	482	102	142	8	3	0	45	.295	274	429	25	.966
1985—Midland†		Texas	2B-SS	117	458	80	124	17	6	2	46	.271	301	339	19	.971
1986—Midland		Texas	2B	63	237	54	75	9	1	1	29	.316	155	194	13	.964
1986—Edmonton		P. C.	2B	73	286	41	79	13	1	0	23	.276	173	215	7	.982
1986—California		Amer.	2B	5	4	0	0	0	0	0	0	.000	3	10	0	1.000
Major League Totals—1 Year				5	4	0	0	0	0	0	0	.000	3	10	0	1.000

Selected by California Angels' organization in 9th round of free-agent draft, June 7, 1982.
†On disabled list, May 15 to May 27, 1985.

JOE CRAIG McMURTRY

(Known by middle name.)
Born November 5, 1959, at Troy, Tex.
Height, 6.05. Weight, 195.
Throws and bats righthanded.
Attended McLennan Community College, Waco, Tex.

Major League saves: 1985 (1).
Tied for International League lead in games started by pitchers with 32 in 1982.
Named National League Rookie Pitcher of the Year by THE SPORTING NEWS, 1983.
Named International League Pitcher of the Year, 1982.

Year	Club	League	G.	IP.	W.	L.	Pct.	H.	R.	ER.	SO.	BB.	ERA.
1980—Savannah		Southern	14	86	7	4	.636	82	40	34	37	35	3.56
1981—Savannah		Southern	28	202	*15	11	.577	168	87	62	111	95	2.76
1982—Richmond		Int'national	32	*210	*17	9	.654	198	98	89	96	107	3.81
1983—Atlanta		National	36	224⅔	15	9	.625	204	86	77	105	88	3.08
1984—Atlanta		National	37	183⅓	9	17	.346	184	100	88	99	102	4.32
1985—Atlanta		National	17	45	0	3	.000	56	36	33	28	27	6.60
1985—Richmond		Int'national	16	107⅓	7	5	.583	88	43	39	74	51	3.27
1986—Atlanta†		National	37	79⅔	1	6	.143	82	46	42	50	43	4.74
1986—Greenville		Southern	3	15	1	1	.500	13	10	10	12	9	6.00
Major League Totals—4 Years			127	532⅔	25	35	.417	526	268	240	282	260	4.06

Selected by Atlanta Braves' organization in 1st round (fourth player selected) of free-agent draft, January 8, 1980.
†On disabled list, July 27 to September 1, 1986; included rehabilitation disability assignment to Greenville, August 14 to September 1, 1986.

HAROLD ABRAHAM McRAE
(Hal)

Born July 10, 1945, at Avon Park, Fla.
Height, 5.11. Weight, 185.
Throws and bats righthanded.
Attended Florida A&M University, Tallahassee, Fla.
Father of Brian McRae, shortstop in Kansas City Royals' organization.

Tied major league record for most long hits, doubleheader, (6), August 27, 1974 (5 doubles, 1 home run).
Major League stolen bases: 1968 (1), 1971 (3), 1973 (2), 1974 (11), 1975 (11), 1976 (22), 1977 (18), 1978 (17), 1979 (5), 1980 (10), 1981 (3), 1982 (4), 1983 (2). Total—109.
Led American League in being hit by pitch with 13 in 1977.
Named designated hitter on THE SPORTING NEWS American League All-Star Team, 1976, 1977 and 1982.
Named designated hitter on THE SPORTING NEWS American League Silver Slugger team, 1982.

Year	Club	League	Pos.	G.	AB.	R.	H.	2B.	3B.	HR.	RBI.	B.A.	PO.	A.	E.	F.A.
1965—Tampa		Fla. St.	OF	22	65	3	10	3	0	0	4	.154	19	0	0	1.000
1966—Peninsula†		Carol.	2B	109	394	65	113	19	4	11	56	.287	252	226	*28	.945
1967—Buffalo‡		Int.	2B	73	259	30	65	14	3	10	34	.251	133	208	23	.937
1967—Knoxville		South.	2B	51	186	26	54	10	3	6	25	.290	140	136	12	.958
1968—Indianapolis		P. C.	2B-OF	119	444	64	131	31	11	16	65	.295	222	307	14	.974
1968—Cincinnati		Nat.	2B	17	51	1	10	1	0	0	2	.196	33	30	5	.926
1969—Indianapolis§		A. A.	OF	17	41	2	9	1	0	0	4	.220	0	0	0	.000
1970—Cincinnati		Nat.	OF-3B-2B	70	165	18	41	6	1	8	23	.248	53	7	1	.984
1971—Cincinnati		Nat.	OF	99	337	39	89	24	2	9	34	.264	167	6	6	.966
1972—Cincinnati x		Nat.	OF-3B	61	97	9	27	4	0	5	26	.278	16	14	6	.833
1973—Kansas City		Amer.	OF-3B	106	338	36	79	18	3	9	50	.234	101	6	5	.955
1974—Kansas City		Amer.	OF-3B	148	539	71	167	36	4	15	88	.310	132	3	7	.951
1975—Kansas City		Amer.	OF-3B	126	480	57	147	38	6	5	71	.306	207	7	3	.986
1976—Kansas City		Amer.	OF	149	527	75	175	34	5	8	73	.332	63	2	2	.970
1977—Kansas City		Amer.	OF	●162	641	104	191	*54	11	21	92	.298	81	8	4	.957
1978—Kansas City		Amer.	OF	156	623	90	170	39	5	16	72	.273	3	1	0	1.000
1979—Kansas City y		Amer.	DH	101	393	55	113	32	4	10	74	.288	0	0	0	.000
1980—Kansas City z		Amer.	DH	124	489	73	145	39	5	14	83	.297	17	0	0	1.000
1981—Kansas City		Amer.	OF	101	389	38	106	23	2	7	36	.272	10	0	1	.909
1982—Kansas City a		Amer.	OF	159	613	91	189	●46	8	27	*133	.308	1	0	1	.500
1983—Kansas City		Amer.	DH	157	589	84	183	41	6	12	82	.311	0	0	0	.000
1984—Kansas City		Amer.	DH	106	317	30	96	13	4	3	42	.303	0	0	0	.000
1985—Kansas City b		Amer.	DH	112	320	41	83	19	0	14	70	.259	0	0	0	.000
1986—Kansas City		Amer.	DH	112	278	22	70	14	0	7	37	.252	0	0	0	.000
National League Totals—4 Years				247	650	67	167	35	3	22	85	.257	269	57	18	.948
American League Totals—14 Years				1819	6536	868	1914	446	63	168	1003	.293	615	27	23	.965
Major League Totals—18 Years				2066	7186	935	2081	481	66	190	1088	.290	884	84	41	.959

Selected by Cincinnati Reds' organization in 6th round of free-agent draft, June, 1965.
†On disabled list, June 23 to July 6, 1966.
‡On disabled list, April 26 to May 7, 1967.
§On disabled list, April 18 to May 28 and July 4 to August 5, 1969.
xTraded with Pitcher Wayne Simpson to Kansas City Royals for Pitcher Roger Nelson and Outfielder Richie Scheinblum, November 30, 1972.
yOn disabled list, June 11 to August 2, 1979.
zOn disabled list, May 13 to June 2, 1980.
aGranted free agency, November 10, 1982; re-signed by Royals, November 15, 1982.
bGranted free agency, November 12, 1985; re-signed by Royals, December 8, 1985.

DIVISION SERIES RECORD

Year	Club	League	Pos.	G.	AB.	R.	H.	2B.	3B.	HR.	RBI.	B.A.	PO.	A.	E.	F.A.
1981—Kansas City	Amer.	DH	3	11	0	1	1	0	0	0	.091	0	0	0	.000

CHAMPIONSHIP SERIES RECORD

Established Championship Series record for most runs, five-game Series (6), 1977.
Tied Championship Series record for most doubles, total Series (7).

Year	Club	League	Pos.	G.	AB.	R.	H.	2B.	3B.	HR.	RBI.	B.A.	PO.	A.	E.	F.A.
1970—Cincinnati	Nat.	PH-OF	2	4	0	0	0	0	0	0	.000	2	0	0	1.000
1972—Cincinnati	Nat.	PH	1	0	0	0	0	0	0	0	.000	0	0	0	.000
1976—Kansas City	Amer.	DH	5	17	2	2	1	1	0	1	.118	5	1	0	1.000
1977—Kansas City	Amer.	OF-DH	5	18	6	8	3	0	1	2	.444	2	1	0	1.000
1978—Kansas City	Amer.	DH	4	14	0	3	0	0	0	2	.214	0	0	0	.000
1980—Kansas City	Amer.	DH	3	10	0	2	0	0	0	0	.200	0	0	0	.000
1984—Kansas City	Amer.	PH	2	2	0	2	1	0	0	1	1.000	0	0	0	.000
1985—Kansas City	Amer.	DH	6	23	1	6	2	0	0	3	.261	0	0	0	.000
Championship Series Totals—8 Years....			28	88	9	23	7	1	1	9	.261	9	2	0	1.000

WORLD SERIES RECORD

Year	Club	League	Pos.	G.	AB.	R.	H.	2B.	3B.	HR.	RBI.	B.A.	PO.	A.	E.	F.A.
1970—Cincinnati	Nat.	OF	3	11	1	5	2	0	0	3	.455	2	1	0	1.000
1972—Cincinnati	Nat.	PH-OF	5	9	1	4	1	0	0	2	.444	4	0	0	1.000
1980—Kansas City	Amer.	DH	6	24	3	9	3	0	0	1	.375	0	0	0	.000
1985—Kansas City	Amer.	PH	3	1	0	0	0	0	0	0	.000	0	0	0	.000
World Series Totals—4 Years			17	45	5	18	6	0	0	6	.400	6	1	0	1.000

ALL-STAR GAME RECORD

Year	League	Pos.	AB.	R.	H.	2B.	3B.	HR.	RBI.	B.A.	PO.	A.	E.	F.A.
1975—American	PH	1	0	0	0	0	0	0	.000	0	0	0	.000
1976—American	PH	1	0	0	0	0	0	0	.000	0	0	0	.000
1982—American	PH	0	0	0	0	0	0	0	.000	0	0	0	.000
All-Star Game Totals—3 Years		2	0	0	0	0	0	0	.000	0	0	0	.000

WALTER KEVIN McREYNOLDS

(Known by middle name.)
Born October 16, 1959, at Little Rock, Ark.
Height, 6.01. Weight, 205.
Throws and bats righthanded.
Attended University of Arkansas, Fayetteville, Ark.

Major League stolen bases: 1983 (2), 1984 (3), 1985 (4), 1986 (8). Total—17.
Led National League outfielders in total chances with 436 in 1984 and 445 in 1985.
Led Pacific Coast League in total bases with 328 in 1983.
Named Minor League Player of the Year by THE SPORTING NEWS, 1983.
Named Pacific Coast League Player of the Year, 1983.
Named California League Most Valuable Player, 1982.
Received reported $125,000 bonus to sign with San Diego Padres, 1982.
Named outfielder on THE SPORTING NEWS College Baseball All-America Team, 1981.

Year	Club	League	Pos.	G.	AB.	R.	H.	2B.	3B.	HR.	RBI.	B.A.	PO.	A.	E.	F.A.
1982—Reno	Calif.	OF	90	338	83	127	17	5	★28	98	★.376	52	7	3	.952
1982—Amarillo	Texas	OF	40	162	30	57	8	3	5	39	.352	76	3	2	.975
1983—Las Vegas	P. C.	OF	113	446	98	168	★46	9	●32	116	.377	257	3	9	.967
1983—San Diego	Nat.	OF	39	140	15	31	3	1	4	14	.221	87	4	1	.989
1984—San Diego	Nat.	OF	147	525	68	146	26	6	20	75	.278	★422	10	4	.991
1985—San Diego	Nat.	OF	152	564	61	132	24	4	15	75	.234	★430	12	3	.993
1986—San Diego†	Nat.	OF	158	560	89	161	31	6	26	96	.288	332	9	8	.977
Major League Totals—4 Years			496	1789	233	470	84	17	65	260	.263	1271	35	16	.988

Selected by Milwaukee Brewers' organization in 18th round of free-agent draft, June 6, 1978.
Selected by San Diego Padres' organization in 1st round (sixth player selected) of free-agent draft, June 8, 1981.
†Traded with Pitcher Gene Walter and Infielder Adam Ging to New York Mets for Outfielders Shawn Abner, Stanley Jefferson and Kevin Mitchell and Pitchers Kevin Armstrong and Kevin Brown, December 11, 1986.

CHAMPIONSHIP SERIES RECORD

Year	Club	League	Pos.	G.	AB.	R.	H.	2B.	3B.	HR.	RBI.	B.A.	PO.	A.	E.	F.A.
1984—San Diego	Nat.	OF	4	10	2	3	0	0	1	4	.300	10	0	0	1.000

LARRY DEAN McWILLIAMS

Born February 10, 1954, at Wichita, Kan.
Height, 6.05. Weight, 181.
Throws and bats lefthanded.
Attended Paris Junior College, Paris, Tex.

Tied major league record for most strikeouts by batter, inning (2), April 22, 1979 (fourth inning).
Major League saves: 1982 (1), 1984 (1). Total—2.
Named lefthanded pitcher on THE SPORTING NEWS National League All-Star Team, 1983.

Year	Club	League	G.	IP.	W.	L.	Pct.	H.	R.	ER.	SO.	BB.	ERA.
1974—Greenwood†	W. Carol.	11	64	4	3	.571	64	26	20	61	23	2.81

Year Club	League	G.	IP.	W.	L.	Pct.	H.	R.	ER.	SO.	BB.	ERA.
1975—Greenwood‡	W. Carol.	17	93	8	4	.667	83	36	29	71	18	2.81
1976—Greenwood	W. Carol.	8	48	2	2	.500	40	19	14	44	13	2.63
1976—Savannah	Southern	16	74	3	8	.273	82	41	38	37	33	4.62
1977—Savannah	Southern	26	158	8	9	.471	153	70	59	139	64	3.36
1978—Richmond	Int'national	15	108	6	5	.545	87	36	34	78	41	2.83
1978—Atlanta	National	15	99	9	3	.750	84	38	31	42	35	2.82
1979—Atlanta§	National	13	66	3	2	.600	69	41	41	32	22	5.59
1980—Atlanta	National	30	164	9	14	.391	188	97	90	77	39	4.94
1981—Richmond	Int'national	29	178	●13	10	.565	174	98	●86	157	79	4.35
1981—Atlanta	National	6	38	2	1	.667	31	13	13	23	8	3.08
1982—Atlanta x-Pittsburgh	National	46	159⅓	8	8	.500	158	79	68	118	44	3.84
1983—Pittsburgh	National	35	238	15	8	.652	205	99	86	199	87	3.25
1984—Pittsburgh	National	34	227⅓	12	11	.522	226	86	74	149	78	2.93
1985—Pittsburgh y	National	30	126⅓	7	9	.438	139	70	66	52	62	4.70
1986—Pittsburgh	National	49	122⅓	3	11	.214	129	75	70	80	49	5.15
Major League Totals—9 Years		258	1240⅓	68	67	.504	1229	598	539	772	424	3.91

Selected by Atlanta Braves' organization in 1st round (sixth player selected) of free-agent draft, January 9, 1974.
†On disabled list, July 22 to September 25, 1974.
‡On disabled list, April 11 to June 3, 1975.
§On disabled list, May 18 to June 15 and July 7 to September 1, 1979.
xTraded to Pittsburgh Pirates for Pitcher Pascual Perez and a player to be named later, June 30, 1982; Atlanta Braves' organization acquired Shortstop Carlos Rios to complete deal, September 8, 1982.
yOn disabled list, May 17 to June 8 and August 18 to September 3, 1985.

ROBERT ANDREW MEACHAM
(Bobby)

Born August 25, 1960, at Los Angeles, Calif.
Height, 6.01. Weight, 180.
Throws right and bats left and righthanded.
Attended San Diego State University, San Diego, Calif.

Major League stolen bases: 1983 (8), 1984 (9), 1985 (25), 1986 (3). Total—45.
Led American League in sacrifice hits with 14 in 1984 and 23 in 1985.
Named shortstop on THE SPORTING NEWS College Baseball All-America Team, 1981.

Year Club	League	Pos.	G.	AB.	R.	H.	2B.	3B.	HR.	RBI.	B.A.	PO.	A.	E.	F.A.
1981—Gastonia	S. Atl.	SS	74	274	24	50	8	2	1	18	.182	107	235	25	.932
1982—St. Petersburg†	Fla. St.	SS	120	421	57	109	15	4	0	37	.259	201	306	★47	.915
1983—Columbus	Int.	SS	120	423	58	111	18	3	9	60	.262	206	348	30	.949
1983—New York	Amer.	SS-3B	22	51	5	12	2	0	0	4	.235	16	64	6	.930
1984—Nashville	South.	SS	8	31	3	9	0	0	0	3	.290	16	25	1	.976
1984—Columbus	Int.	SS	46	187	35	53	13	●6	2	13	.283	67	133	14	.935
1984—New York	Amer.	SS-2B	99	360	62	91	13	4	2	25	.253	140	272	19	.956
1985—New York	Amer.	SS	156	481	70	105	16	2	1	47	.218	236	390	24	.963
1986—New York	Amer.	SS	56	161	19	36	7	1	0	10	.224	70	149	12	.948
1986—Columbus	Int.	SS-2B	46	150	14	21	0	5	0	11	.140	81	133	12	.947
Major League Totals—4 Years			333	1053	156	244	38	7	3	86	.232	462	875	61	.956

Selected by Chicago White Sox' organization in 14th round of free agent draft, June 6, 1978.
Selected by St. Louis Cardinals' organization in 1st round (eighth player selected) of free-agent draft, June 8, 1981.
†Traded with Outfielder Stan Javier to New York Yankees' organization for Pitchers Marty Mason and Steve Fincher and Outfielder Bob Helsom, December 14, 1982.

MICHAEL RAY MEADOWS
(Louie)

Born April 29, 1961, in Onslow County, N.C.
Height, 5.11. Weight, 190.
Throws and bats lefthanded.
Attended North Carolina State University, Raleigh, N.C.

Major League stolen bases: 1986 (1).

Year Club	League	Pos.	G.	AB.	R.	H.	2B.	3B.	HR.	RBI.	B.A.	PO.	A.	E.	F.A.
1982—Asheville	S. Atl.	OF	66	228	43	72	9	1	10	41	.316	87	4	13	.875
1983—Daytona Beach	Fla. St.	OF	112	382	68	112	25	14	9	71	.293	169	5	4	.978
1984—Daytona Beach	Fla. St.	OF-1B	70	252	49	76	14	10	6	44	.302	323	17	5	.986
1984—Columbus	South.	OF-1B	65	225	33	63	17	4	8	36	.280	150	6	3	.981
1985—Columbus	South.	OF-1B	140	476	76	111	16	8	14	67	.233	514	32	12	.978
1986—Tucson	P. C.	OF-1B	82	290	42	87	14	8	10	52	.300	203	15	9	.960
1986—Houston	Nat.	OF	6	6	1	2	0	0	0	0	.333	0	0	0	.000
Major League Totals—1 Year			6	6	1	2	0	0	0	0	.333	0	0	0	.000

Selected by Houston Astros' organization in 2nd round of free-agent draft, June 7, 1982.

DAVID DONALD MEADS III
(Dave)

Born January 7, 1964, at Montclair, N.J.
Height, 6.00. Weight, 175.
Throws and bats lefthanded.
Attended Middlesex County College, Edison, N.J.

Year Club	League	G.	IP.	W.	L.	Pct.	H.	R.	ER.	SO.	BB.	ERA.
1984—Sarasota Astros	Gulf Coast	7	29⅓	2	2	.500	22	11	4	28	2	1.23
1984—Auburn†	NYP	10	28	5	1	.833	31	17	16	29	12	5.14
1985—Gastonia	S. Atlantic	33	146⅓	3	10	.231	160	91	71	118	50	4.37
1986—Asheville	S. Atlantic	19	54⅓	4	3	.571	51	25	12	50	14	1.99
1986—Osceola	Florida St.	11	15⅓	2	4	.333	24	14	13	10	7	7.63
1986—Columbus	Southern	16	22⅓	1	1	.500	22	11	11	26	13	4.43

Selected by Houston Astros' organization in 6th round of free-agent draft, January 17, 1984.

†Loaned to Gastonia (Independent), April 4, 1985; returned, October 15, 1985.

SCOTT HOWARD MEDVIN

Born September 16, 1961, at North Olmsted, O.
Height, 6.00. Weight, 190.
Throws and bats righthanded.
Received bachelor of arts degree in management from Baldwin-Wallace College, Berea, O.

Year Club	League	G.	IP.	W.	L.	Pct.	H.	R.	ER.	SO.	BB.	ERA.
1984—Wausau†	Midwest	40	65⅔	4	2	.667	62	36	26	53	35	3.56
1985—Lakeland‡	Florida St.	31	51⅔	5	4	.556	48	20	16	47	20	2.79
1985—Birmingham	Southern	13	23	3	3	.500	14	10	8	17	12	3.13
1986—Shreveport	Texas	49	93⅔	8	6	.571	71	32	25	68	42	2.40

Signed as free agent by Detroit Tigers' organization, September 27, 1983.

†Loaned to Wausau (Seattle Mariners' organization), April 4, 1984; returned, September 5, 1984.

‡Traded to San Francisco Giants, December 11, 1985, completing deal in which San Francisco traded Pitchers Dave LaPoint and Eric King and Catcher Matt Nokes to Detroit Tigers for Pitcher Juan Berenguer, Catcher Bob Melvin and a player to be named later, October 7, 1985.

FRANCISCO JAVIER MELENDEZ (VILLEGAS)

Born January 25, 1964, at Rio Piedras, Puerto Rico.
Height, 6.00. Weight, 185.
Throws and bats lefthanded.
Led Pacific Coast League first basemen in putouts with 1,085 in 1984.
Led Eastern League first basemen in putouts with 1,081, total chances with 1,166 and double plays with 99 in 1983.

Year Club	League	Pos.	G.	AB.	R.	H.	2B.	3B.	HR.	RBI.	B.A.	PO.	A.	E.	F.A.
1981—Peninsula	Carol.	1B-OF	32	74	6	10	3	0	0	6	.135	154	13	6	.965
1981—Spartanburg	S. Atl.	1B-OF	85	306	44	82	13	1	3	36	.268	760	57	17	.980
1982—Peninsula	Carol.	1B	118	424	54	124	★33	3	4	69	.292	739	75	11	.987
1983—Reading	East.	1B-OF	126	450	81	134	17	4	5	75	.298	1082	73	12	.990
1984—Portland	P. C.	★1B-OF	128	506	63	158	36	8	3	65	.312	1090	85	11	★.991
1984—Philadelphia	Nat.	1B	21	23	0	3	0	0	0	2	.130	37	4	0	1.000
1985—Portland	P. C.	●1B-OF	130	397	41	111	25	2	2	54	.280	974	69	●15	.986
1986—Portland	P. C.	1B-OF	96	356	47	113	21	2	4	57	.318	778	68	12	.986
1986—Philadelphia	Nat.	1B	9	8	0	2	0	0	0	0	.250	1	0	0	1.000
Major League Totals—2 Years			30	31	0	5	0	0	0	2	.161	38	4	0	1.000

Signed as free agent by Philadelphia Phillies' organization, October 4, 1980.

ROBERT PAUL MELVIN
(Bob)

Born October 28, 1961, at Palo Alto, Calif.
Height, 6.04. Weight, 205.
Throws and bats righthanded.
Attended University of California, Berkeley, Calif.,
and Canada College, Redwood City, Calif.

Major League stolen bases: 1986 (3).

Year Club	League	Pos.	G.	AB.	R.	H.	2B.	3B.	HR.	RBI.	B.A.	PO.	A.	E.	F.A.
1981—Macon	S. Atl.	C	114	412	56	112	19	1	14	64	.272	456	67	2	★.996
1982—Birmingham†	South.	★C-1B-3B	98	364	33	86	12	1	13	52	.236	638	54	9	★.987
1983—Birmingham	South.	C-1B-2B	78	285	43	82	14	2	10	56	.288	404	30	2	.995
1983—Evansville	A. A.	C-1B	45	142	10	27	6	0	2	11	.190	213	16	1	.996
1984—Evansville	A. A.	C-1B	44	141	12	35	13	0	0	11	.248	214	21	1	.996
1984—Birmingham	South.	C-1B-3B	69	271	34	73	14	1	2	33	.269	341	38	4	.990
1985—Nashville	A. A.	C-1B-OF	53	177	27	48	7	1	9	24	.271	276	28	2	.993
1985—Detroit‡	Amer.	C	41	82	10	18	4	1	0	4	.220	175	13	2	.989
1986—San Francisco	Nat.	C-3B	89	268	24	60	14	2	5	25	.224	443	60	6	.988
American League Totals—1 Year			41	82	10	18	4	1	0	4	.220	175	13	2	.989
National League Totals—1 Year			89	268	24	60	14	2	5	25	.224	443	60	6	.988
Major League Totals—2 Years			130	350	34	78	18	3	5	29	.223	618	73	8	.989

Selected by Baltimore Orioles' organization in 3rd round of free-agent draft, June 5, 1979.

Selected by Detroit Tigers' organization in secondary phase of free-agent draft, January 13, 1981.

†On disabled list, May 1 to May 25, 1982.

‡Traded with Pitcher Juan Berenguer and a player to be named later to San Francisco Giants for Pitchers Dave LaPoint and Eric King and Catcher Matt Nokes, October 7, 1985; San Francisco acquired Pitcher Scott Medvin to complete deal, December 11, 1985.

ANTONIO GUSTAVO MENENDEZ
(Tony)

Born February 20, 1965, at Havana, Cuba.
Height, 6.02. Weight, 189.
Throws and bats righthanded.

Year Club	League	G.	IP.	W.	L.	Pct.	H.	R.	ER.	SO.	BB.	ERA.
1984—Sarasota White Sox	Gulf Coast	6	37	3	2	.600	26	19	13	30	13	3.16
1985—Appleton	Midwest	24	148	13	4	.765	134	67	45	100	55	2.74
1985—Buffalo	Am. Assoc.	1	2⅓	0	1	.000	9	5	5	2	1	19.29
1986—Birmingham	Southern	17	96⅓	7	8	.467	132	71	61	52	50	5.70

Selected by Chicago White Sox' organization in 1st round (20th player selected) of free-agent draft, June 4, 1984.

ORLANDO MERCADO (RODRIGUEZ)

Born November 7, 1961, at Arecibo, Puerto Rico.
Height, 6.00. Weight, 195.
Throws and bats righthanded.

Major League stolen bases: 1983 (2), 1984 (1). Total—3.
Led Eastern League in passed balls with 23 in 1980.
Led California League in passed balls with 24 in 1979.

Year Club	League	Pos.	G.	AB.	R.	H.	2B.	3B.	HR.	RBI.	B.A.	PO.	A.	E.	F.A.
1978—Bellingham	N'west	C	38	49	7	6	2	0	0	5	.122	184	20	4	.981
1979—San Jose	Calif.	C-1B	110	335	53	86	18	2	10	54	.257	629	71	17	.976
1980—Lynn	East.	C-1B	117	396	55	101	25	6	11	71	.255	607	78	11	.984
1981—Spokane	P. C.	C-OF	95	312	32	67	21	2	4	31	.215	446	60	13	.975
1982—Salt Lake City	P. C.	C-O-1-3	90	321	43	90	19	2	16	66	.280	497	43	13	.976
1982—Seattle	Amer.	C	9	17	1	2	0	0	1	6	.118	31	1	0	1.000
1983—Seattle	Amer.	C	66	178	10	35	11	2	1	16	.197	342	27	2	.995
1983—Salt Lake City	P. C.	C-3B	26	88	12	20	2	1	2	12	.227	131	13	2	.986
1984—Seattle	Amer.	C	30	78	5	17	3	1	0	5	.218	118	10	1	.992
1984—Salt Lake City†	P. C.	C-1B-OF	29	109	18	39	9	2	6	22	.358	169	18	2	.989
1985—Oklahoma City‡	A. A.	C	59	206	20	52	7	1	8	29	.252	268	26	4	.987
1986—Oklahoma City	A. A.	C	48	172	20	47	11	1	3	25	.273	234	29	8	.970
1986—Texas	Amer.	C	46	102	7	24	1	1	1	7	.235	240	25	1	.996
Major League Totals—4 Years			151	375	23	78	15	4	3	34	.208	731	63	4	.995

Signed as free agent by Seattle Mariners' organization, January 6, 1978.
†Traded to Texas Rangers' organization for Catcher Donnie Scott, April 4, 1985.
‡On disabled list, July 10 to September 19, 1985.

RONALD KNOX MERIDITH
(Ron)

Born November 26, 1956, at San Pedro, Calif.
Height, 6.00. Weight, 175.
Throws and bats lefthanded.
Attended Oral Roberts University, Tulsa, Okla.

Major League saves: 1985 (1).
Led American Association in wild pitches with 13 in 1986.

Year Club	League	G.	IP.	W.	L.	Pct.	H.	R.	ER.	SO.	BB.	ERA.
1978—Sarasota Astros	Gulf Coast	2	12	2	0	1.000	12	6	4	6	3	3.00
1978—Daytona Beach	Florida St.	9	56	3	6	.333	59	28	27	31	17	4.34
1979—Columbus	Southern	26	149	9	11	.450	150	75	71	63	78	4.29
1980—Columbus	Southern	25	145	9	5	.643	143	48	41	82	40	2.54
1981—Tucson†	P. Coast	34	132	7	6	.538	166	93	80	70	63	5.45
1982—Hawaii	P. Coast	37	111⅓	6	2	.750	105	53	47	68	41	3.80
1983—Tucson‡§	P. Coast	37	91	2	3	.400	128	74	65	59	33	6.43
1984—Iowa	Am. Assoc.	49	93⅔	7	3	.700	88	33	33	78	33	3.17
1984—Chicago	National	3	5⅓	0	0	.000	6	5	2	4	2	3.38
1985—Iowa	Am. Assoc.	25	41	4	1	.800	29	9	6	29	7	1.32
1985—Chicago	National	32	46⅓	3	2	.600	53	24	23	23	24	4.47
1986—Iowa x-Oklahoma City	Am. Assoc.	34	118	7	7	.500	125	63	58	60	52	4.42
1986—Texas	American	5	3	1	0	1.000	2	1	1	2	1	3.00
National League Totals—2 Years		35	51⅔	3	2	.600	59	29	25	27	26	4.35
American League Totals—1 Year		5	3	1	0	1.000	2	1	1	2	1	3.00
Major League Totals—3 Years		40	54⅔	4	2	.667	61	30	26	29	27	4.28

Selected by Houston Astros' organization in 4th round of free-agent draft, June 6, 1978.
†Loaned to Hawaii (San Diego Padres' organization), April 6, 1982; returned, September 17, 1982.
‡Traded to Atlanta Braves' organization for Pitcher Jose Alvarez, February 16, 1984.
§Traded to Chicago Cubs' organization for Pitcher Terry Leach, April 4, 1984.
xTraded to Texas Rangers for Pitcher Bryan Dial and a player to be named later, July 26, 1986; Chicago Cubs' organization acquired Pitcher Rich Surhoff to complete deal, July 28, 1986.

BILLIE DAVID MERRIFIELD

Born May 7, 1962, at Waukegan, Ill.
Height, 6.04. Weight, 195.
Throws and bats righthanded.
Attended Wake Forest University, Winston-Salem, N.C.

Led Texas League in sacrifice flies with 12 in 1985.
Led Texas League third basemen in double plays with 34 in 1985.
Led Midwest League third basemen in putouts with 122, fielding percentage with .958 and total chances with 406 in 1984.

Year	Club	League	Pos.	G.	AB.	R.	H.	2B.	3B.	HR.	RBI.	B.A.	PO.	A.	E.	F.A.
1983—Peoria		Midw.	3B	80	289	38	72	19	1	10	40	.249	47	168	25	.896
1984—Peoria		Midw.	3B-1B	●138	523	78	142	34	0	29	97	.272	147	268	17	.961
1985—Midland		Texas	3B-1B-SS	133	507	77	142	28	3	15	83	.280	196	274	28	.944
1986—Midland		Texas	3B-1B-SS	67	253	43	73	19	0	8	53	.289	66	116	11	.943
1986—Edmonton		P. C.	3B-1B-OF	55	188	32	53	12	1	9	38	.282	171	77	6	.976

Selected by Pittsburgh Pirates' organization in 36th round of free-agent draft, June 3, 1980.
Selected by California Angels' organization in 2nd round of free-agent draft, June 6, 1983.

JOSE RAMON MESA

Born May 22, 1966, at Azua, Dominican Republic.
Height, 6.03. Weight, 170.
Throws and bats righthanded.

Led Gulf Coast League in shutouts with 3 in 1982.
Tied for Carolina League lead in hit batsmen with 9 in 1985.

Year	Club	League	G.	IP.	W.	L.	Pct.	H.	R.	ER.	SO.	BB.	ERA.
1982—Bradenton Blue Jays		Gulf Coast	13	83⅓	6	4	.600	58	34	25	40	20	2.70
1983—Florence		S. Atlantic	28	141⅓	6	12	.333	153	★116	86	91	93	5.48
1984—Florence		S. Atlantic	7	38⅓	4	3	.571	38	24	16	35	25	3.76
1984—Kinston†		Carolina	10	50⅔	5	2	.714	51	23	22	24	28	3.91
1985—Kinston		Carolina	30	106⅔	5	10	.333	110	89	73	71	79	6.16
1986—Ventura County		California	24	142⅓	10	6	.625	141	71	61	113	58	3.86

Signed as free agent by Toronto Blue Jays' organization, October 31, 1981.
†On disabled list, August 27, 1984 through remainder of season.

TANNER JOE MEYER JR.

(Joey)

Born May 10, 1962, at Kailua, Haw.
Height, 6.03. Weight, 250.
Throws and bats righthanded.
Attended University of Hawaii, Honolulu, Haw.

Led Midwest League in total bases with 264 in 1984.
Named Midwest League Most Valuable Player, 1984.

Year	Club	League	Pos.	G.	AB.	R.	H.	2B.	3B.	HR.	RBI.	B.A.	PO.	A.	E.	F.A.
1984—Beloit		Midw.	1B	128	475	73	152	22	0	★30	★102	★.320	560	34	11	.982
1985—El Paso		Texas	1B	131	506	79	154	17	2	★37	123	.304	252	15	6	.978
1986—Vancouver		P. C.	1B	126	451	65	115	16	0	24	98	.255	784	41	15	.982

Selected by California Angels' organization in 8th round of free-agent draft, June 8, 1981.
Selected by Milwaukee Brewers' organization in 5th round of free-agent draft, June 6, 1983.

DARRELL KEITH MILLER

Born February 26, 1959, at Washington, D.C.
Height, 6.02. Weight, 200.
Throws and bats righthanded.
Attended California State Poly University, Pomona, Calif.
Brother of Cheryl Miller, member of 1984 U.S. Olympic Gold Medal women's basketball team;
and Reggie Miller, forward at University of California at Los Angeles.

Year	Club	League	Pos.	G.	AB.	R.	H.	2B.	3B.	HR.	RBI.	B.A.	PO.	A.	E.	F.A.
1979—Idaho Falls		Pion.	C-1B	60	205	35	55	10	2	6	34	.268	254	40	12	.961
1980—Salinas		Calif.	C-1B-OF	64	195	26	56	6	3	4	28	.287	289	57	8	.977
1980—Salt Lake City		P. C.	C	30	101	10	30	2	2	0	11	.297	113	18	6	.956
1981—Holyoke		East.	C-OF-1B	126	443	61	117	26	9	10	62	.264	507	50	24	.959
1982—Holyoke†		East.	OF	119	450	76	118	25	★10	11	60	.262	187	8	8	.961
1983—Edmonton‡		P. C.	O-C-1-3	51	142	29	43	5	1	2	23	.303	146	24	8	.955
1984—Edmonton§		P. C.	C-OF-1B	92	328	65	107	19	9	10	67	.326	270	27	4	.987
1984—California		Amer.	1B-OF	17	41	5	7	0	0	0	1	.171	92	7	1	.990
1985—California x		Amer.	OF-C-3B	51	48	8	18	2	1	2	7	.375	39	3	2	.955
1985—Edmonton		P. C.	OF-C	17	71	10	20	3	1	1	6	.282	43	5	1	.980
1986—California		Amer.	OF-C	33	57	6	13	2	1	0	4	.228	30	3	0	1.000
1986—Edmonton		P. C.	OF-C-1B	63	212	37	65	8	7	8	30	.307	39	0	2	.951
Major League Totals—3 Years				101	146	19	38	4	2	2	12	.260	161	13	3	.983

Selected by California Angels' organization in 9th round of free-agent draft, June 5, 1979.
†On disabled list, May 6 to May 20, 1982.
‡On disabled list, May 4 to May 31, 1983.
§On disabled list, July 17 to August 7, 1984.
xOn disabled list, June 13 to July 5, 1985.

KEITH ALAN MILLER

Born June 12, 1963, at Midland, Mich.
Height, 5.11. Weight, 175.
Throws and bats righthanded.
Attended Oral Roberts University, Tulsa, Okla.

Tied for Texas League lead in being hit by pitch with 7 in 1986.

Year Club	League	Pos.	G.	AB.	R.	H.	2B.	3B.	HR.	RBI.	B.A.	PO.	A.	E.	F.A.
1985—Lynchburg	Carol.	3B-2B-OF	89	325	51	98	16	5	7	54	.302	103	203	25	.924
1985—Jackson	Texas	2B-SS	46	165	17	37	8	1	3	22	.224	108	132	8	.968
1986—Jackson†	Texas	2B	94	353	80	116	23	4	5	36	.329	198	272	19	.961

Selected by Cleveland Indians' organization in 24th round of free-agent draft, June 5, 1981.
Selected by New York Yankees' organization in 2nd round of free-agent draft, June 4, 1984 (contract was later voided after it was discovered he had a pre-existing knee injury).
Signed as free agent by New York Mets' organization, September 6, 1984.
†On disabled list, April 8 to May 20, 1986.

EDDIE JAMES MILNER JR.

Born May 21, 1955, at Columbus, O.
Height, 5.11. Weight, 170.
Throws and bats lefthanded.
Attended Muskingum College, New Concord, O., and received bachelor of science degree
in business from Central State University, Wilberforce, O. in 1978.
Brother of Hobson Milner, 12th round selection of Minnesota Vikings in 1982 NFL draft;
cousin of John Milner, first baseman-outfielder with New York Mets,
Pittsburgh Pirates and Montreal Expos, 1971 through 1982.
Major League stolen bases: 1982 (18), 1983 (41), 1984 (21), 1985 (35), 1986 (18). Total—133.
Tied for Pioneer League lead in double plays by outfielders with 1 in 1976.
Named Florida State League Most Valuable Player, 1978.

Year Club	League	Pos.	G.	AB.	R.	H.	2B.	3B.	HR.	RBI.	B.A.	PO.	A.	E.	F.A.
1976—Billings	Pion.	OF	67	231	51	59	14	3	2	27	.255	*149	*12	7	.958
1977—Shelby	W. Car.	OF	110	414	62	111	15	8	3	30	.268	254	10	10	.964
1978—Tampa	Fla. St.	OF	133	497	79	141	16	*16	8	44	.284	283	7	6	.980
1979—Indianapolis	A. A.	OF	30	98	9	18	0	2	0	5	.184	49	2	2	.962
1979—Nashville	South.	OF	104	369	70	97	12	12	11	51	.263	259	9	5	.982
1980—Indianapolis	A. A.	OF	130	468	63	118	11	7	5	37	.252	*363	6	7	.981
1980—Cincinnati	Nat.	PH-PR	6	3	1	0	0	0	0	0	.000	0	0	0	.000
1981—Indianapolis	A. A.	OF	127	453	69	130	14	6	3	42	.287	228	12	4	.984
1981—Cincinnati	Nat.	OF	8	5	0	1	1	0	0	1	.200	2	0	0	1.000
1982—Cincinnati†	Nat.	OF	113	407	61	109	23	5	4	31	.268	215	8	3	.987
1983—Cincinnati	Nat.	OF	146	502	77	131	23	6	9	33	.261	392	9	4	.990
1984—Cincinnati‡	Nat.	OF	117	336	44	78	8	4	7	29	.232	285	8	5	.983
1985—Cincinnati	Nat.	OF	145	453	82	115	19	7	3	33	.254	340	12	6	.983
1986—Cincinnati	Nat.	OF	145	424	70	110	22	6	15	47	.259	292	6	3	.990
Major League Totals—7 Years			680	2130	335	544	96	28	38	174	.255	1526	43	21	.987

Selected by Cincinnati Reds' organization in 21st round of free-agent draft, June 8, 1976.
†On disabled list, August 11 to September 7, 1982.
‡On disabled list, June 30 to August 6, 1984.

GREGORY BRIAN MINTON
(Greg)

Born July 29, 1951, at Lubbock, Tex.
Height, 6.02. Weight, 191.
Throws right and bats left and righthanded.
Attended San Diego Mesa College, San Diego, Calif.
Major League saves: 1979 (4), 1980 (19), 1981 (21), 1982 (30), 1983 (22), 1984 (19), 1985 (4), 1986 (5). Total—124.
Led National League in intentional bases on balls issued with 20 in 1984 and 18 in 1985.
Led National League in games finished in relief with 44 in 1981 and 66 in 1982.
Led Pacific Coast League in wild pitches with 18 in 1977.
Led Pacific Coast League in balks with 6 in 1975.

Year Club	League	G.	IP.	W.	L.	Pct.	H.	R.	ER.	SO.	BB.	ERA.
1970—Billings†	Pioneer	16	40	1	4	.200	37	23	14	36	16	3.15
1971—Waterloo	Midwest	27	124	11	6	.647	118	52	42	117	55	3.05
1972—San Jose‡	California	28	178	12	12	.500	182	117	78	153	77	3.94
1973—Phoenix	P. Coast	5	13	0	0	.000	11	6	6	4	8	4.15
1973—Amarillo	Texas	38	122	5	11	.313	138	87	61	77	48	4.50
1974—Fresno	California	13	96	10	1	.909	85	32	24	81	18	2.25
1974—Amarillo	Texas	6	29	1	4	.200	42	26	19	21	10	5.90
1975—Phoenix	P. Coast	42	177	10	6	.625	178	73	51	76	76	2.59
1975—San Francisco	National	4	17	1	1	.500	19	14	13	6	11	6.88
1976—San Francisco	National	10	26	0	3	.000	32	18	14	7	12	4.85
1976—Phoenix§	P. Coast	13	74	4	5	.444	91	57	46	31	32	5.59
1977—Phoenix	P. Coast	29	161	14	6	*.700	188	93	87	77	70	4.86
1977—San Francisco	National	2	14	1	1	.500	14	8	7	5	4	4.50
1978—Phoenix	P. Coast	14	92	7	4	.636	97	54	46	32	38	4.50
1978—San Francisco	National	11	16	0	1	.000	22	14	14	6	8	7.88
1979—San Francisco x	National	46	80	4	3	.571	59	25	16	33	27	1.80
1980—San Francisco	National	68	91	4	6	.400	81	28	25	42	34	2.47
1981—San Francisco	National	55	84	4	5	.444	84	28	27	29	36	2.89
1982—San Francisco	National	78	123	10	4	.714	108	29	25	58	42	1.83
1983—San Francisco	National	73	106⅔	7	11	.389	117	51	42	38	47	3.54
1984—San Francisco	National	74	124⅓	4	9	.308	130	60	52	48	57	3.76
1985—San Francisco	National	68	96⅔	5	4	.556	98	42	38	37	54	3.54
1986—San Francisco y	National	48	68⅔	4	4	.500	63	35	30	34	34	3.93
Major League Totals—12 Years		537	847⅓	44	52	.458	827	352	303	343	366	3.22

Selected by Kansas City Royals' organization in 3rd round of free-agent draft, January 17, 1970.
†Appeared in two games as an outfielder with one putout.
‡Traded to San Francisco Giants for Catcher Fran Healy, April 2, 1973.
§On disabled list, July 24 to August 5, 1976.
xOn disabled list, March 26 to May 31, 1979.
yOn disabled list, July 22 to August 14, 1986.

ALL-STAR GAME RECORD

Year League	IP.	W.	L.	Pct.	H.	R.	ER.	SO.	BB.	ERA.
1982—National	⅔	0	0	.000	0	0	0	0	1	0.00

PAUL THOMAS MIRABELLA

Born March 20, 1954, at Belleville, N. J.
Height, 6.02. Weight, 196.
Throws and bats lefthanded.
Attended Montclair State University, Upper Montclair, N. J.

Major League saves: 1982 (3), 1984 (3). Total—6
Tied for Pacific Coast League lead in balks with 4 in 1978.
Tied for Texas League lead in shutouts with 4 and games started by pitchers with 26 in 1977.
Tied for Western Carolinas League lead in balks with 5 in 1976.

Year Club	League	G.	IP.	W.	L.	Pct.	H.	R.	ER.	SO.	BB.	ERA.
1976—Asheville	W. Carol.	22	149	10	7	.588	149	77	66	★136	69	3.99
1977—Tulsa	Texas	26	176	12	7	.632	167	90	75	112	70	3.83
1978—Tucson	P. Coast	22	143	9	6	.600	158	77	63	85	68	3.97
1978—Texas†	American	10	28	3	2	.600	30	18	18	23	17	5.79
1979—Columbus	Int'national	22	144	11	7	.611	129	75	62	98	50	3.88
1979—New York‡	American	10	14	0	4	.000	16	15	14	4	10	9.00
1980—Syracuse	Int'national	4	31	1	2	.333	28	13	9	23	8	2.61
1980—Toronto	American	33	131	5	12	.294	151	73	63	53	66	4.33
1981—Syracuse	Int'national	22	153	11	7	.611	150	63	52	79	53	3.06
1981—Toronto§x	American	8	15	0	0	.000	20	16	12	9	7	7.20
1982—Texas y	American	40	50⅔	1	1	.500	46	28	27	29	22	4.80
1983—Rochester	Int'national	19	76⅓	3	5	.375	87	44	31	32	29	3.66
1983—Baltimore z	American	3	9⅔	0	0	.000	9	6	6	4	7	5.59
1983—Portland a	P. Coast	5	14⅓	0	1	.000	19	13	12	11	10	7.53
1984—Seattle	American	52	68	2	5	.286	74	39	33	41	32	4.37
1985—Calgary	P. Coast	53	68⅓	5	4	.556	84	34	31	42	29	4.08
1985—Seattle	American	10	13⅔	0	0	.000	9	4	2	8	4	1.32
1986—Seattle	American	8	6½	0	0	.000	13	7	6	6	3	8.53
1986—Calgary b	P. Coast	47	68¼	3	4	.429	92	48	45	42	24	5.93
Major League Totals—9 Years		174	336⅓	11	24	.314	368	206	181	177	168	4.84

Selected by Minnesota Twins' organization in 16th round of free-agent draft, June 4, 1975.
Selected by Texas Rangers' organization in secondary phase of free-agent draft, January 7, 1976.
†Traded with Pitchers Mike Griffin and Dave Righetti and Outfielders Juan Beniquez and Greg Jemison to New York Yankees for Pitchers Sparky Lyle, Larry McCall and Dave Rajsich, Catcher Mike Heath, Shortstop Domingo Ramos and cash, November 10, 1978.
‡Traded with First Baseman Chris Chambliss and Infielder Damaso Garcia to Toronto Blue Jays for Catcher Rick Cerone, Pitcher Tom Underwood and Outfielder Ted Wilborn, November 1, 1979.
§Traded to Chicago Cubs' organization for a player to be named later, December 28, 1981; Toronto Blue Jays' organization acquired Pitcher Dave Geisel to complete deal, March 25, 1982.
xTraded with a player to be named later and cash to Texas Rangers for Second Baseman Bump Wills, March 26, 1982; Texas organization acquired Pitcher Paul Semall to complete deal, April 21, 1982.
yReleased, March 26, 1983; signed by Rochester (Baltimore Orioles' organization), April 16, 1983.
zSold to Portland (Philadelphia Phillies' organization), August 12, 1983.
aGranted free agency, October 20, 1983; signed by Seattle Mariners, January 23, 1984.
bGranted free agency, October 15, 1986.

JOHN KYLE MITCHELL

Born August 11, 1965, at Dickson, Tenn.
Height, 6.02. Weight, 165.
Throws and bats righthanded.
Brother of Charlie Mitchell, pitcher in Minnesota Twins' organization.

Led Florida State League in wild pitches with 21 in 1984.
Named International League Pitcher of the Year, 1986.

Year Club	League	G.	IP.	W.	L.	Pct.	H.	R.	ER.	SO.	BB.	ERA.
1983—Elmira	NYP	16	75⅓	5	6	.455	78	57	41	72	41	4.90
1984—Winter Haven	Florida St.	27	★183⅔	16	9	.640	160	84	64	109	66	3.14
1985—New Britain†	Eastern	26	190⅓	12	8	.600	143	71	57	108	61	2.70
1986—Tidewater	Int'national	27	172⅓	12	9	.571	162	78	65	83	59	3.39
1986—New York	National	4	10	0	1	.000	10	4	4	2	4	3.60
Major League Totals—1 Year		4	10	0	1	.000	10	4	4	2	4	3.60

Selected by Boston Red Sox' organization in 7th round of free-agent draft, June 6, 1983.
†Traded with Pitchers Bob Ojeda, Tom McCarthy and Chris Bayer to New York Mets for Pitchers Calvin Schiraldi and Wes Gardner and Outfielders John Christensen and LaSchelle Tarver, November 13, 1985.

KEVIN DARRELL MITCHELL

Born January 13, 1962, at San Diego, Calif.
Height, 5.11. Weight, 210.
Throws and bats righthanded.

Major League stolen bases: 1986 (3).
Led International League third basemen in assists with 215 in 1984.

Year Club	League	Pos.	G.	AB.	R.	H.	2B.	3B.	HR.	RBI.	B.A.	PO.	A.	E.	F.A.
1981—Kingsport	Appal.	3B-OF	62	221	39	74	9	2	7	45	.335	44	102	18	.890
1982—Lynchburg†	Carol.	3B	29	85	19	27	5	1	1	16	.318	11	33	10	.815
1983—Jackson	Texas	★3B-OF	120	441	75	132	25	2	15	85	.299	81	★224	21	.936
1984—Tidewater	Int.	3B-1B-OF	120	432	51	105	21	3	10	54	.243	114	220	22	.938
1984—New York	Nat.	3B	7	14	0	3	0	0	0	1	.214	1	4	1	.833
1985—Tidewater‡	Int.	★3B-1B	95	348	44	101	24	2	9	43	.290	56	209	★22	.923
1986—New York§	Nat.	O-S-3-1	108	328	51	91	22	2	12	43	.277	158	69	10	.958
Major League Totals—2 Years			115	342	51	94	22	2	12	44	.275	159	73	11	.955

Signed as free agent by New York Mets' organization, November 16, 1980.
†On disabled list, July 21, 1982 through remainder of season.
‡On disabled list, July 12 to July 30, 1985.
§Traded with Outfielders Shawn Abner and Stanley Jefferson and Pitchers Kevin Armstrong and Kevin Brown to San Diego Padres for Outfielder Kevin McReynolds, Pitcher Gene Walter and Infielder Adam Ging, December 11, 1986.

CHAMPIONSHIP SERIES RECORD

Year Club	League	Pos.	G.	AB.	R.	H.	2B.	3B.	HR.	RBI.	B.A.	PO.	A.	E.	F.A.
1986—New York	Nat.	OF	2	8	1	2	0	0	0	0	.250	3	0	0	1.000

WORLD SERIES RECORD

Year Club	League	Pos.	G.	AB.	R.	H.	2B.	3B.	HR.	RBI.	B.A.	PO.	A.	E.	F.A.
1986—New York	Nat.	PH-O-DH	5	8	1	2	0	0	0	0	.250	0	2	0	1.000

JOHN JOSEPH MIZEROCK

Name pronounced MIZZ-rock.
Born December 8, 1960, at Punxsutawney, Pa.
Height, 5.11. Weight, 190.
Throws right and bats lefthanded.

Led Southern League in intentional bases on balls received with 12 in 1982.
Led Southern League catchers in putouts with 762 and total chances with 865 in 1982.
Led Florida State League catchers in fielding percentage with .993 and passed balls with 13 in 1981.
Tied for Florida State League lead in double plays by catchers with 8 in 1980.

Year Club	League	Pos.	G.	AB.	R.	H.	2B.	3B.	HR.	RBI.	B.A.	PO.	A.	E.	F.A.
1979—Daytona Beach	Fla. St.	C	53	152	13	39	6	1	3	12	.257	255	25	5	.982
1980—Daytona Beach	Fla. St.	C	99	299	37	66	11	1	2	39	.221	532	52	9	.985
1981—Daytona Beach	Fla. St.	C-1B-OF	92	304	36	67	11	0	1	42	.220	515	50	4	.993
1981—Columbus	South.	C	11	35	6	8	2	0	0	2	.229	80	11	2	.979
1982—Columbus	South.	★C-1B	128	420	46	96	14	1	12	48	.229	785	★87	17	.981
1983—Houston†	Nat.	C	33	85	8	13	4	1	1	10	.153	154	24	6	.967
1983—Tucson	P. C.	C-1B	53	176	18	46	12	2	5	31	.261	298	29	5	.985
1984—Columbus‡	South.	C-O-1-3	61	181	19	43	7	0	4	23	.238	165	19	5	.974
1985—Tucson	P. C.	C	75	223	24	47	11	1	1	19	.211	333	43	5	.987
1985—Houston	Nat.	C	15	38	6	9	4	0	0	6	.237	77	8	3	.966
1986—Houston	Nat.	C	44	81	9	15	1	1	1	6	.185	221	12	3	.987
1986—Tucson§	P. C.	C-1B	20	56	2	9	3	0	0	5	.161	87	10	4	.960
Major League Totals—3 Years			92	204	23	37	9	2	2	22	.181	452	44	12	.976

Selected by Houston Astros' organization in 1st round (eighth player selected) of free-agent draft, June 5, 1979.
†On disabled list, July 3 to July 26, 1983.
‡On Houston disabled list, April 1 to June 20, 1984; included rehabilitation disability assignment to Columbus, May 31 to June 19, 1984.
§Released, October 24, 1986; signed by Montreal Expos' organization, December 9, 1986.

DALE ROBERT MOHORCIC

Name pronounced Muh-HORR-sick.
Born January 25, 1956, at Cleveland, O.
Height, 6.03. Weight, 205.
Throws and bats righthanded.

Tied major league record for most consecutive games pitched as relief pitcher (13), August 6 through 20, 1986.
Major league saves: 1986 (7).
Tied for Northwest League lead in shutouts with 2 in 1978.

Year Club	League	G.	IP.	W.	L.	Pct.	H.	R.	ER.	SO.	BB.	ERA.
1978—Victoria†	Northwest	14	98	6	5	.545	84	39	22	73	36	2.02
1979—Dunedin‡	Florida St.	23	106	4	7	.364	134	59	52	52	27	4.42
1980—Salem	Carolina	47	111	7	5	.583	91	38	27	85	32	2.18
1981—Portland	P. Coast	40	93	5	3	.625	103	54	45	39	41	4.35
1982—Buffalo§	Eastern	44	57⅔	2	8	.200	71	41	32	40	23	4.99
1983—Lynn	Eastern	18	34⅔	3	1	.750	35	20	14	13	17	3.63
1983—Hawaii	P. Coast	15	69	6	6	.500	90	42	38	30	21	4.96

Year Club	League	G.	IP.	W.	L.	Pct.	H.	R.	ER.	SO.	BB.	ERA.
1984—Hawaii x	P. Coast	9	57⅓	1	3	.250	67	29	25	21	17	3.92
1985—Oklahoma City y	Amer. Assoc.	40	84⅔	3	7	.300	72	32	27	47	21	2.87
1986—Oklahoma City	Amer. Assoc.	16	37⅔	4	4	.500	34	16	10	24	11	2.39
1986—Texas	American	58	79	2	4	.333	86	25	22	29	15	2.51
Major League Totals—1 Year		58	79	2	4	.333	86	25	22	29	15	2.51

Signed as free agent by Victoria, June 11, 1978.
†Sold to Toronto Blue Jays' organization, September 25, 1978.
‡Released, January 8, 1980; signed by Pittsburgh Pirates' organization, April 5, 1980.
§On disabled list, May 27 through July 2, 1982.
xGranted free agency, October 15, 1984; signed by Oklahoma City (Texas Rangers' organization), May 19, 1985.
yGranted free agency, October 15, 1985; re-signed by Oklahoma City (Texas Rangers' organization), February 18, 1986.

PAUL LEO MOLITOR

Born August 22, 1956, at St. Paul, Minn.
Height, 6.00. Weight, 175.
Throws and bats righthanded.
Attended University of Minnesota, Minneapolis, Minn.

Hit three home runs in a game, May 12, 1982.
Major League stolen bases: 1978 (30), 1979 (33), 1980 (34), 1981 (10), 1982 (41), 1983 (41), 1984 (1), 1985 (21), 1986 (20). Total—231.
Led American League third basemen in errors with 29 and double plays with 48 in 1982.
Named American League Rookie Player of the Year by THE SPORTING NEWS, 1978.
Named Midwest League Most Valuable Player, 1977.
Received reported $100,000 bonus to sign with Milwaukee Brewers, 1977.
Named shortstop on THE SPORTING NEWS College Baseball All-America Team, 1977.

Year Club	League	Pos.	G.	AB.	R.	H.	2B.	3B.	HR.	RBI.	B.A.	PO.	A.	E.	F.A.
1977—Burlington	Midw.	SS	64	228	52	79	12	0	8	50	.346	83	207	28	.912
1978—Milwaukee	Amer.	2B-SS-3B	125	521	73	142	26	4	6	45	.273	253	401	22	.967
1979—Milwaukee	Amer.	2B-SS	140	584	88	188	27	16	9	62	.322	309	440	16	.979
1980—Milwaukee†	Amer.	2B-SS-3B	111	450	81	137	29	2	9	37	.304	260	336	20	.968
1981—Milwaukee‡	Amer.	OF	64	251	45	67	11	0	2	19	.267	119	4	3	.976
1982—Milwaukee	Amer.	3B-SS	160	★666	★136	201	26	8	19	71	.302	134	350	32	.938
1983—Milwaukee	Amer.	3B	152	608	95	164	28	6	15	47	.270	105	343	16	.966
1984—Milwaukee§	Amer.	3B	13	46	3	10	1	0	0	6	.217	7	21	2	.933
1985—Milwaukee x	Amer.	3B	140	576	93	171	28	3	10	48	.297	126	263	19	.953
1986—Milwaukee y	Amer.	3B-OF	105	437	62	123	24	6	9	55	.281	86	171	15	.945
Major League Totals—9 Years			1010	4139	676	1203	200	45	79	390	.291	1399	2329	145	.963

Selected by St. Louis Cardinals' organization in 28th round of free-agent draft, June 5, 1974.
Selected by Milwaukee Brewers' organization in 1st round (third player selected) of free-agent draft, June 7, 1977.
†On disabled list, June 24 to July 18, 1980.
‡On disabled list, May 3 to August 12, 1981.
§On disabled list, May 2, 1984 through remainder of season.
xOn disabled list, August 13 to August 28, 1985.
yOn disabled list, May 10 to May 30, June 2 to June 17 and June 19 to July 8, 1986.

DIVISION SERIES RECORD

Year Club	League	Pos.	G.	AB.	R.	H.	2B.	3B.	HR.	RBI.	B.A.	PO.	A.	E.	F.A.
1981—Milwaukee	Amer.	OF	5	20	2	5	0	0	1	1	.250	12	7	0	1.000

CHAMPIONSHIP SERIES RECORD

Tied American League Championship Series record for most home runs, five-game Series (2), 1982.

Year Club	League	Pos.	G.	AB.	R.	H.	2B.	3B.	HR.	RBI.	B.A.	PO.	A.	E.	F.A.
1982—Milwaukee	Amer.	3B	5	19	4	6	1	0	2	5	.316	4	11	2	.882

WORLD SERIES RECORD

Established World Series records for most hits, game (5), October 12, 1982; most one-base hits, game (5), October 12, 1982.
Tied World Series records for most at-bats, nine-inning game (6), October 12, 1982; most hits, two consecutive games, one Series (7), October 12, 13, 1982.

Year Club	League	Pos.	G.	AB.	R.	H.	2B.	3B.	HR.	RBI.	B.A.	PO.	A.	E.	F.A.
1982—Milwaukee	Amer.	3B	7	31	5	11	0	0	0	3	.355	4	9	0	1.000

ALL-STAR GAME RECORD

Year League		Pos.	AB.	R.	H.	2B.	3B.	HR.	RBI.	B.A.	PO.	A.	E.	F.A.
1985—American		3B-OF	1	0	0	0	0	0	0	.000	0	0	0	.000

Named to American League All-Star Team in 1980; replaced due to injury.

RAFAEL MONTALVO (TORRES)

Born March 31, 1964, at Santurce, Puerto Rico.
Height, 6.00. Weight, 185.
Throws and bats righthanded.

Year Club	League	G.	IP.	W.	L.	Pct.	H.	R.	ER.	SO.	BB.	ERA.
1980—Lethbridge	Pioneer	14	31	4	2	.667	37	21	17	18	16	4.94
1981—Lethbridge	Pioneer	13	20	0	0	.000	28	19	12	11	13	5.40

Year Club	League	G.	IP.	W.	L.	Pct.	H.	R.	ER.	SO.	BB.	ERA.
1982—Lodi†	California	39	70⅔	3	3	.500	68	31	27	38	33	3.44
1983—Vero Beach	Florida St.	43	75⅓	5	5	.500	61	18	-13	55	31	1.55
1984—San Antonio	Texas	20	22⅔	0	1	.000	17	8	5	7	12	1.99
1984—Albuquerque	P. Coast	45	63⅓	3	3	.500	73	42	31	46	40	4.41
1985—Albuquerque‡-Tucson	P. Coast	52	75	2	7	.222	97	39	35	42	53	4.20
1986—Houston	National	1	1	0	0	.000	1	1	1	0	2	9.00
1986—Tucson	P. Coast	47	77	5	3	.625	78	39	33	31	21	3.86
Major League Totals—1 Year		1	1	0	0	.000	1	1	1	0	2	9.00

Signed as free agent by Los Angeles Dodgers' organization, February 2, 1980.

†On temporarily inactive list, July 1 to July 13, 1982.

‡Traded with a player to be named later to Houston Astros' organization for Infielder Enos Cabell, July 10, 1985; Houston organization acquired Third Baseman German Rivera to complete deal, July 15, 1985.

JOHN JOSEPH MONTEFUSCO JR.

Name pronounced Mon-tuh-FYOOS-koh.

Born May 25, 1950, at Long Branch, N. J.
Height, 6.01. Weight, 185.
Throws and bats righthanded.
Attended Brookdale Community College, Lincroft, N. J.

Pitched 9-0 no-hit victory against Atlanta Braves, September 29, 1976.
Hit home run on first official major league time at bat, September 3, 1974.
Struck out eight consecutive batters against Salt Lake City, August 11, 1974.
Major League saves: 1981 (1), 1983 (4). Total—5.
Tied for National League lead in shutouts by pitchers with 6 in 1976.
Led Texas League in shutouts with 4 in 1974.
Tied for Pacific Coast League lead in shutouts with 3 in 1974.
Named National League Rookie of the Year by Baseball Writers' Association of America, 1975.
Named National League Rookie Pitcher of the Year by THE SPORTING NEWS, 1975.

Year Club	League	G.	IP.	W.	L.	Pct.	H.	R.	ER.	SO.	BB.	ERA.
1973—Decatur	Midwest	24	120	9	2	.818	94	40	29	126	44	2.18
1974—Amarillo	Texas	19	144	8	9	.471	143	61	50	107	37	3.13
1974—Phoenix	P. Coast	11	77	7	3	.700	60	35	28	90	26	3.27
1974—San Francisco	National	7	39	3	2	.600	41	22	21	34	19	4.85
1975—San Francisco	National	35	244	15	9	.625	210	85	78	215	86	2.88
1976—San Francisco	National	37	253	16	14	.533	224	90	80	172	74	2.85
1977—San Francisco†	National	26	157	7	12	.368	170	82	61	110	46	3.50
1978—San Francisco	National	36	239	11	9	.550	233	110	101	177	68	3.80
1979—San Francisco‡	National	22	137	3	8	.273	145	64	60	76	51	3.94
1980—San Francisco§x	National	22	113	4	8	.333	120	61	55	85	39	4.38
1981—Atlanta y	National	26	77	2	3	.400	75	32	30	34	27	3.51
1982—San Diego	National	32	184⅓	10	11	.476	177	93	82	83	41	4.00
1983—San Diego z	National	31	95⅓	9	4	.692	94	38	35	52	32	3.30
1983—New York	American	6	38	5	0	1.000	39	14	14	15	10	3.32
1984—New York a	American	11	55⅓	3	5	.625	55	26	22	23	13	3.58
1984—Columbus	Int'national	3	13	1	0	1.000	6	1	1	7	1	0.69
1985—New York bc	American	3	7	0	0	.000	12	8	8	2	2	10.29
1986—New York d	American	4	12⅓	0	0	.000	9	3	3	3	5	2.19
National League Totals—10 Years		274	1538⅔	80	80	.500	1489	677	603	1038	483	3.53
American League Totals—4 Years		24	112⅔	10	3	.769	115	51	47	43	30	3.75
Major League Totals—13 Years		298	1651⅓	90	83	.520	1604	728	650	1081	513	3.54

Signed as free agent by San Francisco Giants' organization, October 6, 1972.

†On disabled list, May 27 to July 6, 1977.

‡On disabled list, April 26 to June 13, 1979.

§On disabled list, July 17 to August 24, 1980.

xTraded with Outfielder Craig Landis to Atlanta Braves for Pitcher Doyle Alexander, December 12, 1980.

yGranted free agency, November 13, 1981; signed by San Diego Padres, March 6, 1982.

zTraded to New York Yankees for two players to be named later, August 26, 1983; San Diego Padres acquired Pitcher Dennis Rasmussen and Second Baseman Edwin Rodriguez to complete deal, September 12, 1983.

aOn disabled list, April 29 to August 16, 1984; included rehabilitation disability assignment to Columbus, August 4 to August 16, 1984.

bOn disabled list, April 1 to April 29 and May 15, 1985 through remainder of season.

cReleased, November 12, 1985; re-signed by Yankees, March 17, 1986.

dOn disabled list, May 2, 1986 through remainder of season.

ALL-STAR GAME RECORD

Year League	IP.	W.	L.	Pct.	H.	R.	ER.	SO.	BB.	ERA.
1976—National	2	0	0	.000	0	0	0	2	2	0.00

RICHARD MONTELEONE
(Rich)

Born March 22, 1963, at Tampa, Fla.
Height, 6.02. Weight, 205.
Throws and bats righthanded.
Led Appalachian League pitchers in home runs allowed with 8 in 1982.

Year Club	League	G.	IP.	W.	L.	Pct.	H.	R.	ER.	SO.	BB.	ERA.
1982—Bristol	Ap'lachian	12	71⅔	4	6	.400	66	41	31	52	23	3.89
1983—Lakeland	Florida St.	24	142⅓	9	8	.529	146	80	65	124	80	4.11
1983—Birmingham	Southern	3	15	1	1	.500	25	12	12	9	6	7.20
1984—Birmingham	Southern	19	123⅔	7	8	.467	116	69	64	74	67	4.66
1984—Evansville	Am. Assoc.	11	64	5	3	.625	64	33	32	42	36	4.50
1985—Nashville†	Am. Assoc.	27	145⅓	6	12	.333	149	89	82	97	87	5.08
1986—Calgary	P. Coast	39	158⅔	8	12	.400	177	108	93	101	★89	5.28

Selected by Detroit Tigers' organization in 1st round (20th player selected) of free-agent draft, June 7, 1982.
†Traded to Seattle Mariners for Third Baseman Darnell Coles, December 12, 1985.

REGINALD LAVANCE MONTGOMERY
(Reggie)

Born August 4, 1962, at Los Angeles, Calif.
Height, 6.04. Weight, 220.
Throws and bats righthanded.
Attended University of Southern California, Los Angeles, Calif.

Year Club	League	Pos.	G.	AB.	R.	H.	2B.	3B.	HR.	RBI.	B.A.	PO.	A.	E.	F.A.
1983—Salem	N'west	OF-1B	68	265	39	81	10	4	5	★47	.306	140	18	7	.958
1984—Redwood	Calif.	OF	120	447	81	130	28	1	14	79	.291	152	5	3	★.981
1985—Midland†	Texas	OF	112	450	57	130	23	1	22	101	.289	119	15	5	.964
1986—Edmonton	P. C.	OF	127	470	73	134	22	3	18	82	.285	266	15	5	.983

Selected by Chicago White Sox' organization in 1st round (eighth player selected) of free-agent draft, January 13, 1981.
Selected by California Angels' organization in 1st round (26th player selected) of free-agent draft, June 8, 1981.
Selected by California Angels' organization in 25th round of free-agent draft, June 6, 1983.
†On disabled list, August 8, 1985 through remainder of season.

WILLIAM CRAIG MOONEYHAM
(Bill)

Born August 16, 1960, at Livermore, Calif.
Height, 6.00. Weight, 175.
Throws and bats righthanded.
Attended Merced Community College, Merced, Calif.

Major League saves: 1986 (2).

Year Club	League	G.	IP.	W.	L.	Pct.	H.	R.	ER.	SO.	BB.	ERA.
1980—Salinas	California	12	74	4	7	.364	66	44	31	88	64	3.77
1981—Holyoke	Eastern	25	135	9	11	.450	124	90	68	155	★131	4.53
1982—Holyoke†	Eastern	8	49	2	3	.400	44	26	23	46	24	4.22
1983—Nashua	Eastern	19	110	8	6	.571	99	67	56	76	83	4.58
1983—Edmonton	P. Coast	7	35⅔	2	0	1.000	51	39	39	26	22	9.84
1984—Edmonton‡§	P. Coast	16	72⅔	5	3	.625	99	55	48	40	46	5.94
1985—Modesto	California	8	14⅓	2	0	1.000	9	3	2	13	8	1.26
1985—Huntsville	Southern	10	36⅓	2	1	.667	27	13	8	28	15	1.98
1985—Tacoma	P. Coast	21	60⅓	2	6	.250	56	28	28	49	38	4.18
1986—Tacoma	P. Coast	1	4⅓	0	1	.000	8	6	6	4	2	12.46
1986—Oakland	American	45	99⅔	4	5	.444	103	53	50	75	67	4.52
Major League Totals—1 Year		45	99⅔	4	5	.444	103	53	50	75	67	4.52

Selected by Montreal Expos' organization in 6th round of free-agent draft, June 6, 1978.
Selected by St. Louis Cardinals' organization in secondary phase of free-agent draft, January 9, 1979.
Selected by New York Mets' organization in secondary phase of free-agent draft, June 5, 1979.
Selected by Seattle Mariners' organization in secondary phase of free-agent draft, January 8, 1980.
Selected by California Angels' organization in secondary phase of free-agent draft, June 3, 1980.
†On disabled list, March 26 to July 22, 1982.
‡On disabled list, May 1 to May 21, 1984.
§Released, March 31, 1985; signed by Modesto (Oakland A's organization), April 26, 1985.

CHARLES WILLIAM MOORE JR.
(Charlie)

Born June 21, 1953, at Birmingham, Ala.
Height, 5.11. Weight, 180.
Throws and bats righthanded.
Attended Mesa Junior College, Mesa, Ariz., and University of Alabama, Birmingham, Ala.
Son of Charles William Moore, Sr., minor league pitcher, 1948 through 1952.

Major League stolen bases: 1974 (3), 1975 (1), 1976 (1), 1977 (1), 1978 (4), 1979 (8), 1980 (10), 1981 (1), 1982 (2), 1983 (11), 1985 (4), 1986 (5). Total—51.
Hit for the cycle, October 1, 1980.
Led American League outfielders in double plays with 6 in 1982.
Led American League in passed balls with 14 in 1977.
Led Midwest League catchers in putouts with 721, assists with 91, double plays with 12 and tied for lead in passed balls with 30 in 1972.
Led New York-Pennsylvania League in passed balls with 16 in 1971.

Year Club	League	Pos.	G.	AB.	R.	H.	2B.	3B.	HR.	RBI.	B.A.	PO.	A.	E.	F.A.
1971—Newark	NYP	C	60	209	36	62	12	3	6	27	.297	★439	★34	5	.990
1972—Danville	Midw.	★C-1B	106	348	56	90	14	4	12	44	.259	723	92	★25	.970
1973—Shreveport	Texas	C	76	271	47	69	14	2	8	45	.255	402	46	14	.970

Year Club	League	Pos.	G.	AB.	R.	H.	2B.	3B.	HR.	RBI.	B.A.	PO.	A.	E.	F.A.
1973—Evansville	A. A.	C	50	178	27	52	9	1	7	25	.292	274	30	2	.993
1973—Milwaukee............	Amer.	C	8	27	0	5	0	1	0	3	.185	48	5	1	.981
1974—Milwaukee............	Amer.	C	72	204	17	50	10	4	0	19	.245	229	28	4	.985
1975—Milwaukee............	Amer.	C-OF	73	241	26	70	20	1	1	29	.290	234	23	10	.963
1976—Milwaukee............	Amer.	C-O-3	87	241	33	46	7	4	3	16	.191	249	45	9	.970
1977—Milwaukee............	Amer.	C	138	375	42	93	15	6	5	45	.248	566	78	●13	.980
1978—Milwaukee............	Amer.	C	96	268	30	72	7	1	5	31	.269	314	41	6	.983
1979—Milwaukee............	Amer.	C	111	337	45	101	16	2	5	38	.300	414	58	10	.979
1980—Milwaukee............	Amer.	C	111	320	42	93	13	2	2	30	.291	319	28	4	.989
1981—Milwaukee............	Amer.	C-OF	48	156	16	47	8	3	1	9	.301	160	7	5	.973
1982—Milwaukee............	Amer.	OF-C-2B	133	456	53	116	22	4	6	45	.254	317	23	7	.980
1983—Milwaukee............	Amer.	OF-C	151	529	65	150	27	6	2	49	.284	309	10	7	.979
1984—Milwaukee†...........	Amer.	OF-C	70	188	13	44	7	1	2	17	.234	145	3	3	.980
1985—Milwaukee............	Amer.	C-OF	105	349	35	81	13	4	0	31	.232	511	54	13	.978
1986—Milwaukee‡...........	Amer.	C-OF-2B	80	235	24	61	12	3	3	39	.260	429	45	4	.992
Major League Totals—14 Years..............			1283	3926	441	1029	177	42	35	401	.262	4244	458	96	.980

Selected by Milwaukee Brewers' organization in 4th round of free-agent draft, June 8, 1971.
†On disabled list, July 6 to July 23, 1984.
‡Granted free agency, November 12, 1986.

DIVISION SERIES RECORD

Year Club	League	Pos.	G.	AB.	R.	H.	2B.	3B.	HR.	RBI.	B.A.	PO.	A.	E.	F.A.
1981—Milwaukee............	Amer.	DH-OF	4	9	0	2	0	0	0	1	.222	7	0	0	1.000

CHAMPIONSHIP SERIES RECORD

Year Club	League	Pos.	G.	AB.	R.	H.	2B.	3B.	HR.	RBI.	B.A.	PO.	A.	E.	F.A.
1982—Milwaukee............	Amer.	OF	5	13	3	6	0	0	0	0	.462	7	1	0	1.000

WORLD SERIES RECORD

Tied World Series record for most putouts by right fielder, inning (3), October 12, 1982 (eighth inning).

Year Club	League	Pos.	G.	AB.	R.	H.	2B.	3B.	HR.	RBI.	B.A.	PO.	A.	E.	F.A.
1982—Milwaukee............	Amer.	OF	7	26	3	9	3	0	0	2	.346	13	0	0	1.000

DONNIE RAY MOORE

Born February 13, 1954, at Lubbock, Tex.
Height, 6.00. Weight, 185.
Throws right and bats lefthanded.
Attended Ranger Junior College, Ranger, Tex.
Cousin of Hubie Brooks, shortstop with Montreal Expos.

Major League saves: 1978 (4), 1979 (1), 1982 (1), 1983 (6), 1985 (31), 1986 (21). Total—80.
Led American Association in home runs allowed with 25 in 1976.
Led Texas League pitchers in games started with 27 and tied for lead in shutouts with 3 and home runs allowed with 16 in 1975.
Received reported $50,000 bonus to sign with Chicago Cubs, 1973.

Year Club	League	G.	IP.	W.	L.	Pct.	H.	R.	ER.	SO.	BB.	ERA.
1973—Bradenton Cubs	Gulf Coast	4	10	0	1	.000	9	5	4	6	6	3.60
1974—Key West†	Florida St.	26	174	11	12	.478	167	73	54	97	69	2.79
1974—Midland	Texas	5	22	0	4	.000	32	18	17	9	5	6.95
1975—Midland	Texas	28	●185	14	8	.636	191	79	61	123	67	2.97
1975—Chicago	National	4	9	0	0	.000	12	4	4	8	4	4.00
1976—Wichita	Am. Assoc.	24	152	7	11	.389	170	96	80	92	61	4.74
1977—Wichita	Am. Assoc.	11	66	4	4	.500	68	38	36	34	22	4.91
1977—Chicago	National	27	49	4	2	.667	51	27	22	34	18	4.04
1978—Chicago	National	71	103	9	7	.563	117	55	47	50	31	4.11
1979—Wichita	Am. Assoc.	5	29	1	3	.250	29	26	26	16	20	8.07
1979—Chicago‡	National	39	73	1	4	.200	95	46	42	43	25	5.18
1980—St. Louis	National	11	22	1	1	.500	25	15	15	10	5	6.14
1980—Springfield	Am. Assoc.	14	85	6	5	.545	74	32	29	49	32	3.07
1981—Springfield§xy	Am. Assoc.	21	108	8	6	.571	115	49	41	47	31	3.42
1981—Milwaukee	American	3	4	0	0	.000	4	3	3	2	4	6.75
1982—Richmond	Int'national	36	55	5	3	.625	51	17	14	45	18	2.29
1982—Atlanta	National	16	27⅔	3	1	.750	32	13	13	17	7	4.23
1983—Richmond	Int'national	12	16⅔	0	2	.000	12	6	6	9	7	3.24
1983—Atlanta z	National	43	68⅔	2	3	.400	72	30	28	41	10	3.67
1984—Atlanta ab	National	47	64⅓	4	5	.444	63	27	21	47	18	2.94
1985—California c	American	65	103	8	8	.500	91	28	22	72	21	1.92
1986—California d	American	49	72⅔	4	5	.444	60	28	24	53	22	2.97
National League Totals—8 Years......................		258	416⅔	24	23	.511	467	217	192	250	118	4.15
American League Totals—3 Years		117	179⅔	12	13	.480	155	59	49	127	47	2.45
Major League Totals—11 Years		375	596⅓	36	36	.500	622	276	241	377	165	3.64

Selected by Boston Red Sox' organization in 12th round of free-agent draft, June 6, 1972.
Signed as free agent by Chicago Cubs' organization, June 3, 1973.
†Appeared in two games as an outfielder with two putouts.
‡Traded to St. Louis Cardinals for Second Baseman Mike Tyson, October 17, 1979.
§On temporary inactive list, April 14 to May 11, 1981.
xSold conditionally to Milwaukee Brewers, September 3, 1981; returned, October 23, 1981.
yTraded to Atlanta Braves' organization for Pitcher Dan Morogiello, February 1, 1982.

zOn disabled list, August 3 to August 24, 1983.
aOn disabled list, April 19 to May 24, 1984.
bSelected by California Angels in player compensation pool draft, January 24, 1985. (California received compensation for Baltimore Orioles' signing free agent Outfielder Fred Lynn, a Type A player, December 11, 1984.)
cGranted free agency, November 12, 1985; re-signed by Angels, January 8, 1986.
dOn disabled list, May 25 to June 30, 1986.

CHAMPIONSHIP SERIES RECORD

Year—Club	League	G.	IP.	W.	L.	Pct.	H.	R.	ER.	SO.	BB.	ERA.
1982—Atlanta	National	2	2⅔	0	0	.000	2	0	0	1	0	0.00
1986—California	American	3	5	0	1	.000	8	4	4	0	2	7.20
Championship Series Totals—2 Years		5	7⅔	0	1	.000	10	4	4	1	2	4.70

ALL-STAR GAME RECORD

Year—League	IP.	W.	L.	Pct.	H.	R.	ER.	SO.	BB.	ERA.
1985—American	2	0	0	.000	0	0	0	1	0	0.00

MICHAEL WAYNE MOORE
(Mike)

Born November 26, 1959, at Eakly, Okla.
Height, 6.04. Weight, 205.
Throws and bats righthanded.
Attended Oral Roberts University, Tulsa, Okla.

Major League saves: 1986 (1).
Tied for American League lead in games started by pitchers with 37 in 1986.
Received reported $100,000 bonus to sign with Seattle Mariners, 1981.
Named righthanded pitcher on THE SPORTING NEWS College Baseball All-America Team, 1981.

Year—Club	League	G.	IP.	W.	L.	Pct.	H.	R.	ER.	SO.	BB.	ERA.
1981—Lynn	Eastern	13	94	6	5	.545	83	42	38	81	34	3.64
1982—Seattle	American	28	144⅓	7	14	.333	159	91	86	73	79	5.36
1982—Salt Lake City	P. Coast	1	8	0	0	.000	9	4	4	6	5	4.50
1983—Seattle	American	22	128	6	8	.429	130	75	67	108	60	4.71
1983—Salt Lake City	P. Coast	11	82⅓	4	4	.500	78	48	33	80	54	3.61
1984—Seattle	American	34	212	7	17	.292	236	127	117	158	85	4.97
1985—Seattle	American	35	247	17	10	.630	230	100	95	155	70	3.46
1986—Seattle	American	38	266	11	13	.458	•279	141	127	146	94	4.30
Major League Totals—5 Years		157	997⅓	48	62	.436	1034	534	492	640	388	4.44

Selected by St. Louis Cardinals' organization in 3rd round of free-agent draft, June 6, 1978.
Selected by Seattle Mariners' organization in 1st round (first player selected) of free-agent draft, June 8, 1981.

WILLIAM ROSS MOORE
(Bill)

Born October 10, 1960, at Los Angeles, Calif.
Height, 6.01. Weight, 185.
Throws left and bats righthanded.
Attended California State University, Fullerton, Calif.

Led Florida State League in total bases with 245, bases on balls received with 112, slugging percentage with .506, game-winning RBIs with 17 and tied for lead in intentional bases on balls received with 11 in 1984.
Tied for American Association lead in being hit by pitch with 9 in 1986.

Year—Club	League	Pos.	G.	AB.	R.	H.	2B.	3B.	HR.	RBI.	B.A.	PO.	A.	E.	F.A.
1983—Calgary	Pion.	OF-1B	59	199	63	72	19	1	13	51	.362	125	12	6	.958
1984—W. Palm Beach	Fla. St.	OF-1B	•143	484	•102	145	26	4	•22	94	.300	300	14	7	.978
1985—Jacksonville	South.	OF-1B	140	509	83	132	30	2	33	104	.259	311	21	9	.974
1986—Indianapolis	A. A.	OF-1B	122	407	70	104	23	0	23	82	.256	237	16	6	.977
1986—Montreal	Nat.	1B-OF	6	12	0	2	0	0	0	0	.167	22	1	0	1.000
Major League Totals—1 Year			6	12	0	2	0	0	0	0	.167	22	1	0	1.000

Selected by Kansas City Royals' organization in 10th round for free-agent draft, June 5, 1979.
Selected by Montreal Expos' organization in 6th round of free-agent draft, June 6, 1983.

BOBBY KEITH MORELAND
(Known by middle name.)

Born May 2, 1954, at Dallas, Tex.
Height, 6.00. Weight, 200.
Throws and bats righthanded.
Attended University of Texas, Austin, Texas.

Major League stolen bases: 1980 (3), 1981 (1), 1984 (1), 1985 (12), 1986 (3). Total—20.
Led American Association in sacrifice flies with 10 in 1978 and with 13 in 1979.
Led American Association catchers in double plays with 10 in 1978.
Led American Association in passed balls with 11 in 1979 and tied for lead with 10 in 1978.
Led Eastern League in passed balls with 18 in 1977.
Tied for Carolina League lead in double plays by third basemen with 19 in 1976.

Year—Club	League	Pos.	G.	AB.	R.	H.	2B.	3B.	HR.	RBI.	B.A.	PO.	A.	E.	F.A.
1975—Spartanburg	W. Car.	3B	69	246	28	68	13	1	1	41	.276	52	128	17	.914
1976—Peninsula	Carol.	•3B-SS	78	294	38	83	12	2	4	47	.282	50	221	•26	.912
1976—Reading	East.	3B-2B	61	199	7	52	5	0	0	7	.261	62	99	13	.925

Year Club	League	Pos.	G.	AB.	R.	H.	2B.	3B.	HR.	RBI.	B.A.	PO.	A.	E.	F.A.
1977—Reading	East.	C-3B	104	401	61	131	19	1	8	55	.327	339	60	8	.980
1977—Oklahoma City	A. A.	C	7	13	3	1	0	0	0	1	.077	17	1	0	1.000
1978—Oklahoma City	A. A.	C-1-3-O	130	501	73	145	25	4	16	98	.289	641	75	13	.982
1978—Philadelphia	Nat.	C	1	2	0	0	0	0	0	0	.000	4	0	0	1.000
1979—Oklahoma City	A. A.	C-3B-OF	130	494	86	149	●34	3	20	109	.302	397	44	13	.971
1979—Philadelphia	Nat.	C	14	48	3	18	3	2	0	8	.375	71	3	0	1.000
1980—Philadelphia	Nat.	C-OF	62	159	13	50	8	0	4	29	.314	186	22	7	.967
1981—Philadelphia†	Nat.	C-3-1-O	61	196	16	50	7	0	6	37	.255	267	31	9	.971
1982—Chicago	Nat.	OF-C-3B	138	476	50	124	17	2	15	68	.261	384	38	8	.981
1983—Chicago	Nat.	OF-C	154	533	76	161	30	3	16	70	.302	244	7	6	.977
1984—Chicago	Nat.	O-1-3-C	140	495	59	138	17	3	16	80	.279	393	30	10	.977
1985—Chicago	Nat.	O-1-3-C	161	587	74	180	30	3	14	106	.307	313	29	13	.963
1986—Chicago	Nat.	O-3-C-1	156	586	72	159	30	0	12	79	.271	340	58	9	.978
Major League Totals—9 Years			887	3082	363	880	142	13	83	477	.286	2202	218	62	.975

Selected by Philadelphia Phillies' organization in 7th round of free-agent draft, June 4, 1975.
†Traded with Pitchers Dan Larson and Dickie Noles to Chicago Cubs for Pitcher Mike Krukow and cash, December 8, 1981.

DIVISION SERIES RECORD

Year Club	League	Pos.	G.	AB.	R.	H.	2B.	3B.	HR.	RBI.	B.A.	PO.	A.	E.	F.A.
1981—Philadelphia	Nat.	C	4	13	2	6	0	0	1	3	.462	30	2	1	.970

CHAMPIONSHIP SERIES RECORD

Year Club	League	Pos.	G.	AB.	R.	H.	2B.	3B.	HR.	RBI.	B.A.	PO.	A.	E.	F.A.
1980—Philadelphia	Nat.	C-PH	2	1	0	0	0	0	0	1	.000	0	0	0	.000
1984—Chicago	Nat.	OF	5	18	3	6	2	0	0	2	.333	9	0	0	1.000
Championship Series Totals—2 Years			7	19	3	6	2	0	0	3	.316	9	0	0	1.000

WORLD SERIES RECORD

Year Club	League	Pos.	G.	AB.	R.	H.	2B.	3B.	HR.	RBI.	B.A.	PO.	A.	E.	F.A.
1980—Philadelphia	Nat.	DH	3	12	1	4	0	0	0	1	.333	0	0	0	.000

ARMANDO MORENO (CLEMENTE)

Born December 25, 1963, at Santurce, Puerto Rico.
Height, 5.10. Weight, 160.
Throws and bats righthanded.

Year Club	League	Pos.	G.	AB.	R.	H.	2B.	3B.	HR.	RBI.	B.A.	PO.	A.	E.	F.A.
1982—Calgary	Pion.	2B	66	213	52	72	18	1	5	42	.338	138	163	★23	.929
1983—Gastonia	S. Atl.	2B	115	367	89	120	19	1	8	63	.327	218	262	30	.941
1984—Jacksonville	South.	2B	126	400	51	92	12	1	10	55	.230	255	375	26	.960
1985—Jacksonville†	South.	2B	105	371	67	106	25	0	8	32	.286	262	258	14	.974
1986—Jacksonville	South.	2B	133	456	79	142	24	6	15	61	.311	265	279	17	.970

Signed as free agent by Montreal Expos' organization, August 28, 1981.
†On disabled list, July 8 to August 1, 1985.

OMAR RENAN MORENO (QUINTERO)

Born October 24, 1953, at Puerto Armuelles, Panama.
Height, 6.03. Weight, 185.
Throws and bats lefthanded.

Major League stolen bases: 1975 (1), 1976 (15), 1977 (53), 1978 (71), 1979 (77), 1980 (96), 1981 (39), 1982 (60), 1983 (37), 1984 (20), 1985 (1), 1986 (17). Total—487.
Led National League in caught stealing with 33 in 1980 and 14 in 1981.
Led National League in stolen bases with 71 in 1978 and 77 in 1979.
Led National League outfielders in total chances with 514 in 1979 and 499 in 1980.
Tied for National League lead in caught stealing with 26 in 1982.
Led Carolina League in stolen bases with 77 in 1973.
Led Eastern League in stolen bases with 67 in 1974.
Named outfielder on THE SPORTING NEWS National League All-Star Team, 1979.

Year Club	League	Pos.	G.	AB.	R.	H.	2B.	3B.	HR.	RBI.	B.A.	PO.	A.	E.	F.A.
1969—Bradenton Pir.	Gulf C.	OF	25	62	7	18	1	0	0	4	.290	22	0	3	.880
1970—Bradenton Pir.	Gulf C.	OF-1B	51	219	32	51	7	4	1	19	.233	129	9	8	.945
1970—Niagara Falls	NYP	OF	10	23	1	4	0	0	0	3	.174	10	0	0	1.000
1971—Bradenton Pir.	Gulf C.	OF	38	101	11	33	5	2	0	9	.327	35	4	2	.951
1972—Gastonia	W. Car.	OF	51	144	18	31	5	2	1	17	.215	95	3	3	.970
1972—Niagara Falls	NYP	OF	68	259	52	75	11	6	2	34	.290	87	4	5	.948
1973—Salem	Carol.	OF	136	529	★112	150	22	8	9	56	.284	242	14	13	.952
1973—Charleston	Int.	OF	3	12	1	4	0	1	1	3	.333	4	0	0	1.000
1974—Thetford Mines	East.	OF	112	407	88	122	15	6	7	39	.300	193	13	9	.958
1974—Charleston	Int.	OF	23	82	16	18	3	0	0	4	.220	40	2	1	.977
1975—Charleston	Int.	OF	130	447	73	127	20	2	9	51	.284	★328	10	6	.983
1975—Pittsburgh	Nat.	OF	6	6	1	1	0	0	0	0	.167	0	0	1	.000
1976—Charleston	Int.	OF	94	330	70	104	11	7	3	36	.315	200	★17	1	★.955
1976—Pittsburgh	Nat.	OF	48	122	24	33	4	1	2	12	.270	93	3	4	.960
1977—Pittsburgh	Nat.	OF	150	492	69	118	19	9	7	34	.240	366	10	9	.977
1978—Pittsburgh	Nat.	OF	155	515	95	121	15	7	2	33	.235	409	9	7	.984
1979—Pittsburgh	Nat.	OF	162	★695	110	196	21	12	8	69	.282	★490	11	13	.975

Year	Club	League	Pos.	G	AB	R	H	2B	3B	HR	RBI	B.A.	PO.	A.	E.	F.A.
1980—Pittsburgh	Nat.		OF	162	★676	87	168	20	●13	2	36	.249	★479	15	5	.990
1981—Pittsburgh	Nat.		OF	103	434	62	120	18	8	1	35	.276	302	6	1	.997
1982—Pittsburgh†	Nat.		OF	158	645	82	158	18	9	3	44	.245	396	10	7	.983
1983—Houston‡	Nat.		OF	97	405	48	98	12	11	0	25	.242	251	8	6	.977
1983—New York	Amer.		OF	48	152	17	38	9	1	1	17	.250	120	1	1	.992
1984—New York	Amer.		OF	117	355	37	92	12	6	4	38	.259	262	9	4	.985
1985—N.Y.§-K.C. x	Amer.		OF	58	136	21	30	5	4	3	16	.221	86	3	0	1.000
1986—Atlanta y	Nat.		OF	118	359	46	84	18	6	4	27	.234	151	8	5	.970
National League Totals—10 Years				1159	4349	624	1097	145	76	29	315	.252	2937	80	58	.981
American League Totals—3 Years				223	643	75	160	26	11	8	71	.249	468	13	5	.990
Major League Totals—12 Years				1382	4992	699	1257	171	87	37	386	.252	3405	93	63	.982

Signed as free agent by Pittsburgh Pirates' organization, March 30, 1969.

†Granted free agency, November 10, 1982; signed by Houston Astros, December 10, 1982.

‡Traded to New York Yankees for Outfielder Jerry Mumphrey, August 10, 1983.

§Released, August 16, 1985; signed by Kansas City Royals, September 3, 1985.

xReleased, November 15, 1985; signed by Atlanta Braves' organization, April 1, 1986.

yReleased, October 13, 1986.

CHAMPIONSHIP SERIES RECORD

Year	Club	League	Pos.	G	AB	R	H	2B	3B	HR	RBI	B.A.	PO.	A.	E.	F.A.
1979—Pittsburgh	Nat.		OF	3	12	3	3	0	1	0	0	.250	7	0	0	1.000

WORLD SERIES RECORD

Tied World Series record for most at bats, seven-game Series (33), 1979.

Year	Club	League	Pos.	G	AB	R	H	2B	3B	HR	RBI	B.A.	PO.	A.	E.	F.A.
1979—Pittsburgh	Nat.		OF	7	33	4	11	2	0	0	3	.333	20	1	0	1.000

MICHAEL THOMAS MORGAN
(Mike)

Born October 8, 1959, at Tulare, Calif.
Height, 6.02. Weight, 185.
Throws and bats righthanded.

Major League saves: 1986 (1).
Tied for International League lead in shutouts with 4 in 1984.
Received reported $50,000 bonus to sign with Oakland A's, 1978.

Year	Club	League	G	IP.	W.	L.	Pct.	H.	R.	ER.	SO.	BB.	ERA.
1978—Oakland	American		3	12	0	3	.000	19	12	10	0	8	7.50
1978—Vancouver	P. Coast		14	92	5	6	.455	109	67	57	31	54	5.58
1979—Ogden	P. Coast		13	101	5	5	.500	93	48	39	42	49	3.48
1979—Oakland	American		13	77	2	10	.167	102	57	51	17	50	5.96
1980—Ogden†‡	P. Coast		20	115	6	9	.400	135	79	69	46	77	5.40
1981—Nashville§	Southern		26	169	8	7	.533	164	97	83	100	83	4.42
1982—New York x	American		30	150⅓	7	11	.389	167	77	73	71	67	4.37
1983—Toronto y	American		16	45⅓	0	3	.000	48	26	26	22	21	5.16
1983—Syracuse	Int'national		5	19⅓	0	3	.000	20	12	12	17	13	5.59
1984—Syracuse z	Int'national		34	★185⅔	13	11	.542	167	●101	84	105	●100	4.07
1985—Seattle a	American		2	6	1	1	.500	11	8	8	2	5	12.00
1985—Calgary	P. Coast		1	2	0	0	.000	3	1	1	0	0	4.50
1986—Seattle	American		37	216⅓	11	●17	.393	243	122	109	116	86	4.53
Major League Totals—6 Years			101	507	21	45	.318	590	302	277	228	237	4.92

Selected by Oakland A's organizaton in 1st round (fourth player selected) of free-agent draft, June 6, 1978.

†On disabled list, May 14 to June 27, 1980.

‡Traded to New York Yankees for Shortstop Fred Stanley and a player to be named later, November 3, 1980; Oakland A's acquired Second Baseman Brian Doyle to complete deal, November 17, 1980.

§On disabled list, April 9 to April 22, 1981.

xTraded with Outfielder-First Baseman Dave Collins, First Baseman Fred McGriff and a reported $400,000 to Toronto Blue Jays for Pitcher Dale Murray and Outfielder-Catcher Tom Dodd, December 9, 1982.

yOn disabled list, July 2 to August 23, 1983; included rehabilitation disability assignment to Syracuse, August 1 to August 18, 1983.

zDrafted by Seattle Mariners, December 3, 1984.

aOn disabled list, April 17, 1985 through remainder of season; included rehabilitation disability assignment to Calgary, July 19 to July 22, 1985.

RUSSELL LEE MORMAN
(Russ)

Born April 28, 1962, at Independence, Mo.
Height, 6.04. Weight, 215.
Throws and bats righthanded.
Attended Iowa Western Community College, Clarinda, Ia.,
and Wichita State University, Wichita, Kan.

Tied major league record for most hits, inning, first major league game (2), August 3, 1986 (fourth inning).

Major League stolen bases: 1986 (1).

Led Eastern League in slugging percentage with .512 in 1985.

Led Midwest League in game-winning RBIs with 15 in 1984.

Led American Association third basemen in double plays with 23 in 1986.

Led Eastern League first basemen in assists with 79 in 1985.
Named first baseman on THE SPORTING NEWS College Baseball All-America Team, 1983.

Year	Club	League	Pos.	G.	AB.	R.	H.	2B.	3B.	HR.	RBI.	B.A.	PO.	A.	E.	F.A.
1983—Glens Falls	East.		1B	71	233	29	57	9	1	3	32	.245	591	43	7	.989
1984—Appleton	Midw.		1B-OF	122	424	68	111	17	7	7	80	.262	823	43	10	.989
1985—Glens Falls	East.		★1-3-OF	119	422	64	131	24	5	17	81	.310	905	81	12	★.988
1985—Buffalo	A. A.		1B	21	64	16	19	3	1	7	14	.297	144	7	2	.987
1986—Buffalo	A. A.		3B-OF	106	365	52	97	17	2	13	57	.266	87	201	24	.923
1986—Chicago	Amer.		1B	49	159	18	40	5	0	4	17	.252	342	26	4	.989
Major League Totals—1 Year				49	159	18	40	5	0	4	17	.252	342	26	4	.989

Selected by Kansas City Royals' organization in 7th round of free-agent draft, January 13, 1981.
Selected by Chicago White Sox' organization in 1st round (28th player selected) of free-agent draft, June 6, 1983.

JOHN DANIEL MORRIS

Born February 23, 1961, at Freeport, N.Y.
Height, 6.01. Weight, 185.
Throws and bats lefthanded.
Attended Seton Hall University, South Orange, N.J.

Major League stolen bases: 1986 (6).
Led Southern League outfielders in total chances with 343 in 1985.
Named Southern League Most Valuable Player, 1983.
Named outfielder on THE SPORTING NEWS College Baseball All-America Team, 1982.

Year	Club	League	Pos.	G.	AB.	R.	H.	2B.	3B.	HR.	RBI.	B.A.	PO.	A.	E.	F.A.
1982—Fort Myers	Fla. St.		OF	45	137	21	39	7	2	2	17	.285	64	2	2	.971
1983—Jacksonville	South.		OF	140	490	96	141	27	8	23	92	.288	260	8	3	★.989
1984—Omaha	A. A.		OF	148	492	77	133	24	4	15	60	.270	★359	7	4	★.989
1985—Omaha†-Louis.	A. A.		OF	130	466	64	117	25	6	5	50	.251	★330	11	2	★.994
1986—Louisville‡	A. A.		OF	60	213	30	50	13	7	1	24	.235	132	6	2	.986
1986—St. Louis	Nat.		OF	39	100	8	24	0	1	1	14	.240	68	0	1	.986
Major League Totals—1 Year				39	100	8	24	0	1	1	14	.240	68	0	1	.986

Selected by Kansas City Royals' organization in 1st round (10th player selected) of free-agent draft, June 7, 1982.
†Traded to St. Louis Cardinals' organization for Outfielder Lonnie Smith, May 17, 1985.
‡On disabled list, May 7 to August 4, 1986.

JOHN SCOTT MORRIS
(Jack)

Born May 16, 1955, at St. Paul, Minn.
Height, 6.03. Weight, 200.
Throws and bats righthanded.
Attended Brigham Young University, Provo, Utah.

Tied American League record for most seasons leading league, wild pitches (3).
Pitched 4-0 no-hit victory against Chicago White Sox, April 7, 1984.
Led American League in shutouts with 6 in 1986.
Led American League in wild pitches with 18 in 1983, 14 in 1984 and 15 in 1985.
Named American League Pitcher of the Year by THE SPORTING NEWS, 1981.
Named righthanded pitcher on THE SPORTING NEWS American League All-Star Team, 1981.

Year	Club	League	G.	IP.	W.	L.	Pct.	H.	R.	ER.	SO.	BB.	ERA.
1976—Montgomery		Southern	12	36	2	3	.400	37	31	25	18	36	6.25
1977—Evansville		Am. Assoc.	20	135	6	7	.462	141	68	54	95	42	3.60
1977—Detroit		American	7	46	1	1	.500	38	20	19	28	23	3.72
1978—Detroit		American	28	106	3	5	.375	107	57	51	48	49	4.33
1979—Evansville		Am. Assoc.	5	34	2	2	.500	22	13	9	28	18	2.38
1979—Detroit		American	27	198	17	7	.708	179	76	72	113	59	3.27
1980—Detroit		American	36	250	16	15	.516	252	125	116	112	87	4.18
1981—Detroit		American	25	198	●14	7	.667	153	69	67	97	★78	3.05
1982—Detroit		American	37	266⅓	17	16	.515	247	131	120	135	96	4.06
1983—Detroit†		American	37	★293⅔	20	13	.606	257	117	109	★232	83	3.34
1984—Detroit		American	35	240⅓	19	11	.633	221	108	96	148	87	3.60
1985—Detroit‡		American	35	257	16	11	.593	212	102	95	191	110	3.33
1986—Detroit§		American	35	267	21	8	.724	229	105	97	223	82	3.27
Major League Totals—10 Years			302	2122⅓	144	94	.605	1895	910	842	1327	754	3.57

Selected by Detroit Tigers' organization in 5th round of free-agent draft, June 8, 1976.
†Appeared in seven games as a pinch-runner.
‡Appeared in one game as a pinch-runner.
§Granted free agency, November 12, 1986; re-signed by Tigers, December 19, 1986.

CHAMPIONSHIP SERIES RECORD

Year	Club	League	G.	IP.	W.	L.	Pct.	H.	R.	ER.	SO.	BB.	ERA.
1984—Detroit		American	1	7	1	0	1.000	5	1	1	4	1	1.29

WORLD SERIES RECORD

Established World Series record for most putouts, pitcher, five-game Series (5), 1984.
Tied World Series record for most wild pitches, game (2), October 13, 1984.

Year	Club	League	G.	IP.	W.	L.	Pct.	H.	R.	ER.	SO.	BB.	ERA.
1984—Detroit		American	2	18	2	0	1.000	13	4	4	13	3	2.00

Year	League	IP.	W.	L.	Pct.	H.	R.	ER.	SO.	BB.	ERA.
1981—American		2	0	0	.000	2	0	0	2	1	0.00
1984—American		2	0	0	.000	2	0	0	2	1	0.00
1985—American		2⅔	0	1	.000	5	2	2	1	1	6.75
All-Star Game Totals—3 Years		6⅔	0	1	.000	9	2	2	5	3	2.70

JAMES FORREST MORRISON

(Jim)

Born September 23, 1952, at Pensacola, Fla.
Height, 5.11. Weight, 185.
Throws and bats righthanded.
Attended Georgia Southern College, Statesboro, Ga.

Established major league record for fewest chances accepted by third baseman, season, 150 or more games (349), 1986.

Tied major league record for fewest three-base hits, most at-bats, season (0 and 604), 1980.
Major League stolen bases: 1978 (1), 1979 (11), 1980 (9), 1981 (3), 1982 (2), 1983 (2), 1985 (3), 1986 (9). Total—40.
Led American League second basemen in assists with 481, total chances with 932 and double plays with 117 in 1980.
Led Carolina League in total bases with 239 in 1975.
Led American Association third basemen in assists with 236 in 1977.
Led American Association third basemen in double plays with 22 in 1976.
Led Carolina League third basemen in assists with 311, errors with 32 and double plays with 35 in 1975.

Year	Club	League	Pos.	G.	AB.	R.	H.	2B.	3B.	HR.	RBI.	B.A.	PO.	A.	E.	F.A.
1974—Spartanburg	W. Car.		3B	3	8	1	3	1	0	1	3	.375	4	5	1	.900
1974—Rocky Mount	Carol.		3B	72	265	30	67	9	1	4	24	.253	54	157	19	.917
1975—Rocky Mount	Carol.		3B-SS	140	497	★98	143	24	6	★20	88	.288	135	331	35	.930
1976—Oklahoma City	A. A.		★3B-SS	126	422	79	122	17	6	18	71	.289	100	★239	24	.934
1977—Oklahoma City	A. A.		3B-2B-OF	127	452	72	133	23	4	12	71	.294	99	272	25	.937
1977—Philadelphia	Nat.		3B	5	7	3	3	0	0	0	1	.429	0	7	1	.875
1978—Oklahoma City	A. A.		2B-3B-1B	54	189	37	52	6	1	10	28	.275	111	134	10	.961
1978—Philadelphia	Nat.		2B-3B-OF	53	108	12	17	1	1	3	10	.157	88	97	6	.969
1979—Oklahoma City†	A. A.		2B-3B-OF	79	281	59	90	15	0	22	61	.320	129	226	17	.954
1979—Chicago	Amer.		2B-3B	67	240	38	66	14	0	14	35	.275	121	185	9	.971
1980—Chicago	Amer.		★2B-SS	162	604	66	171	40	0	15	57	.283	★422	482	★29	.969
1981—Chicago	Amer.		3B-2B	90	290	27	68	8	1	10	34	.234	64	200	12	.957
1982—Chicago‡	Amer.		3B	51	166	17	37	7	3	7	19	.223	19	87	10	.914
1982—Pittsburgh	Nat.		3-2-O-S	44	86	10	24	4	1	4	15	.279	17	43	2	.968
1983—Pittsburgh	Nat.		2B-3B-SS	66	158	16	48	7	2	6	25	.304	56	99	7	.957
1984—Pittsburgh	Nat.		3-2-S-1	100	304	38	87	14	2	11	45	.286	86	166	10	.962
1985—Pittsburgh	Nat.		3B-2B-OF	92	244	17	62	10	0	4	22	.254	73	121	5	.975
1986—Pittsburgh	Nat.		3B-2B-SS	154	537	58	147	35	4	23	88	.274	92	258	20	.946
National League Totals—7 Years				514	1444	154	388	71	10	51	206	.269	412	791	51	.959
American League Totals—4 Years				370	1300	148	342	69	4	46	145	.263	626	954	60	.963
Major League Totals—10 Years				884	2744	302	730	140	14	97	351	.266	1038	1745	111	.962

Selected by Pittsburgh Pirates' organization in 5th round of free-agent draft, January 12, 1972.
Selected by Pittsburgh Pirates' organization in secondary phase of free-agent draft, June 6, 1972.
Selected by Philadelphia Phillies' organization in 5th round of free-agent draft, June 5, 1974.
†Traded to Chicago White Sox, July 10, 1979, completing deal in which Chicago traded Pitcher Jack Kucek to Philadelphia Phillies for a player to be named later, April 13, 1979.
‡Traded to Pittsburgh Pirates for Pitcher Eddie Solomon, June 14, 1982.

CHAMPIONSHIP SERIES RECORD

Year	Club	League	Pos.	G.	AB.	R.	H.	2B.	3B.	HR.	RBI.	B.A.	PO.	A.	E.	F.A.
1978—Philadelphia	Nat.		PH	1	1	0	0	0	0	0	0	.000	0	0	0	.000

LLOYD ANTHONY MOSEBY

Born November 5, 1959, at Portland, Ark.
Height, 6.03. Weight, 200.
Throws right and bats lefthanded.

Major League stolen bases: 1980 (4), 1981 (11), 1982 (11), 1983 (27), 1984 (39), 1985 (37), 1986 (32). Total—161.
Led Florida State League in total bases with 237 and tied for lead in being hit by pitch with 10 in 1979.
Led Pioneer League in being hit by pitch with 11 and tied for lead in caught stealing with 7 in 1978.
Named outfielder on THE SPORTING NEWS American League All-Star Team, 1983.
Named outfielder on THE SPORTING NEWS American League Silver Slugger team, 1983.

Year	Club	League	Pos.	G.	AB.	R.	H.	2B.	3B.	HR.	RBI.	B.A.	PO.	A.	E.	F.A.
1978—Medicine Hat	Pion.		OF	67	253	65	77	12	4	10	38	.304	76	3	6	.929
1979—Dunedin	Fla. St.		OF	129	446	★89	★148	23	6	18	84	.332	190	11	9	.957
1980—Syracuse	Int.		OF	37	146	28	47	8	6	3	19	.322	83	1	3	.966
1980—Toronto	Amer.		OF	114	389	44	89	24	1	9	46	.229	208	12	4	.982
1981—Toronto	Amer.		OF	100	378	36	88	16	2	9	43	.233	259	4	3	.989
1982—Toronto	Amer.		OF	147	487	51	115	20	9	9	52	.236	361	4	3	.992
1983—Toronto	Amer.		OF	151	539	104	170	31	7	18	81	.315	399	10	7	.983
1984—Toronto	Amer.		OF	158	592	97	166	28	●15	18	92	.280	473	8	5	.990
1985—Toronto	Amer.		OF	152	584	92	151	30	7	18	70	.259	394	7	8	.980
1986—Toronto	Amer.		OF	152	589	89	149	24	5	21	86	.253	371	6	6	.984
Major League Totals—7 Years				974	3558	513	928	173	46	102	470	.261	2465	51	36	.986

Selected by Toronto Blue Jays' organization in 1st round (second player selected) of free-agent draft, June 6, 1978.

CHAMPIONSHIP SERIES RECORD

Year Club	League	Pos.	G.	AB.	R.	H.	2B.	3B.	HR.	RBI.	B.A.	PO.	A.	E.	F.A.
1985—Toronto	Amer.	OF	7	31	5	7	1	0	0	4	.226	16	0	0	1.000

ALL-STAR GAME RECORD

Year League	Pos.	AB.	R.	H.	2B.	3B.	HR.	RBI.	B.A.	PO.	A.	E.	F.A.
1986—American	OF	0	0	0	0	0	0	0	.000	0	0	0	.000

JOHN WILLIAM MOSES

Born August 9, 1957, at Los Angeles, Calif.
Height, 5.09. Weight, 165.
Throws left and bats left and righthanded.
Attended Golden West College, Huntington Beach, Calif., and
University of Arizona, Tucson, Ariz.

Major League stolen bases: 1982 (5), 1983 (11), 1984 (1), 1985 (5), 1986 (25). Total—47.
Tied for American League lead in caught stealing with 18 in 1986.
Led Midwest League in caught stealing with 21 and bases on balls received with 103 in 1981.
Tied for Midwest League lead in sacrifice hits with 13 in 1981.
Led Eastern League outfielders in double plays with 6 in 1982.

Year Club	League	Pos.	G.	AB.	R.	H.	2B.	3B.	HR.	RBI.	B.A.	PO.	A.	E.	F.A.
1980—Bellingham	N'west	OF	60	227	55	60	5	2	2	32	.264	92	6	3	.970
1981—Wausau	Midw.	OF	123	429	*102	120	24	3	3	48	.280	204	10	5	.977
1982—Lynn	East.	OF	128	466	87	133	25	6	6	52	.285	259	*20	0	*1.000
1982—Seattle	Amer.	OF	22	44	7	14	5	1	1	3	.318	16	2	1	.947
1983—Seattle	Amer.	OF	93	130	19	27	4	1	0	6	.208	87	8	2	.979
1983—Salt Lake City	P. C.	OF	16	65	14	17	4	0	0	10	.262	26	0	0	1.000
1984—Chattanooga	South.	OF	53	182	27	46	6	3	0	12	.253	107	4	2	.982
1984—Salt Lake City	P. C.	OF	70	276	45	76	11	5	0	27	.275	161	8	1	.994
1984—Seattle	Amer.	OF	19	35	3	12	1	1	0	2	.343	26	1	0	1.000
1985—Calgary	P. C.	OF-1B	113	473	75	152	*37	1	5	47	.321	316	12	4	.988
1985—Seattle	Amer.	OF	33	62	4	12	0	0	0	3	.194	35	1	0	1.000
1986—Calgary	P. C.	OF	39	148	31	48	3	1	3	18	.324	93	3	1	.990
1986—Seattle	Amer.	OF-1B	103	399	56	102	16	3	3	34	.256	249	11	5	.981
Major League Totals—5 Years			270	670	89	167	26	6	4	48	.249	413	23	8	.982

Selected by Seattle Mariners' organization in 16th round of free-agent draft, June 3, 1980.

DARRYL DeWAYNE MOTLEY

Born January 21, 1960, at Muskogee, Okla.
Height, 5.09. Weight, 196.
Throws and bats righthanded.

Major League stolen bases: 1981 (1), 1983 (2), 1984 (10), 1985 (6). Total—19.

Year Club	League	Pos.	G.	AB.	R.	H.	2B.	3B.	HR.	RBI.	B.A.	PO.	A.	E.	F.A.
1978—Sarasota Royals	Gulf C.	OF	10	41	10	20	1	0	2	9	.488	23	1	1	.960
1978—Fort Myers	Fla. St.	OF	49	151	13	36	3	2	0	12	.238	100	1	4	.962
1979—Fort Myers	Fla. St.	3B	123	447	47	106	20	2	8	45	.237	*109	183	●29	.910
1980—Fort Myers†	Fla. St.	3B-OF-SS	32	119	20	36	7	0	4	24	.303	33	56	9	.908
1980—Jacksonville‡	South.	3B	51	182	30	58	15	1	5	31	.319	43	100	10	.935
1981—Omaha	A. A.	OF	109	410	63	118	18	5	18	64	.288	201	7	3	.986
1981—Kansas City	Amer.	OF	42	125	15	29	4	0	2	8	.232	88	3	3	.968
1982—Omaha§	A. A.	OF	114	409	51	104	12	6	8	52	.254	216	4	3	.987
1983—Evansville	A. A.	OF	130	506	89	142	32	5	16	60	.281	282	14	5	.983
1983—Kansas City	Amer.	OF	19	68	9	16	1	2	3	11	.235	42	2	1	.978
1984—Kansas City	Amer.	OF	146	522	64	148	25	6	15	70	.284	301	7	5	.984
1985—Kansas City	Amer.	OF	123	383	45	85	20	1	17	49	.222	198	4	7	.967
1986—Kansas City	Amer.	OF	72	217	22	44	9	1	7	20	.203	92	2	2	.979
1986—Omaha x	A. A.	OF	23	77	10	18	4	1	0	8	.234	11	0	1	.917
1986—Atlanta	Nat.	OF	5	10	1	2	1	0	0	0	.200	5	0	0	1.000
American League Totals—5 Years			402	1315	155	322	59	10	44	158	.245	721	18	18	.976
National League Totals—1 Year			5	10	1	2	1	0	0	0	.200	5	0	0	1.000
Major League Totals—5 Years			407	1325	156	324	60	10	44	158	.245	726	18	18	.976

Selected by Kansas City Royals' organization in 2nd round of free-agent draft, June 6, 1978.
†On disabled list, April 11 to May 18, 1980.
‡On disabled list, August 9, 1980 through remainder of season.
§Loaned to Evansville (Detroit Tigers' organization), April 2, 1983; returned, September 1, 1983.
xTraded to Atlanta Braves for Pitcher Steve Shields, September 23, 1986.

CHAMPIONSHIP SERIES RECORD

Year Club	League	Pos.	G.	AB.	R.	H.	2B.	3B.	HR.	RBI.	B.A.	PO.	A.	E.	F.A.
1984—Kansas City	Amer.	OF	3	12	0	2	0	0	0	1	.167	11	0	0	1.000
1985—Kansas City	Amer.	OF	2	3	1	1	0	0	0	1	.333	4	0	0	1.000
Championship Series Totals—2 Years			5	15	1	3	0	0	0	2	.200	15	0	0	1.000

WORLD SERIES RECORD

Year Club	League	Pos.	G.	AB.	R.	H.	2B.	3B.	HR.	RBI.	B.A.	PO.	A.	E.	F.A.
1985—Kansas City	Amer.	OF-PH	5	11	1	4	0	0	1	3	.364	4	0	0	1.000

JAMIE MOYER

Born November 18, 1962, at Sellersville, Pa.
Height, 6.01. Weight, 170.
Throws and bats lefthanded.
Attended St. Joseph's University, Philadelphia, Pa.

Year Club	League	G.	IP.	W.	L.	Pct.	H.	R.	ER.	SO.	BB.	ERA.
1984—Geneva	NYP	14	★104⅔	●9	3	.750	59	27	22	★120	31	1.89
1985—Winston-Salem	Carolina	12	94	8	2	.800	82	36	24	94	22	2.30
1985—Pittsfield	Eastern	15	96⅔	7	6	.538	99	49	40	51	32	3.72
1986—Pittsfield	Eastern	6	41	3	1	.750	27	10	4	42	16	0.88
1986—Iowa	Am. Assoc.	6	42⅓	3	2	.600	25	14	12	25	11	2.55
1986—Chicago	National	16	87⅓	7	4	.636	107	52	49	45	42	5.05
Major League Totals—1 Year		16	87⅓	7	4	.636	107	52	49	45	42	5.05

Selected by Chicago Cubs' organization in 6th round of free-agent draft, June 4, 1984.

TERENCE JOHN MULHOLLAND
(Terry)

Born March 9, 1963, at Uniontown, Pa.
Height, 6.03. Weight, 200.
Throws left and bats righthanded.
Attended Marietta College, Marietta, O.

Led Texas League in shutouts with 3 in 1985.

Year Club	League	G.	IP.	W.	L.	Pct.	H.	R.	ER.	SO.	BB.	ERA.
1984—Fresno	California	9	42⅔	5	2	.714	32	17	14	39	36	2.95
1985—Shreveport	Texas	26	176⅔	9	8	.529	166	79	57	77	87	2.90
1986—Phoenix	P. Coast	17	111	8	5	.615	112	60	55	77	56	4.46
1986—San Francisco	National	15	54⅔	1	7	.125	51	33	30	27	35	4.94
Major League Totals—1 Year		15	54⅔	1	7	.125	51	33	30	27	35	4.94

Selected by San Francisco Giants' organization in 1st round (24th player selected) of free-agent draft, June 4, 1984.

STEVEN RANCE MULLINIKS

Name pronounced MUL-in-iks.

(Known by middle name.)

Born January 15, 1956, at Tulare, Calif.
Height, 6.00. Weight, 170.
Throws right and bats lefthanded.
Son of Harvey Mulliniks, pitcher in New York Yankees' organization, 1956 and 1957.

Major League stolen bases: 1977 (1), 1978 (2), 1982 (3), 1984 (2), 1985 (2), 1986 (1). Total—11.
Led American League third basemen in fielding percentage with .968 in 1984.
Led Pacific Coast League shortstops in fielding percentage with .968 in 1979.

Year Club	League	Pos.	G.	AB.	R.	H.	2B.	3B.	HR.	RBI.	B.A.	PO.	A.	E.	F.A.
1974—Idaho Falls	Pion.	SS	66	202	28	44	8	3	0	24	.218	★110	★170	★33	.895
1975—Quad Cities	Midw.	SS	52	186	34	50	6	2	1	21	.269	82	136	17	.928
1975—Salinas	Calif.	SS-2B	59	209	38	54	8	0	0	10	.258	88	146	14	.944
1976—El Paso†	Texas	SS-2B	90	333	81	105	22	4	7	51	.315	140	247	20	.951
1977—Salt Lake City	P. C.	SS	58	220	48	68	17	3	11	51	.309	116	207	15	.956
1977—California	Amer.	SS	78	271	36	73	13	2	3	21	.269	112	229	13	.963
1978—Salt Lake City	P. C.	SS	34	127	34	39	6	2	3	21	.307	65	109	12	.935
1978—California	Amer.	SS	50	119	6	22	3	1	1	6	.185	68	93	8	.953
1979—Salt Lake City	P. C.	SS-2B	116	402	94	138	21	7	3	59	.343	204	331	17	.969
1979—California‡	Amer.	SS	22	68	7	10	0	0	1	8	.147	46	43	4	.957
1980—Kansas City	Amer.	SS-2B	36	54	8	14	3	0	0	6	.259	30	53	1	.988
1981—Kansas City§	Amer.	2B-SS-3B	24	44	6	10	3	0	0	5	.227	25	39	5	.928
1982—Toronto	Amer.	3B-SS	112	311	32	76	25	0	4	35	.244	69	154	14	.941
1983—Toronto	Amer.	3B-SS-2B	129	364	54	100	34	3	10	49	.275	77	185	7	.974
1984—Toronto	Amer.	3B-SS-2B	125	343	41	111	21	5	3	42	.324	67	152	8	.965
1985—Toronto	Amer.	3B	129	366	55	108	26	1	10	57	.295	75	162	7	★.971
1986—Toronto x	Amer.	★3B-2B	117	348	50	90	22	0	11	45	.259	60	176	6	★.975
Major League Totals—10 Years			822	2288	295	614	150	12	43	274	.268	629	1286	73	.963

Selected by California Angels' organization in 3rd round of free-agent draft, June 5, 1974.
†On disabled list, May 4 to June 9 and September 2 to September 24, 1976.
‡Traded with First Baseman Willie Aikens to Kansas City Royals for Outfielder Al Cowens, Shortstop Todd Cruz and a player to be named later, December 6, 1979; California Angels acquired Pitcher Craig Eaton to complete deal, April 1, 1980.
§Traded to Toronto Blue Jays for Pitcher Phil Huffman, March 25, 1982.
xOn disabled list, August 6 to September 1, 1986.

CHAMPIONSHIP SERIES RECORD

Year Club	League	Pos.	G.	AB.	R.	H.	2B.	3B.	HR.	RBI.	B.A.	PO.	A.	E.	F.A.
1985—Toronto	Amer.	PH-3B	5	11	1	4	1	0	1	3	.364	1	4	0	1.000

FRANCIS JOSEPH MULLINS
(Fran)

Born May 14, 1957, at Oakland, Calif.
Height, 6.00. Weight, 180.
Throws and bats righthanded.
Received bachelor of science degree in accounting from
University of Santa Clara, Santa Clara, Calif. in 1979.

Major League stolen bases: 1984 (3).
Tied for American Association lead in being hit by pitch with 8 in 1983.
Named shortstop on THE SPORTING NEWS College Baseball All-America Team, 1979.

Year Club	League	Pos.	G.	AB.	R.	H.	2B.	3B.	HR.	RBI.	B.A.	PO.	A.	E.	F.A.
1979—Knoxville	South.	SS	53	164	21	44	5	1	4	22	.268	57	150	17	.924
1980—Glens Falls	East.	SS-2B	59	212	46	64	7	2	12	39	.302	109	197	20	.939
1980—Iowa	A. A.	3B-2B-SS	53	201	25	51	12	1	6	35	.254	41	88	8	.942
1980—Chicago	Amer.	3B	21	62	9	12	4	0	0	3	.194	15	36	1	.981
1981—Edmonton†	P. C.	SS-2B-3B	77	238	46	58	8	1	8	27	.244	125	257	11	.972
1982—Edmonton	P. C.	SS	98	309	55	87	15	2	14	57	.282	135	305	29	.938
1983—Denver‡§	A. A.	3B-SS-2B	100	355	65	96	18	2	18	55	.270	98	198	18	.943
1984—San Francisco x	Nat.	SS-3B-2B	57	110	8	24	8	0	2	10	.218	39	101	5	.966
1985—Phoenix y	P. C.	SS-3B-2B	77	232	33	62	13	0	7	30	.267	55	161	5	.977
1986—Maine	Int.	SS	30	107	9	29	8	1	1	8	.271	37	100	4	.972
1986—Cleveland za	Amer.	2B-SS-1B	28	40	3	7	4	0	0	5	.175	23	46	4	.945
American League Totals—2 Years			49	102	12	19	8	0	0	8	.186	38	82	5	.960
National League Totals—1 Year			57	110	8	24	8	0	2	10	.218	39	101	5	.966
Major League Totals—3 Years			106	212	20	43	16	0	2	18	.203	77	183	10	.963

Selected by Detroit Tigers' organization in 3rd round of free-agent draft, June 6, 1978.
Selected by Chicago White Sox' organization in 3rd round of free-agent draft, June 5, 1979.
†On disabled list, April 15 to May 29 and August 1 to August 11, 1981.
‡Traded to Cincinnati Reds for Catcher Steve Christmas, November 21, 1983.
§Drafted by San Francisco Giants, December 5, 1983.
xOn disabled list, May 13 to June 1, July 11 to August 1 and August 7 to August 22, 1984.
ySold to Cleveland Indians, January 23, 1986.
zOn disabled list, July 31 to September 1, 1986.
aReleased, November 15, 1986.

JERRY WAYNE MUMPHREY

Born September 9, 1952, at Tyler, Tex.
Height, 6.02. Weight, 200.
Throws right and bats left and righthanded.

Major League stolen bases: 1976 (22), 1977 (22), 1978 (14), 1979 (8), 1980 (52), 1981 (14), 1982 (11), 1983 (7), 1984 (15), 1985 (6), 1986 (2). Total—173.
Led American Association in stolen bases with 44 and caught stealing with 21 in 1975.
Led Gulf Coast League batters in strikeouts with 45 in 1971.

Year Club	League	Pos.	G.	AB.	R.	H.	2B.	3B.	HR.	RBI.	B.A.	PO.	A.	E.	F.A.
1971—Sarasota Cards	Gulf C.	OF	38	141	20	36	3	2	0	6	.255	52	1	3	.946
1972—Sarasota Cards	Gulf C.	OF	26	111	21	38	5	2	0	12	.342	63	2	0	1.000
1972—Cedar Rapids	Midw.	OF	11	33	6	6	2	0	0	1	.182	15	0	0	1.000
1972—St. Petersburg	Fla. St.	OF	17	44	7	15	2	1	0	1	.341	11	1	1	.923
1973—St. Petersburg	Fla. St.	OF	142	*556	*93	*159	20	•9	5	52	.286	210	6	4	.982
1974—Arkansas	Tex.	OF	130	507	87	147	21	6	10	54	.290	209	11	9	.961
1974—St. Louis	Nat.	OF	5	2	2	0	0	0	0	0	.000	0	0	0	.000
1975—Tulsa	A. A.	OF	127	495	87	141	19	6	6	59	.285	248	7	6	.977
1975—St. Louis	Nat.	OF	11	16	2	6	2	0	0	1	.375	9	0	0	1.000
1976—Tulsa	A. A.	OF	19	68	14	23	9	1	1	8	.338	42	4	0	1.000
1976—St. Louis	Nat.	OF	112	384	51	99	15	5	1	26	.258	261	6	2	.993
1977—St. Louis	Nat.	OF	145	463	73	133	20	10	2	38	.287	291	8	9	.971
1978—St. Louis	Nat.	OF	125	367	41	96	13	4	2	37	.262	178	10	1	.995
1979—St. Louis †‡§	Nat.	OF	124	339	53	100	10	3	3	32	.295	180	3	3	.984
1980—San Diego x	Nat.	OF	160	564	61	168	24	3	4	59	.298	398	10	•11	.974
1981—New York	Amer.	OF	80	319	44	98	11	5	6	32	.307	219	5	•8	.966
1982—New York y	Amer.	OF	123	477	76	143	24	10	9	68	.300	336	5	5	.986
1983—New York z	Amer.	OF	83	267	41	70	11	4	7	36	.262	227	7	4	.983
1983—Houston	Nat.	OF	44	143	17	48	10	2	1	17	.336	103	1	1	.990
1984—Houston	Nat.	OF	151	524	66	152	20	3	9	83	.290	317	5	4	.988
1985—Houston a	Nat.	OF	130	444	52	123	25	2	8	61	.277	248	6	4	.969
1986—Chicago	Nat.	OF	111	359	37	94	11	2	5	32	.304	161	3	3	.982
National League Totals—11 Years			1118	3555	455	1019	150	34	35	386	.287	2146	52	42	.981
American League Totals—3 Years			286	1063	161	311	46	19	22	136	.293	782	17	17	.979
Major League Totals—13 Years			1404	4618	616	1330	196	53	57	522	.288	2928	69	59	.981

Selected by St. Louis Cardinals' organization in 4th round of free-agent draft, June 8, 1971.
†On disabled list, March 29 to April 20, 1979.
‡Traded with Pitcher John Denny to Cleveland Indians for Outfielder Bobby Bonds, December 7, 1979.
§Traded by Cleveland Indians to San Diego Padres for Pitcher Bob Owchinko and Outfielder Jim Wilhelm, February 15, 1980.
xTraded with Pitcher John Pacella to New York Yankees for Outfielders Ruppert Jones and Joe Lefebvre and Pitchers Tim Lollar and Chris Welsh, April 1, 1981.
yOn disabled list, May 10 to June 21, 1982.
zTraded to Houston Astros for Outfielder Omar Moreno, August 10, 1983.

aTraded to Chicago Cubs for Outfielder Billy Hatcher and a player to be named later, December 16, 1985; Houston Astros' organization acquired Pitcher Steve Engel to complete deal, July 24, 1986.

DIVISION SERIES RECORD

Year	Club	League	Pos.	G.	AB.	R.	H.	2B.	3B.	HR.	RBI.	B.A.	PO.	A.	E.	F.A.
1981—New York		Amer.	OF	5	21	2	2	0	0	0	0	.095	15	1	0	1.000

CHAMPIONSHIP SERIES RECORD

Year	Club	League	Pos.	G.	AB.	R.	H.	2B.	3B.	HR.	RBI.	B.A.	PO.	A.	E.	F.A.
1981—New York		Amer.	OF	3	12	2	6	1	0	0	0	.500	4	0	0	1.000

WORLD SERIES RECORD

Year	Club	League	Pos.	G.	AB.	R.	H.	2B.	3B.	HR.	RBI.	B.A.	PO.	A.	E.	F.A.
1981—New York		Amer.	OF	5	15	2	3	0	0	0	0	.200	6	0	0	1.000

ALL-STAR GAME RECORD

Year	League	Pos.	AB.	R.	H.	2B.	3B.	HR.	RBI.	B.A.	PO.	A.	E.	F.A.
1984—National		PH	1	0	0	0	0	0	0	.000	0	0	0	.000

DALE BRYAN MURPHY

Born March 12, 1956, at Portland, Ore.
Height, 6.05. Weight, 215.
Throws and bats righthanded.
Attended Portland Community College, Portland, Ore. and Brigham Young University, Provo, Utah.

Tied major league records for fewest double plays by outfielder, season, 150 or more games (0), 1983; fewest double plays by outfielder, season, for leader in double plays (4), 1981 and 1985.
Major League stolen bases: 1978 (11), 1979 (6), 1980 (9), 1981 (14), 1982 (23), 1983 (30), 1984 (19), 1985 (10), 1986 (7). Total—129.
Hit three home runs in a game, May 18, 1979.
Led National League in bases on balls received with 90 in 1985.
Led National League in total bases with 332 in 1984.
Led National League in slugging percentage with .540 in 1983 and .547 in 1984.
Led National League batters in strikeouts with 145 in 1978, 133 in 1980 and tied for lead with 141 in 1985.
Led National League first basemen in errors with 20 in 1978.
Tied for National League lead in double plays by outfielders with 4 in 1981 and 1985.
Tied for International League lead in total bases with 249 in 1977.
Led International League catchers in putouts with 510, passed balls with 14 and tied for lead in double plays with 7 in 1977.
Named National League Player of the Year by THE SPORTING NEWS, 1982 and 1983.
Named National League Most Valuable Player by Baseball Writers' Association of America, 1982 and 1983.
Named outfielder on THE SPORTING NEWS National League All-Star Team, 1982 through 1985.
Named outfielder on THE SPORTING NEWS National League All-Star fielding team, 1982 through 1986.
Named outfielder on THE SPORTING NEWS National League Silver Slugger team, 1982 through 1985.

Year	Club	League	Pos.	G.	AB.	R.	H.	2B.	3B.	HR.	RBI.	B.A.	PO.	A.	E.	F.A.
1974—Kingsport		Appal.	C	54	181	28	46	7	0	5	31	.254	389	28	7	.983
1975—Greenwood		W. Car.	C-1B	131	443	48	101	20	1	5	48	.228	723	81	18	.978
1976—Savannah		South.	C	104	352	37	94	13	5	12	55	.267	444	40	10	.980
1976—Richmond		Int.	C-OF	18	50	10	13	1	1	4	8	.260	60	9	4	.945
1976—Atlanta		Nat.	C	19	65	3	17	6	0	0	9	.262	100	13	3	.974
1977—Richmond		Int.	C-1B	127	466	71	142	●33	4	22	*90	.305	600	50	15	.977
1977—Atlanta		Nat.	C	18	76	5	24	8	1	2	14	.316	114	11	6	.954
1978—Atlanta		Nat.	1B-C	151	530	66	120	14	3	23	79	.226	1220	105	23	.983
1979—Atlanta†		Nat.	1B-C	104	384	53	106	7	2	21	57	.276	812	57	20	.978
1980—Atlanta		Nat.	OF-1B	156	569	98	160	27	2	33	89	.281	384	15	6	.985
1981—Atlanta		Nat.	OF-1B	104	369	43	91	12	1	13	50	.247	264	11	5	.982
1982—Atlanta		Nat.	OF	●162	598	113	168	23	2	36	●109	.281	407	6	9	.979
1983—Atlanta		Nat.	OF	*162	589	131	178	24	4	36	*121	.302	373	10	6	.985
1984—Atlanta		Nat.	OF	*162	607	94	176	32	8	●36	100	.290	369	10	5	.987
1985—Atlanta		Nat.	OF	●162	616	●118	185	32	2	*37	111	.300	334	8	7	.980
1986—Atlanta		Nat.	OF	160	614	89	163	29	7	29	83	.265	303	6	6	.981
Major League Totals—11 Years				1360	5017	813	1388	214	32	266	822	.277	4680	252	96	.981

Selected by Atlanta Braves' organization in 1st round (fifth player selected) of free-agent draft, June 5, 1974.
†On disabled list, May 25 to July 19, 1979.

CHAMPIONSHIP SERIES RECORD

Year	Club	League	Pos.	G.	AB.	R.	H.	2B.	3B.	HR.	RBI.	B.A.	PO.	A.	E.	F.A.
1982—Atlanta		Nat.	OF	3	11	1	3	0	0	0	0	.273	8	0	0	1.000

ALL-STAR GAME RECORD

Year	League	Pos.	AB.	R.	H.	2B.	3B.	HR.	RBI.	B.A.	PO.	A.	E.	F.A.
1980—National		OF	1	0	0	0	0	0	0	.000	0	0	0	.000
1982—National		OF	2	1	0	0	0	0	0	.000	2	0	0	1.000
1983—National		OF	3	0	1	0	0	0	0	.333	0	0	0	.000
1984—National		OF	3	1	2	0	0	1	1	.667	0	0	0	.000
1985—National		OF	3	0	1	1	0	0	0	.333	1	0	0	1.000
1986—National		OF	2	0	0	0	0	0	0	.000	2	0	0	1.000
All-Star Game Totals—6 Years			14	2	4	1	0	1	2	.286	5	0	0	1.000

DANIEL LEE MURPHY
(Dan)

Born September 18, 1964, at Artesia, Calif.
Height, 6.02. Weight, 195.
Throws and bats righthanded.

Year Club	League	G.	IP.	W.	L.	Pct.	H.	R.	ER.	SO.	BB.	ERA.
1983—Paintsville	Ap'lachian	11	38⅔	3	1	.750	43	22	16	29	26	3.72
1983—Beloit	Midwest	8	24⅔	0	0	.000	21	14	11	22	14	4.01
1984—Beloit	Midwest	26	112⅔	9	4	.692	116	59	45	79	44	3.59
1985—Stockton	California	24	132	9	7	.563	114	65	58	157	84	3.95
1986—El Paso	Texas	18	116⅓	9	2	.818	126	63	57	89	40	4.41

Signed as free agent by Milwaukee Brewers' organization, December 2, 1982.

DWAYNE KEITH MURPHY

Born March 18, 1955, at Merced, Calif.
Height, 6.01. Weight, 185.
Throws right and bats lefthanded.

Tied major league record for fewest double plays by outfielder, season, 150 or more games (0), 1980 and 1985.
Major League stolen bases: 1979 (15), 1980 (26), 1981 (10), 1982 (26), 1983 (7), 1984 (4), 1985 (4), 1986 (3). Total—95.
Led American League in sacrifice hits with 22 in 1980 and game-winning RBIs with 15 in 1981.
Led American League outfielders in total chances with 525 in 1980, 474 in 1982 and 494 in 1984.
Led Southern League in bases on balls received with 97 in 1977.
Tied for Southern League lead in double plays by outfielders with 4 in 1977.
Named outfielder on THE SPORTING NEWS American League All-Star Team, 1981.
Named outfielder on THE SPORTING NEWS American League All-Star fielding team, 1980 through 1985.

Year Club	League	Pos.	G.	AB.	R.	H.	2B.	3B.	HR.	RBI.	B.A.	PO.	A.	E.	F.A.
1973—Lewiston	N'west	OF	68	215	25	50	7	2	3	19	.233	102	★13	6	.950
1974—Burlington†	Midw.	OF	53	150	16	33	6	2	2	10	.220	55	2	3	.959
1975—Modesto	Calif.	OF	126	429	81	125	20	7	8	71	.291	250	7	9	.966
1976—Chattanooga	South.	OF	68	200	32	52	6	0	1	23	.260	138	6	1	.993
1976—Tucson	P. C.	OF	52	179	32	42	7	2	3	11	.235	125	6	4	.970
1977—Chattanooga	South.	OF	132	406	53	104	11	9	5	53	.256	320	14	5	★.985
1978—Vancouver	P. C.	OF-SS	42	148	35	39	4	1	7	17	.264	125	9	3	.978
1978—Oakland	Amer.	OF	60	52	15	10	2	0	0	5	.192	49	1	0	1.000
1979—Oakland‡	Amer.	OF	121	388	57	99	10	4	11	40	.255	322	10	4	.988
1980—Oakland	Amer.	OF	159	573	86	157	18	2	13	68	.274	★507	13	5	.990
1981—Oakland	Amer.	OF	107	390	58	98	10	3	15	60	.251	326	6	5	.985
1982—Oakland	Amer.	★OF-SS	151	543	84	129	15	1	27	94	.238	★452	18	8	.983
1983—Oakland§	Amer.	OF	130	471	55	107	17	2	17	75	.227	365	7	8	.979
1984—Oakland	Amer.	OF	153	559	93	143	18	2	33	88	.256	★474	14	6	.988
1985—Oakland	Amer.	OF	152	523	77	122	21	3	20	59	.233	432	6	5	.989
1986—Oakland x	Amer.	OF	98	329	50	83	11	3	9	39	.252	276	6	2	.993
1986—Modesto	Calif.	OF	2	5	1	1	1	0	0	0	.200	1	0	0	1.000
1986—Madison	Midw.	OF	1	0	0	0	0	0	0	0	.000	1	0	0	1.000
Major League Totals—9 Years			1131	3828	575	948	122	20	145	528	.248	3203	81	43	.987

Selected by Oakland A's organization in 15th round of free-agent draft, June 5, 1973.
†On disabled list, July 16 to September 16, 1974.
‡On disabled list, June 21 to July 14, 1979.
§On disabled list, June 24 to July 11, 1983.
    xOn disabled list, May 12 to July 5, 1986; included rehabilitation disability assignment to Modesto, July 1 to July 3, and to Madison, July 4, 1986.

DIVISION SERIES RECORD

Year Club	League	Pos.	G.	AB.	R.	H.	2B.	3B.	HR.	RBI.	B.A.	PO.	A.	E.	F.A.
1981—Oakland	Amer.	OF	3	11	4	6	1	0	1	2	.545	13	0	0	1.000

CHAMPIONSHIP SERIES RECORD

Year Club	League	Pos.	G.	AB.	R.	H.	2B.	3B.	HR.	RBI.	B.A.	PO.	A.	E.	F.A.
1981—Oakland	Amer.	OF	3	8	1	2	1	0	0	1	.250	9	0	0	1.000

JOHN VINCENT MURPHY

Born May 12, 1962, at Flint, Mich.
Height, 6.03. Weight, 190.
Throws and bats righthanded.
Received degree in business administration from
The Citadel, Charleston, S.C., in 1984.

Year Club	League	Pos.	G.	AB.	R.	H.	2B.	3B.	HR.	RBI.	B.A.	PO.	A.	E.	F.A.
1984—Erie	NYP	OF-3B	60	185	32	52	8	1	4	41	.281	77	29	7	.938
1985—Savannah	S. Atl.	OF	132	464	85	147	17	2	10	51	.317	193	8	6	.971
1986—Springfield	Midw.	OF	89	348	76	113	22	1	13	75	.325	201	2	5	.976

Selected by St. Louis Cardinals' organization in 23rd round of free-agent draft, June 4, 1984.

—DID YOU KNOW—

That in 1986, Cincinnati's Eric Davis joined Rickey Henderson and Joe Morgan as the only players in history to hit 20 homers and steal 60 bases in one season?

MICHAEL CORNELIUS MURPHY
(Mike)

Born February 15, 1963, at Bronx, N.Y.
Height, 6.04. Weight, 230.
Throws and bats righthanded.
Attended Manhattan Community College, New York, N.Y.

Tied for Eastern League lead in shutouts with 3 in 1986.

Year	Club	League	G.	IP.	W.	L.	Pct.	H.	R.	ER.	SO.	BB.	ERA.
1983—Batavia	NYP	17	46	2	2	.500	46	32	24	36	38	4.70
1984—Waterloo	Midwest	17	86	6	4	.600	64	26	23	66	18	2.41
1984—Buffalo	Eastern	9	40⅓	2	4	.333	50	29	28	20	27	6.25
1985—Waterloo†	Midwest	8	51⅔	2	2	.500	60	24	21	40	16	3.66
1986—Waterbury	Eastern	25	118	8	7	.533	107	54	47	62	42	3.58
1986—Maine	Int'national	7	37⅔	1	2	.333	36	22	16	15	19	3.82

Selected by Cleveland Indians' organization in 18th round of free-agent draft, June 6, 1983.
†On disabled list, June 25, 1985 through remainder of season.

ROBERT ALBERT MURPHY JR.
(Rob)

Born May 26, 1960, at Miami, Fla.
Height, 6.02. Weight, 200.
Throws and bats lefthanded.
Attended University of Florida, Gainesville, Fla.

Major League saves: 1986 (1).
Tied for Eastern League lead in saves with 15 in 1984.

Year	Club	League	G.	IP.	W.	L.	Pct.	H.	R.	ER.	SO.	BB.	ERA.
1981—Tampa	Florida St.	25	105	6	8	.429	109	73	53	58	67	4.54
1982—Cedar Rapids	Midwest	31	89	3	7	.300	92	62	40	96	61	4.04
1983—Cedar Rapids	Midwest	36	140⅔	6	10	.375	120	66	52	137	69	3.33
1984—Vermont	Eastern	45	69⅔	2	3	.400	57	23	21	69	35	2.71
1985—Denver	Am. Assoc.	41	84	5	5	.500	94	55	43	66	57	4.61
1985—Cincinnati	National	2	3	0	0	.000	2	2	2	1	2	6.00
1986—Denver	Am. Assoc.	27	42⅔	3	4	.429	33	12	9	36	24	1.90
1986—Cincinnati	National	34	50⅓	6	0	1.000	26	4	4	36	21	0.72
Major League Totals—2 Years		36	53⅓	6	0	1.000	28	6	6	37	23	1.01

Selected by Milwaukee Brewers' organization in 29th round of free-agent draft, June 6, 1978.
Selected by Cincinnati Reds' organization in secondary phase of free-agent draft, January 13, 1981.

EDDIE CLARENCE MURRAY

Born February 24, 1956, at Los Angeles, Calif.
Height, 6.02. Weight, 200.
Throws right and bats left and righthanded.
Attended California State University, Los Angeles, Calif.
Brother of Rich Murray, first baseman with San Francisco Giants, 1980 and 1983;
Leon Murray, first baseman in San Francisco Giants' organization, 1970;
Charles Murray, minor league outfielder, 1962 through 1966
and 1969; and Venice Murray, first baseman in
San Francisco Giants' organization, 1978.

Tied major league records for most games, switch-hit home runs, season (2), 1982; most intentional bases on balls by switch-hitter, season (25), 1984.
Established American League records for most consecutive games, one or more hits by switch-hitter, season (22), 1984; most game-winning runs batted in, lifetime (101).
Major League stolen bases: 1978 (6), 1979 (10), 1980 (7), 1981 (2), 1982 (7), 1983 (5), 1984 (10), 1985 (5), 1986 (3). Total—55.
Hit three home runs in a game, August 29, 1979 (second game), September 14, 1980 (13 innings) and August 26, 1985.
Switch-hit home runs in one game six times: August 3, 1977, August 29, 1979 (two righthanded and one lefthanded); August 16, 1981, April 24, 1982 , August 26, 1982 and August 26, 1985 (two lefthanded and one righthanded).
Led American League in bases on balls received with 107 and game-winning RBIs with 19 in 1984.
Led American League in intentional bases on balls received with 25 in 1984 and tied for lead with 18 in 1982.
Led American League first basemen in double plays with 152 in 1984 and tied for lead with 154 in 1985.
Led American League first basemen in total chances with 1,615 in 1978 and 1,694 in 1984.
Led American League first basemen in putouts with 1,504 in 1978.
Led Florida State League in total bases with 212 in 1974.
Led Florida State League first basemen in double plays with 113 in 1974.
Named American League Rookie of the Year by Baseball Writers' Association of America, 1977.
Named first baseman on THE SPORTING NEWS American League All-Star Team, 1983.
Named first baseman on THE SPORTING NEWS American League All-Star fielding team, 1982 through 1984.
Named first baseman on THE SPORTING NEWS American League Silver Slugger team, 1983 and 1984.
Named Appalachian League Player of the Year, 1973.

Year	Club	League	Pos.	G.	AB.	R.	H.	2B.	3B.	HR.	RBI.	B.A.	PO.	A.	E.	F.A.
1973—Bluefield	Appal.	1B	50	188	34	54	6	0	11	32	.287	421	14	13	.971
1974—Miami	Fla. St.	1B	131	460	64	133	*29	7	12	63	.289	*1114	*51	*25	.979
1974—Asheville	South.	1B	2	7	1	2	2	0	0	2	.286	17	0	0	1.000
1975—Asheville	South.	1B-3B	124	436	66	115	13	5	17	68	.264	637	58	15	.979
1976—Charlotte	South.	1B	88	299	46	89	15	2	12	46	.298	746	45	9	.989
1976—Rochester	Int.	1B-OF-3B	54	168	35	46	6	2	11	40	.274	291	13	5	.984

Year Club	League	Pos.	G.	AB.	R.	H.	2B.	3B.	HR.	RBI.	B.A.	PO.	A.	E.	F.A.
1977—Baltimore	Amer.	OF-1B	160	611	81	173	29	2	27	88	.283	482	20	4	.992
1978—Baltimore	Amer.	1B-3B	161	610	85	174	32	3	27	95	.285	1507	112	6	.996
1979—Baltimore	Amer.	1B	159	606	90	179	30	2	25	99	.295	★1456	107	10	.994
1980—Baltimore	Amer.	1B	158	621	100	186	36	2	32	116	.300	1369	77	9	.994
1981—Baltimore	Amer.	1B	99	378	57	111	21	2	●22	★78	.294	899	★91	1	★.999
1982—Baltimore	Amer.	1B	151	550	87	174	30	1	32	110	.316	1269	97	4	★.997
1983—Baltimore	Amer.	1B	156	582	115	178	30	3	33	111	.306	1393	114	10	.993
1984—Baltimore	Amer.	1B	●162	588	97	180	26	3	29	110	.306	★1538	★143	13	.992
1985—Baltimore	Amer.	1B	156	583	111	173	37	1	31	124	.297	1338	152	★19	.987
1986—Baltimore†	Amer.	1B	137	495	61	151	25	1	17	84	.305	1045	88	13	.989
Major League Totals—10 Years			1499	5624	884	1679	296	20	275	1015	.299	12296	1001	89	.993

Selected by Baltimore Orioles' organization in 3rd round of free-agent draft, June 5, 1973.
†On disabled list, July 10 to August 7, 1986.

CHAMPIONSHIP SERIES RECORD

Tied Championship Series record for most runs, game (4), October 7, 1983.
Tied American League Championship Series record for most bases on balls, four-game Series (5), 1979.

Year Club	League	Pos.	G.	AB.	R.	H.	2B.	3B.	HR.	RBI.	B.A.	PO.	A.	E.	F.A.
1979—Baltimore	Amer.	1B	4	12	3	5	0	0	1	5	.417	44	3	2	.959
1983—Baltimore	Amer.	1B	4	15	5	4	0	0	1	3	.267	34	3	1	.974
Championship Series Totals—2 Years			8	27	8	9	0	0	2	8	.333	78	6	3	.966

WORLD SERIES RECORD

Established World Series record for most double plays started by first baseman, game (2), October 11, 1979.

Year Club	League	Pos.	G.	AB.	R.	H.	2B.	3B.	HR.	RBI.	B.A.	PO.	A.	E.	F.A.
1979—Baltimore	Amer.	1B	7	26	3	4	1	0	1	2	.154	60	7	0	1.000
1983—Baltimore	Amer.	1B	5	20	2	5	0	0	2	3	.250	46	1	1	.979
World Series Totals—2 Years			12	46	5	9	1	0	3	5	.196	106	8	1	.991

ALL-STAR GAME RECORD

Year League	Pos.	AB.	R.	H.	2B.	3B.	HR.	RBI.	B.A.	PO.	A.	E.	F.A.
1981—American	PH-1B	2	0	0	0	0	0	0	.000	2	1	0	1.000
1982—American	PH-1B	1	0	0	0	0	0	0	.000	4	0	0	1.000
1983—American	1B	2	0	0	0	0	0	0	.000	4	0	0	1.000
1984—American	1B	2	0	1	1	0	0	0	.500	3	0	0	1.000
1985—American	1B	3	0	0	0	0	0	0	.000	5	2	0	1.000
All-Star Game Totals—5 Years		10	0	1	1	0	0	0	.100	18	3	0	1.000

Member of American League All-Star Team in 1978 and 1986; did not play.

JEFFREY JOSEPH MUSSELMAN
(Jeff)

Born June 21, 1963, at Doylestown, Pa.
Height, 6.00. Weight, 180.
Throws and bats lefthanded.
Received bachelor of arts degree in economics from Harvard University, Cambridge, Mass., in 1985.
Tied for Pioneer League lead in games started by pitchers with 15 in 1985.

Year Club	League	G.	IP.	W.	L.	Pct.	H.	R.	ER.	SO.	BB.	ERA.
1985—Medicine Hat	Pioneer	16	88	6	4	.600	75	41	39	96	44	3.99
1986—Ventura County	California	26	154⅔	7	7	.500	122	67	52	165	59	3.03
1986—Knoxville	Southern	7	41⅓	5	1	.833	33	17	13	38	25	2.83
1986—Toronto	American	6	5⅓	0	0	.000	8	7	6	4	5	10.13
Major League Totals—1 Year		6	5⅓	0	0	.000	8	7	6	4	5	10.13

Selected by Toronto Blue Jays' organization in 6th round of free-agent draft, June 3, 1985.

GREGORY RICHARD MYERS
(Greg)

Born April 14, 1966, at Riverside, Calif.
Height, 6.01. Weight, 200.
Throws right and bats lefthanded.
Led California League catchers in total chances with 967 in 1986.

Year Club	League	Pos.	G.	AB.	R.	H.	2B.	3B.	HR.	RBI.	B.A.	PO.	A.	E.	F.A.
1984—Medicine Hat	Pion.	C	38	133	20	42	9	0	2	20	.316	216	24	4	.984
1985—Florence	S. Atl.	C	134	489	52	109	19	2	5	62	.223	551	61	7	★.989
1986—Ventura	Calif.	C	124	451	65	133	23	4	20	79	.295	★849	99	19	.980

Selected by Toronto Blue Jays' organization in 3rd round of free-agent draft, June 4, 1984.

RANDALL KIRK MYERS
(Randy)

Born September 19, 1962, at Vancouver, Wash.
Height, 6.01. Weight, 190.
Throws and bats lefthanded.
Attended Clark College, Vancouver, Wash.

Tied for Carolina League lead in complete games with 7 in 1984.
Tied for South Atlantic League lead in games started by pitchers with 28 in 1983.
Tied for Appalachian League lead in games started by pitchers with 13 and balks with 3 in 1982.
Named Carolina League Pitcher of the Year, 1984.

Year Club	League	G.	IP.	W.	L.	Pct.	H.	R.	ER.	SO.	BB.	ERA.
1982—Kingsport	Ap'lachian	13	74⅓	6	3	.667	68	49	34	●86	69	4.12
1983—Columbia	S. Atlantic	28	173⅓	14	10	.583	146	94	70	164	108	3.63
1984—Lynchburg	Carolina	23	157	13	5	.722	123	46	36	171	61	★2.06
1984—Jackson	Texas	5	35	2	1	.667	29	14	8	35	16	2.06
1985—Jackson	Texas	19	120⅓	4	8	.333	99	61	53	116	69	3.96
1985—Tidewater	Int'national	8	44	1	1	.500	40	13	9	25	20	1.84
1985—New York	National	1	2	0	0	.000	0	0	0	2	1	0.00
1986—Tidewater	Int'national	45	65	6	7	.462	44	19	17	79	44	2.35
1986—New York	National	10	10⅔	0	0	.000	11	5	5	13	9	4.22
Major League Totals—2 Years		11	12⅔	0	0	.000	11	5	5	15	10	3.55

Selected by Cincinnati Reds' organization in 3rd round of free-agent draft, January 12, 1982.
Selected by New York Mets' organization in secondary phase of free-agent draft, June 7, 1982.

JERRY AUSTIN NARRON

Born January 15, 1956, at Goldsboro, N. C.
Height, 6.03. Weight, 205.
Throws right and bats lefthanded.
Attends East Carolina University, Greenville, N. C.
Brother of John Narron, Jr., first baseman in New York Yankees' and Chicago White
Sox' organizations, 1974 and 1975; nephew of Sam Narron, catcher with St. Louis Cardinals,
1935, 1942 and 1943; coach, Pittsburgh Pirates, 1951 through 1964; and part-time scout with Pittsburgh Pirates,
1982 through 1985; nephew of Milton Narron, former minor league catcher-outfielder.

Led Pacific Coast League in intentional bases on balls received with 15 in 1983.
Tied for Florida State League lead in being hit by pitch with 10 in 1975.
Led Florida State League catchers in fielding percentage with .986 and double plays with 7 in 1976.
Tied for Pacific Coast League lead in double plays by catchers with 11 in 1978.

Year Club	League	Pos.	G.	AB.	R.	H.	2B.	3B.	HR.	RBI.	B.A.	PO.	A.	E.	F.A.
1974—Johnson City	Appal.	C-OF	66	226	43	68	15	3	7	49	.301	249	19	8	.971
1975—Fort Lauderdale	Fla. St.	1B-C-OF	113	360	39	76	12	0	2	34	.211	425	33	2	.996
1976—Fort Lauderdale	Fla. St.	C-1B	119	412	35	101	17	0	6	56	.245	563	56	8	.987
1977—West Haven	East.	C-1B	121	438	80	131	16	0	28	93	.299	625	40	7	.990
1978—Tacoma	P. C.	C-1B	120	435	67	121	25	1	15	84	.278	552	78	18	.972
1979—New York†	Amer.	C	61	123	17	21	3	1	4	18	.171	167	15	5	.973
1980—Spokane	P. C.	C-1B	67	233	40	66	14	2	9	39	.283	223	19	6	.976
1980—Seattle	Amer.	C	48	107	7	21	3	0	4	18	.196	115	11	1	.992
1981—Seattle‡	Amer.	C	76	203	13	45	5	0	3	17	.222	248	11	1	.996
1982—Spokane	P. C.	C	110	408	60	127	24	2	12	61	.311	446	46	12	.976
1983—Edmonton	P. C.	1B-C	139	532	93	160	30	5	27	102	.301	1298	70	13	.991
1983—California	Amer.	C	10	22	1	3	0	0	1	4	.136	14	3	2	.895
1984—California	Amer.	C-1B	69	150	9	37	5	0	3	17	.247	184	12	1	.995
1985—California	Amer.	C-1B	67	132	12	29	4	0	5	14	.220	146	14	0	1.000
1986—California	Amer.	C	57	95	5	21	3	1	1	8	.221	155	14	2	.988
Major League Totals—7 Years			388	832	64	177	23	2	21	96	.213	1029	80	12	.989

Selected by New York Yankees' organization in 6th round of free-agent draft, June 5, 1974.
†Traded with Outfielder Juan Beniquez and Pitchers Jim Beattle and Rick Anderson to Seattle Mariners for Outfielder Ruppert Jones and Pitcher Jim Lewis, November 1, 1979.
‡Released, March 30, 1982; signed by California Angels' organization, April 1, 1982.

CHAMPIONSHIP SERIES RECORD

Year Club	League	Pos.	G.	AB.	R.	H.	2B.	3B.	HR.	RBI.	B.A.	PO.	A.	E.	F.A.
1986—California	Amer.	C-PH	4	2	1	1	0	0	0	0	.500	1	0	0	1.000

JAMES LLEWELYN NEIDLINGER
(Jim)

Born September 14, 1964, at Vallejo, Calif.
Height, 6.04. Weight, 177.
Throws right and bats left and righthanded.

Pitched 2-0 no-hit victory against Glens Falls, July 1, 1986.
Tied for Carolina League lead in games started by pitchers with 26 in 1985.
Named Eastern League Pitcher of the Year, 1986.

Year Club	League	G.	IP.	W.	L.	Pct.	H.	R.	ER.	SO.	BB.	ERA.
1984—Mason	S. Atlantic	25	166	9	8	.529	138	65	51	113	85	2.77
1985—Prince William	Carolina	26	165⅓	8	●13	.381	141	86	79	143	83	4.30
1986—Nashua	Eastern	22	163⅔	12	7	.632	135	57	44	98	44	★2.42
1986—Hawaii	P. Coast	4	27⅔	2	1	.667	33	14	12	14	9	3.90

Signed as free agent by Pittsburgh Pirates' organization, March 4, 1984.

RICKY LEE NELSON

Born May 8, 1959, at Eloy, Ariz.
Height, 6.00. Weight, 195.
Throws right and bats lefthanded.
Attended Arizona State University, Tempe, Ariz.

Major League stolen bases: 1983 (7), 1986 (1). Total—8.
Tied for California League lead in total bases with 245 and game-winning RBIs with 15 in 1982.

Year Club	League	Pos.	G.	AB.	R.	H.	2B.	3B.	HR.	RBI.	B.A.	PO.	A.	E.	F.A.
1981—Bellingham	N'west	OF	56	197	35	56	5	0	6	37	.284	49	7	3	.949
1982—Bakersfield	Calif.	OF	*140	*566	65	174	*36	1	11	*101	.307	197	13	9	.959
1983—Salt Lake City	P. C.	OF-3B	29	102	20	34	6	3	5	27	.333	55	4	1	.983
1983—Seattle	Amer.	OF	98	291	32	74	13	3	5	36	.254	122	10	4	.971
1984—Salt Lake City†	P. C.	OF	75	310	54	91	11	4	11	42	.294	141	3	2	.986
1984—Seattle	Amer.	OF	9	15	2	3	0	0	1	2	.200	2	0	0	1.000
1985—Calgary	P. C.	OF	120	489	75	131	30	4	16	70	.268	210	5	6	.973
1985—Seattle	Amer.	OF	6	2	2	0	0	0	0	0	.000	1	0	0	1.000
1986—Calgary	P. C.	OF	81	293	38	82	19	2	3	33	.280	120	5	0	1.000
1986—Seattle‡	Amer.	OF	10	12	2	2	0	0	0	1	.167	2	0	1	.667
Major League Totals—4 Years			123	320	38	79	13	3	6	39	.247	127	10	5	.965

Selected by California Angels' organization in 24th round of free-agent draft, June 3, 1980.
Selected by Seattle Mariners' organization in 4th round of free-agent draft, June 8, 1981.
†On disabled list, June 8 to July 19, 1984.
‡Traded to New York Mets' organization for Catcher Doug Gwosdz, December 17, 1986.

ROBERT AUGUSTUS NELSON II
(Rob)

Born May 17, 1964, at Pasadena, Calif.
Height, 6.04. Weight, 215.
Throws and bats lefthanded.
Attended Mount San Antonio College, Walnut, Calif.

Led Pacific Coast League in sacrifice flies with 13 in 1986.
Led Midwest League batters in strikeouts with 140 in 1984.
Led Pacific Coast League first basemen in total chances with 1,359 in 1986.
Led Midwest League first basemen in double plays with 111 and total chances with 1,279 in 1984.

Year Club	League	Pos.	G.	AB.	R.	H.	2B.	3B.	HR.	RBI.	B.A.	PO.	A.	E.	F.A.
1983—Idaho Falls	Pion.	1B	54	196	42	57	12	2	12	38	.291	418	32	6	.986
1984—Madison	Midw.	1B	136	487	71	120	25	2	19	85	.246	*1173	*89	17	.987
1985—Huntsville	South.	1B	140	499	68	116	25	0	32	98	.232	1101	86	*23	.981
1986—Tacoma	P. C.	1B	139	508	77	140	26	4	20	108	.276	*1228	*121	10	.992
1986—Oakland	Amer.	1B	5	9	1	2	1	0	0	0	.222	3	1	1	.800
Major League Totals—1 Year			5	9	1	2	1	0	0	0	.222	3	1	1	.800

Selected by Houston Astros' organization in 27th round of free-agent draft, June 7, 1982.
Selected by Atlanta Braves' organization in secondary phase of free-agent draft, January 11, 1983.
Selected by Oakland A's organization in secondary phase of free-agent draft, June 6, 1983.

WAYLAND EUGENE NELSON II
(Gene)

Born December 3, 1960, at Tampa, Fla.
Height, 6.00. Weight, 172.
Throws and bats righthanded.

Major League saves: 1984 (1), 1985 (2), 1986 (6). Total—9.
Led Florida State League in shutouts with 5 and complete games with 16 in 1980.

Year Club	League	G.	IP.	W.	L.	Pct.	H.	R.	ER.	SO.	BB.	ERA.
1978—Sarasota Rangers	Gulf Coast	14	52	5	0	•1.000	41	18	13	28	20	2.25
1979—Asheville†	W. Carol.	33	155	13	5	*.722	149	77	62	96	44	3.60
1980—Fort Lauderdale	Florida St.	27	196	*20	3	*.870	146	51	43	130	70	1.97
1981—New York‡	American	8	39	3	1	.750	40	24	21	16	23	4.85
1981—Fort Lauderdale	Florida St.	2	10	0	0	.000	9	6	6	8	5	5.40
1981—Columbus§	Int'national	5	32	4	0	1.000	25	9	9	37	14	2.53
1982—Seattle	American	22	122⅔	6	9	.400	133	70	63	71	60	4.62
1982—Salt Lake City	P. Coast	5	37⅔	1	3	.250	36	18	14	22	28	3.35
1983—Salt Lake City x	P. Coast	16	99	9	4	.692	115	65	57	74	28	5.18
1983—Seattle	American	10	32	0	3	.000	38	29	28	11	21	7.88
1984—Salt Lake City y	P. Coast	17	112	6	8	.429	138	75	70	89	54	5.63
1984—Chicago	American	20	74⅔	3	5	.375	72	38	37	36	17	4.46
1985—Chicago z	American	46	145⅔	10	10	.500	144	74	69	101	67	4.26
1986—Chicago a	American	54	114⅔	6	6	.500	118	52	49	70	41	3.85
Major League Totals—6 Years		160	528⅔	28	34	.452	545	287	267	305	229	4.55

Selected by Texas Rangers' organization in 29th round of free-agent draft, June 6, 1978.
†Traded with Pitcher Ray Fontenot to New York Yankees' organization for Pitchers Bob Polinsky, Neal Mersch and Mark Softy, October 8, 1979; completing deal in which New York traded Outfielder Mickey Rivers and three players to be named later to Texas Rangers for Third Baseman Amos Lewis and two players to be named later, August 1, 1979.
‡On disabled list, April 10 to May 4, 1981; included rehabilitation disability assignment to Ft. Lauderdale, April 17 to May 4, 1981.
§Traded with Pitcher Bill Caudill, a player to be named later and cash to Seattle Mariners for Pitcher Shane Rawley, April 1, 1982; Seattle organization acquired Outfielder Bobby Brown to complete deal, April 6, 1982.
xOn disabled list, June 25 to July 31, 1983.
yTraded Pitcher Jerry Don Gleaton to Chicago White Sox for Pitcher Salome Barojas, June 27, 1984.
zHad one at-bat with no hits.
aTraded with a player to be named later to Oakland A's for Infielder Donnie Hill, December 11, 1986; Oakland acquired Pitcher Bruce Tanner to complete deal, December 18, 1986.

GRAIG NETTLES

Born August 20, 1944, at San Diego, Calif.
Height, 6.00. Weight, 187.
Throws right and bats lefthanded.
Attended San Diego State College, San Diego, Calif.
Brother of Jim Nettles, outfielder with Minnesota, Detroit, Kansas City and Oakland,
1970 through 1972, 1974, 1979 and 1981; minor league coach, Oakland A's organization,
1982 and 1983; and minor league manager in Oakland A's organization since 1984.

Established major league records for most assists by third baseman, season (412), and most double plays by third baseman, season (54), 1971.
Tied major league records for most home runs month of April (11), 1974; fewest three-base hits, season, 150 or more games (0), 1972 and 1973.
Established American League record for most home runs by third baseman, lifetime (319).
Tied American League record for most home runs, doubleheader (4), April 14, 1974.
Major League stolen bases: 1969 (1), 1970 (3), 1971 (7), 1972 (2), 1974 (1), 1975 (1), 1976 (11), 1977 (2), 1978 (1), 1979 (1), 1982 (1). Total—31.
Led American League in sacrifice flies with 11 in 1975.
Led American League third basemen in total chances with 587 in 1971, 553 in 1973, 545 in 1974 and 539 in 1976.
Led American League third basemen in double plays with 54 in 1971, 30 in 1976 and tied for lead with 30 in 1978.
Led American League third basemen in assists with 383 in 1976.
Led Southern League third basemen in double plays with 34 in 1967 and led Pacific Coast League third basemen with 20 in 1968.
Named third baseman on THE SPORTING NEWS American League All-Star Team, 1975, 1977 and 1978.
Named third baseman on THE SPORTING NEWS American League All-Star fielding team, 1977 and 1978.

Year	Club	League	Pos.	G.	AB.	R.	H.	2B.	3B.	HR.	RBI.	B.A.	PO.	A.	E.	F.A.
1966—Wis. Rapids	Midw.	2B-3B	117	413	84	111	19	6	★28	75	.269	240	245	28	.945
1967—Charlotte	South.	3B	140	499	69	116	18	4	●19	86	.232	107	★318	24	.947
1967—Minnesota	Amer.	PH	3	3	0	1	1	0	0	0	.333	0	0	0	.000
1968—Denver	P. C.	3B-OF-1B	130	451	84	134	17	●12	22	83	.297	125	266	17	.958
1968—Minnesota	Amer.	OF-3B-1B	22	76	13	17	2	1	5	8	.224	50	9	2	.967
1969—Minnesota†	Amer.	OF-3B	96	225	27	50	9	2	7	26	.222	88	44	2	.985
1970—Cleveland	Amer.	★3B-OF	157	549	81	129	13	1	26	62	.235	135	358	17	★.967
1971—Cleveland	Amer.	3B	158	598	78	156	18	1	28	86	.261	★159	★412	16	.973
1972—Cleveland‡	Amer.	3B	150	557	65	141	28	0	17	70	.253	114	★358	★21	.957
1973—New York	Amer.	3B	160	552	65	129	18	0	22	81	.234	117	★410	26	.953
1974—New York	Amer.	★3B-SS	155	566	74	139	21	1	22	75	.246	★147	377	21	.961
1975—New York	Amer.	3B	157	581	71	155	24	4	21	91	.267	135	★379	19	.964
1976—New York	Amer.	3B-SS	158	583	88	148	29	2	★32	93	.254	137	384	19	.965
1977—New York	Amer.	3B	158	589	99	150	23	4	37	107	.255	132	321	12	.974
1978—New York	Amer.	3B-SS	159	587	81	162	23	2	27	93	.276	110	326	11	.975
1979—New York	Amer.	3B	145	521	71	132	15	1	20	73	.253	110	339	16	.966
1980—New York§	Amer.	3B-SS	89	324	52	79	14	0	16	45	.244	59	183	10	.960
1981—New York	Amer.	3B	103	349	46	85	7	1	15	46	.244	63	214	8	.972
1982—New York x	Amer.	3B	122	405	47	94	11	2	18	55	.232	73	255	23	.934
1983—New York y	Amer.	3B	129	462	56	123	17	3	20	75	.266	78	273	16	.956
1984—San Diego	Nat.	3B	124	395	56	90	11	1	20	65	.228	93	201	20	.936
1985—San Diego	Nat.	3B	137	440	66	115	23	1	15	61	.261	122	229	15	.959
1986—San Diego z	Nat.	3B	126	354	36	77	9	0	16	55	.218	83	174	16	.941
American League Totals—17 Years			2121	7527	1014	1890	273	25	333	1086	.251	1707	4642	239	.964
National League Totals—3 Years			387	1189	158	282	43	2	51	181	.237	298	604	51	.946
Major League Totals—20 Years			2508	8716	1172	2172	316	27	384	1267	.249	2005	5246	290	.962

Selected by Minnesota Twins' organization in 4th round of free-agent draft, June 9, 1965.
†Traded with Pitchers Dean Chance and Robert L. Miller and Outfielder Ted Uhlaender to Cleveland Indians for Pitchers Luis Tiant and Stan Williams, December 12, 1969.
‡Traded with Catcher Jerry Moses to New York Yankees for Catcher-First Baseman John Ellis, Infielder Jerry Kenney and Outfielders Charlie Spikes and Rosendo Torres, November 27, 1972.
§On disabled list, July 27 to October 2, 1980.
xOn disabled list, April 26 to May 17, 1982.
yTraded to San Diego Padres for Pitcher Dennis Rasmussen and a player to be named later, March 30, 1984; New York Yankees' organization acquired Pitcher Darin Cloninger to complete deal, April 26, 1984.
zReleased, December 18, 1986.

DIVISION SERIES RECORD

Year	Club	League	Pos.	G.	AB.	R.	H.	2B.	3B.	HR.	RBI.	B.A.	PO.	A.	E.	F.A.
1981—New York	Amer.	3B	5	17	1	1	0	0	0	1	.059	7	7	0	1.000

CHAMPIONSHIP SERIES RECORD

Established Championship Series records for most hits, inning (2), October 14, 1981; most runs batted in, three-game Series (9), 1981.
Tied Championship Series records for most times reached first base safely, game (5), October 14, 1981; most clubs, total Series (3).
Tied American League Championship Series records for most home runs, five-game Series (2), 1976; highest slugging average, three-game Series (.917), 1981; most Series, one or more home runs (4).

Year	Club	League	Pos.	G.	AB.	R.	H.	2B.	3B.	HR.	RBI.	B.A.	PO.	A.	E.	F.A.
1969—Minnesota	Amer.	PH	1	1	0	1	0	0	0	0	1.000	0	0	0	.000
1976—New York	Amer.	3B	5	17	2	4	1	0	2	4	.235	5	14	0	1.000
1977—New York	Amer.	3B	5	20	1	3	0	0	0	1	.150	2	12	0	1.000
1978—New York	Amer.	3B	4	15	3	5	0	1	1	2	.333	6	7	0	1.000
1980—New York	Amer.	3B-PH	2	6	1	1	0	0	1	1	.167	0	2	0	1.000

Year	Club	League	Pos.	G.	AB.	R.	H.	2B.	3B.	HR.	RBI.	B.A.	PO.	A.	E.	F.A.
1981—New York	Amer.		3B	3	12	2	6	2	0	1	9	.500	4	4	1	.889
1984—San Diego	Nat.		3B	4	14	1	2	0	0	0	2	.143	5	8	0	1.000
Championship Series Totals—7 Years....				24	85	10	22	3	1	5	19	.259	22	47	1	.986

WORLD SERIES RECORD

Established World Series records for most double plays by third baseman, four-game Series (3), 1976; most assists by third baseman, six-game Series (20), 1977; highest fielding average by third baseman, six-game Series, most chances accepted (1.000 and 26), 1978; most double plays by third baseman, total Series (7); most double plays and double plays started by third baseman, six-game Series (3), 1978; most assists by third baseman, total Series (68); most chances accepted by third baseman, total Series (96).

Tied World Series records for most double plays started by third baseman, four-game Series (2), 1976; most double plays started, game (2), October 19, 1976; fewest chances accepted by third baseman, game (0), October 18, 1977.

Year	Club	League	Pos.	G.	AB.	R.	H.	2B.	3B.	HR.	RBI.	B.A.	PO.	A.	E.	F.A.
1976—New York	Amer.		3B	4	12	0	3	0	0	0	2	.250	8	8	0	1.000
1977—New York	Amer.		3B	6	21	1	4	1	0	0	2	.190	2	20	1	.957
1978—New York	Amer.		3B	6	25	2	4	0	0	0	1	.160	8	18	0	1.000
1981—New York	Amer.		3B	3	10	1	4	1	0	0	0	.400	3	10	1	.929
1984—San Diego	Nat.		3B	5	12	2	3	0	0	0	2	.250	7	12	0	1.000
World Series Totals—5 Years				24	80	6	18	2	0	0	7	.225	28	68	2	.980

ALL-STAR GAME RECORD

Year	League	Pos.	AB.	R.	H.	2B.	3B.	HR.	RBI.	B.A.	PO.	A.	E.	F.A.
1975—American		3B	4	0	1	0	0	0	0	.250	2	2	0	1.000
1977—American		3B	2	0	0	0	0	0	0	.000	0	1	0	1.000
1978—American†		3B	0	0	0	0	0	0	0	.000	0	1	0	1.000
1979—American		3B	1	0	1	0	0	0	0	1.000	1	2	0	1.000
1980—American		3B	2	0	0	0	0	0	0	.000	0	1	0	1.000
1985—National		3B	2	0	0	0	0	0	0	.000	0	1	0	1.000
All-Star Game Totals—6 Years			11	0	2	0	0	0	0	.182	3	8	0	1.000

†Originally replaced due to injury by Larry Hisle, then re-named to replace Reggie Jackson.

THOMAS DEAN NEWELL
(Tom)

Born May 17, 1963, at Covina, Calif.
Height, 6.01. Weight, 185.
Throws and bats righthanded.
Attended Lassen College, Susanville, Calif.

Led South Atlantic League in wild pitches with 26 in 1984.

Year	Club	League	G.	IP.	W.	L.	Pct.	H.	R.	ER.	SO.	BB.	ERA.
1985—Spartanburg	S. Atlantic		28	150⅔	7	★13	.350	127	76	64	118	102	3.82
1986—Clearwater	Florida St.		22	85⅓	5	3	.625	68	35	27	64	46	2.85
1986—Portland	P. Coast		5	32⅔	2	2	.500	25	14	11	25	14	3.03

Selected by Philadelphia Phillies' organization in 24th round of free-agent draft, June 6, 1983.

RECORD AS OUTFIELDER

Year	Club	League	Pos.	G.	AB.	R.	H.	2B.	3B.	HR.	RBI.	B.A.	PO.	A.	E.	F.A.
1983—Helena	Pion.		OF	34	113	17	31	6	0	3	13	.274	40	8	4	.923
1984—Bend	N'west		OF	43	135	14	25	2	1	1	10	.185	46	4	3	.943

ALBERT DWAYNE NEWMAN
(Al)

Born June 30, 1960, at Kansas City, Mo.
Height, 5.09. Weight, 175.
Throws right and bats left and righthanded.
Attended Chaffey College, Alta Loma, Calif., and
San Diego State University, San Diego, Calif.

Major League stolen bases: 1985 (2), 1986 (11). Total—13.
Led Southern League in sacrifice hits with 18 in 1982.
Led Texas League shortstops in double plays with 58 in 1984.
Led Southern League second basemen in total chances with 776 in 1982.

Year	Club	League	Pos.	G.	AB.	R.	H.	2B.	3B.	HR.	RBI.	B.A.	PO.	A.	E.	F.A.
1982—Memphis	South.		2B	142	494	85	136	16	8	1	41	.275	★356	●388	★32	.959
1983—Wichita	A. A.		2B	38	124	20	30	6	1	0	16	.242	73	96	5	.971
1983—Memphis††	South.		2B	52	194	18	49	5	2	0	13	.253	111	123	14	.944
1984—Beaumont§	Texas		SS	88	318	69	80	8	0	0	23	.252	138	250	27	.935
1984—Indianapolis	A. A.		2-3-O-S	37	123	13	37	3	0	0	11	.301	49	79	2	.985
1985—Indianapolis	A. A.		2B-SS	87	301	42	85	16	2	0	23	.282	144	250	10	.975
1985—Montreal	Nat.		2B-SS	25	29	7	5	1	0	0	1	.172	19	36	0	1.000
1986—Montreal	Nat.		2B-SS	95	185	23	37	3	0	1	8	.200	98	161	11	.959
Major League Totals—2 Years				120	214	30	42	4	0	1	9	.196	117	197	11	.966

Selected by California Angels' organization in 3rd round of free-agent draft, January 9, 1979.
Selected by Texas Rangers' organization in 3rd round of free-agent draft, January 8, 1980.
Selected by New York Mets' organization in secondary phase of free-agent draft, June 3, 1980.
Selected by Montreal Expos' organization in secondary phase of free-agent draft, June 8, 1981.

†On disabled list, July 23 to August 16, 1983.
‡Traded with Pitcher Scott Sanderson to San Diego Padres for Pitcher Gary Lucas, December 7, 1983.
§Traded to Montreal Expos' organization for Pitcher Greg Harris, July 20, 1984.

CARL EDWARD NICHOLS

Born October 14, 1962, at Los Angeles, Calif.
Height, 6.00. Weight, 184.
Throws and bats righthanded.

Led Southern League catchers in putouts with 693 and total chances with 818 in 1986.
Led California League catchers in total chances with 897 in 1984.
Led New York-Pennsylvania League catchers in assists with 47 and tied for lead in double plays with 6 in 1983.

Year	Club	League	Pos.	G.	AB.	R.	H.	2B.	3B.	HR.	RBI.	B.A.	PO.	A.	E.	F.A.
1980—Bluefield	Appal.	C-1B-OF	37	85	24	18	2	2	0	10	.212	129	13	2	.986
1981—Miami	Fla. St.	C-1-S-3-O	16	31	1	6	0	0	0	3	.194	34	9	6	.878
1981—Hagerstown†	Carol.	C-O-S-2	38	81	8	22	4	0	1	6	.272	131	21	3	.981
1982—Macon	S. Atl.	C-OF-1B	84	257	33	55	10	2	0	30	.214	391	49	21	.954
1983—San Jose	Calif.	C-OF-3B	54	152	16	31	4	0	1	12	.204	204	39	17	.935
1983—Newark	NYP	C-O-3-S	66	217	40	63	14	0	5	26	.290	348	56	10	.976
1984—S.J.‡-Red.§	Calif.	★C-OF	121	389	53	88	14	2	4	54	.226	★769	★112	17	.981
1985—Charlotte	South.	C-OF-1B	115	331	45	78	11	2	2	37	.236	496	71	15	.984
1986—Charlotte	South.	★C-OF	118	439	63	118	26	1	14	72	.269	700	★110	46	.981
1986—Baltimore	Amer.	C	5	5	0	0	0	0	0	0	.000	11	0	0	1.000
Major League Totals—1 Year			5	5	0	0	0	0	0	0	.000	11	0	0	1.000

Selected by Baltimore Orioles' organization in 4th round of free-agent draft, June 3, 1980.
†Loaned to Macon (Detroit Tigers' organization), April 8, 1982; returned, September 15, 1982.
‡Loaned to San Jose (Independent), April 10, 1984; returned, June 9, 1984.
§Loaned to Redwood (California Angels' organization), June 9, 1984; returned, September 10, 1984.

THOMAS REID NICHOLS

(Known by middle name.)

Born August 5, 1958, at Ocala, Fla.
Height, 5.11. Weight, 165.
Throws and bats righthanded.
Attended Snead State Junior College, Boaz, Ala.

Major League stolen bases: 1982 (5), 1983 (7), 1984 (2), 1985 (6), 1986 (5). Total—25.
Led Carolina League in total bases with 227 and being hit by pitch with 12 in 1979.
Led Carolina League outfielders in assists with 23 in 1979.

Year	Club	League	Pos.	G.	AB.	R.	H.	2B.	3B.	HR.	RBI.	B.A.	PO.	A.	E.	F.A.
1976—Elmira	NYP	2B-3B-OF	23	53	8	18	1	0	0	9	.340	11	12	2	.920
1977—Winter Haven	Fla. St.	OF-2B	116	387	41	102	15	7	2	34	.264	166	41	7	.967
1978—Winter Haven	Fla. St.	OF-3B	125	413	52	102	20	1	5	34	.247	200	24	9	.961
1979—Winston-Salem	Carol.	OF-3B	134	★532	★107	★156	25	5	12	59	.293	240	23	10	.963
1980—Pawtucket	Int.	OF	134	511	68	141	27	5	4	42	.276	250	12	6	.978
1980—Boston	Amer.	OF	12	36	5	8	0	1	0	3	.222	24	1	1	.961
1981—Boston	Amer.	OF-3B	39	48	13	9	0	1	0	3	.188	35	4	0	1.000
1982—Boston†	Amer.	OF	92	245	35	74	16	1	7	33	.302	169	9	2	.989
1983—Boston	Amer.	OF-SS	100	274	35	78	22	1	6	22	.285	168	5	1	.994
1984—Boston	Amer.	OF	74	124	14	28	5	1	1	14	.226	79	3	1	.988
1985—Bos.‡-Chic.	Amer.	OF-2B	72	150	23	41	8	1	2	18	.273	85	2	1	.989
1986—Chicago §	Amer.	OF-2B	74	136	9	31	4	0	2	18	.228	90	4	1	.989
Major League Totals—7 Years			463	1013	134	269	55	6	18	111	.266	650	28	7	.990

Selected by Boston Red Sox' organization in 12th round of free-agent draft, June 8, 1976.
†On disabled list, July 21 to August 6, 1982.
‡Traded with a player to be named later to Chicago White Sox for Pitcher Tim Lollar, July 11, 1985.
§On disabled list, June 4 to June 26, 1986.

THOMAS EDWARD NIEDENFUER

Name pronounced NEED-un-fyoor.

(Tom)

Born August 13, 1959, at St. Louis Park, Minn.
Height, 6.04. Weight, 220.
Throws and bats righthanded.
Attended Washington State University, Pullman, Wash.

Major League saves: 1981 (2), 1982 (9), 1983 (11), 1984 (11), 1985 (19), 1986 (11). Total—63.

Year	Club	League	G.	IP.	W.	L.	Pct.	H.	R.	ER.	SO.	BB.	ERA.
1981—San Antonio	Texas	36	90	13	3	★.813	61	19	18	95	34	1.80
1981—Los Angeles	National	17	26	3	1	.750	25	11	11	12	6	3.81
1982—Albuquerque	P. Coast	4	10⅔	2	0	1.000	6	0	0	15	2	0.00
1982—Los Angeles	National	55	69⅔	3	4	.429	71	22	21	60	25	2.71
1983—Los Angeles	National	66	94⅔	8	3	.727	55	22	20	66	29	1.90
1984—Los Angeles†	National	33	47⅓	2	5	.286	39	14	13	45	23	2.47
1985—Los Angeles	National	64	106⅓	7	9	.438	86	32	32	102	24	2.71
1986—Los Angeles ‡	National	60	80	6	6	.500	86	35	33	55	29	3.71
Major League Totals—6 Years		295	424	29	28	.509	362	136	130	340	136	2.76

Selected by Los Angeles Dodgers' organization in 36th round of free-agent draft, June 7, 1977.

Signed as free agent by Los Angeles Dodgers' organization, August 14, 1980.
†On disabled list, July 16 to July 31 and August 5 to September 11, 1984.
‡On disabled list, August 19 to September 3, 1986.

DIVISION SERIES RECORD

Year Club	League	G.	IP.	W.	L.	Pct.	H.	R.	ER.	SO.	BB.	ERA.
1981—Los Angeles	National	1	⅓	0	0	.000	1	0	0	1	1	0.00

CHAMPIONSHIP SERIES RECORD

Tied Championship Series record for most games lost, Series (2), 1985.

Year Club	League	G.	IP.	W.	L.	Pct.	H.	R.	ER.	SO.	BB.	ERA.
1981—Los Angeles	National	1	⅓	0	0	.000	2	0	0	0	0	0.00
1983—Los Angeles	National	2	2	0	0	.000	0	0	0	3	1	0.00
1985—Los Angeles	National	3	5⅔	0	2	.000	5	4	4	5	2	6.35
Championship Series Totals—3 Years		6	8	0	2	.000	7	4	4	8	3	4.50

WORLD SERIES RECORD

Year Club	League	G.	IP.	W.	L.	Pct.	H.	R.	ER.	SO.	BB.	ERA.
1981—Los Angeles	National	2	5	0	0	.000	3	2	0	0	1	0.00

JOSEPH FRANKLIN NIEKRO

Name pronounced NEE-krow.

(Joe)

Born November 7, 1944, at Martins Ferry, O.
Height, 6.01. Weight, 190.
Throws and bats righthanded.
Attended West Liberty State College, West Liberty, W. Va.
Brother of Phil Niekro, pitcher with Cleveland Indians.

Pitched seven-inning, 2-0 perfect game against Tidewater, July 16, 1972 (second game).
Major League saves: 1971 (1), 1972 (1), 1973 (3), 1975 (4), 1977 (5). Total—14.
Led National League pitchers in games started with 38 in 1983 and 1984.
Led National League in wild pitches with 19 in 1982, 14 in 1983, 21 in 1985 and tied for lead with 19 in 1979.
Tied for National League lead in shutouts with 5 in 1979.
Named National League Pitcher of the Year by THE SPORTING NEWS, 1979.
Named righthanded pitcher on THE SPORTING NEWS National League All-Star Team, 1979.

Year Club	League	G.	IP.	W.	L.	Pct.	H.	R.	ER.	SO.	BB.	ERA.
1966—Treasure Valley	Pioneer	1	4	0	0	.000	4	0	0	7	1	0.00
1966—Quincy	Midwest	4	25	1	2	.333	17	7	3	14	6	1.08
1966—Dallas-Fort Worth	Texas	12	79	5	4	.556	71	28	22	50	15	2.51
1967—Chicago	National	36	170	10	7	.588	171	68	63	77	32	3.34
1968—Chicago	National	34	177	14	10	.583	204	93	85	65	59	4.32
1969—Chicago†-San Diego‡	National	41	221	8	18	.308	237	100	91	62	51	3.71
1970—Detroit	American	38	213	12	13	.480	221	107	96	101	72	4.06
1971—Detroit	American	31	122	6	7	.462	136	62	61	43	49	4.28
1972—Toledo§	Int'national	2	14	2	0	1.000	6	1	1	11	3	0.64
1972—Detroit	American	18	47	3	2	.600	62	20	20	24	8	3.83
1973—Toledo x	Int'national	26	143	7	10	.412	148	74	59	77	47	3.71
1973—Atlanta	National	20	24	2	4	.333	23	11	11	12	11	4.13
1974—Richmond	Int'national	30	52	8	1	.889	44	14	12	50	18	2.08
1974—Atlanta y	National	27	43	3	2	.600	36	19	17	31	18	3.56
1975—Iowa	Am. Assoc.	7	9	1	0	1.000	7	6	5	9	7	5.00
1975—Houston	National	40	88	6	4	.600	79	32	30	54	39	3.07
1976—Houston	National	36	118	4	8	.333	107	60	44	77	56	3.36
1977—Houston	National	44	181	13	8	.619	155	66	61	101	64	3.03
1978—Houston	National	35	203	14	14	.500	190	97	87	97	73	3.86
1979—Houston	National	38	264	•21	11	.656	221	102	88	119	107	3.00
1980—Houston	National	37	256	20	12	.625	268	119	101	127	79	3.55
1981—Houston	National	24	166	9	9	.500	150	60	52	77	47	2.82
1982—Houston	National	35	270	17	12	.586	224	79	74	130	64	2.47
1983—Houston	National	38	263⅔	15	14	.517	238	115	102	152	101	3.48
1984—Houston	National	38	248⅓	16	12	.571	223	104	84	127	89	3.04
1985—Houston z	National	32	213	9	12	.429	197	100	88	117	99	3.72
1985—New York a	American	3	12⅓	2	1	.667	14	8	8	4	8	5.84
1986—New York b	American	25	125⅔	9	10	.474	139	84	68	59	63	4.87
National League Totals—16 Years		555	2906	181	157	.536	2723	1225	1078	1425	989	3.34
American League Totals—5 Years		115	520	32	33	.492	572	281	253	231	200	4.38
Major League Totals—20 Years		670	3426	213	190	.529	3295	1506	1331	1656	1189	3.50

Selected by Cleveland Indians' organization in 7th round of free-agent draft, January, 1966.
Selected by Chicago Cubs' organization in 3rd round of free-agent draft, June, 1966.
†Traded with Pitcher Gary Ross and Infielder Francisco Libran to San Diego Padres for Pitcher Dick Selma, April 24, 1969. Libran remained on Cubs' San Antonio farm team but became San Diego property.
‡Traded to Detroit Tigers for Pitcher Pat Dobson and Shortstop-Outfielder Dave Campbell, December 4, 1969.
§On disabled list, August 7 to September 1, 1972.
xSold on waivers to Atlanta Braves, August 7, 1973.
ySold to Houston Astros, April 5, 1975.
zTraded to New York Yankees for Pitcher Jim Deshaies and two players to be named later, September 15, 1985; Houston Astros' organization acquired Infielder Neder Horta, September 24, 1985, and Pitcher Dody Rather, January 11, 1986, to complete deal.

aGranted free agency, November 12, 1985; re-signed by Yankees, January 8, 1986.
bOn disabled list, June 29 to July 17, 1986.

DIVISION SERIES RECORD

Year	Club	League	G.	IP.	W.	L.	Pct.	H.	R.	ER.	SO.	BB.	ERA.
1981—Houston	National	1	8	0	0	.000	7	0	0	4	3	0.00

CHAMPIONSHIP SERIES RECORD

Tied National League Championship Series record for most innings pitched, game (10), October 10, 1980.

Year	Club	League	G.	IP.	W.	L.	Pct.	H.	R.	ER.	SO.	BB.	ERA.
1980—Houston	National	1	10	0	0	.000	6	0	0	2	1	0.00

Appeared as pinch-runner for Detroit Tigers in one game of 1972 Championship Series.

ALL-STAR GAME RECORD

Member of National League All-Star Team for 1979 game; did not play.

PHILIP HENRY NIEKRO

Name pronounced NEE-krow.

(Phil)

Born April 1, 1939, at Blaine, O.
Height, 6.02. Weight, 195.
Throws and bats righthanded.
Brother of Joe Niekro, pitcher with New York Yankees.

Established major league records for fewest sacrifice flies allowed, season, most innings (0 and 284), 1969; most seasons and most consecutive seasons leading major leagues, runs allowed (3); most wild pitches, lifetime (216); most putouts by pitcher, lifetime (373).

Tied major league records for most strikeouts, inning (4), July 29, 1977 (sixth inning); most years, 200 or more innings pitched (19); most seasons and most consecutive seasons leading league, runs allowed (3), 1977 through 1979; most wild pitches, inning (4), August 4, 1979, second game (fifth inning); most seasons and most consecutive seasons leading league, games lost (4), 1977 through 1980.

Tied modern major league record for most wild pitches, game (6), August 4, 1979, second game.

Established National League records for most putouts by pitcher, lifetime (340); most games started, no relief appearances, season (44), 1979.

Established modern National League record for most games lost, lifetime (230).

Pitched 9-0 no-hit victory against San Diego Padres, August 5, 1973.

Major League saves: 1969 (1), 1971 (2), 1973 (4), 1974 (1), 1978 (1), 1980 (1). Total—10.

Led National League in home runs allowed with 40 in 1970, 29 in 1975, 41 in 1979 and 30 in 1980.

Led National League in hit batsmen with 11 in 1975, 13 in 1978 and 11 in 1979.

Led National League in complete games with 18 in 1974, 20 in 1977, 22 in 1978 and 23 in 1979.

Led National League in wild pitches with 19 in 1967, 14 in 1976 and 17 in 1977.

Led National League pitchers in games started with 43 in 1977, 42 in 1978, 44 in 1979, and tied for lead with 38 in 1980.

Led National League batters in sacrifice hits with 18 in 1968.

Tied for National League lead in balks with 3 in 1968 and 3 in 1972.

Named pitcher on THE SPORTING NEWS National League All-Star fielding team, 1978 through 1980, 1982 and 1983.

Year	Club	League	G.	IP.	W.	L.	Pct.	H.	R.	ER.	SO.	BB.	ERA.
1959—Wellsville	NYP	10	35	2	1	.667	47	38	29	16	24	7.46
1959—McCook	Neb. State	★23	52	7	1	.875	35	20	18	48	29	3.12
1960—Jacksonville	Sally	38	84	6	4	.600	66	36	26	52	52	2.79
1960—Louisville	Am. Assoc.	6	10	1	0	1.000	11	5	4	2	9	3.60
1961—Austin	Texas	★51	110	4	4	.500	100	45	36	84	53	2.95
1962—Louisville	Am. Assoc.	49	98	9	6	.600	111	50	42	48	41	3.86
1963—Denver	P. Coast					(In Military Service)						
1964—Milwaukee	National	10	15	0	0	.000	15	10	8	8	7	4.80
1964—Denver	P. Coast	29	172	11	5	.688	172	79	66	119	45	3.45
1965—Milwaukee	National	41	75	2	3	.400	73	32	24	49	26	2.88
1966—Atlanta	National	28	50	4	3	.571	48	32	23	17	23	4.14
1966—Richmond	Int'national	17	54	3	4	.429	43	27	22	36	16	3.67
1967—Atlanta	National	46	207	11	9	.550	164	64	43	129	55	★1.87
1968—Atlanta	National	37	257	14	12	.538	228	83	74	140	45	2.59
1969—Atlanta	National	40	284	23	13	.639	235	93	81	193	57	2.57
1970—Atlanta	National	34	230	12	18	.400	222	124	109	168	68	4.27
1971—Atlanta	National	42	269	15	14	.517	248	112	89	173	70	2.98
1972—Atlanta	National	38	282	16	12	.571	254	112	96	164	53	3.06
1973—Atlanta	National	42	245	13	10	.565	214	103	90	131	89	3.31
1974—Atlanta	National	41	★302	●20	13	.606	249	91	80	195	88	2.38
1975—Atlanta	National	39	276	15	15	.500	285	115	98	144	72	3.20
1976—Atlanta	National	38	271	17	11	.607	249	116	99	173	101	3.29
1977—Atlanta	National	44	★330	16	●20	.444	★315	★166	★148	★262	★164	4.04
1978—Atlanta	National	44	★334	19	★18	.514	★295	★129	●107	248	102	2.88
1979—Atlanta	National	44	★342	●21	★20	.512	★311	★160	129	208	★113	3.39
1980—Atlanta	National	40	275	15	★18	.455	256	119	111	176	85	3.63
1981—Atlanta	National	22	139	7	7	.500	120	56	48	62	56	3.11
1982—Atlanta†	National	35	234⅓	17	4	★.810	225	106	94	144	73	3.61
1983—Atlanta‡	National	34	201⅔	11	10	.524	212	94	89	128	105	3.97
1984—New York	American	32	215⅔	16	8	.667	219	85	74	136	76	3.09

Year	Club	League	G.	IP.	W.	L.	Pct.	H.	R.	ER.	SO.	BB.	ERA.
1985—New York§x		American	33	220	16	12	.571	203	110	100	149	★120	4.09
1986—Cleveland		American	34	210⅓	11	11	.500	241	126	101	81	95	4.32
American League Totals—3 Years			99	646	43	31	.581	663	321	275	366	291	3.83
National League Totals—20 Years			739	4619	268	230	.538	4218	1917	1640	2912	1452	3.20
Major League Totals—23 Years			838	5265	311	261	.544	4881	2238	1915	3278	1743	3.27

Signed as free agent by Milwaukee Braves' organization, July 19, 1958.
†On disabled list, March 31 to April 21, 1982.
‡Released, October 7, 1983; signed by New York Yankees, January 5, 1984.
§Granted free agency, November 12, 1985; re-signed by Yankees, January 8, 1986.
xReleased, March 28, 1986; signed by Cleveland Indians, April 3, 1986.

CHAMPIONSHIP SERIES RECORD

Established Championship Series record for most runs allowed, game (9), October 4, 1969.
Tied Championship Series record for most runs allowed, three-game Series (9), 1969.

Year	Club	League	G.	IP.	W.	L.	Pct.	H.	R.	ER.	SO.	BB.	ERA.
1969—Atlanta		National	1	8	0	1	.000	9	9	4	4	4	4.50
1982—Atlanta		National	1	6	0	0	.000	6	2	2	5	4	3.00
Championship Series Totals—2 Years			2	14	0	1	.000	15	11	6	9	8	3.86

ALL-STAR GAME RECORD

Year	League	IP.	W.	L.	Pct.	H.	R.	ER.	SO.	BB.	ERA.
1969—National		1	0	0	.000	0	0	0	2	0	0.00
1978—National		⅓	0	0	.000	0	0	0	0	0	0.00
All-Star Game Totals—2 Years		1⅓	0	0	.000	0	0	0	2	0	0.00

Member of American League All-Star Team in 1984; did not play.
Member of National League All-Star Team in 1975 and 1982; did not play.

JEFFREY SCOTT NIELSEN
(Known by middle name.)

Born December 18, 1958, at Salt Lake City, Utah.
Height, 6.01. Weight, 190.
Throws and bats righthanded.
Attended Brigham Young University, Provo, Utah.

Year	Club	League	G.	IP.	W.	L.	Pct.	H.	R.	ER.	SO.	BB.	ERA.
1983—Bellingham		Northwest	2	13	2	0	1.000	11	4	3	13	2	2.08
1983—Chattanooga†		Southern	13	63⅓	2	4	.333	81	49	45	24	27	6.39
1984—Fort Lauderdale‡		Florida St.	4	16⅔	2	1	.667	16	8	2	7	5	1.08
1984—Nashville		Southern	10	73⅔	6	3	.667	55	34	20	27	15	2.44
1984—Columbus		Int'national	11	56⅔	5	4	.556	59	27	25	21	23	3.97
1985—Albany§		Eastern	11	73⅓	6	1	.857	60	26	24	31	14	2.95
1986—Fort Lauderdale		Florida St.	6	34⅓	4	0	1.000	32	12	8	10	9	2.10
1986—Columbus		Int'national	19	116⅔	11	7	.611	123	52	45	44	38	3.47
1986—New York		American	10	56	4	4	.500	66	29	25	20	12	4.02
Major League Totals—1 Year			10	56	4	4	.500	66	29	25	20	12	4.02

Selected by Seattle Mariners' organization in 6th round of free-agent draft, June 6, 1983.
†Traded with Pitcher Eric Parent to New York Yankees' organization for Infielder Larry Milbourne, February 14, 1984.
‡On disabled list, April 6 to April 23, 1984.
§On disabled list, May 30 to June 21 and June 27 to September 16, 1985.

RANDY HAROLD NIEMANN

Born November 15, 1955, at Fortuna, Calif.
Height, 6.05. Weight, 215.
Throws left and bats righthanded.
Attended College of the Redwoods, Eureka, Calif.

Major League saves: 1979 (1), 1980 (1), 1982 (1). Total—3.
Tied for American Association lead in games started by pitchers with 29 in 1984.
Tied for Florida State League lead in hit batsmen with 14 in 1976.

Year	Club	League	G.	IP.	W.	L.	Pct.	H.	R.	ER.	SO.	BB.	ERA.
1975—Oneonta		NYP	8	55	3	3	.500	53	26	15	23	20	2.45
1976—Fort Lauderdale		Florida St.	25	190	9	10	.474	173	74	60	79	73	2.84
1977—West Haven†		Eastern	13	62	4	4	.500	73	44	38	18	26	5.52
1977—Columbus		Southern	15	34	0	3	.000	36	22	18	15	19	4.76
1978—Columbus		Southern	29	123	9	5	.643	125	44	28	53	39	2.05
1979—Charleston		Int'national	8	47	3	2	.600	49	25	21	17	10	4.02
1979—Houston		National	26	67	3	2	.600	68	32	28	24	22	3.76
1980—Tucson		P. Coast	9	52	4	1	.800	64	36	28	26	26	4.85
1980—Houston		National	22	33	0	1	.000	40	21	20	18	12	5.45
1981—Tucson‡§x-Portland		P. Coast	10	57	4	2	.667	68	40	31	39	38	4.89
1982—Portland		P. Coast	8	44⅔	3	2	.600	41	22	19	28	26	3.83
1982—Pittsburgh		National	20	35⅓	1	1	.500	34	22	20	26	17	5.09
1983—Pittsburgh		National	8	13⅔	0	1	.000	20	14	14	8	7	9.22
1983—Hawaii y		P. Coast	16	82	2	3	.400	95	49	41	52	45	4.50
1984—Denver		Am. Assoc.	32	★190⅓	10	12	.455	★235	★136	★124	110	86	5.86
1984—Chicago z		American	5	5⅓	0	0	.000	5	1	1	5	5	1.69

Year Club	League	G.	IP.	W.	L.	Pct.	H.	R.	ER.	SO.	BB.	ERA.
1985—Tidewater	Int'national	30	159⅔	11	6	.647	152	65	49	76	51	2.76
1985—New York	National	4	4⅔	0	0	.000	5	0	0	2	0	0.00
1986—New York	National	31	35⅔	2	3	.400	44	17	15	18	12	3.79
1986—Tidewater a	Int'national	7	39	3	1	.750	38	14	14	18	18	3.23
National League Totals—6 Years		111	189⅓	6	8	.429	211	106	97	96	70	4.61
American League Totals—1 Year		5	5⅓	0	0	.000	5	1	1	5	5	1.69
Major League Totals—7 Years		116	194⅔	6	8	.429	216	107	98	101	75	4.53

Selected by Montreal Expos' organization in 5th round of free-agent draft, January 9, 1974.
Selected by Minnesota Twins' organization in 3rd round of free-agent draft, January 9, 1975.
Selected by New York Yankees' organization in secondary phase of free-agent draft, June 4, 1975.
†Traded with Infielder Mike Fischlin and a player to be named later to Houston Astros for Catcher Cliff Johnson, June 15, 1977; Houston Astros acquired First Baseman-Outfielder Dave Bergman to complete deal, November 23, 1977.
‡On Houston disabled list, March 28 to May 11, 1981.
§On disabled list, July 1 to September 1, 1981.
xTraded with Outfielder Kevin Houston to Pittsburgh Pirates' organization, September 9, 1981, completing deal in which Houston Astros traded Second Baseman Johnny Ray and two players to be named later to Pittsburgh for Second Baseman Phil Garner, August 31, 1981.
yTraded to Chicago White Sox for Outfielder Miguel Dilone and Pitcher Mike Maitland, September 7, 1983.
zTraded to New York Mets' organization for Pitcher Ken Reed and Third Baseman Gene Autry, March 30, 1985.
aGranted free agency, November 12, 1986.

THOMAS ANDREW NIETO

Name pronounced Nee-AY-toh.

(Tom)

Born October 27, 1960, at Downey, Calif.
Height, 6.01. Weight, 205.
Throws and bats righthanded.
Attended Cerritos College, Norwalk, Calif., and
Oral Roberts University, Tulsa, Okla.

Tied for American Association lead in being hit by pitch with 8 in 1983.

Year Club	League	Pos.	G.	AB.	R.	H.	2B.	3B.	HR.	RBI.	B.A.	PO.	A.	E.	F.A.
1981—Arkansas	Texas	C	62	184	12	33	2	0	2	19	.179	270	37	8	.975
1982—Arkansas†	Texas	C	96	298	33	72	11	3	5	31	.242	466	58	3	★.994
1983—Louisville	A. A.	C	115	383	44	104	17	1	5	52	.272	605	71	★15	.978
1984—Louisville	A. A.	C	77	253	23	70	12	1	7	34	.277	446	43	8	.984
1984—St. Louis	Nat.	C	33	86	7	24	4	0	3	12	.279	135	18	1	.994
1985—St. Louis‡	Nat.	C	95	253	15	57	10	2	0	34	.225	384	28	4	.990
1986—Montreal§	Nat.	C	30	65	5	13	3	1	1	7	.200	123	11	3	.978
1986—Indianapolis	A. A.	C	53	167	21	50	16	0	3	19	.299	295	25	9	.973
Major League Totals—3 Years			158	404	27	94	17	3	4	53	.233	642	57	8	.989

Selected by Minnesota Twins' organization in 31st round of free-agent draft, June 5, 1979.
Selected by Pittsburgh Pirates' organization in secondary phase of free-agent draft, January 8, 1980.
Selected by St. Louis Cardinals' organization in 3rd round of free-agent draft, June 8, 1981.
†On disabled list, June 19 to June 30, 1982.
‡Traded to Montreal Expos for Infielder Fred Manrique, March 31, 1986.
§On disabled list, August 21 to September 11, 1986; included rehabilitation disability assignment to Indianapolis, September 3 to September 10, 1986.

CHAMPIONSHIP SERIES RECORD

Year Club	League	Pos.	G.	AB.	R.	H.	2B.	3B.	HR.	RBI.	B.A.	PO.	A.	E.	F.A.
1985—St. Louis	Nat.	C	1	3	1	0	0	0	0	0	.000	7	0	0	1.000

WORLD SERIES RECORD

Year Club	League	Pos.	G.	AB.	R.	H.	2B.	3B.	HR.	RBI.	B.A.	PO.	A.	E.	F.A.
1985—St. Louis	Nat.	C	2	5	0	0	0	0	0	1	.000	23	1	0	1.000

JUAN MANUEL NIEVES

Born January 5, 1965, at Santurce, Puerto Rico.
Height, 6.03. Weight, 175.
Throws and bats lefthanded.

Named Texas League Pitcher of the Year, 1985.
Received reported $150,000 bonus to sign with Milwaukee Brewers, 1983.

Year Club	League	G.	IP.	W.	L.	Pct.	H.	R.	ER.	SO.	BB.	ERA.
1983—Beloit	Midwest	12	69⅓	7	1	.875	43	11	10	89	15	1.30
1984—Stockton	California	24	139⅔	10	3	.769	137	75	55	133	63	3.54
1985—El Paso	Texas	17	120	8	2	★.800	106	53	47	91	44	3.53
1985—Vancouver	P. Coast	12	68⅔	8	3	.727	56	30	29	54	44	3.80
1986—Milwaukee	American	35	184⅔	11	12	.478	224	124	101	116	77	4.92
Major League Totals—1 Year		35	184⅔	11	12	.478	224	124	101	116	77	4.92

Signed as free agent by Milwaukee Brewers' organization, July 1, 1983.

ALBERT SAMUEL NIPPER
(Al)

Born April 2, 1959, at San Diego, Calif.
Height, 6.00. Weight, 194.
Throws and bats righthanded.
Attended Northeast Missouri State University, Kirksville, Mo.
Led Florida State League in complete games with 15 in 1981.

Year	Club	League	G.	IP.	W.	L.	Pct.	H.	R.	ER.	SO.	BB.	ERA.
1980—Winter Haven	Florida St.	16	85	6	4	.600	82	29	24	48	49	2.54
1981—Winter Haven	Florida St.	29	*212	14	8	.636	191	59	40	139	60	*1.70
1982—Bristol†	Eastern	19	115	6	7	.462	108	50	47	66	45	3.68
1983—New Britain	Eastern	10	67	4	3	.571	46	26	21	42	25	2.82
1983—Pawtucket	Int'national	18	109⅓	9	4	.692	108	62	54	58	54	4.45
1983—Boston	American	3	16	1	1	.500	17	4	4	5	7	2.25
1984—Boston	American	29	182⅔	11	6	.647	183	86	79	84	52	3.89
1985—Boston‡	American	25	162	9	12	.429	157	83	73	85	82	4.06
1986—Boston§	American	26	159	10	12	.455	186	108	95	79	47	5.38
Major League Totals—4 Years		83	519⅔	31	31	.500	543	281	251	253	188	4.35

Selected by Boston Red Sox' organization in 8th round of free-agent draft, June 3, 1980.
†On disabled list, June 26 to July 25, 1982.
‡On disabled list, March 25 to April 15, 1985; included rehabilitation disability assignment to Pawtucket, March 31 to April 15, 1985.
§On disabled list, May 19 to June 25, 1986.

WORLD SERIES RECORD

Year	Club	League	G.	IP.	W.	L.	Pct.	H.	R.	ER.	SO.	BB.	ERA.
1986—Boston	American	2	6⅓	0	1	.000	10	5	5	2	2	7.11

OTIS JUNIOR NIXON

Born January 9, 1959, at Columbus County, N.C.
Height, 6.02. Weight, 180.
Throws right and bats right and lefthanded.
Attended Louisburg College, Louisburg, N.C.
Brother of Donell Nixon, outfielder in Seattle Mariners' organization.

Major League stolen bases: 1984 (12), 1985 (20), 1986 (23). Total—55.
Led International League in stolen bases with 94 and caught stealing with 29 in 1983.
Led Southern League in bases on balls received with 110 in 1981.
Led South Atlantic League in bases on balls received with 113 and stolen bases with 67 in 1980.
Led Appalachian League in bases on balls received with 57 in 1979.
Led International League outfielders in fielding percentage with .992, putouts with 363 and total chances with 371 in 1983.
Led Appalachian League third basemen in fielding percentage with .945, putouts with 52, assists with 120, and double plays with 12 in 1979.

Year	Club	League	Pos.	G.	AB.	R.	H.	2B.	3B.	HR.	RBI.	B.A.	PO.	A.	E.	F.A.
1979—Paintsville	Appal.	3B-SS	63	203	58	58	10	3	1	25	.286	54	122	11	.941
1980—Greensboro	S. Atl.	3B-SS	136	493	*124	137	12	5	3	48	.278	164	308	36	.929
1981—Nashville	South.	SS	127	407	89	102	9	2	0	20	.251	198	348	*56	.907
1982—Nashville	South.	SS-2B	72	283	47	80	3	2	0	20	.283	126	211	23	.936
1982—Columbus	Int.	2B-SS	59	207	43	58	4	0	0	14	.280	104	169	14	.951
1983—Columbus	Int.	OF-2B	138	*557	*129	*162	11	6	0	41	.291	385	24	4	.990
1983—New York†	Amer.	OF	13	14	2	2	0	0	0	0	.143	14	1	1	.938
1984—Cleveland	Amer.	OF	49	91	16	14	0	0	0	1	.154	81	3	0	1.000
1984—Maine	Int.	OF	72	253	42	70	5	1	0	22	.277	206	7	1	.995
1985—Cleveland	Amer.	OF	104	162	34	38	4	0	3	9	.235	129	5	4	.971
1986—Cleveland	Amer.	OF	105	95	33	25	4	1	0	8	.263	90	3	3	.969
Major League Totals—4 Years		271	362	85	79	8	1	3	18	.218	314	12	8	.976

Selected by Cincinnati Reds' organization in 21st round of free-agent draft, June 6, 1978.
Selected by California Angels' organization in secondary phase of free-agent draft, January 9, 1979.
Selected by New York Yankees' organization in secondary phase of free-agent draft, June 5, 1979.
†Traded with Pitcher George Frazier and a player to be named later to Cleveland Indians for Third Baseman Toby Harrah and a player to be named later, February 5, 1984; New York organization acquired Pitcher Rick Browne and Cleveland organization acquired Pitcher Guy Elston to complete deal, February 8, 1984.

MILCIADES ARTURO NOBOA JR.

Name pronounced Nah-BO-ah.

(Junior)

Born November 10, 1964, at Santo Domingo, D. R.
Height, 5.09. Weight, 160.
Throws and bats righthanded.

Major League stolen bases: 1984 (1).
Led Eastern League in sacrifice hits with 17 in 1984.
Led Midwest League in sacrifice hits with 18 in 1983.
Led Midwest League second basemen in putouts with 257 and double plays with 81 in 1983.

Year	Club	League	Pos.	G.	AB.	R.	H.	2B.	3B.	HR.	RBI.	B.A.	PO.	A.	E.	F.A.
1981—Batavia	NYP	2B	50	162	15	49	8	0	0	6	.302	82	100	*18	.910
1982—Waterloo	Midw.	SS	121	385	69	96	12	5	0	23	.249	*207	306	46	.918

Year Club	League	Pos.	G.	AB.	R.	H.	2B.	3B.	HR.	RBI.	B.A.	PO.	A.	E.	F.A.
1983—Waterloo	Midw.	2B-SS	132	449	64	115	22	3	1	29	.256	260	355	24	.962
1984—Buffalo	East.	2B	117	383	55	97	18	4	1	45	.253	228	305	*18	.967
1984—Cleveland	Amer.	2B	23	11	3	4	0	0	0	0	.364	7	13	0	1.000
1985—Maine	Int.	2B	122	403	62	116	11	2	5	32	.288	270	379	14	.979
1986—Maine	Int.	2B-SS-3B	108	399	44	114	21	1	4	32	.286	160	252	13	.969
Major League Totals—1 Year			23	11	3	4	0	0	0	0	.364	7	13	0	1.000

Signed as free agent by Cleveland Indians' organization, May 26, 1981.

MATTHEW DODGE NOKES
(Matt)

Born October 31, 1963, at San Diego, Calif.
Height, 6.01. Weight, 185.
Throws right and bats lefthanded.

Led Texas League catchers in double plays with 6 in 1985.
Led California League catchers in double plays with 9 in 1983.
Led Pioneer League in passed balls with 19 in 1981.

Year Club	League	Pos.	G.	AB.	R.	H.	2B.	3B.	HR.	RBI.	B.A.	PO.	A.	E.	F.A.
1981—Great Falls	Pion.	C	44	146	14	33	6	2	0	13	.226	288	35	*13	.961
1982—Clinton	Midw.	C	82	247	19	53	12	0	3	23	.215	363	41	13	.969
1983—Fresno	Calif.	C	125	429	62	138	26	6	14	82	.322	595	62	16	.976
1984—Shreveport	Texas	C	97	308	32	89	19	2	11	61	.289	400	31	8	.982
1985—Shreveport	Texas	C	105	344	52	101	24	1	14	56	.294	520	40	12	.979
1985—San Francisco†	Nat.	C	19	53	3	11	2	0	2	5	.208	84	2	2	.977
1986—Nashville	A. A.	C-1B-OF	125	428	55	122	25	4	10	71	.285	502	50	18	.968
1986—Detroit	Amer.	C	7	24	2	8	1	0	1	2	.333	43	2	0	1.000
National League Totals—1 Year			19	53	3	11	2	0	2	5	.208	84	2	2	.977
American League Totals—1 Year			7	24	2	8	1	0	1	2	.333	43	2	0	1.000
Major League Totals—2 Years			26	77	5	19	3	0	3	7	.247	127	4	2	.985

Selected by San Francisco Giants' organization in 20th round of free-agent draft, June 8, 1981.

†Traded with Pitchers Dave LaPoint and Eric King to Detroit Tigers for Pitcher Juan Berenguer, Catcher Bob Melvin and a player to be named later, October 7, 1985; San Francisco Giants acquired Pitcher S2ott Medvin to complete deal, December 11, 1985.

DICKIE RAY NOLES

Born November 19, 1956, at Charlotte, N. C.
Height, 6.02. Weight, 190.
Throws and bats righthanded.

Major League saves: 1980 (6), 1985 (1). Total—7.
Led Eastern League in hit batsmen with 15 in 1978.
Led Carolina League in games started by pitchers with 27 in 1977.
Led Western Carolinas League in hit batsmen with 13 in 1976.
Tied for Carolina League lead in hit batsmen with 11 in 1977.
Tied for Western Carolinas League lead in home runs allowed with 13 in 1976.

Year Club	League	G.	IP.	W.	L.	Pct.	H.	R.	ER.	SO.	BB.	ERA.
1975—Auburn	NYP	9	50	2	2	.500	49	30	20	31	27	3.60
1976—Spartanburg	W. Carol.	24	137	4	*16	.200	166	*110	*90	95	65	5.91
1977—Peninsula	Carolina	27	*199	10	11	.476	188	103	81	114	78	3.66
1978—Reading	Eastern	27	159	12	8	.600	177	100	75	78	72	4.25
1979—Oklahoma City†	Am. Assoc.	12	76	6	4	.600	69	38	33	48	28	3.91
1979—Philadelphia	National	14	90	3	4	.429	80	40	38	42	38	3.80
1979—Reading	Eastern	1	9	0	1	.000	7	5	4	2	4	4.00
1980—Philadelphia	National	48	81	1	4	.200	80	42	35	57	42	3.89
1981—Oklahoma City‡	Am. Assoc.	22	104	6	6	.500	85	45	38	82	46	3.29
1981—Philadelphia§	National	13	58	2	2	.500	57	30	27	34	23	4.19
1982—Chicago x	National	31	171	10	13	.435	180	99	84	85	61	4.42
1983—Chicago y	National	24	116⅓	5	10	.333	133	69	61	59	37	4.72
1983—Quad Cities	Midwest	3	12	0	1	.000	19	11	7	12	5	5.25
1984—Chicago z	National	21	50⅔	2	2	.500	60	29	29	14	16	5.15
1984—Texas	American	18	57⅔	2	3	.400	60	38	33	39	30	5.15
1985—Texas ab	American	28	110⅓	4	8	.333	129	67	62	59	33	5.06
1986—Cleveland c	American	32	54⅔	3	2	.600	56	33	31	32	30	5.10
1986—Maine d	Int'national	3	10	0	1	.000	11	6	5	4	4	4.50
National League Totals—6 Years		151	567	23	35	.397	590	309	274	291	217	4.35
American League Totals—3 Years		78	222⅔	9	13	.409	245	138	126	130	93	5.09
Major League Totals—8 Years		229	789⅔	32	48	.400	835	447	400	421	310	4.56

Selected by Philadelphia Phillies' organization in 4th round of free-agent draft, June 4, 1975.

†On disabled list, April 13 to April 24, 1979.
‡Appeared as outfielder with no chances.
§Traded with Catcher Keith Moreland and Pitcher Dan Larson to Chicago Cubs for Pitcher Mike Krukow and cash, December 8, 1981.
xOn disabled list, June 13 to July 4, 1982.
yOn disabled list, April 12 to June 4, 1983; included rehabilitation disability assignment to Quad Cities, May 21 to June 4, 1983.
zTraded to Texas Rangers for two players to be named later, July 2, 1984; Chicago Cubs' organization acquired Pitcher Tim Henry and Infielder Jorge Gomez to complete deal, December 11, 1984.
aOn disabled list, June 24 to July 14, 1985.

bReleased, December 20, 1985; signed by Maine (Cleveland Indians' organization), February 8, 1986.
cOn disabled list, April 18 to June 18, 1986; included rehabilitation disability assignment to Maine, June 7 to June 18, 1986.
dGranted free agency, November 12, 1986.

DIVISION SERIES RECORD

Year Club	League	G.	IP.	W.	L.	Pct.	H.	R.	ER.	SO.	BB.	ERA.
1981—Philadelphia	National	1	4	0	0	.000	4	2	2	5	2	4.50

CHAMPIONSHIP SERIES RECORD

Year Club	League	G.	IP.	W.	L.	Pct.	H.	R.	ER.	SO.	BB.	ERA.
1980—Philadelphia	National	2	2⅔	0	0	.000	1	0	0	0	3	0.00

WORLD SERIES RECORD

Year Club	League	G.	IP.	W.	L.	Pct.	H.	R.	ER.	SO.	BB.	ERA.
1980—Philadelphia	National	1	4⅔	0	0	.000	5	1	1	6	2	1.93

EDWIN NUNEZ (MARTINEZ)

Name pronounced NOON-yez.

Born May 27, 1963, at Humacao, Puerto Rico.
Height, 6.05. Weight, 235.
Throws and bats righthanded.

Major League saves: 1984 (7), 1985 (16). Total—23.
Led Midwest League in complete games with 13 in 1981.

Year Club	League	G.	IP.	W.	L.	Pct.	H.	R.	ER.	SO.	BB.	ERA.
1979—Bellingham	Northwest	6	39	4	1	.800	39	14	9	30	5	2.08
1980—Wausau	Midwest	22	138	9	7	.563	145	71	57	91	58	3.72
1981—Wausau	Midwest	25	*186	*16	3	.842	143	61	51	*205	58	2.47
1982—Seattle†	American	8	35⅓	1	2	.333	36	18	18	27	16	4.58
1982—Salt Lake City‡	P. Coast	11	55⅓	4	3	.571	40	26	21	42	23	3.42
1983—Seattle	American	14	37	0	4	.000	40	21	18	35	22	4.38
1983—Salt Lake City§	P. Coast	14	77⅓	4	4	.500	99	70	61	52	36	7.10
1984—Salt Lake City x	P. Coast	18	27⅔	3	2	.600	24	12	11	26	12	3.58
1984—Seattle	American	37	67⅔	2	2	.500	55	26	24	57	21	3.19
1985—Seattle	American	70	90⅓	7	3	.700	79	36	31	58	34	3.09
1986—Seattle y	American	14	21⅔	1	2	.333	25	15	14	17	5	5.82
1986—Calgary	P. Coast	6	14	1	2	.333	19	13	11	17	4	7.07
Major League Totals—5 Years		143	252	11	13	.458	235	116	105	194	98	3.75

Signed as free agent by Seattle Mariners' organization, March 17, 1979.
†On disabled list, April 23 to May 15, 1982.
‡On disabled list, June 4 to June 29, 1982.
§On disabled list, June 30 to July 14, 1983.
xOn disabled list, May 12 to June 3, 1984.
yOn disabled list, April 5 to April 29 and May 1 to May 16, 1986.

JOSE NUNEZ

Born January 13, 1964, at Jarabocoa, D. R.
Height, 6.03. Weight, 175.
Throws and bats righthanded.

Year Club	League	G.	IP.	W.	L.	Pct.	H.	R.	ER.	SO.	BB.	ERA.
1984—Charleston	S. Atlantic	25	170	14	8	.636	*167	91	62	106	54	3.28
1985—Fort Myers†	Florida St.	11	44⅓	3	2	.600	32	14	12	23	12	2.44
1986—Memphis	Southern	13	48⅔	2	6	.250	52	43	29	36	51	5.36
1986—Fort Myers‡	Florida St.	14	87⅓	8	2	.800	73	31	24	59	32	2.47

Signed as free agent by Kansas City Royals' organization, November 11, 1983.
†On disabled list, May 30 to June 19 and July 1 to August 24, 1985.
‡Drafted by Toronto Blue Jays, December 9, 1986.

KENNETH RAY OBERKFELL

Name pronounced OH-burk-fell.

(Ken)

Born May 4, 1956, at Maryville, Ill.
Height, 6.01. Weight, 210.
Throws right and bats lefthanded.
Attended Belleville Area Junior College, Belleville, Ill.

Major League stolen bases: 1979 (4), 1980 (4), 1981 (13), 1982 (11), 1983 (12), 1984 (2), 1985 (1), 1986 (7). Total—54.
Led National League third basemen in double plays with 23 and tied for lead in total chances with 338 in 1981.
Led National League second basemen in fielding percentage with .985 in 1979.

Year Club	League	Pos.	G.	AB.	R.	H.	2B.	3B.	HR.	RBI.	B.A.	PO.	A.	E.	F.A.
1975—Johnson City	Appal.	SS	17	54	15	19	3	0	1	8	.352	21	58	4	.952
1975—St. Petersburg	Fla. St.	SS	41	134	14	47	6	1	0	22	.351	71	107	6	.967
1976—Arkansas	Texas	2B-SS	128	456	64	131	19	2	3	47	.287	259	321	18	.970
1977—New Orleans	A. A.	2B-SS	120	418	67	105	18	5	4	32	.251	205	325	17	.969
1977—St. Louis	Nat.	2B	9	9	0	1	0	0	0	1	.111	3	4	0	1.000

Year	Club	League	Pos.	G.	AB.	R.	H.	2B.	3B.	HR.	RBI.	B.A.	PO.	A.	E.	F.A.
1978—Springfield	A. A.	3B-2B-SS	64	242	41	69	13	4	6	38	.285	77	113	6	.969
1978—St. Louis	Nat.	2B-3B	24	50	7	6	1	0	0	0	.120	30	48	1	.987
1979—St. Louis	Nat.	2B-3B-SS	135	369	53	111	19	5	1	35	.301	223	343	9	.984
1980—St. Louis†	Nat.	2B-3B	116	422	58	128	27	6	3	46	.303	227	340	7	.988
1981—St. Louis	Nat.	3B-SS	102	376	43	110	12	6	2	45	.293	77	247	15	.956
1982—St. Louis‡	Nat.	*3B-2B	137	470	55	136	22	5	2	34	.289	80	305	11	*.972
1983—St. Louis	Nat.	*3B-2B-SS	151	488	62	143	26	5	3	38	.293	132	303	18	*.960
1984—St. Louis§-Atl.x	Nat.	3B-2B-SS	100	324	38	87	19	2	1	21	.269	64	173	8	.967
1985—Atlanta	Nat.	3B-2B	134	412	30	112	19	4	3	35	.272	88	257	12	.966
1986—Atlanta	Nat.	3B-2B	151	503	62	136	24	3	5	48	.270	116	335	11	.976
Major League Totals—10 Years			1059	3423	408	970	169	36	20	303	.283	1040	2355	92	.974

Signed as free agent by St. Louis Cardinals' organization, May 4, 1975.
†On disabled list, May 11 to June 20, 1980.
‡On disabled list, March 31 to April 23, 1982.
§Traded to Atlanta Braves for Pitcher Ken Dayley and First Baseman Mike Jorgensen, June 15, 1984.
xOn disabled list, August 27, 1984 through remainder of season.

CHAMPIONSHIP SERIES RECORD

Tied Championship Series record for most at-bats, three-game Series (15).

Year	Club	League	Pos.	G.	AB.	R.	H.	2B.	3B.	HR.	RBI.	B.A.	PO.	A.	E.	F.A.
1982—St. Louis	Nat.	3B	3	15	1	3	0	0	0	2	.200	2	4	1	.857

WORLD SERIES RECORD

Year	Club	League	Pos.	G.	AB.	R.	H.	2B.	3B.	HR.	RBI.	B.A.	PO.	A.	E.	F.A.
1982—St. Louis	Nat.	3B	7	24	4	7	1	0	0	1	.292	3	21	1	.960

CHARLES HUGH O'BRIEN
(Charlie)

Born May 1, 1960, at Tulsa, Okla.
Height, 6.02. Weight, 195.
Throws and bats righthanded.
Attended Wichita State University, Wichita, Kan.

Year	Club	League	Pos.	G.	AB.	R.	H.	2B.	3B.	HR.	RBI.	B.A.	PO.	A.	E.	F.A.
1982—Medford	N'west	C	17	60	11	17	3	0	3	14	.283	116	18	4	.971
1982—Modesto	Calif.	C	41	140	23	42	6	0	3	32	.300	239	44	5	.983
1983—Albany†	East.	C-1B	92	285	50	83	12	1	14	56	.291	478	82	11	.981
1984—Modesto‡	Calif.	C	9	32	8	9	2	0	1	5	.281	41	8	0	1.000
1984—Tacoma	P. C.	C-OF	69	195	33	44	11	0	9	22	.226	260	39	0	1.000
1985—Huntsville	South.	C	33	115	20	24	5	0	7	16	.209	182	29	5	.977
1985—Oakland	Amer.	C	16	11	3	3	1	0	0	1	.273	23	0	1	.958
1985—Modesto	Calif.	C	9	27	5	8	4	1	1	2	.296	33	8	1	.976
1985—Tacoma§	P. C.	C	18	57	5	9	4	0	0	7	.158	110	9	3	.975
1986—Vancouver	P. C.	C	6	17	1	2	0	0	0	1	.118	22	3	2	.926
1986—El Paso	Texas	C-OF-1B	92	336	72	109	20	3	15	75	.324	437	43	4	.992
Major League Totals—1 Year			16	11	3	3	1	0	0	1	.273	23	0	1	.958

Selected by Texas Rangers' organization in 14th round of free-agent draft, June 6, 1978.
Selected by Seattle Mariners' organization in 21st round of free-agent draft, June 8, 1981.
Selected by Oakland A's organization in 5th round of free-agent draft, June 7, 1982.
†On disabled list, July 31, 1983 through remainder of season.
‡On Albany disabled list, April 13 to May 15, 1984.
§Traded with Infielder Steve Kiefer and Pitchers Mike Fulmer and Pete Kendrick to Milwaukee Brewers for Pitcher Moose Haas, March 30, 1986.

PETER MICHAEL O'BRIEN
(Pete)

Born February 9, 1958, at Santa Monica, Calif.
Height, 6.01. Weight, 198.
Throws and bats lefthanded.
Attended Monterrey Peninsula College, Monterrey, Calif.; and
University of Nebraska, Lincoln, Neb.

Tied major league record for most double plays started by first baseman, nine-inning game (3), May 22, 1984.
Major League stolen bases: 1982 (1), 1983 (5), 1984 (3), 1985 (5), 1986 (4). Total—18.
Led American League first basemen in assists with 120 in 1983.

Year	Club	League	Pos.	G.	AB.	R.	H.	2B.	3B.	HR.	RBI.	B.A.	PO.	A.	E.	F.A.
1979—Sarasota Rangers	Gulf C.	1B	50	189	39	46	10	2	0	31	.243	*465	*44	7	.986
1980—Asheville	S. Atl.	1B	134	505	98	149	34	2	17	94	.295	*1227	*96	14	.990
1981—Tulsa	Texas	1B	110	382	57	109	19	3	17	78	.285	973	95	11	.990
1982—Denver	A. A.	OF-1B	128	477	92	148	21	1	25	102	.310	418	37	8	.983
1982—Texas	Amer.	OF-1B	20	67	13	16	4	1	4	13	.239	39	3	0	1.000
1983—Texas	Amer.	1B-OF	154	524	53	124	24	5	8	53	.237	1191	121	11	.992
1984—Texas	Amer.	1B-OF	142	520	57	149	26	2	18	80	.287	1271	105	11	.992
1985—Texas	Amer.	1B	159	573	69	153	34	3	22	92	.267	1457	98	8	.995
1986—Texas	Amer.	1B	156	551	86	160	23	3	23	90	.290	1224	115	11	.992
Major League Totals—5 Years			631	2235	278	602	111	14	75	328	.269	5182	442	41	.993

Selected by Texas Rangers' organization in 15th round of free-agent draft, June 5, 1979.

BRYAN ALOIS OELKERS

Name pronounced ELK-ers.
Born March 11, 1961, at Zaragoza, Spain.
Height, 6.03. Weight, 205.
Throws and bats lefthanded.
Attended Wichita State University, Wichita, Kan.

Major League saves: 1986 (1).
Led Southern League in shutouts with 4 in 1984.
Received reported $69,500 bonus to sign with Minnesota Twins, 1982.

Year Club	League	G.	IP.	W.	L.	Pct.	H.	R.	ER.	SO.	BB.	ERA.
1982—Visalia	California	5	33	2	2	.500	27	15	13	17	17	3.55
1982—Orlando	Southern	3	25	1	0	1.000	16	6	4	14	9	1.44
1983—Minnesota	American	10	34⅓	0	5	.000	56	34	33	13	17	8.65
1983—Toledo	Int'national	17	104⅓	5	7	.417	121	68	60	60	49	5.18
1984—Orlando	Southern	29	219⅔	●16	11	.593	199	★104	83	139	74	3.40
1985—Toledo†	Int'national	12	48	0	4	.000	58	39	36	30	26	6.75
1985—Orlando‡	Southern	6	33	2	3	.400	46	27	22	15	18	6.00
1986—Maine	Int'national	9	52	4	4	.500	49	18	14	28	17	2.42
1986—Cleveland	American	35	69	3	3	.500	70	38	36	33	40	4.70
Major League Totals—2 Years		45	103⅓	3	8	.273	126	72	69	46	57	6.01

Selected by Chicago Cubs' organization in 20th round of free-agent draft, June 5, 1979.
Selected by Minnesota Twins' organization in 1st round (fourth player selected) of free-agent draft, June 7, 1982.
†On disabled list, April 10 to May 22, 1985.
‡Traded with Pitcher Ken Schrom to Cleveland Indians for Pitchers Roy Smith and Ramon Romero, January 7, 1986.

RONALD JOHN OESTER

Name pronounced O-ster.

(Ron)

Born May 5, 1956, at Cincinnati, O.
Height, 6.02. Weight, 190.
Throws right and bats left and righthanded.

Major League stolen bases: 1980 (6), 1981 (2), 1982 (5), 1983 (2), 1984 (7), 1985 (5), 1986 (9). Total—36.
Led National League second basemen in total chances with 861 in 1986.
Led American Association shortstops in double plays with 102 in 1978.
Led Eastern League shortstops in double plays with 84 in 1976.
Led Pioneer League shortstops in double plays with 27 in 1974.

Year Club	League	Pos.	G.	AB.	R.	H.	2B.	3B.	HR.	RBI.	B.A.	PO.	A.	E.	F.A.
1974—Billings	Pion.	SS	53	167	23	52	11	1	0	21	.311	87	141	27	.894
1975—Tampa	Fla. St.	SS	117	375	40	82	3	4	0	25	.219	174	358	34	.940
1976—Three Rivers	East.	SS	138	447	57	110	14	4	0	44	.246	★233	★408	38	.944
1977—Indianapolis	A. A.	SS	134	455	60	116	16	5	3	33	.255	203	★386	39	.938
1978—Indianapolis	A. A.	SS	●135	514	78	133	21	4	7	49	.259	★300	★428	32	.958
1978—Cincinnati	Nat.	SS	6	8	1	3	0	0	0	1	.375	3	9	0	1.000
1979—Indianapolis	A. A.	SS	●136	509	62	143	19	6	2	33	.281	★244	397	31	.954
1979—Cincinnati	Nat.	SS	6	3	0	0	0	0	0	0	.000	1	2	0	1.000
1980—Cincinnati	Nat.	2B-SS-3B	100	303	40	84	16	2	2	20	.277	161	224	10	.975
1981—Cincinnati	Nat.	2B-SS	105	354	45	96	16	7	5	42	.271	213	341	11	.981
1982—Cincinnati	Nat.	2B-SS-3B	151	549	63	143	19	4	9	47	.260	304	403	22	.970
1983—Cincinnati	Nat.	2B	157	549	63	145	23	5	11	58	.264	315	413	17	.977
1984—Cincinnati	Nat.	2B-SS	150	553	54	134	26	3	3	38	.242	357	388	15	.980
1985—Cincinnati	Nat.	2B	152	526	59	155	26	3	1	34	.295	366	457	9	.989
1986—Cincinnati	Nat.	2B	153	523	52	135	23	2	8	44	.258	●367	475	19	.978
Major League Totals—9 Years			980	3368	377	895	149	26	39	284	.266	2087	2712	103	.979

Selected by Cincinnati Reds' organization in 9th round of free-agent draft, June 5, 1974.

BENJAMIN A. OGLIVIE

(Ben)

Born February 11, 1949, at Colon, Panama.
Height, 6.02. Weight, 170.
Throws and bats lefthanded.
Attended Bronx Community College, Bronx, N. Y., Northeastern University, Boston, Mass.,
and Wayne State University, Detroit, Mich.

Tied American League records for longest errorless game and most innings by outfielder, game (25), May 8, finished May 9, 1984 (fielded 24⅓ innings).
Major League stolen bases: 1972 (1), 1973 (1), 1974 (12), 1975 (11), 1976 (9), 1977 (9), 1978 (11), 1979 (12), 1980 (11), 1981 (2), 1982 (3), 1983 (4), 1986 (1). Total—87.
Hit three home runs in a game, July 8, 1979 (first game), June 20, 1982 and May 14, 1983.
Led American League in intentional bases on balls received with 19 in 1980.
Led Eastern League outfielders in double plays with 5 in 1970.
Named outfielder on THE SPORTING NEWS American League All-Star Team, 1980.
Named outfielder on THE SPORTING NEWS American League Silver Slugger team, 1980.

Year Club	League	Pos.	G.	AB.	R.	H.	2B.	3B.	HR.	RBI.	B.A.	PO.	A.	E.	F.A.
1968—Jamestown	NYP	1B-OF	16	45	7	13	1	0	1	5	.289	66	2	2	.971
1969—Greenville	W. Car.	OF	106	363	48	115	15	●7	8	62	.317	128	6	12	.918

Year Club League	Pos.	G.	AB.	R.	H.	2B.	3B.	HR.	RBI.	B.A.	PO.	A.	E.	F.A.
1969—Winter Haven....... Fla. St.	OF	11	32	4	8	1	0	0	5	.250	13	1	1	.933
1970—Pawtucket............ East.	OF	115	391	62	91	15	C	10	51	.233	172	14	5	.974
1971—Louisville............... Int.	OF	134	474	82	144	27	7	17	86	.304	215	★26	12	.953
1971—Boston .... Amer.	OF	14	38	2	10	3	0	0	4	.263	22	1	1	.958
1972—Boston .... Amer.	OF	94	253	27	61	10	2	8	30	.241	98	5	2	.981
1973—Boston† .... Amer.	OF	58	147	16	32	9	1	2	9	.218	56	2	1	.983
1974—Detroit .... Amer.	OF-1B	92	252	28	68	11	3	4	29	.270	162	11	5	.972
1975—Detroit .... Amer.	OF-1B	100	332	45	95	14	1	9	36	.286	232	8	5	.980
1976—Detroit .... Amer.	OF-1B	115	305	36	87	12	3	15	47	.285	234	8	3	.988
1977—Detroit‡.................. Amer.	OF	132	450	63	118	24	2	21	61	.262	236	10	6	.976
1978—Milwaukee........... Amer.	OF-1B	128	469	71	142	29	4	18	72	.303	275	8	6	.979
1979—Milwaukee........... Amer.	OF-1B	139	514	88	145	30	4	29	81	.282	320	10	5	.985
1980—Milwaukee........... Amer.	OF	156	592	94	180	26	2	●41	118	.304	384	18	9	.978
1981—Milwaukee........... Amer.	OF	107	400	53	97	15	2	14	72	.243	211	3	4	.982
1982—Milwaukee........... Amer.	OF	159	602	92	147	22	1	34	102	.244	359	15	7	.982
1983—Milwaukee........... Amer.	OF	125	411	49	115	19	3	13	66	.280	259	8	4	.985
1984—Milwaukee........... Amer.	OF	131	461	49	121	16	2	12	60	.262	256	6	8	.970
1985—Milwaukee........... Amer.	OF	101	341	40	99	17	2	10	61	.290	190	4	7	.965
1986—Milwaukee§.......... Amer.	OF	103	346	31	98	20	1	5	53	.283	105	4	1	.991
Major League Totals—16 Years...............		1754	5913	784	1615	277	33	235	901	.273	3399	121	74	.979

Selected by Boston Red Sox' organization in 7th round of free-agent draft, June 7, 1968.
†Traded to Detroit Tigers for Second Baseman Dick McAuliffe, October 23, 1973.
‡Traded to Milwaukee Brewers for Pitchers Jim Slaton and Rich Folkers, December 9, 1977.
§Granted free agency, November 12, 1986.

DIVISION SERIES RECORD

Year Club League	Pos.	G.	AB.	R.	H.	2B.	3B.	HR.	RBI.	B.A.	PO.	A.	E.	F.A.
1981—Milwaukee............. Amer.	OF	5	18	0	3	1	0	0	1	.167	13	1	0	1.000

CHAMPIONSHIP SERIES RECORD

Year Club League	Pos.	G.	AB.	R.	H.	2B.	3B.	HR.	RBI.	B.A.	PO.	A.	E.	F.A.
1982—Milwaukee............. Amer.	OF	4	15	1	2	0	0	1	1	.133	5	0	2	.714

WORLD SERIES RECORD

Tied World Series records for most putouts by left fielder, inning (3), October 19, 1982 (seventh inning); most consecutive putouts by outfielder (4), October 19, 1982.

Year Club League	Pos.	G.	AB.	R.	H.	2B.	3B.	HR.	RBI.	B.A.	PO.	A.	E.	F.A.
1982—Milwaukee............. Amer.	OF	7	27	4	6	0	1	1	1	.222	13	0	1	.929

ALL-STAR GAME RECORD

Year League	Pos.	AB.	R.	H.	2B.	3B.	HR.	RBI.	B.A.	PO.	A.	E.	F.A.
1980—American	OF	2	0	0	0	0	0	0	.000	1	0	0	1.000
1982—American	PH	1	0	0	0	0	0	0	.000	0	0	0	.000
1983—American	OF	1	0	0	0	0	0	0	.000	0	0	0	.000
All-Star Game Totals—3 Years....................		4	0	0	0	0	0	0	.000	1	0	0	1.000

ROBERT MICHAEL OJEDA

Name pronounced Oh-HEED-a.

(Bob)

Born December 17, 1957, at Los Angeles, Calif.
Height, 6.01. Weight, 190.
Throws and bats lefthanded.
Attended College of the Sequoias, Visalia, Calif.

Major League saves: 1985 (1).
Tied for American League lead in shutouts with 5 in 1984.
Tied for International League lead in balks with 3 in 1980.
Tied for Florida State League lead in games started by pitchers with 29 in 1979.
Named International League Pitcher of the Year, 1981.

Year Club League	G.	IP.	W.	L.	Pct.	H.	R.	ER.	SO.	BB.	ERA.
1978—Elmira.............................. NYP	18	43	1	6	.143	45	32	23	35	43	4.81
1979—Winter Haven............................... Florida St.	29	200	15	7	.682	163	66	54	150	84	2.43
1980—Pawtucket................................ Int'national	19	123	6	7	.462	107	54	44	78	56	3.22
1980—Boston .... American	7	26	1	1	.500	39	20	20	12	14	6.92
1981—Pawtucket................................ Int'national	25	173	12	9	.571	136	52	41	113	73	★2.13
1981—Boston .... American	10	66	6	2	.750	50	25	23	28	25	3.14
1982—Boston† .... American	22	78⅓	4	6	.400	95	53	49	52	29	5.63
1983—Boston .... American	29	173⅔	12	7	.632	173	85	78	94	73	4.04
1984—Boston‡..................................... American	33	216⅔	12	12	.500	211	106	96	137	96	3.99
1985—Boston§..................................... American	39	157⅔	9	11	.450	166	74	70	102	48	4.00
1986—New York................................... National	32	217⅓	18	5	★.783	185	72	62	148	52	2.57
American League Totals—6 Years	140	718⅓	44	39	.530	734	363	336	425	285	4.21
National League Totals—1 Year........................	32	217⅓	18	5	.783	185	72	62	148	52	2.57
Major League Totals—7 Years.....................	172	935⅔	62	44	.585	919	435	398	573	337	3.83

Signed as free agent by Boston Red Sox' organization, May 20, 1978.
†On disabled list, August 20 to September 10, 1982.
‡On disabled list, August 16 to September 1, 1984.
§Traded with Pitchers Tom McCarthy, John Mitchell and Chris Bayer to New York Mets for Pitchers Calvin Schiraldi and Wes Gardner and Outfielders John Christensen and LaSchelle Tarver, November 13, 1985.

CHAMPIONSHIP SERIES RECORD
Tied National League Championship Series record for most hits allowed, game (10), October 9, 1986.

Year Club	League	G.	IP.	W.	L.	Pct.	H.	R.	ER.	SO.	BB.	ERA.
1986—New York	National	2	14	1	0	1.000	15	4	4	6	4	2.57

WORLD SERIES RECORD

Year Club	League	G.	IP.	W.	L.	Pct.	H.	R.	ER.	SO.	BB.	ERA.
1986—New York	National	2	13	1	0	1.000	13	3	3	9	5	2.08

JAMES B. OLANDER
(Jim)

Born February 21, 1963, at Tucson, Ariz.
Height, 6.02. Weight, 175.
Throws and bats righthanded.
Led Carolina League outfielders in total chances with 328 in 1983.

Year Club	League	Pos.	G.	AB.	R.	H.	2B.	3B.	HR.	RBI.	B.A.	PO.	A.	E.	F.A.
1981—Helena	Pion.	OF	61	222	37	72	10	3	6	37	.324	114	5	7	.944
1982—Spartanburg	S. Atl.	OF	121	423	77	129	25	6	12	63	.305	227	16	7	.972
1983—Peninsula	Carol.	OF	126	503	62	125	21	3	15	79	.249	★296	★19	13	.960
1984—Reading	East.	OF-1B	117	362	44	95	12	2	8	47	.262	255	10	9	.967
1985—Portland	P. C.	OF	44	72	6	16	2	0	0	6	.222	23	1	1	.960
1985—Reading	East.	OF	64	208	30	67	15	2	4	39	.322	125	6	2	.985
1986—Reading	East.	OF	129	464	77	151	★33	4	8	68	★.325	320	3	●11	.967

Selected by Philadelphia Phillies' organization in 7th round of free-agent draft, June 8, 1981.

JOSEPH MELTON OLIVER
(Joe)

Born July 24, 1965, at Memphis, Tenn.
Height, 6.03. Weight, 205.
Throws and bats righthanded.
Led Florida State League catchers in assists with 84 and passed balls with 33 in 1985.
Led Midwest League catchers in passed balls with 30 and total chances with 855 in 1984.
Led Pioneer League catchers in putouts with 425, assists with 38 and total chances with 468 in 1983.

Year Club	League	Pos.	G.	AB.	R.	H.	2B.	3B.	HR.	RBI.	B.A.	PO.	A.	E.	F.A.
1983—Billings	Pion.	★C-1B	56	186	21	40	4	0	4	28	.215	426	39	5	★.989
1984—Cedar Rapids	Midw.	C	102	335	34	73	11	0	3	29	.218	★757	85	13	.985
1985—Tampa	Fla. St.	C-1B	112	386	38	104	23	2	7	62	.269	615	94	16	.978
1986—Vermont†	East.	C	84	282	32	78	18	1	6	41	.277	383	62	14	.969

Selected by Cincinnati Reds' organization in 2nd round of free-agent draft, June 6, 1983.
†On disabled list, April 23 to May 6, 1986.

EDWARD R. OLWINE
(Ed)

Born May 28, 1958, at Greenville, O.
Height, 6.02. Weight, 165.
Throws left and bats righthanded.
Attended Morehead State University, Morehead, Ky.
Major League saves: 1986 (1).
Led South Atlantic League in saves with 19 in 1981.

Year Club	League	G.	IP.	W.	L.	Pct.	H.	R.	ER.	SO.	BB.	ERA.
1980—Oneonta	NYP	6	9	2	1	.667	8	4	1	8	6	1.00
1980—Paintsville	Ap'lachian	13	35	5	2	.714	32	11	10	47	11	2.57
1980—Fort Lauderdale	Florida St.	2	1	0	0	.000	5	4	1	0	0	9.00
1981—Greensboro	S. Atlantic	51	75	8	5	.615	67	35	25	73	25	3.00
1982—Fort Lauderdale	Florida St.	39	67⅔	5	4	.556	70	32	25	48	21	3.33
1983—Nashville	Southern	29	82⅔	2	4	.333	90	53	40	66	38	4.35
1983—Columbus†	Int'national	8	10⅓	2	0	1.000	11	11	11	11	6	9.58
1984—Tidewater‡	Int'national	50	68	4	2	.667	47	26	18	50	25	2.38
1985—Tidewater§	Int'national	55	66	4	7	.364	60	23	21	50	26	2.86
1986—Richmond	Int'national	20	24⅔	2	0	1.000	18	2	2	15	9	0.73
1986—Atlanta	National	37	47⅔	0	0	.000	35	20	18	37	17	3.40
Major League Totals—1 Year		37	47⅔	0	0	.000	35	20	18	37	17	3.40

Signed as free agent by New York Yankees' organization, June 15, 1980.
†Drafted by Tidewater (New York Mets' organization), December 6, 1983.
‡Drafted by Philadelphia Phillies, December 3, 1984; returned, March 28, 1985.
§Traded to Atlanta Braves' organization for Pitcher Mike Santiago, April 2, 1986.

THOMAS PATRICK O'MALLEY
(Tom)

Born December 25, 1960, at Orange, N. J.
Height, 6.00. Weight, 185.
Throws right and bats lefthanded.
Major League stolen bases: 1983 (2).

Led International League third basemen in putouts with 90 and fielding percentage with .964 in 1985.

Year—Club	League	Pos.	G.	AB.	R.	H.	2B.	3B.	HR.	RBI.	B.A.	PO.	A.	E.	F.A.
1979—Great Falls	Pion.	2-S-O-3	42	119	13	29	6	1	1	20	.244	41	34	9	.893
1980—Fresno	Calif.	3B	122	435	67	125	20	9	3	74	.287	69	253	22	★.936
1981—Shreveport	Texas	3B	123	467	50	135	23	6	6	53	.289	94	237	15	.957
1982—Phoenix	P. C.	3B	26	96	23	43	11	1	3	15	.448	12	44	6	.903
1982—San Francisco†	Nat.	3B-SS-2B	92	291	26	80	12	4	2	27	.275	60	161	8	.965
1983—San Francisco	Nat.	3B	135	410	40	106	16	1	5	45	.259	70	213	18	.940
1984—Phoenix	P. C.	3B-1B	105	387	44	134	20	2	5	72	.346	227	134	15	.960
1984—San Francisco‡	Nat.	3B	13	25	2	3	0	0	0	0	.120	5	8	0	1.000
1984—Chicago§	Amer.	3B	12	16	0	2	0	0	0	3	.125	2	1	0	1.000
1985—Nashville x	A. A.	3B	33	128	13	39	8	0	1	12	.305	16	62	9	.897
1985—Rochester	Int.	3B-1B	102	358	62	108	13	1	10	44	.302	92	207	11	.965
1985—Baltimore	Amer.	3B	8	14	1	1	0	0	1	2	.071	2	3	1	.833
1986—Rochester	Int.	3B-2B	59	212	36	65	10	0	9	30	.307	46	111	8	.952
1986—Baltimore y	Amer.	3B	56	181	19	46	9	0	1	18	.254	37	98	9	.938
National League Totals—3 Years			240	726	68	189	28	5	7	72	.260	135	382	26	.952
American League Totals—3 Years			76	211	20	49	9	0	2	23	.232	41	102	10	.935
Major League Totals—5 Years			316	937	88	238	37	5	9	95	.254	176	484	36	.948

Selected by San Francisco Giants' organization in 16th round of free-agent draft, June 5, 1979.
†On disabled list, August 16 to September 6, 1982.
‡Traded to Chicago White Sox for two players to be named later, September 1, 1984; San Francisco Giants acquired Pitcher Mike Trujillo and First Baseman Pat Adams to complete deal, September 7, 1984.
§Released, April 1, 1985; signed by Nashville (Detroit Tigers' organization), April 8, 1985.
xTraded to Rochester (Baltimore Orioles' organization) for Catcher Luis Rosado, May 21, 1985.
yGranted free agency, October 15, 1986; signed by Texas Rangers' organization, December 3, 1986.

RANDALL JEFFREY O'NEAL
(Randy)

Born August 30, 1960, at Ashland, Ky.
Height, 6.02. Weight, 195.
Throws and bats righthanded.
Attended Palm Beach Junior College, Lake Worth, Fla.,
and University of Florida, Gainesville, Fla.

Pitched seven-inning, 4-0 no-hit victory against Winter Haven, August 23, 1981 (first game).
Major League saves: 1985 (1), 1986 (2). Total—3.
Tied for American Association lead in balks with 6 in 1984.

Year—Club	League	G.	IP.	W.	L.	Pct.	H.	R.	ER.	SO.	BB.	ERA.
1981—Lakeland	Florida St.	13	69	4	5	.444	59	27	22	31	18	2.87
1982—Birmingham	Southern	27	185	11	7	.611	169	83	70	105	71	3.41
1983—Evansville	Am. Assoc.	23	140⅓	8	10	.444	159	80	66	70	45	4.23
1984—Evansville	Am. Assoc.	25	166⅓	9	10	.474	152	82	66	110	59	3.57
1984—Detroit	American	4	18⅔	2	1	.667	16	7	7	12	6	3.38
1985—Nashville	Am. Assoc.	10	67⅔	5	4	.556	57	29	27	44	19	3.59
1985—Detroit	American	28	94⅓	5	5	.500	82	42	34	52	36	3.24
1986—Detroit	American	37	122⅔	3	7	.300	121	69	59	68	44	4.33
1986—Nashville	Am. Assoc.	4	28⅓	1	2	.333	28	16	15	15	9	4.76
Major League Totals—3 Years		69	235⅔	10	13	.435	219	118	100	132	86	3.82

Selected by Montreal Expos' organization in 4th round of free-agent draft, January 9, 1979.
Selected by Minnesota Twins' organization in secondary phase of free-agent draft, June 5, 1979.
Selected by Milwaukee Brewers' organization in secondary phase of free-agent draft, January 8, 1980.
Selected by Cincinnati Reds' organization in secondary phase of free-agent draft, June 3, 1980.
Selected by Detroit Tigers' organization in secondary phase of free-agent draft, June 8, 1981.

PAUL ANDREW O'NEILL

Born February 25, 1963, at Columbus, O.
Height, 6.04. Weight, 205.
Throws and bats lefthanded.
Attended Otterbein College, Westerville, O.
Son of Charles W. O'Neill, minor league pitcher, 1945 through 1948.

Tied for American Association lead in game-winning RBIs with 13 in 1985.
Led American Association outfielders in assists with 19 and double plays with 8 in 1985.

Year—Club	League	Pos.	G.	AB.	R.	H.	2B.	3B.	HR.	RBI.	B.A.	PO.	A.	E.	F.A.
1981—Billings	Pion.	OF	66	241	37	76	7	2	3	29	.315	87	4	5	.948
1982—Cedar Rapids	Midw.	OF	116	386	50	105	19	2	8	71	.272	137	7	8	.947
1983—Tampa	Fla. St.	OF-1B	121	413	62	115	23	7	8	51	.278	218	14	10	.959
1983—Waterbury	East.	OF	14	43	6	12	0	0	0	6	.279	26	0	0	1.000
1984—Vermont	East.	OF	134	475	70	126	31	5	16	76	.265	246	5	7	.973
1985—Denver	A. A.	OB-1B	★137	★509	63	★155	★32	3	7	74	.305	248	20	7	.975
1985—Cincinnati	Nat.	OF	5	12	1	4	1	0	0	1	.333	3	1	0	1.000
1986—Cincinnati	Nat.	PH	3	2	0	0	0	0	0	0	.000	0	0	0	.000
1986—Denver†	A. A.	OF	55	193	20	49	9	2	5	27	.254	98	7	4	.963
Major League Totals—2 Years			8	14	1	4	1	0	0	1	.286	3	1	0	1.000

Selected by Cincinnati Reds' organization in 4th round of free-agent draft, June 8, 1981.
†On disabled list, May 10 to July 16, 1986.

STEVEN ONTIVEROS
(Steve)

Born March 5, 1961, at Tularosa, N.M.
Height, 6.00. Weight, 180.
Throws and bats righthanded.
Received bachelor of science degree in physical education
from University of Michigan, Ann Arbor, Mich.

Major League saves: 1985 (8), 1986 (10). Total—18.

Year Club	League	G.	IP.	W.	L.	Pct.	H.	R.	ER.	SO.	BB.	ERA.
1982—Medford	Northwest	4	8	1	0	1.000	3	0	0	9	4	0.00
1982—West Haven†	Eastern	16	27	2	2	.500	34	26	19	28	12	6.33
1983—Albany	Eastern	32	129⅔	8	4	.667	131	62	54	91	36	3.75
1984—Tacoma‡	P. Coast	2	11⅓	1	1	.500	18	11	10	6	5	7.94
1985—Madison	Midwest	5	30⅔	3	1	.750	23	10	7	26	6	2.05
1985—Tacoma§	P. Coast	15	33⅔	3	0	1.000	26	13	11	30	21	2.94
1985—Oakland	American	39	74⅔	1	3	.250	45	17	16	36	19	1.93
1986—Oakland xy	American	46	72⅔	2	2	.500	72	40	38	54	25	4.71
Major League Totals—2 Years		85	147⅓	3	5	.375	117	57	54	90	44	3.30

Selected by Oakland A's organization in 2nd round of free-agent draft, June 7, 1982.
†On temporarily inactive list, July 27 to August 6, 1982.
‡On disabled list, April 16 to August 8, 1984.
§On disabled list, April 16 to April 28, 1985.
xAppeared in one game as a pinch-runner.
yOn disabled list, July 24 to September 14, 1986.

JOSE MANUEL OQUENDO

Name pronounced Oh-KEN-doh.
Born July 4, 1963, at Rio Piedras, Puerto Rico.
Height, 5.10. Weight, 156.
Throws right and bats left and righthanded.

Major League stolen bases: 1983 (8), 1984 (10), 1986 (2). Total—20.
Led American Association in sacrifice hits with 15 in 1985.
Led International League in sacrifice hits with 14 in 1982.
Led Carolina League in sacrifice hits with 13 in 1980.
Led American Association shortstops in total chances with 591 in 1985.
Led Northwest League shortstops in errors with 40 in 1979.

Year Club	League	Pos.	G.	AB.	R.	H.	2B.	3B.	HR.	RBI.	B.A.	PO.	A.	E.	F.A.
1979—Grays Harbor	N'west	*SS-2B	64	220	24	50	8	0	1	14	.227	90	177	*40	.870
1980—Lynchburg	Carol.	SS	109	301	38	51	10	3	0	26	.169	126	358	31	*.940
1981—Lynchburg	Carol.	SS	124	393	59	98	8	6	0	38	.249	169	390	23	*.961
1982—Tidewater	Int.	SS	114	337	40	72	8	3	0	22	.214	186	337	25	.954
1983—Tidewater	Int.	SS	13	34	3	4	0	0	0	3	.118	20	23	4	.915
1983—New York	Nat.	SS	120	328	29	70	7	0	1	17	.213	182	326	21	.960
1984—New York	Nat.	SS	81	189	23	42	5	0	0	10	.222	95	152	7	.972
1984—Tidewater†	Int.	SS	38	113	8	18	1	0	1	8	.159	54	111	2	.988
1985—Louisville	A. A.	SS	133	384	38	81	8	1	1	30	.211	*227	341	23	.961
1986—St. Louis	Nat.	S-2-3-O	76	138	20	41	4	1	0	13	.297	52	94	8	.948
Major League Totals—3 Years			277	655	72	153	16	1	1	40	.234	329	572	36	.962

Signed as free agent by New York Mets' organization, April 15, 1979.
†Traded with Pitcher Mark Jason Davis to St. Louis Cardinals' organization for Shortstop Argenis Salazar and Pitcher John Young, April 2, 1985.

JESSE OROSCO

Name pronounced Oh-ROSS-koh.
Born April 21, 1957, at Santa Barbara, Calif.
Height, 6.02. Weight, 185.
Throws left and bats righthanded.
Attended Santa Barbara City College, Santa Barbara, Calif.

Major League saves: 1981 (1), 1982 (4), 1983 (17), 1984 (31), 1985 (17), 1986 (21). Total—91.
Led Appalachian League in intentional bases on balls issued with 5 in 1978.

Year Club	League	G.	IP.	W.	L.	Pct.	H.	R.	ER.	SO.	BB.	ERA.
1978—Elizabethton†	Ap'lachian	20	40	4	4	.500	29	7	5	48	20	1.13
1979—Tidewater	Int'national	16	81	4	4	.500	82	45	35	55	43	3.89
1979—New York	National	18	35	1	2	.333	33	20	19	22	22	4.89
1980—Jackson	Texas	37	71	4	4	.500	52	36	29	85	62	3.68
1981—Tidewater	Int'national	46	87	9	5	.643	80	39	32	81	32	3.31
1981—New York	National	8	17	0	1	.000	13	4	3	18	6	1.59
1982—New York	National	54	109⅓	4	10	.286	92	37	33	89	40	2.72
1983—New York	National	62	110	13	7	.650	76	27	18	84	38	1.47
1984—New York	National	60	87	10	6	.625	58	29	25	85	34	2.59
1985—New York	National	54	79	8	6	.571	66	26	24	68	34	2.73
1986—New York‡	National	58	81	8	6	.571	64	23	21	62	35	2.33
Major League Totals—7 Years		314	518⅓	44	38	.537	402	166	143	428	209	2.48

Selected by St. Louis Cardinals' organization in 7th round of free-agent draft, January 11, 1977.
Selected by Minnesota Twins' organization in 2nd round of free-agent draft, January 10, 1978.
†Traded to New York Mets, February 7, 1979, completing deal in which Minnesota Twins traded Pitcher Greg

Field and a player to be named later to New York for Pitcher Jerry Koosman, December 8, 1978.
‡Appeared in one game as an outfielder with one putout.

CHAMPIONSHIP SERIES RECORD
Established Championship Series record for most games won, Series (3), 1986.

Year Club	League	G.	IP.	W.	L.	Pct.	H.	R.	ER.	SO.	BB.	ERA.
1986—New York	National	4	8	3	0	1.000	5	3	3	10	2	3.38

WORLD SERIES RECORD

Year Club	League	G.	IP.	W.	L.	Pct.	H.	R.	ER.	SO.	BB.	ERA.
1986—New York	National	4	5⅔	0	0	.000	2	0	0	6	0	0.00

ALL-STAR GAME RECORD

Year League	IP.	W.	L.	Pct.	H.	R.	ER.	SO.	BB.	ERA.
1983—National	⅓	0	0	.000	0	0	0	1	0	0.00

Member of National League All-Star Team in 1984; did not play.

JOSEPH MICHAEL ORSULAK
(Joe)

Born May 31, 1962, at Parsippany, N.J.
Height, 6.01. Weight, 186.
Throws and bats lefthanded.

Major League stolen bases: 1984 (3), 1985 (24), 1986 (24). Total—51.
Led Pacific Coast League outfielders in total chances with 367 and double plays with 8 in 1983.
Tied for South Atlantic League lead in double plays by outfielders with 4 in 1981.

Year—Club	League	Pos.	G.	AB.	R.	H.	2B.	3B.	HR.	RBI.	B.A.	PO.	A.	E.	F.A.
1981—Greenwood†	S. Atl.	OF	118	460	80	145	18	8	6	70	.315	249	16	4	★.985
1982—Alexandria	Carol.	OF-1B	129	463	92	134	18	4	14	65	.289	286	7	10	.967
1983—Hawaii	P. C.	OF	139	538	87	154	12	●13	10	58	.286	★341	●18	8	.978
1983—Pittsburgh	Nat.	OF	7	11	0	2	0	0	0	1	.182	2	2	0	1.000
1984—Hawaii	P. C.	OF	98	388	51	110	19	12	3	53	.284	258	6	2	.992
1984—Pittsburgh‡	Nat.	OF	32	67	12	17	1	2	0	3	.254	41	1	0	1.000
1985—Pittsburgh‡	Nat.	OF	121	397	54	119	14	6	0	21	.300	229	10	6	.976
1986—Pittsburgh	Nat.	OF	138	401	60	100	19	6	2	19	.249	193	11	4	.981
Major League Totals—4 Years			298	876	126	238	34	14	2	44	.272	465	24	10	.980

Selected by Pittsburgh Pirates' organization in 6th round of free-agent draft, June 3, 1980.
†On temporarily inactive list, July 10 to July 27, 1981.
‡On disabled list, May 25 to June 9, 1985.

JORGE ORTA (NUNEZ)
Named pronounced OR-ta.

Born November 26, 1950, at Mazatlan, Mexico.
Height, 5.10. Weight, 175.
Throws right and bats lefthanded.

Major League stolen bases: 1972 (3), 1973 (8), 1974 (9), 1975 (16), 1976 (24), 1977 (4), 1978 (1), 1979 (1), 1980 (6), 1981 (4), 1983 (1), 1985 (2). Total—79.
Collected six hits in one game, June 15, 1980.

Year—Club	League	Pos.	G.	AB.	R.	H.	2B.	3B.	HR.	RBI.	B.A.	PO.	A.	E.	F.A.
1968—Fresnillo	Mex. Cen.	2B-SS	20	68	8	18	6	0	0	1	.265	29	39	4	.944
1969—S. Luis Potosi	Mex. C.						(Did not play)								
1970—Puerto Mex.	Mex. S.E.	2B-SS	18	43	6	13	1	0	0	3	.302	29	28	1	.983
1971—S. Luis Potosi	Mex. Cen.	2B	59	182	55	77	17	★7	7	53	★.423	115	108	15	.937
1971—Mexicali†	Mex. No.		58	207	45	75	14	2	16	48	.362	figures unavailable			
1972—Knoxville	South.	2B	53	196	41	62	6	7	7	34	.316	113	142	9	.966
1972—Chicago	Amer.	SS-2B-3B	51	124	20	25	3	1	3	11	.202	50	85	8	.944
1973—Chicago	Amer.	2B-SS	128	425	46	113	9	10	6	40	.266	255	301	18	.969
1974—Chicago	Amer.	2B-SS	139	525	73	166	31	2	10	67	.316	297	313	18	.971
1975—Chicago	Amer.	2B	140	542	64	165	26	10	11	83	.304	354	354	16	.978
1976—Chicago	Amer.	OF-3B	158	636	74	174	29	8	14	72	.274	187	111	15	.952
1977—Chicago	Amer.	2B	144	564	71	159	27	8	11	84	.282	287	335	19	.970
1978—Chicago	Amer.	2B	117	420	45	115	19	2	13	53	.274	290	290	9	.984
1979—Chicago‡	Amer.	2B	113	325	49	85	18	3	11	46	.262	57	75	3	.978
1980—Cleveland	Amer.	OF	129	481	78	140	18	3	10	64	.291	269	10	5	.982
1981—Cleveland§	Amer.	OF	88	338	50	92	14	3	5	34	.272	150	11	1	.994
1982—Los Angeles xy	Nat.	OF	86	115	13	25	5	0	2	8	.217	35	1	2	.947
1983—Toronto z	Amer.	OF	103	245	30	58	6	3	10	38	.237	16	1	0	1.000
1984—Kansas City	Amer.	OF-2B	122	403	50	120	23	7	9	50	.298	48	0	1	.980
1985—Kansas City	Amer.	DH	110	300	32	80	21	1	4	45	.267	0	0	0	.000
1986—Kansas City a	Amer.	DH	106	336	35	93	14	2	9	46	.277	0	0	0	.000
American League Totals—14 Years			1648	5664	717	1585	258	63	126	733	.280	2347	1886	113	.974
National League Totals—1 Year			86	115	13	25	5	0	2	8	.217	35	1	2	.947
Major League Totals—15 Years			1734	5779	730	1610	263	63	128	741	.279	2382	1887	115	.974

Signed as free agent by Fresnillo, June 13, 1968.
†Sold to Appleton (Chicago White Sox' organization), November 30, 1971.
‡Granted free agency, November 1, 1979; signed by Cleveland Indians, December 19, 1979.
§Traded with Catcher Jack Fimple and Pitcher Larry White to Los Angeles Dodgers for Pitcher Rick Sutcliffe and Second Baseman Jack Perconte, December 9, 1981.

xTraded to New York Mets for Pitcher Pat Zachry, December 28, 1982.
yTraded to Toronto Blue Jays for Pitcher Steve Senteney, February 4, 1983.
zTraded to Kansas City Royals for First Baseman Willie Aikens, December 19, 1983.
aReleased, December 22, 1986.

CHAMPIONSHIP SERIES RECORD

Year Club	League	Pos.	G.	AB.	R.	H.	2B.	3B.	HR.	RBI.	B.A.	PO.	A.	E.	F.A.
1984—Kansas City	Amer.	DH	3	10	1	1	0	1	0	1	.100	0	0	0	.000
1985—Kansas City	Amer.	DH-PH	2	5	0	0	0	0	0	0	.000	0	0	0	.000
Championship Series Totals—2 Years			5	15	1	1	0	1	0	1	.067	0	0	0	.000

WORLD SERIES RECORD

Year Club	League	Pos.	G.	AB.	R.	H.	2B.	3B.	HR.	RBI.	B.A.	PO.	A.	E.	F.A.
1985—Kansas City	Amer.	PH	3	3	0	1	0	0	0	0	.333	0	0	0	.000

ALL-STAR GAME RECORD

Named to American League All-Star Team for 1975 game; replaced due to injury.
Member of American League All-Star Team in 1980; did not play.

ADALBERTO ORTIZ JR. (COLON)

Name pronounced Orr-TEEZ.

(Junior)

Born October 24, 1959, at Humacao, Puerto Rico.
Height, 5.11. Weight, 176.
Throws and bats righthanded.
Brother of Alexander Ortiz, minor league outfielder, 1978 and 1979.

Major League stolen bases: 1983 (1), 1984 (1), 1985 (1). Total—3.
Led Pacific Coast League catchers in putouts with 744 and double plays with 17 in 1982.
Led Carolina League catchers in double plays with 12 in 1979.
Tied for Western Carolinas League lead in passed balls with 22 in 1978.

Year Club	League	Pos.	G.	AB.	R.	H.	2B.	3B.	HR.	RBI.	B.A.	PO.	A.	E.	F.A.
1977—Charleston†	W. Car.	C	21	53	2	14	3	0	0	10	.264	93	13	4	.964
1977—Bradenton Pir.	Gulf C.	C	34	118	11	24	5	1	1	12	.203	76	14	4	.957
1978—Charleston‡	W. Car.	C	41	122	12	26	4	0	1	16	213	198	44	7	.972
1979—Salem	Carol.	*C-1B	108	396	35	112	21	2	5	66	.283	632	*84	*17	.977
1980—Buffalo	East.	C	126	515	79	*178	25	1	12	78	★.346	497	91	16	.974
1980—Portland	P. C.	C	8	27	1	3	0	1	0	3	.111	42	10	0	1.000
1981—Portland	P. C.	C	105	346	49	93	14	7	2	46	.269	606	76	15	.978
1982—Portland	P. C.	C-OF-1B	124	449	46	131	22	0	6	57	.292	751	*110	*19	.978
1982—Pittsburgh	Nat.	C	7	15	1	3	1	0	0	0	.200	27	3	0	1.000
1983—Pitt.§-N.Y.	Nat.	C	73	193	11	48	5	0	0	12	.249	293	31	11	.967
1984—New York x	Nat.	C	40	91	6	18	3	0	0	11	.198	136	13	3	.980
1985—Pittsburgh	Nat.	C	23	72	4	21	2	0	1	5	.292	115	14	2	.985
1986—Pittsburgh	Nat.	C	49	110	11	37	6	0	0	14	.336	165	13	3	.983
Major League Totals—5 Years			192	481	33	127	17	0	1	42	.264	736	74	19	.977

Signed as free agent by Pittsburgh Pirates' organization, January 18, 1977.
†On temporary inactive list, June 18 to June 22, 1977.
‡On disabled list, June 16 to September 5, 1978.
§Traded with Pitcher Art Ray to New York Mets for Outfielder Marvell Wynne and Pitcher Steve Senteney, June 14, 1983.
xDrafted by Pittsburgh Pirates, December 3, 1984.

PHILIP ROLAND OUELLETTE

Name pronounced Well-LETT.

(Phil)

Born November 10, 1961, at Salem, Ore.
Height, 6.00. Weight, 190.
Throws right and bats left and righthanded.
Attended Citrus College, Azusa, Calif.
Cousin of Dan Simmons, member of U.S. Olympic ski team, 1980 and 1984.

Year Club	League	Pos.	G.	AB.	R.	H.	2B.	3B.	HR.	RBI.	B.A.	PO.	A.	E.	F.A.
1981—Great Falls	Pion.	C-1B	42	129	17	34	6	1	1	28	.264	234	21	4	.985
1982—Clinton	Midw.	C	109	351	59	96	18	1	13	74	.274	681	65	6	*.992
1983—Fresno†	Calif.	C-1B	71	210	37	57	7	2	5	35	.271	334	18	1	.997
1984—Phoenix	P. C.	C-P	70	171	32	45	8	4	7	29	.263	265	25	3	.990
1985—Phoenix‡	P. C.	C	27	79	7	14	0	0	0	8	.177	114	10	1	.992
1986—Phoenix	P. C.	C	90	294	48	92	21	1	7	41	.313	369	50	8	.981
1986—San Francisco	Nat.	C	10	23	1	4	0	0	0	0	.174	42	3	0	1.000
Major League Totals—1 Year			10	23	1	4	0	0	0	0	.174	42	3	0	1.000

Signed as free agent by San Francisco Giants' organization, May 17, 1981.
†On disabled list, August 2, 1983 through remainder of season.
‡On disabled list, May 27, 1985 through remainder of season.

PITCHING RECORD

Year Club	League	G.	IP.	W.	L.	Pct.	H.	R.	ER.	SO.	BB.	ERA.
1984—Phoenix	P. Coast	3	7⅔	0	1	.000	6	2	2	2	3	2.35

ROBERT DENNIS OWCHINKO

Name pronounced Oh-CHINK-oh.

(Bob)

Born January 1, 1955, at Detroit, Mich.
Height, 6.02. Weight, 195.
Throws and bats lefthanded.
Attended Eastern Michigan University, Ypsilanti, Mich.

Major League saves: 1981 (2), 1982 (3), 1984 (2). Total—7.
Named National League Rookie Pitcher of the Year by THE SPORTING NEWS, 1977.

Year Club	League	G.	IP.	W.	L.	Pct.	H.	R.	ER.	SO.	BB.	ERA.
1976—Amarillo	Texas	13	91	6	2	.750	86	36	33	69	38	3.26
1976—San Diego	National	2	4	0	2	.000	11	8	8	4	3	18.00
1977—Hawaii	P. Coast	6	44	5	1	.833	36	7	7	30	20	1.43
1977—San Diego	National	30	170	9	12	.429	191	93	84	101	67	4.45
1978—San Diego	National	36	202	10	13	.435	198	87	80	94	78	3.56
1979—San Diego†	National	42	149	6	12	.333	144	73	62	66	55	3.74
1980—Cleveland‡§	American	29	114	2	9	.182	138	71	67	66	47	5.29
1981—Oakland	American	29	39	4	3	.571	34	15	14	26	19	3.23
1982—Oakland x	American	54	102	2	4	.333	111	60	59	67	52	5.21
1983—Hawaii	P. Coast	22	137⅔	10	6	.625	150	86	65	124	56	4.25
1983—Pittsburgh y	National	1	0	0	0	.000	2	1	1	0	0	.....
1984—Tampa z	Florida St.	7	12⅔	1	1	.500	4	2	0	13	3	0.00
1984—Cincinnati a	National	49	94	3	5	.375	91	47	43	60	39	4.12
1985—Tacoma bc	P. Coast	16	37⅔	3	5	.375	52	30	24	20	18	5.73
1985—Buffalo d	Am. Assoc.	10	35⅔	1	4	.200	48	21	21	24	15	5.30
1986—Indianapolis	Am. Assoc.	28	150⅔	11	7	.611	156	89	70	104	59	4.18
1986—Montreal e	National	3	15	1	0	1.000	17	6	6	6	3	3.60
National League Totals—7 Years		163	634	29	44	.397	654	315	284	331	245	4.03
American League Totals—3 Years		112	255	8	16	.333	283	146	140	159	118	4.94
Major League Totals—10 Years		275	889	37	60	.381	937	461	424	490	363	4.29

Selected by San Diego Padres' organization in 1st round (fifth player selected) of free-agent draft, June 8, 1976.
†Traded with Outfielder Jim Wilhelm to Cleveland Indians for Outfielder Jerry Mumphrey, February 15, 1980.
‡Traded with Pitchers Victor Cruz and Rafael Vasquez and Catcher Gary Alexander to Pittsburgh Pirates for Pitcher Bert Blyleven and Catcher Manny Sanguillen, December 9, 1980.
§Traded to Oakland A's for cash and a player to be named later, April 6, 1981; Pittsburgh Pirates acquired Pitcher Ernie Camacho to complete deal, April 10, 1981.
xReleased, March 28, 1983; signed by Hawaii (Pittsburgh Pirates' organization), May 2, 1983.
ySold to Cincinnati Reds, November 11, 1983.
zOn Cincinnati disabled list, March 28 to April 18, 1984; included rehabilitation disability assignment to Tampa, April 6 to April 18, 1984.
aGranted free agency, November 8, 1984; signed by Tacoma (Oakland A's organization), April 15, 1985.
bOn disabled list, June 20 to July 17, 1985.
cSold to Buffalo (Chicago White Sox' organization), July 17, 1985.
dReleased, September 24, 1985; signed by Indianapolis (Montreal Expos' organization), February 25, 1986.
eGranted free agency, November 12, 1986.

CHAMPIONSHIP SERIES RECORD

Year Club	League	G.	IP.	W.	L.	Pct.	H.	R.	ER.	SO.	BB.	ERA.
1981—Oakland	American	1	1⅔	0	0	.000	3	1	1	0	0	5.40

DAVE OWEN

Born April 25, 1958, at Cleburne, Tex.
Height, 6.01. Weight, 175.
Throws right and bats left and righthanded.
Attended University of Texas, Arlington, Tex.
Brother of Spike Owen, shortstop with Boston Red Sox.

Major League stolen bases: 1983 (1), 1984 (1), 1985 (1). Total—3.

Year Club	League	Pos.	G.	AB.	R.	H.	2B.	3B.	HR.	RBI.	B.A.	PO.	A.	E.	F.A.
1979—Sarasota Cubs	Gulf C.	SS	10	23	8	7	0	0	0	4	.304	17	26	7	.860
1979—Quad Cities	Midw.	SS	45	129	23	18	3	0	0	4	.140	56	139	11	.947
1980—Midland	Texas	SS	78	257	45	74	8	0	3	31	.288	96	213	32	.906
1980—Quad Cities	Midw.	SS	56	188	43	49	5	1	0	17	.261	88	155	17	.935
1981—Midland	Texas	SS-2B-3B	80	247	40	53	8	1	0	23	.215	109	205	26	.924
1982—Midland	Texas	SS-3B	125	427	59	135	12	9	4	40	.316	183	309	29	.944
1983—Iowa	A. A.	SS	126	425	67	110	21	3	6	39	.259	203	★431	25	★.962
1983—Chicago	Nat.	SS-3B	16	22	1	2	0	1	0	2	.091	10	29	0	1.000
1984—Iowa	A. A.	SS-2B-OF	43	136	18	31	5	1	1	9	.228	65	111	7	.962
1984—Chicago	Nat.	SS-3B-2B	47	93	8	18	2	2	1	10	.194	40	91	7	.949
1985—Iowa	A. A.	2-S-3-O	100	321	60	73	13	5	11	40	.227	157	280	7	.984
1985—Chicago†‡	Nat.	SS-3B-2B	22	19	6	7	0	0	0	4	.368	6	14	2	.909
1986—Oklahoma City	A. A.	S-2-3-1-O	64	188	33	47	8	4	2	22	.250	100	119	10	.956
Major League Totals—3 Years			85	134	15	27	2	3	1	16	.201	56	134	9	.955

Selected by Chicago Cubs' organization in 10th round of free-agent draft, June 5, 1979.
†Traded to San Francisco Giants for Second Baseman Manny Trillo, December 11, 1985.
‡Released, March 24, 1986; signed by Texas Rangers' organization, March 27, 1986.

SPIKE DEE OWEN

Born April 19, 1961, at Cleburne, Tex.
Height, 5.10. Weight, 165.
Throws right and bats left and righthanded.
Attended University of Texas, Austin, Tex.
Brother of Dave Owen, shortstop in Texas Rangers' organization.

Tied modern major league record for most runs, game (6), August 21, 1986.
Major League stolen bases: 1983 (10), 1984 (16), 1985 (11), 1986 (4). Total—41.
Led American League shortstops in total chances with 767 and double plays with 133 in 1986.
Named shortstop on THE SPORTING NEWS College Baseball All-America Team, 1982.

Year Club	League	Pos.	G.	AB.	R.	H.	2B.	3B.	HR.	RBI.	B.A.	PO.	A.	E.	F.A.
1982—Lynn	East.	SS	78	241	32	64	9	2	1	27	.266	106	207	9	.972
1983—Salt Lake City	P. C.	SS	72	256	58	68	8	9	1	32	.266	111	212	14	.958
1983—Seattle	Amer.	SS	80	306	36	60	11	3	2	21	.196	122	233	11	.970
1984—Seattle	Amer.	SS	152	530	67	130	18	8	3	43	.245	245	463	17	.977
1985—Seattle†	Amer.	SS	118	352	41	91	10	6	6	37	.259	196	361	14	.975
1986—Sea.‡-Bos.	Amer.	SS	154	528	67	122	24	7	1	45	.231	279	467	21	.973
Major League Totals—4 Years			504	1716	211	403	63	24	12	146	.235	842	1524	63	.974

Selected by Seattle Mariners' organization in 1st round (sixth player selected) of free-agent draft, June 7, 1982.
†On disabled list, July 15 to August 1, 1985.
‡Traded with Outfielder Dave Henderson to Boston Red Sox for Infielder Rey Quinones, a player to be named later and cash, August 19, 1986; as part of deal, Seattle Mariners claimed Pitchers Mike Brown and Mike Trujillo on waivers from Boston, August 22, 1986. Seattle acquired Outfielder John Christensen to complete deal, September 25, 1986.

CHAMPIONSHIP SERIES RECORD

Tied Championship Series record for most hits, two consecutive games, one Series (6), October 14 and 15, 1986.

Year Club	League	Pos.	G.	AB.	R.	H.	2B.	3B.	HR.	RBI.	B.A.	PO.	A.	E.	F.A.
1986—Boston	Amer.	SS	7	21	5	9	0	1	0	3	.429	12	21	5	.868

WORLD SERIES RECORD

Year Club	League	Pos.	G.	AB.	R.	H.	2B.	3B.	HR.	RBI.	B.A.	PO.	A.	E.	F.A.
1986—Boston	Amer.	SS	7	20	2	6	0	0	0	2	.300	10	13	0	1.000

RICHARD WAYNE OWNBEY
(Rick)

Born October 20, 1957, at Corona, Calif.
Height, 6.03. Weight, 185.
Throws and bats righthanded.
Attended Santa Ana College, Santa Ana, Calif.

Year Club	League	G.	IP.	W.	L.	Pct.	H.	R.	ER.	SO.	BB.	ERA.
1980—Lynchburg	Carolina	12	92	8	1	.889	66	24	19	93	35	1.86
1980—Jackson	Texas	2	13	1	0	1.000	7	3	2	12	7	1.38
1981—Jackson†	Texas	20	133	10	7	.588	110	49	41	125	62	2.77
1982—Tidewater	Int'national	23	150⅓	8	7	.533	107	64	56	122	112	3.35
1982—New York	National	8	50⅓	1	2	.333	44	23	21	28	43	3.75
1983—New York‡	National	10	34⅔	1	3	.250	31	19	18	19	21	4.67
1983—Louisville	Am. Assoc.	16	104	7	5	.583	100	47	42	77	51	3.63
1984—Louisville§	Am. Assoc.	17	96⅓	6	6	.500	75	52	43	111	61	4.02
1984—St. Louis	National	4	19	0	3	.000	23	13	10	11	8	4.74
1985—Louisville x	Am. Assoc.	25	166	10	9	.526	154	68	63	122	74	3.42
1986—St. Louis	National	17	42⅔	1	3	.250	47	20	18	25	19	3.80
1986—Louisville y	Am. Assoc.	10	59	3	3	.500	59	31	29	27	25	4.42
Major League Totals—4 Years		39	146⅔	3	11	.214	145	75	67	83	91	4.11

Selected by Pittsburgh Pirates' organization in 4th round of free-agent draft, January 9, 1979.
Selected by New York Mets' organization in 13th round of free-agent draft, June 3, 1980.
†On disabled list, May 24 to June 9, 1981.
‡Traded with Pitcher Neil Allen to St. Louis Cardinals for First Baseman Keith Hernandez, June 15, 1983.
§On disabled list, April 6 to April 20 and May 3 to June 4, 1984.
xOn St. Louis disabled list, March 28 to May 20, 1985; included rehabilitation disability assignment to Louisville, April 30 to May 20, 1985.
yGranted free agency, October 15, 1986.

JOHN LEWIS PACELLA

Name pronounced Puh-SELL-uh.

Born September 15, 1956, at Brooklyn, N.Y.
Height, 6.02. Weight, 184.
Throws and bats righthanded.

Pitched 3-0 no-hit victory against Tulsa, April 15, 1977.
Major League saves: 1982 (2), 1986 (1). Total—3.
Led American Association in saves with 17 in 1986.

Year Club	League	G.	IP.	W.	L.	Pct.	H.	R.	ER.	SO.	BB.	ERA.
1974—Marion	Ap'lachian	12	43	1	7	.125	48	31	24	19	32	5.02
1975—Wausau	Midwest	19	132	9	8	.529	124	71	56	73	58	3.82
1976—Lynchburg	Carolina	26	185	12	11	.522	151	*97	67	119	83	3.26
1977—Tidewater	Int'national	17	93	7	5	.583	100	50	41	46	54	3.97
1977—Jackson	Texas	11	73	3	4	.429	75	47	33	49	39	4.07

Year Club	League	G.	IP.	W.	L.	Pct.	H.	R.	ER.	SO.	BB.	ERA.
1977—New York	National	3	4	0	0	.000	2	2	0	1	2	0.00
1978—Jackson	Texas	7	48	4	3	.571	31	16	14	44	16	2.63
1978—Tidewater	Int'national	19	102	4	11	.267	110	71	57	77	40	5.03
1979—Tidewater	Int'national	26	142	7	10	.412	129	65	58	95	61	3.61
1979—New York	National	4	16	0	2	.000	16	8	8	12	4	4.50
1980—New York†‡	National	32	84	3	4	.429	89	51	48	68	59	5.14
1981—Columbus	Int'national	27	155	11	9	.550	149	84	77	135	91	4.47
1982—New York§-Minnesota xy	American	24	61⅔	1	3	.250	74	56	50	22	46	7.30
1982—Columbus z	Int'national	6	5⅓	0	2	.000	6	9	4	2	12	6.75
1983—Charlotte	Southern	10	28¼	0	5	.000	34	30	20	17	28	6.35
1984—Charlotte	Southern	12	27⅓	0	0	.000	27	21	13	21	28	4.28
1984—Rochester	Int'national	22	113	6	3	.667	92	45	39	120	48	3.11
1984—Baltimore a	American	6	14⅔	0	1	.000	15	13	11	8	9	6.75
1985—Nashville	Southern	37	122⅔	7	7	.500	90	47	44	79	54	3.23
1986—Nashville	Am. Assoc.	43	68⅓	7	6	.538	63	28	22	55	39	2.90
1986—Detroit	American	5	11	0	0	.000	10	5	5	5	13	4.09
National League Totals—3 Years		39	104	3	6	.333	107	61	56	81	65	4.85
American League Totals—3 Years		35	87⅓	1	4	.200	99	74	66	35	68	6.80
Major League Totals—6 Years		74	191⅓	4	10	.286	206	135	122	116	133	5.74

Selected by New York Mets' organization in 4th round of free-agent draft, June 5, 1974.
†Traded with Infielder Jose Moreno to San Diego Padres for Pitcher Randy Jones, December 15, 1980.
‡Traded by San Diego Padres with Outfielder Jerry Mumphrey and a player to be named later to New York Yankees for Outfielders Ruppert Jones and Joe Lefebvre and Pitchers Tim Lollar and Chris Welsh, April 1, 1981; New York organization acquired Outfielder Dave Stegman to complete deal, April 30, 1981.
§Traded with Infielder Larry Milbourne and Pitcher Pete Filson to Minnesota Twins for Catcher Butch Wynegar and Pitcher Roger Erickson, May 12, 1982.
xOn disabled list, August 8 to September 1, 1982.
yTraded to Texas Rangers for Pitcher Len Whitehouse, November 1, 1982.
zReleased, April 6, 1983; signed by Charlotte (Baltimore Orioles' organization), July 11, 1983.
aReleased, December 10, 1984; signed by Nashville (Detroit Tigers' organization), December 28, 1984.

PATRICK MICHAEL PACILLO
(Pat)

Born July 23, 1963, at Rutherford, N. J.
Height, 6.02. Weight, 205.
Throws and bats righthanded.
Attended Seton Hall University, South Orange, N. J.

Tied for American Association lead in shutouts with 2 in 1986.
Member of 1984 U.S. Olympic baseball team.

Year Club	League	G.	IP.	W.	L.	Pct.	H.	R.	ER.	SO.	BB.	ERA.
1985—Tampa	Florida St.	25	38⅔	8	1	.889	28	17	13	39	28	3.03
1985—Vermont	Eastern	22	36⅔	0	4	.000	27	11	10	39	24	2.45
1986—Denver	Am. Assoc.	25	148	11	6	.647	135	81	71	111	85	4.32

Selected by Cincinnati Reds' organization in 1st round (fifth player selected) of free-agent draft, June 4, 1984.

THOMAS MARIAN PACIOREK
Name pronounced Pah-CHOR-eck.
(Tom)

Born November 2, 1946, at Detroit, Mich.
Height, 6.04. Weight, 205.
Throws and bats righthanded.
Received bachelor of science degree in education from University of Houston, Houston, Tex.
Brother of Jim Paciorek, outfielder in Milwaukee Brewers' organization;
Mike Paciorek, first baseman in Los Angeles Dodgers'
and Atlanta Braves' organizations, 1973 through 1977;
and John Paciorek, outfielder with Houston Astros, 1963.

Major League stolen bases: 1972 (1), 1973 (3), 1974 (1), 1975 (4), 1976 (2), 1977 (1), 1978 (2), 1979 (6), 1980 (3), 1981 (13), 1982 (3), 1983 (6), 1984 (6), 1985 (3), 1986 (1). Total—55.
Led Pacific Coast League in total bases with 310 and tied for lead in sacrifice flies with 12 in 1972.
Named Minor League Player of the Year by THE SPORTING NEWS, 1972.
Named Pacific Coast League Most Valuable Player, 1972.
Named outfielder on THE SPORTING NEWS College Baseball All-America Team, 1967 and 1968.
Selected by Miami Dolphins in 9th round (240th player selected) of 1968 NFL draft.

Year Club	League	Pos.	G.	AB.	R.	H.	2B.	3B.	HR.	RBI.	B.A.	PO.	A.	E.	F.A.
1968—Ogden	Pion.	OF-1B	29	101	25	39	6	3	5	23	.386	45	3	2	.960
1968—Bakersfield	Calif.	OF-1B	38	116	16	32	1	1	0	10	.276	44	1	0	1.000
1969—Bakersfield†	Calif.	OF-3B	91	359	59	114	20	3	15	53	.318	111	44	16	.906
1970—Spokane	P. C.	OF	●146	549	88	179	36	12	17	101	.326	262	5	6	.978
1970—Los Angeles	Nat.	OF	8	9	2	2	1	0	0	0	.222	1	0	0	1.000
1971—Spokane	P. C.	OF-3B	144	564	89	172	31	★14	15	105	.305	240	9	8	.969
1971—Los Angeles	Nat.	OF	2	2	0	0	0	0	0	1	.500	1	0	0	1.000
1972—Albuquerque	P. C.	1B	147	★605	★125	★186	★33	5	★27	107	.307	★1239	80	●13	.990
1972—Los Angeles	Nat.	1B-OF	11	47	4	12	4	0	1	6	.255	53	3	1	.982
1973—Los Angeles	Nat.	OF-1B	96	195	26	51	8	0	5	18	.262	117	3	2	.984
1974—Los Angeles	Nat.	OF-1B	85	175	23	42	8	6	1	24	.240	85	1	5	.945
1975—Los Angeles‡	Nat.	OF	62	145	14	28	8	0	1	5	.193	69	0	2	.972

Year Club	League	Pos.	G.	AB.	R.	H.	2B.	3B.	HR.	RBI.	B.A.	PO.	A.	E.	F.A.
1976—Atlanta	Nat.	OF-1B-3B	111	324	39	94	10	4	4	36	.290	216	10	3	.987
1977—Atlanta§	Nat.	1B-OF-3B	72	155	20	37	8	0	3	15	.239	248	16	5	.981
1978—Atlanta x	Nat.	1B	5	9	2	3	0	0	0	0	.333	21	0	0	1.000
1978—San Jose	P. C.	OF	16	57	7	16	1	2	3	17	.281	32	1	1	.971
1978—Seattle y	Amer.	OF-1B	70	251	32	75	20	3	4	30	.299	115	5	2	.984
1979—Seattle	Amer.	OF-1B	103	310	38	89	23	4	6	42	.287	237	12	1	.996
1980—Seattle	Amer.	OF-1B	126	418	44	114	19	1	15	59	.273	360	22	5	.987
1981—Seattle z	Amer.	OF	104	405	50	132	28	2	14	66	.326	253	10	7	.974
1982—Chicago a	Amer.	1B-OF	104	382	49	119	27	4	11	55	.312	835	66	6	.993
1983—Chicago	Amer.	1B-OF	115	420	65	129	32	3	9	63	.307	629	38	1	.999
1984—Chicago b	Amer.	1B-OF	111	363	35	93	21	2	4	29	.256	596	25	6	.990
1985—Chicago c	Amer.	OF-1B	46	122	14	30	2	0	0	9	.246	76	6	1	.988
1985—New York d	Nat.	OF-1B	46	116	14	33	3	1	1	11	.284	76	3	0	1.000
1986—Texas	Amer.	O-1-3-S	88	213	17	61	7	0	4	22	.286	178	45	4	.982
American League Totals—9 Years			867	2884	344	842	179	19	67	375	.292	3279	229	33	.991
National League Totals—10 Years			498	1177	144	303	50	11	16	116	.257	887	36	18	.981
Major League Totals—17 Years			1365	4061	488	1145	229	30	83	491	.282	4166	265	51	.989

Selected by Los Angeles Dodgers' organization in 42nd round of free-agent draft, June 7, 1968.

†On restricted list, April 3 to June 3, 1969.

‡Traded with Outfielder Jimmy Wynn, Second Baseman Lee Lacy and Infielder Jerry Royster to Atlanta Braves for Outfielder Dusty Baker and First Baseman-Third Baseman Ed Goodson, November 17, 1975.

§Released March 30, 1978; re-signed by Atlanta Braves, April 7, 1978.

xReleased, May 23, 1978; signed by Seattle Mariners' organization, May 31, 1978.

yGranted free agency, November 2, 1978; re-signed by Mariners, January 6, 1979.

zTraded to Chicago White Sox for Catcher Jim Essian, Shortstop Todd Cruz and Outfielder Rod Allen, December 11, 1981.

aOn disabled list, July 27 to August 11 and August 28 to September 17, 1982.

bOn disabled list, June 30 to July 28, 1984.

cTraded to New York Mets for Infielder Dave Cochrane, July 16, 1985.

dReleased, November 13, 1985; signed by Texas Rangers, December 10, 1985.

CHAMPIONSHIP SERIES RECORD

Year Club	League	Pos.	G.	AB.	R.	H.	2B.	3B.	HR.	RBI.	B.A.	PO.	A.	E.	F.A.
1974—Los Angeles	Nat.	PH-OF	1	1	0	1	0	0	0	0	1.000	0	0	0	.000
1983—Chicago	Amer.	1B-OF	4	16	1	4	0	0	0	1	.250	30	3	0	1.000
Championship Series Totals—2 Years.....			5	17	1	5	0	0	0	1	.294	30	3	0	1.000

WORLD SERIES RECORD

Year Club	League	Pos.	G.	AB.	R.	H.	2B.	3B.	HR.	RBI.	B.A.	PO.	A.	E.	F.A.
1974—Los Angeles	Nat.	PH-PR	3	2	1	1	1	0	2	0	.500	0	0	0	.000

ALL-STAR GAME RECORD

Year League	Pos.	AB.	R.	H.	2B.	3B.	HR.	RBI.	B.A.	PO.	A.	E.	F.A.
1981—American	PH	1	0	1	0	0	0	0	1.000	0	0	0	.000

CHRIS PHILLIP PADGET

Born September 20, 1962, at Rochester, N. Y.
Height, 6.01. Weight, 190.
Throws right and bats lefthanded.
Attended George C. Wallace Community College, Dothan, Ala.,
and University of Mississippi, University, Miss.

Tied for Southern League lead in intentional bases on balls received with 9 in 1986.
Tied for Carolina League lead in sacrifice flies with 10 in 1985.

Year Club	League	Pos.	G.	AB.	R.	H.	2B.	3B.	HR.	RBI.	B.A.	PO.	A.	E.	F.A.
1984—Bluefield................	Appal.	OF-2B	34	117	23	36	5	2	5	20	.308	35	6	0	1.000
1984—Newark	NYP	OF	20	67	15	25	6	1	5	26	.373	19	2	0	1.000
1985—Hagerstown	Carol.	1B-OF	136	483	56	134	20	4	7	70	.277	647	56	9	.987
1986—Charlotte................	South.	1B-OF-3B	127	469	77	152	22	7	22	96	.324	553	44	7	.988

Selected by Baltimore Orioles' organization in 7th round of free-agent draft, June 4, 1984.

MICHAEL TIMOTHY PAGLIARULO

Name pronounced Pal-ya-ROO-lo.

(Mike)

Born March 15, 1960, at Medford, Mass.
Height, 6.02. Weight, 195.
Throws right and bats lefthanded.
Attended University of Miami, Coral Gables, Fla.
Son of Charles Pagliarulo, infielder in Chicago Cubs' organization, 1958.

Major League stolen bases: 1986 (4).
Led New York-Pennsylvania League in intentional bases on balls received with 8 in 1981.
Led Southern League third basemen in total chances with 433 in 1983.
Led New York-Pennsylvania League third basemen in total chances with 214 in 1981.

Year Club	League	Pos.	G.	AB.	R.	H.	2B.	3B.	HR.	RBI.	B.A.	PO.	A.	E.	F.A.
1981—Oneonta..................	NYP	3B	72	245	32	53	9	4	2	28	.216	40	★159	15	.930
1982—Greensboro	S. Atl.	3B	123	403	79	113	22	0	22	79	.280	73	★278	27	.929

Year	Club	League	Pos.	G.	AB.	R.	H.	2B.	3B.	HR.	RBI.	B.A.	PO.	A.	E.	F.A.
1983—Nashville	South.		3B	135	450	82	117	19	4	19	80	.260	*98	*315	20	*.954
1984—Columbus	Int.		3B-SS	58	146	24	31	5	1	7	25	.212	27	95	13	.904
1984—New York	Amer.		3B	67	201	24	48	15	3	7	34	.239	44	106	7	.955
1985—New York	Amer.		3B	138	380	55	91	16	2	19	62	.239	67	187	13	.951
1986—New York	Amer.		3B-SS	149	504	71	120	24	3	28	71	.238	104	283	19	.953
Major League Totals—3 Years				354	1085	150	259	55	8	54	167	.239	215	576	39	.953

Selected by New York Yankees' organization in 6th round of free-agent draft, June 8, 1981.

THOMAS ALAN PAGNOZZI
(Tom)

Born July 30, 1962, at Tucson, Ariz.
Height, 6.01. Weight, 190.
Throws and bats righthanded.
Attended Central Arizona College, Coolidge, Ariz.,
and University of Arkansas, Fayetteville, Ark.
Brother of Tim Pagnozzi, shortstop in Philadelphia Phillies' organization, 1976;
and Mike Pagnozzi, pitcher in Baltimore Orioles' organization, 1975 through 1978.

Year	Club	League	Pos.	G.	AB.	R.	H.	2B.	3B.	HR.	RBI.	B.A.	PO.	A.	E.	F.A.
1983—Erie	NYP		C	45	168	28	52	9	1	6	22	.310	183	20	3	.985
1983—Macon	S. Atl.		C	18	57	7	14	2	1	0	6	.246	125	18	8	.947
1984—Springfield	Midw.		C	114	396	57	112	20	4	10	68	.283	667	*90	12	.984
1985—Arkansas	Texas		C-1B	41	139	15	43	7	1	5	29	.309	243	27	1	.996
1985—Louisville	A. A.		C	76	268	29	72	13	2	5	40	.269	266	25	4	.986
1986—Louisville	A. A.		C	30	106	12	31	4	0	1	18	.292	160	19	3	.984

Selected by Milwaukee Brewers' organization in 24th round of free-agent draft, January 12, 1982.
Selected by St. Louis Cardinals' organization in 8th round of free agent draft, June 6, 1983.

ROBERT REY PALACIOS
(Known by middle name.)

Born November 8, 1962, at Brooklyn, N. Y.
Height, 5.10. Weight, 190.
Throws and bats righthanded.
Attended Kingsborough Community College, Brooklyn, N. Y.

Led Eastern League catchers in putouts with 603, assists with 86, errors with 20, total chances with 709 and double plays with 8 in 1986.
Tied for Appalachian League lead in double plays by catchers with 2 in 1984.

Year	Club	League	Pos.	G.	AB.	R.	H.	2B.	3B.	HR.	RBI.	B.A.	PO.	A.	E.	F.A.
1983—Bristol	Appal.		C	47	139	28	42	7	1	7	28	.302	187	22	7	.968
1984—Lakeland†	Fla. St.		3B-1B-C	107	373	44	92	21	4	2	53	.247	285	105	19	.954
1985—Lakeland	Fla. St.		C-1B	85	280	35	65	11	1	2	27	.232	410	45	13	.972
1985—Birmingham	South.		C-3B-1B	35	110	14	29	4	0	2	16	.264	153	43	8	.961
1986—Glens Falls	East.		C-3B-1B	135	461	66	116	20	4	16	66	.252	703	140	26	.970

Signed as free agent by Detroit Tigers' organization, August 16, 1982.
†On disabled list, April 17 to May 21, 1984.

VICENTE PALACIOS (HERNANDEZ)
(Vince)

Born July 19, 1963, at Veracruz, Mex.
Height, 6.03. Weight, 165.
Throws and bats righthanded.

Led Mexican League in balks with 3 in 1983.
Tied for Eastern League lead in balks with 4 in 1985.

Year	Club	League	G.	IP.	W.	L.	Pct.	H.	R.	ER.	SO.	BB.	ERA.
1982—Veracruz	Mexican		(Did not play)										
1983—Veracruz	Mexican	22	165⅓	12	6	.667	121	53	48	125	60	2.61
1984—Veracruz†	Mexican	24	128	7	8	.468	117	64	50	120	79	3.52
1984—Glens Falls	Eastern	5	25⅓	1	2	.333	23	14	7	10	11	2.49
1985—Glens Falls‡	Eastern	8	39⅔	1	1	.500	44	25	21	20	29	4.76
1985—Mexico City Reds	Mexican	13	74⅓	7	2	.778	86	44	32	49	44	3.87
1986—Aguascalientes§xy	Mexican	23	138⅔	5	14	.263	157	75	68	121	78	4.41

Signed as free agent by Veracruz of Mexican League, April 23, 1982.
†Sold to Chicago White Sox' organization, July 20, 1984.
‡Loaned to Mexico City Reds of Mexican League, May 28, 1985; returned, September 3, 1985.
§Loaned to Aguascalientes of Mexican League, April 5, 1986; returned, September 1, 1986.
xReleased, November 10, 1986; signed by Pittsburgh Pirates' organization, December 4, 1986.
yDrafted by Milwaukee Brewers, December 9, 1986.

RAFAEL CORRALES PALMEIRO

Born September 24, 1964, at Havana, Cuba.
Height, 6.00. Weight, 180.
Throws and bats lefthanded.
Attended Mississippi State University, Mississippi State, Miss.

Major League stolen bases: 1986 (1).
Led Eastern League in total bases with 225, sacrifice flies with 13 and intentional bases on balls received with 13 in 1986.

Named outfielder on THE SPORTING NEWS College Baseball All-America Team, 1985.
Named Eastern League Most Valuable Player, 1986.

Year Club	League	Pos.	G.	AB.	R.	H.	2B.	3B.	HR.	RBI.	B.A.	PO.	A.	E.	F.A.
1985—Peoria	Midw.	OF	73	279	34	83	22	4	5	51	.297	113	7	1	.992
1986—Pittsfield	East.	OF	●140	509	66	*156	29	2	12	*95	.306	248	9	3	*.988
1986—Chicago	Nat.	OF	22	73	9	18	4	0	3	12	.247	34	2	4	.900
Major League Totals—1 Year			22	73	9	18	4	0	3	12	.247	34	2	4	.900

Selected by New York Mets' organization in 8th round of free-agent draft, June 7, 1982.
Selected by Chicago Cubs' organization in 1st round (22nd player selected) of free-agent draft, June 3, 1985.

DAVID WILLIAM PALMER JR.

Born October 19, 1957, at Glens Falls, N.Y.
Height, 6.01. Weight, 205.
Throws and bats righthanded.

Pitched five-inning, 4-0 perfect game against St. Louis Cardinals, April 21, 1984 (second game).
Major League saves: 1979 (2).
Tied for Pioneer League lead in home runs allowed with 6 in 1976.

Year Club	League	G.	IP.	W.	L.	Pct.	H.	R.	ER.	SO.	BB.	ERA.
1976—Lethbridge	Pioneer	13	45	0	5	.000	58	49	36	44	28	7.20
1977—West Palm Beach	Florida St.	25	119	6	8	.429	120	49	38	88	44	2.87
1978—West Palm Beach	Florida St.	7	51	4	2	.667	44	23	11	58	4	1.94
1978—Memphis	Southern	19	130	8	10	.444	107	57	44	78	44	3.05
1978—Montreal	National	5	10	0	1	.000	9	4	3	7	2	2.70
1979—Montreal	National	36	123	10	2	.833	110	41	36	72	30	2.63
1980—Montreal†	National	24	130	8	6	.571	124	53	43	73	30	2.98
1981—West Palm Beach‡	Florida St.	3	11	0	0	.000	9	1	1	7	5	0.82
1981—Memphis	Southern	1	0	0	0	.000	0	1	1	0	1	0.00
1982—Memphis	Southern	9	51⅓	3	2	.600	38	21	20	44	33	3.51
1982—Montreal §	National	13	73⅔	6	4	.600	60	34	26	46	36	3.18
1983—West Palm Beach x	Florida St.						(Did not play)					
1984—Montreal y	National	20	105⅓	7	3	.700	101	45	45	66	44	3.84
1985—Montreal za	National	24	135⅔	7	10	.412	128	60	56	106	67	3.71
1986—Atlanta b	National	35	209⅔	11	10	.524	181	98	85	170	102	3.65
Major League Totals—7 Years		157	787⅓	49	36	.576	713	335	294	540	311	3.36

Selected by Montreal Expos' organization in 21st round of free-agent draft, June 8, 1976.
†On disabled list, July 21 to August 27, 1980.
‡On Montreal disabled list, March 25 to August 9, 1981; included rehabilitation disability assignment to West Palm Beach, May 6 to May 25, 1981.
§On disabled list, August 14 to September 27, 1982.
xOn Montreal disabled list, March 28 to September 20, 1983; included rehabilitation disability assignment to West Palm Beach, August 6 to August 26, 1983.
yOn disabled list, August 5 to September 1, 1984.
zOn disabled list, August 9 to September 1, 1985.
aGranted free agency, November 12, 1985; signed by Atlanta Braves' organizaton, February 13, 1986.
bGranted free agency, November 12, 1986; re-signed by Braves, December 19, 1986.

JAMES FRANKLIN PANKOVITS
(Jim)

Born August 6, 1955, at Pennington Gap, Va.
Height, 5.10. Weight, 175.
Throws and bats righthanded.
Attended University of South Carolina, Columbia, S.C.

Major League stolen bases: 1984 (2), 1985 (1), 1986 (1). Total—4.
Led Appalachian League second basemen in assists with 212 and double plays with 47 in 1976.
Named third baseman on THE SPORTING NEWS College Baseball All-America Team, 1976.

Year Club	League	Pos.	G.	AB.	R.	H.	2B.	3B.	HR.	RBI.	B.A.	PO.	A.	E.	F.A.
1976—Covington	Appal.	2B	●70	275	50	68	9	2	5	31	.247	165	212	18	.954
1977—Cocoa†	Fla. St.	SS-3B	91	326	27	74	9	3	2	20	.227	2	3	0	1.000
1978—Columbus	South.	SS	137	509	67	122	19	7	10	43	.240	4	8	2	.857
1978—Charleston	Int.	2B	3	7	0	1	0	0	0	0	.143	5	3	0	1.000
1979—Columbus	South.	SS	92	346	53	91	10	3	10	45	.263	0	13	0	1.000
1979—Charleston	Int.	2B	22	59	7	10	3	1	0	3	.169	43	53	4	.960
1980—Tucson	P. C.	2B-3B-SS	64	213	36	53	8	4	2	26	.249	110	128	9	.964
1981—Tucson	P. C.	O-3-2-S	122	450	83	127	34	9	7	64	.282	93	75	22	.884
1982—Hawaii‡§	P. C.	3B-2B-OF	139	494	84	132	25	7	15	77	.267	192	162	22	.941
1983—Tucson	P. C.	2B	126	450	77	129	25	6	11	62	.287	215	322	25	.956
1984—Tucson	P. C.	2B	49	187	41	62	12	3	7	39	.332	103	176	8	.972
1984—Houston	Nat.	2B-SS-OF	53	81	6	23	7	0	1	14	.284	22	22	3	.936
1985—Houston x	Nat.	O-2-S-3	75	172	24	42	3	0	4	14	.244	81	38	2	.983
1986—Houston	Nat.	2B-OF-C	70	113	12	32	6	1	1	7	.283	42	58	4	.962
Major League Totals—3 Years			198	366	42	97	16	1	6	35	.265	145	118	9	.967

Selected by Houston Astros' organization in 4th round of free-agent draft, June 8, 1976.
†On disabled list, May 22 to June 24, 1977.
‡Loaned to Hawaii (San Diego Padres' organization), March 28, 1982; returned, September 17, 1982.
§Granted free agency, October 22, 1982; re-signed by Astros' organization, January 23, 1983.
xOn disabled list, July 3 to July 18 and July 26 to August 22, 1985.

Year	Club	League	Pos.	G.	AB.	R.	H.	2B.	3B.	HR.	RBI.	B.A.	PO.	A.	E.	F.A.
1986—Houston		Nat.	PH	2	2	0	0	0	0	0	0	.000	0	0	0	.000

ALBERTO JUDAS PARDO
(Al)

Born September 8, 1962, at Oviedo, Spain.
Height, 6.02. Weight, 195.
Throws right and bats left and righthanded.
Brother of Braulio Pardo, minor league catcher, 1980.

Led Southern League in game-winning RBIs with 17 in 1984.

Year	Club	League	Pos.	G.	AB.	R.	H.	2B.	3B.	HR.	RBI.	B.A.	PO.	A.	E.	F.A.
1980—Bluefield	Appal.	C-1B	48	151	26	52	6	2	3	23	.344	66	8	0	1.000	
1981—Miami	Fla. St.	C	91	291	25	63	9	3	3	32	.216	396	41	6	.987	
1981—Hagerstown	Carol.	C	21	76	11	24	3	1	1	7	.316	37	7	2	.957	
1982—Hagerstown	Carol.	C-1B-OF	130	492	76	142	24	4	17	86	.289	685	74	11	.986	
1983—Rochester	Int.	C	69	220	25	56	11	2	1	31	.255	223	18	9	.964	
1983—Charlotte	South.	C	37	141	20	44	11	3	4	19	.312	129	18	4	.974	
1984—Charlotte	South.	C-OF-1B	138	483	72	128	23	2	13	81	.265	397	32	14	.968	
1985—Rochester	Int.	C	60	194	23	49	14	1	8	35	.253	258	19	6	.979	
1985—Baltimore	Amer.	C	34	75	3	10	1	0	0	1	.133	131	7	3	.979	
1986—Rochester	Int.	C	76	253	34	54	12	1	8	34	.213	321	27	3	.991	
1986—Baltimore†	Amer.	C	16	51	3	7	1	0	1	3	.137	70	5	1	.987	
Major League Totals—2 Years			50	126	6	17	2	0	1	4	.135	201	12	4	.982	

Selected by Baltimore Orioles' organization in 2nd round of free-agent draft, June 3, 1980.
†Granted free agency, October 15, 1986; signed by Atlanta Braves' organization, November 17, 1986.

MARK ALAN PARENT

Born September 16, 1961, at Ashland, Ore.
Height, 6.05. Weight, 215.
Throws and bats righthanded.

Led Carolina League catchers in double plays with 16 in 1981.
Led Northwest League catchers in fielding percentage with .979 in 1980.

Year	Club	League	Pos.	G.	AB.	R.	H.	2B.	3B.	HR.	RBI.	B.A.	PO.	A.	E.	F.A.
1979—Walla Walla	N'west	C-OF	40	126	8	24	4	0	1	11	.190	229	34	6	.978	
1980—Reno	Calif.	C	30	99	8	20	3	0	0	12	.202	128	23	2	.987	
1980—Grays Harbor	N'west	C-1B	66	230	29	55	11	2	7	32	.230	381	38	9	.979	
1981—Salem	Carol.	C	123	438	44	103	16	3	6	47	.235	★694	87	★28	.965	
1982—Amarillo	Texas	C	26	89	12	17	3	1	1	13	.191	100	6	2	.981	
1982—Salem	Carol.	C-1B	99	360	39	81	15	2	6	41	.225	475	64	12	.978	
1983—Beaumont†	Texas	C	81	282	38	71	22	1	7	33	.252	464	71	10	★.982	
1984—Beaumont‡	Texas	C-1B	111	380	52	109	24	3	7	60	.287	674	68	7	.991	
1985—Las Vegas	P. C.	C-1B	105	361	36	87	23	3	7	45	.241	586	54	6	.991	
1986—Las Vegas	P. C.	C-1B	86	267	29	77	10	4	5	40	.288	344	40	5	.987	
1986—San Diego	Nat.	C	8	14	1	2	0	0	0	0	.143	16	0	2	.889	
Major League Totals—1 Year			8	14	1	2	0	0	0	0	.143	16	0	2	.889	

Selected by San Diego Padres' organization in 4th round of free-agent draft, June 5, 1979.
†On suspended list, August 27, 1983 through remainder of season.
‡On disabled list, September 4, 1984 through remainder of season.

KELLY JAY PARIS

Born October 17, 1957, at Encino, Calif.
Height, 6.00. Weight, 175.
Throws and bats righthanded.
Brother of Brett Paris, infielder in San Francisco Giants' and
St. Louis Cardinals' organizations, 1975 and 1976.

Led Appalachian League in sacrifice flies with 7 in 1977.
Led Florida State League third basemen in double plays with 24 and tied for lead in errors with 29 in 1979.

Year	Club	League	Pos.	G.	AB.	R.	H.	2B.	3B.	HR.	RBI.	B.A.	PO.	A.	E.	F.A.
1975—Sarasota Cards	Gulf C.	SS	34	123	14	29	2	0	2	13	.236	59	92	14	.915	
1976—Johnson City†	Appal.	1B	●70	247	40	68	7	3	5	30	.275	621	43	7	.990	
1977—St. Petersburg‡	Fla. St.	1B-3B	44	124	14	22	3	0	0	9	.177	269	22	3	.990	
1977—Johnson City‡	Appal.	1B-3B	51	169	32	53	8	1	2	28	.314	355	37	5	.987	
1978—St. Petersburg	Fla. St.	1B	42	155	14	32	6	0	1	12	.206	319	23	5	.986	
1978—Gastonia	W. Car.	1B-3B	79	297	48	75	9	3	2	20	.253	593	49	12	.982	
1979—St. Petersburg	Fla. St.	3B-1B	118	388	52	110	15	3	2	53	.284	291	229	30	.945	
1980—Arkansas	Texas	SS	116	399	63	120	28	3	4	49	.301	181	349	38	.933	
1981—Springfield§	A. A.	SS-3B	90	292	38	78	10	1	6	31	.267	119	237	36	.908	
1982—Louisville	A. A.	SS-3B-1B	129	482	71	158	32	5	11	83	.328	208	364	29	.952	
1982—St. Louis x	Nat.	3B-2B	12	29	1	3	0	0	0	1	.103	9	25	4	.895	
1983—Cincinnati	Nat.	3-2-S-1	56	120	13	30	6	0	0	7	.250	60	62	6	.953	
1983—Indianapolis yz	A. A.	SS-2B-3B	8	35	9	11	1	0	2	9	.314	10	26	0	1.000	
1984—Hawaii a	P. C.	SS-2B	127	460	65	115	26	3	10	58	.250	203	313	32	.942	
1985—Rochester	Int.	S-2-3-O	126	440	69	121	25	2	18	67	.275	169	376	34	.941	
1985—Baltimore	Amer.	2B	5	9	0	0	0	0	0	0	.000	3	3	1	.857	

Year Club League	Pos.	G.	AB.	R.	H.	2B.	3B.	HR.	RBI.	B.A.	PO.	A.	E.	F.A.
1986—Rochester b .... Int.	3B-SS-2B	87	309	43	77	16	2	11	48	.249	92	204	16	.949
1986—Baltimore c .... Amer.	3B	5	10	0	2	0	0	0	0	.200	0	6	1	.857
National League Totals—2 Years		68	149	14	33	6	0	0	8	.221	69	87	10	.940
American League Totals—2 Years		10	19	0	2	0	0	0	0	.105	3	9	2	.857
Major League Totals—4 Years		78	168	14	35	6	0	0	8	.208	72	96	12	.933

Selected by St. Louis Cardinals' organization in 2nd round of free-agent draft, June 4, 1975.
†On temporarily inactive list, April 16 to May 7, 1976.
‡Switch-hitter.
§On disabled list, July 25, 1981 through remainder of season.
xTraded to Cincinnati Reds' organization for Pitcher James Strichek, March 31, 1983.
ySold to Chicago White Sox, November 28, 1983.
zReleased, March 21, 1984; signed by Pittsburgh Pirates' organization, March 28, 1984.
aGranted free agency, October 15, 1984; signed by Rochester (Baltimore Orioles' organization), November 12, 1984.
bOn disabled list, April 16 to May 14, 1986.
cGranted free agency, October 15, 1986.

DAVID GENE PARKER
(Dave)

Born June 9, 1951, at Jackson, Miss.
Height, 6.05. Weight, 230.
Throws right and bats lefthanded.

Tied major league record for most home runs, month of October (4), 1985; fewest errors by outfielder, season, for leader in errors (9), 1986.
Major League stolen bases: 1973 (1), 1974 (3), 1975 (8), 1976 (19), 1977 (17), 1978 (20), 1979 (20), 1980 (10), 1981 (6), 1982 (7), 1983 (12), 1984 (11), 1985 (5), 1986 (1). Total—140.
Led National League in grounding into double plays with 26 in 1985.
Led National League in total bases with 340 in 1978, 350 in 1985 and 304 in 1986.
Led National League in slugging percentage with .541 in 1975 and .585 in 1978.
Led National League in intentional bases on balls received with 23 in 1978 and tied for lead with 24 in 1985.
Tied for National League lead in sacrifice flies with 9 in 1979.
Led National League outfielders in total chances with 430 and double plays with 9 in 1977.
Led Carolina League in total bases with 270 and stolen bases with 38 in 1972.
Tied for Gulf Coast League lead in total bases with 107 in 1970.
Named National League Player of the Year by THE SPORTING NEWS, 1978.
Named National League Most Valuable Player by Baseball Writers' Association of America, 1978.
Named outfielder on THE SPORTING NEWS National League All-Star Team, 1975, 1977, 1978, 1985 and 1986.
Named outfielder on THE SPORTING NEWS National League All-Star fielding team, 1977 through 1979.
Named outfielder on THE SPORTING NEWS National League Silver Slugger team, 1985 and 1986.
Named Carolina League Most Valuable Player, 1972.

Year Club League	Pos.	G.	AB.	R.	H.	2B.	3B.	HR.	RBI.	B.A.	PO.	A.	E.	F.A.
1970—Bradenton Pir. ...... Gulf C.	●OF-P	61	239	34	75	8	3	●6	41	.314	92	11	●8	.928
1971—Waterbury .... East.	OF	30	114	10	26	4	1	0	7	.228	43	5	6	.889
1971—Monroe .... W. Car.	OF	71	268	49	96	16	4	11	48	.358	104	8	10	.918
1972—Salem .... Carol.	OF	135	*523	*91	*162	*30	6	22	*101	*.310	*250	*20	*20	.931
1973—Charleston .... Int.	OF	84	309	44	98	20	7	9	57	.317	144	11	7	.957
1973—Pittsburgh .... Nat.	OF	54	139	17	40	9	1	4	14	.288	77	3	3	.964
1974—Pittsburgh† .... Nat.	OF-1B	73	220	27	62	10	3	4	29	.282	154	8	4	.976
1975—Pittsburgh .... Nat.	OF	148	558	75	172	35	10	25	101	.308	311	7	9	.972
1976—Pittsburgh .... Nat.	OF	138	537	82	168	28	10	13	90	.313	294	13	*14	.956
1977—Pittsburgh‡ .... Nat.	*OF-2B	159	637	107	*215	*44	8	21	88	*.338	*389	*26	*15	.965
1978—Pittsburgh .... Nat.	OF	148	581	102	194	32	12	30	117	*.334	302	12	*13	.960
1979—Pittsburgh .... Nat.	OF	158	622	109	193	45	7	25	94	.310	341	15	*15	.960
1980—Pittsburgh§ .... Nat.	OF	139	518	71	153	31	1	17	79	.295	235	14	9	.965
1981—Pittsburgh§ .... Nat.	OF	67	240	29	62	14	3	9	48	.258	110	1	7	.941
1982—Pittsburgh x .... Nat.	OF	73	244	41	66	19	3	6	29	.270	108	2	5	.957
1983—Pittsburgh y .... Nat.	OF	144	552	68	154	29	4	12	69	.279	282	3	8	.973
1984—Cincinnati .... Nat.	OF	156	607	73	173	28	0	16	94	.285	296	6	8	.974
1985—Cincinnati .... Nat.	OF	160	635	88	198	*42	4	34	*125	.312	329	12	10	.972
1986—Cincinnati .... Nat.	OF	*162	637	89	174	31	3	31	116	.273	278	9	●9	.970
Major League Totals—14 Years		1779	6727	978	2024	397	69	247	1093	.301	3506	130	129	.966

Selected by Pittsburgh Pirates' organization in 14th round of free-agent draft, June 4, 1970.
†On disabled list, June 7 to June 28 and July 5 to July 31, 1974.
‡On disabled list, July 1 to July 16, 1978.
§On disabled list, May 14 to May 29, 1981.
xOn disabled list, May 12 to June 7 and July 29 to September 7, 1982.
yGranted free agency, November 7, 1983; signed by Cincinnati Reds, December 7, 1983.

CHAMPIONSHIP SERIES RECORD

Year Club League	Pos.	G.	AB.	R.	H.	2B.	3B.	HR.	RBI.	B.A.	PO.	A.	E.	F.A.
1974—Pittsburgh.............. Nat.	OF-PH	3	8	0	1	0	0	0	0	.125	4	1	0	1.000
1975—Pittsburgh.............. Nat.	OF	3	10	2	0	0	0	0	0	.000	13	1	0	1.000
1979—Pittsburgh.............. Nat.	OF	3	12	2	4	0	0	0	2	.333	9	0	0	1.000
Championship Series Totals—3 Years....		9	30	4	5	0	0	0	2	.167	26	2	0	1.000

WORLD SERIES RECORD

Year Club League	Pos.	G.	AB.	R.	H.	2B.	3B.	HR.	RBI.	B.A.	PO.	A.	E.	F.A.
1979—Pittsburgh.............. Nat.	OF	7	29	2	10	3	0	0	4	.345	13	1	1	.933

ALL-STAR GAME RECORD

Established All-Star Game record for most assists by outfielder, game (2), July 17, 1979.

Year	League	Pos.	AB.	R.	H.	2B.	3B.	HR.	RBI.	B.A.	PO.	A.	E.	F.A.
1977—National		OF	3	1	1	0	0	0	0	.333	2	0	0	1.000
1979—National		OF	3	0	1	0	0	0	1	.333	0	2	0	1.000
1980—National		OF	2	0	0	0	0	0	0	.000	0	0	0	.000
1981—National		OF	3	1	1	0	0	1	1	.333	1	0	0	1.000
1985—National		OF	2	0	0	0	0	0	0	.000	1	0	0	1.000
1986—National		OF	2	0	1	0	0	0	0	.500	0	0	0	.000
All-Star Game Totals—6 Years			15	2	4	0	0	1	2	.267	4	2	0	1.000

PITCHING RECORD

Year	Club	League	G.	IP.	W.	L.	Pct.	H.	R.	ER.	SO.	BB.	ERA.
1970—Bradenton Pirates		Gulf Coast	1	4	0	0	.000	7	2	2	2	1	4.50

JEFFREY DALE PARRETT
(Jeff)

Born August 26, 1961, at Indianapolis, Ind.
Height, 6.04. Weight, 185.
Throws and bats righthanded.
Attended University of Kentucky, Lexington, Ky.

Year	Club	League	G.	IP.	W.	L.	Pct.	H.	R.	ER.	SO.	BB.	ERA.
1983—Paintsville		Ap'lachian	3	17	2	0	1.000	12	6	4	21	8	2.12
1983—Beloit		Midwest	10	47	2	2	.500	40	26	21	34	29	4.02
1984—Beloit		Midwest	29	91⅔	4	3	.571	76	50	46	95	71	4.52
1985—Stockton†		California	45	127⅔	7	4	.636	97	50	39	120	75	★2.75
1986—Montreal		National	12	20⅓	0	1	.000	19	11	11	21	13	4.87
1986—Indianapolis		Am. Assoc.	25	69	2	5	.286	54	44	38	76	35	4.96
Major League Totals—1 Year			12	20⅓	0	1	.000	19	11	11	21	13	4.87

Selected by Milwaukee Brewers' organization in 9th round of free-agent draft, June 6, 1983.
†Drafted by Montreal Expos, December 10, 1985.

LANCE MICHAEL PARRISH

Born June 15, 1956, at McKeesport, Pa.
Height, 6.03. Weight, 220.
Throws and bats righthanded.

Major League stolen bases: 1979 (6), 1980 (6), 1981 (2), 1982 (3), 1983 (1), 1984 (2), 1985 (2). Total—22.
Led American League in sacrifice flies with 13 in 1983.
Led American League catchers in double plays with 11 in 1984.
Led American League catchers in total chances with 772 in 1983.
Led American League in passed balls with 21 in 1979.
Tied for American League lead in passed balls with 17 in 1980.
Led Appalachian League batters in strikeouts with 92 in 1974.
Led American Association in double plays with 10 and passed balls with 21 in 1977.
Led Southern League in passed balls with 22 in 1976.
Led Florida State League catchers in double plays with 8 and passed balls with 31 in 1975.
Named catcher on THE SPORTING NEWS American League All-Star Team, 1982 and 1984.
Named catcher on THE SPORTING NEWS American League All-Star fielding team, 1983 through 1985.
Named catcher on THE SPORTING NEWS American League Silver Slugger team, 1980, 1982 through 1984 and 1986.

Year	Club	League	Pos.	G.	AB.	R.	H.	2B.	3B.	HR.	RBI.	B.A.	PO.	A.	E.	F.A.
1974—Bristol		Appal.	3B-OF	68	253	45	54	11	1	11	46	.213	36	83	22	.844
1975—Lakeland		Fla. St.	C	100	341	30	75	15	2	5	37	.220	460	50	7	.986
1976—Montgomery		South.	C	107	340	46	75	9	2	14	55	.221	484	71	11	.984
1977—Evansville		A. A.	C	115	416	74	116	21	2	25	90	.279	★722	★82	11	★.987
1977—Detroit		Amer.	C	12	46	10	9	2	0	3	7	.196	76	6	0	1.000
1978—Detroit		Amer.	C	85	288	37	63	11	3	14	41	.219	353	39	5	.987
1979—Detroit		Amer.	C	143	493	65	136	26	3	19	65	.276	707	★79	9	.989
1980—Detroit		Amer.	C-1B-OF	144	553	79	158	34	6	24	82	.286	607	67	7	.990
1981—Detroit		Amer.	C	96	348	39	85	18	2	10	46	.244	407	40	3	.993
1982—Detroit		Amer.	C-OF	133	486	75	138	19	2	32	87	.284	627	76	8	.989
1983—Detroit		Amer.	C	155	605	80	163	42	3	27	114	.269	695	73	4	.995
1984—Detroit		Amer.	C	147	578	75	137	16	2	33	98	.237	720	67	7	.991
1985—Detroit		Amer.	C	140	549	64	150	27	1	28	98	.273	695	53	5	.993
1986—Detroit†‡		Amer.	C	91	327	53	84	6	1	22	62	.257	483	48	6	.989
Major League Totals—10 Years				1146	4273	577	1123	201	23	212	700	.263	5370	548	54	.991

Selected by Detroit Tigers' organization in 1st round (16th player selected) of free-agent draft, June 5, 1974.
†On disabled list, July 31 to September 29, 1986.
‡Granted free agency, November 12, 1986.

CHAMPIONSHIP SERIES RECORD

Year	Club	League	Pos.	G.	AB.	R.	H.	2B.	3B.	HR.	RBI.	B.A.	PO.	A.	E.	F.A.
1984—Detroit		Amer.	C	3	12	1	3	1	0	1	3	.250	21	2	0	1.000

WORLD SERIES RECORD

Year	Club	League	Pos.	G.	AB.	R.	H.	2B.	3B.	HR.	RBI.	B.A.	PO.	A.	E.	F.A.
1984—Detroit		Amer.	C	5	18	3	5	1	0	1	2	.278	30	3	1	.971

Established All-Star Game record for most assists by catcher, game (3), July 13, 1982.

Year League	Pos.	AB.	R.	H.	2B.	3B.	HR.	RBI.	B.A.	PO.	A.	E.	F.A.
1980—American	C	1	0	0	0	0	0	0	.000	0	0	0	.000
1982—American	C	2	0	1	1	0	0	0	.500	2	3	0	1.000
1983—American	C	2	0	0	0	0	0	0	.000	1	0	0	1.000
1984—American	C	2	0	0	0	0	0	0	.000	3	1	1	.800
1986—American	C	3	0	0	0	0	0	0	.000	4	0	0	1.000
All-Star Game Totals—5 Years		10	0	1	1	0	0	0	.100	10	4	1	.933

Named to American League All-Star Team for 1985 game; replaced due to injury by Rich Gedman.

LARRY ALTON PARRISH

Born November 10, 1953, at Winter Haven, Fla.
Height, 6.03. Weight, 215.
Throws and bats righthanded.
Attended Seminole Community College, Sanford, Fla.

Tied major league records for most home runs, bases filled, month (3), July, 1982; most home runs, bases filled, week (3), July 4 through 10 (first game), 1982.
Major League stolen bases' 1975 (4), 1976 (2), 1977 (2), 1978 (2), 1979 (5), 1980 (2), 1982 (5), 1984 (2), 1986 (3). Total—27.
Hit three home runs in a game, May 29, 1977, July 30, 1978, April 25, 1980 and April 29, 1985.
Tied for National League lead in double plays by third basemen with 35 in 1976.
Led Florida State League in sacrifice flies with 9 in 1973.
Led Eastern League third basemen in double plays with 32 in 1974.
Led Florida State League third basemen in putouts with 95 and assists with 285 in 1973.
Named Florida State League Most Valuable Player, 1973.

Year—Club	League	Pos.	G.	AB.	R.	H.	2B.	3B.	HR.	RBI.	B.A.	PO.	A.	E.	F.A.
1972—W. Palm B'ch	Fla. St.	OF	2	4	0	1	0	0	0	0	.250	2	0	0	1.000
1972—Jamestown	NYP	OF	62	223	32	58	4	3	4	28	.260	69	3	3	.960
1973—W. Palm B'ch	Fla. St.	*3B-SS	138	481	82	141	14	6	16	33	.293	100	292	32	*.925
1974—Quebec City	East.	3B	119	437	61	124	14	2	13	77	.284	*108	*277	●31	.925
1974—Montreal	Nat.	3B	25	69	9	14	5	0	0	4	.203	20	51	1	.986
1975—Montreal	Nat.	3B-SS-2B	145	532	50	146	32	5	10	65	.274	105	291	35	.919
1976—Montreal	Nat.	3B	154	543	65	126	28	5	11	61	.232	122	310	25	.945
1977—Montreal	Nat.	3B	123	402	50	99	19	2	11	46	.246	81	225	21	.936
1978—Montreal	Nat.	3B	144	520	68	144	39	4	15	70	.277	122	288	23	.947
1979—Montreal	Nat.	3B	153	544	83	167	39	2	30	82	.307	119	290	23	.947
1980—Montreal†	Nat.	3B	126	452	55	115	27	3	15	72	.254	106	231	18	.949
1981—Montreal‡	Nat.	3B	97	349	41	85	19	3	8	44	.244	*91	141	16	.935
1982—Texas	Amer.	OF-3B	128	440	59	116	15	0	17	62	.264	190	12	8	.962
1983—Texas	Amer.	OF	145	555	76	151	26	4	26	88	.272	215	11	9	.962
1984—Texas	Amer.	OF-3B	156	613	72	175	42	1	22	101	.285	155	35	4	.979
1985—Texas§	Amer.	OF-3B	94	346	44	86	11	1	17	51	.249	111	7	1	.992
1986—Texas x	Amer.	3B	129	464	67	128	22	1	28	94	.276	23	35	4	.935
National League Totals—8 Years			967	3411	421	896	207	24	100	444	.263	866	1827	162	.943
American League Totals—5 Years			652	2418	318	656	117	7	110	396	.271	694	100	26	.968
Major League Totals—13 Years			1619	5829	739	1552	324	31	210	840	.266	1560	1927	188	.949

Signed as free agent by Montreal Expos' organization, May 21, 1972.
†On disabled list, June 2 to June 30, 1980.
‡Traded with First Baseman Dave Hostetler to Texas Rangers for First Baseman-Outfielder Al Oliver, March 31, 1982.
§On disabled list, July 6 to September 1, 1985.
xOn disabled list, May 20 to June 18, 1986.

DIVISION SERIES RECORD

Year Club	League	Pos.	G.	AB.	R.	H.	2B.	3B.	HR.	RBI.	B.A.	PO.	A.	E.	F.A.
1981—Montreal	Nat.	3B	5	20	3	3	1	0	0	1	.150	7	6	0	1.000

CHAMPIONSHIP SERIES RECORD

Year Club	League	Pos.	G.	AB.	R.	H.	2B.	3B.	HR.	RBI.	B.A.	PO.	A.	E.	F.A.
1981—Montreal	Nat.	3B	5	19	2	5	2	0	0	2	.263	3	13	1	.941

ALL-STAR GAME RECORD

Year League	Pos.	AB.	R.	H.	2B.	3B.	HR.	RBI.	B.A.	PO.	A.	E.	F.A.
1979—National	3B	0	0	0	0	0	0	0	.000	0	0	0	.000

SCOTT DONALD PARSONS

Born January 25, 1962, at Livingston, N. J.
Height, 6.05. Weight, 190.
Throws and bats righthanded.
Attended County College of Morris, Randolph Township, N. J.

Year Club	League	Pos.	G.	AB.	R.	H.	2B.	3B.	HR.	RBI.	B.A.	PO.	A.	E.	F.A.
1982—Salem	Carol.	P	26	24	2	4	0	0	0	3	.167	13	18	4	.886
1983—Reno	Calif.	P	29	3	0	0	0	0	0	0	.000	10	27	2	.949
1984—Miami	Fla. St.	P	31	36	2	12	2	1	0	5	.333	8	23	3	.912
1985—Charleston	S. Atl.	OF-1B-P	93	301	30	92	17	0	4	40	.306	146	16	6	.964
1986—Reno	Calif.	OF	60	217	48	87	14	2	13	63	.401	79	3	2	.976
1986—Beaumont	Texas	OF-1B	54	206	32	72	15	0	5	42	.350	229	8	5	.979

Selected by Oakland A's organization in 10th round of free-agent draft, June 3, 1980.
Selected by San Diego Padres' organization in secondary phase of free-agent draft, January 12, 1982.

PITCHING RECORD

Tied for Florida State League in shutouts with 5 in 1984.

Year Club	League	G.	IP.	W.	L.	Pct.	H.	R.	ER.	SO.	BB.	ERA.
1982—Salem	Carolina	19	111	4	10	.286	116	76	60	85	37	4.86
1983—Reno	California	28	187⅓	9	14	.391	★241	★130	★107	118	68	5.14
1984—Miami	Florida St.	29	134	10	9	.526	125	69	53	66	55	3.56
1985—Charleston	S. Atlantic	7	21⅔	1	1	.500	24	17	12	20	10	4.98

DANIEL ANTHONY PASQUA

Name Pronounced PASS-quah.

(Dan)

Born October 17, 1961, at Harrington Park, N.J.
Height, 6.00. Weight, 205.
Throws and bats lefthanded.
Attended William Paterson College, Wayne, N.J.

Major League stolen bases: 1986 (2).
Led International League in slugging percentage with .599 in 1985.
Led Southern League batters in strikeouts with 148 in 1984.
Named International League Player of the Year, 1985.
Named Appalachian League Player of the Year, 1982.

Year Club	League	Pos.	G.	AB.	R.	H.	2B.	3B.	HR.	RBI.	B.A.	PO.	A.	E.	F.A.
1982—Paintsville	Appal.	OF	60	239	43	72	10	2	★16	●63	.301	114	4	4	.967
1982—Oneonta	NYP	OF	4	17	3	5	1	0	2	4	.294	2	1	1	.750
1983—Fort Lauderdale	Fla. St.	OF	131	451	83	123	25	10	19	84	.273	213	8	5	.978
1983—Columbus	Int.	OF	1	3	0	0	0	0	0	0	.000	5	0	0	1.000
1984—Nashville	South.	OF	136	460	78	112	14	3	★33	91	.243	244	11	★12	.955
1985—Columbus	Int.	OF	78	287	52	92	16	5	18	69	.321	141	9	4	.974
1985—New York	Amer.	OF	60	148	17	31	3	1	9	25	.209	72	2	0	1.000
1986—Columbus	Int.	OF	32	110	25	32	3	3	6	20	.291	62	0	3	.954
1986—New York	Amer.	OF-1B	102	280	44	82	17	0	16	45	.293	172	4	2	.989
Major League Totals—2 Years			162	428	61	113	20	1	25	70	.264	244	6	2	.992

Selected by New York Yankees' organization in 3rd round of free-agent draft, June 7, 1982.

FRANK ENRICO PASTORE

Name pronounced Pass-TORR-ee.

Born August 21, 1957, at Alhambra, Calif.
Height, 6.03. Weight, 215.
Throws and bats righthanded.
Attended Cal Poly Pomona State University, Pomona, Calif.; and Stanford University, Palo Alto, Calif.

Major League saves: 1979 (4), 1986 (2). Total—6.

Year Club	League	G.	IP.	W.	L.	Pct.	H.	R.	ER.	SO.	BB.	ERA.
1975—Billings	Pioneer	15	88	5	●7	.417	89	47	25	69	27	2.56
1976—Tampa	Florida St.	21	107	5	7	.417	101	50	37	54	34	3.11
1977—Tampa	Florida St.	14	95	4	5	.444	78	31	24	36	22	2.27
1977—Three Rivers	Eastern	15	94	6	6	.500	98	43	38	51	32	3.64
1978—Indianapolis	Am. Assoc.	4	12	0	2	.000	24	15	9	8	5	6.75
1978—Nashville†	Southern	22	129	6	8	.429	106	58	50	120	46	3.49
1979—Cincinnati	National	30	95	6	7	.462	102	47	45	63	23	4.26
1979—Indianapolis	Am. Assoc.	10	68	7	2	.778	51	21	21	69	17	2.78
1980—Cincinnati‡	National	27	185	13	7	.650	161	72	67	110	42	3.26
1981—Cincinnati	National	22	132	4	9	.308	125	73	59	81	35	4.02
1982—Cincinnati§	National	31	188⅓	8	13	.381	210	86	83	94	57	3.97
1983—Cincinnati	National	36	184⅓	9	12	.429	207	104	100	93	64	4.88
1984—Cincinnati x	National	24	98⅓	3	8	.273	110	74	71	53	40	6.50
1984—Wichita	Am. Assoc.	2	13	0	1	.000	6	4	4	12	8	2.77
1985—Cincinnati yz	National	17	54	2	1	.667	60	23	23	29	16	3.83
1986—Minnesota ab	American	33	49⅓	3	1	.750	54	28	22	18	24	4.01
National League Totals—7 Years		187	937	45	57	.441	975	479	448	523	277	4.30
American League Totals—1 Year		33	49⅓	3	1	.750	54	28	22	18	24	4.01
Major League Totals—8 Years		220	986⅓	48	58	.453	1029	507	470	541	301	4.29

Selected by Cincinnati Reds' organization in 2nd round of free-agent draft, June 4, 1975.
†On disabled list, August 24 to August 31, 1978.
‡On disabled list, July 27 to August 22, 1980.
§On disabled list, June 24 to July 19, 1982.
xOn disabled list, July 9 to July 31, 1984; included rehabilitation disability assignment to Wichita, July 19 to July 31, 1984.
yOn disabled list, July 20, 1985 through remainder of season.
zReleased, April 4, 1986; signed by Minnesota Twins, April 28, 1986.
aOn disabled list, August 11 to September 1, 1986.
bGranted free agency, November 12, 1986.

CHAMPIONSHIP SERIES RECORD

Year Club	League	G.	IP.	W.	L.	Pct.	H.	R.	ER.	SO.	BB.	ERA.
1979—Cincinnati	National	1	7	0	0	.000	7	2	2	1	3	2.57

ROBERT CHANDLER PATTERSON
(Bob)

Born May 16, 1959, at Jacksonville, Fla.
Height, 6.02. Weight, 185.
Throws left and bats righthanded.
Received degree from East Carolina University, Greenville, N.C.

Year Club	League	G.	IP.	W.	L.	Pct.	H.	R.	ER.	SO.	BB.	ERA.
1982—Sarasota Padres	Gulf Coast	8	52	4	3	.571	60	18	17	65	7	2.94
1982—Reno	California	4	25⅓	1	0	1.000	28	11	10	10	5	3.55
1983—Beaumont	Texas	43	116⅔	8	4	.667	107	61	52	97	36	4.01
1984—Las Vegas	P. Coast	*60	143⅓	8	9	.471	129	63	52	97	37	3.27
1985—Las Vegas	P. Coast	42	186⅓	10	11	.476	187	80	65	146	52	3.14
1985—San Diego†	National	3	4	0	0	.000	13	11	11	1	3	24.75
1986—Hawaii	P. Coast	25	156	9	6	.600	146	68	59	*137	44	3.40
1986—Pittsburgh	National	11	36⅓	2	3	.400	49	20	20	20	5	4.95
Major League Totals—2 Years		14	40⅓	2	3	.400	62	31	31	21	8	6.92

Selected by San Diego Padres' organization in 21st round of free-agent draft, June 7, 1982.
†Traded to Pittsburgh Pirates for Outfielder Marvell Wynne, April 3, 1986.

WILLIAM JOSEPH PECOTA
(Bill)

Born February 16, 1960, at Redwood City, Calif.
Height, 6.02. Weight, 195.
Throws and bats righthanded.
Attended De Anza College, Cupertino, Calif.

Led American Association third basemen in assists with 217 and total chances with 337 in 1986.
Led American Association third basemen in total chances with 372 and double plays with 22 in 1985.
Led Southern League third basemen in total chances with 434 in 1984.

Year Club	League	Pos.	G.	AB.	R.	H.	2B.	3B.	HR.	RBI.	B.A.	PO.	A.	E.	F.A.
1981—Sara.Roy.-Blue	Gulf C.	C-3B-2B	61	208	*61	66	11	4	3	22	.317	112	45	6	.963
1982—Fort Myers	Fla. St.	3B	135	482	71	115	16	6	4	49	.239	109	243	15	.959
1983—Fort Myers	Fla. St.	3B	65	234	48	63	7	2	5	33	.269	46	114	7	.958
1983—Jacksonville	South.	3B-SS	72	260	38	63	9	1	5	25	.242	54	135	19	.909
1984—Memphis	South.	3B	145	543	84	131	19	2	9	50	.241	*142	267	25	*.942
1985—Omaha	A. A.	*3-S-O	130	409	47	98	17	3	1	34	.240	*111	*247	14	*.962
1986—Omaha	A. A.	3B-SS-OF	139	474	48	125	26	2	4	54	.264	125	238	11	.971
1986—Kansas City	Amer.	3B-SS	12	29	3	6	2	0	0	2	.207	7	31	1	.974
Major League Totals—1 Year			12	29	3	6	2	0	0	2	.207	7	31	1	.974

Selected by Kansas City Royals' organization in 10th round of free-agent draft, January 13, 1981.

STUART RUSSELL PEDERSON
(Stu)

Born January 28, 1960, at Palo Alto, Calif.
Height, 6.00. Weight, 185.
Throws and bats lefthanded.
Attended University of Southern California, Los Angeles, Calif.

Led Florida State League in total bases with 229 in 1982.
Named Florida State League Most Valuable Player, 1982.

Year Club	League	Pos.	G.	AB.	R.	H.	2B.	3B.	HR.	RBI.	B.A.	PO.	A.	E.	F.A.
1981—Lodi	Calif.	OF	56	182	47	67	14	1	8	35	.368	84	8	1	.989
1982—Vero Beach	Fla. St.	OF	134	464	95	156	16	*18	7	79	.336	211	14	6	.974
1983—San Antonio	Texas	OF	120	406	92	125	21	12	10	66	.308	169	14	3	.984
1983—Albuquerque	P. C.	OF	1	2	0	0	0	0	0	0	.000	0	0	0	.000
1984—San Antonio	Texas	OF-P	131	476	78	137	25	●11	11	86	.288	182	13	7	.965
1985—Albuquerque	P. C.	OF-P	111	287	54	94	20	3	8	55	.328	110	5	8	.935
1985—Los Angeles	Nat.	OF	8	4	1	0	0	0	0	1	.000	2	0	0	1.000
1986—Albuquerque	P. C.	OF	105	357	69	107	25	2	10	63	.300	191	15	7	.967
Major League Totals—1 Year			8	4	1	0	0	0	0	1	.000	2	0	0	1.000

Selected by Los Angeles Dodgers' organization in 9th round of free-agent draft, June 8, 1981.

PITCHING RECORD

Year Club	League	G.	IP.	W.	L.	Pct.	H.	R.	ER.	SO.	BB.	ERA.
1984—San Antonio	Texas	1	1	0	0	.000	0	1	0	1	3	0.00
1985—Albuquerque	P. Coast	1	1	0	0	.000	1	0	0	0	1	0.00

ALFREDO JOSE PEDRIQUE (GARCIA)

Born August 11, 1960, at Aragua, Venezuela.
Height, 6.00. Weight, 155.
Throws and bats righthanded.

Led International League shortstops in fielding percentage with .962, assists with 321, errors with 18, total chances with 478 and double plays with 74 in 1986.
Led Texas League shortstops in fielding percentage with .961 in 1984.

Year Club	League	Pos.	G.	AB.	R.	H.	2B.	3B.	HR.	RBI.	B.A.	PO.	A.	E.	F.A.
1978—Little Falls	NYP	SS	20	54	10	12	4	0	0	2	.222	25	48	6	.924

Year	Club	League	Pos.	G.	AB.	R.	H.	2B.	3B.	HR.	RBI.	B.A.	PO.	A.	E.	F.A.
1979—Lynchburg	Carol.	SS	19	49	2	11	2	0	0	3	.224	22	63	6	.934
1979—Little Falls	NYP	SS-2B	33	92	3	21	0	2	0	11	.228	56	90	19	.885
1980—Lynchburg	Carol.	SS-2B-3B	105	321	37	79	3	2	0	24	.246	120	234	24	.937
1981—Jackson	Texas	SS-2B	115	379	39	91	9	0	0	25	.240	184	324	34	.937
1982—Jackson	Texas	SS	121	392	38	86	13	2	2	36	.219	189	370	23	★.960
1983—Jackson	Texas	SS-2B-3B	102	326	43	78	7	1	0	27	.239	182	292	20	.960
1984—Jackson†	Texas	SS-2B-3B	109	362	47	103	15	5	1	35	.285	198	281	21	.958
1985—Tidewater	Int.	S-3-1-2	110	325	39	82	17	2	2	24	.252	170	261	12	.973
1986—Tidewater	Int.	S-1-3-2	112	379	49	111	13	2	0	41	.293	189	340	19	.965

Signed as free agent by New York Mets' organization, July 21, 1978.
†Granted free agency, October 15, 1984; re-signed by Mets' organization, November 12, 1984.

ADALBERTO PENA (RIVERA)
(Bert)

Born July 11, 1959, at Santurce, Puerto Rico.
Height, 5.11. Weight, 165.
Throws and bats righthanded.

Major League stolen bases: 1986 (1).
Led Southern League shortstops in double plays with 78 in 1980.
Led Florida State League shortstops in double plays with 66 in 1977.

Year	Club	League	Pos.	G.	AB.	R.	H.	2B.	3B.	HR.	RBI.	B.A.	PO.	A.	E.	F.A.
1977—Cocoa	Fla. St.	SS	93	285	28	65	9	2	1	21	.228	161	279	29	.938
1978—Columbus	South.	SS	141	410	24	66	10	0	2	24	.161	★229	352	39	.937
1979—Daytona Beach	Fla. St.	SS	113	341	26	66	11	1	1	23	.194	152	290	★45	.908
1980—Columbus	South.	SS	124	386	47	97	20	0	9	49	.251	193	363	26	.955
1981—Tucson	P. C.	SS	135	468	69	122	24	12	7	66	.261	224	464	39	.946
1981—Houston	Nat.	SS	4	2	0	1	0	0	0	0	.500	1	1	0	1.000
1982—Tucson†	P. C.	SS-OF	97	362	53	78	17	5	5	33	.215	182	299	32	.938
1983—Tucson	P. C.	SS	112	382	45	94	21	3	5	63	.246	166	290	19	★.960
1983—Houston	Nat.	SS	4	8	0	1	0	0	0	0	.125	1	7	0	1.000
1984—Tucson	P. C.	SS	89	281	34	73	10	3	5	35	.260	152	254	14	.967
1984—Houston‡	Nat.	SS	24	39	3	8	1	0	1	4	.205	26	39	3	.956
1985—Tucson§	P. C.	SS-2B	59	204	24	53	10	0	1	19	.260	87	169	17	.938
1985—Houston	Nat.	3B-SS-2B	20	29	7	8	2	0	0	4	.276	9	15	1	.960
1986—Tucson	P. C.	SS	118	457	78	119	23	3	11	60	.260	●206	359	23	.961
1986—Houston	Nat.	SS-3B-2B	15	29	3	6	1	0	0	2	.207	20	24	4	.917
Major League Totals—5 Years			67	107	13	24	4	0	1	10	.224	57	86	8	.947

Signed as free agent by Houston Astros' organization, May 2, 1977.
†On disabled list, August 13 to September 1, 1982.
‡On disabled list, August 4 to August 19, 1984.
§On Houston disabled list, April 8 to May 20 and June 8 to July 19, 1985; included rehabilitation disability assignment to Tucson, April 29 to May 18, 1985.

ALEJANDRO PENA (VASQUEZ)

Born June 25, 1959, at Cambiaso, Dominican Republic.
Height, 6.01. Weight, 205.
Throws and bats righthanded.

Major League saves: 1981 (2), 1983 (1), 1986 (1). Total—4.
Tied for National League lead in shutouts with 4 in 1984.
Led Pacific Coast League in saves with 22 in 1981.

Year	Club	League	G.	IP.	W.	L.	Pct.	H.	R.	ER.	SO.	BB.	ERA.
1979—Clinton	Midwest	21	71	3	3	.500	53	39	33	57	44	4.18
1980—Vero Beach	Florida St.	35	73	10	3	.769	57	32	26	46	41	3.21
1981—Albuquerque	P. Coast	38	56	2	5	.286	36	12	10	40	21	1.61
1981—Los Angeles	National	14	25	1	1	.500	18	8	8	14	11	2.88
1982—Los Angeles	National	29	35⅔	0	2	.000	37	24	19	20	21	4.79
1982—Albuquerque	P. Coast	16	28⅔	1	1	.500	37	18	17	27	10	5.34
1983—Los Angeles	National	34	177	12	9	.571	152	67	54	120	51	2.75
1984—Los Angeles	National	28	199⅓	12	6	.667	186	67	55	135	46	★2.48
1985—Los Angeles†	National	2	4⅓	0	1	.000	7	5	4	2	3	8.31
1986—Vero Beach‡	Florida St.	4	15⅔	0	2	.000	22	15	·13	11	4	7.47
1986—Los Angeles	National	24	70	1	2	.333	74	40	38	46	30	4.89
Major League Totals—6 Years		131	511⅓	26	·21	.553	474	211	178	337	162	3.13

Signed as free agent by Los Angeles Dodgers' organization, September 10, 1978.
†On disabled list, April 8 to September 5, 1985.
‡On Los Angeles disabled list, March 23 to May 26, 1986; included rehabilitation disability assignment to Vero Beach, May 2 to May 19, 1986.

CHAMPIONSHIP SERIES RECORD

Year	Club	League	G.	IP.	W.	L.	Pct.	H.	R.	ER.	SO.	BB.	ERA.
1981—Los Angeles	National	2	2⅓	0	0	.000	1	0	0	0	0	0.00
1983—Los Angeles	National	1	2⅔	0	0	.000	4	2	2	3	1	6.75
Championship Series Totals—2 Years		3	5	0	0	.000	5	2	2	3	1	3.60

ANTONIO FRANCISCO PENA (PADILLA)
(Tony)

Born June 4, 1957, at Monte Cristi, Dominican Republic.
Height, 6.00. Weight, 184.
Throws and bats righthanded.
Brother of Ramon Pena, pitcher in Detroit Tigers' organization.

Major League stolen bases: 1981 (1), 1982 (2), 1983 (6), 1984 (12), 1985 (12), 1986 (9). Total—42.
Tied for National League lead in grounding into double plays with 21 in 1986.
Led National League catchers in assists with 100 in 1985.
Led National League catchers in double plays with 15 in 1984.
Led National League catchers in total chances with 1,075 in 1983, 999 in 1984 and 1,034 in 1985.
Led Eastern League catchers in double plays with 14 in 1979.
Led Carolina League catchers in double plays with 9 in 1977.
Tied for Carolina League lead in passed balls with 16 in 1977.
Named catcher on THE SPORTING NEWS National League All-Star Team, 1983.
Named catcher on THE SPORTING NEWS National League All-Star fielding team, 1983 through 1985.

Year—Club	League	Pos.	G.	AB.	R.	H.	2B.	3B.	HR.	RBI.	B.A.	PO.	A.	E.	F.A.
1976—Bradenton Pir.	Gulf C.	O-1-C-3	33	110	10	23	2	2	1	11	.209	108	14	4	.968
1976—Charleston	W. Car.	C	14	49	4	11	2	0	1	8	.224	64	7	2	.973
1977—Charleston	W. Car.	C	29	101	10	24	4	0	3	16	.238	172	19	6	.970
1977—Salem	Carol.	C	84	319	36	88	15	3	7	46	.276	★470	★66	★17	.969
1978—Shreveport	Texas	C	104	348	34	80	14	0	8	42	.230	637	54	★25	.965
1979—Buffalo	East.	C	134	515	89	161	16	4	34	97	.313	★768	★120	★26	.972
1980—Portland	P. C.	C	124	452	57	148	24	13	9	77	.327	★639	85	●23	.969
1980—Pittsburgh	Nat.	C	8	21	1	9	1	1	0	1	.429	38	2	2	.952
1981—Pittsburgh	Nat.	C	66	210	16	63	9	1	2	17	.300	286	41	5	.985
1982—Pittsburgh	Nat.	C	138	497	53	147	28	4	11	63	.296	763	89	16	.982
1983—Pittsburgh	Nat.	C	151	542	51	163	22	3	15	70	.301	★976	90	9	.992
1984—Pittsburgh	Nat.	C	147	546	77	156	27	2	15	78	.286	★895	★95	9	.991
1985—Pittsburgh	Nat.	C-1B	147	546	53	136	27	2	10	59	.249	925	102	12	.988
1986—Pittsburgh	Nat.	★C-1B	144	510	56	147	26	2	10	52	.288	824	99	★18	.981
Major League Totals—7 Years			801	2872	307	84	140	15	63	340	.286	4707	518	71	.987

Signed as free agent by Pittsburgh Pirates' organization, July 22, 1975.

ALL-STAR GAME RECORD

Year—League	Pos.	AB.	R.	H.	2B.	3B.	HR.	RBI.	B.A.	PO.	A.	E.	F.A.
1982—National	PR-C	1	0	0	0	0	0	0	.000	3	0	0	1.000
1984—National	C	0	0	0	0	0	0	0	.000	2	0	0	1.000
1985—National	C	1	0	0	0	0	0	0	.000	4	1	0	1.000
1986—National	PR	0	0	0	0	0	0	0	.000	0	0	0	.000
All-Star Game Totals—4 Years		2	0	0	0	0	0	0	.000	9	1	0	1.000

HIPOLITO PENA

First name pronounced Ee-PO-lee-to.

Born January 30, 1964, at Cotui, Dominican Republic.
Height, 6.03. Weight, 165.
Throws and bats lefthanded.

Major League saves: 1986 (1).

Year—Club	League	G.	IP.	W.	L.	Pct.	H.	R.	ER.	SO.	BB.	ERA.
1981—Butte	Pioneer	7	33	2	1	.667	21	17	10	22	33	2.73
1982—Pikeville†‡	Ap'lachian	7	21⅓	0	2	.000	23	15	11	23	16	4.64
1983—Aguascalientes	Mexican	17	39⅓	1	4	.200	26	25	19	18	23	4.35
1983—Beloit§	Midwest	1	1	0	0	.000	0	0	0	0	2	0.00
1984—Bradenton Pirates x	Gulf Coast	10	16⅓	1	1	.500	12	8	5	15	9	2.76
1985—Miami	Florida St.	25	71⅓	2	4	.333	69	54	38	73	41	4.79
1985—Prince William	Carolina	20	44	2	1	.667	31	14	14	63	21	2.86
1986—Nashua	Eastern	31	99	7	4	.636	86	47	39	76	43	3.55
1986—Pittsburgh	National	10	8⅓	0	3	.000	7	10	8	6	3	8.64
Major League Totals—1 Year		10	8⅓	0	3	.000	7	10	8	6	3	8.64

Signed as free agent by Milwaukee Brewers' organization, May 30, 1981.
†On temporary inactive list, August 5 to September 2, 1982.
‡Loaned to Aguascalientes of Mexican League, April 2, 1983; returned June 19,1983.
§Released, July 1, 1983; signed by Pittsburgh Pirates' organization, June 21, 1984.
xLoaned to Miami (Independent), April 8, 1985; returned, July 2, 1985.

TERRY LEE PENDLETON

Born July 16, 1960, at Los Angeles, Calif.
Height, 5.09. Weight, 178.
Throws right and bats left and righthanded.
Attended Oxnard College, Oxnard, Calif. and Fresno State University, Fresno, Calif.

Major League stolen bases: 1984 (20), 1985 (17), 1986 (24). Total—61.
Led National League third basemen in total chances with 524 and double plays with 36 in 1986.
Led American Association third basemen in putouts with 88 and fielding percentage with .964 in 1984.

Year—Club	League	Pos.	G.	AB.	R.	H.	2B.	3B.	HR.	RBI.	B.A.	PO.	A.	E.	F.A.
1982—Johnson City	Appal.	2B	43	181	38	58	14	●4	4	27	.320	79	105	17	.915
1982—St. Petersburg	Fla. St.	2B	20	69	4	18	2	1	1	7	.261	41	51	2	.979

Year Club	League	Pos.	G.	AB.	R.	H.	2B.	3B.	HR.	RBI.	B.A.	PO.	A.	E.	F.A.
1983—Arkansas†	Texas	2B	48	185	29	51	10	3	4	20	.276	94	135	7	.970
1984—Louisville	A. A.	3B-2B	91	330	52	98	23	5	4	44	.297	91	157	10	.961
1984—St. Louis	Nat.	3B	67	262	37	85	16	3	1	33	.324	59	155	13	.943
1985—St. Louis‡	Nat.	3B	149	559	56	134	16	3	5	69	.240	129	361	18	.965
1986—St. Louis	Nat.	*3B-OF	159	578	56	138	26	5	1	59	.239	*133	*371	20	.962
Major League Totals—3 Years			375	1399	149	357	58	11	7	161	.255	321	887	51	.959

Selected by St. Louis Cardinals' organization in 7th round of free-agent draft, June 7, 1982.
†On disabled list, April 8 to May 23 and July 16 to September 5, 1983.
‡On disabled list June 15 to June 30, 1985.

CHAMPIONSHIP SERIES RECORD

Year Club	League	Pos.	G.	AB.	R.	H.	2B.	3B.	HR.	RBI.	B.A.	PO.	A.	E.	F.A.
1985—St. Louis	Nat.	3B	6	24	2	5	1	0	0	4	.208	6	18	1	.960

WORLD SERIES RECORD

Tied World Series record for most doubles, driving in three runs, game (1), October 20, 1985.

Year Club	League	Pos.	G.	AB.	R.	H.	2B.	3B.	HR.	RBI.	B.A.	PO.	A.	E.	F.A.
1985—St. Louis	Nat.	3B	7	23	3	6	1	1	0	3	.261	6	14	1	.952

JOHN PATRICK PERCONTE

Name pronounced PURR-con-tee.

(Jack)

Born August 31, 1954, at Joliet, Ill.
Height, 5.10. Weight, 165.
Throws right and bats lefthanded.
Received bachelor of science degree in sociology from
Murray State University, Murray, Ky. in 1976.

Major League stolen bases: 1980 (3), 1981 (1), 1982 (9), 1983 (3), 1984 (29), 1985 (31), 1986 (2). Total—78.

Year Club	League	Pos.	G.	AB.	R.	H.	2B.	3B.	HR.	RBI.	B.A.	PO.	A.	E.	F.A.
1976—Lodi	Calif.	2B	68	252	58	72	7	1	1	19	.286	141	223	12	.968
1977—Lodi	Calif.	2B	131	515	*132	172	21	12	6	58	.334	292	390	22	.969
1978—San Antonio	Texas	2B	134	538	90	148	20	8	2	52	.275	286	357	21	.968
1979—Albuquerque	P. C.	2B	143	521	104	168	25	7	2	68	.322	278	403	*35	.951
1980—Albuquerque	P. C.	2B	120	439	84	143	16	7	2	46	.326	291	320	15	.976
1980—Los Angeles	Nat.	2B	14	17	2	4	0	0	0	2	.235	13	18	0	1.000
1981—Albuquerque	P. C.	2B	127	448	107	155	26	6	1	58	.346	286	321	23	.963
1981—Los Angeles‡	Nat.	OF	8	9	2	2	0	1	0	1	.222	4	13	0	1.000
1982—Cleveland	Amer.	2B	93	219	27	52	4	4	0	15	.237	131	199	8	.976
1983—Charleston	Int.	*2B-3B	94	341	76	118	17	2	4	45	*.346	177	323	6	*.988
1983—Cleveland§	Amer.	2B	14	26	1	7	1	0	0	0	.269	20	37	3	.950
1984—Seattle	Amer.	2B	155	612	93	180	24	4	0	31	.294	303	438	14	.981
1985—Seattle	Amer.	2B	125	485	60	128	17	7	2	23	.264	244	381	9	.986
1985—Calgary x	P. C.	2B	14	52	17	15	2	2	0	9	.288	31	47	2	.975
1986—Buffalo	A. A.	2B-SS	67	231	32	61	11	1	0	15	.264	114	180	5	.983
1986—Chicago y	Amer.	2B	24	73	6	16	1	0	0	4	.219	46	54	1	.990
National League Totals—2 Years			22	26	4	6	0	1	0	3	.231	17	31	0	1.000
American League Totals—5 Years			411	1415	187	383	47	15	2	73	.271	744	1109	35	.981
Major League Totals—7 Years			433	1441	191	389	47	16	2	76	.270	761	1140	35	.982

Selected by Los Angeles Dodgers' organization in 16th round of free-agent draft, June 8, 1976.
†On disabled list, May 18 to June 9, 1980.
‡Traded with Pitcher Rick Sutcliffe to Cleveland Indians for Outfielder Jorge Orta, Catcher Jack Fimple and Pitcher Larry White, December 9, 1981.
§Traded with Outfielder Gorman Thomas to Seattle Mariners for Second Baseman Tony Bernazard, December 7, 1983.
xReleased, April 1, 1986; signed by Chicago White Sox' organization, May 7, 1986.
yReleased, December 20, 1986.

ATANASIO RIGAL PEREZ

Name pronounced PER-ez.

(Tony)

Born May 14, 1942, at Ciego de Avila, Camaguey, Cuba.
Height, 6.02. Weight, 205.
Throws and bats righthanded.

Tied modern major league record for most at bats, game (7), June 13, 1975.
Tied National League records for most home runs through May 31 (18), 1970; fewest errors by first baseman for leader in errors, season (13), 1973.
Major League stolen bases: 1966 (1), 1968 (3), 1969 (4), 1970 (8), 1971 (4), 1972 (4), 1973 (3), 1974 (1), 1975 (1), 1976 (10), 1977 (4), 1978 (2), 1979 (2), 1980 (1), 1983 (1). Total—49.
Led American League in grounding into double plays with 25 in 1980.
Led National League first basemen in double plays with 131 and total chances with 1,416 in 1973.
Led National League third basemen in assists with 304 and total chances with 435 in 1971.
Led National League third basemen in double plays with 35 in 1969 and tied for lead with 33 in 1968.
Led Carolina League third basemen in double plays with 23 in 1962.
Named first baseman on THE SPORTING NEWS National League All-Star Team, 1973.
Named third baseman on THE SPORTING NEWS National League All-Star Team, 1970.
Named Pacific Coast League Most Valuable Player, 1964.

Year Club	League	Pos.	G.	AB.	R.	H.	2B.	3B.	HR.	RBI.	B.A.	PO.	A.	E.	F.A.
1960—Geneva†	NYP	INF-OF	104	384	82	107	21	4	6	43	.279	199	197	31	.927
1961—Geneva	NYP	3B	121	460	110	★160	32	7	27	★132	★.348	107	★232	★42	.890
1962—Rocky Mount‡§	Carol.	3B	100	384	72	112	20	8	18	74	.292	88	178	30	.899
1963—San Diego	P. C.	3B	8	29	4	11	3	1	1	5	.379	6	8	1	.933
1963—Macon x	Sally	3B	69	256	44	79	19	3	11	48	.309	57	100	18	.897
1964—San Diego	P. C.	1B-3B-OF	124	479	96	148	20	8	34	107	.309	816	104	19	.980
1964—Cincinnati	Nat.	1B	12	25	1	2	1	0	0	1	.080	51	0	1	.981
1965—Cincinnati	Nat.	1B	104	281	40	73	14	4	12	47	.260	525	40	6	.989
1966—Cincinnati	Nat.	1B	99	257	25	68	10	4	4	39	.265	530	23	6	.989
1967—Cincinnati	Nat.	3B-1B-2B	156	600	78	174	28	7	26	102	.290	249	234	13	.974
1968—Cincinnati	Nat.	3B	160	625	93	176	25	7	18	92	.282	★151	343	★25	.952
1969—Cincinnati	Nat.	3B	160	629	103	185	31	2	37	122	.294	136	★342	★32	.937
1970—Cincinnati	Nat.	★3B-1B	158	587	107	186	28	6	40	129	.317	167	292	★35	.929
1971—Cincinnati	Nat.	3B-1B	158	609	72	164	22	3	25	91	.269	281	308	20	.967
1972—Cincinnati	Nat.	1B	136	515	64	146	33	7	21	90	.283	1207	68	9	.993
1973—Cincinnati	Nat.	1B	151	564	73	177	33	3	27	101	.314	★1318	85	★13	.991
1974—Cincinnati	Nat.	1B	158	596	81	158	28	2	28	101	.265	1292	75	6	★.996
1975—Cincinnati	Nat.	1B	137	511	74	144	28	3	20	109	.282	1192	72	9	.993
1976—Cincinnati y	Nat.	1B	139	527	77	137	32	6	19	91	.260	1158	73	5	.996
1977—Montreal	Nat.	1B	154	559	71	158	32	6	19	91	.283	1312	110	11	.992
1978—Montreal	Nat.	1B	148	544	63	158	38	3	14	78	.290	1181	82	11	.991
1979—Montreal z	Nat.	1B	132	489	58	132	29	4	13	73	.270	1114	65	11	.991
1980—Boston	Amer.	1B	151	585	73	161	31	3	25	105	.275	1301	87	10	.993
1981—Boston	Amer.	1B	84	306	35	77	11	3	9	39	.252	519	37	4	.993
1982—Boston a	Amer.	1B	69	196	18	51	14	2	6	31	.260	5	1	1	.857
1983—Philadelphia b	Nat.	1B	91	253	18	61	11	2	6	43	.241	514	40	1	.998
1984—Cincinnati c	Nat.	1B	71	137	9	33	6	1	2	15	.241	186	12	2	.990
1985—Cincinnati d	Nat.	1B	72	183	25	60	8	0	6	33	.328	340	22	2	.995
1986—Cincinnati e	Nat.	1B	77	200	14	51	12	1	2	29	.255	398	29	7	.984
National League Totals—20 Years			2473	8691	1146	2443	449	71	339	1477	.281	13302	2315	225	.986
American League Totals—3 Years			304	1087	126	289	56	8	40	175	.266	1825	125	15	.992
Major League Totals—23 Years			2777	9778	1272	2732	505	79	379	1652	.279	15127	2440	240	.987

Signed as free agent by Cincinnati Reds' organization, March 12, 1960.

†On disabled list, June 25 to July 5, 1960.

‡On suspended list, April 13 to April 16, 1962.

§On disabled list, July 30 to September 4, 1962.

xOn suspended list, April 11, 1963; transferred to restricted list, April 23 to June 25, 1963.

yTraded with Pitcher Will McEnaney to Montreal Expos for Pitchers Woodie Fryman and Dale Murray, December 16, 1976.

zGranted free agency, November 1, 1979; signed by Boston Red Sox, November 16, 1979.

aReleased, November 1, 1982; signed by Philadelphia Phillies, January 31, 1983.

bTraded to Cincinnati Reds for a player to be named later, December 5, 1983; deal settled in cash.

cGranted free agency, November 8, 1984; re-signed by Reds, April 10, 1985.

dGranted free agency, November 12, 1985; re-signed by Reds, January 20, 1986.

eOn voluntarily retired list, October 28, 1986; named coach with Cincinnati Reds for 1987 season.

CHAMPIONSHIP SERIES RECORD

Tied Championship Series records for most consecutive games, one or more runs batted in, total Series (4); most at bats, extra-inning game (6), October 9, 1973 (12 innings); most strikeouts, five-game Series (7), 1972.

Year Club	League	Pos.	G.	AB.	R.	H.	2B.	3B.	HR.	RBI.	B.A.	PO.	A.	E.	F.A.
1970—Cincinnati	Nat.	3B-1B	3	12	1	4	2	0	1	2	.333	6	6	1	.923
1972—Cincinnati	Nat.	1B	5	20	0	4	1	0	0	2	.200	45	3	0	1.000
1973—Cincinnati	Nat.	1B	5	22	1	2	0	0	1	2	.091	47	4	0	1.000
1975—Cincinnati	Nat.	1B	3	12	3	5	0	0	1	4	.417	27	5	0	1.000
1976—Cincinnati	Nat.	1B	3	10	1	2	0	0	0	3	.200	27	2	1	.967
1983—Philadelphia	Nat.	PH	1	1	0	1	0	0	0	0	1.000	0	0	0	.000
Championship Series Totals—6 Years			20	77	6	18	3	0	3	13	.234	152	20	2	.989

WORLD SERIES RECORD

Tied World Series record for one or more hits, each game, seven-game Series, 1972; most unassisted double plays by first baseman, game (1), October 11, 1975.

Year Club	League	Pos.	G.	AB.	R.	H.	2B.	3B.	HR.	RBI.	B.A.	PO.	A.	E.	F.A.
1970—Cincinnati	Nat.	3B	5	18	2	1	0	0	0	0	.056	3	13	1	.941
1972—Cincinnati	Nat.	1B	7	23	3	10	2	0	0	2	.435	73	3	1	.987
1975—Cincinnati	Nat.	1B	7	28	4	5	0	0	3	7	.179	66	5	1	.986
1976—Cincinnati	Nat.	1B	4	16	1	5	1	0	0	2	.313	32	4	0	1.000
1983—Philadelphia	Nat.	PH-1B	4	10	0	2	0	0	0	0	.200	13	1	0	1.000
World Series Totals—5 Years			27	95	10	23	3	0	3	11	.242	187	26	3	.986

ALL-STAR GAME RECORD

Year League	Pos.	AB.	R.	H.	2B.	3B.	HR.	RBI.	B.A.	PO.	A.	E.	F.A.
1967—National	3B	2	1	1	0	0	1	1	.500	0	3	0	1.000
1968—National	3B	0	0	0	0	0	0	0	.000	0	1	0	1.000
1969—National	3B	1	0	0	0	0	0	0	.000	1	0	0	1.000
1970—National	3B	3	0	0	0	0	0	0	.000	1	1	0	1.000
1974—National	PH	1	0	0	0	0	0	0	.000	0	0	0	.000
1975—National	1B	1	0	0	0	0	0	0	.000	1	1	0	1.000
1976—National	1B	0	0	0	0	0	0	0	.000	2	0	0	1.000
All-Star Game Totals—7 Years		8	1	1	0	0	1	1	.125	5	7	0	1.000

YORKIS MIGUEL PEREZ

Born September 30, 1967, at Bajos de Haina, D. R.
Height, 6.01. Weight, 185.
Throws and bats lefthanded.

Year Club	League	G.	IP.	W.	L.	Pct.	H.	R.	ER.	SO.	BB.	ERA.
1983—Elizabethton	Ap'lachian	3	4	0	1	.000	5	9	9	6	9	20.25
1984—Elizabethton	Ap'lachian	1	1⅓	0	0	.000	1	0	0	1	1	0.00
1985—Santiago	Dom. Rep.	21	122	6	8	.429	104	58	43	69	63	3.18
1986—Kenosha	Midwest	31	131	4	11	.267	120	81	75	144	88	5.15

Signed as free agent by Minnesota Twins' organization, February 23, 1983.

ANTONIO LLAMAS PEREZCHICA
(Tony)

Born April 20, 1966, at Mexicali, Mex.
Height, 5.10. Weight, 160.
Throws and bats righthanded.

Led Midwest League shortstops in total chances with 599 in 1985.

Year Club	League	Pos.	G.	AB.	R.	H.	2B.	3B.	HR.	RBI.	B.A.	PO.	A.	E.	F.A.
1984—Everett	N'west	SS	33	119	10	23	6	1	0	10	.193	45	73	18	.868
1985—Clinton	Midw.	SS	127	452	54	109	21	●8	4	40	.241	★224	332	43	.928
1986—Fresno	Calif.	SS-3B	126	452	65	126	30	8	9	54	.279	224	303	42	.926

Selected by San Francisco Giants' organization in 3rd round of free-agent draft, June 4, 1984.

GERALD JUNE PERRY

Born October 30, 1960, at Savannah, Ga.
Height, 6.00. Weight, 190.
Throws right and bats lefthanded.
Nephew of Dan Driessen, first baseman with Cincinnati Reds, Montreal
Expos, San Francisco Giants and Houston Astros, 1973 through 1986.

Major League stolen bases: 1984 (15), 1985 (9). Total—24.
Led International League in game-winning RBIs with 17 and tied for lead in intentional bases on balls received with 8 in 1986.
Led Carolina League first basemen in double plays with 109 in 1980.
Led Gulf Coast League first basemen in double plays with 46 in 1978.

Year Club	League	Pos.	G.	AB.	R.	H.	2B.	3B.	HR.	RBI.	B.A.	PO.	A.	E.	F.A.
1978—Bradenton Brav...	Gulf C.	1B	★55	191	32	51	★12	3	1	26	.267	★479	★37	6	★.989
1979—Greenwood	W. Car.	1B	109	400	69	133	17	4	9	71	★.333	881	59	19	.980
1980—Durham	Carol.	1B	138	497	102	124	19	5	15	92	.249	★1296	93	16	.989
1981—Savannah	South.	1B	137	476	71	132	18	3	19	84	.277	1221	86	18	.986
1982—Richmond	Int.	1B	133	492	94	146	22	4	15	92	.297	1110	94	●17	.986
1983—Richmond	Int.	1B	113	423	81	133	21	8	13	71	.314	943	88	11	.989
1983—Atlanta	Nat.	1B-OF	27	39	5	14	2	0	1	6	.359	55	0	1	.982
1984—Atlanta	Nat.	1B-OF	122	347	52	92	12	2	7	47	.265	550	28	12	.980
1985—Atlanta	Nat.	1B-OF	110	238	22	51	5	0	3	13	.214	541	37	9	.985
1986—Richmond	Int.	OF-1B	107	384	69	125	30	5	10	75	.326	394	25	7	.984
1986—Atlanta	Nat.	OF-1B	29	70	6	19	2	0	2	11	.271	24	1	2	.926
Major League Totals—4 Years			288	694	85	176	21	2	13	77	.254	1170	66	24	.981

Selected by Atlanta Braves' organization in 11th round of free-agent draft, June 6, 1978.

WILLIAM PATRICK PERRY
(Pat)

Born February 4, 1959, at Taylorville, Ill.
Height, 6.01. Weight, 170.
Throws and bats lefthanded.
Attended Lincoln Land Community College, Springfield, Ill.

Major League saves: 1986 (2).
Tied for Gulf Coast League lead in shutouts with 2 in 1978.

Year Club	League	G.	IP.	W.	L.	Pct.	H.	R.	ER.	SO.	BB.	ERA.
1978—Sarasota Astros	Gulf Coast	12	35	2	4	.333	29	15	9	35	14	2.31
1979—Daytona Beach	Florida St.	12	51	2	3	.400	64	31	30	30	16	5.29
1979—Sarasota Astros	Gulf Coast	9	49	3	1	.750	55	21	20	24	16	3.67
1980—Daytona Beach	Florida St.	22	115	9	5	.643	121	51	38	54	46	2.97
1981—Columbus	Southern	27	51	3	1	.750	54	40	36	35	38	6.35
1981—Daytona Beach	Florida St.	9	20	2	0	1.000	11	6	6	22	7	2.70
1982—Columbus†	Southern	22	37⅔	4	0	1.000	32	19	17	28	18	4.06
1983—Columbus‡§	Southern	11	49	5	2	.714	60	30	22	27	21	4.04
1983—Buffalo x	Eastern	4	5⅓	0	0	.000	8	5	4	4	4	6.75
1983—Springfield	Midwest	6	24⅓	1	1	.500	17	6	6	31	5	2.22
1984—Arkansas	Texas	25	48⅔	2	2	.667	34	8	6	51	17	1.11
1984—Louisville	Am. Assoc.	21	44⅔	4	3	.571	35	12	11	43	21	2.22
1985—Louisville	Am. Assoc.	45	91	4	3	.571	56	33	24	63	39	2.37
1985—St. Louis	National	6	12⅓	1	0	1.000	3	0	0	6	3	0.00
1986—St. Louis	National	46	68⅔	2	3	.400	59	31	29	29	34	3.80
1986—Louisville	Am. Assoc.	5	11	1	0	1.000	8	6	4	7	6	3.27
Major League Totals—2 Years		52	81	3	3	.500	62	31	29	35	37	3.22

Selected by Houston Astros' organization in 2nd round of free-agent draft, January 10, 1978.
†On disabled list, May 6 to May 24 and August 1, 1982 through remainder of season.
‡On disabled list, May 24 to June 15, 1983.
§Released, June 24, 1983; signed by Buffalo (Cleveland Indians' organization), July 1, 1983.
xReleased, July 12, 1983; signed by Springfield (St. Louis Cardinals' organization), August 3, 1983.

RICHARD DEVIN PETERS
(Rick)

Born November 21, 1955, at Lynwood, Calif.
Height, 5.10. Weight, 160.
Throws right and bats left and righthanded.
Attended Arizona State University, Tempe, Ariz.

Major League stolen bases: 1980 (13), 1981 (1), 1983 (4), 1986 (2). Total—20.

Year Club	League	Pos.	G.	AB.	R.	H.	2B.	3B.	HR.	RBI.	B.A.	PO.	A.	E.	F.A.
1977—Montgomery	South.	OF	38	108	9	33	2	1	0	8	.306	70	3	1	.986
1978—Evansville	A. A.	OF-3B	●135	463	92	128	28	8	2	48	.276	199	5	8	.962
1979—Evansville	A. A.	OF-3B-2B	107	387	88	124	17	10	3	42	.320	125	17	5	.966
1979—Detroit	Amer.	3B-OF	12	19	3	5	0	0	0	2	.263	3	0	2	.600
1980—Detroit	Amer.	OF	133	477	79	139	19	7	2	42	.291	296	1	7	.977
1981—Detroit	Amer.	OF	63	207	26	53	7	3	0	15	.256	103	3	1	.991
1982—Detroit†‡	Amer.						(Did not play)								
1983—Tacoma	P. C.	OF	66	232	50	69	9	3	1	19	.297	166	1	3	.982
1983—Oakland	Amer.	OF	55	178	20	51	7	0	0	20	.287	141	3	2	.986
1984—Tacoma§	P. C.	OF-2B	74	260	38	85	10	4	3	30	.327	186	4	3	.984
1985—Tacoma	P. C.	OF-2B	126	423	73	125	17	6	2	43	.296	260	10	9	.968
1986—Oakland x	Amer.	OF-2B	44	38	7	7	1	0	0	1	.184	29	1	0	1.000
1986—Tacoma y	P. C.	OF	8	27	9	8	1	2	0	6	.296	17	0	0	1.000
Major League Totals—5 Years			307	919	135	255	34	10	2	80	.277	572	8	12	.980

Selected by Minnesota Twins' organization in 18th round of free-agent draft, June 5, 1973.
Selected by Atlanta Braves' organization in 12th round of free-agent draft, June 8, 1976.
Selected by Detroit Tigers' organization in 7th round of free-agent draft, June 7, 1977.
†On disabled list, April 6, 1982 through remainder of season.
‡Released, October 8, 1982; signed by Tacoma (Oakland A's organization), February 2, 1983.
§On disabled list, June 22 to July 14, 1984.
xOn disabled list, July 5 to July 27, 1986; included rehabilitation disability assignment to Tacoma, July 18 to July 27, 1986.
yReleased, July 27, 1986.

EUGENE JAMES PETRALLI JR.
(Geno)

Born September 25, 1959, at Sacramento, Calif.
Height, 6.01. Weight, 180.
Throws right and bats left and righthanded.
Attended Sacramento City College, Sacramento, Calif.
Son of Gene Petralli, minor league first baseman, 1948 through 1951 and 1953.

Major League stolen bases: 1983 (1), 1985 (1), 1986 (3). Total—5.
Led International League catchers in putouts with 633, assists with 86, errors with 19, double plays with 10 and total chances with 738 in 1982.
Tied for Pioneer League lead in passed balls with 27 in 1978.

Year Club	League	Pos.	G.	AB.	R.	H.	2B.	3B.	HR.	RBI.	B.A.	PO.	A.	E.	F.A.
1978—Medicine Hat	Pion.	C-3B	65	242	42	68	14	5	2	40	.281	238	68	19	.942
1979—Dunedin†	Fla. St.	C-3B-OF	52	184	18	53	13	0	1	24	.288	206	42	5	.980
1979—Syracuse	Int.	C	18	56	6	13	0	1	0	7	.232	67	12	1	.988
1980—Knoxville	South.	C-1B-OF	116	382	42	109	20	2	3	38	.285	569	82	18	.973
1981—Syracuse‡	Int.	C	45	151	17	40	11	0	0	16	.265	188	30	6	.973
1982—Syracuse	Int.	C-1B-3B	126	395	57	114	19	3	9	58	.289	674	89	20	.974
1982—Toronto	Amer.	C-3B	16	44	3	16	2	0	0	1	.364	51	4	1	.982
1983—Syracuse	Int.	C-1B	104	327	39	80	9	2	3	40	.245	541	68	7	.989
1983—Toronto	Amer.	C	6	4	0	0	0	0	0	0	.000	7	0	0	1.000
1984—Toronto§	Amer.	C	3	3	0	0	0	0	0	0	.000	1	1	0	1.000
1984—Maine x	Int.	C-O-1	23	83	9	18	3	0	0	5	.217	122	11	6	.957
1985—Maine y	Int.	C	2	7	0	1	0	0	0	1	.143	12	1	1	.929
1985—Oklahoma City	A. A.	C	27	80	11	21	8	0	1	5	.263	108	14	3	.976
1985—Texas	Amer.	C	42	100	7	27	2	0	0	11	.270	179	16	2	.990
1986—Texas	Amer.	C-3B-2B	69	137	17	35	9	3	2	18	.255	163	14	4	.978
Major League Totals—5 Years			136	288	27	78	13	3	2	30	.271	401	35	7	.984

Selected by Toronto Blue Jays' organization in 3rd round of free-agent draft, January 10, 1978.
†On suspended list, April 13 to April 27, 1979.
‡On disabled list, May 6 to June 1 and June 28 to August 18, 1981.
§Sold to Maine (Cleveland Indians' organization), May 8, 1984.
xOn disabled list, July 11, 1984 through remainder of season.
yReleased, April 23, 1985; signed by Oklahoma City (Texas Rangers' organization), May 17, 1985.

DANIEL JOSEPH PETRY

Name pronounced PEE-tree.

(Dan)

Born November 13, 1958, at Palo Alto, Calif.
Height, 6.04. Weight, 200.
Throws and bats righthanded.
Led American League pitchers in games started with 38 and home runs allowed with 37 in 1983.

Year	Club	League	G.	IP.	W.	L.	Pct.	H.	R.	ER.	SO.	BB.	ERA.
1976—Bristol	Ap'lachian	14	79	2	3	.400	54	42	33	51	★56	3.76
1977—Lakeland	Florida St.	25	145	10	11	.476	139	68	55	68	68	3.41
1978—Montgomery	Southern	14	92	6	7	.462	70	38	25	69	41	2.45
1978—Evansville	Am. Assoc.	13	71	4	3	.571	59	38	36	50	33	4.56
1979—Evansville	Am. Assoc.	15	91	4	3	.571	92	60	49	55	37	4.85
1979—Detroit	American	15	98	6	5	.545	90	46	43	43	33	3.95
1980—Evansville	Am. Assoc.	4	30	2	0	1.000	21	11	9	16	12	2.70
1980—Detroit	American	27	165	10	9	.526	156	82	72	88	83	3.93
1981—Detroit	American	23	141	10	9	.526	115	53	47	79	57	3.00
1982—Detroit	American	35	246	15	9	.625	220	98	88	132	100	3.22
1983—Detroit	American	38	266⅓	19	11	.633	256	126	116	122	99	3.92
1984—Detroit	American	35	233⅓	18	8	.692	231	94	84	144	66	3.24
1985—Detroit	American	34	238⅔	15	13	.536	190	98	89	109	81	3.36
1986—Detroit†	American	20	116	5	10	.333	122	78	60	56	53	4.66
1986—Lakeland	Florida St.	3	10⅓	1	1	.500	13	8	8	6	1	6.97
Major League Totals—8 Years		227	1504⅓	98	74	.570	1380	675	599	773	572	3.58

Selected by Detroit Tigers' organization in 4th round of free-agent draft, June 8, 1976.

†On disabled list, June 6 to August 19, 1986; included rehabilitation disability assignment to Lakeland, July 30 to August 19, 1986.

CHAMPIONSHIP SERIES RECORD

Year	Club	League	G.	IP.	W.	L.	Pct.	H.	R.	ER.	SO.	BB.	ERA.
1984—Detroit	American	1	7	0	0	.000	4	2	2	4	1	2.57

WORLD SERIES RECORD

Year	Club	League	G.	IP.	W.	L.	Pct.	H.	R.	ER.	SO.	BB.	ERA.
1984—Detroit	American	2	8	0	1	.000	14	8	8	4	5	9.00

ALL-STAR GAME RECORD

Year	League	IP.	W.	L.	Pct.	H.	R.	ER.	SO.	BB.	ERA.
1985—American		⅓	0	0	.000	0	2	2	1	3	54.00

GARY GEORGE PETTIS

Born April 3, 1958, at Oakland, Calif.
Height, 6.01. Weight, 160.
Throws right and bats left and righthanded.
Attended Laney College, Oakland, Calif.
Brother of Stacey Pettis, outfielder in California Angels' organization.

Established major league record for most strikeouts by switch-hitter, season (132), 1986.
Tied major league record for most putouts by outfielder, game (12), June 4, 1985, 15 innings.
Tied American League record for most chances accepted by outfielder, game (12), June 4, 1985, 15 innings.
Major League stolen bases: 1983 (8), 1984 (48), 1985 (56), 1986 (50). Total—162.
Led American League outfielders in total chances with 478 in 1986.
Led Pacific Coast League in stolen bases with 53 in 1982.
Named outfielder on THE SPORTING NEWS American League All-Star fielding team, 1985 and 1986.

Year	Club	League	Pos.	G.	AB.	R.	H.	2B.	3B.	HR.	RBI.	B.A.	PO.	A.	E.	F.A.
1979—Idaho Falls	Pion.	3B-SS-2B	50	198	39	63	10	●10	3	26	.318	59	94	24	.864
1980—Salinas	Calif.	OF-SS-3B	118	393	71	94	15	3	2	31	.239	206	36	13	.949
1981—Holyoke	East.	OF	120	421	77	112	8	9	3	36	.266	237	5	4	.984
1982—Spokane	P. C.	OF	133	528	108	152	22	★14	1	59	.288	★345	9	6	★.983
1982—California	Amer.	OF	10	5	5	1	0	0	1	1	.200	5	1	0	1.000
1983—Edmonton	P. C.	OF	132	529	★138	151	27	8	11	52	.285	325	10	5	.985
1983—California	Amer.	OF	22	85	19	25	2	3	3	6	.294	49	5	1	.982
1984—California	Amer.	OF	140	397	63	90	11	6	2	29	.227	337	11	6	.983
1985—California†	Amer.	OF	125	443	67	114	10	8	1	32	.257	368	13	4	.990
1986—California	Amer.	OF	154	539	93	139	23	4	5	58	.258	★462	9	7	.985
Major League Totals—5 Years			451	1469	247	369	46	21	12	126	.251	1221	39	18	.986

Selected by California Angels' organization in 6th round of free-agent draft, January 9, 1979.

†On disabled list, July 5 to July 31, 1985.

CHAMPIONSHIP SERIES RECORD

Year	Club	League	Pos.	G.	AB.	R.	H.	2B.	3B.	HR.	RBI.	B.A.	PO.	A.	E.	F.A.
1986—California	Amer.	OF	7	26	4	9	1	0	1	4	.346	28	0	1	.966

—DID YOU KNOW—

That New York Yankee outfielder Henry Cotto's only two major league home runs were hit on the final days of the 1985 and 1986 seasons?

KENNETH ALLEN PHELPS
(Ken)

Born August 6, 1954, at Seattle, Wash.
Height, 6.01. Weight, 204.
Throws and bats lefthanded.
Attended Washington State University, Pullman, Wash.; Mesa Community College,
Mesa, Ariz., and received bachelor of science degree in physical education from
Arizona State University, Tempe, Ariz.

Major League stolen bases: 1984 (3), 1985 (2), 1986 (2). Total—7.
Led American Association in total bases with 320 in 1982.
Led American Association in bases on balls received with 128 in 1980 and 108 in 1982.
Led Southern League in bases on balls received with 99 in 1978.
Tied for American Association lead in intentional bases on balls received with 12 in 1982.
Led American Association first basemen in double plays with 111 in 1979, 103 in 1980 and 108 in 1982.
Named American Association Most Valuable Player, 1982.

Year—Club	League	Pos.	G.	AB.	R.	H.	2B.	3B.	HR.	RBI.	B.A.	PO.	A.	E.	F.A.
1976—Sarasota Royals...	Gulf C.	1B	28	98	20	29	6	3	3	28	.296	166	16	2	.989
1976—Waterloo	Midw.	1B	25	72	12	19	8	0	1	10	.264	205	12	3	.986
1977—Daytona Beach....	Fla. St.	1B	40	145	22	50	7	0	5	32	.345	341	31	8	.979
1977—Jacksonville	South.	1B	81	262	30	51	6	3	5	40	.195	691	38	10	.986
1978—Jacksonville	South.	1B	124	381	65	94	20	0	16	61	.247	1028	66	16	.986
1979—Omaha	A. A.	1B	130	430	71	114	26	3	20	77	.265	★1129	80	★13	.989
1980—Omaha	A. A.	1B	133	442	80	130	30	3	23	72	.294	★1154	51	12	.990
1980—Kansas City	Amer.	1B	3	4	0	0	0	0	0	0	.000	14	0	0	1.000
1981—Kansas City	Amer.	1B	21	22	1	3	0	1	0	1	.136	4	1	0	1.000
1981—Omaha†	A. A.	1B	19	66	9	22	8	1	5	21	.333	169	15	2	.989
1982—Wichita	A. A.	1B	132	453	112	151	23	4	★46	★141	.333	1047	74	14	.988
1982—Montreal‡	Nat.	PH	10	8	0	2	0	0	0	0	.250	0	0	0	.000
1983—Seattle	Amer.	1B	50	127	10	30	4	1	7	16	.236	164	16	0	1.000
1983—Salt Lake City	P. C.	1B	74	270	81	92	29	6	24	82	.341	535	37	7	.988
1984—Seattle§	Amer.	1B	101	290	52	70	9	0	24	51	.241	72	4	1	.987
1984—Salt Lake City	P. C.	1B	12	45	7	14	3	0	3	13	.311	25	5	0	1.000
1985—Seattle	Amer.	1B	61	116	18	24	3	0	9	24	.207	31	2	0	1.000
1986—Seattle	Amer.	1B	125	344	69	85	16	4	24	64	.247	487	34	9	.983
American League Totals—6 Years			361	903	150	212	32	6	64	156	.235	772	57	10	.988
National League Totals—1 Year			10	8	0	2	0	0	0	0	.250	0	0	0	.000
Major League Totals—7 Years			371	911	150	214	32	6	64	156	.235	772	57	10	.988

Selected by Atlanta Braves' organization in 8th round of free-agent draft, June 6, 1972.
Selected by New York Yankees' organization in 1st round (11th player selected) of free-agent draft, January 9, 1974.
Selected by Philadelphia Phillies' organization in secondary phase of free-agent draft, June 5, 1974.
Selected by Kansas City Royals' organization in 15th round of free-agent draft, June 8, 1976.
†Traded to Montreal Expos' organization for Pitcher Grant Jackson, January 19, 1982.
‡Sold to Seattle Mariners, March 31, 1983.
§On disabled list, April 7 to May 18, 1984; included rehabilitation disability assignment to Salt Lake City, May 4 to May 18, 1984.

KEITH ANTHONY PHILLIPS
(Tony)

Born April 25, 1959, at Atlanta, Ga.
Height, 5.10. Weight, 160.
Throws right and bats right and lefthanded.
Attended New Mexico Military Institute, Roswell, N.M.

Tied major league record for most assists by second baseman, nine-inning game (12), July 6, 1986.
Major League stolen bases: 1982 (2), 1983 (16), 1984 (10), 1985 (3), 1986 (15). Total—46.
Hit for the cycle, May 16, 1986.
Led Eastern League in being hit by pitch with 10 in 1981.
Led Southern League in bases on balls received with 98 in 1980.

Year—Club	League	Pos.	G.	AB.	R.	H.	2B.	3B.	HR.	RBI.	B.A.	PO.	A.	E.	F.A.
1978—W. Palm Beach† ..	Fla. St.	3B-SS-2B	32	54	8	9	0	0	0	3	.167	13	33	5	.902
1978—Jamestown	NYP	SS-2B-3B	52	152	24	29	5	2	1	17	.191	73	146	16	.932
1979—W. Palm Beach ..	Fla. St.	2B-SS	60	203	30	47	5	1	0	18	.232	120	156	21	.929
1979—Memphis	South.	SS-2B	52	156	31	44	4	2	3	11	.282	68	134	18	.914
1980—Memphis‡§	South.	★SS-2B	136	502	100	125	18	4	5	41	.249	226	408	★42	.938
1981—West Haven	East.	SS	131	461	79	114	25	3	9	64	.247	200	391	★33	.947
1981—Tacoma	P. C.	2B-SS	4	11	1	4	1	0	0	2	.364	8	10	0	1.000
1982—Tacoma	P. C.	SS	86	300	76	89	18	5	4	47	.297	138	236	30	.926
1982—Oakland	Amer.	SS	40	81	11	17	2	2	0	8	.210	46	95	7	.953
1983—Oakland	Amer.	SS-2B-3B	148	412	54	102	12	3	4	35	.248	218	383	30	.952
1984—Oakland	Amer.	SS-2B-OF	154	451	62	120	24	3	4	37	.266	255	391	28	.958
1985—Tacoma x	P. C.	3B-2B	20	69	9	9	1	0	0	5	.130	15	36	4	.927
1985—Oakland	Amer.	3B-2B	42	161	23	45	12	2	4	17	.280	54	103	3	.981
1986—Oakland y	Amer.	2-3-O-S	118	441	76	113	14	5	5	52	.256	191	326	13	.975
Major League Totals—5 Years			502	1546	226	397	64	15	17	149	.257	764	1298	81	.962

Selected by Seattle Mariners' organization in 16th round of free-agent draft, June 7, 1977.
Selected by Montreal Expos' organization in secondary phase of free-agent draft, January 10, 1978.
†On temporary inactive list, April 11 to May 4, 1978.
‡Traded with cash to San Diego Padres for First Baseman Willie Montanez, August 31, 1980.

CHRISTOPHER FRANCIS PITTARO
(Chris)

Born September 16, 1961, at Trenton, N.J.
Height, 5.11. Weight, 170.
Throws right and bats left and righthanded.
Attended University of North Carolina, Chapel Hill, N.C.
Son of Francis (Sonny) Pittaro, infielder in Washington Senators'
and Minnesota Twins' organizations, 1960 through 1962.

Major League stolen bases: 1985 (1).

Year	Club	League	Pos.	G.	AB.	R.	H.	2B.	3B.	HR.	RBI.	B.A.	PO.	A.	E.	F.A.
1982—Macon	S. Atl.	SS	68	218	25	50	6	0	2	25	.229	99	212	24	.928
1983—Lakeland	Fla. St.	★2B-SS	107	392	43	106	19	4	1	39	.270	224	310	12	★.978
1984—Birmingham	South.	2B-SS	137	517	85	147	27	7	11	61	.284	260	417	22	.969
1985—Detroit†	Amer.	3B-2B	28	62	10	15	3	1	0	7	.242	15	36	6	.895
1985—Nashville‡	A. A.	3B-SS-2B	60	175	22	34	4	1	3	19	.194	63	126	6	.969
1986—Minnesota	Amer.	2B-SS	11	21	0	2	0	0	0	0	.095	15	19	1	.971
1986—Toledo	Int.	SS-2B-3B	107	418	50	107	14	3	8	37	.256	176	326	13	.975
Major League Totals—2 Years				39	83	10	17	3	1	0	7	.205	30	55	7	.924

Selected by Detroit Tigers' organization in 6th round of free-agent draft, June 7, 1982.
†On disabled list, May 27 to June 14, 1985.
‡Traded with Outfielder Alex Sanchez to Minnesota Twins for Catcher Dave Engle, January 16, 1986.

DANIEL THOMAS PLESAC
(Dan)

Born February 4, 1962, at Gary, Ind.
Height, 6.05. Weight, 205.
Throws and bats lefthanded.
Attended North Carolina State University, Raleigh, N.C.

Major League saves: 1986 (14).
Led Appalachian League pitchers in balks with 3 and tied for lead in games started with 14 in 1983.

Year	Club	League	G.	IP.	W.	L.	Pct.	H.	R.	ER.	SO.	BB.	ERA.
1983—Paintsville	Ap'lachian	14	82⅓	★9	1	★.900	76	44	32	★85	57	3.50
1984—Stockton	California	16	108⅓	6	6	.500	106	51	40	101	50	3.32
1984—El Paso	Texas	7	39	2	2	.500	43	19	15	24	16	3.46
1985—El Paso	Texas	25	150⅓	12	5	.706	171	91	83	128	68	4.97
1986—Milwaukee	American	51	91	10	7	.588	81	34	30	75	29	2.97
Major League Totals—1 Year			51	91	10	7	.588	81	34	30	75	29	2.97

Selected by St. Louis Cardinals' organization in 2nd round of free-agent draft, June 3, 1980.
Selected by Milwaukee Brewers' organization in 1st round (26th player selected) of free-agent draft, June 6, 1983.

ERIC VAUGHN PLUNK

Born September 3, 1963, at Wilmington, Calif.
Height, 6.05. Weight, 210.
Throws and bats righthanded.
Attended California State University at Dominguez Hills, Carson, Calif.

Led American League in balks with 6 in 1986.
Tied for Florida State League lead in shutouts with 4 in 1983 and balks with 7 in 1984.

Year	Club	League	G.	IP.	W.	L.	Pct.	H.	R.	ER.	SO.	BB.	ERA.
1981—Bradenton Yankees	Gulf Coast	11	54	3	4	.429	56	29	23	47	20	3.83
1982—Paintsville	Ap'lachian	12	64	6	3	.667	63	35	33	59	30	4.64
1983—Fort Lauderdale†	Florida St.	20	125	8	10	.444	115	55	38	109	63	2.74
1984—Fort Lauderdale‡	Florida St.	28	176⅓	12	12	.500	153	85	56	★152	★123	2.86
1985—Huntsville	Southern	13	79⅓	8	2	.800	61	36	30	68	56	3.40
1985—Tacoma	P. Coast	11	53	0	5	.000	51	41	34	43	50	5.77
1986—Tacoma	P. Coast	6	32⅔	2	3	.400	25	18	17	31	33	4.68
1986—Oakland	American	26	120⅓	4	7	.364	91	75	71	98	102	5.31
Major League Totals—1 Year			26	120⅓	4	7	.364	91	75	71	98	102	5.31

Selected by New York Yankees' organization in 4th round of free-agent draft, June 8, 1981.
†On disabled list, August 11 to August 26, 1983.
‡Traded with Outfielder Stan Javier and Pitchers Jay Howell, Jose Rijo and Tim Birtsas to Oakland A's for Outfielder Rickey Henderson, Pitcher Bert Bradley and cash, December 5, 1984.

GUSTAVO POLIDOR
(Gus)

Born October 26, 1961, at Caracas, Venezuela.
Height, 6.01. Weight, 175.
Throws and bats righthanded.
Led Pacific Coast League shortstops in fielding percentage with .986 in 1986.

Led Pacific Coast League shortstops in double plays with 93 in 1985 and tied for lead with 92 in 1986.
Led Pacific Coast League shortstops in total chances with 669 in 1985.
Tied for Eastern League lead in double plays by shortstops with 69 in 1983.

Year Club	League	Pos.	G.	AB.	R.	H.	2B.	3B.	HR.	RBI.	B.A.	PO.	A.	E.	F.A.
1981—Holyoke	East.	SS	130	479	46	119	17	3	2	47	.248	192	375	32	.947
1982—Holyoke†	East.	SS	56	208	17	47	7	0	2	23	.226	74	149	21	.914
1983—Nashua	East.	*SS-3B	105	329	32	69	7	2	0	21	.210	208	283	★37	.930
1984—Waterbury	East.	*SS-P	119	394	42	88	11	1	1	32	.223	★200	322	27	★.951
1985—Edmonton	P. C.	SS	132	460	56	131	18	7	2	51	.285	★250	★396	23	.966
1985—California	Amer.	SS-OF	2	1	1	1	0	0	0	0	1.000	0	2	0	1.000
1986—Edmonton	P. C.	S-2-1-3	119	476	72	143	27	5	5	61	.300	213	316	7	.987
1986—California	Amer.	2B-SS-3B	6	19	1	5	1	0	0	1	.263	10	13	0	1.000
Major League Totals—2 Years			8	20	2	6	1	0	0	1	.300	10	15	0	1.000

Signed as free agent by California Angels' organization, January 5, 1981.
†On disabled list, June 22 to July 14 and July 26, 1982 through remainder of season.

PITCHING RECORD

Year Club	League	G.	IP.	W.	L.	Pct.	H.	R.	ER.	SO.	BB.	ERA.
1984—Waterbury	Eastern	1	1	0	0	.000	0	0	0	0	1	0.00

LUIS ANDREW POLONIA (ALMONTE)

Born October 12, 1964, at Santiago City, D. R.
Height, 5.08. Weight, 155.
Throws left and bats left and righthanded.
Led Pacific Coast League in caught stealing with 21 in 1986.
Led Midwest League in caught stealing with 24 in 1984.

Year Club	League	Pos.	G.	AB.	R.	H.	2B.	3B.	HR.	RBI.	B.A.	PO.	A.	E.	F.A.
1984—Madison	Midw.	OF	135	*528	103	*162	21	10	8	64	.307	202	9	10	.955
1985—Huntsville	South.	OF	130	515	82	149	15	*18	2	36	.289	236	13	12	.954
1986—Tacoma	P. C.	OF	134	*549	98	*165	20	4	3	63	.301	★318	8	10	.970

Signed as free agent by Oakland A's organization, January 3, 1984.

DARRELL RAY PORTER

Born January 17, 1952, at Joplin, Mo.
Height, 6.01. Weight, 202.
Throws right and bats lefthanded.
Major League stolen bases: 1971 (2), 1973 (5), 1974 (8), 1975 (2), 1976 (2), 1977 (1), 1979 (3), 1980 (1), 1981 (1), 1982 (1), 1983 (1), 1984 (5), 1985 (6), 1986 (1). Total—39.
Led American League in bases on balls received with 121 in 1979.
Led American League catchers in double plays with 15 in 1979.
Led American League in passed balls with 15 in 1975, 9 in 1978 and tied for lead with 12 in 1976.
Tied for American League lead in sacrifice flies with 13 in 1979.
Led Midwest League in passed balls with 19 in 1971.
Named catcher on THE SPORTING NEWS American League All-Star Team, 1979.
Received bonus reported in excess of $70,000 to sign with Milwaukee Brewers, 1970.

Year Club	League	Pos.	G.	AB.	R.	H.	2B.	3B.	HR.	RBI.	B.A.	PO.	A.	E.	F.A.
1970—Clinton	Midw.	C	62	185	24	37	11	0	4	21	.200	380	42	10	.977
1971—Danville	Midw.	C	101	332	75	90	9	7	24	70	.271	674	★69	★19	.975
1971—Milwaukee	Amer.	C	22	70	4	15	2	0	2	9	.214	108	18	3	.977
1972—Evansville	A. A.	C	88	255	37	55	7	2	13	45	.216	541	★56	7	.988
1972—Milwaukee	Amer.	C	18	56	2	7	1	0	1	2	.125	113	8	3	.976
1973—Milwaukee	Amer.	C	117	350	50	89	19	2	16	67	.254	372	47	10	.977
1974—Milwaukee	Amer.	C	131	432	59	104	15	4	12	56	.241	484	60	12	.978
1975—Milwaukee	Amer.	C	130	409	66	95	12	5	18	60	.232	532	82	13	.979
1976—Milwaukee†	Amer.	C	119	389	43	81	14	1	5	32	.208	491	52	4	.975
1977—Kansas City	Amer.	C	130	425	61	117	21	3	16	60	.275	663	61	●13	.982
1978—Kansas City	Amer.	C	150	520	77	138	27	6	18	78	.265	608	62	8	.988
1979—Kansas City	Amer.	C	157	533	101	155	23	10	20	112	.291	628	68	13	.982
1980—Kansas City‡§	Amer.	C	118	418	51	104	14	2	7	51	.249	322	37	8	.978
1981—St. Louis x	Nat.	C	61	174	22	39	10	2	6	31	.224	206	31	5	.979
1982—St. Louis y	Nat.	C	120	373	46	86	18	5	12	48	.231	469	64	9	.983
1983—St. Louis	Nat.	C	145	443	57	116	24	3	15	66	.262	578	70	7	.989
1984—St. Louis	Nat.	C	127	422	56	98	16	3	11	68	.232	620	58	11	.984
1985—St. Louis z	Nat.	C	84	240	30	53	12	2	10	36	.221	386	26	4	.990
1985—Louisville a	A. A.	C	7	20	3	3	0	0	1	2	.150	2	0	0	1.000
1986—Texas bc	Amer.	C	68	155	21	41	6	0	12	29	.265	165	9	1	.994
American League Totals—11 Years			1160	3757	535	946	154	33	127	556	.252	4486	504	98	.981
National League Totals—5 Years			537	1652	211	392	80	15	54	249	.237	2259	249	36	.986
Major League Totals—16 Years			1697	5409	746	1338	234	48	181	805	.247	6745	753	134	.982

Selected by Milwaukee Brewers' organization in 1st round (fourth player selected) of free-agent draft, June 4, 1970.
†Traded with Pitcher Jim Colborn to Kansas City Royals for Outfielder Jim Wohlford, Infielder Jamie Quirk and a player to be named later, December 6, 1976; Milwaukee Brewers acquired Pitcher Bob McClure to complete deal, March 15, 1977.
‡On disabled list, April 4 to May 2, 1980.
§Granted free agency, October 24, 1980; signed by St. Louis Cardinals, December 13, 1980.
xOn disabled list, May 18 to August 19, 1981.
yOn disabled list, May 15 to June 5, 1982.

zOn disabled list, April 12 to April 27 and June 3 to July 16, 1985; included rehabilitation disability assignment to Louisville, July 9 to July 16, 1985.

aReleased, November 14, 1985; signed by Texas Rangers, January 28, 1986.

bOn disabled list, June 16 to July 28, 1986.

cGranted free agency, November 12, 1986; re-signed by Rangers, December 5, 1986.

CHAMPIONSHIP SERIES RECORD

Tied Championship Series record for most two-base hits, three-game Series (3), 1982.
Tied National League Championship Series record for most bases on balls, six-game Series (5), 1985.

Year	Club	League	Pos.	G.	AB.	R.	H.	2B.	3B.	HR.	RBI.	B.A.	PO.	A.	E.	F.A.
1977—Kansas City		Amer.	C	5	15	3	5	0	0	0	0	.333	18	0	0	1.000
1978—Kansas City		Amer.	C	4	14	1	5	1	0	0	3	.357	21	1	0	1.000
1980—Kansas City		Amer.	C	3	10	2	1	0	0	0	0	.100	17	1	0	1.000
1982—St. Louis		Nat.	C	3	9	3	5	3	0	0	1	.556	15	3	0	1.000
1985—St. Louis		Nat.	C	5	15	1	4	1	0	0	0	.267	25	2	1	.964
Championship Series Totals—5 Years				20	63	10	20	5	0	0	4	.317	96	7	1	.990

WORLD SERIES RECORD

Year	Club	League	Pos.	G.	AB.	R.	H.	2B.	3B.	HR.	RBI.	B.A.	PO.	A.	E.	F.A.
1980—Kansas City		Amer.	PH-C	5	14	1	2	0	0	0	0	.143	13	2	0	1.000
1982—St. Louis		Nat.	C	7	28	1	8	2	0	1	5	.286	33	2	0	1.000
1985—St. Louis		Nat.	C	5	15	0	2	0	0	0	0	.133	36	4	0	1.000
World Series Totals—3 Years				17	57	2	12	2	0	1	5	.211	82	8	0	1.000

ALL-STAR GAME RECORD

Year	League	Pos.	AB.	R.	H.	2B.	3B.	HR.	RBI.	B.A.	PO.	A.	E.	F.A.
1978—American		PH	1	0	0	0	0	0	0	.000	0	0	0	.000
1979—American		C	3	0	1	1	0	0	0	.333	2	0	0	1.000
1980—American		C	1	0	0	0	0	0	0	.000	0	1	0	.000
All-Star Game Totals—3 Years			5	0	1	1	0	0	0	.200	2	1	0	1.000

Member of American League All-Star Team in 1974; did not play.

MARK STEVEN PORTUGAL

Born October 30, 1962, at Los Angeles, Calif.
Height, 6.00. Weight, 190.
Throws and bats righthanded.

Major League saves: 1986 (1).
Led Appalachian League in wild pitches with 12, home runs allowed with 11 and tied for lead in hit batsmen with 5 in 1981.

Year	Club	League	G.	IP.	W.	L.	Pct.	H.	R.	ER.	SO.	BB.	ERA.
1981—Elizabethton	Ap'lachian	14	85	7	1	.875	65	41	35	65	39	3.71
1982—Wisconsin Rapids	Midwest	36	119	9	8	.529	110	62	53	95	62	4.01
1983—Visalia	California	24	131⅓	10	5	.667	142	77	61	132	84	4.18
1984—Orlando	Southern	27	196	14	7	.667	171	80	65	110	113	2.98
1985—Toledo†	Int'national	19	128⅔	8	5	.615	129	60	54	89	60	3.78
1985—Minnesota	American	6	24⅓	1	3	.250	24	16	15	12	14	5.55
1986—Toledo	Int'national	6	45	5	1	.833	34	15	13	30	23	2.60
1986—Minnesota	American	27	112⅔	6	10	.375	112	56	54	67	50	4.31
Major League Totals—2 Years		33	137	7	13	.350	136	72	69	79	64	4.53

Signed as free agent by Minnesota Twins' organization, October 23, 1980.
†On disabled list, July 22 to August 2, 1985.

ALONZO SIDNEY POWELL

Born December 12, 1964, at San Francisco, Calif.
Height, 6.00. Weight, 190.
Throws and bats righthanded.

Year	Club	League	Pos.	G.	AB.	R.	H.	2B.	3B.	HR.	RBI.	B.A.	PO.	A.	E.	F.A.
1983—Clinton	Midw.	OF	36	113	14	22	5	1	0	9	.195	66	2	5	.932
1983—Great Falls	Pion.	OF-1B-3B	51	149	13	33	2	2	1	16	.221	127	15	8	.947
1984—Everett	N'west	1B	6	17	2	3	1	0	1	4	.176	38	2	3	.930
1984—Clinton†	Midw.	OF-1B-2B	47	149	22	37	3	2	1	10	.248	166	9	5	.972
1985—San Jose‡	Calif.	★OF-1B	136	473	79	122	27	6	9	62	.258	292	★21	10	.969
1986—W. Palm Beach	Fla. St.	OF	23	76	20	25	7	1	4	18	.329	56	1	0	1.000
1986—Jacksonville	South.	OF	105	402	67	121	21	5	15	80	.301	256	4	3	.989

Signed as free agent by San Francisco Giants' organization, February 3, 1983.
†Loaned to San Jose (Independent), April 9, 1985; returned, September 10, 1985.
‡Traded with Pitcher George Riley to Montreal Expos' organization for Pitcher Bill Laskey, October 24, 1985.

DENNIS CLAY POWELL

Born August 13, 1963, at Moultrie, Ga.
Height, 6.03. Weight, 200.
Throws left and bats righthanded.

Major League saves: 1985 (1).
Led Gulf Coast League in shutouts with 2 in 1983.

Year Club	League	G.	IP.	W.	L.	Pct.	H.	R.	ER.	SO.	BB.	ERA.
1983—Bradenton Dodgers	Gulf Coast	11	74	8	2	.800	52	22	12	*103	23	1.46
1984—Vero Beach	Florida St.	4	26	1	1	.500	19	7	4	14	12	1.38
1984—San Antonio	Texas	24	168	9	8	.529	153	81	63	82	87	3.38
1985—Albuquerque	P. Coast	18	111⅔	9	0	1.000	106	40	34	55	48	2.74
1985—Los Angeles	National	16	29⅓	1	1	.500	30	19	17	19	13	5.22
1986—Los Angeles†	National	27	65½	2	7	.222	65	32	31	31	25	4.27
1986—Albuquerque‡	P. Coast	7	41⅔	3	3	.500	45	23	19	27	15	4.10
Major League Totals—2 Years		43	94⅔	3	8	.273	95	51	48	50	38	4.56

Signed as free agent by Los Angeles Dodgers' organization, May 17, 1983.
†On disabled list, April 30 to June 6, 1986.
‡Traded with Infielder Mike Watters to Seattle Mariners for Pitcher Matt Young, December 10, 1986.

TED HENRY POWER

Born January 31, 1955, at Guthrie, Okla.
Height, 6.04. Weight, 220.
Throws and bats righthanded.
Attended Kansas State University, Manhattan, Kan.

Major League saves: 1983 (2), 1984 (11), 1985 (27), 1986 (1). Total—41.

Year Club	League	G.	IP.	W.	L.	Pct.	H.	R.	ER.	SO.	BB.	ERA.
1976—Lodi	California	13	51	1	3	.250	46	34	26	58	44	4.59
1977—San Antonio†	Texas	12	72	5	3	.625	51	35	31	60	55	3.88
1978—San Antonio‡	Texas	25	101	6	5	.545	92	57	45	97	75	4.01
1979—San Antonio	Texas	10	64	5	1	.833	69	44	37	52	43	5.20
1979—Albuquerque	P. Coast	18	101	5	5	.500	95	59	52	69	82	4.63
1980—Albuquerque	P. Coast	26	155	13	7	.650	160	93	78	113	95	4.53
1981—Albuquerque	P. Coast	27	187	*18	3	*.857	165	84	74	111	*103	3.56
1981—Los Angeles	National	5	14	1	3	.250	16	6	5	7	7	3.21
1982—Los Angeles	National	12	33⅔	1	1	.500	38	27	25	15	23	6.68
1982—Albuquerque§	P. Coast	14	73	5	4	.556	77	51	42	54	49	5.18
1983—Cincinnati	National	49	111	5	6	.455	120	62	56	57	49	4.54
1984—Cincinnati	National	*78	108⅔	9	7	.563	93	37	34	81	46	2.82
1985—Cincinnati	National	64	80	8	6	.571	65	27	24	42	45	2.70
1986—Cincinnati	National	56	129	10	6	.625	115	59	53	95	52	3.70
Major League Totals—6 Years		264	476⅓	34	29	.540	447	218	197	297	222	3.72

Selected by Los Angeles Dodgers' organization in 5th round of free-agent draft, June 8, 1976.
†On disabled list, July 18 to July 29 and August 20 to September 4, 1977.
‡On disabled list, July 5 to July 21, 1978.
§Traded to Cincinnati Reds for cash and Infielder Michael James Ramsey, October 15, 1982.

JAMES ARTHUR PRESLEY
(Jim)

Born October 23, 1961, at Pensacola, Fla.
Height, 6.01. Weight, 200.
Throws and bats righthanded.
Attended Pensacola Junior College, Pensacola, Fla.

Established major league record for fewest putouts by third baseman, season, 150 or more games (82), 1985.
Tied major league record for most home runs, opening day of season (2), April 8, 1986.
Major League stolen bases: 1984 (1), 1985 (2). Total—3.
Hit three home runs in a game, September 1, 1986.
Led Eastern League in game-winning RBIs with 16 in 1982.
Led Midwest League in being hit by pitch with 12 in 1980.
Led Eastern League third basemen in assists with 247 and total chances with 365 in 1982.
Led Southern League third basemen in double plays with 29 in 1983.

Year Club	League	Pos.	G.	AB.	R.	H.	2B.	3B.	HR.	RBI.	B.A.	PO.	A.	E.	F.A.
1979—Bellingham	N'west	SS	48	138	20	27	4	1	1	12	.196	42	127	27	.862
1980—Wausau	Midw.	3-S-2-1	126	429	45	105	21	1	12	52	.245	161	235	22	.947
1981—Wausau	Midw.	3B	57	208	48	58	10	0	12	53	.279	32	105	9	.938
1981—Lynn	East.	3B-2B	64	210	32	54	7	1	8	36	.257	49	110	11	.935
1982—Lynn	East.	*3B-OF	133	462	65	123	24	0	22	79	.266	84	250	*35	.905
1983—Chattanooga	South.	3B-SS	131	461	70	122	31	5	14	90	.265	122	329	27	.944
1984—Salt Lake City	P. C.	3B	69	265	43	84	13	4	13	56	.317	53	140	12	.941
1984—Seattle	Amer.	3B	70	251	27	57	12	1	10	36	.227	48	113	7	.958
1985—Seattle	Amer.	3B	155	570	71	157	33	1	28	84	.275	82	335	17	.961
1986—Seattle	Amer.	3B	155	616	83	163	33	4	27	107	.265	110	308	15	.965
Major League Totals—3 Years			380	1437	181	377	78	6	65	227	.262	240	756	39	.962

Selected by Seattle Mariners' organization in 4th round of free-agent draft, June 5, 1979.

ALL-STAR GAME RECORD
Member of American League All-Star Team in 1986; did not play.

—DID YOU KNOW—

That in a September 25, 1986, doubleheader between Los Angeles and San Diego, the Dodgers' Ken Howell defeated Lance McCullers in the first game and McCullers defeated Howell in the nightcap?

JOSEPH WALTER PRICE
(Joe)

Born November 29, 1956, at Inglewood, Calif.
Height, 6.04. Weight, 220.
Throws left and bats righthanded.
Attended Oklahoma State University, Stillwater, Okla., and
University of Oklahoma, Norman, Okla.

Major League saves: 1981 (4), 1982 (3), 1985 (1). Total—8.

Year Club	League	G.	IP.	W.	L.	Pct.	H.	R.	ER.	SO.	BB.	ERA.
1977—Billings	Pioneer	15	94	6	5	.545	83	50	39	97	42	3.73
1978—Tampa	Florida St.	23	165	10	4	.714	123	40	27	128	51	1.47
1978—Nashville	Southern	2	10	0	0	.000	7	3	3	10	3	2.70
1979—Nashville	Southern	22	109	6	6	.500	101	58	48	69	41	3.96
1980—Indianapolis	Am. Assoc.	11	79	4	4	.500	64	36	34	83	30	3.87
1980—Cincinnati	National	24	111	7	3	.700	95	45	44	44	37	3.57
1981—Cincinnati	National	41	54	6	1	.857	42	19	15	41	18	2.50
1982—Cincinnati	National	59	72⅔	3	4	.429	73	26	23	71	32	2.85
1983—Cincinnati†	National	21	144	10	6	.625	118	46	46	83	46	2.88
1984—Cincinnati	National	30	171⅔	7	13	.350	176	91	80	129	61	4.19
1985—Cincinnati‡	National	26	64⅔	2	2	.500	59	35	28	52	23	3.90
1986—Cincinnati§x	National	25	41⅔	1	2	.333	49	30	25	30	22	5.40
Major League Totals—7 Years		226	659⅔	36	31	.537	612	292	261	450	239	3.56

Selected by Cincinnati Reds' organization in 4th round of free-agent draft, June 7, 1977.
†On disabled list, August 7 to September 1, 1983.
‡On disabled list, July 23 to August 8 and August 29 to September 13, 1985.
§On disabled list, July 17 to September 1, 1986.
xGranted free agency, November 12, 1986.

THOMAS ALBERT PRINCE
(Tom)

Born August 13, 1964, at Kankakee, Ill.
Height, 5.11. Weight, 180.
Throws and bats righthanded.
Attended Kankakee Community College, Kankakee, Ill.

Led Carolina League catchers in total chances with 954 and passed balls with 15 in 1986.
Led South Atlantic League catchers in total chances with 930, double plays with 10 and passed balls with 27 in 1985.

Year Club	League	Pos.	G.	AB.	R.	H.	2B.	3B.	HR.	RBI.	B.A.	PO.	A.	E.	F.A.
1984—Watertown	NYP	C-3B	23	69	6	14	3	0	2	13	.203	155	26	2	.989
1984—Bradenton Pir.	Gulf C.	C-1B	18	48	4	11	0	0	1	6	.229	75	16	4	.958
1985—Macon	S. Atl.	C	124	360	60	75	20	1	10	42	.208	★810	★101	★19	.980
1986—Prince William	Carol.	C	121	395	59	100	34	1	10	47	.253	★821	●113	20	.979

Selected by Atlanta Braves' organization in 8th round of free-agent draft, January 11, 1983.
Selected by Atlanta Braves' organization in secondary phase of free-agent draft, June 6, 1983.
Selected by Pittsburgh Pirates' organization in secondary phase of free-agent draft, January 17, 1984.

GREGORY RUSSELL PRYOR
(Greg)

Born October 2, 1949, at Marietta, O.
Height, 6.00. Weight, 175.
Throws and bats righthanded.
Received bachelor of science degree in industrial management from
Florida Southern College, Lakeland, Fla.
Brother of Jeff Pryor, pitcher in California Angels' organization, 1968 through 1972.

Major League stolen bases: 1978 (3), 1979 (3), 1980 (2), 1982 (2), 1986 (1). Total—11.
Led International League shortstops in assists with 417 and double plays with 87 in 1977.
Tied for Pacific Coast League lead in double plays by shortstop with 90 in 1976.

Year Club	League	Pos.	G.	AB.	R.	H.	2B.	3B.	HR.	RBI.	B.A.	PO.	A.	E.	F.A.
1971—Geneva	NYP	3-2-S-O	60	226	40	64	10	4	4	28	.283	76	138	21	.911
1972—Pittsfield	East.	SS	65	208	23	43	10	2	1	16	.207	89	155	29	.894
1972—Burlington	Carol.	SS-OF	39	119	16	28	2	1	1	15	.235	49	110	11	.935
1973—Rocky Mount	Carol.	SS-2B	126	443	53	130	20	9	2	44	.293	203	349	50	.917
1974—Pittsfield	East.	3B-SS-2B	122	441	61	104	20	1	5	37	.236	113	255	26	.934
1975—Spokane	P. C.	SS-3B-2B	135	481	59	117	21	2	5	53	.243	184	411	33	.947
1976—Sacramento	P. C.	SS	122	495	71	136	21	3	9	51	.275	158	409	32	.947
1976—Texas†	Amer.	2B-3B-SS	5	8	2	3	0	0	0	1	.375	4	8	0	1.000
1977—Syracuse‡	Int.	★S-3-2	124	461	60	125	18	6	7	52	.271	213	420	21	★.968
1978—Chicago	Amer.	2B-3B-SS	82	222	27	58	11	0	2	15	.261	100	202	11	.965
1979—Chicago	Amer.	SS-2B-3B	143	476	60	131	23	3	3	34	.275	218	447	26	.962
1980—Chicago	Amer.	SS-3B-2B	122	338	32	81	18	4	1	29	.240	130	344	16	.967
1981—Chicago§	Amer.	3B-SS-2B	47	76	4	17	1	0	0	6	.224	27	65	6	.939
1982—Kansas City	Amer.	3-2-1-S	73	152	23	41	10	1	2	12	.270	78	112	5	.974
1983—Kansas City	Amer.	3B-1B-2B	68	115	9	25	4	0	1	14	.217	38	100	5	.965
1984—Kansas City x	Amer.	3-2-S-1	123	270	32	71	11	1	4	25	.263	87	190	8	.972
1985—Kansas City	Amer.	3-2-S-1	63	114	8	25	3	0	1	3	.219	47	87	5	.964
1986—Kansas City	Amer.	3-S-2-1	63	112	7	19	4	0	0	7	.170	30	88	6	.952
Major League Totals—10 Years			789	1883	204	471	85	9	14	146	.250	759	1643	88	.965

Selected by Washington Senators' organization in 6th round of free-agent draft, June 8, 1971.
†Traded with Infielder Brian Doyle and cash estimated at $25,000 to New York Yankees for Infielder Sandy Alomar, February 17, 1977.
‡Granted free agency, November 5, 1977; signed by Chicago White Sox, November 28, 1977.
§Traded to Kansas City Royals for Pitcher Jeff Schattinger, March 24, 1982.
xGranted free agency, November 8, 1984; re-signed by Royals, December 20, 1984.

CHAMPIONSHIP SERIES RECORD

Year—Club	League	Pos.	G.	AB.	R.	H.	2B.	3B.	HR.	RBI.	B.A.	PO.	A.	E.	F.A.
1984—Kansas City	Amer.	PR-3B	1	0	0	0	0	0	0	0	.000	1	0	0	1.000

WORLD SERIES RECORD

Year—Club	League	Pos.	G.	AB.	R.	H.	2B.	3B.	HR.	RBI.	B.A.	PO.	A.	E.	F.A.
1985—Kansas City	Amer.	3B	1	0	0	0	0	0	0	0	.000	0	1	0	1.000

KIRBY PUCKETT

Born March 14, 1961, at Chicago, Ill.
Height, 5.08. Weight, 178.
Throws and bats righthanded.
Attended Bradley University, Peoria, Ill., and Triton College, River Grove, Ill.

Tied major league record for most at-bats, season, no sacrifice flies (680), 1986.
Tied modern major league record for most hits, first game in majors, nine innings (4), May 8, 1984.
Major League stolen bases: 1984 (14), 1985 (21), 1986 (20). Total—55.
Hit for the cycle, August 1, 1986.
Led American League outfielders in total chances with 492 in 1985.
Led Appalachian League in total bases with 135 and tied for lead in stolen bases with 43 in 1982.
Led California League outfielders in double plays with 5 in 1983.
Named outfielder on THE SPORTING NEWS American League All-Star Team, 1986.
Named outfielder on THE SPORTING NEWS American League All-Star fielding team, 1986.
Named outfielder on THE SPORTING NEWS American League Silver Slugger team, 1986.
Named California League Player of the Year, 1983.

Year—Club	League	Pos.	G.	AB.	R.	H.	2B.	3B.	HR.	RBI.	B.A.	PO.	A.	E.	F.A.
1982—Elizabethton	Appal.	OF	65	*275	*65	*105	15	3	3	35	*.382	133	*11	5	.966
1983—Visalia	Calif.	OF	138	*548	105	172	29	7	9	97	.314	253	*22	5	.982
1984—Toledo	Int.	OF	21	80	9	21	2	0	1	5	.263	35	1	3	.923
1984—Minnesota	Amer.	OF	128	557	63	165	12	5	0	31	.296	438	*16	3	.993
1985—Minnesota	Amer.	OF	161	*691	80	199	29	13	4	74	.288	*465	19	8	.984
1986—Minnesota	Amer.	OF	161	680	119	223	37	6	31	96	.328	429	8	6	.986
Major League Totals—3 Years			450	1928	262	587	78	24	35	201	.304	1332	43	17	.988

Selected by Minnesota Twins' organization in 1st round (third player selected) of free-agent draft, January 12, 1982.

ALL-STAR GAME RECORD

Year—League	Pos.	AB.	R.	H.	2B.	3B.	HR.	RBI.	B.A.	PO.	A.	E.	F.A.
1986—American	OF	3	0	1	0	0	0	0	.333	5	0	0	1.000

TERRANCE STEPHEN PUHL

Name pronounced Pool.

(Terry)

Born July 8, 1956, at Melville, Saskatchewan, Canada.
Height, 6.02. Weight, 197.
Throws right and bats lefthanded.

Established major league record for highest fielding percentage by outfielder, lifetime, 1,000 or more games (.993).
Tied major league records for highest fielding percentage by outfielder, season, 150 or more games (1.000), 1979; fewest errors by outfielder, season, 150 or more games (0), 1979.
Major League stolen bases: 1977 (10), 1978 (32), 1979 (30), 1980 (27), 1981 (22), 1982 (17), 1983 (24), 1984 (13), 1985 (6), 1986 (3). Total—184.

Year—Club	League	Pos.	G.	AB.	R.	H.	2B.	3B.	HR.	RBI.	B.A.	PO.	A.	E.	F.A.
1974—Covington	Appal.	OF	59	211	42	60	11	0	0	21	.284	89	2	2	.978
1975—Dubuque	Midw.	OF-1B	104	346	57	115	10	2	0	28	.332	230	11	7	.971
1976—Columbus	South.	OF	28	98	13	28	5	0	1	14	.286	76	1	2	.975
1976—Memphis	Int.	OF	105	372	50	99	17	3	1	39	.266	191	5	3	.985
1977—Charleston	Int.	OF	78	285	53	87	12	6	4	33	.305	189	4	3	.985
1977—Houston	Nat.	OF	60	229	40	69	13	5	0	10	.301	119	3	1	.992
1978—Houston	Nat.	OF	149	585	87	169	25	6	3	35	.289	386	6	3	.992
1979—Houston	Nat.	OF	157	600	87	172	22	4	8	49	.287	352	7	0	*1.000
1980—Houston	Nat.	OF	141	535	75	151	24	5	13	55	.282	311	14	3	.991
1981—Houston	Nat.	OF	96	350	43	88	19	4	3	28	.251	185	5	0	●1.000
1982—Houston	Nat.	OF	145	507	64	133	17	9	8	50	.262	257	4	3	.989
1983—Houston	Nat.	OF	137	465	66	136	25	7	8	44	.292	220	4	2	.991
1984—Houston†	Nat.	OF	132	449	66	135	19	7	9	55	.301	213	6	3	.986
1985—Houston‡	Nat.	OF	57	194	34	55	14	3	2	23	.284	92	3	0	1.000
1986—Houston§	Nat.	OF	81	172	17	42	10	0	3	14	.244	65	0	0	1.000
Major League Totals—10 Years			1155	4086	579	1150	188	50	57	363	.281	2200	52	15	.993

Signed as free agent by Houston Astros' organization, September 19, 1973.
†On disabled list, April 13 to April 30, 1984.

‡On disabled list, April 22 to May 7, June 13 to June 28, July 19 to August 15 and August 26, 1985 through remainder of season.

§On disabled list, March 30 to April 15 and July 2 to July 23, 1986.

DIVISION SERIES RECORD

Year Club	League	Pos.	G.	AB.	R.	H.	2B.	3B.	HR.	RBI.	B.A.	PO.	A.	E.	F.A.
1981—Houston	Nat.	OF	5	21	2	4	1	0	0	0	.190	7	1	0	1.000

CHAMPIONSHIP SERIES RECORD

Tied Championship Series records for most at-bats, extra-inning game (6), October 8, 1980; most one-base hits, five-game Series (8), 1980.

Established National League Championship Series records for highest batting average, five-game Series (.526), 1980; most hits, five-game Series (10), 1980.

Tied National League Championship Series record for most hits, game (4), October 12, 1980.

Year Club	League	Pos.	G.	AB.	R.	H.	2B.	3B.	HR.	RBI.	B.A.	PO.	A.	E.	F.A.
1980—Houston	Nat.	PH-OF	5	19	4	10	2	0	0	3	.526	13	0	0	1.000
1986—Houston	Nat.	PH	3	3	0	2	0	0	0	0	.667	0	0	0	.000
Championship Series Totals—2 Years			8	22	4	12	2	0	0	3	.545	13	0	0	1.000

ALL-STAR GAME RECORD

Member of National League All-Star Team for 1978 game; did not play.

CHARLES MICHAEL PULEO

Name pronounced Puh-LAY-oh.

(Charlie)

Born February 7, 1955, at Glen Ridge, N. J.
Height, 6.03. Weight, 190.
Throws and bats righthanded.
Received bachelor of science degree in physical education and science from
Seton Hall University, South Orange, N. J. in 1977.

Pitched seven-inning, 3-0 no-hit victory against St. Petersburg, August 13, 1979 (second game).
Major League saves: 1982 (1).
Tied International League in complete games with 9 in 1986.

Year Club	League	G.	IP.	W.	L.	Pct.	H.	R.	ER.	SO.	BB.	ERA.
1978—Utica	NYP	16	104	10	3	.769	81	46	31	★125	48	2.68
1979—Dunedin	Florida St.	22	123	10	10	.500	126	72	61	77	61	4.46
1980—Knoxville†‡	Southern	19	108	8	7	.533	87	51	34	97	66	2.83
1981—Tidewater	Int'national	26	169	12	9	.571	132	74	65	133	73	3.46
1981—New York	National	4	13	0	0	.000	8	1	0	8	8	0.00
1982—New York§	National	36	171	9	9	.500	179	99	85	98	90	4.47
1983—Cincinnati x	National	27	143⅔	6	12	.333	145	86	78	71	91	4.89
1984—Wichita	Am. Assoc.	19	104⅓	8	9	.471	117	71	62	59	59	5.35
1984—Cincinnati	National	5	22	1	2	.333	27	15	14	6	15	5.73
1985—Denver y	Am. Assoc.	11	61	1	5	.167	70	42	31	40	37	4.57
1985—Richmond	Int'national	16	71	5	4	.556	50	23	22	63	37	2.79
1986—Richmond	Int'national	27	170	★14	7	.667	166	80	66	●124	76	3.79
1986—Atlanta	National	5	24⅓	1	2	.333	13	10	8	18	12	2.96
Major League Totals—5 Years		77	374	17	25	.405	372	211	185	201	216	4.45

Selected by Detroit Tigers' organization in 13th round of free-agent draft, June 5, 1973.
Signed as free agent by Toronto Blue Jays' organization, March 14, 1978.
†On disabled list, April 24 to June 14, 1980.
‡Traded to New York Mets' organization, April 14, 1981; completing deal in which New York traded Pitcher Mark Bomback to Toronto Blue Jays for a player to be named later, April 6, 1981.
§Traded with Catcher Lloyd McClendon and Outfielder Jason Felice to Cincinnati Reds for Pitcher Tom Seaver, December 16, 1982.
xOn disabled list, March 20 to May 2, 1983.
ySold to Richmond (Atlanta Braves' organization), June 6, 1985.

ALFONSO PULIDO (MANZO)

Name pronounced Puh-LEE-doh.

Born January 23, 1959, at Tierra Blanca, Veracruz, Mex.
Height, 5.11. Weight, 175.
Throws and bats lefthanded.

Major League saves: 1986 (1).
Led Pacific Coast League in complete games with 16 and shutouts with 4 in 1984.
Led Mexican Center League in games started by pitchers with 16 in 1978 and tied for lead with 14 in 1977.
Tied for Mexican Center League lead in shutouts with 3 in 1978.

Year Club	League	G.	IP.	W.	L.	Pct.	H.	R.	ER.	SO.	BB.	ERA.
1977—Arandas	Mex. Cent.	14	99	6	6	.500	124	61	48	46	18	4.36
1978—Matamoras	Mex. Cent.	18	111	10	3	.769	103	39	26	81	16	2.11
1978—Cordoba	Mexican	5	12	2	0	1.000	5	1	1	10	2	0.75
1979—Cordoba	Mexican	20	47	3	2	.600	50	22	22	23	19	4.21
1980—Reynosa†	Mexican	26	132	9	6	.600	142	58	52	69	39	3.55
1980—Reynosa‡	Mexican	7	47	3	4	.429	59	18	12	19	13	2.30
1981—Mexico City Reds	Mexican	31	126	5	6	.455	121	46	43	46	25	3.07
1982—Mexico City Reds	Mexican	43	93⅓	8	8	.500	94	34	25	50	31	2.41
1983—Mexico City Reds§	Mexican	29	187⅓	●17	3	.850	170	46	42	83	31	2.02

Year Club	League	G.	IP.	W.	L.	Pct.	H.	R.	ER.	SO.	BB.	ERA.
1983—Pittsburgh	National	1	2	0	0	.000	4	3	2	1	1	9.00
1984—Hawaii	P. Coast	28	*216	18	6	.750	190	73	61	123	46	2.54
1984—Pittsburgh x	National	1	2	0	0	.000	3	2	2	2	1	9.00
1985—Columbus	Int'national	31	146	11	8	.579	154	66	55	67	34	3.39
1986—Columbus	Int'national	23	95⅔	5	8	.385	93	41	31	28	25	2.92
1986—New York	American	10	30⅔	1	1	.500	38	17	16	13	9	4.70
National League Totals—2 Years		2	4	0	0	.000	7	5	4	3	2	9.00
American League Totals—1 Year		10	30⅔	1	1	.500	38	17	16	13	9	4.70
Major League Totals—3 Years		12	34⅔	1	1	.500	45	22	20	16	11	5.19

†20-team season.
‡6-team season.
§Sold to Pittsburgh Pirates, July 22, 1983; remained with Mexico City Reds on loan until September 1, 1983.
xTraded with Infielder Dale Berra and Outfielder Jay Buhner to New York Yankees for Outfielder Steve Kemp, Infielder Tim Foli and $800,000, December 20, 1984.

TIMOTHY MATTHEW PYZNARSKI
(Tim)

Born February 4, 1960, at Chicago, Ill.
Height, 6.02. Weight, 195.
Throws and bats righthanded.
Attended Eastern Illinois University, Charleston, Ill.

Major League stolen bases: 1986 (2).
Led Pacific Coast League batters in strikeouts with 127, game-winning RBIs with 14 and tied for lead in total bases with 278 in 1986.
Led Pacific Coast League first basemen in double plays with 117 in 1986.
Led Eastern League third basemen in putouts with 90, errors with 36, total chances with 336 and double plays with 24 in 1983.
Named Minor League Player of the Year by THE SPORTING NEWS, 1986.
Named Pacific Coast League Player of the Year, 1986.
Named third baseman on THE SPORTING NEWS College Baseball All-America Team, 1981.

Year Club	League	Pos.	G.	AB.	R.	H.	2B.	3B.	HR.	RBI.	B.A.	PO.	A.	E.	F.A.
1981—Modesto	Calif.	OF-3B	53	160	32	36	4	0	5	18	.225	71	29	10	.909
1982—West Haven†	East.	3B-1B	108	294	54	77	18	4	7	34	.262	66	168	31	.883
1983—Albany	East.	*3B-OF	124	416	84	116	15	4	29	79	.279	95	*210	37	.892
1984—Tacoma‡§	P. C.	3B-OF-1B	31	96	12	25	5	0	4	15	.260	6	17	2	.920
1985—Las Vegas	P. C.	1B-OF	115	359	51	102	22	4	7	37	.284	791	76	9	.990
1986—Las Vegas	P. C.	*1-O-3	135	484	93	158	35	8	23	*119	.326	1182	77	*19	.985
1986—San Diego x	Nat.	1B	15	42	3	10	1	0	0	0	.238	118	8	3	.977
Major League Totals—1 Year			15	42	3	10	1	0	0	0	.238	118	8	3	.977

Selected by Oakland A's organization in 1st round (15th player selected) of free-agent draft, June 8, 1981.
†On disabled list, June 10 to June 25, 1982.
†On disabled list, April 7 to April 21, May 10 to June 18 and July 14, 1984 through remainder of season.
§Traded to San Diego Padres' organization for Infielder Joe Lansford, April 3, 1985.
xTraded to Milwaukee Brewers' organization, October 29, 1986, completing deal in which Milwaukee traded Third Baseman Randy Ready to San Diego Padres for a player to be named later, June 12, 1986.

LUIS RAUL QUINONES

Name pronounced Key-NO-nez.
Born April 28, 1962, at Ponce, Puerto Rico.
Height, 5.11. Weight, 165.
Throws right and bats left and righthanded.

Major League stolen bases: 1983 (1), 1986 (3). Total—4.
Led Carolina League shortstops in double plays with 77 in 1981.
Tied for Northwest League lead in double plays by shortstops with 33 in 1980.

Year Club	League	Pos.	G.	AB.	R.	H.	2B.	3B.	HR.	RBI.	B.A.	PO.	A.	E.	F.A.
1980—Grays Harbor	N'west	SS	56	156	33	35	2	2	0	11	.224	70	157	24	.904
1981—Salem	Carol.	●SS-2B	123	455	64	102	10	4	7	37	.224	208	341	●53	.912
1982—Salem	Carol.	SS	41	173	32	48	1	4	5	28	.277	41	99	15	.903
1982—Amarillo†	Texas	SS	95	411	69	120	19	7	11	60	.292	164	288	31	.936
1983—Albany	East.	2B-OF-SS	56	213	35	51	5	0	6	23	.239	101	138	13	.948
1983—Oakland	Amer.	2-O-3-S	19	42	5	8	2	1	0	4	.190	22	24	1	.979
1983—Tacoma‡	P. C.	SS-OF-2B	45	133	14	35	3	1	2	14	.263	62	97	9	.946
1984—Maine	Int.	*SS-OF-2B	131	473	71	127	27	3	8	60	.268	217	330	*43	.927
1985—Maine§	Int.	SS-OF	14	45	4	8	2	1	1	2	.178	19	12	0	1.000
1985—Phoenix	P. C.	SS-2B-3B	85	304	46	78	13	7	8	47	.257	106	236	13	.963
1986—Phoenix	P. C.	SS	14	55	7	14	4	1	0	7	.255	23	37	3	.952
1986—San Francisco x	Nat.	SS-3B-2B	71	106	13	19	1	3	0	11	.179	28	66	8	.922
American League Totals—1 Year			19	42	5	8	2	1	0	4	.190	22	24	1	.979
National League Totals—1 Year			71	106	13	19	1	3	0	11	.179	28	66	8	.922
Major League Totals—2 Years			90	148	18	27	3	4	0	15	.182	50	90	9	.940

Signed as free agent by San Diego Padres' organization, April 28, 1980.
†Drafted by Oakland A's, December 6, 1982.
‡Traded to Cleveland Indians, December 8, 1983, completing deal in which Cleveland traded Catcher Jim Essian to Oakland A's for a player to be named later, December 5, 1983.
§Traded with Pitcher Mike Jeffcoat to San Francisco Giants' organization for Shortstop Johnnie LeMaster, May 7, 1985.
xReleased, November 10, 1986.

REY FRANCISCO QUINONES

Name pronounced Key-NO-nez.

Born November 11, 1963, at Rio Piedras, Puerto Rico.
Height, 5.11. Weight, 160.
Throws and bats righthanded.

Major League stolen bases: 1986 (4).
Led Eastern League in being hit by pitch with 9 in 1985.
Led Carolina League in grounding into double plays with 20 in 1984.
Led Eastern League shortstops in double plays with 75 in 1985.
Led Carolina League shortstops in total chances with 718 and double plays with 84 in 1984.

Year Club	League	Pos.	G.	AB.	R.	H.	2B.	3B.	HR.	RBI.	B.A.	PO.	A.	E.	F.A.
1983—Elmira	NYP	SS	67	234	38	69	11	0	12	55	.295	107	226	27	.925
1984—Winston-Salem	Carol.	SS	132	458	53	128	*30	6	11	69	.279	*240	*428	*50	.930
1985—New Britain	East.	SS	134	439	67	113	19	5	9	50	.257	207	*402	*34	.947
1986—Pawtucket	Int.	SS	24	87	12	23	2	0	4	18	.264	35	67	4	.962
1986—Bos.†-Sea.	Amer.	SS	98	312	32	68	16	1	2	22	.218	143	247	24	.942
Major League Totals—1 Year			98	312	32	68	16	1	2	22	.218	143	247	24	.942

Signed as free agent by Boston Red Sox' organization, September 8, 1982.

†Traded with a player to be named later and cash to Seattle Mariners for Infielder Spike Owen and Outfielder Dave Henderson, August 19, 1986; as part of deal, Seattle claimed Pitchers Mike Brown and Mike Trujillo on waivers from Boston Red Sox, August 22, 1986. Seattle acquired Outfielder John Christensen to complete deal, September 25, 1986.

JAMES PATRICK QUIRK

(Jamie)

Born October 22, 1954, at Whittier, Calif.
Height, 6.04. Weight, 200.
Throws right and bats lefthanded.
Attended Whittier College, Whittier, Calif.

Major League stolen bases: 1980 (3).
Led American Association in passed balls with 23 in 1985.
Led American Association third basemen in double plays with 31 in 1975.
Led Pioneer League shortstops in double plays with 16 in 1972.

Year Club	League	Pos.	G.	AB.	R.	H.	2B.	3B.	HR.	RBI.	B.A.	PO.	A.	E.	F.A.
1972—Billings	Pion.	SS	55	208	29	53	9	4	5	37	.255	*63	*162	*28	*.889
1973—San Jose	Calif.	SS	132	429	58	99	12	7	8	45	.231	160	330	39	.926
1974—Jacksonville	South.	SS	46	163	16	37	7	2	3	21	.227	75	133	20	.912
1974—Omaha	A. A.	SS-3B-2B	53	203	27	57	10	2	10	31	.281	64	141	14	.936
1975—Omaha	A. A.	3B	127	445	62	122	23	4	13	64	.274	109	*254	16	*.958
1975—Kansas City	Amer.	OF-3B	14	39	2	10	0	0	1	5	.256	19	3	2	.917
1976—Kansas City†	Amer.	SS-3B-1B	64	114	11	28	6	0	1	15	.246	9	14	2	.920
1977—Milwaukee	Amer.	OF-3B	93	221	16	48	14	1	3	13	.217	19	4	2	.920
1978—Spokane‡	P. C.	3B-1B	97	343	58	100	20	2	12	63	.292	235	142	20	.950
1978—Kansas City§	Amer.	3B-SS	17	29	3	6	2	0	0	2	.207	11	16	2	.931
1979—Kansas City	Amer.	C-SS-3B	51	79	8	24	6	1	1	11	.304	16	9	1	.960
1980—Kansas City	Amer.	C-3-O-1	62	163	13	45	5	0	5	21	.276	78	66	8	.947
1981—Kansas City	Amer.	C-3-2-O	46	100	8	25	7	0	0	10	.250	63	23	4	.956
1982—Kansas City xy	Amer.	C-1-3-O	36	78	8	18	3	0	1	5	.231	110	12	0	1.000
1983—St. Louis za	Nat.	C-3B-SS	48	86	3	18	2	1	2	11	.209	68	13	6	.931
1984—Denver	A. A.	C-3-O-1-P	70	201	23	42	6	3	2	24	.209	212	67	11	.962
1984—Chi. b-Cle. c	Amer.	3B-C	4	3	1	1	0	0	1	2	.333	1	0	0	1.000
1985—Omaha	A. A.	C-1B-3B	104	324	33	79	5	1	8	48	.244	525	67	14	.977
1985—Kansas City d	Amer.	C-1B	19	57	3	16	3	1	0	4	.281	66	8	1	.987
1986—Kansas City e	Amer.	C-3-1-O	80	219	24	47	10	0	8	26	.215	303	64	4	.989
American League Totals—11 Years			486	1102	97	268	56	3	21	114	.243	695	219	26	.972
National League Totals—1 Year			48	86	3	18	2	1	2	11	.209	68	13	6	.931
Major League Totals—12 Years			534	1188	100	286	58	4	23	125	.241	763	232	32	.969

Selected by Kansas City Royals' organization in 1st round (18th player selected) of free-agent draft, June 6, 1972.

†Traded with Outfielder Jim Wohlford and a player to be named later to Milwaukee Brewers for Pitcher Jim Colborn and Catcher Darrell Porter, December 6, 1976; Milwaukee acquired Pitcher Bob McClure to complete deal, March 15, 1977.

‡Traded to Kansas City Royals for Pitcher Gerry Ako and cash, August 3, 1978.

§On disabled list, August 14 to September 5, 1978.

xOn disabled list, August 10 to September 1, 1982.

yGranted free agency, November 10, 1982; signed by St. Louis Cardinals, February 16, 1983.

zReleased, March 26, 1984; named St. Louis Cardinals coach, April 13, 1984.

aSigned by Chicago White Sox' organization, May 23, 1984.

bSold to Cleveland Indians, September 24, 1984.

cReleased, October 15, 1984; signed by Kansas City Royals' organization, February 25, 1985.

dGranted free agency, November 12, 1985; re-signed by Royals, November 27, 1985.

eGranted free agency, November 12, 1986; re-signed by Royals, December 8, 1986.

CHAMPIONSHIP SERIES RECORD

Year Club	League	Pos.	G.	AB.	R.	H.	2B.	3B.	HR.	RBI.	B.A.	PO.	A.	E.	F.A.
1976—Kansas City	Amer.	PH-DH	4	7	1	1	0	1	0	2	.143	0	0	0	.000
1985—Kansas City	Amer.	PH	1	1	0	0	0	0	0	0	.000	0	0	0	.000
Championship Series Totals—2 Years			5	8	1	1	0	1	0	2	.125	0	0	0	.000

PITCHING RECORD

Year Club	League	G.	IP.	W.	L.	Pct.	H.	R.	ER.	SO.	BB.	ERA.
1984—Denver	Am. Assoc.	2	2	0	0	.000	6	3	3	0	0	13.50

DANIEL RAYMOND QUISENBERRY

Name pronounced QUIZ-en-berry.

(Dan)

Born February 7, 1953, at Santa Monica, Calif.
Height, 6.02. Weight, 180.
Throws and bats righthanded.
Attended Orange Coast College, Costa Mesa, Calif., LaVerne College, LaVerne, Calif.,
and Fresno Pacific College, Fresno, Calif.

Major League saves: 1979 (5), 1980 (33), 1981 (18), 1982 (35), 1983 (45), 1984 (44), 1985 (37), 1986 (12). Total—229.
Led American League in games finished in relief with 68 in both 1980 and 1982, 62 in 1983 and 76 in 1985.
Led American League in saves with 35 in 1982, 45 in 1983, 44 in 1984, 37 in 1985 and tied for lead with 33 in 1980.
Tied for Southern League lead in saves with 15 in 1978.
Named American League Fireman of the Year by THE SPORTING NEWS, 1980 and 1982 through 1985.

Year Club	League	G.	IP.	W.	L.	Pct.	H.	R.	ER.	SO.	BB.	ERA.
1975—Waterloo	Midwest	20	44	3	2	.600	40	16	12	31	6	2.45
1975—Jacksonville	Southern	6	8	0	1	.000	5	3	2	2	4	2.25
1976—Jacksonville	Southern	9	12	0	1	.000	8	6	3	6	2	2.25
1976—Waterloo	Midwest	34	42	2	1	.667	28	4	3	19	9	0.64
1977—Jacksonville	Southern	33	74	3	1	.750	61	18	11	33	11	1.34
1978—Jacksonville	Southern	48	64	4	2	.667	62	22	17	29	12	2.39
1979—Omaha	Am. Assoc.	26	35	2	1	.667	29	15	14	16	10	3.60
1979—Kansas City	American	32	40	3	2	.600	42	16	14	13	7	3.15
1980—Kansas City	American	*75	128	12	7	.632	129	47	44	37	27	3.09
1981—Kansas City	American	40	62	1	4	.200	59	16	12	20	15	1.74
1982—Kansas City	American	72	136⅔	9	7	.563	126	43	39	46	12	2.57
1983—Kansas City	American	*69	139	5	3	.625	118	35	30	48	11	1.94
1984—Kansas City	American	72	129⅓	6	3	.667	121	39	38	41	12	2.64
1985—Kansas City	American	*84	129	8	9	.471	142	41	34	54	16	2.37
1986—Kansas City	American	62	81⅓	3	7	.300	92	30	25	36	24	2.77
Major League Totals—8 Years		506	845⅓	47	42	.528	829	267	236	295	124	2.51

Signed as free agent by Kansas City Royals' organization, June 7, 1975.

DIVISION SERIES RECORD

Year Club	League	G.	IP.	W.	L.	Pct.	H.	R.	ER.	SO.	BB.	ERA.
1981—Kansas City	American	1	1	0	0	.000	1	0	0	0	0	0.00

CHAMPIONSHIP SERIES RECORD

Tied American League Championship Series record for most games pitched, seven-game Series (4), 1985.
Tied American League Championship Series record for most saves, total Series (2), 1985.

Year Club	League	G.	IP.	W.	L.	Pct.	H.	R.	ER.	SO.	BB.	ERA.
1980—Kansas City	American	2	4⅔	1	0	1.000	4	1	0	1	2	0.00
1984—Kansas City	American	1	3	0	1	.000	2	2	1	1	1	3.00
1985—Kansas City	American	4	4⅔	0	1	.000	7	4	2	3	0	3.86
Championship Series Totals—3 Years		7	12⅓	1	2	.333	13	7	3	5	3	2.19

WORLD SERIES RECORD

Established World Series records for most games pitched in relief, six-game Series (6), 1980; most games finished, six-game Series (6), 1980.

Year Club	League	G.	IP.	W.	L.	Pct.	H.	R.	ER.	SO.	BB.	ERA.
1980—Kansas City	American	6	10⅓	1	2	.333	10	6	6	0	3	5.23
1985—Kansas City	American	4	4⅓	1	0	1.000	5	1	1	3	3	2.08
World Series Totals—2 Years		10	14⅔	2	2	.500	15	7	7	3	6	4.30

ALL-STAR GAME RECORD

Year League	IP.	W.	L.	Pct.	H.	R.	ER.	SO.	BB.	ERA.
1982—American	2	0	0	.000	3	1	1	1	0	4.50
1983—American	1	0	0	.000	1	0	0	1	0	0.00
All-Star Game Totals—2 Years	3	0	0	.000	4	1	1	2	0	3.00

Member of American League All-Star Team in 1984; did not play.

TIMOTHY RAINES

(Tim)

Born September 16, 1959, at Sanford, Fla.
Height, 5.08. Weight, 170.
Throws right and bats left and righthanded.
Brother of Ned Raines, minor league outfielder, 1978 through 1980.

Established major league record for highest stolen base percentage, lifetime, 300 or attempts (.870).
Tied major league record for fewest double plays by outfielder, season, for leader in double plays (4), 1985.
Major League stolen bases: 1979 (2), 1980 (5), 1981 (71), 1982 (78), 1983 (90), 1984 (75), 1985 (70), 1986 (70). Total—461.
Led National League in stolen bases with 71 in 1981, 78 in 1982, 90 in 1983 and 75 in 1984.

Led National League outfielders in assists with 21 in 1983.
Led American Association in stolen bases with 77 in 1980.
Won THE SPORTING NEWS Gold Shoe Award, 1984.
Named outfielder on THE SPORTING NEWS National League All-Star Team, 1983 and 1986.
Named outfielder on THE SPORTING NEWS National League Silver Slugger team, 1986.
Named National League Rookie Player of the Year by THE SPORTING NEWS, 1981.
Named Minor League Player of the Year by THE SPORTING NEWS, 1980.

Year	Club	League	Pos.	G.	AB.	R.	H.	2B.	3B.	HR.	RBI.	B.A.	PO.	A.	E.	F.A.
1977—Sarasota Expos	Gulf C.		2B-3B-OF	49	161	28	45	6	2	0	21	.280	79	72	13	.921
1978—W. Palm Beach† ..	Fla. St.		2B-SS	100	359	67	103	10	0	0	23	.287	219	273	24	.953
1979—Memphis................	South.		2B	●145	552	*104	160	25	10	5	50	.290	*341	*413	*23	.970
1979—Montreal	Nat.		PR	6	0	3	0	0	0	0	0	.000	0	0	0	.000
1980—Denver	A. A.		2B	108	429	105	152	23	●11	6	64	*.354	226	338	16	.972
1980—Montreal	Nat.		2B-OF	15	20	5	1	0	0	0	0	.050	15	16	0	1.000
1981—Montreal	Nat.		OF-2B	88	313	61	95	13	7	5	37	.304	162	8	4	.977
1982—Montreal	Nat.		OF-2B	156	647	90	179	32	8	4	43	.277	293	126	8	.981
1983—Montreal	Nat.		OF-2B	156	615	*133	183	32	8	11	71	.298	314	23	4	.988
1984—Montreal	Nat.		OF-2B	160	622	106	192	●38	9	8	60	.309	420	8	6	.986
1985—Montreal	Nat.		OF	150	575	115	184	30	13	11	41	.320	284	8	2	.993
1986—Montreal‡	Nat.		OF	151	580	91	194	35	10	9	62	*.334	270	13	6	.979
Major League Totals—8 Years................				882	3372	604	1028	180	55	48	314	.305	1758	202	30	.985

Selected by Montreal Expos' organization in 5th round of free-agent draft, June 7, 1977.
†On disabled list, May 23 to June 5, 1978.
‡Granted free agency, November 12, 1986.

CHAMPIONSHIP SERIES RECORD

Year	Club	League	Pos.	G.	AB.	R.	H.	2B.	3B.	HR.	RBI.	B.A.	PO.	A.	E.	F.A.
1981—Montreal	Nat.		OF	5	21	1	5	2	0	0	1	.238	9	0	0	1.000

ALL-STAR GAME RECORD

Year	League	Pos.	AB.	R.	H.	2B.	3B.	HR.	RBI.	B.A.	PO.	A.	E.	F.A.
1981—National	PR-OF	0	0	0	0	0	0	0	.000	1	0	0	1.000
1982—National	OF	1	0	0	0	0	0	0	.000	0	0	0	.000
1983—National	OF	3	0	0	0	0	0	0	.000	2	0	0	1.000
1984—National	OF	1	0	0	0	0	0	0	.000	4	0	0	1.000
1985—National	PH-OF	0	1	0	0	0	0	0	.000	0	0	0	.000
1986—National	PH-OF	2	0	0	0	0	0	0	.000	1	0	0	1.000
All-Star Game Totals—6 Years..................		7	1	0	0	0	0	0	.000	8	0	0	1.000

RAFAEL EMILIO RAMIREZ (PEGUERO)
Born February 18, 1959, at San Pedro de Macoris, Dominican Republic.
Height, 6.00. Weight, 170.
Throws and bats righthanded.

Tied major league records for most doubles, game (4), May 21, 1986, 13 innings; most double plays by shortstop, extra-inning game (6), June 27, 1982 (14 innings).
Established National League record for fewest putouts by shortstop, season, for leader in most putouts (251), 1984.
Major League stolen bases: 1980 (2), 1981 (7), 1982 (27), 1983 (16), 1984 (14), 1985 (2), 1986 (19). Total—87.
Led National Stolen League shortstops in double plays with 130 in 1982, 116 in 1983, 115 in 1985 and tied for lead with 94 in 1984.
Led National League shortstops in total chances with 866 in 1982 and 724 in 1984.

Year	Club	League	Pos.	G.	AB.	R.	H.	2B.	3B.	HR.	RBI.	B.A.	PO.	A.	E.	F.A.
1977—Brad. Braves.........	Gulf C.		SS-OF	49	175	20	31	2	1	4	19	.177	52	94	32	.820
1978—Greenwood...........	W. Car.		SS	81	282	54	77	15	3	6	46	.273	119	229	*43	.890
1978—Savannah............	South.		SS	38	131	14	27	4	0	2	13	.206	61	123	15	.925
1979—Savannah†...........	South.		SS	113	386	47	80	17	3	10	39	.207	134	282	*38	.916
1980—Richmond‡..........	Int.		SS	80	281	33	79	15	3	5	38	.281	117	294	23	.947
1980—Atlanta	Nat.		SS	50	165	17	44	6	1	2	11	.267	63	140	11	.949
1981—Atlanta	Nat.		SS	95	307	30	67	16	2	2	20	.218	181	306	*30	.942
1982—Atlanta	Nat.		SS	157	609	74	169	24	4	10	52	.278	*300	528	*38	.956
1983—Atlanta	Nat.		SS	152	622	82	185	13	5	7	58	.297	232	490	*39	.949
1984—Atlanta	Nat.		SS	145	591	51	157	22	4	2	48	.266	*251	443	●30	.959
1985—Atlanta	Nat.		SS	138	568	54	141	25	4	5	58	.248	214	451	*32	.954
1986—Atlanta	Nat.		SS-3B-OF	134	496	57	119	21	1	8	33	.240	156	371	29	.948
Major League Totals—7 Years................				871	3358	365	882	127	21	36	280	.263	1397	2729	209	.952

Signed as free agent by Atlanta Braves' organization, September 28, 1976.
†On disabled list, April 16 to April 27, 1979.
‡On disabled list, June 23 to July 17, 1980.

CHAMPIONSHIP SERIES RECORD

Year	Club	League	Pos.	G.	AB.	R.	H.	2B.	3B.	HR.	RBI.	B.A.	PO.	A.	E.	F.A.
1982—Atlanta	Nat.		SS	3	11	1	2	0	0	1	.182	5	11	1	.941

ALL-STAR GAME RECORD

Member of National League All-Star Team in 1984; did not play.

DOMINGO ANTONIO RAMOS
Born March 29, 1958, at Santiago, Dominican Republic.
Height, 5.10. Weight, 154.
Throws and bats righthanded.

Major League stolen bases: 1983 (3), 1984 (2). Total—5.
Tied for International League lead in sacrifice flies with 6 in 1981.

Year Club	League	Pos.	G.	AB.	R.	H.	2B.	3B.	HR.	RBI.	B.A.	PO.	A.	E.	F.A.
1975—Oneonta	NYP	SS-3B	49	166	29	39	4	1	0	21	.235	60	143	14	.935
1976—Fort Lauderdale	Fla. St.	SS	103	328	34	79	11	3	0	29	.241	150	343	35	.934
1976—Syracuse	Int.	SS	11	39	7	10	2	1	0	8	.256	13	20	2	.943
1977—West Haven	East.	SS	129	431	55	106	18	6	2	50	.246	222	433	23	*.966
1978—Tacoma	P. C.	SS	91	314	43	74	13	3	0	30	.236	155	290	28	.941
1978—West Haven	East.	SS	40	134	16	34	2	2	1	13	.254	40	128	6	.966
1978—New York†‡	Amer.	SS	1	0	0	0	0	0	0	0	.000	0	0	0	.000
1979—Syr.§-Colum. x	Int.	SS	115	376	38	92	11	4	1	28	.245	211	323	26	.954
1980—Syracuse	Int.	SS	84	319	45	80	8	4	4	27	.251	160	240	28	.935
1980—Toronto	Amer.	SS-2B	5	16	0	2	0	0	0	0	.125	5	10	0	1.000
1981—Syracuse y	Int.	SS-3B-2B	96	320	42	82	4	5	0	31	.256	158	248	19	.955
1982—Salt Lake City	P. C.	SS	112	427	75	134	19	8	6	56	.314	174	288	19	.960
1982—Seattle	Amer.	SS	8	26	3	4	2	0	0	1	.154	9	14	2	.920
1983—Seattle	Amer.	2B-SS-3B	53	127	14	36	4	0	2	10	.283	51	109	8	.952
1984—Seattle	Amer.	3-S-1-2	59	81	6	15	2	0	0	2	.185	51	49	5	.952
1985—Seattle	Amer.	S-2-1-3	75	168	19	33	6	0	1	15	.196	87	119	10	.954
1986—Seattle	Amer.	SS-2B-3B	49	99	8	18	2	0	0	5	.182	55	93	6	.961
Major League Totals—7 Years			250	517	50	108	16	0	3	33	.209	258	394	31	.955

Signed as free agent by New York Yankees' organization, May 27, 1975.

†Traded with Pitchers Sparky Lyle, Larry McCall and Dave Rajsich, Catcher Mike Heath and cash to Texas Rangers for Outfielders Juan Beniquez and Greg Jemison and Pitchers Mike Griffin, Paul Mirabella and Dave Righetti, November 10, 1978.

‡Loaned to Toronto Blue Jays' organization, April 5, 1979.

§Loaned to New York Yankees' organization, July 30, 1979; returned to Texas Rangers, September 28, 1979.

xSold to Toronto Blue Jays, November 5, 1979.

yDrafted by Seattle Mariners, December 7, 1981.

WILLIAM LARRY RANDOLPH JR.
(Willie)

Born July 6, 1954, at Holly Hill, S. C.
Height, 5.11. Weight, 163.
Throws and bats righthanded.
Brother of Terry Randolph, defensive back with Green Bay Packers, 1977.

Tied major league record for most assists by second baseman in extra-inning game since 1900 (13), August 25, 1976 (19 innings).

Established American League record for most chances accepted by second baseman in extra-inning game (20), August 25, 1976 (19 innings).

Major League stolen bases: 1975 (1), 1976 (37), 1977 (13), 1978 (36), 1979 (33), 1980 (30), 1981 (14), 1982 (16), 1983 (12), 1984 (10), 1985 (16), 1986 (15). Total—233.

Led American League in bases on balls received with 119 in 1980.
Led American League second basemen in double plays with 128 in 1979 and 112 in 1984.
Led American League second basemen in total chances with 846 in 1979.
Led Eastern League in bases on balls received with 110 in 1974.
Led Western Carolinas League in bases on balls received with 90 and tied for lead in sacrifice flies with 8 in 1973.
Named second baseman on THE SPORTING NEWS American League All-Star Team, 1977 and 1980.
Named second baseman on THE SPORTING NEWS American League Silver Slugger team, 1980.

Year Club	League	Pos.	G.	AB.	R.	H.	2B.	3B.	HR.	RBI.	B.A.	PO.	A.	E.	F.A.
1972—Bradenton Pir.	Gulf C.	SS-OF	44	167	21	53	6	5	0	10	.317	85	116	24	.893
1973—Charleston	W. Car.	2B	121	428	93	120	25	6	8	51	.280	*285	308	*24	.961
1974—Thetford Mines	East.	2B	135	461	*103	117	28	6	12	53	.254	269	319	21	.966
1975—Charleston	Int.	2B	91	313	41	106	13	5	7	42	.339	189	250	16	.965
1975—Pittsburgh†	Nat.	2B-3B	30	61	9	10	1	0	0	3	.164	34	45	6	.929
1976—New York	Amer.	2B	125	430	59	115	15	4	1	40	.267	307	415	19	.974
1977—New York	Amer.	2B	147	551	91	151	28	11	4	40	.274	350	454	16	.980
1978—New York‡	Amer.	2B	134	499	87	139	18	·6	3	42	.279	296	400	16	.978
1979—New York	Amer.	2B	153	574	98	155	15	13	5	61	.270	*355	*478	13	.985
1980—New York	Amer.	2B	138	513	99	151	23	7	7	46	.294	361	401	19	.976
1981—New York	Amer.	2B	93	357	59	83	14	3	2	24	.232	205	268	*11	.977
1982—New York	Amer.	2B	144	553	85	155	21	4	3	36	.280	352	380	14	.981
1983—New York§	Amer.	2B	104	420	73	117	21	1	2	38	.279	265	298	12	.979
1984—New York	Amer.	2B	142	564	86	162	24	2	2	31	.287	334	419	13	.983
1985—New York	Amer.	2B	143	497	75	137	21	2	5	40	.276	303	425	11	.985
1986—New York x	Amer.	2B	141	492	76	136	15	2	5	50	.276	313	381	*20	.972
National League Totals—1 Year			30	61	9	10	1	0	0	3	.164	34	45	6	.929
American League Totals—11 Years			1464	5450	888	1501	215	55	39	448	.275	3441	4319	164	.979
Major League Totals—12 Years			1494	5511	897	1511	216	55	39	451	.274	3475	4364	170	.979

Selected by Pittsburgh Pirates' organization in 7th round of free-agent draft, June 6, 1972.

†Traded with Pitchers Ken Brett and Dock Ellis to New York Yankees for Pitcher Doc Medich, December 11, 1975.

‡On disabled list, June 23 to July 14, 1978.

§On disabled list, June 27 to July 12 and July 13 to August 5, 1983.

xGranted free agency, November 12, 1986.

DIVISION SERIES RECORD

Year Club	League	Pos.	G.	AB.	R.	H.	2B.	3B.	HR.	RBI.	B.A.	PO.	A.	E.	F.A.
1981—New York	Amer.	2B	5	20	0	4	0	0	0	1	.200	7	10	0	1.000

Year Club League	Pos.	G.	AB.	R.	H.	2B.	3B.	HR.	RBI.	B.A.	PO.	A.	E.	F.A.
1975—Pittsburgh .... Nat.	PH-PR-2	2	2	1	0	0	0	0	0	.000	0	1	0	1.000
1976—New York............. Amer.	2B	5	17	0	2	0	0	0	1	.118	8	14	0	1.000
1977—New York............. Amer.	2B	5	18	4	5	1	0	0	2	.278	13	9	0	1.000
1980—New York............. Amer.	2B	3	13	0	5	2	0	0	1	.385	2	9	0	1.000
1981—New York............. Amer.	2B	3	12	2	4	0	0	1	2	.333	12	12	0	1.000
Championship Series Totals—5 Years....		18	62	7	16	3	0	1	6	.258	35	45	0	1.000

WORLD SERIES RECORD

Established World Series record for most bases on balls, six-game Series (9), 1981.
Tied World Series record for fewest chances accepted by second baseman, game (0), October 25, 1981.

Year Club League	Pos.	G.	AB.	R.	H.	2B.	3B.	HR.	RBI.	B.A.	PO.	A.	E.	F.A.
1976—New York............. Amer.	2B	4	14	1	1	0	0	0	0	.071	13	8	0	1.000
1977—New York............. Amer.	2B	6	25	5	4	2	0	1	1	.160	13	14	0	1.000
1981—New York............. Amer.	2B	6	18	5	4	1	1	2	3	.222	13	11	0	1.000
World Series Totals—3 Years		16	57	11	9	3	1	3	4	.158	39	33	0	1.000

ALL-STAR GAME RECORD

Established All-Star Game record for most assists by second baseman, nine-inning game (6), July 19, 1977.
Tied All-Star Game records for most at bats, nine-inning game (5), July 19, 1977; most errors, game (2), July 8, 1980.

Year League	Pos.	AB.	R.	H.	2B.	3B.	HR.	RBI.	B.A.	PO.	A.	E.	F.A.
1977—American.......................	2B	5	0	1	0	0	0	1	.200	2	6	0	1.000
1980—American.......................	2B	4	0	2	0	0	0	0	.500	0	3	2	.600
1981—American.......................	2B	3	0	1	0	0	0	0	.333	0	5	0	1.000
All-Star Game Totals—3 Years..................		12	0	4	0	0	0	1	.333	2	14	2	.888

Named to American League All-Star Team for 1976 game; replaced due to injury.

DENNIS LEE RASMUSSEN

Born April 18, 1959, at Los Angeles, Calif.
Height, 6.07. Weight, 225.
Throws and bats lefthanded.
Attended Creighton University, Omaha, Neb.
Grandson of Wilbur Lee (Bill) Brubaker, infielder with Pittsburgh
Pirates and Boston Braves, 1932 through 1940 and 1943.

Led Eastern League in wild pitches with 18 in 1981.
Tied for International League lead in games started by pitchers with 28 in 1983.

Year Club	League	G.	IP.	W.	L.	Pct.	H.	R.	ER.	SO.	BB.	ERA.
1980—Salinas	California	11	76	4	6	.400	69	51	46	63	52	5.45
1981—Holyoke	Eastern	24	156	8	12	.400	134	95	69	125	99	3.98
1982—Spokane†	P. Coast	27	171⅔	11	8	.579	166	110	96	*113	108	5.03
1983—Columbus‡	Int'national	28	181	●13	10	.565	161	106	92	*187	108	4.57
1983—San Diego§	National	4	13⅔	0	0	.000	10	5	3	13	8	1.98
1984—Columbus	Int'national	6	43⅔	4	1	.800	24	15	15	30	27	3.09
1984—New York	American	24	147⅔	9	6	.600	127	79	75	110	60	4.57
1985—New York	American	22	101⅔	3	5	.375	97	56	45	63	42	3.98
1985—Columbus	Int'national	7	45	0	3	.000	41	24	19	43	25	3.80
1986—New York	American	31	202	18	6	.750	160	91	87	131	74	3.88
National League Totals—1 Year		4	13⅔	0	0	.000	10	5	3	13	8	1.98
American League Totals—3 Years		77	451⅓	30	17	.638	384	226	207	304	176	4.13
Major League Totals—4 Years		81	465	30	17	.638	394	231	210	317	184	4.06

Selected by Pittsburgh Pirates' organization in 18th round of free-agent draft, June 7, 1977.
Selected by California Angels' organization in 1st round (17th player selected) of free-agent draft, June 3, 1980.
†Traded to New York Yankees, November 24, 1982, completing deal in which New York traded Pitcher Tommy John to California Angels for a player to be named later, August 31, 1982.
‡Traded with Second Baseman Edwin Rodriguez to San Diego Padres, September 12, 1983, completing deal in which San Diego traded Pitcher John Montefusco to New York Yankees for two players to be named later, August 26, 1983.
§Traded with a player to be named later to New York Yankees' organization for Third Baseman Graig Nettles, March 30, 1984; New York organization acquired Pitcher Darin Cloninger to complete deal, April 26, 1984.

SHANE WILLIAM RAWLEY

Born July 27, 1955, at Racine, Wis.
Height, 6.00. Weight, 155.
Throws and bats lefthanded.
Attended Indian Hills Community College, Centerville, Ia.

Major League saves: 1978 (4), 1979 (11), 1980 (13), 1981 (8), 1982 (3), 1983 (1). Total—40.
Led American League in intentional bases on balls issued with 16 in 1980.

Year Club	League	G.	IP.	W.	L.	Pct.	H.	R.	ER.	SO.	BB.	ERA.
1974—Sarasota Expos	Gulf Coast	2	12	0	1	.000	12	9	3	16	4	2.25
1974—Kinston	Carolina	5	19	0	2	.000	22	15	13	11	12	6.16
1975—West Palm Beach....................	Florida St.	24	165	8	12	.400	148	80	56	113	73	3.05
1976—Quebec City................................	Eastern	25	164	11	7	.611	143	55	49	113	79	2.69
1977—Denver†-Indianapolis‡§	Am. Assoc.	26	152	6	10	.375	150	89	80	92	68	4.74
1978—Seattle......................................	American	52	111	4	9	.308	114	57	51	66	51	4.14

Year Club	League	G.	IP.	W.	L.	Pct.	H.	R.	ER.	SO.	BB.	ERA.
1979—Seattle x	American	48	84	5	9	.357	88	40	36	48	40	3.86
1980—Seattle	American	59	114	7	7	.500	103	44	42	68	63	3.32
1981—Spokane	P. Coast	3	6	0	0	.000	3	0	0	3	3	0.00
1981—Seattle yz	American	46	68	4	6	.400	64	31	30	35	38	3.97
1982—New York	American	47	164	11	10	.524	165	79	74	111	54	4.06
1983—New York	American	34	238⅓	14	14	.500	246	111	100	124	79	3.78
1984—New York ab	American	11	42	2	3	.400	46	33	29	24	27	6.21
1984—Philadelphia	National	18	120⅓	10	6	.625	117	55	51	58	27	3.81
1985—Philadelphia	National	36	198⅔	13	8	.619	188	82	73	106	81	3.31
1986—Philadelphia c	National	23	157⅔	11	7	.611	166	67	62	73	50	3.54
American League Totals—7 Years		297	821⅓	47	58	.448	826	395	362	476	352	3.97
National League Totals—3 Years		77	476⅔	34	21	.618	471	204	186	237	158	3.51
Major League Totals—9 Years		374	1298	81	79	.506	1297	599	548	713	510	3.80

Selected by Los Angeles Dodgers' organization in 4th round of free-agent draft, January 9, 1974.

Selected by Montreal Expos' organization in secondary phase of free-agent draft, June 5, 1974.

†Traded with Pitcher Angel Torres to Cincinnati Reds' organization, May 27, 1977, completing deal in which Cincinnati traded Pitcher Santo Alcala to Montreal Expos for two players to be named later, May 21, 1977.

‡Appeared with Indianapolis in one game as an outfielder with no chances.

§Traded to Seattle Mariners for Outfielder Dave Collins, December 9, 1977.

xOn disabled list, June 30 to August 21, 1979.

yOn disabled list, April 1 to April 24, 1981; included rehabilitation disability assignment to Spokane, April 16 to April 24, 1981.

zTraded to New York Yankees for Pitchers Gene Nelson and Bill Caudill, a player to be named later and cash, April 1, 1982; Seattle Mariners' organization acquired Outfielder Bobby Brown to complete deal, April 6, 1982.

aOn disabled list, May 20 to June 4, 1984.

bTraded to Philadelphia Phillies for Pitcher Marty Bystrom and Outfielder Keith Hughes, June 30, 1984.

cOn disabled list, July 30, 1986 through remainder of season.

ALL-STAR GAME RECORD

Member of National League All-Star Team in 1986; did not play.

JOHNNY CORNELIUS RAY

Born March 1, 1957, at Chouteau, Okla.
Height, 5.11. Weight, 175.
Throws right and bats right and lefthanded.
Attended Northeastern Oklahoma A & M, Miami, Okla.; and
University of Arkansas, Fayetteville, Ark.

Tied major league record for fewest errors by second baseman, season, 150 or more games (5), 1986.
Major League stolen bases: 1982 (16), 1983 (18), 1984 (11), 1985 (13), 1986 (6). Total—64.
Tied for National League lead in grounding into double plays with 21 in 1986.
Led National League second basemen in total chances with 914 in 1982.
Named National League Rookie Player of the Year by THE SPORTING NEWS, 1982.
Named second baseman on THE SPORTING NEWS National League Silver Slugger team, 1983.

Year Club	League	Pos.	G.	AB.	R.	H.	2B.	3B.	HR.	RBI.	B.A.	PO.	A.	E.	F.A.
1979—Sarasota Astros	Gulf C.	3B-2B	37	132	25	41	8	1	3	25	.311	25	51	11	.874
1979—Daytona Beach	Fla. St.	3B-SS-2B	24	68	6	15	1	2	1	10	.221	21	38	8	.881
1980—Columbus	South.	2B-3B-OF	138	497	86	161	32	6	10	72	.324	203	331	24	.957
1981—Tucson†	P. C.	2B	131	525	111	183	★50	10	5	83	.349	309	369	19	.973
1981—Pittsburgh	Nat.	2B	31	102	10	25	11	0	0	6	.245	52	96	2	.987
1982—Pittsburgh	Nat.	2B	●162	647	79	182	30	7	7	63	.281	★381	★512	★21	.977
1983—Pittsburgh	Nat.	2B	151	576	68	163	●38	7	5	53	.283	319	452	13	.983
1984—Pittsburgh	Nat.	2B	155	555	75	173	●38	6	6	67	.312	331	400	12	.984
1985—Pittsburgh	Nat.	2B	154	594	67	163	33	3	7	70	.274	305	423	18	.976
1986—Pittsburgh	Nat.	2B	155	579	67	174	33	0	7	78	.301	280	479	5	.993
Major League Totals—6 Years			808	3053	366	880	183	23	32	337	.288	1668	2362	71	.983

Selected by Houston Astros' organization in 12th round of free-agent draft, June 5, 1979.

†Traded with two players to be named later to Pittsburgh Pirates for Second Baseman Phil Garner, August 31, 1981; Pittsburgh organization acquired Pitcher Randy Niemann and Outfielder Kevin Houston to complete deal, September 9, 1981.

FLOYD KINNARD RAYFORD

Born July 27, 1957, at Memphis, Tenn.
Height, 5.10. Weight, 195.
Throws and bats righthanded.

Tied American League record for most errors by third baseman, game (4), April 21, 1986.
Major League stolen bases: 1983 (1), 1985 (3). Total—4.
Led International League third basemen in fielding percentage with .942 in 1980.
Led Texas League third basemen in putouts with 95 and in assists with 216 in 1978.
Led California League third basemen in assists with 202, double plays with 21 and fielding percentage with .944 in 1976.
Tied for California League lead in double plays by third basemen with 21 in 1977.

Year Club	League	Pos.	G.	AB.	R.	H.	2B.	3B.	HR.	RBI.	B.A.	PO.	A.	E.	F.A.
1975—Idaho Falls	Pion.	3-C-1-O-S	●72	272	43	77	12	5	2	43	.283	244	100	21	.942
1976—Salinas	Calif.	3B-C-2B	125	462	73	126	19	6	5	67	.273	162	216	16	.959
1977—Salinas	Calif.	3B	51	205	37	53	7	3	6	39	.259	40	117	7	.957
1977—El Paso	Texas	1-2-3-S-O	79	320	65	95	17	3	11	60	.297	427	133	12	.979
1978—El Paso	Texas	3-2-1-S	126	483	78	151	36	2	17	87	.313	113	230	14	.961

Year	Club	League	Pos.	G.	AB.	R.	H.	2B.	3B.	HR.	RBI.	B.A.	PO.	A.	E.	F.A.
1979—Salt Lake City†	P. C.	*3-S-1-2	135	551	98	162	28	6	13	80	.294	134	316	20	*.957
1980—Rochester	Int.	3B-2B-SS	107	387	51	89	22	0	9	46	.230	86	213	19	.940
1980—Baltimore	Amer.	3B-2B	8	18	1	4	0	0	0	1	.222	3	11	2	.875
1981—Rochester	Int.	3B-C-SS	96	311	50	77	18	2	11	45	.248	208	106	11	.966
1982—Baltimore	Amer.	3B-C	34	53	7	7	0	0	3	5	.132	11	43	6	.900
1982—Rochester	Int.	2B	3	12	1	3	0	0	1	2	.250	2	6	0	1.000
1983—Rochester‡	Int.	2B-C-3B	42	140	24	52	16	1	2	38	.371	54	44	5	.951
1983—St. Louis§	Nat.	3B	56	104	5	22	4	0	3	14	.212	13	40	7	.883
1984—Rochester	Int.	C	7	18	1	1	0	0	1	1	.056	25	5	1	.968
1984—Baltimore	Amer.	C-3B-1B	86	250	24	64	14	0	4	27	.256	310	67	6	.984
1985—Baltimore	Amer.	3B-C	105	359	55	110	21	1	18	48	.306	176	152	7	.979
1986—Rochester x	Int.	3B-C	38	137	17	39	11	0	4	17	.285	60	54	3	.974
1986—Baltimore	Amer.	3B-C	81	210	15	37	4	0	8	19	.176	72	117	16	.922
American League Totals—5 Years			314	890	102	222	39	1	33	100	.249	572	390	37	.963
National League Totals—1 Year			56	104	5	22	4	0	3	14	.212	13	40	7	.883
Major League Totals—6 Years			370	994	107	244	43	1	36	114	.245	585	430	44	.958

Selected by California Angels' organization in 4th round of free-agent draft, June 4, 1975.

†Traded with cash to Baltimore Orioles' organization for Outfielder Larry Harlow, June 5, 1979. (Remained on option to Salt Lake City.)

‡Traded to St. Louis Cardinals for a player to be named later, June 13, 1983; Baltimore Orioles purchased Outfielder Tito Landrum to complete deal, August 31, 1983.

§Sold to Baltimore Orioles' organization, March 30, 1984.

xOn Baltimore disabled list, March 29 to April 21, 1986; included rehabilitation disability assignment to Rochester, April 19 to April 21, 1986.

RANDY MAX READY

Born January 8, 1960, at San Mateo, Calif.
Height, 5.11. Weight, 175.
Throws and bats righthanded.
Attended California State University, Hayward,
Calif., and Mesa College, Grand Junction, Colo.

Tied American League record for most innings played by third baseman, game (25), May 8, finished May 9, 1984 (fielded 24⅓ innings).

Major League stolen bases: 1986 (2).

Led Pacific Coast League in bases on balls received with 99 in 1983.

Led Texas League in total bases with 281 in 1982.

Led Texas League third basemen in double plays with 27 and total chances with 456 in 1982.

Led Midwest League third basemen in double plays with 22 in 1981.

Year	Club	League	Pos.	G.	AB.	R.	H.	2B.	3B.	HR.	RBI.	B.A.	PO.	A.	E.	F.A.
1980—Butte	Pion.	SS-2B-3B	61	226	*65	85	*23	4	8	50	*.376	86	174	22	.922
1981—Burlington	Midw.	3B	110	367	74	113	17	0	17	56	.308	72	216	21	*.932
1982—El Paso	Texas	3B	132	475	*122	*178	33	5	20	99	*.375	*115	*312	●29	.936
1983—Vancouver	P. C.	3B	116	407	82	134	28	1	13	59	.329	136	231	24	.939
1983—Milwaukee	Amer.	3B	12	37	8	15	3	2	1	6	.405	5	8	0	1.000
1984—Milwaukee	Amer.	3B	37	123	13	23	6	1	3	13	.187	29	76	6	.946
1984—Vancouver†	P. C.	2B-3B	43	151	48	49	7	4	3	18	.325	74	125	6	.971
1985—Milwaukee‡	Amer.	OF-3B-2B	48	181	29	48	9	5	1	21	.265	93	14	1	.991
1985—Vancouver	P. C.	OF-3B-2B	52	190	33	62	12	3	4	29	.326	60	35	7	.931
1986—Milwaukee§	Amer.	OF-2B-3B	23	79	8	15	4	0	1	4	.190	35	21	3	.949
1986—Las Vegas	P. C.	3B-OF	10	38	5	14	4	0	1	8	.368	12	10	0	1.000
1986—San Diego x	Nat.	3B	1	3	0	0	0	0	0	0	.000	0	2	1	.667
American League Totals—4 Years			120	420	58	101	22	8	6	44	.240	162	119	10	.966
National League Totals—1 Year			1	3	0	0	0	0	0	0	.000	0	2	1	.667
Major League Totals—4 Years			121	423	58	101	22	8	6	44	.239	162	121	11	.963

Selected by Milwaukee Brewers' organization in 5th round of free-agent draft, June 3, 1980.

†On disabled list, August 21, 1984 through remainder of season.

‡On disabled list, April 30 to June 19, 1985; included rehabilitation disability assignment to Vancouver, June 1 to June 19, 1985.

§Traded to San Diego Padres for a player to be named later, June 12, 1986; San Diego traded Infielder Tim Pyznarski to Milwaukee Brewers' organization to complete deal, October 29, 1986.

xOn disabled list, June 19 to July 7, 1986.

JEFFREY JAMES REARDON
(Jeff)

Born October 1, 1955, at Pittsfield, Mass.
Height, 6.01. Weight, 190.
Throws and bats righthanded.
Attended University of Massachusetts, Amherst, Mass.

Major League saves: 1979 (2), 1980 (6), 1981 (8), 1982 (26), 1983 (21), 1984 (23), 1985 (41), 1986 (35). Total—162.

Led National League in saves with 41 in 1985.

Led Carolina League in shutouts with 3 in 1977.

Named National League Fireman of the Year by THE SPORTING NEWS, 1985.

Year	Club	League	G.	IP.	W.	L.	Pct.	H.	R.	ER.	SO.	BB.	ERA.
1977—Lynchburg	Carolina	16	101	8	3	.727	89	42	37	60	30	3.30
1978—Jackson	Texas	28	163	*17	4	*.810	128	56	46	115	65	2.53
1979—Tidewater†	Int'national	30	69	5	2	.714	46	18	16	64	21	2.09

Year	Club	League	G.	IP.	W.	L.	Pct.	H.	R.	ER.	SO.	BB.	ERA.
1979—New York		National	18	21	1	2	.333	12	7	4	10	9	1.71
1980—New York		National	61	110	8	7	.533	96	36	32	101	47	2.62
1981—New York‡-Montreal		National	43	70	3	0	1.000	48	17	17	49	21	2.19
1982—Montreal		National	75	109	7	4	.636	87	28	25	86	36	2.06
1983—Montreal		National	66	92	7	9	.438	87	34	31	78	44	3.03
1984—Montreal		National	68	87	7	7	.500	70	31	28	79	37	2.90
1985—Montreal		National	63	87⅔	2	8	.200	68	31	31	67	26	3.18
1986—Montreal		National	62	89	7	9	.438	83	42	39	67	26	3.94
Major League Totals—8 Years			456	665⅔	42	46	.477	551	226	207	537	246	2.80

Selected by Montreal Expos' organization in 23rd round of free-agent draft, June 5, 1973.
Signed as free agent by New York Mets' organization, June 14, 1977.
†On disabled list, June 13 to June 24 and June 29 to July 26, 1979.
‡Traded with Outfielder Dan Norman to Montreal Expos for Outfielder Ellis Valentine, May 29, 1981.

DIVISION SERIES RECORD

Year	Club	League	G.	IP.	W.	L.	Pct.	H.	R.	ER.	SO.	BB.	ERA.
1981—Montreal		National	3	4⅓	0	1	.000	1	1	1	2	1	2.08

CHAMPIONSHIP SERIES RECORD

Year	Club	League	G.	IP.	W.	L.	Pct.	H.	R.	ER.	SO.	BB.	ERA.
1981—Montreal		National	1	1	0	0	.000	3	3	3	0	0	27.00

ALL-STAR GAME RECORD

Year	League	IP.	W.	L.	Pct.	H.	R.	ER.	SO.	BB.	ERA.
1985—National		1	0	0	.000	1	0	0	1	0	0.00

Member of National League All-Star Team in 1986; did not play.

GARY EUGENE REDUS

Name pronounced REE-dus.
Born November 1, 1956, at Athens, Ala.
Height, 6.01. Weight, 180.
Throws and bats righthanded.
Attended Calhoun Junior College, Decatur, Ala., and Athens State College, Athens, Ala.
Brother of Jeff Redus, outfielder in Kansas City Royals' organization, 1984 and 1985.

Major League stolen bases: 1982 (11), 1983 (39), 1984 (48), 1985 (48), 1986 (25). Total—171.
Led American Association in stolen bases with 54 and tied for lead in sacrifice flies with 9 in 1982.
Led Florida State League in total bases with 220 in 1980.
Led Pioneer League in total bases with 199, stolen bases with 42 and tied for lead in sacrifice flies with 6 in 1978.
Tied for Western Carolinas League lead in errors by second basemen with 20 in 1979.
Named Pioneer League Player of the Year, 1978.

Year	Club	League	Pos.	G.	AB.	R.	H.	2B.	3B.	HR.	RBI.	B.A.	PO.	A.	E.	F.A.
1978—Billings		Pion.	2B	68	253	*100	*117	19	6	17	62	*.462	124	*185	*28	.917
1979—Nashville		South.	OF	36	109	7	19	2	1	0	7	.174	74	3	3	.963
1979—Greensboro		W. Car.	2B-OF	83	309	79	86	17	1	16	52	.278	172	193	21	.946
1980—Tampa		Fla. St.	OF-3B-1B	128	452	78	136	18	9	16	68	.301	213	84	27	.917
1981—Waterbury		East.	OF-1B	138	477	71	119	26	4	20	75	.249	667	34	14	.980
1982—Indianapolis		A. A.	OF	122	439	112	146	29	9	24	93	.333	223	10	7	.971
1982—Cincinnati		Nat.	OF	20	83	12	18	3	2	1	7	.217	29	3	1	.970
1983—Cincinnati		Nat.	OF	125	453	90	112	20	9	17	51	.247	235	11	7	.972
1984—Cincinnati		Nat.	OF	123	394	69	100	21	3	7	22	.254	200	6	7	.967
1985—Cincinnati†		Nat.	OF	101	246	51	62	14	4	6	28	.252	140	3	2	.986
1986—Philadelphia‡		Nat.	OF	90	340	62	84	22	4	11	33	.247	185	8	4	.980
1986—Reading		East.	OF	6	24	4	6	1	0	0	0	.250	11	1	1	.923
Major League Totals—5 Years				459	1516	284	376	80	22	42	141	.248	789	31	21	.975

Selected by Boston Red Sox' organization in 17th round of free-agent draft, June 7, 1977.
Selected by Cincinnati Reds' organization in 15th round of free-agent draft, June 6, 1978.
†Traded with Pitcher Tom Hume to Philadelphia Phillies for Pitchers John Denny and Jeff Gray, December 11, 1985.
‡On disabled list, April 28 to July 1, 1986; included rehabilitation disability assignment to Reading, June 23 to June 30, 1986.

JEFFREY SCOTT REED
(Jeff)

Born November 12, 1962, at Joliet, Ill.
Height, 6.02. Weight, 185.
Throws right and bats lefthanded.
Brother of Curtis Reed, outfielder in San Diego Padres' and
Chicago White Sox' organizations, 1977 through 1984.

Major League stolen bases: 1986 (1).
Led International League catchers in total chances with 720 in 1985.
Led Southern League catchers in total chances with 714 and double plays with 12 in 1983.
Led California League catchers in total chances with 758 and tied for lead in double plays with 9 in 1982.

Year	Club	League	Pos.	G.	AB.	R.	H.	2B.	3B.	HR.	RBI.	B.A.	PO.	A.	E.	F.A.
1980—Elizabethton		Appal.	C	65	225	39	64	15	1	1	20	.284	269	*41	9	.972
1981—Wisconsin Rapids		Midw.	C	106	312	63	73	12	1	4	34	.234	547	*93	7	.989

Year—Club	League	Pos.	G.	AB.	R.	H.	2B.	3B.	HR.	RBI.	B.A.	PO.	A.	E.	F.A.
1981—Orlando	South.	C	3	4	0	1	0	0	0	0	.250	4	1	0	1.000
1982—Visalia	Calif.	C	125	395	69	130	19	2	5	54	.329	★642	●106	10	.987
1983—Orlando	South.	C	118	379	52	100	16	5	6	45	.264	★618	★88	8	★.989
1983—Toledo	Int.	C	14	41	5	7	1	1	0	3	.171	77	6	1	.988
1984—Minnesota	Amer.	C	18	21	3	3	3	0	0	1	.143	41	2	1	.977
1984—Toledo	Int.	C	94	301	30	80	16	3	3	35	.266	546	43	5	★.992
1985—Toledo	Int.	C	122	404	53	100	15	3	5	36	.248	★627	★81	12	.983
1985—Minnesota	Amer.	C	7	10	2	2	0	0	0	0	.200	9	3	0	1.000
1986—Minnesota	Amer.	C	68	165	13	39	6	1	2	9	.236	332	19	2	.994
1986—Toledo	Int.	C	25	71	10	22	5	3	1	14	.310	108	22	2	.985
Major League Totals—3 Years			93	196	18	44	9	1	2	10	.224	382	24	3	.993

Selected by Minnesota Twins' organization in 1st round (12th player selected) of free-agent draft, June 3, 1980.

JERRY MAXWELL REED

Born October 8, 1955, at Bryson City, N.C.
Height, 6.01. Weight, 190.
Throws and bats righthanded.
Received bachelor of science degree in education from
Western Carolina University, Cullowhee, N.C. in 1977.

Major League saves: 1985 (8).
Tied for Eastern League lead in intentional bases on balls issued with 9 in 1979.

Year—Club	League	G.	IP.	W.	L.	Pct.	H.	R.	ER.	SO.	BB.	ERA.
1977—Auburn	NYP	★32	56	3	5	.375	63	35	30	36	24	4.82
1978—Spartanburg	W. Carol.	39	66	7	2	.778	36	22	10	31	34	1.36
1978—Peninsula	Carolina	15	24	1	0	1.000	9	3	2	11	5	0.75
1979—Reading	Eastern	45	80	11	4	.733	67	25	17	37	28	1.91
1980—Oklahoma City	Am. Assoc.	33	97	6	5	.545	128	62	53	36	42	4.92
1980—Reading	Eastern	8	17	1	1	.500	17	6	6	10	10	3.18
1981—Reading	Eastern	56	80	5	4	.556	80	34	29	62	29	3.26
1981—Philadelphia	National	4	5	0	1	.000	7	4	4	5	6	7.20
1982—Oklahoma City	Am. Assoc.	25	131⅔	6	7	.462	135	78	64	73	59	4.37
1982—Philadelphia†	National	7	8⅔	1	0	1.000	11	6	5	1	3	5.19
1982—Cleveland	American	6	15⅔	1	1	.500	15	6	6	10	3	3.45
1983—Charleston	Int'national	21	145⅓	10	6	.625	141	70	58	57	67	3.59
1983—Cleveland	American	7	21⅓	0	0	.000	26	19	17	11	9	7.17
1984—Maine	Int'national	27	179⅓	12	6	.667	★193	86	72	77	57	3.61
1985—Maine	Int'national	14	95⅓	8	5	.615	88	41	36	47	37	3.40
1985—Cleveland‡	American	33	72⅓	3	5	.375	67	41	33	37	19	4.11
1986—Calgary	P. Coast	19	41	2	1	.667	45	24	21	20	17	4.61
1986—Seattle§	American	11	34⅔	4	0	1.000	38	13	12	16	13	3.12
National League Totals—2 Years		11	13⅔	1	1	.500	18	10	9	6	9	5.93
American League Totals—4 Years		57	144	8	6	.571	146	79	68	74	44	4.25
Major League Totals—5 Years		68	157⅔	9	7	.563	164	89	77	80	53	4.40

Selected by Minnesota Twins' organization in 11th round of free-agent draft, June 5, 1973.
Selected by Philadelphia Phillies' organization in 22nd round of free-agent draft, June 7, 1977.
†Traded with Pitcher Roy Smith and Outfielder Wil Culmer to Cleveland Indians for Pitcher John Denny, September 12, 1982.
‡Released, April 1, 1986; signed by Calgary (Seattle Mariners' organization), April 11, 1986.
§On disabled list, August 4, 1986 through remainder of season.

JODY ERIC REED

Born July 26, 1962, at Tampa, Fla.
Height, 5.09. Weight, 170.
Throws and bats righthanded.
Attended Manatee Junior College, Bradenton, Fla., and Florida State University, Tallahassee, Fla.

Led Florida State League in bases on balls received with 94 in 1985.
Led Florida State League shortstops in double plays with 101 in 1985.

Year—Club	League	Pos.	G.	AB.	R.	H.	2B.	3B.	HR.	RBI.	B.A.	PO.	A.	E.	F.A.
1984—Winter Haven	Fla. St.	SS	77	273	46	74	14	1	0	20	.271	128	271	26	.939
1985—Winter Haven	Fla. St.	SS	134	489	★95	157	25	1	0	45	★.321	★256	★478	37	★.952
1986—New Britain	East.	SS	60	218	33	50	12	1	0	11	.229	114	190	14	.956
1986—Pawtucket	Int.	SS	69	227	27	64	11	0	1	30	.282	115	222	12	.966

Selected by Texas Rangers' organization in 3rd round of free-agent draft, January 12, 1982.
Selected by San Francisco Giants' organization in secondary phase of free-agent draft, June 7, 1982.
Selected by Texas Rangers' organization in secondary phase of free-agent draft, June 6, 1983.
Selected by Boston Red Sox' organization in 8th round of free-agent draft, June 4, 1984.

JESSIE THOMAS REID

Born June 1, 1962, at Honolulu, Haw.
Height, 6.01. Weight, 200.
Throws and bats lefthanded.

Year—Club	League	Pos.	G.	AB.	R.	H.	2B.	3B.	HR.	RBI.	B.A.	PO.	A.	E.	F.A.
1980—Great Falls	Pion.	OF-1B	59	227	57	83	15	6	5	48	.366	137	7	4	.973
1981—Fresno	Calif.	OF-1B	124	426	68	105	15	3	1	40	.246	222	13	8	.967
1982—Fresno	Calif.	OF-1B	127	476	78	139	20	5	6	73	.292	385	27	14	.967

Year Club	League	Pos.	G.	AB.	R.	H.	2B.	3B.	HR.	RBI.	B.A.	PO.	A.	E.	F.A.
1983—Shreveport	Texas	OF	125	389	59	101	22	0	13	50	.260	157	7	4	.976
1984—Shreveport	Texas	OF	88	296	33	62	10	1	6	32	.209	129	9	2	.986
1984—Phoenix	P. C.	OF	36	121	13	28	5	0	1	9	.231	70	0	1	.986
1985—Fresno	Calif.	OF-1B	72	254	45	82	14	2	8	55	.323	139	6	4	.973
1985—Phoenix	P. C.	OF	54	179	26	47	6	3	7	32	.263	101	3	3	.972
1986—Phoenix	P. C.	OF	120	428	70	115	26	6	14	61	.269	227	5	7	.971

Selected by San Francisco Giants' organization in 1st round (seventh player selected) of free-agent draft, June 3, 1980.

RICHARD AVINA RENTERIA
ame pronounced Ren-ter-REE-ah.

(Rich)

Born December 25, 1961, at Harbor City, Calif.
Height, 5.09. Weight, 172.
Throws and bats righthanded.
Led South Atlantic League third basemen in errors with 39 in 1981.
Tied for Carolina League in grounding into double plays with 19 in 1982.

Year Club	League	Pos.	G.	AB.	R.	H.	2B.	3B.	HR.	RBI.	B.A.	PO.	A.	E.	F.A.
1980—Bradenton Pir.	Gulf C.	3B-SS	46	176	19	40	6	1	2	23	.227	32	87	16	.882
1981—Greenwood	S. Atl.	3B-SS	127	510	90	146	19	5	4	48	.286	87	232	39	.891
1982—Alexandria	Carol.	2B	127	508	80	*168	24	5	14	*100	*.331	196	346	28	.951
1983—Lynn†	East.	3B	115	424	47	121	25	0	4	40	.285	83	170	19	.930
1984—Nashua	East.	2B	113	443	63	121	22	7	1	34	.273	208	283	12	.976
1984—Hawaii‡	P. C.	2B	19	77	8	19	3	1	0	11	.247	22	45	2	.971
1985—Mex. C. Tigers	Mex.	3B-2B	125	484	89	169	29	11	19	*125	.349	121	241	19	.950
1985—Hawaii	P. C.	2B	7	31	2	6	2	0	0	2	.194	5	15	0	1.000
1986—Hawaii	P. C.	3B-2B	112	389	51	122	20	9	1	51	.314	112	196	13	.960
1986—Pittsburgh§	Nat.	3B	10	12	2	3	1	0	0	1	.250	1	2	2	.600
Major League Totals—1 Year			10	12	2	3	1	0	0	1	.250	1	2	2	.600

Selected by Pittsburgh Pirates' organization in 1st round (20th player selected) of free-agent draft, June 3, 1980.
†On disabled list, May 10 to June 1, 1983.
‡Loaned to Mexico City Tigers, March 11, 1985; returned, August 21, 1985.
§Traded to Seattle Mariners for a player to be named later, December 5, 1986; Pittsburgh Pirates' organization acquired Pitcher Bob Siegel to complete deal, December 10, 1986.

RICKY EUGENE REUSCHEL
Name pronounced RUSH-ul.

(Rick)

Born May 16, 1949, at Quincy, Ill.
Height, 6.03. Weight, 230.
Throws and bats righthanded.
Attended Western Illinois University, Macomb, Ill.
Brother of Paul Reuschel, pitcher with Chicago Cubs and Cleveland Indians, 1975 through 1978.
Tied major league record for most putouts, pitcher, inning (3), April 25, 1975 (third inning).
Major League saves: 1975 (1), 1976 (1), 1977 (1), 1985 (1). Total—4.
Tied for National League lead in hit batsmen with 8 in 1986.
Tied for National League lead in games started by pitchers with 38 in 1980.
Led Northern League pitchers in complete games with 7 and tied for lead in games started with 14 in 1970.
Named righthanded pitcher on THE SPORTING NEWS National League All-Star Team, 1977.
Named National League Comeback Player of the Year by THE SPORTING NEWS, 1985.
Named pitcher on THE SPORTING NEWS National League All-Star fielding team, 1985.

Year Club	League	G.	IP.	W.	L.	Pct.	H.	R.	ER.	SO.	BB.	ERA.
1970—Huron	Northern	14	102	9	2	.818	96	52	40	88	22	3.52
1971—San Antonio†	Texas	16	121	8	4	.667	105	40	31	81	15	2.31
1972—Wichita	Am. Assoc.	12	102	9	2	.818	78	30	15	72	30	1.32
1972—Chicago	National	21	129	10	8	.556	127	46	42	87	29	2.93
1973—Chicago	National	36	237	14	15	.483	244	95	79	168	62	3.00
1974—Chicago	National	41	241	13	12	.520	262	130	115	160	83	4.29
1975—Chicago	National	38	234	11	*17	.393	244	116	97	155	67	3.73
1976—Chicago	National	38	260	14	12	.538	260	*117	100	146	64	3.46
1977—Chicago	National	39	252	20	10	.667	233	84	78	166	74	2.79
1978—Chicago	National	35	243	14	15	.483	235	98	92	115	54	3.41
1979—Chicago	National	36	239	18	12	.600	251	104	96	125	75	3.62
1980—Chicago	National	38	257	11	13	.458	*281	111	97	140	76	3.40
1981—Chicago‡	National	13	86	4	7	.364	87	40	33	53	23	3.45
1981—New York	American	12	71	4	4	.500	75	24	21	22	10	2.66
1982—New York§	American					(Did not play)						
1983—Columbus xy	Int'national	4	16	0	1	.000	21	9	9	7	6	5.06
1983—Quad Cities	Midwest	13	70⅔	3	4	.429	73	29	19	56	9	2.42
1983—Chicago	National	4	20⅔	1	1	.500	18	9	9	9	10	3.92
1984—Chicago za	National	19	92⅓	5	5	.500	123	57	53	43	23	5.17
1985—Hawaii	P. Coast	8	54	6	2	.750	52	18	15	46	12	2.50
1985—Pittsburgh	National	31	194	14	8	.636	153	58	49	138	52	2.27
1986—Pittsburgh	National	35	215⅔	9	16	.360	232	106	95	125	57	3.96
National League Totals—14 Years		424	2700⅔	158	151	.511	2750	1171	1035	1630	749	3.45
American League Totals—1 Year		12	71	4	4	.500	75	24	21	22	10	2.66
Major League Totals—14 Years		436	2771⅔	162	155	.511	2825	1195	1056	1652	759	3.43

Selected by Chicago Cubs' organization in 3rd round of free-agent draft, June 4, 1970.
†On temporary inactive list, July 2, 1971; transferred to military list, July 8, 1971 through April 10, 1972.
‡Traded to New York Yankees for Pitcher Doug Bird, $400,000 and a player to be named later, June 12, 1981; Chicago Cubs acquired Pitcher Mike Griffin to complete deal, August 5, 1981.
§On disabled list, March 23, 1982 through remainder of season.
xOn New York disabled list, April 4 to June 9, 1983; included rehabilitation disability assignment to Columbus, May 23 to June 9, 1983.
yReleased, June 9, 1983; signed by Quad Cities (Chicago Cubs' organization), June 28, 1983.
zOn disabled list, March 27 to April 21 and August 23 to September 1, 1984.
aGranted free agency, November 8, 1984; signed by Pittsburgh Pirates' organization, February 28, 1985.

DIVISION SERIES RECORD

Year Club	League	G.	IP.	W.	L.	Pct.	H.	R.	ER.	SO.	BB.	ERA.
1981—New York	American	1	6	0	1	.000	4	2	2	3	1	3.00

WORLD SERIES RECORD

Year Club	League	G.	IP.	W.	L.	Pct.	H.	R.	ER.	SO.	BB.	ERA.
1981—New York	American	2	3⅔	0	0	.000	7	3	2	2	3	4.91

ALL-STAR GAME RECORD

Year League	IP.	W.	L.	Pct.	H.	R.	ER.	SO.	BB.	ERA.
1977—National	1	0	0	.000	1	0	0	0	0	0.00

JERRY REUSS

Name pronounced Royce.

Born June 19, 1949, at St. Louis, Mo.
Height, 6.05. Weight, 217.
Throws and bats lefthanded.
Attended Southern Illinois University, Carbondale, Ill., Central Missouri State College,
Warrensburg, Mo., and University of California, Santa Barbara, Calif.

Tied major league record for most home runs allowed, bases filled, lifetime (9).
Pitched 8-0 no-hit victory against San Francisco Giants, June 27, 1980.
Major League saves: 1972 (1), 1976 (2), 1979 (3), 1980 (3), 1984 (1). Total—10.
Led National League in shutouts with 6 in 1980.
Led National League in hit batsmen with 10 in 1972.
Tied for National League lead in games started by pitchers with 40 in 1973.
Led American Association pitchers in games started with 29 in 1969.
Led Texas League in wild pitches with 16 in 1968.
Named National League Comeback Player of the Year by THE SPORTING NEWS, 1980.
Received reported $30,000 bonus to sign with St. Louis Cardinals, 1967.

Year Club	League	G.	IP.	W.	L.	Pct.	H.	R.	ER.	SO.	BB.	ERA.
1967—Sarasota Cards	Gulf Coast	2	7	0	0	.000	7	6	4	6	3	5.14
1967—Cedar Rapids	Midwest	9	58	2	5	.286	44	20	12	63	19	1.86
1967—Tulsa	P. Coast	1	1	0	0	.000	2	6	6	1	4	54.00
1968—Arkansas	Texas	17	112	7	8	.467	75	43	27	86	45	2.17
1969—Tulsa	Am. Assoc.	30	★186	●13	11	.542	188	●112	84	★151	116	4.06
1969—St. Louis	National	1	7	1	0	1.000	2	0	0	3	3	0.00
1970—Tulsa	Am. Assoc.	11	85	7	2	.778	69	26	20	69	28	2.12
1970—St. Louis	National	20	127	7	8	.467	132	62	58	74	49	4.11
1971—St. Louis†	National	36	211	14	14	.500	228	125	112	131	109	4.78
1972—Houston	National	33	192	9	13	.409	177	101	89	174	83	4.17
1973—Houston‡	National	41	279	16	13	.552	271	123	116	177	★117	3.74
1974—Pittsburgh	National	35	260	16	11	.593	259	115	101	105	101	3.50
1975—Pittsburgh	National	32	237	18	11	.621	224	73	67	131	78	2.54
1976—Pittsburgh	National	31	209	14	9	.609	209	98	82	108	51	3.53
1977—Pittsburgh	National	33	208	10	13	.435	225	109	95	116	71	4.11
1978—Pittsburgh§	National	23	83	3	2	.600	97	48	45	42	23	4.88
1979—Los Angeles	National	39	160	7	14	.333	178	88	63	83	60	3.54
1980—Los Angeles	National	37	229	18	6	.750	193	74	64	111	40	2.52
1981—Los Angeles	National	22	153	10	4	.714	138	44	39	51	27	2.29
1982—Los Angeles	National	39	254⅔	18	11	.621	232	98	88	138	50	3.11
1983—Los Angeles	National	32	223⅓	12	11	.522	233	94	73	143	50	2.94
1984—Los Angeles x	National	30	99	5	7	.417	102	51	42	44	31	3.82
1985—Los Angeles	National	34	212⅔	14	10	.583	210	78	69	84	58	2.92
1986—Los Angeles y	National	19	74	2	6	.250	96	57	48	29	17	5.84
Major League Totals—18 Years		537	3218⅔	194	163	.543	3206	1438	1251	1744	1018	3.50

Selected by St. Louis Cardinals' organization in 2nd round of free-agent draft, June 6, 1967.
†Traded to Houston Astros for Pitchers Scipio Spinks and Lance Clemons, April 15, 1972.
‡Traded to Pittsburgh Pirates for Catcher Milt May, October 31, 1973.
§Traded to Los Angeles Dodgers for Pitcher Rick Rhoden, April 9, 1979.
xOn disabled list, June 8 to July 12, 1984.
yOn disabled list, July 17 to September 3, 1986.

DIVISION SERIES RECORD

Year Club	League	G.	IP.	W.	L.	Pct.	H.	R.	ER.	SO.	BB.	ERA.
1981—Los Angeles	National	2	18	1	0	1.000	10	0	0	7	5	0.00

CHAMPIONSHIP SERIES RECORD

Established Championship Series records for most games lost, total Series (7); most runs allowed, inning (7), October 13, 1985 (second inning).

Tied Championship Series records for most runs allowed, total Series (25); most games lost, Series (2), 1974, 1983; most bases on balls, four-game Series (8), 1974.

Year Club	League	G.	IP.	W.	L.	Pct.	H.	R.	ER.	SO.	BB.	ERA.
1974—Pittsburgh	National	2	9⅔	0	2	.000	7	4	4	3	8	3.72
1975—Pittsburgh	National	1	2⅔	0	1	.000	4	4	4	1	4	13.50
1981—Los Angeles	National	1	7	0	1	.000	7	4	4	2	1	5.14
1983—Los Angeles	National	2	12	0	2	.000	14	6	6	4	3	4.50
1985—Los Angeles	National	1	1⅔	0	1	.000	5	7	2	0	1	10.80
Championship Series Totals—5 Years		7	33	0	7	.000	37	25	20	10	17	5.45

WORLD SERIES RECORD

Year Club	League	G.	IP.	W.	L.	Pct.	H.	R.	ER.	SO.	BB.	ERA.
1981—Los Angeles	National	2	11⅔	1	1	.500	10	5	5	8	3	3.86

ALL-STAR GAME RECORD

Year League	IP.	W.	L.	Pct.	H.	R.	ER.	SO.	BB.	ERA.
1975—National	3	0	0	.000	3	0	0	2	0	0.00
1980—National	1	1	0	1.000	0	0	0	3	0	0.00
All-Star Game Totals—2 Years	4	1	0	1.000	3	0	0	5	0	0.00

GILBERTO R. REYES (POLANCO)
Name pronounced RAY-us.

(Gil)

Born December 10, 1963, at Santo Domingo, D. R.
Height, 6.03. Weight, 195.
Throws and bats righthanded.

Tied for Pacific Coast League lead in sacrifice flies with 8 in 1985.
Led Pacific Coast League in passed balls with 24 in 1985 and 17 in 1986.
Led Texas League catchers in total chances with 718, double plays with 13 and passed balls with 31 in 1984.
Tied for California League lead in assists by catchers with 106 and double plays with 9 in 1982.

Year Club	League	Pos.	G.	AB.	R.	H.	2B.	3B.	HR.	RBI.	B.A.	PO.	A.	E.	F.A.
1980—Lethbridge	Pion.	1B	6	11	0	2	0	0	0	1	.182	16	0	2	.889
1981—Vero Beach	Fla. St.	1B-C	21	58	3	12	3	0	1	6	.207	71	6	2	.975
1981—Lethbridge	Pion.	C-1B	44	155	28	40	9	0	6	24	.258	240	24	4	.985
1982—Lodi	Calif.	C-3B	127	424	65	119	18	1	15	55	.281	493	106	20	.968
1983—San Antonio†	Texas	C	33	124	10	35	7	0	1	16	.282	167	30	5	.975
1983—Los Angeles	Nat.	C	19	31	1	5	2	0	0	0	.161	59	9	4	.944
1983—Albuquerque	P. C.	C	20	62	8	19	1	2	2	15	.306	103	17	8	.938
1984—San Antonio	Texas	C	120	433	55	131	16	2	10	78	.303	*598	*101	*19	.974
1984—Los Angeles	Nat.	C	4	5	0	0	0	0	0	0	.000	5	0	0	1.000
1985—Albuquerque	P. C.	*C-1B	111	366	35	97	20	0	6	54	.265	439	66	*21	.960
1985—Los Angeles	Nat.	C	6	1	0	0	0	0	0	0	.000	6	4	0	1.000
1986—Albuquerque	P. C.	C-1B	104	306	36	70	13	1	7	36	.229	423	69	14	.972
Major League Totals—3 Years			29	37	1	5	2	0	0	0	.135	70	13	4	.954

Signed as free agent by Los Angeles Dodgers' organization, January 15, 1980.
†On disabled list, May 11 to June 1, 1983.

GORDON CRAIG REYNOLDS
(Known by middle name.)

Born December 27, 1952, at Houston, Tex.
Height, 6.01. Weight, 175.
Throws right and bats lefthanded.
Attended Houston Baptist College, Houston, Tex.

Tied modern major league record for most three-base hits, game (3), May 16, 1981.
Major League stolen bases: 1977 (6), 1978 (9), 1979 (12), 1980 (2), 1981 (3), 1982 (3), 1984 (7), 1985 (4), 1986 (3). Total—49.
Led National League in sacrifice hits with 34 in 1979, 18 in 1981 and 16 in 1984.
Led National League shortstops in assists with 472 in 1984.
Tied for Gulf Coast League lead in sacrifice flies with 4 in 1971.
Led Carolina League shortstops in double plays with 81 in 1973 and tied for International League lead with 64 in 1975.

Year Club	League	Pos.	G.	AB.	R.	H.	2B.	3B.	HR.	RBI.	B.A.	PO.	A.	E.	F.A.
1971—Bradenton Pir.	Gulf C.	SS	48	192	26	61	8	0	0	16	.318	*87	112	*25	.888
1972—Gastonia†	W. Car.	SS	41	146	18	35	4	1	0	9	.240	55	94	12	.925
1973—Salem	Carol.	SS-2B	138	*558	75	*160	18	5	13	86	.287	200	395	50	.922
1973—Charleston	Int.	SS-3B	4	14	2	3	0	0	0	0	.214	4	11	1	.938
1974—Thetford Mines	East.	SS	64	234	31	66	7	0	6	29	.282	76	170	13	.950
1974—Charleston‡	Int.	SS-2B	36	107	12	36	5	0	0	5	.336	44	71	3	.974
1975—Charleston	Int.	SS	108	425	51	131	22	3	6	42	.308	151	287	26	.944
1975—Pittsburgh	Nat.	SS	31	76	8	17	3	0	0	4	.224	43	82	4	.969
1976—Charleston	Int.	SS-2B	126	497	57	144	18	1	2	47	.290	198	262	31	.937
1976—Pittsburgh§	Nat.	SS-2B	7	4	1	1	0	0	1	1	.250	2	6	1	.889
1977—Seattle	Amer.	SS	135	420	41	104	12	3	4	28	.248	197	397	28	.955
1978—Seattle x	Amer.	SS	148	548	57	160	16	7	5	44	.292	243	461	29	.960
1979—Houston	Nat.	SS	146	555	63	147	20	9	0	39	.265	208	428	23	.965
1980—Houston	Nat.	SS	137	381	34	86	9	6	3	28	.226	162	362	17	.969
1981—Houston	Nat.	SS	87	323	43	84	10	●12	4	31	.260	139	261	11	.973

Year	Club	League	Pos.	G.	AB.	R.	H.	2B.	3B.	HR.	RBI.	B.A.	PO.	A.	E.	F.A.
1982—Houston y	Nat.	SS-3B	54	118	16	30	2	3	1	7	.254	45	98	6	.960
1983—Houston	Nat.	2-3-S-O	65	98	10	21	3	0	1	6	.214	37	57	3	.969
1984—Houston	Nat.	SS-3B	146	527	61	137	15	11	6	60	.260	212	473	25	.965
1985—Houston	Nat.	SS-2B	107	379	43	103	18	8	4	32	.272	159	319	11	.978
1986—Houston	Nat.	S-1-3-O-P	114	313	32	78	7	3	6	41	.249	124	209	7	.979
American League Totals—2 Years			283	968	98	264	28	10	9	72	.273	440	858	57	.958
National League Totals—10 Years			894	2774	311	704	87	52	26	249	.254	1131	2295	108	.969
Major League Totals—12 Years			1177	3742	409	968	115	62	35	321	.259	1571	3153	165	.966

Selected by Pittsburgh Pirates' organization in 1st round (22nd player selected) of free-agent draft, June 8, 1971.
†On disabled list, June 6 to August 30, 1972.
‡On disabled list, July 31 to August 21, 1974.
§Traded with Infielder Jim Sexton to Seattle Mariners for Pitcher Grant Jackson, December 7, 1976.
xTraded to Houston Astros for Pitcher Floyd Bannister, December 8, 1978.
yOn disabled list, April 11 to May 5, 1982.

DIVISION SERIES RECORD

Year	Club	League	Pos.	G.	AB.	R.	H.	2B.	3B.	HR.	RBI.	B.A.	PO.	A.	E.	F.A.
1981—Houston	Nat.	PH	2	3	1	1	0	0	0	0	.333	1	0	0	1.000

CHAMPIONSHIP SERIES RECORD

Year	Club	League	Pos.	G.	AB.	R.	H.	2B.	3B.	HR.	RBI.	B.A.	PO.	A.	E.	F.A.
1975—Pittsburgh	Nat.	SS	2	1	0	0	0	0	0	0	.000	0	0	1	.000
1980—Houston	Nat.	SS	4	13	2	2	1	0	0	0	.154	8	12	1	.952
1986—Houston	Nat.	SS-PH	4	12	1	4	0	0	0	0	.333	7	8	2	.882
Championship Series Totals—3 Years			10	26	3	6	1	0	0	0	.231	15	20	4	.897

ALL-STAR GAME RECORD

Year	League	Pos.	AB.	R.	H.	2B.	3B.	HR.	RBI.	B.A.	PO.	A.	E.	F.A.
1979—National		SS	2	0	0	0	0	0	0	.000	0	1	0	1.000

Named to American League All-Star Team for 1978 game; did not play.

PITCHING RECORD

Year	Club	League	G.	IP.	W.	L.	Pct.	H.	R.	ER.	SO.	BB.	ERA.
1986—Houston	National	1	1	0	0	.000	3	3	3	1	2	27.00

HAROLD CRAIG REYNOLDS

Born November 26, 1960, at Eugene, Ore.
Height, 5.11. Weight, 165.
Throws right and bats left and righthanded.
Attended San Diego State University, San Diego, Calif.; Canada College,
Redwood City, Calif., and California State University, Long Beach, Calif.
Brother of Larry Reynolds, shortstop-outfielder in Texas Rangers' and St. Louis Cardinals' organizations,
1979 through 1984; and Don Reynolds, outfielder with San Diego Padres, 1978 and 1979.

Tied major league record for most assists by second baseman, nine-inning game (12), August 27, 1986.
Major League stolen bases: 1984 (1), 1985 (3), 1986 (30). Total—34.
Led American League second basemen in double plays with 111 in 1986.
Led Pacific Coast League in sacrifice hits with 14 in 1983.
Led Eastern League in caught stealing with 20 in 1982.
Led Midwest League in stolen bases with 69 in 1981.
Tied for Pacific Coast League lead in caught stealing with 17 in 1984.
Led Pacific Coast League second basemen in double plays with 104 and total chances with 747 in 1984.
Led Pacific Coast League second basemen in putouts with 286 and total chances with 723 in 1983.
Led Midwest League second basemen in double plays with 82 in 1981.

Year	Club	League	Pos.	G.	AB.	R.	H.	2B.	3B.	HR.	RBI.	B.A.	PO.	A.	E.	F.A.
1981—Wausau	Midw.	2B-OF-3B	127	493	98	146	23	3	11	59	.296	259	386	27	.960
1982—Lynn	East.	2B	102	375	58	102	14	4	2	48	.272	202	232	19	.958
1983—Salt Lake City	P. C.	★2B-SS	136	534	84	165	20	9	1	72	.309	287	★410	★27	.963
1983—Seattle	Amer.	2B	20	59	8	12	4	1	0	1	.203	30	48	2	.975
1984—Salt Lake City	P. C.	2B	135	★558	94	165	22	6	3	54	.296	★326	★396	★25	★.967
1984—Seattle	Amer.	2B	10	10	3	3	0	0	0	0	.300	8	12	0	1.000
1985—Seattle	Amer.	2B	67	104	15	15	3	1	0	6	.144	69	123	8	.960
1985—Calgary	P. C.	2B	52	212	36	77	11	3	5	30	.363	119	171	13	.957
1986—Calgary	P. C.	2B	29	118	20	37	7	0	1	7	.314	64	83	4	.974
1986—Seattle	Amer.	2B	126	445	46	99	19	4	1	24	.222	278	415	16	.977
Major League Totals—4 Years			223	618	72	129	26	6	1	31	.209	385	598	26	.974

Selected by San Diego Padres' organization in 5th round of free-agent draft, June 5, 1979.
Selected by Seattle Mariners' organization in secondary phase of free-agent draft, June 3, 1980.

JEFFREY ALAN REYNOLDS
(Jeff)

Born January 27, 1960, at Charles Town, W. Va.
Height, 6.01. Weight, 195.
Throws and bats righthanded.
Attended Potomac State College, Keyser, W. Va.

Led International League batters in strikeouts with 123 in 1983.

Led South Atlantic League in total bases with 257 and game-winning RBIs with 16 in 1981.
Led International League third basemen in errors with 26 in 1983.
Led South Atlantic League third basemen in double plays with 27 in 1981.
Named South Atlantic League co-Most Valuable Player, 1981.

Year Club	League	Pos.	G.	AB.	R.	H.	2B.	3B.	HR.	RBI.	B.A.	PO.	A.	E.	F.A.
1980—Fort Lauderdale..	Fla. St.	3B	21	63	4	15	2	2	0	7	.238	2	19	2	.913
1980—Oneonta	NYP	3B	70	265	39	75	14	3	7	★56	.283	41	★174	24	.900
1981—Greensboro	S. Atl.	3B	125	474	83	145	28	3	26	★103	.306	●88	★277	25	.936
1982—Nash.†-Knox.	South.	3B	132	471	71	114	30	3	20	63	.242	91	294	35	.917
1983—Syracuse	Int.	3B-1B-SS	128	434	46	95	15	1	13	50	.219	147	211	27	.930
1984—Knoxville‡§x	South.	I-O-P	70	231	33	58	11	2	9	41	.251	206	45	9	.965
1985—Jacksonville	South.	3B-OF	137	499	53	129	30	1	14	69	.259	140	156	21	.934
1986—Jacksonville	South.	3B-P-OF	143	557	85	149	36	0	29	113	.268	101	264	29	.926

Selected by New York Yankees' organization in 4th round of free-agent draft, January 8, 1980.
†Traded with First Baseman Dave Revering to Toronto Blue Jays for First Baseman John Mayberry, May 5, 1982.
‡On disabled list, May 21 to June 5, 1984.
§On suspended list, July 7 to July 13, 1984.
xDrafted by Indianapolis (Montreal Expos' organization), December 4, 1984.

PITCHING RECORD

Year Club	League	G.	IP.	W.	L.	Pct.	H.	R.	ER.	SO.	BB.	ERA.
1984—Knoxville	Southern	2	2	0	0	.000	4	3	3	2	2	13.50
1986—Jacksonville	Southern	4	4	0	0	.000	7	2	2	2	2	4.50

ROBERT JAMES REYNOLDS
(R. J.)

Born April 19, 1959, at Sacramento, Calif.
Height, 6.00. Weight, 180.
Throws right and bats left and righthanded.
Attended Cosumnes River College, Sacramento, Calif.;
and Sacramento City College, Sacramento, Calif.

Tied major league record for fewest errors by outfielder, season, for leader in errors (9), 1986.
Major League stolen bases: 1983 (5), 1984 (7), 1985 (18), 1986 (16). Total—46.
Led Texas League outfielders in double plays with 8 in 1983.
Led Florida State League outfielders in double plays with 6 and total chances with 395 in 1981.
Led California League outfielders in double plays with 6 in 1980.

Year Club	League	Pos.	G.	AB.	R.	H.	2B.	3B.	HR.	RBI.	B.A.	PO.	A.	E.	F.A.
1980—Lodi	Calif.	OF	86	299	33	84	6	3	4	31	.281	188	10	12	.943
1981—Vero Beach	Fla. St.	OF	132	502	62	139	9	11	2	49	.277	★368	20	7	.982
1982—Lodi	Calif.	OF	108	403	67	126	19	3	6	35	.313	212	12	6	.974
1982—San Antonio	Texas	OF	3	12	3	2	0	0	1	2	.167	10	1	0	1.000
1983—San Antonio	Texas	OF	133	504	103	170	25	3	18	89	.337	255	●18	12	.958
1983—Los Angeles	Nat.	OF	24	55	5	13	0	0	2	11	.236	25	2	2	.931
1984—Albuquerque	P. C.	OF	47	199	38	69	10	4	3	30	.347	104	4	6	.947
1984—Los Angeles†	Nat.	OF	73	240	24	62	12	2	2	24	.258	104	4	3	.973
1985—L.A.‡§-Pitt.	Nat.	OF	104	337	44	95	15	7	3	42	.282	159	6	6	.965
1986—Pittsburgh	Nat.	OF	118	402	63	108	30	2	9	48	.269	190	2	●9	.955
Major League Totals—4 Years			319	1034	136	278	57	11	16	125	.269	478	14	20	.961

Selected by Los Angeles Dodgers' organization in 2nd round of free-agent draft, January 8, 1980.
†On disabled list, July 2 to July 17, 1984.
‡On disabled list, April 8 to April 23 and July 18 to August 2, 1985.
§Traded to Pittsburgh Pirates, September 3, 1985, as partial completion of deal in which Los Angeles Dodgers acquired Third Baseman Bill Madlock for three players to be named later, August 31, 1985; Pittsburgh acquired Outfielder Cecil Espy and First Baseman Sid Bream to complete deal, September 9, 1985.

RONN DWAYNE REYNOLDS

Born September 28, 1958, at Wichita, Kan.
Height, 6.00. Weight, 200.
Throws and bats righthanded.
Attended Garden City Community College, Garden City, Kan.,
and University of Arkansas, Fayetteville, Ark.

Tied for Texas League lead in being hit by pitch with 10 in 1982.
Led Texas League catchers in putouts with 583 and total chances with 651 in 1982.

Year Club	League	Pos.	G.	AB.	R.	H.	2B.	3B.	HR.	RBI.	B.A.	PO.	A.	E.	F.A.
1980—Little Falls	NYP	C	15	44	6	8	1	1	1	8	.182	85	3	2	.978
1980—Lynchburg	Carol.	C	36	105	14	21	3	0	2	17	.200	206	23	3	.987
1981—Jackson	Texas	C	88	272	16	64	12	1	2	30	.235	493	67	12	.979
1982—Jackson	Texas	C-3B-OF	123	431	50	110	13	1	10	43	.255	585	57	14	.979
1982—New York	Nat.	C	2	4	0	0	0	0	0	0	.000	3	0	0	1.000
1983—Tidewater	Int.	C	40	128	8	27	8	0	0	9	.211	209	27	1	.996
1983—New York	Nat.	C	24	66	4	13	1	0	0	2	.197	99	14	7	.942
1984—Tidewater	Int.	C-1B	90	280	35	73	11	0	11	46	.261	457	25	7	.986
1985—New York	Nat.	C	28	43	4	9	2	0	0	1	.209	86	9	1	.990
1985—Tidewater†	Int.	C	3	10	0	3	1	0	0	2	.300	5	2	0	1.000
1986—Portland	P. C.	C-1B	51	165	13	38	9	4	2	22	.230	228	23	2	.992
1986—Philadelphia	Nat.	C	43	126	8	27	4	0	3	10	.214	198	16	2	.991
Major League Totals—4 Years			97	239	16	49	7	0	3	13	.205	386	39	10	.977

Selected by Oakland A's organization in 5th round of free-agent draft, June 5, 1979.

Selected by New York Mets' organization in 5th round of free-agent draft, June 3, 1980.

†Traded with Pitcher Jeff Bittiger to Philadelphia Phillies for Pitcher Rodger Cole and First Baseman Ronnie Gideon, January 16, 1986.

RICHARD ALAN RHODEN

Name pronounced ROH-dun.

(Rick)

Born May 16, 1953, at Boynton Beach, Fla.
Height, 6.03. Weight, 195.
Throws and bats righthanded.

Pitched seven-inning, 1-0 no-hit victory against Phoenix, April 23, 1980 (first game).

Major League saves: 1983 (1).

Named pitcher on THE SPORTING NEWS National League Silver Slugger team, 1984 through 1986.

Year Club	League	G.	IP.	W.	L.	Pct.	H.	R.	ER.	SO.	BB.	ERA.
1971—Daytona Beach	Florida St.	11	61	4	6	.400	59	32	27	67	29	3.98
1972—El Paso	Texas	13	87	6	4	.600	70	36	32	89	30	3.31
1972—Albuquerque	P. Coast	13	80	7	1	.875	83	41	34	55	34	3.83
1973—Albuquerque†	P. Coast	20	116	4	9	.308	117	66	58	68	70	4.50
1974—Albuquerque	P. Coast	26	178	9	10	.474	197	103	87	106	65	4.40
1974—Los Angeles	National	4	9	1	0	1.000	5	2	2	7	4	2.00
1975—Los Angeles	National	26	99	3	3	.500	94	40	34	40	32	3.09
1976—Los Angeles	National	27	181	12	3	.800	165	66	60	77	53	2.98
1977—Los Angeles	National	31	216	16	10	.615	223	98	90	122	63	3.75
1978—Los Angeles‡	National	30	165	10	8	.556	160	77	67	79	51	3.65
1979—Pittsburgh§	National	1	5	0	1	.000	5	4	4	2	2	7.20
1980—Portland	P. Coast	10	52	6	3	.667	47	22	17	24	21	2.94
1980—Pittsburgh	National	20	127	7	5	.583	133	58	54	70	40	3.83
1981—Pittsburgh	National	21	136	9	4	.692	147	66	59	76	53	3.90
1982—Pittsburgh	National	35	230⅓	11	14	.440	239	115	106	128	70	4.14
1983—Pittsburgh	National	36	244⅓	13	13	.500	256	95	84	153	68	3.09
1984—Pittsburgh	National	33	238⅓	14	9	.609	216	81	72	136	62	2.72
1985—Pittsburgh x	National	35	213⅓	10	15	.400	254	●119	★106	128	69	4.47
1986—Pittsburgh x	National	34	253⅔	15	12	.556	211	82	80	159	76	2.84
Major League Totals—13 Years		333	2118	121	97	.555	2108	903	818	1177	643	3.48

Selected by Los Angeles Dodgers' organization in 1st round (20th player selected) of free-agent draft, June 8, 1971.

†On disabled list, July 20 to August 15, 1973.

‡Traded to Pittsburgh Pirates for Pitcher Jerry Reuss, April 9, 1979.

§On disabled list, May 12 to October 4, 1979.

xTraded with Pitchers Cecilio Guante and Pat Clements to New York Yankees for Pitchers Doug Drabek, Brian Fisher and Logan Easley, November 26, 1986.

CHAMPIONSHIP SERIES RECORD

Year Club	League	G.	IP.	W.	L.	Pct.	H.	R.	ER.	SO.	BB.	ERA.
1977—Los Angeles	National	1	4⅓	0	0	.000	2	0	0	0	2	0.00
1978—Los Angeles	National	1	4	0	0	.000	2	1	1	3	1	2.25
Championship Series Totals—2 Years		2	8⅓	0	0	.000	4	1	1	3	3	1.08

WORLD SERIES RECORD

Year Club	League	G.	IP.	W.	L.	Pct.	H.	R.	ER.	SO.	BB.	ERA.
1977—Los Angeles	National	2	7	0	1	.000	4	2	2	5	1	2.57

ALL-STAR GAME RECORD

Year League	IP.	W.	L.	Pct.	H.	R.	ER.	SO.	BB.	ERA.
1976—National	1	0	0	.000	1	0	0	0	0	0.00

Member of National League All-Star Team in 1986; did not play.

JAMES EDWARD RICE

(Jim)

Born March 8, 1953, at Anderson, S. C.
Height, 6.02. Weight, 205.
Throws and bats righthanded.

Established major league record for most times grounding into double plays, season (36), 1984.

Tied major league records for most consecutive seasons leading major leagues, total bases (2); fewest double plays by outfielder, season, 150 or more games (0), 1986.

Tied American League records for most consecutive seasons leading league, total bases (3); most years leading league in grounding into double plays (3).

Major League stolen bases: 1975 (10), 1976 (8), 1977 (5), 1978 (7), 1979 (9), 1980 (8), 1981 (2), 1984 (4), 1985 (2). Total—55.

Hit three home runs in a game, August 29, 1977 and August 29, 1983 (second game).

Led American League in grounding into double plays with 29 in 1982, 36 in 1984, 35 in 1985 and tied for lead with 31 in 1983.

Led American League in total bases with 382 in 1977, 406 in 1978, 369 in 1979 and 344 in 1983.

Led American League in slugging percentage with .593 in 1977 and .600 in 1978.

Led American League batters in strikeouts with 123 in 1976.

Led International League in total bases with 249 in 1974.

Led Florida State League in total bases with 240 in 1972.

Named American League Player of the Year by THE SPORTING NEWS, 1978.
Named American League Most Valuable Player by Baseball Writers' Association of America, 1978.
Named outfielder on THE SPORTING NEWS American League All-Star Team, 1975, 1977 through 1979, 1983 and 1986.
Named outfielder on THE SPORTING NEWS American League Silver Slugger team, 1983 and 1984.
Named Minor League Player of the Year by THE SPORTING NEWS, 1974.
Named International League Most Valuable Player, 1974.
Received reported $45,000 bonus to sign with Boston Red Sox, 1971.

Year	Club	League	Pos.	G.	AB.	R.	H.	2B.	3B.	HR.	RBI.	B.A.	PO.	A.	E.	F.A.
1971—Williamsport	NYP	OF	60	223	34	57	9	5	5	27	.256	86	2	6	.936
1972—Winter Haven	Fla. St.	OF	130	*491	*80	*143	20	13	17	87	.291	190	10	9	.957
1973—Bristol	East.	OF	119	423	66	134	25	4	27	93	*.317	169	13	12	.938
1973—Pawtucket	Int.	OF	10	37	7	14	2	0	4	10	.378	21	0	0	1.000
1974—Pawtucket	Int.	OF	117	430	69	145	21	4	*25	*93	*.337	181	10	11	.946
1974—Boston	Amer.	OF	24	67	6	18	2	1	1	13	.269	4	0	1	.800
1975—Boston	Amer.	OF	144	564	92	174	29	4	22	102	.309	162	6	0	1.000
1976—Boston	Amer.	OF	153	581	75	164	25	8	25	85	.282	199	8	7	.967
1977—Boston	Amer.	OF	160	644	104	206	29	15	*39	114	.320	83	4	4	.956
1978—Boston	Amer.	OF	*163	*677	121	*213	25	*15	*46	*139	.315	245	13	3	.989
1979—Boston	Amer.	OF	158	619	117	201	39	6	39	130	.325	241	8	4	.984
1980—Boston†	Amer.	OF	124	504	81	148	22	6	24	86	.294	233	10	3	.988
1981—Boston	Amer.	OF	108	*451	51	128	18	1	17	62	.284	237	9	3	.988
1982—Boston	Amer.	OF	145	573	86	177	24	5	24	97	.309	273	10	9	.969
1983—Boston	Amer.	OF	155	626	90	191	34	1	*39	●126	.305	339	21	6	.984
1984—Boston	Amer.	OF	159	657	98	184	25	7	28	122	.280	336	12	4	.989
1985—Boston	Amer.	OF	140	546	85	159	20	3	27	103	.291	236	8	9	.964
1986—Boston	Amer.	OF	157	618	98	200	39	2	20	110	.324	330	16	8	.977
Major League Totals—13 Years			1790	7127	1104	2163	331	74	351	1289	.303	2918	125	61	.980

Selected by Boston Red Sox' organization in 1st round (15th player selected) of free-agent draft, June 8, 1971.
†On disabled list, June 22 to July 27, 1980.

CHAMPIONSHIP SERIES RECORD

Established American League Championship Series record for most runs, seven-game Series (8), 1986.
Tied American League Championship Series record for most strikeouts, seven-game Series (8), 1986.

Year	Club	League	Pos.	G.	AB.	R.	H.	2B.	3B.	HR.	RBI.	B.A.	PO.	A.	E.	F.A.
1986—Boston	Amer.	OF	7	31	8	5	1	0	2	6	.161	13	1	0	1.000

WORLD SERIES RECORD

Tied World Series record for most at-bats, nine-inning game (6), October 19, 1986.

Year	Club	League	Pos.	G.	AB.	R.	H.	2B.	3B.	HR.	RBI.	B.A.	PO.	A.	E.	F.A.
1986—Boston	Amer.	OF	7	27	6	9	1	1	0	0	.333	16	2	0	1.000

ALL-STAR GAME RECORD

Tied All-Star Game record for most at bats, game (5), July 17, 1979.

Year	League	Pos.	AB.	R.	H.	2B.	3B.	HR.	RBI.	B.A.	PO.	A.	E.	F.A.
1977—American		OF	2	0	1	0	0	0	0	.500	1	0	0	1.000
1978—American		OF	4	0	0	0	0	0	0	.000	2	0	0	1.000
1979—American		OF	5	0	1	1	0	0	0	.200	3	0	0	1.000
1983—American		OF	4	1	2	0	0	1	1	.500	1	0	0	1.000
1984—American		PH-OF	1	0	0	0	0	0	0	.000	1	0	0	1.000
1985—American		OF	3	0	0	0	0	0	0	.000	1	0	0	1.000
1986—American		PH	1	0	0	0	0	0	0	.000	0	0	0	.000
All-Star Game Totals—7 Years			20	1	4	1	0	1	1	.200	9	0	0	1.000

Named to American League All-Star Team in 1980; replaced due to injury.

DAVID ALLAN RIGHETTI
Name pronounced Ri-GET-tee.
(Dave)

Born November 28, 1958, at San Jose, Calif.
Height, 6.03. Weight, 195.
Throws and bats lefthanded.
Attended San Jose City College, San Jose, Calif.
Son of Leo Righetti, minor league infielder, 1944 through 1949 and 1951 through 1957;
Brother of Steven Righetti, third baseman in Texas Rangers' organization, 1977 through 1979.

Established major league record for most saves, season (46), 1986.
Pitched 4-0 no-hit victory against Boston Red Sox, July 4, 1983.
Major League saves: 1982 (1), 1984 (31), 1985 (29), 1986 (46). Total—107.
Led American League in saves with 46 and games finished in relief with 68 in 1986.
Named American League Fireman of the Year by THE SPORTING NEWS, 1986.
Named American League Rookie Pitcher of the Year by THE SPORTING NEWS, 1981.
Named American League Rookie of the Year by Baseball Writers' Association of America, 1981.

Year	Club	League	G.	IP.	W.	L.	Pct.	H.	R.	ER.	SO.	BB.	ERA.
1977—Asheville	W. Carol.	17	109	11	3	*.786	98	47	38	101	53	3.14
1978—Tulsa†‡	Texas	13	91	5	5	.500	66	40	32	127	49	3.16
1979—West Haven§	Eastern	11	69	4	3	.571	45	23	15	78	45	1.96
1979—Columbus x	Int'national	8	40	3	2	.600	22	13	13	44	19	2.93
1979—New York	American	3	17	0	1	.000	10	7	7	13	10	3.71

Year	Club	League	G.	IP.	W.	L.	Pct.	H.	R.	ER.	SO.	BB.	ERA.
1980—Columbus	Int'national	24	142	6	10	.375	124	79	73	139	*101	4.63
1981—Columbus	Int'national	7	45	5	0	1.000	30	8	5	50	26	1.00
1981—New York	American	15	105	8	4	.667	75	25	24	89	38	2.06
1982—New York	American	33	183	11	10	.524	155	88	77	163	*108	3.79
1982—Columbus	Int'national	4	25⅔	1	0	1.000	22	11	8	33	12	2.81
1983—New York	American	31	217	14	8	.636	194	96	83	169	67	3.44
1984—New York y	American	64	96⅓	5	6	.455	79	29	25	90	37	2.34
1985—New York	American	74	107	12	7	.632	96	36	33	92	45	2.78
1986—New York	American	74	106⅔	8	8	.500	88	31	29	83	35	2.45
Major League Totals—7 Years		294	832	58	44	.569	697	312	278	699	340	3.01

Selected by Texas Rangers' organization in 1st round (ninth player selected) of free-agent draft, January 11, 1977.
†On disabled list, July 31 to September 2, 1978.
‡Traded with Pitchers Mike Griffin and Paul Mirabella and Outfielders Juan Beniquez and Greg Jemison to New York Yankees for Pitchers Sparky Lyle, Larry McCall and Dave Rajsich, Catcher Mike Heath, Shortstop Domingo Ramos and cash, November 10, 1978.
§On disabled list, May 21 to June 28, 1979.
xOn disabled list, June 28 to July 20 and August 2 to August 23, 1979.
yOn disabled list, June 17 to July 2, 1984.

DIVISION SERIES RECORD

Year	Club	League	G.	IP.	W.	L.	Pct.	H.	R.	ER.	SO.	BB.	ERA.
1981—New York	American	2	9	2	0	1.000	8	1	1	10	3	1.00

CHAMPIONSHIP SERIES RECORD

Year	Club	League	G.	IP.	W.	L.	Pct.	H.	R.	ER.	SO.	BB.	ERA.
1981—New York	American	1	6	1	0	1.000	4	0	0	4	2	0.00

WORLD SERIES RECORD

Year	Club	League	G.	IP.	W.	L.	Pct.	H.	R.	ER.	SO.	BB.	ERA.
1981—New York	American	1	2	0	0	.000	5	3	3	1	2	13.50

ALL-STAR GAME RECORD

Year	League	IP.	W.	L.	Pct.	H.	R.	ER.	SO.	BB.	ERA.
1986—American	⅔	0	0	.000	2	0	0	0	0	0.00

JOSE ANTONIO RIJO (ABREAU)

Name pronounced REE-ho.

Born May 13, 1965, at San Cristobal, Dominican Republic.
Height, 6.01. Weight, 160.
Throws and bats righthanded.

Major League saves: 1984 (2),1986 (1). Total—3.
Led Pacific Coast League in balks with 11 in 1985.
Led Florida State League in complete games with 15 and tied for lead in shutouts with 4 in 1983.
Named Florida State League Most Valuable Player, 1983.

Year	Club	League	G.	IP.	W.	L.	Pct.	H.	R.	ER.	SO.	BB.	ERA.
1981—Bradenton Yankees	Gulf Coast	11	22	3	3	.500	37	16	11	22	7	4.50
1982—Paintsville	Ap'lachian	13	79⅓	8	4	.667	76	33	22	66	22	2.50
1983—Fort Lauderdale	Florida St.	21	160⅓	*15	5	.750	129	38	30	152	43	*1.68
1983—Nashville	Southern	5	40⅓	3	2	.600	31	12	12	32	22	2.68
1984—New York	American	24	62⅓	2	8	.200	74	40	33	47	33	4.76
1984—Columbus†	Int'national	11	65⅓	3	3	.500	67	35	32	47	40	4.41
1985—Tacoma	P. Coast	24	149	7	10	.412	116	64	48	*179	*108	2.90
1985—Oakland	American	12	63⅔	6	4	.600	57	26	25	65	28	3.53
1986—Oakland	American	39	193⅔	9	11	.450	172	116	100	176	108	4.65
Major League Totals—3 Years		75	319⅔	17	23	.425	303	182	158	288	169	4.45

Signed as free agent by New York Yankees' organization, August 1, 1980.
†Traded with Outfielder Stan Javier and Pitchers Jay Howell, Eric Plunk and Tim Birtsas to Oakland A's for Outfielder Rickey Henderson, Pitcher Bert Bradley and cash, December 5, 1984.

ERNEST RILES

Born October 2, 1960, at Cairo, Ga.
Height, 6.00. Weight, 180.
Throws right and bats lefthanded.
Attended Middle Georgia College, Cochran, Ga.

Major League stolen bases: 1985 (2), 1986 (7). Total—9
Led California League in bases on balls received with 84 in 1982.
Led Texas League shortstops in total chances with 670 and double plays with 77 in 1983.
Led California League shortstops in double plays with 95 and tied for lead in total chances with 692 in 1982.

Year	Club	League	Pos.	G.	AB.	R.	H.	2B.	3B.	HR.	RBI.	B.A.	PO.	A.	E.	F.A.
1981—Butte	Pion.	SS-3B-2B	67	256	63	89	11	2	4	43	.348	97	217	27	.921
1982—Stockton	Calif.	SS	138	447	60	128	23	6	2	56	.286	204	*451	37	.947
1983—El Paso	Texas	SS	130	476	109	166	31	3	13	91	*.349	*193	*445	32	*.952
1984—Vancouver	P. C.	SS	123	424	59	113	19	7	3	54	.267	*190	316	17	.967
1985—Vancouver	P. C.	SS	30	118	19	41	7	1	2	20	.347	47	120	6	.965

Year Club	League	Pos.	G.	AB.	R.	H.	2B.	3B.	HR.	RBI.	B.A.	PO.	A.	E.	F.A.
1985—Milwaukee............	Amer.	SS	116	448	54	128	12	7	5	45	.286	183	310	22	.957
1986—Milwaukee............	Amer.	SS	145	524	69	132	24	2	9	47	.252	212	327	20	.964
Major League Totals—2 Years................			261	972	123	260	36	9	14	92	.267	395	637	42	.961

Selected by Seattle Mariners' organization in 21st round of free-agent draft, June 3, 1980.
Selected by Milwaukee Brewers' organization in secondary phase of free-agent draft, January 13, 1981.

GEORGE MICHAEL RILEY

Born October 6, 1956, at Philadelphia, Pa.
Height, 6.04. Weight, 200.
Throws and bats lefthanded.

Pitched 10-0, seven-inning no-hit victory against Fort Lauderdale, July 11, 1976 (first game).
Led Florida State League in games started with 26 in 1975.

Year Club	League	G.	IP.	W.	L.	Pct.	H.	R.	ER.	SO.	BB.	ERA.
1974—Bradenton Cubs	Gulf Coast	5	21	0	3	.000	18	14	8	16	8	3.43
1975—Key West	Florida St.	28	155	10	10	.500	141	75	62	84	81	3.60
1976—Pompano Beach	Florida St.	20	114	7	10	.412	122	73	49	76	47	3.87
1976—Midland	Texas	8	47	1	5	.167	61	37	34	29	36	6.51
1977—Midland	Texas	30	75	3	1	.750	79	41	36	57	36	4.32
1977—Wichita	Am. Assoc.	9	13	0	0	.000	15	7	7	11	8	4.85
1978—Wichita	Am. Assoc.	24	36	3	5	.375	47	31	29	17	23	7.25
1978—Midland	Texas	10	69	5	3	.625	77	37	34	50	39	4.43
1979—Wichita†	Am. Assoc.	38	74	3	8	.273	75	53	50	53	53	6.08
1979—Chicago	National	4	13	0	1	.000	16	9	8	5	6	5.54
1980—Wichita‡	Am. Assoc.	28	47	3	3	.500	60	23	23	32	19	4.40
1980—Chicago‡	National	22	36	0	4	.000	41	29	23	18	20	5.75
1981—Appleton§	Midwest	7	30	0	3	.000	30	13	12	27	13	3.60
1982—Reading	Eastern	37	58⅔	2	3	.400	56	27	23	46	25	3.53
1983—Reading	Eastern	27	81⅔	8	3	.727	69	27	22	58	44	2.42
1983—Portland	P. Coast	9	47	5	2	.714	48	36	33	27	32	6.32
1984—Portland x	P. Coast	36	163⅔	11	7	.611	127	65	54	138	52	2.97
1984—San Francisco	National	5	29⅓	1	0	1.000	39	14	13	12	7	3.99
1985—Phoenix y	P. Coast	46	89⅓	6	7	.462	97	52	48	64	43	4.84
1986—Montreal z	National	10	8⅔	0	0	.000	7	4	4	5	8	4.15
1986—Indianapolis z	Am. Assoc.	5	9	0	2	.000	13	6	6	4	6	6.00
Major League Totals—4 Years............		41	87	1	5	.167	103	56	48	40	41	4.97

Selected by Chicago Cubs' organization in 4th round of free-agent draft, June 5, 1974.
†On disabled list, April 17 to April 27, 1979.
‡Released, February 26, 1981; signed by Appleton (Chicago White Sox' organization), July 18, 1981.
§Released, March 29, 1982; signed by Reading (Philadelphia Phillies' organization), June 5, 1982.
xTraded with Pitcher Kelly Downs to San Francisco Giants for First Baseman Al Oliver and a player to be named later, August 20, 1984; Philadelphia Phillies acquired Pitcher Renie Martin to complete deal, August 30, 1984.
yTraded with Outfielder Alonzo Powell to Montreal Expos' organization for Pitcher Bill Laskey, October 24, 1985.
zGranted free agency, October 15, 1986.

CALVIN EDWIN RIPKEN JR.
(Cal)

Born August 24, 1960, at Havre de Grace, Md.
Height, 6.04. Weight, 200.
Throws and bats righthanded.
Son of Cal Ripken, manager of Baltimore Orioles;
brother of Billy Ripken, shortstop in Baltimore Orioles' organization;
nephew of Bill Ripken, minor league outfielder, 1947 through 1949.

Established major league record for fewest stolen bases, season, most at-bats (0 and 663), 1983.
Established American League record for most assists by shortstop, season (583), 1984.
Major League stolen bases: 1982 (3), 1984 (2), 1985 (2), 1986 (4). Total—11.
Hit for the cycle, May 6, 1984.
Tied for American League lead in game-winning RBIs with 15 in 1986.
Led American League shortstops in total chances with 831 in 1983 and 906 in 1984.
Led American League shortstops in double plays with 113 in 1983, 122 in 1984 and 123 in 1985.
Tied for Southern League lead in sacrifice flies with 9 in 1980.
Led Southern League third basemen in fielding percentage with .933, putouts with 119, assists with 268, and double plays with 34 in 1980.
Tied for Appalachian League lead in double plays by shortstops with 31 in 1978.
Named Major League Player of the Year by THE SPORTING NEWS, 1983.
Named American League Player of the Year by THE SPORTING NEWS, 1983.
Named American League Most Valuable Player by Baseball Writers' Association of America, 1983.
Named American League Rookie Player of the Year by THE SPORTING NEWS, 1982.
Named American League Rookie of the Year by Baseball Writers' Association of America, 1982.
Named shortstop on THE SPORTING NEWS American League All-Star Team, 1983 through 1985.
Named shortstop on THE SPORTING NEWS Silver Slugger team, 1983 through 1986.

Year Club	League	Pos.	G.	AB.	R.	H.	2B.	3B.	HR.	RBI.	B.A.	PO.	A.	E.	F.A.
1978—Bluefield	Appal.	SS	63	239	27	63	7	1	0	24	.264	★92	204	★33	.900
1979—Miami	Fla. St.	3B-SS-2B	105	393	51	119	★28	1	5	54	.303	149	260	30	.932
1979—Charlotte.............	South.	3B	17	61	6	11	0	1	3	8	.180	13	26	3	.929
1980—Charlotte.............	South.	3B-SS	●144	522	91	144	28	5	25	78	.276	151	341	35	.934
1981—Rochester	Int.	3B-SS	114	437	74	126	31	4	23	75	.288	128	320	21	.955
1981—Baltimore	Amer.	SS-3B	23	39	1	5	0	0	0	0	.128	13	30	3	.935

— 410 —

Year Club League	Pos.	G.	AB.	R.	H.	2B.	3B.	HR.	RBI.	B.A.	PO.	A.	E.	F.A.
1982—Baltimore .... Amer.	SS-3B	160	598	90	158	32	5	28	93	.264	221	440	19	.972
1983—Baltimore .... Amer.	SS	•162	*663	*121	*211	*47	2	27	102	.318	272	*534	25	.970
1984—Baltimore .... Amer.	SS	•162	641	103	195	37	7	27	86	.304	*297	*583	26	.971
1985—Baltimore .... Amer.	SS	161	642	116	181	32	5	26	110	.282	*286	474	26	.967
1986—Baltimore .... Amer.	SS	162	627	98	177	35	1	25	81	.282	240	*482	13	.982
Major League Totals—6 Years		830	3210	529	927	183	20	133	472	.289	1329	2543	112	.972

Selected by Baltimore Orioles' organization in 2nd round of free-agent draft, June 6, 1978.

CHAMPIONSHIP SERIES RECORD

Year Club League	Pos.	G.	AB.	R.	H.	2B.	3B.	HR.	RBI.	B.A.	PO.	A.	E.	F.A.
1983—Baltimore .... Amer.	SS	4	15	5	6	2	0	0	1	.400	7	11	0	1.000

WORLD SERIES RECORD

Year Club League	Pos.	G.	AB.	R.	H.	2B.	3B.	HR.	RBI.	B.A.	PO.	A.	E.	F.A.
1983—Baltimore .... Amer.	SS	5	18	2	3	0	0	0	1	.167	6	14	0	1.000

ALL-STAR GAME RECORD

Year League	Pos.	AB.	R.	H.	2B.	3B.	HR.	RBI.	B.A.	PO.	A.	E.	F.A.
1983—American	SS	0	0	0	0	0	0	0	.000	1	0	0	1.000
1984—American	SS	3	0	0	0	0	0	0	.000	0	0	0	.000
1985—American	SS	3	0	1	0	0	0	0	.333	2	1	0	1.000
1986—American	SS	4	0	0	0	0	0	0	.000	0	1	0	1.000
All-Star Game Totals—4 Years		10	0	1	0	0	0	0	.100	3	2	0	1.000

WILLIAM OLIVER RIPKEN
(Billy)

Born December 16, 1964, at Havre de Grace, Md.
Height, 6.01. Weight, 180
Throws and bats righthanded.
Son of Cal Ripken Sr., manager of Baltimore Orioles; brother of Cal Ripken, Jr.,
infielder with Baltimore Orioles; and nephew of Bill Ripken, minor league outfielder, 1947 through 1949.
Tied for Southern League lead in grounding into double plays with 21 in 1986.
Led Southern League second basemen in total chances with 723 and double plays with 79 in 1986.

Year Club League	Pos.	G.	AB.	R.	H.	2B.	3B.	HR.	RBI.	B.A.	PO.	A.	E.	F.A.
1982—Bluefield................ Appal.	SS-3B-2B	27	45	8	11	1	0	0	4	.244	15	17	3	.914
1983—Bluefield................ Appal.	SS-3B	48	152	24	33	6	0	0	13	.217	82	145	23	.908
1984—Hagerstown† .... Carol.	SS-2B	115	409	48	94	15	3	2	40	.230	187	358	28	.951
1985—Charlotte................ South.	SS	18	51	2	7	1	0	0	3	.137	18	52	4	.946
1985—Daytona Beach‡ .. Fla. St.	SS-3B-2B	67	222	23	51	11	0	0	18	.230	90	198	8	.973
1985—Hagerstown .... Carol.	3B-2B	14	47	9	12	0	1	0	0	.255	14	37	2	.962
1986—Charlotte................ South.	2B	141	530	58	142	20	3	5	62	.268	*305	*395	*23	.968

Selected by Baltimore Orioles' organization in 11th round of free-agent draft, June 7, 1982.
†On disabled list, April 20 to May 3, 1984.
‡On disabled list, June 23 to July 6, 1985.

REGGIE BLAKE RITTER

Born January 23, 1960, at Malvern, Ark.
Height, 6.02. Weight, 195.
Throws right and bats lefthanded.
Attended Henderson State University, Arkadelphia, Ark.

Year Club League	G.	IP.	W.	L.	Pct.	H.	R.	ER.	SO.	BB.	ERA.
1983—Waterloo.. Midwest	31	110	4	7	.364	111	61	45	85	55	3.68
1984—Waterloo.. Midwest	37	128⅔	6	6	.500	145	82	68	89	50	4.76
1985—Waterbury.. Eastern	15	101	7	6	.538	91	40	36	31	33	3.21
1985—Maine†.. Int'national	10	53	4	3	.571	51	26	25	24	17	4.25
1986—Maine.. Int'national	29	97⅔	7	3	*.700	118	60	54	57	37	4.98
1986—Cleveland.. American	5	10	0	0	.000	14	10	7	6	4	6.30
Major League Totals—1 Year..............................	5	10	0	0	.000	14	10	7	6	4	6.30

Signed as free agent by Cleveland Indians' organization, August 12, 1982.
†On disabled list, August 3 to August 14, 1985.

GERMAN RIVERA (DIAZ)

Born July 6, 1960, at Santurce, Puerto Rico.
Height, 6.02. Weight, 170.
Throws and bats righthanded.
Major League stolen bases: 1984 (1).
Led Florida State League in sacrifice flies with 10 in 1980.
Tied for American Association lead in game-winning RBIs with 11 in 1986.
Led American Association third basemen in errors with 25 in 1986.
Led Pacific Coast League third basemen in double plays with 21 in 1985.
Led Pacific Coast League third basemen in assists with 333, double plays with 31 and total chances with 478 in 1983.
Led Texas League third basemen in errors with 29 in 1982.

Tied for Pioneer League lead in double plays by third basemen with 9 in 1978.

Year—Club	League	Pos.	G.	AB.	R.	H.	2B.	3B.	HR.	RBI.	B.A.	PO.	A.	E.	F.A.
1978—Clinton	Midw.	3B-OF	36	108	11	22	3	1	3	13	.204	27	31	5	.921
1978—Lethbridge	Pion.	3B	66	252	61	79	15	2	7	47	.313	50	★120	12	★.934
1979—Lodi	Calif.	3B	36	139	26	26	6	1	1	17	.187	24	84	19	.850
1979—Clinton	Midw.	3B	100	338	43	82	18	5	4	42	.243	74	199	17	.941
1980—Vero Beach	Fla. St.	3B	137	530	77	137	19	10	4	★80	.258	81	203	●29	.907
1981—Lodi	Calif.	3B-SS	128	478	78	127	31	2	13	71	.266	157	419	40	.935
1982—San Antonio†	Texas	SS-3B	136	474	63	137	17	4	15	60	.289	171	342	61	.894
1983—Albuquerque	P. Coast	3B-SS	138	515	109	169	27	5	24	103	.328	116	343	34	.931
1983—Los Angeles	Nat.	3B	13	17	1	6	1	0	0	0	.353	2	11	1	.929
1984—Los Angeles	Nat.	3B	94	227	20	59	12	2	2	17	.260	55	167	15	.937
1984—Albuquerque	P. C.	3B-SS	51	181	30	57	12	3	4	39	.315	53	117	14	.924
1985—Alb.‡-Tucson	P. C.	3B	108	384	45	108	22	2	8	44	.281	76	191	18	★.937
1985—Houston§	Nat.	3B	13	36	3	7	2	1	0	2	.194	7	25	2	.941
1986—Nashville	A. A.	3B-OF-1B	●140	506	86	151	30	2	14	84	.298	136	176	30	.912
Major League Totals—3 Years			120	280	24	72	15	3	2	19	.257	64	203	18	.937

Signed as free agent by Los Angeles Dodgers' organization, December 20, 1977.

†Drafted by Oakland A's, December 6, 1982; returned, March 25, 1983.

‡Traded to Houston Astros' organization, July 15, 1985, completing deal in which Houston traded Infielder Enos Cabell to Los Angeles Dodgers for Pitcher Rafael Montalvo and a player to be named later, July 10, 1985.

§Released, April 1, 1986; signed by Nashville (Detroit Tigers' organization), April 4, 1986.

LUIS ANTONIO RIVERA

Born January 3, 1964, at Cidra, Puerto Rico.
Height, 5.11. Weight, 165.
Throws and bats righthanded.

Major League stolen bases: 1986 (1).

Led Southern League shortstops in total chances with 643 and double plays with 107 in 1985.

Led Florida State League shortstops in assists with 436, errors with 51, total chances with 704 and double plays with 95 in 1983.

Tied for Florida State League lead in total chances by shortstops with 626 in 1984.

Year—Club	League	Pos.	G.	AB.	R.	H.	2B.	3B.	HR.	RBI.	B.A.	PO.	A.	E.	F.A.
1982—San Jose	Calif.	SS	130	476	53	123	20	3	3	49	.258	226	389	55	.918
1983—W. Palm Beach	Fla. St.	SS	129	419	63	95	18	5	5	53	.227	217	436	51	.928
1984—W. Palm Beach	Fla. St.	SS	124	439	54	100	23	0	6	43	.228	★198	★389	39	.938
1985—Jacksonville	South.	SS	138	★538	74	129	20	2	16	72	.240	★198	★412	33	.949
1986—Indianapolis	A. A.	SS	108	407	60	100	17	5	7	43	.246	178	330	24	.955
1986—Montreal	Nat.	SS	55	166	20	34	11	1	0	13	.205	64	119	9	.953
Major League Totals—1 Year			55	166	20	34	11	1	0	13	.205	64	119	9	.953

Signed as free agent by Montreal Expos' organization, September 22, 1981.

BERTRAND ROLAND ROBERGE

Name pronounced ROW-berj.

(Bert)

Born October 3, 1954, at Lewiston, Me.
Height, 6.04. Weight, 190.
Throws and bats righthanded.
Received bachelor of science degree in zoology from
University of Maine, Orono, Me.

Major League saves: 1979 (4), 1982 (3), 1985 (2), 1986 (1). Total—10.

Led National League in balks with 5 in 1985.

Year—Club	League	G.	IP.	W.	L.	Pct.	H.	R.	ER.	SO.	BB.	ERA.
1976—Covington†	Ap'lachian	14	36	2	2	.500	33	21	13	40	12	3.25
1976—Memphis	Int'national	2	10	0	0	.000	11	5	3	8	3	2.70
1977—Columbus	Southern	6	7	0	0	.000	13	5	5	9	3	6.43
1977—Cocoa	Florida St.	33	60	4	5	.444	54	24	17	35	26	2.55
1978—Columbus	Southern	21	32	0	3	.000	37	15	12	24	10	3.38
1979—Columbus	Southern	13	88	7	1	.875	80	34	29	86	37	2.97
1979—Houston‡	National	26	32	3	0	1.000	20	6	6	13	17	1.69
1980—Tucson	P. Coast	34	49	5	3	.625	44	28	26	47	28	4.78
1980—Houston	National	14	24	2	0	1.000	24	16	16	9	10	6.00
1981—Tucson	P. Coast	50	87	5	4	.556	85	43	35	62	32	3.62
1982—Tucson	P. Coast	34	46⅔	4	4	.500	49	21	17	31	23	3.28
1982—Houston	National	22	25⅔	1	2	.333	29	12	12	18	6	4.21
1983—Tucson§	P. Coast	47	68⅔	3	8	.273	66	37	35	63	30	4.59
1984—Denver	Am. Assoc.	26	37	5	1	.833	27	8	8	36	10	1.95
1984—Chicago xy	American	21	40⅔	3	3	.500	36	18	17	25	15	3.76
1985—Montreal z	National	42	68	3	3	.500	58	28	26	34	22	3.44
1985—Indianapolis ab	Am. Assoc.	1	2	0	0	.000	2	1	1	2	1	4.50
1986—Montreal	National	21	28⅔	0	0	.000	33	20	20	20	10	6.28
1986—Indianapolis c	Am. Assoc.	22	43⅓	3	0	1.000	47	12	12	32	17	2.49
National League Totals—5 Years		125	178⅓	9	9	.500	164	82	80	94	65	4.04
American League Totals—1 Year		21	40⅔	3	3	.500	36	18	17	25	15	3.76
Major League Totals—6 Years		146	219	12	12	.500	200	100	97	119	80	3.99

Selected by Houston Astros' organization in 17th round of free-agent draft, June 8, 1976.

†Appeared in one game as outfielder with three putouts.
‡On disabled list, August 16 to September 6, 1979.
§Granted free agency, October 20, 1983; signed by Chicago White Sox, December 5, 1983.
xOn disabled list, June 23 to July 25, 1984; included rehabilitation disability assignment to Denver, July 5 to July 24, 1984.
yTraded to Montreal Expos for Infielder Bryan Little, December 7, 1984.
zOn disabled list, May 30 to July 8, 1985; included rehabilitation disability assignment to Indianapolis, July 4 to July 8, 1985.
aReleased, December 20, 1985; re-signed by Expos' organization, February 14, 1986.
bReleased, April 10, 1986; re-signed by Expos, May 9, 1986.
cReleased, October 7, 1986.

LEON JOSEPH ROBERTS III
(Bip)

Born October 27, 1963, at Berkeley, Calif.
Height, 5.07. Weight, 150.
Throws right and bats left and righthanded.
Attended Chabot College, Hayward, Calif.; and University of Nevada, Las Vegas, Nev.

Major League stolen bases: 1986 (14).
Tied for Eastern League lead in stolen bases with 40 in 1985.
Led Carolina League second basemen in total chances with 654 and double plays with 91 in 1984.
Led South Atlantic League second basemen in fielding percentage with .962 and tied for lead in double plays with 76 in 1983.

Year Club	League	Pos.	G.	AB.	R.	H.	2B.	3B.	HR.	RBI.	B.A.	PO.	A.	E.	F.A.
1982—Bradenton Pir.	Gulf C.	2B	6	23	4	7	1	0	0	1	.304	14	15	0	1.000
1982—Greenwood...........	S. Atl.	2B	33	107	15	23	3	1	0	6	.215	52	82	7	.950
1983—Greenwood...........	S. Atl.	2B-SS	122	438	78	140	20	5	6	63	.320	273	311	24	.961
1984—Prince William	Carol.	2B	134	498	81	*150	25	5	8	77	.301	*282	352	20	*.969
1985—Nashua†‡	East.	2B	105	401	64	109	19	5	1	23	.272	217	249	●29	.941
1986—San Diego§	Nat.	2B	101	241	34	61	5	2	1	12	.253	166	172	10	.971
Major League Totals—1 Year...			101	241	34	61	5	2	1	12	.253	166	172	10	.971

Selected by Pittsburgh Pirates' organization in 5th round of free-agent draft, June 8, 1981.
Selected by Pittsburgh Pirates' organization in secondary phase of free-agent draft, June 7, 1982.
†On suspended list, June 30 to July 3, 1985.
‡Drafted by San Diego Padres, December 10, 1985.
§On disabled list, May 21 to June 5, 1986.

SCOTT ANTHONY ROBERTS

Born October 7, 1959, at Seattle, Wash.
Height, 6.05. Weight, 220.
Throws and bats righthanded.
Attended University of Hawaii, Honolulu, Haw.

Led Pioneer League in hit batsmen with 12 in 1981.

Year Club	League	G.	IP.	W.	L.	Pct.	H.	R.	ER.	SO.	BB.	ERA.
1981—Butte	Pioneer	12	78	6	1	*.857	51	23	16	74	28	1.85
1982—Stockton	California	24	174⅓	14	6	.700	151	65	49	137	41	2.53
1983—Vancouver†	P. Coast	21	109	6	10	.375	135	90	77	69	63	6.36
1984—Vancouver	P. Coast	26	151	8	6	.571	156	72	60	89	74	3.58
1985—Vancouver	P. Coast	12	27⅓	1	2	.333	33	21	19	17	13	6.26
1985—El Paso‡	Texas	12	76	7	2	.778	93	53	48	47	26	5.68
1986—Maine§	Int'national	35	65⅔	4	7	.364	63	38	31	48	20	4.25

Selected by Pittsburgh Pirates' organization in 7th round of free-agent draft, June 6, 1978.
Selected by Milwaukee Brewers' organization in 2nd round of free-agent draft, June 8, 1981.
†On disabled list, May 20 to May 30, 1983.
‡Traded to Cleveland Indians for Pitcher Rich Thompson, December 16, 1985.
§On disabled list, April 20 to May 6, 1986.

WILLIAM JOSEPH ROBIDOUX

Name pronounced ROW-ba-doe.

(Billy Jo)

Born January 13, 1964, at Ware, Mass.
Height, 6.01. Weight, 200.
Throws right and bats lefthanded.

Led Texas League in total bases with 297 and slugging percentage with .577 in 1985.
Led Texas League first basemen in putouts with 1,025, assists with 68, fielding percentage with .988, total chances with 1,106 and double plays with 102 in 1985.
Named Texas League Most Valuable Player, 1985.

Year Club	League	Pos.	G.	AB.	R.	H.	2B.	3B.	HR.	RBI.	B.A.	PO.	A.	E.	F.A.
1982—Pikeville†	Appal.	3B-1B	54	167	28	48	10	1	0	13	.287	57	54	15	.881
1983—Beloit	Midw.	3B-1B-2B	126	435	70	138	30	1	10	61	.317	104	163	25	.914
1984—Stockton	Calif.	3B-1B	97	333	50	93	18	1	5	67	.279	323	98	15	.966
1985—El Paso	Texas	1B-OF-3B	133	515	*111	*176	*46	3	23	*132	*.342	1030	69	15	.987
1985—Milwaukee...........	Amer.	OF-1B	18	51	5	9	2	0	3	8	.176	64	6	0	1.000
1986—Milwaukee‡..........	Amer.	1B	56	181	15	41	8	0	1	21	.227	326	29	5	.986
1986—Beloit	Midw.	1B	7	16	3	4	2	0	0	2	.250	12	2	0	1.000
1986—El Paso..................	Texas	1B	30	114	30	37	9	0	10	34	.325	269	11	1	.996
Major League Totals—2 Years................			74	232	20	50	10	0	4	29	.216	390	35	5	.988

Selected by Milwaukee Brewers' organization in 6th round of free-agent draft, June 7, 1982.
†On disabled list, June 21 to July 1, 1982.
‡On disabled list, May 13 to June 11 and July 8 to August 20, 1986; included rehabilitation disability assignment to Beloit, June 4 to June 11, and to El Paso, August 1 to August 20, 1986.

DON ALLEN ROBINSON

Born June 8, 1957, at Ashland, Ky.
Height, 6.04. Weight, 231.
Throws and bats righthanded.

Major League saves: 1978 (1), 1980 (1), 1981 (2), 1984 (10), 1985 (3), 1986 (14). Total—31.
Tied for National League lead in home runs allowed with 26 in 1982.
Led Western Carolinas League in complete games with 11 in 1976.
Tied for Gulf Coast League lead in hit batsmen with 6 in 1975.
Named National League Rookie Pitcher of the Year by THE SPORTING NEWS, 1978.
Named pitcher on THE SPORTING NEWS National League Silver Slugger team, 1982.

Year	Club	League	G.	IP.	W.	L.	Pct.	H.	R.	ER.	SO.	BB.	ERA.
1975—Bradenton Pirates	Gulf Coast	10	66	2	3	.400	51	23	18	★70	31	2.45
1976—Charleston	W. Carol.	25	★172	12	9	.571	146	79	62	132	64	3.24
1977—Shreveport	Texas	18	112	7	6	.538	113	58	51	103	41	4.06
1977—Columbus†	Int'national	1	5	1	0	1.000	7	0	0	3	1	0.00
1978—Pittsburgh	National	35	228	14	6	.700	203	98	88	135	57	3.47
1979—Pittsburgh	National	29	161	8	8	.500	171	74	69	96	52	3.86
1980—Pittsburgh‡	National	29	160	7	10	.412	157	74	71	103	45	3.99
1981—Pittsburgh§	National	16	38	0	3	.000	47	27	25	17	23	5.92
1982—Pittsburgh	National	38	227	15	13	.536	213	★123	108	165	103	4.28
1983—Pittsburgh x	National	9	36⅓	2	2	.500	43	21	18	28	21	4.46
1983—Lynn	Eastern	2	6⅔	0	1	.000	9	6	6	5	2	8.10
1984—Pittsburgh y	National	51	122	5	6	.455	99	45	41	110	49	3.02
1985—Pittsburgh	National	44	95⅓	5	11	.313	95	49	41	65	42	3.87
1986—Pittsburgh z	National	50	69⅓	3	4	.429	61	27	26	53	27	3.38
1986—Prince William	Carolina	3	12⅔	1	1	.500	13	7	1	13	1	0.71
Major League Totals—9 Years		301	1137	59	63	.484	1089	538	487	772	419	3.85

Selected by Pittsburgh Pirates' organization in 3rd round of free-agent draft, June 4, 1975.
†On disabled list, July 28 to September 6, 1977.
‡On disabled list, March 31 to May 1, 1980.
§On disabled list, May 2 to June 6 and August 2 to August 26, 1981.
xOn disabled list, March 29 to June 10 and July 29 to September 2, 1983; included rehabilitation disability assignment to Lynn, April 29 to May 18, 1983.
yAppeared in one game as an outfielder with two putouts.
zOn disabled list, April 21 to June 7, 1986; included rehabilitation disability assignment to Prince William, May 24 to June 7, 1986.

CHAMPIONSHIP SERIES RECORD

Year	Club	League	G.	IP.	W.	L.	Pct.	H.	R.	ER.	SO.	BB.	ERA.
1979—Pittsburgh	National	2	2	1	0	1.000	0	0	0	3	1	0.00

WORLD SERIES RECORD

Year	Club	League	G.	IP.	W.	L.	Pct.	H.	R.	ER.	SO.	BB.	ERA.
1979—Pittsburgh	National	4	5	1	0	1.000	4	3	3	3	6	5.40

JEFFREY DANIEL ROBINSON
(Jeff)

Born December 13, 1960, at Santa Ana, Calif.
Height, 6.04. Weight, 195.
Throws and bats righthanded.
Attended California State University, Fullerton, Calif.

Major League saves: 1986 (8).
Tied for National League lead in hit batsmen with 7 in 1984.
Tied for Pacific Coast League lead in games started by pitchers with 29 in 1985.

Year	Club	League	G.	IP.	W.	L.	Pct.	H.	R.	ER.	SO.	BB.	ERA.
1983—Fresno	California	14	94⅔	7	6	.538	88	35	24	78	21	2.28
1984—San Francisco	National	34	171⅔	7	15	.318	195	99	87	102	52	4.56
1985—Phoenix	P. Coast	29	161	9	9	.500	192	107	92	80	60	5.14
1985—San Francisco	National	8	12⅓	0	0	.000	16	11	7	8	10	5.11
1986—San Francisco†	National	64	104⅓	6	3	.667	92	46	39	90	32	3.36
Major League Totals—3 Years		106	288⅓	13	18	.419	303	156	133	200	94	4.15

Selected by Toronto Blue Jays' organization in 17th round of free-agent draft, June 5, 1979.
Selected by Detroit Tigers' organization in 14th round of free-agent draft, June 7, 1982.
Selected by San Francisco Giants' organization in 2nd round of free-agent draft, June 6, 1983.
†Appeared in one game as an outfielder with no chances.

JEFFREY MARK ROBINSON
(Jeff)

Born December 14, 1961, at Ventura, Calif.
Height, 6.06. Weight, 210.
Throws and bats righthanded.
Attended Azusa Pacific University, Azusa, Calif.

Year Club	League	G.	IP.	W.	L.	Pct.	H.	R.	ER.	SO.	BB.	ERA.
1983—Lakeland	Florida St.	11	50	2	5	.286	61	38	33	23	19	5.94
1984—Lakeland	Florida St.	10	61⅔	2	3	.400	62	30	23	33	26	3.36
1984—Birmingham	Southern	20	113	6	6	.500	111	64	59	47	56	4.70
1985—Birmingham†	Southern	22	115	4	8	.333	142	79	65	67	59	5.09
1986—Nashville	Am. Assoc.	25	150	10	7	.588	162	85	73	72	72	4.38

Selected by San Diego Padres' organization in 40th round of free-agent draft, June 3, 1980.
Selected by Detroit Tigers' organization in 3rd round of free-agent draft, June 6, 1983.
†On disabled list, June 28 to July 10, 1985.

RONALD DEAN ROBINSON
(Ron)

Born March 24, 1962, at Exeter, Calif.
Height, 6.04. Weight, 200.
Throws and bats righthanded.
Major League saves: 1985 (1), 1986 (14). Total—15.

Year Club	League	G.	IP.	W.	L.	Pct.	H.	R.	ER.	SO.	BB.	ERA.
1980—Tampa	Florida St.	13	76	4	6	.400	76	32	28	44	16	3.32
1981—Cedar Rapids	Midwest	24	169	10	8	.556	136	58	42	165	55	2.24
1982—Waterbury	Eastern	32	178⅓	13	7	.650	166	78	65	149	65	3.28
1983—Waterbury	Eastern	20	142⅔	7	9	.438	132	66	57	82	60	3.60
1983—Indianapolis	Am. Assoc.	4	30⅔	4	0	1.000	22	13	11	20	7	3.23
1984—Wichita	Am. Assoc.	25	150⅓	9	6	.600	168	86	77	98	60	4.61
1984—Cincinnati	National	12	39⅔	1	2	.333	35	18	12	24	13	2.72
1985—Denver	Am. Assoc.	6	39⅔	2	1	.667	39	17	12	24	12	2.72
1985—Cincinnati	National	33	108⅓	7	7	.500	107	53	48	76	32	3.99
1986—Cincinnati	National	70	116⅔	10	3	.769	110	44	42	117	43	3.24
Major League Totals—3 Years		115	264⅔	18	12	.600	252	115	102	217	88	3.47

Selected by Cincinnati Reds' organization in 1st round (19th player selected) of free-agent draft, June 3, 1980.

MICHAEL JOSEPH ROCHFORD
(Mike)

Born March 14, 1963, at Methuen, Mass.
Height, 6.04. Weight, 205.
Throws and bats lefthanded.
Attended Santa Fe Community College, Gainsville, Fla.
Led International League in balks with 5 in 1984.
Tied for Carolina League lead in games started by pitchers with 29 in 1983.

Year Club	League	G.	IP.	W.	L.	Pct.	H.	R.	ER.	SO.	BB.	ERA.
1982—Elmira	NYP	16	85⅔	6	4	.600	99	53	40	66	26	4.20
1983—Winston-Salem	Carolina	29	210⅓	16	11	.593	182	85	70	165	57	3.00
1984—Pawtucket	Int'national	31	141⅓	8	10	.444	156	88	77	73	59	4.90
1985—New Britain	Eastern	14	93⅓	8	5	.615	84	39	31	42	41	2.99
1985—Pawtucket	Int'national	12	72	5	2	.714	74	34	33	47	32	4.13
1986—Pawtucket	Int'national	28	170⅔	11	10	.524	178	76	67	70	50	3.53

Selected by Boston Red Sox' organization in 1st round (17th player selected) of free-agent draft, January 12, 1982.

EDWIN RODRIGUEZ (MORALES)
(Ed)

Born August 14, 1960, at Ponce, Puerto Rico.
Height, 5.10. Weight, 175.
Throws right and bats lefthanded.

Year Club	League	Pos.	G.	AB.	R.	H.	2B.	3B.	HR.	RBI.	B.A.	PO.	A.	E.	F.A.
1980—Bradenton Yanks	Gulf C.	1B-2B	47	157	22	39	4	2	1	16	.248	179	9	6	.969
1981—Oneonta	NYP	2B-3B-SS	50	146	27	45	5	3	0	19	.308	81	120	4	.980
1982—Greensboro	S. Atl.	2B	115	425	88	126	23	3	4	62	.296	227	320	25	.956
1982—Nashville	South.	SS	10	34	4	7	0	1	0	3	.206	19	38	4	.934
1982—New York	Amer.	2B	3	9	2	3	0	0	0	1	.333	2	12	2	.875
1983—Columbus†	Int.	2B-SS-3B	112	393	73	98	7	8	2	54	.249	207	329	25	.955
1983—San Diego	Nat.	2B-SS-3B	7	12	1	2	1	0	0	0	.167	8	8	0	1.000
1984—Las Vegas‡	P. C.	2B-SS-3B	105	341	45	80	10	8	6	35	.235	205	246	14	.970
1985—Las Vegas	P. C.	2B-SS	115	436	78	126	21	6	6	35	.289	207	286	26	.950
1985—San Diego	Nat.	PH	1	1	0	0	0	0	0	0	.000	0	0	0	.000
1986—Las Vegas	P. C.	2-S-O-3	105	309	56	93	14	7	4	32	.301	154	249	19	.955
American League Totals—1 Year			3	9	2	3	0	0	0	1	.333	2	12	2	.875
National League Totals—2 Years			8	13	1	2	1	0	0	0	.154	8	8	0	1.000
Major League Totals—3 Years			11	22	3	5	1	0	0	1	.227	10	20	2	.938

Signed as free agent by New York Yankees' organization, June 3, 1980.
†Traded with Pitcher Dennis Rasmussen to San Diego Padres, September 12, 1983, completing deal in which San Diego traded Pitcher John Montefusco to New York Yankees for two players to be named later, August 26, 1983.
‡On disabled list, May 6 to May 18, 1985.

RICARDO RODRIGUEZ
(Rick)

Born September 21, 1960, at Oakland, Calif.
Height, 6.03. Weight, 190.
Throws and bats righthanded.
Attended Chabot College, Hayward, Calif., and University of California, Riverside, Calif.

Year	Club	League	G.	IP.	W.	L.	Pct.	H.	R.	ER.	SO.	BB.	ERA.
1981—Modesto	California	11	63	2	5	.286	68	51	37	28	28	5.29
1982—Modesto†	California	15	105⅔	8	2	.800	100	38	32	70	41	2.73
1983—Tacoma‡	P. Coast	10	58	1	4	.200	61	32	25	25	28	3.88
1984—Modesto§	California	2	13⅓	0	0	.000	11	3	3	6	5	2.03
1984—Tacoma	P. Coast	6	16⅓	0	1	.000	21	17	16	9	7	8.82
1984—Albany	Eastern	10	42⅔	5	1	.833	59	33	25	29	19	5.27
1985—Modesto	California	16	103⅔	8	1	.889	103	42	38	50	41	3.30
1985—Huntsville	Southern	8	50	2	1	.667	40	18	13	25	13	2.34
1985—Tacoma	P. Coast	7	13⅓	0	1	.000	18	9	6	5	7	4.05
1986—Huntsville	Southern	9	16	0	0	.000	17	11	9	14	7	5.06
1986—Tacoma	P. Coast	26	139	7	8	.467	144	82	61	76	59	3.95
1986—Oakland	American	3	16⅓	1	2	.333	17	12	12	2	7	6.61
Major League Totals—1 Year		3	16⅓	1	2	.333	17	12	12	2	7	6.61

Selected by Oakland A's organization in 2nd round of free-agent draft, June 8, 1981.
†On disabled list, May 15 to July 23, 1982.
‡On disabled list, April 10 to May 14 and July 1, 1983 through remainder of season.
§On Tacoma disabled list, April 7 to May 23 and June 12 to June 22, 1984.

RUBEN DARIO RODRIGUEZ (MARTINEZ)

Born August 4, 1964, at Cabrera, Dominican Republic.
Height, 6.00. Weight, 170.
Throws and bats righthanded.

Led Eastern League in passed balls with 17 in 1985.
Led Eastern League catchers in double plays with 10 in 1984.

Year	Club	League	Pos.	G.	AB.	R.	H.	2B.	3B.	HR.	RBI.	B.A.	PO.	A.	E.	F.A.
1982—Greenwood†	S. Atl.	C	69	218	26	54	13	0	1	15	.248	351	60	19	.956
1983—Alexandria	Carol.	C-1B	79	254	19	58	14	1	4	31	.228	496	70	11	.981
1984—Nashua	East.	C	87	242	26	53	13	1	4	32	.219	409	58	11	.977
1985—Nashua	East.	C	104	341	28	73	9	4	3	40	.214	498	96	11	.982
1985—Hawaii	P. C.	C	1	4	0	1	0	0	0	0	.250	9	0	0	1.000
1986—Nashua	East.	C	53	169	17	31	10	2	0	12	.183	318	47	6	.984
1986—Hawaii	P. C.	C	30	108	11	28	5	2	0	15	.259	201	23	6	.974
1986—Pittsburgh	Nat.	C	2	3	0	0	0	0	0	0	.000	6	1	0	1.000
Major League Totals—1 Year		2	3	0	0	0	0	0	0	.000	6	1	0	1.000

Signed as free agent by Pittsburgh Pirates' organization, November 6, 1981.
†On disabled list, May 10 to May 25, 1982.

GARY STEVEN ROENICKE

Name pronounced RENN-uh-kee.
Born December 5, 1954, at Covina, Calif.
Height, 6.03. Weight, 200.
Throws and bats righthanded.
Attended California Poly State University, Pomona, Calif., Whittier College,
Whittier, Calif., and University of California at Los Angeles, Los Angeles, Calif.
Brother of Ron Roenicke, outfielder with Philadelphia Phillies.

Major League stolen bases: 1979 (1), 1980 (2), 1981 (1), 1982 (6), 1983 (2), 1984 (1), 1985 (2), 1986 (1). Total—16.
Led American Association in being hit by pitch with 13 in 1977.
Led Florida State League in being hit by pitch with 11 in 1974.
Tied for Eastern League lead in being hit by pitch with 12 in 1975.
Tied for Florida State League lead in double plays by third basemen with 32 in 1974.
Named Eastern League Most Valuable Player, 1975.

Year	Club	League	Pos.	G.	AB.	R.	H.	2B.	3B.	HR.	RBI.	B.A.	PO.	A.	E.	F.A.
1973—Jamestown	NYP	3B	68	255	48	76	17	6	3	40	.298	★71	92	11	★.937
1974—W. Palm Beach	Fla. St.	3B-OF-1B	131	470	68	130	24	0	14	★82	.277	152	216	31	.922
1974—Quebec City	East.	3B	1	3	0	1	0	0	0	0	.333	1	2	0	1.000
1975—Quebec City	East.	OF	131	466	67	133	23	0	14	★74	.285	223	★22	10	.961
1976—Denver	A. A.	OF	77	252	56	73	11	5	12	44	.290	110	9	5	.960
1976—Montreal	Nat.	OF	29	90	9	20	3	1	2	5	.222	39	3	2	.955
1977—Denver†	A. A.	OF-3B-1B	124	448	87	144	31	4	11	72	.321	174	113	17	.944
1978—Rochester	Int.	OF-1B-3B	98	329	49	101	15	1	13	64	.307	219	25	2	.992
1978—Baltimore	Amer.	OF	27	58	5	15	3	0	3	15	.259	22	1	0	1.000
1979—Baltimore	Amer.	OF	133	376	60	98	16	1	25	64	.261	246	10	5	.981
1980—Baltimore‡	Amer.	OF	118	297	40	71	13	0	10	28	.239	197	8	0	★1.000
1981—Baltimore	Amer.	OF	85	219	31	59	16	0	3	20	.269	175	2	3	.983
1982—Baltimore	Amer.	OF-1B	137	393	58	106	25	1	21	74	.270	363	13	3	.992
1983—Baltimore	Amer.	OF-1B-3B	115	323	45	84	13	0	19	64	.260	219	9	3	.987
1984—Baltimore	Amer.	OF	121	326	36	73	19	1	10	44	.224	197	6	1	.995

Year Club	League	Pos.	G.	AB.	R.	H.	2B.	3B.	HR.	RBI.	B.A.	PO.	A.	E.	F.A.
1985—Baltimore§	Amer.	OF	114	225	36	49	9	0	15	43	.218	134	6	1	.993
1986—New York x	Amer.	OF-3B-1B	69	136	11	36	5	0	3	18	.265	46	6	0	1.000
American League Totals—9 Years			919	2353	322	591	119	3	109	370	.251	1599	61	16	.990
National League Totals—1 Year			29	90	9	20	3	1	2	5	.222	39	3	2	.955
Major League Totals—10 Years			948	2443	331	611	122	4	111	375	.250	1638	64	18	.990

Selected by Montreal Expos' organization in 1st round (eighth player selected) of free-agent draft, June 5, 1973.

†Traded with Pitchers Joe Kerrigan and Don Stanhouse to Baltimore Orioles for Pitchers Rudy May, Randy Miller and Bryn Smith, December 7, 1977.

‡On disabled list, June 10 to July 15, 1980.

§Traded with a player to be named later to New York Yankees for Pitcher Rich Bordi and Infielder Rex Hudler, December 12, 1985; New York acquired Outfielder Leo Hernandez to complete deal, December 16, 1985.

xGranted free agency, November 12, 1986.

CHAMPIONSHIP SERIES RECORD

Tied Championship Series record for most consecutive games, one or more runs batted in, total Series (4).
Tied American League Championship Series record for most bases on balls, four-game Series (5), 1983.

Year Club	League	Pos.	G.	AB.	R.	H.	2B.	3B.	HR.	RBI.	B.A.	PO.	A.	E.	F.A.
1979—Baltimore	Amer.	OF-PH	2	5	1	1	0	0	0	1	.200	3	1	0	1.000
1983—Baltimore	Amer.	OF-PH	3	4	4	3	1	0	1	4	.750	4	1	0	1.000
Championship Series Totals—2 Years			5	9	5	4	1	0	1	5	.444	7	2	0	1.000

WORLD SERIES RECORD

Year Club	League	Pos.	G.	AB.	R.	H.	2B.	3B.	HR.	RBI.	B.A.	PO.	A.	E.	F.A.
1979—Baltimore	Amer.	OF-PH	6	16	1	2	1	0	0	0	.125	14	1	0	1.000
1983—Baltimore	Amer.	PH-OF	3	7	0	0	0	0	0	0	.000	2	1	0	1.000
World Series Totals—2 Years			9	23	1	2	1	0	0	0	.087	16	2	0	1.000

RONALD JON ROENICKE

Name pronounced RENN-uh-kee.

(Ron)

Born August 19, 1956, at Covina, Calif.
Height, 6.00. Weight, 180.
Throws left and bats left and righthanded.
Attended Mount San Antonio College, Walnut, Calif., and
University of California, Los Angeles, Calif.
Brother of Gary Roenicke, outfielder with Montreal Expos, Baltimore Orioles
and New York Yankees, 1976 and 1978 through 1986.

Major League stolen bases: 1981 (1), 1982 (5), 1983 (9), 1985 (6), 1986 (2). Total—23.

Led Pacific Coast League in on-base percentage with .464, bases on balls received with 110, and sacrifice flies with 16 in 1981.

Led Texas League outfielders in fielding percentage with .993 in 1979.

Year Club	League	Pos.	G.	AB.	R.	H.	2B.	3B.	HR.	RBI.	B.A.	PO.	A.	E.	F.A.
1977—Clinton	Midw.	OF-1B	76	250	35	64	12	0	5	25	.256	253	7	4	.985
1978—Lodi†	Calif.	OF	61	215	61	78	13	5	9	51	.363	100	8	6	.947
1978—San Antonio	Texas	OF	30	109	16	26	2	2	1	11	.239	51	4	2	.965
1979—San Antonio	Texas	OF-1B	130	464	82	140	24	6	13	69	.302	426	18	4	.991
1980—Albuquerque‡	P. C.	OF-1B	77	270	60	80	18	3	7	47	.296	167	9	8	.957
1981—Albuquerque	P. C.	OF-1B	126	411	100	130	23	9	15	94	.316	217	14	4	.983
1981—Los Angeles	Nat.	OF	22	47	6	11	0	0	0	0	.234	38	1	0	1.000
1982—Albuquerque	P. C.	OF	23	78	18	24	5	1	4	15	.308	14	1	0	1.000
1982—Los Angeles	Nat.	OF	109	143	18	37	8	0	1	12	.259	59	1	1	.984
1983—Los Angeles§	Nat.	OF	81	145	12	32	4	0	2	12	.221	75	1	1	.987
1983—Seattle x	Amer.	OF-1B	59	198	23	50	12	0	4	23	.253	168	13	2	.989
1984—Las Vegas y	P. C.	OF-1B	90	290	65	90	14	3	8	45	.310	161	7	1	.994
1984—San Diego z	Nat.	OF	12	20	4	6	1	0	1	2	.300	10	0	0	1.000
1985—Phoenix	P. C.	OF-1B	60	214	36	66	16	0	5	48	.308	130	6	1	.993
1985—San Francisco a ...	Nat.	OF	65	133	23	34	9	1	3	13	.256	63	0	1	.984
1986—Tacoma b	P. C.	OF	20	72	13	16	3	0	0	7	.222	33	1	1	.971
1986—Philadelphia	Nat.	OF	102	275	42	68	13	1	5	42	.247	181	3	2	.989
National League Totals—6 Years			391	763	105	188	35	2	12	81	.246	426	6	5	.989
American League Totals—1 Year			59	198	23	50	12	0	4	23	.253	168	13	2	.989
Major League Totals—6 Years			450	961	128	238	47	2	16	104	.248	594	19	7	.989

Selected by Oakland A's organization in 7th round of free-agent draft, June 5, 1974.

Selected by Detroit Tigers' organization in secondary phase of free-agent draft, January 7, 1976.

Selected by Atlanta Braves' organization in secondary phase of free-agent draft, June 8, 1976.

Selected by Los Angeles Dodgers' organization in secondary phase of free-agent draft, June 7, 1977.

†On disabled list, June 11 to July 17, 1978.

‡On disabled list, July 1 to August 27, 1980.

§Released, July 18, 1983; signed by Seattle Mariners, July 26, 1983.

xReleased, March 23, 1984; signed by Las Vegas (San Diego Padres' organization), April 5, 1984.

yOn disabled list, June 19 to July 29, 1984.

zReleased, March 30, 1985; signed by Phoenix (San Francisco Giants' organization), May 3, 1985.

aReleased, April 1, 1986; signed by Oakland A's organization, April 7, 1986.

bSold to Philadelphia Phillies, May 9, 1986.

Year	Club	League	Pos.	G.	AB.	R.	H.	2B.	3B.	HR.	RBI.	B.A.	PO.	A.	E.	F.A.
1984—San Diego		Nat.	OF-PR	2	0	0	0	0	0	0	0	.000	0	0	0	.000

KENNETH SCOTT ROGERS
(Kenny)

Born November 10, 1964, at Savannah, Ga.
Height, 6.00. Weight, 165.
Throws and bats lefthanded.

Year	Club	League	G.	IP.	W.	L.	Pct.	H.	R.	ER.	SO.	BB.	ERA.
1982—Sarasota Rangers	Gulf Coast	2	3	0	0	.000	0	0	0	4	0	0.00
1983—Sarasota Rangers	Gulf Coast	15	53⅓	4	1	.800	40	21	14	36	20	2.36
1984—Burlington	Midwest	39	92⅔	4	7	.364	87	52	41	93	33	3.98
1985—Daytona Beach	Florida St.	6	10	0	1	.000	12	9	8	9	11	7.20
1985—Burlington	Midwest	33	95	2	5	.286	67	34	30	96	62	2.84
1986—Tulsa†	Texas	10	26⅓	0	3	.000	39	30	29	23	18	9.91
1986—Salem	Carolina	12	66	2	7	.222	75	54	46	46	26	6.27

Selected by Texas Rangers' organization in 39th round of free-agent draft, June 7, 1982.
†On disabled list, April 12 to April 30, 1986.

DANIEL JAY ROHN
(Dan)

Born January 10, 1956, at Alpena, Mich.
Height, 5.09. Weight, 165.
Throws right and bats lefthanded.
Attended Central Michigan University, Mt. Pleasant, Mich.

Major League stolen bases: 1983 (1).
Led International League in bases on balls received with 116 in 1985.
Led Texas League in bases on balls received with 105 in 1979.
Led Florida State League in bases on balls received with 117 in 1978.
Tied for American Association lead in caught stealing with 17 in 1983.
Led American Association second basemen in fielding percentage with .990 in 1983.
Led American Association second basemen in double plays with 104 in 1980.
Led Texas League second basemen in double plays with 120 in 1979.
Led Florida State League second basemen in double plays with 83 in 1978.

Year	Club	League	Pos.	G.	AB.	R.	H.	2B.	3B.	HR.	RBI.	B.A.	PO.	A.	E.	F.A.
1977—Geneva	NYP	2B	21	72	8	15	0	0	1	5	.208	66	63	5	.963
1977—Pompano Beach	Fla. St.	2B-SS	54	173	23	48	6	3	0	22	.277	103	160	9	.967
1978—Pompano Beach	Fla. St.	2B	132	421	★95	116	17	2	2	48	.276	★302	400	26	.964
1979—Midland	Texas	2B	128	489	★122	150	26	6	5	52	.307	★315	★429	19	975
1980—Wichita	A. A.	2B	130	480	81	117	18	1	4	22	.244	★295	★434	●19	.975
1981—Iowa	A. A.	2B-3B	131	488	73	130	23	4	7	43	.266	194	278	10	.979
1982—Iowa	A. A.	2B-3B-SS	107	364	85	100	20	4	8	32	.275	178	241	9	.979
1983—Iowa	A. A.	2-3-S-O-P	117	413	84	130	29	5	8	56	.315	189	315	6	.988
1983—Chicago	Nat.	2B-SS	23	31	3	12	3	2	0	6	.387	12	12	2	.923
1984—Iowa	A. A.	S-2-3-O	109	370	74	99	22	1	8	46	.268	169	298	17	.965
1984—Chicago†	Nat.	3B-2B-SS	25	31	1	4	0	0	1	3	.129	5	15	0	1.000
1985—Maine	Int.	S-3-2-O	137	444	68	116	22	1	9	56	.261	212	373	20	.967
1986—Cleveland‡	Amer.	2B-3B-SS	6	10	1	2	0	0	0	2	.200	4	10	2	.875
1986—Maine§	Int.	S-3-2-O	82	276	38	60	14	0	0	12	.217	126	214	15	.958
National League Totals—2 Years			48	62	4	16	3	2	1	9	.258	17	27	2	.957
American League Totals—1 Year			6	10	1	2	0	0	0	2	.200	4	10	2	.875
Major League Totals—3 Years			54	72	5	18	3	2	1	11	.250	21	37	4	.935

Selected by Chicago Cubs' organization in 4th round of free-agent draft, June 7, 1977.
†Traded to Cleveland Indians' organization for Pitcher Jay Baller, April 1, 1985.
‡On disabled list, May 22 to June 11, 1986.
§Granted free agency, October 15, 1986.

PITCHING RECORD

Year	Club	League	G.	IP.	W.	L.	Pct.	H.	R.	ER.	SO.	BB.	ERA.
1983—Iowa	Am. Assoc.	1	3⅓	0	0	.000	11	8	5	1	3	13.50

JOSE RAFAEL ROMAN
Name pronounced Ro-MON.

Born May 21, 1963, at Santo Domingo, D. R.
Height, 6.00. Weight, 160.
Throws and bats righthanded.
Brother of Miguel Roman, outfielder in Cleveland Indians' organization.

Led New York-Pennsylvania League in home runs allowed with 15 in 1981.

Year	Club	League	G.	IP.	W.	L.	Pct.	H.	R.	ER.	SO.	BB.	ERA.
1981—Batavia	NYP	20	55	0	3	.000	63	45	39	46	27	6.38
1982—Waterloo	Midwest	24	57⅔	2	5	.286	64	42	33	56	37	5.15
1983—Waterloo	Midwest	34	126⅓	6	7	.462	103	49	36	132	56	2.56
1984—Buffalo	Eastern	27	143⅔	14	6	.700	130	69	62	105	63	3.88
1984—Cleveland	American	3	6	0	2	.000	9	12	12	3	11	18.00

Year	Club	League	G.	IP.	W.	L.	Pct.	H.	R.	ER.	SO.	BB.	ERA.
1985—Cleveland	American	5	16⅓	0	4	.000	13	17	12	12	14	6.61
1985—Maine†	Int'national	11	49⅓	4	1	.800	46	23	20	27	30	3.65
1986—Maine	Int'national	16	95⅔	4	5	.444	95	50	45	76	52	4.23
1986—Cleveland	American	6	22	1	2	.333	23	20	16	9	17	6.55
Major League Totals—3 Years		14	44⅓	1	8	.111	45	49	40	24	42	8.12

Signed as free agent by Cleveland Indians' organization, May 23, 1981.
†On disabled list, July 8 to August 6, 1985.

PEDRO MIGUEL ROMAN

Name promounced Ro-MON.

(Known by middle name.)

Born June 18, 1964, at Puerto Plata, D. R.
Height, 6.03. Weight, 170.
Throws right and bats left and righthanded.
Brother of Jose Roman, pitcher in Cleveland Indians' organization.

Led Eastern League in grounding into double plays with 22 in 1986.
Led Midwest League outfielders in total chances with 316 in 1985.

Year	Club	League	Pos.	G.	AB.	R.	H.	2B.	3B.	HR.	RBI.	B.A.	PO.	A.	E.	F.A.
1981—Batavia	NYP	OF	17	35	1	4	0	0	0	1	.114	19	0	1	.950
1982—Batavia	NYP	OF-3B	59	200	21	59	9	2	6	27	.295	64	39	7	.936
1983—Waterloo	Midw.	OF-3B	9	30	2	5	0	0	1	.167	8	1	0	1.000
1983—Batavia	NYP	OF	●75	283	34	71	14	0	9	27	.251	135	9	8	.947
1984—Waterloo	Midw.	OF	32	82	9	19	5	0	2	10	.232	25	2	0	1.000
1984—Batavia	NYP	OF	70	283	48	72	13	1	16	53	.254	143	11	9	.945
1985—Waterloo	Midw.	★OF-3B	136	★548	81	144	19	2	19	76	.263	★299	8	10	.968
1986—Waterbury	East.	OF	133	477	51	127	25	1	6	53	.266	240	11	6	.977

Signed as free agent by Cleveland Indians' organization, May 23, 1981.

RONALD JAMES ROMANICK

Name pronounced RO-manik.

(Ron)

Born November 6, 1960, at Burley, Ida.
Height, 6.04. Weight, 200.
Throws and bats righthanded.
Attended Arizona State University, Tempe, Ariz., and University of Washington, Seattle, Wash.

Pitched 1-0 no-hit victory against Buffalo, April 27, 1982.
Tied for Eastern League lead in games started by pitchers with 27 in 1983.
Received reported $70,000 bonus to sign with California Angels, 1981.

Year	Club	League	G.	IP.	W.	L.	Pct.	H.	R.	ER.	SO.	BB.	ERA.
1981—Redwood	California	28	★207	15	10	.600	173	88	67	178	76	★2.91
1982—Holyoke†	Eastern	16	86⅔	6	3	.667	104	52	41	62	26	4.26
1983—Nashua	Eastern	27	174	9	12	.429	★200	105	94	112	80	4.86
1984—California	American	33	229⅔	12	12	.500	240	107	96	87	61	3.76
1985—California	American	31	195	14	9	.609	210	101	89	64	62	4.11
1986—California	American	18	106⅓	5	8	.385	124	68	65	38	44	5.50
1986—Edmonton‡	P. Coast	8	52	2	3	.400	67	39	33	17	14	5.71
Major League Totals—3 Years		82	531	31	29	.517	574	276	250	189	167	4.24

Selected by Toronto Blue Jays' organization in 3rd round of free-agent draft, June 5, 1979.
Selected by San Diego Padres' organization in secondary phase of free-agent draft, June 3, 1980.
Selected by California Angels' organization in secondary phase of free-agent draft, January 13, 1981.
†On disabled list, May 31 to July 29, 1982.
‡Traded with a player to be named later to New York Yankees' organization for Catcher Butch Wynegar, December 19, 1986.

EDGARDO ROMERO

(Ed)

Born December 9, 1957, at Santurce, Puerto Rico.
Height, 5.11. Weight, 150.
Throws and bats righthanded.

Major League stolen bases: 1980 (2), 1983 (1), 1984 (3), 1985 (1), 1986 (2). Total—9.
Led Pacific Coast League shortstops in double plays with 97 in 1979.
Led Midwest League shortstops in total chances with 647 and double plays with 64 in 1976.

Year	Club	League	Pos.	G.	AB.	R.	H.	2B.	3B.	HR.	RBI.	B.A.	PO.	A.	E.	F.A.
1976—Burlington	Midwest	SS	●129	462	58	101	23	1	1	32	.219	187	★419	41	.937
1977—Holyoke	East.	SS	121	457	63	118	19	6	1	38	.258	203	372	41	.933
1977—Milwaukee	Amer.	SS	10	25	4	7	1	0	0	2	.280	9	24	1	.971
1978—Spokane	P. C.	SS-3B	129	440	73	123	27	2	4	52	.280	221	349	32	.947
1979—Vancouver	P. C.	SS	139	515	65	134	26	6	0	39	.260	215	★414	26	.960
1980—Vancouver	P. C.	SS-2B	50	172	19	47	7	1	0	16	.273	72	153	6	.97
1980—Milwaukee	Amer.	SS-3B-2B	42	104	20	27	7	0	1	10	.260	60	102	12	.93
1981—Milwaukee	Amer.	SS-3B-2B	44	91	6	18	3	0	1	10	.198	61	102	6	.96
1982—Milwaukee	Amer.	2-S-3-O	52	144	18	36	8	0	1	7	.250	103	113	7	.9
1983—Milwaukee	Amer.	S-O-3-2	59	145	17	46	7	0	1	18	.317	59	58	5	.9

Year	Club	League	Pos.	G.	AB.	R.	H.	2B.	3B.	HR.	RBI.	B.A.	PO.	A.	E.	F.A.
1984—Milwaukee............	Amer.	3-S-2-1-O	116	357	36	90	12	0	1	31	.252	141	256	18	.957
1985—Milwaukee†..........	Amer.	S-2-O-3	88	251	24	63	11	1	0	21	.251	157	219	8	.979
1986—Boston.................	Amer.	S-3-2-O	100	233	41	49	11	0	2	23	.210	111	159	12	.957
Major League Totals—8 Years.................			511	1350	166	336	60	1	7	122	.249	701	1033	69	.962

Signed as free agent by Milwaukee Brewers' organization, November 14, 1975.
†Traded to Boston Red Sox for Pitcher Mark Clear, December 11, 1985.

DIVISION SERIES RECORD

Year	Club	League	Pos.	G.	AB.	R.	H.	2B.	3B.	HR.	RBI.	B.A.	PO.	A.	E.	F.A.
1981—Milwaukee............	Amer.	2B	1	2	1	1	0	0	0	0	.500	2	2	0	1.000

CHAMPIONSHIP SERIES RECORD

Year	Club	League	Pos.	G.	AB.	R.	H.	2B.	3B.	HR.	RBI.	B.A.	PO.	A.	E.	F.A.
1986—Boston....................	Amer.	PR-SS	1	2	0	0	0	0	0	0	.000	0	0	0	.000

WORLD SERIES RECORD

Year	Club	League	Pos.	G.	AB.	R.	H.	2B.	3B.	HR.	RBI.	B.A.	PO.	A.	E.	F.A.
1986—Boston....................	Amer.	PR-SS	3	1	0	0	0	0	0	0	.000	0	1	0	1.000

KEVIN ANDREW ROMINE

Name pronounced Ro-MINE.

Born May 23, 1961, at Exeter, N.H.
Height, 5.11. Weight, 185.
Throws and bats righthanded.
Attended Orange Coast College, Costa Mesa, Calif., and
Arizona State University, Tempe, Ariz.

Major League stolen bases: 1985 (1), 1986 (2). Total—3.
Tied for Eastern League lead in double plays by outfielders with 4 in 1983.
Named outfielder on THE SPORTING NEWS College Baseball All-America Team, 1982.

Year	Club	League	Pos.	G.	AB.	R.	H.	2B.	3B.	HR.	RBI.	B.A.	PO.	A.	E.	F.A.
1982—Winter Haven.......	Fla. St.	OF	55	201	24	51	4	4	3	22	.254	97	6	3	.972
1983—New Britain........	East.	OF	132	467	74	122	26	5	11	80	.261	211	12	4	.982
1984—Pawtucket†..........	Int.	OF	113	336	62	85	10	1	12	72	.253	202	12	5	.977
1985—Pawtucket‡..........	Int.	OF	106	403	43	98	20	1	5	33	.243	246	9	8	.970
1985—Boston....................	Amer.	OF	24	28	3	6	2	0	0	1	.214	20	1	0	1.000
1986—Pawtucket.............	Int.	OF	71	257	30	75	8	3	4	32	.292	162	2	2	.988
1986—Boston....................	Amer.	OF	35	35	6	9	2	0	0	2	.257	45	1	0	1.000
Major League Totals—2 Years.................			59	63	9	15	4	0	0	3	.238	65	2	0	1.000

Selected by California Angels' organization in 3rd round of free-agent draft, January 8, 1980.
Selected by Philadelphia Phillies' organization in secondary phase of free-agent draft, June 3, 1980.
Selected by Boston Red Sox' organization in second round of free-agent draft, June 7, 1982.
†On disabled list, July 18 to July 31, 1984.
‡On disabled list, July 6 to July 17, 1985.

ROLANDO AUDLEY ROOMES

Born February 15, 1962, in Jamaica, West Indies.
Height, 6.03. Weight, 180.
Throws and bats righthanded.

Led Midwest League batters in strikeouts with 167 in 1983.
Led New York-Pennsylvania League outfielders in double plays with 4 in 1982.

Year	Club	League	Pos.	G.	AB.	R.	H.	2B.	3B.	HR.	RBI.	B.A.	PO.	A.	E.	F.A.
1980—Sarasota Cubs......	Gulf C.	OF	19	48	11	7	1	0	2	3	.146	19	1	4	.833
1981—Sarasota Cubs......	Gulf C.	OF	63	207	31	48	4	9	2	25	.232	80	7	5	.946
1982—Quad Cities..........	Midw.	OF	31	80	11	12	1	0	3	8	.150	50	1	3	.944
1982—Geneva.................	NYP	OF	65	251	57	80	11	3	22	59	.319	129	8	8	.945
1983—Quad Cities..........	Midw.	OF	122	416	47	89	6	4	9	40	.214	216	★22	14	.944
1984—Lodi.....................	Calif.	OF	116	377	52	100	12	2	13	52	.265	194	11	8	.962
1985—Winston-Salem	Carol.	OF	131	433	57	105	19	6	13	51	.242	254	14	6	.978
1986—Winston-Salem	Carol.	OF	19	68	10	15	3	0	6	14	.238	22	0	0	1.000
1986—Pittsfield	East.	OF	79	191	24	52	5	3	7	42	.272	91	4	7	.931

Signed as free agent by Chicago Cubs' organization, July 14, 1980.

PETER EDWARD ROSE
(Pete)

Born April 14, 1941, at Cincinnati, O.
Height, 5.11. Weight, 203.
Throws right and bats right and lefthanded.
Brother of David Rose, pitcher in Cincinnati Reds' organization, 1967 and 1968.

...d major league records for most games, lifetime (3,562); most singles, lifetime (3,215); most seasons and
...ive seasons, 100 or more games (23); most seasons, 200 or more hits (10); most seasons, 150 or more
...t at-bats, lifetime (14,053); most plate appearances, lifetime (15,890); most consecutive seasons, 600 or
...: most seasons, 600 or more at-bats (17); most plate appearances, season (771), 1974; most hits, lifetime
...les by switch-hitter, season (51), 1978.

Tied major league records for most 20-game hitting streaks, lifetime (7); most consecutive seasons leading major leagues in runs scored (3); fewest sacrifice flies, season, most at-bats (0 and 680), 1973; most hits by switch-hitter, season (230), 1973; most games, first baseman, season (162), 1980 and 1982; most stolen bases, inning (3), May 11, 1980, seventh inning.

Established National League records for most years and most consecutive years played (24); most years playing in all clubs' games (10); most runs, lifetime (2,165); most seasons leading league, hits (7); most doubles, lifetime (746); most singles by switch-hitter, season (181), 1973; fewest stolen bases, season, most at-bats (0 and 662), 1975; most times five or more hits in one game, lifetime (10).

Tied National League records for most consecutive games, one or more hits, season (44), 1978; most games, switch hit home runs, lifetime (2); most seasons leading league in at-bats (4).

Tied modern National League records for most seasons leading league in fielding percentage by outfielder, 100 or more games (3); most consecutive years leading league in fielding percentage by outfielder, 100 or more games (2).

Major League stolen bases: 1963 (13), 1964 (4), 1965 (8), 1966 (4), 1967 (11), 1968 (3), 1969 (7), 1970 (12), 1971 (13), 1972 (10), 1973 (10), 1974 (2), 1976 (9), 1977 (16), 1978 (13), 1979 (20), 1980 (12), 1981 (4), 1982 (8), 1983 (7), 1984 (1), 1985 (8), 1986 (3). Total—198.

Hit three home runs in a game, April 29, 1978.

Tied for National League lead in being hit by pitch with 6 in 1980.

Led Florida State League in total bases with 246 in 1961.

Named Player of the Decade for 1970-79 by THE SPORTING NEWS.

Named Man of the Year by THE SPORTING NEWS, 1985.

Named National League Player of the Year by THE SPORTING NEWS, 1968.

Named National League Most Valuable Player by Baseball Writers' Association of America, 1973.

Named National League Rookie Player of the Year by THE SPORTING NEWS, 1963.

Named National League Rookie of the Year by Baseball Writers' Association of America, 1963.

Named first baseman on THE SPORTING NEWS National League All-Star Team, 1981.

Named third baseman on THE SPORTING NEWS National League All-Star Team, 1978.

Named outfielder on THE SPORTING NEWS National League All-Star Team, 1968 and 1973.

Named second baseman on THE SPORTING NEWS National League All-Star Team, 1965 and 1966.

Named outfielder on THE SPORTING NEWS National League All-Star fielding team, 1969 and 1970.

Named first baseman on THE SPORTING NEWS National League Silver Slugger team, 1981.

Year	Club	League	Pos.	G.	AB.	R.	H.	2B.	3B.	HR.	RBI.	B.A.	PO.	A.	E.	F.A.
1960—Geneva	NYP	2B	85	321	60	89	8	5	1	43	.277	198	193	*36	.916
1961—Tampa	Fla. St.	2B	130	484	105	*160	20	*30	2	77	.331	256	294	21	.963
1962—Macon	Sally	2B	139	540	*136	178	31	*17	9	71	.330	317	368	24	.966
1963—Cincinnati†	Nat.	2B-OF	157	623	101	170	25	9	6	41	.273	360	366	22	.971
1964—Cincinnati	Nat.	2B	136	516	64	139	13	2	4	34	.269	263	301	12	.979
1965—Cincinnati	Nat.	2B	162	*670	117	*209	35	11	11	81	.312	*382	403	20	.975
1966—Cincinnati	Nat.	2B-3B	156	654	97	205	38	5	16	70	.313	409	374	18	.978
1967—Cincinnati	Nat.	OF-2B	148	585	86	176	32	8	12	76	.301	287	93	11	.972
1968—Cincinnati‡	Nat.	●O-2-1	149	626	94	●210	42	6	10	49	*.335	270	●20	3	.990
1969—Cincinnati	Nat.	OF-2B	156	627	●120	218	33	11	16	82	*.348	317	10	4	.988
1970—Cincinnati	Nat.	OF	159	649	120	●205	37	9	15	52	.316	309	8	1	*.997
1971—Cincinnati	Nat.	OF	160	632	86	192	27	4	13	44	.304	306	13	2	●.994
1972—Cincinnati	Nat.	OF	*154	*645	107	*198	31	11	6	57	.307	330	●15	2	.994
1973—Cincinnati	Nat.	OF	160	*680	115	*230	36	8	5	64	*.338	343	15	3	.992
1974—Cincinnati	Nat.	OF	*163	652	*110	185	*45	7	3	51	.284	346	11	1	*.997
1975—Cincinnati	Nat.	3B-OF	●162	662	*112	210	*47	4	7	74	.317	161	230	14	.965
1976—Cincinnati	Nat.	*3B-OF	162	665	*130	*215	*42	6	10	63	.323	115	293	13	*.969
1977—Cincinnati	Nat.	3B	●162	*655	95	204	38	7	9	64	.311	98	268	16	.958
1978—Cincinnati§	Nat.	3B-OF-1B	159	655	103	198	*51	3	7	52	.302	135	256	15	.963
1979—Philadelphia	Nat.	1B-3B-2B	163	628	90	208	40	5	4	59	.331	1429	93	10	.993
1980—Philadelphia	Nat.	1B	162	655	95	185	*42	1	1	64	.282	1427	*123	5	*.997
1981—Philadelphia	Nat.	1B	107	431	73	*140	18	5	0	33	.325	929	91	4	.996
1982—Philadelphia	Nat.	1B	●162	634	80	172	25	4	3	54	.271	1428	123	8	.995
1983—Philadelphia x	Nat.	1B-OF	151	493	52	121	14	3	0	45	.245	827	74	10	.989
1984—Mont. y-Cin.	Nat.	1B-OF	121	374	43	107	15	2	0	34	.286	530	53	8	.986
1985—Cincinnati	Nat.	1B	119	405	60	107	12	2	2	46	.264	870	73	5	.995
1986—Cincinnati za	Nat.	1B	72	237	15	52	8	2	0	25	.219	523	43	6	.990
Major League Totals—24 Years				3562	14053	2165	4256	746	135	160	1314	.303	12394	3349	213	.987

Signed as free agent by Cincinnati Reds' organization, July 8, 1960.

†On military list, October 1, 1963 through March 14, 1964.

‡On disabled list, July 6 to July 27, 1968.

§Granted free agency, November 2, 1978; signed by Philadelphia Phillies, December 5, 1978.

xReleased, October 19, 1983; signed by Montreal Expos, January 20, 1984.

yTraded to Cincinnati Reds for Infielder Tom Lawless, August 16, 1984.

zOn disabled list, April 3 to April 23, 1986.

aReleased as player, November 11, 1986.

DIVISION SERIES RECORD

Year	Club	League	Pos.	G.	AB.	R.	H.	2B.	3B.	HR.	RBI.	B.A.	PO.	A.	E.	F.A.
1981—Philadelphia	Nat.	1B	5	20	1	6	1	0	0	2	.300	29	8	0	1.000

CHAMPIONSHIP SERIES RECORD

Established Championship Series records for most positions played, total Series (4); most consecutive games, one or more hits (15); most hits, total Series (45); most one-base hits, total Series (34); most hits, two consecutive Series (17), 1972 and 1973.

Tied Championship Series records for most times on winning club (6); most one-base hits, five-game Series (8), 1980; most two-base hits, total Series (7); most two-base hits, five-game Series (4), 1972.

Established National League Championship Series records for most games, total Series (28); most Series, played all games (7); highest batting average, total Series, 10 or more games and 30 or more at-bats (.381); most at-bats, total Series (118); most runs, total Series (17); most total bases, total Series (63).

Tied National League Championship Series records for most Series, one or more hits (7); most total bases, five-game Series (15), 1973.

Year Club	League	Pos.	G.	AB.	R.	H.	2B.	3B.	HR.	RBI.	B.A.	PO.	A.	E.	F.A.
1970—Cincinnati	Nat.	OF	3	13	1	3	0	0	0	1	.231	3	0	0	1.000
1972—Cincinnati	Nat.	OF	5	20	1	9	4	0	0	2	.450	10	0	0	1.000
1973—Cincinnati	Nat.	OF	5	21	3	8	1	0	2	2	.381	10	1	0	1.000
1975—Cincinnati	Nat.	3B	3	14	3	5	0	0	1	2	.357	2	1	0	1.000
1976—Cincinnati	Nat.	3B	3	14	3	6	2	1	0	2	.429	2	5	1	.875
1980—Philadelphia	Nat.	1B	5	20	3	8	0	0	0	2	.400	53	7	0	1.000
1983—Philadelphia	Nat.	1B	4	16	3	6	0	0	0	0	.375	29	2	0	1.000
Championship Series Totals—7 Years			28	118	17	45	7	1	3	11	.381	109	16	1	.992

WORLD SERIES RECORD

Tied World Series records for most positions played, total Series (4); most double plays by first baseman, six-game Series (8), 1980; most double plays by first baseman, nine-inning game (4), October 15, 1980; most times awarded first base on catcher's interference, game (1), October 10, 1970; most times home run as leadoff batter in game (1), October 20, 1972.

Year Club	League	Pos.	G.	AB.	R.	H.	2B.	3B.	HR.	RBI.	B.A.	PO.	A.	E.	F.A.
1970—Cincinnati	Nat.	OF	5	20	2	5	1	0	1	2	.250	14	1	1	.938
1972—Cincinnati	Nat.	OF	7	28	3	6	0	0	1	2	.214	14	1	0	1.000
1975—Cincinnati	Nat.	3B	7	27	3	10	1	1	0	2	.370	7	9	0	1.000
1976—Cincinnati	Nat.	3B	4	16	1	3	1	0	0	1	.188	6	3	0	1.000
1980—Philadelphia	Nat.	1B	6	23	2	6	1	0	0	1	.261	49	6	0	1.000
1983—Philadelphia	Nat.	PH-1B-OF	5	16	1	5	1	0	0	1	.313	26	4	0	1.000
World Series Totals—6 Years			34	130	12	35	5	1	2	9	.269	116	24	1	.993

ALL-STAR GAME RECORD

Established All-Star Game record for most positions played, total games (5).

Year League	Pos.	AB.	R.	H.	2B.	3B.	HR.	RBI.	B.A.	PO.	A.	E.	F.A.
1965—National	2B	2	0	0	0	0	0	0	.000	2	4	0	1.000
1967—National	2B	1	0	0	0	0	0	0	.000	1	0	0	1.000
1969—National	OF	1	0	0	0	0	0	0	.000	2	0	0	1.000
1970—National	OF	3	1	1	0	0	0	0	.333	3	0	0	1.000
1971—National	OF	0	0	0	0	0	0	0	.000	0	0	0	.000
1973—National	OF	3	1	0	0	0	0	0	.000	1	0	0	1.000
1974—National	OF	2	0	0	0	0	0	0	.000	1	0	0	1.000
1975—National	OF	4	0	2	0	0	0	1	.500	4	0	0	1.000
1976—National	3B	3	1	2	1	0	0	0	.667	0	1	20	1.000
1977—National	PH-3B	2	0	0	0	0	0	0	.000	0	1	0	1.000
1978—National	3B	4	0	1	1	0	0	0	.250	1	0	0	1.000
1979—National	PH-1B	2	0	0	0	0	0	0	.000	2	0	0	1.000
1980—National	PH	1	0	0	0	0	0	0	.000	0	0	0	.000
1981—National	1B	3	0	1	0	0	0	0	.333	5	0	0	1.000
1982—National	1B	1	0	0	0	0	0	1	.000	4	0	0	1.000
1985—National	PH	1	0	0	0	0	0	0	.000	0	0	0	.000
All-Star Game Totals—16 Years		33	3	7	1	1	0	2	.212	26	6	0	1.000

Named to National League All-Star Team for 1968 game; replaced due to injury.

RECORD AS MANAGER

Year Club	League	Position	W.	L.
1984—Cincinnati†	Nat.	Fifth (W)	19	22
1985—Cincinnati	Nat.	Second (W)	89	72
1986—Cincinnati	Nat.	Second (W)	86	76
Major League Totals—3 Years			194	170

†Replaced Vern Rapp with club in fifth place (record of 51-70), August 16, 1984.

WADE LEE ROWDON

Born September 7, 1960, at Riverhead, N.Y.
Height, 6.02. Weight, 170.
Throws and bats righthanded.
Attended Stetson University, Deland, Fla.

Major League stolen bases: 1986 (2).
Led American Association in total bases with 230 in 1985.
Led Eastern League third basemen in fielding percentage with .940 in 1983.
Led Midwest League third basemen in total chances with 362 and double plays with 24 in 1982.

Year Club	League	Pos.	G.	AB.	R.	H.	2B.	3B.	HR.	RBI.	B.A.	PO.	A.	E.	F.A.
1981—Sarasota W. Sox	Gulf C.	SS	3	6	2	3	0	0	0	1	.500	1	3	0	1.000
1982—Appleton†	Midw.	3B	126	433	75	123	19	8	12	79	.284	81	★264	17	★.953
1983—Waterbury	East.	3B-2B-1B	135	480	62	112	29	1	21	76	.233	173	231	22	.948
1984—Wichita	A. A.	SS-3B	144	479	78	120	30	4	16	72	.251	175	295	28	.944
1984—Cincinnati	Nat.	SS-3B	4	7	0	2	0	0	0	0	.286	3	5	0	1.000
1985—Denver	A. A.	3B-SS-2B	128	457	61	132	31	5	19	78	.289	148	277	25	.944
1985—Cincinnati	Nat.	3B	5	9	2	2	0	0	0	2	.222	1	3	2	.667
1986—Denver	A. A.	3-O-S-1	55	180	36	60	12	4	8	37	.333	56	48	11	.904
1986—Cincinnati	Nat.	3-S-O-2	38	80	9	20	5	1	0	10	.250	22	34	6	.903
Major League Totals—3 Years			47	96	11	24	5	1	0	12	.250	26	42	8	.895

Selected by Chicago White Sox' organization in 8th round of free-agent draft, June 8, 1981.

†Traded with Outfielder Leo Garcia to Cincinnati Reds' organization, September 7, 1982, completing deal in which Cincinnati traded Pitcher Jim Kern to Chicago White Sox for two players to be named later, August 23, 1982.

JERON KENNIS ROYSTER
(Jerry)

Born October 18, 1952, at Sacramento, Calif.
Height, 6.00. Weight, 165.
Throws and bats righthanded.
Attended Healds Business College, Sacramento, Calif.

Major League stolen bases: 1973 (1), 1975 (1), 1976 (24), 1977 (28), 1978 (27), 1979 (35), 1980 (22), 1981 (7), 1982 (14), 1983 (11), 1984 (6), 1985 (6), 1986 (3). Total—185.
Led National League third basemen in putouts with 156 in 1976.
Tied for National League lead in double plays by third basemen with 35 in 1976.
Tied for Pacific Coast League lead in stolen bases with 33 in 1975.
Led Pacific Coast League third basemen in fielding percentage with .962 in 1974.
Led Texas League third basemen in double plays with 26 in 1972.
Named Pacific Coast League Player of the Year in 1975.

Year	Club	League	Pos.	G.	AB.	R.	H.	2B.	3B.	HR.	RBI.	B.A.	PO.	A.	E.	F.A.
1971—Bakersfield	Calif.		3B	7	20	2	2	1	0	0	2	.100	1	5	1	.857
1971—Daytona Beach	Fla. St.		3B-SS-2B	111	371	68	100	13	7	8	42	.270	90	265	29	.925
1972—El Paso	Texas		*3-S-O	127	479	*89	123	28	3	18	59	.257	103	209	*35	.899
1973—Albuquerque	P. C.		3B-SS-OF	122	463	78	140	24	11	6	68	.302	167	222	24	.942
1973—Los Angeles	Nat.		3B-2B	10	19	1	4	0	0	0	2	.211	3	14	3	.850
1974—Albuquerque	P. C.		3B-2B-SS	125	458	69	126	19	1	10	65	.275	121	257	14	.964
1974—Los Angeles	Nat.		2B-OF-3B	6	0	2	0	0	0	0	0	.000	0	3	0	1.000
1975—Albuquerque	P. C.		SS-3B	133	487	*91	162	31	7	10	65	*.333	183	349	38	.933
1975—Los Angeles†	Nat.		O-2-3-S	13	36	2	9	2	1	0	1	.250	12	15	2	.931
1976—Atlanta	Nat.		3B-SS	149	533	65	132	13	1	5	45	.248	158	310	19	.961
1977—Atlanta	Nat.		3-S-2-O	140	445	64	96	10	2	6	28	.216	182	267	28	.941
1978—Atlanta	Nat.		SS-2B-3B	140	529	67	137	17	8	2	35	.259	284	376	23	.966
1979—Atlanta	Nat.		3B-2B	154	601	103	164	25	6	3	51	.273	261	405	22	.968
1980—Atlanta	Nat.		2B-3B-OF	123	392	42	95	17	5	1	20	.242	195	166	18	.953
1981—Atlanta	Nat.		3B-2B	64	93	13	19	4	1	0	9	.204	35	48	4	.954
1982—Atlanta	Nat.		3-O-2-S	108	261	43	77	13	2	2	25	.295	105	112	11	.952
1983—Atlanta‡	Nat.		3-2-O-S	91	268	32	63	10	3	3	30	.235	112	156	10	.964
1984—Atlanta§	Nat.		2-3-S-O	81	227	22	47	13	2	1	21	.207	99	162	9	.967
1985—San Diego	Nat.		2-3-S-O	90	249	31	70	13	2	5	31	.281	130	214	8	.977
1986—San Diego x	Nat.		3-S-2-O	118	257	31	66	12	0	5	26	.257	87	166	14	.948
Major League Totals—14 Years				1287	3910	518	979	149	33	33	324	.250	1663	2414	171	.960

Signed as free agent by Los Angeles Dodgers' organization, August 21, 1970.
†Traded with Outfielder Jimmy Wynn, Second Baseman Lee Lacy and First Baseman-Outfielder Tom Paciorek to Atlanta Braves for Outfielder Dusty Baker and First Baseman-Third Baseman Ed Goodson, November 17, 1975.
‡On disabled list, August 19 to September 9, 1983.
§Granted free agency, November 8, 1984; signed by San Diego Padres, January 3, 1985.
xGranted free agency, November 12, 1986.

CHAMPIONSHIP SERIES RECORD

Year	Club	League	Pos.	G.	AB.	R.	H.	2B.	3B.	HR.	RBI.	B.A.	PO.	A.	E.	F.A.
1982—Atlanta	Nat.		OF-3B	3	11	0	2	0	0	0	0	.182	4	0	0	1.000

DAVID SCOTT ROZEMA

Name pronounced ROZE-mah.

(Dave)

Born August 5, 1956, at Grand Rapids, Mich.
Height, 6.04. Weight, 200.
Throws and bats righthanded.
Attended Grand Rapids Junior College, Grand Rapids, Mich.

Major League saves: 1980 (4), 1981 (3), 1982 (1), 1983 (2), 1985 (7). Total—17.
Tied for Southern League lead in shutouts with 4 in 1976.
Tied for Midwest League lead in shutouts with 5 in 1975.
Named American League Rookie Pitcher of the Year by THE SPORTING NEWS, 1977.

Year	Club	League	G.	IP.	W.	L.	Pct.	H.	R.	ER.	SO.	BB.	ERA.
1975—Clinton	Midwest		27	164	14	5	.737	128	50	38	123	32	2.09
1976—Montgomery†	Southern		19	126	12	4	.750	98	29	22	96	15	*1.57
1977—Detroit	American		28	218	15	7	.682	222	87	75	92	34	3.10
1978—Detroit	American		28	209	9	12	.429	205	83	73	57	41	3.14
1979—Detroit‡	American		16	97	4	4	.500	101	52	38	30	30	3.53
1980—Detroit	American		42	145	6	9	.400	152	68	63	49	49	3.91
1981—Detroit	American		28	104	5	5	.500	99	42	42	46	25	3.63
1982—Detroit§	American		8	27⅔	3	0	1.000	17	5	5	15	7	1.63
1983—Detroit	American		29	105	8	3	.727	100	50	40	63	29	3.43
1984—Detroit x	American		29	101	7	6	.538	110	49	42	48	18	3.74
1985—Texas y	American		34	88	3	7	.300	100	45	41	42	22	4.19
1986—Texas z	American		6	10⅔	0	0	.000	19	9	7	3	3	5.91
1986—Buffalo	Am. Assoc.		13	68⅓	4	4	.500	72	32	30	39	5	3.95
Major League Totals—10 Years			248	1105⅓	60	53	.531	1125	490	426	448	258	3.47

Selected by San Francisco Giants' organization in 22nd round of free-agent draft, June 5, 1974.
Selected by Detroit Tigers' organization in secondary phase of free-agent draft, January 9, 1975.
†On disabled list, May 9 to June 21, 1976.
‡On disabled list, June 16 to August 27, 1979.

DAVID MICHAEL RUCKER

(Dave)

Born September 1, 1957, at San Bernardino, Calif.
Height, 6.01. Weight, 185.
Throws and bats lefthanded.
Attended University of California, Los Angeles, Calif., and
LaVerne College, LaVerne, Calif.

Major League saves: 1985 (1).

Year Club	League	G.	IP.	W.	L.	Pct.	H.	R.	ER.	SO.	BB.	ERA.
1978—Bristol	Ap'lachian	3	7	1	0	1.000	10	5	4	7	2	5.14
1978—Lakeland	Florida St.	18	31	6	3	.667	26	13	11	18	13	3.19
1979—Montgomery	Southern	28	96	4	7	.364	97	56	49	64	66	4.59
1979—Evansville	Am. Assoc.	2	13	1	1	.500	11	4	4	8	1	2.77
1980—Evansville	Am. Assoc.	52	92	7	8	.467	94	53	35	53	52	3.42
1981—Detroit	American	2	4	0	0	.000	3	4	3	2	1	6.75
1981—Evansville	Am. Assoc.	35	67	7	4	.636	60	30	28	36	42	3.76
1982—Evansville	Am. Assoc.	30	58⅓	4	1	.800	53	27	22	42	29	3.39
1982—Detroit	American	27	64	5	6	.455	62	26	24	31	23	3.38
1983—Detroit	American	4	9	1	2	.333	18	17	17	6	8	17.00
1983—Evansville†	Am. Assoc.	18	29⅔	2	4	.333	25	12	11	30	21	3.34
1983—St. Louis	National	34	37	5	3	.625	36	14	10	22	18	2.43
1984—St. Louis‡	National	50	73	2	3	.400	62	23	17	38	34	2.10
1985—Portland	P. Coast	10	16	1	0	1.000	15	9	8	17	4	4.50
1985—Philadelphia	National	39	79⅓	3	2	.600	83	42	38	41	40	4.31
1986—Philadelphia	National	19	25	0	2	.000	34	19	16	14	14	5.76
1986—Portland§	P. Coast	12	69⅔	3	3	.500	71	39	33	36	26	4.26
American League Totals—3 Years		33	77	6	8	.429	83	47	44	39	32	5.14
National League Totals—4 Years		142	214⅓	10	10	.500	215	98	81	115	106	3.40
Major League Totals—6 Years		175	291⅓	16	18	.471	298	145	125	154	138	3.86

Selected by Philadelphia Phillies' organization in 19th round of free-agent draft, June 4, 1975.
Selected by Detroit Tigers' organization in 16th round of free-agent draft, June 6, 1978.
†Traded to St. Louis Cardinals, July 5, 1983, completing deal in which St. Louis traded Pitcher Doug Bair to Detroit Tigers for a player to be named later, June 21, 1983.
‡Traded to Philadelphia Phillies' organization for Pitcher Bill Campbell and Shortstop Ivan DeJesus, April 6, 1985.
§Released, November 12, 1986; signed by Texas Rangers' organization, December 3, 1986.

BRUCE WAYNE RUFFIN

Born October 4, 1963, at Lubbock, Tex.
Height, 6.02. Weight, 205.
Throws and bats lefthanded.
Attended University of Texas, Austin, Tex.

Year Club	League	G.	IP.	W.	L.	Pct.	H.	R.	ER.	SO.	BB.	ERA.
1985—Clearwater	Florida St.	14	97	5	5	.500	87	33	31	74	34	2.88
1986—Reading	Eastern	16	90⅓	8	4	.667	89	41	33	68	26	3.29
1986—Philadelphia	National	21	146⅓	9	4	.692	138	53	40	70	44	2.46
Major League Totals—1 Year		21	146⅓	9	4	.692	138	53	40	70	44	2.46

Selected by Philadelphia Phillies' organization in 31st round of free-agent draft, June 7, 1982.
Selected by Philadelphia Phillies' organization in 2nd round of free-agent draft, June 3, 1985.

VERNON GERALD RUHLE

Name pronounced Rule.

(Vern)

Born January 25, 1951, at Coleman, Mich.
Height, 6.01. Weight, 187.
Throws and bats righthanded.
Attended Olivet College, Olivet, Mich.

Major League saves: 1981 (1), 1982 (1), 1983 (3), 1984 (2), 1985 (3), 1986 (1). Total—11.

Year Club	League	G.	IP.	W.	L.	Pct.	H.	R.	ER.	SO.	BB.	ERA.
1972—Bristol	Ap'lachian	4	28	0	2	.000	24	6	4	30	5	1.29
1972—Rocky Mount	Carolina	13	72	5	8	.385	87	53	38	53	28	4.75
1973—Lakeland	Florida St.	15	96	6	5	.545	81	27	22	67	24	2.06
1973—Montgomery	Southern	10	81	6	2	.750	72	33	26	34	17	2.89
1974—Montgomery	Southern	5	45	5	0	1.000	29	6	3	32	12	0.60
1974—Evansville	Am. Assoc.	22	156	13	5	.722	178	80	70	94	42	4.04
1974—Detroit	American	5	33	2	0	1.000	35	13	10	10	6	2.73
1975—Detroit	American	32	190	11	12	.478	199	104	85	67	65	4.03
1976—Detroit	American	32	200	9	12	.429	227	99	87	88	59	3.92
1977—Evansville†	Am. Assoc.	10	21	1	4	.200	31	19	16	15	9	6.86
1977—Detroit‡§	American	14	66	3	5	.375	83	44	42	27	15	5.73
1978—Columbus	Southern	5	39	4	1	.800	32	9	8	25	8	1.85

Year Club	League	G.	IP.	W.	L.	Pct.	H.	R.	ER.	SO.	BB.	ERA.
1978—Charleston	Int'national	13	94	4	4	.500	89	36	29	48	16	2.78
1978—Houston	National	13	68	3	3	.500	57	17	16	27	20	2.12
1979—Houston x	National	13	66	2	6	.250	64	33	30	33	8	4.09
1980—Houston	National	28	159	12	4	.750	148	51	42	55	29	2.38
1981—Houston y	National	20	102	4	6	.400	97	36	33	39	20	2.91
1982—Houston	National	31	149	9	13	.409	169	81	65	56	24	3.93
1983—Houston z	National	41	114⅔	8	5	.615	107	49	47	43	36	3.69
1984—Houston z	National	40	90⅓	1	9	.100	112	58	46	60	29	4.58
1985—Cleveland ab	American	42	125	2	10	.167	139	65	60	54	30	4.32
1986—San Jose c	California	3	21	2	1	.667	20	10	7	16	4	3.00
1986—Edmonton	P. Coast	8	26	0	1	.000	30	14	12	17	4	4.15
1986—California d	American	16	47⅔	1	3	.250	46	25	22	23	7	4.15
American League Totals—6 Years		141	661⅔	28	42	.400	729	350	306	269	182	4.16
National League Totals—7 Years		186	749	39	46	.459	754	325	279	313	166	3.35
Major League Totals—13 Years		327	1410⅔	67	88	.432	1483	675	585	582	348	3.73

Selected by Detroit Tigers' organization in 17th round of free-agent draft, June 6, 1972.

†On disabled list, July 24 to August 5, 1977.

‡On disabled list, May 21 to June 16, 1977.

§Released, March 27, 1978; signed by Houston Astros' organization, March 29, 1978.

xOn disabled list, May 14 to September 1, 1979.

yOn disabled list, April 30 to May 21, 1981.

zGranted free agency, November 8, 1984; signed by Cleveland Indians, December 22, 1984.

aOn disabled list, April 27 to May 12 and May 29 to June 16, 1985.

bGranted free agency, November 12, 1985; signed by San Jose (Independent), May 24, 1986.

cReleased, June 5, 1986; signed by Edmonton (California Angels' organization), June 5, 1986.

dGranted free agency, November 12, 1986.

DIVISION SERIES RECORD

Year Club	League	G.	IP.	W.	L.	Pct.	H.	R.	ER.	SO.	BB.	ERA.
1981—Houston	National	1	8	0	1	.000	4	2	2	1	2	2.25

CHAMPIONSHIP SERIES RECORD

Year Club	League	G.	IP.	W.	L.	Pct.	H.	R.	ER.	SO.	BB.	ERA.
1980—Houston	National	1	7	0	0	.000	8	3	3	3	1	3.86
1986—California	American	1	⅔	0	0	.000	2	2	1	0	0	13.50
Championship Series Totals—2 Years		2	7⅔	0	0	.000	10	5	4	3	1	4.70

PAUL WILLIAM RUNGE

Name pronounced RUNG-ee.

Born May 21, 1958, at Kingston, N.Y.
Height, 6.00. Weight, 165.
Throws and bats righthanded.
Attended Jacksonville University, Jacksonville, Fla.

Major League stolen bases: 1984 (5).

Led International League in bases on balls received with 95 in 1982 and 92 in 1986.

Tied for International League lead in grounding into double plays with 16 in 1986.

Led International League second basemen in putouts with 269, assists with 383 and total chances with 663 in 1986.

Led International League second basemen in total chances with 747 in 1982.

Led International League shortstops in double plays with 67 in 1981.

Led Appalachian League shortstops in double plays with 38 in 1979.

Year Club	League	Pos.	G.	AB.	R.	H.	2B.	3B.	HR.	RBI.	B.A.	PO.	A.	E.	F.A.
1979—Kingsport	Appal.	SS	66	229	57	67	11	0	6	45	.293	*104	*194	*24	.925
1980—Durham	Carol.	SS	74	245	37	64	8	4	8	37	.261	105	280	25	.939
1980—Savannah	South.	SS	75	248	32	68	11	3	9	34	.274	115	196	17	.948
1981—Richmond	Int.	SS	134	426	49	98	20	5	9	41	.230	191	450	*35	.948
1981—Atlanta	Nat.	SS	10	27	2	7	1	0	0	2	.259	14	27	4	.911
1982—Richmond	Int.	2B	134	507	*106	142	25	6	15	71	.280	*318	412	●17	.977
1982—Atlanta	Nat.	PH-PR	4	2	0	0	0	0	0	0	.000	0	0	0	.000
1983—Richmond	Int.	2B	137	472	76	129	17	4	15	72	.273	269	392	14	.979
1983—Atlanta	Nat.	2B	5	8	0	2	0	0	0	1	.250	4	3	0	1.000
1984—Atlanta	Nat.	2B-SS-3B	28	90	5	24	3	1	0	3	.267	53	101	5	.969
1984—Richmond	Int.	2-3-S-1	91	301	44	72	9	3	8	41	.239	163	264	16	.964
1985—Atlanta	Nat.	3B-SS-2B	50	87	15	19	3	0	1	5	.218	15	66	7	.920
1986—Richmond	Int.	2B-SS	*138	458	76	126	27	1	6	59	.275	275	393	16	.977
1986—Atlanta	Nat.	2B	7	8	1	2	0	0	0	0	.250	5	12	0	1.000
Major League Totals—6 Years			104	222	23	54	7	1	1	11	.243	91	209	16	.949

Selected by Atlanta Braves' organization in 8th round of free-agent draft, June 5, 1979.

THOMAS WILLIAM RUNNELLS
(Tom)

Born April 17, 1955, at Greeley, Colo.
Height, 6.00. Weight, 175.
Throws right and bats right and lefthanded.
Received bachelor of arts degree in physical education from
University of Northern Colorado, Greeley, Colo.

Led American Association second basemen in total chances with 654 and double plays with 83 in 1985.

Led American Association second basemen in fielding percentage with .993 in 1984.

Year Club	League	Pos.	G.	AB.	R.	H.	2B.	3B.	HR.	RBI.	B.A.	PO.	A.	E.	F.A.
1977—Great Falls†	Pion.	2-3-O-S	63	241	61	70	8	1	1	53	.290	117	144	16	.942
1978—Fresno	Calif.	2B-SS-3B	139	564	83	163	15	7	0	55	.289	289	437	37	.952
1979—Shreveport	Texas	SS	128	435	45	102	10	2	4	32	.234	190	413	19	*.969
1980—Shreveport	Texas	SS	73	258	27	50	4	1	0	10	.194	117	240	18	.952
1980—Phoenix	P. C.	SS-2B	37	149	21	45	4	0	0	10	.302	51	121	4	.977
1981—Phoenix	P. C.	SS-OF-2B	131	467	40	128	11	2	0	51	.274	240	392	28	.958
1982—Phoenix	P. C.	S-3-2-O	108	347	52	93	8	11	0	48	.268	164	259	23	.948
1983—Phoenix‡§	P. C.	SS-2B-1B	74	244	43	74	11	4	1	28	.303	119	188	13	.959
1984—Wichita	A. A.	2-3-O-S	125	438	67	108	21	3	6	61	.247	229	350	5	.991
1985—Denver	A. A.	2B	114	466	55	135	22	8	5	51	.290	256	*391	7	*.989
1985—Cincinnati	Nat.	SS-2B	28	35	3	7	1	0	0	0	.200	10	22	0	1.000
1986—Denver	A. A	2-S-O-3	95	298	34	68	12	4	3	28	.228	159	248	10	.976
1986—Cincinnati	Nat.	2B-3B	12	11	1	1	1	0	0	0	.091	4	5	0	1.000
Major League Totals—2 Years			40	46	4	8	2	0	0	0	.174	14	27	0	1.000

Signed as free agent by San Francisco Giants' organization, June 16, 1977.
†Batted righthanded.
‡On disabled list, July 24, 1983 through remainder of season.
§Granted free agency, October 20, 1983; signed by Indianapolis (Cincinnati Reds' organization), October 30, 1983.

JEFFREY LEE RUSSELL
(Jeff)

Born September 2, 1961, at Cincinnati, O.
Height, 6.04. Weight, 200.
Throws and bats righthanded.
Attended Gulf Coast Community College, Panama City, Fla.

Major League saves: 1986 (2).

Year Club	League	G.	IP.	W.	L.	Pct.	H.	R.	ER.	SO.	BB.	ERA.
1980—Eugene	Northwest	13	90	6	5	.545	80	47	30	75	50	3.00
1981—Tampa	Florida St.	22	143	10	4	.714	109	51	32	92	48	2.01
1982—Waterbury†	Eastern	14	79⅔	6	4	.600	67	27	21	88	23	2.37
1983—Indianapolis	Am. Assoc.	18	119	5	5	.500	106	51	47	98	44	3.55
1983—Cincinnati	National	10	68⅓	4	5	.444	58	30	23	40	22	3.03
1984—Cincinnati	National	33	181⅔	6	*18	.250	186	97	86	101	65	4.26
1985—Denver‡§-Oklahoma City	Am. Assoc.	18	115⅓	7	4	.636	105	55	52	94	51	4.06
1985—Texas	American	13	62	3	6	.333	85	55	52	44	27	7.55
1986—Oklahoma City	Am. Assoc.	11	70⅔	4	1	.800	63	32	31	34	38	3.95
1986—Texas	American	37	82	5	2	.714	74	40	31	54	31	3.40
National League Totals—2 Years		43	250	10	23	.303	244	127	109	141	87	3.92
American League Totals—2 Years		50	144	8	8	.500	159	95	83	98	58	5.19
Major League Totals—4 Years		93	394	18	31	.367	403	222	192	239	145	4.39

Selected by Cincinnati Reds' organization in 5th round of free-agent draft, June 5, 1979.
†On disabled list, May 5 to June 10 and July 28, 1982 through remainder of season.
‡On disabled list, May 22 to June 10, 1985.
§Traded to Texas Rangers' organization, July 23, 1985, completing deal in which Texas traded Third Baseman Buddy Bell to Cincinnati Reds for Outfielder Duane Walker and a player to be named later, July 19, 1985.

JOHN WILLIAM RUSSELL

Born January 5, 1961, at Oklahoma City, Okla.
Height, 6.00. Weight, 200.
Throws and bats righthanded.
Attended University of Oklahoma, Norman, Okla.

Major League stolen bases: 1985 (2).
Led National League in passed balls with 17 in 1986.
Tied for Pacific Coast League lead in passed balls with 13 in 1983.

Year Club	League	Pos.	G.	AB.	R.	H.	2B.	3B.	HR.	RBI.	B.A.	PO.	A.	E.	F.A.
1982—Reading	East.	C-OF-1B	77	263	26	53	10	5	6	30	.202	354	44	12	.971
1983—Portland	P. C.	C-O-3	128	445	71	113	23	3	27	76	.254	551	58	12	.981
1984—Portland	P. C.	OF-1B-C	93	350	75	101	22	5	19	77	.289	182	18	5	.976
1984—Philadelphia	Nat.	OF-C	39	99	11	28	8	1	2	11	.283	51	1	0	1.000
1985—Philadelphia	Nat.	OF-1B	81	216	22	47	12	0	9	23	.218	170	9	4	.978
1985—Portland	P. C.	OF-C-1B	16	49	8	15	2	2	4	11	.306	24	1	1	.962
1986—Philadelphia	Nat.	C	93	315	35	76	21	2	13	60	.241	498	39	13	.976
Major League Totals—3 Years			213	630	68	151	41	3	24	94	.240	719	49	17	.978

Selected by Montreal Expos' organization in 4th round of free-agent draft, June 5, 1979.
Selected by Philadelphia Phillies' organization in 1st round (13th player selected) of free-agent draft, June 7, 1982.

WILLIAM ELLIS RUSSELL
(Bill)

Born October 21, 1948, at Pittsburg, Kan.
Height, 6.00. Weight, 175.
Throws and bats righthanded.
Attended Kansas State College, Pittsburg, Kan.

Established major league records for fewest putouts by shortstop, season, 150 or more games (194), 1974.
Tied major league record for most strikeouts, nine-inning game (5), June 9, 1971; fewest double plays by shortstop, season, 150 or more games (64), 1982.

Major League stolen bases: 1969 (4), 1970 (9), 1971 (6), 1972 (14), 1973 (15), 1974 (14), 1975 (5), 1976 (15), 1977 (16), 1978 (10), 1979 (6), 1980 (13), 1981 (2), 1982 (10), 1983 (13), 1984 (4), 1985 (4), 1986 (7). Total—167.
　　Led National League in intentional bases on balls received with 25 in 1974.
　　Led National League shortstops in double plays with 102 in 1977.
　　Led National League shortstops in total chances with 834 in 1973.
　　Tied for California League lead in double plays by outfielders with 4 in 1968.
　　Named shortstop on THE SPORTING NEWS National League All-Star Team, 1973.

Year	Club	League	Pos.	G.	AB.	R.	H.	2B.	3B.	HR.	RBI.	B.A.	PO.	A.	E.	F.A.
1966—Ogden		Pion.	OF	39	87	19	31	5	1	3	21	.356	25	3	2	.933
1967—Dubuque		Midw.	OF	67	263	29	58	11	1	5	21	.221	98	11	10	.916
1968—Bakersfield		Calif.	OF	115	439	76	123	16	3	17	55	.280	255	★22	7	.975
1969—Los Angeles†		Nat.	OF	98	212	35	48	6	2	5	15	.226	132	4	3	.978
1970—Spokane		P. C.	OF-3B-SS	55	237	48	86	13	5	3	30	.363	112	39	6	.962
1970—Los Angeles‡		Nat.	OF-SS	81	278	30	72	11	9	0	28	.259	167	10	3	.983
1971—Los Angeles§		Nat.	2B-OF-SS	91	211	29	48	7	4	2	15	.227	131	124	8	.970
1972—Los Angeles x		Nat.	★SS-OF	129	434	47	118	19	5	4	34	.272	202	439	★34	.950
1973—Los Angeles		Nat.	SS	●162	615	55	163	26	3	4	56	.265	243	★560	31	.963
1974—Los Angeles		Nat.	★SS-OF	160	553	61	149	17	6	5	65	.269	194	491	★39	.946
1975—Los Angeles y		Nat.	SS	84	252	24	52	9	2	0	14	.206	94	230	11	.967
1976—Los Angeles		Nat.	SS	149	554	53	152	17	3	5	65	.274	251	476	28	.963
1977—Los Angeles		Nat.	SS	153	634	84	176	28	6	4	51	.278	234	523	29	.963
1978—Los Angeles		Nat.	SS	155	625	72	179	32	4	3	46	.286	245	533	31	.962
1979—Los Angeles		Nat.	SS	153	627	72	170	26	4	7	56	.271	218	452	30	.957
1980—Los Angeles		Nat.	SS	130	466	38	123	23	2	3	34	.264	179	387	19	.968
1981—Los Angeles		Nat.	SS	82	262	20	61	9	2	0	22	.233	128	261	14	.965
1982—Los Angeles		Nat.	SS	153	497	64	136	20	2	3	46	.274	216	502	29	.961
1983—Los Angeles		Nat.	SS	131	451	47	111	13	1	1	30	.246	192	392	22	.964
1984—Los Angeles z		Nat.	SS-OF-2B	89	262	25	70	12	1	0	19	.267	115	173	9	.970
1985—Los Angeles		Nat.	S-O-2-3	76	169	19	44	6	1	0	13	.260	60	82	10	.934
1986—Los Angeles ab		Nat.	O-S-2-3	105	216	21	54	11	0	0	18	.250	103	84	5	.974
Major League Totals—18 Years				2181	7318	796	1926	293	57	46	627	.263	3104	5723	355	.961

Selected by Los Angeles Dodgers' organization in 37th round of free-agent draft, June 12, 1966.
†On military list, August 1 to August 19, 1969.
‡On military list, July 3 to July 19, 1970.
§On military list, June 19 to July 3, 1971.
xOn military list, July 7 to July 22, 1972.
yOn disabled list, April 13 to May 6 and May 11 to June 30, 1975.
zOn disabled list, May 14 to June 4 and August 12 to August 27, 1984.
aOn voluntarily retired list, October 24, 1986.
bReleased, November 12, 1986; named coach of Los Angeles Dodgers for 1987 season.

DIVISION SERIES RECORD

Year	Club	League	Pos.	G.	AB.	R.	H.	2B.	3B.	HR.	RBI.	B.A.	PO.	A.	E.	F.A.
1981—Los Angeles		Nat.	SS	5	16	1	4	1	0	0	2	.250	10	15	2	.926

CHAMPIONSHIP SERIES RECORD

Established Championship Series record for most one-base hits, four-game Series (7), 1974.

Year	Club	League	Pos.	G.	AB.	R.	H.	2B.	3B.	HR.	RBI.	B.A.	PO.	A.	E.	F.A.
1974—Los Angeles		Nat.	SS	4	18	1	7	0	0	0	3	.389	13	16	0	1.000
1977—Los Angeles		Nat.	SS	4	18	3	5	1	0	0	2	.278	11	12	2	.920
1978—Los Angeles		Nat.	SS	4	17	1	7	1	0	0	2	.412	4	14	0	1.000
1981—Los Angeles		Nat.	SS	5	16	2	5	0	1	0	1	.313	10	13	0	1.000
1983—Los Angeles		Nat.	SS	4	14	1	4	0	0	0	0	.286	4	10	1	.933
Championship Series Totals—5 Years				21	83	8	28	2	1	0	8	.337	42	65	3	.973

WORLD SERIES RECORD

Established World Series record for most assists by shortstop, six-game Series (26), 1981.
Tied World Series record for one or more hits, each game, six-game Series, 1978.

Year	Club	League	Pos.	G.	AB.	R.	H.	2B.	3B.	HR.	RBI.	B.A.	PO.	A.	E.	F.A.
1974—Los Angeles		Nat.	SS	5	18	0	4	0	1	0	2	.222	4	11	1	.938
1977—Los Angeles		Nat.	SS	6	26	3	4	0	1	0	2	.154	9	21	0	1.000
1978—Los Angeles		Nat.	SS	6	26	1	11	2	0	0	2	.423	11	20	3	.912
1981—Los Angeles		Nat.	SS	6	25	1	6	0	0	0	2	.240	4	26	1	.968
World Series Totals—4 Years				23	95	5	25	2	2	0	8	.263	28	78	5	.955

ALL-STAR GAME RECORD

Year	League	Pos.	AB.	R.	H.	2B.	3B.	HR.	RBI.	B.A.	PO.	A.	E.	F.A.
1973—National		SS	2	0	0	0	0	0	0	.000	0	2	0	1.000
1976—National		SS	1	0	0	0	0	0	0	.000	1	2	0	1.000
1980—National		SS	2	0	0	0	0	0	0	.000	0	2	0	1.000
All-Star Game Totals—3 Years			5	0	0	0	0	0	0	.000	1	6	0	1.000

—DID YOU KNOW—

That the 1986 Cincinnati Reds hit home runs in their first 12 games, falling one game short of the record set by the 1954 Chicago Cubs?

RICHARD DAVID RUTHVEN
(Dick)

Born March 27, 1951, at Sacramento, Calif.
Height, 6.03. Weight, 190.
Throws and bats righthanded.
Attended Fresno State University, Fresno, Calif.
Brother-in-law of Tommy Hutton, first baseman-outfielder with Los Angeles, Philadelphia,
Toronto and Montreal, 1966, 1969 and 1972 through 1981, and broadcaster with Montreal Expos since 1982.

Tied National League record for most putouts by pitcher, nine-inning game (5), April 19, 1978.
Major League saves: 1973 (1).
Tied for National League lead in balks with 5 in 1976.
Named righthanded pitcher on THE SPORTING NEWS College Baseball All-America Team, 1972.

Year—Club	League	G.	IP.	W.	L.	Pct.	H.	R.	ER.	SO.	BB.	ERA.
1973—Philadelphia†	National	25	128	6	9	.400	125	69	60	98	75	4.22
1974—Philadelphia	National	35	213	9	13	.409	182	106	95	153	116	4.01
1975—Toledo	Int'national	23	153	10	12	.455	148	72	54	114	69	3.18
1975—Philadelphia‡	National	11	41	2	2	.500	37	22	19	26	22	4.17
1976—Atlanta	National	36	240	14	●17	.452	255	★112	112	142	90	4.20
1977—Atlanta§	National	25	151	7	13	.350	158	86	71	84	62	4.23
1978—Atlanta x-Philadelphia	National	33	232	15	11	.577	214	95	87	120	56	3.38
1979—Philadelphia y	National	20	122	7	5	.583	121	59	58	58	37	4.28
1980—Philadelphia	National	33	223	17	10	.630	241	99	88	86	74	3.55
1981—Philadelphia	National	23	147	12	7	.632	162	★94	★84	80	54	5.14
1982—Philadelphia	National	33	204⅓	11	11	.500	189	99	86	115	59	3.79
1983—Philadelphia z-Chicago	National	32	183	13	12	.520	202	101	89	99	38	4.38
1984—Chicago a	National	23	126⅔	6	10	.375	154	75	71	55	41	5.04
1984—Lodi	California	2	9	1	0	1.000	9	4	4	8	2	4.00
1985—Chicago b	National	20	87⅓	4	7	.364	103	49	44	26	37	4.53
1986—Chicago c	National	6	10⅔	0	0	.000	12	9	6	3	6	5.06
Major League Totals—14 Years		355	2109	123	127	.492	2155	1075	970	1155	767	4.14

Selected by Baltimore Orioles' organization in 20th round of free-agent draft, June 5, 1969.
Selected by Minnesota Twins' organization in 1st round (eighth player selected) of free-agent draft, June 6, 1972.
Selected by Philadelphia Phillies' organization in secondary phase of free-agent draft, January 10, 1973.
†On disabled list, August 3 to September 1, 1973.
‡Traded with Pitcher Roy Thomas and Infielder-Outfielder Alan Bannister to Chicago White Sox for Pitcher Jim Kaat and Shortstop Mike Buskey, December 10, 1975. Traded with Outfielder Ken Henderson and Pitcher Danny Osborn by Chicago White Sox to Atlanta Braves for Outfielder Ralph Garr and Infielder Larvell Blanks, December 12, 1975.
§On disabled list, May 2 to July 4, 1977.
xTraded to Philadelphia Phillies for Pitcher Gene Garber, June 15, 1978.
yOn disabled list, July 2 to July 25 and August 16 to October 4, 1979.
zTraded with Pitcher Bill Johnson to Chicago Cubs for Pitcher Willie Hernandez, May 22, 1983.
aOn disabled list, May 20 to July 15, 1984; included rehabilitation disability assignment to Lodi, June 29 to July 15, 1984.
bOn disabled list, August 11 to October 1, 1985.
cReleased, May 6, 1986.

DIVISION SERIES RECORD

Year—Club	League	G.	IP.	W.	L.	Pct.	H.	R.	ER.	SO.	BB.	ERA.
1981—Philadelphia	National	1	4	0	1	.000	3	3	2	0	1	4.50

CHAMPIONSHIP SERIES RECORD

Year—Club	League	G.	IP.	W.	L.	Pct.	H.	R.	ER.	SO.	BB.	ERA.
1978—Philadelphia	National	1	4⅔	0	1	.000	6	3	3	3	0	5.79
1980—Philadelphia	National	2	9	1	0	1.000	3	2	2	4	5	2.00
Championship Series Totals—2 Years		3	13⅔	1	1	.500	9	5	5	7	5	3.29

WORLD SERIES RECORD

Year—Club	League	G.	IP.	W.	L.	Pct.	H.	R.	ER.	SO.	BB.	ERA.
1980—Philadelphia	National	1	9	0	0	.000	9	3	3	7	0	3.00

ALL-STAR GAME RECORD

Year—League		IP.	W.	L.	Pct.	H.	R.	ER.	SO.	BB.	ERA.
1981—National		⅓	0	0	.000	0	0	0	0	0	0.00

Member of National League All-Star Team in 1976; did not play.

MARK DWAYNE RYAL

Name pronounced Rile.

Born April 28, 1960, at Henryetta, Okla.
Height, 6:01. Weight, 185.
Throws and bats lefthanded.

Major League stolen bases: 1986 (1).
Led Pacific Coast League in intentional bases on balls received with 10 in 1986.
Led American Association in grounding into double plays with 21 in 1983.
Tied for American Association lead in intentional bases on balls received with 12 in 1982.

Year—Club	League	Pos.	G.	AB.	R.	H.	2B.	3B.	HR.	RBI.	B.A.	PO.	A.	E.	F.A.
1978—Sarasota Royals...	Gulf C.	OF	27	83	11	20	0	1	0	10	.241	37	4	0	1.000
1979—Fort Myers..........	Fla. St.	OF	107	360	27	79	12	1	4	34	.219	199	15	3	.986
1980—Fort Myers..........	Fla. St.	OF	123	440	60	117	21	3	5	51	.266	174	8	2	.989
1981—Jacksonville........	South.	OF	123	457	50	122	15	2	14	69	.267	237	8	11	.957
1981—Omaha.................	A. A.	OF	6	19	2	4	0	0	0	1	.211	9	1	0	1.000
1982—Omaha.................	A. A.	★OF-1B	129	473	69	135	27	2	20	77	.285	242	★18	6	.977
1982—Kansas City..........	Amer.	OF	6	13	0	1	0	0	0	0	.077	9	0	1	.900
1983—Omaha.................	A. A.	OF-1B	132	454	61	118	28	5	9	57	.260	203	11	8	.964
1984—Omaha†..............	A. A.	1B-OF	131	435	56	103	18	1	13	64	.237	680	58	16	.979
1985—Buffalo................	A. A.	OF	106	392	50	104	21	1	13	66	.265	175	10	2	.989
1985—Chicago‡	Amer.	OF	12	33	4	5	3	0	0	3	.152	21	0	0	1.000
1986—Edmonton.............	P. C.	1B-OF	127	479	72	163	33	4	14	84	.340	734	50	7	.991
1986—California.............	Amer.	OF-1B	13	32	6	12	0	0	2	5	.375	32	2	1	.971
Major League Totals—3 Years.................			31	78	10	18	3	0	2	8	.231	62	2	2	.970

Selected by Kansas City Royals' organization in 3rd round of free-agent draft, June 6, 1978.

†Released, September 4, 1984, signed by Chicago White Sox' organization, December 28, 1984.

‡Granted free agency, October 15, 1985; signed by California Angels, January 21, 1986.

LYNN NOLAN RYAN JR.

(Known by middle name.)

Born January 31, 1947, at Refugio, Tex.
Height, 6.02. Weight, 195.
Throws and bats righthanded.
Attended Alvin Junior College, Alvin, Tex.

Established major league records for most strikeouts, lifetime (4,277); most games, 15 or more strikeouts, lifetime (19); most games, 10 or more strikeouts, lifetime (162); most seasons, 300 or more strikeouts (5); most games, 10 or more strikeouts, season (23), 1973; most strikeouts, three consecutive games (including extra innings—27⅓) (47), August 12, 16 and 20, 1974; most strikeouts by losing pitcher, extra-inning game (19), August 20, 1974 (11 innings); most seasons leading league, bases on balls allowed (8); most bases on balls, lifetime (2,268); most no-hit games, lifetime (5).

Established modern major league records for most consecutive seasons, 300 or more strikeouts (3); most strikeouts, season (383), 1973.

Tied major league records for striking out side on nine pitches, April 19, 1968 (third inning) and July 9, 1972 (second inning); most no-hit games, season (2), 1973; most clubs shut out, season (8), 1972; most consecutive seasons leading major leagues, bases on balls allowed (3); most strikeouts, three consecutive nine-inning games (41), August 7, 12 and 16, 1974.

Established American League record for most games, 10 or more strikeouts, lifetime (114); most games, 15 or more strikeouts, lifetime (19).

Tied American League records for most consecutive strikeouts, game (8), July 9, 1972 and July 15, 1973; most strikeouts, two consecutive games (32), August 7 (13), 12 (19), 1974; most low-hit (no-hit and one-hit) games, season (3), 1973; most wild pitches, season (21), 1977; most seasons leading league, errors by pitcher (4); most seasons leading league, wild pitches (3).

Pitched 5-0 no-hit victory against Los Angeles Dodgers, September 26, 1981.
Pitched 1-0 no-hit victory against Baltimore Orioles, June 1, 1975.
Pitched 4-0 no-hit victory against Minnesota Twins, September 28, 1974.
Pitched 6-0 no-hit victory against Detroit Tigers, July 15, 1973.
Pitched 3-0 no-hit victory against Kansas City Royals, May 15, 1973.
Major League saves: 1969 (1), 1970 (1), 1973 (1). Total—3.
Led National League in hit batsmen with 8 in 1982.
Led National League in wild pitches with 16 in 1981 and 15 in 1986.
Led American League in shutouts with 9 in 1972, 7 in 1976, and tied for lead with 5 in 1979.
Led American League in wild pitches with 18 in 1972, 21 in 1977 and 13 in 1978.
Tied for American League lead in complete games with 22 in 1977.
Tied for National League lead in sacrifice hits by batters with 14 in 1985.
Led Western Carolinas League pitchers in games started with 28 in 1966.
Tied for Appalachian League lead in hit batsmen with 8 in 1965.
Named American League Pitcher of the Year by THE SPORTING NEWS, 1977.
Named righthanded pitcher on THE SPORTING NEWS American League All-Star Team, 1977.
Named Western Carolinas Pitcher of the Year, 1966.

Year—Club	League	G.	IP.	W.	L.	Pct.	H.	R.	ER.	SO.	BB.	ERA.
1965—Marion....................	Ap'lachian	13	78	3	6	.333	61	47	38	115	56	4.38
1966—Greenville................	W. Carol.	29	183	★17	2	.895	109	59	51	★272	★127	2.51
1966—Williamsport............	Eastern	3	19	0	2	.000	9	6	2	35	12	0.95
1966—New York...............	National	2	3	0	1	.000	5	5	5	6	3	15.00
1967—Winter Haven†.........	Florida St.	1	4	0	0	.000	1	1	1	5	2	2.25
1967—Jacksonville‡...........	Int'national	3	7	1	0	1.000	3	1	0	18	3	3.00
1968—New York§.............	National	21	134	6	9	.400	93	50	46	133	75	3.09
1969—New York...............	National	25	89	6	3	.667	60	38	35	92	53	3.54
1970—New York...............	National	27	132	7	11	.389	86	59	50	125	97	3.41
1971—New York x............	National	30	152	10	14	.417	125	78	67	137	116	3.97
1972—California................	American	39	284	19	16	.543	166	80	72	★329	★157	2.28
1973—California................	American	41	326	21	16	.568	238	113	104	★383	★162	2.87
1974—California................	American	42	★333	22	16	.579	221	127	107	★367	★202	2.89
1975—California................	American	28	198	14	12	.538	152	90	76	186	132	3.45
1976—California................	American	39	284	17	★18	.486	193	117	106	★327	★183	3.36
1977—California................	American	37	299	19	16	.543	198	110	92	★341	★204	2.77
1978—California y.............	American	31	235	10	13	.435	183	106	97	★260	★148	3.71
1979—California z.............	American	34	223	16	14	.533	169	104	89	★223	114	3.59
1980—Houston..................	National	35	234	11	10	.524	205	100	87	200	★98	3.35
1981—Houston..................	National	21	149	11	5	.688	99	34	28	140	68	★1.69

Year Club	League	G.	IP.	W.	L.	Pct.	H.	R.	ER.	SO.	BB.	ERA.
1982—Houston	National	35	250⅓	16	12	.571	196	100	88	245	*109	3.16
1983—Houston a	National	29	196½	14	9	.609	134	74	65	183	101	2.98
1984—Houston b	National	30	183⅔	12	11	.522	143	78	62	197	69	3.04
1985—Houston	National	35	232	10	12	.455	205	108	98	209	95	3.80
1986—Houston c	National	30	178	12	8	.600	119	72	66	194	82	3.34
National League Totals—12 Years		320	1933⅓	115	105	.523	1470	796	697	1861	966	3.24
American League Totals—8 Years		291	2182	138	121	.533	1520	847	743	2416	1302	3.06
Major League Totals—20 Years		611	4115⅓	253	226	.528	2990	1643	1440	4277	2268	3.15

Selected by New York Mets' organization in 8th round of free-agent draft, June, 1965.
†On military list, January 3 to May 13, 1967.
‡On disabled list, July 16 to August 30, 1967.
§On disabled list, July 30 to August 30, 1968.
xTraded with Pitcher Don Rose, Outfielder Leroy Stanton and Catcher Francisco Estrada to California Angels for Infielder Jim Fregosi, December 10, 1971.
yOn disabled list, June 14 to July 5, 1978.
zGranted free agency, November 1, 1979; signed by Houston Astros, November 19, 1979.
aOn disabled list, March 25 to April 17 and May 3 to June 6, 1983.
bOn disabled list, June 2 to June 17 and June 18 to July 3, 1984.
cOn disabled list, June 1 to June 24 and July 28 to August 12, 1986.

DIVISION SERIES RECORD
Year Club	League	G.	IP.	W.	L.	Pct.	H.	R.	ER.	SO.	BB.	ERA.
1981—Houston	National	2	15	1	1	.500	6	4	3	14	3	1.80

CHAMPIONSHIP SERIES RECORD
Established Championship Series record for most strikeouts by relief pitcher, game (7), October 6, 1969.
Tied Championship Series records for most clubs, total Series (3); most earned runs allowed, five-game Series (8), 1980; most consecutive strikeouts, start of game (4), October 3, 1979.
Established National League Championship Series records for most runs allowed, five-game Series (8), 1980; most hits allowed, five-game Series (16), 1980.

Year Club	League	G.	IP.	W.	L.	Pct.	H.	R.	ER.	SO.	BB.	ERA.
1969—New York	National	1	7	1	0	1.000	3	2	2	7	2	2.57
1979—California	American	1	7	0	0	.000	4	3	1	8	3	1.29
1980—Houston	National	2	13⅓	0	0	.000	16	8	8	14	3	5.40
1986—Houston	National	2	14	0	1	.000	9	6	6	17	1	3.86
Championship Series Totals—4 Years		6	41⅓	1	1	.500	32	19	17	46	9	3.70

WORLD SERIES RECORD
Year Club	League	G.	IP.	W.	L.	Pct.	H.	R.	ER.	SO.	BB.	ERA.
1969—New York	National	1	2⅓	0	0	.000	1	0	0	3	2	0.00

ALL-STAR GAME RECORD
Year League	IP.	W.	L.	Pct.	H.	R.	ER.	SO.	BB.	ERA.
1973—American	2	0	0	.000	2	2	2	2	2	9.00
1979—American	2	0	0	.000	5	3	3	2	1	13.50
1981—National	1	0	0	.000	0	0	0	1	0	0.00
1985—National	3	0	0	.000	2	0	0	2	2	0.00
All-Star Game Totals—4 Years	8	0	0	.000	9	5	5	7	5	5.63

Member of American League All-Star Team for the 1972 and 1975 games; did not play.
Named to American League All-Star Team to replace Frank Tanana for 1977 game; declined.

BRET WILLIAM SABERHAGEN
Born April 13, 1964, at Chicago Heights, Ill.
Height, 6.01. Weight, 160.
Throws and bats righthanded.

Major League saves: 1984 (1).
Named American League Pitcher of the Year by THE SPORTING NEWS, 1985.
Won American League Cy Young Memorial Award, 1985.
Named righthanded pitcher on THE SPORTING NEWS American League All-Star Team, 1985.

Year Club	League	G.	IP.	W.	L.	Pct.	H.	R.	ER.	SO.	BB.	ERA.
1983—Fort Myers	Florida St.	16	109⅔	10	5	.667	98	34	28	82	19	2.30
1983—Jacksonville	Southern	11	77⅓	6	2	.750	66	31	25	48	29	2.91
1984—Kansas City†	American	38	157⅔	10	11	.476	138	71	61	73	36	3.48
1985—Kansas City	American	32	235⅓	20	6	.769	211	79	75	158	38	2.87
1986—Kansas City‡	American	30	156	7	12	.368	165	77	72	112	29	4.15
Major League Totals—3 Years		100	549	37	29	.561	514	227	208	343	103	3.41

Selected by Kansas City Royals' organization in 19th round of free-agent draft, June 7, 1982.
†Appeared in one game as a pinch-runner.
‡On disabled list, August 10 to September 1, 1986.

CHAMPIONSHIP SERIES RECORD
Year Club	League	G.	IP.	W.	L.	Pct.	H.	R.	ER.	SO.	BB.	ERA.
1984—Kansas City	American	1	8	0	0	.000	6	3	2	5	1	2.25
1985—Kansas City	American	2	7⅓	0	0	.000	12	5	5	6	2	6.14
Championship Series Totals—2 Years		3	15⅓	0	0	.000	18	8	7	11	3	4.11

Year	Club	League	G.	IP.	W.	L.	Pct.	H.	R.	ER.	SO.	BB.	ERA.
1985—Kansas City		American	2	18	2	0	1.000	11	1	1	10	1	0.50

CHRISTOPHER ANDREW SABO
(Chris)

Born January 19, 1962, at Detroit, Mich.
Height, 6.00. Weight, 170.
Throws and bats righthanded.
Attended University of Michigan, Ann Arbor, Mich.

Led Eastern League third basemen in assists with 236 in 1985.
Led Eastern League third basemen in fielding percentage with .943 in 1984.
Named third baseman on THE SPORTING NEWS College Baseball All-America Team, 1983.

Year	Club	League	Pos.	G.	AB.	R.	H.	2B.	3B.	HR.	RBI.	B.A.	PO.	A.	E.	F.A.
1983—Cedar Rapids	Midw.		3B	77	274	43	75	11	6	12	37	.274	43	130	9	.951
1984—Vermont	East.		3B-2B	125	441	44	94	19	1	5	38	.213	80	210	21	.932
1985—Vermont	East.		3B-SS	124	428	66	119	19	0	11	46	.278	97	236	18	.949
1986—Denver	A. A.		3B	129	432	83	118	26	2	10	60	.273	83	202	9	*.969

Selected by Montreal Expos' organization in 30th round of free-agent draft, June 3, 1980.
Selected by Cincinnati Reds' organization in 2nd round of free-agent draft, June 6, 1983.

RANDY ANTHONY ST. CLAIRE

Born August 23, 1960, at Glens Falls, N.Y.
Height, 6.03. Weight, 180.
Throws and bats righthanded.
Son of Ebba St. Claire, catcher with Boston Braves,
Milwaukee Braves and New York Giants, 1951 through 1954;
and brother of Steve St. Claire, pitcher in Montreal Expos' organization.

Major League saves: 1986 (1).
Led Southern League in intentional bases on balls issued with 14 in 1984.

Year	Club	League	G.	IP.	W.	L.	Pct.	H.	R.	ER.	SO.	BB.	ERA.
1979—Calgary	Pioneer	6	33	1	2	.333	30	22	16	17	15	4.36
1980—Calgary	Pioneer	21	57	5	7	.417	65	36	27	51	23	4.26
1981—Jamestown	NYP	13	51	4	1	.800	53	22	11	36	17	1.94
1982—San Jose	California	9	61	2	5	.286	58	32	28	44	20	4.13
1982—West Palm Beach	Florida St.	19	65	3	8	.273	74	41	38	38	17	5.26
1983—West Palm Beach	Florida St.	42	98	5	7	.417	72	33	23	77	31	2.11
1984—Jacksonville	Southern	48	75	10	7	.588	64	35	24	56	29	2.88
1984—Indianapolis	Am. Assoc.	13	17⅔	1	1	.500	15	2	2	17	6	1.02
1984—Montreal	National	4	8	0	0	.000	11	4	4	4	2	4.50
1985—Indianapolis†	Am. Assoc.	11	19⅔	0	1	.000	21	5	4	11	3	1.83
1985—Montreal	National	42	68⅔	5	3	.625	69	32	30	25	26	3.93
1986—Indianapolis	Am. Assoc.	*57	99⅓	5	7	.417	105	49	44	72	29	3.99
1986—Montreal	National	11	19	2	0	1.000	13	5	5	21	6	2.37
Major League Totals—3 Years		57	95⅔	7	3	.700	93	41	39	50	34	3.67

Signed as free agent by Montreal Expos' organization, September 9, 1978.
†On disabled list, May 7 to May 17, 1985.

LENN HARUKI SAKATA

Name pronounced Lenn Ha-ROO-key Sah-KAH-tah.
Born June 8, 1953, at Honolulu, Haw.
Height, 5.09. Weight, 160.
Throws and bats righthanded.
Attended Treasure Valley Community College, Ontario, Ore. and
Gonzaga University, Spokane, Wash.

Major League stolen bases: 1977 (1), 1978 (1), 1980 (2), 1981 (4), 1982 (7), 1983 (8), 1984 (4), 1985 (3). Total—30.

Year	Club	League	Pos.	G.	AB.	R.	H.	2B.	3B.	HR.	RBI.	B.A.	PO.	A.	E.	F.A.
1975—Thetford Mines†	East.		2B	121	421	63	108	9	3	9	43	.257	243	304	16	.972
1976—Spokane	P. C.		2B	141	510	64	143	23	5	10	70	.280	*327	428	●22	.972
1977—Spokane	P. C.		2B	94	345	52	105	19	4	4	73	.304	221	352	13	*.978
1977—Milwaukee	Amer.		2B	53	154	13	25	2	0	2	12	.162	102	159	4	.985
1978—Spokane	P. C.		2B	45	156	24	42	14	3	0	20	.269	73	160	5	.979
1978—Milwaukee	Amer.		2B	30	78	8	15	4	0	0	3	.192	50	66	3	.975
1979—Vancouver‡	P. C.		2B-3B	118	454	59	136	21	3	6	64	.300	266	409	14	.980
1979—Milwaukee§	Amer.		2B	4	14	1	7	2	0	0	1	.500	10	13	0	1.000
1980—Rochester x	Int.		2B	26	93	19	32	6	1	3	8	.344	45	87	4	.971
1980—Baltimore	Amer.		2B-SS	43	83	12	16	3	2	1	9	.193	55	73	2	.985
1981—Baltimore y	Amer.		SS-2B	61	150	19	34	4	0	5	15	.227	82	148	7	.970
1982—Baltimore	Amer.		2B-SS	136	343	40	89	18	1	6	31	.259	182	299	16	.968
1983—Baltimore	Amer.		2B-C	66	134	23	34	7	0	3	12	.254	84	117	2	.990
1984—Baltimore	Amer.		2B-OF	81	157	23	30	1	0	3	11	.191	80	161	3	.988
1985—Baltimore	Amer.		2B	55	97	15	22	3	0	3	6	.227	58	87	6	.960
1985—Rochester z	Int.		2B	16	56	7	12	1	0	0	2	.214	28	48	3	.962
1986—Tacoma	P. C.		2B-3B	110	399	66	125	27	3	2	48	.313	170	292	10	.979
1986—Oakland a	Amer.		2B	17	34	4	12	2	0	0	5	.353	21	39	1	.984
Major League Totals—10 Years			546	1244	158	284	46	3	23	105	.228	724	1162	44	.977

Selected by San Francisco Giants' organization in 14th round of free-agent draft, June 6, 1972.
Selected by San Diego Padres' organization in 5th round of free-agent draft, June 5, 1974.
Selected by Milwaukee Brewers' organization in secondary phase of free-agent draft, January 9, 1975.
†On disabled list, August 26 to September 5, 1975.
‡On disabled list, April 30 to May 18, 1979.
§Traded to Baltimore Orioles for Pitcher John Flinn, December 6, 1979.
xOn suspended list, April 16 to April 21, 1980.
yOn disabled list, November 9, 1980 through May 28, 1981.
zGranted free agency, November 12, 1985; signed by Tacoma (Oakland A's organization), February 1, 1986.
aGranted free agency, November 12, 1986; signed by New York Yankees, December 16, 1986.

WORLD SERIES RECORD

Year Club	League	Pos.	G.	AB.	R.	H.	2B.	3B.	HR.	RBI.	B.A.	PO.	A.	E.	F.A.
1983—Baltimore	Amer.	PR-2B	1	1	0	0	0	0	0	0	.000	2	2	0	1.000

MARK BRUCE SALAS

Name pronounced SAL-us.
Born March 8, 1961, at Montebello, Calif.
Height, 6.00. Weight, 180.
Throws right and bats lefthanded.

Major League stolen bases: 1986 (3).
Tied for Florida State League lead in sacrifice flies with 10 in 1981.
Tied for Appalachian League lead in passed balls with 10 in 1979.

Year Club	League	Pos.	G.	AB.	R.	H.	2B.	3B.	HR.	RBI.	B.A.	PO.	A.	E.	F.A.
1979—Johnson City	Appal.	C	53	144	23	35	4	2	5	23	.243	194	19	6	.973
1980—Gastonia.................	S. Atl.	C	98	267	42	67	8	3	9	46	.251	452	41	5	★.990
1981—St. Petersburg.......	Fla St.	●C-1B	100	321	26	78	9	2	2	52	.243	387	66	●13	.972
1982—Arkansas................	Texas	C	27	76	4	17	4	0	0	5	.224	88	15	1	.990
1982—Louisville†.............	A. A.	C	7	22	1	4	0	0	0	1	.182	16	3	1	.950
1982—Nashville...............	South.	C	43	137	19	35	7	0	6	20	.255	267	24	7	.977
1983—Arkansas................	Texas	C-OF	131	473	76	144	25	4	20	82	.304	334	41	4	.989
1984—Louisville	A. A.	C-OF	95	316	28	77	20	2	12	48	.244	260	28	7	.976
1984—St. Louis‡..............	Nat.	C-OF	14	20	1	2	1	0	0	1	.100	13	2	0	1.000
1985—Minnesota.............	Amer.	C	120	360	51	108	20	5	9	41	.300	529	39	5	.991
1986—Minnesota§...........	Amer.	C	91	258	28	60	7	4	8	33	.233	358	32	8	.980
National League Totals—1 Year.............			14	20	1	2	1	0	0	1	.100	13	2	0	1.000
American League Totals—2 Years			211	618	79	168	27	9	17	74	.272	887	71	13	.987
Major League Totals—3 Years			225	638	80	170	28	9	17	75	.266	900	73	13	.987

Selected by St. Louis Cardinals' organization in 18th round of free-agent draft, June 5, 1979.
†Loaned to Nashville (New York Yankees' organization), June 30, 1982; returned, September 13, 1982.
‡Drafted by Minnesota Twins, December 3, 1984.
§On disabled list, May 24 to June 17, 1986.

ARGENIS ANTONIO SALAZAR
(Angel)

Born November 4, 1961, at El Tigre, Venezuela.
Height, 6.00. Weight, 173.
Throws and bats righthanded.

Major League stolen bases: 1984 (1), 1986 (1). Total—2.
Tied for Pioneer League lead in double plays by shortstops with 45 in 1981.

Year Club	League	Pos.	G.	AB.	R.	H.	2B.	3B.	HR.	RBI.	B.A.	PO.	A.	E.	F.A.
1980—W. Palm Beach†....	Fla. St.					(Did not play)									
1980—Calgary	Pion.	S-2-1-C	51	169	29	41	2	0	0	11	.243	60	126	17	.916
1981—Calgary	Pion.	SS	63	259	37	64	5	3	2	25	.247	89	★228	13	★.961
1982—W. Palm Beach....	Fla. St.	SS	112	408	63	109	15	2	2	36	.267	176	★364	35	.939
1983—Wichita	A. A.	SS	98	341	47	103	23	7	1	54	.302	152	256	24	.944
1983—Montreal	Nat.	SS	36	37	5	8	1	1	0	1	.216	28	28	2	.966
1984—Montreal	Nat.	SS	80	174	12	27	4	2	0	12	.155	88	155	10	.960
1984—Indianapolis‡§	A. A.	SS-3B	50	156	11	43	8	1	1	14	.276	54	117	3	.983
1985—Tidewater xy........	Int.	SS-2B	84	230	25	58	10	1	0	18	.252	119	244	16	.958
1986—Kansas City..........	Amer.	SS-2B	117	298	24	73	20	2	0	24	.245	121	284	9	.978
National League Totals—2 Years.............			116	211	17	35	5	3	0	13	.166	116	183	12	.961
American League Totals—1 Year			117	298	24	73	20	2	0	24	.245	121	284	9	.978
Major League Totals—3 Years.................			233	509	41	108	25	5	0	37	.212	237	467	21	.971

Signed as free agent by Montreal Expos' organization, January 20, 1980.
†On temporarily inactive list, April 10 to June 1, 1980.
‡Selected by St. Louis Cardinals' organization in player compensation pool draft, January 24, 1985. (St. Louis received compensation for Atlanta Braves' signing of free agent Pitcher Bruce Sutter, a Type A player, December 7, 1984.)
§Traded with Pitcher John Young to New York Mets' organization for Shortstop Jose Oquendo and Pitcher Mark Jason Davis, April 2, 1985.
xOn disabled list, April 13 to April 27 and June 16 to July 2, 1985.
yTraded to Kansas City Royals for Pitcher Tony Ferreira, April 1, 1986.

LUIS ERNESTO SALAZAR

Born May 19, 1956, at Barcelona, Venezuela.
Height, 6.00. Weight, 185.
Throws and bats righthanded.

Major League stolen bases: 1980 (11), 1981 (11), 1982 (32), 1983 (24), 1984 (11), 1985 (14). Total—103.
Led National League third basemen in errors with 26 and tied for lead in double plays with 28 in 1982.
Led Eastern League outfielders in putouts with 312 and tied for lead in double plays with 3 in 1979.

Year	Club	League	Pos.	G.	AB.	R.	H.	2B.	3B.	HR.	RBI.	B.A.	PO.	A.	E.	F.A.
1974—Sarasota Royals†	Gulf C.	SS	2	4	0	1	0	0	0	1	.250	0	2	0	1.000
1976—Niagara Falls	NYP	SS-OF	42	151	18	36	3	4	1	17	.238	71	49	17	.876
1977—Salem	Carol.	SS-3B-2B	116	433	72	117	17	5	11	48	.270	157	294	45	.909
1978—Salem	Carol.	OF-3B-SS	126	472	55	138	20	4	3	49	.292	160	77	19	.926
1979—Buffalo	East.	OF-3B	★139	★561	★108	★181	17	5	27	86	.323	321	42	13	.965
1980—Port.‡-Hawaii	P. C.	OF	127	497	91	157	23	15	9	64	.316	304	11	8	.975
1980—San Diego	Nat.	3B-OF	44	169	28	57	4	7	1	25	.337	39	88	7	.948
1981—San Diego	Nat.	3B-OF	109	400	37	121	19	6	3	38	.303	108	191	14	.955
1982—San Diego	Nat.	3B-SS-OF	145	524	55	127	15	5	8	62	.242	133	326	29	.941
1983—San Diego	Nat.	3B-SS	134	481	52	124	16	2	14	45	.258	122	274	21	.950
1984—San Diego§x	Nat.	3B-OF-SS	93	228	20	55	7	2	3	17	.241	87	97	6	.968
1985—Chicago	Amer.	OF-3B-1B	122	327	39	80	18	2	10	45	.245	180	57	10	.960
1986—Appleton y	Midw.	3B	21	79	9	16	1	0	2	4	.203	9	39	5	.906
1986—Chicago	Amer.	DH-PH	4	7	1	1	0	0	0	0	.143	0	0	0	.000
National League Totals—5 Years			525	1802	192	484	61	22	29	187	.269	489	976	77	.950
American League Totals—2 Years			126	334	40	81	18	2	10	45	.243	180	57	10	.960
Major League Totals—7 Years			651	2136	232	565	79	24	39	232	.265	669	1033	87	.951

Signed as free agent by Kansas City Royals' organization, November 29, 1973.
†Released, July 8, 1974; signed by Pittsburgh Pirates' organization, November 23, 1975.
‡Traded with Outfielder Rick Lancellotti to San Diego Padres' organization for Infielder Kurt Bevacqua and a player to be named later, August 4, 1980; Pittsburgh Pirates' organization acquired Pitcher Mark Lee to complete deal, August 12, 1980.
§On disabled list, May 15 to June 11, 1984.
xTraded with Pitchers Tim Lollar and Bill Long and Shortstop Ozzie Guillen to Chicago White Sox for Pitchers LaMarr Hoyt, Kevin Kristan and Todd Simmons, December 6, 1984.
yOn Chicago disabled list, April 4 to August 8, August 16 to September 1 and September 8, 1986 through remainder of season; included rehabilitation disability assignment to Appleton, July 17 to August 6, 1986.

CHAMPIONSHIP SERIES RECORD

Year	Club	League	Pos.	G.	AB.	R.	H.	2B.	3B.	HR.	RBI.	B.A.	PO.	A.	E.	F.A.
1984—San Diego	Nat.	3B-PH-OF	3	5	0	1	0	1	0	0	.200	1	3	0	1.000

WORLD SERIES RECORD

Year	Club	League	Pos.	G.	AB.	R.	H.	2B.	3B.	HR.	RBI.	B.A.	PO.	A.	E.	F.A.
1984—San Diego†	Nat.	3B-OF	4	3	0	1	0	0	0	0	.333	1	0	0	1.000

†Also appeared as a pinch-runner and pinch-hitter.

JOSEPH CHARLES SAMBITO

Name pronounced Sam-BEET-oh.

(Joe)

Born June 28, 1952, at Brooklyn, N.Y.
Height, 6.01. Weight, 190.
Throws and bats lefthanded.
Attended Adelphi University, Garden City, N.Y.

Major League saves: 1976 (1), 1977 (7), 1978 (11), 1979 (22), 1980 (17), 1981 (10), 1982 (4), 1986 (12). Total—84.
Led Southern League in wild pitches with 14 and tied for lead in games started by pitchers with 28 in 1975.
Tied for Appalachian League lead in shutouts with 2 in 1973.

Year	Club	League	G.	IP.	W.	L.	Pct.	H.	R.	ER.	SO.	BB.	ERA.
1973—Columbus	Southern	1	2	0	0	.000	4	4	4	2	1	18.00
1973—Covington	Ap'lachian	11	55	4	2	.667	32	18	9	13	13	1.47
1974—Cedar Rapids	Midwest	23	156	11	8	.579	133	59	52	182	49	3.00
1975—Columbus	Southern	30	★209	12	9	.571	★200	85	70	★140	85	3.01
1976—Memphis	Int'national	5	27	3	0	1.000	37	19	19	17	13	6.33
1976—Columbus	Southern	12	100	8	2	.800	77	27	20	61	23	1.80
1976—Houston	National	20	53	3	2	.600	45	21	21	26	14	3.57
1977—Houston	National	54	89	5	5	.500	77	34	23	67	24	2.33
1978—Houston	National	62	88	4	9	.308	85	32	30	96	32	3.07
1979—Houston	National	63	91	8	7	.533	80	20	18	83	23	1.78
1980—Houston	National	64	90	8	4	.667	65	26	22	75	22	2.20
1981—Houston	National	49	64	5	5	.500	43	17	13	41	22	1.83
1982—Houston†	National	9	12⅔	0	0	.000	7	2	1	7	2	0.71
1983—Houston‡	National						(Did not play)					
1984—Tucson§	P. Coast	8	8	0	0	.000	5	2	2	5	4	2.25
1984—Houston x	National	32	47⅓	0	0	.000	39	16	16	26	16	3.02
1985—New York	National	8	10⅔	0	0	.000	21	18	15	3	8	12.66
1985—Tidewater y	Int'national	19	20⅔	0	3	.000	31	15	10	12	11	4.35
1986—Boston z	American	53	44⅔	2	0	1.000	54	26	24	30	16	4.84
National League Totals—10 Years		361	546	33	32	.508	462	186	159	424	163	2.62
American League Totals—1 Year		53	44⅔	2	0	1.000	54	26	24	30	16	4.84
Major League Totals—11 Years		414	590⅔	35	32	.522	516	212	183	454	179	2.79

Selected by Houston Astros' organization in 17th round of free-agent draft, June 5, 1973.
†On disabled list, May 20, 1982 through remainder of season.
‡On disabled list, March 30, 1983 through remainder of season.
§On Houston disabled list, April 2 to May 25, 1984; included rehabilitation disability assignment to Tucson, May 9 to May 25, 1984.
xReleased, April 8, 1985; signed by New York Mets, April 26, 1985.
yReleased, August 23, 1985; signed by Pawtucket (Boston Red Sox' organization), January 31, 1986.
zGranted free agency, November 12, 1986; re-signed by Red Sox, December 5, 1986.

DIVISION SERIES RECORD

Year Club	League	G.	IP.	W.	L.	Pct.	H.	R.	ER.	SO.	BB.	ERA.
1981—Houston	National	2	1⅔	1	0	1.000	5	3	3	2	2	16.20

CHAMPIONSHIP SERIES RECORD

Year Club	League	G.	IP.	W.	L.	Pct.	H.	R.	ER.	SO.	BB.	ERA.
1980—Houston	National	3	3⅔	0	1	.000	4	2	2	6	2	4.91
1986—Boston	American	3	⅔	0	0	.000	1	0	0	0	1	0.00
Championship Series Totals—2 Years		6	4⅓	0	1	.000	5	2	2	6	3	4.15

WORLD SERIES RECORD

Year Club	League	G.	IP.	W.	L.	Pct.	H.	R.	ER.	SO.	BB.	ERA.
1986—Boston	American	2	⅓	0	0	.000	2	1	1	0	2	27.00

ALL-STAR GAME RECORD

Year League	IP.	W.	L.	Pct.	H.	R.	ER.	SO.	BB.	ERA.
1979—National	⅔	0	0	.000	0	0	0	0	1	0.00

WILLIAM AMOS SAMPLE
(Billy)

Born April 2, 1955, at Roanoke, Va.
Height, 5.09. Weight, 175.
Throws and bats righthanded.
Received bachelor of science degree in psychology from
James Madison University, Harrisonburg, Va.

Tied major league records for highest fielding percentage by outfielder, season, 100 or more games (1.000), 1979; most assists by outfielder, inning (2), April 28, 1979 (fourth inning).
Major League stolen bases: 1979 (8), 1980 (8), 1981 (4), 1982 (10), 1983 (44), 1984 (18), 1985 (2), 1986 (4). Total—98.
Led Pacific Coast League in bases on balls received with 109 in 1978.
Led Gulf Coast League in total bases with 86 in 1976.
Led Texas League second basemen in errors with 23 in 1977.

Year—Club	League	Pos.	G.	AB.	R.	H.	2B.	3B.	HR.	RBI.	B.A.	PO.	A.	E.	F.A.
1976—Sarasota Rang.	Gulf C.	2B	45	152	35	58	7	∗9	1	33	∗.382	81	113	8	.960
1977—Tulsa	Texas	2B-OF-3B	113	408	86	142	26	∗13	7	72	.348	169	122	26	.918
1978—Tucson	P. C.	OF-2B	131	483	∗141	170	27	13	18	99	.352	234	11	6	.976
1978—Texas	Amer.	OF	8	15	2	7	2	0	0	3	.467	0	0	0	.000
1979—Texas	Amer.	OF	128	325	60	95	21	2	5	35	.292	173	7	0	1.000
1980—Texas	Amer.	OF	99	204	29	53	10	0	4	19	.260	105	2	3	.973
1981—Texas†	Amer.	OF	66	230	36	65	16	0	3	25	.283	132	4	1	.993
1981—Wichita	A. A.	OF	3	14	2	5	1	0	0	2	.357	9	0	0	1.000
1982—Texas	Amer.	OF	97	360	56	94	14	2	10	29	.261	196	6	4	.981
1983—Texas	Amer.	OF	147	554	80	152	28	3	12	57	.274	329	8	4	.988
1984—Texas‡	Amer.	OF	130	489	67	121	20	2	5	33	.247	285	3	4	.986
1985—New York§	Amer.	OF	59	139	18	40	5	0	1	15	.288	89	1	1	.989
1986—Atlanta x	Nat.	OF-2B	92	200	23	57	11	0	6	14	.285	69	1	1	.986
American League Totals—8 Years			734	2316	348	627	116	9	40	216	.271	1309	31	17	.987
National League Totals—1 Year			92	200	23	57	11	0	6	14	.285	69	1	1	.986
Major League Totals—9 Years			826	2516	371	684	127	9	46	230	.272	1378	32	18	.987

Selected by Texas Rangers' organization in 28th round of free-agent draft, June 5, 1973.
Selected by Texas Rangers' organization in 10th round of free-agent draft, June 8, 1976.
†On disabled list, May 6 to June 2, 1981; included rehabilitation disability assignment to Wichita, May 28 to June 2, 1981.
‡Traded with a player to be named later to New York Yankees for Third Baseman Toby Harrah, February 27, 1985; New York organization acquired Pitcher Eric Dersin to complete deal, July 14, 1985.
§Traded to Atlanta Braves for Infielder Miguel Sosa, December 6, 1985.
xGranted free agency, November 12, 1986.

JUAN MILTON SAMUEL

Name pronounced SAHM-well.

Born December 9, 1960, at San Pedro de Macoris, D.R.
Height, 5.11. Weight, 170.
Throws and bats righthanded.

Established major league records for most at-bats by righthander, season (701), 1984; fewest sacrifice hits, most at-bats, season (0 and 701), 1984.
Tied major league record for most assists by second baseman, nine-inning game (12), April 20, 1985.
Established National League record for most at-bats, season (701), 1984.
Major League stolen bases: 1983 (3), 1984 (72), 1985 (53), 1986 (42). Total—170.
Led National League batters in strikeouts with 168 in 1984, 142 in 1986 and tied for lead with 141 in 1985.

— 434 —

Led Carolina League in total bases with 283 and tied for lead in being hit by pitch with 15 in 1982.
Led Northwest League batters in strikeouts with 87 and caught stealing with 10 in 1980.
Led Carolina League second basemen in double plays with 82 and total chances with 721 in 1982.
Led South Atlantic League second basemen in double plays with 82 and total chances with 737 in 1981.
Named National League Rookie Player of the Year by THE SPORTING NEWS, 1984.
Named Carolina League Most Valuable Player, 1982.

Year	Club	League	Pos.	G.	AB.	R.	H.	2B.	3B.	HR.	RBI.	B.A.	PO.	A.	E.	F.A.
1980—Cen. Oregon	N'west	2B	69	*298	66	84	11	2	17	44	.282	162	188	*30	.921
1981—Spartanburg	S. Atl.	2B	135	512	88	127	22	8	11	74	.248	*280	*409	*50	.932
1982—Peninsula	Carol.	2B	135	494	*111	158	29	6	28	94	.320	*244	*442	*35	.951
1983—Reading	East.	2B	47	184	36	43	10	0	11	39	.234	121	127	14	.947
1983—Portland	P. C.	2B	65	261	59	86	14	8	15	52	.330	110	168	15	.949
1983—Philadelphia	Nat.	2B	18	65	14	18	1	2	2	5	.277	44	54	9	.916
1984—Philadelphia	Nat.	2B	160	*701	105	191	36	●19	15	69	.272	388	438	*33	.962
1985—Philadelphia	Nat.	2B	161	*663	101	175	31	13	19	74	.264	*389	463	15	.983
1986—Philadelphia†	Nat.	2B	145	591	90	157	36	12	16	78	.266	290	440	*25	.967
Major League Totals—4 Years			484	2020	310	541	104	46	52	226	.268	1111	1395	82	.968

Signed as free agent by Philadelphia Phillies' organization, April 29, 1980.
†On disabled list, April 13 to May 2, 1986.

CHAMPIONSHIP SERIES RECORD

Year	Club	League	Pos.	G.	AB.	R.	H.	2B.	3B.	HR.	RBI.	B.A.	PO.	A.	E.	F.A.
1983—Philadelphia	Nat.	PR	1	0	0	0	0	0	0	0	.000	0	0	0	.000

WORLD SERIES RECORD

Year	Club	League	Pos.	G.	AB.	R.	H.	2B.	3B.	HR.	RBI.	B.A.	PO.	A.	E.	F.A.
1983—Philadelphia	Nat.	PR-PH	3	1	0	0	0	0	0	0	.000	0	0	0	.000

ALL-STAR GAME RECORD

Member of National League All-Star Team in 1984; did not play.

ALEJANDRO SANCHEZ (PIMENTEL)
(Alex)

Born February 26, 1959, at San Pedro, Dominican Republic.
Height, 6.00. Weight, 175.
Throws and bats righthanded.

Tied American League record for most home runs by pinch-hitter, consecutive at-bats (2), July 20 and 23, 1985.
Major League stolen bases: 1984 (2), 1985 (2). Total—4.
Led Pacific Coast League in total bases with 294 in 1984.
Tied for International League lead in double plays by outfielders with 3 in 1986.
Named Pacific Coast League Player of the Year, 1984.

Year	Club	League	Pos.	G.	AB.	R.	H.	2B.	3B.	HR.	RBI.	B.A.	PO.	A.	E.	F.A.
1978—Helena	Pion.	OF	6	24	4	5	0	1	0	5	.208	2	1	0	1.000
1978—Auburn	NYP	OF	58	242	30	58	9	5	4	28	.240	120	6	*14	.900
1979—Cen. Oregon	N'west	OF	54	204	31	55	10	2	3	38	.270	97	6	5	.954
1980—Spartanburg	S. Atl.	OF	127	490	84	140	26	8	15	76	.286	223	15	●16	.937
1981—Reading	East.	OF	138	495	77	136	19	*17	13	76	.275	216	13	15	.939
1982—Oklahoma City†	A. A.	OF	88	320	57	98	24	7	13	46	.306	155	10	●9	.948
1982—Philadelphia	Nat.	OF	7	14	3	4	1	0	2	4	.286	7	0	0	1.000
1983—Portland	P. C.	OF	125	458	75	113	21	5	17	74	.247	219	●18	*12	.952
1983—Philadelphia‡	Nat.	OF	8	7	2	2	0	0	0	2	.286	1	0	1	.500
1984—Phoenix	P. C.	OF	135	532	98	169	29	9	26	108	.318	249	10	12	.956
1984—San Francisco§	Nat.	OF	13	41	3	8	0	1	0	2	.195	18	2	1	.952
1985—Nashville	A. A.	OF	10	38	6	9	1	0	2	5	.237	17	0	0	1.000
1985—Detroit x	Amer.	OF	71	133	19	33	6	2	6	12	.248	35	1	3	.923
1986—Minnesota	Amer.	OF	8	16	1	2	0	0	0	1	.125	0	0	0	.000
1986—Toledo	Int.	OF	99	349	47	95	19	1	10	47	.272	176	9	10	.949
National League Totals—3 Years			28	62	8	14	1	1	2	8	.226	26	2	2	.933
American League Totals—2 Years			79	149	20	35	6	2	6	13	.235	35	1	3	.923
Major League Totals—5 Years			107	211	28	49	7	3	8	21	.232	61	3	5	.928

Signed as free agent by Philadelphia Phillies' organization, April 10, 1978.
†On disabled list, July 1 to August 5, 1982.
‡Traded to San Francisco Giants' organization for First Baseman Dave Bergman, March 24, 1984.
§Traded to Detroit Tigers' organization for Pitcher Roger Mason, April 5, 1985.
xTraded with Infielder Chris Pittaro to Minnesota Twins for Catcher Dave Engle, January 16, 1986.

ISRAEL SANCHEZ JR.

Born August 20, 1963, at Falcon, Cuba.
Height, 5.09. Weight, 170.
Throws and bats lefthanded.

Year	Club	League	G.	IP.	W.	L.	Pct.	H.	R.	ER.	SO.	BB.	ERA.
1982—Sarasota Royals	Gulf Coast	12	61	3	5	.375	63	41	31	49	36	4.57
1983—Charleston	S. Atlantic	30	163	10	6	.625	172	92	65	130	70	3.59
1984—Fort Myers†	Florida St.	14	66⅔	3	3	.500	62	30	27	63	29	3.65
1985—Fort Myers‡	Florida St.	28	98⅓	8	6	.571	72	32	23	86	27	2.11
1986—Memphis	Southern	28	184⅓	13	7	.650	190	97	71	141	55	3.47
1986—Omaha	Am. Assoc.	1	3	0	1	.000	4	3	3	2	2	9.00

Selected by Kansas City Royals' organization in 9th round of free-agent draft, June 7, 1982.
†On disabled list, May 26 to June 18 and June 29 to August 22, 1984.
‡On disabled list, April 12 to May 1, 1985.

ZOILO PARAHOY SANCHEZ

Born August 27, 1964, at Santo Domingo, D. R.
Height, 6.01. Weight, 175.
Throws and bats righthanded.

Led Carolina League third basemen in total chances with 413 in 1986.
Led South Atlantic League third basemen in total chances with 388 in 1985.
Led Gulf Coast League shortstops in putouts with 50, total chances with 154, double plays with 9 and tied for lead in errors with 19 in 1983.

Year Club	League	Pos.	G.	AB.	R.	H.	2B.	3B.	HR.	RBI.	B.A.	PO.	A.	E.	F.A.
1983—Sarasota Mets	Gulf C.	3B-SS	57	164	21	39	5	2	0	24	.238	51	85	20	.872
1984—Kingsport	Appal.	3B-2B	50	158	25	41	8	0	4	30	.259	66	92	15	.913
1984—Columbia	S. Atl.	2B	5	12	2	2	1	0	0	1	.167	8	8	1	.941
1985—Columbia	S. Atl.	3B	129	496	68	117	21	3	15	94	.236	80	*276	32	*.918
1986—Lynchburg	Carol.	3B	128	459	78	136	25	6	14	85	.296	88	*300	25	.939

Signed as free agent by New York Mets' organization, February 4, 1983.

RYNE DEE SANDBERG

Born September 18, 1959, at Spokane, Wash.
Height, 6.01. Weight, 175.
Throws and bats righthanded.

Tied major league records for most assists by second baseman, nine-inning game (12), June 12, 1983; fewest errors by second baseman, season, 150 or more games (5), 1986.
Established National League record for highest fielding average by second baseman, season (.994), 1986.
Major League stolen bases: 1982 (32), 1983 (37), 1984 (32), 1985 (54), 1986 (34). Total—189.
Led National League second basemen in total chances with 914 in 1983 and 870 in 1984.
Led National League second basemen in assists with 571 and double plays with 126 in 1983.
Led Eastern League shortstops in fielding percentage with .964, assists with 386 and double plays with 81 in 1980.
Led Western Carolinas League shortstops in double plays with 80 in 1979.
Led Pioneer League shortstops in double plays with 39 in 1978.
Named Major League Player of the Year by THE SPORTING NEWS, 1984.
Named National League Player of the Year by THE SPORTING NEWS, 1984.
Named National League Most Valuable Player by Baseball Writers' Association of America, 1984.
Named second baseman on THE SPORTING NEWS National League All-Star Team, 1984.
Named second baseman on THE SPORTING NEWS National League All-Star fielding team, 1983 through 1986.
Named second baseman on THE SPORTING NEWS National League Silver Slugger team, 1984 and 1985.
Received reported $30,000 bonus to sign with Philadelphia Phillies, 1978.

Year Club	League	Pos.	G.	AB.	R.	H.	2B.	3B.	HR.	RBI.	B.A.	PO.	A.	E.	F.A.
1978—Helena	Pion.	SS	56	190	34	59	6	6	1	23	.311	92	*200	24	.924
1979—Spartanburg	W. Car.	SS	*138	*539	83	133	21	7	4	47	.247	134	*467	35	*.945
1980—Reading	East.	SS-3B	129	490	95	152	21	12	11	79	.310	156	388	20	.965
1981—Oklahoma City	A. A.	SS-2B	133	519	78	152	17	5	9	62	.293	229	396	21	.967
1981—Philadelphia†	Nat.	SS-2B	13	6	2	1	0	0	0	0	.167	7	7	0	1.000
1982—Chicago	Nat.	3B-2B	156	635	103	172	33	5	7	54	.271	136	373	12	.977
1983—Chicago	Nat.	*2B-SS	158	633	94	165	25	4	8	48	.261	330	572	13	*.986
1984—Chicago	Nat.	2B	156	636	*114	200	36	●19	19	84	.314	314	*550	6	*.993
1985—Chicago	Nat.	2B-SS	153	609	113	186	31	6	26	83	.305	353	501	12	.986
1986—Chicago	Nat.	2B	154	627	68	178	28	5	14	76	.284	309	*492	5	*.994
Major League Totals—6 Years			790	3146	494	902	153	39	74	345	.287	1449	2495	48	.988

Selected by Philadelphia Phillies' organization in 20th round of free-agent draft, June 6, 1978.
†Traded with Shortstop Larry Bowa to Chicago Cubs for Shortstop Ivan DeJesus, January 27, 1982.

CHAMPIONSHIP SERIES RECORD

Year Club	League	Pos.	G.	AB.	R.	H.	2B.	3B.	HR.	RBI.	B.A.	PO.	A.	E.	F.A.
1984—Chicago	Nat.	2B	5	19	3	7	2	0	0	2	.368	13	18	1	.969

ALL-STAR GAME RECORD

Year League	Pos.	AB.	R.	H.	2B.	3B.	HR.	RBI.	B.A.	PO.	A.	E.	F.A.
1984—National	2B	4	0	1	0	0	0	0	.250	0	0	0	.000
1985—National	2B	1	1	0	0	0	0	0	.000	0	3	0	1.000
1986—National	2B	3	0	0	0	0	0	0	.000	0	2	1	.667
All-Star Game Totals—3 Years		8	1	1	0	0	0	0	.125	0	5	1	.833

SCOTT DOUGLAS SANDERSON

Born July 22, 1956, at Dearborn, Mich.
Height, 6.05. Weight, 198.
Throws and bats righthanded.
Attended Vanderbilt University, Nashville, Tenn.

Tied National League record for most consecutive home runs allowed, inning (3), July 11, 1982 (second inning).
Major League saves: 1979 (1), 1983 (1), 1986 (1). Total—3.

Year Club	League	G.	IP.	W.	L.	Pct.	H.	R.	ER.	SO.	BB.	ERA.
1977—West Palm Beach	Florida St.	10	57	5	2	.714	58	22	17	37	23	2.68
1978—Memphis............................	Southern	9	58	5	3	.625	55	32	26	44	19	4.03
1978—Denver	Am. Assoc.	9	49	4	2	.667	47	35	33	36	30	6.06
1978—Montreal	National	10	61	4	2	.667	52	20	17	50	21	2.51
1979—Montreal	National	34	168	9	8	.529	148	69	64	138	54	3.43
1980—Montreal	National	33	211	16	11	.593	206	76	73	125	56	3.11
1981—Montreal	National	22	137	9	7	.563	122	50	45	77	31	2.96
1982—Montreal	National	32	224	12	12	.500	212	98	86	158	58	3.46
1983—Montreal‡..........................	National	18	81⅓	6	7	.462	98	50	42	55	20	4.65
1984—Chicago§	National	24	140⅔	8	5	.615	140	54	49	76	24	3.14
1984—Lodi	California	1	5	0	1	.000	7	2	2	2	0	3.60
1985—Chicago x...........................	National	19	121	5	6	.455	100	49	42	80	27	3.12
1986—Chicago	National	37	169⅔	9	11	.450	165	85	79	124	37	4.19
Major League Totals—9 Years..............................		229	1313⅔	78	69	.531	1243	551	497	883	328	3.40

Selected by Kansas City Royals' organization in 11th round of free-agent draft, June 5, 1974.
Selected by Montreal Expos' organization in 3rd round of free-agent draft, June 7, 1977.
†On disabled list, July 5 to September 1, 1983.
‡Traded with Infielder Al Newman to San Diego Padres for Pitcher Gary Lucas, December 7, 1983; Traded by San Diego to Chicago Cubs for First Baseman Carmelo Martinez, Pitcher Craig Lefferts and Third Baseman Fritz Connally, December 7, 1983.
§On disabled list, June 1 to July 5, 1984; included rehabilitation disability assignment to Lodi, June 29 to July 5, 1984.
xOn disabled list, August 14, 1985 through remainder of season.

DIVISION SERIES RECORD

Year Club	League	G.	IP.	W.	L.	Pct.	H.	R.	ER.	SO.	BB.	ERA.
1981—Montreal	National	1	2⅔	0	0	.000	4	4	2	2	2	6.75

CHAMPIONSHIP SERIES RECORD

Year Club	League	G.	IP.	W.	L.	Pct.	H.	R.	ER.	SO.	BB.	ERA.
1984—Chicago	National	1	4⅔	0	0	.000	6	3	3	2	1	5.79

RAFAEL FRANCISCO SANTANA (DeLaCRUZ)

Born January 31, 1958, at La Romana, Dominican Republic.
Height, 6.01. Weight, 156.
Throws and bats righthanded.

Established National League record for fewest assists by shortstop, season, 150 or more games (396), 1985.
Major League stolen bases: 1985 (1).
Led New York-Pennsylvania League in sacrifice hits with 8 in 1977.
Led Texas League shortstops in fielding percentage with .955 and tied for lead in double plays with 79 in 1981.

Year Club	League	Pos.	G.	AB.	R.	H.	2B.	3B.	HR.	RBI.	B.A.	PO.	A.	E.	F.A.
1977—Oneonta............	NYP	SS	60	157	26	41	5	0	0	23	.261	62	162	★27	.892
1978—Fort Lauderdale ..	Fla. St.	SS	131	431	37	111	8	5	0	35	.258	166	372	★48	.918
1979—Fort Lauderdale ..	Fla. St.	SS-3B-2B	133	472	62	124	9	6	0	41	.263	160	351	16	.970
1980—Nashville............	South.	SS	86	275	33	64	4	3	0	20	.233	125	247	25	.937
1980—Fort Lauderdale†	Fla. St.	SS	51	168	20	38	2	0	1	17	.226	81	158	9	.964
1981—Arkansas............	Texas	SS-3B-2B	110	326	34	76	14	3	0	19	.233	154	350	23	.956
1981—Springfield..........	A. A.	SS-3B	2	8	3	4	1	0	1	2	.500	1	8	3	.750
1982—Louisville............	A. A.	3B-2B-SS	121	430	65	123	15	3	3	53	.286	163	275	11	.976
1983—St. Louis............	Nat.	2B-SS-3B	30	14	1	3	0	0	0	2	.214	3	8	4	.733
1983—Louisville‡..........	A. A.	3-2-S-1	45	167	19	47	9	1	0	20	.281	60	117	10	.947
1984—Tidewater............	Int.	S-3-2-1	77	255	34	71	6	0	1	23	.278	107	232	14	.960
1984—New York§..........	Nat.	SS	51	152	14	42	11	1	1	12	.276	92	104	6	.970
1985—New York............	Nat.	SS	154	529	41	136	19	1	1	29	.257	★301	396	25	.965
1986—New York............	Nat.	SS-2B	139	394	38	86	11	0	1	28	.218	203	369	16	.973
Major League Totals—4 Years................			374	1089	94	267	41	2	3	71	.245	599	877	51	.967

Signed as free agent by New York Yankees' organization, August 31, 1976.
†Traded to St. Louis Cardinals for a player to be named later, February 16, 1981; New York Yankees' organization acquired Pitcher George Frazier to complete deal, June 7, 1981.
‡Released, January 17, 1984; signed by Tidewater (New York Mets' organization), January 17, 1984.
§On disabled list, August 25 to September 9, 1984.

CHAMPIONSHIP SERIES RECORD

Year Club	League	Pos.	G.	AB.	R.	H.	2B.	3B.	HR.	RBI.	B.A.	PO.	A.	E.	F.A.
1986—New York............	Nat.	SS	6	17	0	3	0	0	0	0	.176	13	18	0	1.000

WORLD SERIES RECORD

Year Club	League	Pos.	G.	AB.	R.	H.	2B.	3B.	HR.	RBI.	B.A.	PO.	A.	E.	F.A.
1986—New York............	Nat.	SS	7	20	3	5	0	0	0	2	.250	11	17	1	.966

BENITO SANTIAGO (RIVERA)

Born September 3, 1965, at Ponce, P.R.
Height, 6.01. Weight, 180.
Throws and bats righthanded.

Led Pacific Coast League catchers in total chances with 655 in 1986.
Led Texas League in passed balls with 16 in 1985.
Led Florida State League catchers in double plays with 12 and passed balls with 26 in 1983.

Year Club	League	Pos.	G.	AB.	R.	H.	2B.	3B.	HR.	RBI.	B.A.	PO.	A.	E.	F.A.
1983—Miami	Fla. St.	C	122	429	34	106	25	3	5	56	.247	471	★69	★21	.963
1984—Reno	Calif.	C	114	416	64	116	20	6	16	83	.279	692	96	25	.969
1985—Beaumont†	Texas	★C-1B-3B	101	372	55	111	16	6	5	52	.298	525	★78	15	.976
1986—Las Vegas	P. C.	C	117	437	55	125	26	3	17	71	.286	★563	71	★21	.968
1986—San Diego	Nat.	C	17	62	10	18	2	0	3	6	.290	80	7	5	.946
Major League Totals—1 Year..................			17	62	10	18	2	0	3	6	.290	80	7	5	.946

Signed as free agent by San Diego Padres' organization, September 1, 1982.
†On disabled list, June 21 to July 2, 1985.

MACKEY DANIEL SASSER

Born August 3, 1962, at Fort Gaines, Ga.
Height, 6.01. Weight, 190.
Throws right and bats lefthanded.
Attended George C. Wallace Community College, Dothan, Ala.,
and Troy State University, Troy, Ala.
Led Texas League in intentional bases on balls received with 13 in 1986.
Led California League in total bases with 245 and tied for lead in game-winning RBIs with 16 in 1985.
Led California League in passed balls with 19 in 1985.

Year Club	League	Pos.	G.	AB.	R.	H.	2B.	3B.	HR.	RBI.	B.A.	PO.	A.	E.	F.A.
1984—Clinton..................	Midw.	1-3-O-C	118	428	57	125	20	5	6	65	.292	526	95	17	.973
1984—Fresno	Calif.	OF-3B-1B	16	62	8	17	1	0	6	.274	24	15	4	.907
1985—Fresno	Calif.	O-C-1-3	133	497	79	168	27	4	14	102	.338	402	42	14	.969
1986—Shreveport	Texas	C-1B-OF	120	441	52	129	29	5	5	72	.293	577	66	10	.985

Selected by San Francisco Giants' organization in 5th round of free-agent draft, January 17, 1984.

RICHARD D. SAUVEUR

(Rich)

Born November 23, 1963, at Arlington, Va.
Height, 6.04. Weight, 163.
Throws and bats lefthanded.
Attended Manatee Junior College, Bradenton, Fla.
Led Eastern League in balks with 4 in 1984 and tied for lead with 4 in 1985.
Tied for New York-Pennsylvania League lead in balks with 4 in 1983.

Year Club	League	G.	IP.	W.	L.	Pct.	H.	R.	ER.	SO.	BB.	ERA.
1983—Watertown	NYP	16	93⅔	7	5	.593	80	41	24	73	31	2.31
1984—Prince William†	Carolina	10	54⅔	3	3	.500	43	22	19	54	31	3.13
1984—Nashua	Eastern	10	70⅔	5	3	.625	54	27	23	48	34	2.93
1985—Nashua	Eastern	25	157⅓	9	10	.474	146	73	62	85	78	3.55
1986—Nashua	Eastern	5	38	3	1	.750	21	5	5	28	11	1.18
1986—Hawaii	P. Coast	14	92	7	6	.538	73	40	31	68	45	3.03
1986—Pittsburgh.....................................	National	3	12	0	0	.000	17	8	8	6	6	6.00
Major League Totals—1 Year..............................		3	12	0	0	.000	17	8	8	6	6	6.00

Selected by Pittsburgh Pirates' organization in 11th round of free-agent draft, January 11, 1983.
Selected by Pittsburgh Pirates' organization in secondary phase of free-agent draft, June 6, 1983.
†On disabled list, May 25 to July 5, 1984.

DAVID JOHN SAX

(Dave)

Born September 22, 1958, at Sacramento, Calif.
Height, 6.00. Weight, 185.
Throws and bats righthanded.
Brother of Steve Sax, second baseman with Los Angeles Dodgers.

Year Club	League	Pos.	G.	AB.	R.	H.	2B.	3B.	HR.	RBI.	B.A.	PO.	A.	E.	F.A.
1978—Lethbridge	Pion.	2-3-S-O	44	145	31	39	10	2	4	31	.269	79	80	13	.924
1979—Clinton..................	Midw.	C-3-O-1	97	282	37	76	18	1	6	49	.270	226	32	7	.974
1980—Lodi	Calif.	C-1-O-3	43	123	9	21	3	0	1	11	.171	159	25	8	.958
1980—Vero Beach	Fla. St.	OF-C-1B	58	193	33	68	8	5	2	33	.352	156	18	2	.989
1981—San Antonio†	Texas	C-OF	62	221	43	68	13	2	4	31	.308	231	17	5	.980
1982—Albuquerque	P. C.	C-3-1-O	117	417	71	132	29	1	12	75	.317	403	57	12	.975
1982—Los Angeles	Nat.	OF	2	2	0	0	0	0	0	0	.000	1	0	0	1.000
1983—Albuquerque	P. C.	C-1B	75	280	59	96	22	3	8	59	.343	159	18	3	.983
1983—Los Angeles	Nat.	C	7	8	0	0	0	0	1	.000	11	0	1	.917
1984—Albuquerque‡	P. C.	C-O-1-3	106	294	54	76	14	1	10	41	.259	297	27	11	.967
1985—Boston	Amer.	C-OF	22	36	2	11	3	0	0	6	.306	66	0	1	.985
1985—Pawtucket	Int.	C-OF-3B	20	61	6	13	2	0	1	4	.213	42	9	2	.962
1986—Pawtucket	Int.	3B-C-1B	99	322	31	93	19	1	9	49	.289	225	105	17	.951
1986—Boston	Amer.	C-1B	4	11	1	5	1	0	1	1	.455	14	1	0	1.000
National League Totals—2 Years			9	10	0	0	0	0	0	1	.000	12	0	1	.923
American League Totals—2 Years			26	47	3	16	4	0	1	7	.340	80	1	1	.988
Major League Totals—4 Years..............			35	57	3	16	4	0	1	8	.281	92	1	2	.979

Signed as free agent by Los Angeles Dodgers' organization, June 16, 1978.
†On disabled list, July 3 to September 15, 1981.
‡Granted free agency, October 15, 1984; signed by Pawtucket (Boston Red Sox' organization), January 23, 1985.

STEPHEN LOUIS SAX
(Steve)

Born January 29, 1960, at Sacramento, Calif.
Height, 5.11. Weight, 185.
Throws and bats righthanded.
Brother of David Sax, catcher in Boston Red Sox' organization.

Major League stolen bases: 1981 (5), 1982 (49), 1983 (56), 1984 (34), 1985 (27), 1986 (40). Total—211.
Led National League in caught stealing with 30 in 1983.
Led Florida State League second basemen in double plays with 91 in 1980.
Named second baseman on THE SPORTING NEWS National League All-Star Team, 1986.
Named second baseman on THE SPORTING NEWS National League Silver Slugger team, 1986.
Named National League Rookie of the Year by Baseball Writers' Association of America, 1982.
Named Texas League Most Valuable Player, 1981.

Year	Club	League	Pos.	G.	AB.	R.	H.	2B.	3B.	HR.	RBI.	B.A.	PO.	A.	E.	F.A.
1978—Lethbridge		Pion.	SS	39	131	24	43	6	3	0	21	.328	21	40	9	.871
1979—Clinton		Midw.	OF-2B-3B	115	386	64	112	15	2	2	52	.290	111	75	18	.912
1980—Vero Beach		Fla. St.	★2B-OF	●139	●530	78	150	18	8	3	61	.283	★360	★438	20	★.976
1981—San Antonio		Texas	2B	115	485	94	168	23	3	8	52	★.346	255	298	17	.970
1981—Los Angeles		Nat.	2B	31	119	15	33	2	0	2	9	.277	64	93	4	.975
1982—Los Angeles		Nat.	2B	150	638	88	180	23	7	4	47	.282	347	452	19	.977
1983—Los Angeles		Nat.	2B	155	623	94	175	18	5	5	41	.281	331	399	★30	.961
1984—Los Angeles		Nat.	2B	145	569	70	138	24	4	1	35	.243	318	450	21	.973
1985—Los Angeles†		Nat.	★2B-3B	136	488	62	136	8	4	1	42	.279	330	358	★22	.969
1986—Los Angeles		Nat.	2B	157	633	91	210	43	4	6	56	.332	●367	432	16	.980
Major League Totals—6 Years				774	3070	420	872	118	24	19	230	.284	1757	2184	112	.972

Selected by Los Angeles Dodgers' organization in 9th round of free-agent draft, June 6, 1978.
†On disabled list, April 19 to May 4, 1985.

DIVISION SERIES RECORD

Year	Club	League	Pos.	G.	AB.	R.	H.	2B.	3B.	HR.	RBI.	B.A.	PO.	A.	E.	F.A.
1981—Los Angeles		Nat.	2B	1	0	0	0	0	0	0	0	.000	0	0	0	.000

CHAMPIONSHIP SERIES RECORD

Year	Club	League	Pos.	G.	AB.	R.	H.	2B.	3B.	HR.	RBI.	B.A.	PO.	A.	E.	F.A.
1981—Los Angeles		Nat.	2B	1	0	0	0	0	0	0	0	.000	0	1	0	1.000
1983—Los Angeles		Nat.	2B	4	16	0	4	0	0	0	0	.250	11	12	0	1.000
1985—Los Angeles		Nat.	2B	6	20	1	6	3	0	0	1	.300	11	21	0	1.000
Championship Series Totals—3 Years				11	36	1	10	3	0	0	1	.278	22	34	0	1.000

WORLD SERIES RECORD

Year	Club	League	Pos.	G.	AB.	R.	H.	2B.	3B.	HR.	RBI.	B.A.	PO.	A.	E.	F.A.
1981—Los Angeles		Nat.	PH-PR-2	2	1	0	0	0	0	0	0	.000	0	0	0	.000

ALL-STAR GAME RECORD

Year	League	Pos.	AB.	R.	H.	2B.	3B.	HR.	RBI.	B.A.	PO.	A.	E.	F.A.
1982—National		PR-2B	1	0	1	0	0	0	0	1.000	2	0	1	.667
1983—National		2B	3	1	1	0	0	0	1	.333	2	0	1	.667
1986—National		2B	1	0	1	0	0	0	1	1.000	0	1	0	1.000
All-Star Game Totals—3 Years			5	1	3	0	0	0	2	.600	4	1	2	.714

ROBERT GUY SCANLAN JR.
(Bob)

Born August 9, 1966, at Los Angeles, Calif.
Height, 6.07. Weight, 200.
Throws and bats righthanded.
Attended University of California, Los Angeles, Calif.

Year	Club	League	G.	IP.	W.	L.	Pct.	H.	R.	ER.	SO.	BB.	ERA.
1984—Sarasota Phillies		Gulf Coast	13	33⅓	0	2	.000	43	31	24	17	30	6.48
1985—Spartanburg		S. Atlantic	26	152⅓	8	12	.400	160	95	70	108	53	4.14
1986—Clearwater		Florida St.	24	125⅔	8	12	.400	146	73	58	51	45	4.15

Selected by Philadelphia Phillies' organization in 25th round of free-agent draft, June 4, 1984.

DANIEL ERNEST SCHATZEDER

Name pronounced Shotz-AY-dur.

(Dan)

Born December 1, 1954, at Elmhurst, Ill.
Height, 6.00. Weight, 195.
Throws and bats lefthanded.
Received degree in business administration from University of Denver, Denver, Colo., in 1976.

Major League saves: 1979 (1), 1983 (2), 1984 (1), 1986 (2). Total—6.

Year	Club	League	G.	IP.	W.	L.	Pct.	H.	R.	ER.	SO.	BB.	ERA.
1976—West Palm Beach		Florida St.	10	64	5	3	.625	49	22	19	49	20	2.67
1976—Quebec City		Eastern	5	28	2	3	.400	38	16	14	19	10	4.50
1977—Quebec City		Eastern	8	62	5	3	.625	39	20	19	59	15	2.76

Year Club	League	G.	IP.	W.	L.	Pct.	H.	R.	ER.	SO.	BB.	ERA.
1977—Denver†	Am. Assoc.	9	36	2	2	.500	45	25	24	28	14	6.00
1977—Montreal	National	6	22	2	1	.667	16	6	6	14	13	2.45
1978—Denver	Am. Assoc.	4	28	3	0	1.000	24	11	9	19	11	2.89
1978—Montreal	National	29	144	7	7	.500	108	54	49	69	68	3.06
1979—Montreal‡	National	32	162	10	5	.667	136	57	51	106	59	2.83
1980—Detroit§	American	32	193	11	13	.458	178	88	86	94	58	4.01
1981—Detroit x	American	17	71	6	8	.429	74	49	48	20	29	6.08
1982—San Francisco y-Montreal	National	39	69⅓	1	6	.143	84	46	41	33	24	5.23
1982—Phoenix	P. Coast	1	3⅔	0	0	.000	10	6	5	1	3	12.27
1983—Montreal z	National	58	87	5	2	.714	88	34	31	48	25	3.21
1984—Montreal	National	36	136	7	7	.500	112	44	41	89	36	2.71
1985—Montreal a	National	24	104⅓	3	5	.375	101	52	44	64	31	3.80
1985—Indianapolis	Am. Assoc.	1	3	0	0	.000	2	0	0	3	1	0.00
1986—Montreal b-Philadelphia	National	55	88⅓	6	5	.545	81	43	32	47	35	3.26
National League Totals—8 Years		279	813	41	38	.519	726	336	295	470	291	3.27
American League Totals—2 Years		49	264	17	21	.447	252	137	134	114	87	4.57
Major League Totals—10 Years		328	1077	58	59	.496	978	473	429	584	378	3.58

Selected by Montreal Expos' organization in 3rd round of free-agent draft, June 8, 1976.
†On disabled list, July 5 to August 30, 1977.
‡Traded to Detroit Tigers for Outfielder Ron LeFlore, December 7, 1979.
§On disabled list, May 27 to June 17, 1980.
xTraded with Pitcher Mike Chris to San Francisco Giants for Outfielder Larry Herndon, December 9, 1981.
ySold to Montreal Expos, June 15, 1982.
zGranted free agency, November 7, 1983; re-signed by Expos, December 19, 1983.
aOn disabled list, June 21 to July 23 and August 7 to September 1, 1985; included rehabilitation disability assignment to Indianapolis, July 19 to July 23, 1985.
bTraded with Infielder Skeeter Barnes to Philadelphia Phillies for Infielder Tom Foley and Pitcher Lary Sorensen, July 24, 1986.

WILLIAM JOSEPH SCHERRER

Named pronounced SHURR-ur.

(Bill)

Born January 20, 1958, at Tonawanda, N. Y.
Height, 6.04. Weight, 180.
Throws and bats lefthanded.
Attended University of Nevada, Las Vegas, Nev.

Major League saves: 1983 (10), 1984 (1). Total—11.
Led American League in intentional bases on balls issued with 13 in 1985.
Tied for American Association lead in shutouts with 2 in 1982.
Tied for Northwest League lead in shutouts with 2 in 1978.

Year Club	League	G.	IP.	W.	L.	Pct.	H.	R.	ER.	SO.	BB.	ERA.
1977—Shelby	W. Carol.	27	158	9	9	.500	132	87	62	122	105	3.53
1978—Shelby	W. Carol.	10	31	0	2	.000	27	19	14	18	26	4.06
1978—Eugene	Northwest	13	84	6	4	.600	61	43	33	87	42	3.54
1979—Tampa	Florida St.	25	159	12	3	.800	126	43	32	140	65	1.81
1980—Waterbury	Eastern	25	151	7	8	.467	139	58	56	84	58	3.34
1981—Waterbury	Eastern	50	119	5	9	.357	121	70	57	89	62	4.31
1982—Tampa	Florida St.	7	47⅓	3	2	.600	37	13	12	45	18	2.28
1982—Waterbury	Eastern	5	31	1	3	.250	30	15	13	18	15	3.77
1982—Indianapolis	Am. Assoc.	19	88⅔	6	4	.600	68	43	40	81	32	4.06
1982—Cincinnati	National	5	17⅓	0	1	.000	17	7	5	7	0	2.60
1983—Cincinnati	National	73	92	2	3	.400	73	31	28	57	33	2.74
1984—Cincinnati†	National	36	52⅓	1	1	.500	64	31	29	35	15	4.99
1984—Wichita‡§	Am. Assoc.	10	16⅔	2	3	.400	16	6	6	14	11	3.24
1984—Detroit	American	18	19	1	0	1.000	14	4	4	16	8	1.89
1985—Detroit	American	48	66	3	2	.600	62	35	32	46	41	4.36
1986—Nashville	Am. Assoc.	31	58⅔	5	2	.714	60	36	33	49	28	5.06
1986—Detroit x	American	13	21	0	1	.000	19	19	17	16	22	7.29
National League Totals—3 Years		114	161⅔	3	5	.375	154	69	62	99	48	3.45
American League Totals—3 Years		79	106	4	3	.571	95	58	53	78	71	4.50
Major League Totals—5 Years		193	267⅔	7	8	.467	249	127	115	177	119	3.87

Selected by Cleveland Indians' organization in 6th round of free-agent draft, June 8, 1976.
Selected by Cincinnati Reds' organization in secondary phase of free-agent draft, January 11, 1977.
†On disabled list, April 18 to May 3, 1984.
‡On disabled list, July 31 to August 10, 1984.
§Traded to Detroit Tigers for cash and a player to be named later, August 27, 1984; Cincinnati Reds acquired Pitcher Carl Willis to complete deal, September 1, 1984.
xGranted free agency, October 15, 1986.

—DID YOU KNOW—

That when the 1986 Atlanta Braves defeated Los Angeles, 6-5, June 23, they stranded 18 baserunners, tying a National League record set in 1897?

Year Club	League	G.	IP.	W.	L.	Pct.	H.	R.	ER.	SO.	BB.	ERA.
1984—Detroit	American	3	3	0	0	.000	5	1	1	0	0	3.00

CALVIN DREW SCHIRALDI

Born June 16, 1962, at Houston, Tex.
Height, 6.04. Weight, 200.
Throws and bats righthanded.
Attended University of Texas, Austin, Tex.

Major League saves: 1986 (9).
Named Texas League Pitcher of the Year, 1984.

Year Club	League	G.	IP.	W.	L.	Pct.	H.	R.	ER.	SO.	BB.	ERA.
1983—Jackson	Texas	7	38⅔	3	3	.500	41	28	25	26	29	5.82
1983—Lynchburg	Carolina	6	30⅓	4	1	.800	28	16	15	41	17	4.45
1984—Jackson	Texas	23	156⅓	●14	3	*.824	118	58	50	131	69	2.88
1984—Tidewater	Int'national	4	31⅓	3	1	.750	18	6	4	24	10	1.15
1984—New York	National	5	17⅓	0	2	.000	20	13	11	16	10	5.71
1985—Tidewater	Int'national	17	100⅓	4	5	.444	91	50	39	76	56	3.50
1985—New York†‡	National	10	26⅓	2	1	.667	43	27	26	21	11	8.89
1986—Pawtucket	Int'national	31	44	4	3	.571	32	19	14	59	20	2.86
1986—Boston	American	25	51	4	2	.667	36	8	8	55	15	1.41
National League Totals—2 Years		15	43⅔	2	3	.400	63	40	37	37	21	7.63
American League Totals—1 Year		25	51	4	2	.667	36	8	8	55	15	1.41
Major League Totals—3 Years		40	94⅔	6	5	.545	99	48	45	92	36	4.28

Selected by Chicago White Sox' organization in 17th round of free-agent draft, June 3, 1980.
Selected by New York Mets' organization in 1st round (27th player selected) of free-agent draft, June 6, 1983.
†On disabled list, May 15 to May 30, 1985.
‡Traded with Pitcher Wes Gardner and Outfielders John Christensen and LaSchelle Tarver to Boston Red Sox for Pitchers Bob Ojeda, Tom McCarthy, John Mitchell and Chris Bayer, November 13, 1985.

CHAMPIONSHIP SERIES RECORD

Tied American League Championship Series records for most games pitched, seven game Series (4), 1986; most strikeouts by a relief pitcher, game (5), October 15, 1986.

Year Club	League	G.	IP.	W.	L.	Pct.	H.	R.	ER.	SO.	BB.	ERA.
1986—Boston	American	4	6	0	1	.000	5	2	1	9	3	1.50

WORLD SERIES RECORD

Tied World Series record for most games lost, seven-game Series (2), 1986.

Year Club	League	G.	IP.	W.	L.	Pct.	H.	R.	ER.	SO.	BB.	ERA.
1986—Boston	American	3	4	0	2	.000	7	7	6	2	3	13.50

DAVID JOSEPH SCHMIDT
(Dave)

Born April 22, 1957, at Niles, Mich.
Height, 6.01. Weight, 185.
Throws and bats righthanded.
Attended Los Angeles Valley College, Van Nuys, Calif., and University of California, Los Angeles, Calif.

Major League saves: 1981 (1), 1982 (6), 1983 (2), 1984 (12), 1985 (5), 1986 (8). Total—34.

Year Club	League	G.	IP.	W.	L.	Pct.	H.	R.	ER.	SO.	BB.	ERA.
1979—Sarasota Rangers	Gulf Coast	7	30	2	2	.500	30	19	14	27	8	4.20
1980—Asheville	S. Atlantic	12	91	8	1	.889	76	32	20	67	13	1.98
1980—Tulsa	Texas	12	73	4	6	.400	90	42	36	46	28	4.44
1981—Tulsa	Texas	3	24	1	1	.500	17	5	5	17	6	1.88
1981—Texas	American	14	32	0	1	.000	31	11	11	13	11	3.09
1981—Wichita	Am. Assoc.	12	87	2	5	.286	90	47	47	49	26	4.86
1982—Texas	American	33	109⅔	4	6	.400	118	45	39	69	25	3.20
1983—Texas†	American	31	46⅓	3	3	.500	42	20	20	29	14	3.88
1984—Texas	American	43	70⅓	6	6	.500	69	30	20	46	20	2.56
1985—Texas‡	American	51	85⅔	7	6	.538	81	36	30	46	22	3.15
1986—Chicago§	American	49	92⅓	3	6	.333	94	37	34	67	27	3.31
Major League Totals—6 Years		221	436⅓	23	28	.451	435	179	154	270	119	3.18

Selected by Texas Rangers' organization in 26th round of free-agent draft, June 5, 1979.
†On disabled list, March 25 to May 1, 1983.
‡Traded with Infielder Wayne Tolleson to Chicago White Sox for Pitcher Ed Correa, Infielder Scott Fletcher and a player to be named later, November 25, 1985; Texas Rangers acquired Infielder Jose Mota to complete deal, December 12, 1985.
§Released, December 20, 1986.

MICHAEL JACK SCHMIDT
(Mike)

Born September 27, 1949, at Dayton, O.
Height, 6.02. Weight, 203.
Throws and bats righthanded.
Received bachelor of arts degree in business administration from Ohio University, Athens, O. in 1971.

Established major league records for most total bases, extra-inning game (17), April 17, 1976 (10 innings); most home runs by third baseman, season (48), 1980.

Tied major league records for most home runs, extra-inning game (4), April 17, 1976 (10 innings); most consecutive home runs, extra-inning game (4), April 17, 1976 (10 innings); most home runs, consecutive plate appearances (4), April 17, 1976 and July 6 and 7, 1979; most extra bases on long hits, game (12), April 17, 1976 (10 innings); most home runs, two consecutive games (5), April 17 and 18, 1976; most home runs, three consecutive games (6), April 17-20, 1976; most home runs, month of April (11), 1976; most consecutive seasons leading major leagues in strikeouts (3), 1974 through 1976; most home runs, month of October (4), 1980.

Established National League records for most years leading league in home runs (8); most years leading league in extra bases on long hits (7); most assists, third baseman, season (404), 1974; fewest singles, season, 150 or more games (63), 1979.

Tied National League records for most years leading league in runs batted in (4); most home runs, bases full, one month, 2, June, 1973; most home runs through July 31 (36), 1979; most home runs, five consecutive games, one or more homer each game (7), July 6 through 10, 1979; most consecutive years leading league in extra bases on long hits (3, performed twice); most consecutive years leading league in bases on balls (3); most years leading league in assists by third baseman (7).

Hit three home runs in a game, July 7, 1979.

Hit home runs in all 12 National League parks, 1979.

Major League stolen bases: 1973 (8), 1974 (23), 1975 (29), 1976 (14), 1977 (15), 1978 (19), 1979 (9), 1980 (12), 1981 (12), 1982 (14), 1983 (7), 1984 (5), 1985 (1), 1986 (1). Total—169.

Led National League in intentional bases on balls received with 18 in 1981 and 25 in 1986.

Led National League in total bases with 306 in 1976, 342 in 1980 and 228 in 1981.

Led National League in slugging percentage with .546 in 1974, .624 in 1980, .644 in 1981 and .547 in 1982 and 1986.

Led National League batters in strikeouts with 138 in 1974, 180 in 1975, 149 in 1976 and 148 in 1983.

Led National League in bases on balls received with 120 in 1979, 73 in 1981, 107 in 1982 and 128 in 1983.

Led National League in sacrifice flies with 13 in 1980 and tied for lead with 9 in 1979.

Tied for National League lead in being hit by pitch with 11 in 1976.

Led National League third basemen in fielding percentage with .980 in 1986.

Led National League third basemen in total chances with 537 in 1976, 521 in 1977, 497 in 1980, 457 in 1982 and tied for lead with 338 in 1981 and 458 in 1983.

Led National League third basemen in double plays with 34 in 1978, 36 in 1979, 31 in 1980, 29 in 1983 and tied for lead with 28 in 1982.

Led National League third basemen in assists with 396 in 1977 and 332 in 1983.

Led Pacific Coast League batters in strikeouts with 145 in 1972.

Named National League Player of the Year by THE SPORTING NEWS, 1980 and 1986.

Named National League Most Valuable Player by Baseball Writers' Association of America, 1980, 1981 and 1986.

Named third baseman on THE SPORTING NEWS National League All-Star Team, 1974, 1976, 1977 and 1979 through 1984 and 1986.

Named third baseman on THE SPORTING NEWS National League All-Star fielding team, 1976 through 1984 and 1986.

Named third baseman on THE SPORTING NEWS National League Silver Slugger team, 1980 through 1984 and 1986.

Named shortstop on THE SPORTING NEWS College Baseball All-America Team, 1971.

Year	Club	League	Pos.	G.	AB.	R.	H.	2B.	3B.	HR.	RBI.	B.A.	PO.	A.	E.	F.A.
1971—Reading	East.	SS-3B	74	237	27	50	7	1	8	31	.211	100	224	23	.934
1972—Eugene	P. C.	2B-3B-SS	131	436	80	127	23	6	26	91	.291	271	324	25	.960
1972—Philadelphia†	Nat.	3B-2B	13	34	2	7	0	0	1	3	.206	10	25	2	.946
1973—Philadelphia‡	Nat.	3-2-1-S	132	367	43	72	11	0	18	52	.196	119	256	18	.954
1974—Philadelphia	Nat.	3B	162	568	108	160	28	7	*36	116	.282	134	*404	26	.954
1975—Philadelphia	Nat.	3B-SS	158	562	93	140	34	3	*38	95	.249	139	390	26	.953
1976—Philadelphia	Nat.	3B	160	584	112	153	31	4	*38	107	.262	139	*377	21	.961
1977—Philadelphia	Nat.	3B-SS-2B	154	544	114	149	27	11	38	101	.274	109	401	20	.962
1978—Philadelphia	Nat.	3B-SS	145	513	93	129	27	2	21	78	.251	98	325	16	.964
1979—Philadelphia	Nat.	3B-SS	160	541	109	137	25	4	45	114	.253	115	363	23	.954
1980—Philadelphia	Nat.	3B	150	548	104	157	25	8	*48	*121	.286	98	*372	27	.946
1981—Philadelphia	Nat.	3B	102	354	*78	112	19	2	*31	*91	.316	74	*249	15	.956
1982—Philadelphia§	Nat.	3B	148	514	108	144	26	3	35	87	.280	110	*324	23	.950
1983—Philadelphia	Nat.	3B-SS	154	534	104	136	16	4	*40	109	.255	108	333	19	.959
1984—Philadelphia	Nat.	3B-1B-SS	151	528	93	146	23	4	●36	●106	.277	93	330	26	.942
1985—Philadelphia	Nat.	1B-3B-SS	158	549	89	152	31	5	33	93	.277	911	193	18	.984
1986—Philadelphia	Nat.	3B-1B	160	552	97	160	29	1	*37	*119	.290	347	238	8	.987
Major League Totals—15 Years			2107	7292	1347	1954	352	57	495	1392	.268	2604	4580	288	.961

Selected by Philadelphia Phillies' organization in 2nd round of free-agent draft, June 8, 1971.

†On disabled list, August 21 to September 2, 1972.

‡On disabled list, March 28 to April 21, 1973.

§On disabled list, April 14 to April 29, 1982.

DIVISION SERIES RECORD

Year	Club	League	Pos.	G.	AB.	R.	H.	2B.	3B.	HR.	RBI.	B.A.	PO.	A.	E.	F.A.
1981—Philadelphia	Nat.	3B	5	16	3	4	1	0	1	2	.250	6	10	1	.941

CHAMPIONSHIP SERIES RECORD

Established Championship Series record for most at-bats, five-game Series (24), 1980.

Tied Championship Series records for highest batting average, four-game Series (.467), 1983; most at-bats, extra-inning game (6), October 8, 1980; most two-base hits, total Series (7).

Year	Club	League	Pos.	G.	AB.	R.	H.	2B.	3B.	HR.	RBI.	B.A.	PO.	A.	E.	F.A.
1976—Philadelphia	Nat.	3B	3	13	1	4	2	0	0	2	.308	4	9	1	.929
1977—Philadelphia	Nat.	3B	4	16	2	1	0	0	1	1	.063	4	15	0	1.000
1978—Philadelphia	Nat.	3B	4	15	1	3	2	0	0	1	.200	3	18	2	.913
1980—Philadelphia	Nat.	3B	5	24	1	5	1	0	0	1	.208	3	17	1	.952
1983—Philadelphia	Nat.	3B	4	15	5	7	2	0	1	2	.467	6	7	1	.929
Championship Series Totals—5 Years			20	83	10	20	7	0	1	7	.241	20	66	5	.945

WORLD SERIES RECORD

Tied World Series record for fewest chances accepted by third baseman, game (0), October 21, 1980.

Year—Club	League	Pos.	G.	AB.	R.	H.	2B.	3B.	HR.	RBI.	B.A.	PO.	A.	E.	F.A.
1980—Philadelphia	Nat.	3B	6	21	6	8	1	0	2	7	.381	9	8	0	1.000
1983—Philadelphia	Nat.	3B	5	20	0	1	0	0	0	0	.050	1	10	1	.917
World Series Totals—2 Years			11	41	6	9	1	0	2	7	.220	10	18	1	.966

ALL-STAR GAME RECORD

Year—League	Pos.	AB.	R.	H.	2B.	3B.	HR.	RBI.	B.A.	PO.	A.	E.	F.A.
1974—National	PH-3B	0	1	0	0	0	0	0	.000	0	1	0	1.000
1976—National	3B	1	0	0	0	0	0	0	.000	0	0	0	.000
1977—National	PR	0	0	0	0	0	0	0	.000	0	0	0	.000
1979—National	3B	3	2	2	1	1	0	1	.667	1	1	1	.667
1981—National	3B	4	1	2	1	0	1	2	.500	0	2	1	.667
1982—National	3B	1	0	0	0	0	0	0	.000	0	0	0	.000
1983—National	3B	3	0	0	0	0	0	0	.000	0	0	1	.000
1984—National	3B	3	0	0	0	0	0	0	.000	0	4	0	1.000
1986—National	3B	1	0	0	0	0	0	0	.000	0	0	0	.000
All-Star Game Totals—9 Years		16	4	4	2	1	1	3	.250	1	8	3	.750

Named to National League All-Star Team in 1980; replaced due to injury by Ray Knight.

RICHARD CRAIG SCHOFIELD
(Dick)

Born November 21, 1962, at Springfield, Ill.
Height, 5.10. Weight, 175.
Throws and bats righthanded.
Son of John Richard (Dick) Schofield, infielder with St. Louis Cardinals, Pittsburgh, San Francisco, New York Yankees, Los Angeles Dodgers, Boston and Milwaukee Brewers, 1953 through 1971.
Major League stolen bases: 1984 (5), 1985 (11), 1986 (23). Total—39.
Led Pioneer League in bases on balls received with 68 in 1981.
Received reported $100,000 bonus to sign with California Angels, 1981.

Year—Club	League	Pos.	G.	AB.	R.	H.	2B.	3B.	HR.	RBI.	B.A.	PO.	A.	E.	F.A.
1981—Idaho Falls	Pion.	*SS-2B	66	226	59	63	10	1	6	31	.279	*102	201	22	.932
1982—Danville	Midw.	SS	92	308	80	111	21	*10	12	53	*.360	129	249	23	.943
1982—Redwood	Calif.	SS	33	102	15	25	3	1	1	8	.245	35	103	3	.979
1982—Spokane	P. C.	SS-3B	7	30	4	9	4	1	1	12	.300	7	20	0	1.000
1983—Edmonton	P. C.	SS-3B	139	521	91	148	30	7	16	94	.284	220	402	30	.954
1983—California	Amer.	SS	21	54	4	11	2	0	3	4	.204	24	67	7	.929
1984—California†	Amer.	SS	140	400	39	77	10	3	4	21	.193	218	420	12	*.982
1985—California	Amer.	SS	147	438	50	96	19	3	8	41	.219	261	397	25	.963
1986—California	Amer.	SS	139	458	67	114	17	6	13	57	.249	246	389	18	.972
Major League Totals—4 Years			447	1350	160	298	48	12	28	123	.221	749	1273	62	.970

Selected by California Angels' organization in 1st round (third player selected) of free-agent draft, June 8, 1981.
†On disabled list, July 1 to July 24, 1984.

CHAMPIONSHIP SERIES RECORD

Year—Club	League	Pos.	G.	AB.	R.	H.	2B.	3B.	HR.	RBI.	B.A.	PO.	A.	E.	F.A.
1986—California	Amer.	SS	7	30	4	9	1	0	1	2	.300	13	23	2	.947

ALFRED WILLIAM SCHROEDER III
Name pronounced SHRO-der.

(Bill)

Born September 7, 1958, at Baltimore, Md.
Height, 6.02. Weight, 210.
Throws and bats righthanded.
Attended Clemson University, Clemson, S. C.
Major League stolen bases: 1986 (1).
Led Pacific Coast League batters in strikeouts with 136 and game-winning RBIs with 15 in 1982.
Led California League batters in strikeouts with 141 in 1980.
Led Pioneer League in total bases with 170 in 1979.
Led California League catchers in total chances with 759 in 1980.
Tied for Pacific Coast League lead in passed balls with 13 in 1983.

Year—Club	League	Pos.	G.	AB.	R.	H.	2B.	3B.	HR.	RBI.	B.A.	PO.	A.	E.	F.A.
1979—Butte	Pion.	C-1B	65	242	73	86	16	7	18	77	.355	474	50	9	.983
1980—Stockton	Calif.	*C-1B	123	437	68	117	20	3	18	97	.268	669	96	7	*.991
1981—El Paso	Texas	C-OF	95	335	41	87	20	2	15	61	.260	511	49	10	.982
1982—Vancouver	P. C.	C	116	425	66	113	16	3	22	77	.266	569	77	7	*.989
1983—Vancouver	P. C.	C	82	304	51	87	13	3	20	70	.286	399	68	6	*.987
1983—Milwaukee	Amer.	C	23	73	7	13	2	1	3	7	.178	92	5	2	.980
1984—Milwaukee	Amer.	C-1B	61	210	29	54	6	0	14	25	.257	277	24	4	.987
1985—Milwaukee†	Amer.	C-1B	53	194	18	47	8	0	8	25	.242	216	23	3	.988
1986—El Paso‡	Texas	C	8	26	5	6	3	0	1	2	.231	26	2	0	1.000
1986—Milwaukee	Amer.	C-1B	64	217	32	46	14	0	7	19	.212	307	25	1	.997
Major League Totals—4 Years			201	694	86	160	30	1	32	76	.231	892	77	10	.990

Selected by Milwaukee Brewers' organization in 8th round of free-agent draft, June 5, 1979.
†On disabled list, May 15 to June 14 and June 22 to July 19, 1985.
‡On Milwaukee disabled list, March 29 to May 4, 1986; included rehabilitation disability assignment to El Paso, April 24 to May 4, 1986.

KENNETH MARVIN SCHROM
(Ken)

Born November 23, 1954, at Grangeville, Ida.
Height, 6.02. Weight, 195.
Throws and bats righthanded.
Attended University of Idaho, Moscow, Ida.

Major League saves: 1980 (1).
Tied for Texas League lead in home runs allowed with 24 in 1978.

Year Club	League	G	IP	W	L	Pct.	H	R	ER.	SO.	BB.	ERA.
1976—Idaho Falls	Pioneer	16	48	1	5	.167	42	31	20	46	32	3.75
1977—Quad Cities	Midwest	16	44	3	1	.750	22	10	7	40	20	1.43
1977—Salinas	California	15	21	1	1	.500	22	8	8	22	11	3.43
1977—El Paso	Texas	10	18	1	0	1.000	14	4	4	7	8	2.00
1978—El Paso	Texas	33	165	9	6	.600	180	93	86	126	52	4.69
1979—El Paso	Texas	25	168	7	8	.467	204	111	97	107	75	5.20
1979—Salt Lake City	P. Coast	3	4	0	0	.000	3	0	0	3	3	0.00
1980—Salt Lake City†	P. Coast	14	23	0	1	.000	32	25	20	11	17	7.83
1980—Syracuse	Int'national	26	46	0	2	.000	41	19	17	32	20	3.33
1980—Toronto	American	17	31	1	0	1.000	32	18	18	13	19	5.23
1981—Syracuse	Int'national	42	104	4	6	.400	86	44	43	72	41	3.72
1982—Syracuse	Int'national	27	98	4	5	.444	102	61	56	49	41	5.14
1982—Toronto‡	American	6	15⅓	1	0	1.000	13	11	10	8	15	5.87
1983—Toledo	Int'national	5	31⅔	3	1	.750	30	19	16	20	14	4.55
1983—Minnesota§	American	33	196⅓	15	8	.652	196	92	81	80	80	3.71
1984—Orlando x	Southern	2	10	0	0	.000	10	8	3	10	6	2.70
1984—Minnesota	American	25	137	5	11	.313	156	75	68	49	41	4.47
1985—Minnesota y	American	29	160⅔	9	12	.429	164	95	89	74	59	4.99
1986—Cleveland	American	34	206	14	7	.667	217	118	104	87	49	4.54
Major League Totals—6 Years		144	746⅓	45	38	.542	778	409	370	311	263	4.46

Selected by Minnesota Twins' organization in 10th round of free-agent draft, June 5, 1973.
Selected by California Angels' organization in 17th round of free-agent draft, June 8, 1976.
†Traded to Toronto Blue Jays' organization, June 10, 1980, completing deal in which Toronto traded Pitcher Dave Lemanczyk to California Angels for a player to be named later, June 3, 1980.
‡Released, August 30, 1982; signed by Minnesota Twins' organization, December 1, 1982.
§Appeared in one game as a pinch-runner.
xOn Minnesota disabled list, March 29 to May 22, 1984; included rehabilitation disability assignment to Orlando, April 18 to April 26, 1984.
yTraded with Pitcher Bryan Oelkers to Cleveland Indians for Pitchers Roy Smith and Ramon Romero, January 7, 1986.

ALL-STAR GAME RECORD
Member of American League All-Star Team in 1986; did not play.

RICHARD SPENCER SCHU

Name pronounced Shoo.

(Rick)

Born January 26, 1962, at Philadelphia, Pa.
Height, 6.00. Weight, 170.
Throws and bats righthanded.
Attended Sacramento City College, Sacramento, Calif.
Son of Ken Schu, minor league pitcher, 1955 and 1956.

Major League stolen bases: 1985 (8), 1986 (2). Total—10.
Led Pacific Coast League third basemen in total chances with 390 in 1984.

Year Club	League	Pos.	G.	AB.	R.	H.	2B.	3B.	HR.	RBI.	B.A.	PO.	A.	E.	F.A.
1981—Bend	N'west	3B-2B-SS	68	258	41	69	10	0	2	42	.267	55	137	24	.889
1982—Spartanburg	S. Atl.	3B-2B-SS	125	429	78	117	28	1	12	60	.273	157	257	45	.902
1983—Peninsula	Carol.	3B-SS-2B	122	444	69	119	22	3	14	63	.268	82	252	30	.918
1983—Portland	P. C.	3B-SS	9	29	7	11	2	1	1	3	.379	6	12	2	.900
1984—Portland	P. C.	3B	140	552	70	166	35	●14	12	82	.301	★109	★254	★27	.931
1984—Philadelphia	Nat.	3B	17	29	12	8	2	1	2	5	.276	7	13	1	.952
1985—Portland	P. C.	SS-3B	42	150	19	42	8	3	4	22	.280	36	91	11	.920
1985—Philadelphia	Nat.	3B	112	416	54	105	21	4	7	24	.252	86	191	20	.933
1986—Philadelphia	Nat.	3B	92	208	32	57	10	1	8	25	.274	42	94	13	.913
Major League Totals—3 Years			221	653	98	170	33	6	17	54	.260	135	298	34	.927

Signed as free agent by Philadelphia Phillies' organization, November 25, 1980.

DONALD ARTHUR SCHULZE

Name pronounced SHULL-zee.

(Don)

Born September 27, 1962, at Roselle, Ill.
Height, 6.04. Weight, 230.
Throws and bats righthanded.

Led Gulf Coast League in complete games with 3 in 1980.
Tied for American Association lead in shutouts with 2 in 1983.

Year Club	League	G.	IP.	W.	L.	Pct.	H.	R.	ER.	SO.	BB.	ERA.
1980—Sarasota Cubs	Gulf Coast	12	66	2	7	.222	58	38	30	30	36	4.09
1981—Quad Cities†	Midwest	17	105	8	5	.615	89	33	27	61	51	2.31
1982—Salinas	California	24	165	13	7	.650	150	61	52	122	59	2.84
1983—Iowa	Am. Assoc.	25	168⅔	11	9	.550	170	88	80	103	63	4.27
1983—Chicago	National	4	14	0	1	.000	19	11	11	8	7	7.07
1984—Iowa	Am. Assoc.	13	79	5	5	.500	79	40	38	44	29	4.33
1984—Chicago‡	National	1	3	0	0	.000	8	4	4	2	1	12.00
1984—Maine	Int'national	2	9⅓	1	1	.500	14	12	9	7	3	8.68
1984—Cleveland	American	19	85⅔	3	6	.333	105	53	46	39	27	4.83
1985—Cleveland	American	19	94⅓	4	10	.286	128	75	63	37	19	6.01
1985—Maine	Int'national	15	115⅓	6	4	.600	105	41	34	45	29	2.65
1986—Cleveland§	American	19	84⅔	4	4	.500	88	48	47	33	34	5.00
1986—Maine	Int'national	3	10	0	1	.000	12	7	7	7	4	6.30
National League Totals—2 Years		5	17	0	1	.000	27	15	15	10	8	7.94
American League Totals—3 Years		57	264⅔	11	20	.355	321	176	156	109	80	5.30
Major League Totals—4 Years		62	281⅔	11	21	.344	348	191	171	119	88	5.46

Selected by Chicago Cubs' organization in 1st round (11th player selected) of free-agent draft, June 3, 1980.

†On disabled list, June 22 to July 16, 1981.

‡Traded with Outfielders Mel Hall and Joe Carter and Pitcher Darryl Banks to Cleveland Indians for Catcher Ron Hassey and Pitchers Rick Sutcliffe and George Frazier, June 13, 1984.

§On disabled list, July 22 to September 1, 1986; included rehabilitation disability assignment to Maine, August 20 to September 1, 1986.

MICHAEL LORRI SCIOSCIA

Name pronounced SO-sha.

(Mike)

Born November 27, 1958, at Upper Darby, Pa.
Height, 6.02. Weight, 200.
Throws right and bats lefthanded.
Attended Pennsylvania State University, University Park, Pa.

Major League stolen bases: 1980 (1), 1982 (2), 1984 (2), 1985 (3), 1986 (3). Total—11.
Led National League in passed balls with 11 in 1981.
Tied for Pacific Coast League lead in being hit by pitch with 7 in 1979.
Led Pacific Coast League catchers in double plays with 19 and passed balls with 22 in 1979.
Led Midwest League catchers in errors with 20 and double plays with 12 in 1978.

Year Club	League	Pos.	G.	AB.	R.	H.	2B.	3B.	HR.	RBI.	B.A.	PO.	A.	E.	F.A.
1976—Bellingham	N'west.	C	46	151	25	42	6	0	7	26	.278	202	35	14	.944
1977—Clinton	Midw.	C-1B	121	364	58	92	20	1	7	44	.253	764	95	22	.975
1978—San Antonio†	Texas	C	58	204	29	61	16	0	2	34	.299	214	17	4	.983
1979—Albuquerque	P. C.	C	143	461	80	155	34	0	3	68	.336	★690	★86	★15	.981
1980—Albuquerque	P. C.	C	52	160	33	53	11	1	3	33	.331	207	19	5	.978
1980—Los Angeles‡	Nat.	C-3B	54	134	8	34	5	1	1	8	.254	226	26	2	.992
1981—Los Angeles	Nat.	C	93	290	27	80	10	0	2	29	.276	493	48	7	.987
1982—Los Angeles	Nat.	C	129	365	31	80	11	1	5	38	.219	631	57	10	.986
1983—Los Angeles§	Nat.	C	12	35	3	11	3	0	1	7	.314	55	4	0	1.000
1984—Los Angeles x	Nat.	C	114	341	29	93	18	0	5	38	.273	701	64	12	.985
1985—Los Angeles	Nat.	C	141	429	47	127	26	3	7	53	.296	818	66	●13	.986
1986—Los Angeles y	Nat.	C	122	374	36	94	18	1	5	26	.251	756	64	15	.982
Major League Totals—7 Years			665	1968	181	519	91	6	26	199	.264	3680	329	59	.985

Selected by Los Angeles Dodgers' organization in 1st round (19th player selected) of free-agent draft, June 8, 1976.

†On disabled list, May 19 to August 4, 1978.

‡On disabled list, April 10 to April 20, 1980.

§On disabled list, May 15, 1983 through remainder of season.

xOn disabled list, May 6 to May 21, 1984.

yOn disabled list, June 10 to July 15, 1986.

DIVISION SERIES RECORD

Year Club	League	Pos.	G.	AB.	R.	H.	2B.	3B.	HR.	RBI.	B.A.	PO.	A.	E.	F.A.
1981—Los Angeles	Nat.	C	4	13	0	2	0	0	0	1	.154	21	3	0	1.000

CHAMPIONSHIP SERIES RECORD

Year Club	League	Pos.	G.	AB.	R.	H.	2B.	3B.	HR.	RBI.	B.A.	PO.	A.	E.	F.A.
1981—Los Angeles	Nat.	C	5	15	1	2	0	0	1	1	.133	27	1	0	1.000
1985—Los Angeles	Nat.	C	6	16	2	4	0	0	0	1	.250	31	4	1	.972
Championship Series Totals—2 Years			11	31	3	6	0	0	1	2	.194	58	5	1	.984

WORLD SERIES RECORD

Year Club	League	Pos.	G.	AB.	R.	H.	2B.	3B.	HR.	RBI.	B.A.	PO.	A.	E.	F.A.
1981—Los Angeles	Nat.	C-PH	3	4	1	1	0	0	0	0	.250	7	1	0	1.000

MICHAEL WARREN SCOTT

(Mike)

Born April 26, 1955, at Santa Monica, Calif.
Height, 6.03. Weight, 215.
Throws and bats righthanded.
Attended Pepperdine University, Malibu, Calif.

Tied major league record for most strikeouts, inning (4), September 3, 1986 (fifth inning).
Pitched 2-0 no-hit victory against San Francisco Giants, September 25, 1986.
Major League saves: 1982 (3).
Tied for National League lead in shutouts with 5 in 1986.
Led Texas League in complete games with 14 and tied for lead in balks with 3 in 1977.
Tied for International League lead in games started by pitchers with 29 in 1978 and balks with 3 in 1980.
Named National League Pitcher of the Year by THE SPORTING NEWS, 1986.
Won National League Cy Young Memorial Award, 1986.
Named righthanded pitcher on THE SPORTING NEWS National League All-Star Team, 1986.

Year Club	League	G.	IP.	W.	L.	Pct.	H.	R.	ER.	SO.	BB.	ERA.
1976—Jackson	Texas	7	44	3	3	.500	34	20	14	19	14	2.86
1977—Jackson	Texas	25	★187	★14	10	.583	132	77	61	97	55	2.94
1977—Tidewater	Int'national	2	2	0	1	.000	4	5	4	0	3	18.00
1978—Tidewater	Int'national	29	192	10	10	.500	196	105	84	93	83	3.94
1979—Tidewater	Int'national	18	99	8	4	.667	103	37	35	40	27	3.18
1979—New York	National	18	52	1	3	.250	59	35	31	21	20	5.37
1980—Tidewater	Int'national	27	170	13	7	.650	165	69	56	88	64	2.96
1980—New York	National	6	29	1	1	.500	40	14	14	13	8	4.34
1981—New York	National	23	136	5	10	.333	130	65	59	54	34	3.90
1982—New York†	National	37	147	7	13	.350	185	100	84	63	60	5.14
1983—Houston‡	National	24	145	10	6	.625	143	67	60	73	46	3.72
1984—Houston	National	31	154	5	11	.313	179	96	80	83	43	4.68
1985—Houston	National	36	221⅔	18	8	.692	194	91	81	137	80	3.29
1986—Houston	National	37	★275⅓	18	10	.643	182	73	68	★306	72	★2.22
Major League Totals—8 Years		212	1160	65	62	.512	1112	541	477	750	363	3.70

Selected by New York Mets' organization in 2nd round of free-agent draft, June 8, 1976.
†Traded to Houston Astros for Outfielder-First Baseman Danny Heep, December 10, 1982.
‡On disabled list, April 5 to May 4, 1983.

CHAMPIONSHIP SERIES RECORD

Established Championship Series record for most complete games, Series (2), 1986.
Tied Championship Series record for most strikeouts, game (14), October 8, 1986.
Established National League Championship Series records for most innings pitched, six-game Series (18), 1986;
most consecutive scoreless innings, Series and total Series (16), 1986; most strikeouts, Series (19), 1986.
Tied National League Championship Series record for most complete games, total Series (2).

Year Club	League	G.	IP.	W.	L.	Pct.	H.	R.	ER.	SO.	BB.	ERA.
1986—Houston	National	2	18	2	0	1.000	8	1	1	19	1	0.50

ALL-STAR GAME RECORD

Year League	IP.	W.	L.	Pct.	H.	R.	ER.	SO.	BB.	ERA.
1986—National	1	0	0	.000	1	1	1	2	0	9.00

TIMOTHY DALE SCOTT
(Tim)

Born November 16, 1966, at Hanford, Calif.
Height, 6.02. Weight, 185.
Throws and bats righthanded.
Tied for Pioneer League lead in shutouts with 2 in 1984.

Year Club	League	G.	IP.	W.	L.	Pct.	H.	R.	ER.	SO.	BB.	ERA.
1984—Great Falls	Pioneer	13	78	5	4	.556	90	58	38	44	38	4.38
1985—Bakersfield†	California	12	63⅔	3	4	.429	84	46	41	31	28	5.80
1986—Vero Beach‡	Florida St.	20	95⅓	5	4	.556	113	44	36	37	34	3.40

Selected by Los Angeles Dodgers' organization in 2nd round of free-agent draft, June 4, 1984.
†On disabled list, July 23, 1985 through remainder of season.
‡On Bakersfield disabled list, April 11 to May 15, 1986.

RODNEY GRANT SCURRY

Name pronounced SKUR-ee.

(Rod)

Born March 17, 1956, at Sacramento, Calif.
Height, 6.02. Weight, 180.
Throws and bats lefthanded.
Cousin of Joe Rose, tight end with Miami Dolphins.
Pitched seven-inning, 2-0 no-hit victory against Richmond, July 25, 1977.
Major League saves: 1981 (7), 1982 (14), 1983 (7), 1984 (4), 1985 (3), 1986 (2). Total—37.
Led Carolina League pitchers in games started with 26 in 1975.
Led New York-Pennsylvania League in hit batsmen with 7 in 1974.

Year Club	League	G.	IP.	W.	L.	Pct.	H.	R.	ER.	SO.	BB.	ERA.
1974—Niagara Falls	NYP	14	89	5	6	.455	55	36	34	102	★74	3.44
1975—Salem	Carolina	26	150	9	12	.429	128	79	61	143	118	3.66
1976—Shreveport	Texas	24	123	8	8	.500	120	71	53	83	83	3.88
1977—Shreveport	Texas	18	113	3	11	.214	97	54	36	111	48	2.87
1977—Columbus	Int'national	8	37	3	2	.600	30	31	19	39	32	4.62
1978—Columbus†	Int'national	16	63	3	3	.500	69	44	40	57	43	5.71
1978—Shreveport	Texas	5	29	1	4	.200	27	19	15	38	24	4.66
1979—Portland‡	P. Coast	35	122	5	5	.500	121	64	56	94	72	4.13

Year Club	League	G.	IP.	W.	L.	Pct.	H.	R.	ER.	SO.	BB.	ERA.
1980—Pittsburgh	National	20	38	0	2	.000	23	12	9	28	17	2.13
1981—Pittsburgh	National	27	74	4	5	.444	74	33	31	65	40	3.77
1982—Pittsburgh	National	76	103⅔	4	5	.444	79	26	20	94	64	1.74
1983—Pittsburgh	National	61	68	4	9	.308	63	45	42	67	53	5.56
1984—Pittsburgh§	National	43	46⅓	5	6	.455	28	14	13	48	22	2.53
1985—Pittsburgh x	National	30	47⅔	0	1	.000	42	22	17	43	28	3.21
1985—New York	American	5	12⅔	1	0	1.000	5	4	4	17	10	2.84
1986—New York y	American	31	39⅓	1	2	.333	38	18	16	36	22	3.66
1986—Fort Lauderdale z	Florida St.	7	7⅓	1	0	1.000	7	3	3	16	7	3.68
National League Totals—6 Years		257	377⅔	17	28	.378	309	152	132	345	224	3.15
American League Totals—2 Years		36	52	2	2	.500	43	22	20	53	32	3.46
Major League Totals—7 Years		293	429⅔	19	30	.388	352	174	152	398	256	3.18

Selected by Pittsburgh Pirates' organization in 1st round (11th player selected) of free-agent draft, June 5, 1974.

†On disabled list, June 12 to July 11, 1978.

‡On disabled list, August 4 to August 14, 1979.

§On disabled list, April 7 to May 13 and August 5 to August 27, 1984.

xSold to New York Yankees, September 14, 1985.

yOn disabled list, May 13 to July 25, 1986; included rehabilitation disability assignment to Fort Lauderdale, July 7 to July 25, 1986.

zGranted free agency, November 12, 1986; re-signed by Yankees, December 6, 1986.

RAYMOND MARK SEARAGE
(Ray)

Born May 1, 1955, at Freeport, N.Y.
Height, 6.01. Weight, 180.
Throws and bats lefthanded.
Attended West Liberty State College, West Liberty, W. Va.

Major League saves: 1981 (1), 1984 (6), 1985 (1), 1986 (1). Total—9.
Led International League in wild pitches with 14 in 1982.

Year Club	League	G.	IP.	W.	L.	Pct.	H.	R.	ER.	SO.	BB.	ERA.
1976—Sara. W. Sox-Sara. Cards	Gulf Coast	11	32	1	3	.250	24	17	15	31	22	4.22
1977—St. Petersburg	Florida St.	13	19	0	0	.000	11	7	6	12	12	2.84
1977—Johnson City	Ap'lachian	8	41	3	2	.600	38	23	22	27	21	4.83
1978—Gastonia	W. Carol.	39	110	8	3	.727	86	40	34	86	68	2.78
1979—Arkansas†	Texas	42	89	10	4	.714	73	27	22	63	46	2.22
1980—Tidewater	Int'national	19	30	1	0	1.000	35	24	23	20	20	6.90
1980—Jackson	Texas	14	70	4	5	.444	54	32	26	71	26	3.34
1981—Tidewater	Int'national	18	27	2	0	1.000	29	10	7	23	13	2.33
1981—New York‡	National	26	37	1	0	1.000	34	16	15	16	17	3.65
1982—Charleston§	Int'national	38	114	2	7	.222	112	73	62	87	87	4.89
1983—Charleston x	Int'national	31	134	7	7	.500	146	94	84	77	76	5.64
1984—Vancouver	P. Coast	33	76⅓	6	3	.667	62	29	26	59	44	3.07
1984—Milwaukee	American	21	38⅓	2	1	.667	20	3	3	29	16	0.70
1985—Milwaukee	American	33	38	1	4	.200	54	27	25	36	24	5.92
1985—Vancouver	P. Coast	23	26	2	0	1.000	22	10	7	31	12	2.42
1986—Milwaukee yz-Chicago	American	46	51	1	1	.500	44	20	19	36	28	3.35
1986—Vancouver	P. Coast	20	25	2	0	1.000	12	5	4	20	8	1.44
National League Totals—1 Year		26	37	1	0	1.000	34	16	15	16	17	3.65
American League Totals—3 Years		100	127⅓	4	6	.400	118	50	47	101	68	3.32
Major League Totals—4 Years		126	164⅓	5	6	.455	152	66	62	117	85	3.40

Selected by St. Louis Cardinals' organization in 22nd round of free-agent draft, June 8, 1976.

†Traded to New York Mets' organization for Catcher Jody Davis, December 10, 1979.

‡Traded to Cleveland Indians for Shortstop Tom Veryzer, January 8, 1982.

§Traded on a conditional basis to San Diego Padres for a player to be named later, December 15, 1982; returned, March 28, 1983.

xGranted free agency, October 20, 1983; signed by Vancouver (Milwaukee Brewers' organization), November 4, 1983.

yLoaned to Buffalo (Chicago White Sox' organization), July 17, 1986; returned, July 23, 1986.

zTraded to Chicago White Sox for Pitcher Al Jones and Outfielder Tom Hartley, July 23, 1986.

GEORGE THOMAS SEAVER
(Tom)

Born November 17, 1944, at Fresno, Calif.
Height, 6.01. Weight, 210.
Throws and bats righthanded.
Attended Fresno City College, Fresno, Calif., and received bachelor of science degree in public relations from University of Southern California, Los Angeles, Calif. in 1974.
Son of Charles Seaver, former U.S. Walker Cup golfer.

Established major league records for most seasons, 200 or more strikeouts (10); most consecutive seasons, 200 or more strikeouts (9), 1968 through 1976; most consecutive strikeouts, game (10), April 22, 1970; most times pitched opening game of season (16).

Established National League records for lowest earned run average, 200 or more games won, lifetime (2.73); most strikeouts, by righthanded pitcher, lifetime (3,272).

Tied National League records for most season opening games won, lifetime (6); most strikeouts, game (19), April 22, 1970.

Pitched 4-0 no-hit victory against St. Louis Cardinals, June 16, 1978.

Led National League in shutouts with 7 in 1977.
Tied for National League lead in shutouts with 5 in 1979.
Tied for National League lead in complete games with 18 in 1973.
Led International League pitchers in games started with 32 in 1966.
Named National League Pitcher of the Year by THE SPORTING NEWS, 1969 and 1975.
Won National League Cy Young Memorial Award, 1969, 1973 and 1975.
Named National League Rookie of the Year by Baseball Writers' Association of America, 1967.
Named righthanded pitcher on THE SPORTING NEWS National League All-Star Team, 1969, 1973, 1975 and 1981.

Year	Club	League	G.	IP.	W.	L.	Pct.	H.	R.	ER.	SO.	BB.	ERA.
1966—Jacksonville	Int'national	34	210	12	12	.500	184	87	73	188	66	3.13
1967—New York	National	35	251	16	13	.552	224	85	77	170	78	2.76
1968—New York	National	36	278	16	12	.571	224	73	68	205	48	2.20
1969—New York	National	36	273	★25	7	★.781	202	75	67	208	82	2.21
1970—New York	National	37	291	18	12	.600	230	103	91	★283	83	★2.81
1971—New York	National	36	286	20	10	.667	210	61	56	★289	61	★1.76
1972—New York	National	35	262	21	12	.636	215	92	85	249	77	2.92
1973—New York	National	36	290	19	10	.655	219	74	67	★251	64	★2.08
1974—New York	National	32	236	11	11	.500	199	89	84	201	75	3.20
1975—New York	National	36	280	★22	9	.710	217	81	74	★243	88	2.38
1976—New York	National	35	271	14	11	.560	211	83	78	★235	77	2.59
1977—New York†-Cincinnati	National	33	261	21	6	.778	199	78	75	196	66	2.59
1978—Cincinnati	National	36	260	16	14	.533	218	97	83	226	89	2.87
1979—Cincinnati	National	32	215	16	6	★.727	187	85	75	131	61	3.14
1980—Cincinnati‡	National	26	168	10	8	.556	140	74	68	101	59	3.64
1981—Cincinnati	National	23	166	★14	2	★.875	120	51	47	87	66	2.55
1982—Cincinnati§	National	21	111⅓	5	13	.278	136	75	68	62	44	5.50
1983—New York x	National	34	231	9	14	.391	201	104	91	135	86	3.55
1984—Chicago	American	34	236⅔	15	11	.577	216	108	104	131	61	3.95
1985—Chicago	American	35	238⅔	16	11	.593	223	103	84	134	69	3.17
1986—Chicago yz-Boston a	American	28	176⅓	7	13	.350	180	83	79	103	56	4.03
National League Totals—17 Years		559	4130⅓	273	170	.616	3352	1380	1254	3272	1204	2.73
American League Totals—3 Years		97	651⅔	38	35	.521	619	294	267	368	186	3.69
Major League Totals—20 Years		656	4782	311	205	.603	3971	1674	1521	3640	1390	2.86

Selected by Los Angeles Dodgers' organization in 22nd round of free-agent draft, June, 1965.
Signed by Atlanta Braves to Richmond contract for reported $40,000 bonus, February, 1966; subsequently, Commissioner William Eckert nullified the contract because the signing violated the college rule. However, since the University of Southern California then declared Seaver ineligible, Eckert decreed that any club other than the Braves which was willing to match terms of his Richmond contract would be eligible to draw for negotiation rights. Cleveland Indians, Philadelphia Phillies and New York Mets expressed that willingness, and Eckert drew the name of the Mets in a special drawing, April 3, 1966; Mets then signed Seaver to Jacksonville contract for reported $50,000 bonus.
†Traded to Cincinnati Reds for Infielder Doug Flynn, Pitcher Pat Zachry and Outfielders Dan Norman and Steve Henderson, June 15, 1977.
‡On disabled list, July 1 to August 4, 1980.
§Traded to New York Mets for Pitcher Charlie Puleo, Catcher Lloyd McClendon and Outfielder Jason Felice, December 16, 1982.
xSelected by Chicago White Sox in player compensation pool draft, January 20, 1984. (Chicago received compensation for Toronto Blue Jays' signing of Pitcher Dennis Lamp, a Type A player, January 10, 1984.
yOn disabled list, May 18 to June 4, 1986.
zTraded to Boston Red Sox for Outfielder Steve Lyons, June 29, 1986.
aGranted free agency, November 12, 1986.

CHAMPIONSHIP SERIES RECORD
Established Championship Series record for most strikeouts, five-game Series (17), 1973.

Year	Club	League	G.	IP.	W.	L.	Pct.	H.	R.	ER.	SO.	BB.	ERA.
1969—New York	National	1	7	1	0	1.000	8	5	5	2	3	6.43
1973—New York	National	2	16⅔	1	1	.500	13	4	3	17	5	1.62
1979—Cincinnati	National	1	8	0	0	.000	5	2	2	5	2	2.25
Championship Series Totals—3 Years		4	31⅔	2	1	.667	26	11	10	24	10	2.84

WORLD SERIES RECORD

Year	Club	League	G.	IP.	W.	L.	Pct.	H.	R.	ER.	SO.	BB.	ERA.
1969—New York	National	2	15	1	1	.500	12	5	5	9	3	3.00
1973—New York	National	2	15	0	1	.000	13	4	4	18	3	2.40
World Series Totals—2 Years		4	30	1	2	.333	25	9	9	27	6	2.70

ALL-STAR GAME RECORD

Year	League	IP.	W.	L.	Pct.	H.	R.	ER.	SO.	BB.	ERA.
1967—National	1	0	0	.000	0	0	0	1	1	0.00
1968—National	2	0	0	.000	2	0	0	5	0	0.00
1970—National	3	0	0	.000	1	0	0	4	0	0.00
1973—National	1	0	0	.000	0	0	0	1	0	0.00
1975—National	1	0	0	.000	2	3	3	2	1	27.00
1976—National	2	0	0	.000	2	1	1	1	0	4.50
1977—National	2	0	0	.000	4	3	2	2	1	9.00
1981—National	1	0	0	.000	3	1	1	1	0	9.00
All-Star Game Totals—8 Years	13	0	0	.000	14	8	7	16	4	4.85

Member of National League All-Star Team for 1969, 1971, 1972 and 1978 games; did not play.

ROBERT BUSH SEBRA
(Bob)

Born December 11, 1961, at Ridgewood, N.J.
Height, 6.02. Weight, 200.
Throws and bats righthanded.
Attended University of Nebraska, Lincoln, Neb.

Tied for American Association lead in home runs allowed with 17 in 1985.

Year	Club	League	G.	IP.	W.	L.	Pct.	H.	R.	ER.	SO.	BB.	ERA.
1983—Tri-Cities		Northwest	12	58⅓	4	3	.571	48	36	26	70	29	4.01
1984—Tulsa		Texas	17	100⅓	10	5	.667	86	45	38	90	41	3.41
1984—Oklahoma City		Am. Assoc.	9	53⅓	4	4	.500	37	23	20	38	25	3.38
1985—Oklahoma City		Am. Assoc.	22	138⅔	10	6	.625	121	62	59	84	57	3.83
1985—Texas†		American	7	20⅓	0	2	.000	26	17	17	13	14	7.52
1986—Indianapolis		Am. Assoc.	20	126	9	2	.818	108	59	48	91	70	3.43
1986—Montreal		National	17	91⅓	5	5	.500	82	39	36	66	25	3.55
American League Totals—1 Year			7	20⅓	0	2	.000	26	17	17	13	14	7.52
National League Totals—1 Year			17	91⅓	5	5	.500	82	39	36	66	25	3.55
Major League Totals—2 Years			24	111⅔	5	7	.417	108	56	53	79	39	4.27

Selected by Detroit Tigers' organization in 4th round of free-agent draft, June 3, 1980.
Selected by Texas Rangers' organization in 5th round of free-agent draft, June 6, 1983.
†Traded with Infielder Jim Anderson to Montreal Expos for Outfielder Pete Incaviglia, November 2, 1985.

RALPH LAWRENCE SEE
(Larry)

Born June 20, 1960, at Norwalk, Calif.
Height, 6.00. Weight, 200.
Throws and bats righthanded.
Attended Cerritos Junior College, Norwalk, Calif.

Led Texas League in being hit by pitch with 16 in 1983.
Tied for Pacific Coast League lead in total bases with 278 in 1986.
Led Pacific Coast League first basemen in fielding percentage with .993 in 1986.
Led Texas League third basemen in putouts with 98, errors with 38 and total chances with 327 in 1983.
Led Pioneer League third basemen in total chances with 196 and tied for lead in double plays with 10 in 1980.

Year	Club	League	Pos.	G.	AB.	R.	H.	2B.	3B.	HR.	RBI.	B.A.	PO.	A.	E.	F.A.
1980—Lethbridge		Pion.	3B	68	252	41	87	19	2	4	44	.345	★55	★119	22	★.888
1981—Lodi†		Calif.						(Did not play)								
1982—Vero Beach		Fla. St.	3B	132	455	74	120	★29	1	12	●85	.264	★118	228	36	.906
1983—San Antonio		Texas	3B-1B	132	445	72	130	38	2	17	91	.292	150	195	39	.898
1984—Albuquerque		P. C.	3B-1B	58	217	32	63	11	1	8	44	.290	41	117	16	.908
1984—San Antonio		Texas	3B-1B	77	254	56	72	17	1	17	50	.283	85	137	26	.895
1985—San Antonio		Texas	1B	99	373	55	100	17	1	15	58	.268	879	57	●14	.985
1985—Albuquerque		P. C.	3B	23	77	7	20	3	1	3	9	.260	25	29	6	.900
1986—Albuquerque		P. C.	1B-3B	★142	536	83	155	★38	2	27	106	.289	1089	118	11	.991
1986—Los Angeles		Nat.	1B	13	20	1	5	2	0	0	2	.250	41	6	1	.979
Major League Totals—1 Year				13	20	1	5	2	0	0	2	.250	41	6	1	.979

Selected by San Diego Padres' organization in 5th round of free-agent draft, January 9, 1979.
Selected by Los Angeles Dodgers' organization in 3rd round of free-agent draft, January 8, 1980.
†On disabled list, April 10, 1981 through entire season.

KEVIN LEE SEITZER

Born March 26, 1962, at Springfield, Ill.
Height, 5.11. Weight, 180.
Throws and bats righthanded.
Attended Eastern Illinois University, Charleston, Ill.

Led South Atlantic League in bases on balls received with 118 in 1984.
Tied for American Association lead in being hit by pitch with 9 in 1986.
Led South Atlantic League third basemen in total chances with 409 in 1984.
Led Pioneer League third basemen in assists with 122 and total chances with 172 in 1983.
Named South Atlantic League Most Valuable Player, 1984.

Year	Club	League	Pos.	G.	AB.	R.	H.	2B.	3B.	HR.	RBI.	B.A.	PO.	A.	E.	F.A.
1983—Butte		Pion.	3B-SS	68	238	60	82	14	1	2	45	.345	52	124	21	.893
1984—Charleston		S. Atl.	3B	●141	489	★96	★145	26	5	8	79	.297	80	★279	★50	.878
1985—Fort Myers		Fla. St.	1B-3B	90	290	61	91	10	5	3	46	.314	569	88	9	.986
1985—Memphis		South.	3B-1B-OF	52	187	26	65	6	2	1	20	.348	79	51	10	.929
1986—Omaha		A. A.	OF-1B-3B	129	432	86	138	20	11	13	74	.319	338	39	9	.977
1986—Kansas City		Amer.	1B-OF-3B	28	96	16	31	4	1	2	11	.323	224	19	3	.988
Major League Totals—1 Year				28	96	16	31	4	1	2	11	.323	224	19	3	.988

Selected by Kansas City Royals' organization in 11th round of free-agent draft, June 6, 1983.

JEFFREY DOYLE SELLERS
(Jeff)

Born May 11, 1964, at Compton, Calif.
Height, 6.01. Weight, 175.
Throws and bats righthanded.

Led Eastern League in shutouts with 5 and complete games with 15 in 1985.
Led Florida State League pitchers in games started with 29 in 1984.

— 449 —

Year Club	League	G.	IP.	W.	L.	Pct.	H.	R.	ER.	SO.	BB.	ERA.
1982—Elmira	NYP	17	61⅔	1	4	.200	55	31	21	45	39	3.06
1983—Winter Haven	Florida St.	21	117⅔	8	9	.471	149	77	59	68	47	4.51
1984—Winter Haven	Florida St.	29	182	12	10	.545	182	87	69	94	80	3.41
1985—New Britain	Eastern	25	184⅔	●14	7	.667	165	67	57	115	67	2.78
1985—Boston	American	4	22⅓	2	0	1.000	24	10	9	6	7	3.63
1986—Pawtucket	Int'national	15	106	7	4	.636	95	50	44	74	59	3.74
1986—Boston	American	14	82	3	7	.300	90	56	45	51	40	4.94
Major League Totals—2 Years		18	104⅓	5	7	.417	114	66	54	57	47	4.66

Selected by Boston Red Sox' organization in 8th round of free-agent draft, June 7, 1982.

RAMON SERNA

Born December 1, 1962, at Ciudad Juarez, Mex.
Height, 6.00. Weight, 190.
Throws and bats righthanded.

Tied for Mexican League lead in games started by pitchers with 29 in 1985.

Year Club	League	G.	IP.	W.	L.	Pct.	H.	R.	ER.	SO.	BB.	ERA.
1983—Juarez	Mexican	27	183⅓	14	8	.636	183	81	68	141	82	3.34
1984—Juarez	Mexican	19	100⅔	5	6	.455	128	67	60	71	38	5.36
1985—Union Laguna†‡	Mexican	30	★236⅓	16	12	.571	222	103	83	★200	61	3.61
1986—Monterrey	Mexican	21	148⅓	12	8	.600	161	76	64	94	40	3.88

†Signed by Vancouver (Milwaukee Brewers' organization), March 26, 1986.
‡Loaned to Monterrey of Mexican League, March 26, 1986; returned, September 1, 1986.

MICHAEL HAROLD SHADE
(Mike)

Born March 7, 1961, at Pottstown, Pa.
Height, 6.02. Weight, 205.
Throws and bats righthanded.
Attended West Chester University, West Chester, Pa.

Year Club	League	G.	IP.	W.	L.	Pct.	H.	R.	ER.	SO.	BB.	ERA.
1982—Erie	NYP	13	45⅓	3	4	.429	38	24	20	63	16	3.97
1983—Springfield	Midwest	47	78⅔	9	5	.643	69	39	25	85	32	2.86
1984—St. Petersburg	Florida St.	28	45⅔	0	2	.000	35	12	7	43	26	1.38
1984—Arkansas	Texas	27	46⅔	2	4	.333	35	18	16	48	30	3.09
1984—Louisville	Am. Assoc.	2	2⅔	0	1	.000	5	4	3	3	3	10.13
1985—Louisville	Am. Assoc.	14	31⅓	0	2	.000	23	20	20	31	29	5.74
1985—Arkansas	Texas	32	41	0	7	.000	44	27	20	36	20	4.39
1986—Louisville	Am. Assoc.	5	9⅔	1	0	1.000	14	11	11	4	14	10.24
1986—Arkansas†	Texas	11	13⅓	1	3	.250	13	12	11	10	15	7.43
1986—Orlando	Southern	17	43⅔	1	1	.500	44	17	13	36	28	2.68

Selected by St. Louis Cardinals' organization in 4th round of free-agent draft, June 7, 1982.
†Released, June 25, 1986; signed by Orlando (Minnesota Twins' organization), July 22, 1986.

MICHAEL TYRONE SHARPERSON
(Mike)

Born October 4, 1960, at Orangeburg, S.C.
Height, 6.01. Weight, 175.
Throws and bats righthanded.
Attended DeKalb Community College South, Decatur, Ga.

Led International League second basemen in putouts with 286 and total chances with 666 in 1985.
Led Southern League second basemen in total chances with 775 and double plays with 103 in 1984.

Year Club	League	Pos.	G.	AB.	R.	H.	2B.	3B.	HR.	RBI.	B.A.	PO.	A.	E.	F.A.
1982—Florence	S. Atl.	SS-3B	111	326	51	83	16	1	3	33	.255	136	261	33	.923
1983—Kinston†	Carol.	S-3-2-C	90	361	55	96	8	1	5	41	.266	148	286	19	.958
1984—Knoxville	South.	2B	140	542	86	165	25	7	4	48	.304	★331	★423	21	.973
1985—Syracuse	Int.	2B-SS	134	★536	★86	★155	19	★7	1	59	.289	291	372	17	.975
1986—Syracuse	Int.	2B-3B	133	519	★86	★150	18	★9	4	45	.289	258	376	18	.972

Selected by Pittsburgh Pirates' organization in 41st round of free-agent draft, June 5, 1979.
Selected by Montreal Expos' organization in secondary phase of free-agent draft, January 8, 1980.
Selected by Detroit Tigers' organization in 4th round of free-agent draft, January 13, 1981.
Selected by Toronto Blue Jays' organization in secondary phase of free-agent draft, June 8, 1981.
†On disabled list, August 14, 1983 through remainder of season.

THEODORE SHAW JR.
(Theo)

Born May 30, 1962, at Cook County, Ill.
Height, 6.00. Weight, 185
Throws and bats righthanded

Year Club	League	G.	IP.	W.	L.	Pct.	H.	R.	ER.	SO.	BB.	ERA.
1980—Sarasota Royals-Gold	Gulf Coast	13	61	5	7	.417	61	34	23	29	24	3.39
1981—Charleston	S. Atlantic	6	30	1	2	.333	27	15	13	24	25	3.90
1981—Fort Myers	Florida St.	14	86	7	1	.875	66	29	20	60	49	2.09
1982—Jacksonville†	Southern	20	128⅔	7	5	.583	80	53	40	114	79	2.80

Year	Club	League	G.	IP.	W.	L.	Pct.	H.	R.	ER.	SO.	BB.	ERA.
1983—Jacksonville‡	Southern	16	105⅔	5	7	.417	102	60	52	68	69	4.43
1984—Omaha	Am. Assoc.	19	73	3	10	.231	81	75	70	40	77	8.63
1984—Memphis	Southern	6	30	1	2	.333	32	27	27	21	31	8.10
1986—Omaha§	Am. Assoc.	21	98⅓	5	9	.357	82	51	42	62	70	3.84

Selected by Kansas City Royals' organization in 16th round of free-agent draft, June 3, 1980.
†On disabled list, July 2 to August 12, 1982.
‡On Omaha disabled list, July 3, 1983 through remainder of season.
§On disabled list, April 10 to May 9, 1986.

RECORD AS OUTFIELDER

Year	Club	League	Pos.	G.	AB.	R.	H.	2B.	3B.	HR.	RBI.	B.A.	PO.	A.	E.	F.A.
1985—Fort Myers	Fla. St.	OF	80	240	24	49	12	0	3	37	.204	51	2	3	.946

DANNY TODD SHEAFFER

Born August 2, 1961, at Jacksonville, Fla.
Height, 6.00. Weight, 185.
Throws and bats righthanded.
Attended Harrisburg Area Community College, Harrisburg, Pa.,
and Clemson University, Clemson, S.C.

Led Florida State League catchers in errors with 14 in 1982.

Year	Club	League	Pos.	G.	AB.	R.	H.	2B.	3B.	HR.	RBI.	B.A.	PO.	A.	E.	F.A.
1981—Elmira	NYP	C	62	198	39	57	9	0	8	29	.288	220	35	5	.981
1981—Bristol	East.	C-2B	8	12	0	0	0	0	0	1	.000	16	3	0	1.000
1982—Winter Haven†	Fla. St.	C-3B	82	260	20	65	4	0	5	25	.250	316	51	16	.958
1983—Winston-Salem	Carol.	C-1B-OF	112	380	48	105	14	2	15	63	.276	427	44	6	.987
1984—New Britain	East.	C-OF	93	303	33	73	10	0	1	27	.241	438	47	6	.988
1985—Pawtucket	Int.	C	77	243	24	63	9	0	8	33	.259	289	18	6	.981
1986—Pawtucket	Int.	C-OF	79	265	34	90	16	1	2	30	.340	380	39	5	.988

Selected by Boston Red Sox' organization in 1st round (20th player selected) of free-agent draft, January 13, 1981.
†On disabled list, May 3 to May 14, 1982.

LARRY KENT SHEETS

Born December 6, 1959, at Staunton, Va.
Height, 6.04. Weight, 210.
Throws right and bats lefthanded.
Attended Eastern Mennonite College, Harrisonburg, Va.

Major League stolen bases: 1986 (2).
Led International League outfielders in double plays with 5 in 1984.

Year	Club	League	Pos.	G.	AB.	R.	H.	2B.	3B.	HR.	RBI.	B.A.	PO.	A.	E.	F.A.
1978—Bluefield	Appal.	OF-1B	67	225	32	60	9	2	11	★48	.267	121	8	4	.970
1979—Miami†	Fla. St.				(Did not play)										
1979—Bluefield	Appal.	OF	3	12	2	4	2	0	0	2	.333	1	0	0	1.000
1980—Bluefield‡	Appal.	OF	37	124	29	47	9	1	★14	47	.379	40	3	2	.956
1980—Charlotte	South.	OF	13	48	1	9	4	0	0	5	.188	4	1	0	1.000
1981—Rochester§	Int.				(Did not play)										
1982—Rochester x	Int.				(Did not play)										
1982—Hagerstown y	Carol.	OF	88	324	46	96	21	0	18	59	.296	123	5	6	.955
1983—Charlotte	South.	OF-1B	138	503	72	145	★37	3	●25	87	.288	256	15	7	.975
1983—Rochester	Int.	OF	3	13	1	2	1	0	0	2	.154	5	0	1	.833
1984—Rochester	Int.	OF	134	431	76	130	26	4	13	67	.302	201	★19	2	.991
1984—Baltimore	Amer.	OF	8	16	3	7	1	0	1	2	.438	12	1	0	1.000
1985—Baltimore	Amer.	OF-1B	113	328	43	86	8	0	17	50	.262	12	1	1	.929
1986—Baltimore z	Amer.	O-1-3-C	112	338	42	92	17	1	18	60	.272	90	8	3	.970
Major League Totals—3 Years			233	682	88	185	26	1	36	112	.271	114	10	4	.969

Selected by Baltimore Orioles' organization in 2nd round of free-agent draft, June 6, 1978.
†On suspended list, May 1 to August 29, 1979.
‡On restricted list, June 18 to June 23, 1980.
§On restricted list, April 14 to May 28 and June 18, 1981 through remainder of season.
xOn suspended list, April 13, 1982; then transferred to restricted list, April 23 to May 13, 1982.
yOn disabled list, August 23, 1982 through remainder of season.
zOn disabled list, June 30 to July 17, 1986.

JOHN T. SHELBY

Born February 23, 1958, at Lexington, Ky.
Height, 6.01. Weight, 175.
Throws right and bats right and lefthanded.
Attended Columbia State Community College, Columbia, Tenn.

Major League stolen bases: 1981 (2), 1983 (15), 1984 (12), 1985 (5), 1986 (18). Total—52.
Led Florida State League outfielders in double plays with 7 in 1979.
Led Appalachian League outfielders in double plays with 3 in 1978.

Year	Club	League	Pos.	G.	AB.	R.	H.	2B.	3B.	HR.	RBI.	B.A.	PO.	A.	E.	F.A.
1977—Bluefield	Appal.	OF	60	211	28	54	9	1	0	1	.256	90	●12	7	.936
1978—Miami	Fla. St.	OF	13	26	4	6	1	0	0	3	.231	14	2	2	.889
1978—Bluefield	Appal.	OF	64	248	49	70	9	1	6	25	.282	128	★11	6	.959
1979—Miami	Fla. St.	OF	132	478	50	96	11	6	3	38	.201	★252	●22	8	.972

Year Club	League	Pos.	G.	AB.	R.	H.	2B.	3B.	HR.	RBI.	B.A.	PO.	A.	E.	F.A.
1980—Charlotte	South.	OF	134	*560	66	135	27	11	6	51	.241	*361	21	*16	.960
1981—Charlotte	South.	OF	62	251	40	59	11	4	2	21	.235	120	3	10	.925
1981—Rochester	Int.	OF	76	326	42	86	21	8	3	32	.264	189	8	6	.970
1981—Baltimore	Amer.	OF	7	2	2	0	0	0	0	0	.000	1	0	0	1.000
1982—Rochester	Int.	OF	133	*548	92	153	26	6	16	52	.279	331	13	8	.977
1982—Baltimore	Amer.	OF	26	35	8	11	3	0	1	2	.314	20	1	0	1.000
1983—Baltimore	Amer.	OF	126	325	52	84	15	2	5	27	.258	200	9	4	.981
1984—Baltimore	Amer.	OF	128	383	44	80	12	5	6	30	.209	261	9	2	.993
1985—Rochester	Int.	OF	52	206	31	59	16	4	8	21	.286	124	4	1	.992
1985—Baltimore	Amer.	OF-2B	69	205	28	58	6	2	7	27	.283	148	4	3	.981
1986—Baltimore	Amer.	OF	135	404	54	92	14	4	11	49	.228	222	5	5	.978
Major League Totals—6 Years			491	1354	188	325	50	13	30	135	.240	852	28	14	.984

Selected by Baltimore Orioles' organization in 1st round (19th player selected) of free-agent draft, January 11, 1977.

CHAMPIONSHIP SERIES RECORD

Year Club	League	Pos.	G.	AB.	R.	H.	2B.	3B.	HR.	RBI.	B.A.	PO.	A.	E.	F.A.
1983—Baltimore	Amer.	OF-PH	3	9	1	2	0	0	0	0	.222	3	0	0	1.000

WORLD SERIES RECORD

Year Club	League	Pos.	G.	AB.	R.	H.	2B.	3B.	HR.	RBI.	B.A.	PO.	A.	E.	F.A.
1983—Baltimore	Amer.	PH-OF	5	9	1	4	0	0	0	1	.444	10	0	0	1.000

RONALD WAYNE SHEPHERD
(Ron)

Born October 27, 1960, at Longview, Tex.
Height, 6.04. Weight, 180.
Throws and bats righthanded.
Attended Kilgore College, Kilgore, Tex.

Major League stolen bases: 1985 (3).

Year Club	League	Pos.	G.	AB.	R.	H.	2B.	3B.	HR.	RBI.	B.A.	PO.	A.	E.	F.A.
1979—Medicine Hat	Pion.	OF	49	178	21	37	6	2	3	20	.208	92	5	8	.924
1980—Kinston	Carol.	OF	110	384	53	80	16	4	11	61	.208	239	7	●13	.950
1981—Kinston	Carol.	OF	135	486	71	114	15	3	16	66	.235	*280	9	12	.960
1982—Knoxville	South.	OF	136	482	62	119	19	8	15	65	.247	260	4	9	.967
1983—Syracuse	Int.	OF	119	404	60	110	20	3	13	62	.272	254	6	4	.985
1984—Syracuse	Int.	OF	113	363	37	80	16	3	12	50	.220	241	7	10	.961
1984—Toronto	Amer.	OF	12	4	0	0	0	0	0	0	.000	2	1	0	1.000
1985—Toronto†	Amer.	OF	38	35	7	4	2	0	0	1	.114	24	0	0	1.000
1985—Syracuse	Int.	OF	37	133	23	41	12	2	2	16	.308	60	0	3	.952
1986—Syracuse	Int.	OF	34	128	14	27	4	0	3	17	.211	80	3	2	.976
1986—Toronto	Amer.	OF	65	69	16	14	4	0	2	4	.203	30	0	0	1.000
Major League Totals—3 Years			115	108	23	18	6	0	2	5	.167	56	1	0	1.000

Selected by Toronto Blue Jays' organization in 2nd round of free-agent draft, June 5, 1979.
†On disabled list, April 7 to April 22, 1985.

PATRICK ARTHUR SHERIDAN
(Pat)

Born December 4, 1957, at Ann Arbor, Mich.
Height, 6.03. Weight, 180.
Throws right and bats lefthanded.
Attended Eastern Michigan University, Ypsilanti, Mich.
Son of Arthur Sheridan, minor league pitcher, 1952 through 1956.

Major League stolen bases: 1983 (12), 1984 (19), 1985 (11), 1986 (9). Total—51.

Year Club	League	Pos.	G.	AB.	R.	H.	2B.	3B.	HR.	RBI.	B.A.	PO.	A.	E.	F.A.
1979—Fort Myers	Fla. St.	OF	67	235	25	66	4	3	0	16	.281	142	8	1	.993
1980—Fort Myers	Fla. St.	OF-C	20	79	17	32	1	0	1	13	.405	37	4	1	.976
1980—Jacksonville†	South.	OF	97	367	63	112	17	7	5	42	.305	201	7	9	.959
1981—Omaha‡	A. A.	OF	86	315	49	94	15	8	5	31	.298	193	2	3	.985
1981—Kansas City	Amer.	OF	3	1	0	0	0	0	0	0	.000	2	0	0	1.000
1982—Omaha§	A. A.	OF	41	135	8	34	8	1	0	13	.252	92	3	0	1.000
1983—Omaha	A. A.	OF	20	75	16	23	4	5	4	14	.307	53	2	0	1.000
1983—Kansas City	Amer.	OF	109	333	43	90	12	2	7	36	.270	237	6	3	.988
1984—Kansas City	Amer.	OF	138	481	64	136	24	4	8	53	.283	273	8	4	.986
1985—Kansas City x	Amer.	OF	78	206	18	47	9	2	3	17	.228	116	3	2	.983
1985—Omaha y	A. A.	OF	8	28	1	10	1	0	0	1	.357	8	1	0	1.000
1986—Nashville	A. A.	OF	9	35	4	10	2	0	1	5	.286	16	0	0	1.000
1986—Detroit	Amer.	OF	98	236	41	56	9	1	6	19	.237	172	1	4	.977
Major League Totals—5 Years			426	1257	166	329	54	9	24	125	.262	800	18	13	.984

Selected by Cincinnati Reds' organization in 36th round of free-agent draft, June 8, 1976.
Selected by Kansas City Royals' organization in 3rd round of free-agent draft, June 5, 1979.
†On disabled list, May 16 to June 2, 1980.
‡On disabled list, May 25 to June 25, 1981.
§On disabled list, April 27 to June 25 and June 27 to July 19, 1982.
xOn disabled list, June 19 to July 4 and August 5 to September 3, 1985; included rehabilitation disability assignment to Omaha, August 26 to September 3, 1985.
yReleased, March 28, 1986; signed by Detroit Tigers, April 25, 1986.

Tied Championship Series record for most home runs by pinch-hitter, game (1), October 9, 1985.

Year	Club	League	Pos.	G.	AB.	R.	H.	2B.	3B.	HR.	RBI.	B.A.	PO.	A.	E.	F.A.
1984—Kansas City		Amer.	OF	3	6	1	0	0	0	0	0	.000	9	0	1	.900
1985—Kansas City		Amer.	OF-PH	7	20	4	3	0	0	2	3	.150	13	0	0	1.000
Championship Series Totals—2 Years				10	26	5	3	0	0	2	3	.115	22	0	1	.957

WORLD SERIES RECORD

Year	Club	League	Pos.	G.	AB.	R.	H.	2B.	3B.	HR.	RBI.	B.A.	PO.	A.	E.	F.A.
1985—Kansas City		Amer.	PH-OF	5	18	0	4	2	0	0	1	.222	6	0	0	1.000

STEPHEN MACK SHIELDS
(Steve)

Born November 30, 1958, in Etowah County, Ala.
Height, 6.05. Weight, 220.
Throws and bats righthanded.
Tied for International League lead in shutouts with 3 and hit batsmen with 8 in 1985.
Tied for Eastern League lead in complete games with 13 and shutouts with 3 in 1982.
Tied for Eastern League lead in intentional bases on balls issued with 10 in 1981.

Year	Club	League	G.	IP.	W.	L.	Pct.	H.	R.	ER.	SO.	BB.	ERA.
1977—Elmira		NYP	15	81	1	6	.143	72	45	37	108	37	4.11
1978—Winter Haven†		Florida St.	14	51	3	3	.500	52	14	11	34	9	1.94
1979—Winston-Salem		Carolina	24	152	11	8	.579	149	78	51	152	80	3.02
1980—Bristol		Eastern	39	113	5	6	.455	128	79	61	63	77	4.86
1981—Bristol		Eastern	29	126	5	*14	.263	136	75	65	87	65	4.64
1982—Bristol		Eastern	29	170⅓	10	13	.435	172	100	67	125	71	3.54
1983—Pawtucket‡		Int'national	36	143	4	12	.250	171	94	74	115	63	4.66
1984—Richmond		Int'national	39	110	9	4	.692	122	69	58	101	39	4.75
1985—Richmond		Int'national	18	133	6	7	.462	110	53	39	88	54	2.64
1985—Atlanta		National	23	68	1	2	.333	86	46	39	29	32	5.16
1986—Richmond		Int'national	21	149⅓	9	8	.529	133	55	43	●124	55	2.59
1986—Atlanta§		National	6	12⅔	0	0	.000	13	10	10	6	7	7.11
1986—Kansas City x		American	3	8⅔	0	0	.000	3	3	2	2	4	2.08
National League Totals—2 Years			29	80⅔	1	2	.333	99	56	49	35	39	5.47
American League Totals—1 Year			3	8⅔	0	0	.000	3	3	2	2	4	2.08
Major League Totals—2 Years			32	89⅓	1	2	.333	102	59	51	37	43	5.14

Selected by Boston Red Sox' organization in 10th round of free-agent draft, June 7, 1977.
†On disabled list, April 10 to June 14, 1978.
‡Granted free agency, October 20, 1983; signed by Richmond (Atlanta Braves' organization), October 26, 1983.
§Traded to Kansas City Royals for Outfielder Darryl Motley, September 23, 1986.
xTraded with Pitcher Scott Bankhead and Outfielder Mike Kingery to Seattle Mariners for Outfielder Danny Tartabull and Pitcher Rick Luecken, December 19, 1986.

CRAIG BARRY SHIPLEY

Born January 7, 1963, at Parramatta, Australia.
Height, 6.01. Weight, 175.
Throws right and bats left and righthanded.
Attended University of Alabama, University, Ala.

Year	Club	League	Pos.	G.	AB.	R.	H.	2B.	3B.	HR.	RBI.	B.A.	PO.	A.	E.	F.A.
1984—Vero Beach†		Fla. St.	SS	85	293	56	82	11	2	0	28	.280	137	216	17	.954
1985—Albuquerque		P. C.	SS	124	414	50	100	9	2	0	30	.242	202	367	21	.964
1986—Albuquerque		P. C.	SS	61	203	33	59	8	2	0	16	.291	99	173	18	.938
1986—Los Angeles		Nat.	SS-2B-3B	12	27	3	3	1	0	0	4	.111	16	18	3	.919
Major League Totals—1 Year				12	27	3	3	1	0	0	4	.111	16	18	3	.919

Signed as a free agent by Los Angeles Dodgers' organization, May 28, 1984.
†Batted righthanded.

ROBERT CHARLES SHIRLEY
(Bob)

Born June 25, 1954, at Oklahoma City, Okla.
Height, 5.11. Weight, 180.
Throws left and bats righthanded.
Attended University of Oklahoma, Norman, Okla.
Major League saves: 1978 (5), 1980 (7), 1981 (1), 1985 (2), 1986 (3). Total—18.

Year	Club	League	G.	IP.	W.	L.	Pct.	H.	R.	ER.	SO.	BB.	ERA.
1976—Amarillo		Texas	16	111	9	5	.643	113	55	41	90	39	3.32
1976—Hawaii		P. Coast	13	81	5	5	.500	91	62	47	47	24	5.22
1977—San Diego		National	39	214	12	18	.400	215	107	88	146	100	3.70
1978—San Diego		National	50	166	8	11	.421	164	75	68	102	61	3.69
1979—San Diego		National	49	205	8	16	.333	196	89	77	117	59	3.38
1980—San Diego†		National	59	137	11	12	.478	143	58	54	67	54	3.55
1981—St. Louis‡		National	28	79	6	4	.600	78	42	36	36	34	4.10
1982—Cincinnati§		National	41	152⅔	8	13	.381	138	74	61	89	73	3.60
1983—New York		American	25	108	5	8	.385	122	71	61	53	36	5.08
1984—New York		American	41	114⅓	3	3	.500	119	47	43	48	38	3.38

Year Club	League	G.	IP.	W.	L.	Pct.	H.	R.	ER.	SO.	BB.	ERA.
1985—New York	American	48	109	5	5	.500	103	34	32	55	26	2.64
1986—New York x	American	39	105⅓	0	4	.000	108	60	59	64	40	5.04
National League Totals—6 Years		266	953⅔	53	74	.417	934	445	384	557	381	3.62
American League Totals—4 Years		153	436⅔	13	20	.394	452	212	195	220	140	4.02
Major League Totals—10 Years		419	1390⅓	66	94	.413	1386	657	579	777	521	3.75

Selected by Los Angeles Dodgers' organization in 38th round of free-agent draft, June 6, 1972.
Selected by San Francisco Giants' organization in 5th round of free-agent draft, June 4, 1975.
Selected by San Diego Padres' organization in secondary phase of free-agent draft, January 7, 1976.
†Traded with Pitcher Rollie Fingers, Catcher-First Baseman Gene Tenace and a player to be named later to St. Louis Cardinals for Catchers Terry Kennedy and Steve Swisher, Pitchers John Littlefield, Al Olmsted, John Urrea and Kim Seaman and Infielder Mike Phillips, December 8, 1980; St. Louis organization acquired Catcher Bob Geren to complete deal, December 10, 1980.
‡Traded to Cincinnati Reds for Pitchers Jeff Lahti and Jose Brito, April 1, 1982.
§Granted free agency, November 10, 1982; signed by New York Yankees, December 10, 1982.
xReleased, December 22, 1986.

ERIC VAUGHN SHOW
Name rhymes with Chow.

Born May 19, 1956, at Riverside, Calif.
Height, 6.01. Weight, 185.
Throws and bats righthanded.
Attended University of California, Riverside, Calif.

Major League saves: 1981 (3), 1982 (3). Total—6.
Led Texas League in hit batsmen with 10 in 1980.

Year Club	League	G.	IP.	W.	L.	Pct.	H.	R.	ER.	SO.	BB.	ERA.
1978—Walla Walla	Northwest	11	60	5	2	.714	47	28	19	43	20	2.85
1979—Reno	California	28	169	13	9	.591	144	79	67	186	92	3.57
1980—Amarillo	Texas	26	166	12	6	.667	141	81	69	144	81	3.74
1981—Hawaii	P. Coast	34	85	7	3	.700	67	30	24	70	35	2.54
1981—San Diego	National	15	23	1	3	.250	17	9	8	22	9	3.13
1982—San Diego	National	47	150	10	6	.625	117	49	44	88	48	2.64
1983—San Diego	National	35	200⅔	15	12	.556	201	97	93	120	74	4.17
1984—San Diego	National	32	206⅔	15	9	.625	175	88	78	104	88	3.40
1985—San Diego	National	35	233	12	11	.522	212	95	80	141	87	3.09
1986—San Diego†	National	24	136⅓	9	5	.643	109	47	45	94	69	2.97
Major League Totals—6 Years		188	949⅔	62	46	.574	831	385	348	569	375	3.30

Selected by Minnesota Twins' organization in 36th round of free-agent draft, June 5, 1974.
Selected by San Diego Padres' organization in 18th round of free-agent draft, June 6, 1978.
†On disabled list, July 8 to July 31 and August 28, 1986 through remainder of season.

CHAMPIONSHIP SERIES RECORD
Tied Championship Series record for most earned runs allowed, five-game Series (8), 1984.
Tied National League Championship Series record for most runs allowed, five-game Series (8), 1984.

Year Club	League	G.	IP.	W.	L.	Pct.	H.	R.	ER.	SO.	BB.	ERA.
1984—San Diego	National	2	5⅓	0	1	.000	8	8	8	2	4	13.50

WORLD SERIES RECORD
Year Club	League	G.	IP.	W.	L.	Pct.	H.	R.	ER.	SO.	BB.	ERA.
1984—San Diego	National	1	2⅔	0	1	.000	4	4	3	2	1	10.13

RICHARD FREDERICK SIEBERT
(Rick)

Born October 13, 1963, at East Cleveland, O.
Height, 6.02. Weight, 165.
Throws and bats righthanded.
Attended Kent State University, Kent, O.

Tied for Carolina League lead in balks with 7 in 1986.

Year Club	League	G.	IP.	W.	L.	Pct.	H.	R.	ER.	SO.	BB.	ERA.
1984—Pulaski	Ap'lachian	14	68	4	3	.571	66	39	29	78	30	3.84
1985—Sumter	S. Atlantic	28	147	7	8	.467	149	93	82	145	72	5.02
1986—Durham	Carolina	30	151⅓	11	9	.550	172	103	92	104	64	5.47

Selected by Atlanta Braves' organization in 8th round of free-agent draft, June 4, 1984.

RUBEN ANGEL SIERRA (GARCIA)
Born October 6, 1965, at Rio Piedras, Puerto Rico.
Height, 6.01. Weight, 175.
Throws right and bats left and righthanded.

Major League stolen bases: 1986 (7).
Switch-hit home runs in one game, September 13, 1986.

Year Club	League	Pos.	G.	AB.	R.	H.	2B.	3B.	HR.	RBI.	B.A.	PO.	A.	E.	F.A.
1983—Sarasota Ran.†	Gulf C.	OF	48	182	26	44	7	3	1	26	.242	67	6	4	.948
1984—Burlington	Midw.	OF	●138	482	55	127	33	5	6	75	.263	239	18	★20	.928
1985—Tulsa	Texas	OF	★137	★545	63	138	34	★8	13	74	.253	234	12	★15	.943

Year	Club	League	Pos.	G.	AB.	R.	H.	2B.	3B.	HR.	RBI.	B.A.	PO.	A.	E.	F.A.
1986—Oklahoma City	A. A.		OF	46	189	31	56	11	2	9	41	.296	114	4	2	.983
1986—Texas	Amer.		OF	113	382	50	101	13	10	16	55	.264	200	7	6	.972
Major League Totals—1 Year				113	382	50	101	13	10	16	55	.264	200	7	6	.972

Signed as free agent by Texas Rangers' organization, November 21, 1982.

†Batted righthanded.

ULISES SIERRA (PIZARRO)
(Candy)

Born March 27, 1967, at Rio Piedras, Puerto Rico.
Height, 6.02. Weight, 190.
Throws and bats righthanded.

Pitched seven-inning, 2-0 no-hit victory against Modesto, June 15, 1984 (first game).

Year	Club	League	G.	IP.	W.	L.	Pct.	H.	R.	ER.	SO.	BB.	ERA.
1983—Spokane		Northwest	23	37	1	5	.167	44	33	22	31	21	5.35
1984—Reno		California	28	135⅓	11	4	.733	133	67	56	106	57	3.72
1985—Beaumont		Texas	23	104⅓	3	6	.333	109	65	55	93	60	4.74
1986—Beaumont		Texas	16	90⅔	4	5	.444	104	53	49	60	37	4.86

Signed as free agent by San Diego Padres' organization, May 29, 1983.

TED LYLE SIMMONS

Born August 9, 1949, at Highland Park, Mich.
Height, 6.00. Weight, 200.
Throws right and bats left and righthanded.
Attended Wayne State University, Detroit, Mich. and
University of Michigan, Ann Arbor, Mich.

Tied major league record for most intentional bases on balls by switch-hitter, season (25), 1977.

Established National League records for most home runs by switch hitter, career (176); fewest errors by catcher, season, for leader in errors (15), 1975.

Tied National League record for most games, switch-hit home runs, season (1), April 17, 1975 and June 11, 1979; most games switch-hit home runs, league (2).

Established American League records for longest errorless game and most innings played by first baseman, game (25), May 8, finished May 9, 1984 (fielded 24⅓ innings).

Major League stolen bases: 1970 (2), 1971 (1), 1972 (1), 1973 (2), 1975 (1), 1977 (2), 1978 (1), 1980 (1), 1983 (4), 1984 (3), 1985 (1), 1986 (1). Total—20.

Switch-hit home runs in one game three times: April 17, 1975, June 11, 1979 and May 2, 1982.

Led National League in intentional bases on balls received with 19 in 1976 and 25 in 1977.

Led National League in grounding into double plays with 29 in 1973.

Led National League catchers in putouts with 842 in 1972 and 888 in 1973.

Led National League catchers in assists with 78 in 1972 and 74 in 1973.

Led National League catchers in total chances with 928 in 1972, 975 in 1973 and 880 in 1975.

Led National League in passed balls with 25 in 1973, 28 in 1975 and 14 in 1979.

Led California League catchers in putouts with 984 in 1968.

Tied for California League lead in being hit by pitch with 9 in 1968.

Named catcher on THE SPORTING NEWS National League All-Star Team, 1977 through 1979.

Named catcher on THE SPORTING NEWS National League Silver Slugger team, 1980.

Named California League Most Valuable Player, 1968.

Received reported $50,000 bonus to sign with St. Louis Cardinals, 1967.

Year	Club	League	Pos.	G.	AB.	R.	H.	2B.	3B.	HR.	RBI.	B.A.	PO.	A.	E.	F.A.
1967—Sarasota Cards	Gulf C.	C	6	20	5	7	1	1	2	8	.350	33	0	0	1.000
1967—Cedar Rapids	Midw.	OF-C	47	171	15	46	11	2	4	34	.269	119	8	3	.977
1968—Modesto	Calif.	★C-OF	136	493	86	163	30	2	28	★117	★.331	989	79	★16	.985
1968—St. Louis	Nat.	C	2	3	0	1	0	0	0	0	.333	3	1	0	1.000
1969—Tulsa	A. A.	C-3-O-1	129	499	80	158	33	4	16	88	.317	463	92	19	.967
1969—St. Louis†	Nat.	C	5	14	0	3	0	1	0	3	.214	22	0	1	.957
1970—Tulsa	A. A.	C	15	51	10	19	4	1	1	8	.373	99	7	0	1.000
1970—St. Louis	Nat.	C	82	284	29	69	8	2	3	24	.243	466	37	5	.990
1971—St. Louis‡	Nat.	C	133	510	64	155	32	4	7	77	.304	747	52	9	.989
1972—St. Louis	Nat.	C-1B	152	594	70	180	36	6	16	96	.303	967	93	13	.988
1973—St. Louis	Nat.	C-1B-OF	161	619	62	192	36	2	13	91	.310	932	78	14	.986
1974—St. Louis	Nat.	C-1B	152	599	66	163	33	6	20	103	.272	813	87	15	.984
1975—St. Louis	Nat.	★C-1B-OF	157	581	80	193	32	3	18	100	.332	818	64	★15	.983
1976—St. Louis	Nat.	C-1-O-3	150	546	60	159	35	3	5	75	.291	726	88	10	.988
1977—St. Louis	Nat.	C-OF	150	516	82	164	25	3	21	95	.318	683	75	10	.987
1978—St. Louis	Nat.	★C-OF	152	516	71	148	40	5	22	80	.287	703	★88	10	.988
1979—St. Louis§	Nat.	C	123	448	68	127	22	0	26	87	.283	606	69	10	.985
1980—St. Louis x	Nat.	C-OF	145	495	84	150	33	2	21	98	.303	528	71	10	.984
1981—Milwaukee	Amer.	C-1B	100	380	45	82	13	3	14	61	.216	333	41	8	.979
1982—Milwaukee	Amer.	C	137	539	73	145	29	0	23	97	.269	570	62	3	★.995
1983—Milwaukee y	Amer.	C	153	600	76	185	39	3	13	108	.308	395	41	11	.975
1984—Milwaukee	Amer.	1B-3B	132	497	44	110	23	2	4	52	.221	352	52	8	.981
1985—Milwaukee z	Amer.	1B-C-3B	143	528	60	144	28	2	12	76	.273	291	26	3	.991
1986—Atlanta	Nat.	1B-C-3B	76	127	14	32	5	0	4	25	.252	167	18	6	.969
National League Totals—14 Years			1640	5852	750	1736	337	37	176	954	.297	8181	821	128	.986
American League Totals—5 Years			665	2544	298	666	132	10	66	394	.262	1941	222	33	.985
Major League Totals—19 Years			2305	8396	1048	2402	469	47	242	1348	.286	10122	1043	161	.986

Selected by St. Louis Cardinals' organization in 1st round (10th player selected) of free-agent draft, June 6, 1967.

†On military list, December 12, 1969 through May 9, 1970.
‡On military list, June 19 to July 4, 1971.
§On disabled list, June 25 to July 24, 1979.
xTraded with Pitchers Rollie Fingers and Pete Vuckovich to Milwaukee Brewers for Pitchers Lary Sorensen and Dave LaPoint and Outfielders Sixto Lezcano and David Green, December 12, 1980.
yGranted free agency, November 7, 1983; re-signed by Brewers, January 16, 1984.
zTraded to Atlanta Braves for Catcher Rick Cerone, Pitcher David Clay and Shortstop Flavio Alfaro, March 5, 1986.

DIVISION SERIES RECORD

Year Club	League	Pos.	G.	AB.	R.	H.	2B.	3B.	HR.	RBI.	B.A.	PO.	A.	E.	F.A.
1981—Milwaukee	Amer.	C	5	18	1	4	1	0	1	4	.222	23	2	1	.962

CHAMPIONSHIP SERIES RECORD

Year Club	League	Pos.	G.	AB.	R.	H.	2B.	3B.	HR.	RBI.	B.A.	PO.	A.	E.	F.A.
1982—Milwaukee	Amer.	C	5	18	3	3	0	0	0	1	.167	36	3	0	1.000

WORLD SERIES RECORD

Tied World Series record for fewest putouts by catcher, game (1), October 15, 1982.

Year Club	League	Pos.	G.	AB.	R.	H.	2B.	3B.	HR.	RBI.	B.A.	PO.	A.	E.	F.A.
1982—Milwaukee	Amer.	C	7	23	2	4	0	0	2	3	.174	28	2	1	.968

ALL-STAR GAME RECORD

Year League	Pos.	AB.	R.	H.	2B.	3B.	HR.	RBI.	B.A.	PO.	A.	E.	F.A.
1973—National	PH-C	1	0	0	0	0	0	0	.000	1	1	0	1.000
1977—National	C	3	0	0	0	0	0	0	.000	5	0	0	1.000
1978—National	C	3	0	1	0	0	0	0	.333	4	1	0	1.000
1981—American	PH	1	0	1	0	0	0	1	1.000	0	0	0	.000
1983—American	C	2	0	0	0	0	0	0	.000	4	0	0	1.000
All-Star Game Totals—5 Years		10	0	2	0	0	0	1	.200	14	2	0	1.000

Member of National League All-Star Team for 1972 and 1974 games; did not play.
Named to National League All-Star Team for 1979 game; replaced due to injury.

ROBERT LEE SIMONSON
(Bob)

Born May 30, 1964, at Grant, Mich.
Height, 6.02. Weight, 220.
Throws and bats righthanded.
Attended Taft College, Taft, Calif.

Led Midwest League batters in strikeouts with 145 in 1986.

Year Club	League	Pos.	G.	AB.	R.	H.	2B.	3B.	HR.	RBI.	B.A.	PO.	A.	E.	F.A.
1984—Paintsville	Appal.	OF	48	153	36	38	6	2	8	23	.248	3	0	1	.750
1985—Beloit	Midw.	OF	9	24	1	3	1	0	0	2	.125	10	2	0	1.000
1985—Helena	Pion.	OF	51	166	39	44	6	1	8	27	.265	44	1	1	.978
1986—Beloit†	Midw.	OF	133	*522	86	145	18	6	27	95	.278	209	7	8	.964

Selected by Milwaukee Brewers' organization in 2nd round of free-agent draft, June 4, 1984.
†Drafted by Montreal Expos, December 9, 1986.

DOUGLAS RANDALL SISK
(Doug)

Born September 26, 1957, at Renton, Wash.
Height, 6.02. Weight, 210.
Throws and bats righthanded.
Attended Green River Community College, Auburn, Wash. and received bachelor of science degree
in criminal justice from Washington State University, Pullman, Wash.

Major League saves: 1982 (1), 1983 (11), 1984 (15), 1985 (2), 1986 (1). Total—30.
Led Appalachian League pitchers in games started with 15 in 1980.

Year Club	League	G.	IP.	W.	L.	Pct.	H.	R.	ER.	SO.	BB.	ERA.
1980—Kingsport	Ap'lachian	15	*98	●8	5	.615	*91	46	29	41	45	2.66
1981—Lynchburg	Carolina	36	83	3	2	.600	78	35	30	61	32	3.25
1981—Jackson	Texas	14	25	3	0	1.000	23	11	10	15	12	3.60
1982—Jackson	Texas	44	138	11	8	.611	136	59	41	53	58	*2.67
1982—New York	National	8	8⅔	0	1	.000	5	1	1	4	4	1.04
1983—New York	National	67	104⅓	5	4	.556	88	38	26	33	59	2.24
1984—New York†	National	50	77⅔	1	3	.250	57	24	18	32	54	2.09
1985—New York	National	42	73	4	5	.444	86	48	43	26	40	5.30
1985—Tidewater	Int'national	4	15	0	2	.000	15	12	12	4	13	7.20
1986—Tidewater	Int'national	9	30	2	3	.400	34	16	14	19	9	4.20
1986—New York	National	41	70⅔	4	2	.667	77	31	24	31	31	3.06
Major League Totals—5 Years		208	334⅓	14	15	.483	313	142	112	126	188	3.01

Signed as free agent by New York Mets' organization, June 10, 1980.
†On disabled list, August 9 to August 29, 1984.

CHAMPIONSHIP SERIES RECORD

Year Club	League	G.	IP.	W.	L.	Pct.	H.	R.	ER.	SO.	BB.	ERA.
1986—New York	National	1	1	0	0	.000	1	0	0	0	1	0.00

Year Club	League	G.	IP.	W.	L.	Pct.	H.	R.	ER.	SO.	BB.	ERA.
1986—New York	National	1	⅔	0	0	.000	0	0	0	1	1	0.00

JOEL PATRICK SKINNER

Born February 21, 1961, at San Diego, Calif.
Height, 6.04. Weight, 205.
Throws and bats righthanded.
Attended San Diego Mesa College, San Diego, Calif.
Son of Bob Skinner, outfielder-first baseman with Pittsburgh Pirates, Cincinnati Reds and St. Louis
Cardinals, 1954 through 1966; manager, Philadelphia Phillies, 1968 and 1969, manager,
San Diego Padres, 1977; coach, San Diego Padres, 1977; coach, California Angels, 1978;
and coach with Pittsburgh Pirates, 1979 through 1985.

Major League stolen bases: 1984 (1), 1986 (1). Total—2.
Led American Association batters in strikeouts with 115 and tied for lead in grounding into double plays with 16 in 1985.
Led American Association catchers in total chances with 698 and double plays with 13 in 1985.
Tied for South Atlantic League lead in double plays by catchers with 7 in 1980.

Year Club	League	Pos.	G.	AB.	R.	H.	2B.	3B.	HR.	RBI.	B.A.	PO.	A.	E.	F.A.
1980—Shelby	S. Atl.	C	100	324	36	73	15	2	7	27	.225	536	63	18	.971
1981—Greenwood†‡	S. Atl.	C	117	428	48	114	25	2	11	63	.266	766	42	★22	.974
1982—Glens Falls	East.	C	120	422	49	107	11	6	7	65	.254	726	80	12	.985
1983—Denver	A. A.	C	108	361	55	94	15	5	12	50	.260	550	54	5	.992
1983—Chicago	Amer.	C	6	11	2	3	0	0	0	1	.273	20	4	1	.960
1984—Denver§	A. A.	C	42	141	27	40	6	0	10	27	.284	255	24	5	.982
1984—Chicago	Amer.	C	43	80	4	17	2	0	0	3	.213	171	11	2	.989
1985—Buffalo	A. A.	C	115	390	47	94	13	0	12	59	.241	★623	★65	10	.986
1985—Chicago	Amer.	C	22	44	9	15	4	1	1	5	.341	94	8	3	.971
1986—Chi.x-N.Y.	Amer.	C	114	315	23	73	9	1	5	37	.232	507	37	9	.984
Major League Totals—4 Years			185	450	38	108	15	2	6	46	.240	792	60	15	.983

Selected by Pittsburgh Pirates' organization in 36th round of free-agent draft, June 5, 1979.
†On disabled list, June 1 to June 13, 1981.
‡Selected by Chicago White Sox' organization in player compensation pool draft, February 2, 1982. (Chicago received compensation for Philadelphia Phillies' signing of free agent Pitcher Ed Farmer, a Type A player, January 28, 1982.)
§On disabled list, July 23, 1984 through remainder of season.
xTraded with Outfielder-Designated Hitter Ron Kittle and Infielder Wayne Tolleson to New York Yankees for Catcher Ron Hassey, Shortstop Carlos Martinez and a player to be named later, July 30, 1986; New York traded Catcher Bill Lindsey to Chicago White Sox' organization to complete deal, December 24, 1986.

MICHAEL ROSS SKINNER

(Mike)

Born August 5, 1964, at Teaneck, N.J.
Height, 6.01. Weight, 195.
Throws and bats righthanded.
Attended County College of Morris, Randolph Township,
N.J., and Jacksonville University, Jacksonville, Fla.

Led International League in home runs allowed with 23 in 1986.
Tied for New York-Pennsylvania League lead in complete games with 7 in 1983.

Year Club	League	G.	IP.	W.	L.	Pct.	H.	R.	ER.	SO.	BB.	ERA.
1983—Bluefield	Ap'lachian	7	22⅔	2	1	.667	13	9	9	30	14	3.57
1984—Bluefield	Ap'lachian	3	14	1	1	.500	25	13	7	13	7	4.50
1984—Newark	NYP	11	79⅓	7	2	.778	65	25	18	55	25	2.04
1985—Hagerstown	Carolina	11	74	5	4	.556	69	40	37	70	16	4.50
1985—Charlotte	Southern	16	111⅓	11	1	★.917	97	37	32	70	43	2.59
1986—Rochester	Int'national	26	161⅓	10	8	.556	166	87	75	96	58	4.18

Selected by Baltimore Orioles' organization in 12th round of free-agent draft, June 6, 1983.

JAMES MICHAEL SLATON

(Jim)

Born June 19, 1950, at Long Beach, Calif.
Height, 6.00. Weight, 185.
Throws and bats righthanded.
Attended Antelope Valley College, Lancaster, Calif.

Pitched 5-0 no-hit victory against Wichita, August 3, 1972.
Major League saves: 1982 (6), 1983 (5), 1985 (1), 1986 (2). Total—14.

Year Club	League	G.	IP.	W.	L.	Pct.	H.	R.	ER.	SO.	BB.	ERA.
1969—Billings	Pioneer	2	8	1	0	1.000	1	0	0	16	0	0.00
1969—Clinton	Midwest	13	82	6	3	.667	65	27	26	83	34	2.85
1970—Clinton†	Midwest	2	18	1	1	.500	9	4	3	15	5	1.50
1971—Evansville	Am. Assoc.	4	32	1	0	1.000	22	9	5	26	9	1.39
1971—Milwaukee	American	26	148	10	8	.556	140	67	62	71	71	3.77
1972—Evansville	Am. Assoc.	16	114	11	2	.846	97	39	37	68	37	2.92
1972—Milwaukee	American	9	44	1	6	.143	50	31	27	17	21	5.52
1973—Milwaukee	American	38	276	13	15	.464	266	127	114	134	99	3.72
1974—Milwaukee	American	40	250	13	16	.448	255	117	109	126	102	3.92

Year Club	League	G.	IP.	W.	L.	Pct.	H.	R.	ER.	SO.	BB.	ERA.
1975—Milwaukee	American	37	217	11	18	.379	238	129	109	119	90	4.52
1976—Milwaukee	American	38	293	14	15	.483	•287	•126	112	138	94	3.44
1977—Milwaukee‡	American	32	221	10	14	.417	223	104	88	104	77	3.58
1978—Detroit§	American	35	234	17	11	.607	235	117	107	92	85	4.12
1979—Milwaukee	American	32	213	15	9	.625	229	95	86	80	54	3.63
1980—Milwaukee x	American	3	16	1	1	.500	17	10	8	4	5	4.50
1981—Milwaukee	American	24	117	5	7	.417	120	60	57	47	50	4.38
1982—Milwaukee y	American	39	117⅔	10	6	.625	117	48	43	59	41	3.29
1983—Milwaukee z	American	46	112⅓	14	6	.700	112	57	54	38	56	4.33
1984—California	American	32	163	7	10	.412	192	95	90	67	56	4.97
1985—California	American	29	148⅓	6	10	.375	162	82	72	60	63	4.37
1986—California a-Detroit b	American	36	113⅓	4	6	.400	130	70	64	43	40	5.08
Major League Totals—16 Years		496	2683⅔	151	158	.489	2773	1335	1202	1191	1004	4.03

Selected by Seattle Pilots' organization in 14th round of free-agent draft, June 5, 1969.
†On military list, May 8, 1970 through remainder of season.
‡Traded with Pitcher Rich Folkers to Detroit Tigers for Outfielder Ben Oglivie, December 9, 1977.
§Granted free agency, November 2, 1978; signed by Milwaukee Brewers, November 28, 1978.
xOn disabled list, May 25 to October 1, 1980.
yOn disabled list, April 1 to April 23, 1982.
zTraded to California Angels for Outfielder Bobby Clark, December 20, 1983.
aReleased, June 30, 1986; signed by Detroit Tigers, July 14, 1986.
bReleased, October 15, 1986.

DIVISION SERIES RECORD

Year Club	League	G.	IP.	W.	L.	Pct.	H.	R.	ER.	SO.	BB.	ERA.
1981—Milwaukee	American	4	6	0	0	.000	6	2	2	2	0	3.00

CHAMPIONSHIP SERIES RECORD

Year Club	League	G.	IP.	W.	L.	Pct.	H.	R.	ER.	SO.	BB.	ERA.
1982—Milwaukee	American	2	4⅔	0	0	.000	3	2	1	3	1	1.93

WORLD SERIES RECORD

Year Club	League	G.	IP.	W.	L.	Pct.	H.	R.	ER.	SO.	BB.	ERA.
1982—Milwaukee	American	2	2⅔	1	0	1.000	1	0	0	1	2	0.00

ALL-STAR GAME RECORD

Member of American League All-Star Team in 1977; did not play.

DONALD MARTIN SLAUGHT
(Don)

Born September 11, 1959, at Long Beach, Calif.
Height, 6.00. Weight, 185.
Throws and bats righthanded.
Attended El Camino College, Torrance, Calif., and
University of California, Los Angeles, Calif.
Major League stolen bases: 1983 (3), 1985 (5), 1986 (3). Total—11.

Year Club	League	Pos.	G.	AB.	R.	H.	2B.	3B.	HR.	RBI.	B.A.	PO.	A.	E.	F.A.
1980—Fort Myers	Fla. St.	C	50	176	13	46	9	0	2	16	.261	175	34	4	.981
1981—Jacksonville	South.	C-1B	96	379	45	127	21	2	6	44	.335	482	61	9	.984
1981—Omaha†	A. A.	C	22	71	10	21	4	0	2	8	.296	91	7	3	.970
1982—Omaha‡	A. A.	C	53	206	29	55	10	1	4	16	.267	216	25	5	.980
1982—Kansas City	Amer.	C	43	115	14	32	6	0	3	8	.278	156	7	1	.994
1983—Kansas City§	Amer.	C	83	276	21	86	13	4	0	28	.312	299	18	12	.964
1984—Kansas City x	Amer.	C	124	409	48	108	27	4	4	42	.264	547	44	11	.982
1985—Texas y	Amer.	C	102	343	34	96	17	4	8	35	.280	550	33	6	.990
1986—Texas z	Amer.	C	95	314	39	83	17	1	13	46	.264	533	40	4	.993
1986—Oklahoma City	A. A.	C	3	12	2	4	1	0	0	1	.333	6	1	0	1.000
Major League Totals—5 Years			447	1457	156	405	80	13	28	159	.278	2085	142	34	.985

Selected by Milwaukee Brewers' organization in 19th round of free-agent draft, June 5, 1979.
Selected by Kansas City Royals' organization in 7th round of free-agent draft, June 3, 1980.
†On disabled list, August 16 to September 29, 1981.
‡On disabled list, April 21 to May 15, 1982.
§On disabled list, May 16 to June 1, 1983.
xTraded to Texas Rangers as part of a six-player, four-team deal in which Kansas City Royals acquired Catcher Jim Sundberg from Milwaukee Brewers, New York Mets' organization acquired Pitcher Frank Wills from Kansas City, Milwaukee acquired Pitcher Danny Darwin and a player to be named later from Texas and Pitcher Tim Leary from New York, January 18, 1985; Milwaukee organization acquired Catcher Bill Hance from Texas to complete deal, January 30, 1985.
yOn disabled list, August 9 to August 26, 1985.
zOn disabled list, May 18 to July 4, 1986; included rehabilitation disability assignment to Oklahoma City, July 1 to July 4, 1986.

CHAMPIONSHIP SERIES RECORD

Year Club	League	Pos.	G.	AB.	R.	H.	2B.	3B.	HR.	RBI.	B.A.	PO.	A.	E.	F.A.
1984—Kansas City	Amer.	C	3	11	0	4	0	0	0	0	.364	17	0	3	.850

ROY FREDERICK SMALLEY III

Born October 25, 1952, at Los Angeles, Calif.
Height, 6.01. Weight, 182.
Throws right and bats left and righthanded.
Attended Los Angeles City Community College, Los Angeles, Calif., and
University of Southern California, Los Angeles, Calif.
Son of Roy Smalley, Jr., infielder with Chicago Cubs, Milwaukee Braves and
Philadelphia Phillies, 1948 through 1958; nephew of Gene Mauch, manager of California Angels.

Tied major league record for most strikeouts, two consecutive games (8), August 28 and 29, 1976 (26 innings).
Major League stolen bases: 1975 (4), 1976 (2), 1977 (5), 1978 (2), 1979 (2), 1980 (3), 1983 (3), 1984 (3), 1986 (1). Total—25.
Switch-hit home runs in one game, September 5, 1982 and May 30, 1986.
Led American League in sacrifice hits with 25 in 1976.
Led American League shortstops in double plays with 116 in 1977, with 121 in 1978 and with 144 in 1979.
Led American League shortstops in putouts with 296 in 1979.
Led American League shortstops in total chances with 792 in 1977, 839 in 1978 and 897 in 1979.
Named shortstop on THE SPORTING NEWS American League All-Star Team, 1979.
Received reported $100,000 bonus to sign with Texas Rangers, 1974.

Year—Club	League	Pos.	G.	AB.	R.	H.	2B.	3B.	HR.	RBI.	B.A.	PO.	A.	E.	F.A.
1974—Pittsfield	East.	SS	125	406	74	102	22	5	14	42	.251	146	376	*42	.926
1975—Spokane	P. C.	SS-2B	43	162	26	55	8	1	2	19	.340	88	151	10	.960
1975—Texas	Amer.	SS-2B-C	78	250	22	57	8	0	3	33	.228	108	232	20	.944
1976—Tex.†-Minn.	Amer.	SS-2B	144	513	61	133	18	3	3	44	.259	274	447	26	.965
1977—Minnesota	Amer.	SS	150	584	93	135	21	5	6	56	.231	255	*504	33	.958
1978—Minnesota	Amer.	SS	158	586	80	160	31	3	19	77	.273	*287	*527	25	.970
1979—Minnesota	Amer.	*SS-1B	●162	621	94	168	28	3	24	95	.271	305	*572	29	.968
1980—Minnesota	Amer.	SS-1B	133	486	64	135	24	1	12	63	.278	226	448	17	.990
1981—Minnesota	Amer.	SS-1B	56	167	24	44	7	1	7	22	.263	62	89	8	.950
1982—Minn.‡-N.Y.	Amer.	SS-3B-2B	146	499	57	127	15	2	20	67	.255	142	367	15	.971
1983—New York	Amer.	SS-3B-1B	130	451	70	124	24	1	18	62	.275	289	295	21	.965
1984—N.Y.§-Chic. x	Amer.	3B-SS-1B	114	344	32	73	12	1	11	39	.212	90	158	16	.939
1985—Macon	Amer.	SS-3B-1B	129	388	57	100	20	0	12	45	.258	70	133	3	.985
1986—Minnesota	Amer.	SS-3B	143	459	59	113	20	4	20	57	.246	14	34	1	.980
Major League Totals—12 Years			1543	5348	713	1369	228	24	155	660	.256	2122	3806	214	.965

Selected by Montreal Expos' organization in 35th round of free-agent draft, June 4, 1970.
Selected by Boston Red Sox' organization in secondary phase of free-agent draft, January 13, 1971.
Selected by St. Louis Cardinals' organization in secondary phase of free-agent draft, June 8, 1971.
Selected by Boston Red Sox' organization in secondary phase of free-agent draft, January 12, 1972.
Selected by Texas Rangers' organization in 1st round (first player selected) of free-agent draft, January 9, 1974.
†Traded with Pitchers Bill Singer and Jim Gideon, Infielder Mike Cubbage, and $250,000 cash to Minnesota Twins for Pitcher Bert Blyleven and Shortstop Danny Thompson, June 1, 1976.
‡Traded to New York Yankees for Pitchers Ron Davis and Paul Boris, Shortstop Greg Gagne and a reported $400,000, April 10, 1982.
§Traded to Chicago White Sox for two players to be named later, July 18, 1984; New York Yankees' organization acquired Pitchers Kevin Hickey and Doug Drabek to complete deal, August 13, 1984.
xTraded to Minnesota Twins for First Baseman Randall Stuart (Randy) Johnson and outfielder Ron Scheer, February 19, 1985.

ALL-STAR GAME RECORD

Year League	Pos.	AB.	R.	H.	2B.	3B.	HR.	RBI.	B.A.	PO.	A.	E.	F.A.
1979—American	SS	3	0	0	0	0	0	0	.000	2	2	0	1.000

JOHN PATRICK SMILEY

Born March 17, 1965 at Phoenixville, Pa.
Height, 6.04. Weight, 180.
Throws and bats lefthanded.

Tied for Gulf Coast League lead in home runs allowed with 5 in 1983.

Year—Club	League	G.	IP.	W.	L.	Pct.	H.	R.	ER.	SO.	BB.	ERA.
1983—Bradenton Pirates	Gulf Coast	12	65⅓	3	4	.429	69	45	43	42	27	5.92
1984—Macon†	S. Atlantic	21	130	5	11	.313	119	73	57	73	41	3.95
1985—Prince William	Carolina	10	56	2	2	.500	64	36	32	45	45	5.14
1985—Macon	S. Atlantic	16	88⅔	3	8	.273	84	55	46	70	37	4.67
1986—Prince William	Carolina	48	90	2	4	.333	64	35	31	93	40	3.10
1986—Pittsburgh	National	12	11⅔	1	0	1.000	4	6	5	9	4	3.86
Major League Totals—1 Year		12	11⅔	1	0	1.000	4	6	5	9	4	3.86

Selected by Pittsburgh Pirates' organization in 12th round of free-agent draft, June 6, 1983.
†On disabled list, April 27 to May 27, 1984.

BRICK DUDLEY SMITH

Born May 2, 1959, at Charlotte, N. C.
Height, 6.04. Weight, 225.
Throws and bats righthanded.
Received bachelor of arts degree in communications from
Wake Forest University, Winston-Salem, N. C., in 1981.

Tied for Northwest League lead in game-winning RBIs with 7 in 1981.
Led Southern League first basemen in fielding percentage with .993 in 1984.

Year—Club	League	Pos.	G.	AB.	R.	H.	2B.	3B.	HR.	RBI.	B.A.	PO.	A.	E.	F.A.
1981—Bellingham	N'west	1B	60	204	48	59	10	0	11	47	.289	510	35	9	.984
1982—Bakersfield	Calif.	1B	96	348	59	90	20	1	12	58	.259	911	83	13	.987
1983—Bakersfield	Calif.	1B	137	493	84	150	26	2	19	88	.304	1084	92	11	.990
1984—Chattanooga†	South.	1B-C	100	334	36	83	13	0	5	35	.249	881	79	9	.991
1985—Chattanooga‡	South.	1B-3B	80	275	38	72	7	0	8	37	.262	563	46	8	.987
1986—Chattanooga	South.	1B-3B	128	474	80	163	*38	2	23	101	*.344	1023	94	7	.994

Selected by San Francisco Giants' organization in 11th round of free-agent draft, June 3, 1980.
Selected by Seattle Mariners' organization in 5th round of free-agent draft, June 8, 1981.
†On disabled list, August 10 to September 4, 1984.
‡On disabled list, April 11 to May 31, 1985.

BRYN NELSON SMITH

First name pronounced Brin.

Born August 11, 1955, at Marietta, Ga.
Height, 6.02. Weight, 200.
Throws and bats righthanded.
Attended Allan Hancock College, Santa Maria, Calif.

Major League saves: 1982 (3), 1983 (3). Total—6.
Tied for American Association lead in complete games with 9 in 1981.
Tied for Southern League lead in complete games with 16 in 1977 and 12 in 1980.
Named American Association Pitcher of the Year, 1981.

Year—Club	League	G.	IP.	W.	L.	Pct.	H.	R.	ER.	SO.	BB.	ERA.
1975—Miami	Florida St.	26	139	11	7	.611	117	48	33	93	59	2.14
1976—Miami	Florida St.	23	164	10	10	.500	140	72	51	119	62	2.80
1977—Charlotte†	Southern	27	*206	*15	11	.577	*195	78	63	103	57	2.75
1978—Denver	Am. Assoc.	11	54	0	6	.000	79	48	41	25	14	6.83
1978—Memphis‡	Southern	11	69	4	6	.400	53	28	19	48	31	2.48
1979—Memphis	Southern	27	184	11	10	.524	175	80	69	115	74	3.38
1980—Memphis	Southern	27	181	10	9	.526	179	75	56	110	54	2.78
1981—Denver	Am. Assoc.	29	*183	*15	5	*.750	166	80	62	127	42	3.05
1981—Montreal	National	7	13	1	0	1.000	14	4	4	9	3	2.77
1982—Wichita	Am. Assoc.	3	23⅔	2	0	1.000	21	5	5	15	2	1.90
1982—Montreal	National	47	79⅓	2	4	.333	81	43	37	50	23	4.20
1983—Montreal	National	49	155⅓	6	11	.353	142	51	43	101	43	2.49
1984—Montreal	National	28	179	12	13	.480	178	72	66	101	51	3.32
1985—Montreal	National	32	222⅓	18	5	.783	193	85	72	127	41	2.91
1986—Montreal§	National	30	187⅓	10	8	.556	182	101	82	105	63	3.94
Major League Totals—6 Years		193	836⅓	49	41	.544	790	356	304	493	224	3.27

Selected by St. Louis Cardinals' organization in the 49th round of free-agent draft, June 5, 1973.
Signed as free agent by Baltimore Orioles' organization, December 18, 1974.
†Traded with Pitchers Rudy May and Randy Miller by Baltimore Orioles' organization to Montreal Expos' organization for Pitchers Don Stanhouse and Joe Kerrigan and Outfielder Gary Roenicke, December 7, 1977.
‡On disabled list, August 5 to August 17, 1978.
§Released, December 19, 1986.

DAVID LEE SMITH

Born October 20, 1962, at Lynwood, Calif.
Height, 6.02. Weight, 175.
Throws and bats righthanded.
Attended University of California, Riverside, Calif.

Year—Club	League	Pos.	G.	AB.	R.	H.	2B.	3B.	HR.	RBI.	B.A.	PO.	A.	E.	F.A.
1984—Newark	NYP	SS-2B-3B	71	229	38	55	9	1	1	31	.240	101	223	22	.936
1985—Hagerstown	Carol.	SS	122	393	48	92	16	1	0	29	.234	186	*394	22	*.963
1986—Charlotte	South.	SS	89	299	44	72	15	2	5	34	.241	129	236	15	.961

Selected by Baltimore Orioles' organization in 6th round of free-agent draft, June 4, 1984.

DAVID STANLEY SMITH JR.

(Dave)

Born January 21, 1955, at San Francisco, Calif.
Height, 6.01. Weight, 195.
Throws and bats righthanded.
Attended San Diego State University, San Diego, Calif.

Major League saves: 1980 (10), 1981 (8), 1982 (11), 1983 (6), 1984 (5), 1985 (27), 1986 (33). Total—100.

Year—Club	League	G.	IP.	W.	L.	Pct.	H.	R.	ER.	SO.	BB.	ERA.
1976—Covington	Ap'lachian	15	97	5	5	.500	80	40	29	71	28	2.69
1977—Cocoa	Florida St.	14	93	7	5	.583	97	40	32	81	31	3.10
1977—Columbus	Southern	9	54	3	5	.375	52	2	21	29	24	3.50
1978—Columbus	Southern	26	181	10	13	.435	170	89	70	114	88	3.48
1979—Charleston	Int'national	34	160	7	8	.467	159	80	65	90	44	3.66
1980—Houston	National	57	103	7	5	.583	90	24	22	85	32	1.92
1981—Houston	National	42	75	5	3	.625	54	26	23	52	23	2.76
1982—Houston†	National	49	63⅓	5	4	.556	69	30	27	28	31	3.84
1983—Houston	National	42	72⅔	3	1	.750	72	32	25	41	36	3.10
1984—Houston	National	53	77⅓	5	4	.556	60	22	19	45	20	2.21
1985—Houston	National	64	79⅓	9	5	.643	69	26	20	40	17	2.27
1986—Houston	National	54	56	4	7	.364	39	17	17	46	22	2.73
Major League Totals—7 Years		361	526⅔	38	29	.567	453	177	153	337	181	2.61

Selected by Houston Astros' organization in 8th round of free-agent draft, June 8, 1976.
†On disabled list, June 27 to July 18, 1982.

DIVISION SERIES RECORD

Year Club	League	G.	IP.	W.	L.	Pct.	H.	R.	ER.	SO.	BB.	ERA.
1981—Houston	National	2	2⅓	0	0	.000	2	1	1	4	0	3.86

CHAMPIONSHIP SERIES RECORD

Year Club	League	G.	IP.	W.	L.	Pct.	H.	R.	ER.	SO.	BB.	ERA.
1980—Houston	National	3	2⅓	1	0	1.000	4	1	1	4	2	3.86
1986—Houston	National	2	2	0	1	.000	2	2	2	2	3	9.00
Championship Series Totals—2 Years		5	4⅓	1	1	.500	6	3	3	6	5	6.23

ALL-STAR GAME RECORD

Member of National League All-Star Team in 1986; did not play.

JOHN DWIGHT SMITH

(Known by middle name.)
Born November 8, 1963, at Tallahassee, Fla.
Height, 5.11. Weight, 175.
Throws right and bats lefthanded.
Attended Spartanburg Methodist College, Spartanburg, S.C.

Led Appalachian League in stolen bases with 47 in 1984.
Led Midwest League outfielders in total chances with 296 in 1986.
Tied for Appalachian League lead in double plays by outfielders with 3 in 1984.

Year Club	League	Pos.	G.	AB.	R.	H.	2B.	3B.	HR.	RBI.	B.A.	PO.	A.	E.	F.A.
1984—Pikeville	Appal.	OF	61	195	42	46	6	2	1	17	.236	77	8	•9	.904
1985—Geneva	NYP	OF	73	232	44	67	11	2	4	32	.289	81	4	7	.924
1986—Peoria	Midw.	OF	124	471	92	146	22	★11	11	57	.310	★272	11	13	.956

Selected by Toronto Blue Jays' organization in 3rd round of free-agent draft, January 17, 1984.
Selected by Chicago Cubs' organization in secondary phase of free-agent draft, June 4, 1984.

LEE ARTHUR SMITH

Born December 4, 1957, at Jamestown, La.
Height, 6.05. Weight, 220.
Throws and bats righthanded.
Attended Northwestern State University, Natchitoches, La.

Major League saves: 1981 (1), 1982 (17), 1983 (29), 1984 (33), 1985 (33), 1986 (31). Total—144.
Led National League in games finished in relief with 57 in 1985 and tied for lead with 56 in 1983.
Led National League in saves with 29 in 1983.
Tied for American Association lead in wild pitches with 16 in 1980.
Named National League co-Fireman of the Year by THE SPORTING NEWS, 1983.

Year Club	League	G.	IP.	W.	L.	Pct.	H.	R.	ER.	SO.	BB.	ERA.
1975—Bradenton Cubs	Gulf Coast	10	62	3	5	.375	35	23	16	35	★49	2.32
1976—Pompano Beach	Florida St.	26	101	4	8	.333	120	76	60	52	74	5.35
1977—Pompano Beach	Florida St.	26	130	10	4	.714	131	67	62	82	85	4.29
1978—Midland	Texas	30	155	8	10	.444	161	122	103	71	★128	5.98
1979—Midland	Texas	35	104	9	5	.643	122	65	57	46	85	4.93
1980—Wichita	Am. Assoc.	50	90	4	7	.364	70	49	37	63	56	3.70
1980—Chicago	National	18	22	2	0	1.000	21	9	7	17	14	2.86
1981—Chicago	National	40	67	3	6	.333	57	31	26	50	31	3.49
1982—Chicago	National	72	117	2	5	.286	105	38	35	99	37	2.69
1983—Chicago	National	66	103⅓	4	10	.286	70	23	19	91	41	1.65
1984—Chicago	National	69	101	9	7	.563	98	42	41	86	35	3.65
1985—Chicago	National	65	97⅔	7	4	.636	87	35	33	112	32	3.04
1986—Chicago†	National	66	90⅓	9	9	.500	69	32	31	93	42	3.09
Major League Totals—7 Years		396	598⅓	36	41	.468	507	210	192	548	232	2.89

Selected by Chicago Cubs' organization in 2nd round of free-agent draft, June 4, 1975.
†On disabled list, April 21 to May 6, 1986.

CHAMPIONSHIP SERIES RECORD

Year Club	League	G.	IP.	W.	L.	Pct.	H.	R.	ER.	SO.	BB.	ERA.
1984—Chicago	National	2	2	0	1	.000	3	2	2	3	0	9.00

ALL-STAR GAME RECORD

Year League	IP.	W.	L.	Pct.	H.	R.	ER.	SO.	BB.	ERA.
1983—National	1	0	0	.000	2	2	1	1	0	9.00

LEROY PURDY SMITH III
(Roy)

Born September 6, 1961, at Mt. Vernon, N.Y.
Height, 6.03. Weight, 205.
Throws and bats righthanded.
Attended Fordham University, Bronx, N.Y.

Tied for Carolina League lead in shutouts with 3 in 1980.
Named Carolina League Pitcher of the Year, 1980.

Year Club	League	G.	IP.	W.	L.	Pct.	H.	R.	ER.	SO.	BB.	ERA.
1979—Helena	Pioneer	5	36	5	0	1.000	21	16	10	42	16	2.50
1980—Peninsula	Carolina	27	163	*17	6	.739	101	54	47	134	63	2.60
1981—Reading	Eastern	27	161	11	8	.579	123	92	79	117	97	4.42
1982—Reading†	Eastern	26	166	10	8	.556	141	81	71	122	82	3.85
1983—Charleston	Int'national	27	155⅓	6	8	.429	166	101	89	95	75	5.16
1984—Maine	Int'national	12	80⅔	5	4	.556	77	47	39	48	29	4.35
1984—Cleveland	American	22	86⅓	5	5	.500	91	49	44	55	40	4.59
1985—Maine	Int'national	15	109⅓	10	4	.714	84	33	29	65	29	2.39
1985—Cleveland‡§	American	12	62⅓	1	4	.200	84	40	37	28	17	5.34
1986—Minnesota	American	5	10⅓	0	2	.000	13	8	8	8	5	6.97
1986—Toledo x	Int'national	9	53⅔	2	1	.667	42	12	9	39	16	1.51
Major League Totals—3 Years		39	159	6	11	.353	188	97	89	91	62	5.04

Selected by Philadelphia Phillies' organization in 3rd round of free-agent draft, June 5, 1979.

†Traded with Pitcher Jerry Reed and Outfielder Wil Culmer to Cleveland Indians for Pitcher John Denny, September 12, 1982.

‡On disabled list, July 3 to August 1, 1985; included rehabilitation disability assignment to Maine, July 27 to July 30, 1985.

§Traded with Pitcher Ramon Romero to Minnesota Twins for Pitchers Ken Schrom and Bryan Oelkers, January 7, 1986.

xReleased, December 19, 1986.

LONNIE SMITH

Born December 22, 1955, at Chicago, Ill.
Height, 5.09. Weight, 170.
Throws and bats righthanded.

Tied major league record for fewest double plays by outfielder, season, for leader in double plays (4), 1983.
Tied modern National League record for most stolen bases, game, (5), September 4, 1982.
Major League stolen bases: 1978 (4), 1979 (2), 1980 (33), 1981 (21), 1982 (68), 1983 (43), 1984 (50), 1985 (52), 1986 (26). Total—299.
Led National League in being hit by pitch with 9 in 1982 and 1984 and tied for lead with 9 in 1983.
Tied for National League lead in caught stealing with 26 in 1982.
Tied for National League lead in double plays by outfielders with 4 in 1983.
Led American Association in stolen bases with 66 and caught stealing with 19 in 1978.
Led Western Carolinas League in stolen bases with 56 and tied for lead in caught stealing with 14 in 1975.
Led American Association outfielders in double plays with 5 in 1978.
Named National League Rookie Player of the Year by THE SPORTING NEWS, 1980.
Named outfielder on THE SPORTING NEWS National League All-Star Team, 1982.

Year Club	League	Pos.	G.	AB.	R.	H.	2B.	3B.	HR.	RBI.	B.A.	PO.	A.	E.	F.A.
1974—Auburn	NYP	OF	61	210	48	60	10	4	5	27	.286	143	6	●9	.943
1975—Spartanburg	W. Car.	OF	131	465	*114	*150	23	4	7	40	.323	*317	9	11	.967
1976—Oklahoma City	A. A.	OF	134	483	*93	149	24	9	8	54	.308	200	4	*14	.936
1977—Oklahoma City	A. A.	OF	125	477	91	132	14	10	4	41	.277	231	8	*13	.948
1978—Oklahoma City†	A. A.	OF	125	480	103	151	20	5	7	43	.315	274	*21	*12	.961
1978—Philadelphia	Nat.	OF	17	4	6	0	0	0	0	0	.000	5	1	0	1.000
1979—Oklahoma City	A. A.	OF	110	451	*106	149	26	9	7	44	.330	268	13	*12	.959
1979—Philadelphia	Nat.	OF	17	30	4	5	2	0	0	3	.167	19	1	0	1.000
1980—Philadelphia	Nat.	OF	100	298	69	101	14	4	3	20	.339	121	2	4	.969
1981—Philadelphia‡	Nat.	OF	62	176	40	57	14	3	2	11	.324	91	10	3	.971
1982—St. Louis§	Nat.	OF	156	592	*120	182	35	8	8	69	.307	303	●16	10	.970
1983—St. Louis§	Nat.	OF	130	492	83	158	31	5	8	45	.321	225	14	*15	.941
1984—St. Louis	Nat.	OF	145	504	77	126	20	4	6	49	.250	184	*18	●11	.948
1985—St. Louis x	Nat.	OF	28	96	15	25	2	2	0	7	.260	43	1	0	1.000
1985—Kansas City	Amer.	OF	120	448	77	115	23	4	6	41	.257	195	10	9	.958
1986—Kansas City yz	Amer.	OF	134	508	80	146	25	7	8	44	.287	245	5	9	.965
National League Totals—8 Years			655	2192	414	654	118	26	27	204	.298	991	63	43	.961
American League Totals—2 Years			254	956	157	261	48	11	14	85	.273	440	15	18	.962
Major League Totals—9 Years			909	3148	571	915	166	37	41	289	.291	1431	78	61	.961

Selected by Philadelphia Phillies' organization in 1st round (third player selected) of free-agent draft, June 5, 1974.

†On disabled list, April 14 to April 25, 1978.

‡Traded with a player to be named later to Cleveland Indians for Catcher Bo Diaz, November 20, 1981; Traded by Cleveland to St. Louis Cardinals for Pitchers Lary Sorensen and Silvio Martinez, November 20, 1981. Cleveland organization acquired Pitcher Scott Munninghoff to complete first deal, December 9, 1981.

§On disabled list, June 11 to July 8, 1983.

xTraded to Kansas City Royals for Outfielder John Morris, May 17, 1985.

yOn disabled list, April 13 to May 4, 1986.

Granted free agency, November 12, 1986.

DIVISION SERIES RECORD

Club	League	Pos.	G.	AB.	R.	H.	2B.	3B.	HR.	RBI.	B.A.	PO.	A.	E.	F.A.
'adelphia	Nat.	OF	5	19	1	5	1	0	0	0	.263	6	1	0	1.000

CHAMPIONSHIP SERIES RECORD

Championship Series record for most clubs, total Series (3).

Club	League	Pos.	G.	AB.	R.	H.	2B.	3B.	HR.	RBI.	B.A.	PO.	A.	E.	F.A.
...hia	Nat.	PR-OF	3	5	2	3	0	0	0	0	.600	2	1	0	1.000
	Nat.	OF	3	11	1	3	0	0	0	1	.273	2	0	0	1.000
	Amer.	OF	7	28	2	7	2	0	0	1	.250	8	3	1	.917
Series Totals—3 Years			13	44	5	13	2	0	0	2	.295	12	4	1	.941

Tied World Series record for most clubs, total Series (3).

Year	Club	League	Pos.	G.	AB.	R.	H.	2B.	3B.	HR.	RBI.	B.A.	PO.	A.	E.	F.A.
1980—Philadelphia		Nat.	PR-O-DH	6	19	2	5	1	0	0	1	.263	4	1	0	1.000
1982—St. Louis		Nat.	OF-DH	7	28	6	9	4	1	0	1	.321	11	0	0	1.000
1985—Kansas City		Amer.	OF	7	27	4	9	3	0	0	4	.333	7	2	0	1.000
World Series Totals—3 Years				20	74	12	23	8	1	0	6	.311	22	3	0	1.000

ALL-STAR GAME RECORD

Year	League	Pos.	AB.	R.	H.	2B.	3B.	HR.	RBI.	B.A.	PO.	A.	E.	F.A.
1982—National		OF	0	0	0	0	0	0	0	.000	1	0	0	1.000

MICHAEL ANTHONY SMITH
(Mike)

Born February 23, 1961, at Jackson, Miss.
Height, 6.01. Weight, 195.
Throws right and bats right and lefthanded.
Attended Utica Junior College, Utica, Miss.

Led Florida State League in saves with 21 in 1982.

Year	Club	League	G.	IP.	W.	L.	Pct.	H.	R.	ER.	SO.	BB.	ERA.
1981—Billings		Pioneer	22	46	5	5	.500	39	21	7	52	19	1.37
1982—Tampa		Florida St.	48	80⅓	7	1	.875	55	17	11	80	42	1.23
1983—Waterbury†		Eastern	22	28⅔	2	5	.286	18	13	9	16	25	2.83
1984—Cincinnati		National	8	10⅓	1	0	1.000	12	6	6	7	5	5.23
1984—Wichita		Am. Assoc.	12	18	3	2	.600	17	8	8	20	13	4.00
1984—Vermont		Eastern	35	51	3	3	.500	51	28	19	49	20	3.35
1985—Denver		Am. Assoc.	47	68⅔	5	4	.556	65	40	37	67	38	4.85
1985—Cincinnati		National	2	3⅓	0	0	.000	2	2	2	2	1	5.40
1986—Denver‡-Indianapolis		Am. Assoc.	40	76⅔	6	3	.667	95	54	46	50	44	5.40
1986—Cincinnati§		National	2	3⅓	0	0	.000	7	5	5	1	1	13.50
Major League Totals—3 Years			12	17	1	0	1.000	21	13	13	10	7	6.88

Signed as free agent by Cincinnati Reds' organization, May 11, 1981.
†On disabled list, June 28, 1983 through remainder of season.
‡Loaned to Indianapolis (Montreal Expos' organization), July 24, 1986; returned, September 10, 1986.
§Traded to Montreal Expos for a player to be named later, December 1, 1986; Cincinnati Reds' organization acquired Pitcher Bill Cutshall to complete deal, December 9, 1986.

MICHAEL ANTHONY SMITH
(Mike)

Born October 31, 1963, at San Antonio, Tex.
Height, 6.03. Weight, 180.
Throws and bats righthanded.
Attended Ranger Junior College, Ranger, Tex.

Tied for Midwest League lead in wild pitches with 19 in 1986.

Year	Club	League	G.	IP.	W.	L.	Pct.	H.	R.	ER.	SO.	BB.	ERA.
1984—Sarasota Reds		Gulf Coast	11	67	2	4	.333	65	33	27	65	24	3.63
1985—Billings		Pioneer	7	33⅔	2	2	.500	24	15	11	24	24	2.94
1985—Cedar Rapids		Midwest	8	44⅓	5	1	.833	38	20	16	28	22	3.25
1986—Cedar Rapids		Midwest	28	*191	10	10	.500	155	88	71	172	106	3.35

Selected by San Diego Padres' organization in 4th round of free-agent draft, January 11, 1983.
Selected by Cincinnati Reds' organization in 5th round of free-agent draft, January 17, 1984.

OSBORNE EARL SMITH
(Ozzie)

Born December 26, 1954, at Mobile, Ala.
Height, 5.10. Weight, 150.
Throws right and bats left and righthanded.
Received degree from California Polytechnic State University, San Luis Obispo, Calif.

Established major league record for most assists by shortstop, season (621), 1980.
Tied major league records for most years with 500 or more assists, shortstop (6); most double plays by shortstop, extra-inning game (6), August 25, 1979 (19 innings).
Tied National League records for most years (5) and most consecutive years (4) leading league in assists, shortstop; most years leading league in chances accepted, shortstop (5).
Major League stolen bases: 1978 (40), 1979 (28), 1980 (57), 1981 (22), 1982 (25), 1983 (34), 1984 (35), 1985 (31), 1986 (31). Total—303.
Led National League in sacrifice hits with 28 in 1978 and 23 in 1980.
Led National League shortstops in total chances with 933 in 1980, 658 in 1981, 844 in 1983 and 827 in 1985.
Led National League shortstops in double plays with 113 in 1980 and tied for lead with 94 in 1984 and 96 in 1986.
Led Northwest League in stolen bases with 30 in 1977.
Led Northwest League shortstops in double plays with 40 in 1977.
Named shortstop on THE SPORTING NEWS National League All-Star Team, 1982 and 1984 through 1986.
Named shortstop on THE SPORTING NEWS National League All-Star fielding team, 1980 through 1986.

Year Club	League	Pos.	G.	AB.	R.	H.	2B.	3B.	HR.	RBI.	B.A.	PO.	A.	E.	F.A.
1977—Walla Walla	N'west	SS	•68	*287	*69	87	10	2	1	35	.303	130	*254	23	*.943
1978—San Diego	Nat.	SS	159	590	69	152	17	6	1	46	.258	264	548	25	.970
1979—San Diego	Nat.	SS	156	587	77	124	18	6	0	27	.211	256	*555	20	.976
1980—San Diego	Nat.	SS	158	609	67	140	18	5	0	35	.230	*288	*621	24	.974
1981—San Diego†	Nat.	SS	•110	*450	53	100	11	2	0	21	.222	220	*422	16	*.976
1982—St. Louis	Nat.	SS	140	488	58	121	24	1	2	43	.248	279	*535	13	*.984
1983—St. Louis	Nat.	SS	159	552	69	134	30	6	3	50	.243	*304	519	21	.975
1984—St. Louis‡	Nat.	SS	124	412	53	106	20	5	1	44	.257	233	437	12	*.982
1985—St. Louis	Nat.	SS	158	537	70	148	22	3	6	54	.276	264	*549	14	*.983
1986—St. Louis	Nat.	SS	153	514	67	144	19	4	0	54	.280	229	453	15	*.978
Major League Totals—9 Years			1317	4739	583	1169	179	38	13	374	.247	2337	4639	160	.978

Selected by Detroit Tigers' organization in 7th round of free-agent draft, June 8, 1976.
Selected by San Diego Padres' organization in 4th round of free-agent draft, June 7, 1977.
†Traded to St. Louis Cardinals for Shortstop Garry Templeton, February 11, 1982.
‡On disabled list, July 14 to August 19, 1984.

CHAMPIONSHIP SERIES RECORD

Established National League Championship Series records for highest batting average (.435) and most hits (10), six-game Series, 1985.
Tied National League Championship Series record for most singles, six-game Series (7), 1985.

Year Club	League	Pos.	G.	AB.	R.	H.	2B.	3B.	HR.	RBI.	B.A.	PO.	A.	E.	F.A.
1982—St. Louis	Nat.	SS	3	9	0	5	0	0	0	3	.556	4	11	0	1.000
1985—St. Louis	Nat.	SS	6	23	4	10	1	1	1	3	.435	6	16	0	1.000
Championship Series Totals—2 Years			9	32	4	15	1	1	1	6	.469	10	27	0	1.000

WORLD SERIES RECORD

Established World Series record for most putouts by shortstop, seven-game Series (22), 1982.
Tied World Series record for fewest chances accepted, shortstop, game (0), October 23, 1985.

Year Club	League	Pos.	G.	AB.	R.	H.	2B.	3B.	HR.	RBI.	B.A.	PO.	A.	E.	F.A.
1982—St. Louis	Nat.	SS	7	24	3	5	0	0	1	1	.208	22	17	0	1.000
1985—St. Louis	Nat.	SS	7	23	1	2	0	0	0	0	.087	10	16	1	.963
World Series Totals—2 Years			14	47	4	7	0	0	1	1	.149	32	33	1	.985

ALL-STAR GAME RECORD

Year League	Pos.	AB.	R.	H.	2B.	3B.	HR.	RBI.	B.A.	PO.	A.	E.	F.A.
1981—National	SS	0	0	0	0	0	0	0	.000	1	0	0	1.000
1982—National	PR-SS	0	0	0	0	0	0	0	.000	0	1	0	1.000
1983—National	SS	2	1	1	0	0	0	0	.500	0	0	0	.000
1984—National	SS	3	0	0	0	0	0	0	.000	3	0	0	1.000
1985—National	SS	4	0	0	0	0	0	0	.000	1	3	0	1.000
1986—National	SS	1	0	0	0	0	0	0	.000	3	2	0	1.000
All-Star Game Totals—6 Years		10	1	1	0	0	0	0	.100	8	6	0	1.000

PETER JOHN SMITH
(Pete)

Born February 27, 1966, at Abington, Mass.
Height, 6.02. Weight, 185.
Throws and bats righthanded.

Year Club	League	G.	IP.	W.	L.	Pct.	H.	R.	ER.	SO.	BB.	ERA.
1984—Sarasota Phillies	Gulf Coast	8	37	1	2	.333	28	11	6	35	16	1.46
1985—Clearwater†	Florida St.	26	153	12	10	.545	135	68	56	86	80	3.29
1986—Greenville	Southern	24	104⅔	1	8	.111	117	88	68	64	78	5.85

Selected by Philadelphia Phillies' organization in 1st round (21st player selected) of free-agent draft, June 4, 1984.
†Traded with Catcher Ozzie Virgil to Atlanta Braves for Pitcher Steve Bedrosian and Outfielder Milt Thompson, December 10, 1985.

ZANE WILLIAM SMITH

Born December 28, 1960, at Madison, Wis.
Height, 6.02. Weight, 195.
Throws and bats lefthanded.
Attended Indiana State University, Terre Haute, Ind.

Major League saves: 1986 (1).

Year Club	League	G.	IP.	W.	L.	Pct.	H.	R.	ER.	SO.	BB.	ERA.
1982—Anderson	S. Atlantic	12	63	5	3	.625	65	53	48	32	34	6.86
1983—Durham	Carolina	27	170⅔	9	•15	.375	183	109	93	126	83	4.90
1984—Greenville	Southern	9	60	7	0	1.000	47	13	11	35	23	1.65
1984—Richmond	Int'national	19	123⅔	7	4	.636	113	62	57	68	65	4.15
1984—Atlanta	National	3	20	1	0	1.000	16	7	5	16	13	2.25
1985—Atlanta†	National	42	147	9	10	.474	135	70	62	85	80	3.80
1986—Atlanta	National	38	204⅔	8	16	.333	209	109	92	139	105	4.05
Major League Totals—3 Years		83	371⅔	18	26	.409	360	186	159	240	198	3.85

Selected by Atlanta Braves' organization in 3rd round of free-agent draft, June 7, 1982.
†On disabled list, August 5 to September 1, 1985.

BILLY MIKE SMITHSON
(Known by middle name.)

Born January 21, 1955, at Centerville, Tenn.
Height, 6.08. Weight, 215.
Throws right and bats lefthanded.
Attended University of Tennessee, Knoxville, Tenn.

Led American League in hit batsmen with 15 in 1985.
Led American League in home runs allowed with 35 in 1984.
Tied for American League lead in games started by pitchers with 36 in 1984 and 37 in 1985.
Tied for International League lead in intentional bases on balls issued with 13 in 1980.

Year Club	League	G.	IP.	W.	L.	Pct.	H.	R.	ER.	SO.	BB.	ERA.
1976—Winter Haven	Florida St.	11	64	4	3	.571	63	27	22	29	20	3.09
1977—Winter Haven	Florida St.	25	172	13	8	.619	170	56	53	92	41	2.77
1977—Bristol	Eastern	1	3	0	1	.000	8	7	7	1	0	21.00
1978—Bristol	Eastern	27	160	11	10	.524	178	92	81	86	76	4.56
1979—Bristol	Eastern	*48	132	8	12	.400	128	82	69	89	53	4.70
1980—Pawtucket	Int'national	*50	99	5	9	.357	95	50	32	73	45	2.91
1981—Pawtucket†	Int'national	34	91	2	4	.333	74	44	39	82	45	3.86
1982—Denver	Am. Assoc.	29	152⅔	11	7	.611	149	82	77	*144	47	4.54
1982—Texas‡	American	8	46⅔	3	4	.429	51	26	26	24	13	5.01
1983—Texas‡	American	33	223⅓	10	14	.417	233	102	97	135	71	3.91
1984—Minnesota	American	36	252	15	13	.536	246	113	103	144	54	3.68
1985—Minnesota	American	37	257	15	14	.517	264	134	*124	127	78	4.34
1986—Minnesota	American	34	198	13	14	.481	234	123	105	114	57	4.77
Major League Totals—5 Years		148	977	56	59	.487	1028	498	455	544	273	4.19

Selected by Boston Red Sox' organization in 5th round of free-agent draft, June 8, 1976.

†Traded to Texas Rangers' organization for Pitcher John Henry Johnson, April 9, 1982.

‡Traded with Pitcher John Butcher and Catcher Sam Sorce to Minnesota Twins for Outfielder Gary Ward, December 7, 1983.

NATHANIEL SNELL
(Nate)

Born September 2, 1952, at Orangeburg, S.C.
Height, 6.04. Weight, 190.
Throws and bats righthanded.
Attended Tennessee State University, Nashville, Tenn.

Major League saves: 1985 (5).
Led Southern League in games finished in relief with 48 and tied for lead in saves with 17 in 1984.
Led Southern League in home runs allowed with 20 in 1978.

Year Club	League	G.	IP.	W.	L.	Pct.	H.	R.	ER.	SO.	BB.	ERA.
1977—Miami	Florida St.	16	106	7	7	.500	106	41	20	68	15	1.70
1978—Charlotte	Southern	28	193	7	13	.350	*193	91	78	97	44	3.64
1979—Charlotte	Southern	10	65	5	2	.714	65	30	27	42	29	3.74
1979—Rochester†‡	Int'national	12	76	4	7	.364	72	44	37	35	22	4.38
1980—Shreveport§	Texas	33	64	4	4	.500	77	38	32	44	18	4.50
1981—Charlotte	Southern	8	38	1	2	.333	32	14	11	19	10	2.61
1981—Rochester	Int'national	15	41	1	3	.250	33	14	12	20	7	2.63
1982—Rochester x	Int'national	37	83½	4	6	.400	83	40	34	31	26	3.67
1983—Charlotte	Southern	15	22⅔	1	0	1.000	15	0	0	7	6	0.00
1983—Rochester y	Int'national	39	70	6	2	.750	71	29	28	46	17	3.60
1984—Rochester	Int'national	6	9⅓	0	2	.000	13	6	5	6	7	4.82
1984—Charlotte	Southern	52	81⅔	9	4	.692	68	30	22	45	28	2.42
1984—Baltimore	American	5	7⅔	1	1	.500	8	2	2	7	1	2.35
1985—Baltimore z	American	43	100⅓	3	2	.600	100	44	30	41	30	2.69
1985—Rochester	Int'national	2	4⅔	0	0	.000	4	0	0	3	0	0.00
1986—Rochester	Int'national	16	24⅓	2	2	.500	25	13	12	9	12	4.44
1986—Baltimore a	American	34	72⅓	2	1	.667	69	36	31	29	22	3.86
Major League Totals—3 Years		82	180⅓	6	4	.600	177	82	63	77	53	3.14

Selected by Baltimore Orioles' organization in 18th round of free-agent draft, June 6, 1972.

Selected by Atlanta Braves' organization in 22nd round of free-agent draft, June 4, 1975.

Signed as free agent by Baltimore Orioles' organization, September 5, 1976.

†On disabled list, July 17 to August 5, 1979.

‡Drafted by Phoenix (San Francisco Giants' organization), December 4, 1979.

§Released, March 27, 1981; signed by Charlotte (Baltimore Orioles' organization), May 26, 1981.

xOn disabled list, May 3 to June 9, 1982.

yGranted free agency, October 20, 1983; re-signed by Orioles, January 17, 1984.

zOn disabled list, July 10 to August 9, 1985; included rehabilitation disability assignment to Rochester, August 2 to August 7, 1985.

aReleased, December 19, 1986.

VAN VOORHEES SNIDER

Born August 11, 1963, at Birmingham, Ala.
Height, 6.03. Weight, 185.
Throws right and bats lefthanded.
Attended Gadsden State Junior College, Gadsden, Ala.

Tied for Southern League lead in intentional bases on balls received with 9 in 1986.
Led South Atlantic League outfielders in double plays with 7 in 1983.

Tied for Pioneer League lead in double plays by outfielder with 2 in 1982.

Year	Club	League	Pos.	G.	AB.	R.	H.	2B.	3B.	HR.	RBI.	B.A.	PO.	A.	E.	F.A.
1982—Butte	Pion.		OF	67	237	46	71	13	5	9	53	.300	99	*14	9	.926
1983—Charleston	S. Atl.		OF	123	467	86	136	26	2	20	94	.291	207	17	*22	.911
1983—Jacksonville	South.		OF	13	33	2	6	3	0	0	2	.182	28	0	2	.933
1984—Memphis	South.		OF	132	488	52	120	23	9	7	62	.246	319	*24	4	*.988
1985—Memphis†	South.		OF	85	292	43	69	15	4	8	39	.236	166	9	*13	.931
1986—Memphis	South.		OF	134	492	79	133	27	5	26	81	.270	276	*23	6	.980
1986—Omaha	A. A.		OF	4	13	5	4	2	1	0	3	.308	7	0	0	1.000

Signed as free agent by Kansas City Royals' organization, November 2, 1981.
†On disabled list, May 3 to July 1, 1985.

JAMES CORY SNYDER
(Known by middle name.)

Born November 11, 1962, at Canyon Country, Calif.
Height, 6.04. Weight, 175.
Throws and bats righthanded.
Attended Brigham Young University, Provo, Utah.

Major League stolen bases: 1986 (2).
Led Eastern League in total bases with 255, game-winning RBIs with 14 and sacrifice flies with 12 in 1985.
Led Eastern League third basemen in putouts with 132, total chances with 391 and double plays with 26 in 1985.
Named Eastern League Most Valuable Player, 1985.
Member of 1984 U.S. Olympic baseball team.
Named shortstop on THE SPORTING NEWS College Baseball All-America Team, 1984.

Year	Club	League	Pos.	G.	AB.	R.	H.	2B.	3B.	HR.	RBI.	B.A.	PO.	A.	E.	F.A.
1985—Waterbury	East.		3B-SS	*139	512	77	144	25	1	*28	*94	.281	134	231	33	.917
1986—Maine	Int.		3B-SS	49	192	25	58	19	0	9	32	.302	46	87	8	.943
1986—Cleveland	Amer.		OF-SS-3B	103	416	58	113	21	1	24	69	.272	213	84	10	.967
Major League Totals—1 Year				103	416	58	113	21	1	24	69	.272	213	84	10	.967

Selected by Cleveland Indians' organization in 1st round (fourth player selected) of free-agent draft, June 4, 1984.

RAYMOND JOHN SOFF JR.
(Ray)

Born October 31, 1958, at Adrian, Mich.
Height, 6.00. Weight, 185.
Throws and bats righthanded.
Attended Central Michigan University, Mt. Pleasant, Mich.

Year	Club	League	G.	IP.	W.	L.	Pct.	H.	R.	ER.	SO.	BB.	ERA.
1979—Geneva	NYP		9	56	3	2	.600	48	26	23	38	34	3.70
1980—Quad Cities	Midwest		40	66	1	8	.111	61	49	35	59	32	4.77
1981—Quad Cities†	Midwest		32	51	3	0	1.000	49	27	21	39	24	3.71
1982—Salinas	California		43	82⅔	10	7	.588	74	36	29	80	30	3.16
1983—Midland	Texas		45	76⅓	4	3	.571	98	63	58	41	37	6.84
1984—Midland ‡§x	Texas		10	41⅓	2	1	.667	36	12	7	17	12	1.52
1985—Arkansas y	Texas		19	26	5	3	.625	16	5	4	26	9	1.38
1986—Arkansas	Texas		18	21⅓	3	2	.600	19	7	3	17	7	1.27
1986—Louisville	Am. Assoc.		21	42⅔	3	2	.600	34	13	8	31	15	1.69
1986—St. Louis	National		30	38⅓	4	2	.667	37	17	14	22	13	3.29
Major League Totals—1 Year			30	38⅓	4	2	.667	37	17	14	22	13	3.29

Selected by Chicago Cubs' organization in 11th round of free-agent draft, June 5, 1979.
†On temporary inactive list, August 7 to September 7, 1981.
‡On disabled list, May 1 to June 4, 1984.
§On suspended list, June 14, 1984 through remainder of season.
xReleased, April 1, 1985; signed by Arkansas (St. Louis Cardinals' organization), June 29, 1985.
yGranted free agency, October 15, 1985; re-signed by Cardinals' organization, January 18, 1986.

JULIO CESAR SOLANO

Born January 8, 1960, at Agua Blanca, Dominican Republic.
Height, 6.01. Weight, 155.
Throws and bats righthanded.

Led South Atlantic League in hit batsmen with 11 and tied for lead in games started by pitchers with 27 and shutouts with 3 in 1982.

Year	Club	League	G.	IP.	W.	L.	Pct.	H.	R.	ER.	SO.	BB.	ERA.
1980—Sarasota Astros-Orange	Gulf Coast		18	38	5	2	.714	31	16	11	29	23	2.61
1981—Sarasota Astros-Blue	Gulf Coast		17	74	4	4	.500	71	47	32	45	36	3.89
1982—Asheville	S. Atlantic		28	178	10	7	.588	165	89	70	163	116	3.54
1983—Houston	National		4	6	0	2	.000	5	5	4	3	4	6.00
1983—Tucson	P. Coast		29	161⅔	10	7	.588	183	104	89	123	71	4.95
1984—Tucson	P. Coast		17	80⅔	3	5	.375	74	41	23	55	37	2.57
1984—Houston	National		31	50⅔	1	3	.250	31	13	11	33	18	1.95
1985—Houston	National		20	33⅔	2	2	.500	34	13	13	17	13	3.48
1985—Tucson	P. Coast		23	31⅔	2	3	.400	25	16	14	23	21	3.98
1986—Tucson	P. Coast		27	71⅓	6	4	.600	64	24	15	54	27	1.89
1986—Houston	National		16	32	3	1	.750	39	28	27	21	22	7.59
Major League Totals—4 Years			71	122⅓	6	8	.429	109	59	55	74	57	4.05

Signed as free agent by Houston Astros' organization, November 21, 1979.

ALAN MARTIN SONTAG

Born October 21, 1963, at Valley Stream, N.Y.
Height, 6.05. Weight, 195.
Throws and bats righthanded.
Attended Indian River Community College, Fort Pierce, Fla.

Led Midwest League in shutouts with 6 and complete games with 15 in 1985.

Year	Club	League	G.	IP.	W.	L.	Pct.	H.	R.	ER.	SO.	BB.	ERA.
1984—Kenosha	Midwest		20	143⅓	7	7	.500	118	51	44	110	57	2.76
1985—Kenosha	Midwest		28	★220⅓	15	11	.577	171	65	57	★213	59	2.33
1986—Orlando	Southern		26	171	9	12	.429	188	101	92	81	85	4.84

Selected by Baltimore Orioles' organization in 9th round of free-agent draft, January 11, 1983.
Selected by Baltimore Orioles' organization in secondary phase of free-agent draft, June 6, 1983.
Selected by Minnesota Twins' organization in secondary phase of free-agent draft, January 17, 1984.

MICHAEL DAVIS SOPER

(Mike)

Born May 23, 1965, at Miami, Fla.
Height, 6.01. Weight, 165.
Throws and bats righthanded.

Led Gulf Coast League in being hit by pitch with 7 in 1983.
Led Midwest League shortstops in total chances with 568 in 1984.

Year	Club	League	Pos.	G.	AB.	R.	H.	2B.	3B.	HR.	RBI.	B.A.	PO.	A.	E.	F.A.
1983—Sarasota W. Sox	Gulf C.		SS	53	199	22	55	11	0	0	26	.276	65	150	17	.927
1984—Appleton	Midw.		SS	128	444	47	105	18	2	1	48	.236	★189	★350	29	.949
1985—Glens Falls†	East.		SS	132	480	50	142	16	0	4	49	.296	208	325	31	.945
1986—Columbus	Int.		SS	55	179	11	35	3	2	0	12	.196	101	157	11	.959
1986—Albany	East.		SS	41	131	13	28	6	0	1	7	.214	72	102	11	.941

Selected by Chicago White Sox' organization in 3rd round of free-agent draft, June 6, 1983.
†Traded with Pitcher Britt Burns and Outfielder Glen Braxton to New York Yankees for Catcher Ron Hassey and Pitcher Joe Cowley, December 12, 1985.

MARIO MELVIN SOTO

Born July 12, 1956, Bani, Dominican Republic.
Height, 6.00. Weight, 185.
Throws and bats righthanded.

Tied major league records for most strikeouts, inning (4), May 17, 1984 (third inning); most home runs allowed, inning (4), April 29, 1986 (fourth inning).
Major League saves: 1980 (4).
Led National League in complete games with 18 in 1983 and 13 in 1984.
Led National League in home runs allowed with 28 in 1983, 30 in 1985 and tied for lead with 13 in 1981.
Tied for National League lead in games started by pitchers with 25 in 1981.
Led Florida State League in balks with 6 in 1976.
Tied for American Association lead in balks with 6 in 1978.

Year	Club	League	G.	IP.	W.	L.	Pct.	H.	R.	ER.	SO.	BB.	ERA.
1974—Billings†	Pioneer						(Did not play)						
1975—Eugene	Northwest		5	30	2	3	.400	33	21	14	11	18	4.20
1976—Tampa	Florida St.		26	★197	13	7	.650	142	54	41	★124	80	1.87
1977—Indianapolis	Am. Assoc.		18	123	11	5	.688	100	51	42	109	61	3.07
1977—Cincinnati	National		12	61	2	6	.250	60	38	36	44	26	5.31
1978—Indianapolis	Am. Assoc.		26	160	9	12	.429	129	102	89	121	95	5.01
1978—Cincinnati	National		5	18	1	0	1.000	13	5	5	13	13	2.50
1979—Indianapolis‡	Am. Assoc.		15	25	1	1	.500	20	11	11	38	18	3.96
1979—Cincinnati	National		25	37	3	2	.600	33	25	22	32	30	5.35
1980—Cincinnati	National		53	190	10	8	.556	126	72	65	182	84	3.08
1981—Cincinnati	National		25	175	12	9	.571	142	69	64	151	61	3.29
1982—Cincinnati	National		35	257⅔	14	13	.519	202	88	80	274	71	2.79
1983—Cincinnati	National		34	273⅔	17	13	.567	207	96	82	242	95	2.70
1984—Cincinnati	National		33	237⅓	18	7	.720	181	102	93	185	87	3.53
1985—Cincinnati	National		36	256⅔	12	15	.444	196	109	102	214	104	3.58
1986—Cincinnati§	National		19	105	5	10	.333	113	61	55	67	46	4.71
Major League Totals—10 Years			277	1611⅓	94	83	.531	1273	665	604	1404	617	3.37

Signed as free agent by Cincinnati Reds' organization, December 3, 1973.
†On disabled list, July 1 to September 17, 1974.
‡On disabled list, April 13 to May 21, 1979.
§On disabled list, May 24 to June 8, June 20 to July 18 and August 16, 1986 through remainder of season.

CHAMPIONSHIP SERIES RECORD

Year	Club	League	G.	IP.	W.	L.	Pct.	H.	R.	ER.	SO.	BB.	ERA.
1979—Cincinnati	National		1	2	0	0	.000	0	0	0	1	0	0.00

ALL-STAR GAME RECORD

Year	League	IP.	W.	L.	Pct.	H.	R.	ER.	SO.	BB.	ERA.
1982—National		2	0	0	.000	3	0	0	4	0	0.00
1983—National		2	0	1	.000	2	2	0	2	2	0.00
1984—National		2	0	0	.000	0	0	0	1	0	0.00
All-Star Game Totals—3 Years		6	0	1	.000	5	2	0	7	2	0.00

ROBERT CLIFFORD SPECK
(Cliff)

Born August 8, 1956, at Portland, Ore.
Height, 6.04. Weight, 195.
Throws and bats righthanded.

Tied for Appalachian League lead in games started by pitchers with 13 in 1974.

Year	Club	League	G.	IP.	W.	L.	Pct.	H.	R.	ER.	SO.	BB.	ERA.
1974—Marion	Ap'lachian	13	79	4	4	.500	58	34	26	70	48	2.96
1975—Wausau†	Midwest	8	38	2	6	.250	36	33	28	28	37	6.63
1976—Lynchburg‡	Carolina	10	55	4	2	.667	37	32	26	31	47	4.25
1977—Lynchburg§	Carolina	20	91	5	7	.417	90	62	54	49	64	5.34
1978—Peninsula	Carolina	29	97	7	4	.636	88	43	34	67	47	3.15
1979—Peninsula	Carolina	26	77	6	3	.667	65	30	24	58	39	2.81
1979—Reading	Eastern	9	56	3	5	.375	60	33	27	39	21	4.34
1980—Reading	Eastern	9	51	4	3	.571	39	25	22	43	25	3.88
1980—Oklahoma City x	Am. Assoc.	20	74	1	5	.167	81	58	50	27	52	6.08
1981—Charlotte	Southern	12	33	1	0	1.000	29	11	10	24	11	2.73
1981—Rochester y	Int'national	27	76	6	3	.667	81	35	32	51	37	3.79
1982—Rochester	Int'national	31	156⅔	8	10	.444	148	77	60	88	72	3.45
1983—Rochester z	Int'national	29	148⅓	8	12	.400	136	95	83	130	105	5.04
1984—Denver	Am. Assoc.	29	176⅔	12	11	.522	186	117	102	148	73	5.20
1985—Buffalo ab	Am. Assoc.	21	122⅓	6	7	.462	113	66	66	88	67	4.86
1986—Richmond	Int'national	24	120⅓	8	5	.615	98	43	37	102	51	2.77
1986—Atlanta	National	13	28⅓	2	1	.667	25	13	13	21	15	4.13
Major League Totals—1 Year		13	28⅓	2	1	.667	25	13	13	21	15	4.13

Selected by New York Mets' organization in 1st round (17th player selected) of free-agent draft, June 5, 1974.
†On disabled list, June 12 to July 12, 1975.
‡On disabled list, June 17, 1976 through remainder of season.
§Released, April 1, 1978; signed by Peninsula (Philadelphia Phillies' organization), April 13, 1978.
xReleased, January 15, 1981; signed by Charlotte (Baltimore Orioles' organization), March 13, 1981.
yOn disabled list, July 3 to July 13, 1981.
zGranted free agency, October 20, 1983; signed by Chicago White Sox, December 16, 1983.
aOn Chicago disabled list, March 25 to May 20, 1985.
bGranted free agency, October 15, 1985; signed by Richmond (Atlanta Braves' organization), November 15, 1985.

CHRIS EDWARD SPEIER

Name pronounced Spire.

Born June 28, 1950, at Alameda, Calif.
Height, 6.01. Weight, 175.
Throws and bats righthanded.
Attended University of Santa Barbara, Santa Barbara, Calif.

Major League stolen bases: 1971 (4), 1972 (9), 1973 (4), 1974 (3), 1975 (4), 1976 (2), 1977 (1), 1978 (1), 1981 (1), 1982 (1), 1983 (2), 1985 (1), 1986 (2). Total—35.
Hit for the cycle, July 20, 1978.
Led Texas League shortstops in putouts with 223 and assists with 325 in 1970.
Named shortstop on THE SPORTING NEWS National League All-Star Team, 1972.

Year	Club	League	Pos.	G.	AB.	R.	H.	2B.	3B.	HR.	RBI.	B.A.	PO.	A.	E.	F.A.
1970—Amarillo	Texas	SS-3B-OF	129	460	44	130	20	5	6	46	.283	224	327	38	.935
1971—San Francisco	Nat.	SS	157	601	74	141	17	6	8	46	.235	239	517	●33	.953
1972—San Francisco	Nat.	SS	150	562	74	151	25	2	15	71	.269	243	★517	20	.974
1973—San Francisco	Nat.	●SS-2B	153	542	58	135	17	4	11	71	.249	255	471	●33	.957
1974—San Francisco	Nat.	SS-2B	141	501	55	125	19	5	9	53	.250	215	453	21	.970
1975—San Francisco	Nat.	★SS-3B	141	487	60	132	30	5	10	69	.271	247	421	12	★.982
1976—San Francisco	Nat.	S-2-3-1	145	495	51	112	18	4	3	40	.226	241	464	19	.974
1977—S.F.†-Mont	Nat.	SS	145	548	59	128	31	6	5	38	.234	239	455	23	.968
1978—Montreal	Nat.	SS	150	501	47	126	18	3	5	51	.251	245	467	18	.975
1979—Montreal‡	Nat.	SS	113	344	31	78	13	1	7	26	.227	194	355	17	.970
1980—Montreal	Nat.	SS-3B	128	388	35	103	14	4	1	32	.265	187	397	21	.965
1981—Montreal§	Nat.	SS	96	307	33	69	10	2	2	25	.225	175	280	17	.964
1982—Montreal	Nat.	SS	156	530	41	136	26	4	7	60	.257	291	405	13	.982
1983—Montreal x	Nat.	SS-3B-2B	88	261	31	67	12	2	2	22	.257	117	203	14	.958
1984—Mont. y-St.L. z	Nat.	SS-3B	63	158	10	27	7	1	3	9	.171	56	152	4	.981
1984—Minnesota ab	Amer.	SS	12	33	2	7	0	0	0	1	.212	14	28	1	.977
1985—Chicago	Nat.	SS-3B-2B	106	218	16	53	11	0	4	24	.243	87	177	11	.960
1986—Chicago c	Nat.	3B-SS-2B	95	155	21	44	8	0	6	23	.284	62	106	3	.982
National League Totals—16 Years		2027	6598	696	1627	276	49	98	660	.247	3093	5840	279	.970
American League Totals—1 Year		12	33	2	7	0	0	0	1	.212	14	28	1	.977
Major League Totals—16 Years		2039	6631	698	1634	276	49	98	661	.246	3107	5868	280	.970

Selected by Washington Senators' organization in 11th round of free-agent draft, June 7, 1968.
Selected by San Francisco Giants' organization in secondary phase of free-agent draft, January 17, 1970.
†Traded to Montreal Expos for Shortstop Tim Foli, April 27, 1977.
‡On disabled list, July 8 to July 27, 1979.
§Granted free agency, November 13, 1981; re-signed by Expos, January 12, 1982.
xOn disabled list, May 29 to June 13, 1983.
yTraded with cash to St. Louis Cardinals for Infielder Mike Ramsey, July 1, 1984.
zTraded to Minnesota Twins for a player to be named later and cash, August 19, 1984; St. Louis Cardinals' organization acquired Pitcher Jay Pettibone to complete deal, October 2, 1984.

aOn disabled list, August 22 to September 7, 1984.
bGranted free agency, November 8, 1984; signed by Chicago Cubs, April 8, 1985.
cGranted free agency, November 12, 1986; signed by San Francisco Giants, December 10, 1986.

DIVISION SERIES RECORD

Year Club	League	Pos.	G.	AB.	R.	H.	2B.	3B.	HR.	RBI.	B.A.	PO.	A.	E.	F.A.
1981—Montreal	Nat.	SS	5	15	4	6	2	0	0	3	.400	16	15	0	1.000

CHAMPIONSHIP SERIES RECORD

Year Club	League	Pos.	G.	AB.	R.	H.	2B.	3B.	HR.	RBI.	B.A.	PO.	A.	E.	F.A.
1971—San Francisco	Nat.	SS	4	14	4	5	1	0	1	1	.357	3	14	1	.944
1981—Montreal	Nat.	SS	5	16	0	3	0	0	0	0	.188	15	16	2	.939
Championship Series Totals—2 Years			9	30	4	8	1	0	1	1	.267	18	30	3	.941

ALL-STAR GAME RECORD

Year League	Pos.	AB.	R.	H.	2B.	3B.	HR.	RBI.	B.A.	PO.	A.	E.	F.A.
1972—National	SS	2	0	0	0	0	0	0	.000	1	5	0	1.000
1973—National	SS	2	0	0	0	0	0	0	.000	1	1	0	1.000
All-Star Game Totals—2 Years		4	0	0	0	0	0	0	.000	2	6	0	1.000

Member of National League All-Star Team in 1974 game; did not play.

WILLIAM HARRY SPILMAN

(Known by middle name.)

Born July 18, 1954, at Albany, Ga.
Height, 6.01. Weight, 190.
Throws right and bats lefthanded.
Son of Harry Spilman, catcher in Los Angeles Dodgers' organization, 1952.

Led Eastern League in total bases with 277 and intentional bases on balls received with 19 in 1977.
Named Eastern League Most Valuable Player, 1977.

Year Club	League	Pos.	G.	AB.	R.	H.	2B.	3B.	HR.	RBI.	B.A.	PO.	A.	E.	F.A.
1974—Billings	Pion.	1B-3B	54	178	29	55	12	2	2	30	.309	92	8	3	.971
1975—Tampa	Fla. St.	1B	115	348	33	90	13	1	1	38	.259	946	56	●17	.983
1976—Tampa	Fla. St.	1B	118	361	50	90	12	5	6	35	.249	986	70	16	.985
1977—Three Rivers	East.	1B	133	493	*94	*184	*39	3	16	78	*.373	1095	78	7	.994
1978—Indianapolis	A. A.	3B-1B	133	488	95	144	26	4	13	79	.295	262	184	23	.951
1978—Cincinnati	Nat.	PH	4	4	1	1	0	0	0	0	.250	0	0	0	.000
1979—Indianapolis	A. A.	3B-1B	71	267	42	77	13	3	3	27	.288	154	92	8	.969
1979—Cincinnati	Nat.	1B-3B-OF	43	56	7	12	3	0	0	5	.214	64	11	0	1.000
1980—Cincinnati	Nat.	1-3-O-C	65	101	14	27	4	0	4	19	.267	132	15	2	.987
1981—Cinc.†-Hou.	Nat.	1B	51	58	9	14	1	0	0	4	.241	62	5	1	.985
1982—Tucson	P. C.	1B-3B	53	190	34	63	16	3	6	33	.332	307	13	3	.991
1982—Houston	Nat.	1B	38	61	7	17	2	0	3	11	.279	86	5	1	.989
1983—Houston	Nat.	1B-C	42	78	7	13	3	0	1	9	.167	138	8	0	1.000
1984—Houston‡	Nat.	1B-C	32	72	14	19	2	0	2	15	.264	143	9	3	.981
1985—Houston§	Nat.	1B-C	44	66	3	9	1	0	1	4	.136	134	4	0	1.000
1986—Detroit x	Amer.	3B-1B-C	24	49	6	12	2	0	3	8	.245	7	1	0	1.000
1986—San Francisco y	Nat.	1-3-2-O-C	58	94	12	27	7	0	2	22	.287	140	17	2	.987
National League Totals—9 Years			377	590	74	139	23	0	13	89	.236	899	74	9	.991
American League Totals—1 Year			24	49	6	12	2	0	3	8	.245	7	1	0	1.000
Major League Totals—9 Years			401	639	80	151	25	0	16	97	.236	906	75	9	.991

Signed as free agent by Cincinnati Reds' organization, June 25, 1974.
†Traded to Houston Astros for Second Baseman Rafael Landestoy, June 8, 1981.
‡On disabled list, July 16, 1984 through remainder of season.
§Granted free agency, November 12, 1985; signed by Nashville (Detroit Tigers' organization), February 18, 1986.
xReleased, June 12, 1986; signed by San Francisco Giants, June 13, 1986.
yGranted free agency, November 12, 1986; re-signed by Giants, December 9, 1986.

DIVISION SERIES RECORD

Year Club	League	Pos.	G.	AB.	R.	H.	2B.	3B.	HR.	RBI.	B.A.	PO.	A.	E.	F.A.
1981—Houston	Nat.	PH	1	1	0	0	0	0	0	0	.000	0	0	0	.000

CHAMPIONSHIP SERIES RECORD

Year Club	League	Pos.	G.	AB.	R.	H.	2B.	3B.	HR.	RBI.	B.A.	PO.	A.	E.	F.A.
1979—Cincinnati	Nat.	PH	2	2	0	0	0	0	0	0	.000	0	0	0	.000

ROBERT MICHAEL STANLEY

(Mike)

Born May 25, 1963, at Fort Lauderdale, Fla.
Height, 6.01. Weight, 185.
Throws and bats righthanded.
Attended University of Florida, Gainesville, Fla.

Major League stolen bases: 1986 (1).

Year Club	League	Pos.	G.	AB.	R.	H.	2B.	3B.	HR.	RBI.	B.A.	PO.	A.	E.
1985—Salem	Carol.	1B-C	4	9	2	5	0	0	0	3	.556	19	1	1
1985—Burlington	Midw.	C-1B-OF	13	42	8	13	2	0	1	6	.310	45	2	0

Year Club	League	Pos.	G.	AB.	R.	H.	2B.	3B.	HR.	RBI.	B.A.	PO.	A.	E.	F.A.
1985—Tulsa	Texas	C-1-O-2	46	165	24	51	10	0	3	17	.309	289	18	6	.981
1986—Tulsa	Texas	C-1B-3B	67	235	41	69	16	2	6	35	.294	379	45	2	.995
1986—Texas	Amer.	3B-C-OF	15	30	4	10	3	0	1	1	.333	14	8	1	.957
1986—Oklahoma City	A. A.	C-3B-1B	56	202	37	74	13	3	5	49	.366	206	55	9	.967
Major League Totals—1 Year			15	30	4	10	3	0	1	1	.333	14	8	1	.957

Selected by Texas Rangers' organization in 16th round of free-agent draft, June 3, 1985.

ROBERT WILLIAM STANLEY
(Bob)

Born November 10, 1954, at Portland, Me.
Height, 6.04. Weight, 205.
Throws and bats righthanded.

Established American League record for most innings pitched by relief pitcher, season (168⅓), 1982.
Major League saves: 1977 (3), 1978 (10), 1979 (1), 1980 (14), 1982 (14), 1983 (33), 1984 (22), 1985 (10), 1986 (16). Total—123.
Led Eastern League in hit batsmen with 11 and tied for lead in games started by pitchers with 27 in 1976.
Led New York-Pennsylvania League pitchers in games started with 15 in 1974.
Tied for Florida State League lead in games started by pitchers with 26 in 1975.

Year Club	League	G.	IP.	W.	L.	Pct.	H.	R.	ER.	SO.	BB.	ERA.
1974—Elmira	NYP	15	86	6	6	.500	94	57	44	45	40	4.60
1975—Winter Haven	Florida St.	27	169	5	*17	.227	136	76	55	73	74	2.93
1976—Bristol†	Eastern	27	186	15	9	.625	176	76	55	78	83	2.66
1977—Boston	American	41	151	8	7	.533	176	74	67	44	43	3.99
1978—Boston	American	52	142	15	2	.882	142	50	41	38	34	2.60
1979—Boston	American	40	217	16	12	.571	250	110	96	56	44	3.98
1980—Boston	American	52	175	10	8	.556	186	75	66	71	52	3.39
1981—Boston	American	35	99	10	8	.556	110	46	42	28	38	3.82
1982—Boston	American	48	168⅓	12	7	.632	161	60	58	83	50	3.10
1983—Boston	American	64	145⅓	8	10	.444	145	56	46	65	38	2.85
1984—Boston	American	57	106⅔	9	10	.474	113	57	42	52	23	3.54
1985—Boston	American	48	87⅔	6	6	.500	76	30	28	46	30	2.87
1986—Boston	American	66	82⅓	6	6	.500	109	48	40	54	22	4.37
Major League Totals—10 Years		503	1374⅓	100	76	.568	1468	606	526	537	374	3.44

Selected by Los Angeles Dodgers' organization in 9th round of free-agent draft, June 5, 1973.
Selected by Boston Red Sox' organization in secondary phase of free-agent draft, January 9, 1974.
†On disabled list, June 19 to June 24, 1976.

CHAMPIONSHIP SERIES RECORD

Year Club	League	G.	IP.	W.	L.	Pct.	H.	R.	ER.	SO.	BB.	ERA.
1986—Boston	American	3	5⅔	0	0	.000	7	4	3	1	3	4.76

WORLD SERIES RECORD

Year Club	League	G.	IP.	W.	L.	Pct.	H.	R.	ER.	SO.	BB.	ERA.
1986—Boston	American	5	6⅓	0	0	.000	5	0	0	4	1	0.00

ALL-STAR GAME RECORD

Year League	IP.	W.	L.	Pct.	H.	R.	ER.	SO.	BB.	ERA.
1979—American	2	0	0	.000	1	1	1	0	0	4.50
1983—American	2	0	0	.000	2	0	0	0	0	0.00
All-Star Game Totals—2 Years	4	0	0	.000	3	1	1	0	0	2.25

DAVID LESLIE STAPLETON
(Dave)

Born January 16, 1954, at Fairhope, Ala.
Height, 6.01. Weight, 170.
Throws and bats righthanded.
Attended Faulkner State Junior College, Bay Minette, Ala., and
received bachelor of science degree in education from
University of South Alabama, Mobile, Ala.

Major League stolen bases: 1980 (3), 1982 (2), 1983 (1). Total—6.
...ed International League in total bases with 249 in 1979.
...med International League co-Most Valuable Player, 1979.

Club	League	Pos.	G.	AB.	R.	H.	2B.	3B.	HR.	RBI.	B.A.	PO.	A.	E.	F.A.
...ter Haven	Fla. St.	2B-SS-OF	56	199	23	48	8	1	1	14	.241	106	143	14	.947
...ter Haven	Fla. St.	3-2-1-S-O	118	400	67	115	13	2	4	38	.288	164	248	17	.960
...l	East.	2B-3B	86	304	52	93	21	4	8	28	.306	147	174	14	.958
...cket	Int.	3-1-2-S-O	25	74	9	18	5	0	1	9	.243	34	29	2	.969
...ket†	Int.	3-2-1-S	113	432	69	112	26	3	11	49	.259	155	224	21	.948
...t	Int.	1-3-2-O-S	140	*553	*88	*169	*33	1	15	64	.306	651	231	9	.990
...t	Int.	1-2-3-O	37	150	25	51	3	1	3	19	.340	239	53	8	.973
...	Amer.	2-1-O-3	106	449	61	144	33	5	7	45	.321	269	338	12	.981
...	Amer.	S-3-2-1	93	355	45	101	17	1	10	42	.285	260	204	17	.965
...	Amer.	1-S-2-3-O	150	538	66	142	28	1	14	65	.264	1032	179	13	.989
...	Amer.	1B-2B	151	542	54	134	31	1	10	66	.247	1249	105	10	.993
...	Amer.	1B	13	39	4	9	2	0	0	1	.231	86	8	0	1.000

.A.
.952
1.000

Year	Club	League	Pos.	G.	AB.	R.	H.	2B.	3B.	HR.	RBI.	B.A.	PO.	A.	E.	F.A.
1985—Boston§	Amer.	2B-1B	30	66	4	15	6	0	0	2	.227	41	36	1	.987
1985—Pawtucket	Int.	3B	5	14	1	3	1	0	0	0	.214	2	11	0	1.000
1986—Boston x	Amer.	1B-3B-2B	39	39	4	5	1	0	0	3	.128	85	16	0	1.000
Major League Totals—7 Years			582	2028	238	550	118	8	41	224	.271	3022	886	53	.987

Selected by Boston Red Sox' organization in 10th round of free-agent draft, June 4, 1975.
†On disabled list, April 10 to May 5, 1978.
‡On disabled list, April 29, 1984 through remainder of season.
§On disabled list, May 16 to June 7, 1985; included rehabilitation disability assignment to Pawtucket, May 31 to June 7, 1985.
xGranted free agency, November 12, 1986; signed by Seattle Mariners, December 23, 1986.

CHAMPIONSHIP SERIES RECORD

Year	Club	League	Pos.	G.	AB.	R.	H.	2B.	3B.	HR.	RBI.	B.A.	PO.	A.	E.	F.A.
1986—Boston	Amer.	1B-PR	4	3	2	2	0	0	0	0	.667	12	1	0	1.000

WORLD SERIES RECORD

Year	Club	League	Pos.	G.	AB.	R.	H.	2B.	3B.	HR.	RBI.	B.A.	PO.	A.	E.	F.A.
1986—Boston	Amer.	1B-PR	3	1	0	0	0	0	0	0	.000	3	2	0	1.000

MATTHEW SCOTT STARK
(Matt)

Born January 21, 1965, at Whittier, Calif.
Height, 6.04. Weight, 225.
Throws and bats righthanded.

Led Southern League catchers in double plays with 12 in 1986.

Year	Club	League	Pos.	G.	AB.	R.	H.	2B.	3B.	HR.	RBI.	B.A.	PO.	A.	E.	F.A.
1983—Medicine Hat	Pion.	C	60	206	29	58	6	0	8	49	.282	215	19	10	.959
1984—Florence†	S. Atl.	C	69	205	24	46	7	1	3	27	.224	383	36	12	.972
1985—Florence	S. Atl.	C	110	381	66	113	15	0	13	70	.297	392	36	17	.962
1985—Knoxville	South.	C	18	53	3	13	1	0	1	3	.245	85	8	4	.959
1986—Knoxville	South.	C	120	424	63	125	21	0	17	72	.295	665	73	16	.979

Selected by Toronto Blue Jays' organization in 1st round (ninth player selected) of free-agent draft, June 6, 1983.
† On disabled list, July 7, 1984 through remainder of season.

JAMES EARL STEELS
(Jim)

Born May 30, 1961, at Jackson, Miss.
Height, 5.10. Weight, 185.
Throws and bats lefthanded.

Named Texas League Most Valuable Player, 1984.

Year	Club	League	Pos.	G.	AB.	R.	H.	2B.	3B.	HR.	RBI.	B.A.	PO.	A.	E.	F.A.
1980—Reno†	Calif.	OF	73	285	42	86	8	4	3	27	.302	78	9	5	.946
1981—Amarillo	Texas	OF-1B	127	485	58	138	28	5	3	59	.285	206	14	8	.965
1982—Amarillo	Texas	1B	86	371	61	118	16	8	6	57	.318	789	61	★20	.977
1982—Hawaii	P. C.	OF-1B	52	196	33	49	10	6	4	26	.250	103	2	4	.963
1983—Las Vegas	P. C.	OF-1B	28	95	17	23	5	1	1	14	.242	47	4	0	1.000
1983—Beaumont	Texas	OF-1B	83	313	57	84	17	4	10	61	.268	188	10	7	.966
1984—Beaumont	Texas	OF-P-1B	127	474	90	161	26	10	12	81	★.340	195	15	5	.977
1985—Las Vegas‡	P. C.	OF	111	394	39	103	19	4	5	46	.261	163	12	3	.983
1986—Las Vegas	P. C.	OF	126	482	87	148	28	9	8	64	.307	228	●16	12	.953

Selected by San Diego Padres' organization in 8th round of free-agent draft, June 5, 1979.
†On disabled list, April 29 to June 16, 1980.
‡On disabled list, July 6 to July 24, 1985.

PITCHING RECORD

Year	Club	League	G.	IP.	W.	L.	Pct.	H.	R.	ER.	SO.	BB.	ERA.
1984—Beaumont	Texas	3	4⅔	0	0	.000	3	4	4	2	10	7.71

JOHN ROBERT STEFERO

Born September 22, 1959, at Sumter, S.C.
Height, 5.08. Weight, 185.
Throws right and bats lefthanded.

Tied for Appalachian League lead in errors by third baseman with 18 in 1979.

Year	Club	League	Pos.	G.	AB.	R.	H.	2B.	3B.	HR.	RBI.	B.A.	PO.	A.	E.	F.A.
1979—Bluefield	Appal.	3B-C	59	200	37	55	11	2	8	42	.275	58	95	19	.890
1980—Miami	Fla. St.	C	101	307	32	66	9	4	5	30	.215	352	63	★14	.967
1981—Hagerstown†	Carol.	C-3B-OF	111	338	69	97	16	2	25	82	.287	630	74	16	.978
1982—Charlotte	South.	C-OF-3B	115	357	45	82	9	2	17	60	.230	435	51	17	.966
1983—Charlotte	South.	C-OF	61	205	33	63	9	0	16	34	.307	261	40	12	.962
1983—Baltimore	Amer.	C	9	11	2	5	1	0	0	4	.455	20	3	2	.920
1983—Rochester	Int.	C	35	97	13	19	5	0	2	5	.196	153	26	4	.978
1984—Rochester	Int.	C	5	15	0	1	0	0	0	1	.067	18	1	2	.905
1984—Hagerstown	Carol.	C-OF	41	134	9	28	3	0	1	17	.209	171	21	2	.990
1984—Charlotte‡	South.	C	51	164	25	34	6	1	7	14	.207	195	30	3	.987

Year Club	League	Pos.	G.	AB.	R.	H.	2B.	3B.	HR.	RBI.	B.A.	PO.	A.	E.	F.A.
1985—Charlotte	South.	C-OF	57	169	31	37	8	0	7	19	.219	203	30	0	1.000
1985—Rochester	Int.	C	49	128	16	24	5	0	10	23	.188	192	24	4	.982
1986—Baltimore	Amer.	C-2B	52	120	14	28	2	0	2	13	.233	221	20	4	.984
1986—Rochester§	Int.	C	25	62	8	16	1	0	2	7	.258	117	13	0	1.000
Major League Totals—2 Years			61	131	16	33	3	0	2	17	.252	241	23	6	.978

Signed as free agent by Baltimore Orioles' organization, June 26, 1979.
†On disabled list, August 31 to September 11, 1981.
‡On disabled list, August 28 to September 4, 1984.
§Traded to Montreal Expos for a player to be named later, December 8, 1986; Baltimore Orioles acquired Infielder Rene Gonzales to complete deal, December 16, 1986.

TERRY LEE STEINBACH

Born March 2, 1962, at New Ulm, Minn.
Height, 6.01. Weight, 195.
Throws and bats righthanded.
Attended University of Minnesota, Minneapolis, Minn.
Brother of Tom Steinbach, outfielder in Seattle Mariners' organization, 1983.
Tied major league record by hitting home run in first major league at-bat, September 12, 1986.
Led Southern League in passed balls with 22 in 1986.
Led Midwest League third basemen in double plays with 31 in 1984.
Led Northwest League third basemen in assists with 122 and tied for lead in errors with 17 in 1983.
Named Southern League Most Valuable Player, 1986.

Year Club	League	Pos.	G.	AB.	R.	H.	2B.	3B.	HR.	RBI.	B.A.	PO.	A.	E.	F.A.
1983—Medford	N'west	3B-OF-1B	62	219	42	69	16	0	6	38	.315	105	124	21	.916
1984—Madison	Midw.	3B-1B-P	135	474	57	140	24	6	11	79	.295	107	257	27	.931
1985—Huntsville	South.	C-3-1-O-P	128	456	64	124	31	3	9	72	.272	187	43	6	.975
1986—Huntsville	South.	C-1B-3B	138	505	113	164	33	2	24	*132	.325	620	73	14	.980
1986—Oakland	Amer.	C	6	15	3	5	0	0	2	4	.333	21	4	1	.962
Major League Totals—1 Year			6	15	3	5	0	0	2	4	.333	21	4	1	.962

Selected by Cleveland Indians' organization in 16th round of free-agent draft, June 3, 1980.
Selected by Oakland A's organization in 9th round of free-agent draft, June 6, 1983.

PITCHING RECORD

Year Club	League	G.	IP.	W.	L.	Pct.	H.	R.	ER.	SO.	BB.	ERA.
1984—Madison	Midwest	2	3	0	0	.000	2	4	3	0	4	9.00
1985—Huntsville	Southern	1	1	0	0	.000	0	0	0	0	0	0.00

MICHAEL STEVEN STENHOUSE
(Mike)

Born May 29, 1958, at Pueblo, Colo.
Height, 6.01. Weight, 185.
Throws right and bats lefthanded.
Received bachelor of arts degree in economics from Harvard University, Cambridge, Mass.
Son of David Stenhouse, pitcher with Washington Senators, 1962 through 1964;
brother of David Stenhouse, Jr., catcher in Toronto Blue Jays' organization.
Major League stolen bases: 1985 (1).
Led American Association in slugging percentage with .681 in 1983.
Led Florida State League in game-winning RBIs with 12 and bases on balls received with 123 in 1980.
Named American Association Most Valuable Player, 1983.
Named designated hitter on THE SPORTING NEWS College Baseball All-America Team, 1979.

Year Club	League	Pos.	G.	AB.	R.	H.	2B.	3B.	HR.	RBI.	B.A.	PO.	A.	E.	F.A.
1980—W. Palm Beach	Fla. St.	1B-OF	133	439	77	120	17	7	13	71	.273	912	56	12	.988
1980—Memphis	South.	OF-1B	1	3	0	0	0	0	0	0	.000	2	0	0	1.000
1981—Memphis†	South.	OF-1B	118	397	64	108	25	7	14	72	.272	407	26	6	.986
1982—Wichita	A. A.	OF	134	436	94	126	25	3	25	80	.289	243	6	6	.976
1982—Montreal	Nat.	PH	1	1	0	0	0	0	0	0	.000	0	0	0	.000
1983—Wichita	A. A.	1B-OF	109	361	93	128	33	5	25	93	*.355	681	48	8	.989
1983—Montreal	Nat.	OF-1B	24	40	2	5	1	0	0	2	.125	37	2	0	1.000
1984—Montreal	Nat.	OF-1B	80	175	14	32	8	0	4	16	.183	118	5	2	.984
1984—Indianapolis‡	A. A.	1B-OF	27	93	22	31	4	2	8	27	.333	128	16	4	.973
1985—Minnesota§	Amer.	OF-1B	81	179	23	40	5	0	5	21	.223	83	10	3	.969
1986—Pawtucket	Int.	1B-OF	49	166	28	43	9	2	5	23	.259	62	1	1	.984
1986—Boston x	Amer.	OF-1B	21	21	1	2	1	0	0	1	.095	23	3	0	1.000
National League Totals—3 Years			105	216	16	37	9	0	4	18	.171	155	7	2	.988
American League Totals—2 Years			102	200	24	42	6	0	5	22	.210	106	13	3	.975
Major League Totals—5 Years			207	416	40	79	15	0	9	40	.190	261	20	5	.983

Selected by Oakland A's organization in 1st round (26th player selected) of free-agent draft, June 5, 1979.
Selected by Montreal Expos' organization in secondary phase of free-agent draft, January 8, 1980.
†On disabled list, April 9 to April 29, 1981.
‡Traded to Minnesota Twins for Pitcher Jack O'Connor, January 9, 1985.
§Traded to Boston Red Sox for Pitcher Charlie Mitchell, December 12, 1985.
xGranted free agency, October 15, 1986.

DAVID KEITH STEWART
(Dave)

Born February 19, 1957, at Oakland, Calif.
Height, 6.02. Weight, 200.
Throws and bats righthanded.

Major League saves: 1981 (6), 1982 (1), 1983 (8), 1985 (4). Total—19.
Led Pacific Coast League pitchers in games started with 29 in 1980.
Tied for Texas League lead in games started by pitchers with 28 in 1978.
Tied for Midwest League lead in complete games with 15, shutouts with 3 and balks with 3 in 1977.

Year Club	League	G.	IP.	W.	L.	Pct.	H.	R.	ER.	SO.	BB.	ERA.
1975—Bellingham	Northwest	22	49	0	5	.000	59	46	30	37	49	5.51
1976—Danville	Midwest	4	10	0	2	.000	17	20	18	10	16	16.20
1976—Bellingham	Northwest	24	50	1	1	.500	47	35	28	53	58	5.04
1977—Clinton	Midwest	24	176	*17	4	*.810	152	52	42	144	72	2.15
1977—Albuquerque	P. Coast	1	6	1	0	1.000	4	3	3	3	6	4.50
1978—San Antonio	Texas	28	*193	14	12	.538	181	99	79	130	97	3.68
1978—Los Angeles	National	1	2	0	0	.000	1	0	0	1	0	0.00
1979—Albuquerque	P. Coast	28	170	11	12	.478	198	112	99	105	81	5.24
1980—Albuquerque	P. Coast	31	*202	●15	10	.600	189	94	83	125	89	3.70
1981—Los Angeles	National	32	43	4	3	.571	40	13	12	29	14	2.51
1982—Los Angeles	National	45	146⅓	9	8	.529	137	72	62	80	49	3.81
1983—Los Angeles†	National	46	76	5	2	.714	67	28	25	54	33	2.96
1983—Texas	American	8	59	5	2	.714	50	15	14	24	17	2.14
1984—Texas	American	32	192⅓	7	14	.333	193	106	101	119	87	4.73
1985—Texas‡	American	42	81⅓	0	6	.000	86	53	49	64	37	5.42
1985—Philadelphia	National	4	4⅓	0	0	.000	5	4	3	2	4	6.23
1986—Philadelphia§	National	8	12⅓	0	0	.000	15	9	9	9	4	6.57
1986—Tacoma	P. Coast	1	3	0	0	.000	4	1	0	3	1	0.00
1986—Oakland	American	29	149⅓	9	5	.643	137	67	62	102	65	3.74
National League Totals—6 Years		136	284	18	13	.581	265	126	111	175	104	3.52
American League Totals—4 Years		111	482	21	27	.438	466	241	226	309	206	4.22
Major League Totals—7 Years		247	766	39	40	.494	731	367	337	484	310	3.96

Selected by Los Angeles Dodgers' organization in 16th round of free-agent draft, June 4, 1975.
†Traded with a player to be named later to Texas Rangers for Pitcher Rick Honeycutt, August 19, 1983; Texas acquired Pitcher Ricky Wright to complete deal, September 16, 1983.
‡Traded to Philadelphia Phillies for Pitcher Rick Surhoff, September 13, 1985.
§Released, May 9, 1986; signed by Tacoma (Oakland A's organization), May 23, 1986.

DIVISION SERIES RECORD

Year Club	League	G.	IP.	W.	L.	Pct.	H.	R.	ER.	SO.	BB.	ERA.
1981—Los Angeles	National	2	⅔	0	2	.000	4	3	3	1	0	40.50

WORLD SERIES RECORD

Year Club	League	G.	IP.	W.	L.	Pct.	H.	R.	ER.	SO.	BB.	ERA.
1981—Los Angeles	National	2	1⅔	0	0	.000	1	0	0	1	2	0.00

HECTOR TORRES STEWART

Born September 30, 1963, at Ponce, Puerto Rico.
Height 6.02. Weight, 210.
Throws and bats lefthanded.
Attended Indian River Community College, Fort Pierce, Fla.,
and University of Puerto Rico, Rio Piedras, Puerto Rico.

Tied for Eastern League lead in saves with 18 in 1986.

Year Club	League	G.	IP.	W.	L.	Pct.	H.	R.	ER.	SO.	BB.	ERA.
1983—Elmira	NYP	14	89⅓	6	5	.545	96	52	40	76	16	4.03
1984—Winston-Salem	Carolina	27	142	6	●13	.316	155	94	77	95	62	4.88
1985—Winter Haven	Florida St.	37	147	10	7	.588	149	56	46	52	37	2.82
1986—New Britain	Eastern	45	68⅔	7	6	.538	64	21	15	46	32	1.97

Signed as free agent by Boston Red Sox' organization, June 7, 1983.

SAMUEL LEE STEWART JR.
(Sammy)

Born October 28, 1954, at Asheville, N.C.
Height, 6.03. Weight, 208.
Throws and bats righthanded.
Attended Montreat-Anderson Junior College, Montreat, N.C.

Established major league record for most consecutive strikeouts, first major league game (7), September 1, 1978 (second game).
Pitched seven-inning, 1-0 no-hit victory against Winter Haven, July 20, 1976.
Major League saves: 1979 (1), 1980 (3), 1981 (4), 1982 (5), 1983 (7), 1984 (13), 1985 (9). Total—42.

Year Club	League	G.	IP.	W.	L.	Pct.	H.	R.	ER.	SO.	BB.	ERA.
1975—Bluefield	Ap'lachian	18	43	3	3	.500	62	44	29	29	26	6.07
1976—Miami	Florida St.	23	182	12	8	.600	147	65	49	79	*86	2.42
1977—Rochester	Int'national	10	54	0	5	.000	68	41	38	28	35	6.33
1977—Charlotte	Southern	16	117	9	6	.600	93	32	27	56	45	*2.08
1978—Rochester	Int'national	27	173	13	10	.565	168	90	73	111	93	3.80

Year Club	League	G.	IP.	W.	L.	Pct.	H.	R.	ER.	SO.	BB.	ERA.
1978—Baltimore	American	2	11	1	1	.500	10	5	4	11	3	3.27
1979—Baltimore	American	31	118	8	5	.615	96	47	46	71	71	3.51
1980—Baltimore	American	33	119	7	7	.500	103	51	47	78	60	3.55
1981—Baltimore	American	29	112	4	8	.333	89	33	29	57	57	2.33
1982—Baltimore†	American	38	139	10	9	.526	140	68	64	69	62	4.14
1982—Hagerstown	Carolina	2	8	0	0	.000	8	2	2	6	1	2.25
1983—Baltimore‡	American	58	144⅓	9	4	.692	138	60	58	95	67	3.62
1984—Baltimore	American	60	93	7	4	.636	81	42	34	56	47	3.29
1985—Baltimore§	American	56	129⅔	5	7	.417	117	60	52	77	66	3.61
1986—Boston xy	American	27	63⅔	4	1	.800	64	33	31	47	48	4.38
Major League Totals—9 Years		334	929⅔	55	46	.545	838	399	365	561	481	3.53

Selected by Kansas City Royals' organization in 28th round of free-agent draft, June 5, 1974.

Signed as free agent by Baltimore Orioles' organization, June 15, 1975.

†On disabled list, June 22 to July 15, 1982; included rehabilitation disability assignment to Hagerstown, July 7 to July 15, 1982.

‡Appeared in one game as a pinch-runner.

§Traded to Boston Red Sox for Shortstop Jackie Gutierrez, December 17, 1985.

xOn disabled list, June 9 to July 14, 1986.

yGranted free agency, November 12, 1986.

CHAMPIONSHIP SERIES RECORD

Year Club	League	G.	IP.	W.	L.	Pct.	H.	R.	ER.	SO.	BB.	ERA.
1983—Baltimore	American	2	4⅓	0	0	.000	2	0	0	2	1	0.00

WORLD SERIES RECORD

Year Club	League	G.	IP.	W.	L.	Pct.	H.	R.	ER.	SO.	BB.	ERA.
1979—Baltimore	American	1	2⅔	0	0	.000	4	0	0	0	1	0.00
1983—Baltimore	American	3	5	0	0	.000	2	0	0	6	2	0.00
World Series Totals—2 Years		4	7⅔	0	0	.000	6	0	0	6	3	0.00

DAVID ANDREW STIEB

Name pronounced Steeb.

(Dave)

Born July 22, 1957, at Santa Ana, Calif.
Height, 6.01. Weight, 185.
Throws and bats righthanded.
Attended Santa Ana College, Santa Ana, Calif., and
Southern Illinois University, Carbondale, Ill.
Brother of Steve Stieb, catcher in Atlanta Braves' organization, 1979 through 1981.

Major League saves: 1986 (1).

Led American League in hit batsmen with 14 in 1983, 11 in 1984, 15 in 1986 and tied for lead with 11 in 1981.

Led American League in complete games with 19 and shutouts with 5 in 1982.

Named American League Pitcher of the Year by THE SPORTING NEWS, 1982.

Named righthanded pitcher on THE SPORTING NEWS American League All-Star Team, 1982.

Named outfielder on THE SPORTING NEWS College Baseball All-America Team, 1978.

Year Club	League	G.	IP.	W.	L.	Pct.	H.	R.	ER.	SO.	BB.	ERA.
1978—Dunedin	Florida St.	4	26	2	0	1.000	23	10	6	8	1	2.08
1979—Dunedin	Florida St.	8	51	5	0	1.000	54	30	24	38	28	4.24
1979—Syracuse	Int'national	7	51	5	2	.714	39	15	12	20	14	2.12
1979—Toronto	American	18	129	8	8	.500	139	70	62	52	48	4.33
1980—Toronto†	American	34	243	12	15	.444	232	108	100	108	83	3.70
1981—Toronto	American	25	184	11	10	.524	148	70	65	89	61	3.18
1982—Toronto	American	38	★288⅓	17	14	.548	★271	116	104	141	75	3.25
1983—Toronto	American	36	278	17	12	.586	223	105	94	187	93	3.04
1984—Toronto	American	35	★267	16	8	.667	215	87	84	198	88	2.83
1985—Toronto	American	36	265	14	13	.519	206	89	73	167	96	★2.48
1986—Toronto‡	American	37	205	7	12	.368	239	128	108	127	87	4.74
Major League Totals—8 Years		259	1859⅓	102	92	.526	1673	773	690	1069	631	3.34

Selected by Toronto Blue Jays' organization in 5th round of free-agent draft, June 6, 1978.

†Appeared in one game as outfielder with no chances.

‡Appeared in one game as a pinch-runner.

CHAMPIONSHIP SERIES RECORD

Tied Championship Series record for most games started, Series (3), 1985.

Established American League Championship Series records for most bases on balls (10) and most strikeouts (18), seven-game Series, 1985.

Year Club	League	G.	IP.	W.	L.	Pct.	H.	R.	ER.	SO.	BB.	ERA.
1985—Toronto	American	3	20⅓	1	1	.500	11	7	7	18	10	3.10

ALL-STAR GAME RECORD

Tied All-Star Game record for most wild pitches, inning and game (2), July 8, 1980 (seventh inning).

Year League		IP.	W.	L.	Pct.	H.	R.	ER.	SO.	BB.	ERA.
1980—American		1	0	0	.000	1	1	0	0	2	0.00
1981—American		1⅔	0	0	.000	1	0	0	1	1	0.00
1983—American		3	1	0	1.000	0	1	0	4	1	0.00

Year	League	IP.	W.	L.	Pct.	H.	R.	ER.	SO.	BB.	ERA.
1984—American		2	0	1	.000	3	2	1	2	0	4.50
1985—American		1	0	0	.000	0	0	0	2	1	0.00
All-Star Game Totals—5 Years		8⅔	1	1	.500	5	4	1	9	5	1.04

RECORD AS OUTFIELDER

Year	Club	League	Pos.	G.	AB.	R.	H.	2B.	3B.	HR.	RBI.	B.A.	PO.	A.	E.	F.A.
1978—Dunedin		Fla. St.	OF-P	35	99	10	19	3	0	1	9	.192	85	7	3	.968

KURT ANDREW STILLWELL

Born June 4, 1965, at Glendale, Calif.
Height, 5.11. Weight, 165.
Throws right and bats left and righthanded.
Son of Ron Stillwell, infielder with Washington Senators, 1961 and 1962.

Major League stolen bases: 1986 (6).

Year	Club	League	Pos.	G.	AB.	R.	H.	2B.	3B.	HR.	RBI.	B.A.	PO.	A.	E.	F.A.
1983—Billings	Pion.		SS	65	250	47	81	10	1	2	44	.324	73	137	⋆30	.875
1984—Cedar Rapids	Midw.		SS	112	382	63	96	15	1	4	33	.251	156	245	25	.941
1985—Denver†	A. A.		SS-3B	59	182	28	48	7	4	1	22	.264	103	135	25	.905
1986—Cincinnati	Nat.		SS	104	279	31	64	6	1	0	26	.229	107	205	16	.951
1986—Denver	A. A.		SS	10	30	2	7	0	0	0	2	.233	14	21	5	.875
Major League Totals—1 Year				104	279	31	64	6	1	0	26	.229	107	205	16	.951

Selected by Cincinnati Reds' organization in 1st round (second player selected) of free-agent draft, June 6, 1983.
†On disabled list, August 9, 1985 through remainder of season.

ROBERT LYLE STODDARD

(Bob)

Born March 8, 1957, at Morgan Hill, Calif.
Height, 6.01. Weight, 190.
Throws and bats righthanded.
Attended Gavilan College, Gilroy, Calif., and
Fresno State University, Fresno, Calif.

Major League saves: 1985 (1), 1986 (1). Total—2.

Year	Club	League	G.	IP.	W.	L.	Pct.	H.	R.	ER.	SO.	BB.	ERA.
1978—Stockton	California		10	51	1	6	.143	46	36	31	47	39	5.47
1979—Stockton	California		20	120	7	5	.583	78	45	40	104	58	3.00
1980—Spokane†	P. Coast		21	124	4	9	.308	147	84	68	84	53	4.94
1981—Spokane‡	P. Coast		19	121	10	4	.714	117	47	39	70	41	2.90
1981—Seattle	American		5	35	2	1	.667	35	10	10	22	9	2.57
1982—Salt Lake City	P. Coast		24	147	7	11	.389	158	91	85	86	65	5.20
1982—Seattle	American		9	67⅓	3	3	.500	48	22	18	24	18	2.41
1983—Seattle	American		35	175⅔	9	17	.346	182	95	86	87	58	4.41
1984—Seattle	American		27	79	2	3	.400	86	51	45	39	37	5.13
1984—Salt Lake City	P. Coast		9	58⅔	4	4	.500	47	34	32	29	20	4.91
1985—Calgary§x	P. Coast		7	39⅔	1	3	.250	55	31	26	33	13	5.90
1985—Nashville	Am. Assoc.		22	30⅔	2	1	.667	15	3	2	31	14	0.59
1985—Detroit y	American		8	13⅓	0	0	.000	15	11	10	11	5	6.75
1986—Tacoma z-Las Vegas	P. Coast		39	51⅓	6	3	.667	52	26	23	51	19	4.03
1986—San Diego a	National		18	23⅓	1	0	1.000	20	7	6	17	11	2.31
American League Totals—5 Years			84	370⅓	16	24	.400	366	189	169	183	127	4.11
National League Totals—1 Year			18	23⅓	1	0	1.000	20	7	6	17	11	2.31
Major League Totals—6 Years			102	393⅔	17	24	.415	386	196	175	200	138	4.00

Selected by Milwaukee Brewers' organization in 19th round of free-agent draft, June 4, 1975.
Selected by Atlanta Braves' organization in secondary phase of free-agent draft, January 7, 1976.
Selected by Oakland A's organization in secondary phase of free-agent draft, June 8, 1976.
Selected by Seattle Mariners' organization in 10th round of free-agent draft, June 6, 1978.
†On disabled list, April 10 to April 24 and May 14 to May 26, 1980.
‡On disabled list, April 15 to April 27, June 7 to June 19 and July 24 to August 9, 1981.
§On disabled list, May 27 to June 28, 1985.
xReleased, June 28, 1985; signed by Nashville (Detroit Tigers' organization), July 1, 1985.
yReleased, October 8, 1985; signed by Tacoma (Oakland A's organization), January 29, 1986.
zTraded with Outfielder Kevin Russ to San Diego Padres' organization for Outfielder Kerry Tillman, April 18, 1986.
aReleased, November 1, 1986.

TIMOTHY PAUL STODDARD

(Tim)

Born January 24, 1953, at East Chicago, Ind.
Height, 6.07. Weight, 250.
Throws and bats righthanded.
Attended North Carolina State University, Raleigh, N. C.

Major League saves: 1979 (3), 1980 (26), 1981 (7), 1982 (12), 1983 (9), 1984 (7), 1985 (1). Total—65.
Tied for Southern League lead in wild pitches with 17 in 1977.

Year	Club	League	G.	IP.	W.	L.	Pct.	H.	R.	ER.	SO.	BB.	ERA.
1975—Knoxville	Southern		31	66	3	4	.429	66	40	31	37	43	4.23
1975—Chicago	American		1	1	0	0	.000	2	1	1	0	0	9.00

Year	Club	League	G.	IP.	W.	L.	Pct.	H.	R.	ER.	SO.	BB.	ERA.
1976—Knoxville	Southern	20	140	9	8	.529	147	55	45	62	60	2.89
1976—Iowa†	Am. Assoc.	12	29	0	2	.000	37	20	18	20	15	5.59
1977—Charlotte	Southern	36	174	10	7	.588	175	75	62	94	66	3.21
1978—Rochester‡	Int'national	45	76	7	3	.700	80	28	22	70	32	2.61
1978—Baltimore	American	8	18	0	1	.000	22	17	12	14	8	6.00
1979—Baltimore§	American	29	58	3	1	.750	44	12	11	47	19	1.71
1980—Baltimore	American	64	86	5	3	.625	72	27	24	64	38	2.51
1981—Baltimore	American	31	37	4	2	.667	38	16	16	32	18	3.89
1982—Baltimore xy	American	50	56	3	4	.429	53	26	25	42	29	4.02
1982—Rochester	Int'national	5	6	0	0	.000	2	1	1	6	2	1.50
1983—Baltimore za	American	47	57⅔	4	3	.571	65	39	39	50	29	6.09
1984—Chicago b	National	58	92	10	6	.625	77	41	39	87	57	3.82
1985—San Diego	National	44	60	1	6	.143	63	35	31	42	37	4.65
1986—San Diego c	National	30	45⅓	1	3	.250	33	20	19	47	34	3.77
1986—New York	American	24	49⅓	4	1	.800	41	23	21	34	23	3.83
American League Totals—8 Years		254	363	23	15	.605	337	161	149	283	164	3.69
National League Totals—3 Years		132	197⅓	12	15	.444	173	96	89	176	128	4.06
Major League Totals—10 Years		386	560⅓	35	30	.538	510	257	238	459	292	3.82

Selected by Texas Rangers' organization in 24th round of free-agent draft, June 5, 1974.
Selected by Chicago White Sox' organization in secondary phase of free-agent draft, January 9, 1975.
†Released, March 28, 1977; signed by Charlotte (Baltimore Orioles' organization), April 8, 1977.
‡On disabled list, June 15 to July 9, 1978.
§On disabled list, July 21 to September 1, 1979.
xOn disabled list, March 31 to May 5, 1982; included rehabilitation disability assignment to Rochester, April 27 to May 5, 1982.
yOn disabled list, September 7, 1982 through remainder of season.
zTraded to Oakland A's for Third Baseman Wayne Gross, December 9, 1983.
aTraded to Chicago Cubs for Pitcher Stan Kyles and a player to be named later, March 26, 1984; Oakland A's acquired Outfielder Stan Boderick to complete deal, March 31, 1984.
bGranted free agency, November 8, 1984; signed by San Diego Padres, January 8, 1985.
cTraded to New York Yankees for Pitcher Ed Whitson, July 9, 1986.

CHAMPIONSHIP SERIES RECORD

Year	Club	League	G.	IP.	W.	L.	Pct.	H.	R.	ER.	SO.	BB.	ERA.
1984—Chicago	National	2	2	0	0	.000	1	2	1	2	2	4.50

WORLD SERIES RECORD

Year	Club	League	G.	IP.	W.	L.	Pct.	H.	R.	ER.	SO.	BB.	ERA.
1979—Baltimore	American	4	5	1	0	1.000	6	3	3	3	1	5.40

JEFFERY GLEN STONE
(Jeff)

Born December 26, 1960, at Kennett, Mo.
Height, 6.00. Weight, 175.
Throws right and bats lefthanded.

Major League stolen bases: 1983 (4), 1984 (27), 1985 (15), 1986 (19). Total—65.
Led Carolina League in stolen bases with 94 in 1982.
Led South Atlantic League in being hit by pitch with 15 and stolen bases with 123 in 1981.
Led South Atlantic League outfielders in total chances with 290 in 1981.
Named Eastern League Most Valuable Player, 1983.

Year	Club	League	Pos.	G.	AB.	R.	H.	2B.	3B.	HR.	RBI.	B.A.	PO.	A.	E.	F.A.
1980—Central Oregon	N'west	OF	55	241	52	63	12	4	0	19	.261	116	4	4	.968
1981—Spartanburg	S. Atl.	OF	134	516	*108	143	13	9	3	53	.277	*264	11	15	.948
1982—Peninsula	Carol.	OF	*137	*559	110	166	18	*13	2	50	.297	●276	9	8	.973
1983—Reading†	East.	OF	125	492	*109	156	25	10	9	67	.317	226	6	9	.963
1983—Philadelphia	Nat.	OF	9	4	2	3	0	2	0	3	.750	0	0	0	.000
1984—Portland	P. C.	OF	82	355	59	109	15	●14	7	34	.307	194	7	12	.944
1984—Philadelphia‡	Nat.	OF	51	185	27	67	4	6	1	15	.362	75	1	7	.916
1985—Philadelphia	Nat.	OF	88	264	36	70	4	3	3	11	.265	82	4	3	.966
1985—Portland	P. C.	OF	67	252	58	83	16	8	2	28	.329	103	6	6	.948
1986—Portland	P. C.	OF	31	118	25	40	4	1	2	9	.339	60	0	1	.984
1986—Philadelphia	Nat.	OF	82	249	32	69	6	4	6	19	.277	103	8	2	.982
Major League Totals—4 Years		230	702	97	209	14	15	10	48	.298	260	13	12	.958

Signed as free agent by Philadelphia Phillies' organization, August 26, 1979.
†On disabled list, May 11 to May 21, 1983.
‡On disabled list, July 7 to August 6, 1984; included rehabilitation disability assignment to Portland, August 2 to August 6, 1984.

TODD VERNON STOTTLEMYRE

Born May 20, 1965, at Yakima, Wash.
Height, 6.03. Weight, 185.
Throws right and bats lefthanded.
Attended Yakima Valley College, Yakima, Wash.
Son of Mel Stottlemyre, Sr., pitcher with New York Yankees, 1964 through 1974; minor league pitching instructor, Seattle Mariners' organization, 1977 through 1981; and coach with New York Mets since 1984; nephew of Jeff Stottlemyre, pitcher in Seattle Mariners' organization, 1980 through 1983, and with Nuevo Laredo of Mexican League, 1984; and brother of Mel Stottlemyre, Jr., pitcher in Houston Astros' organization.

Year	Club	League	G.	IP.	W.	L.	Pct.	H.	R.	ER.	SO.	BB.	ERA.
1986—Ventura County		California	17	103⅔	9	4	.692	76	39	28	104	36	2.43

Selected by New York Yankees' organization in 5th round of free-agent draft, June 6, 1983.
Selected by St. Louis Cardinals' organization in secondary phase of free-agent draft, January 9, 1985.
Selected by Toronto Blue Jays' organization in secondary phase of free-agent draft, June 3, 1985.

LESTER P. STRAKER
(Les)

Born October 10, 1959, at Ciudad Bolivar, Venezuela.
Height, 6.01. Weight, 178.
Throws and bats righthanded.

Pitched 4-0 no-hit victory against Winter Haven, July 17, 1982.
Led Southern League in complete games with 12 and tied for lead in shutouts with 3 in 1985.
Tied for Pioneer League lead in shutouts with 1 in 1978.

Year	Club	League	G.	IP.	W.	L.	Pct.	H.	R.	ER.	SO.	BB.	ERA.
1977—Eugene		Northwest	7	26	1	2	.333	25	10	8	18	20	2.77
1978—Billings		Pioneer	12	69	7	2	.778	46	29	18	54	37	2.35
1979—Greensboro		W. Carol.	29	141	7	10	.412	123	83	62	121	75	3.96
1980—Cedar Rapids		Midwest	34	135	6	5	.545	135	74	56	89	66	3.73
1981—Waterbury†		Eastern	19	45	1	5	.167	50	35	32	33	34	6.40
1982—Tampa		Florida St.	25	154⅓	9	9	.500	137	58	44	99	60	2.57
1983—Waterbury‡§		Eastern	3	10	0	2	.000	16	10	10	5	6	9.00
1984—Albany x		Eastern	28	95⅔	6	5	.545	97	55	45	60	43	4.23
1985—Orlando		Southern	27	*193	16	6	.727	164	75	66	106	79	3.08
1986—Toledo y		Int'national	18	107⅓	6	7	.462	102	46	41	50	44	3.44

Signed as free agent by Cincinnati Reds' organization, February 10, 1977.
†On Tampa disabled list, August 3, 1981 through remainder of season.
‡On disabled list, May 5, 1983 through remainder of season.
§Granted free agency, October 20, 1983; signed by Tacoma (Oakland A's organization), November 26, 1983.
xReleased, December 12, 1984; signed by Orlando (Minnesota Twins' organization), January 10, 1985.
yOn disabled list, April 11 to May 23, 1986.

DARRYL EUGENE STRAWBERRY

Born March 12, 1962, at Los Angeles, Calif.
Height, 6.05. Weight, 190.
Throws and bats lefthanded.
Brother of Michael Strawberry, outfielder in Los Angeles Dodgers' organization, 1980 and 1981.

Hit three home runs in a game, August 5, 1985.
Major League stolen bases: 1983 (19), 1984 (27), 1985 (26), 1986 (28). Total—100.
Led Texas League in slugging percentage with .602, bases on balls received with 100 and caught stealing with 22 in 1982.
Named National League Rookie Player of the Year by THE SPORTING NEWS, 1983.
Named National League Rookie of the Year by Baseball Writers' Association of America, 1983.
Named Texas League Most Valuable Player, 1982.
Received reported $200,000 bonus to sign with New York Mets, 1980.

Year	Club	League	Pos.	G.	AB.	R.	H.	2B.	3B.	HR.	RBI.	B.A.	PO.	A.	E.	F.A.
1980—Kingsport		Appal.	OF	44	157	27	42	5	2	5	20	.268	55	4	3	.952
1981—Lynchburg		Carol.	OF	123	420	84	107	22	6	13	78	.255	173	8	13	.933
1982—Jackson		Texas	OF	129	435	93	123	19	9	*34	97	.283	211	8	9	.961
1983—Tidewater		Int.	OF	16	57	12	19	4	1	3	13	.333	22	0	4	.846
1983—New York		Nat.	OF	122	420	63	108	15	·7	26	74	.257	232	8	4	.984
1984—New York		Nat.	OF	147	522	75	131	27	4	26	97	.251	276	11	6	.980
1985—New York†		Nat.	OF	111	393	78	109	15	4	29	79	.277	211	5	2	.991
1986—New York		Nat.	OF	136	475	76	123	27	5	27	93	.259	226	10	6	.975
Major League Totals—4 Years				516	1810	292	471	84	20	108	343	.260	945	34	18	.982

Selected by New York Mets' organization in 1st round (first player selected) of free-agent draft, June 3, 1980.
†On disabled list, May 12 to June 28, 1985.

CHAMPIONSHIP SERIES RECORD

Established National League Championship Series record for most strikeouts, six-game Series (12), 1986.

Year	Club	League	Pos.	G.	AB.	R.	H.	2B.	3B.	HR.	RBI.	B.A.	PO.	A.	E.	F.A.
1986—New York		Nat.	OF	6	22	4	5	1	0	2	5	.227	9	0	0	1.000

WORLD SERIES RECORD

Year	Club	League	Pos.	G.	AB.	R.	H.	2B.	3B.	HR.	RBI.	B.A.	PO.	A.	E.	F.A.
1986—New York		Nat.	OF	7	24	4	5	1	0	1	1	.208	19	0	0	1.000

ALL-STAR GAME RECORD

Year	League	Pos.	AB.	R.	H.	2B.	3B.	HR.	RBI.	B.A.	PO.	A.	E.	F.A.
1984—National		OF	2	0	1	0	0	0	0	.500	0	0	0	.000
1985—National		OF	1	2	1	0	0	0	0	1.000	3	0	0	1.000
1986—National		OF	2	0	1	0	0	0	0	.500	1	0	0	1.000
All-Star Game Totals—3 Years			5	2	3	0	0	0	0	.600	4	0	0	1.000

FRANKLIN LEE STUBBS

Born October 21, 1960, at Laurinburg, N.C.
Height, 6.02. Weight, 205.
Throws and bats lefthanded.
Attended Virginia Tech., Blacksburg, Va.

Major League stolen bases: 1984 (2), 1986 (7). Total—9.
Named first baseman on THE SPORTING NEWS College Baseball All-America Team, 1982.

Year Club	League	Pos.	G.	AB.	R.	H.	2B.	3B.	HR.	RBI.	B.A.	PO.	A.	E.	F.A.
1982—Vero Beach†	Fla. St.	1B	16	54	6	11	1	1	3	5	.204	134	3	3	.979
1983—San Antonio	Texas	1B-OF	47	173	35	54	8	3	12	52	.312	425	23	5	.989
1983—Albuquerque	P. C.	OF-1B	76	267	49	74	16	3	16	58	.277	106	3	6	.948
1984—Albuquerque	P. C.	OF-1B	29	108	26	35	5	5	6	24	.324	36	4	2	.952
1984—Los Angeles	Nat.	1B-OF	87	217	22	42	2	3	8	17	.194	417	37	4	.991
1985—Albuquerque	P. C.	1B-OF	132	421	86	118	23	5	32	93	.280	945	87	14	.987
1985—Los Angeles	Nat.	1B	10	9	0	2	0	0	0	2	.222	11	0	0	1.000
1986—Los Angeles	Nat.	OF-1B	132	420	55	95	11	1	23	58	.226	244	14	7	.974
Major League Totals—3 Years			229	646	77	139	13	4	31	77	.215	672	51	11	.985

Selected by Los Angeles Dodgers' organization in 1st round (19th player selected) of free-agent draft, June 7, 1982.
†On disabled list, July 5, 1982 through remainder of season.

MARC COOPER SULLIVAN

Born July 25, 1958, at Quincy, Mass.
Height, 6.04. Weight, 198.
Throws and bats righthanded.
Attended University of Florida, Gainesville, Fla.

Son of Haywood Sullivan, catcher with Boston Red Sox and Kansas City A's, 1955, 1957 and 1959 through 1963;
manager, Kansas City A's, 1965; Vice-President of Player Personnel, Boston Red Sox, 1966 through 1977;
Executive Vice-President, General Manager and General Partner, Boston Red Sox,
1978 through 1984; and Chief Executive Officer, Boston Red Sox, since 1985.

Led International League catchers in putouts with 574 in 1984.
Led Eastern League catchers in double plays with 13 in 1982.
Led Carolina League catchers in putouts with 788 in 1981.
Named catcher on THE SPORTING NEWS College Baseball All-America Team, 1979.

Year Club	League	Pos.	G.	AB.	R.	H.	2B.	3B.	HR.	RBI.	B.A.	PO.	A.	E.	F.A.
1979—Winter Haven	Fla. St.	C	31	92	8	19	2	1	0	10	.207	146	20	2	.988
1980—Winter Haven	Fla. St.	C-1B	94	293	32	66	8	3	4	30	.225	482	75	11	.981
1981—Winston-Salem	Carol.	★C-OF-1B	120	406	67	109	21	1	14	64	.268	792	★114	15	★.984
1982—Bristol	East.	★C-1B	117	369	31	75	8	2	1	33	.203	728	★89	13	.984
1982—Pawtucket	Int.	C	4	10	0	2	0	0	0	1	.200	19	4	1	.958
1982—Boston	Amer.	C	2	6	0	2	0	0	0	0	.333	9	2	0	1.000
1983—New Britain	East.	C-1B	73	231	30	53	15	1	7	43	.229	503	32	7	.987
1983—Pawtucket†	Int.	C-1B	27	70	9	13	3	0	1	7	.186	107	14	2	.984
1984—Pawtucket	Int.	C-1B	116	383	54	78	14	1	15	63	.204	600	59	9	.987
1984—Boston	Amer.	C	2	6	1	3	0	0	1	1	.500	19	0	1	.950
1985—Boston‡	Amer.	C	32	69	10	12	2	0	2	3	.174	129	8	1	.993
1985—Pawtucket	Int.	C	2	4	0	1	0	0	0	0	.250	10	0	0	1.000
1986—Boston	Amer.	C	41	119	15	23	4	0	1	14	.193	203	13	3	.986
Major League Totals—4 Years			77	200	26	40	6	0	3	18	.200	360	23	5	.987

Selected by Boston Red Sox' organization in 2nd round of free-agent draft, June 5, 1979.
†On disabled list, August 15, 1983 through remainder of season.
‡On disabled list, June 1 to June 20 and July 3 to July 30, 1985; included rehabilitation disability assignment to Pawtucket, June 16 to June 20, 1985.

JAMES HOWARD SUNDBERG
(Jim)

Born May 18, 1951, at Galesburg, Ill.
Height, 6.00. Weight, 196.
Throws and bats righthanded.
Attended University of Iowa, Iowa City, Iowa.

Tied major league records for most seasons leading league in assists by catcher (6); most assists by catcher, inning (3), September 3, 1976 (fifth inning); fewest errors by catcher, season (4), 1979.
Established American League record for highest fielding percentage by catcher, season (.995), 1979.
Tied American League record for most games, catcher, season (155), 1975.
Major League stolen bases: 1974 (2), 1975 (3), 1977 (2), 1978 (2), 1979 (3), 1980 (2), 1981 (2), 1982 (2), 1984 (1), 1986 (1). Total—20.
Led American League in passed balls with 8 in 1981 and 16 in 1982.
Led American League catchers in total chances with 909 in 1975, 822 in 1976, 909 in 1977, 863 in 1978, 833 in 1979 and 936 in 1980.
Led American League catchers in double plays with 15 in 1974, 11 in 1976 and 15 in 1982.
Tied for American League lead in passed balls with 17 in 1980.
Tied for American League lead in double plays by catchers with 12 in 1977 and 14 in 1978.
Named catcher on THE SPORTING NEWS American League All-Star Team, 1978 and 1981.
Named catcher on THE SPORTING NEWS American League All-Star fielding team, 1976 through 1981.

Year Club	League	Pos.	G.	AB.	R.	H.	2B.	3B.	HR.	RBI.	B.A.	PO.	A.	E.	F.A.
1973—Pittsfield	East.	C	91	242	39	72	14	0	5	40	.298	449	52	3	★.994
1974—Texas	Amer.	C	132	368	45	91	13	3	3	36	.247	722	69	8	.990

Year Club	League	Pos.	G.	AB.	R.	H.	2B.	3B.	HR.	RBI.	B.A.	PO.	A.	E.	F.A.
1975—Texas	Amer.	C	155	472	45	94	9	0	6	36	.199	★791	★101	17	.981
1976—Texas	Amer.	C	140	448	33	102	24	2	3	34	.228	★719	★96	7	★.991
1977—Texas	Amer.	C	149	453	61	132	20	3	6	65	.291	★801	★103	5	★.994
1978—Texas	Amer.	C	149	518	54	144	23	6	6	58	.278	★769	★91	3	★.997
1979—Texas	Amer.	C	150	495	50	136	23	4	5	64	.275	★754	75	4	★.995
1980—Texas	Amer.	C	151	505	59	138	24	1	10	63	.273	★853	★76	7	.993
1981—Texas	Amer.	★C-OF	102	339	42	94	17	2	3	28	.277	465	★52	2	★.996
1982—Texas	Amer.	C-OF	139	470	37	118	22	5	10	47	.251	612	69	6	.991
1983—Texas†	Amer.	C	131	378	30	76	14	0	2	28	.201	618	56	5	.993
1984—Milwaukee‡§	Amer.	C	110	348	43	91	19	4	7	43	.261	556	55	3	★.995
1985—Kansas City	Amer.	C	115	367	38	90	12	4	10	35	.245	572	41	5	.992
1986—Kansas City	Amer.	C	140	429	41	91	9	1	12	42	.212	686	46	4	★.995
Major League Totals—13 Years			1763	5590	578	1397	229	35	83	579	.250	8918	930	76	.992

Selected by Oakland A's organization in 14th round of free-agent draft, June 5, 1969.
Selected by Texas Rangers' organization in 8th round of free-agent draft, June 6, 1972.
Selected by Texas Rangers' organization in secondary phase of free-agent draft, January 10, 1973.
†Traded to Milwaukee Brewers for Catcher Ned Yost and Pitcher Dan Scarpetta, December 8, 1983.
‡On disabled list, August 6 to September 1, 1984.
§Traded to Kansas City Royals as part of a six-player, four-team deal in which Texas Rangers acquired Catcher Don Slaught from Kansas City, New York Mets' organization acquired Pitcher Frank Wills from Kansas City, Milwaukee Brewers acquired Pitcher Danny Darwin and a player to be named later from Texas and Pitcher Tim Leary from New York, January 18, 1985; Milwaukee organization acquired Catcher Bill Hance from Texas to complete deal, January 30, 1985.

CHAMPIONSHIP SERIES RECORD

Year Club	League	Pos.	G.	AB.	R.	H.	2B.	3B.	HR.	RBI.	B.A.	PO.	A.	E.	F.A.
1985—Kansas City	Amer.	C	7	24	3	4	1	1	1	6	.167	41	2	1	.977

WORLD SERIES RECORD

Year Club	League	Pos.	G.	AB.	R.	H.	2B.	3B.	HR.	RBI.	B.A.	PO.	A.	E.	F.A.
1985—Kansas City	Amer.	C	7	24	6	6	2	0	0	1	.250	47	3	0	1.000

ALL-STAR GAME RECORD

Year League	Pos.	AB.	R.	H.	2B.	3B.	HR.	RBI.	B.A.	PO.	A.	E.	F.A.
1978—American	C	0	0	0	0	0	0	0	.000	2	1	0	1.000
1984—American	C	1	0	0	0	0	0	0	.000	6	0	0	1.000
All-Star Game Totals—2 Years		1	0	0	0	0	0	0	.000	8	1	0	1.000

Member of American League All-Star Team in 1974 game; did not play.

WILLIAM JAMES SURHOFF
(B. J.)

Born August 4, 1964, at Rye, N.Y.
Height, 6.01. Weight, 185.
Throws right and bats lefthanded.
Attended University of North Carolina, Chapel Hill, N.C.
Son of Dick Surhoff, forward with New York Knicks and Milwaukee Hawks of the
National Basketball Association, 1952-53 and 1953-54; and brother of
Rich Surhoff, pitcher in Chicago Cubs' organization.

Tied for Pacific Coast League lead in double plays by catchers with 10 in 1986.
Named College Player of the Year by THE SPORTING NEWS, 1985.
Member of 1984 U. S. Olympic baseball team.
Named catcher on THE SPORTING NEWS College Baseball All-America Team, 1985.

Year Club	League	Pos.	G.	AB.	R.	H.	2B.	3B.	HR.	RBI.	B.A.	PO.	A.	E.	F.A.
1985—Beloit	Midw.	C	76	289	39	96	13	4	7	58	.332	475	44	3	.994
1986—Vancouver	P. C.	C	116	458	71	141	19	3	5	59	.308	539	70	7	★.989

Selected by New York Yankees' organization in 5th round of free-agent draft, June 7, 1982.
Selected by Milwaukee Brewers' organization in 1st round (first player selected) of free-agent draft, June 3, 1985.

RICHARD LEE SUTCLIFFE
(Rick)

Born June 21, 1956, at Independence, Mo.
Height, 6.06. Weight, 200.
Throws right and bats lefthanded.
Brother of Terry Sutcliffe, pitcher in Los Angeles Dodgers' organization, 1979 through 1981.

Major League saves: 1980 (5), 1982 (1). Total—6.
Led California League pitchers in games started with 28 in 1975.
Tied for Northwest League lead in shutouts with 2 in 1974.
Named National League Pitcher of the Year by THE SPORTING NEWS, 1984.
Won National League Cy Young Memorial Award, 1984.
Named righthanded pitcher on THE SPORTING NEWS National League All-Star Team, 1984.
Named National League Rookie Pitcher of the Year by THE SPORTING NEWS, 1979.
Named National League Rookie of the Year by Baseball Writers' Association of America, 1979.
Received reported $80,000 bonus to sign with Los Angeles Dodgers, 1974.

Year Club	League	G.	IP.	W.	L.	Pct.	H.	R.	ER.	SO.	BB.	ERA.
1974—Bellingham	Northwest	17	95	10	3	.769	79	42	35	69	48	3.32

Year Club	League	G.	IP.	W.	L.	Pct.	H.	R.	ER.	SO.	BB.	ERA.
1975—Bakersfield	California	28	193	8	*16	.333	*214	*115	*89	91	68	4.15
1976—Waterbury	Eastern	30	187	10	11	.476	*187	90	66	121	45	3.18
1976—Los Angeles	National	1	5	0	0	.000	2	0	0	3	1	0.00
1977—Albuquerque†	P. Coast	17	77	3	10	.231	96	67	55	48	63	6.43
1978—Albuquerque	P. Coast	30	184	13	6	.684	179	101	91	99	92	4.45
1978—Los Angeles	National	2	2	0	0	.000	2	0	0	0	1	0.00
1979—Los Angeles	National	39	242	17	10	.630	217	104	93	117	97	3.46
1980—Los Angeles	National	42	110	3	9	.250	122	73	68	59	55	5.56
1981—Los Angeles‡§	National	14	47	2	2	.500	41	24	21	16	20	4.02
1982—Cleveland	American	34	216	14	8	.636	174	81	71	142	98	*2.96
1983—Cleveland	American	36	243⅓	17	11	.607	251	131	116	160	102	4.29
1984—Cleveland x	American	15	94⅓	4	5	.444	111	60	54	58	46	5.15
1984—Chicago y	National	20	150⅓	16	1	*.941	123	53	45	155	39	2.69
1985—Chicago z	National	20	130	8	8	.500	119	51	46	102	44	3.18
1986—Chicago a	National	28	176⅔	5	14	.263	166	92	91	122	96	4.64
National League Totals—8 Years		166	863	51	44	.537	792	397	364	574	353	3.80
American League Totals—3 Years		85	553⅔	35	24	.593	536	272	241	360	246	3.92
Major League Totals—10 Years		251	1416⅔	86	68	.558	1328	669	605	934	599	3.84

Selected by Los Angeles Dodgers' organization in 1st round (21st player selected) of free-agent draft, June 5, 1974.
†On disabled list, May 3 to May 24, 1977.
‡On disabled list, August 14 to September 5, 1981.
§Traded with Second Baseman Jack Perconte to Cleveland Indians for Outfielder Jorge Orta, Catcher Jack Fimple and Pitcher Larry White, December 9, 1981.
xTraded with Catcher Ron Hassey and Pitcher George Frazier to Chicago Cubs for Outfielders Mel Hall and Joe Carter and Pitchers Don Schulze and Darryl Banks, June 13, 1984.
yGranted free agency, November 8, 1984; re-signed by Cubs, December 14, 1984.
zOn disabled list, May 20 to June 7, July 8 to July 23 and July 29 to September 27, 1985.
aOn disabled list, June 30 to August 3, 1986.

CHAMPIONSHIP SERIES RECORD

Tied Championship Series records for hitting home run in first Series at-bat, October 2, 1984; most home runs hit by pitcher, total Series (1); most bases on balls, five-game Series (8), 1984.

Year Club	League	G.	IP.	W.	L.	Pct.	H.	R.	ER.	SO.	BB.	ERA.
1984—Chicago	National	2	13⅓	1	1	.500	9	6	5	10	8	3.38

ALL-STAR GAME RECORD

Member of American League All-Star Team in 1983; did not play.

HOWARD BRUCE SUTTER

Name pronounced SUIT-er.

(Known by middle name.)

Born January 8, 1953, at Lancaster, Pa.
Height, 6.02. Weight, 190.
Throws and bats righthanded.

Tied major league record by striking out side on 9 pitches, September 8, 1977 (ninth inning).
Established National League records for most saves, lifetime (286); most saves, season (45), 1984.
Tied National League records for most consecutive strikeouts by relief pitcher, game (6), September 8, 1977.
Major League saves: 1976 (10), 1977 (31), 1978 (27), 1979 (37), 1980 (28), 1981 (25), 1982 (36), 1983 (21), 1984 (45), 1985 (23), 1986 (3). Total—286.
Led National League in saves with 37 in 1979, 28 in 1980, 25 in 1981, 36 in 1982 and 45 in 1984.
Led National League in games finished in relief with 63 in 1984.
Tied for Texas League lead in saves with 13 in 1975.
Won National League Cy Young Memorial Award, 1979.
Named National League Fireman of the Year by THE SPORTING NEWS, 1979, 1981, 1982 and 1984.

Year Club	League	G.	IP.	W.	L.	Pct.	H.	R.	ER.	SO.	BB.	ERA.
1972—Bradenton Cubs	Gulf Coast	2	5	0	0	.000	3	0	0	4	0	0.00
1973—Quincy	Midwest	40	85	3	3	.500	94	52	39	76	27	4.13
1974—Key West†	Florida St.	18	40	1	5	.167	26	9	6	50	13	1.35
1974—Midland	Texas	8	25	1	2	.333	22	6	4	14	6	1.44
1975—Midland	Texas	41	67	5	7	.417	64	26	16	50	21	2.15
1976—Wichita	Am. Assoc.	7	12	2	1	.667	9	3	2	16	4	1.50
1976—Chicago	National	52	83	6	3	.667	63	27	25	73	26	2.71
1977—Chicago‡	National	62	107	7	3	.700	69	21	16	129	23	1.35
1978—Chicago	National	64	99	8	10	.444	82	44	35	106	34	3.18
1979—Chicago	National	62	101	6	6	.500	67	29	25	110	32	2.23
1980—Chicago§	National	60	102	5	8	.385	90	35	30	76	34	2.65
1981—St. Louis	National	48	82	3	5	.375	64	24	24	57	24	2.63
1982—St. Louis	National	70	102⅓	9	8	.529	88	38	33	61	34	2.90
1983—St. Louis	National	60	89⅓	9	10	.474	90	45	42	64	30	4.23
1984—St. Louis x	National	71	122⅔	5	7	.417	109	26	21	77	23	1.54
1985—Atlanta	National	58	88⅓	7	7	.500	91	46	44	52	29	4.48
1986—Atlanta y	National	16	18⅔	2	0	1.000	17	9	9	16	9	4.34
Major League Totals—11 Years		623	995⅓	67	67	.500	830	344	304	821	298	2.75

Selected by Washington Senators' organization in 21st round of free-agent draft, June 4, 1970.
Signed as free agent by Chicago Cubs' organization, September 9, 1971.
†On disabled list, May 22 to July 28, 1974.
‡On disabled list, August 2 to August 23, 1977.

xGranted free agency, November 8, 1984; signed by Atlanta Braves, December 7, 1984 (Shortstop Argenis Salazar selected from player compensation pool by St. Louis Cardinals' organization, January 24, 1985).

yOn disabled list, May 28, 1986 through remainder of season.

CHAMPIONSHIP SERIES RECORD

Year	Club	League	G.	IP.	W.	L.	Pct.	H.	R.	ER.	SO.	BB.	ERA.
1982—St. Louis	National		2	4⅓	1	0	1.000	0	0	0	1	0	0.00

WORLD SERIES RECORD

Year	Club	League	G.	IP.	W.	L.	Pct.	H.	R.	ER.	SO.	BB.	ERA.
1982—St. Louis	National		4	7⅔	1	0	1.000	6	4	4	6	3	4.70

ALL-STAR GAME RECORD

Year	League	IP.	W.	L.	Pct.	H.	R.	ER.	SO.	BB.	ERA.
1978—National		1⅔	1	0	1.000	0	0	0	2	0	0.00
1979—National		2	1	0	1.000	2	0	0	3	2	0.00
1980—National		2	0	0	.000	0	0	0	1	1	0.00
1981—National		1	0	0	.000	0	0	0	1	0	0.00
All-Star Game Totals—4 Years		6⅔	2	0	1.000	2	0	0	7	3	0.00

Member of National League All-Star Team in 1984; did not play.
Named to National League All-Star Team in 1977; replaced due to injury.

DONALD HOWARD SUTTON
(Don)

Born April 2, 1945, at Clio, Ala.
Height, 6.01.   Weight, 190.
Throws and bats righthanded.
Attended Gulf Coast Community College, Panama City, Fla.;
Mississippi College, Clinton, Miss.; University of Southern California, Los Angeles, Calif.
and Whittier College, Whittier, Calif.

Established major league records for most consecutive games lost to one club, lifetime (13), 1966 through 1969, (vs. Chicago); most years and most consecutive years with 100 or more strikeouts (21).
Tied National League record for most consecutive home runs allowed, inning (3), May 27, 1980 (third inning).
Tied modern National League record for most one-hit games, lifetime (5).
Major League saves: 1971 (1), 1979 (1), 1980 (1). Total—3.
Led National League pitchers in games started with 40 in 1974.
Led National League in shutouts with 9 in 1972.
Tied for National League lead in balks with 3 in 1968.
Named National League Rookie Pitcher of the Year by THE SPORTING NEWS, 1966.
Named righthanded pitcher on THE SPORTING NEWS National League All-Star Team, 1976.
Named Texas League Player of the Year, 1965.

Year	Club	League	G.	IP.	W.	L.	Pct.	H.	R.	ER.	SO.	BB.	ERA.
1965—Santa Barbara	California		10	84	8	1	.889	59	18	14	101	15	1.50
1965—Albuquerque	Texas		21	165	15	6	*.714	151	60	51	138	30	2.78
1966—Los Angeles	National		37	226	12	12	.500	192	82	75	209	52	2.99
1967—Los Angeles	National		37	233	11	15	.423	223	106	102	169	57	3.94
1968—Spokane	P. Coast		2	16	1	1	.500	11	2	2	19	5	1.13
1968—Los Angeles	National		35	208	11	15	.423	179	64	60	162	59	2.60
1969—Los Angeles	National		41	293	17	18	.486	269	123	113	217	91	3.47
1970—Los Angeles	National		38	260	15	13	.536	251	127	●118	201	78	4.08
1971—Los Angeles	National		38	265	17	12	.586	231	85	75	194	55	2.55
1972—Los Angeles	National		33	273	19	9	.679	186	78	63	207	63	2.08
1973—Los Angeles	National		33	256	18	10	.643	196	78	69	200	56	2.43
1974—Los Angeles	National		40	276	19	9	.679	241	111	99	179	80	3.23
1975—Los Angeles	National		35	254	16	13	.552	202	87	81	175	62	2.87
1976—Los Angeles	National		35	268	21	10	.677	231	98	91	161	82	3.06
1977—Los Angeles	National		33	240	14	8	.636	207	93	85	150	69	3.19
1978—Los Angeles	National		34	238	15	11	.577	228	109	94	154	54	3.55
1979—Los Angeles	National		33	226	12	15	.444	201	109	96	146	61	3.82
1980—Los Angeles†	National		32	212	13	5	.722	163	56	52	128	47	*2.21
1981—Houston	National		23	159	11	9	.550	132	51	46	104	29	2.60
1982—Houston‡	National		27	195	13	8	.619	169	75	65	139	46	3.00
1982—Milwaukee	American		7	54⅓	4	1	.800	55	21	20	36	18	3.29
1983—Milwaukee	American		31	220⅓	8	13	.381	209	109	100	134	54	4.08
1984—Milwaukee§	American		33	212⅔	14	12	.538	224	103	89	143	51	3.77
1985—Oakland x-California y	American		34	226	15	10	.600	221	101	97	107	59	3.86
1986—California	American		34	207	15	11	.577	192	93	86	116	49	3.74
National League Totals—17 Years			584	4082	254	192	.570	3501	1532	1384	2895	1041	3.05
American League Totals—5 Years			139	920⅔	56	47	.544	901	427	392	536	231	3.83
Major League Totals—21 Years			723	5002⅔	310	239	.565	4402	1959	1776	3431	1272	3.20

Signed as free agent by Los Angeles Dodgers' organization, September 11, 1964.

†Granted free agency, October 23, 1980; signed by Houston Astros, December 4, 1980.

‡Traded to Milwaukee Brewers for three players to be named later, August 30, 1982; Houston Astros acquired Pitchers Frank DiPino and Mike Madden and Outfielder Kevin Bass to complete deal, September 3, 1982.

§Traded to Oakland A's for Pitchers Ray Burris, Eric Barry and a player to be named later, December 7, 1984; Milwaukee Brewers' organization acquired Pitcher Ed Myers to complete deal, March 25, 1985.

xTraded to California Angels for two players to be named later, September 10, 1985; Oakland A's organization acquired Pitcher Robert Sharpnack and Outfielder Jerome Nelson to complete deal, September 25, 1985.

yGranted free agency, November 12, 1985; re-signed by Angels, December 5, 1985.

CHAMPIONSHIP SERIES RECORD

Established Championship Series records for most consecutive scoreless innings, Series (15⅔), 1974; most innings pitched, four-game Series (17), 1974.

Tied Championship Series records for most clubs, total Series (3); most games won, Series (2), 1974; most games won, total Series (4).

Established National League Championship Series record for most consecutive scoreless innings, total Series (15⅔).

Tied National League Championship Series records for most games won, total Series (3); most complete games, total Series (2); most strikeouts four-game Series (13), 1974.

Year Club	League	G.	IP.	W.	L.	Pct.	H.	R.	ER.	SO.	BB.	ERA.
1974—Los Angeles	National	2	17	2	0	1.000	7	1	1	13	2	0.53
1977—Los Angeles	National	1	9	1	0	1.000	9	1	1	4	0	1.00
1978—Los Angeles	National	1	5⅔	0	1	.000	7	7	4	0	2	6.35
1982—Milwaukee	American	1	7⅔	1	0	1.000	8	3	3	9	2	3.52
1986—California	American	2	9⅔	0	0	.000	6	2	2	4	1	1.86
Championship Series Totals—5 Years		7	49	4	1	.800	37	14	11	30	7	2.02

WORLD SERIES RECORD

Tied World Series records for most consecutive home runs allowed, inning (2), October 16, 1977 (eighth inning); most runs allowed, six-game Series (10), 1978.

Year Club	League	G.	IP.	W.	L.	Pct.	H.	R.	ER.	SO.	BB.	ERA.
1974—Los Angeles	National	2	13	1	0	1.000	9	4	4	12	3	2.77
1977—Los Angeles	National	2	16	1	0	1.000	17	7	7	6	1	3.94
1978—Los Angeles	National	2	12	0	2	.000	17	10	10	8	4	7.50
1982—Milwaukee	American	2	10⅓	0	1	.000	12	11	9	5	1	7.84
World Series Totals—4 Years		8	51⅓	2	3	.400	55	32	30	31	9	5.26

ALL-STAR GAME RECORD

Year League	IP.	W.	L.	Pct.	H.	R.	ER.	SO.	BB.	ERA.
1972—National	2	0	0	.000	1	0	0	2	0	0.00
1973—National	1	0	0	.000	0	0	0	0	0	0.00
1975—National	2	0	0	.000	3	0	0	1	0	0.00
1977—National	3	1	0	1.000	1	0	0	4	1	0.00
All-Star Game Totals—4 Years	8	1	0	1.000	5	0	0	7	1	0.00

DALE CURTIS SVEUM

Name pronounced Swaim.
Born November 23, 1963, at Richmond, Calif.
Height, 6.02. Weight, 185.
Throws right and bats left and righthanded.

Major League stolen bases: 1986 (4).
Led American League third basemen in errors with 26 in 1986.
Led Texas League in total bases with 256 in 1984.
Led Texas League third basemen in putouts with 111 in 1984.
Led California League third basemen in assists with 261 in 1983.

Year Club	League	Pos.	G.	AB.	R.	H.	2B.	3B.	HR.	RBI.	B.A.	PO.	A.	E.	F.A.
1982—Pikeville	Appal.	SS-3B	58	223	29	52	13	1	2	21	.233	84	158	36	.871
1983—Stockton	Calif.	3B-SS	135	533	70	139	26	5	5	70	.261	105	281	40	.906
1984—El Paso	Texas	*3B-SS	131	523	92	*172	*41	8	9	84	.329	113	259	*30	.925
1985—Vancouver	P. C.	3B-SS	122	415	42	98	17	3	6	48	.236	81	200	26	.915
1986—Vancouver	P. C.	3B	28	105	16	31	3	2	1	23	.295	22	54	4	.950
1986—Milwaukee†	Amer.	3B-SS-2B	91	317	35	78	13	2	7	35	.246	92	179	30	.900
Major League Totals—1 Year			91	317	35	78	13	2	7	35	.246	92	179	30	.900

Selected by Milwaukee Brewers' organization in 1st round (25th player selected) of free-agent draft, June 7, 1982.
†On disabled list, July 23 to August 9, 1986.

WILLIAM DAVID SWAGGERTY
(Bill)

Born December 5, 1956, at Sanford, Fla.
Height, 6.02. Weight, 190.
Throws and bats righthanded.
Attended St. John's River Community College, Palatka, Fla., and Stetson University, Deland, Fla.

Led International League in complete games with 10 in 1985 and tied for lead with 9 in 1986.

Year Club	League	G.	IP.	W.	L.	Pct.	H.	R.	ER.	SO.	BB.	ERA.
1979—Bluefield	Ap'lachian	17	68	5	3	.625	76	45	36	36	28	4.79
1980—Miami	Florida St.	19	43	3	1	.750	39	16	11	25	22	2.30
1980—Charlotte	Southern	26	51	3	6	.333	47	20	14	23	24	2.47
1981—Charlotte†	Southern	35	49	8	5	.615	35	15	11	26	19	2.02
1982—Rochester‡	Int'national	29	92	6	5	.545	111	63	55	27	59	5.38

Year Club	League	G.	IP.	W.	L.	Pct.	H.	R.	ER.	SO.	BB.	ERA.
1983—Rochester§	Int'national	25	118⅓	9	6	.600	136	67	61	25	37	4.64
1983—Baltimore	American	7	21⅔	1	1	.500	23	8	7	7	6	2.91
1984—Rochester	Int'national	11	64⅓	6	2	.750	53	25	19	22	30	2.66
1984—Baltimore x	American	23	57	3	2	.600	68	41	33	18	21	5.21
1985—Rochester	Int'national	30	★189	11	●13	.458	★187	73	68	58	52	3.24
1985—Baltimore	American	1	1⅔	0	0	.000	3	1	1	2	2	5.40
1986—Rochester	Int'national	26	175⅔	12	7	.632	★204	92	●83	56	52	4.25
1986—Baltimore y	American	1	1	0	0	.000	6	2	2	1	1	18.00
Major League Totals—4 Years		32	81⅓	4	3	.571	100	52	43	28	30	4.76

Selected by Baltimore Orioles' organization in 25th round of free-agent draft, June 5, 1979.
†On disabled list, June 1 to June 24, 1981.
‡On disabled list, August 27, 1982 through remainder of season.
§On disabled list, April 12 to May 6, 1983.
xAppeared in one game as a pinch-runner.
yGranted free agency, October 15, 1986; signed by Kansas City Royals' organization, November 15, 1986.

WILLIAM CHARLES SWIFT
(Bill)

Born December 27, 1961, at Portland, Maine.
Height, 6.00. Weight, 170.
Throws and bats righthanded.
Attended University of Maine, Orono, Maine.

Member of 1984 U.S. Olympic baseball team.

Year Club	League	G.	IP.	W.	L.	Pct.	H.	R.	ER.	SO.	BB.	ERA.
1985—Chattanooga†	Southern	7	39	2	1	.667	34	16	16	21	21	3.69
1985—Seattle	American	23	120⅔	6	10	.375	131	71	64	55	48	4.77
1986—Seattle	American	29	115⅓	2	9	.182	148	85	70	55	55	5.46
1986—Calgary	P. Coast	10	57	4	4	.500	57	33	25	29	22	3.95
Major League Totals—2 Years		52	236	8	19	.296	279	156	134	110	103	5.11

Selected by Minnesota Twins' organization in 2nd round of free-agent draft, June 6, 1983.
Selected by Seattle Mariners' organization in 1st round (second player selected) of free-agent draft, June 4, 1984.
†On disabled list, May 6 to May 21, 1985.

FOREST GREGORY SWINDELL
(Greg)

Born January 2, 1965, at Austin, Tex.
Height, 6.02. Weight, 225.
Throws left and bats righthanded.
Attended University of Texas, Austin, Tex.

Named lefthanded pitcher on THE SPORTING NEWS College Baseball All-America Team, 1985 and 1986.

Year Club	League	G.	IP.	W.	L.	Pct.	H.	R.	ER.	SO.	BB.	ERA.
1986—Waterloo	Midwest	3	18	2	1	.667	12	2	2	25	3	1.00
1986—Cleveland	American	9	61⅔	5	2	.714	57	35	29	46	15	4.23
Major League Totals—1 Year		9	61⅔	5	2	.714	57	35	29	46	15	4.23

Selected by Cleveland Indians' organization in 1st round (second player selected) of free-agent draft, June 2, 1986.

PATRICK SEAN TABLER
(Pat)

Born February 2, 1958, at Hamilton, O.
Height, 6.03. Weight, 185.
Throws and bats righthanded.

Major League stolen bases: 1983 (2), 1984 (3), 1986 (3). Total—8.
Led Southern League in game-winning RBIs with 13 in 1980.
Led American Association third basemen in total chances with 361 in 1982.
Tied for American Association lead in sacrifice flies with 9 in 1982.

Year Club	League	Pos.	G.	AB.	R.	H.	2B.	3B.	HR.	RBI.	B.A.	PO.	A.	E.	F.A.
1976—Oneonta	NYP	3B-OF	65	238	27	55	3	0	1	20	.231	79	71	12	.926
1977—Fort Lauderdale	Fla. St.	3B	110	391	35	93	7	1	1	36	.238	87	209	★35	.894
1978—Fort Lauderdale	Fla. St.	1B-3B-OF	138	455	56	124	9	5	5	70	.273	855	88	15	.984
1979—Fort Lauderdale	Fla. St.	O-3-2-1	75	247	39	78	12	4	2	33	.316	102	41	11	.929
1979—West Haven	East.	2B-OF	56	190	33	57	15	3	6	36	.300	124	169	13	.958
1980—Nashville	South.	2B	136	479	56	142	38	8	16	83	.296	262	361	★27	.958
1981—Columbus†‡	Int.	2B-3B	52	179	41	53	14	3	11	33	.296	66	116	14	.929
1981—Iowa	A. A.	2B	63	222	41	68	13	3	6	37	.306	110	141	4	.984
1981—Chicago	Nat.	2B	35	101	11	19	3	1	1	5	.188	70	93	3	.982
1982—Iowa	A. A.	★3B-1B	129	441	89	151	32	★11	17	105	.342	★112	★215	★34	.906
1982—Chicago§x	Nat.	3B	25	85	9	20	4	2	1	7	.235	23	33	3	.949
1983—Charleston	Int.	3B	4	14	2	3	0	1	0	2	.214	2	4	3	.667
1983—Cleveland	Amer.	OF-3B-2B	124	430	56	125	23	5	6	65	.291	197	55	11	.958
1984—Cleveland	Amer.	1-O-3-2	144	473	66	137	21	3	10	68	.290	532	89	7	.989
1985—Cleveland	Amer.	1B-3B-2B	117	404	47	111	18	3	5	59	.275	744	77	14	.983

Year Club League	Pos.	G.	AB.	R.	H.	2B.	3B.	HR.	RBI.	B.A.	PO.	A.	E.	F.A.
1986—Cleveland y .... Amer.	1B	130	473	61	154	29	2	6	48	.326	846	84	9	.990
1986—Maine...................... Int.	DH	3	12	5	3	1	0	0	1	.250	0	0	0	.000
National League Totals—2 Years............		60	186	20	39	7	3	2	12	.210	93	126	6	.973
American League Totals—4 Years		515	1780	230	527	91	13	27	240	.296	2319	305	41	.985
Major League Totals—6 Years.................		575	1966	250	566	98	16	29	252	.288	2412	431	47	.984

Selected by New York Yankees' organization in 1st round (16th player selected) of free-agent draft, June 8, 1976.

†Loaned to Iowa (Chicago Cubs' organization), June 12, 1981; returned, August 19, 1981.

‡Acquired on waivers by Chicago Cubs for two players to be named later, August 19, 1981; New York Yankees acquired Pitcher Bill Caudill, April 1, 1982, and New York organization acquired Pitcher Jay Howell, August 2, 1982, to complete deal.

§Traded with Pitchers Dick Tidrow and Randy Martz and Infielder Scott Fletcher to Chicago White Sox for Pitchers Steve Trout and Warren Brusstar, January 25, 1983.

xTraded to Cleveland Indians for Shortstop Jerry Dybzinski, April 1, 1983.

yOn disabled list, June 11 to June 30, 1986; included rehabilitation disability assignment to Maine, June 26 to June 30, 1986.

GREGORY ROLAND TALAMANTEZ
(Greg)

Born October 17, 1965, at Idaho Falls, Ida.
Height, 6.02. Weight, 190.
Throws and bats righthanded.

Tied for New York-Pennsylvania League lead in games started by pitchers with 15 and wild pitches with 15 in 1985.

Year Club League	G.	IP.	W.	L.	Pct.	H.	R.	ER.	SO.	BB.	ERA.
1984—Bluefield .... Ap'lachian	12	75	6	4	.600	57	36	29	•93	31	3.48
1985—Hagerstown .... Carolina	10	47⅓	3	3	.500	46	30	25	38	46	4.75
1985—Newark .... NYP	15	88⅔	4	7	.364	76	56	43	87	★77	4.36
1986—Hagerstown .... Carolina	26	148⅔	12	6	.667	131	93	72	124	★102	4.36

Selected by Baltimore Orioles' organization in 3rd round of free-agent draft, June 4, 1984.

FRANK DARYL TANANA
Name rhymes with Banana.

Born July 3, 1953, at Detroit, Mich.
Height, 6.03. Weight, 195.
Throws and bats lefthanded.
Attended California State University, Fullerton, Calif.
Son of Frank Richard Tanana, minor league outfielder, 1952 through 1956.

Established American League record for most balks, season (8), 1978.
Tied American League record for most consecutive hits allowed, start of game (5), May 18, 1980.
Led American League in balks with 8 in 1978 and tied for lead with 4 in 1984.
Led American League in shutouts with 7 in 1977.
Led Texas League in complete games with 15 in 1973.
Named American League Rookie Pitcher of the Year by THE SPORTING NEWS, 1974.
Named lefthanded pitcher on THE SPORTING NEWS American League All-Star Team, 1976 and 1977.
Named Texas League Pitcher of the Year, 1973.

Year Club League	G.	IP.	W.	L.	Pct.	H.	R.	ER.	SO.	BB.	ERA.
1971—Idaho Falls† .... Pioneer	....	....	....	....	.....	....	....	....	....	....	.....
1972—Quad Cities .... Midwest	19	129	7	2	.778	111	48	40	134	57	2.79
1973—El Paso.......................... Texas	26	★206	16	6	.727	170	72	62	★197	63	2.71
1973—Salt Lake City .... P. Coast	2	14	1	0	1.000	11	5	4	15	2	2.57
1973—California........................ American	4	26	2	2	.500	20	11	9	22	8	3.12
1974—California........................ American	39	269	14	19	.424	262	104	93	180	77	3.11
1975—California........................ American	34	257	16	9	.640	211	80	75	★269	73	2.63
1976—California........................ American	34	288	19	10	.655	212	88	78	261	73	2.44
1977—California........................ American	31	241	15	9	.625	201	72	68	205	61	★2.54
1978—California........................ American	33	239	18	12	.600	239	108	97	137	60	3.65
1979—California‡........................ American	18	90	7	5	.583	93	44	39	46	25	3.90
1980—California§........................ American	32	204	11	12	.478	223	107	94	113	45	4.15
1981—Boston x .... American	24	141	4	10	.286	142	70	63	78	43	4.02
1982—Texas.............................. American	30	194⅓	7	●18	.280	199	102	91	87	55	4.21
1983—Texas.............................. American	29	159½	7	9	.438	144	70	56	108	49	3.16
1984—Texas.............................. American	35	246⅓	15	15	.500	234	104	89	141	81	3.25
1985—Texas y-Detroit................ American	33	215	12	14	.462	220	112	102	159	57	4.27
1986—Detroit............................ American	32	188⅓	12	9	.571	196	95	87	119	65	4.16
Major League Totals—14 Years........................	408	2758⅓	159	153	.510	2596	1180	1041	1925	772	3.40

Selected by California Angels' organization in 1st round (13th player selected) of free-agent draft, June 8, 1971.

†Appeared in one game as pinch-runner (did not pitch due to a sore arm).

‡On disabled list, July 9 to September 4, 1979.

§Traded with Pitcher Jim Dorsey and Outfielder Joe Rudi to Boston Red Sox for Outfielder Fred Lynn and Pitcher Steve Renko, January 23, 1981.

xGranted free agency, November 13, 1981; signed by Texas Rangers, January 6, 1982.

yTraded to Detroit Tigers for Pitcher Duane James, June 20, 1985.

CHAMPIONSHIP SERIES RECORD
Year Club League	G.	IP.	W.	L.	Pct.	H.	R.	ER.	SO.	BB.	ERA.
1979—California................ American	1	5	0	0	.000	6	2	2	3	2	3.60

Year League	IP.	W.	L.	Pct.	H.	R.	ER.	SO.	BB.	ERA.
1976—American	2	0	0	.000	3	3	3	0	1	6.00

Named to American League All-Star Team for the 1977 game; replaced due to injury.
Named to American League All-Star Team for 1978 game; did not play.

BRUCE MATTHEW TANNER

Born December 9, 1961, at New Castle, Pa.
Height, 6.03. Weight, 220.
Throws right and bats lefthanded.
Attended Florida State University, Tallahassee, Fla.
Son of Chuck Tanner, manager of Atlanta Braves; and brother of Mark Tanner, pitcher in
Chicago Cubs', Chicago White Sox' and Texas Rangers' organizations, 1972 through 1975.

Year Club	League	G.	IP.	W.	L.	Pct.	H.	R.	ER.	SO.	BB.	ERA.
1983—Niagara Falls	NYP	16	25	2	3	.400	30	16	10	31	17	3.60
1983—Glens Falls	Eastern	5	6	0	0	.000	2	1	1	1	5	1.50
1983—Appleton	Midwest	4	3	0	1	.000	3	1	1	1	3	3.00
1984—Appleton	Midwest	37	123⅔	12	4	.750	96	32	27	91	30	*1.96
1985—Buffalo...	Am. Assoc.	20	109⅓	5	7	.417	99	49	42	49	44	3.46
1985—Chicago	American	10	27	1	2	.333	34	17	16	9	13	5.33
1986—Buffalo†	Am. Assoc.	23	158	8	10	.444	165	83	73	81	53	4.16
Major League Totals—1 Year...............................		10	27	1	2	.333	34	17	16	9	13	5.33

Selected by Chicago Cubs' organization in 33rd round of free-agent draft, June 3, 1980.
Selected by Chicago White Sox' organization in 4th round of free-agent draft, June 6, 1983.
†Traded to Oakland A's, December 18, 1986, completing deal in which Oakland traded Infielder Donnie Hill to
Chicago White Sox for Pitcher Gene Nelson and a player to be named later, December 11, 1986.

DANILO TARTABULL (MORA)
(Danny)

Born October 30, 1962, at San Juan, P.R.
Height, 6.01. Weight, 185.
Throws and bats righthanded.
Son of Jose Tartabull, outfielder with Kansas City A's, Boston Red Sox and Oakland A's, 1962 through 1970;
and Yucatan of Mexican League, 1972; and minor league manager,
Houston Astros' organization, 1982 through 1984.

Major League stolen bases: 1985 (1), 1986 (4). Total—5.
Led Pacific Coast League in slugging percentage with .615 and total bases with 291 in 1985.
Led Pacific Coast League shortstops in errors with 35 in 1985.
Led Pacific Coast League shortstops in double plays with 68 in 1984.
Led Florida State League third basemen in errors with 29 in 1981.
Named Pacific Coast League Player of the Year, 1985.
Named Florida State League Most Valuable Player, 1981.

Year Club	League	Pos.	G.	AB.	R.	H.	2B.	3B.	HR.	RBI.	B.A.	PO.	A.	E.	F.A.
1980—Billings	Pion.	3B-OF-2B	59	157	33	47	10	0	2	27	.299	34	54	14	.863
1981—Tampa	Fla. St.	3B-2B	127	422	86	131	*28	10	14	81	*.310	150	248	39	.911
1982—Waterbury†	East.	2B	126	409	64	93	17	3	17	63	.227	237	306	*32	.944
1983—Chattanooga	South.	2B	128	481	95	145	32	7	13	66	.301	252	405	23	.966
1984—Salt Lake City.......	P. C.	SS	116	418	69	127	22	9	13	73	.304	181	333	24	.955
1984—Seattle....................	Amer.	SS-2B	10	20	3	6	1	0	2	7	.300	8	21	2	.935
1985—Calgary	P. C.	SS-3B	125	473	102	142	14	3	*43	*109	.300	181	399	36	.942
1985—Seattle....................	Amer.	SS-3B	19	61	8	20	7	1	1	7	.328	28	43	4	.947
1986—Seattle‡§...............	Amer.	OF-2B-3B	137	511	76	138	25	6	25	96	.270	233	111	18	.950
Major League Totals—3 Years................			166	592	87	164	33	7	28	110	.277	269	175	24	.949

Selected by Cincinnati Reds' organization in 3rd round of free-agent draft, June 3, 1980.
†Selected by Seattle Mariners' organization in player compensation pool draft, January 20, 1983. (Seattle received
compensation for Chicago White Sox' signing of free-agent Pitcher Floyd Bannister, December 13, 1982.)
‡On disabled list, May 15 to May 30, 1986.
§Traded with Pitcher Rick Luecken to Kansas City Royals for Pitchers Scott Bankhead and Steve Shields and
Outfielder Mike Kingery, December 10, 1986.

LaSCHELLE TARVER

Born January 30, 1959, at Modesto, Calif.
Height, 5.11. Weight, 165.
Throws and bats lefthanded.
Attended Reedley College, Reedley, Calif., and California State University, Sacramento, Calif.

Year Club	League	Pos.	G.	AB.	R.	H.	2B.	3B.	HR.	RBI.	B.A.	PO.	A.	E.	F.A.
1981—Shelby	S. Atl.	OF	110	427	78	134	14	5	0	27	.314	247	9	4	.985
1981—Lynchburg.............	Carol.	OF	5	22	3	10	2	0	0	3	.455	10	0	0	1.000
1982—Lynchburg.............	Carol.	OF	99	399	75	123	14	2	1	34	.308	140	3	8	.947
1982—Jackson	Texas	OF	24	74	15	15	2	0	0	8	.203	18	0	0	1.000
1982—Tidewater.............	Int.	OF	3	8	1	2	0	0	0	0	.250	4	0	1	.800
1983—Jackson	Texas	OF	121	481	95	152	19	2	0	36	.316	127	3	7	.949
1983—Tidewater.............	Int.	DH	3	10	4	5	1	0	0	0	.500	0	0	0	.000
1984—Tidewater.............	Int.	OF	108	368	63	120	13	1	0	26	.326	97	0	0	1.000
1985—Tidewater†...........	Int.	OF	126	457	73	142	17	3	1	40	.311	151	5	5	.969

Year	Club	League	Pos.	G.	AB.	R.	H.	2B.	3B.	HR.	RBI.	B.A.	PO.	A.	E.	F.A.
1986—Pawtucket		Int.	OF	97	375	68	120	19	2	2	26	.320	205	6	6	.972
1986—Boston		Amer.	OF	13	25	3	3	0	0	0	1	.120	16	0	0	1.000
Major League Totals—1 Year				13	25	3	3	0	0	0	1	.120	16	0	0	1.000

Selected by California Angels' organization in 32nd round of free-agent draft, June 7, 1977.
Signed as free agent by New York Mets' organization, August 18, 1980.
†Traded with Pitchers Calvin Schiraldi and Wes Gardner and Outfielder John Christensen to Boston Red Sox for Pitchers Bob Ojeda, Tom McCarthy, John Mitchell and Chris Bayer, November 13, 1985.

DONALD C. TAYLOR
(Dorn)

Born August 11, 1958, at Abington, Pa.
Height, 6.02. Weight, 180.
Throws and bats righthanded.

Year	Club	League	G.	IP.	W.	L.	Pct.	H.	R.	ER.	SO.	BB.	ERA.
1982—Greenwood		S. Atlantic	27	164⅔	9	8	.529	128	57	42	133	92	*2.30
1983—Alexandria		Carolina	28	35⅓	2	7	.222	38	33	31	22	30	7.90
1983—Greenwood		S. Atlantic	12	81⅔	6	3	.667	73	35	32	79	40	3.53
1984—Prince William		Carolina	25	161⅓	11	5	.688	133	68	61	148	67	3.40
1985—Nashua†		Eastern	26	112⅔	6	9	.400	101	63	54	64	57	4.31
1986—Nashua‡		Eastern	33	62⅔	2	2	.500	42	13	11	57	26	1.58
1986—Hawaii		P. Coast	5	31⅓	3	1	.750	22	10	7	29	12	2.01

Signed as free agent by Pittsburgh Pirates' organization, December 11, 1981.
†On disabled list, July 5 to July 21, 1985.
†On disabled list, April 11 to April 21, 1986.

DWIGHT BERNARD TAYLOR

Born March 24, 1960, at Los Angeles, Calif.
Height, 5.09. Weight, 166.
Throws and bats lefthanded.
Attended University of Arizona, Tucson, Ariz.

Led International League in stolen bases with 52 in 1985.
Led Eastern League in stolen bases with 95 in 1983.
Tied for American Association lead in stolen bases with 67 in 1986.

Year	Club	League	Pos.	G.	AB.	R.	H.	2B.	3B.	HR.	RBI.	B.A.	PO.	A.	E.	F.A.
1981—Waterloo		Midw.	OF	49	153	25	33	4	0	0	13	.216	51	6	2	.966
1982—Waterloo		Midw.	OF	27	101	28	27	4	1	0	6	.267	49	3	1	.981
1982—Chattanooga		South.	OF	110	426	71	123	10	9	2	33	.289	256	9	14	.950
1983—Buffalo		East.	OF	131	451	95	136	13	4	8	38	.302	223	10	9	.963
1984—Maine†		Int.	OF	108	406	64	110	16	2	4	50	.271	234	9	3	.988
1985—Maine‡		Int.	OF	118	427	67	107	7	4	2	32	.251	266	4	11	.961
1986—Kansas City		Amer.	OF	4	2	1	0	0	0	0	0	.000	0	0	0	.000
1986—Omaha		A. A.	OF	114	428	75	111	12	11	0	23	.259	339	6	5	*.986
Major League Totals—1 Year				4	2	1	0	0	0	0	0	.000	0	0	0	.000

Selected by Philadelphia Phillies' organization in 11th round of free-agent draft, June 6, 1978.
Selected by Cleveland Indians' organization in 7th round of free-agent draft, June 8, 1981.
†On disabled list, June 1 to June 20, 1984.
‡Traded to Kansas City Royals' organization, October 3, 1985, completing deal in which Kansas City traded Pitcher Keith Creel to Cleveland Indians for a player to be named later, March 19, 1985.

TERRY DERRELL TAYLOR

Born July 28, 1964, at Crestview, Fla.
Height, 6.01. Weight, 180.
Throws and bats righthanded.

Led Southern League in wild pitches with 16 in 1986.
Tied for Southern League lead in hit batsmen with 16 in 1985.

Year	Club	League	G.	IP.	W.	L.	Pct.	H.	R.	ER.	SO.	BB.	ERA.
1982—Bellingham		Northwest	14	86⅔	6	4	.600	75	53	42	61	54	4.36
1983—Wausau		Midwest	24	130⅔	9	9	.500	131	94	79	118	79	5.44
1984—Salinas		California	17	104⅓	7	6	.538	87	48	34	73	55	2.93
1985—Chattanooga		Southern	28	165⅓	4	15	.211	171	*114	*97	107	96	5.28
1986—Chattanooga		Southern	27	177	12	8	.600	164	88	79	*164	90	4.02

Selected by Seattle Mariners' organization in 4th round of free-agent draft, June 7, 1982.

WILLIAM HOWELL TAYLOR
(Billy)

Born October 16, 1961, at Monticello, Fla.
Height, 6.08. Weight, 200.
Throws right and bats left and righthanded.
Attended Abraham Baldwin Agricultural College, Tifton, Ga.

Year	Club	League	G.	IP.	W.	L.	Pct.	H.	R.	ER.	SO.	BB.	ERA.
1980—Asheville		S. Atlantic	6	14	0	2	.000	24	24	17	12	9	10.93
1980—Sarasota Rangers		Gulf Coast	14	35	0	0	.000	36	14	9	22	16	2.31
1981—Asheville		S. Atlantic	14	64	1	7	.175	76	43	33	44	35	4.64

Year Club	League	G.	IP.	W.	L.	Pct.	H.	R.	ER.	SO.	BB.	ERA.
1981—Sarasota Rangers†	Gulf Coast	13	35	1	3	.250	28	13	5	13	16	1.29
1982—Wausau-Burlington	Midwest	37	112	7	9	.438	100	64	52	95	63	4.18
1983—Salem	Carolina	7	41⅔	1	1	.500	30	34	29	42	42	6.26
1983—Tulsa	Texas	21	76	5	8	.385	86	65	58	75	51	6.87
1984—Tulsa	Texas	42	80	5	3	.625	65	38	34	80	51	3.83
1985—Tulsa	Texas	20	103⅔	3	9	.250	84	55	40	87	48	3.47
1986—Oklahoma City	Am. Assoc.	16	101⅔	5	5	.500	94	56	52	68	57	4.60

Selected by Texas Rangers' organization in 2nd round of free-agent draft, January 8, 1980.
†Loaned to Wausau (Seattle Mariners' organization), April 5, 1982; returned, June 23, 1982.

WILFREDO ARISTIDES TEJADA (ANDUJAR)

(Wil)

Born November 12, 1962, at Santo Domingo, D.R.
Height, 6.00, Weight, 175.
Throws and bats righthanded.

Tied for South Atlantic League lead in being hit by pitch with 12 in 1983.

Year Club	League	Pos.	G.	AB.	R.	H.	2B.	3B.	HR.	RBI.	B.A.	PO.	A.	E.	F.A.
1982—Helena	Pion.	C	26	57	4	11	3	0	0	4	.193	152	17	8	.955
1983—Spartanburg	S. Atl.	C	90	273	33	68	14	2	2	29	.249	483	63	13	.977
1984—Peninsula	Carol.	C	45	127	13	34	6	1	2	16	.268	262	27	11	.963
1984—Reading	East.	C	28	72	7	24	7	0	0	15	.333	107	22	9	.935
1985—Reading†	East.	C-1B	69	210	24	57	7	0	3	25	.271	295	30	4	.988
1986—Jacksonville	South.	C	107	382	49	103	11	5	13	46	.270	576	65	*19	.971
1986—Montreal	Nat.	C	10	25	1	6	1	0	0	2	.240	40	8	0	1.000
Major League Totals—1 Year			10	25	1	6	1	0	0	2	.240	40	8	0	1.000

Signed as free agent by Philadelphia Phillies' organization, June 10, 1982.
†Drafted by Indianapolis (Montreal Expos' organization), December 11, 1985.

KENTON CHARLES TEKULVE

Name pronounced Tuh-KULL-vee.

(Kent)

Born March 5, 1947, at Cincinnati, O.
Height, 6.04. Weight, 175.
Throws and bats righthanded.
Received bachelor of science degree in physical education
from Marietta College, Marietta, O.

Tied major league records for most intentional bases on balls allowed, season (23), 1982; most consecutive games won by relief pitcher, three consecutive games (3), May 6, 7, 9, 1980.
Established National League record for most games pitched, lifetime (853).
Major league saves: 1975 (5), 1976 (9), 1977 (7), 1978 (31), 1979 (31), 1980 (21), 1981 (3), 1982 (20), 1983 (18), 1984 (13), 1985 (14), 1986 (4). Total—176.
Led National League in intentional bases on balls issued with 20 in 1979, 23 in 1982 and tied for lead with 16 in 1980.
Led National League in games finished in relief with 65 in 1978, 67 in 1979 and tied for lead with 56 in 1983.

Year Club	League	G.	IP.	W.	L.	Pct.	H.	R.	ER.	SO.	BB.	ERA.
1969—Geneva	NYP	9	53	6	2	.750	40	15	10	60	22	1.70
1970—Salem	Carolina	41	79	4	6	.400	68	29	17	51	51	1.94
1971—Salem	Carolina	47	75	11	5	.688	77	36	29	62	31	3.48
1971—Waterbury	Eastern	2	3	0	0	.000	3	0	0	0	2	0.00
1972—Sherbrooke	Eastern	31	72	7	6	.538	61	24	21	54	22	2.63
1972—Charleston	Int'national	9	22	2	1	.667	22	10	10	9	10	4.09
1973—Sherbrooke	Eastern	*57	94	●12	4	*.750	70	24	16	89	35	1.53
1974—Charleston	Int'national	35	60	6	3	.667	50	20	15	38	21	2.25
1974—Pittsburgh	National	8	9	1	1	.500	12	6	6	6	5	6.00
1975—Charleston	Int'national	24	71	5	4	.556	47	23	14	46	19	1.77
1975—Pittsburgh	National	34	56	1	2	.333	43	20	14	28	23	2.25
1976—Pittsburgh	National	64	103	5	3	.625	91	30	28	68	25	2.45
1977—Pittsburgh	National	72	103	10	1	.909	89	41	35	59	33	3.06
1978—Pittsburgh	National	*91	135	8	7	.533	115	44	35	77	55	2.33
1979—Pittsburgh†	National	*94	134	10	8	.556	109	46	41	75	49	2.75
1980—Pittsburgh	National	78	93	8	12	.400	96	39	35	47	40	3.39
1981—Pittsburgh	National	45	65	5	5	.500	61	19	18	34	17	2.49
1982—Pittsburgh	National	*85	128⅔	12	8	.600	113	47	41	66	46	2.87
1983—Pittsburgh‡	National	76	99	7	5	.583	78	27	18	52	36	1.64
1984—Pittsburgh	National	72	88	3	9	.250	86	30	26	36	33	2.66
1985—Pittsburgh §-Philadelphia	National	61	75⅔	4	10	.286	74	35	30	40	30	3.57
1986—Philadelphia	National	73	110	11	5	.688	99	35	31	57	25	2.54
Major League Totals—13 Years		853	1199⅓	85	76	.528	1066	419	358	645	417	2.69

Signed as free agent by Pittsburgh Pirates' organization, July 16, 1969.
†Appeared in one game as an outfielder with one putout.
‡Granted free agency, November 7, 1983; re-signed by Pirates, December 22, 1983.
§Traded to Philadelphia Phillies for Pitchers Al Holland and Frankie Griffin, April 20, 1985.

CHAMPIONSHIP SERIES RECORD

Year Club	League	G.	IP.	W.	L.	Pct.	H.	R.	ER.	SO.	BB.	ERA.
1975—Pittsburgh	National	2	1⅓	0	0	.000	3	1	1	2	1	6.75
1979—Pittsburgh	National	2	2⅔	0	0	.000	2	1	1	2	2	3.38
Championship Series Totals—2 Years		4	4	0	0	.000	5	2	2	4	3	4.50

WORLD SERIES RECORD

Established World Series record for most saves, seven-game Series (3), 1979.

Year Club	League	G.	IP.	W.	L.	Pct.	H.	R.	ER.	SO.	BB.	ERA.
1979—Pittsburgh	National	5	9⅓	0	1	.000	4	3	3	10	3	2.89

ALL-STAR GAME RECORD

Member of National League All-Star Team in 1980; did not play.

GARRY LEWIS TEMPLETON

Born March 24, 1956, at Lockey, Tex.
Height, 5.11. Weight, 190.
Throws right and bats left and righthanded.
Brother of Ken Templeton, outfielder in Oakland A's organization, 1972 through 1974; son of
Spiavia Templeton, former infielder in the Negro Leagues.

Tied major league records by collecting 100 or more hits righthanded and lefthanded, season, 1979; most consecutive seasons leading league, three-base hits (3), 1977 through 1979; most intentional bases on balls, game (4), July 5, 1985 (12 innings).

Tied modern major league record for most three-base hits by switch hitter, season, (19), 1979; most intentional bases on balls, game (4), July 5, 1985 (12 innings).

Major League stolen bases: 1976 (11), 1977 (28), 1978 (34), 1979 (26), 1980 (31), 1981 (8), 1982 (27), 1983 (16), 1984 (8), 1985 (16), 1986 (10). Total—215.

Led National League in intentional bases on balls received with 23 in 1984 and tied for lead with 24 in 1985.
Led National League shortstops in total chances with 848 in 1978 and 851 in 1979.
Led National League shortstops in double plays with 108 in 1978.
Tied for National League lead in caught stealing with 24 in 1977.
Tied for National League lead in double plays by shortstops with 102 in 1979.
Named shortstop on THE SPORTING NEWS National League All-Star Team, 1977, 1979 and 1980.
Named shortstop on THE SPORTING NEWS National League Silver Slugger team, 1980 and 1984.
Received reported $40,000 bonus to sign with St. Louis Cardinals, 1974.

Year—Club	League	Pos.	G.	AB.	R.	H.	2B.	3B.	HR.	RBI.	B.A.	PO.	A.	E.	F.A.
1974—Sarasota Cards	Gulf C.	SS	18	71	11	19	1	0	3	10	.268	15	41	3	.949
1974—St. Petersburg	Fla. St.	SS	23	95	3	20	1	0	0	2	.211	42	64	7	.938
1975—St. Petersburg	Fla. St.	SS	82	349	50	92	7	8	1	32	.264	130	253	29	.930
1975—Arkansas	Texas	SS	42	177	36	71	9	4	2	20	.401	60	131	18	.914
1976—Tulsa	A. A.	★S-3-O	106	443	65	142	24	★15	6	38	.321	★178	319	34	.936
1976—St. Louis	Nat.	SS	53	213	32	62	8	2	1	17	.291	111	172	24	.922
1977—St. Louis	Nat.	SS	153	621	94	200	19	★18	8	79	.322	285	453	32	.958
1978—St. Louis	Nat.	SS	155	647	82	181	31	★13	2	47	.280	★285	523	★40	.953
1979—St. Louis	Nat.	SS	154	672	105	★211	32	★19	9	62	.314	★292	525	★34	.960
1980—St. Louis†	Nat.	SS	118	504	83	161	19	9	4	43	.319	223	451	★29	.959
1981—St. Louis‡§	Nat.	SS	80	333	47	96	16	8	1	33	.288	160	272	18	.960
1982—San Diego	Nat.	SS	141	563	76	139	25	8	6	64	.247	220	422	26	.961
1983—San Diego x	Nat.	SS	126	460	39	121	20	2	3	40	.263	219	355	24	.960
1984—San Diego	Nat.	SS	148	493	40	127	19	3	2	35	.258	225	407	26	.960
1985—San Diego	Nat.	SS	148	546	63	154	30	2	6	55	.282	245	460	23	.968
1986—San Diego	Nat.	SS	147	510	42	126	21	2	2	44	.247	207	358	20	.966
Major League Totals—11 Years			1423	5562	703	1578	240	86	44	519	.284	2472	4398	296	.959

Selected by St. Louis Cardinals' organization in 1st round (13th player selected) of free-agent draft, June 5, 1974.
†On disabled list, July 24 to August 14 and August 24 to September 8, 1980.
‡On suspended list, August 26, 1981; then transferred to disabled list, August 28 to September 14, 1981.
§Traded to San Diego Padres for Shortstop Ozzie Smith, February 11, 1982.
xOn disabled list, April 28 to May 17, 1983.

CHAMPIONSHIP SERIES RECORD

Year Club	League	Pos.	G.	AB.	R.	H.	2B.	3B.	HR.	RBI.	B.A.	PO.	A.	E.	F.A.
1984—San Diego	Nat.	SS	5	15	2	5	1	0	0	2	.333	19	11	1	.968

WORLD SERIES RECORD

Year Club	League	Pos.	G.	AB.	R.	H.	2B.	3B.	HR.	RBI.	B.A.	PO.	A.	E.	F.A.
1984—San Diego	Nat.	SS	5	19	1	6	1	0	0	0	.316	8	11	0	1.000

ALL-STAR GAME RECORD

Year League	Pos.	AB.	R.	H.	2B.	3B.	HR.	RBI.	B.A.	PO.	A.	E.	F.A.
1977—National	SS	1	1	1	0	0	0	0	1.000	1	2	1	.750
1985—National	PH	1	0	1	0	0	0	0	1.000	0	0	0	.000
All-Star Game Totals—2 Years		2	1	2	1	0	0	0	1.000	1	2	1	.750

Named to National League All-Star Team for 1979 game; declined.

—DID YOU KNOW—

That the first 10 games for both Los Angeles and San Diego in 1986 were decided by one run?

CHARLES WALTER TERRELL

Name pronounced TEAR-el.

(Walt)

Born May 11, 1958, at Jeffersonville, Ind.
Height, 6.02. Weight, 205.
Throws right and bats lefthanded.
Received degree from Morehead State University, Morehead, Ky. in 1980.

Tied for International League lead in intentional bases on balls issued with 9 in 1982.
Named International League Pitcher of the Year, 1983.

Year	Club	League	G.	IP.	W.	L.	Pct.	H.	R.	ER.	SO.	BB.	ERA.
1980—Sarasota Rangers	Gulf Coast	7	38	3	2	.600	20	11	6	23	12	1.42
1980—Asheville	S. Atlantic	3	8	1	1	.500	11	9	6	5	8	6.75
1981—Tulsa†	Texas	27	174	●15	7	.682	158	74	60	123	63	3.10
1982—Tidewater‡	Int'national	21	138⅔	7	8	.467	130	69	61	74	72	3.96
1982—New York	National	3	21	0	3	.000	22	12	8	8	14	3.43
1983—Tidewater	Int'national	12	86⅔	10	1	★.909	76	34	30	58	44	3.12
1983—New York	National	21	133⅔	8	8	.500	123	57	53	59	55	3.57
1984—New York§	National	33	215	11	12	.478	232	99	84	114	80	3.52
1985—Detroit	American	34	229	15	10	.600	221	107	98	130	95	3.85
1986—Detroit	American	34	217⅓	15	12	.556	199	116	110	93	98	4.56
National League Totals—3 Years		57	369⅔	19	23	.452	377	168	145	181	149	3.53
American League Totals—2 Years		68	446⅓	30	22	.577	420	223	208	223	193	4.19
Major League Totals—5 Years		125	816	49	45	.521	797	391	353	404	342	3.89

Selected by New York Mets' organization in 15th round of free-agent draft, June 5, 1979.
Selected by Texas Rangers' organization in 33rd round of free-agent draft, June 3, 1980.
†Traded with Pitcher Ron Darling to New York Mets' organization for Outfielder Lee Mazzilli, April 1, 1982.
‡On disabled list, July 19 to August 2, 1982.
§Traded to Detroit Tigers for Third Baseman Howard Johnson, December 7, 1984.

SCOTT RAY TERRY

Born November 11, 1959, at Hobbs, N.M.
Height, 5.10. Weight, 185.
Throws and bats righthanded.
Attended Southwestern University, Georgetown, Tex.

Tied for American Association lead in games started by pitchers with 28 and wild pitches with 14 in 1985.
Led Eastern League in shutouts with 6 in 1984.

Year	Club	League	G.	IP.	W.	L.	Pct.	H.	R.	ER.	SO.	BB.	ERA.
1983—Tampa	Florida St.	30	59⅓	3	3	.500	60	34	28	52	30	4.25
1984—Vermont	Eastern	20	144	14	3	★.824	110	31	24	100	43	★1.50
1984—Wichita†	Am. Assoc.	2	9⅓	0	0	.000	13	6	6	6	7	5.79
1985—Denver	Am. Assoc.	28	178⅔	11	12	.478	★203	★105	★88	101	76	4.43
1986—Denver	Am. Assoc.	10	19⅓	1	2	.333	22	13	5	13	8	2.33
1986—Cincinnati	National	28	55⅔	1	2	.333	66	40	38	32	32	6.14
Major League Totals—1 Year		28	55⅔	1	2	.333	66	40	38	32	32	6.14

Selected by Cincinnati Reds' organization in 12th round of free-agent draft, June 3, 1980.
†On disabled list, August 8 to September 18, 1984.

RECORD AS OUTFIELDER

Year	Club	League	Pos.	G.	AB.	R.	H.	2B.	3B.	HR.	RBI.	B.A.	PO.	A.	E.	F.A.
1980—Billings	Pion.	OF	67	251	39	65	9	3	4	45	.259	104	●10	5	.958
1981—Cedar Rapids	Midw.	OF	113	351	32	68	9	0	5	31	.194	147	.5	5	.968
1982—Cedar Rapids	Midw.	OF	108	335	50	85	16	3	12	54	.254	156	10	8	.954
1983—Tampa	Fla. St.	OF-P	66	105	14	25	6	2	0	12	.238	60	16	3	.962

MICKEY LEE TETTLETON

Born September 16, 1960, at Oklahoma City, Okla.
Height, 6.02. Weight, 200.
Throws right and bats left and righthanded.
Attended Oklahoma State University, Stillwater, Okla.

Major League stolen bases: 1985 (2), 1986 (7). Total—9.
Tied for Eastern League lead in intentional bases on balls received with 8 in 1984.

Year	Club	League	Pos.	G.	AB.	R.	H.	2B.	3B.	HR.	RBI.	B.A.	PO.	A.	E.	F.A.
1981—Modesto	Calif.	C-OF-1B	48	138	28	34	3	0	5	19	.246	235	31	14	.950
1982—Modesto†	Calif.	C-OF	88	253	44	63	18	0	8	37	.249	424	36	8	.983
1983—Modesto	Calif.	C-OF	124	378	55	92	18	2	7	62	.243	582	46	11	.983
1984—Albany	East.	★C-O-1-3-S	86	281	32	65	18	0	5	47	.231	368	42	3	★.993
1984—Oakland	Amer.	C	33	76	10	20	2	1	1	5	.263	112	10	1	.992
1985—Oakland‡	Amer.	C	78	211	23	53	12	0	3	15	.251	344	24	4	.989
1985—Modesto	Calif.	C	4	14	1	3	0	0	0	2	.214	20	1	0	1.000
1986—Oakland§	Amer.	C	90	211	26	43	9	0	10	35	.204	463	32	8	.984
1986—Modesto	Calif.	C	15	42	14	10	1	0	2	8	.238	40	3	2	.956
Major League Totals—3 Years		201	498	59	116	23	1	14	55	.233	919	66	13	.987

Selected by Oakland A's organization in 5th round of free-agent draft, June 8, 1981.
†On disabled list, July 16 to August 13, 1982.

‡On disabled list, August 4 to August 25, 1985; included rehabilitation disability assignment to Modesto, August 21 to August 25, 1985.

§On disabled list, May 9 to June 16, 1986; included rehabilitation disability assignment to Modesto, May 23 to June 13, 1986.

TIMOTHY SHAWN TEUFEL

Name pronounced TUFF-el.

(Tim)

Born July 7, 1958, at Greenwich, Conn.
Height, 6.00. Weight, 175.
Throws and bats righthanded.
Attended St. Petersburg Junior College, St. Petersburg, Fla.,
and Clemson University, Clemson, S. C.

Established American League record for fewest double plays by second baseman, season, 150 or more games (81), 1984.

Major League stolen bases: 1984 (1), 1985 (4), 1986 (1). Total—6.

Led International League second basemen in putouts with 304, assists with 394, total chances with 711 and double plays with 109 in 1983.

Named International League Player of the Year, 1983.

Named second baseman on THE SPORTING NEWS College Baseball All-America Team, 1980.

Year Club	League	Pos.	G.	AB.	R.	H.	2B.	3B.	HR.	RBI.	B.A.	PO.	A.	E.	F.A.
1980—Orlando	South.	2B	86	287	38	76	15	3	11	47	.265	196	246	17	.963
1981—Orlando	South.	2B	128	416	69	103	21	5	17	60	.248	312	376	20	.972
1982—Orlando	South.	2B	100	340	52	96	12	4	9	56	.282	231	185	15	.965
1982—Toledo	Int.	2B	45	149	25	42	10	4	6	20	.282	99	139	3	.988
1983—Toledo	Int.	2B-SS	136	471	103	152	27	6	27	100	.323	306	401	14	.981
1983—Minnesota	Amer.	2B-SS	21	78	11	24	7	1	3	6	.308	47	58	1	.991
1984—Minnesota	Amer.	2B	157	568	76	149	30	3	14	61	.262	315	★485	13	.984
1985—Minnesota†	Amer.	2B	138	434	58	113	24	3	10	50	.260	237	352	12	.980
1986—New York	Nat.	2B-1B-3B	93	279	35	69	20	1	4	31	.247	143	174	9	.972
American League Totals—3 Years			316	1080	145	286	61	7	27	117	.265	599	895	26	.983
National League Totals—1 Year			93	279	35	69	20	1	4	31	.247	143	174	9	.972
Major League Totals—4 Years			409	1359	180	355	81	8	31	148	.261	742	1069	35	.981

Selected by Milwaukee Brewers' organization in 16th round of free-agent draft, June 6, 1978.

Selected by Chicago White Sox' organization in secondary phase of free-agent draft, June 5, 1979.

Selected by Minnesota Twins' organization in 2nd round of free-agent draft, June 3, 1980.

†Traded with Outfielder Pat Crosby to New York Mets for Outfielder Billy Beane and Pitchers Bill Latham and Joe Klink, January 16, 1986.

CHAMPIONSHIP SERIES RECORD

Year Club	League	Pos.	G.	AB.	R.	H.	2B.	3B.	HR.	RBI.	B.A.	PO.	A.	E.	F.A.
1986—New York	Nat.	2B	2	6	0	1	0	0	0	0	.167	2	8	0	1.000

WORLD SERIES RECORD

Year Club	League	Pos.	G.	AB.	R.	H.	2B.	3B.	HR.	RBI.	B.A.	PO.	A.	E.	F.A.
1986—New York	Nat.	2B	3	9	1	4	1	0	1	1	.444	3	3	1	.857

ROBERT ALAN TEWKSBURY

(Bob)

Born November 30, 1960, at Concord, N. H.
Height, 6.04. Weight, 200.
Throws and bats righthanded.
Attended Rutgers University, New Brunswick, N.J., and St. Leo College, St. Leo, Fla.

Led Florida State League in shutouts with 5 and tied for lead in complete games with 13 in 1982.

Year Club	League	G.	IP.	W.	L.	Pct.	H.	R.	ER.	SO.	BB.	ERA.
1981—Oneonta	NYP	14	85	7	3	.700	85	43	34	62	37	3.40
1982—Fort Lauderdale	Florida St.	24	182⅓	★15	4	.789	146	46	38	92	47	★1.88
1983—Fort Lauderdale†	Florida St.	2	16	2	0	1.000	6	1	0	5	1	0.00
1983—Nashville	Southern	7	51	5	1	.833	49	20	16	15	10	2.82
1984—Nashville‡	Southern	26	172	11	9	.550	185	69	54	78	42	2.83
1985—Albany§	Eastern	17	106⅔	6	5	.545	101	48	42	63	19	3.54
1985—Columbus	Int'national	6	44	3	0	1.000	27	5	5	21	5	1.02
1986—New York	American	23	130⅓	9	5	.643	144	58	48	49	31	3.31
1986—Columbus	Int'national	2	10	1	0	1.000	6	3	3	4	2	2.70
Major League Totals—1 Year		23	130⅓	9	5	.643	144	58	48	49	31	3.31

Selected by New York Yankees' organization in 19th round of free-agent draft, June 8, 1981.

†On disabled list, April 8 to June 7, 1983.

‡On disabled list, April 9 to April 27, 1984.

§On disabled list, June 10 to June 25, 1985.

ROBERT THOMAS THIGPEN

(Bobby)

Born July 17, 1963, at Tallahassee, Fla.
Height, 6.03. Weight, 195.
Throws and bats righthanded.
Attended Seminole Community College, Sanford, Fla., and
Mississippi State University, Mississippi State, Miss.

Led Southern League in hit batsmen with 11 in 1986.

Year Club	League	G.	IP.	W.	L.	Pct.	H.	R.	ER.	SO.	BB.	ERA.
1985—Niagara Falls	NYP	28	52⅓	2	3	.400	30	12	10	74	19	1.72
1985—Appleton	Midwest	1	2⅔	1	0	1.000	1	0	0	4	1	0.00
1986—Birmingham	Southern	25	159⅔	8	11	.421	182	97	83	90	54	4.68
1986—Chicago	American	20	35⅔	2	0	1.000	26	7	7	20	12	1.77
Major League Totals—1 Year		20	35⅔	2	0	1.000	26	7	7	20	12	1.77

Selected by Milwaukee Brewers' organization in 7th round of free-agent draft, January 11, 1983.
Selected by Chicago White Sox' organization in 4th round of free-agent draft, June 3, 1985.

ANDRES PERES THOMAS

Born November 10, 1963, at Boca Chica, Dominican Republic.
Height, 6.01. Weight, 170.
Throws and bats righthanded.

Major League stolen bases: 1986 (4).

Year Club	League	Pos.	G.	AB.	R.	H.	2B.	3B.	HR.	RBI.	B.A.	PO.	A.	E.	F.A.
1982—Bradenton Brav...	Gulf C.	SS	44	143	18	37	2	1	1	14	.259	61	136	20	.908
1983—Anderson	S. Atl.	SS	61	251	33	79	8	4	1	20	.315	61	197	24	.915
1983—Durham	Carol.	SS	70	290	17	72	14	0	2	41	.248	107	222	32	.911
1984—Durham†	Carol.	SS	114	460	64	121	18	4	7	44	.263	156	361	34	.938
1985—Greenville	South.	SS-OF	114	458	53	114	18	4	9	59	.249	155	339	31	.941
1985—Richmond	Int.	SS	11	28	3	5	0	0	1	6	.179	15	30	3	.938
1985—Atlanta	Nat.	SS	15	18	6	5	0	0	0	2	.278	6	17	2	.920
1986—Atlanta	Nat.	SS	102	323	26	81	17	2	6	32	.251	143	290	19	.958
Major League Totals—2 Years			117	341	32	86	17	2	6	34	.252	149	307	21	.956

Signed as free agent by Atlanta Braves' organization, December 16, 1981.
†On suspended list, August 28, 1984 through remainder of season.

JAMES GORMAN THOMAS III

(Known by middle name.)

Born December 12, 1950, at Charleston, S. C.
Height, 6.03.   Weight, 200.
Throws and bats righthanded.
Attended Baptist College, Charleston, S. C.

Tied major league records for most strikeouts, two consecutive games (8), July 27 and 28, 1975; most strikeouts, three consecutive games (10), July 27 through 29, 1975.
Tied American League records for most consecutive strikeouts (8), July 27 through 29, 1975; most strikeouts, season (175), 1979; most years with 400 or more putouts, outfielder (4).
Hit three home runs in a game, April 11, 1985.
Major League stolen bases: 1973 (5), 1974 (4), 1975 (4), 1976 (2), 1978 (3), 1979 (1), 1980 (8), 1981 (4), 1982 (3), 1983 (10), 1985 (3), 1986 (3). Total—50.
Led American League batters in strikeouts with 175 in 1979, 170 in 1980 and tied for lead with 133 in 1978.
Led Pacific Coast League in total bases with 320 in 1977.
Led Pacific Coast League batters in strikeouts with 175 in 1974.
Led Texas League batters in strikeouts with 171 in 1972.
Led Midwest League batters in strikeouts with 170 in 1971.
Tied for Texas League lead in double plays by outfielders with 4 in 1972.
Named outfielder on THE SPORTING NEWS American League All-Star Team, 1982.
Named American League Comeback Player of the Year by THE SPORTING NEWS, 1985.

Year Club	League	Pos.	G.	AB.	R.	H.	2B.	3B.	HR.	RBI.	B.A.	PO.	A.	E.	F.A.
1969—Billings	Pion.	SS-1B	41	142	23	42	10	3	4	28	.296	94	82	27	.867
1970—Clinton†	Midw.	SS-3B-2B	85	297	36	63	5	4	8	39	.212	105	186	28	.912
1971—Danville	Midw.	OF-3B	121	457	82	112	20	4	★31	83	.245	195	14	10	.954
1972—San Antonio	Texas	★OF-1B	135	465	70	112	22	2	★26	68	.241	★305	★24	6	★.982
1973—Evansville	A. A.	OF	46	146	26	31	6	0	8	18	.212	66	3	4	.945
1973—Milwaukee	Amer.	OF-3B	59	155	16	29	7	1	2	11	.187	87	1	4	.957
1974—Sacramento	P. C.	OF	138	474	117	141	15	1	51	122	.297	302	16	10	.970
1974—Milwaukee	Amer.	OF	17	46	10	12	4	0	2	11	.261	26	0	0	1.000
1975—Milwaukee	Amer.	OF	121	240	34	43	12	2	10	28	.179	215	5	9	.961
1976—Milwaukee	Amer.	OF-3B	99	227	27	45	9	2	8	36	.198	211	4	4	.982
1977—Spokane‡§	P. C.	OF	143	500	114	161	41	5	36	114	.322	325	13	7	★.980
1978—Milwaukee	Amer.	OF	137	452	70	111	24	1	32	86	.246	345	5	6	.983
1979—Milwaukee	Amer.	OF	156	557	97	136	29	0	★45	123	.244	435	4	4	.991
1980—Milwaukee	Amer.	OF	162	628	78	150	26	3	38	105	.239	455	6	7	.985
1981—Milwaukee	Amer.	OF	103	363	54	94	22	0	21	65	.259	221	8	5	.979
1982—Milwaukee	Amer.	OF	158	567	96	139	29	1	●39	112	.245	427	11	4	.991
1983—Milw. x-Clev. y	Amer.	OF	152	535	72	112	23	1	22	69	.209	439	7	7	.985
1984—Seattle z	Amer.	OF	35	108	6	17	3	0	1	13	.157	45	2	0	1.000
1985—Seattle a	Amer.	DH	135	484	76	104	16	1	32	87	.215	0	0	0	.000
1986—Sea.b-Mil.c	Amer.	1B	101	315	45	59	8	1	16	36	.187	47	3	1	.980
Major League Totals—13 Years			1435	4677	681	1051	212	13	268	782	.225	2953	56	51	.983

Selected by Seattle Pilots' organization in 1st round (21st player selected) of free-agent draft, June 5, 1969.
†On restricted list, March 4 to May 30, 1970.
‡Traded to Texas Rangers, October 25, 1977, completing deal in which Texas traded Outfielder-First Baseman Ed Kirkpatrick to Milwaukee Brewers for a player to be named later, August 20, 1977.
§Sold to Milwaukee Brewers, February 8, 1978.

xTraded with Pitchers Jamie Easterly and Ernie Camacho to Cleveland Indians for Outfielder Rick Manning and Pitcher Rick Waits, June 6, 1983.

yTraded with Second Baseman Jack Perconte to Seattle Mariners for Second Baseman Tony Bernazard, December 7, 1983.

zOn disabled list, May 16, 1984 through remainder of season.

aOn disabled list, May 22 to June 11, 1985.

bReleased, June 25, 1986; signed by Milwaukee Brewers, July 16, 1986.

cReleased, October 16, 1986.

DIVISION SERIES RECORD

Year Club	League	Pos.	G.	AB.	R.	H.	2B.	3B.	HR.	RBI.	B.A.	PO.	A.	E.	F.A.
1981—Milwaukee............	Amer.	OF	5	18	2	2	0	0	1	1	.111	12	0	0	1.000

CHAMPIONSHIP SERIES RECORD

Tied Championship Series record for hitting home run in first Series at-bat, October 5, 1982.

Year Club	League	Pos.	G.	AB.	R.	H.	2B.	3B.	HR.	RBI.	B.A.	PO.	A.	E.	F.A.
1982—Milwaukee............	Amer.	OF	5	16	1	1	0	0	1	3	.063	13	0	0	1.000

WORLD SERIES RECORD

Tied World Series record for most at-bats, inning (2), October 16, 1982 (seventh inning).

Year Club	League	Pos.	G.	AB.	R.	H.	2B.	3B.	HR.	RBI.	B.A.	PO.	A.	E.	F.A.
1982—Milwaukee............	Amer.	OF	7	26	0	3	0	0	0	3	.115	15	0	0	1.000

ALL-STAR GAME RECORD

Year League	Pos.	AB.	R.	H.	2B.	3B.	HR.	RBI.	B.A.	PO.	A.	E.	F.A.
1981—American	PH	1	0	0	0	0	0	0	.000	0	0	0	.000

ROY JUSTIN THOMAS

Born June 22, 1953, at Quantico, Va.
Height, 6.05. Weight, 215.
Throws and bats righthanded.
Attended University of Tampa, Tampa, Fla., and De Anza College, Cupertino, Calif.

Pitched seven-inning, 2-0 no-hit victory against West Haven, August 20, 1974 (second game).
Major League saves: 1978 (3), 1979 (1), 1983 (1), 1984 (1), 1985 (1). Total—7.
Led Pacific Coast League in wild pitches with 27 and tied for lead in hit batsmen with 10 in 1983.
Led American Association in wild pitches with 17 in 1976.
Led Eastern League in games started by pitchers with 27 in 1974.
Led Carolina League in shutouts with 6 in 1973.
Received reported $75,000 bonus to sign with Philadelphia Phillies, 1971.

Year—Club	League	G.	IP.	W.	L.	Pct.	H.	R.	ER.	SO.	BB.	ERA.
1971—Walla Walla	Northwest	7	12	0	3	.000	19	22	14	8	16	10.50
1972—Spartanburg....................	W. Carol.	24	152	11	7	.611	128	67	58	128	62	3.43
1973—Rocky Mount...................	Carolina	26	169	●15	8	.652	119	53	42	★193	77	★2.24
1973—Reading.........................	Eastern	2	16	2	0	1.000	11	2	2	14	7	1.13
1974—Reading.........................	Eastern	27	●191	14	11	.560	154	77	55	★168	89	2.59
1974—Toledo............................	Int'national	2	7	0	0	.000	5	3	1	5	2	1.29
1975—Toledo............................	Int'national	19	119	4	9	.308	112	63	53	95	49	4.01
1975—Reading†	Eastern	10	67	6	3	.667	50	22	19	53	29	2.55
1976—Iowa‡§	Am. Assoc.	27	168	6	11	.353	167	89	70	103	72	3.75
1977—Charleston	Int'national	44	168	11	6	.647	151	63	59	71	65	3.16
1977—Houston.........................	National	4	6	0	0	.000	5	2	2	4	3	3.00
1978—Charleston x	Int'national	28	66	9	4	.692	63	28	23	40	30	3.14
1978—St. Louis........................	National	16	28	1	1	.500	21	14	12	16	16	3.86
1979—Springfield....................	Am. Assoc.	17	74	5	6	.455	79	55	48	85	31	5.84
1979—St. Louis........................	National	26	77	3	4	.429	66	29	25	44	24	2.92
1980—St. Louis........................	National	24	55	2	3	.400	59	32	29	22	25	4.75
1980—Springfield y..................	Am. Assoc.	19	37	5	1	.833	34	18	14	36	18	3.41
1981—Tacoma z........................	P. Coast	36	165	12	8	.600	137	61	56	111	49	3.05
1982—Salt Lake City	P. Coast	33	156⅔	8	9	.471	195	112	98	96	84	5.63
1983—Seattle...........................	American	43	88⅔	3	1	.750	95	44	34	77	32	3.45
1984—Seattle a........................	American	21	49⅔	3	2	.600	52	33	29	42	37	5.26
1984—Salt Lake City b	P. Coast	7	18⅓	0	0	.000	15	10	8	13	12	3.93
1985—Calgary..........................	P. Coast	15	29⅔	2	2	.500	29	15	15	40	13	4.55
1985—Seattle...........................	American	40	93⅔	7	0	1.000	66	37	35	70	48	3.36
1986—Seattle cd......................	American					(Did not play)						
National League Totals—4 Years......................		70	166	6	8	.429	151	77	68	86	68	3.69
American League Totals—3 Years		104	232	13	3	.813	213	114	98	189	117	3.80
Major League Totals—7 Years		174	398	19	11	.633	364	191	166	275	185	3.75

Selected by Philadelphia Phillies' organization in 1st round (sixth player selected) of free-agent draft, June 8, 1971.

†Traded with Pitcher Dick Ruthven and Infielder-Outfielder Alan Bannister by Philadelphia Phillies to Chicago White Sox for Pitcher Jim Kaat and Shortstop Mike Buskey, December 10, 1975.

‡Selected by Seattle Mariners in American League expansion draft, November 5, 1976.

§Traded to Houston Astros for Infielder Larry Milbourne, March 30, 1977.

xSold on waivers to St. Louis Cardinals, June 23, 1978.

yDrafted by Oakland A's, December 8, 1980.

zTraded to Seattle Mariners' organization for Outfielder Rusty McNealy and Pitcher Tim Hallgren, December 9, 1981.

aOn disabled list, June 12 to July 4, 1984.

bGranted free agency, October 15, 1984; signed by Calgary (Seattle Mariners' organization), February 28, 1985.
cOn disabled list, April 3, 1986 through entire season.
dReleased, December 19, 1986.

JASON DOLPH THOMPSON

Born July 6, 1954, at Hollywood, Calif.
Height, 6.03. Weight, 210.
Throws and bats lefthanded.
Attended California State University, Northridge, Calif.

Major League stolen bases: 1976 (2), 1979 (2), 1980 (2), 1982 (1), 1983 (1). Total—8.
Led National League first basemen in total chances with 1,425 in 1984.
Led American League first basemen in double plays with 153 in 1978.
Led American League first basemen in total chances with 1,712 in 1977.

Year Club	League	Pos.	G.	AB.	R.	H.	2B.	3B.	HR.	RBI.	B.A.	PO.	A.	E.	F.A.
1975—Montgomery	South.	1B	75	222	42	72	12	1	10	38	.324	633	47	10	.986
1976—Evansville	A. A.	1B	4	16	3	5	0	0	3	6	.313	29	7	0	1.000
1976—Detroit	Amer.	1B	123	412	45	90	12	1	17	54	.218	1157	88	8	.994
1977—Detroit	Amer.	1B	158	585	87	158	24	5	31	105	.270	*1599	97	16	.991
1978—Detroit	Amer.	1B	153	589	79	169	25	3	26	96	.287	1503	92	11	.993
1979—Detroit	Amer.	1B	145	492	58	121	16	1	20	79	.246	1176	91	8	.994
1980—Det.†-Calif.‡	Amer.	1B	138	438	69	126	19	0	21	90	.288	679	51	0	1.000
1981—Pittsburgh	Nat.	1B	86	223	36	54	13	0	15	42	.242	590	46	7	.989
1982—Pittsburgh	Nat.	1B	156	550	87	156	32	0	31	101	.284	1395	105	10	.993
1983—Pittsburgh	Nat.	1B	152	517	70	134	20	1	18	76	.259	1266	89	9	.993
1984—Pittsburgh	Nat.	1B	154	543	61	138	22	0	17	74	.254	*1337	74	*14	.990
1985—Pittsburgh§	Nat.	1B	123	402	42	97	17	1	12	61	.241	995	82	9	.992
1986—Montreal x	Nat.	1B	30	51	6	10	4	0	0	4	.196	121	4	5	.962
American League Totals—5 Years			717	2516	338	664	96	10	115	424	.264	6114	419	43	.993
National League Totals—6 Years			701	2286	302	589	108	2	93	358	.258	5704	400	54	.991
Major League Totals—11 Years			1418	4802	640	1253	204	12	208	782	.261	11818	819	97	.992

Selected by Los Angeles Dodgers' organization in 15th round of free-agent draft, June 6, 1972.
Selected by Detroit Tigers' organization in 4th round of free-agent draft, June 4, 1975.
†Traded to California Angels for Outfielder Al Cowens, May 27, 1980.
‡Traded to Pittsburgh Pirates for Catcher Ed Ott and Pitcher Mickey Mahler, April 1, 1981.
§Traded to Montreal Expos for two players to be named later, April 4, 1986; Pittsburgh Pirates' organization acquired Outfielder Ben Abner and Infielder Ronnie Giddens to complete deal, April 7, 1986.
xReleased, June 30, 1986.

ALL-STAR GAME RECORD

Year League	Pos.	AB.	R.	H.	2B.	3B.	HR.	RBI.	B.A.	PO.	A.	E.	F.A.
1978—American	PH	1	0	0	0	0	0	0	.000	0	0	0	.000
1982—National	PH	1	0	0	0	0	0	0	.000	0	0	0	.000
All-Star Game Totals—2 Years		2	0	0	0	0	0	0	.000	0	0	0	.000

Member of American League All-Star Team in 1977; did not play.

MILTON BERNARD THOMPSON
(Milt)

Born January 5, 1959, at Washington, D.C.
Height, 5.11. Weight, 160.
Throws right and bats lefthanded.
Attended Howard University, Washington, D.C.

Major League stolen bases: 1984 (14), 1985 (9), 1986 (19). Total—42.
Led International League outfielders in total chances with 341 in 1984.
Led Southern League in stolen bases with 68 and caught stealing with 19 in 1982.
Led Southern League outfielders in total chances with 336 in 1982.

Year Club	League	Pos.	G.	AB.	R.	H.	2B.	3B.	HR.	RBI.	B.A.	PO.	A.	E.	F.A.
1979—Greenwood	W. Car.	OF	53	145	31	27	4	1	2	16	.186	85	8	3	.969
1979—Kingsport	Appol.	OF	26	94	22	31	8	4	1	11	.330	58	4	1	.984
1980—Durham	Carol.	OF	68	255	49	74	12	3	2	36	.290	159	8	5	.971
1980—Savannah	South.	OF	71	278	35	83	7	3	1	15	.299	133	11	6	.960
1981—Savannah	South.	OF	140	493	92	135	18	2	4	31	.274	226	17	8	.968
1982—Savannah	South.	OF	●144	526	83	132	20	7	6	45	.251	*312	10	14	.958
1982—Richmond	Int.	OF	3	6	2	1	0	0	0	0	.167	4	0	0	1.000
1983—Richmond	Int.	OF	12	32	12	8	1	0	0	3	.250	30	0	1	.968
1983—Savannah	South.	OF-1B	115	386	84	117	21	4	5	36	.303	295	15	7	.978
1984—Richmond	Int.	OF	134	503	●91	145	11	3	4	40	.288	*317	13	11	.968
1984—Atlanta	Nat.	OF	25	99	16	30	1	0	2	4	.303	37	6	2	.956
1985—Richmond	Int.	OF	82	312	52	98	10	1	2	22	.314	209	3	4	.981
1985—Atlanta†	Nat.	OF	73	182	17	55	7	2	0	6	.302	78	2	3	.964
1986—Philadelphia	Nat.	OF	96	299	38	75	7	1	6	23	.251	212	1	2	.991
1986—Portland	P. C.	OF	41	161	26	56	10	2	1	16	.348	101	1	1	.990
Major League Totals—3 Years			194	580	71	160	15	3	8	33	.276	327	9	7	.980

Selected by Atlanta Braves' organization in 2nd round of free-agent draft, January 9, 1979.
†Traded with Pitcher Steve Bedrosian to Philadelphia Phillies for Catcher Ozzie Virgil and Pitcher Pete Smith, December 10, 1985.

ROBERT RANDALL THOMPSON
(Rob)

Born May 10, 1962, at West Palm Beach, Fla.
Height, 5.11. Weight, 165.
Throws and bats righthanded.
Attended Palm Beach Junior College, Lake Worth, Fla.,
and University of Florida, Gainesville, Fla.

Major League stolen bases: 1986 (12).
Established major league record for most times caught stealing, game (4), June 27, 1986, 12 innings.
Led National League in sacrifice hits with 18 in 1986.
Named National League Rookie Player of the Year by THE SPORTING NEWS, 1986.
Led Texas League second basemen in putouts with 291, total chances with 664 and double plays with 91 in 1985.

Year Club	League	Pos.	G.	AB.	R.	H.	2B.	3B.	HR.	RBI.	B.A.	PO.	A.	E.	F.A.
1983—Fresno	Calif.	2B	64	220	33	57	8	1	4	23	.259	118	185	11	.965
1984—Fresno	Calif.	2B-SS-3B	102	325	53	81	11	0	8	43	.249	182	280	24	.951
1985—Shreveport	Texas	*2B-SS	121	449	85	117	20	7	9	40	.261	292	366	12	*.982
1986—San Francisco	Nat.	2B-SS	149	549	73	149	27	3	7	47	.271	255	451	17	.976
Major League Totals—1 Year			149	549	73	149	27	3	7	47	.271	255	451	17	.976

Selected by Oakland A's organization in 2nd round of free-agent draft, January 12, 1982.
Selected by Seattle Mariners' organization in secondary phase of free-agent draft, June 7, 1982.
Selected by San Francisco Giants' organization in secondary phase of free-agent draft, June 6, 1983.

RICHARD WILLIAM THON
(Dickie)

Born June 20, 1958, at South Bend, Ind.
Height, 5.11. Weight, 150.
Throws and bats righthanded.
Grandson of Fred Thon, minor league pitcher, 1940.

Tied National League record for fewest triples, season, for league leader in triples (10), 1982.
Major League stolen bases: 1980 (7), 1981 (6), 1982 (37), 1983 (34), 1985 (8), 1986 (6). Total—98.
Led National League in game-winning RBIs with 18 in 1983.
Named shortstop on THE SPORTING NEWS National League All-Star Team, 1983.
Named shortstop on THE SPORTING NEWS National League Silver Slugger team, 1983.

Year Club	League	Pos.	G.	AB.	R.	H.	2B.	3B.	HR.	RBI.	B.A.	PO.	A.	E.	F.A.
1976—Quad Cities	Midw.	SS	69	246	46	68	11	4	1	32	.276	96	193	32	.900
1977—Salinas	Calif.	SS	56	225	48	71	13	2	4	44	.316	95	162	13	.952
1977—Salt Lake City	P. C.	SS	77	274	47	79	9	3	8	43	.288	129	242	26	.935
1978—Salt Lake City	P. C.	2B-SS	130	439	67	113	17	3	1	47	.257	273	380	26	.962
1979—Salt Lake City	P. C.	SS-2B	38	162	25	47	3	1	2	21	.290	70	120	11	.945
1979—California	Amer.	2B-SS-3B	35	56	6	19	3	0	0	8	.339	38	46	8	.913
1980—Salt Lake City	P. C.	2B-SS	40	155	28	61	14	2	2	28	.394	81	107	12	.940
1980—California†	Amer.	S-2-3-1	80	267	32	68	12	2	0	15	.255	70	124	10	.951
1981—Houston	Nat.	2B-SS-3B	49	95	13	26	6	0	0	3	.274	53	63	6	.951
1982—Houston	Nat.	SS-3B-2B	136	496	73	137	31	*10	3	36	.276	183	412	17	.972
1983—Houston	Nat.	SS	154	619	81	177	28	9	20	79	.286	258	*533	28	.966
1984—Houston‡	Nat.	SS	5	17	3	6	0	1	0	1	.353	8	13	0	1.000
1985—Houston§x	Nat.	SS	84	251	26	63	6	1	6	29	.251	106	218	11	.967
1986—Houston y	Nat.	SS	106	278	24	69	13	1	3	21	.248	142	210	10	.972
American League Totals—2 Years			115	323	38	87	15	2	0	23	.269	108	170	18	.939
National League Totals—6 Years			534	1756	220	478	84	22	32	169	.272	750	1449	72	.968
Major League Totals—8 Years			649	2079	258	565	99	24	32	192	.272	858	1619	90	.965

Signed as free agent by California Angels' organization, November 23, 1975.
†Traded to Houston Astros for Pitcher Ken Forsch, April 1, 1981.
‡On disabled list, April 9, 1984 through remainder of season.
§On disabled list, May 19 to June 8, 1985.
xGranted free agency, November 12, 1985; re-signed by Astros, January 7, 1986.
yOn disabled list, June 6 to June 23, 1986.

DIVISION SERIES RECORD

Year Club	League	Pos.	G.	AB.	R.	H.	2B.	3B.	HR.	RBI.	B.A.	PO.	A.	E.	F.A.
1981—Houston	Nat.	SS-PH	4	11	0	2	0	0	0	0	.182	5	10	1	.938

CHAMPIONSHIP SERIES RECORD

Year Club	League	Pos.	G.	AB.	R.	H.	2B.	3B.	HR.	RBI.	B.A.	PO.	A.	E.	F.A.
1979—California	Amer.	PR-SS	1	0	1	0	0	0	0	0	.000	0	0	0	.000
1986—Houston	Nat.	SS-PH	6	12	1	3	0	0	1	1	.250	6	9	0	1.000
Championship Series Totals—2 Years			7	12	2	3	0	0	1	1	.250	6	9	0	1.000

ALL-STAR GAME RECORD

Year League	Pos.	AB.	R.	H.	2B.	3B.	HR.	RBI.	B.A.	PO.	A.	E.	F.A.
1983—National	PH-SS	3	0	1	0	0	0	0	.333	0	2	0	1.000

—DID YOU KNOW—

That the 1986 Atlanta Braves turned the franchise's first triple play since 1978?

ANDRE THORNTON

Born August 13, 1949, at Tuskegee, Ala.
Height, 6.02. Weight, 205.
Throws and bats righthanded.
Attended Cheyney State College, Cheyney, Pa.
Brother-in-law of Pat Kelly, outfielder with Minnesota, Kansas City, Chicago AL,
Baltimore and Cleveland, 1967 through 1981.

Tied major league record for most assists, first baseman, inning (3), August 22, 1975 (5th inning).
Major League stolen bases: 1974 (2), 1975 (3), 1976 (4), 1977 (3), 1978 (4), 1979 (5), 1981 (3), 1982 (6), 1983 (4), 1984 (6), 1985 (3), 1986 (4). Total—47.
Hit for the cycle, April 22, 1978.
Tied for American League lead in intentional bases on balls received with 18 in 1982.
Led Western Carolinas League first basemen in errors with 19 in 1969.
Led Northwest League first basemen in double plays with 35 in 1968.
Tied for Eastern League lead in caught stealing with 8 in 1971.
Named American League Comeback Player of the Year by THE SPORTING NEWS, 1982.
Named designated hitter on THE SPORTING NEWS American League Silver Slugger team, 1984.

Year	Club	League	Pos.	G.	AB.	R.	H.	2B.	3B.	HR.	RBI.	B.A.	PO.	A.	E.	F.A.
1967—Huron†		North.	3B-OF	19	55	3	10	1	2	1	3	.182	7	9	10	.615
1968—Eugene‡		N'west.	1B	56	185	27	46	9	2	5	31	.249	★427	★24	10	★.978
1969—Spartanburg§		W. Car.	1B-3B-OF	90	299	56	75	13	4	13	51	.251	701	45	20	.974
1970—Peninsula x		Carol.	1B	67	193	24	48	7	2	5	23	.249	499	30	5	.991
1971—Reading y		East.	1B	116	367	67	98	18	1	26	76	.267	1006	48	15	.986
1972—Eugene z		P. C.	1B-3B	46	141	22	45	8	2	6	29	.319	224	46	11	.961
1972—Richmond abc		Int.	1B-OF	49	159	30	42	5	0	14	36	.264	379	33	6	.986
1973—Richmond d		Int.	3B-1B-0F	16	49	8	10	2	0	4	8	.204	67	17	5	.944
1973—Wichita		A. A.	1B	40	135	34	39	2	0	17	45	.289	362	23	1	.997
1973—Chicago		Nat.	1B	17	35	3	7	3	0	0	2	.200	81	10	1	.989
1974—Chicago		Nat.	1B-3B	107	303	41	79	16	4	10	46	.261	760	70	7	.992
1975—Chicago e		Nat.	1B-3B	120	372	70	109	21	4	18	60	.293	984	77	13	.988
1976—Chi. f-Mont. gh		Nat.	1B-OF	96	268	28	52	11	2	11	38	.194	542	46	6	.990
1977—Cleveland		Amer.	1B	131	433	77	114	20	5	28	70	.263	1026	71	6	.995
1978—Cleveland		Amer.	1B	145	508	97	133	22	4	33	105	.262	1327	106	7	.995
1979—Cleveland		Amer.	1B	143	515	89	120	31	1	26	93	.233	1089	82	7	.994
1980—Cleveland i		Amer.					(Did not play)									
1981—Cleveland j		Amer.	1B	69	226	22	54	12	0	6	30	.239	67	5	1	.986
1982—Cleveland		Amer.	1B	161	589	90	161	26	1	32	116	.273	76	5	0	1.000
1983—Cleveland		Amer.	1B	141	508	78	143	27	1	17	77	.281	201	21	2	.991
1984—Cleveland k		Amer.	1B	155	587	91	159	26	0	33	99	.271	86	9	2	.979
1985—Cleveland l		Amer.	DH	124	461	49	109	13	0	22	88	.236	0	0	0	.000
1986—Cleveland		Amer.	DH	120	401	49	92	14	0	17	66	.229	0	0	0	.000
American League Totals—9 Years				1189	4228	642	1085	191	12	214	744	.257	3872	299	25	.994
National League Totals—4 Years				340	978	142	247	51	10	39	146	.252	2367	203	27	.990
Major League Totals—13 Years				1529	5206	784	1332	242	22	253	890	.256	6239	502	52	.992

Signed as free agent by Philadelphia Phillies' organization, August 6, 1967.
†On military list, December 29, 1967 through May 1, 1968.
‡On temporary inactive list, June 1 to July 2, 1968.
§On temporary inactive list, June 4 to June 24, 1969.
xOn temporary inactive list, June 11 to June 30, 1970.
yOn temporary inactive list, June 7 to June 26, 1971.
zTraded with Pitcher Joe Hoerner to Atlanta Braves for Pitchers Jim Nash and Gary Neibauer, June 15, 1972.
aOn temporary inactive list, June 28 to July 1, 1972.
bOn disabled list, July 5 to July 16, 1972.
cOn temporary inactive list, August 1 to August 4, 1972.
dTraded to Chicago Cubs for First Baseman Joe Pepitone, May 19, 1973.
eOn disabled list, April 1 to May 4, 1975.
fTraded to Montreal Expos for Pitcher Steve Renko and Outfielder-First Baseman Larry Biittner, May 17, 1976.
gOn disabled list, June 10 to July 1, 1976.
hTraded to Cleveland Indians for Pitcher Jackie Brown, December 10, 1976.
iOn disabled list, March 28 to June 19 and June 19 to October 13, 1980.
jOn disabled list, March 30 to April 17 and August 24 to September 8, 1981.
kGranted free agency, November 8, 1984; re-signed by Indians, December 4, 1984.
lOn disabled list, March 24 to April 25, 1985.

ALL-STAR GAME RECORD

Year	League	Pos.	AB.	R.	H.	2B.	3B.	HR.	RBI.	B.A.	PO.	A.	E.	F.A.
1982—American		PH	1	0	0	0	0	0	0	.000	0	0	0	.000
1984—American		PH	1	0	1	0	0	0	0	1.000	0	0	0	.000
All-Star Game Totals—2 Years			2	0	1	0	0	0	0	.500	0	0	0	.000

LOUIS THORNTON JR.

(Lou)

Born April 26, 1963, at Montgomery, Ala.
Height, 6.00. Weight, 175.
Throws right and bats lefthanded.

Major League stolen bases: 1985 (1).
Led Appalachian League outfielders in errors with 9 in 1982.

Year	Club	League	Pos.	G.	AB.	R.	H.	2B.	3B.	HR.	RBI.	B.A.	PO.	A.	E.	F.A.
1981—Kingsport		Appal.	1B	48	153	23	32	7	0	2	17	.209	338	43	16	.960

Year Club	League	Pos.	G.	AB.	R.	H.	2B.	3B.	HR.	RBI.	B.A.	PO.	A.	E.	F.A.
1982—Kingsport..............	Appal.	OF-1B-3B	57	210	29	44	9	2	5	29	.210	182	7	13	.940
1983—Columbia	S. Atl.	OF	119	448	80	120	24	6	11	73	.268	193	18	11	.950
1984—Lynchburg†..........	Carolina	OF-1B	131	505	78	139	25	7	6	67	.275	250	13	11	.960
1985—Toronto	Amer.	OF	56	72	18	17	1	1	1	8	.236	44	0	2	.957
1986—Syracuse	Int.	OF	64	231	34	60	4	2	2	28	.260	114	5	4	.967
Major League Totals—1 Year....................			56	72	18	17	1	1	1	8	.236	44	0	2	.957

Selected by New York Mets' organization in 19th round of free-agent draft, June 8, 1981.
†Drafted by Toronto Blue Jays, December 3, 1984.

CHAMPIONSHIP SERIES RECORD

Year Club	League	Pos.	G.	AB.	R.	H.	2B.	3B.	HR.	RBI.	B.A.	PO.	A.	E.	F.A.
1985—Toronto	Amer.	PR	2	0	1	0	0	0	0	0	.000	0	0	0	.000

GARY MONTEZ THURMAN JR.

Born November 12, 1964, at Indianapolis, Ind.
Height, 5.10. Weight, 165.
Throws and bats righthanded.

Led Florida State League in stolen bases with 70 in 1985.
Led Gulf Coast League batters in strikeouts with 58 in 1983.
Tied for South Atlantic League lead in caught stealing with 17 in 1984.
Led Gulf Coast League outfielders in total chances with 143 in 1983, South Atlantic League outfielders with 329 in 1984 and Florida State League outfielders with 396 in 1985.

Year Club	League	Pos.	G.	AB.	R.	H.	2B.	3B.	HR.	RBI.	B.A.	PO.	A.	E.	F.A.
1983—Sarasota Royals...	Gulf C.	OF	59	203	32	52	8	2	0	19	.256	*127	*13	3	.979
1984—Charleston............	S. Atl.	OF	129	478	71	109	6	8	6	51	.228	*311	5	13	.960
1985—Fort Myers...........	Fla. St.	OF	134	453	68	137	9	9	0	45	.302	*368	18	10	.975
1986—Memphis...............	South.	OF	131	525	88	164	24	12	7	62	.312	277	5	11	.962
1986—Omaha...................	A. A.	OF	3	2	1	1	0	0	0	0	.500	2	0	0	1.000

Selected by Kansas City Royals' organization in 1st round (21st player selected) of free-agent draft, June 6, 1983.

MARK ANTHONY THURMOND

Born September 12, 1956, at Houston, Tex.
Height, 6.00. Weight, 190.
Throws and bats lefthanded.
Received bachelor of science degree in finance from
Texas A&M University, College Station, Tex. in 1979.

Major League saves: 1985 (2).
Named lefthanded pitcher on THE SPORTING NEWS National League All-Star Team, 1984.
Tied for Texas League lead in games started by pitchers with 27 in 1981.

Year Club	League	G.	IP.	W.	L.	Pct.	H.	R.	ER.	SO.	BB.	ERA.
1979—Amarillo...............	Texas	17	62	3	5	.375	89	52	39	46	31	5.66
1980—Amarillo†..............	Texas	26	156	10	9	.526	164	80	67	125	61	3.87
1981—Amarillo...............	Texas	27	193	12	5	.706	202	86	70	128	56	3.26
1982—Hawaii..................	P. Coast	28	194⅓	12	10	.545	202	88	77	106	58	3.57
1983—Las Vegas............	P. Coast	19	63	6	1	.857	63	28	23	38	24	3.29
1983—San Diego	National	21	115⅓	7	3	.700	104	40	34	49	33	2.65
1984—San Diego	National	32	178⅔	14	8	.636	174	70	59	57	55	2.97
1985—San Diego	National	36	138⅓	7	11	.389	154	70	61	57	44	3.97
1986—San Diego‡	National	17	70⅔	3	7	.300	96	58	51	32	27	6.50
1986—Detroit	American	25	51⅔	4	1	.800	44	13	11	17	17	1.92
National League Totals—4 Years.......................		106	503	31	29	.517	528	238	205	195	159	3.67
American League Totals—1 Year		25	51⅔	4	1	.800	44	13	11	17	17	1.92
Major League Totals—4 Years		131	554⅔	35	30	.538	572	251	216	212	176	3.50

Selected by San Diego Padres' organization in 24th round of free-agent draft, June 6, 1978.
Selected by San Diego Padres' organization in 5th round of free-agent draft, June 5, 1979.
†On disabled list, July 5 to July 16, 1980.
‡Traded to Detroit Tigers for Pitcher Dave LaPoint, July 9, 1986.

CHAMPIONSHIP SERIES RECORD

Year Club	League	G.	IP.	W.	L.	Pct.	H.	R.	ER.	SO.	BB.	ERA.
1984—San Diego	National	1	⅔	0	1	.000	7	4	4	1	2	9.82

WORLD SERIES RECORD

Year Club	League	G.	IP.	W.	L.	Pct.	H.	R.	ER.	SO.	BB.	ERA.
1984—San Diego	National	2	5⅓	0	1	.000	12	6	6	2	3	10.13

JAY LINDSEY TIBBS

Born January 4, 1962, at Birmingham, Ala.
Height, 6.03. Weight, 185.
Throws and bats righthanded.

Year Club	League	G.	IP.	W.	L.	Pct.	H.	R.	ER.	SO.	BB.	ERA.
1980—Kingsport...................................	Ap'lachian	12	76	3	7	.300	88	54	37	45	32	4.38
1981—Lynchburg..................................	Carolina	15	72	2	7	.222	89	65	55	41	34	6.88
1981—Shelby	W. Carol.	13	89	4	8	.333	87	56	38	57	33	3.84
1982—Lynchburg†................................	Carolina	7	38⅓	2	4	.333	42	28	24	31	23	5.63

Year Club	League	G.	IP.	W.	L.	Pct.	H.	R.	ER.	SO.	BB.	ERA.
1982—Jackson	Texas	1	3⅓	0	0	.000	2	1	0	3	1	0.00
1983—Lynchburg‡	Carolina	28	203⅔	14	8	.636	172	94	66	170	96	2.92
1984—Jackson	Texas	6	37⅓	1	2	.333	28	15	13	31	19	3.13
1984—Tidewater§	Int'national	8	41⅓	3	5	.375	44	27	24	27	23	5.23
1984—Wichita	Am. Assoc.	4	27⅔	3	0	1.000	22	13	11	14	8	3.58
1984—Cincinnati	National	14	100⅔	6	2	.750	87	34	32	40	33	2.86
1985—Cincinnati	National	35	218	10	16	.385	216	111	95	98	83	3.92
1985—Denver x	Am. Assoc.	4	31⅔	1	2	.333	20	10	8	15	12	2.27
1986—Montreal	National	35	190⅓	7	9	.438	181	96	84	117	70	3.97
Major League Totals—3 Years		84	509	23	27	.460	484	241	211	255	186	3.73

Selected by New York Mets' organization in 2nd round of free-agent draft, June 3, 1980.

†On disabled list, July 21 to August 29, 1982.

‡Drafted by Philadelphia Phillies, December 5, 1983; returned, March 29, 1984.

§Traded with Third Baseman Eddie Williams and Pitcher Matt Bullinger to Cincinnati Reds' organization for Pitcher Bruce Berenyi, June 15, 1984.

xTraded with Pitchers Andy McGaffigan and John Stuper and Catcher Dann Bilardello to Montreal Expos for Pitcher Bill Gullickson and Catcher Sal Butera, December 19, 1985.

KERRY JEROME TILLMAN
(Rusty)

Born August 29, 1960, at Jacksonville, Fla.
Height, 6.00. Weight, 175.
Throws and bats righthanded.
Attended Florida Junior College, Temple Terrace, Fla.

Major League stolen bases: 1986 (2).

Year Club	League	Pos.	G.	AB.	R.	H.	2B.	3B.	HR.	RBI.	B.A.	PO.	A.	E.	F.A.
1979—Little Falls	NYP	OF	6	22	4	7	0	1	0	4	.318	4	1	0	1.000
1979—Grays Harbor	N'west	OF	60	217	33	64	10	1	3	30	.295	140	7	5	.967
1980—Lynchburg	Carol.	OF	135	526	94	166	27	11	8	79	.316	173	10	5	★.973
1981—Jackson	Texas	OF-1B	122	464	66	129	21	4	6	59	.278	126	8	4	.971
1982—Tidewater	Int.	OF	108	404	60	130	10	6	5	54	.322	156	10	3	.982
1982—New York	Nat.	OF	12	13	4	2	1	0	0	0	.154	2	0	0	1.000
1983—Tidewater	Int.	OF	126	483	67	123	20	7	8	63	.255	220	13	7	.971
1984—Tidewater†	Int.	OF-3B	44	151	17	33	5	1	3	13	.219	56	8	2	.970
1984—Denver‡	A. A.	OF	75	255	43	78	6	3	9	43	.306	114	8	5	.961
1985—Las Vegas	P. C.	O-1-3-P	115	412	66	139	27	7	12	75	.337	193	7	6	.971
1986—L.V.§-Tac.	P. C.	OF	74	261	42	82	19	2	3	42	.314	128	6	1	.993
1986—Oakland x	Amer.	OF	22	39	6	10	1	0	1	6	.256	20	0	1	.952
National League Totals—1 Year			12	13	4	2	1	0	0	0	.154	2	0	0	1.000
American League Totals—1 Year			22	39	6	10	1	0	1	6	.256	20	0	1	.952
Major League Totals—2 Years			34	52	10	12	2	0	1	6	.231	22	0	1	.957

Selected by New York Mets' organization in 10th round of free-agent draft, January 9, 1979.

†Loaned to Denver (Chicago White Sox' organization), June 14, 1984; returned, September 16, 1984.

‡Traded to San Diego Padres' organization for Outfielder-First Baseman Rick Lancellotti, March 31, 1985.

§Traded to Oakland A's organization for Pitcher Bob Stoddard and Outfielder Kevin Russ, April 18, 1986.

xOn disabled list, August 29 to September 13, 1986.

PITCHING RECORD

Year Club	League	G.	IP.	W.	L.	Pct.	H.	R.	ER.	SO.	BB.	ERA.
1985—Las Vegas	P. Coast	1	1	0	0	.000	5	6	3	1	1	27.00

FREDDIE LEE TOLIVER
(Fred)

Born February 3, 1961, at Natchez, Miss.
Height, 6.01. Weight, 170.
Throws and bats righthanded.

Major League saves: 1985 (1).

Year Club	League	G.	IP.	W.	L.	Pct.	H.	R.	ER.	SO.	BB.	ERA.
1979—Oneonta	NYP	13	77	★10	2	.833	46	28	18	71	66	2.10
1980—Fort Lauderdale	Florida St.	3	8	0	2	.000	14	15	13	4	10	14.63
1980—Greensboro†	S. Atlantic	20	126	6	8	.429	98	60	40	96	89	2.86
1981—Greensboro‡§	S. Atlantic	17	80	5	3	.625	67	38	31	62	56	3.49
1982—Cedar Rapids	Midwest	23	115	6	7	.462	114	77	54	117	66	4.23
1982—Indianapolis	Am. Assoc.	4	20⅔	2	2	.500	20	10	9	19	13	3.92
1983—Indianapolis	Am. Assoc.	26	166⅔	8	10	.444	151	93	84	112	★110	4.54
1984—Wichita	Am. Assoc.	32	164	11	6	.647	142	90	88	113	★116	4.83
1984—Cincinnati	National	3	10	0	0	.000	7	2	1	4	7	0.90
1985—Denver xy	Am. Assoc.	19	122⅓	11	3	.786	113	50	44	84	56	3.24
1985—Philadelphia	National	11	25	0	4	.000	27	15	13	23	17	4.68
1986—Portland	P. Coast	6	26⅔	1	3	.250	31	23	22	15	14	7.43
1986—Philadelphia z	National	5	25⅔	0	2	.000	28	14	10	20	11	3.51
Major League Totals—3 Years		19	60⅔	0	6	.000	62	31	24	47	35	3.56

Selected by New York Yankees' organization in 3rd round of free-agent draft, June 5, 1979.

†On disabled list, May 23 to June 6, 1980.

‡On disabled list, April 9 to May 27, 1981.

§Traded to Cincinnati Reds' organization, December 10, 1981, completing deal in which Cincinnati traded Outfielder Ken Griffey to New York Yankees for Pitcher Brian Ryder and a player to be named later, November 4, 1981.

xOn disabled list, July 5 to August 10, 1985.

yTraded to Philadelphia Phillies, August 27, 1985, completing deal in which Philadelphia traded Catcher Bo Diaz and Pitcher Greg Simpson to Cincinnati Reds for Shortstop Tom Foley, Catcher Alan Knicely, a player to be named later and cash, August 8, 1985.

zOn disabled list, May 30 to June 25 and July 8, 1986 through remainder of season.

JIMMY WAYNE TOLLESON

(Known by middle name.)
Born November 22, 1955, at Spartanburg, S. C.
Height, 5.09. Weight, 160.
Throws right and bats left and righthanded.
Attended Western Carolina University, Cullowhee, N. C.
Brother of Mike Tolleson, outfielder in Cleveland Indians' organization, 1984.

Major League stolen bases: 1981 (2), 1982 (1), 1983 (33), 1984 (22), 1985 (21), 1986 (17). Total—96.

Year	Club	League	Pos.	G.	AB.	R.	H.	2B.	3B.	HR.	RBI.	B.A.	PO.	A.	E.	F.A.
1978—Asheville	W. Car.	3B-SS	70	212	35	57	4	1	0	21	.269	85	175	20	.929
1979—Tulsa	Texas	SS	130	418	43	98	9	7	1	36	.234	179	413	*41	.935
1980—Tulsa	Texas	SS	131	452	69	124	19	7	1	30	.274	161	395	31	.947
1981—Wichita	A. A.	3-S-2-O	107	375	58	98	9	4	3	38	.261	96	259	15	.959
1981—Texas	Amer.	3B-SS	14	24	6	4	0	0	0	1	.167	5	8	0	1.000
1982—Texas	Amer.	SS-3B-2B	38	70	6	8	1	0	0	2	.114	47	70	5	.959
1982—Denver	A. A.	SS	71	266	48	64	9	3	4	27	.241	97	195	6	.980
1983—Texas	Amer.	2B-SS	134	470	64	122	13	2	3	20	.260	268	372	17	.974
1984—Texas	Amer.	2-S-3-O	118	338	35	72	9	2	0	9	.213	195	287	10	.980
1985—Texas†	Amer.	SS-2B-3B	123	323	45	101	9	5	1	18	.313	149	255	14	.967
1986—Chi.‡-N.Y.	Amer.	S-3-2-O	141	475	61	126	16	5	3	43	.265	147	327	14	.971
Major League Totals—6 Years			568	1700	217	433	48	14	7	93	.255	811	1319	60	.973

Selected by Pittsburgh Pirates' organization in 12th round of free-agent draft, June 7, 1977.

Selected by Texas Rangers' organization in 8th round of free-agent draft, June 6, 1978.

†Traded with Pitcher Dave Schmidt to Chicago White Sox for Pitcher Ed Correa, Infielder Scott Fletcher and a player to be named later, November 25, 1985; Texas Rangers acquired Infielder Jose Mota to complete deal, December 12, 1985.

‡Traded with Outfielder-Designated Hitter Ron Kittle and Catcher Joel Skinner to New York Yankees for Catcher Ron Hassey, Shortstop Carlos Martinez and a player to be named later, July 30, 1986; New York traded Catcher Bill Lindsey to Chicago White Sox' organization to complete deal, December 24, 1986.

TIMOTHY LEE TOLMAN

(Tim)

Born April 20, 1956, at Santa Monica, Calif.
Height, 6.00. Weight, 190.
Throws and bats righthanded.
Attended University of Southern California, Los Angeles, Calif.

Major League stolen bases: 1986 (1).
Led Gulf Coast League in being hit by pitch with 5 in 1978.
Led Southern League first basemen in assists with 90 in 1980.
Led Florida State League first basemen in errors with 17 in 1979.

Year	Club	League	Pos.	G.	AB.	R.	H.	2B.	3B.	HR.	RBI.	B.A.	PO.	A.	E.	F.A.
1978—Sarasota Astros	Gulf C.	1B	39	122	25	42	5	6	0	23	*.344	292	21	4	.987
1978—Daytona Beach	Fla. St.	OF-1B	7	25	2	7	2	0	0	5	.280	24	2	0	1.000
1979—Daytona Beach	Fla. St.	1B-3B-OF	131	422	62	122	13	3	1	53	.289	688	93	26	.968
1980—Columbus	South.	1B-OF	139	481	67	142	37	4	7	73	.295	980	93	15	.986
1981—Tucson	P. C.	OF-1B	137	479	85	154	28	8	14	99	.322	735	49	10	.987
1981—Houston	Nat.	OF	4	8	0	1	0	0	0	0	.125	2	0	0	1.000
1982—Tucson	P. C.	OF-1B-3B	125	473	93	143	31	6	15	82	.302	525	46	15	.974
1982—Houston	Nat.	OF-1B	15	26	4	5	2	0	1	3	.192	17	1	0	1.000
1983—Houston	Nat.	1B-OF	43	56	4	11	4	0	2	10	.196	55	2	0	1.000
1983—Tucson	P. C.	1B-OF	7	24	4	9	2	0	1	6	.375	31	3	0	1.000
1984—Tucson	P. C.	OF-1B-3B	102	363	63	106	27	7	9	54	.292	299	25	13	.961
1984—Houston	Nat.	OF-1B	14	17	2	3	1	0	0	0	.176	6	0	0	1.000
1985—Houston	Nat.	OF	31	43	4	6	1	0	2	8	.140	12	0	0	1.000
1985—Tucson†	P. C.	OF-1B	40	149	30	45	10	1	4	27	.302	133	5	4	.972
1986—Nashville	A. A.	OF-1B	139	484	68	144	23	4	11	71	.298	371	23	6	.985
1986—Detroit	Amer.	OF-1B	16	34	4	6	1	0	0	2	.176	23	0	0	1.000
National League Totals—5 Years			107	150	14	26	8	0	5	21	.173	92	3	0	1.000
American League Totals—1 Year			16	34	4	6	1	0	0	2	.176	23	0	0	1.000
Major League Totals—6 Years			123	184	18	32	9	0	5	23	.174	115	3	0	1.000

Selected by Houston Astros' organization in 12th round of free-agent draft, June 6, 1978.

†Released, November 13, 1985; signed by Nashville (Detroit Tigers' organization), February 10, 1986.

DAVID ALLEN TOMLIN

(Dave)

Born June 22, 1949, at Maysville, Ky.
Height, 6.02. Weight, 185.
Throws and bats lefthanded.

— 498 —

Led Appalachian League pitchers in games started with 13 and tied for lead in complete games with 6 in 1967.
Major League saves: 1973 (1), 1974 (2), 1975 (1), 1977 (3), 1978 (4), 1979 (1). Total—12.

Year	Club	League	G.	IP.	W.	L.	Pct.	H.	R.	ER.	SO.	BB.	ERA.
1967—Wytheville	Ap'lachian	14	85	●7	6	.538	★93	55	41	47	43	4.34
1968—Tampa	Florida St.	37	56	6	3	.667	47	19	15	38	16	2.41
1969—Tampa	Florida St.	23	44	5	1	.833	34	18	14	25	22	2.86
1970—Asheville	Southern	25	139	6	10	.375	135	62	48	73	58	3.11
1971—Indianapolis	Am. Assoc.	41	61	7	4	.636	46	19	15	50	24	2.23
1972—Indianapolis	Am. Assoc.	36	90	5	6	.455	83	30	28	86	36	2.79
1972—Cincinnati	National	3	4	0	0	.000	7	4	4	2	1	9.00
1973—Indianapolis	Am. Assoc.	25	31	1	3	.250	29	15	12	26	11	3.52
1973—Cincinnati†	National	16	28	1	2	.333	24	15	15	20	15	4.82
1974—Hawaii	P. Coast	25	48	5	1	.833	33	10	9	48	20	1.69
1974—San Diego	National	47	58	2	0	1.000	59	29	28	29	30	4.34
1975—San Diego	National	67	83	4	2	.667	87	38	30	48	31	3.25
1976—San Diego	National	49	73	0	1	.000	62	24	23	43	20	2.84
1977—San Diego‡§	National	76	102	4	4	.500	98	38	34	55	32	3.00
1978—Cincinnati	National	57	62	9	1	.900	88	54	40	32	30	5.81
1979—Cincinnati	National	53	58	2	2	.500	59	29	17	30	18	2.64
1980—Cincinnati x	National	27	26	3	0	1.000	38	17	16	6	11	5.54
1981—Syracuse y	Int'national	38	57	2	3	.400	67	25	23	36	19	3.63
1982—Indianapolis z	Am. Assoc.	★64	91⅔	9	2	.818	96	39	36	67	30	3.53
1982—Montreal	National	1	2	0	0	.000	1	1	1	2	1	4.50
1983—Wichita a	Am. Assoc.	41	52⅓	4	1	.800	44	21	21	44	18	3.61
1983—Pittsburgh b	National	5	4	0	0	.000	6	4	3	5	1	6.75
1984—Hawaii	P. Coast	22	50⅔	3	2	.600	45	17	15	43	21	2.66
1985—Hawaii	P. Coast	33	82	8	2	.800	62	22	19	65	35	2.09
1985—Pittsburgh c	National	1	1	0	0	.000	1	0	0	0	1	0.00
1986—Indianapolis	Am. Assoc.	38	72⅔	7	5	.583	56	24	22	70	38	2.72
1986—Montreal de	National	7	10⅓	0	0	.000	13	8	6	6	7	5.23
Major League Totals—13 Years		409	511⅓	25	12	.676	543	261	217	278	198	3.82

Selected by Cincinnati Reds' organization in 29th round of free-agent draft, June 6, 1967.
†Traded with Outfielder Bobby Tolan to San Diego Padres for Pitcher Clay Kirby, November 9, 1973.
‡Traded with $125,000 to Texas Rangers for Pitcher Gaylord Perry, February 15, 1978.
§Sold to Cincinnati Reds, March 28, 1978.
xReleased, September 2, 1980; signed by Syracuse (Toronto Blue Jays' organization), February 26, 1981.
yReleased, April 8, 1982; signed by Indianapolis (Cincinnati Reds' organization), April 22, 1982.
zSold to Montreal Expos, September 8, 1982.
aSold to Pittsburgh Pirates, August 2, 1983.
bGranted free agency, November 7, 1983; re-signed by Pirates' organization, January 12, 1984.
cGranted free agency, October 15, 1985; signed by Indianapolis (Montreal Expos' organization), November 12, 1985.
dOn disabled list, August 22 to September 12, 1986.
eReleased, October 21, 1986.

CHAMPIONSHIP SERIES RECORD

Year	Club	League	G.	IP.	W.	L.	Pct.	H.	R.	ER.	SO.	BB.	ERA.
1973—Cincinnati	National	1	1⅔	0	0	.000	5	3	3	1	1	16.20
1979—Cincinnati	National	3	3	0	0	.000	3	1	0	3	2	0.00
Championship Series Totals—2 Years		4	4⅔	0	0	.000	8	4	3	4	3	5.79

JAMES JOSEPH TRABER
(Jim)

Born December 26, 1961, at Columbus, O.
Height, 6.00. Weight, 194.
Throws and bats lefthanded.
Attended Oklahoma State University, Stillwater, Okla.

Led Appalachian League in game-winning RBIs with 10 in 1982.
Led Carolina League first basemen in putouts with 1,006, double plays with 96 and total chances with 1,070 in 1983.
Led Appalachian League first basemen in double plays with 44 and total chances with 581 in 1982.

Year	Club	League	Pos.	G.	AB.	R.	H.	2B.	3B.	HR.	RBI.	B.A.	PO.	A.	E.	F.A.
1982—Bluefield	Appal.	1B	61	235	41	76	18	3	9	●63	.323	★540	★34	7	.988
1982—Hagerstown	Carol.	OF-1B	7	26	1	9	2	0	0	2	.346	12	0	0	1.000
1983—Hagerstown	Carol.	★1B-OF	128	449	73	123	22	1	14	79	.274	1012	54	10	★.991
1984—Hagerstown†	Carol.	1B	48	165	33	59	15	0	2	29	.358	361	30	7	.982
1984—Charlotte	South.	1B	75	296	50	104	17	2	16	56	.351	663	44	7	.990
1984—Baltimore	Amer.	DH-PH	10	21	3	5	0	0	0	2	.238	0	0	0	.000
1985—Rochester‡	Int.	OF-1B	80	279	32	74	13	2	7	37	.265	220	22	4	.984
1986—Rochester	Int.	1B-OF	87	323	46	90	19	2	12	55	.279	592	56	3	.995
1986—Baltimore	Amer.	1B-OF	65	212	28	54	7	0	13	44	.255	243	23	5	.982
Major League Totals—2 Years			75	233	31	59	7	0	13	46	.253	243	23	5	.982

Selected by Baltimore Orioles' organization in 21st round of free-agent draft, June 7, 1982.
†On suspended list, June 7 to June 17, 1984.
‡On disabled list, May 21 to July 8, 1985.

—DID YOU KNOW—

That when Chicago's Joe Cowley held California hitless September 19, it marked the ninth time that the Angels' Reggie Jackson had played in a major league no-hitter?

ALAN STUART TRAMMELL

Name pronounced TRAM-mull.

Born February 21, 1958, at Garden Grove, Calif.
Height, 6.00. Weight, 170.
Throws and bats righthanded.

Major League stolen bases: 1978 (3), 1979 (17), 1980 (12), 1981 (10), 1982 (19), 1983 (30), 1984 (19), 1985 (14), 1986 (25). Total—149.
Led American League in sacrifice hits with 16 in 1981 and 15 in 1983.
Named American League Comeback Player of the Year by THE SPORTING NEWS, 1983.
Named shortstop on THE SPORTING NEWS American League All-Star fielding team, 1980, 1981, 1983 and 1984.
Named Southern League Most Valuable Player, 1977.

Year	Club	League	Pos.	G.	AB.	R.	H.	2B.	3B.	HR.	RBI.	B.A.	PO.	A.	E.	F.A.
1976—Bristol	Appal.	SS	41	140	27	38	2	2	0	7	.271	59	131	12	.941
1976—Montgomery	South.	SS	21	56	4	10	0	0	0	2	.179	40	64	2	.981
1977—Montgomery	South.	SS	134	454	78	132	9	*19	3	50	.291	188	397	27	.956
1977—Detroit	Amer.	SS	19	43	6	8	0	0	0	0	.186	15	34	2	.961
1978—Detroit	Amer.	SS	139	448	49	120	14	6	2	34	.268	239	421	14	.979
1979—Detroit	Amer.	SS	142	460	68	127	11	4	6	50	.276	245	388	26	.961
1980—Detroit	Amer.	SS	146	560	107	168	21	5	9	65	.300	225	412	13	.980
1981—Detroit	Amer.	SS	105	392	52	101	15	3	2	31	.258	181	347	9	.983
1982—Detroit	Amer.	SS	157	489	66	126	34	3	9	57	.258	259	459	16	.978
1983—Detroit†	Amer.	SS	142	505	83	161	31	2	14	66	.319	236	367	13	.979
1984—Detroit†	Amer.	SS	139	555	85	174	34	5	14	69	.314	180	314	10	.980
1985—Detroit	Amer.	SS	149	605	79	156	21	7	13	57	.258	225	400	15	.977
1986—Detroit	Amer.	SS	151	574	107	159	33	7	21	75	.277	238	445	22	.969
Major League Totals—10 Years			1289	4631	702	1300	214	42	90	504	.281	2043	3587	140	.976

Selected by Detroit Tigers' organization in 2nd round of free-agent draft, June 8, 1976.
†On disabled list, July 9 to July 31, 1984.

CHAMPIONSHIP SERIES RECORD

Year	Club	League	Pos.	G.	AB.	R.	H.	2B.	3B.	HR.	RBI.	B.A.	PO.	A.	E.	F.A.
1984—Detroit	Amer.	SS	3	11	2	4	0	1	1	3	.364	1	8	0	1.000

WORLD SERIES RECORD

Tied World Series records for batting in all club's runs, game, most (4), October 13, 1984; most hits, five-game Series (9), 1984.

Year	Club	League	Pos.	G.	AB.	R.	H.	2B.	3B.	HR.	RBI.	B.A.	PO.	A.	E.	F.A.
1984—Detroit	Amer.	SS	5	20	5	9	1	0	2	6	.450	8	9	1	.944

ALL-STAR GAME RECORD

Year	League	Pos.	AB.	R.	H.	2B.	3B.	HR.	RBI.	B.A.	PO.	A.	E.	F.A.
1980—American		SS	0	0	0	0	0	0	0	.000	0	0	0	.000
1985—American		SS	1	0	0	0	0	0	0	.000	0	0	0	.000
All-Star Game Totals—2 Years			1	0	0	0	0	0	0	.000	0	0	0	.000

Named to American League All-Star Team for 1984 game; replaced due to injury by Alfredo Griffin.

HUGH JEFFREY TREADWAY
(Jeff)

Born January 22, 1963, at Columbus, Ga.
Height, 6.00. Weight, 175.
Throws right and bats lefthanded.
Attended Middle Georgia College, Cochran, Ga.,
and University of Georgia, Athens, Ga.

Year	Club	League	Pos.	G.	AB.	R.	H.	2B.	3B.	HR.	RBI.	B.A.	PO.	A.	E.	F.A.
1984—Tampa	Fla. St.	3B-2B	119	372	44	115	16	0	0	44	.309	128	184	25	.926
1985—Vermont	East.	2B	129	431	63	130	17	1	2	49	.302	271	332	15	.976
1986—Vermont	East.	2B	33	122	18	41	8	1	1	16	.336	68	102	5	.971
1986—Denver	A. A.	2B-3B	72	204	20	67	11	4	3	23	.328	75	153	6	.974

Selected by Montreal Expos' organization in 18th round of free-agent draft, January 13, 1981.
Signed as free agent by Cincinnati Reds' organization, January 29, 1984.

ALEJANDRO TREVINO (CASTRO)
(Alex)

Born August 26, 1957, at Monterrey, Nuevo Leon, Mex.
Height, 5.10. Weight, 165.
Throws and bats righthanded.
Attended University of Nuevo Leon, Monterrey, Mexico.
Brother of Bobby Trevino, outfielder with California Angels, 1968; outfielder in Mexican League,
1970 through 1979; manager, Tabasco, 1977, Tampico, 1979, and Toluca, 1980.

Major League stolen bases: 1979 (2), 1981 (3), 1982 (3), 1984 (5). Total—13.
Led Midwest League catchers in putouts with 847 and assists with 102 in 1977.
Led Carolina League in passed balls with 18 in 1976.

Year	Club	League	Pos.	G.	AB.	R.	H.	2B.	3B.	HR.	RBI.	B.A.	PO.	A.	E.	F.A.
1973—Victoria†	Mx. Cen.	C-OF	12	26	3	6	1	0	0	2	.231	26	5	1	.969
1974—Marion	Appal.	C-SS	12	16	0	1	0	0	0	1	.063	15	0	0	1.000

Year	Club	League	Pos.	G.	AB.	R.	H.	2B.	3B.	HR.	RBI.	B.A.	PO.	A.	E.	F.A.
1975—Marion	Appal.	C-2B-OF	22	60	10	12	1	0	0	3	.200	96	8	6	.963
1976—Lynchburg	Carol.	C-3-2-S	94	284	17	57	11	2	0	31	.201	400	130	18	.967
1977—Wausau	Midw.	C-2-1-3	128	422	57	100	10	0	2	36	.237	865	110	15	.985
1978—Tidewater	Int.	C-3B	87	262	44	77	13	2	5	37	.294	303	68	11	.971
1978—New York	Nat.	C-3B	6	12	3	3	0	0	0	0	.250	12	4	0	1.000
1979—New York	Nat.	C-3B-2B	79	207	24	56	11	1	0	20	.271	229	71	9	.971
1980—New York‡	Nat.	C-3B-2B	106	355	26	91	11	2	0	37	.256	450	76	16	.970
1981—New York‡	Nat.	C-2-O-3	56	149	17	39	2	0	0	10	.262	215	25	9	.964
1982—Cincinnati	Nat.	★C-3B	120	355	24	89	10	3	1	33	.251	725	61	★17	.979
1983—Cincinnati	Nat.	C-3B-2B	74	167	14	36	8	1	1	13	.216	359	32	5	.987
1984—Cinc.§-Atl.	Nat.	C	85	272	36	66	16	0	3	28	.243	403	61	5	.989
1985—Atl. x-S.F. y	Nat.	C-3B	57	157	17	34	10	1	6	19	.217	299	19	7	.978
1986—Los Angeles	Nat.	C-1B	89	202	31	53	13	0	4	26	.262	304	46	11	.970
Major League Totals—9 Years			672	1876	192	467	81	8	15	186	.249	2996	395	79	.977

Signed as free agent by Victoria, May 16, 1973.

†Sold to New York Mets' organization, May 22, 1974.

‡Traded with Pitchers Jim Kern and Greg Harris to Cincinnati Reds for Outfielder George Foster, February 10, 1982.

§Traded to Atlanta Braves for player to be named later, April 24, 1984; deal settled with reported $50,000 in July, 1984.

xTraded to San Francisco Giants for Catcher-Outfielder John Rabb, April 17, 1985.

yTraded to Los Angeles Dodgers for Outfielder Candy Maldonado, December 11, 1985.

JESUS MANUEL TRILLO (MARCANO)

Name pronounced TREE-yo.

(Manny)

Born December 25, 1950, at Caritito, Monagas, Venezuela.

Height, 6.01. Weight, 164.

Throws and bats righthanded.

Attended Colegio Libertador Bolivar, Maturin, Monagas, Venz.

Established major league records for most consecutive errorless games by second baseman, season (89), 1982; most consecutive errorless chances accepted by second baseman, season (479), 1982.

Major League stolen bases: 1975 (1), 1976 (17), 1977 (3), 1979 (4), 1980 (8), 1981 (10), 1982 (8), 1983 (1), 1985 (2). Total—54.

Led National League second basemen in double plays with 99 in 1978.

Led National League second basemen in total chances with 822 in 1977 and 878 in 1978.

Led Pacific Coast League second basemen in double plays with 113 in 1973.

Named second baseman on THE SPORTING NEWS National League All-Star Team, 1980 through 1982.

Named second baseman on THE SPORTING NEWS National League All-Star fielding team, 1979, 1981 and 1982.

Named second baseman on THE SPORTING NEWS National League Silver Slugger team, 1980 and 1981.

Year	Club	League	Pos.	G.	AB.	R.	H.	2B.	3B.	HR.	RBI.	B.A.	PO.	A.	E.	F.A.
1968—Huron†	North.	SS-3B-C	35	92	8	24	2	1	0	4	.261	35	48	5	.943
1969—Spartanburg‡	W. Car.	3-C-S-2	83	275	41	77	18	0	1	26	.280	188	98	12	.960
1970—Birmingham	South.	3B-2B-SS	84	241	26	63	10	1	2	19	.261	101	130	14	.943
1971—Birmingham§	South.	3B-SS	107	371	37	104	18	1	5	44	.280	110	212	31	.912
1972—Iowa	A. A.	3B-2B-SS	133	509	67	153	27	6	9	53	.301	176	304	28	.945
1973—Tucson	P. C.	★2B-OF	135	519	76	162	25	7	8	78	.312	★304	★373	19	★.973
1973—Oakland	Amer.	2B	17	12	0	3	2	0	0	3	.250	15	17	2	.941
1974—Tucson	P. C.	2B	85	320	31	81	19	1	2	39	.253	198	256	12	.974
1974—Oakland x	Amer.	2B	21	33	3	5	0	0	0	2	.152	31	43	4	.949
1975—Chicago	Nat.	★2B-SS	154	545	55	135	12	2	7	70	.248	350	★509	★29	.967
1976—Chicago	Nat.	★2B-SS	158	582	42	139	24	3	4	59	.239	350	★527	17	.981
1977—Chicago	Nat.	2B	152	504	51	141	18	5	7	57	.280	330	★467	★25	.970
1978—Chicago y	Nat.	2B	152	552	53	144	17	5	4	55	.261	354	★505	19	.978
1979—Philadelphia z	Nat.	2B	118	431	40	112	22	1	6	42	.260	270	368	10	.985
1980—Philadelphia a	Nat.	2B	141	531	68	155	25	9	7	43	.292	★360	467	11	.987
1981—Philadelphia	Nat.	2B	94	349	37	100	14	3	6	36	.287	★245	286	7	.987
1982—Philadelphia b	Nat.	2B	149	549	52	149	24	1	0	39	.271	343	441	5	★.994
1983—Cleveland cd	Amer.	2B	88	320	33	87	13	1	1	29	.272	172	269	5	.989
1983—Montreal e	Nat.	2B	31	121	16	32	8	0	2	16	.264	57	86	3	.979
1984—San Francisco f	Nat.	2B-3B	98	401	45	102	21	1	4	36	.254	218	294	6	.988
1985—San Francisco g	Nat.	2B-3B	125	451	36	101	16	2	3	25	.224	263	361	13	.980
1986—Chicago h	Nat.	3B-1B-2B	81	152	22	45	10	0	1	19	.296	114	63	5	.973
American League Totals—3 Years			126	365	36	95	15	1	1	34	.260	218	329	11	.980
National League Totals—12 Years			1453	5168	517	1355	211	32	51	497	.262	3254	4374	150	.981
Major League Totals—14 Years			1579	5533	553	1450	226	33	52	531	.262	3472	4703	161	.981

Signed as free agent by Philadelphia Phillies' organization, January 26, 1968.

†On disabled list, August 16 to September 3, 1968.

‡Drafted by Birmingham (Oakland Athletics' organization), December 1, 1969.

§On disabled list, May 1 to May 20, 1971.

xTraded with Pitchers Darold Knowles and Bob Locker to Chicago Cubs for First Baseman-Outfielder Billy Williams, October 23, 1974.

yTraded with Outfielder Greg Gross and Catcher Dave Rader to Philadelphia Phillies for Outfielder Jerry Martin, Catcher Barry Foote, Second Baseman Ted Sizemore and Pitchers Derek Botelho and Henry Mack, February 23, 1979.

zOn disabled list, May 4 to June 16, 1979.

aOn disabled list, April 20 to May 7, 1980.

bTraded with Outfielder George Vukovich, Infielder Julio Franco, Pitcher Jay Baller and Catcher Jerry Willard to Cleveland Indians for Outfielder Von Hayes, December 9, 1982.

cOn disabled list, July 24 to August 8, 1983.
dTraded to Montreal Expos for outfielder Don Carter and cash, August 17, 1983.
eGranted free agency, November 7, 1983; signed by San Francisco Giants, December 20, 1983.
fOn disabled list, May 13 to July 7, 1984.
gTraded to Chicago Cubs for Infielder Dave Owen, December 11, 1985.
hOn disabled list, June 3 to July 11, 1986.

DIVISION SERIES RECORD

Year Club	League	Pos.	G.	AB.	R.	H.	2B.	3B.	HR.	RBI.	B.A.	PO.	A.	E.	F.A.
1981—Philadelphia	Nat.	2B	5	16	1	3	0	0	0	1	.188	15	10	0	1.000

CHAMPIONSHIP SERIES RECORD

Year Club	League	Pos.	G.	AB.	R.	H.	2B.	3B.	HR.	RBI.	B.A.	PO.	A.	E.	F.A.
1974—Oakland..................	Amer.	PR	1	0	1	0	0	0	0	0	.000	0	0	0	.000
1980—Philadelphia	Nat.	2B	5	21	1	8	2	1	0	4	.381	18	25	1	.977
Championship Series Totals—2 Years.....			6	21	2	8	2	1	0	4	.381	18	25	1	.977

WORLD SERIES RECORD

Year Club	League	Pos.	G.	AB.	R.	H.	2B.	3B.	HR.	RBI.	B.A.	PO.	A.	E.	F.A.
1980—Philadelphia	Nat.	2B	6	23	4	5	2	0	0	2	.217	14	25	1	.975

ALL-STAR GAME RECORD

Year League	Pos.	AB.	R.	H.	2B.	3B.	HR.	RBI.	B.A.	PO.	A.	E.	F.A.
1977—National	2B	1	0	0	0	0	0	0	.000	0	1	0	1.000
1981—National	2B	2	0	0	0	0	0	0	.000	1	1	0	1.000
1982—National	2B	2	0	1	0	0	0	0	.500	0	1	0	1.000
1983—American	2B	3	1	1	0	0	0	0	.333	3	1	0	1.000
All-Star Game Totals—4 Years..................	8	1	2	0	0	0	0	.250	4	4	0	1.000

STEVEN RUSSELL TROUT
(Steve)

Born July 30, 1957, at Detroit, Mich.
Height, 6.04. Weight, 195.
Throws and bats lefthanded.
Son of Paul (Dizzy) Trout, pitcher with Detroit Tigers, Boston Red Sox and
Baltimore Orioles, 1939 through 1952 and 1957.

Major League saves: 1979 (4).
Led American League in hit batsmen with 9 in 1980.

Year Club	League	G.	IP.	W.	L.	Pct.	H.	R.	ER.	SO.	BB.	ERA.
1976—Sarasota White Sox.....................	Gulf Coast	9	38	1	3	.250	28	18	11	35	29	2.61
1977—Appleton	Midwest	21	111	6	8	.429	113	66	50	101	66	4.05
1977—Iowa	Am. Assoc.	5	24	0	4	.000	27	16	15	14	11	5.63
1978—Knoxville	Southern	12	71	8	3	.727	46	16	13	48	33	1.65
1978—Iowa	Am. Assoc.	9	55	3	4	.429	57	36	32	38	22	5.24
1978—Chicago	American	4	22	3	0	1.000	19	10	10	11	11	4.09
1979—Iowa	Am. Assoc.	4	27	3	1	.750	24	10	9	12	19	3.00
1979—Chicago	American	34	155	11	8	.579	165	77	67	76	59	3.89
1980—Chicago	American	32	200	9	16	.360	229	102	82	89	49	3.69
1981—Chicago	American	20	125	8	7	.533	122	53	48	54	38	3.46
1982—Chicago†	American	25	120⅓	6	9	.400	130	76	57	62	50	4.26
1983—Chicago	National	34	180	10	14	.417	217	105	93	80	59	4.65
1984—Chicago‡	National	32	190	13	7	.650	205	80	72	81	59	3.41
1985—Chicago§	National	24	140⅔	9	7	.563	142	57	53	44	63	3.39
1986—Chicago	National	37	161	5	7	.417	184	88	85	69	78	4.75
American League Totals—5 Years		115	622⅓	37	40	.481	665	318	264	292	207	3.82
National League Totals—4 Years		127	671⅔	37	35	.514	748	330	303	274	259	4.06
Major League Totals—9 Years		242	1294	74	75	.497	1413	648	567	566	466	3.94

Selected by Chicago White Sox' organization in 1st round (eighth player selected) of free-agent draft, June 8, 1976.
†Traded with Pitcher Warren Brusstar to Chicago Cubs for Pitchers Dick Tidrow and Randy Martz and Infielders Scott Fletcher and Pat Tabler, January 25, 1983.
‡Granted free agency, November 8, 1984; re-signed by Cubs, December 7, 1984.
§On disabled list, July 23 to August 23, 1985.

CHAMPIONSHIP SERIES RECORD

Year Club	League	G.	IP.	W.	L.	Pct.	H.	R.	ER.	SO.	BB.	ERA.
1984—Chicago	National	2	9	1	0	1.000	5	2	2	3	3	2.00

MICHAEL ANDREW TRUJILLO
Name pronounced Tru-HEEY-O.

(Mike)

Born January 12, 1960, at Denver, Colo.
Height, 6.01. Weight, 180.
Throws and bats righthanded.
Attended University of Northern Colorado, Greeley, Colo.

Major League saves: 1985 (1), 1986 (1). Total—2.

Led International League in games finished in relief with 36 and tied for lead in intentional bases on balls issued with 6 in 1986.

Led Midwest League pitchers in games started with 29 and tied for lead in complete games with 11 in 1983.

Year Club	League	G.	IP.	W.	L.	Pct.	H.	R.	ER.	SO.	BB.	ERA.
1982—Sarasota White Sox	Gulf Coast	1	7⅓	0	0	.000	1	2	1	6	4	1.23
1982—Niagara Falls	NYP	12	79	5	4	.556	54	33	21	100	25	2.39
1983—Appleton	Midwest	29	*198⅔	15	8	.652	146	75	53	148	63	2.40
1984—Glens Falls	Eastern	20	121⅔	13	3	.813	107	47	32	69	25	2.37
1984—Denver†	Am. Assoc.	8	30	2	5	.286	38	27	26	9	20	7.80
1985—Boston	American	27	84	4	4	.500	112	55	45	19	23	4.82
1986—Pawtucket	Int'national	42	84⅔	8	9	.471	76	29	25	45	27	2.66
1986—Boston§-Seattle	American	14	47	3	2	.600	39	17	17	23	21	3.26
Major League Totals—2 Years		41	131	7	6	.538	151	72	62	42	44	4.26

Selected by Chicago White Sox' organization in 7th round of free-agent draft, June 7, 1982.

†Traded with First Baseman Pat Adams to San Francisco Giants, September 7, 1984, completing deal in which San Francisco traded Infielder Tom O'Malley to Chicago White Sox for two players to be named later, September 1, 1984.

‡Drafted by Boston Red Sox, December 3, 1984.

§Claimed with Pitcher Mike Brown on waivers by Seattle Mariners from Boston Red Sox, August 22, 1986, as part of deal in which Seattle traded Infielder Spike Owen and Outfielder Dave Henderson to Boston for Infielder Rey Quinones, a player to be named later and cash, August 19, 1986. Seattle acquired Outfielder John Christensen to complete deal, September 25, 1986.

GREGORY ALAN TUBBS

(Greg)

Born August 31, 1962, at Smithville, Tenn.
Height, 5.09. Weight, 180.
Throws and bats righthanded.
Attended Austin Peay State University, Clarksville, Tenn.

Year Club	League	Pos.	G.	AB.	R.	H.	2B.	3B.	HR.	RBI.	B.A.	PO.	A.	E.	F.A.
1984—Bradenton Brav...	Gulf C.	OF	18	58	13	21	4	3	0	3	.362	24	2	0	1.000
1984—Anderson	S. Atl.	OF	50	174	25	53	5	2	2	11	.305	88	7	3	.969
1985—Sumter	S. Atl.	OF	61	239	53	85	11	7	6	36	.356	93	6	4	.961
1985—Durham	Carol.	OF	70	266	44	75	15	6	8	32	.282	188	3	2	.990
1986—Greenville	South.	OF	*144	536	95	144	21	7	5	56	.269	371	7	4	*.990

Selected by Atlanta Braves' organization in 22nd round of free-agent draft, June 4, 1984.

JOHN THOMAS TUDOR

Born February 2, 1954, at Schenectady, N.Y.
Height, 6.00. Weight, 185.
Throws and bats lefthanded.
Attended North Shore Community College, Beverly, Mass. and received bachelor of science degree in criminal justice from Georgia Southern College, Statesboro, Ga.

Pitched seven-inning, 2-0 no-hit victory against Reading, June 28, 1977.
Major League saves: 1981 (1).
Led National League in shutouts with 10 in 1985.
Named lefthanded pitcher on The Sporting News National League All-Star Team, 1985.

Year Club	League	G.	IP.	W.	L.	Pct.	H.	R.	ER.	SO.	BB.	ERA.
1976—Winston-Salem	Carolina	25	82	5	2	.714	77	26	25	76	28	2.74
1977—Bristol	Eastern	27	115	6	5	.545	113	57	45	78	35	3.52
1977—Pawtucket	Int'national	4	4	1	1	.500	5	1	1	1	3	2.25
1978—Pawtucket	Int'national	26	105	7	4	.636	100	46	36	83	56	3.09
1979—Pawtucket	Int'national	25	163	10	11	.476	145	73	53	103	52	2.93
1979—Boston	American	6	28	1	2	.333	39	23	20	11	9	6.43
1980—Pawtucket	Int'national	12	74	4	5	.444	67	36	30	51	33	3.65
1980—Boston	American	16	92	8	5	.615	81	35	31	45	31	3.03
1981—Boston	American	18	79	4	3	.571	74	44	40	44	28	4.56
1982—Boston	American	32	195⅔	13	10	.565	215	90	79	146	59	3.63
1983—Boston†	American	34	242	13	12	.520	236	122	110	136	81	4.09
1984—Pittsburgh‡	National	32	212	12	11	.522	200	81	77	117	56	3.27
1985—St. Louis	National	36	275	21	8	.724	209	68	59	169	49	1.93
1986—St. Louis§	National	30	219	13	7	.650	197	81	71	107	53	2.92
American League Totals—5 Years		106	636⅔	39	32	.549	645	314	280	382	208	3.96
National League Totals—3 Years		98	706	46	26	.639	606	230	207	393	158	2.64
Major League Totals—8 Years		204	1342⅔	85	58	.594	1251	544	487	775	366	3.26

Selected by New York Mets' organization in 21st round of free-agent draft, June 4, 1975.
Selected by Boston Red Sox' organization in secondary phase of free-agent draft, January 7, 1976.

†Traded to Pittsburgh Pirates for Outfielder Mike Easler, December 6, 1983.

‡Traded with Outfielder Brian Harper to St. Louis Cardinals for Outfielder-First Baseman George Hendrick and Catcher Steve Barnard, December 12, 1984.

§On disabled list, September 16, 1986 through remainder of season.

CHAMPIONSHIP SERIES RECORD

Year Club	League	G.	IP.	W.	L.	Pct.	H.	R.	ER.	SO.	BB.	ERA.
1985—St. Louis	National	2	12⅔	1	1	.500	10	5	4	8	3	2.84

WORLD SERIES RECORD

Year	Club	League	G.	IP.	W.	L.	Pct.	H.	R.	ER.	SO.	BB.	ERA.
1985—St. Louis	National	3	18	2	1	.667	15	6	6	14	7	3.00

BYRON LEE TUNNELL

Name pronounced TUNN-ul.
(Known by middle name.)
Born October 30, 1960, at Tyler, Tex.
Height, 6.00. Weight, 180.
Throws and bats righthanded.
Attended Baylor University, Waco, Tex.

Major League saves: 1984 (1).

Year	Club	League	G.	IP.	W.	L.	Pct.	H.	R.	ER.	SO.	BB.	ERA.
1981—Bradenton Pirates	Gulf Coast	1	4	0	0	.000	0	0	0	6	1	0.00
1981—Buffalo	Eastern	12	71	5	5	.500	76	38	35	45	37	4.44
1982—Portland	P. Coast	28	189⅔	12	9	.571	182	93	73	112	91	3.46
1982—Pittsburgh	National	5	18⅓	1	1	.500	17	8	8	4	5	3.93
1983—Pittsburgh	National	35	177⅔	11	6	.647	167	81	72	95	58	3.65
1984—Pittsburgh†	National	26	68⅓	1	7	.125	81	44	40	51	40	5.27
1985—Pittsburgh	National	24	132⅓	4	10	.286	126	70	59	74	57	4.01
1985—Hawaii	P. Coast	7	46⅔	4	1	.800	32	12	12	29	24	2.31
1986—Hawaii‡	P. Coast	27	142⅓	4	11	.267	180	106	95	95	81	6.01
Major League Totals—4 Years		90	396⅔	17	24	.415	391	203	179	224	160	4.06

Selected by Pittsburgh Pirates' organization in 2nd round of free-agent draft, June 8, 1981.
†On disabled list, July 2 to July 23, 1984.
‡Released, December 22, 1986.

WILLIE CLAY UPSHAW

Born April 27, 1957, at Blanco, Tex.
Height, 6.00. Weight, 185.
Throws and bats lefthanded.
Cousin of Gene Upshaw, guard with Oakland Raiders, 1967 through 1981;
and currently executive director of NFL Players Association; and Marvin Upshaw,
lineman with Cleveland Browns, Kansas City Chiefs and St. Louis Cardinals, 1968 through 1976.

Tied major league record for most errors by first baseman, inning (3), July 1, 1986 (fifth inning).
Major League stolen bases: 1978 (4), 1980 (1), 1981 (2), 1982 (8), 1983 (10), 1984 (10), 1985 (8), 1986 (23). Total—66.
Led American League first basemen in total chances with 1,556 in 1982.

Year	Club	League	Pos.	G.	AB.	R.	H.	2B.	3B.	HR.	RBI.	B.A.	PO.	A.	E.	F.A.
1975—Oneonta	NYP	OF	29	91	8	8	1	0	0	4	.088	7	1	0	1.000
1976—Fort Lauderdale	Fla. St.	OF	84	263	20	60	6	0	3	22	.228	22	0	0	1.000
1977—Fort Lauderdale	Fla. St.	1B-OF	87	335	38	92	13	7	3	29	.275	358	31	14	.965
1977—West Haven†	East.	OF-1B	41	157	20	47	5	2	4	22	.299	40	0	4	.909
1978—Toronto	Amer.	OF-1B	95	224	26	53	8	2	1	17	.237	131	4	7	.951
1979—Syracuse	Int.	OF-1B	140	526	71	131	25	8	12	68	.249	544	24	14	.976
1980—Syracuse	Int.	OF-1B	100	358	55	91	13	7	9	52	.254	355	19	7	.982
1980—Toronto	Amer.	1B-OF	34	61	10	13	3	1	1	5	.213	51	7	1	.983
1981—Toronto	Amer.	1B-OF	61	111	15	19	3	1	4	10	.171	72	6	0	1.000
1982—Toronto	Amer.	1B	160	580	77	155	25	7	21	75	.267	★1438	101	★17	.989
1983—Toronto	Amer.	1B	160	579	99	177	26	7	27	104	.306	1294	117	★21	.985
1984—Toronto	Amer.	1B	152	569	79	158	31	9	19	84	.278	1246	103	14	.990
1985—Toronto	Amer.	1B	148	501	79	138	31	5	15	65	.275	1157	104	10	.992
1986—Toronto	Amer.	1B	155	573	85	144	28	6	9	60	.251	1314	131	12	.992
Major League Totals—8 Years		965	3198	470	857	155	38	97	420	.268	6703	573	82	.989

Selected by New York Yankees' organization in 5th round of free-agent draft, June 4, 1975.
†Drafted by Toronto Blue Jays, December 5, 1977.

CHAMPIONSHIP SERIES RECORD

Year	Club	League	Pos.	G.	AB.	R.	H.	2B.	3B.	HR.	RBI.	B.A.	PO.	A.	E.	F.A.
1985—Toronto	Amer.	1B	7	26	2	6	2	0	0	1	.231	53	7	1	.984

JOSE ALTA URIBE

(Name pronounced Oo-REE-bay.)
(Formerly known as Jose Alta Gonzalez.)

Born January 21, 1959, at San Cristobal, D.R.
Height, 5.10. Weight, 156.
Throws right and bats left and righthanded.

Major League stolen bases: 1984 (1), 1985 (8), 1986 (22). Total—31.
Led American Association in sacrifice hits with 14 in 1983.
Led American Association shortstops in total chances with 720 and double plays with 96 in 1984.
Led American Association shortstops in total chances with 664 and double plays with 90 in 1983.
Led Texas League shortstops in double plays with 88 in 1982.

Year	Club	League	Pos.	G.	AB.	R.	H.	2B.	3B.	HR.	RBI.	B.A.	PO.	A.	E.	F.A.
1981—St. Petersburg†	Fla. St.	SS	128	463	54	124	15	2	0	40	.268	171	★387	32	.946
1982—Arkansas	Texas	SS	123	465	73	115	17	7	0	41	.247	185	385	36	.941
1982—Louisville	A. A.	SS	8	28	5	10	2	0	0	4	.357	15	18	1	.971

Year Club League	Pos.	G.	AB.	R.	H.	2B.	3B.	HR.	RBI.	B.A.	PO.	A.	E.	F.A.
1983—Louisville .... A. A.	SS	122	423	64	120	19	6	3	44	.284	206	425	★33	.950
1984—Louisville .... A. A.	SS	145	484	68	135	20	2	3	46	.279	★233	★455	★32	★.956
1984—St. Louis‡........... Nat.	SS-2B	8	19	4	4	0	0	0	3	.211	7	15	1	.957
1985—San Francisco ...... Nat.	SS-2B	147	476	46	113	20	4	3	26	.237	209	438	26	.961
1986—San Francisco ...... Nat.	SS	157	453	46	101	15	1	3	43	.223	249	444	16	.977
Major League Totals—3 Years.................		312	948	96	218	35	5	6	72	.230	465	897	43	.969

Signed as free agent by New York Yankees' organization, February 18, 1977.

†Released, July 5, 1977; signed by St. Louis Cardinals' organization, August 18, 1980.

‡Traded with First Basemen David Green and Gary Rajsich and Pitcher Dave LaPoint to San Francisco Giants for Outfielder-First Baseman Jack Clark, February 1, 1985.

SERGIO SANCHEZ VALDEZ

Born September 7, 1964, at Elias Pina, D.R.
Height, 6.00. Weight, 165.
Throws and bats righthanded.

Tied for Florida State League lead in shutouts with 4 in 1986.
Tied for New York-Pennsylvania League lead in games started by pitchers with 15 in 1985.

Year Club League	G.	IP.	W.	L.	Pct.	H.	R.	ER.	SO.	BB.	ERA.
1983—Calgary .... Pioneer	13	72⅔	6	3	.667	88	55	45	41	31	5.57
1984—West Palm Beach† .... Florida St.	5	11⅓	0	0	.000	15	11	11	6	8	8.74
1984—Jamestown .... NYP	13	76	2	7	.222	78	47	34	46	33	4.03
1985—Utica .... NYP	15	105⅔	6	5	.545	98	53	36	86	36	3.07
1986—West Palm Beach .... Florida St.	24	145⅔	★16	6	.727	119	48	40	108	46	2.47
1986—Montreal .... National	5	25	0	4	.000	39	20	19	20	11	6.84
Major League Totals—1 Year..............................	5	25	0	4	.000	39	20	19	20	11	6.84

Signed as free agent by Montreal Expos' organizaton, June 18, 1983.

†On disabled list, May 17 to June 3, 1984.

FERNANDO VALENZUELA (ANGUAMEA)

Name pronounced Val-en-ZWAY-luh.

Born November 1, 1960, at Navajoa, Sonora, Mexico.
Height, 5.11. Weight, 180.
Throws and bats lefthanded.

Tied modern major league record for most shutout games won or tied, rookie year (8), 1981.
Tied National League record for fewest assists by pitcher, season, for leader in assists (47), 1986.
Major League saves: 1980 (1).
Led National League in complete games with 11 in 1981 and 20 in 1986.
Led National League in shutouts with 8 in 1981.
Tied for National League lead in games started by pitchers with 25 in 1981.
Led Mexican Center League in wild pitches with 13 in 1978.
Named Major League Player of the Year by THE SPORTING NEWS, 1981.
Named National League Pitcher of the Year by THE SPORTING NEWS, 1981.
Won National League Cy Young Memorial Award, 1981.
Named National League Rookie Pitcher of the Year by THE SPORTING NEWS, 1981.
Named National League Rookie of the Year by Baseball Writers' Association of America, 1981.
Named lefthanded pitcher on THE SPORTING NEWS National League All-Star Team, 1981 and 1986.
Named pitcher on THE SPORTING NEWS National League All-Star fielding team, 1986.
Named pitcher on THE SPORTING NEWS National League Silver Slugger team, 1981 and 1983.

Year Club League	G.	IP.	W.	L.	Pct.	H.	R.	ER.	SO.	BB.	ERA.
1978—Guanajuato .... Mex. Cent.	16	93	5	6	.455	88	46	23	★91	46	2.23
1979—Yucatan† .... Mexican	26	181	10	12	.455	157	68	50	141	70	2.49
1979—Lodi .... California	3	24	1	2	.333	21	10	3	18	3	1.13
1980—San Antonio..................... Texas	27	174	13	9	.591	156	70	60	★162	70	3.10
1980—Los Angeles .... National	10	18	2	0	1.000	8	2	0	16	5	0.00
1981—Los Angeles .... National	25	★192	13	7	.650	140	55	53	★180	61	2.48
1982—Los Angeles‡ .... National	37	285	19	13	.594	247	105	91	199	83	2.87
1983—Los Angeles .... National	35	257	15	10	.600	245	★122	107	189	99	3.75
1984—Los Angeles .... National	34	261	12	17	.414	218	109	88	240	★106	3.03
1985—Los Angeles .... National	35	272⅓	17	10	.630	211	92	74	208	101	2.45
1986—Los Angeles .... National	34	269⅓	★21	11	.656	226	104	94	242	85	3.14
Major League Totals—7 Years.....................	210	1554⅔	99	68	.593	1295	589	507	1274	540	2.94

†Sold to Los Angeles Dodgers' organization, July 6, 1979.

‡Appeared in one game as an outfielder with no chances.

DIVISION SERIES RECORD

Year Club League	G.	IP.	W.	L.	Pct.	H.	R.	ER.	SO.	BB.	ERA.
1981—Los Angeles .... National	2	17	1	0	1.000	10	2	2	10	3	1.06

CHAMPIONSHIP SERIES RECORD

Established National League Championship Series records for most bases on balls (10) and most strikeouts (13), six-game Series, 1985; most bases on balls, game (8), October 14, 1985.

Year Club League	G.	IP.	W.	L.	Pct.	H.	R.	ER.	SO.	BB.	ERA.
1981—Los Angeles .... National	2	14⅔	1	1	.500	10	4	4	10	5	2.45
1983—Los Angeles .... National	1	8	1	0	1.000	7	1	1	5	4	1.13
1985—Los Angeles .... National	2	14⅓	1	0	1.000	11	3	3	13	10	1.88
Championship Series Totals—3 Years.................	5	37	3	1	.750	28	8	8	28	19	1.95

Year Club	League	G.	IP.	W.	L.	Pct.	H.	R.	ER.	SO.	BB.	ERA.
1981—Los Angeles	National	1	9	1	0	1.000	9	4	4	6	7	4.00

ALL-STAR GAME RECORD

Tied All-Star Game record for most consecutive strikeouts, game (5), July 15, 1986.

Year League	IP.	W.	L.	Pct.	H.	R.	ER.	SO.	BB.	ERA.
1981—National...............................	1	0	0	.000	2	0	0	0	0	0.00
1982—National...............................	⅔	0	0	.000	0	0	0	0	2	0.00
1984—National...............................	2	0	0	.000	2	0	0	3	0	0.00
1985—National...............................	1	0	0	.000	0	0	0	1	1	0.00
1986—National...............................	3	0	0	.000	1	0	0	5	0	0.00
All-Star Game Totals—5 Years............	7⅔	0	0	.000	5	0	0	9	3	0.00

Member of National League All-Star Team in 1983; did not play.

DAVID VALLE

Name pronounced Valley.

(Dave)

Born October 30, 1960, at Bayside, N. Y.
Height, 6.02. Weight, 200.
Throws and bats righthanded.
Brother of John Valle, minor league outfielder, 1972 through 1984.

Led Northwest League catchers in double plays with 6 and tied for lead in passed balls with 23 in 1978.

Year Club	League	Pos.	G.	AB.	R.	H.	2B.	3B.	HR.	RBI.	B.A.	PO.	A.	E.	F.A.
1978—Bellingham	N'west	C	57	167	12	34	2	0	2	21	.204	*338	65	10	.976
1979—Alexandria†	Carol.	C	58	169	17	36	5	0	6	25	.213	290	44	11	.968
1980—San Jose	Calif.	C	119	430	81	126	14	0	12	70	.293	570	*102	17	.975
1981—Lynn‡	East.	C	93	318	38	82	16	0	11	54	.258	445	56	6	.988
1982—Salt Lake City......	P. C.	C-1B	75	234	28	49	11	1	4	28	.209	347	49	11	.973
1983—Chattanooga§	South.	C-1B	53	176	20	42	11	0	3	22	.239	239	24	4	.985
1984—Salt Lake City x ...	P. C.	C	86	284	54	79	13	1	12	54	.278	433	34	6	.987
1984—Seattle y	Amer.	C	13	27	4	8	1	0	1	4	.296	56	5	0	1.000
1985—Seattle	Amer.	C	31	70	2	11	1	0	0	4	.157	117	7	3	.976
1985—Calgary	P. C.	C	42	131	17	45	8	0	6	26	.344	202	11	1	.995
1986—Calgary	P. C.	C	105	353	71	110	21	2	21	72	.312	404	61	6	.987
1986—Seattle..................	Amer.	C-1B	22	53	10	18	3	0	5	15	.340	90	3	2	.979
Major League Totals—3 Years...............			66	150	16	37	5	0	6	23	.247	263	15	5	.982

Selected by Seattle Mariners' organization in 2nd round of free-agent draft, June 6, 1978.
†On disabled list, July 26 to August 25, 1979.
‡On disabled list, June 24 to July 3, 1981.
§On disabled list, April 13 to June 20 and June 27 to July 7, 1983.
xOn disabled list, May 4 to May 17 and June 9 to June 25, 1984.
yOn disabled list, April 26 to July 19, 1985; included rehabilitation disability assignment to Calgary, June 26 to July 12, 1985.

PITCHING RECORD

Year Club	League	G.	IP.	W.	L.	Pct.	H.	R.	ER.	SO.	BB.	ERA.
1980—San Jose	California	1	1	0	0	.000	1	0	0	2	2	0.00

EDWARD JOHN VANDE BERG

(Ed)

Born October 26, 1958, at Redlands, Calif.
Height, 6.01. Weight, 170.
Throws left and bats righthanded.
Attended San Bernardino Valley, San Bernardino, Calif. and Arizona State University, Tempe, Ariz.

Major League saves: 1982 (5), 1983 (5), 1984 (7), 1985 (3). Total—20.
Named American League Rookie Pitcher of the Year by THE SPORTING NEWS, 1982.

Year Club	League	G.	IP.	W.	L.	Pct.	H.	R.	ER.	SO.	BB.	ERA.
1980—Bellingham	Northwest	14	101	9	0	*1.000	82	40	32	78	46	2.85
1981—Spokane	P. Coast	49	62	4	3	.571	62	33	26	49	29	3.77
1982—Seattle............................	American	*78	76	9	4	.692	54	21	20	60	32	2.37
1983—Seattle............................	American	68	64⅓	2	4	.333	59	32	24	49	22	3.36
1984—Seattle†...........................	American	50	130⅓	8	12	.400	165	76	69	71	50	4.76
1985—Seattle‡...........................	American	76	67⅔	2	1	.667	71	30	28	34	31	3.72
1986—Los Angeles§.....................	National	60	71⅓	1	5	.167	83	32	27	42	33	3.41
American League Totals—4 Years		272	338⅓	21	21	.500	349	159	141	214	135	3.75
National League Totals—1 Year............................		60	71⅓	1	5	.167	83	32	27	42	33	3.41
Major League Totals—5 Years............................		332	409⅔	22	26	.458	432	191	168	256	168	3.69

Selected by San Diego Padres' organization in 3rd round of free-agent draft, January 10, 1978.
Selected by St. Louis Cardinals' organization in secondary phase of free-agent draft, June 6, 1978.
Selected by Seattle Mariners' organization in 13th round of free-agent draft, June 3, 1980.
†Appeared in one game as a pinch-runner.
‡Traded to Los Angeles Dodgers for Catcher Steve Yeager, December 11, 1985.
§Released, December 17, 1986.

DAVID THOMAS VAN GORDER
(Dave)

Born March 27, 1957, at Los Angeles, Calif.
Height, 6.02. Weight, 205.
Throws and bats righthanded.
Attended University of Southern California, Los Angeles, Calif.

Major League stolen bases: 1982 (1).
Led American Association catchers in putouts with 666, total chances with 736 and double plays with 14 in 1983.
Led American Association catchers in putouts with 705, total chances with 785, and fielding percentage with .991 in 1981.
Named catcher on THE SPORTING NEWS College Baseball All-America Team, 1978.

Year Club	League	Pos.	G.	AB.	R.	H.	2B.	3B.	HR.	RBI.	B.A.	PO.	A.	E.	F.A.
1978—Nashville..............	South.	C	73	217	23	57	10	0	1	25	.263	396	38	5	.989
1979—Nashville..............	South.	C	137	461	58	131	27	1	6	64	.284	★726	★74	6	★.993
1980—Indianapolis†	A. A.	★C-1B	71	253	11	57	12	1	3	26	.225	442	45	4	★.992
1981—Indianapolis	A. A.	C-1B	123	432	50	108	21	0	15	66	.250	712	75	8	.990
1982—Indianapolis	A. A.	C	54	174	21	46	7	0	4	29	.264	260	36	3	.990
1982—Cincinnati.............	Nat.	C	51	137	4	25	3	1	0	7	.182	273	18	4	.986
1983—Indianapolis	A. A.	★C-OF	117	380	38	86	17	0	5	48	.226	673	68	3	★.996
1984—Wichita..................	A. A.	C-1B	67	205	26	54	14	1	4	36	.263	350	26	4	.989
1984—Cincinnati.............	Nat.	C-1B	38	101	10	23	2	0	0	6	.228	194	11	0	1.000
1985—Cincinnati‡...........	Nat.	C	73	151	12	36	7	0	2	24	.238	255	11	3	.989
1986—Denver§................	A. A.	C-1B	66	180	26	41	6	1	1	19	.228	269	29	0	1.000
1986—Cincinnati x	Nat.	C	9	10	0	0	0	0	0	0	.000	20	0	0	1.000
Major League Totals—4 Years.................			171	399	26	84	12	1	2	37	.211	742	40	7	.991

Selected by Philadelphia Phillies' organization in 9th round of free-agent draft, June 4, 1975.
Selected by Cincinnati Reds' organization in 2nd round of free-agent draft, June 6, 1978.
†On disabled list, July 10 to September 30, 1980.
‡On disabled list, July 6 to July 20, 1985.
§On Cincinnati disabled list, March 24 to May 19, 1986; included rehabilitation disability assignment to Denver, April 30 to May 19, 1986.
xReleased, November 11, 1986.

ANDREW JAMES VAN SLYKE
(Andy)

Born December 21, 1960, at Utica, N.Y.
Height, 6.01. Weight, 190.
Throws right and bats lefthanded.

Tied Major League record for fewest double plays by outfielder, season, for leader in double plays (4), 1985.
Major League stolen bases: 1983 (21), 1984 (28), 1985 (34), 1986 (21). Total—104.
Tied for National League lead in double plays by outfielders with 4 in 1985.
Received reported $50,000 bonus to sign with St. Louis Cardinals, 1979.

Year Club	League	Pos.	G.	AB.	R.	H.	2B.	3B.	HR.	RBI.	B.A.	PO.	A.	E.	F.A.
1979—Johnson City†........	Appal.						(Did not play)								
1980—Gastonia..............	S. Atl.	OF	126	426	62	115	15	4	8	59	.270	177	16	●16	.923
1981—St. Petersburg‡.....	Fla. St.	OF	94	282	42	62	11	3	1	25	.220	168	10	5	.973
1982—Arkansas...............	Texas	OF	123	416	83	116	13	★11	16	70	.279	266	17	7	.976
1983—Louisville	A. A.	3B-1B-OF	54	220	52	81	21	4	6	41	.368	201	78	16	.946
1983—St. Louis...............	Nat.	OF-3B-1B	101	309	51	81	15	5	8	38	.262	203	59	6	.978
1984—St. Louis...............	Nat.	OF-3B-1B	137	361	45	88	16	4	7	50	.244	357	82	8	.982
1985—St. Louis...............	Nat.	OF-1B	146	424	61	110	25	6	13	55	.259	237	13	1	.996
1986—St. Louis...............	Nat.	OF-1B	137	418	48	113	23	7	13	61	.270	415	34	8	.982
Major League Totals—4 Years.................			521	1512	205	392	79	22	41	204	.259	1212	188	23	.984

Selected by St. Louis Cardinals' organization in 1st round (sixth player selected) of free-agent draft, June 5, 1979.
†On disabled list, June 8, 1979 through remainder of season.
‡On disabled list, April 10 to May 14, 1981.

CHAMPIONSHIP SERIES RECORD

Year Club	League	Pos.	G.	AB.	R.	H.	2B.	3B.	HR.	RBI.	B.A.	PO.	A.	E.	F.A.
1985—St. Louis..................	Nat.	OF-PR	5	11	1	1	0	0	0	1	.091	6	0	0	1.000

WORLD SERIES RECORD

Year Club	League	Pos.	G.	AB.	R.	H.	2B.	3B.	HR.	RBI.	B.A.	PO.	A.	E.	F.A.
1985—St. Louis..................	Nat.	O-PH-PR	6	11	0	1	0	0	0	0	.091	8	0	0	1.000

WILLIAM McKINLEY VENABLE JR.
(Max)

Born June 6, 1957, at Phoenix, Ariz.
Height, 5.10. Weight, 185.
Throws right and bats lefthanded.

Major League stolen bases: 1979 (3), 1980 (8), 1981 (3), 1982 (9), 1983 (15), 1984 (1), 1985 (11), 1986 (7). Total—57.

Year Club	League	Pos.	G.	AB.	R.	H.	2B.	3B.	HR.	RBI.	B.A.	PO.	A.	E.	F.A.
1976—Bellingham†	N'west	OF	51	162	25	35	2	0	1	16	.216	58	4	8	.886
1977—Clinton..................	Midw.	OF-2B	125	425	72	115	19	4	9	63	.271	149	13	13	.926
1978—Lodi‡	Calif.	OF	●140	566	134	180	30	9	17	101	.318	220	8	8	.966

Year Club League	Pos.	G.	AB.	R.	H.	2B.	3B.	HR.	RBI.	B.A.	PO.	A.	E.	F.A.
1979—San Francisco ...... Nat.	OF	55	85	12	14	1	1	0	3	.165	30	2	3	.914
1979—Shreveport .... Texas	OF	18	69	11	16	1	2	0	3	.232	28	2	1	.968
1979—Phoenix................ P. C.	OF	38	150	27	46	5	4	0	11	.307	96	4	3	.971
1980—Phoenix................ P. C.	OF	78	312	52	89	10	10	5	40	.285	179	7	4	.979
1980—San Francisco ...... Nat.	OF	64	138	13	37	5	0	0	10	.268	61	0	0	1.000
1981—Phoenix§............... P. C.	OF	104	428	81	122	24	10	8	48	.285	263	6	3	.989
1981—San Francisco ...... Nat.	OF	18	32	2	6	0	2	0	1	.188	12	0	0	1.000
1982—San Francisco x... Nat.	OF	71	125	17	28	2	1	1	7	.224	66	6	1	.986
1982—Phoenix................ P. C.	OF	8	32	5	8	1	2	0	3	.250	16	0	0	1.000
1983—San Francisco y... Nat.	OF	94	228	28	50	7	4	6	27	.219	141	5	1	.993
1984—Indianapolis .... A. A.	OF	99	330	57	82	13	3	9	47	.248	183	4	4	.979
1984—Montreal .... Nat.	OF	38	71	7	17	2	0	2	7	.239	33	0	0	1.000
1985—Indy. z-Den. .... A. A.	OF	46	172	27	42	7	5	4	19	.244	93	2	1	.990
1985—Cincinnati............. Nat.	OF	77	135	21	39	12	3	0	10	.289	60	3	0	1.000
1986—Cincinnati............. Nat.	OF	108	147	17	31	7	1	2	15	.211	63	0	2	.969
Major League Totals—8 Years................		525	961	117	222	36	12	11	80	.231	466	16	7	.986

Selected by Los Angeles Dodgers' organization in 3rd round of free-agent draft, June 8, 1976.
†On disabled list, June 26 to July 10, 1976.
‡Drafted by San Francisco Giants, December 4, 1978.
§On disabled list, April 23 to May 16, 1981.
xOn disabled list, April 21 to June 1, 1982; included rehabilitation disability assignment to Phoenix, May 22 to June 1, 1982.
yTraded to Montreal Expos' organization, March 31, 1984, completing deal in which Montreal traded First Baseman Al Oliver to San Francisco Giants for Pitcher Fred Breining and a player to be named later, February 27, 1984. (San Francisco traded Pitcher Andy McGaffigan to Montreal, March 31, 1984, as compensation for the injury that Breining arrived with. Breining remained with Montreal.)
zTraded to Cincinnati Reds' organization for Infielder Skeeter Barnes, April 26, 1985.

FRANK JOHN VIOLA JR.

Name pronounced Vy-OH-luh.

Born April 19, 1960, at Hempstead, N.Y.
Height, 6.04. Weight, 209.
Throws and bats lefthanded.
Attended St. John's University, Jamaica, N.Y.

Tied for American League lead in games started by pitchers with 37 in 1986.

Year Club	League	G.	IP.	W.	L.	Pct.	H.	R.	ER.	SO.	BB.	ERA.
1981—Orlando	Southern	17	97	5	4	.556	112	47	37	50	33	3.43
1982—Toledo	Int'national	8	58	2	3	.400	61	27	25	34	18	3.88
1982—Minnesota.....................................	American	22	126	4	10	.286	152	77	73	84	38	5.21
1983—Minnesota.....................................	American	35	210	7	15	.318	242	★141	★128	127	92	5.49
1984—Minnesota.....................................	American	35	257⅔	18	12	.600	225	101	92	149	73	3.21
1985—Minnesota.....................................	American	36	250⅔	18	14	.563	262	★136	114	135	68	4.09
1986—Minnesota.....................................	American	37	245⅔	16	13	.552	257	136	123	191	83	4.51
Major League Totals—5 Years...........................		165	1090	63	64	.496	1138	591	530	686	354	4.38

Selected by Kansas City Royals' organization in 16th round of free-agent draft, June 6, 1978.
Selected by Minnesota Twins' organization in 2nd round of free-agent draft, June 8, 1981.

OSVALDO JOSE VIRGIL JR.

(Ozzie)

Born December 7, 1956, at Mayaguez, P. R.
Height, 6.01. Weight, 195.
Throws and bats righthanded.
Son of Ozzie Virgil, infielder-catcher with New York N.L., Detroit, Kansas City, Baltimore, Pittsburgh and San Francisco, 1956 through 1958, 1960 through 1962, 1965, 1966 and 1969; coach, San Francisco Giants, 1970 through 1972, 1974 and 1975; scout, San Francisco Giants, 1973; coach, Montreal Expos, 1976 through 1981; and coach with San Diego Padres since 1982.

Major League stolen bases: 1984 (1), 1986 (1). Total—2.
Led Carolina League in total bases with 234 in 1978.
Named Carolina League Most Valuable Player, 1978.

Year Club League	Pos.	G.	AB.	R.	H.	2B.	3B.	HR.	RBI.	B.A.	PO.	A.	E.	F.A.
1976—Auburn .... NYP	C	39	113	10	16	1	2	1	10	.142	153	14	5	.971
1977—Spartanburg.......... W. Car.	C	107	365	53	103	21	1	14	54	.282	502	★68	18	.969
1978—Peninsula.............. Carol.	C	126	409	79	124	21	1	★29	★98	.303	581	45	8	.987
1979—Reading................. East.	C	128	429	57	99	17	1	8	66	.231	532	64	12	.980
1980—Reading................. East.	C-1B	135	456	92	123	15	2	28	★104	.270	592	62	16	.976
1980—Philadelphia .... Nat.	C	1	5	1	1	0	0	0	0	.200	4	0	0	1.000
1981—Oklahoma City†... A. A.	C	83	275	41	63	11	2	11	44	.229	201	28	4	.983
1981—Philadelphia .... Nat.	C	6	6	0	0	0	0	0	0	.000	2	0	0	1.000
1982—Philadelphia .... Nat.	C	49	101	11	24	6	0	3	8	.238	173	14	7	.964
1983—Philadelphia .... Nat.	C	55	140	11	30	7	0	6	23	.214	228	24	9	.966
1984—Philadelphia .... Nat.	C	141	456	61	119	21	2	18	68	.261	722	58	6	.992
1985—Philadelphia‡....... Nat.	C	131	426	47	105	16	3	19	55	.246	667	52	4	★.994
1986—Atlanta .... Nat.	C	114	359	45	80	9	0	15	48	.223	682	93	13	.984
Major League Totals—7 Years................		497	1493	176	359	60	5	61	202	.240	2478	241	39	.986

Selected by Philadelphia Phillies' organization in 6th round of free-agent draft, June 8, 1976.
†On disabled list, April 14 to April 27 and June 2 to June 29, 1981.

‡Traded with Pitcher Pete Smith to Atlanta Braves for Pitcher Steve Bedrosian and Outfielder Milt Thompson, December 10, 1985.

CHAMPIONSHIP SERIES RECORD

Year Club League	Pos.	G.	AB.	R.	H.	2B.	3B.	HR.	RBI.	B.A.	PO.	A.	E.	F.A.
1983—Philadelphia .... Nat.	PH	1	1	0	0	0	0	0	0	.000	0	0	0	.000

WORLD SERIES RECORD

Year Club League	Pos.	G.	AB.	R.	H.	2B.	3B.	HR.	RBI.	B.A.	PO.	A.	E.	F.A.
1983—Philadelphia .... Nat.	PH-C	3	2	0	1	0	0	0	1	.500	1	0	0	1.000

ALL-STAR GAME RECORD

Year League	Pos.	AB.	R.	H.	2B.	3B.	HR.	RBI.	B.A.	PO.	A.	E.	F.A.
1985—National	C	1	0	1	0	0	0	2	1.000	3	0	0	1.000

DAVID VON OHLEN
(Dave)

Born October 25, 1958, at Flushing, N.Y.
Height, 6.02. Weight, 200.
Throws and bats lefthanded.

Major League saves: 1983 (2), 1984 (1), 1986 (1). Total—4.

Year Club	League	G.	IP.	W.	L.	Pct.	H.	R.	ER.	SO.	BB.	ERA.
1976—Marion................................	Ap'lachian	5	20	1	0	1.000	11	5	3	12	6	1.35
1976—Wausau..............................	Midwest	9	31	1	4	.200	42	27	16	18	21	4.65
1977—Lynchburg.........................	Carolina	37	65	6	3	.667	75	39	34	49	28	4.71
1978—Lynchburg.........................	Carolina	34	72	6	7	.462	62	28	23	54	22	2.88
1979—Jackson..............................	Texas	37	34	4	1	.800	28	11	7	26	10	1.85
1980—Tidewater...........................	Int'national	45	87	5	4	.556	88	40	31	44	27	3.21
1981—Jackson..............................	Texas	11	29	4	0	1.000	20	3	3	24	4	0.93
1981—Tidewater†.........................	Int'national	10	25	0	4	.000	30	22	16	18	11	5.76
1982—Tidewater‡.........................	Int'national	36	64⅓	4	1	.800	64	22	20	44	25	2.80
1983—Louisville	Am. Assoc.	12	15⅓	1	0	1.000	16	8	8	13	5	4.70
1983—St. Louis............................	National	46	68⅓	3	2	.600	71	27	25	21	25	3.29
1984—Louisville	Am. Assoc.	22	43⅓	1	3	.250	30	11	11	22	18	2.28
1984—St. Louis§..........................	National	27	34⅔	1	0	1.000	39	13	12	19	8	3.12
1985—Cleveland x	American	26	43⅓	3	2	.600	47	20	14	12	20	2.91
1985—Maine y	Int'national	4	23⅔	2	1	.667	26	11	10	7	2	3.80
1986—Miami z	Florida St.	15	61	6	2	.750	54	14	11	32	17	1.62
1986—Tacoma..............................	P. Coast	13	20⅓	2	1	.667	15	5	4	11	9	1.77
1986—Oakland..............................	American	24	15⅓	0	3	.000	18	7	6	4	7	3.52
National League Totals—2 Years........................		73	103	4	2	.667	110	40	37	40	33	3.23
American League Totals—2 Years.....................		50	58⅔	3	5	.375	65	27	20	16	27	3.07
Major League Totals—4 Years............................		123	161⅔	7	7	.500	175	67	57	56	60	3.17

Selected by New York Mets' organization in 17th round of free-agent draft, June 8, 1976.
†On disabled list, July 19 to September 1, 1981.
‡Granted free agency, October 22, 1982; signed by St. Louis Cardinals, December, 1982.
§Released, November 9, 1984; signed by Cleveland Indians' organization, January 9, 1985.
xOn disabled list, May 16 to September 1, 1985; included rehabilitation disability assignment to Maine, June 12 to July 2, 1985.
yReleased, March 28, 1986; signed by Miami (Independent), April 3, 1986.
zSold to Tacoma (Oakland A's organization), June 1, 1986.

EDWARD JOHN VOSBERG
(Ed)

Born September 28, 1961, at Tucson, Ariz.
Height, 6.01. Weight, 190.
Throws and bats lefthanded.
Attended University of Arizona, Tucson, Ariz.

Tied for Texas League lead in games started by pitchers with 27 in 1984 and 1985.

Year Club	League	G.	IP.	W.	L.	Pct.	H.	R.	ER.	SO.	BB.	ERA.
1983—Reno	California	15	97⅔	6	6	.500	111	61	42	70	39	3.87
1983—Beaumont...........................	Texas	1	7	1	0	1.000	2	0	0	1	2	0.00
1984—Beaumont...........................	Texas	27	183⅔	13	●11	.542	196	87	70	100	74	3.43
1985—Beaumont...........................	Texas	27	175	9	11	.450	178	92	76	124	69	3.91
1986—Las Vegas..........................	P. Coast	25	129⅔	7	8	.467	136	80	68	93	64	4.72
1986—San Diego...........................	National	5	13⅔	0	1	.000	17	11	10	8	9	6.59
Major League Totals—1 Year...........................		5	13⅔	0	1	.000	17	11	10	8	9	6.59

Selected by St. Louis Cardinals' organization in 3rd round of free-agent draft, June 5, 1979.
Selected by Toronto Blue Jays' organization in 11th round of free-agent draft, June 7, 1982.
Selected by San Diego Padres' organization in 3rd round of free-agent draft, June 6, 1983.

—DID YOU KNOW—

That when Boston's Rich Gedman hit a pinch-hit grand slam on August 10, 1986, it was the first by a Red Sox player since Vic Wertz performed the feat in 1960?

PETER DENNIS VUCKOVICH

Name pronounced VOO-ko-vitch.

(Pete)

Born October 27, 1952, at Johnstown, Pa.
Height, 6.04. Weight, 220.
Throws and bats righthanded.
Attended Clarion State College, Clarion, Pa.

Major League saves: 1977 (8), 1978 (1), 1980 (1). Total—10.
Won American League Cy Young Memorial Award, 1982.

Year	Club	League	G.	IP.	W.	L.	Pct.	H.	R.	ER.	SO.	BB.	ERA.
1974—Appleton	Midwest	5	15	1	0	1.000	10	2	2	22	3	1.20
1974—Knoxville	Southern	13	47	2	5	.286	50	32	22	42	29	4.21
1975—Denver	Am. Assoc.	19	116	11	4	●.733	103	63	56	86	54	4.34
1975—Chicago	American	4	10	0	1	.000	17	15	15	5	7	13.50
1976—Chicago†	American	33	110	7	4	.636	122	59	57	62	60	4.66
1977—Toronto‡	American	53	148	7	7	.500	143	64	57	123	59	3.47
1978—St. Louis	National	45	198	12	12	.500	187	65	56	149	59	2.55
1979—St. Louis	National	34	233	15	10	.600	229	108	93	145	64	3.59
1980—St. Louis§	National	32	222	12	9	.571	203	96	84	132	68	3.41
1981—Milwaukee	American	24	150	●14	4	★.778	137	61	59	84	57	3.54
1982—Milwaukee	American	30	223⅔	18	6	●.750	234	96	83	105	102	3.34
1983—Milwaukee x	American	3	14⅔	0	2	.000	15	9	8	10	10	4.91
1984—Milwaukee y	American					(Did not play)						
1985—Milwaukee za	American	22	112⅔	6	10	.375	134	74	69	55	48	5.51
1986—Vancouver	P. Coast	6	28⅔	2	1	.667	17	6	4	19	7	1.26
1986—Milwaukee b	American	6	32½	2	4	.333	33	18	11	12	11	3.06
American League Totals—8 Years		175	801⅓	54	38	.587	835	396	359	456	354	4.03
National League Totals—3 Years		111	653	39	31	.557	619	269	233	426	191	3.21
Major League Totals—11 Years		286	1454⅓	93	69	.574	1454	665	592	882	545	3.66

Selected by Chicago White Sox' organization in 3rd round of free-agent draft, June 5, 1974.
†Selected by Toronto Blue Jays in American League expansion draft, November 5, 1976.
‡Traded with a player to be named later to St. Louis Cardinals for Pitchers Tom Underwood and Victor Cruz, December 6, 1977. St. Louis organization acquired Outfielder John Scott to complete deal, December 16, 1977.
§Traded with Pitcher Rollie Fingers and Catcher Ted Simmons to Milwaukee Brewers for Outfielders Sixto Lezcano and David Green and Pitchers Lary Sorensen and Dave LaPoint, December 12, 1980.
xOn disabled list, March 24 to August 22, 1983.
yOn disabled list, March 27, 1984 through entire season.
zOn disabled list, May 11 to June 4, 1985.
aGranted free agency after refusing to report to minors, November 21, 1985; re-signed by Brewers' organization, August 1, 1986.
bReleased, October 21, 1986; invited to Milwaukee Brewers' spring training for 1987.

DIVISION SERIES RECORD

Year	Club	League	G.	IP.	W.	L.	Pct.	H.	R.	ER.	SO.	BB.	ERA.
1981—Milwaukee	American	2	5⅓	1	0	1.000	2	1	0	4	3	0.00

CHAMPIONSHIP SERIES RECORD

Year	Club	League	G.	IP.	W.	L.	Pct.	H.	R.	ER.	SO.	BB.	ERA.
1982—Milwaukee	American	2	14⅓	0	1	.000	15	7	7	8	7	4.40

WORLD SERIES RECORD

Year	Club	League	G.	IP.	W.	L.	Pct.	H.	R.	ER.	SO.	BB.	ERA.
1982—Milwaukee	American	2	14	0	1	.000	16	9	7	4	5	4.50

THOMAS DAVID WADDELL

Name pronounced WADD-ell.

(Tom)

Born September 17, 1958, at Dundee, Scotland.
Height, 6.01. Weight, 185.
Throws and bats righthanded.
Received bachelor of science degree in education from Manhattan College, Bronx, N.Y. in 1980.
Cousin of Peter Lorimer, former Scottish/English soccer player.

Major League saves: 1984 (6), 1985 (9). Total—15.

Year	Club	League	G.	IP.	W.	L.	Pct.	H.	R.	ER.	SO.	BB.	ERA.
1981—Bradenton Braves	Gulf Coast	2	10	0	1	.000	5	2	1	7	1	0.90
1981—Anderson	S. Atlantic	13	63	6	3	.667	57	24	20	51	12	2.86
1982—Anderson	S. Atlantic	4	9⅓	0	0	.000	9	5	5	13	6	4.82
1982—Durham	Carolina	42	74⅓	5	3	.625	44	20	12	102	26	1.45
1983—Savannah†	Southern	29	44⅓	8	2	.800	32	11	7	40	13	1.42
1983—Richmond‡	Int'national	13	24⅔	5	0	1.000	26	12	12	29	6	4.38
1984—Cleveland	American	58	97	7	4	.636	68	35	33	59	37	3.06
1985—Cleveland	American	49	112⅔	8	6	.571	104	61	61	53	39	4.87
1986—Maine§	Int'national	3	8	0	0	.000	12	6	6	4	3	6.75
Major League Totals—2 Years		107	209⅔	15	10	.600	172	96	94	112	76	4.03

Signed as free agent by Atlanta Braves' organization, April 1, 1981.

†On disabled list, May 17 to May 31, 1983.
‡Drafted by Cleveland Indians, December 5, 1983.
§On Cleveland disabled list, March 31, 1986 through entire season; included rehabilitation disability assignment to Maine, April 23 to May 2 and June 17 to June 28, 1986.

ROBERT VERNON WALK
(Bob)

Born November 26, 1956, at Van Nuys, Calif.
Height, 6.03. Weight, 200.
Throws and bats righthanded.
Attended College of the Canyons, Valencia, Calif.

Major League saves: 1986 (2).
Led Pacific Coast League in complete games with 12 in 1985.
Led International League in complete games with 11 and tied for lead in games started by pitchers with 28 and home runs allowed with 22 in 1983.
Led Carolina League in hit batsmen with 13 in 1978.

Year Club	League	G.	IP.	W.	L.	Pct.	H.	R.	ER.	SO.	BB.	ERA.
1977—Spartanburg	W. Carol.	15	99	6	9	.400	90	55	40	66	46	3.64
1977—Peninsula	Carolina	8	36	0	2	.000	44	31	17	23	20	4.25
1978—Peninsula	Carolina	26	187	13	8	.619	147	58	44	150	64	2.12
1979—Reading	Eastern	24	185	12	7	.632	156	62	46	*135	77	*2.24
1980—Oklahoma City	Am. Assoc.	8	49	5	1	.833	39	21	16	36	17	2.94
1980—Philadelphia†	National	27	152	11	7	.611	163	82	77	94	71	4.56
1981—Atlanta‡	National	12	43	1	4	.200	41	25	22	16	23	4.60
1981—Richmond	Int'national	4	22	2	1	.667	18	7	6	13	11	2.45
1982—Atlanta	National	32	164⅓	11	9	.550	179	101	89	84	59	4.87
1983—Richmond	Int'national	28	*185	11	12	.478	179	*119	*107	123	102	5.21
1983—Atlanta§	National	1	3⅔	0	0	.000	7	3	3	4	2	7.36
1984—Hawaii	P. Coast	18	127⅓	9	5	.643	100	39	32	85	42	*2.26
1984—Pittsburgh x	National	2	10⅓	1	1	.500	8	5	3	10	4	2.61
1985—Hawaii	P. Coast	24	173	*16	5	.762	143	57	51	124	61	*2.65
1985—Pittsburgh	National	9	58⅔	2	3	.400	60	27	24	40	18	3.68
1986—Pittsburgh	National	44	141⅔	7	8	.467	129	66	59	78	64	3.75
Major League Totals—7 Years		127	573⅔	33	32	.508	587	309	277	326	241	4.35

Selected by California Angels' organization in 5th round of free-agent draft, January 1, 1975.
Selected by Philadelphia Phillies' organization in 5th round of free-agent draft, January 7, 1976.
Selected by Philadelphia Phillies' organization in secondary phase of free-agent draft, June 8, 1976.
†Traded to Atlanta Braves for Outfielder Gary Matthews, March 25, 1981.
‡On disabled list, May 26 to August 9, 1981.
§Released, March 26, 1984; signed by Pittsburgh Pirates' organization, April 3, 1984.
xOn disabled list, July 23, 1984 through remainder of season.

CHAMPIONSHIP SERIES RECORD

Year Club	League	G.	IP.	W.	L.	Pct.	H.	R.	ER.	SO.	BB.	ERA.
1982—Atlanta	National	1	1	0	0	.000	2	1	1	1	1	9.00

WORLD SERIES RECORD

Year Club	League	G.	IP.	W.	L.	Pct.	H.	R.	ER.	SO.	BB.	ERA.
1980—Philadelphia	National	1	7	1	0	1.000	8	6	6	3	3	7.71

ANTHONY BRUCE WALKER
(Tony)

Born July 1, 1960, at San Diego, Calif.
Height, 6.02. Weight, 205.
Throws and bats righthanded.

Major League stolen bases: 1986 (11).

Year Club	League	Pos.	G.	AB.	R.	H.	2B.	3B.	HR.	RBI.	B.A.	PO.	A.	E.	F.A.
1981—Waterbury	East.	OF	17	22	2	2	0	0	0	0	.091	9	0	1	.900
1981—Tampa	Fla. St.	OF	18	40	11	12	3	2	0	3	.300	21	0	0	1.000
1981—Eugene	N'west	OF	18	58	16	22	1	1	1	4	.379	22	1	1	.958
1982—Tampa†‡	Fla. St.	OF	128	499	73	136	9	5	2	28	.273	277	●23	*12	.962
1983—Daytona Beach‡	Fla. St.	OF	92	350	84	114	8	2	0	41	.326	196	4	3	.985
1983—Columbus‡	South.	OF	44	171	22	38	7	1	0	10	.222	83	4	0	1.000
1984—Columbus‡	South.	OF	132	408	65	101	18	4	3	35	.248	281	15	8	.974
1985—Columbus‡	South.	OF	135	530	88	156	23	5	12	65	.294	335	16	7	.980
1986—Houston	Nat.	OF	84	90	19	20	7	0	2	10	.222	73	0	1	.986
1986—Tucson	P. C.	OF	29	84	8	17	1	2	0	8	.202	62	4	3	.957
Major League Totals—1 Year			84	90	19	20	7	0	2	10	.222	73	0	1	.986

Signed as free agent by Cincinnati Reds' organization, March 22, 1981.
†Traded with Pitcher Bill Dawley to Houston Astros for Catcher Alan Knicely, March 31, 1983.
‡Switch-hitter.

CLEOTHA WALKER
(Chico)

Born November 25, 1957, at Jackson, Miss.
Height, 5.09. Weight, 170.
Throws right and bats left and righthanded.

Major League stolen bases: 1980 (3), 1985 (1), 1986 (15). Total—19.
Led American Association in total bases with 258, caught stealing with 22 and tied for lead in game-winning RBIs with 11 and stolen bases with 67 in 1986.
Led International League in intentional bases on balls received with 9 in 1984.
Led Eastern League in caught stealing with 16 in 1979.
Led American Association outfielders in assists with 16 in 1986.
Tied for International League lead in double plays by second basemen with 74 in 1980.

Year—Club	League	Pos.	G.	AB.	R.	H.	2B.	3B.	HR.	RBI.	B.A.	PO.	A.	E.	F.A.
1976—Elmira	NYP	2B	22	28	9	5	1	2	0	1	.179	9	18	3	.900
1977—Elmira	NYP	2B-SS	64	227	26	50	4	3	1	14	.220	122	196	15	.955
1978—Winter Haven	Fla. St.	SS-3B-2B	133	480	66	134	10	6	3	52	.279	172	380	42	.929
1979—Bristol†	East.	2B	123	498	75	132	19	*12	8	57	.265	252	357	23	.964
1980—Pawtucket	Int.	2B	139	536	59	146	18	7	8	52	.272	252	*394	*21	.969
1980—Boston	Amer.	2B	19	57	3	12	0	0	1	5	.211	15	31	2	.958
1981—Pawtucket	Int.	OF-2B-3B	138	535	50	148	21	5	17	68	.277	209	178	13	.968
1981—Boston	Amer.	2B	6	17	3	6	0	0	0	2	.353	4	10	0	1.000
1982—Pawtucket	Int.	O-2-3-S	133	494	71	124	22	2	15	66	.251	209	48	11	.959
1983—Pawtucket	Int.	3-O-S-2	125	442	78	119	18	1	18	56	.269	122	126	16	.939
1983—Boston	Amer.	OF	4	5	2	2	0	2	0	1	.400	4	1	0	1.000
1984—Pawtucket	Int.	2B-OF-3B	130	499	●91	131	26	5	18	51	.263	223	241	20	.959
1984—Boston‡	Amer.	2B	3	2	0	0	0	0	0	1	.000	0	1	0	1.000
1985—Iowa	A. A.	OF-3B	89	331	47	94	17	8	5	46	.284	177	6	5	.973
1985—Chicago	Nat.	OF-2B	21	12	3	1	0	0	0	0	.083	4	0	0	1.000
1986—Iowa	A. A.	OF-2B	138	530	97	●158	30	11	16	65	.298	286	38	8	.976
1986—Chicago	Nat.	OF	28	101	21	28	3	2	1	7	.277	42	1	2	.956
American League Totals—4 Years			32	81	8	20	0	2	1	9	.247	23	43	2	.971
National League Totals—2 Years			49	113	24	29	3	2	1	7	.257	46	1	2	.959
Major League Totals—6 Years			81	194	32	49	3	4	2	16	.253	69	44	4	.966

Selected by Boston Red Sox' organization in 22nd round of free-agent draft, June 8, 1976.
†On disabled list, August 22 to September 19, 1979.
‡Granted free agency, October 15, 1984; signed by Iowa (Chicago Cubs' organization), November 9, 1984.

GREGORY LEE WALKER
(Greg)

Born October 6, 1959, at Douglas, Ga.
Height, 6.03. Weight, 210.
Throws right and bats lefthanded.

Major League stolen bases: 1983 (2), 1984 (8), 1985 (5), 1986 (1). Total—16.
Led Midwest League first basemen in double plays with 108 in 1980.

Year—Club	League	Pos.	G.	AB.	R.	H.	2B.	3B.	HR.	RBI.	B.A.	PO.	A.	E.	F.A.
1977—Auburn†	NYP	1B	33	98	12	25	1	2	2	8	.255	5	0	0	1.000
1978—Spartanburg	W. Car.	1B-3B-C	100	341	51	71	16	2	11	47	.208	538	50	13	.978
1979—Peninsula‡	Carol.	1B	122	446	59	125	*27	4	10	61	.280	973	53	19	.982
1980—Appleton	Midw.	1B	135	464	88	130	20	3	21	*98	.280	*1298	*88	10	*.993
1981—Glens Falls	East.	1B	135	508	*117	*163	*33	2	22	86	.321	*1215	77	11	.992
1982—Edmonton§	P. C.	1B	35	117	18	41	8	0	3	12	.350	94	11	0	1.000
1982—Chicago	Amer.	DH	11	17	3	7	2	1	2	7	.412	0	0	0	.000
1983—Chicago	Amer.	1B	118	307	32	83	16	3	10	55	.270	426	19	7	.985
1984—Chicago	Amer.	1B	136	442	62	130	29	2	24	75	.294	791	51	4	.995
1985—Chicago	Amer.	1B	*163	601	77	155	38	4	24	92	.258	1217	97	8	.994
1986—Chicago x	Amer.	1B	78	282	37	78	10	6	13	51	.277	670	57	5	.993
Major League Totals—5 Years			506	1649	211	453	95	16	73	280	.275	3104	224	24	.993

Selected by Philadelphia Phillies' organization in 20th round of free-agent draft, June 7, 1977.
†On disabled list, June 21, 1977 through remainder of season.
‡Drafted by Iowa (Chicago White Sox' organization), December 4, 1979.
§On disabled list, April 23 to July 27, 1982.
xOn disabled list, April 15 to May 14 and August 3, 1986 through remainder of season.

CHAMPIONSHIP SERIES RECORD

Year—Club	League	Pos.	G.	AB.	R.	H.	2B.	3B.	HR.	RBI.	B.A.	PO.	A.	E.	F.A.
1983—Chicago	Amer.	PH-1B	2	3	0	1	0	0	0	0	.333	7	1	0	1.000

TIMOTHY CHARLES WALLACH
(Tim)

Born September 14, 1957, at Huntington Park, Calif.
Height, 6.03. Weight, 220.
Throws and bats righthanded.
Attended Saddleback Junior College, Mission Viejo, Calif., and California State University, Fullerton, Calif.

Tied major league record by hitting home run in first major league at-bat, September 6, 1980.
Major League stolen bases: 1982 (6), 1984 (3), 1985 (9), 1986 (8). Total—26.
Led National League in being hit by pitch with 10 in 1986.
Led National League third basemen in total chances with 515 in 1984 and 549 in 1985.
Led National League third basemen in double plays with 29 in 1984 and 34 in 1985.
Led American Association in total bases with 295, game-winning RBIs with 16 and tied for lead in sacrifice flies with 9 in 1980.
Named third baseman on THE SPORTING NEWS National League All-Star Team, 1985.

Named third baseman on THE SPORTING NEWS National League All-Star fielding team, 1985.
Named third baseman on THE SPORTING NEWS National League Silver Slugger team, 1985.
Named College Player of the Year by THE SPORTING NEWS, 1979.
Received reported $90,000 bonus to sign with Montreal Expos, 1979.
Named first baseman on THE SPORTING NEWS College Baseball All-America Team, 1979.

Year	Club	League	Pos.	G.	AB.	R.	H.	2B.	3B.	HR.	RBI.	B.A.	PO.	A.	E.	F.A.
1979—Memphis	South.		1B-3B	75	257	50	84	16	4	18	51	.327	290	35	4	.988
1980—Denver	A. A.		3B-OF-1B	134	512	103	144	29	7	36	124	.281	222	147	21	.946
1980—Montreal	Nat.		OF-1B	5	11	1	2	0	0	1	2	.182	12	0	0	1.000
1981—Montreal	Nat.		OF-1B-3B	71	212	19	50	9	1	4	13	.236	207	31	1	.996
1982—Montreal	Nat.		★3-O-1	158	596	89	160	31	3	28	97	.268	★132	287	23	.948
1983—Montreal	Nat.		3B	156	581	54	156	33	3	19	70	.269	★151	265	19	.956
1984—Montreal	Nat.		★3B-SS	160	582	55	143	25	4	18	72	.246	★162	★332	21	.959
1985—Montreal	Nat.		3B	155	569	70	148	36	3	22	81	.260	★148	★383	18	.967
1986—Montreal	Nat.		3B	134	480	50	112	22	1	18	71	.233	94	270	16	.958
Major League Totals—7 Years				839	3031	338	771	156	15	110	406	.254	906	1568	98	.962

Selected by California Angels' organization in 8th round of free-agent draft, June 6, 1978.
Selected by Montreal Expos' organization in 1st round (10th player selected) of free-agent draft, June 5, 1979.

DIVISION SERIES RECORD

Year	Club	League	Pos.	G.	AB.	R.	H.	2B.	3B.	HR.	RBI.	B.A.	PO.	A.	E.	F.A.
1981—Montreal	Nat.		OF	4	4	1	1	1	0	0	0	.250	4	0	0	1.000

CHAMPIONSHIP SERIES RECORD

Year	Club	League	Pos.	G.	AB.	R.	H.	2B.	3B.	HR.	RBI.	B.A.	PO.	A.	E.	F.A.
1981—Montreal	Nat.		PH	1	1	0	0	0	0	0	0	.000	0	0	0	.000

ALL-STAR GAME RECORD

Year	League	Pos.	AB.	R.	H.	2B.	3B.	HR.	RBI.	B.A.	PO.	A.	E.	F.A.
1984—National		3B	1	0	0	0	0	0	0	.000	0	0	0	.000
1985—National		3B	2	1	1	1	0	0	0	.500	1	1	0	1.000
All-Star Game Totals—2 Years			3	1	1	1	0	0	0	.333	1	1	0	1.000

DENNIS MARTIN WALLING
(Denny)

Born April 17, 1954, at Neptune, N.J.
Height, 6.01. Weight, 185.
Throws right and bats lefthanded.
Attended Brookdale Community College, Lincroft, N.J., and
Clemson University, Clemson, S.C.
Brother of Gregory Walling, minor league outfielder, 1967.

Major League stolen bases: 1978 (9), 1979 (3), 1980 (4), 1981 (2), 1982 (4), 1983 (2), 1984 (7), 1985 (5), 1986 (1). Total—37.

Named outfielder on THE SPORTING NEWS College Baseball All-America Team, 1975.

Year	Club	League	Pos.	G.	AB.	R.	H.	2B.	3B.	HR.	RBI.	B.A.	PO.	A.	E.	F.A.
1975—Oakland	Amer.		OF	6	8	0	1	1	0	0	2	.125	3	0	0	1.000
1976—Chattanooga	South.		OF	115	369	48	95	15	5	9	42	.257	241	8	2	★.992
1976—Oakland	Amer.		OF	3	11	1	3	0	0	0	0	.273	8	0	1	.889
1977—San Jose†‡	P. C.		OF	3	10	1	3	0	0	0	4	.300	8	0	0	1.000
1977—Charleston	Int.		OF	29	89	17	31	4	1	4	14	.348	66	0	0	1.000
1977—Houston	Nat.		OF	6	21	1	6	0	1	0	6	.286	14	0	0	1.000
1978—Houston	Nat.		OF	120	247	30	62	11	3	3	36	.251	140	4	3	.980
1979—Houston	Nat.		OF	82	147	21	48	8	4	3	31	.327	65	2	1	.985
1980—Houston	Nat.		1B-OF	100	284	30	85	6	5	3	29	.299	525	31	6	.989
1981—Houston	Nat.		1B-OF	65	158	23	37	6	0	5	23	.234	226	9	2	.992
1982—Houston	Nat.		OF-1B	85	146	22	30	4	1	1	14	.205	167	11	1	.994
1983—Houston§	Nat.		1B-3B-OF	100	135	24	40	5	3	3	19	.296	134	29	6	.964
1984—Houston x	Nat.		3B-1B-OF	87	249	37	70	11	5	3	31	.281	116	102	7	.969
1985—Houston	Nat.		3B-1B-OF	119	345	44	93	20	1	7	45	.270	326	124	12	.974
1986—Houston	Nat.		3B-OF-1B	130	382	54	119	23	1	13	58	.312	108	161	9	.968
American League Totals—2 Years				9	19	1	4	1	0	0	2	.210	11	0	1	.917
National League Totals—10 Years				894	2114	286	590	94	24	41	292	.279	1821	473	47	.980
Major League Totals—12 Years				903	2133	287	594	95	24	41	294	.278	1832	473	48	.980

Selected by San Francisco Giants' organization in 8th round of free-agent draft, June 5, 1974.
Selected by Oakland A's organization in secondary phase of free-agent draft, June 4, 1975.
†On disabled list, April 18 to June 15, 1977.
‡Traded with cash to Houston Astros' organization for Outfielder Willie Crawford, June 15, 1977.
§Granted free agency, November 7, 1983; re-signed by Astros, December 20, 1983.
xOn disabled list, May 2 to May 24, 1984.

DIVISION SERIES RECORD

Year	Club	League	Pos.	G.	AB.	R.	H.	2B.	3B.	HR.	RBI.	B.A.	PO.	A.	E.	F.A.
1981—Houston	Nat.		PH-1B	3	6	0	2	0	0	0	1	.333	6	1	1	.875

Year	Club	League	Pos.	G.	AB.	R.	H.	2B.	3B.	HR.	RBI.	B.A.	PO.	A.	E.	F.A.
1980—Houston	Nat.		1-O-PH	3	9	2	1	0	0	0	2	.111	6	0	0	1.000
1986—Houston	Nat.		3B-PH	5	19	1	3	1	0	0	2	.158	3	6	0	1.000
Championship Series Totals—2 Years				8	28	3	4	1	0	0	4	.143	9	6	0	1.000

GENE WINSTON WALTER

Born November 22, 1960, at Chicago, Ill.
Height, 6.04. Weight, 200.
Throws and bats lefthanded.
Received degree from Eastern Kentucky University, Richmond, Ky.

Major League saves: 1985 (3), 1986 (1) Total—4.

Year	Club	League	G.	IP.	W.	L.	Pct.	H.	R.	ER.	SO.	BB.	ERA.
1982—Walla Walla	Northwest	17	72⅔	4	4	.500	73	55	39	61	46	4.83
1983—Miami	Florida St.	42	121⅓	6	13	.316	114	73	51	105	61	3.78
1984—Miami	Florida St.	9	59	3	5	.375	43	22	15	70	27	2.29
1984—Beaumont	Texas	34	76	7	3	.700	53	25	22	71	40	2.61
1985—Las Vegas†	P. Coast	45	95	7	5	.583	75	34	29	107	35	2.75
1985—San Diego	National	15	22	0	2	.000	12	6	5	18	8	2.05
1986—San Diego‡	National	57	98	2	2	.500	89	47	42	84	49	3.86
Major League Totals—2 Years		72	120	2	4	.333	101	53	47	102	57	3.53

Selected by Montreal Expos' organization in 25th round of free-agent draft, June 8, 1981.
Selected by San Diego Padres' organization in 29th round of free-agent draft, June 7, 1982.
†Appeared in one game as an outfielder with one putout.
‡Traded with Outfielder Kevin McReynolds and Infielder Adam Ging to New York Mets for Outfielders Shawn Abner, Stanley Jefferson and Kevin Mitchell and Pitchers Kevin Armstrong and Kevin Brown, December 11, 1986.

COLIN NORVAL WARD

Born November 22, 1960, at Los Angeles, Calif.
Height, 6.03. Weight, 190.
Throws and bats lefthanded.
Attended Citrus College, Azusa, Calif., and
University of California, Los Angeles, Calif.

Year	Club	League	G.	IP.	W.	L.	Pct.	H.	R.	ER.	SO.	BB.	ERA.
1982—Lakeland	Florida St.	11	63	2	2	.500	55	29	24	37	44	3.43
1983—Birmingham†	Southern	26	150⅔	10	3	.769	139	81	69	71	★109	4.12
1984—Phoenix	P. Coast	46	126⅔	7	8	.467	143	85	74	95	71	5.26
1985—Phoenix‡	P. Coast	22	41⅓	3	0	1.000	45	27	27	31	30	5.88
1985—San Francisco§	National	6	12⅓	0	0	.000	10	6	6	8	7	4.38
1986—Shreveport	Texas	4	24⅔	1	1	.500	20	9	7	17	16	2.55
1986—Phoenix	P. Coast	22	122⅔	8	11	.421	133	73	70	93	63	5.14
Major League Totals—1 Year		6	12⅓	0	0	.000	10	6	6	8	7	4.38

Selected by San Francisco Giants' organization in 32nd round of free-agent draft, June 3, 1980.
Selected by Detroit Tigers' organization in 3rd round of free-agent draft, June 7, 1982.
†Traded to San Francisco Giants' organization for Pitcher Pat Larkin, February 8, 1984.
‡On disabled list, April 11 to June 24, 1985.
§Traded to Cincinnati Reds' organization for Pitcher Bob Buchanan, November 11, 1985; trade voided, January 27, 1986.

GARY LAMELL WARD

Born December 6, 1953, at Los Angeles, Calif.
Height, 6.02. Weight, 207.
Throws and bats righthanded.

Major League stolen bases: 1981 (5), 1982 (13), 1983 (8), 1984 (7), 1985 (26), 1986 (12). Total—71.
Hit for the cycle, September 18, 1980 (first game).
Led American League outfielders in double plays with 4 in 1981.
Led New York-Pennsylvania League first basemen in errors with 12 in 1973.
Tied for Midwest League lead in assists by outfielders with 18 in 1974.

Year	Club	League	Pos.	G.	AB.	R.	H.	2B.	3B.	HR.	RBI.	B.A.	PO.	A.	E.	F.A.
1973—Geneva	NYP	1B-OF-3B	61	211	36	57	13	1	10	38	.270	336	20	14	.962
1974—Wis. Rapids	Midw.	OF-1B	126	★467	★104	122	12	5	26	78	.261	184	19	11	.949
1975—Orlando	South.	OF-C	124	438	45	117	18	5	8	71	.267	204	10	4	.982
1976—Orlando	South.	OF	132	475	50	119	17	2	9	65	.251	235	●16	●10	.962
1977—Tacoma	P. C.	OF-3B	125	413	62	97	15	8	8	43	.235	212	34	10	.961
1978—Toledo	Int.	★O-1-3	139	511	82	150	20	12	14	79	.294	260	6	★13	.953
1979—Toledo	Int.	OF	134	506	75	133	16	9	13	67	.263	323	12	●11	.968
1979—Minnesota	Amer.	DH-PH	10	14	2	4	0	0	0	1	.286	0	0	0	.000
1980—Toledo†	Int.	OF-1B	128	496	82	140	22	8	13	66	.282	269	14	8	.973
1980—Minnesota	Amer.	OF	13	41	11	19	6	2	1	10	.463	14	0	0	1.000
1981—Minnesota	Amer.	OF	85	295	42	78	7	6	3	29	.264	185	8	5	.975
1982—Minnesota	Amer.	OF	152	570	85	165	33	7	28	91	.289	343	13	4	.989
1983—Minnesota‡	Amer.	OF	157	623	76	173	34	5	19	88	.278	374	★24	9	.978
1984—Texas	Amer.	OF	155	602	97	171	21	7	21	79	.284	376	11	5	.987
1985—Texas	Amer.	OF	154	593	77	170	28	7	15	70	.287	304	11	10	.969
1986—Texas§	Amer.	OF	105	380	54	120	15	2	5	51	.316	237	8	1	.996
Major League Totals—8 Years			831	3118	444	900	144	36	92	419	.289	1833	75	34	.982

— 514 —

Signed as free agent by Minnesota Twins' organization, August 29, 1972.

†On disabled list, April 16 to April 26, 1980.

‡Traded to Texas Rangers for Pitchers Mike Smithson and John Butcher and Catcher Sam Sorce, December 7, 1983.

§Granted free agency, November 12, 1986; signed by New York Yankees, December 24, 1986.

ALL-STAR GAME RECORD

Year League	Pos.	AB.	R.	H.	2B.	3B.	HR.	RBI.	B.A.	PO.	A.	E.	F.A.
1983—American	PH	1	0	0	0	0	0	0	.000	0	0	0	.000
1985—American	PH	1	0	0	0	0	0	0	.000	0	0	0	.000
All-Star Game Totals—2 Years		2	0	0	0	0	0	0	.000	0	0	0	.000

ROY DUANE WARD

(Known by middle name.)
Born May 28, 1964, at Parkview, N.M.
Height, 6.04. Weight, 185.
Throws and bats righthanded.

Year Club	League	G.	IP.	W.	L.	Pct.	H.	R.	ER.	SO.	BB.	ERA.
1982—Bradenton Braves	Gulf Coast	8	45⅔	2	3	.400	45	25	23	31	24	4.53
1982—Anderson	S. Atlantic	5	23⅔	1	2	.333	24	16	14	18	15	5.32
1983—Durham	Carolina	28	178⅓	11	13	.458	165	103	85	115	75	4.29
1984—Greenville†	Southern	21	104⅔	4	9	.308	108	71	58	54	57	4.99
1985—Greenville	Southern	28	150	11	10	.524	141	83	70	100	★105	4.20
1985—Richmond	Int'national	5	5⅓	0	1	.000	8	9	7	3	8	11.81
1986—Atlanta	National	10	16	0	1	.000	22	13	13	8	8	7.31
1986—Richmond‡-Syracuse	Int'national	20	117⅔	7	5	.583	125	56	52	67	52	3.98
1986—Toronto	American	2	2	0	1	.000	3	4	3	1	4	13.50
National League Totals—1 Year		10	16	0	1	.000	22	13	13	8	8	7.31
American League Totals—1 Year		2	2	0	1	.000	3	4	3	1	4	13.50
Major League Totals—1 Year		12	18	0	2	.000	25	17	16	9	12	8.00

Selected by Atlanta Braves' organization in 1st round (ninth player selected) of free-agent draft, June 7, 1982.

†On disabled list, May 7 to May 29 and July 14 to August 7, 1984.

‡Traded to Toronto Blue Jays for Pitcher Doyle Alexander, July 6, 1986.

CURTIS RAY WARDLE

(Curt)

Born November 16, 1960, at Downey, Calif.
Height, 6.05. Weight, 220.
Throws and bats lefthanded.
Attended San Bernardino Valley, San Bernardino, Calif., and
University of California, Riverside, Calif.

Major League saves: 1985 (1).
Tied for Southern League lead in saves with 17 in 1984.

Year Club	League	G.	IP.	W.	L.	Pct.	H.	R.	ER.	SO.	BB.	ERA.
1981—Wisconsin Rapids	Midwest	16	53	4	3	.571	49	27	19	41	32	3.23
1982—Visalia	California	28	79⅓	3	4	.429	114	66	59	42	56	6.69
1983—Visalia	California	49	146	8	6	.571	118	52	43	134	55	2.65
1984—Orlando	Southern	45	78	6	1	.857	41	10	6	75	30	0.69
1984—Minnesota	American	2	4	0	0	.000	3	2	2	5	0	4.50
1985—Minnesota†-Cleveland	American	50	115	8	9	.471	127	83	79	84	62	6.18
1986—Maine	Int'national	34	113	7	10	.412	113	58	52	71	57	4.14
Major League Totals—2 Years		52	119	8	9	.471	130	85	81	89	62	6.13

Selected by St. Louis Cardinals' organization in 45th round of free-agent draft, June 6, 1978.

Selected by California Angels' organization in secondary phase of free-agent draft, January 9, 1979.

Selected by San Diego Padres' organization in 2nd round of free-agent draft, January 8, 1980.

Selected by Minnesota Twins' organization in 3rd round of free-agent draft, June 8, 1981.

†Traded with Outfielder Jim Weaver, Infielder Jay Bell and a player to be named later to Cleveland Indians for Pitcher Bert Blyleven, August 1, 1985; Cleveland organization acquired Pitcher Rich Yett to complete deal, September 17, 1985.

CLAUDELL WASHINGTON

Born August 31, 1954, at Los Angeles, Calif.
Height, 6.00. Weight, 190.
Throws and bats lefthanded.
Brother of Don Washington, outfielder in Los Angeles Dodgers' and
Oakland A's organizations, 1975 through 1977.

Hit three home runs in a game, July 14, 1979 and June 22, 1980.

Major League stolen bases: 1974 (6), 1975 (40), 1976 (37), 1977 (21), 1978 (5), 1979 (19), 1980 (21), 1981 (12), 1982 (33), 1983 (31), 1984 (21), 1985 (14), 1986 (10). Total—270.

Led Midwest League in total bases with 218 in 1973.

Year Club	League	Pos.	G.	AB.	R.	H.	2B.	3B.	HR.	RBI.	B.A.	PO.	A.	E.	F.A.
1972—C's Bay-N. Bend	N'west.	OF	33	111	13	31	3	2	2	15	.279	37	1	6	.864
1973—Burlington	Midw.	OF	108	447	★92	144	25	5	13	81	.322	149	10	★15	.914
1974—Birmingham	South.	OF	74	294	64	106	23	4	11	55	.361	116	5	13	.903
1974—Oakland	Amer.	OF	73	221	16	63	10	5	0	19	.285	63	2	1	.985
1975—Oakland	Amer.	OF	148	590	86	182	24	7	10	77	.308	305	8	7	.978

Year Club	League	Pos.	G.	AB.	R.	H.	2B.	3B.	HR.	RBI.	B.A.	PO.	A.	E.	F.A.
1976—Oakland†‡	Amer.	●OF	134	490	65	126	20	6	5	53	.257	276	10	●11	.963
1977—Texas§	Amer.	OF	129	521	63	148	31	2	12	68	.284	255	11	6	.978
1978—Tex. x-Chi. y	Amer.	OF	98	356	34	90	16	5	6	33	.253	170	6	8	.957
1979—Chicago	Amer.	OF	131	471	79	132	33	5	13	66	.280	256	7	7	.974
1980—Chicago z	Amer.	OF	32	90	15	26	4	2	1	12	.289	41	1	3	.933
1980—New York a	Nat.	OF	79	284	38	78	16	4	10	42	.275	123	12	3	.978
1981—Atlanta b	Nat.	OF	85	320	37	93	22	3	5	37	.291	145	5	1	.993
1982—Atlanta	Nat.	OF	150	563	94	150	24	6	16	80	.266	221	9	12	.950
1983—Atlanta	Nat.	OF	134	496	75	138	24	8	9	44	.278	218	8	6	.974
1984—Atlanta c	Nat.	OF	120	416	62	119	21	2	17	61	.286	170	4	6	.967
1985—Atlanta	Nat.	OF	122	398	62	110	14	6	15	43	.276	122	3	5	.962
1986—Atlanta de	Nat.	OF	40	137	17	37	11	0	5	14	.270	44	1	2	.957
1986—New York f	Amer.	OF	54	135	19	32	5	0	6	16	.237	66	0	1	.985
American League Totals—8 Years			799	2874	377	799	143	32	53	344	.278	1432	45	44	.971
National League Totals—7 Years			730	2614	385	725	132	29	77	321	.277	1043	42	35	.969
Major League Totals—13 Years			1529	5488	762	1524	275	61	130	665	.278	2475	87	79	.970

Signed as free agent by Oakland A's organization, July 7, 1972.

†On disabled list, August 16 to September 1, 1976.

‡Traded to Texas Rangers for Pitcher Jim Umbarger, Infielder Rodney Scott and cash estimated at $100,000, March 26, 1977.

§On disabled list, May 27 to June 11, 1977.

xTraded with Outfielder Rusty Torres and cash to Chicago White Sox for Outfielder Bobby Bonds, May 16, 1978.

yOn disabled list, May 22 to June 16, 1978.

zTraded to New York Mets for Pitcher Jesse Anderson, June 7, 1980.

aGranted free agency, October 31, 1980; signed by Atlanta Braves, November 15, 1980.

bOn disabled list, June 5 to August 9, 1981.

cOn disabled list, May 30 to June 14, 1984.

dOn disabled list, May 18 to June 16, 1986.

eTraded with Shortstop Paul Zuvella to New York Yankees for Outfielder Ken Griffey, June 30, 1986.

fGranted free agency, November 12, 1986; re-signed by Yankees, December 7, 1986.

CHAMPIONSHIP SERIES RECORD

Year Club	League	Pos.	G.	AB.	R.	H.	2B.	3B.	HR.	RBI.	B.A.	PO.	A.	E.	F.A.
1974—Oakland	Amer.	OF-PH	4	11	1	3	1	0	0	0	.273	11	0	0	1.000
1975—Oakland	Amer.	OF-DH	3	12	1	3	1	0	0	1	.250	1	0	2	.333
1982—Atlanta	Nat.	OF	3	9	0	3	0	0	0	0	.333	5	1	0	1.000
Championship Series Totals—3 Years			10	32	2	9	2	0	0	1	.281	17	1	2	.900

WORLD SERIES RECORD

Tied World Series record for most positions played, Series (3), 1974 (all three outfield positions).

Year Club	League	Pos.	G.	AB.	R.	H.	2B.	3B.	HR.	RBI.	B.A.	PO.	A.	E.	F.A.
1974—Oakland	Amer.	OF-PH	5	7	1	4	0	0	0	0	.571	3	0	0	1.000

ALL-STAR GAME RECORD

Year League	Pos.	AB.	R.	H.	2B.	3B.	HR.	RBI.	B.A.	PO.	A.	E.	F.A.
1975—American	PR-OF	1	0	1	0	0	0	0	1.000	1	0	0	1.000
1984—National	OF	2	0	1	1	0	0	0	.500	1	0	0	1.000
All-Star Game Totals—2 Years		3	0	2	1	0	0	0	.667	2	0	0	1.000

RONALD WASHINGTON
(Ron)

Born April 29, 1952, at New Orleans, La.
Height, 5.11. Weight, 160.
Throws and bats righthanded.
Attended Manatee Junior College, Bradenton, Fla.

Major League stolen bases: 1977 (1), 1981 (4), 1982 (3), 1983 (10), 1984 (1), 1985 (5), 1986 (1). Total—25.

Year Club	League	Pos.	G.	AB.	R.	H.	2B.	3B.	HR.	RBI.	B.A.	PO.	A.	E.	F.A.
1971—Sara. Royals†	Gulf C.	C	38	127	29	37	2	●6	1	23	.291	★213	23	3	★.987
1972—Waterloo	Midw.	C-OF-3B	76	241	37	55	3	1	1	30	.228	424	48	8	.983
1973—Waterloo	Midw.	SS	85	289	35	80	13	5	6	34	.277	130	198	29	.919
1974—San Jose‡	Calif.	2B-SS-C	109	425	49	104	16	3	2	41	.245	233	266	33	.938
1975—Jacksonville§	South.	2-3-S-1	96	267	22	61	7	1	0	20	.228	133	199	22	.938
1976—Waterbury x	East.	3B-2B	115	436	61	128	9	10	4	32	.294	170	249	26	.942
1977—San Antonio y	Texas	SS	39	158	24	44	8	4	0	13	.278	78	92	12	.934
1977—Albuquerque	P. C.	SS	85	359	71	116	17	8	8	59	.323	204	250	★33	.932
1977—Los Angeles	Nat.	SS	10	19	4	7	0	0	0	1	.368	4	14	3	.857
1978—Albuquerque z	P. C.	3B	31	122	26	42	10	3	5	32	.344	23	58	8	.910
1979—Aguila	Mex.	3B	42	165	22	43	3	3	0	14	.261	35	96	10	.929
1979—Tidewater a	Int.	3B-SS	83	273	18	72	13	4	1	26	.264	77	157	13	.947
1980—Toledo	Int.	3B-2B-SS	114	407	62	117	●31	5	3	36	.287	131	268	30	.930
1981—Toledo	Int.	3B-OF-SS	138	★544	84	157	27	8	15	54	.289	130	287	26	.941
1981—Minnesota	Amer.	SS-OF	28	84	8	19	3	1	0	5	.226	64	80	8	.947
1982—Minnesota	Amer.	SS-2B-3B	119	451	48	122	17	6	5	39	.271	201	269	13	.973
1983—Minnesota	Amer.	SS-2B-3B	99	317	28	78	7	3	4	26	.246	140	246	16	.960
1984—Minnesota	Amer.	SS-2B-3B	88	197	25	58	11	5	3	23	.294	77	134	4	.981
1985—Minnesota	Amer.	S-2-3-1	70	135	24	37	6	4	1	14	.274	55	100	7	.957

Year	Club	League	Pos.	G.	AB.	R.	H.	2B.	3B.	HR.	RBI.	B.A.	PO.	A.	E.	F.A.
1986—Minnesota	Amer.	2B-SS-3B	48	74	15	19	3	0	4	11	.257	12	20	2	.941
1986—Toledo	Int.	2B-3B-SS	49	198	22	53	6	1	3	19	.268	79	112	9	.955
National League Totals—1 Year			10	19	4	7	0	0	0	1	.368	4	14	3	.857
American League Totals—6 Years			452	1258	148	333	47	19	17	118	.265	549	849	50	.965
Major League Totals—7 Years			462	1277	152	340	47	19	17	119	.266	553	863	53	.964

Signed as free agent by Kansas City Royals' organization, July 17, 1970.
†On military list, September 30, 1971 through March 3, 1972.
‡On temporary inactive list, July 4 to July 25, 1974.
§On disabled list, June 19 to June 30, 1975.
xTraded to Los Angeles Dodgers' organization for Catcher Steve Patchin, November 2, 1976.
yOn temporary inactive list, April 12 to April 22, 1977.
zOn disabled list, May 12 to June 26 and July 17 to September 10, 1978.
aTraded to Minnesota Twins' organization for Infielder Wayne Caughey, March 26, 1980.

U. L. WASHINGTON

Born October 27, 1953, at Atoka, Okla.
Height, 5.11. Weight, 175.
Throws right and bats left and righthanded.
Attended Murray State College, Tishomingo, Okla.

Switch-hit home runs in one game, September 21, 1979.
Major League stolen bases: 1977 (1), 1978 (12), 1979 (10), 1980 (20), 1981 (10), 1982 (23), 1983 (40), 1984 (4), 1985 (6), 1986 (6). Total—132.
Led American Association batters in strikeouts with 145 in 1975.
Led Appalachian League in sacrifice flies with 8 in 1973.
Led Appalachian League shortstops in double plays with 29 in 1973.

Year	Club	League	Pos.	G.	AB.	R.	H.	2B.	3B.	HR.	RBI.	B.A.	PO.	A.	E.	F.A.
1973—Kingsport	Appal.	SS	68	244	47	69	14	4	5	51	.283	89	176	36	.880
1974—San Jose	Calif.	SS-2B	68	245	38	61	9	2	6	21	.249	81	201	34	.892
1974—Jacksonville	South.	SS	47	167	29	43	11	1	2	20	.257	71	172	17	.935
1975—Omaha	A. A.	SS	128	475	60	113	11	8	5	37	.238	195	367	★46	.924
1976—Omaha†	A. A.	SS	30	120	20	30	3	2	4	16	.250	48	102	15	.909
1977—Omaha	A. A.	★SS-2B	131	★514	82	131	13	10	2	37	.255	218	391	★48	.927
1977—Kansas City	Amer.	SS	10	20	0	4	1	1	0	1	.200	13	21	5	.872
1978—Kansas City	Amer.	SS-2B	69	129	10	34	2	1	0	9	.264	79	92	9	.950
1979—Kansas City	Amer.	SS-2B-3B	101	268	32	68	12	5	2	25	.254	174	243	18	.959
1980—Kansas City	Amer.	SS	153	549	79	150	16	11	6	53	.273	237	467	32	.957
1981—Kansas City	Amer.	SS	98	339	40	77	19	1	2	29	.227	135	297	12	.973
1982—Kansas City‡	Amer.	SS	119	437	64	125	19	3	10	60	.286	173	371	22	.961
1983—Kansas City	Amer.	SS	144	547	76	129	19	6	5	41	.236	201	448	★36	.947
1984—Kansas City§x	Amer.	SS	63	170	18	38	6	0	1	10	.224	81	166	10	.961
1985—Montreal yz	Nat.	2B-SS-3B	68	193	24	48	9	4	1	17	.249	76	130	7	.967
1986—Hawaii	P. C.	SS	36	120	27	29	3	2	2	15	.242	54	90	15	.906
1986—Pittsburgh a	Nat.	SS-2B	72	135	14	27	0	4	0	10	.200	50	97	8	.948
American League Totals—8 Years			757	2459	319	625	94	28	26	228	.254	1093	2105	144	.957
National League Totals—2 Years			140	328	38	75	9	8	1	27	.229	126	227	15	.959
Major League Totals—10 Years			897	2787	357	700	103	36	27	255	.251	1219	2332	159	.957

Signed as free agent by Kansas City Royals' organization, August 4, 1972.
†On disabled list, May 21 to September 6, 1976.
‡On disabled list, May 3 to May 26, 1982.
§On disabled list, March 28 to April 12, July 18 to August 2 and August 16, 1984 through remainder of season.
xTraded to Montreal Expos for Outfielder Ken Baker and Pitcher Mike Kinnunen, January 7, 1985.
yOn disabled list, June 8 to June 24 and June 28 to July 18, 1985.
zGranted free agency, November 12, 1985; signed by Pittsburgh Pirates' organization, April 24, 1986.
aReleased, November 7, 1986.

DIVISION SERIES RECORD

Year	Club	League	Pos.	G.	AB.	R.	H.	2B.	3B.	HR.	RBI.	B.A.	PO.	A.	E.	F.A.
1981—Kansas City	Amer.	SS	3	9	0	2	0	0	0	0	.222	7	11	1	.947

CHAMPIONSHIP SERIES RECORD

Year	Club	League	Pos.	G.	AB.	R.	H.	2B.	3B.	HR.	RBI.	B.A.	PO.	A.	E.	F.A.
1980—Kansas City	Amer.	SS	3	11	1	4	1	0	0	1	.364	5	7	0	1.000
1984—Kansas City	Amer.	PH-PR	2	1	0	0	0	0	0	0	.000	0	0	0	.000
Championship Series Totals—2 Years			5	12	1	4	1	0	0	1	.333	5	7	0	1.000

WORLD SERIES RECORD

Year	Club	League	Pos.	G.	AB.	R.	H.	2B.	3B.	HR.	RBI.	B.A.	PO.	A.	E.	F.A.
1980—Kansas City	Amer.	SS	6	22	1	6	0	0	0	2	.273	8	20	1	.966

MARK THOMAS WASINGER

Born August 4, 1961, at Monterey, Calif.
Height, 6.00. Weight, 165.
Throws and bats righthanded.
Attended Old Dominion University, Norfolk, Va.

Led Texas League in sacrifice hits with 16 in 1984.
Led Texas League second basemen in fielding percentage with .977 in 1984.

Named second baseman on The Sporting News College Baseball All-America Team, 1983.

Year Club	League	Pos.	G.	AB.	R.	H.	2B.	3B.	HR.	RBI.	B.A.	PO.	A.	E.	F.A.
1982—Reno	Calif.	2B	60	220	36	70	18	0	2	32	.318	108	184	9	.970
1983—Reno	Calif.	2B	83	308	46	102	13	5	4	53	.331	164	241	9	.978
1984—Beaumont†	Texas	2B-SS	106	362	54	103	20	0	3	48	.285	220	358	14	.976
1985—Beaumont	Texas	3B-2B-SS	114	411	71	124	13	0	8	52	.302	93	240	22	.938
1986—Las Vegas..............	P. C.	2B-3B	103	378	68	116	22	5	1	34	.307	136	241	11	.972
1986—San Diego	Nat.	3B-2B	3	8	0	0	0	0	0	1	.000	2	2	3	.571
Major League Totals—1 Year..................			3	8	0	0	0	0	0	1	.000	2	2	3	.571

Selected by San Diego Padres' organization in 3rd round of free-agent draft, June 7, 1982.
†On disabled list, May 16 to May 27 and August 31, 1984 through remainder of season.

LEONARD EARL WATTS
(Len)

Born July 21, 1965, at Galveston, Tex.
Height, 6.00. Weight, 160.
Throws and bats lefthanded.

Year Club	League	G.	IP.	W.	L.	Pct.	H.	R.	ER.	SO.	BB.	ERA.
1984—Sarasota Phillies..................	Ap'lachian	7	11⅔	0	0	.000	12	8	6	13	5	4.63
1985—Clearwater	Florida St.	22	71⅔	5	3	.625	56	25	17	57	30	2.13
1985—Reading................................	Eastern	6	31⅓	1	3	.250	39	24	21	27	20	6.03
1986—Reading................................	Eastern	22	114⅔	9	3	.750	106	51	46	86	50	3.61

Signed as a free agent by Philadelphia Phillies' organization, July 2, 1984.

MITCHELL DEAN WEBSTER
(Mitch)

Born May 16, 1959, at Larned, Kan.
Height, 6.01. Weight, 170.
Throws left and bats left and righthanded.

Major League stolen bases: 1985 (15), 1986 (36). Total—51.
Led International League outfielders in double plays with 5 and total chances with 385 in 1982.

Year Club	League	Pos.	G.	AB.	R.	H.	2B.	3B.	HR.	RBI.	B.A.	PO.	A.	E.	F.A.
1977—Lethbridge	Pion.	OF	55	168	45	59	4	0	0	31	.351	81	3	8	.913
1978—Clinton	Midw.	OF	45	157	18	38	3	1	0	9	.242	92	6	7	.933
1978—Lethbridge	Pion.	OF	55	182	58	58	5	1	0	18	.319	77	3	0	*1.000
1979—Clinton†	Midw.	OF	123	473	95	*154	17	7	2	40	*.326	*272	10	10	.966
1980—Syracuse	Int.	OF	49	161	23	35	4	2	1	12	.217	112	3	5	.958
1980—Kinston...................	Carol.	OF	65	258	43	76	7	3	0	28	.295	129	8	5	.965
1981—Knoxville	South.	OF	140	554	89	163	26	6	1	42	.294	317	7	10	.970
1982—Syracuse	Int.	OF	137	513	95	144	21	7	13	68	.281	*367	16	2	*.995
1983—Syracuse	Int.	OF-1B	135	462	77	120	26	8	9	45	.260	266	16	10	.966
1983—Toronto	Amer.	OF	11	11	2	2	0	0	0	0	.182	5	0	0	1.000
1984—Toronto	Amer.	OF-1B	26	22	9	5	2	1	0	4	.227	16	0	2	.889
1984—Syracuse	Int.	OF	95	360	60	108	22	5	3	25	.300	239	7	7	.972
1985—Toronto	Amer.	OF	4	1	0	0	0	0	0	0	.000	0	0	0	.000
1985—Syracuse‡	Int.	OF	47	189	32	52	5	3	3	23	.275	83	10	1	.989
1985—Montreal	Nat.	OF	74	212	32	58	8	2	11	30	.274	133	3	1	.993
1986—Montreal	Nat.	OF	151	576	89	167	31	*13	8	49	.290	325	12	8	.977
American League Totals—3 Years			41	34	11	7	2	1	0	4	.206	21	0	2	.913
National League Totals—2 Years.............			225	788	121	225	39	15	19	79	.286	458	15	9	.981
Major League Totals—4 Years.................			266	822	132	232	41	16	19	83	.282	479	15	11	.978

Selected by Los Angeles Dodgers' organization in 23rd round of free-agent draft, June 7, 1977.
†Drafted by Syracuse (Toronto Blue Jays' organization), December 4, 1979.
‡Traded to Montreal Expos for a player to be named later, June 22, 1985; Toronto Blue Jays' organization acquired Pitcher Cliff Young to complete deal, September 10, 1985.

WILLIAM EDWARD WEGMAN
(Bill)

Born December 19, 1962, at Cincinnati, O.
Height, 6.05. Weight, 200.
Throws and bats righthanded.

Led Pacific Coast League in home runs allowed with 21 in 1985.
Led California League in balks with 5 and tied for lead in complete games with 15 and shutouts with 4 in 1983.

Year Club	League	G.	IP.	W.	L.	Pct.	H.	R.	ER.	SO.	BB.	ERA.
1981—Butte	Pioneer	14	82	6	5	.545	94	51	38	47	44	4.17
1982—Beloit	Midwest	25	179⅔	12	6	.667	176	77	56	129	38	2.81
1983—Stockton....................................	California	24	186⅔	*16	5	.762	149	33	27	135	45	*1.30
1984—El Paso	Texas	10	64	4	5	.444	62	25	19	42	15	2.67
1984—Vancouver†	P. Coast	6	27⅔	0	3	.000	30	11	6	16	8	1.95
1985—Vancouver..................................	P. Coast	28	188	10	11	.476	187	93	84	113	52	4.02
1985—Milwaukee..................................	American	3	17⅔	2	0	1.000	17	8	7	6	3	3.57
1986—Milwaukee‡...............................	American	35	198⅓	5	12	.294	217	120	113	82	43	5.13
Major League Totals—2 Years.............................		38	216	7	12	.368	234	128	120	88	46	5.00

Selected by Milwaukee Brewers' organization in 5th round of free-agent draft, June 8, 1981.
†On disabled list, June 18 to August 11, 1984.
‡Appeared in two games as a pinch-runner.

ROBERT LYNN WELCH
(Bob)

Born November 3, 1956, at Detroit, Mich.
Height, 6.03. Weight, 190.
Throws and bats righthanded.
Attended Eastern Michigan University, Ypsilanti, Mich.

Major League saves: 1978 (3), 1979 (5). Total—8.

Year Club	League	G.	IP.	W.	L.	Pct.	H.	R.	ER.	SO.	BB.	ERA.
1977—San Antonio	Texas	14	71	4	5	.444	94	44	35	56	17	4.44
1978—Albuquerque	P. Coast	11	69	5	1	.833	72	33	29	53	19	3.78
1978—Los Angeles	National	23	111	7	4	.636	92	28	25	66	26	2.03
1979—Los Angeles	National	25	81	5	6	.455	82	42	36	64	32	4.00
1980—Los Angeles	National	32	214	14	9	.609	190	85	78	141	79	3.28
1981—Los Angeles	National	23	141	9	5	.643	141	56	54	88	41	3.45
1982—Los Angeles†	National	36	235⅔	16	11	.593	199	94	88	176	81	3.36
1983—Los Angeles	National	31	204	15	12	.556	164	73	60	156	72	2.65
1984—Los Angeles	National	31	178⅔	13	13	.500	191	86	75	126	58	3.78
1985—Los Angeles‡	National	23	167⅓	14	4	.778	141	49	43	96	35	2.31
1985—Vero Beach	Florida St.	3	17	0	0	.000	15	4	4	9	1	2.12
1986—Los Angeles	National	33	235⅔	7	13	.350	227	95	86	183	55	3.28
Major League Totals—9 Years		257	1568⅓	100	77	.565	1427	608	545	1096	479	3.13

Selected by Chicago Cubs' organization in 14th round of free-agent draft, June 5, 1974.
Selected by Los Angeles Dodgers' organization in 1st round (20th player selected) of free-agent draft, June 7, 1977.
†Appeared in one game as outfielder with no chances.
‡On disabled list, April 29 to June 5, 1985; included rehabilitation disability assignment to Vero Beach, May 21 to June 5, 1985.

DIVISION SERIES RECORD

Year Club	League	G.	IP.	W.	L.	Pct.	H.	R.	ER.	SO.	BB.	ERA.
1981—Los Angeles	National	1	1	0	0	.000	0	0	0	1	1	0.00

CHAMPIONSHIP SERIES RECORD

Tied Championship Series record for most bases on balls, inning (4), October 12, 1985 (first inning).

Year Club	League	G.	IP.	W.	L.	Pct.	H.	R.	ER.	SO.	BB.	ERA.
1978—Los Angeles	National	1	4⅓	1	0	1.000	2	1	1	5	0	2.08
1981—Los Angeles	National	3	1⅔	0	0	.000	2	1	1	2	0	5.40
1983—Los Angeles	National	1	1⅓	0	1	.000	0	2	1	0	2	6.75
1985—Los Angeles	National	1	2⅔	0	1	.000	5	4	2	2	6	6.75
Championship Series Totals—4 Years		6	10	1	2	.333	9	8	5	9	8	4.50

WORLD SERIES RECORD

Year Club	League	G.	IP.	W.	L.	Pct.	H.	R.	ER.	SO.	BB.	ERA.
1978—Los Angeles	National	3	4⅓	0	1	.000	4	3	3	6	2	6.23
1981—Los Angeles	National	1	0	0	0	.000	3	2	2	0	1	....
World Series Totals—2 Years		4	4⅓	0	1	.000	7	5	5	6	3	10.38

ALL-STAR GAME RECORD

Year League	IP.	W.	L.	Pct.	H.	R.	ER.	SO.	BB.	ERA.
1980—National	3	0	0	.000	5	2	2	4	1	6.00

BRAD EUGENE WELLMAN

Born August 17, 1959, at Lodi, Calif.
Height, 6.00. Weight, 165.
Throws and bats righthanded.
Attended Chabot College, Hayward, Calif.

Major League stolen bases: 1983 (5), 1984 (10), 1985 (5). Total—20.

Year Club	League	Pos.	G.	AB.	R.	H.	2B.	3B.	HR.	RBI.	B.A.	PO.	A.	E.	F.A.
1979—Sarasota Royals	Gulf C.	SS	48	170	24	44	6	0	2	24	.259	79	159	20	.922
1980—Fort Myers	Fla. St.	2B-SS	105	390	67	130	15	7	1	39	.333	175	301	27	.946
1981—Jacksonville	South	2B-SS	135	498	72	131	25	2	6	47	.263	286	368	25	.963
1982—Omaha†	A. A.	2B	6	24	5	7	3	0	1	3	.292	14	23	0	1.000
1982—Phoenix	P. C.	2B-3B	102	339	64	110	19	7	4	42	.324	201	257	14	.970
1982—San Francisco	Nat.	2B	6	4	1	1	0	0	0	0	.250	0	1	0	1.000
1983—Phoenix	P. C.	2B-SS	45	167	32	52	6	4	2	28	.311	79	123	4	.981
1983—San Francisco	Nat.	2B-SS	82	182	15	39	3	0	1	16	.214	94	167	9	.967
1984—Phoenix	P. C.	2B	43	159	26	47	8	1	0	11	.296	91	123	6	.973
1984—San Francisco	Nat.	2B-SS-3B	93	265	23	60	9	1	2	25	.226	151	258	11	.974
1985—San Francisco‡	Nat.	2B-3B-SS	71	174	16	41	11	1	0	16	.236	66	107	9	.951
1986—San Francisco	Nat.	SS-3B-2B	12	13	0	2	0	0	0	1	.154	3	10	0	1.000
1986—Phoenix§	P. C.	2B-SS-3B	79	262	31	74	17	1	2	30	.282	145	221	13	.966
Major League Totals—5 Years			264	638	55	143	23	2	3	58	.224	314	543	29	.967

Signed as free agent by Kansas City Royals' organization, August 27, 1978.
†Traded to San Francisco Giants' organization, April 19, 1982, completing deal in which San Francisco traded Pitchers Vida Blue and Bob Tufts to Kansas City Royals for Pitchers Atlee Hammaker, Craig Chamberlain and Renie Martin and a player to be named later, March 30, 1982.
‡On disabled list, May 30 to June 28, 1985.
§Granted free agency, October 15, 1986; signed by Albuquerque (Los Angeles Dodgers' organization), December 5, 1986.

CHRISTOPHER CHARLES WELSH
(Chris)

Born April 14, 1955, at Wilmington, Del.
Height, 6.02. Weight, 185.
Throws and bats lefthanded.
Received bachelor of arts degree in marketing from
University of South Florida, Tampa, Fla.

Led New York-Pennsylvania League in complete games with 12, shutouts with 4 and tied for lead in games started by pitchers with 14 in 1977.
Tied for Eastern League lead in wild pitches with 18 and balks with 2 in 1978.

Year	Club	League	G.	IP.	W.	L.	Pct.	H.	R.	ER.	SO.	BB.	ERA.
1977—Oneonta	NYP	14	*112	8	5	.615	77	40	31	*125	54	2.49
1978—Fort Lauderdale	Florida St.	2	15	1	1	.500	5	5	1	13	10	0.60
1978—West Haven	Eastern	24	164	11	9	.550	159	88	63	115	68	3.46
1979—Columbus	Int'national	36	114	8	4	.667	120	67	59	79	48	4.70
1980—Columbus†	Int'national	29	158	9	12	.429	134	78	48	84	68	2.73
1981—San Diego	National	22	124	6	7	.462	122	55	52	51	41	3.77
1982—San Diego‡	National	28	139⅓	8	8	.500	146	88	76	48	63	4.91
1983—San Diego§-Montreal	National	23	59	0	2	.000	59	35	29	22	20	4.42
1983—Wichita	Am. Assoc.	11	56⅔	3	6	.333	72	47	44	27	29	6.99
1984—Indianapolis x	Am. Assoc.	29	167⅔	13	4	.765	165	63	56	87	80	*3.01
1985—Texas	American	25	76⅓	2	5	.286	101	40	35	31	25	4.13
1985—Oklahoma City y	Am. Assoc.	8	52	6	1	.857	49	26	26	22	27	4.50
1986—Denver	Am. Assoc.	10	53⅔	5	2	.714	58	26	24	18	14	4.02
1986—Cincinnati za	National	24	139⅓	6	9	.400	163	79	74	40	40	4.78
National League Totals—4 Years		97	461⅔	20	26	.435	490	257	231	161	164	4.50
American League Totals—1 Year		25	76⅓	2	5	.286	101	40	35	31	25	4.13
Major League Totals—5 Years		122	538	22	31	.415	591	297	266	192	189	4.45

Selected by New York Yankees' organization in 24th round of free-agent draft, June 8, 1976.
Selected by New York Yankees' organization in 21st round of free-agent draft, June 7, 1977.
†Traded with Outfielders Ruppert Jones and Joe Lefebvre and Pitcher Tim Lollar to San Diego Padres for Outfielder Jerry Mumphrey and Pitcher John Pacella, April 1, 1981.
‡On disabled list, March 23 to April 27, 1982.
§Sold to Montreal Expos, May 4, 1983.
xTraded to Texas Rangers' organization for First Baseman Dave Hostetler, November 7, 1984.
yReleased, November 9, 1985; signed by Cincinnati Reds' organization, April 4, 1986.
zOn disabled list, July 18 to August 8, 1986.
aReleased, November 11, 1986.

DAVID LEE WEST

Born September 1, 1964, at Memphis, Tenn.
Height, 6.06. Weight, 205.
Throws and bats lefthanded.

Won 3-0 no-hit victory against Spartanburg, August 14, 1985.
Led New York-Pennsylvania League in wild pitches with 16 in 1984.

Year	Club	League	G.	IP.	W.	L.	Pct.	H.	R.	ER.	SO.	BB.	ERA.
1983—Sarasota Mets	Gulf Coast	12	53⅔	2	4	.333	41	28	17	56	52	2.85
1984—Columbia	S. Atlantic	12	60⅔	3	5	.375	41	47	42	60	68	6.23
1984—Little Falls	NYP	13	62	6	4	.600	43	35	23	79	62	3.34
1985—Columbia	S. Atlantic	26	150	10	9	.526	105	97	76	194	*111	4.56
1986—Lynchburg	Carolina	13	75	1	6	.143	76	50	43	70	53	5.16

Selected by New York Mets' organization in 4th round of free-agent draft, June 6, 1983.

MATTHEW TERRY WEST
(Matt)

Born January 13, 1960, at Santa Monica, Calif.
Height, 6.04. Weight, 195.
Throws right and bats left and righthanded.
Attended Cabrillo College, Aptos, Calif. and received bachelor of arts degree
in political science from California State University, Long Beach, Calif. in 1981.

Pitched 1-0 no-hit loss against Jacksonville, May 21, 1982.
Tied for Southern League lead in balks with 3 in 1982.

Year	Club	League	G.	IP.	W.	L.	Pct.	H.	R.	ER.	SO.	BB.	ERA.
1981—Bradenton Braves	Gulf Coast	9	44	3	4	.429	32	19	13	44	24	2.66
1982—Savannah†	Southern	22	115⅔	6	8	.429	97	70	59	91	91	4.59
1983—Durham‡	Carolina	12	65⅓	2	5	.286	66	51	31	42	48	4.27
1984—Greenville	Southern	26	145	10	7	.588	143	81	72	102	75	4.47
1985—Richmond§	Int'national	23	133⅓	8	9	.471	122	64	55	73	64	3.71
1986—Richmond x	Int'national					(Did not play)						

Signed as free agent by Atlanta Braves' organization, June 29, 1981.
†On disabled list, June 1 to July 1, 1982.
‡On disabled list, July 16, 1983 through remainder of season.
§On disabled list, June 8 to July 1, 1985.
xOn disabled list, April 11, 1986 through entire season.

LOUIS RODMAN WHITAKER
(Lou)

Born May 12, 1957, at Brooklyn, N.Y.
Height, 5.11. Weight, 160.
Throws right and bats lefthanded.

Major League stolen bases: 1977 (2), 1978 (7), 1979 (20), 1980 (8), 1981 (5), 1982 (11), 1983 (17), 1984 (6), 1985 (6), 1986 (13). Total—95.

Led American League second basemen in total chances with 811 and double plays with 120 in 1982.
Led Florida State League second basemen in double plays with 30 in 1976.
Named second baseman on THE SPORTING NEWS American League All-Star Team, 1983 and 1984.
Named second baseman on THE SPORTING NEWS American League All-Star fielding team, 1983 through 1985.
Named second baseman on THE SPORTING NEWS American League Silver Slugger team, 1983 through 1985.
Named American League Rookie of the Year by Baseball Writers' Association of America, 1978.
Named Florida State League Most Valuable Player, 1976.

Year Club	League	Pos.	G.	AB.	R.	H.	2B.	3B.	HR.	RBI.	B.A.	PO.	A.	E.	F.A.
1975—Bristol	Appal.	3B-SS	42	114	17	27	6	1	1	17	.237	38	82	16	.882
1976—Lakeland	Fla. St.	3B	124	343	*70	129	12	5	1	62	.297	*99	*267	*30	*.924
1977—Montgomery†	South.	2B	107	396	*81	111	13	4	3	48	.280	208	285	15	.970
1977—Detroit	Amer.	2B	11	32	5	8	1	0	0	2	.250	17	18	0	1.000
1978—Detroit	Amer.	2B	139	484	71	138	12	7	3	58	.285	301	458	17	.978
1979—Detroit‡	Amer.	2B	127	423	75	121	14	8	3	42	.286	280	369	9	.986
1980—Detroit	Amer.	2B	145	477	68	111	19	1	1	45	.233	340	428	12	.985
1981—Detroit	Amer.	2B	●109	335	48	88	14	4	5	36	.263	227	*354	9	.985
1982—Detroit	Amer.	2B	152	560	76	160	22	8	15	65	.286	331	*470	10	*.988
1983—Detroit	Amer.	2B	161	643	94	206	40	6	12	72	.320	299	447	13	.983
1984—Detroit	Amer.	2B	143	558	90	161	25	1	13	56	.289	290	405	15	.979
1985—Detroit	Amer.	2B	152	609	102	170	29	8	21	73	.279	314	414	11	.985
1986—Detroit	Amer.	2B	144	584	95	157	26	6	20	73	.269	276	421	11	.984
Major League Totals—10 Years			1283	4705	724	1320	202	49	93	522	.281	2475	3784	107	.983

Selected by Detroit Tigers' organization in 5th round of free-agent draft, June 4, 1975.
†On disabled list, May 3 to May 14, 1977.
‡On disabled list, June 13 to June 28, 1979.

CHAMPIONSHIP SERIES RECORD

Year Club	League	Pos.	G.	AB.	R.	H.	2B.	3B.	HR.	RBI.	B.A.	PO.	A.	E.	F.A.
1984—Detroit	Amer.	2B	3	14	3	2	0	0	0	0	.143	5	6	0	1.000

WORLD SERIES RECORD

Tied World Series record for most runs, five-game Series (6), 1984.

Year Club	League	Pos.	G.	AB.	R.	H.	2B.	3B.	HR.	RBI.	B.A.	PO.	A.	E.	F.A.
1984—Detroit	Amer.	2B	5	18	6	5	2	0	0	0	.278	15	18	0	1.000

ALL-STAR GAME RECORD

Year League	Pos.	AB.	R.	H.	2B.	3B.	HR.	RBI.	B.A.	PO.	A.	E.	F.A.
1983—American	PH-2B	1	1	1	0	1	0	2	1.000	1	0	0	1.000
1984—American	2B	3	0	2	1	0	0	0	.667	0	5	0	1.000
1985—American	2B	2	0	0	0	0	0	0	.000	1	1	0	1.000
1986—American	2B	2	1	1	0	0	1	2	.500	0	3	0	1.000
All-Star Game Totals—4 Years		8	2	4	1	1	1	4	.500	2	9	0	1.000

DAVID W. WHITE
(Dave)

Born December 18, 1961, at Olympia Fields, Ill.
Height, 6.04. Weight, 210.
Throws and bats righthanded.
Attended College of St. Francis, Joliet, Ill.

Tied for Gulf Coast League lead in complete games with 3 in 1984.

Year Club	League	G.	IP.	W.	L.	Pct.	H.	R.	ER.	SO.	BB.	ERA.
1984—Niagara Falls	NYP	1	1⅔	0	0	.000	3	3	2	2	2	10.80
1984—Sarasota White Sox	Gulf Coast	13	82⅓	9	3	.750	81	32	23	58	7	2.51
1985—Appleton	Midwest	53	91⅓	9	4	.692	74	23	14	83	22	1.38
1986—Birmingham	Southern	50	128⅔	11	3	.786	120	51	44	69	62	3.08

Selected by Chicago White Sox' organization in 36th round of free-agent draft, June 4, 1984.

DEVON MARKES WHITE

First name pronounced De-VON.

Born December 29, 1962, at Kingston, Jamaica.
Height, 6.01. Weight, 170.
Throws right and bats left and righthanded.

Major League stolen bases: 1985 (3), 1986 (6). Total—9.
Led Pacific Coast League in stolen bases with 42 in 1986.
Led Pacific Coast League outfielders in total chances with 339 in 1986.
Led California League outfielders in total chances with 351 in 1984.
Led Midwest League outfielders in total chances with 286 in 1983.

Year Club	League	Pos.	G.	AB.	R.	H.	2B.	3B.	HR.	RBI.	B.A.	PO.	A.	E.	F.A.
1981—Idaho Falls	Pion.	OF-3B-1B	30	106	10	19	2	0	0	10	.179	33	10	3	.935
1982—Danville†	Midw.	OF	57	186	21	40	6	1	1	11	.215	89	3	8	.920
1983—Peoria	Midw.	OF	117	430	69	109	17	6	13	66	.253	267	8	11	.962
1983—Nashua	East.	OF	17	70	11	18	7	2	0	2	.257	37	0	3	.925
1984—Redwood	Calif.	OF	138	520	101	147	25	5	7	55	.283	*322	16	13	.963
1985—Midland	Texas	OF	70	260	52	77	10	4	4	35	.296	176	10	4	.979
1985—Edmonton	P. C.	OF	66	277	53	70	16	5	4	39	.253	205	6	2	.991
1985—California	Amer.	OF	21	7	7	1	0	0	0	0	.143	10	1	0	1.000
1986—Edmonton‡	P. C.	OF	112	461	84	134	25	10	14	60	.291	317	●16	6	.982
1986—California	Amer.	OF	29	51	8	12	1	1	1	3	.235	49	0	2	.961
Major League Totals—2 Years			50	58	15	13	1	1	1	3	.224	59	1	2	.968

Selected by California Angels' organization in 6th round of free-agent draft, June 8, 1981.
†On suspended list, June 11 to June 12 and July 19, 1982 through remainder of season.
‡On disabled list, May 12 to May 22, 1986.

CHAMPIONSHIP SERIES RECORD

Year Club	League	Pos.	G.	AB.	R.	H.	2B.	3B.	HR.	RBI.	B.A.	PO.	A.	E.	F.A.
1986—California	Amer.	OF-PR	4	2	2	1	0	0	0	0	.500	3	0	0	1.000

FRANK WHITE JR.

Born September 4, 1950, at Greenville, Miss.
Height, 5.11. Weight, 170.
Throws and bats righthanded.
Attended Manatee Junior College, Bradenton, Fla., and
Longview Community College, Lee's Summit, Mo.

Hit for the cycle, September 26, 1979 and August 3, 1982.
Major League stolen bases: 1973 (3), 1974 (3), 1975 (11), 1976 (20), 1977 (23), 1978 (13), 1979 (28), 1980 (19), 1981 (4), 1982 (10), 1983 (13), 1984 (5), 1985 (10), 1986 (4). Total—166.
Led American League second basemen in total chances with 849 in 1985.
Led Gulf Coast League in stolen bases with 18 in 1971.
Led Gulf Coast League shortstops in double plays with 27 in 1971.
Named second baseman on THE SPORTING NEWS American League All-Star Team, 1978.
Named second baseman on THE SPORTING NEWS American League All-Star fielding team, 1977 through 1982 and 1986.
Named second baseman on THE SPORTING NEWS American League Silver Slugger team, 1986.

Year Club	League	Pos.	G.	AB.	R.	H.	2B.	3B.	HR.	RBI.	B.A.	PO.	A.	E.	F.A.
1971—Sara. Royals	Gulf C.	SS	50	158	31	39	6	3	1	21	.247	70	*149	17	*.928
1972—San Jose	Calif.	SS	49	187	44	55	7	2	10	26	.294	77	138	14	.939
1972—Jacksonville	South.	SS	91	333	34	84	12	2	2	23	.252	124	306	31	.933
1973—Omaha	A. A.	2B-SS	86	348	49	92	19	2	4	32	.264	163	221	21	.948
1973—Kansas City	Amer.	SS-2B	51	139	20	31	6	1	0	5	.223	71	121	12	.941
1974—Kansas City	Amer.	2B-SS-3B	99	204	19	45	6	3	1	18	.221	119	189	12	.963
1975—Kansas City	Amer.	2-S-3-C	111	304	43	76	10	2	7	36	.250	182	275	12	.974
1976—Kansas City	Amer.	2B-SS	152	446	39	102	17	6	2	46	.229	296	479	23	.971
1977—Kansas City	Amer.	*2B-SS	152	474	59	116	21	5	5	20	.245	310	437	8	*.989
1978—Kansas City	Amer.	2B	143	461	66	127	24	6	7	50	.275	325	385	16	.978
1979—Kansas City†	Amer.	2B	127	467	73	124	26	4	10	48	.266	317	332	12	.982
1980—Kansas City	Amer.	2B	154	560	70	148	23	4	7	60	.264	395	448	10	.988
1981—Kansas City	Amer.	2B	94	364	35	91	17	1	9	38	.250	226	263	6	.988
1982—Kansas City	Amer.	2B	145	524	71	156	45	6	11	56	.298	*361	389	*17	.978
1983—Kansas City	Amer.	2B	146	549	52	143	35	6	11	77	.260	*390	442	8	*.990
1984—Kansas City‡	Amer.	2B	129	479	58	130	22	5	17	56	.271	299	425	11	.985
1985—Kansas City	Amer.	2B	149	563	62	140	25	1	22	69	.249	342	*490	*17	.980
1986—Kansas City	Amer.	2B-SS-3B	151	566	76	154	37	3	22	84	.272	317	441	10	.987
Major League Totals—14 Years			1803	6100	743	1583	314	53	131	693	.260	3950	5116	174	.981

Signed as free agent by Kansas City Royals' organization, July 2, 1970.
†On disabled list, May 9 to June 11, 1979.
‡On disabled list, July 6 to July 21, 1984.

DIVISION SERIES RECORD

Year Club	League	Pos.	G.	AB.	R.	H.	2B.	3B.	HR.	RBI.	B.A.	PO.	A.	E.	F.A.
1981—Kansas City	Amer.	2B	3	11	1	2	0	0	0	0	.182	5	6	1	.917

CHAMPIONSHIP SERIES RECORD

Year Club	League	Pos.	G.	AB.	R.	H.	2B.	3B.	HR.	RBI.	B.A.	PO.	A.	E.	F.A.
1976—Kansas City	Amer.	2B-PR	4	8	2	1	0	0	0	0	.125	6	11	0	1.000
1977—Kansas City	Amer.	2B	5	18	1	5	1	0	0	2	.278	13	16	0	1.000
1978—Kansas City	Amer.	2B	4	13	1	3	0	0	0	2	.231	9	12	0	1.000
1980—Kansas City	Amer.	2B	3	11	3	6	1	0	1	3	.545	9	10	1	.950
1984—Kansas City	Amer.	2B	3	11	1	1	0	0	0	0	.091	7	3	0	1.000
1985—Kansas City	Amer.	2B	7	25	1	5	0	0	0	3	.200	9	28	0	1.000
Championship Series Totals—6 Years			26	86	9	21	2	0	1	10	.244	53	80	1	.993

WORLD SERIES RECORD

Tied World Series records for fewest runs, Series (0), 1980; most at-bats, nine-inning game, no hits (5), October 18, 1980; most unassisted double plays by second baseman, game (1), October 17, 1980; fewest chances accepted, second baseman, game (0), October 20, 1985.

Year Club League	Pos.	G.	AB.	R.	H.	2B.	3B.	HR.	RBI.	B.A.	PO.	A.	E.	F.A.
1980—Kansas City.......... Amer.	2B	6	25	0	2	0	0	0	0	.080	13	21	2	.944
1985—Kansas City.......... Amer.	2B	7	28	4	7	3	0	1	6	.250	10	20	0	1.000
World Series Totals—2 Years		13	53	4	9	3	0	1	6	.170	23	41	2	.970

ALL-STAR GAME RECORD

Tied All-Star Game record for most home runs by pinch-hitter, game (1), July 15, 1986.

Year League	Pos.	AB.	R.	H.	2B.	3B.	HR.	RBI.	B.A.	PO.	A.	E.	F.A.
1978—American	2B	1	0	0	0	0	0	0	.000	1	2	0	1.000
1979—American	2B	2	0	0	0	0	0	0	.000	2	2	0	1.000
1981—American	PR-2B	1	0	0	0	0	0	0	.000	1	0	0	1.000
1982—American	2B	1	0	0	0	0	0	0	.000	2	1	0	1.000
1986—American	PH-2B	2	1	1	0	0	1	1	.500	1	1	0	1.000
All-Star Game Totals—5 Years....................		7	1	1	0	0	1	1	.143	7	6	0	1.000

JEROME CARDELL WHITE
(Jerry)

Born August 23, 1952, at Shirley, Mass.
Height, 5.11. Weight, 172.
Throws right and bats left and righthanded.
Attended City College of San Francisco, San Francisco, Calif.

Year Club League	Pos.	G.	AB.	R.	H.	2B.	3B.	HR.	RBI.	B.A.	PO.	A.	E.	F.A.
1970—Bradenton Expos Gulf C.	OF	55	201	32	58	10	2	1	16	.289	102	5	5	.955
1971—W. Palm Beach.... Fla. St.	OF	130	505	71	132	17	4	2	32	.261	222	4	●13	.946
1972—Quebec City†........ East.	OF	26	56	4	13	1	0	0	2	.232	46	1	0	1.000
1972—W. Palm Beach.... Fla. St.	OF	27	96	13	28	1	1	1	13	.292	63	1	2	.970
1973—Peninsula‡............. Int.	OF	112	360	50	99	10	6	1	30	.275	182	7	5	.974
1974—Quebec City.......... East.	OF	21	69	13	17	2	2	0	5	.246	35	2	1	.974
1974—Memphis................ Int.	OF	77	175	28	45	6	2	3	17	.257	87	5	1	.989
1974—Montreal .... Nat.	OF	9	10	0	4	1	1	0	2	.400	6	0	0	1.000
1975—Memphis................ Int.	OF	98	354	44	105	16	5	10	45	.297	223	6	6	.974
1975—Montreal .... Nat.	OF	39	97	14	29	4	1	2	7	.299	81	1	2	.976
1976—Montreal .... Nat.	OF	114	278	32	68	11	1	2	21	.245	157	4	3	.982
1977—Denver .... A. A.	OF-1B	123	463	92	145	32	9	14	57	.313	235	7	6	.976
1977—Montreal .... Nat.	OF	16	21	4	4	0	0	0	1	.190	5	0	0	1.000
1978—Denver .... A. A.	OF	27	100	22	29	4	0	5	19	.290	53	0	1	.981
1978—Chi.§-Mtl. x .... Nat.	OF	77	146	24	39	6	0	1	10	.267	102	4	2	.981
1979—Montreal .... Nat.	OF	88	138	30	41	7	1	3	18	.297	55	2	1	.983
1980—Montreal .... Nat.	OF	110	214	22	56	9	3	7	23	.262	101	5	6	.946
1981—Montreal .... Nat.	OF	59	119	11	26	5	1	3	11	.218	58	2	3	.952
1982—Montreal y............ Nat.	OF	69	115	13	28	6	1	2	13	.243	40	1	0	1.000
1983—Montreal .... Nat.	OF	40	34	4	5	1	0	0	0	.147	13	0	0	1.000
1983—Wichita z............. A. A.	OF	32	101	18	25	7	2	1	8	.248	45	2	0	1.000
1984—Seibu.................... Japan					Figures unavailable									
1985—Seibu a............. Japan					Figures unavailable									
1986—St. Louis b .... Nat.	OF	25	24	1	3	0	0	1	3	.125	5	0	0	1.000
1986—San Jose c .... Calif.	OF-3B-2B	40	149	21	39	6	6	1	22	.262	45	8	4	.930
Major League Totals—11 Years...............		646	1194	155	303	50	9	21	109	.254	623	19	17	.974

Selected by Montreal Expos' organization in 14th round of free-agent draft, June 4, 1970.
†On temporary inactive list, April 22 to June 24, 1972.
‡On temporary inactive list, July 28 to August 14, 1973.
§Traded to Chicago Cubs, June 23, 1978, completing deal in which Chicago traded Pitcher Woodie Fryman to Montreal Expos for a player to be named later, June 9, 1978.
xTraded with Infielder-Outfielder Rodney Scott to Montreal Expos for Outfielder Sam Mejias, December 14, 1978.
yOn disabled list, June 30 to July 15, 1982.
zGranted free agency, November 7, 1983; signed by Seibu Lions of Japanese baseball for 1984 season.
aSigned by Louisville (St. Louis Cardinals' organization), December 15, 1985.
bReleased, June 12, 1986; signed by San Jose (Independent), July 21, 1986.
cNamed coach in Montreal Expos' organization, November, 1986.

DIVISION SERIES RECORD

Year Club League	Pos.	G.	AB.	R.	H.	2B.	3B.	HR.	RBI.	B.A.	PO.	A.	E.	F.A.
1981—Montreal .... Nat.	OF	5	18	3	3	1	0	0	1	.167	11	0	0	1.000

CHAMPIONSHIP SERIES RECORD

Year Club League	Pos.	G.	AB.	R.	H.	2B.	3B.	HR.	RBI.	B.A.	PO.	A.	E.	F.A.
1981—Montreal .... Nat.	OF	5	16	2	5	1	0	1	3	.313	6	0	0	1.000

TERRY BERTLAND WHITFIELD

Born January 12, 1953, at Blythe, Calif.
Height, 6.01. Weight, 200.
Throws right and bats lefthanded.

Major League stolen bases: 1975 (1), 1977 (2), 1978 (5), 1979 (5), 1980 (4), 1984 (1). Total—18.
Led International League batters in strikeouts with 129 in 1974.
Led Carolina League in total bases with 234 in 1973.
Led Appalachian League in total bases with 125 in 1971.
Tied for International League lead in double plays by outfielders with 3 in 1976.
Named Carolina League Player of the Year, 1973.

Named Appalachian League co-Player of the Year, 1971.

Year Club	League	Pos.	G.	AB.	R.	H.	2B.	3B.	HR.	RBI.	B.A.	PO.	A.	E.	F.A.
1971—Johnson City	Appal.	OF	67	252	42	73	14	4	★10	★43	.290	104	6	●9	.924
1972—Fort Lauderdale	Fla. St.	OF	49	153	21	25	3	5	1	15	.163	57	4	5	.924
1972—Oneonta	NYP	OF	●70	256	★65	70	6	●11	7	47	.273	120	7	3	.977
1973—Kinston	Carol.	OF	129	451	94	151	25	2	●18	81	★.335	197	9	11	.949
1974—Syracuse	Int.	OF	140	499	71	129	25	4	17	71	.259	★345	12	5	.986
1974—New York	Amer.	OF	2	5	0	1	0	0	0	0	.200	0	0	0	.000
1975—Syracuse	Int.	OF	111	390	47	106	24	4	11	69	.272	208	10	10	.956
1975—New York	Amer.	OF	28	81	9	22	1	1	0	7	.272	42	3	1	.978
1976—Syracuse	Int.	OF	●138	★525	81	152	25	6	16	89	.290	208	13	15	.936
1976—New York†	Amer.	OF	1	0	0	0	0	0	0	0	.000	0	0	0	.000
1977—San Francisco	Nat.	OF	114	326	41	93	21	3	7	36	.285	167	4	5	.972
1978—San Francisco	Nat.	OF	149	488	70	141	20	2	10	32	.289	249	7	3	.988
1979—San Francisco	Nat.	OF	133	394	52	113	20	4	5	44	.287	167	10	8	.957
1980—San Francisco‡	Nat.	OF	118	321	38	95	16	2	4	26	.296	140	11	2	.987
1981—Seibu	Pacific	OF	123	469	....	148	....	....	22	100	.316	Figures unavailable			
1982—Seibu	Pacific	OF	122	453	....	123	....	....	25	71	.272	Figures unavailable			
1983—Seibu§	Pacific	OF	129	485	....	135	....	....	38	109	.278	Figures unavailable			
1984—Los Angeles x	Nat.	OF	87	180	15	44	8	0	4	18	.244	76	4	1	.988
1985—Los Angeles	Nat.	OF	79	104	8	27	7	0	3	16	.260	23	2	2	.926
1986—Los Angeles y	Nat.	OF	19	14	0	1	0	0	0	0	.071	1	0	0	1.000
1986—San Jose	Calif.	OF	19	64	18	25	3	0	1	6	.391	38	3	3	.932
American League Totals—3 Years			31	86	9	23	1	1	0	7	.267	42	3	1	.978
National League Totals—7 Years			699	1827	224	514	92	11	33	172	.281	823	38	21	.976
Major League Totals—10 Years			730	1913	233	537	93	12	33	179	.281	865	41	22	.976

Selected by New York Yankees' organization in 1st round (19th player selected) of free-agent draft, June 8, 1971.
†Traded to San Francisco Giants for Second Baseman Marty Perez, March 14, 1977.
‡Sold to Seibu Lions of Japanese baseball, March 4, 1981.
§Signed as free agent by Los Angeles Dodgers, January 13, 1984.
xOn disabled list, August 21 to September 5, 1984.
yReleased, May 24, 1986; signed by San Jose (Independent), July 12, 1986.

CHAMPIONSHIP SERIES RECORD

Year Club	League	Pos.	G.	AB.	R.	H.	2B.	3B.	HR.	RBI.	B.A.	PO.	A.	E.	F.A.
1985—Los Angeles	Nat.	PH	1	0	0	0	0	0	0	0	.000	0	0	0	.000

EDDIE LEE WHITSON
(Ed)

Born May 19, 1955, at Johnson City, Tenn.
Height, 6.03. Weight, 200.
Throws and bats righthanded.

Major League saves: 1978 (4), 1979 (1), 1982 (2), 1983 (1). Total—8.
Led Carolina League in complete games with 16 in 1976.
Led Western Carolinas League in hit batsmen with 15 in 1975.

Year Club	League	G.	IP.	W.	L.	Pct.	H.	R.	ER.	SO.	BB.	ERA.
1974—Bradenton Pirates	Gulf Coast	8	44	1	4	.200	45	28	21	25	15	4.30
1975—Charleston	W. Carol.	24	142	8	★15	.348	140	★96	★80	120	99	5.07
1976—Salem	Carolina	26	★203	●15	9	.625	168	75	57	★186	65	2.53
1977—Columbus	Int'national	26	175	8	13	.381	175	74	65	120	68	3.34
1977—Pittsburgh	National	5	16	1	0	1.000	11	6	6	10	9	3.38
1978—Columbus	Int'national	7	51	2	2	.500	56	25	21	55	10	3.71
1978—Pittsburgh	National	43	74	5	6	.455	66	31	27	64	37	3.28
1979—Pittsburgh†-San Francisco	National	37	158	7	11	.389	151	83	72	93	75	4.10
1980—San Francisco	National	34	212	11	13	.458	222	88	73	90	56	3.10
1981—San Francisco‡	National	22	123	6	9	.400	130	61	55	65	47	4.02
1982—Cleveland§	American	40	107⅔	4	2	.667	91	43	39	61	58	3.26
1983—San Diego x	National	31	144⅓	5	7	.417	143	73	69	81	50	4.30
1983—Las Vegas	P. Coast	3	12	1	0	1.000	15	9	9	11	5	6.75
1984—San Diego y	National	31	189	14	8	.636	181	72	68	103	42	3.24
1985—New York	American	30	158⅔	10	8	.556	201	100	86	89	43	4.88
1986—New York za	American	14	37	5	2	.714	54	37	31	27	23	7.54
1986—San Diego	National	17	75⅓	1	7	.125	85	48	47	46	37	5.59
National League Totals—8 Years		220	992	50	61	.450	989	462	417	552	353	3.78
American League Totals—3 Years		84	303⅓	19	12	.613	346	180	156	177	124	4.63
Major League Totals—10 Years		304	1295⅓	69	73	.486	1335	642	573	729	477	3.98

Selected by Pittsburgh Pirates' organization in 6th round of free-agent draft, June 5, 1974.
†Traded with Pitchers Fred Breining and Al Holland to San Francisco Giants for Infielders Bill Madlock and Lenny Randle and Pitcher Dave Roberts, June 28, 1979.
‡Traded to Cleveland Indians for Second Baseman Duane Kuiper, November 16, 1981.
§Traded to San Diego Padres for Pitcher Juan Eichelberger and First Baseman-Outfielder Broderick Perkins, November 18, 1982.
xOn disabled list, April 18 to May 28, 1983; included rehabilitation disability assignment to Las Vegas, May 10 to May 28, 1983.
yGranted free agency, November 8, 1984; signed by New York Yankees, December 27, 1984.
zOn disabled list, April 30 to May 21, 1986.
aTraded to San Diego Padres for Pitcher Tim Stoddard, July 9, 1986.

Year Club	League	G.	IP.	W.	L.	Pct.	H.	R.	ER.	SO.	BB.	ERA.
1984—San Diego	National	1	8	1	0	1.000	5	1	1	6	2	1.13

WORLD SERIES RECORD

Year Club	League	G.	IP.	W.	L.	Pct.	H.	R.	ER.	SO.	BB.	ERA.
1984—San Diego	National	1	⅔	0	0	.000	5	3	3	0	0	40.50

ALL-STAR GAME RECORD

Member of National League All-Star Team in 1980; did not play.

LEO ERNEST WHITT
(Ernie)

Born June 13, 1952, Detroit, Mich.
Height, 6.02. Weight, 200.
Throws right and bats lefthanded.
Attended Macomb County Community College, Warren, Mich.

Major League stolen bases: 1980 (1), 1981 (5), 1982 (3), 1983 (1), 1985 (3). Total—13.
Led International League in passed balls with 16 in 1978.
Led Eastern League catchers in fielding percentage with .992 in 1974.
Tied for Carolina League lead in double plays by catchers with 7 in 1973.

Year Club	League	Pos.	G.	AB.	R.	H.	2B.	3B.	HR.	RBI.	B.A.	PO.	A.	E.	F.A.
1972—Williamsport	NYP	1B	1	4	1	2	1	0	0	0	.500	8	1	0	1.000
1972—Winter Haven	Fla. St.	C-1B-OF	31	82	3	15	1	1	0	7	.183	151	14	5	.971
1973—Winston-Salem	Carol.	C-OF-1B	130	424	63	123	23	3	1	50	.290	686	70	15	.980
1974—Bristol	East.	C-OF-1B	111	385	55	96	10	1	9	56	.249	557	50	6	.990
1975—Bristol†	East.	C-OF	82	252	29	64	9	1	2	19	.254	357	36	7	.982
1976—Bristol	East.	C	26	87	12	19	2	3	1	10	.218	127	25	1	.993
1976—Rhode Island	Int.	C-1-O-3	90	304	33	81	16	2	7	42	.266	487	59	9	.984
1976—Boston‡	Amer.	C	8	18	4	4	2	0	1	3	.222	24	0	0	1.000
1977—Charleston	Int.	C-3B	29	94	12	24	6	0	0	7	.255	129	28	7	.957
1977—Toronto§	Amer.	C	23	41	4	7	3	0	0	6	.171	62	4	0	1.000
1978—Syracuse	Int.	C-1B-OF	121	399	50	98	16	3	12	53	.246	673	79	7	.991
1978—Toronto	Amer.	C	2	4	0	0	0	0	0	0	.000	7	1	0	1.000
1979—Syracuse	Int.	*C-OF-3B	114	382	32	95	18	4	7	43	.249	494	69	3	*.995
1980—Toronto	Amer.	C	106	295	23	70	12	2	6	34	.237	436	56	7	.986
1981—Toronto	Amer.	C	74	195	16	46	9	0	1	16	.236	297	46	3	.991
1982—Toronto	Amer.	C	105	284	28	74	14	2	11	42	.261	406	30	8	.982
1983—Toronto	Amer.	C	123	344	53	88	15	2	17	56	.256	554	50	5	.992
1984—Toronto x	Amer.	C	124	315	35	75	12	1	15	46	.238	583	40	4	.994
1985—Toronto	Amer.	C	139	412	55	101	21	2	19	64	.245	649	38	8	.988
1986—Toronto yz	Amer.	C	131	395	48	106	19	2	16	56	.268	709	41	7	.991
Major League Totals—10 Years			835	2303	266	571	107	11	86	323	.248	3727	306	42	.990

Selected by Boston Red Sox' organization in 15th round of free-agent draft, June 6, 1972.
†On disabled list, April 11 to June 13, 1975.
‡Selected by Toronto Blue Jays in American League expansion draft, November 5, 1976.
§On disabled list, August 17 to September 27, 1977.
xOn disabled list, June 16 to July 1, 1984.
yOn disabled list, April 15 to April 30, 1986; included rehabilitation disability assignment to Syracuse, April 28 to April 30, 1986.
zGranted free agency, November 12, 1986.

CHAMPIONSHIP SERIES RECORD

Year Club	League	Pos.	G.	AB.	R.	H.	2B.	3B.	HR.	RBI.	B.A.	PO.	A.	E.	F.A.
1985—Toronto	Amer.	C	7	21	1	4	1	0	0	2	.190	50	3	0	1.000

ALL-STAR GAME RECORD

Year League	Pos.	AB.	R.	H.	2B.	3B.	HR.	RBI.	B.A.	PO.	A.	E.	F.A.
1985—American	C	0	0	0	0	0	0	0	.000	2	0	0	1.000

ALAN ANTHONY WIGGINS

Born February 17, 1958, at Los Angeles, Calif.
Height, 6.02. Weight, 160.
Throws right and bats left and righthanded.
Attended Pasadena City College, Pasadena, Calif.

Tied modern National League record for most stolen bases, game (5), May 17, 1984.
Major League stolen bases: 1981 (2), 1982 (33), 1983 (66), 1984 (70), 1985 (30), 1986 (21). Total—222.
Led National League in caught stealing with 21 in 1984.
Led California League in stolen bases with 120 in 1980.
Tied for Pioneer League lead in sacrifice hits with 5 in 1977.

Year Club	League	Pos.	G.	AB.	R.	H.	2B.	3B.	HR.	RBI.	B.A.	PO.	A.	E.	F.A.
1977—Idaho Falls	Pion.	2B	63	225	64	61	3	1	1	23	.271	137	163	28	.915
1978—Quad Cities†‡	Midw.	2B	49	169	30	34	3	0	1	12	.201	96	130	12	.950
1979—Clinton	Midw.	S-O-1-2-3	95	296	57	76	3	1	0	27	.257	196	198	32	.925
1980—Lodi§	Calif.	O-2-1-S	135	513	108	148	10	5	0	35	.288	365	76	23	.950
1981—Hawaii	P. C.	OF-2B	133	513	97	155	17	8	0	33	.302	234	26	7	.974
1981—San Diego	Nat.	OF	15	14	4	5	0	0	0	0	.357	6	0	2	.750

Year Club	League	Pos.	G.	AB.	R.	H.	2B.	3B.	HR.	RBI.	B.A.	PO.	A.	E.	F.A.
1982—Hawaii	P. C.	OF	19	77	14	24	2	4	1	4	.312	33	4	0	1.000
1982—San Diego x	Nat.	OF-2B	72	254	40	65	3	3	1	15	.256	140	8	5	.967
1983—San Diego	Nat.	OF-1B	144	503	83	139	20	2	0	22	.276	572	35	8	.987
1984—San Diego	Nat.	2B	158	596	106	154	19	7	3	34	.258	★391	410	32	.962
1985—San Diego y	Nat.	2B	10	37	3	2	1	0	0	0	.054	22	21	0	1.000
1985—Las Vegas	P. C.	2B	2	8	2	2	0	0	0	1	.250	2	6	0	1.000
1985—Rochester	Int.	2B	6	22	1	4	1	0	0	1	.182	18	15	2	.943
1985—Baltimore z	Amer.	2B	76	298	43	85	11	4	0	21	.285	148	186	14	.960
1986—Baltimore	Amer.	2B	71	239	30	60	3	1	0	11	.251	121	151	6	.978
1986—Rochester	Int.	2B	17	44	2	9	2	0	0	3	.205	18	20	1	.974
National League Totals—5 Years			399	1404	236	365	43	12	4	71	.260	1131	474	47	.972
American League Totals—2 Years			147	537	73	145	14	5	0	32	.270	269	337	20	.968
Major League Totals—6 Years			546	1941	309	510	57	17	4	103	.263	1400	811	67	.971

Selected by California Angels' organization in 1st round (seventh player selected) of free-agent draft, January 11, 1977.

†On suspended list, June 8 to June 10, 1978.

‡Released, June 10, 1978; signed by Los Angeles Dodgers' organization, January 26, 1979.

§Drafted by San Diego Padres, December 8, 1980.

xOn disabled list, July 21 to September 19, 1982.

yTraded to Baltimore Orioles' organization for Pitcher Roy Lee Jackson and a player to be named later, June 27, 1985; San Diego Padres acquired Pitcher Rich Caldwell to complete deal, September 16, 1985.

zOn disabled list, June 27 to July 5, 1985; included rehabilitation disability assignment to Rochester, June 27 to July 5, 1985.

CHAMPIONSHIP SERIES RECORD

Year Club	League	Pos.	G.	AB.	R.	H.	2B.	3B.	HR.	RBI.	B.A.	PO.	A.	E.	F.A.
1984—San Diego	Nat.	2B	5	19	4	6	0	0	0	1	.316	11	11	0	1.000

WORLD SERIES RECORD

Year Club	League	Pos.	G.	AB.	R.	H.	2B.	3B.	HR.	RBI.	B.A.	PO.	A.	E.	F.A.
1984—San Diego	Nat.	2B	5	22	2	8	1	0	1	1	.364	13	6	2	.905

MILTON EDWARD WILCOX
(Milt)

Born April 20, 1950, at Honolulu, Hawaii.
Height, 6.02. Weight, 215.
Throws and bats righthanded.

Pitched seven-inning, 2-0 no-hit victory against Evansville, July 4, 1970.
Major League saves: 1970 (1), 1971 (1), 1974 (4). Total—6.
Led American Association in shutouts with 5 in 1970 and tied for lead with 3 in 1971.
Named American Association Pitcher of the Year, 1970.

Year Club	League	G.	IP.	W.	L.	Pct.	H.	R.	ER.	SO.	BB.	ERA.
1968—Tampa	Florida St.	8	47	3	3	.500	28	11	7	48	18	1.34
1968—Sarasota Reds	Gulf Coast	6	33	3	2	.600	24	10	4	33	11	1.09
1969—Tampa†‡	Florida St.	15	46	4	1	.800	53	30	28	38	29	5.48
1970—Indianapolis	Am. Assoc.	28	168	12	10	.545	144	58	53	110	53	2.84
1970—Cincinnati	National	5	22	3	1	.750	19	6	6	13	7	2.45
1971—Indianapolis	Am. Assoc.	16	102	8	5	.615	84	29	25	62	22	2.20
1971—Cincinnati§	National	18	43	2	2	.500	43	22	16	21	17	3.35
1972—Cleveland	American	32	156	7	14	.333	145	67	59	90	72	3.40
1973—Cleveland xy	American	26	134	8	10	.444	143	90	87	82	68	5.84
1974—Cleveland za	American	41	71	2	2	.500	74	42	37	33	24	4.69
1975—Wichita	Am. Assoc.	8	48	4	3	.571	56	31	23	18	15	4.31
1975—Chicago	National	25	38	0	1	.000	50	27	24	21	17	5.68
1976—Wichita b-Evansville	Am. Assoc.	27	130	6	7	.462	141	72	55	94	63	3.81
1977—Evansville	Am. Assoc.	14	107	9	4	.692	89	38	29	69	40	2.44
1977—Detroit	American	20	106	6	2	.750	96	46	43	82	37	3.65
1978—Detroit	American	29	215	13	12	.520	208	94	90	132	68	3.77
1979—Detroit	American	33	196	12	10	.545	201	105	95	109	73	4.36
1980—Detroit	American	32	199	13	11	.542	201	112	99	97	68	4.48
1981—Detroit	American	24	166	12	9	.571	152	61	56	79	52	3.04
1982—Detroit c	American	29	193⅔	12	10	.545	187	91	78	112	85	3.62
1983—Detroit d	American	26	186	11	10	.524	164	89	82	101	74	3.97
1983—Evansville e	Am. Assoc.	2	8	0	1	.000	8	5	3	5	6	3.38
1984—Detroit	American	33	193⅔	17	8	.680	183	99	86	119	66	4.00
1985—Detroit fg	American	8	39	1	3	.250	51	24	21	20	14	4.85
1986—Seattle h	American	13	55⅔	0	8	.000	74	38	34	26	28	5.50
National League Totals—3 Years		48	103	5	4	.556	112	55	46	55	41	4.02
American League Totals—13 Years		346	1911	114	109	.511	1879	958	867	1082	729	4.08
Major League Totals—16 Years		394	2014	119	113	.513	1991	1013	913	1137	770	4.08

Selected by Cincinnati Reds' organization in 2nd round of free-agent draft, June 7, 1968.

†On military list, April 16 to May 9, 1969.

‡On temporary inactive list, June 11 to July 1, 1969.

§Traded to Cleveland Indians for Outfielder Ted Uhlaender, December 6, 1971.

xOn military list, June 16 to June 30, 1973.

yOn disabled list, July 24 to August 15, 1973.

zOn military list, July 20 to August 4, 1974.

aTraded to Chicago Cubs for Pitcher Dave LaRoche and Outfielder Brock Davis, February 28, 1975.

bSold to Detroit Tigers, June 10, 1976.
cOn disabled list, July 19 to August 9, 1982.
dOn disabled list, August 1 to September 1, 1983; included rehabilitation disability assignment to Evansville, August 12 to September 1, 1983.
eGranted free agency, November 7, 1983; re-signed by Tigers, December 29, 1983.
fOn disabled list, June 13, 1985 through remainder of season.
gReleased, December 20, 1985; signed by Calgary (Seattle Mariners' organization), February 5, 1986.
hReleased, June 14, 1986.

CHAMPIONSHIP SERIES RECORD

Year Club	League	G.	IP.	W.	L.	Pct.	H.	R.	ER.	SO.	BB.	ERA.
1970—Cincinnati	National	1	3	1	0	1.000	1	0	0	5	2	0.00
1984—Detroit	American	1	8	1	0	1.000	2	0	0	8	2	0.00
Championship Series Totals—2 Years		2	11	2	0	1.000	3	0	0	13	4	0.00

WORLD SERIES RECORD

Year Club	League	G.	IP.	W.	L.	Pct.	H.	R.	ER.	SO.	BB.	ERA.
1970—Cincinnati	National	2	2	0	1	.000	3	2	2	2	0	9.00
1984—Detroit	American	1	6	1	0	1.000	7	1	1	4	2	1.50
World Series Totals—2 Years		3	8	1	1	.500	10	3	3	6	2	3.38

DAVID SCOTT WILDER
(Dave)

Born October 14, 1960, at Oakland, Calif.
Height, 6.01. Weight, 185.
Throws and bats righthanded.
Attended Contra Costa College, San Pablo, Calif.,
and California State University, Fullerton, Calif.

Year Club	League	Pos.	G.	AB.	R.	H.	2B.	3B.	HR.	RBI.	B.A.	PO.	A.	E.	F.A.
1982—Idaho Falls	Pion.	OF	46	136	30	48	5	3	2	24	.353	70	4	6	.925
1983—Madison	Midw.	OF	115	356	71	86	13	3	6	39	.242	189	16	10	.953
1984—Madison	Midw.	OF-2B	48	167	28	42	10	1	2	25	.251	173	95	10	.964
1984—Albany	East.	OF	70	199	47	52	10	6	1	25	.261	132	6	3	.979
1985—Modesto	Calif.	OF	70	239	48	62	15	2	7	37	.259	120	9	8	.942
1985—Huntsville	South.	OF	29	68	11	11	5	0	2	8	.162	39	1	4	.909
1986—Huntsville	South.	OF	126	445	91	134	23	6	11	85	.301	239	13	6	.977

Selected by California Angels' organization in 8th round of free-agent draft, January 8, 1980.
Selected by Kansas City Royals' organization in secondary phase of free-agent draft, June 3, 1980.
Signed as free agent by Oakland A's organization, June 21, 1982.

ROBERT DONALD WILFONG
(Rob)

Born September 1, 1953, at Pasadena, Calif.
Height, 6.01. Weight, 185.
Throws right and bats lefthanded.
Attended Mount San Antonio Junior College, Walnut, Calif.
Brother of James Wilfong, outfielder in Detroit Tigers' organization, 1978.

Major League stolen bases: 1977 (10), 1978 (8), 1979 (11), 1980 (10), 1981 (2), 1982 (4), 1984 (3), 1985 (4), 1986 (1). Total—53.
Led American League in sacrifice hits with 25 in 1979.
Led American League second basemen in fielding percentage with .995 in 1980.

Year Club	League	Pos.	G.	AB.	R.	H.	2B.	3B.	HR.	RBI.	B.A.	PO.	A.	E.	F.A.
1972—Charlotte†	W. Car.	2B	102	363	64	107	18	2	2	35	.295	212	224	16	.965
1973—Lynchburg	Carol.	2B	131	520	94	143	13	9	7	37	.275	*323	326	18	.973
1974—Orlando	South.	2B	109	403	58	99	7	4	3	23	.246	249	303	8	*.986
1975—Orlando	South.	2B	125	403	54	99	14	1	4	37	.246	274	347	16	.975
1976—Tacoma	P. C.	2B	69	220	41	67	8	3	3	16	.305	163	191	6	.983
1977—Tacoma	P. C.	2B	34	123	26	40	8	1	2	17	.325	83	101	8	.958
1977—Minnesota	Amer.	2B	73	171	22	42	1	1	1	13	.246	114	164	12	.959
1978—Minnesota‡	Amer.	2B	92	199	23	53	8	0	1	11	.266	152	196	5	.986
1979—Minnesota	Amer.	2B-OF	140	419	71	131	22	6	9	59	.313	287	379	14	.979
1980—Minnesota	Amer.	2B-OF	131	416	55	103	16	5	8	45	.248	245	338	4	.993
1981—Minnesota	Amer.	2B	93	305	32	75	11	3	3	19	.246	183	268	9	.980
1982—Minn.§-Calif.	Amer.	2-3-O-S	80	183	24	38	5	2	1	16	.208	69	155	5	.978
1983—California	Amer.	2B-3B-SS	65	177	17	45	7	1	2	17	.254	107	144	2	.992
1984—California x	Amer.	2B-SS	108	307	31	76	13	2	6	33	.248	162	268	12	.973
1985—California	Amer.	2B	83	217	16	41	3	0	4	13	.189	124	216	5	.986
1986—California	Amer.	2B	92	288	25	63	11	3	3	33	.219	135	257	7	.982
Major League Totals—10 Years			957	2682	316	667	97	23	38	259	.249	1578	2385	75	.981

Selected by Minnesota Twins' organization in 13th round of free-agent draft, June 8, 1971.
†On disabled list, May 22 to June 2, 1972.
‡On disabled list, March 22 to April 7, 1978.
§Traded with Pitcher Doug Corbett to California Angels for Outfielder Tom Brunansky, Pitcher Mike Walters and cash, May 12, 1982.
xGranted free agency, November 8, 1984; re-signed by Angels, January 10, 1985.

Year Club League	Pos.	G.	AB.	R.	H.	2B.	3B.	HR.	RBI.	B.A.	PO.	A.	E.	F.A.
1982—California.............. Amer.	PH-PR	2	1	0	0	0	0	0	0	.000	0	0	0	.000
1986—California.............. Amer.	2B-PH	4	13	1	4	1	0	0	2	.308	8	10	0	1.000
Championship Series Totals—2 Years.....		6	14	1	4	1	0	0	2	.286	8	10	0	1.000

CURTIS VERNON WILKERSON
(Curt)

Born April 26, 1961, at Petersburg, Va.
Height, 5.09. Weight, 160.
Throws right and bats left and righthanded.

Major League stolen bases: 1983 (3), 1984 (12), 1985 (14), 1986 (9). Total—38.
Tied for Texas League lead in sacrifice hits with 11 in 1982.

Year Club League	Pos.	G.	AB.	R.	H.	2B.	3B.	HR.	RBI.	B.A.	PO.	A.	E.	F.A.
1980—Sarasota Rangers Gulf C.	SS-2B	37	105	15	20	2	0	0	8	.190	38	86	17	.879
1981—Asheville................ S. Atl.	SS-2B	106	333	45	68	7	3	0	19	.204	188	372	28	.952
1982—Burlington .... Midw.	SS-2B	56	198	18	50	6	0	0	13	.253	78	159	16	.937
1982—Tulsa .... Texas	SS	72	266	32	71	6	3	2	14	.267	102	225	18	.948
1983—Oklahoma City†... A. A.	SS	89	343	51	107	19	4	3	31	.312	135	272	19	.955
1983—Texas................... Amer.	SS-2B-3B	16	35	7	6	0	1	0	1	.171	18	31	1	.980
1984—Texas................... Amer.	SS-2B	153	484	47	120	12	0	1	26	.248	227	391	30	.954
1985—Texas................... Amer.	SS-2B	129	360	35	88	11	6	0	22	.244	165	328	21	.959
1986—Texas................... Amer.	2B-SS	110	236	27	56	10	3	0	15	.237	125	199	13	.961
Major League Totals—4 Years................		408	1115	116	270	33	10	1	64	.242	535	949	65	.958

Selected by Texas Rangers' organization in 4th round of free-agent draft, June 3, 1980.
†On disabled list, May 19 to June 21, 1983.

WILLIAM CARL WILKINSON
(Bill)

Born August 10, 1964, at Greybull, Wyo.
Height, 5.10. Weight, 160.
Throws left and bats righthanded.

Year Club League	G.	IP.	W.	L.	Pct.	H.	R.	ER.	SO.	BB.	ERA.
1983—Bellingham .... Northwest	13	63⅔	4	5	.444	54	41	24	87	54	3.39
1984—Wausau........................... Midwest	19	103⅓	6	4	.600	79	47	38	117	52	3.31
1985—Salinas .... California	9	59⅔	6	1	.857	47	19	18	75	23	2.72
1985—Calgary†......................... P. Coast	9	57⅓	5	1	.833	44	21	17	42	25	2.67
1985—Seattle............................. American	2	6	0	2	.000	8	9	9	5	6	13.50
1986—Calgary .... P. Coast	23	143	8	8	.500	146	82	76	86	51	4.78
Major League Totals—1 Year..................	2	6	0	2	.000	8	9	9	5	6	13.50

Selected by Seattle Mariners' organization in 4th round of free-agent draft, June 6, 1983.
†On disabled list, July 18, 1985 through remainder of season.

GERALD DUANE WILLARD JR.
(Jerry)

Born March 14, 1960, at Oxnard, Calif.
Height, 6.02. Weight, 200.
Throws right and bats lefthanded.
Attended Oxnard College, Oxnard, Calif.

Major League stolen bases: 1984 (1).
Led International League catchers in assists with 78 in 1983.

Year Club League	Pos.	G.	AB.	R.	H.	2B.	3B.	HR.	RBI.	B.A.	PO.	A.	E.	F.A.
1980—Central Oregon .... N'west	C	65	231	53	85	21	1	5	59	.368	283	37	★18	.947
1981—Peninsula.............. Carol.	C	107	334	43	87	17	1	12	60	.260	319	28	3	.991
1982—Reading................. East.	C	81	281	43	82	10	1	12	51	.292	534	64	13	.979
1982—Oklahoma City†... A. A.	C	36	95	13	22	5	0	2	14	.232	169	35	8	.962
1983—Charleston........... Int.	C-3B-OF	127	396	61	119	22	2	19	77	.301	613	79	12	.983
1984—Cleveland.............. Amer.	C	87	246	21	55	8	1	10	37	.224	335	35	7	.981
1985—Cleveland.............. Amer.	C	104	300	39	81	13	0	7	36	.270	427	52	5	.990
1985—Maine‡................. Int.	C	11	40	5	9	3	0	1	4	.225	56	11	2	.971
1986—Tacoma................. P. C.	C	22	62	7	16	5	0	1	12	.258	100	7	1	.991
1986—Oakland................ Amer.	C	75	161	17	43	7	0	4	26	.267	300	12	2	.994
Major League Totals—3 Years............		266	707	77	179	28	1	21	99	.253	1062	99	14	.988

Signed as free agent by Philadelphia Phillies' organization, December 20, 1979.
†Traded with Second Baseman Manny Trillo, Infielder Julio Franco, Outfielder George Vukovich and Pitcher Jay Baller to Cleveland Indians for Outfielder Von Hayes, December 9, 1982.
‡Released, April 1, 1986; signed by Oakland A's organization, April 4, 1986.

EDWARD LAQUAN WILLIAMS
(Eddie)

Born November 1, 1964, at Shreveport, La.
Height, 6.00. Weight, 175.
Throws and bats righthanded.

Led Midwest League in being hit by pitch with 15 in 1985.
Named Midwest League Most Valuable Player, 1985.

Year	Club	League	Pos.	G.	AB.	R.	H.	2B.	3B.	HR.	RBI.	B.A.	PO.	A.	E.	F.A.
1983—Little Falls	NYP	3B	50	190	30	50	6	2	6	28	.263	50	53	13	.888
1984—Columbia†	S. Atl.	3B	43	152	17	28	4	2	3	24	.184	24	76	16	.862
1984—Tampa	Fla. St.	3B	50	138	20	35	8	0	2	16	.254	25	43	11	.861
1985—Cedar Rapids‡	Midw.	3B	119	406	71	106	13	3	20	83	.261	83	204	33	.897
1986—Cleveland	Amer.	OF	5	7	2	1	0	0	0	1	.143	0	0	0	.000
1986—Waterbury	East.	3B	62	214	24	51	10	0	7	30	.238	39	100	15	.903
Major League Totals—1 Year			5	7	2	1	0	0	0	1	.143	0	0	0	.000

Selected by New York Mets' organization in 1st round (fourth player selected) of free-agent draft, June 6, 1983.
†Traded with Pitchers Matt Bullinger and Jay Tibbs to Cincinnati Reds for Pitcher Bruce Berenyi, June 15, 1984.
‡Drafted by Cleveland Indians, December 10, 1985.

FRANK LEE WILLIAMS

Born February 13, 1958, at Seattle, Wash.
Height, 6.01. Weight, 180.
Throws and bats righthanded.
Attended Shoreline Community College, Seattle, Wash.,
and Lewis-Clark State College, Lewiston, Ida.

Major League saves: 1984 (3), 1986 (1) Total—4.
Led California League in hit batsmen with 18 in 1980 and 13 in 1981.
Led Pioneer League in hit batsmen with 9 in 1979.
Tied for Texas League lead in hit batsmen with 13 in 1982.
Tied for California League lead in complete games with 14 in 1981.

Year	Club	League	G.	IP.	W.	L.	Pct.	H.	R.	ER.	SO.	BB.	ERA.
1979—Great Falls	Pioneer	13	91	6	•7	.462	85	53	34	81	53	3.36
1980—Fresno	California	21	114	12	3	.800	105	53	42	80	70	3.32
1981—Fresno	California	27	187	14	9	.609	170	81	70	170	85	3.37
1982—Shreveport	Texas	27	169⅔	11	9	.550	143	96	74	145	99	3.93
1983—Shreveport	Texas	21	42	7	2	.778	22	14	8	54	25	1.71
1983—Phoenix	P. Coast	25	47⅔	5	3	.625	45	22	19	37	24	3.59
1984—San Francisco	National	61	106⅓	9	4	.692	88	49	42	91	51	3.55
1985—San Francisco	National	49	73	2	4	.333	65	39	34	54	35	4.19
1985—Phoenix	P. Coast	9	13⅔	1	1	.500	10	8	6	10	14	3.95
1986—Phoenix	P. Coast	27	38	1	1	.500	28	10	9	41	17	2.13
1986—San Francisco	National	36	52⅓	3	1	.750	35	8	7	33	21	1.20
Major League Totals—3 Years		146	231⅔	14	9	.609	188	96	83	178	107	3.22

Selected by San Francisco Giants' organization in 11th round of free-agent draft, June 5, 1979.

KENNETH ROYAL WILLIAMS
(Ken)

Born April 6, 1964, at Berkeley, Calif.
Height, 6.02. Weight, 187.
Throws and bats righthanded.
Attended Stanford University, Stanford, Calif.

Major League stolen bases: 1986 (1).
Received reported $165,000 bonus to sign with Chicago White Sox, 1982.

Year	Club	League	Pos.	G.	AB.	R.	H.	2B.	3B.	HR.	RBI.	B.A.	PO.	A.	E.	F.A.
1982—Sarasota W. Sox	Gulf C.	OF	31	104	19	31	2	1	1	11	.298	61	2	0	1.000
1983—Appleton	Midw.	OF	124	415	60	96	18	2	12	53	.231	218	10	10	.958
1984—Appleton	Midw.	OF	38	147	23	42	11	2	5	26	.286	58	5	2	.969
1984—Glens Falls	East.	OF	97	309	35	76	7	5	8	47	.246	173	10	5	.973
1985—Glens Falls	East.	OF	133	★520	★87	130	16	6	16	66	.250	296	★20	★14	.958
1986—Buffalo	A. A.	OF	50	189	21	40	4	2	4	15	.212	100	8	1	.991
1986—Birmingham	South.	OF	68	272	41	90	16	5	6	40	.331	192	3	8	.961
1986—Chicago	Amer.	OF	15	31	2	4	0	0	1	1	.129	18	1	0	1.000
Major League Totals—1 Year			15	31	2	4	0	0	1	1	.129	18	1	0	1.000

Selected by Chicago White Sox' organization in 3rd round of free-agent draft, June 7, 1982.

MITCHELL STEVEN WILLIAMS
(Mitch)

Born November 17, 1964, at Santa Ana, Calif.
Height, 6.03. Weight, 180.
Throws and bats lefthanded.
Brother of Bruce Williams, pitcher in Milwaukee Brewers' organization, 1981 through 1985.

Major League saves: 1986 (8).
Established major league record for most games pitched by rookie (80), 1986.
Led Northwest League pitchers in wild pitches with 14 and tied for lead in games started with 14 and balks with 2 in 1983.

Year	Club	League	G.	IP.	W.	L.	Pct.	H.	R.	ER.	SO.	BB.	ERA.
1982—Walla Walla	Northwest	12	58⅓	3	4	.429	37	37	31	66	★72	4.78
1983—Reno	California	11	58	1	7	.125	58	56	46	44	60	7.14
1983—Spokane	Northwest	14	92⅓	7	6	.538	84	51	•46	87	55	4.48
1984—Reno†‡	California	26	164	9	8	.529	163	113	91	165	127	4.99

Year Club	League	G.	IP.	W.	L.	Pct.	H.	R.	ER.	SO.	BB.	ERA.
1985—Salem	Carolina	22	99	6	9	.400	57	64	60	138	*117	5.45
1985—Tulsa	Texas	6	33	2	2	.500	17	24	17	37	48	4.64
1986—Texas	American	*80	98	8	6	.571	69	39	39	90	79	3.58
Major League Totals—1 Year		80	98	8	6	.571	69	39	39	90	79	3.58

Selected by San Diego Padres' organization in 8th round of free-agent draft, June 7, 1982.
†Drafted by Texas Rangers, December 3, 1984; returned, April 6, 1985.
‡Traded to Texas Rangers for Third Baseman Randy Asadoor, April 6, 1985.

REGINALD DEWAYNE WILLIAMS
(Reggie)

Born August 29, 1960, at Memphis, Tenn.
Height, 5.11. Weight, 185.
Throws and bats righthanded.
Received bachelor of science degree in business
from Southern University, New Orleans, La.
Major League stolen bases: 1985 (1), 1986 (9). Total—10.

Year Club	League	Pos.	G.	AB.	R.	H.	2B.	3B.	HR.	RBI.	B.A.	PO.	A.	E.	F.A.
1982—Lethbridge	Pion.	OF	67	253	40	76	8	2	3	33	.300	*141	12	7	.956
1983—Vero Beach†	Fla. St.	OF	81	293	53	83	11	3	4	32	.283	142	3	8	.948
1984—Vero Beach‡	Fla. St.	OF	60	222	31	53	5	2	0	19	.239	87	5	1	.989
1985—San Antonio	Texas	OF	120	436	73	127	17	4	10	53	.291	209	14	11	.953
1985—Los Angeles	Nat.	OF	22	9	4	3	0	0	0	0	.333	8	1	1	.900
1986—Los Angeles	Nat.	OF	128	303	35	84	14	2	4	32	.277	179	5	3	.984
1986—Albuquerque	P. C.	OF	11	44	6	13	1	1	1	4	.295	18	0	0	1.000
Major League Totals—2 Years			150	312	39	87	14	2	4	32	.279	187	6	4	.980

Selected by St. Louis Cardinals' organization in 6th round of free-agent draft, June 8, 1981.
Selected by Los Angeles Dodgers' organization in 13th round of free-agent draft, June 7, 1982.
†On disabled list, June 22 to August 11, 1983.
‡On disabled list, April 6 to June 28, 1984.

MARK ALAN WILLIAMSON

Born July 21, 1959, at Lemon Grove, Calif.
Height, 6.00. Weight, 155.
Throws and bats righthanded.
Received degree from San Diego State University, San Diego, Calif.
Tied for Pacific Coast League lead in saves with 16 in 1986.
Tied for California League lead in intentional bases on balls issued with 10 in 1984.

Year Club	League	G.	IP.	W.	L.	Pct.	H.	R.	ER.	SO.	BB.	ERA.
1982—Reno	California	26	41	7	5	.583	34	24	20	30	18	4.39
1983—Beaumont	Texas	47	82⅔	6	3	.667	90	45	37	39	30	4.03
1984—Reno	California	56	93	10	12	.455	105	41	30	69	23	2.90
1985—Beaumont	Texas	42	78⅔	10	9	.526	72	27	25	64	23	2.86
1986—Las Vegas	P. Coast	*65	104⅓	10	3	*.769	103	47	39	81	36	3.36

Selected by Kansas City Royals' organization in 12th round of free-agent draft, June 8, 1981.
Selected by San Diego Padres' organization in 4th round of free-agent draft, June 7, 1982.

CARL BLAKE WILLIS

Born December 28, 1960, at Danville, Va.
Height, 6.03. Weight, 210.
Throws right and bats lefthanded.
Attended University of North Carolina, Wilmington, N.C.
Major League saves: 1984 (1), 1985 (1). Total—2.

Year Club	League	G.	IP.	W.	L.	Pct.	H.	R.	ER.	SO.	BB.	ERA.
1983—Bristol	Ap'lachian	2	2⅔	0	1	.000	0	1	1	3	4	3.38
1983—Lakeland	Florida St.	4	9⅔	3	0	1.000	6	0	0	7	5	0.00
1983—Birmingham	Southern	14	20⅓	3	1	.750	16	9	9	13	7	3.98
1984—Evansville	Am. Assoc.	40	60⅓	5	3	.625	59	26	25	27	20	3.73
1984—Detroit†	American	10	16	0	2	.000	25	13	13	4	5	7.31
1984—Cincinnati	National	7	9⅔	0	1	.000	8	4	4	3	2	3.72
1985—Cincinnati	National	11	13⅔	1	0	1.000	21	18	14	6	5	9.22
1985—Denver‡	Am. Assoc.	37	78	4	4	.500	82	39	36	27	30	4.15
1986—Denver	Am. Assoc.	20	32⅔	1	3	.250	29	22	17	16	16	4.68
1986—Cincinnati	National	29	52⅓	1	3	.250	54	29	26	24	32	4.47
American League Totals—1 Year		10	16	0	2	.000	25	13	13	4	5	7.31
National League Totals—3 Years		47	75⅔	2	4	.333	83	51	44	33	39	5.23
Major League Totals—3 Years		57	91⅔	2	6	.250	108	64	57	37	44	5.60

Selected by San Francisco Giants' organization in 31st round of free-agent draft, June 7, 1982.
Selected by Detroit Tigers' organization in 23rd round of free-agent draft, June 6, 1983.
†Traded to Cincinnati Reds, September 1, 1984, completing deal in which Cincinnati traded Pitcher Bill Scherrer to Detroit Tigers for cash and a player to be named later, August 27, 1984.
‡Drafted by California Angels, December 10, 1985; returned, April 6, 1986.

FRANK LEE WILLS JR.

Born October 26, 1958, at New Orleans, La.
Height, 6.02. Weight, 200.
Throws and bats righthanded.
Attended Tulane University, New Orleans, La.

Pitched seven-inning, 1-0 no-hit victory against Tacoma, May 31, 1985 (first game).
Major League saves: 1985 (1), 1986 (4). Total—5.
Tied for Southern League lead in wild pitches with 15 in 1981.
Named righthanded pitcher on THE SPORTING NEWS College Baseball All-America Team, 1980.

Year Club	League	G.	IP.	W.	L.	Pct.	H.	R.	ER.	SO.	BB.	ERA.
1980—Sarasota Royals-Blue	Gulf Coast	4	23	2	0	1.000	18	7	5	20	8	1.96
1980—Charleston	S. Atlantic	9	57	2	5	.286	59	33	23	48	32	3.63
1981—Jacksonville	Southern	27	192	9	14	.391	199	104	85	174	91	3.98
1982—Omaha	Am. Assoc.	41	107⅓	7	10	.412	110	71	62	77	*81	5.20
1983—Jacksonville	Southern	8	54⅓	5	2	.714	44	19	15	40	23	2.48
1983—Omaha	Am. Assoc.	16	95	4	11	.267	96	56	50	65	45	4.74
1983—Kansas City	American	6	34⅔	2	1	.667	35	17	16	23	15	4.15
1984—Omaha	Am. Assoc.	15	89⅔	7	4	.636	75	32	28	69	49	2.81
1984—Kansas City†‡§	American	10	37	2	3	.400	39	21	21	21	13	5.11
1985—Calgary	P. Coast	9	46⅓	4	3	.571	44	27	25	31	25	4.86
1985—Seattle x	American	24	123	5	11	.313	122	85	82	67	68	6.00
1986—Maine y	Int'national	22	31⅓	4	3	.571	37	10	10	21	10	2.87
1986—Cleveland	American	26	40⅓	4	4	.500	43	23	22	32	16	4.91
Major League Totals—4 Years		66	235	13	19	.406	239	146	141	143	112	5.40

Selected by Kansas City Royals' organization in 1st round (16th player selected) of free-agent draft, June 3, 1980.
†On disabled list, August 1 to August 16, 1984.
‡Traded to New York Mets' organization as part of a six-player, four-team deal in which Kansas City Royals acquired Catcher Jim Sundberg from Milwaukee Brewers, Texas Rangers acquired Catcher Don Slaught from Kansas City, Milwaukee acquired Pitcher Danny Darwin and a player to be named later from Texas and Pitcher Tim Leary from New York, January 18, 1985; Milwaukee organization acquired Catcher Bill Hance from Texas to complete deal, January 30, 1985.
§Traded to Seattle Mariners' organization for Pitcher Wray Bergendahl, March 29, 1985.
xReleased, March 20, 1986; signed by Cleveland Indians' organization, March 27, 1986.
yOn disabled list, May 4 to May 31, 1986.

GLENN DWIGHT WILSON

Born December 22, 1958, at Baytown, Tex.
Height, 6.01. Weight, 190.
Throws and bats righthanded.
Attended Sam Houston State University, Huntsville, Tex.

Tied major league record for fewest double plays by outfielder, season, for leader in double plays (4), 1985.
Major League stolen bases: 1982 (2), 1983 (1), 1984 (7), 1985 (7), 1986 (5). Total—22.
Led National League outfielders in double plays with 5 in 1986 and tied for lead with 4 in 1985.
Received reported $60,000 bonus to sign with Detroit Tigers, 1980.
Named third baseman on THE SPORTING NEWS College Baseball All-America Team, 1980.

Year Club League	Pos.	G.	AB.	R.	H.	2B.	3B.	HR.	RBI.	B.A.	PO.	A.	E.	F.A.
1980—Montgomery .... South.	3B	77	284	36	75	16	2	7	31	.264	56	189	*33	.881
1981—Birmingham .... South.	OF	124	496	77	152	24	6	18	82	.306	292	18	5	.984
1981—Evansville .... A. A.	OF-1B	10	37	5	9	2	0	2	7	.243	16	2	0	1.000
1982—Detroit.................. Amer.	OF	84	322	39	94	15	1	12	34	.292	215	8	3	.987
1982—Evansville† .... A. A.	OF	42	165	24	46	7	2	10	33	.279	96	6	3	.971
1983—Detroit‡ .... Amer.	OF	144	503	55	135	25	6	11	65	.268	225	12	3	.988
1984—Philadelphia .... Nat.	OF-3B	132	341	28	82	21	3	6	31	.240	153	7	7	.958
1985—Philadelphia .... Nat.	OF	161	608	73	167	39	5	14	102	.275	343	*18	*12	.968
1986—Philadelphia .... Nat.	OF	155	584	70	158	30	4	15	84	.271	331	*20	4	.989
American League Totals—2 Years		228	825	94	229	40	7	23	99	.278	440	20	6	.987
National League Totals—3 Years		448	1533	171	407	90	12	35	217	.265	827	45	23	.974
Major League Totals—5 Years		676	2358	265	636	130	19	58	316	.270	1267	65	29	.979

Selected by Detroit Tigers' organization in 1st round (18th player selected) of free-agent draft, June 3, 1980.
†On disabled list, May 27 to June 9 and June 17 to June 27, 1982.
‡Traded with Catcher-First Baseman John Wockenfuss to Philadelphia Phillies for First Baseman Dave Bergman and Pitcher Willie Hernandez, March 24, 1984.

ALL-STAR GAME RECORD

Year League	Pos.	AB.	R.	H.	2B.	3B.	HR.	RBI.	B.A.	PO.	A.	E.	F.A.
1985—National	PH	1	0	0	0	0	0	0	.000	0	0	0	.000

PHILLIP FRANKLYN WILSON
(Phil)

Born June 1, 1963, at Bamberg, S.C.
Height, 5.08. Weight, 160.
Throws right and bats left and righthanded.
Attended University of South Carolina, Columbia, S.C.
Brother of Mookie Wilson, outfielder with New York Mets;
and John Wilson, outfielder in New York Mets' organization.

Led Southern League in being hit by pitch with 9 in 1986.

Year Club	League	Pos.	G.	AB.	R.	H.	2B.	3B.	HR.	RBI.	B.A.	PO.	A.	E.	F.A.
1984—Kenosha†	Midw.	OF	104	399	58	79	10	4	4	33	.198	210	9	15	.936
1985—Visalia†	Calif.	OF	127	492	92	146	12	5	2	46	.297	298	11	5	.984
1986—Orlando	South.	OF	129	526	88	154	12	8	6	42	.293	294	9	10	.968

Selected by Minnesota Twins' organization in 5th round of free-agent draft, January 17, 1984.
†Batted righthanded.

WILLIAM HAYWARD WILSON
(Mookie)

Born February 9, 1956, at Bamberg, S. C.
Height, 5.10. Weight, 170.
Throws right and bats right and lefthanded.
Attended Spartanburg Methodist College, Spartanburg, S. C.,
and University of South Carolina, Columbia, S. C.
Brother of John Wilson, outfielder in New York Mets' organization; and
Phil Wilson, outfielder in Minnesota Twins' organization.

Major League stolen bases: 1980 (7), 1981 (24), 1982 (58), 1983 (54), 1984 (46), 1985 (24), 1986 (25). Total—238.
Led National League outfielders in double plays with 6 in 1984.

Year Club	League	Pos.	G.	AB.	R.	H.	2B.	3B.	HR.	RBI.	B.A.	PO.	A.	E.	F.A.
1977—Wausau	Midw.	OF	68	245	50	71	10	2	6	32	.290	150	8	9	.946
1978—Jackson	Texas	OF	132	497	72	145	13	*15	7	72	.292	282	10	7	.977
1979—Tidewater	Int.	OF	*141	529	84	141	22	10	5	36	.267	317	11	7	.979
1980—Tidewater	Int.	OF	132	515	*92	*152	11	*14	4	44	.295	*350	11	7	.981
1980—New York	Nat.	OF	27	105	16	26	5	3	0	4	.248	72	1	2	.973
1981—New York	Nat.	OF	92	328	49	89	8	8	3	14	.271	226	3	4	.983
1982—New York	Nat.	OF	159	639	90	178	25	9	5	55	.279	415	12	5	.988
1983—New York	Nat.	OF	152	*638	91	176	25	6	7	51	.276	422	5	7	.984
1984—New York	Nat.	OF	154	587	88	162	28	10	10	54	.276	396	8	4	.990
1985—New York†	Nat.	OF	93	337	56	93	16	8	6	26	.276	216	0	8	.964
1986—Tidewater	Int.	OF	9	31	4	8	1	0	0	4	.258	19	1	0	1.000
1986—New York‡	Nat.	OF	123	381	61	110	17	5	9	45	.289	228	7	5	.979
Major League Totals—7 Years			800	3015	451	834	124	49	40	249	.277	1975	36	35	.983

Selected by Los Angeles Dodgers' organization in 4th round of free-agent draft, January 7, 1976.
Selected by New York Mets' organization in 2nd round of free-agent draft, June 7, 1977.
†On disabled list, July 2 to September 1, 1985.
†On New York disabled list, March 30 to May 9, 1986; included rehabilitation disability assignment to Tidewater, April 26 to May 9, 1986.

CHAMPIONSHIP SERIES RECORD
Tied Championship Series record for most at-bats, game (7), October 15, 1986 (16 innings).

Year Club	League	Pos.	G.	AB.	R.	H.	2B.	3B.	HR.	RBI.	B.A.	PO.	A.	E.	F.A.
1986—New York	Nat.	OF	6	26	2	3	0	0	0	1	.115	16	1	0	1.000

WORLD SERIES RECORD

Year Club	League	Pos.	G.	AB.	R.	H.	2B.	3B.	HR.	RBI.	B.A.	PO.	A.	E.	F.A.
1986—New York	Nat.	OF	7	26	3	7	1	0	0	0	.269	15	2	0	1.000

WILLIE JAMES WILSON

Born July 9, 1955, at Montgomery, Ala.
Height, 6.03. Weight, 187.
Throws right and bats left and righthanded.

Established major league records for most at-bats season (705), 1980; most at-bats by switch-hitter, season (705), 1980.
Tied major league records by collecting 100 or more hits righthanded and lefthanded, season, 1980; for most hits by switch-hitter, season (230), 1980.
Established American League records for most triples by switch-hitter, season (21), 1985; highest stolen base percentage, lifetime, 300 or more attempts (.841); fewest times, grounded into double play, season (1), 1979.
Tied American League records for most consecutive stolen bases without caught stealing (32); fewest times caught stealing, season, 50 or more stolen bases (8), 1983.
Major League stolen bases: 1976 (2), 1977 (6), 1978 (46), 1979 (83), 1980 (79), 1981 (34), 1982 (37), 1983 (59), 1984 (47), 1985 (43), 1986 (34). Total—470.
Switch-hit home runs in one game, June 15, 1979.
Led American League in stolen bases with 83 in 1979.
Led Gulf Coast League in stolen bases with 24 in 1974, Midwest League with 76 in 1975 and American Association with 74 in 1977.
Led Midwest League in being hit by pitch with 13 in 1975.
Named outfielder on THE SPORTING NEWS American League All-Star fielding team, 1980.
Named outfielder on THE SPORTING NEWS American League Silver Slugger team, 1980 and 1982.
Named Midwest League Most Valuable Player, 1975.
Received reported $90,000 bonus to sign with Kansas City Royals, 1974.

Year Club	League	Pos.	G.	AB.	R.	H.	2B.	3B.	HR.	RBI.	B.A.	PO.	A.	E.	F.A.
1974—Sarasota Royals	Gulf C.	OF	47	155	30	39	3	5	1	14	.252	92	8	4	.962
1975—Waterloo	Midw.	OF	127	486	92	*132	18	4	8	73	.272	249	●17	*17	.940
1976—Jacksonville	South.	OF	107	388	54	98	13	6	1	35	.253	273	5	8	.972
1976—Kansas City	Amer.	OF	12	6	0	1	0	0	0	0	.167	6	1	1	.875
1977—Omaha	A. A.	OF	132	495	67	139	10	6	4	47	.281	*278	7	11	.963
1977—Kansas City	Amer.	OF	13	34	10	11	2	0	0	1	.324	24	0	1	.960
1978—Kansas City	Amer.	OF	127	198	43	43	8	2	0	16	.217	171	6	4	.978

Year	Club	League	Pos.	G.	AB.	R.	H.	2B.	3B.	HR.	RBI.	B.A.	PO.	A.	E.	F.A.
1979—Kansas City	Amer.		OF	154	588	113	185	18	13	6	49	.315	384	12	6	.985
1980—Kansas City	Amer.		OF	161	★705	★133	★230	28	●15	3	49	.326	482	9	6	.988
1981—Kansas City	Amer.		OF	102	439	54	133	10	7	1	32	.303	299	★14	4	.987
1982—Kansas City	Amer.		OF	136	585	87	194	19	★15	3	46	★.332	215	8	3	.987
1983—Kansas City†‡	Amer.		OF	137	576	90	159	22	8	2	33	.276	354	3	9	.975
1984—Kansas City	Amer.		OF	128	541	81	163	24	9	2	44	.301	383	6	4	.990
1985—Kansas City	Amer.		OF	141	605	87	168	25	★21	4	43	.278	378	4	2	.995
1986—Kansas City	Amer.		OF	156	631	77	170	20	7	9	44	.269	408	4	3	.993
Major League Totals—11 Years				1267	4908	775	1457	176	99	30	357	.297	3104	67	43	.987

Selected by Kansas City Royals' organization in 1st round (18th player selected) of free-agent draft, June 5, 1974.
†On disabled list, August 21 to September 6, 1983.
‡On suspended list, December 15, 1983 through May 15, 1984.

DIVISION SERIES RECORD

Year	Club	League	Pos.	G.	AB.	R.	H.	2B.	3B.	HR.	RBI.	B.A.	PO.	A.	E.	F.A.
1981—Kansas City	Amer.		OF	3	13	0	4	0	0	0	1	.308	6	0	0	1.000

CHAMPIONSHIP SERIES RECORD

Year	Club	League	Pos.	G.	AB.	R.	H.	2B.	3B.	HR.	RBI.	B.A.	PO.	A.	E.	F.A.
1978—Kansas City	Amer.		PR-OF	3	4	0	1	0	0	0	0	.250	2	0	0	1.000
1980—Kansas City	Amer.		OF	3	13	2	4	2	1	0	4	.308	6	1	0	1.000
1984—Kansas City	Amer.		OF	3	13	0	2	0	0	0	0	.154	10	0	0	1.000
1985—Kansas City	Amer.		OF	7	29	5	9	0	0	1	2	.310	12	0	0	1.000
Championship Series Totals—4 Years				16	59	7	16	2	1	1	6	.271	30	1	0	1.000

WORLD SERIES RECORD

Established World Series record for most strikeouts, six-game and any length Series (12), 1980.
Tied World Series record for most at bats, inning (2), October 18, 1980 (first inning).

Year	Club	League	Pos.	G.	AB.	R.	H.	2B.	3B.	HR.	RBI.	B.A.	PO.	A.	E.	F.A.
1980—Kansas City	Amer.		OF	6	26	3	4	1	0	0	0	.154	15	1	0	1.000
1985—Kansas City	Amer.		OF	7	30	2	11	0	1	0	3	.367	19	1	0	1.000
World Series Totals—2 Years				13	56	5	15	1	1	0	3	.268	34	2	0	1.000

ALL-STAR GAME RECORD

Year	League	Pos.	AB.	R.	H.	2B.	3B.	HR.	RBI.	B.A.	PO.	A.	E.	F.A.
1982—American		OF	2	0	0	0	0	0	0	.000	1	0	0	1.000
1983—American		OF	1	0	1	1	0	0	1	1.000	2	0	0	1.000
All-Star Game Totals—2 Years			3	0	1	1	0	0	1	.333	3	0	0	1.000

ROBERT PAUL WINE JR.
(Robbie)

Born July 13, 1962, at Norristown, Pa.
Height, 6.02. Weight, 190.
Throws and bats righthanded.
Attended Oklahoma State University, Stillwater, Okla.
Son of Bobby Wine Sr., shortstop with Philadelphia Phillies and Montreal Expos, 1960 and 1962 through 1972;
coach, Philadelphia Phillies, 1972 through 1983; coach with Atlanta Braves, 1985;
interim manager, Atlanta Braves, August 26, 1985 through remainder of season;
and scout, Atlanta Braves, 1984 and 1986.
Led Southern League catchers in putouts with 502 and passed balls with 18 in 1985.
Led Florida State League catchers in assists with 124, double plays with 14, passed balls with 25 and total chances with 743 in 1984.
Tied for Pacific Coast League lead in double plays by catchers with 10 in 1986.
Named College Player of the Year by THE SPORTING NEWS, 1983.
Named catcher on THE SPORTING NEWS College Baseball All-America Team, 1983.

Year	Club	League	Pos.	G.	AB.	R.	H.	2B.	3B.	HR.	RBI.	B.A.	PO.	A.	E.	F.A.
1983—Auburn	NYP		C	53	198	32	48	15	3	5	22	.242	35	6	6	.984
1984—Daytona Beach	Fla. St.		C-3B	124	430	66	105	★36	2	13	79	.244	601	126	18	.976
1985—Columbus	South.		C-OF	109	384	53	73	13	2	21	55	.190	503	63	8	.986
1986—Tucson	P. C.		C	106	347	42	79	24	2	10	44	.228	459	★76	7	.987
1986—Houston	Nat.		C	9	12	2	3	1	0	0	0	.250	28	5	0	1.000
Major League Totals—1 Year				9	12	2	3	1	0	0	0	.250	28	5	0	1.000

Selected by Houston Astros' organization in 1st round (eighth player selected) of free-agent draft, June 6, 1983.

DAVID MARK WINFIELD
(Dave)

Born October 3, 1951, at St. Paul, Minn.
Height, 6.06. Weight, 220.
Throws and bats righthanded.
Attended University of Minnesota, Minneapolis, Minn.
Major League stolen bases: 1974 (9), 1975 (23), 1976 (26), 1977 (16), 1978 (21), 1979 (15), 1980 (23), 1981 (11), 1982 (5), 1983 (15), 1984 (6), 1985 (19), 1986 (6). Total—195.
Led National League in total bases with 333 and intentional bases on balls received with 24 in 1979.
Named outfielder on THE SPORTING NEWS American League All-Star Team, 1982 through 1984.

Named outfielder on The Sporting News National League All-Star Team, 1979.
Named outfielder on The Sporting News American League All-Star fielding team, 1982 through 1985.
Named outfielder on The Sporting News National League All-Star fielding team, 1979 and 1980.
Received outfielder on The Sporting News American League Silver Slugger team, 1981 through 1985.
Received reported $100,000 bonus to sign with San Diego Padres, 1973.
Selected by Atlanta Hawks in 5th round (79th player selected) of 1973 NBA draft.
Selected by Utah Stars in 6th round (58th player selected) of 1973 ABA draft.
Selected by Minnesota Vikings in 17th round (429th player selected) of 1973 NFL draft.
Named outfielder on The Sporting News College Baseball All-America Team, 1973.

Year Club	League	Pos.	G.	AB.	R.	H.	2B.	3B.	HR.	RBI.	B.A.	PO.	A.	E.	F.A.
1973—San Diego	Nat.	OF-1B	56	141	9	39	4	1	3	12	.277	65	1	3	.957
1974—San Diego	Nat.	OF	145	498	57	132	18	4	20	75	.265	276	11	●12	.960
1975—San Diego	Nat.	OF	143	509	74	136	20	2	15	76	.267	302	9	9	.972
1976—San Diego	Nat.	OF	137	492	81	139	26	4	13	69	.283	304	★15	6	.982
1977—San Diego	Nat.	OF	157	615	104	169	29	7	25	92	.275	368	15	11	.972
1978—San Diego	Nat.	OF-1B	158	587	88	181	30	5	24	97	.308	328	8	7	.980
1979—San Diego	Nat.	OF	159	597	97	184	27	10	34	★118	.308	344	14	5	.986
1980—San Diego†	Nat.	OF	162	558	89	154	25	6	20	87	.276	273	20	4	.987
1981—New York	Amer.	OF	105	388	52	114	25	1	13	68	.294	196	1	3	.985
1982—New York‡	Amer.	OF	140	539	84	151	24	8	37	106	.280	279	★17	8	.974
1983—New York	Amer.	OF	152	598	99	169	26	8	32	116	.283	313	5	7	.978
1984—New York§	Amer.	OF	141	567	106	193	34	4	19	100	.340	306	3	2	.994
1985—New York	Amer.	OF	155	633	105	174	34	6	26	114	.275	316	13	3	.991
1986—New York	Amer.	OF-3B	154	565	90	148	31	5	24	104	.262	292	9	5	.984
National League Totals—8 Years			1117	3997	599	1134	179	39	154	626	.284	2260	93	57	.976
American League Totals—6 Years			847	3290	536	949	174	32	151	608	.288	1702	48	28	.984
Major League Totals—14 Years			1964	7287	1135	2083	353	71	305	1234	.286	3962	141	85	.980

Selected by Baltimore Orioles' organization in 40th round of free-agent draft, June 5, 1969.
Selected by San Diego Padres' organization in 1st round (fourth player selected) of free-agent draft, June 5, 1973.
†Granted free agency, October 22, 1980; signed by New York Yankees, December 15, 1980.
‡On disabled list, May 20 to June 4, 1982.
§On disabled list, April 16 to May 1, 1984.

DIVISION SERIES RECORD

Year Club	League	Pos.	G.	AB.	R.	H.	2B.	3B.	HR.	RBI.	B.A.	PO.	A.	E.	F.A.
1981—New York	Amer.	OF	5	20	2	7	3	0	0	0	.350	10	1	0	1.000

CHAMPIONSHIP SERIES RECORD

Year Club	League	Pos.	G.	AB.	R.	H.	2B.	3B.	HR.	RBI.	B.A.	PO.	A.	E.	F.A.
1981—New York	Amer.	OF	3	13	2	2	1	0	0	2	.154	6	0	0	1.000

WORLD SERIES RECORD

Tied World Series record for fewest runs, Series (0), 1981.

Year Club	League	Pos.	G.	AB.	R.	H.	2B.	3B.	HR.	RBI.	B.A.	PO.	A.	E.	F.A.
1981—New York	Amer.	OF	6	22	0	1	0	0	0	1	.045	13	1	0	1.000

ALL-STAR GAME RECORD

Established All-Star Game record for most doubles, lifetime (5).
Tied All-Star Game record for most at bats, game (5), July 17, 1979.

Year League	Pos.	AB.	R.	H.	2B.	3B.	HR.	RBI.	B.A.	PO.	A.	E.	F.A.
1977—National	OF	2	0	2	1	0	0	2	1.000	1	0	0	1.000
1978—National	OF	2	1	1	0	0	0	0	.500	1	0	0	1.000
1979—National	OF	5	1	1	1	0	0	1	.200	3	0	0	1.000
1980—National	OF	2	0	0	0	0	0	1	.000	2	0	0	1.000
1981—American	OF	4	0	0	0	0	0	0	.000	0	1	0	1.000
1982—American	OF	2	0	1	0	0	0	0	.500	0	0	0	.000
1983—American	OF	3	2	3	1	0	0	1	1.000	3	0	0	1.000
1984—American	OF	4	0	1	1	0	0	0	.250	2	1	0	1.000
1985—American	OF	3	0	1	0	0	0	0	.333	0	0	0	.000
1986—American	OF	1	1	1	1	0	0	0	1.000	0	0	0	.000
All-Star Game Totals—10 Years		28	5	11	5	0	0	5	.393	12	2	0	1.000

JAMES FRANCIS WINN
(Jim)

Born September 23, 1959, at Stockton, Calif.
Height, 6.03. Weight, 190.
Throws and bats righthanded.
Attended John Brown University, Siloam Springs, Ark.

Major League saves: 1984 (1), 1986 (3). Total—4.

Year Club	League	G.	IP.	W.	L.	Pct.	H.	R.	ER.	SO.	BB.	ERA.
1981—Bradenton Pirates	Gulf Coast	1	4	0	0	.000	1	0	0	6	0	0.00
1981—Buffalo	Eastern	12	65	2	5	.286	60	40	33	44	23	4.57
1982—Buffalo†	Eastern	3	6⅔	0	2	.000	6	7	4	7	5	5.40
1982—Alexandria	Carolina	7	28	1	2	.333	31	17	12	20	11	3.86
1983—Pittsburgh	National	7	11	0	0	.000	12	9	9	3	6	7.36
1983—Hawaii	P. Coast	31	38⅔	0	1	.000	49	23	17	22	22	3.96
1984—Hawaii	P. Coast	21	44⅔	6	1	.857	44	19	17	28	28	3.43
1984—Pittsburgh	National	9	18⅔	1	0	1.000	19	8	8	11	9	3.86

Year Club	League	G.	IP.	W.	L.	Pct.	H.	R.	ER.	SO.	BB.	ERA.
1985—Hawaii	P. Coast	7	42⅔	5	2	.714	31	19	16	33	20	3.38
1985—Pittsburgh	National	30	75⅔	3	6	.333	77	45	44	22	31	5.23
1986—Pittsburgh	National	50	88	3	5	.375	85	44	35	70	38	3.58
Major League Totals—4 Years		96	193⅓	7	11	.389	193	106	96	106	84	4.47

Selected by Pittsburgh Pirates' organization in 1st round (14th player selected) of free-agent draft, June 8, 1981.
†On disabled list, April 12 to May 24 and June 8 to July 16, 1982.

HERMAN S. WINNINGHAM JR.
(Herm)

Born December 1, 1961, at Orangeburg, S.C.
Height, 6.00. Weight, 165.
Throws right and bats lefthanded.
Attended DeKalb Community College South, Decatur, Ga.

Major League stolen bases: 1984 (2), 1985 (20), 1986 (12). Total—34.

Year Club	League	Pos.	G.	AB.	R.	H.	2B.	3B.	HR.	RBI.	B.A.	PO.	A.	E.	F.A.
1981—Kingsport	Appal.	OF	58	204	44	52	7	4	2	14	.255	128	3	2	*.985
1982—Lynchburg	Carol.	OF	120	430	65	127	20	5	6	61	.295	235	6	5	.980
1983—Jackson	Texas	OF	78	288	54	102	13	6	4	41	.354	157	5	6	.964
1983—Tidewater†	Int.	OF	29	113	18	30	5	2	1	11	.265	70	1	3	.959
1984—Tidewater	Int.	OF	115	406	50	114	20	3	3	47	.281	228	8	4	.983
1984—New York‡	Nat.	OF	14	27	5	11	1	1	0	5	.407	7	0	0	1.000
1985—Montreal§	Nat.	OF	125	312	30	74	6	5	3	21	.237	229	6	4	.983
1985—Indianapolis	A. A.	OF	11	35	3	6	0	0	0	2	.171	22	0	1	.957
1986—Montreal	Nat.	OF-3B	90	185	23	40	6	3	4	11	.216	97	2	2	.980
1986—Indianapolis	A. A.	OF-3B	51	201	35	54	5	7	4	24	.269	106	3	1	.991
Major League Totals—3 Years			229	524	58	125	13	9	7	37	.239	333	8	6	.983

Selected by Pittsburgh Pirates' organization in 38th round of free-agent draft, June 5, 1979.
Selected by Milwaukee Brewers' organization in secondary phase of free-agent draft, January 8, 1980.
Selected by Montreal Expos' organization in secondary phase of free-agent draft, June 3, 1980.
Selected by New York Mets' organization in secondary phase of free-agent draft, January 13, 1981.
†On disabled list, August 9 to September 20, 1983.
‡Traded with Infielder Hubie Brooks, Catcher Mike Fitzgerald and Pitcher Floyd Youmans to Montreal Expos for Catcher Gary Carter, December 10, 1984.
§On disabled list, June 24 to July 13, 1985; included rehabilitation disability assignment to Indianapolis, July 4 to July 13, 1985.

MICHAEL ALLEN WISHNEVSKI
(Mike)

Born March 29, 1961, at Johnstown, Pa.
Height, 6.00. Weight, 207.
Throws and bats lefthanded.
Attended Indiana Central University, Indianapolis, Ind.

Year Club	League	Pos.	G.	AB.	R.	H.	2B.	3B.	HR.	RBI.	B.A.	PO.	A.	E.	F.A.
1982—Wausau	Midw.	OF	59	176	25	51	7	2	4	14	.290	38	2	3	.930
1983—Wausau	Midw.					(Did not play)									
1984—Wausau	Midw.	OF	110	361	52	96	18	0	11	57	.266	127	13	8	.946
1985—Salinas	Calif.	OF	119	414	70	125	26	6	13	91	.302	189	8	6	.970
1986—Chattanooga	South.	OF	130	461	80	113	21	3	17	72	.245	185	13	9	.957

Selected by Seattle Mariners' organization in 2nd round of free-agent draft, June 7, 1982.

MICHAEL ATWATER WITT
(Mike)

Born July 20, 1960, at Fullerton, Calif.
Height, 6.07. Weight, 185.
Throws and bats righthanded.
Attending Cypress Junior College, Cypress, Calif.

Pitched 1-0 perfect game against Texas Rangers, September 30, 1984.
Major League saves: 1983 (5).
Tied for American League lead in hit batsmen with 11 in 1981.

Year Club	League	G.	IP.	W.	L.	Pct.	H.	R.	ER.	SO.	BB.	ERA.
1978—Idaho Falls	Pioneer	13	86	7	1	.875	88	45	34	79	26	3.56
1979—Salinas	California	30	141	8	10	.444	156	96	80	94	70	5.11
1980—Salinas	California	13	90	7	3	.700	85	30	21	76	35	2.10
1980—El Paso	Texas	12	70	5	5	.500	72	53	45	64	39	5.79
1981—California	American	22	129	8	9	.471	123	60	47	75	47	3.28
1982—California	American	33	179⅔	8	6	.571	177	77	70	85	47	3.51
1983—California	American	43	154	7	14	.333	173	90	84	77	75	4.91
1984—California	American	34	246⅔	15	11	.577	227	103	95	196	84	3.47
1985—California	American	35	250	15	9	.625	228	115	99	180	98	3.56
1986—California	American	34	269	18	10	.643	218	95	85	208	73	2.84
Major League Totals—6 Years		201	1228⅓	71	59	.546	1146	540	480	821	424	3.52

Selected by California Angels' organization in 4th round of free-agent draft, June 6, 1978.

Year	Club	League	G.	IP.	W.	L.	Pct.	H.	R.	ER.	SO.	BB.	ERA.
1982—California		American	1	3	0	0	.000	2	2	2	3	2	6.00
1986—California		American	2	17⅔	1	0	1.000	13	5	5	8	2	2.55
Championship Series Totals—2 Years			3	20⅔	1	0	1.000	15	7	7	11	4	3.05

ALL-STAR GAME RECORD

Member of American League All-Star Team in 1986; did not play.

ROBERT ANDREW WITT
(Bobby)

Born May 11, 1964, at Canton, Mass.
Height, 6.02. Weight, 190.
Throws and bats righthanded.
Attended University of Oklahoma, Norman, Okla.

Established American League record for most wild pitches, season (22), 1986.
Led American League in wild pitches with 22 in 1986.
Named as righthanded pitcher on THE SPORTING NEWS College Baseball All-America Team, 1985.
Member of 1984 U.S. Olympic baseball team.

Year	Club	League	G.	IP.	W.	L.	Pct.	H.	R.	ER.	SO.	BB.	ERA.
1985—Tulsa		Texas	11	35	0	6	.000	26	26	25	39	44	6.43
1986—Texas		American	31	157⅔	11	9	.550	130	104	96	174	★143	5.48
Major League Totals—1 Year			31	157⅔	11	9	.550	130	104	96	174	143	5.48

Selected by Cincinnati Reds' organization in 7th round of free-agent draft, June 7, 1982.
Selected by Texas Rangers' organization in 1st round (third player selected) of free-agent draft, June 3, 1985.

JAMES EUGENE WOHLFORD
(Jim)

Born February 28, 1951, at Visalia, Calif.
Height, 5.11. Weight, 175.
Throws and bats righthanded.
Attended College of the Sequoias, Visalia, Calif.

Major League stolen bases: 1973 (1), 1974 (16), 1975 (12), 1976 (22), 1977 (17), 1978 (3), 1979 (6), 1980 (1), 1982 (8), 1984 (3). Total—89.
Led Pioneer League in stolen bases with 32 in 1970.
Led American Association second basemen in errors with 27 in 1972.
Led Pioneer League shortstops in errors with 33 in 1970.

Year	Club	League	Pos.	G.	AB.	R.	H.	2B.	3B.	HR.	RBI.	B.A.	PO.	A.	E.	F.A.
1970—Billings		Pion.	SS-2B-3B	62	221	42	68	7	2	3	37	.308	72	158	36	.865
1971—San Jose		Calif.	2B-SS	120	491	82	149	27	6	11	41	.303	193	327	30	.945
1972—Omaha		A. A.	2B-3B-OF	132	475	75	138	13	10	7	47	.291	247	292	32	.944
1972—Kansas City		Amer.	2B	15	25	3	6	1	0	0	0	.240	7	12	1	.950
1973—Omaha		A. A.	OF	65	246	30	76	9	4	3	30	.309	91	5	2	.980
1973—Kansas City		Amer.	OF	45	109	21	29	1	3	2	10	.266	31	2	0	1.000
1974—Kansas City		Amer.	OF	143	501	55	136	16	7	2	44	.271	273	7	5	.982
1975—Kansas City		Amer.	OF	116	353	45	90	10	5	0	30	.255	175	9	9	.953
1976—Kansas City†		Amer.	OF-2B	107	293	47	73	10	2	1	24	.249	190	8	5	.975
1977—Milwaukee		Amer.	OF-2B	129	391	41	97	16	3	2	36	.248	246	7	5	.981
1978—Milwaukee		Amer.	OF	46	118	16	35	7	2	1	19	.297	52	2	1	.982
1979—Milwaukee‡		Amer.	OF	63	175	19	46	13	1	1	17	.263	126	0	4	.969
1980—San Francisco		Nat.	OF-3B	91	193	17	54	6	4	1	24	.280	89	3	2	.979
1981—San Francisco		Nat.	OF	50	68	4	11	3	0	1	7	.162	3	1	0	1.000
1982—San Francisco§		Nat.	OF	97	250	37	64	12	1	2	25	.256	122	4	1	.992
1983—Montreal		Nat.	OF	83	141	7	39	8	0	1	14	.277	80	2	1	.988
1984—Montreal x		Nat.	OF-3B	95	213	20	64	13	2	5	29	.300	85	4	1	.989
1985—Montreal		Nat.	OF	70	125	7	24	5	1	1	15	.192	58	1	0	1.000
1986—Montreal y		Nat.	OF-3B	70	94	10	25	4	2	1	11	.266	22	6	0	1.000
American League Totals—8 Years				664	1965	247	512	74	23	9	190	.261	1100	47	30	.975
National League Totals—7 Years				556	1084	102	281	51	10	12	125	.259	459	21	5	.990
Major League Totals—15 Years				1220	3049	349	793	125	33	21	315	.260	1559	68	35	.979

Selected by California Angels' organization in 11th round of free-agent draft, June 5, 1969.
Selected by Kansas City Royals' organization in secondary phase of free-agent draft, January 17, 1970.
†Traded with Infielder Jamie Quirk and a player to be named later to Milwaukee Brewers for Pitcher Jim Colborn and Catcher Darrell Porter, December 6, 1976; Milwaukee acquired Pitcher Bob McClure to complete deal, March 15, 1977.
‡Granted free agency, November 1, 1979; signed by San Francisco Giants, November 28, 1979.
§Traded to Montreal Expos for Infielder Chris Smith, February 2, 1983.
xGranted free agency, November 8, 1984; re-signed by Expos, January 11, 1985.
yReleased, November 1, 1986.

CHAMPIONSHIP SERIES RECORD

Year	Club	League	Pos.	G.	AB.	R.	H.	2B.	3B.	HR.	RBI.	B.A.	PO.	A.	E.	F.A.
1976—Kansas City		Amer.	OF-PH	5	11	3	2	0	0	0	0	.182	7	0	0	1.000

EDWARD DAVID WOJNA

Name pronounced WOHJ-nuh.

(Ed)

Born August 20, 1960, at Bridgeport, Conn.
Height, 6.01. Weight, 195.
Throws and bats righthanded.
Attended Indian River Community College, Ft. Pierce, Fla.

Led Eastern League in hit batsmen with 9 in 1983.
Tied for Pacific Coast League lead in wild pitches with 16 in 1984.

Year Club	League	G.	IP.	W.	L.	Pct.	H.	R.	ER.	SO.	BB.	ERA.
1981—Spartanburg	S. Atlantic	27	178	11	13	.458	181	●107	●82	130	69	4.15
1982—Peninsula	Carolina	27	176⅔	12	8	.600	156	79	57	116	49	2.90
1983—Reading†	Eastern	28	161⅔	13	7	.650	147	80	66	83	78	3.67
1984—Las Vegas	P. Coast	29	159⅓	14	8	.636	182	99	90	95	81	5.08
1985—Las Vegas	P. Coast	18	111⅓	5	8	.385	121	63	55	66	43	4.45
1985—San Diego	National	15	42	2	4	.333	53	35	27	18	19	5.79
1986—Las Vegas	P. Coast	25	175⅓	12	7	.632	181	81	70	102	50	3.59
1986—San Diego	National	7	39	2	2	.500	42	19	14	19	16	3.23
Major League Totals—2 Years		22	81	4	6	.400	95	54	41	37	35	4.56

Selected by Baltimore Orioles' organization in 6th round of free-agent draft, January 8, 1980.
Selected by Philadelphia Phillies' organization in secondary phase of free-agent draft, June 3, 1980.
†Traded with Pitchers Marty Decker, Darren Burroughs and Lance McCullers to San Diego Padres, September 20, 1983, as partial completion of deal in which San Diego traded Outfielder Sixto Lezcano and a player to be named later to Philadelphia Phillies for four players to be named later, August 31, 1983; Philadelphia organization acquired Pitcher Steve Fireovid to complete deal, October 11, 1983.

MICHAEL CARY WOODARD

(Mike)

Born March 2, 1960, at Melrose Park, Ill.
Height, 5.09. Weight, 155.
Throws right and bats lefthanded.

Major League stolen bases: 1985 (6), 1986 (7). Total—13.
Led Eastern League in stolen bases with 54 in 1982.
Led Eastern League in caught stealing with 23 in 1981.
Led Pacific Coast League second basemen in total chances with 702 and double plays with 89 in 1985.
Led Northwest League second basemen in double plays with 34 in 1978.

Year Club	League	Pos.	G.	AB.	R.	H.	2B.	3B.	HR.	RBI.	B.A.	PO.	A.	E.	F.A.
1978—Bend	N'west	2B	62	231	45	79	8	1	0	12	.342	141	136	●20	.933
1979—Modesto	Calif.	2B	118	431	90	124	8	3	2	31	.288	230	253	★30	.942
1980—Modesto	Calif.	2B-OF	73	289	52	86	8	1	0	32	.298	177	165	19	.947
1980—West Haven†	East.	2B	6	13	2	0	0	0	0	0	.000	8	9	2	.895
1981—West Haven	East.	2B	133	427	59	96	9	3	1	25	.225	249	299	19	.967
1982—West Haven‡	East.	2B-3B	104	348	55	95	13	1	1	43	.273	198	208	13	.969
1983—Tacoma	P. C.	2B-SS-3B	122	323	45	78	7	1	0	27	.241	120	236	12	.967
1984—Albany	East.	2B	23	96	19	34	2	0	0	9	.354	62	72	6	.957
1984—Tacoma§	P. C.	2B-OF-SS	95	325	47	89	8	2	1	17	.274	191	229	6	.986
1985—Phoenix	P. C.	2B	140	★573	85	★181	16	9	3	63	.316	★283	★404	15	.979
1985—San Francisco	Nat.	2B	24	82	12	20	1	0	0	9	.244	49	46	1	.990
1986—Phoenix	P. C.	2B-3B	62	248	45	79	7	2	0	27	.319	116	165	8	.972
1986—San Francisco	Nat.	2B-3B-SS	48	79	14	20	2	1	1	5	.253	28	43	2	.973
Major League Totals—2 Years			72	161	26	40	3	1	1	14	.248	77	89	3	.982

Selected by Oakland A's organization in 4th round of free-agent draft, June 6, 1978.
†On disabled list, July 8, 1980 through remainder of season.
‡On disabled list, July 4 to July 14 and July 20 to July 31, 1982.
§Granted free agency, October 15, 1984; signed by Phoenix (San Francisco Giants' organization), November 20, 1984.

ALVIS WOODS

(Al)

Born August 8, 1953, at Oakland, Calif.
Height, 6.03. Weight, 195.
Throws and bats lefthanded.
Attended Laney Junior College, Oakland, Calif.

Major League stolen bases: 1977 (8), 1978 (1), 1979 (6), 1980 (4), 1981 (3), 1982 (1). Total—23.
Hit home run as pinch-hitter first at bat in major leagues, April 7, 1977.

Year Club	League	Pos.	G.	AB.	R.	H.	2B.	3B.	HR.	RBI.	B.A.	PO.	A.	E.	F.A.
1973—Geneva	NYP	OF	35	116	17	35	6	1	2	10	.302	47	3	5	.909
1974—Wis. Rapids	Midw.	OF	111	405	87	126	17	5	18	77	.311	207	6	5	.977
1975—Orlando†	South.	OF	123	411	55	108	11	4	6	50	.263	248	9	4	.985
1976—Tacoma‡§	P. C.	OF	121	416	60	118	15	4	6	74	.284	219	11	9	.962
1977—Toronto	Amer.	OF	122	440	58	125	17	4	6	35	.284	215	6	7	.969
1978—Syracuse	Int.	OF	81	287	47	89	13	1	11	49	.310	145	7	4	.974
1978—Toronto	Amer.	OF	62	220	19	53	12	3	3	25	.241	131	2	3	.978
1979—Toronto	Amer.	OF	132	436	57	121	24	4	5	36	.278	251	10	9	.967
1980—Toronto	Amer.	OF	109	373	54	112	18	2	15	47	.300	205	5	2	.991
1981—Toronto	Amer.	OF	85	288	20	71	15	0	1	21	.247	179	4	5	.973

Year Club League	Pos.	G.	AB.	R.	H.	2B.	3B.	HR.	RBI.	B.A.	PO.	A.	E.	F.A.
1982—Toronto xy .... Amer.	OF	85	201	20	47	11	1	3	24	.234	96	2	3	.970
1983—Syracuse .... Int.	OF	47	153	18	39	6	4	3	23	.255	22	0	2	.917
1984—Syracuse za .... Int.	OF	85	258	33	64	16	1	8	41	.248	119	4	2	.984
1985—Toledo .... Int.	OF-1B	96	315	54	89	12	2	14	48	.283	73	1	0	1.000
1986—Toledo .... Int.	DH	72	205	24	55	12	1	5	32	.268	0	0	0	.000
1986—Minnesota bc .... Amer.	DH	23	28	5	9	1	0	2	8	.321	0	0	0	.000
Major League Totals—7 Years................		618	1986	233	538	98	14	35	196	.271	1077	29	29	.974

Selected by Montreal Expos' organization in 32nd round of free-agent draft, June 8, 1971.
Selected by Minnesota Twins' organization in secondary phase of free-agent draft, June 6, 1972.
†On disabled list, May 29 to June 8, 1975.
‡On disabled list, April 17 to April 27, 1976.
§Selected by Toronto Blue Jays in American League expansion draft, November 5, 1976.
xTraded to Oakland A's for Designated Hitter Cliff Johnson, November 5, 1982.
yReleased, March 28, 1983; signed by Syracuse (Toronto Blue Jays' organization), July 7, 1983.
zOn disabled list, May 24 to June 5, 1984.
aReleased, September 4, 1984; signed by Toledo (Minnesota Twins' organization), December 8, 1984.
bOn disabled list, May 27 to June 12, 1986.
cGranted free agency, November 12, 1986.

TRACY MICHAEL WOODSON

Born October 5, 1962, at Richmond, Va.
Height, 6.03. Weight, 215.
Throws and bats righthanded.
Attended North Carolina State University, Raleigh, N. C.

Led Texas League third basemen in total chances with 413 in 1986.
Led Florida State League third basemen in putouts with 111, fielding percentage with .926 and total chances with 408 in 1985.

Year Club League	Pos.	G.	AB.	R.	H.	2B.	3B.	HR.	RBI.	B.A.	PO.	A.	E.	F.A.
1984—Vero Beach........... Fla. St.	1B	76	256	29	56	9	0	4	36	.219	630	38	9	.987
1985—Vero Beach........... Fla. St.	3B-1B	138	504	55	126	30	4	9	62	.250	131	270	30	.930
1986—San Antonio........... Texas	*3B-SS	131	495	65	133	27	3	18	90	.269	*135	259	22	*.947

Selected by Los Angeles Dodgers' organization in 3rd round of free-agent draft, June 4, 1984.

ROBERT JOHN WOODWARD
(Rob)

Born September 28, 1962, at Hanover, N.H.
Height, 6.03. Weight, 185.
Throws and bats righthanded.

Led International League in shutouts with 4 in 1986.
Led Eastern League pitchers in hit batsmen with 12 and tied for lead in games started with 27 in 1984.
Tied for Carolina League lead in games started by pitchers with 29 in 1983.

Year Club League	G.	IP.	W.	L.	Pct.	H.	R.	ER.	SO.	BB.	ERA.
1981—Elmira.............. NYP	12	77	4	3	.571	77	38	29	47	23	3.39
1982—Winter Haven.............. Florida St.	27	126⅔	7	9	.438	140	85	72	50	62	5.12
1983—Winston-Salem .... Carolina	30	197⅔	13	11	.542	177	103	91	157	100	4.14
1984—New Britain .... Eastern	28	166	10	●12	.455	167	87	73	100	65	3.96
1985—New Britain .... Eastern	12	86⅓	7	5	.583	71	42	34	54	36	3.54
1985—Pawtucket .... Int'national	15	82⅔	3	8	.273	79	46	41	70	41	4.46
1985—Boston.............. American	5	26⅔	1	0	1.000	17	8	5	16	9	1.69
1986—Pawtucket.............. Int'national	18	127⅔	9	6	.600	114	55	45	73	42	3.17
1986—Boston.............. American	9	35⅔	2	3	.400	46	26	21	14	11	5.30
Major League Totals—2 Years..............	14	62⅓	3	3	.500	63	34	26	30	20	3.75

Selected by Boston Red Sox' organization in 3rd round of free-agent draft, June 8, 1981.

TODD ROLAND WORRELL

Name pronounced Wor-RELL.

Born September 28, 1959, at Arcadia, Calif.
Height, 6.05. Weight, 215.
Throws and bats righthanded.
Received bachelor of science degree in Christian education from
Biola College, La Mirada, Calif.

Established major league record for most saves by rookie (36), 1986.
Major League saves: 1985 (5), 1986 (36). Total—41.
Led National League in games finished in relief with 60, saves with 36 and intentional bases on balls issued with 16 in 1986.
Named National League Rookie Pitcher of the Year by THE SPORTING NEWS, 1986.
Named National League Rookie of the Year by Baseball Writers' Association of America, 1986.
Named National League Fireman of the Year by THE SPORTING NEWS, 1986.
Named righthanded pitcher on THE SPORTING NEWS College Baseball All-America Team, 1982.

Year Club League	G.	IP.	W.	L.	Pct.	H.	R.	ER.	SO.	BB.	ERA.
1982—Erie .... NYP	9	51⅔	4	1	.800	52	23	19	57	15	3.31
1983—Louisville............... Am. Assoc.	15	79⅔	4	2	.667	76	49	42	46	42	4.74
1983—Arkansas............... Texas	10	70⅓	5	2	.714	57	33	24	74	37	3.07
1984—Arkansas............... Texas	18	100⅓	3	10	.231	109	72	50	88	67	4.49
1984—St. Petersburg............... Florida St.	8	47⅓	3	2	.600	41	22	11	33	24	2.09

Year Club	League	G.	IP.	W.	L.	Pct.	H.	R.	ER.	SO.	BB.	ERA.
1985—Louisville	Am. Assoc.	34	127⅔	8	6	.571	114	59	51	*126	47	3.60
1985—St. Louis	National	17	21⅔	3	0	1.000	17	7	7	17	7	2.91
1986—St. Louis†	National	74	103⅔	9	10	.474	86	29	24	73	41	2.08
Major League Totals—2 Years		91	125⅓	12	10	.545	103	36	31	90	48	2.23

Selected by St. Louis Cardinals' organization in 1st round (21st player selected) of free-agent draft, June 7, 1982.
†Appeared in two games as an outfielder with no chances.

CHAMPIONSHIP SERIES RECORD

Year Club	League	G.	IP.	W.	L.	Pct.	H.	R.	ER.	SO.	BB.	ERA.
1985—St. Louis	National	4	6⅓	1	0	1.000	4	1	1	3	2	1.42

WORLD SERIES RECORD

Tied World Series record for most consecutive strikeouts, game (6), October 24, 1985.

Year Club	League	G.	IP.	W.	L.	Pct.	H.	R.	ER.	SO.	BB.	ERA.
1985—St. Louis	National	3	4⅔	0	1	.000	4	2	2	6	2	3.86

GEORGE DEWITT WRIGHT

Born December 22, 1958, at Oklahoma City, Okla.
Height, 5.11. Weight, 185.
Throws right and bats right and lefthanded.
Major League stolen bases: 1982 (3), 1983 (8), 1985 (4), 1986 (4). Total—19.
Led Western Carolinas League outfielders in double plays with 6 in 1979.
Tied for Texas League lead in double plays by outfielders with 4 in 1980.

Year Club	League	Pos.	G.	AB.	R.	H.	2B.	3B.	HR.	RBI.	B.A.	PO.	A.	E.	F.A.
1977—Sarasota Rangers	Gulf C.	OF	31	87	11	16	0	2	0	8	.184	44	4	1	.980
1978—Asheville	W. Car.	OF	110	335	66	83	16	1	1	27	.248	203	15	7	.969
1979—Asheville	W. Car.	OF	115	379	53	97	17	4	4	40	.256	*245	*22	7	.974
1980—Tulsa	Texas	OF	●136	458	60	126	22	5	5	65	.275	*319	22	11	.969
1981—Tulsa	Texas	OF	●133	489	58	127	29	8	11	58	.260	286	8	7	.977
1982—Texas	Amer.	OF	150	557	69	147	20	5	11	50	.264	398	14	8	.981
1983—Texas	Amer.	OF	●162	634	79	175	28	6	18	80	.276	460	6	7	.985
1984—Texas†	Amer.	OF	101	383	40	93	19	4	9	48	.243	175	3	3	.983
1984—Oklahoma City	A. A.	DH	8	30	7	10	2	1	1	8	.333	0	0	0	.000
1985—Texas	Amer.	OF	109	363	21	69	13	0	2	18	.190	213	8	2	.991
1985—Oklahoma City	A. A.	OF	39	142	22	36	4	2	8	27	.254	108	2	1	.991
1986—Texas‡	Amer.	OF	49	106	10	23	3	1	2	7	.217	61	2	2	.969
1986—Montreal	Nat.	OF	56	117	12	22	5	2	0	5	.188	48	2	0	1.000
1986—Indianapolis§	A. A.	OF	14	52	9	17	3	0	5	21	.327	30	2	1	.970
American League Totals—5 Years			571	2043	219	507	83	16	42	203	.248	1307	33	22	.984
National League Totals—1 Year			56	117	12	22	5	2	0	5	.188	48	2	0	1.000
Major League Totals—5 Years			627	2160	231	529	88	18	42	208	.245	1355	35	22	.984

Selected by Texas Rangers' organization in 4th round of free-agent draft, June 7, 1977.
†On disabled list, June 12 to July 12, 1984; included rehabilitation disability assignment to Oklahoma City, June 14 to July 12, 1984.
‡Traded to Montreal Expos for a player to be named later, June 18, 1986.
§Released, December 19, 1986.

JAMES RICHARD WRIGHT
(Ricky)

Born November 22, 1958, at Paris, Tex.
Height, 6.03. Weight, 190.
Throws and bats lefthanded.
Attended Paris Junior College, Paris, Tex.,
and University of Texas, Austin, Tex.
Nephew of Larry Click, minor league outfielder, 1957 through 1962.
Pitched 4-2 no-hit victory against Portland, May 4, 1983.
Led Texas League in wild pitches with 17 and tied for lead in balks with 4 in 1980.

Year Club	League	G.	IP.	W.	L.	Pct.	H.	R.	ER.	SO.	BB.	ERA.
1980—San Antonio†	Texas	23	152	8	10	.444	144	85	71	127	85	4.20
1981—Albuquerque	P. Coast	27	155	14	6	.700	141	81	73	112	90	4.24
1982—Albuquerque‡	P. Coast	15	60⅓	4	3	.571	63	45	38	57	36	5.67
1982—Los Angeles	National	14	32⅔	2	1	.667	28	12	11	24	20	3.03
1983—Albuquerque	P. Coast	33	83⅓	7	6	.538	75	60	45	68	58	4.86
1983—Los Angeles§	National	6	6⅓	0	0	.000	5	2	2	5	2	2.84
1983—Texas	American	1	2	0	0	.000	0	0	0	2	1	0.00
1984—Oklahoma City x	Am. Assoc.	31	48⅔	2	1	.667	37	14	13	38	24	2.40
1984—Texas	American	8	14⅔	0	2	.000	20	10	10	6	11	6.14
1985—Oklahoma City y	Am. Assoc.	17	82⅔	5	4	.556	67	30	25	55	37	2.72
1985—Texas	American	5	7⅔	0	0	.000	5	4	4	7	5	4.70
1986—Texas za	American	21	39⅓	1	0	1.000	44	22	22	23	21	5.03
1986—Oklahoma City b	Am. Assoc.	8	26	1	1	.500	28	22	20	18	16	6.92
National League Totals—2 Years		20	39	2	1	.667	33	14	13	29	22	3.00
American League Totals—4 Years		35	63⅔	1	2	.333	69	36	36	38	38	5.09
Major League Totals—5 Years		55	102⅔	3	3	.500	102	50	49	67	60	4.30

Selected by St. Louis Cardinals' organization in 2nd round of free-agent draft, June 7, 1977.

Selected by Los Angeles Dodgers' organization in secondary phase of free-agent draft, January 8, 1980.
†On temporary inactive list, July 26 to August 14, 1980.
‡On disabled list, April 5 to May 10, 1982.
§Traded to Texas Rangers, September 16, 1983, completing deal in which Los Angeles Dodgers traded Pitcher Dave Stewart and a player to be named later to Texas for Pitcher Rick Honeycutt, August 19, 1983.
xOn disabled list, July 28 to August 13, 1984.
yOn disabled list, May 6 to June 18, 1985.
zAppeared in two games as a pinch-runner.
aOn disabled list, June 26 to July 29 and August 6 to September 3, 1986; included rehabilitation disability assignment to Oklahoma City, July 10 to July 29 and August 16 to September 3, 1986.
bReleased, December 16, 1986.

HAROLD DELANO WYNEGAR JR.
Name pronounced WY-nuh-ger.
(Butch)

Born March 14, 1956, at York, Pa.
Height, 6.00. Weight, 194.
Throws right and bats left and righthanded.

Major League stolen bases: 1977 (2), 1978 (1), 1979 (2), 1980 (3), 1983 (1), 1984 (1). Total—10.
Led American League catchers in double plays with 13 in 1980.
Led California League in bases on balls received with 142 in 1975.
Led Appalachian League catchers in double plays with 9 in 1974.
Named American League Rookie Player of the Year by THE SPORTING NEWS, 1976.

Year Club	League	Pos.	G.	AB.	R.	H.	2B.	3B.	HR.	RBI.	B.A.	PO.	A.	E.	F.A.
1974—Elizabethton	Appal.	C	60	191	32	66	10	0	8	51	★.346	344	39	5	★.987
1975—Reno	Calif.	C	●139	468	106	147	18	6	19	★112	.314	★734	★99	9	★.989
1976—Minnesota	Amer.	C	149	534	58	139	21	2	10	69	.260	650	78	★16	.978
1977—Minnesota	Amer.	C-3B	144	532	76	139	22	3	10	79	.261	676	84	5	.993
1978—Minnesota	Amer.	C-3B	135	454	36	104	22	1	4	45	.229	582	70	8	.988
1979—Minnesota	Amer.	C	149	504	74	136	20	0	7	57	.270	653	65	6	.992
1980—Minnesota	Amer.	C	146	486	61	124	18	3	5	57	.255	670	72	9	.988
1981—Minnesota†	Amer.	C	47	150	11	37	5	0	0	10	.247	162	24	1	.995
1982—Minn.‡-N.Y. §	Amer.	C	87	277	36	74	12	1	4	28	.267	523	26	5	.991
1983—New York x	Amer.	C	94	301	40	89	18	2	6	42	.296	480	29	8	.985
1984—New York	Amer.	C	129	442	48	118	13	1	6	45	.267	757	59	6	.993
1985—New York yz	Amer.	C	102	309	27	69	15	0	5	32	.223	547	34	6	.990
1986—New York abc	Amer.	C	61	194	19	40	4	1	7	29	.206	325	22	2	.994
Major League Totals—11 Years			1343	4183	486	1069	170	14	64	493	.256	6025	563	72	.989

Selected by Minnesota Twins' organization in 2nd round of free-agent draft, June 5, 1974.
†On disabled list, April 6 to May 16 and August 26 to September 11, 1981.
‡Traded with Pitcher Roger Erickson to New York Yankees for Infielder Larry Milbourne and Pitchers John Pacella and Pete Filson, May 12, 1982.
§On disabled list, July 25 to September 1, 1982.
xOn disabled list, May 12 to May 27, 1983.
yOn disabled list, June 18 to July 18 and July 22 to August 2, 1985.
zGranted free agency, November 12, 1985; re-signed by Yankees, January 8, 1986.
aOn disabled list, April 21 to May 6, 1986.
bOn restricted list, August 1, 1986 through remainder of season.
cTraded to California Angels for Pitcher Ron Romanick and a player to be named later, December 19, 1986.

ALL-STAR GAME RECORD

Year League	Pos.	AB.	R.	H.	2B.	3B.	HR.	RBI.	B.A.	PO.	A.	E.	F.A.
1976—American	PH	0	0	0	0	0	0	0	.000	0	0	0	.000
1977—American	C	2	1	1	0	0	0	0	.500	3	0	0	1.000
All-Star Game Totals—2 Years		2	1	1	0	0	0	0	.500	3	0	0	1.000

MARVELL WYNNE
Name pronounced Win.

Born December 17, 1959, at Chicago, Ill.
Height, 5.11. Weight, 176.
Throws and bats lefthanded.

Major League stolen bases: 1983 (12), 1984 (24), 1985 (10), 1986 (11). Total—57.
Led South Atlantic League in total bases with 256 in 1980.
Led South Atlantic League outfielders in assists with 17 in 1980.
Tied for International League lead in game-winning RBIs with 14 in 1982.
Tied for Gulf Coast League lead in being hit by pitch with 5 in 1979.

Year Club	League	Pos.	G.	AB.	R.	H.	2B.	3B.	HR.	RBI.	B.A.	PO.	A.	E.	F.A.
1979—Sarasota Royals	Gulf C.	OF	50	190	21	54	6	4	4	28	.284	108	9	4	.967
1980—Charleston†	S. Atl.	OF-2B-3B	137	★547	106	152	20	★15	18	98	.278	281	19	13	.958
1981—Jackson	Texas	OF	127	497	69	142	29	2	4	50	.286	267	21	6	.980
1982—Tidewater	Int.	OF	130	512	76	118	15	7	10	65	.230	283	13	12	.961
1983—Tidewater‡	Int.	OF	51	175	32	50	13	1	3	29	.286	114	5	2	.983
1983—Pittsburgh	Nat.	OF	103	366	66	89	16	2	7	26	.243	223	3	4	.983
1984—Pittsburgh	Nat.	OF	154	653	77	174	24	11	0	39	.266	373	8	4	.990
1985—Pittsburgh§x	Nat.	OF	103	337	21	69	6	3	2	18	.205	229	7	3	.987
1986—San Diego	Nat.	OF	137	288	34	76	19	2	7	37	.264	203	3	3	.986
Major League Totals—4 Years			497	1644	198	408	65	18	16	120	.248	1028	21	14	.987

Signed as free agent by Kansas City Royals' organization, September 3, 1978.
†Traded with Pitcher John Skinner to New York Mets' organization for Pitcher Juan Berenguer, March 31, 1981.
‡Traded with Pitcher Steve Senteney to Pittsburgh Pirates for Catcher Junior Ortiz and Pitcher Arthur Ray, June 14, 1983.
§On disabled list, April 20 to May 5 and June 3 to June 18, 1985.
xTraded to San Diego Padres for Pitcher Bob Patterson, April 3, 1986.

STEPHEN WAYNE YEAGER

Name pronounced YAY-gur.

(Steve)

Born November 24, 1948, at Huntington, W. Va.
Height, 6.00. Weight, 200.
Throws and bats righthanded.
Nephew of retired Air Force Brigadier General Chuck Yeager, first man to break sound barrier.

Tied major league record for most putouts, extra-inning game, catcher (22), August 8, 1972 (19 innings).
Established National League record for most chances accepted, extra-inning game, catcher (24), August 8, 1972 (19 innings).
Major League stolen bases: 1973 (1), 1974 (2), 1975 (2), 1976 (3), 1977 (1), 1979 (1), 1980 (2), 1983 (1), 1984 (1). Total—14.

Year	Club	League	Pos.	G.	AB.	R.	H.	2B.	3B.	HR.	RBI.	B.A.	PO.	A.	E.	F.A.
1967—Ogden		Pion.	C	1	0	0	0	0	0	0	0	.000	0	0	0	.000
1967—Dubuque		Midw.	C-1B	14	35	0	6	0	0	0	2	.171	67	3	3	.959
1968—Daytona Beach		Fla. St.	C	59	144	17	22	3	1	1	6	.153	314	23	9	.974
1969—Bakersfield		Calif.	C	22	65	8	10	1	0	0	2	.154	145	26	4	.977
1969—Albuquerque		Texas	PH	1	1	0	0	0	0	0	0	.000	0	0	0	.000
1970—Albuquerque		Texas	C-OF-3B	55	151	23	42	5	1	3	24	.278	224	29	5	.981
1971—Albuquerque		Texas	C	107	339	49	93	16	5	8	53	.274	678	84	★14	.982
1972—Albuquerque		P. C.	C	82	257	46	72	6	6	13	45	.280	494	26	9	.983
1972—Los Angeles		Nat.	C	35	106	18	29	0	1	4	15	.274	220	19	4	.984
1973—Los Angeles		Nat.	C	54	134	18	34	5	0	2	10	.254	230	24	5	.981
1974—Los Angeles		Nat.	C	94	316	41	84	16	1	12	41	.266	552	58	5	.992
1975—Los Angeles		Nat.	C	135	452	34	103	16	1	12	54	.228	★806	62	7	.992
1976—Los Angeles		Nat.	C	117	359	42	77	11	3	11	35	.214	522	★77	9	.985
1977—Los Angeles		Nat.	C	125	387	53	99	21	2	16	55	.256	690	89	★18	.977
1978—Los Angeles†		Nat.	C	94	228	19	44	7	0	4	23	.193	373	55	5	.988
1979—Los Angeles		Nat.	C	105	310	33	67	9	2	13	41	.216	513	56	9	.984
1980—Los Angeles		Nat.	C	96	227	20	48	8	0	2	20	.211	382	36	7	.984
1981—Los Angeles		Nat.	C	42	86	5	18	2	0	3	7	.209	142	13	1	.994
1982—Los Angeles‡		Nat.	C	82	196	13	48	5	2	2	18	.245	338	42	4	.990
1983—Los Angeles§		Nat.	C	113	335	31	68	8	3	15	41	.203	579	63	10	.985
1984—Los Angeles		Nat.	C	74	197	16	45	4	0	4	29	.228	317	30	2	.994
1985—Los Angeles xy		Nat.	C	53	121	4	25	4	1	0	9	.207	212	28	2	.992
1986—Seattle za		Amer.	C	50	130	10	27	2	0	2	12	.208	234	22	0	1.000
National League Totals—14 Years				1219	3454	347	789	116	16	100	398	.228	5876	652	88	.987
American League Totals—1 Year				50	130	10	27	2	0	2	12	.208	234	22	0	1.000
Major League Totals—15 Years				1269	3584	357	816	118	16	102	410	.228	6110	674	88	.987

Selected by Los Angeles Dodgers' organization in 4th round of free-agent draft, June 6, 1967.
†On disabled list, August 8 to August 25, 1978.
‡On disabled list, July 12 to August 9, 1982.
§On disabled list, August 1 to August 23, 1983.
xGranted free agency, November 12, 1985; re-signed by Dodgers, November 26, 1985.
yTraded to Seattle Mariners for Pitcher Ed Vande Berg, December 11, 1985.
zOn disabled list, June 18 to July 3, 1986.
aGranted free agency, November 12, 1986.

DIVISION SERIES RECORD

Year	Club	League	Pos.	G.	AB.	R.	H.	2B.	3B.	HR.	RBI.	B.A.	PO.	A.	E.	F.A.
1981—Los Angeles		Nat.	PH-C	2	5	1	2	1	0	0	0	.400	6	0	0	1.000

CHAMPIONSHIP SERIES RECORD

Tied National League Championship Series record for most Series played, one club (6).

Year	Club	League	Pos.	G.	AB.	R.	H.	2B.	3B.	HR.	RBI.	B.A.	PO.	A.	E.	F.A.
1974—Los Angeles		Nat.	C	3	9	1	0	0	0	0	0	.000	14	1	0	1.000
1977—Los Angeles		Nat.	C	4	13	1	3	0	0	0	2	.231	22	1	0	1.000
1978—Los Angeles		Nat.	C	4	13	2	3	0	0	1	2	.231	21	2	0	1.000
1981—Los Angeles		Nat.	PH-C	1	2	1	1	0	0	0	0	.500	2	0	0	1.000
1983—Los Angeles		Nat.	C	2	6	0	1	1	0	0	0	.167	7	1	0	1.000
1985—Los Angeles		Nat.	PH-C	1	2	0	0	0	0	0	0	.000	4	0	0	1.000
Championship Series Totals—6 Years				15	45	5	8	1	0	1	4	.178	70	5	0	1.000

WORLD SERIES RECORD

Tied World Series record for most at-bats, inning (2), October 28, 1981 (sixth inning).

Year	Club	League	Pos.	G.	AB.	R.	H.	2B.	3B.	HR.	RBI.	B.A.	PO.	A.	E.	F.A.
1974—Los Angeles		Nat.	C	4	11	0	4	1	0	0	1	.364	32	4	1	.973
1977—Los Angeles		Nat.	C	6	19	2	6	1	0	2	5	.316	32	6	0	1.000
1978—Los Angeles		Nat.	C	5	13	2	3	1	0	0	0	.231	23	2	0	1.000
1981—Los Angeles		Nat.	PH-C	6	14	2	4	1	0	2	4	.286	20	0	0	1.000
World Series Totals—4 Years				21	57	6	17	4	0	4	10	.298	107	12	1	.992

RICHARD MARTIN YETT
(Rich)

Born October 6, 1962, at Pomona, Calif.
Height, 6.02. Weight, 187.
Throws and bats righthanded.

Major League saves: 1986 (1).
Led International League in wild pitches with 16 in 1985.

Year Club	League	G.	IP.	W.	L.	Pct.	H.	R.	ER.	SO.	BB.	ERA.
1980—Elizabethton	Ap'lachian	10	52	3	4	.429	46	30	25	35	19	4.33
1981—Wisconsin Rapids	Midwest	25	164	12	6	.667	147	87	67	121	77	3.68
1982—Visalia	California	27	196⅔	16	9	.640	183	98	80	121	97	3.66
1983—Orlando†	Southern	24	162	8	10	.444	153	82	68	93	78	3.78
1984—Toledo	Int'national	26	174⅔	12	9	.571	159	71	63	129	66	3.25
1985—Minnesota	American	1	⅓	0	0	.000	1	1	1	0	2	27.00
1985—Toledo‡-Maine	Int'national	25	165	9	11	.450	162	82	76	99	*101	4.15
1986—Maine	Int'national	1	6	0	0	.000	7	3	3	2	2	4.50
1986—Cleveland	American	39	78⅔	5	3	.625	84	48	45	50	37	5.15
Major League Totals—2 Years		40	79	5	3	.625	85	49	46	50	39	5.24

Selected by Minnesota Twins' organization in 26th round of free-agent draft, June 3, 1980.
†On disabled list, April 8 to April 25, 1983.
‡Traded to Cleveland Indians' organization, September 17, 1985, completing deal in which Cleveland traded Pitcher Bert Blyleven to Minnesota Twins for Pitcher Curt Wardle, Outfielder Jim Weaver, Infielder Jay Bell and a player to be named later, August 1, 1986.

FLOYD EVERETT YOUMANS JR.

Name pronounced YOH-muns.

Born May 11, 1964, at Tampa, Fla.
Height, 6.02. Weight, 180.
Throws and bats righthanded.

Year Club	League	G.	IP.	W.	L.	Pct.	H.	R.	ER.	SO.	BB.	ERA.
1982—Kingsport	Ap'lachian	10	39⅓	2	4	.333	35	39	27	31	39	6.18
1983—Columbia	S. Atlantic	23	134⅓	12	3	.800	112	77	51	117	73	3.42
1984—Lynchburg	Carolina	7	39⅔	5	2	.714	31	19	16	45	27	3.63
1984—Jackson†‡	Texas	16	86	6	7	.462	75	47	44	87	74	4.60
1985—Jacksonville	Southern	14	85⅔	7	3	.700	65	35	32	86	57	3.36
1985—Montreal	National	14	77	4	3	.571	57	27	21	54	49	2.45
1985—Indianapolis	Am. Assoc.	6	37⅔	3	2	.600	19	14	13	38	26	3.11
1986—Montreal	National	33	219	13	12	.520	145	93	86	202	*118	3.53
Major League Totals—2 Years		47	296	17	15	.531	202	120	107	256	167	3.25

Selected by New York Mets' organization in 2nd round of free-agent draft, June 7, 1982.
†On disabled list, June 11 to June 21, 1984.
‡Traded with Infielder Hubie Brooks, Catcher Mike Fitzgerald and Outfielder Herm Winningham to Montreal Expos for Catcher Gary Carter, December 10, 1984.

CLIFFORD RAPHAEL YOUNG
(Cliff)

Born August 2, 1964, at Willis, Tex.
Height, 6.04. Weight, 195.
Throws and bats lefthanded.

Led Southern League in games started by pitchers with 31 in 1986.
Led Florida State League in home runs allowed with 13 in 1986.

Year Club	League	G.	IP.	W.	L.	Pct.	H.	R.	ER.	SO.	BB.	ERA.
1983—Calgary	Pioneer	13	79⅓	7	1	.875	98	55	45	72	32	5.11
1984—Gastonia†	S. Atlantic	24	144⅓	8	10	.444	117	77	67	121	68	4.18
1985—West Palm Beach‡	Florida St.	25	153⅔	15	5	.750	149	77	68	112	57	3.98
1986—Knoxville§	Southern	31	*203⅔	12	*14	.462	*232	111	88	121	71	3.89

Selected by Montreal Expos' organization in 5th round of free-agent draft, June 6, 1983.
†On suspended list, May 23 to May 30, 1984.
‡Traded to Toronto Blue Jays' organization, September 10, 1985, completing deal in which Toronto traded Outfielder Mitch Webster to Montreal Expos for a player to be named later, June 22, 1985.
§Drafted by Oakland A's, December 9, 1986.

CURTIS ALLEN YOUNG
(Curt)

Born April 16, 1960, at Saginaw, Mich.
Height, 6.01. Weight, 175.
Throws left and bats righthanded.
Attended Central Michigan University, Mt. Pleasant, Mich.

Led California League pitchers in games started with 28 in 1982.

Year Club	League	G.	IP.	W.	L.	Pct.	H.	R.	ER.	SO.	BB.	ERA.
1981—Medford	Northwest	8	53	2	2	.500	45	27	25	49	32	4.25
1981—Modesto	California	5	31	2	1	.667	28	15	12	22	16	3.48
1982—Modesto	California	28	205	15	8	.652	189	90	79	162	81	3.47
1983—Tacoma	P. Coast	27	158⅔	12	9	.571	175	94	89	109	52	5.05

Year	Club	League	G.	IP.	W.	L.	Pct.	H.	R.	ER.	SO.	BB.	ERA.
1983—Oakland	American.	8	9	0	1	.000	17	17	16	5	5	16.00
1984—Tacoma	P. Coast	14	95⅓	6	4	.600	88	45	40	61	28	3.78
1984—Oakland	American	20	108⅔	9	4	.692	118	53	49	41	31	4.06
1985—Oakland†	American	19	46	0	4	.000	57	38	37	19	22	7.24
1985—Modesto	California	2	5⅔	0	0	.000	7	4	3	3	6	4.76
1985—Tacoma	P. Coast	3	15	2	0	1.000	10	7	6	8	7	3.60
1986—Tacoma	P. Coast	4	27	4	0	1.000	16	7	6	28	6	2.00
1986—Oakland	American	29	198	13	9	.591	176	88	76	116	57	3.45
Major League Totals—4 Years		76	361⅔	22	18	.550	368	196	178	181	115	4.43

Selected by Oakland A's organization in 4th round of free-agent draft, June 8, 1981.

†On disabled list, May 3 to July 5, 1985; included rehabilitation disability assignment to Modesto, June 29 to July 5, 1985.

GERALD ANTHONY YOUNG

Born October 22, 1964, in Tele, Honduras.
Height, 6.02. Weight, 185.
Throws right and bats left and righthanded.

Led Southern League in stolen bases with 54 and caught stealing with 27 in 1986.
Tied for Appalachian League lead in being hit by pitch with 6 in 1982.
Led Appalachian League shortstops in errors with 38 in 1982.
Tied for Florida State League lead in double plays by outfielders with 5 in 1985.

Year	Club	League	Pos.	G.	AB.	R.	H.	2B.	3B.	HR.	RBI.	B.A.	PO.	A.	E.	F.A.
1982—Kingsport	Appal.	SS-2B-3B	59	197	27	35	6	1	0	15	.178	79	170	39	.865
1983—Sarasota Mets	Gulf C.	OF-SS	56	177	34	42	7	2	1	14	.237	88	9	7	.933
1984—Columbia†	S. Atl.	OF	124	396	69	84	14	3	1	52	.212	254	7	4	.985
1985—Osceola	Fla. St.	OF	133	474	88	121	20	9	3	48	.255	251	11	5	.981
1986—Columbus	South.	OF	136	539	101	151	30	4	9	62	.280	317	22	13	.963

Selected by New York Mets' organization in 5th round of free-agent draft, June 7, 1982.

†Traded with Infielder Manny Lee to Houston Astros, August 31, 1984, as partial completion of deal in which New York Mets acquired Infielder Ray Knight for three players to be named later, August 28, 1984; Houston acquired Pitcher Mitch Cook to complete deal, September 10, 1984.

MATTHEW JOHN YOUNG
(Matt)

Born August 9, 1958, at Pasadena, Calif.
Height, 6.03. Weight, 200.
Throws and bats lefthanded.
Attended Pasadena City College, Pasadena, Calif., and
University of California, Los Angeles, Calif.

Major League saves: 1985 (1), 1986 (13). Total—14.

Year	Club	League	G.	IP.	W.	L.	Pct.	H.	R.	ER.	SO.	BB.	ERA.
1980—Bellingham	Northwest	12	73	4	5	.444	73	46	40	53	62	4.93
1981—Lynn	Eastern	14	81	3	9	.250	80	47	36	57	38	4.00
1982—Salt Lake City	P. Coast	29	176	12	10	.545	192	113	91	118	75	4.65
1983—Seattle	American	33	203⅔	11	15	.423	178	86	74	130	79	3.27
1984—Seattle†	American	22	113⅓	6	8	.429	141	81	72	73	57	5.72
1984—Salt Lake City	P. Coast	6	41⅔	6	0	1.000	32	9	7	37	20	1.51
1985—Seattle	American	37	218⅓	12	*19	.387	242	135	119	136	76	4.91
1986—Seattle‡	American	65	103⅔	8	6	.571	108	50	44	82	46	3.82
Major League Totals—4 Years		157	639	37	48	.435	669	352	309	421	258	4.35

Selected by Boston Red Sox' organization in 2nd round of free-agent draft, January 10, 1978.
Selected by Seattle Mariners' organization in 2nd round of free-agent draft, June 3, 1980.

†On disabled list, July 4 to July 29, 1984.

‡Traded to Los Angeles Dodgers for Pitcher Dennis Powell and Infielder Mike Watters, December 10, 1986.

ALL-STAR GAME RECORD

Year	League	IP.	W.	L.	Pct.	H.	R.	ER.	SO.	BB.	ERA.
1983—American		1	0	0	.000	0	0	0	1	0	0.00

MICHAEL DARREN YOUNG
(Mike)

Born March 20, 1960, at Hayward, Calif.
Height, 6.02. Weight, 195.
Throws right and bats left and righthanded.
Attended St. Mary's College, Moraga, Calif.; and Chabot College, Hayward, Calif.

Switch-hit home runs in one game, August 13, 1985.
Major League stolen bases: 1983 (1), 1984 (6), 1985 (1), 1986 (3). Total—11.
Led International League batters in strikeouts with 140 in 1982.
Tied for Florida State League lead in double plays by outfielders with 4 in 1980.

Year	Club	League	Pos.	G.	AB.	R.	H.	2B.	3B.	HR.	RBI.	B.A.	PO.	A.	E.	F.A.
1980—Miami	Fla. St.	OF	115	393	72	105	13	8	5	52	.267	212	*17	7	.970
1981—Miami	Fla. St.	OF	63	235	32	81	19	6	3	34	.345	135	7	1	.993
1981—Charlotte	South.	OF	75	275	58	88	16	3	12	45	.320	190	5	5	.975
1981—Rochester	Int.	OF	1	3	0	1	0	0	0	0	.000	1	0	0	1.000

Year Club League	Pos.	G.	AB.	R.	H.	2B.	3B.	HR.	RBI.	B.A.	PO.	A.	E.	F.A.
1982—Rochester .... Int.	OF	137	502	86	133	22	11	16	62	.265	291	7	11	.964
1982—Baltimore .... Amer.	OF	6	2	2	0	0	0	0	0	.000	1	0	0	1.000
1983—Rochester .... Int.	OF	102	373	62	106	14	8	14	66	.284	198	4	6	.971
1983—Baltimore .... Amer.	OF	25	36	5	6	2	1	0	2	.167	25	1	2	.929
1984—Rochester .... Int.	OF	20	72	17	24	6	1	4	15	.333	39	0	3	.929
1984—Baltimore .... Amer.	OF	123	401	59	101	17	2	17	52	.252	216	4	4	.982
1985—Baltimore .... Amer.	OF	139	450	72	123	22	1	28	81	.273	190	6	5	.975
1986—Baltimore .... Amer.	OF	117	369	43	93	15	1	9	42	.252	149	1	6	.962
1986—Rochester .... Int.	OF	32	97	14	27	2	0	5	21	.278	58	3	2	.968
Major League Totals—5 Years.................		410	1258	181	323	56	5	54	177	.257	581	12	17	.972

Selected by Cleveland Indians' organization in 7th round of free-agent draft, June 6, 1978.
Selected by Baltimore Orioles' organization in secondary phase of free-agent draft, January 8, 1980.

JOEL RANDOLPH YOUNGBLOOD III

Born August 28, 1951, at Houston, Tex.
Height, 5.11. Weight, 175.
Throws and bats righthanded.

Established major league record for most clubs, one or more hits for, one day (2), August 4, 1982.
Tied major league record for most clubs played, one day (2), August 4, 1982.
Major League stolen bases: 1976 (1), 1977 (1), 1978 (4), 1979 (18), 1980 (14), 1981 (2), 1982 (2), 1983 (7), 1984 (5), 1985 (3), 1986 (1). Total—58.
Led National League third basemen in errors with 36 in 1984.
Led National League outfielders in double plays with 6 in 1980.
Led Northern League second basemen in errors with 19 in 1970.
Tied for Northern League lead in being hit by pitch with 5 in 1970.

Year Club League	Pos.	G.	AB.	R.	H.	2B.	3B.	HR.	RBI.	B.A.	PO.	A.	E.	F.A.
1970—Tampa.................... Fla. St.	SS	17	54	7	12	0	0	0	3	.222	22	40	9	.873
1970—Sioux Falls............. North.	2B-3B-SS	65	236	27	53	11	1	0	17	.225	110	134	26	.904
1971—Tampa.................... Fla. St.	3B-SS-OF	136	443	75	113	25	4	5	44	.255	159	207	26	.934
1972—Three Rivers......... East.	OF-3B	104	366	57	106	15	5	12	60	.290	118	80	30	.868
1973—Indianapolis......... A. A.	OF-SS-3B	124	451	88	143	24	9	11	50	.317	136	112	28	.899
1974—Indianapolis†........ A. A.	OF	103	316	55	90	17	4	13	49	.285	115	6	4	.968
1975—Indianapolis......... A. A.	OF-2B	123	418	65	110	21	●9	6	51	.263	201	13	7	.968
1976—Cincinnati‡........... Nat.	1-O-C-2	55	57	8	11	1	1	0	1	.193	15	3	1	.947
1977—St.L.§-N.Y.............. Nat.	2B-OF-3B	95	209	17	51	13	1	0	12	.244	107	94	8	.962
1978—New York............. Nat.	O-2-3-S	113	266	40	67	12	8	7	30	.252	160	96	13	.952
1979—New York............. Nat.	OF-2B-3B	158	590	90	162	37	5	16	60	.275	337	57	9	.978
1980—New York............. Nat.	OF-3B-2B	146	514	58	142	26	2	8	69	.276	318	65	13	.967
1981—New York x........... Nat.	OF	43	143	16	50	10	2	4	25	.350	70	6	3	.962
1982—N.Y. y-Mont. z ...... Nat.	O-2-S-3	120	292	37	70	14	0	3	29	.240	149	23	7	.961
1983—San Francisco ..... Nat.	2B-3B-OF	124	373	59	109	20	3	17	53	.292	147	182	19	.945
1984—San Francisco ..... Nat.	3B-OF-2B	134	469	50	119	17	1	10	51	.254	102	206	37	.893
1985—San Francisco a... Nat.	OF-3B	95	230	24	62	6	0	4	24	.270	103	6	6	.948
1986—San Francisco ..... Nat.	O-1-3-2-S	97	184	20	47	12	0	5	28	.255	68	14	3	.965
Major League Totals—11 Years...............		1180	3327	419	890	168	23	74	382	.268	1576	752	119	.951

Selected by Cincinnati Reds' organization in 2nd round of free-agent draft, January 17, 1970.
†On disabled list, June 7 to June 19, 1974.
‡Traded to St. Louis Cardinals for Pitcher Bill Caudill, March 28, 1977.
§Traded to New York Mets for Shortstop Mike Phillips, June 15, 1977.
xOn disabled list, June 6 to August 1 and August 15 to September 15, 1981.
yTraded to Montreal Expos for a player to be named later, August 4, 1982; New York Mets' organization acquired Pitcher Tom Gorman to complete deal, August 14, 1982.
zGranted free agency, November 10, 1982; signed by San Francisco Giants, February 7, 1983.
aReleased, December 20, 1985; re-signed by Giants, March 20, 1986.

ALL-STAR GAME RECORD

Year League	Pos.	AB.	R.	H.	2B.	3B.	HR.	RBI.	B.A.	PO.	A.	E.	F.A.
1981—National..............................	PH	1	0	0	0	0	0	0	.000	0	0	0	.000

ROBIN R. YOUNT

Born September 16, 1955, at Danville, Ill.
Height, 6.00. Weight, 170.
Throws and bats righthanded.
Brother of Larry Yount, pitcher with Houston Astros, 1971.

Major League stolen bases: 1974 (7), 1975 (12), 1976 (16), 1977 (16), 1978 (16), 1979 (11), 1980 (20), 1981 (4), 1982 (14), 1983 (12), 1984 (14), 1985 (10), 1986 (14). Total—166.
Led American League in total bases with 367 and slugging percentage with .578 in 1982.
Led American League outfielders in fielding percentage with .997 in 1986.
Led American League shortstops in double plays with 104 and total chances with 831 in 1976.
Named Major League Player of the Year by THE SPORTING NEWS, 1982.
Named American League Player of the Year by THE SPORTING NEWS, 1982.
Named American League Most Valuable Player by Baseball Writers' Association of America, 1982.
Named shortstop on THE SPORTING NEWS American League All-Star team, 1978, 1980 and 1982.
Named shortstop on THE SPORTING NEWS American League All-Star fielding team, 1982.
Named shortstop on THE SPORTING NEWS American League Silver Slugger team, 1980 and 1982.

Year Club League	Pos.	G.	AB.	R.	H.	2B.	3B.	HR.	RBI.	B.A.	PO.	A.	E.	F.A.
1973—Newark................. NYP	SS	64	242	29	69	15	3	3	25	.285	43	85	18	.877

Year	Club	League	Pos.	G.	AB.	R.	H.	2B.	3B.	HR.	RBI.	B.A.	PO.	A.	E.	F.A.
1974—Milwaukee	Amer.	SS	107	344	48	86	14	5	3	26	.250	148	327	19	.962
1975—Milwaukee	Amer.	SS	147	558	67	149	28	2	8	52	.267	273	402	★44	.939
1976—Milwaukee	Amer.	●SS-OF	●161	638	59	161	19	3	2	54	.252	●290	510	31	.963
1972—Milwaukee	Amer.	SS	154	605	66	174	34	4	4	49	.288	256	449	29	.964
1978—Milwaukee†	Amer.	SS	127	502	66	147	23	9	9	71	.293	246	453	30	.959
1979—Milwaukee	Amer.	SS	149	577	72	154	26	5	8	51	.267	267	517	25	.969
1980—Milwaukee	Amer.	SS	143	611	121	179	★49	10	23	87	.293	239	455	28	.961
1981—Milwaukee	Amer.	SS	96	377	50	103	15	5	10	49	.273	161	370	8	★.985
1982—Milwaukee	Amer.	SS	156	635	129	★210	●46	12	29	114	.331	253	★489	24	.969
1983—Milwaukee	Amer.	SS	149	578	102	178	42	★10	17	80	.308	256	420	19	.973
1984—Milwaukee	Amer.	SS	160	624	105	186	27	7	16	80	.298	199	402	18	.971
1985—Milwaukee	Amer.	OF-1B	122	466	76	129	26	3	15	68	.277	267	5	8	.971
1986—Milwaukee	Amer.	OF-1B	140	522	82	163	31	7	9	46	.312	365	9	2	.995
Major League Totals—13 Years				1811	7037	1043	2019	380	82	153	827	.287	3220	4808	282	.966

Selected by Milwaukee Brewers' organization in 1st round (third player selected) of free-agent draft, June 5, 1973.
†On disabled list, March 28 to May 3, 1978.

DIVISION SERIES RECORD

Year	Club	League	Pos.	G.	AB.	R.	H.	2B.	3B.	HR.	RBI.	B.A.	PO.	A.	E.	F.A.
1981—Milwaukee	Amer.	SS	5	19	4	6	0	1	0	1	.316	6	16	1	.957

CHAMPIONSHIP SERIES RECORD

Year	Club	League	Pos.	G.	AB.	R.	H.	2B.	3B.	HR.	RBI.	B.A.	PO.	A.	E.	F.A.
1982—Milwaukee	Amer.	SS	5	16	1	4	0	0	0	0	.250	11	12	1	.958

WORLD SERIES RECORD

Established World Series record for most games, Series, four or more hits (2), 1982.
Tied World Series record for most at-bats, nine-inning game (6), October 12, 1982.

Year	Club	League	Pos.	G.	AB.	R.	H.	2B.	3B.	HR.	RBI.	B.A.	PO.	A.	E.	F.A.
1982—Milwaukee	Amer.	SS	7	29	6	12	3	0	1	6	.414	20	19	3	.929

ALL-STAR GAME RECORD

Year	League	Pos.	AB.	R.	H.	2B.	3B.	HR.	RBI.	B.A.	PO.	A.	E.	F.A.
1980—American	SS	2	0	0	0	0	0	0	.000	3	2	0	1.000
1982—American	SS	3	0	0	0	0	0	0	.000	0	2	0	1.000
1983—American	SS	2	1	0	0	0	0	1	.000	0	1	0	1.000
All-Star Game Totals—3 Years		7	1	0	0	0	0	1	.000	3	5	0	1.000

LLOYD JEFFREY ZASKE

Name pronounced ZASS-kee.

(Jeff)

Born October 6, 1960, at Seattle, Wash.
Height, 6.05. Weight, 193.
Throws and bats righthanded.
Attended Edmonds Community College, Lynnwood, Wash.

Led Pacific Coast League in wild pitches with 17 in 1986.
Led Eastern League in saves with 24 and games finished in relief with 44 in 1983.

Year	Club	League	G.	IP.	W.	L.	Pct.	H.	R.	ER.	SO.	BB.	ERA.
1979—Shelby	W. Carol.	25	100	5	10	.333	91	80	58	88	96	5.22
1980—Salem	Carolina	26	132	8	10	.444	101	68	62	103	★116	4.23
1981—Buffalo	Eastern	4	10	0	1	.000	10	6	4	4	8	3.60
1981—Alexandria	Carolina	21	110	5	9	.357	105	64	54	75	72	4.42
1982—Alexandria	Carolina	48	74⅔	7	4	.636	63	30	24	84	29	2.89
1983—Lynn	Eastern	48	70⅓	5	3	.625	54	20	17	72	38	2.18
1983—Hawaii	P. Coast	6	6	1	0	1.000	6	4	4	4	6	6.00
1984—Hawaii	P. Coast	37	60⅓	2	4	.333	51	28	24	60	40	3.58
1984—Pittsburgh	National	3	5	0	0	.000	4	0	0	2	1	0.00
1985—Hawaii	P. Coast	46	68⅔	2	7	.222	51	28	26	75	57	3.41
1986—Hawaii†	P. Coast	40	113⅔	5	5	.500	104	54	52	87	78	4.12
Major League Totals—1 Year		3	5	0	0	.000	4	0	0	2	1	0.00

Selected by Pittsburgh Pirates' organization in 27th round of free-agent draft, June 6, 1978.
†Traded to Texas Rangers for Pitcher Randy Kramer, September 30, 1986.

STEPHEN GRAELING ZIEM

(Steve)

Born October 24, 1961, at Milwaukee, Wis.
Height, 6.02. Weight, 210.
Throws and bats righthanded.
Attended California State Poly University, Pomona, Calif.

Year	Club	League	G.	IP.	W.	L.	Pct.	H.	R.	ER.	SO.	BB.	ERA.
1983—Pulaski	Ap'lachian	20	54	6	4	.600	43	27	20	52	22	3.33
1984—Durham	Carolina	49	67⅓	5	4	.556	49	30	29	55	26	3.88
1984—Greenville	Southern	8	21	2	1	.667	12	1	0	14	9	0.00
1985—Greenville	Southern	48	157⅓	5	14	.263	158	87	73	86	73	4.18

Year Club	League	G.	IP.	W.	L.	Pct.	H.	R.	ER.	SO.	BB.	ERA.
1986—Greenville	Southern	31	74⅔	7	2	.778	73	44	39	54	32	4.70
1986—Richmond	Int'national	15	96⅓	8	5	.615	88	38	33	48	34	3.08

Selected by Chicago Cubs' organization in 29th round of free-agent draft, June 5, 1979.
Selected by Detroit Tigers' organization in 12th round of free-agent draft, June 7, 1982.
Selected by Atlanta Braves' organization in 8th round of free-agent draft, June 6, 1983.

PAUL ZUVELLA

Name pronounced Zoo-VELL-uh.
Born October 31, 1958, at San Mateo, Calif.
Height, 6.00. Weight, 170.
Throws and bats righthanded.
Received bachelor of arts degree in communications
from Stanford University, Stanford, Calif.

Major League stolen bases: 1985 (2).
Led International League in being hit by pitch with 8 in 1984.
Led International League shortstops in total chances with 644 and double plays with 85 in 1984.
Led Southern League shortstops in total chances with 661 in 1981.

Year Club	League	Pos.	G.	AB.	R.	H.	2B.	3B.	HR.	RBI.	B.A.	PO.	A.	E.	F.A.
1980—Bradenton Brav...	Gulf C.	SS	2	8	0	1	0	0	0	1	.125	4	9	1	.929
1980—Durham†	Carol.	SS	48	149	21	47	7	0	2	19	.315	58	140	12	.943
1981—Savannah	South.	SS	138	485	61	145	17	2	11	68	.299	220	★406	35	.947
1982—Richmond	Int.	SS	133	455	63	128	15	2	9	54	.281	245	335	22	.963
1982—Atlanta	Nat.	SS	2	1	0	0	0	0	0	0	.000	0	4	1	.800
1983—Richmond	Int.	SS	117	415	53	119	13	2	6	64	.287	169	324	18	★.965
1983—Atlanta	Nat.	SS	3	5	0	0	0	0	0	0	.000	1	2	1	.750
1984—Richmond	Int.	SS	127	462	77	140	18	•6	6	55	.303	★219	★409	16	★.975
1984—Atlanta	Nat.	2B-SS	11	25	2	5	1	0	0	1	.200	13	21	0	1.000
1985—Richmond	Int.	SS	8	32	3	7	0	0	1	3	.219	10	30	3	.930
1985—Atlanta	Nat.	2B-SS-3B	81	190	16	48	8	1	0	4	.253	112	173	8	.973
1986—Rich.‡-Col.	Int.	SS-2B	89	334	56	101	13	1	2	31	.302	149	231	10	.974
1986—New York	Amer.	SS	21	48	2	4	1	0	2	2	.083	30	54	3	.966
National League Totals—4 Years			97	221	18	53	9	1	0	5	.240	126	200	10	.970
American League Totals—1 Year			21	48	2	4	1	0	0	2	.083	30	54	3	.966
Major League Totals—5 Years			118	269	20	57	10	1	0	7	.212	156	254	13	.969

Selected by Milwaukee Brewers' organization in 11th round of free-agent draft, June 5, 1979.
Selected by Atlanta Braves' organization in 15th round of free-agent draft, June 3, 1980.
†On disabled list, August 27, 1980 through remainder of season.
‡Traded with Outfielder Claudell Washington to New York Yankees for Outfielder Ken Griffey, June 30, 1986.

PLAYER MOVES

The following player deals involve players in the Register with the transactions occurring after January 4, 1987 and including January 12.

BERENGUER, JUAN: Signed by Minnesota Twins, January 9, 1987.

BURLESON, RICK: Signed by Baltimore Orioles, January 7, 1987.

CLANCY, JIM: Re-signed by Toronto Blue Jays, January 6, 1987.

DeCINCES, DOUG: Re-signed by California Angels, January 8, 1987.

DOWNING, BRIAN: Re-signed by California Angels, January 8, 1987.

FILSON, PETE: Traded with Infielder Randy Velarde to New York Yankees for Pitcher Scott Nielsen and Infielder Mike Soper, January 5, 1987.

FIMPLE, JACK: Signed by Edmonton (California Angels' organization), January 7, 1987.

GARNER, PHIL: Re-signed by Astros, January 7, 1987.

HOYT, LaMARR: Released by San Diego Padres, January 7, 1987.

JOHN, TOMMY: Re-signed by New York Yankees, January 8, 1987.

MILNER, EDDIE: Traded to San Francisco Giants for Pitchers Frank Williams, Timber Mead and Mike Villa, January 8, 1987.

NIELSEN, SCOTT: Traded with Infielder Mike Soper to Chicago White Sox for Pitcher Pete Filson and Infielder Randy Velarde, January 5, 1987.

RANDOLPH, WILLIE: Re-signed by New York Yankees, January 8, 1987.

SOPER, MIKE: Traded with Pitcher Scott Nielsen to Chicago White Sox for Pitcher Pete Filson and Infielder Randy Velarde, January 5, 1987.

WHITT, ERNIE: Re-signed by Toronto Blue Jays, January 8, 1987.

WILLIAMS, FRANK: Traded with Pitchers Timber Mead and Mike Villa to Cincinnati Reds for Outfielder Eddie Milner, January 8, 1987.

Major League Managers

GEORGE LEE ANDERSON
(Sparky)
Detroit Tigers

Born February 22, 1934, at Bridgewater, S. D.
Height, 5.09. Weight, 168.
Threw and batted righthanded.

Major League stolen bases: 1959 (6).
Led Western League in sacrifice hits with 20 in 1954 and International League with 15 in 1960.
Led Texas League second basemen in double plays with 117 in 1955, Pacific Coast League with 135 in 1957 and International League with 104 in 1958 and 89 in 1960.
Led California League shortstops in double plays with 83 in 1953.
Tied for Texas League lead in sacrifice hits with 22 in 1955 and International League lead with 15 in 1960.

Year	Club	League	Pos.	G	AB	R	H	2B	3B	HR	RBI	B.A.	PO	A.	E.	F.A.
1953—Santa Barbara	Calif.		SS	●141	★598	98	157	21	4	5	55	.263	★277	395	32	.955
1954—Pueblo	West.		2B	147	497	72	147	13	5	0	62	.296	★397	432	20	●.976
1955—Fort Worth	Texas		2B	158	594	86	158	24	1	0	42	.266	★456	★469	18	★.981
1956—Montreal	Int.		2B	140	453	65	135	17	5	0	47	.298	372	391	15	.981
1957—Los Angeles	P. C.		★●2B-SS	●168	619	74	161	15	0	2	35	.260	★524	★488	●15	★.985
1958—Montreal†	Int.		2B	●155	580	78	156	35	5	2	56	.269	★387	★464	10	★.983
1959—Philadelphia	Nat.		2B	152	477	42	104	9	3	0	34	.218	343	403	12	.984
1960—Toronto	Int.		2B	148	543	67	123	11	5	5	21	.227	319	★416	12	.984
1961—Toronto	Int.		2B	97	275	30	66	17	0	0	22	.240	189	203	6	.985
1962—Toronto	Int.		2B	124	432	56	111	18	2	2	38	.257	282	327	8	★.987
1963—Toronto	Int.		2B	116	358	56	89	12	5	3	25	.249	226	256	6	★.988
Major League Totals—1 Year				152	477	42	104	9	3	0	34	.218	343	403	12	.984

†Recalled by Los Angeles Dodgers; traded to Philadelphia Phillies for Pitchers Jim Golden and Gene Snyder and Outfielder Eldon (Rip) Repulski, December 23, 1958.

RECORD AS MANAGER

Year	Club	League	Position	W.	L.		Year	Club	League	Position	W.	L.
1964—Toronto	Int.	Fifth	80	72			1977—Cincinnati	Nat.	Second(W)	88	74	
1965—Rock Hill	W. Carol.	Eighth	24	40			1978—Cincinnati	Nat.	Second(W)	92	69	
(Second Half)		†First	35	23			1979—Detroit z	Amer.	Fifth(E)	56	50	
1966—St. Petersburg	Fla. St.	Second	42	24			1980—Detroit	Amer.	Fifth(E)	84	78	
(Second Half)		‡First	49	21			1981—Detroit a	Amer.		60	49	
1967—Modesto	Calif.	§Second	38	32			1982—Detroit	Amer.	Fourth(E)	83	79	
(Second Half)		xFirst	41	29			1983—Detroit	Amer.	Second(E)	92	70	
1968—Asheville	South.	First	86	54			1984—Detroit	Amer.	First(E)	104	58	
1970—Cincinnati	Nat.	First(W)	102	60			1985—Detroit	Amer.	Third(E)	84	77	
1971—Cincinnati	Nat.	yFourth(W)	79	83			1986—Detroit	Amer.	Third(E)	87	75	
1972—Cincinnati	Nat.	First(W)	95	59			American League Totals—8 Years			650	536	
1973—Cincinnati	Nat.	First(W)	99	63			National League Totals—9 Years			863	586	
1974—Cincinnati	Nat.	Second(W)	98	64			Major League Totals—17 Years			1513	1122	
1975—Cincinnati	Nat.	First(W)	108	54								
1976—Cincinnati	Nat.	First(W)	102	60								

†Won playoff against Salisbury (First Half winner), two games to none.
‡Lost playoff against Leesburg (First Half winner), three games to two.
§Tied for position with Santa Barbara.
xLost playoff against San Jose (First Half winner), two games to none.
yTied for position with Houston Astros.
zReplaced Les Moss (and interim manager Dick Tracewski) with club in fifth place (record of 29-26), June 14, 1979.
aFirst Half.... Fourth (E) (record of 31-26); Second Half.... Third (E) (record of 29-23).
Coach, San Diego Padres, 1969.
Manager, American League All-Star Team, 1985.
Manager, National League All-Star Team, 1971, 1973, 1976 and 1977.
Coach, National League All-Star Team, 1974.
Coach, American League All-Star Team, 1982 and 1984.

CHAMPIONSHIP SERIES RECORD

Year	Club	League	W.	L.
1970—Cincinnati	National	3	0
1972—Cincinnati	National	3	2
1973—Cincinnati	National	2	3
1975—Cincinnati	National	3	0
1976—Cincinnati	National	3	0
1984—Detroit	American	3	0
Championship Series Totals—6 Years		17	5

WORLD SERIES RECORD

Year	Club	League	W.	L.
1970—Cincinnati	National	1	4
1972—Cincinnati	National	3	4
1975—Cincinnati	National	4	3
1976—Cincinnati	National	4	0
1984—Detroit	American	4	1
World Series Totals—5 Years		16	12

—DID YOU KNOW—

That Tri-Cities of the Northwest League, trailing 10-1 with two out in the ninth inning, rallied for nine runs to tie the game and then scored four more in the 11th for a 14-10 victory over Spokane?

LAWRENCE ROBERT BOWA
(Larry)
San Diego Padres

Born December 6, 1945, at Sacramento, Calif.
Height, 5.10. Weight, 155.
Threw right and batted left and righthanded.
Attended Sacramento City College, Sacramento, Calif.
Son of Paul Bowa, infielder in St. Louis Cardinals' organization, 1944 and 1946; manager,
St. Louis Cardinals' organization, 1947; nephew of Frank Bowa, minor
league infielder, 1944 through 1949.

Established major league records for highest fielding percentage by shortstop, lifetime, 1,000 or more games (.980); highest fielding percentage by shortstop, season (.991), 1979; most years leading league in fielding average by shortstop, 100 or more games (6).

Tied modern major league record for most at bats, game (7), July 12, 1975.

Established National League records for most games by shortstop, lifetime (2,222); fewest errors, season, 150 or more games, by shortstop (9), 1972; most seasons leading league in fielding percentage by shortstop, 100 or more games (6), 1971, 1972, 1974, 1978, 1979 and 1983.

Major League stolen bases: 1970 (24), 1971 (28), 1972 (17), 1973 (10), 1974 (39), 1975 (24), 1976 (30), 1977 (32), 1978 (27), 1979 (20), 1980 (21), 1981 (16), 1982 (8), 1983 (7), 1984 (10), 1985 (5). Total—318.

Led National League in sacrifice hits with 18 in 1972.
Led National League shortstops in total chances with 843 in 1971.
Tied for National League lead in double plays by shortstops with 97 in 1971.
Led Pacific Coast League in stolen bases with 48 in 1969.
Led Pacific Coast League shortstops in putouts with 468 in 1969.
Led Eastern League shortstops in double plays with 77 in 1968.
Named shortstop on THE SPORTING NEWS National League All-Star Team, 1975 and 1978.
Named shortstop on THE SPORTING NEWS National League All-Star fielding team, 1972 and 1978.

Year Club	League	Pos.	G.	AB.	R.	H.	2B.	3B.	HR.	RBI.	B.A.	PO.	A.	E.	F.A.
1966—Spartanburg	W. Car.	SS	97	429	70	134	14	4	2	36	.312	138	284	12	★.972
1966—San Diego	P. C.	SS	5	19	0	6	0	1	0	1	.316	13	20	2	.943
1967—Bakersfield†	Calif.	SS-2B	7	32	4	6	2	0	0	3	.188	15	12	1	.964
1967—Reading	East.	SS	22	89	11	25	4	0	0	9	.281	35	79	9	.927
1968—Reading	East.	SS	133	480	47	116	14	2	3	36	.242	192	●395	24	.961
1969—Eugene	P. C.	★SS-2B	135	568	80	163	11	6	1	26	.287	★215	469	18	★.974
1970—Philadelphia	Nat.	SS-2B	145	547	50	137	17	6	0	34	.250	202	418	13	.979
1971—Philadelphia	Nat.	SS	159	★650	74	162	18	5	0	25	.249	272	★560	11	★.987
1972—Philadelphia	Nat.	SS	152	579	67	145	11	★13	1	31	.250	212	494	9	.987
1973—Philadelphia‡	Nat.	SS	122	446	42	94	11	3	0	23	.211	191	361	12	.979
1974—Philadelphia	Nat.	SS	162	669	97	184	19	10	1	36	.275	256	462	12	★.984
1975—Philadelphia§	Nat.	SS	136	583	79	178	18	9	2	38	.305	227	403	25	.962
1976—Philadelphia	Nat.	SS	156	624	71	155	15	9	0	49	.248	180	492	17	.975
1977—Philadelphia	Nat.	SS	154	624	93	175	19	3	4	41	.280	222	518	13	.983
1978—Philadelphia	Nat.	SS	156	654	78	192	31	5	3	43	.294	224	502	10	★.986
1979—Philadelphia x	Nat.	SS	147	539	74	130	17	11	0	31	.241	229	448	6	★.991
1980—Philadelphia	Nat.	SS	147	540	57	144	16	4	2	39	.267	225	449	17	.975
1981—Philadelphia y	Nat.	SS	103	360	34	102	14	3	0	31	.283	117	309	11	.975
1982—Chicago	Nat.	SS	142	499	50	123	15	7	0	29	.246	210	396	17	.973
1983—Chicago	Nat.	SS	147	499	73	133	20	5	2	43	.267	230	464	11	★.984
1984—Chicago	Nat.	SS	133	391	33	87	14	2	0	17	.223	217	378	16	.974
1985—Chi z-N.Y. a	Nat.	SS-2B	86	214	15	50	7	4	0	15	.234	109	210	11	.967
Major League Totals—16 Years			2247	8418	987	2191	262	99	15	525	.260	3323	6864	211	.980

Signed as free agent by Philadelphia Phillies' organization, October 12, 1965.
†On military list, March 7 to July 18, 1967.
‡On disabled list, July 26 to September 1, 1973.
§On disabled list, May 27 to June 23, 1975.
xOn disabled list, May 25 to June 9, 1979.
yTraded with Infielder Ryne Sandberg to Chicago Cubs for Shortstop Ivan DeJesus, January 27, 1982.
zReleased, August 13, 1985; signed by New York Mets, August 20, 1985.
aGranted free agency, November 12, 1985; named minor league manager in San Diego Padres' organization, November 14, 1985.

DIVISION SERIES RECORD

Year Club	League	Pos.	G.	AB.	R.	H.	2B.	3B.	HR.	RBI.	B.A.	PO.	A.	E.	F.A.
1981—Philadelphia	Nat.	SS	5	17	0	3	1	0	0	1	.176	12	9	1	.955

CHAMPIONSHIP SERIES RECORD

Year Club	League	Pos.	G.	AB.	R.	H.	2B.	3B.	HR.	RBI.	B.A.	PO.	A.	E.	F.A.
1976—Philadelphia	Nat.	SS	3	8	1	1	1	0	0	1	.125	2	11	0	1.000
1977—Philadelphia	Nat.	SS	4	17	2	2	0	0	0	1	.118	0	17	0	1.000
1978—Philadelphia	Nat.	SS	4	18	2	6	0	0	0	0	.333	5	16	0	1.000
1980—Philadelphia	Nat.	SS	5	19	2	6	0	0	0	0	.316	4	11	1	.938
1984—Chicago	Nat.	SS	5	15	1	3	1	0	0	1	.200	8	15	0	1.000
Championship Series Totals—5 Years			21	77	8	18	2	0	0	3	.234	19	70	1	.989

WORLD SERIES RECORD

Established World Series record for most double plays started by shortstop, six-game Series (7), 1980.
Tied World Series record for most double plays started by shortstop, nine-inning game (3), October 15, 1980.

Year Club	League	Pos.	G.	AB.	R.	H.	2B.	3B.	HR.	RBI.	B.A.	PO.	A.	E.	F.A.
1980—Philadelphia	Nat.	SS	6	24	3	9	1	0	0	2	.375	5	18	0	1.000

ALL-STAR GAME RECORD

Year League	Pos.	AB.	R.	H.	2B.	3B.	HR.	RBI.	B.A.	PO.	A.	E.	F.A.
1974—National	SS	2	0	0	0	0	0	0	.000	2	0	0	1.000
1975—National	SS	0	1	0	0	0	0	0	.000	2	0	0	1.000
1976—National	SS	1	0	0	0	0	0	0	.000	2	1	0	1.000
1978—National	SS	3	1	2	0	0	0	0	.667	2	4	0	1.000
1979—National	SS	2	0	0	0	0	0	0	.000	1	3	0	1.000
All-Star Game Totals—5 Years		8	2	2	0	0	0	0	.250	9	8	0	1.000

RECORD AS MANAGER

Year Club	League	Position	W.	L.
1986—Las Vegas	P. C.	Third(S)	36	34
(Second Half)†		First(S)	44	28

†Won Southern Division Championship from Phoenix, three games to two; won league championship from Vancouver, three games to two.

PATRICK CORRALES

Name pronounced Corr-AL-ees.

(Pat)

Cleveland Indians

Born March 20, 1941, at Los Angeles, Calif.
Height, 6.00. Weight, 195.
Threw and batted righthanded.
Attended Fresno City College, Fresno, Calif.

Tied major league record for most times awarded first base on catcher's interference, game (2), September 29, 1965.

Major League stolen bases: 1966 (1).

Led Florida State League catchers in double plays with 18 in 1960 and tied for Sally League lead with 10 in 1963.

Year Club	League	Pos.	G.	AB.	R.	H.	2B.	3B.	HR.	RBI.	B.A.	PO.	A.	E.	F.A.
1959—Bakersfield	Calif.	C	5	5	0	0	0	0	0	0	.000	4	2	1	.857
1959—Johnson City	Appal.	C	23	74	10	18	4	0	2	13	.243	124	5	3	.977
1960—Tampa	Fla. St.	C	128	386	73	95	18	5	1	60	.246	*1011	83	23	*.979
1961—Des Moines	I.I.I.	C	104	333	33	103	18	0	3	36	.309	707	42	*19	.975
1962—Dallas-Ft. W.	A. A.	C	42	121	10	27	6	1	2	14	.223	180	16	3	.985
1962—Williamsport	East.	C-OF	42	136	9	26	1	0	1	10	.191	237	24	7	.974
1963—Chattanooga	Sally	C	127	415	42	108	15	1	3	51	.260	715	59	17	.979
1964—Arkansas	P. C.	C	101	335	36	102	19	1	9	48	.304	682	51	7	.991
1964—Philadelphia	Nat.	PH	2	1	1	0	0	0	0	0	.000	0	0	0	.000
1965—Philadelphia†	Nat.	C	63	174	16	39	8	1	2	15	.224	358	24	7	.982
1965—Arkansas	P. C.	C	28	85	6	16	4	0	0	4	.188	181	14	2	.990
1966—St. Louis	Nat.	C	28	72	5	13	2	0	0	3	.181	133	23	4	.975
1967—Tulsa‡	P. C.	C-1B	130	435	55	119	18	1	10	54	.274	714	69	8	.990
1968—Indianapolis	P. C.	C-1B	77	242	26	66	11	3	6	34	.273	461	42	5	.990
1968—Cincinnati	Nat.	C	20	56	3	15	4	0	0	6	.268	101	8	1	.991
1969—Cincinnati	Nat.	C	29	72	10	19	5	0	1	5	.264	133	7	2	.986
1970—Cincinnati	Nat.	C	43	106	9	25	5	1	1	10	.236	167	11	3	.983
1971—Cincinnati	Nat.	C	40	94	6	17	2	0	0	6	.181	145	4	3	.980
1972—Indianapolis	A. A.	C	30	98	9	31	4	0	1	12	.316	193	10	0	1.000
1972—Cinn.§-S. Diego	Nat.	C	46	120	6	23	0	0	0	6	.192	251	23	2	.993
1973—San Diego	Nat.	C	29	72	7	15	2	1	0	3	.208	130	6	2	.986
1974—Hawaii x	P. C.	C	53	169	21	42	6	0	5	24	.249	324	17	3	.991
1975—Alexandria	Texas	C-1B	1	0	0	0	0	0	0	0	.000	4	0	0	1.000
Major League Totals—9 Years			300	767	63	166	28	3	4	54	.216	1418	106	24	.984

†Traded with Pitcher Art Mahaffey and Outfielder Alex Johnson to St. Louis Cardinals for First Baseman Bill White, Shortstop Dick Groat and Catcher Bob Uecker, October 27, 1965.

‡Recalled by St. Louis Cardinals; traded to Cincinnati Reds' organization with Infielder Jim Williams for Catcher John Edwards, February 8, 1968.

§Traded to San Diego Padres for Catcher Bob Barton, June 11, 1972.

xReleased, September 27, 1974.

WORLD SERIES RECORD

Year Club	League	Pos.	G.	AB.	R.	H.	2B.	3B.	HR.	RBI.	B.A.	PO.	A.	E.	F.A.
1970—Cincinnati	Nat.	PH	1	1	0	0	0	0	0	0	.000	0	0	0	.000

RECORD AS MANAGER

Year Club	League	Position	W.	L.	Year Club	League		W.	L.
1975—Alexandria	Texas	Fourth(E)	58	72	1984—Cleveland	Amer.	Sixth(E)	75	87
1978—Texas†	Amer.	‡Second(W)	1	0	1985—Cleveland	Amer.	Seventh(E)	60	102
1979—Texas	Amer.	Third(W)	83	79	1986—Cleveland	Amer.	Fifth(E)	84	78
1980—Texas	Amer.	Fourth(W)	76	85	American League Totals—7 Years			409	463
1982—Philadelphia	Nat.	Second(E)	89	73	National League Totals—2 Years			132	115
1983—Philadelphia§	Nat.	First(E)	43	42	Major League Totals—8 Years			541	578
1983—Cleveland x	Amer.	Seventh(E)	30	32					

†Replaced Billy Hunter with club tied for second place (record of 86-75), October 1, 1978.

‡Tied for position with California Angels.

§Replaced by Paul Owens, July 18, 1983.

xReplaced Mike Ferraro with club in seventh place (record of 40-60), July 31, 1983.

Coach, Texas Rangers, part of 1975 through September 30, 1978.
Coach, American League All-Star Team, 1979 and 1986.
Coach, National League All-Star Team, 1983.

ROGER LEE CRAIG
San Francisco Giants

Born February 17, 1931, at Durham, N. C.
Height, 6.04. Weight, 196.
Threw and batted righthanded.
Attended North Carolina State College, Raleigh, N. C.

Tied major league record for most 1-0 games lost, season (5), 1963.
Tied National League record for most consecutive losses, season (18), May 4 through August 4, 1963, inclusive.
Tied for National League lead in shutouts with 4 in 1959.

Year—Club	League	G.	IP.	W.	L.	Pct.	H.	R.	ER.	SO.	BB.	ERA.
1950—Newport News	Piedmont	6	19	0	1	.000	22	17	15	7	23	7.11
1950—Valdosta	Ga.-Fla.	23	167	14	7	.667	136	86	58	152	150	3.13
1951—Newport News	Piedmont	38	21	14	11	.560	175	109	90	119	★175	3.67
1952-53—Elmira	Eastern							(In Military Service)				
1954—Elmira	Eastern	3	2	0	0	.000	4	6	2	1	2	9.00
1954—Pueblo	Western	6	14	1	1	.500	14	17	15	8	19	9.64
1954—Newport News	Piedmont	20	125	8	3	.727	107	44	35	108	56	2.50
1955—Montreal	Int'national	22	117	10	2	.833	105	48	46	68	64	3.54
1955—Brooklyn	National	21	91	5	3	.625	81	37	28	48	43	2.77
1956—Brooklyn	National	35	199	12	11	.522	169	90	82	109	87	3.71
1957—Brooklyn	National	32	111	6	9	.400	102	58	57	69	47	4.62
1958—Los Angeles	National	9	32	2	1	.667	30	20	16	16	12	4.50
1958—St. Paul	Am. Assoc.	28	182	5	●17	.227	180	100	79	119	77	3.91
1959—Spokane	P. Coast	14	96	6	7	.462	86	39	34	46	26	3.19
1959—Los Angeles	National	29	153	11	5	.688	122	49	35	76	45	2.06
1960—Los Angeles	National	21	116	8	3	.727	99	48	42	69	43	3.26
1961—Los Angeles†	National	40	113	5	6	.455	130	87	77	63	52	6.13
1962—New York	National	42	233	10	★24	.294	261	133	117	118	70	4.52
1963—New York‡	National	46	236	5	★22	.185	249	117	99	108	58	3.78
1964—St. Louis§	National	39	166	7	9	.438	180	76	60	84	35	3.25
1965—Cincinnati x	National	40	64	1	4	.200	74	33	26	30	25	3.66
1966—Philadelphia	National	14	23	2	1	.667	31	15	14	13	5	5.48
1966—Seattle	P. Coast	6	22	0	1	.000	15	11	6	11	9	2.45
1968—Albuquerque	Texas	1	4	0	0	.000	3	0	0	2	2	0.00
Major League Totals—12 Years		368	1537	74	98	.430	1528	763	653	803	522	3.82

†Selected by New York Mets in National League expansion draft, October 10, 1961.
‡Traded to St. Louis Cardinals for Pitcher Bill Wakefield and Outfielder George Altman, November 4, 1963.
§Traded to Cincinnati Reds with Outfielder Charlie James for Pitcher Bob Purkey and a player to be named later, December 14, 1964.
xReleased by Cincinnati Reds and signed by Philadelphia Phillies, April 11, 1966.

WORLD SERIES RECORD

Year—Club	League	G.	IP.	W.	L.	Pct.	H.	R.	ER.	SO.	BB.	ERA.
1955—Brooklyn	National	1	6	1	0	1.000	4	2	2	4	5	3.00
1956—Brooklyn	National	2	6	0	1	.000	10	8	8	4	3	12.00
1959—Los Angeles	National	2	9⅓	0	1	.000	15	9	9	8	5	8.68
1964—St. Louis	National	2	5	1	0	1.000	2	0	0	9	3	0.00
World Series Totals—3 Years		7	26⅓	2	2	.500	31	19	19	25	16	6.49

RECORD AS MANAGER

Year—Club	League	Position	W.	L.
1968—Albuquerque	Texas	Second(W)	70	69
1978—San Diego	Nat.	Fourth(W)	84	78
1979—San Diego	Nat.	Fifth(W)	68	93
1985—San Francisco†	Nat.	Sixth(W)	6	12
1986—San Francisco	Nat.	Third(W)	83	79
Major League Totals—4 Years			241	262

†Replaced Jim Davenport with club in sixth place (record of 56-88), September 18, 1985.
Scout, Los Angeles Dodgers, 1967; coach, San Diego Padres, 1969 through 1972; minor league pitching instructor, Los Angeles Dodgers, 1973; coach, Houston Astros, 1974 and 1975; coach, San Diego Padres, 1976 and 1977; named manager of Padres (replacing Alvin Dark), March 21, 1978; coach, Detroit Tigers, 1980 through 1983; scout, Detroit Tigers, March 2, 1985 through September 18, 1985.

JOHN FREDERICK FELSKE
Name pronounced FELL-skee.
Philadelphia Phillies

Born May 30, 1942, at Chicago, Ill.
Height, 6.04. Weight, 225.
Threw and batted righthanded.
Attended University of Illinois, Urbana, Ill.

Led American Association catchers in double plays with 12 in 1971.
Led Texas League catchers in double plays with 14 in 1964 and tied for lead with 8 in 1966.

Led Northern League in passed balls with 19 in 1963.
Led Florida State League catchers in double plays with 9 in 1962.

Year Club	League	Pos.	G.	AB.	R.	H.	2B.	3B.	HR.	RBI.	B.A.	PO.	A.	E.	F.A.
1962—Palatka	Fla. St.	C	94	269	29	50	12	1	5	32	.186	546	60	11	*.982
1962—St. Cloud	North.	C	5	9	0	0	0	0	0	1	.000	22	2	0	1.000
1963—St. Cloud	North.	C	117	396	52	99	22	2	12	58	.250	656	*86	8	.989
1964—Fort Worth	Texas	C	108	319	28	58	15	1	6	28	.182	528	*86	11	.982
1965—Salt Lake City	P. C.	C	41	124	10	23	4	0	3	11	.185	226	21	0	1.000
1965—Dallas-Ft.Worth	Texas	C	74	231	21	51	8	1	2	18	.221	383	41	7	.984
1966—Tacoma	P. C.	C	2	5	1	0	0	0	0	0	.000	0	0	0	.000
1966—Dallas-Ft. Worth	Texas	C	73	220	18	44	10	0	6	24	.200	456	49	7	.986
1967—Dallas-Ft. W.†	Texas	C-OF	68	203	18	53	3	1	3	20	.261	352	31	7	.982
1968—Tacoma	P. C.	C-OF	84	249	19	53	9	1	7	29	.213	388	41	7	.984
1968—Chicago	Nat.	C	4	2	0	0	0	0	0	0	.000	5	0	1	.833
1969—San Antonio	Texas	C-1B-OF	91	265	25	72	14	1	9	44	.272	438	48	7	.986
1970—Portland	P. C.	*C-1B	131	432	70	136	25	2	18	75	.315	*778	60	●10	.988
1971—Evansville	A. A.	1-C-O-3	119	402	54	118	20	4	14	68	.294	802	92	9	.990
1972—Evansville	A. A.	C-1B	33	113	14	27	5	2	1	16	.239	211	20	1	.996
1972—Milwaukee	Amer.	C-1B	37	80	6	11	3	0	1	5	.138	124	9	3	.978
1973—Milwaukee‡	Amer.	C-1B	13	22	1	3	0	1	0	4	.136	41	4	0	1.000
National League Totals—1 Year			4	2	0	0	0	0	0	0	.000	5	0	1	.833
American League Totals—2 Years			50	102	7	14	3	1	1	9	.137	165	13	3	.983
Major League Totals—3 Years			54	104	7	14	3	1	1	9	.135	170	13	4	.979

†On disabled list, August 22 to September 4, 1967.
‡Released, October 23, 1973.

RECORD AS MANAGER

Named Pacific Coast League Manager of the Year, 1983.

Year Club	League	Position	W.	L.
1974—Newark	NYP	†Fifth	30	36
1975—Thetford Mines	East.	Fifth	28	35
(Second Half)		Eighth	31	45
1976—Berkshire	East.	Third(N)	68	68
1977—Spokane	P. C.	Second(W)	75	69
1978—Spokane	P. C.	Fourth(W)	64	75
1979—Vancouver	P. C.	Third(N)	39	36
(Second Half)		‡First(N)	40	32
1982—Reading	East	Third(S)	33	31
(Second Half)		Third(S)	30	44
1983—Portland	P. C.	Third(N)	34	38
(Second Half)		§First(N)	41	29
1985—Philadelphia	Nat.	Fifth(E)	75	87
1986—Philadelphia	Nat.	Second(E)	86	75
Major League Totals—2 Years			161	162

†One tie.
‡Lost playoff to Hawaii, two games to one.
§Won Northern Division Championship from Edmonton, three games to one; won league championship from Albuquerque, three games to none; lost in Triple A World Series playoff.
Coach, Toronto Blue Jays, 1980 and 1981.
Coach, Philadelphia Phillies, 1984.

JAMES LOUIS FREGOSI

Name Pronounced Free-GO-see.

(Jim)

Chicago White Sox

Born April 4, 1942, at San Francisco, Calif.
Height, 6.02. Weight, 197.
Threw and batted righthanded.
Attended Menlo College, Menlo Park, Calif.
Father of Jim Fregosi, Jr., shortstop in St. Louis Cardinals' organization.

Tied major league records for most double plays started by shortstop, nine-inning game (5), May 1, 1966 (first game); fewest stolen bases, 150 or more games, season (0), 1970.
Led American League in sacrifice hits with 15 in 1965.
Led American League shortstops in double plays with 125 in 1966 and tied for lead with 92 in 1968.
Tied for American Association lead in double plays by shortstops with 100 in 1961.
Named shortstop on THE SPORTING NEWS American League All-Star Team, 1964 and 1967.
Named shortstop on THE SPORTING NEWS American League All-Star fielding team, 1967.

Year Club	League	Pos.	G.	AB.	R.	H.	2B.	3B.	HR.	RBI.	B.A.	PO.	A.	E.	F.A.
1960—Alpine†	Soph.	INF-OF	112	404	96	108	17	7	6	58	.267	198	261	39	.922
1961—Dal.-Ft. Worth	A. A.	SS	150	516	54	131	18	4	6	50	.254	247	*495	*53	.933
1961—Los Angeles	Amer.	SS	11	27	7	6	0	0	0	3	.222	12	22	2	.944
1962—Dal.-Ft. Worth	A. A.	SS-OF	64	219	25	62	9	3	1	14	.283	94	164	22	.921
1962—Los Angeles	Amer.	SS	58	175	15	51	3	4	3	23	.291	96	150	15	.943
1963—Los Angeles	Amer.	SS	154	592	83	170	29	12	9	50	.287	271	446	27	.964
1964—Los Angeles	Amer.	SS	147	505	86	140	22	9	18	72	.277	225	421	23	.966
1965—California	Amer.	SS	161	602	66	167	19	7	15	64	.277	*312	481	26	.968
1966—California	Amer.	*SS-1B	162	611	78	154	32	7	13	67	.252	299	*531	●35	.960
1967—California	Amer.	SS	151	590	75	171	23	6	9	56	.290	258	435	25	.965
1968—California	Amer.	SS	159	614	77	150	21	*13	9	49	.244	273	454	29	.962
1969—California	Amer.	SS	161	580	78	151	22	6	12	47	.260	255	465	21	.972
1970—California	Amer.	SS	158	601	95	167	33	5	22	82	.278	313	475	20	.975
1971—California‡§	Amer.	SS-1B-OF	107	347	31	81	15	1	5	33	.233	241	251	22	.957
1972—New York	Nat.	3B-SS-1B	101	340	31	79	15	4	5	32	.232	91	162	15	.944
1973—New York x	Nat.	S-3-1-O	45	124	7	29	4	1	0	11	.234	47	70	9	.929
1973—Texas	Amer.	3B-1B-SS	45	157	25	42	6	2	6	16	.268	98	53	5	.968

Year	Club	League	Pos.	G.	AB.	R.	H.	2B.	3B.	HR.	RBI.	B.A.	PO.	A.	E.	F.A.
1974—Texas	Amer.		1B-3B	78	230	31	60	5	0	12	34	.261	331	73	5	.988
1975—Texas	Amer.		1B-3B	77	191	25	50	5	0	7	33	.262	356	35	6	.985
1976—Texas	Amer.		1B-2B	58	133	17	31	7	0	2	12	.233	183	18	2	.990
1977—Texas yz	Amer.		1B	13	28	4	7	1	0	1	5	.250	31	4	0	1.000
1977—Pittsburgh	Nat.		1B-3B	36	56	10	16	1	1	3	16	.286	99	5	2	.981
1978—Pittsburgh a	Nat.		3B-1B-2B	20	20	3	4	1	0	0	1	.200	14	4	2	.900
American League Totals—16 Years				1700	5983	793	1598	243	72	143	646	.267	3554	4314	263	.968
National League Totals—4 Years				202	540	51	128	21	6	8	60	.237	251	241	28	.946
Major League Totals—18 Years				1902	6523	844	1726	264	78	151	706	.265	3805	4555	291	.966

†Selected by Los Angeles Angels off Boston Red Sox roster in American League expansion draft, December 14, 1960.

‡On disabled list, July 12 to August 5, 1971.

§Traded to New York Mets for Pitchers Nolan Ryan and Don Rose, Outfielder Leroy Stanton and Catcher Francisco Estrada, December 10, 1971.

xTraded to Texas Rangers for a player to be named later, July 11, 1973; deal settled with cash.

yOn disabled list, April 22 to May 12, 1977.

zTraded to Pittsburgh Pirates for First Baseman-Catcher Ed Kirkpatrick, June 15, 1977.

aReleased, June 1, 1978 (in order to accept managerial position with California Angels).

ALL-STAR GAME RECORD

Year	League	Pos.	AB.	R.	H.	2B.	3B.	HR.	RBI.	B.A.	PO.	A.	E.	F.A.
1964—American		SS	4	1	1	0	0	0	1	.250	4	1	0	1.000
1966—American		SS	2	0	0	0	0	0	0	.000	0	1	0	1.000
1967—American		SS	4	0	1	0	0	0	0	.250	2	3	0	1.000
1968—American		SS	3	0	1	1	0	0	0	.333	1	6	0	1.000
1969—American		SS	1	0	0	0	0	0	0	.000	0	0	0	.000
1970—American		PH	1	0	0	0	0	0	0	.000	0	0	0	.000
All Star Game Totals—6 Years			15	1	3	1	0	0	1	.200	7	11	0	1.000

RECORD AS MANAGER

Named Minor League Manager of the Year by THE SPORTING NEWS, 1985.
Named American Association co-Manager of the Year, 1985.
Named American Association Manager of the Year, 1983.

Year	Club	League	Position	W.	L.	Year	Club	League	Position	W.	L.
1978—California†	Amer.	‡Second(W)		62	54	1984—Louisville	A. A.	yFourth		79	76
1979—California	Amer.	First (W)		88	74	1985—Louisville	A. A.	zFirst(E)		74	68
1980—California	Amer.	Sixth(W)		65	95	1986—Louisville	A. A.	Third(E)		32	34
1981—California§	Amer.	Fourth(W)		22	25	1986—Chicago a	Amer.	Fifth(W)		45	51
1983—Louisville	A. A.	xFirst(E)		78	57	Major League Totals—5 Years				282	299

†Replaced Dave Garcia with club in third place (record of 25-21), June 1, 1978.

‡Tied for position with Texas Rangers.

§Replaced by Gene Mauch, May 28, 1981.

xWon playoff from Oklahoma City, three games to two; lost championship playoff to Denver, four games to none.

yWon playoff from Indianapolis, four games to two; won championship playoff from Denver, four games to one.

zWon championship playoff from Oklahoma City, four games to one.

aReplaced manager Tony LaRussa (record of 26-38) and interim manager Doug Rader (record of 1-1) with club in fifth place (combined record of 27-39), June 22, 1986.

CHAMPIONSHIP SERIES RECORD

Year	Club	League	W.	L.
1979—California		American	1	3

DORREL NORMAN ELVERT HERZOG
(Relly or Whitey)

(Named "Relly" by mother from his first name; "Whitey" by Bill Speith, McAlester sportscaster, because of light hair.)

St. Louis Cardinals

Born November 9, 1931, at New Athens, Ill.
Height, 5.11. Weight, 187.
Threw and batted lefthanded.

Major League stolen bases: 1956 (8), 1957 (1), 1959 (1), 1961 (1), 1962 (2). Total—13.

Year	Club	League	Pos.	G.	AB.	R.	H.	2B.	3B.	HR.	RBI.	B.A.	PO.	A.	E.	F.A.
1949—McAlester	Soo. St.		OF	96	398	53	111	19	7	0	31	.279	222	14	0	*1.000
1950—McAlester	Soo. St.		OF	132	467	107	164	36	10	4	85	.351	272	15	7	*.976
1951—Norfolk	Pied.		OF	5	17	5	1	0	0	0	2	.059	13	0	1	.926
1951—Joplin	W. A.		OF-1B	113	418	99	119	14	8	7	48	.285	454	19	9	.981
1952—Beaumont	Texas		OF	35	121	11	24	4	1	0	9	.198	83	3	5	.945
1952—Quincy	I. I. I.		OF	68	225	53	65	9	6	7	44	.289	131	9	5	.966
1952—Kansas City	A. A.		OF-1B	14	27	5	8	1	0	1	5	.296	21	1	1	.957
1953-54—								(In Military Service.)								
1955—Denver†	A. A.		OF-1B	149	515	101	149	24	7	21	98	.289	324	10	4	.988
1956—Washington	Amer.		OF-1B	117	421	49	103	13	7	4	35	.245	274	10	7	.976
1957—Washington	Amer.		OF	36	78	7	13	3	0	0	4	.167	53	0	1	.981
1957—Miami	Int.		OF	77	257	48	70	14	5	2	25	.272	114	5	4	.967
1958—Wash.‡-K.C.	Amer.		OF-1B	96	101	11	23	1	2	0	9	.228	146	6	3	.981

Year	Club	League	Pos.	G.	AB.	R.	H.	2B.	3B.	HR.	RBI.	B.A.	PO.	A.	E.	F.A.
1959—Kansas City	Amer.		OF-1B	38	123	25	36	7	1	1	9	.293	87	2	3	.967
1960—Kansas City§	Amer.		OF-1B	83	252	43	67	10	2	8	38	.266	137	6	4	.973
1961—Baltimore	Amer.		OF	113	323	39	94	11	6	5	35	.291	143	2	0	1.000
1962—Baltimore x	Amer.		OF	99	263	34	70	13	1	7	35	.266	132	4	3	.978
1963—Detroit	Amer.		1B-OF	52	53	5	8	2	1	0	7	.151	44	1	1	.978
Major League Totals—8 Years				634	1614	213	414	60	20	25	172	.257	1016	31	22	.979

†Traded to Washington Senators with Pitcher Bob Wiesler, Catcher Lou Berberet, Second Baseman Herb Plews and Outfielder Dick Tettelbach for pitcher Maury McDermott and Shortstop Bob Kline (assigned to the Yankees' American Association farm club—Denver). Other players in deal assigned February 8, 1956; Herzog, April 2, 1956.

‡Sold to Kansas City Athletics, May 14, 1958.

§Traded to Baltimore Orioles with Outfielder Russ Snyder and a player to be named at later date, for Pitcher Jim Archer, Catcher Clint Courtney, First Baseman Bob Boyd, Infielder Wayne Causey and Outfielder Al Pilarcik, January 24, 1961; Courtney returned to the Orioles, April 15, 1961, to complete deal.

xTraded to Detroit Tigers with Catcher Gus Triandos for Catcher Dick Brown, November 26, 1962.

RECORD AS MANAGER

Named Man of the Year by THE SPORTING NEWS, 1982.
Named Major League Manager of the Year by THE SPORTING NEWS, 1982.

Year	Club	League	Position	W.	L.	Year	Club	League	Position	W.	L.
1973—Texas†	Amer.	Sixth(W)		47	91	1982—St. Louis	Nat.		First(E)	92	70
1974—California‡	Amer.	Sixth(W)		2	2	1983—St. Louis	Nat.		Fourth(E)	79	83
1975—Kansas City§	Amer.	Second(W)		41	25	1984—St. Louis	Nat.		Third(E)	84	78
1976—Kansas City	Amer.	First(W)		90	72	1985—St. Louis	Nat.		First(E)	101	61
1977—Kansas City	Amer.	First(W)		102	60	1986—St. Louis	Nat.		Third(E)	79	82
1978—Kansas City	Amer.	First(W)		92	70	National League Totals—7 Years				532	452
1979—Kansas City	Amer.	Second(W)		85	77	American League Totals—7 Years				459	397
1980—St. Louis xy	Nat.	Fourth(E)		38	35	Major League Totals—14 Years				991	849
1981—St. Louis z	Nat.			59	43						

†Replaced by Billy Martin, September 8, 1973 (Del Wilber served as interim manager, September 7).
‡Served as interim manager, June 27 to June 30, 1974 after Dick Williams replaced Bobby Winkles, June 26.
§Replaced Jack McKeon with club in second place (record of 50-46), July 24, 1975.
xReplaced Ken Boyer (and interim manager Jack Krol) with club in sixth place (record of 18-33), June 9, 1980.
yNamed General Manager, August 28, 1980, with Red Schoendienst serving as manager remainder of season.
zFirst Half. . . . Second(E) (record of 30-20); Second Half. . . . Second(E) (record of 29-23).
Scout, Kansas City Athletics, 1964.; coach, Kansas City Athletics, 1965; New York Mets, 1966; California Angels, 1974 and part of 1975.
Director of Player Development, New York Mets, 1967 through 1972.
Manager, National League All-Star Team, 1983 and 1986.
Coach, American League All-Star Team, 1973, 1974 and 1978.

CHAMPIONSHIP SERIES RECORD

Year	Club	League	W.	L.
1976—Kansas City	American		2	3
1977—Kansas City	American		2	3
1978—Kansas City	American		1	3
1982—St. Louis	National		3	0
1985—St. Louis	National		4	2
Championship Series Totals—5 Years			12	11

WORLD SERIES RECORD

Year	Club	League	W.	L.
1982—St. Louis	National		4	3
1985—St. Louis	National		3	4
World Series Totals—2 Years			7	7

RICHARD DALTON HOWSER
(Dick)
Kansas City Royals

Born May 14, 1937, at Miami, Fla.
Height, 5.09. Weight, 155.
Threw and batted righthanded.
Received bachelor of science degree in education from
Florida State University, Tallahassee, Fla.

Tied American League record for most games played by shortstop, season (162), 1964.
Major League stolen bases: 1961 (37), 1962 (19), 1963 (9), 1964 (20), 1965 (17), 1966 (2), 1967 (1). Total—105.
Tied for American League lead in sacrifice hits with 6 in 1964.
Led Three-I League in stolen bases with 31 in 1959.
Named American League Rookie of the Year by THE SPORTING NEWS, 1961.
Received reported $21,000 bonus to sign with Kansas City Athletics, 1958.

Year	Club	League	Pos.	G.	AB.	R.	H.	2B.	3B.	HR.	RBI.	B.A.	PO.	A.	E.	F.A.
1958—Winona	I.I.I.		SS	83	333	80	96	16	1	6	30	.288	152	233	28	.932
1959—Sioux City	I.I.I.		2B-SS	111	392	●107	109	17	5	4	39	.278	240	289	33	.941
1960—Sioux City	I.I.I.		SS	44	149	59	52	15	1	5	21	.349	63	130	20	.906
1960—Shreveport	South.		SS	88	331	78	112	20	6	4	38	.338	189	270	31	.937
1961—Kansas City	Amer.		SS	158	611	108	171	29	6	3	45	.280	*299	427	*38	.950
1962—Kansas City†	Amer.		SS	83	286	53	68	8	3	6	34	.238	138	191	13	.962
1963—K.C.‡-Cleve.	Amer.		SS	64	203	29	48	5	0	1	11	.236	101	113	11	.951
1964—Cleveland	Amer.		SS	162	637	101	163	23	4	3	52	.256	291	463	20	.974
1965—Cleveland	Amer.		SS-2B	107	307	47	72	8	2	1	6	.235	144	211	7	.981
1966—Cleveland§	Amer.		SS-2B	67	140	18	32	9	1	2	4	.229	53	95	5	.967
1967—New York x	Amer.		2B-3B-SS	63	149	18	40	6	0	0	10	.268	64	76	3	.979
1968—New York	Amer.		2B-3B-SS	85	150	24	23	2	1	0	3	.153	61	106	3	.982
Major League Totals—8 Years				789	2483	398	617	90	17	16	165	.248	1151	1682	100	.966

†On disabled list, June 26 to August 10, 1962.
‡Traded to Cleveland Indians with Catcher Jose Azcue for Catcher Howard Edwards and reported $100,000, May 25, 1963.
§Traded to New York Yankees for Pitcher Gil Downs and cash, December 20, 1966.
xOn disabled list, July 17 to September 1, 1967.

ALL-STAR GAME RECORD

Year League	Pos.	AB.	R.	H.	2B.	3B.	HR.	RBI.	B.A.	PO.	A.	E.	F.A.
1961—American (first game)	3B	1	0	0	0	0	0	0	.000	0	1	0	1.000

Member of American League All-Star Team in 1961 (second game); did not play.

RECORD AS MANAGER

Year Club	League	Position	W.	L.
1980—New York	Amer.	First(E)	103	59
1981—Kansas City†‡	Amer.		20	13
1982—Kansas City	Amer.	Second(W)	90	72
1983—Kansas City	Amer.	Second(W)	79	83
1984—Kansas City	Amer.	First(W)	84	78
1985—Kansas City	Amer.	First(W)	91	71
1986—Kansas City§	Amer.	Fourth(W)	40	48
Major League Totals—7 Years			507	424

†Replaced Jim Frey with club in third place during second half (record of 10-10), August 31, 1981.
‡Second Half. . . . First(W) (record of 20-13).
§Replaced by Mike Ferraro after illness was discovered, July 18, 1986.
Coach, New York Yankees, 1969 through 1978, scout, New York Yankees, November 21, 1980 through August 30, 1981.
Baseball coach at Florida State University, 1979. Record: 43 wins, 17 losses, 1 tie.
Manager, American League All-Star Team, 1986.
Coach, American League All-Star Team, 1982 and 1985.

DIVISION SERIES RECORD

Year Club	League	W.	L.
1981—Kansas City	American	0	3

CHAMPIONSHIP SERIES RECORD

Year Club	League	W.	L.
1980—New York	American	0	3
1984—Kansas City	American	0	3
1985—Kansas City	American	4	3
Championship Series Totals—3 Years		4	9

WORLD SERIES RECORD

Year Club	League	W.	L.
1985—Kansas City	American	4	3

DAVID ALLEN JOHNSON
(Dave)
New York Mets

Born January 30, 1943, at Orlando, Fla.
Height, 6.01. Weight, 182.
Threw and batted righthanded.
Attended Texas A&M University, College Station, Tex., received bachelor of
science degree in mathematics from Trinity University, San Antonio, Tex.,
and attended Johns Hopkins University, Baltimore, Md.

Established major league record for most home runs by second baseman, season, (42), 1973.
Tied major league records for fewest triples, season (150 or more games), (0), 1973; most home runs, bases filled, season, pinch-hitter (2), 1978.
Major League stolen bases: 1965 (3), 1966 (3), 1967 (4), 1968 (7), 1969 (3), 1970 (2), 1971 (3), 1972 (1), 1973 (5), 1974 (1), 1977 (1). Total—33.
Tied for American League lead in sacrifice flies with 8 in 1967.
Led National League second basemen in total chances with 877 and tied for lead in double plays with 106 in 1973.
Led American League second basemen in double plays with 103 in 1971.
Led California League shortstops in double plays with 63 in 1962.
Named National League Comeback Player of the Year by THE SPORTING NEWS, 1973.
Named second baseman on THE SPORTING NEWS National League All-Star Team, 1973.
Named second baseman on THE SPORTING NEWS American League All-Star Team, 1970.
Named second baseman on THE SPORTING NEWS American League All-Star fielding team, 1969 through 1971.

Year Club	League	Pos.	G.	AB.	R.	H.	2B.	3B.	HR.	RBI.	B.A.	PO.	A.	E.	F.A.
1962—Stockton	Calif.	SS	97	343	58	106	18	●12	10	63	.309	135	307	40	★.917
1963—Elmira	East.	SS-2B	63	233	47	76	11	6	13	42	.326	115	155	12	.957
1963—Rochester	Int.	2B-OF	63	211	31	52	9	3	6	22	.246	141	138	11	.962
1964—Rochester	Int.	2B-SS	●155	590	87	156	29	14	19	73	.264	326	445	39	.952
1965—Baltimore	Amer.	3B-2B-SS	20	47	5	8	3	0	0	1	.170	11	37	3	.941
1965—Rochester	Int.	SS	52	193	29	58	9	3	4	22	.301	96	161	10	.963
1966—Baltimore	Amer.	★2B-SS	131	501	47	129	20	3	7	56	.257	294	357	★20	.970
1967—Baltimore	Amer.	2B-3B	148	510	62	126	30	3	10	64	.247	344	351	14	.980
1968—Baltimore	Amer.	2B-SS	145	504	50	122	24	4	9	56	.242	294	370	15	.978
1969—Baltimore	Amer.	2B-SS	142	511	52	143	34	1	7	57	.280	294	370	12	.984
1970—Baltimore	Amer.	●2B-SS	149	530	68	149	27	1	10	53	.281	●382	391	8	.990
1971—Baltimore	Amer.	2B	142	510	67	144	26	1	18	72	.282	361	367	12	.984
1972—Baltimore†	Amer.	2B	118	376	31	83	22	3	5	32	.221	286	307	6	★.990

Year Club League	Pos.	G.	AB.	R.	H.	2B.	3B.	HR.	RBI.	B.A.	PO.	A.	E.	F.A.
1973—Atlanta .... Nat.	2B	157	559	84	151	25	0	43	99	.270	383	464	*30	.966
1974—Atlanta .... Nat.	1B-2B	136	454	56	114	18	0	15	62	.251	789	231	11	.989
1975—Atlanta‡ .... Nat.	PH	1	1	0	1	1	0	0	1	1.000	0	0	0	.000
1975—Yomiuri............... Central	3B-SS	91	289	29	57	7	0	13	38	.197	85	157	11	.957
1976—Yomiuri§.............. Central	2B-3B-1B	108	371	48	102	16	2	26	74	.275	226	28	11	.979
1977—Philadelphia x...... Nat.	1B-2B-3B	78	156	23	50	9	1	8	36	.321	299	31	0	1.000
1978—Phil. y-Chi. z.......... Nat.	3B-2B-1B	68	138	19	32	3	1	4	20	.232	61	63	11	.919
1979—Miami .... Int.-Am.	1B	10	25	7	6	2	0	1	2	.240	Figures Unavailable			
American League Totals—8 Years		995	3489	382	904	186	16	66	391	.259	2330	2550	90	.982
National League Totals—5 Years		440	1308	182	348	56	2	70	218	.266	1532	789	52	.978
Major League Totals—13 Years..............		1435	4797	564	1252	242	18	136	609	.261	3862	3339	142	.981

†Traded with Pitchers Pat Dobson and Roric Harrison and Catcher Johnny Oates to Atlanta Braves for Catcher Earl Williams and Infielder Taylor Duncan, November 30, 1972.

‡Released, April 11, 1975; signed by Yomiuri Giants of Japanese baseball.

§Released, January 21, 1977; signed as free agent with Philadelphia Phillies, February 3, 1977.

xOn supplemental disabled list, June 15 to July 1, 1977.

yTraded to Chicago Cubs for Pitcher Larry Anderson, August 6, 1978.

zReleased, October 17, 1978.

CHAMPIONSHIP SERIES RECORD

Tied American League Championship Series record for most home runs, three-game Series (2), 1970.

Year Club League	Pos.	G.	AB.	R.	H.	2B.	3B.	HR.	RBI.	B.A.	PO.	A.	E.	F.A.
1969—Baltimore .... Amer.	2B	3	13	2	3	0	0	0	0	.231	5	11	0	1.000
1970—Baltimore .... Amer.	2B	3	11	4	4	0	0	2	4	.364	4	4	0	1.000
1971—Baltimore .... Amer.	2B	3	10	2	3	2	0	0	0	.300	5	6	1	.917
1977—Philadelphia .... Nat.	1B	1	4	0	1	0	0	0	2	.250	8	0	0	1.000
Championship Series Totals—4 Years.....		10	38	8	11	2	0	2	6	.289	29	21	1	.980

WORLD SERIES RECORD

Established World Series record for highest fielding average by second baseman, four-game Series (1.000 with 24 chances), 1966.

Year Club League	Pos.	G.	AB.	R.	H.	2B.	3B.	HR.	RBI.	B.A.	PO.	A.	E.	F.A.
1966—Baltimore .... Amer.	2B	4	14	1	4	1	0	0	1	.286	12	12	0	1.000
1969—Baltimore .... Amer.	2B	5	16	1	1	0	0	0	0	.063	8	15	0	1.000
1970—Baltimore .... Amer.	2B	5	16	2	5	2	0	0	2	.313	15	9	0	1.000
1971—Baltimore .... Amer.	2B	7	27	1	4	0	0	0	3	.148	18	12	0	1.000
World Series Totals—4 Years		21	73	5	14	3	0	0	6	.192	53	48	0	1.000

ALL-STAR GAME RECORD

Year League	Pos.	AB.	R.	H.	2B.	3B.	HR.	RBI.	B.A.	PO.	A.	E.	F.A.
1968—American	2B	1	0	0	0	0	0	0	.000	1	1	0	1.000
1970—American	2B	5	0	1	0	0	0	0	.200	5	1	0	1.000
1973—National	2B	1	0	0	0	0	0	0	.000	1	1	0	1.000
All-Star Game Totals—3 Years..................		7	0	1	0	0	0	0	.143	7	3	0	1.000

Named to American League All-Star Team for 1969 game; replaced due to injury.

RECORD AS MANAGER

Year Club League	Position	W.	L.	Year Club League	Position	W.	L.
1979—Miami .... Inter-Amer.	First	43	17	1984—New York............... Nat.	Second(E)	90	72
(Second Half)	First	8	4	1985—New York............... Nat.	Second(E)	98	64
1981—Jackson .... Texas	†First(E)	39	27	1986—New York............... Nat.	First(E)	108	54
(Second Half)	Third(E)	29	39	Major League Totals—3 Years..................		296	190
1983—Tidewater .... Int.	‡Fourth	71	68				

†Defeated Tulsa, two games to one, and San Antonio (finals), three games to none, for championship.

‡Defeated Columbus, three games to two, and Richmond (finals), three games to one, for championship.

Coach, National League All-Star Team, 1986.

Instructor, New York Mets' organization, 1982.

CHAMPIONSHIP SERIES RECORD					WORLD SERIES RECORD			
Year Club League		W.	L.		Year Club League		W.	L.
1986—New York.................. National		4	2		1986—New York.................. National		4	3

JAY THOMAS KELLY
(Tom)
Minnesota Twins

Born August 15, 1950, at Graceville, Minn.
Height, 5.11. Weight, 185.
Threw and batted lefthanded.
Attended Mesa Community College, Mesa, Ariz., and Monmouth College, West Long Branch, N. J.
Son of Joe Kelly, former pitcher in St. Louis Cardinals'
and New York Giants' organizations.

Led International League in bases on balls received with 91 in 1978.
Led New York-Pennsylvania League in stolen bases with 16 in 1968.
Led Pacific Coast League outfielders in double plays with 6 in 1972.

Year Club	League	Pos.	G.	AB.	R.	H.	2B.	3B.	HR.	RBI.	B.A.	PO.	A.	E.	F.A.
1968—Newark	NYP	OF	65	218	50	69	11	4	2	10	.317	*144	*9	3	.981
1969—Clinton	Midw.	OF	100	269	47	60	10	2	6	35	.223	158	15	4	.977
1970—Jacksonville††‡	South.	OF-1B	93	266	33	64	10	1	8	38	.241	204	19	4	.982
1971—Charlotte	South.	1B-OF	100	303	50	89	17	0	6	41	.294	508	38	9	.984
1972—Tacoma	P. C.	OF-1B	132	407	76	114	19	2	10	52	.280	282	19	10	.968
1973—Tacoma	P. C.	OF-1B	114	337	67	87	10	2	17	49	.258	200	20	6	.973
1974—Tacoma	P. C.	OF-1B	115	357	68	110	16	0	18	69	.308	514	41	3	.985
1975—Tacoma	P. C.	OF-1B	62	202	38	51	5	0	9	29	.252	185	12	6	.970
1975—Minnesota	Amer.	1B-OF	49	127	11	23	5	0	1	11	.181	360	28	6	.985
1976—Rochester	Int.	OF-1B	127	405	71	117	19	3	18	70	.289	323	28	4	.989
1977—Tacoma xyz	P. C.	1B-OF-P	113	363	80	99	12	1	12	64	.273	251	15	6	.978
1978—Toledo ab	Int.	1B-OF	119	325	47	74	13	0	10	49	.228	556	46	5	.992
Major League Totals—1 Year			49	127	11	23	5	0	1	11	.181	360	28	6	.985

†On temporary inactive list, April 16 to April 20, April 25 to April 30 and August 21, 1970 through remainder of season.

‡Released, April 6, 1971; signed by Charlotte (Minnesota Twins' organization), April 28, 1971.

§Loaned to Rochester (Baltimore Orioles' organization), April 5, 1976; returned, September 22, 1976.

xOn temporary inactive list, April 15 to April 19, 1977.

yPlayer-manager.

zOn disabled list, July 25 to August 4, 1977.

aPlayer-coach.

bReleased, December 18, 1978.

PITCHING RECORD

Year Club	League	G.	IP.	W.	L.	Pct.	H.	R.	ER.	SO.	BB.	ERA.
1977—Tacoma	P. Coast	1	3	0	0	.000	2	2	2	0	3	6.00

RECORD AS MANAGER

Named Southern League Manager of the Year, 1981.
Named California League Co-Manager of the Year, 1980.
Named California League Manager of the Year, 1979.

Year Club	League	Position	W.	L.	Year Club	League	Position	W.	L.
1977—Tacoma†	P. Coast	Third(W)	28	26	1981—Orlando	South.	xFirst(E)	42	27
1979—Visalia	Calif.	‡First(S)	44	26	(Second Half)		Third(E)	37	36
(Second Half)		Second(S)	42	28	1982—Orlando	South.	Fifth(E)	31	38
1980—Visalia	Calif.	Fourth(S)	27	43	(Second Half)		Second(E)	43	32
(Second Half)		§First(S)	44	26	1986—Minnesota y	Amer.	Sixth(W)	12	11
					Major League Totals—1 Year			12	11

†Replaced Del Wilber (record of 40-49), June, 1977.

‡Lost to San Jose, two games to one in semifinals.

§Defeated Fresno, two games to none in semifinals, and lost to Stockton, three games to none for championship.

xDefeated Savannah, three games to one in semifinals, and defeated Nashville, three games to one for championship.

yReplaced Ray Miller with club in seventh place (record of 59-80), September 12, 1986.
Coach, Minnesota Twins, 1983 through September 11, 1986.

HAROLD CLIFTON LANIER
(Hal)
Houston Astros

Born July 4, 1942, at Denton, N.C.
Height, 6.02. Weight, 186.
Threw and batted righthanded.
Son of Max Lanier, pitcher with St. Louis Cardinals, New York Giants
and St. Louis Browns, 1938 through 1953.

Major League stolen bases: 1964 (2), 1965 (2), 1966 (1), 1967 (2), 1968 (2), 1970 (1), 1972 (1). Total—11.
Led Eastern League second basemen in double plays with 85 in 1963.
Received reported $50,000 bonus to sign with San Francisco Giants, 1961.

Year Club	League	Pos.	G.	AB.	R.	H.	2B.	3B.	HR.	RBI.	B.A.	PO.	A.	E.	F.A.
1961—Quincy	Midw.	SS	73	295	61	93	7	5	1	25	.315	112	204	18	.946
1962—Fresno	Calif.	2B	133	555	89	173	20	4	5	49	.312	*358	*321	23	*.967
1963—Springfield	East.	2B	138	*577	77	*163	27	9	6	49	.282	*359	*379	18	*.976
1964—Tacoma	P. C.	2B-SS	61	254	33	83	17	1	4	28	.327	140	152	9	.970
1964—San Francisco	Nat.	2B-SS	98	383	40	105	16	3	2	28	.274	226	298	11	.979
1965—San Francisco	Nat.	2B-SS	159	522	41	118	15	9	0	39	.226	294	445	18	.976
1966—San Francisco	Nat.	2B-SS	149	459	37	106	14	2	3	37	.231	303	423	13	.982
1967—San Francisco	Nat.	2B-SS	151	525	37	112	16	3	0	42	.213	253	519	20	.975
1968—San Francisco	Nat.	SS	151	486	37	100	14	1	0	27	.206	*282	496	17	*.979
1969—San Francisco	Nat.	SS	150	495	37	113	9	1	0	35	.228	252	530	25	.969
1970—San Francisco	Nat.	SS-2-1	134	438	33	101	13	1	2	41	.231	263	399	22	.968
1971—San Francisco†	Nat.	3-2-S-1	109	206	21	48	8	0	1	13	.233	91	130	6	.974
1972—New York	Amer.	3-S-2	60	103	5	22	3	0	0	6	.214	32	87	4	.967
1973—New York‡	Amer.	S-2-3	35	86	9	18	3	0	0	5	.209	45	81	4	.969
1974—Tulsa	A. A.	2-3-S	103	357	45	96	15	0	1	32	.269	158	203	10	.973
1975—Tulsa§x	A. A.	3B-2B	21	74	11	15	1	1	1	7	.203	26	50	0	1.000
1979—Springfield	A. A.	SS	1	2	0	1	0	0	0	0	.500	3	1	0	1.000
National League Totals—8 Years			1101	3514	283	803	105	20	8	262	.229	1964	3240	132	.975
American League Totals—2 Years			95	189	14	40	6	0	0	11	.212	77	168	8	.968
Major League Totals—10 Years			1196	3703	297	843	111	20	8	273	.228	2041	3408	140	.975

CHAMPIONSHIP SERIES RECORD

Year	Club	League	Pos.	G.	AB.	R.	H.	2B.	3B.	HR.	RBI.	B.A.	PO.	A.	E.	F.A.
1971—San Francisco	Nat.		3B	1	1	0	0	0	0	0	0	.000	1	0	0	1.000

RECORD AS MANAGER

Named Major League Co-Manager of the Year by THE SPORTING NEWS, 1986.
Named Minor League Manager of the Year by THE SPORTING NEWS, 1980.
Named Western Carolinas League Manager of the Year, 1977.

Year	Club	League	Position	W.	L.	Year	Club	League	Position	W.	L.
1976—St. Petersburg	Fla. St.	Third(N)	70	71		1979—Springfield	A. A.	Second(E)	73	63
1977—Gastonia†	W.Car.	‡Second	37	32		1980—Springfield y	A. A.	First(E)	75	61
(Second Half)		First	45	25		1986—Houston	Nat.	First(W)	96	66
1978—St. Petersburg§	Fla. St.	First(N)	41	25		Major League Totals—1 Year			96	66
(Second Half)		Second(N)	x43	31						

†Won championship playoff from Greenwood, three games to one.
‡Tied for postion.
§Lost playoff to Lakeland, one game to none.
xOne tie game.
yLost championship playoff to Denver, four games to one.
Coach, St. Louis Cardinals, 1981 through 1985.

CHAMPIONSHIP SERIES RECORD

Year	Club	League	W.	L.
1986—Houston	National		2	4

ANTHONY LaRUSSA JR.
(Tony)
Oakland A's

Born October 4, 1944, at Tampa, Fla.
Height, 6.00. Weight, 185.
Threw and batted righthanded.
Attended University of Tampa, Tampa, Fla., and received degree in industrial management from
University of Southern Florida, Tampa, Fla.; and received law degree from
Florida State University, Tallahassee, Fla. in 1980.

Led International League in being hit by pitch with 11 in 1972.
Received reported $50,000 bonus to sign with Kansas City A's, 1962.

Year	Club	League	Pos.	G.	AB.	R.	H.	2B.	3B.	HR.	RBI.	B.A.	PO.	A.	E.	F.A.
1962—Daytona Beach	Fla. St.	SS	64	225	37	58	7	0	1	32	.258	135	173	38	.890
1962—Binghamton	East.	SS-2B	12	43	3	8	0	0	0	4	.186	20	27	8	.855
1963—Kansas City	Amer.	SS-2B	34	44	4	11	1	1	0	1	.250	29	25	2	.964
1964—Lewiston†	N'west	2B-SS	90	329	50	77	22	1	1	25	.234	188	218	18	.958
1965—Birmingham‡	South.	2B	75	259	24	50	11	2	1	18	.193	202	161	21	.945
1966—Modesto	Calif.	2B	81	316	67	92	20	1	7	54	.291	201	212	20	.954
1966—Mobile	South.	2B	51	170	20	50	9	4	4	26	.294	117	133	10	.962
1967—Birmingham§	South.	2B	41	139	12	32	6	1	5	22	.230	88	120	5	.977
1968—Oakland	Amer.	PH	5	3	0	1	0	0	0	0	.333	0	0	0	.000
1968—Vancouver	P. C.	2B	122	455	55	109	16	8	5	29	.240	249	321	14	★.976
1969—Iowa	A. A.	2B	67	235	37	72	11	1	4	27	.306	177	222	15	.964
1969—Oakland	Amer.	PH	8	8	0	0	0	0	0	0	.000	0	0	0	.000
1970—Iowa	A. A.	2B	22	88	13	22	5	0	2	5	.250	52	59	3	.974
1970—Oakland	Amer.	2B	52	106	6	21	4	1	0	6	.198	67	89	5	.969
1971—Iowa	A. A.	2-3-S-O	28	107	21	31	5	1	2	11	.290	70	85	2	.987
1971—Oakland x	Amer.	2B-SS-3B	23	8	3	0	0	0	0	0	.000	8	7	2	.882
1971—Atlanta	Nat.	2B	9	7	1	2	0	0	0	0	.286	8	6	1	.933
1972—Richmond y	Int.	2B	122	389	68	120	13	2	10	42	.308	305	289	20	.967
1973—Wichita	A. A.	2B-1B-3B	106	392	82	123	16	0	5	75	.314	423	213	26	.961
1973—Chicago z	Nat.	PR	1	0	1	0	0	0	0	0	.000	0	0	0	.000
1974—Charleston a	Int.	2B	139	457	50	119	17	1	8	35	.260	262	★378	17	.974
1975—Denver	A. A.	3-O-S-2	118	354	87	99	23	2	7	46	.280	95	91	10	.949
1976—Iowa bc	A. A.	INF-O-P	107	332	53	86	11	0	4	34	.259	132	160	22	.930
1977—New Orleans de	A. A.	2B-3B	50	128	17	24	2	2	3	6	.188	66	87	7	.956
American League Totals—5 Years			122	169	13	33	5	2	0	7	.195	104	121	9	.962
National League Totals—2 Years			10	7	2	2	0	0	0	0	.286	8	6	1	.933
Major League Totals—6 Years			132	176	15	35	5	2	0	7	.199	112	127	10	.960

PITCHING RECORD

Year Club	League	G.	IP.	W.	L.	Pct.	H.	R.	ER.	SO.	BB.	ERA.
1976—Iowa	Am. Assoc.	3	3	0	0	.000	3	1	1	0	0	3.00

RECORD AS MANAGER

Tied major league record for most clubs managed, season (2), 1986.
Named Major League Manager of the Year by THE SPORTING NEWS, 1983.

Year Club	League	Position	W.	L.	Year Club	League	Position	W.	L.
1978—Knoxville	South.	First(W)	49	21	1983—Chicago	Amer.	First(W)	99	63
(Second Half)†		Third(W)	4	4	1984—Chicago	Amer.	yFifth(W)	74	88
1979—Iowa‡	A. A.	Second(E)	54	52	1985—Chicago	Amer.	Third(W)	85	77
1979—Chicago§	Amer.	Fifth(W)	27	27	1986—Chicago z	Amer.	Sixth(W)	26	38
1980—Chicago	Amer.	Fifth(W)	70	90	1986—Oakland a	Amer.	bThird(W)	45	34
1981—Chicago x	Amer.		54	52	Major League Totals—8 Years			567	544
1982—Chicago	Amer.	Third(W)	87	75					

†Replaced by Joe Jones, July 3, 1978.
‡Replaced by Joe Sparks, August 3, 1979.
§Replaced Don Kessinger with club in fifth place (record of 46-60), August 3, 1979.
xFirst Half. . . . Third (W) (record 31-22); Second Half. . . . Sixth (W) (record of 23-30).
yTied for position with Seattle Mariners.
zReplaced by interim manager Doug Rader, June 20, 1986.
aReplaced manager Jackie Moore (record of 29-44) and interim manager Jeff Newman (record of 2-8) with club in seventh place (combined record of 31-52), July 7, 1986.
bTied for position with Kansas City Royals.
Coach, Chicago White Sox, July 3 through remainder of 1978 season.
Coach, American League All-Star Team, 1984.

CHAMPIONSHIP SERIES RECORD

Year Club	League	W.	L.
1983—Chicago	American	1	3

THOMAS CHARLES LASORDA

Name pronounced Luh-SORR-duh.

(Tom)

Los Angeles Dodgers

Born September 22, 1927, at Norristown, Pa.
Height, 5.09. Weight, 195.
Threw and batted lefthanded.

Tied National League record by making three wild pitches in an inning, first inning, May 5, 1955.
Led International League in complete games with 16 and tied for lead in shutouts with 5 in 1958.
Led Canadian-American League in wild pitches with 20 in 1948 and led International League with 14 in 1953.
Named International League Pitcher of the Year, 1958.

Year Club	League	G.	IP.	W.	L.	Pct.	H.	R.	ER.	SO.	BB.	ERA.
1945—Concord	N. C. St.	27	121	3	12	.200	115	84	55	91	100	4.09
1946-47—†	E. Shore					(In Military Service)						
1948—Schenectady‡§	Can.-Am.	32	192	9	12	.429	180	122	99	195	153	4.64
1949—Greenville	Sally	45	178	7	7	.500	141	81	58	151	138	2.93
1950—Montreal	Int'national	31	146	9	4	.692	136	73	60	85	82	3.70
1951—Montreal	Int'national	31	165	12	8	.600	145	75	64	80	87	3.49
1952—Montreal	Int'national	33	182	14	5	.737	156	90	74	77	93	3.66
1953—Montreal	Int'national	36	208	17	8	.680	171	77	65	122	94	2.81
1954—Montreal	Int'national	23	154	14	5	.737	142	66	60	75	79	3.51
1954—Brooklyn	National	4	9	0	0	.000	8	5	5	5	5	5.00
1955—Brooklyn	National	4	4	0	0	.000	5	6	6	4	6	13.50
1955—Montreal x	Int'national	22	143	9	8	.529	125	58	52	92	62	3.27
1956—Kansas City y	American	18	45	0	4	.000	40	38	31	28	45	6.20
1956—Denver	Am. Assoc.	16	83	3	4	.429	94	54	46	54	34	4.99
1957—Denver z	Am. Assoc.	6	17	0	2	.000	29	25	23	8	6	12.18
1957—Los Angeles	P. Coast	29	132	7	10	.412	134	73	57	72	59	3.90
1958—Montreal	Int'national	34	*230	*18	6	.750	191	77	64	126	76	2.50
1959—Montreal	Int'national	29	188	12	8	.600	192	93	80	64	77	3.83
1960—Montreal a	Int'national	12	45	2	5	.286	79	48	41	17	24	8.20
American League Totals—1 Year		18	45	0	4	.000	40	38	31	28	45	6.20
National League Totals—2 Years		8	13	0	0	.000	13	11	11	9	11	7.62
Major League Totals—3 Years		26	58	0	4	.000	53	49	42	37	56	6.52

†On National Defense list, May 14, 1946 through February 2, 1948.
‡On disabled list, July 9 to July 19, 1948.
§Drafted by Nashua (Brooklyn Dodgers' organization) from Philadelphia Phillies' organization, November 24, 1948.
xSold by Brooklyn Dodgers' organization to Kansas City Athletics for an estimated $35,000, March 2, 1956.
yTraded to New York Yankees for Pitcher Wally Burnette and cash, July 11, 1956.
zSold by New York Yankees' organization to Brooklyn Dodgers' organization, May 26, 1957.
aReleased, July 9, 1960.

RECORD AS MANAGER

Named Minor League Manager of the Year by THE SPORTING NEWS, 1970.
Named Pacific Coast League co-Manager of the Year, 1970.
Named Pioneer League Manager of the Year, 1967.

Year Club	League	Position	W.	L.	Year Club	League	Position	W.	L.
1965—Pocatello	Pion.	†Second	33	33	1978—Los Angeles	Nat.	First(W)	95	67
1966—Ogden	Pion.	First	39	27	1979—Los Angeles	Nat.	Third(W)	79	83
1967—Ogden	Pion.	First	41	25	1980—Los Angeles	Nat.	Second(W)	92	71
1968—Ogden	Pion.	First	39	25	1981—Los Angeles y	Nat.		63	47
1969—Spokane	P. C.	Second(N)	71	73	1982—Los Angeles	Nat.	Second(W)	88	74
1970—Spokane	P. C.	‡First(N)	94	52	1983—Los Angeles	Nat.	First(W)	91	71
1971—Spokane	P. C.	Third(N)	69	76	1984—Los Angeles	Nat.	Fourth(W)	79	83
1972—Albuquerque	P. C.	§First(E)	92	56	1985—Los Angeles	Nat.	First(W)	95	67
1976—Los Angeles x	Nat.	Second(W)	2	2	1986—Los Angeles	Nat.	Fifth(W)	73	89
1977—Los Angeles	Nat.	First(W)	98	64	Major League Totals—11 Years			855	718

†Tied for position with Magic Valley.
‡Won championship playoff against Hawaii, four games to none.
§Won championship playoff against Eugene, three games to one.
xReplaced retiring Walter Alston with club in second place (record of 90-68), September 29, 1976.
yFirst Half. . . . First(W) (record of 36-21); Second Half. . . . Fourth(W) (record of 27-26).
Scout, Los Angeles Dodgers, 1961 through 1965; manager Los Angeles farm team in Arizona Instructional League, 1969; coach, Los Angeles Dodgers, 1973 through 1976.
Manager, National League All-Star Team, 1978, 1979 and 1982.
Coach, National League All-Star Team, 1977, 1983, 1984 and 1986.

DIVISION SERIES RECORD

Year Club	League	W.	L.
1981—Los Angeles	National	3	2

CHAMPIONSHIP SERIES RECORD

Year Club	League	W.	L.
1977—Los Angeles	National	3	1
1978—Los Angeles	National	3	1
1981—Los Angeles	National	3	2
1983—Los Angeles	National	1	3
1985—Los Angeles	National	2	4
Championship Series Totals—5 Years		12	11

WORLD SERIES RECORD

Year Club	League	W.	L.
1977—Los Angeles	National	2	4
1978—Los Angeles	National	2	4
1981—Los Angeles	National	4	2
World Series Totals—3 Years		8	10

JAMES RICHARD LEYLAND

Named pronounced LEE-lund.

(Jim)

Pittsburgh Pirates

Born December 15, 1944, at Toledo, O.
Height, 5.11. Weight, 170.
Threw and batted righthanded.

Year Club	League	Pos.	G.	AB.	R.	H.	2B.	3B.	HR.	RBI.	B.A.	PO.	A.	E.	F.A.
1964—Lakeland†	Fla. St.	C	52	129	8	25	0	1	0	8	.194	268	17	6	.979
1964—Cocoa Tigers	Rookie	C	24	52	2	12	1	1	0	4	.231	122	15	3	.979
1965—Jamestown	NYP	C-3B-P	82	211	18	50	7	2	1	21	.237	318	36	6	.983
1966—Rocky Mount	Carol.	C	67	173	24	42	6	0	0	16	.243	369	23	1	.997
1967—Montgomery	South.	C	62	171	11	40	3	0	1	16	.234	350	25	6	.984
1968—Montgomery	South.	C-3B-SS	81	264	19	51	3	0	1	20	.193	511	43	7	.988
1969—Montgomery	South.	C	16	39	1	8	0	0	0	1	.205	64	6	3	.959
1969—Lakeland	Fla. St.	C-P	60	179	20	43	8	0	1	16	.240	321	28	4	.989
1970—Montgomery‡	South.	C	2	3	0	0	0	0	0	0	.000	6	0	1	.857

Signed as free agent by Detroit Tigers' organization, September 21, 1963.
†On disabled list, June 15 to June 27, 1964.
‡Player-coach.

PITCHING RECORD

Year Club	League	G.	IP.	W.	L.	Pct.	H.	R.	ER.	SO.	BB.	ERA.
1965—Jamestown	NYP	1	2	0	0	.000	2	0	0	1	0	0.00
1969—Lakeland	Florida St.	1	2	0	0	.000	4	2	2	1	0	9.00

RECORD AS MANAGER

Named American Association Manager of the Year, 1979.
Named Florida State League Manager of the Year, 1977 and 1978.

Year Club	League	Position	W.	L.	Year Club	League	Position	W.	L.
1971—Bristol	Appal.	Third(S)	31	35	1977—Lakeland	Fla. St.	§First(N)	85	53
1972—Clinton	Midw.	Fifth(N)	22	41	1978—Lakeland	Fla. St.	Fourth(N)	31	38
(Second Half)		Fourth(N)	27	36	(Second Half)		xFirst(N)	47	22
1973—Clinton	Midw.	Second(N)	36	26	1979—Evansville	A. A.	yFirst(E)	78	58
(Second Half)		†First(N)	37	25	1980—Evansville	A. A.	Second(E)	61	74
1974—Montgomery	South.	Third(W)	61	76	1981—Evansville	A. A.	zFirst(E)	73	63
1975—Clinton	Midw.	Fourth(S)	29	31	1986—Pittsburgh	Nat.	Sixth(E)	64	98
(Second Half)		Second(S)	38	30	Major League Totals—1 Year			64	98
1976—Lakeland	Fla. St.	‡Second(N)	74	64					

— 559 —

GENE WILLIAM MAUCH
California Angels

Born November 18, 1925, at Salina, Kan.
Height, 5.10. Weight, 173.
Threw and batted righthanded.
Brother-in-law of Roy Smalley, Jr., infielder with Chicago Cubs, Milwaukee Braves and Philadelphia Phillies, 1948 through 1958; Uncle of Roy Smalley III, infielder with Minnesota Twins; and Harry Mauch, minor league outfielder, 1978 and 1980.

Major League stolen bases: 1948 (1), 1949 (3), 1950 (1), 1957 (1). Total—6.

Year Club	League	Pos.	G.	AB.	R.	H.	2B.	3B.	HR.	RBI.	B.A.	PO.	A.	E.	F.A.
1943—Durham	Pied.	SS	32	115	19	37	5	1	0	14	.322	77	81	19	.893
1943—Montreal	Int.	2B-SS	31	77	5	13	1	0	0	4	.169	36	41	12	.865
1944—Brooklyn	Nat.	SS	5	15	2	2	1	0	0	2	.133	7	9	0	1.000
1944—Montreal†	Int.	SS	14	53	12	15	0	0	0	2	.283	25	39	8	.889
1945—Brooklyn	Nat.					(In Military Service)									
1946—St. Paul‡	A. A.	SS	149	536	74	133	19	3	6	55	.248	296	★417	★64	.918
1947—Pittsburgh	Nat.	2B-SS	16	30	8	9	0	0	0	1	.300	18	20	3	.927
1947—Indianapolis§	A. A.	2B	58	217	37	65	13	4	0	16	.300	176	174	12	.967
1948—Brook.x-Chicago	Nat.	2B-SS	65	151	19	30	3	2	1	7	.199	90	105	12	.942
1949—Chicago y	Nat.	2B-SS-3B	72	150	15	37	6	2	1	7	.247	98	125	9	.961
1950—Boston	Nat.	2B-3B-SS	48	121	17	28	5	0	1	15	.231	83	85	7	.960
1951—Boston	Nat.	SS-3B-2B	19	20	5	2	0	0	0	1	.100	16	16	1	.970
1951—Milwaukee za	A. A.	INF	37	109	30	33	2	0	1	16	.303	76	89	7	.959
1952—St. Louis b	Nat.	SS	7	3	0	0	0	0	0	0	.000	1	0	1	.500
1952—Milwaukee	A. A.	SS-2B	102	327	58	106	24	3	4	60	.324	202	258	12	.975
1953—Atlanta c	South.	2B	111	340	65	91	23	3	9	51	.268	200	239	18	.961
1954—Los Angeles	P. C.	2B	153	565	81	162	26	2	11	58	.287	354	380	19	.975
1955—Los Angeles	P. C.	★2B-3B	155	584	93	173	37	4	8	49	.296	★436	375	18	.978
1956—Los Angeles d	P. C.	2B-3B	146	566	123	197	29	3	20	84	.348	348	403	24	.969
1956—Boston	Amer.	2B	7	25	4	8	0	0	1	1	.320	12	17	2	.935
1957—Boston	Amer.	2B	65	222	23	60	10	3	2	28	.270	127	153	11	.962
1958—Minneapolis	A. A.	2B-3B	65	210	25	51	12	2	3	29	.243	108	136	16	.938
1959—Minneapolis	A. A.	PH	8	8	1	4	0	0	0	0	.500	0	0	0	.000
American League Totals—2 Years			72	247	27	68	10	3	2	29	.275	139	170	13	.960
National League Totals—7 Years			232	490	66	108	15	4	2	33	.220	313	360	33	.953
Major League Totals—9 Years			304	737	93	176	25	7	5	62	.239	452	530	46	.955

†Entered Military Service in May, 1944.
‡Recalled by Brooklyn Dodgers and traded to Pittsburgh Pirates with Pitchers Kirby Higbe and Cal McLish and Catcher Homer (Dixie) Howell for Outfielder Al Gionfriddo and reported $100,000, May 3, 1947.
§Recalled by Pittsburgh Pirates and traded to Brooklyn Dodgers with Pitcher Elwin (Preacher) Roe and Shortstop Billy Cox for Pitchers Hal Gregg and Vic Lombardi and Outfielder Fred (Dixie) Walker, December 7, 1947.
xSold to Chicago Cubs, June 17, 1948.
yTraded to Boston Braves with cash for Pitcher Bill Voiselle, December 14, 1949.
zDrafted by New York Yankees from Milwaukee (Boston Braves' organization), November 19, 1951.
aSold via waivers by New York Yankees to St. Louis Cardinals, March 26, 1952.
bReturned by Cardinals to Milwaukee (Boston Braves' organization), May 21, 1952.
cReleased to Los Angeles (Chicago Cubs' organization), September 28, 1953.
dReleased to Boston Red Sox, September 10, 1956.

RECORD AS MANAGER

Established major league record for most consecutive years, no championships won as manager (25), 1960 through 1982 and 1985.
Established National League record for most years, no championships won as manager (16), 1960 through 1975.
Named American Association Manager of the Year, 1958 and 1959.
Named Major League Manager of the Year by THE SPORTING NEWS, 1973.

Year Club	League	Position	W.	L.	Year Club	League	Position	W.	L.
1953—Atlanta	South.	Third	84	70	1969—Montreal	Nat.	Sixth(E)	52	110
1958—Minneapolis	A. A.	†Third	82	71	1970—Montreal	Nat.	Sixth(E)	73	89
1959—Minneapolis	A. A.	‡Second(E)	95	67	1971—Montreal	Nat.	Fifth(E)	71	90
1960—Philadelphia§	Nat.	Eighth	58	94	1972—Montreal	Nat.	Fifth(E)	70	86
1961—Philadelphia	Nat.	Eighth	47	107	1973—Montreal	Nat.	Fourth(E)	79	83
1962—Philadelphia	Nat.	Seventh	81	80	1974—Montreal	Nat.	Fourth(E)	79	82
1963—Philadelphia	Nat.	Fourth	87	75	1975—Montreal	Nat.	zFifth(E)	75	87
1964—Philadelphia	Nat.	xSecond	92	70	1976—Minnesota	Amer.	Third(W)	85	77
1965—Philadelphia	Nat.	Sixth	85	76	1977—Minnesota	Amer.	Fourth(W)	84	77
1966—Philadelphia	Nat.	Fourth	87	75	1978—Minnesota	Amer.	Fourth(W)	73	89
1967—Philadelphia	Nat.	Fifth	82	80	1979—Minnesota	Amer.	Fourth(W)	82	80
1968—Philadelphia y	Nat.	Fifth	28	27	1980—Minnesota a	Amer.	Fourth(W)	54	71

Year	Club	League	Position	W.	L.
1981—California bc	Amer.			29	34
1982—California	Amer.	First(W)		93	69
1985—California	Amer.	Second(W)		90	72
1986—California	Amer.	First(W)		92	70

American League Totals—9 Years 682 639
National League Totals—16 Years 1146 1311

Major League Totals—25 Years 1828 1950

†Won playoffs by defeating Wichita, four games to two and Denver, four games to none; won Junior World Series by defeating Montreal (International League), four games to none.

‡Won playoffs by defeating Omaha, four games to two and Fort Worth, four games to three; lost Junior World Series to Havana (International League), four games to three.

§Replaced Eddie Sawyer, who resigned after managing Phils in season opener (Coach Andy Cohen served as acting manager for second game), April 15, 1960.

xTied for position with Cincinnati Reds.

yReplaced by Bob Skinner, June 16, 1968.

zTied for position with Chicago Cubs.

aReplaced by John Goryl, August 24, 1980.

bFirst Half. . . . Fourth(W) (record of 9-4); Second Half. . . . Seventh(W) (record of 20-30).

cReplaced Jim Fregosi with club in fourth place (record of 22-25), May 28, 1981.

Manager, National League All-Star Team, 1965.

Coach, National League All-Star Team, 1961 (first game), 1963 and 1973; American League All-Star Team, 1976; Director of Player Personnel, California Angels, 1983 and 1984.

CHAMPIONSHIP SERIES RECORD

Year	Club	League	W.	L.
1982—California	American		2	3
1986—California	American		3	4

Championship Series Totals—2 Years......... 5 7

JOHN FRANCIS McNAMARA
Boston Red Sox

Born June 4, 1932, at Sacramento, Calif.
Height, 5.10. Weight, 175.
Threw and batted righthanded.
Attended Sacramento State College, Sacramento, Calif.

Led Northwest League in sacrifice hits with 18 in 1959.
Led Northwest League catchers in double plays with 15 in 1958, 10 in 1959 and 14 in 1962.

Year	Club	League	Pos.	G.	AB.	R.	H.	2B.	3B.	HR.	RBI.	B.A.	PO.	A.	E.	F.A.
1951—Fresno	Calif.	C	60	182	20	38	2	0	0	12	.209	284	46	11	.968
1952—Houston	Texas	....	6	13	0	1	0	0	0	0	.077	....	....	....	....
1952—Lynchburg	Pied.	C	102	303	25	54	8	0	0	19	.178	489	57	8	★.986
1953—Winston-Salem	Carol.						(In Military Service)									
1954—Omaha†	West.						(In Military Service)									
1955—Lewiston	N'west	C	129	427	49	102	24	4	1	54	.239	544	★93	●15	.977
1956—Sacramento	P. C.	C	76	181	22	31	5	1	1	18	.171	256	25	0	1.000
1956—Albuquerque	West.	C	29	83	11	23	2	2	1	9	.277	191	23	1	.995
1957—Tulsa	Texas	C	19	47	5	7	2	0	0	5	.149	92	9	2	.981
1957—Amarillo	West.	C	43	93	17	26	8	0	0	21	.280	177	13	3	.984
1958—Lewiston	N'west	C	133	439	62	117	20	2	2	63	.276	★892	★76	9	★.991
1959—Lewiston	N'west	C	141	491	74	122	25	4	1	44	.248	714	★84	8	.990
1960—Lewiston	N'west	C	120	387	62	98	19	2	0	42	.253	★726	48	7	★.991
1961—Lewiston	N'west	C	77	204	28	54	6	0	0	27	.265	368	37	4	.990
1962—Lewiston	N'west	C	93	281	41	77	11	2	1	33	.274	670	74	8	★.989
1963—Binghamton	East.	C	69	199	19	45	10	1	0	24	.226	483	34	2	.996
1964—Dallas	P. C.	C-3B	13	13	1	6	0	0	0	1	.194	58	7	0	1.000
1965—Birmingham	South.						(Did Not Play)									
1966—Mobile	South.	C	8	17	3	4	0	0	0	0	.235	44	1	0	1.000
1967—Birmingham	South.	C	2	6	1	0	0	0	0	1	.000	10	1	0	1.000

†Released by St. Louis Cardinals' organization, April 16, 1955.

PITCHING RECORD

Year	Club	League	G.	IP.	W.	L.	Pct.	H.	R.	ER.	SO.	BB.	ERA.
1960—Lewiston	Northwest	5	....	0	0	.000	....	....	....	....	....	....
1961—Lewiston	Northwest	4	....	0	0	.000	....	....	....	....	....	....
1962—Lewiston	Northwest	4	9	0	0	.000	13	6	6	3	2	6.00
1963—Binghamton	Eastern	1	1	0	0	.000	0	0	0	0	0	0.00

RECORD AS MANAGER

Named Major League Co-Manager of the Year by THE SPORTING NEWS, 1986.

Year	Club	League	Position	W.	L.	Year	Club	League	Position	W.	L.
1959—Lewiston	N'west	Second	36	34	1962—Lewiston	N'west	Fifth	31	38		
(Second Half)		Third	39	32	(Second Half)		Fourth	35	37		
1960—Lewiston	N'west	Third	38	29	1963—Binghamton	East.	Fourth	65	75		
(Second Half)		Third	40	34	1964—Dallas	P. C.	Sixth(E)	53	104		
1961—Lewiston	N'west	†First	41	25	1965—Birmingham	South.	Eighth	54	85		
(Second Half)		Second	43	31	1966—Mobile	South.	First	88	52		

Year	Club	League	Position	W.	L.	Year	Club	League	Position	W.	L.
1967—Birmingham	South.	First	84	55		1981—Cincinnati x	Nat.			66	42
1969—Oakland‡	Amer.	Second(W)	8	5		1982—Cincinnati y	Nat.	Sixth(W)		34	58
1970—Oakland	Amer.	Second(W)	89	73		1983—California	Amer.	zFifth		70	92
1974—San Diego	Nat.	Sixth(W)	60	102		1984—California	Amer.	zSecond(W)		81	81
1975—San Diego	Nat.	Fourth(W)	71	91		1985—Boston	Amer.	Fifth(E)		81	81
1976—San Diego	Nat.	Fifth(W)	73	89		1986—Boston	Amer.	First(E)		95	66
1977—San Diego§	Nat.	Fifth(W)	20	28		American League Totals—6 Years				424	398
1979—Cincinnati	Nat.	First(W)	90	71		National League Totals—8 Years				503	554
1980—Cincinnati	Nat.	Third(W)	89	73		Major League Totals—14 Years				927	952

†Won playoff by defeating Yakima (Second Half winner), four games to one.
‡Replaced Hank Bauer with club in second place (record of 80-69), September 19, 1969.
§Replaced by Alvin Dark, May 30, 1977 (Bob Skinner served as interim manager, May 29).
xFirst Half....Second (W) (record of 35-21); Second Half....Second (W) (record of 31-21).
yReplaced by Russ Nixon, July 21, 1982.
zTied for position with Minnesota Twins.
Coach, Oakland Athletics, 1968 and 1969; San Francisco Giants, 1971 through 1973; California Angels, 1978.
Coach, American League All-Star Team, 1986.
Coach, National League All-Star Team, 1976, 1980 and 1982.

CHAMPIONSHIP SERIES RECORD

Year	Club	League	W.	L.
1979—Cincinnati	National		0	3
1986—Boston	American		4	3
Championship Series Totals—2 Years			4	6

WORLD SERIES RECORD

Year	Club	League	W.	L.
1986—Boston	American		3	4

EUGENE RICHARD MICHAEL
(Gene)
Chicago Cubs

Born June 2, 1938, at Kent, O.
Height, 6.02. Weight, 183.
Threw right and batted left and righthanded.
Received bachelor of science degree in education from Kent State University, Kent, O.

Led Northern League shortstops in double plays with 87 in 1959 and 90 in 1960; led Sophomore League with 85 in 1961 and International League with 78 in 1965.
Led International League in sacrifice hits with 16 in 1965.

Year	Club	League	Pos.	G.	AB.	R.	H.	2B.	3B.	HR.	RBI.	B.A.	PO.	A.	E.	F.A.
1959—Grand Forks	North.	SS	124	480	54	109	11	3	1	43	.227	★225	370	★56	.914
1960—Savannah	Sally	3B-SS	3	10	1	1	1	0	0	0	.100	1	6	1	.875
1960—Grand Forks	North.	SS	121	428	47	88	15	2	2	41	.206	★232	360	★55	.915
1961—Hobbs	Soph.	SS	121	★513	121	166	25	7	5	79	.324	★195	★391	51	.920
1962—Kinston	Carol.	SS-3B	138	474	58	102	11	3	1	36	.215	169	253	38	.917
1963—Kinston	Carol.	S-3-2-P	125	421	73	128	17	6	1	57	.304	202	238	26	.944
1964—Columbus	Int.	SS-2B	131	407	43	90	13	3	3	19	.221	235	343	23	.962
1965—Columbus	Int.	SS	138	443	53	96	14	0	1	30	.217	★254	362	26	.960
1966—Columbus	Int.	SS	78	277	38	80	9	2	3	21	.289	126	244	14	.964
1966—Pittsburgh†	Nat.	SS-2B-3B	30	33	9	5	2	1	0	2	.152	10	20	3	.909
1967—Los Angeles‡	Nat.	SS	98	223	20	45	3	1	0	7	.202	117	204	17	.950
1968—New York	Amer.	SS-P	61	116	8	23	3	0	1	8	.198	68	103	11	.940
1969—New York	Amer.	SS	119	412	41	112	24	4	2	31	.272	205	365	19	.968
1970—New York	Amer.	★S-3-2	134	435	42	93	10	1	2	38	.214	259	390	★28	.959
1971—New York	Amer.	SS	139	456	36	102	15	0	3	35	.224	243	474	20	.973
1972—New York	Amer.	SS	126	391	29	91	7	4	1	32	.233	218	437	21	.969
1973—New York	Amer.	SS	129	418	30	94	11	1	3	47	.225	208	433	23	.965
1974—New York§	Amer.	2B-SS-3B	81	177	19	46	9	0	0	13	.260	122	170	9	.970
1975—Detroit x	Amer.	SS-2B-3B	56	145	15	31	2	0	3	13	.214	63	125	10	.949
1976—Boston y	Amer.					(Did not play)									
American League Totals—8 Years			845	2550	220	592	81	10	15	217	.232	1386	2497	141	.965
National League Totals—2 Years			128	256	29	50	5	2	0	9	.195	127	224	20	.946
Major League Totals—10 Years			973	2806	249	642	86	12	15	226	.229	1513	2721	161	.963

†Traded with Third Baseman Bob Bailey to Los Angeles Dodgers for Shortstop Maury Wills, December 1, 1966.
‡Sold to New York Yankees, November 30, 1967.
§Released, January 21, 1975; signed as free agent by Detroit Tigers, January 28, 1975.
xReleased, October 22, 1975; signed as free agent by Boston Red Sox, February 15, 1976.
yReleased, May 8, 1976.

PITCHING RECORD

Year	Club	League	G.	IP.	W.	L.	Pct.	H.	R.	ER.	SO.	BB.	ERA.
1962—Kinston	Carolina	1	2	0	0	.000	0	0	0	1	0	0.00
1963—Kinston	Carolina	16	53	1	3	.250	71	47	40	48	36	6.79
1964—Columbus	Int'national	2	4	0	0	.000	5	4	4	2	1	9.00
1968—New York	American	1	3	0	0	.000	5	5	0	3	0	0.00
Major League Totals—1 Year			1	3	0	0	.000	5	5	0	3	0	0.00

RECORD AS MANAGER

Year	Club	League	Position	W.	L.
1979—Columbus................	Int.	†First	85	54
1981—New York ‡§..........	Amer.		48	34
1982—New York xy.........	Amer.	Fifth(E)	44	42
1986—Chicago z................	Nat.	Fifth(E)	46	56
American League Totals—2 Years.............				92	76
National League Totals—1 Year...................				46	56
Major League Totals—3 Years......................				138	132

†Won playoff against Tidewater, three games to one; won championship playoff from Syracuse, four games to three.

‡First Half . . . First (E) (record of 34-22); Second Half . . . Fourth (E) (record of 14-12).

§Replaced by Bob Lemon, September 6, 1981.

xReplaced Bob Lemon with club tied for fourth place (record of 6-8), April 25, 1982.

yReplaced by Clyde King, August 4, 1982.

zReplaced manager Jim Frey (record of 23-33) and interim manager George Vukovich (record of 1-1) with club in fifth place (combined record of 24-34), June 14, 1986.

Coach, New York Yankees, June 4, 1976 through June 13, 1977, 1978 and 1984 through June 13, 1986; General Manager, New York Yankees, 1980; Scout, New York Yankees, 1983.

LOUIS VICTOR PINIELLA

Name pronounced Pin-ELLA.

(Lou)

New York Yankees

Born August 28, 1943, at Tampa, Fla.
Height, 6.02. Weight, 199.
Threw and batted righthanded.
Attended University of Tampa, Tampa, Fla.
Cousin of Dave Magadan, third baseman in New York Mets' organization.

Tied major league record for most assists by outfielder, inning (2), May 27, 1974 (third inning).

Major League stolen bases: 1969 (2), 1970 (3), 1971 (5), 1972 (7), 1973 (5), 1974 (1), 1977 (2), 1978 (3), 1979 (3), 1983 (1). Total—32.

Led American League in grounding into double plays with 25 in 1972.

Named American League Rookie of the Year by Baseball Writers' Association of America, 1969.

Year	Club	League	Pos.	G.	AB.	R.	H.	2B.	3B.	HR.	RBI.	B.A.	PO.	A.	E.	F.A.
1962—Selma†	Ala.-Fl.	OF	70	278	40	75	10	5	8	44	.270	94	6	9	.917
1963—Peninsula................	Carol.	OF	143	548	71	170	29	4	16	77	.310	271	★23	8	.974
1964—Aberdeen‡§	North.	OF	20	74	8	20	8	3	0	12	.270	37	1	1	.974
1964—Baltimore	Amer.	PH	4	1	0	0	0	0	0	0	.000	0	0	0	.000
1965—Elmira x	East.	OF	126	490	64	122	29	6	11	64	.249	176	5	7	.963
1966—Portland.................	P. C.	OF	133	457	47	132	22	3	7	52	.289	177	11	11	.945
1967—Portland.................	P. C.	OF	113	396	49	122	20	1	8	56	.308	199	7	6	.972
1968—Portland.................	P. C.	OF	88	331	49	105	15	3	13	62	.317	167	6	7	.961
1968—Cleveland yz	Amer.	OF	6	5	1	0	0	0	0	1	.000	1	0	0	1.000
1969—Kansas City	Amer.	OF	135	493	43	139	21	6	11	68	.282	278	13	7	.977
1970—Kansas City.............	Amer.	OF-1B	144	542	54	163	24	5	11	88	.301	250	6	4	.985
1971—Kansas City a	Amer.	OF	126	448	43	125	21	5	3	51	.279	201	6	3	.986
1972—Kansas City	Amer.	OF	151	574	65	179	★33	4	11	72	.312	275	8	7	.976
1973—Kansas City b	Amer.	OF	144	513	53	128	28	1	9	69	.250	196	9	3	.986
1974—New York	Amer.	OF-1B	140	518	71	158	26	0	9	70	.305	270	16	3	.990
1975—New York c	Amer.	OF	74	199	7	39	4	1	0	22	.196	65	5	1	.986
1976—New York.............	Amer.	OF	100	327	36	92	16	6	3	38	.281	199	10	4	.981
1977—New York.............	Amer.	OF-1B	103	339	47	112	19	3	12	45	.330	86	3	2	.978
1978—New York.............	Amer.	OF	130	472	67	148	34	5	6	69	.314	213	4	7	.969
1979—New York.............	Amer.	OF	130	461	49	137	22	2	11	69	.297	204	13	4	.982
1980—New York.............	Amer.	OF	116	321	39	92	18	0	2	27	.287	157	8	5	.971
1981—New York d	Amer.	OF	60	159	16	44	9	0	5	18	.277	69	2	1	.986
1982—New York	Amer.	OF	102	261	33	80	17	1	6	37	.307	68	2	0	1.000
1983—New York e	Amer.	OF	53	148	19	43	9	1	2	16	.291	67	4	3	.959
1984—New York fg.........	Amer.	OF	29	86	8	26	4	1	1	6	.302	40	3	0	1.000
Major League Totals—18 Years.............				1747	5867	651	1705	305	41	102	766	.291	2639	112	54	.981

Signed as free agent by Cleveland Indians' organization, June 9, 1962.

†Drafted by Washington Senators, November 26, 1962.

‡On military list, March 9 to July 20, 1964.

§Traded to Baltimore Orioles' organization, August 4, 1964, completing deal in which Baltimore traded Pitcher Lester (Buster) Narum to Washington Senators for cash and a player to be named later, March 31, 1964.

xTraded to Cleveland Indians' organization for Catcher Cam Carreon, March 10, 1966.

ySelected by Seattle Pilots in expansion draft, October 15, 1968.

zTraded by Seattle Pilots to Kansas City Royals for Outfielder Steve Whitaker and Pitcher John Gelnar, April 1, 1969.

aOn disabled list, May 5 to June 8, 1971.

bTraded with Pitcher Ken Wright to New York Yankees for Pitcher Lindy McDaniel, December 7, 1973.

cOn disabled list, June 17 to July 6, 1975.

dOn disabled list, August 23 to September 7, 1981.

eOn disabled list, March 30 to April 22, 1983.

fOn voluntarily retired list, June 17, 1984.

gNamed New York Yankees coach, June 25, 1984 through 1985.

DIVISION SERIES RECORD

Year Club	League	Pos.	G.	AB.	R.	H.	2B.	3B.	HR.	RBI.	B.A.	PO.	A.	E.	F.A.
1981—New York.............	Amer.	DH-PH	4	10	1	2	1	0	1	3	.200	0	0	0	.000

CHAMPIONSHIP SERIES RECORD

Year Club	League	Pos.	G.	AB.	R.	H.	2B.	3B.	HR.	RBI.	B.A.	PO.	A.	E.	F.A.
1976—New York.............	Amer.	DH-PH	4	11	1	3	1	0	0	0	.273	0	0	0	.000
1977—New York.............	Amer.	OF-DH	5	21	1	7	3	0	0	2	.333	9	1	0	1.000
1978—New York.............	Amer.	OF	4	17	2	4	0	0	0	0	.235	13	0	0	1.000
1980—New York.............	Amer.	OF	2	5	1	1	0	0	1	1	.200	5	0	0	1.000
1981—New York.............	Amer.	PH-D-O	3	5	2	3	0	0	1	3	.600	0	0	0	.000
Championship Series Totals—5 Years....			18	59	7	18	4	0	2	6	.305	27	1	0	1.000

WORLD SERIES RECORD

Tied World Series record for one or more hits, each game, six-game Series, 1978.

Year Club	League	Pos.	G.	AB.	R.	H.	2B.	3B.	HR.	RBI.	B.A.	PO.	A.	E.	F.A.
1976—New York.............	Amer.	D-O-PH	4	9	1	3	1	0	0	0	.333	1	0	0	1.000
1977—New York.............	Amer.	OF	6	22	1	6	0	0	0	3	.273	16	1	1	.944
1978—New York.............	Amer.	OF	6	25	3	7	0	0	0	4	.280	14	1	0	1.000
1981—New York.............	Amer.	OF-PH	6	16	2	7	1	0	0	3	.438	7	0	0	1.000
World Series Totals—4 Years			22	72	7	23	2	0	0	10	.319	38	2	1	.976

ALL-STAR GAME RECORD

Year League	Pos.	AB.	R.	H.	2B.	3B.	HR.	RBI.	B.A.	PO.	A.	E.	F.A.
1972—American...............................	PH	1	0	0	0	0	0	0	.000	0	0	0	.000

RECORD AS MANAGER

Year Club	League	Position	W.	L.
1986—New York...............	Amer.	Second(E)	90	72

CALVIN EDWIN RIPKEN SR.
(Cal)
Baltimore Orioles

Born December 17, 1935, at Aberdeen, Md.
Height, 5.11. Weight, 170.
Threw and batted righthanded.
Brother of Bill Ripken, minor league outfielder, 1947 through 1949; father of Cal Ripken Jr.,
infielder with Baltimore Orioles; and Billy Ripken, shortstop in Baltimore Orioles' organization.

Year Club	League	Pos.	G.	AB.	R.	H.	2B.	3B.	HR.	RBI.	B.A.	PO.	A.	E.	F.A.
1957—Phoenix................	Ar.-Mx.	OF-C-3B	112	398	68	109	15	6	7	60	.274	220	54	17	.942
1958—Wilson†..................	Carol.	★C-OF-3B	118	393	40	85	20	2	4	38	.216	655	★72	5	★.993
1959—Pensacola............	Ala.-Fla.	C-P	61	219	36	64	14	3	2	35	.292	378	31	6	.986
1959—Amarillo...............	Texas	C	30	69	6	14	2	0	0	3	.203	111	10	0	1.000
1960—Fox Cities	I.I.I.	★C-OF	107	356	59	100	20	4	9	74	.281	619	34	7	★.989
1961—Little Rock	South.	C	32	81	6	15	2	1	1	8	.185	120	12	0	1.000
1961—Leesburg‡............	Fla. St.	C-P	52	127	20	30	3	0	1	13	.236	286	32	1	.997
1961—Rochester	Int.	C	11	24	2	2	0	0	1	2	.083	36	0	0	1.000
1962—Fox Cities‡...........	Midw.	C-P	58	143	25	39	9	0	4	36	.273	311	20	4	.988
1963—Aberdeen§............	North.						(Did not play)								
1964—Aberdeen‡............	North.		2	1	0	0	0	0	0	0	.000	....	....	....	....

†Released by Baltimore Orioles' organization, April 20, 1959; re-signed by Orioles' organization, April 25, 1959.
‡Player-manager.
§On disabled list, April 27 to September 17, 1963.

PITCHING RECORD

Year Club	League	G.	IP.	W.	L.	Pct.	H.	R.	ER.	SO.	BB.	ERA.
1959—Pensacola.....................	Ala.-Fla.	1	....	0	0	.000	....	....	....	....	....	....
1961—Leesburg†.....................	Florida St.	2	....	0	0	.000	....	....	....	....	....	....
1962—Fox Cities†	Midwest	3	15	0	0	.000	22	15	11	3	7	6.60

†Player-manager.

RECORD AS MANAGER

Year Club	League	Position	W.	L.	Year Club	League	Position	W.	L.
1961—Leesburg†................	Fla. St.	Seventh	8	5	1967—Miami......................	Fla. St.	Third(E)	31	39
(Second Half)‡		Third	30	31	(Second Half)		Second(E)	34	37
1962—Fox Cities	Midw.	Ninth	25	36	1968—Elmira......................	East.	Third	77	63
(Second Half)		Third	36	27	1969—Rochester	Int.	Fifth	71	69
1963—Aberdeen................	North.	Second	65	55	1970—Rochester	Int.	Third	76	64
1964—Aberdeen................	North.	§First	80	57	1971—Dallas-Ft.W.	Texas	Second(W)	82	59
1965—Tri-City....................	N'west.	Fourth	34	36	1972—Asheville.................	South.	yFirst(E)	81	58
(Second Half)		xFirst	47	22	1973—Asheville.................	South.	Second(W)	71	69
1966—Aberdeen................	North.	Second	47	22	1974—Asheville.................	South.	Second(W)	70	67

†Replaced Billy DeMars, June 7, 1961.
‡Assigned to Rochester as a player, August 17, 1961.
§Won Baukol Playoff (based on last 30 days of regular season) with record of 19 wins, 10 losses and 1 tie.
xWon playoff against Lewiston (First Half winner), three games to none.
yLost playoff to Montgomery, three games to none.
Scout, Baltimore Orioles, 1975; coach, Baltimore Orioles, 1976 through 1986.

ROBERT LEROY RODGERS
(Bob or Buck)
Montreal Expos

Born August 16, 1938, at Delaware, O.
Height, 6.01. Weight, 190.
Threw right and batted left and righthanded.
Attended Ohio Wesleyan University, Delaware, O., and Ohio Northern
University, Ada, O.

Established American League record for most games, by catcher, rookie season (150), 1962.
Tied American League record for fewest assists by catcher, season, 150 or more games (73), 1962.
Major League stolen bases: 1962 (1), 1963 (2), 1964 (4), 1965 (4), 1966 (3), 1967 (1), 1968 (2). Total—17.
Led American League catchers in double plays with 14 in 1962 and 14 in 1964.

Year	Club	League	Pos.	G.	AB.	R.	H.	2B.	3B.	HR.	RBI.	B.A.	PO.	A.	E.	F.A.
1956—Jamestown	Pony	OF	48	153	28	36	8	1	6	26	.235	43	6	3	.942
1957—Erie	NYP	★C-OF	114	430	79	127	26	4	12	80	.295	568	★77	★25	.963
1958—Lancaster	East.	C	19	63	8	16	3	0	3	8	.254	111	11	2	.984
1958—Idaho Falls	Pion.	★C-OF	99	378	73	115	15	6	12	74	.304	524	45	★20	.966
1959—Birmingham	South.	C	3	13	1	1	0	1	0	2	.077	28	0	1	.966
1959—Knoxville	Sally	★C-OF	105	355	53	102	18	6	7	55	.287	565	60	★13	.980
1960—Denver	A. A.	C	23	84	12	20	7	1	3	12	.238	127	15	4	.973
1960—Birmingham	South.	C	93	313	36	77	14	1	5	38	.246	456	★68	7	.987
1961—Dallas-Ft. W.†	A. A.	C	124	427	55	122	22	3	3	62	.286	★595	★70	11	.984
1961—Los Angeles	Amer.	C	16	56	8	18	2	0	2	13	.321	71	11	3	.965
1962—Los Angeles	Amer.	C	155	565	65	146	34	6	6	61	.258	826	73	●10	.989
1963—Los Angeles	Amer.	C	100	300	24	70	6	0	4	23	.233	416	48	★10	.979
1964—Los Angeles	Amer.	C	148	514	38	125	18	3	4	54	.243	884	★87	★13	.987
1965—California	Amer.	C	132	411	33	86	14	3	1	32	.209	682	52	7	.991
1966—California	Amer.	C	133	454	45	107	20	3	7	48	.236	662	★69	6	.992
1967—California	Amer.	★C-OF	139	429	29	94	13	3	6	41	.219	728	★73	7	.991
1968—California	Amer.	C	91	258	13	49	6	0	1	14	.190	407	50	7	.985
1969—Hawaii	P. C.	C-3B	44	145	15	37	5	0	0	12	.255	215	26	4	.984
1969—California	Amer.	C	18	49	4	9	1	0	0	2	.196	74	9	0	1.000
1975—Salinas‡	Calif.	PH	4	3	1	1	0	0	0	0	.333	0	0	0	.000
1977—El Paso§	Texas	PH	1	0	0	0	0	0	0	0	.000	0	0	0	.000
Major League Totals—9 Years			932	3033	259	704	114	18	31	288	.232	4750	472	63	.988

†Selected by Los Angeles Angels from Detroit Tigers in American League expansion draft, December 14, 1960.
‡Player-manager, August 24 through September 15, 1975.
§Player-manager, July 15 through August 14, 1977.

RECORD AS MANAGER

Named Minor League Manager of the Year by THE SPORTING NEWS, 1984.
Named American Association Manager of the Year, 1984.
Named Texas League Manager of the Year, 1977.

Year	Club	League	Position	W.	L.	Year	Club	League	Position	W.	L.
1975—Salinas	Calif.	Fifth	35	35	1984—Indianapolis	A. A.	zFirst	91	63
(Second Half)			Sixth	32	38	1985—Montreal	Nat.	Third(E)	84	77
1977—El Paso	Texas	First(W)	38	24	1986—Montreal	Nat.	Fourth(E)	78	83
(Second Half)		†First(W)	40	28	American League Totals—3 Years			124	102
1980—Milwaukee‡	Amer.	Third(E)	39	31	National League Totals—2 Years			162	160
1981—Milwaukee§	Amer.		62	47	Major League Totals—5 Years			286	262
1982—Milwaukee x	Amer.	yFifth(E)	23	24						

†Lost league championship to Arkansas, two games to none.
‡Began season as interim manager for ill George Bamberger who returned June 6, 1980, with club in second place
(record of 26-21); named manager when Bamberger retired with club tied for fourth place (record of 73-66), September
7, 1980.
§First Half . . . Third (E) (record of 31-25); Second Half . . . First (E) (record of 31-22).
xReplaced by Harvey Kuenn, June 2, 1982.
yTied for position with Baltimore Orioles.
zLost semifinal playoff series to Louisville, four games to two.
Coach, Minnesota Twins, 1970 through 1974; San Francisco Giants, 1976; Milwaukee Brewers, 1978 through 1980.

DIVISION SERIES RECORD

Year	Club	League	W.	L.
1981—Milwaukee	American	2	3

Pete Rose's managerial record is listed under his playing record beginning on page 420.

CHARLES WILLIAM TANNER JR.
(Chuck)
Atlanta Braves

Born July 4, 1929, at New Castle, Pa.
Height, 6.00. Weight, 185.
Threw and batted lefthanded.

— 565 —

Father of Mark Tanner, pitcher in Chicago Cubs', Chicago White Sox' and Texas Rangers' organizations, 1972 through 1975; and Bruce Tanner, pitcher in Oakland A's organization.

Tied major league record by hitting home run in first time at bat in major leagues, eighth inning, April 12, 1955. Major League stolen bases: 1958 (1), 1960 (1). Total—2.

Year Club	League	Pos.	G.	AB.	R.	H.	2B.	3B.	HR.	RBI.	B.A.	PO.	A.	E.	F.A.
1946—Evansville	I.I.I.	OF	2	1	0	0	0	0	0	0	.000	0	0	1	.000
1946—Owensboro	Kitty	OF	23	80	15	20	3	1	0	7	.250	50	3	4	.930
1947—Owensboro	Kitty	OF	25	104	32	35	9	3	0	20	.337	47	3	2	.962
1947—Eau Claire	North.	OF	40	151	29	49	6	3	7	27	.325	76	3	9	.898
1948—Eau Claire	North.	OF	67	263	60	95	22	5	7	52	.361	89	4	9	.912
1948—Pawtucket	N. Eng.	OF	46	171	26	47	1	6	2	20	.275	60	6	5	.930
1949—Denver	West.	OF	124	467	92	146	32	5	5	53	.313	206	13	12	.948
1950—Denver	West.	OF	154	619	111	*195	34	9	7	86	.315	248	16	14	.950
1951—Atlanta	South.	OF	134	506	84	161	28	6	4	44	.318	286	6	4	.986
1952—Milwaukee	A. A.	OF	11	27	2	4	1	1	0	4	.148	11	1	0	1.000
1952—Atlanta	South.	OF	117	440	64	152	18	11	2	65	.345	212	9	6	.974
1953—Toledo	A. A.	OF	17	52	5	10	3	0	2	5	.192	29	2	0	1.000
1953—Atlanta	South.	OF	126	465	71	148	29	11	6	57	.318	220	8	3	.987
1954—Atlanta	South.	OF	●155	594	109	192	35	12	20	101	.323	290	21	7	.978
1955—Milwaukee	Nat.	OF	97	243	27	60	9	3	6	27	.247	101	4	2	.981
1956—Milwaukee	Nat.	OF	60	63	6	15	2	0	1	4	.238	4	0	1	.800
1957—Mil.†-Chi.	Nat.	OF	117	387	47	108	19	2	9	48	.279	191	5	2	.990
1958—Chicago‡	Nat.	OF	73	103	10	27	6	0	4	17	.262	21	0	1	.955
1959—Minneapolis§	A. A.	OF	152	549	79	175	*41	10	12	78	.319	194	5	4	.980
1959—Cleveland	Amer.	OF	14	48	6	12	2	0	1	5	.250	18	0	0	1.000
1960—Cleveland	Amer.	OF	21	25	2	7	1	0	0	4	.280	5	0	0	1.000
1960—Toronto	Int.	OF	28	92	13	27	5	2	4	14	.293	40	1	0	1.000
1961—Toronto x	Int.	OF	70	218	19	49	5	3	6	22	.225	84	7	3	.968
1961—Dallas-Ft. Worth	A. A.	OF	48	170	28	51	12	5	1	18	.300	74	5	5	.940
1961—Los Angeles	Amer.	OF	7	8	0	1	0	0	0	0	.125	0	0	0	.000
1962—Los Angeles	Amer.	OF	7	8	0	1	0	0	0	0	.125	0	0	0	.000
1962—Dallas-Ft. Worth	A. A.	OF	114	359	43	113	28	2	5	41	.315	181	16	8	.961
1968—El Paso	Texas	PH	1	1	0	0	0	0	0	0	.000	0	0	0	.000
American League Totals—4 Years			49	89	8	21	3	0	1	9	.236	23	0	0	1.000
National League Totals—4 Years			347	796	90	210	36	5	20	96	.264	317	9	6	.982
Major League Totals—8 Years			396	885	98	231	39	5	21	105	.261	340	9	6	.983

†Sold on waivers to Chicago Cubs, June 8, 1957.
‡Traded to Boston Red Sox for Pitcher Robert W. Smith, March 9, 1959.
§Purchased from Boston Red Sox by Cleveland Indians, September 9, 1959.
xSold by Cleveland Indians to Los Angeles Angels, September 8, 1961.

RECORD AS MANAGER

Named Major League Manager of the Year by THE SPORTING NEWS 1972.
Named Pacific Coast League co-Manager of the Year, 1970.

Year Club	League	Position	W.	L.
1963—Quad Cities	Midw.	Fourth	29	32
(Second Half)		Second	37	25
1964—Quad Cities	Midw.	Eighth	24	31
(Second Half)		Second	38	25
1965—El Paso	Texas	Third(W)	53	87
1966—El Paso	Texas	Fifth	62	78
1967—Seattle	P. C.	Fifth(W)	69	79
1968—El Paso	Texas	†First(W)	77	60
1969—Hawaii	P. C.	Third(S)	74	72
1970—Hawaii	P. C.	‡First(S)	98	48
1970—Chicago§	Amer.	Sixth(W)	3	13
1971—Chicago	Amer.	Third(W)	79	83
1972—Chicago	Amer.	Second(W)	87	67
1973—Chicago	Amer.	Fifth(W)	77	85
1974—Chicago	Amer.	Fourth(W)	80	80
1975—Chicago	Amer.	Fifth(W)	75	86

Year Club	League	Position	W.	L.
1976—Oakland x	Amer.	Second(W)	87	74
1977—Pittsburgh	Nat.	Second(E)	96	66
1978—Pittsburgh	Nat.	Second(E)	88	73
1979—Pittsburgh	Nat.	First(E)	98	64
1980—Pittsburgh	Nat.	Third(E)	83	79
1981—Pittsburgh y	Nat.		46	56
1982—Pittsburgh	Nat.	Fourth(E)	84	78
1983—Pittsburgh	Nat.	Second(E)	84	78
1984—Pittsburgh	Nat.	Sixth(E)	75	87
1985—Pittsburgh	Nat.	Sixth(E)	57	104
1986—Atlanta	Nat.	Sixth(W)	72	89
National League Totals—10 Years			783	774
American League Totals—7 Years			488	488
Major League Totals—17 Years			1271	1262

†Won playoff by defeating Arkansas, three games to one.
‡Lost playoff to Spokane, four games to none.
§Replaced Don Gutteridge (and interim manager Billy Adair) with club in sixth place (record of 53-93), September 14, 1970.
xTraded to Pittsburgh Pirates for Catcher Manny Sanguillen and $100,000 cash, November 5, 1976.
yFirst Half. . . . Fourth(E) (record of 25-23); Second Half. . . . Sixth(E) (record of 21-33).
Manager, National League All-Star Team, 1980.
Coach, American League All-Star Team, 1973.
Coach, National League All-Star Team, 1978, 1982 and 1984.

CHAMPIONSHIP SERIES RECORD

Year Club	League	W.	L.
1979—Pittsburgh	National	3	0

WORLD SERIES RECORD

Year Club	League	W.	L.
1979—Pittsburgh	National	4	3

THOMAS LYNN TREBELHORN
(Tom)
Milwaukee Brewers

Born January 27, 1948, at Portland, Ore.
Height, 5.11. Weight, 178.
Threw right and batted lefthanded.
Received bachelor of science degree in history and teaching
from Portland State University, Portland, Ore. in 1970.

Led Northwest League catchers in fielding percentage with .997 in 1971.
Led National League catchers in double plays with 5 in 1970.
Tied for Northwest League lead in double plays by catchers with 3 in 1972.

Year	Club	League	Pos.	G.	AB.	R.	H.	2B.	3B.	HR.	RBI.	B.A.	PO.	A.	E.	F.A.
1970—Bend		N'west	C-3-2-O	68	198	33	48	4	1	4	32	.242	296	48	12	.966
1971—Bend		N'west	C-OF	51	149	28	47	13	3	3	38	.315	282	33	2	.994
1972—Walla Walla†		N'west	C	42	124	17	25	5	1	2	20	.202	272	19	4	.986
1973—Birmingham		South.	3B-C-1B	33	89	9	18	5	0	2	13	.202	87	31	8	.937
1973—Burlington		Midw.	C-1B	43	146	23	33	6	0	2	20	.226	298	25	5	.985
1974—Birmingham		South.	C-3B	8	9	1	2	1	0	0	0	.222	13	1	1	.933
1974—Lewiston‡§		N'west	P	7	2	0	0	0	0	0	0	.000	1	2	0	1.000

Signed as free agent by Hawaii (Pacific Coast League), June 4, 1970.
†Sold to Oakland A's organization, September 2, 1972.
‡Player-coach.
§Released, June 17, 1975.

PITCHING RECORD

Year	Club	League	G.	IP.	W.	L.	Pct.	H.	R.	ER.	SO.	BB.	ERA.
1974—Lewiston		Northwest	5	12	1	0	1.000	7	1	1	2	2	0.75

RECORD AS MANAGER

Year	Club	League	Position	W.	L.	Year	Club	League	Position	W.	L.
1975—Boise		N'west	Third(S)	39	39	1983—Hawaii		P. C.	†Fourth(S)	32	40
1976—Boise		N'west	Third(S)	33	38		(Second Half)		Second(S)	40	31
1977—Modesto		Calif.	Fourth	31	39	1985—Vancouver‡		P. C.	Second(N)	38	34
	(Second Half)		Sixth	22	48		(Second Half)		First(N)	41	30
1979—Batavia		NYP	Third(W)	37	34	1986—Milwaukee§		Amer.	Sixth(E)	6	3
1982—Portland		P. C.	Fifth(N)	32	39		Major League Totals—1 Year				6	3
	(Second Half)		Fifth(N)	33	40							

†Tied for position with Phoenix.
‡Won division championship from Calgary, three games to none; won league championship from Phoenix, three games to none.
§Replaced retiring manager George Bamberger with club in sixth place (record of 71-81), September 26, 1986.
Coach, Cleveland Indians' organization, 1978; coach, Pittsburgh Pirates' organization, 1980 and 1981; coach, Milwaukee Brewers, 1984 and beginning of 1986 season through September 25, 1986.

ROBERT JOHN VALENTINE
(Bobby)
Texas Rangers

Born May 13, 1950, at Stamford, Conn.
Height, 5.10. Weight, 185.
Threw and batted righthanded.
Attended Arizona State University, Tempe, Ariz., and University of Southern California, Los Angeles, Calif.
Son-in-law of Ralph Branca, pitcher with Brooklyn Dodgers, Detroit Tigers
and New York Yankees, 1944 through 1954 and 1956.

Major League stolen bases: 1971 (5), 1972 (5), 1973 (6), 1974 (8), 1975 (1), 1978 (1), 1979 (1). Total—27.
Led Pioneer League in stolen bases with 20 in 1968.
Led Pacific Coast League in total bases with 324, sacrifice flies with 10 and double plays by shortstops with 106 in 1970.
Named Pacific Coast League Player of the Year in 1970.

Year	Club	League	Pos.	G.	AB.	R.	H.	2B.	3B.	HR.	RBI.	B.A.	PO.	A.	E.	F.A.
1968—Odgen		Pion.	*OF-SS	62	224	*62	63	14	4	6	26	.281	*111	●10	6	.953
1969—Spokane		P. C.	*SS-OF	111	402	61	104	19	5	3	35	.259	166	254	*38	.917
1969—Los Angeles		Nat.	PR	5	0	3	0	0	0	0	0	.000	0	0	0	.000
1970—Spokane		P. C.	*SS-2B	●146	*621	*122	*211	*39	*16	14	80	*.340	*217	474	*54	.928
1971—Spokane		P. C.	SS	7	30	7	10	2	0	1	2	.333	13	18	3	.912
1971—Los Angeles		Nat.	S-3-2-O	101	281	32	70	10	2	1	25	.249	123	176	16	.949
1972—Los Angeles†		Nat.	2-3-O-S	119	391	42	107	11	2	3	32	.274	178	245	23	.948
1973—California‡		Amer.	SS-OF	32	126	12	38	5	2	1	13	.302	63	75	6	.958
1974—California§x		Amer.	OF-SS-3B	117	371	39	97	10	3	3	39	.261	160	116	17	.942
1975—Charleston		Int.	3B	56	175	27	41	4	0	1	17	.234	44	74	6	.952
1975—Salt Lake City		P. C.	1-O-3-2	46	147	29	45	6	1	0	17	.306	92	14	3	.972
1975—California y		Amer.	1B-3B-OF	26	57	5	16	2	0	0	5	.281	27	1	2	.933
1975—San Diego		Nat.	OF	7	15	1	2	0	0	1	1	.133	4	0	0	1.000
1976—Hawaii		P. C.	1-O-3-S	120	395	67	120	23	2	13	89	.304	578	47	4	.994
1976—San Diego		Nat.	OF-1B	15	49	3	18	4	0	0	4	.367	55	6	0	1.000
1977—S.D.z-N.Y.		Nat.	SS-1B-3B	86	150	13	23	4	0	2	13	.153	119	64	3	.984

Year	Club	League	Pos.	G.	AB.	R.	H.	2B.	3B.	HR.	RBI.	B.A.	PO.	A.	E.	F.A.
1978—New York a		Nat.	2B-3B	69	160	17	43	7	0	1	18	.269	78	109	6	.969
1979—Seattle b		Amer.	S-O-2-3-C	62	98	9	27	6	0	0	7	.276	32	38	2	.972
National League Totals—7 Years				402	1046	111	263	36	4	8	93	.251	557	600	48	.960
American League Totals—4 Years				237	652	65	178	23	5	4	64	.273	282	230	27	.950
Major League Totals—10 Years				639	1698	176	441	59	9	12	157	.260	839	830	75	.957

Selected by Los Angeles Dodgers' organization in 1st round (fifth player selected) of free-agent draft, June 7, 1968.

†Traded with Infielder Billy Grabarkewitz, Outfielder Frank Robinson and Pitchers Bill Singer and Mike Strahler to California Angels for Pitcher Andy Messersmith and Third Baseman Ken McMullen, November 28, 1972.

‡On disabled list, May 17, 1973 through remainder of season.

§On disabled list, May 29 to June 13, 1974.

xLoaned to Charleston (Pittsburgh Pirates' organization), April 4, 1975; returned, June 20, 1975.

yTraded with a player to be named later to San Diego Padres for Pitcher Gary Ross, September 17, 1975; San Diego acquired Infielder Rudy Meoli to complete deal, November 4, 1975.

zTraded with Pitcher Paul Siebert to New York Mets for Infielder-Outfielder Dave Kingman, June 15, 1977.

aReleased, March 26, 1979; signed by Seattle Mariners, April 10, 1979.

bGranted free agency, November 1, 1979.

RECORD AS MANAGER

Year	Club	League	Position	W.	L.
1985—Texas†		Amer.	Seventh(W)	53	76
1986—Texas		Amer.	Second(W)	87	75
Major League Totals—2 Years				140	151

†Replaced Doug Rader with club in seventh place (record of 9-23), May 16, 1985.

Scout and minor league instructor, San Diego Padres, 1981; minor league instructor, New York Mets, 1982; coach, New York Mets, 1983 through May 15, 1985.

JAMES FRANCIS WILLIAMS
(Jimy)
Toronto Blue Jays

Born October 4, 1943, at Santa Maria, Calif.
Height, 5.11. Weight, 170.
Threw and batted righthanded.
Received bachelor of science degree in agribusiness from Fresno State College, Fresno, Calif.

Year	Club	League	Pos.	G.	AB.	R.	H.	2B.	3B.	HR.	RBI.	B.A.	PO.	A.	E.	F.A.
1965—Waterloo†		Midw.	SS	115	435	64	125	19	3	2	31	.287	173	★312	26	★.949
1966—St. Louis‡		Nat.	SS-2B	13	11	1	3	0	0	0	3	.273	2	5	0	1.000
1967—Arkansas		Texas	SS	28	101	8	21	1	1	0	8	.208	49	80	2	.985
1967—Tulsa		P. C.	SS	61	164	18	37	2	0	1	21	.226	87	156	26	.903
1967—St. Louis§		Nat.	SS	1	2	0	0	0	0	0	0	.000	6	1	0	1.000
1968—Indianapolis x		P. C.	SS-2B	120	403	38	91	19	5	2	34	.226	198	323	27	.951
1969—Vancouver y		P. C.	3B-OF-SS	35	66	7	17	1	1	0	9	.258	17	23	2	.952
1970—Buf. z-Winn.		Int.	SS-2B-3B	109	361	49	83	15	0	3	18	.230	178	244	30	.934
1971—Winn. ab-Tide. c		Int.	SS-3B-2B	105	327	40	84	7	4	5	31	.257	120	219	22	.939
1975—El Paso de		Texas	DH	6	17	3	2	0	0	0	2	.118	0	0	0	.000
Major League Totals—2 Years				14	13	1	3	0	0	0	1	.231	8	6	0	1.000

†Drafted by St. Louis Cardinals from Toronto (Boston Red Sox' organization), November 29, 1965.

‡In military service, July 24, 1966 through remainder of season.

§Traded with Catcher Pat Corrales to Cincinnati Reds for Catcher John Edwards, February 8, 1968.

xRecalled by Cincinnati Reds; selected by Montreal Expos from Cincinnati in expansion draft, October 14, 1968.

yOn disabled list, May 13 to May 30 and June 24 to September 2, 1969.

zFranchise transferred from Buffalo to Winnipeg, June 4, 1970.

aOn suspended list, June 7 to June 16, 1971.

bSold to New York Mets' organization, June 16, 1971.

cOn temporary inactive list, August 12 to August 16, 1971.

dPlayer-manager.

eOn disabled list, May 15 to July 17 and July 29 to August 20, 1975.

RECORD AS MANAGER

Named Pacific Coast League Manager of the Year, 1976 and 1979.

Year	Club	League	Position	W.	L.
1974—Quad Cities		Midw.	First(S)	33	26
(Second Half)			†Third(S)	32	32
1975—El Paso		Texas	Third(W)	62	71
1976—Salt Lake City		P. C.	‡First(E)	90	54
1977—Salt Lake City		P. C.	Second(E)	74	65
1978—Springfield		A. A.	Third(E)	70	66
1979—Salt Lake City		P. C.	Fourth(S)	34	40
(Second Half)			§First(S)	46	28
1986—Toronto		Amer.	Fourth (E)	86	76
Major League Totals—1 Year				86	76

†Lost playoff to Danville, two games to one.

‡Lost championship playoff to Hawaii, three games to two.

§Won playoff from Albuquerque, two games to none; won championship playoff from Hawaii, three games to none.

Coach, Toronto Blue Jays, 1980 through 1985.

RICHARD HIRSHFELD WILLIAMS
(Dick)
Seattle Mariners

Born May 7, 1929, at St. Louis, Mo.
Height, 6.00. Weight, 190.
Threw and batted righthanded.
Attended Pasadena City College, Pasadena, Calif.
Father of Ricky Williams, pitcher in Montreal Expos' organization, 1977 through 1980;
and minor league instructor and coach in Montreal Expos' organization since 1981.

Major League stolen bases: 1956 (5), 1957 (3), 1959 (4). Total—12.

Year	Club	League	Pos.	G.	AB.	R.	H.	2B.	3B.	HR.	RBI.	B.A.	PO.	A.	E.	F.A.
1947—Santa Barbara	Calif.		OF-3B	79	313	47	77	20	2	4	50	.246	165	36	5	.976
1948—Santa Barbara	Calif.		OF	97	385	82	129	29	2	16	90	.335	245	19	9	.967
1948—Fort Worth	Texas		OF-3B	41	140	16	29	1	0	4	16	.207	60	2	1	.984
1949—Fort Worth	Texas		*O-2-3	154	562	109	174	30	6	23	114	.310	*446	18	8	.983
1950—Fort Worth	Texas		OF	144	510	69	153	30	1	11	72	.300	401	20	6	.986
1951—Brooklyn†	Nat.		OF	23	60	5	12	3	1	1	5	.200	21	1	0	1.000
1952—Brooklyn	Nat.		OF-1B-3B	36	68	13	21	4	1	0	11	.309	51	3	0	1.000
1953—Brooklyn	Nat.		OF	30	55	4	12	2	0	2	5	.218	24	0	2	.923
1953—Montreal	Int.		OF	66	230	28	64	12	1	2	33	.278	111	3	2	.983
1954—Brooklyn	Nat.		OF	16	34	5	5	0	0	1	2	.147	12	0	0	1.000
1954—St. Paul	A. A.		OF-1B	49	162	23	40	8	0	6	18	.247	212	15	3	.987
1955—Fort Worth	Texas		OF-1B	153	596	82	189	29	4	24	91	.317	580	22	7	.989
1956—Brooklyn	Nat.		PH	7	7	0	2	0	0	0	0	.286	0	0	0	.000
1956—Montreal‡	Int.		1B	13	50	3	13	3	0	0	6	.260	106	17	4	.969
1956—Baltimore	Amer.		O-1-2-3	87	353	45	101	18	4	11	37	.286	249	17	4	.985
1957—Balt.§-Cleve.x	Amer.		OF-3B-1B	114	372	49	97	17	2	7	34	.261	244	72	8	.975
1958—Baltimore y	Amer.		O-3-1-2	128	409	36	113	17	0	4	32	.276	359	61	8	.981
1959—Kansas City	Amer.		3-1-O-2	130	488	72	130	33	1	16	75	.266	349	181	13	.976
1960—Kansas City z	Amer.		3B-1B-OF	127	420	47	121	31	0	12	65	.288	376	131	11	.979
1961—Baltimore	Amer.		OF-1B-3B	103	310	37	64	15	2	8	24	.206	209	16	3	.987
1962—Baltimore ab	Amer.		OF-1B-3B	82	178	20	44	7	1	1	18	.247	180	13	0	1.000
1963—Boston	Amer.		3B-1B-OF	79	136	15	35	8	0	2	12	.257	64	28	1	.989
1964—Boston	Amer.		1B-3B-OF	61	69	10	11	2	0	5	11	.159	50	21	1	.986
American League Totals—9 Years				911	2735	331	716	148	10	66	308	.262	2080	540	49	.982
National League Totals—5 Years				112	224	27	52	9	2	4	23	.232	108	4	2	.982
Major League Totals—13 Years				1023	2959	358	768	157	12	70	331	.260	2188	544	51	.982

†On National Defense Service List, February 7 to May 29, 1951.
‡Recalled by Brooklyn Dodgers and sold to Baltimore Orioles, June 25, 1956.
§Traded to Cleveland Indians for Outfielder Jim Busby, June 13, 1957.
xTraded with Pitcher Bud Daley and Outfielder Gene Woodling to Baltimore Orioles for Pitcher Don Ferrarese and Outfielder Larry Doby, April 1, 1958.
yTraded to Kansas City Athletics for Shortstop Chico Carrasquel, October 2, 1958.
zTraded with Pitcher Dick Hall to Baltimore Orioles for Pitcher Jerry Walker and Outfielder Chuck Essegian, April 13, 1961.
aSold to Houston Colts, October 12, 1962.
bTraded by Houston Colts to Boston Red Sox for Outfielder Carroll Hardy, December 10, 1962.

WORLD SERIES RECORD

Year	Club	League	Pos.	G.	AB.	R.	H.	2B.	3B.	HR.	RBI.	B.A.	PO.	A.	E.	F.A.
1953—Brooklyn	Nat.		PH	3	2	0	1	0	0	0	0	.500	0	0	0	.000

RECORD AS MANAGER

Tied major league record for most clubs managed, lifetime (6).
Named Major League Manager of the Year by The Sporting News, 1967.

Year	Club	League	Position	W.	L.	Year	Club	League	Position	W.	L.
1965—Toronto	Int.	†Third	81	64		1978—Montreal	Nat.	Fourth(E)	76	86
1966—Toronto	Int.	‡Second	82	65		1979—Montreal	Nat.	Second(E)	95	65
1967—Boston	Amer.	First	92	70		1980—Montreal	Nat.	Second(E)	90	72
1968—Boston	Amer.	Fourth	86	76		1981—Montreal ab	Nat.		44	37
1969—Boston§	Amer.	Third(E)	82	71		1982—San Diego	Nat.	Fourth(W)	81	81
1971—Oakland	Amer.	First(W)	101	60		1983—San Diego	Nat.	Fourth(W)	81	81
1972—Oakland	Amer.	First(W)	93	62		1984—San Diego	Nat.	First(W)	92	70
1973—Oakland x	Amer.	First(W)	94	68		1985—San Diego	Nat.	cThird(W)	83	79
1974—California y	Amer.	Sixth(W)	36	48		1986—Seattle d	Amer.	Seventh(W)	58	75
1975—California	Amer.	Sixth(W)	72	89						
1976—California z	Amer.	Fourth(W)	39	57		National League Totals—9 Years			717	658
1977—Montreal	Nat.	Fifth(E)	75	87		American League Totals—10 Years			753	676
						Major League Totals—19 Years			1470	1334

†Won playoffs by defeating Atlanta, four games to none and Columbus, four games to one.
‡Tied for position during regular season. Won playoffs by defeating Columbus, three games to two and Richmond, four games to one.
§Replaced by interim manager Eddie Popowski, September 23, 1969.
xQuit as manager of the Oakland Athletics following 1973 World Series. Signed contract to manage New York Yankees but American League President Joe Cronin ruled that Williams must honor the two years remaining on his Oakland contract.
yReplaced Bobby Winkles (and interim manager Whitey Herzog) with club in sixth place (record of 32-46), July 1, 1974.
zReplaced by Norm Sherry, July 23, 1976.

aFirst Half . . . . Third (E) (record of 30-25); Second Half . . . . Second (E) (record of 14-12).
bReplaced by Jim Fanning, September 8, 1981.
cTied for position with Houston Astros.
dReplaced manager Chuck Cottier (record of 9-19) and interim manager Marty Martinez (record of 0-1) with club in sixth place (combined record of 9-20), May 9, 1986.
Coach, Montreal Expos, 1970.
Manager, National League All-Star Team, 1985.
Manager, American League All-Star Team, 1968, 1973 and 1974.
Coach, American League All-Star Team, 1972.
Coach, National League All-Star Team, 1981.

<table>
<tr><td colspan="6">CHAMPIONSHIP SERIES RECORD</td></tr>
<tr><td>Year</td><td>Club</td><td>League</td><td>W.</td><td>L.</td></tr>
<tr><td>1971—Oakland</td><td></td><td>American</td><td>0</td><td>3</td></tr>
<tr><td>1972—Oakland</td><td></td><td>American</td><td>3</td><td>2</td></tr>
<tr><td>1973—Oakland</td><td></td><td>American</td><td>3</td><td>2</td></tr>
<tr><td>1984—San Diego</td><td></td><td>National</td><td>3</td><td>2</td></tr>
<tr><td>Championships Series Totals—4 Years</td><td></td><td></td><td>9</td><td>9</td></tr>
</table>

WORLD SERIES RECORD				
Year	Club	League	W.	L.
1967—Boston		American	3	4
1972—Oakland		American	4	3
1973—Oakland		American	4	3
1984—San Diego		National	1	4
World Series Totals—4 Years			12	14

1987 Hall of Fame Inductees

JAMES AUGUSTUS HUNTER
(Catfish)

(Nicknamed by Charlie Finley, owner of Oakland A's.)
Born April 8, 1946, at Hertford, N. C.
Height, 6.00. Weight, 195.
Threw and batted righthanded.

Established American League record for most home runs allowed, lifetime (374).
Tied major league record for most home runs allowed, inning (4), June 17, 1977 (first inning).
Pitched 4-0 perfect game victory against Minnesota Twins, May 8, 1968.
Led American League pitchers in complete games with 30 in 1975.
Led American League in home runs allowed with 39 in 1973 and 28 in 1976.
Tied for American League lead in games started by pitchers with 40 in 1970.
Named American League Pitcher of the Year by THE SPORTING NEWS, 1974.
Won American League Cy Young Memorial Award, 1974.
Named righthanded pitcher on THE SPORTING NEWS American League All-Star Team, 1974.
Received reported $75,000 bonus to sign with Kansas City Athletics, 1964.
Named to Hall of Fame, 1987.

Year Club	League	G.	IP.	W.	L.	Pct.	H.	R.	ER.	SO.	BB.	ERA.
1964—Daytona Beach†	Florida St.					(Did not play)						
1965—Kansas City	American	32	133	8	8	.500	124	68	63	82	46	4.26
1966—Kansas City‡	American	30	177	9	11	.450	158	87	79	103	64	4.02
1967—Kansas City§	American	35	260	13	17	.433	209	91	81	196	84	2.80
1968—Oakland	American	36	234	13	13	.500	210	99	*87	172	69	3.35
1969—Oakland	American	38	247	12	15	.444	210	99	92	150	85	3.35
1970—Oakland	American	40	262	18	14	.563	253	124	111	178	74	3.81
1971—Oakland	American	37	274	21	11	.656	225	103	90	181	80	2.96
1972—Oakland	American	38	295	21	7	*.750	200	74	67	191	70	2.04
1973—Oakland	American	36	256	21	5	*.808	222	105	95	124	69	3.34
1974—Oakland x	American	41	318	●25	12	.676	268	97	88	143	45	*2.49
1975—New York	American	39	*328	●23	14	.622	248	107	94	177	83	2.58
1976—New York	American	36	299	17	15	.531	268	126	117	173	68	3.52
1977—New York y	American	22	143	9	9	.500	137	83	75	52	47	4.72
1978—New York z	American	21	118	12	6	.667	98	49	47	56	35	3.58
1979—New York a	American	19	105	2	9	.182	128	68	62	34	34	5.31
Major League Totals—15 Years		500	3449	224	166	.574	2958	1380	1248	2012	954	3.26

Signed as free agent by Kansas City A's organization, June 8, 1964.
†On disabled list, June 11 to July 10, 1964.
‡On disabled list, July 26 to August 31, 1966.
§Appeared as first baseman in one game.
xDeclared a free agent by an arbitration panel, December 16, 1974; signed by New York Yankees for an estimated $2.85 million, December 31, 1974.
yOn disabled list, April 13 to May 4, 1977.
zOn disabled list, May 28 to June 17 and June 23 to July 17, 1978.
aOn voluntarily retired list, October 19, 1979.

CHAMPIONSHIP SERIES RECORD

Established Championship Series records for most innings pitched, total Series (69⅓); most games started, total Series (10); most home runs allowed, total Series (12).

Tied Championship Series records for most series pitched (6); most games won, total Series (4); most home runs allowed, game (4), October 4, 1971.

Tied American League Championship Series records for most games lost, total Series (3); most games won, Series (2), 1973.

Year Club	League	G.	IP.	W.	L.	Pct.	H.	R.	ER.	SO.	BB.	ERA.
1971—Oakland	American	1	8	0	1	.000	7	5	5	6	2	5.63
1972—Oakland	American	2	15⅓	0	0	.000	10	2	2	9	5	1.17
1973—Oakland	American	2	16⅓	2	0	1.000	12	3	3	6	5	1.65
1974—Oakland	American	2	11⅔	1	1	.500	11	6	6	6	2	4.63
1976—New York	American	2	12	1	1	.500	10	6	6	5	1	4.50
1978—New York	American	1	6	0	0	.000	7	3	3	5	3	4.50
Championship Series Totals—6 Years		10	69⅓	4	3	.571	57	25	25	37	18	3.25

WORLD SERIES RECORD

Established World Series record for most home runs allowed, total Series (9).

Year Club	League	G.	IP.	W.	L.	Pct.	H.	R.	ER.	SO.	BB.	ERA.
1972—Oakland	American	3	16	2	0	1.000	12	5	5	11	6	2.81
1973—Oakland	American	2	13⅓	1	0	1.000	11	3	3	6	4	2.03
1974—Oakland	American	2	7⅔	1	0	1.000	5	1	1	5	2	1.17
1976—New York	American	1	8⅔	0	1	.000	10	4	3	5	4	3.12
1977—New York	American	2	4⅓	0	1	.000	6	5	5	1	0	10.38
1978—New York	American	2	13	1	1	.500	13	6	6	5	1	4.15
World Series Totals—6 Years		12	63	5	3	.625	57	24	23	33	17	3.29

JIM 'CATFISH' HUNTER

Tied All-Star Game records for most games lost (2); most home runs allowed, total games (4).

Year	League	IP.	W.	L.	Pct.	H.	R.	ER.	SO.	BB.	ERA.
1967—American		5	0	1	.000	4	1	1	4	0	1.80
1970—American		⅓	0	0	.000	3	3	3	0	0	81.00
1973—American		1⅓	0	0	.000	1	0	0	1	0	0.00
1974—American		2	0	0	.000	2	1	1	3	1	4.50
1975—American		2	0	1	.000	3	2	2	2	0	9.00
1976—American		2	0	0	.000	2	2	2	3	0	9.00
All-Star Game Totals—6 Years		12⅔	0	2	.000	15	9	9	13	1	6.39

Member of American League All-Star Team for 1966 and 1972 games; did not play.

BILLY LEO WILLIAMS

Born June 15, 1938, at Whistler, Ala.
Height, 6.01. Weight, 170.
Threw right and batted lefthanded.

Established major league record for most games by outfielder, season (164), 1965.

Tied major league records for most home runs two consecutive games (5), September 8 and 10, 1968; most consecutive doubles, game (4), April 9, 1969; most times, four long hits, game, season (2), April 9 and September 5, 1969.

Established National League record for most games played consecutive, league (1,117), September 22, 1963 through September 2, 1970.

Hit three home runs in game, September 10, 1968.

Led National League in total bases with 321 in 1968, 373 in 1970 and 348 in 1972.

Led National League in slugging percentage with .606 in 1972.

Named National League Rookie Player of the Year by THE SPORTING NEWS and National League Rookie of the Year by Baseball Writers' Association, 1961.

Named THE SPORTING NEWS Major League Player of the Year, 1972.

Named THE SPORTING NEWS National League Player of the Year, 1972.

Named outfielder on THE SPORTING NEWS National League All-Star Team, 1964, 1968, 1970 and 1972.

Named to Hall of Fame, 1987.

Year	Club	League	Pos.	G.	AB.	R.	H.	2B.	3B.	HR.	RBI.	B.A.	PO.	A.	E.	F.A.
1956—Ponca City†	Soo. St.	OF	13	17	4	4	0	0	0	4	.235	6	0	1	.857
1957—Ponca City	Soo. St.	OF	●126	451	87	140	★40	3	17	95	.310	211	21	★25	.903
1958—Pueblo‡	West.	OF	21	80	9	20	2	1	2	11	.250	30	1	2	.939
1958—Burlington	I.I.I.	OF	61	214	38	65	7	0	10	38	.304	93	4	4	.960
1959—San Antonio	Tex.	1B-OF	94	371	57	118	22	7	10	79	.318	578	54	21	.968
1959—Fort Worth	A. A.	OF	5	21	7	10	4	1	1	5	.476	10	2	1	.923
1959—Chicago	Nat.	OF	18	33	0	5	0	1	0	2	.152	18	0	0	1.000
1960—Houston§	A. A.	OF	126	473	74	153	28	3	26	80	.323	207	7	7	.968
1960—Chicago	Nat.	OF	12	47	4	13	0	2	2	7	.277	25	0	1	.962
1961—Chicago	Nat.	OF	146	529	75	147	20	7	25	86	.278	220	9	★11	.954
1962—Chicago	Nat.	OF	159	618	94	184	22	8	22	92	.298	273	18	10	.967
1963—Chicago	Nat.	OF	161	612	87	175	36	9	25	95	.286	298	13	4	.987
1964—Chicago	Nat.	OF	162	645	100	201	39	2	33	98	.312	233	14	13	.950
1965—Chicago	Nat.	OF	●164	645	115	203	39	6	34	108	.315	296	10	10	.968
1966—Chicago	Nat.	OF	●162	648	100	179	23	5	29	91	.276	319	9	8	.976
1967—Chicago	Nat.	OF	162	634	92	176	21	12	28	84	.278	271	3	3	.989
1968—Chicago	Nat.	OF	★163	642	91	185	30	8	30	98	.288	261	4	9	.967
1969—Chicago	Nat.	OF	★163	642	103	188	33	10	21	95	.293	250	15	12	.957
1970—Chicago	Nat.	OF	●161	636	★137	●205	34	4	42	129	.322	259	13	3	.989
1971—Chicago	Nat.	OF	157	594	86	179	27	5	28	93	.301	284	8	7	.977
1972—Chicago	Nat.	OF-1B	150	574	95	191	34	6	37	122	★.333	275	13	4	.986
1973—Chicago	Nat.	OF-1B	156	576	72	166	22	2	20	86	.288	420	34	6	.987
1974—Chicago xy	Nat.	1B-OF	117	404	55	113	22	0	16	68	.280	635	53	11	.984
1975—Oakland	Amer.	1B	155	520	68	127	20	1	23	81	.244	30	3	1	.971
1976—Oakland z	Amer.	OF	120	351	36	74	12	0	11	41	.211	0	0	0	.000
National League Totals—16 Years			2213	8479	1306	2510	402	87	392	1354	.296	4337	216	112	.976
American League Totals—2 Years			275	871	104	201	32	1	34	122	.231	30	3	1	.971
Major League Totals—18 Years			2488	9350	1410	2711	434	88	426	1476	.290	4367	219	113	.976

†On disabled list, July 17 to August 18, 1956.

‡On temporary inactive list, June 7 to July 2, 1958.

§On disabled list, August 8 to September 5, 1960.

xOn disabled list, August 19 to September 3, 1974.

yTraded to Oakland Athletics for Pitchers Darold Knowles and Bob Locker and Second Baseman Manny Trillo, October 23, 1974.

zReleased, November 9, 1976.

Batting instructor, Chicago Cubs, 1978, 1979, 1982 and 1986; coach, Chicago Cubs, 1980 and 1981; coach, Oakland A's, 1983 through 1985.

CHAMPIONSHIP RECORD

Year	Club	League	Pos.	G.	AB.	R.	H.	2B.	3B.	HR.	RBI.	B.A.	PO.	A.	E.	F.A.
1975—Oakland	Amer.	DH-PH	3	8	0	0	0	0	0	0	.000	0	0	0	.000

ALL-STAR GAME RECORD

Year	League	Pos.	AB.	R.	H.	2B.	3B.	HR.	RBI.	B.A.	PO.	A.	E.	F.A.
1962—National (second game)		OF	1	0	0	0	0	0	1	.000	2	0	0	1.000
1964—National		OF	4	1	1	0	0	1	1	.250	1	0	0	1.000
1965—National		PH	1	0	0	0	0	0	0	.000	0	0	0	.000

BILLY WILLIAMS

Year	League	Pos.	AB.	R.	H.	2B.	3B.	HR.	RBI.	B.A.	PO.	A.	E.	F.A.
1968—National		PH	1	0	0	0	0	0	0	.000	0	0	0	.000
1972—National		OF	2	1	1	0	0	0	0	.500	0	0	0	.000
1973—National		OF	2	0	1	0	0	0	0	.500	0	0	0	.000
All-Star Game Totals—6 Years			11	2	3	0	0	1	2	.273	3	0	0	1.000

NOTES